The Broadview Anthology of

BRITISH LITERATURE

Volume 1
The Medieval Period
Second Edition

The Broadview Anthology of British Literature

The Medieval Period
The Renaissance and the Early Seventeenth Century
The Restoration and the Eighteenth Century
The Age of Romanticism
The Victorian Era
The Twentieth Century and Beyond

The Broadview Anthology of

BRITISH LITERATURE

Volume 1
The Medieval Period
Second Edition

GENERAL EDITORS

Joseph Black, University of Massachusetts
Leonard Conolly, Trent University
Kate Flint, Rutgers University
Isobel Grundy, University of Alberta
Don LePan, Broadview Press
Roy Liuzza, University of Tennessee
Jerome J. McGann, University of Virginia
Anne Lake Prescott, Barnard College
Barry V. Qualls, Rutgers University
Claire Waters, University of California, Davis

broadview press

LIBRARY AND ARCHIVES CANADA CATALOGUING IN PUBLICATION

  The Broadview anthology of British Literature: volume 1: the medieval period / general editors Joseph Black ... [et al].
— 2nd ed.

Includes bibliographical references and index.
ISBN 978-1-55111-965-6

  1. Literature, Medieval. 2. English literature—Old English, ca. 450-1100. 3. English literature—Middle English, 1100-1500.
I. Black, Joseph Laurence, 1962–

PRII20.B76   2009   820.8'001   C2009-901366-5

Broadview Press is an independent, international publishing house, incorporated in 1985. Broadview believes in shared ownership, both with its employees and with the general public; since the year 2000 Broadview shares have traded publicly on the Toronto Venture Exchange under the symbol BDP.

We welcome comments and suggestions regarding any aspect of our publications—please feel free to contact us at the addresses below or at broadview@broadviewpress.com.

North America
PO Box 1243,
Peterborough, Ontario
Canada K9J 7H5

2215 Kenmore Road,
Buffalo, NY, USA 14207
Tel: (705) 743-8990;
Fax: (705) 743-8353
email: customerservice@broadviewpress.com

UK, Ireland, and continental Europe
NBN International
Estover Road
Plymouth
UK PL6 7PY
Tel: +44 (0) 1752 202301;
Fax: +44 (0) 1752 202331;
Fax Order Line: +44 (0) 1752 202333;
Cust Ser: enquiries@nbninternational.com
Orders: orders@nbninternational.com

Australia and New Zealand
New South Books,
University of New South Wales
Sydney, NSW, 2052
Australia
Tel: 61 2 9664 0999;
Fax: 61 2 9664 5420
email: info.press@unsw.edu.au

www. broadviewpress.com
Broadview Press acknowledges the financial support of the Government of Canada through the Book Publishing Industry Development Program (BPIDP) for our publishing activities.

Cover design by Lisa Brawn

PRINTED IN CANADA

Contributing Editors and Writers

MANAGING EDITOR · Don LePan
EDITORIAL COORDINATOR · Jennifer McCue
DEVELOPMENTAL EDITOR · Laura Cardiff
GENERAL ACADEMIC AND TEXTUAL EDITORS · Colleen Franklin, Morgan Rooney
DESIGN COORDINATOR · Kathryn Brownsey

CONTRIBUTING EDITORS

Katherine O. Acheson
Sandra Bell
Emily Bernhard Jackson
Joseph Black
Robert Boenig
Michael Calabrese
Laura Cardiff
Noel Chevalier
Mita Choudhury
Thomas J. Collins
Leonard Conolly
Dianne Dugaw
Michael Faletra
Christine Fitzgerald
Stephen Glosecki
Amanda Goldrick-Jones

Douglas Hayes
John Holmes
Michael Keefer
Scott Kleinman
Gary Kuchar
Don LePan
Roy Liuzza
Marie Loughlin
D.L. Macdonald
Hugh Magennis
Anne McWhir
Tobias Menely
Britt Mize
David Oakleaf
Jude Polsky

Anne Lake Prescott
Joyce Rappaport
Herbert Rosengarten
Jason Rudy
Janice Schroeder
John T. Sebastian
Emily Steiner
David Swain
Andrew Taylor
Peggy Thompson
Fred Waage
Craig Walker
Claire Waters
David Watt
James Winny

CONTRIBUTING WRITERS

Laura Cardiff
Jude Polsky
Victoria Abboud
Jane Beal
Jennifer Beauvais
Rachel Bennett
Emily Bernhard Jackson
Rebecca Blasco
Julie Brennan
Andrew Bretz
Emily Cargan
Adrienne Eastwood
Wendy Eberle-Sinatra
Peter Enman
Joanne Findon

Jane Grove
Camille Isaacs
Erik Isford
Stephanie King
Gabrielle L'Archeveque
Don LePan
Anna Lepine
John McIntyre
Carrie Nartkler
Byron Nelson
Robin Norris
Kenna Olsen
Kendra O'Neal Smith
Laura Pellerine
Jason Rudy

Anne Salo
Janice Schroeder
Carrie Shanafelt
Nicole Shukin
James Soderholm
Anne Sorbie
Martha Stoddard-Holms
Jenna Stook
Candace Taylor
David van Belle
Shari Watling
Matthew Williams
bj Wray
Nicole Zylstra

LAYOUT AND TYPESETTING

Kathryn Brownsey   Susan Chamberlain

ILLUSTRATION FORMATTING AND ASSISTANCE

Cheryl Baldwin   Lisa Brawn

Contents

Please note that the full *Broadview Anthology of British Literature* includes material both in the six bound-book volumes and the anthology's website component located at **www.broadviewpress.com/babl**.

PREFACE

A FRESH APPROACH

The publication of the first edition of this anthology in 2006 was widely hailed as an exciting achievement, with many academics concluding that its comprehensiveness, its consistency, its visual appeal, and its fresh approach made the Broadview edition the "new standard" in anthologies of British literature. We are also taking a fresh approach in issuing new editions of the anthology's volumes. Rather than publishing a second edition of each of the six volumes simultaneously, we plan to publish a new edition of one of the six volumes each year. Each volume will thus appear in a new edition every six years. We recognize that our two main competitors have in recent years made it a practice to issue new editions much more frequently, but our feeling is that it is better to allow several years to elapse between editions—not least of all as a new edition may represent a considerable inconvenience to academics teaching from the anthology. (The approach also has real practical advantages for a smaller publisher such as Broadview; rather than gearing up for a massive process of revision every few years and then gearing down again in the wake of publication, we can proceed at a steady pace with the work of updating and revising.)

For the second edition of this volume a considerable number of changes have been made. From the Anglo-Saxon period, a substantial excerpt from Gildas's *The Ruin of Britain* is now included, as is an excerpt from Pseudo-Nennius's *History of the Britons* (the latter in the online component of the anthology). The Old English *Life of Saint Mary of Egypt* is now part of the anthology, and the Middle English *Life of Saint Margaret* will soon be added to the anthology's website component. The inclusion of Michael Faletra's fine translation of Geoffrey of Monmouth's *A History of the King's of Britain* is another feature new to this edition. Coverage of the Ricardian period has been considerably expanded through the inclusion of William Langland (previously represented only by brief excerpts) and John Gower, as

well as by the addition of Chaucer's "Parliament of Fowles." Literature of the late medieval period is also more fully represented, with Thomas Hoccleve and the "Scots Makars" now included; we also plan to add writings by John Lydgate to the anthology's website component. Coverage of medieval romance is considerably enriched through the inclusion of *Sir Launfal* in the online component. And coverage of medieval drama has been extended as well; additions include two of the York plays and the Towneley *Last Judgement*, with more planned for the future. (In this as in other areas, the online component of the anthology allows for virtually unlimited flexibility.) Nothing has been cut from the first edition, though some material has been shifted to the website component from the bound book—perhaps most notably the English translation of *Everyman*, long a staple of British literature survey courses but now increasingly acknowledged to be of less than central importance to the development of British literature or drama.

A further change to the drama segment of the anthology is the re-ordering of the biblical plays; given the uncertainty surrounding their provenance, we felt that arranging these plays according to biblical sequence might make more sense (pedagogically as well as intellectually) than trying to order them chronologically by estimating dates of composition or first performance.

In the preparation of the new material we have received invaluable assistance from a number of academics who are now among the anthology's contributing editors and writers. Among these are Michael Calabrese of California State University, Los Angeles; Michael Faletra of Reed College; Joanne Findon of Trent University; Christina Fitzgerald of the University of Toledo; Douglas Hayes of Lakehead University; Britt Mize of Texas A&M University; John T. Sebastian of Loyola University, New Orleans; Emily Steiner of the University of Pennsylvania; and David Watt of the University of Manitoba.

Inviting these academics to contribute to the new edition is entirely consistent with the approach we have followed from the start. Rather than dividing up the vast amount of work entailed in preparing such a large anthology among a relatively small number of academics, and asking each of them to handle on their own the work of choosing, annotating, and preparing introductions to texts in their own areas of specialization, we chose to involve a large number of contributors in the process (as the pages following the title page to this volume attest), and to encourage a high degree of collaboration at every level. First and foremost are the distinguished academics who serve as our General Editors for the project, but in all there have literally been hundreds of people involved at various stages in researching, drafting headnotes or annotations, reviewing material, editing material, and carrying out the work of designing and typesetting the texts and other materials. That approach allowed us to draw on a diverse range of talent, and to prepare the first edition of a large anthology with extraordinary efficiency. It has also facilitated the maintenance of a high degree of consistency. Material has been reviewed and revised in-house at Broadview, by outside editors, by a variety of academics with an extraordinarily diverse range of backgrounds and academic specialities, and by our team of General Editors for the project as a whole. The aim has been not only to ensure accuracy but also to make sure that the same standards be applied throughout the anthology to matters such as coverage provided in introductions, level of annotation, tone of writing, and student accessibility.

As with the first edition, our General Editors have throughout taken the lead in the process of making selections for the anthology. Along the way we have been guided by several core principles. We have endeavored to provide a selection that is broadly representative, while also being mindful of the importance of choosing texts that have the capacity to engage readers' interest today. We have for the most part made it a policy to include long works in their entirety or not at all; readers will find complete in these pages works such as *Utopia*, *Confessions of an English Opium Eater*, *In Memoriam* and *A Room of One's Own* that are often excerpted in other anthologies. Where inexpensive editions of works are available in our series of paperback Broadview Editions, we have often decided to omit them here, on the grounds that those wishing to teach one or more such works may easily order them in a combination package with the anthology; on these grounds we have decided against including *Frankenstein*, *Pride and Prejudice*, or *Heart of Darkness*. (For both Mary Shelley and Jane Austen we have made exceptions to our general policy regarding excerpts, however, including selections from *The Last Man* to represent Shelley and the first four chapters of *Pride and Prejudice*, together with a complete shorter work, *Lady Susan*, to represent Austen.)

Any discussion of what is distinctive about *The Broadview Anthology of British Literature* must focus above all on the contents. In every volume of the anthology there is material that is distinctive and fresh—including not only selections by lesser-known writers but also less familiar selections from canonical writers. The anthology takes a fresh approach too to a great many canonical texts. The first volume of the anthology includes not only Roy Liuzza's translation of *Beowulf* (widely acclaimed as the most engaging and reliable translation available), but also new translations by Liuzza of many other works of Old English poetry and prose. Unique to the first volume of this anthology are a verse translation of *Judith* by Stephen Glosecki, and new translations by Claire Waters of several of the *Lais* of Marie de France. The second volume includes *King Lear* not only in the full Folio version but also with three key scenes from the Quarto version; readers are thus invited to engage first-hand with the question of how textual issues may substantially affect larger issues of meaning. And so on through all six volumes.

In a number of these cases the distinctive form of the anthology facilitates the presentation of content in an engaging and practical fashion. Notably, the adoption of a two-column format allows for some translations (the Marie de France *Lais*, the James Winny translation of *Sir Gawain and the Green Knight*) to be presented in parallel column format alongside the original texts, allowing readers to experience something of the flavor of the original, while providing convenient access to an accessible translation. Similarly, scenes from the Quarto version of *King Lear* are presented alongside the comparable sections of the Folio text, and passages from four translations of the Bible are laid out parallel to each other for ready comparison.

The large trim-size, two-column format also allows

for greater flexibility in the presentation of visual materials. Throughout our intent is to make this an anthology that is fully alive to the connections between literary and visual culture, from the discussion of the CHI-RHO page of the Lindisfarne Gospels in the first volume of the anthology (and the accompanying color illustration) to the inclusion in Volume 6 of a number of selections (including Graham Greene's "The Basement Room," Hanif Kureishi's "My Son the Fanatic," Tom Stoppard's "Professional Foul," and several skits from "Monty Python's Flying Circus") that may be discussed in connection with film or television versions. Along the way appear several full-page illustrations from the Ellesmere manuscript of Chaucer's *Canterbury Tales* and illustrations to a wide variety of other works, from *Robinson Crusoe* and *Gulliver's Travels* to *A Christmas Carol* and *The Road to Wigan Pier*.

CONTEXTUAL MATERIALS

Visual materials are also an important component of the background materials that form the anthology. These materials are presented in two ways. Several "Contexts" sections on particular topics or themes appear in each volume of the anthology, presented independently of any particular text or author. These include broadly based groupings of material on such topics as "Religion and Spiritual Life," "Print Culture," "India and the Orient," "The Abolition of Slavery," "The New Art of Photography," and "The End of Empire." The groups of "In Context" materials each relate to a particular text or author. They range from the genealogical tables provided as a supplement to *Beowulf*; to materials on "The Eighteenth-Century Sexual Imagination" (presented in conjunction with Haywood's *Fantomina*); to a selection of materials relating to the Peterloo massacre (presented in conjunction with Percy Shelley's "The Mask of Anarchy"); to materials on "'The Vilest Scramble for Loot' in Central Africa" (presented in conjunction with Conrad's "An Outpost of Progress"). For the most part these contextual materials are, as the word suggests, included with a view to setting texts in their broader literary, historical, and cultural contexts;

in some cases, however, the materials included in "Contexts" sections are themselves literary works of a high order. The autobiographical account by Eliza M. of nineteenth-century life in Cape Town, for example (included in the section in Volume 5 on "Race and Empire"), is as remarkable for its literary qualities as it is for the light it sheds on the realities of colonial life. In the inclusion of texts such as these, as well as in other ways, the anthology aims to encourage readers to explore the boundaries of the literary and the non-literary, and the issue of what constitutes a "literary text."

WOMEN'S PLACE

A central element of the broadening of the canon of British literature in recent generations has of course been a great increase in the attention paid to texts by women writers. As one might expect from a publisher that has played an important role in making neglected works by women writers widely available, this anthology reflects the broadening of the canon quantitatively, by including a substantially larger number of women writers than have earlier anthologies of British literature. But it also reflects this broadening in other ways. In many anthologies of literature (anthologies of British literature, to be sure, but also anthologies of literature of a variety of other sorts) women writers are set somewhat apart, referenced in introductions and headnotes only in relation to issues of gender, and treated as important only for the fact of their being women writers. *The Broadview Anthology* strenuously resists such segregation; while women writers are of course discussed in relation to gender issues, their texts are also presented and discussed alongside those by men in a wide variety of other contexts, including seventeenth-century religious and political controversies, the abolitionist movement, and World War I pacifism. Texts by women writers are front and center in the discussion of the development of realism in nineteenth-century fiction. And when it comes to the twentieth century, both Virginia Woolf and Dorothy Richardson are included alongside James Joyce as practitioners of groundbreaking modernist narrative techniques.

"BRITISH," "ENGLISH," "IRISH," "SCOTTISH," "WELSH," "OTHER"

The broadening of English Studies, in conjunction with the expansion and subsequent contraction of British power and influence around the world, has considerably complicated the issue of exactly how inclusive anthologies should be. In several respects this anthology (like its two main competitors) is significantly more inclusive than its title suggests, including a number of non-British writers whose works connect in important ways with the traditions of British literature. We endeavor to portray the fluid and multilingual reality of the medieval period through the inclusion not only of works in Old and Middle English but also, where other cultures interacted with the nascent "English" language and "British" culture, works in Latin, in French, and in Welsh. In later periods the word "British" becomes deeply problematic in different respects, but on balance we have preferred it to the only obvious alternative, "English." There are several objections to the latter in this context. Perhaps most obviously, "English" excludes authors or texts not only from Ireland but also from Scotland and from Wales, both of which retain to this day cultures quite distinct from that of the English. "English literature," of course, may also be taken to mean "literature written in English," but since the anthology does not cover *all* literature written in English (most obviously in excluding American literature), the ambiguity would not in this case be helpful.

The inclusion of Irish writers presents a related but even more tangled set of issues. At the beginning of the period covered by the six volumes of this anthology we find works, such as the *Book of Kells*, that may have been created in what is now England, in what is now Scotland, in what is now Ireland—or in some combination of these. Through most of the seventeenth, eighteenth, and nineteenth centuries almost the whole of Ireland was under British control—but for the most part unwillingly. In the period covered in the last of the six volumes Ireland was partitioned, with Northern Ireland becoming a part of the United Kingdom and the Republic of Ireland declared independent of Britain on 6 December 1921. Less than two months earlier, James Joyce had completed *Ulysses*, which was first published

as a complete work the following year (in Paris, not in Britain). It would be obviously absurd to regard Joyce as a British writer up to just before the publication of *Ulysses*, and an Irish writer thereafter. And arguably he and other Irish writers should never be regarded as British, whatever the politics of the day. If on no other grounds than their overwhelming influence on and connection to the body of literature written in the British Isles, however, we have included Irish writers—among them Swift, Sheridan, Wilde, Shaw, Beckett, Bowen, Muldoon, and Heaney as well as Joyce —throughout this anthology. We have also endeavored to give a real sense in the introductions to the six volumes of the anthology, in the headnotes to individual authors, and in the annotations to the texts themselves, of the ways in which the histories and the cultures of England, Ireland, Scotland and Wales, much as they interact with one another, are also distinct.

Also included in this anthology are texts by writers from areas that are far removed geographically from the British Isles but that are or have been British possessions. Writers such as Mary Rowlandson, Olaudah Equiano, and Phillis Wheatley are included, as they spent all or most of their lives living in what were then British colonial possessions. Writers who came of age in an independent United States, on the other hand, are not included, unless (like T.S. Eliot) they subsequently put down roots in Britain and became important British literary figures. Substantial gray areas, of course, surround such issues. One might well argue, for example, that Henry James merits inclusion in an anthology of British literature, or that W.H. Auden and Thom Gunn are more American poets than British ones. But the chosen subject matter of James's work has traditionally been considered to mark him as having remained an American writer, despite having spent almost two-thirds of his life in England. And both Auden and Gunn so clearly made a mark in Britain before crossing the Atlantic that it would seem odd to exclude them from these pages on the grounds of their having lived the greater part of their adult lives in America. One of our competitors includes Sylvia Plath in their anthology of British literature; Plath lived in England for only five of her thirty years, though, and her poetry is generally agreed to have more in common with the traditions of

Lowell, Merwin and Sexton than with the currents of British poetry in the 1950s and '60s.

As a broad principle, we have been open to the inclusion of twentieth- and twenty-first century work in English not only by writers from the British Isles but also by writers from British possessions overseas, and by writers from countries that were once British possessions and have remained a part of the British Commonwealth. In such cases we have often chosen selections that relate in one way or another to the tradition of British litera- ture and the British colonial legacy. Of the Judith Wright poems included here, several relate to her coming to terms with the British colonial legacy in Australia; similarly, both the Margaret Atwood and the Alice Munro selections include work in which these Canadian authors attempt to recreate imaginatively the experience of British emigrants to Canada in the nine- teenth century; the Chinua Achebe story in the anthol- ogy concerns the divide between British colonial culture and traditional Nigerian culture; and so on. For conve- nience we have also grouped most of the post-World War II non-British authors together, following the "Contexts: The End of Empire" section. (For the most part, the table of contents for the anthology is arranged chronologically according to the birthdate of each author.)

THE HISTORY OF LANGUAGE, AND OF PRINT CULTURE

Among the liveliest discussions we had at meetings of our General Editors were those concerning the issue of whether or not to bring spelling and punctuation into accord with present-day practice. We finally decided that, in the interests of making the anthology accessible to the introductory student, we should *in most cases* bring spelling and punctuation in line with present-day practice. An important exception has been made for works in which modernizing spelling and punctuation would alter the meaning or the aural and metrical qualities. In practice this means that works before the late sixteenth century tend to be presented either in their original form or in translation, whereas later texts tend to have spelling and punctuation modernized. But where spelling and punctuation choices in later texts are

known (or believed on reliable authority) to represent conscious choice on the part of the author rather than simply the common practice of the time, we have in those cases, too, made an exception and retained the original spelling and punctuation. (Among these are texts by Edmund Spenser, by William Cowper, by William Blake, John Clare, and several other poets of the Romantic era, by George Bernard Shaw, and by contemporary figures such as Linton Kwesi Johnson.)

Beyond this, we all agreed that we should provide for readers a real sense of the development of the language and of print culture. To that end we have included in each volume examples of texts in their original form—in some cases through the use of pages shown in facsimile, in others by providing short passages in which spelling and punctuation have not been modernized. A list of these appears near the beginning of each volume of the anthology.

We have also included a section of the history of the language as part of the introduction to each volume. And throughout the anthology we include materi- als—visual as well as textual—relating to the history of print culture.

A DYNAMIC AND FLEXIBLE ANTHOLOGY

Almost all major book publishing projects nowadays are accompanied by an adjunct website, and most large- scale anthologies are accompanied by websites that provide additional background materials in electronic form. The website component of this anthology, on the other hand, is precisely that—a *component* of the anthology itself. The notion of a website of this sort grew organically out of the process of trying to winnow down the contents of the first edition of the anthology to a manageable level—the point at which all the material to be included would fit within the covers of bound books that would not be overwhelmingly heavy. And we simply could not do it. After we had made a very substantial round of cuts we were still faced with a table of contents in which each volume was at least 200 or 300 pages longer than our agreed-upon maximum. Our solution was not to try to cut anything more, but rather to select a range of material to be made available in a website component of the anthology. This material is in every way produced according to the same high standards of the material in the bound books; the editorial standards, the procedures for annotation, the author introductions, and the page design and layout—all are the same. The texts on the web, in short, are not "extra" materials; they are an integral part of the full anthology. In accordance with that principle, we have been careful to include a wide range of texts by lesser-known writers within the bound books, and a number of texts by canonical writers within the web component of the anthology.

The latter may be used in a variety of ways. Most obviously, readings from the web component are available to any purchaser of the book. Instructors who adopt *The Broadview Anthology of British Literature* as a course text are also granted permission to reproduce any web material for which Broadview holds copyright in a supplementary coursepack. An alternative for instructors who want to "create their own" anthology is to provide the publisher with a desired table of contents; Broadview will then make available to students through their university bookstore a custom-made coursepack with precisely those materials included. Other options are available too. Volumes of the anthology itself may of course be shrink-wrapped together at special prices in any desired combination. They may also (for a modest additional charge) be combined in a shrink-wrapped package with one or more of the over 300 volumes in the Broadview Editions series.

We anticipate that over the years the web-based component of the anthology will continue to grow—every year there will be a greater choice of web-based texts in the anthology. But we never foresee a day when the web will be the only option; we expect physical books always to remain central to Broadview's approach to publishing.

The Broadview List

One of the reasons we were able to bring a project of this sort to fruition in a relatively short time was that we were able to draw on the resources of the full Broadview list: the many titles in the Broadview Editions series, and also the considerable range of other Broadview anthologies. As the contributors'

pages and the permissions acknowledgments pages indicate, a number of Broadview authors have acted as contributing editors to this volume, providing material from other volumes that has been adapted to suit the needs of the present anthology; we gratefully acknowledge their contribution.

As it has turned out, the number of cases where we have been able to draw on the resources of the Broadview list in the full sense, using in these pages texts and annotations in very much the same form in which they appear elsewhere, has been relatively small; whether because of an issue such as the level of textual modernization or one of style of annotation, we have more often than not ended up deciding that the requirements of this anthology were such that we could not use material from another Broadview source as-is. But even in these cases we often owe a debt of gratitude to the many academics who have edited outstanding editions and anthologies for Broadview. For even where we have not drawn directly from them, we have often been inspired by them—inspired to think of a wider range of texts as possibilities than we might otherwise have done, inspired to think of contextual materials in places where we might otherwise not have looked, inspired by the freshness of approach that so many of these titles exemplify.

Editorial Procedures and Conventions, Apparatus

The in-house set of editorial guidelines for *The Broadview Anthology of British Literature* runs to over 40 pages, covering everything from conventions for the spacing of marginal notes, to the use of small caps for the abbreviations CE and BCE, to the approach we have adopted to references in author headnotes to name changes. Perhaps the most important core principle in the introductions to the various volumes, in the headnotes for each author, in the introductions in "Contexts" sections, and in annotations throughout the anthology, is to endeavor to provide a sufficient amount of information to enable students to read and interpret these texts, but without making evaluative judgments or imposing particular interpretations. In practice that is all a good deal more challenging than it sounds; it is often extremely difficult to describe why a particular author is considered to be important without using language that verges on the interpretive or the evaluative. But it is a fine line that we have all agreed is worth trying to walk; we hope that readers will find that the anthology achieves an appropriate balance.

ANNOTATION: It is also often difficult to make judgments as to where it is appropriate to provide an explanatory annotation for a word or phrase. Our policy has been to annotate where we feel it likely that most first- or second-year students are likely to have difficulty understanding the denotative meaning. (We have made it a practice not to provide notes discussing connotative meanings.) But in practice the vocabularies and levels of verbal facility of first- and second-year students may vary enormously, both from institution to institution and within any given college or university class. On the whole, we provide somewhat more annotation than our competitors, and somewhat less interpretation. Again, we hope that readers will find that the anthology has struck an appropriate balance.

THE ETHICS AND POLITICS OF ANNOTATION: On one issue regarding annotation we have felt that principles are involved that go beyond the pedagogical. Most anthologies of British literature allow many words or phrases of a racist, sexist, anti-Semitic, or homophobic nature either to pass entirely without comment, or to be glossed with apologist comments that leave the impression that such comments were excusable in the past, and may even be unobjectionable in the present. Where derogatory comments about Jewish people and money-lending are concerned, for example, anthologies often leave the impression that money-lending was a pretty unsavory practice that Jewish people entered by choice; it has been all too rare to provide readers with any sense of the degree to which English society consistently discriminated against Jews, expelling them entirely for several centuries, requiring them to wear physical marks identifying their Jewish status, prohibiting them from entering most professions, and so on. *The Broadview Anthology* endeavors in such cases, first of all, not to allow such words and phrases to pass without comment; and second, to gloss without glossing over.

DATES: We make it a practice to include the date when a work was first made public, whether publication in print or, in the case of dramatic works, made public through the first performance of the play. Where that date is known to differ substantially from the date of composition, a note to this effect is included in parentheses. With medieval works, where there is no equivalent to the "publication" of later eras, where texts often vary greatly from one manuscript copy to another, and where knowledge as to date of original composition is usually imprecise, the date that appears at the end of each work is an estimate of the date of the work's origin in the written form. Earlier oral or written versions are of course in some cases real possibilities.

TEXTS: Where translations appear in this anthology, a note at the bottom of the first page indicates what translation is being used. Similar notes also address overall textual issues where choice of copy text is particularly significant. Reliable editions of all works are listed in the bibliography for the anthology, which is included as part of the website component rather than in the bound books, to facilitate ready revision. (In addition to information as to reliable editions, the bibliography provides for each author and for each of the six periods select lists of important or useful historical and critical works.) Copyright information for texts not in the public domain, however, is provided within the bound books in a section listing Permissions Acknowledgments.

INTRODUCTIONS: In addition to the introductory headnotes for each author included in the anthology, each "Contexts" section includes a substantial introduction, and each volume includes an introduction to the period as a whole. These introductions to the six volumes of the anthology endeavor to provide a sense not only of the broad picture of literary developments in the period, but also of the historical, social, and political background, and of the cultural climate. Readers should be cautioned that, while there is inevitably some overlap between information presented here and information presented in the author headnotes, an effort has been made to avoid such repetition as much as possible; the general introduction to each period should thus be read in conjunction with the author headnotes. The general introductions aim not only to provide an overview of ways in which texts and authors included in these pages may connect with one another, but also to give readers a sense of connection with a range of other writers and texts of the period.

READING POETRY: For much of the glossary and for the "Reading Poetry" section that appears as part of the appendices to each volume we have drawn on the superb material prepared by Herbert Rosengarten and Amanda Goldrick-Jones for *The Broadview Anthology of Poetry*; this section provides a concise but comprehensive introduction to the study of poetry. It includes discussions of diction, imagery, poetic figures, and various poetic forms, as well as offering an introduction to prosody.

MAPS: Also appearing within each of the bound books are maps especially prepared for this anthology, including, for each volume, a map of Britain showing towns and features of relevance during the pertinent period; a map showing the counties of Britain and of Ireland; maps both of the London area and of the inner city; and world maps indicating the locations of some of the significant places referenced in the anthology, and for later volumes showing the extent of Britain's overseas territories.

GLOSSARY: Some other anthologies of British literature include both glossaries of terms and essays introducing students to various political and religious categories in British history. Similar information is included in *The Broadview Anthology of British Literature*, but we have adopted a more integrated approach, including political and religious terms along with literary ones in a convenient general glossary. While we recognize that "googling" for information of this sort is often the student's first resort (and we recognize too the value of searching the web for the wealth of background reference information available there), we also recognize that information culled from the Internet is often far from reliable; it is our intent, through this glossary, through our introductions and headnotes, and through the wealth of accessible annotation in the anthology, to provide as part of the anthology a reliable core of information in the most convenient and accessible form possible.

OTHER MATERIALS: A chart of Monarchs and Prime Ministers is also provided within these pages. A range of other adjunct materials may be accessed through *The Broadview Anthology of British Literature* website. "Texts and Contexts" charts for each volume provide a convenient parallel reference guide to the dates of literary texts and historical developments. "Money in Britain" provides a thumbnail sketch of the world of pounds, shillings, and pence, together with a handy guide to estimating the current equivalents of monetary values from earlier eras. And the website offers, too, a variety of aids for the student and the instructor. An up-to-date list of these appears on the site.

ACKNOWLEDGMENTS

The names of the General Editors that shaped this anthology appear on the title page, and those of the many who contributed directly to the writing, editing, and production of the project on the following two pages. Special acknowledgment should go to Jennifer McCue, who as Editorial Coordinator has been instrumental in tying together all the vast threads of this project and in making it a reality; to Laura Cardiff and Jude Polsky, who have carried larger loads than any others in drafting introductory materials and annotations, and who have done so with great skill and unfailing grace; to Kathryn Brownsey, who has been responsible for design and typesetting, and has continued to do a superb job and to maintain her good spirits even when faced with near-impossible demands; to Colleen Franklin, for the range of her scholarship as well as for her keen eye as our primary copy editor for the entire project; to Emily Cargan, Jennifer Elsayed and Amy Nimegeer who have together done superb work on the vast job of clearing permissions for the anthology; and to Michelle Lobkowicz and Anna Del Col, who have ably and enthusiastically taken the lead with marketing matters.

The General Editors and all of us in-house at Broadview owe an enormous debt of gratitude to the hundreds of academics who have offered assistance at various stages of this project. In particular we would like to express our appreciation and our thanks to the following:

Rachel Ablow, University of Rochester
Bryan Alexander, Middlebury College
James Allard, Brock University
Sharon Alker, Whitman College
Laurel Amtower, San Diego State University
Rob Anderson, Oakland University
Christopher Armitage, University of North Carolina, Chapel Hill
Clinton Atchley, Henderson State University
John Baird, University of Toronto
William Baker, Northern Illinois University
Karen Bamford, Mount Allison University
John Batchelor, University of Newcastle
Lynn Batten, University of California, Los Angeles
Alexandra Bennett, Northern Illinois University
John Beynon, California State University, Fresno
Robert E. Bjork, Arizona State University
Rita Bode, Trent University
Robert Boenig, Texas A & M University
Rick Bowers, University of Alberta
David Brewer, Ohio State University

William Brewer, Appalachian State University
Susan Brown, University of Guelph
Sylvia Brown, University of Alberta
Sheila Burgar, University of Victoria
Catherine Burroughs, Wells College
Rebecca Bushnell, University of Pennsylvania
Michael Calabrese, California State University
Elizabeth Campbell, Oregon State University
Cynthia Caywood, University of San Diego
Jane Chance, Rice University
Ranita Chatterjee, California State University, Northridge
Nancy Cirillo, University of Illinois, Chicago
Eric Clarke, University of Pittsburgh
Jeanne Clegg, University of Aquila, Italy
Thomas J. Collins, University of Western Ontario
Kevin Cope, Louisiana State University
David Cowart, University of South Carolina
Catherine Craft-Fairchild, University of St. Thomas
Carol Davison, University of Windsor
Alex Dick, University of British Columbia

Len Diepeveen, Dalhousie University
Mary Dockray-Miller, Lesley College
Frank Donoghue, Ohio State University
Chris Downs, Saint James School
Julie Early, University of Alabama, Huntsville
Siân Echard, University of British Columbia
Garrett Epp, University of Alberta
Daniel Fischlin, University of Guelph
Verlyn Flieger, University of Maryland
Robert Forman, St. John's University
Lorcan Fox, University of British Columbia
Roberta Frank, Yale University
Jeff Franklin, University of Colorado, Denver
Maria Frawley, George Washington University
Mark Fulk, Buffalo State College
Andrew Galloway, Cornell University
Michael Gamer, University of Pennsylvania
Barbara Gates, University of Delaware
Daniel Gonzalez, University of New Orleans
Jan Gorak, University of Denver
Chris Gordon-Craig, University of Alberta
Ann-Barbara Graff, Georgia Tech University
Michael Griffin, formerly of Southern Illinois
    University
Elisabeth Gruner, University of Richmond
Stephen Guy-Bray, University of British Columbia
Ruth Haber, Worcester State College
Margaret Hadley, University of Calgary
Robert Hampson, Royal Holloway University of
    London
Michael Hanly, Washington State University
Lila Harper, Central Washington State University
Joseph Harris, Harvard University
Anthony Harrison, North Carolina State University
Douglas Hayes, Winona State University
Jennifer Hellwarth, Allegheny University
Peter Herman, San Diego State University
Kathy Hickock, Iowa State University
John Hill, US Naval Academy
Thomas Hill, Cornell University
Laura Hodges
Elizabeth Hodgson, University of British Columbia
Joseph Hornsby, University of Alabama
Scott Howard, University of Denver
Tara Hyland-Russell, St. Mary's College

Catherine Innes-Parker, University of Prince Edward
    Island
Jacqueline Jenkins, University of Calgary
John Johansen, University of Alberta
Richard Juang, Susquehanna University
Michael Keefer, University of Guelph
Sarah Keefer, Trent University
Jon Kertzer, University of Calgary
Helen Killoran, Ohio University
Gordon Kipling, University of California, Los Angeles
Anne Klinck, University of New Brunswick
Elizabeth Kraft, University of Georgia
Mary Kramer, University of Massachusetts, Lowell
Linda Leeds, Bellevue Community College
Mary Elizabeth Leighton, University of Victoria
William Liston, Ball State University
Sharon Locy, Loyola Marymount University
Ross MacKay, Malaspina University College
Peter Mallios, University of Maryland
Arnold Markley, Penn State University
Pamela McCallum, University of Calgary
Kristen McDermott, Central Michigan University
John McGowan, University of North Carolina
Thomas McLean, University of Otago, New Zealand
Susan McNeill-Bindon, University of Alberta
Rod Michell, Thompson Rivers University
Kitty Millett, San Francisco State University
Richard Moll, University of Western Ontario
Monique Morgan, McGill University
Lucy Morrison, Salisbury University
Byron Nelson, West Virginia University
Carolyn Nelson, West Virginia University
Claudia Nelson, Southwest Texas State University
Holly Faith Nelson, Trinity Western University
John Niles, University of Wisconsin, Madison
Michael North, University of California, Los Angeles
Mary Anne Nunn, Central Connecticut State University
David Oakleaf, University of Calgary
Tamara O'Callaghan, Northern Kentucky University
Karen Odden, Assistant Editor for *Victorian Literature
    and Culture* (formerly of University of Wisconsin,
    Milwaukee)
Erika Olbricht, Pepperdine University
Patrick O'Malley, Georgetown University
Patricia O'Neill, Hamilton College

Delilah Orr, Fort Lewis College
Cynthia Patton, Emporia State University
Russell Perkin, St. Mary's University
Marjorie G. Perloff, Stanford University
John Peters, University of North Texas
Alexander Pettit, University of North Texas
Jennifer Phegley, The University of Missouri,
    Kansas City
John Pollock, San Jose State University
Mary Poovey, New York University
Gautam Premnath, University of Massachusetts, Boston
Regina Psaki, University of Oregon
Jonathan Quick, Texas A&M University
Katherine Quinsey, University of Windsor
Geoff Rector, University of Ottawa
Margaret Reeves, Atkinson College, York University
Cedric Reverand, University of Wyoming
Gerry Richman, Suffolk University
David Robinson, University of Arizona
Laura Rotunno, Pennsylvania State University, Altoona
Nicholas Ruddick, University of Regina
Jason Rudy, University of Maryland
Donelle Ruwe, Northern Arizona University
Michelle Sauer, Minot State University
SueAnn Schatz, Lock Haven University of Pennsylvania
Dan Schierenbeck, Central Missouri State University
Norbert Schürer, California State University,
    Long Beach
David Seed, University of Liverpool
Karen Selesky, University College of the Fraser Valley
Carol Senf, Georgia Tech University
Judith Slagle, East Tennessee State University
Sharon Smulders, Mount Royal College
Malinda Snow, Georgia State University
Goran Stanivukovic, St. Mary's University
Richard Stein, University of Oregon

Eric Sterling, Auburn University Montgomery
James Stokes, University of Wisconsin, Stevens Point
Mary-Ann Stouck, Simon Fraser University
Nathaniel Strout, Hamilton College
Lisa Surridge, University of Victoria
Beth Sutton-Ramspeck, Ohio State University
Nanora Sweet, University of Missouri, St. Louis
Dana Symons, Simon Fraser University
Andrew Taylor, University of Ottawa
Elizabeth Teare, University of Dayton
Doug Thorpe, University of Saskatchewan
Jane Toswell, University of Western Ontario
Kim Trainor, University of British Columbia
Herbert Tucker, University of Virginia
John Tucker, University of Victoria
Mark Turner, King's College, University of London
Eleanor Ty, Wilfrid Laurier University
Deborah Tyler-Bennett, Loughborough University
Kirsten Uszkalo, University of Alberta
Lisa Vargo, University of Saskatchewan
Gina Luria Walker, The New School, New York City
Kim Walker, Victoria University of Wellington
Miriam Wallace, New College of Florida
Hayden Ward, West Virginia State University
Ruth Wehlau, Queen's University
Lynn Wells, University of Regina
Chris Willis, Birkbeck University of London
Lisa Wilson, SUNY College at Potsdam
Anne Windholz, Augustana College
Susan Wolfson, Princeton University
Kenneth Womack, Pennsylvania State University
Carolyn Woodward, University of New Mexico
Julia Wright, Wilfrid Laurier University
Julian Yates, University of Delaware
Arlene Young, University of Manitoba
Lisa Zeitz, University of Western Ontario

THE MEDIEVAL PERIOD

From a medieval perspective, the very title of this collection is interestingly problematic. The implication of deliberate choice in the term "anthology" (as opposed, for example, to a "miscellany") reminds us that in any such collection decisions have been made about what does and does not "fit," about lines of influence between works, and about defining the boundaries of a literary tradition. Medieval literature written in England, for instance, was by no means entirely, nor indeed mostly, written in English; works in Latin, Anglo-Norman French, Middle Welsh, and Old Irish all survive alongside works in the languages now known to us as Old and Middle English. Many of these non-English texts had a profound influence on the literary tradition in English; to the extent that we have had to omit such works here, we have created gaps in the story this anthology tries to tell.

The anthology's designation of its literature as "British," moreover, raises a terminological difficulty that is almost as old as the Middle Ages itself. "British" and "English" are by no means interchangeable terms in the medieval period, and the uses of these terms as labels for a language and literary tradition have always been entwined with political realities and national identities. Broadly speaking, the word "British" derives from the Roman name for early Celtic settlers in what we now call the British Isles; "English" refers to the Germanic invaders and settlers who began arriving in the fifth century, pushed the Celtic inhabitants to the west and the north (now Wales and Scotland) and eventually ruled the central part of the island. For many centuries, the English defined themselves by their difference from the British, and *vice versa*. At the same time, those who attempted to claim legitimate rulership of England made strategic use of the "British" tradition, perhaps most obviously in the ongoing traditions surrounding King Arthur, whose origins lie deep in British legendary history. But the intercultural appropriation between "British" and "English" has often worked both ways, and continues to do so: the Anglo-Irish poet Seamus Heaney laces his modern translation of *Beowulf*, a decidedly "English" poem, with idiosyncratic Ulsterisms and Celtic turns of phrase.

Finally, the very word "literature" (deriving from the Latin *litterae*, "letters") implies an existence in writing, but a great deal of what remains in written form from the Middle Ages had a prior existence as, or owes enormous debts to, oral forms. Most of what we now read as literature, from romances to lyrics to sermons, was written to be heard, not read. Texts of vernacular works in the Middle Ages are by no means as solidly fixed—as "textual"—as works of modern literature, or of medieval works in Latin, for that matter; the circumstances of their creation and reception are, at least ostensibly, performative and communal, not silent and solitary like a modern student reading this book. Modern literary culture tends to regard the written text, fixed and inert, as the primary or "real" form of a literary work; for some medieval works, especially those from the earlier Middle Ages, the written text seems to be almost an afterthought, little more than an aid to the memory of the reader/performer who recreates the "real" work by voicing the text out loud.

At the same time, however, the concept of a collection that gathers the authoritative examples of a cultural tradition would have been very familiar to medieval readers, who made extensive use of such collections. Medieval manuscripts that contain multiple works may be anything from carefully planned volumes presented to a patron, to somewhat haphazard gatherings of texts, to collections composed by an individual for his or her own use; our current knowledge of medieval literary culture could rightly be said to rest on medieval anthologies. Thus a reader who first encounters these texts in an anthologized form will encounter them in a format not so unlike their original manuscript context. The single-text "monograph"—one work between two covers—is by no means the most common mode of transmission for medieval texts, and the effort to determine the relationships between texts in medieval manuscripts, the intentions of the creators of such compilations and their effect upon readers, is one of the most interesting and important areas of contemporary medieval literary studies.

The drawing of artificial lines, whether geographical or temporal, is a profound limitation on one's understanding of the history of western literature. At the same time, we cannot simply ignore the geographical facts—which are historical and political facts as well, insofar as the unity of the island of Britain was imagined and achieved—or the differences between one age and another, although the borders (both of historical periods and of kingdoms) may always be contested. This collection likewise relies on distinctions—sometimes arbitrary, sometimes necessary, some obvious and some obscure—to give it shape and contour, form and structure. In English literary history one of the most obvious divisions lies between the literature of the Anglo-Saxons—the English before the Norman Conquest (1066)—and that of the English after the Conquest. Within these two broadly drawn periods further divisions can be made: early Old English literature, as far as we can reconstruct it, differs markedly from literature after the reign of Alfred the Great (d. 899), who sought to begin a program of vernacular literacy and bestowed a certain royal authority on English as a quasi-official written language.

After the Conquest, although English manuscripts were produced and read in somewhat reduced numbers, Norman French was the language of courtly culture in England. In the absence of schools and pedagogical traditions, English began to manifest the changes that characterize "Middle" English. After this period of "early" Middle English—roughly from the century after the Conquest until the beginning of the fourteenth century—English began to take its place alongside the culturally more prestigious Latin (the language of the church) and French (the language of the court, of law, and of administration); authors increasingly chose to write literary texts in English for aristocratic readers. The fifteenth century saw a gradual re-development of a written "standard" English, and an outpouring of literary works (particularly of a devotional nature) that fostered and responded to rising literacy rates. With the advent of printing in the later fifteenth century, books became ever more widely available and the language increasingly standardized; in the sixteenth century, with the wider spread of printing in England, the standard became more and more fixed, even as the language was rapidly changing again, into what linguists call early Modern English.

HISTORY, NARRATIVE, CULTURE

Even a set of very broad periodizations like these raises questions about the relation between historical events and literary developments, or more generally speaking between culture and the imagination. Can we understand these literary works better by learning more about their historical context? Or can these works of the imagination shed light on that context and help us fill in its blank spaces? Which partner in the inseparable pairing of text and context will serve as the solid ground from which we can survey the other—which one is beyond interpretation? Has the human imagination changed so much that we only have access to it historically, and not immediately? On the other hand, what can we really *know* about the past, except what is said about it?

These questions vexed the minds of many medieval authors as well. Most modern scholars, like their medieval predecessors such as Isidore of Seville (a Spanish bishop who lived c. 560–636), are careful to note that history is not simply "what happened" in the past, but the *stories we tell* about what happened in the past. Events, objects, even stories, do not speak for themselves; they have to be arranged and explained, looked at and looked into, and gradually placed in a context constructed from our interpretations of other objects, events and stories. In this sense, no matter how great our respect for objectivity or how carefully balanced our analysis may be, our study of the past says as much about us as it does about the past we try to study. And texts help us understand their context as much as contexts help us understand texts.

In his poem *Ars Poetica* the modern author Archibald MacLeish insisted that "a poem should not mean / But be," but readers of literature from the distant past cannot indulge in the soothing luxury of that misconception. A rock can simply "be"; the remains of a stone wall, however, must "mean" something—they mark a boundary, claim a space, indicate a settlement. A rough diamond lying underground might "be"; but when it has been mined, cut, polished, weighed, set, valued, bought, and worn as jewelry, it is no longer "palpable and mute / as a globed fruit"; it has entered the noisy world of meaning. Similarly, a poem like *Beowulf* or *Sir Gawain and the Green Knight* does not simply exist as a self-evident story; like any work of the human imagination, it responds to and acts on the world in which it was created. Objects and events—the Sutton Hoo ship burial, Durham Cathedral, the Magna Carta, the Black Death of the fourteenth century—positively hum with meaning and intention and human consequences; they are inextricably caught in the web of signification and interpretation. Nothing goes without saying. Even a thing of astonishing beauty that we may enjoy simply for the aesthetic pleasure it gives us is not a self-contained object; it had a function in the society that made it, and part of its meaning—even the meaning of its beauty—lies in that function, which might range from the deepest of spiritual blessings to the purest gaudy display of its owner's ability to possess and appreciate expensive objects. To ignore the cultures that surrounded, created, and consumed these objects—whether they are artifacts in a museum or texts in a book—would be a fundamental mistake.

The famous CHI-RHO page of the early eighth-century Lindisfarne Gospels (London, British Library, MS Cotton Nero D.iv, a color illustration of which appears elsewhere in this volume), offers one example of the kinds of context we might consider when looking at a medieval artifact. We may begin by admiring its beauty, enjoying its exotic strangeness or Celtic "alterity," and marveling at the skill of its creators (whose names, as it happens, are recorded in the manuscript). Such an image could have a number of different effects on its viewers: it might impress those who can't read with the beauty and value of God's Word; it might attest to the devotion of the artists who made such a complex design, as well as their sophistication and expertise as craftsmen; it might display a religious house's capability for such "conspicuous consumption" in the service of God. As we consider it more closely, we may find ourselves puzzled by the presence of a Greek monogram in a Latin text decorated in a distinctively "Insular" style in Northumbria c. 700. At least three cultures are on display here. The page insists on the intersection of English, Irish, and Latin cultures—as intricately woven together as the knotty patterns of its own design. Looking more closely, we can see an English interlinear gloss to the Latin text, written in much smaller script, added some 200 years later. Its presence creates yet another layer of meaning and raises further questions. Who would write in such a rich and beautiful book? Is the gloss a necessary addition, suggesting that the Latin text was not sufficiently accessible to those using the book? What might its presence tell us about the status of Latin as a learned language, or a sacred one, in medieval England? The questions arising from this single page of a manuscript remind us that it is not simply a work of remarkable beauty, but a complex artifact of cultural history.

Saint Luke, Lindisfarne Gospels. This page and a decorative "carpet page" precede the text of the gospel itself.

First text page, Gospel of Saint Luke, Lindisfarne Gospels. The text reads as follows: "Quoniam quidem multi conati sunt ordinare narrationem," "Since many have undertaken to put in narrative order …"

Note: A reproduction of the CHI-RHO page from the Lindisfarne Gospels appears in the section of color illustrations.

The CHI-RHO page embodies, in a particularly striking way, the reciprocal relationship of text and context; while it has much to tell us about the world of its creators, what we know about their world must also be brought to bear on our understanding of the manuscript. To take another example, the poem *Beowulf* has been used to explain other texts (or objects, in the case of the early East Saxon ship-burial at Sutton Hoo; the poem was introduced as evidence in the inquest that determined the ownership and disposition of the priceless objects unearthed from that site in 1939); conversely, other texts and objects can be brought to bear on the obscurities of the text of *Beowulf* and used as explanatory tools. And of course the poem has a place in a series of cultural moments—the unknown moment of its creation, the moment of its transcription into the manuscript in which it survives, the moment of its rediscovery and publication, the modern moment in which it is studied today. Each of these contributes, in some way, to the "meaning" of *Beowulf*, and however tempting it may be to give priority to the more distant (and hence less familiar) contexts, no one of these cultural moments, strictly speaking, has a greater claim on the poem than another. We may wish to regard material objects as somehow more "real" than stories, but from the distant perspective from which we observe them now, they are not: these bright objects on a blank background are as mute and as meaningful, as mysterious and as communicative, as the anonymous stories surviving in single manuscripts by unknown hands.

So the questions we might ask as we approach these texts involve less what they "are" than what they "do," what they might mean not only to their imagined original audience(s) but to us, and how that meaning might change as our knowledge develops. What draws us to these old tales? What do we derive from them? Can we understand them in anything like their original form, with our inevitably modern minds? To what extent can we negotiate the difference between the present and the past? This is a constant problem, a challenge for any reader of early literature. A reader of a contemporary novel is seldom aware of the complex web of cultural assumptions that sustains the narrative; these assumptions are transparent and automatic. For readers of early literature the assumptions are solid, opaque, at times impenetrable—but this awareness of the alterity of the reader to the text is, we think, a very healthy thing. It is always good to be reminded that meanings are not simply "there" in the text, waiting for the reader to stumble over them; they are kindled by the friction between the reader, the story, and the world they both inhabit. Medieval texts force this awareness upon us, but it serves us well as readers of any literary work.

The cultures of the Middle Ages are as varied as they are numerous, and diverse as well in the ways in which they interacted with one another. Moreover, the medieval period was one of continual change. Such change tended to occur at a slower pace than it does in our own time, but the medieval era saw vast and violent upheavals, and great cultural and social developments. From long habit, however, we refer to the millennium following the collapse of the Roman Empire in the fifth century CE as one period, the Middle Ages (or, using the Latinized form of the same phrase, the medieval period). At the end of this long expanse of time falls what we still sometimes call the Renaissance (or "rebirth"). This term reflects Renaissance writers' and thinkers' view of their own time. Many modern historians and literary scholars see the Renaissance of the fourteenth to sixteenth centuries as representing the final flowering of medieval culture rather than a dramatic break with the past; where historians *in* the Renaissance saw difference and division, historians *of* the period tend to see continuity and development.

Even so, many readers coming to the study of medieval literature or culture for the first time will be struck by a sense of strangeness in much of what they encounter. They will enter worlds in which nature is malevolent, not benign; in which Christ fights as a warrior; in which the walls of an ancient city are said to have been broken by fate; in which it is possible to have one's head sliced off and carry it around before putting it back on; in which doubtful legal claims may be decided by the judgment of God through trial by ordeal or by battle; in which water may be thought to flow upward; and in which the middle of a literary text can be said to be inherently better from a moral point of view than the beginning or the end. Much as this introduction aims to convey, and offer a context for, the complexity and sophistication that often characterize medieval texts, it will also recognize that it is difficult —and perhaps even undesirable—for modern readers to lose entirely their sense of strangeness and even wonder in experiencing the products of medieval literature and medieval culture.

Just as the literature of the Middle Ages may seem unusual to us, many modern readers may be surprised by the marginal political status of England and the English language in the Middle Ages. Britain was geographically on the edge of the world, and at the periphery of the political life of the continent; England was for many centuries the object rather than the subject of imperial ambitions. The status of English varied considerably from one century to another, but it was never at any time the dominant global force it is today. The ways in which an extraordinarily diverse cultural and linguistic mix began, over the course of the Middle Ages, to produce the works presented here—as well as, ultimately, the language of this introduction—will be a major theme of these pages.

ENGLAND BEFORE THE NORMAN CONQUEST

ROMAN AND CELTIC BRITAIN

We know little or nothing of the inhabitants of Britain before 500 BCE, when groups of people that we now call the Celts began to migrate from continental Europe to Britain and Ireland. We have come to think of these peoples as a unified group in large part because the artistic and literary heritage of Celtic culture that has come down to us displays considerable unity in the characteristics of its narratives, in the bold decorative style of its visual arts, and in the close ties among Celtic languages. But the Celts, who had spread throughout much of Europe in the centuries before they began to inhabit Britain, were very much a loose grouping of societies, often at odds with one another, with no overarching administrative authority or social coherence.

The Romans invaded and conquered Celtic Britain in the first century CE. Britain lay at the edge of the Roman Empire; the Romans never managed to conquer Ireland or what is now Scotland, then largely inhabited by a Celtic or possibly pre-Celtic people of particularly fierce reputation known as the Picts. (In the early second century CE the Romans constructed the rampart known as "Hadrian's Wall" across the island as a defense against them.) Throughout most of what is now England and Wales, however, the Romans were successful in establishing administrative structures that made *Britannia* a province of the Roman Empire. Though far from the heart of the Empire, Britain was clearly a rich and valuable province, and much of the population, at least in the center of the island, was thoroughly Romanized. It is now thought that the island was densely populated; it enjoyed a thriving money economy and commerce, with a number of large urban centers including a settlement on the banks of the Thames River named *Londinium*, a network of roads, large villas in the Roman style, heated baths, water and sewage service in some areas, and sturdy traditions of Roman administration, education, and literacy. When Christianity spread throughout the Roman empire, it spread in Britain as well—Christian mosaics have been discovered on the site of a large fourth-century villa, and in 314 three British bishops attended a council in Arles, France. In the early years of the fifth century Saint Patrick, a Roman Briton, traveled through Ireland as a missionary bishop, spearheading the conversion of that island. In many respects Britain in the fourth century had a prosperity it would not see again until the fourteenth century.

Roman Britain was highly fortified and well defended from its hostile neighbors, but at the turn of the fifth century the Roman legions stationed in Britain were withdrawn for deployment in the heart of the Empire, in part to defend Rome from the various barbarian tribes pouring across its eastern frontiers. Soon afterwards, the Scots and the Picts began to encroach upon the territories of the Romanized British. It is unclear who ruled the island during these years or how it was defended; the Britons were left to their own devices, and tradition portrays them as hapless and virtually helpless. The traditional story, told among other places in the writing of a sixth-century Briton named Gildas, tells how the Britons turned to the Germanic peoples of continental Europe for assistance. The Angles, Saxons, and Jutes, Germanic tribes who occupied the coastal areas of what is now northwestern Germany and Denmark, were quite willing to work as soldiers for hire, but once they had established themselves in Britain as allies of the Britons, they began to demand land of their own, seized power from their employers, slaughtered and dispossessed them, and soon established themselves in the eastern parts of the island.

Contemporary archaeological evidence suggests, however, that the Germanic migrations actually took place in numerous waves from the later fourth century on. Relations between these Germanic invaders, who were probably not numerous, and the British are hard to reconstruct, but it appears that British culture was eventually supplanted not simply because the British were driven out. Many of them intermingled with their Germanic conquerors and adopted the dress, language, and culture of their new ruling class so that whatever their cultural heritage, they became, to later archaeologists and historians, indistinguishable from the Germanic Angles and Saxons. When the Romans had ruled, the Britons were Romanized; when the Saxons ruled, they were Saxonized. There are few words of British origin in Old English, the language of the Germanic invaders, and it is certainly significant that the Old English word *wealh* means both "slave" and "Welshman."

Whatever the reasons for its erosion, by around 600 CE a distinctively British culture was largely confined to Wales and Cornwall. On the continent a parallel series of events occurred, with groups of Franks pushing the Celtic peoples of Gaul to the geographical margin of Brittany. Although they had been marginalized geographically and politically, however, the Celtic peoples continued to exert a powerful shaping influence on what would become English literature. Their influence persisted even after the Norman Conquest, in the retelling of Irish and Welsh legends, in the survival of the genre of story known as the "Breton lay," and in the fragmentary memories of British kings and warlords who led a temporarily successful resistance against the Saxon invaders—stories that formed the kernel of truth at the heart of the legends of King Arthur, arguably the great political myth of the Middle Ages.

MIGRATION AND CONVERSION

The culture of the Angles, Saxons, and Jutes was quite different from that of the Romanized Britons. Though there is some evidence for continuing populations in Roman cities, the Germanic migrants were largely rural rather than urban, and built primarily in wood rather than stone—most of the great buildings of the Romans fell into ruin or were plundered for building materials. Society was apparently organized, at least during the migration period, around a male leader and warrior band rather than the hearth and family, or the city or state. If the characterization of the first century CE Roman historian Tacitus is to be believed, the continental Germanic tribes were a notably warlike culture: "they are not so easily persuaded to plow the earth and to wait for the year's produce as they are to challenge an enemy and earn the honor of wounds," Tacitus comments. "They actually think it tame and stupid to acquire by the sweat of toil what they might win by their blood." Certainly later centuries regarded the Germanic tribes as particularly fierce. The Angles and Saxons had a writing system—runic carvings—but no culture of literacy in which it might be put to more than the simplest uses. Their economy was based on barter and gift-exchange, not money. Perhaps most importantly, the Angles and Saxons were pagan, worshipping a pantheon of northern gods such as Woden and Thor, and as they came to dominate Britain so the influence of Christianity moved (with the Britons themselves) to the margins.

But Christianity did not disappear as Britain became England (from *engla-land*, the land of the Angles). When Pope Gregory the Great sent Augustine (now known as Augustine of Canterbury, not to be confused with the more famous Augustine, bishop of Hippo in north Africa) on a mission to convert the English in 597, he met with extraordinary early success, in part no doubt because Christianity already had a strong presence in Britain. King Æthelberht of Kent, for example, who was Augustine's first notable convert, was married to a Frankish Christian named Bertha. The expansion of English power over the west and southwest of the island undoubtedly brought many British Christians under English rule. Apart from any question of spiritual benefit, conversion to Christianity offered the appeal of new political alliances with other Christian kings, and the considerable power of Latin literacy, law, science, philosophy, and education. Nonetheless conversion was a significant cultural change, and the momentum of conversion wavered back and forth for a century or so, with large areas of resistance and a good deal of backsliding; Christianized England was not everywhere peaceful and prosperous or even thoroughly converted. By the beginning of the eighth century, however, the English were Christian enough to send missionaries like St. Boniface to preach the gospel to the pagan Saxons in Germany.

Alongside the Franks, the native British Christians, and the Roman missionaries, the Irish were busy in this period establishing monasteries in northern England. St. Columba founded the important monastery of Iona in Scotland in the mid-sixth century. This early insular monastic culture produced the extraordinary flourishing of Christian decorative art that finds its greatest expression in the Book of Kells. Tensions between the churches of the Roman mission and the idiosyncratic and relatively independent Irish churches were often high, but many of the most enduring Christian documents from the first centuries following the conversion of Britain, even those made in Northumbrian monasteries after the official rejection of the "Irish" model of Christianity at the Synod of Whitby (664), are manuscripts in the Celtic tradition.

One of the most remarkable of these is the Lindisfarne Gospels, mentioned above, dating from around 700. (A full-page illustration appears in the color pages in this volume.) Like the Book of Kells, this manuscript of the gospels is remarkable for the profusion and richness of its detailed illustrations; the motifs of intertwined lions of different colors, the zoomorphic shapes, and the sheer density of intricate detail of these gospel manuscripts make them central documents in the history both of Christian and of Celtic art. It would be misleading to mention the visually impressive Lindisfarne Gospels, however, without placing it in context with other manuscripts such as the Codex Amiatinus, a massive (75 lbs) copy of the Bible now in Florence. This manuscript, though visually more sedate than the Lindisfarne Gospels, contains a biblical text so closely similar to the original Latin translation of St. Jerome (known as the Vulgate Bible) that today it forms the basis for the scholarly reconstruction of Jerome's text. The Codex Amiatinus was made at the same time as the Lindisfarne Gospels, in the monastery of Wearmouth-Jarrow. While the Lindisfarne Gospels are a strong testimony to the Irish influence on Christian culture in England, the Codex Amiatinus is a powerful statement of Northumbrian monasticism's aspirations to pure *romanitas* as opposed to the provincial practices of the Irish and British. Between the

Page from the Gospel of St. Mark, Book of Kells (ninth century). The page size of the original is 9 ½ inches by 12 ½ inches. Like many early Insular manuscripts, the provenance of this book is uncertain. The monastery at Kells in County Meath, Ireland, was established by monks from the large monastery at Iona, off the coast of Scotland at the time of the Viking invasions early in the ninth century. Among the many hypotheses as to the book's origin are theories that the monks brought the book with them from Iona in its present (unfinished) state; that some work was done at Iona, some at Kells; and even that the book originated at Lindisfarne in the northeast of England. This uncertainty indicates the high degree of interaction among the monasteries of Ireland, Scotland, and northern England during this period.

shifting forces of these various traditions—the ideals of Roman orthodoxy, the influence of the Irish monasteries, the political pull of the Frankish world, and the remnants, however tattered, of the native British church—England became a Christian nation.

When the Northumbrian historian Bede wrote his *Ecclesiastical History of the English People* around 725, in fact, religion was the only unity the English had; political unity had to grow out of this unity of religious practice. Near the beginning of his history, Bede lists the various languages of Britain: "At the present time [i.e., the early 700s], there are five languages in Britain, English, British, Irish, Pictish, and Latin, just as the divine law is written in five books, each in its own way devoted to seeking out and setting forth one and the same knowledge of sublime truth and true sublimity. The Latin tongue, through the study of the Scriptures, has become common to all the rest." By "English" Bede refers to what we now call Old English; by "British" he means the Celtic language of the Britons, ancestor of modern Welsh. The fact that Bede counts Latin, the learned language of religion and science, among the languages of Britain, however, suggests that he is not speaking of cultures or ethnic divisions in the modern sense. His point is not so much anthropological as it is spiritual—Britain was the fortunate recipient of the unifying force of Latin Christianity—but it does remind us of the linguistic, cultural, and intellectual diversity to be found in Anglo-Saxon England.

The story that Bede recounts of the period from 597 to 700 is in some respects parallel to the story of Britain under Roman rule. As it had been under the Romans, the island became an outpost at the edge of an empire—in this case, however, an empire founded on religion rather than on secular power. Just as Roman administrators in Britain had reported to their superiors in Rome, so too the archbishops of Canterbury and of York (the two pre-eminent centers of Christianity in Britain, as ordained by Pope Gregory the Great) derived their authority from the pope in Rome; the Roman church had inherited many of the bureaucratic systems, and some of the universalizing aspirations, of the Roman Empire and the Pope assumed the role and name of *pontifex maximus* (from which he retains the modern title "Pontiff"), the sacerdotal aspect of imperial

power. England's was, to be sure, a missionary church, not always willing or able to follow the Roman church in all respects; the English church developed in a relationship, with varying degrees of tension and accommodation, between Christian conversion and secular Germanic culture, and from an early date the English church displayed distinctively local features. As a purely practical matter, too, communication was an enormous challenge in an era when a courier traveling across Europe on horseback could typically cover little more than thirty miles (fifty kilometers) per day. To send a message from London to Rome and receive a reply could thus be expected to take the better part of two months. And yet many people made the journey, and were expected to make it—the roads between England and Rome were familiar to bishops, pilgrims, penitents, monks, messengers, and merchants. Within Britain, too, transportation and communication—and thus any form of centralized control—were made problematic by purely logistical considerations.

It was also in accordance with the church's own inclinations to make some effort to preserve traditional culture and customs, reinvesting existing practices with a Christian meaning. Bede's *Ecclesiastical History* preserves a letter written by Pope Gregory to the Abbot Mellitus in 601, as the latter was going to join Augustine's mission in Britain; Gregory instructs him to tell Augustine that

the temples of the idols in that nation ought not to be destroyed; but let the idols that are in them be destroyed; let holy water be made and sprinkled in the said temples, let altars be erected, and relics placed. For if those temples are well built, it is requisite that they be converted from the worship of devils to the service of the true God; that the nation, seeing that their temples are not destroyed, may remove error from their hearts, and knowing and adoring the true God, may the more familiarly resort to the places to which they have been accustomed. And because they have been used to slaughter many oxen in the sacrifices to devils, some solemnity must be exchanged for them on this account, as that on the day of the dedication, or the nativities of the holy martyrs, whose relics are there deposited, they may build themselves huts of the boughs of trees, about those churches which have been turned to that use from temples, and celebrate the solemnity with religious feasting, and no more offer beasts to the Devil, but kill cattle to the praise of God in their eating, and return thanks to the Giver of all things for their sustenance; to the end that, whilst some gratifications are outwardly permitted them, they may the more easily consent to the inward consolations of the grace of God.

Gregory may not be entirely clear on the precise nature of English paganism—he seems to imagine England to be like Rome, with temples and priesthoods—but his strategy permits many sorts of accommodations of Christian practice to English culture, and *vice versa*. Doubtless this hastened the process of conversion; Bede himself, writing barely a century after the beginning of the Roman mission to England, does not seem to regard lingering paganism among the English as a contemporary problem worth mentioning. The old pagan gods of the north were abandoned along with pagan temples and rituals—though remnants of their importance persisted, as they do today in our days of the week: *Wednesday* is "Woden's day," *Thursday* is "Thor's Day," and so on. But the Anglo-Saxons managed to adopt the civilization offered by Christianity and at the same time adapt it to their own Germanic heritage. From the perspective of literary history, this policy of "cleansing the temples" fostered an amazing interpenetration of Germanic and Christian ideas; each is re-thought and revised in terms of the other, and it is impossible as well as inappropriate to separate "Christian" from "pagan" elements in the literature of the Anglo-Saxons. A longing for the heavenly home could be expressed in the tones of traditional elegy, Christ could be portrayed as a mighty warrior and his crucifixion as a heroic battle, and the pagan past could be depicted with regretful admiration and poignant sadness in a long poem like *Beowulf*.

Throughout this period monasteries were the most important outposts of Christian culture in England. The institutions of monasticism had their roots in the ascetic tradition of early Christianity, the belief that one could serve God best by living apart from the world in a state of constant prayer and self-denial. A monastery, as the concept developed in the third and fourth centuries CE,

was a place where ascetically minded Christians could live together, supporting one another in prayer and penitential practice while mitigating some of the harsher aspects of the solitary life. As monastic communities grew various rules were devised, some no more than collections of observations and advice. In the sixth century the *Rule* of St. Benedict outlined a clear and codified plan for the communal life, a plan that is still followed today in monastic communities around the world. The Benedictine rule—which, however rigorous it might seem to a modern reader, was meant to curb some of the ascetic extremes seen in Benedict's own time—was the foundation on which the great monastic establishments were built, where work, communal prayer, and study comprised the *Opus Dei* or "work of God," and which spread what Jean Leclercq has called "the love of learning and the desire for God" throughout early medieval Europe.

Many different rules and monastic orders developed throughout the Middle Ages; their practices differed from one order to another and one house to the next, but the general principles were constant. Monks were not usually ordained as priests, and had no pastoral responsibilities to minister to a congregation (though monasteries often did, especially in the early Middle Ages, provide pastoral care in areas without an established system of parishes). Monks were obliged to give up worldly wealth, their position in society, and their connections with family and friends so as to live in a community of individuals devoted to the same goals; at the same time, however, abbots were often from the same families as the secular rulers, and became powerful rulers and possessors of great wealth. Monastic communities always observed, at least in theory, a strict separation of the sexes, but the monastic life was open to women as much as to men; the English practice in the century before Bede was to have double monastic houses of monks and nuns, in almost all cases headed by an abbess such as the famous and noble Hild of Whitby. The monasteries, as the most important locus for intellectual activity and for the preservation and creation of cultural artifacts, became essential to the continuance of Latin culture, the practices of literacy, and the texts both of the church fathers and of classical authors, which were copied and read even as they were sometimes regarded with suspicion. Monastic culture flourished so vigorously in the north of England that one scholar has described Northumbria in the generations around 700 as a "veritable monastic Riviera."

INVASION AND UNIFICATION

This came to a dramatic end in the 790s with the first wave of invasions by the various Scandinavian peoples known to history as "Vikings," and organized monastic life in England seems to have fallen into a state of more or less complete disrepair in the course of the ninth century. (It would be restored in the later tenth century by the reformers Oswald, Dunstan, and Æthelwold; by this time, however, the centers of monastic culture were in Canterbury, Winchester, and Glastonbury rather than the far north, which was thoroughly Danish and in some places re-paganized.) Among the first targets of Viking attack were the holy island of Lindisfarne, which fell in 793, and Bede's monastery at Jarrow, which was destroyed in 794; the raids would continue on and off for two centuries. The Vikings were in many ways an extraordinary group of peoples. Whereas previous invaders such as the Angles, Saxons, and Jutes traveled relatively short distances, the Vikings constructed longships that proved capable of crossing the Atlantic; the remains of a Viking settlement at L'anse Aux Meadows in Newfoundland, dating from about 1000, are evidence that they traveled even to the New World. They established settlements in Iceland and Greenland, and settled in Ireland, Scotland, and Normandy as well as in England (the territory of Normandy takes its name from the "northmen"). The popular image of the Vikings is one of raiders who would arrive, plunder, and return to their homeland; in fact, Viking raids were followed in most areas by invasion and settlement, and gradually Viking groups were absorbed into local populations. For most of the tenth century Viking raids ceased; the former raiders had become farmers, and had begun to intermarry with Anglo-Saxons in a process of cultural and linguistic assimilation that continued through the eleventh century.

The ruins at Lindisfarne.

The Viking presence contributed significantly to the unification of the Anglo-Saxon kingdoms and the first stirrings of what might be called, for lack of a better term, national feeling, both in Scotland and in England. The centers of political power shifted southward, to Mercia in the eighth century and Wessex in the ninth; smaller kingdoms formed alliances and larger ones expanded their rule, until most of England was united under King Alfred the Great of Wessex, who reigned from 871 to 899. Alfred was able to raise a substantial army and stop the Vikings militarily; while the Vikings maintained control over the north and northeast of England, Alfred and his successors controlled most of the remainder of the country.

With peace secured, Alfred began promoting education and literary culture. What is of incalculable importance for the history of English literature is that he proposed to encourage the translation of Latin works into English and the cultivation of vernacular literacy. Alfred surrounded himself with a learned circle of advisors after the manner of the Frankish emperor Charlemagne (d. 814), and was himself literate in Latin—he translated several works from Latin, including Boethius's *Consolation of Philosophy*, though probably with a great deal of assistance from his advisors. He sets out the reasoning behind his policy of

English translation in the Preface to his translation of Gregory the Great's *Pastoral Care*—and it is significant that he announces his program of education and translation in a book on how to rule and govern:

> I recalled how the law was first composed in the Hebrew language, and thereafter, when the Greeks learned it, they translated it all into their own language, and all other books as well. And so too the Romans, after they had mastered them, translated them all through myriad interpreters into their own language.... Therefore it seemed better to me ... that we too should turn certain books which are the most necessary for all men to know into a language that we can all understand.

Alfred's educational program was designed primarily to help him govern, but one of its legacies is the relatively large quantity of literary, historical, legal, spiritual, and political writing in English (about 30,000 lines of poetry and about ten times as much prose) that has survived, almost all of it in manuscripts from the tenth and eleventh centuries. Under Alfred the *Anglo-Saxon Chronicle* was probably begun; to this year-by-year historical record we owe a great deal of our knowledge of the period.

The authority of even the most capable and ambitious rulers in the early Middle Ages was seldom able to survive long after their deaths. More often than not family feuding would undo much of what had been accomplished, as happened when fighting among Charlemagne's three sons led to the tripartite division of the Carolingian empire. Alfred had rather better luck with his descendants, who were able to consolidate his accomplishments and even extend them somewhat; his descendant Edgar (r. 959–75) commanded the allegiance of all of the most important English lords, had ties to the most important families on the Continent, and had in his control all senior church appointments. Under the weaker leadership of the next generation, however, in particular Æthelred II (r. 978–1016), and in the face of a renewed series of Viking attacks (dramatically depicted in the poetic *Battle of Maldon*, written some time after the actual battle in 991), the allegiance of the great lords and landholders to the king loosened, and the shameful decline of the English nobility described in the *Anglo-Saxon Chronicle* culminated in the Danish King Cnut (r. 1016–35) taking the English throne.

The end of the tenth century was by no means entirely a period of decline, however; it was also a time of such literary figures as the homilist and grammarian Ælfric, the archbishop Wulfstan, and the scholar Byrhtferth of Ramsey; during these years a number of *de luxe* decorated manuscripts were produced, and important works such as the *Rule* of St. Benedict and the Gospels were translated into English. It is a tribute to the strength of Alfred's reforms that much of the administrative, military, and church structures he had put into place survived the conquest of England by a Danish king—as, indeed, they would in part survive the conquest fifty years later by the Normans. That these conquests did not cause more destruction than they did must also be attributed in part to the fact that these invading cultures were far from alien to English culture. In the centuries between the early Viking invasions and the reign of Cnut, Christianity had reached Scandinavia; whereas the early Vikings had raided and destroyed monasteries, Cnut was a Christian who continued to support the monasteries much as Alfred and his descendants had done. Similarly, while the Vikings had conquered Normandy in the early tenth century, by the time the Normans invaded Britain in 1066, the Viking culture there had largely been assimilated to that of Christian France.

ENGLAND AFTER THE NORMAN CONQUEST

THE NORMANS AND FEUDALISM

The Norman Conquest of England in 1066 was the next in the long series of invasions and migrations—Celts, Romans, Angles, Saxons, Jutes, and Vikings—that have shaped English culture. That it has held a special place as a focal point in English history is no doubt partly due to its timing, almost exactly at the point where many scholars see larger forces creating a dividing line between the early and the later Middle Ages. French language and culture never threatened to extinguish the existing Anglo-Saxon culture and English

From the Bayeux Tapestry (late eleventh century). This object is actually an embroidered banner, around 20 inches high and 230 feet long, rather than a woven tapestry. It was probably created by English embroiderers, who were particularly skilled in this kind of work. This section of the tapestry shows the Norman ships landing at Pevensy, Sussex, 28 September; several ships have already landed on the beach, and horses are being unloaded from another ship that has just arrived. The text of the tapestry at this point (translated from the Latin) reads as follows: Here the horses are getting out of the ships. And here the soldiers [hurry to Hastings to seize supplies].

language, although they did exert enormous and lasting influence on them. The contrast with the Anglo-Saxon migrations is striking: these effectively and permanently imposed an English culture on Britain, while conquest by the Normans never permanently imposed French culture on England. But the Norman invasion helped to change Britain in fundamental ways—most obviously in language, but also in social and economic structure.

For all its far-reaching consequences, the invasion itself was a relatively modest affair. When Harold was crowned as king following the death of King Edward, the succession was disputed by William, Duke of Normandy, who settled the matter militarily; with a force probably numbering no more than 8,000, he crossed the channel, and had soon defeated and killed Harold in a day-long battle just outside Hastings. His victory brought England under the rule of a French-speaking king with substantial territorial claims in France, a situation that would persist for roughly the next three hundred years. Despite this obvious shift, and despite the triumphant narrative of the Bayeux tapestry (probably made within a generation of the battle for a Norman patron), the effects of the Conquest, particularly as it was viewed at close range rather than years later, apparently did not always loom so large. In

this connection it is interesting to compare the five different accounts in different manuscripts of the *Anglo-Saxon Chronicle* that have come down to us. At one extreme is the remarkably brief account of a scribe writing at Winchester in the manuscript known as the Parker MS: "In this year King Edward died and Earl Harold succeeded to the kingdom, and held it forty weeks and one day; and in this year William came and conquered England. And in this year Christ Church was built and a comet appeared on 18 April." By contrast, a scribe writing a generation or more later in Peterborough presents a much fuller account of how Harold was forced to fight a Norse invader in the north of the country before meeting William at Hastings, and conveys more of the immediate effects of William's conquest. Yet even here one has the sense that the death of a local abbot is regarded as being of almost as much importance as the Norman invasion:

And King Harold was informed [of the victory of a Norse King near the town of York], and he came with a very great force of English men and met him at Stamford Bridge, and killed him and Earl Tostig and valiantly overcame all the invaders. Meanwhile

Count William landed at Hastings on Michaelmas Day, and Harold came from the north and fought with him before all of the army had come and there he fell and his two brothers Gyrth and Leofwine; and William conquered this country, and came to Westminster, and Archbishop Aldred consecrated him king, and people paid taxes to him, and gave him hostages and afterwards bought their land. And Leofric, Abbot of Peterborough, was at that campaign and fell ill there, and came home and died soon after, on the Eve of All Saints. God have mercy on his soul. In his day there was every happiness and every good at Peterborough, and he was beloved by everyone, so that the King gave to Saint Peter and him the Abbacy of Burton and that of Coventry which Earl Leofric, who was his uncle, had built, and that of Crowland and that of Thorne. And he did much for the benefit of the monastery of Peterborough with gold and silver and vestments and land, more indeed than any before or after him.

Significant here is the mention of people paying taxes to William and "buying" their lands. William exacted tribute from the conquered both in the immediate aftermath of his invasion and on an ongoing basis, keeping as much as a fifth of English lands for himself and dividing much of the rest among members of his family and the barons who had supported him, who in turn maintained their own followers. While neither the lords nor the peasants of Anglo-Saxon England had held legal title to their land in quite the way that we conceive of it today, they had in practice exercised rights over that land similar to those that we would describe as the rights of ownership. Under the Normans, by contrast, nobles held the land that they occupied not on any permanent basis but as part of a system of exchange. The king granted land to a nobleman as a *fief*; in return for the right to its use the nobleman was obliged to perform services for the king, including making payments at various times and providing armed knights whenever the king might demand them. The nobleman, in his turn, would grant land—again, as a fief—to a knight, who in return would owe to the nobleman military service and other dues. The knight would typically retain a substantial portion of this land, and then divide the rest among the peasantry. There were

obligations in the other direction, as well: knights were obliged to provide protection for the peasantry, nobles for the knights, and the king for the nobles. The relationship at each level was, in theory at least, entirely voluntary and often publicly proclaimed, with the "vassal" (or holder of the fief) kneeling and promising homage and fealty to his lord, and a kiss between the two then sealing their mutual obligation.

The institution of this new system was marked in a unique way by William through the compilation of the Domesday Book, so-called in reference to the "Day of Judgment" at the end of the world, an extraordinary survey on a county-by-county basis of all the lands held by the king and by his vassals, recording all the obligations of the landholders. Without the sort of commitment to record keeping and enforcement that the Domesday Book represented (a commitment made possible, it must be said, by the underlying social order inherited from the Anglo-Saxons), the Normans might not have succeeded to such a great degree in imposing a new network of obligation on the conquered people. It must be noted, however, that the Domesday Book was seldom used to settle disputes or clarify owner-ship—the two functions for which, one might suppose, such a comprehensive census would be undertaken—in the first century of its existence. The eleventh-century ability to make records outpaced the development of a system in which to exploit them, and it would take some time before the mechanisms of government could make efficient use of such burdensome archives of documents. It has been argued that the Domesday Book, for all the impressive bureaucracy that brought it about, reflects a mistaken idea of the nature of written obligations: William may have imagined that the island of Britain could be granted to him by a written charter, like any other piece of land, and that recording the disposition of property and population would somehow fix them permanently in that state. But even if Domesday was more symbolic than useful, the imposition of feudal obligations was fairly thorough in England; the Anglo-Saxon nobles were quickly assimilated, dispossessed, or killed, leaving William in effective control of England. The Norman conquests of Wales and Scotland, however, were much slower and more piecemeal, and the Anglo-Norman kings never exercised very much control over Ireland.

The late eleventh century in England saw the arrival of the Jews as well as the French invaders. Christian disdain for moneylending—although there were certainly Christian usurers—and the exclusion of Jews from some other professions meant that they tended to become strongly associated with, and very important in, the financial workings of the kingdom. In the twelfth and thirteenth centuries, until their expulsion in 1290, they served at times as a financial last resort for the king; their relatively unprotected status as non-Christians made them vulnerable to much more severe forms of taxation and the abrogation of debts incurred by Christians but never repaid. Another important development of the later eleventh century, which would become much more central to civic life in the late Middle Ages, was the rise of guilds—initially merchant guilds that exercised a monopoly over the trade in a particular area, but later craft guilds that established regulations allowing them to control who could practice a given craft and that offered social and financial support to their members, as well as regulating the quality of production. While guilds and confraternities of some description, often purely religious in orientation, had existed since perhaps the seventh century, they became increasingly important in the course of the twelfth and thirteenth centuries, particularly in England, and their rise coincided with the growth of urban centers and of new forms of religious devotion.

Henry II and an International Culture

If William was the key figure in establishing Norman and feudal rule in England, his great-grandson Henry II (r. 1154–89) was the key figure in its preservation and extension through the later Middle Ages. Henry's coming to the throne in 1154 brought to an end almost twenty years of civil war under the disputed kingship of Stephen, in the course of which barons and church leaders had taken advantage of the collapse of royal authority to expand local powers. Many of them began to encroach on land claimed by the crown, and to build private castles to protect their domains. Henry put a stop to these practices, taking back the lands, tearing down the castles, and reorganizing royal authority in a fashion that was increasingly supported by standardized records and documents. Central authority over legal matters, which had previously been largely restricted to capital cases, was now extended to legal matters of all sorts; the first legal textbook was composed in Henry's reign. The expansion of the crown's legal control came in part at the expense of the church, and provoked one of the most famous incidents of Henry's reign, his clash with Thomas Becket (1118–70), Archbishop of Canterbury, who wanted the clergy to retain their right to be tried in church courts independent of the secular legal system. The Archbishop was subsequently murdered, allegedly on the orders of Henry, an event that exercised a tremendous hold on the contemporary imagination. As John of Salisbury tells the story (in the earliest surviving account of the murder, written in 1171), Becket was standing before the altar when the knights who had come in pursuit of him arrived and told him that it was his time to die. John writes:

> Steadfast in speech as in spirit, he replied: "I am prepared to die for my God, to preserve justice and my church's liberty. But if you seek my head, I forbid you on behalf of God almighty and on pain of anathema to do any hurt to any other man, monk, clerk or layman, of high or low degree. ... I embrace death readily, so long as peace and liberty for the Church follow from the shedding of my blood." ...
> He spoke, and saw that the assassins had drawn their swords; and bowed his head like one in prayer. His last words were "To God and St. Mary and the saints who protect and defend this church, and to the blessed Denis, I commend myself and the church's cause." ... A son's affection forbids me to describe each blow the savage assassins struck, spurning all fear of God, forgetful of all fealty and any human feeling. They defiled the cathedral and the holy season with a bishop's blood and with slaughter.

It remains unclear whether or not Henry ordered Becket's murder. What is clear is that the outcry was so great that Henry was forced to perform public penance—and to accept that the church would, to some extent, remain outside the realm of royal authority. Becket's martyrdom created the Canterbury shrine that was the goal of Chaucer's pilgrims, among many others.

Plan for Canterbury Cathedral, c. 1160.

Canterbury Cathedral, the seat of the Archbishop of Canterbury, head of the English Church, is a kind of time capsule of Christianity in Britain since Anglo-Saxon times. The earliest church known to have stood on this site was that of St. Augustine of Canterbury, who arrived as a missionary in 597 CE; traces of this building are believed to lie beneath the current structure. An Anglo-Saxon church was built over that of Augustine in the ninth or tenth century; it was destroyed by fire in 1067 and rebuilt by the Normans shortly afterward, and this construction still forms the basic fabric of the existing church, although it was modified and decorated further in the succeeding centuries. The plan shows the extensive monastic buildings as well as the cathedral itself. The lines shown connecting the buildings represent the plumbing system. At the top left the vineyard and orchard are indicated. The murder of St. Thomas Becket, then Archbishop, on the Cathedral's altar, made Canterbury a major pilgrimage shrine.

Durham Cathedral, begun in 1093, is regarded as one of the finest examples of Norman architecture in Europe; this style, a form of the Romanesque, is characterized by round arches (as here, along the sides of the nave) and vast but relatively spare interiors. Durham also displays some features (such as the pointed vaulting) that came to characterize the Gothic style of many later cathedrals.

Lincoln Cathedral, Galilee Porch.

Begun in 1072 and substantially rebuilt in the late twelfth and early thirteenth centuries, Lincoln Cathedral shows some of the classic features of both Romanesque and Gothic architecture. The Gothic Galilee Porch dates from c. 1230.

Salisbury Cathedral (thirteenth century). With a spire of 404 feet, this was until the 1960s the tallest building in England. It is a classic example of the high Gothic style, with its pointed arches, flying buttresses to support a higher vault, and greater intricacy of design, including decorative features such as exterior sculpture and stained glass windows.

If Henry's extension of the power of the English throne throughout the realm were unprecedented—though not, as the example of Becket suggests, entirely unopposed—so too was his extension of that power beyond the British Isles. Like previous Anglo-Norman monarchs, Henry controlled much of what is now northern France as well as England. With his marriage to Eleanor of Aquitaine in 1152 he had acquired control of much of southern France; he also exerted control over most of Scotland and Wales and in 1171 he invaded and took control of Ireland, where he quickly imposed the same feudal structures and judicial system on the Irish people as he had on the English. Despite England's political control over Ireland—which itself was of varying strength over the next centuries—there was relatively little cultural assimilation, and the English nobles ruling in Ireland formed to a large extent a self-contained enclave. Like Scotland and Wales, with which it formed intermittent alliances, Ireland throughout this period pursued its own political strategies in the British Isles and on the continent. And despite the efforts of Henry and the kings who followed him, the English presence in France was far less enduring than its presence in Ireland. By 1453, at the close of the Hundred Years' War between France and England, the port town of Calais was the only remnant of English control over France.

Henry II and Eleanor of Aquitaine sailing across the English Channel. Detail of illustration from Matthew Paris, *Historia Major* (c. 1240). The king and queen made the crossing many times as they traveled between their French and English kingdoms.

The period around the Norman Conquest also coincided with important developments in learned culture. England had produced outstanding scholars at various points in the early Middle Ages—among them Bede, the Latin poet Aldhelm, Ælfric, Byrhtferth, and most famously Alcuin of York, a monk of York who became master of Charlemagne's palace school—and in the eleventh century was home to the illustrious Anselm of Bec (1033–1109), one of the founders of scholastic thought, whose career demonstrates the international culture of the church and the schools, both of which used Latin, an international language. Born in Italy, Anselm became abbot of a monastery in Normandy, and was eventually appointed Archbishop of Canterbury —the leading church position in England. His development of the ontological argument for the existence of God in his *Why God Became Man* (excerpted in this volume) is a good example of scholastic ways of thinking, proceeding on the basis of deductive logic to new theological conclusions. While there were outstanding individual thinkers at this time, however, the universities were still in their infancy; in most of Europe, schools had existed for the most part only in association with cathedrals or monasteries and their chief purpose was to provide training for clerics. In the wake of monastic and ecclesiastical reform in the tenth and eleventh centuries, these schools began to expand their curricula to provide a more highly educated clergy at all levels. Already by the end of the eleventh century there was some form of instruction taking place at Oxford, and by the end of the twelfth century it was a substantial enough center of learning to have attracted its first foreign student, and to benefit when Henry II forbade English scholars to study at the university of Paris. The university of Bologna was also already in existence at this time, and these three were soon followed by others across Europe.

The British Isles in the twelfth century also saw the rise of new modes of historical writing, including works such as William of Malmesbury's *Gesta Regum Anglorum* or "Deeds of the English Kings," Henry of Huntingdon's *Chronicle*, and Geoffrey of Monmouth's *Historia Regum Britanniae* or "History of the Kings of Britain." These writers' approach to history emphasized, as their titles suggest, the deeds of kings and the rise and fall of nations; in this they departed from predecessors more interested in depicting the Christian framework of history. The period also illustrates the political uses of literature. While Henry II—unlike, for example, King Alfred—is not particularly remembered for his own literary activities, numerous works in Anglo-Norman are associated with him as a patron or dedicatee, and his desire to solidify and extend his claims on both French and English lands was one of the things that made him an important figure for literary history. Henry and his descendants are known as the Angevin (or Plantagenet) kings, a reference to Henry's father, Geoffrey "Plantagenet" of Anjou, and this designation accurately represents their ongoing political and cultural interest in France. Henry's reign saw the production and wide dissemination of numerous literary and historical works that proved foundational for British literature, especially the development of the Arthurian legend.

Geoffrey of Monmouth's *History*, completed around 1139, offers an account of the history of the realm going back to its mythical Trojan founder, Brutus (from whom the name Britain supposedly derived), and provided the foundation for the Arthurian stories of the later Middle Ages. Henry II, the descendant of Normans who, like the mythical British under Arthur, had battled the Saxons for control of Britain, was only the first in a long line of kings to find this legend, with its potential to offer an authoritative and legitimizing history, an appealing subject; Arthur's imperial ambitions, as told in this version of the tale, also offered a supposed historical precedent for English claims to rule on the continent.[1] Geoffrey's *History* was popular throughout Europe, and in the British Isles alone was translated into Middle Welsh, Anglo-Norman, and Middle English. The Anglo-Norman version *Brut*, by the poet Wace, was dedicated to Henry's queen, Eleanor of Aquitaine, a further suggestion of the story's royal allure. Later in the century, French authors—most notably Chrétien de Troyes (c. 1150–90)—inserted into the legendary history of Arthur episodes that focused on

the individual achievements of knights and on romantic (sometimes adulterous) love, creating a considerably greater role for female characters. Their works took their name from the language in which they were written, *roman* (French, from which we derive the modern literary term *romance* as well as the name for the *romance* languages), as opposed to Latin a choice that reflected the growing audience for vernacular poetry in the European courts.

A form closely related to the romance, and also written in the vernacular, was the Breton lay, a short narrative with, usually, a significant element of the marvelous and a central emphasis on a romantic relationship rather than large-scale political or military events. The lays' emphasis on the supernatural, which is often attributed to their origin in the Celtic culture of Brittany, is reminiscent at times of the early-twelfth-century prose tales of the *Mabinogi* from medieval Wales—which also, however, show notable chivalric and courtly features. By far the most famous medieval lays are those by an Anglo-Norman author who calls herself simply "Marie" and who apparently wrote in England in Henry's time; her twelve short tales—two of which are set in the world of Arthurian legend—offer a particularly careful attention to women's role in the conflicts of loyalty that often characterize romance narratives, and are one of the relatively few medieval works by a named female author, the Marie who wrote the lays is usually identified with the "Marie de France" who composed a collection of fables and an account of a knight's visionary journey to purgatory. Romance and the lays took some time to make their way into English; Layamon translated Wace's *Brut* into English around the turn of the thirteenth century, but most Middle English romances date from the late-thirteenth and fourteenth centuries, probably reflecting the linguistic tendencies of their primary audience, the French-speaking nobility, before the fourteenth century.

As had happened centuries earlier in the wake of Alfred's rule, royal authority was scaled back under Henry's successors, who included two of his sons: first Richard I (the Lionheart), who ruled from 1189 to 1199, and then John, who ruled until 1216. In order to raise money in his struggle against Phillip II of France for territory on the continent, John imposed extra-

---

[1] *Arthur's imperial ... continent*   Although the Normans may have liked to associate themselves with the British side in the Arthurian legends, Welsh poets of the time, whose culture was the more direct descendant of the early British, cast the Normans in the role of the despised English.

ordinary taxes on English barons and other nobles; the barons rebelled and forced the king to sign a document setting out the rights and obligations both of the nobles and of the king himself, and making explicit that the king was not to contravene these customary arrangements without consulting the barons. The document also reaffirmed the freedom of the English church, particularly the freedom from royal interference in the election of bishops or other officeholders. Under this "great charter" or Magna Carta, the power of the king was for the first time limited by the terms of a written document.

THE THIRTEENTH CENTURY

1215 was a momentous year in medieval Europe. In addition to the signing of Magna Carta—whose ultimately far-reaching effects were at the time felt only in England—this year witnessed the Fourth Lateran Council, a major gathering of church leaders under the guidance of the energetic Pope Innocent III. Lateran IV represented an extraordinarily far-reaching attempt to unify Christian practice and raise standards of Christian observance. The Canons of the Council covered almost all aspects of Christian life, and their effects on both religious practice and religious instruction resounded through the rest of the Middle Ages. Christians from now on were required to confess their sins formally and receive Communion at least once a year, and the sacrament of the altar was officially declared to involve transubstantiation, meaning that the body and blood of Christ were actually present in, rather than merely represented by, the bread and wine consecrated at the Mass (a doctrine that became a matter of serious dispute, however, in later medieval England). A new network of regulation was put into place to govern marriages, with secret marriages prohibited and marriage itself declared a sacrament.

Associated with the increased emphasis on the importance of priests administering sacraments to the faithful were increased efforts to ensure that members of the clergy were educated and competent; one of the canons involved the maintenance of cathedral schools free to clerics. Bishops were required to preach in their dioceses or ensure that there were others who could do

so in their stead, and clergy were forcefully reminded of the requirement of clerical celibacy. Individual Christians, for their part, were expected to be able to recite a small number of prayers, but there was no thought of encouraging widespread education of a sort that would enable the populace to read the word of God on their own. On the contrary, it was considered important to keep the Bible at a remove from the common people so that it could be safely interpreted to them through church intermediaries. The controversy that later developed over this issue would extend over several centuries and become a crucial concern for the Lollard or Wycliffite sect in fourteenth- and fifteenth-century England, as well as a central distinguishing point between the Roman Catholic Church and the various Protestant faiths in the Reformation.

As this suggests, the reforms of the Fourth Lateran Council aimed to strengthen the Christian community, but with a new emphasis on differentiating, excluding, and penalizing unorthodox believers and non-Christians. The canons include extensive commentary on the need to control and excommunicate heretics; they require Jews and "Saracens" (Muslims) to wear distinctive clothing lest they be mistaken for Christians; they prohibit Jews from holding public office, and make provisions to encourage crusading against Muslim control of the Holy Land. The English joined whole-heartedly in the Crusades and the restrictions placed on Jews. There had been massacres of Jews, particularly at York, already in the late twelfth century; expulsions from various cities by the local lords became widespread as early as the 1230s; and in 1290 Edward I expelled all Jews from England. It is not surprising, in view of this, that anti-Jewish miracle stories became popular across Europe during this period; Chaucer's *Prioress's Tale* is a later example of this genre. Heresy remained a concern throughout Europe, although in this period the persecutions were more severe in France and other parts of the continent than in England.

The Fourth Lateran Council was in part a response to increased lay devotion and interest in religion, which offered a challenge to the sometimes inadequate pastoral care provided by the clergy. In the early thirteenth century, for example, the records of the Bishop of Winchester show numerous priests being forced to declare that they will learn the Creed, the Ten Commandments, the Seven Deadly Sins, and various other basic Christian doctrines within the space of a year, or pay a fine of forty shillings, a far from unusual instance which suggests that their preparation was not all that could have been wished. We may note, however, that some of the greatest works of Middle English religious literature survive in a closely related group of texts from around this same time: the *Ancrene Riwle* (Rule for Anchoresses) and the saints' lives and other spiritual-guidance texts that accompany it in the manuscripts testify to the presence of learned and committed religious men and women in early thirteenth-century England.

The new religious movements that arose in the course of the twelfth and thirteenth centuries—movements often instigated by the laity—were in some cases accepted by the church, though others were declared heretical; the growth in such movements was so great that the Council decreed that no new religious orders could be instituted after 1215, a decree that was largely observed. Among the new groups, the most significant, particularly for literary history, were the fraternal orders or friars (terms that derive from the Latin and French words for "brother"): the Augustinian hermits, Carmelites, and, especially, Dominicans and Franciscans. Like the monks of the early church, the members of these new movements embraced poverty and learning. Unlike previous monks of any era, however, they devoted themselves to carrying religion directly to the people, rather than living an enclosed life; their aim was to pursue the "vita apostolica," the way of life of the Apostles. Founded in the first part of the thirteenth century, they spread with great rapidity, and had a substantial presence in the British Isles by around 1250.

The friars' considerable success and speedy growth derived in no small part from their practice of preaching and establishing foundations in urban centers. The tremendous growth in the European economy from the eleventh century onward had fostered the development of ever-larger towns and cities. Urban growth in turn made possible an increasing specialization of labor that is reflected in the rise of craft guilds and, in another sense, in the friars themselves. The religious and civic cultures that each represented were deeply entwined. Guilds, which by this time were at the center of civic

life, had patron saints and made religious fellowship a central part of their collective identities; their later sponsorship of the great cycle plays of the fourteenth to sixteenth centuries was a natural outgrowth of this melding. And although St Francis, the founder of the Franciscans, had entirely rejected his merchant background upon his conversion, the preachers of his order and the others found the towns, with their concentrated populations and alleged moral turpitude, an ideal place for their work.

Builders at work. Detail of illustration to Matthew Paris, *Historia Major* (c. 1240). Matthew Paris, a monk at the famous Benedictine Abbey of St. Alban's, near London, took over the chronicle kept by his abbey in 1235 and continued it until his death in 1259. He is one of the liveliest sources for all kinds of information on the mid-thirteenth century, and was among those who commented (with some disapproval) on the spread of the friars and, among other things, their extensive building projects as their orders grew ever larger.

Ornamental belt buckle (early 7ᵗʰ century CE) from the Sutton Hoo burial site. Twentieth century excavations at Sutton Hoo in southeast England uncovered a remarkable collection of artifacts from an Anglo-Saxon ship-burial. In addition to this buckle, 40 other gold objects were discovered in the burial mound, together with human remains, the bones of horses, weaponry, silverware, and the remains of large open ships.

CHI-RHO page from the Lindisfarne Gospels (c. 698 CE). See the introduction for a discussion of this page.

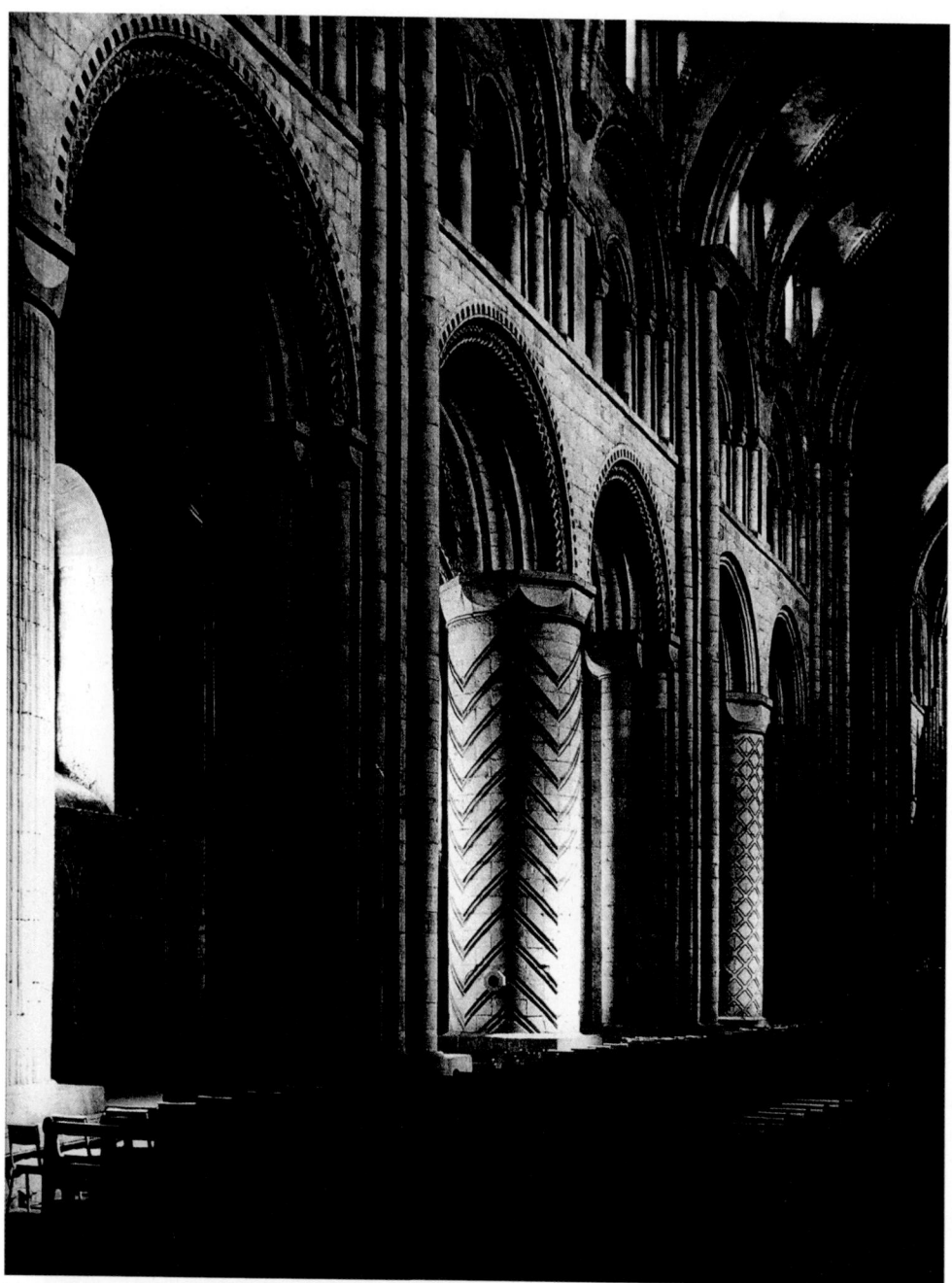

Nave, Durham Cathedral (1093–1133). One of the largest and most imposing of English cathedrals, Durham was built by Norman bishops over a remarkably short period. A shrine for Saint Cuthbert, it also houses the bones of the Venerable Bede.

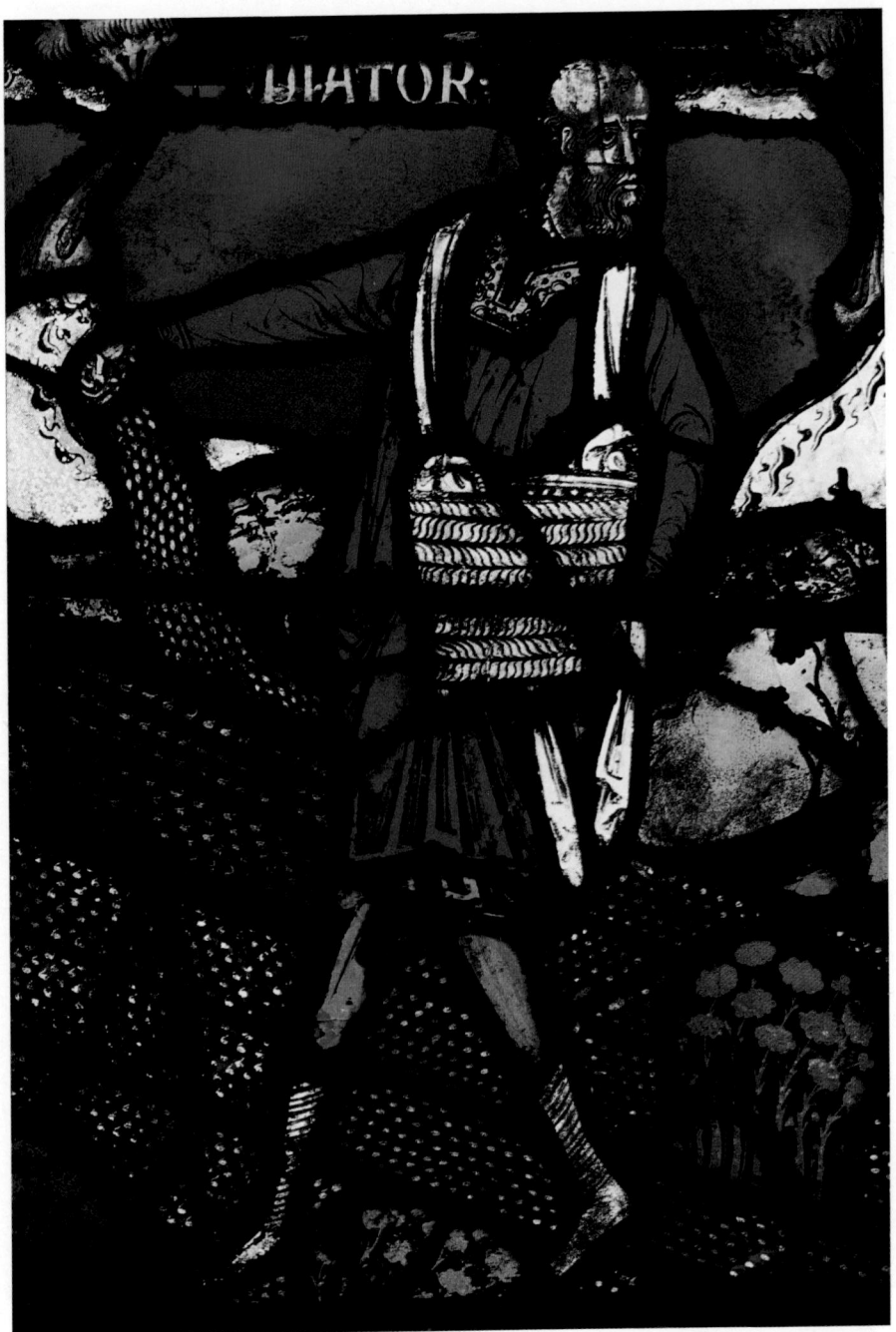

"The Parable of the Sower" (detail), stained glass, Canterbury Cathedral (early 13ᵗʰ century). The extensive use of stained glass in church architecture began in the twelfth century; when Abbot Suger of Saint-Denis in France rebuilt sections of his church c. 1135. He commissioned stained glass windows, the light from which he believed would assist worshipers to raise themselves to "the purity of heaven."

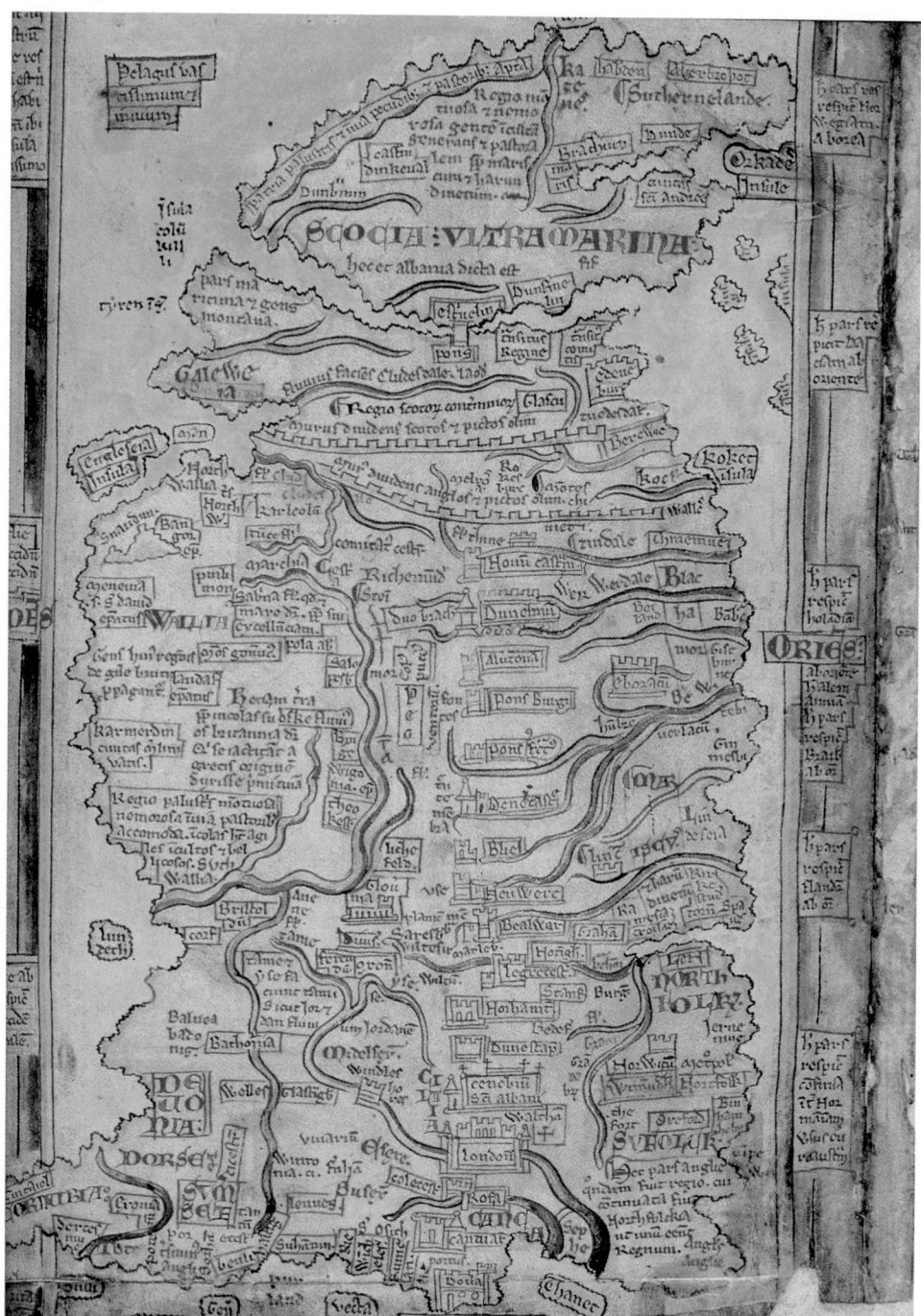

Map of Britain (c. 1250), drawn by Matthew Paris for his history of England, *Historia Major*. As well as counties and major towns, Matthew identifies features such as Hadrian's Wall, noting that it "once divided the English and the Picts."

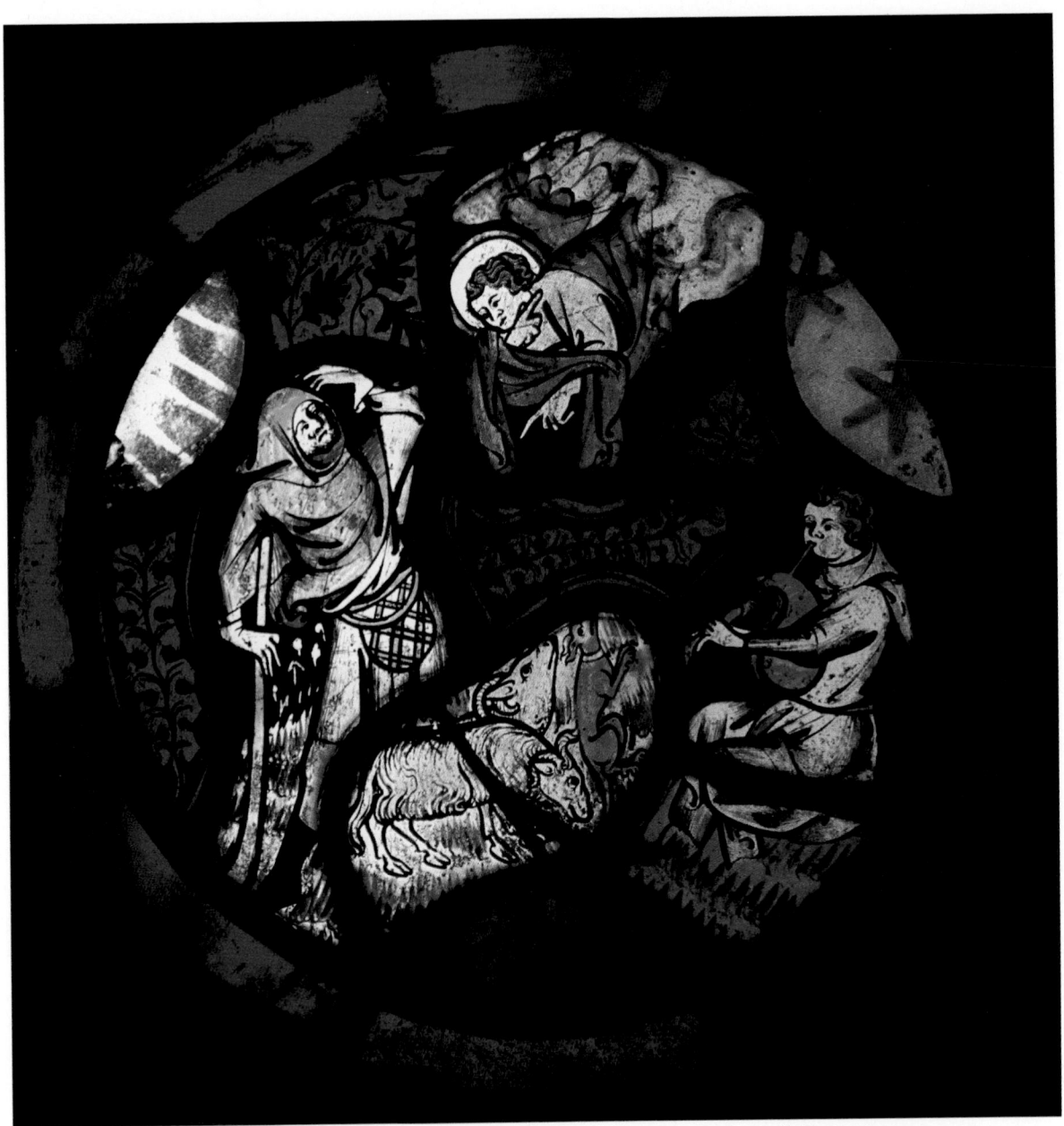

"Annunciation to the Shepherds," stained glass (later 14ᵗʰ century), Victoria and Albert Museum.

"Virgin and Child," stained glass (14th century),
Eaton Bishop Church, Herefordshire.

"Sir James Berners," stained glass (later 14th century), St. Mary's
Church, West Horseley, Surrey. This knight, who was beheaded
in 1388, is shown here wearing armor typical of the period.

Opening page of the Prologue to *The Wife of Bath's Tale*, Ellesmere manuscript.
(This item is reproduced by permission of the *Huntington Library*, San Marino, California. EL26C9F72r.)

In the British Isles as elsewhere, the friars proved popular and controversial in almost equal measure; a fierce critique of them by the Irish bishop Richard FitzRalph (c. 1299–1360) survives in over seventy manuscripts from every part of Europe, and their influence at the University of Paris in the mid-thirteenth century so infuriated the other clerics there that the pope had to intervene. Their preaching was widely admired, however, perhaps especially by lay audiences, and while they quickly became part of the church and university hierarchies, they also claimed a particular affinity for pastoral work. Their mission thus promoted the translation and dissemination of religious teaching among the laity, and their energy in this activity made their writings an important influence on the development of literature in the vernacular languages of Europe, including England. Their emergence and quick expansion both coincided with and furthered the rise of lay involvement in religious life, whether this took the form of pilgrimage, of spiritual reading or writing, of attendance at sermons and church services, or of devotion to saints' cults, particularly that of the Virgin Mary. Nor were the friars the only force for increased religious education; English churchmen were particularly active in their response to the canons of the Fourth Lateran Council, and many works of spiritual instruction for the clergy or the laity, in Latin, Anglo-Norman, or English, attempted to disseminate the basic tenets of the faith. The *Speculum Confessionis* usually attributed to the learned Robert Grosseteste (c. 1170–1253), bishop of Lincoln, is one example of the new works that responded to the requirement of yearly confession; another is the Anglo-Norman *Manuel des Pechiez* (c. 1270), the source for Robert Mannyng's *Handlyng Synne* (1303), which aimed to give laypeople the knowledge they needed to live in accordance with Christian teaching. Just as the influence of the French aristocracy after the Norman Conquest brought French language and literature into the realm of English literary history, so the broader emphasis on basic Christian instruction in the thirteenth century and beyond made Latin works and church teachings increasingly available to vernacular audiences.

The growing lay participation in religion is reflected in the growth of certain characteristic literary genres.

The *exemplum*, or illustrative short story, most famously characteristic of medieval sermons, often provided a narrative argument for avoiding particular sins or emulating certain virtues; the closely related form of the *miraculum*, or miracle story, aimed to impress the reader or hearer with a sense of wonder. In the later Middle Ages *exempla* and other short narratives were often especially associated with the preaching of the friars; such stories were thought to be appealing to laypeople, who might need help with the fine points of doctrine and would find narrative more accessible. These tales were sometimes criticized for being more entertaining than instructive, and indeed are not always very different from the genres of fable or fabliau—the latter being a "funny short story in verse," often dealing with sexual or economic deception and valuing cleverness over morality. Popular in French, fabliaux are essentially non-existent in (written) English until Chaucer, whose *Miller's, Reeve's,* and *Shipman's Tales,* among others, are based on this genre.

Saints' lives, another widely popular literary form, are also one of the oldest genres in English literature; the Old English *Martyrology* of the ninth century is a particularly comprehensive example, but some of the earliest texts in Middle English are the lives of three virgin martyrs (Juliana, Katherine, and Margaret), all dating from the early thirteenth century. Intriguingly, lives of women martyrs of the early church were extremely popular in late-medieval England; Chaucer's *Second Nun's Tale,* which recounts the life of St. Cecilia, is another well-known (later) example. As with the Bible, even texts that do not center on the life or deeds of a saint may invoke the saints or briefly recount their miracles; they were part of the common knowledge of the time, and widely represented in art. Saints were regarded as protectors and intercessors, and the retelling of their lives was part of the effort to promote their cults and gain their assistance; their stories could provide points of contact with the sacred, particularly since they came from many walks of life.

The growing attention to pastoral care further stimulated the need for clerical education, and the worldly duties of the clergy—from the care of souls (including the writing of sermons) to administration of lands or finances—made studies in logic, rhetoric, and other subjects beyond theology or canon law an important part of their training. At the same time, contact with Arab scholars made both Arabic learning and the writings of classical philosophers—Aristotle most influential among them—newly available in western Europe. The need to assimilate these traditions and bring them into accord with Christian teaching fostered the development of the scholastic method, or scholasticism, which gathered the evidence of various authorities and worked to synthesize it, usually by means of a debate form, into a single coherent authority. The structure of university study was quite different from its modern descendant, though not unrecognizably so. A student would first study the seven liberal arts, around which higher education was organized throughout the later Middle Ages: grammar, rhetoric, and logic (or dialectic), collectively known as the trivium, and arithmetic, music, astronomy and geometry, called the quadrivium. Students who wished to continue could pursue further studies in theology, medicine, or law—roughly the equivalent of modern graduate schools.

Despite the intellectual flowering of the eleventh to thirteenth centuries, education remained in essence a luxury for most of the population. Not only laborers, but many of the nobility and even some of the clergy never learned to read, although the widespread practice of reading or reciting aloud—both secular and religious works—and of course the experience of hearing sermons meant that those who could not read were not cut off from literate culture. Our own inevitable focus on the written sources that survive should not blind us to the ways in which those who could not themselves read or write still had considerable access to the great narratives and images of their culture.

THE ENGLISH MONARCHY

The religious and cultural energy of the thirteenth century in England was not particularly reflected in its monarchs; the period's important political developments tended to arise, as we have seen in the case of John and Magna Carta, from limitations on the king's power rather than, as with William the Conqueror or Henry II, his exercise of that power. The reign of John's son

Henry III (1216–72) was long but not particularly successful; he came to the throne as a child and by the end of his reign his son held effective power. Under his rule the monarchy lost ground to both external and internal forces. The French dauphin Louis controlled the southern part of England upon Henry's accession, but was expelled in 1217; later in the century, however, Henry had to sell most of his French possessions to pay war debts, and the English barons continually challenged the king's authority, culminating in his effective deposition in 1264–65 by the forces led by the baron Simon de Montfort, who as regent convened a kind of proto-Parliament. Simon's death in 1265 at the hands of Henry's troops made him a martyr to many of the English, and both praise-poems and laments in his honor survive from the period. The most significant legacy of the barons' increased power was the consolidation of the principle of the king's limited rulership and the idea that the people of the realm (primarily the nobility) should take some part in its governance. The losses of French territory had contributed to a growing tendency for the ruling inhabitants of England to regard themselves as *English* (rather than Norman, Angevin, French, and so on); the broader participation in government in the course of the century may have solidified this tendency. By the early fourteenth century language could be seen as a unifying force in the nation: "both the learned and unlearned man who were born in England can understand English," asserts one commentator of the period.

Henry's son Edward I, a much more successful ruler than his father, managed to mend the relationship between monarchy and people, in part by strengthening administrative structures related to law (Chancery), finances (the Exchequer), and governance (the Council); in this he built on the legacy of Henry II and the achievements of the baronial challenge, and the meetings of his Council were the first to bear the name of Parliaments. He also conquered Wales, which never fully regained its independence, although resistance to English rule continued. Like other English monarchs, however, he was unable to gain much control over Ireland, and despite diplomatic and military attempts, he never managed to conquer Scotland, which remained officially independent of England until the eighteenth century. A significant outcome of the ongoing English-Scots conflict was the growth of a sense of national identity among the Scots at least as marked as that among the English; we see this in the declaration of Arbroath (1320), sent to the pope by the nobles of Scotland as a group, in which they declared that they were speaking for "the community of the realm" and that "for so long as one hundred men remain alive, we shall never under any conditions submit to the domination of the English." Edward's attempts to subdue Scotland demonstrated once more the political usefulness of legendary history: in putting forward the English claim on Scottish territory, he made reference to the historical assertions of Layamon's *Brut*, the Middle English translation of the legends gathered in Geoffrey of Monmouth's *History of the Kings of Britain*.

The strong, if sometimes brutal, kingship of Edward I contrasts sharply with the troubled rule of his son Edward II (1307–27), who was frequently at odds with his nobles and eventually was deposed by his French queen, Isabella, and her lover, Roger Mortimer, an English baron. Edward was succeeded by his son Edward III (1327–77), whose long reign provided a certain stability but involved considerable losses for England. Edward III forcefully reasserted his claims to French territory through his French mother, and began the long-lasting conflict that came to be known as the Hundred Years' War (1337–1453). This conflict displayed the ongoing contradictoriness of medieval English attitudes toward France: Edward's embrace of a French-derived chivalric culture and claim to the French throne tended to link the nobility of both countries, who exchanged hostages and diplomatic missions, while at the same time the battles provided a focus for anti-French sentiment (which went back to the Norman Conquest) and for renewed claims for English as a valued national language. This was not, of course, a sudden development; already in the thirteenth century a writer could assert that "common men know no French, among a hundred scarcely one," and similar claims become increasingly common in the fourteenth century. Despite considerable early success in the war, meanwhile, England's French holdings dwindled almost to nothing by the time of Edward III's death, and his continuing demand for funds to pursue his military projects put considerable strain on the economy, already weakened by the northern European famine of 1315–18.

Even more significant than the famine was the great plague of 1348–49, the "Black Death," which had a lasting impact on the demography, the economy, and ultimately the culture of Britain and of Europe more generally. It is believed that roughly one-third of western Europe's population died in the plague, though not evenly across all areas; the population of London is estimated to have fallen by almost half, from perhaps 70,000 to about 40,000. In the wake of the plague, there was—not surprisingly—a severe labor shortage; this facilitated a certain amount of social mobility as people were able to take higher-paying work, and the countryside suffered further depopulation as laborers left for the towns. Some employers competed for scarce labor by improving wages or conditions of labor, but the Statute of Laborers of 1351 officially restricted both wages and labor mobility; it became a cause of long-standing friction between the working population of England and its large landholders. Some of that tension found violent expression early in the reign of Edward's successor, his grandson Richard II (r. 1377–99) who inherited the throne at the age of only ten. (His father, the Black Prince, had died in 1376.) Severe taxation and limits on wages imposed in the wake of the Black Death caused considerable distress among the general populace, and helped to spark the Rising of 1381 (at which time the kingdom was still under the regency of John of Gaunt, Richard's uncle), in which groups from all over the country challenged the legislative and fiscal policies of the nobility, although they declared their allegiance to King Richard. While this uprising was easily quelled, it was a tremendous shock to the political and cultural establishment and foreshadowed the struggles for legitimacy that continued throughout the early fifteenth century; it also left behind an unusually rich record of non-nobles' views on the political economy of their day. The general unrest, exacerbated by Richard's autocratic style and struggles with his nobles for control of the country, made the last quarter of the fourteenth century a politically fragile time in England. The king's preference for his own favorites over other, more powerful lords led these "Lords Appellant," as they called themselves, to challenge his authority. Eventually, they succeeded in severely circumscribing his power—and, in 1388, in executing several of his closest advisors. A major source of the conflict between these lords and the king was Richard's desire to make peace with France; the king did eventually succeed in instituting a truce in 1396 through his marriage to the French princess Isabella (his beloved first wife, Anne of Bohemia, had died in 1394). In his later years he regained much of his control, in part through the help of his uncle John of Gaunt, but became increasingly despotic and took harsh revenge on the lords who had threatened his power. The contest culminated in the usurpation of the throne in 1399 by the Lancastrian Henry Bolingbroke (Henry IV), who had earlier been banished from the kingdom; Henry took advantage of Richard's absence in Ireland, where he was continuing his fruitless efforts to bring it under English control. Richard was later murdered in prison, echoing the fate of his deposed great-grandfather, Edward II.

CULTURAL EXPRESSION IN THE FOURTEENTH CENTURY

Richard's rulership may not have been a great success, but he is known, like Henry II, for his deep interest in artistic and cultural production and for the extraordinary literary output that took place during his reign —output that was, unlike that of Henry's reign, as likely to be in English as in French. The writers of the period, some of the best-known figures of medieval English literature, include John Gower, Geoffrey Chaucer, the *Gawain*-poet, and William Langland; because they all thrived under Richard II they are sometimes referred to as the "Ricardian poets." Despite their contemporaneity, however, their writings by no means reflect a unified literary culture. There are certainly overlaps and, in the case of Chaucer and Gower, even mutual references between some of their works, but the main thing they have in common apart from historical era is that they all wrote in English. As this introduction has tried to suggest, this in itself is a striking fact; only at the end of the fourteenth century do we begin to see the major works of later-medieval English literature participating, often deliberately, in the project of making English a literary language considered worthy of taking its place alongside Latin and the illustrious continental vernacu-

lars, particularly French and Italian, and of being accorded to a position of renewed prominence and respect in its native country after a perceived period of neglect. At the same time, these authors were anything but removed from non-English influences. Gower composed works in Latin and French as well as English; Chaucer translated French and Italian works, and borrowings from continental and Latin traditions shape all his poetry; Langland's *Piers Plowman* contains numerous lines in Latin and is strongly influenced by monastic Latin literary forms, while in its use of personification allegory it echoes a popular pan-European mode (also seen in the hugely influential French *Romance of the Rose*); in *Sir Gawain and the Green Knight*, the legendary history of Arthur is blended with borrowings from Celtic sources and Christian chivalric culture.

This brings us to an important point about medieval writers—one that applies to all the works in this volume, but that is usefully demonstrated by the Ricardian poets: they did not regard originality in the modern sense as an essential component of a literary work's value. While a medieval poet or preacher or chronicler certainly aimed to tell their story or convey their message in the best possible way, he or she would willingly draw on, combine, borrow from, translate, and rewrite the work of previous authors or storytellers. (The same could, of course, be said of Shakespeare.) Indeed, a link to authoritative sources—which could be written or oral—is often a crucial component of a medieval composition's own claims to authority. The increasing availability of Latin works, through preaching or written translation into the vernacular, or French ones, through performance or translation into English, along with Welsh, Breton, and Irish story material and works in other continental vernaculars, thus provided a rich trove from which Middle English authors constructed their writings.

The tendency of the "big four" Ricardian poets to attract so much attention can overshadow their debts to, and continuity with, the century that preceded them. *Sir Gawain* is part of a substantial tradition of Middle English romance—Arthurian and other—that includes *Sir Orfeo*, *Sir Launfal*, and the *Alliterative* and *Stanzaic Morte Arthure*, among many others. These vary in form but show the tendency of romance, too, to draw on a wide range of traditions for its subject matter. The lay

Sir Orfeo, for example, reworks the story of Orpheus and Eurydice into a form with both Celtic and chivalric aspects: the classical underworld of Hades becomes a fairy land ruled by a powerful lord. The *Alliterative* and the *Stanzaic Morte Arthure*, meanwhile, each recount the fall of Arthur's kingdom, but with very different emphases—the *Alliterative Morte* sees imperial ambition and family treachery as essential elements, while the *Stanzaic* focuses on the adulterous love of Lancelot and Guinevere and the clash of blood brotherhood with the fraternal ties of the Round Table. Chaucer mocks traditional romance forms in his parodic *Tale of Sir Thopas* from *The Canterbury Tales*, and was all too aware of the challenges posed to idealized chivalry by the military realities of the fourteenth century. But as a member of the royal court, he could appreciate the virtues of what has rightly been called "the principal secular literature of entertainment" of the later Middle Ages and the appeal to an idealized past or a magic-laden landscape, the conflicts of loyalties or contests for love that characterize many romances and help to structure works as otherwise diverse as the *Franklin's*, *Wife of Bath's*, *Knight's* and *Merchant's Tales*.

Religious belief and practice are another crucial context for much late-fourteenth-century writing. Early in the century, the poet and canon Robert Mannyng (fl. 1288–1338) translated a handbook on basic Christian teachings from Anglo-Norman to English, titling it *Handlyng Synne* (1303) and illustrating it lavishly with *exempla*. There was a growing audience for such spiritual "self-help" works in the English vernacular, and it has been suggested that *Handlyng Synne* also influenced many later works, including Gower's *Confessio Amantis*, Chaucer's *Canterbury Tales*, and Langland's *Piers Plowman*. Whether or not Mannyng's work formed part of their background, the authors were all able to draw on extensive knowledge of biblical material and Christian history, as well as on the wealth of exemplary narratives that characterized many works designed for religious instruction in the vernacular.

The late fourteenth century also sees the first records of the biblical drama of late-medieval England. Though little is certain regarding the origins of such drama, we do know that in the late fourteenth century substantial groups of plays presenting biblical subject matter began to be performed in several English towns, often in conjunction with festival days of late spring or summer such as Whitsun ("White Sunday"), or Pentecost (the seventh Sunday after Easter), and the Feast of Corpus Christi (a celebration of the Eucharist, held eleven days later); such plays continued to be performed until their suppression in the late sixteenth century. We know too that the presentation of the plays (which have variously been termed "miracle plays," "mystery plays," and "cycle plays"—designations that are all problematic in one way or another as blanket terms) varied. The texts that survive from the northern towns of York and Chester consist of more-or-less unified sequences of short plays—often called "pageants," like the wagons in which they were performed—that present the full sweep of biblical history. The sequence of plays from Coventry is in some respects similar, but includes only New Testament material. Two much more disparate manuscript collections of plays also exist; these are known as "the N-Town plays" and "the Towneley plays." No firm evidence suggests that either group of plays was ever performed as a sequence—or, indeed, that there was ever any intention to perform the collected plays as a sequence. The N-Town collection contains what was once a separate play on the childhood of Mary as well as a two-part Passion Play. The Towneley collection is of particular interest for a small group of remarkable plays traditionally ascribed to the "Wakefield Master." (Three of these plays contain textual allusions to the area of Wakefield.)

Individual biblical plays, particularly in the northern sequences, were generally produced by particular craft guilds, representing a large outlay of time and money; in addition to providing religious instruction and entertainment, the plays reflected and emphasized the guilds' central importance to civic life at this time, as well as the growth of lay power in the governance of many towns. But production of biblical drama was not restricted to annual guild-sponsored performances in towns; some plays were produced by local parishes and some plays performed in the halls of great houses, often by troupes of traveling players.

The scope of late-medieval English drama is similarly diverse. The body of surviving religious drama deriving from some other areas, such as East Anglia, includes not only biblical plays but also a large number of plays depicting the lives of saints or the performance of miracles. Passion plays and Christmas plays were also frequently performed in the late medieval period, as were interludes (typically, short comic sketches, intended for performance at court); mummings (dumb shows with masked performers); folk plays (featuring music and dance as well as dialogue, typically depicting the death and revival of a legendary hero); and Robin Hood plays.

A fifteenth- and sixteenth-century form that has attracted particular interest is the genre conventionally referred to as the "morality play." Plays in this genre (such as *Mankind* and *The Castle of Perseverance*) depict in allegorical form the struggles of a universal human figure; vices and virtues are personified as characters and participate fully in the action of the play. Morality plays were clearly intended to encourage devout individuals to consider their own moral position and to maintain a keen awareness of the state of their souls. But morality plays could also offer a broad range of entertainment—as the humor and energy of *Mankind* amply demonstrate.

The continuing growth of lay participation in spiritual matters that we see reflected in a work such as *Handlyng Synne* or in the biblical dramas became, in other contexts, one of the most contentious issues in fourteenth- and fifteenth-century England. The critiques of the clergy, and particularly of monks and friars, that had accompanied ecclesiastical reform movements from the tenth century onward were strongly endorsed in the works of the Oxford theologian John Wyclif (c. 1324–84). In the course of a long and influential writing career, he attacked the church for its enormous wealth and criticized clerics for their moral failings, questioned the doctrine of transubstantiation, and moved toward a view that all laypeople should have direct access to the Bible and could communicate directly with God, needing no priestly intermediation (although he was in many cases sympathetic to parish priests). His views, some of which were declared heretical by the Archbishop of Canterbury's council in 1382, were nonetheless widely shared, including by some of the nobility at Richard II's court. Wyclif provided much of the intellectual foundation for the English sect known as Wycliffites or Lollards, and had an enormous

influence on the religious, literary, and political culture of late-medieval England. Many of the issues that aroused his wrath are addressed also in Langland's *Piers Plowman*, a text highly critical of clerical and ecclesiastical shortcomings (though unlike the writings of Wyclif and his followers it was not generally regarded as heretical).

Yet another aspect of fourteenth-century spirituality is evident in the *Showings* of the anchoress Julian of Norwich, one of the most important visionary texts of the Middle Ages. Julian's theologically complex and deeply learned account of her experience forms part of both a long tradition of women's visionary literature in medieval Europe (going back at least to the twelfth-century German abbess Hildegard of Bingen) and of a flowering of vernacular religious writing in late-fourteenth-century England that also includes authors such as Richard Rolle and Walter Hilton. And to set Julian's image of the created world as a hazelnut in the palm of God's hand alongside *Sir Gawain and the Green Knight*'s richly detailed hunting scenes or the mysterious John Mandeville's accounts of satyrs, the phoenix, and the exotic kingdoms of the east is to be reminded of the enormous diversity of the literature of late-medieval England. As we noted at the beginning of this introduction, moreover, medieval manuscripts would in many cases have kept this diversity immediately present to readers, recording texts of very different genres alongside one another: saints' lives with confessional manuals, fabliaux with satirical poetry, romances with recipes. Such compilations are reflected in miniature, as it were, by "compilation poems" like the *Canterbury Tales*, which place stories from varied genres and traditions within a unifying frame, or *Piers Plowman*, which blends social critique, personification allegory, and anti-clerical satire into a visionary autobiography.

FIFTEENTH-CENTURY TRANSITIONS

Writers in fifteenth-century England were deeply aware of the rich and authoritative literary tradition that immediately preceded them, drawing on and praising the works of their predecessors even as they devised a distinctive tradition of their own. In political and religious terms as well, the fifteenth century was not immune to the turmoil of the late fourteenth, beginning with a crisis of royal authority as the "usurper" Henry IV tried to solidify his claims to the throne and to contain a major nationalist rebellion in Wales led by Owain Glyndwr (Owen Glendower). Religious legitimacy was also at issue, as ongoing Wycliffite (or Lollard) challenges to current church practices caused aggressive responses on the part of the ecclesiastical and secular hierarchies—most notably the royal decree *De heretico comburendo* of 1401, ordering that recalcitrants be burnt at the stake as heretics (the first institution of such punishment in England), and the famous *Constitutions* (1407–09) of Thomas Arundel, Archbishop of Canterbury, which declared that the making or owning of Bibles in English was forbidden and set strict limits on acceptable religious composition in the vernacular. William Thorpe's testimony during his trial for heresy before Archbishop Arundel, an excerpt from which appears on the website to this volume, demonstrates the depth of commitment and the high level of religious understanding that the Lollards brought to this struggle, which both sides regarded as a matter of eternal life and death as well as immediate political importance. The religious and political threats came together in the short-lived rebellion led by Sir John Oldcastle in 1413, in which he and other Londoners tried to depose the new King Henry V; the fact that Oldcastle had at this time already been convicted of heresy (as a Lollard) solidified the link many secular and church lords made between religious and worldly sedition. While Henry V's military success in France—most famously at the battle of Agincourt in 1415—and his strength as a ruler eased some of the strain, anxiety about the monarchy's legitimacy and about composition in the vernacular are evident in much of the literary production of the century.

One of the modes in which these anxieties were expressed was an outpouring of carefully orthodox religious literature in English, often in forms such as saints' lives, visionary narratives, or meditations on the life of the Virgin or on Christ's Passion. The great religious foundations of Henry V, Sheen Charterhouse and Syon Abbey, were important centers for both the dissemination of fourteenth-century writings and the creation of new works (many of which were translations from Latin or French); when Henry VI came to the throne after his father's early death, his own devout tendencies reinforced the link between the Lancastrian court and monastic spirituality. Religious devotion was far from limited to the elite, however; probably the most famous English text of the first half of the fifteenth century is the *Book of Margery Kempe*, composed by a laywoman living in the world as an account of her spiritual experiences, visions, pilgrimages, and trials for heresy. Margery's frequent conversations with divine and saintly personages show her to be simultaneously extraordinary in and typical of her time; fifteenth-century devotion, particularly in the vernacular, often emphasized emotional connection to and a sense of familiarity with the figures of salvation history.

The intense spirituality of figures such as Margery Kempe contrasts sharply in tone with many of the historical events of the later part of the century. The civil war between the Lancastrian and Yorkist factions—known to us as the Wars of the Roses from the two groups' emblems—pitted descendants of Edward III against one another as claimants to the throne. Begun under the weak kingship of Henry VI, who was deposed by the Yorkist faction in 1460, returned briefly to the throne in 1470, and was executed in 1471, the struggle went on until 1485 when Henry Tudor, a Lancastrian descendant (on his mother's side) of Edward III, defeated Richard III of the house of York and united the warring houses by marrying Elizabeth, daughter of the Yorkist king Edward IV (1461–70, 1471–83). Henry's direct descent, on his father's side, from the twelfth-century Welsh prince Rhys made his rulership the apparent fulfillment of longstanding Welsh prophecies that a Briton would rule England once more.

The chaos and disillusionment that attended the period of civil war echo through the *Morte Darthur* of Thomas Malory, who drew on Middle English and French works to create his massive cycle of Arthurian romances. This text, a kind of summation of the Arthurian obsessions of late-medieval England, became one of the first printed books in England when William Caxton published it in 1485. In his preface, Caxton—who gave Malory's work the title by which we know it—described the *Morte Darthur* as recounting "noble chivalry, courtesy, humanity, friendliness, hardiness, love, friendship, cowardice, murder, hate, virtue and sin," a catalogue whose ending echoes the often dark tone of Malory's work. The *Morte Darthur* seems to reflect and perhaps comment upon the decline of the chivalric world that Malory, a knight who apparently fought on both sides in the Wars of the Roses, would have known well, and its account of the competing loyalties that eventually destroy Arthur and his kingdom would surely have resonated with contemporary events.

The printing of Malory's work by Caxton was only one small piece of the latter's enormous output. Between about 1475 and his death in 1491, he published almost a hundred different works, many of them his own translations; the most famous of the latter is his *Golden Legend*, an English version of a monumentally influential thirteenth-century Latin compendium of saints' lives. He is probably best known, however, for his awareness of and influence on the canon of British literature; works by Chaucer, Lydgate, and Gower were among his most important productions, with Malory joining them not long after. His attention to the ever-growing market for vernacular literature and his admiration for the great authors of the past made his professional life one of the great shaping forces on the development of the British tradition, as well as, of course, the instrument of England's entry into the world of printed books.

Caxton's (numerous) early readers included members of the Paston family, a wealthy Norfolk clan. Their extensive surviving letters, which range in date from 1422 to 1529, deal not with legendary heroism or magical encounters, but with the minutiae of everyday

Table of contents and woodcut illustration from *The Game and Play of Chesse*, printed by William Caxton (2nd edition, 1481).

life: bills, quarrels with neighbors, marriages, deaths, political gossip. Like the Tudor dynasty, the civic dramas and the early print culture of England carry us forward into the sixteenth century, and offer a glimpse of the kinds of everyday events and concerns that formed the original contexts for all the works presented here.

Advertisement issued by William Caxton (c. 1477).

LANGUAGE AND PROSODY

Old English poetry differs in important ways from later English poetry. Whereas a modern poem can be written in any of a number of forms—sonnets, blank verse, ballad meter, free verse, and so on—all surviving Old English poetry is written in essentially the same meter and form. Lines in modern English metrical poetry are built out of a fixed number of feet, each of which has (in principle) the same sequence of stressed and unstressed syllables; in Old English poetry, apart from a small number of extended or hypermetric lines appearing irregularly throughout the corpus of surviving verse and a handful of isolated "half-lines" that may or may not be errors, every line consists of two half-lines containing (usually) two stressed syllables each and a varying number of unstressed syllables. The two half-lines are linked by alliteration between one or both stressed syllables in the first half-line and the first stressed syllable of the second half-line. Alliteration and stress held the lines of an Old English poem together, as meter and rhyme hold together the lines of a Shakespearean sonnet; they were not decorative, as they are in modern poetry, but necessary structural elements.

The opening lines of the poem *Beowulf* illustrate this poetic structure:

Hwæt: We gardena   in geardagum
þeodcyninga   þrym gefrunon,
hu ða æþelingas   ellen fremedon!
Oft Scyld Scefing   sceaþena þreatum
5   monegum mægþum   meodosetla ofteah,
egsode eorl,   syððan ærest wearð
feasceaft funden.   He þæs frofre gebad,
weox under wolcnum,   weorðmyndum þah,
oð þæt him æghwylc   þara ymbsittendra
10 ofer hronrade   hyran scolde,
gomban gyldan.   Þæt wæs god cyning.
Ðæm eafera wæs   æfter cenned
geong in geardum,   þone God sende
folce to frofre.   Fyrenðearfe ongeat
15 þæt hie ær drugon   aldorlease
lange hwile.   Him þæs Liffrea,
wuldres wealdend,   woroldare forgeaf.
Beowulf wæs breme,   blæd wide sprang,
Scyldes eafera   Scedelandum in.
20 Swa sceal geong guma   gode gewyrcean,
fromum feohgiftum   on fæder bearme,
þæt hine on ylde   eft gewunigen
wilgesiþas,   þonne wig cume,
leode gelæsten.   Lofdædum sceal
25 in mægþa gehwære   man geþeon.

Most of this passage (to *fæder*, line 21) is on fol. 129r of the *Beowulf* manuscript, which is reproduced on p. 46. Old English script is relatively easy to read, though some letter forms are different from those of modern printed English (especially the round *d*, the open *g*, the long *f*, *r*, and *s*, the short *t*, the p-shaped *w* called *wynn*, and the *ae* ligature called *aesc* or "ash") and some letters have not survived (the crossed *d* called *eth* and the long *p*-shaped letter called *thorn*, both of which represent the sound spelled *th* in Modern English). As with other surviving Old English poems, the scribe does not put each line of verse on its own line but writes straight across the page verse on its own line. Abbreviations in this text are rare, consisting mostly of a line over a final vowel to indicate that it is followed by the consonant *m* or *n* (e.g., *monegū* in line 5 for the adjective *monegum* "many"). Punctuation is much lighter than in modern English, and the divisions between what modern linguists recognize as words is not always clear, so that the scribe combines a preposition with the word that follows it, and divides the two parts of a compound word to write *ingear dagum* in line 1, or combines two short words to write *hu ða* in line 3.

Though many thousands of words have changed their shape, disappeared, or been added to the lexicon over the past millennium, Old English is still recognizably the ancestor of Modern English. The most common words have changed hardly at all: pronouns such as *we*, *he*, *him*, and *that* (though it is spelled *þæt* in Old English), prepositions such as *in*, *under*, and *over* (spelled *ofer*, but pronounced just like modern English *over*), and adverbs such as *hu* (how) and *oft*. Many other words are either the same as modern English words though spelled differently (*god* "good," *wæs* "was") or related to surviving words: *geardagum* is recognizable as "yore-days," i.e., "days of yore"; *wolcnum*, an inflected plural form of the noun *wolcn*, survives as the archaic word "welkin" and still means "the heavens"; *funden* is the past participle of *findan*, which is the modern word "find"; *hyran* is the ancestor of modern "hear," though it means "obey" as well as "hear" in Old English. Some other words, however, especially those in the aristocratic or poetic register, vanished from the language soon after the arrival of the Normans—examples here include *æþelingas* "noblemen," *ellen* "brave (deeds)," *þrym* "glory," and *frofre* "consolation."

Other important differences between Old and Modern English are found in word order and inflection. A literal translation of these lines into Modern English clearly reveals this (words in parentheses are grammatical particles required in Modern English but expressed by inflectional endings in Old English):

> What! We (of the) spear-Danes   in yore-days
> of people's-kings   glory heard
> how those noblemen   brave-deeds did!
> Often Scyld Son-of-Sheaf   (of) enemies (from) troops
> 5   (from) many tribes   mead-benches took away
> terrified (the) noblemen,   after first (he) was
> penniless found.   He (for) that comfort awaited,
> grew under (the) skies,   (in) honors prospered,
> until (to) him each   (of those) surrounding-sitters
> 10   over (the) whale's-riding-place   to obey had to,
> tribute pay.   That was (a) good king.
> (To) that (one) (a) son was   afterwards born
> young in (the) yards,   whom God sent
> (the) people to comfort.   Severe-need (he) perceived
> 15   that they before endured   lord-less
> (a) long while.   (To) him (for) that (the) Life-lord,
> (of) glory (the) wielder,   world-honor gave.
> Beowulf was famous,   fame widely sprang,
> (of) Scyld (the) son   Scandinavian-lands in.
> 20   So shall (a) young man   good make-happen
> (with) pious gifts   from (his) father's coffers,
> so that him in old-age   afterwards might support
> willing-companions,   when war (should) come,
> the people (might) support. (With) praise-deeds shall
> 25   in tribes each one   (a) man prosper.

If we compare this literal rendering to the translation included in this volume (see page 47 and below), we can see that Old English tended to place verbs after direct objects and at the ends of clauses, while modern English requires a fairly strict subject-verb-object order:

> *Listen!*
> *We have heard of the glory in bygone days*
> *of the folk-kings of the spear-Danes,*
> *how those noble lords did lofty deeds.*
> 5   *Often Scyld Scefing seized the mead-benches*
> *from many tribes, troops of enemies,*
> *struck fear into earls. Though he first was*

> *found a waif, he awaited solace for that—*
> *he grew under heaven and prospered in honor*
> 10   *until every one of the encircling nations*
> *over the whale's-riding had to obey him,*
> *grant him tribute. That was a good king!*
> *A boy was later born to him,*
> *young in the courts, whom God sent*
> 15   *as a solace to the people—He saw their need,*
> *the dire distress they had endured, lordless,*
> *for such a long time. The Lord of Life,*
> *Wielder of Glory, gave him worldly honor;*
> *Beowulf, the son of Scyld, was renowned,*
> 20   *his fame spread far and wide in Scandinavian lands.*
> *Thus should a young man bring about good*
> *with pious gifts from his father's possessions,*
> *so that later in life loyal comrades*
> *will stand beside him when war comes,*
> 25   *the people will support him—with praiseworthy deeds*
> *a man will prosper among any people.*

Old English, then, expresses most grammatical relationships by inflection, while Modern English requires grammatical particles such as prepositions and definite articles. Sentence elements could be multiplied without explicit connections such as "and" or "or": *gardena* and *þeodcyninga* in line 2 are both plural possessives modifying *þrym*, and the whole phrase means something like "the glory of the spear-Danes (who were) the kings of the people"; *sceapena þreatum* and *monegum mægþum* in lines 4–5 are both plural datives modifying the verb *ofteah*, so the phrase means "took away from troops of enemies (who were) from many tribes." The sentence beginning *he þæs frofre* on line 7 has three verbs, *gebad*, *weox*, and *þah*; it can be translated "He awaited consolation for that (as he) grew under the heavens (and) prospered in honors"—even though the three verbs are in one sense a temporal series (first he waited, then he grew, and finally he prospered), they are (more importantly) three variations of one idea (the consolation, the growing, and the prospering are all the same thing). As this example suggests, Old English poetry can be considerably more compressed than a modern translation, and its unlinked chains of multiple statements often require the reader's time and consideration to unfold their full meaning.

The borrowings of French words into the English vocabulary are many, and generally seem to have been culturally motivated; thus, English borrows words for government (*peace, justice, court, judge, sentence*—though *gallows* is an English word) and culture (*noble, dame, gentle, honor, courtesy, polite, manners*). One effect of all this borrowing is that English has a great flexibility in its synonyms; we can express things in several different ways using words from different origins: we can *ask* or *question* someone, and get an *answer* or a *response*, which may make us *glad* or *pleased*, or it may make us *mad* or *angry*, and lead to a *fight* or *dispute* (or even an *altercation*). Often the English and French words for the same thing have come to differ in meaning: it has long been observed, for example, that animals used for meat are called by their English names when they are in the field—*cow, calf, pig, sheep, deer*—and by their French names on the table—*beef, veal, pork, mutton, venison*. This linguistic development reflects the social situation of post-Conquest England, in which the lower-class English raised the animals and the upper-class French ate them; it may also have something to do with the superiority of French over English cooking, which was recognized even a thousand years ago.

Alongside this generous borrowing of vocabulary and literary forms, one of the most important changes in Middle English was the wearing-away of the complex inflectional system of Old English, which had already begun to disappear by the end of the tenth century in some dialects, and the concomitant fixing of word-order into something more like its modern form. Another was the representation of many different regional dialects in written Middle English; Old English had regional varieties, but by far the majority of surviving manuscripts are written in some approximation of the standard West Saxon of the late tenth century. In the absence of a strong educational system teaching a standard for English spelling, regional dialects were much more fully represented in written Middle English. The differences between Old and Middle English can be seen in the following two passages, each translating the opening verses of Psalm 23; the former is from the Old English "Paris Psalter" of the ninth century, the latter from the Wycliffite translation of the Bible in the later

fourteenth century (the same verses from the modern Douay-Rheims Bible, also translated from the Latin Vulgate, appear after the two passages):

Drihten me ræt, ne byð me nanes godes wan, and he me geset on swyðe good feohland. And fedde me be wætera staðum, and min mod gehwyrfde of unrotnesse on gefean. He me gelædde ofer þa wegas rihtwisnesse, for his naman.

The Lord gouerneth me, and no thing schal faile to me; in the place of pasture there he hath set me. He nurschide me on the watir of refreischyng; he conuertide my soule. He ledde me forth on the pathis of rigtfulnesse; for his name.

The LORD ruleth me; and I shall want nothing. He hath set me in a place of pasture: he hath brought me up, on the water of refreshment. He hath converted my soul. He hath led me on the paths of justice, for his own name's sake.

Even in these few lines the differences are notable: considerable developments in vocabulary (*Drihten > Lord, ræt > gouerneth, feohland > the place of pasture, mod > soule, gehwyrfde > conuertide, wegas > pathis*), changes in word order (*Drihten me ræt > The Lord gouerneth me, he me geset > he hath set me, min mod gehwyrfde > he conuertide my soule*) and the erosion of inflectional endings (*be wætera sta<u>ðum</u> > on the watir of refreischyng, for his nama<u>n</u> > for his name*) all indicate the movement of English toward its present state. The Middle English passage is nearly identical to the early Modern English of the Douay-Rheims version. To understand something of the dialect diversity in written Middle English, however, one should compare the Wycliffe version to the same passage in two other Middle English texts, the *West Midlands Psalter* and the Yorkshire version of Richard Rolle, both written around the middle of the fourteenth century:

(*West Midlands Psalter*) Our Lord gouerneþ me, and noþyng shal defailen to me; in þe stede of pasture he sett me þer. He norissed me vp water of fyllyng; he turned my soule fram þe fende. He lad me vp þe bistiges of rigtfulnes for his name.

(*Richard Rolle Psalter*) Lord gouerns me and naþyng
sall me want; in sted of pasture þare he me sett. On
þe watere of rehetynge forþ he me broght; my saule
he turnyd. He led me on þe stretis of rightwisnes;
for his name.

By the end of the thirteenth century English began
to appear once again as a language of official documents
and public occasions. In 1337 a lawyer addressed the
Parliament in English for the first time, as a chronicle
says, "so that he might be better understood by all"; in
1362 Parliament ordered all lawsuits to be conducted in
English. There is some indication that at the beginning
of the fourteenth century the nobility had to be taught
French—the language still held prestige, but it was by
no means the native tongue of those born on English
soil. Not surprisingly, it is in the same period, the
fourteenth century, that English literary output becomes
significant again. But the language that emerged had
been strongly altered by two centuries of "underground" existence and the shaping pressure from the
dominant French language and literary culture. It is
thought that the use of alliterative verse in the Old
English style may have persisted through the twelfth and
thirteenth centuries, though evidence of this is scarce
and ambiguous. In the fourteenth century alliterative
verse reappears in written form throughout much of
England, and is used for subjects as varied as Arthurian
legendary history (the *Alliterative Morte Arthure*),
Christian dream vision (*Pearl*), and satiric commentary
(Langland's *Piers Plowman*), among others. Rhymed,
metrical, non-alliterative poetry such as that of Chaucer
and Gower was largely inspired by French traditions.

The literary flowering of the second half of the
fourteenth century was by no means restricted to one
region. Chaucer wrote in the dialect of London and the
east Midlands which, more than any other, is the
ancestor of modern English; the author of *Sir Gawain
and the Green Knight*, on the other hand, wrote in a
dialect of the northwest midlands. As Chaucer himself
put it, there was great "diversitee in English and in
writing of our tonge." With the coming of the printing
press in the fifteenth century, the printed language
began to take on more and more common characteristics, though it would be not until the late eighteenth

and early nineteenth centuries that grammar, spelling,
and punctuation were standardized.

In reading Old and Middle English (in whatever
dialect) it is important to be aware of the major ways in
which the language differs from our own. For any
historical period of English the reconstruction of
pronunciation is only approximate, but a careful study
of sound changes, spelling, cognate languages and word
histories allows scholars to make highly educated guesses
about the way Old and Middle English sounded. Old
English used some letters not found in the Latin alphabet, including *thorn* (þ), *eth* (ð), and *yogh* (ȝ); the first
two survived into Middle English, where thorn gradually came to be written much like the letter *y* (giving rise
to the common misreading of "ye" for "the" in faux-
antique signs like "ye olde shoppe"). Some Old English
consonant clusters were pronounced in unusual ways; *sc*
was pronounced like *sh* and *cg* like *dg*, so that OE *scip*
and *ecg* sounded much like their modern descendants
ship and *edge*. The consonants *c* and *g* were pronounced
differently depending on their position in a word; the
Old English words *gold* and *camb* were pronounced
much as in Modern English *gold* and *comb*, but *geat* was
pronounced with a *y* as if it were roughly *yat*, and *ciric*
was pronounced with *ch* sounds as in its modern descendant *church*.

One way in which Old and Middle English are
dramatically different from Modern English is in
sounding all consonants, including those in combinations such as *kn, gn, lk,* and *wr* that have become largely
or entirely silent in modern English. The word
"knight," for example, is pronounced something like "k-
ni*cht*" (with the *i* short). Final unstressed *e* in words is
always sounded in Old English, and sounded far more
frequently in Middle English than is the case in modern
English—though during the late-medieval period the
sounding of the final *e* was beginning to die out, and
scholars continue to dispute how frequently the final *e*
should be sounded in Chaucerian English. Vowels are
pronounced roughly as in French or Spanish—the
modern English values are the result of a "Great Vowel
Shift" that began in the fifteenth century. The long *a* in
words such as "made," for example, was pronounced like
the *a* in "father"; the long *e* in words such as "sweete"
was sounded like the *a* in "mate"; the long *i* (or *y*) in

words such as "lif" and "myn" was pronounced in the same way we sound the *i* in "machine"; the long *o* in words such as "do" and "spoon" was sounded as we pronounce the *o* in "note"; and the long *u* (or *ou* or *ow*) in words such as "flowr" was sounded as we would pronounce the *oo* in "boot."

While Middle English is far less inflected than Old English, meaning that fewer grammatical differences are signaled in the form of words, matters are, as noted above, complicated by dialect. Third person singular formations of verbs, for example, tend to end in *-s* or *-ys* in northern dialects, and in *-th* or *-ith* (later *-eth*) in southern dialects. "She has" is thus a form deriving from northern Middle English dialects, and "she hath" from southern English forms (cf. Richard Rolle's "Lord gouerns me" where the Wycliffite version has "The Lord gouerneth me"). When the sheep thief Mak in *The Second Shepherds' Play* pretends to be from southern England he says "ich be" instead of "I am" as northerners then (and all English speakers nowadays) would say. Word order in Middle English is often substantially different from modern practice, with the verb often coming later in the sentence than is our custom in statements, but coming at the beginning at the sentence in questions, as is the practice in many Romance languages. Many Middle English words are of course unfamiliar to the modern reader, but there are also many "false friends"—words that look identical or very similar to modern English words but carry significantly different denotations. *Lewd*, which in Old English means "secular, not relating to the clergy," comes in Middle English to mean "unlearned," but without any suggestion of a sexual character. *Sely*, though the ancestor of the modern "silly," can mean "poor," "miserable," or "innocent" as well as "strange" or "foolish." Even at the level of a single word, one might say, we can see the peculiar and provocative mixture of strangeness and familiarity, the haunting family resemblances and the disconcerting dissonances, that make the study of medieval literary culture so compelling and rewarding. We hope that in this collection of works you will come to know its powerful appeal.

History of the Language
and of Print and Manuscript Culture

In an effort to provide for readers a direct sense of the development of the language and of print culture, examples of texts in their original form have been provided in each volume. A list of these within the present volume appears below.

An overview of developments in the history of language during this period appears on pages LVI–LXI.

Beowulf, lines 1–21: p. 46.

Anglo-Saxon Chronicle, Preface to the Peterborough manuscript: p. 126.

Alfred's "Preface" to *Pastoral Care*, opening lines: p. 130.

Wulfstan, *Sermo Lupi ad Anglos*, opening page: p. 153.

Lindisfarne Gospels, pages from the Gospel of St. Luke: p. XXX, XXXI; CHI-RHO, color insert.

Book of Kells, opening page from the Gospel of St. Matthew: front cover; page from the Gospel of St. Mark: p. XXXV.

"Sumer is icumen in," Harley Manuscript 978: p. 211.

Sir Orfeo, lines 417–34: p. 245.

Sir Gawayn and the Grene Knyght, illustrations from the original manuscript: p. 327.

The Game and Play of Chesse, printed by William Caxton, Table of Contents and illustration: p. LVI.

Paston Letters, passage in original spelling and punctuation: p. 371

Chaucer, *The Canterbury Tales*, pages from the Ellesmere Manuscript: p. 380, 398, 415–16, 449, 462 (and color insert), 483, 502, 518–19, 531–32, 538–39.

The Travels of Sir John Mandeville, woodcut illustrations to the 1481 edition: p. 571, 575, 580.

Decorative pages, various gospels: p. 629–31.

Lambeth Bible, illuminated page showing the Virgin Mary: p. 634.

The Wakefield Master, *The Second Shepherds' Play*, opening page: p. 713.

Everyman, title page, first edition: (www.broadviewpress.com/babl)

Malory, *Morte Darthur*: passage in original spelling and punctuation: p. 788–89; illustrations from William Caxton's 1498 edition: p. 799.

GILDAS
c. 494 or 516 – c. 570

Saint Gildas was a sixth-century British monk and is one of the very few contemporary sources for information about fifth- and sixth-century Britain. While modern scholars consider Gildas's work to be inaccurate historically, two very prominent medieval historians rely on him as a source for their own work: Bede and Geoffrey of Monmouth. In *Historia Ecclesiastica Gentis Anglorum* (*Ecclesiastical History of the English People*), Bede's account of fifth- and sixth-century British history is adapted largely from Gildas's Latin text, *De excidio Britanniae* ("The Ruin of Britain"), and Geoffrey of Monmouth borrows from Gildas, sometimes almost verbatim, in *Historia Regum Brittaniae* (*The History of the Kings of Britain*), specifically in his initial description of Britain, his account of the Roman withdrawal, and his depiction of some of King Arthur's successors.

While Gildas's importance for both Bede and Geoffrey of Monmouth is clear, many of his biographical details are uncertain due to the existence of two biographies that disagree on the details of his life, although both identify his birthplace as what is known as Strathclyde in modern Scotland. The first Life, known as the *Vita Gildae auctore monacho Ruiensi* (*The Life of Gildas written by a monk of Rhuys*) is dated to the eleventh century. The second Life is dated to the early or mid-twelfth century and was written by a contemporary of Geoffrey of Monmouth, Caradoc of Llancarvan. Gildas himself provides some clues about his life, but he does not always provide sufficient detail. For example, he explains that he was born in the year of the battle of Badon Hill, but he does not provide a date for the battle; modern historians debate the exact date of the battle, placing it sometime between 490 and 520.

Particulars about Gildas's later life are also uncertain. He was a clergyman, but it is not clear if he was a monk or a member of the secular clergy. Although the first Life indicates that Gildas studied at a Welsh monastic school under Saint Illtud in the company of Saint Samson of Dol and Saint Paul Aurelian, the second Life has him educated in Gaul; both Lives indicate that he spent at least some time in his later life living in Ireland. While the facts of Gildas's life are uncertain, most scholars agree that his major work, *De excidio Britanniae* ("The Ruin of Britain") was probably written around 547. In "The Ruin of Britain," Gildas aims to denounce contemporary rulers—Constantine of Dumnonia, Aurelius Caninus, Vortiporius of the Demetae, Cuneglas and Maglocunus—for their greed, cruelty, and sinfulness. He also admonishes the clergy, condemning them for sloth and simony, and provides a narrative of the period from the Roman invasion to his own time. Although the historical accuracy of the narrative is suspect—Gildas was not attempting to write a history in the contemporary sense, but rather to identify and chastise what he considered to be the wrongs of his time—the text remains an important one for modern scholars because it is one of the very few surviving works from sixth-century Britain.

Gildas died around 570; according to the first Life, his body was set adrift on a boat, found intact three months later and then buried at Rhuys. The second Life identifies Gildas's final resting place as Glastonbury Abbey. His relics were venerated at the monastery that he founded at Rhuys until the tenth century, at which point they were moved to Berry for safety; in the eighteenth century, they were said to be in the cathedral of Vannes.

⌘⌘⌘

from *The Ruin of Britain*[1]

In this epistle I lament far more than I denounce. But I do not blame me if my style is lowly, for my intentions are pure. Let no one think that I scorn all men or esteem myself too highly, but understand that I bewail the loss of the common good and the accumulation of evils through grievous conflicts. I feel my country's hardships and am looking for ways to assuage them....

... The Isle of Britain lies at almost the very brink of the world, toward the west and northwest. When weighed in the divine scales that, we are told, hold the entire earth in balance, it stretches out from the southwest toward the North Pole. It is eight hundred miles long and two hundred miles wide, not counting the great promontories that enclose curving bays of the ocean. As I mentioned, it is protected by a vast and impassable circle of the sea on all sides except the south, where one can travel across the straits to Belgic Gaul. The mouths of the two noble rivers Thames and Severn extend like arms and improve the terrain, as do a number of other rivers, and many luxury items were once conveyed by ship upstream. Twenty-eight cities and numerous fortresses also adorned the island, and they were suitably equipped with walls, gates, houses, and watchtowers whose pointed spires jutted up menacingly from the solid walls. Like a bride bejeweled with various fineries, Britain is ornamented with wide expanses of fields and rolling hills in a lovely landscape that is exceedingly good for the cultivation of crops. Mingled with these are mountain pastures that are perfectly fit for the grazing of livestock. Flowers of many different colors grace the ground wherever one goes, presenting the beholder with lovely vistas. The land is watered by clear springs whose steady waters wash snow-white pebbles into the bright, gently murmuring rivers that meander down with the promise of delicious rest to those who lie on their banks, and into lakes that overflow with the cool torrent of fresh water.

Since the days of its earliest settlement, Britain has been over-proud in mind and spirit, rebellious against God, against its own citizens, and even occasionally against kings and peoples from across the sea. What human deeds, either now or in the future, can be more depraved and wicked than to deny the proper fear to God or the proper charity to one's good countrymen? What could be more depraved and wicked than to deny the obligation one has to those in a higher position, provided that there is no harm done to the Faith? What could be more depraved and wicked than to break faith with both God and man, or to slough one's fear of both heaven and earth and allow oneself to be ruled by one's personal desires?

I will pass over the ancient errors that were common to all peoples before they were absolved by the advent of Christ in the flesh, nor shall I recount the devilish portents infesting the land, whose number almost surpasses that of the plagues of Egypt, some deformed traces of which can still be seen unchanged in men's gloomy faces, both within the abandoned city walls and beyond them. Nor shall I enumerate all the mountains and hills and rivers, which are now put to such decent use but which were once so treacherous when blind pagans gathered in those places to worship. I shall therefore be silent about those monstrous tyrants of ancient times, whose deeds were so widely sung abroad that Porphyry[2]—that mad dog of the East and enemy of the Church—pompously added these words to his ravings: "Britain is a land abundant in tyrants." I shall instead attempt to set down those things that have occurred in Britain since the days of the Roman emperors, describing the evils that Britain has inflicted upon others, even those in far-flung lands. I have had to rely for the most part not on the antiquarian writings of native historians, which—if they ever even existed—have long since been burnt by the flames of foes or carried off in the ships of exiles, but upon accounts from abroad, though even these have too many gaps to be useful sources. ...

... Christ's teachings were received by the native Britons only halfheartedly at first, though they more or less remained unaltered there until the nine-year-long persecution under the tyrannical Diocletian.[3] Churches were then torn down all over the world, and all the Holy

---

[2] *Porphyry*   Porphyry of Tyre (c. 233–c. 309), Phoenician neo-platonic philosopher.

[3] *Diocletian*   Roman emperor (c. 244–311), who ruled from 284 to 305.

Scriptures were burnt in the town squares whenever they were found, and the chosen priests of the Lord's flock were slaughtered along with their innocent sheep so that, if it could be done, no trace of the Christian religion was left in many provinces. The history of the Church relates what escapes occurred in those days, what executions, what doom for apostates, what crowns of glorious martyrdom, what angry persecutors there were, as well as what patience existed among the saints, who so eagerly and in such numbers turned their backs to the shadows of this world and headed for the wondrous kingdom of Heaven, as if the entire Church were taking its appointed seat.

Wishing that all men be saved, God turned His mercy upon us, for He seeks out the sinful just as much as He summons those who think themselves just. During this same persecution, I believe, God granted us a free gift, lest Britain remain benighted in the thick mist of black night: He lit for us the bright lanterns of the holy martyrs. Their graves and the sites of their martyrdoms would have inspired great love in the hearts of those who visited them, but many of these places have been destroyed by the greedy looting of barbarians and the many wicked acts of the British people. I speak especially of St. Alban of Verulamium, of Aaron and Julius of Caerleon, and of the many others of both sexes who in various places exerted their utmost valor in the army of Christ.

Alban, the foremost of these saints, imitated Christ, who gave His life for His sheep. Out of pure love, this Alban harbored a certain confessor who had been followed by persecutors and was about to be arrested. First he hid the man in his house and then he exchanged clothes with him, willingly exposing himself to the pursuers while in his spiritual brother's garb. From the moment of his holy confession until the spilling of his blood by the pagans, who displayed the Roman banners most horribly, Alban was pleasing to God, and God adorned his suffering with a miraculous sign. Just as when the Ark of the Israelite Covenant once stood for a while amid the pebbles on a dry path in the middle of the River Jordan, so did Alban's ardent prayers open up a dry road across the bed of the River Thames while one thousand men walked in it, the swelling waters rising like mountains on either side of them. And when his

first torturer beheld this miracle, he turned from a wolf into a lamb, causing him too to thirst for and receive the triumphal palm of martyrdom.

The other saints I mentioned were tormented in a variety of other ways, and the trophies of their glorious deaths were soon affixed to the splendid gates of Jerusalem. Those who survived took refuge in the forests and deserts and hidden caves, hoping that God, their just Ruler, would one day mete out severe judgment on their tormentors and provide them with protection in the meantime.

After ten years of such storms, the wicked decrees began to slacken and their perpetrators were overtaken by death, while all of Christ's faithful joyously welcomed the serene light of Heaven's breeze as if after a long and stormy winter night. They rebuilt the churches, which had been destroyed to the very last one; they founded, built, and completed chapels to the holy martyrs, proclaiming them everywhere like the banners of victory. They also celebrated the high feast days, carrying out the holy rites with pure hearts and mouths. All the sons of the Church rejoiced as if they were nestled in their mother's bosom.

This harmony between the head and members of Christ's Church remained until the Arian[1] treachery arrived here from across the sea, spitting venom like a vicious serpent upon us, making our brethren who were living together be lethally separated. Then, as if there were a paved road across the ocean, there came to us every type of deadly beast, their horrible mouths pulsing with pestilent heresies, and their fangs inflicting deadly bites upon a country that always longed to hear something new and that could settle on nothing for long.

Thus it came about that the ever-spreading thickets of tyranny were about to burst forth into an enormous forest, and the island remained Roman in name alone, but not by law or custom. Indeed, it was even then that the land cast out a seedling of its own bitter planting, sending Maximus[2] over to Gaul accompanied by a great cohort of accomplices and bearing the imperial insig-

---

[1] *Arian* Arianism, based on the teachings of Arius (c. 250–331) is a sect of Christianity that denied Christ's divinity; at the first Council of Nicaea (325), Arian beliefs were deemed to be heretical.

[2] *Maximus* Possibly Magnus Maximus (c. 335–88), Roman emperor from 383 to 388.

nia—which he was not worthy to possess, having no legal authority and having been raised to the emperorship by a rebellious military, as befits a tyrant. Relying on clever stratagems rather than valor, Maximus first annexed the nearby towns and provinces to his own criminal kingdom and turned them against Rome through lies and perjuries. Then he spread one wing over Spain and another over Italy and, establishing the capital of his illegitimate empire at Trier,[1] he vented such fury upon his masters—the two legal emperors—that he forced them to flee, one from Rome, the other from a life of great piety. Though emboldened by these beastly deeds, Maximus—he who had overthrown the crowned heads of the entire world—soon had his own wicked head lopped off in the city of Aquileia.[2]

By then, Britain had been stripped of all her armed men, all her military forces, all her illustrious commanders, and all her brave youths, for they had all departed with Maximus, never to return. Now that Britain was completely bereft of any who were skilled in the arts of war, the island suffered and was paralyzed for many years, trodden down violently by two savage peoples from across the sea: the Scots from the northwest and the Picts[3] from the north.

Because of their dire conditions in the face of these attacks, the Britons sent messengers to Rome with letters, requesting military aid in avenging their lamentable situation. They thus reconfirmed their complete subjugation and loyalty to the Roman Empire, as long as it could defend them from their enemies. A legion was quickly dispatched, unmindful of Britain's previous calamities but armed heavily enough. It crossed the ocean by ship to our country and gave battle to those grievous foes, destroying a great host of them and driving the rest beyond our borders. The legion thus saved the citizens of Britain from a brutal invasion and almost certain captivity. The Romans then recommended that the Britons construct a wall stretching from sea to sea across the island which, when fully manned, would frighten away their enemies and protect their people. However, because the wall was erected by an aimless and unreasonable rabble, it was made of sod rather than of stone, and so it proved useless in the end.

As soon as the Roman legion returned home, joyous in their great triumph, their same old enemies, the Ambrones,[4] returned. They were like ravenous wolves, leaping with their dry maws into the sheepfold while the shepherd is away. Thus they returned, conveyed by their oars (which were as fast as wings), by the arms of their oarsmen, and by the wind in their sails. They burst through the frontiers, destroying everything they came across, cutting it down like so much corn in the field.

Once more messengers were dispatched. Just like fearful chicks taking shelter under the wings of their steadfast parents, it is said that it was with torn clothes and dust covering their heads that they pleaded with the Romans for help, lest their wretched homeland be destroyed or the Roman name, which even now echoed through their ears as a mere word, be further reviled by the scorn of an alien people. The Romans were as moved as was humanly possible upon hearing the tale of this great tragedy. Like eagles, they hastened the flight of their cavalry across the land and the course of their navy across the sea, and they buried their fearsome talons—the points of their swords—into their heedless foes, and their enemies fell like the leaves in autumn in this slaughter. The Roman forces were like a tempest-swollen mountain torrent, bursting thunderously from its accustomed course. It foams forth splendidly, with furrowed back and fierce brow, with waves as tall, they say, as the storm clouds that darken one's eyes and dazzle them with lines of shimmering lightning, its surge sweeping aside everything in its path. The battalions of our noble, worthy allies thus almost instantly drove those enemies across the sea, if they were able to escape at all, though year after year they had greedily been shipping their plunder across the waters with no one to stand in their way.

The Romans then announced that they would by no means be troubled any longer with such costly expeditions and that it was beneath them to waste their military forces on land and sea dealing with unruly pirates. Instead, they said, the Britons should get into

---

[1] *Trier* City in modern-day Germany.

[2] *Aquileia* City in modern-day Italy.

[3] *Picts* Confederation of tribes that flourished from the time of the Roman empire to about the twentieth century; they lived in present-day Scotland.

[4] *Ambrones* Second-century tribe, associated primarily with the coasts of northern Europe.

the habit of relying upon their own forces; they should manfully defend their own lands, riches, women, children, and, above all, their freedom and way of life. Their enemies were no stronger than the Britons themselves, unless they allowed themselves to become idle and sluggish. The Britons should by no means allow themselves to be conquered and cast into chains without a fight. Instead, their hands should be prepared to kill, armed with shields, swords, and spears. Having made these arguments, the Romans hoped to leave behind something that would prove of further use to the people, and so they constructed a wall quite unlike the first one. This new wall was built in the usual Roman manner, drawing upon both public and private funding and the labor of the inhabitants, and it ran from sea to sea, linking together the cities that had been situated there out of fear of the enemy. They then gave the timid Britons some good advice and left plans for implementing their defenses, recommending that the Britons build a series of watchtowers at fixed intervals all along the southern coast of the ocean, for that is where the Britons kept their merchant fleet and therefore where they should most fear an attack from the bestial barbarians. The Romans then bade them farewell, never to return.[1]

As soon as the Romans had sailed home, filthy bands of Scots and Picts, like the black hordes of worms that creep out of the narrow cracks of rocks when the sun is high in the heavens and the air grows warm, emerged from the coracles[2] that had conveyed them across the valley of Tethys.[3] Although different in many of their customs, these two peoples shared a thirst for bloodshed, and they were both more likely to cover their faces with hair than to cover their genitals or nearby regions with clothing. Now, having learned of the departure of our fellow debtors and the unlikelihood of their ever returning, they acted more boldly than usual and captured from the natives the entire northern region of the land down to the wall. A troop of men was garrisoned there to oppose them, but they proved too lazy to fight and

unable to flee. With their hearts full of fear, the fools sat there day and night, just withering away at their useless posts. In the meantime, the barbed weapons of their naked foes never ceased to strike, and the wretched Britons were shot from the walls and dashed to pieces one by one. Such an untimely demise actually proved a benefit for those who were slain in that way, for by this speedy death they avoided the terrible pains that awaited their brothers and children.

What more can I say? Once their cities and the high wall were abandoned, all the expected exiles swiftly followed, as did desperate dispersions, and persecution by the enemy, and the cruelest slaughter. The miserable Britons were ripped apart by their foes like sheep by a butcher. And they began to live like beasts of the field, for they took to robbing one another, there being only a scanty amount of food to feed that miserable people. All the onslaughts from these foreigners were multiplied by domestic strife, since, due to these frequent disruptions, all the land lacked any food excepting what comforts the art of the hunt brought.

Once again, the miserable remnant sent a letter, this time to Agitius,[4] a powerful man among the Romans, imploring him thus: "O Agitius, thrice consul, hear the groans of the Britons!" And after saying a few more words, they added: "The sea drives us toward the barbarians and the barbarians drive us into the sea. Two different modes of death await us: we will either be drowned or get our throats cut." But they received no help.

Meanwhile, a dire and notorious plague struck at the feeble and wandering Britons, many of whom, utterly defeated, were now compelled to turn over many things into the hands of their cruel oppressors merely in order to obtain a little bit of food to keep themselves alive. Some of the others fared differently: they kept up the fight, attacking from mountains, caves, meadows, and thorny brambles. And then, trusting not in man but in God, they at last slaughtered the men who had been plundering their land for many years. As Philo[5] says: "It is necessary to rely on God when the aid of men fails." Thus the brazenness of our enemies subsided for a brief time, though our own wickedness did not; the enemies

---

[1] *The Romans ... never to return* Many of the lines in this paragraph were reproduced almost verbatim by Geoffrey of Monmouth in Book 6 of *The History of the Kings of Britain*.

[2] *coracles* Type of boat.

[3] *Tethys* I.e., the sea. In classical mythology, Tethys is a sea goddess.

[4] *Agitius* Flavius Aëtius (c. 396–454), Roman general.

[5] *Philo* Hellenistic Jewish philosopher (20 BCE–50 CE).

retreated from the people, but the people did not retreat from their sins.

It was ever the habit of this people, as it still is today, that they were weak at repelling their armed enemies but strong at waging civil wars and carrying the burden of sins; slow, I say, to follow the banners of peace and truth, but swift to turn to wickedness and falsehood. And so the shameless, lazy Scots might go home, but it was not long before they would return. The Picts also returned to the utmost region of the island for the first time then, and there they remained, though they too still made the occasional plundering raids. The desperate Britons' cruel scars began to heal during this cessation of hostilities, but a new famine—far more deadly than the first—was quietly spreading. Now that the invasions had ceased, the island overflowed with such an abundance of goods that no previous age had ever seen the like, and with these things Luxury increased. Its seed soon spread, so that of those times the saying was aptly applied: "It is actually reported that there is fornication here such as is unknown even among the pagans."[1]

It was not the vice of fornication alone that was spreading, but all the other vices to which human nature is prone, especially the one that proves the overthrow of every good state even today: hatred of the truth and of those who tell the truth, love of falsehoods and of falsifiers, adoration of wickedness instead of goodness, desire for the darkness rather than the sun, and the welcoming of Satan as the angel of light. Kings were anointed not by God but because they were crueler than all the rest. They were, in turn, quickly murdered by their anointers with no consideration for the truth, and crueler men still were chosen in their stead. In fact, if any one of them appeared gentler or more inclined to the truth in any small way, it was as if he were overturning all things in Britain, and everyone heedlessly cast their hatred and weapons at him. And the things that were pleasing and displeasing to God hung evenly in the balance, though perhaps those displeasing to Him fared somewhat better. Thus could the words of the prophet, with which he addresses his own slothful people, be deservingly applied to our land: "O sons who deal corruptly, you have forsaken God and have provoked the Holy One of Israel. Why will you still be smitten

that you continue to rebel? The whole head is sick, and the whole heart faint. From the sole of the foot even to the head, there is no soundness in it."[2] And so they acted in all matters in a way that was contrary to their salvation, as though the True Doctor of us all had provided the world with no remedy. And not only laymen but also most of the flock of the Lord and its shepherds, who were supposed to serve as an example to all the people, were lying about in a drunken stupor as if they were sodden with wine. They were so consumed by the kindling of hostility, by the strife of quarrels, by the greedy claws of envy, and by their heedless judgment of good and evil that, as is still true today, they seemed to hold their princes in contempt, and they were led astray by their follies and wandered in the trackless wild.

In the meantime, God desired to purge His family and to erase the stain of these evils with the mere mention of tribulations. Then the pricked ears of all the folk were filled with the winged rumor of the rapid approach of their old enemies, who were now bent, as usual, on the utter devastation and resettlement of the entire island from end to end. But they made nothing of this knowledge and instead, like foolish beasts of burden, they held tight onto the bit of reason with clenched teeth, as the saying goes, forsaking the narrow road to salvation and going headlong down the path that leads through many vices to death.

And so, as Solomon says, "A stubborn servant is not mended by words alone,"[3] and a fool may be flogged and not feel a thing. For then a terrible plague struck brutally at this foolish people. Within a brief time it felled without even a sword such a multitude of people that the living were unable to bury the dead. But even this did not amend them, and the words of the prophet Isaiah were fulfilled yet again: "And God has invoked lamentation and baldness and the donning of the sackcloth. Behold the slaying of the calves and the slaughter of the rams, behold the eating and drinking and the people saying: 'let us eat and drink today, for tomorrow we die.'"[4] Indeed, the time drew near in which all of their iniquities would be complete, as those

---

[1] *It is actually ... pagans* Cf. 1 Corinthians 5.1.

[2] *O sons ... soundness in it* Cf. Isaiah 1.4–6.

[3] *A stubborn servant ... words alone* See Proverbs 29.19.

[4] *let us eat ... we die* See Isaiah 22.12–13.

of the Amorites[1] once were. Then they held a council to decide what would be the best and most helpful way of driving back the cruel and constant invasions and looting by that abovementioned people.

But then all the members of the council, along with their proud tyrant, were blinded: thinking they were devising a means of defense, they instead devised the destruction of the land. Bringing wolves into a sheepfold, they invited to the island those fierce Saxons,[2] whose name should not be said aloud and who were despised by God and man alike, in order to drive away the invaders from the north. Nothing more ruinous or woeful has ever befallen. How deep was the darkness that clouded their senses! How desperate and cruel was the dullness of their minds! For they willingly invited the people whom they feared more than death even when far away to abide under their own roof. Thus, as it is said: "The princes of Zoan are foolish, giving foolish advice to the Pharaoh."[3]

At that point in time a pack of cubs issued forth from the den of the barbarian lioness, arriving in three longships, or cyulas as they are called in their tongue. They sailed there on a favorable wind, and favorable too were their omens and augurs, which had clearly foretold that they would occupy the land toward which they pointed their prows for three hundred years, half of which time—that is, one hundred fifty years—they would frequently lay the country waste. At the bidding of that unfortunate tyrant, they first dug their fearsome claws into the eastern part of the island, acting as if they were fighting for our homeland but in reality fighting against it. When their mother country realized that her first brood had prospered, she sent an even greater contingent of guard dogs, which came by ship and immediately joined up with the other false mercenaries. From this the seed of iniquity, the root of bitterness, the pestilent plant that our deeds merited began to sprout ferocious vines and shoots throughout our soil. Once these barbarians had been introduced to the island, they presented themselves, under false pretences, as soldiers who were willing to undergo great tribulation for their

hosts, and they asked to be given provisions. Once the supplies were distributed, the dog's maw was shut for a long time, so to speak. Then, embellishing certain specific episodes, they made a new complaint that the remuneration they were given was not enough, and that if they were not granted a greater salary they would break their pact and devastate the entire island. They put their threats into effect without delay.

Because of the Britons' previous sins, the fire of just vengeance swept through the entire island from sea to sea, kindled by those unholy easterners, and it ravaged the cities and the fields and farmlands; once lit, it did not die down until it had burnt almost the entire surface of the island and its terrible red flames licked the western ocean. With this invasion, as with the Assyrian[4] attack against Judea[5] of old, was fulfilled for us what the prophet once said in lamentation: "They have burnt Your sanctuary to the ground, and they have polluted the tabernacle of Your Name,"[6] and also "God, a race of gentiles has come into Your inheritance; it has desecrated Your holy temple,"[7] and so on. And so all the towns were destroyed by battering rams. All their citizens—the church leaders, priests, and people too—were cut down everywhere by swords and by the crackling flames. And it was a wonder to see in the middle of the town squares the keystones of towers and walls that had been thrown down, alongside the holy altars and fragments of corpses which were covered, it seemed, with a purple crust of dried blood—all these things appeared as if they had been mixed together in some horrific wine press. There were no burials either, except beneath caved-in buildings or within the bellies of birds or beasts; the only reverence left was to the souls of the pious, if there were many of those found, who were conveyed by the blessed angels up to high heaven. Then the vineyard that had once been good degenerated into bitterness, and, as the prophet says, there was hardly ever to be seen a cluster of grapes or an ear of corn on the backs of the vintners and reapers.[8]

---

[1] *Amorites* Ancient Semitic people who occupied parts of the Middle East in the third millennium BCE.

[2] *Saxons* Confederation of old Germanic tribes.

[3] *The princes ... to the Pharaoh* See Isaiah 19.11.

[4] *Assyrian* Arabic peoples of the Middle East.

[5] *Judea* Modern-day Israel and Palestine.

[6] *They have burnt ... Your Name* Cf. Psalms 73.7.

[7] *God, a race ... holy temple* Cf. Psalms 78.1.

[8] *Then the vineyard ... and reapers* See Obadiah 1.5.

Some of the wretched survivors were captured up in the hills and slain en masse. Many of the others succumbed to their hunger and gave themselves up, offering their hands to their enemies in eternal servitude if they were not slain on the spot, which was, in reality, the greatest of gifts. Others headed across the sea, and, with the wind filling their sails, they sang out great lamentations instead of sea chanties,[1] calling: "You have given us like sheep for the slaughter, and you have scattered us among the nations."[2] Others still anxiously remained in their homeland, dwelling with constant fear in the deep and dangerous fastnesses of the mountains and hills, or in the darkest forests, or by the coasts of the sea.

After a space of time had passed and the cruel marauders had returned home, God granted a new vigor to the survivors. Many miserable people fled to them from all about, as eagerly as honey-bees cluster to the hive when a storm draws near, begging with all their hearts—"burdening heaven with their prayers," as it were—that they not be completely annihilated. Their leader was Ambrosius Aurelius,[3] a gentleman who, perhaps alone of the Roman people, had weathered the onslaught of the recent storms. His family, who had been killed in these troubles, had certainly worn the purple. In our own times, his descendants have greatly degenerated from their ancestor's goodness. Under Ambrosius Aurelius, our people revived its strength and provoked the victors to battle. By the will of the Lord, triumph was theirs.

In those days, the citizens of Britain sometimes emerged victorious, and sometimes their enemies won the day. In this way the Lord tested that people, as is His wont, as if it was a present-day Israel, in order to determine whether it loved Him or not. This state of affairs continued until the year of the siege of Mount Badon,[4] which was the latest (though not the least) of the defeats of those churls. That battle took place during the year of my birth, and I reckon that to be forty-four years and one month ago.

But even today the cities of our land are not as populated as they once were but languish in ruin and disorder, because, though foreign invasions have ceased, civil wars have not. Yet the memory of the hopeless downfall of the island and its unexpected revival has lingered in the minds of those who lived to witness both of these miracles. It was for this reason that kings, public and private citizens, priests, and clergy, all clung to their proper positions. But the generation that succeeds them as they die off remembers nothing of that time and has known only the present state of peace, and hence all the guidelines of truth and justice have been shaken off and cast aside so that barely a trace or memory remains among the orders I have mentioned, except among a few—a very few indeed. A great multitude is lost, and people rush headlong into Hell each day. There are so few now remaining that Holy Mother Church hardly notices them, though they lie in Her bosom, the only true sons She has. It is by these men that we are sustained in our infirmity, and it is by their holy prayers (the pillars and posts of salvation) that we are kept from near collapse. Let no man think that I calumniate their noble lives, which are admired by all and beloved by God, if I speak freely and, indeed, mournfully of those who serve their own bellies or even the devil instead of Christ, Who is the Ever-Blessed God, for I am not so much debating as lamenting. Indeed, why should their compatriots conceal what neighboring countries not only already know about but condemn?

—C. MID-6TH CENTURY

---

[1]   *chanties* I.e., songs.

[2]   *You have ... the nations* Cf. Psalms 44.12.

[3]   *Aurelius* Roman-Briton war general (c. fifth century).

[4]   *Mount Badon* Thought to be c. 490–520.

BEDE

c. 673 – 735

Bede "the Venerable," the most learned writer of the Anglo-Saxon period, was born in Northumbria around 673. At the age of seven he entered the twin monastery of Wearmouth-Jarrow and remained there, except for a few short excursions, until his death. Under the Abbot Ceolfrith, Bede received a thorough education in grammar, rhetoric, mathematics, music, natural science and the study of Scripture; he was ordained a deacon at 19 and a priest at 30. In a brief autobiographical note appended to his *Ecclesiastical History* he describes himself in this manner: "Amid the observance of the discipline of the Rule [of St. Benedict] and the daily task of singing in the church, it has always been my delight to learn or to teach or to write." Over the course of his life Bede produced a body of writing that remains impressive for its clarity, intelligence, range and devotion. His works, which survive in hundreds of manuscripts, were deeply influential and widely copied throughout the Middle Ages. Apart from a brief and enigmatic Old English poem and a lost translation of the Gospel of John he is said to have composed on his deathbed, all Bede's works were written in Latin, then the international language of scholarship and of the Church.

The founder of Jarrow monastery, Benedict Biscop, had traveled extensively and assembled an impressive library; during Bede's lifetime this remote outpost on the northeastern coast of England—founded about the year Bede was born, and scarcely 50 years after the rulers of Northumbria had converted to Christianity—was perhaps the most learned monastic center in all of Europe. Bede's writings include numerous works of Scriptural commentary, many homilies, works on meter and orthography, lives of several saints, books of poetry and hymns, and several treatises on cosmology and timekeeping. He was deeply interested in time and its measurement, a matter of some urgency in his lifetime because the Irish and Roman churches had different methods for calculating the date of Easter. In some years the two churches celebrated the feast on different days, which to Bede was a shocking sign of disunity. In his works promoting the Roman method of reckoning Easter he also helped establish the foundations of medieval astronomy and chronology; Bede is primarily responsible for popularizing the western "BC" and "AD" system of reckoning dates using the *anno domini* or "year of (the birth of) our Lord" as the dividing principle.

It is Bede's historical works, however, that are best known today. His *Historia Ecclesiastica Gentis Anglorum* (*Ecclesiastical History of the English People*), completed in 731, is an extensive history of England which takes as its theme the conversion of the Anglo-Saxon invaders who had displaced the native Britons. The *Ecclesiastical History* imagines an "English" people united not so much by culture or language or geography as by faith, the Roman Christianity brought to the island by Augustine of Canterbury and other missionaries sent by Pope Gregory the Great in 597. This work still provides the foundation for much of our knowledge of England in the fourth, fifth, and sixth centuries. Bede's talent as a historian was his ability to take multiple sources—documents, other histories, local oral traditions and legends—and weave them together into a coherent narrative. Though Bede was not fully a historian in the modern sense, his approach is far less foreign to the modern historical sensibility than that of most medieval chroniclers; unlike many writers of the time, for example, he makes frequent reference to the sources for the material he is recounting. In Bede's narrative, written very much from the Northumbrian point of view, the English are gradually and inevitably brought into the happy embrace of the Roman church, triumphing against the bitterness and treachery of the native Britons, the well-meaning but deluded zeal of the Irish missionaries, and the temporizing and backsliding of one pagan king after another. It is a tribute to Bede's great literary talent that in many ways the story he constructs from whatever meager evidence was available to him is still regarded as a fundamentally accurate account.

The following selections give some of the flavor of Bede's work: a geographical prologue describing the island of Britain; a lively narrative of the coming of the Angles and Saxons derived largely from the early sixth-century Briton Gildas's *De excidio Britonum* ("On The Ruin of Britain"), a passionate work of moral exhortation written from a stridently anti-English perspective; a detailed psychological portrait of the Northumbrian king Edwin's slow movement towards conversion; and an account of two remarkable figures from the monastery of Whitby, the abbess Hild and the lay brother Cædmon. Cædmon's story is far more widely read today. According to Bede, Cædmon receives a miraculous talent for poetic composition and becomes a great composer of religious verse; Cædmon's *Hymn* (which Bede records in Latin, not English) is sometimes treated as the first English Christian poetic work. Bede's account of the life and miracles of the abbess Hild, however, plays a role of equal importance in his larger history; it is included here to suggest that the paired lives of a learned aristocratic woman and an illiterate peasant can tell us a great deal about the boundaries of Bede's narrative and the kinds of material it excludes, about the relationship between history and hagiography, and about the ways in which the cultural roles prescribed by one's gender and class affect the shape of one's spiritual journey.

⌘ ⌘ ⌘

from *Ecclesiastical History of the English People*[1]

1. A DESCRIPTION OF THE ISLAND OF BRITAIN AND ITS INHABITANTS (I.1)

Britain, an island in the ocean, formerly called Albion, is situated in the northwest, opposite the coasts of Germany, France, and Spain, which form the greatest part of Europe, though at a considerable distance from them. It extends 800 miles to the north and is 200 miles broad, except where several promontories extend further in breadth, which makes the circuit of its coastline 3600 miles. To the south lies Belgic Gaul, from which the closest port for travelers is the city of *Rutubi Portus*, corrupted by the English into "Reptacestir."[2] The distance from there across the sea to *Gessoriacum*,[3] the closest point in the land of the Morini, is fifty miles, or as some writers say, 450 *stadia*. Behind the island, where it opens upon the boundless ocean, are the Orkney Islands.

Britain is rich in grain and trees, and is well adapted for feeding cattle and beasts of burden. It also produces vines in some places, and has plenty of land and water-fowls of various kinds; it is remarkable also for its rivers, abounding in fish, particularly salmon and eels, and plentiful springs. Seals and dolphins are frequently taken, and even whales; besides many sorts of shellfish

---

[1] *Ecclesiastical History of the English People* The standard edition of the *Historia Ecclesiastica*, with a modern English translation, is Bertram Colgrave and R.A.B. Mynors, eds., *Bede's Ecclesiastical History of the English People* (Oxford, 1969). This translation, by R.M. Liuzza, relies heavily on that work, as well as the earlier work of L. Stevens (London: J.M. Dent; New York: E.P. Dutton, 1910) and J.M. Wallace-Hadrill's *Bede's Ecclesiastical History of the English People: A Historical Commentary* (Oxford: Clarendon Press, 1991).

[2] *Reptacestir* Richborough.

[3] *Gessoriacum* Boulogne.

such as mussels, in which are often found excellent pearls of all colors, red, purple, violet, and green, but mostly white. There is also a great abundance of cockles, from which a scarlet dye is made, a most beautiful color which never fades from the heat of the sun nor exposure to the rain; but the older it is, the more beautiful it becomes. Britain has salt springs and hot springs, and from them flow rivers which furnish hot baths, suitable for all ages and sexes, arranged for each separately. For water, as St. Basil says,[1] receives the quality of heat when it passes through certain metals, so that it becomes not only hot but scalding. Britain has also many veins of metals, copper, iron, lead, and silver; it produces much excellent jet, which is black and sparkling, burns in fire, and when heated drives away serpents; when it is warmed by rubbing it attracts whatever is applied to it, like amber. The island was once famous for its twenty-eight noble cities, besides innumerable castles which were all strongly secured with walls, towers, gates, and locks.

Because Britain lies almost under the North Pole, the nights are light in summer, so that at midnight it is difficult for those who are watching to tell whether the evening twilight still lingers, or the dawn of morning is coming, since the sun at night returns to the east through the northern regions without passing far below the horizon. For this reason the summer days are extremely long; on the other hand the winter nights are also of great length, namely eighteen hours, for the sun then withdraws into the regions of Africa. In summer too the nights are extraordinarily short, as are the days in winter, each containing only six equinoctial hours,[2] while in Armenia, Macedonia, Italy, and other countries in the same latitude, the longest day or night extends to fifteen hours, and the shortest to nine.

At the present time, there are five languages in Britain, the English, British,[3] Irish, Pictish, and Latin, just as the divine law is written in five books, each in its own way devoted to seeking out and setting forth one and the same knowledge of sublime truth and true sublimity. The Latin tongue, through the study of the Scriptures, has become common to all the rest. At first this island had no other inhabitants than the Britons, from whom it derived its name, and who, coming over into Britain, so it is said, from Armorica,[4] took possession of the southern parts of it. When they had made themselves masters of the greatest part of the island, beginning from the south, it is said that the Pictish race from Scythia,[5] putting to sea in a few long ships, were driven by the winds beyond the shores of Britain and arrived on the northern coast of Ireland. There they found the Irish race and asked to be allowed to settle among them, but their request was refused. Ireland is the largest island next to Britain, and lies to the west of it; but though it is shorter than Britain to the north, yet it runs out far beyond it to the south, opposite to the northern parts of Spain, though a wide sea lies between them. The Picts came to this island, as has been said, by sea and asked that a place be granted them where they might settle. The Irish answered that the island could not hold them both; but they said, "We can give you some good advice as to what to do. We know of another island not far from ours, to the east, which we often see in the distance on a clear day. If you will go there, you can make settlements; but if anyone should oppose you, you shall have our help." And so the Picts, sailing over into Britain, began to occupy the northern parts of the island, because the Britons had seized the southern parts. Now the Picts had no wives, so they asked the Irish for some; they consented to give them women only on condition that, when any difficulty should arise, they should choose a king from the female line rather than the male; this custom, as is well known, has been observed among the Picts to this day. In the course of time Britain received a third nation in addition to the Britons and the Picts, namely the Irish, who came from Ireland under their leader Reuda, and won lands from

---

[1] *St. Basil says* In his *Hexaemeron*, a treatise on the six days of creation.

[2] *equinoctial hours* As Bede explains in his *De temporum ratione* (*The Reckoning of Time*), these hours are those which divide the day evenly into twenty-four parts (i.e., like a modern day); "common" hours divide day and night into twelve hours each of uneven length, so that summer hours are long during the day and short at night, and winter hours are just the reverse.

[3] *British* I.e., Welsh.

[4] *Armorica* Area along the northwest coast of France somewhat larger than modern Brittany.

[5] *Scythia* Irish tradition reports that the Picts come from Thrace; Bede may be following this here, or using "Scythia" to mean the farthest northern regions of the world, Ultima Thule.

the Picts either by fair means or by force of arms. They still possess these lands. They are to this day called *Dalreudini* after their commander—in their language, *Dal* signifies a part.

Ireland far surpasses Britain in breadth and in wholesomeness and serenity of climate, for the snow rarely lies there above three days. No man makes hay in the summer for winter use, or builds stables for his beasts of burden. No reptiles are found there, and no snake can live there; for although serpents have often been carried to Ireland from Britain, as soon as the ship comes near the shore and the scent of the air reaches them, they die. In fact almost everything in the island is good against poison. We have seen how, for example, when people have been bitten by serpents, the leaves of manuscripts from Ireland were scraped, and the scrapings put in water and given to them to drink. These scrapings immediately expelled the spreading poison, and eased the swelling. The island abounds in milk and honey, nor is there any lack of vines, fish, or fowl; and it is noted for deer and goats. It is properly the native land of the Irish; they migrated from there, as has been said, and formed the third nation in Britain in addition to the Britons and the Picts. There is a very wide arm of the sea, which originally divided the nation of the Picts from the Britons; it runs from the west very far into the land, where, to this day, stands the strong city of the Britons, called Alcluith.[1] The Irish settled on the north side of this bay and made their home there.

2. THE COMING OF THE ENGLISH TO BRITAIN

[After the Goths attack Rome in 410, the Roman legions in Britain withdraw, leaving the British defenseless, "utterly ignorant of the arts of war." They are immediately attacked by the Irish from the west and the Picts from the north. Bede's source for this section is the British historian Gildas, whose *De excidio Britonum* ("On the Ruin of Britain") is a stern and prophetic work upbraiding the British for their sins and lamenting the punishments they suffered at the hands of the Saxon invaders. Bede's allegiances are different, of course, but the harsh tone of Gildas's polemic, and his assertion that the coming of the English was ordained by God, is put to good use in Bede's excoriation of the British (Bede's deep dislike of the British arose, ostensibly at least, from their refusal to convert their conquerors to Christianity).]

In the year of our Lord 423, Theodosius the younger became emperor after Honorius, the forty-fifth from Augustus, and governed the Roman empire twenty-six years. In the eighth year of his reign Palladius was sent by Celestinus, the Roman pontiff, to the Irish who believed in Christ, to be their first bishop.[2] In the twenty-third year of his reign Aetius, a man of high rank and a patrician, held his third consulship with Symmachus. The wretched remnants of the Britons sent him a letter which began: "To Aetius, thrice Consul, the groans of the Britons." In the course of the letter they expressed their sorrows: "The barbarians drive us to the sea; the sea drives us back to the barbarians: between them we face two sorts of death—we are either slaughtered or drowned." Yet all this could not procure any assistance from him, because he was engaged in a deadly war with Blædla and Attila, kings of the Huns. And even though Blædla had been murdered the year before this by the treachery of his brother Attila, nevertheless Attila himself remained so dangerous an enemy to the state that he devastated almost all of Europe, attacking and destroying cities and castles. At the same time there was a famine in Constantinople, which was followed shortly afterwards by the plague, and a great part of the walls of that city fell to the ground, along with fifty-seven towers. Many cities also fell into ruins, and the famine and pestilential stench which filled the air destroyed thousands of men and cattle.

Meanwhile this famine afflicted the Britons more and more, leaving a lasting memory of its malice to posterity. It forced many of them to submit themselves to their predatory enemies; others still held out, trusting in divine assistance when none was to be had from men. These continually made raids from the mountains, caves, and forests, and at last they began to inflict severe losses on the enemy who had been plundering their land

---

[1] *Alcluith* Dumbarton.

[2] *Palladius was sent ... bishop* Nothing much is known of Palladius beyond what Bede reports; Bede never mentions St. Patrick, who is generally remembered as the "Apostle to the Irish."

for so many years. The shameless Irish robbers then returned home, intending to come back before long; the Picts, from that time on, remained quiet in the farthest part of the island, though they did not cease to plunder and harass the Britons from time to time.

When the ravages of the enemy finally ceased, there was such an abundance of grain in the island as had never been known before. With abundance came an increase in luxury, which was immediately followed by every sort of crime; in particular, cruelty and hatred of truth and love of falsehood increased so much that if anyone among them happened to be milder than the rest and somewhat inclined to truth, all the rest heaped hatred and missiles upon him, as if he had been the enemy of Britain. Not only were laymen guilty of these things, but even our Lord's own flock and their pastors too; they cast off the light yoke of Christ[1] and thrust their necks under the burden of drunkenness, hatred, argument, strife, envy, and other crimes of this sort. In the meantime a severe plague suddenly fell upon that corrupt generation, and soon destroyed so many of them that there were scarcely enough people left alive to bury the dead: yet those who survived could not be awakened from the spiritual death which their sins had brought upon them, either by the death of their friends or by the fear of their own death. For this reason, a still more severe retribution soon afterwards fell upon this sinful nation for their horrible wickedness. They consulted as to what should be done, and where they should seek help to prevent or repel the very frequent attacks of the northern nations, and they all agreed with their King Vortigern[2] that they should call the Saxons to their aid from across the sea. As events clearly showed, this was ordained by the will of our Lord Himself so that evil might fall upon them for their wicked deeds.

In the year of our Lord 449 Marcian became emperor with Valentinian, the forty-sixth emperor from Augustus, and ruled for seven years. At this time the nation of the Angles or Saxons, being invited by Vortigern, came to Britain in three long ships; they were granted a place to settle in the eastern part of the island so that they might appear to be fighting for their country, but their real intention was to enslave it. Accordingly they first fought against the enemy who attacked from the north, and won the victory. When this became known at home in their own country, and also the fertility of the country and the cowardice of the Britons, a much larger fleet was quickly sent over with a greater number of men; this, added to the troop already there, made an invincible army. The newcomers received a grant of land from the Britons, on condition that they wage war against their enemies for the peace and safety of the country, and the Britons agreed to pay them.

Those who came over were from three powerful tribes in Germany—the Saxons, Angles, and Jutes. From the Jutes are descended the people of Kent and of the Isle of Wight, and that part of the kingdom of the West Saxons just opposite the Isle of Wight, which is still today called the nation of the Jutes. From the country of the Saxons, that is, the region which is now known as Old Saxony, came the East Saxons, the South Saxons, and the West Saxons. From the country of the Angles—that is, the region between the provinces of the Jutes and the Saxons which is called *Angulus*, and which is said to remain deserted from that day to this—came the East Angles, the Middle Angles, the Mercians, and all the Northumbrian race (that is, those people that dwell north of the river Humber), and the other Anglian tribes.[3] Their first commanders are said to have been two brothers, Hengest and Horsa. Horsa was afterwards killed in battle by the Britons, and was buried in the eastern part of Kent, where there is still a monument bearing his name. They were the sons of Wihtgils, son of Witta, son of Woden, from whose stock the royal families of many kingdoms claim their descent.[4]

---

[1] *Not only ... of Christ* See Matthew 11.29.

[2] *King Vortigern* Bede expands on his source Gildas here to supply the name of the king Vortigern (which means "chief lord"—Gildas calls him only *superbus tyrannus*, which basically means the same thing) and the names of the Saxons Hengest and Horsa (both names mean "horse"). Vortigern later has a prominent (though ignominious) role in the Arthurian legends as shaped by Geoffrey of Monmouth's *History of the Kings of Britain*.

[3] *Anglian tribes* Or "English people." In the title of his work, and in its text as well, Bede refers to all the invading tribes as the *gens Anglorum* or "English people."

[4] *They were the ... their descent* Bede is apparently not troubled by the fact that Woden is a Germanic god, suggesting that by his day active worship of Woden was not widespread. In medieval historical writing, the various classical and Germanic gods (when they are not written off as demons masquerading to lead men astray) are usually

In a short time hordes of these peoples flooded into the island, and their numbers increased so much that they became a terror to the natives who had invited them. Then suddenly they joined forces with the Picts, whom they had by this time driven far away by the force of their arms, and began to turn their weapons against their allies. First they made them supply a greater quantity of food; then, seeking an occasion to quarrel, they insisted that unless more plentiful supplies were brought to them, they would break the alliance and ravage the whole island. Nor were they slow in carrying out their threats—to make a long story short, the fire kindled by the hands of these pagans executed God's just revenge on the nation for its crimes, not unlike the fire once kindled by the Chaldeans which consumed the walls and city of Jerusalem.[1] Likewise here in Britain the just Judge ordained that the fire of these brutal conquerors should ravage all the neighboring cities and countryside from the east to the western sea, without opposition, until it covered almost every part of the doomed island. Public and private buildings fell into ruins; priests were everywhere slain before the altars; the prelates and people alike were destroyed with fire and sword regardless of their rank; and there was no one left to bury those who had died in such a cruel slaughter. Some of the miserable remnant were captured in the mountains and butchered in heaps; others, exhausted by hunger, came forward and submitted themselves to the enemy, ready to accept perpetual slavery for the sake of food, if only they were not killed on the spot. Some fled sorrowfully beyond the sea, while others remained in their own land and led a miserable life among the forests, crags, and mountains, always expecting every moment to be their last.

When the victorious army had destroyed and dispersed the native peoples, and returned home to their own settlements,[2] the Britons slowly began to gather strength and courage. They emerged from their hiding places and unanimously prayed for divine assistance that they might not be utterly destroyed. Their leader at that time was Ambrosius Aurelius,[3] a modest man who was, by chance, the sole member of the Roman nation to survive the storm in which his parents, who were of a royal and famous family, had perished. Under his leadership the Britons regained their strength, challenged their victors to battle and, by the help of God, won the victory. From that time on, sometimes the natives, and sometimes their enemies, prevailed, until the year of the siege of Mount Badon, when the Britons made no small slaughter of their enemies, about forty-four years after their arrival in England. But more of this hereafter.

3. The Life and Conversion of Edwin, King of Northumbria; the Faith of the East Angles

[The conversion of Edwin is in many ways the central event in Bede's long history—it sets England firmly on the road to Christianity and represents the crowning achievement of the mission of Augustine of Canterbury, sent by Pope Gregory the Great to convert the island. Bede probably relied on local knowledge and memories for his story; he therefore has to explain why Edwin's conversion is significantly delayed and accomplished with much foot-dragging.

According to Bede's account, Edwin secured his kingship in Northumbria with the help of Rædwald, the king of East Anglia, in 616; later he married Æthelburh, daughter of the Christian king Æthelberht of Kent, in 625. One of the conditions of the marriage was that he put no obstacles in the way of Christian worship in his kingdom, and promise to consider becoming a Christian himself. Æthelburh arrives in Northumbria accompanied by the bishop Paulinus; though Paulinus works diligently to convert Edwin, he is unsuccessful for a long time. When Edwin survives an assassination attempt by the West Saxons on the same day he celebrates the birth of his daughter (whom he allows to be baptized), he promises to convert if God will grant him victory over his enemies. After his campaign against the West Saxons is successful, however, he delays

---

explained as ancient heroes whose exploits and stature were inflated over time until they were worshipped as gods.

[1] *not unlike ... Jerusalem*   See 2 Kings 25.8–10.

[2] *settlements*   I.e., in Britain, not Germany.

[3] *Ambrosius Aurelius*   Bede's information comes from Gildas; no earlier or more reliable source is known for Ambrosius Aurelius, later transformed into King Arthur. The battle of Mount Badon, if it occurred at all, probably took place around 500 CE.

fulfilling his promise for a long time, despite the instruction of Paulinus, the prayers of his wife, and the entreaties of the Pope (Boniface) himself.

Bede's account of Edwin's conversion is sometimes caught between its contradictory impulses towards hagiography (in which conversion is described as a personal journey to faith, punctuated by miracles) and political history (in which conversion is seen as an act of royal policy). But it is marked by a lively sense of scene and character, and vividly conveys the fragile and sometimes dangerous nature of early Anglo-Saxon kingship, the power of the "heroic" code as an ideal of behavior, and the complex implications of conversion; Bede's report (or invention) of the council at which Edwin hears the opinions of his advisors—the unnamed philosophical nobleman, the opportunistic high priest Coifi—is a classic scene, a Christian writer's lyrical, almost elegiac imagination of the pagan heart.]

Such was the letter that Pope Boniface wrote for the salvation of King Edwin and his nation. But a heavenly vision, which God in His mercy had once chosen to reveal to Edwin when he was in exile at the court of Rædwald, king of the Angles, was of greater use in urging him to understand and embrace the counsels of salvation. Paulinus saw how difficult it was for the king's proud mind to bow to the humility of the way of salvation and accept the mystery of the life-giving cross, but at the same time he continued to use both exhortation with men and prayer to God for his and his subjects' salvation. At length, as we may suppose, he was shown in spirit the nature of the vision that had once been revealed to the king. Nor did he lose any time in warning the king to fulfill the vow he had made when he saw the vision, which he had promised to undertake if he should be delivered from the trouble he was in at that time, and ascend to the throne.

His vision was this: when his predecessor Æthelfrith was persecuting him, he wandered secretly for many years through several places and kingdoms, and at last came to Rædwald, asking him for protection against the plots of his powerful persecutor. Rædwald gladly received him, and promised to do what he asked. But when Æthelfrith learned that he had been seen in that kingdom, and had been hospitably entertained by the king and his retainers, he sent messengers to offer Rædwald a great sum of money to kill Edwin. But this had no effect; he sent a second and a third time, offering more and more each time, and threatening to make war on him if he refused. Rædwald, either terrified by his threats or corrupted by his bribes, yielded to his request and promised either to kill Edwin or to give him up to the messengers. A trusty friend of Edwin's found this out, and went into his chamber when he was going to bed, for it was the first hour of the night. He called him outside, told him what the king had promised to do with him, adding, "If you are willing, I will take you from this kingdom right now, and lead you to a place where neither Rædwald nor Æthelfrith will ever find you." Edwin answered, "I thank you for your goodwill, but I cannot do what you suggest, lest I be the first to break the compact I have made with this great king; he has done me no wrong, nor shown me any enmity. If I must die, let it rather be by his hand than by that of some meaner person. For where should I now fly, when I have for so many years been a vagabond through all the kingdoms of Britain, trying to escape the snares of my enemies?" His friend went away, and Edwin remained alone outside; sitting with a heavy heart in front of the palace, he began to be overwhelmed with many thoughts, not knowing what to do or which way to turn.

He remained a long time in silent anguish, brooding over his misfortunes, when suddenly in the dead of night he saw a man approach him whose face and dress were equally strange. He was more than a little frightened at this unexpected sight. The stranger came close, saluted him, and asked why he sat there alone and melancholy on a stone at that time, when everyone else was resting, and fast asleep. Edwin asked in reply what concern it was to him whether he spent the night indoors or out. The stranger replied, "Do not think that I am unaware of the cause of your grief, your sleeplessness, and your sitting alone outside. For I know who you are, and why you grieve, and the evils which you fear will fall upon you. But tell me, what reward would you give the man who would free you from this anguish, and persuade Rædwald neither to harm you himself, nor to give you up to be murdered by your enemies?" Edwin replied that he would give that person all that he was able in return for such a favor. The other continued, "What if he also assured you that you will overcome your enemies, and be a king who surpasses in power not only all your ancestors, but also all who have reigned before you over the English?" Edwin, encouraged by these questions, did not hesitate to promise that he would make a suitable return to anyone who should offer him such great benefits. Then the man said, "If the one who truly foretold so many good things could also give you better and more useful advice for your life and salvation than any of your ancestors or kindred ever heard of, would you consent to obey him, and to follow his saving counsel?" Edwin did not hesitate to promise that he would follow in every detail the directions of the one who could rescue him from so many troubles and raise him to the throne. At this answer the man who was speaking to him laid his hand on his head saying, "When this sign shall come to you, remember this conversation that has passed between us, and do not hesitate to fulfill what you have now promised." Having uttered these words, it is said that he immediately disappeared, so that the king might realize that it was not a man but a spirit that had appeared to him.

The young prince sat there alone for a time, rejoicing in the consolation he had received but deeply troubled and anxiously wondering who it was that had talked to him in that way, or where he had come from. Meanwhile the friend mentioned earlier returned, greeted him pleasantly and said, "Rise, go inside, and let yourself sleep without fear! The king has changed his mind and intends to do you no harm but rather to keep the promise he made you; when he secretly revealed to the queen the plan I told you before, she talked him out of it, warning that was unworthy of so great a king to sell his good friend for gold when he was in such distress, and to sacrifice his own honor, more precious than any ornament, for the love of money." In short, the king did as he had said, and not only refused to betray the banished man to his enemy's messengers, but helped Edwin to recover his kingdom. As soon as the messengers had returned home, he raised a mighty army to overthrow Æthelfrith. Rædwald did not give him time to gather all his forces; he attacked him with a much larger army and killed him on the borders of the kingdom of Mercia, on the east bank of the river Idle. In this

battle Rædwald's son Regenhere was killed. And thus Edwin, in accordance with the vision he had received, not only escaped the snares of the king his enemy, but after his death succeeded him on the throne.

King Edwin hesitated to accept the word of God preached by Paulinus, and for some time, as we have said, used to sit alone for several hours at a time, earnestly debating within himself what he ought to do and what religion he should follow. One day the man of God[1] came to him, laid his right hand on the king's head, and asked him if he recognized this sign. The king, trembling, was about to fall down at his feet but Paulinus raised him up and said in a voice that seemed familiar, "Behold, with God's help you have escaped the hands of the enemies you feared; behold, you have obtained by His gift the kingdom you desired; take heed not to delay what you promised to do—receive the faith and keep the commandments of Him who rescued you from earthly adversity and has raised you to the honor of an earthly kingdom. If, from this time forward, you are willing to follow his will, which is made known to you through me, He will not only deliver you from the everlasting torments of the wicked, but also make you a partaker with Him of His eternal kingdom in heaven."

When the king heard these words, he answered that he was both willing and bound to accept the faith which Paulinus taught, but that he would confer about it with his chief men and counselors so that, if they agreed with him, they might all together be cleansed in Christ, the Fountain of Life. Paulinus agreed, and the king did as he said: holding a meeting with his council of wise men, he asked each one in turn what he thought of this new doctrine, and the new worship of God that had been proclaimed.

Coifi, chief of his own priests, immediately answered, "Consider, O king, this new doctrine that is being preached to us. For I say to you truly that as far as I can tell, the religion we have practiced until now has no virtue in it. None of your people has devoted himself more diligently to the worship of our gods than I, and yet there are many who receive greater favors and greater honor from you than I do, and are more prosperous in all their undertakings. If the gods had any power they would have helped me more readily, since I have been

---

[1] *man of God* I.e., Paulinus.

more careful to serve them. It follows, therefore, that if on examination those new doctrines which are now preached to us are found to be better and more effective, we should accept them immediately and without delay."

Another of the king's chief men agreed with his words and his advice, and then added: "This is how the present life of man, O king, seems to me in comparison with that time which is unknown to us: as if you are sitting in your feasting-hall with your ealdormen and thanes[1] in wintertime, with a good fire burning in the middle of the hall and all inside is warm, while outside the winter storms of rain and snow are raging; and a sparrow flies swiftly through the hall, entering in at one door and quickly flying out at another. While he is within the winter storms cannot touch him; but after the briefest moment of calm he immediately vanishes out of your sight, out of the winter and back into it again. So this life of man appears just for a moment—of what went before, or what is to follow, we know nothing at all. If this new doctrine contains anything more certain, it seems right that we should follow it." The other elders and counselors spoke in the same way, by divine inspiration.

Coifi added that he wanted to listen more attentively to what Paulinus had to say about the God he preached. The king ordered Paulinus to speak and Coifi, hearing his words, cried out, "I have long realized that our religion is worthless—the the more diligently I sought the truth in our worship, the less I found it. But now I freely confess that such truth shines forth clearly in this preaching, which can bestow on us the gift of life, salvation, and eternal happiness. Therefore I advise, O king, that we instantly abandon and set fire to those temples and altars which we have consecrated without reaping any benefit from them." What more is there to say? The king publicly accepted the gospel which Paulinus preached, renouncing idolatry, and confessed his faith in Christ; and when he asked the high priest who should be the first to profane the altars and temples of their idols, together with the enclosures around them, Coifi answered, "I will; for who can more properly than myself destroy those things which I once worshiped in ignorance, through the wisdom which has been given me by the true God, and set an example for others?"

And immediately, casting aside his former superstitions, he asked the king to furnish him with arms and a stallion, and mounting it he set out to destroy the idols. Now the high priest was not allowed to carry arms or to ride on any horse but a mare; but with a sword girded about him and a spear in his hand, he mounted the king's stallion and set off for the idols.[2] The common people, seeing this, thought he was mad; but wasting no time, as soon as he drew near the temple he profaned it by casting into it the spear which he held, and rejoicing in the knowledge of the worship of the true God, he ordered his companions to destroy and set fire to the temple and all its enclosures. This place where the idols once stood is still shown, a short distance east of York beyond the river Derwent. Today it is called Goodmanham, the place where the high priest, by the inspiration of the true God, profaned and destroyed the altars which he had himself consecrated.

So King Edwin and all the nobles of his nation, and a large number of the common people, received the faith and regeneration by holy baptism in the eleventh year of his reign, that is in the year of our Lord 627, and about 180 years after the coming of the English into Britain. He was baptized at York on Easter day, the 12th of April, in the church of St. Peter the Apostle which he himself had built of timber, while he was a catechumen[3] and receiving instruction in order to receive baptism. In the same city he established an episcopal see for his instructor and bishop Paulinus. As soon as he was baptized he began, under the direction of Paulinus, to build a larger and more noble church of stone in the same place, in the midst of which the chapel which he had built first would be enclosed. The foundations were laid and he began to build the church square, surrounding the former chapel, but before the walls were raised to their proper height, the king was cruelly slain[4] and the work was left to his successor Oswald. Paulinus continued to preach the word of the Lord in the king-

---

[1] *ealdormen and thanes* Noblemen.

[2] *Now the high priest ... idols* Bede is our only authority for this custom, or for the existence of "high priests" in Anglo-Saxon pagan religion.

[3] *catechumen* Person preparing to be baptized into the Catholic faith.

[4] *The king was cruelly slain* In battle against Cædwalla, king of the Britons, and Penda, King of the Mercians.

dom for six years, that is, until the end of the king's reign, with his consent and favor, and all who were predestined for eternal life believed and were baptized. Among these were Osfrid and Eadfrid, King Edwin's sons, who were born to him while he was in exile; their mother was Cwenburh, daughter of Ceorl, king of the Mercians.

Other children of his by Queen Æthelburh were baptized later, namely Æthelhun and a daughter Æthelthryth and a second son Uscfrea; the first two were snatched from this life while still in their white garments,[1] and buried in the church at York. Yffi, son of Osfrith, was also baptized, and many more nobles and members of the royal family. It is said that the fervor of the faith and the longing for the washing of salvation was so great among the Northumbrians that once when Paulinus came to the king and queen in their royal palace called *Ad gefrin*,[2] he spent thirty-six days there fully occupied in catechising and baptizing, and during these days, from morning till night, he did nothing but instruct the people who came from every village and region in Christ's saving word. When they were instructed, he washed them with the water of absolution in the river Glen, which is nearby. This palace was abandoned by the kings who followed Edwin and another built instead, at the place called *Mælmin*.[3]

All this happened in the kingdom of Bernicia; but in the kingdom of Deira also, where Paulinus used to stay frequently with the king, he baptized in the river Swale, which runs by the village of Catterick, for in the earliest days of the church there they could not build chapels or baptistries. But in *Campodonum*,[4] where there was also a royal dwelling, he built a church which afterwards was burned down, together with all the buildings, by the pagans who killed King Edwin. In its place later kings built a dwelling for themselves in the region called *Loidis*.[5] The altar, which was made of stone, escaped the fire and is still preserved in the monastery of the most reverend abbot and priest Thrythwulf, which is in the forest of Elmet.

Edwin was so devoted to the true worship that he also persuaded Eorpwald, son of Rædwald and king of the East Saxons, to abandon his idolatrous superstitions and, with his whole kingdom, to accept the Christian faith and sacraments. Indeed his father Rædwald had long before been initiated into the mysteries of the Christian faith in Kent, but in vain; for on his return home, he was seduced by his wife and by certain perverse teachers, and turned back from the sincerity of the faith, so that his last state was worse than his first.[6] Like the ancient Samaritans, he seemed at the same time to serve Christ and the gods whom he had previously served, and in the same temple he had one altar for Christian sacrifice and another small one to offer victims to devils. Ealdwulf, ruler of that kingdom up to our own time, testified that the temple had stood until his time, and that he had seen it when he was a boy. King Rædwald, noble by birth but ignoble in his actions, was the son of Tytil, whose father was Wuffa, from whom the kings of the East Angles are called Wuffings.[7]

Eorpwald, not long after he had embraced the Christian faith, was killed by a heathen called Ricberht; and afterwards the kingdom remained in error for three years, until Eorpwald's brother Sigeberht came to the throne. Sigeberht was a devout Christian and a learned man; he was in exile during his brother's life and went to live in Gaul, where he was admitted to the sacraments of the Christian faith. As soon as he came to the throne he made it his business to see that the whole kingdom shared his faith. His efforts were strongly supported by

---

[1] *white garments* I.e., still wearing the white robe given to those who are newly baptized and worn every day for the first week after the sacrament.

[2] *Ad gefrin* Present-day Yeavering, Northumberland. Archaeologists have excavated the site of Edwin's hall, an impressive complex of large buildings and outdoor spaces on the site of a Neolithic hill fort.

[3] *Mælmin* Near present-day Millfield, Northumberland.

[4] *Campodonum* Roman site near Dewsbury, Yorkshire.

[5] *Loidis* Leeds.

[6] *so that his … his first* See Luke 11.26.

[7] *King Rædwald … Wuffings* Bede's account of Rædwald's incomplete conversion and excessive ecumenism contrasts sharply with that of Edwin's deep, thoughtful and fervent faith; moreover, since he is a Northumbrian, Bede's center of gravity is in the north, not least because his sources of information were probably richer. But the treacherous and backsliding East Saxons should not be underrated: Rædwald is widely thought to be the king honored by the elaborate and richly decorated ship-burial at Sutton Hoo, and the *Wuffings* may or may not be the same as the Swedish *Wylfings* mentioned in *Beowulf*.

Bishop Felix. The bishop had been born and ordained in Burgundy; when he came to Archbishop Honorius and expressed his desires, the archbishop sent him to preach the word of life to this nation of the Angles. Nor were his wishes in vain, for the devoted sower reaped an abundant harvest of believers in this spiritual field—indeed, as his name signified,[1] he delivered all of that kingdom from longstanding evil and unhappiness, brought it to the faith and to the works of righteousness, and gave it the gift of everlasting felicity. He received the see of his bishopric in the city of *Dommoc*,[2] and when he had ruled as bishop over the kingdom for seventeen years, he ended his days there in peace.

Paulinus also preached the word to the kingdom of Lindsey, the first land on the south bank of the river Humber, bordering on the sea. He first converted the prefect of the city of Lincoln, whose name was Blæcca, and his whole family. In this city he also built a stone church of beautiful workmanship; its roof has now either fallen through age or been thrown down by enemies, but the walls are still standing, and every year some miraculous cures are wrought in that place for the benefit of those who seek them in faith. When Justus departed to Christ, in his place Paulinus consecrated Honorius as bishop in that church, as we will later tell in its proper place.

An abbot and priest of the monastery of Partney, a most truthful man whose name was Deda, told me this about the faith of this kingdom: an old man had told him that he himself had been baptized at noon by Bishop Paulinus, in the presence of King Edwin, with a great number of people, in the river Trent, near the city which in English is called *Tiowulfingacæstir*.[3] He also used to describe the appearance of Paulinus: he was tall, a little stooping, with black hair, a thin face, a slender and aquiline nose, and an aspect both venerable and majestic. In his ministry he also had with him a deacon named James, a man of zeal and great reputation in Christ's Church, who survived right up to our days.

It is reported that there was such perfect peace in Britain, wherever the dominion of King Edwin extended, that, as the proverb still says, a woman with a new-born child could walk throughout the island from sea to sea without receiving any harm. The king cared so much for the good of his nation that in various places where he had noticed clear springs near the highways, he had stakes set up with bronze drinking-cups hanging from them, for the convenience of travelers. No one dared to touch them for any other purpose than the one they were designed for, because they feared the king and loved him dearly. His dignity was so great throughout his realm that not only were banners carried before him in battle, but even in time of peace, when he rode about his cities, estates, or regions with his thegns, a standard-bearer always used to go before him, and when he walked along the roads, there used to be carried before him the type of standard which the Romans call a *tufa* and the English a *thuf*.

4. ABBESS HILD OF WHITBY; THE MIRACULOUS POET CÆDMON

In the year of our Lord 680 Hild, the most devout servant of Christ, abbess of the monastery that is called Whitby,[4] departed on the 17th of November after having performed many heavenly works on earth, to receive the rewards of the heavenly life, at the age of sixty-six. She spent her first thirty-three years living most nobly in the secular habit, and more nobly dedicated the remaining half to our Lord in the monastic life. She was of noble birth, being the daughter of Hereric, nephew to King Edwin; in Edwin's company she received the faith and mysteries of Christ at the preaching of Paulinus of blessed memory, the first bishop of the Northumbrians, and she preserved her faith undefiled until she was rewarded with the sight of Him in heaven.

Resolving to give up the secular habit and serve Him alone, she withdrew to the kingdom of the East Angles, for she was related to the king there; she intended to pass over from there into Gaul, leaving her native land and all that she had to live as a stranger for our Lord's sake in the monastery of Chelles, so that she might more easily reach her eternal home in heaven. Her sister

---

[1] *as his name signified* Felix means "fortunate" or "happy" in Latin.

[2] *Dommoc* Dunwich.

[3] *Tiowulfingacæstir* Littleborough.

[4] *Whitby* Bede uses the Old English name "Streaneshalch."

Hereswith, mother of Ealdwulf, king of the East Angles, was at that time living in the same monastery under the discipline of the monastic Rule, waiting for her heavenly crown. Inspired by her example, Hild continued a whole year in the kingdom of the East Angles with the intention of going abroad; Bishop Aidan called her home, however, and gave her enough land to support herself on the north side of the river Wear, where she lived in the monastic life for a year, with a small group of companions.

After this she was made abbess in the monastery called *Heruteu*,[1] which had been founded not long before by Heiu, a devoted handmaid of Christ, who is said to have been the first woman in the kingdom of Northumbria to take the habit and vows of a nun, having been ordained by Bishop Aidan. But soon after she had founded that monastery, Heiu went away to the town of *Calcaria*, which the English call *Kælcacæstir*,[2] and there made her dwelling. Hild, the handmaid of Christ, was appointed to rule over that monastery, and immediately began to establish a rule of life there in all things, as she had been taught by many learned men; for Bishop Aidan and other devout men who knew her visited her frequently, instructed her diligently, and loved her dearly for her innate wisdom and devotion to the service of God.

When she had ruled over this monastery for some years, wholly intent upon establishing a rule of life there, it happened that she also undertook either to found or to reform a monastery in the place called *Streaneshalch*,[3] which she carried out with great industry. She established the same rule in this monastery as in the other, and she taught there the strict observance of justice, piety, chastity, and other virtues, above all peace and charity. After the example of the primitive church, no one there was rich, and no one was poor, for all things were common to all, and none had any private property. Her wisdom was so great that not only ordinary people, but even kings and princes sometimes asked for and received her advice; she obliged those who were under her direction to devote so much time to the study of the Holy Scriptures, and to exercise themselves so much in works of justice, that there might be no difficulty in finding many there who were fit for ecclesiastical duties, that is for the service of the altar.

In fact we have seen five men from that monastery become bishops, all of them men of singular merit and sanctity: Bosa, Ætla, Oftfor, John, and Wilfrid. The first of them, as we related elsewhere, was consecrated bishop of York; of the second, it may be observed that he was appointed bishop of Dorchester. Of the two last we shall later relate that John was consecrated bishop of Hexham and Wilfrid, bishop of York; of Oftfor we will here note that after he applied himself to the reading and observance of the Scriptures in both of Hild's monasteries, being anxious to attain to greater perfection, he went to Kent to join Archbishop Theodore, of blessed memory. After he had spent more time in sacred studies there, he resolved to go to Rome, which in those days was considered to be an act of great merit. After his return to Britain, he went to the province of the Hwicce, where King Osric then ruled, and remained there a long time, preaching the word of faith and setting an example of holy life to all who saw and heard him. At that time Bosel, the bishop of that kingdom, suffered such weakness of body that he could not carry out his episcopal duties; so Oftfor was appointed bishop in his place by universal consent, and was consecrated at King Æthelred's command by Bishop Wilfrid, of blessed memory, who was at that time bishop of the Middle Angles because Archbishop Theodore was dead, and no other bishop had been ordained in his place. Before Bosel, a most learned and industrious man of excellent ability named Tatfrid had been chosen bishop there, also from Hild's monastery, but he had been snatched away by an untimely death before his consecration.

All who knew Abbess Hild, the handmaid of Christ, called her Mother because of her outstanding piety and grace. She was not only an example of holy life to those who lived in her monastery, but provided an opportunity for repentance and salvation to many who lived far away who heard the happy news of her diligence and virtue. This was bound to happen so that the dream which her mother Breguswith had during Hild's infancy should be fulfilled. When her husband Hereric lived in exile under the British king Cerdic, where he was later

1   *Heruteu*   Hartlepool.

2   *Kælcacæstir*   Uncertain; possibly Tadcaster.

3   *Streaneshalch*   Site in northeastern Yorkshire (now Whitby) where the Abbess Hilda founded a double monastery.

poisoned, Breguswith dreamed that she was looking for him most carefully, and could find no sign of him anywhere; but suddenly, after having tried with all her might to find him, she found a most precious necklace under her garment, and as she was gazing at it very attentively, it cast such a blaze of light that it spread throughout all Britain. This dream came true in her daughter Hild, whose life was a bright example, not only to herself, but to many who desired to live well.

After she had governed this monastery many years, it pleased Him who has made such merciful provision for our salvation to subject her holy soul to the trial of a long sickness so that, like the apostle, her strength might be made perfect in weakness.

She was struck by a fever and fell into a violent heat, and for six years was afflicted continually; during all which time she never failed to give thanks to her Maker or to instruct the flock entrusted to her care both in public and in private. From her own experience she admonished everyone to serve the Lord dutifully in health and always to return thanks to Him in adversity or bodily illness. In the seventh year of her illness, she began to suffer internally and approached her last day. Around cock-crow, having received the viaticum of Holy Communion,[1] she called together the handmaids of Christ who were in the monastery, and admonished them to preserve the Gospel peace among themselves and towards all others; and as she was exhorting them she joyfully saw death approaching or, to use the words of our Lord, she passed from death into life.

That same night it pleased Almighty God by a vision to reveal her death in another monastery at some distance from hers called Hackness, which she had built that same year. In that monastery was a nun called Begu, who for thirty years or more had dedicated her virginity to God and served Him in the monastic life. While she was in the dormitory of the sisters, she suddenly heard in the air the familiar sound of the bell which used to awaken the sisters and call them to prayers when any one of them had been taken out of this world. Opening her eyes, she seemed to see the top of the house open, and a strong light pour in from above; looking intently at that light, she saw the soul of the handmaid of the Lord borne into heaven in the midst of that light, attended by angels. Then awaking and seeing the other sisters lying around her, she realized that what she had seen was either a dream or a vision; greatly frightened, she rose immediately and ran to a maiden named Frigyth, who was then presiding over the monastery in place of the abbess. With many tears and sighs, Begu told her that the Abbess Hild, mother of them all, had departed this life, and that she had seen her ascend with a great light, and with angels conducting her, into eternal bliss and the company of the inhabitants of heaven. When Frigyth heard this, she awoke all the sisters, and called them to the church; she ordered them to pray and sing psalms for Hild's soul, which they did for the rest of the night. At break of day, the brothers came from the place she had died with news of her death. They answered that they already knew it, and when they told how and when they had heard it, it was found that her death had been revealed to them in a vision in the very same hour that the brothers said she had died. Thus it was happily ordained by Heaven that when some watched her departure out of this world, others watched her entrance into the eternal life of the spirit. These monasteries are about thirteen miles distant from each other.

It is also reported that her death was made known in a vision the same night to one of the holy maidens who loved her most passionately, in the same monastery where this servant of God died. She saw Hild's soul ascend to heaven in the company of angels; and she declared this, the very same hour it happened, to those servants of Christ who were with her, and awakened them to pray for her soul, even before the rest of the congregation had heard of her death, for it was only made known to the whole monastery the next morning. This same nun was at that time with some other servants of Christ in the remotest part of the monastery, where the women who had recently entered the monastery used to spend their time of probation until they were instructed in the Rule and admitted to the society of the community.

In Hild's monastery was a certain brother specially marked by the grace of God, who used to make pious and religious verses, so that whatever he learned from the holy Scriptures through interpreters, he soon

---

[1] *viaticum … Communion* Communion received by someone who is possibly near death.

afterwards turned into poetry of great sweetness and humility, in English, which was his native language. By his verses the minds of many were often inspired to despise the world and to long for the heavenly life. After him other Englishmen tried to compose religious poems, but none could ever compare with him, for he did not learn the art of poetry from men or through a man,[1] but received the gift of song freely by divine grace. For this reason he never could compose any trivial or foolish poem, but only those which were concerned with devotion and were fitting for his pious tongue to utter.

He had lived in the secular life until he was well advanced in years, and had never learned any verses; therefore sometimes at feasts, when it was agreed for the sake of entertainment that all present should take a turn singing, when he saw the harp coming towards him, he would rise up from the table in the middle of the feast, go out, and return home. On one occasion when he did this, he left the house of feasting and went to the stable, where it was his turn to take care of the animals that night. In due time he stretched out to rest; a person appeared to him in his sleep, saluted him by name, and said, "Cædmon, sing me something." Cædmon answered, "I cannot sing; that is why I left the feast and came here, because I could not sing." The man who was talking to him replied, "Nevertheless, you must sing to me."

"What shall I sing?" he asked. "Sing about the beginning of created things," he replied. At that, Cædmon immediately began to sing verses which he had never heard before in praise of God, whose general sense is this: "We ought now to praise the Maker of the heavenly kingdom, the power of the Creator and his counsel, the deeds of the Father of glory and how He, since He is the eternal God, was the author of all marvels and first, as almighty Guardian of the human race, created heaven as a roof for the sons of men, and then the earth."[2] This is the sense but not the actual order of the words he sang in his sleep, for poetry, no matter how well composed, cannot be literally translated from one language into another without losing much of its beauty and dignity. Awaking from his sleep, Cædmon remembered all that he had sung in his dream, and soon added more verses in the same manner, praising God in a worthy style.

In the morning he went to the steward, his master, and told him of the gift he had received; the steward led him to the abbess, who ordered him, in the presence of many learned men, to recount his dream and repeat his poem, so that they might all decide what it was and where it had come from. It was clear to all of them he had received a gift of heavenly grace from our Lord. Then they explained to him a passage of sacred history or doctrine, and ordered him, if he could, to turn it into verse. He undertook this task and went away; when he returned the next morning he repeated it to them, composed in excellent verse. At this the abbess, recognizing the grace of God in this man, instructed him to renounce the secular habit and take up the monastic life; when this was done she joined him to the rest of the brethren in her monastery and ordered that he should be taught the whole course of sacred history. He learned all that he could by listening, and turned it over in his mind like a clean beast chewing the cud,[3] turned it into the most harmonious verse, and recited it so sweetly that his teachers became in turn his audience. He sang of the creation of the world, the origin of the human race, and all the history of Genesis; and made many verses on the departure of the children of Israel from Egypt, and their entry into the Promised Land, and many other stories from the holy Scriptures; of the Incarnation, Passion, and Resurrection of our Lord, and of His Ascension into heaven, of the coming of the Holy Spirit and the teaching of the apostles, also of the terror of future judgment, the horror of the pains of hell, and the joys of the kingdom of heaven, and many more songs about the divine mercies and judgments by which he tried to turn all men away from the love of vice and to inspire in them the love and practice of good works. He was a very devout man, humbly submissive to the discipline of the

---

[1] *from men or through a man*   See Galatians 1.1.

[2] *We ought now ... the earth*   See below for Cædmon's *Hymn* in Old English. Bede gives only this paraphrase; in two manuscripts of Bede's Latin *Historia* a poem in the Northumbrian dialect of Old English is added in the margins. When Bede's work was translated into Old English at the end of the ninth century, the translators substituted a version of this poem for Bede's paraphrase, and omitted the disclaimer that follows it.

[3] *He learned ... the cud*   See Leviticus 11.3; Deuteronomy 14.6.

monastic rule, but full of zeal against those who behaved otherwise; for this reason his life had a lovely ending.

When the hour of his departure drew near, for fourteen days he was afflicted with a bodily weakness which seemed to prepare the way, yet mild enough that he could talk and walk the whole time. Nearby was the house to which the sick and dying were carried. As evening fell on the night he was going to depart this life, he asked his attendant[1] to prepare a place for him there so he could take his rest. The attendant wondered why he should desire that, because there seemed to be no sign of his dying soon, but did what he had asked. They went there and were talking pleasantly and joyfully with the people who were already in the house; when it was past midnight he asked them whether they had the Eucharist there. They answered, "What need do you have of the Eucharist? You are not likely to die, since you talk so merrily with us, just as though you were in perfect health." "Nevertheless," he said, "bring me the Eucharist." When he had taken it into his hand he asked whether they were all in charity with him, without any complaint or quarrel. They answered that they were all in perfect charity, and free from anger; and likewise asked him whether he felt the same towards them. He answered at once, "My sons, I am in charity with all the servants of God." Then strengthening himself with the heavenly viaticum, he prepared for his entrance into the next life; he asked how near it was to the time when the brothers had to awaken to sing their nightly praise of our Lord. They answered, "It is not far off." He said, "Good; let us wait until then," and signing himself with the sign of the holy cross, he laid his head on the pillow and fell into a slumber, and so ended his life quietly. Thus it came to pass that, just as he had served God

with a simple and pure mind and quiet devotion, so now he departed into His presence and left the world by a quiet death, and his tongue, which had composed so many holy words in praise of the Creator, uttered its last words while he was in the act of signing himself with the cross, and commending his spirit into God's hands; and from what has been said, it seems he had foreknowledge of his death.

5. Cædmon's Hymn in Old and Modern English

Nu sculon herian   heofonrices weard,
Metodes meahta   ond his modgeþanc,
weorc wuldorfæder,   swa he wundra gehwæs,
ece Drihten,   or astealde.
He ærest scop   ielda bearnum
heofon to hrofe,   halig Scieppend;
þa middangeard   manncynnes weard,
ece Drihten,   æfter teode,
firum foldan   Frea ælmihtig.

Now (we) ought to praise Heaven-kingdom's guardian,
the Maker's might and his mind's thoughts,
the work of the glory-father, as he of each of wonders,
eternal Lord, established a beginning.[2]
He first shaped for men's sons
Heaven as a roof, the holy Creator;
then middle-earth mankind's guardian,
eternal Lord, afterwards prepared
the earth for men, the Lord almighty.

—C. 731

---

[1] *his attendant* Older monks were attended by young novices who took care of them.

[2] *Lord ... beginning* I.e., He established the beginning of every wonder.

EXETER BOOK ELEGIES

M ost of the Old English poetry that has survived is contained in only four manuscripts. The richest and most diverse of these is Exeter Cathedral Library MS 3501, a large anthology of secular and religious poems. The Exeter Book was given to the Cathedral library by the bishop Leofric some time before 1072 CE (and has remained there ever since), but it was written probably a century earlier, somewhere in the south of England. Because some pages have been lost from the manuscript, we cannot say how many poems it originally contained, and we do not know the impulse behind its compilation. But the Exeter Book is a fascinating miscellany, ranging from serious religious poetry on the Advent and Ascension of Christ, to verse lives of St. Guthlac and Juliana, to a translation of a Latin poem on the Phoenix, to a collection of almost 100 verse riddles which are sometimes comical or obscene. The poems are probably by many different authors; a poet named Cynewulf encoded his own name (in runes) in two poems, *Juliana* and *Christ II*, but all others are anonymous and untitled.

The Exeter Book includes a group of short philosophical poems, differing in style and outlook but similar in tone, which have come to be known as "elegies": among these are *The Wanderer*, *The Seafarer*, *The Wife's Lament*, *The Ruin*, *Wulf and Eadwacer*, and *The Husband's Message*. The label "elegy" here is potentially misleading. In Greek and Latin literature the term refers to a particular metrical form, and since the sixteenth century the word has been used in English literature to describe a poem of lament or mourning (the most famous English elegies include Milton's *Lycidas*, Shelley's *Adonais*, and Tennyson's *In Memoriam*). But the term "elegy" is sometimes used more loosely to describe any serious meditative poem, and it is in this sense that these Old English poems should be considered elegies. The poems share certain themes and concerns—the passage of time and the transience of earthly things, the pain of exile and separation, the ache of absence and longing—as well as certain images and scenes such as ruined or abandoned buildings, desolate landscapes, storms at sea, darkness, night and the chill of winter. These themes, and the traditional language in which they are presented, are also found in other Old English poems; certain passages of *Beowulf* may be called elegiac, and the contemplation of earthly instability sometimes seems to pervade Old English literature. The tone and language of elegy may have roots deep in the traditions of Germanic poetry, but it is also influenced by late classical works such as Boethius's *Consolation of Philosophy*; the recognition that the "world under the heavens" is a place of tragic impermanence would probably be regarded as equally good Christian doctrine and pagan wisdom. Both *The Wanderer* and *The Ruin* also appear to borrow from the Latin convention of posing "ubi sunt?" questions—in literal translation, "Where are they" or "Where are these things?"

Most of the Old English elegies are monologues spoken by an unidentified character whose situation is unclear but who seems to be cut off from human society and the comforts of home and friendship. But even though they share the poetic language of exile and longing, each poem has its own shape and purpose, and each makes its own statement about the problems and possibilities of earthly life. *The Wanderer* is initially concerned with a wandering warrior who has lost his Lord; the focus of the second half of the poem opens up to lament the passing of a whole way of life, the heroic world of the warrior's hall. *The Wife's Lament* (one of only two poems in the Exeter Book to be written from a woman's point of view) is a poem of intense personal longing for an absent husband or lover. *The Seafarer*, like *The Wanderer*, divides into two parts. The opening lines of the poem consist of a first-person narrative describing the hardships of going to sea, and contrasting them with the comforts of staying at home on land; around line 65 the poem shifts from a narrative to a spiritual meditation that is at times explicitly and even aggressively homiletic and Christian. *The Ruin* describes the remains of an ancient city—most probably an ancient Roman city in Britain, such as Bath, which had been abandoned centuries before the writing of this poem. The poem is detached and dispassionate about the scene it describes, and—in contrast to *The Seafarer*—whatever moral judgments it makes are implicit and indirect.

Each of the four poems presented below has some structural and interpretive difficulties. *The Wanderer* is a dramatic monologue with a prologue and epilogue, but the beginnings and endings of speeches are not indicated in the manuscript and can only be guessed at. *The Seafarer* switches tone so radically that many readers (including Ezra Pound, who translated the poem) have simply rejected the second, more homiletic half. *The Wife's Lament* is obscure more by virtue of its language than its structure—a number of the poem's key terms are ambivalent or uncertain. And the pages of the Exeter Book containing *The Ruin* have been so damaged that the poem is itself a ruin, crumbling into incoherence. The poems develop philosophical arguments and present evidence and conclusions, but Old English poetic language is not necessarily congenial to the demands of precise reasoning; sentence boundaries and relationships between clauses are often uncertain. And yet despite these interpretive problems, the Exeter Book "elegies" are among the most moving and powerful poems in Old English; their vision of life as both infinitely precious and inevitably transitory still strikes a responsive chord in the hearts of many readers.

⌘ ⌘ ⌘

The Wanderer [1]

Always the one alone longs for mercy,
the Maker's mildness, though, troubled in mind,
across the ocean-ways he has long been forced
to stir with his hands the frost-cold sea,
5   and walk in exile's paths. *Wyrd* [2] is fully fixed!

Thus spoke the Wanderer, mindful of troubles,
of cruel slaughters and the fall of dear kinsmen:[3]
"Often alone, every first light of dawn,
I have lamented my sorrows. There is no one living
10   to whom I would dare to reveal clearly
my heart's thoughts. I know it is true

that it is in the lordly nature of a nobleman
to closely bind his spirit's coffer,
hold his treasure-hoard, whatever he may think.
15   The weary mind cannot withstand *wyrd*,
the troubled heart can offer no help,
and so those eager for fame often bind fast
in their breast-coffers a sorrowing soul,
just as I have had to take my own heart—
20   often wretched, cut off from my homeland,
far from dear kinsmen—and bind it in fetters,
ever since long ago I hid my gold-giving friend
in the darkness of earth, and went wretched,
winter-sad, over the ice-locked waves,
25   sought, hall-sick, a treasure-giver,
wherever I might find, far or near,
someone in a meadhall who knew of my people,
or who'd want to comfort me, friendless,
accustom me to joy. He who has come to know
30   how cruel a companion is sorrow
to one who has few dear protectors, will understand
    this:
the path of exile claims him, not patterned gold,
a winter-bound spirit, not the wealth of earth.
He remembers hall-holders and treasure-taking,
35   how in his youth his gold-giving lord
accustomed him to the feast—that joy has all faded.

---

[1] *The Wanderer* The present text has been translated for *The Broadview Anthology of British Literature* by R.M. Liuzza.

[2] *Wyrd* A powerful but not quite personified force; the closest parallel in modern English is "Fate." It is related to the verb "weorthan," meaning roughly "to occur." Its meanings range from a neutral "event" to a prescribed "destiny" to a personified "Fate"; it is useful to think of "wyrd" as "what happens," usually in a negative sense.

[3] *Thus spoke ... kinsmen* The manuscript in which the poem survives does not have quotation marks, or clear indications of where speeches begin and end in this poem; we are not sure whether lines 1–5 are spoken by the same character who speaks the following lines, or whether they are the narrator's opinion on the general situation of the Wanderer.

And so he who has long been forced to forgo
his dear lord's beloved words of counsel will understand:
when sorrow and sleep both together
40 often bind up the wretched exile,
it seems in his mind that he clasps and kisses
his lord of men, and on his knee lays
hands and head, as he sometimes long ago
in earlier days enjoyed the gift-throne.[1]
45 But when the friendless man awakens again
and sees before him the fallow waves,
seabirds bathing, spreading their feathers,
frost falling and snow, mingled with hail,
then the heart's wounds are that much heavier,
50 longing for his loved one. Sorrow is renewed
when the memory of kinsmen flies through the mind;
he greets them with great joy, greedily surveys
hall-companions—they always swim away;
the floating spirits bring too few
55 well-known voices. Cares are renewed
for one who must send, over and over,
a weary heart across the binding of the waves.[2]

And so I cannot imagine for all this world
why my spirit should not grow dark
60 when I think through all this life of men,
how they suddenly gave up the hall-floor,
mighty young retainers. Thus this middle-earth
droops and decays every single day;
and so a man cannot become wise, before he has
    weathered
65 his share of winters in this world. A wise man
    must be patient,
neither too hot-hearted nor too hasty with words,
nor too weak in war nor too unwise in thoughts,
neither fretting nor fawning nor greedy for wealth,
never eager for boasting before he truly understands;
70 a man must wait, when he makes a boast,
until the brave spirit understands truly
whither the thoughts of his heart will turn.
The wise man must realize how ghastly it will be
when all the wealth of this world stands waste,

75 as now here and there throughout this middle-earth
walls stand blasted by wind,
beaten by frost, the buildings crumbling.
The wine halls topple, their rulers lie
deprived of all joys; the proud old troops
80 all fell by the wall. War carried off some,
sent them on the way, one a bird carried off
over the high seas, one the gray wolf
shared with death—and one a sad-faced man
covered in an earthen grave. The Creator
85 of men thus wrecked this enclosure,
until the old works of giants[3] stood empty,
without the sounds of their former citizens.

He who deeply considers, with wise thoughts,
this foundation and this dark life,
90 old in spirit, often remembers
so many ancient slaughters, and says these words:
'Where has the horse gone? where is the rider? where
    is the giver of gold?
Where are the seats of the feast? where are the joys
    of the hall?
O the bright cup! O the brave warrior!
95 O the glory of princes! How the time passed away,
slipped into nightfall as if it had never been!'
There still stands in the path of the dear warriors
a wall wondrously high, with serpentine stains.
A storm of spears took away the warriors,
100 bloodthirsty weapons, *wyrd* the mighty,
and storms batter these stone walls,
frost falling binds up the earth,
the howl of winter, when blackness comes,
night's shadow looms, sends down from the north
105 harsh hailstones in hatred of men.
All is toilsome in the earthly kingdom,
the working of *wyrd* changes the world under heaven.
Here wealth is fleeting, here friends are fleeting,
here man is fleeting, here woman is fleeting,
110 all the framework of this earth will stand empty."
So said the wise one in his mind, sitting apart
    in meditation.

---

[1] *it seems ... gift-throne* The description seems to be of some sort
of ceremony of loyalty, charged with intense regret and longing.

[2] *Cares are ... waves* The grammar and reference of this intense,
almost hallucinatory scene are not entirely clear; the translation
reflects one commonly proposed reading.

---

[3] *works of giants* Ruined buildings are called "the work of giants"
(*enta geweorc*) in several places in Old English literature.

He is good who keeps his word,[1] and the man who
    never too quickly
shows the anger in his breast, unless he already
    knows the remedy
115 a noble man can bravely bring about. It will be
    well for one who seeks mercy,
consolation from the Father in heaven, where for
    us all stability stands.
        —C. 975

The Seafarer [2]

I sing a true song of myself,
  tell of my journeys, how in days of toil
I've often suffered troubled times,
hard heartache, come to know
5 on the keel of a ship many of care's dwellings,
terrible tossing of the waves, where the anxious
night-watch often held me at the ship's stem
when it knocks against the cliffs. Pinched with cold
were my feet, bound by frost
10 in cold fetters, while cares seethed
hot around my heart, hunger tore from within
my sea-weary mind. That man does not know,
he whose lot is fairest on land,
how I, wretched with care, dwelt all winter
15 on the ice-cold sea in the paths of exile,
deprived of dear kinsmen,
hung with icicles of frost while hail flew in showers.
I heard nothing there but the noise of the sea,
the ice-cold waves; the wild swan's song
20 sometimes served as my music, the gannet's call
and the curlew's[3] cry for the laughter of men,
the seagull's singing for mead-drink.
Storms beat the stone cliffs where the tern answered
    them,
icy-feathered; often the eagle screamed,
25 dewy-feathered—no sheltering family

could bring consolation to my desolate soul.
    And so[4] he who has tasted life's joy in towns,
suffered few sad journeys, scarcely believes,
proud and puffed up with wine, what I, weary,
30 have often had to endure in my seafaring.
The night-shadow darkened; snow came from the
    north,
frost bound the ground, hail fell on earth,
coldest of grains. And so[5] they compel me now,
my heart-thoughts, to try for myself
35 the high seas, the tossing salt streams;
my heart's desire urges my spirit
time and again to travel, so that I might seek
far from here a foreign land.
    And so no man on earth is so proud in spirit,
40 nor so gifted in grace or so keen in youth,
nor so bold in deeds, nor so beloved of his lord,
that he never has sorrow over his seafaring,
when he sees what the Lord might have in store for
    him.
He has no thought of the harp or the taking of rings,
45 nor the pleasures of woman or joy in the world,
nor anything else but the tumbling waves—
he always has longing who hastens to sea.
The groves take blossom, the cities grow fair,
the fields brighten, the world rushes on;
50 all these urge the eager-hearted
spirit to travel, when one has a mind
to journey far over the flood-ways.
Even the cuckoo urges with its sad voice,
summer's guardian announces sorrow

---

[1] *who keeps his word* Or "keeps faith." These last lines offer an answer to the Wanderer's unresolved melancholia—the wisdom of self-control and the hope of Christian salvation.

[2] *The Seafarer* The present text has been translated for *The Broadview Anthology of British Literature* by R.M. Liuzza.

[3] *gannet … curlew* Seabirds.

[4] *And so* The repeated connecting word "forthon" is notoriously difficult in this poem—it points forwards and/or backwards, meaning either "therefore" or "thus" or "because." In a poem in which a logical progression is by no means clear or easy to follow this is a significant source of ambiguity. Rendering it with the vague "and so," preserves some of the interpretive difficulty found in the original.

[5] *And so* The disjunction between what has come before and what come after this line is so great that it has been proposed that a second speaker is introduced here (there are no quotation marks in Old English that might clarify this ambiguity). Though this "two-speaker" theory is no longer widely accepted, it reflects the difficulty many critics have reconciling the conflicting attitudes presented in the poem—sea voyage as terrible suffering, sea voyage as longed-for escape, sea-voyage as metaphor for spiritual pilgrimage, or even for life itself.

55 bitter in the breast-hoard. He does not know,
the man blessed with ease, what those endure
who walk most widely in the paths of exile.
    And so now my thought flies out from my breast,
my spirit moves with the sea-flood,
60 roams widely over the whale's home,
to the corners of the earth, and comes back to me
greedy and hungry; the lone flier cries out,
incites my heart irresistibly to the whale's path
over the open sea—because hotter to me
65 are the joys of the Lord than this dead life,
loaned, on land.[1] I will never believe
that earthly goods will endure forever.
Always, for everyone, one of three things
hangs in the balance before its due time:
70 illness or age or attack by the sword
wrests life away from one doomed to die.
And so for every man the praise of posterity,
those coming after, is the best eulogy—
that before he must be on his way, he act
75 bravely on earth against the enemies' malice,
do bold deeds to beat the devil,
so the sons of men will salute him afterwards,
and his praise thereafter live with the angels
forever and ever, in the joy of eternal life,
80 delight among heaven's host. The days are lost,
and all the pomp of this earthly kingdom;
there are now neither kings nor emperors
nor gold-givers as there once were,
when they did the greatest glorious deeds
85 and lived in most lordly fame.
All this noble host is fallen, their happiness lost,
the weaker ones remain and rule the world,
get what they can with toil. Joy is laid low,
the earth's nobility grows old and withers,
90 just like every man throughout middle-earth.
Old age overtakes him, his face grows pale,
the graybeard grieves; he knows his old friends,
offspring of princes, have been given up to the earth.

When life fails him, his fleshly cloak will neither
95 taste the sweet nor touch the sore,
nor move a hand nor think with his mind.
Though a brother may wish to strew his brother's
grave with gold, bury him among the dead
with myriad treasures to take with him,
100 that gold will be useless before the terror of God
for the soul that is full of sin,
the gold he had hidden while he lived here on earth.
    Great is the terror of God, the earth trembles
        before it;
He established the sturdy foundations,
105 the earth's solid surface and the high heavens.
Foolish is he who dreads not the Lord; death will
        find him unprepared.
Blessed is he who lives humbly; that mercy comes
        to him from heaven,
the Maker strengthens his spirit, for he believes in
        His might.
A man must steer a strong mind and keep it stable,
110 steadfast in its promises, pure in its ways;
every man must hold in moderation
his love for a friend and his hatred for a foe,
though he may wish him full of fire …
… or his friend consumed
115 on a funeral pyre.[2] Fate is greater,
the Maker mightier than any man's thoughts.
    Let us consider where we should have our home,
and then think how we may come there,
and let us also strive to reach that place
120 of eternal blessedness,
where life is found in the love of the Lord,
hope in Heaven. Thanks be to the Holy One
that He has so honored us, Ruler of Glory,
Eternal Lord, throughout all time. Amen.[3]

—C. 975

---

[1] *And so … on land* At this point the sea-voyage is revealed to be a journey of spiritual discovery. The hermit-monks of Ireland had a particular penchant for taking to small boats and trusting in God for their safety. Some reached Iceland, some are rumored to have reached the Americas; many others, no doubt, found rest at the bottom of the sea.

[2] *full of fire … funeral pyre* Something is missing from the manuscript here; the translation is conjectural and makes as little sense as the original.

[3] *Let us consider … Amen* The tone of these last lines, different in many respects from the rest of the poem, seems to place the poem finally in a homiletic setting—the exhortation of a preacher rather than the confession of a weathered mariner.

The Wife's Lament [1]

I make this song of myself, deeply sorrowing,
my own life's journey. I am able to tell
all the hardships I've suffered since I grew up,
but new or old, never worse than now—
5   ever I suffer the torment of my exile.

First my lord left his people
over the tumbling waves; I worried at dawn
where on earth my leader of men might be.
When I set out myself in my sorrow,
10   a friendless exile, to find his retainers,
that man's kinsmen began to think
in secret that they would separate us,
so we would live far apart in the world,
most miserably, and longing seized me.

15   My lord commanded me to live here;[2]
I had few loved ones or loyal friends
in this country, which causes me grief.
Then I found that my most fitting man
was unfortunate, filled with grief,
20   concealing his mind, plotting murder
with a smiling face. So often we swore
that only death could ever divide us,
nothing else—all that is changed now;
it is now as if it had never been,
25   our friendship. Far and near, I must
endure the hatred of my dearest one.

They forced me to live in a forest grove,
under an oak tree in an earthen cave.[3]
This earth-hall is old, and I ache with longing;
30   the dales are dark, the hills too high,
harsh hedges overhung with briars,
a home without joy. Here my lord's leaving
often fiercely seized me. There are friends on earth,
lovers living who lie in their bed,
35   while I walk alone in the first light of dawn
under the oak-tree and through this earth-cave,
where I must sit the summer-long day;

there I can weep for all my exiles,
my many troubles; and so I can never
40   escape from the cares of my sorrowful mind,
nor all the longings that seize me in this life.

May the young man always be sad-minded
with hard heart-thoughts, yet let him have
a smiling face along with his heartache,
45   a crowd of constant sorrows. Let to himself
all his worldly joys belong! let him be outlawed
in a far distant land, so my friend sits
under stone cliffs chilled by storms,
weary-minded, surrounded by water
50   in a sad dreary hall! My beloved will suffer
the cares of a sorrowful mind; he will remember
too often a happier home. Woe to the one
who must wait with longing for a loved one.[4]
—c. 975

The Ruin [5]

Wondrous is this foundation—the fates have broken
and shattered this city; the work of giants
   crumbles.
The roofs are ruined, the towers toppled,
frost in the mortar has broken the gate,
5   torn and worn and shorn by the storm,
eaten through with age. The earth's grasp
holds the builders, rotten, forgotten,
the hard grip of the ground, until a hundred
generations of men are gone. This wall, rust-stained
10   and covered with moss, has seen one kingdom after
   another,
stood in the storm, steep and tall, then tumbled.
The foundation remains, felled by the weather,
it fell …. [6]

---

1. *The Wife's Lament*   The present text has been translated for *The Broadview Anthology of British Literature* by R.M. Liuzza.

2. *My lord … to live here*   Or, "take up a dwelling in a grove" or "live in a (pagan) shrine." The precise meaning of the line, like the general meaning of the poem, is a matter of dispute and conjecture.

3. *earthen cave*   Or "an earthen grave" or barrow.

4. *May the young man … loved one*   These difficult lines have been read as a particular reflection, imagining the mental state of her distant beloved, or as a general reflection on the double-faced nature of the world; here, following the reading of some critics, they are taken as a kind of curse.

5. *The Ruin*   The present text has been translated for *The Broadview Anthology of British Literature* by R.M. Liuzza.

6. *it fell ….*   Several lines are lost here; the translation tries to make sense of a few surviving words.

grimly ground up ....

15 ...... cleverly created ....
...... a crust of mud surrounded ...
..... put together a swift
and subtle system of rings; one of great wisdom
wondrously bound the braces together with wires.

20   Bright were the buildings, with many bath-houses,
high noble gables and a great noise of armies,
many a meadhall filled with men's joys,
until mighty fate made an end to all that.
The slain fell on all sides, plague-days came,
25 and death destroyed all the brave swordsmen;
the seats of their idols became empty wasteland,
the city crumbled, its re-builders collapsed
beside their shrines. So now these courts are empty,
and the rich vaults of the vermilion[1] roofs
30 shed their tiles. The ruins toppled to the ground,
broken into rubble, where once many a man
glad-minded, gold-bright, bedecked in splendor,

proud, full of wine, shone in his war-gear,
gazed on treasure, on silver, on sparkling gems,
35 on wealth, on possessions, on the precious stone,[2]
on this bright capital of a broad kingdom.

    Stone buildings stood, the wide-flowing stream
threw off its heat; a wall held it all
in its bright bosom where the baths were,
40 hot in its core, a great convenience.
They let them gush forth .....
the hot streams over the great stones,
under...
until the circular pool .... hot ...
45 ..... where the baths were.
Then ....
..... that is a noble thing,
how .... the city ....[3]
—C. 975

---

[1] *vermilion* Shade of red.

[2] *precious stone* The singular form here is unexpected, but may be nothing more than a collective noun.

[3] *the city ....* The poem, appropriately, trails off into decay.

The Dream of the Rood

The devotional and visionary poem known as *The Dream of the Rood* survives in a manuscript called the Vercelli Book; the manuscript was written in the southeast of England in the later tenth century but was left in the northern Italian town of Vercelli (an important stop on the pilgrimage route from England to Rome) by the end of the eleventh century. The Vercelli Book contains twenty-three prose homilies and six poems; as with most Old English literature, its origins, authorship and audience are not known.

Although the Vercelli book was copied in the tenth century, *The Dream of the Rood* may be considerably older. Several lines from the poem are carved in runic characters on a large stone monument known as the Ruthwell Cross, found in a small church in Dumfriesshire (on the western border of England and Scotland). The Cross, which has been dated to the early eighth century, is elaborately carved with scenes from the Gospels and lives of the saints, antiphons in Latin, and decorative scroll-work; if the runic inscriptions were part of the original monument (and not a later addition), then portions of *The Dream of the Rood* are among the earliest written Old English poems.

The Dream of the Rood tells the story of the Crucifixion of Christ from the point of view of the Cross, which appears to the narrator in a dream and recounts its experiences. Christ is presented as a heroic warrior, eagerly leaping on the Cross to do battle with Death; the Cross is a loyal retainer who is painfully and paradoxically forced to participate in his lord's execution. The narrator who witnesses all then shares his vision, describes the virtues of devotion to the Cross, and looks forward to the time when the righteous, protected by the Cross, will be taken up into the banquet-halls of heaven. The blending of Christian themes and heroic conventions is a striking example of how the Anglo-Saxons vigorously re-imagined Christianity even as they embraced it. *The Dream of the Rood* interweaves biblical, liturgical, and devotional material with the language of heroic poetry and elegy, and something of the ambiguity and wordplay of the *Riddles*; its complex structure of echoes, allusions, repetitions, and verbal parallels makes it one of the most carefully constructed poems in Old English.

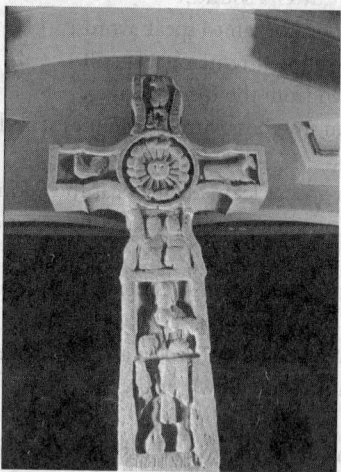

The Ruthwell Cross.

⌘⌘⌘

The Dream of the Rood [1]

Listen! I will speak of the sweetest dream,
what came to me in the middle of the night,
when speech-bearers slept in their rest.

It seemed that I saw a most wondrous tree
5   raised on high, circled round with light,
the brightest of beams. All that beacon was
     covered in gold; gems stood
fair at the earth's corners, and five there were
up on the cross-beam. All the angels of the lord
     looked on,

---

[1] *The Dream of the Rood*   Translated by R.M. Liuzza for *The Broadview Anthology of British Literature*.

fair through all eternity;[1] that was no felon's gallows,
but holy spirits beheld him there,
men over the earth and all this glorious creation.
    Wondrous was the victory-tree, and I was fouled
        by sins,
wounded with guilt; I saw the tree of glory
honored in garments, shining with joys,
bedecked with gold; gems had
covered worthily the creator's tree.
And yet beneath that gold I began to see
an ancient wretched struggle, for it first began
to bleed on the right side. I was all beset with sorrows,
fearful for that fair vision; I saw that eager beacon
change garments and colors—now it was drenched,
stained with blood, now bedecked with treasure.
    And yet, lying there a long while,
I beheld in sorrow the savior's tree,
until I heard it utter a sound;
that best of woods began to speak words:
"It was so long ago—I remember it still—
that I was felled from the forest's edge,
ripped up from my roots. Strong enemies seized me
    there,
made me their spectacle, made me bear their criminals;
they bore me on their shoulders and then set me on a
    hill,
enemies enough fixed me fast. Then I saw the lord of
    mankind
hasten eagerly when he wanted to ascend onto me.
There I dared not bow down or break,
against the lord's word, when I saw
the ends of the earth tremble. Easily I might
have felled all those enemies, and yet I stood fast.
Then the young hero made ready—that was God
    almighty—
strong and resolute; he ascended on the high gallows,
brave in the sight of many, when he wanted to
    ransom mankind.
I trembled when he embraced me, but I dared not
    bow to the ground,
or fall to the earth's corners—I had to stand fast.

I was reared as a cross: I raised up the mighty king,
the lord of heaven; I dared not lie down.
They drove dark nails through me; the scars are
    still visible,
open wounds of hate; I dared not harm any of them.
They mocked us both together; I was all drenched
    with blood
flowing from that man's side after he had sent
    forth his spirit.
    Much have I endured on that hill
of hostile fates: I saw the God of hosts
cruelly stretched out. Darkness had covered
with its clouds the ruler's corpse,
that shining radiance. Shadows spread
grey under the clouds; all creation wept,
mourned the king's fall: Christ on the cross.
And yet from afar men came hastening
to that noble one; I watched it all.
I was all beset with sorrow, yet I sank into their hands,
humbly, eagerly. There they took almighty God,
lifted him from his heavy torment; the warriors then
    left me
standing drenched in blood, all shot through with arrows.
They laid him down, bone-weary, and stood by
    his body's head;
they watched the lord of heaven there, who
    rested a while,
weary from his mighty battle. They began to build a
    tomb for him
in the sight of his slayer; they carved it from bright stone,
and set within the lord of victories. They began to
    sing a dirge for him,
wretched at evening, when they wished to travel hence,
weary, from the glorious lord—he rested there
    with little company.[2]
And as we stood there, weeping, a long while
fixed in our station, the song ascended
from those warriors. The corpse grew cold,
the fair life-house. Then they began to fell us
all to the earth—a terrible fate!
They dug for us a deep pit, yet the lord's thanes,
friends found me there …

---

1 *All the … eternity* These lines are difficult and much debated;
another possible translation is "All creation, eternally fair / beheld
the Lord's angel there," the Lord's angel presumably being the Cross
itself, God's messenger to earth.

---

2 *with little company* I.e., utterly alone.

adorned me with gold and silver.[1]

Now you can hear, my dear hero,
that I have endured the work of evil-doers,
harsh sorrows. Now the time has come
80 that far and wide they honor me,
men over the earth and all this glorious creation,
and pray to this sign. On me the son of God
suffered for a time; and so, glorious now
I rise up under the heavens, and am able to heal
85 each of those who is in awe of me.
Once I was made into the worst of torments,
most hateful to all people, before I opened
the true way of life for speech-bearers.
Lo! the King of glory, guardian of heaven's kingdom
90 honored me over all the trees of the forest,
just as he has also, almighty God, honored
his mother, Mary herself,
above all womankind for the sake of all men.

Now I bid you, my beloved hero,
95 that you reveal this vision to men,
tell them in words that it is the tree of glory
on which almighty God suffered
for mankind's many sins
and Adam's ancient deeds.
100 Death he tasted there, yet the Lord rose again
with his great might to help mankind.
He ascended into heaven. He will come again
to this middle-earth to seek mankind,
on doomsday, almighty God,
105 the lord himself and his angels with him,
and he will judge—he has the power of judgment—
each one of them as they have earned
beforehand here in this loaned life.
No one there may be unafraid
110 at the words which the ruler will speak:
he will ask before the multitude where the man
    might be
who for the lord's name would taste
bitter death, as he did earlier on that tree.
But they will tremble then, and little think
115 what they might even begin to say to Christ.

But no one there need be very afraid
who has borne in his breast the best of beacons;
but through the cross shall seek the kingdom
every soul from this earthly way,
120 whoever thinks to rest with the ruler."

Then I prayed to the tree with a happy heart,
eagerly, there where I was alone
with little company. My spirit longed to start
the journey forth; it has felt
125 so much of longing. It is now my life's hope
that I may seek the tree of victory
alone, more often than all men,
and honor it well. I wish for that
with all my heart, and my hope of protection is
130 fixed on the cross. I have few wealthy friends
on earth; they all have gone forth,
fled from worldly joys and sought the king of glory;
they live now in heaven with the high father,
and dwell in glory, and each day I look forward
135 to the time when the cross of the lord,
on which I have looked while here on this earth,
will fetch me from this loaned life,
and bring me where there is great bliss,
joy in heaven, where the lord's host
140 is seated at the feast, with ceaseless bliss;
and then set me where I may afterwards
dwell in glory, share joy
fully with the saints. May the lord be my friend,
he who here on earth once suffered
145 on the hanging-tree for human sin;
he ransomed us and gave us life,
a heavenly home. Hope was renewed
with cheer and bliss for those who were burning there.[2]
The son was successful in that journey,
150 mighty and victorious, when he came with a multitude,
a great host of souls, into God's kingdom,
the one ruler almighty, the angels rejoicing
and all the saints already in heaven
dwelling in glory, when almighty God,
155 their ruler, returned to his rightful home.
—10TH CENTURY

---

[1] *silver*   There is no gap in the manuscript here, but something is
obviously missing—the story of the Finding of the True Cross, told
(among other places) in the Old English poem *Elene*. The Cross is
buried, hidden, forgotten, then recovered by Helen, mother of the
emperor Constantine; its authenticity is established and it becomes
an object of veneration and sign of victory.

[2] A well-known Christian tradition known as the "Harrowing of Hell"
tells how Jesus, after His death on the Cross, descended into Hell and
broke open its gates, releasing the souls of those unjustly imprisoned
by Satan since the creation of human beings. Jesus conveyed them to
Heaven, then returned to earth for His resurrection.

rume. rode þis nebid snoʒton ʒeɥno cɥæðriʒ wꝥle
wꝥð uton to þam beorhtan næs þe cunnon hicʒan þhtran
þæt ge hwonne leohte uppe mid englum aʒan moton
ʒæstum to ʒeoce þonne ʒod wile swiðan lifes æt ʒe
ƿpican⁊

Hƿæt ic sƿefna cyst secʒan wylle hƿæt me ʒemætte
to midre nihte syðþan reordberend reste wunedon.
þuhte me þæt ic ʒesawe syllicre treow onlyft
lædan leohte beƿunden beama beorhtost eall þæt
beacen ƿæs beʒoten mid ʒolde ʒimmas stodon fæʒere
æt foldan sceatum. sƿylce þær fife ƿæron uppe
onþam eaxleʒespanne beheoldon þær enʒel dryht
nes ealle fæʒere þurh forðʒesceaft ne ƿæs ðær huru
fracodes ʒealʒa. Ac hine þær beheoldon haliʒe ʒastas
men ofer moldan ⁊ eall þeos mære ʒesceaft⁊
Syllic ƿæs se siʒebeam ⁊ ic synnum fah forƿunded
mid ƿommum ʒeseah ic ƿuldres treow. ƿædum ʒeƿeor
ðode ƿynnum scinan ʒeʒyred mid ʒolde ʒimmas hæfdon
beƿriʒene ƿeorðlice ƿealdes treow⁊ hƿæðre ic
þurh þæt ʒold onʒytan meahte earmra ærʒeƿin
þæt hit ærest onʒan sƿætan on þa sƿiðran healfe
eallic ƿæs mid surʒum ʒedrefed. forht ic ƿæs for
þære fæʒran ʒesyhðe ʒeseah ic þæt fuse beacen

O

Lines 1-21 of the Vercelli Book.

THE COTTON MAXIMS

This collection of proverbs is found in an eleventh-century manuscript now in the British Library, BL Cotton Tiberius B.i, commonly known as the Cotton Manuscript after its one-time owner Sir Robert Cotton (1571–1631). It is copied there between a poetic list of liturgical feasts called the *Menologium* and a version of the *Anglo-Saxon Chronicle*; the arrangement creates a fitting progression from the cycle of the Christian year, to the eternal truths of nature and society, to the flow of historical events.

    The loosely-linked collection of proverbial observations is a poetic genre as old as Hesiod's *Works and Days* and the Biblical book of Proverbs. Post-medieval Western culture has tended to look down on clichés (in Shakespeare's *Hamlet*, Polonius's stream of proverbial advice to Laertes is one sign of his foolishness), but such "wisdom literature" was well respected in the ancient and medieval world, and survived well into the modern age in such works as Benjamin Franklin's *Poor Richard's Almanac*. Maxims point to universal facts of life ("fish gotta swim, birds gotta fly," as Jerome Kern and Oscar Hammerstein II would write in *Showboat*) or norms of behavior (e.g., the fish "shall be" in the water spawning, and the king in his hall giving out rings—the implication being that a king in his hall is as natural as a fish in water, and ring-giving generates life as abundantly as a fish spawns fry). In Old English literature proverbial statements are often recognized by their use of the world *sceal* —"shall"—which in this context implies a general tendency (usually translated here as "must" or "belongs," or with the simple present tense, as in the first line).

    The Cotton Maxims are also sometimes referred to as the *Cotton Gnomes* (a "gnome" is a short, pithy statement of a truth) and as the *Maxims II*; a similar, longer collection of maxims or "gnomic verses" appears in the *Exeter Book*. Though *The Cotton Maxims* may seem like—and in places may actually be—a disorganized jumble of random observations, some common threads can be perceived, and if the reader lets go of the demand for paragraph-style unity he or she can appreciate instead the concatenation of associations, similitudes and contrasts that make up the poetic structure. Reading in this spirit, one can also notice a number of recurring motifs, themes that would be perfectly at home in much more widely-appreciated literary works like *The Wanderer*: delight in the manifold and various harmonies in the diversity of the world, acknowledgment of God's power and mystery in establishing and ordaining the world, and recognition of the need for wisdom to balance the destructive forces of human desire.

⌘⌘⌘

Maxims II (The Cotton Maxims)[1]

A king controls his realm. Cities are clear from afar,
ancient ingenious giant-works on the earth,
wondrous foundations of stone. In the sky wind is
    swiftest,
thunder loudest in its time. Great are the glories of Christ,

5   wyrd[2] is most powerful. Winter is coldest,
Lent most frosty, cold for the longest time,
summer most sun-lovely, its sunshine hottest,
autumn most bountiful, and brings to men

[1] The text is taken from E.V.K. Dobbie, *Anglo-Saxon Minor Poems* (New York, 1942), with minor corrections.

[2] *wyrd* A powerful but not quite personified force; the closest parallel in modern English is "Fate." It is related to the verb "weorthan," meaning roughly "to occur." Its meanings range from a neutral "event" to a prescribed "destiny" to a personified "Fate"; it is useful to think of "wyrd" as "what happens," usually in a negative sense.

the fruits of the seasons, sent from God.

10 Truth is trickiest, and treasure, gold, most costly
to every man; and old folks are wisest,
having known many years and endured much—
woe is wondrously clinging, but the clouds glide past.
Good comrades encourage a young nobleman

15 in battle and in bestowing rings.
In the nobleman, courage; the blade endures combat
against the helmet. The hawk belongs on the glove,
though wild; the wolf belongs in his den,
a wretched loner; in the woods the boar,

20 strong with great tusks; a good man belongs at home,
striving for fame. The spear belongs in the hand,
decorated with gold, and jewels in a ring,
standing broad and high. Streams belong in the waves,
mingling with the flood; the mast on a ship,

25 the sailyard hanging heavy. The sword belongs in
        the lap,
a lordly iron; the dragon belongs in his barrow,
old, proud of his finery; the fish in the water,
spawning his own kind, the king in his hall,
handing out rings. The bear belongs on the heath,

30 old and frightening; down from the hills flows
a river, sea-grey. An army sticks together,
a troop firm in glory; trust must be in a nobleman,
wisdom in a man. The woods on the earth
must blossom with leaves, a barrow must stand

35 green on the ground, and God in His Heaven,
judging our deeds. The door belongs in the hall,
broad building-mouth; the boss on the shield,
firm finger-protector. The bird belongs above,
sailing on the wind, the salmon in the water,

40 gliding with the trout. Tempests from the heavens
come into this world, churned by the wind.
A thief goes out in murky weather; a monster
        dwells in the fens[1]
alone in the land; a lady, a woman, must visit her lover
with secret cunning, if she does not want to make
        people think

45 she can be bought with rings.[2] The waves surge salty,
misty clouds and ocean flood flow around every land,
and mountain streams; cattle must breed
and multiply on the earth; the star must shine
bright in the heavens, just as the Maker commanded.

50 Good against evil, youth against age,
life against death, light against darkness,
army against army, enemies against each other,
foe against foe—all must fight to gain ground,
accuse the other of sin. A wise man must always
        consider

55 the contentiousness of the world—the criminal hangs,
rightly pays for the crime he has committed
against mankind. The Maker alone knows
where his soul must travel afterwards;
and all those spirits who travel to God

60 after their death-day await judgment
in the Father's embrace. The shape of the future
is hidden and secret; the Lord alone knows,
the Redeeming Father. No one returns
here under the firmament who will truly

65 say to men what sort of thing God's creation is,
the thrones of the triumphant, where He himself dwells.

—? 10TH CENTURY

---

[1] *fens* Swamps, marshes.

[2] *she can be bought with rings* I.e., if she does not want it to be
rumored that she is a prostitute. This reading, offered by Joseph A.
Dane, "*On folce gebeon*: Note on the Old English *Maxims II* Lines
43–5," *Neuphilologische Mitteilungen* 85 (1984): 61–64, is only one
possible interpretation of a difficult passage which apparently alludes
to social norms we no longer understand. The idea of "buying with
rings" may refer to the custom of giving a "bride-price" as part of a
marriage; the woman's "secret cunning" (*dyrne cræft*) may be an
allusion to the alleged affinity of women and magical charms and
spells. The implication may be that a woman must seek out her own
lover by magical means if she wants to have any control over her
marriage plans at all. Another possible translation is "a lady, a
woman, must find a lover by secret means so that she may be
married, if she does not have a good reputation among her people."
See Audrey L. Meaney, "The *ides* of the Cotton Gnomes," *Medium
Ævum* 48 (1979): 23–39.

Exeter Book Riddles

The Exeter Book manuscript of Old English poetry ends with two sections of short verse riddles. The manuscript is damaged and it is impossible to know how many riddles were in the original collection, but it is likely that there were 100, following the model of the popular Latin *Enigmata* ("Riddles") of Aldhelm and Symphosius. But apart from this, there are few similarities between the Latin and English versions of this popular poetic genre. The *Enigmata* of Aldhelm were apparently used as classroom examples of the principles of Latin versification, but it is unlikely that the English Riddles would have served such a purpose for apprentice English poets. Moreover, very few of the English Riddles depend on the sort of deliberate obscurity common in the *Enigmata*—no. 82 below is an example, but it is closely modeled on one of the Latin Riddles of Symphosius.

Many of the Exeter Book Riddles echo one another's language, especially in the repeated closing line *saga hwæt ic hatte* "say what I am called," but it is unlikely that the whole collection was written by one person. Apart from one Riddle which is found in an earlier version, there is little evidence for the origins and audience of the Riddles, either individually or collectively. A number of the Riddles seem to come from a bookish milieu, probably monastic (see nos. 24 and 45), and others are somewhat philosophical in tone (no. 41), but the presence of about a dozen riddles with obscene double meanings (see nos. 42 and 43 below) still raises a few eyebrows. Unlike the Latin riddles, which give away their solutions in their titles, some of the Old English riddles are apparently meant to be genuinely puzzling and difficult to solve—in fact a few (such as no. 91 below) continue to baffle readers to this day. In many cases, however, the pleasure of the Riddles seems to lie not in obscurity but in observation—they are in essence short lyric poems which show the world at a slightly odd angle, and bring the material and the natural world to new life through metaphor, analogy, wordplay, and misdirection. In the Riddles creatures speak, things express their point of view, everyday objects perform heroic deeds, and innocent household items become obscene projections of human desire. The playful language of the Riddles is a kind of lens through which the wonder, poignancy and wild energy of the created world are brought into focus. Whether they were written for education, inspiration, or amusement, the delight of the Riddles lies in their gift for seeing familiar things with fresh eyes, and compressing these insights in a few short lines which draw the listener into sharing the process of that perception; they help remind us that the poetic landscape of Old English literature was not as gloomy, as pious, or as bloody as is sometimes thought.

⌘ ⌘ ⌘

Riddle 5 [1]

My gown is silent as I thread the seas,
Haunt old buildings or tread the land.

[1] The following riddles are from Craig Williamson's *A Feast of Creatures: Anglo-Saxon Riddle Songs* (Philadelphia: U of Pennsylvania Press, 1982). The Old English text is edited by Craig Williamson, *The Old English Riddles of the "Exeter Book"* (Chapel Hill, NC: University of North Carolina Press, 1977). The numbers are those of Williamson's edition and translation.

Sometimes my song-coat and the supple wind
Cradle me high over the homes of men,
5 And the power of clouds carries me
Windward over cities. Then my bright silks
Start to sing, whistle, roar,
Resound and ring, while I
Sail on untouched by earth and sea,
10 A spirit, ghost and guest, on wing.

Riddle 12

Once I was a plain warrior's weapon—
    Now a stripling prince wraps my body
With bright twists of silver and gold.
Sometimes men kiss me, or carry me to battle
5   Where I call my lord's companions to wage war.
Bright with jewels, I am borne by a horse
Over hard plains, sometimes by the sea-stallion
Over storm waves. Sometimes a woman,
Ring-adorned, fills my breast for the table—
10 Later I lie stripped of sweet treasure,
Hard and headless on the long boards.
Clothed in gold, I may grace the wall
Where men sit drinking, a soldier's gem.
Wound with silver, I sometimes ride
15 A warrior's horse, swallowing soldier's breath,
Blasting battle-song. Sometimes I bring
Bold men to wine, sometimes I sing caution
—Or rescue thieves' catch or scatter foes
For my lord. Say what I am called.

Riddle 23

I am a wonderful help to women,
    The hope of something to come. I harm
No citizen except my slayer.
Rooted I stand on a high bed.
5   I am shaggy below. Sometimes the beautiful
Peasant's daughter, an eager-armed,
Proud woman grabs my body,
Rushes my red skin, holds me hard,
Claims my head. The curly-haired
10 Woman who catches me fast will feel
Our meeting. Her eye will be wet.

Riddle 24

A life-thief stole my world-strength,
    Ripped off flesh and left me skin,
Dipped me in water and drew me out,

Stretched me bare in the tight sun;
5   The hard blade, clean steel, cut,
Scraped-fingers folded, shaped me.
Now the bird's once wind-stiff joy
Darts often to the horn's dark rim,
Sucks wood-stain, steps back again
10 With a quick scratch of power, tracks
Black on my body, points trails.
Shield-boards clothe me and stretched hide,
A skin laced with gold. The bright song
Of smiths glistens on me in filigree tones.
15 Now decorative gold and crimson dye,
Cloisoned jewels and a coat of glory
Proclaim the world's protector far and wide—
Let no fool fault these treasured claims.
If the children of men make use of me,
20 They will be safer and surer of heaven,
Bolder in heart, more blessed in mind,
Wiser in soul: they will find friends,
Companions and kinsmen, more loyal and true,
Nobler and better, brought to new faith—
25 So men shall know grace, honor, glory,
Fortune, and the kind clasp of friends.
Say who I am—glorious, useful to men,
Holy and helpful from beginning to end.

Riddle 41

A noble guest of great lineage dwells
    In the house of man. Grim hunger
Cannot harm him, nor feverish thirst,
Nor age, nor illness. If the servant
5   Of the guest who rules, serves well
On the journey, they will find together
Bliss and well-being, a feast of fate;
If the slave will not as a brother be ruled
By a lord he should fear and follow
10 Then both will suffer and sire a family
Of sorrows when, springing from the world,
They leave the bright bosom of one kinswoman,
Mother and sister, who nourished them.
Let the man who knows noble words
15 Say what the guest and servant are called.

Riddle 42

A small miracle hangs near a man's thigh,
  Full under folds. It is stiff, strong,
Bold, brassy, and pierced in front.
When a young lord lifts his tunic
5 Over his knees, he wants to greet
With the hard head of this hanging creature
The hole it has long come to fill.

Riddle 43

I heard of something rising in a corner,
  Swelling and standing up, lifting its cover.
The proud-hearted bride grabbed at that boneless
Wonder with her hands; the prince's daughter
5 Covered that swelling thing with a swirl of cloth.

Riddle 45

A moth ate songs—wolfed words!
  That seemed a weird dish—that a worm
Should swallow, dumb thief in the dark,
The songs of a man, his chants of glory,
5 Their place of strength. That thief-guest
Was no wiser for having swallowed words.

Riddle 81

S hunning silence, my house is loud
  While I am quiet: we are movement bound
By the Shaper's will. I am swifter,
Sometimes stronger—he is longer lasting,
5 Harder running. Sometimes I rest
While he rolls on. He is the house
That holds me living—alone I die.

Riddle 82

A weird creature came to a meeting of men,
  Hauled itself in to the high commerce
Of the wise. It lurched with one eye,
Two feet, twelve hundred heads,
5 A back and belly—two hands, arms,
Shoulders—one neck, two sides.
Untwist your mind and say what I mean.

Riddle 91

I am noble, known to rest in the quiet
  Keeping of many men, humble and high born.
The plunderers' joy, hauled far from friends,
Rides richly on me, shines signifying power,
5 Whether I proclaim the grandeur of halls,
The wealth of cities, or the glory of God.
Now wise men love most my strange way
Of offering wisdom to many without voice.
Though the children of earth eagerly seek
10 To trace my trail, sometimes my tracks are dim.
—IOTH CENTURY

Solutions: 5, swan; 12, horn (for drinking or hunting); 23, penis or onion; 24, manuscript book (Bible), made of parchment; 41, soul and body; 42, key; 43, dough; 45, book-moth; 81, fish and river; 82, a one-eyed seller of garlic; 91 unsolved.

Old English Metrical Charms

Modern scholars often give the name "charm" to a sort of language, usually in verse, that is used for magical purposes. Most Old English charms were accompanied by some form of physical action, whether a significant gesture, writing words on an object, or the preparation of a medical compound. The precise relation between the words and the action are debatable and probably indefinable. The "charms" below are all intended to do good—settle a swarm of bees or cure a disease—but presumably charms and other magical practices could be used for evil purposes as well, though no examples have survived.

The cultural place of such texts, and their role in the medical theory and practice of the Anglo-Saxons, have generated a great deal of controversy. Hundreds of pages of medical literature have survived from Anglo-Saxon England, most of them containing translations from late-classical sources in Latin (which in turn were translated from medical works in Greek). Manuscripts collecting and organizing medical recipes attest to the sophistication and professionalization of the practice of medicine among the Anglo-Saxons. Only a few works appear to preserve native Germanic practices and beliefs; these have attracted a great deal of attention for the information they might reveal about the religion of the pre-Christian Anglo-Saxons. They represent only a small fraction of the medical literature of the period, but they have a great deal to tell us about the way health and sickness were imagined in the early Middle Ages.

These texts are complicated from any perspective, medical or spiritual, and their cultural significance is easily mistaken. Although some charms—and many prose medical remedies in Old English—involve the use of plants which have been shown to have some therapeutic value, it should be emphasized that the plants in a given remedy were probably not recommended for their chemical properties but because of other qualities, such as those evident in the "Nine Herbs Charm." Modern herbal remedies, though sometimes outside the mainstream of modern medicine, are used within the theoretical frameworks supplied by chemistry, physiology, and pharmacology; Old English charms are not. And although the charms retain traces of pre-Christian thought and belief, such as the mention of the god Woden in the "Nine Herbs Charm," it should not be thought that they are "pagan" or antithetical to Christianity. The efficacy of the "dwarf" charm, for example, depends upon the ready availability of communion wafers, and calls upon the power of the Seven Sleepers of Ephesus, a group of early Christian saints. Many other charms involve Latin prayers and Christian sacramental practices such as the sign of the Cross or the saying of Mass; the "Nine Herbs Charm" invokes the power of Christ more often than that of Woden.

⌘ ⌘ ⌘

The Old English Bee Charm[1]

Against a swarm of bees[2] take earth, cast it with your right hand under your right foot, and say:

I seize it under foot: I've found it now.
Lo! earth has might   over all creatures
5 and against malice   and over mindlessness
and over the mighty man   with his mighty tongue.

And thereupon, when they swarm, throw gravel over them and say:

Victory-wives! sit:[3]   sink to earth now!
Never to the woodland   wild may you fly!
10 Be as mindful   of my fortune
As folks all are   of food and home.

Against a Dwarf

Against a dwarf[4] take seven little wafers like those one offers [at Mass], and write these names on each wafer: Maximianus, Malchus, Johannes, Martimianus, Dionisius, Constantinus, Serafion.[5] Then one should

5 sing the charm follows here, first in the left ear, then in the right ear, then over the person's crown. And then have a virgin go in and hang it around his neck; and do so for three days, and he will soon be well.

Spider creature   came right in here—
10 had his harness in hand: you're his horse, he claimed!
and to your neck tied reins!   Then they began
to rise from the land.
As they left the land   their limbs grew cool.
Then in she dashed—   the dwarf's sister![6]
Then she ended it all   and oaths she swore:
15 no hurt would come   to harm the sick
nor whoever gets the lore   and learns this charm
and knows how to chant   this charm as well.
Amen. Fiat.[7]

For a Sudden Stitch

For a sudden stitch,[8] feverfew and the red nettle that grows in the grain, and plantain; boil in butter.

Loud were they—real loud![9]   when they rode
down mound;

---

[1] *The Old English Bee Charm* The present translations, by Stephen O. Glosecki, for *The Broadview Anthology of British Literature*, are based upon texts as found in E.V.K. Dobbie's *The Anglo-Saxon Minor Poems*.

[2] *Against a swarm of bees* Presumably to make a swarm of bees settle into a *skep* or manmade hive.

[3] *Victory-wives! sit* The meaning of this line is much debated. It may be that the word(s) translated "victory-wives" is actually a verb of command, and the Old English line *sitte ge sige wif sigað to eorþan* actually means "sit you down, settle, women, sink to the earth."

[4] *Against a dwarf* Originally, perhaps, a night demon of some sort; in Old English prose texts translated from Latin medical treatises, however, the word seems to mean nothing more than "fever" (Latin *febrem*), and it is not certain that the word signified much more than a particular kind of disease, just as modern doctors speak of "malaria" and "influenza" without believing that these are caused by bad air or the malign influence of the stars. The vivid poem that accompanies this charm, however, certainly suggests some sort of personified agent of illness, in which the patient is the steed and the evil dwarf—the "spider-creature"—is the rider.

[5] *take seven ... Serafion* Since the dwarf attacks sleeping victims, the charm opens with sympathetic appeal to the Seven Sleepers of Ephesus, an early Christian legend similar to the Rip van Winkle story. Seven young Christian men of Ephesus, fleeing persecution by

the Emperor Decius (249–251), took refuge in a cave, where they were walled in while sleeping. Nearly two hundred years later, after the Roman Empire had officially converted to Christianity, the cave was opened and the Sleepers awoke. Thinking they had been asleep only one night, they went into the city of Ephesus, causing much confusion; eventually the miraculous truth was revealed, whereupon the young men died, praising God. The Seven Sleepers were often invoked in medieval prayers against insomnia and fever.

[6] *the dwarf's sister* The manuscript reads "the animal's sister"—i.e., the spider's?

[7] *Fiat* Latin: so be it.

[8] *For a sudden stitch* The Old English word *færstice* appears only here; considering the seriousness of the invocations, "stabbing pain" might be a better translation. The charm protects against a pain visualized as being caused by a "little spear" (l. 6) shot either by "gods" (OE *esa*, whose meaning is not entirely certain), "elves" (OE *ylfa*) or "witches" (OE *hægtessan*; in German lumbago is still called *Hexenschuss*). Elves were thought to cause pains in humans and cattle by shooting projectiles at them; they were often equated with devils and lesser demons in Christian thought.

[9] *Loud were ... real loud* It is not clear who "they" are, elves or devils or the "mighty women" of l. 8 (who may or may not be the same as the witches mentioned later in the charm), or where the

resolute they were when over land they rode.
5 Shield yourself now: you can shake this attack.
Out! little spear! if inside here!
Under linden[1] I stood, under lambent shield
where those mighty women wielded power:
and screaming spears they sent our way!
10 Now I'll send them another one back—
flying arrow forth against them!
Out! little spear, if inside here!
Sat that smith[2] there, smacked little knife,
[world's best iron][3] with wonder-punch.[4]
15 Out! little spear, if inside here!
Six smiths sat there, slaughter-spear forging.
Out, spear! Not in, spear!
If within here be an iron bit—
wicked witch-work, away must it melt!
20 If you were shot in skin or shot in flesh
or shot in blood [or shot in bone]
or shot in limb: never let your life be harmed.
If it were old gods' shot or elfin shot
or hag-witch shot, I'll help you now.
25 This your cure for old gods' shot! This your cure
  for elfin shot!
This your cure for hag-witch shot! I'll help for sure!
[Fly off, dart-point!] far to cliff-head!
May God help you. Health be with you.

Then take the knife; put it in the potion.[5]

"mound" (OE *hlæw*, which usually denotes a pre-Christian burial mound) is.

[1] *linden* Shield (of lime-wood).

[2] *Sat that smith* In many cultures smiths are perceived as ambivalent, often malevolent or half-magical figures; it is not known who this smith (or the "six smiths" mentioned in l. 16) is supposed to be.

[3] *[world's best iron]* Here and in other half-lines in brackets, there is no gap in the manuscript to indicate a loss, but something seems missing in the meter or sense of the poem. The lines supplied are conjectural.

[4] *with wonder-punch* Or "powerful in wounding."

[5] *potion* Presumably the buttery stew of feverfew, nettle and plantain prescribed at the beginning of the text. It is also possible, however, that the terse instructions (in OE, *ado on wætan*) mean that the knife is to be smeared with the salve and then placed on the part of the body afflicted by the pain.

The Nine Herbs Charm[6]

Mind you, mugwort, how much you showed,
 what you arranged at Rainmelding.[7]
Eldest of herbs, "Una"[8] we call you.
You have might against three, might against thirty,
5 might against all venom and against onfliers;[9]
you have might against the foe who fares
  through the land.
And you, plantain, plant-tribes' mother,
eastward open, inward mighty:
over you carts clattered; over you queans[10] rode;
10 over you brides clamored; over you bulls snorted:
all this you withstood and struck against,
just as you withstand them all: onfliers, venom,
and the loathsome foe who fares through the land.
This herb's called "Stunner," on stone well grown:
15 she stands against poison; she'll stun your pain.
"Valiant" we call her— venom she allays;
she casts out venom, overcomes evil.
This is the plant that pummeled the worm:
she has might against all venom, she has might
  against onfliers,
20 she has might against the foe who fares through
  the land.
Launch them now, cock's-spur: lesser lash bigger;
bigger lash lesser till both be healed.
Mind you, mayweed,[11] how much you showed:
the end you achieved at Alorford:

---

[6] *The Nine Herbs Charm* This translation has been adapted from Stephen Glosecki, "'Blow these vipers from me': Mythic Magic in *The Nine Herbs Charm*," in L.C. Gruber, ed., *Essays On Old, Middle, Modern English and Old Icelandic: In Honor of Raymond P. Tripp, Jr.* (Lewiston, NY: Mellen, 2000), 117–19. The text of the charm is corrupt, its context obscure, and its meaning unclear. The recitation of charms over herbs was expressly condemned in some Anglo-Saxon homilies and law codes; Christian prayers were recommended instead. Such prayers and blessings over plants are not uncommon in Anglo-Saxon medicine, but the botanical animism of this charm is otherwise unknown.

[7] *what you ... Rainmelding* Or, "what you brought about at the Great Proclamation."

[8] *Una* Latin: one.

[9] *onfliers* Flying or airborne diseases.

[10] *queans* Women.

[11] *mayweed* Mayweed is presumably synonymous with chamomile.

25 never will airborne illness   end a lifetime
if one make a meal   from mayweed now.
Known as nettle,   the next herb here—
a seal sent it   over sea ridges
to undo anger   and other venom.
30 These nine have might   against nine venoms.
+ Snake came stealing—   he stung someone![1]
Then Woden grabbed   nine glory-twigs,
knocked that adder   into nine pieces!
There it ended: apple and venom:
35 never would it slither   inside a house!
+ Chervil and fennel,   both full of might:
herbs created   by the all-wise Lord,
holy in heaven,   while hanging there;[2]
He set them and sent them   into seven worlds
40 to remedy all,   the wretched and the blest.
They stand against pain,   they strike against venom,
They have might against three,   might against thirty,
against fiendish fist   and fast attack,
against vile creatures'   vicious witchcraft.
45 + Now these nine herbs have might   against nine
    magic sendings,[3]
against nine venoms   and against nine fliers—
against the red venom,[4]   against the reeking venom,

against the white venom,   against venom in blue,
against the yellow venom,   against venom in green,
50 against the black venom,   against the blue venom,
against the brown venom,   against venom purplish,
against worm-blister,   against water-blister,
against thorn-blister,   against troll-blister,
against ice-blister,   against venom-blister—
55 if there fly in from the east   any oncoming venom
or in from the north   flying in here now
or any from the west   over the world of man.
+ Christ stood over old ones—   each and every
    kind.[5]
I alone fathom   a fast river
60 where the nine adders   are all watching.
Let all plants now   spring up from their roots!
Let the seas divide—   all salt water—
when I blow this poison   right past you now.

Mugwort, plantain that is open to the east, lamb's cress, cock's-spur grass, mayweed, nettle, crabapple, chervil and fennel, old soap. Work the herbs into a powder, mix with the soap and with the pulp of an apple.[6] Make a paste from water and ashes; take fennel, boil it in the paste, and bathe with beaten egg[7] when the salve is applied, both before and after. Sing the charm over each of the herbs, thrice before they are ground up, and also over the apple; and sing the same charm into the man's mouth and into both ears and over the wound before he applies the salve.

[1] *someone* The manuscript reads "no-one" (OE *nan*). Along with the *Sudden Stitch* charm, this is the only reference to non-Christian gods in Anglo-Saxon medical literature, and the only reference anywhere to Woden battling a serpent. Our knowledge of pre-Christian Anglo-Saxon religion is exceptionally sparse, and for all we know this passage may owe as much to the story of Moses and the serpent in the wilderness (Numbers 21.4–9) as to any actual Germanic belief.

[2] *Then Woden ... hanging there* Woden gives way to Christ or is somehow identified with him (or has "Christ" been substituted for an earlier reference to Woden?) whose death on the cross gives rise to healing plants; folk beliefs of several cultures still hold that Good Friday—the day of Christ's crucifixion—is a good day for planting. It may also be relevant here that in Old Norse legend Odin also experienced hanging on Yggdrasil, the "World Tree."

[3] *nine magic sendings* Another possible translation of this line is that the nine herbs have might against "nine of those who fled from glory," i.e., nine demons.

[4] *red venom* Presumably the various venoms and blisters listed refer to different diseases, but none of them can be identified.

[5] *Christ stood ... every kind* The meaning is unknown; other possible translations are "Christ, whose nature was unique, overcame disease" and "Christ stood against every type of illness."

[6] *Mugwort ... an apple* The dazzling and surreal poetry of the charm is followed by a rather prosaic list of ingredients and instructions. But it would be as wrong to discard the "superstition" of the charm in favor of the "rational" recipe as it would be to remove the practical elements of the cure from the "poetic" invocation that accompanies it. Both were presumably important to the readers and users of this text.

[7] *boil it ... beaten egg* Or "boil with the mixture"?

BEOWULF

Only one copy of the poem that modern editors call *Beowulf* has survived, and it probably survived only by accident. A manuscript containing *Beowulf* and a small collection of other texts—a poetic treatment of the Old Testament story of Judith, a prose life of St. Christopher, and two treatises of fantastical geography known as *The Wonders of the East* and *Alexander's Letter to Aristotle*—was copied by two scribes, probably in the decade after 1000, in a monastic center somewhere in the south of England; it lay disregarded for centuries, narrowly escaped destruction by fire in 1731, and is now preserved in the British Library under the shelfmark Cotton Vitellius A.xv.

Beowulf is the longest surviving poem in Old English, consisting of 3,182 extant lines of alliterative verse divided into forty-four sections. Its language is allusive and embellished and its narrative digressive and complex, but its relatively straightforward plot follows the outlines of a folktale: a young hero who fights in isolation from friends and family engages in fabulous battles against monstrous foes, faces three challenges in ascending order of difficulty, and in the end wins glory and fame. The fabulous outlines of the story equally recall the deep undertones of myth: the mighty Beowulf may be a distant cousin of Thor, and his death may contain a hint of Ragnarok, the northern apocalypse.

But whatever its underlying structural patterns, *Beowulf* is neither myth nor folktale; its stories of dragon-slaying and night-battles are set against a complex background of legendary history. The action of the poem unfolds in a recognizable version of Scandinavia: Hrothgar's hall Heorot has been plausibly placed in the village of Lejre on the Danish island of Zealand; Beowulf's tribe of Geats may be the historical Gautar of Southern Sweden; and a number of the poem's characters (Heremod, Hrothgar, Ingeld, and Hygelac) are mentioned in other sources as if they were figures of history rather than fable. Moreover, *Beowulf* is an intensely political poem; the poet seems as intrigued by Danish diplomacy and the bitter feud between the Geats and Swedes as he is by the hero's monster-slaying. Kingdoms and successions, alliances and truces, loyalties and the tragically transient stability of heroic society are the poem's somber subtext, a theme traced less in the clashes of the battlefield than in the patterns of marriage and kin, in stories remembered and retold, in allusion and digression and pointed foreshadowing.

Despite the poem's historical interests, we cannot read *Beowulf* with any modern expectation of historical accuracy. Like many medieval works, *Beowulf* is frustratingly ambivalent—not quite mythical enough to be read apart from the history it purports to contain, nor historical enough to furnish clear evidence for the past it poetically recreates. The action of the poem is set in a somewhat vague heroic *geardagum* ("bygone days"), an age not meant to be counted on a calendar, nor its kingdoms and tribes marked on a map. Nor, undoubtedly, were the monstrous races of Grendels and dragons so clearly distinct in the poet's mind from the real dangers of the real world just beyond the margins of the known. While medieval authors certainly made distinctions between *historia* and *fabula*, the boundaries between these terms are not nearly as impermeable as those of our modern categories "history" and "fable."

Both the ultimate and the immediate origins of *Beowulf* are unknown. Most scholars assume that the single surviving manuscript, written around 1000–20, is a copy of an earlier text, and probably the last in a long chain of copies. But it may be impossible to determine when that chain of texts began, or what cultural and literary milieu gave birth to the poem; proposed dates have ranged from 700 to 1000, and most years in between. The poem seems to arise from a world in which such stories were common, and it presupposes our own position in this world. The poem begins with the assumption that we are hearing a well-known story, or a least a story from a familiar milieu: "We have heard of the glory ... of the folk-kings of the spear-Danes," the poet asserts, and the way he tosses out cryptic allusions throughout the poem suggests that his audience was already familiar with songs and stories of other kings and heroes. But at what time in the history of the Anglo-Saxons did such a world exist? And can we trust the narrator as a faithful reporter of this world, or should we view him as a vivid creator of the illusion of antiquity?

The question of the origin of *Beowulf* is not just philological pedantry: the poem will yield very different meanings if it is imagined to have been produced in the time of Bede (c. 725, just a generation or two after the conversion of the English) or of Alfred (c. 880, a time of nation-building and political centralization) or of Ælfric (c. 1000, after half a century of monastic reform and a decade which saw the demoralizing collapse of national security). The earlier we think the poem to be, the more potentially authentic its historical material; the later we imagine it, the more openly fictional and nostalgic it seems. Moreover, the more closely we try to assign a date and place of origin to the poem, the more closely we read it as a text, the intention of a single author or a reflection of a particular ideology, rather than a product of a poetic art whose composition may have been oral and communal and whose traditional roots are beyond discovery.

Most critics agree that the heroic action of the poem is thoroughly accommodated to a world in which the truths of Christianity are accepted without question; they disagree, often sharply, on the meaning and purpose of that accommodation. Some scholars have argued that *Beowulf* is a type of Christ, because he gives his life for his people; others have read the poem as a condemnation of pagan pride, greed and violence. These two extreme positions capture the poem's deliberate ambivalence: *Beowulf* is a secular Christian poem about pagans which avoids the easy alternatives of automatic condemnation or enthusiastic anachronism. The person responsible for putting *Beowulf* in its final form was certainly a Christian: the technology of writing in the Anglo-Saxon period was almost entirely a monopoly of the church. The manuscript in which *Beowulf* survives contains a saint's legend and a versified Bible story, and the poet indicates a clear familiarity with the Bible and expects the same from his audience. Though the paganism of *Beowulf*'s world is downplayed, however, it is not denied; his age is connected to that of the audience but separated by the gulf of conversion and the seas of migration.

More recent work, rather than trying to define a single source for the poem's complex and peculiar texture (whether that source is pure Germanic paganism or orthodox Augustinian Christianity), recognizes that *Beowulf*, like the culture of the Anglo-Saxons themselves, reflects a variety of interdependent and competing influences and attitudes, even a certain tension inherent in the combination of biblical, patristic, secular Latin, and popular Germanic material. The search for a single unified "audience" of *Beowulf*, and with it a sense of a single meaning, has given way to a recognition that there were many readers in Anglo-Saxon England, often with competing and conflicting interests.

⌘⌘⌘

Beowulf, lines 1–21
(British Library, Ms Cotton Vitellius A.xv, fol. 129r).

Beowulf[1]

PROLOGUE

Listen!
We have heard of the glory in bygone days
of the folk-kings of the spear-Danes,[2]
how those noble lords did lofty deeds.

Often Scyld Scefing[3] seized the mead-benches
5 from many tribes, troops of enemies,
struck fear into earls. Though he first was
found a waif, he awaited solace for that—
he grew under heaven and prospered in honor
until every one of the encircling nations
10 over the whale's-riding[4] had to obey him,
grant him tribute. That was a good king!
A boy was later born to him,
young in the courts, whom God sent
as a solace to the people—He saw their need,
15 the dire distress they had endured, lordless,
for such a long time. The Lord of Life,
Wielder of Glory, gave him worldly honor;
Beowulf,[5] the son of Scyld, was renowned,
his fame spread wide in Scandinavian lands.
20 Thus should a young man bring about good
with pious gifts from his father's possessions,
so that later in life loyal comrades
will stand beside him when war comes,
the people will support him—with praiseworthy deeds
25 a man will prosper among any people.

Scyld passed away at his appointed hour,
the mighty lord went into the Lord's keeping;
they bore him down to the brimming sea,
his dear comrades, as he himself had commanded
30 while the friend of the Scyldings[6] wielded speech—
that dear land-ruler had long held power.
In the harbor stood a ring-prowed ship,
icy, outbound, a nobleman's vessel;
there they laid down their dear lord,
35 dispenser of rings, in the bosom of the ship,
glorious, by the mast. There were many treasures
loaded there, adornments from distant lands;
I have never heard of a more lovely ship
bedecked with battle-weapons and war-gear,
40 blades and byrnies;[7] in its bosom lay
many treasures, which were to travel
far with him into the keeping of the flood.
With no fewer gifts did they furnish him there,
the wealth of nations, than those did who
45 at his beginning first sent him forth
alone over the waves while still a small child.[8]
Then they set a golden ensign
high over his head, and let the waves have him,
gave him to the Deep with grieving spirits,
50 mournful in mind. Men do not know
how to say truly—not trusted counselors,
nor heroes under the heavens—who received that cargo.

1

Then Beowulf Scylding, beloved king,
was famous in the strongholds of his folk
55 for a long while—his father having passed away,
a lord from earth—until after him arose
the great Healfdene, who held the glorious Scyldings
all his life, ancient and fierce in battle.
Four children, all counted up,
60 were born to that bold leader of hosts:
Heorogar, Hrothgar, and Halga the Good,
I heard that …[9] was Onela's queen,

---

[1] *Beowulf* This translation is by R.M. Liuzza from the edition published by Broadview Press.

[2] *spear-Danes* The Danes are described by many different epithets in the poem.

[3] *Scyld Scefing* The name means "Shield, Son of Sheaf" (i.e., of grain). The mysterious origins of Scyld, who seems to arrive providentially from nowhere and is returned to the sea after his death, have occasioned much critical speculation.

[4] *whale's-riding* A condensed descriptive image of the sea—the riding-place of whales. Elsewhere the sea is the "gannet's bath" and the "swan's riding."

[5] *Beowulf* Not the monster-slaying hero of the title, but an early Danish king. Many scholars argue that the original name was *Beow*.

[6] *Scyldings* The Danes, "sons of Scyld."

[7] *byrnie* Coat of ring-mail.

[8] *With no fewer … small child* Scyld was found destitute—this statement is an example of *litotes*, or ironic understatement, not uncommon in Anglo-Saxon poetry.

[9] A name is missing from the manuscript here; it has been conjectured from parallel sources that is should be Yrse, or Ursula. The Swedish ("Scylfing") king Onela appears later in the story, causing much distress to Beowulf's nation.

dear bedfellow of the Battle-Scylfing.

Then success in war was given to Hrothgar,
65 honor in battle, so that his beloved kinsmen
eagerly served him, until the young soldiers grew
into a mighty troop of men. It came to his mind
that he should order a hall-building,
have men make a great mead-house
70 which the sons of men should remember forever,[1]
and there inside he would share everything
with young and old that God had given him,
except for the common land and the lives of men.
Then the work, as I've heard, was widely proclaimed
75 to many nations throughout this middle-earth,
to come adorn the folk-stead. It came to pass
swiftly among men, and it was soon ready,
the greatest of halls; he gave it the name "Heorot,"[2]
he who ruled widely with his words.
80 He remembered his boast; he gave out rings,
treasure at table. The hall towered
high and horn-gabled—it awaited hostile fires,
the surges of war; the time was not yet near
that the sword-hate of sworn in-laws
85 should arise after ruthless violence.[3]

A bold demon who waited in darkness
wretchedly suffered all the while,
for every day he heard the joyful din
loud in the hall, with the harp's sound,
90 the clear song of the scop.[4] He said
who was able to tell of the origin of men
that the Almighty created the earth,
a bright and shining plain, by seas embraced,
and set, triumphantly, the sun and moon
95 to light their beams for those who dwell on land,
adorned the distant corners of the world
with leaves and branches, and made life also,
all manner of creatures that live and move.

---

[1] *a great … forever* Or "a greater meadhall / than the sons of men had ever heard of." The reading adopted here is that of Mitchell and Robinson.

[2] *Heorot* "Hart." An object recovered from the burial-mound at Sutton Hoo, perhaps a royal insignia, is surmounted by the image of a hart.

[3] *it awaited … violence* The hall Heorot is apparently fated to be destroyed in a battle between Hrothgar and his son-in-law Ingeld the Heathobard, a conflict predicted by Beowulf at 2024–69. The battle itself happens outside the action of the poem.

[4] *scop* Poet-singer.

— Thus this lordly people lived in joy,
100 blessedly, until one began
to work his foul crimes—a fiend from Hell.
This grim spirit was called Grendel,
mighty stalker of the marches, who held
the moors and fens; this miserable man
105 lived for a time in the land of giants,
after the Creator had condemned him
among Cain's race—when he killed Abel
the eternal Lord avenged that death.[5]
No joy in that feud—the Maker forced him
110 far from mankind for his foul crime.
From thence arose all misbegotten things,
trolls and elves and the living dead,
and also the giants who strove against God
for a long while—He gave them their reward for that.

2

115 When night descended he went to seek out
the high house, to see how the Ring-Danes
had bedded down after their beer-drinking.
He found therein a troop of nobles
asleep after the feast; they knew no sorrow
120 or human misery. The unholy creature,
grim and ravenous, was ready at once,
ruthless and cruel, and took from their rest
thirty thanes;[6] thence he went
rejoicing in his booty, back to his home,
125 to seek out his abode with his fill of slaughter.
When in the dim twilight just before dawn
Grendel's warfare was made known to men,
then lamentation was lifted up after the feasting,
a great mourning-sound. Unhappy sat
130 the mighty lord, long-good nobleman,
suffered greatly, grieved for his thanes,
once they beheld that hostile one's tracks,
the accursed spirit; that strife was too strong,
loathsome and long.
                                    It was not longer
135 than the next night until he committed
a greater murder, mourned not at all
for his feuds and sins—he was too fixed in them.

---

[5] *Cain … Abel* See Genesis 4.1–16.

[6] *thanes* Companions of a king.

Then it was easy to find a thane
who sought his rest elsewhere, farther away,
140 a bed in the outbuildings,[1] when was pointed out—
truly announced with clear tokens—
that hall-thane's hate; he kept himself afterwards
farther and safer, who escaped the fiend.
So he ruled, and strove against right,
145 one against all, until empty stood
the best of houses. And so for a great while—
for twelve long winters the lord of the Scyldings
suffered his grief, every sort of woe,
great sorrow, for to the sons of men
150 it became known, and carried abroad
in sad tales, that Grendel strove
long with Hrothgar, bore his hatred,
sins and feuds, for many seasons,
perpetual conflict; he wanted no peace
155 with any man of the Danish army,
nor ceased his deadly hatred, nor settled with money,
nor did any of the counselors need to expect
bright compensation from the killer's hands,[2]
for the great ravager relentlessly stalked,
160 a dark death-shadow, lurked and struck
old and young alike, in perpetual night
held the misty moors. Men do not know
whither such whispering demons wander about.
       Thus the foe of mankind, fearsome and solitary,
165 often committed his many crimes,
cruel humiliations; he occupied Heorot,
the jewel-adorned hall, in the dark nights—
he saw no need to salute the throne,
he scorned the treasures; he did not know their love.[3]
170 That was deep misery to the lord of the Danes,
a breaking of spirit. Many a strong man sat

in secret counsel, considered advice,
what would be best for the brave at heart
to save themselves from the sudden attacks.
175 At times they offered honor to idols
at pagan temples, prayed aloud
that the soul-slayer[4] might offer assistance
in the country's distress. Such was their custom,
the hope of heathens—they remembered Hell
180 in their minds, they did not know the Maker,
the Judge of deeds, they did not know the Lord God,
or even how to praise the heavenly Protector,
Wielder of glory. Woe unto him
who must thrust his soul through wicked force
185 in the fire's embrace, expect no comfort,
no way to change at all! It shall be well for him
who can seek the Lord after his deathday
and find security in the Father's embrace.

3

With the sorrows of that time the son of Healfdene[5]
190 seethed constantly; nor could the wise hero
turn aside his woe—too great was the strife,
long and loathsome, which befell that nation,
violent, grim, cruel, greatest of night-evils.
       Then from his home the thane of Hygelac,[6]
195 a good man among the Geats, heard of Grendel's deeds—
he was of mankind the strongest of might
in those days of this life,
noble and mighty. He commanded to be made
a good wave-crosser, said that that war-king
200 he would seek out over the swan's-riding,
the renowned prince, when he was in need of men.
Wise men did not dissuade him at all
from that journey, though he was dear to them;
they encouraged his bold spirit, inspected the omens.
205 From the Geatish nation that good man
had chosen the boldest champions, the best
he could find; one of fifteen,
he sought the sea-wood. A wise sailor
showed the way to the edge of the shore.
210 The time came—the craft was on the waves,

---

[1] *outbuildings* Hrothgar's hall is apparently surrounded by smaller buildings, including the women's quarters (see lines 662–5, 920–4). Under normal circumstances the men sleep together in the hall, ready for battle (1239–50).

[2] *bright compensation* Germanic and Anglo-Saxon law allowed that a murderer could make peace with the family of his victim by paying compensation, or *wergild*. The amount of compensation varied with the rank of the victim.

[3] *Thus the foe … love* This is a much-disputed passage; this reading follows a suggestion made by Fred C. Robinson in "Why is Grendel's Not Greeting the *gifstol a wræc micel*?" and repeated in Mitchell and Robinson's *Beowulf*.

[4] *soul-slayer* The Devil.

[5] *son of Healfdene* I.e., Hrothgar.

[6] *thane of Hygelac* I.e., Beowulf.

moored under the cliffs. Eager men
climbed on the prow—the currents eddied,
sea against sand—the soldiers bore
into the bosom of the ship their bright gear,
215 fine polished armor; the men pushed off
on their wished-for journey in that wooden vessel.
Over the billowing waves, urged by the wind,
the foamy-necked floater flew like a bird,
until in due time on the second day
220 the curved-prowed vessel had come so far
that the seafarers sighted land,
shining shore-cliffs, steep mountains,
wide headlands—then the waves were crossed,
the journey at an end. Thence up quickly
225 the people of the Weders[1] climbed onto the plain,
moored their ship, shook out their mail-shirts,
their battle-garments; they thanked God
that the sea-paths had been smooth for them.
      When from the wall the Scyldings' watchman,
230 whose duty it was to watch the sea-cliffs,
saw them bear down the gangplank bright shields,
ready battle-gear, he was bursting with curiosity
in his mind to know who these men were.
This thane of Hrothgar rode his horse
235 down to the shore, and shook mightily
his strong spear, and spoke a challenge:
"What are you, warriors in armor, wearing
coats of mail, who have come thus sailing
over the sea-road in a tall ship,
240 hither over the waves? Long have I been
the coast-warden, and kept sea-watch
so that no enemies with fleets and armies
should ever attack the land of the Danes.
Never more openly have there ever come
245 shield-bearers here, nor have you heard
any word of leave from our warriors
or consent of kinsmen. I have never seen
a greater earl on earth than that one among you,
a man in war-gear; that is no mere courtier,
250 honored only in weapons—unless his looks belie him,
his noble appearance! Now I must know
your lineage, lest you go hence
as false spies, travel further
into Danish territory. Now, you sea-travelers

255 from a far-off land, listen to my
simple thought—the sooner the better,
you must make clear from whence you have come."

4

      The eldest one answered him,
leader of the troop, unlocked his word-hoard:
260 "We are men of the Geatish nation
and Hygelac's hearth-companions.
My father was well-known among men,
a noble commander named Ecgtheow;
he saw many winters before he passed away,
265 ancient, from the court; nearly everyone
throughout the world remembers him well.
With a friendly heart have we come
seeking your lord, the son of Healfdene,
guardian of his people; be of good counsel to us!
270 We have a great mission to that famous man,
ruler of the Danes; nor should any of it be
hidden, I think. You know, if things are
as we have truly heard tell,
that among the Scyldings some sort of enemy,
275 hidden evildoer, in the dark nights
manifests his terrible and mysterious violence,
shame and slaughter. With a generous spirit
I can counsel Hrothgar, advise him how,
wise old king, he may overcome this fiend—
280 if a change should ever come for him,
a remedy for the evil of his afflictions,
and his seething cares turn cooler;
or forever afterwards a time of anguish
he shall suffer, his sad necessity, while there stands
285 in its high place the best of houses."
      The watchman spoke, as he sat on his horse,
a fearless officer: "A sharp shield-warrior
must be a judge of both things,
words and deeds, if he would think well.
290 I understand that to the Scylding lord
you are a friendly force. Go forth, and bear
weapons and armor—I shall guide your way;
and I will command my young companions
to guard honorably against all enemies
295 your ship, newly-tarred, upon the sand,
to watch it until the curved-necked wood
bears hence across the ocean-streams

---

[1] *Weders* I.e., Geats.

a beloved man to the borders of the Weders—
and such of these good men as will be granted
300 that they survive the storm of battle."
They set off—their vessel stood still,
the roomy ship rested in its riggings,
fast at anchor. Boar-figures shone
over gold-plated cheek-guards,[1]
305 gleaming, fire-hardened; they guarded the lives
of the grim battle-minded. The men hastened,
marched together, until they could make out
the timbered hall, splendid and gold-adorned—
the most famous building among men
310 under the heavens—where the high king waited;
its light shone over many lands.
Their brave guide showed them the bright court
of the mighty ones, so that they might go
straight to it; that fine soldier
315 wheeled his horse and spoke these words:
"Time for me to go. The almighty Father
guard you in his grace,
safe in your journeys! I must to the sea,
and hold my watch against hostile hordes."

5

320 The road was stone-paved, the path led
the men together. Their mail coats shone
hard, hand-linked, bright rings of iron
rang out on their gear, when right to the hall
they went trooping in their terrible armor.
325 Sea-weary, they set their broad shields,
wondrously-hard boards, against the building's wall;
they sat on a bench—their byrnies rang out,
their soldiers' war-gear; their spears stood,
the gear of the seamen all together,
330 a gray forest of ash. That iron troop
was worthy of its weapons.
                    Then a proud warrior[2]

---

[1] *Boar-figures … cheek-guards* The boar was a sacred animal in Germanic mythology; in his *Germania* the Roman historian Tacitus mentions warriors wearing boar-images into battle (ch. 45). Images of boars may have been placed on helmets to protect the wearer from the "bite" of a sword, which was often quasi-personified as a serpent. Archaeologists have unearthed several Anglo-Saxon helmets with various kinds of boar-images on them.

[2] *proud warrior* I.e., Wulfgar.

asked those soldiers about their ancestry:
"From whence do you carry those covered shields,
gray coats of mail and grim helmets,
335 this troop of spears? I am herald and servant
to Hrothgar; never have I seen
so many foreign men so fearless and bold.
For your pride, I expect, not for exile,
and for greatness of heart you have sought out Hrothgar."
340 The courageous one answered him,
proud prince of the Weders, spoke words
hardy in his helmet: "We are Hygelac's
board-companions—Beowulf is my name.
I wish to explain my errand
345 to the son of Healfdene, famous prince,
your lord, if he will allow us,
in his goodness, to greet him."
Wulfgar spoke—a prince of the Wendels,
his noble character was known to many,
350 his valor and wisdom: "I will convey
to the friend of the Danes, lord of the Scyldings,
giver of rings, what you have requested,
tell the famous prince of your travels,
and then quickly announce to you the answer
355 which that good man sees fit to give me."
He hastily returned to where Hrothgar sat
old and gray-haired, with his band of earls;
he boldly went, stood by the shoulder
of the Danish king—he knew the noble custom.
360 Wulfgar spoke to his friend and lord:
"There have arrived here over the sea's expanse,
come from afar, men of the Geats;
the oldest among them, the fighting men
call Beowulf. They have requested
365 that they, my lord, might be allowed
to exchange words with you—do not refuse them
your reply, gracious Hrothgar!
In their war-trappings they seem worthy
of noble esteem; notable indeed is that chief
370 who has shown these soldiers the way hither."

6

Hrothgar spoke, protector of the Scyldings:
"I knew him when he was nothing but a boy—
his old father was called Ecgtheow,

to whom Hrethel the Geat[1] gave in marriage
375 his only daughter; now his daring son
has come here, sought a loyal friend.
Seafarers, in truth, have said to me,
those who brought to the Geats gifts and money
as thanks, that he has thirty
380 men's strength, strong in battle,
in his handgrip. Holy God
in His grace has guided him to us,
to the West-Danes, as I would hope,
against Grendel's terror. To this good man
385 I shall offer treasures for his true daring.
Be hasty now, bid them enter
to see this troop of kinsmen all assembled;
and tell them in your words that they are welcome
to the Danish people."
390   He announced from within:[2]
"My conquering lord commands me to tell you,
ruler of the East-Danes, that he knows your ancestry,
and you are to him, hardy spirits,
welcome hither from across the rolling waves.
395 Now you may go in your war-gear
under your helmets to see Hrothgar,
but let your battle-shields and deadly spears
await here the result of your words."
        The mighty one arose, and many a man with him,
400 powerful thanes; a few waited there,
guarded their battle-dress as the bold man bid them.
They hastened together as the man led them,
under Heorot's roof; [the warrior went][3]
hardy in his helmet, until he stood on the hearth.
405 Beowulf spoke—his byrnie gleamed on him,
war-net sewn by the skill of a smith—:
"Be well, Hrothgar! I am Hygelac's kinsman
and young retainer; in my youth I have done
many a glorious deed. This business with Grendel
410 was made known to me on my native soil;
seafarers say that this building stands,

most excellent of halls, idle and useless
to every man, after evening's light
is hidden under heaven's gleaming dome.
415 Then my own people advised me,
the best warriors and the wisest men,
that I should, lord Hrothgar, seek you out,
because they knew the might of my strength;
they themselves had seen me, bloodstained from battle,
420 come from the fight, when I captured five,
slew a tribe of giants, and on the salt waves
fought sea-monsters by night, survived that tight spot,
avenged the Weders' affliction—they asked for trouble!—
and crushed those grim foes; and now with Grendel,
425 that monstrous beast, I shall by myself have
a word or two with that giant. From you now I wish,
ruler of the Bright-Danes, to request,
protector of the Scyldings, a single favor,
that you not refuse me, having come this far,
430 protector of warriors, noble friend to his people—
that I might alone, O my own band of earls
and this hardy troop, cleanse Heorot.
I have also heard that this evil beast
in his wildness does not care for weapons,
435 so I too will scorn—so that Hygelac,
my liege-lord, may be glad of me—
to bear a sword or a broad shield,
a yellow battle-board, but with my grip
I shall grapple with the fiend and fight for life,
440 foe against foe. Let him put his faith
in the Lord's judgment, whom death takes!
I expect that he will, if he is allowed to win,
eat unafraid the folk of the Geats
in that war-hall, as he has often done,
445 the host of the Hrethmen.[4] You'll have no need
to cover my head—he will have done so,
gory, bloodstained, if death bears me away;
he will take his kill, think to taste me,
will dine alone without remorse,
450 stain his lair in the moor; no need to linger
in sorrow over disposing of my body!
Send on to Hygelac, if battle should take me,
the best battledress, which my breast wears,
finest of garments; it is Hrethel's heirloom,

---

[1] *Hrethel the Geat* Father of Hygelac and grandfather of Beowulf.

[2] *people … within* There is no gap in the manuscript, but the two halves of the line do not alliterate, and something is probably missing from the text at this point. Most editors add two half-lines with the sense "Then Wulfgar went to the door."

[3] *[the warrior went]* A half-line is missing; the translation follows the most innocuous conjecture.

---

[4] *Hrethmen* I.e., Geats.

455 the work of Weland.[1] *Wyrd* always goes as it must!"[2]

7

Hrothgar spoke, protector of the Scyldings:
"For past favors, my friend Beowulf,
and for old deeds, you have sought us out.
Your father struck up the greatest of feuds,
460 when he killed Heatholaf by his own hand
among the Wylfings. When the Weder tribe
would not harbor him for fear of war,
thence he sought the South-Dane people
over the billowing seas, the Honor-Scyldings;
465 then I first ruled the Danish folk
and held in my youth this grand kingdom,
city of treasure and heroes—then Heorogar
was dead, my older brother unliving,
Healfdene's firstborn—he was better than I!
470 Later I settled that feud with fee-money;
I sent to the Wylfings over the crest of the waves
ancient treasures; he swore oaths to me.[3]
It is a sorrow to my very soul to say
to any man what Grendel has done to me—
475 humiliated Heorot with his hateful thoughts,
his sudden attacks. My hall-troop,
my warriors, are decimated; *wyrd* has swept them away
into Grendel's terror. God might easily
put an end to the deeds of this mad enemy!
480 Often men have boasted, drunk with beer,
officers over their cups of ale,
that they would abide in the beerhall
Grendel's attack with a rush of sword-terror.
Then in the morning this meadhall,
485 lordly dwelling, was drenched with blood,
when daylight gleamed, the benches gory,

the hall spattered and befouled; I had fewer
dear warriors when death took them away.
Now sit down at my feast, drink mead in my hall,[4]
490 men's reward of victory, as your mood urges."
Then a bench was cleared in the beerhall
for the men of the Geats all together;
the strong-minded men went to sit down,
proud in their strength. A thane did his service,
495 bore in his hands the gold-bright ale-cup,
poured the clear sweet drink. The scop sang
brightly in Heorot—there was the joy of heroes,
no small gathering of Danes and Geats.

8

Unferth[5] spoke, son of Ecglaf,
500 who sat at the feet of the Scylding lord,
unbound his battle-runes[6]—Beowulf's journey,
that brave seafarer, sorely vexed him,
for he did not wish that any other man
on this middle-earth should care for glory
505 under the heavens, more than he himself:
"Are you the Beowulf who strove with Breca
in a swimming contest on the open sea,
where in your pride you tried the waves
and for a foolish boast risked your life
510 in the deep water? No man, whether
friend or foe, could dissuade you two
from that sad venture, when you swam in the sea;
there you seized in your arms the ocean-streams,
measured the sea-ways, flailed your hands
515 and glided over the waves—the water roiled,
wintry surges. In the keeping of the water
you toiled for seven nights, and he outswam you,
and had more strength. Then in the morning
the swells bore him to the Heathoream shore;
520 from thence he sought his own sweet land,
beloved by his people, the land of the Brondings,
the fair fortress, where he had his folk,

---

[1] *Weland* Legendary blacksmith of the Norse gods. The antiquity of weapons and armor added to their value.

[2] *Wyrd* The Old English word for "fate" is sometimes quasi-personified, though apparently not to the extent that the goddess *Fortuna* was in Roman poetic mythology. The word survives, via Shakespeare's *Macbeth*, as the Modern English word "weird."

[3] *I sent ... me* Hrothgar pays the *wergild* for the man Ecgtheow killed, and Ecgtheow swears an oath of loyalty and support. It is this oath, passed on to the next generation, that Beowulf is fulfilling (at least this is Hrothgar's public sentiment; his thoughts in the privacy of his council are somewhat different).

[4] *Now sit ... hall* The meaning of this line in Old English is disputed.

[5] *Unferth* Unferth's name, which may be significant, means either "un-peace" or "un-reason." In the manuscript it is always spelled "Hunferth," though it alliterates with a vowel. His position at Hrothgar's feet appears to be one of honor.

[6] *unbound his battle-runes* Or "unleashed his hostile secret thoughts." *Run* in Old English often means "secret."

his castle and treasure. He truly fulfilled,
the son of Beanstan, his boast against you.
525 So I expect a worse outcome from you—
though you may have survived the storm of battle,
some grim combats—if for Grendel you dare
to lie in wait the whole night long."
        Beowulf spoke, son of Ecgtheow:
530 "What a great deal, Unferth my friend,
drunk with beer, you have said about Breca,
told his adventures! I will tell the truth—
I had greater strength on the sea,
more ordeals on the waves than any other man.
535 When we were just boys we two agreed
and boasted—we were both still
in our youth—that out on the great ocean
we would risk our lives, and we did just that.
We had bare swords, when we swam in the sea,
540 hard in our hands; we thought to protect
ourselves from whales. Not for anything
could he swim far from me on the sea-waves,
more swiftly on the water, nor would I go from him.
We two were together on the sea
545 for five nights, until the flood drove us apart,
surging waves, coldest of weathers,
darkening night, and a northern wind,
knife-sharp, pushed against us. The seas were choppy;
the fishes of the sea were stirred up by it.
550 There my coat of armor offered help,
hard, hand-locked, against those hostile ones,
my woven battle-dress lay on my breast
adorned with gold. Down to the ocean floor
a grisly foe dragged me, gripped me fast
555 in his grim grasp, yet it was given to me
to stab that monster with the point of my sword,
my war-blade; the storm of battle took away
that mighty sea-beast, through my own hand.

9

"Time and again those terrible enemies
560 sorely threatened me. I served them well
with my dear sword, as they deserved.
They got no joy from their gluttony,
those wicked maneaters, when they tasted me,
sat down to their feast on the ocean floor—
565 but in the morning, wounded by my blade,

they were washed ashore by the ocean waves,
dazed by sword-blows, and since that day
they never hindered the passage of any
sea-voyager. Light shone from the east,
570 God's bright beacon; the waves grew calm,
so that I could see the sea-cliffs,
the windswept capes. *Wyrd* often spares
an undoomed man, when his courage endures!
And so it came about that I was able to kill
575 nine of these sea-monsters. I have never heard
of a harder night-battle under heaven's vault,
nor a more wretched man on the water's stream;
yet I escaped alive from the clutches of my enemies,
weary from my journey. Then the sea washed me up,
580 the currents of the flood, in the land of the Finns,
the welling waters. I have never heard a word
about any such contest concerning you,
such sword-panic. In the play of battle
Breca has never—nor you either—
585 done a deed so bold and daring
with his decorated blade—I would never boast of it!—
though you became your brothers' killer,
your next of kin; for that you needs must suffer
punishment in Hell, no matter how clever you are.[1]
590 I will say it truly, son of Ecglaf,
that never would Grendel have worked such terror,
that gruesome beast, against your lord,
or shames in Heorot, if your courage and spirit
were as fierce as you yourself fancy they are;
595 but he has found that he need fear no feud,
no storm of swords from the Victory-Scyldings,
no resistance at all from your nation;
he takes his toll, spares no one
in the Danish nation, but indulges himself,
600 hacks and butchers and expects no battle
from the Spear-Danes. But I will show him
soon enough the strength and courage
of the Geats in war. Afterwards, let him who will

---

[1] *though you became ... you are* Unferth's fratricide brings the
general theme of kin-slaying, represented by Grendel's descent from
Cain, inside Hrothgar's hall. In reality—at least in the reality of the
heroic world depicted in poetry—it may not have been unthinkable
for kinsmen to find themselves on opposite sides of a battle; loyalty
to one's lord was supposed to outweigh the claims of blood-relation.
The word "Hell" is not in the manuscript, but it is attested by one
of the early transcriptions. Some scholars read *healle*, i.e., "hall."

go bravely to mead, when the morning light
605 of a new day, the sun clothed in glory
shines from the south on the sons of men!"

Then the giver of treasure was greatly pleased,
gray-haired and battle-bold; the Bright-Danes' chief
had faith in his helper; that shepherd of his folk
610 recognized Beowulf's firm resolution.
There was man's laughter, lovely sounds
and winsome words. Wealhtheow went forth,
Hrothgar's queen, mindful of customs;
adorned with gold, she greeted the men in the hall,
615 then that courteous wife offered the full cup
first to the guardian of the East-Danes' kingdom,
bid him be merry at his beer-drinking,
beloved by his people; with pleasure he received
the feast and cup, victorious king.
620 The lady of the Helmings then went about
to young and old, gave each his portion
of the precious cup, until the moment came
when the ring-adorned queen, of excellent heart,
bore the mead-cup to Beowulf;
625 she greeted the Geatish prince, thanked God
with wise words that her wish had come to pass,
that she could rely on any earl for relief
from those crimes. He took the cup,
the fierce warrior, from Wealhtheow,
630 and then eager for battle he made his announcement.
Beowulf spoke, son of Ecgtheow:
"I resolved when I set out over the waves,
sat down in my ship with my troop of soldiers,
that I would entirely fulfill the wishes
635 of your people, or fall slain,
fast in the grip of my foe. I shall perform
a deed of manly courage, or in this meadhall
I will await the end of my days!"
These words well pleased that woman,
640 the boasting of the Geat; she went, the gold-adorned
and courteous folk-queen, to sit beside her lord.

Then, as before, there in that hall were
strong words spoken, the people happy,
the sounds of a victorious nation, until shortly
645 the son of Healfdene wished to seek
his evening rest; he knew that the wretched beast
had been planning to do battle in the high building
from the time they could first see the sunrise

until night fell darkening over all,
650 and creatures of shadow came creeping about
pale under the clouds. The company arose.
One warrior greeted another there,
Hrothgar to Beowulf, and wished him luck,
gave him control of the wine-hall in these words:
655 "I have never entrusted to any man,
ever since I could hold and hoist a shield,
the great hall of the Danes—except to you now.
Have it and hold it, protect this best of houses,
be mindful of glory, show your mighty valor,
660 watch for your enemies! You will have all you desire,
if you emerge from this brave undertaking alive."

10

Then Hrothgar and his troop of heroes,
protector of the Scyldings, departed from the hall;
the war-chief wished to seek Wealhtheow,
665 his queen's bedchamber. The glorious king[1]
had set against Grendel a hall-guardian
— as men had heard said—who did special service
for the king of the Danes, kept a giant-watch.
Surely the Geatish prince greatly trusted
670 his mighty strength, the Maker's favor,
when he took off his iron byrnie,
undid his helmet, and gave his decorated iron,
best of swords, to his servant
and bid him hold his battle-gear.
675 The good man, Beowulf the Geat,
spoke a few boasting words before he lay down:
"I consider myself no poorer in strength
and battle-deeds than Grendel does himself;
and so I will not kill him with a sword,
680 put an end to his life, though I easily might;
he knows no arts of war, no way to strike back,
hack at my shield-boss, though he be brave
in his wicked deeds; but tonight we two will
forgo our swords, if he dare to seek out
685 a war without weapons—and then let the wise Lord
grant the judgment of glory, the holy God,
to whichever hand seems proper to Him."
He lay down, battle-brave; the bolster took
the earl's cheek, and around him many

---

[1] *The glorious king* Or "King of Glory," i.e., God?

690 a bold seafarer sank to his hall-rest.
None of them thought that he should thence
ever again seek his own dear homeland,
his tribe or the town in which he was raised,
for they had heard it said that savage death
695 had swept away far too many of the Danish folk
in that wine-hall. But the Lord gave them
a web of victory, the people of the Weders,
comfort and support, so that they completely,
through one man's craft, overcame their enemy,
700 by his own might. It is a well-known truth
that mighty God has ruled mankind
always and forever.
                      In the dark night he came
creeping, the shadow-goer. The bowmen slept
who were to hold that horned hall—
705 all but one. It was well-known to men
that the demon foe could not drag them under
the dark shadows if the Maker did not wish it;
but he, wakeful, keeping watch for his enemy,
awaited, enraged, the outcome of battle.

II

710 Then from the moor, in a blanket of mist,
Grendel came stalking—he bore God's anger;
the evil marauder meant to ensnare
some of human-kind in that high hall.
Under the clouds he came until he clearly knew
715 he was near the wine-hall, men's golden house,
finely adorned. It was not the first time
he had sought out the home of Hrothgar,
but never in his life, early or late,
did he find harder luck or a hardier hall-thane.
720 To the hall came that warrior on his journey,
bereft of joys. The door burst open,
fast in its forged bands, when his fingers touched it;
bloody-minded, swollen with rage, he swung open
the hall's mouth, and immediately afterwards
725 the fiend strode across the paved floor,
went angrily; in his eyes stood
a light not fair, glowing like fire.
He saw in the hall many a soldier,
a peaceful troop sleeping all together,
730 a large company of thanes—and he laughed inside;
he meant to divide, before day came,

this loathsome creature, the life of each
man from his body, when there befell him
the hope of a feast. But it was not his fate
735 to taste any more of the race of mankind
after that night. The kinsman of Hygelac,
mighty one, beheld how that maneater
planned to proceed with his sudden assault.
Not that the monster[1] meant to delay—
740 he seized at once at his first pass
a sleeping man, slit him open suddenly,
bit into his joints, drank the blood from his veins,
gobbled his flesh in gobbets, and soon
had completely devoured that dead man,
745 feet and fingertips. He stepped further,
and took in his hands the strong-hearted
man in his bed; the monster reached out
towards him with his hands—he quickly grabbed him
with evil intent, and sat up against his arm.
750 As soon as that shepherd of sins discovered
that he had never met on middle-earth,
in any region of the world, another man
with a greater handgrip, in his heart he was
afraid for his life, but none the sooner could he flee.
755 His mind was eager to escape to the darkness,
seek out a host of devils—his habit there
was nothing like he had ever met before.
The good kinsman of Hygelac remembered then
his evening speech, and stood upright
760 and seized him fast. His fingers burst;
the giant turned outward, the earl stepped inward.
The notorious one meant—if he might—
to turn away further and flee, away
to his lair in the fen; he knew his fingers
765 were held in a hostile grip. That was an unhappy journey
that the harm-doer took to Heorot!
The great hall resounded; to the Danes it seemed,
the city's inhabitants, and every brave earl,
like a wild ale-sharing.[2] Both were angry,

---

[1] *monster* The OE word *ǽglǽca*, which literally means "awesome one" or "terror," is elsewhere applied to the dragon-slaying Sigemund (line 892, where it is translated "fierce creature") and to Beowulf himself. Its translation here is admittedly tendentious. The word appears elsewhere, variously translated, in lines 159, 433, 732, 556, etc.

[2] *wild ale-sharing* The general sense of the OE word *ealuscerwen* is "panic" or "terror," but its precise meaning (probably "a dispensing of ale") is unclear; did the Danes think a wild party was going on? Or

770 fierce house-wardens—the hall echoed.
It was a great wonder that the wine-hall
withstood their fighting and did not fall to the ground,
that fair building—but it was fastened
inside and out with iron bands,
775 forged with skill. From the floor there flew
many a mead-bench, as men have told me,
gold-adorned, where those grim foes fought.
The Scylding elders had never expected
that any man, by any ordinary means,
780 could break it apart, beautiful, bone-adorned,
or destroy it with guile, unless the embrace of fire
might swallow it in flames. The noise swelled
new and stark—among the North-Danes was
horrible terror, in each of them
785 who heard through the wall the wailing cry—
God's adversary shrieked a grisly song
of horror, defeated, the captive of Hell
bewailed his pain. He pinned him fast,
he who among men was the strongest of might
790 in those days of this life.

12

That protector of earls would not for anything
let that murderous visitor escape alive—
he did not consider his days on earth
of any use at all. Many an earl
795 in Beowulf's troop drew his old blade,
longed to protect the life of his liege-lord,
the famous captain, however they could.
But they did not know as they entered the fight,
those stern-minded men of battle,
800 and thought to strike from all sides
and seek his soul, that no sword,
not the best iron anywhere in the world,
could even touch that evil sinner,
for he had worked a curse on weapons,
805 every sort of blade. His separation from the world
in those days of this life
would have to be miserable, and that alien spirit
would travel far into the keeping of fiends.
Then he discovered, who had done before

were they dismayed by the loss of their mead-hall? Or does OE *ealu* mean "luck"?

810 so much harm to the race of mankind,
so many crimes—he was marked by God—
that his body could bear it no longer,
but the courageous kinsman of Hygelac
had him in hand—hateful to each
815 was the life of the other. The loathsome creature felt
great bodily pain; a gaping wound opened
in his shoulder-joint, his sinews sprang apart,
his joints burst asunder. Beowulf was given
glory in battle—Grendel was forced
820 to flee, mortally wounded, into the fen-slopes,
seek a sorry abode; he knew quite surely
that the end of his life had arrived,
the sum of his days. The will of the Danes
was entirely fulfilled in that bloody onslaught!
825 He who had come from afar had cleansed,
wise and stout-hearted, the hall of Hrothgar,
warded off attack. He rejoiced in his night-work,
his great courage. That man of the Geats
had fulfilled his boast to the East-Danes,
830 and entirely remedied all their distress,
the insidious sorrows they had suffered
and had to endure from sad necessity,
no small affliction. It was a clear sign,
when the battle-brave one laid down the hand,
835 arm and shoulder—there all together
was Grendel's claw—under the curved roof.

13

Then in the morning was many a warrior,
as I have heard, around that gift-hall,
leaders of the folk came from far and near
840 throughout the wide land to see that wonder,
the loathsome one's tracks. His parting from life
hardly seemed sad to any man
who examined the trail of that inglorious one,
how he went on his weary way,
845 defeated by force, to a pool of sea-monsters,
doomed, put to flight, and left a fatal trail.
The water was welling with blood there—
the terrible swirling waves, all mingled together
with hot gore, heaved with the blood of battle,
850 concealed that doomed one when, deprived of joys,
he laid down his life in his lair in the fen,
his heathen soul—and Hell took him.

Then the old retainers returned from there,
and many a youth on the joyful journey,
855 bravely rode their horses back from the mere,
men on their steeds. There they celebrated
Beowulf's glory: it was often said
that south or north, between the two seas,[1]
across the wide world, there was none
860 better under the sky's expanse
among shield-warriors, nor more worthy to rule—
though they found no fault with their own friendly lord,
gracious Hrothgar, but said he was a good king.
At times the proud warriors let their horses prance,
865 their fallow mares fare in a contest,
wherever the footpaths seemed fair to them,
the way tried and true. At times the king's thane,
full of grand stories, mindful of songs,
who remembered much, a great many
870 of the old tales, found other words
truly bound together; he began again
to recite with skill the adventure of Beowulf,
adeptly tell an apt tale,
and weave his words. He said nearly all
875 that he had heard said of Sigemund's
stirring deeds,[2] many strange things,
the Volsung's strife, his distant voyages
obscure, unknown to all the sons of men,
his feuds and crimes—except for Fitela,
880 when of such things he wished to speak to him,
uncle to nephew[3]—for always they were,

in every combat, companions at need;
a great many of the race of giants
they slaughtered with their swords. For Sigemund
885 no small fame grew after his final day,
after that hardened soldier, prince's son,
had killed a dragon, keeper of a hoard;
alone, he dared to go under gray stones,
a bold deed—nor was Fitela by his side;
890 yet so it befell him that his sword pierced
the wondrous serpent, stood fixed in the wall,
the manly iron; the dragon met his death.
That fierce creature had gone forth in courage
so that he could possess that store of rings
895 and use them at his will; the son of Wæls
loaded his sea-boat, bore the bright treasure
to the ship's hold. The serpent melted in its own heat.

He was the most famous of exiles, far and wide,
among all people, protector of warriors,
900 for his noble deeds—he had prospered for them—
since the struggles of Heremod had ceased,
his might and valor. Among the Eotens[4]
he was betrayed into his enemies' hands,
quickly dispatched. The surging of cares
905 had crippled him too long; he became a deadly burden
to his own people, to all noblemen;
for many a wise man had mourned
in earlier times over his headstrong ways
who had looked to him for relief from affliction,
910 hoped that that prince's son would prosper,
receive his father's rank, rule his people,
hoard and fortress, a kingdom of heroes,
the Scylding homeland. The kinsman of Hygelac
became to all of the race of mankind
915 a more pleasant friend; sin possessed him.[5]

Sometimes, competing, the fallow paths
they measured on horseback. When morning's light
raced on and hastened away, many a retainer,
stout-hearted, went to see the high hall
920 to see the strange wonder; the king himself,
guard of the treasure-hoard, strode glorious
from the woman's chambers with a great entourage,

---

[1] *between the two seas* A conventional expression like Modern English "coast to coast"; probably it originally referred to the North and Baltic seas.

[2] *He said … deeds* Beowulf is praised indirectly, by being compared first to Sigemund, another famous monster-slayer (a different version of whose story is told in the Old Norse *Volsungasaga* and the Middle High German *Nibelungenlied*; there the dragon-slaying is attributed to Sigemund's son Siegfried), and then contrasted to Heremod, an earlier king of the Danes who descended into tyranny (it is sometimes assumed that the disastrous ending of Heremod's reign is the cause of the Danes' lordlessness and distress mentioned at the beginning of the poem). The implication is that Beowulf's deeds place him in the ranks of other exemplary figures. The method of narration is allusive and indirect, as though the audience were expected to know the details of the story and appreciate an elliptical reference to them.

[3] *uncle to nephew* Fitela is actually Sigemund's son by his own sister—either the poet is being discreet, or his version of the story differs from the Norse.

[4] *Eotens* Perhaps "Jutes." The word literally means "giants" and may be a tribal name, or an epithet, or may in fact refer to an actual race of giants.

[5] *sin possessed him* I.e., Heremod.

a chosen retinue, and his royal queen with him
measured the meadhall-path with a troop of maidens.

14

925   Hrothgar spoke—he went to the hall,
stood on the steps, beheld the steep roof
plated with gold, and Grendel's hand:
"For this sight let us swiftly offer thanks
to the Almighty! Much have I endured
930   of dire grief from Grendel, but God may always
work, Shepherd of glory, wonder upon wonder.
It was not long ago that I did not expect
ever in my life to experience relief
from any of my woes, when, stained with blood,
935   this best of houses stood dripping, gory,
a widespread woe to all wise men
who did not expect that they might ever
defend the people's fortress from its foes,
devils and demons. Now a retainer has done
940   the very deed, through the might of God,
which we all could not contrive to do
with all our cleverness. Lo, that woman could say,
whosoever has borne such a son
into the race of men, if she still lives,
945   that the God of Old was good to her
in childbearing. Now I will cherish you,
Beowulf, best of men, like a son
in my heart; hold well henceforth
your new kinship. You shall have no lack
950   of the worldly goods which I can bestow.
Often have I offered rewards for less,
honored with gifts a humbler man,
weaker in battle. Now by yourself
you have done such deeds that your fame will endure
955   always and forever—may the Almighty
reward you with good, as He has already done!"
    Beowulf spoke, son of Ecgtheow:
"Freely and gladly have we fought this fight,
done this deed of courage, daringly faced
960   this unknown power. I would much prefer
that you might have seen the foe himself
decked in his finery,[1] fallen and exhausted!

With a hard grip I hoped to bind him
quickly and keenly on the killing floor,
965   so that for my handgrasp he would have to
lie squirming for life, unless he might slip away;
I could not—the Creator did not wish it—
hinder his going, no matter how hard I held
that deadly enemy; too overwhelming was
970   that fiend's flight. Yet he forfeited his hand,
his arm and shoulder, to save his life,
to guard his tracks—though he got thereby,
pathetic creature, little comfort;
the loathsome destroyer will live no longer,
975   rotten with sin, but pain has seized him,
grabbed him tightly in its fierce grip,
its baleful bonds—and there he shall abide,
guilty of his crimes, the greater judgment,
how the shining Maker wishes to sentence him."
980   Then the son of Ecglaf[2] was more silent
in boasting words about his battle-works
after the noblemen, through the earl's skill,
looked on the hand over the high roof,
the enemy's fingers; at the end of each nail
985   was a sharp tip, most like steel,
heathen talons, the terrible spikes
of that awful warrior; each of them agreed
that not even the hardest of ancient and honorable
irons could touch him, or injure at all
990   the bloody battle-paw of that baleful creature.

15

    Then it was quickly commanded that Heorot
be adorned by hands inside; many there,
men and women, prepared that wine-hall,
the guest-house. Gold-dyed tapestries
995   shone on the walls, many wonderful sights
to any man who might look on them.
That shining building was nearly shattered
inside, entirely, fast in its iron bands,
its hinges sprung; the roof alone survived
1000   unharmed, when that horrible creature,
stained with foul deeds, turned in his flight,
despairing of life. Death is not an easy
thing to escape—try it who will—

---

[1] *in his finery*   Literally "in his adornments," a peculiar phrase since
Grendel is notoriously not armed and unadorned. Perhaps Beowulf
means "covered in a garment of blood"?

[2] *son of Ecglaf*   I.e., Unferth.

but compelled by necessity all must come
1005 to that place set aside for soul-bearers,
children of men, dwellers on earth,
where the body, fast on its bed of death,
sleeps after the feast.   Then was the set time
that the son of Healfdene went to the hall;
1010 the king himself wished to share in the feast.
I have never heard of a greater host
who bore themselves better before their treasure-giver.
Those men in their glory moved to their benches,
rejoiced in the feast; fairly those kinsmen
1015 took many a full mead-cup,
stouthearted in the high hall,
Hrothgar and Hrothulf. Heorot within was
filled with friends—no false treacheries
did the people of the Scyldings plot at that time.[1]
1020 He gave to Beowulf the blade of Healfdene,[2]
a golden war-standard as a reward for victory,
the bright banner, a helmet and byrnie,
a great treasure-sword—many saw them
borne before that man. Beowulf received
1025 the full cup in the hall, he felt no shame
at that gift-giving before his bowmen;
never have I heard tell of four treasures
given more graciously, gold-adorned,
from one man to another on the ale-benches.
1030 On the crown of the helmet as a head-protector
a ridge, wound with wire, stood without,
so that the file-sharp swords might not terribly
harm him, shower-hard, when shield-fighters
had to go against hostile forces.
1035 The protector of earls ordered eight horses
with ornamented bridles led into the building,
in under the eaves; on one sat

a saddle, skillfully tooled, set with gemstones;
that was the warseat of the high-king
1040 when the son of Healfdene sought to perform
his swordplay—the widely-known warrior
never failed at the front, when the slain fell about him.
And the lord of the Ingwines[3] gave ownership
of both of them to Beowulf,
1045 the horses and weapons, bid him use them well.
So manfully did the mighty prince,
hoard-guard of warriors, reward the storm of battle
with such steeds and treasures that none who will speak
the truth rightfully could ever reproach them.

16

1050   Then the lord of earls, to each of those
on the meadbenches who had made with Beowulf
a sea-journey, gave jeweled treasures,
antique heirlooms, and then ordered
that gold be paid for the man whom Grendel
1055 had wickedly slain—he would have done more,
if wise God and one man's courage
had not prevented that fate. The Maker ruled all
of the race of mankind, as He still does.
Therefore understanding is always best,
1060 spiritual foresight—he must face much,
both love and hate, who long here
endures this world in these days of strife.
        Noise and music mingled together
before the leader of Healfdene's forces,
1065 the harp was touched, tales often told,
when Hrothgar's scop was set to recite
among the mead-tables his hall-entertainment
about the sons of Finn, surprised in ambush,
when the hero of the Half-Danes, Hnæf the Scylding
1070 had to fall in a Frisian slaughter.[4]

---

[1] Implicit in this statement is the idea that, at some later time, the people of the Scyldings did plot false treacheries; from other sources it is possible to infer that after the death of Hrothgar, his nephew Hrothulf ruled rather than Hrethric, Hrothgar's son. Many scholars assume that the story of some sort of treacherous usurpation was known to the audience; this gives a special urgency to much of what happens in these scenes of feasting, especially the speeches of Wealhtheow.

[2] *He gave ... Healfdene* The translation follows the reading of Mitchell and Robinson, and see Bruce Mitchell, "Beowulf, line 1020b: *brand* or *bearn*?" The manuscript is usually emended to mean "The son of Healfdene gave to Beowulf."

[3] *Ingwines* I.e., Danes.

[4] *the sons of Finn … Frisian slaughter* The story is obscure; the survival of a fragment of another poem ("The Fight at Finnsburh") telling the same story helps clarify the action somewhat. Hnæf, prince of the Danes, is visiting his sister Hildeburh at the home of her husband Finn, king of the Frisians. While there, the Danish party is treacherously attacked (perhaps by a Jutish contingent among Finn's troops, unless the "Jutes" and Frisians are one and the same people); after five days of fighting Hnæf lies dead, along with many casualties on either side. Hnæf's retainer Hengest is left to lead the remnant of Danish survivors.

Hildeburh, indeed, had no need to praise
the good faith of the Jutes.[1] Guiltless, she was
deprived of her dear ones in that shieldplay,
her sons and brothers—sent forth to their fate,
1075 dispatched by spears; she was a sad lady!
Not without cause did she mourn fate's decrees,
the daughter of Hoc, after daybreak came
and she could see the slaughter of her kin
under the very skies where once she held
1080 the greatest worldly joys. War took away
all of the thanes of Finn, except a few,
so that he could not continue at all
a fight with Hengest on the battlefield,
nor could that woeful remnant drive away
1085 the prince's thane—so they offered them terms:[2]
they would clear out another hall for them,
a house and high-seat, of which they should have
half the control with the sons of the Jutes,
and Folcwalda's son,[3] with feasting and gifts,
1090 should honor the Danes each and every day,
gladden the troops of Hengest with gold rings
and ancient treasures, ornamented gold,
just as often as he would encourage
the hosts of the Frisians in the beerhall.
1095 They swore their pledges then on either side,
a firm compact of peace. With unfeigned zeal
Finn swore his oaths to Hengest, pledged that he,
with the consent of his counselors, would
support with honor those sad survivors,
1100 and that none should break their pact in word or deed,
nor through malice should ever make mention,
though they should serve their ring-giver's slayer,
without a lord, as they were led by need—
and if, provoking, any Frisian spoke
1105 reminding them of all their murderous hate,
then with the sword's edge they should settle it.
The oath[4] was made ready, and ancient gold

was brought from the hoard; the Battle-Scyldings'
best fighting-man was ready for the fire.
1110 It was easy to see upon that pyre
the bloodstained battle-shirt, the gilded swine,
iron-hard boar-images, the noblemen
with fatal wounds—so many felled by war!
Then Hildeburh commanded at Hnæf's pyre
1115 that her own son be consigned to the flames
to be burnt, flesh and bone, placed on the pyre
at his uncle's shoulder; the lady sang
a sad lament. The warrior ascended;
to the clouds coiled the mighty funeral fire,
1120 and roared before their mound; their heads melted,
their gashes burst open and spurted blood,
the deadly body-bites. The flame devoured,
most greedy spirit, those whom war destroyed
of both peoples—their glory departed.

17

1125 The warriors left to seek their native lands,
bereft of friends, to behold Frisia,
their homes and high fortresses. Hengest still
stayed there with Finn that slaughter-stained winter,
unwilling, desolate. He dreamt of home,
1130 though on the frozen sea he could not[5] steer
his ring-prowed ship—the ocean raged with storms,
strove with the wind, and winter locked the waves
in icy bonds, until there came another
year to the courtyard—as it yet does,
1135 always observing its seasons and times,
bright glorious weather. Gone was the winter,
and fair the bosom of earth; the exile burned
to take leave of that court, yet more he thought
of stern vengeance than of sea-voyages,
1140 how he might arrange a hostile meeting,
remind the Jutish sons of his iron sword.
So he did not refuse the world's custom
when the son of Hunlaf[6] placed a glinting sword,

---

[1] *Jutes* I.e., Frisians.

[2] *them terms* The referent of this pronoun in not entirely clear—who offers what to whom? The terms of the truce are unthinkable—no hero could honorably follow the killer of his lord. In the following line "they" refers to the Frisians, "them" to the Danes.

[3] *Folcwalda's son* I.e., Finn.

[4] *oath* Some editors emend to *ad*, "pyre."

[5] *not* OE *ne* "not" is not in the manuscript; most editors and translators add it to make better sense of the passage and of Hengest's character.

[6] *the son of Hunlaf* It is not clear who this is: perhaps Guthlaf or Oslaf (mentioned a few lines later), perhaps not; apparently some retainers remained with Hengest in Finn's hall, nursing their resentment throughout the winter. Some scholars take the OE word

the best of battle-flames, upon his lap;
1145 its edge was not unknown among the Jutes.
And so, in turn, to the bold-minded Finn
befell cruel sword-evil in his own home,
when Guthlaf and Oslaf spoke of their grief,
the fierce attack after their sea voyage,
1150 and cursed their wretched lot—the restless heart
could not restrain itself. The hall was stained
with the lifeblood of foes, and Finn was slain,
the king among his host; the queen was seized.
The Scylding bowmen carried to their ships
1155 all the house property of that earth-king,
whatever they could find in Finn's homestead,
brooches and bright gems. On their sea journey
they bore that noble queen back to the Danes
and led her to her people.
                              The lay was sung,
1160 the entertainer's song. Glad sounds rose again,
the bench-noise glittered, cupbearers gave
wine from wondrous vessels. Wealhtheow came forth
in her golden crown to where the good two
sat, nephew and uncle; their peace was still whole then,
1165 each true to the other. Likewise Unferth, spokesman,[1]
sat at the foot of the Scylding lord; everyone trusted
       his spirit,
that he had great courage, though to his kinsmen he
       had not been
merciful in sword-play. Then the lady of the Scyldings
       spoke:
       "Take this cup, my noble courteous lord,
1170 giver of treasure! Be truly joyful,
gold-friend of men, and speak to the Geats
in mild words, as a man should do!
Be gracious to the Geats, mindful of the gifts
which you now have from near and far.
1175 I have been told that you would take this warrior
for your son. Heorot is cleansed,
the bright ring-hall—use your many rewards
while you can, and leave to your kinsmen
the folk and kingdom, when you must go forth

1180 to face the Maker's decree. I know that my own
dear gracious Hrothulf will hold in honors
these youths, if you should give up the world
before him, friend of the Scyldings;
I expect that he would wish to repay
1185 both our sons kindly, if he recalls all
the pleasures and honors that we have shown him,
in our kindness, since he was a child."
She turned to the bench where her boys sat,
Hrethric and Hrothmund, and the hero's son,
1190 all the youths together; the good man,
Beowulf the Geat, sat between the brothers.

18

The flagon was borne to him, a friendly greeting
conveyed with words, and wound gold
offered with good will, two armlets,
1195 garments and rings, and the greatest neck-collar
ever heard of anywhere on earth.
Under heaven I have not heard tell of a better
hoard-treasure of heroes, since Hama carried off
to the bright city the Brosinga necklace,[2]
1200 the gem and its treasures; he fled the treachery
of Eormanric, chose eternal counsel.
       Hygelac the Geat on his last journey
had that neck-ring,[3] nephew of Swerting,
when under the banner he defended his booty,
1205 the spoils of slaughter. Fate struck him down
when in his pride he went looking for woe,
a feud with the Frisians. He wore that finery,
those precious stones, over the cup of the sea,
that powerful lord, and collapsed under his shield.
1210 Into Frankish hands came the life of that king,
his breast-garments, and the great collar too;
a lesser warrior looted the corpses
mown down in battle; Geatish men

---

hunlafing as the name of a sword.

[1] spokesman The Old English word thyle has been variously
interpreted, from "court jester" to "official speechmaker." The
present translation grants Unferth a measure of dignity and position
to which, perhaps, he is not entitled.

[2] Brosinga necklace The Brosinga necklace had apparently been
worn by the Norse goddess Freya. Nothing much is known of Hama,
who apparently stole the necklace from Eormanric, famous king of
the Goths. The "bright city" and "eternal counsel" may refer to his
retreat into a monastery and Christianity (a story told in the Old
Norse Thidrekssaga), though this is not entirely certain.

[3] Hygelac ... neck-ring The first of several mentions of Hygelac's
ill-fated raid against the Frisians. Later we are told that Beowulf gives
the necklace to Hygd, Hygelac's wife; she apparently let him borrow
it when he went on his piratical raid.

held that killing field.

The hall swallowed the noise.

1215 Wealhtheow stood before the company and spoke:
"Beowulf, beloved warrior, wear this neck-ring
in good health, and enjoy this war-garment,
treasure of a people, and prosper well,
be bold and clever, and to these boys be
1220 mild in counsel—I will remember you for that.
You have made it so that men will praise you
far and near, forever and ever,
as wide as the seas, home of the winds,
surround the shores of earth. Be while you live
1225 blessed, o nobleman! I wish you well
with these bright treasures. Be to my sons
kind in your deeds, keeping them in joys!
Here each earl is true to the other,
mild in his heart, loyal to his liege-lord,
1230 the thanes united, the nation alert;
the troop, having drunk at my table, will do as I bid."

She went to her seat. The best of feasts it was—
the men drank wine, and did not know *wyrd*,
the cruel fate which would come to pass
1235 for many an earl once evening came,
and Hrothgar departed to his own dwelling,
the mighty one to his rest. Countless men
guarded that hall, as they often had before.
They cleared away bench-planks, spread cushions
1240 and bedding on the floor. One of those beer-drinkers
lay down to his rest fated, ripe for death.
They set at their heads their round battle-shields,
bright boards; there on the bench was
easily seen over the noblemen
1245 the high battle-helmet, the ringed byrnie,
the mighty wooden spear. It was their custom
to be always ready, armed for battle,
at home or in the field, every one of them,
on whatever occasion their overlord
1250 had need of them; that was a good troop.

19

They sank into sleep—one paid sorely
for his evening rest, as had often happened
when Grendel guarded that gold-hall,
committed his wrongs until he came to his end,
1255 died for his sins. It was clearly seen,

obvious to all men, that an avenger still
lived on after that enemy for a long time
after that grim battle—Grendel's mother,
monster-woman, remembered her misery,
1260 she who dwelt in those dreadful waters,
the cold streams, ever since Cain
killed with his blade his only brother,
his father's kin; he fled bloodstained,
marked for murder, left the joys of men,
1265 dwelled in the wasteland. From him awoke
many a fateful spirit—Grendel among them,
hateful accursed foe, who found at Heorot
a wakeful warrior waiting for battle.
There the great beast began to seize him,
1270 but he remembered his mighty strength,
the ample gifts which God had given him,
and trusted the Almighty for mercy,
favor and support; thus he overcame the fiend,
subdued the hellish spirit. He went away wretched,
1275 deprived of joy, to find his place of death,
mankind's foe. But his mother still
greedy, grim-minded, wanted to go
on her sorrowful journey to avenge her son's death.

She reached Heorot, where the Ring-Danes
1280 slept throughout the building; sudden turnabout
came to men, when Grendel's mother
broke into the hall. The horror was less
by as much as a maiden's strength,
a woman's warfare, is less than an armed man's
1285 when a bloodstained blade, its edges strong,
hammer-forged sword, slices through
the boar-image on a helmet opposite.[1]
Then in the hall was the hard edge drawn,
swords over seats, many a broad shield
1290 raised in hands—none remembered his helmet
or broad mail-shirt when that terror seized them.
She came in haste and meant to hurry out,
save her life, when she was surprised there,
but she had quickly seized, fast in her clutches,
1295 one nobleman when she went to the fens.
He was the dearest of heroes to Hrothgar
among his comrades between the two seas,
mighty shield-warrior, whom she snatched from his rest,

---

[1] *The horror … opposite* In fact Grendel's mother is a much more
dangerous opponent for Beowulf; the point of these lines is not clear.

a glorious thane. Beowulf was not there,
1300 but another place had been appointed
for the famous Geat after the treasure-giving.
Heorot was in an uproar—she took the famous hand,
covered in gore; care was renewed,
come again to the dwellings. That was no good exchange,
1305 that those on both sides should have to bargain
with the lives of friends.
                                        Then the wise old king,
gray-bearded warrior, was grieved at heart
when he learned that he no longer lived—
the dearest of men, his chief thane, was dead.
1310 Quickly Beowulf was fetched to the chambers,
victory-blessed man. Just before dawn
that noble champion came with his companions,
went with his men to where the old king waited
wondering whether the Almighty would ever
1315 work a change after his tidings of woe.
Across the floor walked the worthy warrior
with his small troop—the hall-wood resounded—
and with his words he addressed the wise one,
lord of the Ingwines, asked him whether
1320 the night had been agreeable, after his urgent summons.

20

Hrothgar spoke, protector of the Scyldings:
"Ask not of joys! Sorrow is renewed
for the Danish people. Æschere is dead,
elder brother of Yrmenlaf,
1325 my confidant and my counselor,
my shoulder-companion in every conflict
when we defended our heads when the footsoldiers
        clashed
and struck boar-helmets. As a nobleman should be,
always excellent, so Æschere was!
1330 In Heorot he was slain by the hand
of a restless death-spirit; I do not know
where that ghoul went, gloating with its carcass,
rejoicing in its feast. She avenged that feud
in which you killed Grendel yesterday evening
1335 in your violent way with a crushing vice-grip,
for he had diminished and destroyed my people
for far too long. He fell in battle,
it cost him his life, and now has come another

mighty evil marauder who means to avenge
1340 her kin, and too far has carried out her revenge,
as it may seem to many a thane
whose spirit groans for his treasure-giver,
a hard heart's distress—now that hand lies dead
which was wont to give you all good things.
1345   I have heard countrymen and hall-counselors
among my people report this:
they have seen two such creatures,
great march-stalkers holding the moors,
alien spirits. The second of them,
1350 as far as they could discern most clearly,
had the shape of a woman; the other, misshapen,
marched the exile's path in the form of a man,
except that he was larger than any other;
in bygone days he was called 'Grendel'
1355 by the local folk. They knew no father,
whether before him had been begotten
any more mysterious spirits. That murky land
they hold, wolf-haunted slopes, windy headlands,
awful fenpaths, where the upland torrents
1360 plunge downward under the dark crags,
the flood underground. It is not far hence
—measured in miles—that the mere stands;
over it hangs a grove hoar-frosted,
a firm-rooted wood looming over the water.
1365 Every night one can see there an awesome wonder,
fire on the water. There lives none so wise
or bold that he can fathom its abyss.
Though the heath-stepper beset by hounds,
the strong-horned hart, might seek the forest,
1370 pursued from afar, he will sooner lose
his life on the shore than save his head
and go in the lake—it is no good place!
The clashing waves climb up from there
dark to the clouds, when the wind drives
1375 the violent storms, until the sky itself droops,
the heavens groan. Now once again all help
depends on you alone. You do not yet know
this fearful place, where you might find
the sinful creature—seek it if you dare!
1380 I will reward you with ancient riches
for that feud, as I did before,
with twisted gold, if you return alive."

21

Beowulf spoke, son of Ecgtheow:
"Sorrow not, wise one! It is always better
1385 to avenge one's friend than to mourn overmuch.
Each of us shall abide the end
of this world's life; let him who can
bring about fame before death—that is best
for the unliving man after he is gone.
1390 Arise, kingdom's guard, let us quickly go
and inspect the path of Grendel's kin.
I promise you this: he[1] will find no protection—
not in the belly of the earth nor the bottom of the sea,
nor the mountain groves—let him go where he will!
1395 For today, you must endure patiently
all your woes, as I expect you will."
The old man leapt up, thanked the Lord,
the mighty God, for that man's speech.
     Then for Hrothgar a horse was bridled
1400 with plaited mane. The wise prince
rode in full array; footsoldiers marched
with shields at the ready. The tracks were seen
far and wide on the forest paths,
a trail through the woods, where she went forth
1405 over the murky moor, bore the young man's
lifeless body, the best of all those
who had held watch over Hrothgar's home.
The son of nobles crossed over
the steep stone cliffs, the constricted climb,
1410 a narrow solitary path, a course unknown,
the towering headlands, home of sea-monsters.
He went before with just a few
wise men to see the way,
until suddenly he saw mountain-trees,
1415 stunted and leaning over gray stone,
a joyless wood; the water went under,
turbid and dreary. To all the Danes,
the men of the Scyldings, many a thane,
it was a sore pain at heart to suffer,
1420 a grief to every earl, when on the seacliff
they came upon the head of Æschere.
The flood boiled with blood—the folk gazed on—
and hot gore. At times a horn sang

its eager war-song. The footsoldiers sat down.
1425 They saw in the water many kinds of serpents,
strange sea-creatures testing the currents,
and on the sloping shores lay such monsters
as often attend in early morning
a sorrowful journey on the sail-road,
1430 dragons and wild beasts. They rushed away
bitter, enraged; they heard the bright noise,
the sound of the battle-horn. A Geatish bowman
cut short the life of one of those swimmers
with a bow and arrow, so that in his body stood
1435 the hard war-shaft; he was a slower swimmer
on the waves, when death took him away.
At once in the water he was assailed
with the barbed hooks of boar-pikes,
violently attacked and dragged ashore,
1440 the strange wave-roamer; the men inspected
this grisly visitor.
     Beowulf geared up
in his warrior's clothing, cared not for his life.
The broad war-shirt, woven by hand,
cunningly made, had to test the mere—
1445 it knew well how to protect his bone-house
so that a battle-grip might not hurt his breast
nor an angry malicious clutch touch his life.
The shining helmet protected his head,
set to stir up the sea's depths,
1450 seek that troubled water, decorated with treasure,
encircled with a splendid band, as a weapon-smith
in days of old had crafted it with wonders,
set boar-images, so that afterwards
no blade or battle-sword might ever bite it.
1455 Not the smallest of powerful supports was that
which Hrothgar's spokesman lent him at need;
that hilted sword was named Hrunting,
unique among ancient treasures—
its edge was iron, etched with poison-stripes,
1460 hardened with the blood of war; it had never failed
any man who grasped it in his hands in battle,
who dared to undertake a dreadful journey
into the very home of the foe—it was not the first time
that it had to perform a work of high courage.
1465 Truly, the son of Ecglaf, crafty in strength,
did not remember what he had said before,
drunk with wine, when he lent that weapon

---

[1] *he* I.e., Grendel's mother. The hero does not note carefully
enough the gender of Grendel's mother, or else the pronoun *he* refers
to OE *magan* "kinsman," a masculine noun.

to a better swordsman; he himself did not dare
to risk his life under the rushing waves,
1470 perform a lordly act; for that he lost honor,
his fame for courage. Not so with the other,
when he had geared himself up for battle.

22

Beowulf spoke, son of Ecgtheow:
"Consider now, famous kinsman of Healfdene,
1475 wise prince, now that I am eager to depart,
gold-friend to men, what we spoke of before:
if ever in your service I should
lose my life, that you would always be
in a father's place to me when I have passed away.
1480 Be a protector to my band of men,
my boon-companions, if battle should take me,
and send on to Hygelac, beloved Hrothgar,
the gifts of treasure which you have given me.
The lord of the Geats will understand by that gold,
1485 the son of Hrethel will see by that treasure,
that I found a ring-giver who was good
in ancient customs and, while I could, enjoyed it.
And let Unferth have that ancient heirloom,
that well-known man have my wave-patterned sword,
1490 hard-edged, splendid; with Hrunting I shall
win honor and fame, or death will take me!"
After these words the Weder-Geat man
hastened boldly, by no means wished to
stay for an answer; the surging sea received
1495 the brave soldier. It was the space of a day[1]
before he could perceive the bottom.
Right away she who held that expanse of water,
bloodthirsty and fierce, for a hundred half-years,
grim and greedy, perceived that some man
1500 was exploring from above that alien land.
She snatched at him, seized the warrior
in her savage clutches, but none the sooner
injured his sound body—the ring-mail encircled him,
so that she could not pierce that war-dress,
1505 the locked coat of mail, with her hostile claws.
Then that she-wolf of the sea swam to the bottom,
and bore the prince of rings into her abode,
so that he might not—no matter how strong—

wield his weapons, but so many wonders
1510 set upon him in the water, many a sea-beast
with battle-tusks tearing at his war-shirt,
monsters pursuing him.[2]
Then the earl perceived
that he was in some sort of battle-hall
where no water could harm him in any way,
1515 and, for the hall's roof, he could not be reached
by the flood's sudden rush—he saw a fire-light,
a glowing blaze shining brightly.
Then the worthy man saw that water-witch,
a great mere-wife; he gave a mighty blow
1520 with his battle-sword—he did not temper that stroke—
so that the ring-etched blade rang out on her head
a greedy battle-song. The guest discovered then
that the battle-flame would not bite,
or wound her fatally—but the edge failed
1525 the man in his need; it had endured many
hand-to-hand meetings, often sheared through helmets,
fated war-garments. It was the first time
that the fame of that precious treasure had fallen.
Again he was stalwart, not slow of zeal,
1530 mindful of glory, that kinsman of Hygelac—
the angry challenger threw away that etched blade,
wrapped and ornamented, so that it lay on the earth,
strong, steel-edged. He trusted his strength,
the might of his handgrip—as a man should do
1535 if by his warfare he thinks to win
long-lasting praise: he cares nothing for his life.
The man of the War-Geats grabbed by the shoulder
Grendel's mother—he had no regret for that feud;
battle-hardened, enraged, he swung her around,
1540 his deadly foe, so she fell to the ground.
Quickly she gave him requital for that
with a grim grasp, and grappled him to her—
weary, he stumbled, strongest of warriors,
of foot-soldiers, and took a fall.
1545 She set upon her hall-guest and drew her knife,
broad, bright-edged; she would avenge her boy,
her only offspring. On his shoulders lay
the linked corselet; it defended his life,
prevented the entrance of point and blade.
1550 There the son of Ecgtheow would have ended his life

---

[1] *It was the space of a day*   Or "it was daylight."

[2] *pursuing him*   Or "attacked their adversary." The Old English
word *æglæcan* may refer here to Beowulf or to the sea-monsters.

under the wide ground, the Geatish champion,
had not his armored shirt offered him help,
the hard battle-net, and holy God
brought about war-victory—the wise Lord,
1555 Ruler of the heavens, decided it rightly,
easily, once he stood up again.

23

He saw among the armor a victorious blade,
ancient giant-sword strong in its edges,
an honor in battle; it was the best of weapons,
1560 except that it was greater than any other man
might even bear into the play of battle,
good, adorned, the work of giants.[1]
The Scyldings' champion seized its linked hilt,
fierce and ferocious, drew the ring-marked sword
1565 despairing of his life, struck in fury
so that it caught her hard in the neck,
broke her bone-rings; the blade cut through
the doomed flesh—she fell to the floor,
the sword was bloody, the soldier rejoiced.
1570   The flames gleamed, a light glowed within
even as from heaven clearly shines
the firmament's candle. He looked around the chamber,
passed by the wall, hefted the weapon
hard by its hilt, that thane of Hygelac,
1575 angry and resolute—nor was the edge useless
to that warrior, but he quickly wished
to pay back Grendel for the many battle-storms
which he had wrought on the West-Danes
much more often than on one occasion,
1580 when Hrothgar's hall-companions
he slew in their beds, devoured sleeping
fifteen men of the Danish folk,
and made off with as many more,
a loathsome booty. He paid him back for that,
1585 the fierce champion, for on a couch he saw
Grendel lying lifeless,
battle-weary from the wound he received
in the combat at Heorot. His corpse burst open
when he was dealt a blow after death,
1590 a hard sword-stroke, and his head chopped off.

---

[1] *the work of giants* Old, highly-praised weapons are often called
"the work of giants"—whether this reference is meant to connect the
sword to the giants "who fought against God" is not clear.

Soon the wise men saw it,
those who kept watch on the water with Hrothgar—
all turbid were the waves, and troubled,
the sea stained with blood. The graybearded
1595 elders spoke together about the good one,
said they did not expect that nobleman
would return, triumphant, to seek
the mighty prince; to many it seemed
that the sea-wolf had destroyed him.
1600 The ninth hour came; the noble Scyldings
abandoned the headland, and home went
the gold-friend of men. The guests[2] sat
sick at heart, and stared into the mere;
they wished, but did not hope, that they would
1605 see their lord himself.
               Then the sword began,
that blade, to waste away into battle-icicles
from the war-blood; it was a great wonder
that it melted entirely, just like ice
when the Father loosens the frost's fetters,
1610 unwraps the water's bonds—He wields power
over times and seasons; that is the true Maker.
The man of the Geats took no more precious treasures
from that place—though he saw many there—
than the head, and the hilt as well,
1615 bright with gems; the blade had melted,
the ornamented sword burned up; so hot was the blood
of the poisonous alien spirit who died in there.
Soon he was swimming who had survived in battle
the downfall of his enemies, dove up through the water;
1620 the sea-currents were entirely cleansed,
the spacious regions, when that alien spirit
gave up life-days and this loaned world.
The defender of seafarers came to land,
swam stout-hearted; he rejoiced in his sea-booty,
1625 the great burden which he brought with him.
That splendid troop of thanes went towards him,
thanked God, rejoiced in their prince,
that they might see him safe and sound.
Then from that bold man helmet and byrnie
1630 were quickly unstrapped. Under the clouds
the mere stewed, stained with gore.
They went forth, followed the trail,
rejoicing in their hearts; they marched along the road,

---

[2] *guests* I.e., the Geats who had come to Heorot with Beowulf.

the familiar path; proud as kings
1635 they carried the head from the sea-cliff
with great trouble, even for two pairs
of stout-hearted men; four of them had to
bear, with some strain, on a battle-pole
Grendel's head to the gold-hall,
1640 until presently fourteen proud
and battle-hardy Geats came to the hall,
warriors marching; the lord of those men,
mighty in the throng, trod the meadhall-plain.
Then the ruler of thanes entered there,
1645 daring in actions, honored in fame,
battle-brave hero, to greet Hrothgar.
Then, where men were drinking, they dragged by its hair
Grendel's head across the hall-floor,
a grisly spectacle for the men and the queen.
1650 Everyone stared at that amazing sight.

24

Beowulf spoke, son of Ecgtheow:
"Look! son of Healfdene, prince of the Scyldings,
we have brought you gladly these gifts from the sea
which you gaze on here, a token of glory.
1655 Not easily did I escape with my life
that undersea battle, did my brave deed
with difficulty—indeed, the battle would have been
over at once, if God had not guarded me.
Nor could I achieve anything at that battle
1660 with Hrunting, though that weapon is good;
but the Ruler of Men granted to me
that I might see on the wall a gigantic old sword,
hanging glittering—He has always guided
the friendless one—so I drew that weapon.
1665 In that conflict, when I had the chance, I slew
the shepherds of that house. Then that battle-sword
burned up with its ornaments, as the blood shot out,
hottest battle-sweat. I have brought the hilt
back from the enemy; I avenged the old deeds,
1670 the slaughter of Danes, as seemed only right.
Now you have my word that you may in Heorot
sleep without care with your company of men,
and every thane, young and old,
in your nation; you need fear nothing,
1675 prince of the Scyldings, from that side,
no deadly manslaughters, as you did before."

Then the golden hilt was placed in the hand
of the gray-haired war-chief, wise old leader,
that old work of giants; it came to the keeping
1680 of the Danish lord after the fall of demons,
a work of wonder-smiths; and when that evil-hearted man,
God's adversary, gave up the world,
guilty of murders—and his mother too—
it passed to the possession of the best
1685 of world-kings between the two seas,
of all those that dealt out treasures in Danish lands.
Hrothgar spoke—he studied the hilt
of the old heirloom, where was written[1] the origin
of ancient strife, when the flood slew,
1690 rushing seas, the race of giants—
they suffered awfully. That was a people alien
to the eternal Lord; a last reward
the Ruler gave them through the raging waters.
Also, on the sword-guard of bright gold
1695 was rightly marked in rune-letters,
set down and said for whom that sword,
best of irons, had first been made,
with scrollery and serpentine patterns. Then spoke
the wise son of Healfdene—all fell silent:
1700 "One may, indeed, say, if he acts in truth
and right for the people, remembers all,
old guardian of his homeland, that this earl was
born a better man! My friend Beowulf,
your glory is exalted throughout the world,
1705 over every people; you hold it all with patient care,
and temper strength with wisdom. To you I shall fulfill
our friendship, as we have said. You shall become a comfort
everlasting to your own people,
and a help to heroes.
                     Not so was Heremod
1710 to the sons of Ecgwala,[2] the Honor-Scyldings;[3]
he grew not for their delight, but for their destruction
and the murder of Danish men.
Enraged, he cut down his table-companions,
comrades-in-arms, until he turned away alone
1715 from the pleasures of men, that famous prince;
though mighty God exalted him in the joys

---

[1] *written* Or "carved." It is not clear whether the scene is visual or
textual, depicted or written in (presumably runic) characters.

[2] *Ecgwala* A king of Danes.

[3] *Honor-Scyldings* I.e., Danes.

of strength and force, advanced him far
over all men, yet in his heart he nursed
a blood-ravenous breast-hoard. No rings did he give
1720 to the Danes for their honor; he endured, joyless,
to suffer the pains of that strife,
a long-lasting harm to his people. Learn from him,
understand virtue! For your sake I have told this,
in the wisdom of my winters.

                            It is a wonder to say
1725 how mighty God in His great spirit
allots wisdom, land and lordship
to mankind; He has control of everything.
At times He permits the thoughts of a man
in a mighty race to move in delights,
1730 gives him to hold in his homeland
the sweet joys of earth, a stronghold of men,
grants him such power over his portion of the world,
a great kingdom, that he himself cannot
imagine an end to it, in his folly.
1735 He dwells in plenty; in no way plague him
illness or old age, nor do evil thoughts
darken his spirit, nor any strife
or sword-hate shows itself, but all the world
turns to his will; he knows nothing worse.

25

1740   "At last his portion of pride within him
grows and flourishes, while the guardian sleeps,
the soul's shepherd—that sleep is too sound,
bound with cares, the slayer too close
who, sinful and wicked, shoots from his bow.[1]
1745 Then he is struck in his heart, under his helmet
with a bitter dart—he knows no defense—
the strange, dark demands of evil spirits.
What he has long held seems too little;
angry and greedy, he gives no golden rings
1750 for vaunting boasts, and his final destiny
he neglects and forgets, since God, Ruler of glories,
has given him a portion of honors.
In the end it finally comes about
that the loaned life-dwelling starts to decay
1755 and falls, fated to die; another follows him

---

[1] *At last … bow* The slayer is sin or vice; the soul's guardian is
reason, conscience or prudence.

who doles out his riches without regret,
the earl's ancient treasure; he heeds no terror.
Defend yourself from wickedness, dear Beowulf,
best of men, and choose the better,
1760 eternal counsel; care not for pride,
great champion! The glory of your might
is but a little while; soon it will be
that sickness or the sword will shatter your strength,
or the grip of fire, or the surging flood,
1765 or the cut of a sword, or the flight of a spear,
or terrible old age—or the light of your eyes
will fail and flicker out; in one fell swoop
death, o warrior, will overwhelm you.

    "Thus, a hundred half-years I held the Ring-Danes
1770 under the skies, and kept them safe from war
from many tribes throughout this middle-earth,
from spears and swords, so that I considered none
under the expanse of heaven my enemy.
Look! Turnabout came in my own homeland,
1775 grief after gladness, when Grendel became
my invader, ancient adversary;
for that persecution I bore perpetually
the greatest heart-cares. Thanks be to the Creator,
eternal Lord, that I have lived long enough
1780 to see that head, stained with blood,
with my own eyes, after all this strife!
Go to your seat, enjoy the feast,
honored in battle; between us shall be shared
a great many treasures, when morning comes."

1785   Glad-hearted, the Geat went at once
to take his seat, as the wise one told him.
Then again as before, a feast was prepared
for the brave ones who occupied the hall
on this new occasion. The dark helm of night
1790 overshadowed the troop. The soldiers arose;
the gray-haired ruler was ready for bed,
the aged Scylding. Immeasurably well
did rest please the Geat, proud shield-warrior;
at once a chamberlain led him forth,
1795 weary from his adventure, come from afar,
he who attended to all the needs
of that thane, for courtesy, as in those days
all battle-voyagers used to have.

    The great-hearted one rested; the hall towered
1800 vaulted and gold-adorned; the guest slept within

until the black[1] raven, blithe-hearted, announced
the joy of heaven. Then light came hurrying
[bright over shadows;] the soldiers hastened,
the noblemen were eager to travel
1805   back to their people; the bold-spirited visitor
wished to seek his far-off ship.

The hardy one ordered Hrunting to be borne
to the son of Ecglaf,[2] bid him take his sword,
lordly iron; he thanked him for the loan,
1810   and said that he regarded it as a good war-friend,
skillful in battle, and the sword's edges
he did not disparage; he was a noble man.
And when the warriors were eager for their way,
equipped in their war-gear, the nobleman went,
1815   the Danes' honor, to the high seat where the other was:
the hero, brave in battle, saluted Hrothgar.

26

Beowulf spoke, son of Ecgtheow:
"Now we seafarers, come from afar,
wish to say that we desire
1820   to seek Hygelac. Here we were honorably
entertained with delights; you have treated us well.
If ever on earth I can do any thing
to earn more of your affection,
than the battle-deeds I have done already,
1825   ruler of men, I will be ready at once.
If ever I hear over the sea's expanse
that your neighbors threaten you with terror
as your enemies used to do,
I will bring you a thousand thanes,
1830   heroes to help you. I have faith in Hygelac—
the lord of the Geats, though he be young,
shepherd of his people, will support me
with words and deeds, that I might honor you well
and bring to your side a forest of spears,
1835   the support of my might, whenever you need men.
If ever Hrethric decides, son of a prince,
to come to the Geatish court, he will find
many friends there; far-off lands

are better sought by one who is himself good."
1840   Hrothgar spoke in answer to him:
"The wise Lord has sent those words
into your heart; I have never heard
a shrewder speech from such a young man.
You are strong in might and sound in mind,
1845   prudent in speech! I expect it is likely
that if it should ever happen that the spear
or the horrors of war take Hrethel's son,[3]
or sickness or sword strike the shepherd of his people,
your lord, and you still live,
1850   that the sea-Geats could not select
a better choice anywhere for king,
hoard-guard of heroes, if you will hold
the realm of your kinsmen. Your character pleases me
better and better, beloved Beowulf.
1855   You have brought it about that between our peoples,
the Geatish nation and the spear-Danes,
there shall be peace, and strife shall rest,
the malicious deeds that they endured before,
as long as I shall rule this wide realm,
1860   and treasures together; many shall greet
another with gifts across the gannet's bath;[4]
the ring-necked ship shall bring over the sea
tribute and tokens of love. I know these nations
will be made fast against friend and foe,
1865   blameless in everything, in the old way."

The protector of heroes, kinsman of Healfdene,
gave him twelve great treasures in the hall;
bid him seek his own dear people in safety
with those gifts, and quickly come again.
1870   Then the good king, of noble kin, kissed
that best of thanes and embraced his neck,
the Scylding prince; tears were shed
by that gray-haired man. He was of two minds—
but in his old wisdom knew it was more likely
1875   that never again would they see one another,
brave in their meeting-place. The man was so dear to him
that he could not hold back the flood in his breast,
but in his heart, fast in the bonds of his thought,
a deep-felt longing for the dear man
1880   burned in his blood. Beowulf from thence,
gold-proud warrior, trod the grassy lawn,

---

[1] *black* Either OE *blac* "shining" or *blæc* "black"; the translation
prefers the irony of the image of the black raven, not otherwise
known as a harbinger of joy, announcing the surprising good news
of a dawn without slaughter.

[2] *Son of Ecglaf* I.e., Unferth.

[3] *Hrethel's son* I.e., Hygelac.

[4] *gannet's bath* I.e., the sea.

exulting in treasure; the sea-goer awaited
its lord and owner, where it rode at anchor.
As they were going, the gift of Hrothgar
1885 was often praised; that king was peerless,
blameless in everything, until old age took from him
—it has injured so many—the joy of his strength.

27

Those men of high courage then came to the sea,
that troop of young retainers, bore their ring-mail,
1890 locked shirts of armor. The coast-guard observed
the return of those earls, as he had once before;
he did not greet those guests with insults
on the clifftop, but he rode towards them,
said that the warriors in their shining armor
1895 would be welcome in their ships to the people of the
      Weders.
The sea-curved prow, the ring-necked ship,
as it lay on the sand was laden with war-gear,
with horses and treasures; the mast towered high
over Hrothgar's hoard-gifts.
1900 To the ship's guardian he[1] gave a sword,
bound with gold, so that on the mead-benches
he was afterwards more honored by that heirloom,
that old treasure. Onward they went, the ship
sliced through deep water, gave up the Danish coast.
1905 The sail by the mast was rigged fast with ropes,
a great sea-cloth; the timbers creaked,
the wind over the sea did not hinder at all
the wave-floater on its way; the sea-goer sped on,
floated foamy-necked, forth upon the waves,
1910 the bound prow over the briny streams,
until they could make out the cliffs of Geatland,
familiar capes; the keel drove forward
thrust by the wind, and came to rest on land.
Right away the harbor-guard was ready at the shore,
1915 who for a long time had gazed far
over the currents, eager for the beloved men;
he moored the broad-beamed ship on the beach
fast with anchor-ropes, lest the force of the waves
should drive away the handsome wooden vessel.
1920 He bade that the nobleman's wealth be borne ashore,
armor and plated gold; they had not far to go

to seek their dispenser of treasure,
Hygelac son of Hrethel, where he dwelt at home
with his companions, near the sea-wall.
1925 The building was splendid, the king quite bold,
high in his hall, Hygd[2] very young,
wise, well-mannered, though few winters
had the daughter of Hæreth passed within
the palace walls—yet not poor for that,
1930 nor stingy of gifts to the Geatish people,
of great treasures. She considered Thryth's pride,[3]
famous folk-queen, and her terrible crimes;
no man so bold among her own retainers
dared to approach her, except as her prince,[4]
1935 or dared to look into her eyes by day;
for he knew that deadly bonds, braided by hand,
were waiting for him—first the hand-grip,
and quickly after a blade appointed,
so that a patterned sword had to settle things,
1940 proclaim the execution. That is no queenly custom
for a lady to perform—no matter how lovely—
that a peace-weaver[5] should deprive of life
a friendly man after a pretended affront.
The kinsman of Hemming[6] put a halt to that:
1945 then ale-drinkers told another tale,
said she caused less calamity to the people,
less malicious evil, after she was
given gold-adorned to the young champion,
fair to that nobleman, when to Offa's floor
1950 she sought a journey over the fallow sea
at her father's wish, where she afterwards

---

[1] *he* I.e., Beowulf.

[2] *Hygd* Hygelac's queen.

[3] *Thryth's pride* These lines are difficult. Some editions and translations read the name as "Modthryth"; the reading adopted here smoothes out a transition that is otherwise abrupt even by the standards of this poem. This "digression" on the character of a queen, with some elements of a folktale, is the counterpoint to the story of Heremod in earlier sections.

[4] *her prince* I.e., as her husband or her father.

[5] *peace-weaver* This epithet reflects the common practice, whose sometimes-tragic consequences are explored at length elsewhere in the poem, of settling intertribal feuds with a marriage between the daughter of one lord and the son of another.

[6] *kinsman of Hemming* Offa I, fourth-century king of the continental Angles, not Offa II, the eighth-century king of Mercia. The elaborate praise offered to Offa I has been taken to suggest that the poem may have been written or circulated in the court of Offa II, but there is otherwise no evidence for this.

on the throne, famous for good things,
used well her life while she had it,
held high love with that chief of heroes,
1955   of all mankind, as men have told me,
the best between the two seas
of all the races of men; therefore Offa,
in gifts and battle, spear-bold man,
was widely honored, and held in wisdom
1960   his own homeland. From him arose Eomer
as a help to heroes, kinsman of Hemming,
grandson of Garmund, skilled in violence.

28

The hardy man[1] with his hand-picked troop
went across the sand, trod the sea-plain,
1965   the wide shore. The world's candle shone,
hastening from the south. They had survived their journey,
went boldly to where they knew
the protector of earls, slayer of Ongentheow,[2]
good young battle-king, gave out rings
1970   in his fortress. To Hygelac
the arrival of Beowulf was quickly reported,
that to the enclosures his battle-companion,
protector of warriors, came walking alive
back to his court, safe from his battle-play.
1975   Quickly, as the powerful one commanded,
the hall was cleared out inside for the foot-guests.
He sat down with him, who had survived the fight,
kinsmen together, after he greeted
his friend and liege-lord with a formal speech,
1980   with courteous words and cups of mead.
The daughter of Hæreth[3] passed through the hall,
cared for the people, bore the cup
to the hand of the hero.[4] Hygelac began
to question his companion courteously
1985   in the high hall—curiosity pressed him
to know how the sea-Geats' adventures were:
"How did you fare, beloved Beowulf,

in your journey, when you suddenly resolved
to seek a far-off strife over the salt sea,
1990   a battle in Heorot? Did you better at all
the well-known woe of Hrothgar,
the famous prince? For that I seethed
with heart-care and distress, mistrusted the adventure
of my beloved man; long I implored
1995   that you not seek that slaughter-spirit at all,
let the south-Danes themselves make
war against Grendel. I say thanks to God
that I might see you again safe and sound."
Beowulf spoke, son of Ecgtheow:
2000   "It is no mystery to many men,
my lord Hygelac—the great meeting,
what a time of great struggle Grendel and I
had in that place where he made so many
sorrows for the victory-Scyldings,
2005   life-long misery—I avenged them all,
so that none of Grendel's tribe needs to boast
anywhere on earth of that uproar at dawn,
whoever lives longest of that loathsome kind,
enveloped in foul evil. First I came there
2010   to the ring-hall to greet Hrothgar;
quickly the famous kinsman of Healfdene,
once he knew of my intentions,
assigned me a seat with his own sons.
That troop was in delight; never in my life
2015   have I seen among hall-sitters, under heaven's vault,
a more joyous feast. At times the famous queen,
bond of peace to nations, passed through the hall,
urged on her young sons; often she gave
twisted rings before she took her seat.
2020   At times before the hall-thanes the daughter of Hrothgar
bore the ale-cup to the earls in the back—
Freawaru, I heard the men in the hall
call her, when the studded treasure-cup
was passed among them. She is promised,
2025   young, gold-adorned, to the gracious son of Froda;[5]
the ruler of the Scyldings has arranged this,
the kingdom's shepherd, and approves the counsel
that he should settle his share of feud and slaughter

---

1   *The hardy man*   I.e., Beowulf.

2   *slayer of Ongentheow*   Hygelac. The death of the Swedish king Ongentheow (at the hands of Wulf and Eofor, retainers of Hygelac) is told below, section 40.

3   *daughter of Hæreth*   I.e., Hygd.

4   *to the hand of the hero*   The manuscript reads "to the hands of heathens," which makes sense, but is usually emended.

5   *the gracious son of Froda*   Ingeld, prince of the Heathobards. His attack on the Danes, alluded to earlier in the poem (80–5), was apparently unsuccessful; another Old English poem, *Widsith*, reports that "Hrothulf and Hrothgar ... humbled Ingeld's battle-array."

with this young woman. But seldom anywhere
2030 after the death of a prince does the deadly spear rest
for even a brief while, though the bride be good!
        "It may, perhaps, displease the Heathobards' prince,
and every retainer among his tribe,
when across the floor, following that woman, goes
2035 a noble son of the Danes, received with honors;
on him glitters an ancestral heirloom,
hard, ring-adorned, once a Heathobard treasure
as long as they were able to wield their weapons.

29

"And then in that deadly shield-play they undid
2040 their beloved comrades and their own lives.
Then an old spear-bearer[1] speaks over his beer,
who sees that ring-hilt and remembers all
the spear-deaths of men—his spirit is grim—
begins, sad-minded, to test the mettle
2045 of a young thane with his innermost thoughts,
to awaken war, and says these words:
        'Can you, my friend, recognize that sword,
which your father bore into battle
in his final adventure beneath the helmet,
2050 that dear iron, when the Danes struck him,
ruled the field of slaughter after the rout of heroes,
when Withergyld[2] fell—those valiant Scyldings?
Now here some son or other of his slayer
walks across this floor, struts in his finery,
2055 brags of the murder and bears that treasure
which ought, by right, to belong to you.'
        He urges and reminds him on every occasion
with cruel words, until the time comes
that Freawaru's thane, for his father's deeds,
2060 sleeps, bloodstained from the bite of a sword,
forfeits his life; from there the other
escapes alive, for he knows the land well.
Then on both sides the sworn oaths of earls
will be broken, once bitter violent hate
2065 wells up in Ingeld, and his wife-love

grows cooler after his surging cares.
Thus I expect that the Heathobards' part
in the Danish alliance is not without deceit,
nor their friendship fast.
                I will speak further
2070 concerning Grendel, so that you might certainly know,
giver of treasure, how it turned out,
the heroic wrestling-match. When heaven's gem
slipped under the ground, the angry spirit came,
horrible, evening-grim, sought us out
2075 where, unharmed, we guarded the hall.
The attack came first against Hondscio[3] there,
deadly to that doomed man—he fell first,
a girded champion; Grendel was
that famous young retainer's devourer,
2080 gobbled up the body of that beloved man.
None the sooner did that slayer, blood in his teeth,
mindful of misery, mean to leave
that gold-hall empty-handed,
but in his mighty strength he tested me,
2085 grabbed with a ready hand. A glove[4] hung
huge, grotesque, fast with cunning clasps;
it was all embroidered with evil skill,
with the devil's craft and dragons' skins.
Inside there, though I was innocent,
2090 that proud evil-doer wanted to put me,
one of many; but it was not to be,
once I angrily stood upright.

30[5]

"It is too long to tell how I handed back payment
to the people's enemy for all his evils—
2095 there, my prince, I did honor to your people
with my actions. He escaped away,
enjoyed his life a little while longer;
yet behind him, guarding his path, was his right

---

[1] *an old spear-bearer* Of the Heathobards, outraged by the presence of his former enemies, the Danes. In heroic poetry when a warrior falls, his killer is often awarded his armor; the sword is a vivid reminder of the fate of its former owner and the duty of revenge which is passed on to the next generation.

[2] *Withergyld* Apparently a famous Heathobard warrior.

[3] *Hondscio* We finally learn the name of the retainer killed in section 11. The name, as in modern German (Handschuh), means "glove."

[4] *glove* It is not clear what this is; apparently a pouch of some kind. It is characteristic of a troll in Norse legend. In any case it does not figure in the narrator's own description of Grendel's attack, and is but one of several discrepancies between the two tellings of the story.

[5] *30* The placement of this section is conjectural; the sectional divisions of the manuscript are confused at this point.

hand in Heorot, and wretched, he went hence,
2100 sad at heart, and sank to the sea-floor.

    For that bloody onslaught the friend of the Scyldings
repaid me greatly with plated gold,
many treasures, when morning came,
and we had gathered together to the feast again.
2105 There was song and joy; the aged Scylding,[1]
widely learned, told of far-off times;
at times the brave warrior touched the song-wood,
delight of the harp, at times made lays
both true and sad, at times strange stories
2110 he recounted rightly. That great-hearted king,
gray-bearded old warrior wrapped in his years,
at times began to speak of his youth again,
his battle-strength; his heart surged within him
when, old in winters, he remembered so much.
2115 And so there inside we took our ease
all day long, until night descended
again upon men. There, quickly ready
with revenge for her griefs, Grendel's mother
journeyed sorrowful; death took her son,
2120 the war-hate of the Weders. That monstrous woman
avenged her son, killed a soldier
boldly at once—there the life of Æschere,
wise old counselor, came to its end.
And when morning came the men of the Danes
2125 were not able to burn his body, death-weary,
with flames, nor place him on a funeral pyre,
beloved man; she bore away his corpse
in her evil embrace under the upland streams.
That, to Hrothgar, was the most wrenching distress
2130 of all those that had befallen that folk-leader.
Then the prince—by your life—implored me,
his mind wracked, that in the roaring waves
I should do a noble deed, put my life in danger,
perform glorious things—he promised me reward.
2135 In the waves I found, as is widely known,
a grim, horrible guardian of the abyss.
There, for a while, we fought hand-to-hand;
the sea foamed with blood, and I severed the head
of Grendel's mother with a mighty sword

2140 in that [battle-]hall;[2] I barely managed
to get away with my life—I wasn't doomed yet—
and the protector of earls once again gave me
many treasures, that kinsman of Healfdene.

31

    "So that nation's king followed good customs;
2145 in no wise have I lost those rewards,
the prize for my strength, but the son of Healfdene
offered me treasures at my own choice,
which I wish to bring to you, o war-king,
to show good will. Still all my joys
2150 are fixed on you alone; I have few
close kinsmen, my Hygelac, except for you."
    He ordered to be borne in the boar standard,
the helmet towering in battle, the gray byrnie,
the decorated sword, and told this story:
2155 "Hrothgar gave me this battle-gear,
wise prince, and commanded particularly
that first I should tell you the story of his gift—
he said that Heorogar the king[3] first had it,
lord of the Scyldings, for a long while;
2160 none the sooner would he give to his own son,
the valiant Heoroward—loyal though he was—
that breast-armor. Use all well!"
Then, as I've heard, four swift horses,
fallow as apples, well-matched, followed
2165 that war-gear; he gave him as a gift
the horses and harness—as kinsman should behave,
never knitting a net of malice for another
with secret plots, preparing death
for his hand-picked comrades. Hygelac's nephew
2170 was loyal to him, hardy in the fight,
and each man to the other mindful of benefits.—
I heard that he gave the necklace to Hygd,
the wondrous ornamented treasure which Wealhtheow
    had given him,
to that lord's daughter, along with three horses
2175 graceful and saddle-bright; her breast was adorned
the more graciously after that ring-giving.
    So the son of Ecgtheow showed himself brave,

---

[1] *the aged Scylding* It is not clear whether this is Hrothgar or not,
or how many storytellers and singers are at this banquet.

[2] *[battle-]hall* A word is missing; other editors and translators
supply different words, such as *grund* or "earth."

[3] *Heorogar the king* Eldest brother of Hrothgar.

renowned for battles and noble deeds,
pursued honor, by no means slew, drunken,
2180 his hearth-companions; he had no savage heart,
but the great gift which God had given him,
the greatest might of all mankind, he held,
brave in battle. He had been long despised,
as the sons of the Geats considered him no good,
2185 nor did the lord of the Weders wish to bestow
many good things upon him on the meadbenches,
for they assumed that he was slothful,
a cowardly nobleman. Reversal came
to the glorious man for all his griefs.
2190   The protector of earls, battle-proud king,
ordered the heirloom of Hrethel[1] brought in,
adorned with gold; among the Geats there was
no finer treasure in the form of a sword.
He laid the sword in Beowulf's lap,
2195 and gave him seven thousand hides of land,[2]
a hall and a princely throne. Both of them held
inherited land in that nation, a home
and native rights, but the wider rule
was reserved to the one who was higher in rank.
2200   Then it came to pass amid the crash of battle
in later days, after Hygelac lay dead,
and for Heardred[3] the swords of battle held
deadly slaughter under the shield-wall,
when the Battle-Scylfings sought him out,
2205 those hardy soldiers, and savagely struck down
the nephew of Hereric[4] in his victorious nation—
then came the broad kingdom
into Beowulf's hands; he held it well
for fifty winters—he was then a wise king,
2210 old guardian of his homeland—until
in the dark nights a dragon began his reign,
who guarded his hoard in the high heaths
and the steep stone barrows; the path below
lay unknown to men. Some sort of man
2215 went inside there, found his way to

the heathen hoard—his hand ...[5]
inlaid with jewels. He[6] got no profit there,
though he had been trapped in his sleep
by a thief's trickery: the whole nation knew,
2220 and all the people around them, that he was enraged.

32

Not for his own sake did he who sorely harmed him
break into that worm-hoard,[7] or by his own will,
but in sad desperation some sort of [slave][8]
of a warrior's son fled the savage lash,
2225 the servitude of a house, and slipped in there,
a man beset by sins. Soon he gazed around
and felt the terror from that evil spirit;
yet ...
    ...made...
2230   ... when the terror seized him
he snatched a jeweled cup.[9]
                    There were many such
antique riches in that earth-hall,
for in ancient days an unknown man
had thought to hide them carefully there,
2235 the rich legacy of a noble race,
precious treasures. In earlier times
death had seized them all, and he who still survived
alone from that nation's army lingered there,
a mournful sentry, expected the same,
2240 that he might enjoy those ancient treasures
for just a little while. A waiting barrow
stood in an open field near the ocean waves,
new on the cape, safe with crafty narrow entrances;
he bore within the noble wealth,
2245 the plated gold, that guardian of rings,
a share worthy of a hoard, and spoke few words:
    "Hold now, o thou earth, for heroes cannot,

---

[1] *Hrethel* Father of Hygelac.

[2] *hides* Units of land, originally the amount of land which could support a peasant and his family; its actual size varied from one region to another. Seven thousand hides is by any measure a very generous area.

[3] *Heardred* Son of Hygelac.

[4] *nephew of Hereric* I.e., Heardred.

[5] The manuscript is damaged here and some text is unreadable. Among many conjectural restorations one thing is clear—a cup is taken from the dragon's hoard.

[6] *He* The thief; "he" in the following line refers to the dragon. These lines are nearly illegible and other readings have been proposed.

[7] *worm-hoard* Dragon's treasure.

[8] *slave* The word is illegible in the manuscript; the translation follows most editions.

[9] *yet ... cup* The manuscript is unreadable at this point.

the wealth of men—lo, from you long ago
those good ones first obtained it! Death in war
2250 and awful deadly harm have swept away
all of my people who have passed from life,
and left the joyful hall. Now have I none
to bear the sword or burnish the bright cup,
the precious vessel—all that host has fled.
2255 Now must the hardened helm of hammered gold
be stripped of all its trim; the stewards sleep
who should have tended to this battle-mask.
So too this warrior's coat, which waited once
the bite of iron over the crack of boards,
2260 molders like its owner. The coat of mail
cannot travel widely with the war-chief,
beside the heroes. Harp-joy have I none,
no happy song; nor does the well-schooled hawk
soar high throughout the hall, nor the swift horse
2265 stamp in the courtyards. Savage butchery
has sent forth many of the race of men!"

        So, grieving, he mourned his sorrow,
alone after all. Unhappy sped
both days and nights, until the flood of death
2270 broke upon his heart. An old beast of the dawn
found that shining hoard standing open—
he who, burning, seeks the barrows,
a fierce and naked dragon, who flies by night
in a pillar of fire; people on earth
2275 fear him greatly. It is his nature to find
a hoard in the earth, where, ancient and proud,
he guards heathen gold, though it does him no good.[1]

        Three hundred winters that threat to the people
held in the ground his great treasury,
2280 wondrously powerful, until one man
made him boil with fury; he[2] bore to his liege-lord
the plated cup, begged for peace
from his lord. Then the hoard was looted,
the hoard of rings fewer, a favor was granted
2285 the forlorn man; for the first time
his lord looked on that ancient work of men.

        When the dragon stirred, strife was renewed;
he slithered along the stones, stark-hearted he found
his enemy's footprint—he had stepped too far

2290 in his stealthy skill, too close to the serpent's head.
Thus can an undoomed man easily survive
wrack and ruin, if he holds to the Ruler's
grace and protection![3] The hoard-guardian
searched along the ground, greedy to find
2295 the man who had sorely harmed him while he slept;
hot, half-mad, he kept circling his cave
all around the outside, but no one was there
in that wilderness to welcome his warfare
and the business of battle. Soon he returned to his barrow,
2300 sought his treasure; he soon discovered
that some man had disturbed his gold,
his great wealth. The hoard-guardian waited
impatiently until evening came;
the barrow's shepherd was swollen with rage,
2305 the loathsome foe would repay with fire
his precious drinking-cup. Then day was departed
to the delight of that worm; he did not linger
on the barrow wall, but took off burning
in a burst of flames. The beginning was terror
2310 to the people on land, and to their ring-giving lord
the ending soon would be sore indeed.

33

        Then that strange visitor began to spew flames
and burn the bright courts; his burning gleams
struck horror in men. That hostile flier
2315 would leave nothing alive.
The worm's warfare was widely seen,
his ferocious hostility, near and far,
how the destroyer hated and harmed
the Geatish people, then hastened to his hoard,
2320 his dark and hidden hall, before the break of day.
He had surrounded the people of that region with fire,
flames and cinders; he took shelter in his barrow,
his walls and warfare—but that trust failed him.
        To Beowulf the news was quickly brought
2325 of that horror—that his own home,
best of buildings, had burned in waves of fire,
the gift-throne of the Geats. To the good man that was
painful in spirit, greatest of sorrows;
the wise one believed he had bitterly offended
2330 the Ruler of all, the eternal Lord,

---

[1] *It is ... good* The association of dragons and hoarded treasure is
ancient and proverbial.

[2] *he* I.e., the thief.

[3] *Thus can ... protection* This is the narrator's version of Beowulf's
comment at lines 572–73.

against the old law; his breast within groaned
with dark thoughts—that was not his custom.
The fire-dragon had found the stronghold of that folk,
that fortress, and had razed it with flames
2335 entirely and from without; for that the war-king,
prince of the Weders, devised revenge.
Then the lord of men bade them make,
protector of warriors, a wondrous war-shield,
all covered with iron; he understood well
2340 that wood from the forest would not help him,
linden against flames. The long-good nobleman
had to endure the end of his loaned days,
this world's life—and so did the worm,
though he had held for so long his hoarded wealth.

2345   Then that prince of rings scorned to seek out
the far-flung flier with his full force of men,
a large army; he did not dread that attack,
nor did he worry much about the dragon's warfare,
his strength or valor, because he had survived
2350 many battles, barely escaping alive
in the crash of war, after he had cleansed,
triumphant hero, the hall of Hrothgar,
and at battle crushed Grendel and his kin,
that loathsome race.

    It was not the least
2355 of hand-to-hand combats when Hygelac was slain,
when the king of the Geats, in the chaos of battle,
the lord of his people, in the land of the Frisians,
the son of Hrethel, died sword-drunk,
beaten by blades. Beowulf escaped from there
2360 through his own strength, took a long swim;
he had in his arms the battle-armor
of thirty men, when he climbed to the cliffs.
By no means did the Hetware[1] need to exult
in that fight, when they marched on foot to him,
2365 bore their linden shields; few came back
from that brave soldier to seek their homes.
The son of Ecgtheow crossed the vast sea,
wretched, solitary, returned to his people,
where Hygd offered him the hoard and kingdom,
2370 rings and royal throne; she did not trust
that her son could hold the ancestral seat
against foreign hosts, now that Hygelac was dead.
But despite their misery, by no means

could they prevail upon that prince at all
2375 that he should become lord over Heardred,
or choose to rule the kingdom.
Yet he upheld him[2] in the folk with friendly counsel,
good will and honors, until he was older,
and ruled the Weder-Geats.

    Wretched exiles,
2380 the sons of Ohthere,[3] sought him out across the seas;
they had rebelled against the Scylfings' ruler,[4]
the best of all the sea-kings
who dispensed treasure in the Swedish lands,
a famous king. That cost him[5] his life:
2385 for his hospitality he took a mortal hurt
with the stroke of a sword, that son of Hygelac;
and the son of Ongentheow afterwards went
to seek out his home, once Heardred lay dead,
and let Beowulf hold the high throne
2390 and rule the Geats—that was a good king.

34

In later days he[6] did not forget
that prince's fall, and befriended Eadgils
the wretched exile; across the open sea
he gave support to the son of Ohthere
2395 with warriors and weapons. He[7] wreaked his revenge
with cold sad journeys, and took the king's life.
    And so the son of Ecgtheow had survived
every struggle, every terrible onslaught,
with brave deeds, until that one day
2400 when he had to take his stand against the serpent.

---

[2] *upheld him* Beowulf upheld Heardred, as champion and in effect a kind of regent.

[3] *sons of Ohthere* I.e., Eanmund and Eadgils.

[4] *Scylfing's ruler* Onela, son of Ongentheow. Ohthere had succeeded his father Ongentheow, but after his death his brother Onela apparently seized the throne and drove the two young men Eanmund and Eadgils into exile. They take refuge at the Geatish court, for which Heardred is attacked and killed by Onela. Later Eanmund is killed by Weohstan (see section 36 below) but Eadgils, with the help of Beowulf, becomes king (section 34).

[5] *him* I.e., Heardred.

[6] *he* I.e., Beowulf, whose revenge for the death of his lord Heardred takes a curiously indirect form—he supports Eadgils' return to Sweden, where Onela is killed.

[7] *He* I.e., Eadgils.

---

[1] *Hetware* A Frankish tribe apparently on the side of the Frisians.

Grim and enraged, the lord of the Geats
took a dozen men[1] to seek out the dragon;
he had found out by then how the feud arose,
the baleful violence; the precious vessel
2405 had come to him through the thief's hands.
He was the thirteenth man among that troop,
who had brought about the beginning of that strife,
a sad-minded captive—wretched and despised
he led the way to that plain. He went against his will
2410 to where he alone knew the earth-hall stood,
an underground cave near the crashing waves,
the surging sea; inside it was full
of gems and metal bands. A monstrous guardian,
eager for combat, kept his gold treasures
2415 ancient under the ground; getting them
was no easy bargain for any man.

    The battle-hardened king sat down on the cape,
then wished good health to his hearth-companions,
the gold-friend of the Geats. His heart was grieving,
2420 restless and ripe for death—the doom was
      immeasurably near
that was coming to meet that old man,
seek his soul's treasure, split asunder
his life and his body; not for long was
the spirit of that noble king enclosed in its flesh.
2425   Beowulf spoke, the son of Ecgtheow:
"In my youth I survived many storms of battle,
times of strife—I still remember them all.
I was seven years old when the prince of treasures,
friend to his people, took me from my father;[2]
2430 Hrethel the king held me and kept me,
gave me gems and feasts, remembered our kinship.
I was no more hated to him while he lived
— a man in his stronghold—than any of his sons,
Herebeald and Hæthcyn and my own Hygelac.
2435 For the eldest,[3] undeservedly,
a death-bed was made by the deeds of a kinsman,
after Hæthcyn with his horn bow
struck down his own dear lord with an arrow—
he missed his mark and murdered his kinsman,

2440 one brother to the other with a bloody shaft.
That was a fight beyond settling, a sinful crime,
shattering the heart; yet it had to be
that a nobleman lost his life unavenged.
    "So it is sad for an old man
2445 to live to see his young son
ride on the gallows[4]—then let him recount a story,
a sorry song, when his son hangs
of comfort only to the ravens, and he cannot,
though old and wise, offer him any help.
2450 Each and every morning calls to mind
his son's passing away; he will not care
to wait for any other heir or offspring
in his fortress, when the first one has
tasted evil deeds and fell death.
2455 He looks sorrowfully on his son's dwelling,
the deserted wine-hall, the windswept home,
bereft of joy—the riders sleep,
heroes in their graves; there is no harp-music,
no laughter in the court, as there had been long before.

35

2460 "He takes to his couch and keens a lament
all alone for his lost one; all too vast to him
seem the fields and townships.
          So the protector of the Weders[5]
bore surging in his breast heartfelt sorrows
for Herebeald. He could not in any way
2465 make amends for the feud with his murderer,
but neither could he hate that warrior
for his hostile deeds, though he was not dear to him.
Then with the sorrow which befell him too sorely,
he gave up man's joys, chose God's light;[6]
2470 he left to his children his land and strongholds
—as a blessed man does—when he departed this life.

---

[1] *a dozen men* Literally "one of twelve"—Beowulf, Wiglaf, and ten others. The thief who leads the way is the thirteenth man.

[2] *took me ... father* Beowulf was brought up as a noble foster-child in the royal court.

[3] *eldest* I.e., Herebeald.

[4] *So it is ... gallows* It is usually suggested that this is a kind of epic simile, comparing Hrethel's grief over his son's death—a death beyond the scope of vengeance—to the grief of a criminal's father, who cannot claim compensation for the execution of his son. Mitchell and Robinson suggest that this is rather a reference to a pagan practice, part of the cult of Odin (also known as "Woden"), in which the body of a man who did not die in battle was ritually hanged on a gallows. If this interpretation is correct, the "old man" is Hrethel himself.

[5] *the protector of ... Weders* I.e., Hrethel.

[6] *God's light* I.e., he died.

Then there was strife between Swedes and Geats,[1]
a quarrel in common across the wide water,
hard hostility after Hrethel died,
2475 until the sons of Ongentheow[2]
were bold and warlike, wanted no peace
over the sea, but around the Hill of Sorrows[3]
they carried out a terrible and devious campaign.
My friends and kinsmen got revenge for those
2480 feuds and evils[4]—as it is said—
although one of them paid for it with his own life,
a hard bargain; that battle was fatal
for Hæthcyn, king of the Geats.
Then, I've heard, the next morning, one kinsman
2485 avenged the other with the sword's edge,[5]
when Ongentheow attacked Eofor;
his battle-helm slipped, the old Scylfing
staggered, corpse-pale; Eofor's hand recalled
his fill of feuds, and did not withhold the fatal blow.

2490 "I have paid in battle for the precious treasures
he[6] gave me, as was granted to me,
with a gleaming sword; he gave me land,
a joyous home. He had no need
to have to go seeking among the Gifthas
2495 or the Spear-Danes or the Swedes
for a worse warrior, or buy one with his wealth;
always on foot I would go before him,
alone in the front line—and all my life
I will wage war, while this sword endures,
2500 which before and since has served me well,
since I slew Dæghrefn, champion of the Hugas,[7]
with my bare hands in front of the whole army.
He could not carry off to the Frisian king

that battle-armor and that breast-adornment,[8]
2505 but there in the field the standard-bearer fell,
a nobleman in his strength; no blade was his slayer,
but my warlike grip broke his beating heart,
cracked his bone-house. Now the blade's edge,
hand and hard sword, shall fight for the hoard."

2510 Beowulf spoke, said boasting words
for the very last time: "I have survived
many battles in my youth; I will yet
seek out, an old folk-guardian, a feud
and do a glorious deed, if only that evildoer
2515 will come out to me from his earth-hall."
Then for the last time he saluted
each of the soldiers, his own dear comrades,
brave in their helmets: "I would not bear a sword
or weapon to this serpent, if I knew any other way
2520 I could grapple with this great beast[9]
after my boast, as I once did with Grendel;
but I expect the heat of battle-flames there,
steam and venom; therefore shield and byrnie
will I have on me. From the hoard's warden
2525 I will not flee a single foot, but for us
it shall be at the wall as *wyrd* decrees,
the Ruler of every man. My mind is firm—
I will forgo boasting against this flying foe.
Wait on the barrow, protected in your byrnies,
2530 men in war-gear, to see which of the two of us
after the bloody onslaught can better
bear his wounds. It is not your way,
nor proper for any man except me alone,
that he should match his strength against this monster,
2535 do heroic deeds. With daring I shall
get that gold—or grim death
and fatal battle will bear away your lord!"

Then that brave challenger stood up by his shield,
stern under his helmet, bore his battle-shirt
2540 under the stone-cliffs, trusted the strength
of a single man—such is not the coward's way.
He saw then by the wall—he who had survived
a great many conflicts, good in manly virtues,
the crash of battles when footsoldiers clashed—
2545 stone arches standing, and a stream

---

[1] *strife ... Geats* This refers to a time a generation before the conflicts of Heardred, Eanmund and Eadgils; the Swedish-Geatish feud is longstanding.

[2] *sons of Ongentheow* I.e., Ohthere and Onela.

[3] *Hill of Sorrows* A hill in Geatland, in OE *Hreosnabeorh*.

[4] *My friends ... evils* The scene of this revenge is apparently Sweden, in a place called "Ravenswood"; this battle is described again in sections 40 and 41.

[5] *one kinsman ... sword's edge* Hygelac avenged the death of Hæthcyn on his slayer Ongentheow—not directly but through his man Eofor.

[6] *he* I.e., Hygelac.

[7] *Hugas* Frankish tribes allied to the Frisians; the battle in question may be the same as Hygelac's fatal raid.

---

[8] *breast-adornment* Possibly the same as the necklace described in 1195–1214.

[9] *great beast* The OE word *æglæcan* is here used of the dragon.

shooting forth from the barrow; its surge
was hot with deadly flames, and near the hoard
he could not survive for very long
unburnt, for the dragon's flaming breath.
2550 Enraged, the ruler of the Weder-Geats
let a word burst forth from his breast,
shouted starkly; the sound entered
and resounded battle-clear under the gray stone.
Hate was stirred up—the hoard-warden recognized
2555 the voice of a man; there was no more time
to sue for peace. First there issued
the steam of that great creature out of the stone,
hot battle-sweat; the earth bellowed.
The warrior in the barrow turned his shield-board
2560 against the grisly stranger, lord of the Geats,
when the writhing beast's heart was roused
to seek combat. The good war-king
had drawn his sword, its edges undulled,
an ancient heirloom; each of the two
2565 hostile ones was horrified by the other.
He stood stouthearted behind his steep shield,
that friend and commander, when the worm coiled itself
swiftly together—he waited in his war-gear.
Then coiled, burning, slithering he came,
2570 rushing to his fate. The shield defended well
the life and limb of the famous lord
for less time than he might have liked;
there on that day for the first time
he faced the outcome,[1] and *wyrd* did not
2575 grant victory in battle. The lord of the Geats
raised his hand, struck that mottled horror
with his ancient sword, so that that edge failed
bright against the bony scales, bit less strongly
than the king of that nation needed it to do,
2580 hard-pressed in battle. Then the barrow-warden
was more savage after that battle-stroke,
and spit out gruesome fire; wide sprang
the battle-flames. The gold-friend of the Geats
did not boast of his glorious victories; his bare sword
2585 failed at need, as it should never have done,
that ancient good iron. It was no easy journey
for the famous son of Ecgtheow to agree
to give up his ground in that place;

he was forced, against his will, to find
2590 a place of rest elsewhere—just as every one of us
must give up these loaned days.

It was not long
until those two great creatures[2] came together again.
The hoard-guard took heart, his breast swelled with breath
once again; he[3] suffered anguish,
2595 trapped by flames, he who had once ruled his folk.
His comrades, hand-chosen, sons of noblemen,
did not take their stand in a troop around him,
with warlike valor—they fled to the woods
and saved their lives. The spirit rose up in sorrow
2600 in the heart of one of them; nothing can overrule
kinship at all, in one who thinks well.

36

He was called Wiglaf, Weohstan's son,
a worthy shield-warrior, a prince of the Scylfings,[4]
kinsman of Ælfhere. He saw his liege-lord
2605 suffer heat under his war-helmet;
he recalled the honors he had received from him,
the wealthy homestead of the Waegmundings,
every folk-right that his father had possessed;
he could not hold back—his hand seized
2610 the pale linden shield, and he drew his old sword.
It was known among men as the heirloom of Eanmund,
son of Ohthere; that friendless exile
was slain in battle with the edge of a sword
by Weohstan, who brought to his kinsman
2615 the burnished helmet, the ringed byrnie,
the old giant-work sword; Onela gave to him
the war-equipment of his young kinsman,
the shining armor—he never spoke of a feud,
though he had slain his brother's son.[5]

---

[1] *for the first time … outcome*   Or "if he could have controlled the outcome for the first time."

[2] *creatures*   OE *æglæcan* again, here referring to Beowulf and the dragon together.

[3] *he*   I.e., Beowulf.

[4] *a prince of the Scylfings*   Wiglaf's nationality is in question—he is both a Swede and a Wægmunding (like Beowulf; see lines 2813–14). His father fought on the Swedish side in their feuds with the Geats. Tribal allegiance is more fluid than modern nationality.

[5] *he never … brother's son*   Onela never spoke of a feud, though Weohstan had killed Onela's brother's son, for he wished him dead. As elsewhere in the poem, a sword is the reminder of both victory and vengeance.

2620 He[1] kept that war-gear for a great many years,
the blade and byrnie, until his boy could
perform brave deeds like his father before him;
he gave him among the Geats that battle-gear,
every piece of it, when, old, he departed this life
2625 and went forth. That was the first time
that the young warrior had to weather
the storm of battle beside his noble lord.
His courage did not melt, nor did his kinsman's legacy
weaken in war; the worm discovered that,
2630 when they began to meet together.
      Wiglaf spoke, said to his companions
many true words—he was mournful at heart—
"I remember the time that we took mead together,
when we made promises to our prince
2635 in the beer-hall—he gave us these rings—
that we would pay him back for this battle-gear,
these helmets and hard swords, if such a need
as this ever befell him. For this he chose us from the army
for this adventure by his own will,
2640 thought us worthy of glory, and gave me these treasures—
for this he considered us good spear-warriors,
proud helmet-wearers, even though our prince,
shepherd of his people, intended to perform
this act of courage all alone,
2645 because he has gained the most glory among men,
reckless heroic deeds. Now the day has come
that our noble lord has need of the support
of good warriors; let us go to it,
help our warlord, despite the heat,
2650 grim fire-terror. God knows for my part
that I would much prefer that the flames should enfold
my body alongside my gold-giving lord.
It seems wrong to me that we should bear shields
back to our land, unless we first might
2655 finish off this foe, defend the life
of the prince of the Weders. I know full well
that he does not deserve to suffer
this torment all alone among the Geatish troop,
or fall in the struggle; now sword and helmet,
2660 byrnie and battle-dress, shall be ours together!"
      He hurried through the deadly fumes, bore his
            helmet
to the aid of his lord, spoke little:

"Dear Beowulf, do all well,
as in your youth you said you would,
2665 that you would never let in your whole life
your fame decline; now firm in deeds,
single-minded nobleman, with all your strength
you must protect your life—I will support you."
After these words the worm came angrily,
2670 terrible vicious creature, a second time,
scorched with surging flames, seeking out his enemies,
the hated men. The hot flames rolled in waves,
burned the shield to its rim; the byrnie was not
of any use to the young soldier,
2675 but he showed his courage under his kinsman's shield,
the young warrior, when his own was
charred to cinders. Still the battle-king
remembered his glory, and with his mighty strength
swung his warblade with savage force,
2680 so that it stuck in the skull. Nægling shattered—
the sword of Beowulf weakened at battle,
ancient and gray. It was not granted to him
that iron-edged weapons might ever
help him in battle; his hand was too strong,
2685 he who, I am told, overtaxed every blade
with his mighty blows, when he bore to battle
a wound-hardened[2] weapon—it was no help to him at all.
      Then that threat to the people for a third time,
fierce fire-dragon, remembering his feud,
2690 rushed on the brave man, hot and bloodthirsty,
when he saw the chance, seized him by the neck
in his bitter jaws; he was bloodied
by his mortal wounds—blood gushed in waves.

37

Then, I have heard, in his king's hour of need
2695 the earl[3] beside him showed his bravery,
the noble skill which was his nature.
He did not heed that head when he helped his kinsman;
that brave man's hand was burned, so that
he struck that savage foe a little lower down,
2700 the soldier in armor, so that his sword plunged in
bejeweled and bloody, so that the fire began
to subside afterwards. The king himself

---

1 *he* I.e., Weohstan.

2 *wound-hardened* Or "wondrously hard"; the OE text is unclear.

3 *earl* I.e., Wiglaf.

still had his wits, drew the war-dagger,
bitter and battle-sharp, that he wore in his byrnie;
2705 the protector of the Weders carved through the
    worm's midsection.
They felled their foe—their force took his life—
and they both together had brought him down,
the two noble kinsmen; a thane at need,
as a man should be! But that, for the prince, was
2710 his last work of victory, by his own will,
of worldly adventures.
               When the wound
which the earth-dragon had worked on him
began to burn and swell, he soon realized
that in his breast, with an evil force,
2715 a poison welled; then the nobleman went,
still wise in thought, so that he sat
on a seat by the wall. On that work of giants he gazed,
saw how stone arches and sturdy pillars
held up the inside of that ancient earth-hall.
2720 Then with his hands the thane, immeasurably good,
bathed with water his beloved lord,
the great prince, spattered with gore,
sated with battle, and unstrapped his helmet.
Beowulf spoke—despite his wound,
2725 that deadly cut; he knew clearly
that his allotted life had run out,
and his joys in the earth; all gone
was his portion of days, death immeasurably near:
    "Now I should wish to give my war-gear
2730 to my son, if there had been such,
flesh of my flesh, if fate had granted me
any heir. I held this people
fifty winters; there was no folk-king,
not any of the neighboring tribes,
2735 who dared to face me with hostile forces
or threaten fear. The decrees of fate
I awaited on earth, held well what was mine;
I sought no intrigues, nor swore many
false or wrongful oaths. For all that I may
2740 have joy, though sick with mortal wounds,
because the Ruler of men need not reproach me
with the murder of kinsmen, when my life
quits my body. Now go quickly
to look at the hoard under the hoary stone,
2745 dear Wiglaf, now that the worm lies dead,

sleeps with his wounds, stripped of his treasure.
Hurry, so I might witness that ancient wealth,
those golden goods, might eagerly gaze on
the bright precious gems, and I might more gently,
2750 for that great wealth, give up my
life and lordship, which I have held so long."

38

    Then swiftly, I have heard, the son of Weohstan
after these words obeyed his lord,
sick with wounds, wore his ring-net,
2755 the woven battle-shirt, under the barrow's roof.
As he went by the seat he saw there, triumphant,
the brave young warrior, many bright jewels,
glittering gold scattered on the ground,
wonders on the walls, and the lair of that worm,
2760 the old dawn-flier—flagons standing,
ancient serving-vessels without a steward,
their trappings all moldered; there was many a helmet
old and rusty, a number of arm-bands
with twisted ornaments.—Treasure may easily,
2765 gold in the ground, give the slip
to any one of us: let him hide it who will![1]—
Likewise he saw an ensign, all golden,
hanging high over the hoard, greatest hand-work,
linked together with skill; light gleamed from it
2770 so that he could see the cave's floor,
survey those strange artifacts. There was no sign
of the serpent there—a sword had finished him off.
Then the hoard in that barrow, as I've heard, was looted,
ancient work of giants, by one man alone;
2775 he piled in his arms cups and plates,
whatever he wanted; he took the ensign too,
brightest of beacons. His aged lord's blade
—its edge was iron— had earlier harmed
the one who was protector of those treasures
2780 for such a long time, who bore his fiery terror
flaming before the hoard, seething fiercely
in the darkest night, until he died a bloody death.
    The messenger rushed out, eager to return,
burdened with treasures; he was burning to know

---

[1] *give the slip ... who will* Or "can get the better of any man—heed [these words] who will!" The OE is uncertain; the translation follows Mitchell and Robinson.

2785 whether, stout-hearted, he would find still alive
the prince of the Weders, weakened by wounds,
in the place where he had left him on that plain.
Then with the treasures he found the famous prince,
his own lord, his life at an end,
2790 all bloody; he began once more
to sprinkle water on him, until the point of a word
escaped from his breast.
Old, full of grief, he looked on the gold:
　　"For all these treasures, I offer thanks
2795 with these words to the eternal Lord,
King of Glory, for what I gaze upon here,
that I was able to acquire such wealth
for my people before my death-day.
Now that I have sold my old lifespan
2800 for this hoard of treasures, they will attend[1]
to the needs of the people; I can stay no longer.
The brave in battle will bid a tomb be built
shining over my pyre on the cliffs by the sea;
it will be as a monument to my people
2805 and tower high on Whale's Head,
so that seafarers afterwards shall call it
'Beowulf's Barrow,' when their broad ships
drive from afar over the darkness of the flood."
　　The boldminded nobleman took from his neck
2810 a golden circlet, and gave it to the thane,
the young spear-carrier, and the gold-covered helmet,
ring and byrnie, bid him use them well:
"You are the last survivor of our lineage,
the Wægmundings; fate has swept away
2815 all of my kinsmen, earls in their courage,
to their final destiny; I must follow them."
That was the last word of the old warrior,
his final thought before he chose the fire,
the hot surging flames—from his breast flew
2820 his soul to seek the judgment of the righteous.[2]

---

[1] *they will attend*   Usually translated "you [Wiglaf] will attend …";
the OE verb may be indicative or imperative, but it is unambigu-
ously plural, and the imperative plural is not used elsewhere in the
poem to address a single person.

[2] *the judgment of the righteous*   Literally "the *dom* (fame) of the
truth-fast," an ambiguous pronouncement. It is not clear whether
this means that Beowulf's soul will receive the sort of judgment that
a righteous soul ought to receive (and so go to Heaven), or that it
will be judged by those "fast in truth" (and so go to Hell as an
unbaptized pagan).

39

Then it came to pass with piercing sorrow
that the young warrior had to watch
his most precious lord fare so pitifully,
his life at an end. Likewise his slayer lay dead,
2825 the awesome earth-dragon deprived of his life,
overcome by force. The coiled serpent
could no longer rule his hoard of rings—
edges of iron did away with him,
the hard, battle-scarred shards of the smithy,
2830 so that the wide-flier, stilled by his wounds,
toppled to the ground near his treasure-house.
No more soaring about in the skies
at midnight, preening in his precious treasures,
showing his face—he fell to earth
2835 through that war-commander's handiwork.
Indeed, few men on earth, no matter how strong,
could succeed at that, as I have heard tell,
though he were daring in every deed,
could rush against the reek of that venomous foe,
2840 or rifle through that ring-hall with his hands,
if he should find a waking warden
waiting in that barrow. Beowulf's share
of that royal treasure was repaid by his death—
each of them had journeyed to the end
2845 of this loaned life.
　　　　　　　It was not long before
the men late for battle left the woods,
ten of those weak traitors all together
who had not dared to hoist their spears
when their lord of men needed them most;
2850 now shamefaced, they carried their shields
and battledress to where the old man lay dead,
to stare at Wiglaf. He sat exhausted,
a foot-soldier at his lord's shoulder,
tried to rouse him with water—but it was no use.
2855 He could not, no matter how much he wanted,
keep the life in the body of his captain,
nor change any bit of the Ruler's decree;
the judgment of God would guide the deeds
of every man, as it still does today.
2860 Then it was easy to get a grim answer
from that youth to those who gave up courage.
Wiglaf spoke, son of Weohstan,
looked, sad-hearted, on those unloved:

"He can say—o yes—who would speak the truth
2865 that the liege-lord who gave you those gifts of treasures,
the military gear that you stand in there,
when on the ale-benches he often handed out
helmets and byrnies to the hall-sitters,
a lord to his followers, whatever he could find
2870 finest anywhere, far or near—
that all that battle-dress he absolutely
and entirely threw away, when war beset him.
Our nation's king had no need to boast
of his comrades-in-arms! But the Ruler of victories
2875 allowed that he, alone with his blade,
might avenge himself when he needed your valor.
Only a little life-protection could I offer
him in battle, but began nevertheless
to support my kinsman beyond my own strength;
2880 ever the worse was the deadly enemy
when I struck with my sword, a fire less severe
surging from his head. Too few supporters
thronged around our prince in his great peril.
Now the getting of treasure, the giving of swords,
2885 and all the happy joys of your homeland
shall end for your race; empty-handed
will go every man among your tribe,
deprived of his land-rights, when noblemen learn
far and wide of your flight,
2890 your inglorious deed. Death is better
for any earl than a life of dishonor!"

40

He bade that the battle-work be announced to
the camp
up by the cliff's edge, where that troop of earls,
shield-bearers, sat sad-minded
2895 all the long morning, expecting either
the final day of their dear lord
or his homecoming. He who rode up to the cape
was not at all silent with his new tidings,
but he spoke truly in the hearing of all:
2900 "Now is the joy-giver of the Geatish people,
the lord of the Weders, laid on his deathbed,
holding a place of slaughter by the serpent's deeds;
beside him lies his life-enemy,
sick with knife-slashes; he could not with his sword

2905 make in the monstrous beast
any kind of wound. Wiglaf sits,
Weohstan's offspring, over Beowulf,
one earl over the other, now dead;
he holds with desperate heart the watch
2910 over friend and foe.
            Now this folk may expect
a time of trouble, when this is manifest
to the Franks and Frisians, and the fall of our king
becomes widespread news. The strife was begun
hard with the Hugas, after Hygelac came
2915 travelling with his ships to the shores of Frisia,
where the Hetware attacked him in war,
advanced with valor and a vaster force,
so that the warrior in his byrnie had to bow down,
and fell amid the infantry; not at all did that lord
2920 give treasure to his troops. Ever after that
the Merovingians have not shown mercy to us.
    "Nor do I expect any peace or truce
from the Swedish nation, but it has been well-known
that Ongentheow ended the life
2925 of Hæthcyn, son of Hrethel, in Ravenswood,
when in their arrogant pride the Geatish people
first sought out the Battle-Scylfings.
Immediately the ancient father of Ohthere,
old and terrifying, returned the attack—
2930 the old warrior cut down the sea-captain,[1]
rescued his wife, bereft of her gold,
Onela's mother and Ohthere's;
and then hunted down his deadly enemies
until they escaped, with some difficulty,
2935 bereft of their lord, into Ravenswood.
With his standing army he besieged those sword-leavings,
weary, wounded; he kept threatening woe
to that wretched troop the whole night through—
in the morning, he said, with the edge of his sword
2940 he would gut them, and leave some on the gallows-tree
as sport for birds. But for those sad-hearted men
solace came along with the sunrise,
after they heard Hygelac's horn and trumpet
sounding the charge, when the good man came
2945 following the trail of that people's troop.

---

[1] *old warrior ... sea-captain* Ongentheow killed Hæthcyn. Hygelac
is not present at this battle, but arrives later.

41

"The bloody swath of the Swedes and Geats,
the slaughter of men, was easily seen,
how the folk had stirred up feud between them.
That good man[1] then departed, old, desperate,
2950 with a small band of kinsmen, sought his stronghold,
the earl Ongentheow turned farther away;
he had heard of proud Hygelac's prowess in battle,
his war-skill; he did not trust the resistance
he might muster against the seafarers' might
2955 to defend from the wave-borne warriors his treasure,
his women and children; he ran away from there,
old, into his fortress. Then the pursuit was offered
to the Swedish people, the standard of Hygelac
overran the place of refuge,
2960 after the Hrethlings thronged the enclosure.
There with the edge of a sword was Ongentheow,
old graybeard, brought to bay,
so that the king of that nation had to yield
to Eofor's will. Angrily he struck;
2965 Wulf the son of Wonred lashed at him with his weapon,
so that with his blow the blood sprang in streams
from under his hair. Yet the ancient Scylfing
was undaunted, and dealt back quickly
a worse exchange for that savage stroke,
2970 once the ruler of that people turned around.
The ready son of Wonred could not
give a stroke in return to the old soldier,
for he had cut through the helmet right on his head
so that he collapsed, covered in blood,
2975 fell to the ground—he was not yet fated to die,
but he recovered, though the cut hurt him.
The hardy thane of Hygelac[2] then let
his broad blade, as his brother lay there,
his ancient giant-made sword, shatter that gigantic helmet
2980 over the shield-wall; then the king stumbled,
shepherd of his people, mortally stricken.
There were many there who bandaged his[3]
kinsman,
quickly raised him up, when a way was clear for them,
so that they had control of that killing field.

---

[1] *good man*   I.e., Ongentheow.

[2] *thane of Hygelac*   I.e., Eofor, Wulf's brother.

[3] *his*   I.e., Eofor's.

2985 Then one warrior plundered another,[4]
took from Ongentheow the iron byrnie,
his hard hilted sword and his helmet too,
and carried the old man's armor to Hygelac.
He[5] took that war-gear and promised him gifts
2990 among his people—and he kept that promise;
the king of the Geats repaid that carnage,
the offspring of Hrethel, when he made it home,
gave to Eofor and Wulf extravagant treasures,
gave them each lands and locked rings,
2995 worth a hundred thousand. Not a man in this world
could
reproach those rewards, since they had won them
with their deeds;
and to Eofor he gave his only daughter,
the pride of his home, as a pledge of his friendship.
"That is the feud and the fierce enmity,
3000 savage hatred among men, that I expect now,
when the Swedish people seek us out
after they have learned that our lord
has perished, who had once protected
his hoard and kingdom against all hostility,
3005 after the fall of heroes, the valiant Scyldings,[6]
worked for the people's good, and what is more,
performed noble deeds. Now we must hurry
and look upon our people's king,
and go with him who gave us rings
3010 on the way to the pyre. No small part
of the hoard shall burn with that brave man,
but countless gold treasures, grimly purchased,
and rings, here at last with his own life
paid for; then the flames shall devour,
3015 the fire enfold—let no warrior wear
treasures for remembrance, nor no fair maiden
have a ring-ornament around her neck,
but sad in mind, stripped of gold, she must
walk a foreign path, not once but often,
3020 now that leader of our troop has laid aside laughter,

---

[4] *one ... another*   Eofor plundered Ongentheow.

[5] *He*   I.e., Hygelac.

[6] *Scyldings*   The manuscript reading ("Scyldings" is a further object of "protected") is often emended to *Scylfingas*, i.e., Swedes, or *scildwigan*, "shield-warriors"; the present reading is that of Mitchell and Robinson. As it stands in the manuscript the Geatish herald is referring to Beowulf's earlier adventures against Grendel and his mother.

his mirth and joy. Thus many a cold morning
shall the spear be grasped in frozen fingers,
hefted by hands, nor shall the sound of the harp
rouse the warriors, but the dark raven,
3025   greedy for carrion, shall speak a great deal,
ask the eagle how he fared at his feast
when he plundered corpses with the wolf."[1]
    Thus that brave speaker was speaking
a most unlovely truth; he did not lie much
3030   in words or facts. The troop of warriors arose;
they went, unhappy, to the Cape of Eagles,
with welling tears to look at that wonder.
There on the sand they found the soulless body
of the one who gave them rings in earlier times
3035   laid out to rest; the last day
had come for the good man, when the war-king,
prince of the Weders, died a wondrous death.
But first they saw an even stranger creature,
a loathsome serpent lying on the plain
3040   directly across from him; grim with his colors
the fire-dragon was, and scorched with his flames.
He was fifty feet long, lying there
stretched out; once he had joy in the air
in the dark night, and then down he would go
3045   to seek his den, but now he was fast in death;
he had come to the end of his cave-dwelling.
Cups and vessels stood beside him,
plates lay there and precious swords,
eaten through with rust, as if in the bosom of the earth
3050   they had lain for a thousand winters;
all that inheritance was deeply enchanted,
the gold of the ancients was gripped in a spell
so that no man in the world would be able to touch
that ring-hall, unless God himself,
3055   the true King of Victories, Protector of men,
granted to whomever He wished to open the hoard,
to whatever person seemed proper to Him.[2]

42

    Then it was plain that the journey did not profit
the one[3] who had wrongfully hidden under a wall
3060   that great treasure. The guardian had slain
that one and few others;[4] then that feud was
swiftly avenged. It is a wonder to say
where a valiant earl should meet the end
of his span of life, when he may no longer
3065   dwell in the meadhall, a man with his kinsmen.
So it was with Beowulf, when he sought the barrow's
    guardian
and a hostile fight; even he did not know
how his parting from life should come to pass,
since until doomsday mighty princes had deeply
3070   pronounced, when they placed it there,
that the man who plundered that place would be
harried by hostile demons, fast in hellish bonds,
grievously tortured, guilty of sins,
unless the Owner's grace had earlier
3075   more readily favored the one eager for gold.[5]
    Wiglaf spoke, son of Weohstan:
"Often many earls must suffer misery
through the will of one man, as we have now seen.
We could not persuade our dear prince,
3080   shepherd of a kingdom, with any counsel,
that he should not greet that gold-guardian,
let him lie there where he long had been,
inhabit the dwellings until the end of the world:
he held to his high destiny. The hoard is opened,
3085   grimly gotten; that fate was too great
which impelled the king of our people thither.
I was in there, and looked over it all,
the hall's ornaments, when a way was open to me;
by no means gently was a journey allowed
3090   in under that earth-wall. In eager haste I seized
in my hands a great mighty burden

---

[1]   *the dark raven ... the wolf*   The eagle, wolf, and raven, the "beasts
of battle," are a recurring motif in Old English poetry.

[2]   *unless God himself ... proper to him*   The power of the pagan spell
can be overruled by the will of the true God.

---

[3]   *the one*   I.e., the dragon.

[4]   *that one and few others*   Or "that one of a few," i.e., "a unique
man" or "a man of rare greatness."

[5]   *favored the one eager for gold*   The OE text is corrupt and the
precise meaning of this passage is not certain; the present translation
tries to incorporate several suggested interpretations. The general
sense seems to be clear enough—the gold was cursed, and only
God's special grace would enable anyone to remove it. What this
implies about Beowulf's failure, and his moral status, is less clear.

of hoard-treasure, and bore it out hither
to my king. He was still conscious then,
thoughtful and alert; he spoke of many things,
3095 an old man in his sorrow, and ordered that I greet you;
he asked that you build a great high barrow
for your prince's deeds, in the place of his pyre,
mighty and glorious, since he was of men
the most worthy warrior throughout the wide world,
3100 while he could enjoy the wealth of a hall.
Let us now make haste for one more time
to see and seek out that store of cunning gems,
the wonder under the wall; I will direct you
so that you can inspect them up close,
3105 abundant rings and broad gold. Let the bier be ready,
quickly prepared, when we come out,
then let us bear our beloved lord,
that dear man, to where he must long
rest in the keeping of the Ruler."

3110   Then the son of Weohstan, brave battle-warrior,
let it be made known to many heroes
and householders that they should bring from afar
the wood for the pyre to that good one,[1]
the leader of his folk: "Now the flames must devour,
3115 the black blaze rise over the ruler of warriors,
who often awaited the showers of iron
when the storm of arrows hurled from bow-strings
shot over the wall, the shafts did their duty
swift on feather-wings, sent on the arrow-heads."

3120   Lo, then the wise son of Weohstan
summoned from that host some of the best
of the king's thanes, seven altogether;
he went, one of eight, under that evil roof;
one of the brave warriors bore in his hands
3125 a flaming torch, and went before them.
It was not chosen by lots who should loot that hoard,[2]
once the men saw it sitting in the hall,
every part of it unprotected,
lying there wasting; there was little lament
3130 that they should have to hurry out with
the precious treasures. They also pushed the dragon,
the worm, over the cliff-wall, let the waves take him,
the flood embrace the guard of that finery;

then the twisted gold, an uncountable treasure,
3135 was loaded in a wagon, and the noble one was carried,
the gray-haired warrior, to the Cape of Whales.

43

The people of the Geats then prepared for him
a splendid pyre upon the earth,
hung with battle-shields and helmets
3140 and bright byrnies, as he had bidden;
there in the middle they laid the mighty prince,
the heroes lamenting their dear lord.
Then the warriors kindled there on the cliff
the greatest of funeral pyres; dark over the flames
3145 the woodsmoke rose, the roaring fire
mingled with weeping—the wind lay still—
until it had broken that bone-house
hot at the heart. With heavy spirits
they mourned their despair, the death of their lord;
3150 and a sorrowful song sang the Geatish woman,[3]
with hair bound up, for Beowulf the king,
with sad cares, earnestly said
that she dreaded the hard days ahead,
the times of slaughter, the host's terror,
3155 harm and captivity. Heaven swallowed the smoke.

    Then the Weder people wrought for him
a barrow on the headland; it was high and broad,
visible from afar to sea-voyagers,
and in ten days they built the beacon
3160 of that battle-brave one; the ashes of the flames
they enclosed with a wall, as worthily
as the most clever of men could devise it.
In the barrow they placed rings and bright jewels,
all the trappings that those reckless men
3165 had seized from the hoard before,
let the earth hold the treasures of earls,
gold in the ground, where it yet remains,
just as useless to men as it was before.
Then round the mound rode the battle-brave men,
3170 offspring of noblemen, twelve in all;
they wished to voice their cares and mourn their king,

---

[1] *that good one* I.e., the dead Beowulf.

[2] *It was not chosen … hoard* I.e., everybody had a share; there was enough for all.

[3] *Geatish woman* The manuscript is damaged throughout this section and the readings in this passage are conjectural; it is not clear who the "Geatish woman" is, though her advanced age is indicated by her bound-up hair. Typically, in Germanic poetry, it is women (and poets) who mourn.

utter sad songs and speak of that man;
they praised his lordship and his proud deeds,
judged well his prowess. As it is proper
3175 that one should praise his lord with words,
should love him in his heart when the fatal hour comes,
when he must from his body be led forth,

so the men of the Geats lamented
the fall of their prince, those hearth-companions;
3180 they said that he was of all the kings of the world
the mildest of men and the most gentle,
the kindest to his folk and the most eager for fame.

In Context

Background Material

Glossary of Proper Names

Abel	slain by his brother **Cain**; the story is told in Genesis 4.1–16
Ælfhere	kinsman of **Wiglaf**
Æschere	a prominent Dane, advisor to **Hrothgar**; slain by Grendel's mother
Battle-Scyldings	see **Scyldings**
Battle-Scylfings	see **Scylfings**
Beanstan	father of **Breca**
Beowulf	(prologue) Danish king, son of **Scyld**
Breca	engaged in a youthful swimming contest with Beowulf
Bright-Danes	see **Danes**
Brondings	the people of **Breca**
Brosinga	makers of the magical necklace of Freya in Norse myth, to which a necklace in the story is compared
Cain	slayer of **Abel** in Genesis 4.1–16; father of the race of monsters
Dæghrefn	a warrior of the **Hugas** slain by Beowulf in hand-to-hand combat during Hygelac's ill-fated raid on **Frisia**
Danes	**Hrothgar**'s people; the **Scyldings**; also called Bright-, Half-, Ring-, Spear-, East-, West-, North-, and South-Danes
Eadgils	son of **Ohthere**, brother of **Eanmund**
Eanmund	son of **Ohthere**, brother of **Eadgils**; slain by **Weohstan**
East-Danes	see **Danes**
Ecglaf	father of **Unferth**
Ecgtheow	father of Beowulf
Ecgwala	a Danish king; the "sons of Ecgwala" are the **Danes**
Eofor	a warrior of the **Geats**; brother of **Wulf**; slayer of **Ongentheow**
Eomer	son of **Offa**
Eormanric	king of the Ostrogoths
Eotens	unclear: perhaps the **Jutes**, perhaps the **Frisians**, perhaps "giants" (the literal meaning of the word) as a nickname for one group or the other
Finn	king of the **Frisians**, husband of **Hildeburh**; killed by **Hengest**
Finns	the people of Finland; the Lapps
Fitela	legendary companion, nephew (and son) of **Sigemund**
Folcwalda	father of **Finn**
Franks	a Germanic tribe; see **Hetware, Hugas, Merovingians**

Freawaru	daughter of **Hrothgar**, betrothed to **Ingeld**
Frisians	a Germanic tribe; **Finn**'s people
Froda	chief of the **Heathobards**, father of **Ingeld**
Garmund	father of **Offa**
Geats	**Hygelac**'s people and **Beowulf**'s; a Germanic tribe; also called War-Geats, Hrethmen, Hrethlings, Weders
Gifthas	an East-Germanic tribe
Grendel	descendent of **Cain**; monstrous marauder of the **Danes**
Guthlaf	a Danish warrior, companion of **Hengest**
Hæreth	father of **Hygd**
Hæthcyn	Geatish prince, second son of **Hrethel**
Half-Danes	see **Danes**
Halga	Danish prince, younger brother of **Hrothgar**
Hama	legendary Goth; stole **Brosinga** necklace
Healfdene	king of the **Danes**, father of **Hrothgar**
Heardred	king of the **Geats**, son of **Hygelac**
Heathobards	**Ingeld**'s people; a Germanic tribe
Heatholaf	a **Wylfing** slain by **Ecgtheow**
Heathoream	a Scandinavian tribe; Norwegians, more or less
Helmings	the family of **Wealhtheow**
Hemming	kinsman of **Offa** and **Eomer**
Hengest	leader of the **Danes**; killed **Finn** in **Frisia**
Heorogar	Dane, eldest brother of **Hrothgar**
Heorot	the great hall of **Hrothgar**
Heoroweard	Dane; son of **Heorogar**
Herebeald	Geatish prince, eldest son of **Hrethel**; killed by his brother **Hæthcyn**
Heremod	king of the **Danes** in the poem's distant past, before the **Scylding** dynasty
Hereric	brother of **Hygd**, uncle of **Heardred**
Hetware	a Frankish tribe, allied with the **Frisians**; fought against **Hygelac**
Hildeburh	sister of the Danish **Hnæf**, wife of the Frisian **Finn**
Hnæf	chief of the **Half-Danes**, brother of **Hildeburh**; killed by **Finn**
Hoc	Dane, father of **Hildeburh** and **Hnæf**
Hondscio	Geatish warrior, comrade of Beowulf; slain by **Grendel**
Honor-Scyldings	see **Scyldings**
Hrethel	king of the **Geats**, father of **Hygelac**, grandfather of Beowulf
Hrethlings	sons of **Hrethel**, i.e., the **Geats**
Hrethmen	the **Geats**
Hrethric	Dane, son of **Hrothgar**
Hrothgar	aged king of the **Danes** beset by **Grendel**; helped by Beowulf
Hrothmund	Dane, son of **Hrothgar**
Hrothulf	Dane, son of **Halga**, nephew of **Hrothgar**; not to be trusted
Hrunting	the sword of **Unferth**
Hugas	the Franks, allies of the **Frisians**
Hunlaf	father of one of the warriors in **Hengest**'s troop
Hygd	queen of the **Geats**, wife of **Hygelac**, daughter of **Hæreth**
Hygelac	king of the **Geats**, uncle of Beowulf
Ingeld	prince of the **Heathobards**, son of **Froda**, betrothed to **Freawaru**; after the events narrated in the poem he burns down the great hall of **Heorot**

Ingwines	the "friends of Ing": the **Danes**
Jutes	allies of the **Frisians**; see **Eotens**
Merovingians	the **Franks**
Nægling	Beowulf's sword
North-Danes	see **Danes**
Offa	king of the Angles, husband of **Thryth**
Ohthere	Swede, son of **Ongentheow**
Onela	Swede, son of **Ongentheow**; usurped throne
Ongentheow	Swedish king; killed by **Wulf** and **Eofor**
Oslaf	a Danish warrior, companion of **Hengest**
Ring-Danes	see **Danes**
Scyld Scefing	legendary founder of the Danish royal family
Scyldings	the Danes; also called Battle-, Honor-, Victory-Scyldings
Scylfings	the Swedes
Sigemund	legendary Germanic hero, son of **Wæls**
South-Danes	see **Danes**
Spear-Danes	see **Danes**
Swerting	uncle of **Hygelac**
Thryth	(often construed as **Modthryth**) wife of **Offa**
Unferth	Danish spokesman ("thyle") and courtier of **Hrothgar**
Victory-Scyldings	see **Scyldings**
Volsung	another name for **Sigemund**, son of **Wæls**
Wægmundings	the family of **Weohstan**, **Wiglaf**, and Beowulf
Wæls	father of **Sigemund**
War-Geats	see **Geats**
Wealhtheow	Danish queen, wife of **Hrothgar**
Weders	the **Geats**
Weland	legendary Germanic smith
Wendels	a Germanic tribe; perhaps the Vandals, perhaps not
Weohstan	father of **Wiglaf**; killed **Eanmund**
West-Danes	see **Danes**
Wiglaf	son of **Weohstan**, young retainer of Beowulf
Withergyld	a dead **Heathobard**
Wonred	a **Geat**, father of **Wulf** and **Eofor**
Wulf	a warrior of the **Geats**, brother of **Eofor**; assisted in killing **Ongentheow**
Wulfgar	a warrior of the **Danes**; herald at the court of **Hrothgar**
Wylfings	a Germanic tribe of which **Heatholaf** was a member, until **Ecgtheow** killed him
Yrmenlaf	a Dane, younger brother of **Æschere**

Genealogies

1. The Danes (Scyldings)

(Heremod)

Scyld Scefing

Beowulf

Healfdene

Heorogar   Hrothgar=Wealtheow   Halga   [daughter]=Onela (Swede)

Heoroweard   Hrothulf

Hrethric   Hrothmund   Freawaru=Ingeld (Heathobard)

2. The Geats

Hrethel

Herebeald   Haethcyn   Hygelac   [daughter]=Ecgtheow

Eofor=[daughter]   Heardred   Beowulf

3. The Swedes (Scylfings)

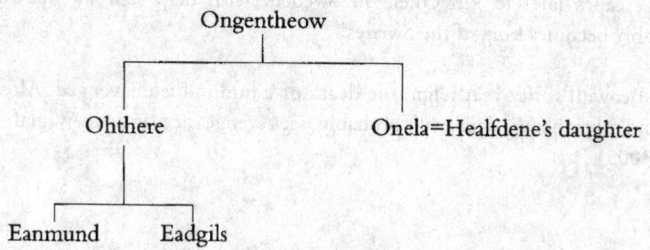

Ongentheow

Ohthere   Onela=Healfdene's daughter

Eanmund   Eadgils

The Geatish-Swedish Wars

When the story of Beowulf's fight with the dragon begins, the narrator leaps over fifty years in one brief passage. It is a tumultuous condensation of a complex chain of events (2200–08):

Then it came to pass amid the crash of battle
in later days, after Hygelac lay dead,
and for Heardred the swords of battle held
deadly slaughter under the shield-wall,
when the Battle-Scylfings sought him out,
those hardy soldiers, and savagely struck down
the nephew of Hereric in his victorious nation—
then came the broad kingdom
into Beowulf's hands …

These events are referred to throughout the last thousand lines of the poem, but they are not told in a straightforward way or in chronological order. The fortunes of the Geatish royal house may be reconstructed as follows:

1. Hæthcyn accidentally kills his brother Herebeald; their father Hrethel dies of grief (2432–71). Hæthcyn becomes king.

2. After the death of Hrethel, Ohthere and Onela, the sons of the Swedish king Ongentheow, attack the Geats (2472–78).

3. In retaliation, Hæthcyn attacks Ongentheow in Sweden (2479–84); at first he is successful, but later is killed at Ravenswood (2922–41). Hygelac's men Wulf and Eofor kill Ongentheow, and Hygelac (Hæthcyn's brother) is victorious (2484–89, 2942–99). Ohthere becomes king of the Swedes.

4. Hygelac is killed in Frisia; his son Heardred becomes king (2354–78).

5. Ohthere's brother Onela seizes the Swedish throne and drives out the sons of Ohthere, Eanmund and Eadgils (2379–84). Heardred takes in these exiles, and Onela attacks Heardred for this hospitality and kills him. Onela allows Beowulf to rule the Geats (2385–90).

6. Around this time Weohstan, father of Wiglaf, kills Eanmund on behalf of Onela (2611–19).

7. Eadgils escapes later to kill Onela in Sweden, with help sent by Beowulf (2391–96); he presumably becomes king of the Swedes.

8. During Beowulf's fifty-year reign, the death of Eanmund is unavenged. After Beowulf's death, Eanmund's brother Eadgils will probably seek vengeance against Wiglaf, son of Weohstan (2999–3005).

JUDITH

This Old English poem survives in the manuscript that also contains the poem *Beowulf* (London, British Library, Cotton Vitellius A.xv). As with most Old English poems, its author is unknown, and the poem is untitled in the manuscript. It is commonly referred to as *Judith* because it takes its subject from the Book of Judith, a text found in the Greek and Latin versions of the Bible and accepted as canonical in Catholic traditions, but placed among the Apocrypha in the Protestant Bible. The book and the poem tell the story of a pious Hebrew widow, Judith, who rescues the people of the besieged city of Bethulia by beheading the Assyrian general Holofernes as he attempts to seduce her.

The beginning of the poem has been lost, and the story begins in mid-sentence just before the raucous banquet in which Holofernes orders Judith to be brought to his tent. It is not known how much is missing prior to the first surviving line of the poem. Although the first numbered section is X—implying that nine previous sections (perhaps some thousand lines) have been lost—some have suggested that this is misleading, and that the surviving poem is nearly complete. Like other Old English Biblical poems, they argue, *Judith* is a heroic ode that focuses on the most crucial episode of the story, the slaying of Holofernes and the rout of the Assyrian army.

Judith is metrically unusual, especially in contrast to the metrical precision of its manuscript neighbor *Beowulf*. The poem abounds in hypermetric lines (lines with more than the four stresses normally found in lines of Old English poetry), in irregular alliteration, and in rhyme, a very rare feature in Old English poetry. This relatively unusual meter has suggested to some scholars that the poem was composed fairly late in the Anglo-Saxon period, but the relationship between metrical strictness and date of composition has not been established with any certainty.

Poetically *Judith* blurs the distinctions between ancient and contemporary, Biblical and Germanic, a characteristic of many other Old English poems such as *Exodus*—Hebrew warriors rage into battle clad in helmets and byrnies (coats of mail), carrying linden shield and ancient swords, while around them circle the traditional Germanic "beasts of battle," the wolf, raven and eagle. Accuracy of historical details mattered less to Anglo-Saxon poets than fidelity to the spirit of the story and the dramatic deployment of their traditional poetic motifs. In contrast to *Exodus*, however, the poem focuses on heroic action rather than complex allegorical interpretation. The choice of a female character as the subject of a heroic poem indicates the relatively high status of women within Anglo-Saxon nobility prior to the Norman invasion of 1066; the poem subtly alters its source to stress the heroine's wisdom and courage rather than the allure of her beauty or the cunning of her plot to seduce Holofernes. Judith is portrayed as a woman of power, and may have been seen by audiences not only as a figure from the Biblical past, but also as a contemporary hero; the homilist Ælfric, who wrote his own prose paraphrase of the Biblical Book of Judith, sees a connection between her time and his own. At the time Ælfric was writing, the Danes were carrying out frequent raids along the English coast; in Ælfric's retelling Judith is not only a Hebrew fighting against the Assyrians but also a saintly Christian queen defending her homeland against pagan invaders. We should therefore not be surprised that, although the poem is set in pre-Christian Israel, Judith prays to the Trinity of Father, Son and Holy Spirit to give her strength to assassinate Holofernes, nor that many of the poem's most dramatic moments seem drawn as much from Christian hagiography as from Old Testament history.

⌘ ⌘ ⌘

Judith [1]

… nor ever upon earth's broad surface[2]   could she be brought to doubt
the grace of God   who gave favor—
renowned Ruler—   when she needed it most:
protection came from the primal Power   against pure terror,
5   help from the highest Judge   when our heavenly Father
in glory bestowed   an outstanding gift,
thanks to her full belief,   her faith in the Almighty forever.
I've heard that Holofernes   then heartily called
for a wine-swilling   with wonders served
10   to senior thanes,°   each sweet delight;   *noblemen*
and the master of men   commanded them come.
Shield-fighters rushed   to their ruling prince—
all his folk-leaders.   That was the fourth day then
since she'd first arrived—   since the radiant lady,
15   elf-lovely[3] Judith,   ingenious had come.

Then to the feast they fared   and found their seats.
Wine-drinkers reveled,   wretched henchmen
in byrnies° bold.   Time after time were bowls so deep   *coats of mail*
down benches borne   brimful to hall-guests,
20   shield-warriors keen.   Likewise were cups and jugs
for the fated filled,   though their fell° ruler,   *cruel*
the fierce warlord,   didn't know fate was near.
Old Holofernes,   heroes' gold-friend,
sunk in wine-joy,   screamed with laughter,

---

[1] *Judith* The poem has been newly translated for this anthology by Stephen O. Glosecki. The translator has asked that the following note be included: "I am grateful to Roy Liuzza and Broadview's four anonymous readers, whose suggestions vastly improved this translation. As far as possible, I follow Classical Germanic rules of prosody (rules equally apparent in Old English, Old Norse, Old Saxon, and Old High German heroic verse). I discuss my alliterative approach in "Skalded Epic (Make It Old)" in Beowulf *in Our Time: Teaching* Beowulf *in Translation*, ed. Mary K. Ramsey, *OEN Subsidia* 31 (Kalamazoo: Medieval Institute Publications, 2002). I rely upon the original as edited in E.V.K. Dobbie's *Beowulf and Judith* (Anglo-Saxon Poetic Records IV. New York: Columbia University Press, 1953). Dobbie's introduction cites the poem's numerous hypermetric halflines. Though unable to preserve their original distribution, I include some long lines to suggest the poem's remarkably ornate versification. But I have simplified its equally ornate syntax. This is unavoidable, since, for instance, verb-final periods, though still grammatical in German, disappeared from English centuries ago (along with a powerful suspended effect, a sort of semantic "crack the whip" when the closing verb clinches the action and the preceding phrases fall into place). The original also includes a surprising amount of end rhyme (a feature Dobbie notes, with line references; this flourish suggests a late date of composition). I therefore take my own liberties with the rhyme, using it to mark pivotal passages in a translation dedicated to my wife Karen Anne Reynolds, *idese alf-scinre minre*."

[2] *… nor ever upon earth's broad surface* The opening of the poem is imperfect, and the translation is conjectural. The manuscript reading is "… doubted the gifts in this wide world."

[3] *elf-lovely* The Old English compound *ælf-scinu* may mean "wonderfully bright"; *Ælf-* is a common element in Old English names, so it presumably had a positive connotation.

25   roared and ranted,   raged and chanted,
      so no man afar   could fail to hear
      him storm with pride   while plunged in mead,
      demanding brave war-deeds   from bench-sitters.
      Treacherous schemer!   For the entire day he
30   drenched his band   with drafts of wine,
      arrogant ring-breaker,   until his band all swooned
      as drunk as death—   doughty veterans
      drained of virtue.   So he kept the drink flowing,
      poured for hall-thanes,   prince of warriors,
35   till dark of night   dropped down on men.
      Festering with evil,   he ordered her fetched—
      brought to his bedstead—   blessed maiden,
      in circlets rich   all ring-adorned.

      The appointed thanes   as their prince ordered—
40   byrnie-troops' chief—   charged off boisterous
      and grabbed Judith   from the guest-house there.
      Then with the wise lady   they went promptly,
      linden-shield° troops   leading her forth—   *shield made of lime-tree wood*
      the bright maiden—   to the mighty tent,[1]
45   towering pavilion   where the tyrant slept
      inside at night   by our Savior loathed—
      old Holofernes.   There flowed round his bed
      a fair curtain,   fly-net all golden,
      wrought so fine that the folk-leader—   fiercely lethal
50   prince of warriors—   could peer through it
      to see whomever   therein might come—
      whichever heroes' sons;   but at him not a one
      from the tribe of men   might take a look
      unless that arrogant lord   should issue commands
55   for counselors to come   from his keen warband.[2]

      Straight to his bed they brought   the brilliant lady.
      Sturdy warriors   strode to tell him
      they'd brought the holy maid   to the high tent then.
      The famous fort-prince   felt fiendish glee:
60   with filth and vice he'd ravish   the radiant lady!
      But the Guardian of Hosts,   glorious Judge,
      our Lord on high   wouldn't allow this thing:

---

[1] *tent* The poet uses the unusual word *træf* for "tent" rather than the more common *geteld*, perhaps because the latter could also mean "tabernacle" and had a more positive connotation.

[2] *There flowed … keen warband* The Biblical source only mentions that Holofernes's bed had a *canopeum*; the poet adds the apparently original detail that it functioned as a sort of see-though mirror, an appropriately sinister detail that aptly reflects the paranoia of those who wield the power of evil.

He stopped outrage;   He restrained evil.
Spawn of devils,   his spirit lustful,
65   he strode toward the bed   with his band of men.
Before that night elapsed   he'd lose honor,
reach the unhappy end   he'd earned before.
Evil-doer!   On earth he'd dwelt
a cruel prince,   oppressing men
70   under the clouds' rooftops.   Then the king collapsed
in midst of bed so drunk on wine   that his wit-locker
was of sense empty.   Off went his soldiers,
wine-glutted troops,   once they'd led that troth-breaker—
loathsome tyrant—   to his last resting.
75   Then the Savior's handmaid,   hearty and strong,
astutely sought   the most certain way
to end that besotted life   before the sinner woke.
Her locks entwined,   she took a sword—[1]
razor-sharp blade,   battle-hardened:
80   the Shaper's maid   from its sheath drew it
with her right hand then.   Heaven's Defender
she addressed by name—   Redeemer of all
in this world dwelling—   and these words then spoke:
"Source of all, great God on high,   and Spirit of holy help,
85   Son of the Almighty: mercy I need now,
Trinitarian strength!   Intensely now
is my heart inflamed: Lord, fierce sorrow
oppresses my soul.   Prince of heaven:
give me triumph and true belief;   let me take this sword
90   and cleave this murder-monger!   Mankind's Ruler,
grant me health and grace: I've never had greater need
for your mercy before.   Almighty Lord,
bright-minded Glory-Giver,   grant me vengeance;
let my mind's fury   inflame my heart!"[2]

95   Then supreme Justice   promptly filled her
with strength and zeal,   as He still will do
for everyone who dwells down here   seeking help for himself
with true faith and much counsel.   Thus her mind was filled
with hope renewed.   She took that heathen man
100   by the hair fast then   and with her fists tugging
stretched him deftly   in deep disgrace,

---

[1] *she took a sword* As in the climactic dragon-fight in *Beowulf*, there is a considerable gap between the drawing of the sword and its use.

[2] *Source of all ... inflame my heart* Judith's prayer to the Trinity makes her more like a Christian saint than a Hebrew heroine, but her prayer for vengeance and courage in battle makes her a warrior rather than a martyr.

wielding control   of the wicked man,
that hapless wretch.   Then with her hair knotted
she hacked fearsome foe   with fateful blade,
105   carved halfway through   his hateful neck,
so that he lay in a drunken swoon   with a deadly wound
though as yet unslain,   with his soul elsewhere.
So she swung the sword   a second time then—
the brave lady   lashed in earnest,
110   and that heathen hound's   whole head unwound—
rolled forth on the floor,   leaving the foul carcass
empty behind it.   Elsewhere the soul went:
under the cliff of death   cast down below,
ever thereafter in torment tied,   to torture bound,
115   with worms wound round   rank under ground:
leashed in hellfire!   lost in darkness!
Never a hope of leaving hell—   hall of serpents!
Throughout endless time   eternally slow
his soul shall stay   enslaved below
120   in that darkest home   no joy to know!

Thus she won foremost fame   as a fighter there:
God gave Judith   glory at war—
the sky's Chieftain   let her achieve triumph.
Into her bag at once   the brilliant maid
125   put the army-hunter's   head all bloody—
in the supply pouch that   her companion had brought
with food for both   when they'd first set out—
fair-faced maiden,   filled with virtue
and astute judgment.   Judith gave her
130   the bloody head   to bear homeward.
She and her young helper—   high-born ladies,
boldly daring,   brave in spirit,
blessed with triumph—   both left quickly,
steadfast maidens,   to steal right through
135   the hostile camp   till they could clearly see
the gleaming walls   of the gorgeous town,
Bethulia indeed!   Adorned with rings,
they hastened forth   on the footpath then,
until, glad-minded,   they made it through
140   to the wall's gateway.   Warriors sat there
holding watch then,   wakeful guardsmen
at the mighty fort—   just as, with mournful heart
but good judgment,   Judith had ordered
before setting forth   filled with courage.
145   Lady so brave!—   back at last now,

famed for valor, to her folk so dear:
at once the clear-minded woman called for someone
to come towards her from the tall fortress
to help them in with utmost haste

150 through the wall's gateway; and these words she spoke
to the victory-folk: "I can confirm for you
something to make us all grateful and end grieving:
mourn no longer: the Measurer exults!
Toward you the Wonder-Prince is well-disposed:

155 over the whole wide world it's well-known now:
to you is glory given and great honor
instead of the dire torment you've endured so long."
All those city-dwellers knew sudden bliss then,
once they'd heard her speak, the holy maid,

160 over the high wall there. The host rejoiced.
To the fortress-gate all the folk hastened,
men with women in multitudes.
The host in hordes all hurried and thronged,
by the thousands pressed toward the Prince's maid—

165 the young and old, each uplifted—
all their minds hopeful in that happy city
where they rejoiced to hear of Judith's return
to her own homeland. Humble, reverent,
with utmost haste they helped her in.

170 Then the deep-minded maid adorned with gold
bade her servant— resourceful companion—
to unveil the man-hunter's head before them—
show the bloody trophy to the townspeople
so all could see her success at war.

175 Then spoke the fine lady to the folk-gathering:
"Victory-famed troops, valiant commanders:
here you can see the heathen warrior's
head before you. Yes, Holofernes
now lies lifeless. Our most loathsome foe,

180 who committed more murder than any man on earth,
caused us grievous pain and had plotted more
grief than before, but God refused
him longer life— didn't let him commit
more atrocity: for I took his life

185 with the help of God. Now, each good man here
in this town dwelling: I tell you all,
shield-bearing men: you must make haste now
and gird for war. When our glorious King,
God the Creator, from the east sends high

190 His shining light, then bear linden shields forth,

boards before breasts   and byrnie-jackets
under gleaming helms   to the host of the foe!
With flashing swords   fell folk-leaders,
their doomed chieftains.   Death is allotted
195   to all your foes   and honor to you,
glory in battle,   as God in his might
through this hand of mine   has made clear now."

Then the eager host   became all ready
to contend bravely.   Thence bold as kings
200   veteran companions   bore victory-flags
forth to the fight—   forth for the right!
Heroes under helmets   left the holy town
at dawn of day   to din of shields
loudly resounding.   And so the lean one rejoiced,
205   the wolf in the woods,   with the wan raven,
corpse-hungry bird.   The beasts both knew
the local troops   would allot them the fated,
let them feast their fill.   There flew in their tracks,
all prey-driven,   the dew-feathered
210   brown-coated eagle,   who sang battle songs
through horn-hooked beak.[1]   The host advanced,
bear-troops[2] to battle   by boards covered,
by the curved linden—   those who not long before
had suffered outlanders'   lashings of scorn,
215   heathen insults.   But that was all repaid—
and repaid fiercely!—   when play of spears
found the Assyrian host   once the Hebrews came
to wage battle   under war-banners
in the invaders' camp.   Keenly they launched
220   arrow-showers   shooting forward
from horn-curved bows—   battle-adders,
stout-headed darts!   Storming loudly
furious warriors   flung forth spears then
into the hardy throng.   Heroes went raging:
225   against that loathsome tribe,   the land-dwellers
stepped stern-minded,   stout in spirit,
unsoft to wake up   old opponents,
all mead-weary.   With mighty hands
thanes pulled from sheath   the patterned sword
230   with sturdy edge   to strike and slay

---

[1] *Then the eager host ... horn-hooked beak* The "beasts of battle" (the raven, wolf, and eagle) are a traditional motif in Old English poetry, signaling the beginning of a scene of slaughter.

[2] *bear-troops* Literally *beornas* or "warriors," but the animal imagery is not inappropriate here.

Assyrian foes,   fearsome warriors.
Their spirits frenzied,   they spared no one
in that army's ranks,   neither rich nor poor,
no man alive   they might subdue.

235 And so in those morning hours   the mighty thanes
fiercely assailed   the foreign troops
until the chief leaders   of that large army
were forced to find   fury drove them!
They showed their strength   with stout sword-swings,
240 Hebrew fighters.   Their foe brought word
to the eldest ranks   of ruling thanes:
to their flag-bearers   they brought fierce tidings:
they woke warlords   with wild stories—
told the mead-weary   of the morning kill,
245 deadly swordplay.   Then soon I'm told
death-fated troops   tossed aside sleep,
and, heavy-hearted,   they huddled round
the mighty tent   of their murderous prince,
old Holofernes.   They'd hoped quickly
250 to warn their lord   that war was near
before the attack itself   brought terror down
with all the armed Hebrews.   They all still thought
the bear-troops' chief   and the bright maiden
in the lovely tent   still lay together—
255 Judith the regal   and their corrupt leader
wickedly lusting.   But of his lords not one
would dare to wake   the war-chief there
or try to find   how the flag-warrior
had behaved himself   with the holy woman,
260 with God's handmaid.   The host approached,
Hebrew folk all   fighting briskly
with their hard weapons,   with haft requiting
old offenses   when the flashing sword
answered old slander.   Assyria watched
265 glory's downfall   in the day's work there—
her pride toppled!   But troops still stood
round the lord's tent then,   intensely alarmed,
their spirits darkening.   Drawn together
they began to murmur, moan,[1]   lament aloud,
270 and grind and gnash: they showed no virtue,
gnashing teeth in fear.   Thus did they forfeit honor,
glory and valor.   They wanted to go waken

---

[1] *murmer, moan* More comically, "cough," "clear their throats." The Old English word *cohhetan* appears only here and its meaning is not known. The hesitation of the retainers is presumably meant to be ironic and bitterly comical.

their beloved leader—   which would do little good!
Sooner or later   someone would have to.
275   So a ring-warrior went   right to the tent—
undaunted enough   when need drove him.
On the bed he found—   blanched, sprawling—
his gold-giver: gone his spirit—
his life taken.   Then he tumbled flat—
280   to the earth frozen;   with frantic mind
he ripped his hair,   rent his garments,
and wailed out words   to warriors around,
unhappy all,   outside waiting:
"Here it's plain to see   ourselves all doomed:
285   we have clear token   our time has come,
evil upon us: now we all must lose,
assailed by strife: here lies sword-stricken—
our lord!—beheaded!"   Thus heavy-minded
they cast down weapons   and went with weary hearts
290   in flight trembling.   But they were attacked from behind
by the mighty host   until most who ran
with that force all lay   felled in battle
on the victory-field,   hacked flat by swords
as wolves would wish   and war-birds too,
295   all corpse-hungry.   Yet they kept fleeing,
shield-foe survivors.   Vying in foot-tracks
came the Hebrew force,   flushed with triumph,
honored with glory: God the Ruler,
our almighty Friend   gave His full support.
300   With bloody swords   they boldly went:
headstrong heroes   hacked a pathway
through the thronging foe.   They thrashed linden;
they slashed shield-wall—   those soldiers raged
with war's frenzy—   furious Hebrews.
305   Those thanes lusted   with a long thirst then
for the spear-thrusting.   There lay spent in dust,
by head-tally,   a high number
of slain nobles,   Assyrian lords,
the chief liege-men   of the loathsome tribe.
310   Few survived to go home!

                        Valiant as kings then
the warriors returned,   tearing through carnage,
reeking corpses.   They found room to loot—
land-dwellers there—   their most loathsome foe,
315   their old enemies,   all unliving.
They took bright booty,   bloody trappings,

board and broadsword,   burnished helmet,
much precious wealth.   Thus they won glory
on the battlefield   when they beat enemies,
320   the land-guardians: they'd laid to sleep
old foes with swords.   In swaths they sprawled,
those whom they loathed the most   among living tribes.
Then the whole nation   of noble clans—
foremost families—   took a full month there,
325   proud, hair-knotted,   to hoist and cart
to Bethulia the bright   beautiful city
helm and hip-sword,   hoary byrnies,
men's war-trappings   all tooled with gold:
they took more treasure   than any man living,
330   no matter how clever,   could recount fully—
all taken by troops   with true valor,
brave under banners,   battling in strife,
thanks to the wise counsel   of the keen Judith,
bold-minded maid.   From their mighty quest
335   spear-brave they gave   gifts of esteem
in her high honor: old Holofernes'
gory helm and broadsword   beside his byrnie so wide,
arrayed in gold so red,   with goods that the ring-warriors' prince
in pride and power had owned: his heirlooms and riches and gems,
340   all his glittering wealth and his rings: this to the radiant lady,
to the one so ingenious they gave.   And Judith devoted it all
to the glorious God of high hosts   who'd given her honor on earth,
renown in the worldly realm,   with reward in heaven to come,
triumph in splendor on high,   thanks to her true belief,
345   her faith in the Almighty forever.   In the end there could be no doubt
about the reward she'd cherished so long.   For this to our Lord so dear
be there glory forever arrayed.   Air and the lofty wind He made,
rolling sky and roomy ground,   rushing streams all tumbling down,
and, through His bounty of merciful love,   bliss in His heaven above.

—LATE 9TH OR EARLY 10TH CENTURY

THE BATTLE OF MALDON

During the reign of King Æthelred "the Unready" (978–1016), England experienced a renewed campaign of Viking attacks, which increased in strength and effect until the Danish King Cnut became King of England in 1016. Æthelred apparently lacked the resources, financial and otherwise, to repel the Vikings, and sources such as the *Anglo-Saxon Chronicle* depict his nobles and advisors as a treacherous, fragmented, and demoralized gang (the King's nickname, which may be a later invention, is in Old English *Un-ræd*, "no counsel," a pun on the name *Æthel-ræd* "noble counsel").

Though the last decade of the tenth century was a period of remarkable literary production by writers such as Ælfric, Wulfstan, and Byrhtferth of Ramsey, and saw the creation of many *de luxe* manuscripts and works of art, it is better remembered for the abysmal failure of Æthelred's policy of Viking appeasement. This began with a payment of £10,000 in 991, followed by £16,000 in 994, £24,000 in 1002, £36,000 in 1007, and £48,000 in 1012; finally, in 1013, the king was forced into exile in Normandy. The idea of buying off the Vikings with "Danegeld" was apparently inspired by the arrival in August of 991 of a fleet of 93 Viking ships; according to the *Anglo-Saxon Chronicle* the Viking army sacked Ipswich, sailed up the river Blackwater (Panta) to Maldon in Essex, and defeated the English army led by Byrhtnoth, ealdorman of Essex. Whether or not this battle was in fact the turning-point in Anglo-Danish relations, a poem was composed to commemorate the battle and the leader of the English army.

The manuscript of *The Battle of Maldon* was apparently already missing its beginning and end before the remaining pages were destroyed in a fire which devastated a portion of the British Library's manuscripts in 1731. Fortunately a transcript had been made before the fire, and this transcript is the only source for the poem. Only 325 lines of the poem survive, and while we do not know how much has been lost, the main action of the battle is complete and fairly clear. The Vikings have beached their boats on a spit of land that is cut off from the shore when the tide is in, but accessible via a causeway at low tide. The English army, ranged on the shore opposite the Vikings, is depicted as being composed of Byrhtnoth's own troops—his "retainers"—and a more or less trained local militia drawn from all ranks of society; a Viking messenger cannily tries to exploit potential differences in class or status among the troops, but the narrator portrays them as united by loyalty to their leader and a desire for honor.

The poem's attitude towards its hero, however, is not entirely celebratory; Byrhtnoth is praised for his bravery and strength, but his decision to allow the Vikings passage across the causeway (so that they might have more room to fight) is said to arise from his *ofermod*, a word which can mean either "pride" or "great courage." Byrhtnoth's loyalty to his king, Æthelred, and his ringing refusal to pay tribute to the Vikings must have had provocative resonance in the last years of the King's reign, assuming the poem was written shortly after the battle. Byrhtnoth fights well but dies quickly, with a desperate prayer on his lips; upon his death the treacherous retainer Godric leaps on Byrhtnoth's horse and gallops away. The men further away from Byrhtnoth assume that it is he who is fleeing, so they do the same, and the army falls apart; the rest of the poem depicts the brave speeches and noble deaths of the men who remain.

The Battle of Maldon is not a news report but a reflection on the complex relation between military victory and moral triumph; it draws on the conventions of heroic poetry to give motive and meaning to the historical facts, and turns the humiliation of Byrhtnoth's death and defeat into a celebration of other virtues such as courage and steadfastness. The poem may idealize the voices and actions of ordinary soldiers facing certain death, but it does not glorify their leaders or their cause; though the Vikings are by no means depicted as heroic, or even for the most part as individuals, the poem's moral absolutes are not arranged as an English "us" against a Viking "them," but as a stark personal choice between courage and cowardice, truth and treachery, which is only made clearer by the impossibility of victory.

⌘ ⌘ ⌘

The Battle of Maldon[1]

... was broken.
Then he ordered every young soldier to send off his
    horse,
drive it far off and go forward,
pay heed to hands and high courage.
5 When the kinsman of Offa first discovered
that the earl would not suffer slackness,
he let fly from his hands his favorite hawk
off to the woods, and advanced to the battle;
by that you knew that the young warrior
10 would not weaken at battle, when he took up weapons.
Likewise Eadric wished to support his leader,
the lord in the fight; forward he went
with his spear to battle. He had a stout heart
as long as he might hold in his hands
15 board and broad sword; he fulfilled his boast
when he had to fight before his lord.
    Then Byrhtnoth began to array the troops,
ordered, instructed, and showed the soldiers
how they should stand and hold the field,
20 told them to hold their shields securely,
firm in their fists, and never be afraid.
When he had properly organized all those men,
he dismounted among the men where he most wanted
to be, where he knew his retinue most loyal and brave.
25   Then on the riverbank, stoutly shouting,
stood a Viking messenger who made a speech,
broadcast the boast of the seafarers
to the earl where he stood on the shore:
"Bold seamen have sent me to thee,
30 commanded me to say that thou must quickly
send us rings for protection; and it is better for you
to buy off this spear-storm with tribute

than for us to share such a hard battle.[2]
We needn't ruin one another, if you're rich enough;
35 we'll call a truce in exchange for gold.
If thou, the richest here, agree to this,
that thou wilt ransom thy people,
give to the seamen all the money they want
in exchange for peace, and take a truce with us,
40 we'll go back to our ships with your gold coins,
sail off on the sea, and hold you in peace."
    Byrhtnoth spoke out, raised his shield,
shook his slender spear and made a speech,
angry and resolute, he gave this answer:
45 "Do you hear, seafarer, what this people says?
they will give you spears for your tribute,
poisoned points and ancient swords,
the heriot[3] that will not help you in battle.
Messenger of the sailors, take back a message,
50 tell your people much more hateful news:
here stands an undisgraced earl with his army,
who will defend this homeland,
the land of Æthelred, my own lord,
the folk and the fields. Fated are heathens
55 to fall in battle—it seems too shameful to me
to let you go with our gold to your ships
without a fight, now that you have come
this far into our country.
You shall not get your treasure so easily;
60 points and blades will settle this business,
grim war-play, before we pay tribute."
    Then he commanded his men to carry their shields
until they all stood on the river's edge.
The water kept each troop from the other
65 when the flood came flowing after the ebb,

---

[1] *The Battle of Maldon* Translated by R.M. Liuzza for *The Broadview Anthology of British Literature.*

[2] *Bold seamen ... hard battle* The translation preserves the use of singular (*thou, thee*) and plural (*you*) pronouns in the original, which may be a deliberate device to indicate that the messenger is trying to drive a wedge between Byrhtnoth and his army.

[3] *heriot* Military equipments.

locking the water-streams.[1] It seemed too long
until they could bring their spears together.
They stood arrayed on the shores of the Panta,
the East-Saxon vanguard and the Viking army;
70   neither side could strike at the other,
unless one might fall from an arrow's flight.
The tide receded; the sailors stood ready,
a great many Vikings eager for battle.
The protector of heroes[2] ordered a hardened warrior
75   to hold the causeway; he was called Wulfstan,
the son of Ceol, brave among his kinsmen;
he shot with his Frankish spear the first man
who stepped most boldly across the bridge.
Beside Wulfstan stood fearless warriors,
80   Ælfere and Maccus, two valiant men
who would not take flight at the ford,
but stoutly defended themselves against the foe
as long as they might wield weapons.
When they perceived this, and clearly saw
85   that they would meet bitter bridge-wardens there,
the hateful visitors hatched a plot—
they asked if they could have access
to lead their footsoldiers across the ford.
   Then the earl in his overconfidence[3] began
90   to allow too much land to that hateful people.
Over the cold water he called out then,
the son of Byrhthelm, while the soldiers listened:
"Here's room enough—now come quickly to us,
bring on the battle; God alone knows

95   who will hold this place of slaughter."
On came the slaughter-wolves, not minding the water,
the Viking troop went west over the Panta,
carried their shields over the shining water,
the seamen bore their linden shields[4] to land.
100   Against the attackers Byrhtnoth and his men
stood ready; he ordered them to raise
the battle-wall with their shields, and stand
fast against the foe. The fight was near,
glory in combat; the time had come
105   when fated men should fall.
The cry was raised, ravens circled,
the eagle longed for prey, and panic was on earth.
They let fly the file-hard spears,
grimly ground spearheads from their grip;
110   the bows were busy, the shield-boards took the arrows.
The attack was bitter, on either hand
warriors fell, young men lay dead.
Wulfmar was wounded, chose his bed of slaughter;
the kinsman of Byrhtnoth, savagely cut
115   to pieces with swords, his sister's son.
Payback was brought to the Vikings for that:
I heard that Edward struck one fiercely
with his sword—not stingy with strokes—
until at his feet fell the doomed soldier;
120   his leader gave thanks for that
to his attendant when he had the chance.
   And so they stood their ground, stouthearted
young men at war, eagerly worked
to see who might be the first to win
125   the life of a doomed man with his spear,
soldiers with weapons; slaughter fell on earth.
They stood steadfast; Byrhtnoth encouraged them,
ordered each young warrior to give thought to war
if he hoped to earn fame from the Danes in the fight.
130   Then came a tough warrior, weapon raised,
his shield for protection, and stepped toward him.[5]
Just as firmly went the earl to the churl;[6]
each of them thought to harm the other.
The sailor sent off his southern spear
135   so that the lord of warriors was wounded;

---

[1]   *locking the water-streams*   The Blackwater (OE Panta) is a tidal
river; when the tide came in the island on which the Vikings have
landed was cut off from the shore. Later, at low tide, a stone
causeway connects it to the shore.

[2]   *The protector of heroes*   Byrhtnoth.

[3]   *overconfidence*   The Old English word "ofermod" is notoriously
ambiguous in this passage—literally it means "too much *mod*"
(spirit, courage), implying a degree of reckless excess in what might
still be an admirable quality, but in later Old English prose it often
translates Latin *superbia* "pride," a deadly sin. It is difficult to argue
that the hero of the poem—if that is what Byrhtnoth is—is guilty of
a deadly sin in deciding to engage the Vikings in battle where they
stood; but part of the poem's enduring interest is its undertone,
which qualifies the moral absolutes in which battles are usually
recounted. Whatever the precise meaning of the word "ofermod,"
and whatever the military necessities under which Byrhtnoth reaches
his decision, his act proves to be a fatal error, as even he seems to
recognize.

[4]   *linden shields*   Shields of lime-tree wood.

[5]   *him*   I.e., Byrhtnoth.

[6]   *churl*   Man without noble rank.

he shoved with his shield so that the shaft broke in two,
and sprung out the spear when the point sprang back.
The warrior was furious—he stabbed with his spear
the proud Viking who gave him that wound.
140 The battle-leader was bold—he let his spear go forth,
his hand threaded it through the young man's neck
and he took the life of his attacker.
Then without waiting he stabbed another
so his armor burst; he was wounded in the breast
145 through his ring-mail, a deadly point
stood at his heart. The earl was the happier;
he laughed, brave man, and thanked his Maker
for the day's work the Lord had allowed him.
    Then one of the Vikings threw a spear from his
        hand,
150 let it fly from his fingers so it went too far,
through the noble thane of Æthelred.[1]
By his side stood a half-grown young warrior,
a boy in the battle, who very boldly
drew out the blood-drenched spear from the man—
155 Wulfstan's son, Wulfmar the young—
and sent the hard spear flying back again;
the point went in, so he lay on the earth,
the one who had grievously wounded his lord.
Then an armored man went to the earl,
160 he wanted to plunder the warrior's gear,
his robes and rings and decorated sword.
Byrhtnoth drew his sword, broad, bright-edged,
from its sheath, and swung at his mail-coat.
Too soon one of the seafarers stopped him
165 with a wound in the earl's arm.
The gold-hilted sword fell to the ground;
he could no longer hold the hardened blade,
or wield a weapon. But still the old warrior
said what he could, encouraged the young men
170 and bade them go forth as good companions.
He could no longer stand steady on his feet;
he gazed up to heaven:
    "I give thee thanks, O Lord of Nations,
for all the joys I have had in this world.
175 Now, gracious Maker, I have most desperate need
that Thou grant grace to my spirit,
so that my soul may journey to Thee
into Thy keeping, King of Angels,

and depart in peace. I implore Thee
180 that the fiends of Hell may not harm it."
Then the heathen savages hacked him up,
and both the men who stood beside him,
Ælfnoth and Wulmar, both lay dead,
and gave up their lives with their lord.
185   Then some unwilling ones bowed out of the battle:
the sons of Odda were the first in the flight,
Godric left the battle, and abandoned the good man
who had often given him many horses;
he leapt on the horse that belonged to his lord,
190 in his riding gear—which was not right!—
and his brothers with him both ran away,
Godwine and Godweg didn't care for battle,
but turned from the war and took to the woods,
fled to safety and saved their lives,
195 and many more beyond any good measure,
if they had remembered all the rewards
he had given them for their services.
So Offa had said, earlier that day
in the assembly, when he held a meeting,
200 that many a man spoke bravely there
who later would not stand firm at need.
    Then the people's leader lay fallen,
Æthelred's earl; all the house-troops
saw that their lord lay dead.[2]
205 Then forward pressed the proud thanes,
uncowardly men hastened eagerly;
they all wanted one of two things—
to give up their lives or avenge their dear lord.
    So the son of Ælfric urged them forward,
210 a warrior young in years spoke his words,
Ælfwine spoke, and bravely said:
"I remember the speeches we made over mead
when we raised our boasts on the benches,
heroes in the hall, about hard struggle;
215 now he who is bold has to prove it.
I will make known my noble descent to all:
I come from a famous family among the Mercians,
my ancestor was called Ealhelm,
a wise nobleman, and prosperous in the world.
220 Thanes will not mock me among my people,

---

1 *thane of Æthelred* Nobleman, i.e., Byrhtnoth.

2 *all the … lay dead* I.e., the troops closest to Byrhtnoth (cf. 23–25) see that he is dead; those further away mistake the fleeing Godric for their lord (236–41).

that I would go away from this army,
seek my homeland, now that my lord lies
cut down in battle. Mine is the greatest grief:
he was both my kinsman and my master."

225 He went forth, remembering revenge,
until with the point of his spear he struck one
of the seamen so that he lay dead on the ground,
cut down by his weapon. He urged his comrades,
friends and companions, to go forth.

230   Offa spoke, shook his ashen spear:
"Indeed, Ælfwine, you have reminded all
the thanes at need, now that our lord lies dead,
the earl on the earth. Each of us
needs to encourage every other

235 warrior to war, as long as his weapon
he can have and hold, the hard blade,
the spear and the good sword. Godric,
wretched son of Odda, has betrayed us all.
When he rode off on that horse, that proud steed,

240 too many men thought that it was our lord;
and so our forces were divided on this field,
the shield-wall broken. Shame on his deed,
by which he caused so many men to flee!"

    Leofsunu spoke and raised his shield,

245 his board for protection, and replied to him:
"I hereby promise that from hence I will not
flee the space of a single foot, but will go further,
avenge in the battle my beloved lord.
The steadfast men of Sturmer need not

250 mock me, now that my lord has fallen,
saying I would go home without my lord,
turn away from war—instead weapons shall take me,
point and iron." Full of ire he went forth,
fought tenaciously; he scorned flight.

255   Dunnere then spoke, shook his spear,
a humble churl, cried out over all,
urged each man to avenge Byrhtnoth:
"He must never weaken, who hopes to revenge
his lord on this people, nor care for his life!"

260 Then they went forth, not fearing for their lives;
the retainers set about fighting fiercely,
the grim spear-bearers, and asked God
that they might avenge their dear lord

and bring about the downfall of their foe.

265 The hostage began to help them eagerly;
he was from a strong family of Northumbrians,
the son of Ecglaf—his name was Æscferth.
He never weakened at the war-play,
but he shot forth arrows ceaselessly;

270 sometimes he struck a shield, sometimes a man,
again and again he gave one a wound,
as long as he was able to wield weapons.

    Still in the front stood Edward the Long,
brave and eager, spoke boastful words

275 that he would not flee a single foot's space,
or turn back now that his better lay dead.
He broke through the shield-wall and did battle
with the seamen, until he had worthily avenged
his treasure-giver, then took his place among the slain.

280 Likewise Ætheric, excellent comrade,
eager, death-ready, fought earnestly.
Sibyrht's brother and many another
split banded shields,[1] boldly defended themselves—
the shield-rim burst, and the byrnie[2] sang

285 its grim horrible song. Then Offa struck
a seafarer in the fight[3] so that he fell to the earth,
and there Gadd's kinsman sought the ground.
In the heat of battle Offa was hacked up,
but he had lived up to his promise to his lord—

290 he had boasted before his ring-giver
that they would ride together into the stronghold,
get home safely, or fall in the slaughter,
die of wounds on the field of war:
he lay like a thane at his lord's side.

295   Then shields were shattered, the sailors advanced,
enraged by battle; spears broke open
many a doomed man's life-house. Then Wistan went
    forth,
Thurstan's son, and fought with them;
he was the killer of three in that crowd,

---

[1] *banded shields* The precise meaning of the OE adjective "cellod," which appears only here, is not known.

[2] *byrnie* Coat of mail.

[3] *Then Offa ... fight* The Old English specifically says "*the* seafarer," as if some particular opponent had already been pointed out; there may be a line or two missing, indicating that Offa stepped forward, fought against an attacker, etc.

300   before Wigelin's son lay down in the slaughter.[1]
       There was keen conflict; the men stood
       firm in the struggle, warriors fell,
       weary with wounds. Slaughter fell on earth.
       Oswold and Eadwold all the while,
305   two brothers, exhorted the troops,
       bade their band of brothers with their words
       that they had to stand steady there at need,
       use their weapons without weakness.
             Byrhtwold spoke, raised his shield—
310   he was an old retainer—and shook his ash-spear;
       he most boldly gave the men a lesson:
       "Spirits must be the harder, hearts the keener,
       courage the greater, as our strength grows less.

       Here lies our lord all hacked to pieces,
315   a good man in the dust. He will mourn evermore
       who thinks to turn back from this war-play now.
       I'm an old man; I will not leave,
       but by the side of my lord—by such
       a beloved man—I intend to lie."
320   So also the son of Æthelgar urged them all,
       Godric, to the battle. Often he let go a spear,
       sent a slaughter-shaft whirling to the Vikings,
       as he advanced foremost among the folk,
       hacked and laid low, until he fell on the field.
325   That was not the Godric who turned away from
             the battle …
       —C. 1000

---

[1] *Wigelin's son … slaughter*   It is not clear how Wistan is both the
son of Thurstan and of Wigelin, unless Wigelin is his mother.
"Matronymic" epithets are rare in Old English, but this may be an
instance of one.

Exodus

The poem now called *Exodus* survives in a manuscript in the Bodleian Library at Oxford (Bodl. Lib. MS Junius 11). The Junius Manuscript contains four Old English poems on Biblical themes (*Genesis A* and *B*, *Exodus*, *Daniel*, and *Christ and Satan*), separately composed but deliberately compiled in a volume that is unique among Old English poetic manuscripts for containing a series of illustrations (though the series was not completed). Together the poems of the Junius Manuscript offer a poetic retelling of redemption history from Satan's fall to the Last Judgment. The subject-matter of this manuscript is remarkably similar to the body of work which Bede ascribes to the poet Cædmon; early readers attributed the whole collection to Cædmon, but it is now generally agreed that the four poems are so different in style that they could not have been written by the same person.

The focus of *Exodus* is on one episode from the Biblical story of Moses, the crossing of the Red Sea, but the poet emphasizes the story's typological associations with the Harrowing of Hell and with baptism; its themes and structure have been plausibly connected to the Easter Vigil liturgy. In this way the poem manages to be both more and less than the Biblical Book of Exodus. It is also a poem of strenuous energy and sweeping action, very much a representative of the heroic style. Drawing on the traditional language of heroic poetry, the poem depicts the Israelites who fled with Moses from the wrath of Pharaoh as a proud triumphant army ready to march into battle. When Pharaoh's army is drowned in the sea, the sea itself is described as a warrior, fighting a divine battle against the enemies of God. At other times the Israelites in the desert are described as sailors and seafarers—appropriately enough, for they will soon be crossing the sea to a new land. In these ways, perhaps, the Anglo-Saxons found a mirror of their own experience, since they too were seafarers and migrants, conquerors of a new land across the ocean. In this sense the poem is a kind of self-portrait of its English audience.

Exodus contains some of the most dazzlingly inventive language of any Old English poem. It is full of metaphoric energy, exuberant wordplay and sound patterns; its syntax is in some places lively to the point of incoherence. It is a notoriously difficult poem, apparently not well preserved—there are gaps in the text, and some passages may be out of sequence—and the same energy that makes the poem's language so exciting and inventive and its narrative so powerful and surprising occasionally makes it difficult to recognize errors in the text, let alone correct them. The present translation is fairly loose in some passages where the text does not make perfect sense; in a few places the translation reflects the obscurity of the original.

⌘ ⌘ ⌘

Exodus[1]

Listen! far and wide throughout the world
we have learned how the laws of Moses,
a marvelous code, were proclaimed to men—
a happy reward in heaven above
5 for every blessed soul's hard struggle,
a lasting counsel for all the living,
heavenly life—let him hear who will!
    He was exalted in the wilderness, where
the Lord of Hosts, the righteous King,
10 endowed him with His own power
and put mighty deeds into his hands.
Beloved of God, lord of his people,
canny and wise, commander of armies,
famous leader—Pharaoh, God's enemy,
15 he bound with a rod, and all his race.
There the God of triumph entrusted and gave
the lives of his kinsmen to that brave leader,
and a habitation in their homeland to Abraham's sons.
Great was the reward, and loyal the Lord,
20 who gave strength to his arms against the enemies' terror;
he conquered many a kingdom on the battlefield
and took dominion over many tribes.[2] In that first time[3]
that the God of Hosts addressed him,
He told him in words many wonderful truths,
25 how the wise Lord wrought the world,
the orb of the earth and the sky above,
established them in glory—and His own name too,
which the sons of men had never known,
wise Patriarchs, though they knew many things.
30   Afterwards, when he had strengthened and exalted
the prince of his people with true powers,
Pharaoh's enemy, for his exodus,

then that nation's army was soon drenched
in death, ancient plagues, and the overthrow
35 of too many of those treasure-hoarders—
their lamentation arose, their hall-joys slaughtered,
their wealth plundered.[4] Those wicked oppressors
He annihilated at midnight, many first-born sons,
the city-guards slain. A killer stalked widely,
40 choked the land with the corpses of the dead,
hostile persecutor of the people—and the host went
    forth.
There was widespread weeping, few worldly joys,
the laughter-smiths' hands were locked shut
when the people were allowed to depart on their
45 harsh journey,[5] the fiend and his hellish host
were despoiled—Heaven descended,
and their demon idols fell. A most famous day
across the earth it was, when that multitude set out,
so they suffered captivity for many years,
50 the accursed people of Egypt,
because they imagined they could ever hold back
the people of Moses, if the Maker had allowed them,
from their beloved and long-awaited journey.
    The army was eager, and bold their leader,
55 a brave commander of that nation of kinsmen.
He passed with his people through many desert lands,
the habitations of hostile men,
narrow passes, unknown paths,
until they bore their arms among the fierce borderers
60 whose lands lay shrouded in a cover of clouds,[6]
their high mountain dwellings. Moses led
his army past these, through many border-lands.

---

[1] *Exodus* The present translation is by R.M. Liuzza and has been prepared especially for *The Broadview Anthology of British Literature.* The translation is based on the text edited by P.J. Lucas, *Exodus* (U of Exeter Press, 1977; 2nd ed. 1994), though considerable freedom has been exercised with regard to Lucas's punctuation, emendations and proposed translations. For advice and assistance the translator expresses gratitude to J.R. Hall, Anne Klinck and Eileen Joy.

[2] *he conquered … tribes* This refers perhaps to a future time when the Hebrews settled in the land of Canaan and displaced the inhabitants.

[3] *In that first time* In the wilderness, in the form of a burning bush (see Exodus 3).

[4] *Afterwards … plundered* A complex and multivalent passage; "treasure," "hall-joys," and "wealth" all refer to the first-born sons of the Egyptians, but they give the impression that the Hebrews somehow conquered them in battle and took possession of their wealth as well.

[5] *He annihilated … journey* The blurring of the Egyptians' death and the Israelites' exodus throughout this passage is a complex *double entendre*, referring both to the Hebrews, reluctantly set free, and to the first-born children, sent to their death. The description recalls the legends of Christ's Harrowing of Hell (undertaken between the Crucifixion and the Resurrection to rescue the souls of the righteous from their imprisonment in Hell).

[6] *shrouded … clouds* Though geographically imprecise, this is probably a reference to the Nubians, whose name was thought to derive from the Latin *nubes* (clouds).

Then two nights after they had escaped their enemies,
He commanded that glorious hero[1] to encamp
65 with all their host around the fortress of Etham,
with great clamor and resounding noise,
a mighty force among those borderlands.
Danger pushed their path northward—
to the south, they knew, lay the Sun-dwellers' land,[2]
70 the sunburnt hillsides of a people browned
by the hot coals of heaven. There Holy God
shielded the people from the scorching heat:
spread a canopy over the searing sky,
hung a holy veil in the burning air.[3]
75 A cloud spread broad across the sky
evenly divided earth and heaven,
went before that company, and heaven's bright fires
were quenched in its heat. The host, most happy people,
marveled at it. The sheltering day-shield
80 glided across the heavens; wise God
unfurled a sail across the course of the sun
whose halyards none could know
nor could the sailyard be seen
by any earth-dweller, no matter how skilled,
85 how that greatest of tabernacles was tied,
when he had honored with glory
those faithful people. The third encampment
was a comfort to them; the army observed
how those holy sails billowed above,
90 radiant miracle aloft; the multitude of Israel,
that people, saw in that place how the Lord,
the Lord of Hosts himself, had come to make camp.
Before them headed the fire and cloud
in the bright sky, twin beams,
95 each of them equally shared
in the high service of the Holy Spirit,
by day and night on the daring journey.
    Then, as I've heard, the next morning,
that bold-hearted people raised their brave trumpets,
100 heralds of glory. The group all arose,

a mighty army eager to set out
as Moses, their great leader, commanded them,
the people of God. Going before them they saw
their life-guide lay out the path of life;
105 the sky set the course, the sailors followed
on the sea-path.[4] The people were joyful,
loud the army's clamor. Each evening arose
a heavenly beacon, second marvelous sign,
wondrously held the setting sun's place
110 and blazed with light above the people,
a gleaming beam. Bright rays
stood blazing above the soldiers,
a shining shield-cover—shadows vanished,
and the deep shades of night could scarcely
115 stay hidden in their dens. Heaven's candle burned,
the new night-watchman had great need
to guard the host, lest the desert horror,
grey heath-stalker, should sever their lives
with the sudden clutch of violent storms.
120 Their forerunner had fiery locks,
bright beams, threatening to burn up
those desert troops with flaming terror,
a blaze of fire on that army, unless
they were brave in heart and obeyed Moses.
125   The bright troops shone, their shields gleamed,
the shield-bearers kept sight of the true path,
the sign above, until the barrier of the sea
at land's end prevented their progress,
their eager advance. Exhausted, they pitched
130 their camp, refreshed themselves with food
served by noble stewards, and restored their strength.
When the trumpets sang, the sailors spread
their field-tents in the hills; this was the fourth camp,
the shield-bearers' rest by the Red Sea.
135   Then terrible news arose among the army—
inland pursuit. Fear of slaughter
spread among the troops, those exiles awaited
their hostile pursuers, who had long punished
those homeless people with harsh affliction
140 and woeful oppression. They ignored their pledge,

---

[1] *glorious hero* I.e., God commanded Moses.

[2] *Sun-dwellers' land* Old English *sigelwara*, usually applied to the Ethiopians, though they are not mentioned in the Biblical story of Exodus.

[3] *spread a canopy ... burning air* This is the pillar of cloud described throughout Exodus. The cloud accompanies the Israelites by day, and a pillar of fire accompanies them by night (lines 93–97).

[4] *Going before ... sea-path* The "life-guide" is the pillar of cloud; the nautical imagery is a somewhat disconcerting way of describing the desert passage of the Hebrews from Egypt, but resonates powerfully in traditional Old English poetry—and will, of course, become more appropriate when the travelers reach the Red Sea.

the promise given by the elder Pharaoh ...[1]

Then he became the custodian of the treasure
of all the Egyptians, and he greatly prospered.
But they forgot all that; the Egyptian nation
145 grew grim and hostile, did not hesitate at all,
carried out crimes against his kinsmen,
stirred up strife and devoured their pledges.
Seething desires surged in their hearts,
mighty passions; they wanted to repay
150 that good with evil, lies and treachery,
so the people of Moses would have paid in blood
for that day's work, if Almighty God
had granted success to their mission of destruction.

　　The men's spirits began to despair
155 when they saw surging up from the south
the army of Pharaoh advancing forward,
a great forest moving, the cavalry gleaming,
with spears ready, the battle swarming,
shields shining, trumpets sounding,
160 banners aloft, an army marching across the border.
Black birds of prey croaked for carrion, greedy for
　　slaughter
and a feast of corpses, dewy-feathered
dark Furies.[2] The wolves howled
a grim evening-song, eager for prey,
165 pitiless beasts, bold scavengers, followed
in their tracks, waiting the warriors' fall.
These border-stalkers bayed in the black of night,
doomed souls grew faint as the people despaired.

　　At times proud thanes° from the host　　*noblemen*
170 measured the miles with their galloping horses;
there the proud king, prince of men,
rode before the border-troop brandishing the standard;

the warriors' warlord fastened his helmet,
strapped on his chinguard as the standard gleamed,
175 ready for battle, he rattled his war-coat,
commanded his chosen troops to stand fast
and hold their formation. The friends[3] watched
the approach of that land-host with eyes full of hate.

　　Around him[4] roved fearless warriors,
180 grey sword-wolves who welcomed battle
with a lust for combat, loyal to their leader.
For the host, he himself had chosen
from that nation two thousand most noble,
and all were kings and royal kinsmen
185 in the old order, esteemed for their ancestry:
each of them in turn had led forth
each and every male soldier
he was able to find on that occasion.
All the kings of that country were there
190 together in formation; the well-known trumpet
announced among the throng where the young men,
a horde of warriors, should bear their weapons.

　　And so those dark legions surged forward,
foe upon foe, a vast multitude of the nation's might,
195 thousands at a time, eager to advance.
They meant with their mighty troops to attack
the people of Israel at the first light of day,
destroy them with swords in revenge for their brothers.
And so there was weeping and wailing in the camps,
200 a grim song at evening, terror spreading;
they put on their war-coats when panic seized them,
and fled the fearful tidings. The enemy was united,
the army war-bright, until the mighty angel
who protected the multitude repelled those proud ones,
205 so that those two enemies were no longer able
to see one another: their ways were separated.

　　The exiles experienced a night-long reprieve,
though enemies loomed on either side—
the army or the sea, and no other way out.
210 Giving up hope for their homeland,
they sat among the sloping hills in somber clothing,
expecting sorrow. Watchful, they awaited,
all that company of kinsmen together,
the greater forces, until in the first light of dawn
215 Moses bade the heralds with brass trumpets

---

[1] *Pharaoh ...*　　There is a gap of perhaps four pages in the manuscript here; the missing lines apparently recounted how an earlier
Pharaoh had given Joseph authority over all Egypt (Genesis 41), but
when a new Pharaoh arose who knew nothing of Joseph, the
oppression of the Israelites began (Exodus 1). Dramatically the
passage, emphasizing the treachery of the Egyptians, is a delaying
device between the first mention of their pursuit and their visible
approach.

[2] *dark Furies*　　The meter is defective here but no proposed solution
is entirely satisfactory. The word translated here as "Furies" is
wælceasega, "chooser of the slain," a word cognate with the "Valky-
rie" of Norse mythology but also used in Old English to gloss
classical figures like the Fates and Furies.

[3] *The friends*　　I.e., the Israelites.

[4] *him*　　I.e., the Pharaoh.

to assemble the people, and soldiers to arise,
put on their mail coats and consider their courage,
bear the bright armor, and with banners summon
the war-band to the shore. Swiftly the defenders
220 heeded the battle-call, the host was alerted;
they heard the trumpets, and the sailors hurried
over the hills from their tents, a troop in haste.
Then they assigned twelve troops to stand
against the vicious attack of the advancing enemy,
225 brave-spirited men whose courage was stirred.
In each one, fifty companies were chosen
from the most noble families among the nations,
assembled in battalions to bear arms;
and each hand-picked company of that famous host
230 was composed of ten hundred spear-carriers
and fighting men, gloriously favored—
a warlike host! The army's commanders
did not welcome the weak among their ranks,
the young who were not yet able
235 to defend themselves against the treacherous foe
in the shelter of a shield and a mail-shirt,
or those who had not known a sharp wound
over the edge of a shield, or bore battle-scars
from boasting spear-play. Nor could the old,
240 greybearded warriors, hold their own in battle
if their might had diminished among the brave men.
Instead, they selected battalions by their stature,
how their courage would endure honorably
among the people, and how powerfully
245 their skilled hands could grasp a spear.
When the stalwart army was assembled,
eager to advance, the ensign° rode on high,[1]   *flag*
brightest of beams; there they abided
until their guide, glittering above their shields,
250 burst through the gates of the air by the sea.
    Then the herald leapt up before that host,
bold battle-crier, raised up his shield
and ordered the commanders to quiet the army
so all could listen to their leader's speech.
255 That kingdom's guardian wanted to counsel
the hand-picked troops. With his holy voice,
the leader of that host spoke with worthy words:
"Do not be afraid, even though Pharaoh

has brought a vast army of sword-warriors,
260 countless men. The almighty Lord
intends today, through my hand,
to pay them back for their past deeds,
so that they shall no longer survive
to keep the people of Israel in misery.
265 You will not fear those dead foot-soldiers
in their doomed bodies—their brief lease on life
has come to an end. God's counsel
has fled your heart; I have a better way:
that you should always praise the Prince of Glory,
270 pray for the grace of the Lord of Life
and the salvation of victory as you set forth.
It is the eternal God of Abraham,
the Lord of Creation, lofty and powerful,
who guards this host with his Almighty Hand."
275   Then the lord of the living lifted up his voice
and spoke before the army to all the nation:
"Behold! most beloved of people, now you see
with your own eyes a most awesome wonder,
now with this green rod[2] in my right hand
280 I myself have struck the depths of the sea:
the waves ascend, and swiftly the waters
form a sturdy wall. The ways are dry,
a glistening road, the deep has revealed
its ancient foundations, where no man before,
285 as I have heard tell, has ever traveled,
mottled plains which always remain
forever hidden by the foaming waves.
A south wind, breath of the ocean, has unsealed
the sea's depths, the waves are split,
290 the surf churns out sand. Well I know
that Almighty God has shown mercy to you,
happy as in days of old. Now hurry,
that you may escape the embrace of your enemies,
now that the Ruler has raised up
295 red sea-streams as a sheltering rampart.
The retaining walls of this wondrous wave-road
are fairly raised to the roof of the heavens."
    With these words, all the host arose,
a courageous force. The sea lay calm;

---

[1] *the ensign rode on high* I.e., the pillar, which at this point is "of
fire and of the cloud" (Exodus 14.24).

[2] *green rod* The Old English phrase is *grene tacn*, literally "green (*or*
living) sign," which has occasioned much comment. The phrase may
simply be an error for *grene tane* "green rod" (corresponding to the
Latin *virga* [rod], the staff of Moses mentioned in Exodus 14.16).

upon the sand the hand-picked troops raised
their banners and bright shields. The sea-wall
stood upright alongside the Israelites
for an entire day.[1]

That troop of earls was of one mind,
kept their covenant in close embrace—
they did not despise their dear lord's
holy teaching, when his sweet words were still
and his voice silent by their path through the sea.[2]

The fourth tribe was the first to lead them,
an army of men marching through the waves
upon the green sea bed.[3] The soldiers of Judah
hastened alone down that unknown path
before all their brothers. And so Almighty God
gave them a great reward for that day's work—
glorious deeds of victory were granted to them,
so that later they might have lordship
over kingdoms, and rule their kinsmen.
When they entered the sea they raised their ensign,
a battle-standard high above their shields,
among the mass of spears those most lordly men
lifted up a golden lion, bravest of beasts.
With it, those warriors would not long suffer
insult or injury from any lord living,
as long as they could lift a spear in battle
against any nation. Ahead lay the attack,
hard hand-play, young men brave
in the carnage of weapons, fearless warriors,
bloody wounds and the rush of battle,
the grim grinding of helmets, when Judah advanced.

After that army the sailor followed boldly,
the son of Reuben; those sea-dwellers[4]
bore their shields over the salty marsh,

a multitude of men, a mighty legion
went forth fearlessly. In sinful deeds
he[5] squandered his lordship, and so he marched
in his beloved's footsteps—his brother had taken
his natural rights as first-born of that nation,
his wealth and status—yet still he was no coward.

After them, among the throng of peoples,
the sons of Simeon advanced in troops,
the third tribe. Their banners waving,
the battalion pressed on, spear-points flashing
and shafts gleaming. The glimmer of day
came over the crest of the sea, God's bright beacon,
the glorious morning. The multitude went forth
there while one family followed after another,
in iron-clad armies—one man led these,
greatest in might, for which he became famous
on their march—beneath the pillar of cloud,
kin after kin; each one observed
the rights of each tribe and the rank of earls,
as Moses instructed them. They had one father,
a beloved prince, dear to his people,
ancient and wise, who held the land-right;
that great patriarch begat a line
of brave noblemen, a holy nation,
the race of Israel, righteous before the Lord.
This is how ancient writers in their wisdom
tell it, who know most about these tribes,
each one's lineage, origin and ancestry:

Over new seas Noah[6] sailed,[7]
glorious prince, together with his three sons,
over the deepest of drenching floods
that had ever come over the earth.
He had in his heart a holy faith,
and so he steered over the ocean streams

---

[1]   *entire day* A half-line is apparently missing here (or after the following line?); various suggestions, none compellingly plausible, have been made to fill the gap, but none is adopted here.

[2]   *sea* The original is obscure here; this is a guess at its probable meaning.

[3]   *green sea bed* The description of the sea floor as "green" has occasioned much debate; elsewhere in Old English poetry the road to Paradise is described as "green," and the poem may be pointing towards the moment's typological or allegorical significance.

[4]   *sea-dwellers* Literally, "sea-vikings." It is by no means certain that the word had any of its later connotations in this passage, and a more neutral translation (reflecting Old English *wic* "dwelling") is given here.

[5]   *he* I.e., Reuben.

[6]   *Noah* The story of Noah and the ark is found in Genesis 5–9.

[7]   *Over new ... sailed* Many readers and editors have felt the transition to be abrupt, and assumed that this passage originally belonged somewhere else. But the overarching nautical imagery connects it to the action described in the rest of the poem, and the typological connections found in the Easter Vigil liturgy make the linkage of Noah, Abraham, and Moses less peculiar to an early medieval reader than it might be to a modern one. The sense of narrative unity found here might be thought of as "liturgical" rather than "dramatic," and sequence less important than significance.

the greatest treasure-chest[1] I have ever heard tell of.
The wise sea-prince, to save the lives
of all who dwell upon on earth,
370 had reckoned up a lasting remnant,
a first generation, father and mother
of all who bear offspring, more diverse
than men can imagine. Likewise the heroes brought
into the bosom of the ship every kind of seed
375 for which men have use beneath the heavens.

   And so the words of wise men tell us
that the ninth in lineage from Noah
was Abraham's father among that folk.
This is the Abraham[2] to whom the God of angels
380 gave a new name; and near and far
entrusted the holy tribes into his keeping,
and lordship over nations. He lived in exile.
Later, he led the most beloved of creatures
at the Lord's behest; into the highlands
385 climbed the two kinsmen, up to Mount Sion.
They found the Covenant there, gazed on God's glory,
the holy pledge, as men have heard tell.

   In that same place the wise son of David,[3]
glorious king, through the counsel of the prophet
390 later built the temple of the Lord,
a holy shrine, highest and holiest—
the wisest among the world's kingdoms
of all earthly rulers, most renowned among men—
the greatest and most glorious that the sons of men
395 in all nations on earth ever made with their hands.[4]

   To the appointed meeting-place he led his son,
Abraham took Isaac; up blazed the pyre,
most deadly slayer—but he was not doomed to die[5]—
he intended to offer his offspring to the flames,
400 his best of children to the blazing pyre,
his sweet son as a sacrifice for victory,
his only heir upon the earth,
his life's consolation, which he had long awaited,
his lasting hope for the nation's legacy.

405 He made it clear, when he took the child
fast in his hands, and the famous man drew
his ancient heirloom (its edge rasping),
that he did not hold his son's life dearer
than his obedience to the King of Heaven.

410   Up he rose,[6]
ready to slay his only son,
still a boy, with his bloody blade,
put his child to the sword, if God had not stopped him;
the Bright Father would not take the boy
415 as a holy sacrifice, but laid His hands upon him.[7]
Then to restrain him came a voice from the heavens,
a sound of glory, and spoke these words:
"Abraham! do not slay your own child,
your son, with a sword. The truth is known,
420 now that the King of all Creation has tested you,
that you have kept your covenant with God,
a firm faith, which shall be a protector
for you all the days of your life
forever and ever, unfailing.
425 Why should the Son of Man need a stronger pledge?
Heaven and earth cannot confine
the words of His glory, wider and broader
than all the ends of the earth can enfold,
the orb of the world and the firmament above,
430 the depths of the sea and the yearning sky.[8]
The King of Angels, God of Hosts,
Ruler of destinies, righteous in victory,
swears you an oath by His own life,
that men across the earth, in all their wisdom,
435 will never know how to count the number
of all your tribe and offspring,
shield-bearing warriors, nor say it truly
unless someone might grow so wise in spirit
that he alone might reckon the number
440 of stones on the earth, stars in the heavens,
the sands of the sea-swell's salty waves;

---

[1] *treasure-chest*   I.e., the ark and its contents, usually identified with the Church in medieval readings of Genesis.

[2] *Abraham*   See Genesis 17 and forward.

[3] *wise son of David*   I.e., Solomon.

[4] *temple ... hands*   See 1 Kings 6.

[5] *most deadly ... to die*   Or "the foremost life-slayer (i.e., Satan) was no happier for that."

[6] *Up he rose*   A half-line is usually assumed to be missing here, but (as at line 304) the text makes sense as it stands, so nothing has been invented to fill the "gap."

[7] *Bright Father ... him*   "Father" and "His" refer equally to Moses and to God.

[8] *yearning sky*   It is not clear why the sky is described as *geomre* (sad or dreary) at this particular moment—the phrase, which is much better suited to the North Sea than the Middle East, may be traditional, but it does not occur elsewhere in Old English poetry.

But your people, most noble of nations,
free-born of their father, will occupy
the land of Canaan, between the two seas

445 even unto the borders of Egypt."…[1]
　All that folk[2] fell into a panic; fear of the flood
filled their wretched hearts, and the sea wreaked death.
The steep sea-slopes were soaked with blood,
the sea spewed gore, chaos was in the waves,

450 the water full of weapons, a death-mist arose.
The Egyptians were thrown into retreat:
they fled terrified, felt the sudden terror,
cowards, deserters, they sought out their homes—
their boasts were milder. The wild tossing waves

455 darkened over them again: none of that army
came home again, but fate cut off their retreat
and locked them in the waves. Where a road lay before,
the ocean raged, that host was overwhelmed,
the sea flowed forth. A storm arose[3]

460 up to high heaven, a great outcry of despair,
the enemies shrieked, the sky grew dark
with doomed voices, the flood was blood-muddy.
The shield-walls were shattered, and the greatest of
　　sea-deaths
lashed the sky; those proud kings and their legions

465 were slain. Their screams grew silent,
the waves at an end; war-shields gleamed.
High above those heroes rushed a wall of water,
a mighty sea-stream. That multitude was caught
fast in death's fetters, deprived of escape,

470 snagged in their armor. The sands awaited
their ordained fate, when the flowing waves,
the ice-cold sea, the salty billows,
bare bringer of doom, driven from its course
might come seeking again its ancient bed,

475 an angry wandering spirit smiting his enemies.
With blood was the blue air defiled,

the flood threatened bloody terror wild
on the seafarers' march, while the true Maker
revealed his fury through the hand of Moses.

480 Ravaging, seething, the surging flood swept them away
in its deadly clutches; doomed men dropped,
the sea fell upon the land, the sky was shaken.
The ramparts gave way, the waves burst,
the sea-columns melted, when the Mighty One,

485 Heavenly Guardian, struck with His holy Hand
those wretched warriors of a proud nation[4]—
no restraining the course of the saving waters,
the might of the sea-streams; He wrecked the multitudes
in shrieking terror. The raging ocean

490 towered high, glided over them, terror mounted,
murderous waves gushed, and God's handiwork,
foamy-bosomed, fell upon the battle-path
from the heights of heaven; the flood's Guardian
struck the unprotected way with an ancient sword,

495 so that at the death-blow the legions slept,
a sinful throng, fast shut in,
lost their lives, an army flood-pale,
when they were buried under the brown water,
the proud and mighty waves.[5] The force all fell,

500 the afflicting ones, the legions of Egypt,
Pharaoh and all his army. God's adversary
quickly found as he sank to the sea-floor
that the Guardian of the waves was stronger than he—
angry and enraged, he had intended to settle

505 the battle in a deadly embrace. For that day's work
the Egyptians received an overwhelming reward,
for none of that army, vast beyond number,
ever survived to return home again
to tell of his fate, or proclaim in the cities

510 the worst tidings to the wives of those warriors,
the fall of their treasure's protectors,
but a mighty sea-death swallowed their legions
and their heralds with them. He who has power
drained the boasts of men—they fought against God.

---

[1] *Egypt …* A page is missing in the manuscript here; it probably would have told the story found in Exodus 14.23–26: the people of Israel cross the Red Sea; the Egyptians pursue them; when Moses stretches out his hands the sea returns to its former place and the army of Pharaoh is destroyed.

[2] *that folk* I.e., Egyptians.

[3] *A storm arose* Some critics have interpreted these lines differently, but it seems best to read the passage as an example (by no means the only one in Old English poetry) of synaesthesia—the uproar of the drowning army is described as a storm which darkens the sky.

---

[4] *The ramparts … nation* These lines are difficult and no single solution is entirely satisfactory; the translation is fairly loose. The vivid impressionistic style of the passage seems almost to have gone out of control, and the chaos of the scene described has shaken the syntax of the description itself.

[5] *fast shut in … waves* These lines are difficult and this translation is conjectural.

515   Then Moses, man of noble virtue,
gave a holy speech on the shore of the sea,
spoke eternal wisdom to the Israelites
and deep counsel. Even now the nations speak
of that day's work, discover in Scripture
520 every law which the Lord, in words of truth,
ordained for them on that journey.
If the interpreter of Life will unlock,
the body's Guardian radiant in the breast,
these expansive blessings with the keys of the spirit,
525 the mysteries will be clear and good counsel will emerge,
for it has words of wisdom in its keeping,
and earnestly seeks to instruct our heart
so we will not lack for fellowship with God,
the Maker's mercy. He will enlighten us even more;
530 for now, scholars inform us of the better
and more lasting joys of Heaven. Here pleasure fades,
cursed with sin, allotted to exiles,
a wretched time of waiting. Homeless,
we anxiously inhabit this guest-house,
535 mourning in spirit, mindful of the house of pain
fast under the earth, a place of fire and worms,
the den of every kind of evil ever open,
while here those arch-thieves divide up their domain,
old age and early death. The day of reckoning draws near,
540 greatest of all glories, upon the earth,
a day marked by deeds: in the meeting-place
the Lord Himself will judge the multitude,
when He will lead into Heaven above
the souls of the righteous, blessed spirits,
545 where there is light and life and the joy of bliss.[1]
In delight that troop will praise the Lord,
King of Glory, God of Hosts, for all eternity.

     And so he spoke, mindful of wise counsel,
mildest of men made strong in might,
550 in a loud voice—awaiting their leader's will
the army stood silent, perceived that wonder,
his brave words of salvation. He said to the multitude:
"Mighty is this multitude, great our Commander,
the strongest of Supports who guides our journey.

555 He has given over to us the tribes of Canaan,
their cities and treasures and spacious kingdoms;
He will now fulfill what He long ago promised
with sworn oaths, the Lord of Angels,
to our fathers' generations in ancient days,
560 if you will only hold His holy precepts,
that you will overcome each of your enemies
and hold, rich in victory, the feast-halls of heroes
between the two seas: great will be your glory."
     At these words the whole host was glad,
565 trumpets of victory sounded, standards were raised
to the lovely sound. The folk had reached land;
the pillar of glory had guided the host,
the holy troop, under God's protection.
The shield-warriors exulted that they had escaped alive
570 from the power of their enemies, though they had
          passed boldly
under the roof of the waves, and seen the walls standing;
the sea through which they had borne their armor
          seemed brimming blood.
They rejoiced with war-songs when they escaped
          that army;
the battalions and legions lifted up a loud voice,
575 gave praise to God, raised a song of glory
for that day's work. The women opposite them,
greatest of gatherings, chanted a battle anthem
with voiced raised, sang of all these many wonders.
Then it was easy to see the African woman,[2]
580 adorned with gold at the edge of the sea,
her hands grasping neck-adornments;
they rejoiced, seeing their reward,
received the spoils of war[3]—their bondage was released.
They divided up the sea's leavings, ancient treasures,
585 along the shore by each tribe's ensign,
robes and shields; they divided rightly
gold and good cloth, the treasures of Joseph,
glorious possessions of men, whose guardians lay,
greatest of armies, fast in the arms of death.
—?8TH CENTURY

---

[1] *Then Moses, man of ... joy of bliss* Lines 515–48 have struck many critics as a later addition to the poem; they interrupt the speech of Moses (which resumes at 553) and may well be misplaced here, but no compelling alternative to the existing text has been proposed.

[2] *African woman* Perhaps Zipporah, Moses's Ethiopian wife (Numbers 12.1), who figures in medieval exegesis as an image of the Christian Church.

[3] *spoils of war* I.e., the armor and jewels of the drowned Egyptian army, washed up on the shores of the Red Sea.

The Anglo-Saxon Chronicle

The Anglo-Saxon Chronicle is not a single work, but a group of interrelated manuscripts. It is presumed to have originated during the reign of Alfred the Great, whose court scholars compiled a year-by-year record of important events from the birth of Christ to their own day. Their compilation was based on Bede's *Ecclesiastical History*, other written sources, some local traditions, and the annotations (called "annals") made in monastic Easter tables to record the most memorable events of each year—the death of an abbot, the appearance of a comet, a notably bad famine. From these unpromising bits and pieces the authors of the *Chronicle* assembled an essentially coherent narrative which tells a story of England from the time of the Romans to that of the heroic struggles of Alfred himself against the terror of the Viking raids. In this sense *The Chronicle* is a work of propaganda, designed to inspire the English to resist the Viking invasions.

The completed record was sent to various places across England around 892. Each copy was supplemented, interpolated into, and continued, sometimes annually as events were unfolding, and each represents the interests and narrow views of the place in which it was written. Some copies include records of local events, often no more than a line or two; others have lengthy continuations and elaborate histories of the monasteries in which they were kept. Scholars have discerned several different threads of continuations, interwoven in various ways (surviving manuscripts are often copies of copies of the originals, and a great deal of cross-borrowing and collating has taken place in the history of the *Chronicle* texts). A version from Peterborough was continued by two different scribes well into the twelfth century, providing an invaluable witness not only to the period of transition from English to Norman rule but also to the gradual shift of the English language from Old to Middle English.

It would be unwise to take every word of the *Chronicle* as a reliable or unbiased historical account, but it remains the most important source for our knowledge of Anglo-Saxon history. Among its sometimes bare annals are some sparks of political wisdom, narrative flair, historical insight, and even authorial wit; it offers not only a sturdy context in which to read Old English literature but a fascinating literary experience in itself.

⌘ ⌘ ⌘

from *The Anglo-Saxon Chronicle*[1]

A. The Coming of the Angles and Saxons to Britain (449–495)

449.[2] Here[3] Martianus and Valentinian succeeded to the empire, and reigned seven winters. In their days Hengest and Horsa,[4] invited by Vortigern, king of the Britons, landed in Britain in a place that is called

---

[1] *The Anglo-Saxon Chronicle* The present text, prepared by R.M. Liuzza for this volume, draws on various manuscripts; most entries follow the text of the Peterborough Chronicle (known as E to scholars) or the Winchester text (A). The translation draws heavily on those by James Ingram (1823) and J.A. Giles (1847); the translation of Michael Swanton (2000) has also been consulted.

[2] *449* This story of the arrival of the Angles and Saxons is mostly from Bede's *Ecclesiastical History* with a few added details presumably from popular legend or local tradition.

[3] *Here* Each year's entry begins with the word "here," i.e., "in this place on the page," reflecting the origins of the work as a series of annotations in annals.

[4] *Hengest and Horsa* Both names mean "horse" in Old English and are probably not their given names.

Ipwin's-fleet;[1] first of all to support the Britons, but they later fought against them. The king directed them to fight against the Picts, and they did so, winning victory wherever they went. They then sent word to Angeln[2] asking them to send more assistance; they described the worthlessness of the Britons and the richness of the land. They then sent them greater support—the men came from three powers of Germany: the Old Saxons, the Angles, and the Jutes. From the Jutes are descended the men of Kent, the Wightware—that is, the tribe that now lives in the Isle of Wight—and that race in Wessex that is still called the race of the Jutes. From the Old Saxons came the East Saxons and the South Saxons and the West Saxons. From Angeln, which has remained a wasteland ever since between the Jutes and the Saxons, came the East Angles, the Middle Angles, the Mercians, and all of those north of the Humber. Their war-leaders were two brothers, Hengest and Horsa, the sons of Wihtgils; Wihtgils was the son of Witta, Witta the son of Wecta, Wecta the son of Woden.[3] From this Woden arose all our royal kindred, and that of the Southumbrians also.

455. Here Hengest and Horsa fought with Vortigern the king on the spot that is called Aylesford, and his brother Horsa was killed there. Hengest afterwards succeeded to the kingdom with his son Æsc.

457. Here Hengest and Æsc fought with the Britons in the place that is called Crayford, and there killed four thousand men. The Britons then abandoned the land of Kent, and in great terror fled to London.

465. Here Hengest and Æsc fought with the Welsh near Wipped's-fleet; and there killed twelve Welsh chieftains. On Hengest's side a thane[4] whose name was Wipped was killed there.

473. Here Hengest and Æsc fought with the Welsh, and took countless spoils. and the Welsh fled from the English like fire.

477. Here came Ælla to Britain with his three sons, Cymen, and Wlencing, and Cissa, in three ships. They landed at a place that is called Cymen's Shore, and there slew many Welsh and drove some in flight into the wood that is called Andredsley.[5]

485. Here Ælla fought with the Welsh near Mearcred's Burn.

488. Here Æsc succeeded to the kingdom, and was king of the men of Kent twenty-four winters.[6]

490. Here Ælla and Cissa besieged the city of Andred,[7] and killed everyone who lived there—not one Briton was left there afterwards.

495. Here came two leaders into Britain, Cerdic and his son Cynric, with five ships, at a place that is called Cerdic's Shore, and they fought with the Welsh that same day.[8]

B. THE STORY OF CYNEWULF AND CYNEHEARD (755)

755.[9] Here Cynewulf, with the consent of the West-Saxon council, deprived his relative Sigebriht of his kingdom, except Hampshire, because of his unrighteous deeds; and he retained Hampshire until he slew the ealdorman[10] who remained the longest with him. Then

---

[1] *Ipwin's-fleet* Modern Ebbsfleet in Kent.

[2] *Angeln* Narrow land between modern Germany and Denmark, roughly modern Schleswig.

[3] *Their war-leaders … Woden* Most Anglo-Saxon royal genealogies trace the king's family back to a god, presumably as a way of emphasizing the king's status and power; later the genealogy of the West Saxon kings will incorporate Biblical figures as well.

[4] *thane* Like a knight.

[5] *Andredsley* The Weald.

[6] *twenty-four winters* One manuscript reads "xxx.iiii." rather than "xx.iiii."

[7] *Andred* Roman coastal fort near Pevensey, Sussex.

[8] *Here came … same day* Cerdic is the leader of the West Saxons and ancestor of Alfred the Great.

[9] *755* This entry, whose source is unknown, suggests that long before their history was officially transcribed, prose tales of notable events circulated as part of Anglo-Saxon popular tradition. The story, whose chronology is unlike that of most other annals, is a finely-wrought and tightly-narrated saga in miniature, portraying conflicts between loyalty and power in desperate circumstances.

[10] *ealdorman* High-ranking nobleman.

Cynewulf drove him to the forest of Andred, and he remained there until a swineherd stabbed him by the stream at Privett—and the swineherd revenged the Ealdorman Cumbra.[1] The same Cynewulf fought many hard battles with the Welsh; and, about thirty-one winters after he had the kingdom, he wanted to expel a prince called Cyneheard, who was the brother of Sigebriht. And then he[2] learned that the king was gone with a small troop to visit a woman at Merton, and he rode after him, and surrounded the chamber from outside before the men who were with the king were aware of him.

When the king realized this, he went out the door and defended himself bravely until his eyes fell on the nobleman, and then he rushed out upon him and wounded him severely. Then they were all fighting against the king until they killed him. And then from the woman's screams the king's men became aware of the disturbance, and they ran to the spot, as quickly as they could get ready. The nobleman immediately offered each of them life and rewards, and none of them would accept it, but continued fighting until they all lay dead except for one British hostage, and he was severely wounded.

In the morning, the king's men who had been left behind heard that the king was slain. Then they rode to the spot—Osric his Ealdorman, and Wiferth his thane, and the men that he had left behind; and they met the nobleman at the enclosure[3] where the king lay dead. They had locked the gates against them, and they went up to them. He[4] promised them as much money and land as they wanted, if they would grant him the kingdom; and let them know that their kinsmen were already with him, who would never desert him. And then they said that no kinsman could be dearer to them than their lord, and they would never follow his murderer. Then they asked their kinsmen to depart from

him, safe and sound, and they replied that the same offer had been made to their companions who were with the king. They said that they would pay no more attention to that "than your companions did who were killed beside the king."[5] And they were fighting at the gates until they forced their way in and killed the nobleman and all the men who were with him, except one, who was the godson of the ealdorman,[6] and he spared his life, though he was often wounded.

This Cynewulf reigned thirty-one winters. His body lies at Winchester, and that of the nobleman at Axminster. Their paternal ancestry goes directly back to Cerdic.

C. KING ALFRED'S EARLY YEARS (871–78)

871.   Here the army[7] came to Reading in Wessex; and three nights afterwards two jarls[8] rode up; they were met by Ealdorman Æthelwulf at Englefield and fought with them, and obtained the victory. There one of them was slain, whose name was Sidroc. About four nights after this, King Æthelred and Alfred his brother led their main army to Reading, where they fought with the enemy; and there was much slaughter on either hand, Ealdorman Æthelwulf being among the slain; and the Danes held possession of the field. And about four nights after this, King Æthelred and Alfred his brother fought with all the army on Ashdown, and the Danes were overcome. They had two heathen kings, Bagsecg and Halfdan, and many jarls; and they were in two divisions, in one of which were Bagsecg and Halfdan, the heathen kings, and in the other were the jarls. King Æthelred fought with the troops of the kings, and King Bagsecg was killed; Alfred his brother fought with the troops of the jarls, and there Jarl Sidroc the Ealdorman, Jarl Sidroc the younger, Jarl Osbern, Jarl Frene, and Jarl Harold were killed. They put both troops to flight; there

---

[1] *Ealdorman Cumbra* I.e., the one whom Sigebriht had killed in Hampshire.

[2] *he* I.e., Cyneheard.

[3] *enclosure* The scene should be imagined as a small building (a *burh*) surrounded by a wall (a *byrig*). The king's fight took place inside the enclosure; the king's men ride up to the outside of it and fight there.

[4] *He* I.e., Cyneheard.

[5] *They said … the king* The dramatic shift from indirect to direct discourse is striking; it may well be a mark of the story's origins in oral tradition.

[6] *ealdorman* I.e., Osric.

[7] *Here the army* In *The Chronicle* "the army" (Old English *here*) almost always means the Vikings.

[8] *jarls* This spelling has been preferred to the modern English "earl" as a way of indicating its use within the *Chronicle*.

were many thousands killed, and they kept fighting until nightfall. Within two weeks, King Æthelred and Alfred his brother fought with the army at Basing, and there the Danes had the victory. About two months after this, King Æthelred and Alfred his brother fought with the army at Merton. They were in two bands, and they put them both to flight, and had the victory for most of the day; and there was much slaughter on either hand, but the Danes became masters of the field; and there Bishop Heahmund was killed, along with many other good men. After this fight came a vast army in the summer to Reading. And after the Easter of this year King Æthelred died. He reigned five years, and his body lies at Wimborne Minster.

Then Alfred, his brother, the son of Æthelwulf, became king of Wessex. And within a month of this, King Alfred fought against all the army with a small force at Wilton, and long pursued them during the day; but the Danes got possession of the field. In this year there were nine general battles fought with the army in the kingdom south of the Thames, besides those skirmishes in which Alfred the king's brother, and every single ealdorman, and the thanes of the king often rode against them, which were not counted. Here also were slain nine jarls, and one king; and the same year the West-Saxons made peace with the army.

872. Here the army went to London from Reading, and there chose their winter-quarters. Then the Mercians made peace with the army.

873. Here the army went against the Northumbrians, and fixed their winter quarters at Torksey in Lindsey. And the Mercians again made peace with the army.

874. Here the army went from Lindsey to Repton, and there took winter quarters, and drove the king, Burhred, across the sea, when he had reigned about twenty-two winters, and subdued all that land. He then went to Rome, and there remained to the end of his life. And his body lies in the church of St. Mary, in the English Quarter. And the same year they gave Ceolwulf, a foolish king's thane, the kingdom of Mercia to hold; and he swore oaths to them, and gave hostages, that it should be ready for them whenever they wanted it, and

he would be ready with himself, and with all those that would remain with him, at the service of the army.

875. Here the army went from Repton; and Halfdan advanced with some of the army against the Northumbrians, and fixed his winter-quarters by the river Tine. The army then subdued that land, and often raided among the Picts and the Britons of Strathclyde. Meanwhile the three kings, Guthrum, Oscytel, and Anwind, went from Repton to Cambridge with a vast army, and settled there for one year. And that summer King Alfred went out to sea with an armed fleet, and fought against seven ships, and captured one of them and dispersed the others.

876. Here the army stole into Wareham, a fort of the West-Saxons. The king afterwards made peace with them; and they gave him as hostages those who were worthiest in the army; and swore with oaths on the holy bracelet, which they had never done before to any nation, that they would quickly go from his kingdom. Then, under cover of this, their cavalry stole by night into Exeter. The same year Halfdan divided the land of the Northumbrians, so that they were ploughing and providing for themselves.

877. Here the Danish army came into Exeter from Wareham, while the navy sailed west until they met with a great storm at sea, and 120 ships were lost at Swanage. Meanwhile King Alfred with his army rode after the cavalry as far as Exeter; but he could not overtake them before their arrival in the fortress, where they could not be attacked. There they gave him as many hostages as he required, swearing with solemn oaths to hold the strictest peace. In the fall the army entered Mercia, and divided some of it among themselves, and gave some to Ceolwulf.

878. Here about mid-winter, after twelfth-night, the Danish army stole out to Chippenham, and rode over the land of the West-Saxons and occupied it, driving many of the people over sea; and the greatest part of the others they rode down and subdued to their will, except for Alfred the king, who went with a little band with great difficulty into the woods and fastnesses of the

moors. And in the winter of this same year a brother of Ivar and Halfdan landed in Wessex, in Devonshire, with twenty-three ships, and was killed there, and eight hundred men with him, and forty of his army. There also was taken the banner which they called "The Raven." In the Easter of this year King Alfred with his little force raised a stronghold at Athelney, from which he assailed the army, assisted by that part of Somersetshire which was nearest to it. Then, in the seventh week after Easter, he rode to Brixton by the eastern side of Selwood, and there came out to meet him all the people of Somerset, and Wiltshire, and that part of Hampshire which is on this side of the sea; and they were very glad to see him. Then within one night he went from this retreat to Hey; and within one night after he proceeded to Heddington; and there fought with all the army and put them to flight, riding after them as far as the fortress, where he remained a fortnight. Then the army gave him hostages, and swore with many oaths that they would go out of his kingdom. They told him also that their king would receive baptism, and they fulfilled that promise. Three weeks later King Guthrum, attended by some thirty of the worthiest men in his army, came to the king at Aller, which is near Athelney, and there the king became his sponsor in baptism; and his chrism-loosing[1] was at Wedmore. He was there twelve nights with the king, who honored him and his companions with many gifts.

D. KING ÆTHELRED'S TROUBLES (980–93)

980. In this year on the 2nd of May Æthelgar was consecrated bishop for the bishopric of Selsey; and in the same year Southampton was plundered by a raiding ship-army, and most of the population slain or imprisoned. And the same year the Isle of Thanet was overrun, and the county of Chester was plundered by the raiding ship-army of the North.

981. In this year St. Petroc's-stow was plundered; and in the same year much harm was done everywhere along the sea-coast, both in Devonshire and Cornwall.

982. In this year three ships of Vikings came up in Dorsetshire and plundered in Portland. The same year London was burned. And in the same year died two ealdormen, Æthelmær in Hampshire and Edwin in Sussex. Æthelmær's body lies in the New Minster at Winchester, and Edwin's in the monastery at Abingdon. …

987. Here the port of Watchet was plundered.

988. Here Goda, the thane of Devonshire, was slain, and a great number with him; and Dunstan, the holy archbishop, departed this life, and sought a heavenly one. Bishop Æthelgar succeeded him in the archbishopric; but he lived only a little while after, one year and three months.

989. Here Abbot Edwin died, and Abbot Wulfgar succeeded to the abbacy. Sigeric was ordained archbishop this year, and went to Rome to receive his pallium.[2]

991. Here Ipswich was plundered; and very soon afterwards Ealdorman Byrhtnoth was slain at Maldon. In this same year it was decided that tribute should be given for the first time to the Danes, because of the great terror they caused along the sea-coast. That was at first 10,000 pounds. Archbishop Sigeric first advised this measure.

992. Here the blessed Archbishop Oswald departed this life, and sought a heavenly one; and in the same year died Ealdorman Æthelwin. Then the king and all his council resolved that all the ships that were of any account should be gathered together at London; and the king placed the army under the command of Ealdorman Ælfric, and Earl Thorod, and Bishop Ælfstan, and Bishop Æscwig, and told them that they should try to find a way to entrap the enemy. Then Ealdorman Ælfric sent and gave warning to the enemy; and on the night preceding the day of battle he scuttled away from the army, to his great disgrace. The enemy then escaped, except for the crew of one ship, who were slain on the

---

[1] *chrism-loosing* Ceremony which takes place a week after baptism.

[2] *pallium* Vestment, like a stole, bestowed by the pope on an archbishop as a sign of his office.

spot. Then the enemy met the ships from East Anglia and from London; and a great slaughter was made there, and they took the ship, all armed and rigged, that held the ealderman. Then after the death of Archbishop Oswald, Ealdwulf, Abbot of Peterborough, succeeded to the sees[1] of York and of Worcester; and Cenwulf to the abbacy of Peterborough.

993. Here in this year Bamburgh was destroyed, and much plunder was there taken. Afterwards the army came to the mouth of the Humber, and did much evil both in Lindsey and in Northumbria. Then a very great army was gathered, but when the armies should have come together, the generals were the first to set the example of flight; namely, Fræne and Godwin and Frithugist. In this same year the king ordered Ælfgar, son of Ealderman Ælfric, to be blinded.

994. Here in this year Olaf and Swein came to London, on the feast of the Nativity of St. Mary, with ninety-four ships, and they closely besieged the city, and they also wanted to set it on fire; but there they suffered more harm and evil than they ever supposed any citizens could inflict on them. The Holy Mother of God on that day showed her mercy to the citizens, and rescued them from their enemies. They went from there and wrought the greatest evil that ever any army could do, in burning and plundering and manslaughter, not only on the seacoast in Essex, but in Kent and in Sussex and in Hampshire. Next they took themselves horses, and rode as widely as they wanted, and committed unspeakable evil. Then the king and his council resolved to send to them and offer them tribute and provision if they would stop their plunder. They accepted the terms, and the whole army came to Southampton, and there set up their winter quarters; they were fed by all the subjects of the West-Saxon kingdom, and were paid 16,000 pounds. Then the king sent Bishop Ælfeah and Ealderman Æthelweard after king Olaf, and left hostages with the ships; they led Olaf with great pomp to the king at Andover. And King Æthelred received him at the bishops' hands, and honored him with royal gifts. In return Olaf promised—and he fulfilled that prom-

ise—that he would never come back to England in a hostile manner.

E. THE LIFE AND DEATH OF
WILLIAM THE CONQUEROR (1086)

1086. One thousand and eighty-seven winters after the birth of our Lord and Savior Jesus Christ, in the twenty-first year after William began to govern and direct England, as God granted him, there was a very heavy and pestilent season in this land. Such a sickness came on men that nearly every other man had the worst disorder, that is, a fever, and so dreadfully that many men died from it. Afterwards, through the bad weather we mentioned, came so great a famine over all England that many hundreds of men died a miserable death through hunger. Alas! how wretched and how rueful a time was there! When poor wretches lay nearly driven to premature death, and then came sharp hunger to dispatch them completely! Who will not be pierced with grief at such a season? or who is so hardhearted as not to weep at such misfortune? Yet such things happen for the sins of the people, who will not love God and righteousness. So it was in those days, that little righteousness was in this land among any men except the monks alone, wherever they fared well. The king and the powerful men loved much, and too much, covetousness in gold and in silver; and did not care how sinfully it was obtained, provided it came to them. The king leased his land at the highest rate he possibly could; then came some other person, and offered more than the former, and the king leased it to the man that offered him more. Then came a third, and offered even more, and the king leased it to whomever offered most of all; and he did not care how very sinfully the stewards got it from wretched men, nor how many unlawful deeds they did; but the more men talked about just law, the more unjustly they acted. They raised unjust tolls, and many other unjust things they did, that are difficult to reckon.

Also in the same year, before harvest, the holy minster[2] of St. Paul, the episcopal see in London, was completely burned, with many other minsters, and the greatest and richest part of the whole city. So also, about the same time, almost every chief port in England was

---

[1] *sees* Cities in which bishops or archbishops reside and have authority.

[2] *minster* Church.

entirely burned. Alas! rueful and woeful was the fate of the year that brought forth so many misfortunes. In the same year also, before the Feast of the Assumption, King William went from Normandy into France with an army, and made war upon his own lord King Philip, and killed many of his men, and burned the town of Mante, and all the holy minsters that were in the town; and two holy men that served God, living in anchorite's[1] cells, were burned there. This being done, King William returned to Normandy. He did a pitiful thing, but an even more pitiful thing befell him. How more pitiful? He fell sick and was severely afflicted.

What shall I say? Sharp death, that spares neither rich men nor poor, seized him also. He died in Normandy, the day after the Nativity of St. Mary, and he was buried at Caen in St. Stephen's minster, which he had formerly raised, and afterwards endowed with many gifts. Alas! how false and how uncertain is this world's fortune! He that was before a rich king, and lord of many lands, then had no more land than a space of seven feet! and he that was once enshrouded in gold and gems lay there covered with dirt! He left behind him three sons: the eldest, called Robert, who was earl in Normandy after him; the second, called William, who wore the crown after him in England; and the third, called Henry, to whom his father bequeathed immense treasure.

If any person wants to know what kind of man he was, or what honor he had, or of how many lands he was lord, then we will write about him as well as we understand him: we who often looked upon him, and once lived in his court. This King William we speak of was a very wise man, and very rich; more splendid and powerful than any before him. He was mild to the good men that loved God, and harsh beyond all measure to men that opposed his will. On that same spot where God granted that he should gain England, he raised a mighty minster, and set monks therein, and endowed it well. In his days the great monastery in Canterbury was built, and also very many others over all England. This land was moreover well filled with monks, who modeled their lives after the rule of St. Benedict,[2] and such was

the state of Christianity in his time that each man who wanted to followed what pertained to his order.

He was also very dignified. Three times each year he wore his crown, as often as he was in England. At Easter he wore it in Winchester, at Pentecost in Westminster, at midwinter in Gloucester. And then with him were all the rich men over all England, archbishops and bishops, abbots and earls, thanes and knights. He was also a very stern man, and very hot-tempered, such that no man dared do anything against his will. He had earls in his bonds who acted against his will; bishops he threw from their bishoprics, and abbots from their abbeys, and thanes into prison. At length he did not spare his own brother Odo, who was a very rich bishop in Normandy. His bishopric was at Bayeux, and he was the foremost man of all next to the king. He had an earldom in England, and when the king was in Normandy, he was the mightiest man in this land: William confined him to prison. But among other things it should not be forgotten that he made good peace in this land, so that a man who was of any status might travel all over his kingdom, even with his pockets full of gold, unharmed. No man dared to slay another, no matter how much evil he had done to the other, and if any churl[3] lay with a woman against her will, he soon lost the same limb that he played with.

William truly reigned over England, and in his astuteness so thoroughly surveyed it that there was not a hide of land in England that he did not know who owned it, or what it was worth, and afterwards set it down in his book. The land of the Britons was in his power; and he built castles within it; and controlled that nation. So also he subdued Scotland by his great strength. Normandy was his native land, but he ruled also over the earldom of Maine; and if he might have lived two years more, he would have won Ireland by his shrewdness without any weapons. Assuredly in his time had men much distress, and very many sorrows.

Castles he had built, and crushed the poor.
The king himself was very stark,
and seized from his subjects many marks
of gold, and many hundred pounds of silver;

---

[1] *anchorite* Hermit.

[2] *rule of St. Benedict* Monastic rule, i.e., for the ordering of monastic life, composed by St. Benedict (480–543), founder of the monastic Order of St. Benedict.

[3] *churl* Man without noble rank; at this time, a serf (following the Conquest).

which he took of his people, for little need, justly and
  unjustly.
He was fallen into avarice, and loved greed above all.
He made many deer-parks, and set laws for them;
so that whosoever slew a hart, or a hind,[1]
should be blinded.
He forbade hunting of harts, and also of boars;
and he loved the tall deer as if he were their father.
Likewise he decreed that the hares should go free.
His rich men bemoaned it, and the poor men
  complained of it.
But he was so stern that he cared nothing about the
  hatred of them all;
for they must follow the king's will,
if they wanted to live, or have land,
or possessions, or even his peace.
Alas! that any man should presume to puff himself up so,
and boast over all men.
May the Almighty God have mercy on his soul,
and grant him forgiveness of his sins!

We have written these things concerning him, both
good and evil, so that men may choose the good after
their goodness, and flee from the evil entirely, and go
in the way that leads us to the kingdom of heaven.

    We could write many things that were done in this
same year. So it was in Denmark that the Danes, a
nation that was formerly accounted the truest of all,
were turned aside to the greatest untruth, and to the
greatest treachery that ever could be. They chose and
submitted to King Cnut, and swore him oaths, and
afterwards basely killed him in a church. It happened
also in Spain that the heathens went and made inroads
upon the Christians, and reduced much of the country to their dominion. But the king of the Christians,
who was called Alfonso, sent everywhere into each
land asking for assistance. And they came to his
support from every Christian land, and killed or drove
out all the heathen folk, and won their land again,
with God's assistance. In this land also, in the same
year, many rich men died: Stigand, Bishop of
Chichester, and the Abbot of St. Augustine, and the
Abbot of Bath, and the Abbot of Pershore, and the
lord of them all, William, King of England, that we
spoke of before. After his death his son, also called
William, took to the kingdom, and was consecrated
king by Archbishop Lanfranc at Westminster three
days before Michaelmas. And all the men in England
submitted to him, and swore oaths to him. When this
was done the king went to Winchester, and inspected
the treasury and the treasures that his father had
gathered: gold, and silver, and vases, and purple cloth,
and gems, and many other valuable things that are
difficult to enumerate. Then the king did as his father
asked him before his death, and distributed treasures
for his father's soul to each monastery that was in
England; to some he gave ten marks of gold, to some
six, to each country church sixty pence. And into each
shire were sent a hundred pounds of money to distribute to the poor, for William's soul. And before he died
he commanded that they should release all the men
that were in prison under his power. And the king was
in London that midwinter.

—9TH–11TH CENTURIES

---

[1] *hart, or a hind* Male or female deer, stag or doe.

Preface to a manuscript of the *Anglo-Saxon Chronicle*
England, Peterborough Abbey, c. 1121 (Bodleian, Ms. Laud 636).

ALFRED THE GREAT, KING OF WESSEX
849 – 899

When Alfred became ruler of the West Saxons (871–99) his kingdom had been reduced and threatened by wave upon wave of Viking attacks; at one point he was forced to hide in the Somerset marshes to avoid capture. He ended his reign as a wealthy and successful "King of the Anglo-Saxons"—first by negotiating peace with his enemies and arranging the baptism of the Viking leader Guthrum, and then by strengthening the system of garrisons and military service, and building up the English naval forces. Alfred also extended his power beyond the boundaries of his own West Saxon kingdom into Mercia and the southeast, gaining control of neighboring kingdoms through a series of alliances and military coalitions. For keeping England from being placed entirely under Viking control, and for his wise and clever use of the powers of church and state to secure, strengthen and expand his kingdom, Alfred has long been called "The Great."

Part of his reputation rests on his support of learning and the arts. Most kings are presumed to have had scribes for writing documents and singer/poets for entertainment; in Alfred's court literary and artistic activity was far more extensive. Somewhat in the manner of Charlemagne, Alfred gathered to his court an assembly of international scholars and clerics who worked with him to promote English as a language of learning, teaching, religion and government. It is remarkable to consider (as Alfred himself does in some of his writings) that the ruler of a busy and often threatened kingdom would often spend whatever spare moments he had with a tutor, laboriously reading and translating Latin. But his biographer Asser testifies to Alfred's lifelong practices of prayer and study, and he undoubtedly recognized the need to rebuild the intellectual foundations of England after nearly a century of decline. Education in English was, he argued, both necessary (due to the dismal condition of Latin learning in England) and useful for promoting new values and ideas to a broader audience. It is generally agreed that Alfred himself translated Boethius's *Consolation of Philosophy*, St. Augustine's *Soliloquies*, and the first fifty Psalms; in each of these works he presumably relied on the advice of a circle of scholars and assistants, but each bears his distinctive, somewhat discursive style and characteristic vocabulary. It is likely that Alfred commissioned the translation of other works, including Bede's *Ecclesiastical History*, Orosius's *Historiae adversus paganos* (a work of world history showing how God's Providence has guided the fates of nations), and the *Dialogues* of Gregory the Great (a collection of stories of the miracles of the saints). Alfred was also undoubtedly responsible for initiating the *Anglo-Saxon Chronicle* and for commissioning his own biography.

For Alfred, as of course for most people in his day, there was no "separation of church and state"—a well-run kingdom was built upon Christian principles, and the public good depended on the ruler's piety. Alfred's law code was founded on the Biblical Ten Commandments, and when he announced his policy of promoting translation of important works of learning—what he calls "those books most necessary for all men to know"—into English, he began with Pope Gregory the Great's *Regula Pastoralis* ("Pastoral Care"), a handbook for bishops and priests. For Alfred, the work was a "how-to" manual for those in power, a compelling vision of how the social and moral diversity of society might be put in order by wise rulers and by a conflation of duty and devotion that would make spiritual development almost a civic obligation and "pastoral care" a model of political organization. In the prefatory letter attached to this translation Alfred justifies and explains his policy on vernacular education: bishops were expected to require their priests to be more learned, and royal officials were required to learn to read, or they would lose their positions.

King Alfred is responsible as much as any single person could be for the development of English into a language that could be used for literary and public documents, a language that soon came to be perceived as a worthy companion to Latin. If Bede imagined the "English People" united by their common faith, Alfred worked to build a "Kingdom of the English" around their common language. The policy set out in Alfred's "Preface" to the *Pastoral Care* was apparently somewhat unevenly applied during his own lifetime, but it laid the groundwork for a great flowering of learning—much of it created or preserved in English—in the next century.

⌘ ⌘ ⌘

Alfred's "Preface" to the Old English Version of Gregory the Great's Pastoral Care

King Alfred bids Bishop Wærferth to be greeted with his loving and friendly words;[1] and bids you know that it has come very often to my mind what wise men there once were throughout England,[2] both in the sacred and the secular orders; and how happy the times were then throughout England; and how the kings who had power over the people in those days were obedient to God and His ministers; and they maintained their peace, morality and power within their borders, and also enlarged their kingdom abroad; and how they prospered both in war and in wisdom; and also the sacred orders, how zealous they were about teaching, learning, and all the services that they should do for God; and how men from abroad sought wisdom and learning in this land, and how we now have had to acquire them from abroad if we would have them at all. It[3] was so completely decayed in England that there were very few on this side of the Humber[4] who could understand their services in English,[5] or even translate a letter from Latin into English; and I think that there were not many beyond the Humber. There were so few of them that I cannot think of even a single one south of the Thames when I first came to the throne. Thanks be to Almighty God that we now have any supply of teachers. Therefore I command you to do, as I believe you wish to do, that you empty yourself of worldly affairs as often as you can, so that wherever you can apply the wisdom that God gave you, you eagerly apply it. Consider what punishments befell us in this world when we neither loved it[6] ourselves, nor left it to others; we loved only the name of Christians, and very few of the practices.

Then when I remembered all this, then I also remembered how I saw, before it had all been ravaged and burnt,[7] how the churches throughout all England stood filled with treasures and books, and also a great many of God's servants; and they had very little benefit from those books, because they could not understand anything in them, because they were not written in their own language. It is as if they had said, "Our elders, who formerly held these places, loved wisdom, and through it they obtained riches and left it to us. Here we can still see their tracks, but we cannot follow after them. And therefore we have now lost both the wealth and the wisdom, because we would not bend down to their tracks with our minds." Then when I remembered all this, then I wondered greatly at the good wise men who were once throughout England, and who had completely learned all those books, that they would not translate any part of them into their own language. But I answered myself at once and said: "They did not think that men would ever become so careless and learning so decayed: they deliberately avoided it, and intended that

---

[1] *King Alfred … words* The letter begins formally in the third person but shifts quickly to a more personal voice.

[2] *England* Alfred consistently calls his kingdom *angelcynn*, "the race of the Angles," though he himself was a Saxon.

[3] *It* I.e., Wisdom.

[4] *Humber* River in northern England.

[5] *who … English* Either the mass or the monastic Liturgy of the Hours, both said in Latin throughout the Middle Ages (and well into the modern age).

[6] *it* I.e., Wisdom.

[7] *it had all … burnt* By the Vikings, whose attacks began in 793 and continued in waves of increasing frequency and ferocity to Alfred's own day.

the more languages we knew, the more wisdom would be here in this land."

Then I remembered how the law[1] was first established in the Hebrew language, and afterwards, when the Greeks learned it, they turned it all into their own language, and also all other books;[2] and later likewise the Romans, when they had learned them, turned all of them through wise translators into their own language. And also all other Christian peoples turned some part of them into their own language. Therefore it seems better to me, if it seems so to you, that we also turn certain books which are most necessary for all people to know into that language that we all can understand, and bring it about, as we very easily may with God's help (if we have peace), that all the youth of free men now in England who have the means to apply themselves to it, be set to learning, as long as they cannot be set to any other use, until the time when they know well how to read English writing. One may further teach in Latin those whom one wishes to teach further, and wants to promote to a higher order.[3]

Then when I remembered before this time how the knowledge of the Latin language was decayed through-out England, and yet many knew how to read English writing, I began among the other various and manifold duties of this kingdom to turn into English the book that is called in Latin *Pastoralis*, and in English *Shepherd's Book*, sometimes word for word, sometimes sense for sense, just as I had learned it from Plegmund my archbishop and from Asser my bishop and from Grimbold my masspriest and from John my masspriest. After I had learned it, I translated it into English, just as I understood it and as I could most meaningfully construe it. And I wish to send one to each bishopric in my kingdom, and in each will be an *æstel*[4] worth fifty mancuses. And I command in God's name that no one take the *æstel* from the book nor the book from the church; it is unknown how long there may be such learned bishops as now, thanks be to God, are nearly everywhere. Therefore I would like it always to be in that place, unless the bishop wishes to have it with him, or it is loaned out somewhere, or someone is making a copy of it.

—LATE 9TH CENTURY

---

[1] *law* I.e., the Law of Moses, the *Torah* or first five books of the Bible.

[2] *all other books* I.e., the other books of the Bible. Like many medieval writers, Alfred is not consistent in referring to the Bible as singular or plural. The Bible was both one book and many.

[3] *higher order* I.e., the religious life of the priesthood or monastery.

[4] *æstel* Usually thought to be a kind of pointer used to keep one's place while reading a book. A pointer worth fifty mancuses (one mancus was worth 30 silver pennies) would be very valuable. The intricately inlaid piece known as the Alfred Jewel in the Ashmolean Museum in Oxford may be the surviving knob of such an "æstel," with the shaft of its wooden pointer now lost.

The beginning of Alfred's "Preface" to the translation of *Pastoral Care* (Ms. [Manuscript] Hatton 20, folio 1r).

ÆLFRIC OF EYNSHAM

c. 945 – ca. 1010

Æ lfric, monk of Cerne Abbas in Dorset and later abbot of the monastery of Eynsham in Oxfordshire, was a prolific writer of homilies, sermons, and saints' lives. He was born around 945, just at the beginning of a tenth-century monastic reform movement that fostered a renaissance in arts and letters in later Anglo-Saxon England. Inspired by developments on the Continent, the Benedictine reformers in England founded new monasteries and rebuilt and reorganized old ones; a close alliance between the king and the clergy, and a period of relative peace and national unity, created an environment rich in material and intellectual wealth. It was during this period, roughly the second half of the tenth century, that the manuscripts containing most of the surviving Old English poetry were copied, and many works translated from Latin into English including the *Rule of St. Benedict* and several books of the Bible. Ælfric was educated at the Cathedral school of Winchester under Abbot Æthelwold, one of the leaders of the reform movement; his prodigious literary output reflects the high standards of pastoral care, doctrinal accuracy, scholarship and stylistic fluency that he learned there.

In the last decade of the tenth century, however, England entered a period of decline. King Æthelred suffered military defeats during a new wave of Danish invasions, treachery among his demoralized advisors, and a loss of support from rich landowners and noblemen. Unlike his contemporary Wulfstan, Ælfric was not really active in the royal centers of power; instead he spent his career in relatively isolated monasteries which had been founded by his patrons, the nobleman Æthelweard and his son Æthelmær. Before his death sometime around 1010 Ælfric wrote many works, most of them in connection with his monastic and pastoral duties as teacher and preacher: two long series of homilies to be read on Sundays and major feasts throughout the year, many lives of saints for liturgical and private reading, translations of parts of the Bible, a Latin grammar in English, a *Colloquy* or conversational exercise for teaching Latin, and other pedagogical and pastoral works. But it would be wrong to imagine that Ælfric was unaware of or untroubled by the political decline that was evident around the turn of the millennium. Often, as in the saint's life translated below, his works deal with urgent issues of war and peace, violence and sanctity, heroism and right government—questions that must have been on many minds as Æthelred's kingship gradually crumbled into ruin.

Ælfric's *Life of St. Edmund* commemorates a king of the East Angles who was killed by the Danes in 869 and whose martyrdom was celebrated on 20 November. Ælfric's source is the Latin *Passio Sancti Edmundi* by Abbo of Fleury (c. 945–1004), reworked by Ælfric in an elaborate rhythmical prose style as an expression of a Christian ideal of kingship. Ælfric is careful to anchor the saint's legend in plausible historical report, tracing the story back to its source or relying on common consensus to justify his extraordinary claims for Edmund's power. The story is evenly divided between accounts of the saint's death and tales of his miraculous power after death; the miracles of the saints, signs of God's favor, were regarded as a proof of the truth of Christianity as opposed to the violent paganism of the Vikings and what Ælfric regarded as the stubbornness of the Jews. (Though it is not likely that there were any actual Jews in England during Ælfric's time, they served as a powerful metaphor for those who could accept Christianity but refused to do so.)

As Ælfric tells it, Edmund's story reminds his audience that even among the English, and even in the secular world, there are figures of ideal holiness worthy of remembrance, just as there are ideal figures like Beowulf to represent the highest values of the heroic life. Edmund's paradoxically heroic act of refusing to fight his enemies placed him in the company of other great saints—and, of course, for any Christian, the greatest exemplary figure of all, Jesus Christ. In a country threatened by war, and a culture rooted in ideals of violent, heroic self-assertion, this image of kingship as (literal) sacrifice may have offered a puzzling but powerful alternative to the political realities of the day.

⌘⌘⌘

The Passion of Saint Edmund, King and Martyr[1]

A certain very learned monk came from the south over the sea from St. Benedict's place, in the days of King Æthelred, to Archbishop Dunstan three years before he died; the monk was named Abbo. They were in conversation; Dunstan related the story of St. Edmund, just as Edmund's sword-bearer had related it to King Athelstan when Dunstan was a young man and the sword-bearer was a very old man. Then the monk set down that whole narrative in a book, and afterward, when the book came to us a few years later, we translated it into English, just as appears below. Within two years, the monk Abbo returned home to his monastery, and was quickly appointed abbot of the same monastery.

The blessed Edmund, King of the East Angles, was wise and honorable, and always honored Almighty God with noble customs. He was humble and virtuous, and remained so steadfast that he would not turn to shameful sins, nor turn away on either side from his good practices, but was always mindful of that true teaching, "You are appointed ruler? do not exalt yourself, but be among men as one of them."[2] He was generous to the poor and widows like a father, and with benevolence always guided his people to righteousness, restrained the violent, and lived blessedly in the true faith.

It eventually happened that the Danish people came with their fleet, pillaging and killing throughout the land, as is their custom. The principal leaders of the fleet were Ivar and Ubbi, united by the devil, and they landed in Northumbria with warships, and laid waste the land and killed the people. Then Ivar turned eastwards with his ships, and Ubbi remained in Northumbria, having won the victory with his savagery. Then Ivar came sailing to the East Angles in the year when Prince Alfred, who later became the famous king of the West Saxons, was twenty-one. Ivar violently prowled about the land like a wolf, and slew the people, men and women and innocent children, and shamefully tormented the innocent Christians.

He then immediately sent the King a boastful message that he must submit to his service, if he cared for his life. The messenger came to King Edmund and quickly announced Ivar's message: "Ivar our King, brave and victorious on sea and land, has command of many people, and has now suddenly landed here with an army so that he might have winter quarters here with his troops. He now commands you to share your hidden treasures and your ancestral wealth with him without delay, and be his under-king, if you wish to live, for you do not have the power to resist him."

Then, indeed, King Edmund summoned a bishop who was nearby and considered with him how he should answer the fierce Ivar. The bishop was afraid for the King's life in this sudden turn of events, and said that it seemed advisable to him that he should submit to what Ivar demanded of him. Then the King fell silent and looked at the ground, and then said regally to him: "Alas, Bishop! the wretched people of this land are treated shamefully, and I would rather fall in battle, so long as my people could enjoy their native land." And the bishop said, "Alas, dear King! your people lie slain, and you do not have the forces to be able to fight, and these pirates will come and bind you alive, unless you save your life by fleeing, or save yourself by submitting to them." Then King Edmund said, very brave as he was: "I desire and wish in my heart that I alone should not survive after my dear thanes, who have been violently slain in their beds with their children and wives by these pirates. It has never been my custom to flee, but I would rather die, if I must, for my own land, and the Almighty God knows that I will never turn away from his service nor from his true love, whether I live or die."

After these words he turned to the messenger whom Ivar had sent to him and said to him, undaunted:

---

[1] *The Passion of Saint Edmund King and Martyr* Translated by R.M. Liuzza for *The Broadview Anthology of British Literature.*

[2] *You are ... them* See Ecclesiasticus 32.1.

"Indeed you would be now worthy of death, but I will not defile my clean hands with your foul blood, because I follow Christ, who gave us such an example; and I will gladly be slain by you if God so decrees it. Go now very quickly and tell your fierce lord, 'Edmund will never in his life submit to Ivar, a heathen chieftain, unless he first submit with faith to Christ the Savior in this land.'"

Then the messenger went away quickly and met the bloodthirsty Ivar along the way, hastening to Edmund with all his band, and told the dishonorable man how he had been answered. Then Ivar boldly commanded the army that they should seize only the King, who had despised his commands, and bind him quickly. And then, indeed, King Edmund, when Ivar came, stood within his hall, mindful of the Savior, and threw away his weapons; he wished to imitate the example of Christ, who forbade Peter to fight with weapons against the bloodthirsty Jews.[1] And then, indeed, these dishonorable men bound Edmund and insulted him shamefully and beat him with cudgels, and afterwards led the faithful King to a tree set fast in the earth and tied him to it with strong bonds, and again lashed him with whips for a long time; and he constantly cried out, between the strokes, with true faith to Christ the Savior. And then the heathens, because of his faith, became furiously angry, because he called on Christ to help him. They shot at him with spears, as if for their sport, until he was entirely covered by their shots like the bristles of a hedgehog, just as Sebastian was.[2]

When Ivar, the wicked pirate, saw that the noble King would not forsake Christ, but with steadfast faith continually cried out to Him, he commanded him to be beheaded, and the heathens did so. While he was still calling out to Christ, the heathens dragged the holy man to his death, and struck off his head with one blow, and his soul went blessed to Christ. There was a certain man nearby, kept hidden from the heathens by God, who overheard all this and afterwards told it, just as we tell it here.

Then, indeed, the pirates went back to their ship,

and hid the head of holy Edmund in thick brambles, so that it would not be buried. Then after a while, when they had gone away, the people of that land—those who were left—came to the place where their lord's headless body lay, and they were very sorry in their hearts for his death, and more so because they did not have the head for the body. Then the eyewitness who had seen it said that the pirates took the head with them, and it seemed to him, as indeed was very true, that they had hidden the head somewhere in the woods.

Then they all went together into the woods, searching everywhere through bushes and brambles, to see if they could find the head anywhere. It was also a great wonder that a wolf was sent by the guidance of God to guard the head day and night against other wild beasts. Then they went searching and continually crying out, as people who often go into the woods always do, "Where are you now, companion?" and the head answered them: "Here, here, here!" And so it called out frequently, answering them all whenever any of them called, until by means of that shouting they all came to it. There lay the gray wolf that watched over the head, and between his two paws he clasped the head, greedy and hungry, and did not dare, for God's sake, to taste the head, but guarded it against wild beasts. They were amazed at the wolf's care, and carried the holy head home with them, thanking the Almighty for all His wonders. But the wolf followed along with the head until they came to the village, as if he were tame, and then he turned back to the woods. The people of the land afterwards laid the head beside the holy body and buried it as best they could in such haste, and immediately built a church above it.

Eventually, many years later, when the pillaging stopped and peace was granted to the afflicted people, they banded together and built a church worthy of the saint, because miracles had frequently taken place at his grave in the chapel where he was buried. They wished to transport the holy body with public ceremony and lay it inside the church. It was great wonder then that he was just as whole as if he were alive, with an uncorrupted body, and his neck was healed which had been severed, and there was something like a red silken thread around his neck, to show people how he had been slain. Likewise the wounds which the bloodthirsty heathens had

---

[1] *And then ... Jews* See John 18.10–11.

[2] *They shot ... Sebastian was* St. Sebastian, whose feast is celebrated on 20 January, was a Roman soldier who was martyred under the Emperor Diocletian. According to legend he was riddled with arrows by a team of archers—but he recovered from this ordeal and returned to the Emperor, who then ordered him to be beaten to death with cudgels.

made on his body with their repeated shots had been healed by the Heavenly God; and he lies uncorrupted like this until this present day, awaiting the resurrection and eternal glory. His body, which lies undecayed, shows us that he lived here in the world without fornication, and journeyed to Christ with a pure life. A certain widow named Oswyn dwelt at the saint's tomb in prayers and fasting for many years afterwards; she would cut the saint's hair every year and pare his nails carefully with devotion, and keep them in a shrine as relics on the altar. So the people of that region venerated the saint with true faith, and Bishop Theodred richly endowed the church with gifts of gold and silver, in honor of the saint.

There came at a certain time eight unlucky thieves one night to the reverend saint, wishing to steal the treasures people had brought there, and craftily conniving how they might get in. One struck the hasps hard with a sledgehammer, one of them filed around them with a rasp, one even dug under the door with a spade, one of them with a ladder tried to unlock the window, but they toiled in vain and fared miserably, because the holy man miraculously bound them, each one as he stood there struggling with his tool, so that none of them could commit his crime, nor escape, but they stood in that manner until morning. People were amazed at how the criminals were hanging—one on a ladder, one bending down to dig, each bound fast in his labor. Then they were all brought to the bishop, who commanded that they should all hang on a high gallows; but he was not mindful how the merciful God spoke through his prophet these words that stand here, *Eos qui ducuntur ad mortem eruere ne cesses,* "always release those who are led to death";[1] and also the holy canons forbid those in holy orders, both bishops and priests, to concern themselves with thieves, for it is not fitting that those who are chosen to serve God should have a hand in any man's death, if they are the Lord's servants. Later, when Bishop Theodred had examined his books, he repented with lamentation that he had passed such a cruel sentence on the unfortunate thieves, and he always regretted it until the end of his life, and earnestly asked the people if they would fast with him for three whole days, asking the Almighty to have mercy on him.

In that region was a certain man named Leofstan,

powerful in the world and foolish before God, who rode to the saint's shrine with great arrogance, and very insolently commanded them to show him the holy saint to see if he was undecayed; but as soon as he saw the saint's body, he immediately went mad and roared savagely, and wretchedly ended with an evil death. This is similar to what the faithful Pope Gregory said in his narrative about Saint Lawrence, who lies in the city of Rome—that men, both good and evil, were always wanting to examine how he lay, but God restrained them, so that once seven men died there together when they were looking at him, and then others stopped examining the martyr with their human foolishness.

We have heard many miracles in popular report concerning the holy Edmund, which we will not set down in writing, but everyone knows them. By this saint and by others like him, it is clear that Almighty God is able to raise man again on Judgment Day uncorrupted from the earth, He who keeps Edmund whole in his body until that great day, though he came from the earth. Because of that worthy saint the place is worthy, that men should honor it and provide it well with pure servants of God in the service of Christ, because the saint is greater than men can conceive.

The English nation is not lacking in the Lord's saints, when in England there lie such saints as this holy King, and the blessed Cuthbert, and Æthelthryth in Ely, and also her sister, sound in body as a confirmation of the faith. There are also many other saints in the English nation who perform many miracles, as is widely known, for the praise of the Almighty in whom they believed. Christ reveals to mankind through His famous saints that He is Almighty God who does such miracles, though the wretched Jews completely rejected him, wherefore they are accursed, just as they wished upon themselves.[2] No miracles are performed at their tombs, because they do not believe in the living Christ, but Christ reveals to mankind where the true faith is, when He works such miracles through His saints widely throughout this earth. Wherefore to Him be glory forever with His Heavenly Father and the Holy Ghost. Amen.

—C. EARLY 11TH CENTURY

---

[1]   *always release ... death*   See Proverbs 24.11.

[2]   *though the wretched ... themselves*   See Matthew 27.25.

Saint Mary of Egypt

c. 344 – 421

Hagiography, or writing about the saints, was one of the most popular forms of literature throughout the Middle Ages, and there are over one hundred lives of saints extant in Old English prose and verse. Anglo-Saxon authors composed biographies of English saints, such as King Edmund and Abbess Hilda of Whitby, but they also imported many Latin saints' lives from the continent. Some of these were translated into Old English, including the *Life of Mary of Egypt*, because vernacular versions of such texts could reach an audience illiterate in Latin, whether preached as a sermon or read in private devotion.

Saints were venerated all year long, but each saint also had a special commemoration on a particular day of the year; for example, modern calendars still include St. Valentine's Day on 14 February and St. Patrick's Day on 17 March. The feast day is the saint's *dies natalis*, or "day of birth," but this actually refers to the date the saint died (and was thereby born into eternal life). Saints' lives were often compiled in anthologies and organized by feast day in order of the church year, beginning with Christmas. Mary of Egypt's feast day was 9 April —the saint herself records her name and the date of her death so that her feast day may be commemorated properly—and churchgoers on that day may have heard the life of the saint preached during the service, while monks or nuns may have heard the life read aloud at meals. Anglo-Saxon Christians believed it was important to commemorate a saint on his or her feast day because the saint could intercede for the believer by praying to God on his or her behalf. Mary of Egypt's closest relationship to the divine is through the Virgin Mary, who was considered the greatest intercessor of all.

The death of every saint served not only to establish the saint's feast day, but it is also crucial for the genre of the saint's life. Historically, the first saints were the martyrs, who died for their faith, but after Christianity became a mainstream religion in the Roman empire, the persecution ceased. Sainthood could no longer rely only on those who died a holy death, and new candidates were found among those who had lived a holy life, including the "desert fathers" who left society to live in ascetic isolation. The holy deaths of the martyrs and holy lives of the "confessors"—those who "confessed" (i.e., professed) exemplary Christian faith and virtue in both words and deeds—form two distinct subgenres of hagiographic writing, distinguished in Latin by the terms *passio* (which refers to the "passion" or suffering of a martyred saint) and *uita* (which recounts the "life" of a saint who dies of natural causes). However, the Anglo-Saxon hierarchy of holiness among the saints consists of not two but three levels: male martyrs, male confessors, and virgins, a category that includes every female saint, regardless of the manner of her death or the genre of her life, including wives, widows, and even Mary of Egypt. Technically, then, the *Life of Mary of Egypt* may be considered the *uita* of a virgin.

Her story is told from the point of view of Zosimus, a monk who has gone into the desert in search of a new role model because he thinks he cannot perfect himself further in a monastery. Meanwhile, Mary of Egypt fled to the desert to repent her life of sexual depravity in the city. Mary, who is naked and blackened by the sun, initially flees from Zosimus, but he chases her before offering his cloak. Mary's account of her sinful past is punctuated both by Zosimus's tears and his demands for more detail about her past temptations. Because Mary has lived alone in the desert for 47 years, she asks Zosimus to bring her communion in one year's time, which he does. Then, when Zosimus returns for their next annual rendezvous, he finds Mary dead. However, she has left a message written in the sand to tell him her name, which he had never asked, and the date of her death, which took place on the night of their last meeting.

This relatively simple story, notable for the complicated perspectives of its narrative frame, contains a number of elements that are common in other saints' lives. A standard miracle in many *uitae* is that the saint receives divine foreknowledge of her exact time of death and shares this information with a follower, who becomes the saint's mourner. Although Zosimus begins to cry before he even meets Mary, and he does not stop until after she is dead and buried, there is ample evidence to suggest that Mary knew her death was approaching and made preparations far in advance. Zosimus's emotional reaction to Mary repays consideration, as does his function in the creation and transmission of the text. What is his role in the telling of this saint's life, and what is Mary's? What lessons did Mary impart to Zosimus? What lessons would a medieval Christian audience learn from a sermon like this? Why must Mary recount her past sins in such detail? What ideas about sexuality and the body does the text transmit? What different meanings might the story hold for various audiences—secular, monastic, clerical, male, female—in the Middle Ages? Interestingly, Ælfric of Eynsham may have read a Latin version of *Mary of Egypt* when selecting saints' lives to translate into Old English; why didn't he choose this one?

These questions have only been raised recently for this story. For many years, scholars did not consider Old English prose saints' lives to be truly "literary" works; poetry like *Beowulf*—not prose—is the privileged form of Anglo-Saxon literature. Mary of Egypt herself probably never existed (in fact, her life may be a spin-off from the legend of Mary Magdalene), so it is inaccurate to think of this text as a biography, but to call the text "fictional" also seems anachronistic and runs counter to medieval devotion to the saints. To make matters worse, the Old English *Life of Mary of Egypt* is a close translation of a Latin text, rather than the creative work of an independent author (and, in turn, what is presented here is a present-day English translation of the Old English text).

⌘ ⌘ ⌘

The Passing of Mary of Egypt[1]

Paul the worthy deacon of the church at holy Naples translated from the Greek language into Latin the most praiseworthy conversion, both in deeds and in morals, and the great repentance and very brave struggle of the worthy Mary of Egypt, how she completed the days of her life in the desert.

Truly it is read that Raphael the archangel spoke to Tobit after the loss of his eyes and again after their glorious re-enlightenment and after the passing of the dangers from which he was preserved, and he said this: "In truth it is very injurious that one should reveal secrets of one's kin, and yet it is a great disgrace to the soul that one should keep secret the glorious works of God."

Because of such things, on no account will I conceal this holy story in silence. He has made clear to me that I may fall headlong into the ignominious sentence of the lazy servant who hid in the ground without increase the talent which he had received from his lord. But let no one be too disbelieving of me as I write concerning the things I heard and found out about in this matter; and far be it from me that I should engage in falsification in the details of the holy narrative or that I should conceal the telling of it in silence.

FURTHER ACCOUNT OF THE SAME

There was a man in a monastery in the region of Palestine. He was very much adorned with regard to the conduct of his life. From childhood he had been in-

[1]   *The Passing of Mary of Egypt*   Translated by Hugh Magennis for *The Broadview Anthology of British Literature.*

structed and trained in monastic customs in a profound manner. He was called Zosimus.

This man, thus, as I have already said, lived his life from the beginning in a monastery in Palestine, and in works of abstinence he became the most accomplished in all the rules of the monastery. Blamelessly he kept all the requirements of the rule and the perfection of the monastic service, and he also added for himself there similar practices as well, since he wished to subject his flesh to the spirit. Indeed, so much was he perfected in all monastic customs that very often monks came to him from distant places and monasteries, in order that they might attach themselves to his example and his teachings and subject themselves to emulation of his abstinence.

He devoted himself entirely to these practices, and he never diverted his mind from meditations upon Holy Scriptures. And all the benefits that he enjoyed he would use in a spiritual manner; and he had one task unconcealed by silence and never tired of—that was the singing of psalms, exaltation, and the study of Holy Scriptures. Very often also too, as they recounted, he was made worthy of divine enlightenment through revelation from God of the holy vision—which is no marvel nor moreover an unbelievable matter: concerning this the Lord himself said, "Blessed are the pure in heart, for they shall see God." So much the more shall those people behold the manifestation of divine enlightenment who constantly purify their bodies with abstinent behaviour and vigilant mind, who will receive hereafter their coming reward in eternal blessedness.

As Zosimus himself said, then, he was entrusted by himself into that monastery from the time his mother gave birth to him, and until his fifty-third year he remained there living by the rule. And after this he was oppressed by certain thoughts to the effect that he might be perfect in all things and might need no further teaching or example in his mind. And he would speak thus: "Can it be that there is any monk on earth who can teach me anything new or help me in any matters that I myself do not know or that I myself have not perfected in monastic works, or is there anyone among those who love the desert who is superior to me in his actions?"

As he pondered these things and others like them, there stood by him an angel, and it said to him, "O Zosimus, you have succeeded in a most praiseworthy manner. However, there is no person who may show himself perfect. Much greater is the struggle that lies ahead of you than that which has passed, though you do not know it. But in order that you may be able to perceive and understand how great are other paths to salvation, go out from your land and come to the monastery which is situated near the Jordan."

Then, indeed, he went at once away from the monastery in which he had dwelt from his childhood, and he came to the Jordan, the holiest of all rivers. He then went inside the monastery to which the angel had directed him. Then he began to speak first to the monk in charge of the gate of the monastery, who announced him to the abbot and led him to him.

After he [Zosimus] had received his blessing, as it is customary among monks, he [the abbot] said to him, "When did you come here, brother, or for what reasons have you associated yourself with such humble monks?"

Zosimus answered him, "There is no need, father, for me to tell you where I have come from, but I have sought you out here for reasons of learning, because I have heard about many spiritual practices among you here, and they are beyond expression pleasing to God."

The abbot said to him, "May God, who alone cares about and heals so many weaknesses, strengthen you and us in his divine precepts and direct us to attend to the works that are pleasing to him. No man can uplift another unless he constantly pays attention to himself and with sober understanding works towards that same thing himself, with God as his guide. Nonetheless, since you have said that true love of Christ has led you here to us, to seek us out as a humble monk, remain here with us then, if you have come for that reason, and may the Good Shepherd feed us all together with the grace of the Holy Spirit."

These words having been spoken by the abbot, Zosimus bent his knees and, after receiving his blessing, he remained in the monastery, where he truly beheld all the elders shining in their behaviour and deeds, enthusiastic in spirit and serving the Lord. Every day and also at night there was unceasing steadfastness there in the praising of God. And there were never any idle conversations there, nor was there thought of gold and silver or of other riches—of which the very names were unknown to them; but the one goal that they hastened to most was that each of them should be dead in body and living in spirit.

At the same time, they had food which never fails, that is, the divine discourses; their bodies, in truth, they fed with the bare necessities alone, that is, with bread and water, with the intention that they should show themselves the keener in the true love of God.

When Zosimus beheld these practices, he eagerly applied himself to perfection among his co-workers, who renewed divine paradise without ceasing.

Then after this the season of the Lenten fast drew near, which is established for all Christians to celebrate and for them to purify themselves in honour of the divine passion and resurrection. In truth the gate of the monastery was never opened but was always shut up, and thus they fulfilled their routine without any disturbance; nor was it ever to be opened unless perchance some monk went out for some necessary purpose. The locality was so desolate and so hidden that not only was it uninhabited but it was also even unknown to the people of the country themselves. In this way the rule was kept from ancient times, and from these practices it is to be believed that God led Zosimus to that monastery.

Now I will relate next how a tradition of the monastery was kept. On the Lord's day of the first week of the fast, which we call Holy Day, the divine sacramental rites were performed in the usual way, and then they participated in the communion of the living and undefiled body of our Lord Jesus Christ, and after that, having taken a little to eat, they were then all gathered together in the oratory, and on bended knees and with humble prayer each of them greeted the other and humbly asked for the blessing of their abbot, so that they might be the more firmly strengthened for the divine struggle. When these things had been completed, the gates of the monastery were opened, and they then sang this psalm together: "*Dominus illuminatio mea et salus mea; quem*

timebo?"[1] And so they went out together. They left one or two behind in the monastery, not at all for the purpose of guarding the valuables they had acquired—there was nothing of such a kind there—but so that they would not leave the oratory without the divine solemnities. And each one of them provided food for himself according as he could or wished to: one took with him a sufficient supply for the body, another fruits from the palm-trees, another beans soaked in water, another nothing except only his body and clothing; but they were nourished [when] the necessity of nature required, that is, with the plants that grew in the desert; and each one bound himself to abstinence there as seemed good to himself, in such a way that none of them knew the conduct or deeds of another.

When they had crossed over the river Jordan, then each one separated himself far from the others, and none of them joined up with his companions again, but if anyone of them saw another in the distance coming towards him, he immediately turned away from the path of his journey and went in another direction, and lived and remained by himself in continuous prayers and fasts. Having fulfilled the fast in this manner, then, they returned again to the monastery before the Lord's day of the resurrection, that is, on the feast-day that we traditionally call Palm-day. Each one kept in his own conscience within himself the witness of his own toil, as to what he had been occupied with and of what labours he had sowed the seeds; and none of them asked another in what manner he had fulfilled the struggle of his toil.

This was, then, the rule of the monastery, and so perfectly did each one conduct himself, as I have already said, that he united himself with God in the desert, and they strove in themselves to please not men but God himself.

Then, following the traditional law of the monastery, Zosimus crossed over the river Jordan, bringing with him some little for the body's necessities, and he made his way through the desert in observance of the rule, taking the necessities at meal-time and according to the requirements of nature, and at night sitting on

---

[1] *Dominus … quem timebo* Latin: "The Lord is my light and my salvation; whom should I fear?" (Psalms 27.1)

the ground and resting a little; and he would sleep wherever nightfall found him, and in the early morning [he would be] proceeding on his way again, in accordance with the course on which he was unceasingly set, and travelling on—because he desired, as he himself said afterwards, to come across some father in the desert, who might edify him in certain matters which he himself was not aware of before. And so for twenty-six days he continued on that journey, as though he were purposefully travelling to some particular person.

When it came to the hour of midday, he stopped for some length of time, breaking off his journey and turning to the east, and he prayed in the usual manner, for he was accustomed at the set times of the day to fix the course of his journey and to stand and sing and to pray on his bended knees.

Now, while he sang and with keen regard looked up and gazed at the sky, he noticed then to his right, as he stood at his prayers, as though he ...[1] appearing in human physical form, and he was at first greatly frightened, because he thought that it might be a phantom of some spirit that he saw there; but immediately, however, he strengthened himself with the sign of the cross of Christ and threw off his fear from him. And when the end of his prayer had been completed, he then turned his eyes and really saw there a human being hastening westwards in the desert, and it was actually a woman that appeared there. She was extremely black in her body because of the sun's heat, and the hair of her head was as white as wool and no longer than down to her neck.

Zosimus kept gazing intently at these details, and because of the longed-for loveliness of that glorious sight, filled with joy he ran speedily in the direction in which he had seen hastening that which had appeared to him there. Truly, in all the days before he had not seen the sight of any human being or the appearance of any animals or birds or wild beasts, and therefore he ran eagerly and desired to learn what kind of wild beast that might be which appeared to him.

As soon as Zosimus saw her, overcoming his old age and taking no notice of the difficulty of his path, he ran

exerting himself with a very rapid onward course, because he desired to unite himself with that which fled there. He kept pursuing her and she kept fleeing; then as each of them kept on their courses little by little Zosimus got to be closer. When he was near enough that she could hear his voice, he began then to send forth the following speech in a loud cry, weeping and speaking thus: "Why, you handmaid of God, do you flee from me, a sinner worn out with old age? Wait for me, for the sake of the hope of the reward for which you have striven so much. Stop and give me the blessing of your prayer, in the name of the God who casts no one away from him."

Zosimus uttered these words amidst his tears. Then she came running to a particular spot in which was marked out, as it were, a dried-up stream. When they got there, she darted into the stream and up onto the other side again. Zosimus stood then on the other side of the stream which was apparent there, calling out and getting no further on in any direction; and he added tears to tears and multiplied his groans with sighs, so that nothing was heard there except the lamentation of his grief.

Then, indeed, the figure which was fleeing sent forth the following speech and said this: "Abbot Zosimus, have pity on me for God's sake, I beg you, because I cannot show myself and turn towards you, for I am a person of the female sex and am completely bereft of bodily clothing, as you yourself see, and I have the shame of my body uncovered. But if you wish to grant me, a wretched sinner, your salutary blessings, then throw here to me your cloak which you are wearing, so that I can cover up my womanly frailty and turn to you and receive your prayers."

Then an intense dread and fear seized Zosimus, because he heard that she called him by his name, whom she had never seen previously or heard tell of before—except that he perceived clearly that she had been enlightened with divine foreknowledge. Unhesitatingly he did as she instructed, took off the cloak he was wearing [and], with his back turned, threw it to her. She grabbed hold of it then and put it over her body, and covered herself up in the parts she was most able to and which there was most need to conceal. She then turned

---

[1] *as though he ...*   There is no gap in the manuscript here, but the sense requires something meaning "saw a shadow."

to Zosimus and said to him, "Why, O abbot Zosimus, was there so great a need for you to see me, a sinful woman, or what do you wish to have from me or to learn, to the extent that you did not slacken in exercising so much toil on my account?"

He then immediately prostrated himself on the ground and asked for her blessing. She in turn prostrated herself and asked for his blessing.

Then after a period of many hours the woman said to Zosimus, "It befits you, abbot Zosimus, to pray and to bless, because you are sustained by the special knowledge of the priesthood, and you fathom the sacramental rites of Christ with the gifts of godly things, serving for many years at his holy altar."

These words really brought great dread and fear upon Zosimus, and he kept trembling and was suffused with drops of sweat. Then he began to sigh, as though completely overcome with weakness and gasping for breath, and he spoke as follows: "O spiritual mother, reveal now what you are in your appearance, for you are truly God's handmaid. Intercede for me now, you who have been made dead to this world with regard to the concerns of youth. In this above all divine love is manifest in you, that you called me by my name, whom you had never before seen. But since grace is not recognized on grounds of rank but is accustomed to indicate itself by the works of the soul, you bless me, for the Lord's sake, I beg you, and grant me the inalienable blessing of your perfection."

Then she began to take pity on the old man's persistence and said, "Blessed be God, who works for the salvation of souls."

Then she gave Zosimus [her blessing] and he answered "Amen."

Then they both arose from the ground. Thereupon the woman began to speak to the old man again, saying this: "O sir, for what reason have you come to me in my sinfulness? However, since the grace of the Holy Spirit has guided you for the purpose that you may do some service to the benefit of my little body, tell me how now today Christ's people are ruled in the world and how the emperors are, or how the flock of Christ's true-believing congregation are now looked after."

Zosimus answered her, "O holy mother, in accordance with your holy prayers, God has granted a firm peace ... of a monk,[1] and for God's sake [pray] for the world and for me in my sinfulness, so that the toil of this journey and the path over so great a desert may not become [fruitless] to me."

Then she said, "[It befits you,] abbot Zosimus, to pray for me and for all, since ..., as I said before, ... and since we have the requirement ... will I shall do."

And speaking thus, she ... with eyes raised on high and outstretched arms, began to pray, moving her lips in silence, so that no voice at all could be heard there that one could perceive. Thus Zosimus could make out nothing of the prayer. As he himself said, he stood trembling and looking at the ground and saying nothing at all. In fact, he swore, proposing God as witness of his words, that while she continued thus with her prayer, he raised his eyes a little from the ground to see her elevated just the height of a man's forearm above the ground, and she began to pray hanging in the air. When he saw this he was seized then with great fear, and he prostrated himself on the ground, and he was covered in sweat and very much agitated. He did not dare to speak, except that within himself he said only. ...

As he lay stretched out on the ground, then ... it could possibly be a spirit that was praying there in some sort of pretence. The woman turned then and raised up the monk, speaking as follows: "Why, abbot, do you vex your thoughts to take offence with me, as though I were some spirit engaging in prayer deceitfully? But know, sir, that I am a sinful woman, although protected from without by holy baptism, and I am no spirit but dust and ashes and wholly flesh, and nothing spirit-like ..."

... spoke, she blessed her face with the holy sign of the cross, and she fortified her eyes and lips and also her breast with that blessing, and said this: "May God deliver us, abbot Zosimus, from our enemy and from his incitement, because his malice against us is great." When the old man heard these words he stretched himself downwards ....

... "... the things concerning me, you will at once flee from me in the way one might flee from a serpent. But

---

[1] *firm peace ... of a monk* Ellipses in this section indicate words missing in the manuscript.

nonetheless I will tell you, and I will hide nothing; and first I beg you not to cease to pray for me, so that I may merit and find some degree of mercy on Judgement Day."

The old man began to weep bitterly, suffused with tears. Then the woman began to relate and recount all the things that happened concerning her, speaking as follows: "I had a brother and my homeland in Egypt, and I lived there with my parents. In the twelfth year of my age I began then to spurn their love, and I went to the city of Alexandria. But it shames me now to recount how in the beginning I first defiled my maidenhood and how unceasingly and licentiously I lay enslaved to the vices of desires for sin. This is now to be recounted briefly, but I reveal it nonetheless the more readily so that you may appreciate the illicit fire of the vices to which I was subject in my love of sexual depravity. But have pity on me, abbot; for all of seventeen years I roamed openly through the crowd of the population, lying in the fire of promiscuity. Nor did I lose my maidenhood at all in exchange for gifts from anyone or in fact that I might receive anything from any people who wished to give me anything, but I was very much on fire with the passion of desire for sin, so that I desired that they might rush to me the more numerously without payment, my purpose being to satisfy the more easily the disgraceful desires of my sexual depravity. Do not imagine at all that I undertook anything for any wealth, but I always lived in poverty, because I had, as I have said already, insatiable desires, so that I unceasingly defiled myself in the mire of wicked promiscuity; and that was my misery. And that I counted as life, that I should unceasingly perpetrate wrongs against nature."

"While I lived thus, on a particular occasion I saw a large crowd of Africans and Egyptians hurrying together as if to the sea. I quickly fell in with one of them then and asked him where he thought the crowd intended to hasten to. He answered me and said this, that they intended to go to Jerusalem for the honouring of the holy cross, which would be celebrated after not many days. Then I said to him, 'Do you think they will be willing to take me, if I wish to go with them?' He said, 'If you have the fare-money, none of them will stop you.' Then I said to him, 'Brother, in truth I have no fare-money to give, but I intend to go and board one of the ships, even though they don't wish to support me, and I will give myself over to them, and instead of the fare-money they may have my body in their power, so that they may receive me the more readily.' Pity me, abbot, because I desired to go with them in order to have more fellow-workers in the passion of my lusting for pleasure. I said to you before, 'Have pity on me, you holy man, that you don't compel me to relate my shamefulness.' God knows that, because these words of mine defile both you and the air itself, I am frightened of them."

Soaking the ground with his tears Zosimus then said to her, "O spiritual mother, tell for God's sake, I beg you, and do not leave off the continuation of so salutary a story."

And she spoke thus: "The young man straightaway heard the shamefulness of my words and he went off laughing away from me. At once then I threw from me the whip that I was seldom accustomed to have in my hands, and ran towards the sea, where I saw them gathered. Then I saw ten young men standing together by the shore, good-looking enough in body and in demeanour, and admirable indeed, it seemed to me, for the pleasure of my body. Shamelessly then, as was my custom, I mingled amongst them and said to them, 'Take me on your journey with you. I will not be unpleasing to you.' And straightaway I excited them all then to wicked sins and shameful bouts of sniggering, with many other dirty and lewd expressions.

"When they saw my shameless behaviour, then, they took me with them on board their ship and sailed forth. O Zosimus, how can I recount to you, or what tongue can say it or what ear can hear the vile deeds that were enacted on that voyage and on that journey, and how I compelled to sin both the wretches who were willing and the wretches who gave to me. There is no form of obscenity, speakable or unspeakable, of a kind that I did not incite and teach, after becoming its instigator. O be assured of this now, for I marvel how the sea endured and put up with those wicked lusts of mine, or how it was that the earth did not open its mouth and plunge me into hell alive as I was, I who led so many souls into the trap of perdition—but I expect that it was because God looked for my repentance, he who lets no one perish but causes all to be safe who believe in him, for truly he wishes not the death of the sinner but patiently waits for his conversion.

"Thus with great speed then we travelled to Jerusalem, and for as many days as I stayed in the city before the feast of the cross, I engaged in impure bodily acts, and even worse. I wasn't content with the young men with whom I had had sex on the sea or on the journey, but I also polluted likewise in the works of my iniquities many foreigners and townspeople whom I had gathered together and seduced.

"When the feast of the exaltation of the holy precious cross arrived, I went about as before enticing the young men into the trap of perdition. Then in the early morning I saw them all running eagerly to the church. I began to run then with those who were running, and along with them I strove to get to the front of the temple. When the time came to venerate the holy cross, then in the midst of the people I began to push forcefully against the crowd, and so with great difficulty I, in my wretched state, got to the temple door with those who went in there. When I expected to enter the door, they began to go in without any impediment; truly, divine power hindered my passage, and I was immediately pushed away from all the people, until I alone stood in the courtyard by myself. Then I began to think that this had happened to me because of my womanly weakness, and I began again to mingle in with the others, so that in some way I would push in; but I laboured in vain when I touched the threshold of the door.

"And they were all received inside without any hinderance, while I alone was thrust out. But as if some strong host stood in front of me to bar entry for me, so God's vengeance suddenly blocked the door, until again I was left standing in the courtyard of the temple. Thus three or four times I attempted to see and also attain what I wished, and when I didn't succeed at all then I began earnestly to think it over, and my body was tired out with the force of the pushing. So then I went away from there, and I stood alone in a particular corner of the courtyard, and in my mind I earnestly pondered and considered for what reason it was that the sight of the life-giving tree was being denied me. Then truly knowl-

edge of salvation touched my mind and the eyes of my heart, when I reflected that the inexpiable circumstances of my misdeeds had closed the entrance against me. Then I began to weep bitterly and to beat my breast in great tribulation and, as I lamented from deep in my heart, to bring forth sorrowful sighs.

"Then from the place where I stood I noticed an image of the holy mother of God set up, and I earnestly spoke to her, beholding her unswervingly and saying, 'O glorious lady, who bore the true God in bodily childbirth, I fully know that it is not proper or fitting that I who am so dire a sinner should look upon and pray to your image, with eyes in so many ways defiled. You were always known as a virgin who kept your body pure and unstained; for that reason it really is quite right for me, being so polluted, to be excluded and cast out from your pure spotlessness. But nevertheless, since I have heard that the God whom you yourself bore became man for this reason, to call sinners to repentance, aid me now, alone as I am, bereft of every help. Allow me and give me leave to open the entrance of your holy church, so that I may not be made a stranger to the sight of the precious cross, on which was fastened the Saviour of all the world, whom you conceived as a virgin and also likewise gave birth to as a virgin, he who shed his own blood for my redemption. But command now, O glorious lady, the door to be unfastened for me in my unworthiness to greet the divine cross, and I will commit myself to you and choose you as my advocate against your Son, and I promise both of you that never after this will I defile my body in the terrible shameful lust of wicked promiscuity, but as soon as I see, holy virgin, the cross of your Son, I will at that moment forsake this world and its works along with everything that is in it, and afterwards I will go wherever you guide me as my advocate.'

"Saying this, I was led then with the heat of faith and touched with belief, and becoming bold with the mercy of the gracious mother of God, I stirred myself from the same place where I had spoken this prayer and I joined myself again with those who were going in. From now on there was nothing that pushed me out or hindered me from the temple door, and I entered with those who were going in. Then in truth a powerful fear seized me, and I was trembling all over in excitement when I again came to the door where entry had previously been closed to me—it was just as if all the force that previously had guarded the door against my entry, afterwards prepared the entry for my path.

"So I was filled with the spiritual mysteries within the temple, and I was deemed worthy to pay reverence to the mysteries of the precious and life-giving cross. When I saw there the holy mysteries of God, how he is always ready to receive those who repent, then I threw myself forth on the floor and kissed the holy ground.

"When I had gone out, I arrived back again at the place from which I had previously seen the image of the holy mother, and I bent my knees before the holy countenance, asking with these words: 'O most benign lady, who showed to me your gracious mercy and did not cast my unworthy prayer away from you, I have seen the glory which we sinful people do not see by our deserts. Glory be to God Almighty, who through you accepts the repentance and penitence of sinners and wrong-doers. What more can I, who am wretched and despaired of, think or tell? Now is the time to fulfill and accomplish what I said with respect to your worthy surety. Direct me now on the road according to your wish. Be now a guide to salvation appearing to me and a source of truthfulness, going before me on the road that leads to penitence.'

"When I spoke thus, I heard then from afar a voice calling out, 'If you cross over the river Jordan, there you will experience and obtain good repose.'

"When I heard this utterance and realized that it had been called out on my account, I spoke weeping and gazing at the likeness of the holy mother of God, crying out again, 'O lady, queen of all the world, through you salvation came to all the human race. Do not forsake me.'

"Speaking thus, I went out from the courtyard of the temple and went hurriedly on my way. Then I met someone, and he gave me three pennies, with which I bought myself three loaves, which I took as subsistence for the blessing of my journey. Then I asked the person from whom I bought the loaves which was the road that led most directly to the river Jordan. When I found out the way, I ran weeping on my journey, twisting always enquiry onto enquiry, and in this way, weeping, I

completed the day's journey. Now, it was morning-time of the day when I strove to get to see the holy precious cross, and the sun was sinking to its setting and it was approaching nightfall by the time I arrived at the church of St. John the Baptist, situated by the Jordan. And I went in there and prayed, and, immediately after, I descended into the Jordan and washed my hands and face with the holy water, and I partook in the life-giving and undefiled sacrament of our Lord the Saviour Christ in that same church of the holy Precursor and Baptist John; and there I ate half of one loaf and drank some of the water, and I rested there for the night, and early the next morning I went across the river. Then I began again to ask my guide Saint Mary to direct me to where she wished.

"So I came to this desert, and from then until this present day I have kept apart, always fleeing away, waiting and hoping for my God, who delivers from the danger of this world all those who turn to him."

Zosimus said to her, "O my lady, how many years have there been now, that you have lived in this desert?"

The woman answered him, "It has been forty-seven years, according to my reckoning, since I went out from the holy city."

Zosimus said to her, "And what could you find for yourself to eat, or with what things did you feed yourself until now?"

She answered him, "I brought two and a half loaves here with me when I crossed over the Jordan. After no length of time they dried up just like stone, and became hard, and I subsisted on those, making use of them for some time."

Zosimus said to her, "And were you able to pass the length of so many seasons without thinking longingly of the burning of the instinctive pull of the flesh?"

In a troubled state then, she answered him, "Now you are asking me about things of which I myself am exceedingly afraid, if all the dangers that I endured and the unwise thoughts that often oppressed me come into my mind, namely that I may again experience some tribulation from those same thoughts."

Zosimus said, "O lady, do not leave out anything that you may not reveal to me, but divulge everything in its proper order."

Then she said, "Abbot, believe me, for seventeen years I struggled against the lusts of appetites of the placid and irrational wild animals. When I began to feel hungry, then my desires were for meats. I longed for the fish that I used to have in Egypt. I desired the wine in which formerly I loved to indulge to the point of drunkenness, and now likewise it is still very much in my desires, because formerly I indulged in it to excess, when I was in the world. I was also very thirsty here because of the desert's lack of water, and was hardly able to bear the terrible need. Likewise I had an excessive desire for lewd songs [that] troubled me, when they brought it into my mind to sing the devil's songs which I had learned formerly in the world. But when this happened I would weep and beat my breast with my hands, and I would remind myself of my vow and of the surety I had previously chosen; and so eagerly I would come in my thoughts before the image of the good and the holy mother of God, who had previously received me in covenant with her. And weeping in front of her I would ask that she would drive away from me the foul thoughts that afflicted my wretched soul. Then indeed I wept in my overwhelming grief, and as I beat my breast hard I saw then a light shining everywhere about me, and at once a secure peace came upon me then.

"Pardon me now, abbot. How can I reveal my thoughts to you, which I feared might drive me again to sexual depravity, causing an intense fire to burn up my unhappy body from within? When I felt such thoughts arising in me, which completely tormented me with the thought of intercourse, then I stretched myself out on the ground and drenched my cheeks with tears, because I hoped in truth that she would stand beside me, whom I ... myself from the ground before that sweet voice shone upon me as usual and drove my troubled thoughts away from me. Constantly in truth I raised up the eyes of my heart to my guarantor in my necessity, begging her that in this desert she might help me to proper penitence, she who gave birth to the source of all chastity. And thus for the course of seventeen years, I have been, as I said before, struggling in all respects against perils of many kinds, until this present day; and the holy mother of God was my help and the guide of my ways."

Zosimus said to her, "And did you not need any food or clothing?"

She answered him and said, "For seventeen years, as I have told you already, I used the loaves, and afterwards I lived on the plants that I found in this desert. The clothing I had at the time when I crossed over the Jordan wore out, torn to pieces with extreme old age, and afterwards I suffered hardships of many kinds, sometimes from the icy coldness of winter, sometimes from the intense scorching of the sun's heat. I was terribly seared from the great burning and again by the extreme frosty coldness of winter, so that very often I lay down on the ground, almost completely motionless without breath.

"So for a long time I was struggling and striving with many and various kinds of distresses and with inordinate temptations, and afterwards until this present day divine power has preserved me and my wretched soul and my body, while I have constantly reflected in myself from how many evils it had delivered me. Truly I am nourished to satiety with most abundant sustenance, that is, with the hope of my salvation, and I am clothed with the garment of the word of God, who embraces and encompasses all things. Man does not live by bread alone but from every word that comes forth from God's mouth."

Now when Zosimus heard that she produced sayings out of the holy books, both from the gospel and from many others, he said to her, "O mother, did you ever learn the psalms or other holy scriptures?"

When she heard this, then she smiled towards him, speaking as follows: "Believe me, I have never seen any person except you, neither wild beast nor animal of any kind, since I crossed over the river Jordan and came here into this desert; nor indeed have I learned letters or listened to those who studied and read. But God's word is living and keen, and teaches this human understanding from within.

"And this is the end now of all the things that were accomplished concerning me. Now I beg and beseech you through the incarnate word of God to pray for me, a wretched harlot."

When she said this, then the old man hastened towards her on bended knees in order to throw himself to the ground, calling out loudly amidst his doleful tears, "Blessed be God, who alone brings about wonders of many kinds; and may you be blessed, Lord God, who have revealed to me the glory that you grant to those who fear you. Now I truly know that you do not abandon any of those who seek you."

She forestalled the old man, however, and did not let him prostrate himself fully on the ground, but said to him, "The things that you have heard, sir, I implore you through the Lord Saviour Christ, our Redeemer, not to tell to anyone, before God releases me from the fetters of the flesh. But now that everything has been disclosed, go home in peace. And within the space of a year I will appear to you again at this same time, and you will see me. And truly indeed, do as I now command you: when the holy fast of Lent comes round next year, do not cross over the Jordan at all, as people from your monastery usually do."

Then Zosimus began to marvel again that she knew the rule of the monastery with such particularity, and he said nothing else, [except] that he glorified God, who when he is entreated gives so abundantly to people who love him.

Then she said again, "Remain now, Zosimus, in your monastery, because in fact even though you may wish ahead of time to go anywhere, you will not be able to. Then on the holy evening of the Holy Supper, that is on the holy Thursday before the Lord's Easter Day, put into a consecrated vessel a portion of the Lord's body and of the life-giving blood, and bring it with you, and wait for me on the side of the Jordan that relates to the world, until I come to you to receive the life-giving sacramental elements. Truthfully, from the time when I participated in the Lord's body and his blood in the church of the blessed Precursor before I crossed over the Jordan, never since then have I partaken of or received the sacrament; and therefore I ask that you do not refuse my request, but rather that you bring to me the divine and life-giving sacramental elements at the time when the Saviour made his followers sharers in the divine Supper. Point out also to John, the abbot of the monastery where you are, that he should pay attention to himself and also to his flock, because there are some practices to correct and amend. But I do not want you to disclose these matters to him at this time before God tells you."

Speaking thus, she also asked for a prayer from the old man, and rapidly hastened to the inner desert.

Zosimus then stretched himself forward and kissed the ground on which her feet had stood, glorifying God and expressing many thanks; and as he went back he kept praising and blessing our Lord Saviour Christ. And he went back by the same path through the desert by which he had arrived there previously, and he got to the monastery at the very time when they were assembled together for their Easter observances.

And all that year he carefully kept silent about the vision, daring to say the least amount possible of what he had seen, but unceasingly within himself he prayed earnestly to God that he might show him that longed-for countenance again, and with frequent sighs he waited out the slowness of the year's course.

When the holy season of the Lenten fast came round, on the Lord's day that we call Holy Day [Sunday], the brothers went out after their customary prayers and psalms, while he himself was left behind in the monastery, and he remained there, detained by some physical illness; and he, Zosimus, remembered too, very well, the message of the saint, when she told him that even if he wanted to go out from his monastery he would not be able to. Nonetheless, after not many days he recovered from the illness and engaged in life in the monastery.

Now, when the monks returned home and gathered themselves together on the holy evening of the Supper, then he did as he had been instructed earlier and put into a small chalice a portion of the undefiled body and the precious blood of our Lord Saviour Christ, and he took in his hand a little basket filled with dried figs and with palm-tree-fruits, which we call finger-fruits [dates], and a few lentils soaked in water; and in the evening he came to the banks of the river Jordan, and sorrowing he waited for the arrival of the holy woman, when she would get there.

Zosimus did not doze at all, and eagerly surveyed the desert, and he considered within himself and thought, saying this: "O, will she come here and not notice me, and has she turned from me and departed?"

As he said this, he wept bitterly, and raising his eyes up to heaven he humbly prayed to God, speaking as follows: "Do not keep me, Lord, from the vision which formerly you showed to me, so that I do not depart from here in vain, bearing my sins in reproach."

As he prayed tearfully, another thought occurred to him again, and he said this: "And if she does come, how is she to cross this river, since there is no ship here so that she can come to me in my unworthiness? O unhappy me, kept away as I am from so righteous a sight."

As he thought this, he noticed then where she stood on the other side of the river. Seeing her, Zosimus now rose up with great happiness and joy, glorifying God, though he was uncertain in his mind how she would be able to cross the waters of the Jordan. Then, however, he noticed that she blessed the waters of the Jordan with the sign of the cross of Christ. Truly, the brightness of the moon lit up the darkness of the whole night, as soon as she plunged the sign of the cross into the waters. Thus she made her way towards him on top of the soft waves, walking as though on dry land. As Zosimus marvelled and made to bend his knees towards her, she began to call out and restrain him, and she spoke as follows: "What are you doing, abbot? Remember that you are a priest of God and you have the divine sacramental elements with you."

He obeyed her at once then and got up. As soon as she arrived from the waters, she said to him, "Father, bless me."

Now, extreme astonishment came upon him at so magnificent a glory, and then he said this: "O righteous one, good is he who has promised that those who have first purified themselves will be like himself. Glory be to you, Lord God, who have shown me through this servant of yours how much in my own estimation I [am inferior] in comparison to the perfection of those others."

When he had spoken thus, then she, Mary, asked that she might begin the prayer of true faith, that is *Credo in Deum*, and after that the Lord's Prayer, *Pater noster*.[1] These having been completed, she offered the old man the kiss of peace, as is customary, and there she

received the holy sacramental elements of Christ's body and blood, with outstretched hands. And looking towards heaven and sorrowing tearfully, she spoke as follows: "Lord, let now your servant go in peace according to your word, for my eyes have seen your salvation."[2]

And then she said to the old man, "Have mercy on me, abbot, and carry out another prayer which I request. Go now to your monastery guided with the peace of God, and come then after the course of a year to the stream where the two of us first spoke together. I ask you in the name of God not to refuse this, but to come, and you will see me then, in accordance with God's will."

Then he said to her, "O that I might be allowed to follow in your footsteps and enjoy the sight of your precious face! But I ask you, mother, to grant a little request from me, an old man, namely that you condescend to accept from me some little of what I have brought here."

And he said this: "Pass to me here the basket I brought with me."

Then at once she touched the lentils, which are peas, with the tips of her fingers, and she put the amount of three grains in her mouth, and said that this gift was sufficient to keep the condition of the soul undefiled. And she said to the old man, "Pray for me, and protect me in my unhappiness."

Straightaway amidst his tears he touched her feet, asking that she pray in respect of the holy church of God. And then weeping and sighing she left him, and he did not dare to hinder her in any respect; in no respect could she be hindered.

Then she began to touch the Jordan again by dipping the holy cross in it, and she went over the soft waves of the river, just as she had done before on the way there. So Zosimus returned then with great joy, and he was suddenly filled with great awe. He sorrowfully blamed himself severely that he had not asked the name of the saint; however, he hoped that he would learn it the following year.

---

[1] *Credo in Deum … Pater noster* The first words of the Creed (profession of faith) and Our Father, respectively: "I believe in one [God]" and "Our Father [Who art in Heaven]." Both prayers are said at mass and were among the prayers that lay people were expected to know in the early Middle Ages.

[2] *Lord, let now … salvation* Luke 2.29. This verse was used as the cantide *Nunc dimittis* and sung during Compline in Benedictine monastic communities.

Then when the course of the year had passed, he came into the vast desert and eagerly hastened to the glorious vision, and he travelled for a long time seeking hither and thither, until he perceived some clear sign of the longed-for vision and the place of his desire, as he eagerly looked both to the right and to the left with the keenness of his eyes, just like the most skilful hunter, seeing if he might be able to catch there the sweetest wild animal. When he could not find anything that moved, then he began to soak himself with tears, and with upraised eyes he prayed and said, "Reveal to me, Lord, that hidden treasure of gold which formerly you condescended to show to me—I ask you, Lord, for the sake of your glory."

When he had prayed thus, he arrived then at the place where the stream was marked out, where they had first spoken, and he saw there situated on the other side what looked just like a shining sun and the body of the holy woman lying lifeless, and the hands were arranged as was proper for them to be, and it was turned to the east. He ran there at once then and washed her feet with his tears; in truth he did not dare to touch any other part of the body. And with much lamentation he performed a service for burial, with psalm-singing and other prayers that pertained to the occasion. Then he began to consider whether this would be pleasing to her. As he was considering this, there was a written message marked out on the ground, expressed as follows: "Abbot Zosimus, bury and have mercy on the body of Mary. Commit to the earth that which belongs to it, and add dust to dust. Also pray for me, moreover, departing from this world on the ninth night of the month of April, that is, the Ides of April, on the day of the Lord's Supper, and after partaking in the Eucharist."

When the old man read those letters, he wondered at first who had written them, since she herself had said formerly that she had never learned any such thing. However, he realized, rejoicing very much about it, that he knew her name; and he perceived clearly that as soon as she had received the divine elements of the sacrament at the Jordan, at that same time she had come here and had at once departed from the world; and the journey that Zosimus had travelled in twenty days with much

hardship, Mary had fully completed in the course of one hour, and had immediately departed to the Lord. Truly Zosimus glorified God then, and he soaked his own body with tears, and said, "Now is the time, Zosimus, unfortunate wretch, for you to carry out what has been asked of you. But what am I [to do] now in my unhappiness, for I do not know what to dig with, since both spade and mattock are so lacking to me."

When he said this secretly in his heart, then he saw lying there some bit of wood or other, and a small one at that. He began to dig there, really very busily. But the ground was very hard and he could not dig, for he was very much weakened both with fasting and from the long toil, and he was oppressed with sighs, and he groaned from the depths of his heart.

As he looked around him, he saw a lion of enormous size standing beside the body of the saint, and it was licking the soles of her feet. Then he became terrified with fear of the enormous wild beast, and especially because the holy woman had told him previously that she had not seen any wild beast there. But at once he armed himself on all sides with the sign of the cross and with the power of the person lying there. Then the lioness began to fawn at the old man and to greet him with its moving limbs. Zosimus then said to the lion, "O greatest wild beast, if you were sent here by God in order that you should commit the body of this holy servant of God to the earth, perform now the task of your duty. In truth I am weakened with old age, so that I cannot dig; nor have I anything suitable to carry out this task, nor am I able to rush away on so great a journey to bring anything here. But you do this task with your claws, in accordance with the divine command, until the two of us have committed this holy body to the earth."

Immediately after his words the lioness made a pit with the claws of its forelegs, as big as was suitable for burying the saint, while he washed her feet with his tears, and as he poured forth his tears he offered manifold prayers that she would intercede for all; and so he covered over the body in the earth, as naked as when he first met her, except for the protection of the torn garment which Zosimus had formerly thrown to her, with which Mary had covered some part of her body. And they went away together, the lion heading into the inner desert, just like the gentlest lamb. Then Zosimus departed to his monastery, glorifying and blessing God and extolling him with praises.

As soon as he arrived at the monastery he related the matter to them all from the beginning, and concealed nothing of all the things that he had seen or heard, so that they all exalted the glories of God and celebrated the day of the passing of the saint. John indeed per-

ceived that some of the practices of the monastery had to be corrected, just as the saint had previously mentioned, but with the help of God he immediately corrected them. Zosimus served in that monastery for a hundred years and then departed to the Lord. Glory be to our Lord Saviour Christ, who lives and reigns for ever, world without end. Amen.

—C. 450–1100

WULFSTAN
c. 960 – 1023

Wulfstan the Homilist (so called to avoid confusion with others of that name: an earlier Archbishop of York, a saintly Bishop of Worcester, and a monk of Winchester known as "Wulfstan the Cantor" for his musical accomplishments) was probably born in the East Midlands, became Bishop of London in 996, and simultaneously Bishop of Worcester and Archbishop of York in 1002. He died in 1023. As a bishop rather than an abbot he was directly involved in secular politics during an intensely troubled period in English history, but he still found time to write a great number of works, all in a powerfully distinctive style. The exact number of his sermons is not known—at least 23 English works and a number of Latin ones are acknowledged as his—but fragments and revisions abound, all of which can be attributed to him because of his idiosyncratic style. Wulfstan also wrote a guide to secular and clerical government (*The Institutes of Polity*), a set of canons for secular clergy, and treatises on the management of large landholdings and estates, and he had a hand in the law codes of Æthelred and of Cnut. According to one report (in the twelfth-century *Liber Eliensis*), "he was loved as a brother and honored as a father, and frequently summoned to the highest affairs of the realm" by these kings, and his position as well as his personality placed him in the center of political life.

Wulfstan's work, unlike the homilies and textbooks of the more scholarly Ælfric, often addresses practical and political matters, speaks directly to contemporary conditions, and is deeply concerned with the organization and right governance of the state. But, like Ælfric, Wulfstan was first and foremost a pastor, and in his homilies one can see how his political and civil interests are woven into his spiritual concerns. Also like Ælfric, Wulfstan was a deliberate stylist of English prose who exploited all the resources of vernacular poetry— alliteration, rhythm, variation, balance—and of hortatory rhetoric to bring his audience into his theme. The vigorous *Sermo Lupi ad Anglos* (signed with the Latin name *Lupus*, "wolf," a play on his English name) is written in strongly rhythmical prose. In it Wulfstan considers the Viking attacks as divine retribution for the sins of the English; he adopts the historical attitude of the sixth-century British writer Gildas, whose *De excidio Britonum* similarly lamented the arrival of the English as a retribution upon the British. In doing so Wulfstan places contemporary events into a Biblical historiography which sees the rise and fall of nations as a reflection of their moral status. Even pagans may be instruments of God's justice, as the pagan English were to the Christian Britons: Wulfstan rebukes the English, now Christian, with the observation that pagans practice their religion more faithfully and with more morality than Christians do. His eloquently savage portrait of his age is presumably meant to rouse his audience to repentance rather than despair; his answer to the terrors and moral collapse of his nation combines spiritual and political perspectives—do justice, obey the law, keep faith, and remember the waiting torments of Hell.

⌘ ⌘ ⌘

Sermo Lupi ad Anglos[1]

The Sermon of "Wolf" to the English, when the Danes were greatly persecuting them, which was in the 1014th year after the Incarnation of our Lord Jesus Christ.

Dear people, recognize what is true: this world is in haste and it draws near its end. And therefore in this world things get worse and worse, and so it needs must be that because of the people's sins things will get very much worse before the coming of the Antichrist; and then it will indeed be terrible and grim widely throughout the world. Understand well, too, that the Devil has led this nation too far astray for many years, and there has been little loyalty among men, though they might speak well, and too many wrongs have ruled this land, and there were never many men who sought the remedy as eagerly as they should, but every day they added one evil to another, and raised up wrong and injustice too widely throughout this entire land.

And therefore we have also suffered many injuries and insults, and if we are to expect any remedy then we must deserve better of God than we have done previously. For with great demerit we have earned the miseries that oppress us, and with very great merits we must obtain the remedy from God, if things are to improve henceforth. Indeed, we know full well that a great breach requires a great remedy, and a great fire needs no little water, if one is to quench that fire at all. And the necessity is great for every man henceforth diligently to heed God's law, and pay God's dues justly. Among heathen peoples no one dares withhold little or much of that which is pledged to the worship of false gods, and everywhere we withhold God's dues all too often. And among heathen people no one dares diminish, inside the temple or out, anything brought to the false gods and given over as an offering; and we have completely stripped the houses of God, inside and out, and the servants of God are everywhere deprived of respect and protection. And among heathen people no one dare abuse the servants of the false gods in any way, just as is now done too widely to the servants of God, where Christians ought to observe God's laws and protect God's servants.

But what I say is true: there is need of a remedy, because God's dues have decreased for too long in this land in every region, and the laws of the people have deteriorated all too much, and sanctuaries are commonly violated, and the houses of God are entirely stripped of ancient dues and are despoiled within of everything decent. And widows are wrongfully forced to take a husband, and too many are reduced to poverty and greatly humiliated; and poor men are sorely betrayed and cruelly defrauded, and widely sold out of this land into the power of foreigners, even though they are completely innocent; and with cruel injustice children in the cradle are enslaved for petty theft commonly throughout this nation; and the rights of freemen are taken away and the rights of slaves restricted, and the right to alms curtailed, and to speak briefly, the laws of God are hated and His teaching scorned; therefore through God's anger we all are frequently put to shame, let him know it who can. And although one might not imagine it, the harm will become common to all this nation, unless God protects us.

For it is clear and evident in us all that we have hitherto more often transgressed than we have amended, and therefore many things have fallen upon this nation. For a long time now, nothing has prospered either at home or abroad, but there has been plunder and famine, burning and bloodshed in every region time and again. And stealing and slaughter, plague and pestilence, murrain[2] and disease, slander and hatred, and the thievery of robbers has harmed us severely. And excessive taxes have greatly afflicted us, and bad weather has often caused crop failures, for there have been in this land, so it seems, many years now of injustices and unstable loyalties among men everywhere. Now very often a kinsman will not protect a kinsman any more than a foreigner, nor the father his children, nor sometimes the child his own father, nor one brother the other. Nor has any of us ordered his life as he should, neither the cleric according to the rule nor the layman according to the law. But all too frequently we have made lust into law for us, and have kept neither the teachings nor the laws of God or men as we should.

---

[1] *Sermo Lupi ad Anglos* The present text is translated by R.M. Liuzza for *The Broadview Anthology of British Literature*.

[2] *murrain* Disease afflicting domestic animals such as sheep and cattle.

Neither has anyone had loyal intentions toward others as justly as he should, but almost all men have betrayed and injured others by word and deed; and indeed almost everyone unjustly stabs the other in the back with shameful assaults, and worse, if he can.

For there are here in this land great disloyalties towards God and towards the state, and there are also in this country many who betray their lords in various ways, and the greatest of all betrayals of one's lord in the world is that a man betrays his lord's soul. And it is also a great betrayal of one's lord in the world when a man plots against his lord's life, or, living, drives him from the land, and both have happened in this country. They plotted against Edward and then killed, and afterwards burned him; and Æthelred was driven out of his country. And too many godparents and godchildren have been destroyed widely throughout this nation, and likewise too many other innocent people have been too commonly slain. And also far too many holy places have fallen down because previously certain men have been placed in them who ought not to have been, if one wished to show respect to God's sanctuary. And too many Christian people have been sold out of this land, all the time now, and all this is hateful to God, let him believe it who will. And it is shameful to speak of what happens too commonly, and dreadful to know what too many often do, who practice a wretched deed: they pool their money together and buy a woman in common as a joint purchase, and with the one woman commit foul sin, one after another and each after the other, just like dogs who do not care about filth, and then for a price they sell out of the land into the hands of the enemy this creature of God, His own purchase that He bought so dearly.

Also we know well where the crime has occurred that a father has sold his son for a price, and a son his mother, and one brother has sold another into the hands of foreigners; and all those are serious and terrible deeds, let him understand it who will. And yet that which is injuring this nation is still greater and more manifold: many are forsworn and greatly perjured, and vows are broken time and again, and it is evident in this nation that God's anger violently oppresses us, let him know it who can.

And indeed, how can greater shame befall men through the wrath of God than frequently does us for our own deeds? Though a slave should escape from his lord and, leaving Christendom become a Viking, and it afterwards happens that armed combat takes place between thane and slave, if the slave should slay the thane,[1] he will lie without payment to any of his family; but if the thane kills the slave that he had previously owned, he must pay the price of a thane. Utterly shameful laws and disgraceful tributes are common among us, because of God's anger, let him understand it who is able; and many misfortunes befall this nation time and again. For a long time now nothing has prospered at home or abroad, but there has been devastation and hatred in every region time and again, and for a long time now the English have been entirely without victory and too much disheartened through God's wrath, and the pirates so strong through God's consent that often in battle one drives away ten, sometimes less and sometimes more, all because of our sins. And often ten or twelve, one after the other, will disgracefully put to shame a thane's wife, and sometimes his daughter or close kinswomen, while he looks on, he who considered himself brave and strong and good enough before that happened. And often a slave will bind fast the thane who had been his lord, and make him a slave through God's anger. Alas the misery, and alas the public shame that the English now suffer, all because of God's anger! Often two seamen, or sometimes three, will drive the droves of Christian men all through this nation from sea to sea, huddled together as a public shame for us all, if we could in earnest properly feel any. But all the disgrace we often suffer we repay with honour to those who shame us: we pay them continually, and they humiliate us daily. They ravage and they burn, plunder and rob and carry off to the ship; and indeed, what else is there in all these events than the wrath of God on this nation, clear and evident?

It is no wonder that misfortune should befall us, because we know full well that for many years now men have not cared what they did in word or deed. Rather it seems this nation has become thoroughly corrupted through manifold sins and many misdeeds: through acts of murder and evil, through avarice and greed, through theft and thievery, through slavery and pagan abuses, through treachery and trickery, through the breach of

---

[1] *thane* Nobleman.

law and order, through mayhem upon kinsmen and manslaughter, through crimes against clergy and adulteries, through incest and various fornications. And everywhere, as we said before, by the breaking of oaths and by various lies many more than should be are lost and betrayed, and breaches of feasts and fasts are widely and frequently committed. And here in this land also there are far too many degenerate apostates, hostile enemies of the Church, and cruel tyrants, and widespread scorners of divine law and Christian custom, and everywhere in the nation foolish mockers, most often of those things that the messengers of God command, and especially those things which always by right belong to God's law. And therefore it has now come far and wide to such an evil state that men are nowadays more ashamed of good deeds than of misdeeds; because too often good deeds are dismissed with derision and God-fearing men are reviled all too much, and especially mocked and treated with contempt are those who love justice and fear God to any extent. And because men behave thus, blaming all that they should praise and hating too much all that they ought to love, they bring all too many to evil intentions and wicked deeds, so that they are never ashamed even though they sin greatly and commit wrongs against God himself. But because of idle assaults they are ashamed to atone for their misdeeds as the books teach, like those fools who for pride will not guard themselves against injury, until they cannot do so even though they wish to.

Here, so it seems, too many in this country are sorely injured by the stains of sin. Here there are slayers of men and slayers of kinsmen, and murderers of priests and enemies of monasteries, and here are perjurers and murderers, and here there are whores and child-killers and many foul fornicating adulterers, and here there are wizards and sorceresses,[1] and here there are robbers and thieves and plunderers, and, to be brief, countless numbers of crimes and misdeeds. And we are not ashamed of it at all, but we are greatly ashamed to begin the remedy as the books teach us, and that is obvious in this wretched and sinful nation. Alas, many could easily call to mind much more in addition, which one man could not hastily devise, how wretchedly things have gone all the time now widely throughout this nation. And indeed let each one examine himself well, and not delay it all too long.

But lo! in God's name, let us do what is necessary for us, defend ourselves as best we may, lest we all perish together. There was a historian in the time of the Britons named Gildas, who wrote about their misdeeds, how they with their sins angered God so exceedingly that He finally allowed the army of the English to conquer their land and completely destroy the nobility of the Britons.[2] And this came about, he said, through robbery by the powerful and the coveting of ill-gotten gains, through the people's lawlessness and evil judgements, through the slackness of bishops and the abject cowardice of God's heralds, who too often kept silent from the truth and mumbled in their jaws when they should have cried out. Likewise, through the foul excesses of the people and through gluttony and manifold sins they destroyed their nation and themselves perished. But let us do what is needful—warn ourselves by such things; and what I say is true, we know of worse deeds among the English than we have ever heard of among the Britons. And therefore it is very necessary that we consider ourselves and earnestly plead with God Himself. And let us do what is necessary for us—bow to justice, and in some measure abandon injustice, and repair carefully what we have broken; and let us love God and follow God's laws, and earnestly practice what we promised when we received baptism, or those who were our sponsors at baptism; and let us arrange our words and deeds rightly, and cleanse our conscience thoroughly, and carefully keep our oaths and pledges, and have some faith between ourselves without deceit. And let us frequently consider the great judgment to which we all must come, and eagerly defend ourselves against the surging fires of the torments of hell, and earn for ourselves the glories and delights which God has prepared for those who do His will in the world. May God help us. Amen.

—1014

---

[1] *sorceresses* Wulfstan uses the word "wæl-cyrian," literally "choosers of the slain," related to the Norse Valkyries. But the word does not seem to have much mythological resonance here: as the context indicates, he apparently means only "female sorcerers" or "witches."

[2] *Britons* I.e., the Welsh, the Romano-Celtic Christian inhabitants of the island whom the Angles and Saxons displaced.

The first page of the manuscript text of *Sermo Lupi ad Anglos* (MS Cotton Nero Ai, fol. 110).

BLICKLING HOMILIES

The *Blickling Homilies* are a collection of English vernacular sermons from the end of the tenth century, surviving in a manuscript now in the Scheide Library in Princeton, New Jersey. These nineteen sermons cover many of the most important days in the liturgical calendar—Lent, Palm Sunday, Easter, Rogation Days (the three days of prayer and fasting before Ascension Thursday), the Ascension, the Annunciation and the Assumption of Mary. Other items cover the lives of saints such as John the Baptist, Peter and Paul, and Andrew. In the manuscript that has come down to us the texts are arranged in order of the liturgical year, but this may not be the original order of the items.

The collection is anonymous. Its contents are often unfavorably compared to the more polished and learned work of Ælfric or the rhetorical energy of Wulfstan; it is generally thought that the *Blickling Homilies* reflect the state of English preaching in the generation before Ælfric—more colloquial and anecdotal, more hortatory and sensational, less exegetical and scriptural. They are not necessarily less learned—the homily below draws on sermons of Caesarius of Arles and Gregory the Great for some passages—but they are, broadly speaking, more general, and seem to have been designed for a wider audience. These early homilies are primarily for reading aloud; their style and structure are more aural than textual, designed for listening rather than study and meditation.

Homily 10, probably intended for the third of the three Rogation Days before the feast of the Ascension, combines two powerful and popular themes: the decay of society, which signals the approaching end of the world, and the decay of the body which demonstrates the worthlessness of worldly things. It is apocalyptic only in a general sense, however, and bears few traces of the panic that is alleged to have gripped Christian Europe in the years surrounding 1000. It is really best thought of as a catechetical work, encouraging faith and fidelity to true doctrine and promising mercy to those who repent and put their lives in order. The sermon is particularly notable for its powerful theme of death and decay—the appeal of which can hardly be understated in this period—and for its use of the elegiac *ubi sunt* (Latin: "where are they") motif as it laments the lost world of the past, a rhetorical flourish found also in the poem *The Wanderer*.

⌘⌘⌘

Blickling Homily 10[1]

Beloved men, listen! I now admonish and instruct every person, both men and women, both young and old, both wise and foolish, both the rich and the poor, that everyone should examine and understand himself, and whatever great sins or small he has committed, he should turn immediately to better things and to the true medicine; then we may have God Almighty merciful to us, because the Lord desires all men should be healthy and sound, and turn to the true knowledge,

as David said, "Humble and fearing and trembling and quaking hearts, and those fearing their Creator, God will never despise nor disregard, but He hears their prayers when they cry to Him and ask Him for mercy."[2]

We can now see and recognize and very easily understand that the end of this world is very near; and many calamities have appeared and men's crimes and woes are greatly multiplied; and from one day to another we hear of monstrous torments and unnatural deaths that have come upon men throughout the country, and we often perceive that nation arises against nation, and unfortunate fighting gives rise to evil deeds;

---

[1] *Blickling Homily 10*   The present translation, prepared for this volume by R.M. Liuzza, is adapted from that of R. Morris.

[2] *Humble ... for mercy*   See Psalms 51.17.

and we often and frequently hear tell of the death of powerful men whose life was dear to men, and whose life seemed fair and beautiful and pleasant. And we are also informed of various diseases in many places of the world, and of growing famine. And we hear of many evils becoming more common and flourishing here in this life, and no good abides here, and all worldly things are very sinful, and too greatly cools the love that we ought to have for Our Lord, and we abandon those good works that we should undertake for our souls' health.

These tokens I have just described of this world's tribulations and perils are just as Christ Himself said to His disciples, that all these things should happen before the end of this world.[1] Let us now strive with all the might of good works and be eager for God's mercy, now that we can perceive that the time of the world's destruction is approaching, and therefore I admonish and warn everyone to consider carefully his own deeds, so that here in the world he may live rightly, before God and in the sight of the highest King. We should be generous to poor men, and charitable to the poor, as God Himself commanded us, to observe true peace and have concord among ourselves. And let those who have children instruct them in right discipline and teach them the way of life and the right way to Heaven. And if they in any way live their life wickedly, let them then at once be converted from their wickednesses and turn from their unrighteousness, that we thereby may all please God, as it stands required of all believing people, and not just of those who have subjected themselves to God in exalted positions—bishops and kings, and mass-priests, and archdeacons, but is also indeed required of subdeacons and monks.

And to all men it is necessary and profitable that they observe well their baptismal vows. Let no man here in this worldly kingdom be too proud in his thoughts, nor too strong in his body, nor too eager for malice, nor too bold in wickedness, nor too full of tricks, nor too fond of guile, neither given to making accusations nor to laying snares. Nor should anyone think that his body can or will make up for the burdens of sin in the grave; but there he will rot into dust and there await his fate, when the Almighty God will bring about an end to this world, and when He will draw His fiery sword and strike through all this world, and pierce through the bodies, and cut apart this middle-earth; and the dead will rise up, then shall the fleshly garment be as transparent as glass, and no trace of unrighteousness can be concealed at all.

Therefore it is needful for us that we not pursue foolish works too long, but we must make our peace with God and men, and establish firmly the right belief in our hearts, that it may and can dwell there, and there grow and bloom; and we must confess the true belief in the Lord God and our Savior Jesus Christ, His only-begotten Son, and in the Holy Ghost, who is co-eternal with the Father and Son. And we must trust in God's holy Church, and in those that have right belief; and we must believe in the forgiveness of sins and the resurrection of the body on the Day of Judgment, and we must believe in the everlasting life, and in the heavenly kingdom that is promised to all that are now workers of good. This is the right faith, which it behooves every man well to hold and perform, for no worker may perform good works before God without love and belief. And it is very necessary that we ourselves consider and bear this in mind, and then most diligently when we hear God's books explained and read to us, and the gospel declared, and His glories made known to men. Let us then diligently strive to be afterwards the better and the happier for the teaching that we have often heard.

Oh, beloved men, listen! we must take care not to love too greatly what we ought to leave behind, nor yet to give up too quickly what we ought to hold eternally. Let us now notice very carefully that no man in the world has such wealth, nor such magnificent riches here in the world, that he will not come to an end in a brief interval; and he shall leave behind all that was pleasant to him before in this world and most dear to possess and to hold; and no man is so dear to his kinsmen and his friends in the world, nor none of them loves him so greatly that he shall not immediately afterwards shrink from him, when the body and the spirit are separated, and his fellowship will seem loathsome and foul to him. That is no marvel; for, behold! what else is the flesh after the eternal portion, that is the soul, is removed? Lo! what else remains but the food of worms? Where then

---

[1]   *These tokens ... world*   See Luke 21.9.

shall be his riches and his feasts? Where then shall be his pride and his arrogance? Where then shall be his vain garments? Where then shall be the ornaments and the grand attire with which he previously adorned his body? Where then shall be his desire and his sinful lusts which he followed here in the world? Behold, then he must with his soul alone atone to God Almighty for all that he here in this world wickedly committed.

Let us now hear related a story[1] of a certain rich and powerful man: he possessed in this world great wealth and very splendid and manifold treasures, and lived in comfort. Then it happened that his life ended, and there came to him a sudden end of this transitory life. There was then a certain one of his kinsmen and earthly friends that loved him more than any other man; on account of the longing and sorrow caused by the other's death he could no longer stay in that country, but, with a sorrowful mind, he departed from his native land and from his dwelling-place, and dwelt in that land many years; and his longing never diminished, but greatly oppressed and afflicted him. Then after a time he began to long for his native land again, for he wished to see and examine the tomb again, to see what he was like whom formerly he had often seen beautiful in face and stature....[2] The bones of the dead man called to him, and thus said, "Why have you come hither to look at us? Now you may see here a portion of dust, and the leavings of worms, where before you saw a beautiful garment interwoven with gold. Behold now dust and dry bones, where before you saw, after the nature of flesh, limbs fair to look upon. Oh, my friend and kinsman, be mindful of this, and convince yourself that you are now what I once was, and after a time you will be what I now am. Remember this, and know that my riches that I once had are all vanished and decayed, and my dwellings have crumbled and perished. But turn to yourself and incline your heart to good counsel, and deserve that your prayers be acceptable to God Al-

mighty." Then, so sad and grieving, he departed from this spectacle of dust and turned himself away from all the affairs of this world; and he began to learn the praise of God and to teach it, and to love spiritual virtues, and thereby earned for himself the grace of the Holy Spirit; and he delivered also the other's soul from punishment and released him from torments.

Let us, then, beloved men, keep this in mind, and set this example in our hearts, that we should not love the adornments of the world too greatly, nor this middle-earth itself; because the world is all corruptible, and perishable, and subject to decay, and unstable; and this world is all transitory. Let us then carefully consider and know in regard to the beginning of this world, that when it was first formed it was full of all beauty, and was blooming in itself with many and various pleasures; and in that time it was pleasant to men upon earth, and healthful, and complete serenity was upon the earth, and an abundance of peace, and excellent progeny; and in that time this world was so fair and so delightful that it drew men to it by its beauty and pleasantness, away from Almighty God. And when it was thus fair and thus pleasant, it withered away in the hearts of Christ's holy people, and is now blooming in our hearts, as is fit. Now there is lamentation and weeping on all sides; now there is mourning everywhere, and breach of peace; now there is evil and slaughter everywhere; and everywhere this middle-earth flees from us with great bitterness, and we follow it as it flies from us, and love it as it passes away.

Listen! we may perceive by this that this world is fleeting and transitory. Let us then be mindful of this while we may and can, so that we may gladly submit to God. Let us obey Our Lord readily, and give thanks to Him for all His gifts and all his mercies, and for all His kindness and benefits that He has always shown to us, the Heavenly King that lives and reigns forever and ever, world without end, in eternity. Amen.

—LATE IOTH CENTURY

---

[1] *a story*   What follows is an *exemplum* or example, a narrative that illustrates the sermon's lesson.

[2] *stature* ...   A line is missing here, apparently telling how the traveler returned home and saw the decaying corpse of his deceased friend.

GEOFFREY OF MONMOUTH

c. 1100 — c. 1154

Geoffrey of Monmouth was born at Monmouth and died at Llandaff. He may have been a Benedictine monk. After arriving in Llandaff in 1140, he became Archdeacon of St. Teilo's, and he was ordained a priest in 1151–52. He was elected Bishop of St. Asaph and consecrated at Lambeth by the Archbishop of Canterbury, but he died before he could enter his diocese. Geoffrey of Monmouth is best known for his chronicle, *The History of the Kings of Britain* (*Historia regum britanniae*), which he composed in Latin for an educated audience. His *Historia* appeared before 1139, but the chronicler continued to revise, reissuing his completed work in 1147. He also wrote a version of the *Prophecies of Merlin* and perhaps a life of Merlin (*Vita Merlini*) as well.

In his *Historia*, Geoffrey aimed to recount the history of the kings of Britain from before the time of Christ to the time of Cadwallader (689 CE). His version of the myth of the origins of his island nation begins with Brutus, the great-grandson of Aeneas, who ostensibly arrives in Albion in the late twelfth century BCE. With his Trojan followers, Brutus defeats the giants inhabiting the land, and his compatriots rename the island "Britain" in his honor. After this, Geoffrey follows the line of British kings up to the time of Julius Caesar and the Roman invasions. By the fifth century, after Rome has departed from Britain (c. 410 CE), Geoffrey is ready to introduce Arthur, to whom he devotes approximately one-quarter of his *Historia*.

Geoffrey depicts Arthur as the son of Uther Pendragon and Ygerna, the wife of Gorlois, Duke of Cornwall. According to the *Historia*, Uther fell in love with Ygerna and wanted her for himself. In order to obtain her, Uther brought his army to attack the Duke, her husband. While Gorlois fought, Merlin cast a spell over Uther so that he would look exactly like Gorlois and thus be able to enter Tintagel, Gorlois's stronghold, and sleep with his wife. It was on this occasion that Arthur was conceived. Meanwhile, Gorlois died fighting against Uther's army, so Uther was soon able to resume his natural appearance and marry Ygerna.

With such a magical beginning, it is no surprise that Geoffrey's Arthur turns out to do extraordinary things. He becomes king as a young man and engages in a series of successful battles, defeating the Saxons, the Picts, and the Scots (with the help of his sword Caliburn), and conquering Ireland and Iceland as well. He marries Guinevere, a lady of Roman descent, and establishes an internationally famous order of knighthood which includes such men as Kay, Bedivere, and Gawain. After years of peace, he attacks and conquers Norway, Denmark, and much of Gaul. He holds court at Caerleon in Wales. But when Lucius, the western Emperor of Rome, demands tribute and the return of conquered lands, Arthur goes back to the continent to fight the Romans and defeats them in Burgundy. He might have continued his conquests except that news reaches him that his nephew Mordred has declared himself king, seduced the Queen, and made a pact with the Saxons. So Arthur returns to do battle with Mordred and routs him near the River Camel in Cornwall. Unluckily, Arthur is badly wounded in the fray. He is taken to the Isle of Avalon to recover from his wounds, but he transfers his crown to his cousin Constantine before his departure. Geoffrey does not record Arthur's death, leaving room for the belief in the future return of Arthur as King of Britain.

Geoffrey certainly used more than one source to create his fabulous *Historia*. He himself claimed that his chronicle was a translation of "a certain very ancient book written in the British language" that had been given to him by Walter, the Archdeacon of Oxford, but this book does not appear to have survived (and some doubt that it ever existed). Geoffrey's other sources include such historians as Gildas, Bede, and Nennius, and his account of Arthur also may have had a Welsh source.

Geoffrey's own imagination must be given credit, too, for his *Historia* reflects creative, if not always historically accurate, thinking.

Geoffrey's imagination and his status as an historian have been the subject of much debate. In his chronicle of 1151, Alfred of Beverly questioned why other historians do not acknowledge the deeds of the Britons celebrated by Geoffrey of Monmouth. In 1198, the historian William of Newburgh concluded that the Arthur and Merlin who appear in Geoffrey's *Historia* are fictitious characters, not historical ones, and he condemned Geoffrey as the "father of lies." William of Malmesbury, perhaps thinking of Geoffrey of Monmouth, complained that Arthur was the one about whom the Welsh tell "deceitful fables," and Ranulf Higden, the fourteenth-century compiler of the Latin *Polychronicon*, dismissed Geoffrey's portrayal of Arthur as improbable. Ranulf explained Geoffrey's glorification of Arthur by saying that each people likes to have its own hero and to praise him excessively; the Greeks have Alexander, for example, and the French have Charlemagne. Modern historians, beginning with the Renaissance historian Polydore Vergil, an Italian living in England who authored the *Anglica historia* (1534), have confirmed that Geoffrey of Monmouth departed from historical truth more often than he stuck to it. Nevertheless, Geoffrey's *Historia* exercised a tremendous influence not only on historical accounts of Britain, but also on romance narratives in medieval England and France.

Vernacular translations of Geoffrey's *Historia* abounded in the Middle Ages. Gaimar and Wace translated the work into Anglo-Norman, while Layamon and Robert of Gloucester translated it into English. Once translated into French, Geoffrey's *Historia* influenced French romance traditions dealing with the "Matter of Britain," including, perhaps most significantly, the works of Chrétien de Troyes. Geoffrey's *Historia* influenced both historical chronicles (the "Brut" tradition) and romance narratives such as the fourteenth-century alliterative poem *Morte Arthure* and the stanzaic *Le Morte Arthur* as well. In later centuries, it also helped to shape such works as Sir Thomas Malory's *Morte d'Arthur*, Tennyson's "Idylls of the King," and numerous modern novels that retell Arthurian legends.

⌘ ⌘ ⌘

from *A History of the Kings of Britain*[1]

from BOOK 1

Britain is the best of isles, situated in the western ocean between France and Ireland.[2] Stretching eight hundred miles north to south and two hundred miles east to west, it supplies ceaseless abundance for every human necessity. It is rich in every type of metal and likewise has wide fields and hills, which are well-suited for widespread agriculture. The soil in its richness brings forth many types of crops, each in its proper season. The island also has forests filled with all types of wild beasts and pastures filled with domestic animals and with all colors of flowers that offer their nectar to the flying bees. It also possesses the greenest fields stretching pleasantly beneath lofty mountains, in which sparkling waters flow by in sweetly murmuring streams, promising sweet slumbers on their banks. Moreover, Britain is watered with lakes and rivers full of fish, and on its southern edge by a channel over which one can sail to France.

Three noble rivers—the Thames, the Severn, and the Humber—extend like three arms, bringing in the commerce of the sea from all countries. Twenty-eight cities once adorned the land. Some of these cities, their walls leveled, now lie in ruin; in others, still standing, there tower high the most beautiful steepled churches of the saints, in which groups of religious men and women

---

[1] *The History of the Kings of Britain*   The translation from the Latin of Geoffrey's *Historia regum britanniae* excerpted here is that prepared by Michael Faletra for the Broadview edition of *The History of the Kings of Britain*; Faletra's annotations have also been drawn on extensively here.

[2] *Britain ... Ireland*   The description of Britain here follows those of Gildas and Bede, often almost verbatim.

give praise to God according to the Christian teaching. In latter days, five peoples have inhabited the island: the Normans, the Britons, the Saxons, the Picts, and the Scots. Of these, the Britons first settled the island from sea to sea, until divine vengeance, on account of their overweening pride, sent the Picts and Saxons[1] to drive them out. The story of their origins and arrival now remains to be explained.

After the Trojan War, Aeneas fled the fall of Troy with his son Ascanius[2] and then sailed on to Italy. There he was most honorably received by King Latinus.[3] Turnus, the King of the Rutuli, grew jealous and fought against him. They met together in combat, wherein Aeneas prevailed and slew Turnus, thus winning the kingdom of Italy, as well as the hand of Lavinia, King Latinus's daughter. After Aeneas had breathed his last, Ascanius took on the royal authority. He built Alba Longa on an island in the Tiber[4] and had a son whose name was Silvius. This son, indulging in secret pleasures, wed a certain granddaughter of Lavinia and fathered a child on her. When this was made known to Ascanius, he ordered his court wizards to ascertain the sex of the child. The wizards revealed, in no uncertain terms, that the girl would bear a son who would kill both his father and his mother, but that he would also wander in exile through many lands until he had finally achieved the highest honor. In this prophecy the wizards were not mistaken, for when the day of the child's birth arrived, the woman indeed bore a son and died in childbirth. The boy was taken by the midwife and named Brutus. When fifteen years had passed, this young man came upon his father while hunting and unintentionally killed him with an arrow: for it hap-

pened that, while his servants were leading a group of deer towards him, Brutus attempted to shoot at them, but his missile struck his father in the chest instead.[5]

Brutus's relatives were horrified by the crime he had committed, and he was expelled from Italy. …

[Brutus wanders collecting followers and showing his prowess as a leader, eventually reaching "Albion."]

In those days, the island was named Albion, and was uninhabited except by a few giants.[6] It was a beautiful place, filled with forests and with rivers that teemed with fish. It inspired Brutus and his companions with a great desire to settle there. As they explored the various regions of the island, the Trojans discovered giants who had fled to caves in the mountains. With the approval of their leader, the Trojans then partitioned the land among themselves. They began to cultivate the fields and construct buildings, so that, after a short space of time, you would think that they had lived there forever. Then Brutus called the island Britain, after his own name, and he called his comrades Britons. In devising these names, he hoped to be remembered forever. Thus in later days, the language of the people, which was originally called Trojan or crooked Greek, was known as British.[7] But Corineus called the portion of the realm that fell by lot to him Corinea after himself, and his people followed his example and called themselves the Corineans. When all the provinces of Britain were to be divided up, Corineus had been allowed to choose his portion before everyone else, and he preferred that region which is now called Cornwall, either from the fact that it is the horn of Britain or from corruption of

---

[1] *Britons* Celtic inhabitants of Great Britain at the time of the Roman invasions; *Saxons* West Germanic groups that invaded Great Britain sporadically in the fifth and sixth centuries; *Picts* Ancient Celtic people, early inhabitants of what is now Scotland.

[2] *Trojan War* Ten-year war between the Trojans and Greeks, caused by Paris's abduction of Helen, and ending in the destruction of Troy; *Aeneas* Trojan hero who escaped the city's fall, wandering for seven years before founding Rome; *Ascanius* Aeneas's son.

[3] *King Latinus* King of Latium, a pre-Roman city in Italy.

[4] *Alba* Alba Longa, ancient pre-Roman city destroyed in the twelfth century BCE, shortly after Troy; *Tiber* Principal river of central Italy, flowing through Rome.

[5] *while hunting … instead* This incident doubtless resonated with Geoffrey's contemporaries, since King William Rufus of England was also slain in a hunting accident (in the New Forest, in 1100).

[6] *Albion* The name is an ancient one, known to the Greeks and Romans. It is unclear, however, whether the indigenous peoples of Britain ever used the term at such an early date.

[7] *British* Geoffrey here uses the word *Britannica*, a term that in twelfth-century Latin was regularly used to describe the Celtic languages of Wales, Brittany, and Cornwall alike. The term "crooked Greek" here derives from a Welsh folk etymology in which the name of the Welsh language, *Cymraeg* in Welsh, is derived from *cam groeg*, "crooked Greek."

the word Corinea.[1]

Corineus himself took great relish in fighting against the giants who seemed to thrive in his homeland more than in that of any of his comrades. There was among them a certain giant by the name of Gogmagog who stood some twelve cubits[2] tall. This Gogmagog was so strong that he once uprooted an oak tree as if it were a hazel-shoot. One day, when Brutus was celebrating a feast at the place where the Trojans had first landed, Gogmagog came with twenty other giants and caused great slaughter among the Britons. The Britons managed to band together and defeat the invaders, killing all of them except for Gogmagog. Brutus insisted that he be kept alive, for he greatly desired to see a wrestling match between him and Corineus, who enjoyed fighting giants above all other sport. Corineus arrived most jubilantly. He rolled up his sleeves, threw aside his weapons and provoked the giant to wrestle. At first Corineus, then the giant, prevailed as they struggled together, locked in each other's embrace. The very air vibrated with the groaning of their mighty breaths. Eventually Gogmagog exerted all his strength on Corineus and broke three of his ribs, two on the right side, and one on the left. This infuriated Corineus: he put forth all of his own strength, slung the giant over his shoulders, and made as fast as he could under the weight to the edge of the sea. There, at the pinnacle of a great cliff, he shook himself out of the giant's grip, heaved up the deadly creature that he carried on his shoulders, and cast him into the sea. Gogmagog, falling against the sharp rocks below, was dashed into a thousand pieces. The tide was red with his blood. That place derived its name from the giant's fall and is still called Gogmagog's Leap up to the present day.

After dividing up the realm, Brutus decided to build a city. To carry out this plan, he traveled all around the island looking for the perfect location. Coming eventually to the River Thames, he wandered its banks until he found a spot that was well suited to his purposes. He built a city there and called it *Troia Nova*, New Troy. From this name it was called in latter days, through the corruption of tongues, *Trinovant*. But in years to come, Lud—the brother of that Cassibelaunus who fought against Julius Caesar[3]—took control of the kingdom, and he surrounded that city with mighty walls and towers constructed with the most cunning artifice. He ordered the city to be called Caer Lud after himself. There afterwards arose great strife between him and his other brother Nennius, who bore it ill that Lud should want to erase the name of Troy from their land. The historian Gildas describes the dispute between them at length; I shall therefore choose to pass over these matters, lest I spoil with my humbler diction that which such a great writer discusses so elegantly.[4]

After Brutus built this city, he dedicated it to the citizens as their birthright, and he gave them a law code with which they could maintain the peace. In those days, the High Priest Eli ruled in Judaea, and the Ark of the Covenant was captured by the Philistines.[5] In Troy, the sons of Hector reigned, having expelled the descendants of Antenor. Silvius Aeneas, the son of Aeneas, ruled in Italy.[6] He was Brutus's uncle and the third king of the Latins.

---

1 *Cornwall … Corinea* Geoffrey's usual Latin term for Cornwall is *Cornubia*, and he usually refers to its inhabitants as *Cornubienses*; here he employs the appellation *Corineiensem*, in order to emphasize the derivation of their name from Corineus. Historically, the name of the land likely derives from the *Cornovii*, a Celtic British tribe mentioned by Roman authorities. The resemblance of the shape of the Cornish peninsula to a horn has led some to claim that the Celtic term *corn* ("horn") underlies the word.

2 *cubit* Unit of measurement, equal to the distance between the elbow and the fingertips.

---

3 *Julius Caesar* Roman general, emperor, and historian (100–44 BCE) who invaded Britain in the first century CE, and who was assassinated by political enemies.

4 *great strife … elegantly* Gildas's account of the relations between Rome and Britain in his *Ruin of Britain* makes no mention of this fraternal strife.

5 *Judea* Ancient kingdom composed of modern-day southern Israel and southwestern Jordan; *Ark of the Covenant* Sacred chest in which the ancient Hebrews stored the tablets on which the Ten Commandments were inscribed. Insofar as these Biblical events are historical, they are thought to have occurred in the eleventh century BCE.

6 *Troy … Italy* Geoffrey here touches on incidents from the Trojan War, which holds a central place in Greek legend. The events of the war were taken by the ancient Greeks (and by medieval chroniclers) to be historical fact, with the events believed to have taken place in the thirteenth or twelfth centuries BCE.

from Book 2

[Geoffrey proceeds to discuss the genealogy and history of many of the kings of England, including the legendary King Leir—whose story appears here in a rather different form than Shakespeare gives it in *King Lear*.]

... With Bladud thus consigned to his doom, his son Leir was elevated to the kingship and ruled the land for sixty years. Leir built a city on the banks of the Soar which derives its name from him in the British tongue as Kaer Leir and in the Saxon tongue as Leicester. Denied any male offspring, he nonetheless had three daughters whose names were Goneril, Regan, and Cordelia.[1] Their father loved them all greatly, but he loved his youngest daughter, Cordelia, most of all. And so, when he began to grow old he thought about how to divide his kingdom among them and he sought to find such husbands as would share the rule of the land with them. In order to determine which of his three daughters was more worthy of the greater part of the kingdom, he went and asked them one by one who loved him the best. Posed this question by her father, Goneril the eldest daughter took the gods in heaven as witness that she bore for him a greater love than she bore for the soul that was in her own body. Her father then said to her, "Since in my old age you place me above all else, I shall marry you, my most beloved daughter, to whatever young man you should choose, and I shall give you a third of the kingdom of Britain." Then Regan, the second daughter, taking heed of her sister's example and hoping to insinuate her way into her father's good graces, answered him with many oaths, swearing that she could by no means express how much she loved him, except to say that she loved him above all other creatures. Thus gulled, her father granted her the same dignity as her sister and promised to find her a husband and give her another third of his kingdom.

But when Cordelia, the youngest daughter, perceived that her father was content with her sisters' flattery, she thought she would test him and decided to answer him quite differently. "Is there, my father," she asked, "a daughter anywhere who can presume to love her father more than is fitting? I do not think that there is any daughter who would dare to confess this, unless she is seeking to conceal the truth with empty words. Indeed, I have always loved you as my father and even now my feelings do not waver. And if you insist on wrenching any more out of me, remember the constancy of the love I have held for you and cease your questioning. You truly have as much of my love as you are worth: that's how much I love you." Then her father grew exceedingly angry and indignant about this answer that she had given from the bottom of her heart. He did not delay in expressing himself thus: "Because you hold your aged father in such contempt and do not deign to love me as your sisters do, I refuse to let you share any part of this realm with your sisters. Since you are my daughter, however, I am not saying that I wouldn't marry you off to some foreigner if Fortune should permit it. But I assure you that I shall never seek to marry you with the same honor that I showed your sisters. Of course, while I had loved you until today more than your sisters, you have in fact loved me far less than they do."

Without delay, Leir followed the advice of his noble counsellors and married his two oldest daughters to the Duke of Cornwall and the Duke of Alban, along with half the island to rule between them as long as he lived. After his death, they would possess sovereignty over all of Britain.

Then it happened that Aganippus, the king of the Franks,[2] having heard great tidings of Cordelia's beauty, sent messengers to the king asking for his daughter's hand in marriage. Her father, steadfast in his anger, answered that he would give her to him freely, but without land or dowry, for he had already partitioned his kingdom, along with all his gold and silver, to his daughters Goneril and Regan. When this settlement was announced to Aganippus, he was even more greatly inflamed with love for the girl. He sent again to Leir, saying that he had gold and silver and lands enough, for

---

[1]   *three daughters ... Cordelia*   Geoffrey's account of Leir and his three daughters is the earliest known version of the story that formed the basis of Shakespeare's *King Lear*. The story passed from Geoffrey into the writings of various medieval chroniclers, before finding its way into Holinshed's *Chronicles*, Shakespeare's primary source.

[2]   *Franks*   Geoffrey's use of the term *Franks* rather than *Gauls* to refer to the inhabitants of France may reflect his having turned here from one source to another.

he possessed a third of Gaul. So he obtained the girl in this way in order to produce heirs with her. When the agreement was reached, Cordelia was sent to Gaul and married off to Aganippus.

After a long space of time, old age began to wear Leir down, and the dukes to whom he had partitioned the kingdom and married his daughters rose up against him. They seized from him the kingdom and the sovereign power that he had hitherto wielded bravely and gloriously. They avoided an all-out civil war, however, because one of his sons-in-law, Maglaurus the Duke of Alban, maintained Leir with one hundred forty knights so that the king would not appear dishonored. When two years had passed with Leir in residence there, his daughter Goneril became impatient with the great crowd of her father's retainers because they made trouble with her own servants, always insisting on more sumptuous rations. Her husband therefore decided that her father should be content with a retinue of thirty, and he dismissed the remainder.

Leir became so indignant at this treatment that he left Maglaurus and sought out Henwin, the Duke of Cornwall, whom he had married to his second daughter, Regan. Although the duke welcomed him honorably, not a year had passed before there was again friction between the household and Leir's attendants. Regan became angry because of this and ordered her father to dismiss all of his men, except for five who should remain to serve him. Her father was then greatly anguished, and he went back to his first daughter to see if he could move her to pity and allow him to keep all of his retainers. But Goneril was not moved at all and rekindled her former hostility. She swore by the gods in heaven that he could not lodge with her unless he dismissed all his men and would be content with a single retainer. She chided the old man, who now had nothing, for expecting to maintain such a following. Since she would in no way agree to anything he wanted, he yielded to her and dismissed the others and remained with one single servant.

But when Leir cast his memory back upon his former dignity, he began to detest the misery of his current state and thought about going to entreat his youngest daughter who lived across the ocean. He feared that she would not help him at all since he had

married her off so ungraciously, yet he could tolerate his abjection no longer and set sail for Gaul. While crossing the sea, he noticed that he was accounted third among the princes there on the ship, and he lamented with crying and sobbing in these words: "O, you unbendable chain of Fate! you who keep to such an unswerving and narrow path! Why did you ever elevate me to an unstable happiness when it is a greater pain to revisit good times lost than to be oppressed by the sorrows to come? Indeed, the mere memory of that time when I was attended by a hundred thousand knights, when I was accustomed to cast down city walls and lay waste the lands of my enemies, grieves me more than the calamity of my present state. Fate has driven those who once lay beneath my feet to forsake me now in my weakness. O vengeful Fortune, will the day ever come when I will be able to repay those who have deserted me in my present state of poverty? O Cordelia, how true were those words you spoke when I asked what kind of love you bore me! You said 'I love you with as much of my love as you are worth.' While I was still able to give, I was worth much to them who were friends not to me but to my gifts. All the while they loved me but loved my riches more, for when the handouts went away so did they. But, dearest daughter, how will I dare to beg from you? Because of your words, I chose to marry you off more poorly than your sisters, who now, after receiving their inheritance, have reduced me to an exile and beggar."

Leir was saying these and similar things, and he came to Caritia where his daughter was dwelling. Waiting outside the city, he sent a messenger ahead to announce how he had fallen upon such hard times. And since Leir had neither food nor clothing, the messenger begged her to grant mercy upon the king. When her father was presented in this way, Cordelia was moved to bitter tears and she inquired as to how many men he had with him. He sent answer that he had only the one man who waited outside with him. At this, Cordelia seized all the gold and silver at hand and gave it to the messenger, instructing him to bring her father to a nearby city. There the messenger should treat the king as if he were ill, and he should provide Leir with baths, food, and shelter. Cordelia also arranged that her father retain forty well-dressed and fully-armed knights and that, after a time, he should send for King Aganippus and his own daughter.

When the messenger returned to King Leir, he brought him to another city and hid him there, carrying out all the things that Cordelia had commanded. As soon as Leir was arrayed in kingly attire and had established his new household, he sent messages to Aganippus and Cordelia, explaining that he had been cast out of Britain by his own sons-in-law and that he was coming now to seek their aid in recovering his realm. And so Aganippus and Cordelia came to him with their counselors and retinue, and they treated him with great honor and restored him to the power and high dignity he had once commanded in his own kingdom. In the meantime, Aganippus sent messengers all throughout Gaul to muster every armed soldier for assistance in restoring the kingdom of Britain to his father-in-law. Once Aganippus had done this, Leir led Cordelia and the assembled host and fought against his sons-in-law and defeated them. Three years after he had regained all of his former power, he died. Aganippus, king of the Franks, had also died by then. So Leir's daughter Cordelia assumed the governance of the kingdom, and she buried her father in an underground chamber which she had had built beneath the River Soar downstream from Leicester. This crypt was built in honor of the two-faced god Janus.[1] There, on the god's feast day, all the craftsmen of the city came to begin the first of the works that they would undertake for the entire year.

from BOOK 6

[This book is largely concerned with Britain at the end of the Roman period (when Rome held only a tenuous grasp of much of the island), and the period immediately following the withdrawal of Roman forces.]

When Gratianus the freedman learned of the death of Maximianus, he seized the crown of the realm and declared himself king. From that moment on, he oppressed the people with such great tyranny that the common folk organized themselves and attacked and

killed him.[2] As word of this event reached other countries, the above-mentioned enemies, Wanius and Melga, returned from Ireland. Leading an army of Scots, Norsemen, and Danes, they ravaged the kingdom with fire and sword from sea to sea. Because of this terrible infestation and oppression, messengers were sent to Rome with letters, tearfully imploring the Romans to lend military aid so that they could avenge themselves; they also vowed their own eternal subjection to Rome, if only their enemies could be held at bay. In response, a legion that had not been involved with the recent ills in Britain was dispatched at once. It was shipped across the ocean to Britain and engaged the enemy in hand-to-hand combat. Overthrowing that great host, they drove the rest of the foreigners out of the land and thus delivered the oppressed people of Britain from destruction. The Romans then advised the Britons to construct a wall between Alban and Deira[3] stretching from coast to coast. Though requiring a multitude of workers, such a wall would protect them from their enemies and would instill fear in any invaders, thus providing a defense for the Britons. Indeed, Alban in those days was completely overrun with barbarians, and any enemy force that landed there could always find a warm welcome. Therefore, drawing upon both private and public support, the local inhabitants pressed on in their labor and erected the wall.

The Romans then announced that they would by no means be troubled any longer with such costly expeditions and that it was beneath them to waste their military forces on land and sea dealing with unruly pirates. Instead, they said, the Britons should get into the habit of relying upon their own forces; they should act like men and defend their own lands, riches, women, children, and, above all, their freedom and way of life. Having issued this warning, they summoned all the men of the island who could bear arms back to London, for they themselves were preparing to return to Rome.

---

[2] *Gratianus ... killed him* Geoffrey's description of Gratianus is based on a similarly terse account in Bede (*Ecclesiastical History* 1.11).

[3] *wall ... Deira* The ancient kingdoms of Deira and Bernicia were later merged into the kingdom of Northumbria. The wall referred to here, now known as Hadrian's Wall, was in fact constructed in the second century CE (at the instigation of the Roman Emperor Hadrian), not in the fifth century, as Geoffrey's account implies.

---

[1] *Janus* In Roman mythology, God of doorways and gates, traditionally represented with two faces looking in opposing directions.

When all the men were assembled, word was sent to Guithelin, the bishop of London, who addressed the Britons with these words: "Because of the command of the princes gathered around me, I feel obliged to address you. But I feel more like weeping than giving you some fancy speech; for I bewail the weakness and lack of guidance that has beset us since Maximianus bereaved this realm of all its armed forces and young men. You, a people unskilled in the waging of war, are all that is left, you who whose real business lies in the tilling of fields or the trading of wares. When invaders came from foreign lands, you went running like sheep without a shepherd, abandoning your folds until the power of the Romans restored your possessions. Will your hope always lie in outside protection? Will you not equip your own hands with shields and swords and spears against thieves who would by no means be stronger than you if you would only shake off your own sloth and sluggishness? The Romans have grown weary of running constantly about and taking the trouble to fight our enemies for us. They would rather forego whatever tribute they used to collect than continue to waste their efforts defending us by land and by sea. So now what? If you had only been a humble folk back when you were at the height of your former military power, do you think that all mankind would have fled from you? Can real men not be born of humble stock? Can a soldier not be born into a farmer's family, or a farmer from a military family? A soldier can indeed come from a shopkeeper's family and a shopkeeper from a soldier's. Since it is not unusual, then, that a man of one type can come from a different type of stock, I do not believe that you people can forget how to be real men. Since you are men, act like men! Call upon Christ to grant you the courage to defend your own homes!" When he had finished speaking, the people broke out in such a clamor that you might say that their courage was restored in that very moment.

After this, the Romans gave the timid Britons some good advice and left plans for the construction of defenses. They recommended that the Britons build a series of watchtowers at fixed intervals all along the southern coast of the ocean, for that is where the Britons kept their merchant fleet and therefore where they should most fear a barbarian attack. But it is easier to make a kite hunt like a sparrow-hawk than to instruct a farmer in the art of war. He who tries to explain complex matters to such a person might as well toss a pearl among swine. For as soon as the Romans bade their farewell, never to return, their old enemies emerged once again from the ships in which they had fled to Ireland. They brought with them hideous hosts of Scots and Picts and Norsemen and Danes and many others, and they captured all of Alban down to the Wall. Now that they had learned about the withdrawal of the Romans and their intention never to return, they were far more confident and threatened to ravage the entire island. The farm-folk defended the walls against them, but they were useless in battle, unable even to flee because of their faint-heartedness, and a poor defense they made perched up in their look-out posts all day and all night. All the while, the enemy continued to shoot the wretched Britons with barbed missiles, which flung them from the walls and dashed them to the ground. This untimely death was actually a blessing, for with such an end they avoided the awful torments that their brethren and loved ones would soon suffer. O how God punishes past evils! Alas, that Maximianus in his folly took away so many strong warriors! If they had been there when such a disaster hit, there would have been no enemy host that could not have been repelled. What was now clear about the Roman occupation is that they had been able to protect far-off lands with their military might and that they had ruled Britain peacefully. This is what happens when the defense of a kingdom falls upon its common-folk. What more can I say? Once their cities and the High Wall were abandoned, all the usual exiles swiftly followed, as did desperate dispersions, and persecution by the enemy, and the cruelest slaughter. The miserable Britons were plucked off by their foes like sheep by a wolf.

And so once again, the miserable remnant sent letters to Agitius, a powerful man among the Romans, imploring him thus: "O Agitius, thrice consul, hear the groans of the Britons!" And after saying a few more words, they added: "The sea drives us toward the barbarians and the barbarians drive us into the sea. Two different modes of death await us: we will either be drowned or get our throats slashed."[1] But, not receiving any aid from the Romans, the messengers returned home sadly to relate the sorry news to their countrymen.

Taking counsel together, the Britons decided that Guithelin, the Archbishop of London, should go to Brittany, which was then called Armorica or Letavia, to seek help from their fellow Britons there. At that time, Aldroenus was king of Brittany, the fourth since that Conan to whom Maximianus had granted that land, as has been related above. Seeing a man of such high reverence as Guithelin approaching, Aldroenus welcomed him with great ceremony and asked the reason for his visit. Guithelin answered: "It is clear enough that pity can move you and your noble retainers to tears over what we, your fellow Britons, have suffered since Maximianus despoiled our island of all its soldiers and ordered them to inhabit the land which you rule. May you yet rule over it in peace for many long years. However, all the peoples who dwell near our island have risen up against us, the destitute remainder of your own British people. They have completely emptied our island realm of its store of riches. The British folk now have no food at all except what they can catch by hunting. There is no one who can stop them since no one remains among us who is skilled in the arts of war. You see, the Romans grew weary of defending us and went home, depriving us of all support. We are now bereft of all other hope, and we come to beg for your mercy. We beg you to take command and defend the kingdom that rightfully belongs to you from barbarian invasion. Who else but you whom we implore should wear the crown of Constantine and Maximianus, the crown your own grandfathers and great-grandfathers wore? Prepare your fleet and come: I place the kingdom of Britain in your hands."

To these words Aldroenus responded: "There was once a time when I would not have refused the isle of Britain if it had been offered to me. Truly, I do not deem any country more prosperous than Britain when it enjoyed peace and tranquility. But now that misfortune has overtaken the land, it becomes less appealing to me and completely loathsome to my vassals. Above all, the evil power of the Romans has harmed Britain, so much so that no king can now maintain his power there unless he abrogates his freedom and accepts servitude to Rome. Who, then, would not prefer to reign quietly but freely over another land rather than possess the riches of Britain under the yoke of servitude? The kingdom that is now under my power is one I hold honorably, paying no homage to anyone higher than myself. I cherish it above all other lands, for I govern it in liberty. However, since my grandfathers and great-grandfathers did indeed once hold sway over the island of Britain, I will send with you my brother Constantine[2] and two thousand soldiers so that, by God's mercy, he may liberate the country from the barbarian upstarts and attain the crown of the kingdom for himself. In fact, this very brother of mine, whose name I have already mentioned, is most skilled in the affairs of war and in many other matters. I do not hesitate to commit him to you, along with the abovementioned number of troops, if you are pleased to receive him. I can dispatch no more troops than that because the unruliness of the Gauls poses a constant threat."

As soon as he finished speaking, the archbishop thanked him, and, summoning Constantine, smiled and said: "Christ triumphs, Christ is king, Christ reigns! Behold the king of desolate Britain, with the help of Christ! Behold our defense! Behold our hope and joy!" What more can I say? While the fleet was made ready, soldiers were mustered from the various parts of Brittany and handed over to Guithelin. When everything was in order, they crossed the sea and landed in the port of Totnes. They at once mustered together the remaining youth of the island and, meeting their enemies in battle, were led to victory by the merits of that blessed man. Then the Britons, who had been scattered all about, began to flock together. Convening at Silchester, they made Constantine their king and placed the crown of the realm upon his head. They also gave him a wife from a noble family, whom Guithelin had personally raised. And when he knew her, she produced three sons whose names were Constans, Aurelius Ambrosius, and

---

[1] *O Agitius … slashed*   The letter is taken almost verbatim from Gildas's *The Ruin of Britain*.

[2] *Constantine*   Geoffrey derived the character of Constantine from Bede (*Ecclesiastical History* 1.11), though in this case he has altered his source significantly. Bede's Constantine is "a common trooper of no merit" who moves from being a tyrant over Britain to the Roman Emperorship, where he is soon executed.

Uther Pendragon. The eldest, Constans,[1] was dedicated to the Church of Amphybalus in Winchester and took monastic orders there. The other two, Aurelius and Uther Pendragon, were committed to Guithelin for their fostering. But later, after ten years had passed, a Pict in Constantine's service sought to have a private conversation with the king. Once the king was separated from all his other companions in a thicket of trees, the Pict stabbed him to death.

Upon the death of Constantine, there was unrest among the nobility over who was to be elevated to the throne. Some of them proclaimed Aurelius Ambrosius, some proclaimed Uther Pendragon, while others still supported various other relatives. While they were arguing for one over the other claimant, Vortigern, the leader of the Gewissei and a man who exerted every effort to obtain the throne for himself, came forth.[2] …

[Here follows an extended recounting of the machinations of Vortigern to win the throne.]

Now that Vortigern saw no rival in the kingdom, he placed the royal crown upon his own head, declaring his authority over all the other nobles. When his treachery was made known, the peoples of the neighboring islands, whom the Picts had invited into Albania, rose up against him. The Picts were angry indeed that their compatriots had been executed on account of the death of Constans, and now they sought vengeance. Because of this, Vortigern worried every day about his army sustaining heavy losses in a battle against the Picts. He was also concerned about Aurelius Ambrosius and his brother Uther Pendragon, who, as was related above, had fled to Brittany because of him. Every day, more-

over, rumors filled his ears that these two were now grown up and that they were building a fleet and preparing their return to their rightful kingdom.

In the meantime, three *ceolas*, which we call long-ships,[3] came ashore in Kent. They were filled with armed men under the leadership of the two brothers Horsa and Hengist. At that moment, Vortigern happened to be in Durobernia, which is now called Canterbury, for habit often led him to visit that city. When messengers came to him announcing that an unknown people of mighty stature had landed in longships, he granted them safe transit and ordered them to be brought before him. As soon as they arrived in his presence, his eyes fell upon the two brothers, for they stood out among the rest on account of their noble bearing. After he had looked long and hard upon the rest of them, he asked what country they were from and why they had come into his kingdom. Hengist began to answer for them, for he was older and wiser than the rest: "Most noble king of foreign peoples, the land of Saxony reared us, which is one of the regions of Germany. The cause of our coming is to offer our service to you or to some other foreign prince. Indeed, we have been exiled from our homeland for no other reason except that the custom of that land demands such an action. For the custom of our homeland is that, whenever there is a surplus population of men, the princes of the entire realm gather together, bringing the youth of the realm with them. They then cast lots[4] to decide who among the stronger and more experienced of us must seek his fortune in another country. In this way our country is relieved of its excess population. Our land has just recently become overpopulated again, and so our leaders have cast lots and chosen the band of young men whom you see before you, and they ordered us to honor that custom passed down from ancient times. We two brothers are the leaders of these men, for we are born of a noble house: I am Hengist and this is Horsa. Obeying our hallowed ancient traditions, we have sailed the sea

---

[1] *Constans* As with Constantine, Geoffrey derives Constans from Bede, but elaborates greatly on Bede's brief description. Bede describes Constans merely as "a monk whom Constantine had created Caesar" and who was assassinated by a rival, presumably in Rome.

[2] *Vortigern* Vortigern, a figure known under the name of *Gurtheyrn* in the Welsh genealogies as one of the ancestors of the Welsh rulers of Powys, is the first figure in *The History of the Kings of Britain* to have been mentioned extensively in other historical sources, appearing in Bede and Nennius, as well as in the work of Geoffrey's contemporaries William of Malmesbury and Henry of Huntington.

[3] *ceolas … longships* Geoffrey borrows the Anglo-Saxon term *ceolas*.

[4] *cast lots* Choosing by lot was a common method of making decisions. Typically, objects bearing the mark of competitors were placed in a receptacle and the first one to be drawn out (or to fall out) would be the first selected.

and, by the will of Mercury,[1] we have come upon your kingdom."

At the mention of Mercury, King Vortigern raised an eyebrow and inquired about their religion. Hengist replied: "We worship the gods of our country, including Saturn, Jove, and all the others who govern this world. But the greatest god of all is Mercury, whom we call Woden in our tongue.[2] To him our forefathers dedicated the fourth day of the week, which we even today know by the name of *Wodnesdei*. After him we venerate the most powerful of the goddesses. Her name is Frea and to her we have dedicated the sixth day of the week, which we call *Fridei* in honor of her." Hearing this, Vortigern said: "Your belief—or, rather, unbelief—grieves me terribly. But I do rejoice in your arrival, for either God or some other power has sent you to me in the hour of my need. My enemies are pressing upon me from all sides, and, if you would care to share the labor of my battles, I will treat you honorably here in my kingdom and will give you gifts and land." The barbarians agreed to these terms, a treaty was drawn up, and they took up residence in Vortigern's court. The Picts soon after sent out a great force from Alban and began to ravage the northern regions of the island. When this news was related to Vortigern, he mustered his troops and crossed the Humber to engage them. They met in close, hand-to-hand combat; back and forth, the Britons and their enemies fought most bitterly. But the Britons themselves did not need to fight much, for the Saxons who had accompanied them fought so valiantly that they speedily repulsed the Picts, who had hitherto been so used to winning.

Securing this victory through the aid of the Saxons, Vortigern distributed generous gifts among his Saxon allies, and he granted their leader Hengist broad tracts of land in Lindsey where he could maintain his men. Then Hengist, who was a wise and clever man, recognizing the friendship that the king was offering him, addressed Vortigern in these words: "Lord, your enemies are everywhere burning with hatred for you and for your subjects who love you. Everyone is threatened, and now you are told that Aurelius Ambrosius will be leading a force of men from Brittany to oust you and set himself up as king. By your leave, allow us to send word to our homeland and invite soldiers from there, so that our numbers will be able to support you in a fight. There is one more request I would beg to ask you in your clemency, if I did not fear it would be refused." To this, Vortigern answered: "Go ahead and send word to your allies in Germany and invite whom you will. Now tell me what else you desire and you will not be denied." Hengist bowed his head and thanked the king. Then he said: "You have invested me with great lands and estates, but not, however, with the honor that befits a leader of noble blood. Perhaps along with these other things I should also be given cities and castles so that I will be respected by the other peers of your realm. The title of Earl or Prince should be granted to me, seeing as I spring from a people that has both of these ranks." Vortigern answered: "I am forbidden to give you a gift of this sort, for you and your men are both foreign-born and pagans. And I do not yet understand your customs and character well enough to consider you the equal of my people. Even if I considered you to be true citizens, I could never treat you as such because of the disapproval of the British nobility." "Then at least," Hengist said, "grant to me, your servant, as much land as can be encircled by a single thong on land on which I can build a fortress and where, if the need arises, I can find safe refuge. I am loyal to you, and I have been and will continue to be loyal to you. What I now desire to do, I shall likewise do in complete loyalty to you."

The king was moved by these words to acquiesce to this request. Hengist sent messengers into Germany to invite more warriors from that land to come quickly and lend their aid. As soon as the messengers had departed, Hengist took the hide of a bull and made it into a single leather thong. Then, in a rocky place which he had chosen with much thought, he walked around with this thong and began to build a castle within this measured-out space. Once built, it took its name from the thong with which it had been surveyed. For it was later called Kaercarrei in the British tongue, Thanchester in the

---

[1] *Mercury* Roman messenger god, and god of travellers.

[2] *Saturn* Roman god of agriculture; *Jove* Supreme Roman deity; *Woden* Supreme Anglo-Saxon deity, god of wisdom, war, and culture. Since at least as early as Tacitus's *Germania* (first century CE), it had been customary to equate the Germanic gods with members of the Roman pantheon.

Saxon tongue, and Castrum Corrigiae in Latin.[1]

In the meantime, the Saxon messengers had returned from their mission, bringing eighteen ships full of the choicest soldiers. They also brought with them Hengist's daughter Renwein, whose beauty was second to none. After their arrival, Hengist invited King Vortigern to his house to inspect the new fortress and fresh soldiers. Coming there in secret, the king praised how quickly the castle had been erected, and he retained the soldiers who had been invited. Once the royal feast had been served, the girl Renwein came out of her chamber carrying a goblet of wine. Approaching the king, she curtsied and said: "*Lauerd king, Waesseil!*" When Vortigern saw the girl's face, he marveled greatly at her beauty and grew inflamed with desire for her. Then he asked his interpreter what the girl had said and how he should answer. The interpreter explained: "She called you 'lord king' and honored you with a word of greeting. You should answer '*Drincheil*'." The king said "*Drincheil*," and commanded the girl to drink. He then took the goblet from her hand, kissed her, and drank. From that day until the present time it has been the custom of the table in Britain that whoever drinks should say "*Waesseil*" to his fellow. And whoever receives the drink next should say "*Drincheil*."[2]

Vortigern got rather drunk because of the different types of drinks he had imbibed. At that point Satan entered his heart, and he fell in love with the girl and asked her father for her hand. I say that Satan entered his heart because, though he was a Christian, he desired to sleep with a pagan woman. Hengist, who was no fool, had taken note of the king's mood. He consulted his brother Horsa and the other elders who were there, asking how they should respond to the king's request. They were all of one mind that the girl should be given to the king and that they should be given the province of Kent as a bride-price. She was thus given to the king at once and Hengist was invested with Kent, despite the

fact that Earl Gorangon currently held those lands.[3] The king wed the pagan girl that very night, for he found her pleasing beyond measure. Because of this, he earned the immediate enmity of both his vassals and his sons, for Vortigern had already sired three sons whose names were Vortimer, Katigern, and Paschent.

from Book 8

[Vortigern, unpopular because of his Saxon ties, is eventually challenged for the kingdom by his son Vortimer, who has the people's support, but after Vortimer is poisoned, Vortigern regains his throne. Ultimately, however, he is defeated by Aurelius Ambrosius, who in this account is the brother of Uther Pendragon and the uncle of Arthur. He and Uther jointly fight off the Saxon hordes and their allies.]

… While these events were occurring in Winchester, a star of great size and brightness appeared, shining forth in a single beam. At the end of the beam was a globe of fire shaped like a dragon, and from the dragon's mouth two more beams were emanating. The length of one of the beams could be seen stretching out beyond the shores of Gaul; the other stretched toward the Irish Sea in seven smaller beams. This star appeared three times, inspiring fear and wonder in all who beheld it. Even the king's brother Uther, who was engaging the enemy force in Wales at the time, was struck with considerable trepidation, and he sought out wise men to explain what the star portended. He especially desired that Merlin be summoned, for Merlin had come with the army in order that their war strategies could benefit from his counsel. When Merlin stood before him, Uther ordered him to explain the meaning of the star. Merlin began weeping, but then, summoning forth his spirit, exclaimed: "Woe for the irreversible damage! Woe for the orphaned folk of Britain! Woe for the passing of our most noble king! That renowned king of Britain, Aurelius Ambrosius, has died; we shall all perish with him unless God lends us His aid. Hasten now, Uther, our most noble leader! Do not shirk from the fight against your enemies now. The

---

[1] *Thanchester … Latin* The location of Hengist's Thanchester is unknown and has been the subject of considerable dispute.

[2] *until the present … Drincheil* "Wassail" remains in occasional use in Britain as a salutation used when presenting a cup of wine to a guest; "drink-hail," however, has fallen into disuse.

[3] *Kent … those lands* Bede documents the fact that Kent was the initial area of Anglo-Saxon settlement in Britain.

victory will be in your hand and you will be the king of all Britain. Indeed, this star signifies you, as does the fiery dragon beneath the star. That beam which is stretched out toward the shores of Gaul indicates your future son, a most powerful man, whose might shall hold sway over all the lands he will protect. The other ray signifies a daughter, whose sons and grandsons will later rule the kingdom of Britain."[1]

Then Uther, though he doubted whether Merlin really spoke the truth, advanced on the enemy host in hopes of capturing it. And he came into the vicinity of Menevia, where he intended to rest for half a day. When Uther's presence there was reported to Gillomanius, Pascent, and the Saxons who were there, they left the city to fight with him. As soon as the two hosts spied each other, they both drew up their battle-lines and fell upon each other in close combat. Clashing in that way, soldiers of both sides were slain left and right, as would be usual in such a battle. Uther finally prevailed and seized the victory, but only after most of the day had passed and he had slain both Pascent and Gillomanius. The barbarians fell back to their ships as quickly as they could, but the Britons cut them down as they fled. With Christ's favor, a complete victory was granted to Uther, who then made his way as speedily as he could to Winchester, for messengers had arrived announcing that the king had indeed died and that he had just been buried near the abbey of Ambrius within the Ring of Giants which, in life, he had had erected.[2] Hearing of the king's death, the bishops and abbots and all the other clergy of that region had gathered in the city of Winchester and had overseen his funeral rites, as befitted such a king. Because Aurelius had once commanded that he be buried in the cemetery that he himself had established, they carried him there and buried him in royal pomp.

And so Uther, the brother of Aurelius, in the presence of both the clergy and the common folk, took the crown of the island and was elevated to the kingship. Remembering Merlin's explanation of the star, Uther ordered two dragons to be fashioned from gold in the likeness of the dragon that he had seen in the beam of the star. These were made with wondrous skill. He presented one to the parishioners of the cathedral church of Winchester; the other one he carried with him into battle. And it was from that time on that he was called Uther Pendragon, by which in the British tongue we mean "head of the dragon." Uther received this title on account of the fact that Merlin had foreseen his kingship in the dragon....

... As Easter approached, Uther summoned all the nobility of the realm to London so that he could receive the crown and celebrate the holy day with honor. All the nobility gathered just before the feast day, arriving from all the various cities of the kingdom. The king celebrated the feast itself with great solemnity as he had planned, and then made merry with his vassals. All the guests enjoyed themselves, for Uther had welcomed them gladly. The noblemen had even brought their wives and daughters to that joyous feast. Among the nobles present there was Gorlois, the duke of Cornwall, with his wife Igerna, whose beauty surpassed that of all the other women of Britain. When the king beheld her there among the other women, he was suddenly consumed with such love that he forgot all else and could think of nothing but her. Igerna alone it was to whom Uther continually directed the serving trays, Igerna alone it was to whom he sent his personal attendants with goblets of wine. He smiled at her many times, and engaged her in pleasant conversation. When her husband noticed this, he became quite angry and left the court without permission. No one there could persuade Gorlois to stay, for he feared losing the one thing that he loved above all else. Uther grew furious and ordered Gorlois to return to the court so that Uther could obtain justice for the insult he had suffered. But Gorlois continued to flee, and this infuriated Uther even more. He swore that he would ravage all of Gorlois's lands unless the duke gave him immediate satisfaction. While this feud was still hot between them, Uther wasted no time in assembling a great army, and he made for Cornwall, setting flame to every city and town along the way. Gorlois, however, did not dare to engage Uther in

---

[1] *that beam ... kingdom of Britain* Merlin's prophecy refers to the continental conquests of Uther's future son, King Arthur, and to the reigns of Arthur's successors.

[2] *Ring of Giants ... had erected* The ruins now known as Stonehenge are located approximately 20 miles northwest of Winchester. According to a legend recounted by Geoffrey, Merlin arranged for the Ring of Giants to be transported magically from Ireland.

battle, since his own army was far smaller; instead, he decided to fortify his castles until help could arrive from Ireland. Because he was more concerned about his wife's safety than his own, he placed her in the castle of Tintagel by the sea, for it was his best-protected stronghold. He, on the other hand, took refuge in the castle of Dimilioc so that, if any misfortune occurred, they would not both be in danger.[1]

When this was announced to the king, he came to the castle where Gorlois was and laid siege to it, barring every exit. Uther still remembered his love for Igerna, and so, after a week had passed, he summoned his old comrade-at-arms, Ulfin of Rhyddcaradoc, and told him what he was feeling in these words: "I burn with love for Igerna, and I hold myself in bodily peril unless I can have her. Advise me as to how I can quench my desire, or else I shall perish from this torment within." Ulfin answered: "What advice can anyone give you? There is no way to get to where Igerna is kept in the castle of Tintagel. That fortress is surrounded by the sea on three sides, and there is no means of access other than a narrow causeway. It only takes three armed knights to defend that approach, even if you brought the entire kingdom of Britain against them. If only the prophet Merlin would set his mind to this problem. Only then do I think you will be able to achieve your desire."

The hopeful king then summoned Merlin to him; for even Merlin had come along with Uther's army. Merlin soon stood before the king, who commanded him to offer his advice as to how he could sate his desire for Igerna. When Merlin perceived the torment that the king suffered for his great love of that woman, he said: "For your wish to be fulfilled, it will be necessary to employ new arts that are unheard of in this day and age. By means of certain concoctions of mine, I will be able to give you the appearance of Gorlois, so that you will look exactly like him to all eyes. If you follow my instructions, I shall make you look just like him, and I shall make Ulfin look like Jordan of Tintagel, Gorlois's servant. I too shall assume a different guise and come

with the two of you. In this way, you will be able to gain safe access to Igerna in her castle."

The king agreed to this plan, and followed all of Merlin's instructions diligently. After handing over command of the siege to his officers, he submitted himself to Merlin's craft and was transformed in appearance to look just like Gorlois. Ulfin was changed into Jordan, and Merlin himself took on the form of Britahel so that no one would be able to perceive who they really were. They then took the road up toward Tintagel and reached the castle at dusk. Once the warden there was notified that the duke had arrived, the castle gates were opened and the three men were allowed to pass inside. Who would have thought anything but that Gorlois himself had come home? The king spent the entire night with Igerna, making love with her and thus sating his desire. Indeed, even Igerna herself was taken in by the false shape that the king had assumed. He deceived her with many lying words that he had taken great care in devising. He also told her that he had come secretly from his besieged stronghold at Dimilioc just to check up on his beloved wife and his castle. She, of course, believed everything that Uther told her. That very night they conceived Arthur, that renowned man who in later days won great repute for his extraordinary prowess.

In the meantime, when it was noticed that the king was not present at the siege of Dimilioc, the army, acting without permission, attempted to raze the walls and thereby provoke the besieged duke to battle. Acting just as rashly, Gorlois issued forth with his troops, thinking that he would be able to fight off so many armed men with his meager force. Gorlois, however, was among the first to be killed in the course of the skirmish, and his soldiers were scattered. Castle Dimilioc was then captured, though the treasure there was divided most unevenly, for everyone just snatched up whatever spoils he could according to his own strength or good fortune. Only after these outrageous acts of violence had settled down did messengers come to Igerna to inform her of the death of the duke and the outcome of the siege. But when they beheld the king, who sat next to Igerna still wearing the duke's form, they turned red and marveled greatly that the man whom they had left for dead could have gotten to Tintagel safe and sound. They knew nothing of the

---

[1] *the castle ... danger* Geoffrey's geography of the northern coast of Cornwall is reasonably accurate and would seem to rely upon an eyewitness account; it is quite possible that Geoffrey himself had visited the region. Both Tintagel Castle and Dimilioc Castle existed in Geoffrey's day.

concoctions that Merlin had prepared. The king smiled at these rumors and embraced the duchess, saying: "I am of course not slain, but am still living, as you can plainly see. But I do regret the destruction of my castle and the slaughter of so many of my men. We must be wary that the king does not come here and capture us in this castle. I will go now to meet with him and will make my peace with him so that nothing worse happens to us." He then left the castle and came to his own camp and, shedding the form of Gorlois, he turned back into Uther Pendragon. When he learned of all that had occurred, he did indeed bemoan the death of Gorlois, but he also rejoiced that Igerna was now freed from the bond of marriage. Returning to Tintagel, he captured the castle and took Igerna to him, thus achieving his desire. From that day on, Uther and Igerna lived together as equals bound by mutual affection, and they had a son and a daughter. The son's name was Arthur and the daughter's was Anna. …

from Book 9

After the death of Uther Pendragon, the leaders of all the various provinces of Britain gathered together in the city of Silchester. They urged Dubricius, the archbishop of Caerleon to consecrate Uther's son Arthur as the next king.[1] Indeed, necessity dictated this action, since the Saxons had heard of Uther's death and were now summoning more of their countrymen out of Germany under the leadership of Colgrim, and they hoped to exterminate the Britons. The Saxons had in fact already subdued all the lands that lay from the River Humber to where Caithness meets the sea.

Dubricius, greatly concerned about the calamity about to befall the land, summoned all the other bishops and invested Arthur with the crown of the kingdom. Although Arthur was only fifteen years old at the time, he was a youth of outstanding virtue and largesse. His innate goodness made him exhibit such grace that he was beloved by almost all the people. On being invested with the royal insignia, Arthur upheld the ancient custom and dispensed gifts to one and all. Such a great number of soldiers flocked to him that he began to run out of gifts to give them. Yet for a man in whom great generosity dwells in the company of great courage, such empty-handedness can last only for a time, and habitual poverty cannot afflict him. Thus Arthur, who indeed possessed both great courage and generosity, was determined to attack the Saxons so that he could distribute their riches among his men. Justice spurred him on as well, since by right of inheritance he ought to have had control over the entire island. …

[Here follows a long series of battles in which Arthur defeats enemies foreign and domestic, ending with the Scots, who beg for mercy.]

Having pardoned the Scots, the king headed for York to celebrate the feast of Christmas, which was drawing near. As he entered the city, he was grieved that all the holy churches had been abandoned, for Archbishop Samson had been driven out, as had all the other men of faith there, and the half-burnt churches no longer celebrated their services to God. The fury of the pagans had indeed prevailed there. Arthur therefore gathered the clergy and the people together and appointed his chaplain Piramus as the new archbishop. Arthur then rebuilt all the churches that had been destroyed and established communities of religious men and women there. He also restored titles and property to all those who had been driven out by the Saxon occupation.

With him there were three brothers of royal blood: Loth, Urien, and Anguselus.[2] They had been eminent men before the coming of the Saxons and had the governance of those regions. Desiring to honor the decrees of his own father, Arthur gave Anguselus royal power over the Scots, and he gave Urien the scepter of Moray. Back in the days of Aurelius Ambrosius, Loth had married the king's sister Anna, by whom he fathered

---

[1] *Arthur … next king* Geoffrey's account of King Arthur is the first known attempt, aside from the brief catalogue of Arthur's battles in the ninth century *Historia Britorum* (traditionally ascribed to the Welsh monk Nennius) to treat Arthur as an historical figure and to describe the king's entire career from birth to death. Falling in line with certain Welsh traditions, Geoffrey is the first historian to describe Arthur as a king rather than a victorious general.

[2] *Loth … Anguselus* The origins of the figures of Loth and Anguselus are obscure, but Urien derives from the sixth-century Brittonic hero Urien Rheged. The poet Taliesin was connected to Urien's court, and several of his poems in praise of Urien survive.

Gawain and Mordred. Arthur now granted him the earldom of Lothian and the other neighboring lands that had once belonged to him. Finally, having restored the entire kingdom to its former state of pristine dignity, Arthur married a woman by the name of Guinevere, who sprang from a noble Roman family.[1] She had been brought up in the household of Duke Cador and surpassed all the other women of the island in beauty.

… At long last, having pacified all the cities and peoples of Gaul, he returned to Britain at the first approach of spring.

When the solemn feast of Pentecost began to draw near, Arthur, rejoicing in his triumph, decided to hold court and place the crown of the kingdom of Britain upon his head. He summoned all the kings and dukes who were subject to him to this feast so that he could celebrate it all the more honorably and renew the pacts with his vassals all the more effectively. Informing his household of his plans, he took their advice to hold the court in Caerleon.[2] This city was located in Glamorganshire on the river Usk, at a lovely site not far from where the Severn empties into the sea. It had a great abundance of riches, above all that of the other cities, and thus was an excellent place to hold a high feast. On one side of the city, moreover, the noble Usk flowed in such a way that the kings and princes who were coming from across the sea would be able to get there by ship. On the other side, which was surrounded by fields and royal forests, the buildings were so impressive that the golden gables of their roofs seemed to rival Rome. There were also two great churches there. One had been erected in honor of the martyr Julius, and it was adorned with a choir of the most beautiful virgins who had dedicated themselves to God. The other church had been founded in the name of Aaron, the blessed companion of Julius.

It was served by a house of canons and was the site of the third metropolitan see of Britain. It also had a school with two hundred philosophers who were most learned in astronomy and other arts. They diligently observed the motion of the stars, and, employing reasonable arguments, they would explain to King Arthur the omens of things to come. Caerleon, then, which was endowed with so many fine things, was made ready for the great feast.

And so messengers were sent to invite the vassals from the various realms. Both those from Gaul as well as those from the neighboring islands had to come to the court. And so there arrived Anguselus, the king of Alban, which is now called Scotland; and Urien, the king of Moray; Cadvan, the king of Venedotia, which is now called North Wales; Eddelin, the king of Demetia, which is now called South Wales; and King Cador of Cornwall. The three archbishops of the metropolitan sees of London, York, and Caerleon also came, and Dubricius was the archbishop of Caerleon. He was the foremost prelate in Britain, and he held the apostolic see with such piety that he was able to relieve the pain of the suffering through his very words. The earls of the noble cities also attended: Morvid, the earl of Gloucester; Mauron of Worcester; Anarawd of Salisbury; Arthgal of Caer Gweir, which is now called Warwick; Jugin of Leicester; Cursalem of Chester; Kinmarc of Durham; Galluc of Winchester; Urgennius of Bath; Jonathal of Dorchester; and Boso of Rydychen, that is, Oxford. In addition to these earls came other noble heroes: Donaut map Papo; Cheneus map Coil; Pederur map Peredur; Gruffudd map Nogoid; Regin map Clawd; Eddelein map Cledauc; Kingar map Bangan; Kinmarc; Gorbonian map Sgoit; Clofaut; Rhun map Neton; Kinbelin map Trunat; Cathleus map Cadell; Kinlith map Nethon; and many others whom it would take too long to enumerate here.[3] From the outlying islands came Gillamorius, the king of Ireland; Malvasius, the king of Iceland; Doldavius, the king of Gothland; Gunuasius, the king of the Orkneys; King Loth of

---

[1] *Guinevere … family*   This is the earliest extant mention of Guinevere in a Latin text. Geoffrey draws her name, at least, from Welsh traditions concerning Arthur's wife *Gwenhwyfar* (literally "White Phantom").

[2] *Caerleon*   Geoffrey's detailed description of the city of Caerleon probably reflects his intimate knowledge of the areas along the Welsh border. His association of King Arthur with Caerleon continues into the later romance traditions; Arthur's more famous court at Camelot does not appear until the romance *Lancelot, or, The Knight of the Cart* (*Le chevalier de la charrette*), written by Chrétien de Troyes in the later twelfth century.

[3] *noble heroes … enumerate here*   All the "noble heroes" mentioned here have distinctively Welsh names, many incorporating the Welsh patronymic *map* ("son of"). This list of Arthur's men resembles—in style, though not in content—the vast catalogs of Arthur's heroes in Welsh texts such as *Culhwch and Olwen* (c. 11th century) or *The Dream of Rhonabwy* (c. 12th or 13th century).

Norway; and King Aschill of Denmark. From other distant lands across the sea came Holdwin, the duke of the Ruteni; Leodegarius, the count of Bologna; Bedivere the Cup-Bearer, the duke of Normandy; Borrellus of Cenomania; Kay the Seneschal,[1] the duke of Anjou; and Guitard of Poitou; along with the twelve peers of the Gauls, who were led by Gerin of Chartres.[2] Duke Hoel of the Armorican Britons was also there with his vassals. They all came with such a train of equipment and mules and horses that it is well-nigh impossible to describe. There did not remain one prince of any merit on this side of Spain who did not attend this court when summoned. And this is no wonder, for Arthur's generosity was renowned all over the world, and this made all men love him.

Once everyone had gathered together in the city in order to celebrate the solemn feast, the archbishops arrived at the palace to bestow the royal crown. Since Dubricius was the prelate of the dicoese where the court was being held, he made ready to celebrate the high mass. The king, as soon as he was robed, was led with great ceremony to the church of the metropolitan see. On both his right and left he was escorted by an archbishop. Ahead of him marched the four kings of Alban, Cornwall, Demetia, and Venedotia. It was their duty to walk before him carrying golden swords. A great company of clerics also preceded him, chanting in wondrous harmony. From the opposite direction, the archdeacons and priests escorted the queen in all her regalia to the church of the devoted virgins. The four queens of the abovementioned kings came with her, carrying morning-doves, as was the custom. All the other women who were there marched in her train with great delight. As the procession drew to a halt, there was such beautiful music and singing coming from both churches that the knights who were there did not know which church they should attend first. They crowded together first towards one, then toward the other; if the entire day had passed in this

kind of celebration they would not have grown bored.

After the holy mass was celebrated in both churches, the king and queen put aside their crowns and adopted less formal garments. The king then retired to his hall to feast with the men, while the queen withdrew to hers with the women, for they still maintained the Trojan custom of celebrating feast days separately, the men with the men and the women with the women. Once they were all seated according to their proper rank, Kay the Seneschal, clothed all in ermine, brought in the food, accompanied by one thousand young nobles who were also clad in ermine.[3] On the other side of the king's hall, Bedivere the Cup-Bearer, followed by another thousand young men all clad in miniver,[4] distributed the drinks in different chalices of various styles and shapes. In the queen's hall, countless attendants in different types of fine clothing, performed their duties, each having his own particular task. If I were to describe every detail of this feasting, I would draw my history out far too long.

Britain had at that point attained such a state of dignity that it surpassed all other kingdoms in its courtliness, in the extravagance of its fineries, and in the polished manners of its citizens. Every individual knight of fame and virtue in the kingdom bore a livery and arms of a unique color. The women of those days had a similar style of dress. And those ladies would only grant their love to a man who had thrice proven his worth in battle. They were therefore made all the more chaste and the men all the more virtuous out of love for them.

Finishing their meals, the men went down to the fields outside the city, organizing themselves into groups for the playing of various games. The knights quickly matched off for competitions on horseback and arranged a mock battle. The ladies looked on from atop the city walls: the games inspired them with the maddening flames of love. Some of the other men whiled away their time at archery, others with spear-throwing; some cast heavy rocks and stones, while others still played at dice and a host of other amusements. What's more, they had put aside all ill-will toward one another. Whoever achieved victory in a contest received the most

---

[1] *Kay the Seneschal* In later renditions of Arthurian legend (but not in Geoffrey), Kay is also identified as foster-brother to Arthur. Kay is said to act as Arthur's seneschal (or steward) in the vast majority of the legends.

[2] *twelve peers of the Gauls* The Twelve Peers of France were Charlemagne's vassals and companions in the French cycles of *chansons de geste*. Geoffrey's inclusion of them here implicitly places Arthur above even Charlemagne.

[3] *ermine* I.e., dressed in the highly valued furs of ermines, which are of the weasel family.

[4] *miniver* Unspotted white fur derived from ermines; like ermine, miniver was traditionally worn by members of the medieval nobility.

generous gifts from Arthur himself. Three whole days passed by in this way. On the morning of the fourth day, Arthur summoned everyone to him who had performed service in whatever office that he held. Each man was granted possession of cities and castles, bishoprics and archbishoprics, and many other high honors. ...

[Into this happy scene come Roman ambassadors, demanding tribute from Arthur. He refuses, deciding instead to attempt to defeat Rome. He assembles a fleet to sail across to the continent, and war ensues.]

from BOOK 10

When Arthur heard of the Romans' advance, he yielded Britain to the custodianship of his nephew Mordred[1] and Queen Guinevere. Then he made his way with the army to Southampton, where he set out across the sea amid stormy winds. Around midnight that same evening, while the king's ship sailed amid the innumerable ships of his fleet as they plowed the waves with good winds and high spirits, a portentous dream befell the king. Sound asleep, Arthur dreamt that he saw a bear flying through the air, whose growling made all the coastlands tremble. Then he saw a terrible dragon flying towards him from out of the west, and the light from the dragon's eyes lit up all the land. As these two creatures came together, they engaged in a furious battle. But the dragon attacked the bear many times with his flaming breath, and the bear finally fell to the earth, burnt to a crisp. This awakened the king, and he immediately related his dream to those who were standing about. Interpreting the dream, they said that the dragon symbolized him, while the bear must represent some giant that he would fight with; the fight between the dragon and the bear portended the battle that would occur between them, and the dragon's victory, they claimed, indicated Arthur's victory. Arthur, on the other hand, believed that the vision referred to the imminent

war between himself and the Roman emperor. As the night wore on and the red dawn approached, they landed in Barfleur. They pitched their tents at once and awaited the arrival of the kings of the islands and of the leaders of the provinces of Gaul.

In the meantime, news came to King Arthur that a certain giant of marvelous size had come up from Spain and had kidnapped Helen, the niece of Duke Hoel of Brittany, fleeing with her to the top of that hill that is now called Mont-St.-Michel.[2] The knights of the region had gone in pursuit, but to no avail. Whether they attacked him by sea or by land, the giant would either sink their ships with heavy rocks or would finish them off with other sundry weapons. Indeed, he had even captured many of them and eaten them while still half-alive. So on the following night, two hours past midnight, King Arthur woke up Kay his seneschal and Bedivere his cup-bearer and secretly left the camp, stealing his way up toward the mountain. For King Arthur possessed such strength and courage that he scoffed at bringing the entire army against such monsters. He wanted to impress his men by vanquishing the creature himself.

As they approached the mountain, they perceived a fire burning atop it and another fire on a hill nearby. So the king ordered Bedivere the Cup-Bearer to sail over to the mountain; there was no other way across since the hill rose up out of the sea. While he was attempting to climb up, Bedivere heard a woman's screams issuing from above him. At first he was struck with horror, fearing that the monster was drawing near. But his courage soon returned, and he drew his sword. When he reached the summit, at first he saw nothing at all except for the fire that he had sighted earlier. But then he noticed a recently dug grave and beside it an old woman who was moaning and bewailing. When she saw him, however, she ceased her lament at once and spoke to him thus: "O unlucky man! What ill fortune has led you to this place? Oh, you will suffer a death of the most unspeakable agonies! I do pity you, for this very night

---

[1] *Mordred* Mordred is mentioned in the *Annales Cambriae* (c. 970) as falling, along with Arthur, at the Battle of Camlann in 537. There, as elsewhere in the Welsh genealogies and triads, his name appears as *Medrawt*. The form *Mordred* is distinctly Cornish, which may indicate Geoffrey's familiarity with Cornish sources or local folklore.

[2] *Mont-St.-Michel* Located off the coast of France between Normandy and Brittany, Mont St. Michel was the site of an impressive abbey and town, which is to this day surrounded by water when the tide is high. The story of the giant who plagued the area perhaps reflects Geoffrey's knowledge of local folklore, though no extant story antedates this one.

that most detestable monster will devour the flower of your youth! For soon that most wicked and nameless giant will be here. He carried the two of us up to this mountain—Duke Hoel's niece, whom I have just buried here, and myself her nurse—and without delay he will mete you out some unspeakable death."

"Alas!" she continued, "How terrible was my dear girl's fate! When this wicked creature gathered her into his embrace, such fear seized her tender breast that it ended her life, which should have seen many more years. However, since in unclean union he failed to lay with her—she who was my kindred spirit, my life, all my sweetness and light—he instead raped me. He did this, I confess, with great force and violence, in spite of God and my old age. Flee, my dear! Flee before he returns to have his way with me again. When he sees you he will tear you up most hideously."

Bedivere was moved as much as is humanly possible. He calmed the woman with kind words and promised to hurry back with help. So he hastened back to Arthur and told him everything that had happened, whereupon Arthur, groaning over the girl's fate, announced that he would attack the giant by himself and would call for them to assist him only if necessary. They then made their way to the higher hill and, entrusting their horses to their squires, began to climb up. Arthur led the ascent.

There by his fire was that inhuman creature, his mouth stained with the gore of half-eaten pigs. Some of them he had gobbled up, while others he had roasting on spits over the fire. The giant was caught off guard by the approach of the men and made immediately for his cudgel, which was itself so heavy that two young men could scarcely lift it off the ground. The king then unsheathed his sword, drew his shield up before him, and made a rush for the giant before he could get hold of the cudgel. But the giant noticed the king's hostile intention. He seized the club and struck the king against his shield with such force that the sound of the blow reverberated across the waters and caused the king himself to go deaf. The king now burned with a bitter anger. He lifted up his sword and dealt the giant such a blow that, though not lethal, made the blood gush all over his face and eyes, blinding him. The giant had, however, fended off the main force of the blow with his

club and so avoided a mortal wound to his forehead. Unable to see because of the bleeding and now even angrier than before, the giant rose up and, just as a cornered boar will turn on the hunter, threw himself at the king's sword. He grabbed the king by his middle and forced him to kneel on the ground. Recovering his strength, the king quickly wriggled out of his grasp and began swiftly lashing out with his sword, now here, now there, not ceasing until he had dealt a mortal blow by driving his sword into the giant's head at that point where the brain is protected by the skull. The evil creature screamed and finally fell with the greatest tumult, like an oak uprooted by blasts of great winds.

The king then laughed in relief. Bedivere came up and cut off the giant's head and gave it to one of the squires to carry back down to the camp for everyone to behold. The king then said that he had never encountered anyone of such strength since he slew the giant Retho[1] atop Mount Aravius. This Retho had summoned Arthur to fight in single combat and had been collecting the beards of kings with which to make a fur coat. He had sent a message to Arthur that requested that the king rip his own beard out and send the ripped-out beard up to him. He promised that, since Arthur was eminent above all other kings, he would find Arthur's beard a place of honor among the other beards. If Arthur refused, he would challenge the king to combat: whichever of the two proved stronger would receive the loser's coat and beard. Arthur won the day soon after the contest began, and so he received the other's beard and coat. Since that day, Arthur maintained, he had met no one stronger than Retho.

Having secured this victory as noted above, they returned to their tents with the giant's head just before daybreak. The men all crowded around to see it, giving great praise to him who had freed the land from such a gluttonous monster. But Hoel, mourning over the death of his niece, ordered a church to be built upon the grave of that girl who now lay upon the hilltop. The church took its name from the girl's burial site, and is still called Helen's Tomb in the present day. ...

[1] *Retho* The giant Retho appears in Welsh traditions as Rhita Mawr.

[Several more encounters between British and Roman forces ensue, and Geoffrey tells of a British victory in a major battle fought in "a lowland by the name of Saussy" near the town of Autun.]

Having achieved this victory, Arthur commanded the bodies of his own chief vassals to be separated from the enemy corpses. Once this was done, he had their bodies prepared for burial as if they were kings, and then had each carried to the abbey of his native territory and honorably interred. Bedivere the Cup-Bearer, however, was carried off by the Neustrians with great lamentation to the city of Bayeux, which his great-grandfather, Bedivere I, had founded. There he was laid to an honorable rest in a cemetery in the southern part of the city near the walls. Kay, on the other hand, who was grievously wounded, was brought to Chinon, a fortress that he himself had built. He succumbed to his wounds shortly thereafter, and was buried, as befit the leader of the Angevins, at an anchorage in the forest, not far from his castle. Holdwin, the duke of the Ruteni, was borne to Flanders and laid to rest in his city of Thérouanne. Other earls and vassals, on Arthur's orders, were brought to nearby abbeys. Taking pity on his enemies, Arthur ordered their bodies to be buried in their native soil as well, and he had the body of Lucius conveyed to the Roman Senate, telling them to expect no other tribute from Britain.

King Arthur wintered in those parts and spent his time subduing the cities of the Allobroges. As summer approached, he desired to head for Rome. However, just as he was about to cross the mountains, news reached Arthur that his nephew Mordred, in whose keeping he had left the governance of Britain, had proven himself to be a tyrant and a traitor. Mordred had seized the throne of Britain and now took his wicked pleasure with Guinevere, who had broken her marriage vows. ...

from BOOK 11

My noble Earl,[1] Geoffrey of Monmouth does not fall silent here. Instead, drawing on the abovementioned source in the British tongue as well as on the assistance of Walter of Oxford, a man most expert in historical matters,[2] I will now in my humble style briefly relate the battles that this famous king fought with his nephew upon returning to Britain after his great victory.

When the news of the wicked deed reached King Arthur's ears, he immediately postponed the campaign that he had hoped to wage against Leo, emperor of the Romans. Placing Hoel, the duke of the Armorican Britons, in charge of the armies in Gaul in order to pacify those regions, Arthur returned to Britain accompanied by only the insular kings and their forces. Meanwhile, that most wicked traitor Mordred had sent the Saxon Chelric into Germany in order to muster whatever allies he could and to bring them back as swiftly as possible to Britain. He even promised to give Chelric that part of the island that lay north of the Humber up to the borders of Scotland, as well as all the domains in Kent that Hengist and Horsa had once held under King Vortigern. Chelric, fulfilling his side of the bargain, brought eight hundred ships filled with armed pagan men, who obeyed that traitor as if he were the real king. Mordred had also made alliances with the Scots, Picts, and Irish, all of whom had long nurtured a hatred for his uncle. All counted, Mordred's troops numbered around eight hundred thousand and were composed of pagan and Christian alike.

Placing his trust in the enormous army he had amassed, Mordred marched out to meet Arthur as he attempted to land in Richborough. The two forces met in battle, and Mordred's troops inflicted great slaughter on the others, who were still in the process of disembarking. King Anguselus of Scotland, the king's nephew Gawain, and countless others fell on the field of battle that day. Anguselus was succeeded in Scotland by Ywain, the son of his brother Urien.[3] This Ywain later distinguished himself through many valiant deeds during the wars that followed. At last, through great

---

1   *noble Earl*   Robert, Earl of Gloucester (d. 1147), son of Henry I of England and patron to whom Geoffrey dedicates his *History*.

2   *Walter ... historical matters*   Archbishop of Oxford and a friend of Geoffrey's, Walter of Oxford (died c. 1150) reputedly lent Geoffrey the Welsh book he alludes to above (the existence of which is entirely unsubstantiated).

3   *Urien*   Owein ap Urien is an historical, sixth-century Welsh hero. The figure of Ywain would later appear prominently in the cycle of Arthurian romances, beginning with *Yvain* (c. 1175) by Chrétien de Troyes.

effort, Arthur's forces managed to come ashore, returning the terrible onslaught that they had suffered and
setting Mordred's army to flight. Being used to constant
warfare, they had arranged their forces partly on foot
and partly on horseback: whenever the infantry needed
to attack or retreat, the cavalry would charge at an angle,
thus attempting to break the enemy lines and force
them to retreat. The traitor Mordred regrouped his
troops and entered Winchester the next night. When
this was reported to Queen Guinevere, she gave up hope
and fled from York to Caerleon, where she joined the
nuns at the Church of St. Julius the Martyr and was
determined to live chastely.

Arthur was now kindled with an even greater wrath,
having lost so many hundreds of his men. Three days
later, after having given his fallen warriors a decent
burial, he approached Winchester and besieged the
wretched traitor who had taken refuge there. But
Mordred did not wish to abandon all of his plans yet,
and so, exhorting his men in various ways, he issued out
of the city with his troops in formation and pitched a
battle against his uncle. As the fighting began, great
slaughter befell both sides. But Mordred's men got the
worst of it, and he was forced to abandon the field.
Caring little for the burial of his dead, Mordred at once
took to flight by boat, making his way towards Cornwall.[1] Arthur, on the other hand, was greatly concerned
that so many of the enemy had escaped. He pursued
them with great haste into Cornwall and awaited their
arrival at the River Camlann.[2] Mordred, since he was a
bold man and ever swift to attack in battle, quickly
arranged his troops. He hoped either to be victorious or
to perish in the attempt, not desiring to flee any longer.
Sixty thousand armed soldiers still remained of his allies,

and he placed them in six battle-groups, assigning 6,666
to each group. Then he formed one last group from the
remainder. He assigned commanders to all of the
divisions, and took personal command of the last
division. With the troops now arranged, Mordred
encouraged them, promising them the possessions of
their enemies if they were able to emerge triumphant
from this battle.

Arthur was also arranging his troops on the other
side of the field. He divided them into nine companies
of infantrymen, each of which was arranged in a square,
with a left wing and a right wing. Then, appointing
commanders to each division, he urged them all to
destroy the thieves and traitors who had been brought to
their land by his treacherous nephew and who still
hoped to take away all of their possessions. He told
them that many of these barbarians from various kingdoms were unwarlike by nature and completely ignorant
of the arts of war. It would be nothing at all, he said, for
worthy men as expert in war as themselves to emerge
victorious if they rushed bravely onto the field and
fought valiantly.

Both Arthur and Mordred exhorted their own troops
in this way. Then, in a sudden onslaught, the two
armies advanced upon the field and strove to inflict one
another with many dire blows. Great carnage was
suffered on both sides, countless groans issued from the
dying men. Indeed, the clashing of these warriors is
almost too grievous and laborious to describe. Men all
around inflicted wounds and were wounded in turn,
killed and were killed.

After they had passed much of the day in this way,
Arthur rushed in with a battalion of 6,666 men against
the company where he knew Mordred to be. Clearing
the way with their swords, they penetrated Mordred's
bodyguard and inflicted the most fearsome slaughter.
The traitor finally fell there, and many thousands with
him. However, the rest of the enemy force did not flee
the field because of Mordred's death, but instead
gathered together from all around the battlefield and
made a last stand with all the boldness they could
muster. They fought most bitterly, for almost all the
commanders from both sides were there with their men.
On Mordred's side there fell that day the Saxon leaders
Chelric, Elafius, Egbrict, and Bruniggus; the Irish

---

[1] *took to flight ... Cornwall* Geoffrey's geography is a bit murky
here. Winchester is neither on the sea nor on a major waterway.
Moreover, the traditional sites for the subsequent Battle of Camlann
place that battlefield on the northern side of Cornwall, surely out of
Mordred's direct escape route.

[2] *River Camlann* Camlann was, according to long-standing Welsh
traditions, the site of Arthur's last battle; the *Annales Cambriae* states
that it occurred in the year 537 and that both Arthur and Mordred
fell there. Geoffrey seems to be the first to identify the spot with the
River Camel in Cornwall. Certain Welsh traditions pre-dating
Geoffrey attribute the cause of the battle to a dispute between
Gwenhwyfar (Guinevere) and an otherwise unknown woman named
Gwenhwyfach.

leaders Gillapatric, Gillabor, Gillafer, and Gillarum; as well as all the Scottish and Pictish leaders along with everyone they commanded. On Arthur's side, there fell King Olberic of Norway, King Aschill of Denmark, Cador Limenic, and Cassibelaunus, along with many soldiers of both British and foreign origin whom he had brought with him. However, even the illustrious King Arthur was mortally wounded. He was carried away to be healed of his wounds on the isle of Avalon, and he gave the crown of Britain to his kinsman Constantine, son of Duke Cador of Cornwall, in the year of our Lord 542....

from BOOK 12

[Having recounted the fates of the kings who followed Arthur, Geoffrey turns to the subject of the Britons' decline and the fall of Cadwallader, the last British king.]

... And so, as I had begun to say, the Britons were afflicted with a lamentable civil discord, and they destroyed the well-being of their country with their terrible divisiveness. Then yet another misfortune struck them: a dire and infamous famine afflicted them so badly that they were deprived of the support of any food at all; their only solace remained in the art of hunting. A deadly plague followed on the heels of this famine, striking down such a multitude of people in so short a space of time that the living were unable to bury the dead.[1] The wretched survivors gathered together in companies and fled from their homeland, seeking out lands across the seas. Beneath the swollen sails of their ships, they lamented greatly, crying out: "You gave us up, O God, like we were sheep for the slaughter, and dispersed us among the heathens!"[2] Even King Cadwallader himself, taking a wretched ship over to Armorica, added his voice to their lament, saying: "Woe unto us sinners for the many wicked deeds with which

we did not hesitate to offend God while we believed we still had time to repent. Now, snatching us out of our native land, the vengeance of His might falls upon us whom neither the Romans nor the Scots nor Picts nor even the treasonous wiles of the Saxons were able to exterminate. In vain, however, have we recovered our homeland from them so many times, since it was not God's will that we would reign here for all time. He is the True Judge, and when He saw that we did not wish to refrain from our wickedness in the least and that no foreign people could dislodge us from our land, He directed his righteous indignation upon us fools, and now we desert our own homeland in droves. Come back, Romans! Come back, Scots and Picts! Come back, Huns and Saxons! Behold! Britain now lies open for you, for the wrath of God has emptied that which you could not empty. Your force has not expelled us, but rather the might of the King of Kings, Whom we have never ceased to offend." When Cadwallader arrived upon the shores of Armorica, lamenting in this way, he made his way with all his host to King Alan, the grandson of King Solomon, who gave him an honorable welcome.

For eleven years, Britain was completely abandoned by all the Britons, except for those few who were spared from death in certain districts of Wales. The land was abhorred by the Britons, and even the Saxons who remained there during this trying period continued to die without any hope of relief. But when this terrible plague finally abated, the Saxons, preserving their ancient custom, sent word to their compatriots back in Germany that the island was now emptied of its native people and would be easy to subdue if they came to dwell there. When this news was reported to them, that wicked folk gathered together a great host of men and women and landed in the province of Northumbria, and they took up residence in the deserted provinces of Scotland and Cornwall. No one was there to prevent their settlement, except for the meager remnant of the Britons who had survived but had now withdrawn to the remote forests of Wales.

From that moment forth the power of the Britons in the isle of Britain came to a close and the Angles then began to rule. After a little time, the Britons began to regain their strength, so Cadwallader turned his atten-

---

[1] *deadly plague ... the dead*   The *Annales Cambriae* place this plague in the year 682; it has been suggested that the *Annales* are erroneously referring to the Great Plague of 664 recorded by Bede.

[2] *You gave us up ... heathens*   Psalms 44.11: "You made us like sheep for food, and have scattered us among the nations."

tion once more to his kingdom, which had now been cleansed of the plague. He went to Brittany to ask King Alan there for aid in restoring him to his former power. Cadwallader was determined on this course of action, but the voice of an Angel called to him just as the fleet was getting underway. It told him to abandon his plans: God did not want the Britons to reign in Britain any longer, not before the day that Merlin had foretold to Arthur should arrive. The Angel commanded him to go to Pope Sergius in Rome to do penance so that he might be numbered among the blessed. The Angel told him further that the British people would regain the island through their great faith in days to come after the predestined time had passed. And that day, moreover, would not come until the Britons could recover the holy relics that they had lost during the invasions of the pagans.

When that blessed man heard the Angel's message, he went at once to King Alan and explained what had been revealed to him. Then Alan consulted various prophetical tomes concerned with the Eagle of Shaftesbury, as well as books of the verses of the Sybil and of Merlin, to see whether Cadwallader's vision conformed to one of the recorded prophecies. Since he could discover no discrepancy, he believed Cadwallader's vision to be a divine dispensation. Cadwallader therefore acted on the advice that the Angel had given him and laid Britain aside. He directed his son Yvor and his nephew Yni to rule over the Britons who remained on the island, lest the descendants of that ancient race lose their freedom because of the foreign invasions. Then Cadwallader himself, putting aside the concerns of this world, journeyed to Rome on account of the Lord and the Eternal Kingdom, and he was confirmed in his faith by Pope Sergius. There he was seized by an unexpected illness. On the first day of May in the year of our Lord 689, Cadwallader left behind the weakness of this flesh and entered the great hall of the Kingdom of Heaven.

So Yvor and Yni gathered ships together and, summoning all the men that they could, sailed to the island. For seventy-nine years they fought with great ferocity against the Angles but with little success, for the abovementioned plague and famine, as well as their own penchant for civil war, had caused this once proud people to degenerate to such a degree that they could no longer fend off their enemies. Through their habitual barbarity, they were no longer called Britons but "Welsh," a term derived either from their leader Gualo or from Queen Galaes or indeed from their own barbarity.[1] But the Saxons acted more wisely. They established peace and concord among themselves, and they tilled the fields and rebuilt the cities and towns. Casting aside the power of the Britons, they ruled all of Logres under their leader, Athelstan, who was the first to wear the royal crown.[2]

Having degenerated from the nobility they had enjoyed as Britons, the Welsh never again regained the kingship of the island. They instead persisted foolishly in their quarrels with the Saxons or among themselves and were hence constantly engaged in foreign wars and civil unrest.

I leave it to my contemporary Caradoc of Llancarvan to record the kings who continued to rule in Wales, and to William of Malmesbury and Henry of Huntington to discuss the kings of the Saxons.[3] But I insist that they all be silent in regard to the kings of the Britons, since they do not have that book in the British tongue which Walter the Archdeacon of Oxford obtained from Wales. This same book, which deals so truthfully with the honor of the native princes, I have endeavored to translate into Latin as accurately as I possibly could.

—C. 1138

---

[1] *Welsh ... own barbarity* The Anglo-Saxon word *wealh*, which is the ancestor of the modern term *Welsh*, meant "foreigner" or "slave"; hence, Geoffrey's etymology is not far from the mark.

[2] *Athelstan ... crown* King Athelstan of Wessex (reigned 924–40) was the grandson of King Alfred and was erroneously believed by various medieval writers to have been the first sovereign over all England.

[3] *Caradoc ... the Saxons* Caradoc of Llancarvan was the author of a twelfth-century life of Gildas. The Welsh *Chronicle of the Princes* (*Brut y Tywysogion*) had long been attributed to him, perhaps on Geoffrey's authority, but modern scholarship has proven that authorship impossible. The famed historian William of Malmesbury (1080–1142) was the author of *The Deeds of the Bishops of England* (*Gesta Pontificum Angliae*) and *The Deeds of the Kings of England* (*Gesta Regum Angliae*). Henry of Huntington (1084–1155) was composing his own *History of the English* (*Historia Anglorum*) at the same time that Geoffrey was writing *The History of the Kings of Britain*.

MARIE DE FRANCE
c. 1155 – 1215

Although she is widely credited with being the earliest female poet in France, and was arguably the leading female writer of the Middle Ages, little is known about Marie de France; no surviving documents refer to her life outside of her literary activity. What has come down to us are three works, which vary widely in genre: the *Lais* (c. 1155–70), a collection of short romance narratives; the *Ysopet* or *Fables* (c. 1167–89), a collection commonly accepted as the earliest translation of Aesop into French; and the less-studied *Espurgatoire de Saint Patrice* (*Legend of the Purgatory of Saint Patrick*, c. 1189), a didactic tale in which Patrick, an Irish knight, makes a spiritual journey through Purgatory.

Her name is known from the self-identification she makes in each of her texts; this occurs most forcefully and descriptively in the epilogue of the *Ysopet*:

> I shall name myself so that it will be remembered;
> Marie is my name, I am of France.
> It may be that many clerks
> will take my labor on themselves.
> I don't want any of them to claim it.

"France" itself is a slippery designation here, since it had multiple possible meanings in this period; it may be intended to convey that she was from Continental Europe instead of England, for instance, or from northern France instead of the southern Languedoc. The Norman dialect in which her works are composed suggests that Marie was native to Normandy, and lived during the latter part of the 12th century. The "King Henry" to whom she dedicates her *Lais* is usually identified as Henry II, the Angevin French king of England from 1154–89, and Marie is thought to have been a member of his court, which spoke the form of Norman dialect in which her works come down to us. It has sometimes been suggested that she was Henry's illegitimate sister Marie, who became Abbess of Shaftesbury around 1181, and who died in 1216, but without any other corroborating documents, such theories are no more than intriguing speculation. It seems very likely, however, that she was attached to the court of Henry II and his wife, Eleanor of Aquitaine, and was of noble birth; her works reveal a level of education and culture that would not usually have been available to a layperson of lower rank during this time. It is clear that she was educated in Latin, as well as French, and perhaps even in the Breton language, since she claims to have translated her *Lais* from that tongue.

The *Lais* of Marie de France are brief narratives written in octosyllabic rhyming couplets, which was the conventional literary vehicle for French romance during this time. This collection is made up of twelve stories, each prefaced by a short prologue in which Marie reveals that she is translating into French for the first time a number of "Breton *lais*." The *lais* were Celtic tales of romance that often involved elements of the fantastic. The compressed space of the form requires Marie to handle her material with considerable finesse and she recounts her tales with an economy of words and a tight narrative control that lend the romances a down-to-earth precision without sacrificing meaning or nuance.

Many of the *lais* have a strongly female focus, and in this regard offer a certain contrast to the romances of Marie's contemporaries. The works of male romancers, while treating the subject of love, often emphasized the tension between love and chivalric pursuits, and the need to balance the two in order to fulfill both personal needs and social responsibilities. Marie is largely uninterested in such concerns, and focuses instead on the personal desires of her characters, especially those of her female characters. Her *lais* often depict intensely intimate love relationships set against a backdrop of a threatening society in which unfulfilling marriages, the arbitrary dictates of court life, and oppressive social practices hold sway.

 Lanval and *Chevrefoil* are *lais* drawn from the larger literary universe of Arthurian legend. The former recounts the tale of a knight whose inherent worth is unrecognized by the Arthurian court, and who is able to escape this uncaring and arbitrary society through the love of an otherworldly fairy figure, while the latter presents an episode involving the doomed lovers Tristan and Isolde and explores frustrated love, the grief of separation, and the transcendence of artistic expression. The other two *lais* presented here, like Marie's *Fables*, implicitly use the animal world to approach human emotion and relationships. In *Laüstic*, the love affair between a knight and his neighbor's wife raises the issues of violent jealousy, marital betrayal, and loss. In *Bisclavret*, the title character makes a startling confession to his wife that leads us into an examination of the clash between his innate nobility and his dangerous appearance, and the ability of loyalty and generosity to resolve this conflict.

⌘⌘⌘

Bisclavret (The Werewolf)[1]

Quant de lais faire m'entremet,	Since I have undertaken to compose lais,
ne voil ublïer Bisclaveret.	I don't want to forget *Bisclavret*.
Bisclaveret ad nun en bretan,	*Bisclavret* is the name in Breton;
Garwaf l'apelent li Norman.	the Normans call it *Garwaf*.
5 Jadis le poeit hume oïr,	There was a time when one would hear,
e sovent suleit avenir,	and it often used to happen,
humes plusurs garual devindrent	that many people became werewolves
e es boscages meisun tindrent.	and kept house in the woods.[2]
Garualf, c'est beste salvage:	The werewolf is a wild beast:
10 tant cum il est en cele rage,	when it is in that frenzy,
hummes devure, grant mal fait,	it devours people and does great harm.
es granz fore[z] converse e vait.	It lives in and roams the great forests.
Cest afere les ore ester;	Now I let this matter be;
del biclaveret [vus] voil cunter.	I want to tell you about the *bisclavret*.
15 En Bretaine maneit un ber,	In Brittany there lived a baron,
merveille l'ai oï loër;	whom I have heard marvelously praised;
beaus chevalers e bons esteit	he was a handsome, good knight

---

[1]   *Bisclavret, Lanval, Laüstic,* and *Chevrefoil* have all been newly translated for this anthology by Claire M. Waters. The Anglo-Norman text is based on British Library MS Harley 978, and emendations are marked by square brackets.

[2]   *Since … woods*   When referring to werewolves generally in her opening lines, Marie uses the name she has identified as Norman: "garual/garwaf." After this, in talking about her protagonist, she uses the Breton "bisclaveret." This translation signals the change in terms at line 14, where she switches to "bisclaveret," but thereafter translates "bisclaveret" as "werewolf" when it is used with a definite article or seems to be a generic term, and as "Bisclavret" (a name) when it specifically designates the protagonist himself—which is usually at key moments in the story.

e noblement se cunteneit.
De sun seinur esteit privez
20   e de tuz ses veisins amez.
Femme ot espuse mut vailant
e que mut feseit beu semblant.
Il amot li e ele lui,
mes d'une chose ert grant ennui:
25   que en la semeine le deperdeit
treis jurs entiers, que ele ne saveit
u deveneit në u alout,
ne nul des soens nïent n'e[n] sout.
Une feiz esteit repeirez
30   a sa meisun joius e liez.
Demandé li ad e enquis:
"Sire," fait ele, "beau duz amis,
une chose vus demandasse
mut volenters, si jeo osasse;
35   mes jeo creim tant vostre curuz,
que nule rien tant ne redut."
Quant il l'oï, [si] l'acola,
vers li la traist, si la beisa.
"Dame," fait il, "[or] demandez!
40   Ja cele chose ne [querrez],
si jo la sai, ne la vus die."
"Par fei," fet ele, "ore sui garie!
Sire, jeo sui en tel effrei
les jurs quant vus partez de mei,
45   el [quor] en ai mut grant dolur
e de vus perdre tel poür,
si jeo n'en ai hastif cunfort,
bien tost en puis aver la mort.
Kar me dites u vus alez,
50   u vus estes, u vus conversez!
Mun escïent que vus amez,
e si si est, vus meserrez."
"Dame," fet il, "pur Deu, merci!
Mal m'en vendra si jol vus di,
55   kar de m'amur vus partirai
e mei memes en perdirai."
Quant la dame l'ad entendu,
ne l'ad neent en gab tenu.
Suventefeiz li demanda;
60   tant le blandi e losenga
que s'aventure li cunta;
nule chose ne li cela.

and conducted himself nobly.
He was dear to his lord
and beloved by all his neighbors.
He had married a most noble wife
who made him good cheer.
He loved her and she him,
but she was greatly troubled by one thing:
each week she lost him
for three whole days, when she did not know
what became of him nor where he went,
nor did any of his people know anything about it.
One day he returned
to his house joyful and happy.
She questioned him and made an inquiry:
"Lord," she said, "fair sweet beloved,
I would very much like to ask you
one thing, if I dared;
but I am so afraid of your anger
that nothing frightens me more."
When he heard this, he embraced her,
drew her toward him and kissed her.
"Lady," he said, "go ahead and ask!
There is nothing you can ask that,
if I know, I will not tell you."
"By my faith," she said, "now I am cured!
Lord, I am so anxious
on those days when you leave me,
I have such great sorrow in my heart
and such fear of losing you,
that if I do not get reassurance shortly,
very soon I may die of it.
So do tell me where you go,
where you are, where you live!
It is my belief you are in love,
and if it is so, you do wrong."
"Lady," he said, "mercy, by God!
Trouble will come to me if I tell you,
for I will divide you from my love
and destroy myself in doing so."
When the lady heard him,
she considered it no joke.
Many times she asked him;
she cajoled and flattered him so much
that he told her what happened to him;
he hid nothing from her.

"Dame, jeo devienc besclaveret:
en cele grant forest me met,
65 al plus espés de la gaudine,
s'i vif de preie e de ravine."
Quant il li aveit tut cunté,
enquis li ad e demaundé
se il se despuille u vet vestu.
70 "Dame," fet il, "jeo vois tut nu."
"Di mei, pur Deu, u sunt voz dras."
"Dame, ceo ne dirai jeo pas;
kar si jeo les eüsse perduz
e de ceo feusse aparceüz
75 bisclaveret sereie a tuz jurs;
jamés n'avereie mes sucurs,
de si k'il me fussent rendu.
Pur ceo ne voil k'il seit seü."
"Sire," la dame li respunt,
80 "Jeo vus eim plus que tut le mund:
nel me devez nïent celer,
ne [mei] de nule rien duter;
ne semblereit pas amisté.
Qu'ai jeo forfait? pur queil peché
85 me dutez vus de nule rien?
Dites [le] mei, si ferez bien!"
Tant l'anguissa, tant le suzprist,
ne pout el faire, si li dist.
"Dame," fet il, "[delez] cel bois,
90 lez le chemin par unt jeo vois,
une vielz chapele i esteit,
ke meintefeiz grant bien me feit:
la est la piere cruose e lee
suz un buissun, dedenz cavee;
95 mes dras i met suz le buissun,
tant que jeo revi[e]nc a meisun."
La dame oï cele merveille;
de poür fu tute vermeille.
De l'aventure se esfrea.
100 E[n] maint endreit se purpensa
cum ele s'en puïst partir;
ne voleit mes lez lui gisir.
Un chevaler de la cuntree,
que lungement l'aveit amee
105 e mut preié[e] e mut requise
e mut duné en sun servise—
ele ne l'aveit unc amé

"Lady, I become a werewolf:
I go into that great forest,
to the deepest part of the woods,
and live on prey and plunder."
When he had told her everything,
she inquired and asked him
whether he undressed or went clothed.
"Lady," he said, "I go quite naked."
"Tell me, by God, where your clothes are."
"Lady, that I will not tell;
for if I should lose them
and were discovered through this
I would be a werewolf always;
there would never again be hope for me,
until they were returned to me.
For this reason I don't want it known."
"Sir," the lady replied to him,
"I love you more than all the world:
you must hide nothing from me,
nor mistrust me in any way;
that would not seem like friendship.
What have I done wrong? For what misdeed
do you mistrust me in any way?
You will do well to tell me!"
She so tormented and nagged him
that he could not do otherwise, and so he told her.
"Lady," he said, "near this wood,
beside the path by which I travel,
there is an old chapel,
which many times has been a great help to me:
there is a broad, carved-out stone
which is hollow inside, below a bush;
I put my clothes under the bush
until I return home."
The lady heard this marvel;
she turned quite red with fear.
She was terrified by this adventure.
Many times she thought hard
about how she could get away;
she did not want to lie beside him any more.
A knight of that land,
who had loved her a long time
and greatly implored and courted her
and greatly devoted himself to her service—
she had never loved him

ne de s'amur aseüré—
celui manda par sun message,
110 si li descoveri sun curage.
"Amis," fet ele, "seez leéz!
Ceo dunt vus estes travaillez
vus otri jeo sanz nul respit:
ja n'i averez nul cuntredit.
115 M'amur e mun cors vus otrei:
vostre drue fetes de mei!"
Cil l'en mercie bonement
e la fiance de li prent;
e ele le met par serement.
120 Puis li cunta cumfaitement
ses sires ala e k'il devint;
tute la veie kë il tint
vers la forest l[i] enseigna;
pur sa despuille l'enveia.
125 Issi fu Bisclaveret trahiz
e par sa femme maubailiz.
Pur ceo que hum le perdeit sovent,
quidouent tuz communalment
que dunc s'en fust del tut alez.
130 Asez fu quis e demandez,
mes n'en porent mie trover;
si lur estuit lesser ester.
La dame ad cil dunc espusee,
que lungement aveit amee.
135   Issi remist un an entier,
tant que li reis ala chacier;
a la forest ala tut dreit,
la u li bisclaveret esteit.
Quant li chiens furent descuplé,
140 le bisclaveret unt encuntré;
a lui cururent tutejur
e li chien e li veneür,
tant que pur poi ne l'eurent pris
e tut deciré e maumis,
145 de si qu'il ad le rei choisi;
vers lui curut quere merci.
Il l'aveit pris par sun estrié,

or promised him her love—
she sent to this man by messenger
and revealed her feelings to him.
"Friend," she said, "rejoice!
That for which you have labored
I grant you without delay:
you will find no resistance.
I grant you my love and my body;
take me as your lover!"
He thanks her warmly
and accepts her promise,
and she binds him to her by oath.
Then she told him just how
her lord went away and what became of him;
she taught him the whole path
he took to the forest;
she sent him to the discarded clothes.
Thus Bisclavret was betrayed
and brought to ruin by his wife.
Since men often had known him to be missing,
everyone generally believed
that he had gone away for good.
He was widely sought and asked after,
but they could not find him at all,
so they had to let it be.
The lady then married him
who had loved her for a long time.
   Things remained this way for a whole year,
until the king went hunting;
he went straight to the forest
where the werewolf was.
When the hounds were unleashed,
they found the werewolf;
the hounds and hunters
chased it all day,
so that they very nearly caught it
and completely tore it to shreds and destroyed it,
until it saw the king;
it ran to him to ask mercy.[1]
It took him by the stirrup,

---

[1] Although the noun "bisclaveret" is masculine, here the werewolf is referred to in English as "it" when it is in wolf form; the human protagonist Bisclavret, who is of course the same "person," is "he." This both helps to distinguish the wolf from the king and other masculine characters and conveys his dual nature; it also helps to account for the term "beast," which is several times applied to the wolf, and which is feminine in Old French. Only at the end, when the wise counselor seems to assume that the werewolf is indeed also the man Bisclavret, is the werewolf called "he" in the translation (ll. 283–92).

la jambe li baise e le pié.
Li reis le vit, grant poür ad;
150 ses cumpainuns tuz apelad.
"Seignurs," fet il, "avant venez!
Ceste merveillë esgardez,
cum ceste beste se humilie!
Ele ad sen de hume, merci crie.
155 Chacez mei tuz ces chiens arere,
si gardez quë hum ne la fiere!
Ceste beste ad entente e sen.
Espleitez vus! Alum nus en!
A la beste durrai ma pes;
160 kar jeo ne chacerai hui mes."
    Li reis s'en est turné atant.
Le bisclaveret li vet siwant;
mut se tint pres, n'en vout partir,
il n'ad cure de lui guerpir.
165 Li reis l'en meine en sun chastel;
mut en fu liez, mut li est bel,
kar unke mes tel n'ot veü.
A grant merveille l'ot tenu
e mut le tient a grant chierté.
170 A tuz les suens ad comaundé
que sur s'amur le gardent bien
e li ne mesfacent de rien,
ne par nul de eus ne seit feruz;
bien seit abevreiz e [peüz].
175 Cil le garderent volenters.
Tuz jurs entre les chevalers
e pres del rei se alout cuchier.
N'i ad celui que ne l'ad chier;
tant esteit franc e deboneire,
180 unc ne volt a rien mesfeire.
U ke li reis deüst errer,
il n'out cure de deseverer;
ensemble od li tuz jurs alout:
bien s'aparceit quë il l'amout.
185   Oëz aprés cument avint.
A une curt ke li rei tint
tuz les baruns aveit mandez,
ceus ke furent de li cha[s]ez,
pur aider sa feste a tenir
190 e lui plus beal faire servir.
Li chevaler i est alez,
richement e bien aturnez,

it kisses his leg and his foot.
The king sees this and is very much afraid;
he called all his companions.
"Lords," he said, "come here at once!
Look at this wonder,
how this beast humbles itself!
It has human understanding, it begs mercy.
Get all these dogs away from me,
make sure that no one strikes it!
This beast has intelligence and understanding.
Hurry up! Let's go!
I will extend my peace to the beast;
for I will hunt no more."
    The king turned back at once.
The werewolf went along following him;
it stayed very close, it would not leave,
it had no desire to part from him.
The king led it into his castle;
he was very happy with it, it delighted him,
for he had never seen such a thing.
He considered it a great wonder
and held it very dear.
He commanded all his people
to take good care of it for love of him
and not ill-treat it in any way,
nor should any of them strike it;
it should be well fed and watered.
They took care of it gladly.
Every day it went to sleep
among the knights and close to the king.
There was no one who did not hold it dear;
it was so noble and kind,
it never wished to do wrong in any way.
Wherever the king had to go
it did not care to be apart from him;
it always went along with him:
he could see well that it loved him.
    Listen to what happened afterwards.
One time when the king held court
he had sent for all his barons,
those who were his vassals,
to help him celebrate
and to serve him as pleasingly as possible.
The knight who had Bisclavret's wife
went along there,

ki la femme Bisclaveret ot.
Il ne saveit ne ne quidot
195   que il le deüst trover si pres.
Si tost cum il vint al paleis
e le bisclaveret le aparceut,
de plain esleis vers li curut;
as denz le prist, vers lui le trait.
200   Ja li eüst mut grant leid fait,
ne fust li reis ki l'apela,
de une verge le manaça.
Deus feiz le vout mordrë al jur.
Mut s'esmerveillent li plusur,
205   kar unkes tel semblant ne fist
vers nul hume k'il veïst.
Ceo dïent tut par la meisun
ke il nel fet mie sanz reisun:
mesfait li ad, coment que seit,
210   kar volenters se vengereit.
A cele feiz remist issi,
tant que la feste departi
e li barun unt pris cungé;
a lur meisun sunt repeiré.
215   Alez s'en est li chevaliers,
mien escïent tut as premers,
que le bisclaveret asailli;
n'est merveille s'il le haï.
     Ne fu puis gueres lungement,
220   ceo m'est avis, si cum j'entent,
que a la forest ala li reis,
que tant fu sages e curteis
u li bisclaveret fu trovez;
e il i est od li alez.
225   La nuit quant il s'en repeira,
en la cuntree herberga.
La femme le bisclaveret le sot.
Avenantment se appareilot;
al demain vait al rei parler,
230   riche present li fait porter.
Quant Bisclaveret la veit venir,
nul hum nel poeit retenir;
vers li curut cum enragiez.
Oiez cum il est bien vengiez:
235   le neis li esracha del vis!
Quei li p[e]üst il faire pis?
De tutes parz l'unt manacié;

well and richly dressed.
He did not know nor imagine
that he would find Bisclavret so close.
As soon as he arrived at the palace
and the werewolf saw him,
it ran at him full tilt;
it grabbed him with its teeth and dragged him down.
It would have done him great injury,
were it not for the king, who called to it
and threatened it with a staff.
Twice that day it tried to bite him.
Everyone was astonished,
for it had never acted like this
toward anyone it saw.
Everyone in the household said
that surely it did this for a reason:
the knight had in some way done it wrong
and now it was eager to avenge itself.
Things went along this way
until the festivities broke up
and the barons took their leave;
they went back to their houses.
The knight the werewolf had attacked
went away, I believe,
among the first;
it's no wonder if it hated him.
     It was not long after,
it seems to me, as I understand it,
that the king, who was so wise and courteous,
went to the forest
where the werewolf was found,
and it went with him.
That night, when he was returning from there,
he took lodging in the countryside.
The werewolf's wife found this out.
She dressed herself becomingly;
the next day she went to talk to the king,
she had rich gifts brought to him.
When Bisclavret sees her coming,
no one could hold him back;
he ran toward her as though he were mad.
Hear how well he avenged himself:
he tore the nose from her face!
What worse could he have done to her?
They threatened him from all sides;

	ja l'eüssent tut depescié,
	quant un sages hum dist al rei,
240	"Sire," fet il, "entent a mei!
	Ceste beste ad esté od vus;
	n'i ad ore celui de nus
	que ne l'eit veü lungement
	e pres de li alé sovent.
245	Unke mes humme ne tucha
	ne felunie ne mustra,
	fors a la dame que ici vei.
	Par cele fei ke jeo vus dei,
	aukun curuz ad il vers li,
250	e vers sun seignur autresi.
	Ceo est la femme al chevaler
	que taunt par suliez aveir chier,
	que lung tens ad esté perduz;
	ne s[e]ümes [qu']est devenuz.
255	Kar metez la dame en destreit,
	se aucune chose vus direit,
	pur quei ceste beste la heit;
	fetes li dire se ele le seit!
	Meinte merveille avum veü
260	quë en Bretaigne est avenu."
	Li reis ad sun cunseil creü:
	le chevaler ad retenu;
	de l'autre part ad la dame prise
	e en mut grant destresce mise.
265	Tant par destresce e par poür
	tut li cunta de sun seignur:
	coment ele l'aveit trahi
	e sa despoille li toli,
	l'aventure qu'il li cunta,
270	e quei devint e u ala.
	Puis que ses dras li ot toluz,
	ne fud en sun païs veüz.
	Tresbien quidat e bien creeit
	que la beste Bisclaveret seit.
275	Le reis demande la despoille;
	u bel li seit u pas nel voille,
	ariere la fet aporter,
	al bisclaveret la fist doner.
	Quant il les urent devant li mise,
280	Ne se prist garde en nule guise.
	Li produme le rei apela,
	cil ki primes le cunseilla:

they would have torn him all to pieces,
when a wise man said to the king,
"Sire," he said, "listen to me!
This beast has been living with you;
there is not one of us
who has not watched it for a long time
and often been near it.
It has never touched anyone
nor shown any wickedness,
except to the lady I see here.
By the faith I owe you,
it has some cause for anger against her,
and also against her husband.
This is the wife of the knight
whom you used to hold so dear,
who has been missing for a long time;
we never knew what became of him.
Put the lady under duress about this,
to see if she will tell you anything
about why this beast hates her;
make her tell it if she knows!
We have seen many a wonder
come to pass in Brittany."
The king had faith in his counsel:
he had the knight arrested;
moreover he had the lady taken
and put to severe torture.
On account of such torture and out of fear
she told him all about her lord:
how she had betrayed him
and taken his clothes away,
the adventure that he had told her,
and what he became and where he went.
Since she had taken away his clothes,
he had not been seen in his lands.
She fully believed and supposed
that this beast was Bisclavret.
The king demanded the clothes he had left;
whether she liked it or not,
she had them brought back
and given to the werewolf.
When they were put in front of it,
it would not take any notice at all.
The wise man, the one
who had first advised the king, addressed him:

"Sire, ne fetes mie bien:
cist nel fereit pur nule rien,
285   que devant vus ses dras reveste
ne mute la semblance de beste.
Ne savez mie que ceo munte:
mut durement en ad grant hunte.
En tes chambres le fai mener
290   e la despoille od li porter;
une grant piece l'i laissums.
S'il devient hum, bien le verums."
Li reis memes le mena
e tuz les hus sur li ferma.
295   Al chief de piece i est alez,
deuz baruns ad od li menez;
en la chambrë entrent tut trei.
Sur le demeine lit al rei
trova il dormant le chevaler.
300   Li reis le curut enbracier;
plus de cent feiz l'acole e baise.

Si tost cum il pot aver aise,
tute sa tere li rendi;
plus li duna ke jeo ne di.
305   La femme ad del païs ostee
e chacie hors de la cuntree.
Cil s'en alat ensemble od li,
pur ki sun seignur ot trahi.
Enfanz en ad asés eüz;
310   puis unt esté bien cuneüz
[e] del semblant e del visage:
plusurs [des] femmes del lignage,
c'est verité, senz nes sunt [nees]
e [si] viveient esnasees.
315   L'aventure ke avez oïe
veraie fu, n'en dutez mie.
De *Bisclaveret* fu fet li lais
pur remembrance a tutdis mais.

"Sire, you are not doing this right:
he wouldn't, for anything,
put his clothing back on in front of you
nor change his animal appearance.
You have no idea what this means for him:
he feels terrible shame about it.
Have him led into your rooms
and take the clothing with him;
we'll leave him there for a while.
We shall see if he becomes a man."
The king himself led him in
and closed all the doors behind him.
After a time he went there,
taking two barons with him;
all three of them entered the chamber.
On the king's own bed
he found the knight sleeping.
The king ran to embrace him;
more than a hundred times he embraces and
    kisses him.
As soon as he was able,
he returned all his lands to him;
he gave him more than I say.
He banished his wife from the land
and chased her out of the country.
The man for whom she had betrayed her lord
went along with her.
She had a number of children,
who were quite recognizable
in face and appearance:
most of the women of that line,
in truth, were born without noses
and lived noseless.
    The adventure you have heard
was true, have no doubt.
The lai of *Bisclavret* was made
to be remembered forevermore.

Lanval

L'aventure d'un autre lai,
cum ele avient, vus cunterai.
Fait fu d'un mut gentil vassal;
en bretans l'apelent Lanval.

I shall tell you the adventure
of another lay, just as it happened.
It was made about a very noble vassal;
in Breton they call him Lanval.

5	A Kardoel surjurnot li reis	The king was staying at Cardoel—
	Artur, li pruz e li curteis,	Arthur, the valiant and courteous—
	pur les Escoz e pur les Pis,	on account of the Scots and Picts
	que destrui[ei]ent le païs;	who were ravaging the country:
	en la tere de Loengre entroënt	they came into the land of Logres[1]
10	e mut suvent la damagoënt.	and repeatedly caused destruction there.
	A la Pentecuste en esté	At Pentecost, in the summer,
	i aveit li reis sujurné.	the king had taken up residence there.
	Asez i duna riches duns	He gave many rich gifts
	e as cuntes e as baruns.	both to counts and to noblemen.
15	A ceus de la table runde—	To the members of the Round Table—
	n'ot tant de teus en tut le munde—	they had no equal in all the world—
	femmes e tere departi	he shared out wives and land
	par tut, fors un ki l'ot servi:	among all except one who had served him:
	ceo fu Lanval, ne l'en sovient,	that was Lanval, whom he did not remember,
20	ne nul de[s] soens bien ne li tient.	nor did any of his men favor him.
	Pur sa valur, pur sa largesce,	For his valor, his generosity,
	pur sa beauté, pur sa prüesce	his beauty, his prowess,
	l'envioënt tut li plusur;	most people envied him;
	tel li mustra semblant d'amur,	many a one pretended to love him
25	se al chevaler mesavenist,	who wouldn't have complained for a moment
	ja une feiz ne l'en pleinsist.	if something bad had befallen the knight.
	Fiz a rei fu de haut parage,	He was a king's son, of high lineage,
	mes luin ert de sun heritage.	but he was far from his heritage.
	De la meisné le rei fu.	He was part of the king's household.
30	Tut sun aveir ad despendu,	He had spent all his wealth,
	kar li reis rien ne li dona	for the king gave him nothing,
	ne Lanval rien ne li demanda.	nor did Lanval ask him for anything.
	Ore est Lanval mut entrepris,	Now Lanval is very unhappy,
	mut est dolent e mut pensis.	very sorrowful and anxious.
35	Seignurs, ne vus esmerveillez:	Lords, do not wonder:
	hume estrange descunseillez	a foreign man without support
	mut est dolent en autre tere,	is very sorrowful in another land
	quant il ne seit u sucurs quere.	when he does not know where to seek help.
	Le chevaler dunt jeo vus di,	The knight of whom I'm telling you,
40	que tant aveit le rei servi,	who had served the king so well,
	un jur munta sur sun destrer,	got on his horse one day
	si s'est alez esbaneer.	and went off to enjoy himself.
	Fors de la vïlë est eissuz,	He went out of the town
	tut sul est en un pre venuz;	and came, all alone, to a meadow;
45	sur une ewe curaunt descent—	he got down beside running water—
	mes sis cheval tremble forment.	but his horse trembled terribly.
	Il le descengle, si s'en vait;	He unsaddled it and went off;
	en mi le pre vuiltrer le lait.	he let it roll around in the middle of the meadow.

---

[1] *Logres*   The Celtic word for England.

Le pan de sun mantel plia

50   desuz sun chief puis le cucha.

Mut est pensis pur sa mesaise;

il ne veit chose ke li plaise.

La u il gist en teu maniere,

garda aval lez la riviere,

55   [si] vit venir deus dameiseles;

unc n'en ot veü[es] plus beles.

Vestues ierent richement,

lacie[es] mut estreitement

en deus blians de purpre bis;

60   mut par aveient bel le vis.

L'eisnee portout un[s] bacins,

doré furent, bien faiz e fins;

le veir vus en dirai sans faile.

L'autre portout une tuaile.

65   Eles s'en sunt alees dreit

la u li chevaler giseit.

Lanval, que mut fu enseigniez,

cuntre eles s'en levad en piez.

Celes l'unt primes salué,

70   lur message li unt cunté:

"Sire Lanval, ma dameisele,

que tant est pruz e sage e bele,

ele nus enveit pur vus;

kar i venez ensemble od nus!

75   Sauvement vus i cundurums:

veez, pres est li paveilluns!"

Le chevalers od eles vait;

de sun cheval ne tient nul plait,

que devant li pe[ssei]t al pre.

80   Treskë al tref l'unt amené,

que mut fu beaus e bien asis.

La reïne Semiramis,

quant ele ot unkes plus aveir

e plus pussaunce e plus saveir,

85   ne l'emperere Octovïen

n'esligasent le destre pan.

Un aigle d'or ot desus mis;

de cel ne sai dire le pris,

ne des cordes ne des peissuns

90   que del tref tienent les giruns;

suz ciel n'ad rei ki[s] esligast

pur nul aver k'il i donast.

Dedenz cel tref fu la pucele:

He folded the end of his mantle

and lay down with it under his head.

He is very worried by his difficult situation;

he sees nothing that pleases him.

As he lay there like this,

he looked down toward the bank

and saw two maidens coming;

he had never seen any more beautiful.

They were richly dressed

and very tightly laced

in tunics of dark purple;

they had exceedingly lovely faces.

The elder was carrying basins

of gold, fine and well made;

I shall tell you the truth without fail.

The other carried a towel.

They went right along

to where the knight was lying.

Lanval, who was very well bred,

got to his feet to meet them.

They greeted him first

and told him their message:

"Sir Lanval, my lady,

who is most noble, wise, and beautiful,

sent us for you;

now come along with us!

We will convey you safely to her.

Look, the pavilion is right here!"

The knight goes with them;

he takes no heed of his horse,

who was off grazing in the meadow.

They led him up to the tent,

which was very beautiful and well situated.

Not Queen Semiramis,

when she was at her richest

and most powerful and wisest,

nor the emperor Octavian

could have bought the right flap.

A golden eagle was set on top of it;

I can't tell its value,

nor of the cords or the stakes

that held the sides of the tent;

no king under heaven could buy them

for any wealth he might offer.

Inside the tent was the maiden:

flur de lis [e] rose nuvele,
95 quant ele pert al tens d'esté,
trespassot ele de beauté.
Ele jut sur un lit mut bel—
li drap valeient un chastel—
en sa chemise senglement.
100 Mut ot le cors bien fait e gent.
Un cher mantel de blanc hermine,
covert de purpre alexandrine,
ot pur le chaut sur li geté.
Tut ot descovert le costé,
105 le vis, le col e la peitrine;
plus ert blanche que flur d'espine.
    Le chevaler avant ala,
e la pucele l'apela;
il s'est devant le lit asis.
110 "Lanval," fet ele, "beus amis,
pur vus vienc jeo fors de ma tere;
de luinz vus sui venu[e] quere.
Se vus estes pruz e curteis,
emperere ne quens ne reis
115 n'ot unkes tant joie ne bien;
kar jo vus aim sur tute rien."
Il l'esgarda, si la vit bele;
amurs le puint de l'estencele,
que sun quor alume e esprent.
120 Il li respunt avenantment.
"Bele," fet il, "si vus pleiseit
e cele joie me aveneit
que vus me vousissez amer,
ja [ne savrïez] rien commander
125 que jeo ne face a mien poeir,
turt a folie u a saveir.
Jeo frai voz comandemenz;
pur vus guerpirai tutes genz.
Jamés ne queor de vus partir:
130 ceo est la rien que plus desir."
Quant la meschine l'oï parler,
celui que tant la peot amer,
s'amur e sun cors li otreie.
Ore est Lanval en dreite veie!
135 Un dun li ad duné aprés:
ja cele rien ne vudra mes
quë il nen ait a sun talent;
doinst e despende largement,

her beauty surpassed
the lily and the new rose
when they bloom in summer.
She lay on a very beautiful bed—
the sheets were worth a castle—
in nothing but her shift.
Her body was very elegant and comely.
She had thrown on for warmth
a costly mantle of white ermine,
lined with alexandrine silk.
Her side was entirely uncovered,
her face, her neck, and her breast;
she was whiter than hawthorn blossom.
    The knight went forward,
and the maiden called to him;
he sat down in front of the bed.
"Lanval," she said, "handsome friend,
for you I have come out of my own land;
I have come from afar to look for you.
If you are valiant and courteous,
no emperor, count, or king
ever had such joy or good fortune;
for I love you more than anything."
He looked at her, and saw she was beautiful;
love stung him with a spark
that lit and inflamed his heart.
He responded fittingly.
"Beautiful one," he said, "if it pleased you
that such joy should come to me
as to have you consent to love me,
you could never command anything
that I would not do to the best of my power,
be it folly or wisdom.
I will do what you command;
for you I will give up everyone.
I never wish to part from you:
this is what I most desire."
When the maiden heard him speak,
he who could love her so well,
she granted him her love and her body.
Now Lanval is on the right path!
She gave him still one more gift:
he will never again want anything
without having as much of it as he likes;
let him give and spend generously,

	ele li troverat asez.	she will provide him with enough.
140	Mut est Lanval bien herbergez:[1]	Lanval is very well situated:
	cum plus despendra richement,	the more richly he spends,
	plus averat or e argent.	the more gold and silver he will have.
	"Ami," fet ele, "ore vus chasti,	"Friend," she said, "now I warn you,
	si vus comant e si vus pri,	I command and beg you,
145	ne vus descoverez a nul humme!	tell no one about this!
	De ceo vus dirai ja la summe:	I will tell you the whole truth:
	a tuz jurs m'avrïez perdue,	you would lose me forever
	se ceste amur esteit seüe;	if this love should be known;
	jamés ne me purriez veeir	you could never see me again
150	ne de mun cors seisine aveir."	or have possession of my body."
	Il li respunt que bien tendra	He replies that he will certainly hold to
	ceo que ele li comaundera.	what she commands.
	Delez li s'est al lit cuchiez:	He lay down beside her on the bed:
	ore est Lanval bien herbergez.	now Lanval is well lodged.
155	Ensemble od li la relevee	All afternoon he stayed with her
	demurat tresque a l[a] vespree,	until the evening,
	e plus i fust, së il poïst	and he would have stayed longer, if he could
	e s'amie lui cunsentist.	and his beloved had consented.
	"Amis," fet ele, "levez sus!	"Friend," she said, "get up!
160	Vus n'i poëz demurer plus.	You can't stay here any more.
	Alez vus en, jeo remeindrai;	You go on, I will remain—
	mes un[e] chose vus dirai:	but one thing I will tell you:
	quant vus vodrez od mei parler,	when you want to talk with me,
	ja ne saverez cel liu penser,	there is no place you can think of
165	u nuls puïst aver sa amie	where one could have his beloved
	sanz reproece, sanz vileinie,	without reproach or villainy
	que jeo ne vus seie en present	that I will not be with you at once
	a fere tut vostre talent;	to do all your will;
	nul humme fors vus ne me verra	no man but you will see me
170	ne ma parole nen orra."	or hear my words."
	Quant il l'oï, mut en fu liez;	When he heard this, he was delighted;
	il la baisa, puis s'est dresciez.	he kissed her, then got up.
	Celes quë al tref l'amenerent	The maidens who had brought him to the tent
	de riches dras le cunreerent;	covered him with rich clothes;
175	quant il fu vestu de nuvel,	when he was newly dressed,
	suz ciel nen ot plus bel dancel.	there was no handsomer young man under heaven.
	N'esteit mie fous ne vileins.	He was not at all foolish or base.
	L'ewe li donent a ses meins	They gave him water for his hands
	e la tuaille a [es]suier;	and the towel to dry them;
180	puis li portent a manger.	then they brought him to the table.

---

1 *Mut ... herbergez* Other manuscripts have here, "mut est Lanval bien *assenez*" (Lanval is very well provided for) and some editors prefer this reading, since the line as it stands is repeated below at l. 154.

Od s'amie prist le super:
ne feseit mie a refuser.
Mut fu servi curteisement,
e il a grant joie le prent.
185 Un entremés i ot plener,
que mut pleiseit al chevalier:
kar s'amie baisout sovent
e acolot estreitement.

Quant del manger furent levé,
190 sun cheval li unt amené.
Bien li unt la sele mise;
mut ad trové riche servise.
Il prent cungé, si est muntez;
vers la cité s'en est alez.
195 Suvent esgarde ariere sei.
Mut est Lanval en grant esfrei;
de s'aventure vait pensaunt
e en sun curage d[o]taunt.
Esbaïz est, ne seit que creir,

200 il ne la quide mie a veir.
Il est a sun ostel venuz;
ses hummes treve bien vestuz.
Icele nuit bon estel tient;
mes nul ne sot dunt ceo li vient.
205 N'ot en la vile chevalier
ki de surjur ait grant mestier,
që il ne face a lui venir
e richement e bien servir.
Lanval donout les riches duns,
210 Lanval aquitout les prisuns,
Lanval vesteit les jugleürs,
Lanval feseit les granz honurs:
n'i ot estrange ne privé
a ki Lanval nen ust doné.
215 Mut ot Lanval joie e deduit:
u seit par jur u seit par nuit,
s'amie peot veer sovent,
tut est a sun comandement.

Ceo m'est avis, memes l'an,
220 aprés la feste seint Johan,
d'ici qu'a trente chevalier
si erent alé esbanïer
en un vergier desuz la tur
u la reïne ert a surjur.

He took supper with his beloved:
he by no means refused.
He was served very courteously,
and accepted it with great joy.
There was an excellent extra dish
that greatly pleased the knight,
for he often kissed his lady
and embraced her closely.

When they had gotten up from the table,
they brought him his horse.
They have put its saddle on well;
it has been richly looked after.
He took his leave and mounted;
he went toward the city.
Several times he looks back.
Lanval is greatly troubled;
he goes along thinking about his adventure
and worrying to himself.
He is astonished, he doesn't know what to
think,
he doesn't believe he will see her again.
He arrives at his lodging;
he finds his men handsomely dressed.
That night he keeps a rich table,
but no one knew where he got this from.
There was no knight in the town
who greatly needed sustenance
whom Lanval does not have brought to him
and well and richly served.
Lanval gave rich gifts,
Lanval ransomed prisoners,
Lanval clothed minstrels,
Lanval did great honor:
there was no stranger or dear friend
to whom Lanval did not give.
Lanval had great joy and pleasure:
he can see his beloved often,
whether by day or by night;
she is entirely at his command.

That same year, as I understand,
after the feast of St. John,
as many as thirty knights
were going out to enjoy themselves
in a garden below the tower
where the queen was staying.

225 Ensemble od eus [esteit] Walwains
e sis cusins, li beaus Ywains.
E dist Walwains, li francs, li pruz,
que tant se fist amer de tuz:
"Par Deu, seignurs, nus feimes mal
230 de nostre cumpainun Lanval,
que tant est larges e curteis,
e sis peres est riches reis,
que od nus ne l'avum amené."
Atant se sunt ariere turné;
235 a sun ostel rev[u]nt ariere,
Lanval ameinent par preere.

A une fenestre entaillie
s'esteit la reïne apuïe[e];
treis dames ot ensemble od li.
240 La maisné [le rei] choisi;
Lanval choisi e esgarda.
Une des dames apela;
par li manda ses dameiseles,
les plus quointes [e] les plus beles:
245 od li si irrunt esbainïer
la u cil sunt al vergier.
Trente en menat od li e plus;
par les degrez descendent jus.
Les chevalers encuntre vunt,
250 que pur eles grant joïe unt.
Il les unt prises par les mains;
cil [parlemenz] ni ert pas vilains.
Lanval s'en vait a une part,
mut luin des autres. Ceo li est tart
255 que s'amie puïst tenir,
baiser, acoler e sentir;
l'autrui joie prise petit,
si il n'ad le suen delit.
Quant la reïne sul le veit,
260 al chevaler en va tut dreit;
lunc lui s'asist, si l'apela,
tut sun curage li mustra:
"Lanval, mut vus ai honuré
e mut cheri e mut amé.
265 tute m'amur poëz aveir;
kar me dites vostre voleir!
Ma drüerie vus otrei;
mut devez estre lié de mei."
"Dame," fet il, "lessez m'ester!

Gawain was with them
and his cousin, the handsome Yvain.
Gawain, the noble, the valiant,
who made himself so beloved by everyone, said,
"By God, my lords, we have done wrong
not to have brought along with us
our companion Lanval,
who is so generous and courteous,
and whose father is a rich king."
They turned back at once;
they go back to his lodging
and persuade Lanval to accompany them.

The queen was leaning
on a window ledge;
she had three ladies along with her.
She saw the king's household;
she saw Lanval and noticed him.
She called one of her ladies;
she got her to send for her maidens,
the most elegant and lovely:
they will go to enjoy themselves with her
there where the men are in the orchard.
She took thirty or more of them with her;
they go down by the stairs.
The knights, who are delighted to see them,
go to meet them.
They took the ladies by the hand;
the conversation was not unrefined.
Lanval wanders off by himself,
quite far from the others. It seems long to him
until he might have his beloved,
kiss, embrace, and touch her;
he values little another's joy
if he does not have what pleases him.
When the queen sees him alone,
she goes right to the knight;
she sat by him and spoke to him,
she showed him all her feelings:
"Lanval, I have honored you greatly
and loved you and held you very dear.
You can have all my love;
tell me your desire!
I am willing to be your lover;
you should be delighted with me."
"Lady," he said, "let me be!

270	Jeo n'ai cure de vus amer.
	Lungement ai servi le rei;
	ne li voil pas mentir ma fei.
	Ja pur vus ne pur vostre amur
	ne mesfrai a mun seignur."
275	La reïne s'en curuça;
	irie[e] fu, si mesparla.
	"Lanval," fet ele, "bien le quit,
	vuz n'amez gueres cel delit.
	Asez le m'ad humme dit sovent
280	que des femmez n'avez talent.
	Vallez avez bien afeitiez,
	ensemble od eus vus deduiez.
	Vileins cüarz, mauveis failliz,
	mut est mi sires maubailliz
285	que pres de lui vus ad suffert;
	mun escïent que Deus en pert!"
	Quant il l'oï, mut fu dolent;
	del respundre ne fu pas lent.
	Teu chose dist par maltalent
290	dunt il se repenti sovent.
	"Dame," dist il, "de cel mestier
	ne me sai jeo nïent aidier;
	mes jo aim, [e] si sui amis
	cele ke deit aver le pris
295	sur tutes celes que jeo sai.
	E une chose vus dirai,
	bien le sachez a descovert:
	une de celes ke la sert,
	tute la plus povre meschine,
300	vaut meuz de vus, dame reïne,
	de cors, de vis e de beauté,
	d'enseignement e de bunté."
	La reïne s'en par[t] atant,
	en sa chambrë en vait plurant.
305	Mut fu dolente e curuciee
	de ceo k'il [l']out [si] avilee.
	En sun lit malade cucha;
	jamés, ceo dit, ne levera,
	si li reis ne l'en feseit dreit
310	de ceo dunt ele se plein[d]reit.
	Li reis fu del bois repeiriez;
	mut out le jur esté haitiez.
	As chambres la reïne entra.
	Quant ele le vit, si se clamma;

I have no interest in loving you.
For a long time I have served the king;
I don't want to betray my faith to him.
Never for you or for your love
shall I wrong my lord."
The queen became furious at this;
in her anger, she spoke wrongly.
"Lanval," she said, "it's quite clear to me
you have no interest in that pleasure.
People have often told me
that you're not interested in women.
You have shapely young men
and take your pleasure with them.
Base coward, infamous wretch,
my lord is very badly repaid
for allowing you to remain in his presence;
I believe that he will lose God by it!"
When he heard this, he was very distressed;
he was not slow to respond.
Out of anger he said something
that he would often regret.
"Lady," he said, "I know nothing
about that line of work;
but I love, and am loved by,
one who should be valued more highly
than all the women I know.
And I'll tell you one thing,
know it well and openly:
any one of her servants,
even the poorest maid,
is worth more than you, lady queen,
in body, face, and beauty,
in manners and goodness."
The queen leaves at once
and goes into her chamber, crying.
She was very upset and angry
that he had insulted her in this way.
She took to her bed, sick;
never, she said, would she get up
if the king did not do the right thing
about the complaint she would make to him.
The king returned from the woods;
he had had a very pleasant day.
He went into the queen's rooms.
When she saw him, she made her appeal;

315	as piez li chiet, merci crie,
	e dit que Lanval l'ad hunie.
	De drüerie la requist;
	pur ceo que ele l'en escundist,
	mut [la] laidi e avila.
320	De tele amie se vanta,
	que tant iert cuinte e noble e fiere
	que meuz valut sa chamberere,
	la plus povre que [la] serveit,
	que la reïne ne feseit.
325	Li reis s'en curuçat forment;
	juré en ad sun serement:
	si il ne s'en peot en curt defendre,
	il le ferat arder u pendre.
	Fors de la chambre eissi li reis,
330	de ses baruns apelat treis;
	il les enveit pur Lanval,
	quë asez ad dolur e mal.
	A sun [o]stel fu revenuz;
	il s'est[eit] bien aparceüz
335	qu'il aveit perdue s'amie:
	descovert ot la drüerie.
	En une chambre fu tut suls,
	pensis esteit e anguissus;
	s'amie apele mut sovent,
340	mes ceo ne li valut neent.
	Il se pleigneit e suspirot,
	d'ures en autres se pasmot;
	puis li crie cent feiz merci
	que ele par[ol]t a sun ami.
345	Sun quor e sa buche maudit;
	ceo est merveille k'il ne s'ocit.
	Il ne seit tant crïer ne braire
	ne debatre ne sei detraire
	que ele en veulle merci aveir
350	sul tant que la puisse veeir.
	Oi las, cument se cuntendra?
	Cil ke li reis ci enveia,
	il sunt venu, si li unt dit
	que a la curt voise sanz respit:
355	li reis l'aveit par eus mandé,
	la reïne l'out encusé.
	Lanval i vait od sun grant doel;
	il l'eüssent ocis [sun] veoil.
	Il est devant le rei venuz;

she falls at his feet and asks for mercy
and says that Lanval has shamed her.
He asked her to be his lover;
because she refused him,
he insulted her greatly and said ugly things.
He boasted of such a beloved,
one who was so elegant, noble, and proud,
that her chambermaid,
the poorest girl who served her,
was worth more than the queen.
The king got extremely angry;
he swore an oath that
if Lanval cannot defend himself in court,
he will have him burnt or hanged.
The king went out of the chamber
and called three of his nobles;
he sends them for Lanval,
who has sorrow and trouble enough.
He had gone back to his lodging;
it was quite evident to him
that he had lost his beloved:
he had revealed their love.
He went into a chamber by himself,
anxious and distraught;
he calls on his beloved over and over,
and it does him no good at all.
He lamented and sighed,
he fainted repeatedly;
then a hundred times he begs her to have pity
and appear to her beloved.
He cursed his heart and his mouth;
it's a wonder he does not kill himself.
He cannot cry out or wail
or reproach or torment himself
enough to make her take pity on him,
even enough that he might see her.
Alas, what will he do?
    Those the king sent there
arrived, and said to him
that he must go to the court without delay:
the king had sent the order through them,
the queen had accused him.
Lanval goes there in his great sorrow;
they could have killed him for all he cared.
He came before the king;

360	mut fu dolent, taisanz e mu,	he was very sorrowful, silent and unspeaking,
	de grant dolur mustre semblant.	showing the appearance of great sorrow.
	Li reis li dit par maltalant,	The king says to him angrily,
	"Vassal, vus me avez mut mesfait!	"Vassal, you have done me a great wrong!
	Trop començastes vilein plait	You began too base a suit
365	de mei hunir e aviler	to shame and revile me
	e la reïne lendengier.	and insult the queen.
	Vanté vus estes de folie:	You boasted foolishly:
	trop par est noble vostre amie,	your beloved is far too exalted
	quant plus est bele sa meschine	when her maid is more beautiful
370	e plus vaillante que la reïne."	and worthy than the queen."
	Lanval defent la deshonur	Lanval denies the dishonor
	e la hunte de sun seignur	and shame of his lord
	de mot en mot, si cum il dist,	word by word, just as he said it,
	que la reïne ne requist;	for he had not requested the queen's love;
375	mes de ceo dunt il ot parlé	but he acknowledged the truth
	reconut il la verité,	of what he had said
	de l'amur dunt il se vanta:	concerning the love about which he boasted:
	dolent en est, perdue l'a.	he is sorrowful, for he has lost her.
	De ceo lur dit qu'il en ferat	Concerning this he says that he will do
380	quanque la curt esgarderat.	whatever the court judges best.
	Li reis fu mut vers li irez;	The king was quite furious with him;
	tuz ses hummes ad enveiez	he sent for all his men
	pur dire dreit que il en deit faire,	to say rightly what he must do,
	que hum ne li puis[se] a mal retraire.	so that no one would speak ill of it.
385	Cil unt sun commandement fait,	They did what he ordered,
	u eus seit bel, u eus seit lait.	whether they liked it or not.
	Comunement i sunt alé	They all went off together
	e unt jugé e esgardé	and judged and decided
	que Lanval deit aveir un jur;	that Lanval should have his day in court;
390	mes plegges truisse a sun seignur	but he must provide guarantees for his lord
	qu'il atendra sun jugement	that he will await his judgment
	e revendra en sun present:	and return to his presence:
	si serat la curt esforcie[e],	a larger court will be gathered,
	kar n'i ot dunc fors la maisne[e].	for now there was no one there but the household.
395	Al rei revienent li barun,	The nobles return to the king
	si li mustrent la reisun.	and explain to him their judgment.
	Li reis ad plegges demandé.	The king demanded guarantees.
	Lanval fu sul e esgaré;	Lanval was alone and in great distress;
	n'i aveit parent në ami.	he had no family or friends.
400	Walwain i vait, ki l'a plevi,	Gawain goes to act as a guarantor for Lanval,
	e tuit si cumpainun aprés.	and all his companions after him.
	Li reis lur dit: "E jol vus les	The king says to them: "I commend him to you
	sur quanke vus tenez de mei,	on the basis of whatever you may hold of me,

teres e fieus, chescun par sei."

405   Quant plevi fu, dunc n'[i] ot el;

alez s'en est a sun ostel.
Li chevaler l'unt conveé;
mut l'unt blasmé e chastïé
k'il ne face si grant dolur,
410 e maudïent si fol'amur.
Chescun jur l'aloënt veer,
pur ceo k'il voleient saveir
u il beüst, u il mangast;
mut dotouent k'il s'afolast.

415   Al jur que cil orent numé
li barun furent asemblé.
Li reis e la reïne i fu,
e li plegge unt Lanval rendu.
Mut furent tuz pur li dolent:
420 jeo quid k'il en i ot teus cent
ki feïssent tut lur poeir
pur lui sanz pleit delivre aveir;
il iert retté a mut grant tort.
Li reis demande le recort
425 sulunc le cleim e les respuns;
ore est trestut sur les baruns.
Il sunt al jugement alé,
mut sunt pensifz e esgaré
del franc humme d'autre païs
430 quë entre eus ert si entrepris.
Encumbrer le veulent plusur
pur la volenté sun seignur.
Ceo dist li quoens de Cornwaille:
"Ja endreit [nus] n'i avera faille;
435 kar ki que en plurt e ki que en chant,
le dreit estuet aler avant.
Li reis parla vers sun vassal,
que jeo vus oi numer Lanval;
de felunie le retta
440 e d'un mesfait l'acheisuna,

d'un'amur dunt il se vanta,
e ma dame s'en curuça.
Nuls ne l'apele fors le rei;
par cele fei ke jeo vus dei,
445 ki bien en veut dire le veir,

lands and fiefs, each one for himself."

Once the pledge was made, there was
nothing more to do;
Lanval went off to his lodging.
The knights went along with him;
they greatly rebuked and counseled him
not to be in such sorrow,
and they cursed such mad love.
Every day they went to see him,
for they wanted to know
if he was drinking, if he was eating;
they greatly feared that he would do himself
harm.

  On the day that they had named
the nobles gathered.
The king and queen were there,
and the guarantors brought Lanval.
Everyone was very sad for him:
I believe that there were some hundred there
who would have done anything in their power
to free him without a trial;
he was very wrongly accused.
The king demands the verdict
according to the charges and the defense;
now it is entirely up to the nobles.
They went to sit in judgment,
very anxious and dismayed
over the noble man from another country
who was in such trouble among them.
Many want to find him guilty
according to their lord's wishes.
The count of Cornwall said,
"We must not fall short,
for whoever may weep or sing,
the law must take precedence.
The king has spoken against his vassal,
whom I hear you call Lanval;
he accused him of a crime
and brought charges of wrongdoing against
him,
concerning a love of which he boasted,
which made my lady angry.
No one accuses him but the king;
by the faith I owe you,
whoever wants to speak the truth,

	ja n'i deüst respuns aveir,	there would not even be a case
	si pur ceo nun que a sun seignur	except that to the name of his lord
	deit [hum] par tut fairë honur.[1]	a man should do honor in everything.
	Un serement l'engagera,	Lanval can affirm this by oath,
450	e li reis le nus pardura.	and the king will turn him over to us for judgment.
	E s'il peot aver sun guarant	And if he can have his guarantor—
	e s'amie venist avant	if his lady should come forward
	e ceo fust veir k'il en deïst,	and what he said about her,
	dunt la reïne se marist,	which made the queen angry, was true—
455	de ceo avera il bien merci,	then he will certainly receive mercy,
	quant pur vilté nel dist de li.	since he did not say it out of baseness.
	E s'il ne peot garant aveir,	And if he cannot produce proof,
	ceo li devum faire saveir:	we must make him understand this:
	tut sun servise perde del rei,	he loses all his service to the king
460	e sil deit cungeer de sei."	and must take his leave of him."
	Al chevaler unt enveé,	They sent to the knight,
	si li unt dit e nuntïé	and they told him and announced
	que s'amie face venir	that he should make his beloved come
	pur lui tencer e garentir.	to defend and bear witness for him.
465	Il lur dit qu'il ne poeit:	He told them that he could not:
	ja pur li sucurs nen avereit.	he would never get help from her.
	Cil s'en rev[un]t as jugeürs,	They go back to the judges,
	ki n'i atendent nul sucurs.	who expect no help from that quarter.
	Li reis les hastot durement	The king urged them fiercely
470	pur la reïne kis atent.	for the sake of the queen who was waiting.
	Quant il deveient departir,	Just as they were about to make their ruling,
	deus puceles virent venir	they saw two maidens coming
	sur deus beaus palefreiz amblanz.	on two beautiful brisk palfreys.
	Mut par esteient avenanz;	They were extremely lovely;
475	de cendal purpre sunt vestues	they were dressed in purple taffeta
	tut senglement a lur char nues.	down to their bare skin.
	Cil les esgardou volenters.	Everyone gazed at them eagerly.
	Walwain, od li treis chevalers,	Gawain, and three knights with him,
	vait a Lanval, si li cunta;	went to Lanval and told him;
480	les deus puceles li mustra.	he showed him the two maidens.
	Mut fu haitié, forment li prie	He was very happy, and begged him
	qu'il li deïst si ceo ert [s]'amie.	to say whether this was his beloved.
	Il lur ad dit ne seit ki sunt	Lanval tells them that he does not know who they are
	ne dunt vienent ne u eles vunt.	or where they come from or where they are going.
485	Celes sunt alees avant	The maidens went along

---

[1] *d'un'amur … honur* Lines 441–49 appear in a different order in the manuscript: 443–48, 442, 441. This emendation is made by most editors.

tut a cheval; par tel semblant
descendirent devant le deis,
la u seeit Artur li reis.
Eles furent de grant beuté,
490   si unt curteisement parlé:
"Reis, fai tes chambers delivrer
e de pa[il]es encurtiner,
u ma dame puïst descendre
si ensemble od vus veut ostel prendre."
495   Il lur otria mut volenters,
si appela deus chevalers:
as chambres les menerent sus.
A cele feiz ne distrent plus.
      Li reis demande a ses baruns
500   le jugement e les respuns
e dit que mut l'unt curucié
de ceo que tant l'unt delaié.
"Sire," funt il, "nus departimes
pur les dames que nus veïmes;
505   [nus n'i avum] nul esgart fait.
Or recumencerum le plait."
Dunc assemblerent tut pensif;
asez i ot noise e estrif.
Quant il ierent en cel esfrei,
510   deus puceles de gent cunrei—
vestues de deus pa[il]es freis,
chevauchent deus muls espanneis—
virent venir la rue aval.
Grant joie en eurent li vassal;
515   entre eus dïent que ore est gariz
Lanval li pruz e li hardiz.
Yweins i est a lui alez,
ses cumpainuns i ad menez.
"Sire," fet il, "rehaitiez vus!
520   Pur amur Deu, parlez od nus!
Ici vienent deus dameiseles
mut acemées e mut beles:
ceo est vostre amie vereiment!"
Lanval respunt hastivement
525   e dit qu'il pas nes avuot
ne il nes cunut ne nes amot.
Atant furent celes venues,
devant le rei sunt descendues.
Mut les loërent li plusur
530   de cors, de vis e de colur;

on their horses; in this fashion
they got down in front of the dais
where King Arthur was sitting.
They were very beautiful
and spoke courteously:
"King, make your chambers ready
and spread out silks
where my lady can step
if she wants to take lodging with you."
He very willingly granted this to them,
and called two knights:
they led them up to the chambers.
At that time they said no more.
      The king asks his nobles
for the judgment and the verdict
and says that they have made him very angry
by delaying for so long.
"Sire," they say, "we broke off our discussion
on account of the ladies that we saw;
we have not made a decision.
Now we will resume the trial."
Then they gathered, quite concerned;
there was a great deal of noise and debate.
While they were in this disarray,
they saw coming down the road
two maidens of noble bearing,
dressed in cool silks,
riding two Spanish mules.
The vassals were delighted by this;
they say to each other that now Lanval,
the bold and strong, is cured.
Yvain went to him,
taking his companions with him.
"Sir," he said, "rejoice!
For the love of God, speak to us!
Here come two maidens,
very elegant and beautiful:
surely it is your beloved!"
Lanval answers hastily
and says that he neither claimed them
nor knew them nor loved them.
Just then the maidens arrived
and dismounted before the king.
Many people greatly praised
their bodies, faces and coloring;

	n'i ad cele meuz ne vausist	both of them were certainly worth
	que unkes la reïne ne fist.	more than the queen ever was.
	L'aisnee fu curteise e sage,	The elder was courteous and wise;
	avenantment dist sun message:	she spoke her message becomingly:
535	"Reis, kar nus fai chambres baillier	"King, make ready rooms for us
	a oés ma dame herbergier;	to receive my lady;
	ele vient ici a tei parler."	she is coming here to speak to you."
	Il les cumandë a mener	He orders that they be taken
	od les autres quë ainceis viendrent.	to the others who had arrived previously.
540	Unkes des muls nul plai[t] ne tindrent.	They need not worry about the mules.
	Quant il fu d'eles deliverez,	When he had sent them off,
	puis ad tuz ses baruns mandez	he ordered all his nobles
	que le jugement seit renduz:	that the judgment be given:
	trop ad le jur esté tenuz.	too much of the day had been taken up.
545	La reïne s'en curuceit,	The queen was getting angry
	que si lunges les atendeit.	that she was kept waiting so long by them.
	Ja departissent a itant,	They were about to take a decision,
	quant par la vile vient errant	when through the town comes
	tut a cheval une pucele:	a maiden riding on a horse:
550	en tut le secle n'ot plus bele.	there was no lady in the world more beautiful.
	Un blanc palefrei chevachot,	She was riding a white palfrey,
	que bel e süef la portot.	which carried her well and gently.
	Mut ot bien fet e col e teste:	It had a well-shaped neck and head:
	suz ciel nen ot plus bele beste.	there was no more beautiful animal under heaven.
555	Riche atur ot al palefrei:	The palfrey was richly harnessed:
	suz ciel nen ad quens ne rei	no count or king under heaven
	ki tut [le] p[e]üst eslegier	could have afforded it all
	sanz tere vendre u engagier.	without selling or mortgaging land.
	Ele iert vestue en itel guise:	She was dressed in this manner:
560	de chainsil blanc e de chemise,	in a shift of white linen,
	que tuz les costez li pareient,	which let both her sides be seen,
	que de deus parz laciez esteient.	as it was laced on either side.
	Le cors ot gent, basse la hanche,	She had a lovely body, a long waist,
	le col plus blanc que neif sur branche,	a neck whiter than snow on a branch,
565	les oilz ot vairs e blanc le vis,	grey-green eyes and white skin,
	bele buche, neis bien asis,	a beautiful mouth, a well-formed nose,
	les surcilz bruns e bel le frunt	dark eyebrows and a lovely forehead
	e le chef cresp e aukes blunt;	and curling golden hair;
	fil d'or ne gette tel luur	no golden thread casts such a gleam
570	cum sun chevel cuntre le jur.	as did her hair in the sun.
	Sis manteus fu de purpre bis;	Her mantle was dark purple;
	les pans en ot entur li mis.	she had wrapped its ends around her.
	Un espervier sur sun poin tient,	She holds a falcon on her fist,
	e un leverer aprés lui vient.	and a greyhound runs behind her.
575	Il n'ot al burc petit ne grant	There was no one in the town, great or small,

	ne li veillard ne li enfant	not the old men or the children,
	que ne l'alassent esgarder.	who did not go to look at her.
	Si cum il la veent errer,	As they saw her pass,
	de sa beauté n'iert mie gas.	there was no joking about her beauty.
580	Ele veneit meins que le pas.	She came along quite slowly.
	Li jugeür, que la veeient,	The judges, who saw her,
	a [grant] merveille le teneient;	considered it a great marvel;
	il n'ot un sul ki l'esgardast	there was not one who looked at her
	de dreite joie ne s'eschaufast.	who did not grow warm with sheer joy.
585	Cil ki le chevaler amoënt	Those who loved the knight
	a lui veneient, si li cuntouent	came to him, and told him
	de la pucele ki veneit,	of the maiden who was coming,
	si Deu plest, que le delivereit:	who, if it pleased God, would set him free:
	"Sire cumpain, ci en vient une,	"Sir companion, here comes one
590	mes ele n'est pas fave ne brune;	who is not tawny nor dark;
	ceo'st la plus bele del mund,	she is the loveliest in the world,
	de tutes celes kë i sunt."	of all the women who live."
	Lanval l'oï, sun chief dresça;	Lanval heard this, he lifted his head;
	bien la cunut, si suspira.	he knew her well, and sighed.
595	Li sanc li est munté al vis;	The blood rose to his face;
	de parler fu aukes hastifs.	he was very quick to speak.
	"Par fei," fet il, "ceo est m'amie!	"In faith," he said, "it is my beloved!
	Or m'en est gueres ki m'ocie,	Now I care little who may kill me,
	si ele n'ad merci de mei;	if she does not take pity on me;
600	kar gariz sui, quant jeo la vei."	for I am cured when I see her."
	La damë entra al palais;	The lady entered the palace;
	unc si bele n'i vient mais.	such a beauty had never come there.
	Devant le rei est descendue	She dismounted before the king
	si que de tuz iert bien [veüe].	so that she was quite visible to all.
605	Sun mantel ad laissié ch[e]eir,	She let her mantle fall
	que meuz la puïssent veer.	so that they could see her better.
	Li reis, que mut fu enseigniez,	The king, who was very well-bred,
	il s'est encuntre lui dresciez,	got up to meet her,
	e tuit li autre l'enurerent,	and all the others honored her
610	de li servir se presenterent.	and offered themselves to serve her.
	Quant il l'orent bien esgardee	When they had looked at her well
	e sa beauté forment loëe,	and greatly praised her beauty,
	ele parla en teu mesure,	she spoke in this way,
	kar de demurer nen ot cure:	for she did not wish to delay:
615	"Reis, jeo ai amé un tuen vassal:	"King, I have fallen in love with one of your vassals:
	veez le ici, ceo est Lanval!	you see him here, it is Lanval!
	Acheisuné fu en ta curt.	He was accused in your court.
	Ne vuil mie que a mal li turt	I do not wish it to be held against him,
	de ceo qu'il dist; ceo sachez tu	concerning what he said; you should know

620	que la reïne ad tort eü:	that the queen was wrong:
	unc nul jur ne la requist.	he never asked for her love.
	De la vantance kë il fist,	And concerning the boast he made,
	si par me peot estre aquitez,	if he can be acquitted by me,
	par voz baruns seit deliverez!”	let your nobles set him free!”
625	Ceo qu'il jugerunt par dreit	The king grants that it should be so,
	li reis otrie ke issi seit.	that they should judge rightly.
	N'i ad un sul que n'ait jugié	There was not one who did not judge
	que Lanval ad tut desrainié.	that Lanval was completely exonerated.
	Deliverez est par lur esgart,	He is freed by their judgment,
630	e la pucele s'en depart.	and the maiden takes her leave.
	Ne la peot li reis retenir;	The king cannot detain her;
	asez gent ot a li servir.	she had enough people to serve her.
	Fors de la sale aveient mis	Outside the hall was set
	un grant perrun de marbre bis,	a great block of dark marble,
635	u li pesant humme muntoënt,	where heavy men mounted,
	que de la curt le rei [aloënt]:	who were leaving the king's court:
	Lanval esteit munté desus.	Lanval got up on it.
	Quant la pucele ist fors a l'us,	When the maiden came through the gate,
	sur le palefrei, detriers li,	with one leap Lanval
640	de plain eslais Lanval sailli.	jumped on the palfrey, behind her.
	Od li s'en vait en Avalun,	With her he went to Avalon,
	ceo nus recuntent li Bretun,	so the Bretons tell us,
	en un isle que mut est beaus;	to a very beautiful island;
	la fu ravi li dameiseaus.	the young man was carried off there.
645	Nul hum n'en oï plus parler,	No one ever heard another word of him,
	ne jeo n'en sai avant cunter.	and I can tell no more.

Laüstic (The Nightingale)

	Une aventure vus dirai	I shall tell you an adventure
	dunt li Bretun firent un lai.	of which the Bretons made a lai.
	Laüstic ad nun, ceo m'est avis—	Its name is Laüstic, I believe—
	si l'apelent en lur païs;	so they call it in their country;
5	ceo est “[russignol]” en franceis	that is “rossignol” in French
	e “nihtegale” en dreit engleis.	and “nightingale” in proper English.
	[En] Seint Mallo en la cuntree	In the region of St. Malo
	ot une vile renumee.	there was a well-known town.
	Deus chevalers ilec manëent	Two knights lived there,
10	e deus for[z] maisuns aveient.	and had two strong houses.
	Pur la bunté des deus baruns	Because of the goodness of the two men
	fu de la vile bons li nuns.	the town had a good name.
	Li uns aveit femme espusee,	One of them had married a woman
	sage, curteise, mut acemee;	who was wise, courteous, and very gracious;

15	a merveille se teneit chiere	she had a great deal of self-respect
	sulunc l'usage e la manere.	according to custom and usage.
	Li autres fu un bachelers	The other was a young knight,
	bien conu entre ses pers	well regarded among his peers
	de prüesce, de grant valur,	for prowess and great bravery,
20	e volenters feseit honur:	and he willingly behaved honorably:
	mut turnëot e despendeit	he went tourneying a great deal and spent a lot
	e bien donot ceo qu'il aveit.	and gave out generously what he had.
	La femme sun veisin ama.	The woman loved her neighbor.
	Tant la requist, tant la preia,	He had so often asked and implored her,
25	e tant par ot en lui grant bien	and there was such great good in him,
	que ele l'ama sur tute rien,	that she loved him above all things,
	tant pur le bien que ele oï,	partly for the good that she heard of him,
	tant pur ceo qu'il iert pres de li.	partly because he was near to her.
	Sagement e bien s'entreamerent,	They loved one another wisely and well,
30	mut se covrirent e esgarderent	they dissembled and took good care
	qu'il ne feussent aparceüz	not to be perceived
	ne desturbez ne mescreüz;	nor disturbed nor suspected;
	e eus le poeient bien fere,	and they could easily do this,
	kar pres esteient lur repere.	because they lived close to one another.
35	Preceines furent lur maisuns	Their houses were neighboring,
	e lur sales e lur dunguns;	both their halls and their keeps;
	n'i aveit bare ne devise	there was no obstacle or barrier
	fors un haut mur de piere bise.	except a high wall of grey stone.
	Des chambres u la dame jut	From the room where the lady slept,
40	quant a la fenestre s'estut,	when she was at the window,
	poeit parler a sun ami	she could talk to her beloved
	de l'autre part, e il a li,	on the other side, and he to her,
	e lur aveirs entrechangier	and they could exchange things
	e par geter e par lancier.	by tossing or throwing them.
45	N'unt gueres rien que lur despleise,	There was hardly anything that displeased them,
	mut esteient amdui a eise—	they were both very much at ease—
	fors tant k'il ne poënt venir	except that they could not be together
	del tut ensemble a lur pleisir,	entirely at their pleasure,
	kar la dame ert estrei[t] gardee	for the lady was closely guarded
50	quant cil esteit en la cuntree.	when her husband was at home.
	Mes de tant aveient retur,	But at least they had the consolation,
	u fust par nuit u fust par jur,	whether at night or during the day,
	que ensemble poeient parler.	of talking to one another.
	Nul nes poeit de ceo garder	No one could prevent them
55	que a la fenestre n'i venissent	from coming to the window
	e iloec s'entreveïssent.	and seeing one another there.
	Lungement se sunt entreamé,	They loved one another for a long time,
	tant que ceo vient a un esté,	until there came a summer
	que bruil e pré sunt rever[d]i	when the woods and meadow were all green

60	e li vergier ierent fluri;
	cil oiselet par grant duçur
	mainent lur joie en sum la flur.
	Ki amur ad a sun talent,
	n'est merveille s'il i entent!
65	Del chevaler vus dirai veir:
	il i entent a sun poeir
	e la dame de l'autre part,
	e de parler e de regart.
	Les nuiz, quant la lune luseit
70	e ses sires cuché esteit,
	de juste li sovent levot
	e de sun mantel se afublot;
	a la fenestre ester veneit
	pur sun ami qu'el i saveit
75	que autreteu vie demenot:
	le plus de la nuit veillot.
	Delit aveient al veer,
	quant plus ne poeient aver.
	Tant i estut, tant i leva,
80	que ses sires s'en curuça
	e meintefeiz li demanda
	pur quei levot e u ala.
	"Sire," la dame li respunt,
	"il nen ad joië en cest mund
85	ki nen ot le laüstic chanter.
	Pur ceo me vois ici ester.
	Tant ducement le oi la nuit
	que mut me semble grant deduit;
	tant me delit[e] e tant le voil
90	que jeo ne puis dormir de l'oil."
	Quant li sires ot que ele dist,
	de ire e maltalent en rist.
	De une chose se purpensa:
	que le laüstic enginnera.
95	Il n'ot vallet en sa meisun
	ne face engin, reis u la[ç]un;
	puis les mettent par le vergier.
	N'i ot codre ne chastainier
	u il ne mettent laz u glu,
100	tant que pri[s] l'unt et retenu.
	Quant le laüstic eurent pris,
	al seignur fu rendu tut vis.
	Mut en fu liez, quant il le tient;
	as chambres la dame vient.

and the orchards were flowering;
the little birds with great sweetness
expressed their joy among the flowers.
It is no wonder if one who has a mind to love
gives it his attention!
I shall tell you truly about the knight:
he attended to it with all his might,
and the lady did so on the other side,
both with words and with looks.
At night, when the moon shone
and her husband was in bed,
often she got up from beside him
and put on her mantle;
she would go stand at the window
on account of her beloved, who, she knew,
led a similar life:
he was awake most of the night.
They delighted in seeing one another,
when they could have no more.
She was there so much, she got up so often,
that her husband became angry
and asked her many times
why she got up and where she went.
"Sir," the lady answered,
"he has no joy in this world
who does not hear the nightingale sing.
That is why you see me here.
I hear him so sweetly here at night
that it seems a great pleasure to me;
it delights me so and I desire it so
that I cannot close my eyes in sleep."
When her husband heard what she said,
he laughed out of anger and ill will.
He fixed his thoughts on one thing:
entrapping the nightingale.
There was no servant in his house
who did not make a trap, net or snare;
then they put them in the orchard.
There was no hazel tree or chestnut
where they did not put a snare or birdlime,
until they took and captured it.
When they had caught the nightingale alive,
they took it to the lord.
He was very happy when he had it;
he came to the lady's chamber.

105	"Dame," fet il, "u estes vus?
	Venez avant, parlez a nus!
	Jeo ai le laüstic englué
	pur quei vus avez tant veillé.
	Des ore poëz gisir en peis:
110	il ne vus esveillerat meis."
	Quant la dame l'ad entendu,
	dolente e cureçuse fu.
	A sun seignur l'ad demandé,
	e il l'ocist par engresté:
115	le col li rumpt a ses deus meins.
	De ceo fist il ke trop vileins.
	Sur la dame le cors geta,
	se que sun chainse ensanglanta
	un poi desur le piz devant;
120	de la chambre s'en ist a tant.
	La dame prent le cors petit;
	durement plure e si maudit
	tuz ceus ki le laüstic traïrent,
	e les engins e les laçuns firent,
125	kar mut li unt toleit grant hait.
	"Lasse," fet ele, "mal m'estait!
	Ne purrai mes la nuit lever
	ne aler a la fenestre ester,
	u jeo suleie mun ami veer.
130	Une chose sai jeo de veir:
	il quidra ke jeo me feigne.
	De ceo m'estuet que cunseil preigne.
	Le laüstic li trameterai;
	l'aventure li manderai."
135	En une piece de samit
	a or brusdé e tut escrit
	ad l'oiselet envulupé;
	un sun vatlet ad apelé,
	sun message li ad chargié,
140	a sun ami l'ad enveié.
	Cil est al chevalier venuz;
	de part sa dame li dist saluz,
	tut sun message li cunta,
	e le laüstic li presenta.
145	Quant tut li ad dit e mustré
	e il l'aveit bien escuté,
	de l'aventure esteit dolenz;
	mes ne fu pas vileins ne lenz.
	Un vasselet ad fet forgeer;

"Lady," he said, "where are you?
Come here, talk to me!
I have caught the nightingale
for which you stayed awake so long.
From now on you can rest in peace:
he will wake you no more."
When the lady had heard this,
she was sorrowful and angry.
She asked her lord for it,
and he killed it out of spite:
he broke its neck with his two hands.
In this he behaved most basely.
He threw the body at the lady,
so that her shift was bloodied
a bit above the breast in front;
with that he left the room.
The lady takes the little body;
she weeps bitterly and curses all those
who betrayed the nightingale
by making traps and snares,
for they have taken a great happiness from her.
"Alas," she said, "it goes ill with me!
I can no longer get up at night
nor go to stand by the window,
where I was accustomed to see my beloved.
I know one thing for certain:
he will think that I am deceiving him.
I must give thought to this matter.
I will convey the nightingale to him;
I will let him know of the adventure."
In a piece of samite
embroidered and inscribed all over with gold
she wrapped the little bird;
she called a servant of hers,
charged him with her message,
sent him to her beloved.
He came to the knight;
he greeted him on behalf of his lady,
told him all her message,
and presented him with the nightingale.
When he had told and shown everything
and the knight had listened well,
he was sorrowful over the adventure;
but he was not ill-bred or slow.
He had a small casket made;

150 unc n'i ot fer ne acer,
tut fu de or fin od bones pieres,
mut precïuses e mut cheres;
covercle i ot tres bien asis.
Le laüstic ad dedenz mis,
155 puis fist la chasse enseeler.
Tuz jurs l'ad fet[e] od li porter.

    Cele aventure fu cuntee,
ne pot estre lunges celee.
Un lai en firent li Bretun:
160 Le Laüstic l'apelent hum.

it contained not a bit of iron or steel,
it was made all of fine gold with valuable gems,
most precious and costly;
it had a very well-fitting cover.
He put the nightingale inside,
then had the coffer sealed.
He carried it with him always.

    This adventure was told;
it could not long be hidden.
The Bretons made a lai of it;
men call it Laüstic.

Chevrefoil (The Honeysuckle)

Asez me plest e bien le voil
del lai que humme nume *Chevrefoil*
que la verité vus en cunt,
pur quei il fu fet e dunt.
5 Plusurs le me unt cunté e dit
e jeo l'ai trové en escrit
de Tristram e de la reïne,
de lur amur que tant fu fine,
dunt il eurent meinte dolur,
10 puis mururent en un jur.

    Li reis Markes esteit curucié,
vers Tristram sun nevuz irié;
de sa tere le cungea
pur la reïne qu'il ama.
15 En sa cuntree en est alez.
En Suhtwales, u il fu nez,
un an demurat tut entier;
ne pot ariere repeirier.
Mes puis se mist en abandun
20 de mort e de destructïun.
Ne vus esmerveilliez neent,
kar ki eime mut lëalment
mut est dolenz e trespensez,
quant il nen ad ses volentez.
25 Tristram est dolent e trespensis:
pur ceo se met de sun païs.
En Cornwaille vait tut dreit,
la u la reïne maneit.
En la forest tut sul se mist;
30 ne voleit pas que hum le veïst.

It pleases me well and I truly wish
to tell you the truth of the lai
that men call *Chevrefoil*,
why it was made and how it originated.
Many have told and recounted it to me
and I have found it written
about Tristan and the queen,
and their love that was so true,
for which they had great sorrow
and then died the same day.

    King Mark was angry,
enraged against his nephew Tristan;
he sent him away from his land
on account of the queen, whom he loved.
Tristan went into his own lands.
In South Wales, where he was born,
he stayed a full year;
he could not go back again.
But then he gave up caring
about death and destruction.
Don't be astonished by this,
for he who loves most loyally
is most sorrowful and despondent
when he does not have his wishes.
Tristan is sorrowful and despondent;
for this reason he leaves his country.
He goes straight to Cornwall,
where the queen was staying.
He went into the forest quite alone;
he did not wish anyone to see him.

	En la vespree s'en eisseit,	In the evening he went out
	quant tens de herberger esteit;	when it was time to find lodging;
	od païsanz, od povre gent	with peasants, with poor people,
	perneit la nuit herbergement.	he took lodging that night.
35	Les noveles lur enquereit	He asked them for news
	del rei, cum il se cunteneit.	of the king and how he was behaving.
	Ceo li dïent qu'il unt oï	They said that they had heard
	que li barun erent bani.	that the lords were banished.[1]
	A Tintagel deivent venir;	They were to go to Tintagel;
40	li reis i veolt sa curt tenir,	the king wanted to hold court there,
	a pentecuste i serunt tuit.	at Pentecost they would all be there.
	Mut i avera joie e deduit,	There would be great joy and delight,
	e la reïnë i sera.	and the queen would be there.
	Tristram l'oï, mut se haita:	Tristan heard this and was very glad:
45	ele ne purrat mie aler	there was no way she could go
	k'il ne la veie trespasser.	without him seeing her pass by.
	Le jur que li rei fu meüz,	The day that the king had set out,
	e Tristram est al bois venuz:	Tristan came to the wood:
	sur le chemin qu'il saveit	beside the road that he knew
50	que la reine passer deveit,	the queen must pass along,
	une codre trencha par mi,	he split a hazel tree along its length
	tute quarreie la fendi.	and squared it off.
	Quant il ad paré le bastun,	When he had prepared the staff,
	de sun cutel escrit sun nun.	with his knife he wrote his name.
55	[S]e la reïne s'aparceit,	If the queen should notice it,
	que mut grant gardë s'en perneit—	as she was keeping careful watch—
	autre feiz li fu avenu	it had happened other times
	que si l'aveit aparceü—	that she had seen it—
	de sun ami bien conustra	she would surely recognize the staff
60	le bastun quant ele le verra.	of her beloved when she saw it.
	Ceo fu la summe de l'escrit	This was the sum of the writing
	qu'il li aveit mandé e dit:	that he had sent and said:
	que lunges ot ilec esté	that he had been there a long time
	e atendu e surjurné	and waited and sojourned
65	pur [espïer] e pur saver	to have a glimpse and to know
	coment il la pust veer,	how he might see her,
	kar ne pot nent vivre sanz li.	for he could not live without her.
	D'euls deus fu il autresi	For the two of them it was just
	cum del chevrefoil esteit	as it is with the honeysuckle
70	ki a la codre se perneit:	that holds to the hazel tree:
	quant il est si laciez e pris	when it is entwined and attached in this way
	e tut entur le fust s'est mis,	and has established itself all around,
	ensemble po[ë]nt bien durer;	they can endure well together,
	mes ki puis les volt desevrer,	but if someone then wishes to separate them,

---

[1] That is, the lords who had made accusations of adultery against Tristan and the queen.

75	li codres muert hastivement
	e li chevrefoil ensemblement.
	"Bele amie, si est de nus:
	ne vus sanz mei, ne mei sanz vus."
	La reïne vait chevachant;
80	ele esgardat tut un pendant.
	Le bastun vit, bien l'aparceut,
	tutes les lettres i conut.
	Les chevalers que la menoënt,
	quë ensemblë od li erroënt,
85	cumanda tuz [a] arester:
	descendre vot e resposer.
	Cil unt fait sun commandement.
	Ele s'en vet luinz de sa gent;
	sa meschine apelat a sei,
90	Brenguein, que mut fu de bone fei.
	Del chemin un poi s'esluina;
	dedenz le bois celui trova
	que plus l'amot que rien vivant.
	Entre eus meinent joie grant.
95	A lui parlat tut a leisir,
	e ele li dit sun pleisir;
	puis li mustre cumfaitement
	del rei avrat acordement,
	e que mut li aveit pesé
100	de ceo qu'il [l]'ot si cungïé;
	par encusement l'aveit fait.
	Atant s'en part, sun ami lait,
	mes quant ceo vient al desevrer,
	dunc comenc[er]ent a plurer.
105	Tristram a Wales s'en rala,
	tant que sis uncles le manda.
	Pur la joie qu'il ot eüe
	de s'amie qu'il ot veüe
	e pur ceo k'il aveit escrit—
110	si cum la reïne l'ot dit,
	pur les paroles remembrer—
	Tristram, ki bien saveit harper,
	en aveit fet un nuvel lai;
	Asez brevement le numerai:
115	*Gotelef* l'apelent en engleis,
	Chevrefoil le nument en franceis.
	Dit vus en ai la verité
	del lai que j'ai ici cunté.

the hazel tree dies quickly
and the honeysuckle along with it.
"Sweet beloved, so it is with us:
neither you without me, nor me without you."
     The queen came riding along;
she looked all along the slope of the road.
She spotted the staff, she saw it well,
she recognized all the letters.
The knights who attended her,
who were traveling with her,
she commanded to stop:
she wished to dismount and rest.
They did as she commanded.
She went far from her people;
she summoned her maid,
Brangain, who was truly faithful.
She went a little way from the road;
in the wood she found him
who loved her more than any living thing.
They had great joy together.
She spoke to him quite at leisure,
and told him her pleasure;
then she showed him just how
he could be reconciled with the king,
and said it had weighed on him greatly
that he had sent Tristan away as he had;
he had done it because of the accusation.[1]
Then she departed, left her beloved—
but when it came time to separate,
they both began to weep.
     Tristan went back to Wales,
until his uncle should send for him.
Because of the joy that he had had
from seeing his beloved,
and because of what he had written—
just as the queen had told him,
in order to remember the words—
Tristan, who was a gifted harper,
made of it a new lai.
I will name it very briefly:
they call it *Goat-leaf* in English,
and in French it is named *Chevrefoil*.
I have told you the truth
of the lai I have recounted here.

---

[1] That is, the accusation of adultery between Tristan and the queen that some of the lords had made.

MIDDLE ENGLISH LYRICS

The Middle English poems in this section are for the most part difficult to date with any precision. In some cases they draw on relatively sophisticated lyric traditions from continental sources, but very largely they seem to be rooted in popular traditions that were probably already old when the earliest surviving copies of these poems were made. Like most short medieval poems that have survived, they are anonymous. From the familiarity with medieval Latin exhibited in some of the poems and their survival in manuscripts containing Latin alongside English (and French) texts, we may infer that many were read and quite possibly written by clerics—though even in these cases the authors may well have been adapting existing popular materials. Such poems have by convention been referred to for centuries as "medieval lyrics," though the term has been thought by some to be both anachronistic (the earliest appearance of the word "lyric" in English is in 1581) and somewhat misleading; in tone and subject matter many of these poems have little in common with the poems we have become accustomed to think of as "lyrical."

The majority of medieval lyrics that have survived deal with religious subjects, the most common being devotion to Jesus or the Virgin Mary (or both), often with a focus on Christ's Passion as it is linked to the theme of salvation and sacrifice, or Mary's roles as intercessor and suffering mother ("Now skrinketh rose and lily-flour," "Stond well, moder, under Rode"). Other religious lyrics contemplate Adam's fall and the transitory nature of life ("Farewell this world, I take my leve forever," "To dy, to dy / What haue I"), or the importance of constancy in faith. A number of religious lyrics draw on the conventions of secular literature, employing the topoi of so-called courtly love. Such is the case, for example, in "I sing of a maiden," in which Christ appears as a lover-knight and Mary is depicted as an unblemished maiden who chooses Christ as her son in the way that a secular poem might depict a lady bestowing her favor on a lover.

Modern readers may find a more immediate appeal in the lyrics that deal with secular themes. Earthly love is a frequent subject of these poems, sometimes dwelling on the perceived virtue and attractiveness of the beloved ("Betwene Mersh and Averil"), sometimes employing lewd word play ("I have a gentil cock"), and often taking the form of a lover's lament or complaint about a beloved's absence ("My lefe is faren in a lond"). Satires against women (such as "Of all creatures women be best") are common; most authorities think it probable that these medieval lyrics were all (or almost all) written by men, even those written in a woman's voice (such as "I lovede a child of this cuntree").

The range of emotion and expression in the lyrics is remarkably wide. Some poems are light-hearted celebrations of the pleasures of the ale-house ("Bring us in good ale") or the simple joy of experiencing nature's abundance ("Sumer is icumen in"). There is a refreshing directness (and sometimes a refreshing crudity) to many of these poems. Yet even those lyrics that clearly aim at comic entertainment can employ sophisticated poetic devices, such as internal rhyme, wordplay and allegory. Some lyrics (such as "Foweles in the frith") are ambiguous and perhaps ambivalent in their content, capable of both secular and religious readings.

We do not know how many of these poems were set to music, but the practice was apparently common; several manuscripts have come down to us that provide music to accompany their lyrics.

⌘ ⌘ ⌘

Harley Manuscript 978, now in the British Museum, is a miscellany dating from the second half of the thirteenth century; it was compiled and transcribed by monks at Reading Abbey. The page shown here provides the music as well as the English words to "Sumer is icumen in," which remains perhaps the best known of all medieval lyrics. Between the lines alternative words in Latin (focused on the "celicus agricola," or heavenly farmer) are provided by the monks.

Sumer is icumen in[1]

S umer° is icumen° in   summer / has come
    Sing, cuccu, nu.[2] Sing, cuccu.
    Sing, cuccu. Sing, cuccu, nu.

5   Sumer is icumen in—
    Lhude° sing, cuccu.   loudly
    Groweth sed° and bloweth° med°   seed / blooms / meadow
    And springth the wude° nu[3]—   wood
    Sing, cuccu.

10 Awe° bleteth after lomb,   ewe
    Lhouth after calve cu,[4]
    Bulluc sterteth, bucke verteth,
    Murie° sing,[5] cuccu.   merry
    Cuccu, cuccu,
    Well singes thu,° cuccu—   thou
15 Ne swik thu naver nu![6]
    —EARLIER 13TH CENTURY

Now goth sonne under wod

N ow goth sonne under wod:°   wood (of the Cross)
    Me reweth,° Mary, thy faire rode.°   pity / face, complexion
    Now goth sonne under Tree:
    Me reweth, Mary, thy sonne and thee.
    —EARLIER 13TH CENTURY

Foweles in the frith

F oweles° in the frith,°   birds / wood
    The fisses° in the flod,°   fishes / river, stream

And I mon waxe wod:[7]
Much sorw I walk with
5   For beste of bon and blod.[8]
    —LATER 13TH CENTURY

Betwene Mersh and Averil

B etwene Mersh° and Averil,°   March / April
    When spray beginneth to springe,[9]
The lutel° fowl hath hire will   little
On hire lud to singe.[10]
5   Ich libbe° in love-longinge   I live
For semlokest° of alle thinge—   the most fair, seemly
He° may me blisse bringe;   she
Ich am in hire baundoun.°   power, control

An hendy hap ich habbe ihent![11]
10 Ichot° from Hevene it is me sent.   I know
From alle wimmen my love is lent,
And light on Alisoun.[12]

On hue hire hair is fair enough,
Hire browe browne, hire eye blake;
15 With lossum chere he° on me logh,[13] she
With middle small and well imake.°   fashioned
Bote° he me wolle° to hire take,   unless / will
For to ben hire owen make,[14]
Longe to liven ichulle° forsake,   I shall
20 And feye fallen adoun.[15]

Nightes when I wende° and wake—   twist, turn
Forthy mine wonges waxeth won[16]—

---

[7] *mon ... wod* Must go mad.

[8] *For ... blod* For beast of bone and blood.

[9] *When ... springe* When twigs/shoots begin to grow.

[10] *The lutel ... singe* The little bird has her wish to sing in her language.

[11] *An hendy ... ihent* I have received a fair fortune!

[12] *From alle ... on Alisoun* My love is taken from all women, and falls upon Alisoun.

[13] *With lossum ... logh* With beautiful face she laughed at me.

[14] *For to ... make* To be her own lover/companion.

[15] *Longe ... adoun* I shall not live long, and fated to die, fall down.

[16] *Forthy ... won* Therefore my cheeks grow pale.

---

[1] *Sumer is icumen in* In the preparation of the texts of this lyric and the others reproduced here, several editions have been consulted, among them those of R.T. Davies, Thomas G. Duncan, and Theodore Silverstein.

[2] *cuccu, nu* Cuckoo, now.

[3] *Groweth sed ... wude nu* Seed grows and meadow blooms, and the wood now brings forth growth.

[4] *Lhouth ... cu* The cow lows after the calf.

[5] *Bulluc ... sing* The bullock starts, the buck breaks wind, sing merrily!

[6] *Well singes ... naver nu* You sing well, cuckoo—now never cease!

Levedy,° all for thine sake,   *lady*
Longinge is ilent me on.[1]
25 In world nis non so witer mon
That all hire bounte tell con:[2]
Hire swire is whittore then the swon,[3]
And fairest may in toun.[4]

Ich am for wowing° all forwake,°   *wooing / exhausted*
30 Wery so water in wore,[5]
Lest eny reve me my make,
Ich habbe iyirned yore.[6]
Betere is tholien while sore
Then mournen evermore.[7]
35 Geynest° under gore,[8]   *fairest*
Herkne to my roun!°   *song, cry*
—LATER 13TH CENTURY–EARLY 14TH CENTURY

Now skrinketh rose and lily-flour

Now skrinketh° rose and lily-flour,°   *fade / lily-flower*
That whilen° ber° that swete savour,   *at one time / bore*
In somer,° that swete tide.°   *summer / time*
Ne is no quene so stark ne stour,
5 Ne no levedy so bright in bour,[9]
That Ded ne shall by glide.[10]
Whoso° wol flesh lust forgon   *whoever*

---

[1] *Longinge … on* Longing has fallen on me.

[2] *In world … con* In the world there is no man so wise that he could tell all her virtue.

[3] *Her swire … swon* Her neck is whiter than the swan.

[4] *And … in toun* And she is the fairest maiden in town.

[5] *Ich am … in wore* I am all wearied from wooing, as weary as water on the shore.

[6] *Lest … yore* Lest any deprive me of my beloved, whom I have yearned for for so long.

[7] *Betere … evermore* It is better to suffer miserably for a while than to mourn forever.

[8] *Geynest under gore* Loveliest under clothing (a common expression meaning "most beautiful").

[9] *Ne is … bour* There is no queen so severe and fierce, nor lady so bright in her chamber.

[10] *That … glide* That Death shall not come to her.

And Hevene blis abide,[11]
On Jesu be his thoght anon,°   *at once*
10 That therled° was his side.   *pierced*

From Petresbourgh in o morewening,°   *morning*
As I me wende o° my pleying,   *went about*
On my folye° I thoghte.   *folly*
Menen I gon my mourning
15 To hire that ber the Hevene King,
Of mercy hire besoghte:[12]
"Ledy, preye° thy sone for ous,°   *pray to / us*
That us dere bought,[13]
And shild° us from the lothe° hous   *shield / hateful*
20 That to the Fend is wroghte."°   *made*
Mine herte of dedes wes fordred,
Of sinne that I have my flesh fed
And folewed all my time:[14]
That I not° whider I shall be led   *know not*
25 When I lie on dethes bed,
In joy or into pyne.°   *pining, sorrow*
On o° ledy myn hope is,   *one*
Moder and virgine;
We shulen° into hevene° bliss   *shall [go] / heavenly*
30 Thurgh hire° medicine.   *through her*

Betere is hire medicine
Then any mead or any wyn.
Hire erbes smulleth swete;
From Catenas° into Dyvelyn°   *Caithness / Dublin*
35 Nis ther non leche so fyn
Oure serewes to bete.[15]
Mon that feleth eny sor,
Ant his folie wol lete,[16]
Without gold other° eny tresor°   *or / treasure*
40 He may be sound° and sete.°   *healthy / content*

---

[11] *Whoso wol … abide* Whoever will forgo fleshly lust, and wait for the bliss of Heaven.

[12] *Menen … besoghte* I began to make my mourning complaint to her that bore the King of Heaven, and sought her mercy.

[13] *That … bought* Who redeemed us at great cost.

[14] *Mine herte … my time* My heart was full of dread for my deeds of sin that I have fed my body (on) and followed all my life.

[15] *Nis ther … bete* There is no doctor so able to make our troubles better.

[16] *Mon … wol lete* Anyone who feels pain and will leave behind his own folly.

Of penaunce is his plaster° all,   *remedy*
And ever serven hire I shall,
Now and all my live;°   *life*
Now is free that ere wes thrall°   *slave*
45 Al thourh that levedy gent° and small   *noble lady*
Heried° be hir joyes five!   *praised*
Wher-so eny sek is,
Thider hie blyve;[1]
Thurh hire beoth ybroht° to bliss   *are brought*
50 Bo° maiden ant wive.   *both*

For he that dude° his body on tree,   *put*
Of° oure sinnes have piete°   *for / pity*
That weldes heovene boures![2]
Wimmon,° with thy jolyfte,°   *woman / merrymaking*
55 Thou thench on° Godes shoures!°   *think about / suffering*
Thagh thou be whyt and bryth on ble,°   *face*
Falewen shule thy floures.[3]
Jesu, haue mercy of vs,
That° all this world honoures.   *[you] whom*
—LATER 13TH CENTURY—EARLY 14TH CENTURY

Lenten is come with love to toune

Lenten° is come with love to toune,°   *spring / town*
     With blosmen° and with briddes
          roune,[4]   *blossoms, flowers*
That all this blisse bringeth.
Dayeseyes° in this dales,°   *daisies / valleys*
5   Notes swete of nightegales,
Uch° fowl song singeth.   *each*
The threstelcok him threteth oo.[5]
Away is huere° winter wo   *their*
When woderofe° springeth.   *woodruff*
10 This fowles singeth ferly fele,[6]

---

[1] *Wher-so ... hie blyve* Wherever there is anyone sick, (let him) hasten to that place.

[2] *That weldes heovene boures* That rules the bowers of heaven.

[3] *Thagh thou ... floures* Even if you are fair and bright of face, your flowers shall fade.

[4] *briddes roune* Song of birds.

[5] *The threstelcok ... oo* The song thrush always quarrels.

[6] *This fowles ... fele* These many birds sing wonderfully.

And wliteth on huere wynne wele,[7]
That all the wode° ringeth.   *wood*

The rose raileth° hire rode,°   *adorns / face, complexion*
The leves on the lighte° wode   *bright*
15 Waxen all with wille.[8]
The mone mandeth hire ble,[9]
The lilye is lossom° to se,   *lovely*
The fennel and the fille.°   *thyme*
Wowes this[10] wilde drakes,
20 Miles murgeth huere makes,[11]
Ase strem that striketh stille.[12]
Mody meneth, so doth mo;[13]
Ichot° ich am on of tho[14]   *I know*
For love that likes ille.°   *goes badly*

25 The mone mandeth hire light,
So doth the semly° sonne bright,   *lovely, beautiful*
When briddes singeth breme.°   *loudly*
Deawes donketh the dounes,[15]
Deores° with huere derne rounes[16]   *animals*
30 Domes for to deme.[17]
Wormes woweth under cloude,°   *earth*
Wimmen waxeth wounder[18] proude,
So well it wol hem seme.[19]
Yef me shall wonte wille of on,[20]
35 This wunne wele I wole forgon,[21]
And wiht° in wode be fleme.°   *quickly / in exile*
—LATER 13TH CENTURY—EARLY 14TH CENTURY

[7] *And wliteth ... wele* And warble about their abundance of joys.

[8] *Waxen ... wille* Grow with joy.

[9] *The mone ... ble* The moon sends her light.

[10] *Wowes this* Woo these.

[11] *Miles ... makes* Animals are happy with their mates.

[12] *Ase ... stille* Like a stream that flows softly.

[13] *Mody ... mo* The passionate man mourns, so do others.

[14] *ich ... tho* I am one of those.

[15] *Deawes ... dounes* Dews wet the hills.

[16] *Derne rounes* Mysterious cries.

[17] *Domes ... deme* In making their judgments.

[18] *waxeth wounder* Grow wondrously.

[19] *hem seme* Appear to them.

[20] *Yef me ... of on* If I shall lack pleasure of one.

[21] *This wunne ...forgon* I will give up this abundance of joys.

Stond well, moder, under Rode

"Stond well, moder,° under Rode.°   *mother / rood, cross*
Behold thy sone with glade mode°—   *mind, heart*
Blithe° moder might thou be."   *joyful*
"Sone, how shulde I blithe stonde?
5 I se thine fet,° I se thine honde,°   *feet / hands*
Nailed to the harde Tree."

"Moder, do wey° thy wepinge.   *away*
I thole° deth for monkinde—   *suffer*
For my gult° thole I non."   *sin*
10 "Sone, I fele the dedestounde:°   *hour of death*
The swerd is at mine herte grounde,
That me bihet Simeon."[1]

"Moder, thou rewe all of thy bern:[2]
Thou woshe° away the blody tern°—   *wash / tears*
15 It doth me worse then my ded."°   *death*
"Sone, how may I teres werne?[3]
I se the blody stremes erne°   *run*
From thine herte to my fet."

"Moder, now I may thee seye,°   *say*
20 Betere is that ich one deye[4]
Then all monkunde° to helle go."   *mankind*
"Sone, I se thy body beswungen,°   *hung*
Fet and honden thourhout stongen°—   *pierced*
No wonder thah me be wo."[5]

25 "Moder, now I shall thee telle,
Yef I ne deye thou gost to helle:[6]
I thole ded for thine sake."
"Sone, thou art so meke and minde,[7]

Ne wit me naht, it is my kinde[8]
30 That I for thee this sorewe make."

"Moder, mercy, let me deye!
For Adam out of helle beye,°   *to redeem*
And his kun that is forlore."[9]
"Sone, what shall me to rede?[10]
35 My peine pineth me to dede.[11]
Lat° me deye thee before."   *let*

"Moder, now thou might well leren°   *learn*
Whet sorewe haveth that children beren,[12]
Whet sorewe it is with childe gon."
40 "Sorewe, iwis,° I con thee telle!   *indeed, truly*
Bote it be the pine of helle,
More sorewe wot° I non."   *know*

"Moder, rew of moder care,[13]
For now thou wost of moder fare,[14]
45 Thou thou be clene maiden-mon."[15]
"Sone, help at alle nede
Alle tho that to me grede,°   *cry out*
Maiden, wif and fol wimmon."°   *prostitutes*

"Moder, may I no lengore° dwelle.   *longer*
50 The time is come I shall to helle.
The thridde° day I rise upon."   *third*
"Sone, I will with thee founden.°   *go*
I deye, iwis, for° thine wounden,°   *of / wounds*
So soreweful ded nes never non."[16]

55 When he ros tho° fell hire sorewe,   *then*
Hire blisse sprong the thridde morewe:°   *morrow, morning*
Blithe moder were thou tho.

---

[1] *The swerd ... Simeon* The sword that Simeon promised me has pierced the bottom of my heart. See Luke 2.25–35.

[2] *rewe ... bern* Have pity on your child.

[3] *how ... werne* How may I deny my tears?

[4] *Betere ... deye* It is better that I alone die.

[5] *No wonder ... wo* No wonder though I grieve.

[6] *Yef ... helle* If I do not die you will go to hell.

[7] *meke and minde* Gentle and thoughtful.

[8] *Ne wit ... kinde* Do not blame me, it is my nature.

[9] *kun ... forlore* Kin that is lost.

[10] *what shall ... rede* What shall I do?

[11] *peine ... dede* Pain tortures me to death.

[12] *sorewe ... beren* Sorrow they have who bear children.

[13] *rew ... care* Pity a mother's care.

[14] *wost ... fare* Know of motherhood.

[15] *clene maiden-mon* Pure virgin.

[16] *So soreweful ... non* There was never such a sorrowful death.

Levedy, for that ilke blisse,[1]
Besech thy sone of sunnes lisse—[2]
60 Thou be oure sheld ayein oure fo.[3]

Blessed be thou, full of blisse,
Let us never Hevene misse,
Thourh thy swete sones might.
Louerd,° for that ilke blod   *Lord*
65 That thou sheddest on the Rod,
Thou bring us into Hevene light.
Amen.
—LATER 13TH CENTURY–EARLY 14TH CENTURY

Maiden in the mor lay

Maiden in the mor° lay,   *wilds*
In the mor lay;
Sevenight° fulle,   *seven nights, one week*
Sevenight fulle,
5 Maiden in the mor lay;
In the mor lay,
Sevenightes fulle and a day.

Welle° was hire mete.°   *good / food*
What was hire mete?
10 The primerole[4] and the—
The primerole and the—
Welle was hire mete.
What was hire mete?
The primerole and the violet.

15 Welle was hire dring.°   *drink*
What was hire dring?
The chelde° water of the—   *cold*
The chelde water of the—
Welle was hire dring.
20 What was hire dring?
The chelde water of the welle-spring.

Welle was hire bowr.°   *chamber*
What was hire bowr?
The rede rose and the—
25 The rede rose and the—
Welle was hire bowr.
What was hire bowr?
The rede rose and the lilye flour.
—EARLIER 14TH CENTURY

I lovede a child of this cuntree

Were it undo that is ido,
I wolde bewar.[5]

I lovede a child of this cuntree,°   *country*
And so I wende° he had do me;[6]   *thought*
Now myself the sothe° I see,   *truth*
That he is far.°   *far away, remote*

He seide to me he wolde be true,
And change me for non other new;
Now I sikke° and am pale of hue,   *sigh*
10 For he is far.

He said his sawes° he wolde fulfille: *promises*
Therfore I let him have all his wille;
Now I sikke and mourn stille,[7]
For he is far.
—C. 14TH CENTURY

Erthe tok of erthe erthe with woh

Erthe tok° of erthe erthe with woh;°   *took / evil, wrong*
Erthe other erthe to the erthe droh;°   *pulled, added*
Erthe leide erthe in erthene throh.°   *grave, coffin*
Tho hevede erthe of erthe erthe inoh.[8]
—C. 14TH CENTURY

---

[1] *Levedy ... blisse* Lady, for that same joy.

[2] *of sunnes lisse* Relief of sins.

[3] *ayein oure fo* Against our foe.

[4] *primerole* Early spring flowers (e.g., daisy and primrose).

[5] *Were it ... bewar* If whatever done could be undone, I would be careful (possibly a refrain to be repeated following each stanza).

[6] *I lovede ... do me* I loved a young man of this country, and so I believed he also loved me.

[7] *stille* Continually.

[8] *Tho hevede ... inoh* Then had earth of earth, earth enough.

When Adam delf

When Adam delf,°   *dug*
And Eve span,°   *spun*
Spir, if thou will spede,[1]
Whare was than
5 The pride of man
That now merres° his mede?°   *restricts / reward*
Of erth and slame,°   *slime*
Als° was Adam,   *as*
Maked° to noyes° and nede,   *made / misfortune*
10 Ar we als he
Maked to be,
Whil we this lif shall lede.
With I and E,
Born ar we,
15 Als Salomon us hight,°   *promised*
To travel here,
Whils we ar fere,°   *alive*
Als fowls° to the flight.   *birds*

In worlde we ware°   *were*
20 Cast for to care,
To° we be broght to wende°   *until / go*
Till wele or wa—[2]
An of tha twa—[3]
To won° withouten ende.   *live, dwell*
25 Forthy,° whils thou   *therefore*
May helpe thee now,
Amend thee and haf minde
When thou shall ga°   *go*
He bese thy fa[4]
30 That ar° was here thy frende.   *before*
With E and I,
I rede,° forthy,   *advise*
Thou think upon these three,
What we are,
35 And what we ware,
And what we shall be.

War thou als wise,
Praised in price,°   *excellence, esteem*
Als was Salomon,
40 Fairer fode°   *child*
Of bone and blode
Then° was Absalon,   *than*
Strengthy and strang°   *strong*
To wreke° thy wrang   *avenge*
45 Als ever was Sampson,
Thou ne might a day,
Na mare then thay,
Dede° withstand allon.[5]   *death*
With I and E,
50 Dede to thee
Shall com, als I thee kenne.°   *know, teach*
Thou ne wate[6]
In what state,
How, ne whare, ne when.

55 Of erth aght°   *anything*
That thee was raght[7]
Thou shall not have, I hete,°   *promise*
Bot seven fote
Therin to rote,°   *rot*
60 And thy windingshete.°   *winding-sheet, shroud*
Forthy gif
Whils thou may lif,
Or all gase that thou gete—
Thy gast fra God,
65 Thy godes olod,
Thy flesh fouled under fete.[8]
With I and E,
Siker° thou be   *certain*
That thy secutours°   *executor*
70 Of thee ne will rek,°   *care*
Bot skelk and skek[9]
Full boldly in thy bowrs.°   *dwellings*

---

[1] *Spir ... spede*   Ask, for your success/advantage.

[2] *Till wele or wa*   To happiness or woe.

[3] *An of tha twa*   One of those two.

[4] *He bese ... fa*   He will be your foe/enemy.

[5] *Thou ne might ... allon*   No more than they were, would you be able to stand in the way of death even for a day.

[6] *Thou ne wate*   You do not know.

[7] *That thee ... raght*   That was given to you.

[8] *Forthy gif ... under fete*   Therefore give (what is due to God), while you still live, or all you receive will go—your spirit from God, your goods scattered, and your flesh trampled in the grave.

[9] *Bot skelk and skek*   But mock and attack.

Of welth and wit
This shall be hitt,°   *be fulfilled*
75 In world that thou here wroght.
Reckon thou mon
And yelde reson
Of thing that thou here thoght.[1]
May no falas°   *fallacy, sophism*
80 Help in this case,
Ne counsel getes thou noght;
Gift ne grace
Nane thare gase,
Bot brok als thou hase boght.[2]
85 With I and E,
The Boke biddes thee,
Man, beware of thy werkes:
Terme° of the yere   *time*
Hase thou nan here,[3]
90 Thy mede bese ther thy merkes.[4]

What may this be
That I here se,
The fairehede° of thy face?   *beauty*
Thy ble° so bright,   *complexion*
95 Thy main,° thy might,   *strength*
Thy mouth that miry mas?[5]
All mon als was
To powder passe,
To dede, when thou gase;[6]
100 A grisely geste°   *guest*
Bese than thy breste
In armes til° enbrase.   *to*
With I and E,
Siker thou be
105 Thare es nane, I thee hete,°   *promise*
Of all thy kith°   *kin*

---

[1] *Reckon thou ... here thoght*   Think on yourself and give reasons for what you thought here.

[2] *Gift ne ... boght*   No gift or favor works there; you will get what you have bought (i.e., you'll get what you deserve).

[3] *Terme of ... here*   The end of your days does not come here (on earth).

[4] *Thy mede ... merkes*   Your reward will be final (?).

[5] *miry mas*   Rejoices.

[6] *All mon ... gase*   All men who have lived turn to dust in death, when you die (i.e., as you will also).

Wald slepe thee with
A night under shete.
—14TH CENTURY?

The Lady Dame Fortune is both frende and foe

The Lady Dame Fortune is both frende and foe:
Of pore hee maketh riche and ryche of pore also;[7]
Hee turneth woe to wele° and wele also to woe.   *happiness*
Ne trist noght to hir word, the whele turneth so.[8]
—MID-14TH CENTURY

I have a gentil cock

I have a gentil° cock,   *noble*
Croweth° me day: *who crows*
He doth° me risen erly   *makes*
My matins° for to say.   *morning prayers*

5 I have a gentil cock,
Comen he is of gret:°   *great or noble family*
His comb° is of° red coral,   *crest / like*
His tail is of jet.

I have a gentil cock,
10 Comen he is of kinde:
His comb is of red coral,
His tail is of inde.°   *indigo*

His legges ben of asor,[9]
So gentle and so smale;
15 His spores° arn of silver whit   *spurs*
Into the wortewale.[10]

His eynen° arn of cristal,   *eyes*
Loken° all in aumber:°   *set / amber*

---

[7] *Of pore ... pore also*   She makes the poor rich, and also the rich poor.

[8] *Ne trist ... turneth so*   Do not trust her word, because the wheel (Fortune's wheel) turns so.

[9] *ben of asor*   Are like azure.

[10] *Into the wortewale*   Up to the root (of the cock's spur).

And every night he percheth him
20 In mine ladye's chaumber.
—EARLIER 15TH CENTURY

I sing of a maiden

I sing of a maiden
  That is makeles:°   *matchless, unique*
King of alle kinges
To here sone she ches.[1]

5 He cam also° stille°   *as / quietly, gently*
Ther his moder was,
As dew in Aprille
That falleth on the grass.

He cam also stille
10 To his moderes bowr,°   *chamber*
As dew in Aprille
That falleth on the flowr.

He cam also stille
Ther his moder lay,
15 As dew in Aprille
That falleth on the spray.

Moder and maiden
Was never non but she:[2]
Well may swich° a lady   *such*
20 Godes moder be.
—EARLIER 15TH CENTURY

Adam lay ibounden

A dam lay ibounden,°   *bound*
  Bounden in a bond:
Foure thousand winter
Thought he not too long.
5 And all was for an apple,

---

[1] *To here ... ches* She chose for her son.

[2] *Moder ... but she* Never was any but she both mother and maiden.

An apple that he tok,
As clerkes° finden   *scholars*
Wreten in here° book.   *their*

Ne hadde the apple take ben,[3]
10 The apple taken ben,
Ne hadde never our Lady
A ben Hevene Quen.[4]
Blissed be the time
That apple take was!
15 Therfore we moun° singen,   *may*
"Deo gracias!"[5]
—EARLIER 15TH CENTURY

Farewell this world, I take my leve forever

F arewell this world, I take my leve forever,
  I am arrestid° to appere affore°   *at rest, waiting / before*
    Godis face.
O mercyfull God, Thow knowest that I had lever°   *rather*
Than all this worldis good to haue an owre° space   *hour*
5 For to make aseth° for my gret trespace.   *amends*
My harte, alas, is brokyn for that sorow.
Som be this day that shall not be tomorow.

This world, I see, is but a chery fayre,[6]
All thyngis passith and so moste I algate.°   *inevitably*
10 This day I satt full royally in a chayre
Tyll sotyll° deth knokkid at my gate   *subtle*
And vnavised° he said to me, "Chekmate!"   *unexpected*
Loo,° how sodynly he maketh a devorce°   *look / separation*
And wormes to fede° here he hath layde my
    corse.°   *feed / corpse*

15 Speke softe, ye folkis,° for I am layde a° slepe.   *folks / to*
I haue my dreme,° in triste is myche   *dream, vision*
    treason.[7]

---

[3] *Ne hadde ... ben* Had the apple never been taken.

[4] *A ben ... Quene* Been Queen of Heaven.

[5] *"Deo gracias!"* I.e., *Deo gratias*. Latin: Thanks be to God!

[6] *is but ... fayre* Is only a cherry festival (i.e., is passing or transient, like the time of cherry harvest).

[7] *in triste ... treason* Proverbial: "in trust is much treason," i.e., confidence is often deceived.

From dethis° hold fayn° wold I make a lepe   *death's / glad*
But my wisdom ys torned into feble° reason: *weak*
I see this worldis joye lastith but a season.
20 Wold God I had remembrid this beforne!
I say no more but beware of an horne.°   *summons (?)*

This febyll world, so false and so vnstable,
Promoteth his lovers but for a lytill while,
But at last he geveth them a bable°   *bauble, toy*
25 Whan his payntid trowth° is torned into
gile.°   *painted truth / deceit*
Experence cawsith° me the trowth to
compile,°   *causes / gather*
Thynkyng this: to° late, alas, that I began;   *too*
For foly and hope disseyveth° many a man.   *tricks, deceives*

Farewell my frendis, the tide° abidith°   *time / waits for*
no man;
30 I moste departe hens° and so shall ye,   *hence*
But in this passage° the beste songe that I can   *journey*
Is Requiem Eternam.[1] I pray God grant it me.
Whan I haue endid all myn adversite°   *adversity*
Graunte me in paradise to haue a mancyon,°   *mansion*
35 That shede his blode for my redempcion.
Beati mortui qui in Domino moriuntur.
Humiliatus sum vermis.[2]

—15TH CENTURY

To dy, to dy. What haue I

To dy°, to dy. What° haue I   *die / how*
Offendit,° that deth° is so
hasty?   *offended, displeased / death*

O marcyfull God, maker of all mankynd,
What menyth° dethe in hys mynd   *intends, means*
5 And I so young of age?
Now deth is unkynd
For he seyth, "Man, stop thy wynde."°   *complaint*
Thus he doth rage.

—LATE 15TH–EARLY 16TH CENTURY

[1] *Requiem Eternam* Latin: Eternal rest (a requiem is a mass sung for
the dead).

[2] *Beati … vermis* Latin: Blessed are the dead who die in the Lord.
I am humbled by (or with) worms.

Bring us in good ale

Bring us in good ale, and bring us in good ale,
Fore our blessed Lady sak,° bring us in   *sake*
good ale.

Bring us in no browne bred, fore that is mad of brane;[3]
Nor bring us in no whit bred, fore therin is no game:
5 But bring us in good ale.

Bring us in no befe, for ther is many bones;
But bring us in good ale, for that goth downe at
ones,°   *once*
And bring us in good ale.

Bring us in no bacon, for that is passing fat;
10 But bring us in good ale, and give us inought°   *enough*
of that,
And bring us in good ale.

Bring us in no mutton, for that is ofte lene;[4]
Nor bring us in no tripes, for they be seldom clene:
But bring us in good ale.

15 Bring us in no egges, for ther ar many shelles;
But bring us in good ale, and give us nothing elles,°   *else*
And bring us in good ale.

Bring us in no butter, for therin ar many heres;°   *hairs*
Nor bring us in no pigges flesh, for that will mak
us bores:°   *boars*
20 But bring us in good ale.

Bring us in no podinges, for therin is all gotes blod;[5]
Nor bring us in no venison, for that is not for our good:
But bring us in good ale.

Bring us in no capon's° flesh, for that is ofte
der;°   *fowl's / dear, costly*

[3] *mad of brane* Made of bran.

[4] *ofte lene* Often lean.

[5] *gotes blod* I.e., goat's blood puddings.

25 Nor bring us in no dokes° flesh for they slobber in
    the mer:°   *ducks' / pond*
But bring us in good ale.
    —LATER 15TH CENTURY

Of all creatures women be best

Of all creatures women be best,
Cuius contrarium verum est.[1]

In every place ye may well see
  That women be trewe° as tirtill° on tree,   *true / turtledove*
Not liberal° in langage but ever in secree,[2]   *licentious*
And gret joye amonge them is for to be.

5 The stedfastnes of women will never be don,
So gentil,° so curtes,° they be everichon,[3]   *noble / courteous*
Meke° as a lambe, still° as a stone,   *meek / quiet*
Croked° nor crabbed° find ye none.   *perverse / twisted*

Men be more cumbers° a thousandfold,   *troublesome*
10 And I mervail° how they dare be so bold   *marvel*
Against women for to hold,
Seeing them so pascient,° softe and cold.   *patient*

For tell a woman all your counsaile
And she can kepe it wonderly well:
15 She had lever° go quik° to hell   *rather/ alive*
Than to her neighbour she wold it tell.

Now say well by women or elles° be still,   *else*
For they never displesed man by ther will:
To be angry or wroth they can no skill,[4]
20 For I dare say they think non° ill.   *no*

Trow ye that women list to smater,[5]
Or against ther husbondes for to clater?°   *make noise*

Nay! they had lever fast, bred and water,
Then for to dele° in suche a matter.   *deal, act*

25 To the tavern they will not go,
Nor to the alehous never the mo,°   *more*
For, God wot,° ther hartes wold be wo°   *knows / sorry*
To spende ther husbondes money so.
    —LATER 15TH CENTURY

My lefe is faren in a lond [6]

My lefe is faren in a lond—
  Alas! why is she so?
And I am so sore bound
I may nat com her to.
5 She hath my hert in hold,°   *imprisoned*
Where-ever she ride or go,
With trew love a thousandfold.
    —LATER 15TH CENTURY

A god and yet a man

A god and yet a man,
  A maide and yet a mother:
Wit° wonders what wit can   *human knowledge, wit*
Conceave this or the other.

5 A god and can he die?
A dead man, can he live?
What wit can well reply?
What reason reason give?

God, Truth itself, doth teach it.
10 Man's wit senkis° too far under   *sinks*
By reason's power to reach it:
Believe and leave to wonder.
    —16TH CENTURY

---

[1] *Cuius … est* Latin: The opposite of this is true.

[2] *in secree* In secret, i.e., discreet.

[3] *they be everychon* Is each one.

[4] *can no skill* Are completely unable.

[5] *Trow ye … smater* Do you believe that women enjoy chattering?

---

[6] *My lefe … lond* My love has gone away (to another land). This lyric is referred to in Chaucer's *Nun's Priest's Tale* (1.112).

THE CRISES OF THE FOURTEENTH CENTURY

CONTEXTS

Britain in the fourteenth century suffered an unprecedented series of crises and catastrophes. The first of these was the great famine of 1315-18. Whereas we tend to think of famine as resulting from drought, the famine of the early fourteenth century was the result of too much water rather than too little. In Britain, as in the rest of Europe, a pattern of extraordinarily wet weather was repeated for several years; as the chronicle account below details, rot was followed by hunger, pestilence, and universal hardship.

The next great upheaval was the series of conflicts that eventually became known as the Hundred Years' War. Since the time of Henry II in the early thirteenth century, the English had held considerable territory in what is now France, and English kings continued to nurture ambitions of increasing their power on the other side of the English Channel. The French nobles' refusal to recognize Edward III's claim to the French throne acted as a spark to ignite conflict, and hostilities broke out in 1337 and would not truly end until 1453. With the help of the new technology of the longbow English forces at first enjoyed great success—most notably at the battles of Crécy (1346) and Poitiers (1356) under the leadership of Edward the Black Prince. Under the leadership of Henry V they inflicted a massive defeat upon the French armies at Agincourt (1415), but with the death of Henry V in 1422 and the extraordinary rise to military glory of the sixteen-year-old peasant Jeanne D'Arc (who is credited with leading the French to victory at Orléans in 1429) the tide of the conflict turned. By 1450 the English had abandoned almost all their possessions on the Continent, and the map of France had come to resemble closely its present-day shape. France had been left exhausted and impoverished by the struggle, but the events of the previous century helped to nurture a national myth that before long carried the French nation to new prosperity. The war gave rise to a national mythology in England too; the fact that the British had lost a vast expanse of territory was largely forgotten, while the famous victories of the Black Prince and of Henry V provided an ongoing source of nourishment for national pride.

The upheaval caused by the plague known as the Black Death that swept across Europe in the 1340s turned out to be just as long-lasting as that of the Hundred Years' War—and even more severe in its effects. The Black Death (so named for the color of the sores it brought with it) probably originated in China in 1320. Initially its spread was gradual, but once it reached the Crimean port of Calla in 1346 it began to spread much more rapidly; by the end of 1347 it was devastating much of continental Europe, and in the summer of 1348 it reached Britain. In many areas of Europe close to half the population succumbed; in some areas the figure exceeded seventy percent. The toll in Britain is believed to be in the range of a third of the people dead; not until a century later did the population begin to recover substantially. As the documents below indicate, the effects of such a vast and sudden demographic event were wide-ranging. One of the most significant was a persistent shortage of labor, which in turn contributed to scarcities and price increases. The almost universal response from the authorities was to attempt to impose wage and price controls, with mixed results; the aftershocks of the plague continued to ripple through the economic system, contributing significantly to the destabilizing and eventual disappearance of the feudal order.

Both the Hundred Years' War and the Black Death were underlying causes for another great fourteenth-century upheaval—the Uprising of 1381, sometimes called the Peasants' Revolt (though many non-peasants were involved). The shortage of labor caused by the Black Death—and the attempts of the authorities to suppress it, most notably Edward III's 1351 Statute of Laborers—had created a climate of restlessness among the peasantry. Thirty years on, when Parliament responded to the mounting costs of the wars with France by imposing a new tax on all adults (termed a "poll tax"), the action sparked the first widespread rebellion of commoners in English history. Though the revolt was suppressed, in its wake the peasantry were emboldened in dealing with their lords; feudal relationships of outright servitude began to die out, replaced by lease-hold arrangements under the terms of which peasants paid rent for the land they farmed.

⌘ ⌘ ⌘

The Great Famine

The chronicle excerpt below is of interest for its comments about such matters as price controls and relations between the Scots and the English as well as for its description of the effects of the famine.

from Anonymous (the "Monk of Malmesbury"), *Life of Edward the Second* (fourteenth century)

In this parliament [of February–March, 1315], because merchants going about the country selling victuals charged excessively, the earls and barons, looking to the welfare of the state, appointed a remedy for this malady; they ordained a fixed price for oxen, pigs and sheep, for fowls, chickens, and pigeons, and for other common foods.... These matters were published throughout the land, and publicly proclaimed in shire courts and boroughs....

By certain portents the hand of God appears to be raised against us. For in the past year there was such plentiful rain that men could scarcely harvest the corn or bring it safely to the barn. In the present year worse has happened. For the floods of rain have rotted almost all the seed, so that the prophecy of Isaiah might seem now to be fulfilled; for he says that "ten acres of vineyard shall yield one little measure and thirty bushels of seed shall yield three bushels":[1] and in many places the hay lay so long under water that it could neither be mown nor gathered. Sheep generally died and other animals were killed in a sudden plague. It is greatly to be feared that if the Lord finds us incorrigible after these visitations, he will destroy at once both men and beasts; and I firmly believe that unless the English Church had

interceded for us, we should have perished long ago. ...

After the feast of Easter [in 1316] the dearth of corn[2] was much increased. Such a scarcity has not been seen in our time in England, nor heard of for a hundred years. For a measure of wheat sold in London and the neighboring places for forty pence, and in other less thickly populated parts of the country thirty pence was a common price. Indeed during this time of scarcity a great famine appeared, and after the famine came a severe pestilence, of which many thousands died in many places. I have even heard it said by some, that in Northumbria dogs and horses and other unclean things were eaten. For there, on account of the frequent raids of the Scots, work is more irksome, as the accursed Scots despoil the people daily of their food. Alas, poor England! You who once helped other lands from your abundance, now poor and needy are forced to beg. Fruitful land is turned into a salt-marsh; the inclemency of the weather destroys the fatness of the land; corn is sown and tares[3] are brought forth. All this comes from the wickedness of the inhabitants. Spare, O Lord, spare thy people! For we are a scorn and a derision to them who are around us. Yet those who are wise in astrology say that these storms in the heavens have happened naturally; for Saturn, cold and heedless, brings rough weather that is useless to the seed; in the ascendant now for three years he has completed his course, and mild Jupiter duly succeeds him. Under Jupiter these floods of rain will cease, the valleys will grow rich in corn, and the fields will be filled with abundance. For the Lord shall give that which is good and our land shall yield her increase....

---

[1] *ten acres ... bushels* Cf. Isaiah 5.10.

[2] *corn* Grain.

[3] *tares* Weeds.

[In 1318] the dearth that had so long plagued us ceased, and England became fruitful with a manifold abundance of good things. A measure of wheat, which the year before was sold for forty pence, was now freely offered to the buyer for sixpence.…

The Hundred Years' War

The *Chronicle* of Jean Froissart of Valenciennes is among the most valuable historical records we possess of the course of fourteenth-century history. Froissart (c. 1337–c. 1404) was in direct contact with many of the nobility on both sides of the conflict between France and England. His *Chronicle* appeared in four volumes between 1370 and 1400, and survives in over one hundred manuscript copies. The excerpt below describes the battle fought at Crécy in 1346, beginning with a French lord's unsuccessful attempt to give the French King, Philip VI, good tactical advice.

The second excerpt below may perhaps be regarded as an early equivalent of a newspaper; it is from a letter sent by Edward the Black Prince to the people of London, recounting the story of the English victory at Poitiers (1356).

from Jean Froissart, *Chronicle* (late fourteenth century)

The lord Moyne said [to the king of France], "Sir, I will speak, since it pleases you to order me, but with the assistance of my companions. We have advanced far enough to reconnoitre your enemies. Know, then, that they are drawn up in three battalions and are awaiting you. I would advise, for my part (submitting, however, to better counsel), that you halt your army here and quarter them for the night; for before the rear shall come up and the army be properly drawn out, it will be very late. Your men will be tired and in disorder, while they will find your enemies fresh and properly arrayed. On the morrow, you may draw up your army more at your ease and may reconnoitre at leisure on what part it will be most advantageous to begin the attack; for, be assured, they will wait for you."

The king commanded that it should be so done; and the two marshals rode, one towards the front, and the other to the rear, crying out, "Halt banners, in the name of God and St. Denis." Those that were in the front halted; but those behind said they would not halt until they were as far forward as the front. When the front perceived the rear pushing on, they pushed forward; and neither the king nor the marshals could stop them, but they marched on without any order until they came in sight of their enemies. As soon as the foremost rank saw them, they fell back at once in great disorder, which alarmed those in the rear, who thought they had been fighting. There was then space and room enough for them to have passed forward, had they been willing to do so. Some did so, but others remained behind.

All the roads between Abbeville and Crécy were covered with common people, who, when they had come within three leagues of their enemies, drew their swords, crying out, "Kill, kill"; and with them were many great lords who were eager to make show of their courage. There is no man, unless he had been present, who can imagine, or describe truly, the confusion of that day, especially the bad management and disorder of the French, whose troops were beyond number.

The English, who were drawn up in three divisions and seated on the ground, on seeing their enemies advance, arose boldly and fell into their ranks. That of the Prince was the first to do so, whose archers were formed in the manner of a portcullis, or harrow, and the men-at-arms in the rear.[1] The earls of Northampton and Arundel, who commanded the second division, had posted themselves in good order on his wing to assist and succor the Prince, if necessary.

You must know that these kings, dukes, earls, barons, and lords of France did not advance in any regular order, but one after the other, or in any way most pleasing to themselves. As soon as the King of France came in sight of the English his blood began to boil, and he cried out to his marshals, "Order the

---

[1]   *archers were formed … in the rear* A portcullis (a kind of gate) and a harrow (a farming implement) both have prongs or teeth; in this formation, lines of bowmen would probably have advanced like the arms of a V ahead of the main troops. Lines of bowmen were roughly "vertical" in relation to the "horizontal" line of men-at-arms.

Genoese[1] forward, and begin the battle, in the name of God and St. Denis." There were about fifteen thousand Genoese cross-bowmen; but they were quite fatigued, having marched on foot that day six leagues, completely armed, and with their cross-bows. They told the constable that they were not in a fit condition to do any great things that day in battle. The Earl of Alençon, hearing this, said, "This is what one gets by employing such scoundrels, who fail when there is any need for them."

During this time a heavy rain fell, accompanied by thunder and a very terrible eclipse of the sun; and before this rain a great flight of crows hovered in the air over all those battalions, making a loud noise. Shortly afterwards it cleared up and the sun shone very brightly; but the Frenchmen had it in their faces, and the English at their backs.

When the Genoese were somewhat in order they approached the English and set up a loud shout in order to frighten them; but the latter remained quite still and did not seem to hear it. They then set up a second shout and advanced a little forward; but the English did not move. They hooted a third time, advancing with their cross-bows presented, and began to shoot. The English archers then advanced one step forward and shot their arrows with such force and quickness that it seemed as if it snowed.

When the Genoese felt these arrows, which pierced their arms, heads, and through their armor, some of them cut the strings of their cross-bows, others flung them on the ground, and all turned about and retreated, quite discomfited. The French had a large body of men-at-arms on horseback, richly dressed, to support the Genoese. The King of France, seeing them fall back, cried out, "Kill me those scoundrels; for they stop up our road, without any reason." You would then have seen the above-mentioned men-at-arms lay about them, killing all that they could of these runaways.

The English continued shooting as vigorously and quickly as before. Some of their arrows fell among the horsemen, who were sumptuously equipped, and, killing and wounding many, made them caper and fall among the Genoese, so that they were in such confusion they could never rally again. In the English army there were some Cornish- and Welshmen on foot who had armed themselves with large knives. These, advancing through the ranks of the men-at-arms and archers, who made way for them, came upon the French when they were in this danger and, falling upon earls, barons, knights and squires, slew many, at which the king of England was afterwards much exasperated.[2]

From a fifteenth-century manuscript of Froissart's *Chronicle*, "The Battle of Crécy."

From a fifteenth-century manuscript of Froissart's *Chronicle*, "The Battle of Poitiers."

---

[1] *Genoese* The Genoese (from Genoa, in Italy) are here fighting for the French as mercenaries; hence the comment of the Earl of Alençon, below.

[2] *slew many ... much exasperated* It would have been typical at this time to capture aristocratic enemy fighters and return them for ransom, rather than killing them.

Late after vespers,[1] the King of France had not more about him than sixty men, every one included. Sir John of Hainault, who was of the number, had once re-mounted the king; for the latter's horse had been killed under him by an arrow. He said to the king, "Sir, retreat while you have an opportunity, and do not expose yourself so needlessly. If you have lost this battle, another time you will be the conqueror." After he had said this, he took the bridle of the king's horse and led him off by force; for he had before entreated him to retire.

The king rode on until he came to the castle of La Broyes, where he found the gates shut, for it was very dark. The king ordered the governor of it to be summoned. He came upon the battlements and asked who it was that called at such an hour. The king answered, "Open, open, governor; it is the fortune of France." The governor, hearing the king's voice, immediately de-scended, opened the gate, and let down the bridge. The king and his company entered the castle; but he had with him only five barons—Sir John Hainault, the lord Charles of Montmorency, the lord of Beaujeu, the lord of Aubigny, and the lord of Montfort. The king would not bury himself in such a place as that, but, having taken some refreshments, set out again with his atten-dants about midnight, and rode on, under the direction of guides who were well acquainted with the country, until, about daybreak, he came to Amiens, where he halted.

This Saturday the English never quitted their ranks in pursuit of anyone, but remained on the field, guard-ing their positions and defending themselves against all who attacked them. The battle was ended at the hour of vespers. When, on this Saturday night, the English heard no more hooting or shouting, nor any more crying out to particular lords, or their banners, they looked upon the field as their own and their enemies as beaten.

They made great fires and lighted torches because of the darkness of the night. King Edward [III] then came down from his post, who all that day had not put on his helmet, and, with his whole battalion, advanced to the prince of Wales [Edward the "Black Prince"], whom he embraced in his arms and kissed, and said, "Sweet son, God give you good preference. You are my son, for most loyally have you acquitted yourself this day. You are worthy to be a sovereign." The prince bowed down very low and humbled himself, giving all honor to the king his father.

The English, during the night, made frequent thanksgivings to the Lord for the happy outcome of the day, and without rioting; for the King had forbidden all riot or noise.

from Prince Edward, Letter to the People of London (1356)

Very dear and very much beloved: As concerning news in the parts where we are, know that since the time when we informed our most dread lord and father, the King [Edward III], that it was our purpose to ride forth against the enemies in the parts of France, we took our road through the country of Périgueux and of Limousin, and straight on towards Bourges in Vienne, where we expected to have found the [French] king's son, the count of Poitiers. ....[2]

And then our people pursued them as far as Chau-vigny, full three leagues further; for which reason we were obliged that day to take up our quarters as near to that place as we could, that we might collect our men. And on the morrow we took our road straight towards the king, and sent out our scouts, who found him with his army; set himself[3] in battle array at one league from Poitiers, in the fields; and we went as near to him as we could take up our post, we ourselves on foot and in battle array, and ready to fight with him.

Where came the said Cardinal [Talleyrand], request-ing very earnestly for a little respite, that so there might parley together certain persons of either side, and so attempt to bring about an understanding and good peace; the which he undertook that he would bring about to a good end. Whereupon we took counsel, and granted him his request; upon which there were ordered

---

[1] *vespers* The hour for evening service in monastic practice; probably around 6:00 in the evening. This is one of the "canonical hours" used for telling time in monasteries.

[2] *the King's son ... Poitiers* I.e., the French king, who at this time was Jean II, son of Philip VI; his son, the Dauphin, was later to become Charles V.

[3] *set himself* I.e., the French king.

certain persons of the one side and the other to treat upon this matter; which treating was of no effect. And then the said Cardinal wished to obtain a truce, by way of putting off the battle at his pleasure; to which truce we would not assent. And the French asked that certain knights on the one side and the other should take equal shares, so that the battle might not in any manner fail: and in such manner was that day delayed; and the battalions on the one side and the other remained all night, each one in its place, and until the morrow, about half prime;[1] and as to some troops that were between the said main armies, neither would give any advantage in commencing the attack upon the other. And for default of victuals, as well as for other reasons, it was agreed that we should take our way, flanking them, in such manner that if they wished for battle or to draw towards us, in a place that was not very much to our disadvantage, we should be the first; and so forthwith it was done. Whereupon battle was joined, on [September 19,] the eve of the day before St. Matthew; and, God be praised for it, the enemy was discomfited, and the King was taken, and his son; and a great number of other great people were both taken and slain; as our very dear bachelor Messire Neele Lorraine, our chamberlain, the bearer hereof, who has very full knowledge thereon, will know how to inform and show you more fully, as we are not able to write to you. To him you should give full faith and credence; and may our Lord have you in his keeping. Given under our privy seal, at Bordeaux, the 22nd day of October.

The Black Death

The excerpted letter below by Ralph of Shrewsbury, Bishop of Bath and a distinguished scholar as well as an administrator, was sent to several of his subordinates just after the plague had begun. The second excerpt, from the *Chronicle* of Henry Knighton, provides a much more wide-ranging sense of the devastation wrought by the Black Death.

from Ralph of Shrewsbury, Letter (17 August 1348)

… Since the disaster of such a pestilence has come from the eastern parts to a neighboring kingdom, it is greatly to be feared, and being greatly to be feared, it is to be prayed devoutly and without ceasing that such a pestilence not extend its poisonous growth to the inhabitants of this kingdom, and torment and consume them.

Therefore, to each and all of you we mandate, with firm enjoining, that in your churches you publicly announce this present mandate in the vulgar tongue[2] at opportune times, and that in the bowels of Jesus Christ you exhort your subordinates—regular, secular, parishioners, and others—or have them exhorted by others, to appear before the Face of the Lord in confession, with psalms and other works of charity.

Remember the destruction that was deservedly pronounced by prophetic utterance on those who, doing penance, were mercifully freed from the destruction threatened by the judgment of God.…

from Henry Knighton, *Chronicle* (1378–96)

In that year and the following year there was a universal mortality of men throughout the world. It began first in India, then in Tarsus, then it reached the Saracens and finally the Christians and Jews.…

On a single day 1,312 people died in Avignon, according to a calculation made in the pope's presence. On another day more than 400 died. 358 of the Dominicans in Provence died during Lent. At Montpellier only seven friars survived out of 140. At Magdalen seven survived out of 160, which is quite enough. From 140 Minorites [i.e., Franciscans] at Marseilles not one remained to carry the news to the rest.… At the same time the plague raged in England. It began in the autumn in various places and after racing across the country it ended at the same time in the following year.

… Then the most lamentable plague penetrated the coast through Southampton and came to Bristol, and virtually the whole town was wiped out. It was as if sudden death had marked them down beforehand, for few lay sick for more than two or three days, or even for

---

[1] *half prime* About 9:30 in the morning. Like vespers, prime is part of the monastic way of measuring time, the "canonical hours."

[2] *vulgar tongue* I.e., the vernacular (the language of the land) rather than Latin.

half a day. Cruel death took just two days to burst out all over a town. At Leicester, in the little parish of St. Leonard, more than 380 died; in the parish of Holy Cross more than 400; in the parish of St. Margaret 700; and a great multitude in every parish. The Bishop of Lincoln sent word through the whole diocese, giving general power to every priest (among the regular as well as the secular clergy) to hear confession and grant absolution with full and complete authority except only in cases of debt.[1] In such cases the penitent, if it lay within his power, ought to make satisfaction while he lived, but certainly others should do it from his goods after his death. Similarly the Pope granted plenary remission of all sins to those at the point of death, the absolution to be for one time only, and the right to each person to choose his confessor as he wished.[2] This concession was to last until the following Easter.

In the same year there was a great murrain[3] of sheep throughout the realm, so much so that in one place more than 5,000 sheep died in a single pasture, and their bodies were so corrupt that no animal or bird would touch them. And because of the fear of death everything fetched a low price. For there were very few people who cared for riches, or indeed for anything else. A man could have a horse previously valued at 40s. for half a mark, a good fat ox for 4s., a cow for 12d., a bullock for 6d., a fat sheep for 4d., a ewe for 3d., a lamb for 2d., a large pig for 5d., a stone of wool for 9d. And sheep and cattle roamed unchecked through the fields and through the standing corn, and there was no one to chase them and round them up. For want of watching animals died in uncountable numbers in the fields and in bye-ways and hedges throughout the whole country;

for there was so great a shortage of servants and laborers that there was no one who knew what needed to be done. There was no memory of so inexorable and fierce a mortality since the time of Vortigern, King of the Britons, in whose time, as Bede testifies in his *De gestis Anglorum*,[4] there were not enough living to bury the dead. In the following autumn it was not possible to hire a reaper for less than 8d. and his food, or a mower for 12d. with his food.[5] For which reason many crops rotted unharvested in the fields; but in the year of the pestilence, as mentioned above, there was so great an abundance of all types of grain that no one cared.

The Scots, hearing of the cruel plague of the English, declared that it had befallen them through the revenging hand of God, and they took to swearing "by the foul death of England"—or so the common report resounded in the ears of the English. And thus the Scots, believing that the English were overwhelmed by the terrible vengeance of God, gathered in the forest of Selkirk with the intention of invading the whole realm of England. The fierce mortality came upon them, and the sudden cruelty of a monstrous death winnowed the Scots. Within a short space of time around 5,000 died, and the rest, weak and strong alike, decided to retreat to their own country. But the English, following, surprised them and killed many of them. …

After the aforesaid pestilence many buildings of all sizes in every city fell into total ruin for want of inhabitants. Likewise, many villages and hamlets were deserted, with no house remaining in them, because everyone who had lived there was dead, and indeed many of these villages were never inhabited again. In the following winter there was such a lack of workers in all areas of activity that it was thought that there had hardly ever been such a shortage before; for a man's farm animals and other livestock wandered about without a shepherd and all his possessions were left unguarded. And as a result all essentials were so expensive that something which had previously cost 1d. was now worth 4d. or 5d.

---

[1] *among the regular … cases of debt* "Regular" clergy are those bound by a rule of communal life (i.e., most commonly, monks), who ordinarily would not have the "care of souls," that is, the duty of hearing confession or other interactions with lay people. That was the job of the "secular" clergy, the clergy who lived and worked in the outside world, such as parish priests or bishops.

[2] *the right … as he wished* Like the call for regular clergy to take on the care of souls, the concessions on remission (i.e., forgiveness) of sins and on the right to choose a confessor reflect the church's anxiety about the salvation of the faithful in a time of crisis. Ordinarily one would have been expected to confess to one's parish priest.

[3] *murrain* Infectious disease of livestock.

[4] *Bede … Anglorum De Gestis Anglorum (On the Deeds of the English)* by Venerable Bede (673–735), English scholar.

[5] *In the following autumn … with his food* Before the Black Death, laborers were typically hired for 2 or 3 pence per day, so these wages represent a roughly four-fold increase. (The abbreviation "d." is of the Latin denarius, or penny.)

Confronted by this shortage of workers and the scarcity of goods the great men of the realm, and the lesser landowners who had tenants, remitted part of the rent so that their tenants did not leave. Some remitted half the rent, some more and some less; some remitted it for two years, some for three and some for one—whatever they could agree with their tenants. Likewise those whose tenants held by the year, by the performance of labor services (as is customary in the case of serfs), found that they had to release and remit such works, and either pardon rents completely or levy them on easier terms, otherwise houses would be irretrievably ruined and land left uncultivated. And all victuals and other necessities were extremely dear.

Fourteenth-century manuscript: plague victims.

The Uprising of 1381

The following excerpts from a 1350 set of London wage and price regulations and from the Statute of Laborers imposed the following year by King Edward III provide some sense of the economic background for the Uprising of 1381 (or the "Peasants' Revolt"). As the Statute of 1363 demonstrates, regulations continued to tighten thereafter in an attempt to maintain traditional social distinctions between ranks, which were threatened by the economic upheaval that followed the plague. The passage by Froissart recounts a sermon by one of the leading figures of the rebellion, John Ball, and the letter that follows was allegedly written by Ball as a coded message to those sympathetic to the uprising. The extended passage from the *Chronicle* of Henry Knighton, a canon of St. Mary's Abbey in the city of Leicester, provides a vivid account of the climax of the rebellion.

from Regulations, London (1350)

To amend and redress the damages and grievances which the good folks of the city, rich and poor, have suffered and received within the past year, by reason of masons, carpenters, plasterers, tilers, and all manner of laborers, who take immeasurably more than they have been wont to take, by assent of Walter Turk, mayor, the aldermen, and all the commonalty of the city, the points under-written are ordained, to be held and firmly observed for ever; that is to say:

In the first place, that the masons, between the Feasts of Easter and St. Michael,[1] shall take no more by the working-day than 6d., without victuals or drink; and from the Feast of St. Michael to Easter, for the working-day, 5d. And upon Feast Days, when they do not work, they shall take nothing. And for the making or mending of their implements they shall take nothing.

Also, that the carpenters shall take, for the same time, in the same manner.

Also, that the plasterers shall take the same as the masons and carpenters take.

Also, that the tilers shall take for the working-day, from the Feast of Easter to St. Michael 5 ½ d., and from the Feast of St. Michael 4 ½ d.

Also, that the laborers shall take in the first half year 3 ½ d., and in the other half 3d. ...

Also, that the tailors shall take for making a gown, garnished with fine cloth and silk, 18d.

Also, for a man's gown, garnished with linen thread and with buckram, 14d.

Also, for a coat and hood, 10d.

Also, for a long gown for a woman, garnished with fine cloth or with silk, 2s. 6d.

Also, for a pair of sleeves, to change, 4d.

Also, that the porters of the city shall not take more for their labor than they used to take in olden time, on

---

[1] *St. Michael*   The Feast of St. Michael the Archangel is held on 29 September.

pain of imprisonment.

Also, that no vintner shall be so daring as to sell the gallon of wine of Vernaccia for more than 2s., and wine of Crete, wine of the River, Piement, and Clare, and Malveisin, at 16d. …

Also, that a pair of spurs shall be sold for 6d., and a better pair for 8d., and the best at 10d. or 12d., at the very highest.

Also, that a pair of gloves of sheepskin shall be sold for one penny, and a better pair at 1 ½ d., and a pair at 2d., so going on to the very highest.

Also, that the shearmen shall not take more than they were wont to take; that is to say, for a short cloth 12d., and for a long cloth 2s.; and for a cloth of striped serge, for getting rid of the stripes, and shearing the same, 2s.

Also, that the farriers[1] shall not take more than they were wont to take before the time of the pestilence, on pain of imprisonment and heavy ransom; that is to say, for a horse-shoe of six nails 1½ 2d., and for a horse-shoe of eight nails 2d.; and for taking off a horse-shoe of six nails or of eight, one halfpenny; and for the shoe of a courser 2 ½ d., and the shoe of a charger 3d.; and for taking off the shoe of a courser or charger, one penny.

Also, if any workman or laborer will not work or labor as is above ordained, let him be taken and kept in prison until he shall have found good surety, and have been sworn to do that which is so ordained. And if anyone shall absent himself, or go out of the city, because he does not wish to work and labor, as is before mentioned, and afterwards by chance be found within the city, let him have imprisonment for a quarter of the year, and forfeit his chattels which he has in the city, and then let him find surety, and make oath, as is before stated. And if he will not do this, let him forswear the city for ever.

from Statute of Laborers (1351)

Because a great part of the people and especially of the workers and servants has now died in the pestilence, some, seeing the needs of the masters and the scarcity of servants, are not willing to serve unless they receive excessive wages, and others, rather than gain their living through labor, prefer to beg in idleness. We, considering the grave inconveniences which might come from such a shortage, especially of ploughmen and such laborers, have held deliberation and discussion concerning this with the prelates and nobles and other learned men sitting by us, by whose consenting counsel we have seen fit to ordain that every man and woman of our kingdom of England, of whatever condition, whether serf or free, who is able bodied and below the age of 60 years, not living from trade or carrying on a definite craft, or having private means of living or private land to cultivate, and not serving another—if such a person is sought after to serve in a suitable service appropriate to that person's status, that person shall be bound to serve whomever has seen fit so to offer such employment, and shall take only the wages, liveries, reward or salary usually given in that place in the twentieth year of our reign in England, or the usual year of the five or six preceding ones. This is provided so that in thus retaining their service, lords are preferred before others by their serfs or land tenants, so that such lords nevertheless thus retain as many as shall be necessary, but not more. And if any man or woman, being thus sought after for service, will not do this, the fact being proven by two faithful men before the sheriffs or the bailiffs of our Lord the King, or the constables of the town where this happens to be done, immediately through them, or some one of them, that person shall be taken and sent to the next jail, and remain there in strict custody until offering security for serving in the aforesaid form. And if a reaper or mower, or other worker or servant, of whatever standing or condition, who is retained in the service of anyone, departs from the said service before the end of the agreed term without permission or reasonable cause, that person shall undergo the penalty of imprisonment, and let no one, under the same penalty, presume to receive or retain such a person for service. Let no one, moreover, pay or permit to be paid to anyone more wages, livery, reward or salary than was customary, as has been said.

… Likewise saddlers, skinners, tawyers,[2] cordwainers,[3] tailors, smiths, carpenters, masons, tilers, shipwrights, carters and all other artisans and laborers

---

[1] *farriers* Smiths who shoe horses.

[2] *tawyers* Producers of white leather.

[3] *cordwainers* Shoemakers.

shall not take for their labor and handiwork more than what, in the places where they happen to labor, was customarily paid to such persons in the said twentieth year and in the other usual years preceding, as has been said. And anyone who takes more shall be committed to the nearest jail in the aforesaid manner.

Likewise, let butchers, fishmongers, innkeepers, brewers, bakers, those dealing in foodstuffs and all other vendors of any victuals, be bound to sell such victuals for a reasonable price, having regard for the price at which such victuals are sold in the adjoining places, so that such vendors may have moderate gains, and not excessive ones, according as the distance of the places from which such victuals are carried may seem reasonably to require. And if anyone sells such victuals in another manner, and is convicted of it in the aforesaid way, that person shall pay double what was received to the injured party, or in default of the injured party, to another who shall be willing to prosecute in this behalf. ...

And because many sturdy beggars refuse to labor so long as they can live from begging alms, giving themselves up to idleness and sin and, at times, to robbery and other crimes, let no one, under the aforesaid pain of imprisonment, presume, under color of piety or alms, to give anything to those who can very well work, or to cherish them in their sloth, so that thus they may be compelled to work for the necessities of life.

from Statute (1363)

... Item. Regarding the outrageous and excessive apparel of diverse people, violating their estate and degree, to the great destruction and impoverishment of the whole land, it is ordained that grooms (both servants of lords and those employed in crafts) shall be served meat or fish once a day, and the remaining occasions shall be served milk, butter, and cheese, and other such food, according to their estate. They shall have clothes for their wear worth no more than two marks, and they shall wear no cloth of higher price which they have bought themselves or gotten in some other way. Nor shall they wear anything of silver, embroidered items, nor items of silk, nor anything pertaining to those things. Their wives, daughters, and children shall be of

the same condition in their clothing and apparel, and they shall wear no veils worth more than 12 pence a veil.

Item. Artisans and yeomen[1] shall not take or wear cloth for their clothing or stockings of a higher price than 40 shillings for the whole cloth, by way of purchase or by any other means. Nor may they take or wear silk, silver, or jeweled cloth, nor shall they take or wear silver or gold belts, knives, clasps, rings, garters, or brooches, ribbons, chains, or any manner of silk apparel which is embroidered or decorated. And their wives, daughters and children are to be of the same condition in their dress and apparel. And they are to wear no veils made of silk, but only of yarn made within the kingdom, nor are they to wear any manner of fur or of budge,[2] but only of lamb, rabbit, cat, or fox. ...

Item. Knights who have land or rent valued up to 200 marks a year shall take and wear clothes of cloth valued at 6 marks for the whole cloth, and nothing of more expensive cloth. And they shall not wear cloth of gold or mantles or gowns furred with pure miniver[3] or ermine, or any apparel embroidered with jewels or anything else. Their wives, daughters, and children will be of the same condition. And they shall not wear ermine facings or lettice[4] or any jeweled apparel, except on their heads. All knights and ladies, however, who have land or rent of more than 400 marks a year, up to the sum of 1,000 marks, shall wear what they like, except ermine and lettice, and apparel with jewels and pearls, unless on their heads.

Item. Clergy who have any rank in a church, cathedral, college, or schools, or a cleric of the King who has an estate that requires fur, will wear and use it according to the constitution of the same. All other clergy who have 200 marks from land a year will wear and do as knights who receive the same rent. Other clergy with the same rent will wear what the esquires who have 100 pounds in rent wear. All of them, both clergy and knights, may wear fur in winter, and in the same manner will wear linure[5] in summer.

---

[1] *yeomen* Freeholders; those who farm their own land.

[2] *budge* Lamb's wool fur.

[3] *miniver* Ermine when taken in its white winter coat.

[4] *lettice* White-gray fur.

[5] *linure* Fine linen.

Item. Carters, ploughmen, ploughdrivers, cowherds, shepherds, swineherds, and all other keepers of animals, wheat threshers and all manner of people of the estate of a groom occupied in husbandry, and all other people who do not have 40 shillings' worth of goods or chattels will not take or wear any kind of cloth but blanket, and russet worth 12 pence, and shall wear belts of linen according to their estate. And domestic servants shall come to eat and drink in the manner pertaining to them, and not excessively. And it is ordained that if anyone wears or does contrary to the above, that person will forfeit to the King all the apparel thus worn against this ordinance.

Item. In order to maintain this ordinance and keep it in all points without exception, it is ordained that all makers of cloth within the realm, both men and women, shall confirm that they make their cloth according to the price set by this ordinance. And all the clothmakers shall buy and sell their varieties of cloth according to the same price, so that a great supply of such cloths will be made and put up for sale in every city, borough, and merchant town and elsewhere in the realm, so that no lack of supply of such cloths shall cause the violation of this ordinance. And to that end the said clothmakers will be constrained in any way that shall seem best to the King and his council. And this ordinance on new apparel shall take effect at the next Candlemas.[1]

from Jean Froissart, *Chronicle* (late fourteenth century), Account of a Sermon by John Ball

There was a foolish priest in the county of Kent called John Ball, who, for his foolish words, had been three times in the Archbishop of Canterbury's prison; for this priest used oftentimes, on the Sundays after Mass, when the people were going out of the minster,[2] to go into the cloister[3] and preach, and made the people to assemble about him, and would say thus, "Ah, ye good people, things are not going well in England, nor shall they do so till everything be common, and till there be no villeins[4] nor gentlemen, but we be all united together, and the lords be no greater masters than we be. What have we deserved, or why should we be kept thus in serfdom? We be all come from one father and one mother, Adam and Eve; whereby can they say or show that they be greater lords than we be, except that they cause us to earn and labor for what they spend? They are clothed in velvet and camlet furred with gris,[5] and we be vestured with poor cloth; they have their wines, spices, and good bread, and we have the drawing out of the chaff and drink water; they dwell in fair houses and we have the pain and travail, rain and wind in the fields; and by what cometh of our labors they keep and maintain their estates: we be called their bondmen, and unless we readily do them service, we be beaten; and we have no sovereign to whom we may complain, nor that will hear us and do us right. Let us go to the King—he is young—and show him what serfage we be in, and show him how we will have it otherwise, or else we will provide us with some remedy, either by fairness or otherwise."[6] Thus John Ball said on Sundays, when the people issued out of the churches in the villages; wherefore many of the lowly people loved him, and said how he said truth; and so they would murmur one with another in the fields and in the ways as they went together, affirming how John Ball spoke the truth.

---

[1] *Candlemas* The Feast of the Purification of the Virgin Mary, celebrated on 2 February.

[2] *minster* Cathedral church.

[3] *cloister* Here, covered walkway connecting buildings of the Cathedral.

[4] *villeins* Peasants subject to lords or attached to manors.

[5] *camlet furred with gris* Fabric imported from the East and trimmed with gray fur.

[6] *the King … fairness or otherwise* The young King mentioned here is Richard II, who had come to the throne at the age of only ten years old, after the death of his grandfather, Edward III, in 1377; for the first three years of his kingship the kingdom was actually ruled by a council of nobles. This problematic royal transition contributed to the general uncertainties and tensions in England.

John Ball, Letter to the Common People of Essex, 1381[1]

Johan Schep[2] sometime[3] Seynte Marie's priest of York[4] and now of Colchester, greeteth wel Johan Nameless, and Johan the Millere, and Johon Cartere, and biddeth them that they be ware of gyle in borough,[5] and stondeth togidre in God's name, and biddeth Peres Ploughman[6] go to his werk, and chastise wel Hobbe the Robbere,[7] and taketh with you Johan Trewman, and alle his felowes, and no mo,[8] and look schappe you to one head,[9] and no mo.

Johan the Millere hath ygrounde smal,°   *ground finely*
    smal, smal;
The Kyng's Sone of Hevene schal paye for al.
Be ware or° ye be woe;   *before*
Knoweth your freend fro your foe;
Haveth ynow and seith 'Hoo';[10]
And do wel and bettre,[11] and fleeth sinne,
And seeketh peace, and hold you therinne;

And so biddeth Johan Trewman and alle his felowes.

---

[1] *John Ball's Letter … 1381* Text has been modernized for *The Broadview Anthology* from *Fourteenth Century Verse and Prose*, ed. Kenneth Sisam (Oxford: Clarendon, 1970).

[2] *Johan Schep* Alias for John Ball; priests were often referred to as shepherds. The various Johns named in this letter are probably allegorical aliases for figures involved in the revolt.

[3] *sometime* Formerly.

[4] *Seynte Marie's priest of York* Priest of Saint Mary's Church in New York.

[5] *gyle in borough* Trickery in town.

[6] *Peres Ploughman* This is a reference to William Langland's poem *Piers Plowman*, which contains sharp criticism of abuses by both ecclesiastical and secular powers.

[7] *Hobbe the Robbere* This figure appears in *Piers Plowman*, Passus 5.1.463; "Hobbe" is a nickname for Robert.

[8] *mo* More.

[9] *look schappe you to one head* Be sure that you follow one head, i.e., one leader.

[10] *Haveth … 'Hoo'* I.e., have what you need and say, "Enough."

[11] *do wel and bettre* Dowel and Dobet (Do-Well and Do-Better) are characters in *Piers Plowman*.

from Henry Knighton, *Chronicle* (1378–96)

In the year 1381, the second of the reign of King Richard II, during the month of May … that impious band began to assemble from Kent, from Surrey, and from many other surrounding places. Apprentices also, leaving their masters, rushed to join these. And so they gathered on Blackheath, where, forgetting themselves in their multitude, and neither contented with their former cause nor appeased by smaller crimes, they unmercifully planned greater and worse evils and determined not to desist from their wicked undertaking until they should have entirely extirpated the nobles and great men of the kingdom.

So at first they directed their course of iniquity to a certain town of the Archbishop of Canterbury called Maidstone, in which there was a jail of the said Archbishop, and in the said jail was a certain John Ball, a chaplain who was considered among the laity to be a very famous preacher; many times in the past he had foolishly spread abroad the word of God, by mixing tares with wheat, too pleasing to the laity and extremely dangerous to the liberty of ecclesiastical law and order, execrably introducing into the Church of Christ many errors among the clergy and laymen. For this reason he had been tried as a clerk and convicted in accordance with the law, being seized and assigned to this same jail for his permanent abiding place. On [June 12,] the Wednesday before the Feast of the Consecration, they came into Surrey to the jail of the King at Marshalsea, where they broke the jail without delay, forcing all imprisoned there to come with them to help them; and whomsoever they met, whether pilgrims or others of whatever condition, they forced to go with them.

On [June 14,] the Friday following the Feast of the Consecration, they came over the bridge to London; here no one resisted them, although, as was said, the citizens of London knew of their advance a long time before; and so they directed their way to the Tower where the King was surrounded by a great throng of knights, esquires, and others. It was said that there were in the Tower about one hundred and fifty knights together with one hundred and eighty others. …

John Leg and a certain John, a Minorite, a man active in warlike deeds, skilled in natural sciences, an intimate friend of Lord John, duke of Lancaster, hastened with three others to the Tower for refuge, intending to hide themselves under the wings of the King. The people had determined to kill the Archbishop and the others above mentioned with him; for this reason they came to this place, and afterwards they fulfilled their vows. The King, however, desired to free the Archbishop and his friends from the jaws of the wolves, so he sent to the people a command to assemble outside the city, at a place called Mile End, in order to speak with the King and to treat with him concerning their designs. The soldiers who were to go forward, consumed with folly, lost heart, and gave up, on the way, their boldness of purpose. Nor did they dare to advance but, unfortunately, struck as they were by fear, like women, kept themselves within the Tower.

But the King advanced to the assigned place, while many of the wicked mob kept following him.... More, however, remained where they were. When the others had come to the King they complained that they had been seriously oppressed by many hardships and that their condition of servitude was unbearable, and that they neither could nor would endure it longer. The King, for the sake of peace, and on account of the violence of the times, yielding to their petition, granted to them a charter with the great seal, to the effect that all men in the kingdom of England should be free and of free condition, and should remain both for themselves and their heirs free from all kinds of servitude and villeinage forever. This charter was rejected and decided to be null and void by the King and the great men of the kingdom in the Parliament held at Westminster in the same year, after the Feast of St. Michael.

While these things were going on, behold those degenerate sons, who still remained, summoned their father the Archbishop with his above-mentioned friends without any force or attack, without sword or arrow, or any other form of compulsion, but only with force of threats and excited outcries, inviting those men to death. But they did not cry out against it for themselves, nor resist, but, as sheep before the shearers, going forth barefooted with uncovered heads, ungirt, they offered themselves freely to an undeserved death, just as if they had deserved this punishment for some murder or theft. And so, alas! before the King returned, seven were killed at Tower Hill, two of them lights of the kingdom, the worthy with the unworthy. John Leg and his three associates were the cause of this irreparable loss. Their heads were fastened on spears and sticks in order that they might be told from the rest....

Whatever representatives of the law they found or whatever men served the kingdom in a judicial capacity, these they slew without delay.

On the following day, which was Saturday, they gathered in Smithfield, where there came to them in the morning the King, who although only a youth in years yet was in wisdom already well versed. Their leader, whose real name was Wat Tyler, approached him; already they were calling him by the other name of Jack Straw. He kept close to the King, addressing him for the rest. He carried in his hand an unsheathed weapon which they call a dagger, and, as if in childish play, kept tossing it from one hand to the other in order that he might seize the opportunity, if the King should refuse his requests, to strike the King suddenly (as was commonly believed); and from this thing the greatest fear arose among those about the King as to what might be the outcome.

They begged from the King that all the warrens, well waters, park, and wood, should be common to all, so that a poor man as well as a rich should be able freely to hunt animals everywhere in the kingdom—in the streams, in the fish ponds, in the woods, and in the forest; and that he might be free to chase the hare in the fields, and that he might do these things and others like them without objection. When the King hesitated about granting this concession Jack Straw came nearer, and, speaking threatening words, seized with his hand the bridle of the horse of the King very daringly. When John de Walworth, a citizen of London, saw this, thinking that death threatened the King, he seized a sword and pierced Jack Straw in the neck. Seeing this, another soldier, by name Radulf Standyche, pierced his side with another sword. He sank back, slowly letting go with his hands and feet, and then died. A great cry and much mourning arose: "Our leader is slain." When this dead man had been meanly dragged along by the hands and feet into the church of St. Bartholomew, which was near by, many withdrew from the band, and, vanishing, betook themselves to flight, to the number it is believed of ten thousand....

After these things had happened and quiet had been restored, the time came when the King caused the offenders to be punished. So Lord Robert Tresillian, one of the judges, was sent by order of the King to inquire into the uprisings against the peace and to punish the guilty. Wherever he came he spared no one, but caused great slaughter. . . .

For whoever was accused before him in this said cause, whether justly or as a matter of spite, he immediately passed upon him the sentence of death. He ordered some to be beheaded, others to be hanged, still others to be dragged through the city and hanged in four different parts thereof; others to be disemboweled, and the entrails to be burned before them while they were still alive, and afterwards to be decapitated, quartered, and hanged in four parts of the city according to the greatness of the crime and its desert. John Ball was captured at Coventry and led to St. Albans, where, by order of the King, he was drawn and hanged, then quartered, and his quarters sent to four different places.

From a fifteenth-century manuscript of Froissart's *Chronicle*,
"The Death of Wat Tyler."

SIR ORFEO

c. 1325

The Breton *lai* is a poetic form that evolved in England and France during the twelfth century. Originally composed in Anglo-Norman, these relatively brief poems ostensibly originated in the oral legends of Brittany. The Breton *lais* generally retain the themes of longer chivalric poems—tales of adventure and noble love often colored by the supernatural—but their overall structure is much more concise and they are notable for the ways in which they often call attention to their own supposed origins in Breton stories. It is possible that the recitation of the tales was accompanied by music—the *lai* proper—and that (as in *Sir Orfeo*) the narrative originally served as something like a frame for a musical performance.

Eventually, English writers began to produce these works in their own language; *Sir Orfeo* is considered by many critics to be one of the best examples of the Breton *lai* in any language. As with many medieval English poems, the author of *Sir Orfeo* is unknown; the poem shows some signs of having been translated from a French original. The poem exists in three separate manuscripts, the earliest of which dates from the second quarter of the fourteenth century, the other two from the fifteenth century.

Sir Orfeo consists of a mixture of classical, romance, and Celtic elements. Its plot structure and main characters mirror those of the Greek myth of Orpheus and Eurydice, familiar to the Middle Ages particularly through versions in Ovid and Virgil. But the setting has been "domesticated" (the ancient city of Thrace is identified with Winchester) and many of the story's most distinctive plot elements have been altered to align it with romance rather than with classical myth. Whereas in the classical version Orpheus attempts to rescue Eurydice from Hades, the land of the dead, in this English version Sir Orfeo's task is to rescue Heurodis from the land of the fairies. The queen is not dead but merely "taken"; the king's descent into the wilderness precedes rather than follows his attempted rescue of the queen. Most strikingly, while the classical versions end in tragedy and loss—as he leads Eurydice from Hades, Orpheus glances back at her and thereby loses her forever—*Sir Orfeo* ends in reunion, recuperation and recovery. The couple are reunited, the king regains his kingdom, and all live happily ever after. We cannot say with any certainty whether the author knowingly replaced the tragic ending of the classical version with this happier one, or why he did so, or whether readers of the story would have recognized or appreciated such a striking reversal. But these puzzling uncertainties about sources and form do not detract from the skill of the storytelling, in which even the most familiar plot devices are presented with precision, grace, and admirable narrative economy.

The poem was influential not only in its time (Chaucer's *Franklin's Tale* and *Wife of Bath's Tale* drew on some of the story material of *Sir Orfeo*) but also in the twentieth century; J.R.R. Tolkien studied the poem extensively and may well have been influenced by it in writing some portions of *The Lord of the Rings*.

⌘ ⌘ ⌘

Sir Orfeo [1]

We redeth oft and findeth y-write,° *written*
And this clerkes° wele it wite,° *scholars / know*
Layes that ben in harping° *are in song*
Ben y-founde of ferli thing:° *composed about marvelous things*
5 Sum bethe of wer° and sum of wo,° *some are of war / grief*
And sum of joie° and mirthe also, *gaiety*
And sum of trecherie and of gile,° *deceit (or, trickery)*
Of old aventours° that fel while;° *adventures / happened once*
And sum of bourdes° and ribaudy,° *jokes / ribaldry*
10 And mani ther beth of fairy.[2]
Of al thinges that men seth,° *relate*
Mest o° love, forsothe,° they beth. *most of / in truth*
In Breteyne this° layes were wrought,° *Brittany these / made*
First y-founde° and forth y-brought,° *composed / produced*
15 Of aventours that fel bi dayes,° *happened in olden times*
Wherof Bretouns maked her° layes. *their*
When kinges might our y-here° *anywhere hear*
Of ani mervailes° that ther were, *marvels*
Thai token° an harp in gle° and game *took / minstrelsy*
20 And maked a lay and gaf° it name. *gave*
Now of this aventours that weren y-falle° *have happened*
Y° can tel sum, ac° nought alle. *I / but*
Ac herkneth,° lordinges that ben trewe, *but listen*
Ichil° you telle of "Sir Orfewe." *I will*
25 Orfeo mest° of ani thing *most*
Lovede the gle° of harping.[3] *glee or music*
Siker° was everi gode° harpour *sure / good*
Of him to have miche° honour. *much*
Himself he lerned forto° harp, *he taught himself to*
30 And leyd° theron his wittes scharp; *applied*
He lerned so ther nothing° was *in no way*
A better harpour in no plas.° *anywhere*
In al the warld was no man bore° *born*
That ones° Orfeo sat before— *once*
35 And° he might of his harping here— *if / could*

Bot he schuld thenche° that he were *think*
In on° of the joies of Paradis, *one*
Swiche melody in his harping is.
Orfeo was a king,
40 In Inglond an heighe° lording, *high*
A stalworth man and hardi bo;° *brave as well*
Large° and curteys[4] he was also. *generous*
His fader was comen° of King Pluto, *descended from*
And his moder of King Juno,[5]
45 That sum time° were as godes *who once*
yhold° *considered to be gods*
For aventours that thai dede° and told. *did*
This king sojourndy° in Traciens, *dwelled*
That was a cité of noble defens—° *fortifications*
For Winchester was cleped° tho° *called / then*
50 Traciens,[6] withouten no.° *denial*
The king hadde a quen of priis° *queen of excellence*
That was y-cleped° Dame Heurodis, *called*
The fairest levedi, for the nones,° *lady indeed*
That might gon on° bodi and bones, *walk about in*
55 Ful of love and godenisse—° *goodness*
Ac no man may telle hir fairnise.° *beauty*

Bifel° so in the comessing° of May *it happened / beginning*
When miri° and hot is the day, *merry (pleasant)*
And oway° beth winter schours, *away*
60 And everi feld° is ful of flours, *field*
And blosme breme° on everi bough *blossoms bright*
Over al wexeth° miri anought,° *everywhere grow / enough*
This ich° quen, Dame Heurodis *same*
Tok to° maidens of priis, *two*
65 And went in an undrentide° *late morning*
To play° bi an orchardside, *enjoy themselves*
To se the floures sprede and spring
And to here the foules° sing. *birds*
Thai sett hem° doun al thre *sat themselves*

---

[1] *Sir Orfeo* For this anthology the text used is that prepared by Anne Laskaya and Eve Salisbury for their edition (published by Medieval Institute Publications, Kalamazoo).

[2] *fairy* The word "fairy" here and elsewhere in the poem means "land of the fays" or the "fays" themselves. The word "fay" comes from Old French "fée" derived from the Latin "fata," "the Fates."

[3] *Orfeo … harping* Orfeo's name had a long tradition of being associated with music, art, and the power of eloquence; his name had been understood to mean "beautiful voice."

[4] *curteys* In medieval texts this word carries much greater weight than today's "courteous" or "polite"; it connotes courtly, elite, valuable, and cultured behavior as well as generosity.

[5] *King Pluto … King Juno* Pluto was, according to classical myth, god of the underworld. Juno was a goddess, the wife of Jupiter, not a king.

[6] *This king … Traciens* Because the poet has set the poem in England, classical and medieval places are conflated; hence, Winchester, the old capital, becomes Thrace.

70	Under a fair ympe-tre,°	*grafted tree*
	And wel sone° this fair quene	*very quickly*
	Fel on slepe° opon the grene.	*asleep*
	The maidens durst° hir nought awake,	*dared*
	Bot lete hir ligge° and rest take.	*let her lie*
75	So sche slepe til after none,°	*noon*
	That undertide° was al y-done.°¹	*until midday / past*
	Ac, as sone as sche gan° awake,	*began (to)*
	Sche crid, and lothli bere gan make;°	*terrible outcry made*
	Sche froted° hir honden° and hir fete,	*rubbed / hands*
80	And crached hir visage°—it bled	
	wete—°	*scratched her face / profusely*
	Hir riche robe hye al to-rett°	*she tore all to pieces*
	And was reveyd° out of hir wit.	*driven*
	The two maidens hir biside	
	No durst with hir no leng° abide,	*longer*
85	Bot ourn° to the palays ful right°	*ran / immediately*
	And told bothe squier and knight	
	That her° quen awede wold,°	*their / was going mad*
	And bad° hem go and hir at-hold.°	*bade / seize*
	Knightes urn° and levedis also,	*ran*
90	Damisels sexti and mo.°	*numbering sixty and more*
	In the orchard to the quen hye come,°	*they came*
	And her up in her armes nome,°	*their arms took*
	And brought hir to bed atte last,	
	And held hir there fine fast.°	*very securely*
95	Ac ever she held in o° cri	*persisted in one*
	And wold° up and owy.°	*wished (to go) / away*
	When Orfeo herd° that tiding	*heard*
	Never him nas wers for	
	nothing.°	*had he been as grieved by anything*
	He come with knightes tene°	*ten*
100	To chaumber, right bifor the quene,	
	And bi-held,° and seyd with grete pité,°	*beheld her / sorrow*
	"O lef liif,° what is te,°	*dear life / with you*
	That° ever yete° hast ben so stille°	*who / yet / calm*
	And° now gredest wonder schille?°	*but / cries strangely shrilly*
105	Thy bodi, that was so white y-core,°	*exquisitely*
	With thine nailes is all to-tore.°	*torn to pieces*
	Allas! thy rode,° that was so red,	*face*
	Is al wan, as° thou were ded;	*pale as (if)*
	And also thine fingres smale°	*slender*
110	Beth al blodi and al pale.	
	Allas! thy lovesum eyyen to°	*lovely two eyes*

	Loketh so° man doth on his fo!°	*as / foe*
	A, dame, ich biseche,° merci!	*I beg you*
	Lete ben° al this reweful° cri,	*let be / pitiful*
115	And tel me what the is,° and	
	hou,°	*what's bothering you / how*
	And what thing may the help now."	
	Tho° lay sche stille atte last	*then*
	And gan to wepe swithe fast,°	*very hard*
	And seyd thus the King to:	
120	"Allas, mi lord, Sir Orfeo!	
	Sethen° we first togider were,	*since*
	Ones wroth never we	
	nere;°	*we were never once angry with each other*
	Bot ever ich have yloved the	
	As mi liif and so thou me;	
125	Ac now we mot delen ato;°	*must separate*
	Do thi best, for y mot° go."	*I must*
	"Allas!" quath he, "forlorn icham!°	*I am utterly lost*
	Whider wiltow° go, and to wham?°	*where will you / whom*
	Whider thou gost, ichil° with the,	*I will go*
130	And whider y go, thou schalt with me."²	
	"Nay, nay, Sir, that nought nis!°	*cannot be*
	Ichil the telle al hou° it is:	*all how*
	As ich lay this undertide	
	And slepe under our orchardside,	
135	Ther come to me to fair knightes,	
	Wele y-armed al to rightes,°	*quite properly*
	And bad me comen an heighing°	*in haste*
	And speke with her lord the king.	
	And ich answerd at° wordes bold,	*with*
140	Y durst nought, no y nold.°	*dared not, nor did I want to*
	Thai priked oyain as thai might drive;³	
	Tho° com her king, also blive,°	*then / as quickly*
	With an hundred knightes and mo,	
	And damisels an hundred also,	
145	Al on snowe-white stedes;	
	As white as milke were her wedes.°⁴	*their garments*
	Y no seighe° never yete bifore	*saw*

---

¹ *So sche slepe … al y-done* Midday, or noon, was considered a perilous time in both folktales and Christian literature.

² *Whider … with me* Cf. Ruth 1.16: "Wither thou goest I will go, and where thou lodgest, I will lodge." Although Ruth speaks these words not to her husband but to her mother-in-law, Naomi, the lines were frequently associated with marriage.

³ *Thai … drive* They rode back again as fast as they could.

⁴ *Al … her wedes* The white horse and the white clothes worn by those who escort or meet the protagonists at the boundary of the Otherworld are common in romance and dream vision literature.

So fair creatours y-core.

The king hadde a croun on hed;

150 It nas of silver, no of gold red,

Ac it was of a precious ston—

As bright as the sonne it schon.

And as son as he to me cam,

Wold ich, nold ich, he me
nam,°   *whether I wished or not he took me*

155 And made me with him ride

Opon a palfray° bi his side;   *horse*

And brought me to his palays,

Wele atird° in ich ways,°   *adorned / every way*

And schewed me castels and tours,°   *towers*

160 Rivers, forestes, frith with flours,°   *woods with flowers*

And his riche stedes ichon.°   *gorgeous steeds each one*

And sethen° me brought oyain hom° *afterwards / back home*

Into our owhen° orchard,   *own*

And said to me thus afterward,

165 "Loke, dame, tomorwe thatow° be   *that you*

Right here under this ympe-tre,

And than thou schalt with ous° go   *us*

And live with ous evermo.

And yif thou makest ous y-let,°   *a hindrance for us*

170 Whar° thou be, thou worst y-fet,° *wherever / will be fetched*

And totore° thine limes° al   *torn apart / limbs*

That nothing help the no schal;

And thei thou best so totorn,° *though (even if) you are so torn*

Yete thou worst with ous y-born."° *will be carried with us*

175 When King Orfeo herd this cas,°   *matter*

"O we!"° quath he, "Allas, allas!   *woe*

Lever me were to lete° mi liif   *I'd rather lose*

Than thus to lese° the quen, mi wiif!"   *lose*

He asked conseyl at ich man,°   *advice from each person*

180 Ac no man him help no can.

Amorwe° the undertide is come   *the next day*

And Orfeo hath his armes y-nome,°   *taken*

And wele ten hundred knightes with him,

Ich y-armed, stout° and grim;°   *strong / fierce*

185 And with the quen wenten he

Right unto that ympe-tre.

Thai made scheltrom[1] in
ich a side   *a rank of armed men*

And sayd thai wold there abide

And dye° ther everichon,°   *die / everyone*

190 Er° the quen schuld fram° hem gon.   *before / from*

Ac yete amiddes hem ful right° *yet amidst them straightaway*

The quen was oway y-twight,°   *snatched*

With fairi° forth y-nome.°   *enchantment / taken*

Men wist never° wher sche was bicome.° *never knew / gone*

195 Tho° was ther criing, wepe and wo!   *then*

The king into his chaumber is go,°   *went*

And oft swoned° opon the ston,° *swooned / stone (i.e., floor)*

And made swiche diol° and swiche mon° *such lament / moan*

That neighe° his liif was y-spent—°   *almost / ended*

200 Ther was non amendement.°   *no remedy (for it)*

He cleped° togider his barouns,   *called*

Erls, lordes of renouns,

And when thai al y-comen were,

"Lordinges," he said, "bifor you here

205 Ich ordainy° min heighe steward[2]   *I ordain*

To wite° mi kingdom afterward;°   *rule / henceforth*

In mi stede° ben he schal   *place*

To kepe mi londes overal.

For now ichave° mi quen y-lore,°   *I have / lost*

210 The fairest levedi that ever was bore,

Never eft y nil no woman
se.°   *never again will I see another woman*

Into wildernes ichil te°   *I will go*

And live ther evermore

With wilde bestes in holtes hore;°   *woods grey*

215 And when ye understond that y be spent,°   *dead*

Make you than a parlement,

And chese° you a newe king.   *choose*

Now doth° your best with al mi thing."°   *do / affairs*

Tho was ther wepeing in the halle

220 And grete cri among hem alle;

Unnethe° might old or yong°   *hardly / young*

For wepeing speke a word with tong.

Thai kneled adoun al y-fere°   *together*

---

[1] *scheltrom* From the OE "scyld-truma," a tribal battle formation in which warriors used their shields to create a wall of defence.

[2] *steward* High court official from the nobility.

And praid° him, yif his wille were,   *prayed*
225 That he no schuld nought fram hem go.
     "Do way!"° quath he, "It schal be so!"   *enough!*
     Al his kingdom he forsoke;
     Bot° a sclavin° on him he toke.[1]   *only / pilgrim's mantle*
     He no hadde kirtel no hode,°   *had neither tunic nor hood*
230 Schert,° ne no nother gode,°   *shirt / goods*
     Bot his harp he tok algate°   *at any rate*
     And dede him barfot° out atte gate;   *passed barefoot*
     No man most° with him go.   *might*
     O way! What ther was wepe and wo,
235 When he that hadde ben king with croun
     Went so poverlich out of
          toun!°   *in such poverty out of his town*
     Thurth° wode and over heth°   *through / heath*
     Into the wildernes he geth.°   *goes*
     Nothing he fint° that him° is ays,°   *finds / for him / comfort*
240 Bot ever he liveth in gret malais.°   *distress*
     He that hadde y-werd the fowe and
          griis,°   *worn the variegated and grey fur*
     And on bed the purper biis,°   *purple linen*
     Now on hard hethe he lith,°   *lies*
     With leves and gresse he him writh.°   *covers himself*
245 He that hadde had castels and tours,
     River, forest, frith with flours,
     Now, thei it comenci° to snewe° and
          frese,°   *although it begins / snow / freeze*
     This king mot° make his bed in mese.°   *must / moss*
     He that had y-had knightes of priis
250 Bifor him kneland,° and levedis,   *kneeling*
     Now seth he nothing that him liketh,
     Bot wilde wormes° bi him striketh.°   *snakes / glide*
     He that had y-had plenté
     Of mete and drink, of ich deynté,°   *delicacy*
255 Now may he al day digge° and wrote°   *dig / grub*
     Er he finde his fille of rote.°   *roots*
     In somer he liveth bi wild frut,°   *fruit*
     And berien bot gode lite;°   *berries of little worth*
     In winter may he nothing finde
260 Bot rote, grases, and the rinde.°   *bark*

Al his bodi was oway dwine°   *away dwindled*
     For missays,° and al to-chine.°   *hardship / chapped*
     Lord! who may telle the sore°   *sorrow*
     This king sufferd ten yere and more?
265 His here° of his berd,° blac and rowe,°   *hair / beard / rough*
     To his girdel-stede° was growe.   *waist*
     His harp, whereon was al his gle,°   *pleasure*
     He hidde in an holwe° tre;   *hollow*
     And when the weder° was clere and bright,   *weather*
270 He toke his harp to him wel right
     And harped° at his owhen wille.°   *played / own desire*
     Into alle the wode the soun gan
          schille,°   *sound began to resound*
     That alle the wilde bestes that ther beth
     For joie abouten him thai teth,°   *gathered*
275 And alle the foules° that ther were   *birds*
     Come and sete° on ich a brere°   *sat / every briar*
     To here his harping a-fine—
     So miche° melody was therin;   *much*
     And when he his harping lete wold,°   *would leave off*
280 No best° bi him abide nold.°[2]   *beast / would remain*
          He might se him bisides,°   *nearby*
     Oft in hot undertides,
     The king o fairy with his rout°   *company*
     Com to hunt him al about
285 With dim cri and bloweing,°   *blowing (of horns)*
     And houndes also with him berking;°   *barking*
     Ac no best thai no nome,°   *but they took no beast (game)*
     No never he nist whider they
          bicome.°   *nor did he ever know where they went*
     And other while° he might him se   *at other times*
290 As a gret ost° bi him te,°   *army / went*
     Wele atourned,° ten hundred knightes,   *equipped*
     Ich y-armed to his rightes,°   *all properly armed*
     Of cuntenaunce° stout and fers,   *appearance*
     With mani desplaid° baners,   *unfurled*
295 And ich his swerd y-drawe hold—
     Ac never he nist whider° thai
          wold.°   *knew not whither / went*
     And otherwile he seighe° other thing: *saw*
     Knightes and levedis com daunceing

---

[1] *Al his kingdom ... he toke* Among scholars, considerable disagreement surrounds Orfeo's exile. It has been seen as an act of despair, atonement, or spiritual retreat, as part of a process of initiation for Orfeo, as an expression of the great love (or too great a love) Orfeo has for Heurodis.

[2] *He toke his harp ... abide nold* The tradition of harping as a way of "taming" the animals has roots in pre-Christian material as well as in the classical myth of Orpheus and in the Biblical story of David.

In queynt° atire, gisely,°   *elegant / skilfully*
300 Queynt pas° and softly;   *graceful steps*
Tabours and trunpes yede° hem
   bi,   *drums and trumpets went*
And al maner menstraci.°   *sorts of minstrelsy*

   And on a day° he seighe him biside   *on a certain day*
Sexti° levedis on hors ride,   *sixty*
305 Gentil and jolif as brid on ris;°   *lively as a bird on bough*
Nought o man amonges hem ther
   nis;°   *not a single man was with them*
And ich a faucoun on hond
   bere,°   *each a falcon on her hand bore*
And riden on haukin bi o° rivere.   *a-hawking by a*
Of game thai founde wel gode haunt—°   *great plenty*
310 Maulardes,° hayroun,° and
   cormeraunt;°   *mallards / heron / cormorant*
The foules of the water ariseth,
The faucouns hem wele deviseth;°   *marked*
Ich faucoun his pray slough—°   *prey killed*
That seigh Orfeo, and lough:°   *laughed*
315 "Parfay!"° quath he, "ther is fair game;   *by my faith*
Thider ichil,° bi Godes name;   *I'll go*
Ich was y-won swiche werk to se!"[1]
He aros, and thider gan te.°   *began to approach*
To a levedi he was y-come,
320 Biheld, and hath wele undernome,°   *perceived*
And seth bi al thing that it is
His owhen quen, Dam Heurodis.
Yern° he biheld hir, and sche him eke,°   *eagerly / also*
Ac noither° to other a word no speke;   *neither*
325 For messais° that sche on him seighe,   *sadness*
That° had ben so riche and so heighe,   *who*
The teres fel out of her eighe.°   *eye*
The other levedis this y-seighe
And maked hir oway to ride—
330 Sche most with him no lenger abide.
"Allas!" quath he, "now me is wo!"
Whi nil° deth now me slo?°   *will not / slay*
Allas, wreche, that y no might
Dye now after this sight!
335 Allas! to long last° mi liif,   *too long lasts*
When y no dar nought with mi wiif,
No hye° to me, o° word speke.   *nor she / one*
Allas! Whi nil min hert breke!

Parfay!" quath he, "tide wat bitide,°   *come what may*
340 Whiderso this° levedis ride,   *wherever these*
The selve° way ichil streche—°   *same / hasten*
Of liif no° deth me no reche."°   *nor / I do not care*
His sclavain he dede on also
   spac°   *pilgrim's gown he put on quickly*
And henge his harp opon his bac,
345 And had wel gode wil to gon—°   *great desire to go*
He no spard° noither stub° no ston.   *avoided / stump*
In at a roche° the levedis rideth,   *Into a rock*
And he after, and nought abideth.
When he was in the roche y-go,°   *gone*
350 Wele thre mile other mo,
He com into a fair cuntray°   *country*
As bright so sonne on somers° day,   *as sun on summer's*
Smothe and plain° and al grene—   *smooth and level*
Hille no dale nas ther non y-sene.°   *was not to be seen*
355 Amidde the lond a castel he sighe,
Riche and real° and wonder heighe.°   *royal / wondrously high*
Al the utmast wal°   *all of the outermost wall*
Was clere and schine° as cristal;   *bright*
An hundred tours ther were about,
360 Degiselich and batayld stout.[2]
The butras° com out of the diche°   *buttresses / moat*
Of rede gold y-arched riche.
The vousour° was avowed° al   *vaulting / adorned*
Of ich maner divers aumal.°   *with every kind of enamel*
365 Within ther wer wide wones,°   *spacious dwellings*
Al of precious stones;
The werst piler on to biholde
Was al of burnist° gold.   *burnished*
Al that lond was ever° light,   *always*
370 For when it schuld be therk° and night,   *dark*
The riche stones light gonne°   *stone's light shone*
As bright as doth at none° the sonne.   *noon*
No man may telle, no thenche° in thought,   *nor think*
The riche° werk that ther was wrought.°   *exquisite / made (done)*
375 Bi al thing him think° that it is   *it seems to him*
The proude court of Paradis.
In this castel the levedis alight;°   *dismounted*
He wold in after, yif° he might.   *wished to enter if*
   Orfeo knokketh atte gate;
380 The porter was redi therate
And asked what he wold hav y-do.°   *wanted (to do)*

---

[1] *Ich … se!* I was accustomed to seeing such sport!

[2] *Degiselich and bataild stout* Wonderful with strong battlements.

"Parfay!" quath he, "icham° a minstrel, lo!   *I am*
To solas° thi lord with mi gle,°   *entertain / minstrelsy*
Yif his swete wille be."
385 The porter undede° the gate anon   *undid*
And lete him into the castel gon.

Than he gan bihold about al,°   *look all around*
And seighe liggeand° within the wal   *remaining, living*
Of folk that were thider y-brought
390 And thought dede, and nare
     nought.°   *believed to be dead, but were not*
Sum stode° withouten hade,°   *stood / head*
And sum non armes nade,°   *had no arms*
And sum thurth° the bodi hadde wounde,   *through*
And sum lay wode,° y-bounde,   *mad*
395 And sum armed on hors sete,°   *sat*
And sum astrangled as thai ete;°   *they ate*
And sum were in water adreynt,°   *drowned*
And sum with fire al forschreynt.°   *shriveled*
Wives ther lay on childe bedde,
400 Sum ded and sum awedde,°   *driven mad*
And wonder fele° ther lay bisides   *wondrous many*
Right as° thai slepe her° undertides;   *just as / their*
Eche was thus in this warld y-nome,°   *taken*
With fairi thider y-come.°   *enchantment brought there*
405 Ther he seighe his owhen wiif,
Dame Heurodis, his lef liif,°   *dear life*
Slepe under an ympe-tre—
Bi her clothes he knewe that it was he.°   *she*
And when he hadde bihold this mervails
     alle,°   *all these marvels*
410 He went into the kinges halle.
Than seighe he ther a semly° sight,   *fair*
A tabernacle blisseful° and bright,   *canopy beautiful*
Therin her maister king sete
And her quen, fair and swete.
415 Her crounes, her clothes schine so bright
That unnethe° bihold he him might.   *scarcely*
When he hadde biholden al that thing,
He kneled adoun bifor the king:
"O lord," he seyd, "yif it thi wille were,
420 Mi menstraci thou schust y-here."°   *should hear*
The king answered, "What man artow,°   *are you*
That art hider y-comen now?
Ich, no non° that is with me,   *neither I, nor no one*

No sent never after the.°   *you*
425 Sethen° that ich here regni° gan,   *since / reign*
Y no fond never so folehardi° man   *foolhardy*
That hider to ous durst wende°   *to us dared come*
Bot that ic him wald ofsende."[1]
"Lord," quath he, "trowe° ful wel,   *believe*
430 Y nam bot a pover menstrel;
And, sir, it is the maner of ous
To seche mani° a lordes hous—   *seek many*
Thei° we nought welcom no be,   *although (even if)*
Yete we mot proferi° forth our gle."   *must offer*

435 Bifor the king he sat adoun
And tok his harp so miri° of soun,°   *merry / sound*
And tempreth° his harp, as he wele
     can,°   *tunes / knows well how to do*
And blisseful notes he ther gan,°   *began*
That al that in the palays were
440 Com to him forto here,°   *to listen*
And liggeth° adoun to his fete—   *lie*
Hem thenketh° his melody so swete.   *they think*
The king herkneth° and sitt ful stille;°   *listens / sits quietly*
To here his° gle he° hath gode
     wille.   *his (Orfeo's) / he (the king)*
445 Gode bourde° he hadde of his gle;°   *great pleasure / songs*
The riche quen also hadde he.°   *she*
When he hadde stint° his harping,   *stopped*
Than seyd to him the king,
"Menstrel, me liketh° wel thi gle.   *pleases me*
450 Now aske of me what it be,°   *whatever you wish*
Largelich° ichil the pay;   *generously*
Now speke, and tow might asay."°   *if you wish to find out*
"Sir," he seyd, "ich biseche the°   *beseech you*
Thatow° woldest give me   *that you*
455 That ich° levedi, bright on ble,   *same / of complexion*
That slepeth under the ympe-tre."
"Nay!" quath the king, "that nought
     nere!°   *that could never be*
A sori° couple of you it were,   *ill-matched*
For thou art lene, rowe° and blac,   *lean, rough*
460 And sche is lovesum,° withouten lac;°   *beautiful / blemish*
A lothlich° thing it were, forthi,°   *loathly / therefore*
To sen° hir in thi compayni."   *see*
"O sir!" he seyd, "gentil king,

---

1 *Bot that ... ofsende* Unless I wished him summoned.

Yete were it a wele fouler thing°   *much more disgraceful*
465 To here a lesing of° thi mouthe!   *hear a lie from*
So, sir, as ye seyd nouthe,°   *just now*
What ich wold aski,° have y
   schold,°   *wished to ask for / I should*
And nedes° thou most thi word hold."   *by necessity*
The king seyd, "Sethen it is so,
470 Take hir bi the hond and go;
Of° hir ichil thatow be
   blithe."°   *with / I wish that you be happy*
He kneled adoun and thonked him swithe.°   *quickly*
His wiif he tok bi the hond,°   *hand*
And dede° him swithe out of that lond,°   *went / land*
475 And went him out of that thede—°   *country*
Right as he come, the way he yede.°   *went*
So long he hath the way y-nome°   *taken*
To Winchester he is y-come,
That was his owhen cité;
480 Ac no man knewe that it was he.
No forther° than the tounes ende   *further*
For knoweleche no durst he wende,[1]
Bot with a begger, y-bilt ful
   narwe,°   *whose house was very small*
Ther he tok his herbarwe°   *lodging*
485 To him and to° his owhen wiif   *for himself and for*
As a minstrel of pover liif,
And asked tidinges of that lond,
And who the kingdom held in hond.
The pover begger in his cote°   *cottage*
490 Told him everich a grot:°   *every scrap*
Hou her quen was stole owy,°   *away*
Ten yer gon,° with fairy,°   *ago / by magic*
And hou her king en° exile yede,°   *into / went*
But no man nist° in wiche thede;°   *no one knew / country*
495 And how the steward the lond gan hold,
And other mani thinges him told.

Amorwe, oyain nonetide,°   *the next day, towards noon*
He maked his wiif ther abide;°   *stay there*
The beggers clothes he borwed anon
500 And heng his harp his rigge° opon,   *back*
And went him into that cité
That men might him bihold and se.

Erls and barouns bold,
Buriays° and levedis him gun bihold.   *burgesses (citizens)*
505 "Lo!" thai seyd, "swiche a man!
Hou long the here° hongeth him opan!°   *hair / upon*
Lo! Hou his berd hongeth to his kne!
He is y-clongen also° a tre!"   *gnarled like*
And, as he yede in the strete,
510 With his steward he gan mete,
And loude he° sett on him° a
   crie: *he (Orfeo) / him (the steward)*
"Sir steward!" he seyd, "merci!
Icham° an harpour of hethenisse;°   *I am / from heathendom*
Help me now in this destresse!"
515 The steward seyd, "Com with me, come;
Of that ichave,° thou schalt have some.   *what I have*
Everich gode harpour is welcom me to
For mi lordes love, Sir Orfeo."
In the castel the steward sat atte mete,°   *table*
520 And mani lording was bi him sete;
Ther were trompours° and tabourers,°   *trumpeters / drummers*
Harpours fele,° and crouders—[2]   *many*
Miche melody thai maked alle.
And Orfeo sat stille in the halle
525 And herkneth; when thai ben al stille,
He toke his harp and tempred schille;°   *tuned it loudly*
The blissefulest° notes he harped there   *most beautiful*
That ever ani man y-herd with ere—
Ich man liked wele his gle.
530 The steward biheld and gan y-se,°   *began to perceive*
And knewe the harp als blive.°   *at once*
"Menstrel!" he seyd, "so mot thou
   thrive,°   *if you wish to thrive*
Where hadestow° this harp, and hou?°   *did you get / how*
Y pray that thou me telle now."
535 "Lord," quath he, "in uncouthe° thede   *unknown*
Thurth a wildernes as y yede,
Ther y founde in a dale
With lyouns a man totorn smale,°   *torn in small pieces*
And wolves him frete° with teth so scharp.   *had devoured*
540 Bi him y fond this ich° harp;   *same*

---

[1] *For knoweleche … wende* He did not dare go lest he be recognized.

[2] *crouders* "Croud-players." The word probably derives from the Welsh "crwth," a Celtic string instrument which was played with a bow and plucked with the fingers. However, the *MED* refers to this line in *Sir Orfeo* and interprets the word as "one who plays the crowd."

Wele ten yere it is y-go."
"O!" quath the steward, "now me is wo!
That was mi lord, Sir Orfeo!
Allas, wreche, what schal y do,
545 That have swiche a lord y-lore?°   lost
A, way° that ich was y-bore!   O, woe
That him° was so hard grace
   y-yarked,°   to him / bitter fortune allotted
And so vile deth y-marked!"°   (a) death was ordained
Adoun he fel aswon° to grounde;   in a faint
550 His barouns him tok up in that stounde°   moment
And telleth him how it° geth—   it (the world)
"It is no bot of mannes
   deth!"   there is no remedy for man's death!
   King Orfeo knewe wele bi than
His steward was a trewe man
555 And loved him as he aught to do,
And stont up, and seyt thus, "Lo,
Steward, herkne now this thing:
Yif ich were Orfeo the king,
And hadde y-suffred ful yore°   very long ago
560 In wildernisse miche sore,°   much sorrow
And hadde ywon mi quen o-wy
Out of the lond of fairy,
And hadde y-brought the levedi hende°   gracious
Right here to the tounes ende,
565 And with a begger her in y-nome,°   had placed her
And were mi-self hider y-come
Poverlich to the, thus stille,
For to asay° thi gode wille,   test
And ich founde the thus trewe,
570 Thou no schust it never rewe.°   should never regret it
Sikerlich,° for love or ay,°   surely / fear
Thou schust° be king after mi day;   should
And yif° thou of mi deth hadest ben
   blithe,°   but if / happy

Thou schust have voided, also
   swithe."°   been banished immediately
575 Tho all tho° that therin sete   then all those
That it was King Orfeo underyete,   recognized that it was
And the steward him wele knewe—
Over and over the bord he threwe,°   overturned the table
And fel adoun to his° fet;   his (Sir Orfeo)
580 So dede everich lord that ther sete,
And all thai seyd at o criing:°   in one cry
"Ye beth our lord, sir, and our king!"
Glad thai were of his live;°   life
To chaumber thai ladde him als belive°   led him immediately
585 And bathed him and schaved his berd,
And tired° him as a king apert;°   clothed / openly
And sethen,° with gret processioun,   afterwards
Thai brought the quen into the toun
With al maner menstraci—
590 Lord! ther was grete melody!
For joie thai wepe with her eighe
That hem so sounde y-comen seighe.
Now King Orfeo newe coround° is,   newly crowned
And his quen, Dame Heurodis,
595 And lived long afterward,
And sethen° was king the steward.   and after that
Harpours in Bretaine after than
Herd hou this mervaile bigan,
And made herof° a lay of gode
   likeing,°   made of it / great delight
600 And nempned° it after the king.   named
That lay "Orfeo" is y-hote;°   called
Gode is the lay, swete is the note.
Thus com Sir Orfeo out of his care:°   sorrow
God graunt ous alle wele to fare! Amen!

Explicit.°   the end
—C. 1325

The Auchinleck Manuscript (National Library of Scotland, Advocates' MS. 19.2.1), fol. 302r, the last 26 lines of the first column (lines 417–34).

THE MABINOGI

The group of tales that are known as *The Mabinogi* form the core of the earliest known major collection of Welsh literature. They provide a unique window into the world of pre-literate Celtic culture that came to assume a vital role in the literature of England as well as that of Scotland, Ireland, and Wales. (Indeed, they connect in various ways with several of the major works of Middle English literature—from *Sir Gawain and the Green Knight* to Malory's Arthurian romances.) But *The Mabinogi* are also remarkable works in themselves—remarkable in the richness of the quasi-mythical world they evoke, in the intensely human conflicts and dilemmas they present, and in the sheer narrative interest of their story material.

The written form of these tales dates from the early fourteenth century; the manuscript referred to as the *White Book of Rhydderch*, which provides a near-complete manuscript of the four tales known as *The Mabinogi*, together with seven other early Welsh tales, dates from c. 1325. But it has generally been concluded (from both internal and external evidence) that the tales were in all likelihood shaped through several centuries of oral transmission before this. An early twelfth-century manuscript includes fragments of the tales, and some linguistic and cultural evidence suggests that they may well have existed in something resembling their present form in the eleventh and twelfth centuries.

By the period 1000–1250, the Celtic peoples, who in pre-Roman times had populated a good deal of what is now England, had been driven first by the Romans and later by the Anglo-Saxons into the further reaches of the British Isles: Wales, Scotland, and Ireland. Though the language and culture of the people developed various individual characteristics in each of these areas, they also retained a recognizably Celtic character. Free-spirited and tempestuous, colorful, as fond of storytelling as of feasting and of other physical pleasures, yet deeply imbued with a sense of the supernatural world—in such terms have the Celtic peoples often been characterized, by themselves as often as by outsiders, and the appeal of these tales has doubtless rested in no small part on the degree to which they convey that spirit in vivid and elemental fashion. Just as much, though, the appeal of the tales is rooted in a narrative strength that partakes of myth, folklore and history.

Many parallels to these stories exist in early Irish literature (as, for example, in the *Fled Bricrend* tale that was a key source for the Gawain poet): ritualized competitions between two noblemen to win the hand of a lady; ritualized missions or "errands," always involving some request; battles in which the combatants are pledged to return to the same place in exactly a year's time; elaborate tricks in which the participants make similar arrangements; repeated chains of events in which the supernatural figures prominently. As well, in the versions that have come down to us the Welsh tales seem to be touched by something of the chivalric spirit. The Welsh language did not import new words to denote such concepts as "knight" and "armor" (instead adapting exiting vocabulary to serve additional purposes or take on new connotations), and it is thus difficult to speak with any certainty of the extent to which the chivalric world permeates the world of *The Mabinogi*. In the other direction, however, we do know that Malory and other writers of Middle English romance borrowed here and there from the old Welsh tales; Malory, for example, borrows the names of Bedivere and Guinevere, and the Gawain poet evidently drew on the story of Pwyll being tempted by the availability of Arrawn's wife during the year in which he and Arrawn assumed each other's appearance.

"Pwyll Lord of Dyved" is the first of a group of four tales with which all manuscript versions of the early Welsh tales open; each of these four ends with a close variant of the expression "So ends this part [or "branch"] of the mabinogi [or "tale"]." Like other tales in the group, "Pwyll Lord of Dyved" includes several more or less self-contained narratives. The four are generally thought to display a sufficient degree of structural and thematic affinity so as to justify the supposition that one individual was involved in shaping the written form we now know. The other seven tales included in the early manuscripts are more diverse, and for the most part less clear in their narrative structure. (Charlotte Guest, who in the nineteenth century was instrumental in introducing the tales to the English-speaking world, applied a word she invented, "Mabinogion," to the entire collection of eleven tales, and since then they have continued to be referred to most frequently in that way.)

Even in a tale such as "Pwyll Lord of Dyved" there are numerous loose ends and inconsistencies—especially in the last of the three narratives that comprise the tale. Why and by whom is the baby abducted? Why is he abandoned with Teirnyon? What significance do the horses have? Why is the boy given away almost as soon as he has been returned to Pwyll and Rhiannon? None of this is made clear. It has been suggested that the presence of this sort of narrative inconsistency in even the most tightly structured of the tales is an indication of the degree to which they represent a long process of oral transmission in which elements of story material may be altered, combined and recombined many times over. Unquestionably the stories of *The Mabinogi* are often inconsistent, and often seem incomplete. Yet they continue to convey a mythic and narrative resonance; the tales continue to hold for readers a fascination that is at least as much literary as it is anthropological.

⌘⌘

Pwyll,[1] Prince of Dyfed

Pwyll,[2] Prince of Dyfed, was lord of the seven cantrefs[3] of Dyfed. Once upon a time he was at Arberth, his chief court, and he was seized by the desire to go hunting. The part of his dominions in which he wished to hunt was Glyn Cuch, so he set forth from Arberth that night, and went as far as Llwyn Diarwyd. And that night he stayed there, and early the next day he rose and came to Glyn Cuch; there he let loose the dogs in the wood, and sounded the horn, and began the chase. And as he followed the dogs, he lost his companions, and while he listened to the hounds, he heard the cry of other hounds, a different cry, and coming from the opposite direction.

Pwyll beheld a glade in the wood forming a level plain, and as his dogs came to the edge of the glade he saw a stag in front of the other dogs. As it reached the middle of the glade, the dogs that had been following it overtook it and brought it down. Then he looked at the color of the dogs (not paying any attention to the stag); of all the hounds that he had seen in the world, he had never seen any like these. Their hair was of a brilliant shining white, and their ears were red, and as the whiteness of their bodies shone, so did the redness of their ears glisten. And he came towards the dogs, and drove away those that had brought down the stag, and set his own dogs upon the dying animal.

As he was urging on his dogs he saw a horseman coming towards him, upon a large light-gray steed, with a hunting horn around his neck, and clad in garments of gray woolen in the fashion of a hunter. The horseman drew near and spoke to him. "Chieftain," said he, "I know who you are, and I refuse to greet you."

"Perhaps," said Pwyll, "you are of such high position that you feel it would be inappropriate to do so."

"God knows," answered he, "it is not my dignity that prevents me."

"What is it then, chieftain?" asked Pwyll.

"By heaven, it is by reason of your own rudeness and want of courtesy."

"What discourtesy, chieftain, have you seen in me?"

"Greater discourtesy I have never seen," said he, "than to drive away the dogs that were killing the stag, and to set your dogs upon it. This was discourteous, and though I will not take revenge upon you, yet I declare to heaven that I will claim dishonor on you to the value of one hundred stags."

---

[1] *Pwyll, Prince of Dyfed* The present text, prepared for *The Broadview Anthology of British Literature*, is based very largely upon the English translation of Charlotte Guest. Certain passages referring to expressions of sexuality that were omitted from the Guest translation are here restored, and the text has been substantially modernized. Certain spellings have also been returned to their usual Welsh form.

[2] *Pwyll* Welsh: good sense, judgment.

[3] *cantrefs* Districts each containing a hundred townships.

"Chieftain," Pwyll replied, "if I have done wrong I will win your friendship."

"How will you do that?"

"According to your rank—but who are you?"

"A crowned king am I in the land from which I have come."

"Lord," said Pwyll, "may the day prosper with you. And from what land do you come?"

"From Annwn," he answered: "Arawn, King of Annwn, am I."

"Lord," said Pwyll, "how may I gain your friendship?"

"In this way," he said. "There is a man whose dominions border directly on mine, and who is always making war against me. His name is Hafgan, and he too is a king of Annwn. By ridding me of this oppression, which you can easily do, you shall gain my friendship."

"Gladly will I do this," said Pwyll. "Show me how I may."

"I will show you. I will make a firm friendship with you, and I will do the following. I will send you to Annwn in my place, and I will give you the fairest lady you ever beheld as your companion, and I will put my form and appearance upon you, so that not a page of the chamber, nor the steward, nor any other man that has followed me shall know that you are not I. This shall be for the space of a year from tomorrow, and then we will meet in this place."

"Yes," said Pwyll, "but when I have been there for a space of a year, how shall I recognize the man you are speaking of?"

"One year from this night," he answered, "it has already been arranged that he and I will meet at the ford; assume my appearance and take my place there, and with one stroke that you give him, he shall no longer live. And if he asks you to give him another, do not do so, no matter how much he may entreat you. For when I did so, he fought with me the next day as well as he had ever done before."

"Very well," said Pwyll, "but what shall I do concerning my kingdom if I must be away from it for a twelvemonth?"

Arawn said, "I will make sure that no one in your dominions, neither man nor woman, will know that I am not you; I will take on your appearance, and act in your place."

"Gladly then," said Pwyll, "I will set forward."

"Your path shall be clear, and nothing will detain you until you come into my dominions, and I myself will be your guide."

So Arawn conducted Pwyll until he came in sight of the court and its dwellings. "The court and the kingdom," he said, "are now in your power. Enter the court; there is no one there who will know you, and when you observe how things are done there, you will know the customs of the court."

So Pwyll went forward to the court, and when he came there he beheld sleeping rooms, and halls, and chambers—the most beautiful buildings ever seen. He went into the hall to change, and youths and pages came to dress him, and all as they entered saluted him. Two knights came and removed his hunting dress, and clothed him in a vesture of silk and gold. The hall was prepared, and behold he saw the household and the troops come in, the most refined and noble troops that he had ever seen. With them came the queen, who was the fairest woman he had ever yet beheld; she had on a yellow robe of silk and gold. They washed and went to the table and sat down, the queen upon one side of him, and one who seemed to be an earl on the other side.

Pwyll began to speak with the queen, and he thought from her speech that she was the most gracious, lively, and most noble lady he had ever spoken with. And they partook of food and drink, and there were songs and celebrations. Of all the courts upon the earth, this was the best supplied with food and drink, all served in vessels of gold, decorated with royal jewels.

When the time came for them to go to bed, Pwyll and the queen retired. As soon as they got into the bed, he turned away from her, and from then until the next day he did not speak a word to her. The next day they spoke affectionately to each other, but however tender they were to each other during the day, each night was like the first.

Pwyll spent the year before the night that had been fixed for the conflict in hunting, feasting, singing, dancing, and enjoying himself with his companions. When that night finally came, it was remembered even by those who lived in the most distant parts of his dominions. He went to the meeting, and the nobles of the kingdom went with him. When he came to the ford, a knight rode up to him and spoke. "Good men," he said, "listen well. It is between two kings that this meeting is, and between them only. Each has made a claim on the other's land and territory; all of you must stand aside and leave the fight to be between them."

Thereupon the two kings approached each other in the middle of the ford, and prepared to do battle. And from first thrust, the man who was taking the place of Arawn struck Hafgan on the centre of the boss of his shield, so that it was split in two, and his armor was broken, and Hafgan himself was thrown to the ground an arm's and a spear's length over the back of his horse, and he received a deadly blow. "Oh chieftain," said Hafgan, "what right have you to cause my death? I was doing you no harm, and I know not why you would slay me. But, for the love of heaven, since you have begun to slay me, finish the job."

"Ah, chieftain," he replied, "I may yet repent this, but, whoever else may slay you now, I will not do so."

"My trusted lords," said Hafgan, "take me away from here. My death has come. I shall not be able to uphold you any longer."

"My nobles," said the one who was in Arawn's place, "take counsel and know who ought to be my subjects."

"Lord," they said, "all should be your subjects, for there is no king ruling over the whole of Annwn but you."

"Agreed," he replied. "It is right that he who comes humbly should be received graciously—but he that does not come with obedience shall be compelled by the force of swords."

Thereupon he received the homage of the men, and he began to conquer the country, and the next day by noon the two kingdoms were in his power. And thereupon he went to keep his tryst, and came to Glyn Cuch. When he came there, the king of Annwn was there to meet him; the two rejoiced to see each other. "Truly," said Arawn, "may heaven reward you for your friendship towards me; I have heard what you have done."

"When you return to your own land," said Pwyll, "you will see what I have done for you."

"Whatever you have done for me," said Arawn, "may heaven repay you for it."

Then Arawn gave back to Pwyll Prince of Dyfed his proper form and semblance, and he himself resumed his own form and semblance, and Arawn set forth towards the court of Annwn. He rejoiced when he beheld his troops and his household, whom he had not seen for so long—but they had not known of his absence, and wondered no more at his coming than they would have on any other day. That day was spent on joy and merriment as Arawn sat and conversed with his wife and his nobles. And when it was time for them to go to bed rather than carouse, they retired.

Arawn's wife then came to him in bed, and he spoke to her and they joined each other in love and pleasure. It had been a year since she had been treated in this way, and for a long time she thought to herself, "How he differs now from what he had been!" Eventually he awoke and spoke to her—once, twice, three times—but she provided no answer. "Why do you not reply?" he asked her. To which she replied, "For one year now I have said nothing in this place."

"What can you mean?" asked her husband. "We always talk in bed."

"For the past year this bed has seen no words and no pleasure between us, or even you turning your face towards me, let alone anything else that might have happened." And Arawn thought for a moment and then said, "Oh God, how faithful is this one I have taken for a friend!" To his wife he said, "My lady, I am not to blame, for I have not been with you or slept beside you for the space of one full year." He then told her all that had happened, and she said, "To God I declare it: the bond between you and your friend must have been strong for him to resist temptation and remain loyal to you."

"My lady, such were my own thoughts when I was silent." "No wonder," she replied. Meanwhile, Pwyll Prince of Dyfed had come to his country and dominions, and had begun to ask the nobles of the land how his rule had been during the previous year, compared with what it had been before. "Lord," they said, "your wisdom was never so great, and you were never so kind or so free in bestowing gifts, and justice was never more seen than it has been in this past year."

"By heaven," said Pwyll, "for all the good you have enjoyed, you should thank the one who has been with you; thus has this matter been." Thereupon Pwyll related everything to them.

"Truly, lord," they said, "let us give thanks unto heaven that you have such a friendship. We ask you not to withhold from us a continuation of the sort of rule that we have enjoyed for the past year."

"I take heaven as my witness that I will not withhold it," answered Pwyll. And thenceforth Arawn and Pwyll made strong the friendship that was between them, and each sent unto the other horses, and greyhounds, and hawks, and such jewels as they thought would be pleasing to each other. And by reason of having lived a year in Annwn, and having ruled there so prosperously and united the two kingdoms in one day by his valor and prowess, Pwyll lost the name Pwyll Prince of Dyfed and was called Pwyll Head of Annwn from that time forward.

One day Pwyll was at Arberth, his chief court, where a feast had been prepared for him, and with him was a great host of men. And after the first part of the feast Pwyll arose to walk, and he went to the top of a mound that was above the court, and was called Gorsedd Arberth.

"My lord," said one of the court, "it is peculiar to the mound that whatever nobly born man sits upon it cannot leave without either receiving wounding blows, or else seeing a wonder."

"I fear not to receive wounding blows in the midst of such a host as this," said Pwyll, "but as to the wonder, gladly would I see it. I will therefore go and sit upon the mound."

And upon the mound he sat. And while he sat there, they all saw a lady on a great white horse, with a garment of shining gold around her, coming along the road that led past the mound. And the horse seemed to move at a slow and even pace, and to be coming up towards the mound. "Men," asked Pwyll, "is there any among you who knows that lady on horseback?"

"There is not, my lord," said they.

"One of you go and meet her," Pwyll commanded, "so that we may know who she is." One of the men arose, and as he came upon the road to meet her, she passed by. He followed as fast as he could on foot, but the more he increased his speed, the further she was from him. And when he saw that it was no use to follow her, he returned to Pwyll and said to him, "Lord, it is useless for anyone in the world to follow her on foot."

"In that case," said Pwyll, "go unto the court, and take the fleetest horse that you see, and go after her."

The man to whom Pwyll had spoken took the horse and went forward as he had been told. And he came to an open level plain, and put spurs to his horse; and the more he urged on his horse, the further was the mysterious lady in front of him. Yet she held the same pace as she had at first. His horse began to fail, and when his horse's feet failed him, he returned to the place where Pwyll was. "My lord," said he, "it will be useless for anyone to follow yonder lady. I know of no horse in these realms swifter than this one, and it was no help to me as I tried to pursue her."

"Of a truth," said Pwyll, "there must be some illusion here. Let us go towards the court." So to the court they went, and they spent that night there. And the next day they arose, and that day also they spent at court until it was time to go to meat.

And after the first part of the feast Pwyll began to speak. "Of a truth," said Pwyll, "we will go to the same place as yesterday, to the top of the mound. And you," he commanded one of his young men, "take the swiftest horse that you know in the field." And this the young man did. They went towards the mound, taking the horse with them. And as they were sitting down they beheld the lady on the same horse as she had ridden before, and in the same clothing, coming along the same road. "Behold," said Pwyll, "here is the lady of yesterday on horseback. Make ready, young man, to learn who she is."

"My lord," said he, "that I will gladly do." And thereupon the lady on horseback came alongside them. So the youth mounted his horse; and before he had settled himself in the saddle, she passed by, and there was a clear space between them. But her speed was no greater than it had been the day before. Then he put his horse into a trot, and thought that, despite the gentle pace at which his horse went, he would soon overtake her. But he was proved wrong, so he broke into a gallop. And still he came no nearer to her than if he had been on foot. The more he urged on his horse, the further she was from him. Yet she did not ride faster than before. When he saw that it was useless to follow her, he returned to where Pwyll was. "Lord," said he, "the horse can do no more than you have seen."

"I see indeed that it is useless for anyone to try and follow her," said Pwyll. "By heaven," he said, "she must have a message for someone on this plain if only she were willing to give it! Let us go back to the court." And to court they went, and they spent that night in songs and in feasting, as it pleased them.

And the next day they amused themselves until it was time to go to meat. When the feasting was ended Pwyll said, "Where are the troops that went with me yesterday and the day before to the top of the mound?"

"Lord, we are here," said they.

"Let us go," he said, "to the mound, to sit there. And you," said he to the page who tended his horse, "saddle my horse and hasten with him to the road, and bring my spurs with you." And the youth did this.

They went and sat upon the mound, and they had been there only a short time before they saw the lady on horseback coming by the same road, and in the same clothing, and at the same pace. "Young man," said Pwyll, "I see the lady on horseback coming; give me my horse!" No sooner had he mounted his horse than she passed. And he turned after her and followed her. And he let his horse go bounding energetically, and thought that at the second step or the third he would catch up with her. But he came no nearer to her than at first. Then he urged his horse to its utmost speed, and still he found that it brought him no closer. Then Pwyll said, "Oh maiden, for the sake of the one whom you love best, wait for me."

"I will do so gladly," said she. "It would have been better for your horse if you had asked this of me much earlier." So the maiden stopped, and she threw back that part of her headdress that covered her face, and fixed her eyes upon him, and began to talk with him.

"Lady," he asked, "where do you come from, and where do you journey to?"

"I travel on my own errand," said she, "and very glad I am to see you."

"And I am glad to see you," said he. Already he was beginning to think that the beauty of all the women and girls he had ever seen was as nothing compared to her beauty. "Lady," he said, "will you tell me anything concerning your purpose?"

"Between myself and God, I will," said she. "My chief quest was to seek you out."

"By heaven," said Pwyll, "that is to me the most pleasing quest on which you could have come. Will you tell me who you are?"

"I will tell you, lord," said she. "I am Rhiannon,[1] the daughter of Hefeydd Hên. They sought to give me to a husband against my will, but no husband would I have, and that because of my love for you. Nor will I yet have one now, unless you reject me. Hither have I come to hear your answer."

"By heaven," said Pwyll, "this is my answer: if I could choose from all the women and girls in the world, you are the one I would choose."

"Truly," said she, "if you mean what you say, make a pledge to meet me before I am given to another."

"The sooner I may do so, the more pleasing it will be to me," said Pwyll. "Wherever you wish, there will I meet you."

"Then meet me on this day a year from now at the court of Hefeydd Hên. I will cause a feast to be prepared, and it will be ready for your arrival."

"Gladly," said he, "will I keep this tryst."

"My lord," said she, "remain in health, and remember to keep your promise. Now I will go from here." So they parted, and he went back to his troops and the people of his household, and whenever they asked him questions about the damsel, he always turned the talk to other matters.

When a year had passed, he caused one hundred knights to equip themselves and to go with him to the court of Hefeydd Hên. And he came to the court, and there was great joy concerning him; there had been vast preparations for his coming, and the people milled about amongst great rejoicing. And the whole court was placed under his command.

The hall was decorated, and they sat down to dinner. Hefeydd Hên was on one side of Pwyll, and Rhiannon on the other, and all the rest according to their rank. And they ate and feasted and talked one with another, and at the beginning of the carousing after the meal there entered a tall auburn-haired youth of royal bearing, clothed in a garment of satin brocaded silk. When he came to the hall, he saluted Pwyll and his companions.

"The greeting of heaven be unto you," said Pwyll,

---

[1] *Rhiannon* The character of Rhiannon appears in several of the early Welsh tales; like Arawn, she is always portrayed as a being who is to a greater or lesser degree otherworldly, and is possessed of magical powers. She is particularly associated with the horse-goddess Epona.

"come and sit down."

"No," said he, "I come with a request, and I will do my errand."

"Do so freely," said Pwyll.

"My lord," said the stranger, "my errand is with you; it is to make a request of you that I have come."

"Whatever favour you ask of me," said Pwyll, "so far as I am able to grant it, it shall be yours."

"Ah!" said Rhiannon, "why ever did you give that answer?"

"Has he not said this in the presence of all these nobles?" asked the young stranger.

"Sir," said Pwyll, "tell me what is the favor you request."

"The lady I love best is to sleep with you this night; I have come to ask you for her to be given to me with this wedding feast."

And Pwyll sat for a long time in silence because of the answer he had given. "You may well be silent," said Rhiannon. "Never did a man make worse use of his wits than you have just done."

"My lady," said Pwyll to her, "I did not know who he was, or what he would ask for."

"He is the man to whom they would have given me against my will," said she. "He is Gwawl the son of Clud, a man of great power and wealth. Now you have given him your word, and you are obliged to bestow me upon him, or shame will befall you."

"My lady," said he, "I do not understand your answer. Never can I do as you say."

"Bestow me upon him," said Rhiannon, "and I will make sure that I shall never be his."

"How can you make that happen?" asked Pwyll.

"In your hand I will place a small bag," she said. "See that you keep it well. He has asked you for this banquet, but the preparations for it are not in your power to give. For the knights and the rest of the household I prepared this feast—such will be your answer respecting this. And as for myself, I will agree to sleep with him on this night in a year's time. At the end of the year, return here," said she, "and bring this bag with you, and let your one hundred knights be in the orchard over there. And when he is in the midst of joy and feasting, come in by yourself, clad in ragged clothes, and holding your bag in your hand. Ask nothing but a bag full of food, and I will so arrange things that if all the meat and drink in these seven cantrefs were put into the bag, it would be no fuller than before. And after a great deal has been put in the bag, he will ask you whether your bag will ever be full. Say then that it never will, until a man of noble birth and of great wealth shall arrive and shall press down on everything that is in the bag with both his feet, saying, 'Enough has now been put herein'; and I will cause him to go and press down on the food in the bag. When he does so, you must turn the bag so that he is in over his head, and then you must tie a knot with the thongs of the bag. Make sure you have a good horn around your neck, and as soon as you have bound him in the bag, put wind in your horn, and let that be a signal between you and your knights. When they hear the sound of the horn, let them come down upon the court."

The two had been talking quietly between themselves; now Gwawl spoke up, saying to Pwyll, "My lord, I must have an answer to my request."

"As much of what you have asked for as it is in my power to give, you shall have," replied Pwyll.

"My lord," added Rhiannon to Gwawl, "as for the feast and the banquet that are laid out here, I have bestowed them upon the men of Dyfed, and the household and the warriors that are with us. These things I cannot allow to be given to any others. But in a year from tonight a banquet shall be prepared for you in this court when you sleep with me."

So Gwawl went forth to his lands, and Pwyll went back to Dyfed. In their own lands they both spent that year, and at the end of the twelvemonth it was time for the feast at the court of Hefeydd Hên. Then Gwawl the son of Clud set out to the feast that had been prepared for him, and he came to the court, and he was received there with rejoicing. Pwyll head of Annwn came to the orchard with his one hundred knights, as Rhiannon had commanded him, and he had brought the bag with him. And Pwyll was clad in coarse and ragged clothes, and wore large clumsy old shoes upon his feet. When he knew that the carousing after the meal had begun, he went towards the hall, and when he came into the hall he saluted Gwawl the son of Clud, and his company, both men and women.

"Heaven prosper you," said Gwawl, "and the greeting of heaven be unto you."

"My lord," said Pwyll, "may heaven reward you! I

have an errand with you."

"Welcome to you and to your errand; if you ask of me something which is just, you shall be granted what you wish."

"That is only fair," answered Pwyll. "I ask only from need; the favor that I ask is to have this small bag that you see filled with meat and drink."

"This is a reasonable request," said Gwawl, "and gladly shall I grant it. Bring him food." A great number of attendants arose and began to fill the bag, but no matter how much they put into it, it was no fuller than at first. "Friend," said Gwawl, "will your bag ever be full?"

"It will not, I declare to heaven," said Pwyll, "unless one who is possessed of land and many valuables shall arise and tread down with both his feet the food that is within the bag and shall say, 'Enough has been put herein.'"

Then Rhiannon said to Gwawl the son of Clud, "rise up quickly."

"I will willingly arise," said Gwawl. So he rose up and put his two feet into the bag. And Pwyll turned up the sides of the bag, so that Gwawl was over his head in it. And Pwyll shut it up quickly and slipped a knot upon the thongs, and blew his horn. And behold, thereupon his household came down upon the court. And they seized all the host that had come with Gwawl, and took each one prisoner. And Pwyll threw off his rags, and his old shoes, and his tattered clothes; and as they came in, every one of Pwyll's knights struck a blow upon the bag, and asked, "What is here?"

"A badger," another would say. And in this manner they played, each of them striking the bag, either with his foot or with a staff. And thus they played with the bag. Everyone as he came in asked, "What game are you playing at?"

"The game of badger in the bag," he would be told. And then was the game of badger-in-the-bag first played.

"Lord," said the man in the bag, "if you would only listen to me! I do not deserve to be slain in a bag."

Then said Hefeydd Hên, "My lord, he speaks truth. It is fitting that you listen to him; he does not deserve this death."

"Truly," said Pwyll to Rhiannon and Hefeydd, "I will take your advice concerning him."

"My lord, this then is my counsel," said Rhiannon to Pwyll. "You are now in a position in which it behooves you to satisfy petitioners and minstrels; let Gwawl give unto them in your place, and take a pledge from him that he will never seek to avenge what has been done to him. This will be punishment enough."

"I will do this gladly," said Gwawl from within the bag.

"And gladly will I accept your assurance," said Pwyll, "if this is what Hefeydd Hên and Rhiannon counsel me to do."

"Such is our counsel," they answered.

"I accept it," said Pwyll. "But surely we should demand some bond to guarantee his good behavior."

"We will answer for him," said Hefeydd, "until his men are free to do so." And upon this Gwawl was let out of the bag and his liegemen were also freed. "Let us now demand of Gwawl his bond," said Hefeydd. "We know what should be taken from him." And Hefeydd listed the sureties. Said Gwawl, "You may draw up the agreement yourself."

"It will be enough that all shall be as Rhiannon said," answered Pwyll. So on those terms were the sureties pledged.

"Truly, my lord," said Gwawl, "I am greatly hurt, and I have many wounds. I am in need of healing; with your permission I will now go forth. I will leave nobles in my place to answer for me in everything that you require."

"Willingly," said Pwyll, "will we allow you to do this." So Gwawl went off towards his own lands.

The hall was then set in order for Pwyll and the men of his company, and also for the people of the court, and they went to the tables and sat down; as they had sat at the same time twelve months earlier, so they sat that night. And they ate, and feasted, and spent the night in mirth and tranquillity. And the time came that they should retire, and Pwyll and Rhiannon went to their chamber, and for them the night was a time of pleasure and delight.

Next morning at the break of day Rhiannon said, "My lord, arise and begin to give your gifts to the minstrels. Refuse no one today that may ask you to be generous."

"Gladly shall it be done," said Pwyll, "both today and every day while this feast shall last." So Pwyll arose, and he caused silence to be proclaimed, and he instructed all the petitioners and the minstrels to show and to point out what gifts they desired. This being done, the feast went on, and he denied no one while it lasted. And when the feast was ended, Pwyll said unto Hefeydd, "My lord, with your permission, I will set out for Dyfed tomorrow."

"Certainly," said Hefeydd. "May heaven help you to prosper. Fix also a time when Rhiannon may follow you."

"By heaven," said Pwyll, "we will leave here together."

"Is that your will, my lord?" said Hefeydd.

"Yes, by heaven," answered Pwyll.

The next day they set out for Dyfed, and journeyed to the court of Arberth, where a feast was made ready for them. And there came to them great numbers of the most important men and most noble ladies of the land, and of these there was none to whom Rhiannon did not give some rich gift, either a bracelet, a ring or a precious stone. And Pwyll and Rhiannon ruled the land prosperously both that year and the next.

In the third year the nobles of the land began to be sorrowful at seeing a man whom they loved so much, and who was their lord and their foster-brother, without an heir, and they came to him. The place where they met was Preseleu, in Dyfed. "Lord," said they, "we know that you are not so young as some of the men in this country, and we fear that you may not be provided with an heir by the wife you have taken. Take therefore another wife–one by whom you may have heirs. You cannot always remain with us, and though you desire things to stay as they are, we do not wish to stand idly by."

"Truly," said Pwyll, "Rhiannon and I have not long been joined together, and many things may yet happen. Grant me a year from this time; for the space of twelve months the two of us will remain together and after that I will abide by your wishes if nothing has changed." So they agreed. And before the end of a year a son was born unto Pwyll, and in Arberth was he born. On the night that he was born, women were brought to watch the mother and the boy. And the women slept, as did also Rhiannon and her son. And the number of the women that were brought into the chamber was six. They

watched for a good portion of the night, and then before midnight every one of them fell asleep. Towards break of day they awoke, and when they awoke they looked to where they had put the boy, and behold, he was not there. "Oh," said one of the women, "the boy is lost!"

"Yes," said another, "and we will be lucky if we are merely burnt to death for losing him!"

"Is there any counsel for us in the world in this matter?" asked another of the women.

"There is," answered another, "I offer you good counsel."

"What is that?" all the others asked.

"There is a deer-hound nearby, and she has a litter of puppies. Let us kill some one of them and rub the blood on the face and the hands of Rhiannon as she sleeps, and lay the bones before her, and say when she wakes that she herself has killed her son; she alone will not be able to go against the word of all six of us." According to this counsel it was settled.

Towards morning Rhiannon awoke, and she said, "Women, where is my son?"

"Lady," they said, "do not ask us about your son. We are still nursing the blows and the bruises we got while struggling with you; truly we never saw any woman so violent as you were. It was of no use to struggle with you. Did you not yourself destroy your own son? Do not therefore ask us for him."

"Oh wretched creatures!" said Rhiannon, "for the sake of the Lord God who knows all things, do not bring false charges against me. God, who knows all things, knows that this accusation is not true. If you are telling me this because you are afraid, I swear before heaven I will protect you."

"Truly," they said, "we would not bring evil on ourselves for anyone in the world."

"Oh wretched creatures," said Rhiannon, "you will receive no evil by telling the truth." But for all her words, whether kind or harsh, Rhiannon received the same answer from the women.

And Pwyll the head of Annwn arose, and so did his knights and those in his household. The death of the child could not be concealed, but the story went forth throughout the land, and all the nobles heard it. And the nobles came to Pwyll, and beseeched him to send his wife away for the great crime that she had done. Pwyll answered them, saying that they had put forward no reason to blame his wife other than her having had no children. "There was no reason given to put aside my wife except that she was childless. But a child she now has had, and therefore I will not send her away. If she has done any wrong, let her do penance for it."

So Rhiannon sent for the teachers and the wise men, and, since she preferred doing penance to contending with the women, she took upon herself a penance. The penance that was imposed upon her was this: that she should remain in that court of Arberth until the end of seven years, and that she should sit every day near a horse-block that was outside the gate. She had to relate the story to all who should come there whom she might suppose not to know it already, and she should make the offer to all guests and strangers, that if they would permit her to do so, she would carry them upon her back to the court. But it rarely happened that any would permit this. And thus did she spend the next part of the year.

Now at that time, Teyrnon Twryf Lliant was lord of Gwent-Ys-Coed, and he was the best man in the world. And unto his house belonged a mare more beautiful than any other horse in the kingdom. And on the night of the first of May[1] every year she foaled, and no one knew what became of the foals. And one night Teyrnon said to his wife, "Wife, we are fools that our mare should foal every year, and that we never have any of her colts."

"What can be done in the matter?" she asked.

"This is the night of the first of May," said he. "The vengeance of heaven be upon me if I am not able to learn what misfortune it is that takes away the colts." So he caused the mare to be brought into a house, and he armed himself, and that night he began to watch. And in the beginning of the night the mare gave birth to a large and beautiful colt, and it stood up in that place. And Teyrnon got up and looked at the size of the colt, and as he did so he heard a great commotion. And behold, after the commotion an arm ending in a claw came through the window into the house, and it seized the colt by the mane. Then Teyrnon drew his sword, and struck off the arm at the elbow, so that a portion of

the arm, together with the colt, remained in the house with him, and then did he hear a tumult and wailing, both at once. And he went out of the door in the direction of the noise, and he could not see the cause of the tumult because of the darkness of the night, but he rushed after it, following the noise. Then he remembered that he had left the door open and he returned. And behold, at the door there was an infant boy in swaddling clothes, wrapped in a mantle of brocaded silk. And Teyrnon took up the boy, and beheld that he was very strong for such a small baby.

Then he shut the door, and went into the chamber where his wife was. "My lady," he said, "are you sleeping?"

"No, my lord," said she. "I was asleep, but as you came in I did awake."

"Behold, here is a child for you if you will take him," said Teyrnon, "since you have never had one."

"My lord," said she, "what adventure has led to this?"

"It happened in this way," said Teyrnon, and he told her how it all had befallen.

"Truly, lord," said she, "what sort of garments are there upon the child?"

"A mantle of brocaded silk," said he.

"He is then a boy of noble birth," she replied. "My lord," she said, "if you will permit it, I should like to play a trick that will bring us great comfort and pleasure. I would like to get the support of my women, and say that I had been pregnant."

"I will readily let you do this," he answered. And so they did, and they caused the boy to be baptized with the ceremony that they used in that time, and the name which they gave to him was Gwri Wallt Euryn, because what hair was on his head was as yellow as gold.[2] And they had the boy raised in the court until he was a year old. Before the year was over he could walk stoutly, and he was stronger than a boy of three years old, even one of great growth and size. And the boy was raised the second year, and then he was as large as a child six years old. And before the end of his fourth year, he would bribe the grooms to allow him to take the horses to water.

"My lord," said his wife to Teyrnon, "where is the colt which you saved on the night that we got the boy?"

---

[1] The first day in May (or "May eve") in the Celtic calendar marked the beginning of summer. On the night before the first day of May, visits from the otherworld were often said to occur.

[2] *Wallt Euryn* Welsh: golden hair.

"I have commanded the grooms of the horses to take care of him," he said.

"Would it not be well, my lord," said she, "for you to cause him to be broken in, and given to the boy, seeing that on the same night that you found the boy the colt was foaled and you saved him?"

"I will not go against you in this matter," said Teyrnon. "I will allow you to give the colt to the boy."

"My lord," said she, "may heaven reward you; I will give it to him." So the horse was given to the boy. Then she went to the grooms and those who tended the horses and commanded them to be careful of the horse, so that it might be broken in by the time the boy could ride it.

And while these things were going forward, Teyrnon and his wife heard tidings of Rhiannon and her punishment. And Teyrnon Twryf Lliant, by reason of what he had heard, began to listen for news and inquired closely, until he had heard laments from many of those who had been to the court about Rhiannon's wretched fate and her penance. Then Teyrnon, often lamenting this sad history, pondered within himself, and looked steadfastly on the boy. As he looked upon him, it seemed that he had never beheld so great a likeness between father and son as the likeness he saw now between the boy and Pwyll the head of Annwn. The appearance of Pwyll was well known to Teyrnon, for he had long before been one of Pwyll's followers.

And immediately he began to regret the wrong that he had done, in keeping with him a boy whom he knew to be the son of another man. And the first time after that that he was alone with his wife, he asked her if it was right that they should keep the boy with them, and allow so excellent a lady as Rhiannon to be punished so greatly on his account; the boy was the son of Pwyll the head of Annwn. And Teyrnon's wife agreed with him that they should send the boy to Pwyll. "Three things, my lord," said she, "shall we gain by doing this: thanks and gratitude for releasing Rhiannon from her punishment; and thanks from Pwyll for raising his son and restoring him unto him; and thirdly, if the boy is of gentle nature he will be our foster-son, and he will do for us all the good that is in his power." So it was settled according to this counsel.

And no later than the next day Teyrnon equipped himself and set off with two other knights accompanying him. The boy was the fourth in their company, riding upon the horse that Teyrnon had given him. And they journeyed towards Arberth, and it was not long before they reached that place. And as they drew near to the court, they saw Rhiannon sitting beside a horse-block, and when they were opposite her she said, "Chieftain, do not go any further. I will carry every one of you who shall permit it to the court; this is my penance for slaying my own son and destroying him."

"Ah, fair lady," said Teyrnon, "I don't think a single one of us shall be carried upon your back."

"Let him go who wants to, but I will not," said the boy.

"Upon my soul, truly we will not have you carry us," said Teyrnon. So they went forward to the court, and there was great joy at their coming. At the court a feast had been prepared, because Pwyll had come back from the confines of Dyfed. And they went into the hall and washed, and Pwyll welcomed Teyrnon. And in this order they sat: Teyrnon between Pwyll and Rhiannon, and Teyrnon's two companions on the other side of Pwyll, with the boy between them. And after they had eaten their meat they began to carouse and to talk. And Teyrnon's talk was of the adventure of the mare and the boy, and how he and his wife had nursed and reared the child as their own. "And behold, here is your son, my lady," said Teyrnon to Rhiannon. "Whoever told that lie about you has done wrong. When I heard of your sorrow, I was troubled and grieved. And I believe that there is none of the company here who will not perceive that this boy is the son of Pwyll."

"There is none," said they all, "who is not certain of this."

"I declare to heaven," said Rhiannon, "that if this be true, there is indeed an end to my trouble."

"My lady," said Pendaran Dyfed,[1] "well have you named your son Pryderi,[2] and the name of Pryderi, son of Pwyll, head of Annwn, well becomes him."

"Look," said Rhiannon, "will not his own name be more suitable?"

"What name is that?" asked Pendaran Dyfed.

"Gwri Wallt Euryn is the name that we gave him."

"His name should be Pryderi," said Pendaran.

---

[1] *Pendaran Dyfed* Either a title ("Chieftain of Dyfed") or a proper name.

[2] *Pryderi* Welsh: worry, anxiety.

"It would be more appropriate," said Pwyll, "for the boy to take his name from the word his mother spoke when she received the joyful tidings of him." And thus it was arranged.

"Teyrnon," said Pwyll, "heaven reward you for bringing up the boy to his time; it would be fitting for him to repay you for it."

"My lord," said Teyrnon, "it was my wife who raised him, and there is no one in the world so saddened as she is at parting with him. It were well that he should bear in mind what I and my wife have done for him."

"I call heaven to witness," said Pwyll, "that while I live I will give support to you and your land. If it so pleases you, and pleases my nobles, I shall decree that, as you have raised the boy up to the present time, he may be brought up by Pendaran Dyfed from now on. And you shall be companions, and both be foster-parents unto him."

"This is good counsel," they all said. So the boy was given to Pendaran Dyfed, and the nobles of the land formed an alliance with him. Teyrnon Twryf Lliant and his companions then set out for his own country, with love and with gladness. And he went not without being offered the fairest jewels and the fairest horses, and the choicest dogs, but he would take none of them.

Thereafter they all remained in their own dominions, and Pryderi, the son of Pwyll the head of Annwn, was cared for well, so that he became the fairest youth and the most handsome, and the most skilled in games of any in the kingdom. And in this way years and years passed until the end of Pwyll the head of Annwn's life came, and he died.

And Pryderi ruled the seven cantrefs of Dyfed prosperously, and he was beloved by his people, and by all around him. And at length he added unto them the three cantrefs of Ystrad Twyi, and the four cantrefs of Ceredigion, and these seven cantrefs were called Seisyllwch. And when he added these lands to his territory, Pryderi the son of Pwyll the head of Annwn desired to take a wife, and the wife he chose was Cigfa the daughter of Gwynn Gohoyw, the son of Gloyw Lydan, the son of Casnar Wledic, one of the nobles of this island.

And thus ends this branch of the Mabinogi.

—? 12TH CENTURY

SIR GAWAIN AND THE GREEN KNIGHT

Little is known about *Sir Gawain and the Green Knight* apart from what the poem itself tells us. Its author is anonymous. The work is preserved in a single manuscript copy that was originally bound up with three other poems, *Pearl*, *Cleanness*, and *Patience*, which are generally regarded as having the same author. Like *Sir Gawain and the Green Knight* they are written in alliterative verse. The collection is known to have belonged to a private library in Yorkshire during the late sixteenth and early seventeenth centuries. It came to light in the nineteenth century, and *Sir Gawain and the Green Knight* was edited and printed for the first time in 1839. By the middle of the twentieth century the great interest and imaginative power of the poem had been generally acknowledged, and had attracted an increasing number of scholarly studies and commentaries.

The poem is written in a regional dialect characteristic of northwestern England at the time of its probable composition during the last quarter of the fourteenth century. That would mean that the *Gawain*-poet was a contemporary of Chaucer, who died in 1400; but even a brief comparison of their work shows how widely they were separated linguistically and culturally.

In the northern country reflected in the wintry landscapes of *Sir Gawain and the Green Knight*, an older literary language seems to have persisted, relatively unmarked by French, a language which the poet associates with the elaborately courtly manners displayed by Gawain and his hostess. In Chaucer a reader may gain the impression that the English and French components of his language have formed a comfortable liaison, so much so that he uses both indifferently and without reserving either for particular tasks. *Sir Gawain and the Green Knight* creates a different impression: that the two elements have not yet reached an accommodation, and that the poet and his audience are sufficiently alive to the nuances of words still novel and alien to their regional culture that French words tend to be used for distinctive purposes.

The poem is composed in a unique stanza form, made up of a varying number of long alliterative lines followed by a "bob and wheel": five short lines rhyming a b a b a, of which the first consists of only two syllables. The number of stressed alliterative words in each long line also varies, the norm being three.

Evidently it suits the poet's purposes to present himself as a simple popular entertainer whose occasional comments to his audience—"I schal telle yow how thay wroght"—and explanatory remarks about incidents in the story—"Wyt ye wel, hit watz worth wele ful hoge"—create an impression of the close relationship that a storyteller must maintain with his listeners. In oral narration such remarks would arise spontaneously, but here they are contrived as part of a deliberate purpose. It is not difficult to understand why the poet should have adopted the manner of an oral tale in a written work. Alliterative poetry is addressed to the ear, not to the eye, and its effects are not fully realized unless what Chaucer called the "rum-ram-ruf" of its pounding consonants is heard. Until displaced by rhyming verse it was also the established form of English poetry, and it seems evident from *Sir Gawain and the Green Knight* that its author felt a strong attachment to native tradition and culture. That may explain why he adopted the persona of a popular storyteller in addressing his audience, when the tale itself—particularly the three episodes in Gawain's bedchamber—prove him unusually cultivated and well acquainted with the literature of courtly manners and ideals.

Sir Gawain and the Green Knight represents the close fusion of three separate stories which may have been individually familiar to the poet's audience, but which have not survived in any similar combination in England or any other country. The first is the legend of the beheading game, which provides the opening and closing episodes of the poet's story. The second is the "exchange of winnings" proposed by Gawain's host in the central episodes of his adventure, which overlaps with the third motif, the sexual testing of Gawain. Combining these three elements into a single romance was not in itself a remarkable feat. The poet's achievement lies in having amalgamated them in such a way that while they appear unrelated, the outcome of one is determined by Gawain's behavior in the quite separate circumstances of the other.

In *Sir Gawain and the Green Knight* the story takes substantially the same form as in *Fled Bricrend* (see *Contexts* below), but with many changes of detail. The giant is no longer terrifying and ugly but physically attractive, splendidly dressed, and mounted on a horse which like himself is emerald green. He makes his challenge on New Year's Day and requires his opponent to stand the return blow a year and a day later at the Green Chapel, which must be found without directions. Gawain is chosen as the court's representative, promises to meet the Green Knight as stipulated, and decapitates him. The victim picks up his head, leaps into his saddle, and after reminding Gawain of his undertaking gallops away. At the Green Chapel a year later Gawain stands three swings from the Green Knight's axe. The first two are checked just short of his neck, and the third gashes the flesh as punishment for Gawain's dishonesty in a matter which has no evident connection with the beheading game. In this and other respects *Sir Gawain and the Green Knight* is a much more elaborate and ingenious reworking of the legend, but its dependence upon that primitive story is obvious. There are reasons for supposing that the major changes in the *Gawain*-poet's version of the tale—the challenger's color, the midwinter setting, and the year's interval between blows, for instance—were of his own devising, for these are not inconsequential details but parts of the imaginative purpose that integrates the whole poem.

None of the analogues of the temptation theme used by the poet are very closely related to his story of Gawain's attempted seduction, and no source of the motif has been found in legend. In the Welsh *Mabinogi* Pwyll spends a year at the court of Arawn in his friend's likeness, sleeping beside the queen but respecting her chastity; but while his self-restraint is tested no attempt is made to seduce him. The story is one of many legends which require the hero or heroine to undergo a trial of patience, forbearance or self-denial, usually in preparation for some task that demands special powers. The French romance of *Le Chevalier à l'Épée* is distantly related to this theme, and one of several works which seem to have contributed to the *Gawain*-poet's version of the temptation story.

The James Winny translation of the poem which appears below has been widely praised for its sensitivity to nuances of meaning; given the facing-text presentation, the translator has not felt it necessary to imitate the alliterative qualities of the Middle English verse, and has thus been able to convey the sense of the original as clearly as possible for the modern reader.

⌘⌘

Sir Gawayn and the Grene Knyght

FITT 1

Sithen the sege and the assaut watz sesed at Troye,
The borgh brittened and brent to brondez and askez,
The tulk that the trammes of tresoun ther wroght
Watz tried for his tricherie, the trewest on erthe.

Sir Gawain and the Green Knight[1]

PART 1

When the siege and the assault were ended at Troy,
The city laid waste and burnt into ashes,
The man who had plotted the treacherous scheme
Was tried for the wickedest trickery ever.

---

[1] *Sir Gawain and the Green Knight*   The translation is that of James Winny.

5 Hit watz Ennias the athel[1] and his highe kynde
   That sithen depreced provinces, and patrounes bicome
   Welneghe of al the wele in the west iles.
   Fro riche Romulus to Rome ricchis hym swythe;
   With gret bobbaunce that burghe he biges upon fyrst,
10 And nevenes hit his aune nome, as hit now hat;
   Ticius to Tuskan and teldes bigynnes,
   Langaberde in Lumbardie lyftes up homes,
   And fer over the French flod Felix Brutus
   On mony bonkkes ful brode Bretayn he settez
15   with wynne;
          Where werre and wrake and wonder
          Bi sythez hatz wont therinne,
          And oft both blysse and blunder
          Ful skete hatz skyfted synne.

20 Ande quen this Bretayn watz bigged bi this burn rych,
   Bolde bredden therinne, baret that lofden,
   In mony turned tyme tene that wroghten.
   Mo ferlyes on this folde han fallen here oft
   Then in any other that I wot, syn that ilk tyme.
25 Bot of alle that here bult, of Bretaygne kynges,
   Ay watz Arthur the hendest, as I haf herde telle.
   Forthi an aunter in erde I attle to schawe,
   That a selly in syght summe men hit holden,
   And an outtrage awenture of Arthurez wonderez.
30 If ye wyl lysten this laye bot on little quile
   I schal telle hit as-tit, as I in toun herde,[2]
          with tonge,[3]
          As hit is stad and stoken[4]
          In stori stif and stronge,
35   With lel letteres loken,
          In londe so hatz ben longe.

   This kyng lay at Camylot upon Krystmasse
   With mony luflych lorde, ledez of the best,
   Rekenly of the Rounde Table alle tho rich brether,
40 With rych revel oryght and rechles merthes.

5 It was princely Aeneas and his noble kin
   Who then subdued kingdoms, and came to be lords
   Of almost all the riches of the western isles.
   Afterwards noble Romulus hastens to Rome;
   With great pride he gives that city its beginnings,
10 And calls it by his own name, which it still has.
   Ticius goes to Tuscany and sets up houses,
   Langobard in Lombardy establishes homes,
   And far over the French sea Felix Brutus
   On many broad hillsides settles Britain
15   with delight;
          Where war and grief and wonder
          Have visited by turns,
          And often joy and turmoil
          Have alternated since.

20 And when Britain had been founded by this noble lord,
   Valiant men bred there, who thrived on battle.
   In many an age bygone they brought about trouble.
   More wondrous events have occurred in this country
   Than in any other I know of, since that same time.
25 But of all those who dwelt there, of the British kings
   Arthur was always judged noblest, as I have heard tell.
   And so an actual adventure I mean to relate
   Which some men consider a marvelous event,
   And a prodigious happening among tales about Arthur.
30 If you will listen to this story just a little while
   I will tell it at once, as I heard it told
          in court.
          As it is written down
          In story brave and strong,
35   Made fast in truthful words,
          That had endured long.

   The king spent that Christmas at Camelot
   With many gracious lords, men of great worth,
   Noble brothers-in-arms worthy of the Round Table,
40 With rich revelry and carefree amusement, as was right.

---

[1] *Ennias the athel* Here *athel* is used as a title appropriate to a prince (Aeneas), but at 2065 the word is applied to Gawain's guide.

[2] *as I in toun herde* It seems unlikely that the poet had either read or heard this particular tale recited. Although the beheading game figures in an Irish legend and the test of chastity has many analogues, no other surviving story combines them in a single narrative. But originality was not expected of medieval storytellers.

[3] *with tonge* Compare *wyth syght*, 197 and 226, and *meled with his muthe,* 447, for similar constructions.

[4] *stad and stoken* Set down and fixed.

Ther tournayed tulkes by tymez ful mony,
Justed ful jolilé thise gentyle knightes,
Sythen kayred to the court caroles to make.
For ther the fest watz ilyche ful fifteen dayes,
45 With alle the mete and the mirthe that men couthe avyse;
Such glaume and gle glorious to here,
Dere dyn upon day, daunsyng on nyghtes,
Al watz hap upon heghe in hallez and chambrez
With lordez and ladies, as levest him thoght.
50 With all the wel of the worlde thay woned ther samen,
The most kyd knyghtez under Krystes selven,
And the lovelokkest ladies that ever lif haden,
And he the comlokest kyng that the court haldes;
For al watz this fayre folk in her first age,[1]
55   on sille,
     The hapnest under heven,
     Kyng hyghest mon of wylle;
     Hit were now gret nye to neven
     So hardy a here on hille.

60 Wyle Nwe Yer watz so yep that hit watz nwe cummen,
That day doubble on the dece watz the douth served.
Fro the kyng watz cummen with knyghtes into the halle,
The chauntré of the chapel cheved to an ende,
Loude crye watz ther kest of clerkez and other,
65 Nowel[2] nayted onewe, nevened ful ofte;
And sythen riche forth runnen to reche hondeselle,
Yeghed yeres-giftes on high, yelde hem bi hond,[3]
Debated busyly aboute tho giftes;
Ladies laghed ful loude, thogh thay lost haden,
70 And he that wan watz not wrothe, that may ye wel trawe.[4]
Alle this mirthe thay maden to the mete tyme;
When thay had waschen worthyly thay wenten to sete,
The best burne ay abof,[5] as hit best semed,
Whene Guenore, ful gay, graythed in the myddes,
75 Dressed on the dere des, dubbed al aboute,
Smal sendal bisides, a selure hir over
Of tryed tolouse, of tars tapites innoghe,

There knights fought in tournament again and again,
Jousting most gallantly, these valiant men,
Then rode to the court for dancing and song.
For there the festival lasted the whole fifteen days
45 With all the feasting and merry-making that could be devised:
Such sounds of revelry splendid to hear,
Days full of uproar, dancing at night.
Everywhere joy resounded in chambers and halls
Among lords and ladies, whatever pleased them most.
50 With all of life's best they spent that time together,
The most famous warriors in Christendom,
And the loveliest ladies who ever drew breath,
And he the finest king who rules the court.
For these fair people were then in the flower of youth
55   in the hall.
     Luckiest under heaven,
     King of loftiest mind;
     Hard it would be
     Bolder men to find.

60 When New Year was so fresh that it had hardly begun,
Double helpings of food were served on the dais that day.
By the time the king with his knights entered the hall
When the service in the chapel came to an end,
Loud cries were uttered by the clergy and others,
65 "Nowel" repeated again, constantly spoken;
And then the nobles hurried to hand out New Year's gifts,
Cried their wares noisily, gave them by hand,
And argued excitedly over those gifts.
Ladies laughed out loud, even though they had lost,
70 And the winner was not angry, you may be sure.
All this merry-making went on until feasting time.
When they had washed as was fit they took their places,
The noblest knight in a higher seat, as seemed proper;
Queen Guenevere gaily dressed and placed in the middle,
75 Seated on the upper level, adorned all about;
Fine silk surrounding her, a canopy overhead
Of costly French fabric, silk carpets underfoot

---

[1] *in her first age* In their youth.

[2] *Nowel* I.e., Noël, a Christmas greeting.

[3] *And sythen … hond* Some have suggested that *hondeselle* are given to servants and *yeres-giftes* to equals. But Arthur is said figuratively to have received a *hanselle* at 491.

[4] *Ladies … trawe* The lines refer to some kind of Christmas game, perhaps involving guesses and paying a forfeit of kisses when the guess is wrong.

[5] *The best burne ay abof* Members of the court are seated according to social degree, at the *hyghe table*, 107, or at *sidbordez*, 115. The reference to *lordes and ladis that longed to the Table*, 2515, suggests that the poet saw the Round Table as a social institution.

That were enbrawded and beten wyth the best gemmes
That myght be preved of prys[1] wyth penyes to bye,
80   in daye.[2]
        The comlokest to discrye
        Ther glent with yghen gray,[3]
        A semloker that ever he syghe
        Soth moght no mon say.

85 Bot Arthure wolde not ete til al were served,
    He watz so joly of his joyfnes, and sumquat childgered:
    His lif liked hym lyght, he lovied the lasse
    Auther to longe lye or to longe sitte,
    So bisied him his yonge blod and his brayn wylde.
90 And also an other maner meved him eke
    That he thurgh nobelay had nomen, he wolde never ete
    Upon such a dere day er hym devised were
    Of sum aventurus thyng an uncouthe tale,
    Of sum mayn mervayle, that he myght trawe,
95 Of alderes, of armes, of other aventurus,
    Other sum segg hym bisoght of sum siker knyght
    To joyne wyth hym in justyng, in jopardé to lay
    Lede, lif for lyf, leve uchon other,
    As fortune wolde fulsun hom, the fayrer to have.
100 This watz the kynges countenaunce where he in court were,
    At uch farande fest among his fre meny
                in halle.
        Therfore of face so fere
        He stightlez stif in stalle,
105   Ful yep in that Nw Yere
        Much mirthe he mas withalle.

    Thus ther stondes in stale the stif kyng hisselven,
    Talkkande bifore the hyghe table of trifles ful hende.
    There gode Gawan[4] watz graythed Gwenore bisyde,
110 And Agravain à la dure mayn on that other syde sittes,
    Bothe the kynges sistersunes and ful siker knightes;
    Bischop Bawdewyn abof biginez the table,
    And Ywan, Uryn son, ette with hymselven.
    Thise were dight on the des and derworthly served,
115 And sithen mony siker segge at the sidbordez.

That were embroidered and studded with the finest gems
That money could buy at the highest price
80   anywhere.
        The loveliest to see
        Glanced round with eyes blue-grey;
        That he had seen a fairer one
        Truly could no man say.

85 But Arthur would not eat until everyone was served,
    He was so lively in his youth, and a little boyish.
    He hankered after an active life, and cared very little
    To spend time either lying or sitting,
    His young blood and restless mind stirred him so much.
90 And another habit influenced him too,
    Which he had made a point of honor: he would never eat
    On such a special day until he had been told
    A curious tale about some perilous thing,
    Of some great wonder that he could believe,
95 Of princes, of battles, or other marvels;
    Or some knight begged him for a trustworthy foe
    To oppose him in jousting, in hazard to set
    His life against his opponent's, each letting the other,
    As luck would assist him, gain the upper hand.
100 This was the king's custom when he was in court,
    At each splendid feast with his noble company
                in hall.
        Therefore with proud face
        He stands there, masterful,
105   Valiant in that New Year,
        Joking with them all.

    So there the bold king himself keeps on his feet,
    Chatting before the high table of charming trifles.
    There good Gawain was seated beside Guenevere,
110 And Agravain à la Dure Main on the other side;
    Both the king's nephews and outstanding knights.
    Bishop Baldwin heads the table in the highest seat,
    And Ywain, son of Urien, dined as his partner.
    These knights were set on a dais and sumptuously served,
115 And after them many a true man at the side tables.

---

[1] *preved of prys* Proved of value.

[2] *in daye* Literally, ever.

[3] *yghen gray* Virtually obligatory in medieval heroines.

[4] *gode Gawan* So characterized throughout the story, even after his
disgrace. The spelling of the hero's name varies considerably. He is
Gawan consistently throughout Part 1. Later the poet or his scribe
prefers the form *Gawayn* or *Gawayne*, which is used throughout Part
4. For alliterative purposes he is occasionally referred to as *Wawan,
Wawen, Wowayn,* or *Wowen.* Less frequently he is *Gavan* or *Gavayn.*

Then the first cors come with crakkyng of trumpes,
Wyth mony baner ful bryght that therbi henged;
Nwe nakryn noyse with the noble pipes,
Wylde werbles and wyght wakned lote,
120 That mony hert ful highe hef at her towches.
Dayntés dryven therwyth of ful dere metes,
Foysoun of the fresche, and on so fele disches
That pine to fynde the place the peple biforne
For to sette the sylveren that sere sewes halden
125   on clothe.
       Iche lede as he loved hymselve
       Ther laght withouten lothe;
       Ay two had disches twelve,
       Good ber and bryght wyn bothe.

130 Now wyl I of hor servise say yow no more,
For uch wyghe may wel wit no wont that ther were.
An other noyse ful newe neghed bilive
That the lude myght haf leve liflode to cache;[1]
For unethe watz the noyce not a whyle sesed,
135 And the fyrst cource in the court kyndely served,
Ther hales in at the halle dor an aghlich mayster,
On the most[2] on the molde on mesure hyghe;
Fro the swyre to the swange so sware and so thik,
And his lyndes and his lymes so longe and so grete,
140 Half etayn in erde I hope that he were,
Bot mon most I algate mynn hym to bene,
And that the myriest in his muckel that myght ride;
For of his bak and his brest al were his bodi sturne,
Both his wombe and his wast were worthily smale,
145 And alle his fetures folyande, in forme that he hade,
       ful clene;
       For wonder of his hwe men hade,
       Set in his semblaunt sene;
       He ferde as freke were fade,
150   And overal enker-grene.

And al grathed in grene this gome and his wedes:
A strayte cote ful streght, that stek on his sides,
A meré mantile abof, mensked withinne
With pelure pured apert, the pane ful clene
155 With blythe blaunner ful bryght, and his hode bothe,
That watz laght fro his lokkez and layde on his schulderes;

Then the first course was brought in with trumpets blaring,
Many colorful banners hanging from them.
The novel sound of kettledrums with the splendid pipes
Waked echoes with shrill and tremulous notes,
120 That many hearts leapt at the outburst of music.
At the same time servings of such exquisite food,
Abundance of fresh meat, in so many dishes
That space could hardly be found in front of the guests
To set down the silverware holding various stews
125   on the board.
       Each man who loved himself
       Took ungrudged, pair by pair,
       From a dozen tasty dishes,
       And drank good wine or beer.

130 Now I will say nothing more about how they were served,
For everyone can guess that no shortage was there.
Another noise, quite different, quickly drew near,
So that the king might have leave to swallow some food.
For hardly had the music stopped for a moment,
135 And the first course been properly served to the court,
When there bursts in at the hall door a terrible figure,
In his stature the very tallest on earth.
From the waist to the neck so thick-set and square,
And his loins and his limbs so massive and long,
140 In truth half a giant I believe he was,
But anyway of all men I judge him the largest,
And the most attractive of his size who could sit on a horse.
For while in back and chest his body was forbidding,
Both his belly and waist were becomingly trim,
145 And every part of his body equally elegant
       in shape.
       His hue astounded them,
       Set in his looks so keen;
       For boldly he rode in,
150   Completely emerald green.

And all arrayed in green this man and his clothes:
A straight close-fitting coat that clung to his body,
A pleasant mantle over that, adorned within
With plain trimmed fur, the facing made bright
155 With gay shining ermine, and his hood of the same
Thrown back from his hair and laid over his shoulders.

---

[1] *haf leve liflode to cache* Arthur will not eat until he has *sen a selly*, 475, which is about to arrive.

[2] *On the most* Not "one of the biggest" but "the very biggest."

Heme wel-haled hose of that same,
That spenet on his sparlyr, and clene spures under
Of bryght golde, upon silk bordes barred ful ryche,
160 And scholes under schankes[1] there the schalk rides;
And all his vesture verayly watz clene verdure,
Bothe the barres of his belt and other blythe stones,
That were richely rayled in his aray clene
Aboutte hymself and his sadel, upon silk werkez.
165 That were to tor for to telle of tryfles[2] the halve
That were enbrauded abof, wyth bryddes and flyghes,
With gay gaudi of grene, the gold ay inmyddes.
The pendauntes of his payttrure, the proude cropure,
His molaynes, and alle the metail anamayld was thenne,
170 The steropes that he stod on stayned of the same,
And his arsounz al after and his athel skyrtes,
That ever glemered and glent al of grene stones;
The fole that he ferkkes on fyn of that ilke,
            sertayn.
175   A grene hors gret and thikke,
        A stede ful stif to strayne,
        In brawden brydel quik;
        To the gome he watz ful gayn.

Wel gay watz this gome gered in grene,
180 And the here of his hed of his hors swete.
Fayre fannand fax umbefoldes his schulderes;
A much berd as a busk over his brest henges,
That wyth his highlich here that of his hed reches
Watz evesed al umbetorne abof his elbowes,
185 That half his armes ther-under were halched in the wyse
Of a kyngez capados[3] that closes his swyre;
The mane of that mayn hors much to hit lyke,
Wel cresped and cemmed, wyth knottes ful mony
Folden in with a fildore aboute the fayre grene,
190 Ay a herle of the here, an other of golde;
The tayl and his toppyng twynnen of a sute,
And bounden bothe wyth a bande of a bryght grene,
Dubbed wyth ful dere stonez, as the dok lasted,
Sythen thrawen wyth a thwong a thwarle knot alofte,
195 Ther mony bellez ful bryght of brende golde rungen.
Such a fole upon folde, ne freke that hym rydes,

Neat tightly-drawn stockings colored to match
Clinging to his calf, and shining spurs below
Of bright gold, over embroidered and richly striped silk;
160 And without shoes on his feet there the man rides.
And truly all his clothing was brilliant green,
Both the bars on his belt and other gay gems
That were lavishly set in his shining array
Round himself and his saddle, on embroidered silk.
165 It would be hard to describe even half the fine work
That was embroidered upon it, the butterflies and birds,
With lovely beadwork of green, always centered upon gold.
The pendants on the breast-trappings, the splendid crupper,
The bosses on the bit, and all the metal enameled.
170 The stirrups he stood in were colored the same,
And his saddlebow behind him and his splendid skirts
That constantly glittered and shone, all of green gems;
The horse that he rides entirely of that color,
            in truth.
175   A green horse huge and strong,
        A proud steed to restrain,
        Spirited under bridle,
        But obedient to the man.

Most attractive was this man attired in green,
180 With the hair of his head matching his horse.
Fine outspreading locks cover his shoulders;
A great beard hangs down over his chest like a bush,
That like the splendid hair that falls from his head
Was clipped all around above his elbows,
185 So that his upper arms were hidden, in the fashion
Of a royal capados that covers the neck.
That great horse's mane was treated much the same,
Well curled and combed, with numerous knots
Plaited with gold thread around the fine green,
190 Always a strand of his hair with another of gold.
His tail and his forelock were braided to match,
Both tied with a ribbon of brilliant green,
Studded with costly gems to the end of the tail,
Then tightly bound with a thong to an intricate knot
195 Where many bright bells of burnished gold rang.
No such horse upon earth, nor such a rider indeed,

---

[1] scholes under schankes   Meaning that he was not wearing the steel shoes belonging to a suit of armor; see 574. The Green Knight's feet are covered by the wel-haled hose of 157.

[2] tryfles   Decorative emblems, such as are embroidered on Gawain's silk uryson, 611–12, and on the old lady's headdress, 960.

[3] capados   Hood.

Watz never sene in that sale wyth syght er that tyme,
        with yghe.
    He loked as layt so lyght,
200   So sayd al that hym syghe;
    Hit semed as no mon myght
    Under his dynttez dryghe.

Whether hade he no helme ne no hawbergh[1] nauther,
Ne no pysan ne no plate that pented to armes,
205 Ne no schafte ne no schelde to schwve ne to smyte,
Bot in his on honde he hade a holyn bobbe,
That is grattest in grene when grevez ar bare,
And an ax in his other, a hoge and unmete,
A spetos sparthe to expoun in spelle, quoso myght.
210 The lenkthe of an elnyerde the large hede hade,
The grayn al of grene stele and of golde hewen,
The bit burnyst bryght, with a brod egge
As wel schapen to schere as scharp rasores,
The stele of a stif staf the sturne hit bi grypte,
215 That watz wounden wyth yrn to the wandez ende,
And al bigraven with grene in gracios werkes;
A lace lapped aboute, that louked at the hede,
And so after the halme halched ful ofte,
Wyth tryed tasselez therto tacched innoghe
220 On botounz of the bryght grene brayden ful ryche.
This hathel heldez hym in and the halle entres,
Drivande to the heghe dece, dut he no wothe,
Haylsed he never one, bot heghe he over loked.
The fyrst word that he warp, "Where is," he sayd,
225 "The governour of this gyng? Gladly I wolde
Se that segg in syght, and with hymself speke
        raysoun."[2]
    To knyghtez he kest his yghe,
    And reled hym up and doun;
230   He stemmed, and con studie
    Quo walt ther most renoun.

Ther watz lokyng on lenthe the lude to beholde,
For uch mon had mervayle quat hit mene myght

Had any man in that hall before thought to see
        with his eyes.
    His glance was lightning swift,
200   All said who saw him there;
    It seemed that no one could
    His massive blows endure.

Yet he had no helmet nor hauberk either,
No neck-armour or plate belonging to arms,
205 No spear and no shield to push or to strike;
But in one hand he carried a holly-branch
That is brilliantly green when forests are bare,
And an axe in the other, monstrously huge;
A cruel battle-axe to tell of in words, if one could.
210 The great head was as broad as a measuring-rod,
The spike made entirely of green and gold steel,
Its blade brightly burnished, with a long cutting-edge
As well fashioned to shear as the keenest razor.
The grim man gripped the handle, a powerful staff,
215 That was wound with iron to the end of the haft
And all engraved in green with craftsmanly work.
It had a thong wrapped about it, fastened to the head,
And then looped round the handle several times,
With many splendid tassels attached to it
220 With buttons of bright green, richly embroidered.
This giant bursts in and rides through the hall,
Approaching the high dais, disdainful of peril,
Greeting none, but haughtily looking over their heads.
The first words he spoke, "Where is," he demanded,
225 "The governor of this crowd? Glad should I be
To clap eyes on the man, and exchange with him
        a few words."
    He looked down at the knights,
    As he rode up and down,
230   Then paused, waiting to see
    Who had the most renown.

For long there was only staring at the man,
For everyone marveled what it could mean

---

[1] hawbergh I.e., hauberk, coat of chain mail.

[2] raysoun Words, implicit in speke but evidently idiomatic.

That a hathel and a horse myght such a hwe lach

235 As growe gren as the gres and grener hit semed,

Then grene aumayl on golde glowande bryghter.

Al studied that ther stod, and stalked hym nerre

With al the wonder of the worlde what he worche schulde.

For fele sellyez had thay sen, bot such never are;

240 Forthi for fantoun and fayryye the folk there hit demed.

Therfore to answare watz arghe mony athel freke,

And al stouned at his steven and stonstil seten

In a swogh sylence thurgh the sale riche;

As al were slypped upon slepe so slaked hor lotez

245   in hyghe;

    I deme hit not al for doute,

    Bot sum for cortaysye,

    Bot let hym that al schulde loute

    Cast unto that wyghe.

250 Thenne Arthour bifore the high dece that aventure byholdez,

And rekenly hym reverenced, for rad was he never,

And sayde, "Wyghe, welcum iwys to this place,

The hede of this ostel Arthour I hat;

Lyght luflych adoun and lenge, I the praye,

255 And quat-so thy wylle is we schal wyt after."

"Nay, as help me," quoth the hathel, "he that on hygh syttes,

To wone any quyle in this won hit watz not myn ernde;

Bot for the los of the, lede, is lyft up so hyghe,

And thy burgh and thy burnes best ar holden,

260 Stifest under stel-gere on stedes to ryde,

The wyghtest and the worthyest of the worldes kynde,

Preve for to playe wyth in other pure laykez,

And here is kydde cortaysye, as I haf herd carp,

And that hatz wayned me hider, iwyis, at this tyme.

265 Ye may be seker bi this braunch that I bere here

That I passe as in pes, and no plyght seche;

For had I founded in fere in feghtyng wyse,

I have a hauberghe at home and a helme bothe,

A schelde and a scharp spere, schinande bryghte,

270 Ande other weppenes to welde, I wene wel, als;

Bot for I wolde no were, my wedez ar softer.

Bot if thou be so bold as alle burnez tellen,

Thou wyl grant me godly the gomen that I ask

        bi ryght."

275   Arthour con onsware,

    And sayd, "Sir cortays knyght,

That a knight and a horse might take such a color

235 And become green as grass, and greener it seemed

Than green enamel shining brightly on gold.

All those standing there gazed, and warily crept closer,

Bursting with wonder to see what he would do;

For many marvels they had known, but such a one never;

240 So the folk there judged it phantasm or magic.

For this reason many noble knights feared to answer:

And stunned by his words they sat there stock-still,

While dead silence spread throughout the rich hall

As though everyone fell asleep, so was their talk stilled

245   at a word.

    Not just for fear, I think,

    But some for courtesy;

    Letting him whom all revere

    To that man reply.

250 Then Arthur confronts that wonder before the high table,

And saluted him politely, for afraid was he never,

And said, "Sir, welcome indeed to this place;

I am master of this house, my name is Arthur.

Be pleased to dismount and spend some time here, I beg,

255 And what you have come for we shall learn later."

"No, by heaven," said the knight, "and him who sits there,

To spend time in this house was not the cause of my coming,

But because your name, sir, is so highly regarded,

And your city and your warriors reputed the best,

260 Dauntless in armor and on horseback afield,

The most valiant and excellent of all living men,

Courageous as players in other noble sports,

And here courtesy is displayed, as I have heard tell,

And that has brought me here, truly, on this day.

265 You may be assured by this branch that I carry

That I approach you in peace, seeking no battle.

For had I traveled in fighting dress, in warlike manner,

I have a hauberk at home and a helmet too,

A shield and a keen spear, shining bright,

270 And other weapons to brandish, I assure you, as well;

But since I look for no combat I am not dressed for battle.

But if you are as courageous as everyone says,

You will graciously grant me the game that I ask for

        by right."

275   In answer Arthur said,

    "If you seek, courteous knight,

If thou crave batayl bare,[1]
Here faylez thou not to fyght."

"Nay, frayst I no fyght, in fayth I the telle,
280 Hit arn aboute on this bench bot berdlez chylder.
If I were hasped in armes on a heghe stede,
Here is no mon me to mach, for myghtez so wayke.
Forthy I crave in this court a Crystemas gomen,[2]
For hit is Yol and Nwe Yer, and here ar yep mony.
285 If any so hardy in this hous holdez hymselven,
Be so bolde in his blod, brayn[3] in hys hede,
That dar stifly strike a strok for an other,
I schal gif hym of my gyft thys giserne ryche,
This ax, that is hevé innogh, to hondele as hym lykes,
290 And I schal bide the fyrst bur as bare as I sitte.[4]
If any freke be so felle to fonde that I telle,
Lepe lyghtly me to, and lach this weppen,
I quit-clayme hit for ever, kepe hit as his awen,
And I schal stonde hym a strok, stif on this flet,
295 Ellez thou wyl dight me the dom to dele hym an other
barlay;[5]
And yet gif hym respite
A twelmonyth and a day;
Now hyghe, and let se tite
300 Dar any herinne oght say."

If he hem stouned upon fyrst, stiller were thanne
Alle the heredmen in halle, the hyghe and the lowe.
The renk on his rouncé hym ruched in his sadel,
And runischly his red yghen he reled aboute,
305 Bende his bresed browez, blycande grene,
Wayved his berde for to wayte quo-so wolde ryse.
When non wolde kepe hym with carp he coghed ful hyghe,
Ande rimed hym ful richely, and ryght hym to speke:
"What, is this Arthures hous?" quoth the hathel thenne,
310 "That al the rous rennes of thurgh ryalmes so mony?
Where is now your sourquydrye and your conquestes,
Your gryndellayk and your greme, and your grete wordes?

A combat without armor,
You will not lack a fight."

"No, I seek no battle, I assure you truly;
280 Those about me in this hall are but beardless children.
If I were locked in my armor on a great horse,
No one here could match me with their feeble powers.
Therefore I ask of the court a Christmas game,
For it is Yule and New Year, and here are brave men in plenty.
285 If anyone in this hall thinks himself bold enough,
So doughty in body and reckless in mind
As to strike a blow fearlessly and take one in return,
I shall give him this marvelous battle-axe as a gift,
This ponderous axe, to use as he pleases;
290 And I shall stand the first blow, unarmed as I am.
If anyone is fierce enough to take up my challenge,
Run to me quickly and seize this weapon,
I renounce all claim to it, let him keep it as his own,
And I shall stand his blow unflinching on this floor,
295 Provided you assign me the right to deal such a one
in return;
And yet grant him respite
A twelvemonth and a day.
Now hurry, and let's see
300 What any here dare say."

If he petrified them at first, even stiller were then
All the courtiers in that place, the great and the small.
The man on the horse turned himself in his saddle,
Ferociously rolling his red eyes about,
305 Bunched up his eyebrows, bristling with green,
Swung his beard this way and that to see whoever would rise.
When no one would answer he cried out aloud,
Drew himself up grandly and started to speak.
"What, is this Arthur's house?" said the man then,
310 "That everyone talks of in so many kingdoms?
Where are now your arrogance and your victories,
Your fierceness and wrath and your great speeches?

---

[1] *batayl bare* Either "without armor" (compare 290) or—as suggested by *thre bare mote*, 1141—"in single combat."

[2] *a Crystemas gomen* In earlier times the midwinter festival included many games and sports now forgotten. Many of them involved mock-violence, of which traces remained in Blind Man's Buff, played by striking a blindfolded victim and inviting him to guess who had struck him. Others exposed a victim to ridicule by playing a trick on him.

[3] *brayn* Crazy, reckless; usually *braynwod*, as at 1461.

[4] *as bare as I sitte* Without the protection of armor.

[5] *barlay* An obscure term, possibly meaning "by law," or here, "by agreement."

Now is the revel and the renoun of the Rounde Table
Overwalt wyth a worde of on wyghes speche,
315 For al dares for drede withoute dynt schewed!"
Wyth this he laghes so loude that the lorde greved;
The blod schot for scham into his schyre face
      and lere;
    He wex as wroth as wynde,
320   So did alle that ther were.
    The kyng as kene bi kynde
    Then stod that stif mon nere,

And sayde, "Hathel, by heven, thy askyng is nys,
And as thou foly hatz frayst, fynde the behoves.
325 I know no gome that is gast of thy grete wordes,
Gif me now thy geserne, upon Godez halve,
And I schal baythen thy bone that thou boden habbes."
Lyghtly lepez he him to, and laght at his honde,
Then feersly that other freke upon fote lyghtis.
330 Now hatz Arthure his axe, and the halme grypez,
And sturnely sturez hit aboute, that stryke wyth hit thoght.
The stif mon hym bifore stod upon hyght,
Herre then ani in the hous by the hede and more.
With sturne schere ther he stod he stroked his berde,
335 And wyth a countenaunce dryghe he drogh doun his cote,
No more mate ne dismayd for hys mayn dintez[1]
Then any burne upon bench hade broght hym to drynk
      of wyne.
    Gawan, that sate bi the quene,
340   To the kyng he can enclyne:
    "I beseche now with sayez sene
    This melly mot be myne."[2]

"Wolde ye, worthilych lorde," quoth Wawan to the kyng,
"Bid me boghe fro this benche, and stonde by yow there,
345 That I wythoute vylanye myght voyde this table,
And that my legge lady lyked not ille,[3]
I wolde com to your counseyl bifore your cort riche.
For me think hit not semly, as hit is soth knawen,
Ther such an askyng is hevened so hyghe in your sale,
350 Thagh ye yourself be talenttyf, to take hit to yourselven,
Whil mony so bolde yow aboute upon bench sytten
That under heven I hope non hagherer of wylle,
Ne better bodyes on bent ther baret is rered.

---

[1] *for hys mayn dintez* Because of Arthur's great practice blows.

[2] *This melly mot be myne* Let this be my combat.

Now the revelry and repute of the Round Table
Are overthrown with a word from one man's mouth,
315 For you all cower in fear before a blow has been struck!"
Then he laughs so uproariously that the king took offense;
The blood rushed into his fair face and cheek
      for shame.
    Arthur grew red with rage,
320   As all the others did.
    The king, by nature bold,
    Approached that man and said,

"Sir, by heaven, what you demand is absurd,
And since you have asked for folly, that you deserve.
325 No man known to me fears your boastful words;
Hand over your battle-axe, in God's name,
And I shall grant the wish that you have requested."
He quickly goes to him and took the axe from his hand.
Then proudly the other dismounts and stands there.
330 Now Arthur has the axe, grips it by the shaft,
And grimly swings it about, as preparing to strike.
Towering before him stood the bold man,
Taller than anyone in the court by more than a head.
Standing there grim-faced he stroked his beard,
335 And with an unmoved expression then pulled down his coat,
No more daunted or dismayed by those powerful strokes
Than if any knight in the hall had brought him a measure
      of wine.
    Seated by Guenevere
340   Then bowed the good Gawain:
    "I beg you in plain words
    To let this task be mine."

Said Gawain to the king, "If you would, noble lord,
Bid me rise from my seat and stand at your side,
345 If without discourtesy I might leave the table,
And that my liege lady were not displeased,
I would offer you counsel before your royal court.
For it seems to me unfitting, if the truth be admitted,
When so arrogant a request is put forward in hall,
350 Even if you are desirous, to undertake it yourself
While so many brave men sit about you in their places
Who, I think, are unrivalled in temper of mind,
And without equal as warriors on field of battle.

---

[3] *that my legge lady lyked not ille* That the Queen (beside whom Gawain is sitting) would not be offended if I left her side.

I am the wakkest, I wot, and of wyt feblest,
355 And lest lur of my lyf, quo laytes the sothe:
Bot for as much as ye are myn em I am only to prayse,
No bounté bot your blod I in my bodé knowe;
And sythen this note is so nys that noght hit yow falles,
And I have frayned hit at yow fyrst, foldez hit to me;
360 And if I carp not comlyly, let alle this cort rych
      bout blame."
        Ryche togeder con roun,
        And sythen thay redden alle same,
        To ryd the kyng wyth croun
365   And gif Gawan the game.

Then comaunded the kyng the knyght for to ryse;
And he ful radly upros, and ruchched hym fayre,
Kneled doun bifore the kyng, and cachez that weppen;
And he luflyly hit hym laft, and lyfte up his honde
370 And gef hym Goddez blessyng, and gladly hym biddes
That his hert and his honde schulde hardi be bothe.
"Kepe the, cosyn," quoth the kyng, "that thou on kyrf sette,
And if thou redez hym ryght, redly I trowe
That thou schal byden the bur[1] that he schal bede after."
375 Gawan gotz to the gome with giserne in honde,
And he baldly hym bydez, he bayst never the helder.
Then carppez to Sir Gawan the knyght in the grene,
"Refourme we oure forwardes, er we fyrre passe.
Fyrst I ethe the, hathel, how that thou hattes
380 That thou me telle truly, as I tryst may."
"In god fayth," quoth the goode knyght, "Gawan I hatte,
That bede the this buffet, quat-so bifallez after,
And at this tyme twelmonyth take at the an other
Wyth what weppen so thou wylt, and wyth no wygh ellez
385   on lyve."
        That other onswarez agayn,
        "Sir Gawan, so mot I thryve,
        As I am ferly fayn
        This dint that thou schal dryve.

390 "Bigog," quoth the grene knyght, "Sir Gawan, me lykes
That I schal fange at thy fust that I haf frayst here.[2]
And thou hatz redily rehersed, bi resoun ful trwe,
Clanly al the covenaunt that I the kynge asked,
Saf that thou schal siker me, segge, bi thi trawthe,

I am the weakest of them, I know, and the dullest-minded,
355 So my death would be least loss, if truth should be told;
Only because you are my uncle am I to be praised,
No virtue I know in myself but your blood;
And since this affair is so foolish and unfitting for you,
And I have asked you for it first, it should fall to me.
360 And if my request is improper, let not this royal court
      bear the blame."
        Nobles whispered together
        And agreed on their advice,
        That Arthur should withdraw
365   And Gawain take his place.

Then the king commanded Gawain to stand up,
And he did so promptly, and moved forward with grace,
Kneeled down before the king and laid hold of the weapon;
And Arthur gave it up graciously, and lifting his hand
370 Gave Gawain God's blessing, and cheerfully bids
That he bring a strong heart and firm hand to the task.
"Take care, nephew," said the king, "that you strike one blow,
And if you deal it aright, truly I believe
You will wait a long time for his stroke in return."
375 Gawain approaches the man with battle-axe in hand,
And he waits for him boldly, with no sign of alarm.
Then the knight in the green addresses Gawain,
"Let us repeat our agreement before going further.
First I entreat you, sir, that what is your name
380 You shall tell me truly, that I may believe you."
"In good faith," said that virtuous knight, "I am called Gawain,
Who deals you this blow, whatever happens after,
On this day next year to accept another from you
With what weapon you choose, and from no other person
385   on earth."
        The other man replied,
        "Sir Gawain, as I live,
        I am extremely glad
        This blow is yours to give.

390 By God," said the Green Knight, "Sir Gawain, I am pleased
That I shall get from your hands what I have asked for here.
And you have fully repeated, in exact terms,
Without omission the whole covenant I put to the king;
Except that you shall assure me, sir, on your word,

---

[1] *thou schal byden the bur* You'll be kept waiting for his blow.

[2] *"Bigog,"... here* The Green Knight does not explain why he is especially pleased that Gawain accepts the challenge.

395 That thou schal seche me thiself, where-so thou hopes
I may be funde upon folde, and foch the such wages
As thou deles me to-day bifore this douthe ryche."
"Where schulde I wale the?" quoth Gawan, "Where is thy
      place?
I wot never where thou wonyes, bi hym that me wroght,
400 Ne I know not the, knyght, thy cort ne thi name.
Bot teche me truly therto, and telle me how thou hattes,
And I schal ware alle my wyt to wynne me theder,
And that I swere the for sothe, and by my seker traweth."
"That is innogh in Nwe Yer,[1] hit nedes no more,"
405 Quoth the gome in the grene to Gawan the hende;
"Yif I the telle trwly quen I the tape have,
And thou me smothely hatz smyten, smartly I the teche
Of my hous and my home and myn owen nome,
Then may thou frayst my fare and forwardez holde;
410 And if I spende no speche, thenne spedez thou the better,
For thou may leng in thy londe and layt no fyrre—
        bot slokes!
     Ta now thy grymme tole to the,
     And lat se how thou cnokez."
415   "Gladly, sir, for sothe,"
     Quoth Gawan: his ax he strokes.

The grene knyght upon grounde graythely hym dresses,
A littel lut with the hed, the lere he discoverez,
His longe lovelych lokkez he layd over his croun,
420 Let the naked nec to the note schewe.
Gawan gripped to his ax and gederes hit on hyght,
The kay fot on the folde he before sette,
Let hit doun lyghtly lyght on the naked,
That the scharp of the schalk schyndered the bones,
425 And schrank thurgh the schyire grece, and schade hit in twynne,
That the bit of the broun[2] stel bot on the grounde.
The fayre hede fro the halce hit to the erthe,
That fele hit foyned wyth hir fete, there hit forth roled;
The blod brayed from the body, that blykked on the grene;
430 And nawther faltered ne fel the freke never the helder,
Bot stythly he start forth upon styf schonkes,
And runyschly he raght out, there as renkkez stoden,
Laght to his lufly hed, and lyft hit up sone;
And sythen bowez to his blonk, the brydel he cachchez,

395 That you will seek me yourself, wherever you think
I may be found upon earth, to accept such payment
As you deal me today before this noble gathering."
"Where shall I find you?" said Gawain, "Where is your
      dwelling?
I have no idea where you live, by him who made me;
400 Nor do I know you, sir, your court nor your name.
Just tell me truly these things, and what you are called,
And I shall use all my wits to get myself there,
And that I swear to you honestly, by my pledged word."
"That is enough for the moment, it needs nothing more,"
405 Said the man in green to the courteous Gawain,
"If I answer you truly after taking the blow,
And you have dextrously struck me, I will tell you at once
Of my house and my home and my proper name,
Then you can pay me a visit and keep your pledged word;
410 And if I say nothing, then you will fare better,
For you may stay in your country and seek no further—
        but enough!
     Take up your fearsome weapon
     And let's see how you smite."
415   Said Gawain, "Gladly, indeed,"
     Whetting the metal bit.

The Green Knight readily takes up his position,
Bowed his head a little, uncovering the flesh,
His long lovely hair he swept over his head,
420 In readiness letting the naked neck show.
Gawain grasped the axe and lifts it up high,
Setting his left foot before him on the ground,
Brought it down swiftly on the bare flesh
So that the bright blade slashed through the man's spine
425 And cut through the white flesh, severing it in two,
So that the shining steel blade bit into the floor.
The handsome head flew from the neck to the ground,
And many courtiers kicked at it as it rolled past.
Blood spurted from the trunk, gleamed on the green dress,
430 Yet the man neither staggered nor fell a whit for all that,
But sprang forward vigorously on powerful legs,
And fiercely reached out where knights were standing,
Grabbed at his fine head and snatched it up quickly,
And then strides to his horse, seizes the bridle,

---

[1] *innogh in Nwe Yer* Literally, "enough for this New Year's Day"; meaning that Gawain need say nothing more, as the Green Knight goes on to say.

[2] *broun* Burnished.

435 Steppez into stelbawe and strydez alofte,
And his hede by the here in his honde haldez.
And as sadly the segge hym in his sadel sette
As non unhap had hym ayled, thagh hedlez he were
                                    in stedde.
440   He brayde his bulk aboute,
       That ugly bodi that bledde;
       Moni on of hym had doute
       Bi that his resounz were redde.

For the hede in his honde he haldez up even,
445 Toward the derrest on the dece he dressez the face,
And hit lyfte up the yghe-lyddez and loked ful brode,
And meled thus much with his muthe, as ye may now
                                    here:
"Loke, Gawan, thou be graythe to go as thou hettez,
And layte as lelly til thou me, lude, fynde,
450 As thou hatz hette in this halle, herande thise knyghtes;
To the grene chapel thou chose, I charge the, to fotte
Such a dunt as thou hatz dalt, disserved thou habbez
To be yederly yolden on Nw Yeres morn.
The knyght of the grene chapel men knowen me mony,
455 Forthi me for to fynde if thou fraystez, faylez thou never.
Therfore com, other recreaunt be calde thou behoves."
With a runisch rout the raynez he tornez,
Halled out at the hal dor, his hed in his hande,
That the fyr of the flynt flaghe fro fole hoves.
460 To quat kyth he becom knwe non there,
Never more then thay wyste from quethen he watz wonnen.
          What thenne?
       The kyng and Gawan thare
       At that grene thay laghe and grenne;
465   Yet breved watz hit ful bare
       A mervayl among tho menne.

Thagh Arther the hende kyng at hert hade wonder,
He let no semblaunt be sene, bot sayde ful hyghe
To the comlych quene wyth cortays speche,
470 "Dere dame, to-day demay yow never;
Wel bycommes such craft[1] upon Cristmasse,
Laykyng of enterludez, to laghe and to syng,
Among thise kynde caroles of knyghtez and ladyez.
Never the lece to my mete I may me wel dres,

435 Puts foot into stirrup and swings into his seat,
His other hand clutching his head by the hair;
And the man seated himself on horseback as firmly
As if he had suffered no injury, though headless he sat
                                    in his place.
440   He turned his body round,
       That gruesome trunk that bled;
       Many were struck by fear
       When all his words were said.

For he holds up the head in his hand, truly,
445 Turns its face towards the noblest on the dais,
And it lifted its eyelids and glared with wide eyes,
And the mouth uttered these words, which you shall now
                                    hear:
"See, Gawain, that you carry out your promise exactly,
And search for me truly, sir, until I am found,
450 As you have sworn in this hall in the hearing of these knights.
Make your way to the Green Chapel, I charge you, to get
Such a blow as you have dealt, rightfully given,
To be readily returned on New Year's Day.
As the Knight of the Green Chapel I am widely known,
455 So if you make search to find me you cannot possibly fail.
Therefore come, or merit the name of craven coward."
With a fierce jerk of the reins he turns his horse
And hurtled out of the hall door, his head in his hand,
So fast that flint-fire sparked from the hoofs.
460 What land he returned to no one there knew,
Any more than they guessed where he had come from.
          What then?
       Seeing that green man go,
       The king and Gawain grin;
465   Yet they both agreed
       They had a wonder seen.

Although inwardly Arthur was deeply astonished,
He let no sign of this appear, but loudly remarked
To the beautiful queen with courteous speech,
470 "Dear lady, let nothing distress you today.
Such strange goings-on are fitting at Christmas,
Putting on interludes, laughing and singing,
Mixed with courtly dances of ladies and knights.
None the less, I can certainly go to my food,

---

[1] *such craft* Display of skill. Arthur speaks as though the beheading had been a conjuring trick.

475 For I haf sen a selly, I may not forsake."
He glent upon Sir Gawen, and gaynly he sayde,
"Now sir, heng up thyn ax,[1] that hatz innogh hewen."
And hit watz don abof the dece on doser to henge,
Ther alle men for mervayl myght on hit loke,
480 And bi trwe tytel therof to telle the wonder.
Thenne thay bowed to a borde thise burnes togeder,
The kyng and the gode knyght, and kene men hem served
Of alle dayntyez double, as derrest myght falle;
Wyth alle maner of mete and mynstralcie bothe,
485 Wyth wele walt thay that day, til worthed an ende
          in londe.
      Now thenk wel, Sir Gawan,
      For wothe that thou ne wonde
      This aventure for to frayn
490   That thou hatz tan on honde.

FITT 2

This hanselle hatz Arthur of aventurus on fyrst
In yonge yer, for he yerned yelpyng to here.
Thagh hym wordez were wane[2] when thay to sete wenten,
Now ar thay stoken of sturne werk, stafful her hond.
495 Gawan watz glad to begynne those gomnez in halle,
Bot thagh the ende be hevy haf ye no wonder;
For thagh men ben mery quen thay han mayn drynk,
A yere yernes ful yerne, and yeldez never lyke,
The forme to the fynisment foldez ful selden.
500 Forthi this Yol overyede, and the yere after,
And uche sesoun serlepes sued after other:
After Crystenmasse com the crabbed lentoun
That fraystez flesch wyth the fysche and fode more symple;
Bot thenne the weder of the worlde wyth wynter hit threpez,[3]
505 Colde clengez adoun,[4] cloudez upliften,
Schyre schedez the rayn in schowrez ful warme,
Fallez upon fayre flat, flowrez there schewen,
Bothe-groundez and the grevez grene ar her wedez,
Bryddez busken to bylde, and bremlych syngen

475 For I have witnessed a marvel, I cannot deny."
He glanced at Sir Gawain, and aptly he said,
"Now sir, hang your axe up, for it has severed enough."
And it was hung above the dais, on a piece of tapestry,
Where everyone might gaze on it as a wonder,
480 And the living proof of this marvelous tale.
Then these two men together walked to a table,
The king and the good knight, and were dutifully served
With delicious double helpings befitting their rank.
With every kind of food and minstrelsy
485 They spent that day joyfully, until daylight ended
          on earth.
      Now take good care, Gawain,
      Lest fear hold you back
      From leaving on the quest
490   You have sworn to undertake.

PART 2

This wonder has Arthur as his first New Year's gift
When the year was newborn, for he loved hearing challenges.
Though words were wanting when they sat down at table,
Now a grim task confronts them, their hands are cram-full.
495 Gawain was glad enough to begin those games in the hall,
But if the outcome prove troublesome don't be surprised;
For though men are light-hearted when they have strong drink,
A year passes swiftly, never bringing the same;
Beginning and ending seldom take the same form.
500 And so that Yule went by, and the year ensuing,
Each season in turn following the other.
After Christmas came mean-spirited Lent,
That tries the body with fish and plainer nourishment;
But then the weather on earth battles with winter,
505 The cold shrinks downwards, clouds rise higher,
And shed sparkling rain in warming showers,
Falling on smiling plains where flowers unfold.
Both open fields and woodlands put on green dress;
Birds hasten to build, and rapturously sing

---

[1] *heng up thyn ax* Arthur *gaynly* or aptly quotes a proverbial saying, meaning "end your strife."

[2] *wordez were wane* Because the Green Knight had taken their breath away.

[3] *wyth wynter hit threpez* The seasons do not simply follow each other quietly but fight for succession: see 525, where autumn wind *wrastelez with the sunne.*

[4] *Colde clengez adoun* Winter is driven down into the earth, waiting to emerge again.

510 For solace of the softe somer that sues therafter
         bi bonk;
     And blossumez bolne to blowe
     Bi rawez rych and ronk,
     Then notez noble innoghe
515   Ar herde in wod so wlonk.

     After the sesoun of somer wyth the soft wyndez,
     Quen Zeferus[1] syflez hymself on sedez and erbez,
     Wela wynne is the wort that waxes theroute,
     When the donkande dewe dropez of the levez,
520 To bide a blysful blusch of the bryght sunne.
     Bot then hyghes hervest, and hardenes hym sone,
     Warnez hym for the wynter to wax ful rype.
     He dryves wyth droght the dust for to ryse
     Fro the face of the folde to flyghe ful hyghe;
525 Wrothe wynde of the welkyn wrastelez with the sunne,
     The levez lancen fro the lynde and lyghten on the grounde,
     And al grayes the gres that grene watz ere.
     Thenne al rypez and rotez that ros upon fyrst,
     And thus yirnez the yere in yisterdayez mony,
530 And wynter wyndez agayn, as the worlde askez,
             no fage;
         Til Meghelmas[2] mone
         Watz cumen wyth wynter wage;
         Then thenkkez Gawan ful sone
535   Of his anious vyage.

     Yet quyl Al-hal-day[3] with Arther he lenges;
     And he made a fare on that fest for the frekez sake,
     With much revel and ryche of the Rounde Table.
     Knyghtez ful cortays and comlych ladies
540 Al for luf of that lede in longynge thay were,
     Bot never the lece ne the later thay nevened bot merthe;
     Mony joylez for that jentyle japez ther maden.
     And aftter mete with mournyng he melez to his eme,
     And spekez of his passage, and pertly he sayde,
545 "Now, lege lorde of my lyf, leve I yow ask;
     Ye knowe the cost of this cace, kepe I no more
     To telle yow tenez therof, never bot trifel;
     Bot I am boun to the bur barely to-morne
     To sech the gome of the grene, as God wyl me wysse."
550 Then the best of the burgh bowed togeder,

[1] *Zeferus* God of the West Wind.

[2] *Meghelmas* I.e., Michaelmas, the feast of St. Michael, celebrated
on 29 September.

510 For joy of gentle summer that follows next
         on the slopes.
     And flowers bud and blossom
     In hedgerows rich with growth,
     And many splendid songs
515   From woodlands echo forth.

     Then comes the summer season with gentle winds,
     When Zephirus blows softly on seeding grasses and plants,
     Beautiful is the growth that springs from the seed,
     When the moistening dew drips from the leaves
520 To await a joyful gleam of the bright sun.
     But then autumn comes quickly and urges it on,
     Warns it to ripen before winter's approach.
     Dry winds of autumn force the dust to fly
     From the face of the earth high into the air;
525 Fierce winds of heaven wrestle with the sun,
     Leaves are torn from the trees and fall to the ground,
     And all withered is the grass that was green before.
     Then all ripens and rots that had sprung up at first,
     And in so many yesterdays the year wears away,
530 And winter comes round again, as custom requires,
             in truth;
         Until the Michaelmas moon
         Brought hint of winter's frost;
         And into Gawain's mind
535   Come thoughts of his grim quest.

     Yet until All Saints' Day he lingers in court,
     And Arthur made a feast on that day to honor the knight,
     With much splendid revelry at the Round Table.
     The most courteous of knights and beautiful ladies
540 Grieved out of love for that noble man,
     But no less readily for that spoke as if unconcerned.
     Many troubled for that nobleman made joking remarks.
     And after the feast sorrowfully he addressed his uncle,
     Raised the matter of his quest, and openly said,
545 "Liege lord of my being, I must ask for your leave;
     You know the terms of this matter, and I have no wish
     To bother you with them, saving one small point;
     But tomorrow without fail I set out for the blow,
     To seek this man in green, as God will direct me."
550 Then the noblest in the court gathered together,

Aywan and Errik, and other ful mony,
Sir Doddinaval de Savage, the duc of Clarence,
Launcelot and Lyonel, and Lucan the gode,
Sir Boos and Sir Bydver, big men bothe,
555   And mony other menskful, with Mador de la Port.
Alle this compayny of court com the kyng nerre
For to counseyl the knyght, with care at her hert.
There watz much derve doel driven in the sale
That so worthé as Wawan schulde wende on that ernde,
560   To dryve a delful dynt, and dele no more
          wyth bronde.
     The knyght mad ay god chere,
     And sayde, "Quat schuld I wonde?
     Of destinés derf and dere
565   What may mon do bot fonde?"

He dowellez ther al that day, and dressez on the morn,
Askez erly hys armez, and alle were thay broght.
Fyrst a tulé tapit tyght over the flet,
And miche watz the gild gere that glent theralofte.
570   The stif mon steppez theron, and the stel hondelez,
Dubbed in a dublet of a dere tars,
And sythen a crafty capados, closed aloft,
That wyth a bryght blaunner was bounden withinne.
Thenne set thay the sabatounz upon the segge fotez,
575   His legez lapped in stel with luflych greves,
With polaynez piched therto, policed ful clene,
Aboute his knez knaged wyth knotez of golde;
Queme quyssewes then, that coyntlych closed
His thik thrawen thyghez, with thwonges to tachched;
580   And sythen the brawden bryné of bryght stel ryngez
Umbeweved that wygh upon wlonk stuffe,
And wel bornyst brace upon his bothe armes,
With gode cowters and gay, and glovez of plate,
And alle the godlych gere that hym gayn schulde
585   that tyde;
     Wyth ryche cote-armure
     His gold sporez spend with pryde,
     Gurde wyth a bront ful sure
     With silk sayn umbe his syde.

590   When he watz hasped in armes, his harnays watz ryche:
The lest lachet other loupe lemed of golde.
So harnayst as he watz he herknez his masse,
Offred and honoured at the heghe auter.
Sythen he come to the kyng and to his cort-ferez,

Ywain and Eric, and many others,
Sir Dodinal le Sauvage, the duke of Clarence,
Lancelot and Lionel, and Lucan the good,
Sir Bors and Sir Bedevere, both powerful men,
555   And several other worthy knights, including Mador de la Port.
This group of courtiers approached the king,
To give advice to Gawain with troubled hearts.
Much deep sorrowing was heard in the hall
That one as noble as Gawain should go on that quest,
560   To stand a terrible blow, and never more brandish
          his sword.
     Keeping an unchanged face,
     "What should I fear?" he said;
     "For whether kind or harsh
565   A man's fate must be tried."

He stays there all that day, and makes ready the next,
Calls early for his accouterment, and all was brought in.
First a crimson carpet was stretched over the floor,
A heap of gilded armor gleaming brightly piled there.
570   The brave knight steps on it and examines his armour,
Dressed in a costly doublet of silk
Under a well-made capados, fastened at the top
And trimmed with white ermine on the inside.
Then they fitted metal shoes upon the knight's feet,
575   Clasped his legs in steel with elegant greaves
With knee-pieces attached to them, highly polished
And fastened to his knees with knots of gold.
Next fine cuisses that neatly enclosed
His thick muscular thighs, with thongs attached,
580   And then the linked mail-shirt made of bright steel rings
Covered that man and his beautiful clothes:
Well burnished braces on both his arms,
With fine elbow-pieces and gloves of steel plate,
And all the splendid equipment that would benefit him
585   at that time;
     With costly coat-armor,
     His gold spurs worn with pride,
     Girt with a trusty sword,
     A silk belt round him tied.

590   All locked in his armor his gear looked noble:
The smallest fastening or loop was gleaming with gold.
In armor as he was, he went to hear mass
Offered and celebrated at the high altar.
Then he comes to the king and his fellows at court,

595 Lachez lufly his leve at lordez and ladyez;
And thay him kyst and conveyed, bikende hym to Kryst.
Bi that watz Gryngolet grayth, and gurde with a sadel
That glemed ful gayly with mony golde frenges,
Ayquere naylet ful nwe, for that note ryched;
600 The brydel barred aboute, with bryght golde bounden,
The apparayl of the payttrure and of the proude skyrtez,
The cropore and the covertor, acorded wyth the arsounez;
And al watz rayled on red ryche golde naylez,
That al glytered and glent as glem of the sunne.
605 Thenne hentes he the helme, and hastily hit kysses,
That watz stapled stifly, and stoffed wythinne.
Hit watz hyghe on his hede, hasped bihynde,
Wyth a lyghtly urysoun over the aventayle,
Enbrawden and bounden wyth the best gemmez
610 On brode sylkyn borde, and bryddez on semez,
As papjayez paynted pervyng bitwene,
Tortors and trulofez entayled so thyk
As mony burde theraboute had ben seven wynter
      in toune.
615   The cercle watz more o prys
       That umbeclypped hys croun,
       Of diamauntez a devys
       That bothe were bryght and broun.[1]

Then thay schewed hym the schelde, that was of schyr goulez,
620 Wyth the pentangel depaynt of pure gold hwez.
He braydez hit by the bauderyk, aboute the hals kestes,
That bisemed the segge semlyly fayre.
And quy the pentangel apendez to that prynce noble
I am in tent yow to telle, thof tary hyt me schulde:
625 Hit is a syngne that Salomon set sumquyle
In bytoknyng of trawthe, bi tytle that hit habbez,
For hit is a figure that haldez fyve poyntez,
And uche lyne umbelappez and loukez in other,
And ayquere hit is endelez; and Englych hit callen
630 Overal, as I here, the endeles knot.[2]
Forthy hit acordez to this knyght and to his cler armez,
For ay faythful in fyve and sere fyve sythez
Gawan watz for gode knawen, and as golde pured,
Voyded of uche vylany, wyth vertuez ennourned
635   in mote;

595 Graciously takes his leave of lords and ladies;
And they kissed and escorted him, commending him to Christ.
By then Gringolet was ready, fitted with a saddle
That splendidly shone with many gold fringes,
Newly studded all over for that special purpose;
600 The bridle striped all along, and trimmed with bright gold;
The adornment of the trapping and the fine saddle-skirts,
The crupper and the horse-cloth matched the saddle-bows,
All covered with gold studs on a background of red,
So that the whole glittered and shone like the sun.
605 Then Gawain seizes his helmet and kisses it quickly,
That was strongly stapled and padded inside.
It stood high on his head, fastened at the back
With a shining silk band over the mailed neck-guard,
Embroidered and studded with the finest gems
610 On a broad border of silk with birds covering the seams—
Popinjays depicted between periwinkles,
Turtledoves and true-love flowers embroidered so thick
As if many women had worked on it seven years
      in town.
615   A circlet still more precious
       Was ringed about his head,
       Made with perfect diamonds
       Of every brilliant shade.

Then they brought out the shield of shining gules,
620 With the pentangle painted on it in pure gold.
He swings it over his baldric, throws it round his neck,
Where it suited the knight extremely well.
And why the pentangle should befit that noble prince
I intend to explain, even should that delay me.
625 It is a symbol that Solomon designed long ago
As an emblem of fidelity, and justly so;
For it is a figure consisting of five points,
Where each line overlaps and locks into another,
And the whole design is continuous, and in England is called
630 Everywhere, I am told, the endless knot.
Therefore it suits this knight and his shining arms,
For always faithful in five ways, and five times in each case,
Gawain was reputed as virtuous, like refined gold,
Devoid of all vice, and with all courtly virtues
635   adorned.

---

[1]   *bryght and broun* Clear and colored.

[2]   *the endeles knot* No other use of this phrase is known. Like the
poet's claim to have heard the story recited, and his closing of reference to its place in *the best boke of romaunce*, 2521, the remark should
probably be regarded as poetic license. The line does not alliterate.

Forthy the pentangel nwe
He ber in schelde and cote,
As tulk of tale most trwe
And gentylest knyght of lote.

640 Fyrst he watz funden fautlez in his fyve wyttez,
And eft fayled never the freke in his fyve fyngres,
And alle his afyaunce upon folde watz in the fyve woundez
That Cryst caght on the croys, as the crede tellez;
And quere-so-ever thys mon in melly watz stad,
645 His thro thoght watz in that, thurgh alle other thyngez,
That alle his forsnes he feng at the fyve joyez
That the hende heven-quene had of hir chylde;
At this cause the knyght comlyche hade
In the inore half of his schelde hir image depaynted,
650 That quen he blusched therto his belde never payred.
The fyft fyve that I fynde that the frek used
Watz fraunchyse and felaghschyp forbe al thyng,
His clannes and his cortaysye croked were never,
And pité,[1] that passez alle poyntez: thyse pure fyve
655 Were harder happed on that hathel then on any other.
Now alle these fyve sythez, for sothe, were fetled on this
        knyght,
And uchone halched in other, that non ende hade,
And fyched upon fyve poyntez, that fayld never,
Ne samned never in no syde, ne sundred nouther,
660 Withouten ende at any noke I oquere fynde,
Whereever the gomen bygan, or glod to an ende.
Therfore on his schene schelde schapen watz the knot
Ryally wyth red golde upon rede gowlez,
That is the pure pentaungel wyth the peple called
665   with lore.
        Now graythed is Gawan gay,
        And laght his launce ryght thore,
        And gef them alle goud day,
        He wende for evermore.

670 He sperres the sted with the spurez and sprong on his way,
So stif that the ston-fyr stroke out therafter.
Al that sey that semly syked in hert,
And sayde sothly[2] al same segges til other,
Carande for that comly, "Bi Kryst, hit is scathe
675 That thou leude, schal be lost, that art of lyf noble!

So this new-painted sign
He bore on shield and coat,
As man most true of speech
And fairest-spoken knight.

640 First he was judged perfect in his five senses,
And next his five fingers never lost their dexterity;
And all his earthly faith was in the five wounds
That Christ suffered on the cross, as the creed declares.
And wherever this man found himself in battle
645 His fixed thought was that, above all other things,
All his fortitude should come from the five joys
That the mild Queen of Heaven found in her child.
For this reason the gracious knight had
Her image depicted on the inside of his shield,
650 So that when he glanced at it his heart never quailed.
The fifth group of five the man respected, I hear,
Was generosity and love of fellow-men above all;
His purity and courtesy were never lacking,
And surpassing the others, compassion: these noble five
655 Were more deeply implanted in that man than any other.
Now truly, all these five groups were embodied in that
        knight,
Each one linked to the others in an endless design,
Based upon five points that was never unfinished,
Not uniting in one line nor separating either;
660 Without ending anywhere at any point that I find,
No matter where the line began or ran to an end.
Therefore the knot was fashioned on his bright shield
Royally with red gold upon red gules,
That is called the true pentangle by learned people
665   who know.
        Now Gawain, lance in hand,
        Is ready to depart;
        He bade them all farewell,
        Not to return, he thought.

670 He set spurs to his horse and sprang on his way
So vigorously that sparks flew up from the stones.
All who watched that fair knight leave sighed from the heart,
And together whispered one to another,
Distressed for that handsome one, "What a pity indeed
675 That your life must be squandered, noble as you are!

----

[1] *pité* Cannot readily be translated in one word, as it means both
pity and piety.

[2] *sothly* A dialect term meaning "quietly."

To fynde hys fere upon folde, in fayth, is not ethe.
Warloker to haf wroght had more wyt bene,
And haf dyght yonder dere a duk to have worthed;
A lowande leder of ledez in londe hym wel semez,
680 And so had better haf ben then britned to noght,
Hadet wyth an alvisch mon, for angardez pryde.
Who knew ever any kyng such counsel to take
As knyghtez in cavelaciounz on Crystmasse gomnez!"
Wel much watz the warme water that waltered of yghen,
685 When that semly syre soght fro tho wonez
          thad daye.
          He made non abode,
          Bot wyghtly went hys way;
          Mony wylsum way he rode,
690   The bok as I herde say.

Now ridez this renk thurgh the ryalme of Logres,[1]
Sir Gawan, on Godez halve, thagh hym no gomen thoght.
Oft leudlez and alone he lengez on nyghtez
Ther he fonde noght hym byfore the fare that he lyked.
695 Hade he no fere bot his fole by frythez and dounez,
Ne no gome bot God bi gate wyth to carp,
Til that he neghed ful neghe into the Northe Walez.
Alle the iles of Anglesay on lyft half he haldez,
And farez over the fordez by the forlondez,
700 Over at the Holy Hede, til he hade eft bonk
In the wyldrenesse of Wyrale; wonde ther bot lyte
That auther God other gome wyth goud hert lovied.
And ay he frayned as he ferde, at frekez that he met,
If thay hade herde any karp of a knyght grene,
705 In any grounde theraboute, of the grene chapel;
And al nykked hym wyth nay, that never in her lyve
Thay seye never no segge that watz of suche hwez
          of grene.
          The knyght tok gates straunge
710   In mony a bonk unbene,
          His cher ful oft con chaunge
          That chapel er he myght sene.

Mony klyf he overclambe in contrayez straunge,
Fer floten fro his frendez fremedly he rydez.
715 At uche warthe other water ther the wyghe passed
He fonde a foo hym byfore, bot ferly hit were,
And that so foule and so felle that feght hym byhode.

To find his equal on earth is not easy, in faith.
To have acted more cautiously would have been much wiser,
And have appointed that dear man to become a duke:
To be a brilliant leader of men, as he is well suited,
680 And would better have been so than battered to nothing,
Beheaded by an ogrish man out of excessive pride.
Whoever knew a king to take such foolish advice
As knights offer in arguments about Christmas games?"
A great deal of warm water trickled from eyes
685 When that elegant lord set out from the city
          that day.
          He did not linger there,
          But swiftly went his way;
          Taking perplexing roads
690   As I have heard books say.

Now rides this knight through the realm of England,
Sir Gawain, in God's name, though he found it no pleasure.
Often friendless and alone he passes his nights,
Finding before him no food that he liked.
695 He had no fellow but his horse by forest and hill,
And no one but God to talk to on the way,
Until he came very close to the north part of Wales.
All the islands of Anglesey he keeps on his left,
And crosses over the fords at the headlands,
700 There at the Holyhead, and came ashore again
In the wilderness of Wirral. There few people lived
Whom either God or good-hearted men could love.
And always as he rode he asked those whom he met
If they had heard anyone speak of a green knight
705 Or of a green chapel in any place round about;
And they all answered him no, that never in their lives
Had they ever seen a man who had such color
          of green.
          Strange roads the knight pursued
710   Through many a dreary space,
          Turning from side to side
          To find the meeting-place.

Many fells he climbed over in territory strange,
Far distant from his friends like an alien he rides.
715 At every ford or river where the knight crossed
He found an enemy facing him, unless he was in luck,
And so ugly and fierce that he was forced to give fight.

---

1 *Logres* Celtic name for England.

So mony mervayl bi mount ther the mon fyndez,
Hit were to tore for to telle of the tenthe dole.
720 Sumwhyle wyth wormez he werrez, and with wolves als,
Sumwhyle wyth wodwos that woned in the knarrez,
Bothe wyth bullez and berez, and borez otherquyle,
And etaynez that hym anelede of the heghe felle;
Nade he ben dughty and dryghe, and Dryghtyn had served,
725 Douteles he hade ben ded and dreped ful ofte.
For werre wrathed hym not so much that wynter nas wors,
When the colde cler water fro the cloudez schadde,
And fres er hit falle myght to the fale erthe.
Ner slayn wyth the slete he sleped in his yrnes
730 Mo nyghtez then innoghe in naked rokkez,
Ther as claterande fro the crest the colde borne rennez,
And henged heghe over his hede in hard iisse-ikkles.
Thus in peryl and payne and plytes ful harde
Bi contray caryez this knyght, tyl Krystmasse even,
735   al one;
        The knyght wel that tyde
        To Mary made his mone,
        That ho hym red to ryde
        And wysse hym to sum wone.

740 Bi a mounte on the morne meryly he rydes
Into a forest ful dep, that ferly watz wylde;
Highe hillez on uche a halve, and holtwodez under
Of hore okez ful hoge a hundreth togeder;
The hasel and the haghthorne were harled al samen,
745 With roghe raged mosse rayled aywhere,
With mony bryddez unblythe upon bare twyges,
That pitosly ther piped for pyne of the colde.
The gome upon Gryngolet glydez hem under,
Thurgh mony misy and myre, mon al hym one,
750 Carande for his costes, lest he ne kever schulde
To se the servyse of that syre, that on that self nyght
Of a burde watz borne, our baret to quelle;
And therfore sykyng he sayde, "I beseche the, lorde,
And Mary, that is myldest moder so dere,
755 Of sum herber ther heghly I myght here masse,
And thy matynez[1] to-morne, mekely I ask,
And therto prestly I pray my pater and ave
            and crede."

So many wonders befell him in the hills,
It would be tedious to recount the least part of them.
720 Sometimes he fights dragons, and wolves as well,
Sometimes with wild men who dwelt among the crags;
Both with bulls and with bears, and at other times boars,
And ogres who chased him across the high fells.
Had he not been valiant and resolute, trusting in God,
725 He would surely have died or been killed many times.
For fighting troubled him less than the rigorous winter,
When cold clear water fell from the clouds
And froze before it could reach the faded earth.
Half dead with the cold Gawain slept in his armor
730 More nights than enough among the bare rocks,
Where splashing from the hilltops the freezing stream runs,
And hung over his head in hard icicles.
Thus in danger, hardship and continual pain
This knight rides across the land until Christmas Eve
735   alone.
        Earnestly Gawain then
        Prayed Mary that she send
        Him guidance to some place
        Where he might lodging find.

740 Over a hill in the morning in splendor he rides
Into a dense forest, wondrously wild;
High slopes on each side and woods at their base
Of massive grey oaks, hundreds growing together;
Hazel and hawthorn were densely entangled,
745 Thickly festooned with coarse shaggy moss,
Where many miserable birds on the bare branches
Wretchedly piped for torment of the cold.
The knight on Gringolet hurries under the trees,
Through many a morass and swamp, a solitary figure,
750 Troubled about his plight, lest he should be unable
To attend mass for that lord who on that same night
Was born of a maiden, our suffering to end;
And therefore sighing he prayed, "I beg of you, Lord,
And Mary, who is gentlest mother so dear,
755 For some lodging where I might devoutly hear mass
And your matins tomorrow, humbly I ask;
And to this end promptly repeat my Pater and Ave
            and Creed."[2]

---

[1] *matynez* I.e., matins, morning prayer, but here a church service specifically devoted to Mary as the mother of Jesus Christ ("matins of the blessed Virgin Mary").

[2] *Pater ... Creed Pater* Latin: father, i.e., "The Lord's Prayer" ("Our Father, who art in Heaven ..."); *Ave* Latin: hail, i.e., Ave Maria ("Hail Mary"); *Creed* Latin: I believe ("The Creed").

He rode in his prayere,

760 And cryed for his mysdede,

He sayned hym in sythes sere,[1]

And sayde, "Cros Kryst me spede!"

Nade he sayned hymself, segge, bot thrye,

Er he watz war in the wod of a wone in a mote,

765 Abof a launde, on a lawe, loken under boghez

Of mony borelych bole aboute bi the diches:

A castle the comlokest that ever knyght aghte,

Pyched on a prayere, a park al aboute,

With a pyked palays pyned ful thik,

770 That umbeteye mony tre mo then two myle.

That holde on that on syde the hathel avysed

As hit schemered and schon[2] thurgh the schyre okez;

Thenne hatz he hendly of his helme, and heghly he thonkez

Jesus and sayn Gilyan,[3] that gentyle ar bothe,

775 That cortaysly had hym kydde, and his cry herkened.

"Now bone hostel,"[4] cothe the burne, "I beseche yow yette!"

Thenne gerdez he to Gryngolet with the gilt helez,

And he ful chauncely hatz chosen to the chef gate,

That broght bremly the burne to the bryge ende

780   in haste.

          The bryge watz breme upbrayde,

          The gatez were stoken faste,

          The wallez were wel arayed

          Hit dut no wyndez blaste.

785 The burne bode on blonk, that on bonk hoved

Of the depe double dich that drof to the place;

The walle wod in the water wonderly depe,

And eft a ful huge heght hit haled upon lofte

Of harde hewen ston up to the tablez,

790 Enbaned under the abataylment in the best lawe;

And sythen garytez ful gaye gered bitwene,

Wyth mony luflych loupe that louked ful clene:

A better barbican that burne bluschede upon never.

And innermore he behelde that halle ful hyghe,

795 Towres telded bytwene, trochet ful thik,

Fayre fylyolez that fyghed, and ferlyly long,

Bewailing his misdeeds,

760 And praying as he rode,

He often crossed himself

Crying, "Prosper me, Christ's cross!"

Hardly had he crossed himself, that man, three times,

Before he caught sight through the trees of a moated building

765 Standing over a field, on a mound, surrounded by boughs

Of many a massive tree-trunk enclosing the moat:

The most splendid castle ever owned by a knight,

Set on a meadow, a park all around,

Closely guarded by a spiked palisade

770 That encircled many trees for more than two miles.

That side of the castle Sir Gawain surveyed

As it shimmered and shone through the fine oaks;

Then graciously takes off his helmet, and devoutly thanks

Jesus and St. Julian, who kindly are both,

775 Who had treated him courteously, and listened to his prayer.

"Now good lodging," said the man, "I beg you to grant!"

Then he urged Gringolet forward with his gilt spurs,

And by good chance happened upon the main path

That led the knight directly to the end of the drawbridge

780   with speed.

          The bridge was drawn up tight,

          The gates were bolted fast.

          The walls were strongly built,

          They feared no tempest's blast.

785 The knight sat on his horse, pausing on the slope

Of the deep double ditch that surrounded the place.

The wall stood in the water incredibly deep,

And then soared up above an astonishing height,

Made of squared stone up to the cornice,

790 With coursings under battlements in the latest style.

At intervals splendid watch-towers were placed,

With many neat loop-holes that could be tightly shut:

Better outworks of a castle the knight had never seen.

Further inside he noticed a lofty hall

795 With towers set at intervals, richly ornate,

Splendid pinnacles fitted into them, wonderfully tall,

---

[1]   *in sythes sere*   Every time he prayed.

[2]   *hit schemered and schon*   See also *that blenked ful quyte*, 799.

[3]   *sayn Gilyan*   I.e., St. Julian, patron saint of hospitality.

[4]   *bone hostel*   "Good lodging," a traditional invocation to St. Julian.

With corvon coprounez craftyly sleghe.[1]
Chalkwhyt chymnees ther ches he innoghe[2]
Upon bastel rovez, that blenked ful quyte;
800 So mony pynakle paynted watz poudred ayquere,
Among the castel carnelez clambred so thik
That pared out of papure[3] purely hit semed.
The fre freke on the fole hit fayre innoghe thoght,
If he myght kever to com the cloyster wythinne,
805 To herber in that hostel whyl halyday lested,
      avinant.
    He calde, and son ther com
    A porter pure plesaunt,
    On the wal his ernde he nome,
810   And haylsed the knyght erraunt.

"Gode sir," quoth Gawan, "woldez thou go myn ernde,
To the hegh lorde of this hous, herber to crave?"
"Ye, Peter,"[4] quoth the porter, "and purely I trowee
That ye be, wyghe, welcum to wone quyle yow lykez."
815 Then yede the wyghe yerne and com agayn swythe,
And folke frely hym wyth, to fonge the knyght.
Thay let doun the grete draght and derely out yeden,
And kneled doun on her knes upon the colde erthe
To welcum this ilk wygh as worthy hom thoght;
820 Thay yolden hym the brode gate, yarked up wyde,
And he hem raysed rekenly, and rod over the brygge.
Sere segges hym sesed by sadel, quel he lyght,
And sythen stabled his stede stif men innoghe.
Knyghtez and swyerez comen doun thenne
825 For to bryng this buurne wyth blys into halle;
Quen he hef up his helme, ther hyghed innoghe
For to hent it at his honde, the hende to serven;
His bronde and his blasoun both thay token.
Then haylsed he ful hendly tho hathelez uchone,
830 And mony proud mon ther presed that prynce to honour.
Alle hasped in his hegh wede to halle thay hym wonnen,

Topped by carved crocketing, skillfully worked.
Chalk-white chimneys he saw there without number
On the roofs of the towers, that brilliantly shone.
800 So many painted pinnacles were scattered everywhere,
Thickly clustered among the castle's embrasures,
That, truly, the building seemed cut out of paper.
To the noble on the horse it was an attractive thought
That he might gain entrance into the castle,
805 To lodge in that building during the festival days
      at his ease.
    A cheerful porter came
    In answer to his shout,
    Who stationed on the wall
810   Greeted the questing knight.

"Good sir," said Gawain, "will you carry my message
To the master of this house, to ask for lodging?"
"Yes, by St. Peter," said the porter, "and I truly believe
That you are welcome, sir, to stay as long as you please."
815 Then the man went speedily and quickly returned,
Bringing others with him, to welcome the knight.
They lowered the great drawbridge and graciously came out,
Kneeling down on their knees upon the cold ground
To welcome this knight in the way they thought fit.
820 They gave him passage through the broad gate, set open wide,
And he courteously bade them rise, and rode over the bridge.
Several men held his saddle while he dismounted,
And then strong men in plenty stabled his horse.
Knights and squires came down then
825 To escort this man joyfully into the hall.
When Gawain took off his helmet, several jumped forward
To receive it from his hand, serving that prince.
His sword and his shield they took from him both.
Then he greeted politely every one of these knights,
830 And many proud men pressed forward to honor that noble.
Still dressed in his armor they brought him into hall,

---

[1] *craftyly sleghe* The castle architecture abounds with crafts-manship. *Sleghe*, meaning skillful, intricate, subtle, is a term of some significance in the poem. Gawain's fellow-guests hope to see *sleghtez of thewez*, 916, skillful displays of good manners; and after creeping into his bedchamber the lady calls him *a sleper unslyghe*, 1209 or unwary, a related term. On being told that he cannot be killed *for slyght upon erthe*, 1854, while wearing the belt, Gawain tells himself that such a *sleght were noble*, 1858. Here the word shades off towards modern "sleight," with overtones of trickery or deceit appropriate to

the story. But many passages of the poem illustrate the poet's fondness for the elaborate craftsmanship or *wylyde werke* that is evident in his own writing, particularly in the *entrelacement* of Part 3.

[2] *ches he innoghe* He saw enough of them, meaning there were very many.

[3] *papure* Paper, a word newly introduced into English, perhaps by the poet.

[4] *Peter* I.e., St. Peter, one of Christ's twelve apostles and, traditionally, the gate-keeper of Heaven.

Ther fayre fyre upon flet fersly brenned.
Thenne the lorde of the lede loutez fro his chambre
For to mete wyth menske the mon on the flor;
835 He sayde, "Ye ar welcum to welde as yow lykez
That here is: al is yowre awen, to have at yowre wylle
                and welde."
        "Graunt mercy," quoth Gawayn,
        "Ther Kryst hit yow foryelde."
840   As frekez that semed fayn
        Ayther other in armez con felde.

Gawan glynte on the gome that godly hym gret,
And thught hit a bolde burne that the burgh aghte;
A hoge hathel for the nonez, and of hyghe eldee;
845 Brode, bryght, watz his berde, and al bever-hwed,
Sturne, stif on the stryththe on stalworth schonkez,
Felle face as the fyre, and fre of hys speche,
And wel hym semed, for sothe, as the segge thught,
To lede a lortschyp in lee of leudez ful gode.
850 The lorde hym charred to a chambre, and chefly cumaundez
To delyver hym a leude, hym lowly to serve;
And there were boun at his bode burnez innoghe,
That broght hym to a bryght boure, ther beddyng was
                noble,
Of cortynes of clere sylk wyth cler golde hemmez,
855 And covertorez ful curious with comlych panez
Of bryght blaunner above, enbrawded bisydez,
Rudelez rennande on ropez, red golde ryngez,
Tapitez tyght to the wowe of tuly and tars,
And under fete, on the flet, of folyande sute.
860 Ther he watz dispoyled, wyth speches of myerthe,
The burne of his bruny and of his bryght wedez.
Ryche robes ful rad renkkez hym broghten,
For to charge and to chaunge, and chose of the best.
Sone as he on hent, and happed therinne,
865 That sete on hym semly wyth saylande skyrtez,
The ver by his visage verayly hit semed
Welnegh to uche hathel, alle on hwes
Lowande and lufly alle his lymmez under,
That a comloker knyght never Kryst made,
870   hem thoght.
        Whethen in worlde he were,
        Hit semed as he moght

Where a blazing fire was fiercely burning.
Then the lord of that company comes down from his chamber,
To show his respect by meeting Gawain there.
835 He said, "You are welcome to do as you please
With everything here: all is yours, to have and command
                as you wish."
        Said Gawain, "Thanks indeed,
        Christ repay your noblesse."
840   Like men overjoyed
        Each hugged the other close.

Gawain studied the man who greeted him courteously,
And thought him a bold one who governed the castle,
A great-sized knight indeed, in the prime of life;
845 Broad and glossy was his beard, all reddish-brown,
Stern-faced, standing firmly on powerful legs;
With a face fierce as fire, and noble in speech,
Who truly seemed capable, it appeared to Gawain,
Of being master of a castle with outstanding knights.
850 The lord led him to a chamber and quickly orders
A man to be assigned to him, humbly to serve;
And several attendants stood ready at his command
Who took him to a fine bedroom with marvelous
                bedding:
Curtains of pure silk with shining gold borders,
855 And elaborate coverlets with splendid facing
Of bright ermine on top, embroidered all around;
Curtains on golden rings, running on cords,
Walls covered with hangings from Tharsia and Toulouse
And underfoot on the floor of a matching kind.
860 There he was stripped, with joking remarks,
That knight, of his mail-shirt and his fine clothes.
Men hurried to bring him costly robes
To choose from the best of them, change and put on.
As soon as he took one and dressed himself in it,
865 Which suited him well with its flowing skirts,
Almost everyone truly supposed from his looks
That spring had arrived in all its colors;
His limbs so shining and attractive under his clothes
That a handsomer knight God never made,
870   it seemed.
        Wherever he came from,
        He must be, so they thought,

Be prynce withouten pere
In felde ther felle men foght.

A prince unparalleled
In field where warriors fought.

875 A cheyer[1] byfore the chemné, ther charcole brenned,
Watz grathed for Sir Gawan graythely with clothez,
Whyssynes upon queldepoyntes that koynt wer bothe;
And thenne a meré mantyle watz on that mon cast
Of a broun bleeaunt, enbrauded ful ryche
880 And fayre furred wythinne with fellez of the best,
Alle of ermyn in erde, his hode of the same;
And he sette in that settel semlych ryche,
And achaufed hym chefly, and thenne his cher mended.
Sone watz telded up a tabil on trestez ful fayre,
885 Clad wyth a clene clothe that cler quyt schewed,
Sanap, and salure, and sylverin sponez.
The wyghe wesche at his wylle and went to his mete:
Seggez hym served semly innoghe,
Wyth sere sewes and sete, sesounde of the best,
890 Double-felde, as hit fallez, and fele kyn fischez,[2]
Summe baken in bred, summe brad on the gledez,
Summe sothen, summe in sewe savered with spyces,
And ay sawes so sleghe that the segge lyked.
The freke calde hit a fest ful frely and ofte
895 Ful hendely, quen alle the hatheles rehayted hym at onez,
        as hende,
    "This penaunce now ye take,
    And eft hit schal amende."
    That mon much merthe con make,
900   For wyn in his hed that wende.

Thenne watz spyed and spured upon spare wyse
Bi prevé poyntez of that prynce, put to hymselven,
That he biknew cortaysly of the court that he were
That athel Arthure the hende haldez hym one,
905 That is the ryche ryal kyng of the Rounde Table,
And hit watz Wawen hymself that in that won syttez,
Comen to that Krystmasse, as case hym then lymped.
When the lorde hade lerned that he the leude hade,
Loude laghed he therat, so lef hit hym thoght,

875 A chair before the fireplace where charcoal glowed
Was made ready with coverings for Gawain at once:
Cushions set on quilted spreads, both skilfully made,
And then a handsome robe was thrown over the man
Made of rich brown material, with embroidery rich,
880 And well fur-lined inside with the very best pelts,
All of ermine in fact, with a matching hood.
Becomingly rich in attire he sat in that chair,
Quickly warmed himself, and then his expression softened.
Soon a table was deftly set up on trestles,
885 Spread with a fine tablecloth, brilliantly white,
With overcloth and salt-cellar, and silver spoons.
When he was ready Gawain washed and sat down to his meal.
Men served him with every mark of respect,
With many excellent dishes, wonderfully seasoned,
890 In double portions, as is fitting, and all kinds of fish:
Some baked in pastry, some grilled over coals,
Some boiled, some in stews flavored with spices,
Always with subtle sauces that the knight found tasty.
Many times he graciously called it a feast,
895 Courteously when the knights all urged him together,
        as polite,
    "Accept this penance now,
    Soon you'll be better fed."
    Gawain grew full of mirth
900   As wine went to his head.

Then he was tactfully questioned and asked
By discreet enquiry addressed to that prince,
So that he must politely admit he belonged to the court
Which noble Arthur, that gracious man, rules alone,
905 Who is the great and royal king of the Round Table;
And that it was Gawain himself who was sitting there,
Having arrived there at Christmas, as his fortune chanced.
When the lord of the castle heard who was his guest,
He laughed loudly at the news, so deeply was he pleased;

---

[1] *A cheyer* Chairs were relatively rare, and to be given one was a mark of respect. The usual form of seat is indicated by the Green Knight's reference to knights *aboute on this bench*, 280, and by Gawain's request for permission to *boghe fro this benche*, 344.

[2] *fele kyn fischez* Many kinds of fish. Because Christmas Eve is a fast-day, no red meat is served. The meal is jokingly referred to as penance, 897, and Gawain is promised something better on the next day, 898.

910 And alle the men in that mote maden much joye
To apere in his presense prestly that tyme,
That alle prys and prowes and pured thewes[1]
Apendes to hys persoun, and praysed is ever;
Byfore alle men upon molde his mensk is the most.
915 Uch segge ful softly sayde to his fere:
"Now schal we semlych se sleghtez of thewez
And the teccheles termes of talkyng noble,
Wich spede is in speche unspurd may we lerne,[2]
Syn we haf fonged that fyne fader of nurture.
920 God hatz geven us his grace godly for sothe,
That such a gest as Gawan grauntez us to have,
When burnez blythe of his burthe schal sitte
     and synge.
     In menyng of manerez mere
925   This burne now schal us bryng,
     I hope that may hym here
     Schal lerne of luf-talkyng."

Bi that the diner watz done and the dere up
Hit watz negh at the niyght neghed the tyme.
930 Chaplaynez to the chapeles chosen the gate,
Rungen ful rychely, ryght as thay schulden,
To the hersum evensong of the hyghe tyde.
The lorde loutes therto, and the lady als,
Into a cumly closet coyntly ho entrez.
935 Gawan glydez ful gay and gos theder sone;
The lorde laches hym by the lappe and ledez hym to sytte,
And couthly hym knowez and callez hym his nome,
And sayde he watz the welcomest wyghe of the worlde;
And he hym thonkked throly, and ayther halched other,
940 And seten soberly samen the servise quyle.
Thenne lyst the lady to loke on the knyght,
Thenne com ho of hir closet with mony cler burdez.
Ho watz the fayrest in felle,[3] of flesche and of lyre,
And of compas and colour and costes, of all other,
945 And wener then Wenore, as the wyght thoght.
Ho ches thurgh the chaunsel to cheryche that hende:
An other lady hir lad bi the lyft honde,
That watz alder then ho, an auncian hit semed,
And heghly honowred with hathelez aboute.

910 And all the men in the castle were overjoyed
To make the acquaintance quickly then
Of the man to whom all excellence and valor belongs,
Whose refined manners are everywhere praised,
And whose fame exceeds any other person's on earth.
915 Each knight whispered to his companion,
"Now we shall enjoy seeing displays of good manners,
And the irreproachable terms of noble speech;
The art of conversation we can learn unasked,
Since we have taken in the source of good breeding.
920 Truly, God has been gracious to us indeed,
In allowing us to receive such a guest as Gawain,
Whose birth men will happily sit down and celebrate
     in song.
     In knowledge of fine manners
925   This man has expertise;
     I think that those who hear him
     Will learn what love-talk is."

When dinner was finished and Gawain had risen,
The time had drawn on almost to night:
930 Chaplains made their way to the castle chapels,
Rang their bells loudly, just as they should,
For devout evensong on that holy occasion.
The lord makes his way there, and his lady too,
Who gracefully enters a finely carved pew.
935 Gawain hastens there, smartly dressed, and quickly arrives;
The lord takes him by the sleeve and leads him to a seat,
And greets him familiarly, calling him by his name,
And said he was the welcomest guest in the world.
Gawain thanked him heartily, and the two men embraced,
940 And sat gravely together while the service lasted.
Then the lady wished to set eyes on the knight
And left her pew with many fair women.
She was the loveliest on earth in complexion and features,
In figure, in coloring and behavior above all others,
945 And more beautiful than Guenevere, it seemed to the knight.
She came through the chancel to greet him courteously,
Another lady leading her by the left hand,
Who was older than she, an aged one it seemed,
And respectfully treated by the assembled knights.

---

[1] *alle prys and prowes and pured thewes* Great excellence, military valor, and refined manners.

[2] *Wich spede is in speche unspurd may we lerne* We may learn without asking what success in conversation consists of.

---

[3] *the fayrest in felle* Literally, the most beautiful in skin.

950 Bot unlyke on to loke tho ladyes were,
For if the yonge watz yep, yolwe watz that other;
Riche red on that on rayled ayquere,
Rugh ronkled chekez that other on rolled;
Kerchofes of that on, wyth mony cler perlez,
955 Hir brest and hir bryght throte bare displayed,
Schon schyrer then snawe that schedez on hillez;
That other wyth a gorger watz gered over the swyre,
Chymbled over hir blake chyn with chalkquyte vayles,
Hir frount folden in sylk, enfoubled ayquere,
960 Toreted and treleted with tryfles aboute,
That noght watz bare of that burde bot the blake browes,
The tweyne yghen and the nase, the naked lyppez,
And those were soure to se and sellyly blered;
A mensk lady on molde mon may hire calle,
965   for Gode!
    Hir body watz schort and thik,
    Hir buttokez balgh and brode,
    More lykkerwys on to lyk
    Watz that scho hade on lode.

970 When Gawayn glent on that gay, that graciously loked,
Wyth leve laght of the lorde he lent hem agaynes;
The alder he haylses, heldande ful lowe,
The loveloker he lappez a lyttel in armez,
He kysses hir comlyly, and knyghtly he melez.
975 Thay kallen hym of aquoyntaunce, and he hit quyk askez
To be hir servaunt sothly, if hemself lyked.
Thay tan hym bytwene hem, wyth talkyng hym leden
To chambre, to chemné, and chefly thay asken
Spycez,[1] that unsparely men speded hom to bryng,
980 And the wynnelych wyne therwith uche tyme.
The lorde luflych aloft lepez ful ofte,
Mynned merthe to be made upon mony sythez,
Hent heghly of his hode, and on a spere henged,
And wayned hom to wynne the worchip therof,
985 That most myrthe myght meve that Crystenmasse whyle:[2]
"And I schal fonde, bi my fayth, to fylter wyth the best
Er me wont the wede, with help of my frendez."
Thus wyth laghande lotez the lorde hit tayt makez,
For to glade Sir Gawayn with gomnez in halle
990   that nyght,

950 But very different in looks were those two ladies,
For where the young one was fresh, the other was withered;
Every part of that one was rosily aglow:
On that other, rough wrinkled cheeks hung in folds.
Many bright pearls adorned the kerchiefs of one,
955 Whose breast and white throat, uncovered and bare,
Shone more dazzling than snow new-fallen on hills;
The other wore a gorget over her neck,
Her swarthy chin wrapped in chalkwhite veils,
Her forehead enfolded in silk, muffled up everywhere,
960 With embroidered hems and lattice-work of tiny stitching,
So that nothing was exposed of her but her black brows,
Her two eyes and her nose, her naked lips,
Which were repulsive to see and shockingly bleared.
A noble lady indeed you might call her,
965   by God!
    With body squat and thick,
    And buttocks bulging broad,
    More delectable in looks
    Was the lady whom she led.

970 Gawain glanced at that beauty, who favored him with a look,
And taking leave of the lord he walked towards them.
The older one he salutes with a deep bow,
And takes the lovelier one briefly into his arms,
Kisses her respectfully and courteously speaks.
975 They ask to make his acquaintance, and he quickly begs
Truly to be their servant, if that would please them.
They place him between them and lead him, still chatting,
To a private room, to the fireplace, and immediately call
For spiced cakes, which men hurried to bring them unstinted,
980 Together with marvelous wine each time they asked.
The lord jumps up politely on several occasions,
Repeatedly urging his guests to make merry;
Graciously pulled off his hood and hung it on a spear,
And encouraged them to gain honor by winning it,
985 So that the Christmas season would abound with mirth.
"And I shall try, on my word, to compete with the best,
Before I lose my hood, with the help of my friends."
Thus with laughing words the lord makes merry,
To keep Sir Gawain amused with games in hall
990   that night,

---

1   Spycez   Spiced cakes, still a Christmas tradition. Cloves, ginger, and cinnamon were available.

2   Hent heghly … Crystenmasse whyle   Another Christmas game, evidently a jumping contest, typically boisterous in character.

Til that hit watz tyme
The lord comaundet lyght;
Sir Gawen his leve con nyme
And to his bed hym dight.

995 On the morne, as uch mon mynez that tyme
That Dryghtyn for oure destyné to deye watz borne,
Wele waxez in uche a won in world for his sake;
So did hit there on that day thurgh dayntés mony.
Bothe at mes and at mele messes ful quaynt[1]
1000 Derf men upon dece drest of the best.
The olde auncian wyf heghest ho syttez,
The lorde lufly her by lent, as I trowe;
Gawan and the gay burde togeder thay seten,
Even inmyddez, as the messe metely come,
1005 And sythen thurgh al the sale as hem best semed.
Bi uche grome at his degré graythely watz served,
Ther watz mete, ther watz myrthe, ther watz much joye,
That for to telle therof hit me tene were,
And to poynte hit yet I pyned me paraventure.
1010 Bot yet I wot that Wawen and the wale burde
Such comfort of her compaynye caghten togeder
Thurgh her dere dalyaunce of her derne wordez,
Wyth clene cortays carp closed fro fylthe,
That hor play watz passande uche prynce gomen,
1015   in vayres.
     Trumpes and nakerys,
     Much pypyng ther repayres;
     Uche mon tented hys,[2]
     And thay two tented thayres.

1020 Much dut watz ther dryven that day and that other,
And the thryd as thro thronge in therafter;
The joye of sayn Jonez day[3] watz gentyle to here,
And watz the last of the layk, leudez ther thoghten.
Ther wer gestes to go upon the gray morne,
1025 Forthy wonderly thay woke, and the wyn dronken,
Daunsed ful dreghly wyth dere carolez.
At the last, when hit watz late, thay lachen her leve,
Uchon to wende on his way that watz wyghe straunge.[4]

Until it was so late
That lights were ordered in;
Then taking courteous leave
To chamber went Gawain.

995 On the next day, when everyone remembers the time
When God who died for our salvation was born,
Joy spreads through every dwelling on earth for his sake.
So did it there on that day, through numerous pleasures;
Both light meals and great dishes cunningly prepared
1000 And of exquisite quality bold men served on the dais.
The ancient lady sits in the place of honor,
The lord politely taking his place by her, I believe.
Gawain and the lovely lady were seated together,
Right in the middle of the table, where food duly came,
1005 And was then served throughout the hall in proper sequence.
By the time each man had been served according to rank,
Such food and such merriment, so much enjoyment were there
That to tell you about it would give me much trouble,
Especially if I tried to describe it in detail.
1010 Yet I know that Gawain and his beautiful partner
Found such enjoyment in each other's company,
Through a playful exchange of private remarks,
And well-mannered small-talk, unsullied by sin,
That their pleasure surpassed every princely amusement,
1015   for sure.
     Trumpets, kettledrums
     And piping roused all ears.
     Each man fulfilled his wishes,
     And those two followed theirs.

1020 Great joy filled that day and the one following,
And a third as delightful came pressing after;
The revelry on St. John's Day was glorious to hear,
And was the end of the festivities, the people supposed.
The guests were to leave early next morning,
1025 And so they reveled all night, drinking the wine
And ceaselessly dancing and caroling songs.
At last, when it was late, they take their leave,
Each one who was a guest there to go on his way.

---

[1] *messes ful quaynt* Finely prepared meals, set out (*drest*) on the high table. Elsewhere *koynt*, 877 is a variant spelling, again indicating skillfully made things.

[2] *Uche mon tented hys* Each man attended to his own needs or pleasures.

[3] *sayn Jonez day* 27 December, but three days later it is New Year's Eve—a day too early. Some editors have suggested a line may be missing here.

[4] *wyghe straunge* Stranger or visitor to the castle.

Gawan gef hym god day, the godmon hym lachchez,
1030 Ledes hym to his awen chambre, the chemné bysyde,
And there he drawez hym on dryghe, and derely hym thonkkez
Of the wynne worschip that he hym wayved hade,
As to honour his hous on that hygh tyde,
And enbelyse his burgh with his bele chere.[1]
1035 "Iwysse, sir, quyl I leve, me worthez the better
That Gawayn hatz ben my gest at Goddez awen fest."
"Grant merci, sir," quoth Gawayn, "in god fayth hit is yowrez,
Al the honour is your awen——the heghe kyng yow yelde!
And I am wyghe at your wylle to worch youre hest,
1040 As I am halden therto, in hyghe and in lowe,
        bi right.
    The lorde fast can hym payne
    To holde lenger the knyght;
    To hym answarez Gawayn
1045 Bi non way that he myght.[2]

Then frayned the freke ful fayre at himselven
Quat derve dede had hym dryven at that dere tyme
So kenly fro the kyngez kourt to kayre al his one,
Er the halidayez holly were haler[3] out of toun.
1050 "For sothe, sir," quoth the segge, "ye sayn bot the trawthe,
A heghe ernde and a hasty me hade fro tho wonez,
For I am sumned myselfe to sech to a place,
I ne wot in the worlde whederwarde to wende hit to fynde.
I nolde bot if I hit negh myght on Nw Yeres morne
1055 For alle the londe inwyth Logres, so me oure lorde help!
Forthy, sir, this enquest I require yow here,
That ye telle me with trawthe if ever ye tale herde
Of the grene chapel, quere hit on grounde stondez,
And of the knyght that hit kepes, of colour of grene.
1060 Ther watz stabled bi statut a steven us bitwene
To mete that mon at that mere, yif I myght last;
And of that ilk Nw Yere bot neked now wontez,
And I wolde loke on that lede, if God me let wolde,
Gladloker, bi Goddez sun, then any god welde!
1065 Forthi, iwysse, bi yowre wylle, wende me bihoves,
Naf I now to busy bot bare thre dayez,
And me als fayn to falle feye as fayly of myyn ernde."
Thenne laghande quoth the lorde, "Now leng the byhoves,

Gawain bids goodbye to his host, who takes hold of him,
1030 Leads him to his own room, beside the fire,
And there he detains him, thanks him profusely
For the wonderful kindness that Gawain had shown
By honoring his house at that festive time,
And by gracing the castle with his charming presence.
1035 "Indeed, sir, as long as I live I shall be the better
Because Gawain was my guest at God's own feast."
"All my thanks, sir," said Gawain, "in truth it is yours,
All the honor falls to you, and may the high king repay you!
And I am at your commandment to act on your bidding,
1040 As I am duty bound to in everything, large or small,
        by right.
    The lord tried strenuously
    To lengthen Gawain's stay,
    But Gawain answered him
1045 That he could not delay.

Then the lord politely enquired of the knight
What pressing need had forced him at that festive time
So urgently from the royal court to travel all alone,
Before the holy days there had completely passed.
1050 "Indeed, sir," said the knight, "you are right to wonder;
A task important and pressing drove me into the wild,
For I am summoned in person to seek out a place
With no idea whatever where it might be found.
I would not fail to reach it on New Year's morning
1055 For all the land in England, so help me our Lord!
Therefore, sir, this request I make of you now,
That you truthfully tell me if you ever heard talk
Of a Green Chapel, wherever it stands upon earth,
And of a knight who maintains it, who is colored green.
1060 A verbal agreement was settled between us
To meet that man at that place, should I be alive,
And before that New Year little time now remains;
And I would face that man, if God would allow me,
More gladly, by God's son, than come by great wealth!
1065 With your permission, therefore, I must indeed leave:
I have now for my business only three short days,
And would rather be struck dead than fail in my quest."
Then the lord said, laughing, "Now you must stay,

---

[1] *enbelyse ... bele chere* Bertilak (Gawain's host) makes an uncharacteristic sortie into courtly French terms.

[2] *Bi non way that he myght* He could not by any means.

[3] *Er the halidayez holly were halet* Before the holidays were completely over. A curious remark. Gawain reaches the castle, Hautdesert, after a long journey (*towen fro ferre*, 1093) as the festivities are reaching their height, having left Camelot long before the holiday season began.

For I schal teche yow to that terme bi the tymes ende,
1070 The grene chapayle upon grounde greve yow no more;
Bot ye schal be in yowre bed, burne, at thyn ese,
Quyle forth dayez, and ferk on the fyrst of the yere,
And cum to that merk at mydmorn, to make quat yow likez
   in spenne.
1075 Dowellez whyle New Yeres daye,
 And rys, and raykez thenne,
 Mon schal yow sette in waye,
 Hit is not two myle henne."

Thenne watz Gawan ful glad, and gomenly he laghed:
1080 "Now I thonk yow thryvandely thurgh alle other thynge,
Now acheved is my chaunce, I schal at your wylle
Dowelle, and ellez do quat ye demen."
Thenne sesed hym the syre and set hym bysyde,
Let the ladiez be fette to lyke hem the better.
1085 Ther watz seme solace by hemself stille;
The lorde let for luf lotez so myry
As wygh that wolde of his wyte, ne wyst quat he myght.
Thenne he carped to the knyght, criande loude,
"Ye han demed to do the dede that I bidde;
1090 Wyl ye halde this hes here at thys onez?"
"Ye, sir, for sothe," sayd the segge trwe,
"Whyl I byde in yowre borghe, be bayn to yowre hest."
"For ye haf travayled," quoth the tulk, "towen fro ferre,
And sythen waked me wyth, ye arn not wel waryst
1095 Nauther of sostnaunce ne of slepe, sothly I knowe;
Ye schal lenge in your lofte, and lyghe in your ese
To-morn quyle the messequyle, and to mete wende
When ye wyl, wyth my wyf, that wyth yow schal sitte
And comfort yow with compayny, til I to cort torne;
1100   ye lende,
 And I schal erly ryse,
 On huntyng wyl I wende."
 Gavayn grantez alle thyse,
 Hym heldande, as the hende.

1105 "Yet firre," quoth the freke, "a forwarde we make:
Quat-so-ever I wynne in the wod hit worthez to yourez,
And quat chek so ye acheve[1] chaunge me therforne.
Swete, swap we so, sware with trawthe,

---

[1] *quat chek so ye acheve* Whatever fortune you win. The remark is equivocal. *Chek* also has the sense of misfortune—see 1857 and 2195.

For I shall direct you to your meeting at the year's end.
1070 Let the whereabouts of the Green Chapel worry you no more;
For you shall lie in your bed, sir, taking your ease
Until late in the day, and leave on the first of the year,
And reach that place at midday, to do whatever pleases you
   there.
1075 Stay till the year's end,
 And leave on New Year's Day;
 We'll put you on the path,
 It's not two miles away."

Then Gawain was overjoyed, and merrily laughed:
1080 "Now I thank you heartily for this, above everything else,
Now my quest is accomplished, I shall at your wish
Remain here, and do whatever else you think fit."
Then the host seized him, set Gawain by his side,
And bid the ladies be fetched to increase their delight.
1085 They had great pleasure by themselves in private;
In his excitement the lord uttered such merry words
Like a man out of his mind, not knowing what he did.
Then he said to the knight exuberantly,
"You have agreed to carry out whatever deed I ask;
1090 Will you keep this promise now, at this very instant?"
"Yes, sir, assuredly," said the true knight,
"While I am under your roof, I obey your bidding."
"You have wearied yourself," said the man, "traveling from far,
And then reveled all night with me: you have not recovered
1095 Either your lost sleep or your nourishment, I am sure.
You shall stay in your bed and lie at your ease
Tomorrow until mass-time, and then go to dine
When you like, with my wife, who will sit at your side
And be your charming companion until I come home.
1100   You stay;
 And I shall rise at dawn
 And hunting will I go."
 All this Gawain grants,
 With a well-mannered bow.

1105 "Yet further," said the man, "let us make an agreement:
Whatever I catch in the wood shall become yours,
And whatever mishap comes your way give me in exchange.
Dear sir, let us swap so, swear me that truly,

Quether, leude, so lymp, lere other better."[1]

1110 "Bi God," quoth Gawayn the gode, "I grant thertylle,
And that yow lyst for to layke, lef hit me thynkes."
"Who bryngez uus this beverage, this bargayn is maked":
So sayde the lorde of that lede; thay laghed uchone,
Thay dronken and dalyeden and dalten untyghtel,
1115 Thise lordez and ladyez, quyle that hem lyked;
And sythen with Frenkysch fare[2] and fele fayre lotez
Thay stoden and stemed and stylly speken,
Kysten ful comlyly and kaghten her leve.
With mony leude ful lyght and lemande torches
1120 Uche burne to his bed watz broght at the laste,
　　　ful softe.
　　　To bed yet er thay yede,
　　　Recorded covenauntez ofte;
　　　The olde lorde of that leude
1125　　　Cowthe wel halde layk alofte.

Whatever falls to our lot, worthless or better."

1110 "By God," said the good Gawain, "I agree to that,
And your love of amusement pleases me much."
"If someone brings us drink, it will be an agreement,"
Said the lord of that company: everyone laughed.
They drank wine and joked and frivolously chatted
1115 For as long as it pleased them, these lords and ladies;
And then with exquisite manners and many gracious words
They stood at a pause, conversing quietly,
Kissed each other affectionately and then took their leave.
With many brisk servingmen and gleaming torches
1120 Each man was at last escorted to a bed
　　　downy soft.
　　　Yet first, and many times
　　　Again the terms were sworn;
　　　The master of those folk
1125　　　Knew how to foster fun.

FITT 3

Ful erly bifore the day the folk uprysen,
Gestes that go wolde hor gromez thay calden,
And thay busken up bilyve blonkkez to sadel,
Tyffen her takles, trussen her males,
1130 Richen hem the rychest, to ryde alle arayde,
Lepen up lightly, lachen her brydeles,
Uche wyghe on his way ther hym wel lyked.
The leve lorde of the londe watz not the last
Arayed for the rydyng, with renkkes ful mony;
1135 Ete a sop hastyly, when he hade herde masse,
With bugle to bent-felde he buskez bylyve.
By that any daylyght lemed upon erthe
He with his hatheles on hyghe horsses weren.
Thenne thise cacheres that couthe cowpled hor houndez,
1140 Unclosed the kenel dore and calde hem theroute,
Blwe bygly in buglez thre bare mote;[3]
Braches bayed therfor and breme noyse maked;
And thay chastysed and charred on chasyng that went,

PART 3

Early before daybreak the household arose;
Guests who were leaving called for their grooms,
And they hurried quickly to saddle horses,
Make equipment ready and pack their bags.
1130 The noblest prepare themselves to ride finely dressed,
Leap nimbly into saddle, seize their bridles,
Each man taking the path that attracted him most.
The well-loved lord of the region was not the last
Prepared for riding, with a great many knights;
1135 Snatched a hasty breakfast after hearing mass,
And makes ready for the hunting-field with bugles blowing.
By the time the first glimmers of daylight appeared
He and his knights were mounted on horse.
Then experienced huntsmen coupled the hounds,
1140 Unlocked the kennel door and ordered them out,
Loudly blowing three long notes on their horns.
Hounds bayed at the sound and made a fierce noise;
And those who went straying were whipped in and turned back,

---

[1] *Quether, leude, so lymp, lere other better* Whichever man wins
something worthless or better. The literal sense of *lymp* is "falls to
his lot."

[2] *Frenkysch fare* Refined manners, modeled on courtly French
behavior.

[3] *thre bare mote* Three single notes on the horn, ordering the
release of the hounds.

A hundreth of hunteres, as I haf herde telle,
1145   of the best.
      To trystors vewters yod,[1]
      Couples huntes of kest;
      Ther ros for blastez gode
      Gret rurd in that forest.

1150 At the fyrst quethe of the quest quaked the wylde;
      Der drof in the dale, doted for drede,
      Highed to the hyghe, bot heterly thay were
      Restayed with the stablye, that stoutly ascryed.
      Thay let the herttez haf the gate, with the hyghe hedes,
1155 The breme bukkez also with hor brode paumez;
      For the fre lorde hade defende in fermysoun tyme
      That ther schulde no mon meve to the male dere.
      The hindez were halden in with hay! and war!
      The does dryven with gret dyn to the depe sladez.
1160 Ther myght mon se, as thay slypte, slenting of arwes—
      At uche wende under wande wapped a flone—
      That bigly bote on the broun with ful brode hedez.
      What! thay brayen and bleden, bi bonkkez thay deyen,
      And ay rachches in a res radly hem folwes,
1165 Hunterez wyth hyghe horne hasted hem after
      Wyth such a crakkande kry as klyffes haden brusten.
      What wylde so atwaped wyghes that schotten
      Watz al toraced and rent at the resayt,
      Bi thay were tened at the hyghe and taysed to the wattres;
1170 The ledez were so lerned at the lowe trysteres,
      And the grehoundez so grete, that geten hem bylyve
      And hem tofylched, as fast as frekez myght loke,
            ther-ryght.
            The lorde for blys abloy
1175   Ful ofte con launce and lyght,
            And drof that day wyth joy
            Thus to the derk nyght.

Thus laykez this lorde by lynde-wodez evez,
And Gawayn the god mon in gay bed lygez,
1180 Lurkkez[2] quyl the daylyght lemed on the wowes,
Under covertour ful clere, cortyned aboute;
And as in slomeryng he slode, sleghly he herde
A littel dyn at his dor, and dernly upon;
And he hevez up his hed out of the clothes,

By a hundred hunters, as I have been told,
1145   of the best.
      With keepers at their posts
      Huntsmen uncoupled hounds;
      Great clamor in the woods
      From mighty horn-blasts sounds.

1150 At the first sound of the hunt the wild creatures trembled;
      Deer fled from the valley, frantic with fear,
      And rushed to the high ground, but were fiercely turned back
      By the line of beaters, who yelled at them savagely.
      They let the stags with their tall antlers pass,
1155 And the wonderful bucks with their broad horns;
      For the noble lord had forbidden in the close season
      Anyone to interfere with the male deer.
      The hinds were held back with shouts of hay! and war!
      The does driven with great noise into the deep valleys.
1160 There you might see, as they ran, arrows flying—
      At every turn in the wood a shaft whistled through the air—
      Deeply piercing the hide with their wide heads.
      What! they cry out and bleed, on the slopes they are slaughtered,
      And always swiftly pursued by the rushing hounds;
1165 Hunters with screaming horns gallop behind
      With such an ear-splitting noise as if cliffs had collapsed.
      Those beasts that escaped the men shooting at them
      Were all pulled down and killed at the receiving points,
      As they were driven from the high ground down to the streams.
1170 The men at the lower stations were so skilful,
      And the greyhounds so large, that they seized them quickly
      And tore them down as fast as men could number,
            right there.
            On horseback and on foot
1175   The lord, filled with delight,
            Spent all that day in bliss
            Until the fall of night.

Thus this nobleman sports along the edges of woods,
And the good man Gawain lies in his fine bed,
1180 Lying snug while the daylight gleamed on the walls,
Under a splendid coverlet, shut in by curtains.
And as he lazily dozed, he heard slily made
A little noise at his door and it stealthily open;
And he raised up his head from the bedclothes,

---

1 *To trystors vewters yod* Keepers of hounds went to their hunting-stations.

2 *Lurkkez* Lay snug; but the term has pejorative overtones that are heard again at 1195.

1185	A corner of the cortyn he caght up a lyttel,
	And waytez warly thiderwarde quat hit be myght.
	Hit watz the ladi, loflyest to beholde,
	That drow the dor after hir ful dernly and stylle,
	And bowed towarde the bed; and the burne schamed,[1]
1190	And layde hym doun lystyly and let as he slepte;
	And ho stepped stilly and stel to his bedde,
	Kest up the cortyn and creped withinne,
	And set hir ful softly on the bed-syde,
	And lenged there selly longe to loke quen he wakened.
1195	The lede lay lurked a ful longe quyle,
	Compast in his concience to quat that cace myght
	Meve other mount—to mervayle hym thoght,
	Bot yet he sayde in hymself, "More semly hit were
	To aspye wyth my spelle in space quat ho wolde."
1200	Then he wakenede, and wroth, and to hir warde torned,
	And unlouked his yghe-lyddez, and let as hym wondered,
	And sayned hym, as bi his saghe the saver to worthe,
	with hande.
	Wyth chynne and cheke ful swete,
1205	Both quit and red in blande,
	Ful lufly con ho lete
	Wyth lyppez smal laghande.

"God moroun, Sir Gawayn," sayde that gay lady,
"Ye ar a sleper unslyghe, that mon may slyde hider;
1210 Now ar ye tan as-tyt![2] Bot true uus may schape,
I schal bynde yow in your bedde, that be ye trayst."
Al laghande the lady lanced tho bourdez.
"Goud moroun, gay," quoth Gawayn the blythe,
"Me schal worthe at your wille, and that me wel lykez,[3]
1215 For I yelde me yederly, and yeghe after grace,
And that is the best, be my dome, for me byhovez nede":
And thus he bourded agayn with mony a blythe laghter.
"Bot wolde ye, lady lovely, then leve me grante,
And deprece your prysoun, and pray hym to ryse,
1220 I wolde bowe of this bed, and busk me better;
I schulde kever the more comfort to karp yow wyth."
"Nay, for sothe, beau sire," sayde that swete,

1185	Lifted a corner of the curtain a little,
	And takes a glimpse warily to see what it could be.
	It was the lady, looking her loveliest,
	Who shut the door after her carefully, not making a sound,
	And came towards the bed. The knight felt confused,
1190	And lay down again cautiously, pretending to sleep;
	And she approached silently, stealing to his bed,
	Lifted the bed-curtain and crept within,
	And seating herself softly on the bedside,
	Waited there strangely long to see when he would wake.
1195	The knight shammed sleep for a very long while,
	Wondering what the matter could be leading to
	Or portend. It seemed an astonishing thing,
	Yet he told himself, "It would be more fitting
	To discover straightway by talking just what she wants."
1200	Then he wakened and stretched and turned towards her,
	Opened his eyes and pretended surprise,
	And crossed himself as if protecting himself by prayer
	and this sign.
	With lovely chin and cheek
1205	Of blended color both,
	Charmingly she spoke
	From her small laughing mouth.

"Good morning, Sir Gawain," said that fair lady,
"You are an unwary sleeper, that one can steal in here:
1210 Now you are caught in a moment! Unless we agree on a truce,
I shall imprison you in your bed, be certain of that!"
Laughing merrily the lady uttered this jest.
"Good morning, dear lady," said Gawain gaily,
"You shall do with me as you wish, and that pleases me much,
1215 For I surrender at once, and beg for your mercy,
And that is best, in my judgment, for I simply must."
Thus he joked in return with a burst of laughter.
"But if, lovely lady, you would grant me leave
And release your captive, and ask him to rise,
1220 I would get out of this bed and put on proper dress,
And then take more pleasure in talking with you."
"No, indeed not, good sir," said that sweet one,

---

[1] *and the burne schamed*   And the knight was embarrassed.

[2] *Now ar ye tan as-tyt!*   Now are you captured in a moment! There may be a suggestion here of another traditional game, played by women on Hock Monday, the week after Easter. It consisted of seizing and binding men, who were released after paying a small sum of money.

[3] *that me wel lykez*   That pleases me very much.

"Ye schal not rise of your bedde, I rych yow better.
I schal happe yow here that other half als,
1225 And sythen karp wyth my knyght that I kaght have;
For I wene wel, iwysse, Sir Wowen ye are,
That alle the worlde worchipez quere-so ye ride;
Your honour, your hendelayk is hendely praysed
With lordez, wyth ladyes, with alle that lyf bere.
1230 And now ye are here, iwysse, and we bot oure one;
My lorde and his ledez ar on lenthe faren,
Other burnez in her bedde, and my burdez als,
The dor drawen and dit with a derf haspe;
And sythen I have in this hous hym that al lykez,
1235 I schal ware my whyle wel, quyl hit lastez,
                with tale.
        Ye ar welcum to my cors,[1]
        Yowre awen won to wale,
        Me behovez of fyne force
1240   Your servaunt be, and schale."

"In god fayth," quoth Gawayn, "gayn hit me thynkkez,
Thagh I be not now he that ye of speken;
To reche to such reverence as ye reherce here
I am wyghe unworthy, I wot wel myselven.
1245 Bi God, I were glad, and yow god thoght,
At saghe other at servyce that I sette myght
To the plesaunce of your prys[2]—hit were a pure joye."
"In god fayth, Sir Gawayn," quoth the gay lady,
"The prys and the prowes that plesez al other,
1250 If I hit lakked other set at lyght, hit were little daynté;
Bot hit ar ladyes innoghe that lever were nowthe
Haf the, hende, in hor holde, as I the habbe here,
To daly with derely your daynté wordez,
Kever hem comfort and colen her carez,
1255 Then much of the garysoun other gold that thay haven.
Bot I louve that ilk lorde that the lyfte haldez
I have hit holly in my honde that al desyres,
                thurghe grace."
        Scho made hym so gret chere,
1260   That watz so fayr of face,
        The knyght with speches skere
        Answered to uche a case.

"You shall not leave your bed, I intend something better.
I shall tuck you in here on both sides of the bed,
1225 And then chat with my knight whom I have captured.
For I know well, in truth, that you are Sir Gawain,
Whom everyone reveres wherever you go;
Your good name and courtesy are honorably praised
By lords and by ladies and all folk alive.
1230 And now indeed you are here, and we two quite alone,
My husband and his men have gone far away,
Other servants are in bed, and my women too,
The door shut and locked with a powerful hasp;
And since I have under my roof the man everyone loves,
1235 I shall spend my time well, while it lasts,
                with talk.
        You are welcome to me indeed,
        Take whatever you want;
        Circumstances force me
1240   To be your true servant."

"Truly," replied Gawain, "I am greatly honored,
Though I am not in fact such a man as you speak of.
To deserve such respect as you have just described
I am completely unworthy, I know very well.
1245 I should be happy indeed, if you thought it proper,
That I might devote myself by words or by deed
To giving you pleasure: it would be a great joy."
"In all truth, Sir Gawain," replied the beautiful lady,
"If the excellence and gallantry everyone admires
1250 I were to slight or disparage, that would hardly be courteous;
But a great many ladies would much rather now
Hold you, sir, in their power as I have you here,
To spend time amusingly with your charming talk,
Delighting themselves and forgetting their cares,
1255 Than much of the treasure or wealth they possess.
But I praise that same lord who holds up the heavens,
I have completely in my grasp the man everyone longs for,
                through God's grace."
        Radiant with loveliness
1260   Great favor she conferred;
        The knight with virtuous speech
        Answered her every word.

---

[1] *Ye are welcum to my cors* A suggestive ambiguity that cannot be translated. *My cors* may mean "me," just as "your honor" or "your worship" mean "you." But the literal sense of the phrase, "my body," is present.

---

[2] *To the plesaunce of your prys* To pleasing you, or to carrying out your wishes, *your prys* meaning your noble self.

"Madame," quoth the myry mon, "Mary yow yelde,
For I haf founden, in god fayth, yowre fraunchis nobele,
1265 And other ful much of other folk fongen bi hor dedez,
Bot the daynté that thay delen, for my disert nys even,
Hit is the worchyp of yourself, that noght bot wel connez."
"Bi Mary," quod the menskful, "me thynk hit an other;
For were I worth al the wone of wymmen alyve,
1270 And al the wele of the worlde were in my honde,
And I schulde chepen and chose to cheve me a lorde,
For the costes that I haf knowen upon the, knyght, here,
Of bewté and debonerté and blythe semblaunt,
And that I haf er herkkened and halde hit here trwee,
1275 Ther schulde no freke upon folde bifore yow be chosen."
"Iwysse, worthy," quoth the wyghe, "ye haf waled wel
        better,[1]
Bot I am proude of the prys that ye put on me,
And soberly your servaunt, my soverayn I holde yow,
And yowre knyght I becom, and Kryst yow foryelde."
1280 Thus thay meled of muchquat til mydmorn paste,
And ay the lady let lyk as hym loved mych.
The freke ferde with defence, and feted ful fayre;
Thagh ho were burde bryghtest the burne in mynde hade,[2]
The lasse luf in his lode for lur that he soght
1285   bout hone—
        The dunte that schulde hym deve,
        And nedez hit most be done.
        The lady thenn spek of leve,
        He granted hir ful sone.

1290 Thenne ho gef hym god day, and wyth a glent laghed,
And as ho stod, ho stonyed hym wyth ful stor wordez:
"Now he that spedez uche spech this disport yelde yow!
Bot that ye be Gawan, hit gotz in mynde."
"Querfore?" quoth the freke, and freschly he askez,
1295 Ferde lest he hade fayled in fourme of his castes;
Bot the burde hym blessed, and "Bi this skyl" sayde:
"So god as Gawayn gaynly is halden,
And cortaysye is closed so clene in hymselven,
Couth not lightly haf lenged so long wyth a lady,
1300 Bot he had craved a cosse, bi his courtayse,

"Lady," said the man pleasantly, "may Mary repay you,
For I have truly made proof of your great generosity,
1265 And many other folk win credit for their deeds;
But the respect shown to me is not at all my deserving:
That honor is due to yourself, who know nothing but good."
"By Mary," said the noble lady, "to me it seems very different;
For if I were the worthiest of all women alive,
1270 And held all the riches of the earth in my hand,
And could bargain and pick a lord for myself,
For the virtues I have seen in you, sir knight, here,
Of good looks and courtesy and charming manner—
All that I have previously heard and now know to be true—
1275 No man on earth would be picked before you."
"Indeed, noble lady," said the man, "you have chosen
        much better,
But I am proud of the esteem that you hold me in,
And in all gravity your servant, my sovereign I consider you,
And declare myself your knight, and may Christ reward you."
1280 So they chatted of this and that until late morning,
And always the lady behaved as if loving him much.
The knight reacted cautiously, in the most courteous of ways,
Though she was the loveliest woman he could remember:
He felt small interest in love because of the ordeal he must face
1285   very soon—
        To stand a crushing blow,
        In helpless sufferance.
        Of leaving then she spoke,
        The knight agreed at once.

1290 Then she bade him goodbye, glanced at him and laughed,
And as she stood astonished him with a forceful rebuke:
"May he who prospers each speech repay you this pleasure!
But that you should be Gawain I very much doubt."
"But why?" said the knight, quick with his question,
1295 Fearing he had committed some breach of good manners;
But the lady said "Bless you" and replied, "For this cause:
So good a knight as Gawain is rightly reputed,
In whom courtesy is so completely embodied,
Could not easily have spent so much time with a lady
1300 Without begging a kiss, to comply with politeness,

---

[1] *ye haf waled wel better* You have made a much better choice; reminding the lady that she has a husband.

[2] *Thagh ho were burde bryghtest the burne in mynde hade* The frightening prospect facing Gawain (*the lur that he soght*, 1284) does

not allow him to become distracted by the lady's beauty, though her loveliness surpasses anything he can remember. The manuscript reading of this line, *Thagh I were burde bryghtest the burde in mynde hade,* is usually amended as shown.

Bi sum towch of summe tryfle at sum talez ende."
Then quoth Wowen, "Iwysse, worthe as yow lykez;
I schal kysse at your comaundement, as a knyght fallez,
And fire, lest he displese yow, so plede hit no more."
1305 Ho comes nerre with that and cachez hym in armez,
Loutez luflych adoun and the leude kysses.
Thay comly bykennen to Kryst ayther other;
Ho dos hir forth at the dore withouten dyn more;
And he ryches hym to ryse and rapes hym sone,
1310 Clepes to his chamberlayn, choses his wede,
Bowez forth, quen he watz boun, blythely to masse;
And thenne he meved to his mete that menskly hym keped,
And made myry al day, til the mone rysed,
          with game.
1315   Watz never freke fayrer fonge
       Bitwene two so dyngne dame,
       The alder and the yonge;
       Much solace set thay same.

And ay the lorde of the londe is lent on his gamnez,
1320 To hunt in holtez and hethe at hyndez barayne;
Such a sowme he ther slowe bi that the sunne heldet,
Of dos and of other dere, to deme were wonder.
Thenne fersly thay flokked in folk at the laste,
And quykly of the quelled dere a querré thay maked.
1325 The best bowed therto with burnez innoghe,
Gedered the grattest of gres that ther were,
And didden hem derely undo as the dede askez;
Serched hem at the asay summe that ther were,
Two fyngeres thay fonde of the fowlest of alle.
1330 Sythen thay slyt the slot, sesed the erber,
Schaved wyth a scharp knyf, and the schyre knitten;
Sythen rytte thay the four lymmes, and rent of the hyde,
Then brek thay the balé, the bowelez out token
Lystily for laucyng the lere of the knot;
1335 Thay gryped to the gargulun, and graythely departed
The wesaunt fro the wynt-hole, and walt out the guttez;
Then scher thay out the schulderez with her scharp knyvez,
Haled hem by a lyttel hole to have hole sydes.
Sithen britned thay the brest and brayden hit in twynne,
1340 And eft at the gargulun bigynez on thenne,
Ryvez hit up radly ryght to the byght,
Voydez out the avanters, and verayly therafter
Alle the rymez by the rybbez radly thay lance;
So ryde thay of by resoun bi the rygge bonez,

By some hint or suggestion at the end of a remark."
Then Gawain said, "Indeed, let it be as you wish;
I will kiss at your bidding, as befits a knight,
And do more, rather than displease you, so urge it no further."
1305 With that she approaches him and takes him in her arms,
Stoops graciously over him and kisses the knight.
They politely commend each other to Christ's keeping:
She goes out of the room without one word more.
And he prepares to get up as quickly as he can,
1310 Calls for his chamberlain, selects his clothes,
Makes his way, when he was ready, contentedly to mass;
And then went to his meal that worthily awaited him,
And made merry all day until the moon rose
          with games.
1315   Never knight was entertained
       By such a worthy pair,
       One old, the other young;
       Much pleasure did they share.

And still the lord of that land is absorbed his sport,
1320 Chasing through woodland and heath after barren hinds.
What a number he killed by the time the day ended
Of does and other deer would be hard to imagine.
Then proudly the hunters flocked together at the end,
And quickly made a quarry of the slaughtered deer.
1325 The noblest pressed forward with many attendants,
Gathered together the fattest of the deer,
And neatly dismembered them as ritual requires.
Some of those who examined them at the assay
Found two inches of flesh in the leanest of them.
1330 Then they slit the base of the throat, took hold of the gullet,
Scraped it with a sharp knife and knotted it shut;
Next they cut off the four legs and ripped off the hide,
Then broke open the belly and took out the entrails
Carefully to avoid loosening the ligature of the knot.
1335 They took hold of the throat, and quickly separated
The gullet from the windpipe, and threw out the guts.
Then they cut round the shoulders with their keen knives,
Drawing them through an aperture to keep the sides whole.
Next they cut open the breast and split it in two,
1340 And then one of them turns again to the throat
And swiftly lays open the body right to the fork,
Throws out the neck-offal, and expertly then
Quickly severs all the membranes on the ribs.
So correctly they cut off all the offal on the spine

1345 Evenden to the haunche, that henged al samen,
And heven it up al hole, and hwen hit of there,
And that thay neme for the noumbles bi nome, as I trowe,
        bi kynde;
    Bi the byght al of the thyghes
1350   The lappez thay lance bihynde;
    To hewe hit in two thay hyghes,
    Bi the bakbon to unbynde.

Bothe the hede and the hals thay hwen of thenne,
And sythen sunder thay the sydez swyft fro the chyne,
1355 And the corbeles fee[1] thay kest in a greve;
Thenn thurled they ayther thik side thurgh bi the rybbe,
And henged thenne ayther bi hoghes of the fourchez,
Uche freke for his fee, as fallez for to have.
Upon a felle of the fayre best fede thay thayr houndes
1360 Wyth the lyver and the lyghtez, the lether of the paunchez,
And bred bathed in blod blende theramongez.
Baldely thay blw prys,[2] bayed thayr rachchez,
Sythen fonge thay her flesche, folden to home,
Strakande ful stoutly mony stif motez.
1365 Bi that the daylyght watz done the douthe watz al wonen
Into the comly castel, ther the knyght bidez
        ful stille,
    Wyth blys and bryght fyr bette.
    The lorde is comen thertylle;
1370   When Gawayn wyth hym mette
    Ther watz bot wele at wylle.

Thenne comaunded the lorde in that sale to samen alle the
        meny,
Bothe the ladyes on lowe to lyght with her burdes
Bifore alle the folk on the flette, frekez he beddez
1375 Verayly his venysoun to fech hym byforne,
And al godly in gomen Gawayn he called,
Techez hym to the tayles[3] of ful tayt bestes,
Schewez hym the schyree grece schorne upon rybbes.
"How payez yow this play? Haf I prys wonnen?
1380 Have I thryvandely thonk thurgh my craft served?"
"Ye, iwysse," quoth that other wyghe, "here is wayth fayrest
That I sey this seven yere in sesoun of wynter."
"And al I gif yow, Gawayn," quoth the gome thenne,

1345 Right down to the haunches, in one unbroken piece,
And lifted it up whole, and cut it off there;
And to that they give the name of numbles, I believe,
        as is right.
    Then where the hind legs fork
1350   At the back they cut the skin,
    Then hacked the carcass in two,
    Swiftly along the spine.

Both the head and the neck they cut off next,
And then rapidly separate the sides from the chine;
1355 And the raven's fee in a thicket they threw.
Then they pierced both thick sides through the ribs,
Hanging each of them by the hocks of their legs,
For each man's payment, as his proper reward.
They put food for their hounds on a fine beast's skin—
1360 The liver and lights, the lining of the stomach,
And bread soaked in blood, mixed up together.
Noisily they blew capture, their hounds barking,
Then shouldering their venison they started for home,
Vigorously sounding many loud single notes.
1365 By the time daylight failed they had ridden back
To the splendid castle, where the knight waits
        undisturbed,
    With joy and bright fire warm.
    Then into hall the lord
1370   Came, and the two men met
    In joyfullest accord.

Then the lord commanded the household to assemble in
        hall,
And both ladies to come downstairs with their maids.
In front of the gathering he orders his men
1375 To lay out his venison truly before him;
And with playful courtesy he called Gawain to him,
Reckons up the tally of well-grown beasts,
Points out the splendid flesh cut from the ribs.
"Does this game please you? Have I won your praise?
1380 Do I deserve hearty thanks for my hunting skill?"
"Yes indeed," said the other, "this is the finest venison
That I have seen for many years in the winter season."
"And I give it all to you, Gawain," said the man then,

---

[1]   *the corbeles fee*   A piece of gristle thrown to the birds as part of the
ritual.

[2]   *blw prys*   A blast on the horn when the quarry is taken.

[3]   *the tayles*   Left on the carcasses to facilitate the tally, or count.

"For by acorde of covenaunt ye crave hit as your awen."
1385 "This is soth," quoth the segge, "I say yow that ilke:
That I haf worthyly wonnen this wonez wythinne,
Iwysse with as god wylle hit worthez to yourez."
He hasppez his fayre hals his armez wythinne,
And kysses hym as comlyly as he couthe awyse:
1390 "Tas yow there my chevicaunce, I cheved no more;
I wowche hit saf fynly, thagh feler hit were."
"Hit is god," quoth the godmon, "grant mercy therfore.
Hit may be such hit is the better, and ye me breve wolde
Where ye wan this ilk wele bi wytte of yorselven."
1395 "That watz not forward," quoth he, "frayst me no more.
For ye haf tan that yow tydez, trawe non other
          ye mowe."
          Thay laghed, and made hem blythe
          Wyth lotez that were to lowe;
1400   To soper thay yede as-swythe,
          Wyth dayntés nwe innowe.

And sythen by the chymné in chamber thay seten,
Wyghez the walle wyn weghed to hem oft,
And efte in her bourdyng thay baythen in the morn
1405 To fylle the same forwardez that thay byfore maden:
Wat chaunce so bytydez hor chevysaunce to chaunge,
What nwez so thay nome, at naght quen thay metten.
Thay acorded of the covenauntez byfore the court alle;
The beverage watz broght forth in bourde at that tyme,
1410 Thenne thay lovelych leghten leve at the last,
Uche burne to his bedde busked bylyve.
Bi that the coke hade crowen and cakled bot thryse[1]
The lorde watz lopen of his bedde, the leudez uchone;
So that the mete and the masse watz metely delyvered,
1415 The douthe dressed to the wod er any day sprenged,
          to chace;
          Hegh with hunte and hornez
          Thurgh playnez thay passe in space,
          Uncoupled among tho thornez
1420   Rachez that ran on race.

Sone thay calle of a quest in a ker syde,
The hunt rehayted the houndez that hit fyrst mynged,
Wylde wordez hym warp wyth a wrast noyce;
The howndez that hit herde hastid thider swythe,

"For by the terms of our compact you may claim it as yours."
1385 "That is true," said the knight, "and I say the same to you:
What I have honorably won inside this castle,
With as much good will truly shall be yours."
He takes the other's strong neck in his arms,
And kisses him as pleasantly as he could devise.
1390 "Take here my winnings, I obtained nothing else;
I bestow it on you freely, and would do so were it more."
"It is excellent," said the lord, "many thanks indeed.
It could be even better if you would inform me
Where you won this same prize by your cleverness."
1395 "That was not in our agreement," said he, "ask nothing else;
For you have had what is due to you, expect to receive
          nothing more."
          They laughed and joked awhile
          In speech deserving praise;
1400   Then quickly went to sup
          On new delicacies.

Afterwards they sat by the fire in the lord's chamber,
And servants many times brought in marvelous wine;
And once again in their jesting they agreed the next day
1405 To observe the same covenant as they had made before:
Whatever fortune befell them, to exchange what they won,
Whatever new things they were, at night when they met.
They renewed the agreement before the whole court—
The pledge-drink was brought in with jokes at that time—
1410 Then they graciously took leave of each other at last,
Every man hastening quickly to bed.
By the time cock-crow had sounded three times
The lord had leapt out of bed and each of his men,
So that breakfast and mass were duly done,
1415 And long before daybreak they were all on their way
          to the chase.
          Through fields they canter soon,
          Loud with hunting-horns;
          Headlong the hounds run
1420   Uncoupled among the thorns.

Soon they give tongue at the edge of a marsh;
The huntsman urged on the hounds that found the scent first,
Shouting at them wildly in a loud voice.
The hounds who heard him raced there in haste

---

[1] *crowen ... bot thryse* Cocks supposedly crowed at midnight, 3 a.m., and 6 a.m.

1425 And fellen as fast to the fuyt, fourty at ones;
Thenne such a glaver ande glam of gedered rachchez
Ros that the rocherez rungen aboute;
Hunterez hem hardened with horne and wyth muthe.
Then al in a semblé sweyed togeder
1430 Bitwene a flosche in that fryth and a foo cragge;
In a knot bi a clyffe, at the kerre syde,
Ther as the rogh rocher unrydely was fallen,
Thay ferden to the fyndyng, and frekez hem after;
Thay umbekesten the knarre and the knot bothe,
1435 Wyghez, whyl thay wysten wel wythinne hem it were,
The best that ther breved watz wyth the blodhoundez.
Thenne thay beten on the buskez, and bede hym upryse,
And he unsoundyly out soght seggez overthwert;
On the sellokest swyn swenged out there,
1440 Long sythen fro the sounder that sighed for olde,
For he watz borelych and brode, bor alther-grattest,
Ful grymme quen he gronyed; thenne greved mony,
For thre at the fyrst thrast he thryght to the erthe,
And sparred forth good sped boute spyt more.
1445 Thise other halowed hyghe! ful hyghe, and hay! hay!
        cryed,
Haden hornez to mouthe, heterly rechated;
Mony watz the myry mouthe of men and of houndez
That buskkez after this bor with bost and wyth noyse
        to quelle.
1450   Ful ofte he bydez the baye,
        And maymez the mute inn melle;
        He hurtez of the houndez, and thay
        Ful yomerly yaule and yelle.

Schalkez to shote at hym schowen to thenne,
1455 Haled to hym of her arewez, hitten hym oft;
Bot the poyntez payred at the pyth that pyght in his scheldez,
And the barbez of his browe bite non wolde;
Thagh the schaven schafte schyndered in pieces,
The hede hypped agayn were-so-ever hit hitte.
1460 Bot quen the dyntez hym dered of her dryghe strokez,
Then, braynwod for bate, on burnez he rasez,
Hurtz hem ful heterly ther he forth hyghez,
And mony arghed therat, and on lyte droghen.
Bot the lorde on a lyght horce launces hym after,
1465 As burne bolde upon bent his bugle he blowez,
He rechated, and rode thurgh ronez ful thyk,
Suande this wylde swyn til the sunne schafted.

1425 And rushed towards the trail, forty of them together.
Then such a deafening babel from gathered hounds rose
That the rocky bank echoed from end to end.
Huntsmen encouraged them with horn-blasts and shouts;
And then all in a throng they rushed together
1430 Between a pool in that thicket and a towering crag.
On a wooded knoll near a cliff at the edge of the marsh
Where fallen rocks were untidily scattered,
They ran to the dislodging, with men at their heels.
The hunters surrounded both the crag and the knoll
1435 Until they were certain that inside their circle
Was the beast which had made the bloodhounds give tongue.
Then they beat on the bushes and called him to come out;
And he broke cover ferociously through a line of men.
An incredible wild boar charged out there,
1440 Which long since had left the herd through his age,
For he was massive and broad, greatest of all boars,
Terrible when he snorted. Then many were dismayed,
For three men in one rush he threw on their backs,
And made away fast without doing more harm.
1445 The others shouted "hi!" and "hay, hay!" at the tops of
        their voices,
Put horns to mouth and loudly sounded recall.
Many hunters and hounds joyfully gave tongue,
Hurrying after this boar with outcry and clamor
        to kill.
1450   Often he stands at bay,
        And maims the circling pack,
        Wounding many hounds
        That piteously yelp and bark.

Men press forward to shoot at him then,
1455 Loosed their arrows at him, hit him many times;
But those that struck his shoulders were foiled by their toughness,
And none of them could pierce through the bristles on his brow.
Although the polished shaft shivered into pieces,
The head rebounded away wherever it struck.
1460 But when the hits hurt him with their constant blows,
Frenzied with fighting he turns headlong on the men,
And injures them savagely when he charges out,
So that many grew fearful and drew back further.
But the lord on a lively horse races after him,
1465 Like a valiant hunter, blowing his horn.
He urged the hounds on, and through dense thickets rode
Following this wild boar until the sun went down.

This day wyth this ilk dede thay dryven on this wyse,
Whyle oure luflych lede lys in his bedde,
1470 Gawayn graythely at home, in gerez ful ryche
of hewe.
The lady noght forgate
Com to hym to salue;
Ful erly ho watz hym ate[1]
1475 His mode for to remwe.

Ho commes to the cortyn, and at the knyght totes.
Sir Wawen her welcumed worthy on fyrst,
And ho hym yeldez agayn ful yerne of hir wordez,
Settez hir softly by his syde, and swythely ho laghez,
1480 And wyth a luflych loke ho layde hym thyse wordez:
"Sir, yif ye be Wawen, wonder me thynkkez,
Wyghe that is so wel wrast alway to god,
And connez not of compaynye[2] the costez undertake;
And if mon kennes yow hom to knowe, ye kest hom of
our mynde;
1485 Thou hatz foryeten yederly that yisterday I taght te
Bi alder-trest token of talk that I cowthe."
"What is that?" quoth the wyghe, "Iwysse I wot never;
If hit be sothe that ye breve, the blame is myn awen."
"Yet I kende yow of kyssyng," quoth the clere thenne,
1490 "Quere-so countenaunce is couthe[3] quikly to clayme;
That bicumes uche a knyght that cortaysy uses."
"Do way," quoth that derf mon, "my dere, that speche;
For that durst I not do, lest I devayed[4] were.
If I were werned, I were wrang, iwysse, yif I profered."
1495 "Ma fay,"[5] quoth the meré wyf, "ye may not be werned,
Ye ar stif innoghe to constrayne wyth strenkthe, yif yow lykez,
Yif any were so vilanous that yow devaye wolde."
"Ye, be God," quoth Gawayn, "good is your speche;
Bot threte is unthryvande in thede ther I lende,
1500 And uche gift that is geven not with goud wylle.
I am at your comaundement, to kysse quen yow lykez,
Ye may lach quen yow lyst, and leve quen yow thynkkez,
in space."
The lady loutez adoun
1505 And comlyly kysses his face;

So they spent the day in this manner, in this wild chase,
While our gracious knight lies in his bed:
1470 Gawain, happily at home amid bright-colored bedding
so rich.
Nor did the lady fail
To wish her guest good day;
Early she was there
1475 His mood to mollify.

She comes to the curtain and peeps in at the knight.
Sir Gawain welcomes her politely at once,
And she returns his greeting with eager speech,
Seats herself gently at his side and quickly laughs,
1480 And with a charming glance at him uttered these words:
"Sir, if you are Gawain, it astonishes me
That a man always so strongly inclined to good,
Cannot grasp the rules of polite behavior,
And if someone instructs him, lets them drop out of
mind.
1485 You have quickly forgotten what I taught you yesterday,
By the very truest lesson I could put into words."
"What was that?" said the knight, "Indeed, I don't know at all.
If what you say is true, the blame is all mine."
"Yet I told you about kissing," the fair lady replied,
1490 "To act quickly wherever a glance of favor is seen;
That befits every knight who practises courtesy."
"Dear lady, enough of such talk," said that brave man,
"For I dare not do that, lest I were refused.
If repulsed, I should be at fault for having presumed."
1495 "Ma foi," said the gay lady, "you could not be refused;
You are strong enough to force your will if you wish,
If any woman were so ill-mannered as to reject you."
"Yes, indeed," said Gawain, "what you say is quite true;
But in my country force is considered ignoble,
1500 And so is each gift that is not freely given.
I am at your disposal, to kiss when it pleases you,
You may take one when you like, and stop as seems good,
in a while."
She bends down over him
1505 And gives the knight a kiss;

---

1 *watz hym ate* At him in one of two senses or both: in his bedchamber, and bothering him.

2 *compaynye* Critics have suggested that the term may have amorous connotations.

3 *Quere-so countenaunce is couthe* Wherever looks of favor are shown.

4 *devayed* Denied, refused: a neologism from Old French, repeated by the lady at 1497.

5 *"Ma fay"* I.e., *ma foi*, French: "by my faith," as asseveration.

Much speche thay ther expoun
Of druryes greme and grace.

"I woled wyt at yow, wyghe," that worthy then sayde,
"And yow wrathed not therwyth, what were the skylle
1510 That so yong and so yepe as ye at this tyme,
So cortayse, so knyghtly, as ye ar knowen oute—
And of alle chevalry to chose, the chef thyng alosed
Is the lel layk of luf, the lettrure of armes;
For to telle of this tevelyng of this trwe knyghtez,
1515 Hit is the tytelet token and tyxt of her werkkez;
How ledes for her lel lufe hor lyvez han auntered,
Endured for her drury dulful stoundez,
And after wenged with her walour and voyded her care,
And broght blysse into boure[1] with bountees hor awen—
1520 And ye ar knyght comlokest kyd of your elde,
Your worde and your worchip walkez ayquere,
And I haf seten by yourself here sere twyes,
Yet herde I never of your hed helde no wordez
That ever longed to luf, lasse ne more;
1525 And ye, that are so cortays and coynt of your hetes,[2]
Oghe to a yonke thynk yern to schewe
And teche sum tokenez of trweluf craftes.
Why, ar ye lewed, that alle the los weldez?
Other elles ye demen me to dille your dalyaunce to herken?
1530   For schame!
    I com hider sengel, and sitte
    To lerne at yow sum game;
    Dos, techez me of your wytte
    Whil my lorde is fro hame."

1535 "In goud faythe," quoth Gawayn, "God yow foryelde!
Gret is the gode gle, and gomen to me huge,
That so worthy as ye wolde wynne hidere,
And pyne yow with so pouer a man, as play wyth your
    knyght
With anyskynnez countenaunce, hit keverez me ese;
1540 Bot to take the torvayle to myself to trwluf expoun,
And towche the temez of tyxt and talez of armez
To yow that, I wot wel, weldez more slyght
Of that art, bi the half, or a hundreth of seche
As I am, other ever schal, in erde ther I leve,
1545 Hit were a folé felefolde, my fre, by my trawthe.

For long they then discuss
Love's misery and bliss.

"I would learn from you, sir," said that gentle lady,
"If the question was not irksome, what the reason was
1510 That someone as young and valiant as yourself,
So courteous and chivalrous as you are known far and wide—
And of all the aspects of chivalry, the thing most praised
Is the true practice of love, knighthood's very lore;
For to speak of the endeavors of true knights,
1515 The written heading and text of their deeds is that:
How knights have ventured their lives for true love,
Suffered for their love-longings dismal times,
And later taken revenge on their misery through valor,
Bringing joy to their ladies through their personal merits—
1520 And you are the outstanding knight of your time,
Your fame and your honor are known everywhere,
And I have sat by you here on two separate occasions
Yet never heard from your mouth a solitary word
Referring to love, of any kind at all.
1525 And you, who make such courteous and elegant vows,
Should be eager to instruct a youthful creature,
And teach her some elements of skill in true love.
What, are you ignorant, who enjoy such great fame?
Or do you think me too silly to take in courtly chat?
1530   For shame!
    I come here alone, and sit
    To learn your special play;
    Show me your expertise
    While my husband is away."

1535 "In good faith," said Gawain, "may God reward you!
It gives me great gladness and pleases me hugely
That one as noble as yourself should make your way here,
And trouble yourself with a nobody, trifling with your
    knight
With any kind of favor: it gives me delight.
1540 But to take the task on myself of explaining true love,
And treat the matter of romance and chivalric tales
To you whom—I know well—have more expertise
In that subject by half than a hundred such men
As myself ever can, however long I may live,
1545 Would be absolute folly, noble lady, on my word.

---

[1] *into boure*   Into the lady's bower.

[2] *coynt of your hetes*   Gracious in your promises of knightly service.

I wolde yowre wylnyng worche at my myght,
As I am hyghly bihalden, and evermore wylle
Be servaunt to yourselven, so save me Dryghtyn!"
Thus hym frayned that fre, and fondet hym ofte,
1550 For to haf wonnen hym to woghe,[1] what-so scho thoght ellez;
Bot he defended hym so fayr that no faut semed,
Ne non evel on nawther halve, nawther thay wysten
      bot blysse.
    Thay laghed and layked long;
1555   At the last scho con hym kysse,
    Hir leve fayre con scho fonge,
    And went hir waye, iwysse.

Then ruthes hym the renk and ryses to the masse,
And sithen hor diner watz dyght and derely served.
1560 The lede with the ladyez layked alle day,
Bot the lorde over the londez launced ful ofte,
Swez his uncely swyn, that swyngez bi the bonkkez
And bote the best of his braches the bakkez in sunder
Ther he bode in his bay, tel bawemen hit breken,
1565 And madee hym mawgref his hed[2] for to mwe utter,
So felle flonez ther flete when the folk gedered.
Bot yet the styffest to start bi stoundez he made,
Til at the last he watz so mat he myght no more renne,
Bot in the hast that he myght he to a hole wynnez
1570 Of a rasse bi a rokk ther rennez the boerne.
He gete the bonk at his bak, bigynez to scrape,[3]
The frothe femed at his mouth unfayre bi the wykez,
Whettez his whyte tuschez; with hym then irked
Alle the burnez so bolde that hym by stoden
1575 To nye hym on-ferum, bot neghe hym non durst
      for wothe;
    He hade hurt so mony byforne
    That al thught thenne ful lothe
    Be more wyth his tusches torne
1580   That breme watz and braynwode bothe.

Til the knyght com hymself, kachande his blonk,
Sygh hym byde at the bay, his burnez bysyde;
He lyghtes luflych adoun, levez his corsour,
Braydez out a bryght bront and bigly forth strydez,
1585 Foundez fast thurgh the forth ther the felle bydez.

I will carry out your desires with all my power,
As I am in all duty bound, and always will be
The servant of your wishes, may God preserve me!"
Thus that lady made trial of him, tempting him many times
1550 To have led him into mischief, whatever her purpose;
But he defended himself so skillfully that no fault appeared,
Nor evil on either side, nor anything did they feel
      but delight.
    They laughed and bantered long;
1555   Then she kissed her guest;
    Charmingly took her leave,
    And went her way at last.

Then Gawain rouses himself and dresses for mass,
And afterwards dinner was cooked and splendidly served.
1560 The knight diverted himself with the ladies all day,
But the lord raced ceaselessly over the countryside,
After his menacing boar, that scurries over the hills,
And bit the backs of his bravest hounds asunder
Where he stood at bay, until archers broke it,
1565 And forced him unwillingly to move into the open;
So thickly the arrows flew when the hunters gathered.
But yet he made the bravest of them flinch at times,
Until at last he was so tired that he could run no more,
And as fast as he can he makes his way to a hole
1570 By a rocky ledge overlooking the stream.
He gets the river-bank at his back, begins to scrape—
The froth foamed hideously at the corners of his mouth—
And whets his white tusks. Then it grew irksome
For all the bold men who surrounded him trying
1575 To wound him from afar, but for the danger none dared
      to get close;
    So many had been hurt
    That no one wished to risk
    To be more savaged by
1580   A maddened boar's tusk.

Until the lord himself came, spurring his horse,
Saw the boar standing at bay, ringed by his men;
He nimbly dismounts, leaving his courser,
Unsheathes a bright sword and mightily strides,
1585 Hastens quickly through the stream towards the waiting boar.

---

[1] *to haf wonnen hym to woghe* It is uncertain whether *woghe* means "wrong" or "woo."

[2] *mawgref his hed* In spite of himself.

[3] *bigynez to scrape* Angrily scrapes (the earth with his feet).

The wylde watz war of the wyghe with weppen in honde,
Hef heghly the here, so hetterly he fnast
That fele ferde for the freke, lest felle hym the worre.
The swyn settez hym out on the segge even,
1590 That the burne and the bor were both upon hepez
In the wyghtest of the water: the worre hade that other,
For the mon merkkez hym wel, as thay mette fyrst,
Set sadly the scharp in the slot even,
Hit hym up to the hult, that the hert schyndered,
1595 And he yarrande hym yelde, and yedoun the water
        ful tyt.
    A hundreth houndez hym hent,
    That bremely con hym bite,
    Burnez him broght to bent,
1600   And doggez to dethe endite.

There watz blawyng of prys in mony breme horne,
Heghe halowing on highe with hathelez that myght;
Brachetes bayed that best, as bidden the maysterez
Of that chargeaunt chace that were chef huntes.
1605 Thenne a wyghe that watz wys upon wodcraftez
To unlace this bor lufly bigynnez.
Fyrst he hewes of his hed and on highe settez,
And sythen rendez him al roghe bi the rygge after,
Braydez out the boweles, brennez hom on glede,
1610 With bred blent therwith his braches rewardez.
Sythen he britnez out the brawen in bryght brode cheldez,
And hatz out the hastlettez, as hightly bisemez;
And yet hem halchez al hole the halvez togeder,
And sythen on a stif stange stoutly hem henges.
1615 Now with this ilk swyn thay swengen to home;
The bores hed watz borne bifore the burnes selven
That him forferde in the forthe thurgh forse of his honde
        so stronge.
    Til he seye Sir Gawayne
    In halle hym thoght ful longe;
1620 He calde, and he com gayn
    His feez ther for to fonge.

The lorde ful lowde with lote and laghter myry,
When he seye Sir Gawayn, with solace he spekez;
1625 The goude ladyez were geten, and gedered the
        meyny,
He schewez hem the scheldez, and schapes hem the tale
Of the largesse and the lenthe, the lithemez alse

The beast saw the man with his weapon in hand,
Raised his bristles erect, and so fiercely snorted
That many feared for the man, lest he got the worst of it.
The boar charged out, straight at the man,
1590 So that he and the beast were both in a heap
Where the water was swiftest. The other had the worse;
For the man takes aim carefully as the two met,
And thrust the sword firmly straight into his throat,
Drove it up to the hilt, so that the heart burst open,
1595 And squalling he gave up, and was swept through the water
        downstream.
    Seized by a hundred hounds
    Fierce and sharp of tooth,
    Men dragged him to the bank,
1600   And dogs do him to death.

There was sounding of capture from many brave horns,
Proud shouting by knights as loud as they could,
Hounds bayed at that beast, as bidden by the masters
Who were the chief huntsmen of that wearisome chase.
1605 Then a man who was expert in hunting practice
Skilfully begins to dismember this boar.
First he cuts off the head and sets it on high,
And then roughly opens him along the spine,
Throws out the entrails, grills them over embers,
1610 And rewards his hounds with them, mixed with bread.
Next he cuts out the boar's-meat in broad glistening slabs,
And takes out the innards, as properly follows;
Yet he fastens the two sides together unbroken,
And then proudly hangs them on a strong pole.
1615 Now with this very boar they gallop towards home;
Carrying the boar's head before the same man
Who had killed it in the stream by force of his own
        strong hand.
    Until he saw Gawain
    It seemed a tedious time,
1620 He gladly came when called,
    His due reward to claim.

The lord, noisy with speech and merry laughter,
Joyfully exclaims at the sight of Sir Gawain.
1625 The good ladies were brought down and the household
        assembled;
He shows them the sides of meat, and gives an account
Of the boar's huge size and the ferocity

Of the were of the wylde swyn in wod ther he fled.
That other knyght ful comly comended his dedez,
1630 And praysed hit as a gret prys that he proved hade,
For suche a brawne of a best, the bolde burne sayde,
Ne such sydes of a swyn segh he never are.
Thenne hondeled thay the hoge hed, the hende mon hit praysed,
And let lodly therat the lorde for to here.
1635 "Now, Gawayn," quoth the godmon, "this gomen is your awen
By fyn forwarde and faste, faythely ye knowe."
"Hit is sothe," quoth the segge, "and as siker trwe
Alle my get I schal yow gif agayn, bi my trawthe."
He hent the hathel aboute the halse, and hendely hym kysses,
1640 And eftersones of the same he served hym there.
"Now ar we even," quoth the hathel, "in this eventide,
Of alle the covenauntes that we knyt, sythen I com hider, bi lawe."
  The lorde sayde, "Bi saynt Gile,
1645 Ye ar the best that I knowe!
  Ye ben ryche in a whyle,
  Such chaffer and ye drowe."[1]

Thenne thay teldet tablez trestes alofte,
Kesten clothez upon; clere lyght thenne
1650 Wakned by wowes, waxen torches;
Segges sette and served in sale al aboute;
Much glam and gle glent up therinne
Aboute the fyre upon flet, and on fele wyse
At the soper and after, mony athel songez,
1655 As coundutes of Krystmasse and carolez newe,
With al the manerly merthe that mon may of telle.
And ever oure luflych knyght the lady bisyde,
Such semblaunt to that segge semly ho made
Wyth stille stollen countenaunce, that stalworth to plese,
1660 That al forwondered watz the wyghe, and wroth with hymselven,
Bot he nolde not for his nurture nurne hir agaynez,
Bot dalt with hir al in daynté, how-se-ever the dede turned towrast.
  Quen thay hade played in halle
1665 As longe as hor wylle hom last,

Of the fight with the beast in the wood where he fled.
The other knight warmly commended his deeds,
1630 And praised his action as proof of his excellence,
For such boar's-meat, the brave knight declared,
And such sides of wild boar he had never seen before.
Then they picked up the huge head, the polite man praised it
And pretended to feel horror, to honor the lord.
1635 "Now, Gawain," said his host, "this quarry is all yours,
By fully ratified covenant, as you well know."
"That is so," said the knight, "and just as truly indeed
I shall give you all I gained in return, by my pledged word."
He grasped the lord round the neck and graciously kisses him,
1640 And then a second time treated him in the same way.
"Now we are quit," said Gawain, "at the end of the day,
Of all the agreements we have made since I came here, in due form."
  The lord said, "By St. Giles,
1645 You're the best man I know!
  You'll be a rich one soon
  If you keep on trading so."

Then tables were set up on top of trestles,
And tablecloths spread on them: bright light then
1650 Glittered on the walls from waxen torches.
Attendants laid table and served throughout hall.
A great noise of merry-making and joking arose
Round the fire in the center; and of many kinds,
At supper and afterwards, noble songs were sung,
1655 Such as Christmas carols and the newest dances,
With all the fitting amusement that could be thought;
Our courteous knight sitting with the lady throughout.
Such a loving demeanor she displayed to that man,
Through furtive looks of affection to give him delight,
1660 That he was utterly astonished and angry inside;
But he could not in courtesy rebuff her advances,
But treated her politely, even though his actions might be misconstrued.
  When the revelry in hall
1665 Had lasted long enough,

---

[1] *Such chaffer and ye drowe* If you carry on such a trade (since on the second day Gawain has doubled his takings). Bertilak makes another joking allusion to marketing at the third exchange: see 1938–9.

To chambre he con hym calle,
And to the chemné thay past.

Ande ther thay dronken, and dalten, and demed eft nwe
To norne on the same note on Nwe Yerez even;
1670 Bot the knyght craved leve to kayre on the morn,
For hit watz neghe at the terme that he to schulde.
The lorde hym letted of that, to lenge hym resteyed,
And sayde, "As I am trwe segge, I siker my trawthe
Thou schal cheve to the grene chapel thy charres to make,
1675 Leude, on Nw Yeres lyght, longe bifore pryme.[1]
Forthy thow lye in thy loft and lach thyn ese,
And I schal hunt in this holt, and halde the towchez,[2]
Chaunge wyth the chevisaunce, bi that I charre hider;
For I haf fraysted the twys, and faythful I fynde the.
1680 Now 'thrid tyme throwe best' thenk on the morne,
Make we mery quyl we may and mynne upon joye,
For the lur may lach when-so mon lykez."
This watz graythely graunted, and Gawayn is lenged,
Blithe broght watz hym drynk, and thay to bedde yeden
1685   with light.
        Sir Gawayn lis and slepes
        Ful stille and softe al night;
        The lorde that his craftez kepes,[3]
        Ful erly he watz dight.

1690 After messe a morsel he and his men token;
Miry watz the mornyng, his mounture he askes.
Alle the hatheles that on horse schulde helden hym after
Were boun busked on hor blonkkez bifore the halle gatez.
Ferly fayre watz the folde, for the forst clenged;
1695 In red rudede upon rak rises the sunne,
And ful clere castez the clowdes of the welkyn.
Hunteres unhardeled bi a holt syde,
Rocheres roungen bi rys for rurde of her hornes;
Summe fel in the fute ther the fox bade,
1700 Traylez ofte a traveres[4] bi traunt of her wyles;
A kenet kryes therof, a hunt on hym calles;
His felawes fallen hym to, that fnasted ful thike,
Runnen forth in a rabel in his ryght fare,

To the fireside in his room
The lord took Gawain off.

And there they drank and chatted, and spoke once again
To repeat the arrangement on New Year's Eve;
1670 But the knight begged leave to depart the next day,
For it was near time for the appointment that he had to keep.
The lord held him back, begging him to remain,
And said, "As I am an honest man, I give you my word
That you shall reach the Green Chapel to settle your affairs,
1675 Dear sir, on New Year's Day, well before nine.
Therefore lie in your bed enjoying your ease,
And I shall hunt in the woods, and keep the compact,
Exchange winnings with you when I return here;
For I have tested you twice, and find you trustworthy.
1680 Now tomorrow remember, 'Best throw third time';
Let us make merry while we can and think only of joy,
For misery can be found whenever a man wants it."
This was readily agreed, and Gawain is stayed;
Drink was gladly brought to him, and with torches they went
            to their beds.
        Sir Gawain lies and sleeps
        All night taking his rest;
        While eager for his sport
        By dawn the lord was dressed.

1690 After mass he and his men snatched a mouthful of food:
The morning was cheerful, he calls for his horse.
All the knights who would ride after him on horses
Were ready arrayed in the saddle outside the hall doors.
The countryside looked splendid, gripped by the frost;
1695 The sun rises fiery through drifting clouds,
And then dazzling bright drives the rack from the sky.
At the edge of a wood hunters unleashed the hounds;
Among the trees rocks resounded with the noise of their horns.
Some picked up the scent where a fox was lurking,
1700 Search back and forwards in their cunning practice.
A small hound gives tongue, the huntsman calls to him,
His fellows rally around, panting loudly,
And dash forward in a rabble right on the fox's track.

---

[1] *Thou schal cheve … bifore pryme* Prime begins either at 6 a.m. or at sunrise. At 1073 Bertilak promises that Gawain will *cum to that merk at mydmorn*, meaning at 9 a.m. In fact the sun rises when he is on the way to the Green Chapel, 2085–86. In northwest England midwinter sunrise would not occur before 8 a.m. Two hours earlier it would be completely dark.

[2] *halde the towchez* Keep the terms of the agreement.

[3] *that his craftez kepes* Who attends to his pursuits.

[4] *Traylez ofte a traveres* Track the scent by working back and forth across the line.

And he fyskez hem byfore; thay founden hym sone,
1705 And quen thay seghe hym with syght thay sued hym fast,
Wreghande hym ful weterly with a wroth noyse;
And he trantes and tornayeez thurgh mony tene greve,
Havilounez, and herkenez bi hegges ful ofte.
At the last bi a littel dich he lepez over a spenne,
1710 Stelez out ful stilly bi a strothe rande,
Went half wylt of the wode[1] with wylez fro the houndes;
Thenne watz he went, er he wyst, to a wale tryster,
Ther thre thro at a thrich thrat hym at ones,
        al graye.
1715   He blenched agayn bilyve,
        And stifly start on-stray,[2]
        With alle the wo on lyve
        To the wod he went away.

Thenne watz hit list upon lif to lythen the houndez,
1720 When alle the mute hade hym met, menged togeder:
Such a sorwe at that syght thay sette on his hede
As alle the clamberande clyffes hade clatered on hepes;
Here he watz halawed, when hathelez hym metten,
Loude he watz yayned with yarande speche;
1725 Ther he watz threted and ofte thef called,
And ay the titleres at his tayl, that tary he ne myght.
Ofte he watz runnen at, when he out rayked,
And ofte reled in agayn, so Reniarde[3] watz wylé.
And ye, he lad hem bi lagmon,[4] the lorde and his meyny,
1730 On this maner bi the mountes quyle myd-over-under,[5]
Whyle the hende knyght at hom holsumly slepes
Withinne the comly cortynes, on the colde morne.
Bot the lady for luf let not to slepe,
Ne the purpose to payre that pyght in hir hert,
1735 Bot ros hir up radly, rayked hir theder,
In a mery mantyle, mete to the erthe,
That watz furred ful fyne with fellez wel pured;
No hwez[6] goud on hir hede bot the hagher stones
Trased aboute hir tressour by twenty in clusteres;
1740 Hir thryven face and hir throte throwen al naked,

He scampers ahead of them, they soon found his trail,
1705 And when they caught sight of him followed fast,
Abusing him furiously with an angry noise.
He twists and dodges through many a dense copse,
Often doubling back and listening at the hedges.
At last he jumps over a fence by a little ditch,
1710 Creeps stealthily by the edge of a bush-covered marsh,
Thinking to escape from the wood and the hounds by his wiles.
Then he came, before he knew it, to a well-placed station,
Where three fierce greyhounds flew at him at once
        in a rush.
1715   Undaunted changing course
        He quickly swerved away,
        Pursued into the woods
        With hideous outcry.

Then it was joy upon earth to hear the hounds giving tongue
1720 When all the pack had come upon him, mingled together:
Such a cursing at that sight they called down on his head
As if all the clustering cliffs had crashed down in a mass.
Here he was yelled at when hunters happened upon him,
Loudly he was greeted with chiding speech;
1725 There he was reviled and often called thief,
And always the hounds at his tail, that he could not pause.
Many times he was run at when he made for the open,
And many times doubled back, so cunning was Reynard.
And yes! strung out he led them, the lord and his followers,
1730 Across the hills in this manner until mid-afternoon,
While the knight in the castle takes his health-giving sleep
Behind splendid bed-curtains on the cold morn.
But out of love the lady did not let herself sleep,
Nor the purpose to weaken that was fixed in her heart;
1735 But rose from her bed quickly and hastened there
In a charming mantle reaching to the ground,
That was richly lined with well-trimmed furs:
No modest coif on her head, but skillfully cut gems
Arranged about her hair-fret in clusters of twenty;
1740 Her lovely face and throat displayed uncovered,

---

[1] *Went haf wylt of the wode* Thought to have escaped out of the wood.

[2] *on-stray* In a different direction.

[3] *Reniarde* Renard was the crafty fox hero of a series of old French poems.

[4] *he lad hem bi lagmon* The critic Norman Davis explains *lagmon* as "the last man in a line of reapers," who would advance diagonally across a field; hence "strung out."

[5] *quyle myd-over-under* Variously explained as mid-morning, midday, or afternoon. When the fox is killed it is *niegh nyght* (1922).

[6] *hwez* So the manuscript; some critics prefer *hwef*. The sense of the passage is that the lady is not wearing the headdress of a married woman.

Hir brest bare bifore, and bihinde eke.
Ho comez withinne the chambre dore, and closes hit hir after,
Wayvez up a wyndow, and on the wyghe callez,
And radly thus rehayted hym with hir riche wordes,
1745   with chere:
       "A, mon, how may thou slepe,
       This morning is so clere?"
       He watz in drowping depe,
       Bot thenne he con hir here.

1750 In dregh droupyng of dreme draveled that noble,[1]
       As mon that watz in mornyng of many thro thoghtes,
       How that destiné schulde that day dele hym his wyrde
       At the grene chapel, when he the gome metes,
       And bihoves his buffet abide withoute debate more;
1755 Bot quen that comly com he kevered his wyttes,
       Swenges out of the swevenes, and swarez with hast.
       The lady luflych com laghande swete,
       Felle over his fayre face, and fetly hym kyssed;
       He welcumez hir worthily with a wale chere.
1760 He sey hir so glorious and gayly atyred,
       So fautles of hir fetures and of so fyne hewes,
       Wight wallande joye warmed his hert.
       With smothe smylyng and smolt thay smeten into merthe,
       That al watz blis and bonchef that breke hem bitwene,
1765   and wynne.
           Thay lanced wordes gode,
           Much wele then watz therinne;
           Gret perile bitwene hem stod,
           Nif Maré of hir knyght mynne.

1770 Fo that prynces of pris depressed hym so thikke,
       Nurned hym so neghe the thred, that nede hym bihoved
       Other lach ther hir luf other lodly refuse.
       He cared for his cortaysye, lest crathayn he were,
       And more for his meschef yif he schulde make synne,
1775 And be traytor to that tolke that that telde aght.
       "God schylde," quoth the schalk, "that schal not befalle!"
       With luf-laghyng a lyt he layd hym bysyde
       Alle the spechez of specialté that sprange of her mouthe.
       Quoth that burde to the burne, "Blame ye disserve
1780 Yif ye luf not that lyf that ye lye nexte,

Her breast was exposed, and her shoulders bare.
She enters the chamber and shuts the door after her,
Throws open a window and calls to the knight,
Rebuking him at once with merry words
1745   in play:
       "Ah, sir, how can you sleep?
       The morning is so clear!"
       Deep in his drowsiness
       Her voice broke in his ear.

1750 In the stupor of a dream that nobleman muttered,
       Like a man overburdened with troublesome thoughts;
       How destiny would deal him his fate on the day
       When he meets the man at the Green Chapel,
       And must stand the return blow without any more talk:
1755 But when that lovely one spoke he recovered his wits,
       Broke out of his dreaming and hastily replied.
       The gracious lady approached him, laughing sweetly,
       Bent over his handsome face and daintily kissed him.
       He welcomes her politely with charming demeanor;
1760 Seeing her so radiant and attractively dressed,
       Every part of her so perfect, and in color so fine,
       Hot passionate feeling welled up in his heart.
       Smiling gently and courteously they made playful speech,
       So that all that passed between them was happiness, joy
1765   and delight.
           Gracious words they spoke,
           And pleasure reached its height.
           Great peril threatened, should
           Mary not mind her knight.

1770 For that noble lady so constantly pressed,
       Pushed him so close to the verge, that either he must
       Take her love there and then or churlishly reject it.
       He felt concerned for good manners, lest he behaved like a boor,
       And still more lest he shame himself by an act of sin,
1775 And treacherously betray the lord of the castle.
       "God forbid!" said the knight, "That shall not come about!"
       With affectionate laughter he put to one side
       All the loving inducements that fell from her mouth.
       Said that lady to the knight, "You deserve rebuke
1780 If you feel no love for the person you are lying beside,

---

[1] *In dregh ... that noble* A literal translation—"In a heavy troubled
sleep that nobleman muttered"—misses the grinding effect of the
alliterated words.

Bifore alle the wyghez in the worlde wounded in hert,
Bot if ye haf a lemman, a lever, that yow lykez better,
And folden fayth to that fre, festned so harde
That yow lausen ne lyst—and that I leve nouthe;
1785 And that ye telle me that now trwly I pray yow,
For alle the lufez upon lyve layne not the sothe
       for gile."
     The knyght sayde, "Be sayn Jon,"
     And smethely con he smyle,
1790   "In fayth I welde right non,
     Ne non wil welde the quile."

"That is a worde," quoth that wyght, "that worst is of alle,
Bot I am swared for sothe, that sore me thinkkez.
Kysse me now comly, and I schal cach hethen,
1795 I may bot mourne upon molde, as may that much lovyes."
Sykande ho sweghe doun and semly hym kyssed,
And sithen ho severes hym fro, and says as ho stondes,
"Now, dere, at this departyng do me this ese,
Gif me sumquat of thy gifte, thi glove if hit were,
1800 That I may mynne on the, mon, my mournyng to lassen."
"Now iwysse," quoth that wyghe, "I wolde I hade here
The levest thing for thy luf that I in londe welde,
For ye haf deserved, for sothe, sellyly ofte
More rewarde bi resoun then I reche myght;
1805 Bot to dele yow for drurye that dawed bot neked,
Hit is not your honour to haf at this tyme
A glove for a garysoun of Gawaynez giftez;
And I am here an erande in erdez uncouthe,
And have no men wyth no males with menskful thingez;
1810 That mislykez me, ladé, for luf at this tyme,
Iche tolke mon do as he is tan, tas to non ille
      ne pine."
     "Nay, hende of hyghe honours,"
     Quoth that lufsum under lyne,
1815   "Thagh I hade noght of yourez,
     Yet schulde ye have of myne."

Ho raght hym a riche rynk of red golde werkez,
With a starande ston stondande alofte
That bere blusshande bemez as the bryght sunne—
1820 Wyt ye wel, hit watz worth wele ful hoge.
Bot the renk hit renayed, and redyly he sayde,
"I wil no giftez, for God, my gay, at this tyme;
I haf none yow to norne, ne noght wyl I take."

More than anyone on earth wounded in her heart;
Unless you have a mistress, someone you prefer,
And have plighted troth with that lady, so strongly tied
That you wish not to break it—which now I believe;
1785 And I beg you now to confess that honestly:
For all the loves in the world hide not the truth
       in guile."
     The knight said, "By St. John,"
     And gave a pleasant smile,
1790   "In truth I have no one,
     Nor seek one for this while."

"That remark," said the lady, "is the worst you could make,
But I am answered indeed, and painfully, I feel.
Kiss me now lovingly, and I will hasten from here,
1795 I must spend my life grieving, as a woman deeply in love."
Sighing she stooped down and kissed him sweetly,
And then moves away from him and says, standing there,
"Now, dear sir, do me this kindness at parting,
Give me something as a present, for instance your glove,
1800 That I may remember you by, to lessen my sorrow."
"Now truly," said that man, "I wish I had here
The dearest thing in the world I possess for your love,
For you have truly deserved, wonderfully often,
More recompense by right than I could repay.
1805 But to give you as love-token something worth little
Would do you no honor, or to have at this time
A glove for a keepsake, as Gawain's gift.
I am here on a mission in unknown country,
And have no servants with bags full of precious things;
1810 That grieves me, lady, for your sake at this time,
But each man must do as conditions allow; take no offense
      or pain."
     "No, most honored sir,"
     Then said that lady free,
1815   "Though I get no gift from you,
     You shall have one from me."

She held out a precious ring of finely worked gold
With a sparkling jewel standing up high,
Its facets flashing as bright as the sun:
1820 Take my word, it was worth an enormous sum.
But the knight would not accept it, and straightaway said,
"I want no gifts, I swear, dear lady, at this time;
I have nothing to offer you, and nothing will I take."

Ho bede hit hym ful bysily, and he hir bode wernes,
1825 And swere swyfte by his sothe that he hit sese nolde,
And ho soré that he forsoke, and sayde therafter,
"If ye renay my rynk, to ryche for hit semez,
Ye wolde not so hyghly halden be to me,
I schal gif yow my girdel, that gaynes yow lasse."
1830 Ho lacht a lace lyghtly that leke umbe hir sydez,
Knit upon hir kyrtel under the clere mantyle;
Gered hit watz with grene sylke and with golde schaped,
Noght bot arounde brayden,[1] beten with fyngrez;
And that ho bede to the burne, and blythely bisoght,
1835 Thagh hit unworthi were, that he hit take wolde.
And he nay that he nolde neghe in no wyse
Nauther golde ne garysoun, er God hym grace sende
To acheve to the chaunce that he hade chosen there.
"And therfore, I pray yow, displese yow noght,
1840 And lettez be your bisinesse, for I baythe hit yow never
            to graunte.
        I am derely to yow biholde
        Bicause of your sembelaunt,
        And ever in hot and colde
1845   To be your trwe servaunt."

"Now forsake ye this silke," sayde the burde thenne,
"For hit is symple in hitself? and so wel hit semez.
Lo, so hit is littel, and lasse hit is worthy;
But who-so knew the costes that knit ar therinne,
1850 He wolde hit prayse at more prys, paraventure.
For quat gome so is gorde with this grene lace,
While he hit hade hemely halched aboute,
Ther is no hathel under heven tohewe hym that myght,
For he myght not be slayn for slyght upon erthe."
1855 Then kest the knyght, and hit come to his hert
Hit were a juel for the jopardé that hym jugged were:
When he acheved to the chapel his chek for to fech,
Myght he haf slypped to be unslayn, the sleght were noble.
Thenne he thulged with hir threpe and tholed hir to speke,
1860 And ho bere on hym the belt and bede hit hym swythe—
And he granted and hym gafe with a goud wylle—
And bisoght hym, for hir sake, discever hit never,
Bot to lelly layne fro hir lorde; the leude hym acordez
That never wyghe schulde hit wyt, iwysse, bot thay twayne
1865   for noghte.

---

[1] *Noght bot arounde brayden*   No part of which was not embroidered at the edges.

She pressed him insistently, and he declines her request,
1825 Swearing quickly on his word that he would never touch it,
And she was grieved that he refused it, and said to him then,
"If you reject my ring because you think it too precious,
And wish not to be so deeply indebted to me,
I shall give you my girdle, that profits you less."
1830 Quickly she unbuckled a belt clipped round her waist,
Fastened over her kirtle beneath the fine mantle;
It was woven of green silk and trimmed with gold,
Embroidered at the edges and decorated by hand;
And this she offered to the knight, and sweetly implored him
1835 That despite its slight value he would accept it.
And he declared absolutely that he would never agree
To take either gold or keepsake before God gave him grace
To finish the task he had undertaken.
"And therefore I beg you, do not be displeased,
1840 And cease your insisting, for I shall never be brought
            to consent.
        I am deeply in your debt
        Because of your kind favor,
        And will through thick and thin
1845   Remain your servant ever."

"Now, do you refuse this belt," the lady said then,
"Because it is worth little? and so truly it appears.
See, it is indeed a trifle, and its worth even less;
But anyone who knew the power woven into it
1850 Would put a much higher price on it, perhaps.
For whoever is buckled into this green belt,
As long as it is tightly fastened about him
There is no man on earth who can strike him down,
For he cannot be killed by any trick in the world."
1855 Then the knight reflected, and it flashed into his mind
This would be a godsend for the hazard he must face
When he reached the chapel to receive his deserts;
Could he escape being killed, the trick would be splendid.
Then he suffered her pleading and allowed her to speak,
1860 And she pressed the belt on him, offering it at once—
And he consented and gave way with good grace—
And she begged him for her sake never to reveal it,
But loyally hide it from her husband. Gawain gives his word
That no one should ever know of it, not for anything,
1865   but themselves.

He thonkked hir oft ful swythe,
Ful thro with hert and thoght.
Bi that on thrynne sythe
Ho hatz kyst the knyght so toght.

1870 Thenne lachchez ho hir leve, and levez hym there,
For more myrthe of that mon moght ho not gete,
When ho watz gon, Sir Gawayn gerez hym sone,
Rises and riches him in araye noble,
Lays up the luf-lace the lady hym raghte,
1875 Hid hit ful holdely, ther he hit eft fonde.
Sythen chevely to the chapel choses he the waye,
Prevély aproched to a prest, and prayed hym there
That he wolde lyste his lyf [1] and lern hym better
How his sawle schulde be saved when he schuld seye hethen.
1880 There he schrof hym schyrly and schewed his mysdedez,
Of the more and the mynne, and merci besechez,
And of absolucioun he on the segge calles;
And he asoyled hym surely and sette hym so clene
As domezday schulde haf ben dight on the morn.
1885 And sythen he mace hym as mery among the fre ladyes,
With comelych caroles and alle kynnes joye,
As never he did bot that daye, to the derk nyght,
    with blys.
    Uche mon hade daynté thare
1890   Of hym, and sayde, "Iwysse,
    Thus mery he watz never are,
    Syn he com hider, er this."

Now hym lenge in that lee, ther luf hym bityde!
Yet is the lorde on the launde ledande his gomnes.
1895 He hatz forfaren this fox that he folwed longe;
As he sprent over a spenne to spye the schrewe,
Ther as he herd the howndes that hasted hym swythe,
Renaud com richchande thurgh a roghe greve,
And alle the rabel in a res ryght at his helez.
1900 The wyghe watz war of the wylde, and warly abides,
And braydez out the bryght bronde, and at the best castez.
And he schunt for the scharp, and schulde haf
    arered;

He gave her heartfelt thanks
With earnest mind and sense;
By then she has three times
Kissed that valiant prince.

1870 Then she takes her departure, leaving him there,
For more pleasure from that man was not to be had.
When she had gone, Gawain quickly makes himself ready,
Gets up and dresses himself in splendid array,
Puts away the love-token the lady gave him,
1875 Hid it carefully where he could find it again.
Then quickly to the chapel he makes his way,
Approached a priest privately, and besought him there
To hear his confession and instruct him more clearly
How his soul could be saved when he leaves this world.
1880 There he confessed himself honestly and admitted his sins,
Both the great and the small, and forgiveness begs,
And calls on the priest for absolution.
And the priest absolved him completely, and made him as clean
As if the Judgment were appointed for the next day.
1885 And then Gawain makes merry with the noble ladies,
With charming dance-songs and gaiety of all kinds,
As he never did before that day, until darkness fell,
    with joy.
    Each man had courtesy
1890   From him, and said, "Sure,
    So merry since he came
    He never was before."

Let him stay in that shelter, and love come his way!
But still the lord is afield, enjoying his sport.
1895 He has headed off the fox that he pursued so long;
As he leapt over a hedge to look for the villain,
Where he heard the hounds barking as they chased him fast,
Reynard came running through a rough thicket
With the pack howling behind him, right at his heels.
1900 The man caught sight of the fox, and warily waits,
Unsheathes his bright sword and slashes at the beast;
And he swerved away from the blade and would have
    turned back.

---

[1] *lyste his lyf*   Hear his confession. Much ink has been spilt over the passage. If Gawain tells the priest about his love-token he would be obliged to return it; if he does not reveal the liaison he cannot be *schrof schyrly* or given absolution.

A rach rapes hym to, ryght er he myght,
And ryght bifore the hors fete thay fel on hym alle,
1905 And woried me this wyly[1] wyth a wroth noyse.
The lorde lyghtez bilyve, and lachez hym sone,
Rased hym ful radly out of the rach mouthes,
Haldez heghe over his hede, halowez faste,
And ther bayen aboute hym mony brath houndez.
1910 Huntes hyghed hem theder with hornez ful mony,
Ay rechatande aryght til thay the renk seyen.
Bi that watz comen his compeyny noble
Alle that ever ber bugle blowed at ones,
And alle thise other halowed that had no hornes;
1915 Hit watz the myriest mute that ever men herde,
The rich rurd that ther watz raysed for Renaude saule
          with lote.
      Hor houndez thay ther rewarde,
      Her hedez thay fawne and frote,
1920   And sythen thay tan Reynarde
      And tyrven of his cote.

And thenne thay helden to home, for hit watz niegh nyght,
Strakande ful stoutly in hor store hornez.
The lorde is lyght at last at hys lef home,
1925 Fyndez fire upon flet, the freke ther-byside,
Sir Gawayn the gode, that glad watz withalle,
Among the ladies for luf he ladde much joye.
He were a bleaunt of blwe that bradde to the erthe,
His surkot semed hym wel that softe watz forred,
1930 And his hode of that ilke henged on his schulder,
Blande al of blaunner were bothe al aboute.
He metez me this godmon inmyddez the flore,
And al with gomen he hym gret, and goudly he sayde,
"I schal fylle upon fyrst oure forwardez nouthe,
1935 That we spedly han spoken, ther spared watz no drynk."
Then acoles he the knyght and kysses hym thryes,
As saverly and sadly as he hem sette couthe.
"Bi Kryst," quoth that other knyght, "ye cach much sele
In chevisaunce of this chaffer, yif ye hade goud chepez."[2]

A hound rushed at him before he could turn,
And right at the horse's feet the pack fell on him all,
1905 Tearing at the wily one with an enraged noise.
The lord swiftly dismounts, grabs the fox at once,
Lifted it quickly out of the hounds' mouths,
Holds it high over his head, halloos loudly,
And many fierce hounds surround him there, baying.
1910 Hunters hurried towards him with many horns blowing,
Sounding rally in proper fashion until they saw the lord.
When his noble company was all assembled,
Everyone carrying a bugle blew it at once,
And the others, without horns, raised a great shout.
1915 It was the most glorious baying that man ever heard,
The noble clamor set up there for Reynard's soul
          with din.
      Hunters reward their hounds,
      Heads they rub and pat;
1920   And then they took Reynard
      And stripped him of his coat.

And then they set off for home, for it was nearly night,
Stridently sounding their mighty horns.
At last the lord dismounts at his well-loved home,
1925 Finds a fire burning in hall, the knight waiting beside,
Sir Gawain the good, completely content,
Taking great pleasure from the ladies' affection.
He wore a blue mantle of rich stuff reaching the ground;
His softly furred surcoat suited him well,
1930 And his hood of the same stuff hung on his shoulder,
Both trimmed with ermine along the edges.
He meets his host in the middle of the hall,
Laughingly greeted him, and courteously said,
"Now I shall first carry out the terms of our covenant,
1935 Which we readily agreed on when wine was not spared."
Then he embraces the lord and gives him three kisses,
With as much relish and gravity as he could contrive.
"By God," said that other knight, "you had much luck
In winning this merchandise, if the price was right."

---

[1] *woried me this wyly* Tore at the fox. The ethic dative *me* is colloquial. Other examples occur at 2014 and 2144.

[2] *yif ye hade goud chepez* If you struck a good bargain.

1940 "Ye, of the chepe no charg," quoth chefly that other,
"As is pertly payed the porchaz that I aghte."
"Mary," quoth that other man, "myn is bihynde,
For I haf hunted al this day, and noght haf I geten
Bot this foule fox felle—the fende haf the godez!
1945 And that is ful pore for to pay for suche prys thinges
As ye haf thryght me here thro, suche thre cosses
      so gode."
    "Inogh," quoth Sir Gawayn,
    "I thonk yow, bi the rode";[1]
1950   And how the fox watz slayn
    He tolde hym as thay stode.

With merthe and mynstralsye, wyth metez at hor wylle,
Thay maden as mery as any men moghten
With laghyng of ladies, with lotez of bordez.
1955 Gawayn and the godemon so glad were thay bothe
Bot if the douthe had doted, other dronken ben other.[2]
Both the mon and the meyny maden mony japez
Til the sesoun watz seghen that thay sever moste;
Burnez to hor bedde behoved at the laste.
1960 Thenne lowly his leve at the lorde fyrst
Fochchez this fre mon, and fayre he hym thonkkez:
"Of such a selly sojorne as I haf hade here,
Your honour at this hyghe fest, the hyghe kyng yow yelde!
I gef yow me for on of yourez, if yowreself lykez,
1965 For I mot nedes, as ye wot, meve to-morne,
And ye me take sum tolke to teche, as ye hyght,
The gate to the grene chapel,[3] as God wyl me suffer
To dele on Nw Yerez day the dome of my wyrdes."[4]
"In god faythe," quoth the godmon, "wyth a goud wylle
1970 Al that ever I yow hyght halde schal I redé."
Ther asyngnes he a servaunt to sette hym in the waye,
And coundue hym by the downez, that he no drechch had,
For to ferk thurgh the fryth[5] and fare at the gaynest
    bi greve.

1940 "Oh, never mind the price," replied the other quickly,
"So long as the goods I got have been honestly paid."
"Marry," said the other man, "mine don't compare,
For I have hunted all day, and yet have caught nothing
But this stinking fox pelt—the devil take the goods!
1945 And that is a meager return for such precious things
As you have warmly pressed on me, three such kisses
      so good."
    "Enough," said Gawain,
    "I thank you, by the Rood";
1950   And how the fox was killed
    He heard as there they stood.

With mirth and minstrelsy, and all the food they would wish,
They made as much merriment as any men could
With laughter of ladies and jesting remarks.
1955 Both Gawain and the lord were ravished with joy
As if the company had gone crazy or taken much drink.
Both the lord and his retainers played many tricks
Until the time came round when they must separate:
Folk to their beds must betake them at last.
1960 Then humbly this noble knight first takes leave
Of the lord, and graciously gives him thanks:
"For such a wonderful stay as I have had here,
Honored by you at this holy feast, may God repay you!
I offer myself as your servant, if you agree,
1965 For I am compelled, as you know, to leave tomorrow,
If you will assign someone to show me, as you promised,
The road to the Green Chapel, as God will allow me,
To get what fate ordains for me on New Year's Day."
"In good faith," said the lord, "very willingly,
1970 Everything I ever promised you I shall readily give."
There he appoints a servant to put Gawain on the road
And guide him over the fells, so that he would not be delayed,
To ride through the woods and take the shortest path
    in the trees.

---

1   *bi the rode* I.e., by the Cross (on which Christ was crucified).

2   *Gawayn ... other* The syntax of these two lines seems erratic. Instead of following *so glad* with a comparison "as if" the poet continues *Bot if*, meaning unless. The intended sense of the passage seems to be, "They could only have been more deliriously happy if the whole company had gone crazy or got drunk."

3   *I gef yow ... grene chapel* Gawain politely offers to become Bertilak's servant (*on of yourez*) if he will give him a man (*take sum tolke*) to guide him to the Green Chapel.

4   *the dome of my wyrdes* The judgment of my fate.

5   *to ferk thurgh the fryth* To ride through the wood, as Gawain does at 2084. *Bi greve* refers to it again.

1975   The lorde Gawayn con thonk,
      Such worchip he wolde hym weve.
      Then at tho ladyez wlonk
      The knyght hatz tan his leve.

      With care and wyth kyssyng he carppez hem tille,
1980   And fele thryvande thonkkez he thrat hom to have,
      And thay yelden hym agayn yeply that ilk.
      Thay bikende hym to Kryst with ful colde sykyngez.
      Sythen fro the meyny he menskly departes;
      Uche mon that he mette, he made hem a thonke
1985   For his servyse and his solace and his sere pyne,
      That thay wyth busynes had ben aboute hym to serve;
      And uche segge as soré to sever with hym there
      As thay hade wonde worthyly with that wlonk ever.
      Then with ledes and lyght he watz ladde to his chambre,
1990   And blythely broght to his bedde to be at his rest.
      Yif he ne slepe soundyly say ne dar I,
      For he hade muche on the morn to mynne, yif he wolde,
         in thoght.
         Let hym lyghe there stille,
1995   He hatz nere that he soght;
         And ye wyl a whyle be stylle[1]
         I schal telle yow how thay wroght.

Fitt 4

      Now neghez the Nw Yere, and the nyght passez,
      The day dryvez to the derk, as Dryghtyn biddez;
2000   Bot wylde wederez of the worlde wakned theroute,
      Clowdes kesten kenly the colde to the erthe,
      Wyth nyghe innoghe of the northe the naked to tene.
      The snawe snitered ful snart, that snayped the wylde;
      The werbelande wynde wapped fro the hyghe,
2005   And drof uche dale ful of dryftes ful grete.
      The leude lystened ful wel that ley in his bedde,
      Thagh he lowkez his liddez, ful lyttel he slepes;
      Bi uch kok that crue he knwe wel the steven.
      Deliverly he dressed up, er the day sprenged,
2010   For there watz lyght of a laumpe that lemed in his chambre;
      He called to his chamberlayn, that cofly hym swared,

---

[1] *stille ... stylle* Literary convention of the time allowed homonyms to be used as rhyme-words different in sense; here "without moving," 1994, and "without noise," 1996.

1975   Gawain thanked the lord,
      Paying him great respect;
      Then from those noble ladies
      Took leave, as was correct.

      With tears and with kisses he addresses them both,
1980   And begged them to accept many profuse thanks,
      And they immediately returned the same words to him.
      They commended him to Christ with many deep sighs.
      Then from the household he takes courteous leave;
      To each man whom he met he expressed his thanks
1985   For his service and kindness and the personal pains
      They had taken in busying themselves for his sake;
      And each man was as sorry to part from him there
      As if they had honorably lived with that nobleman ever.
      Then with attendants and torches he was led to his room,
1990   And cheerfully brought to his bed and his rest.
      Whether or not he slept soundly I dare not say,
      For he had much about the next day to turn over, if he wished,
         in his mind.
         Let him lie there undisturbed,
1995   He is close to what he sought;
         Be quiet a short while,
         And I'll tell how things turned out.

Part 4

      Now the New Year approaches and the night wears away,
      The dawn presses against the darkness, as the Creator bids,
2000   But rough weather blows up in the country outside,
      Clouds empty their bitter cold contents on the earth,
      With enough malice from the north to torment the ill-clad.
      Snow pelted down spitefully, stinging the wild creatures;
      The wind shrilly whistled down from the fells,
2005   Choking the valleys with enormous drifts.
      The knight lay in bed listening intently,
      Although his eyelids are shut very little he sleeps;
      Each cock-crow reminded him of his undertaking.
      He got up quickly before the day dawned,
2010   For there was light from a lamp burning in his room;
      He called to his chamberlain, who answered him promptly,

And bede hym bryng hym his bruny and his blonk sadel;
That other ferkez hym up and fechez hym his wedez,
And graythez me Sir Gawayn upon a grett wyse.
2015 Fyrst he clad hym in his clothez the colde for to were,
And sythen his other harnays, that holdely watz keped,
Bothe his paunce and his platez, piked ful clene,
The ryngez rokked of the roust of his riche bruny;
And al watz fresch as upon fyrst, and he watz fayn thenne
2020   to thonk.
          He hade upon uche pece,
          Wypped ful wel and wlonk;
          The gayest unto Grece
          The burne bede bryng his blonk.

2025 Whyle the wlonkest wedes he warp on hymselven—
His cote wyth the conysaunce of the clere werkez
Ennurned upon velvet, vertuus stonez
Aboute beten and bounden, enbrauded semez,
And fayre furred withinne wyth fayre pelures—
2030 Yet laft he not the lace, the ladiez gifte,
That forgat not Gawayn for gode of hymselven.
Bi he hade belted the bronde upon his balghe haunchez,
Thenn dressed he his drurye double hym aboute,
Swythe swethled umbe his swange swetely that knyght
2035 The gordel of the grene silk, that gay wel bisemed,
Upon that ryol red clothe that ryche watz to schewe.
Bot wered not this ilk wyghe for wele this gordel,
For pryde of the pendauntez, thagh polyst thay were,
And thagh the glyterande golde glent upon endez,
2040 Bot for to saven hymself, when suffer hym byhoved,
To byde bale withoute dabate of bronde hym to were
               other knyffe.
          Bi that the bolde mon boun
          Wynnez theroute bilyve,
2045   Alle the meyny of renoun
          He thonkkez ofte ful ryve.

Thenne watz Gryngolet graythe, that gret watz and huge,
And hade ben sojourned saverly and in a siker wyse,
Hym lyst prik for poynt, that proude hors thenne.
2050 The wyghe wynnez hym to and wytez on his lyre,
And sayde soberly hymself and by his soth swerez:
"Here is a meyny in this mote that on menske thenkkez,
The mon hem mayntines, joy mot thay have;
The leve lady on lyve luf hir bityde;

Bade him bring his mail-shirt and saddle his horse.
The man leaps out of bed and fetches him his clothes,
And gets Gawain ready in splendid attire.
2015 First he puts clothing on him to keep out the cold,
And then the rest of his gear, that had been well looked after,
His body-armor and his plate, all polished clean,
The rings of his fine mail-shirt rocked free of rust;
Everything unstained as at first, for which he gladly
2020   gave thanks.
          Wearing each metal piece
          Rubbed clean of stain and spot,
          The best-dressed man on earth
          Ordered his horse be brought.

2025 While he dressed himself in his noblest clothes—
His coat with its finely embroidered badge
Set upon velvet, with stones of magical power
Inlaid and clasped round it, with embroidered seams,
And richly lined on the inside with beautiful furs—
2030 He did not leave out the belt, the lady's present:
For his own good Gawain did not forget that.
When he had buckled his sword on his curving hips,
That noble knight bound his love-token twice
Closely wrapped round his middle, with delight;
2035 The girdle of green silk, whose color went well
Against that splendid red surcoat that showed so fine.
But the knight did not wear the belt for its costliness,
Or for pride in its pendants, however they shone,
Or because its edges gleamed with glittering gold,
2040 But to safeguard himself when he had to submit,
To await death without sword to defend himself
               or blade.
          When he was fully dressed
          The knight hurries outside,
2045   And pays that noble household
          His debt of gratitude.

Then Gringolet was ready, that great horse and huge,
Who had been stabled securely, keeping him safe;
In such fine condition that he was eager to gallop.
2050 The knight walks up to him and examines his coat,
And said gravely to himself, swearing by his true word,
"There is a company in the castle that keeps courtesy in mind;
And a lord who supports them, may he have joy,
And may the dear lady be loved all her life!

2055 Yif thay for charyté cherysen a gest,
And halden honour in her honde, the hathel hem yelde
That haldez the heven upon hyghe, and also yow alle!
And yif I myght lyf upon londe lede any quyle,
I schuld rech yow sum rewarde redyly, if I myght."
2060 Thenn steppez he into stirop and strydez alofte;
His schalk schewed hym his schelde, on schulder he hit laght,
Gordez to Gryngolet with his gilt helez,
And he startez on the ston, stod he no lenger
            to praunce.
2065   His hathel on hors watz thenne,
        That bere his spere and launce.
        "This kastel to Kryst I kenne":
        He gef hit ay god chaunce.[1]

The brygge watz brayed doun, and the brode gatez
2070 Unbarred and born open upon bothe halve.
The burne blessed hym bilyve, and the brede passed—
Prayses the porter bifore the prynce kneled,
Gef hym God and goud day, that Gawayn he save—
And went on his way with his wyghe one,
2075 That schulde teche hym to tourne to that tene place
Ther the ruful race he schulde resayve.
Thay bowen bi bonkkez ther boghez ar bare,
Thay clomben bi clyffez ther clengez the colde.
The heven watz uphalt, bot ugly ther-under;
2080 Mist muged on the mor, malt on the mountez,
Uche hille hade a hatte, a myst-hakel huge.
Brokez byled and breke bi bonkkez about,
Schyre schaterande on schorez ther thay doun showved.
Wela wylle watz the way ther thay bi wod schulden,
2085 Til hit watz sone sesoun that the sunne ryses
            that tyde.
        Thay were on a hille ful hyghe,
        The quyte snaw lay bisyde;
        The burne that rod hym by
2090   Bede his mayster abide.

"For I haf wonnen yow hider, wyghe, at this tyme,
And now nar ye not fer fro that note place
That ye han spied and spuryed so specially after;
Bot I schal say yow for sothe, sythen I yow knowe,

2055 If out of kindliness they cherish a guest
And dispense hospitality, may the noble lord
Who holds up heaven repay them, and reward you all!
And were I to live any long time on earth
I would gladly recompense you, if I could."
2060 Then he sets foot in stirrup and vaults on to his horse;
His servant gave him his shield, he slung it on his shoulder,
Strikes spurs into Gringolet with his gilt heels,
And he leaps forward on the paving, he waited no longer
            to prance.
2065   His man was mounted then,
        Carrying his spear and lance.
        "I commend this house to God,
        May it never meet mischance."

The drawbridge was lowered, and the broad gates
2070 Unbarred and pushed open upon both sides.
The knight blessed himself quickly and rode over the planks,
Praises the porter who knelt before him
Commending Gawain to God, that he should the knight save,
And went on his way with his single guide,
2075 Who would show him the way to that perilous place
Where he must submit to a fearful stroke.
They struggled up hillsides where branches are bare,
They climbed up past rock-faces gripped by the cold.
The clouds were high up, but murky beneath them,
2080 Mist shrouded the moors, melted on the hills.
Each summit wore a hat, a huge cloak of mist.
Streams foamed and splashed down the slopes around them,
Breaking white against the banks as they rushed downhill.
Very wandering was the way they must take to the wood,
2085 Until soon it was time for sunrise at that point
            of the year.
        They were high up in the hills,
        By snow surrounded then;
        The servant at his side
2090   Bade Gawain draw rein.

"For I have guided you here, sir, on this day,
And now you are not far from that notorious place
That you have searched and enquired for so specially.
But I shall tell you truly—since I know who you are,

---

[1] *He gef hit ay god chaunce*   Either Gawain wishes the castle lasting
good fortune or, continuing his prayer in the previous line, hopes
that Christ will do so, *He gef* then meaning "May he give."

2095	And ye are a lede upon lyve that I wel lovy,
	Wolde ye worch bi my wytte, ye worthed the better.
	The place that ye prece to ful perelous is halden;
	Ther wonez a wyghe in that waste, the worst upon erthe,
	For he is stiffe and sturne, and to strike lovies,
2100	And more he is then any mon upon myddelerde,
	And his body bigger then the best fowre
	That ar in Arthurez hous, Hestor, other other.
	He chevez that chaunce at the chapel grene,
	Ther passes non bi that place so proude in his armes
2105	That he ne dyngez hym to dethe with dynt of his honde;
	For he is a mon methles, and mercy non uses,
	For be hit chorle other chaplayn that bi the chapel rydes,
	Monk other masseprest, other any mon elles,
	Hym thynk as queme hym to quelle as quyk go hymselven.
2110	Forthy I say the, as sothe as ye in sadel sitte,
	Com ye there, ye be kylled, I may the knyght rede;[1]
	Trawe ye me that trwely, thagh ye had twenty lyves
	to spende.
	He hatz wonyd here ful yore,
2115	On bent much baret bende,
	Agayn his dyntez sore
	Ye may not yow defende.

"Forthy, goude Sir Gawayn, let the gome one,
And gotz away sum other gate, upon Goddez halve!
2120 Cayrez bi sum other kyth, ther Kryst mot yow spede,
And I schal hygh me hom agayn, and hete yow fyrre
That I schal swere bi God and alle his gode halwez,
As help me God and the halydam, and othez innoghe,
That I schal lelly yow layne,[2] and lance never tale
2125 That ever ye fondet to fle for freke that I wyst."
"Grant merci," quoth Gawayn, and gruchyng he sayde,
"Wel worth the, wyghe, that woldez my gode,
And that lelly me layne I leve wel thou woldez.
Bot helde thou hit never so holde, and I here passed,
2130 Founded for ferde for to fle, in fourme that thou tellez,
I were a knyght kowarde, I myght not be excused.
Bot I wyl to the chapel, for chaunce that may falle,
And talk wyth that ilk tulk the tale that me lyste,

And you are a man whom I love dearly—
If you would follow my advice, it would be better for you.
The place you are going to is extremely dangerous;
There lives a man in that wilderness, the worst in the world,
For he is powerful and grim, and loves dealing blows,
And is bigger than any other man upon earth:
His body is mightier than the four strongest men
In Arthur's household, Hector or any other.
He so brings it about at the Green Chapel
That no one passes that place, however valiant in arms,
Who is not battered to death by force of his hand;
For he is a pitiless man who never shows mercy.
For whether peasant or churchman passes his chapel,
Monk or mass-priest, or whatever man else,
To him killing seems as pleasant as enjoying his own life.
Therefore I tell you, as sure as you sit in your saddle,
If you go there you'll be killed, I warn you, sir knight,
Believe that for certain, though you had twenty lives
to lose.
He has dwelt there long,
And brought about much strife;
Against his brutal blows
Nothing can save your life.

"Therefore, good Sir Gawain, let the man be,
And for God's sake get away from here by some other road!
Ride through some other country, where Christ be your help,
And I will make my way home again, and further I vow
That I shall swear by God and all his virtuous saints—
As help me God and the holy thing, and many more oaths—
That I shall keep your secret truly, and never reveal
That ever you took flight from a man that I knew."
"Many thanks," replied Gawain, and grudgingly he spoke,
"Good luck to you, man, who wishes my good,
And that you would loyally keep my secret I truly believe.
But however closely you kept it, if I avoided this place,
Took to my heels in fright, in the way you propose,
I should be a cowardly knight, and could not be excused.
But I will go to the chapel, whatever may chance,
And discuss with that man whatever matter I please,

---

1 *I may the knyght rede* I can tell you, knight. The original text does not include the first personal pronoun.

2 *I schal lelly yow layne* The guide repeats Gawain's promise to the lady at 1863.

Worthe hit wele other wo, as the wyrde lykez
2135   hit hafe.
        Thaghe he be a sturn knape
        To stightel, and stad with stave,
        Ful wel con Dryghtyn schape
        His servauntez for to save."

2140 "Mary!" quoth that other man, "now thou so much spellez
That thou wylt thyn awen nye nyme to thyselven,
And the lyste lese thy lyf, the lette I ne kepe.
Haf here thi helme on thy hede, thi spere in thi honde,
And ryde me doun this ilke rake bi yon rokke syde,
2145 Til thou be broght to the bothem of the brem valay;
Thenne loke a littel on the launde, on thy lyfte honde,
And thou schal se in that slade the self chapel,
And the borelych burne on bent that hit kepez.
Now farez wel, on Godez half, Gawayn the noble!
2150 For alle the golde upon grounde I nolde go wyth the,
Ne bere the felaghschip thurgh this fryth on fote fyrre."
Bi that the wyghe in the wod wendez his brydel,
Hit the hors with the helez as harde as he myght,
Lepez hym over the launde, and levez the knyght there
2155   al one.
        "Bi Goddez self," quoth Gawayn,
        "I wyl nauther grete ne grone;
        To Goddez wylle I am ful bayn,
        And to hym I haf me tone."

2160 Thenne gyrdez he to Gryngolet, and gederez the rake,
Schowvez in bi a schore at a schawe syde,
Ridez thurgh the roghe bonk ryght to the dale;
And thenne he wayted hym aboute, and wylde hit hym thoght,
And seye no syngne of resette bisydez nowhere,
2165 Bot hyghe bonkkez and brent upon bothe halve,
And rughe knokled knarrez with knorned stonez;
The skwez of the scowtes skayned hym thoght.
Thenne he hoved, and wythhylde his hors at that tyde,
And ofte chaunged his cher the chapel to seche:
2170 He seye non suche in no syde, and selly hym
          thoght,
Save, a lyttle on a launde, a lawe as hit were;
A balgh berw bi a bonke the brymme bysyde,
Bi a forgh of a flode that ferked thare;
The borne blubred therinne as hit boyled hade.
2175 The knyght kachez his caple and com to the lawe,

Whether good or ill come of it, as destiny
2135   decides.
        Though an opponent grim
        To deal with, club in hand,
        His faithful servants God
        Knows well how to defend."

2140 "Marry!" said the other man, "since your words make it clear
That you will deliberately bring harm on yourself,
And lose your life by your own wish, I won't hinder you.
Put your helmet on your head, take your spear in your hand,
And ride down this track beside the rock over there
2145 Until it brings you to the bottom of the wild valley;
Then look to your left, some way off in the glade,
And you will see in that dale the chapel itself,
And the giant of a man who inhabits the place.
Now in God's name, noble Gawain, farewell!
2150 For all the wealth in the world I would not go with you,
Nor keep you company through this wood one further step."
With that the man at his side tugs at his bridle,
Struck his horse with his heels as hard as he could,
Gallops over the hillside and leaves the knight there
2155   alone.
        Said Gawain, "By God himself,
        I shall not moan or cry;
        My life is in his hands,
        His will I shall obey."

2160 Then he sets spurs to Gringolet and picks up the path,
Makes his way down a slope at the edge of a wood,
Rides down the rugged hillside right to the valley,
And then looked about him, and it seemed a wild place,
And saw no sign of a building anywhere near,
2165 But high and steep hillsides upon both sides,
And rough rocky crags of jagged stones:
The clouds grazing the jutting rocks, as it seemed.
Then he halted, and checked his horse for a while,
Often turning his face to look for the chapel.
2170 He saw nothing of the kind anywhere, which he thought
          strange,
Except a way off in a glade, something like a mound;
A rounded hillock on the bank of a stream,
Near the bed of a torrent that tumbled there;
The water foamed in its course as though it had boiled.
2175 The knight urges his horse and comes to the mound,

Lightez doun luflyly, and at a lynde tachez	Alights nimbly, and makes fast to a tree
The rayne and his riche with a roghe braunche.	The reins and his noble steed with a rough branch.
Thenne he bowez to the berwe, aboute hit he walkez,	Then he goes to the mound and walks around it,
Debatande with hymself quat hit be myght.	Wondering to himself what it could be.
2180 Hit hade a hole on the ende and on ayther syde,	2180 It had a hole at the end and on either side,
And overgrowen with gresse in glodes aywhere,	And was covered all over with patches of grass,
And al watz holw inwith, nobot an olde cave,[1]	And was all hollow inside; nothing but an old cave,
Or a crevisse of an olde cragge, he couthe hit noght deme	Or a fissure in an old rock: what to call it he hardly
with spelle.	could tell.
2185 "We, lorde!" quoth the gentyle knyght,	2185 "Good lord!" said the noble knight,
"Whether this be the grene chapelle?	"Can the Green Chapel be this place?
Here myght aboute mydnyght	Here probably at midnight
The dele his matynnes telle!	The devil his matins says!
"Now iwysse," quoth Wowayn, "wysty is here;	"Now truly," said Gawain, "this is a desolate place;
2190 This oritore is ugly, with erbez overgrowen;	2190 This chapel looks evil, with grass overgrown;
Wel bisemez the wyghe wruxled in grene	Here fittingly might the man dressed in green
Dele here his devocioun on the develez wyse.	Perform his devotions, in devilish ways.
Now I fele hit is the fende, in my fyve wyttez,	Now all my senses tell me that the devil himself
That hatz stoken me this steven to strye me here.	Has forced this agreement on me, to destroy me here!
2195 This is a chapel of meschaunce, that chekke hit bytyde!	2195 This is a chapel of disaster, may ill-luck befall it!
Hit is the corsedest kyrk that ever I com inne!"	It is the most damnable church I was ever inside."
With hegh helme on his hede, his launce in his honde,	With tall helmet on head, his lance in his hand,
He romez up to the roffe of the rogh wonez.	He climbs to the top of that primitive dwelling.
Thene herde he of that hyghe hil, in a harde roche	Then he heard up the hillside, from behind a great rock,
2200 Biyonde the broke, in a bonk, a wonder breme noyse:	2200 On the slope across the stream, a deafening noise:
Quat! hit clatered in the clyff, as hit cleve schulde,	What! it echoed in the cliffs, as though they would split,
As one upon a gryndelston hade grounden a sythe.	As if someone with a grindstone were sharpening a scythe.
What! hit wharred and whette, as water at a mulne;	What! it whirred and sang, like water at a mill;
What! hit rusched and ronge, rawthe to here.	What! it rasped and it rang, terrible to hear.
2205 Thenne "Bi Godde," quoth Gawayn, "that gere, as I trowe,	2205 Then said Gawain, "By God, these doings, I suppose,
Is ryched at the reverence me, renk, to mete	Are a welcoming ceremony, arranged in my honor
bi rote.[2]	as a knight.
Let God worche! 'We loo'	God's will be done: 'Alas'
Hit helppez me not a mote.	Helps me no whit here.
2210 My lif thagh I forgoo,	2210 Although my life be lost,
Drede dotz me no lote."	Noise cannot make me fear."
Thenne the knyght con calle ful hyghe,	Then the knight shouted at the top of his voice,
"Who stightlez in this sted me steven to holde?	"Who is master of this place, to keep tryst with me?

---

[1] *nobot an olde cave*   An unlikely guess. The hollow mound half-covered with grass, with *a hole on the ende and on ayther syde*, has the characteristic form of a prehistoric burial chamber.

[2] *Is ryched … bi rote*   Is intended in honor of me, in order to meet a knight with due ceremony; or, if *renk* means a field of combat or a dueling-place, the noise is intended to mark (*mete*) it out ceremoniously.

For now is gode Gawayn goande ryght here.[1]
2215 If any wyghe oght wyl, wynne hider fast,
Other now other never, his nedez to spede."
"Abyde," quoth on on the bonke aboven his hede,
"And thou schal haf al in hast that I the hyght ones."
Yet he rusched on that rurde rapely a throwe,
2220 And wyth quettyng awharf, er he wolde lyght;
And sythen he keverez bi a cragge, and comez of a hole,
Whyrlande out of a wro wyth a felle weppen,
A denez ax nwe dyght, the dynt with to yelde,
With a borelych bytte bende bi the halme,
2225 Fyled in a fylor, fowre foot large—
Hit watz no lasse bi the lace that lemed ful bryght—[2]
And the gome in the grene gered as fyrst,
Bothe the lyre and the leggez, lokkez and berde,
Save that fayre on his fote he foundez on erthe,
2230 Sette the stele to the stone, and stalked bysyde.
When he wan to the watter, ther he wade nolde,
He hypped over on hys ax, and orpedly strydez,
Bremly brothe on a bent that brode watz aboute,
        on snawe.
2235   Sir Gawayn the knyght con mete,
        He ne lutte hym nothyng lowe;
        That other sayde, "Now, sir swete,
        Of steven mon may the trowe.

"Gawayn," quoth that grene gome, "God the mot loke!
2240 Iwysse thou art welcom, wyghe, to my place,
And thou hatz tymed thi travayl as truee mon schulde,
And thou knowez the covenauntez kest uus bytwene:
At this tyme twelmonyth thou toke that the falled,
And I schulde at this Nwe Yere yeply the quyte.
2245 And we ar in this valay verayly oure one;
Here are no renkes us to rydde, rele as uus lykez.
Haf thy helme of thy hede, and haf here thy pay.
Busk no more debate then I the bede thenne
When thou wypped of my hede at a wap one."
2250 "Nay, bi God," quoth Gawayn, "that me gost lante,

For now is good Gawain waiting right here.
2215 If anyone wants something, let him hurry here fast,
Either now or never, to settle his affairs."
"Wait," said someone on the hillside above,
"And you shall quickly have all that I promised you once."
Yet he kept making that whirring noise for a while,
2220 And turned back to his whetting before he would come down;
And then makes his way among the rocks, bursting out of a hole,
Whirling out of a nook with a fearsome weapon—
A Danish axe newly made—for dealing the blow,
With a massive blade curving back on the shaft,
2225 Honed with a whetstone, four feet across—
No less than that, despite the gleaming green girdle—
And the man in the green, dressed as at first,
Both his flesh and his legs, hair and beard,
Except that grandly on foot he stalked on the earth,
2230 Set the handle to the ground and walked beside it.
When he came to the stream he refused to wade:
He hopped over on his axe and forcefully strides,
Fiercely grim on a clearing that stretched wide about,
        under snow.
2235   Sir Gawain met the knight,
        Made him a frosty bow;
        The other said, "Good sir,
        A man may trust your vow.

"Gawain," said that green man, "may God protect you!
2240 You are indeed welcome, sir, to my place;
You have timed your journey as a true man should,
And you know the agreement settled between us:
A twelvemonth ago you took what fell to your lot,
And I was to repay you promptly at this New Year.
2245 And we are in this valley truly by ourselves,
With no knights to separate us, so we can fight as we please.
Take your helmet off your head, and here get your pay.
Make no more argument than I offered you then,
When you slashed off my head with a single stroke."
2250 "No, by God," said Gawain, "who gave me a soul,

---

[1] *goande ryght here* Walking right here, with a suggestion of being ready to leave immediately if no one answers.

[2] *Hit watz no lasse bi that lace that lemed ful bryght* Commentators disagree about which lace the poet is referring to. The axe used by Gawain has *a lace lapped aboute, that louked at the hede*, 217 as part of its decoration. But the axe which the Green Knight has just finished sharpening is a different weapon, newly made and not apparently decorated. The other lace is the green girdle or *luf-lace*,

see 1830, *a lace ... that leke umbe hir sydez*, and 2030, *the lace, the ladiez gifte*. The belt is so designated at least eight times between 1830 and 2505, while lace in the first sense is not clearly mentioned again after 217. The more likely reading of the line is that the axe seemed enormous to Gawain, despite the assurance of the green belt, whose *glyterande golde* decoration explains *lemed ful bryght*.

I schal gruch the no grwe for grem that fallez.
Bot styghtel the upon on strok, and I schal stonde stylle
And warp the no wernyng to worch as the lykez,
nowhare."[1]
2255 He lened with the nek, and lutte,
And schewed that schyre al bare,
And lette as he noght dutte;
For drede he wolde not dare.

Then the gome in the grene graythed hym swythe,
2260 Gederez up hys grymme tole Gawayn to smyte;
With alle the bur in his body he ber hit on lofte,
Munt as maghtyly as marre hym he wolde;
Hade hym dryven adoun as dregh as he atled,
Ther hade ben ded of his dynt that doghty watz ever.[2]
2265 Bot Gawayn on that giserne glyfte hym bysyde,
As hit com glydande adoun on glode hym to schende,
And schranke a lytel with the schulderes for the scharp yrne.
That other schalk wyth a schunt the schene wythhaldez,
And thenne repreved he the prynce with mony prowde wordez:
2270 "Thou art not Gawayn," quoth the gome, "that is so goud
halden,
That never arghed for no here by hylle ne be vale,
And now thou fles for ferde er thou fele harmez!
Such cowardise of that knyght cowthe I never here.
Nawther fyked I ne flaghe, freke, quen thou myntest,
2275 Ne kest no cavelacioun in kyngez hous Arthor.
My hede flagh to my fote, and yet flagh I never;
And thou, er any harme hent, arghez in hert.
Wherfore the better burne me burde be called
therfore."
2280 Quoth Gawayn, "I schunt onez,
And so wyl I no more;
Bot thagh my hede falle on the stonez,
I con not hit restore.

"But busk, burne, bi thi fayth, and bryng me to the poynt.
2285 Dele to me my destiné, and do hit out of honde,[3]
For I schal stonde the a strok, and start no more
Til thy ax have me hitte: haf here my trawthe."
"Haf at the thenne!" quoth that other, and hevez hit alofte,
And waytez as wrothely as he wode were.

I shall bear you no grudge at all, whatever hurt comes about.
Just limit yourself to one blow, and I will stand still
And not resist whatever it pleases you to do
at all."
2255 He bent his neck and bowed,
Showing the flesh all bare,
And seeming unafraid;
He would not shrink in fear.

Then the man dressed in green quickly got ready,
2260 Raised his terrible axe to give Gawain the blow;
With all the strength in his body he heaved it in the air,
Swung it as fiercely as if meaning to mangle him.
Had he brought the axe down as forcibly as he acted,
That courageous knight would have been killed by the blow;
2265 But Gawain glanced sideways at that battle-axe
As it came sweeping down to destroy him there,
And hunched his shoulders a little to resist the sharp blade.
The other man checked the bright steel with a jerk,
And then rebuked the prince with arrogant words:
2270 "You're not Gawain," said the man, "who is reputed so
good,
Who never quailed from an army, on valley or on hill,
And now flinches for fear before he feels any hurt!
I never heard of such cowardice shown by that knight.
I neither flinched nor fled, sir, when you aimed one at me,
2275 Nor raised any objections in King Arthur's house.
My head fell to the floor, yet I gave no ground;
But you, though not wounded, are trembling at heart,
So I deserve to be reckoned the better man
for that."
2280 Gawain said, "I flinched once,
But won't twice hunch my neck,
Though if my head should fall
I cannot put it back.

"But hurry up, man, by your faith, and come to the point.
2285 Deal out my fate to me, and do it out of hand,
For I shall let you strike a blow, and not move again
Until your axe has hit me, take my true word."
"Have at you then!" said the other, and raises it up,
Contorting his face as though he were enraged.

---

[1] *nowhare* Anywhere you like. Gawain is only concerned that the
Green Knight shall restrict himself to one stroke (2253).

[2] *that doghty watz ever* The man who was always brave.

[3] *out of honde* I.e., out of hand: at once. The first recorded use of
the phrase.

2290 He myntez at hym maghtyly, bot not the mon rynez,
Withhelde heterly his honde er hit hurt myght.
Gawayn graythely hit bydez, and glent with no membre,
Bot stode stylle as the ston, other a stubbe auther
That ratheled is in roché grounde with rotez a hundreth.
2295 Then muryly efte con he mele, the mon in the grene,
"So, now thou hatz thi hert holle, hitte me bihovs.
Halde the now the hyghe hode that Arthur the raght,
And kepe thy kanel at this kest, yif hit kever may."
Gawayn ful gryndelly with greme thenne sayde:
2300 "Wy! thresch on, thou thro mon, thou thretez to longe;
I hope that thi hert arghe wyth thyn awen selven."
"For sothe," quoth that other freke, "so felly thou spekez,
I wyl no lenger on lyte lette thin ernde[1]
        right nowe."
2305   Thenne tas he hym strythe to stryke,
        And frounsez bothe lyppe and browe,
        No mervayle thagh hym myslyke
        That hoped of no rescowe.

He lyftes lyghtly his lome, and let hit doun fayre
2310 With the barbe of the bitte bi the bare nek;
Thagh he homered heterly, hurt hym no more
Bot snyrt hym on that on syde, that severed the hyde.
The scharp schrank to the flesche thurgh the schyre grece,
That the schene blod over his schulderes schot to the erthe;
2315 And quen the burne sey the blode blenk on the snawe,
He sprit forth a spenne-fote[2] more then a spere lenthe,
Hent heterly his helme, and his hed cast,
Schot with his schulderes his fayre schelde under,
Braydez out a bryght sworde, and bremly he spekez—
2320 Never syn that he watz burne borne of his moder
Watz he never in this worlde wyghe half so blythe—
"Blynne, burne, of thy bur, bede me no mo!
I haf a stroke in this sted withoute stryf hent,
And if thow rechez me any mo, I redyly schal quyte,
2325 And yelde yederly agayn—and therto ye tryst—
        and foo.
        Bot on stroke here me fallez—
        The covenaunt ryght schop so,
        Fermed in Arthurez hallez—
2330   And therfore, hende, now hoo!"

2290 He swings the axe at him savagely, without harming the man,
Checked his blow suddenly before it could inflict hurt.
Gawain awaits it submissively, not moving a limb,
But stood as still as a stone, or the stump of a tree
Anchored in rocky ground by hundreds of roots.
2295 Then the man in green spoke mockingly again,
"So, now you have found courage it is time for the blow.
Now may the order of knighthood given you by Arthur
Preserve you and your neck this time, if it has power!"
Then Gawain replied angrily, mortified deeply,
2300 "Why, strike away, you fierce man, you waste time in threats;
I think you have frightened yourself with your words."
"Indeed," said that other man, "you speak so aggressively
That I will no longer delay or hinder your business
        at all."
2305   He takes his stance to strike,
        Puckering mouth and brow;
        No wonder if Gawain feels
        No hope of rescue now.

He swiftly raises his weapon, and brings it down straight
2310 With the cutting edge of the blade over Gawain's bare neck;
Although he struck fiercely, he hurt him no more
Than to slash the back of his neck, laying open the skin.
The blade cut into the body through the fair flesh
So that bright blood shot over his shoulders to the ground.
2315 And when the knight saw his blood spatter the snow
He leapt forward with both feet more than a spear's length,
Snatched up his helmet and crammed it on his head,
Jerked his shoulders to bring his splendid shield down,
Drew out a gleaming sword and fiercely he speaks—
2320 Never since that man was born of his mother
Had he ever in the world felt half so relieved—
"Hold your attack, sir, don't try it again!
I have passively taken a blow in this place,
And if you offer me another I shall repay it promptly
2325 And return it at once—be certain of that—
        with force.
        One single blow is due;
        The contract is my proof,
        Witnessed in Arthur's hall;
2330   And therefore, sir, enough!"

---

[1] *I wyl no lenger on lyte lette thin ernde*   Literally: I will no longer in delay hinder your mission.

[2] *spenne-fote*   With feet together.

The hathel heldet hym fro, and on his ax rested,
Sette the schaft upon schore, and to the scharp lened,
And loked to the leude that on the launde yede,
How that doghty, dredles, dervely ther stondez
2335 Armed, ful aghles: in hert hit hym lykez.
Thenn he melez muryly wyth a much steven,
And with a rynkande rurde he to the renk sayde:
"Bolde burne, on this bent be not so gryndel.
No mon here unmanerly the mysboden habbez,
2340 Ne kyd bot as covenaunde at kyngez kort schaped.
I hyght the a strok and thou hit hatz, halde the wel payed;
I relece the of the remnaunt of ryghtes alle other.
Iif I deliver had bene, a boffet paraunter
I couthe wrotheloker haf waret, to the haf wroght anger.
2345 Fyrst I mansed the muryly with a mynt one,
And rove the wyth no rofe-sore, with ryght I the profered
For the forwarde that we fest in the fyrst nyght,[1]
And thou trystyly the trawthe and trwly me haldez,
Al the gayne thow me gef, as god mon schulde.
2350 That other munt for the morne, mon, I the profered,
Thou kyssedes my clere wyf—the cosses me raghtez.
For bothe two here I the bede bot two bare myntes
           boute scathe.[2]
      Trwe mon trwe restore,
2355   Thenne thar mon drede no wathe.
      At the thrid thou fayled thore,
      And therfore that tappe ta the.

"For hit is my wede that thou werez, that ilke woven girdel,
Myn owen wyf hit the weved, I wot wel for sothe.
2360 Now know I wel thy cosses, and thy costes als,
And the wowyng of my wyf: I wroght it myselven.
I sende hir to asay the, and sothly me thynkkez
On the fautlest freke that ever on fote yede;
As perle bi the quite pese is of prys more,
2365 So is Gawayn, in god fayth, bi other gay knyghtez.
Bot here yow lakked a lyttel, sir, and lewté yow wonted;
Bot that watz for no wylde werke,[3] ne wowyng nauther,
Bot for ye lufed your lyf; the lasse I yow blame."
That other stif mon in study[4] stod a gret whyle,
2370 So agreved for greme he gryed withinne;
Alle the blod of his brest blende in his face,

The knight kept his distance, and rested on his axe,
Set the shaft on the ground and leaned on the blade,
Contemplating the man before him in the glade;
Seeing how valiant, fearlessly bold he stood there
2335 Armed and undaunted, he admired him much.
Then he spoke to him pleasantly in a loud voice,
And said to the knight in a resounding tone,
"Brave sir, don't act so wrathfully in this place.
No one has discourteously mistreated you here,
2340 Or acted contrary to the covenant sworn at the king's court.
I promised you a blow and you have it; think yourself well paid;
I free you from the rest of all other obligations.
Had I been more dextrous, maybe I could
Have dealt you a more spiteful blow, to have roused your anger.
2345 First I threatened you playfully with a pretence,
And avoided giving you a gash, doing so rightly
Because of the agreement we made on the first night,
When you faithfully and truly kept your pledged word,
Gave me all your winnings, as an honest man should.
2350 That other feint, sir, I gave you for the next day,
When you kissed my lovely wife and gave me those kisses.
For both occasions I aimed at you two mere mock blows
           without harm.
      True man must pay back truly,
2355   Then he need nothing fear;
      You failed me the third time
      And took that blow therefore.

"For it is my belt you are wearing, that same woven girdle,
My own wife gave it to you, I know well in truth.
2360 I know all about your kisses, and your courteous manners,
And my wife's wooing of you: I arranged it myself.
I sent her to test you, and to me truly you seem
One of the most perfect men who ever walked on the earth.
As pearls are more valuable than the white peas,
2365 So is Gawain, in all truth, before other fair knights.
Only here you fell short a little, sir, and lacked fidelity,
But that was not for fine craftsmanship, nor wooing either,
But because you wanted to live: so I blame you the less."
That other brave man stood speechless a long while,
2370 So mortified and crushed that he inwardly squirmed;
All the blood in his body burned in his face,

---

[1] *fyrst nyght* The night before the first hunt.

[2] *boute scathe* Without injury, unscathed.

[3] *wylyde werke* Intricate workmanship (of the belt).

[4] *in study* Lost in thought, speechless.

That al he schranke for schome that the schalk talked.
The forme worde upon folde that the freke meled:
"Corsed worth cowarddyse and covetyse bothe!
2375 In yow is vylany and vyse that vertue disstryez."
Thenne he kaght to the knot, and the kest lawsez,
Brayde brothely the belt to the burne selven:
"Lo, ther the falssyng, foule mot hit falle!
For care of thy knokke cowardyse me taght
2380 To acorde me with covetyse, my kynde to forsake,
That is larges and lewté that longez to knyghtez.
Now am I fawty and falce, and ferde haf ben ever
Of trecherye and untrawthe: bothe bityde sorwe
                         and care!
2385   I biknowe yow, knyght, here stylle,
        Al fawty is my fare;
        Letez me overtake your wylle
        And efte I schal be ware."

The loghe that other leude and luflyly sayde,
2390 "I halde hit hardily hole, the harme that I hade.[1]
Thou art confessed so clene, beknowen of thy mysses,
And hatz the penaunce apert of the poynt of myn egge,
I halde the polysed of that plyght, and pured as clene
As thou hadez never forfeted sythen thou watz fyrst borne;
2395 And I gif the, sir, the gurdel that is golde-hemmed;
For hit is grene as my goune, Sir Gawayn, ye maye
Thenk upon this ilke threpe, ther thou forth thryngez
Among prynces of prys, and this a pure token
Of the chaunce of the grene chapel at chevalrous
                         knyghtez.
2400 And ye schal in this Nwe Yer agayn to my wonez,
And we schyn revel the remnaunt of this ryche fest
         ful bene."
        Ther lathed hym fast the lorde
        And sayde, "Wyth my wyf, I wene,
2405   We schal yow wel acorde,
        That watz your enmy kene."

"Nay, for sothe," quoth the segge, and sesed hys helme,
And hatz hit of hendely, and the hathel thonkkez,
"I haf sojorned sadly; sele yow bytyde
2410 And he yelde hit yow yare that yarkkez al menskes!
And comaundez me to that cortays, your comlych fere,
Bothe that on and that other, myn honoured ladyez,

So that he winced with shame at what the man said.
The first words that the knight uttered there
Were, "A curse upon cowardice and coveteousness!
2375 You breed boorishness and vice that ruin virtue."
Then he took hold of the knot and looses the buckle,
Flung the belt violently towards that man:
"There it is, the false thing, may the devil take it!
For fear of your blow taught me cowardice,
2380 To give way to covetousness, be false to my nature,
The generosity and fidelity expected of knights.
Now I am false and unworthy, and have always dreaded
Treachery and deceit: may misfortune and grief
                         befall both!
2385   Sir, humbly I confess
        My good name is marred.
        Let me regain your trust,
        Next time I'll be on guard."

Then the other man laughed, and graciously said,
2390 "The wrong you did me I consider wiped out.
You have so cleanly confessed yourself, admitted your fault,
And done honest penance on the edge of my blade.
I declare you absolved of that offence, and washed as clean
As if you had never transgressed since the day you were born.
2395 And I make you a gift, sir, of my gold-bordered belt;
Since it is green like my gown, Sir Gawain, you may
Remember this meeting in the world where you mingle
With princes of rank: it will be a true token
Of the exploit of the Green Chapel among chivalrous
                         knights.
2400 And you shall come back to my castle at this New Year,
And we will see out the revelry of this high feast
         with joy."
        He pressed him earnestly
        And said, "We shall, I know,
2405   Reconcile you with my wife,
        Who was your cunning foe."

"No, indeed," said the knight, and seizing his helmet
Takes it off politely and gives the lord thanks;
"I have stayed long enough: good fortune attend you,
2410 And may he who gives all honors soon send you reward!
And commend me to that gracious one, your lovely wife,
Both the one and the other of those honorable ladies

---

[1]   *the harme that I hade*   I.e., being cheated of his winnings.

That thus hor knyght wyth hor kest han koyntly bigyled.
Bot hit is no ferly thagh a fole madde,
2415 And thurgh wyles of wymmen be wonen to sorwe,
For so watz Adam in erde with one bygyled,
And Salamon with fele sere, and Samson eftsonez—
Dalyda dalt hym hys wyrde—and Davyth therafter
Watz blended with Barsabe, that much bale tholed.[1]
2420 Now these were wrathed wyth her wyles, hit were a wynne huge
To luf hom wel and leve hem not, a leude that couthe.
For thes wer forne the freest, that folwed alle the sele
Exellently of alle thyse other, under hevenryche
          that mused;
2425   And alle thay were biwyled
          With wymmen that thay used.
          Thagh I be now bigyled
          Me think me burde be excused.

"Bot your gordel," quoth Gawayn, "God yow foryelde!
2430 That wyl I welde wyth goud wylle, not for the wynne golde,
Ne the saynt, ne the sylk, ne for syde pendaundes,
For wele ne for worchyp, ne for the wlonk werkkez,
Bot in syngne of my surfet I schal se hit ofte,
When I ride in renoun, remorde to myselven
2435 The faut and the fayntyse of the flesche crabbed,
How tender hit is to entyse teches of fylthe;
And thus, quen pryde schal me pryk for prowes of armes,
The loke to this luf-lace schal lethe my hert.
Bot on I wolde yow pray, displeses yow never:
2440 Syn ye be lorde of the yonder londe her I haf lent inne
Wyth yow wyth worschyp—the wyghe hit yow yelde
That uphaldez the heven and on hygh sittez—
How norne ye yowre ryght nome, and thenne no more?"
"That schal I telle the trwly," quoth that other thenne,
2445 "Bertilak de Hautdesert I hat in this londe.
Thurgh myght of Morgne la Faye, that in my hous lenges,
And koyntyse of clergye, bi craftes wel lerned,
The maystrés of Merlyn mony hatz taken—
For ho hatz dalt drwry ful dere sumtyme
2450 With that conable klerk, that knowes alle your knyghtez
          at hame.
          Morgne the goddes
          Therfore hit is hir name:
          Weldez non so hyghe hawtesse
2455   That ho ne con make ful tame—

Who have so cleverly deluded their knight with their game.
But it is no wonder if a fool acts insanely
2415 And is brought to grief through womanly wiles;
For so was Adam beguiled by one, here on earth,
Solomon by several women, and Samson was another—
Delilah was cause of his fate—and afterwards David
Was deluded by Bathsheba, and suffered much grief.
2420 Since these were ruined by their wiles, it would be a great gain
To love women and not trust them, if a man knew how.
For these were the noblest of old, whom fortune favored
Above all others on earth, or who dwelt
          under heaven.
2425   Beguiled were they all
          By women they thought kind.
          Since I too have been tricked
          Then I should pardon find.

"But for your belt," said Gawain, "God repay you for that!
2430 I accept it gratefully, not for its wonderful gold,
Nor for the girdle itself nor its silk, nor its long pendants,
Nor its value nor the honor it confers, nor its fine workmanship,
But I shall look at it often as a sign of my failing,
And when I ride in triumph, recall with remorse
2435 The corruption and frailty of the perverse flesh,
How quick it is to pick up blotches of sin.
And so, when pride in my knightly valor stirs me,
A glance at this girdle will humble my heart.
Just one thing I would ask, if it would not offend you,
2440 Since you are the lord of the country that I have dwelt in,
Honorably treated in your house—may he reward you
Who holds up the heavens and sits upon high!—
What do you call yourself rightly, and then no more demands?"
"I will tell you that truthfully," replied that other man,
2445 "Bertilak of Hautdesert I am called in this land.
Through the power of Morgan le Fay, who lives under my roof,
And her skill in learning, well taught in magic arts,
She has acquired many of Merlin's occult powers—
For she had love-dealings at an earlier time
2450 With that accomplished scholar, as all your knights know
          at home.
          Morgan the goddess
          Therefore is her name;
          No one, however haughty
2455   Or proud she cannot tame.

---

[1] *For so watz Adam ... tholed* Famous stories of female betrayal from the Old Testament.

"Ho wayned me upon this wyse to your wynne halle
For to assay the surquidré, yif hit soth were
That rennes of the grete renoun of the Rounde Table.
Ho wayned me this wonder your wyttez to reve,
2460 For to have greved Gaynour and gart hir to dyghe
With glopnyng of that ilke gome that gostlych speked
With his hede in his honde bifore the hyghe table.
That is ho that is at home, the auncian lady;
Ho is even thyn aunt, Arthurez half-suster,
2465 The duches doghter of Tyntagelle, that dere Uter after
Hade Arthur upon, that athel is nowthe.
Therfore I ethe the, hathel, to com to thyn aunt,
Make myry in my hous; my meny the lovies,
And I wol the as wel, wyghe, bi my faythe,
2470 As any gome under God for thy grete trauthe."
And he nikked hym naye, he nolde bi no wayes.
Thay acolen and kyssen and kennen ayther other
To the prynce of paradise, and parten ryght there
        on coolde;
2475   Gawayn on blonk ful bene
        To the kyngez burgh buskez bolde,
        And the knyght in the enker-grene
        Whiderwarde-so-ever he wolde.

Wylde wayez in the worlde Wowen now rydez
2480 On Gryngolet, that the grace hade geten of his lyve;
Ofte he herbered in house and ofte al theroute,
And mony aventure in vale, and venquyst ofte,
That I ne tyght at this tyme in tale to remene.
The hurt watz hole that he hade hent in his nek,
2485 And the blykkande belt he bere theraboute
Abelef as a bauderyk bounden by his syde,
Loken under his lyfte arme, the lace, with a knot,
In tokenyng he watz tane in tech of a faute.
And thus he commes to the court, knyght al in sounde.
2490 Ther wakned wele in that wone when wyst the grete
That gode Gawayn watz commen; gayn hit hym thoght.
The kyng kysses the knyght, and the whene alce,
And sythen mony syker knyght that soght hym to haylce,
Of his fare that hym frayned; and ferlyly he telles,
2495 Biknowez alle the costes of care that he hade,
The chaunce of the chapel, the chere of the knyght,
The luf of the ladi, the lace at the last.
The nirt in the neck he naked hem schewed

"She sent me in this shape to your splendid hall
To make trial of your pride, and to judge the truth
Of the great reputation attached to the Round Table.
She sent me to drive you demented with this marvel,
2460 To have terrified Guenevere and caused her to die
With horror at that figure who spoke like a specter
With his head in his hand before the high table.
That is she who is in my castle, the very old lady,
Who is actually your aunt, Arthur's half-sister,
2465 The duchess of Tintagel's daughter, whom noble Uter
Afterwards begot Arthur upon, who now is king.
So I entreat you, good sir, to visit your aunt
And make merry in my house: my servants all love you,
And so will I too, sir, on my honor,
2470 As much as any man on earth for your great truth."
But Gawain told him no, not for any persuasion.
They embrace and kiss, and commend each other
To the prince of paradise, and separate there
        in the cold;
2475   On his great horse Gawain
        To the king's court quickly goes,
        And the knight in emerald green
        Went wheresoever he chose.

Over wild country Gawain now makes his way
2480 On Gringolet, after his life had been mercifully spared.
Sometimes he lodged in a house and often out of doors,
And was vanquisher often in many encounters
Which at this time I do not intend to relate.
The injury he had received in his neck was healed,
2485 And over it he wore the gleaming belt
Across his body like a baldric, fastened at his side,
And this girdle tied under his left arm with a knot,
To signify he had been dishonored by a slip.
And so safe and sound he arrives at the court.
2490 Joy spread through the castle when the nobles learnt
That good Gawain had returned: they thought it a wonder.
The king kisses the knight, and the queen too,
And then many true knights who came to embrace him,
Asking how he had fared; he tells a marvelous story,
2495 Describes all the hardships he had endured,
What happened at the chapel, the Green Knight's behavior,
The lady's wooing, and finally the belt.
He showed them the scar on his bare neck

2500 That he laght for his unleuté at the leudes hondes
  for blame.
   He tened quen he schulde telle,
   He groned for gref and grame;
   The blod in his face con melle,
   When he hit schulde schewe, for schame.

2505 "Lo, lorde," quoth the leude, and the lace hondeled,
"This is the bende of this blame I bere in my nek,
This is the lathe and the losse that I laght have
Of cowardise and covetyse that I haf caght thare,
This is the token of untrawthe that I am tane inne,
2510 And I mot nedez hit were wyle I may last;
For mon may hyden his harme, bot unhap ne may hit,
For ther hit onez is tachched twynne wil hit never."
The kyng comfortez the knyght, and alle the court als
Laghen loude therat, and luflyly acorden
2515 That lordes and ladis that longed to the Table,
Uche burne of the brotherhede, a bauderyk schulde have,
A bende abelef hym aboute of a bryght grene,
And that, for sake of that segge, in swete to were.
For that watz acorded the renoun of the Rounde Table,
2520 And he honoured that hit hade evermore after,
As hit is breved in the best boke of romaunce.
Thus in Arthurus day this aunter bitidde,
The Brutus bokez therof beres wyttenesse;
Sythen Brutus, the bolde burne, bowed hider fyrst,
2525 After the segge and the asaute watz sesed at Troye,[1]
  iwysse,
   Mony aunterez here-biforne
   Haf fallen suche er this.
   Now that bere the croun of thorne
2530   He bryng uus to his blysse! AMEN.

HONY SOYT QUI MAL PENCE.[2]

2500 That he received for his dishonesty at the lord's hands
  in rebuke.
   Tormented by his tale
   He groaned for grief and hurt;
   The blood burned in his face
   When he showed the shameful cut.

2505 "See, my lord," said the man, and held up the girdle,
"This belt caused the scar that I bear on my neck;
This is the injury and damage that I have suffered
For the cowardice and covetousness that seized me there;
This is the token of the dishonesty I was caught committing,
2510 And now I must wear it as long as I live.
For a man may hide his misdeed, but never erase it,
For where once it takes root the stain can never be lifted."
The king consoles the knight, and the whole court
Laughs loudly about it, and courteously agrees
2515 That lords and ladies who belong to the Table,
Each member of the brotherhood, should wear such a belt,
A baldric of bright green crosswise on the body,
Similar to Sir Gawain's and worn for his sake:
And that became part of the renown of the Round Table,
2520 And whoever afterwards wore it was always honored,
As is set down in the most reputable books of romance.
So in the time of Arthur this adventure happened,
And the chronicles of Britain bear witness to it;
After the brave hero Brutus first arrived here,
2525 When the siege and the assault were ended at Troy,
  indeed.
   Many exploits before now
   Have happened much like this.
   Now may the thorn-crowned God
2530   Bring us to his bliss! AMEN.

HONI SOIT QUI MAL Y PENSE.

---

[1] *After the segge and the asaute watz sesed at Troye* The last long line of the poem repeats the first one, as though bringing the story full circle after its hundred and one stanzas.

[2] *Hony Soyt Qui Mal Pence* Old French: evil be to him who evil thinks, the motto embroidered on the blue velvet garter worn by Knights of the Garter, the highest order of English knighthood bestowed by the sovereign. According to Froissart, the order was instituted about 1344. The poet's use of the motto has not been accounted for.

In Context

Fled Bricrend

The earliest known example of the beheading-game legend appears in the Irish story *Fled Bricrend*, written down about the year 1100 but probably a good deal older. It tells how a terrifying ogre enters the hall where several heroes are gathered, carrying a huge club in one hand and an enormous axe in the other. He explains that he is searching for a man who will deal with him fairly, and that the reputation of the Ulaid has brought him there in the hope of finding one. The terms of fair play that he proposes are that he will cut off the head of one of the heroes, who on the following night will decapitate him. This arrangement is not accepted, and the ogre agrees to reverse the conditions by standing a blow forthwith and returning on the next day to give one in return. One of the heroes accepts the challenge and cuts off the ogre's head, filling the hall with blood; but the ogre rises, picks up his head and the axe, and leaves the hall, still bleeding profusely. When he returns on the following night his opponent shirks his undertaking to stand the return blow. Two further heroes take up the challenge with the same result, but when the ogre returns on the fourth night contemptuous of the false and cowardly Ulaid, Cú Chulaind (Cuchulainn) is present. He too decapitates the ogre and smashes the head for good measure. On the next night Cú Chulaind places his neck on the block to receive the return blow, and is mocked by the ogre because his neck does not cover the enormous block. Cú Chulaind rebukes the ogre for tormenting him, and insists on being despatched at once. The ogre raises the huge axe and brings it down on Cú Chulaind's neck with the blade uppermost. After praising Cú Chulaind's courage and fidelity the ogre vanishes. In a shorter version of the story he swings the axe at Cú Chulaind three times, each time with the blade reversed.

from *Fled Bricrend/Bricriu's Feast*

Once, when the Ulaid were at Emuin Machae, tired after the fair and the games, Conchubur and Fergus and the other Ulaid chieftains returned from the playing field to sit in Conchubur's Cráebrúad. Lóegure and Conall and Cú Chulaind were not there that evening, but the best of the other warriors of Ulaid were. As night drew on, they saw a huge, ugly churl coming towards them in the house, and it seemed to them that there was not in all Ulaid a warrior half as tall. His appearance was frightful and terrifying: a hide against his skin, and a dun cloak round him, and a great bushy tree overhead where a winter shed for thirty calves could fit. Each of his two yellow eyes was the size of an ox-cauldron; each finger was as thick as a normal man's wrist. The tree trunk in his left hand would have been a burden for twenty yoked oxen; the axe in his right hand, whence had gone three fifties of glowing metal pieces, had a handle that would have been a burden for a team of oxen, yet it was sharp enough to cut hairs against the wind.

He came in this guise and stood beneath the forked beam at one end of the fire. "Do you find the house so narrow," said Dubthach Dóeltenga, "that there is no place to stand but under the forked beam? You may wish to contest the position of house candlebearer, but you are more likely to burn the house than to illuminate the company inside." "Although that is my gift," the churl replied, "perhaps you will grant that, despite my height, the entire household may be lit without the house's being burnt. But that is not my primary gift, and I have others. That which I have come to seek I have not found in Ériu or the Alps or Europe or Africa or Asia or Greece or Scythia or Inis Orc or the Pillars of Hercules or Tor mBregoind or Inis Gaid. Nowhere have I found a man to keep my bargain. Since you Ulaid surpass the hosts of every land in anger and prowess and weaponry, in rank and pride and dignity, in honor and generosity and excellence, let one of you keep faith with me in the matter over which I have come."

"It is not right," said Fergus, "to dishonor a province because of one man's failure to keep his word—perhaps death is no nearer to him than it is to you." "It is not I who shirk death," replied the churl. "Then let us hear your proposal," said Fergus. "Only if I am allowed fair play," said the churl. "It is right to allow him that," said Senchae son of Ailill, "for it would be no fair play if a great host broke faith with a completely unknown individual. Besides, it would seem to us that if you are to find the man you seek, you will find him here." "I exempt Conchubur, for he is the king, and I exempt Fergus, for he is of equal rank," said the churl. "Whoever else may dare, let him come that I may cut off his head tonight, he mine tomorrow."

"After those two," said Dubthach, "there is certainly no warrior here worthy of that." "Indeed, there is," said Muinremur son of Gerrgend, and he sprang into the center of the house. Now, Muinremur had the strength of one hundred warriors, and each arm had the strength of one hundred. "Bend down, churl," he said, "that I may cut off your head tonight—you may cut off mine tomorrow night." "I could make that bargain anywhere," said the churl. "Let us rather make the bargain I proposed: I will cut off your head tonight, and you will avenge that by cutting off my head tomorrow night." "I swear by what my people swear by," said Dubthach Dóeltenga, "such a death would not be pleasant if the man you killed tonight clung to you tomorrow. But you alone have the power to be killed one night and to avenge it the next." "Then whatever conditions you propose I will fulfil, surprising as you may find that," said the churl, whereupon he made Muinremur pledge to keep his part of the bargain the following night.

With that, Muinremur took the churl's axe, whose two edges were seven feet apart. The churl stretched his neck out on the block, and Muinremur so swung the axe that it stuck in the block underneath; the head rolled to the foot of the forked beam, and the house was filled with blood. At once, the churl rose, gathered his head and his block and his axe and clutched them to his chest, and left the house, blood streaming from the neck and filling the Cráebrúad on every side. The household were horrorstruck by the wondrousness of the event they had witnessed. "I swear by what my people swear by," said Dubthach Dóeltenga, "if that churl returns tomorrow after having been killed tonight, not a man in Ulaid will be left alive."

The following night, the churl returned, but Muinremur avoided him. The churl complained, saying "Indeed, it is not fair of Muinremur to break his part of the bargain." Lóegure Búadach, however, was present that night, and when the churl continued, "Who of the warriors who contest the champion's portion of Ulaid will fulfil this bargain with me tonight? Where is Lóegure Búadach?", Lóegure said, "Here I am!" The churl pledged Lóegure as he had pledged Muinremur, but Lóegure, like Muinremur, failed to appear the following night. The churl then pledged Conall Cernach, and he too failed to appear and keep his pledge.

When he arrived on the fourth night, the churl was seething with rage. All the women of Ulaid had gathered there that night to see the marvel that had come to the Cráebrúad, and Cú Chulaind had come as well. The churl began to reproach them, then, saying, "Men of Ulaid, your skill and courage are no more. Your warriors covet the champion's portion, yet they are unable to contest it. Where is that pitiful stripling you call Cú Chulaind? Would his word be better than that of his companions?" "I want no bargain with you," said Cú Chulaind. "No doubt you fear death, wretched fly," said the churl. At that, Cú Chulaind sprang towards the churl and dealt him such a blow with the axe that his head was sent to the rafters of the Cráebrúad, and the entire house shook. Cú

Chulaind then struck the head with the axe once more, so that he shattered it into fragments. The churl rose nonetheless.

The following day, the Ulaid watched Cú Chulaind to see if he would avoid the churl the way his companions had done; they saw that he was waiting for the churl, and they grew very dejected. It seemed to them proper to begin his death dirge, for they feared greatly that he would live only until the churl appeared. Cú Chulaind, ashamed, said to Conchubur, "By my shield and by my sword, I will not go until I have fulfilled my pledge to the churl—since I am to die, I will die with honor."

Towards the end of the day, they saw the churl approaching them. "Where is Cú Chulaind?" he asked. "Indeed, I am here," said Cú Chulaind. "You speak low, tonight, wretch, for you fear death greatly," said the churl. "Yet for all that, you have not avoided me." Cú Chulaind rose and stretched his neck out on the block, but its size was such that his neck reached only halfway across. "Stretch out your neck, you wretch," said the churl. "You torment me," said Cú Chulaind. "Kill me quickly. I did not torment you last night. Indeed, I swear, if you torment me now, I will make myself as long as a heron above you." "I cannot dispatch you, not with the length of the block and the shortness of your neck," said the churl.

Cú Chulaind stretched himself, then, until a warrior's foot would fit between each rib, and he stretched his neck until it reached the other side of the block. The churl raised his axe so that it reached the rafters of the house. What with the creaking of the old hide that he wore and the swish of his axe as he raised it with the strength of his two arms, the sound he made was like that of a rustling forest on a windy night. The churl brought the axe down, then, upon Cú Chulaind's neck—with the blade turned up. All the chieftains of Ulaid saw this.

"Rise, Cú Chulaind!" the churl then said. "Of all the warriors in Ulaid and Ériu, whatever their merit, none is your equal for courage and skill and honor. You are the supreme warrior of Ériu, and the champion's portion is yours, without contest; moreover, your wife will henceforth enter the drinking house before all the other women of Ulaid. Whoever might dispute this judgment, I swear by what my people swear by, his life will not be long." After that, the churl vanished. It was Cú Rui son of Dáre, who in that guise had come to fulfil the promise he had made to Cú Chulaind.

Illustrations from the Original Manuscript

In the manuscript in which *Sir Gawain and the Green Knight* appears the text is accompanied by four illustrations. Two of these are reproduced below. The first, which appears before the text in the original manuscript, brings together two scenes from the poem in a single illustration. Gawain is shown both taking the axe from King Arthur (who appears with the Queen on his left), and holding the axe (having just decapitated the Green Knight); the Green Knight is shown on horseback, holding his head.

In the second illustration reproduced here, the lady of the castle is shown visiting Gawain. (The two lines appearing above the illustration were written in a hand other than that of the manuscript scribe, and are not connected to the poem.)

The two illustrations not reproduced here are somewhat indistinct in the manuscript; they portray Gawain at the Green Chapel with the Green Knight above, axe in hand, and Gawain kneeling in front of Arthur and Guenevere.

The Thorn and the Yogh

The "original" text of *Sir Gawain and the Green Knight* as provided above substitutes modern English letters for two letters in Middle English that have now died out. One of these, the letter þ ("thorn"), was sounded very much as we sound the letters "th" today. The other, ȝ ("yogh"), various represented sounds that we represent with "gh," "y," and "z." Following is the first part of the poem with Middle English letters.

> Siþþen þe sege and þe assaut watz sesed at Troye,
> Þe borȝ brittened and brent to brondeȝ and askez,
> Þe tulk þat þe trammes of tresoun þer wroȝt
> Watz tried for his tricherie, þe trewest on erþe:
> Hit watz Ennias þe athel, and his highe kynde,
> Þat siþþen depreced prouinces, and patrounes bicome
> Welneȝe of al þe wele in þe west iles.
> Fro riche Romulus to Rome ricchis hym swyþe,
> With gret bobbaunce þat burȝe he biges vpon fyrst,
> And neuenes hit his aune nome, as hit now hat;
> Tirius to Tuskan and teldes bigynnes,
> Langaberde in Lumbardie lyftes vp homes,
> And fer ouer þe French flod Felix Brutus
> On mony bonkkes ful brode Bretayn he settez wyth wynne,
> Where werre and wrake and wonder
> Bi syþez hatz wont þerinne,
> And oft boþe blysse and blunder
> Ful skete hatz skyfted synne.

John Gower

c. 1330 – 1408

In Southwark Cathedral, across the Thames from the old, medieval City of London, lies the tomb of the poet John Gower, a friend and contemporary of Chaucer. Gower was a prolific writer who was praised throughout the fifteenth and sixteenth centuries as one of the most masterful English poets. His popularity was not sustained, however, and his reputation has since been overshadowed by that of Chaucer, who famously christened his friend "moral Gower" for his simple, direct style and his progressive views. This epithet has stayed with Gower and perhaps contributed to the sense many readers have that his work is dry and solemn. More and more, however, Gower has been receiving critical attention not just as a contemporary of Chaucer but as a powerful poet in his own right, and one whose wide learning and moral poetics bear powerful witness to the literary and ethical achievements of English medieval authors.

JOHN GOWER,
POET LAUREAT to KING HENRY 4th
OR 1400, Born 1326.
*Taken from his Monumental Effigy
in S.t Mary Overies Church Southwark.*
Published as the Act directs May 17.97. by J.SIMCO Print & Printseller
N.º II. Great Queen Street Lincolns Inn Fields London

Outside of his literary biography, little is known of Gower's life. Records indicate that a man named John Gower, likely the poet, came from the gentry in Kent. He may have been educated at the Inns of the Court of London, and he seems to have been quite successful, even affluent, if his land purchases are any indication. He is known to have taken up residence in the precincts of St. Mary's Overie in Southwark, where he would have had access to a library, in a church that now, after many demolitions and restorations, has become the cathedral where he is buried. Gower married Agnes Grouldold in 1398. He lived with her for 10 years and died in 1408; his will mentions no children but records copious and generous gifts to the church and to hospitals in and around Southwark.

Gower was a prolific writer who composed poems in the three languages—Latin, French (Anglo-Norman), and English—that were widely used in England in his time, although the literary use of French was on the decline and Gower was the last medieval English author to write major works in that language. His three most important works (on which his tombstone depicts him resting his head) are each composed in a different language. The earliest, *Mirour de l'omme* (*The Mirror of Man*), is a nearly 30,000-word poem in Anglo-Norman, written c. 1378; it survives unfinished in a single extant manuscript. Derived from penitential texts, the same tradition that produced Chaucer's *Parson's Tale*, the poem, as Gower said, treats "of the vices and virtues and the various classes of this world" and undertakes "to teach by what right path the sinner who has transgressed ought to return to a recognition of his creator."

Gower's second major work, in Latin, is the *Vox Clamantis* or "voice of one crying [in the wilderness]" (Isaiah 40.3). Books 2 through 7 (of 7) confront the evils of the three estates—clergy, knighthood, and peasantry—while the much more famous first book, added later, chronicles the Peasants' Revolt of 1381.

Gower's reputation as a poet, however, primarily rests on the third of his major works, which he wrote in Middle English. *Confessio amantis* (*Confession of a Lover*) is a study of personal governance that is threatened and disrupted by sin. For Gower, as for many medieval and renaissance authors, the individual is a kingdom that must be administered with wisdom and moderation. The *Confessio*, like Gower's other works, consistently engages the personal and political as interdependent; the salvation of the soul and the health of society are bound together and depend upon just moral governance of the will, a theme Gower's work shares with that of his contemporary William Langland, the author of *Piers Plowman*.

Though Gower has always been treated by critics and literary historians as subordinate to Chaucer, his literary associations with that poet have nonetheless helped to sustain critical interest in his work. Recent scholarship has particularly emphasized the early reception history of Gower's work, which was widely copied by well-known, accomplished scribes working to provide vernacular texts, both historical and imaginative, for educated readers. It seems likely, then, that Gower's contemporaries appreciated the depth and variety of his work as well as its exploration of how the soul seeks to know and govern itself and to find a home in society, kingdom, nature, and ultimately heaven.

⌘ ⌘ ⌘

from *Confessio Amantis*

Gower's best-known work, *Confessio Amantis*, is a 33,000 line dream vision, a frame narrative in the tradition of the *Romance of the Rose* and Boethius's *Consolation of Philosophy*. Fifteenth-century copies of the book were often lavishly produced by prominent scribes and artists. Though the poem is written primarily in Middle English, Latin verse is interspersed throughout—a testament to a cultural trilingualism that is the hallmark of post-conquest England. Excerpted below are some of the *Confessio*'s best-known and liveliest tales, two of which are also told by Chaucer. Despite these similarities in tales, Gower's achievement is highly individual, and his purposes within the frame-tale structure of his own poem differ from those of Chaucer.

In its combination of various literary genres, the *Confessio* recalls the thematic and generic scope of the *Canterbury Tales* and Boccaccio's *Decameron*. However, the structural constant running through Gower's work is the theme of sin and confession; each book and the stories therein treat of a sin and are offered for the benefit of a "lover," Amant, whom we finally learn is John Gower, entrapped by a dangerous, idolatrous passion and in need of the healing remedies for love. Here the narrative evokes the last installment of the Roman poet Ovid's "arts of love," the *Remedia Amoris*, designed to heal a destructive passion before it kills. As in the great medieval model for such works, Boethius's *Consolation*, a supernatural intervention occurs and the goddess Venus appears to counsel the lover; she summons her priest "Genius," who will hear the Lover's confession and instruct him so that he may recover himself and "rule the lost kingdom of the soul." Genius serves Nature, which is essentially good, and the Lover's crimes are against Nature, for his self-indulgent love and self pity serve no personal, social, or natural function; they cut him off from all the work he must do, all the work that healthy, productive love does in the world of Nature. Thus, the stories that ensue allow the Lover to see his misuse of creative energy, as well as that of others before him throughout history. In Gower's dynamic and sometimes quite oblique use of exempla, readers can see how medieval writers could draw from a collective European literary and cultural past, summoning classical and biblical learning for ethical instruction.

The *Confessio* fiercely confronts issues of family, gender, incest, and desire as the work explores not only the errors but also the perfectibility of human love. In its use of the sacramental processes of self-confrontation and awareness, the work is deeply Christian and pious; in its broad embrace of knowledge from the classical as well as the biblical past of a sort that would have been a mark of learning for men such as Gower and Chaucer—knowledge of human destinies and of natural and of social responsibilities, it is also deeply humanist.

Gower wrote in the same London dialect of Middle English that we find in Chaucer, and like Chaucer in *The Canterbury Tales*, Gower employs rhymed couplets. The *Confessio*, however, is written in octosyllabic lines that are much more in the mainstream of the Middle English poetic tradition than are Chaucer's decasyllabic lines. Gower himself characterized his style as plain, and many since have agreed—some ascribing to it a praiseworthy purity, others disparaging what they perceive as its lack of variety. The eight narrative books of the *Confessio* are framed by a prologue and epilogue, in which Gower surveys the world around him, decrying the sins and the shortcomings of each of the three estates (much as he had done in the *Vox Clamantis*) and prescribing remedies. As the frame makes clear, the narratives that form the heart of the *Confessio* are to be read as part of a broader social vision that is dark and purposeful.

[from Book 5]

Book Five concerns Avarice, and the tale of Jason and Medea in particular exemplifies Perjury. Before this tale, Genius the Confessor has shown Amant that lying to women to attain their love is a type of avarice, for it employs deceit and falsehood to gain a profit. Genius labors throughout the poem to display for Amant the nexus of desire where many vices merge. Here, as throughout the *Confessio*, we learn that to purify love, we must know the craft of every vice that perverts it. Amant boasts that he would never lie to his love, but he nonetheless lets Genius continue his regimen of stories. Jason, nephew of the Greek king, travels to the island of Colchis with a troop (including Hercules) after hearing of a "golden fleece." He greets the King Oetes and informs him that he intends to take the prize. The story that ensues explores both the irrational power of love that consumes Medea, who is a witch, and also the ambition for glory and fame that compels Jason to promise marriage to Medea in order to ensure her magical support of his bold quest. No one vice in the *Confessio* exists in isolation; they relate in compound ways to each other and of course to Amant's love obsession. Medea's acts—gathering magical herbs and venoms, restoring Jason's father's youth—are a dramatic *tour de force*. Like Ovid, his ultimate source, Gower emphasizes these aspects of the myth, and what little attention he pays to Medea's murder of her children does not seem to minimize her role as the victim of false male

promises. As we pick up the tale, a concerned King Oetes warns Jason of the danger of attempting to attain the heavily guarded fleece.

[The Tale of Jason and Medea]

"Jason, thou art a worthi kniht,
Bot it lith in no mannes myht
3345 To don that thou art come fore.
Ther hath be many a kniht forlore°   destroyed
Of that thei wolden it assaie."°   attempt
Bot Jason wolde him noght esmaie,°   not be disconcerted
And seide, "Of every worldes cure°   care
3350 Fortune stant in aventure,
Per aunter wel,° per aunter wo.   (Whether) for good luck
Bot hou as evere that it go,
It schal be with myn hond assaied."
The king tho hield him noght wel
        paied,°   then was not well pleased
3355 For he the Grekes sore dredde,°   feared
In aunter, if Jason ne spedde,°   should not succeed
He mihte therof bere° a blame.   bear
For tho was al the worldes fame
In Grece, as for to speke of armes.°   military strength
3360 Forthi he dredde him of his
        harmes,°   feared he might be harmed
And gan to preche him and to preie.°   plead with him
Bot Jason wolde noght obeie,
Bot seide he wolde his porpos holde
For ought that eny° man him tolde.   Regardless of what any
3365 The king, whan he thes wordes herde,
And sih hou that this kniht ansuerde,
Yit for he wolde make him glad,
After Medea gon he bad,°   He called for Medea
Which was his dowhter, and sche cam.
3370 And Jason, which good hiede nam,°   heed took
Whan he hire sih,° agein hire goth;   saw, toward her goes
And sche, which was him nothing
        loth,°   who was not loathsome to him
Welcomede him into that lond,
And softe tok him be the hond,
3375 And doun thei seten bothe same.°   together
Sche hadde herd spoke of his name
And of his grete worthinesse.
Forthi sche gan hir yhe impresse

Upon his face and his stature,
3380 And thoghte hou nevere creature
Was so wel farende° as was he.   *handsome*
And Jason riht in such degré
Ne mihte noght withholde his lok,
Bot so good hiede on hire he tok,
3385 That him ne thoghte under the hevene
Of beauté sawh he nevere hir evene,°   *match*
With al that fell to wommanhiede.°   *pertained to womanliness*
Thus ech of other token hiede,
Thogh ther no word was of record.
3390 Here hertes bothe of on acord
Ben set to love, bot as tho
Ther mihten be no wordes mo.
The king mad him gret joie and feste,
To alle his men he gaf an heste,°   *order*
3395 So as thei wolde his thonk deserve,
That thei scholde alle Jason serve,
Whil that he wolde there duelle.
And thus the dai, schortly to telle,
With manye merthes thei despente,
3400 Til nyht was come, and tho thei wente,
Echon of other tok his leve,
Whan thei no lengere myhten leve.°   *remain*
I not hou° Jason that nyht slep,   *do not know how*
Bot wel I wot that of the schep,
3405 For which he cam into that yle,
He thoghte bot a litel whyle;
Al was Medea that he thoghte,
So that in many a wise° he soghte   *manner*
His witt wakende er° it was day,   *waking before*
3410 Som time yee, som time nay,
Som time thus, som time so,
As he was stered° to and fro   *tossed*
Of° love, and ek of his conqueste   *By*
As he was holde of° his beheste.°   *beholden to / promise*
3415 And thus he ros up be the morwe
And tok himself Seint John to borwe,[1]
And seide he wolde ferst beginne

At love, and after for to winne
The flees of gold, for which he com,
3420 And thus to him good herte he nom.°   *took*
Medea riht the same wise,
Til dai cam that sche moste arise,
Lay and bethoughte° hire al the nyht,   *pondered*
Hou sche that noble worthi kniht
3425 Be eny weie mihte wedde.
And wel sche wiste,° if he ne spedde°   *knew / should not succeed*
Of thing which he hadde undertake,
Sche mihte hirself no porpos
    take;°   *she herself would not benefit*
For if he deide of his bataile,
3430 Sche moste thanne algate° faile   *altogether*
To geten him, whan he were ded.
Thus sche began to sette red°   *to use her wisdom*
And torne aboute hir wittes alle,
To loke hou that it mihte falle
3435 That sche with him hadde a leisir°   *leisure*
To speke and telle of hir desir.
And so it fell that same day
That Jason with that suete may°   *sweet maiden*
Togedre sete and hadden space°   *had leisure*
3440 To speke, and he besoughte hir grace.
And sche his tale goodli° herde,   *willingly*
And afterward sche him ansuerde
And seide, "Jason, as thou wilt,
Thou miht be sauf,° thou miht be spilt;°   *safe / destroyed*
3445 For wite° wel that nevere man,   *know*
Bot if he couthe that I can,°   *knows what I know*
Ne mihte that fortune achieve
For which thou comst: bot as I lieve,°   *believe*
If thou wolt holde covenant
3450 To love, of al the remenant°   *from everything else*
I schal thi lif and honour save,
That thou the flees of gold schalt have."
He seide, "Al at youre oghne wille,
Ma dame, I schal treuly fulfille
3455 Youre heste, whil mi lif mai laste."
Thus longe he preide, and ate laste
Sche granteth, and behihte° him this,   *promised*
That whan nyht comth and it time is,
Sche wolde him sende certeinly
3460 Such on° that scholde him prively°   *Such a person / secretly*
Alone into hire chambre bringe.

---

[1] *Seint John to borwe* I.e., committed himself to St. John's care. St. John was a visionary; the implication may be that Jason lends himself to (or puts himself in the hands of) what may come, which only St. John might foresee. Given Jason's assertion that "he wolde ferst beginne / At love" (lines 3417–18), it is possible, too, that Gower intends a parodic allusion to "God is love" (1 John 4.8) to define Jason's hypocrisy.

He thonketh hire of that tidinge,
For of that grace him is begonne
Him thenkth alle othre thinges wonne.[1]
3465 The dai made ende and lost his lyht,
And comen was the derke nyht,
Which al the daies yhe blente.°   *Day's eye (sun) concealed*
Jason tok leve and forth he wente,
And whan he cam out of the pres,°   *crowd*
3470 He tok to conseil Hercules,
And tolde him hou it was betid,°   *what was what*
And preide it scholde wel ben hid,°   *kept secret*
And that he wolde loke aboute,
Therwhiles that he schal ben oute.
3475 Thus as he stod and hiede nam,°   *took heed*
A mayden° fro Medea cam   *maidservant (lady-in-waiting)*
And to hir chambre Jason ledde,
Wher that he fond redi to bedde°   *for bed*
The faireste and the wiseste eke;
3480 And sche with simple chiere° and meke,   *facial expression*
Whan sche him sih, wax al aschamed.
Tho was here tale newe
          entamed;°   *Then their conversation was resumed*
For sikernesse° of mariage   *security*
Sche fette° forth a riche ymage,   *brought*
3485 Which was figure of Jupiter,
And Jason swor and seide ther,
That also wiss god scholde° him helpe,   *as sure as*
That if Medea dede him helpe,
That he his pourpos myhte winne,
3490 Thei scholde nevere parte atwinne,°   *separate*
Bot evere whil him lasteth lif,
He wolde hire holde for his wif.[2]
And with that word thei kisten bothe.
And for° thei scholden hem unclothe,°   *because / undress*
3495 Ther cam a maide, and in hir wise
Sche dede hem bothe full servise,
Til that thei were in bedde naked.
I wot° that nyht was wel bewaked;°   *know / kept sleepless*

---

[1]   *For of that ... wonne* I.e., because of this good fortune that had come upon him, he thinks that he will succeed in all matters at hand.

[2]   *Sche fette ... his wif* Medea's piety here is notable. Their mutual consent and solemn vows at the altar of God would be taken, according to medieval custom, as the basis of a true and binding marriage, which is important to subsequent details in their relationship, as Jason proves unfaithful and destroys all.

Thei hadden bothe what thei wolde.°   *desired*
3500 And thanne of leisir sche him tolde,
And gan fro point to point enforme
Of his bataile° and al the forme,°   *conflict / details*
Which as he scholde finde there,
Whan he to th'yle° come were.   *the island*
3505 Sche seide, at entre° of the pas°   *beginning / passage (adventure)*
Hou Mars, which god of armes was,
Hath set tuo oxen sterne° and stoute,   *two fierce oxen*
That caste fyr and flamme aboute
Bothe at the mouth and ate nase,°   *nose*
3510 So that thei setten al on blase°   *on fire*
What thing that passeth hem betwene,
And forthermore upon the grene°   *green*
Ther goth the flees of gold to kepe
A serpent, which mai nevere slepe.
3515 Thus who that evere scholde it winne,
The fyr to stoppe he mot° beginne,   *must*
Which that the fierce bestes caste,
And daunte he mot hem° ate laste,   *must control them*
So that he mai hem yoke and dryve;
3520 And therupon he mot as blyve°   *quickly*
The serpent with such strengthe assaile,
That he mai slen him be bataile;
Of which he mot the teth outdrawe,°   *extract*
As it belongeth to that lawe,
3525 And thanne he mot tho° oxen yoke,   *those*
Til thei have with a plowh tobroke
A furgh° of lond, in which arowe°   *furrow / in a row*
The teth of th'addre° he moste sowe,   *the serpent (adder)*
And therof schule arise knihtes
3530 Wel armed up at alle rihtes.°   *completely*
Of hem is noght to taken hiede,
For ech of hem in hastihiede
Schal other slen with dethes wounde:°   *lethal wound*
And thus whan thei ben leid to grounde,
3535 Than mot he to the goddes preie,°   *pray*
And go so forth and take his preie.°   *prey*
Bot if he faile in eny wise°   *any way*
Of that ye hiere me devise,
Ther mai be set non other weie,
3540 That he ne moste algates deie.
          "Nou have I told the peril al:
I wol you tellen forth withal,"
Quod Medea to Jason tho,°   *then*

"That ye schul knowen er ye go,
3545 Agein the venym and the fyr
What schal ben the recoverir.°   antidote
Bot, sire, for it is nyh day,
Ariseth up, so that I may
Delivere you what thing I have,
3550 That mai youre lif and honour save."
Thei weren bothe loth to rise,
Bot for thei weren bothe wise,
Up thei arisen ate laste.
Jason his clothes on him caste°   put on
3555 And made him redi riht anon,
And sche hir scherte dede upon
And caste on hire a mantel clos,
Withoute more and thanne aros.
Tho tok sche forth a riche tye°   splendid casket
3560 Mad al of gold and of perrie,°   jewels
Out of the which sche nam° a ring,   took
The ston was worth al other thing.
Sche seide, whil he wolde it were,°   wear
Ther myhte no peril him dere,°   harm
3565 In water mai it noght be dreynt,°   drowned
Wher as it comth the fyr is queynt,°   extinguished
It daunteth ek the cruel beste,
Ther may no qued° that man areste,°   evil / impede
Wher so he be on see or lond,
3570 Which hath that ring upon his hond:
And over that sche gan to sein,°   say
That if a man wol ben unsein,°   unseen
Withinne his hond hold clos the ston,
And he mai invisible gon.
3575 The ring to Jason sche betauhte,°   entrusted
And so forth after sche him tauhte
What sacrifise he scholde make;
And gan out of hire cofre take
Him thoughte an hevenely figure,
3580 Which al be charme° and be   by magical spell
    conjure°   incantation
Was wroght, and ek it was thurgh write
With names, which he scholde wite,
As sche him tauhte tho to rede;°   understand
And bad him, as he wolde spede,
3585 Withoute reste of eny while,
Whan he were londed in that yle,
He scholde make his sacrifise

And rede his carecte° in the wise   recite his charm
As sche him tauhte, on knes doun bent,
3590 Thre sithes toward orient;[1]
For so scholde he the goddes plese
And winne himselven mochel ese.
And whanne he hadde it thries rad,°   read, recited
To opne a buiste° sche him bad,   box
3595 Which sche ther tok him in present,°   gave him as a present
And was full of such oignement,
That ther was fyr ne venym non°   neither fire nor poison
That scholde fastnen him upon,
Whan that he were enoynt withal.
3600 Forthi sche tauhte him hou he schal
Enoignte his armes al aboute,
And for he scholde nothing doute,
Sche tok° him thanne a maner glu,°   gave / kind of glue
The which was of so gret vertu,
3605 That where a man it wolde caste,
It scholde binde anon so faste
That no man mihte it don aweie.
And that sche bad be alle weie°   completely
He scholde into the mouthes throwen
3610 Of tho tweie oxen that fyr blowen,
Therof to stoppen the malice;
The glu schal serve of that office.
And over that hir oignement,
Hir ring and hir enchantement
3615 Agein the serpent scholde him were,°   defend
Til he him sle° with swerd or spere.   slew
And thanne he may saufliche ynowh°   safely enough
His oxen yoke into the plowh
And the teth sowe in such a wise,
3620 Til he the knyhtes se° arise,   should see
And ech of other doun be leid
In such manere as I have seid.
Lo, thus Medea for Jason
Ordeigneth, and preith therupon
3625 That he nothing forgete scholde,
And ek sche preith him that he wolde,
Whan he hath alle his armes don,°   trials completed
To grounde knele and thonke anon

---

[1] *Thre sithes toward orient* Genius gives Medea a good Hebrew
sense of prayerful validation. (See Daniel 6.10: "Daniel opening the
windows in his upper chamber towards Jerusalem … knelt down
three times a day, and adored, and gave thanks before his God, as he
had been accustomed to do before.")

The goddes, and so forth be° ese   *with (by)*
The flees of gold he scholde sese.°   *seize*
3630

And whanne he hadde it sesed so,
That thanne he were sone ago
Withouten eny tariynge.
Whan this was seid, into wepinge
Sche fell, as sche that was thurgh
3635   nome°   *thoroughly overwhelmed*
With love, and so fer° overcome,   *far*
That al hir world on him sche sette.
Bot whan sche sih ther was no lette,°   *delaying (him)*
That he mot nedes parte hire fro,
3640
Sche tok him in hire armes tuo,
An hundred time and gan him kisse,
And seide, "O, al mi worldes blisse,
Mi trust, mi lust, mi lif, min hele,°   *health*
To be thin helpe in this querele°   *trial*
3645
I preie unto the goddes alle."
And with that word sche gan doun falle
On swoune, and he hire uppe nam,°   *took her up*
And forth with that the maiden cam,
And thei to bedde anon hir broghte,
3650
And thanne Jason hire besoghte,
And to hire seide in this manere:
"Mi worthi lusti ladi dere,
Conforteth you, for be my trouthe
It schal noght fallen in mi slouthe°   *not be because of my sloth*
3655
That I ne wol thurghout fulfille°   *If I do not completely fulfill*
Youre hestes° at youre oghne wille.   *instructions*
And yit I hope to you bringe
Withinne a while such tidinge,
The which schal make ous bothe game."°   *glad*
3660
Bot for he wolde kepe hir name,°   *reputation*
Whan that he wiste° it was nyh dai,°   *knew / nearly*
He seide, "A dieu, mi swete mai."°   *maiden*
And forth with him he nam his gere,°   *took his equipment*
Which as sche hadde take him there,
3665
And strauht unto his chambre he wente,
And goth to bedde and slep him hente,°   *seized him*
And lay, that no man him awok,
For Hercules hiede of him tok,
Til it was undren hih and more.°   *between 9 and 10 a.m.*
3670
And thanne he gan to sighe sore
And sodeinliche abreide of slep;°   *started from*
And thei that token of him kep,°   *attended to him*

His chamberleins, be sone there,
And maden redi al his gere,
3675   And he aros and to the king
He wente, and seide hou to that thing
For which he cam he wolde go.
The king therof was wonder wo,
And for he wolde him fain withdrawe,°   *gladly discourage him*
3680   He tolde him many a dredful sawe,°   *tale*
Bot Jason wolde it noght recorde,°   *pay heed*
And ate laste thei acorde.
Whan that he wolde noght abide,[1]
A bot was redy ate tyde,
3685   In which this worthi kniht of Grece
Ful armed up at every piece,
To his bataile which belongeth,
Tok ore° on honde and sore him longeth,°   *oar / sorely he longs*
Til he the water passed were.
3690   Whan he cam to that yle° there,   *island*
He set him on his knes doun strauht,
And his carecte,° as he was tawht,   *charm*
He radde,° and made his sacrifise,   *recited aloud*
And siththe enoignte him° in   *then anointed himself*
           that wise
3695   As Medea him hadde bede;°   *commanded*
And thanne aros up fro that stede,°   *place*
And with the glu the fyr he queynte,°   *quenched*
And anon° after he atteinte°   *quickly / overtook*
The grete serpent and him slowh.°   *slew*
3700   Bot erst he hadde sorwe ynowh,
For that serpent made him travaile
So harde and sore of his bataile,
That nou he stod and nou he fell.
For longe time it so befell,
3705   That with his swerd ne with his spere
He mihte noght that serpent dere.°   *harm*
He was so scherded al aboute,°   *covered with scales*
It hield all eggetol° withoute,   *withstood all swords ("edge-toll")*
He was so ruide° and hard of skin,   *rough*
3710   Ther mihte nothing go therin;
Venym and fyr togedre he caste,
That he Jason so sore ablaste,°   *so sorely blasted*
That if ne were° his oignement,   *if it were not for*
His ring and his enchantement,

---

1 *When that … abide* I.e., when it became clear that Jason insisted
on undertaking the adventure.

3715 Which Medea tok him tofore,°   gave him previously
     He hadde with that worm be
        lore;°   by that dragon would have been destroyed
     Bot of vertu which therof cam
     Jason the dragon overcam.
     And he anon the teth outdrouh,
3720 And sette his oxen in a plouh,°   plow
     With which he brak a piece of lond
     And sieu hem° with his oghne hond.   sowed them
     Tho mihte he gret merveile se:
     Of every toth in his degré°   "by process" or "in rank"
3725 Sprong up a kniht with spere and schield,
     Of whiche anon riht in the field
     Ech on slow other;° and with that   Each one slew the other
     Jason Medea noght forgat,
     On bothe his knes he gan doun falle,
3730 And gaf thonk to the goddes alle.
     The flees he tok and goth to bote,°   goes to the boat
     The sonne schyneth bryhte and hote,
     The flees of gold schon forth withal,
     The water glistreth overal.
3735 Medea wepte and sigheth ofte,
     And stod upon a tour° alofte: tower
     Al prively withinne hirselve,
     Ther herde it nouther ten ne tuelve,
     Sche preide, and seide, "O, god him spede,
3740 The kniht which hath mi maidenhiede!"°   virginity
     And ay sche loketh toward th'yle.
     Bot whan sche sih withinne a while
     The flees glistrende agein the sonne,
     Sche saide, "Ha lord, now al is wonne.
3745 Mi kniht the field hath overcome.
     Nou wolde god he were come,
     Ha lord, that he ne were alonde!"
     Bot I dar take this on honde,°   daresay
     If that sche hadde wynges tuo,
3750 Sche wolde have flowe unto him tho
     Strawht ther he was into the bot.
     The dai was clier, the sonne hot,
     The Gregeis weren in gret doute,°   fear
     The whyle that here lord was oute.
3755 Thei wisten noght what scholde
        tyde,°   knew not what would happen
     Bot waiten evere upon the tyde,
     To se what ende scholde falle.

     Ther stoden ek the nobles alle
     Forth with the comun° of the toun;   citizenry
3760 And as thei loken up and doun,
     Thei weren war withinne a throwe,°   after a time
     Wher cam the bot, which thei wel knowe,
     And sihe hou Jason broghte his preie.
     And tho thei gonnen alle seie,°   began to speak
3765 And criden alle with o stevene,°   one voice
     "Ha, wher was evere under the hevene
     So noble a knyht as Jason is?"
     And wel nyh alle seiden this,
     That Jason was a faie° kniht,   an enchanted
3770 For it was nevere of mannes miht
     The flees of gold so for to winne;
     And thus to talen° thei beginne.   gossip (converse)
     With that the king com forth anon,
     And sih° the flees, hou that it schon;°   saw / shone
3775 And whan Jason cam to the lond,
     The king himselve tok his hond
     And kist him, and gret joie him made.
     The Gregeis weren wonder glade,
     And of that thing riht merie hem thoghte,
3780 And forth with hem the flees thei broghte,
     And ech on other gan to leyhe;°   laugh
     Bot wel was him° that mihte   he was merry who
        neyhe,°   come near
     To se therof the propreté.
     And thus thei passen° the cite   pass through
3785 And gon unto the paleis straght.
     Medea, which° forgat him naght,   who
     Was redy there, and seide anon,
     "Welcome, O worthi kniht Jason."
     Sche wolde have kist him wonder fayn,°   eagerly
3790 Bot schame tornede hire agayn;°   turned her away
     It was noght the manere as tho,°   at that time
     Forthi sche dorste° noght do so.[1]   dared
     Sche tok hire leve, and Jason wente
     Into his chambre, and sche him sente
3795 Hire maide to sen hou he ferde;
     The which whan that sche sih° and herde,   saw
     Hou that he hadde faren oute

---

[1] *Forthi … do so* The narrator's praise of Medea's restraint and sense of propriety is ironic given her murder of her children after Jason's betrayal. Her relative victimhood is one of the complexities of the myth and of its countless medieval retellings.

And that it stod wel al aboute,
Sche tolde hire ladi what sche wiste,
3800 And sche for joie hire maide kiste.
The bathes weren thanne araied,°   *prepared*
With herbes tempred and assaied,°   *tested*
And Jason was unarmed sone
And dede as it befell to done.°   *did as one normally would do*
3805 Into his bath he wente anon
And wyssh him° clene as eny bon;° *washed himself / any bone*
He tok a sopp,° and oute he cam,   *had a snack (light repast)*
And on his beste aray he nam, °   *put on his best clothes*
And kempde° his hed, whan he was clad,   *combed*
3810 And goth him forth al merie and glad
Riht strawht into the kinges halle.
The king cam with his knihtes alle
And maden him glad welcominge;
And he hem tolde the tidinge
3815 Of this and that, hou it befell,
Whan that he wan the schepes fell.°   *won the sheep's fleece*
Medea, whan sche was asent,°   *sent for*
Com sone to that parlement,
And whan sche mihte Jason se,
3820 Was non so glad of alle as sche.
Ther was no joie for to seche:
Of him mad every man a speche;°   *everyone made a speech*
Som man seid on, som man seide other.
Bot thogh° he were goddes brother   *even if*
3825 And mihte make fyr° and thonder,   *lightning*
Ther mihte be no more wonder
Than was of him in that cité.
Ech on° tauhte other, "This is he,   *Each one*
Which hath in his pouer withinne
3830 That al the world ne mihte winne.° *What no one else on earth*
Lo, hier the beste of alle goode."°   *best of all good (people)*
Thus saiden thei that there stode,
And ek that walkede up and doun,
Bothe of the court and of the toun.
3835 The time of souper cam anon,
Thei wisshen,° and therto thei gon.   *clean up (wash)*
Medea was with Jason set.°   *seated beside*
Tho was ther many a deynté fet°   *gourmet food brought*
And set tofore hem° on the bord,°   *before them / table*
3840 Bot non so likinge° as the word   *pleasing to them*
Which was ther spoke among hem
     tuo,°   *between the two of them*

So as thei dorste° speke tho.°   *dared / then*
Bot thogh thei hadden litel space,
Yit thei acorden° in that place   *agreed*
3845 Hou Jason scholde come at nyht,
Whan every torche and every liht
Were oute, and thanne of other thinges
Thei spieke aloud for supposinges°   *(purpose of) deluding*
Of hem that stoden there aboute.
3850 For love is everemore in doute,°   *fear (and therefore cautious)*
If that it be wisly governed
Of hem that ben of love lerned.
Whan al was don, that dissh and cuppe
And cloth and bord and al was uppe,
3855 Thei waken whil hem lest to
     wake,°   *stayed awake as long as it pleased them*
And after that thei leve take
And gon to bedde for to reste.
And whan him thoghte for the beste,
That every man was faste aslepe,
3860 Jason, that wolde his time kepe,°   *bide his time*
Goth forth stalkende al prively°   *stealthily*
Unto the chambre, and redely°   *eagerly*
Ther was a maide, which him kepte.°   *who awaited him*
Medea wok and nothing slepte,
3865 Bot natheles sche was abedde,
And he with alle haste him spedde°   *came quickly*
And made him naked and al warm.
Anon he tok hire in his arm:
What nede is for to speke of ese?
3870 Hem list ech other for to plese,° *They wanted to please each other*
So that thei hadden joie ynow.°   *enough*
And tho thei setten° whanne and how   *planned*
That sche with him awey schal stele.
With wordes suche and othre fele°   *many others*
3875 Whan al was treted° to an ende,   *arranged*
Jason tok leve and gan forth wende°   *went*
Unto his oughne chambre in pes.°   *contentedly (quietly)*
Ther wiste° it non bot Hercules.   *knew*
He slepte and ros whan it was time,
3880 And whanne it fell towardes
     prime,°   *first part of the day (6-9 a.m.)*
He tok to him suche as he triste°   *trusted*
In secre,° that non other wiste,   *secrecy*
And told hem of his conseil there,
And seide that his wille were

3885	That thei to schipe hadde alle thinge	
	So priveliche in th'evenynge,	
	That no man mihte here dede° aspie	*their deed*
	Bot tho° that were of compaignie:	*those*
	For he woll go withoute leve,	
3890	And lengere° woll he noght beleve;°	*longer / remain*
	Bot he ne wolde at thilke throwe°	*wished not at that time*
	That king or queene scholde it knowe.	
	Thei° saide, "Al this schal wel	*They (i.e., Hercules and others)*
	be do."	
	And Jason truste wel therto.	
3895	Medea in the menewhile,	
	Which thoghte hir fader to beguile,	
	The tresor which hir fader hadde	
	With hire al priveli sche ladde,	
	And with Jason at time set	
3900	Awey sche stal° and fond no let,°	*stole / hindrance*
	And straght sche goth hire unto schipe	
	Of Grece with that felaschipe,	
	And thei anon drowe up the seil.	
	And al that nyht this was conseil,°	*secret*
3905	Bot erly, whan the sonne schon,	
	Men syhe° hou that thei were agon,	*saw*
	And come unto the king and tolde.	
	And he the sothe° knowe wolde,	*truth*
	And axeth° where his dowhter was.	*asked*
3910	Ther was no word bot "Out, allas!"	
	Sche was ago. The moder wepte,	
	The fader as a wod man° lepte,	*madman*
	And gan the time for to warie,°	*curse*
	And swor his oth he wol noght tarie,	
3915	That with caliphe and with galeie°	*(two kinds of boats)*
	The same cours, the same weie,	
	Which Jason tok, he wolde take,	
	If that he mihte him overtake.	
	To this thei seiden alle "Yee."	
3920	Anon thei weren ate see,°	*sea*
	And alle, as who seith, at a word	
	Thei gon withinne schipes bord,°	*aboard ship*
	The sail goth up, and forth thei strauhte.°	*set out*
	Bot non espleit° therof thei cauhte,	*no success*
3925	And so thei tornen hom agein,	
	For al that labour was in vein.	
	Jason to Grece with his preie°	*plunder*
	Goth thurgh the see the rihte° weie:	*most direct*

	Whan he ther com and men it tolde,	
3930	Thei maden joie yonge and olde.	
	Eson, whan that he wiste of this,	
	Hou that his sone comen is,	
	And hath achieved that he soughte	
	And hom with him Medea broughte,	
3935	In al the wyde world was non	
	So glad a man as he was on.	
	Togedre ben these lovers tho,	
	Til that thei hadden sones tuo,	
	Wherof thei weren bothe glade;	
3940	And olde Eson gret joie made	
	To sen th'encress of his lignage,	
	For he was of so gret an age,	
	That men awaiten every day	
	Whan that he scholde gon away.°	*(i.e., die)*
3945	Jason, which sih his fader old,	
	Upon Medea made him bold,°	*(i.e., addressed her confidently)*
	Of art magique, which sche couthe,°	*knew*
	And preith hire that his fader youthe°	*father's youth*
	Sche wolde make ageinward newe:	
3950	And sche, that was toward him trewe,	
	Behihte° him that sche wolde it do,	*Promised*
	Whan that sche time sawh therto.	
	Bot what sche dede in that matiere	
	It is a wonder thing to hiere.°	*hear*
3955	Bot yit for the novellerie	
	I thenke tellen a partie.	
	Thus it befell upon a nyht,	
	Whan ther was noght bot sterreliht,	
	Sche was vanyssht riht as hir liste,	
3960	That no wyht° bot hirself it wiste,°	*person / knew*
	And that was ate mydnyht tyde.°	*time*
	The world was stille on every side;	
	With open hed° and fot° al bare,	*bare head / feet*
	Hir her tosprad° sche gan to fare,	*hair spread out*
3965	Upon hir clothes gert sche was,	
	Al specheles and on° the gras	*And all speechless on*
	Sche glod forth as an addre doth.	
	Non otherwise sche ne goth,	
	Til sche cam to the freisshe flod,°	*ocean*
3970	And there a while sche withstod.°	*stood in*
	Thries sche torned hire aboute,	
	And thries ek sche gan doun loute°	*bow*
	And in the flod° sche wette hir her,°	*water / wet her hair*

And thries on the water ther
3975 Sche gaspeth with a drecchinge onde,°   *drowning wave*
And tho sche tok hir speche on honde.°   *utilized her speech*
Ferst sche began to clepe and calle°   *call and cry out*
Upward unto the sterres° alle,   *stars*
To wynd, to air, to see, to lond
3980 Sche preide, and ek hield up hir hond,
To Echates and gan to crie,°   *And began to call to Hecate*
Which is goddesse of sorcerie.[1]
Sche seide, "Helpeth at this nede,
And as ye maden me to spede,
3985 Whan Jason cam the flees to seche,°   *seek*
So help me nou, I you beseche."
With that sche loketh and was war,
Doun fro the sky ther cam a char,°   *chariot*
The which Dragouns aboute drowe:
3990 And tho sche gan hir hed doun bowe,
And up sche styh,° and faire and wel   *ascended*
Sche drof forth bothe char and whel
Above in th'air among the skyes.
The lond of Crete and tho parties
3995 Sche soughte, and faste gan hire hye,°   *hasten*
And there upon the hulles hyhe°   *high hills*
Of Othrin and Olimpe also,
And ek of othre hulles mo,
Sche fond and gadreth herbes suote,°   *sweet*
4000 Sche pulleth up som be the rote,
And manye with a knyf sche scherth,°   *cuts off*
And alle into hir char sche berth.
Thus whan sche hath the hulles sought,
The flodes° ther forgat sche nought,   *rivers*
4005 Eridian and Amphrisos,
Peneie and ek Spercheidos,
To hem sche wente and ther sche nom°   *took*
Bothe of the water and the fom,°   *foam*
The sond and ek the smale stones,
4010 Whiche as sche ches out for the nones,°   *for the occasion*
And of the Rede See a part,
That was behovelich to hire art,
Sche tok, and after that aboute
Sche soughte sondri sedes° oute   *seeds*

4015 In feldes and in many greves,°   *groves*
And ek a part sche tok of leves:
Bot thing which mihte hire most availe
Sche fond in Crete and in Thessaile.
In daies and in nyhtes nyne,
4020 With gret travaile and with gret pyne,°   *pain*
Sche was pourveid of every
    piece,°   *fully supplied with every necessity*
And torneth homward into Grece.
Before the gates of Eson
Hir char sche let awai to gon,
4025 And tok out ferst that was therinne;
For tho sche thoghte to beginne
Such thing as semeth impossible,
And made hirselven invisible,
As sche that was with air enclosed
4030 And mihte of no man be desclosed.°   *revealed*
Sche tok up turves° of the lond   *clods*
Withoute helpe of mannes hond,
Al heled° with the grene gras,   *covered*
Of which an alter mad° ther was   *altar made*
4035 Unto Echates the goddesse
Of art magique and the maistresse,
And eft another to Juvente,°   *the goddess of youth*
As sche which dede° hir hole° entente. *Accomplished / whole*
Tho tok sche fieldwode and verveyne,°   *medicinal herbs*
4040 Of herbes be noght betre tueyne,°   *two*
Of which anon withoute let°   *hindrance*
These alters ben aboute set.
Tuo sondri puttes° faste by   *Two different pits*
Sche made, and with that hastely
4045 A wether° which was blak sche slouh,°   *sheep / slew*
And out therof the blod sche drouh°   *drew*
And dede into the pettes tuo;
Warm melk° sche putte also therto   *milk*
With hony meynd:° and in such wise   *mixed*
4050 Sche gan to make hir sacrifice,
And cride and preide forth withal
To Pluto the god infernal,
And to the queene Proserpine.
And so sche soghte out al the line°   *lineage*
4055 Of hem that longen to that
    craft,°   *those who are skilled in occult arts*
Behinde was no name laft,
And preide hem alle, as sche wel couthe,°   *knew*

---

1 *Echates … of sorcerie* Hecate, the goddess of night, is the deity to
whom witches commonly pray; see *Macbeth* 3.5, where Hecate tells
the three sisters of Macbeth's approach, and 4.1, where she appears
with prophecies for Macbeth.

To grante Eson his ferste youthe.
This olde Eson broght forth was tho.
4060 Awei sche bad alle othre go°   *told all others to leave*
Upon peril that mihte falle;°   *(i.e., because of potential danger)*
And with that word thei wenten alle,
And leften there hem tuo alone.
And tho sche gan to gaspe and gone,°   *gasp and gape*
4065 And made signes many on,°   *many a one*
And seide hir wordes therupon;
So that with spellinge° of hir charmes°   *chanting / incantations*
Sche tok Eson in bothe hire armes,
And made him for to slepe faste,
4070 And him upon hire herbes caste.
The blake wether tho sche tok,
And hiewh the fleissh,° as doth a cok;°   *minced / as a cook does*
On either alter part sche leide,
And with the charmes that sche seide
4075 A fyr doun fro the sky alyhte
And made it for to brenne lyhte.°   *burn brightly*
Bot whan Medea sawh it brenne,°   *burn*
Anon sche gan to sterte and renne°   *run*
The fyri aulters al aboute:
4080 Ther was no beste° which goth oute   *beast*
More wylde than sche semeth ther.
Aboute hir schuldres hyng hir her°   *hung her hair*
As thogh sche were oute of hir mynde
And torned in another kynde.°   *creature*
4085 Tho lay ther certein wode cleft,°   *chopped wood*
Of which the pieces nou and eft°   *now and again (repeatedly)*
Sche made hem in the pettes wete,°   *pits wet*
And put hem in the fyri hete,
And tok the brond° with al the blase,°   *firebrand / flame*
4090 And thries sche began to rase°   *race*
Aboute Eson, ther as he slepte;
And eft with water, which sche kepte,
Sche made a cercle aboute him thries,
And eft with fyr of sulphre twyes.°   *twice*
4095 Ful many another thing sche dede,
Which is noght writen in this stede.°   *place*
Bot tho sche ran so up and doun,
Sche made many a wonder soun,°   *sound*
Somtime lich unto the cock,
4100 Somtime unto the laverock,°   *lark*
Somtime kacleth as an hen,
Somtime spekth as don the men.

And riht so as hir jargoun
strangeth,°   *just as her speech becomes more strange*
In sondri wise hir forme changeth,
4105 Sche semeth faie° and no womman;   *fairy-like*
For with the craftes that sche can°   *knows*
Sche was, as who seith, a goddesse;
And what hir liste,° more or lesse,   *desired*
Sche dede, in bokes as we finde,
4110 That passeth over manneskinde.°   *What exceeds human nature*
Bot who that wole of wondres hiere,
What thing sche wroghte in this matiere,
To make an ende of that sche gan,
Such merveile herde nevere man.
4115 Apointed° in the newe mone,°   *Prescribed by / moon*
Whan it was time for to done,
Sche sette a caldron on the fyr,
In which was al the hole atir,°   *were all the necessary supplies*
Wheron the medicine stod,
4120 Of jus,° of water, and of blod,   *herbal extract*
And let it buile° in such a plit,   *boil*
Til that sche sawh the spume whyt;°   *white froth (spume)*
And tho sche caste in rynde and rote,
And sed° and flour that was for bote,°   *seed / remedy*
4125 With many an herbe and many a ston,
Wherof sche hath ther many on.
And ek Cimpheius the serpent
To hire hath alle his scales lent,
Chelidre° hire gaf his addres skin,   *A poisonous snake*
4130 And sche to builen caste hem in;
A part ek of the horned oule,°   *owl*
The which men hiere on nyhtes houle;°   *howl*
And of a raven, which was told
Of nyne hundred wynter old,
4135 Sche tok the hed with al the bile;
And as the medicine it wile,°   *medicinal formula dictates*
Sche tok therafter the bouele°   *bowel*
Of the seewolf,° and for the hele°   *shark / healing*
Of Eson, with a thousand mo
4140 Of thinges that sche hadde tho,
In that Caldroun togedre as blyve°   *forthwith*
Sche putte, and tok thanne of olyve
A drie branche hem with to stere,°   *stir*
The which anon gan floure° and bere   *flower*
4145 And waxe al freissh and grene agein.
Whan sche this vertu hadde sein,

Sche let the leste drope of alle
Upon the bare flor doun falle;
Anon ther sprong up flour and gras,
Where as the drope falle was,
4150 And wox anon° al medwe° grene,   *grew swiftly / meadow*
So that it mihte wel be sene.
Medea thanne knew and wiste°   *understood*
Hir medicine is for to triste,°   *trustworthy*
4155 And goth to Eson ther he lay,
And tok a swerd was of assay,°   *of proven quality*
With which a wounde upon his side
Sche made, that therout mai slyde
The blod withinne, which was old
4160 And sek° and trouble° and fieble°   *sick / murky / feeble*
    and cold.
And tho sche tok unto his us°   *made use of*
Of herbes al the beste jus,
And poured it into his wounde;
That made his veynes fulle and sounde.
4165 And tho sche made his wounde clos,
And tok his hand, and up he ros,
And tho sche gaf him drinke a drauhte,
Of which his youthe agein he cauhte,°   *caught*
His hed, his herte, and his visage
4170 Lich unto twenty wynter age.
Hise hore heres were away,°   *gray hair disappeared*
And lich unto the freisshe Maii,
Whan passed ben the colde schoures,
Riht so recovereth he his floures.°   *youthfulness*
4175 Lo, what mihte eny man devise,
A womman schewe in eny wise
Mor hertly love in every stede,
Than Medea to Jason dede?
Ferst sche made him the flees to winne,
4180 And after that fro kiththe and kinne
With gret tresor with him sche stal,
And to his fader forth withal
His elde hath torned into youthe,
Which thing non other womman couthe.°   *knew (how to do)*
4185 Bot hou it was to hire aquit,
The remembrance duelleth yit.
King Peleus his em° was ded,   *uncle*
Jason bar corone on his hed,
Medea hath fulfild his wille.
4190 Bot whanne he scholde of riht fulfille
The trouthe,° which to hire afore°   *pledge / before*

He hadde in th'yle of Colchos swore,°   *sworn*
Tho was Medea most deceived.
For he another hath received,°   *took up with another woman*
4195 Which dowhter was to King Creon.
Creusa sche hihte,° and thus Jason,   *was named*
As he that was to love untrewe,
Medea lefte and tok a newe.
Bot that was after sone aboght:°   *soon paid for*
4200 Medea with hire art hath wroght
Of cloth of gold a mantel riche,
Which semeth worth a kinges riche,°   *worthy of a kingdom*
And that was unto Creusa sent
In name of gifte and of present,
4205 For sosterhode hem was betuene;
And whan that yonge freisshe queene
That mantel lappeth hire aboute,
Anon therof the fyr sprong oute
And brente hir bothe fleissh and bon.
4210 Tho cam Medea to Jason
With bothe his sones on hire hond,
And seide, "O thou of every lond
The moste untrewe creature,
Lo, this schal be thi forfeture."
4215 With that sche bothe his sones slouh
Before his yhe, and he outdrouh
His swerd and wold have slayn hir tho,
Bot farewel, sche was ago
Unto Pallas the court° above,[1]   *Pallas's court*
4220 Wher as sche pleigneth° upon love,   *bewails*
As sche that was with that goddesse,
And he was left in gret destresse.
Thus miht thou se what sorwe it doth
To swere an oth which is noght soth,°   *true*
4225 In loves cause namely.
Mi sone, be wel war° forthi,   *well-cautioned*
And kep that° thou be noght forswore:°   *take care / perjured*
For this, which I have told
    tofore,°   *(i.e., concerning this story I just told)*
Ovide[2] telleth everydel.°   *every part*
—1390

---

1   *Pallas ... above* The court of Pallas Athena is the suitable residence for Medea to retire. Pallas is the goddess of wisdom, invention, and ingenuity, reputed for her prowess in warfare—all qualities characteristic of Medea.

2   *Ovide* Ovid. Gower proudly reveals one of his sources, included below in "Gower in Context."

IN CONTEXT

from Geoffrey Chaucer, *The Legend of Good Women* (c. 1386)

Distinctly different from Ovid's treatment of the subject, Chaucer's version of the Medea story takes its part in his *Legends of Good Women*, a dynamic and sometimes ironic send-up of classical heroes and heroines, written by Chaucer supposedly to compensate for his crimes against woman in *The Romaunt of the Rose* and *Troilus and Criseyde*, which offended Richard's Queen Anne. Chaucer focuses, therefore, not on Medea's evil but, more akin to Gower, on the crimes of Jason, who distinguishes himself in the annals of male evil by falsifying not one but two women, Medea and Hypsipyle. Chaucer accordingly suppresses Medea's crimes and depicts her as a victim. The different "Medeas" that emerge in Middle English literature testify to the attraction of Ovid's character and witness the complexities of gender, violence, and sin with which the medieval Christian poet wrestles. As humanists and mythographers, the poets were drawn to the classical tale of adventure, magic and intrigue; as male clerics, they knew of the evil associated with woman in Scripture and in myth; and as Christians, they knew the price of damnable sin. Gower's and Chaucer's treatments of the seductive Medea betray these conflicting inheritances and imperatives. Medea is the *femme fatale* they love to hate and yet struggle somehow to redeem.

THE LEGEND OF HYPSIPYLE AND MEDEA

Thow rote° of false lovers, Duc Jasoun,   *root*
    Thow sly devourere and confusioun
1370 Of gentil wemen, tender creatures,
    Thou madest thy recleymyng and thy lures[1]
    To ladyes of thy statly aparaunce,
    And of thy wordes, farced° with plesaunce,   *filled*
    And of thy feyned trouthe and thy manere,
1375 With thyn obeÿsaunce and humble cheere,
    And with thy contrefeted peyne and wo.
    There othere falsen oon, thow falsest two!
    O, often swore thow that thow woldest dye
    For love, whan thow ne feltest maladye
1380 Save foul delyt, which that thow callest love!
    Yif that I live, thy name shal be shove
    In English that thy sekte shal be knowe!
    Have at thee, Jason! now thyn horn is blowe!
    But certes, it is bothe routhe and wo
1385 That love with false lovers werketh so;
    For they shal have wel betere love and chere
    Than he that hath abought his love ful dere,
    Or hadde in armes many a blody box.°   *blow, buffet*
    For evere as tendre a capoun et the fox,

---

[1] *lures* A lure that "calls back" a hawk in hunting.

1390 Thow he be fals and hath the foul betrayed,
      As shal the good-man that therefore hath payed.
      Al have he to the capoun skille and ryght,
      The false fox wol have his part at nyght.[1]
      On Jason this ensaumple is wel ysene
1395 By Isiphile and Medea the queene.[2]

THE LEGEND OF MEDEA

      ...

1580 To Colcos comen is this duc Jasoun,
      That is of love devourer and dragoun.
      As mater apetiteth forme alwey,
      And from forme into forme it passen may,[3]
      Or as a welle that were botomles,
1585 Ryght so can false Jason have no pes.
      For, to desyren, thourgh his apetit,
      To don with gentil women his delyt,
      This is his lust and his felicite.
          Jason is romed forth to the cyte,
1590 That whilom cleped was Jaconitos,
      That was the mayster-toun of al Colcos,
      And hath ytold the cause of his comyng
      Unto Oetes,[4] of that contre kyng,
      Preyinge hym that he moste don his assay
1595 To gete the fles of gold, if that he may;
      Of which the kyng assenteth to his bone,
      And doth hym honour, as it was to done,
      So fer forth that his doughter and his eyr,
      Medea, which that was so wis and fayr
1600 That fayrer say there nevere man with ye,
      He made hire don to Jason companye
      At mete, and sitte by hym in the halle.
          Now was Jason a semely man withalle,°   *very handsome man*
      And lyk a lord, and hadde a gret renoun,
1605 And of his lok as real as a leoun,
      And goodly of his speche, and familer,
      And coude of love al the art and craft pleyner
      Withoute bok, with everych observaunce.
      And, as Fortune hire oughte° a foul myschaunce,   *owed to her*

---

[1] *Thow he … at nyght*   I.e., Jason is a fox who will find a way to attain his prey, despite the efforts of the "good man" who protects his chickens.

[2] *By Isiphile … queene*   Hypsipyle was queen of Lemnos; she welcomed the Argonauts, married Jason, and bore him two sons.

[3] *from forme … passen may*   The complex idea from medieval physics suggests that, just as matter desires to "take form," Jason is inclined by his nature to pursue, consume, and discard women.

[4] *Oetes*   The King of Colchis.

1610   She wex enamoured upon this man.
        "Jason," quod she, "for ought I se or can,
        As of this thyng the whiche ye ben aboute,
        Ye han youreself yput in moche doute.
        For whoso wol this aventure acheve,
1615   He may nat wel asterten, as I leve,
        Withouten deth, but I his helpe be.
        But natheles, it is my wylle," quod she,
        "To fortheren yow, so that ye shal nat die,
        But turnen sound hom to youre Tessalye."
1620   "My ryghte lady," quod this Jason tho,
        "That ye han of my deth or of my wo
        Any reward, and don me this honour,
        I wot wel that my myghte ne my labour
        May nat disserve it in my lyves day.
1625   God thanke yow, there I ne can ne may!
        Youre man I am, and lowely yow beseche
        To ben my helpe, withoute more speche;
        But, certes, for my deth shal I nat spare."[1]
            Tho gan this Medea to hym declare
1630   The peril of this cas, from poynt to poynt,
        And of his batayle, and in what disjoynt°   *peril*
        He mote stonde, of which no creature,
        Save only she, ne myghte his lyf assure.
        And, shortly to the poynt ryght for to go,
1635   They been acorded ful bytwixe hem two
        That Jason shal hire wedde, as trewe knyght;
        And terme set to come sone at nyght
        Unto hire chamber and make there his oth
        Upon the goddes, that he for lef or loth°   *i.e., for no reason*
1640   Ne sholde nevere hire false, nyght ne day,
        To ben hire husbonde whil he lyve may,
        As she that from his deth hym saved here.
        And hereupon at nyght they mette in-feere,
        And doth his oth, and goth with hire to bedde;
1645   And on the morwe upward he hym spedde,
        For she hath taught hym how he shal nat fayle
        The fles to wynne, and stynten his batayle;
        And saved hym his lyf and his honour;
        And gat hym a name right as a conquerour,
1650   Ryght through the sleyghte of hire enchauntement.
            Now hath Jason the fles, and hom is went
        With Medea, and tresor ful gret won;
        But unwist of° hire fader is she gon   *unknown to*
        To Tessaly, with Duk Jason hire lef,
1655   That afterward hath brought hire to myschef.

---

[1] *But, certes … spare* I.e., only death will prevent me from keeping my commitment to you.

For as a traytour he is from hire go,
And with hire lafte his yonge children two,
And falsly hath betraysed hire, allas!
As evere in love a chef traytour he was;
1660   And wedded yit the thridde wif anon,
That was the doughter of the kyng Creon.
    This is the mede of lovynge and guerdoun
That Medea receyved of Jasoun
Ryght for hire trouthe and for hire kyndenesse,
1665   That lovede hym beter than hireself, I gesse,
And lafte hire fader and hire heritage.
And of Jason this is the vasselage,°   *knighthood*
That, in his dayes, nas ther non yfounde
So fals a lovere goinge on the grounde.
1670   And therefore in hire letter[1] thus she seyde
Fyrst, whan she of his falsnesse hym upbreyde:
"Whi lykede me thy yelwe her to se
More than the boundes of myn honeste?
Why lykede me thy youthe and thy fayrnesse,
1675   And of thy tonge, the infynyt graciousnesse?
O, haddes thow in thy conquest ded ybe,
Ful mikel untrouthe hadde ther deyd with the!"
Wel can Ovyde hire letter in vers endyte,
Which were as now to long for me to wryte.

---

[1] *letter* The letter refers to Medea's missive to Jason found in Ovid's *Heroides*.

WILLIAM LANGLAND
c. 1325 – 1390

Geoffrey Chaucer is perhaps the most accessible medieval author for modern readers. We can identify the places he worked, the woman he married, and the men he served. For his part, he acknowledges his debts to the great Italian poets, and he shamelessly cites his own works, as in his famous "Retraction," in which he outlines his entire oeuvre for future readers. Chaucer's literary successors, such as the poet John Lydgate (c. 1370–1449), or England's first printer, William Caxton (c. 1415–92), ensured his posterity: Lydgate through flattering imitation, and Caxton through the wide circulation of *The Canterbury Tales*.

The 7,000-line religious allegory, *Piers Plowman*, written and revised between c. 1370 and 1386, gives us exactly the opposite view of what it meant to write and to be read in medieval England. Whereas Chaucer's life appears legible to the modern eye, the author of *Piers Plowman*, whom we call, for convenience, William Langland (c. 1325–90), left no records. With the exception of a marginal note in a copy of an Irish manuscript, which attributes the poem to William Langland, son of Stacy de Rokayle of Oxfordshire, we have little information about the poet other than what we can glean from the poem itself. The dialect of *Piers Plowman* places the poet somewhere in the West Midlands —about 120 miles north-west of London—and the Malvern Hills in Worcestershire provide the spectacular setting for the Prologue. Manuscript evidence suggests, however, that the poem may have circulated first among a readership of lawyers, notaries, and bureaucrats in London and Westminster, places with which the poet was, at the very least, extremely familiar.

The author's failure to stamp the poem with his own name was no doubt partly due to its form: long alliterative poems like *Piers Plowman* tended to circulate anonymously. It may also have had something to do with its content. As in the case of other "self-help" works from this period, such as the popular penitential manual the *Prick of Conscience* (c. 1360), the poem's huge seriousness of purpose—how, it asks, can all of us be saved?—along with its concern about addressing a diverse audience may have eclipsed any sense of the poet's personal connections. On the other hand, *Piers Plowman* enjoyed a political currency unprecedented for a poem written in English. By 1381, it had become a rallying cry for the low-born rebels of the Peasants' Revolt, and by the turn of the fifteenth century, it had inspired a vernacular literature committed to critiquing the excesses of the institutional church, the suffering of the poor, and the corruption of justice. As a result, medieval readers turned the poem's ideological leanings into a form of authorship; more than one early reader assigned the poem to Piers the Plowman, the near-allegorical character—sometime laborer, reeve, pope, and Christ—who appears intermittently in the poem to lead the people to Truth. The temporal reach of *Piers Plowman* was much more limited than that of the *Canterbury Tales*—both its dialect and its meter sounded old-fashioned to early modern readers, for whom London English and rhymed verse had already become literary standards. William Caxton chose not to publish it. Yet it struck a chord with sixteenth-century Protestant Reformers, who regarded it as a vehicle for Church reform, and who sometimes attributed it to their favorite fourteenth-century heresiarch, John Wycliffe (d. 1384).

Modern readers take for granted, rightly or wrongly, the existence of a stable text called the *Canterbury Tales*, and despite the fact that we have no manuscripts produced during the author's lifetime, it appears as if Chaucer exercised some control over the dissemination of his work. By contrast, the rangier *Piers Plowman* contests assumptions about textual stability and authorial control, surviving in at least three substantially modified versions, which modern editors label A, B, and C. Although most scholars detect the hand of the poet in its various versions, the order and significance of those versions is hotly debated. Some scholars believe, for example, that the A-text (Prologue and 11 passus), B-text (Prologue and 20 passus), and C-text (Prologue and 22 passus) represent Langland's ongoing expansion of his poem, as well as his increasingly deeper engagement with some of the issues raised. Other scholars, observing that manuscripts of the A-text postdate those of the C-text, speculate that A may have really been a later recension of both B and C commissioned for a particular audience. While many scholars believe that the C-text, generally less contentious and more streamlined than B, reflects the poet's conservative turn in the 1380s, recently, one scholar has shown that medieval scribes used manuscripts of C to correct what has been traditionally called the B-text, suggesting that the version of B that has come down to us may actually postdate C. Medieval scribes of *Piers Plowman* tolerated the existence of different versions admirably well, several of them fashioning composite versions of the text, adding a C-ending to an A-opening, and so forth.

Although the textual variability of *Piers Plowman* often confounds modern readers, it is nevertheless a poem keenly aware of its own project, constantly questioning what it takes to speak and write about the good life. This poetic self-awareness is exemplified by Langland's alter ego, his dreamer-narrator, whose status, as the opening lines of the Prologue show, is never quite certain, and whose moral authority is often in doubt. To be sure, he is learned, well-versed in biblical interpretation, and trained to be a cleric, as most educated medieval men were. He is peculiarly removed, however, from academic life and possesses neither the bureaucratic office nor ecclesiastical benefice that would keep him otherwise grounded. Consequently, he wanders like a minstrel or actor, living off the kindness of the gentry, who give him room and board in return for prayers, devout conversation, and other services. The poet often pokes fun at his dreamer, comparing him to "lewd hermits" and other folk who consider themselves special and unique ("singular"), but who, without the benefit of institutional discipline, such as a monastic rule, are tempted by the world in the worst possible ways. Yet, in the C-text, passus 9, and elsewhere, the poet imagines a brand-new category of person, a "minstrel of God" or a "holy beggar," a person whose itinerancy is a reflection, not of avid self-interest but of a sincere attempt to find a life pleasing to God.

Although Langland's dreaming persona is a fictionalized ideal of a life, it may end up telling us a good deal about the poet and his work. It seems likely, for one thing, that a poet who wrote at least three versions of an extremely long alliterative poem had the luxury of time to do so: a project underwritten, perhaps, by the income of his own estates or by the protective interests of a patron. Such a patron might resemble John de Dalton, who supported the solitary mystic Richard Rolle (c. 1300–49), or Sir Thomas Berkeley, the great lord who funded the ambitious translator John Trevisa (fl. 1385–98). Like his dreamer, in other words, Langland may have used his education to serve a patron in various capacities, including the writing of vernacular religious poetry. Further, like his dreamer, Langland is well-versed in Latin—for all intents and purposes, *Piers Plowman* is a bilingual poem. Although it is true that you could cover up the Latin (usually distinguished in manuscripts by red ink or a grander font) and still understand much of the poem, the poem's Latin quotations are indispensable to its project, constituting a search engine for its clerkly readers; an imaginative structure for individual episodes, many of which arise from commentaries on biblical verses, such as "Man can not live by bread alone" (Matthew 4.4) or "The fool says in his heart, 'there is no God'" (Psalms 14.1); and an entirely new form of inter-lingual poetry, at once scholarly and affecting.

Like its dreamer, *Piers Plowman* is an experimental work made up of a dizzying array of medieval genres. Its texture is unrhymed alliterative verse, a meter composed of two half-lines bound by alliteration (aa/ax), with two stressed syllables in each half line. But *Piers Plowman* conspicuously lacks the ornate vocabulary of other alliterative romances, such as *Sir Gawain and the Green Knight* (c. late fourteenth century), which have hundreds of synonyms for armor, horse, and sword, preferring instead what early readers praised as Langland's "plain" style, one that uses the vocabulary of everyday life. *Piers Plowman* also borrows heavily from that most conventional of medieval genres, the allegorical dream-vision, in which a sleeper has a vision, converses with personifications, and eventually reaches his goal, usually sex with a noble lady, heavenly salvation, or a privileged vision of the afterlife. Both allegorical dream-visions and alliterative romances are, however, linear narratives, expansive enough to include theological debates, treatises on sin, and social commentary, but, at the same time, inexorably committed to progress. *Piers Plowman*, despite the fact that it is divided into twenty passus (Latin for "steps"), does not go anywhere at all except progressively deeper into itself.

Piers Plowman is also an experimental work because it asks big questions by taking extreme measures with the literary and cultural forms available to its author. In the Prologue, for example, the poet wonders whether a sinner can be a visionary, and if so, what view of the world his vision would reveal. Would its institutions and hierarchies, its most cherished traditions, require entirely new modes of description? In passus 5, the poet considers what would happen if the Seven Deadly Sins confessed: would the result be merely satirical, humorous treatises on medieval vice, or would the sins' self-negation be tantamount to the obliteration of the entire human disposition to sin? In passus 7, Langland imagines a new genre of social critique, a legal pardon sent from on high, according to which everyone of every social station would have the chance to be saved. In passus 18, the account of Christ's death, the poet asks, what would it mean to write a sacred narrative so fragmentary and rich that belief itself, with its weird logic and mysterious rites, could become a thing of art?

Piers Plowman takes some effort to understand, not only because it is written in a 700-year-old version of the English language, but also because it repeatedly attempts to capture what is most meaningful about its own densely wrought historical moment. Like James Joyce's *Ulysses* (1922), indeed, like the best experimental art, *Piers Plowman* is provocative and searching. It is also, very often, beautiful, and a worthy example of the best of medieval English verse.

⌘ ⌘ ⌘

from *Piers Plowman*[1]

B. PROLOGUE

In summertime, when the sun was fine,
I clothed myself in garments as if I were a sheep.
Outfitted like a hermit whose works are unholy,
I traveled widely in the world to hear about wonders.[2]
5   And on a May morning on the Malvern Hills
I encountered a marvel; it seemed supernatural!
I was all tired out and decided to rest
Against a broad bank by the side of a stream;
And as I lay, and leaned, and gazed on the water
10   I nodded off to sleep, it flowed so merrily.

Then I began to dream a marvelous dream:
I was in a wilderness, I knew not where.
As I looked toward the east in the direction of the sun,
I saw on a hill a tower finely built,
15   A deep valley beneath it, a dungeon inside,
With pits deep, and dark, and dreadful to see.
Between them I discovered a fair field of folk
Of all kinds of people, the poor and the rich,
Working and wandering as the world demands.

20   Some took up the plow, very seldom played,
Worked very hard at planting and sowing,
And won what those wasters destroy in their gluttony.
Some took up a life of pride, dressed accordingly,
Came all decked out in superficial show.
25   Some took up a life of prayers and penance,
Lived austerely, entirely for the love of our Lord,
In the hope to have heavenly bliss:
Such as anchorites and hermits[3] who remain in their cells,

Have no desire to traipse about the country
30   To find extravagant food with which to please their
        bodies.

And some took up trade; they did well for themselves
It seems to me that such men thrive.
And some took up entertainment, the kind that
        minstrels know,
And get gold for their performance—blameless, I guess.
35   But tricksters and jokesters, Judas's[4] children,
Make up stories and make others into fools,
And have their wit on hand to use when they like.[5]
What Paul says about them I won't demonstrate here:
Whoever speaks evil is Lucifer's servant.[6]

40   Beggars and bidders made the rounds quickly
'Till their belly and bag were filled to the brim;
They faked [injury] to get food, fought at the ale.
In gluttony, God knows, they go to bed,
And rise with obscenity, those Robert's[7] knaves!
45   Sleep and shameful sloth follow them always.

Pilgrims and palmers together vowed
To seek Saint James and the saints in Rome,[8]
Went forth on their way with many wise tales
And had excuse to lie for the rest of their life.
50   I saw some who said they had sought out saints:

---

[1]   *Piers Plowman*   Translated by Emily Steiner for *The Broadview Anthology of British Literature*.

[2]   *I traveled ... wonders*   The narrator immediately establishes himself as a curious conflation of two kinds of wanderers: the knight errant of medieval romance and the itinerant religious, a frequent object of criticism in estates satire. Although it is the desire to wander that allows the narrator to experience marvels, the same desire marks him as someone who has strayed from institutionally-sanctioned paths.

[3]   *anchorites and hermits*   Sometimes used interchangeably in the poem, anchorites and hermits refer to those medieval Christians pursuing a solitary life of religious "athleticism," living apart from a religious community and maintaining an ascetic personal regimen.

Traditionally, anchorites are confined to cells, usually attached to churches or monasteries, whereas hermits were supposed to live a solitary life but are not confined to cells.

[4]   *Judas's*   Judas Iscariot was one of the twelve apostles and Christ's betrayer.

[5]   *But tricksters ... they like*   Throughout the poem, the poet is concerned to distinguish between good entertainment, which educates and inspires the audience, and bad entertainment, which wastes speech, corrupts the audience, and takes away alms from the deserving poor.

[6]   *Whoever speaks ... servant*   See Ephesians 5.4 and Colossians 3.18.

[7]   *Robert's*   A generic name for a robber.

[8]   *To seek ... in Rome*   Another form of religious "athleticism" was pilgrimage, making the arduous journey to the shrines of saints, for example, across the Pyrenees to St. James of Compostela in Spain, or to the city of Rome, or even by ship to Jerusalem. Like hermits, pilgrims were criticized for taking on religious apparel for the wrong reasons; in this case, to have adventures to relate when they get back home.

With every tale they told their tongue was tuned more
    to lie
Than to tell the truth, at least it seemed by their speech.

A heap of hermits with hooked staffs
Went to Walsingham, their mistresses in tow:
55 Big, tall lubbers, who were reluctant to work,
Dressed themselves in cloaks to set themselves apart
And passed themselves off as hermits to live the easy life.

I found friars there, all four orders,
Preaching to the people to benefit themselves.[1]
60 [They] expounded the gospel however they saw fit,
Construed it as they liked to get themselves cloaks.
Many of these master friars can wear what they want
Because their profession and their money march together.
Ever since Charity has become a dealer, and mainly to
    confess lords,
65 Many strange marvels have occurred in the last few years.
Unless [the friars] and Holy Church support each
    other better
The biggest disaster on earth is just around the corner![2]

A pardoner preached there as if he were a priest.[3]
He brought forth a bull with bishops' seals,
70 And said that he had the power to absolve them all
Of [their] broken fasts and broken vows.
Laymen readily believed him and liked his words;
They came up kneeling to kiss his bulls.
He struck them with his letter and bleared their eyes,

75 And caught rings with his ragman[4] and brooches too.
Thus you help gluttons by giving away your gold,
And handing it over to rascals who routinely fornicate!
If the bishop was blessed and worth both his ears,
His seal would not be sent to deceive the people.
80 But the fellow doesn't preach through permission of
    the bishop;
Rather, the pardoner and the priest split the silver,
Which the poor people of the parish ought to have
    instead.

Parsons and parish priests complained to the bishop
That their parishes have been poor since the time of
    the plague,
85 To have a license and leave to live in London,[5]
And to sing there for simony,[6] because silver is sweet.
Bishops and scholars, bachelors, masters, and doctors
    [of divinity]—
Who have care of souls under Christ and tonsure[7] as proof
And sign that they should confess their parishioners,
90 Preach and pray for them, and feed the poor—
Reside in London, at Lent and other times too.
Some of them serve the King, and count up his silver:
In the Exchequer and Chancery[8] they prosecute his fines

---

[1] *I found friars … benefit themselves* Dominicans, Franciscans, Carthusians, Carmelites, and Augustinians. Like many of his contemporaries, the poet repeatedly satirizes the mendicant friars (religious orders that rejected both individual and communal poverty), who traveled around preaching and hearing confession, and whose dependence on alms tended to put a strain on the resources of charitable laypeople.

[2] *The biggest disaster … corner* The narrator emphasizes the seriousness of his critique by referencing the conventions of visionary prophecy, a literature that claims to reveal divine truths as well as imminent future events.

[3] *A pardoner … a priest* Pardoners carried grants of indulgence, offering remittance of purgatorial punishment, in exchange for good works. These works often took the form of collections or fundraising for special Church projects (see Passus 5). Pardoners were notoriously corrupt.

[4] *ragman* A ragman refers to a document—here, the papal bull carried by the pardoner—that had a raggedy appearance due to the seals hanging from the bottom of the document by strips of parchment. The poem's medieval readers probably would have also noted the pun: a ragman also referred to the Devil, who was sometimes imagined to carry with him a list of sinners or their offences.

[5] *Parsons and parish … in London* I.e., rural priests are buying up benefices (appointments) in London, which will guarantee them both property and income. The plague (or Black Death, c. 1349–50) devastated the populations of the countryside, and, as a result, priests receive fewer tithes from their parishioners.

[6] *simony* The exchange of spiritual for temporal goods; here, it refers to the practice, condemned by medieval reformers, of paying for ecclesiastical offices.

[7] *tonsure* I.e., the bare part of a priest's or monk's head as a result of shaving.

[8] *Exchequer and Chancery* Departments or "courts" of the royal household, which dealt with finance and law, respectively. The Exchequer collected and disbursed revenue. Chancery was an administrative office, which also served as a court where the king could prosecute claims—for example, his claim to the wardship of a feudal heir (noble guardianship entitled the king to the income from a fief during the minority of an heir).

From wards and ward-meetings,[1] "waifs and strays."[2]
95   And some serve as servants to lords and ladies,
And in place of stewards, sit and judge.[3]
Their mass, and their matins, and many of their hours
Are performed without devotion; the dreaded
            outcome is
That Christ at Judgment Day will curse many in his Court.

100   I thought about the power that was entrusted to Peter—
To bind and unbind, as Scripture reports—
How he lovingly bequeathed it, as Our Lord commanded,
To the four virtues, most virtuous of all the virtues,
Which are called "cardinals"[4] and "closing gates,"
105   To close and to shut the kingdom of Christ
Or to open it up and reveal heavenly bliss.
But of the Cardinals at court who assume the same name
And take for granted the power to make a Pope
Who has the same power that Peter had, I won't speak
            badly—
110   For love and learning pertain to the election [of a pope].
Therefore I both can and cannot speak more about
            the court.

Then a King arrived; Knighthood led him;
Might of the Commons allowed him to reign.
And then Kind Wit[5] came along and invented clerics
115   To counsel the King and save the Commons.
The King, and Knighthood, and Clergy together

Arranged for the Commons to provide them with food.
The Commons improvised through Kind Wit's skills,
And, for profit of all the people, ordained plowmen
120   To till and to work as true life demands.
The King and the Commons and Kind Wit all three
Created law and justice, so each life could know its own.[6]

Then a lunatic looked up, a skinny thing, too,
And kneeling in front of the King, he said like a cleric,
125   "Christ protect you and your kingdom, Sir King,
And let you rule your land so that Justice loves you.
And for your just ruling be rewarded in heaven!"

And then high up in the air a heavenly angel
Came down to speak in Latin—because laymen didn't
            know how
130   To argue or judge to defend themselves,
But only to suffer and serve—therefore the angel said,
"I am King, I am Ruler'; but in the future you may be
            neither,
O you who preside over the special law of Christ the King,
So that you may do [your job] better—you are just, so be
            conscientious!
135   *Naked law needs to be dressed by you with mercy.*
Sow only the amount of grain that you wish to gather:
If the law is stripped bare [by you], then it shall be meted
            out to you according to naked law!
If you sow mercy, you will gather according to mercy."

Then a goliard[7] grew angry, a glutton of words,
140   And to the angel on high he answers,
"Just as 'king' is said to take its name from 'to rule,'
He has the name without the thing unless he strives to
            maintain the law."

And then the whole Commons began to cry in a Latin
            verse
To the King's council—understand he who will—
145   *"The king's precepts have for us the binding force of law."*

---

[1] *wards and ward-meetings* Courts of the wards (i.e., of urban districts), which drew up lists of adulterers and prostitutes; the fines they imposed were collected by Exchequer clerks.

[2] *waifs and strays* Moveable property that has no obvious owner and therefore can be confiscated.

[3] *And in place ... judge* Some clerics used their literate skills to work as officials on manorial estates, even serving as the lords' deputies in manorial courts. The poet criticizes these and other clerics for neglecting the official public prayer of the Church.

[4] *cardinals* The poet is making a pun on the word "cardinal," which refers both to the cardinal virtues of prudence, justice, temperance, and fortitude (the four ethical virtues, as opposed to the three theological virtues of faith, hope, and charity), and to the powerful Roman bishops who assisted the pope in papal administration and finance, and who had the power to choose a new pope, usually from among their members.

[5] *Kind Wit* A recurrent figure in the poem, usually referring to the natural ability to make sense of the world through lived experience. Here, it seems to carry the additional meaning of the ability of human societies to maintain order through responsible governance.

[6] *own* I.e., one's share or due, what belongs to a person, and what a person's rights and privileges are under the law.

[7] *goliard* Satirical poet of Latin verse (generally clerical students residing in Germany, England, and France during the twelfth and thirteenth centuries).

With that a pack of rats ran out at once
And small mice with them. More than a thousand
Came to a council for the common profit.
It seems a cat from the court went wherever he liked,
150　And pounced on them indifferently and caught them
　　　　at will,
And played with them dangerously and tossed them
　　　　about.[1]

For fear of all kinds of dangers we hardly dare to look!
And if we complain about his game, he will injure us all,
Scratch us, or claw us, or hold us in his clutches,
155　So that our life becomes loathsome by the time he
　　　　releases us.
If we could find a strategy to foil his desire,
We might be lords on high and live at our ease.

A famous rat, most eloquent of tongue,
Came up with a perfect remedy for them all.
160　"I have seen men," he said, "in the city of London,
Wear shiny necklaces around their necks,
And some wear collars skillfully made; they go unleashed
Both in warren and in wasteland, wherever they like,
And at other times elsewhere, as I have heard tell.[2]
165　By Jesus, it seems to me, if there was a bell on their
　　　　necklace,
Men would know where they went and to where they
　　　　had run.
And therefore," said that rat, "it makes sense to me
To buy a bell made of brass or of bright silver
And attach it to a collar for the common profit
170　And hang it around the cat's neck. Then we could hear
Where he rides, or rests, or goes out to play;
And if he wishes to amuse himself, we can look

And appear in his presence for that period of time,
And if he becomes angry, we'll be cautious and stay
　　　　out of his way."

175　The whole pack of rats agreed to this plan.
Yet, though the bell was bought and fastened to the collar,
There was no rat in all the pack, for the kingdom of
　　　　France,
That dared hang the bell from the neck of the cat,
Nor drape it around his neck, for to win all of England,
180　And they thought themselves cowardly and their
　　　　counsel feeble,
And they held their labor lost and their long deliberations.

A mouse with good judgment, as it seemed to me,
Strode forward sternly and stood before them all,
And to the pack of rats made the following speech:
185　"Even if we had killed the cat, another one would come
To scratch us and all our kind, though we crept under
　　　　benches.
Therefore I advise the whole commune to let the cat be,
And never attempt to show him the bell.
As long as he catches rabbits, he doesn't want our flesh;
190　[He] feeds himself game instead. We should never
　　　　dishonor him,
Because it's better to have a little loss than a long sorrow.
Even if we got rid of the rascal, we'd have total chaos.
I heard my father say seven years ago,
'Where the cat is a kitten, the court is very wretched!'
195　Holy Scripture supports that, whoever wishes to read it,
'Woe to the land where a child is king.'[3]
Further, no one would rest because of rats at night
Because we mice would destroy many men's malt,
And you tribe of rats would shred men's clothes,
200　Were it not for the court cat who keeps you
　　　　continually in check.
Even if you rats had power you couldn't rule yourselves.

"I speak for myself," said the mouse, "I'll tell you one
　　　　thing for sure:
Neither the cat nor the kitten will be oppressed by my
　　　　counsel,
Nor by my talking about this collar, which cost me
　　　　nothing.

---

[1] *With that ... them about* This popular rats and mice fable is deployed here to satirize the Good Parliament of 1376. At the time, Edward III was in failing health; his grandson, Richard, who would succeed him the following year, was only 9 years old, and the Court party was largely controlled by Richard's powerful uncle, John of Gaunt, Duke of Lancaster, represented in this allegory by the cat. In 1376, the parliamentary Commons, headed by the audacious speaker Sir Peter de la Mare (the rat), successfully, if temporarily, curbed the influence of Gaunt over the royal party.

[2] *some wear collars ... tell* A reference to livery collars, collars worn by medieval men to indicate their allegiance to a particular patron, such as the well-known "SS" collars associated with the House of Lancaster.

[3] *Woe ... is king* See Ecclesiastics 10.16.

205   And even if it did cost me something, I would never
          mention it,
But allow him to do exactly what he wants,
Whether leashed or unleashed, to catch what [he] can.
Thus I warn every wise man to look out for himself."

What this dream signifies, you men who are merry,
210   Interpret yourselves—I don't dare—by dear God in
          heaven!

And yet, a hundred still lingered there in silken caps,
Sergeants, it seemed, who served at the Bar,
Who pleaded the law for pennies and pounds,
And wouldn't once unloose their lips for love of our Lord.
215   You'd have a better chance of measuring the mist on
          Malvern Hills
Than getting a "mum" from their mouths, before they
          see the money.

Barons, and burgesses, and bondsmen, too,
I saw in this assembly, as you shall hear next:
Bakers, and brewers, and butchers aplenty,
220   Weavers of wool, and weavers of linen,
Tailors, and tinkers, and toll-takers in markets,
Masons, and miners, and many other types.
Of all living laborers, some stood out,
Such as dikers, and diggers, who do their work badly,
225   And drive forth the day with "God save you, Dame
          Emme."[1]
Cooks and their boys cried out, "Hot pies, hot!
Good geese and pork! Let's get some dinner!"
Innkeepers touted the same sort of thing,
"White wine of Alsace and wine of Gascony,
230   Of the Rhine, and La Rochelle, to digest the roast!"
All this I saw sleeping, and seven times more.
          —C. 1377–79

---

¹ *God save you, Dame Emme*   A popular song, possibly referring to Dame Emma of Shoreditch, perhaps a healer of some sort.

PASSUS 18

With wool shirt and wet feet I went forth afterwards
          Like a reckless man who cares little about
          hardship.[2]
And I wandered like a drifter my entire life,
Until I grew weary of the world and wished then to sleep,
5   And I lay down until Lent, and for a long time slept,[3]
Rested there and snored soundly until *Palm Sunday*.[3]
I dreamed splendidly of children and of "*Glory, praise*"
And how old people sang "*Hosanna*" to the organ,
Leading up to the passion of Christ and his penance.

10   Someone resembling the Samaritan, and somewhat
          Piers the Plowman,
Came riding barefoot and bootless on the back of an ass.
Lacking spurs and spear, he looked very eager,
As in the case of a knight on his way to be dubbed,
To get golden spurs on slashed shoes.[4]

15   Then Faith was in a window, and cried, "*A! Son of David!*"
As does a herald of arms does when adventurers come to
          joust.
Old Jews of Jerusalem sang for joy,
"*Blessed be he who comes in the name of the Lord.*"[5]

---

² *With wool … hardship*   By this point in the poem, the dreamer has forged a complex identity for himself. He is at once the wayward and often combative social critic who we see in the Prologue as well as the spiritual seeker who cares little for the conventions and comforts of the world following the model of Piers Plowman in Passus 7.

³ *And I wandered … Palm Sunday*   Passus 18 recounts the life and death of Christ, from his Entry into Jerusalem to the Harrowing of Hell. It does so both narratively, by stitching together fragments from the four Gospels and the Psalms, and ritually, by invoking the events and liturgy of Holy Week. It begins with the dreamer's vision of people singing *Laudamus Te Deum* on Palm Sunday and concludes with a waking moment in which the dreamer hears the church bells ring for Easter Sunday.

⁴ *Someone resembling … slashed shoes*   Importantly, for the poet, Jesus is of noble birth, and his Crucifixion is not an ignoble death but a chivalric joust, or perhaps a trial by combat, in which he triumphs even in death. In these lines, his noble apparel refers not only to his high status but also to what the poet calls his "kynde"—that is, the divine assumption of human nature.

⁵ *Blessed be he … the Lord*   See Matthew 21.9.

Then I asked Faith what all the fanfare meant,
And who was jousting in Jerusalem. "Jesus," he said,
20   "And [he] will fetch what the devil claims: Piers the
        Plowman's fruit."[1]

"Is Piers in this place," said I, and he winked at me.

"This Jesus will joust in Piers's arms,
In his helmet and his mail coat, *human nature*.
So that Christ won't be revealed here in his *absolute divinity*,
25   In Piers the Plowman's jacket this knight will ride,
For no blow will hurt him here as in *God the Father*.[2]

"Who will joust with Jesus," said I, "Jews or scribes?"

"No," said Faith, "the devil, and false sentence of death.
Death says he shall destroy and bring down
30   All that live or look in land or in water.
Life says he lies, and lays down his life as guarantee,
That, for all that Death can do, in three days he'll walk
And deliver from the devil the fruit of Piers the
        Plowman,
And put it where it pleases him, and bind Lucifer,
35   And destroy and bring down baleful death forever:
'*O Death, I will be your death!*'"[3]

Then came *Pilate* with a crowd, *sitting in front of the
        tribunal*,[4]
To see how bravely Death would act, and judge who
        was in the right.
The Jews and the judge were against Jesus,
And the whole court cried shrilly, "*Crucify!*"

40   Then they appointed an accuser, who said in front of
        Pilate,
"This Jesus mocked and insulted the temple of us Jews,
[Said he would] raze it in one day, and three days later,
Build it anew—here he stands who said it!—
And yet make it as great in every dimension,
45   Both as broad and as large, from the top to the bottom."

"*Crucify*," said a tax-collector, "I warrant he's a witch."

"*Away with him, away with him*,"[5] said another, and
        took some sharp thorns,
And with the sharp thorns began to make a garland,
And set it on his head, and said with spite,
50   "*Hail, Rabbi*,"[6] said that scoundrel, and scourged him
        with reeds,
With three nails nailed him naked on the cross,
And they put to his lips [a cup of] poison on a pole,
And told him to drink his evil death—his days were over—
And said, "If you're so clever, help yourself now!
55   If you are Christ and a king's son, come down from the
        cross;
Then we will believe that Life loves you and won't let
        you die."

"*It is finished*,"[7] said Christ, and began to swoon,
Piteously and pale, like a prisoner dying,
The lord of life and light then closed his eyes.
60   The day withdrew for fear, and dark became the sun.
The walls shuddered and cracked, and the whole world
        shook.
Dead men came out of deep graves on account of the noise,
And explained why the tempest endured for so long.

"Because of a bitter battle," the dead body said,
65   "Life and Death in this darkness, each annihilating the
        other.
No person knows for sure who will have the upper hand
Before Sunday at sunrise"—and with that, sank into the
        earth.

---

[1]   *And [he] will … Plowman's fruit*   A reference to the beginning of
Passus 16, in which Piers cultivates an Edenic apple tree, only to
have the Devil confiscate the "fruit"; the event symbolically alludes
to humanity's condemnation to hell by Original Sin before the
coming of Christ.

[2]   *For no blow … Father*   I.e., Jesus cannot be hurt in the divine
nature that he shares with God the Father. Knights in the medieval
romance tradition often disguised themselves for jousts only to have
their true identities revealed through their deeds. Here, Christ,
disguised in Piers's arms, fools the Jews into thinking that he is
merely mortal when, in fact, as the miraculous healing of Longinus
shows below, his nature is both human and divine.

[3]   *O Death … your death*   See Hosea 13.14.

[4]   *Then came Pilate … tribunal*   See Acts 25.

[5]   *Away with him, away with him*   See John 19.15.

[6]   *Hail, Rabbi*   See Matthew 26.49.

[7]   *It is finished*   See John 19.30.

Some said he was God's son, who died so well:
"*Truly [this man] was the son of God.*"[1]
And some said he was a witch: "It would be a good idea
   to test
70 Whether he be dead or no, before he's taken down."

Two thieves also suffered death at that time
Upon a cross next to Christ—according to the common
   law.[2]
An officer came by and cracked both their legs,
And then the arms of each of the two thieves.
75 But there was no person bold enough to touch God's body;
Because he was a knight and king's son, God granted it
   that time
That no rogue was brave enough to lay a hand on him.

But a knight stepped up with a sharply ground spear,
Called Longinus, as the text tells [us], who long before
   had lost his sight.[3]
80 He stood near Pilate and the other people in that place;
And despite his objections he was forced that time
To joust with Jesus, this blind Jew Longinus.
For everyone else was too timid, who stood or sat on
   horseback,
To touch him, or feel him, or take him down from the
   cross,
85 Except this blind knight, who stabbed him through the
   heart.
The blood sprang out from the spear and unsealed the
   knight's eyes.

The knight fell on his knees then and asked Jesus for mercy:
"It was against my will, Lord, to wound you so badly!"
He sighed and said, "It pains me to think about it!
90 For the deed I have done I throw myself on your grace.
Have pity on me, righteous Jesus!"—and right with that
   he wept.

Then Faith fiercely began to chide the false Jews,
Called them slaves condemned forever:[4]
"For this foul villainy [may there be] vengeance upon
   you all!
95 To have a blind man assault a bound man—that was a
   rogue's counsel!
Accursed wretches! It has never been noble
To attack a dead body by day or by night.
Yet he has received the prize, despite his great wound,

"Because your champion knight, the best knight of you all,
100 Declares himself beaten, just as Jesus wills.
For this darkness is at an end, Death has been
   vanquished,
And you, rascals, have lost, for Life will prevail,
And your condition, once free, has now fallen into
   servitude,
And you, churls, and your children, shall never flourish,
105 Nor have dominion in the land, nor till the soil,
But you will be entirely barren, and use usury,
Which is the life that Our Lord has cursed in all his laws.
Now your good times are over, as Daniel prophesied:
When Christ came their kingdom would lose its crown,
'*When the saint of saints comes, your anointed kingship
   will cease.*'"[5]

110 For fear of this marvel and of the false Jews,
I withdrew myself into darkness and *descended into hell*,
And there I saw truly, *following scripture*,[6]

---

[4] *Then Faith ... condemned forever* Medieval Christian writers long
debated the "problem" of the Jews in their midst, who did not
accept the messiah of the dominant religious culture in the West
and, as a consequence, suffered enormous persecution in the form of
legal restrictions, religious propaganda, physical attacks, and, in
1290 in England, expulsion from the country. Jews were prohibited in
many territories from holding land, but they were permitted and
even encouraged by the governing classes to practice usury (a
practice condemned by the Church).

[5] *When the saint ... will cease* See Daniel 9.24.

[6] *For fear ... following scripture* The poet traces Christ's descent
into hell, detailed in the *Gospel of Nicodemus* (from the *Acts of Pilate*,
c. 150–255 CE), and is probably inspired by the line that the poet
quotes from the fifth article of the Apostles Creed (or the 38th
article of the Athanasian Creed): "He descended into hell; the third
day He rose again from the dead." *The Gospel of Nicodemus*, now
considered apocryphal, circulated widely in the fourteenth century,
both in Latin and in English prose and poetic versions, as well as in
the fifteenth-century biblical cycle plays. In *Piers Plowman*, the four

---

[1] *Truly ... son of God* See Matthew 27.54.

[2] *Upon a cross ... common law* The customary practice at that time
and place.

[3] *Called Longinus ... his sight* Longinus (or Longeus) presented
here as the reluctant champion of the Jews in the "joust" against
Jesus, is the name given by popular tradition to a unnamed Roman
soldier in the Gospels. In Langland's poem, as in later medieval texts
such as the widely-known *Golden Legend* (c. 1260), the touch of
Jesus's blood restores Longinus's sight.

Out from the West, a girl, it seemed to me,
Came walking on that path; she looked towards hell.
115 The girl was named Mercy, gentle through and through,
A very gracious lady, and humble of speech.

Her sister, so it seemed, came quietly walking
Straight from the East, and she looked to the West.
A very comely creature and pure; her name was Truth.
120 Thanks to the quality that she stood for she was never
    afraid.

When these maidens met, Mercy and Truth,
Each asked the other about this great wonder—
About the noise and the darkness, and how the day was
    unfolding,
And how a light and a glow lay before hell.

125 "I am baffled, in faith, by these goings on," said Truth,
"And I am going to find out what this wonder means."

"Don't be amazed," said Mercy, "it signifies joy.
A maiden called Mary, [who became] a mother without
    sex
With any natural creature, conceived through speech
130 And grace of the Holy Ghost. [She] grew big with child;
She, without blemish, brought him into the world.
And I take God to witness that my story is true.

"Thirty winters have passed since this child was born,
Who died and suffered death about midday today.
135 And that is the cause of the solar eclipse,
A sign that humanity will be delivered from darkness,
While this light and this glow will blind Lucifer.
"Indeed, patriarchs and prophets have preached of this
    often:
That a man shall save mankind through a maiden's help.
140 And that which was lost through a tree will be won back
    through a tree,
And those whom Death brought down, a death shall
    release."

"What you are talking about," said Truth, "is just a tale
    of hogwash!
As for Adam, and Eve, and Abraham, among other

Patriarchs and prophets who lie in pain,
145 Never believe that that light will bring them above ground,
Nor rescue them from Hell. Hold your tongue, Mercy!
This is rubbish of which you speak—I, Truth, know the
    truth.
For once something is in hell, it's never coming out.
The prophet Job refutes what you say:
'*Because in hell there is no redemption.*'"[1]

150 Then Mercy very gently spoke the following words:
"Through experience," said she, "I know that they'll be
    saved,
Because venom counters venom—and I will prove that
    through reason.
For the deadliest of all venoms is that of the scorpion;
No medicine can cure the place where it stings,
155 Until it dies and is placed there—it destroys the evil,
The first poison, through its own power.
So shall this death destroy—I wager my life—
Everything that Death first did through the enticement
    of the Devil.
And just as man was first beguiled through the beguiler's
    guile,
160 So shall grace, which began everything, make a good end,
And beguile the beguiler—and that's a good trick:
'*Thus art is deceived by art.*'"[2]

"Let's be quiet now," said Truth, "I see, as it seems to me,
Out of the cold of the North, not very far from here,
Righteousness comes running. Let's rest here awhile,
165 For she knows more than we do—she was around
    before either of us."

"That is true," said Mercy, "and from here I can see
    from the South
Where Peace comes playing, clothed in patience.

---

[1] *Because in hell … redemption* Response from the Office of the Dead, with allusion to Job 7.9: "Sic qui descenderit ad infernos non ascenderet." (So he who goes down into hell shall not come up.)

[2] *Thus art … by art* From Fortunatus, "Pange Lingua," used in the Good Friday liturgy; also a source for a legend of the Cross, in which the Cross of the Crucifixion was carved from the Tree of Knowledge. This is the beginning of a series of arguments, offered by Mercy and Peace, and later, by Christ himself, regarding the legality and fittingness of the Atonement. At stake for the four daughters of God is whether God is fundamentally merciful or just.

---

daughters of God—Mercy, Truth, Justice (or Righteousness), and Peace—anticipate and debate the legality of the Harrowing of Hell.

Love has wanted her a long time—I have no reason not
    to believe
That he has sent her a certain letter. She will tell us
170 What this light means, thus suspended over Hell."

When Peace, clothed in patience, approached the two of
    them,
Righteousness esteemed her for her fine clothing,
And asked Peace to tell her where she was going,
And in her lovely garments whom she intended to greet.

175 "My desire is to go," said she, "and welcome all those whom
I haven't seen for a long time, because of the darkness of
    sin:
Adam, and Eve, and many others in Hell,
Moses and many more shall have mercy,
And I shall dance [in celebration]—join in, sister!
180 For Jesus jousted well, joy begins to dawn:
'*In the evening, weeping shall have place, and in the
    morning, gladness.*'[1]

Love, who is my lover, sent me letters about this:
That Mercy, my sister, and I should save mankind,
And that God has given and granted me, Peace, and
    Mercy,
To be man's surety for evermore after.
185 Look, here's the patent," said Peace, '*In peace in the
    selfsame,*'
And that this deed shall last, '*I shall sleep and I shall rest.*'"[2]

"What, are you raving," said Righteousness, "or are you
    completely drunk?
Do you really believe that the light over there could
    unlock Hell
And save man's soul? Sister, don't believe it.
190 God Himself gave the judgment at the beginning,
That Adam and Eve, and all those who came after them,
Should die outright and live in pain forever,
If they touched a tree and ate its fruit.
Afterwards, Adam, against [God's] prohibition,
195 Devoured that fruit, and forsook, as it were,
Both the love and instruction of Our Lord,

And followed the Devil's teaching, and his companion's
    desire,[3]
Against reason. I, Righteousness, proclaim thus with Truth
That their pain will be perpetual, and no prayer can
    help them.
200 Therefore let them chew what they have chosen, and
    let's not argue, sisters,
For it's an incurable woe, the bite they have eaten."

"And I shall pray," said Peace, "that their pain might end,
And [that their] woe might finally turn into joy.[4]
After all, if they hadn't known woe, they wouldn't know
    joy,
205 For no one can know joy who has never suffered woe,
Nor what searing hunger is, who has never had lack.
If there were no night, I believe, no man
Would know for sure what day is to mean.
No rich man can ever really know, one who lives in rest
    and ease,
210 What suffering is, or what it means to die.
In the same way, God who created all through his good
    will
Became man through a virgin to save mankind,
And let himself to be sold, in order to see the sorrow of
    dying,
From which all care is unwoven and from which rest begins.
215 For until a *little* meets with us, I may well declare it,
No man knows, I suspect, what is meant by enough.

"Therefore God, in his goodness, the first man, Adam,
Created in comfort and in total joy.
And then He allowed him to sin, in order to feel sorrow,
220 To know what affliction was, to comprehend it fully.
And later, God ventured Himself and assumed Adam's
    nature,
To know what he had experienced in three different
    places:
In heaven, and on earth, and now into Hell He plans to go,
To understand total woe, He who knows of total joy.

---

[1] *In the evening … gladness* See Psalms 29.6.

[2] *I shall … rest* See Psalms 4.9.

[3] *companion's desire* I.e., Eve.

[4] *And I shall … into joy* Peace offers an explanation for the
fittingness of both the Incarnation and the Harrowing of Hell. God
became man to experience pain and sadness; likewise, God allowed
humanity to be punished, and then released from punishment, so
that man, too, could know both sorrow and joy.

225 "Likewise it will happen to these folk: their folly and
       their sin
    Shall teach them what pain is and bliss without end.
    No person can know what war is who lives where peace
       reigns,
    Nor truly what is joy until 'woe is me' teaches him."

    Then a creature was there with two wide eyes;
230 Book was the old man's name, a man bold of speech.
    "By God's body," said this Book,[1] "I will bear witness
    That when this child was born, a star blazed there,
    From which all the wise men of the world concluded
      together
    That such a child was born in the city of Bethlehem
235 Who would save man's soul and destroy sin.

    "And all the elements," said Book, "bear witness to this.
    The sky first showed that He was God who made all;
    Those who were in heaven took a *comet*
    And lit it like a torch to celebrate His birth.
240 The light followed the Lord into the low earth.
    The water witnessed that he was God, because He walked
      upon it.
    Peter the Apostle noticed His gait,
    And as He walked on the water, recognized Him, saying,
    '*Bid me come to you upon the waters.*'[2]
    And lo, how the sun began to lock up the light in herself
245 When she saw him suffer, who made the sun and sea.
    The earth in sorrow that he had to suffer
    Quaked like a living thing and pounded the rocks.

    "Lo, Hell itself couldn't hold, but opened when God
      suffered,
    And let Simeon's sons out to watch Him hang on the
      cross.[3]

---

[1] *Book* Here, not simply the sacred text (the books of the Bible), but also the idea that true belief in the mystery of the Atonement depends upon the perfect identification of witness and text. Book, with his two big eyes, can attest to the miracles of Christ's ministry and the marvels that occurred at his death because he (Book) was "there."

[2] *Bid me come ... the waters* See Matthew 14.28.

[3] *Simeon's sons ... the cross* In Luke 2.25–35, Simeon is a witness to the infant Jesus and among the first to recognize him as Christ; in the *Gospel of Nicodemus*, he is identified with his sons as witnesses to the Harrowing. From this, the poet imagines that Simeon's sons witnessed the Crucifixion, an idea apparently not otherwise attested

250 And now Lucifer must believe it, though it seems
      loathsome to him;
    For *Gigas*[4] the giant has contrived with an engine
    To break and beat down those who are against Jesus.
    "And I, Book, will be burned, if Jesus doesn't rise to live
    In all the power of his manhood, and gladden his mother,
255 And comfort all his kin, and bring them out of hardship,
    And unjoin and unlock all the joy of the Jews;
    And, unless they revere his cross and resurrection,
    And accept a new law, [they will] be lost, body and soul!"

    "Let's be quiet," said Truth. "I both hear and see
260 A spirit speaking to Hell and asking it to open the gates."
    "*Lift up your gates.*"
    A loud voice in the light cried out to Lucifer,
    "Princes of this place, unbolt and unlock,
    For here comes with a crown he who is King of Glory."

    Then sighed Satan, and said to all of Hell,
265 "This very light, against our leave, made off with Lazarus.
    Hardship and misfortune are coming to us all.
    If this king comes in, he will abduct mankind,
    And lead it where Lazarus is, and tie me up without delay.
    Patriarchs and prophets have talked about this a long time,
270 That such a lord and a light shall lead them all away.

    "Listen," said Lucifer, "because I know this lord;
    Both this lord and this light—I knew them long ago—
    No death can hurt this lord, and no devil's ruse.[5]
    And what he wants, he gets, but let him beware of the
      dangers.
275 If he deprives me of my rights, he robs me by force,

---

to in the *Nicodemus* tradition.

[4] *Gigas* Perhaps a reference to Christ himself (see Psalms 18.6: "exultavit ut gigans ad currendam viam suam" [He has rejoiced as a giant to run the way]).

[5] *No death ... devil's ruse* The lines that follow refer to a number of medieval theories about God's right to reclaim humanity from hell, theories that the poet represents as compatible, even interdependent, rather than antagonistic: 1) God successfully tricked the devil by appearing in human form; 2) God sacrificed himself in order to pay back the devil, and/or he ransomed his followers; 3) the devil forfeited his right to humanity by deceiving Adam and Eve in Paradise, and therefore his claim to possess them has no legal justification. Significantly, Lucifer's explanation of the "devil's rights" theory is no literary fiction, but rather a summary of serious and longstanding theological debates.

For the people who are here, by right and by reason,
Are mine, body and soul, both good and bad.
For he himself said, who is the lord of heaven,
That if Adam ate the apple, everyone would die,
280 And dwell in sorrow with us devils—he made this threat.
And since he who is Truthfulness itself said these words,
And I subsequently took possession for 7,000 winters,
I am sure the law won't give me an inch."[1]

"That is true," said Satan, "but I am very worried,
285 Because you got him with guile and broke into his garden,
And, disguised as a serpent, you sat on the apple tree,
And egged them on to eat, Eve when alone,
And told her a tale composed of treasonous words.
And so you carried them away and [brought] them here in
    the end.
290 A [thing] is not licitly acquired, if guile is at the root!"

"For God," said Goblin, "will not be beguiled or tricked.
We have no true title to them, because they were damned
    through treason."

"Of course, I'm afraid," said the Devil, "that Truth wants
    to take them.
For the last thirty winters, I understand, he went about
    and preached.
295 I have assailed him with temptation, and once I asked
If he were God or God's son (he gave me short answer),
And thus has he wandered these thirty winters.
And when I saw what was happening, I went while she slept
To warn Pilate's wife what kind of man Jesus was,
300 For the Jews hated him and had him sentenced to death.
I wanted to lengthen his life, for I believed, if he died,
That his soul would tolerate no sin in its sight.
For the body, while it went on bones, was ever busy
To save men from sin, as long as they were willing.
305 "And now I see where a soul comes sailing this way,

With glory and great light—it is God, I know for sure.
I suggest we flee," he said, "let's make a run for it,
For it were better that we were gone than we were seen
    by him.
On account of your lies, Lucifer, our prey is lost.
310 Thanks to you, we fell from heaven so high;
Because we believed your lies, we leapt out altogether
    with you.
And thanks to your last lie, we have [now] lost Adam,
And our whole dominion, I believe, on land and on water:
'Now shall the prince of this world be cast out.'"[2]

Then the light demanded entry, and Lucifer answered,
"Who is it?
315 What lord are you?" said Lucifer. The light promptly
    answered,
"The King of Glory,
The lord of might and of main and of every kind of virtue,
The Lord of Virtues.[3]
Dukes of this dark place, unlatch these gates at once
So that Christ may come in, the King of Heaven's son!"

And with that breath, hell broke, along with Belial's bars,
320 In spite of any man or guard, the gates [burst] wide open.
Patriarchs and prophets, the people in darkness,[4]
Sang Saint John's song, "Behold the Lamb of God."[5]
Lucifer couldn't look, the light blinded him so.

And those that our Lord loved, he caught into his light,
325 And said to Satan, "Behold, here's my soul a compensation
For all sinful souls, to save the ones who are worthy—
They are mine and of me—so I may better claim them.
Although reason maintains, and my own justice,
That if they ate the apple, all should die,
330 I didn't promise them Hell here forever
For the deed that they did. Your deceit prompted it;
You got them with guile, against all reason.
For in my palace, Paradise, in the shape of an adder,
You snatched away falsely the thing that I loved.

---

1 *And I subsequently ... an inch* Contained within these theological
arguments offered by the devils, and later by Christ, is a legal
argument about property: if you have physically taken possession of
real or moveable property and have successfully held on to it for
some time, it becomes irrevocably yours despite prior written claims.
The arguments in this Passus about God's and the Devil's rights
revolve around a fundamental belief that it is the job of lawgivers to
uphold the law that they themselves create. How can one claim, as
Christ does here, to uphold the law and yet override the judgment
that one has given oneself?

2 *Now shall ... cast out* See John 12.31.

3 *The Lord of Virtues* See Psalms 23.10.

4 *the people in darkness* See Matthew 4.16.

5 *Behold the Lamb of God* See Matthew 9.2.

335 Thus like a snake with a lady's face,
You robbed me like a thief.[1] The Old Law permits
Beguilers to be beguiled—and that makes good sense:
'*Tooth for a tooth, and an eye for an eye.*'[2]
Therefore soul shall avenge soul, and sin match sin,
All that man has done wrong, I, a man, shall put right.
340 Member for member was how the Old Law made
satisfaction,
And also life for life—and by that law I claim
Adam and all his issue under my control, from now on.[3]
And those whom Death killed, my death shall bring to life,
And both revive and avenge what was drowned through sin;
345 And [to accept that] grace destroys guile requires good faith.
"So Lucifer, don't believe that I seize them against the law;
By right and reason, rather, I now ransom my lieges:
'*I come here not to destroy the law but to fulfill it.*'[4]

You seized mine in my place against all reason,
Falsely and felonously. Good faith taught me
350 To recover them through ransom, and by no other means.
"So that which you got with guile, through grace it is won.
You, Lucifer, in the likeness of a wicked adder,
Got by guile the thing that God loved,
And I, in likeness of a man, who am the Lord of Heaven,
355 Have graciously paid back your guile—go guile against guile!
And just as Adam and everyone died through a tree,
So Adam and everyone through a tree shall turn and live.
And guile is beguiled, and fallen into his guile:
'*And he has fallen into the hole that he made.*'[5]
Now your guile is beginning to turn against you
360 And my grace to grow ever greater and far-reaching.
"The bitterness that you have brewed, now enjoy it
yourself;
You who are doctor of death, drink what you've made.

Since I am lord of life, love is my drink,
And for that drink today, I died on earth.
365 I fought for it, yet I still thirst, for the sake of man's soul:
May no drink refresh me, nor slake my thirst,
Until the grapes be harvested in the vale of Josaphat.
What I drink must be fully ripened; *the resurrection of the
dead.*[6]
And then shall I come as a king, crowned, with angels,
370 And take back from Hell all men's souls.

"Major fiends and minor fiends shall stand before me,
And be at my bidding, wherever I like.
But to be merciful to man, then, my nature demands it,
For we are brethren of one blood, but not all in baptism.
375 But those who are my whole brothers, both in blood and
in baptism,
Shall not be damned to everlasting death:
'*To you only I have sinned.*'[7]

"It is not the custom on earth to hang a felon
More than one time, even if he was a traitor.
And if the king of that kingdom should come that time
380 Where the felon was about to suffer death or some other
punishment,
The law is that the king gives him life if he looks upon him.
And I, who am the king of kings, shall come at such a time,
Where the sentence of death damns all wicked,
And if I want to invoke that law, it lies in my power,
385 [To decide] whether they die or not for what they did
wrong.[8]

---

[6] *resurrection of the dead* See *Nicene Creed* (c. 325).

[7] *To you ... sinned* See Psalms 50.6. In these and the following lines,
Christ offers rejoinders to the devils' objections that Christ is acting
against the law: kinship is a law unto itself, and divine mercy is an
extension of the kinship of blood that Christ feels with all humanity.
Additionally, kings should uphold the laws of the land, but there are
laws in place that allow kings to make exceptions, such as in the case
of a king who arrives on the scene of capital punishment. By analogy,
God has both ordinate and absolute powers: his ordinate power
compels him to abide by the laws he has made, and his absolute power
enables him to "fulfill" the law by going beyond it.

[8] *Where the felon ... did wrong* Christ notes, first, that English
customary law prevented a person from being hanged twice, even for
a serious crime like treason, and, second, that a king, if physically
present at an execution, could pardon the criminal. By theological
analogy, the first principle argues that a baptized person does not
have to suffer Hell twice; after the Last Judgment, he or she deserves
resurrection. The second principle, by analogy, argues for God's

---

[1] *You robbed ... thief* The Passus as a whole offers an interesting
comparison to the cycle plays that flourished in the fifteenth
century. In the Draper's play of the Chester cycle, the devil claims
he will deceive Eve by assuming a snake's body and woman's face.

[2] *Tooth for ... an eye* See Exodus 21.24.

[3] *Therefore soul shall ... now on* Although Christ's use of Old
Testament justice, as embodied by the law of retribution would seem
to work counter to New Testament charity, in these lines it provides
more fodder for the idea of Atonement reciprocity so crucial to the
Passus as a whole.

[4] *I come here ... fulfill it* See Matthew 5.17.

[5] *And he has ... made* See Psalms 7.16.

If there is any way the boldness of their sins can be
    redeemed,
I can still be merciful and just, and still maintain the truth
    of all my words.
"And although Holy Writ wants me to avenge myself on
    those who did wrong—
'*No evil should go unpunished*'—
They shall be cleansed clearly and washed clean of their sins
390 In my prison, Purgatory, until it is called '*Spare [me]*'[1]
And my mercy shall be showed to many of my brothers.
For blood may suffer blood to be both hungry and cold,
But blood can't see blood bleed, without feeling compassion:

'*I heard secret words, which are not permitted to man to
    speak.*'[2]

But my righteousness and right shall rule all Hell,
395 And [my] mercy [rule] mankind before me in heaven.
For I would be an unnatural king if I didn't help my kin,
And namely those in great need, where there is need:
'*Enter not into judgment with your servant.*'[3]

Thus by law," said our Lord, "I will lead away from here
Those people whom I loved and who believed in my
    coming.
400 And as for your lie, Lucifer, that you told to Eve,
You shall pay for it dearly," and bound him in chains.

As troth and all the rest hid themselves away;
Even the least didn't dare to look at our Lord,
But they let him lead away whom he wished and do what
    he liked.

405 Many hundreds of angels played the harp and sang,
"*Flesh sins, flesh purges, God flesh within.*"[4]

Then Peace piped a note of poetry:
"*The sun is usually brighter after the biggest cloud;*

And after enmity, brighter is love.*"[5]
"After the sharpest showers," said Peace, "most radiant is
    the sun;
No weather is ever warmer than after watery clouds;
No love dearer, nor dearer friends,
410 Than after war and woe, when Love and Peace are masters.
There was never war in this world, no wickedness so keen,
That Love couldn't turn it into laughter, when he chose,
And Peace, through patience, make all danger cease."

"Truce!" said Truth, "you speak the truth, by Jesus.
415 Let's seal it with a kiss, and each embrace the other."

"And let no people," said Peace, "perceive that we argued;
For nothing is impossible to Him that is almighty."

"You say right," said Righteousness, and reverently kissed
    her;
[She kissed] Peace, and Peace her, *forever and ever.*
"*Mercy and Truth have met each other; justice and peace
    have kissed.*"[6]

420 Truth trumpeted then and sang "*We Praise You God,*"
And Love, in a loud voice, sang to the lute
"*Behold how good and how pleasant [it is for brothers to
    dwell together]...*"[7]

These damsels caroled to the break of dawn,
When men rang bells for the Resurrection—and I woke
    up at once,
And called Kitty my wife and Calotte my daughter:
425 "Arise and go reverence God's resurrection,
And crawl on your knees to the cross, and kiss it like a
    jewel.
For it bore God's blessed body for our remedy,
And it scares off the fiend—for such is its power.
May no grisly ghost glide where its shadow falls!"
—C. 1377–79

---

absolute power.
[1] *Spare [me]*   See Job 7.16.
[2] *I heard secret ... speak*   See 2 Corinthians 12.4.
[3] *Enter not ... your servant*   See Psalms 142.2.
[4] *Flesh sins ... within*   See *Aeterne rex altissime,* stanza 4, Roman
Breviary, Matins Ascension Hymn.

[5] *The sun ... is love*   See Alanus de Isulis, *Liber parabolorum.*
[6] *Mercy and Truth ... kissed*   See Psalms 84.11.
[7] *Behold how good ... together*   See Psalms 132.1.

LOVE AND MARRIAGE IN MEDIEVAL BRITAIN
CONTEXTS

Most Old English literature focuses on the bonds between men, whether heroic retainers and their lords or pious saints and their God, and there seems to have been little interest in depicting domestic relationships and values. Even the elegiac lyric known as "The Wife's Lament" uses the language of heroic loyalty and service to express the female speaker's longing for her absent lover. Domestic life certainly existed, of course, and we may assume that men and women had various types of close and meaningful relationships; these did not, however, generally attract the interest of the authors of surviving literary works, at any rate not to the extent that they would fascinate later centuries. Apart from a few isolated passages, and the domestic scenes depicted from the peculiar perspective of the Exeter Book *Riddles*, the realm of private or personal feelings in the Anglo-Saxon period is closed to us. Several sets of laws from the early medieval period, however, give some sense of the social customs and attitudes surrounding marriage in the Anglo-Saxon world.

The literary traditions of courtly love that appeared in the south of France in the twelfth century spread rapidly throughout Europe, and had enormous impact both on literature and on the culture of European courts. It seems likely, however, that the ideology of romantic love was not shared by most members of society during this period; the early Middle English *Owl and the Nightingale* recounts, tongue in cheek, a debate on the moral implications of courtly love, and texts such as *Piers Plowman* convey some of the realities of love and marriage for the English in the later medieval period.

From its earliest days the Church had an interest in regularizing private behavior, but in general, marriage and divorce in the early medieval world appear to have been as much a matter of secular custom as of law or religion. With the Fourth Lateran Council of 1215 marriage procedures began much more widely to be brought under ecclesiastical control, but the status of marriage as one of the seven sacraments in the Roman Catholic Church was not firmly established until the late medieval period (at the Councils of Florence and of Trent in 1439 and 1547 respectively). Arranged marriages, often at a very young age, were common among the upper classes in the later medieval period, and the letter below concerning Elizabeth Paston's situation in the mid-fifteenth century speaks to the seriousness of the consequences if the arrangements were resisted. Arranged marriages of this sort were almost certainly much less common among the peasantry, who constituted the vast majority of the population.

Evidence concerning same-sex love in the Middle Ages is for the most part scant and inconclusive. Specific accounts of sexual activity (such as that attributed to Robert Grosseteste) are rare—indeed, in the case of female same-sex sexual activity, entirely unknown. The term "sodomy" begins to be widely used by Christian theologians beginning in the eleventh and twelfth centuries, but it is often unclear precisely what sorts of activity are being condemned; the term often comes to be applied to all sexual practices that by their nature cannot lead to procreation (including masturbation), and even to heterosexual intercourse in an unconventional position. As the excerpts below from the letters of Anselm attest, expressions of same-sex love could be highly eroticized even when no explicitly sexual element was acknowledged.

The reputation the English acquired in later centuries as being less romantically inclined than, for example, the French or the Italians, may well have had no basis in fact in any age; the views on this matter expressed by an Italian traveler in the late fifteenth century may nevertheless be of interest.

⌘ ⌘ ⌘

Anglo-Saxon Laws

from The Laws of Æthelberht (c. 600 CE)

At the height of his power Æthelberht of Kent (560–616) controlled almost all of Britain south of the Humber River. With his permission Augustine of Canterbury began his missionary work during this period, and Æthelberht himself converted to Christianity, no doubt motivated in part by familiarity with the new faith: his wife Bertha was a Frankish Christian. His exposure to Christianity and the Latin culture that accompanied it was presumably the inspiration for the recording of his laws in writing, but Æthelberht's code of law contains few explicit references to Christianity. Æthelberht's laws were probably recorded some time around 600, though they survive only in a twelfth-century copy; they are the oldest extant vernacular laws in a Germanic language, and the earliest legal text from Britain. The laws set out an elaborate system of compensation for injury, varying according to the status of the injured person and the seriousness of the injury. Such monetary payments, called *wergild*, were meant to prevent the escalation of acts of revenge.

The translation is adapted from that of Dorothy Whitelock. See also Lisi Oliver, "The Laws of Æthelberht: A Student Edition," *Old English Newsletter* 38.1 (2004), 58–72, for a newly-edited text and very useful commentary.

16. If anyone lies with a maiden belonging to the king, he is to pay 50 shillings compensation. If she is a grinding slave,[1] he is to pay 25 shillings compensation; [if a slave of] the third [class], 12 shillings.

17. The king's *fedesl*[2] is to be paid for with 20 shillings.

18. If anyone kills a man on a nobleman's estate, he is to pay 12 shillings compensation.

19. If anyone lies with a nobleman's serving-woman, he is to pay 12 shillings compensation.[3]

20. A free peasant's protection is six shillings.

21. If anyone lies with a free peasant's serving-woman, he is to pay six shillings compensation; [if] with a slave-woman of the second [class], 50 *sceattas*; [if with one of] the third [class], 30 *sceattas*.[4] …

31. If a freeman lies with the wife of another freeman, he is to atone with his wergild,[5] and to obtain another wife with his own money, and bring her to the other's home. …

72. If a freewoman with control of a household[6] commits any misconduct, she is to pay 30 shillings compensation.

73. The compensation for [injury to] a maiden is to be as for a freeman.

---

[2] *fedesl*   The meaning of *fedesl* is not known; it may mean a boarder in the king's household, under royal protection. It may also refer to the duty of subjects to provide food and drink for the king; if one defaults on this obligation, he owes twenty shillings.

[3] *If anyone … compensation*   I.e., to the nobleman, not the woman.

[4] *sceattas*   In Kent at this period a *shilling* was a gold piece containing 20 *sceattas*; a *sceatta* was a smaller gold piece equal in weight to a grain of barley.

[5] *his wergild*   Or "her wergild"; the Old English is ambiguous. *Wergild* is the monetary valuation placed on the worth of an individual in order to assign compensation in the event of wrongdoing.

[6] The Old English words *friwif locbore* are not clearly understood. It has often been interpreted as referring to an unmarried young woman who did not need to bind up her hair; more recently it has been suggested that it refers to a woman "in charge of the locks," i.e., the provisions.

---

[1] *grinding slave*   A "grinding slave" was presumably one whose job it was to prepare meal from grain; she had a higher status than a simple house slave, but a lower status than the king's own slaves.

74. [Breach of] guardianship over a noble-born widow of the highest class is to be compensated for with 50 shillings; over one of the second class, with 20 shillings; over one of the third class, with 12 shillings; over one of the fourth, with six shillings.

75. If a man takes a widow who does not belong to him, the [penalty for breach of the] guardianship is to be doubled.

76. If anyone buys a maiden with a payment, if there is no fraud, then let the transaction stand. If, however, there is any fraud, she is to be taken back home, and he is to be given back his money. If she bears a living child, she is to inherit half the goods if her husband dies first. If she wishes to remain with the children,[1] she is to inherit half the goods. If she wishes to take [another] husband, [she is to inherit the same share] as a child. If she does not bear a child, [her] paternal kinsmen are to have [her] goods and the morning-gift.[2]

77. If anyone carries off a maiden by force, [he is to pay] to the owner[3] 50 shillings, and afterwards buy from the owner his consent [to the marriage]. If she is betrothed to another man at a [bride] price, he is to pay 20 shillings compensation. If a return [of the woman] takes place, [he is to pay] 35 shillings, and 15 shillings to the king.

78. If anyone lies with the woman of a poor freeman while her husband is alive, he is to pay a two-fold compensation.

---

[1] *If she wishes to remain with the children* I.e., after her husband's death. This phrase has sometimes been translated "if she wishes to go away with the children," but there is no real evidence for Anglo-Saxon divorce laws, and the sequence of ideas suggests that the translation offered here (which is that of Carole Hough in *Anglo-Saxon England* 23 [1994], 19–34, and Lisi Oliver) is more likely.

[2] *If she wishes to take … the morning-gift* This apparently means that the dowry originally paid by her paternal kin is returned, and they also keep the "morning gift" given to her by her husband when the marriage has been consummated.

[3] *owner* Or possibly "protector."

from The Laws of Cnut (c. 1021)

Cnut (r. 1016–35) was a Danish prince who defeated Æthelred in 1016 to become king of England; he was also king of Denmark from 1018 until his death in 1035. He secured the goodwill of the English and minimized opposition to his reign through strong policy, generous patronage, and a marriage to Emma, the widow of Æthelred. His law code was drafted in part by the homilist and archbishop Wulfstan. Though there is a much stronger Christian presence in these laws than in those of Æthelberht from some four centuries earlier, there are many points of similarity; the increasing strictness in the laws concerning the sexual conduct of women, however, suggests that the state was taking a greater interest in regulating the moral lives of its subjects.

51. If anyone commit adultery, let him make amends for it as the deed may be. It is a wicked adultery when a married man commits fornication with a single woman, and much worse with another's wife, or with a consecrated nun.

52. If anyone commit incest, let him make amends for it according to the degree of kinship [between them] with wergild or punishment or [by the forfeiture] of all his possessions. The cases are by no means alike whether a man lie with a sister, or with a distant relative.

53. If anyone rapes a widow, let him make amends for it with his wergild. If anyone rapes a maiden, let him make amends for it with his wergild.

54. If a woman commits adultery with another man while her husband is alive, and it becomes public, she shall be disgraced, and let her lawful husband have all that she possesses; and let her then lose both her nose and her ears: and if it be a prosecution,[4] and the attempt to refute it fails, let the bishop use his power, and judge severely.

---

[4] *If a woman commits adultery … prosecution* Presumably, if there is some doubt, as opposed to getting caught *in flagrante*.

55. If a married man commits adultery with his own slave, let him lose her, and make amends for himself to God and to men: and he who has a lawful wife, and also a concubine,[1] let no priest administer to him any of those rites which ought to be administered to a Christian man before he desist, and make amends as seriously as the bishop may instruct him; and let him ever afterwards desist from such things.

56. If foreigners will not correct their fornications,[2] let them be driven from the land with their possessions, departing in sin. ...

74. And let every widow continue husbandless for twelve months: afterwards let her choose what she wishes. And if she choooses a husband within the space of a year, then let her forfeit her morning-gift and all the possessions which she inherited through her first husband; and let the nearest kinsmen take the land and the possessions that she had before. And let the husband be liable for his wergild to the king, or to whomever has jurisdiction over him. And even if she is taken forcibly, let her forfeit the possessions, unless she be willing to go home again from the man, and never again be his. And let not a widow take the veil too hastily. And let every widow pay her heriot[3] without penalty within twelve months, unless it be convenient to her earlier.

75. And let no one compel either a woman or maiden to marry someone whom she herself dislikes, nor exchange her for money, unless he is willing to give anything voluntarily.[4]

---

[1] *lawful wife, and also a concubine* In the early Middle Ages a married man could legally have a concubine as a servant. Surprisingly, the church accepted such practices for many centuries, though it did not endorse them.

[2] *If foreigners will not correct their fornications* I.e., regularize their state as married couples.

[3] *heriot* A death-tax consisting of the return of the weapons with which a lord had outfitted his man. The heriot of a lesser-class thane in Wessex was a horse, its trappings, and a set of personal weapons (spear, shield, helmet, and coat of mail); in some parts of England this could be commuted into a cash payment.

[4] *And let no one compel ... unless he is willing to give anything voluntarily* I.e., unless a man is willing to offer money to the bride's family of his own accord.

"King Canute and Queen Aelfgyfu give the cross," from the *Liber Vitae* of New Minster (London, British Library, MS Stowe 944, Fol. 6r).

from The Canons of the Fourth Lateran Council (1215)

As discussed more fully elsewhere in this volume, the Fourth Lateran Council did much to regularize Christian law and practice. On the subject of marriage the Council devoted considerable space to the issue of consanguinity: to what degree should marriages between those related by blood be permitted? As the following articles detail, the Council was also at pains to extend and formalize the general authority of the church over marriage, and to combat the fairly widespread practice of priests having "wives" or concubines, a situation that, as the canon notes, was treated differently in different regions.

14. In order that the morals and general conduct of clerics may improve, let them all, particularly those in sacred orders, strive to live chastely and virtuously. Let them guard against every vice of desire, especially that on account of which the anger of God came from heaven upon the children of unbelief,[1] so that they may perform their duties in the sight of Almighty God with a pure heart and a chaste body. But lest the ease of obtaining pardon should become an incentive to do wrong, we decree that whoever may be found to indulge in the vice of incontinence shall, in proportion to the gravity of his sin, be punished in accordance with the canonical statutes. We command that these statutes be strictly and rigorously observed, so that if the fear of God does not restrain a man from evil, he may at least be held back from sin by an earthly punishment. If, therefore, anyone suspended for this reason should presume to celebrate the divine mysteries [i.e., perform mass], let him not only be deprived of his ecclesiastical benefices but for this twofold offense let him be forever deposed [from the priesthood]. Prelates who dare support such men in their iniquities, especially with an eye to money or other temporal advantages, shall be subject to a similar punishment. But those who, in accordance with the practice of their region, have not renounced the marriage bond should be punished more severely if they fall into the vice of impurity, since they can lawfully be married.

51. Since the prohibition against marriage in the three remotest degrees has been revoked, we wish it to be strictly observed in the other degrees. Following in the footsteps of our predecessors, we altogether forbid clandestine marriages and we forbid any priest to presume to be present at such a marriage. Extending the special custom of certain regions to other regions generally, we decree that when marriages are to be contracted they shall be publicly announced in the churches by priests, with a suitable time being fixed beforehand within which whoever wishes and is able to may adduce a lawful impediment. The priests themselves shall also investigate whether there is any impediment. When there appears a credible reason why the marriage should not be contracted, the contract shall be expressly forbidden until there has been established from clear documents what ought to be done in the matter. If any persons presume to enter into clandestine marriages of this kind, or forbidden marriages within a prohibited degree, even if done in ignorance, the offspring of the union shall be deemed illegitimate and shall have no help from their parents' ignorance, since the parents in contracting the marriage could be considered as not devoid of knowledge, or even as affecters of ignorance. Likewise the offspring shall be deemed illegitimate if both parents know of a legitimate impediment and yet dare to contract a marriage in the presence of the church, contrary to every prohibition. Moreover the parish priest who refuses to forbid such unions, or even any member of the regular clergy who dares to attend them, shall be suspended from office for three years and shall be punished even more severely if the nature of the fault requires it. Those who presume to be united in this way, even if it is within a permitted degree, are to be given a suitable penance. Anybody who maliciously proposes an impediment in order to prevent a legitimate marriage will not escape the church's vengeance.

---

[1] *children of unbelief* The inhabitants of Sodom and Gomorrah, whose destruction is told in Genesis 19.

en vn lit enfamble.

Lancelot and Guinevere in bed, from
Le Livre de Lancelot del Lac (c. 1316, f. 312v).

from Andreas Capellanus, *The Art of Courtly Love* (c. 1180)

The Art of Courtly Love (in Latin, *De Amore*) was one of the most wide-ranging and influential treatises on the subject, although it should not be taken at face value as a depiction of social practices at the time. Andreas addressed the work to a young man named Walter, promising to make known to him "the way in which a state of love between two lovers may be kept unharmed, and likewise how those who do not love may get rid of the darts of Venus that are in their hearts." Little is known of Andreas himself, though he is believed to have been a chaplain with some connection to the court of Marie de Champagne. The work is divided into three books, the first of which offers a wide range of definitions and descriptions as well as a series of entertaining dialogues between men trying to seduce women and the women who cleverly fend them off, the second advice on how to behave in a love affair, and the third (under the heading "The Rejection of Love") reasons why one should in fact never conduct love affairs of the sort described in the second book.

from BOOK 1

Chapter 1. What Love Is

Love is a certain inborn suffering derived from the sight of and excessive meditation upon the beauty of the opposite sex, which causes each one to wish above all things the embraces of the other and by common desire to carry out all of love's precepts in the other's embrace.

Chapter 3. Where Love Gets Its Name

Love gets its name *(amor)* from the word for hook *(amus),* which means "to capture" or "to be captured," for he who is in love is captured in the chains of desire and wishes to capture someone else with his hook. Just as a skillful fisherman tries to attract fishes by his bait and to capture them on his crooked hook, so the man who is a captive of love tries to attract another person by his allurements and exerts all his efforts to unite two different hearts with an intangible bond, or if they are already united he tries to keep them so forever.

Chapter 4. What the Effect of Love Is

Now it is the effect of love that a true lover cannot be degraded with any avarice. Love causes a rough and uncouth man to be distinguished for his handsomeness; it can endow a man even of the humblest birth with nobility of character; it blesses the proud with humility; and the man in love becomes accustomed to performing many services gracefully for everyone. O what a wonderful thing is love, which makes a man shine with so many virtues and teaches everyone, no matter who he is, so many good traits of character! There is another thing about love that we should not praise in few words: it adorns a man, so to speak, with the virtue of chastity, because he who shines with the light of one love can hardly think of embracing another woman, even a beautiful one. For when he thinks deeply of his beloved the sight of any other woman seems to his mind rough and rude.

Chapter 8. The Love of Nuns

You may be interested enough to ask what we have to say regarding the love of nuns. What we say is that their solaces must be absolutely avoided just as though they were a pestilence of the soul, because from them comes the great wrath of our heavenly Father and the civil authorities are greatly stirred up and threaten the most severe punishments, and by all of this we become infamous among men and our good reputation is destroyed. Even Love's commandment warns us not to choose for our love any woman whom we may not properly seek to marry.[1] ...

Chapter 9. Love Got with Money

Now let us see whether real love can be got with money or any other gift. Real love comes only from the affection of the heart and is granted out of pure grace and genuine liberality, and this most precious gift of love cannot be paid for at any set price or be cheapened by a matter of money. If any woman is so possessed with a feeling of avarice as to give herself to a lover for the sake of pay, let no one consider her a lover, but rather a counterfeiter of love, who ought to join those shameful women in the brothel. Indeed the wantonness of such women is more polluted than the passion of harlots who ply their trade openly, for they do what one expects them to, and they deceive no one since their intentions are perfectly obvious. But those others who pretend to be fine ladies of the very best breeding force men to languish for love of them, and under the false veil of affection they gleefully rob of all their wealth those who have been smitten by Cupid's arrow. Men are deceived by their fallacious looks, outwitted by their crafty beckonings, and impelled by their clever and deceitful demands; they are kept busy giving them as many good things as they can, and they get more pleasure out of what they give away than from what they keep for their own use. These women have all sorts of ways of asking for things, and so long as they see that a man can respond to their greedy desire for gifts, they say that he is their adored lover, and they never cease to drain away his property or ruin him by their constant demands. But when his substance is gone and his patrimony is exhausted they despise and hate him and cast him aside like an unproductive bee, and then they begin to appear

in their real colors. Any man who would seek for the love of women like these ought to be classed with shameless dogs and deserves no help from anybody. ...

Chapter 11. The Love of Peasants

But lest you should consider that what we have already said about the love of the middle class applies also to farmers, we will add a little about their love. We say that it rarely happens that we find farmers serving in Love's court, but naturally, like a horse or a mule, they give themselves up to the work of Venus, as nature's urging teaches them to do. For a farmer hard labor and the uninterrupted solaces of plough and mattock are sufficient. And even if it should happen at times, though rarely, that contrary to their nature they are stirred up by Cupid's arrows, it is not expedient that they should be instructed in the theory of love, lest while they are devoting themselves to conduct which is not natural to them the kindly farms which are usually made fruitful by their efforts may through lack of cultivation prove useless to us. And if you should, by some chance, fall in love with some of their women, be careful to puff them up with lots of praise and then, when you find a convenient place, do not hesitate to take what you seek and to embrace them by force. For you can hardly soften their outward inflexibility so far that they will grant you their embraces quietly or permit you to have the solaces you desire unless first you use a little compulsion as a convenient cure for their shyness. We do not say these things, however, because we want to persuade you to love such women, but only so that, if through lack of caution you should be driven to love them, you may know, in brief compass, what to do.

from BOOK 2: THE RULES OF LOVE

1. Marriage is no real excuse for not loving.
2. He who is not jealous cannot love.
3. No one can be bound by a double love.
4. It is well known that love is always increasing or decreasing.
5. That which a lover takes against the will of his beloved has no relish.
6. Boys do not love until they arrive at the age of maturity.

---

[1] *Even Love's commandment ... properly seek to marry* As will become clear below, Andreas does not here include women who are already married; instead, he means those whom, for reasons of class, religious status, or moral shortcomings, a man would avoid marrying on principle.

7. When one lover dies, a widowhood of two years is required of the survivor.

8. No one should be deprived of love without the very best of reasons.

9. No one can love unless he is impelled by the persuasion of love.

10. Love is always a stranger in the home of avarice.

11. It is not proper to love any woman whom one should be ashamed to seek to marry.

12. A true lover does not desire to embrace in love anyone except his beloved.

13. When made public love rarely endures.

14. The easy attainment of love makes it of little value; difficulty of attainment makes it prized.

15. Every lover regularly turns pale in the presence of his beloved.

16. When a lover suddenly catches sight of his beloved his heart palpitates.

17. A new love puts to flight an old one.

18. Good character alone makes any man worthy of love.

19. If love diminishes, it quickly fails and rarely revives.

20. A man in love is always apprehensive.

21. Real jealousy always increases the feeling of love.

22. Jealousy, and therefore love, are increased when one suspects his beloved.

23. He whom the thought of love vexes, eats and sleeps very little.

24. Every act of a lover ends within the thought of his beloved.

25. A true lover considers nothing good except what he thinks will please his beloved.

26. Love can deny nothing to love.

27. A lover can never have enough of the solaces of his beloved.

28. A slight presumption causes a lover to suspect his beloved.

29. A man who is vexed by too much passion usually does not love.

30. A true lover is constantly and without intermission possessed by the thought of his beloved.

31. Nothing forbids one woman being loved by two men or one man by two women.

Anonymous, Images of Troubadours: illustrations for a song by Bernart de Ventadorn (13th century). The figure here is believed to be Bernart.

Royal Couples

For the first century and a half after the Norman conquest most English monarchs were buried in their French territories, not their English ones. The first illustration below shows the tombs at the abbey of Fontevrault of Henry II (on the right), Eleanor of Aquitaine (in the center), and their son Richard I the Lion-Hearted (on the left). Eleanor and Henry's son John, who also became king of England, was buried at Worcester Cathedral, but the tomb of his wife, Isabella of Angoulême, is at Fontevrault.

The second illustration is of two of the Lewes chess pieces, found on the island of Lewes in Scotland's Outer Hebrides in the early nineteenth century. Carvings in the same style have also been found in Scandinavia and East Anglia; it is not known whether the carvings were made in Scandinavia or in Britain.

The tombs of the Plantagenets at Fontrevault.   Lewes Chess Pieces: King and Queen (12th century).

from Christine de Pizan, "Seulete sui" (Alone I am) (c. 1395)

Christine de Pizan (1365–c. 1429) is sometimes considered the first professional woman writer. The daughter of an Italian physician and astrologer who served at the court of the French King Charles V, she lost her father in the late 1380s and her beloved husband, Etienne de Castel, in 1390, after fifteen years of marriage. Left with three children and other family members to support, she began to write lyric poetry in the early 1390s and, later, many other works including proverbs and moral instruction, dream visions on governance and universal history, advice to princes, a biography of Charles V, and works defending women's moral virtue and intelligence; the best known of the latter is her *Book of the City of Ladies* (c. 1404). "Seulete sui" ("Alone I am") is one of her early lyrics and reflects both her sorrow at the loss of her husband and her ability to express that sorrow in a form that gained her patronage and respect in France and England, where many of her works were translated and enjoyed great popularity throughout the fifteenth century.

Seulete sui[1]

Seulete sui et seulete vueil estre,   Alone I am and alone I wish to be,
Seulete m'a mon douz ami laissiee;   Alone has my sweet friend left me;
Seulete sui, sanz compaignon ne maistre,   Alone I am, without companion or teacher,
Seulete sui, dolente et courrouciee,   Alone I am, sorrowful and in distress,
Seulete sui, en langueur mesaisiee,   Alone I am, languishing in wretchedness,
Seulete sui, plus que nulle esgaree,   Alone I am, more lost than anyone,
Seulete sui, sanz ami demouree.   *Alone I am, left without a friend.*
Seulete sui a uis ou a fenestre,   Alone I am at the door or at the window,

5

---
[1] *Seulete sui*   Text from Marcel Braunschvig, ed. *Notre Littérature étudiée dans les textes.*

10 Seulete sui en un anglet muciee,
Seulete sui pour moi de pleurs repaistre,
Seulete sui, dolente ou apaisiee;
Seulete sui, rien n'est qui tant messiee;
Seulete suis, en ma chambre enserree,
Seulete sui, sanz ami demouree.

Alone I am, hidden in a corner,
Alone I am, to nourish myself with tears,
Alone I am, sorrowing or calm;
Alone I am, there is nothing that goes so badly;
Alone I am, shut up in my room,
Alone I am, left without a friend.

15 Seulete sui partout et en tout estre;
Seulete sui, ou je voise ou je siee;
Seulete sui plus qu'aultre riens terrestre,
Seulete sui, de chascun delaissiee,
Seulete sui durement abaissiee,
20 Seulete sui, souvent toute esplouree,
Seulete sui, sanz ami demouree.

Alone I am everywhere and in every place;
Alone I am, whether I go or stay;
Alone I am, more than any earthly thing,
Alone I am, abandoned by everyone,
Alone I am, drooping woefully,
Alone I am, often drowning in tears,
Alone I am, left without a friend.

Prince, or est ma douleur commenciee:
Seulete sui, de tout deuil manaciee,
Seulete sui, plus teinte que moree:
Seulete sui, sanz ami demouree.

Prince, now my sorrow has begun:
Alone I am, threatened with every sadness,
Alone I am, duller than deep purple,
Alone I am, left without a friend.

from *The Paston Letters*

A large body of the fifteenth-century correspondence of the Paston family of Norfolk has survived; it is a rich source of information about many aspects of English life in this period.

The first of the two letters below concerns twenty-year old Elizabeth Paston (referred to by the letter-writer, Elizabeth Clere, as "my cousin your sister"), whose family wished her to marry fifty-year old Stephen Scrope. (In the end the marriage did not occur, though at one point Elizabeth indicated a willingness to accede to the family's demands.)

The second letter concerns the clandestine marriage a generation later of Margery Paston to Richard Calle, the family steward. Such marriages were deeply disapproved of, particularly when, as in this case, there was a considerable difference in social standing between the two participants. The church did consider such unions to be valid, however, unless it could be shown after the fact that some "impediment" existed, such as the two being too closely related or one being already married.

from Letter from Agnes Paston to her son John Paston I (not later than 1449)

Son, I greet you well with God's blessing and mine and to let you know that my cousin [Elizabeth] Clere wrote to me that she has spoken with [Stephen] Scrope after he had been with me at Norwich, and told her what hospitality I had given him, and he said to her he very much liked the reception I gave him.

He told my cousin Clere that unless you gave him a warm reception and comforting words at London, he would speak no more of the matter.

My cousin Clere thinks that it would be folly to forsake him unless you knew of another as good or better; and I have consulted your sister and I've never found her so willing toward anyone as she is to him, if it be the case that his land stands clear.[1] ...

---

[1] *land stands clear* I.e., is not pledged as collateral on a debt.

original spelling

Soon, I grete ȝow wel wyth Goddys blyssyng and myn; and I latte ȝow wette þat my cosyn Clere wrytted to me þat sche spake wyth Schrowpe aftyre þat he had byen wyth me at Norwyche, and tolde here what chere þat I had made hym; and he seyde to here he lyked wel by þe chere þat I made hym. He had swyche wordys to my cosyn Clere þat lesse þan ȝe made hym good chere and ȝaf hym wordys of conforth at London he wolde no more speke of þe matyre. My cosyn Clere thynkyth þat it were a foly to forsake hym lesse þan ȝe knew of on owdyre as good ore bettere, and I haue assayde ȝowre sustere and I fonde here neuer so wylly to noon as sche is to hym, ȝyf it be so þat his londe stande cleere. I sent ȝow a letter by Brawnton fore sylke and fore þis matyre be-fore my cosyn Clere wrote to me, þe qwyche was wrytten on þe Wednysday nexȝt aftyre Mydsomere Day. Ser Herry Ynglows is ryȝth besy a-bowt Schrowpe fore on of his doȝthteres. I prey ȝow fore-ȝette noȝth to brynge me my mony fro Horwelbery as ȝe com fro London, edyre all ore a grete parte. þe dew dette was at Crystemesse last paste, no thynge a-lowyd, vij li. xiiij s. viij d., and at þis Mydsomere it is v li. more; and thow I a-low hym all his askyng it is but xxvj s. vj d. lesse, but I am noȝth so avysyth ȝytt. As fore þe frere, he hath byen at Sent Benettys and at Norwyche, and made grete bowste of þe sewte þat he hath a-ȝens me, and bowȝthe many boxes, to what jntent I wett neuer. It is well doen to be ware at London in drede ȝyf he bryng ony syse at Sent Margaretys tyme. I kan no more, but Almyȝty God be owre good lorde, who have ȝow euer in kepyng. Wryten at Oxnede in grete hast on þe Satyr-[day] next aftyre Mydsomere. By ȝowre modyre A. P.

from Letter from Richard Calle to Margery Paston (1469)

My own lady and mistress, and before God my very true wife, with a heart full of sorrow I recommend me to you, as one that cannot be merry, nor shall be until it be otherwise with us than it now is. For this life that we now lead is neither pleasing to God nor to the world, considering the great bond of matrimony that is between us, and also the great love that has been, and I trust is still between us, and on my part has never been greater. On this account I beseech almighty God to comfort us as soon as it pleases him, for we who ought by right to be together are torn apart; it seems to me that it is a thousand years since I spoke with you. I would rather be with you than have all the goods in the world. Alas, alas, good lady, consider little them and what they do to keep us apart. Four times in the year they who obstruct matrimony are cursed. It causes many men to reflect inwardly who have a great conscience in matters other than matrimony. But, lady, suffer as you must and make merry as you can, for certainly, lady, in the long run God will from his righteousness help his servants who mean well and wish to live according to his laws, etc.

I understand, lady, that you have had as much sorrow for me as any gentlewoman has had in the world. I wish to God that all the sorrow that you have had rested upon me, so that you would be free of it. For certainly, lady, it is like death for me to hear that you are being treated otherwise than you ought to be. This is a painful life that we lead. I cannot live thus without it being a great displeasure to God.

Also, I would like you to know that I had sent you a letter from London by my lad, and he told me he was not allowed to speak with you, and was made to wait there for you a long time. He told me that John Thresher came to him in your name and said that you sent him to my lad for a letter or a token which I should have sent you. But he didn't trust him and he would not deliver anything to him. After that he brought him a ring, saying that you sent it to him, commanding him that he should deliver the letter or token to him, which I have affirmed by my lad was not sent by you, but was sent by my mistress and on Sir James Gloys' advice. Alas, what do they intend? I suppose that they consider us not to be pledged together. And if they think that, I am amazed, for then they are not well advised, remembering the plainness with which I broke the matter to my mistress at the very beginning, and I suppose by you as well, if you did as you ought to have done by right. And if you have done the contrary, as I have been informed you have done, you did it neither from conscience nor to God's pleasure, unless you did it from fear and to please for the time those who were around you. And if you did so for this reason it was a reasonable cause, considering the great and unbearable demands you had, and the many untrue tales being told you about me, which God knows I was never guilty of.

My lad told me that my mistress your mother asked him if he had brought any letter to you, and she insinuated many other things to him. Among all the others she said to him, that I would not tell her about it at the beginning but she supposed I would at the end. And as to that, God knows she knew of it first from me and no other. I do not know what her ladyship means, for upon my word there is no gentlewoman alive whom my heart cherishes more than her, nor is more loathe to displease, except only your person, which by right I ought to cherish and love best, for I am bound to you by the law of God, and so I will do while I am alive, whatsoever results from it. I suppose if you told them plainly the truth they would not damn their souls for us. Although I tell them the truth, they will not believe me as well as they will you. And therefore, good lady, at the reverence of God be plain to them and tell the truth. And if they will by no means agree to it, it will be between God, the devil, and them, and the peril that we should be in, I beg God that it may lie on them and not upon us. I am grieving and sorry to remember their disposition. God send them grace to guide all things well, as well as I wish they did. God be their guide, and send them peace and rest, etc.

I marvel greatly that they should take this matter so hard, as I understand they do, remembering that it is a situation that cannot be remedied. My desire on behalf of everyone is for it to be thought there is no obstacle against it and also that their honor is not in your marriage; it is in their own marriage, which I pray God send them such as may be to their honor and pleasing to God, and to ease their hearts, for otherwise it would be a great pity. Mistress, I am afraid to write to you, for I understand you have shown my letters that I have sent you previously, but I ask you to let no one see this letter. As soon as you have read it, let it be burned for I wish that no man should see it in any way. You have had no letters from me for these two years, nor will I send you any more. Therefore I send this whole matter to your wisdom. Almighty Jesus preserve, keep, and give you your heart's desire, which I know well to be God's pleasure, etc.

This letter was written with as great pain as was anything I ever wrote, I think, in my whole life, for in good faith I have been sick and am not yet very well recovered, God amend it, etc.

from William Langland, *The Vision of Piers the Plowman* (late 14th century)

Langland's fiercely satirical poem speaks out against many abuses, including the corruption of many members of the clergy, and also comments on many aspects of the social world of his time, from professions to education to church practice. The following excerpt discusses and offers advice concerning love and marriage, and shows an approval of and interest in ordinary married people ("true wedded living folk") that is in line with much of the poem's view of the laity as potential models of Christian behavior, although, typically for Langland, it also has much to say about lay failings.

In this world is Do-well true wedded living folk,
   For they mote° work and win and the world *must*
     sustain.
For of hir° kind they come that confessors *this*
    been nempned°, *called*
Kings and knights, kaysers° and clerks°, *rulers / clerics*
5 Maidens and martyrs—out of one man come.
The wife was made the wye° for to help work, *man*
And thus was wedlock wrought with a mene° *intermediary*
    person—
First by the father's will and the friends' counsel,
And sithenes° by assent of himself, as they two *then*
    might accord,° *agree*
10 And thus was wedlock wrought, and God himself
    it made;° *made it*
In earth the heaven is—himself was the witness.
   Ac° false folk faithless, thieves and liars, *but*
Wasters and wretches out of wedlock, I trowe,° *believe*
Conceived been in evil time, as Cain was on Eve.
15 Of switch° sinful shrews° the *such / wretches*
    Sauter° maketh mind: *psalter*

Concepit dolorem et peperit iniquitatem[1]
And all that come of that Cain[2] come to evil end.
    For God sent to Seth and said by° an angel,   *through*
'Thine issue in thine issue, I will that they be wedded,
20 And not thy kind with Cain's coupled ne° spoused.' *nor*
Yet some, against the sonde° of our   *commandment*
    saviour of heaven,
Cain's kind and his° kind coupled together—   *their*
Till God wrathed° with hir° works, and *grew angry / their*
    such a word said,
'That I maked man, now it me forthinketh.'[3]
25 *Penitet me fecisse hominem.*[4]
    And came to Noah anon° and bade him   *at once*
    nought let:[5]
'Swith° go shape a ship of shides² and *quickly / planks*
    of boards.
Thyself and thy sons three and sithen your wifes,
Busketh° you to that boat and bideth° therein *hurry / stay*
30 Till forty days be fulfilled, that flood have washed
Clean away the cursed blood° that Cain   *lineage*
    hath maked.
    'Beasts that now been shall ban° the time   *curse*
That ever that cursed Cain come on this earth.
All shall die for his deeds by dales and hills,
35 And the fowls that fly forth with other beasts,
Except oonliche° of each kind a couple   *only*
That in thy shingled ship shall be saved.'
    Here abought° the bairns the belsires'   *paid for*
    guilts,°   *ancestors' sins*
And all for hir forefathers they fared the worst.
40 The gospel is hereagainst in o degree,[6] I find:
Filius non portabit iniquitatem patris et pater non portabit
    iniquitatem filii.[7]
Ac I find, if the father be false and a shrew,°   *wretch*

That somdel° the son shall have the sire's   *somewhat*
    tacches.°   *qualities*
Impe° on an alder, and if thine apple be sweet   *graft*
45 Muchel° marvel me thinketh; and more of a shrew *much*
That bringeth forth any bairn, but if he be the same
And have a savour after the sire —selde seestow other:[8]
Numquam colligunt de spinis uvas nec de tribulis ficus.[9]
    And thus through cursed Cain came care°   *trouble*
    upon earth,
50 And all for° they wrought wedlock against   *because*
    God's will.
Forthi have they maugre of their marriages, that marry
    so their children.[10]
For some, as I see now, sooth° for to tell   *truth*
For coveting of cattle unkindly been wedded.[11]
As careful° conception cometh of swich   *sorrowful*
    marriages
55 As befell other folk that I before of told.[12]
For good should wed good, though° they no   *even if*
    goods have;
'I am *via et veritas*,'[13] saith Christ. 'I may advance all.'
    It is an uncomely couple, by Christ! as me
    thinketh–
To yeven° a young wench to an old feeble° *give / weak man*
60 Or wed any widow for wealth of her goods
That never shall bairn bear but if it be in arms![14]
In jealousy joyless and jangling° on bed,   *quarreling*
Many a pair sithen° the pestilence have   *since*
    plight° them together.   *joined*
The fruits that they bring forth are many foul words;
65 Have they no children but cheeste° and   *fighting*
    chops° them between …   *blows*

---

[1] *Concepit dolorem et peperit iniquitatem* Latin: He has conceived sorrow, and brought forth iniquity.

[2] *all that come of that Cain* All of Cain's descendants.

[3] *it me forthinketh* I regret it.

[4] *Penitet me fecisse hominem* Latin: I regret that I created humankind.

[5] *bade him nought let* Told him not to delay.

[6] *hereagainst in o degree* Against this in one way.

[7] *Filius non portabit iniquitatem patris et pater non portabit iniquitatem filii* The son shall not bear the father's iniquity, and the father shall not carry the son's iniquity.

[8] *have a savour … other* Taste like (i.e., have qualities like) his parent—you seldom see [it happen] otherwise.

[9] *Numquam colligunt de spinis uvas nec de tribulis ficus* Latin: Men never gather grapes from thorn bushes, or figs from thistles.

[10] *Forthi … their children* Thus those who allow their children to be married in this way will be blamed for their marriages.

[11] *For coveting of cattle unkindly been wedded* Out of a desire for wealth have married unnaturally.

[12] *As befell other folk that I before of told* As happened to the people that I told of before (i.e., those that were destroyed in the Flood).

[13] *via et veritas* Latin: the way and the truth.

[14] *never shall bairn bear but if it be in arms* Never shall bear a child except by carrying it in her arms.

Forthi° I counsel all Christians covet not [to] be
      wedded   *therefore*
For coveting of cattle ne of kindred rich;
Ac maidens and maydens,° match you   *bachelors*
      together;
Widowers and widows, work the same;
70 For no lands, but for love, look ye be wedded,
And then get ye the grace of God, and goods enough to
      live with.
      And every manner secular° that may not   *layperson*
         continue [chaste],
Wisely go wed, and ware° him[1] from sin;   *guard*
For lechery in liking is limeyard of hell.[2]
75 Whiles thou art young, and thy weapon keen,°   *sharp*
Wreak° thee with wiving, if thou   *give vent to [your lust]*
      will be excused;[3]
Dum sis vir fortis, ne des tua robora scortis.
Scribitur in portis, meretrix est ianua mortis.[4]
      "When you have wived, be wary, and work in
         time[5] —
80 Not as Adam and Eve when Cain was engendered.
For in un-time, truly, between man and woman
Ne should no bed-board be: but if they both were clean
Of life and in soul, and in law also,
That ilk derne° deed do no man ne should.   *private, secret*
85 Ac if they lead thus their life, it liketh° God   *pleases*
      almighty,
For he made wedlock first and himself it said:
Bonum est ut unusquisque uxorem suam habeat propter
      fornicacionem.[6]

---

[1] *ware him* Guard himself from.

[2] *For lechery ... of hell* For taking pleasure in lechery is the snare
of hell.

[3] *if thou will be excused* If you want an excuse [for your lustful
behavior].

[4] *Dum sis vir fortis, ne des tua robora scortis. Scribitur in portis,
meretrix est ianua mortis* Latin: While you are a strong man, do not
give your strength to harlots. For as it is written on the gates, a
harlot is the entrance to death.

[5] *work in time* Have sex at the proper time.

[6] *Bonum est ut unusquisque uxorem suam habeat propter
fornicacionem* Latin: It is good that every man have his own wife
in order to avoid fornication.

"That othergates been gotten, for gedelings are
      holden,[7]
And false folk, fondlings,° faitours° and   *bastards / deceivers*
      liars,
90 Ungracious° to get good or love of the   *unsuccessful (at)*
      people;
Wander and waste what they catch mowe.°   *can acquire*
Against Do-well they do evil and the devil serve,
And after hir death-day shall dwell with the same
But° God give them grace here themselves to   *unless*
      amend."

from Robert Grosseteste (attr.), *Speculum Confessionis* (early 13th century)

The work on confession in which the following
passages appear is attributed to Robert Grosseteste,
Bishop of Lincoln from 1235 to 1253. One of the
most important thinkers and church leaders of his
day, he left important writings in both science and
theology and demanded a high level of learning
from the clergy under his direction. The *Speculum*
reflects the self-scrutiny that confession required of
the penitent.

Often I stroked forbidden members, shameful
members, both on me and on others ... often I
returned my hand to my lap, caressing the flesh and
weakening it and rendering it more prone to titillation
and excitement from touches of this kind. [...] I also
oftentimes provoked others to evil, either by a light
touch or more brashly and irreverently, because I
exposed myself to him, showing him my erection, or by
a gesture of my body, or by some other means which is
too disgusting to mention, whence those who were
previously innocent afterwards, at my provocation, were
violently tempted or perhaps cast down, and this
because of me.

---

[7] *That othergates ... holden* Those who are otherwise begotten
(i.e., are born out of wedlock) are considered vagabonds.

from Eadmer, *The Life of Saint Anselm* (early 12th century)

Anselm of Bec, who was born in Italy, later became abbot at a monastery in Normandy, Archbishop of Canterbury, and one of the most respected theologians of the age. Anselm was a defender of the then-common practice of oblation, in which families placed children in the care of religious houses as oblates or "offerings"—a move that was generally binding on the child for life. He was also, however, a voice of moderation on the issue of how the boys should be treated.

The language that Anselm and other monks sometimes employed with one another may strike modern readers as homoerotic, but would probably not have been read in the same fashion in the eleventh or early twelfth centuries. Anselm sometimes used a similarly fervid devotional style both in addressing female correspondents and in speaking of the Virgin Mary—and numerous others followed his lead. The wording of the Benedictine Rule, however, is perhaps an indication that the possibility of overtly sexual behavior between males was tacitly acknowledged.

1.4 *How he left his native land because of his father's great hostility to him*

From that time, with health of body, youth, and worldly well-being smiling upon him, he began little by little to cool in the fervor of his desire for a religious life—so much so that he began to desire to go the way of the world rather than to leave the world for a monastic life. He gradually turned from study, which had formerly been his chief occupation, and began to give himself up to youthful amusements. His love and reverence for his mother held him back to some extent from these paths, but she died and then the ship of his heart had as it were lost its anchor and drifted almost entirely among the waves of the world. But almighty God, foreseeing what he was going to make of him, stirred up for him a hateful and domestic strife, lest in enjoying a transitory peace he should lose his soul. That

is to say, he stirred up in his father's mind so keen a hatred against him that he persecuted him as much, or even more, for the things he did well as for those which he did ill. Nor could he soften his father by any degree of humility, but the more humble he showed himself towards his father, the sharper did he feel his father's anger towards him. When he saw that this was becoming more than he could bear, he feared that worse might come of it, and he chose rather to renounce both his patrimony and his country than to bring some disgrace upon either himself or his father by continuing to live with him. He gathered together those things that were necessary for the journey, and left his country, with a clerk as his companion and servant. As they were crossing Mount Cenis, he grew weary and his strength failed him, being unequal to the toil. He tried to revive himself by eating snow, for there was nothing else at hand that he could eat. His servant was grieved to see this and began to make a careful search in the bag that was carried on the ass's back to see if by chance there was anything to eat. Soon, against all expectation, he found some bread of exceptional whiteness and, having eaten and been refreshed, Anselm set out once more on the road with renewed strength....

1.11 *The reason for his giving more attention to the training of young men than of others*

Nevertheless his chief care was for the youths and young men, and when men asked him why this was, he replied by way of a simile. He compared the time of youth to a piece of wax of the right consistency for the impress of a seal. "For if the wax," he said, "is too hard or too soft it will not, when stamped with the seal, receive a perfect image. But if it preserves a mean between these extremes of hardness and softness, when it is stamped with the seal, it will receive the image clear and whole. So it is with the ages of men. Take a man who has been sunk in the vanity of this world from infancy to extreme old age, knowing only earthly things, and altogether set in these ways. Converse with such a man about spiritual things, talk to him about the fine points of divine contemplation, show him how to explore heavenly mysteries, and you will find he cannot see the things you wish him to. And no wonder. He is the hardened wax; his life has not moved in these paths; he has learnt to follow other ways. Now consider a boy of tender years and little knowledge, unable to distinguish between good and evil, or even to understand you when you talk about such things. Here indeed the wax is soft, almost liquid, and incapable of taking an image of the seal. Between these extremes is the youth and young man, aptly tempered between the extremes of softness and hardness. If you teach him, you can shape him as you wish. Realizing this, I watch over the young men with greater solicitude, taking care to nip all their faults in the bud, so that being afterwards properly instructed in the practice of holy exercises they may form themselves in the image of a spiritual man." ...

1.22 *Concerning the discretion that he taught a certain abbot to practice toward boys who were being educated in his school*

On one occasion then, a certain abbot, who was considered to be a sufficiently religious man, was talking with him about matters of monastic discipline, and among other things he said something about the boys brought up in the cloister, adding: "What, I ask you, is to be done with them? They are incorrigible ruffians. We never give over beating them day and night, and they only get worse and worse." Anselm replied with astonishment: "You never give over beating them? And what are they like when they grow up?" "Stupid brutes," he said. To which Anselm retorted, "You have spent your energies in rearing them to good purpose: from men you have reared beasts." "But what can we do about it?" he said. "We use every means to force them to get better, but without success." "You force them? Now tell me, my lord abbot, if you plant a tree-shoot in your garden, and straightway shut it in on every side so that it has no space to put out its branches, what kind of tree will you have in after years when you let it out of its confinement?" "A useless one, certainly, with its branches all twisted and knotted." "And whose fault would this be, except your own for shutting it in so unnaturally? Without doubt, this is what you do with your boys. At their oblation they are planted in the garden of the church, to grow and bring forth fruit for God. But you terrify them and hem them in on all sides with threats and blows so that they are utterly deprived of their liberty. And being thus injudiciously oppressed, they harbor and welcome and nurse within themselves evil and crooked thoughts like thorns, and cherish these thoughts so passionately that they doggedly reject everything which could minister to their correction. Hence, feeling no love or pity, good-will or tenderness in your attitude towards them, they have in future no faith in your goodness but believe that all your actions proceed from hatred and malice against them. The deplorable result is that as they grow in body so their hatred increases, together with their apprehension of evil, and they are forward in all crookedness and vice. They have been brought up in no true charity towards anyone, so they regard everyone with suspicion and jealousy." ...

from Letters of Anselm to fellow monks (late 11th century)

Brother Anselm to Dom Gilbert, brother, friend, beloved lover [*dilecto dilectori*] ... sweet to me, sweetest friend, are the gifts of sweetness, but they cannot begin to console my desolate heart for want of your love. Even if you sent every scent of perfume, every glitter of metal, every precious gem, every texture of clothes, still it would not make up to my soul for this separation unless it returned the separated half. The anguish of my heart just thinking about this bears witness, as do the tears dimming my eyes and wetting my face and the fingers writing this. You recognized, as I do know, my love for you, but I did not. Our separation from one another has shown me how much I love you; a man does not in fact have knowledge of good and evil unless he has experienced both. Not having experienced your absences, I did not realize how sweet it was to be with you and how bitter it was to be without you. But you have gained from our separation the company of someone else, whom you love no less—or even more—than [you love] me; while I have lost you, and there is no one to take your place. You are thus enjoying your consolation, while nothing is left to me but heartbreak.

[Anselm] To Gondulph— I put no other or longer salutations at the head of my letter, because I can say nothing more to him whom I love. All who know Gondulph and Anselm know well what this means, and how much love is understood in these two names. ... How could I forget thee? Can a man forget one who is placed like a seal upon his heart? In thy silence I know that thou lovest me; and thou also, when I say nothing, thou knowest that I love thee. Not only have I no doubt of thee, but I answer for thee that thou art sure of me. What can my letter tell thee that thou knowest not already, thou who art my second soul? Go into the secret place of thy heart, look there at thy love for me, and thou shalt see mine for thee. ... Thou knewest how much I love thee, but I knew it not. He who has separated us has alone instructed me how dear to me thou wert. No, I knew not before the experience of thy absence how sweet it was to have thee, how bitter to have thee not. Thou hast another friend whom thou hast loved as much or more than me to console thee, but I have no longer thee, thou understandest? and nothing to replace thee. Those who rejoice in the possession of thee may perhaps be offended by what I say. Ah, I let them content themselves with their joy, and permit me to weep for him whom I ever love.

from *The Rule of Saint Benedict*, Chapter 22: How the Brothers [or Sisters] Are to Sleep

Let each one sleep in a separate bed. Let them receive bedding suitable to their manner of life, according to the abbot's directions. If possible let all sleep in one place; but if the number does not allow this, let them take their rest by tens or twenties with the seniors who have charge of them.

A candle shall be kept burning in the room until morning.

Let them sleep clothed and girded with belts or cords—but not with their knives at their sides, lest they cut themselves in their sleep—and thus be always ready to rise without delay when the signal is given and hasten to be before one another at the Work of God, yet with all gravity and decorum. The younger shall not have beds next to one another, but among those of the older ones. When they rise for the Work of God let them gently encourage one another, that the drowsy may have no excuse.

from Anonymous, *A Relation, or Rather a True Account, of the Island of England, with Sundry Particulars of the Customs of these People, and of the Royal Revenues under King Henry the Seventh* (late 15th century)

The report from which the following extract is taken was written by an official from Venice who visited England in 1496–97.

[The English] have an antipathy to foreigners, and imagine that they never come into their island, but to make themselves masters of it, and to usurp their goods; neither have they any sincere and solid friendships amongst themselves, insomuch that they do not trust each other to discuss either public or private affairs together, in the confidential manner we do in Italy. And although their dispositions are somewhat licentious, I never have noticed anyone, either at court or amongst the lower orders, to be in love; whence one must necessarily conclude, either that the English are the most discreet lovers in the world, or that they are incapable of love. I say this of the men, for I understand it is quite the contrary with the women, who are very violent in their passions. Howbeit the English keep a very jealous guard over their wives, though anything may be compensated in the end, by the power of money.

The want of affection in the English is strongly manifested towards their children; for after having kept them at home till they arrive at the age of 7 or 9 years at the utmost, they put them out, both males and females, to hard service in the houses of other people, binding them generally for another 7 or 9 years. And these are called apprentices, and during that time they perform all the most menial offices; and few are born who are exempted from this fate, for everyone, however rich he may be, sends away his children into the houses of others, whilst he, in return, receives those of strangers into his own. And on inquiring their reason for this severity, they answered that they did it in order that their children might learn better manners. But I, for my part, believe that they do it because they like to enjoy all their comforts themselves, and that they are better served by strangers than they would be by their own children. Besides which the English being great epicures, and very avaricious by nature, indulge in the most delicate fare themselves and give their household the coarsest bread, and beer, and cold meat baked on Sunday for the week, which, however, they allow them in great abundance. If they had their own children at home, they would be obliged to give them the same food they made use of for themselves. . . .

GEOFFREY CHAUCER
c. 1343 – 1400

Little is known about the private life of the greatest English author of the Middle Ages, but because Geoffrey Chaucer spent most years of his adult life in service to the Crown and the government, medieval records tell us much about his working life. These records, in which Chaucer's name is mentioned some 500 times, document decades of work for various royal households—as a page, a controller of customs, and a justice of the peace, among other positions. What they fail to provide are any details about Chaucer's education, literary life, or personal life.

As the author of the exquisite *Troilus and Criseyde* and of a variety of shorter poems and prose works, Chaucer would be regarded among the most important medieval English writers. But it is *The Canterbury Tales* that has secured his place as one of the greatest English authors of any era. From the time of its first appearance in the late fourteenth century, this linked series of stories has remained one of the most popular works of literature of the Middle Ages. The *Tales* were, in fact, among the first works ever printed in England, after William Caxton introduced the printing press to the country in 1476, some two decades after Gutenberg's invention of moveable type. In his Preface to *Fables Ancient and Modern* (1700), John Dryden called Chaucer the "father of English poetry," not only for his great influence upon future generations, but also for the fact that he was one of the first poets to compose his works in English, rather than French, Latin, or Anglo-Norman. Indeed, like Dante before him, Chaucer used the everyday language of the common people and proved its poetic capacity.

Chaucer was born at a time that saw the beginnings of a breakdown in strict divisions between the aristocracy, the Church, and the commoners. Although he was not born into the noble class, he was able to transcend the restrictions of the old social order and to procure a variety of high positions. Chaucer was born to Agnes Copton and John Chaucer just a few years before the beginning of the Hundred Years' War between France and England; his childhood also saw the outbreak of bubonic plague in England (which eventually killed between thirty and forty per cent of the population). Both of his parents held court positions at various times, but his father was primarily a prosperous wine merchant in London. With his knowledge of Latin, French, and Italian, the young Chaucer was likely educated in a good London grammar school; later he may have attended university. Court documents show that in his early teens he held a position as page in the household of the Countess of Ulster and Prince Lionel, son of the ruling monarch, Edward III.

In 1359 Chaucer took part in the war in France and was captured and ransomed to the king, who procured his release in 1360. Speculation has it that during this period on the continent Chaucer began his literary career, translating from the French the popular and influential allegorical poem *Le Roman de la Rose* (*The Romance of the Rose*), written by Guillaume de Lorris and Jean de Meun. In 1366 Chaucer married Philippa Roet, a lady-in-waiting to the queen. The couple had at least two children; Chaucer addressed *A Treatise on Astrolabe* (1391) to "little Lewis," and another son, Thomas, was eventually knighted.

The first page of Chaucer's *Tale of Melibee*, from the Ellesmere manuscript of *The Canterbury Tales*. The figure on horseback is generally taken to be a representation of Chaucer. The actual size of pages in the Ellesmere manuscript is approximately 15¾ x 11⅛". (Reprinted by permission of *The Huntington Library, San Marino, California*. EL26C9F72r.)

Over the course of the next twenty years, Chaucer continued his work for the royal household, serving in the army in France under John of Gaunt and in 1372 traveling on a diplomatic mission to Italy, where he probably acquired his knowledge of the works of Dante, Petrarch, and Boccaccio. *The Book of the Duchess* (1368), written when he was about twenty-five, is already an accomplished work. After his trip to Italy, however, Chaucer's writing began to show a new level of maturity and innovative technique, as well as a vast knowledge of both classical and contemporary literature and the various languages associated with these writings. *The House of Fame* (c. 1377) owes a debt to Dante, *The Parliament of Fowls* (1380) to Boccaccio and Cicero, and *Troilus and Criseyde* (c. 1385) again to Boccaccio; it is a reworking of Boccaccio's *Il Filostrato*.

Troilus, a long romantic poem recounting the fateful love of the Trojan Prince Troilus for Criseyde, has often been considered the most perfectly realized of all Chaucer's works. Although it exhibits less range than *The Canterbury Tales*, its elegant and supple verse, sustained narrative accomplishment, and depth of characterization are unsurpassed in medieval poetry in English.

In his next (and unfinished) work, *The Legend of Good Women*, written as a series of tales, Chaucer parodies his own authorial persona, taking himself to task for the writing of Criseyde's betrayal of Troilus by telling the stories of famous women who were themselves deceived by men.

Although the beginning of the 1380s were difficult times for Chaucer and for the country (he was accused of abduction or rape by a young woman named Cecilia Chaumpaigne, and 1381 saw the uprising against the poll tax), he seemed to regain inspiration in the latter part of the decade, at the same time as he held some important positions in the court. He became Controller of Customs and Justice of the Peace, and in 1386 was elected Member of Parliament for Kent; in 1389 Chaucer was appointed Clerk of the King's Works, a vital and challenging position in which he oversaw repairs and maintenance of government buildings. During these years he began work on *The Canterbury Tales*, generally considered his masterpiece. Rather than adapting old legends or reworking ancient stories of heroes, as was the norm, Chaucer told the stories of a gallery of English characters, from knight to clerk, parson to cook, nobility and commoners alike. Frequently hilarious, sometimes bawdy, and often revealing, *The Canterbury Tales* claims to be a series of stories told by a group of pilgrims on their way from London to Canterbury to visit the shrine of the martyr St. Thomas Becket. Similar framing devices had been used by other writers of the Middle Ages, but Chaucer's inclusion of such a wide range of classes and types of people, as well as his tonal range and his melding of diverse styles, were without precedent in English.

Although the work as it stands includes 24 tales and runs to over 17,000 lines, *The Canterbury Tales* was far from complete at the end of Chaucer's life. *The General Prologue*, in which the narrator introduces some thirty pilgrims, suggests that Chaucer intended to write more than 100 tales, with each narrator telling two tales on the journey to Canterbury and two on the way back. Chaucer must have known that such a plan was entirely unrealistic, however. Perhaps he allowed it to stand in the *General Prologue*, which he probably revised on several occasions, to indicate that *The Canterbury Tales* was a work that could never be finished. The narratives we do have are fleshed out by linking passages recounting exchanges among the pilgrims. Although these characters are fictional, the text provides a wealth of insight into the customs and practices of the time. Many of the pilgrims are medieval "types," but by varying narrative style with each speaker, Chaucer breathes imaginative life into the characters as individuals and into their world as a whole.

Chaucer's moral stance in *The Canterbury Tales* has been the subject of much discussion. The *Retraction* that follows *The Parson's Tale* disavows on moral grounds not only the *Tales*, but virtually all his more secular writings. Is this "Geoffrey Chaucer" merely another imaginary personage, or did the aging author truly repent of all "worldly vanitees"? At so great a remove as we are from medieval sensibilities, it is impossible to be sure. It can be said, however, that through most of *The Canterbury Tales* the author refrains from moralizing or casting judgment. The whole notion of a religious pilgrimage is frequently undermined by the actions of the characters, many of whom show themselves to be more interested in carnal than spiritual quests. Other characters, such as the Pardoner, may seem at first to be of high moral character, but deliberately or unwittingly expose their own compromised morality as they tell their stories. More broadly, there is an ongoing and unresolved tension in the tales between the spiritual and the worldly. This tension operates not only within many of the individual tales but also in the work as a whole, with the elevated tone of *The Knight's Tale*, for example, standing in marked contrast to the bawdiness of *The Miller's Tale*, the irreverence of the Wife of Bath's fantasy, or the elaborate pretense of artlessness in the fable recounted by the Nun's Priest. There is tension as well between the social classes represented among the pilgrims, between different religious views, between the sexes, and over the extent to which the traditions and conventions of the past should still be respected and adhered to. *The Canterbury Tales* is of all the classics of English literature one of the most entertaining and also one of the most open: open-minded in its underlying sensibilities, and open to an extraordinary range of interpretation.

The final year of Chaucer's life saw great upheaval in England's monarchy. In 1399, Richard II, who had supported Chaucer, was overthrown by Henry Bolingbroke (Henry IV), the oldest son of Richard's uncle, John of Gaunt, Duke of Lancaster, who had also been one of Chaucer's patrons. It may have been due to his gifts as a poet that Chaucer managed to retain the favor of the new regime, which was anxious for respectability. Chaucer wrote his final poem, "Complaint to His Purse," as a plea to King Henry to pay income owing from Richard II's reign; while the king did promise payment, Chaucer never collected the money. He died in October of 1400 and was buried in the south transept of Westminster Abbey. A century and a half later a monument to Chaucer was erected on the spot; thus began the tradition of the abbey's "Poets' Corner."

⌘ ⌘ ⌘

To Rosemounde
A Balade

Madame, ye ben of al beaute shryne°   *shrine*
  As fer as cercled° is the   *rounded*
    mapamounde,°[1]   *map of the world*
For as the cristal glorious ye shyne,
And lyke ruby ben your chekes rounde.
5 Therwith ye ben so mery and so jocounde° *pleasant, joyful*
That at a revel° whan that I see you daunce,   *festival*
It is an oynement° unto my wounde,   *ointment*
Thogh ye to me ne do no daliaunce.[2]

For thogh I wepe of teres ful a tyne,°   *barrel*
10 Yet may that wo myn herte nat confounde;°   *destroy*
Your semy° voys that ye so smal out   *small, high*
    twyne°   *twist out*
Maketh my thoght in joy and blis habounde.° *abound, be full of*
So curtaysly I go with love bounde
That to myself I sey in my penaunce,
15 "Suffyseth me to love you, Rosemounde,
Thogh ye to me ne do no daliaunce."[3]

Nas never pyk walwed° in galauntyne[4]   *immersed*
As I in love am walwed and ywounde,°   *wound*

---

[1] *ye ben of al ... mapamounde* You are the shrine of all beauty throughout the world.

[2] *Thogh ... daliaunce* Even though you give me no encouragement.

[3] *daliaunce* Sociable interaction, or more explicitly amorous or sexual exchange.

[4] *Nas ... galauntyne* No pike was ever steeped in galantine sauce.

For which ful ofte I of myself devyne° *discover, understand*
20 That I am trewe Tristam[1] the secounde.
My love may not refreyde° nor   *grow cold*
   affounde,°   *founder, grow numb*
I brenne° ay in an amorous plesaunce.°   *burn / desire*
Do what you lyst,° I wyl your thral be founde,[2]   *wish*
Thogh ye to me ne do no daliaunce.

tregentil————————//————————chaucer[3]
—C. 1477

Parliament of Fowles[4]

The lyfe so shorte, the crafte so longe to lerne,[5]
Th'assay° so hard, so sharpe the conquerynge,   *attempt*
The dredful° ioye always that slyd° so   *fearful / slides away*
   yerne:°   *quickly*
All this mene I by loue, that my felynge° *consciousness, emotions*
5 Astonyeth° with his wonderful workynge   *bewilders*
So sore, ywys,° that whan I on° hym thynke   *indeed / of*
Not wote I[6] well where° that I flete°   *whether / float*
   or synke.°   *swim / sink*

For all be that I knowe not loue in dede,
Ne wote how that he quyteth folke here hyre,[7]
10 Yet happeth me ful ofte[8] in bokes° to rede°   *books / read*
Of his myracles and his cruell yre.°   *anger*
There rede I well he wyll° be lorde and syre;° *wishes to / master*
I dar not say, his strokes ben° so sore,   *blows are*

But[9] "God saue suche a lorde"—I can°   *know (or, can say)*
   no more.
15 Of usage°—what for luste what for lore[10]—   *customarily*
On bokes rede I ofte, as I you tolde.
But wherfore that I speke all this? Nat yore
Agon[11] it happed me for to beholde°   *gaze*
Upon a boke, was wryte with letters olde,
20 And there vpon a certayne° thynge   *particular, significant*
   to lerne,
The longe day ful faste I redde and yerne.[12]

For out of olde feldes,° as men sayth,   *fields*
Cometh all this newe corne fro° yere to yere,   *from*
And out of olde bokes, in good fayth,[13]
25 Cometh all this newe scyence° that men lere.° *knowledge / learn*
But now to purpose° as of this   *the point*
   matere:°   *matter, discussion*
To rede forth hit gan me so delyte[14]
That all that day me thought° but a lyte.°   *seemed to me / little*

This boke of whiche I make mencyon
30 Entytuled° was all there, as I shal tell: *titled*
"Tullius of the dreme of Cypyon."[15]
Chapytrees° sevene it hadde, of heuen and hell *topics, sections*
And erthe, and soules that therin dwell,
Of whiche, as shortly as I can trete,
35 Of his° sentence° I wyll yow seyn the   *its / content*
   grete.°   *main part*

---

[1] *Tristam* Tristan, lover of Isolde, often presented as the ideal lover in medieval romance.

[2] *I … founde* I will remain your servant.

[3] *tregentil … chaucer* Although the words appear joined (or separated) by a line or flourish in the manuscript, the status of *tregentil* is uncertain. It may be an epithet (French: very gentle) or a proper name.

[4] *Parliament of Fowles* The text has been drawn primarily from the 1530 edition with the *Riverside Chaucer* as a reference for modernization and spelling.

[5] *The … lerne* Proverbial.

[6] *Not wote I* I know not.

[7] *quyteth folke here hyre* Rewards people for their efforts.

[8] *happeth me ful ofte* It very often happens to me.

[9] *I … But* Because his punishments are so painful, I dare not say anything but.

[10] *what … lore* Partly for pleasure, partly for learning.

[11] *Nat yore / Agon* Not long since.

[12] *The …yerne* I read very quickly and eagerly for the whole day.

[13] *in good fayth* Truly.

[14] *To … delyte* To read on pleased me so much.

[15] *Tullius* Marcus Tullius Cicero (106–43 BCE), Roman statesperson; *Cypyon* Scipio Africanus the Younger (185–129 BCE), Roman general; *dreme of Cypyon* "Dream of Scipio," the final part of Cicero's *Republic* in which Scipio the Younger dreams that he meets his grandfather, Scipio the Elder (236–183 BCE), who was famous for his defeat of Hannibal in the Second Punic War. In the following stanzas, *Cypyon* is Scipio the Younger while *Aufrycan* refers to Scipio the Elder.

Fyrst telleth it, whan Cypyon was come
In Aufryke, how he mette Messymysse,[1]
That hym for ioye in armes hathe ynome;°   *taken*
Than telleth it her° speche and all the blysse   *their*
40   That was betwix° them tyll the day gan mysse°   *between / ended*
And how his auncestre, Aufrycan so dere,
Gan in his slepe that nyght to hym appere.

Than telleth it that, fro a sterry° place,   *starry*
How Aufrycan hathe hym Cartage[2] shewed,
45   And warned hym before of all his grace,°   *fortune, future*
And sayd hym what° man, lerned other lewed,[3]   *whatever*
That loueth comune profyte,° well ythewed,[4]   *public good*
He shulde° into a blysfull place wende°   *would / go*
There as° ioye is that last withouten ende.   *Where*

50   Than asked he° yf folke that here been dede   *Scipio the Younger*
Haue lyfe and dwellynge in another place.
And Aufrycan sayd, "Ye° withoute drede,"°   *yes / certainly*
And that oure present worldes lyues space[5]
Nis° but a maner° dethe, what°   *is nothing / form of / whatever*
      wey we trace;
55   And ryghtfull° folke shall gon, after they dye,   *righteous*
To heuen; and shewed hym the Galaxye.°   *Milky Way*

Than shewed he hym the lytell erthe that here is
At regarde of° the heuens quantyte;°   *compared to / size*
And after shewed he hym the nyne sperys;[6]
60   And after that the melodye herde he
That cometh of thylke sperys[7] thryes thre,°   *three times three*

That well° is of musyke and melodye   *source*
In this worlde here, and cause of armonye.

Than bade° he hym, syn° erthe was so lyte°   *urged / since / little*
65   And dissevable° and full of harde grace,°   *deceptive / bad fortune*
That he ne shulde hym in the worlde delyte.[8]
Than tolde he hym, in certayne yeres space[9]
That euery sterre shulde come into his place
There it was fyrste, and all shulde out of mynde
70   That in this worlde is done of all mankynde.[10]

Than prayed° hym Cypyon to tell hym all   *asked*
The waye to come into that heuens blysse.
And he sayd, "Knowe thyselfe fyrst immortall,
And loke ay besyly thou worke and wysse
75   To comune profyte,[11] and thou shalte not mysse°   *fail*
To come swyftly to that place dere
That full of blysse is and soules clere.°   *bright, pure*

"But brekers of the lawe, sothe for to sayne,[12]
And lecherous folke, after that they ben deed,
80   Shall whirle aboute th'erthe alwey in peyne,°   *pain*
Tyll many a worlde° be passed, out of   *many ages*
      drede,°   *certainly*
And than, forgyuen all theyr wycked dede,
Than shall they come into that blysfull place,
To whiche to comen God the sende his grace."[13]

85   The day gan fayle, and the derke nyght
That reueth° bestes from theyr busynesse   *steals*
Byrefte° me my boke for lacke of lyght,   *took away (from)*

---

[1] *Messymysse*   Masinissa (c. 240–c. 148 BCE), a king of Numidia, which is now Libya.

[2] *Cartage*   Carthage, a city in northern Africa which was the center of the Carthaginian Empire. The Romans destroyed the city in the Third Punic War.

[3] *lerned other lewed*   Educated or uneducated.

[4] *well ythewed*   Possessed of good characteristics.

[5] *present worldes lyues space*   Lifetime in the present world.

[6] *nyne sperys*   According to classical and medieval models, the universe was made up of eight or nine concentric spheres revolving around the stationary earth.

[7] *melodye herde ... sperys*   He heard the melody that comes from those spheres. The movement of the spheres was believed to create music that was perfectly harmonious. This music of the spheres was

thought to be the source and model of all other music, although it was typically inaudible to those on earth.

[8] *That he ... delyte*   That he should not take pleasure in the world.

[9] *in certayne yeres space*   In a certain amount of time. In this case, the thousands of years until the heavenly bodies return to their starting places. This year is referred to as the great year.

[10] *all shulde out ... mankynde*   All the deeds of mankind in this world would be forgotten.

[11] *loke ay besyly ... profyte*   See to it that you always work diligently and direct yourself to the public good.

[12] *sothe for to sayne*   To tell the truth.

[13] *To whiche ... his grace*   (May) God send you his grace so that you come there (i.e., to heaven).

And to my bed I gan me for to dresse,[1]
Fulfylled° of thought and busy   *filled full*
   heuynesse;°   *anxious sorrow*
90 For bothe I had thynge whiche that I nolde,°   *did not want*
And eke° I ne had[2] that thynge that I wolde.°   *also / wanted*

But fynally my spyryte at the laste,
Forwery of[3] my laboure all the daye,
Toke rest, that made me to slepe faste;°   *soundly, heavily*
95 And in my slepe I mette,° as that I lay,   *dreamed*
How Aufrycan, ryght° in the selfe aray° *exactly / same appearance*
That Cypyon hym sawe before that tyde,°   *time*
Was comen and stode ryght at my beddes syde.

The wery hunter, slepynge in his bed,
100 To woode agayne his mynde gothe anone;°   *quickly*
The iudge dremeth how his pleys been
   sped;°   *cases have turned out*
The carter dremeth how his carte is gone;
The ryche, of golde; the knyght fyght° with his   *fights*
   fon;°   *foe*
The seke° meteth° he drynketh of the   *sick man / dreams*
   tonne;°   *cask*
105 The louer meteth he hathe his lady wonne.

Can I not° say yf that the cause were   *I cannot*
For° I hadde red of Aufrycan beforne   *because*
That made me to mete that he stode there;
But thus sayd he: "Thou hast the so well borne[4]
110 In lokynge of° myne olde boke totorn,°   *considering / tattered*
Of whiche Macrobye[5] rought° not a lyte,°   *cared / little*
That somdele° of thy laboure wolde I quyte."° *a part / reward*

Cytherea,° thou blysfull lady swete,   *Venus*
That with thy fyrbrond° dauntest° whome   *torch / subdue*

the leste[6]
115 And madest me this sweuen° for to mete,° *dream / dream*
Be thou my helpe in this, for thou mayste
   beste!°   *can best (do so)*
As wisly° as I sey the° north-north-west,[7] *surely, truly / saw you*
Whan I beganne my sweuen° for to wryte,   *dream*
So gyue me myght° to ryme and endyte!° *power, ability / compose*

120 This foresayd° Aufrycan me hente°   *aforesaid / seized*
   anone°   *straightaway*
And forth with hym vnto a gate brought,
Ryght of a parke walled with grene° stone;   *mossy*
And ouer the gate, with letters large ywrought,°   *worked*
There were verses wryten, as me thought,
125 On eyther halfe,° of full great dyfference,[8]   *each side*
Of whiche I shall you saye the playne sentence:° *clear meaning*

"Thrughe me men go into that blysfull place
Of hertes hele° and deedly woundes cure;°   *health, happiness*
Thrughe me men go vnto the well of grace,
130 There grene and lusty° Maye shall euer endure. *pleasing, lively*
This is the waye to all good auenture.°   *fortune*
Be glad, thou reder, and thy sorowe of-caste;° *dismiss, throw off*
All open am I—passe in, and sped° the faste!"° *hurry / quickly*

"Thrughe me men go," than spake that other syde,
135 "Vnto the mortall° stroke of the spere   *deadly*
Of whiche Dysdayne and Daunger° *standoffishness and resistance*
   is the gyde,
There nevere tre shal fruyt ne leues bere.[9]
This streme you ledeth to the sorowfull were° *weir, small dam*
There as° the fysshe in pryson is all drye;°   *where*
140 Th'eschewynge° is only the° remedy!"   *avoidance / the sole*

---

[1] *And to my ... to dresse* And I went to my bed.

[2] *ne had* Did not have. Pronounced *n'ad*.

[3] *Forwery of* Tired out by.

[4] *Thou hast ... well borne* You have conducted yourself so well.

[5] *Macrobye* Ambrosius Theodosius Macrobius (fl. 395–423 CE), author of a long commentary on "The Dream of Scipio" through which the work was transmitted to the Middle Ages.

[6] *whome the leste* Whomever you please.

[7] *north-north-west* Some scholars argue that this phrase can be used to help date the poem; Venus is not seen so far north as north-northwest from London, but can rarely be seen in a position which may loosely be described this way. Others suggest that the phrase means that Venus is seen in an unusual, indirect way or not seen at all.

[8] *of full great dyfference* Of (very) greatly different meaning.

[9] *There nevere ... bere* Where no tree will ever bear fruit or leaves. In Middle English, the double (or even triple) negative is sometimes used to intensify negation, rather than canceling it as is the case in modern English.

These verses of golde and blacke ywryten° were,   *written*
Of whiche I gan astoned to beholde.°   *beheld with astonishment*
For with that one encreased ay° my fere   *always*
And with that other gan myne herte bolde;°   *grew bold*
145   That one me hette,° that other dyd me colde;   *warmed*
No wytte had I, for erroure, for to chese[1]
To entre or fle, or me to saue or lese.°   *destroy*

Ryght as° bytwene adamantes° two   *just as / magnetic stones*
Of euen myght,° a pyece of yron sette   *equal strength, power*
150   Ne hathe no myght° to meue° to ne fro—   *power / move*
For what that one may hale,° that other   *call, attract*
        lette°—   *repels*
Ferde I, that nyste whether me was bette[2]
To entre or leue, tyll Aufrycan, my gyde,
Me hente° and shofe° in at the gates wyde,   *seized / shoved*

155   And sayd, "It standeth wryten in thy face,
Thyne erroure, thoughe thou tell it not to me;
But drede the not° to come into this place,   *do not fear*
For this wrytynge nys° nothynge ment by° the,[3]   *is not / about*
Ne° by none but° he loues seruaunt be: *nor / unless*
160   For thou of loue hase lost thy tast, I gesse,°   *suppose*
As seke° man hathe of swete and bytternesse.   *sick*

"But nethles,° all though that° thou   *nevertheless / even though*
        be dull,
Yit that° thou can not do, yet° may thou se.   *yet what / still*
For many a man that may not stande a pull[4]
165   Yet lyketh hym at wrastlynge for to be,
And demeth° yet wher° he do bette°   *judges / whether / better*
        or he.[5]
And yf thou haddest conynge° for   *skill, ability*
        t'endyte,°   *to compose*
I shall the shewe matter° of to wryte."   *material, subject matter*

With that my hande in his he toke anone,°   *at once*
170   Of whiche I conforte caught,° and went in faste.   *took comfort*
But, Lorde, so I was glad and well begoon!°   *in a good situation*
For ouer all where° that I myne eyes caste   *wherever*
Were trees clad with leues that aye° shall laste,   *always*
Eche in his kynde,° of coloure fresshe   *according to its nature*
        and grene
175   As emerawde, that ioye was to sene.°   *see*

The bylder° oke, and eke° the hardy asshe;   *builder / also*
The pyler[6] elme, the cofer° vnto carayne;°   *coffin / corpses*
The boxtre° pipere,[7] holme° to whyppes   *boxwood / holly*
        lasshe;
The saylynge fyrre;° the cypresse, dethe to   *fir*
        playne;°   *lament, mourn*
180   The shetere ewe; the aspe for shaftes playne;[8]
The olyue of peas,° and eke the dronke vyne;   *peace*
The victor palme, the laurer° to deuyne.°   *laurel / make prophecies*

A garden sawe I full of blosomed bowis°   *boughs, branches*
Vpon a ryuer,° in a grene mede,°   *riverbank / meadow*
185   There as swetenes euermore ynoughe is,[9]
With floures whyte, blewe, yelowe, and rede,
And colde well-stremes,° nothynge   *springs*
        deed,°   *not slow-moving*
And swymmynge full of small fysshes lyght,°   *quick*
With fynnes reed° and scales syluer bryght.   *red fins*

190   On euery bough the byrdes herde I synge,
With voyce of angell in theyr armonye;°   *harmony*
Some busyed them° theyr byrdes°   *made themselves busy / fledglings*
        forthe to brynge;
The lytell conyes° to theyr play gan hye;°   *rabbits / hurried*
And further al aboute I gan espye°   *saw all around*
195   The drefull roo,° the bucke,° the   *timid deer / male deer*
        herte° and hynde,°   *male red deer / female deer*
Squyrells, and beestes small of gentyll kynde.°   *noble nature*

---

[1] *No wytte … chese* I could not (i.e., I had not ability to) choose, for (fear of) error.

[2] *Ferde I, that … was bette* (So) I behaved, not knowing whether it was better for me.

[3] *this wrytynge … by the* This writing does not apply to you at all.

[4] *stande a pull* Compete in a wrestling match.

[5] *And demeth … he* And judges whether one (contestant) does better or the other.

[6] *pyler* Pillar. The description likely refers to the tendency of elm to be covered by vines.

[7] *boxtre pipere* Boxwood was used to make flutes or pipes.

[8] *The shetere … shaftes playne* Yew was used to make bows, aspen for smooth arrows.

[9] *There as … ynoughe is* Where there is eternally abundant sweetness.

On instrumentes of strynge in acorde°   *harmony*
Herde I so playe a rauyshynge swetenesse,
That God, that maker is of all and lorde,
200 Ne herde neuer better, as I gesse.
Therwith° a wynde, vneth° it myght be lesse,   *Moreover / hardly*
Made in the leues grene a noyse softe
Acordynge to° the foules° songe on   *harmonious with / birds'*
        lofte.°   *above*

Th'ayre of that place so attempred° was   *temperate*
205 That neuer was greuaunce° of hote ne colde.   *annoyance*
There wex° ek° euery holsome spyce and   *grew / also*
        gras;°   *herb*
No man may there wexe° seke° ne olde;   *become / sick*
Yet was there ioye more a
        thousandefolde°   *a thousand times more joy*
Than man can tell; ne neuer wolde it nyght,°   *become night*
210 But ay° clere day to ony mannes syght.   *always*

Under a tree, besyde a well, I saye°   *saw*
Copide,° our lorde, his arowes forge and   *Cupid*
        fyle;°   *make and sharpen*
And at his fete, his bowe all redy laye;
And Wyll, his doughter, tempered[1] all the whyle
215 The hedes in the well, and with hire wile°   *skill, craft*
She couched° them after° they   *positioned, placed / according as*
        shulde serue,
Some for to sle,° and some to wounde and kerue.°   *slay / cut*

Tho was I ware of Pleasaunce anone ryght,[2]
And of Araye,° and Lust,° and Curtesye,   *Adornment / Desire*
220 And of the Crafte° that can° and hathe   *Guile / knows how*
        the myght°   *power*
To don by force a wyght to do folye—[3]
Dysfygured was she, I shall not lye;
And by hymselfe, vnder an oke, I gesse,
Sawe I Delyte, that stode with Gentylnesse.°   *Nobility*

225 I saw Beaute without ony atyre,°   *clothing*
And Youthe, full of game° and iolyte;° *playfulness / merriment*
Foolehardynesse,° Flatery, and Desyre,   *Recklessness*
Massagery,° and Mede,°   *Sending messages / Reward, Bribery*
        and other thre—[4]
Theyr names shall not here be tolde for me—
230 And vpon pylers great of iasper longe
I sawe a temple of bras founded stronge.°   *firmly set*

Aboute the temple daunced alway
Women ynowe,° of whiche some ther were   *enough*
Fayre of themselfe, and some of them were
        gay;°   *richly, brightly dressed*
235 In kyrtles,° all dyssheueled,° *simple dresses / with unbound hair*
        went they there:
That was theyr offyce° always, yere by yere.   *occupation*
And on the temple, of dowves whyte and fayre
Saw I syttynge many an hundreth payre.

Before the temple dore full sobrelye
240 Dame Peas sate, with a curtayne[5] in her honde,
And by her syde, wonder dyscretlye,° *with wonderful courtesy*
Dame Pacyence syttynge there I fonde,
With face pale, vpon an hyll of sonde;°   *sand*
And aldernexte,° within and ek°   *right next to them / also*
        withoute,
245 Beheste,° and Arte,° and of theyr folke a   *Promise / Skill*
        route.°   *crowd*

Within the temple, of syghes hote as fyre
I herde a swogh° that gan aboute   *sound of wind*
        renne,°   *ran about*
Whiche syghes were engendred with desyre
That made euery auter° for to brenne°   *altar / burn*
250 Of newe flamme; and wel espyed I thenne
That all the cause of sorowes that they drye°   *endure, suffer*
Come of the bytter goddes Ialosye.°   *goddess Jealousy*

---

[1] *Wyll* Sexual Desire; *tempered* In blacksmithing, tempering
refers to the hardening of newly forged pieces.

[2] *Tho was I ... anone ryght* Then suddenly I noticed (became aware
of) Pleasure.

[3] *To don by ... do folye* To force a person to act wrongly.

---

[4] *other thre* These three figures are unnamed, and it is not clear
what they are meant to represent.

[5] *curtayne* The meaning here is uncertain. Chaucer could have in
mind a temple curtain or a bed curtain.

The god Pyrapus[1] sawe I, as I wente,
Within the temple in souerayne° place stande,   *superior*
255 In suche aray° as whan the asse hym   *state*
      shente°   *disgraced, ruined*
With crye by nyght, and with his ceptre in hande.[2]
Full besyly° men ganne assaye°   *very diligently, eagerly / attempted*
      and fonde°   *tried*
Vpon his heed to sette, of sondry hewe,°   *various colors*
Garlandes full of fresshe floures newe.

260 And in a preuy° corner in   *private, hidden*
      dysporte°   *entertaining themselves*
Founde I Venus and her porter Rychesse,°   *Abundance*
That was full° noble and hauteyne° of her   *very / dignified*
      porte;°   *manner*
Derke° was that place, and afterwarde   *dark*
      lyghtnesse°   *brightness*
I sawe a lyte,° vnneth° it myght be lesse—   *little / scarcely*
265 And on a bedde of golde she laye to reste,
Tyll that the hote sonne gan to west.°   *moved westward*

Her gylte heers° with a golde threed   *golden hair*
Ibounden° were, vntressed° as she laye,   *tied / falling loosely*
And naked fro the breest vnto the heed
270 Men myght hire se; and, sothly° for to say,   *truly*
The remanent° was wel couered to   *remainder*
      pay° my   *approval, satisfaction*
Ryght with a subtyll keuerchesse° of   *delicate piece of cloth*
      Valence—[3]
There was no thycker clothe of no defence.[4]

The place gaue a thousande sauoures swote,°   *sweet scents*
275 And Bacchus, god of wyne, sate her besyde
And Ceres[5] nexte, that dothe of hunger
      bote,°   *brings relief of hunger*
And, as I sayd, amyddes lay Cypride,°   *Venus*
To whome on knees two yonge folke ther cryde
To be theyr helpe. But thus I let her lye,
280 And ferther in the temple I gan espye

That, in despyte of° Dyane the chaste,   *as an insult to*
Full many a bowe ybroke° hanged on the wall   *broken bow*
Of maydens suche as gan theyr tymes waste
In her seruyce;[6] and peynted ouer all°   *all over*
285 Ful many a story, of whiche I touche° shall   *touch upon*
A fewe, as of Calyxte and Athalante,[7]
And many a mayde of whiche the name I
      wante.°   *whose name I do not know*

Semiramus, Candace, and Hercules,[8]
Byblys, Dido, Tesbe, and Piramus,[9]

---

[1] *Pyrapus*   Statue of Priapus, god of fruitfulness in both flora and fauna.

[2] *as whan the asse ... hande*   The reference here is to Ovid (perhaps via Boccaccio), who tells the story of Priapus and the ass. Priapus is rejected by the nymph Lotis and so attempts to take advantage of her while she sleeps. An ass's bray awakens her before he can complete his plan; she awakens in time to throw him out and raise an alarm. Others respond in time to ridicule him when they discover him unclothed and aroused.

[3] *Valence*   Cloth from the French city of Valence, which was known for textile production.

[4] *There was no ... defence*   There was no thicker cloth offering any (additional) protection.

[5] *Ceres*   Goddess of the harvest and agriculture.

[6] *Dyane the chaste ... seruyce*   Diana is goddess of the hunt and chastity. Her followers were required to remain chaste also; the broken bows represent their broken vows.

[7] *Calyxte*   Callisto, a follower of Diana who was raped by Zeus and became pregnant. Diana turned her into a bear as punishment; eventually she was turned into the constellation Ursa Major (her son by Zeus is Ursa Minor); *Athalante*   Atalanta, a follower of Diana whose father ordered her to marry. She made a bargain with him that she would only marry a suitor who defeated her in a footrace. Venus aided the successful suitor by providing him with the golden apples, which he dropped throughout the race to slow Atalanta as she picked them up.

[8] *Semiramus*   Semiramis, an Assyrian queen famous for lust; *Candace*   Reference either to Candace, the Indian queen who loved Alexander or Canace, who was sentenced to death by her father for loving her brother; *Hercules*   Mythical Greek hero who was given a shirt stained with poisoned blood by his wife Deianira. The poison caused his flesh to burn with such agony that he threw himself on a pyre and died.

[9] *Byblys*   Depending on the source, Biblis either loved or was loved by her brother, and her fate was either that she was turned into a nymph, or was consumed by her own tears and became a fountain; *Dido*   Queen of Carthage, her doomed love for Aeneas is told in Chaucer's *Legend of Good Women*; *Tesbe, and ... Piramus*   Pyramus and Thisbe are famous tragic lovers whose Romeo-and-Juliet story is told in the *Legend of Good Women*.

290 Trystram, Ysoude, Parys, and Achylles,[1]
Heleyne, Cleopatre, and Troylus,[2]
Sylla, and eke° the mother of Romulus:[3]   *also*
All these were paynted on that other syde,
And all theyr loue, and in what plyte°   *plight, condition*
    they dyed.

295 Whan I was come agayne into the place
That I of spake, that was so swete and grene,
Forthe walked I tho° myselfe to   *then*
    solace.°   *comfort, give pleasure*
Tho° was I ware° where that there sate a quene   *then / aware*
That, as of lyght the somer sonne shene
300 Passeth the sterre, ryght so ouer mesure°   *immeasurably*
She fayrer was than ony creature.[4]

And in a launde,° vpon an hyll of flowres,   *glade, clearing*
Was set this noble goddes Nature.
Of braunches were her halles and her bowres°   *inner rooms*
305 Ywrought after her cast° and her   *design*
    mesure;°   *specifications, measurements*
Ne there nas foule that cometh of engendrure[5]
That they ne were preste° in her presence   *prepared*
To take her dome° and gyue her audyence.°   *judgment / hearing*

For this was on saynt Valentynes day,
310 Whan euery foule cometh there to chose his make,°   *mate*
Of euery kynde that men thynke maye,
And that so huge a noyse gan they make

That erthe, and eyr,° and tree, and euery lake   *air*
So full was that vnneth° was other space   *scarcely*
315 For me to stande, so full was al the place.

And ryght° as Alayne, in the Pleynt of Kynde,   *exactly, just*
Deuyseth Nature of araye and face,[6]
In suche araye° men myght her there fynde.   *clothing*
This noble empresse, full of grace,
320 Bade° euery foule to take his owne place,   *commanded*
As they were wonte° alway fro yere to yere,   *accustomed*
Saynt Valentynes day, to stande there.

That is to saye, the foules of rauyne°   *birds of prey*
Were hyghest set, and than the foules smale
325 That eten, as hem° Nature wolde enclyne,   *them*
As worme or thynge of whiche I tell no tale;
But water-foule sate lowest in the dale;°   *valley*
And foule that lyueth by sede° sate on the   *seed*
    grene,°   *grass, lawn*
And that so fele° that wonder was to sene.   *many*

330 There myght° men the royall egle fynde,   *could*
That with his sharpe loke° perceth°   *vision / pierces, sees into*
    the sonne,
And other egles of a lower kynde,°   *type, nature*
Of which that clerkes well deuysen
    konne.°   *know well how to describe*
There was the tyraunte with his fethers donne°   *greyish brown*
335 And grey—I mene the goshauke that dothe pyne°   *harm*
To byrdes for his outragyous rauayne.°   *greed*

The gentyll faucon,° that with his feet   *noble falcon*
    dystreyneth°   *grasps*
The kynges hande;[7] the sperhauke eke,°   *sparrowhawk also*
The quayles fo;° the merlyon,[8] that   *quail's enemy*
    peyneth°   *endeavors*

---

[1] *Trystram, Ysoude* Tristan and Isolde, famous adulterous and tragic lovers; *Parys* Paris abducted Helen (*Heleyne*) with the help of Venus and so started the Trojan War; *Achylles* Achilles was a Greek hero of the Trojan War. In some versions, he was ambushed and killed in the temple of Apollo during his wedding to Polixena.

[2] *Cleopatre* Cleopatra's story is told in the *Legend of Good Women*; *Troylus* Troilus, the faithful, betrayed lover whose story is told in Chaucer's *Troilus and Criseyde*.

[3] *Sylla* Silla betrayed her father for love; her story is told in the *Legend of Good Women*; *mother of Romulus* Rhea Silvia, a vestal virgin (chaste priestess) who was raped by Ares.

[4] *as of lyght … creature* Just as the summer sun shines brighter than a star, so she was immeasurably more beautiful than any other creature.

[5] *Ne there nas … engendrure* Nor was there any bird produced by procreation.

---

[6] *Alayne, in the … face* Just as Alan (of Lille), in the *Complaint of Nature*, describes Nature's face and clothing. Alan of Lille (or Alanus de Insulis) wrote his influential *De Planctu naturae* in the late twelfth century. In it, the goddess complains of human crimes against natural law.

[7] *that with his … kynges hande* In falconry the bird is carried on the falconer's hand or fist.

[8] *merlyon* Merlin, a type of small falcon.

340 Hymselfe full ofte° the larke for to seke;°   *frequently / seek*
There was the douue° with her eyes meke;°   *dove / gentle, humble*
The ielouse swanne, ayenst° his dethe that   *shortly before*
     syngeth;
The oule° eke, that of dethe the bode°   *owl / warning*
     bryngeth;

The crane, the geaunte,° with his trompes   *giant*
     soun;°   *trumpet sound*
345 The thefe, the choughe;[1] and eke° the   *also*
     ianglynge pye;°   *chattering magpie*
The skornynge iaye; the eles fo, herowne;°   *heron, the eel's enemy*
The fals° lapwynge, full of trechery;   *deceitful*
The stare,° that the counseyle° can   *starling / secrets*
     bewrye;°   *betray, tell*
The tame ruddoke,° and the cowarde kytte;°   *robin / kite, vulture*
350 The cocke,° that orloge° is of thorpes   *rooster / timekeeper*
     lyte;°   *small villages*

The sparowe, Venus sone;[2] the nyghtyngale,
That clepyth° forth the grene leues newe;   *calls*
The swalowe, mordrer° of the foules smale   *murderer, eater*
That maken hony of floures fresshe of
     hewe;°   *fresh, colorful flowers*
355 The wedded turtle,° with hire herte trewe;   *turtledove*
The pecocke, with his angels fethers bryght;[3]
The fesaunte,° scorner of the cocke by nyght;   *pheasant*

The waker° goos; the cukkowe euer vnkynde;[4]   *watchful*
The popyniay,° full of delycasye;°   *parrot / wantonness*
360 The drake,° stroyere° of his owne kynde;[5]   *male duck / destroyer*
The storke, wreker° of auowtrye;°   *punisher / adultery*

The hote° cormeraunte[6] of glotenye;   *eager, keen*
The rauen wys; the crowe with voyce of care;°   *sad voice*
The throstle° olde; the frosty feldfare.[7]   *thrush*

365 What shulde I say? Of foules euery kynde
That in this worlde haue fethers and stature°   *shape, form*
Men myghten in that place assembled fynde
Before that noble goddes Nature,
And yche° of them dyd his besy cure[8]   *each*
370 Benyngly° to chose or for to take,   *courteously, genially*
By her acorde,° his formell° or his   *consent / female (bird)*
     make.°   *mate*

But to the poynt: Nature helde on her honde
A formall° egle, of shape the   *female*
     gentyllest°   *noblest, most excellent*
That euer she ymonge° her workes fonde,°   *among / found*
375 The most benynge° and the   *gracious*
     goodlyest.°   *most beautiful, pleasing*
In her was euery vertue at his rest,°   *at home*
So ferforthe° that Nature herselfe had   *to such an extent*
     blysse°   *happiness*
To loke on her, and ofte her beke to kysse.

Nature, the vyker° of the almyghty Lorde,   *deputy*
380 That hote, colde, heuy, lyght, moyste, and drye[9]
Hathe knytte° by euen nombres of acorde,[10]   *combined, joined*
In esy° voyce began to speke and saye,   *gentle*
"Foules, take hede of my sentence,° I praye,   *words, meaning*
And for your ease,° in furtherynge of your nede,   *relief, benefit*
385 As fast as I may speke, I wyll yow spede.°   *help*

"Ye knowe well how, on Saynt Valentynes day,
By my statute° and thrugh my gouernaunce,   *law*

---

[1] *choughe*   The chough, a member of the crow family notorious for its thievery.

[2] *The sparowe, Venus sone*   The sparrow had a reputation for lechery, hence the moniker *Venus sone*.

[3] *The pecocke ... fethers bryght*   There was an artistic tradition of depicting angels' wings as made up of peacock feathers.

[4] *vnkynde*   The cuckoo is called *vnkynde*, meaning both "unkind" and "unnatural," because it lays its eggs in the nests of other birds; the young cuckoos then drive the original young out of the nest.

[5] *drake, stroyere ... kynde*   Refers either to a belief that male ducks would kill their own young, or that they inadvertently kill the female during mating due to their lack of restraint.

[6] *cormeraunte*   The cormorant, a marine bird with a reputation for greediness.

[7] *olde*   The thrush has a white chest, which can resemble a beard, and it was believed to live to advanced age; *frosty feldfare*   The fieldfare, a type of thrush, also has a white chest and underside and is found in England in winter.

[8] *dyd his besy cure*   Exerted himself vigorously.

[9] *hote, colde ... drye*   This list presents the commonly accepted fundamental qualities of matter.

[10] *euen nombres of acorde*   Harmonious proportions.

Ye come for to chose—and fle° your way—   *fly*

Your makes,° as I prycke° you with   *mates / incite*

plesaunce;°   *desire*

390 But nethles,° my ryghtfull ordenaunce°   *nevertheless / just decree*

May I not let° for all this worlde to wynne,   *abandon*

That he that most is worthy shall begynne.

"The tercell° egle, as that ye knowe well,   *male eagle or hawk*

The foule° royall, aboue you in degre,°   *bird / social rank*

395 The wyse and worthy, secrete,° true as stele,   *discreet*

Whiche I haue fourmed, as ye may wel se,

In euery parte as it best lyketh me—

It nedeth not his shappe you to deuyse—[1]

He shall fyrst chose and speke in his gyse.°   *usual manner*

400 "And after hym by ordre° shall ye chese,°   *rank / choose*

After° your kynde, eueryche° as you   *according to / each one*

lyketh,

And as your happe° is, shall ye wynne or lese.°   *luck / lose*

But whiche of you that loue moste entryketh,°   *ensnares*

God sende hym her that sorest° for hym   *most intensely*

syketh!"°   *sighs, pines*

405 And therwithall° the tercell gan she calle,°   *with that / she began to*

And sayd, "My sone, the choys is to the yfalle.°   *falls to you*

"But netheles,° in this condycyon   *nonetheless*

Must be the choys of eueryche° that is here,   *everyone*

That she agre to his eleccyon,°   *choice*

410 Whoso° he be that shulde° be her fere.°   *whoever / would / mate*

This is oure vsage° always, fro yere to yere,   *custom*

And whoso° maye at this tyme haue his   *whoever*

grace°   *good fortune*

In blysfull tyme he came into this place!"

With heed° enclyned and with full humble   *head*

chere°   *expression*

415 This royall tercell spake,° and taryed   *spoke*

nought:°   *did not delay*

"Vnto my souereygne lady, and not my fere,°   *equal*

I chese, and chesse° with wyll, and herte, and thought,   *choose*

The formell° on your hande, so well   *female*

iwrought,°   *made, fashioned*

Whose I am all, and euer wyll her serue,

420 Do what her lust,° to do me lyue or sterue;°[2]   *pleases / die*

"Besechynge her of mercy and of grace,

As she that is my lady souerayne;

Or let me dye present° in this place.   *at once, straightaway*

For certes,° longe may I not lyue in payne,   *certainly*

425 For in myne herte is koruen° euery veyne.   *carved, cut*

Hauynge rewarde° only to my trouthe,°   *regard / faithfulness*

My dere herte, haue on my wo some ruthe.°   *pity*

"And yf that I be founde to her vntrewe,°   *unfaithful*

Dysobeysaunte,° or wylfull   *disobedient*

neclygent,°   *willfully negligent*

430 Auauntour,° or in processe° loue a newe,   *boaster / time*

I pray to you this be my iudgment:

That with° these foules I be all torent,°   *by / torn apart*

That ylke° day that euer she me fynde   *very, same*

To her vntrewe, or in my gylte° vnkynde.   *deliberately*

435 "And syth that° none loueth her so well as I,   *since*

Al be° she neuer of loue me behette,°   *even though / promised*

Than ought she be myne thrugh her mercy,

For other bonde can I none on her knette.°   *fasten*

Ne neuer for no wo ne shall I lette°   *cease*

440 To serue her, how ferre° so that she wende;°   *however far / go*

Say what thou lest,° my tale is at an ende."   *wish, like*

Ryght as° the fresshe, reed rose newe   *just as*

Ayenst° the somer sonne coloured is,   *in the presence of*

Ryght so for shame° all wexen gan° the hewe   *modesty / became*

445 Of this formell,° whan she herde all this;   *female*

She neyther answered well,° ne sayd   *favorably*

amys,°   *unfavorably*

So sore abasshed° was she, tyll   *intensely embarrassed, disconcerted*

that Nature

Sayd, "Doughter, drede you not,° I you assure."   *do not fear*

Another tercell egle spake anone,°   *at once*

450 Of lower kynde, and sayd, "That shal not be!

I loue her bet than ye do, by Saynt Iohan,[3]

---

[1] *It nedeth not ... deuyse* It is not necessary to describe his shape to you.

[2] *Do what her ... sterue* Whether it pleases her to make me live or die.

[3] *Saynt Iohan* Saint John the Evangelist.

Or at the lest I loue her as well as ye,

And lenger haue serued her in my degre;° — *station*

And yf she shulde haue loued for° longe louynge, — *because of*

455 To me alone had be the guerdonynge.° — *reward*

"I dare eke° say, yf she me fynde fals, — *also*

Vnkynde, iangler,° or rebell ony wyse,° — *a gossip / in any way*

Or ialouse, do me hange by the hals!° — *neck*

And, but° I bere° me in her seruyse — *unless / conduct*

460 As well as that my wytte can me suffyse,° — *be sufficient*

Fro poynt in poynt,° her honoure for to saue, — *in every part*

Take she my lyfe and all the good° I haue!" — *wealth, possessions*

The thyrde tercell egle answered tho,° — *then*

"Now, syrs, ye seen the lytell layser° here; — *limited time*

465 For euery foule cryeth out to be ago° — *gone, departed*

Forthe with his make, or with his lady dere;

And eke Nature herselfe ne wyll not here,° — *hear*

For taryenge° here, not halfe that I wolde say; — *delaying*

And but° I speke, I must for sorowe dey.° — *But unless / die*

470 "Of longe seruyce auaunte I me nothynge;° — *I make no boast*

But as possyble is me to dye to-day

For wo as he that hathe ben languysshynge

This twenty wynter, and well happen may;[1]

A man may serue bet° and more to pay° — *better / pleasingly*

475 In halfe a yere, although it were no more,

Than some man dothe that hathe serued full
yore.° — *for a long time*

"I say not this by me, for I ne can

Do no seruyce that may my lady plese;

But I dare say, I am her truest man

480 As to my dome,[2] and faynest° wolde her
ese.° — *most eagerly / comfort, entertain*

At shorte wordes, tyll that dethe me sese° — *seizes*

I wyll be hers, wheder° I wake or wynke,° — *whether / sleep*

And true in all that herte may bethynke." — *imagine*

Of° all my lyfe, syn° that day I was borne, — *In / since*

485 So gentyll ple° in loue or other thynge — *noble a plea*

Ne herde neuer no man° me beforne— — *No man ever heard*

Who° that had leyser° and connynge° — *If one / opportunity / ability*

For to rehers her chere° and her spekynge; — *their expression*

And from the morwe° gan this speche laste — *morning*

490 Tyll downewarde wente the sonne wonder° faste. — *amazingly*

The noyse of fowles for to be delyuered° — *released, dismissed*

So loude range,° "Haue doone,° and let vs
wende!"° — *rang / finish up / go*

That well wende° I the wood hadde° — *thought / wood would have*
all to-shyuered.° — *splintered*

"Come of!"° they cryed, "alas, ye wyll vs
shende!° — *come on / destroy*

495 Whan shall your cursed pletynge° haue an ende? — *argument*

How shulde a iudge eyther party leue° — *believe*

For ye or nay without ony preue?"° — *proof*

The goos,° the cokkow,° and the doke° also — *goose / cuckoo / duck*

So cryed, "Keke keke! cukkowe! queke queke!" hye,° — *loudly*

500 That thrugh myn eeres the noyse wente tho.° — *then*

The goos sayd, "All this nys not worthe a flye![3]

But I can shape hereof a remedye,

And I wyll say my verdyte fayre and
swythe° — *verdict clearly and quickly*

For water-foule, whoso° be wroth° or
blythe!"° — *whoever / angry / glad*

505 "And I for worme-foule," sayd the fol° cuckow, — *foolish*

"For I wyll of myne owne auctoryte,° — *authority*

For comune spede,° take on the
charge° now, — *common good / matter*

For to delyuer vs is great charyte." — *kindness*

"Ye may abyde a whyle yet, parde!"° — *by God*

510 Quod° the turtle,° "Yf it be your wyll — *said / turtledove*

A whyght may speke, hym were as fayr be styll.[4]

---

[1]   *But as … happen may*   But it is as possible for me to die of woe today as it is for someone who has been languishing for the past twenty years, and it may well happen.

[2]   *As to my dome*   In my judgment.

---

[3]   *not worthe a flye*   Idiomatic expression meaning "worthless."

[4]   *Yf it be … be styll*   There are multiple ways to interpret these lines, depending on how they are punctuated. In this case, the meaning is "If I have permission to speak, I would say that it would be best if the cuckoo kept quiet." Some alternative examples include: "With your permission, a man may say what he is better off keeping quiet about"; "If it be your [the cuckoo's] wish for someone to speak, it would be just as well for him to keep quiet."

"I am a sede-foule,° one the vnworthyest, — *seed bird*
That wote° I well, and lytell of — *know*
   connynge.° — *of limited understanding*
But bet° is that a wyghtes° tongue rest — *better / person's*
515 Then entremete hym of° suche doynge, — *concern himself with*
Of whiche he neyther rede° can nor synge; — *advise*
And whoso° hit dothe full foule hymselfe — *whoever*
   acloyeth,° — *overburdens*
For offyce vncommytted° ofte anoyeth." — *unasked*

Nature, whiche that alway had an ere
520 To murmure of the lewdnesse° behynde, — *coarse behavior*
With faconde° voyce sayd, "Holde your — *eloquent*
   tongues there!
And I shall soone, I hope, a counsell fynde
You to delyuer, and from this noyse vnbynde:
I iudge, of euery folke° men shall one call — *group*
525 To say the verdyte° for you foules all." — *verdict*

Assented were to this conclusyon
The byrdes all; and foules of rauyne° — *birds of prey*
Haue chosen fyrst, by playne eleccyon,° — *simple vote*
The tercelet° of the faucon° to — *young male / falcon*
   dyffyne° — *specify*
530 All her sentence,° and as hym lust,° to — *their opinion / pleased*
   termyne;° — *reach a conclusion*
And to Nature hym gonne to present,° — *presented*
And she accepteth hym with glad entent.° — *goodwill*

The tercelet sayd then in this manere:
"Full harde were it to preue by reason
535 Who loueth beste this gentyll formell° here; — *noble female*
For eueryche° hath suche replycacyon° — *each one / replies*
That non° by skylles° may be brought — *none / arguments, reasons*
   adoune.° — *refuted*
I can not se that argumentes auayle:° — *help, are of use*
Then semeth it there must be batayle."° — *trial by combat*

540 "All redy!"° quod these egles tercelles tho.° — *Right! / said / then*
"Nay syrs," quod he, "yf that I durst° it say, — *dare*
Ye do me wronge, my tale is not ydo!° — *finished*
For, syrs—taketh not agrefe° I pray— — *do not be annoyed*
It may not gon as ye wolde in this way;
545 Ours is the voyce that haue the charge in honde,

And to the iudges dome ye moten stonde.[1]

"And therfore pes!° I say, as to my wyt,° — *peace / in my opinion*
Me wolde thynke how that the worthyest
Of knyghthode, and lengest had
   vsed it,° — *who had practiced it longest*
550 Most of estate,° of blode the gentyllest,° — *highest in rank / noblest*
Were syttyngest° for hire, yf that her lest;° — *most suitable / pleases*
And of these thre she wote° herselfe, I trowe,° — *knows / think*
Whiche that he be, for it is lyght° to knowe." — *easy*

The water-foules haue theyr hedes layde
555 Togyder, and of° a shorte auysement,° — *after / debate*
Whan eueryche had his large golee° sayde, — *mouthful*
They sayd sothely,° all by one assent, — *truly*
How that the goos, with her faconde gent,° — *refined eloquence*
"That so desyreth to pronounce our nede,° — *case*
560 Shall tell our tale," and prayed "God her spede."

And for these water-foules tho° began — *then*
The goos to speke, and in her cakelynge
She sayd, "Pes!° Now take kepe° — *Peace!, Quiet / pay attention*
   euery man,
And herkeneth° whiche a reason[2] I shall forth brynge! — *hear*
565 My wytte is sharpe; I loue no taryenge;° — *delays*
I say I rede° hym, thoughe he were my brother, — *advise*
But° she wyll loue hym, let hym loue another!" — *Unless*

"Lo, here a perfyte reson of a goos!"
Quod the sperhauke; "Neuer mote she thee![3]
570 Lo, suche it is to haue a tongue loos!
Now parde,° fole,° yit° were it bet° — *indeed / fool / yet / better*
   for the
Haue holde thy peas[4] than shewed° thy — *shown*
   nycete.° — *foolishness*
It lyeth not in his wytte, ne in his wyll,
But sothe° is sayd, 'a foole can not be styll.'"° — *truth / silent*

---

[1] *Ours is the … stonde* We (birds of prey) are the ones who have the floor, and you must abide by the judge's decision.

[2] *whiche a reason* What sort of reason.

[3] *Lo, here … she thee* "Ah, what a perfectly goosey argument!" said the sparrowhawk; "May she never thrive!"

[4] *holde thy peas* Kept quiet.

575   The laughter arose of gentyll° foules all,   *noble*
And ryght anone° the sede-foules chosen had   *without delay*
The turtle° true, and gonne° her to   *turtledove / did*
   them call,
And preyeden° her to saye the sothe sad°   *beseeched / sober truth*
Of this mater, and asked what she rad.°   *would advise*
580   And she answered that playnly her intent
She wolde shewe,° and sothly° what she ment.   *reveal / truly*

"Nay, God forbede a louer shulde chaunge!"
The turtle sayd, and wexe° for shame all reed,°   *grew / red*
"Though that° his lady euermore be   *Even if*
   straunge,°   *distant, reserved*
585   Yet lete hym serue her ever, tyll he be deed.°   *dead*
Forsothe,° I prayse nat the goses reed;°   *indeed / goose's advice*
'For, though she dyed I wolde° non other   *would want*
   make;°   *mate*
I wyll be hers, tyll that the dethe me take.'"

"Well bourded,"° quod° the ducke,   *Good joke / said*
   "by my hat!
590   That men shulde louen alway
   causelesse!°   *without encouragement*
Who can a reason fynde or wytte° in that?   *wisdom*
Daunceth he mery that is myrthlesse?
Who shulde recke of that is rechelesse?"[1]
"Ye queke,"° seyde the goos, "full well   *quack, speak*
   and fayre!°   *prettily*
595   There been mo sterres, God wote, than a payre!"[2]

"Now fy, chorle,"° quod° the gentyll   *peasant / said*
   tercelette,°   *noble male falcon*
"Out of the donghyll° came that worde°   *dunghill / decree*
   full ryght!°   *certainly*
Thou canst not seen whiche thynge is well bysette!°   *proper*
Thou farest by° loue as owles do by° lyght: *act / concerning*
600   The day them blent,° full well they se by nyght.   *blinds*
Thy kynde is of so lowe a wretchednesse
That what loue is, thou canst nouther°   *neither*
   seen ne gesse."

Tho° gan the cuckow put hym° forth in   *then / himself*
   preas°   *the crowd*
For foule° that eteth worme, and   *On behalf of the birds*
   sayd blyue:°   *quickly*
605   "So° I," quod° he, "may haue my   *provided that / said*
   make° in peas,   *mate*
I reche° not how longe that ye stryue.°   *care / quarrel*
Let yche of them be soleyne° all theyr lyue!   *alone, single*
This is my reed,° syth° they may not   *advice / since*
   acorde;°   *come to an agreement*
This shorte lesson nedeth not recorde."[3]

"Ye, haue the gloton° fylled ynoughe his   *glutton*
610   paunche,°   *belly*
Than are we well!" sayd the emerlyon;°   *merlin*
"Thou murderer of the haysoge° on   *hedge sparrow*
   the braunche
That brought the forth, thou rufullest°   *most contemptible*
   gloton!
Lyue thou soleyne, wormes corrupcyon,
615   For no force is of lacke of thy nature![4]
Go, lewde° be thou whyle the world   *ignorant, foolish*
   may dure!"°   *last*

"Now peas," quod Nature, "I commaunde here!
For I haue herde all your opynyon,
And in effecte yet be we neuer the nere.[5]
620   But fynally, this is my conclusyon,
That she herselfe° shall haue her eleccyon°   *the formel / choice*
Of whome her lust;° whoso be wrothe°   *likes / angry*
   or blythe,°   *glad*
Hym that she cheseth,° he shall hire   *chooses*
   han° as swythe.°   *have / without delay*

"For syth° it may not here dyscussed° be   *since / determined*
625   Who loueth her best, as sayd the tercelet,
Than wyll I do hire this fauoure, that she
Shall haue ryght° hym on whom her herte is set,   *exactly*
And he her that his herte hath on her knet;°   *fastened, joined*

---

[1] *Daunceth he mery … rechelesse?* Does he who is unhappy dance merrily? Who should care for someone who is uncaring?

[2] *There been mo … payre!* There are more stars in the sky, God knows, than a pair (i.e., there are more possible mates than this one).

[3] *This shorte lesson … recorde* This simple lesson does not need to be learned (i.e., it is obvious).

[4] *no force … nature* No one cares if all your kind die out.

[5] *neuer the nere* No closer to a solution.

This iudge I, Nature, for I may not lye;
630 To none estate° I haue none other eye.   *rank*

"But as for counseyle° to chese° a
    make,°   *advice / choose*
Yf I were Reason, than wolde I   *mate*
Counseyle you the royall tercell take,
As sayd the tercelet full skylfully,°   *reasonably*
635 As for the gentyllest° and most worthy,   *noblest*
Whiche I haue wrought so well to my
    pleasaunce°   *delight, pleasure*
That to yow hit ought to been a suffysaunce."°   *sufficiency*

With dredefull° voyce the formell her answerde,   *timid*
"My ryghtfull lady, goddes of Nature!
640 Sothe is° that I am euer vnder your yerde°   *It is true / authority*
As is euery other creature,
And must be youres whyle my lyfe may dure;°   *last*
And therfore graunte me my fyrst boone,°   *request*
And myne entent° I wol you say°   *plan, intention / tell*
    ryght soone."

645 "I graunte it you," quod she; and ryght anone°   *straightaway*
This formell egle spake in this degre:°   *manner*
"Almyghty quene, unto° this yere be done,   *until*
I ask respyte° for to aduyse me,°   *a period of delay / consider*
And after that to haue my choys all fre.°   *without restriction*
650 This all and some that I wolde speke and sey;
Ye gete no more, allthough ye do me dey!

"I wyll not serue Venus ne Cupyde
Forsothe° as yet, by no maner way."   *indeed*
"Now, syth° it may none otherwayes betyde,"°   *since / happen*
655 Quod Nature, "here is no more to say.
Than wolde° I that these foules were awaye,°   *wish / gone*
Yche with his make, for° taryenge longer here!"   *to prevent*
And sayd them thus, as ye shall after here.

"To you speke I, ye tercelettes," quod Nature,
660 "Beth of good herte, and serueth all thre.
A yere is not so longe to endure,
And yche of you peyne hym in his degre[1]
For to do well, for, God wote, quyte° is she   *free*

Fro you this yere; what after so
    befall,°   *whatever may happen afterward*
665 This entremesse[2] is dressed° for you all."   *prepared*

And whan this werke all brought was to an ende,
To euery foule Nature gaue his make
By euen acorde,° and on theyr way they   *mutual agreement*
    wende.°   *went*
And, Lorde, the blysse and ioye that they make!
670 For yche of them gan other in wynges take,
And with theyr neckes yche gan other wynde,°   *entwine*
Thankynge alway the noble goddes of kynde.°   *nature*

But fyrst were chosen foules for to synge,
As yere by yere was alway theyr vsaunce°   *custom*
675 To synge a roundell[3] at theyr departynge,
To do Nature honoure and plesaunce[4]
The note,° I trowe,° ymaked°   *melody / believe / made*
    was in Fraunce,
The wordes were suche as ye may here fynde,
The nexte verse, as I now haue in mynde.
680 Que bien ayme atard oblye.[5]

"Now welcome, somer, with thy sonne softe,
That hast thes wintres wedres overshake,
And driven away the longe nyghtes blake!

"Saynt Valentyn, that art ful hy on-lofte,
685 Thus syngen smale foules for thy sake:
[Now welcome, somer, with thy sonne softe,
That hast thes wintres wedres overshake.]

"Wel han they cause for to gladen ofte,
Sith ech of hem recovered hath hys make,
690 Ful blissful mowe they synge when they wake:
[Now welcome, somer, with thy sonne softe,
That hast thes wintres wedres overshake,
And driven away the longe nyghtes blake!"]

---

1 *peyne hym in his degre* Endeavor according to your rank.

2 *entremesse* A dish served between the main courses of a meal.

3 *roundell* The rondel is a French form in which one (or more) opening lines reoccur at the middle and/or end, having only two rhymes.

4 *To do ... pleasaunce* To honor and entertain Nature.

5 *Que bien ... oblye* French: who loves well forgets slowly.

And with the shoutyng, whan the songe was do°   *done*
695 That foules maden at theyr flyght away,
I woke, and other bokes toke me to,
To rede vpon, and yet I rede alway.
I hope, ywys,° to rede so some day   *indeed*
That I shall mete° some thynge for to fare   *dream*
700 The bet,° and thus to rede I nyl not° spare.   *better / will not*

Explicit parliamentum Auium in die sancti Valentini tentum,
secundum Galfridum Chaucers. Deo gracias.[1]
—C. 1478

The Canterbury Tales

It is some indication of its popularity that *The Canterbury Tales* survives in so many manuscripts: fifty-five complete or nearly complete collections and a further twenty-eight manuscripts that contain one or more tales. Of these manuscripts, two of the earliest, the Hengwrt, now in the National Library in Wales, and the Ellesmere, now in the Huntington Library in Pasadena, California, have provided the basis for most editions. The two manuscripts were copied by the same scribe, Adam Pynkhurst, in the first few years after Chaucer's death in 1400, or just possibly in the last year or two of Chaucer's life. The differences between the two manuscripts raise one of the great puzzles in Chaucerian scholarship: how close Chaucer came to finishing *The Canterbury Tales*. Ellesmere, generally agreed to be slightly later, presents the tales in an order that many modern readers have found to make strong artistic sense; Ellesmere also contains material—most notably the *Canon's Yeoman's Tale*, an account of a fraudulent alchemical workshop—that is missing from Hengwrt. On the other hand, many individual lines in Ellesmere contain small errors or are missing words. Why Pynkhurst, having managed to get an accurate (although incomplete) text from which to copy when he was writing the Hengwrt manuscript, should then have failed to do so when writing Ellesmere remains unclear. This edition reproduces the text of the Ellesmere manuscript, preserving its spellings and

modifying only its word division and punctuation. Where the text of the Ellesmere is clearly deficient or does not make sense, the editors have drawn on Hengwrt. In each case, these alterations are noted.

The Ellesmere manuscript includes a considerable number of marginal notes, or glosses. In the tales included in this anthology, these glosses are particularly numerous in *The Wife of Bath's Tale* and in *The Franklin's Tale*. Who first composed these glosses is still an open question, although there are strong grounds for believing that Chaucer himself composed quite a few of them. In these pages the texts of a number of the more interesting marginal glosses have been included in the notes at the bottom of the page.

The Ellesmere manuscript is large, its pages measuring roughly 15 by 11 inches, and elegantly decorated. It is the kind of luxury volume that might have been commissioned by an aristocrat, a prosperous London merchant, or a senior civil servant of the early fifteenth century. Various personal inscriptions in the manuscript indicate that it once belonged to John de Vere, who became the twelfth earl of Oxford in 1417, and whose guardians (possibly the book's first owners) were Thomas Beaufort, Duke of Exeter (one of the sons of John of Gaunt) and Henry IV's third son, John, Duke of Bedford, a great book collector.

The General Prologue

Chaucer's account of meeting a group of twenty-nine pilgrims at the Tabard Inn in Southwark, on the south bank of the Thames, has such an air of verisimilitude that it was once read as an account of an actual pilgrimage, with much attention devoted to determining just when it took place (1387 being the most favored date), how many days it took the pilgrims to get to Canterbury, and who the pilgrims were in real life. In fact, *The Canterbury Tales* draws on a tradition of medieval estates satire, poems that describe members of the three estates (those who pray, i.e., monks and nuns; those who fight, i.e., knights; and those who work, i.e., peasants) in terms of their characteristic vices. Many of Chaucer's most memorable and vivid characters, including his Friar and the Wife of Bath, are drawn from satirical figures found in such works as *Le Roman de la Rose* (*The Romance of the Rose*), in which a lover's quest for his lady (the rose) serves as an occasion for broad social commentary. Chaucer knew the work well, having translated it from

---

[1] *Explicit ... gracias*   Latin: here ends the Parliament of Birds held on Saint Valentine's Day, according to Geoffrey Chaucer. Thanks be to God.

French, and also knew the major example of English estates satire, William Langland's *Piers Plowman*, which Langland composed and then repeatedly reworked in the 1370s and 1380s.

Chaucer includes a Knight and a Plowman among his pilgrims, but for the most part they are drawn from the middle ranks of society, including prosperous members of the clergy, or first estate, such as the Friar, the Monk, and the Prioress, and those of the third estate who no longer fitted among the peasantry, such as the five prosperous Guildsmen, the Wife of Bath, the Merchant, the Physician, the Sergeant of Law, and the Manciple. Energetic and often clever, or at least sophisticated, the pilgrims are all professionally successful and—with a few exceptions—they thrive in the vibrant money economy of the later fourteenth century. To describe these people, Chaucer employs an affable and naively enthusiastic narrator, who mingles easily with them, admiring and even echoing their speeches, all apparently uncritically. As George Lyman Kittredge has observed, however, Chaucer was a professional tax collector and "a naïf collector of Customs would be a paradoxical monster." The poet and his narrator must not be confused.

The framing device of the pilgrimage allows Chaucer to explore the social tensions and moral debates of his day more freely than would otherwise be possible, transposing all conflict into an apparently innocent tale-telling competition. The question of who will tell the tale that offers the "best sentence and moost solaas" (line 798), i.e., the best moral meaning and the most enjoyment, is a standing invitation to probe beneath the surface and ask what the meaning of each tale really is. The pilgrimage frame also allows Chaucer to experiment with almost every major literary genre of his day and to assemble an encyclopedic compilation of ancient wisdom, history, and moral lessons. The learned aspect of this compilation is reinforced in the Ellesmere manuscript by the large number of marginal glosses, which identify the source for quotations and draw attention to particularly sententious passages.

Opening page of *The General Prologue*, Ellesmere manuscript. (Reprinted by permission of the *Huntington Library, San Marino, California*. EL26C9F72r.)

from *The Canterbury Tales*[1]

THE GENERAL PROLOGUE

Whan that Aprill with hise shoures° / *showers*
soote° / *sweet*
The droghte° of March hath perced° to the / *drought / pierced*
roote / *drought / pierced*
And bathed every veyne° in swich° licour° / *vein / such / liquid*
Of which vertu° engendred is the flour;° / *power / flower*
5 Whan Zephirus[2] eek° with his sweete breeth / *also*
Inspired hath in every holt° and heeth° / *wood / heath*
The tendre croppes;and the yonge sonne
Hath in the Ram[3] his half cours yronne° ; / *run*
And smale foweles° maken melodye / *birds*
10 That slepen al the nyght with open eye,
So priketh° hem nature in hir corages;° / *excites / their hearts*
Thanne longen folk to goon° on pilgrimages / *go*
And palmeres° for to seken° straunge / *pilgrims / seek / shores*
strondes° / *pilgrims / seek / shores*
To ferne halwes° kowthe° in sondry / *far-off shrines / known*
londes. / *far-off shrines / known*
15 And specially, fram° every shires° ende / *from / shire's*
Of Engelond to Caunterbury they wende,° / *travel*
The hooly blisful martir[4] for to seke
That hem° hath holpen° whan that they were / *them / helped / sick*
seeke.° / *them / helped / sick*
Bifil° that in that seson° on a day / *it happened / season*
20 In Southwerk[5] at the Tabard[6] as I lay

Redy to wenden° on my pilgrymage / *travel*
To Caunterbury with ful devout corage,° / *heart*
At nyght were come into that hostelrye° / *inn*
Wel nyne° and twenty in a compaignye / *nine*
25 Of sondry° folk by aventure yfalle[7] / *various*
In felaweshipe, and pilgrimes were they alle
That toward Caunterbury wolden° ryde. / *would*
The chambres° and the stables weren wyde,° / *bedrooms / wide*
And wel we weren esed° atte beste. / *fed*
30 And shortly, whan the sonne was to reste,
So hadde I spoken with hem° everichon° / *them / everyone*
That I was of hir° felaweshipe anon° / *their / soon*
And made forward° erly° for to ryse / *a pact / early*
To take oure wey ther as I yow devyse.° / *as I will tell you*
35 But nathelees,° whil I have tyme and space / *nevertheless*
Er that I ferther° in this tale pace,° / *further / go*
Me thynketh it° acordaunt° to resoun / *it seems to me / according*
To telle yow al the condicioun° / *i.e., character and estate*
Of ech of hem,° so as it semed me, / *each of them*
40 And whiche they were and of what degree° / *rank*
And eek° in what array° that they were inne, / *also / clothing*
And at a knyght than wol I first bigynne.
   A Knyght ther was and that a worthy man,
That fro the tyme that he first bigan
45 To riden out, he loved chivalrie,
Trouthe and honour, fredom and curteisie.[8]
Ful worthy was he in his lordes werre° / *war*
And therto hadde he riden no man ferre° / *further*
As wel in Cristendom as in hethenesse° / *pagan lands*
50 And evere honoured for his worthynesse.
At Alisaundre he was whan it was wonne.
Ful ofte tyme he hadde the bord bigonne[9]
Aboven alle nacions in Pruce.
In Lettow hadde he reysed° and in Ruce, / *raided*
55 No Cristen man so ofte of his degree.
In Gernade at the seege eek° hadde he be / *also*
Of Algezir, and riden in Belmarye.

---

[1] *The Canterbury Tales* The present text of introductions to, and quotations for *the Canterbury Tales* have been prepared for *The Broadview Anthology of British Literature* by Robert Boenig and Andrew Taylor from their forthcoming Broadview edition of the *Tales*.

[2] *Zephirus* The name given to the personified west wind.

[3] *Ram* The sign of the Zodiac for the early spring.

[4] *The hooly blisful martir* St. Thomas Becket, Archbishop of Canterbury, was killed on 29 December 1170 during a dispute with his King, Henry II, by four knights who thought the king wished his death.

[5] *Southwerk* Southwark is the region, now officially part of London but not so during Chaucer's time, on the southern bank of the Thames, directly across from the old city of London.

[6] *Tabard* This is the name of Harry Bailly's inn. A "tabard" was a type of tunic often worn over chain-mail armor.

[7] *yfalle* Encountered by chance.

[8] *Trouthe … curteisie* Keeping one's word, preserving one's reputation or honor, generosity, and courtesy or courtly manners are central values in the code of chivalry.

[9] *hadde the bord bigonne* Sat at the first table—an honor in victory banquets.

At Lyeys was he and at Satalye
Whan they were wonne and in the Grete See.
60 At many a noble armee° hadde he be.   *army*
At mortal batailles hadde he been fiftene
And foughten for oure feith° at Tramyssene   *faith*
In lystes° thries—and ay slayn his foo.   *jousting arenas*
This ilke° worthy knyght hadde been also   *same*
65 Somtyme with the lord of Palatye
Agayn another hethen° in Turkye,[1]   *heathen*
And everemoore he hadde a sovereyn° prys.° *sovereign / reputation*
And though that he were worthy,° he was wys,° *brave / prudent*
And of his port° as meeke as is a mayde.   *behavior*
70 He nevere yet no vileynye ne sayde
In al his lyf unto no maner wight.[2]
He was a verray,° parfit,° gentil° knyght.   *true / perfect / noble*
But for to tellen yow of his array,°   *appearance*
His hors° weren goode, but he was nat gay.°   *horses / gaudy*
75 Of fustian° he wered a gypon°   *rough cloth / tunic*
Al bismotered° with his habergeon,°   *soiled / mail coat*
For he was late ycome° from his viage°   *arrived / voyage*
And wente for to doon° his pilgrymage.   *do*
   With hym ther was his sone, a yong Squier,[3]
80 A lovyere° and a lusty° bacheler   *lover / vigorous*
With lokkes crulle° as they were leyd in presse.   *curled locks*
Of twenty yeer of age he was, I gesse.°   *guess*
Of his stature he was of evene lengthe°   *moderate height*

And wonderly delyvere° and of greet strengthe.   *quick*
85 And he hadde been somtyme in chyvachie°   *calvary expedition*
In Flaundres, in Artoys, and Pycardie[4]
And born hym weel as of so litel space°   *in so short a time*
In hope to stonden° in his lady grace.°   *stand / lady's favor*
Embrouded° was he as it were a meede,°   *embroidered / meadow*
90 Al ful of fresshe floures whyte and reede.°   *white and red*
Syngynge he was or floytynge° al the day.   *playing the flute*
He was as fressh as is the monthe of May.
Short was his gowne with sleves longe and wyde.
Wel koude he sitte on hors and faire ryde.
95 He koude songes make and wel endite,°   *compose verse*
Juste and eek daunce and weel putreye° and write.   *draw*
So hoote° he lovede, that by nyghtertale°   *hotly / nighttime*
He slepte namoore° than dooth a nyghtyngale.   *no more*
Curteis he was, lowely,° and servysable°   *humble / helpful*
100 And carf° biforn his fader at the table.   *carved (meat)*
   A Yeman[5] hadde he and servantz namo°   *no more*
At that tyme for hym liste° ride so,   *desired*
And he was clad in cote° and hood of grene.   *coat*
A sheef of pecok arwes° bright and kene° *peacock arrows / sharp*
105 Under his belt he bar ful thriftily.°   *very carefully*
Wel koude he dresse his takel° yemanly.   *equipment*
His arwes drouped° noght with fetheres° lowe, *drooped / feathers*
And in his hand he baar° a myghty bowe.   *bore*
A not heed° hadde he, with a broun visage.°   *curly head / face*
110 Of wodecraft wel koude° he al the usage.°   *knew / customs*
Upon his arm he baar° a gay bracer,°   *bore / leather bracelet*
And by his syde a swerd° and a bokeler°   *sword / small shield*
And on that oother syde a gay° daggere   *bright*
Harneised wel° and sharpe as point of spere;   *well-sheathed*
115 A cristophere° on his brest of silver
   sheene.°   *St. Christopher medal / bright*
An horn he bar;° the bawdryk° was of grene. *bore / shoulder-belt*
A forster° was he, soothly° as I gesse.°   *forester / truly / guess*

---

[1] *Alisaundre ... Turkye* The locations of the Knight's battles are as follows: Alexandria in Egypt (1365), Prussia, Lithuania, Russia (the scenes of much fighting against hold-out pagans in the last decades of the fourteenth century), Grenada (in Spain) whose city Algezir was captured in 1344, Banu Merin (in North Africa), Ayash (Lyeys in Syria, captured in 1367), Antalya (Satalye, in modern Turkey, captured in 1361), Tlemcen (in modern Algeria), Balat (Palatye, in modern Turkey, involved in campaigning in both the 1340s and 1365), and Turkey. The places not identified with a specific date of battle saw protracted hostilities between Christians and non-Christians during the period in question. The "great sea" is the Mediterranean. It would, of course, have been impossible for a knight to have taken part in all these campaigns.

[2] *In ... wight* He was never rude to anyone. Middle English often uses double or even triple negatives to intensify each other rather than to cancel each other out.

[3] *yong Squier* A squire would serve a knight, especially by helping to arm him, and would fight with him in battle. In some cases, as here, squires were young men training to be knights, but squires could also be older men, such as Chaucer.

[4] *In ... Pycardie* These places in Flanders saw military action in 1383, as the English troops fought for Pope Urban VI against his rival, Anti-Pope Clement VII. The campaign, led by the war-loving Bishop of Norwich, was a great disaster for the English.

[5] *A Yeman* Yeoman, a small landholder or tenant farmer, often prosperous enough to serve as an infantryman or archer in a knight's retinue.

Ther was also a Nonne,° a Prioresse,[1]   *nun*
That of hir smylyng was ful° symple and coy.°   *very / modest*
120 Hire gretteste ooth was but "By Seint Loy!"[2]
And she was cleped° Madame Eglentyne.[3]   *called*
Ful weel she soong° the service dyvyne,[4]   *sung*
Entuned°in hir nose ful semely.°   *intoned / seemly*
And Frenssh she spak ful faire and fetisly°   *elegantly*
125 After the scole° of Stratford atte Bowe:[5]   *school*
For Frenssh of Parys was to hire unknowe.°   *unknown*
At mete° wel ytaught° was she withalle.   *dinner / taught*
She leet° no morsel from hir lippes falle,   *let*
Ne wette hir fyngres in hir sauce depe.
130 Wel koude she carie a morsel and wel kepe,°   *take care*
That no drope ne fille upon hire brist.°   *breast*
In curteisie° was set ful muchel° hir list.° *courtesy / much / pleasure*
Hir over-lippe° wyped° she so clene,°   *upper lip / wiped / clean*
That in hir coppe° ther was no ferthyng°
    sene   *cup / coin-sized spot*
135 Of grece° whan she dronken hadde hir draughte.° *grease / draft*
Ful semely after hir mete° she raughte.°   *food / reached*
And sikerly° she was of greet desport°   *surely / geniality*
And ful plesaunt and amyable° of port° *amiable / disposition*
And peyned° hire to counterfete cheere°   *took pains / manners*
140 Of court and to been estatlich° of manere   *stately*

And to ben holden° digne° of reverence.   *held / worthy*
But for to speken° of hire conscience,°   *speak / conscience*
She was so charitable and so pitous,°   *compassionate*
She wolde wepe° if that she saugh° a mous° *weep / saw / mouse*
145 Kaught in a trappe if it were deed° or bledde.° *dead / bleeding*
Of smale houndes hadde she that she fedde
With rosted flessh or milk and wastel breed.[6]
But soore wepte she if any of hem were deed°   *dead*
Or if men smoot it with a yerde° smerte.° *yardstick / smartly*
150 And al was conscience and tendre herte.°   *tender heart*
Ful semyly hir wympul[7] pynched was;
Hir nose tretys,° hir eyen° greye as glas,   *shapely / eyes*
Hir mouth ful smal, and therto softe and reed.°   *red*
But sikerly, she hadde a fair forheed.
155 It was almoost a spanne brood,° I
    trowe,°   *a hand's span across / believe*
For hardily° she was nat undergrowe.° *certainly / not undergrown*
Full fetys° was hir cloke, as I was war.°   *elegant / aware*
Of smal coral aboute hire arm she bar
A peire° of bedes, gauded° al with grene,[8]   *pair / divided*
160 And theron heng a brooch of gold ful sheene,°   *very shiny*
On which ther was first write° a crowned "A"   *written*
And after, "Amor vincit omnia."[9]
    Another Nonne with hire hadde she
That was hir chapeleyne,° and Preestes° thre. *chaplain / priests*
165 A Monk ther was, a fair for the maistrie,° *i.e., better than all*
An outridere[10] that lovede venerie,°   *hunting*
A manly man, to been an abbot able.
Ful many a deyntee° hors hadde he in stable.   *fine*
And whan he rood, men myghte his brydel heere°   *hear*
170 Gynglen° in a whistlynge wynd als cleere° *jingling / as clear*

---

[1] *Prioresse* A prioress is either the second-in-command of an abbey, a large convent governed by an abbess, or is in charge of a priory, a smaller convent.

[2] *Seint Loy* St. Eligius, a seventh-century Bishop of Noyon in France. He is patron saint of both goldsmiths and blacksmiths.

[3] *Eglentyne* Eglantine, also known as sweet briar, is an early species of rose. It is known for its sweet, apple-like smell (which even the leaves emit if crushed) and five-petaled coral flowers, which appear once a year, in spring. Eglantine was not a common name in the Middle Ages.

[4] *service dyvyne* Divine service; the phrase refers to the Office (or Canonical Hours)—the round of services dominated by psalm-singing that monks and nuns perform on a daily basis. The names of the individual services are Matins, Lauds, Prime, Terce, Sext, None, Vespers, and Compline.

[5] *Stratford atte Bowe* Stratford-at-Bow is in Middlesex, just to the west of London. Chaucer's point, elaborated in the next line, is that the Prioress does not speak French properly but with a provincial accent. The Benedictine Priory of St. Leonard's was at Stratford-at-Bow and in Chaucer's day it had nine nuns, one of them named Argentine. The similarity of the names is suggestive, but Argentine was not the prioress there.

[6] *wastel breed* White bread (which, in the Middle Ages, was a delicacy reserved for the nobility).

[7] *wympul* Cloth folded cover the neck sides of the head, leaving only the face exposed. It was worn by both nuns and lay women.

[8] *A ... grene* She carries a set of coral rosary beads, a chain of prayer-beads. These are divided at intervals by green beads. The green beads indicated the end of the "decade," one set of prayers, and the beginning of the next.

[9] *Amor vincit omnia* Latin: love conquers all.

[10] *An outridere* An outrider was a monk whose job was to leave the cloister (which, as Chaucer makes clear below, was not the ideal thing for a monk to do) to take care of his monastery's business in the world at large. One of the common accusations made against monks was that they loved the secular world more than the cloister.

And eek as loude as dooth the chapel belle
Theras° this lord was kepere of the celle.[1]   *since*
The Reule° of Seint Maure or of Seint Beneit,[2]   *rule*
Bycause that it was old and somdel streit,°   *somewhat restrictive*
175 This ilke monk leet olde thynges pace°   *pass*
And heeld after the newe world the space.°   *course*
He yaf nat° of that text a pulled° hen   *gave not / plucked*
That seith that hunters beth nat hooly° men,   *not holy*
Ne that° a monk whan he is recchelees°   *nor when / reckless*
180 Is likned til° a fissh that is waterlees.   *likened to*
This is to seyn,° a monk out of his cloystre.°   *say / cloister*
But thilke° text heeld he nat worth an oystre.   *that same*
And I seyde his opinioun was good.
What° sholde he studie and make hymselven
     wood°   *why / crazy*
185 Upon a book in cloystre° alwey to poure°   *cloister / poor*
Or swynken° with his handes and laboure°   *work / labor*
As Austyn[3] bit?° How shal the world be served?   *commanded*
Lat Austyn have his owene swynk° to hym reserved!   *work*
Therfore he was a prikasour aright.°   *hard rider*
190 Grehoundes he hadde as swift as fowel° in flight.   *bird*
Of prikyng° and of huntyng for the hare   *riding*
Was al his lust.° For no cost wolde he spare.   *pleasure*
I seigh his sleves° ypurfiled° at the hond°   *sleeves / lined / hand*
With grys—and that the fyneste° of a
     lond.°   *expensive gray fur / finest / the land*
195 And for to festne° his hood under his chyn°   *fasten / chin*
He hadde of gold ywroght° a ful° curious pyn:°   *made / very / pin*
A love knotte in the gretter° ende ther was.   *bigger*
His heed was balled,[4] that shoon as any glas,

And eek his face as it hadde been enoynt.°   *anointed*
200 He was a lord ful fat and in good poynt,[5]
Hise eyen° stepe° and rollynge in his heed,   *eyes / bright*
That stemed as a forneys° of a leed,   *furnace*
His bootes souple,° his hors in greet estaat.°   *supple / in best shape*
Now certeinly he was a fair prelaat.°   *prelate*
205 He nas nat° pale as a forpyned goost.°   *was not / distressed ghost*
A fat swan loved he best of any roost.°   *roast*
His palfrey[6] was as broun as is a berye.°   *berry*
   A Frere° ther was, a wantowne° and a
     merye,°   *friar / pleasure-seeking / merry*
A lymytour,[7] a ful solempne° man.   *distinguished*
210 In alle the ordres foure[8] is noon° that kan°   *no one / knows*
So muchel° of daliaunce° and fair langage.   *much / flirtation*
He hadde maad° ful many a mariage   *made*
Of yonge wommen at his owene cost.
Unto his ordre he was a noble post!°   *pillar*
215 And wel biloved and famulier was he
With frankeleyns° ever al in his contree   *franklins (gentry)*
And with worthy wommen of the toun,
For he hadde power of confessioun,
As seyde hymself, moore than a curat,°   *curate (local priest)*
220 For of his ordre he was licenciat.°   *licensed*
Ful swetely° herde he confessioun,   *sweetly*
And plesaunt was his absolucioun.
He was an esy° man to yeve° penaunce,   *easy / give*
Theras° he wiste° to have a good
     pitaunce.°   *where / thought / donation*
225 For unto a povre° ordre for to yive°   *poor / give*
Is signe that a man is wel yshryve.°   *confessed*
For if he yaf,° he dorste° make avaunt,°   *gave / dared / assert*

---

[1] *celle* Priory or outlying house governed by the central monastery.

[2] *Seint Maure ... Seint Beneit* Monks. St. Benedict, a sixth-century Italian monk and abbot, compiled the famous Rule that goes by his name. It became normative for most of Western monasticism. St. Maurus, by legend one of his monks, was credited with bringing his Rule to France.

[3] *Austyn* "Austin" is the typical Middle English abbreviation for Augustine, the great Doctor of the Church and Bishop of Hippo in Northern Africa (354–430 CE). He was famous for his theological writings, particularly *The City of God* and *The Confessions*, the latter his spiritual autobiography. He is also credited with writing the Rule (followed by Augustinian canons and monks) to which this passage alludes.

[4] *His heed was balled* Monks shaved the crowns of their heads in a haircut known as a tonsure.

---

[5] *in good poynt* Idiomatic: in good condition.

[6] *palfrey* Everyday horse, as opposed to a destrier (war-horse) or a plowhorse.

[7] *lymytour* Friar licensed to preach, minister, and hear confessions in a specified, limited area.

[8] *In ... foure* There were four main orders of friars in the later Middle Ages—the Franciscans, the Dominicans, the Carmelites, and the Augustinians. Like monks, the friars took vows of poverty, chastity, and obedience, but they were supposed to go out in the world and preach to the laity, whereas monks were supposed to live apart from the world and devote themselves to prayer.

He wiste that a man was repentaunt.[1]

For many a man so hard is of his herte,

230 He may nat wepe° althogh hym soore
    smerte.°   *weep / sorely hurts*

Therfore instede of wepynge° and preyeres,° *weeping / prayers*

Men moote yeve° silver to the povre freres! *should give*

His typet[2] was ay farsed° ful of knyves   *stuffed*

And pynnes° for to yeven yonge
    wyves.°   *pins / give to young women*

235 And, certeinly, he hadde a murye note;°   *merry melody*

Wel koude he synge and pleyen on a rote.°   *play on a lyre*

Of yeddynges° he baar outrely° the
    pris.°   *songs / completely / prize*

His nekke° whit° was as the flour-de-lys.° *neck / white / lily*

Therto he strong was as a champion.

240 He knew the tavernes wel° in al the toun   *well*

And everich hostiler and
    tappestere°   *each innkeeper and barmaid*

Bet° than a lazar° or a beggestere.° *better / leper / female beggar*

For unto swich° a worthy man as he   *such*

Acorded nat as by his facultee[3]

245 To have with sike lazars aqueyntaunce.° *sick lepers acquaintance*

It is nat honeste,° It may nat avaunce,° *respectable / advance (one)*

For to deelen° with no swich poraille°   *deal / poor folk*

But al with riche° and selleres of vitaille.° *rich / sellers of food*

And overal theras profit sholde arise,

250 Curteis he was and lowely° of servyse.   *humble*

Ther nas no° man nowher so vertuous;   *was not*

He was the beste beggere in his hous.°[4]   *convent*

For thogh a wydwe° hadde noght a sho,° *widow / not a shoe*

So plesaunt was his "In principio,"[5]

255 Yet wolde he have a ferthyng° er he wente.   *farthing (coin)*

His purchas° was wel bettre than his rente,° *income / expenses*

And rage° he koude as it were right a whelp.° *cavort / dog*

In love-dayes ther koude he muchel° help, *could he (offer) much*

For ther he was nat lyk a cloystrer°   *monk*

260 With a thredbare cope° as is a povre scoler,° *cloak / poor student*

But he was lyk a maister or a pope.

Of double worstede° was his semycope° *thick cloth / short-cloak*

That rounded as a belle out of the presse.°   *mold*

Somwhat he lipsed° for his wantownesse° *lisped / affectation*

265 To make his Englissh sweete upon his tonge.

And in his harpyng, whan that he hadde songe,

Hise eyen° twynkled in his heed aryght°   *eyes / aright*

As doon° the sterres° in the frosty nyght.   *do / stars*

This worthy lymytour was cleped Huberd.   *limiter*

270   A Marchant was ther with a forked berd;°   *beard*

In motlee° and hye° on horse he sat, *multi-colored cloth / high*

Upon his heed a Flaundryssh° bevere° hat, *Flemish / beaver*

His bootes clasped faire and fetisly.

Hise resons° he spak ful solempnely,   *opinions*

275 Sownynge° alwey th'encrees° of his
    wynnyng.°   *concerning / increase / profit*

He wolde° the see° were kept for anythyng   *wished / sea*

Bitwixe° Middelburgh and Orewelle.[6]   *between*

Wel koude he in eschaunge° sheeldes selle.[7]   *exchange*

This worthy man ful wel his wit bisette;°   *employed*

280 Ther wiste no wight that he was in dette,[8]

So estatly° was he of his governaunce,° *dignified / management*

With his bargaynes and with his
    chevyssaunce.°   *commerce for interest*

Forsothe,° he was a worthy man withalle.° *truly / for all that*

But sooth to seyn, I noot how men hym calle.[9]

---

[1] *For ... repentaunt* For if a man gave money then he (the Friar) knew that man was repentant. The Friar is imposing a light penance in exchange for a donation to his order.

[2] *typet* Long ornamental piece of cloth worn either as a kind of scarf or as part of a hood or as sleeves. It provided a convenient place to put small objects.

[3] *For ... facultee* It was not appropriate according to his profession.

[4] The Hengwrt manuscript at this point includes the following two lines, usually numbered 252b and 252c: "And yaf a certeyn ferme for the graunt / Noon of his bretheren cam ther in his haunt" (And he paid a certain annual amount for the rights [to beg] / so that none of his brother friars came into his territory).

[5] *In principio* Latin: "in the beginning was the Word," the opening line of the Gospel of John.

---

[6] *Middelburgh and Orewelle* These two ports were in the Netherlands and in England respectively. There was much trade in the late Middle Ages between the two countries, particularly in textiles.

[7] *sheeldes selle* A shield, or *écu*, was a French coin. This kind of trade between national currencies was regarded with suspicion. It was often illegal and could be used as a way of surreptitiously charging interest on a loan (which the Church condemned as usury).

[8] *Ther ... dette* The syntax is ambiguous. Either "No one knew that he was in debt" (implying he was) or "No one knew him to be in debt" (implying he was not) or, since merchants were normally in debt, "No one knew how much he was in debt."

[9] *sooth ... calle* To tell the truth, I don't know what he was called.

285   A Clerk ther was of Oxenford° also[1]   *Oxford*
       That unto logyk hadde longe ygo,°   *who had [committed himself] to*
       And leene° was his hors as is a rake.   *lean*
       And he nas nat right° fat, I undertake,°   *was not very | declare*
       But looked holwe° and therto sobrely.°   *hollow | soberly*
290   Ful thredbare was his overeste courtepy,°   *overcoat*
       For he hadde geten hym yet no benefice[2]
       Ne was so worldly for to have office.
       For hym was levere° have at his beddes
          heed°   *would rather | bed's head*
       Twenty bookes clad° in blak or reed°   *bound | red*
295   Of Aristotle and his philosophie
       Than robes riche or fithele° or gay sautrie.°   *fiddle | psaltery*
       But al be that he was a philosophre,
       Yet hadde he but litel gold in cofre.°[3]   *little gold in a chest*
       But al that he myghte of his freendes° hente,°   *friends | obtain*
300   On bookes and on lernynge° he it spente   *learning*
       And bisily° gan for the soules preye°   *busily | prayed*
       Of hem° that yaf° hym wherwith to
          scoleye.°   *them | gave | the means to study*
       Of studie took he moost cure° and moost heede.   *care*
       Noght o° word spak he moore than was neede,   *one*
305   And that was seyd in forme° and reverence   *formally*
       And short and quyk and ful of hy sentence.°   *meaning*
       Sownynge in° moral vertu was his speche,   *tending towards*
       And gladly wolde he lerne and gladly teche.

       A Sergeant of the Lawe[4] war° and wys°   *shrewd | wise*
310   That often hadde been at the Parvys[5]
       Ther was also, ful riche of excellence.
       Discreet he was and of greet reverence.
       He semed swich, his wordes weren so wise.
       Justice° he was ful often in assise°   *judge | court*
315   By patente and by pleyn commissioun,[6]
       For his science° and for his heigh renoun.° *knowledge | renown*
       Of fees and robes hadde he many oon;°   *many a one*
       So greet a purchasour[7] was nowher noon.°   *nowhere at all*
       Al was fee symple[8] to hym in effect.
320   His purchasyng myghte nat been infect.°   *invalidated*
       Nowher so bisy° a man as he ther nas,°   *busy | was not*
       And yet he semed bisier° than he was.   *seemed busier*
       In termes° hadde he caas° and doomes
          alle°   *files | cases | judgments*
       That from the tyme° of Kyng William[9] were
          yfalle.°   *time | given*
325   Therto he koude endite° and make a thyng.°   *write | brief*
       Ther koude no wight° pynchen° at his
          writyng.   *nobody | quibble*
       And every statut koude he pleyn by rote.°   *recite by heart*
       He rood but hoomly° in a medlee° cote,   *simply | multi-colored*
       Girt with a ceint° of silk with barres° smale. *belt | ornaments*
330   Of his arraye tell I no lenger tale.

---

[1] *Clerk* The term clerk can mean student or professor, priest or priest's assistant, or learned man or philosopher, depending on the context. University students were supposed to be preparing for the priesthood. Some became priests, which required a vow of celibacy, and could then win promotion in the ranks of the Church. Others only took minor orders (which meant they could marry), and either remained at university or, in many cases, became members of the growing royal, baronial, and civic administration. Chaucer's Clerk, who is studying advanced logic, is roughly the equivalent of a graduate student or junior professor.

[2] *benefice* Position as a priest or clergyman. In the Middle Ages there had developed a much-criticized custom of granting the income from some benefices to people who would apportion a small amount of the income to a poorer clergyman to do the work and then live off the rest. This practice made some bishops with multiple benefices very wealthy, and it became a means of supporting a well-connected scholar at one of the universities.

[3] *But ... cofre* Chaucer is punning on the word philosopher, which can also mean alchemist. The search for the Philosopher's Stone, thought to be the key to turning metal to gold, was a particular study of alchemists.

[4] *Sergeant of the Lawe* In late fourteenth-century England, a Sergeant of Law was not simply a lawyer; he was one of about twenty or so lawyers who functioned as legal advisors to the king and served as judges.

[5] *Parvys* Shortened form of "Paradise," a name given to the porch in front of large churches. Here the reference is to the porch of Saint Paul's Cathedral in London, where lawyers would meet with their clients, the lawyer's office being unknown to late-fourteenth-century England.

[6] *By ... commissioun* Letters patent were royal letters of appointment that were open, i.e., public, documents that anyone was allowed to read. The full commission gives the Sergeant the right to hear all legal cases in the Court of Assizes, circuit courts that would move from county to county.

[7] *purchasour* I.e., purchaser, someone who acquired feudal property by money rather than feudal service.

[8] *fee symple* Ownership without feudal obligations.

[9] *Kyng William* William the Conqueror, who ruled England from 1066 to 1087. His reign marked a turning point in English governance.

A Frankeleyn[1] was in his compaignye.
Whit° was his heed° as is a dayesye.°   *white / head / daisy*
Of his complexioun he was sangwyn;[2]
Wel loved he by the morwe a sope in wyn.[3]

335   To lyven° in delit° was evere his wone,°   *live / delight / custom*
For he was Epicurus[4] owene sone°   *son*
That heeld opinioun that pleyn delit°   *full delight*
Was verray° felicitee parfit.°   *true / perfect happiness*
An housholdere and that a greet was he;

340   Seint Julian[5] was he in his contree.
His breed,° his ale was always after oon;[6]   *bread*
A bettre envyned man° was nevere noon.   *man stocked with wine*
Withoute bake mete° was nevere his hous   *baked food*
Of fissh and flessh, and that so plentevous°   *plentiful*

345   It snewed° in his hous of mete and drynke,   *snowed*
Of alle deyntees° that men koude thynke.   *delicacies*
After the sondry° sesons° of the yeer   *various / seasons*
So chaunged he his mete° and his soper.°   *food / meals*
Ful° many a fat partrich° hadde he in
     muwe°   *very / partridge / coop*

350   And many a breem° and many a luce° in
     stuwe.°   *bream / pike / pond*
Wo° was his cook but if° his sauce were   *woe / unless*
Poynaunt° and sharpe° and redy al his
     geere.°   *pungent / spicy / utensils*

His table dormant[7] in his halle alway
Stood redy covered al the longe day.

355   At sessiouns° ther was he lord and sire;   *court sessions*
Ful ofte tyme he was Knyght of the Shire.[8]
An anlaas° and a gipser° al of silk   *dagger / pouch*
Heeng° at his girdel whit° as morne°
     milk.   *hung / white / morning*
A shirreve° hadde he been and countour.°   *sheriff / tax-collector*

360   Was nowher swich a worthy vavasour.°   *feudal land holder*
     An Haberdasshere[9] and a Carpenter,
A Webbe,° a Dyere, and a Tapycer,°   *weaver / tapestry-maker*
And they were clothed alle in o° lyveree[10]   *one*
Of a solempne and a greet fraternitee.[11]

365   Ful fressh and newe hir geere° apiked° was.   *equipment / polished*
Hir knyves were chaped° noght° with bras°   *mounted / not / brass*
But al with silver, wroght ful clene° and weel   *made very elegantly*
Hire girdles° and hir pouches everydeel.°   *belts / every bit*
Wel semed° ech of hem a fair burgeys°   *seemed / citizen*

370   To sitten in a yeldehalle° on a deys.°   *guildhall / raised platform*
Everich° for the wisdom that he kan°   *everyone / knew*

---

[1] *Frankeleyn* From the word franc or free, a wealthy independent landowner and a member of the minor gentry.

[2] *Of … sangwyn* The Franklin's physiological makeup is dominated by blood, one of the four humors, which makes him red-faced and cheerful.

[3] *Wel … wyn* He greatly loved in the morning bread soaked in wine. Such was the preferred breakfast for those wealthy enough to afford wine, which had to be imported from Gascony, the sole remaining territory England retained in what we now call France.

[4] *Epicurus* The Greek philosopher Epicurus (341–270 BCE) maintained that the pursuit of pleasure was the natural state of humankind.

[5] *Seint Julian* St. Julian, the patron saint of hospitality in the Middle Ages. Julian set up a way-station for travelers in penance for unwittingly killing his parents, who had unknowingly lodged in his house while journeying.

[6] *after oon* Consistent, i.e., consistently good.

[7] *His table dormant* Always standing. Most medieval tables on which meals were set were trestle tables, i.e., a long board placed on top of what we would call saw-horses. After the meal was over, the table would normally be taken down. Not so the Franklin's.

[8] *Knyght of the Shire* Official designation for people chosen to represent their region in Parliament. Chaucer himself, while he was never knighted and only held the rank of squire, served as Knight of the Shire for Kent in 1386, the year before the fictitious pilgrimage to Canterbury takes place. The Franklin has also presided at the sessions of the Justices of the Peace (line 355) and served as Sheriff, the chief royal officer in a county who was responsible for collecting its taxes, and as the county auditor, who assisted the Sheriff.

[9] *Haberdasshere* Seller of ribbons, buttons, hats, gloves, and small articles of clothing.

[10] *lyveree* Uniform. Members of craft or religious guilds, as well as retainers of various lords, wore liveries. At this time the wearing of liveries encouraged factionalism and attendant violence, and there were some legal attempts to curb abuses.

[11] *fraternitee* Trade guilds or religious guilds. The trade guilds regulated who was allowed to follow a given trade in a given town, and the religious guilds functioned as mutual aid societies, burying their dead and helping members who were sick or had fallen into poverty. These guildsmen, though identified by their trades, are members of a religious guild, since trade guilds admitted only members of a single trade.

Was shaply° for to been an alderman.[1] *suitable*

For catel° hadde they ynogh° and rente,° *belongings / enough / rent*

And eek hir wyves° wolde it wel assente° *wives / agree*

375 And elles° certeyn were they to blame. *otherwise*

It is ful fair to been ycleped° "Madame" *called*

And goon to vigilies[2] al bifore

And have a mantel roialliche ybore.° *cloak royally carried*

   A Cook° they hadde with hem° for the
nones° *cook / them / occasion*

380 To boille° the chiknes° with the
marybones° *boil / chickens / marrowbones*

And poudre-marchant tart and galyngale.[3]

Wel koude he knowe a draughte of Londoun ale.

He koude rooste and sethe° and boille° and frye, *simmer / boil*

Maken mortreux° and wel bake a pye. *stews*

385 But greet harm° was it as it thoughte me° *pity / seemed to me*

That on his shyne° a mormal° hadde he. *shin / ulcer*

For blankmanger[4] that made he with the beste.

   A Shipman was ther wonynge° fer by
weste.° *living / far in the west*

For aught I woot,° he was of Dertemouthe.[5] *all I know*

390 He rood° upon a rouncy° as he kouthe° *rode / nag / could*

In a gowne of faldyng° to the knee. *woollen cloth*

A daggere hangynge on a laas° hadde he *lace*

About his nekke under his arm adoun.° *downwards*

The hoote° somer hadde maad° his hewe°
al broun, *hot / made / color*

395 And certeinly he was a good felawe.

Ful many a draughte° of wyn° had he
drawe° *draft / wine / drawn*

Fro Burdeuxward whil that the chapman° sleepe.[6] *merchant*

Of nyce° conscience took he no keepe.° *scrupulous / notice*

If that he faught° and hadde the hyer
hond,° *if he fought / upper hand*

400 By water he sente hem hoom° to every lond.[7] *home*

But of his craft° to rekene° wel his tydes,° *ability / reckon / tides*

His stremes° and his daungers° hym
bisides,° *currents / dangers / all around him*

His herberwe° and his moone,° his
lodemenage,° *harborage / moon / piloting*

Ther nas noon swich° from Hull to
Cartage.[8] *was not such a one*

405 Hardy he was and wys to undertake;° *wise in his endeavors*

With many a tempest hadde his berd° been
shake.° *beard / shaken*

He knew alle the havenes° as they were *havens*

Fro Gootlond to the Cape of Fynystere[9]

And every cryke° in Britaigne° and in
Spayne.° *inlet / Brittany / Spain*

410 His barge ycleped was the Maudelayne.

   With us ther was a Doctour of Physik.[10]

In al this world ne was ther noon hym
lik° *there was no one like him*

To speke of phisik° and of surgerye, *medicine*

For he was grounded in astronomye.[11]

415 He kepte° his pacient a ful greet deel *watched over*

---

[1] *alderman* In late medieval England, as in some cities today, the board of aldermen governs under the mayor. The five guildsmen have prospered, rising from artisans to masters. They are successful businessmen who run their own shop or shops, participate in civic government, and aspire, with their wives, to the status of the lesser gentry.

[2] *vigilies* Church services held the night before an important holy day. The aldermen and their wives would lead the procession, with their cloaks carried by a servant.

[3] *And … galyngale* And tart ground spice and aromatic roots (such as ginger).

[4] *blankmanger* Stew of milk, rice, almonds, and chicken or fish.

[5] *Dertemouthe* I.e., Dartmouth, a port on the English Channel in the southwest of England, near Plymouth.

[6] *Ful … sleepe* Sailing home from Bordeaux with a cargo of wine, the Shipman would secretly steal some while the wine merchant (chapman) was asleep.

[7] *By … lond* I.e., he threw his defeated opponents overboard.

[8] *Hull to Cartage* Hull is a port in northern England; Cartage is either Carthage on the Mediterranean coast of North Africa or Cartagena in Spain.

[9] *Fro … Fynystere* Gotland is an island in the Baltic Sea off the coast of southern Sweden; Cape Finisterre is the point of land that juts out into the Atlantic Ocean in northwest Spain.

[10] *Doctour of Physik* Physician. The term "doctor" means "teacher," as everyone in the Middle Ages knew, so the type of doctor who taught medicine and sometimes practiced it needed to be distinguished from other types of doctors, who taught academic subjects in the universities.

[11] *For … astronomye* In the Middle Ages, physicians often based their schedules of treatment on astrological tables.

In houres by his magyk natureel.[1]
Wel koude he fortunen the ascendent°   *calculate a planet's position*
Of hise ymages[2] for his pacient.
He knew the cause of everich° maladye,   *every*
420 Were it of hoot or coold or moyste or drye,[3]
And where they engendred and of what humour.
He was a verray, parfit praktisour:°   *practitioner*
The cause yknowe° and of his harm the roote,°   *known / root*
Anon he yaf° the sike man his boote.°   *gave / remedy*
425 Ful redy hadde he hise apothecaries°   *pharmacists*
To sende hym drogges° and his letuaries,°   *drugs / syrups*
For ech° of hem° made oother for to wynne.°*each / them / profit*
Hir° frendshipe nas nat newe° to
     bigynne.°   *their / recently / begun*
Wel knew he the olde Esculapius[4]
430 And Deyscorides and eek Rufus,
Olde Ypocras, Haly, and Galyen,

Serapion, Razis, and Avycen,
Averrois, Damascien, and Constantyn,
Bernard and Gatesden and Gilbertyn.
435 Of his diete° mesurable° was he,   *diet / moderate*
For it was of no superfluitee°   *excess*
But of greet norissyng° and digestible.   *nourishment*
His studie was but litel on the Bible.[5]
In sangwyn° and in pers° he clad was al,   *red / blue*
440 Lyned with taffata and with sendal.[6]
And yet he was but esy of dispence.°   *moderate in spending*
He kepte that he wan° in pestilence.°[7]   *what he earned / plague*
For gold in phisik° is a cordial.°   *medicine / heart-medicine*
Therfore he lovede gold in special.°   *especially*
445 A good Wif was ther of biside Bathe,[8]
But she was somdel deef,° and that was
     scathe.°   *somewhat deaf / a shame*
Of clooth makyng she hadde swich an haunt,°   *skill*
She passed hem of Ypres and of Gaunt.[9]
In al the parisshe° wif ne was ther noon   *parish*
450 That to the offrynge°[10] bifore hire sholde goon.   *offering*
And if ther dide, certeyn so wrooth° was she,   *angry*
That she was out of alle charitee.
Hir coverchiefs° ful fyne were of ground°—   *kerchiefs / texture*
I dorste swere° they weyeden° ten pound—   *dare swear / weighed*
455 That on a Sonday weren upon hir heed.
Hir hosen weren of fyn° scarlet reed,°   *fine / red*
Ful streite yteyd° and shoes ful moyste° and
     newe.   *tightly laced / supple*

[1] *In … natureel* Hours are the times in the day when the various planetary influences were pronounced, when the Physician watched over (kepte) his patient. Natural magic is opposed to black magic, which involves contact with malicious spirits.

[2] *Of hise ymages* The practice of astrologically-based medicine involved the use of images of the planets as talismans.

[3] *He … drye* Medieval medicine was also based on a theory, traceable back to Greek physicians such as the ones Chaucer mentions below, of the balance of the four bodily humors (blood, phlegm, black bile, and yellow bile) and their qualities of hot, cold, moist, and dry mentioned in this line.

[4] *Wel … Esculapius* Aesculapius was a mythological demi-god, son to Apollo. Dioscorides, Rufus of Ephesus, Hippocrates (associated with the Hippocratic Oath physicians still swear), and Galen were famous Greek physicians. Galen (129–199) was particularly influential, since he set out the theory of four humors which was the basis of medieval medicine. "Haly" is probably the Persian physician Ali Ben el-Abbas (d. 994). Rhazes (d. c. 930) was an Arab astronomer and physician. Avicenna, or Ibn Sina (980–1037), and Averroes (1126–98) were Islamic philosophers and physicians. John of Damascus was a Syrian physician of the ninth century. Constantine the African came from Carthage, converted to Christianity, became a Benedictine monk, and taught at Salerno in Italy in the eleventh century. His work on aphrodisiacs earns him the title the "cursed monk" in *The Merchant's Tale*, line 1810. Islamic science was widely influential in the Middle Ages; it first brought Greek thought to the Latin West. The last three authorities are British. Bernard Gordon was a Scottish physician who taught at Montpellier in the fourteenth century. John Gaddesden (d. c. 1349) taught at Oxford and served as court doctor to Edward II. Gilbert was an English physician in the thirteenth century and the author of a major medical treatise.

[5] *His … Bible* In the Middle Ages physicians were often thought to be religious skeptics, partly because of their knowledge of classical astronomy.

[6] *Lyned … sendal* Taffeta and sendal are types of silk cloth; silk, imported from Asia, was a mark of status and wealth.

[7] *He … pestilence* Possibly a reference to the Black Death, which killed at least a third of the population of England between 1348 and 1349, although there were later outbreaks of plague in 1362, 1369, and 1376.

[8] *Bathe* I.e., Bath, a town in southwest England near Bristol. It is famous for its hot springs (hence its name) and Roman ruins. The parish of St. Michael's, just north of Bath, was famous for its weavers.

[9] *Ypres … Gaunt* Cities in Flanders (now north-western Belgium) known for cloth trading. There were also skilled weavers from these cities working in England.

[10] *offrynge* In eucharistic services, gifts are brought to the altar during the Offering, or Offertory.

Boold° was hir face and fair and reed of hewe.°   *bold / color*

She was a worthy womman al hir lyve.

460 Housbondes at chirche dore° she hadde fyve,°[1] *church door / five*

Withouten° oother compaignye in youthe.   *apart from*

But therof nedeth nat to speke as nowthe.°   *for now*

And thries° hadde she been at Jerusalem.[2]   *three times*

She hadde passed many a straunge strem.°   *foreign water*

465 At Rome she hadde been and at Boloigne,

In Galice at Seint Jame and at Coloigne.

She koude muchel of wandrynge by the weye.[3]

Gat-tothed was she, soothly for to seye.[4]

Upon an amblere° esily° she sat,   *saddle-horse / easily*

470 Ywympled[5] wel, and on hir heed° an hat   *head*

As brood° as is a bokeler or a targe,°   *broad / shields*

A foot mantel° aboute hir hipes large   *outer skirt*

And on hir feet a paire of spores° sharpe.   *spurs*

In felaweshipe wel koude she laughe and carpe.°   *joke*

475 Of remedies of love she knew perchaunce,°   *as it happened*

For she koude° of that art the olde daunce.   *knew*

   A good man was ther of religioun

And was a povre Persoun° of a toun,   *poor parson*

But riche he was of hooly thoght° and werk.° *holy thought / work*

480 He was also a lerned man, a clerk,

That Cristes° gospel trewely wolde preche.°   *Christ's / preach*

Hise parisshens° devoutly wolde he teche.   *parishioners*

Benygne° he was and wonder diligent   *benign*

And in adversitee ful pacient,

485 And swich° he was preved° ofte sithes.° *such / proven / many times*

Ful looth° were hym to cursen° for hise

 tithes,[6]   *reluctant / excommunicate*

But rather wolde he yeven° out of doute°   *give / without doubt*

Unto his povre parisshens aboute

Of his offryng and eek of his substaunce.

490 He koude in litel thyng have suffisaunce.[7]

Wyd° was his parisshe and houses fer asonder,° *wide / far apart*

But he ne lefte° nat for reyn° ne thonder   *did not neglect / rain*

In siknesse nor in meschief° to visite   *trouble*

The ferreste° in his parisshe muche and

 lite,°   *farthest / of greater or lesser (rank)*

495 Upon his feet and in his hand a staf.°   *staff*

This noble ensample° to his sheepe he yaf,   *example*

That firste he wroghte° and afterward that he taughte. *acted*

Out of the gospel he tho° wordes caughte,°   *those / took*

And this figure° he added eek therto,°   *figure of speech / to it*

500 "That if gold ruste, what shal iren° do?"   *iron*

For if a preest be foul on whom we truste,

No wonder is a lewed man° to ruste,   *layman*

And shame it is if a preest take keepe°—   *heed*

A shiten° shepherde and a clene°

 sheepe.   *soiled with excrement / clean*

505 Wel oghte° a preest ensample for to yeve   *ought*

By his clennesse how that his sheepe sholde lyve.

He sette nat° his benefice to hyre   *did not offer*

And leet° his sheepe encombred° in the myre° *left / stuck / mud*

And ran to Londoun unto Seint Poules[8]

510 To seken hym° a chauntrie° for soules   *seek for himself / chantry*

Or with a bretherhed° to been withholde,°[9]   *guild / hired*

But dwelleth at hoom and kepeth wel his

 folde°   *sheepfold (i.e., flock)*

---

[1] *Housbondes ... fyve* Marriage vows were exchanged on the church steps and were followed by a Mass inside the church.

[2] *And ... Jerusalem* Jerusalem was the greatest of all pilgrimages. From England, a trip there and back could take a couple of years. The other pilgrimages mentioned below are Rome, where the Apostles Peter and Paul were buried; Boulogne-sur-mer in France, famous for its miraculous image of the Blessed Virgin; Compostella in Galicia, where the relics of St. James were venerated; and Cologne, where the relics of the Three Kings (or Three Magi) were kept.

[3] *She ... weye* She knew much about wandering along the road.

[4] *Gat-tothed ... seye* According to medieval physiognomy, a gap between the teeth was a sign that a woman was bold, lecherous, faithless, and suspicious.

[5] *Ywympled* Wearing a wimple.

---

[6] *tithes* Periodic assessments made to determine one tenth of a person's goods, harvest, and animals, which would then be claimed by the Church. Parish priests could excommunicate parishioners who would not pay them.

[7] *He ... suffisaunce* He was able to have enough in little things.

[8] *Seint Poules* St. Paul's Cathedral in London. The custom Chaucer refers to is related to the issue of benefices. A chantry is an endowed position, usually at large churches and cathedrals, in which a priest sings masses for the soul of the person who left money for the endowment. It involved very little work, unlike the Parson's toil described in his section of the General Prologue.

[9] *Or ... withholde* The brotherhood here is a guild. Guilds hired priests to serve as their chaplains.

So that the wolf ne made° it nat

    myscarie.°   *would not make / come to grief*

He was a shepherde and noght° a mercenarie,°   *not / mercenary*

515 And though he hooly were and vertuous,

He was nat to synful men despitous,°   *scornful*

Ne of his speche daungerous° ne digne,°   *proud / haughty*

But in his techyng discreet and benygne,°   *kind*

To drawen folk to hevene by fairnesse,

520 By good ensample. This was his bisynesse.

But it were any persone obstinat,[1]

Whatso° he were of heigh or lough estat,°   *whether / low class*

Hym wolde he snybben° sharply for the

    nonys.°   *rebuke / occasion*

A bettre preest I trowe° that nowher noon ys.   *believe*

525 He waiteth after° no pompe and reverence,   *expected*

Ne maked° hym a spiced° conscience.   *affected / overly fastidious*

But Cristes loore° and hise apostles twelve   *teaching*

He taughte, but first he folwed it hymselve.

    With hym ther was a Plowman, was° his brother, *(who) was*

530 That hadde ylad° of dong ful many a fother.° *hauled / cartload*

A trewe swynkere° and a good was he,   *true worker*

Lyvynge in pees and parfit charitee.

God loved he best with al his hoole herte

At alle tymes, thogh he gamed or smerte,[2]

535 And thanne° his neighebore right° as hymselve. *then / just*

He wolde thresshe° and therto dyke° and

    delve°   *thresh / dig / shovel*

For Cristes sake for every povre wight°   *poor person*

Withouten hire° if it lay in his myght.   *pay*

Hise tithes payde he ful faire and wel,

540 Bothe of his propre swynk° and his catel.° *own work / possessions*

In a tabard° he rood upon a mere.°   *over-shirt / mare*

    Ther was also a Reve° and a Millere,   *reeve*

A Somnour°[3] and a Pardoner[4] also,   *summoner*

A Maunciple°[5] and myself. Ther were namo.° *manciple / no more*

545 The Millere was a stout carl° for the nones. *sturdy fellow*

Ful byg he was of brawn and eek of bones.

That proved wel,° for overal ther° he

    cam°   *was clear / everywhere / came*

At wrastlynge° he wolde have alwey the ram.[6] *wrestling*

He was short-sholdred,° brood,° a thikke

    knarre.°   *stocky / broad / thick fellow*

550 Ther was no dore that he ne wolde heve of harre[7]

Or breke it at a rennyng° with his heed.   *by running at it*

His berd as any sowe° or fox was reed,   *sow*

And therto brood as though it were a spade.

Upon the cope° right of his nose he hade   *ridge*

555 A werte° and theron stood a toft of herys,° *wart / tuft of hairs*

Reed as the brustles° of a sowes erys.°   *bristles / sow's ears*

Hise nosethirles° blake were and wyde.°   *nostrils / wide*

A swerd and a bokeler bar° he by his syde.   *bore*

His mouth as greet was as a greet forneys.° *furnace*

560 He was a janglere° and a goliardeys,[8]   *joker*

And that was moost of synne° and harlotries.° *sin / obscenities*

Wel koude he stelen° corn° and tollen

    thries,°   *steal / grain / take his toll (percentage) thrice*

And yet he hadde a thombe° of gold,

    pardee.°   *thumb / by God*

A whit cote° and a blew° hood wered° he. *white coat / blue / wore*

565 A baggepipe wel koude he blowe and sowne,° *sound*

And therwithal he broghte us out of towne.

    A gentil° Maunciple was ther of a temple *gracious*

Of which achatours° myghte take exemple *buyers*

For to be wise in byynge° of vitaille.°,   *buying / food*

570 For wheither that he payde or took by taille,° *credit*

Algate he wayted so in his achaat

That he was ay biforn and in good staat.[9]

---

[1] *But ... obstinat* But if anyone were obstinate.

[2] *At ... smerte* At all times, whether he gamed (i.e., did pleasant things) or hurt.

[3] *A Somnour* Deliverer of legal summonses to either secular or ecclesiastical courts, although more often the latter. The ecclesiastical courts were run by the Church and had jurisdiction over all clerics but also over any lay person charged with a moral offense such as adultery or fornication.

[4] *Pardoner* Seller of indulgences, which were writs authorized by the Church to raise money for charitable causes. Indulgences usually promised reduction of time in penance and, after death, in Purgatory.

---

[5] *Maunciple* Servant at one of the Inns of Court, the legal brotherhoods in London. The Inns of Court were also called temples.

[6] *ram* Typical prize for victors at trade fairs.

[7] *Ther ... harre* There was not a door that he would not heave off its hinges.

[8] *goliardeys* The reference is to Goliards, wandering scholars in the eleventh and twelfth centuries who were known for their rowdy life.

[9] *Algate ... staat* He was always so watchful in his purchasing (achaat) / That he always came out ahead (biforn) and did well.

Now is nat that of God a ful faire grace

That swich a lewed° mannes wit shal pace°   *unlearned / surpass*

575   The wisdom of an heepe° of lerned men?   *heap*

Of maistres hadde he mo° than thries ten°   *more / three times ten*

That weren° of lawe° expert and curious,°   *were / law / skilled*

Of whiche ther weren a duszeyne° in that hous   *dozen*

Worthy to been stywardes° of rente and lond   *stewards*

580   Of any lord that is in Engelond,

To maken hym lyve by his propre good°   *own means*

In honour dettelees°—but if he were wood—   *without debt*

Or lyve as scarsly° as hym list desire,°   *frugally / as he wanted*

And able for to helpen al a shire°   *an entire county*

585   In any caas° that myghte falle or happe,°   *situation / happen*

And yet this Manciple sette hir aller cappe.°   *cheated them all*

     The Reve was a sclendre,° colerik° man.[1]   *slender / angry*

His berd was shave° as ny° as ever he kan,   *shaven / closely*

His heer° was by his erys° ful round yshorn.°   *hair / ears / cut*

590   His tope was dokked° lyk a preest biforn.[2]   *clipped*

Ful longe were his legges and ful lene°—   *lean*

Ylyk° a staf° ther was no calf ysene.°   *like / staff / seen*

Wel koude he kepe a gerner° and a bynne;°   *granary / bin*

Ther was noon auditour koude of hym wynne.°   *get the better of*

595   Wel wiste° he by the droghte° and by the reyn°   *knew / drought / rain*

The yeldynge° of his seed and of his greyn.°   *yield / grain*

His lordes sheepe, his neet,° his dayerye,°   *cattle / dairy cows*

His swyn,° his hors, his stoor,° and his pultrye°   *swine / livestock / poultry*

Was hoolly° in this Reves governyng,   *wholly*

600   And by his covenant° yaf the rekenyng°   *contract / reckoning*

Syn° that his lord was twenty yeer of age.   *since*

Ther koude no man brynge hym in arrerage.°   *arrears*

Ther nas baillif ne hierde nor oother hyne,

That he ne knew his sleighte and his covyne.[3]

605   They were adrad° of hym as of the deeth.°[4]   *afraid / death*

His wonyng° was ful faire upon an heeth;°   *dwelling / heath*

With grene trees shadwed was his place.

He koude bettre than his lord purchace.°   *buy land*

Full riche he was, astored pryvely.°   *privately stocked*

610   His lord wel koude he plesen subtilly,°   *please subtly*

To yeve and lene° hym of his owene good°   *loan / goods*

And have a thank and yet a gowne and hood.[5]

In youthe he hadde lerned° a good myster:°   *learned / craft*

He was a wel good wrighte,° a carpenter.   *craftsman*

615   This Reve sat upon a ful good stot°   *farm horse*

That was al pomely° grey and highte° Scot.   *dappled / named*

A long surcote° of pers upon he hade,   *overcoat*

And by his syde he baar a rusty blade.

Of Northfolk° was this Reve of which I telle,   *Norfolk*

620   Biside a toun men clepen Baldeswelle.[6]

Tukked° he was as is a frere° aboute,[7]   *belted / friar*

And ever he rood the hyndreste° of oure route.°   *last / company*

     A Somonour was ther with us in that place

That hadde a fyr reed,° cherubynnes° face,[8]   *fire red / cherub-like*

625   For saucefleem° he was with eyen narwe.°   *blotchy / narrow eyes*

As hoot he was and lecherous as a sparwe,°[9]   *sparrow*

With scaled browes blake and piled berd.[10]

Of his visage° children were aferd.°   *face / afraid*

---

[1]   *The ... man* A reeve was someone, often originally a peasant, who served as a supervisor on a lord's estate. Among other things, reeves collected the portion of the harvest due to the lords and made sure peasants performed their customary labor for the lords. They were much resented. Chaucer's Reeve is dominated by choler, or yellow bile, which makes him suspicious and irritable.

[2]   *His ... biforn* The top of his head was cut short in the front like a priest's haircut. This would have been an unfashionable cut for a layman, and suitable to a man who was poor, or miserly, or austere.

[3]   *Ther nas ... covyne* There was not a bailiff (foreman), herdsman, or other worker whose tricks and deception he did not know.

[4]   *adrad ... deeth* Death in general, or possibly the plague.

[5]   *His lord ... hood* This reeve cheats his lord by storing away the lord's goods as his own and then using them to provide loans to the lord, receiving payment and thanks. Payment in the Middle Ages was most often in tangible goods, like the clothing mentioned here, rather than in money.

[6]   *Baldeswelle* I.e., Bawdeswell, a town in the northern part of Norfolk, the northernmost county in East Anglia on the east coast of England.

[7]   *Tukked ... aboute* Franciscan friars wore habits tied about the waist with ropes.

[8]   *That ... face* Cherubim, the second highest order of angels, were bright red. See Ezekiel 1.13.

[9]   *sparwe* Since sparrows travel in flocks, they had a reputation in the Middle Ages for being lecherous, similar to the more modern reputation of rabbits.

[10]   *With ... berd* The Summoner's eyebrows have a disease called the scall, and his beard has been losing tufts of hair.

Ther nas quyksilver, lytarge, ne brymstoon,
630 Boras, cerice, ne oille of Tartre noon,[1]
Ne oynement° that wolde clense° and
    byte°   *ointment / cleanse / bite*
That hym myghte helpen of the whelkes° white   *blemishes*
Nor of the knobbes sittynge° on his chekes.°   *sitting / cheeks*
Wel loved he garleek, oynons, and eek lekes°   *leeks*
635 And for to drynken strong wyn reed as blood.
Thanne wolde he speke and crie° as he were wood.   *yell*
And whan that he wel dronken hadde the wyn,
Thanne wolde he speke no word but Latyn.
A fewe termes hadde he, two or thre,
640 That he had lerned out of som decree.°   *legal document*
No wonder is, he herde it al the day,
And eek ye knowen wel how that a jay°   *chattering bird*
Kan clepen "Watte"° as wel as kan the Pope.   *Walter*
But whoso koude in oother thyng him grope,°   *examine*
645 Thanne hadde he spent al his philosophie.
Ay° "Questio quid iuris!"[2] wold he crie.   *always*
He was a gentil harlot and a kynde;°   *noble and kindly scoundrel*
A bettre felawe° sholde men noght° fynde.   *fellow / not*
He wolde suffre for a quart of wyn
650 A good felawe to have his concubyn°   *mistress*
A twelf monthe° and excuse hym atte fulle.°   *a year / fully*
Ful prively° a fynch° eek koude he pulle.[3]   *secretly / finch*
And if he foond° owher° a good felawe,   *found / anywhere*
He wolde techen° hym to have noon awe°   *teach / no respect*
655 In swich caas of the Ercedekenes curs—[4]
But if° a mannes° soule were in his purs.°   *unless / man's / purse*
For in his purs he sholde ypunysshed be:°   *be punished*
Purs is the Ercedekenes Helle, seyde he.
But wel I woot° he lyed° right in dede.°   *know / lied / indeed*
660 Of cursyng° oghte ech gilty man him drede;   *excommunication*
For curs wol slee° right as° assoillyng°   *kill / just as / absolution*

savith.
And also war° him of a "Significavit"![5]   *beware*
In daunger° hadde he at his owene gise°   *power / pleasure*
The yonge girles[6] of the diocise°   *diocese*
665 And knew hir conseil° and was al hir reed.[7]   *their secrets*
A gerland° hadde he set upon his heed   *garland*
As greet as it were for an ale stake.[8]
A bokeleer hadde he, maad° hym of a cake.°   *made / loaf of bread*
    With hym ther was a gentil° Pardoner   *noble*
670 Of Rouncivale,[9] his freend and his compeer,°   *companion*
That streight° was comen fro the court of Rome.   *straight*
Ful loude he soong "Com Hider, Love, to Me;"[10]
This Somonour bar to hym a stif burdoun.[11]
Was nevere trompe° of half so greet a soun!   *trumpet*
675 This Pardoner hadde heer as yelow as wex,°   *wax*
But smothe it heeng as dooth a strike° of flex.°   *bunch / flax*
By ounces° henge hise lokkes that he hadde,   *strands*
And therwith he hise shuldres°
    overspradde,°   *shoulders / spread over*
But thynne° it lay by colpons° oon° and oon.   *thin / strands / one*
680 But hood for jolitee° wered° he noon,   *fun / wore*
For it was trussed° up in his walet.°   *packed / bag*
Hym thoughte° he rood al of the newe
    jet.°   *it seemed to him / fashion*

---

1 *Ther ... noon* The unsuccessful remedies are mercury (sometimes known as quicksilver), lead monoxide (lytarge), sulfur (sometimes known as brimstone), borax, white lead (cerice), and cream of tartar.

2 *Questio quid iuris* Latin: Question: what point of the law? The expression was often used in the ecclesiastical courts.

3 *Ful ... pulle* Obscene expression that meant, literally, "to pluck a bird."

4 *In ... curs* In such a case of the excommunication (curse) of the archdeacon. An archdeacon was the ecclesiastical official in charge of the ecclesiastical court of a diocese.

5 *Significavit* Latin: it signified. It is the first word in a writ authorizing the civil court to imprison someone who had been excommunicated.

6 *yonge girles* In Middle English, girls can mean young people of both sexes, but here it may just mean young women.

7 *was al hir reed* Was all their advice. Idiomatic: the Summoner was in their confidence.

8 *ale stake* Ale-sign; a long pole that stuck out into the street and showed that ale was being sold on the premises.

9 *Of Rouncivale* The Pardoner belongs to the Hospital of the Blessed Mary of Roncesvalles in London, a dependent house of the larger one at Roncesvalles, the mountain pass between Spain and France which many pilgrims used when they traveled to St. James of Compostela. Hospitals in the Middle Ages were not purely medical facilities; they also served as inns and poor houses.

10 *Com Hider, Love, to Me* This song, "Come Here, Love, to Me," does not survive.

11 *This ... burdoun* The Summoner accompanied him with a strong bass. In medieval carols, each sung verse was separated by a burden, a kind of refrain. Carols originally had many subjects, not just the joys of Christmas.

Dischevelee° save° his cappe° he rood° al
    bare.   *with his hair loose | except | cap | rode*
Swiche glarynge° eyen hadde he as an hare.[1]   *bulging*
685 A vernycle[2] hadde he sowed° upon his cappe;   *sewn*
His walet° biforn° hym in his lappe,°   *wallet | before | lap*
Bretful° of pardoun, comen from Rome al hoot.   *brimful*
A voys° he hadde as smal° as hath a
    goot.°   *voice | high-pitched | goat*
No berd hadde he, ne never sholde° have: *would*
690 As smothe° it was as° it were late yshave.[3]   *smooth | as if | shaven*
I trowe° he were a geldyng° or a mare.[3]   *believe | gelding*
But of his craft fro° Berwyk into Ware[4]   *from*
Ne was ther swich° another pardoner.   *there was not such*
For in his male° he hadde a pilwe beer,°   *bag | pillow-case*
695 Which that he seyde was oure Lady veyl;°[5]   *Virgin Mary's veil*
He seyde he hadde a gobet° of the seyl°   *piece | sail*
That Seint Peter hadde when that he wente
Upon the see til Jhesu Crist hym hente.°[6]   *grabbed him*
He hadde a croys° of latoun° ful of stones,   *cross | brass*
700 And in a glas° he hadde pigges bones.   *glass*
But with thise relikes whan that he fond
A povre person dwellynge upon lond,
Upon a day he gat hym° moore moneye   *got himself*
Than that the person gat in monthes tweye.
705 And thus with feyned° flaterye and japes°   *pretended | jokes*
He made the person and the peple his apes.°   *dupes*
But trewely, to tellen atte laste,
He was in chirche a noble ecclesiaste.°   *churchman*

Wel koude he rede a lessoun° or a
    storie,°   *lesson | story (from the Bible)*
710 But alderbest° he song° an offertorie,[7]   *best of all | sang*
For wel he wiste whan that song was songe
He moste preche° and wel affile° his
    tonge°   *must preach | sharpen | tongue*
To wynne° silver as he ful wel koude.   *acquire*
Therfore he song the murierly° and loude.   *more merrily*
715   Now have I toold yow shortly° in a clause   *briefly*
Th'estaat,° th'array,° the nombre, and eek the
    cause   *social position | appearance*
Why that assembled was this compaignye
In Southwerk at this gentil hostelry
That highte the Tabard, faste by the Belle.[8]
720 But now is tyme to yow° for to telle   *you*
How that we baren° us that ilke nyght   *behaved*
Whan we were in that hostelrie alyght,°   *arrived*
And after wol I tell of oure viage
And al the remenaunt of oure pilgrimage.
725 But first I pray yow of youre curteisye
That ye n'arette it nat my vileynye,[9]
Thogh that I pleynly° speke in this mateere   *plainly*
To telle yow hir wordes and hir cheere,°   *comportment*
Ne thogh I speke hir wordes proprely.°   *exactly*
730 For this ye knowen also wel as I:
Whoso° shal telle a tale after a man,   *whoever*
He moot° reherce as ny° as ever he kan   *should | closely*
Everich a word° if it be in his charge,   *every word*
Al° speke he never so rudeliche° or
    large,°   *although | crudely | freely*
735 Or ellis° he moot° telle his tale untrewe,   *else | must*
Or feyne thyng,° or fynde wordes newe.   *falsify something*
He may nat spare althogh he were his brother;
He moot as wel seye o word as another.

---

[1] *hare* According to medieval lore, hares were hermaphroditic, becoming both male and female in order to reproduce. Bulging eyes were thought to be a sign of lust and folly.

[2] *vernycle* Badge depicting St. Veronica's veil, a relic at Rome. St. Veronica wiped Jesus's face with her veil as he carried the cross, and by miracle his image was imprinted upon it. Pilgrims collected such badges.

[3] *I ... mare* I believe he was either a gelding (a castrated horse) or a mare.

[4] *Berwyk into Ware* Berwick is in the extreme north of England near the border with Scotland; Ware is near London.

[5] *For ... veyl* Chaucer's point is that the Pardoner sells fraudulent relics (sacred objects associated with Jesus or the saints).

[6] *That ... hente* The reference is to Peter's unsuccessful attempt to imitate Christ by walking on the water. Christ had to rescue him. See Matthew 14.22–33.

---

[7] *offertorie* The Offertory was chanted when the congregation was bringing gifts to the altar.

[8] *Belle* Previous editors have capitalized this word, guessing that it was the name of another inn—there were several called the Bell in that area — or perhaps a house of prostitution. Perhaps the word should not be capitalized, as it may imply a notable bell in the neighborhood.

[9] *That ... vileynye* That you not attribute it to my lack of manners. Vileynye does not mean villainy in the modern sense. A villein was originally an inhabitant of a rural village; thus the word signifies the state of being rustic rather than civilized.

Crist spak hymself ful brode° in Hooly
    Writ,°   *freely / Holy Scripture*
740 And wel ye woot no vileynye is it.
Eek Plato seith, whoso kan hym rede,
The wordes moote be cosyn° to the dede.°[1]   *cousin / deed*
Also I prey yow to foryeve° it me   *forgive*
Al° have I nat set folk in hir degree°   *although / according to rank*
745 Heere in this tale as that they sholde stonde.
My wit° is short, ye may wel understonde.   *intelligence*
   Greet chiere° made oure Hoost us everichon,°   *cheer / everyone*
And to the soper sette he us anon.
He served us with vitaille at the beste;
750 Strong was the wyn, and wel to drynke us leste.°   *it pleased us*
A semely° man oure Hoost was withalle   *suitable*
For to been a marchal° in an halle.[2]   *marshal*
A large man he was, with eyen stepe.°   *bright*
A fairer burgeys° was ther noon in Chepe,[3]   *citizen*
755 Boold of his speche and wys and wel ytaught,°   *learned*
And of manhod hym lakked° right naught.°   *lacked / nothing*
Eek therto° he was right a myrie man,   *in addition*
And after soper pleyen° he bigan°   *play / began*
And spak of myrthe amonges othere thynges
760 Whan that we hadde maad oure rekenynges[4]
And seyde thus, "Now lordynges, trewely,
Ye been° to me right welcome hertely.°   *are / heartily*
For by my trouthe, if that I shal nat lye,
I saugh nat this yeer so myrie a compaignye
765 Atones° in this herberwe° as is now.   *at once / inn*
Fayn° wolde I doon yow myrthe, wiste I°   *gladly / if I knew*
    how.
And of a myrthe I am right now bythoght°   *in mind*
To doon yow ese,° and it shal coste   *do you ease*
    noght.°   *nothing*
Ye goon to Caunterbury: God yow
    speede!°   *God bring you success!*

770 The blissful martir quite° yow youre meede!°   *pay / reward*
And wel I woot as ye goon by the weye,
Ye shapen yow° to talen° and to pleye.°   *intend / tell tales / play*
For trewely,° confort° ne myrthe is noon   *truly / comfort*
To ride by the weye doumb as the stoon.[5]
775 And therfore wol I maken yow disport,°   *entertainment*
As I seyde erst,° and doon yow som
    confort.°   *first / bring you some comfort*
And if yow liketh° alle by oon assent°   *pleases you / unanimously*
For to stonden at° my juggement°   *abide by / judgment*
And for to werken° as I shal yow seye,   *proceed*
780 Tomorwe, whan ye riden by the weye,
Now by my fader soule° that is deed,°   *father's soul / dead*
But if ye be myrie, I wol yeve yow myn heed!
Hoold up youre hondes withouten moore speche."
   Oure conseil° was nat° longe for to seche.°   *counsel / not / seek*
785 Us thoughte° it was noght worth to make it wys,[6]   *we thought*
And graunted hym withouten moore avys°   *more debate*
And bad° hym seye his voirdit° as hym
    leste.°   *asked / verdict / as he wanted*
"Lordynges," quod he, "now herkneth for the beste,
But taak it nought, I prey° yow, in desdeyn.°   *beg / disdain*
790 This is the poynt, to speken short and pleyn,
That ech of yow to shorte° with oure weye   *shorten*
In this viage shal telle tales tweye°   *two*
To Caunterburyward,° I mene° it so,   *towards Canterbury / mean*
And homward he shal tellen othere two
795 Of aventures that whilom° han bifalle.°   *once / have happened*
And which of yow that bereth hym° best of
    alle,   *conducts himself*
That is to seyn, that telleth in this caas°   *occasion*
Tales of best sentence° and moost solaas,°   *meaning / enjoyment*
Shal have a soper at oure aller cost°   *at all our cost*
800 Heere in this place, sittynge by this post,
Whan that we come agayn fro Caunterbury.
As for to make yow the moore mury,°   *merry*
I wol myself goodly° with yow ryde,   *gladly*
Right at myn owene cost, and be youre gyde.
805 And whoso wole my juggement withseye°   *resist*
Shal paye al that we spenden by the weye.°   *along the way*
And if ye vouchesauf° that it be so,   *grant*

---

[1] *Eek ... dede* The reference is to Plato's *Timaeus*, the only one of his dialogues available in translation to the Latin West in the Middle Ages. The quotation is found in section 29. The passage is also discussed by Boethius in his *Consolation of Philosophy* (3, prose 12), a work that Chaucer had translated and drew upon frequently.

[2] *For ... halle* A marshal is a steward or chief butler; a hall is a manor house or town house of a lord.

[3] *Chepe* Cheapside was the merchants' district in London.

[4] *Whan ... rekenynges* When we had paid our bills.

[5] *For ... stoon* For truly there is neither comfort nor mirth in riding along as silent as a stone.

[6] *to make it wys* Idiomatic: to make a big deal of it.

Tel me anon withouten wordes mo,

And I wol erly° shape me° therfore."°   *early | get ready | for it*

810   This thyng was graunted and oure othes° swore°   *oaths | sworn*

With ful glad herte, and preyden° hym also   *asked*

That he wolde vouchesauf for to do so

And that he wolde been oure governour

And of oure tales juge° and reportour°   *judge | referee*

815   And sette a soper at a certeyn pris°   *price*

And we wol reuled been at his devys°   *wish*

In heigh and lough.° And thus by oon°   *all matters | one*
        assent

We been acorded° to his juggement,   *agreed*

And therupon the wyn was fet° anon.°   *fetched | immediately*

820   We dronken and to reste wente echon°   *each one*

Withouten any lenger taryynge.°   *longer delaying*

        Amorwe,° whan that day gan° for to
            sprynge,°   *the next day | began | dawn*

Up roos° oure Hoost and was oure aller cok°   *rose | rooster for us all*

And gadrede° us togidre° all in a flok.°   *gathered | together | flock*

825   And forth we ridden,° a litel moore than
            paas,°   *rode | a horse's walking pace*

Unto the Wateryng of Seint Thomas.[1]

And there oure Hoost bigan his hors areste°   *rein in*

And seyde, "Lordynges, herkneth if yow leste!°   *please*

Ye woot youre foreward° and it yow recorde;°   *contract | recall*

830   If evensong° and morwesong° accorde,[2]   *Evensong | Matins*

Lat se° now who shal telle the firste tale.   *let us see*

As evere mote° I drynke wyn or ale,   *might*

Whoso be rebel to my juggement

Shal paye for al that by the wey is spent.

835   Now draweth cut er that we ferrer twynne;[3]

He which that hath the shorteste shal bigynne.

Sire Knyght," quod he, "my mayster and my lord,

Now draweth cut,° for that is myn
            accord.°   *a straw | decision*

840   Cometh neer," quod he, "my lady Prioresse,

And ye, sire Clerk, lat be youre shamefastnesse,°   *shyness*

Ne studieth noght.° Ley° hond° to every
            man."   *stop studying | lay | hand | person*

Anon to drawen every wight° bigan,   *person*

And shortly for to tellen as it was,

Were it by aventure or sort or cas,[4]

845   The sothe° is this: the cut° fil° to the knyght,   *truth | straw | fell*

Of which ful blithe° and glad was every wyght.   *very happy*

And telle he moste his tale as was reso un,°   *reasonable*

By foreward° and by composicioun,°   *agreement | arrangement*

As ye han herd. What nedeth wordes mo?

850   And whan this goode man saugh° that it was so,   *saw*

As he that wys was and obedient

To kepe his foreward by his free assent,

He seyde, "Syn° I shal bigynne the game,   *since*

What, welcome be the cut, a Goddes° name!   *in God's*

855   Now lat us ryde and herkneth what I seye."

And with that word we ryden forth oure weye.

And he bigan with right a myrie cheere°   *cheerful expression*

His tale anon, and seyde in this manere.[5]

---

[1]   *Wateryng of Seint Thomas*   The Watering of St. Thomas was the name given to a brook just outside London on the way to Canterbury.

[2]   *If ... accorde*   I.e., if you still say in the morning what you said last evening.

[3]   *Now ... twynne*   "Now draw a straw before we depart further."

[4]   *Were ... cas*   Adventure, sort, and case mean roughly the same thing: chance.

[5]   *His ... manere*   Hengwrt and some other manuscripts read "and seyde as ye may heere," not "and seyde in this manere," a suggestion that *The Canterbury Tales* were to be read aloud as well as silently.

The Knight's Tale

The Knight has the highest social status of the pilgrims and it is appropriate that he should initiate the tale-telling and do so with a work that reflects the interests of his class, a philosophical romance. As befits the teller, the poem is stately in tone and pace and filled with lengthy descriptions of aristocratic rituals, including the great final tournament and the funeral of one of the two lovers. It offers a fantasy of idealized aristocratic love, set in a world of violence to which the love sometimes contributes. In so doing it also raises questions of free will and astrological determinism, inviting us to ask whether a providential order can be reconciled with the violence and disorder of earthly life.

Chaucer originally composed *The Knight's Tale* as a separate work, probably during the 1380s. His source was Boccaccio's story of Theseus, the *Teseida* (written c. 1340), a work of nearly 10,000 lines, in twelve books, and written in Italian to provide a vernacular rival to Virgil's Latin epic, the *Aeneid*. The 2350 lines of *The Knight's Tale* make it Chaucer's longest single poem after *Troilus and Criseyde*, although it is only a quarter of the length of Boccaccio's *Teseida*.

The Knight's central subject is the love of two young nobles, Palamon and Arcite, for the beautiful Emelye, which follows the conventions of *amour courtois* or courtly love, a refined love that is inspired by the sight of the beloved and is violent in its intensity, demanding absolute devotion and years of painful service. Palamon and Arcite fall in love with Emelye while gazing from their prison window and without exchanging a word with her, their passion remains as intense as ever seven years later. The literature of courtly love often takes a legalistic turn, inviting readers or listeners to join in a debate on a formal question, known as a *demande d'amour*; in this case, the question is whether the lover who can see his lady but do nothing to win her is in a worse position than the lover who can struggle to win her but can never see her.

Chaucer, or his Knight, complicates the basic love story by repeated references to cosmic forces. The three earthly lovers are in the character of pagan gods of love, war, and chastity, whose conflict is ultimately resolved by Saturn, the oldest of the gods and a source of destruction. Chaucer takes the sub-plot of the pagan gods from Boccaccio, but he greatly expands the descriptions of the grim effects of Mars and Saturn on human life, evoking the wars, rebellions, plagues, and devastation of his own day. One might describe this world as a thoroughfare of woe, as Theseus's father Egeus does (line 1987). Alternatively, one could look beyond it to a higher order, as Theseus does, in an evocation of cosmic harmony that draws on one of Chaucer's most important sources, the *Consolation of Philosophy* of the late Roman philosopher Boethius. For Theseus, the principle that maintains this order is either Jupiter, chief of the pagan gods, or the First Mover of Aristotelian philosophy (l. 2127), but Chaucer's readers would have understood this principle in Christian terms. In many respects, Theseus speaks for the Knight's values, but whether the tale always confirms them is more questionable.

Detail, opening page of *The Knight's Tale*, Ellesmere manuscript.
(Reprinted by permission of *The Huntington Library, San Marino, California*. EL26C9F72r.)

Opening page of *The Knight's Tale,* Ellesmere manuscript. (Reprinted by permission of *The Huntington Library, San Marino, California.* EL26C9F72r.)

THE KNIGHT'S TALE

Iamque domos patrias, Scithice post aspera gentis
Prelia, laurigero[1]

HEERE BIGYNNETH THE KNYGHTES TALE

Whilom,° as olde stories tellen us,   *once*
Ther was a duc° that highte° Theseus.   *duke / was named*
Of Atthenes° he was lord and governour,   *Athens*
And in his tyme swich° a conquerour   *such*
5 That gretter° was ther noon° under the sonne.   *greater / none*
Ful many a riche contree hadde he wonne,°   *won*
What with his wysdom and his chivalrie.°   *knightly prowess*
He conquered al the regne of Femenye[2]
That whilom was ycleped° Scithia[3]   *called*
10 And wedded the queene Ypolita°   *Hippolita*
And broghte hire hoom° with hym in° his contree   *home / to*
With muchel° glorie and greet
   solempnytee,°   *much / great ceremony*
And eek° hir faire suster° Emelye.°   *also / sister / Emily*
And thus with victorie and with melodye
15 Lete° I this noble duc to Atthenes ryde   *let*
And al his hoost° in armes hym bisyde.°   *host / beside him*
   And certes,° if it nere to long to
   heere,°   *certainly / were not too long to hear*
I wolde° yow have toold fully the manere°   *would / manner*
How wonnen° was the regne of Femenye   *won*
20 By Theseus and by his chivalrye°   *knights*
And of the grete bataille° for the
   nones°   *great battle / on that occasion*
Bitwixen° Atthenes and Amazones   *between*
And how asseged° was Ypolita,   *besieged*

The faire, hardy queene of Scithia,
25 And of the feste° that was at hir weddynge   *feast*
And of the tempest at hir hoomcomynge.°   *homecoming*
But al that thyng I moot° as now
   forbere.°   *must / for the moment resist (telling)*
I have, God woot,° a large feeld to ere,°   *God knows / plow*
And wayke° been° the oxen in my plough.   *weak / are*
30 The remenant of the tale is long ynough:°   *enough*
I wol nat letten° eek noon° of this route.°   *hinder / none / company*
Lat° every felawe° telle his tale aboute!°   *let / fellow / in turn*
And lat se° now, who shal the soper wynne?   *let us see*
And ther° I lefte I wol ayeyn° bigynne.   *where / again*
35   This duc of whom I make mencioun,
Whan he was come almoost unto the toun
In al his wele° and in his mooste pride,°   *prosperity / great pride*
He was war° as he caste his eye aside   *aware*
Where that ther° kneled° in the weye°   *there / kneeled / road*
40 A compaignye of ladyes tweye and tweye,°   *two by two*
Ech after oother clad in clothes blake.
But swich a cry and swich a wo° they make,   *woe*
That in this world nys° creature lyvynge   *is no*
That herde° swich another waymentynge.°   *heard / sorrowing*
45 And of this cry they nolde° nevere stenten°   *would not / cease*
Til they the reynes of his brydel henten.°   *grasped*
   "What folk been° ye, that at myn homcomynge   *are*
Perturben° so my feste with criynge?"   *disturb*
Quod° Theseus. "Have ye so greet envye°   *said / envy*
50 Of myn honour that thus compleyne and crye?
Or who hath yow mysboden° or offended?   *harmed*
And telleth me if it may been amended
And why that ye been clothed thus in blak."
   The eldeste lady of hem alle spak,
55 Whan she hadde swowned° with a deedly°
   cheere°   *fainted / deathly / face*
That it was routhe° for to seen and heere,   *pity*
And seyde, "Lord to whom fortune hath yeven°   *given*
Victorie and as a conquerour to lyven,°   *live*
Nat greveth us° youre glorie and youre
   honour,   *we are not grieved by*
60 But we biseken° mercy and socour!°   *ask / help*
Have mercy on oure wo° and oure distresse!   *woe*
Som drope of pitee thurgh° thy gentillesse°   *through / nobility*
Upon us wrecched wommen lat thou falle.
For certes,° lord, ther is noon of us alle   *certainly*
65 That she ne hath been a duchesse or a queene.
Now be we caytyves,° as it is wel seene,   *miserable people*

---

[1] *Iamque … laurigero* Latin: "And now Theseus, [drawing near] his native land in a chariot covered with laurels, after fierce battle with the Scythians [is heralded by glad applause and the shouts of the people to the heavens and the merry trumpet celebrating the end of the war]." This passage occurs at the end of Latin poet Statius's epic poem about the Theban War, *The Thebaid*, which was one of Chaucer's sources for *The Knight's Tale*. This passage describes the triumphant return of Theseus at the very end of the poem.

[2] *Femenye* Land of the Amazons, a race of female warriors.

[3] *Scithia* Scythia was an ancient country of nomads who inhabited the Caucasus region and was believed to be the homeland of the Amazons.

Thanked be Fortune and hire false wheel,[1]

That noon estaat assureth to be weel!°   *assures no estate prospers*

And certes, lord, to abyden° youre presence,   *await*

70   Heere in the temple of the goddesse

    Clemence°   *clemency (mercy)*

We han° been waitynge al this

    fourtenyght.°   *have / two-week period*

Now help us, lord, sith° it is in thy myght!   *since*

    "I, wrecche° which that wepe° and crie thus,   *wretched one / weep*

Was whilom wyf to Kyng Cappaneus[2]

75   That starf° at Thebes, cursed be that day!   *died*

And alle we that been in this array°   *condition*

And maken al this lamentacioun,

We losten alle oure housbondes at that toun

Whil° that the seege° theraboute lay.   *while / siege*

80   And yet now the olde Creon,[3] weylaway,°   *alas*

That lord is now of Thebes the citee,

Fulfild of ire° and of iniquitee,°   *filled with anger / wickedness*

He for despit° and for his tirannye   *spite*

To do the dede bodyes vileynye°   *disgrace*

85   Of alle oure lordes whiche that been slawe,°   *killed*

He hath alle the bodyes on an heepe°

    ydrawe°   *heap / gathered together*

And wol nat suffren hem by noon

    assent°   *permit them on any terms*

Neither to been yburyed° nor ybrent,°   *buried / burned*

But maketh houndes° ete° hem in despit!"°   *dogs / eat / spite*

90   And with that word, withouten° moore respit,   *delay*

They fillen gruf° and criden° pitously,   *fell groveling / cried*

"Have on us wrecched wommen som mercy,

And lat oure sorwe synken° in thyn herte!"   *sink*

    This gentil° duc doun from his courser°

    sterte°   *noble / horse / jumped*

95   With herte pitous° whan he herde hem speke.   *pitying*

Hym thoughte that his herte wolde breke

Whan he saugh° hem so pitous and so maat,°   *saw / downcast*

That whilom weren of so greet estaat.

And in his armes he hem alle up hente°   *took*

100   And hem conforteth in ful good entente°   *with good will*

And swoor his ooth as he was trewe knyght

He wolde doon so ferforthly° his myght   *completely*

Upon the tiraunt° Creon, hem to wreke,°   *tyrant / avenge*

That al the peple of Grece sholde speke

105   How Creon was of Theseus yserved°   *dealt with*

As he that hadde his deeth ful wel deserved.

And right anoon° withouten moore abood,°   *immediately / delay*

His baner° he desplayeth and forth rood°   *banner / rode*

To Thebesward° and al his hoost° biside.   *towards Thebes / army*

110   No neer° Atthenes° wolde he go ne° ride   *nearer / Athens / nor*

Ne take his ese° fully half a day,   *rest*

But onward on his wey that nyght he lay

And sente anon Ypolita the queene

And Emelye hir yonge suster sheene°   *bright*

115   Unto the toun of Atthenes to dwelle.

And forth he rit;° ther is namoore to telle.   *rode*

    The rede° statue of Mars with spere° and

    targe°   *red / spear / shield*

So shyneth in his white baner large

That alle the feeldes glyteren° up and doun,   *glitter*

120   And by his baner born° is his penoun°   *carried / pennant*

Of gold ful riche, in which ther was ybete°   *embroidered*

The Mynotaur[4] which that he slough° in Crete.   *killed*

Thus rit this duc. Thus rit this conquerour,

And in his hoost of chivalrie the flour,°   *flower*

125   Til that he cam to Thebes and alighte°   *dismounted*

Faire in a feeld theras° he thoughte fighte.   *where*

But shortly for to speken of this thyng,

With Creon, which° that was of Thebes kyng,   *who*

He faught and slough hym manly as a knyght

130   In pleyn bataille,° and putte the folk to flyght.   *open battle*

And by assaut° he wan° the citee after   *assault / captured*

And rente adoun° bothe wall and sparre° and

    rafter.   *pulled down / beam*

And to the ladyes he restored agayn

The bones of hir housbondes that weren slayn

---

[1] *Fortune ... wheel* The Wheel of Fortune appears in Boethius's *Consolation of Philosophy*, a work Chaucer translated into English. The goddess Fortune turns her Wheel, and those on the top, in prosperity, fall to the bottom, and misery.

[2] *Kyng Cappaneus* King Cappaneus was one of seven leaders who attacked and besieged Thebes.

[3] *Creon* Creon was the king of Thebes and brother of Jocasta, mother of Oedipus.

---

[4] *The Mynotaur* An earlier deed of Theseus's is his killing of the Minotaur, a half-bull, half-human monster, who was kept in the labyrinth on the island of Crete and there given Athenian youths to devour for food. The Cretan King Minos's daughter, Ariadne, helped Theseus in this feat by giving him a ball of thread to roll out behind him so he could find his way out of the labyrinth once his deed was done.

135 To doon obsequies° as was tho the
gyse.°   *funeral rites / then the custom*
But it were al to longe for to devyse°   *narrate*
The grete clamour and the waymentynge°   *lamentation*
That the ladyes made at the brennynge°   *cremation*
Of the bodies and the grete° honour   *great*
140 That Theseus the noble conquerour
Dooth to the ladyes whan they from hym wente;
But shortly for to telle is myn entente.
    Whan that this worthy duc, this Theseus
Hath Creon slayn and wonne Thebes thus,
145 Stille° in that feeld he took al nyght his reste   *quietly*
And dide with al the contree as hym leste.°   *desired*
    To ransake in the taas° of the bodyes dede   *pile*
Hem for to strepe° of harneys° and of
wede°   *strip / armor / clothes*
The pilours° diden bisynesse and cure[1]   *scavengers*
150 After the bataille and disconfiture.°   *defeat*
And so bifel that in the taas they founde,
Thrugh girt° with many a grevous, blody wounde,   *pierced*
Two yonge knyghtes liggynge° by and by,°   *lying / side by side*
Bothe in oon armes wroght ful richely,[2]
155 Of whiche two, Arcita highte° that oon   *was named*
And that oother knyght highte Palamon.
Nat fully quyke° ne fully dede they were,   *alive*
But by hir cote-armures° and by hir gere°   *coat of arms / equipment*
The heraudes° knewe hem best in special°   *heralds / particularly*
160 As they that weren of the blood roial°   *were / royal*
Of Thebes, and of sustren° two yborn.°   *sisters / born*
Out of the taas the pilours han hem torn°   *had pulled them*
And han hem caried softe° unto the tente   *softly*
Of Theseus. And ful soone he hem sente
165 To Atthenes to dwellen in prisoun
Perpetuelly. He nolde° no raunsoun.[3]   *would take*
And whan this worthy duc hath thus ydon,
He took his hoost and hoom he rood anon

---

[1] *diden ... cure* Worked hard.

[2] *Bothe ... richely* Both in one coat of arms fashioned very richly.
As members of the same family, Palamon and Arcite have the same
heraldic markings on a light cloth jacket worn over their armor.

[3] *He ... raunsoun* In the fourteenth century, the custom was to try
to capture enemy soldiers in battle rather than kill them, for
ransoming was profitable. Although the tale is ostensibly set in
classical antiquity, the descriptions of warfare and the social customs
are based on those of Chaucer's own day.

With laurer° crowned as a conquerour.   *laurel*
170 And ther he lyveth in joye and in honour
Terme of lyve.° What nedeth wordes
mo?°   *for the rest of his life / more*
And in a tour° in angwissh° and in wo   *tower / anguish*
This Palamon and his felawe° Arcite   *companion*
For everemoore; ther° may no gold hem
quite.°   *where / buy them back*
175   This passeth yeer by yeer and day by day,
Til it fil° ones° in a morwe° of May   *happened / once / morning*
That Emelye, that fairer was to sene°   *see*
Than is the lylie° upon his stalke grene   *lily*
And fressher than the May with floures newe—
180 For with the rose colour stroof° hire hewe;   *competed*
I noot° which was the fyner° of hem two!—   *know not / finer*
Er it were day, as was hir wone° to do,   *custom*
She was arisen and al redy dight,°   *dressed*
For May wol have no slogardrie° anyght!°   *laziness / at night*
185 The sesoun° priketh° every gentil herte°   *season / incites / heart*
And maketh hym out of his slep to sterte
And seith, "Arys and do thyn observaunce!"°   *pay your respects*
This maked Emelye have remembraunce
To doon honour to May and for to ryse.
190 Yclothed was she fressh for to devyse.
Hir yelow heer° was broyded° in a tresse°   *hair / braided / plait*
Bihynde hir bak, a yerde° long, I gesse.   *yard*
And in the gardyn at the sonne upriste°   *sunrise*
She walketh up and doun, and as hire liste
195 She gadereth° floures, party° white and rede,   *gathers / mingled*
To make a subtil° gerland for hire hede.   *intricate*
And as an aungel hevenysshly° she soong.   *heavenly*
The grete tour that was so thikke and stroong
Which of the castel was the chief dongeoun,[4]
200 Theras° the knyghtes weren in prisoun,   *where*
Of whiche I tolde yow and tellen shal,
Was evene joynaunt° to the gardyn wal   *next to*
Theras this Emelye hadde hir pleyynge.°   *enjoyment*
Bright was the sonne and cleer that morwenynge.
205 And this Palamoun, this woful prisoner,
As was his wone° by leve° of his gayler°   *custom / leave / jailor*
Was risen and romed° in a chambre an heigh°   *roamed / on high*

---

[4] *dongeoun* In the Middle Ages, a tower, often part of a castle.
Dungeons were sometimes indeed used as prisons, as is the case here,
but they had other functions as well, both domestic and military.
The word here does not imply a miserable place of imprisonment.

In which he al the noble citee seigh°   saw
And eek the gardyn ful of braunches grene
210 Theras this fresshe Emelye the shene°   bright
Was in hir walk and romed up and doun.
This sorweful prisoner, this Palamoun
Goth in the chambre romynge° to and fro,   roaming
And to hymself compleynynge of his wo
215 That he was born. Ful ofte he seyde, "Allas!"
And so bifel by aventure° or cas°   chance / accident
That thurgh a wyndow thikke of many a
     barre°   thickly set with bars
Of iren° greet° and square as any sparre,°   iron / great / beam
He caste his eye upon Emelya.
220 And therwithal° he bleynte° and cride, "A!"   with that / went pale
As though he stongen° were unto the herte.   stung
And with that cry Arcite anon up sterte
And seyde, "Cosyn° myn, what eyleth° thee   cousin / ails
That art so pale and deedly° on to see?   deathly
225 Why cridestow?° Who hath thee doon offence?   did you cry
For Goddes love, taak° al° in pacience   take / all
Oure prisoun, for it may noon oother be!°   may not be otherwise
Fortune hath yeven° us this adversitee.   given
Som wikke° aspect or disposicioun   wicked
230 Of Saturne by som constellacioun
Hath yeven us this, although we hadde it sworn.
So stood the hevene whan that we were born.[1]
We moste endure! This is the short and playn!"°   simple (truth)
     This Palamon answerde and seyde agayn,
235 "Cosyn, forsothe° of this opinioun   in truth
Thow hast a veyn° ymaginacioun!°   foolish / misconception
This prison caused me nat for to crye.
But I was hurt right now thurghout myn eye
Into myn herte, that wol my bane° be!   death-blow
240 The fairnesse of that lady that I see
Yond° in the gardyn romen to and fro   yonder
Is cause of al my crying and my wo.
I noot where° she be woman or goddesse,   whether
But Venus[2] is it, soothly° as I gesse!"   truly
245 And therwithal on knees doun° he fil   down

And seyde, "Venus, if it be thy wil,
Yow in this gardyn thus to transfigure°   change shape
Bifore me, sorweful wrecche° creature,   wretched
Out of this prisoun helpe that we may scapen!°   escape
250 And if so be my destynee be shapen°   predetermined
By eterne° word to dyen in prisoun,   eternal
Of oure lynage° have som compassioun   lineage
That is so lowe ybroght by tirannye!"
And with that word Arcite gan espye°   to see
255 Wheras° this lady romed to and fro,   where
And with that sighte hir beautee hurte hym so
That if that Palamon was wounded soore,
Arcite is hurt as muche as he or moore.
And with a sigh he seyde pitously,
260 "The fresshe beautee sleeth me sodeynly
Of hire that rometh in the yonder place,
And but° I have hir mercy and hir grace,   unless
That I may seen hire atte leeste° weye,   at least
I nam° but deed! Ther is namoore° to seye."   am not / no more
265   This Palamon, whan he tho° wordes herde,   those
Dispitously° he looked and answerde,   angrily
"Wheither seistow° this in ernest or in pley?"°   do you say / jest
     "Nay," quod Arcite, "in ernest, by my fey!°   faith
God helpe me so, me list ful yvele pleye!"[3]
270   This Palamon gan knytte° his browes tweye.   knit
"It nere,"° quod he, "to thee no greet honour   were not
For to be fals ne for to be traitour
To me that am thy cosyn and thy brother,
Ysworn° ful depe, and ech of° us til oother,   sworn / each to
275 That nevere, for to dyen in the peyne,[4]
Til that deeth departe shal us tweyne,
Neither of us in love to hyndre° oother   hinder
Ne in noon oother cas, my leeve° brother,   beloved
But that thou sholdest trewely forthren° me   help
280 In every cas as I shal forthren thee.
This was thyn ooth and myn also, certeyn,
I woot° right wel, thou darst it nat withseyn.°   know / deny
Thus artow° of my conseil° out of
     doute,°   are you / counsel / doubtless
And now thow woldest falsly been aboute°   set about
285 To love my lady, whom I love and serve
And evere shal, til that myn herte sterve.°   dies

---

[1] *So ... born* Some evil aspect or alignment of Saturn with some
other constellation has given us this fate, which we must endure
although we had sworn to do otherwise. The stars were arranged that
way when we were born. (Saturn was the Roman god of time and old
age.)

[2] *Venus* Roman goddess of love, reproduction, and peace.

[3] *me ... pleye* I desire to play very little.

[4] *That ... peyne* Even if we were to die by torture.

Nay, certes, false Arcite, thow shalt nat so.
I loved hire first, and tolde thee my wo
As to my conseil° and to my brother sworn — *my counsellor*
290 To forthre° me, as I have toold biforn,° — *help / before*
For which thou art ybounden° as a knyght — *obligated*
To helpen me if it lay in thy might,
Or elles artow fals, I dar wel seyn."
    This Arcite ful proudly spak ageyn.
295 "Thow shalt," quod he, "be rather fals than I.
And thou art fals, I telle thee outrely,° — *completely*
For paramour° I loved hire first er thow.° — *as a lover / you*
What wiltow seyn? Thou wistest nat yet
    now° — *did not yet know just now*
Wheither she be a womman or goddesse!
300 Thyn is affeccioun° of hoolynesse,° — *feeling / religious devotion*
And myn is love, as to a creature,° — *human being*
For which I tolde thee myn aventure
As to my cosyn and my brother sworn.
I pose° that thow lovedest hire biforn: — *suppose*
305 Wostow nat wel the olde clerkes sawe[1]
That 'Who shal yeve° a lovere any lawe?' — *give*
Love is a gretter° lawe, by my pan,° — *greater / skull*
Than may be yeve° of any erthely man. — *given*
And therfore positif lawe[2] and swich decree
310 Is broken alday,° for love in ech degree.° — *daily / social rank*
A man moot nedes love, maugree his heed.° — *despite his intentions*
He may nat flee it thogh he sholde be deed,° — *dead*
Al be she° mayde° or wydwe° or elles° — *even if she is / maiden / widow / else*
    wyf.
And eek, it is nat likly al thy lyf
315 To stonden in hir grace;° namoore° shal I. — *favor / no more*
For wel thou woost° thyselven° verraily° — *know / yourself / truly*
That thou and I be dampned° to prisoun — *condemned*
Perpetuelly. Us gayneth no raunsoun.° — *no ransom will free us*
We stryven° as dide the houndes for the boon;° — *quarrel / bone*
320 They foughte al day, and yet hir° part was noon: — *their*
Ther cam a kyte° whil they weren so wrothe° — *buzzard / angry*
And baar awey° the boon bitwixe hem bothe. — *carried away*
And therfore at the kynges court, my brother,
Ech man for hymself! Ther is noon oother!
325 Love if thee list, for I love and ay° shal. — *always*

[1] *Wostow ... sawe* Do you not know well the old scholar's saying.

[2] *Positif lawe* Positive law is that written into the statute books, as opposed to natural law, which is self-evident from God's creation.

And soothly,° leeve brother, this is al. — *truly*
Heere in this prisoun moote we endure° — *must we remain*
And everich° of us take his aventure!" — *each*
    Greet was the strif and long bitwix hem tweye,
330 If that I hadde leyser° for to seye. — *leisure*
But to th'effect:° It happed on a day, — *result*
To telle it yow as shortly as I may,
A worthy duc that highte Perotheus,
That felawe° was to Duc Theseus — *companion*
335 Syn° thilke° day that they were children lite,[3] — *since / the same / little*
Was come to Atthenes his felawe to visite
And for to pley, as he was won° to do. — *accustomed*
For in this world he loved no man so,
And he loved hym als° tendrely agayn. — *as*
340 So wel they lovede, as olde bookes sayn,
That whan that oon was deed, soothly to telle,
His felawe wente and soughte hym doun in Helle![3]
But of that storie, list me nat° to write. — *I do not desire*
Duc Perotheus loved wel Arcite
345 And hadde hym knowe at Thebes yeer by yere.
And finally at requeste and preyere
Of Perotheus, withouten any raunsoun,
Duc Thesuus hym leet out of prisoun
Frely° to goon wher that hym liste overal — *freely*
350 In swich a gyse° as I you tellen shal. — *such a manner*
    This was the forward,° pleynly for
    t'endite,° — *agreement / to write it plainly*
Bitwixen Theseus and hym Arcite:
That if so were that Arcite were yfounde° — *found*
Evere in his lif by day or nyght or stounde° — *hour*
355 In any contree of this Theseus
And he were caught, it was acorded° thus: — *agreed*
That with a swerd he sholde lese° his heed.° — *lose / head*
Ther nas noon oother remedie ne reed,° — *counsel*
But taketh his leve° and homward he him spedde. — *leave*
360 Lat hym bewar! His nekke lith to wedde!° — *lies as a pledge*
    How greet a sorwe suffreth now Arcite!

[3] *His ... Helle* The classical legend is that Theseus accompanied Pirithous (Chaucer's Perotheus) to the Underworld in his unsuccessful attempt to rescue Proserpina, who had been abducted by Pluto, king of that region. Both men eventually returned alive, although Theseus was imprisoned and rescued by Hercules. The suggestion that Theseus went down to rescue Pirithous because he had died probably comes from the long thirteenth-century medieval allegory *The Romance of the Rose*, which Chaucer translated from French.

The deeth he feeleth thurgh his herte smyte!°   *strike*
He wepeth, wayleth, crieth pitously.
To sleen hymself he waiteth prively.°   *secretly*
365　He seyde, "Allas that day" that he "was born!¹
Now is my prisoun worse than biforn!
Now is me shape° eternally to dwelle   *ordained*
Nat in my Purgatorie but in Helle!
Allas, that evere knew I Perotheus,
370　For elles hadde I dwelled with Theseus
Yfetered° in his prisoun everemo!   *chained*
Thanne hadde I been in blisse and nat in wo!
Oonly the sighte of hire whom that I serve,
Though that I nevere hir grace may deserve,
375　Wolde han suffised right ynough for me!
O deere cosyn Palamon," quod he,
"Thyn is the victorie of this aventure.
Ful blissfully in prisoun maistow dure.°   *may you remain*
In prisoun? certes nay,° but in Paradys!   *no*
380　Wel hath Fortune yturned thee the dys°   *dice*
That hast the sighte of hire, and I th'absence.
For possible is, syn° thou hast hire presence   *since*
And art a knyght, a worthy and an able,
That som cas,° syn Fortune is chaungeable,   *(by) some event*
385　Thow maist to thy desir somtyme atteyne.°   *attain*
But I that am exiled and bareyne°   *lacking*
Of alle grace and in so greet dispeir
That ther nys° erthe, water, fir, ne eir,°   *is not / nor air*
Ne creature that of hem maked is
390　That may me heele° or doon confort° in
　　　this,   *heal / bring comfort*
Wel oughte I sterve in wanhope° and distresse!   *despair*
Farwel my lif,° my lust,° and my gladnesse!   *life / desire*
　　　"Allas, why pleynen° folk so in commune°   *complain / commonly*
On° purveiaunce° of God or of Fortune   *against / foresight*
395　That yeveth hem° ful ofte in many a gyse°   *gives them / way*
Wel bettre than they kan hemself devyse?
Som man desireth for to han richesse
That cause is of his moerdre° or greet siknesse,   *murder*
And som man wolde out of his prisoun fayn°   *gladly (get)*
400　That in his hous is of his meynee° slayn.   *his retinue*

---

¹ *Allas … born* Many editions prefer the reading, found in several
other manuscripts, "Allas the day that I was born." The Ellesmere
variant (which we have preserved, although it may indeed be an
error) would originally have been less awkward, since the quotation
marks are a modern addition.

Infinite harmes been in this mateere.°   *matter*
We witen nat° what we preyen heere;°   *know not / pray for*
We faren° as he that dronke is as a mous.°   *behave / mouse*
A dronke man woot wel that he hath an hous,
405　But he noot° which the righte wey is
　　　thider,°   *does not know / there*
And to a dronke man the wey is slider.°   *slippery*
And certes in this world so faren° we: *fare*
We seken faste° after felicitee,°   *determinedly / happiness*
But we goon wrong ful often, trewely.
410　Thus may we seyn° alle and namely° I,   *see / especially*
That wende° and hadde a greet opinioun   *expected*
That if I myghte escapen from prisoun,
Thanne hadde I been in joye and parfit heele°   *well-being*
That now I am exiled fro my wele,°   *happiness*
415　Syn° that I may nat seen you, Emelye!   *since*
I nam° but deed! Ther nys no remedye!"   *am not*
　　　Upon that oother syde° Palamon,   *side*
Whan that he wiste Arcite was agon,°   *gone*
Swich sorwe° he maketh that the grete tour   *sorrow*
420　Resouned° of his youlyng° and clamour.   *resounded / yowling*
The pure fettres° on his shynes°
　　　grete°   *very chains / shins / swollen*
Weren of his bittre salte teeres wete.°   *wet*
"Allas," quod he, "Arcita, cosyn myn!
Of al oure strif,° God woot, the fruyt° is thyn!   *strife / fruit*
425　Thow walkest now in Thebes at thy large,°   *freely*
And of my wo thow yevest° litel° charge!   *give / little*
Thou mayst, syn° thou hast wisdom and
　　　manhede,°   *since / manhood*
Assemblen alle the folk of oure kynrede°   *kindred*
And make a werre so sharpe on this citee
430　That by som aventure or som tretee°   *treaty*
Thow mayst have hire° to lady and to wyf   *her*
For whom that I moste nedes lese° my lyf.   *lose*
For as by wey of possibilitee,
Sith thou art at thy large of prisoun free
435　And art a lord, greet is thyn avauntage
Moore than is myn that sterve here in a cage.
For I moot° wepe and wayle whil I lyve   *must*
With al the wo that prison may me yeve°   *give*
And eek with peyne that love me yeveth also
440　That doubleth al my torment and my wo!"
Therwith the fyr° of jalousie up sterte   *fire*
Withinne his brest and hente° him by the herte   *grabbed*
So woodly° that he lyk was to biholde   *madly*

The boxtree[1] or the asshen° dede and colde.   ashes

445   Thanne seyde he, "O crueel goddes that governe
This world with byndyng° of youre word eterne   binding
And writen in the table of atthamaunt°   adamant (diamond)
Youre parlement and youre eterne graunt,°   eternal decree
What is mankynde moore unto you holde°   indebted

450   Than is the sheepe that ronketh° in the folde?   huddles
For slayn is man right as another beest
And dwelleth eek in prison and arreest°   arrest
And hath siknesse and greet adversitee
And ofte tymes giltlees,° pardee!°   guiltless / by God

455   What governance is in this prescience
That giltlees tormenteth innocence?[2]
And yet encresseth° this al my penaunce,   increases
That man is bounden to his observaunce
For Goddes sake to letten of° his wille,   restrain

460   Theras° a beest may al his lust fulfille.   whereas
And whan a beest is deed, he hath no peyne,
But after his deeth man moot wepe and pleyne,
Though in this world he have care and wo;
Withouten doute it may stonden so!

465   The answere of this lete° I to dyvynys,°   leave / religious scholars
But wel I woot that in this world greet pyne ys.
Allas, I se° a serpent or a theef°   see / thief
That many a trewe man hath doon mescheef
Goon at his large° and where hym list may turne.   go freely

470   But I moot been in prisoun thurgh Saturne
And eek thurgh Juno,[3] jalous° and eek wood,°   jealous / crazy
That hath destroyed wel ny° al the blood   very nearly
Of Thebes with hise° waste° walles wyde,   its / wasted
And Venus sleeth me on that oother syde

475   For jalousie and fere° of hym Arcite."   fear
Now wol I stynte° of Palamon a lite°   stop (speaking) / little
And lete hym in his prisoun stille° dwelle   quietly
And of Arcita forth I wol yow telle.
The sonne passeth, and the nyghtes longe

480   Encressen doublewise° the peynes stronge   double
Bothe of the lovere and the prisoner.
I noot° which hath the wofuller°
    mester.°   do not know / sadder / profession
For shortly for to seyn,° this Palamoun   say
Perpetuelly is dampned° to prisoun   condemned

485   In cheynes and in fettres to been deed,°   to die
And Arcite is exiled upon his heed°   upon pain of losing his head
Forever mo as out of that contree,
Ne nevere mo he shal his lady see.
Yow loveres, axe° I now this questioun: ask

490   Who hath the worse, Arcite or Palamoun?
That oon may seen his lady day by day,
But in prison he moot dwelle alway.
That oother wher hym list may ride or go,
But seen his lady shal he nevere mo.[4]

495   Now demeth° as you list, ye that kan,   judge
For I wol telle forth as I bigan.

EXPLICIT PRIMA PARS

SEQUITUR PARS SECUNDA[5]

Whan that Arcite to Thebes comen was,
Ful ofte a day he swelte° and seyde, "Allas,"   fainted
For seen his lady shal he nevere mo.

500   And shortly to concluden° al his wo,   summarize
So muche sorwe hadde nevere creature
That is or shal° whil° that the world may
    dure.°   shall be / while / endure
His slepe, his mete,° his drynke is hym biraft° food / taken away
That lene° he wexeth° and drye as is a shaft.° lean / grows / arrow

505   Hise eyen holwe° and grisly° to biholde,   hollow / grim
His hewe° falow° and pale as asshen colde,   complexion / yellow
And solitarie he was and evere allone
And waillynge al the nyght, makynge his mone.°   moan
And if he herde song or instrument,

510   Thanne wolde he wepe. He myghte nat be stent.°   stopped
So feble eek were hise spiritz and so lowe
And chaunged so that no man koude knowe

---

[1]   *The boxtree*   The box tree is known for its light yellow wood.
Palamon is as pale as ashes.

[2]   *What ... innocence*   What governing principle is in this foresight
that torments innocent people who are guiltless?

[3]   *Juno*   In Roman mythology, Juno, wife of Jupiter (king of the
gods), was the goddess of the hearth and of domesticity, and was
frequently jealous of Jupiter's love affairs. Juno hated Thebes
because of Jupiter's love affairs with the Theban women Semele,
mother of Bacchus, and Alcmena, mother of Hercules.

[4]   *But ... mo*   This is a typical *demande d'amour* (French: question
of love) that sets forth a problem in the aristocratic code of love for
courtiers to debate.

[5]   *Explicit ... Secunda*   Latin: Here ends the first part. The second
part follows.

His speche nor his voys,° though men it herde,   *voice*
And in his geere° for al the world he ferde°   *manner / fared*
515 Nat oonly lik the loveris maladye
Of hereos¹ but rather lyk manye°   *mania*
Engendred of humour malencolik²
Biforn his owene celle fantastik.³
And shortly, turned was al up so doun°   *upside-down*
520 Bothe habit and eek disposicioun
Of hym this woful lovere daun Arcite.°   *Sir Arcite*
   What sholde I al day of his wo endite?°   *write*
Whan he endured hadde a yeer or two
This crueel torment and this peyne and wo
525 At Thebes in his countree, as I seyde,
Upon a nyght in sleepe as he hym leyde,°   *lay*
Hym thoughte° how that the wynged god Mercurie⁴   *it seemed*
Biforn hym stood and bad° hym to be murie.°   *commanded / merry*
His slepy yerde° in hond he bar°
   uprighte;   *sleep-producing staff / bore*
530 An hat he werede° upon hise heris° brighte.   *wore / hairs*
Arrayed was this god, as I took keepe,°   *noticed*
As he was whan that Argus⁵ took his sleepe,
And seyde hym thus: "To Atthenes shaltou
   wende.°   *shall you go*
Ther is thee shapen° of thy wo an ende."   *for you ordained*
535 And with that word Arcite wook° and sterte.°   *woke / got up*
"Now trewely, hou° soore° that me
   smerte,"°   *however / sore / it may injure*
Quod he, "to Atthenes right now wol I fare.°   *travel*
Ne for the drede of deeth shal I nat spare°   *avoid*
To se my lady that I love and serve.
540 In hire presence I recche nat° to sterve!"   *care not*
   And with that word he caughte° a greet mirour°   *seized / mirror*

---

¹ *hereos* Hereos or amor hereos was the name given for the "disease" of love.

² *humour malencolik* Melancholic humor is one of the four humors of the body according to classical and medieval medicinal theory. The other humors are the choleric, phlegmatic, and sanguine. Melancholic humor, of course, makes one sad—hence our word "melancholy."

³ *celle fantastik* The portion of the brain where the imagination resided. The other two cells were those of memory and reason.

⁴ *Mercurie* Roman messenger of the gods.

⁵ *Argus* In Roman mythology, Argus had a hundred eyes and bore watch over Io, whom Jupiter loved. Mercury put him to sleep with his staff and then killed him.

And saugh° that chaunged was al his colour   *saw*
And saugh his visage° al in another kynde.°   *face / nature*
And right anon it ran hym in his mynde
545 That sith his face was so disfigured
Of maladye, the which he hadde endured,
He myghte wel, if that he bar hym lowe,°   *acted humbly*
Lyve in Atthenes everemoore unknowe
And seen his lady wel ny day by day.°   *nearly every day*
550 And right anon he chaunged his array°   *dress*
And cladde hym as a povre° laborer.   *poor*
And al allone save only a squier
That knew his privetee° and al his cas,°   *secret / case*
Which was disgised povrely as he was,
555 To Atthenes is he goon the nexte way,°   *shortest way*
And to the court he wente upon a day,
And at the gate he profreth° his servyse   *offered*
To drugge° and drawe° what so men wol
   devyse.°   *drudge / draw (water) / demand*
And shortly of this matere for to seyn,
560 He fil in office° with a chamberleyn°   *was employed / chamberlain*
The which that dwellynge was with Emelye,
For he was wys° and koude soone espye°   *wise / see*
Of every servaunt which that serveth here.°   *her*
Wel koude he hewen° wode and water bere,°   *cut / carry*
565 For he was yong and myghty for the nones.°   *occasion*
And therto he was long° and big of bones   *tall*
To doon that° any wight° kan hym devyse.   *whatever / person*
A yeer or two he was in this servyse,
Page° of the chambre° of Emelye the
   brighte,   *young servant / chamber*
570 And Philostrate⁶ he seyde that he highte.°   *was named*
But half so wel biloved a man as he
Ne was ther nevere in court of his degree.
He was so gentil° of condicioun   *noble*
That thurghout al the court was his renoun.°   *renown*
575 They seyden that it were a charitee°   *would be an act of charity*
That Theseus wolde enhauncen his degree°   *promote him*
And putten hym in worshipful servyse°   *honorable service*
Theras° he myghte his vertu excercise.°   *where / demonstrate*
And thus withinne a while his name is spronge°   *spread about*
580 Bothe of hise dedes and his goode tonge,°   *elegant speech*
That Theseus hath taken hym so neer°   *close (to himself)*

---

⁶ *Philostrate* Greek: one knocked down by love.

That of his chambre[1] he made hym a squier
And gaf° hym gold to mayntene° his
    degree.°   *gave | maintain | rank*
And eek men broghte hym out of his contree
585 From yeer to yeer ful pryvely° his rente.[2]   *privately*
But honestly and slyly° he it spente,   *discreetly*
That no man wondred how that he it hadde.
And thre yeer° in this wise° his lif he ladde°   *years | way | led*
And bar hym° so, in pees° and eek in
    werre,°   *conducted himself | peace | war*
590 Ther was no man that Theseus hath derre.°   *held more dear*
And in this blisse lete I now Arcite
And speke I wole of Palamon a lite.°   *little*
    In derknesse and horrible and strong prisoun
Thise seven yeer hath seten Palamoun
595 Forpyned,° what for wo and for distresse.   *tormented*
Who feeleth double soor° and hevynesse°   *soreness | heaviness*
But Palamon that love destreyneth° so,   *afflicts*
That wood° out of his wit he goth° for wo?   *crazy | goes*
And eek therto he is a prisoner
600 Perpetuelly, noght oonly for a yer.
    Who koude ryme° in Englyssh properly   *rhyme*
His martirdom? Forsothe, it am nat I!
Therfore I passe as lightly° as I may.   *quickly*
    It fel that in the seventhe yer in May,
605 The thridde° nyght, as olde bookes seyn   *third*
That al this storie tellen moore pleyn,°   *plainly*
Were it° by aventure or destynee,   *whether it were*
As whan a thyng is shapen° it shal be,   *ordained*
That soone after the mydnyght Palamoun
610 By helpyng of a freend° brak° his prisoun   *friend | escaped*
And fleeth° the citee faste as he may go.   *flees*
For he hadde yeve° his gayler° drynke so   *given | jailor*
Of a clarree° maad° of a certeyn wyn   *spiced drink | made*
Of nercotikes° and opie° of Thebes fyn°   *narcotics | opium | fine*
615 That al that nyght thogh that men wolde him shake,

This gayler sleepe; he myghte nat awake!
And thus he fleeth as faste as evere he may.
The nyght was short and faste by the day°   *it was almost day*
That nedes cost° he moot° hymselven hyde,   *necessarily | must*
620 And til° a grove faste therbisyde°   *to | nearby*
With dredeful° foot thanne stalketh°
    Palamon.   *fearful | walks quietly*
For shortly, this was his opinion
That in that grove he wolde hym hyde al day,
And in the nyght thanne wolde he take his way
625 To Thebesward,° his freendes for to preye°   *towards Thebes | ask*
On Theseus to helpe hym to werreye.°   *make war*
And shortly outher° he wolde lese° his lif   *either | lose*
Or wynnen° Emelye unto his wyf.   *win*
This is th'effect and his entente pleyn.°   *plain intent*
630   Now wol I turne to Arcite ageyn,°   *again*
That litel wiste how ny° that was his care,   *near*
Til that Fortune had broght him in the snare.
    The bisy larke, messager of day,
Salueth° in hir song the morwe gray,   *salutes*
635 And firy Phebus[3] riseth up so brighte
That al the orient° laugheth of the lighte   *east*
And with hise stremes° dryeth° in the
    greves°   *beams | dries | branches*
The silver dropes hangynge on the leves.°   *leaves*
And Arcita that is in the court roial
640 With Theseus, his squier principal,
Is risen and looketh on the myrie° day.   *merry*
And for to doon his observaunce to May,[4]
Remembrynge on the poynt° of his desir,   *point*
He on a courser° startlynge° as the fir° *war-horse | prancing | fire*
645 Is riden into the feeldes° hym to pleye.   *fields*
Out of the court were it a myle° or tweye,   *mile*
And to the grove of which that I yow tolde
By aventure his wey he gan to holde
To maken hym a gerland of the greves,°   *branches*
650 Were it of wodebynde° or hawethorn
    leves.°   *woodbine | hawthorn leaves*
And loude he song ayeyn the sonne shene,°   *in the bright sunshine*
"May, with alle thy floures and thy grene,°   *green*
Welcome be thou, faire, fresshe May,

---

[1] *That of his chambre* Medieval English kings relied heavily on knights of their chamber for administrative duties of government. Originally servants who performed various domestic functions, these people had honorific titles implying these duties but took on the duties of governmental administration instead.

[2] *From ... rente* The rent here referred to is not something Arcite must pay but what is owed to him. Medieval lords possessed land and were owed various rents and services from those whom they allowed use it. A high lord like Arcite would have had much income from such sources.

---

[3] *Phebus* Name for Apollo, god of the sun.

[4] *And ... May* The custom was for courtly people to rise early in mornings in May and roam about in the countryside to enjoy the good weather that had recently returned.

In hope that I som grene° gete may."   *something green*
655 And from his courser° with a lusty
         herte°   *war-horse | spirited heart*
Into a grove ful hastily he sterte,
And in a path he rometh° up and doun   *roams*
Theras° by aventure this Palamoun   *where*
Was in a bussh that no man myghte hym se,°   *see*
660 For soore aferd of his deeth thanne was he.
Nothyng ne knew he° that it was Arcite.   *he did not know*
God woot, he wolde have trowed° it ful lite!°   *believed | very little*
But sooth is seyd, so sithen° many yeres,°   *after | years*
That "Feeld hath eyen and the wode° hath eres."°   *wood | ears*
665 It is ful fair a man to bere hym evene,
For al day meeteth men at unset stevene.[1]
Ful litel woot Arcite of his felawe
That was so ny to herknen° al his sawe,°   *listen to | speech*
For in the bussh he sitteth now ful stille.
670   Whan that Arcite hadde romed all his fille
And songen al the roundel[2] lustily,
Into a studie° he fil° al sodeynly,   *meditative mood | fell*
As doon thise loveres in hir queynte° geres.°   *curious | customs*
Now in the crope,° now doun in the breres,°   *tree-top | briars*
675 Now up, now doun as boket° in a welle.   *bucket*
Right as the Friday, soothly° for to telle,   *truly*
Now it shyneth, now it reyneth° faste: *rains*
Right so kan geery° Venus overcaste   *fickle*
The hertes of hir folk. Right as hir day[3]
680 Is gereful,° right so chaungeth she array.   *fickle*
Selde° is the Friday al the wowke
         ylike.°   *seldom | like the rest of the week*
    Whan that Arcite had songe,° he gan to sike°   *sung | sigh*
And sette hym doun withouten any moore.
"Allas," quod he, "that day that I was bore!
685 How longe, Juno, thurgh thy crueltee
Woltow werreyen° Thebes the citee?   *make war on*

Allas, ybroght° is to confusioun   *brought*
The blood roial of Cadme and Amphioun[4]—
Of Cadmus which that was the firste man
690 That Thebes bulte,° or first the toun bigan,   *built*
And of the citee first was crouned kyng.
Of his lynage am I and his ofspryng
By verray ligne° as of the stok° roial,   *true lineage | stock*
And now I am so caytyf° and so thral,°   *captive | enslaved*
695 That he that is my mortal enemy
I serve hym as his squier povrely.°   *poorly*
And yet dooth Juno me wel moore° shame,   *much more*
For I dar noght biknowe° myn owene name!   *reveal*
But theras I was wont to highte Arcite,
700 Now highte I Philostrate, noght worth a myte!°   *small coin*
Allas, thou felle° Mars,[5] allas, Juno!   *cruel*
Thus hath youre ire° oure kynrede° al
         fordo,°   *anger | kindred | destroyed*
Save oonly me and wrecched Palamoun
That Theseus martireth° in prisoun.   *martyrs*
705 And over al this to sleen me outrely,°   *completely*
Love hath his firy dart so brennyngly°   *burningly*
Ystiked° thurgh my trewe,° careful° herte,   *stuck | true | sorrowful*
That shapen° was my deeth° erst than my
         sherte.°[6]   *ordained | death | shirt*
Ye sleen me with youre eyen, Emelye!
710 Ye been the cause wherfore that I dye!
Of al the remenant of myn oother care,
Ne sette I nat° the montance° of a tare,°   *I do not set | value | weed*
So that I koude doon aught to youre plesaunce."
And with that word he fil doun in a traunce
715 A longe tyme, and after he up sterte.
    This Palamoun that thoughte that thurgh his herte
He felte a coold swerd sodeynliche° glyde,   *suddenly*
For ire° he quook.° No lenger wolde he
         byde.°   *anger | shook | wait*
And whan that he had herd Arcites tale,
720 As he were wood,° with face deed° and pale,   *crazy | dead*
He stirte hym up out of the buskes° thikke°   *bushes | thick*
And seide, "Arcite, false traytour wikke,°   *wicked*
Now artow° hent° that lovest my lady so,   *are you | caught*

---

[1] *It … stevene* It is very desirable for a man to behave with restraint, for every day people meet at an unexpected time.

[2] *roundel* Type of popular song in both France and England in the fourteenth century. It was characterized by repeated phrases of both music and words.

[3] *Right as hir day* The days of the week were originally devoted to the various gods and goddesses, as our names for them still attest (Saturn's day—Saturday; Thor's day—Thursday). Venus's day was Friday (*Veneris dies*) in the Romance languages; the Germanic goddess most resembling Venus was named Freya.

---

[4] *Cadme and Amphioun* Earlier kings of Thebes.

[5] *Mars* Roman god of war.

[6] *That … sherte* The reference here is probably to the *first* shirt made for Arcite when he was a baby.

For whom that I have al this peyne and wo!
725 And art my blood° and to my conseil°
    sworn, *of my blood / counsel*
As I ful ofte have seyd thee heer biforn,
And hast byjaped° heere Duc Theseus *tricked*
And falsly chaunged hast thy name thus—
I wol be deed or elles thou shalt dye!
730 Thou shalt nat love my lady Emelye!
But I wol love hire oonly and namo,° *no more*
For I am Palamon, thy mortal foo!° *foe*
And though that I no wepene have in this place,
But out of prison am astert° by grace, *escaped*
735 I drede noght° that outher° thow shalt dye *fear not / either*
Or thow ne shalt nat loven Emelye.
Chees° which thou wolt,° or thou shalt nat
    asterte!" *choose / wish*
    This Arcite, with ful despitous° herte, *scornful*
Whan he hym knew° and hadde his tale herd, *recognized*
740 As fiers as leoun pulled out his swerd
And seyd thus: "By God that sit above,
Nere it° that thou art sik° and wood for love, *were it not / sick*
And eek that thow no wepne° hast in this place, *weapon*
Thou sholdest nevere out of this grove pace° *escape*
745 That thou ne sholdest dyen of° myn hond! *by*
For I defye° the seurete° and the bond *defy / promise*
Which that thou seist that I have maad° to thee. *made*
What, verray fool, thynk wel that love is free,
And I wol love hire maugree° al thy myght! *despite*
750 But for as muche thou art a worthy knyght
And wilnest to darreyne hire by bataille,[1]
Have heer° my trouthe:° tomorwe I wol nat faille, *here / vow*
Withoute wityng° of any oother wight,° *the knowledge / person*
That heere I wol be founden as a knyght,
755 And bryngen harneys° right ynough° for thee, *armor / enough*
And chese the best and leve the worste for me.
And mete° and drynke this nyght wol I brynge *food*
Ynough for thee and clothes for thy beddynge.
And if so be that thou my lady wynne° *win*
760 And sle° me in this wode ther I am inne,° *kill / in*
Thow mayst wel have thy lady as for me!"
    This Palamon answerde, "I graunte it thee!"
And thus they been departed til amorwe,° *the next day*

Whan ech of hem had leyd his feith° to
    borwe.° *word / as a pledge*
765 O Cupide,[2] out of all charitee!
O regne,° that wolt no felawe° have with thee! *reign / equal*
Ful sooth is seyd that love ne lordshipe
Wol noght, hir thankes, have no felaweshipe.[3]
Wel fynden that Arcite and Palamoun!
770 Arcite is riden anon unto the toun,
And on the morwe er it were dayes light
Ful prively two harneys° hath he dight,° *suits of armor / prepared*
Bothe suffisaunt° and mete° to
    darreyne° *sufficient / fitting / decide*
The bataille in the feeld bitwix hem tweyne.
775 And on his hors allone as he was born
He carieth al the harneys hym biforn.
And in the grove at tyme and place yset,° *appointed*
This Arcite and this Palamon ben° met. *are*
To chaungen gan the colour in hir° face, *their*
780 Right as the hunters in the regne of
    Trace° *(Greek) kingdom of Thrace*
That stondeth at the gappe° with a spere,° *gap / spear*
Whan hunted is the leoun and the bere° *bear*
And hereth hym come russhyng in the greves° *brush*
And breketh bothe bowes and the leves
785 And thynketh, "Heere cometh my mortal enemy!
Withoute faille, he moot be deed or I!
For outher I moot sleen hym at the gappe
Or he moot sleen me if that me myshappe"°— *I am unlucky*
So ferden° they in chaungyng of hir hewe *fared*
790 As fer as everich of hem oother knewe.° *knew the other*
    Ther nas no° good day ne no saluyng,° *was neither / saluting*
But streight° withouten word or
    rehersyng° *immediately / conversation*
Everich of hem heelpe for to armen oother° *to arm the other*
As freenly° as he were his owene brother. *friendly*
795 And after that with sharpe speres stronge
They foynen° ech at oother wonder° longe. *thrust / wonderfully*
Thou myghtest wene° that this Palamoun *expect*
In his fightyng were a wood leoun,
And as a crueel tigre was Arcite.
800 As wilde bores gonne° they to smyte, *began*

---

1 *And ... bataille* And wish to vindicate your right to her by battle.

2 *Cupide* Cupid, son of Venus, is the Roman god of love.

3 *Ful ... felaweshipe* Truly it is said that neither love nor lordship will willingly have company.

That frothen whit as foom for ire wood.[1]
Up to the anclee° foghte they in hir blood,   *ankle*
And in this wise I lete hem fightyng dwelle°   *still fighting*
And forth I wole of Theseus yow telle.
805   The destinee, ministre° general   *agent*
That executeth in the world over al
The purveiaunce° that God hath seyn° biforn,   *foresight / seen*
So strong it is that though the world had sworn
The contrarie of a thyng by ye or nay,
810   Yet somtyme it shal fallen° on a day   *happen*
That falleth nat eft° withinne a thousand yeere.   *not again*
For certeinly oure appetites heere,
Be it of werre or pees° or hate or love,   *war or peace*
Al is this reuled° by the sighte above.   *ruled*
815   This mene° I now by myghty Theseus,   *mean*
That for to hunten is so desirus,°   *eager*
And namely at the grete hert° in May,   *deer*
That in his bed ther daweth° hym no day   *dawns*
That he nys clad° and redy° for to ryde   *is not clothed / ready*
820   With hunte and horn and houndes hym bisyde,
For in his huntyng hath he swich delit
That it is al his joye and appetit°   *desire*
To been hymself the grete hertes bane.°   *slayer*
For after Mars he serveth now Dyane.[2]
825   Cleer was the day, as I have toold er this,
And Theseus with alle joye and blis
With his Ypolita the faire queene
And Emelye clothed al in grene
On huntyng° be they riden° roially.   *a-hunting / are they riding*
830   And to the grove that stood ful faste by°   *very nearby*
In which ther was an hert, as men hym tolde,
Duc Theseus the streighte wey° hath holde.°   *road / has held*
And to the launde° he rideth hym ful right,°   *clearing / directly*
For thider° was the hert wont° have his flight,   *there / accustomed*
835   And over a brook and so forth in his weye,
This duc wol han a cours° at hym or tweye   *chase*
With houndes swiche as hym list comaunde.°   *to command*
    And whan this duc was come unto the launde
Under the sonne he looketh. And anon
840   He was war° of Arcite and Palamon,   *aware*
That foughten breme° as it were bores° two.   *boldly / boars*

The brighte swerdes wenten to and fro
So hidously that with the leeste strook°   *stroke*
It semed as it wolde fille° an ook!°   *fell / oak*
845   But what they were, nothyng he ne woot.[3]
This duc his courser with his spores° smoot,°   *spurs / struck*
And at a stert° he was bitwix hem two   *in an instant*
And pulled out a swerd and cride, "Hoo!°   *whoa!*
Namoore, upon peyne of lesynge° of youre heed!   *losing*
850   By myghty Mars, he shal anon be deed
That smyteth any strook° that I may seen.   *stroke*
But telleth me what mystiers men ye been[4]
That been so hardy° for to fighten here   *bold*
Withouten juge° or oother officere   *judge (referee)*
855   As it were in a lystes° roially."   *jousting ground*
    This Palamon answerde hastily
And seyde, "Sire, what nedeth wordes mo?
We have the deeth disserved bothe two.[5]
Two woful wrecches been we, two caytyves°   *wretches*
860   That been encombred of° oure owene lyves.   *burdened by*
And as thou art a rightful lord and juge,
Ne yeve° us neither mercy ne refuge.   *do not give*
But sle° me first, for Seinte Charitee,[6]   *slay*
But sle my felawe eek as wel as me.
865   Or sle hym first! For though thow knowest it lite,°   *little*
This is thy mortal foo.° This is Arcite   *foe*
That fro thy lond is banysshed on his heed,[7]
For which he hath deserved to be deed.
For this is he that cam unto thy gate
870   And seyde that he highte Philostrate.
Thus hath he japed° thee ful many a yer,   *fooled*
And thou hast maked hym thy chief squire,
And this is he that loveth Emelye.

---

[1] *That ... wood*   That froth (at the mouth), white as foam, with raging anger.

[2] *Dyane*   Roman goddess of the hunt.

---

[3] *But ... woot*   He did not know anything about who they were.

[4] *But ... been*   But tell me what occupation you follow, i.e., what kind of men you are. Mystiers is cognate with mystery, which in the Middle Ages meant a trade or occupation and gave the name to the religious plays the trade guilds put on in various cities—mystery plays.

[5] *We ... two*   They deserve death because of the terms of their conditional sentence: Palamon must stay in prison or die, while Arcite must remain in exile or die.

[6] *Seinte Charitee*   Holy Charity. Charity is the old word for God's love.

[7] *banysshed on his heed*   Banished with the consequence of losing his head should he return without pardon.

For sith the day is come that I shal dye,

875 I make pleynly° my confessioun — *fully*

That I am thilke° woful Palamoun — *the same*

That hath thy prisoun broken° wikkedly. — *escaped*

I am thy mortal foo, and it am I

That loveth so hoote° Emelye the brighte, — *hotly*

880 That I wol dye,° present in hir sighte. — *die*

Wherfore I axe° deeth and my juwise.° — *ask / sentence*

But sle my felawe in the same wise,

For bothe han we deserved to be slayn!"

    This worthy duc answerde anon agayn

885 And seyde, "This is a short conclusioun!° — *quick decision*

Youre owene mouth by youre confessioun

Hath dampned° yow, and I wol it recorde. — *damned*

It nedeth noght to pyne yow with the corde:[1]

Ye shal be deed, by myghty Mars the rede!"° — *red*

890   The queene anon for verray wommanhede° — *womanhood*

Gan for to wepe and so dide Emelye

And alle the ladyes in the compaignye.

Greet pitee was it as it thoughte hem alle,° — *it seemed to them*

That evere swich a chaunce° sholde falle.° — *event / happen*

895 For gentil men they were, of greet estaat,

And no thyng but for love was this debaat,° — *quarrel*

And saugh hir blody woundes wyde and soore

And alle crieden° bothe lasse and

    moore,° — *cried / the lesser and the greater*

"Have mercy, lord, upon us wommen alle!"

900 And on hir bare knees adoun they falle

And wolde have kist° his feet theras° he stood, — *kissed / where*

Til at the laste aslaked° was his mood. — *calmed*

For pitee renneth° soone in gentil herte. — *runs*

And though he first for ire quook° and sterte, — *shook*

905 He hath considered shortly° in a clause — *briefly*

The trespas° of hem bothe and eek the cause. — *crime*

And although that his ire hir gilt° accused, — *their guilt*

Yet in his resoun° he hem bothe excused — *reason*

As thus: he thoghte wel that every man

910 Wol° helpe hymself in love if that he kan,° — *will*

And eek delivere hymself out of prisoun.

And eek his herte hadde compassioun

Of wommen, for they wepen evere in oon.° — *in unity*

And in his gentil herte he thoughte anon

915 And softe unto hymself he seyde, "Fy° — *shame*

Upon a lord that wol have no mercy

But been a leoun bothe in word and dede

To hem that been in repentaunce and drede,

As wel as to a proud, despitous° man — *scornful*

920 That wol mayntene that he first bigan.

That lord hath litel of discrecioun

That in swich cas kan° no divisioun — *knows*

But weyeth° pride and humblesse after oon."° — *weighs / equally*

And shortly, whan his ire is thus agoon,° — *gone*

925 He gan to looken up with eyen lighte

And spak thise same wordes al on highte:° — *aloud*

"The god of love, a, *benedicite*,°[2] — *bless you*

How myghty and how greet a lord is he!

Ayeyns° his myght ther gayneth° none — *against / prevails*

    obstacles!

930 He may be cleped° a god for hise myracles. — *called*

For he kan maken at his owene gyse° — *in his own way*

Of everich herte as that hym list divyse.° — *as he wishes to arrange*

Lo heere this Arcite and this Palamon,

That quitly° weren out of my prisoun — *freely*

935 And myghte han lyved in Thebes roially,

And witen° I am hir mortal enemy — *know*

And that hir deth lith° in my myght also, — *lies*

And yet hath love maugree hir° eyen two[3] — *despite their*

Broght hem hyder° bothe for to dye. — *here*

940 Now looketh: is nat that an heigh° folye? — *great*

Who may been a fool but if he love?° — *unless he who loves*

Bihoold, for Goddes sake that sit above:

Se how they blede! Be they noght wel arrayed?° — *decorated*

Thus hath hir lord, the god of love, ypayed° — *paid*

945 Hir wages and hir fees for hir servyse!

And yet they wenen for to been ful

    wyse° — *consider (themselves) very wise*

That serven love, for aught that may

    bifalle.° — *anything that may happen*

But this is yet the beste gam° of alle, — *game*

That she for whom they han° this jolitee° — *have / amusement*

950 Kan° hem therfore as muche thank as me. — *owes*

She woot namoore° of al this hoote° — *knows no more / rash / business*

    fare,°

---

1 *It ... corde* There is no need to torture you with a rope (i.e., with a rope twisted about the prisoner's head).

2 *benedicite* Latin: bless you.

3 *maugree ... two* Despite anything they could do.

By God, than woot a cokkow° of an hare.[1]   *cuckoo*
But al moot been assayed,° hoot and coold!   *tried*
A man moot been a fool or yong or oold.[2]
955 I woot it by myself ful yore agon,°   *very long ago*
For in my tyme a servant[3] was I oon,
And therfore syn° I knowe of loves peyne   *since*
And woot hou soore° it kan a man
      distreyne,°   *how painfully | afflict*
As he that hath been caught ofte in his laas,°   *trap*
960 I yow° foryeve° al hoolly° this trespass   *you | forgive | completely*
At requeste of the queene that kneleth heere
And eek of Emelye, my suster deere.°   *dear sister(-in-law)*
And ye shul bothe anon unto me swere
That nevere mo ye shal my contree° dere,°   *country | harm*
965 Ne make werre° upon me nyght ne day   *war*
But been my freendes in al that ye may.
I yow foryeve this trespas every deel."°   *completely*
And they hym sworen his axyng° faire and weel   *asking*
And hym of lordshipe° and of mercy
      preyde,   *his protection as lord*
970 And he hem graunteth grace,° and thus he seyde: *his favor*
      "To speke of roial lynage and richesse,
Though that she were a queene or a princesse,
Ech of you bothe is worthy, doutelees,
To wedden whan tyme is, but nathelees—
975 I speke as for my suster Emelye,
For whom ye have this strif° and jalousye.   *strife*
Ye woot yourself she may nat wedden two
Atones,° though ye fighten everemo.   *at once*
That oon of you, al be hym looth or lief,°   *whether he likes it or not*
980 He moot pipen in an yvy leef.°[4]   *pipe in an ivy leaf*
This is to seyn, she may nat now han bothe,
Al be° ye never so jalouse ne so wrothe.   *although*
And forthy° I yow putte in this degree,°   *therefore | situation*
That ech of yow shal have his destynee
985 As hym is shape,° and herkneth in what wyse;°   *ordained | way*
Lo heere° youre ende of that I shal devyse.   *here is*

"My wyl° is this for plat° conclusioun,   *will | plain*
Withouten any repplicacioun:°   *reply*
If that you liketh, take it for the beste,
990 That everich° of you shal goon where hym leste   *each*
Frely° withouten raunson or daunger,   *freely*
And this day fifty wykes fer ne ner[5]
Everich of you shal brynge an hundred knyghtes
Armed for lystes° up at alle rightes,°[6]   *arena | points*
995 Al redy° to darreyne° hire by bataille.   *ready | decide*
And this bihote° I yow withouten faille°   *promise | fail*
Upon my trouthe and as I am a knyght:
That wheither of yow bothe that hath myght,
This is to seyn, that wheither he or thow
1000 May with his hundred as I spak° of now   *spoke*
Sleen his contrarie° or out of lystes dryve,   *opponent*
Thanne shal I yeve° Emelya to wyve   *give*
To whom that Fortune yeveth so fair a grace.
The lystes shal I maken in this place,
1005 And God so wisly° on my soule rewe,°   *wisely | have mercy*
As I shal evene° juge been and trewe.   *fair*
Ye shul noon oother ende° with me maken,   *resolution*
That oon of yow ne shal be deed or taken.°   *captured*
And if yow thynketh this is weel ysayd,°   *well said*
1010 Seyeth youre avys° and holdeth you apayd.°   *opinion | satisfied*
This is youre ende and youre conclusioun."
      Who looketh lightly now but Palamoun?
Who spryngeth up for joye but Arcite?
Who kouthe° telle or who kouthe endite°   *could | write*
1015 The joye that is maked in the place
Whan Theseus hath doon so fair a grace?°   *behaved so graciously*
But doun on knees wente every maner wight°   *manner of person*
And thonken hym with al hir herte and myght,
And namely the Thebans often sithe.°   *many times*
1020 And thus with good hope and with herte blithe°   *happy*
They taken hir leve and homward gonne° they ride   *began*
To Thebes with hise° olde walles wyde.   *its*

EXPLICIT SECUNDA PARS

---

[1] *of an hare*   Many editors prefer the reading "or a hare," which is found in many manuscripts, but "less than a cuckoo knows about a hare" also makes sense.

[2] *A ... oold*   A man must be a fool, either when he is young or when he is old.

[3] *For ... servant*   I.e., a servant of Cupid.

[4] *pipen in an yvy leef*   I.e., make an attempt at an impossible task.

---

[5] *fifty ... ner*   Fifty weeks from this day, neither more nor less.

[6] *Armed ... rightes*   Lists were the spaces fenced off for a medieval tournament, in which knights fought in two groups, and for individual jousts. The description of the lists set up by Theseus in the lines below, however, is based on accounts of Roman arenas, like the Coliseum in Rome.

SEQUITUR PARS TERTIA[1]

I trowe° men wolde deme° it necligence   *believe / judge*
If I foryete° to tellen the dispence°   *forget / expense*
1025 Of Theseus that gooth so bisily
To maken up the lystes° roially   *arena*
That swich a noble theatre° as it was,   *ampitheater*
I dar wel seyn in this world ther nas.°   *was not*
The circuit a myle was aboute,
1030 Walled of stoon° and dyched° al withoute.   *stone / ditched*
Round was the shape, in manere of compas,
Ful of degrees, the heighte of sixty pas,°   *spaces*
That whan a man was set on o° degree,   *one*
He lette nat° his felawe for to see.   *hindered not*
1035 Estward ther stood a gate of marbul whit,°   *white marble*
Westward right swich another in the opposit.
And shortly to concluden, swich a place
Was noon in erthe° as in so litel space,   *earth*
For in the lond ther was no crafty° man   *skillful*
1040 That geometrie or ars metrik° kan,°   *arithmetic / knew*
Ne portreitour,° ne kervere° of   *portrait-painter / carver /*
      ymages°   *statues*
That Theseus ne yaf° mete° and wages   *did not give / food*
The theatre for to maken and devyse.
And for to doon his ryte° and sacrifise   *ceremonies*
1045 He estward hath upon the gate above
In worshipe of Venus, goddesse of love,
Doon make° an auter° and an oratorie,°   *had made / altar / chapel*
And on the westward in memorie
Of Mars, he maked hath right swich° another,   *just such*
1050 That coste largely of gold a fother.[2]
And northward in a touret° on the wal   *turret*
Of alabastre° whit and reed° coral   *alabaster / red*
An oratorie riche for to see
In worshipe of Dyane of chastitee
1055 Hath Theseus doon wroght in noble wyse.°   *manner*
      But yet hadde I foryeten° to devyse°   *forgotten / describe*
The noble kervyng° and the portraitures,°   *carving / portraits*
The shape, the contenaunce, and the figures
That weren in thise oratories thre.
1060 First, in the temple of Venus maystow se°   *you may see*

Wroght on the wal ful pitous° to biholde   *pitiful*
The broken slepes° and the sikes° colde,   *sleeps / sighs*
The sacred teeris° and the waymentynge,°   *tears / lamentation*
The firy strokes and the desirynge
1065 That loves servantz° in this lyf enduren,   *love's servants*
The othes° that hir covenantz assuren,°   *oaths / assure*
Plesaunce° and Hope, Desir, Foolhardynesse,   *pleasure*
Beautee and Youthe, Bauderie,° Richesse,   *bawdiness*
Charmes and Force, Lesynges,° Flaterye,   *lies*
1070 Despense,° Bisynesse,° and Jalousye,   *spending / anxiety*
That wered° of yelewe° gooldes° a
      gerland   *wore / yellow / marigolds*
And a cokkow° sittynge on hir hand.   *cuckoo*
Festes,° instrumentz, caroles,[3] daunces,   *feasts*
Lust,° and array,° and all the circumstaunces   *pleasure / dress*
1075 Of love, whiche that I rekned° have and rekne shal,   *reckoned*
By ordre weren peynted on the wal,
And mo than I kan make of mencioun.°   *make mention*
For soothly, al the Mount of Citheroun[4]
Ther° Venus hath hir principal dwellynge,   *where*
1080 Was shewed on the wal in portreyynge°   *painting*
With al the gardyn and the lustynesse.
Nat was forgyeten the porter Ydelnesse
Ne Narcisus[5] the faire of yore agon,°   *days of old*
And yet the folye of Kyng Salomon,[6]
1085 And eek the grete strengthe of Ercules,°   *Hercules*
Th'enchauntementz of Medea and Circes,[7]
Ne of Turnus[8] with the hardy fiers corage,
The riche Cresus,[9] kaytyf° in servage.°   *captive / servitude*

---

[1] *Explicit ... Tertia*   Latin: Here ends the second part. The third part follows.

[2] *That ... fother*   That cost many a cart-load of gold.

[3] *caroles*   Dances performed to the accompaniment of singing.

[4] *Mount of Citheroun*   In Roman mythology, Venus rose from the sea fully-formed at the island of Cythera. In a number of medieval texts, including *The Knight's Tale*, Mount Cithaeron is confused with this island.

[5] *Narcisus*   Narcissus fell in love with his own image when he saw it in a pool. See Ovid's *Metamorphoses*.

[6] *folye of Kyng Salomon*   King Solomon, famously the wisest of men, fell into folly under the influence of the many wives and concubines in his harem.

[7] *Medea and Circes*   In Greek mythology, Medea and Circe were sorceresses. They were in love with Jason and Odysseus respectively.

[8] *Turnus*   In the later books of Virgil's *Aeneid*, Turnus is Aeneas's main antagonist and his rival for the hand of Lavinia in marriage.

[9] *The riche Cresus*   In Roman mythology, Croesus, King of Lydia, was fabulously rich but died a wretched death, captured by Cyrus.

Thus may ye seen that wysdom ne richesse,
1090 Beautee ne sleighte,° strengthe, hardynesse   *trickery*
Ne may° with Venus holde
     champartie.°   *may not | equal partnership*
For as hir list,° the world than° may she
     gye.°   *she desires | then | rule*
Lo, alle thise folk so caught were in hir las,°   *snare*
Til they for wo ful ofte seyde, "Allas!"
1095 Suffiseth° heere ensamples° oon or two,   *it is enough | examples*
And though I koude rekene a thousand mo.

   The statue of Venus glorious for to se
Was naked, fletynge° in the large see,°   *floating | sea*
And fro° the navele doun al covered was   *from*
1100 With wawes° grene and brighte as any glas.   *waves*
A citole[1] in hir right hand hadde she,
And on hir heed, ful semely° for to se,   *very beautiful*
A rose gerland fressh and wel smellynge;°   *sweet smelling*
Above hir heed hir dowves° flikerynge.°   *doves | fluttering*
1105 Biforn hire stood hir sone Cupido.
Upon his shuldres wynges hadde he two,
And blynd° he was as it was often seene.   *blind*
A bowe he bar° and arwes° brighte and
     kene.°   *carried | arrows | sharp*
   Why sholde I noght° as wel eek telle yow al   *not*
1110 The portreiture that was upon the wal
Withinne the temple of myghty Mars the rede?
Al peynted was the wal in lengthe and brede°   *breadth*
Lyk to the estres° of the grisly place   *interior*
That highte° the grete temple of Mars in
     Trace°   *was called | Thrace*
1115 In thilke° colde, frosty regioun   *the same*
Theras° Mars hath his sovereyn° mansioun.[2]   *where | chief*
   First on the wal was peynted a forest
In which ther dwelleth neither man ne best,
With knotty, knarry,° bareyne° trees olde,   *gnarled | barren*
1120 Of stubbes° sharpe and hidouse° to biholde,   *stumps | hideous*
In which ther ran a rumbel° and a
     swough°   *rumble | rush of wind*
As though a storm sholde bresten° every bough.   *break*

---

[1] *A citole* Musical instrument that had a fingerboard and was plucked with a plectrum. It was a distant descendant of the classical lyre.

[2] *mansioun* A "mansion" of a god/planet was, in astrological terms, its appropriate region in the sky, but here the reference is to Mars's greatest temple, in Thracia in northern Greece.

And dounward from an hille under a bente,°   *slope*
Ther stood the temple of Mars Armypotente,°   *powerful in arms*
1125 Wroght al of burned° steel of which the
     entree°   *polished | entrance*
Was long and streit° and gastly for to see.   *narrow*
And therout cam a rage° and swich a veze,°   *roar of wind | blast*
That it made al the gate for to rese.°   *shake*
The northren lyght in at the dores° shoon,   *doors*
1130 For wyndowe on the wal ne was ther noon
Thurgh which men myghten any light discerne.
The dore was al of adamant eterne,°   *eternal*
Yclenched° overthwart° and
     endelong°   *supported | crosswise | lengthwise*
With iren tough, and for to make it strong
1135 Every pyler° the temple to sustene   *pillar*
Was tonne-greet° of iren° bright and shene.   *big as a barrel | iron*
   Ther saugh I first the dirke ymaginyng°   *dark plotting*
Of Felonye° and the compassyng,°   *crime | scheming*
The crueel Ire, reed° as any gleede,°   *red | ember*
1140 The pykepurs° and the pale Drede,°   *pick-pocket | dread*
The smylere° with the knyf° under the
     cloke,°   *smiler | knife | cloak*
The shepne° brennynge° with the blake smoke,   *stable | burning*
The tresoun of the mordrynge° in the bedde,°   *murdering | bed*
The open werre° with woundes al bibledde,°   *war | bleeding*
1145 Contek° with blody knyf and sharpe manace;°   *conflict | menace*
Al ful of chirkyng° was that sory° place.[3]   *groaning | sorry*
The sleere of hymself° yet saugh° I ther: *suicide | saw*
His herte blood hath bathed al his heer,°   *hair*
The nayl° ydryven° in the shode°
     anyght,°   *nail | driven | temple | at night*
1150 The colde deeth with mouth gapyng upright.
Amyddes° of the temple sat
     Meschaunce°   *in the middle | misfortune*
With disconfort° and sory contenaunce.   *distress*
Yet saugh I Woodnesse° laughynge in his rage,   *madness*
Armed Compleint,° Outhees,° and fiers
     Outrage,°   *grievance | outcry | violence*
1155 The careyne° in the busk° with throte
     ycorne,°   *corpse | forest | cut throat*
A thousand slayn and nat oon of qualm
     ystorve,°   *killed by plague*

---

[3] *The tresoun … place* The images and statues on the walls of the temple of Mars show the planet's influence, which causes not only war but other sorts of violence and catastrophe.

The tiraunt° with the pray° by force yraft,° *tyrant | prey | seized*
The toun° destroyed: ther was nothyng laft! *town*
Yet saugh I brent° the shippes
    hoppesteres,° *burned | dancing ships*
1160 The hunte° strangled with° the wilde
    beres,° *hunter | killed by | bears*
The sowe° freten° the child right in the cradel, *sow | eat*
The cook yscalded° for al his longe ladel.° *scalded | ladle*
Noght was foryeten° by the infortune° of
    Marte:° *forgotten | adverse influence | Mars*
The cartere,° overryden° with his carte. *carter | run over by*
1165 Under the wheel ful lowe° he lay adoun. *very low*
Ther were also of Martes divisioun° *company*
The laborer and the bocher° and the smyth *butcher*
That forgeth sharpe swerdes° on his styth.°[1] *swords | anvil*
And al above depeynted° in a tour° *painted | tower*
1170 Saugh I Conquest sittynge in greet honour
With the sharpe swerd over his heed
Hangynge by a soutil twynes threed.° *thin twine's thread*
Depeynted° was the slaughtre° of Julius, *painted | assassination*
Of grete Nero and of Antonius.[2]
1175 Al° be that thilke tyme they were
    unborn,° *although | not yet born*
Yet was hir deth° depeynted ther biforn° *death | painted before*
By manasynge° of Mars, right by figure.° *menacing | by horoscope*
So was it shewed in that protreiture
As is depeynted in the certres[3] above
1180 Who shal be slayn or elles deed for love.
Suffiseth° oon ensample in stories olde; *suffices*
I may nat rekene° hem alle, though I wolde.° *count | wanted to*
    The statue of Mars upun a carte° stood *upon a chariot*
Armed, and looked grym° as he were wood.° *looking grim | crazy*
1185 And over his heed ther shynen° two figures *shone*
Of sterres° that been cleped in
    scriptures,° *stars | called in writings*
That oon Puella, that oother Rubeus.[4]
This god of armes was arrayed thus:

A wolf ther stood biforn° hym at his feet *before*
1190 With eyen rede,° and of a man he eet.° *red | ate*
With soutil pencel° was depeynted this storie *brush*
In redoutynge° of Mars and of his glorie.° *honor | glory*
    Now to the temple of Dyane the chaste
As shortly as I kan I wol me haste
1195 To telle yow al the descripsioun.
Depeynted been the walles up and doun
Of huntyng and of shamefast° chastitee. *modest*
Ther saugh I how woful Calistopee,[5]
Whan that Diane agreved° was with here,° *angry | her*
1200 Was turned from a womman til° a bere,° *into | bear*
And after was she maad° the loode sterre.° *made | pole-star*
Thus was it peynted. I kan° sey you no ferre.° *can | further*
Hir sone[6] is eek a sterre, as men may see.
Ther saugh I Dane[7] yturned° til a tree— *turned*
1205 I mene° nat the goddesse Diane, *mean*
But Penneus doghter° which that highte°
    Dane. *Penneus's daughter | named*
Ther saugh I Attheon[8] an hert° ymaked° *deer | made*
For vengeaunce that he saugh Diane al naked.
I saugh how that hise houndes have hym caught
1210 And freeten° hym for that they knewe hym
    naught.° *ate | did not know him*
Yet peynted a litel forthermoor° *further away*
How Atthalante[9] hunted the wilde boor° *boar*

---

[1] *The laborer ... styth* These trades, which all use sharp tools, are under the protection of Mars.

[2] *Depeynted ... Antonius* Julius Caesar, the Emperor Nero, and Marc Antony all met violent deaths.

[3] *As ... certres* Depicted in the astrological certainties.

[4] *Puella ... Rubeus* Patterned figures used in the method of predicting the future known as geomancy—a method of arranging dots into columns according to chance.

[5] *Calistopee* Callisto was a favorite companion of Diana. In order to sleep with Callisto, Jupiter disguised himself as Diana. Diana discovered the trick and forced Callisto from her company. Shortly after she left Diana, she found she was pregnant. She gave birth to a boy, Arcas. Juno, Jupiter's wife, jealously changed Callisto into a bear. When her son Arcas was about to kill her mistakenly in a hunt, Jupiter changed her into the constellation Ursa Major, the Great Bear.

[6] *Hir sone* Callisto's son is Arcas, whom Jupiter transformed into the constellation Ursa Minor, the Little Bear.

[7] *Dane* I.e., Daphne, who was chased by the god Apollo. At her request, the gods turned her into a laurel tree to protect her from him. See Ovid's *Metamorphoses*.

[8] *Attheon* I.e., Actaeon, who saw the naked Diana taking a bath. She changed him into a deer to punish him and he was killed by his own hunting dogs.

[9] *Atthalante* I.e., Atalanta, a maiden, a hunter who acquitted herself well in the Calydonian Boar Hunt.

And Meleagree[1] and many another mo,

For which Dyane wroghte hym° care and wo.   *fashioned for him*

1215 Ther saugh I many another wonder° storie,   *wonderful*

The whiche me list nat drawen to memorie.[2]

   This goddesse on an hert ful wel hye seet,°   *sat very high*

With smale houndes al aboute hir feet,

And undernethe hir feet she hadde a moone.°   *moon*

1220 Wexynge° it was and sholde wanye° soone.   *waxing / wane*

In gaude grene° hir statue clothed was,   *yellow-green*

With bowe in honde and arwes in a cas.°   *quiver*

Hir eyen caste she ful lowe adoun

Ther° Pluto[3] hath his derke regioun.   *where*

1225 A womman travaillynge° was hire biforn,   *in labor*

But for° hir child so longe was unborn   *because*

Ful pitously, "Lucyna!"[4] gan she calle

And seyde, "Helpe! For thow mayst best° of
alle!"   *may best (help)*

Wel koude he peynten lifly° that it wroghte;°   *life-like / made*

1230 With many a floryn° he the hewes°
boghte.°   *gold coin / colors / bought*

   Now been the lystes maad° and Theseus   *made*

That at his grete cost arrayed° thus   *arranged*

The temples and the theatre every deel,°   *part*

Whan it was doon, hym lyked wonder
weel.°   *it pleased him very well*

1235 But stynte° I wole of Theseus a lite   *stop speaking*

And speke of Palamon and of Arcite.

   The day approcheth of hir retournynge

That everich sholde an hundred knyghtes brynge

The bataille to darreyne° as I yow tolde.   *decide*

1240 And til Atthenes,° hir covenantz° for to
holde,   *to Athens / agreement*

Hath everich of hem broght an hundred knyghtes

Wel armed for the werre at alle rightes.°   *in all aspects*

And sikerly,° ther trowed° many a man   *surely / believed*

That nevere sithen° that the world bigan,   *never since*

1245 As for to speke of knyghthod° of hir hond,   *deeds of knighthood*

As fer as God hath maked see or lond

Nas° of so fewe so noble a compaignye.   *there was not*

For every wight° that lovede chivalrye   *person*

And wolde his thankes° han a passant° name   *gladly / surpassing*

1250 Hath preyd° that he myghte been of°
that game.   *prayed / (part) of*

And wel was hym that therto chosen was,

For if ther fille° tomorwe swich a cas,   *befell*

Ye knowen wel that every lusty knyght

That loveth paramours° and hath his myght,   *as a lover*

1255 Were it in Engelond or elleswhere,

They wolde hir thankes° wilnen° to be there   *gladly / wish*

To fighte for a lady, benedicitee.

It were a lusty° sighte for to see!   *pleasant*

   And right so ferden° they with Palamon.   *did*

1260 With hym ther wenten knyghtes many on.°   *one*

Som wol ben° armed in an haubergeon°   *one would be / mail-coat*

And in bristplate° and in light gypon,°   *breast-plate / over-garment*

And somme woln have a paire plates,[5]

And somme woln have a Pruce-sheeld° or a
targe.   *Prussian shield*

1265 Somme woln ben armed on hir legges° weel°   *legs / well*

And have an ax, and somme a mace[6] of steel.

There is no newe gyse° that it nas° old.   *fashion / was not*

Armed were they as I have yow told,

Everych after his opinioun.

1270   Ther maistow seen comynge° with Palamoun   *see coming*

Lygurge[7] hymself, the grete kyng of Trace.

Blak was his berd, and manly was his face.

The cercles of hise eyen in his heed,

They gloweden bitwixen yelow and reed,

1275 And lik a grifphon[8] looked he aboute,

With kempe heeris° on hise browes stoute,°   *combed hairs / large*

Hise lymes° grete, his brawnes° harde and
stronge,   *limbs / muscles*

His shuldres brode,° hise armes rounde and
longe.   *shoulders broad*

And as the gyse° was in his contree,   *fashion*

1280 Ful hye upon a chaar° of gold stood he   *chariot*

---

[1] *Meleagree* Meleager was awarded Atalanta after the hunt for the Calydonian boar, occasioning jealousy between him and his family.

[2] *The ... memorie* Which I do not wish to call to memory.

[3] *Pluto* God of the Underworld, the realm of the dead.

[4] *Lucyna* Lucina is another name for Diana. One of Diana's attributes was the goddess of childbirth.

[5] *paire plates* Plate armor, as opposed to chain-mail armor.

[6] *mace* Here, a spiked metal club.

[7] *Lygurge* King of Sparta, in Greece, known for his austere militarism.

[8] *grifphon* Mythological beast with a lion's hindquarters and an eagle's torso and head.

With foure white boles° in the trays.°   *bulls / harness*
Instede of cote armure° over° his
   harnays,°   *coat of arms / on / armor*
With nayles° yelewe and brighte as any gold,   *nails*
He hadde a beres skyn, col blak for old.°   *coal-black with age*
1285 His longe heer was kembd° bihynde his bak;   *combed*
As any ravenes fethere° it shoon° for blak.   *raven's feather / shone*
A wrethe° of gold, arm-greet,° of huge
   wighte°   *wreath / arm-thick / weight*
Upon his heed, set ful of stones° brighte,   *jewels*
Of fyne rubyes° and of dyamauntz.°   *rubies / diamonds*
1290 Aboute his chaar ther wenten white alauntz,°   *wolfhounds*
Twenty and mo, as grete as any steer
To hunten at the leoun or the deer,
And folwed hym with mosel° faste ybounde,   *muzzle*
Colered° of gold and tourettes° fyled°
   rounde.   *collared / leash-rings / filed*
1295 An hundred lordes hadde he in his route,
Armed ful wel with hertes stierne° and stoute.   *stern*
   With Arcite in stories as men fynde
The grete Emetreus,[1] the kyng of Inde,°   *India*
Upon a steede bay,° trapped in steel,   *bay horse*
1300 Covered in clooth of gold dyapred[2] weel,
Cam ridynge lyk the god of armes, Mars.
His cotearmure° was of clooth of Tars,°   *cloth tunic / Tartary*
Couched° with perles white and rounde and grete.   *decorated*
His sadel° was of brend° gold newe ybete,[3]   *saddle / burnished*
1305 A mantel° upon his shulder hangynge   *tunic*
Bratful° of rubyes rede as fyr sparklynge;   *full to the brim*
His crispe heer° lyk rynges was yronne,°   *curly hair / curled*
And that was yelow and glytered as the sonne.
His nose was heigh, hise eyen bright citryn,°   *lemon-colored*
1310 Hise lippes rounde, his colour was sangwyn;°   *red*
A fewe frakenes° in his face yspreynd,°   *freckles / sprinkled*
Bitwixen yelow and somdel blak°
   ymeynd;°   *somewhat black / mixed*

And as a leoun he his lookyng caste;°   *he looked about*
Of fyve and twenty yeer his age I caste.°   *guess*
1315 His berd was wel bigonne for to sprynge.°   *grow*
His voys was as a trompe thondrynge.°   *thundering trumpet*
Upon his heed he wered° of laurer° grene   *wore / laurel-leaves*
A gerland fressh and lusty° for to sene.   *pleasant*
Upon his hand he bar° for his deduyt°   *carried / pleasure*
1320 An egle° tame as any lilye whyt.   *eagle*
An hundred lordes hadde he with hym there,
Al armed save hir heddes° in al hir gere,° *except their heads / armor*
Ful richely in alle maner thynges.
For trusteth wel that dukes, erles, kynges
1325 Were gadered° in this noble compaignye   *gathered*
For love and for encrees° of chivalrye.   *increase*
Aboute this kyng ther ran on every part
Ful many a tame leoun and leopard,
And in this wise thise lordes alle and some
1330 Been on the Sonday to the citee come
Aboute pryme, and in the toun alight.°   *arrived*
   This Theseus, this duc, this worthy knyght,
Whan he had broght hem into his citee
And inned hem° everich in his
   degree,°   *lodged them / according to his rank*
1335 He festeth° hem and dooth so greet labour   *feasted*
To esen° hem and doon hem al honour,°   *refresh / every honor*
That yet man weneth° that no maner wit   *imagines*
Of noon estaat ne koude amenden it.°   *make it better*
   The mynstralcye,° the service at the feeste, *musical performances*
1340 The grete yiftes° to the meeste and
   leeste,°   *gifts / most and least (important)*
The riche array° of Theseus paleys,   *decoration*
Ne who sat first ne last upon the deys,°   *dais (high table)*
What ladyes fairest been or best daunsynge,
Or which of hem kan dauncen best and synge,
1345 Ne who moost felyngly speketh of love,
What haukes° sitten on the perche above,   *hawks*
What houndes liggen° in the floor adoun,   *lie*
Of al this make I now no mencioun,
But al th'effect° that thynketh me° the
   beste.[4]   *only the general effect / seems to me*
1350 Now cometh the point, and herkneth° if yow
   leste.°   *listen / wish*

---

[1] *The grete Emetreus* King Emetreus is not attested in classical mythology nor is he to be found in Chaucer's sources.

[2] *dyapred* "Diapered" is a technical term drawn from the world of medieval manuscript illumination that indicates the diamond-shaped patterns used as the background for many paintings in medieval books. King Emetreus's horse wears a decorative cloth covered with this type of pattern.

[3] *newe ybete* I.e., newly beaten. A goldsmith works goldplate jewelry into pleasing patterns by beating it with a small hammer.

---

[4] *But ... beste* Here Chaucer offers an example of *occupatio*, the rhetorical figure in which one lists at great length the things one is not going to describe, thus describing them.

The Sonday nyght er day bigan to sprynge,
Whan Palamon the larke herde synge,
Although it nere nat day by houres two,
Yet song the larke and Palamon also.
1355 With hooly herte and with an heigh corage°   *high spirit*
He roos° to wenden° on his pilgrymage   *rose / go*
Unto the blisful Citherea° benigne.°   *Venus / kind*
I mene Venus, honurable and digne.°   *worthy*
And in hir houre he walketh forth a pas°   *slowly*
1360 Unto the lystes ther hire temple was,
And doun he kneleth with ful humble cheere°   *expression*
And herte soor, and seyde in this manere:
      "Faireste of faire, O lady myn, Venus,
Doughter to Jove and spouse of Vulcanus,
1365 Thow gladere° of the mount of Citheron,   *one who delights*
For thilke° love thow haddest to° Adoon,[1]   *the same / for*
Have pitee of my bittre teeris smerte°   *bitter, painful tears*
And taak myn humble preyere at° thyn herte.   *to*
Allas, I ne have no langage° to telle   *words*
1370 Th'effectes ne° the tormentz of myn helle!°   *nor / my hell*
Myn herte may myne harmes° nat biwreye.°   *wrongs / reveal*
I am so confus, that I kan noght seye
But 'Mercy!' Lady bright, that knowest weele
My thought and seest what harmes that I feele,
1375 Considere al this and rewe° upon my soore,°   *have mercy / pain*
As wisly° as I shal for everemore,   *surely*
Emforth° my myght, thy trewe servant be,   *according to*
And holden werre° alwey with chastitee,   *be at war*
That make I myn avow,° so° ye me helpe.   *promise / if*
1380 I kepe noght° of armes for to yelpe,°   *do not care / boast*
Ne I ne axe° nat tomorwe to have victorie   *nor do I ask*
Ne renoun in this cas,° ne veyneglorie°   *event / pride*
Of pris° of armes blowen up and
      doun.°   *reputation / made widely known*
But I wolde have fully possessioun
1385 Of Emelye, and dye in thy servyse.
Fynd thow the manere hou° and in what
      wyse.°   *means how / way*
I recche nat but° it may bettre be   *do not care whether*
To have victorie of hem or they of me,
So that I have my lady in myne armes!
1390 For though so be that Mars is god of armes,
Youre vertu° is so greet in hevene above,   *power*

That if yow list, I shal wel have my love.
Thy temple wol I worshipe everemo,
And on thyn auter, where° I ride or go,   *wherever*
1395 I wol doon sacrifice and fires beete.°   *kindle fires (of sacrifice)*
And if ye wol nat so,° my lady sweete,   *you will not (do) so*
Thanne preye I thee tomorwe with a spere
That Arcita me thurgh the herte bere!°   *pierce*
Thanne rekke° I noght whan I have lost my lyf,   *care*
1400 Though that Arcita wynne hire to° his wyf.   *as*
This is th'effect and ende of my preyere.°   *prayer*
Yif° me my love, thow blisful lady deere."   *give*
      Whan the orison was doon° of Palamon,   *done*
His sacrifice he dide and that anon
1405 Ful pitously with alle circumstaunce,°   *ritual*
Al° telle I noght as now° his observaunce.   *although / for now*
But atte laste the statue of Venus shook
And made a signe wherby that he took
That his preyere accepted was that day.
1410 For thogh the signe shewed a delay,
Yet wiste he wel that graunted was his boone.°   *request*
And with glad herte he wente hym hoom ful soone.
      The thridde houre inequal[2] that Palamon
Bigan to Venus temple for to gon,°   *go*
1415 Up roos the sonne, and up roos Emelye,
And to the temple of Dyane gan hye.°   *went*
Hir maydens,° that she thider with hire
      ladde,°   *ladies-in-waiting / led*
Ful redily with hem the fyr° they
      hadde,.°   *fire (for sacrifice) / carried*
Th'encens,° the clothes, and the remenant al   *the incense*
1420 That to the sacrifice longen shal,°   *belongs*
The hornes° fulle of meeth,° as was the
      gyse;°   *drinking horns / mead / custom*
Ther lakked noght to doon hir sacrifise.
Smokynge° the temple ful of clothes
      faire,°   *incensing / beautiful cloth hangings*

---

[1] *Adoon* Adonis was a youth whom Venus loved. He was killed by
a boar, and Venus transformed his blood into a flower.

[2] *houre inequal* In Chaucer's day there were two ways of dividing
up time into hours. "Artificial" hours are those we use today, where
both day and night are divided into twelve hours equal in amount.
"Unequal" hours, the older system used in an age that did not have
the clocks that made the artificial hours possible, was the division of
the daylight time into twelve hours and the time of dark into twelve.
The length of these hours would change according to the seasons.
They were the same as the artificial hours only at the spring and
autumn equinoxes. Each hour of the day was devoted to one of the
gods/planets.

This Emelye, with herte debonaire,°   *gentle*
1425 Hir body wessh° with water of a welle.   *washed*
But hou° she dide hir ryte,° I dar nat telle,   *how / rite*
But° it be anythyng in general.   *unless*
And yet it were a game° to heeren al.   *joy*
To hym that meneth wel, it were no charge,°   *burden*
1430 But it is good a man been at his large.°   *free (to speak)*
Hir brighte heer was kembd, untressed° al;   *unbraided*
A coroune° of a grene ook° cerial[1]   *crown / oak*
Upon hir heed was set ful fair and meete.°   *fitting*
Two fyres on the auter gan she beete°   *kindled*
1435 And dide hir thynges° as men may biholde   *performed her duties*
In Stace° of Thebes and thise bookes olde.   *Statius*
Whan kyndled was the fyr, with pitous cheere
Unto Dyane she spak as ye may heere:
   "O chaste goddesse of the wodes grene,
1440 To whom bothe hevene and erthe and see° is sene,°   *sea / seen*
Queene of the regne of Pluto derk° and lowe,   *dark*
Goddesse of maydens° that myn herte hast
    knowe°   *maidens / known*
Ful many a yeer, and woost° what I desire,   *knows*
As keepe me fro thy vengeaunce and thyn ire,
1445 That Attheon aboughte° cruelly.   *paid for*
Chaste goddesse, wel wostow° that I   *you know*
Desire to ben a mayden al my lyf.
Ne nevere wol I be no love ne wyf!
I am, thow woost, yet of thy compaignye,
1450 A mayde, and love huntynge° and venerye°   *hunting / the chase*
And for to walken in the wodes wilde
And noght to ben a wyf and be with childe.
Noght° wol I knowe the compaignye of man.   *by no means*
Now helpe me, lady, sith ye may and kan,
1455 For tho° thre formes[2] that thou hast in thee,   *those*
And Palamon that hath swich love to me
And eek Arcite that loveth me so soore,
This grace I preye thee withoute
    moore:°   *without any more (words)*
And sende love and pees° bitwixe hem two,   *peace*
1460 And fro me turne awey hir hertes so
That al hire hoote love and hir desir
And al hir bisy° torment and hir fir°   *intense / fire*

---

[1] *cerial*   Distinct species of oak, *quercus cerris.*

[2] *thre formes*   I.e., three attributes of Diana, goddess of the hunt, of the underworld, and of chastity.

Be queynt° or turned in another place.   *quenched*
And if so be thou wolt do° me no grace,°   *grant / favor*
1465 And if my destynee be shapen so
That I shal nedes° have oon of hem two,   *necessarily*
As sende me hym that moost° desireth me.   *most*
Bihoold, goddesse of clene° chastitee,   *pure*
The bittre teeris that on my chekes falle!
1470 Syn° thou art mayde and kepere° of us alle,   *since / keeper*
My maydenhede° thou kepe and wel
    conserve,°   *virginity / preserve*
And whil I lyve, a mayde I wol thee serve."
   The fires brenne upon the auter cleere°   *bright*
Whil Emelye was thus in hir preyere,
1475 But sodeynly she saugh a sighte queynte.°   *curious*
For right anon oon of the fyres queynte°   *went out*
And quyked agayn,° and after that anon   *kindled again*
That oother fyr was queynt° and al
    agon.°   *quenched / completely gone*
And as it queynte, it made a whistlynge,
1480 As doon thise wete° brondes° in hir brennynge,   *wet / sticks*
And at the brondes ende out ran anon
As it were blody dropes° many oon,°   *bloody drops / many a one*
For which so soore° agast° was Emelye,   *sorely / appalled*
That she was wel ny mad° and gan to crye,   *almost crazy*
1485 For she ne wiste° what it signyfied,   *did not know*
But oonly for the feere° thus hath she cried   *fear*
And weepe, that it was pitee for to heere.
And therwithal° Dyane gan appeere   *with all of this*
With bowe° in honde, right as an hunteresse,   *bow*
1490 And seyde, "Doghter, stynt° thyn hevynesse!°   *stop / laments*
Among the goddes hye,° it is affermed°   *high / affirmed*
And by eterne word writen and confermed:
Thou shalt ben wedded unto oon of tho°   *those*
That han for thee so muchel care and wo,
1495 But unto which of hem, I may nat telle.
Farwel, for I ne may no lenger dwelle.
The fires whiche that on myn auter brenne
Shulle° thee declaren, er that thou go henne,°   *shall / away*
Thyn aventure° of love as in this cas."   *fortune*
1500 And with that word, the arwes in the caas°   *quiver*
Of the goddesse clateren° faste and rynge,°   *clatter / ring*
And forth she wente and made a vanysshynge,°   *vanished*
For which this Emelye astoned° was   *astonished*
And seyde, "What amounteth this,° allas?   *what does this mean*
1505 I putte me in thy proteccioun,
Dyane, and in thy disposicioun."°   *care*

And hoom she goth anon the nexte weye.
This is th'effect. Ther is namoore to seye.
　　The nexte houre of Mars folwynge this,
1510 Arcite unto the temple walked is
Of fierse Mars to doon his sacrifise
With alle the rytes of his payen wyse.°　　　　*rites / pagan customs*
With pitous herte and heigh devocioun
Right thus to Mars he seyde his orisoun:
1515 　"O stronge god that in the regnes° colde　　*kingdoms*
Of Trace honoured art and lord yholde,°　　*considered lord*
And hast in every regne and every lond
Of armes al the brydel in thyn hond,[1]
And hem fortunest° as thee lyst
　　devyse,°　　　　*give fortune to them / wish to arrange*
1520 Accepte of me my pitous° sacrifise.　　　　*pious*
If so be that my youthe may deserve
And that my myght° be worthy for to serve　　*strength*
Thy godhede,° that I may been oon of thyne,　　*divinity*
Thanne preye I thee to rewe° upon my pyne.　　*have pity*
1525 For thilke peyne and thilke hoote fir°　　*the same hot fire*
In which thow whilom° brendest for desir　　*once*
Whan that thow usedest° the beautee　　*used*
Of faire, yonge, fresshe Venus fre°　　*noble*
And haddest hire in armes at thy wille
1530 (Although thee ones° on a tyme mysfille°　*once / had a misfortune*
Whan Vulcanus hadde caught thee in his las°　　*trap*
And foond thee liggynge° by his wyf, allas!)[2]—　　*lying*
For thilke sorwe° that was in thyn herte,　　*sorrow*
Have routhe as wel upon my peynes smerte!°　　*smart*
1535 I am yong and unkonnynge,° as thow
　　woost,°　　　　*unknowing / know*
And, as I trowe,° with love offended° moost　*believe / injured*
That evere was any lyves° creature.　　*living*
For she that dooth° me al this wo endure°　*does / enduring woe*
Ne reccheth° nevere wher° I synke or
　　fleete!°　　*does not care / whether / sink / float*
1540 And wel I woot er° she me mercy heete,°　*before / promise*
I moot with strengthe wynne hire in the place.

And wel I woot withouten helpe or grace
Of thee ne may° my strengthe noght availle.°　*may not / succeed*
Thanne helpe me, lord, tomorwe in my bataille
1545 For thilke fyr that whilom brente° thee　　*once burned*
As wel as° thilke fyr now brenneth me,　　*just as*
And do° that I tomorwe have victorie.　　*cause it*
Myn be the travaille° and thyn be the glorie!　　*trouble*
Thy sovereyn temple wol I moost honouren
1550 Of any place, and alwey moost labouren
In thy plesaunce° and in thy craftes[3] stronge,　　*pleasure*
And in thy temple I wol my baner honge.°　　*hang*
And alle the armes of my compaignye,
And evere mo unto that day I dye
1555 Eterne fir I wol biforn thee fynde,°　　*provide*
And eek to this avow° I wol me bynde:　　*promise*
My beerd, myn heer that hongeth° long adoun　　*hangs*
That nevere yet ne felte offensioun°　　*felt offense (was cut)*
Of rasour° nor of shere° I wol thee yeve°　*razor / scissors / give*
1560 And ben° thy trewe servant whil I lyve.　　*be*
Now, lord, have routhe upon my sorwes soore.
Yif° me the victorie. I aske thee namoore."°　*give / no more*
　　The preyere stynt° of Arcita the stronge.　　*ends*
The rynges on the temple dore that honge,°　　*hung*
1565 And eek the dores, clatereden° ful faste,　　*clattered*
Of which Arcita somwhat hym agaste.°　*was somewhat afraid*
The fyres brenden upon the auter brighte,
That it gan al the temple for to lighte,
And sweete smel the ground anon up yaf.°　*immediately gave*
1570 And Arcita anon his hand up haf°　　*raised*
And moore encens° into the fyr he caste°　*incense / threw*
With othere rytes° mo. And atte laste　　*rites*
The statue of Mars bigan his hauberk° rynge,　　*mail-coat*
And with that soun° he herde a
　　murmurynge°　　*sound / murmuring*
1575 Full lowe and dym,° and seyde thus: "Victorie,"　*low and dim*
For which he yaf° to Mars honour and glorie.　　*gave*
And thus with joye and hope wel° to fare,　　*well*
Arcite anon unto his in° is fare°　　*inn / has gone*
As fayn° as fowel° is of the brighte sonne.　　*happy / bird*
1580 　And right anon swich strif° ther is bigonne　　*strife*
For thilke grauntyng° in the hevene
　　above　　*this granting (of answers to prayers)*
Bitwixe Venus the goddesse of love

---

[1] *Of armes … hond* Mars has complete control (has the bridle, or as might be said now, the reins) of all matters relating to arms.

[2] *Although … allas* Arcite refers here to the story of Vulcan's jealousy over the affair his wife, Venus, had with Mars. As the greatest of smiths, he fashioned an invisible net, which fell upon Mars and Venus when they were in bed together, trapping them for all the gods to see their shame.

---

[3] *craftes* I.e., those that belong to war—wielding the sword and lance and horsemanship foremost among them.

And Mars the stierne° god armypotente,°   *stern / strong in arms*
That Juppiter was bisy it to stente,°   *stop*
1585 Til that the pale Saturnus the colde
That knew so manye of aventures olde
Foond° in his olde experience and art   *found*
That he ful soone hath plesed every part.°   *each side*
As sooth° is seyd, elde° hath greet avantage;   *truly / age*
1590 In elde is bothe wysdom and usage.°   *experience*
Men may the olde atrenne° and noght
    atrede.°   *outrun / not out-wit*
Saturne anon, to stynten strif and drede,°   *stop strife and fear*
Albeit that it is agayn° his kynde,°   *against / nature*
Of al this strif he gan remedie fynde.°   *found a remedy*
1595   "My deere doghter, Venus," quod Saturne,
"My cours° that hath so wyde° for to
    turne   *course (across the sky) / wide*
Hath moore power than woot any man.[1]
Myn is the drenchyng° in the see° so wan.°   *drowning / sea / pale*
Myn is the prison° in the derke cote.°   *imprisonment / dark cell*
1600 Myn is the stranglyng and hangyng by the throte,°   *throat*
The murmure° and the cherles
    rebellyng,°   *murmur / peasants' rebellion*
The groynynge° and the pryvee
    empoysonyng.°   *groaning / secret poisoning*
I do vengeance and pleyn correccioun°   *full punishment*
Whil I dwelle in signe of the leoun.[2]
1605 Myn is the ruyne° of the hye° halles,   *ruin / high*
The fallynge of the toures° and of the walles   *towers*
Upon the mynour° or the carpenter.[3]   *miner*
I slow° Sampsoun shakynge the piler.[4]   *killed*

And myne be the maladyes colde,[5]
1610 The derke tresons° and the castes° olde.   *treasons / plots*
My lookyng is the fader° of pestilence.   *father*
Now weepe namoore. I shal doon diligence°   *take care*
That Palamon, that is thyn owene knyght,
Shal have his lady as thou hast hym hight.°   *promised*
1615 Though Mars shal helpe his knyght, yet nathelees
Bitwixe yow ther moot be somtyme pees,°   *peace*
Al° be ye noght of o compleccioun,°   *although / one temperament*
That causeth al day swich divisioun.
I am thyn aiel,° redy at thy wille.   *your grandfather*
1620 Weepe now namoore. I wol thy lust fulfille."°   *satisfy your desire*
  Now wol I stynten° of the goddes above,   *stop speaking*
Of Mars and of Venus, goddesse of love,
And telle yow as pleynly as I kan
The grete effect° for which that I bygan.   *result*

EXPLICIT TERCIA PARS

SEQUITUR PARS QUARTA[6]

1625   Greet was the feeste in Atthenes that day,
And eek the lusty seson° of that May   *pleasant season*
Made every wight to been in swich plesaunce°   *enjoyment*
That al that Monday justen° they and daunce   *joust*
And spenten it in Venus heigh servyse.
1630 And by the cause° that they sholde ryse°   *because / had to rise*
Eerly for to seen the grete fight,
Unto hir reste wenten they at nyght,
And on the morwe whan that day gan sprynge,
Of hors° and harneys,° noyse and claterynge   *horse / equipment*
1635 Ther was in hostelryes° al aboute,   *inns*
And to the paleys° rood° ther many a route° *palace / rode / crowd*
Of lordes upon steedes and palfreys.
Ther maystow seen divisynge of harneys°   *preparation of gear*
So unkouth° and so riche and wroght so weel   *unusual*
1640 Of goldsmythrye,° of browdynge,° and of
    steel,   *goldsmithery / embroidering*
The sheeldes brighte, testeres,° and
    trappures,°   *horses' headpieces / horse-armor*
Gold-hewen helmes, hauberkes,° cote-armures,   *mail-coats*
Lordes in parementz° on hir courseres,   *robes*

---

[1] *My ... man* Saturn, in the Middle Ages the farthest known planet from the sun, was believed to have a cold and harmful influence. The following speech of Saturn enumerates disasters that he as god and planet (i.e., as an astrological influence) typically causes.

[2] *signe of the leoun* Saturn is most harmful when he is in the astrological house of Leo.

[3] *mynour or the carpenter* Here, military men who helped dig tunnels under besieged walls of towns and castles. The walls would be shored up with timber, and then, at the right time for an attack to start, the timbers would be set on fire, thus insuring the collapse of the walls. The disaster envisioned here is that which would occur if the miners and carpenters did not leave the tunnel in time before the walls collapsed.

[4] *I slow ... piler* Samson, blinded and enslaved by his enemies, pulled down the pillars supporting their temple, killing them and himself as well. See Judges 13–16.

---

[5] *And ... colde* Diseases caused by a preponderance of the cold humor.

[6] *Explicit ... Quarta* Latin: here ends the third part. The fourth part follows.

Knyghtes of retenue and eek squieres

1645 Nailynge the speres° and helmes
bokelynge,°   *nailing spears / buckling helmets*

Giggynge of sheeldes° with layneres
lacynge°   *setting straps / lacing straps*

(Thereas° nede° is, they weren nothyng
ydel°),   *where / need / idle*

The fomy° steedes on the golden brydel°   *foamy / bridle*

Gnawynge,° and faste° the armurers°
also   *gnawing / quickly / armorers*

1650 With fyle° and hamer prikynge° to and fro,   *file / galloping*

Yemen° on foote and communes° many oon   *yeomen / commoners*

With shorte staves thikke° as they may goon,   *densely*

Pypes, trompes,° nakerers,° clariounes,°   *trumpets / drums / bugles*

That in the bataille blowen° blody sounes,°   *blow / bloody sounds*

1655 The paleys ful of peples up and doun,

Heere thre, ther ten, holdynge° hir questioun,   *debating*

Dyvynynge of° thise Thebane knyghtes two.   *guessing about*

Somme seyden thus; somme seyde it shal be so;

Somme helden with° hym with the blake berd;   *sided with*

1660 Somme with the balled,° somme with the thikke
herd;°   *bald / thick-haired*

Somme seyde he looked grymme° and he wolde
fighte;°   *fierce / wanted to fight*

"He hath a sparth° of twenty pound of wighte!"°   *axe / weight*

Thus was the halle ful of divynynge

Longe after that the sonne gan to sprynge.

1665   The grete Theseus that of his sleepe awaked

With mynstralcie° and noyse that was maked   *music*

Heeld yet the chambre of his paleys riche

Til that the Thebane knyghtes, bothe yliche°   *equally*

Honured, were into the paleys fet.°   *fetched*

1670 Duc Theseus was at a wyndow set,

Arrayed right as he were a god in trone.°   *on (his) throne*

The peple preesseth thiderward° ful soone   *towards there*

Hym for to seen and doon heigh reverence

And eek to herkne his heste° and his
sentence.°   *command / decision*

1675 An heraud° on a scaffold made an "Oo!"°   *herald / whoa!*

Til al the noyse of peple was ydo.°   *stopped*

And whan he saugh the noyse of peple al stille,

Tho° shewed he the myghty dukes wille.   *then*

   "The lord hath of his heigh discrecioun

1680 Considered that it were destruccioun

To gentil° blood to fighten in the gyse°   *noble / manner*

Of mortal bataille now in this emprise.°   *enterprise*

Wherfore to shapen° that they shal nat dye,°   *ensure / die*

He wolde his firste purpos modifye.

1685 No man therfore up° peyne of los of lyf   *upon*

No maner shot,° polax,° ne short knyf   *arrow / battle-axe*

Into the lystes sende ne thider brynge,°   *bring there*

Ne short swerd for to stoke° with poynt
bitynge°   *stab / biting point*

Ne man ne drawe ne bere° by his syde.   *carry*

1690 Ne no man shal unto his felawe° ryde   *against his opponent*

But o° cours° with a sharpe ygrounde
spere;°   *one / turn / sharpened spear*

Foyne, if hym list, on foote hymself to were.[1]

And he that is at meschief° shal be take°   *in trouble / taken*

And noght slayn,° but be broght unto the stake   *not killed*

1695 That shal ben ordeyned° on either syde,   *set up*

But thider he shal° by force and there abyde.   *shall (go)*

And if so be the chieftayn° be take°   *leader / taken*

On outher syde or elles sleen° his make,°   *killed / opponent leader*

No lenger shal the turneiynge° laste.   *tourneying*

1700 God spede you! Gooth forth and ley° on faste!   *lay*

With long swerd and with maces fighteth youre fille!

Gooth now youre wey! This is the lordes wille!"

   The voys° of peple touched the hevene,°   *voice / sky*

So loude cride they with murie stevene,°   *merry voice*

1705 "God save swich a lord that is so good!

He wilneth° no destruccion of blood!"   *wills*

Up goon the trompes and the melodye,

And to the lystes rit° the compaignye,   *rides*

By ordinance° thurghout the citee large,   *decree*

1710 Hanged with clooth of gold and nat° with
sarge.°   *not / serge (plain cloth)*

   Ful lik a lord this noble duc gan ryde,

Thise two Thebans upon either syde.

And after rood the queene and Emelye,

And after that another compaignye

1715 Of oon and oother after hir degree.

And thus they passen thurghout the citee

And to the lystes come they by tyme.°   *in time*

---

[1] *Foyne ... were* Let him parry, if he wishes, to protect himself when he is on foot. Knights who had been dismounted in a tournament would often continue to fight on foot. Although set in an arena and conducted under the eyes of the Roman gods, the tournament will follow the customs of Chaucer's own day.

It nas nat° of the day yet fully pryme[1]   was not
Whan set was Theseus ful riche and hye,
1720 Ypolita the queene, and Emelye,
And othere ladys in degrees aboute.
Unto the seetes° preesseth al the route.   seats
And westward thurgh the gates under Marte°   Mars
Arcite, and eek the hondred of his parte,°   party
1725 With baner reed is entred right anon.
And in that selve° moment Palamon   same
Is under Venus estward° in the place   eastward
With baner whyt and hardy chiere and face.
In al the world to seken° up and doun   seek
1730 So evene, withouten variacioun,
Ther nere° swiche compaignyes tweye!   were not
For ther was noon so wys that koude seye
That any hadde of oother° avauntage   (the) other
Of worthynesse ne of estaat ne age,
1735 So evene were chosen for to gesse.°   guess
And in two renges° faire they hem
    dresse°   ranks / arrange themselves
Whan that hir names rad° were everichon,   read
That in hir nombre° gyle° were ther noon.   number / trickery
Tho° were the gates shet° and cried was loude: then / shut
1740 "Do now youre devoir,° yonge° knyghtes proude!" duty / young
    The heraudes lefte hir prikyng° up and doun.   riding
Now ryngen trompes loude and clarioun.°   bugle
Ther is namoore to seyn, but west and est
In goon the speres ful sadly° in arrest;°   firmly / holder
1745 In gooth the sharpe spore° into the syde.   spur
Ther seen men who kan° juste° and who kan
    ryde.   know how (to) / joust
Ther shyveren° shaftes upon sheeldes thikke;   shiver
He feeleth thurgh the herte-spoon° the prikke.° breast / point
Up spryngen speres twenty foot on highte,
1750 Out gooth the swerdes as the silver brighte;
The helmes they tohewen° and toshrede.°   cut up / shred up
Out brest° the blood with stierne stremes rede;   bursts
With myghty maces the bones they tobreste.°   break up
He thurgh the thikkeste of the throng° gan
    threste.°   crowd / thrust
1755 Ther semblen° steedes stronge, and doun gooth al! stumble
He rolleth under foot as dooth a bal.°   ball
He foyneth° on his feet with his tronchon,° parries / spear-shaft

And he hym hurtleth° with his hors adoun.   strikes
He thurgh the body is hurt and sithen
    ytake,°   afterwards captured
1760 Maugree his heed,° and broght unto the
    stake;   despite all he could do
As forward° was, right there he moste abyde.   the agreement
Another lad° is on that oother syde.   led
And somtyme dooth hem° Theseus to reste,   causes them
Hem to fresshen° and drynken if hem
    leste.°   take refreshment / they wanted
1765 Ful ofte° a day han thise Thebanes two   very often
Togydre ymet and wroght° his felawe wo.   caused
Unhorsed hath ech oother° of hem tweye.   each other
Ther nas no tygre in the vale of Galgopheye[2]
Whan that hir whelpe° is stole° whan it is lite   cub / stolen
1770 So crueel on the hunte as is Arcite
For jelous herte° upon this Palamoun,   heart
Ne in Belmarye[3] ther nys so fel leoun°   is not so fierce a lion
That hunted is or for his hunger wood
Ne of his praye° desireth so the blood   prey
1775 As Palamoun to sleen his foo Arcite.
The jelous strokes on hir helmes byte;°   bite
Out renneth blood on bothe hir sydes rede.
    Somtyme an ende ther is of every dede,°   deed
For er the sonne unto the reste wente,
1780 The stronge Kyng Emetreus gan hente°   captured
This Palamon as he faught with Arcite
And made his swerd depe in his flessh to byte.
And by the force of twenty is he take°   taken
Unyolden° and ydrawe° unto the stake.   not yielding / drawn
1785 And in the rescus° of this Palamon   rescue
The stronge Kyng Lygurge is born adoun,°   knocked down
And Kyng Emetreus for al his strengthe
Is born° out of his sadel a swerdes lengthe,   carried
So hitte hym Palamoun er he were take.°   taken
1790 But al for noght.° He was broght to the stake;   nothing
His hardy herte myghte hym helpe naught.°   by no means
He moste abyde° whan that he was caught   had to stay
By force and eek by composicioun.°   agreement
    Who sorweth now but woful Palamoun,
1795 That moot namoore goon agayn° to fighte?   go again

---

[1] *pryme* Roughly three hours after sunrise; i.e., some time towards 9 a.m.

[2] *Galgopheye* I.e., Galgophia, a valley in Greece.

[3] *Belmarye* I.e., Benmarin, a region of Morocco. In the General Prologue, we find that the Knight has fought there.

And whan that Theseus hadde seyn° this sighte,   *seen*
Unto the folk that foghten° thus echon,°   *fought | each one*
He cryde, "Hoo!° Namoore! For it is doon!   *stop!*
I wol be trewe juge and no partie.°   *partisan*
1800 Arcite of Thebes shal have Emelie,
That by his fortune hath hire faire ywonne!"°   *won fairly*
Anon ther is a noyse of peple bigonne
For joye of this so loude and heighe withalle
It semed that the lystes sholde falle.
1805   What kan now faire Venus doon° above?   *do*
What seith she now? What dooth this queene of love
But wepeth so for wantynge° of hir wille   *lack*
Til that hir teeres in the lystes fille?
She seyde, "I am ashamed doutelees!"°   *doubtless*
1810   Saturnus seyde, "Doghter, hoold thy pees!
Mars hath his wille. His knyght hath al his bone.°   *request*
And by my heed, thow shalt been esed° soone!"   *be eased*
    The trompes with the loude mystralcie,°   *music*
The heraudes that ful loude yolle° and crie   *yell*
1815 Been° in hire wele° for joye of Daun° Arcite.   *be | prosperity | sir*
But herkneth me,° and stynteth° now a
    lite   *listen to me | keep quiet*
Which a myracle ther bifel anon.
    This fierse Arcite hath of his helm ydon,°   *removed*
And on a courser for to shewe his face
1820 He priketh endelong° the large place,   *from end to end of*
Lokynge upward upon Emelye.
And she agayn° hym caste a freendlich° eye[1]   *towards | friendly*
And was al his chiere as in his herte.
    Out of the ground a furie infernal sterte,°   *infernal fury arose*
1825 From Pluto sent at requeste of Saturne,
For which his hors for fere° gan to turne   *fear*
And leepe° aside and foundred° as he
    leepe.°   *leap | stumbled | leapt*
And er that Arcite may taken keepe,°   *care*
He pighte hym° on the pomel° of his
    heed,   *knocked himself | crown*
1830 That in the place he lay as he were deed.

His brest tobrosten° with his sadel bowe,   *broken up*
As blak he lay as any cole° or crowe,   *coal*
So was the blood yronnen° in his face.   *run*
Anon he was yborn° out of the place   *carried*
1835 With herte soor° to Theseus paleys.   *sore*
Tho° was he korven° out of his harneys°   *then | cut | armor*
And in a bed ybrought° ful faire and blyve,°   *brought | quickly*
For he was yet in memorie° and alyve°   *conscious | alive*
And alwey criynge° after Emelye.   *crying*
1840   Duc Theseus with al his compaignye
Is comen hoom to Atthenes his citee
With alle blisse and greet solempnitee.°   *ceremony*
Albeit° that this aventure° was
    falle,°   *although | mishap | had happened*
He nolde noght° disconforten° hem alle.   *would not | distress*
1845 Men seyde eek that Arcite shal nat dye.°   *not die*
He shal been heeled° of his maladye!   *be healed*
And of another thyng they weren as fayn,°   *glad*
That of hem alle was ther noon yslayn.°   *killed*
Al° were they soore yhurt and namely
    oon°   *although | especially one*
1850 That with a spere was thirled° his brest
    boon.°   *pierced | breast-bone*
To othere woundes and to broken armes
Somme hadden salves, and somme hadden charmes.[2]
Fermacies° of herbes and eek save°   *medicines | sage*
They dronken, for they wolde hir lymes
    have.°   *to save their limbs*
1855 For which this noble duc, as he wel kan,
Conforteth and honoureth every man
And made revel al the longe nyght
Unto the straunge° lordes, as was right,   *foreign*
Ne ther was holden no disconfitynge
1860 But as a justes or a tourneiynge.[3]
For soothly, ther was no disconfiture.°   *dishonor*
For fallyng nys nat° but an aventure,   *is nothing*
Ne to be lad by force unto the stake
Unyolden° and with twenty knyghtes take,   *unyielded*
1865 O° persone allone withouten mo,   *one*
And haryed° forth by arm, foot and too,°   *dragged | toe*

---

[1] *And ... eye* The following lines occur in most editions of *The Canterbury Tales* after this one: "For wommen, as to speken in comune, / Thei folwen alle the favour of Fortune." Ellesmere and Hengwrt both omit these lines. They are found in Oxford, Corpus Christi College MS 198. Dated c. 1410–20, this manuscript, like Ellesmere and Hengwrt, is a very early witness to the text of *The Canterbury Tales*.

[2] *Somme ... charmes* Some had salves and some had charms. Herbal medicine and medicinal magic were widely practiced in the Middle Ages.

[3] *Ne ... tourneiynge* Nor was it considered a defeat for anyone except of the kind appropriate to a joust or tournament.

And eek his steede dryven forth with staves,°   spears
With footmen, bothe yemen° and eek knaves,°   yeomen / boys
It nas arretted hym no vileynye.[1]
1870 Ther may no man clepen° it cowardye.°   call / cowardice
For which anon Duc Theseus leet crye°   proclaimed
To stynten alle rancour and envye,
The gree° as wel of o° syde as of oother,   victory / one
And eyther syde ylik° as ootheres brother,   either side like
1875 And yaf hem yiftes° after hir degree   gave them gifts
And fully heeld° a feeste dayes three   held
And convoyed° the kynges worthily   accompanied
Out of his toun a journee° largely.   day's ride
And hoom went every man the righte way.
1880 Ther was namoore but "Farewel! Have good day!"
Of this bataille I wol namoore endite
But speke of Palamoun and of Arcite.
    Swelleth° the brest of Arcite, and the soore°   swells / sore
Encreesseth at his herte moore and moore.
1885 The clothered° blood for any lechecraft°   clotted / skill in medicine
Corrupteth° and is in his bouk° ylaft,°   corrupts / chest / left
That neither veyne-blood ne ventusynge[2]
Ne drynke of herbes may ben° his helpynge.°   be / helping
The vertu expulsif[3] or animal
1890 Fro thilke vertu° cleped° natural[4]   power / called
Ne may the venym° voyden° ne expelle.   poison / purge
The pipes of his longes° gonne° to swelle,   lungs / began
And every lacerte° in his brest adoun°   muscle / down
Is shent° with venym° and corrupcioun.   destroyed / poison
1895 Hym gayneth° neither, for to gete° his lif,   it helps him / preserve
Vomyt° upward ne dounward laxatif.°   vomit / laxative
Al is tobrosten thilke regioun;
Nature hath now no dominacioun.
And certeinly ther° nature wol nat wirche,°   where / work
1900 Farewel phisik!° Go ber° the man to
    chirche!°   medicine / carry / church
This al and som:° that Arcita moot dye,   this briefly (means)

For which he sendeth after Emelye
And Palamon, that was his cosyn deere.°   dear cousin
Thanne° seyde he thus, as ye shal after heere: then
1905 "Naught° may the woful spirit in myn herte   by no means
Declare o° point of alle my sorwes smerte°   one / painful sorrows
To yow, my lady that I love moost,
But I biquethe the servyce of my goost°   spirit
To yow aboven every creature,
1910 Syn that my lyf may no lenger dure.°   last
Allas the wo! Allas the peynes stronge
That I for yow have suffred and so longe!
Allas the deeth! Allas, myn Emelye!
Allas, departynge of oure compaignye!
1915 Allas, myn hertes queene! Allas my wyf,[5]
Myn hertes lady, endere of my lyf!°   one who ends my life
What is this world? What asketh men to have?
Now with his love, now in his colde grave,
Allone, withouten any compaignye.
1920 Farewel, my sweete foo, myn Emelye!
And softe, taak° me in youre armes tweye   take
For love of God, and herkneth what I seye:
    I have heer with my cosyn Palamon
Had strif and rancour many a day agon°   past
1925 For love of yow and for my jalousye.
And Juppiter so wys° my soule gye°   wise / guide
To speken of a servaunt° proprely   a servant (of love)
With alle circumstances trewely—
That is to seyn, trouthe, honour, knyghthede,°   knighthood
1930 Wysdom, humblesse,° estaat, and heigh
    kynrede,°   humility / high kindred
Fredom, and al that longeth° to that art—   pertains
So Juppiter have of my soule part
As in this world right now ne knowe I non°   I know none
So worthy to ben loved as Palamon,
1935 That serveth yow and wol doon° al his lyf.   will do
And if that evere ye shul ben a wyf,
Foryet nat° Palamon, the gentil man."   forget not
And with that word his speche faille gan,°   speech began to fail
And from his herte up to his brest was come
1940 The coold of deeth, that hadde hym overcome.
And yet moreover,° for in hise armes two   and that is not all

---

[1] It ... vileynye It was not attributed to him as any dishonor.

[2] veyne-blood ne ventusynge Vein-blood Blood-letting; ventusing Cupping. Two medieval medical procedures.

[3] expulsif The power of the body to expel unhealthy humors, medieval medicine's version of modern immune theory. "Animal" was a term applied to this power, which was supposed to reside in one's brain.

[4] Fro ... natural Natural power in medieval medicine was supposed to reside in the liver, and it too helped combat illness.

---

[5] Allas ... wyf Arcite may simply be thinking of Emily as the woman who is destined to be his wife, but in Boccaccio's *Teseida*, Chaucer's immediate source, Arcite actually marries Emily on his death-bed.

The vital strengthe° is lost and al ago.°   *power of life / gone*
Oonly the intellect withouten moore
That dwelled in his herte syk and soore,
1945   Gan faillen whan the herte felte deeth.[1]
Dusked° hise eyen two, and failled breeth.   *darkened*
But on his lady yet caste he his eye.
His laste word was "Mercy, Emelye!"
His spirit chaunged hous° and wente ther°   *its dwelling / where*
1950   As I can nevere;° I kan nat tellen wher.   *can never know*
Therfore I stynte. I nam no divinistre.°   *theologian*
Of soules fynde I nat in this registre,°   *list*
Ne me ne list° thilke opinions to telle   *I do not wish*
Of hem° though that they writen wher they
dwelle.   *them (other writers)*
1955   Arcite is coold. Ther Mars his soule gye!°   *guide*
Now wol I speken forth of Emelye.
    Shrighte° Emelye, and howleth Palamon,   *shrieks*
And Theseus his suster took anon,
Swownynge,° and baar° hire fro the corps
away.   *fainting / carried*
1960   What helpeth it to tarien forth° the day   *while away*
To tellen how she weepe bothe eve and morwe?°   *morning*
For in swich cas wommen have swich sorwe,
Whan that hir housbond is from hem ago,°   *gone*
That for the moore part they sorwen° so   *sorrow*
1965   Or ellis fallen in swich maladye
That at the laste certeinly they dye.
    Infinite been the sorwes and the teeres
Of olde folk and eek of tendre yeeres°   *(those of) tender years*
In al the toun for deeth of this Theban.
1970   For hym ther wepeth bothe child and man.
So greet a wepyng was ther noon, certayn,
Whan Ector[2] was ybroght al fressh yslayn°   *freshly killed*
To Troye. Allas, the pitee that was ther,
Cracchynge° of chekes, rentynge° eek of
heer!°   *scratching / tearing / hair*
1975   "Why woldestow° be deed," thise wommen crye,   *would you*
"And haddest gold ynough and Emelye?"
    No man myghte gladen° Theseus   *make glad*
Savynge° his olde fader° Egeus,   *except for / father*
That knew this worldes transmutacioun,°   *changing*

As he hadde seyn° it up and doun—   *seen*
1980   Joye after wo and wo after gladnesse—
And shewed hem ensamples° and liknesse.°   *examples / analogies*
"Right as ther dyed° nevere man," quod he,   *died*
"That he ne lyvede° in erthe° in som degree,   *did not live / earth*
1985   Right so ther lyvede never man," he seyde,
"In al this world that somtyme he ne deyde.°   *did not die*
This world nys° but a thurghfare°   *is nothing / thoroughfare*
ful of wo,
And we been pilgrymes passynge to and fro.
Deeth is an ende of every worldes soore."°   *sorrow*
1990   And over al this yet seyde he muchel more
To this effect, ful wisely to enhorte°   *exhort*
The peple that they sholde hem reconforte.°   *comfort themselves*
    Duc Theseus with al his bisy cure°   *anxious care*
Cast° now wher that the sepulture°   *considered / grave*
1995   Of goode Arcite may best ymaked be
And eek moost honurable in his degree.°   *according to his rank*
And at the laste he took conclusioun
That theras° first Arcite and Palamoun   *where*
Hadden for love the bataille hem bitwene,°   *between them*
2000   That in that selve° grove swoote° and grene   *same / sweet*
Theras° he hadde hise amorouse desires,   *where*
His compleynte,° and for love hise hoote° fires,   *lament / hot*
He wolde make a fyr in which the office°   *ceremony*
Funeral he myghte al accomplice,°   *accomplish*
2005   And leet comande° anon to hakke and hewe°   *ordered / cut*
The okes° olde and leye hem on a rewe°   *oaks / row*
In colpons° wel arrayed° forto brenne.   *piles / arranged*
Hise officers with swifte feet they renne°   *run*
And ryden anon at his comandement.°   *commandment*
2010   And after this Theseus hath ysent°   *has sent*
After a beere,° and it al overspradde   *bier*
With clooth of gold, the richeste that he hadde,
And of the same suyte° he cladde° Arcite.   *material / clothed*
Upon his hondes hadde he gloves white,
2015   Eek on his heed a coroune° of laurer° grene,   *crown / laurel*
And in his hond a swerd ful bright and kene.°   *sharp*
He leyde hym, bare the visage,° on the beere,   *bare-faced*
Therwith° he weepe that pitee was to heere.   *thus*
And for the peple sholde seen hym alle,
2020   Whan it was day, he broghte hym to the halle,
That roreth° of the criyng and the soun.°   *roars / sound*
    Tho° cam° this woful Theban Palamoun   *then / came*

---

[1]   *Oonly … deeth*   Only when the heart felt death did the intellect
begin to fail.

[2]   *Ector*   I.e., Hector, the greatest of Trojan warriors, killed by the
Greek Achilles. See Homer's *Iliad*.

With flotery° berd° and rugged, asshy heeres,[1] *fluttering / beard*
In clothes blake,° ydropped° al with teeres, *black / wet*
2025 And passynge° othere of wepynge,° Emelye, *surpassing / weeping*
The rewefulleste° of al the compaignye. *most pitiful*
Inasmuche as the servyce sholde be
The moore noble and riche in his degree,
Duc Theseus leet forth thre steedes brynge,[2]
2030 That trapped° were in steel al gliterynge° *equipped / glittering*
And covered with the armes° of Daun Arcite. *coat of arms*
Upon thise steedes grete and white
Ther sitten folk of whiche oon baar° his sheeld, *carried*
Another his spere in his hondes heeld,
2035 The thridde baar with hym his bowe Turkeys° *Turkish bow*
(Of brend gold was the caas° and eek the harneys), *quiver*
And riden forth a paas° with sorweful cheere *slowly*
Toward the grove, as ye shul after heere.
The nobleste of the Grekes that ther were
2040 Upon hir shuldres caryeden the beere
With slak° paas and eyen rede and wete *slow*
Thurghout the citee by the maister strete,° *main street*
That sprad° was al with blak, and wonder
    hye° *spread / wonderfully high*
Right of the same is the strete ywrye.[3]
2045 Upon the right hond wente olde Egeus,
And on that oother syde Duc Theseus
With vessel° in hir hand of gold ful fyn,° *jar / fine*
Al ful of hony,° milk, and blood, and wyn,° *honey / wine*
Eek Palamon with ful greet compaignye.
2050 And after that cam woful Emelye
With fyr in honde as was that tyme the gyse° *custom*
To do the office of funeral servyse.
    Heigh labour and ful greet apparaillynge° *preparation*
Was at the service and the fyr makynge,° *making of the fire*
2055 That with his grene tope° the hevene raughte°[4] *top / reached*

And twenty fadme° of brede° the armes
    straughte°— *fathoms / breadth / stretched*
This is to seyn, the bowes° weren so brode.° *boughs / broad*
Of stree° first ther was leyd° ful many a lode.° *straw / laid / load*
But how the fyr was maked upon highte° *high*
2060 Ne eek the names that the trees highte°— *were called*
As ook, firre, birch, aspe, alder, holm, popeler,
Wylugh, elm, plane, assh, box, chasteyn, lynde, laurer,
Mapul, thorn, bech, hasel, ew, whippeltree—[5]
How they weren fild° shal nat be toold for me, *cut down*
2065 Ne hou° the goddes ronnen up and doun, *nor how*
Disherited° of hire habitacioun° *disinherited / dwelling*
In whiche they woneden° in reste and pees— *lived*
Nymphus,° fawnes, and amadrides°—[6] *nymphs / hamadryads*
Ne hou the beestes and the briddes° alle *birds*
2070 Fledden° for fere whan the wode° was
    falle,° *fled / wood / cut down*
Ne how the ground agast was° of the light *was frightened*
That was nat wont° to seen the sonne bright, *accustomed*
Ne how the fyr was couched° first with stree° *made / straw*
And thanne with drye stokkes cloven athre° *sticks cut in three*
2075 And thanne with grene wode and spicerye° *spices*
And thanne with clooth of gold° and with
    perrye° *golden cloth / jewels*
And gerlandes hangynge with ful many a flour,
The mirre,° th'encens, withal so greet odour, *myrrh / incense*
Ne how Arcite lay among al this,
2080 Ne what richesse aboute his body is,
Ne how that Emelye, as was the gyse,
Putte in the fyr of funeral servyse,
Ne how she swowned whan men made fyr,
Ne what she spak, ne what was hir desir,
2085 Ne what jeweles men in the fyre caste
Whan that the fyr was greet and brente faste,

---

1 *With … heeres* To throw ashes on one's hair is an ancient form of mourning.

2 *Duc Theseus … brynge* Duke Theseus commanded that three horses be brought out.

3 *ywrye* Draped. The walls of the houses along the main street have been draped high with black cloth, a standard practice in the late Middle Ages for the funerals of great nobles.

4 *That … raughte* The huge pile of trees, with its branches still green, reaches to the sky and is 120 feet (twenty fathoms) wide. Chaucer draws his description of the funeral from Boccaccio's *Teseida* (Book 11) and also probably from the Statius's *Thebaid*

(6.98–106), which in turn draws on Virgil's *Aeneid*. Unlike the warfare, courtship, and tournament in the *Knight's Tale*, the funeral rituals are those of classical antiquity and not of Chaucer's own day.

5 *Ne … whippeltree* Catalogues of trees are a feature of several epic poems from ancient times. The trees here listed are oak, fir, birch, aspen, alder, holm-oak, poplar, willow, elm, plane, ash, boxtree, chestnut, linden, laurel, maple, thorn, beech, hazel, yew, and dogwood.

6 *Disherited … amadrides* In Roman mythology, lesser gods and goddesses like those listed here lived in the woods and fields. Since the grove is cut down for the funeral, the gods and goddesses normally inhabiting it no longer have a home.

Ne how somme caste hir sheeld° and somme hir spere   *some threw in their shields*

And of hire vestimentz° whiche that they were°   *clothing | were wearing*

And coppes° fulle of wyn and milk and blood   *cups*

2090 Into the fyr that brente as it were wood,

Ne how the Grekes with an huge route

Thries° riden al the place about   *thrice*

Upon the left hand° with a loud shoutynge   *counter-clockwise*

And thries with hir speres claterynge,

2095 And thries how the ladyes gonne crye

And how that lad was homward Emelye,

Ne how Arcite is brent to asshen colde,

Ne how that lych-wake° was yholde°   *funeral wake | held*

Al thilke nyght, ne how the Grekes pleye

2100 The wake-pleyes,° ne kepe° I nat to seye   *funeral games | care*

What° wrastleth° best naked with oille enoynt,°   *who | wrestles | anointed*

Ne who that baar hym best in no disjoynt.°   *difficulty*

I wol nat tellen eek how that they goon

Hoom til Atthenes° whan the ple° is doon,   *to Athens | funeral game(s)*

2105 But shortly to the point thanne wol I wende°   *turn*

And maken of my longe tale an ende.

By processe° and by lengthe of certeyn yeres,   *in due course*

Al stynted is the moornynge° and the teres   *mourning*

Of Grekes by oon general assent.

2110 Thanne semed me° ther was a parlement°   *it seemed to me | parliament*

At Atthenes upon certein pointz° and caas,°   *points | cases*

Among the whiche pointz yspoken° was   *spoken*

To have with certein contrees° alliaunce°   *countries | alliance*

And have fully of Thebans obeisaunce,°   *obedience*

2115 For which this noble Theseus anon

Leet senden° after gentil Palamon,   *had sent*

Unwist of hym° what was the cause and why,   *unknown by him*

But in hise blake clothes sorwefully

He cam at his comandement in hye.°   *in haste*

2120 Tho° sente Theseus for Emelye   *then*

Whan they were set and hust° was al the place.   *quieted*

And Theseus abiden° hadde a space   *waited*

Er° any word cam fram his wise brest.   *before*

Hise eyen sette he theras was his lest,°   *where he wished*

2125 And with a sad visage he siked stille,°   *sighed quietly*

And after that right thus he seyde his wille:

"The Firste Moevere[1] of the cause above,

Whan he first made the faire cheyne° of love,   *chain*

Greet was th'effect and heigh was his entente.

2130 Wel wiste he why and what therof he ment.

For with that faire cheyne of love he bond°   *bound*

The fyr, the eyr, the water, and the lond[2]

In certeyn boundes, that they may nat flee.

That same prince and that same Moevere," quod he,

2135 Hath stablissed° in this wrecched° world adoun°   *established | wretched | below*

Certeyne dayes and duracioun°   *duration*

To al that is engendred° in this place,   *born*

Over the which day they may nat pace,°   *not go beyond*

Al mowe° they yet tho° dayes wel abregge.°   *although | those | shorten*

2140 Ther nedeth noght noon auctoritee allegge,[3]

For it is preeved° by experience.   *proven*

But that me list declaren° my sentence.°   *I wish to give | judgment*

Thanne may men by this ordre° wel discerne   *order*

That thilke Moevere stable is and eterne.

2145 Wel may men knowe, but it be° a fool,   *unless (the man) is*

That every part dirryveth° from his hool.°   *derives | its wholeness*

For Nature hath taken his bigynnyng°   *its beginning*

Of no partie° or of cantel° of a thyng,   *part | portion*

But of a thyng that parfit° is and stable,   *perfect*

2150 Descendynge° so til it be corrumpable.°   *descending | corruptible*

And therfor of his wise purveiaunce°   *foresight*

He hath so wel biset° his ordinaunce°   *well established | laws*

That speces° of thynges and progressiouns°   *species | natural processes*

Shullen enduren° by successiouns,°   *last | one after another*

2155 And nat eterne,° withouten any lye.°   *not (be) eternal | lie*

This maystow understonde and seen at eye.°   *see with your eye*

"Loo, the ook° that hath so long a norisshynge°   *oak | growing*

From tyme that it first bigynneth sprynge°   *begins to grow*

And hath so long a lif, as we may see,

---

[1] *The Firste Moevere* I.e., God. According to Aristotle, the First Mover is the principle that sets all other things into motion. The idea that love unites all the elements, each of which is linked to the others in a hierarchical order (the Great Chain of Being), goes back to Plato and is described in Boethius's *Consolation of Philosophy* (Book 2, meter 8), on which this passage is based.

[2] *The ... lond* Four elements from which everything was thought to be made.

[3] *Ther ... allegge* There is no need to cite authority.

2160 Yet at the laste wasted is the tree.
      "Considereth eek how that the harde stoon
      Under oure feet, on which we trede° and goon,°   *tread / go*
      Yet wasteth it° as it lyth by the weye.°   *it wastes / lies along the road*
      The brode ryver° somtyme wexeth dreye,°   *broad river / grows dry*
2165 The grete toures° se° we wane and
          wende;.°   *towers / see / diminishing and changing*
      Thanne may ye se that al this thyng hath ende.
      "Of man and womman seen we wel also
      That nedeth in oon of thise termes two,
      This is to seyn, in youthe or elles age,
2170 He moot be deed—the kyng as shal a page:
      Som in his bed, som in the depe see,
      Som in the large feeld, as men may see.
      Ther helpeth noght.° Al goth that ilke weye.   *nothing can help*
      Thanne may I seyn al this thyng moot deye.
2175   What maketh this° but Juppiter the kyng,[1]   *who does this*
      That is prince and cause of alle thyng,
      Convertynge al unto his propre welle,°   *own source*
      From which it is dirryved,° sooth° to telle?   *derived / truth*
      And heer agayns no creature on lyve
2180 Of no degree availleth for to stryve.[2]
        "Thanne° is it wysdom, as it thynketh me°   *then / seems to me*
      To maken vertu of necessitee
      And take it weel that we may nat eschue,°   *avoid*
      And namely that to us alle is due.
2185 And whoso gruccheth° ought, he dooth
          folye,°   *whoever / complains at all / folly*
      And rebel is to hym that al may gye.°   *who may guide all (Jupiter)*
      And certeinly a man hath moost honour
      To dyen° in his excellence and flour°   *die / flower*
      Whan he is siker° of his goode name: *sure*
2190 Thanne hath he doon° his freend ne hym° no
          shame.   *done / nor himself*
      And gladder oghte° his freend been of his deeth   *ought*
      Whan with honour up yolden° is his breeth   *yielded up*
      Than whan his name apalled° is for age,   *faded*
      For al forgeten is his vassellage.°   *service in arms*
2195 Thanne is it best as for a worthy fame
      To dyen whan that he is best of name.
        "The contrarie of al this is wilfulnesse.

---

[1] *What ... kyng* Theseus here identifies Jupiter, as the King of the
classical gods, with the First Mover.
[2] *And ... stryve* And against this it is of no use for any living
creature, of whatever rank, to struggle.

      Why grucchen° we? Why have we hevynesse°   *complain / sadness*
      That goode Arcite, of chivalrie flour,
2200 Departed is with duetee° and honour   *duty*
      Out of this foule prisoun of this lyf?
      Why grucchen heere his cosyn and his wyf
      Of his welfare, that loved hem so weel?
      Kan he hem thank? Nay, God woot, never a deel,°   *not a bit*
2205 That bothe his soule and eek hemself offende,°   *harm*
      And yet they mowe° hir lustes nat amend.   *can*
      What may I concluden of this longe serye,°   *series of arguments*
      But after wo I rede° us to be merye°   *advise / merry*
      And thanken Juppiter of al his grace?
2210 And er that we departen from this place,
      I rede we make of sorwes two
      O° parfit joye, lastynge everemo.   *one*
      And looketh now, wher° moost sorwe is
          herinne,°   *where / in this matter*
      Ther wol we first amenden° and bigynne.   *amend*
2215   "Suster," quod he, "this is my fulle assent,°   *desire*
      With al th'avys° heere° of my parlement,   *advice / here*
      That gentil Palamon, thyn owene° knyght,   *your own*
      That serveth yow with wille,° herte, and myght   *(all his) will*
      And evere hath doon syn that ye first hym knewe,
2220 That ye shul of youre grace upon hym rewe°   *have pity upon him*
      And taken hym for housbonde and for lord.
      Lene° me youre hond, for this is oure accord.   *give*
      Lat se° now of youre wommanly pitee.   *let (us) see*
      He is a kynges brother sone, pardee,°   *by God*
2225 And though he were a povre bacheler,°   *poor young knight*
      Syn he hath served yow so many a yeer
      And had for yow so greet adversitee,
      It moste been° considered, leeveth me.°   *must be / believe me*
      For gentil mercy oghte to passen right."°   *prevail over justice*
2230   Thanne seyde he thus to Palamon ful right,°   *forthrightly*
      "I trowe ther nedeth litel sermonyng°   *few words*
      To make yow assente to this thyng.
      Com neer, and taak youre lady by the hond!"
      Bitwixen hem was maad° anon the bond   *made*
2235 That highte matrimoigne° or mariage,   *matrimony*
      By al the conseil° and the baronage,°   *council / company of barons*
      And thus with alle blisse and melodye
      Hath Palamon ywedded Emelye.
      And God that al this wyde world hath wroght°   *made*
2240 Sende hym his love that it deere aboght.°   *who purchased it dearly*
      For now is Palamon in alle wele,°   *good fortune*
      Lyvynge in blisse, in richesse, and in heele,°   *health*

And Emelye hym loveth so tendrely,
And he hire serveth so gentilly,°   nobly
2245   That nevere was ther no word hem bitwene
Of jalousie or any oother teene.°   discord

Thus endeth Palamon and Emelye.
And God save al this faire compaignye! Amen.

HEERE IS ENDED THE KNYGHTES TALE

The Miller's Prologue and Tale

When the Knight has finished his tale, much applauded
by the "gentles," the Host turns to the pilgrim who,
after the Prioress, ranks next in the social hierarchy: the
Monk, a senior brother from a wealthy monastery. But the
Miller, who has already placed himself at the head of the
pilgrims to lead them out of town with his discordant
bagpipes, has no respect for social hierarchy. He insists that
he will "quyte" the Knight, that is, repay him or match him,
and his tale does just that. With the insertion of *The Miller's
Tale*, Chaucer breaks decisively from less dynamic frame
narratives such as Boccaccio's *Decameron*, in which the
stories are told by a homogeneous and harmonious group of
aristocrats, and launches a social comedy in which the
various tellers will contest each other's authority and values.

The Miller's Tale belongs to the medieval genre of the
fabliau, a short tale of trickery often set among lower-class
or bourgeois characters. These tales may have circulated
orally, but they were also written down, and the written
versions were enjoyed by aristocratic, not peasant, readers.
Chaucer draws on two well-established *fabliau* plots. In the
first, a young scholar cuckolds an old husband by making
him believe that a second flood is coming; in the second, a
young lover humiliates a rival by tricking him into a misdi-
rected kiss. Chaucer may have drawn on a source that had
already combined these two plots or may have combined
them himself. Early critics, embarrassed by the tale's
vulgarity, tended to regard it as a regrettable lapse and take
Chaucer at his word when he apologizes in *The General
Prologue* for his boorish lower-class characters, whom he
designates as "churls" who insist on telling churlish stories.
But Chaucer devoted all his powers of comic timing, sensual
description, and social satire to expanding the basic story

line into a comic masterpiece, in which the two plots come
together when Nicholas calls for water.

The Miller tells his tale, a "legend or a life" (which
would normally mean a saint's life) of the cuckolding of an
old carpenter, in part to attack the Reeve, who is also a
carpenter—and a professional rival, since reeves were
expected to catch dishonest millers. The Miller's rivalry with
the Knight, however, and his claim that he will "quyte" him,
invite readers to observe how extensively his tale parallels
that of the Knight. These parallels all serve to subvert the
values of *The Knight's Tale*, calling into question its lengthy
tribute to cosmic order, its chivalric dignity, and its depiction of refined love from afar. Whereas Palamon and Arcite
are almost interchangeable, Nicholas, who is "hende" or
handy in so many ways, is completely unlike the squeamish
Absolon; and Alison, in complete contrast to the passive
Emelye, is an energetic schemer, who participates gleefully
in Absolon's humiliation.

Set in Oxford, *The Miller's Tale* gives a vivid sense of
medieval student life and reveals the tensions between the
more prosperous members of the peasantry and cunning
clerics. Most unusually, the butt of the story, the old
cuckolded husband, becomes a complex and often sympathetic character. John the carpenter is allowed to expand
upon his philosophy of life, warning against prying into
God's secrets, just as the Miller warns the Reeve not to pry
into his wife's secrets. With the fast pace of burlesque or a
modern situation comedy, *The Miller's Tale* is filled with
vivid details of domestic life; it could not be more different
from the Knight's, and its insistence that cleverness or
proximity will triumph over high ideals is one of its many
possible morals. The tale offers solace and *sentens*, but
exactly what this *sentens* is remains the source of continual
debate.

Opening page to *The Miller's Tale*, Ellesmere manuscript. (Reprinted by permission of *The Huntington Library, San Marino, California.* EL26C9F72r.)

The Miller's Prologue

Here Folwen the Wordes bitwene the Hoost and the Millere

Whan that the Knyght hath thus his tale ytoold,°   *told*
In al the route° ne was ther° yong
   ne° oold   *company | there was not | nor*
That he ne seyde° it was a noble storie   *did not say*
And worthy for to drawen to memorie,°   *learn by heart*
5   And namely° the gentils°
   everichon.°   *especially | gentlefolk | every one*
Oure Hoost lough° and swoor,° "So moot I
   gon,[1]   *laughed | swore*
This gooth aright!° Unbokeled° is the
   male.°   *goes well | unbuckled | purse*
Lat se,° now, who shal telle another tale?   *let's see*
For trewely, the game is wel bigonne.
10 Now telleth on, Sire Monk, if that ye konne,°   *if you can*
Somwhat to quite with° the knyghtes tale."   *match*
The Millere, that for dronken° was al pale   *being drunk*
So that unnethe° upon his hors he sat,   *scarcely*
He nolde° avalen° neither hood ne hat   *would not | take off*
15 Ne abyde° no man for his curteisie,°   *put up with | courtesy*
But in Pilates[2] voys° he gan° to crie   *voice | began*
And swoor, "By armes and by blood and bones,[3]
I kan° a noble tale for the nones°   *know | occasion*
With which I wol now quite° the Knyghtes tale!"   *match*
20 Oure Hoost saugh° that he was dronke of ale   *saw*
And seyde, "Abyd,° Robyn, my leeve° brother,   *wait | dear*
Som bettre man shal telle us first another.
Abyde, and lat° us werken° thriftily."°   *let | work | respectably*
   "By Goddes soule," quod° he, "that wol° nat I.   *said | will*
25 For I wol speke or elles° go my wey."°   *else | way*
Oure Hoost answerde, "Tel on a devele wey!°   *in the devil's name*
Thou art a fool! Thy wit is overcome!"
   "Now herkneth,"° quod the Millere, "alle and
   some.°   *listen | one and all*

But first I make a protestacioun°   *protest*
30 That I am dronke; I knowe it by my soun.°   *sound*
And therfore if that I mysspeke or seye,°   *say something wrong*
Wyte it° the ale of Southwerk, I preye.°   *blame it on | pray*
For I wol tell a legende and a lyf[4]
Bothe of a carpenter and of his wyf,
35 How that a clerk° hath set the wrightes cappe."[5]   *student*
   The Reve answerde and seyde, "Stynt thy
   clappe!°   *shut your mouth*
Lat be thy lewed,° dronken°
   harlotrye!°   *ignorant | drunken | bawdiness*
It is a synne° and eek° a greet° folye°   *sin | also | great | folly*
To apeyren° any man or hym° defame°   *harm | him | slander*
40 And eek to bryngen wyves in swich° fame.°   *such | dishonor*
Thou mayst ynogh° of othere thynges seyn."°   *enough | speak*
   This dronke° Millere spak° ful° soone
   agayn°   *drunken | spoke | very | again*
And seyde, "Leve brother Osewold,
Who hath no wyf, he is no cokewold.[6]
45 But I sey nat therfore that thou art oon.°   *one*
Ther been ful goode wyves many oon,°   *a one*
And evere a thousand goode ayeyns° oon badde.°   *against | bad*
That knowestow wel° thyself, but if° thou
   madde.°   *you know well | unless | are mad*
Why artow° angry with my tale now?   *are you*
50 I have a wyf, Per Die,° as wel as thow,   *by God*
Yet nolde° I for the oxen in my plogh°   *would not | plow*
Take upon me moore than ynogh,°   *enough*
As demen° of myself that I were oon.°   *judge | one (i.e., a cuckold)*
I wol bileve° wel that I am noon.°   *believe | none*
55 An housbonde shal nat been inquisityf°   *inquisitive*
Of Goddes pryvetee° nor of his wyf.   *secrets*
So he may fynde° Goddes foyson° there,   *find | abundance*
Of the remenant nedeth nat enquere!"°   *he need not inquire*
   What sholde I moore seyn, but this Millere,
He nolde° his wordes for no man
60   forbere,°   *would not | bear patiently*
But tolde his cherles° tale in his manere.°   *boor's | manner*
M'athynketh° that I shal reherce° it heere,   *I regret | repeat*

---

1 *So … goon* I.e., as I hope to live.

2 *But in Pilates* I.e., Pontius Pilate, the Roman governor who condemned Jesus to be crucified. In medieval religious plays he was depicted as a loud, rampaging villain.

3 *By … bones* Swearing during the Middle Ages and Renaissance often involved taking oaths on various parts of God's body—here God's arms, blood, and bones.

4 *legende and a lyf* Normally a "saint's life," or biography of a Christian saint.

5 *set the wrightes cappe* Made a fool of the carpenter.

6 *cokewold* I.e., cuckold: a husband whose wife has sex with another man.

And therfore every gentil° wight° I preye,°   *noble / person / pray*
For Goddes love demeth° nat° that I seye°   *judge / not / speak*
65 Of yvel entente,° but that I moot reherce°   *evil intent / repeat*
Hir° tales, all be they° bettre or werse,   *their / although they be*
Or elles° falsen° som of my mateere.°   *else / falsify / matter*
And therfore,° whoso° list° it nat
     yheere,°   *whoever / wishes / not to hear*
Turne over the leef,° and chese° another tale.   *page / choose*
70 For he shal fynde° ynowe,° grete° and
     smale,°   *find / enough / great / small*
Of storial° thyng that toucheth gentillesse°   *historical / nobility*
And eek moralitee° and hoolynesse.°   *morality / holiness*
Blameth nat me if that ye chese amys.°   *choose wrongly*
The millere is a cherl.° Ye knowe wel this.   *boor*
75 So was the Reve, and othere manye mo,°   *more*
And harlotrie° they tolden bothe two.   *bawdiness*
Avyseth yow;° putteth me out of blame,   *be advised*
And eek men shal nat maken ernest° of game.°   *seriousness / joke*

THE MILLER'S TALE

HEERE BIGYNNETH THE MILLERE HIS TALE

Whilom° ther was dwellynge° at
Oxenford°   *once / living / Oxford*
80 A riche gnof° that gestes° heeld to bord,[1]   *fellow / guests*
And of his craft° he was a carpenter.   *profession*
With hym ther was dwellynge a povre° scoler°   *poor / student*
Hadde lerned° art, but al his fantasye°   *learned / interest*
Was turned for to lerne astrologye,
85 And koude a certeyn of conclusiouns[2]
To demen° by interrogaciouns°   *judge / questions*
If that men asked hym in certein houres[3]
Whan that men sholde have droghte° or elles
     shoures,°   *drought / rain*
Or if men asked hym what sholde bifalle°   *happen*
90 Of every thyng—I may nat rekene° hem° all.   *count up / them*
     This clerk was cleped° hende° Nicholas.   *named / handy*

Of deerne° love he koude° and of solas,°   *secret / knew / pleasure*
And therto he was sleigh° and ful privee°   *sly / very secretive*
And lyk° a mayden meke° for to see.   *like / meek*
95 A chambre° hadde he in that hostelrye,°   *room / lodging*
Allone° withouten any compaignye.   *alone*
Ful fetisly° ydight° with herbes[4]
     swoote,°   *fashionably / decorated / sweet*
And he hymself as swete as is the roote°   *root*
Of lycorys° or any cetewale.[5]   *licorice*
100 His *Almageste*[6] and bookes grete and smale,
His astrelabie[7] longynge for° his art,   *pertaining to*
Hise augrym stones[8] layen° faire apart°   *lay / somewhat away*
On shelves couched° at his beddes heed,°   *arranged / bed's head*
His presse° ycovered° with a faldyng°
     reed,°   *cupboard / covered / cloth / red*
105 And al above ther lay a gay sautrie[9]
On which he made a nyghtes° melodie°   *nightly / melody*
So swetely that al the chambre rong.°   *rang*
And *Angelus ad virginem*[10] he song,
And after that he song *The Kynges Noote*;[11]
110 Full often blessed was his myrie° throte!°   *merry / throat*
And thus this sweete clerk his tyme spente
After his freendes fyndyng[12] and his rente.°   *income*

---

[1] *heeld to bord*   Rented out rooms.

[2] *koude a certeyn of conclusions*   Knew some (astrological) calculations.

[3] *houres*   I.e., astrological hours—times when certain planets exerted a certain influence.

[4] *ydight with herbes*   Spread with dried and sweet smelling herbs.

[5] *cetewale*   The spice zedoary, similar to ginger.

[6] *Almageste*   I.e., *Almagest*, the basic textbook for medieval astronomy. It was the work of Claudius Ptolemy (2nd century CE), who gives his name to the Ptolemaic system, in which the sun revolves around the earth. According to Ptolemy, the heavens comprised nine concentric crystal spheres that revolved and on which the planets and stars were affixed.

[7] *astrelabie*   I.e., astrolabe, a scientific instrument used to measure angles of heavenly bodies. Chaucer wrote *The Treatise on the Astrolabe*, a prose work that is one of the first pieces of technical writing in the English language.

[8] *augrym stones*   I.e., Augrim stones; they were marked with numbers and were used for making mathematical calculations.

[9] *sautrie*   I.e., psaltery, a stringed musical instrument.

[10] *Angelus ad virginem*   Latin: The Angel to the Virgin. The song, an antiphon used in liturgical service, depicts the conversation between the angel Gabriel and the Virgin Mary about the coming birth of Jesus.

[11] *The Kynges Noote*   This song has not survived.

[12] *After his freendes fyndyng*   According to what his friends found to give him.

This carpenter hadde wedded newe° a wyf   *newly married*
Which that he lovede moore than his lyf.
115 Of eighteteene yeer she was of age.
Jalous° he was and heeld hire narwe° in cage,[1]   *jealous / closely*
For she was yong and wylde and he was old,
And demed° hymself been° lik° a
    cokewold.°   *guessed / to be / likely / cuckold*
He knew nat Catoun,[2] for his wit° was
    rude,°   *intelligence / unformed*
120 That bad° man sholde wedde his
    simylitude.°   *who advised / equal*
Men sholde wedden after hire° estaat,°   *their / condition*
For youthe and elde° is often at debaat.°   *age / in dispute*
But sith° that he was fallen in the snare,°   *since / trap*
He moste endure as oother folk his care.°   *sorrow*
125   Fair was this yonge wyf and therwithal
As any wezele° hir body gent° and smal.   *weasel / delicate*
A ceynt° she werede° ybarred° al of silk,   *girdle / wore / striped*
A barmclooth° as whit° as morne° milk   *apron / white / morning*
Upon hir lendes,° ful of many a goore.°   *hips / pleat*
130 Whit° was hir smok° and broyden° al
    bifoore°   *white / undergarment / embroidered / in front*
And eek bihynde on hir coler° aboute   *collar*
Of col-blak° silk withinne and eek withoute.   *coal-black*
The tapes° of hir white voluper°   *ribbons / cap*
Were of the same suyte° of hir coler,   *pattern*
135 Hir filet° brood° of silk and set ful hye,°   *headband / broad / high*
And sikerly° she hadde a likerous° eye.   *certainly / flirtatious*
Ful smale ypulled° were hire browes° two,   *plucked / eyebrows*
And tho° were bent and blake° as any
    sloo.°   *they / black / sloeberry*
She was ful moore blisful° on to see   *much more pleasant*
140 Than is the newe perejonette tree,°   *pear tree*
And softer than the wolle° is of a wether.°   *wool / male sheep*
And by hir girdel° heeng a purs of
    lether°   *belt / hung a purse of leather*
Tasseled with grene° and perled° with
    latoun.°   *green / decorated / brass*
In al this world to seken° up and doun   *seek*

145 Ther nas° no man so wys° that koude
    thenche°   *was not / wise / imagine*
So gay a popelote° or swich a wenche.°   *doll / peasant girl*
Full brighter was the shynyng° of hir hewe°   *shining / complexion*
Than in the Tour° the noble° yforged°
    newe![3]   *tower / gold coin / forged*
But of hir song, it was as loude and yerne°   *eager*
150 As any swalwe° sittynge on a berne.°   *swallow / barn*
Therto she koude skippe° and make game°   *dance / play*
As any kyde° or calf folwynge his dame.°   *kid (young goat) / mother*
Hir mouth was sweete as bragot° or the
    meeth°   *ale / mead (fermented honey)*
Or hoord° of apples leyd° in hey° or
    heeth.°   *hoard / stored / hay / heather*
155 Wynsynge° she was as is a joly° colt,   *skittish / pretty*
Long as a mast and uprighte° as a bolt.°   *straight / arrow*
A brooch° she baar° upon hir loue
    coler°   *broach / wore / low collar*
As brood° as is the boos[4] of a bokeler.°   *broad / shield*
Hir shoes were laced on hir legges hye.°   *high*
160 She was a prymerole,° a piggesnye°   *primrose / pig's eye (flower)*
For any lord to leggen° in his bedde   *lay*
Or yet for any good yeman° to wedde.   *yeoman*
    Now sire° and eft° sire, so bifel° the cas°   *sir / again / befell / event*
That on a day this hende° Nicholas   *handy*
165 Fil° with this yonge wyf to rage° and pleye   *fell / romp*
Whil that hir housbonde was at Oseneye,[5]
As clerkes been ful subtile° and ful queynte,°   *subtle / clever*
And prively° he caughte hire by the queynte°[6]   *secretly / genitals*
And seyde, "Ywis,° but if° ich° have my wille,   *indeed / unless / I*
170 For deerne° love of thee, lemman,° I
    spille,"°   *secret / sweetheart / die*
And heeld hire harde by the haunche bones°   *thighs*

---

1   *in cage*   In a cage; i.e., he guarded her carefully.

2   *Catoun*   I.e., Cato. The *Distichs*, a widely circulating collection of proverbs and wise sayings in verse couplets, often used for teaching Latin in schools, were ascribed in the Middle Ages to the Roman writer Dionysius Cato.

3   *Than ... newe*   Gold coins were forged in the Tower of London.

4   *boos*   I.e., boss, the center bulge of a shield, occasionally used to injure an enemy.

5   *Oseneye*   I.e., Oseney, a small town just to the west of Oxford (now part of the modern city) where there was an abbey.

6   *queynte*   A rhyme on two homonyms (such as *blue / blew* or *guest / guessed*), near homonyms (such as *seke / seke*, i.e., *seek* and *sick* in the General Prologue, lines 18–19) or on two different meanings of the same word, as here with *queynte*, was known as "rime riche" and was much valued by the French court poets of Chaucer's day. The modern term "rich rhyme" has a slightly narrower meaning and is confined to rhymes on homonyms.

And seyde, "Lemman,° love me al at
   ones°   *sweetheart / immediately*
Or I wol dyen,° also° God me save!"   *die / as*
And she sproong° as a colt dooth° in the
   trave,°   *sprang / does / stall*
175 And with hir heed she wryed° faste away.   *twisted*
She seyde, "I wol nat kisse thee, by my fey!°   *faith*
Why, lat be, quod ich,°[1] lat be Nicholas,   *I say*
Or I wol crie 'Out, harrow, and allas!'[2]
Do wey° youre handes, for youre curteisye!"   *let go*
180   This Nicholas gan mercy for to crye
And spak so faire and profred° hire so faste   *urged*
That she hir love hym graunted atte last°   *at last*
And swoor hir ooth,° "By Seint Thomas of
   Kent,"°   *oath / St. Thomas à Becket*
That she wol° been at his comandement   *would*
185 Whan that she may hir leyser° wel espie.°   *leisure / see*
"Myn housbonde is so ful of jalousie
That but° ye wayte° wel and been privee,°   *unless / wait / secretive*
I woot° right wel I nam° but deed," quod she.   *know / am not*
"Ye moste been ful deerne° as in this cas."°   *secretive / business*
190   "Nay, therof care thee noght,"° quod Nicholas,   *have no care*
"A clerk hadde lutherly biset his whyle[3]
But if° he koude a carpenter bigyle."°   *unless / trick*
And thus they been accorded° and ysworn°   *agreed / sworn*
To wayte a tyme° as I have told biforn.°   *wait (for a time) / before*
195   Whan Nicholas had doon° thus everideel°   *done / every bit*
And thakked° hire aboute the lendes° weel,°   *patted / loins / well*
He kiste hire sweete and taketh his sawtrie°   *psaltery*
And pleyeth° faste and maketh melodie.   *plays*
    Thanne fil it° thus that to the paryssh chirche   *it happened*
200 Cristes owene werkes° for to wirche,°   *works / perform*
This goode wyf wente on an haliday.[4]
Hir forheed° shoon° as bright as any day,   *forehead / shone*
So was it wasshen° whan she leet° hir werk.°   *washed / left / work*

Now was ther of that chirche° a parissh clerk[5]   *church*
205 The which that was ycleped° Absolon.[6]   *called*
Crul° was his heer, and as the gold it shoon,   *curled*
And strouted° as a fanne° large and
   brode;°   *stretched out / fan / broad*
Ful streight and evene lay his joly shode.°   *parting of his hair*
His rode° was reed,° hise eyen greye as
   goos,°   *complexion / red / goose*
210 With Poules wyndow[7] corven° on his shoos.°   *carved / shoes*
In hoses° rede° he wente fetisly.°   *stockings / red / elegantly*
Yclad° he was ful smal° and proprely   *clothed / very tightly*
Al in a kirtel° of a lyght waget.°   *tunic / blue*
Ful faire and thikke° been the poyntes° set,   *thick / laces*
215 And therupon he hadde a gay surplys°   *surplice (liturgical garment)*
As whit as is the blosme upon the rys.°   *twig*
A myrie° child° he was, so God me save.   *merry / young man*
Wel koude he laten blood° and clippe and shave[8]   *let blood*
And maken a chartre° of lond° or
   acquitaunce.°   *contract / land / quit-claim*
220 In twenty manere koude he trippe and daunce
After the scole° of Oxenford tho,°   *school / then*
And with his legges casten to and fro
And pleyen songes on a smal
   rubible.°   *rebec (bowed stringed instrument)*
Therto he song somtyme a loud quynyble,°   *falsetto*
225 And as wel koude he pleye on his
   giterne.°   *gittern (plucked stringed instrument)*
In al the toun° nas° brewhous ne taverne   *town / was not*
That he ne visited° with his solas°   *did not visit / comfort*
Ther any gaylard tappestere° was.   *merry bar-maid*
But sooth to seyn, he was somdeel
   squaymous°   *somewhat squeamish*

---

[1] *quod ich* Both Ellesmere and Hengwrt read "ich" here, yet modern editors emend to "she," under the assumption that Chaucer is here slipping in and out of direct discourse. The manuscript readings can be defended on the basis of her uttering these words: "Let me be, I said, let me be, Nicholas…!"

[2] *Out, harrow, and allas* Common cries of alarm to summon assistance.

[3] *lutherly biset his whyle* Wasted his time.

[4] *haliday* I.e., holy day; a saint's day or the day of a major religious celebration.

[5] *a parissh clerk* Absolon is an assistant to the parish priest. He is a member of the clergy and probably in minor orders and might, in due course, be ordained as a priest himself.

[6] *Absolon* The Biblical Absalom, son of King David, was famous for his beauty. Cf. 2 Samuel 14.25–26.

[7] *Poules wyndow* Fancy shoes were sometimes cut to produce a lattice pattern, which Chaucer compares to the stained glass rose window at St. Paul's Cathedral, London, which burned down in the disastrous fire in 1666.

[8] *clippe and shave* Medieval barbers not only worked on one's hair but also did minor surgery like letting blood. This procedure, which involved opening a vein and allowing blood to flow out, was considered important in keeping the body's four humors (one of which was blood) in balance, thus insuring good health.

230 Of fartyng, and of speche daungerous.°   *fastidious*
       This Absolon that jolif° was and gay   *jolly*
     Gooth° with a sencer° on the haliday,[1]   *goes | incense censer*
     Sensynge° the wyves° of the parisshe
           faste.°   *incensing | wives | diligently*
     And many a lovely look on hem° he caste,   *them*
235 And namely° on this carpenteris wyf.   *especially*
     To looke on hire hym thoughte a myrie lyf.
     She was so propre and sweete and likerous,
     I dar wel seyn if she hadde been a mous°   *mouse*
     And he a cat, he wolde hire° hente° anon.   *her | grab*
240 This parissh clerk, this joly Absolon,
     Hath in his herte swich a love longynge
     That of no wyf took he noon offrynge.°   *no offering*
     For curteisie, he seyde, he wolde noon.°   *wanted none*
       The moone, whan it was nyght, ful brighte shoon,
245 And Absolon his gyterne° hath ytake;°   *gittern | taken*
     For paramours° he thoghte for to wake.°   *love's sake | stay awake*
     And forth he gooth, jolif° and amorous,   *jolly*
     Til he cam to the carpenteres hous
     A litel after cokkes° hadde ycrowe°   *roosters | crowed*
250 And dressed° hym up by a
           shot-wyndowe°   *approached | hinged window*
     That was upon the carpenteris wal.°   *wall*
     He syngeth in his voys° gentil° and
           smal,°   *voice | refined | high-pitched*
     "Now deere lady, if thy wille be,
     I pray yow that ye wole thynke on me,"
255 Ful wel acordaunt° to his
           gyternynge.°   *in accord | playing of the gittern*
     This carpenter awook and herde synge
     And spak unto his wyf and seyde anon,
     "What, Alison, herestow nat° Absolon   *don't you hear*
     That chaunteth° thus under oure boures°
           wal?"   *who sings | bedroom's*
260 And she answerde hir housbonde therwithal,
     "Yis, God woot,° John! I heere it every deel."*God knows | every bit*
       This passeth forth. What wol ye bet than
           weel?°   *what more do you want?*
     Fro day to day this joly Absolon
     So woweth° hire that hym is wobigon.°   *woos | filled with woe*
265 He waketh al the nyght and al the day.

He kembeth° hise lokkes° brode and made hym
       gay.   *combs | hair*
He woweth hire by meenes° and brocage°   *go-betweens | agents*
And swoor he wolde been hir owene page.°   *young servant*
He syngeth brokkynge° as a nyghtyngale.   *twittering*
270 He sent hire pyment,° meeth,° and spiced ale *spiced wine | mead*
And wafres° pipyng hoot° out of the
       gleede,°   *wafer cakes | hot | fire*
And for° she was of towne, he profreth meede.° *because | money*
For som folk wol ben wonnen° for richesse,   *won*
And somme for strokes,° and somme for
       gentillesse.°   *force | nobility*
275 Somtyme to shewe his lightnesse° and maistrye° *agility | ability*
He playeth Herodes[2] upon a scaffold° hye.°   *stage | high*
But what availleth hym as in this cas?
She loveth so this hende Nicholas
That Absolon may blowe the bukkes° horn.[3]   *buck's*
280 He ne hadde° for his labour but a scorn.   *did not have*
And thus she maketh Absolon hire ape,
And al his ernest° turneth til a jape.°   *seriousness | joke*
Ful sooth° is this proverbe, it is no lye,°   *true | lie*
Men seyn right thus: "Alwey the nye slye°   *near sly one*
285 Maketh the ferre° leeve° to be looth."° *far | loved one | hated*
For though that Absolon be wood° or wrooth,°   *crazy | angry*
Bycause that he fer° was from hire sighte,   *far*
This nye Nicholas stood in his lighte.
       Now bere° thee wel, thou hende Nicholas,   *bear*
290 For Absolon may waille° and synge "Allas!"   *complain*
And so bifel it° on a Saterday   *it happened*
This carpenter was goon° til Osenay,°   *gone | to Oseney*
And hende Nicholas and Alisoun
Acorded° been to this conclusioun   *agreed*
295 That Nicholas shal shapen° hym a wyle°   *fabricate | scheme*
This sely,° jalous housbonde to bigyle,°   *simple | trick*
And if so be the game wente aright,
She sholde slepen° in his arm al nyght,   *sleep*
For this was his desir and hire° also.   *hers*
300 And right anon, withouten wordes mo,
This Nicholas no lenger wolde tarie,°   *delay*
But dooth ful softe° unto his chambre carie° *quietly | carry*

---

1 *Gooth … holiday* It was and is the custom in liturgical churches
to burn incense in a censer, a metal container which hung from a
chain and was swung about by a cleric called a thurifer.

2 *Herodes* I.e., King Herod. Told of the birth of the Messiah,
Herod ordered the slaughter of all male children born in Bethlehem,
an event depicted in some religious plays.

3 *blowe the bukkes horn* The expression "blow the buck's horn"
more or less means "go whistle."

Bothe mete° and drynke for a day or tweye°   *food | two*
And to hire housbonde bad hire for to seye,°   *asked her to say*

305 If that he axed° after Nicholas,   *asked*
She sholde seye she nyste° where he was;   *did not know*
Of al that day she saugh° hym nat° with eye.   *saw | not*
She trowed° that he was in maladye,°   *believed | sickness*
For° for° no cry hir mayde koude hym calle.   *because | with*

310 He nolde° answere for thyng° that myghte
     falle.°   *would not | anything | happen*
     This passeth forth al thilke° Saterday,   *that same*
That Nicholas stille° in his chambre lay   *quietly*
And eet° and sleepe° or dide what hym
     leste,°   *ate | slept | what he wanted*
Til Sonday that the sonne gooth to reste.

315 This sely carpenter hath greet merveyle°   *wondered greatly*
Of Nicholas or what thyng myghte hym eyle°   *ail (trouble)*
And seyde, "I am adrad,° by Seint Thomas,   *afraid*
It stondeth nat aright with Nicholas.
God shilde° that he deyde° sodeynly!   *forbid | died*

320 This world is now ful tikel,° sikerly.°   *uncertain | certainly*
I saugh today a cors° yborn° to chirche   *body | carried*
That now on Monday last I saugh hym wirche!°   *work*
     Go up," quod he unto his knave°
     anoon,°   *serving boy | immediately*
"Clepe° at his dore or knokke with a stoon.   *call*

325 Looke how it is and tel me boldely."
     This knave gooth hym up ful sturdily
And at the chambre dore whil that he stood,
He cride and knokked as that he were wood,
"What how! What do ye, maister Nicholay?

330 How may ye slepen al the longe day?"
     But al for noght. He herde nat a word.
An hole he foond ful lowe upon a bord°   *board*
Theras° the cat was wont° in for to
     crepe,°   *where | accustomed | creep*
And at that hole he looked in ful depe.

335 Til at the laste he hadde of hym a sighte.
This Nicholas sat capyng evere uprighte°   *gaping upwards*
As he had kiked° on the newe moone.   *looked*
Adoun° he gooth and tolde his maister soone   *down*
In what array° he saugh that ilke° man.   *condition | same*

340 This carpenter to blessen[1] hym bigan°   *began*

And seyde, "Help us, Seinte Frydeswyde![2]
A man woot litel what hym shal bityde!°   *shall happen to him*
This man is falle° with his astromye°   *fallen | astronomy*
In som woodnesse° or in som agonye.°   *madness | fit*

345 I thoghte ay° wel how that it sholde be.   *I always thought*
Men sholde nat knowe of Goddes pryvetee.°   *secrets*
Yblessed° be alwey a lewed° man   *blessed | uneducated*
That noght but oonly° his Bileve[3] kan.°   *nothing other than | knows*
So ferde° another clerk with astromye:°   *it happened | astronomy*

350 He walked in the feeldes° for to prye°   *fields | pry (study foolishly)*
Upon the sterres,° what ther sholde bifalle,   *stars*
Til he was in a marleput[4] yfalle.°   *fallen*
He saugh nat that! But yet by Seint Thomas,
Me reweth° soore of hende Nicholas.   *I have pity*

355 He shal be rated of° his studiyng   *scolded for*
If that I may, by Jhesus hevene° kyng!   *Heaven's*
Get me a staf° that I may underspore,°   *staff | pry*
Whil that thou, Robyn, hevest of the dore.°   *heave off the door*
He shal out of his studiyng, as I gesse."°   *guess*

360 And to the chambre dore° he gan hym dresse.°   *door | approached*
His knave° was a strong carl° for the
     nones,°   *servant | fellow | occasion*
And by the haspe° he haaf it of°
     atones;°   *hinge | heaved it off | at once*
Into° the floor the dore° fil° anon.   *onto | door | fell*
This Nicholas sat ay° as stille as stoon°   *ever | stone*

365 And evere caped° upward into the eir.°   *gaped | air*
This carpenter wende° he were in despeir,   *believed*
And hente° hym by the sholdres° myghtily   *grabbed | shoulders*
And shook hym harde and cride spitously,°   *loudly*
"What Nicholay! What, how! What! Looke adoun!

370 Awake and thenk° on Cristes Passioun!   *think*
I crouche° thee from elves and fro
     wightes."°   *sign with the cross | evil creatures*
Therwith the nyght spel[5] seyde he anonrightes°   *right away*

---

[2] *Seinte Frydeswyde* The Anglo-Saxon St. Frideswide, a young noblewoman who was persecuted for her desire to be a nun, is the patron saint of the town of Oxford. She was abbess of a monastery that was on the site of the present Christ Church, Oxford.

[3] *Bileve* Carpenter John's "Believe" is his Creed—the Apostle's Creed, which, along with the Lord's Prayer, was to be memorized by every Christian.

[4] *marleput* I.e., marl-pit, a ditch on a farm for keeping marl, a type of soil rich in clay and used for fertilizing fields.

[5] *nyght spel* Spell or charm said at night to ward off evil spirits.

---

[1] *blessen* I.e., to bless oneself, to make the sign of the cross.

On foure halves° of the hous aboute   *four corners*
And on the thresshfold° of the dore withoute.   *threshold*
375 "Jhesu Crist and Seint Benedight[1]
Blesse this hous from every wikked wight
For nyghtes nerye° the white Pater Noster:°   *save | Lord's Prayer*
Where wentestow,° Seint Petres soster?"[2]
      And atte laste this hende Nicholas
380 Gan for to sike° soore and seyde, "Allas!   *sigh*
Shal al this world be lost eftsoones° now?"°   *immediately*
      This carpenter answerde, "What seystow?°   *do you say*
What! Thynk on God as we doon, men that swynke."[3]
      This Nicholas answerde, "Fecche° me drynke,   *get*
385 And after wol I speke in pryvetee
Of certeyn thyng that toucheth me and thee.
I wol telle it noon oother° man certeyn."   *(to) no other*
      This carpenter goth doun and comth ageyn°   *comes again*
And broghte of myghty ale a large quart.
390 And whan that ech of hem had dronke his part,
This Nicholas his dore faste shette°   *shut*
And doun the carpenter by hym he sette.
      He seyde, "John, myn hoost, lief° and deere,   *beloved*
Thou shalt upon thy trouthe swere me here
395 That to no wight thou shalt this conseil° wreye,° *counsel | betray*
For it is Cristes conseil that I seye!
And if thou telle man, thou art forlore,°   *lost*
For this vengeaunce thou shalt han therfore:°   *for it*
That if thou wreye° me, thou shalt be wood."   *betray*
400 "Nay, Crist forbede it for his hooly blood!"
Quod tho this sely man, "I nam no labbe.°   *am no blabber*
Ne, though I seye, I am nat lief to gabbe.°   *accustomed to gab*
Sey what thou wolt, I shal it nevere telle
To child ne wyf, by hym that harwed helle!"[4]

405 "Now John," quod Nicholas, "I wol nat lye.
I have yfounde° in myn astrologye   *found*
As I have looked in the moone bright
That now a Monday next° at quarter nyght[5]   *next Monday*
Shal falle a reyn,° and that so wilde and wood   *rain*
410 That half so greet° was nevere Noees° Flood.   *great | Noah's*
This world," he seyde, "in lasse than an hour   *less*
Shal al be dreynt,° so hidous is the shour.°   *drowned | downpour*
Thus shal mankynde drenche° and lese hir lyf."   *drown*
      This carpenter answerde, "Allas, my wyf!
415 And shal she drenche? Allas, my Alisoun!"
For sorwe° of this he fil° almoost adoun   *sorrow | fell*
And seyde, "Is ther no remedie in this cas?"
      "Why, yis, for Gode," quod hende Nicholas.
"If thou wolt werken° after loore° and reed.° *act | teaching | advice*
420 Thou mayst nat werken after thyn owene
      heed,°   *head (intelligence)*
For thus seith Salomon,[6] that was ful trewe:
'Werk° al by conseil and thou shalt nat rewe!'°   *do | regret*
And if thou werken wolt by good conseil,
I undertake withouten mast and seyl°   *sail*
425 Yet shal I saven hire° and thee and me.   *save her*
Hastou nat herd how saved was Noe°   *Noah*
Whan that oure Lord hadde warned hym biforn°   *before*
That al the world with water sholde be lorn?"°   *lost*
      "Yis," quod this carpenter, "ful yoore ago."°   *very long ago*
430 "Hastou nat herd," quod Nicholas, "also,
The sorwe of Noe with his felaweshipe
Er that he myghte brynge his wyf to shipe?[7]
Hym hadde be levere,° I dar° wel
      undertake,°   *he had rather | dare | affirm*
At thilke tyme° than alle hise wetheres
      blake°   *at that time | black sheep*
435 That she hadde had a shipe hirself° allone.   *to herself*
And therfore woostou° what is best to doone?   *do you know*

---

[1] *Seint Benedight* St. Benedict of Nursia was an early sixth-century
abbot who wrote the famous Rule for monasteries.

[2] *For nyghtes ... soster* These lines have never been satisfactorily
explained and probably represent John's mangling of popular charms
or invocations; *Where wentestow* Where did you go; *soster* Sister.

[3] *men that swynke* Men who labor. John is making the old
distinction between the three estates here. The first estate comprises
those who pray (the profession for which Nicholas is studying), the
second, those who fight (the nobility), and the third, those who
work and thus provide the food for all three estates.

[4] *harwed helle* The Harrowing of Hell (another subject of medieval
religious drama) was the victorious entry Christ made into Hell
between his death and resurrection to save the righteous souls held
in limbo.

---

[5] *quarter nyght* One-fourth of the way through the night.

[6] *Salomon* Solomon, the ancient King of Israel, was known for his
wisdom and was thought to be the author of several books of the
Hebrew Bible. The reference here is to Ecclesiasticus 32.24. John
makes a mistake here: Ecclesiasticus, part of the Greek Old Testament considered apocryphal by Protestants or deuterocanonical by
Catholics, was written by Jesus ben Sirach, not Solomon, as Saint
Augustine (among others) noted.

[7] *to shipe* On board. The difficulty Noah has in getting his wife
aboard the Ark is depicted in medieval drama.

This asketh° haste, and of an hastif thyng°   *requires / urgent business*
Men may nat preche or maken tariyng.°   *delay*
   "Anon, go gete us faste into this in°   *house*
440 A knedyng trogh° or ellis a kymelyn°   *kneading pot / tub*
For ech° of us—but looke that they be large—   *each*
In whiche we mowe swymme° as in a barge,   *may float*
And han therinne vitaille suffissant°   *enough food*
But for a day. Fy on° the remenant!   *disregard*
445 The water shal aslake° and goon away   *ebb*
Aboute pryme° upon the nexte day.   *prime (an early hour of prayer)*
But Robyn may nat wite° of this, thy knave,°   *know / servant*
Ne eek thy mayde Gille I may nat save.
Axe nat° why, for though thou aske me,   *ask not*
450 I wol nat tellen Goddes pryvetee.°   *secrets*
Suffiseth thee, but if thy wittes madde,
To han as greet a grace as Noe hadde.[1]
Thy wyf shal I wel saven, out of doute.°   *doubtless*
Go now thy wey, and speed thee heer aboute.
455   "But whan thou hast for hire and thee and me
Ygeten° us thise knedyng tubbes thre,   *gotten*
Thanne shaltow hange hem° in the roof ful hye,   *hang them*
That° no man of oure purveiaunce° spye.   *so that / preparations*
And whan thou thus hast doon as I have seyd
460 And hast oure vitaille faire in hem yleyd,°   *laid*
And eek an ax to smyte the corde° atwo°   *rope / in two*
Whan that the water comth, that we may go,
And breke an hole anheigh° up on the gable   *on high*
Unto the gardynward° over the stable,   *towards the garden*
465 That we may frely passen forth oure way
Whan that the grete shour is goon away.
Thanne shal I swymme as myrie,° I undertake,   *merrily / expect*
As dooth the white doke° after hire drake.°   *duck / male duck*
Thanne wol I clepe,° 'How, Alison! How, John!   *call*
470 Be myrie, for the flood wol passe anon!'
And thou wolt seyn, 'Hayl,° maister Nicholay,   *hail*
Good morwe! I se thee wel, for it is day.'
And thanne shul° we be lordes al oure lyf   *shall*
Of al the world, as Noe and his wyf.
475   "But of o° thyng I warne thee ful right:°   *one / directly*
Be wel avysed on that ilke nyght°   *that same night*
That we ben entred° into shippes bord   *entered*
That noon of us ne speke nat a word,

Ne clepe,° ne crie, but been in his preyere,   *call*
480 For it is Goddes owene heeste° deere.   *commandment*
   "Thy wyf and thou moote hange fer° atwynne,°   *far / apart*
For that bitwixe yow shal be no synne,°   *sin*
Namoore in lookyng than ther shal in deede.
This ordinance° is seyd. Go, God thee speede!   *commandment*
485 Tomorwe at nyght, whan folk ben alle aslepe,
Into oure knedyng tubbes wol we crepe,
And sitten there abidyng Goddes grace.
Go now thy wey. I have no lenger space°   *no more time*
To make of this no lenger sermonyng.°   *speech*
490 Men seyn thus: 'Sende the wise and sey nothing.'
Thou art so wys, it nedeth thee nat to preche.°   *preach*
Go save oure lyf, and that I the biseche."°   *implore*
   This sely carpenter goth forth his wey.
Ful ofte he seith "Allas!" and "Weylawey!"
495 And to his wyf he tolde his pryvetee.°   *secret*
And she was war° and knew it bet° than he   *aware / better*
What al this queynte cast° was for to seye.   *unusual scheme*
But nathelees she ferde as° she wolde deye,   *acted as if*
And seyde, "Allas! Go forth thy wey anon.
500 Help us to scape° or we been lost echon!°   *escape / everyone*
I am thy trewe, verray° wedded wyf.   *faithful*
Go, deere spouse, and help to save oure lyf!"
   Lo, which a greet° thyng is affeccioun!   *what a great*
Men may dyen° of ymaginacioun,°   *die / imagination*
505 So depe° may impressioun be take.°   *deep / taken*
This sely carpenter bigynneth quake.°   *to shake*
Hym thynketh verraily° that he may see   *it truly appears to him*
Noees° Flood come walwynge° as the see   *Noah's / surging*
To drenchen° Alisoun, his hony deere.   *drown*
510 He wepeth, weyleth, maketh sory cheere.°   *a sorry face*
He siketh with ful many a sory swogh.°   *groan*
He gooth and geteth hym a knedyng trogh,
And after that a tubbe and a kymelyn,
And pryvely he sente hem to his in°   *house*
515 And heng hem in the roof in pryvetee.
His owene hand made laddres thre
To clymben by the ronges and the stalkes°   *shafts*
Into the tubbes hangynge in the balkes,°   *beams*
And hem vitailleth,° bothe trogh and tubbe,   *provides food for*
520 With breed and chese and good ale in a jubbe,°   *jug*
Suffisynge right ynogh as for a day.
But er that he hadde maad al this array°   *these preparations*
He sente his knave and eek his wenche also
Upon his nede° to London for to go.   *need*

---

[1] *Suffiseth ... hadde* It is enough for you (i.e., you should be grateful), unless you are insane, to have as much favor as Noah had (by being warned of the Flood).

525 And on the Monday whan it drow to nyght,°	*approached night*
He shette° his dore withoute candel lyght	*shut*
And dresseth° alle thyng as it shal be.	*arranged*
And shortly, up they clomben alle thre.	
They sitten stille, wel a furlong way.[1]	
530 Now, "Pater Noster, clom!"° seyde Nicholay.	*be quiet*
And "Clom," quod John. And "Clom," seyde Alisoun.	
This carpenter seyde his devocioun,°	*prayers*
And stille he sit and biddeth his preyere,°	*offers his prayers*
Awaitynge on the reyn, if he it heere.	
535 The dede° sleepe, for wery° bisynesse,	*dead / weary*
Fil° on this carpenter, right as I gesse,°	*fell / guess*
About corfew° tyme[2] or litel moore.	*curfew*
For travaille° of his goost° he groneth soore	*labor / spirit*
And eft° he routeth,° for his heed°	
myslay.°	*also / snores / head / lay wrong*
540 Doun of the laddre stalketh Nicholay,	
And Alisoun ful softe adoun she spedde.°	*hastens*
Withouten wordes mo they goon to bedde	
Theras° the carpenter is wont to lye.	*where*
Ther was the revel° and the melodye,	*fun*
545 And thus Alison and Nicholas	
In bisynesse of myrthe and of solas	
Til that the belle of laudes[3] gan to rynge	
And freres° in the chauncel[4] gonne synge.°	*friars / began to sing*
This parissh clerk, this amorous Absolon	
550 That is for love alwey so wobigon,°	*sorrowful*
Upon the Monday was at Oseneye	
With a compaignye hym to disporte and	
pleye,°	*play and have fun*
And axed upon cas° a cloistrer°	*asked by chance / monk*
Ful prively° after John the carpenter.	*very secretly*
555 And he drough hym apart° out of the chirche	*drew him aside*
And seyde, "I noot.° I saugh hym heere nat wirche	*don't know*
Syn° Saterday.[5] I trowe° that he be went°	*since / believe / is gone*

For tymber ther° oure abbot hath hym sent,	*timber where*
For he is wont° for tymber for to go	*accustomed*
560 And dwellen° at the grange° a day or two.[6]	*stay / farm-house*
Or elles he is at his hous, certeyn.	
Where that he be, I kan nat soothly seyn."°	*truly say*
This Absolon ful joly was and light	
And thoghte, "Now is tyme wake° al nyght,	*to stay awake*
565 For sikirly,° I saugh hym nat stirynge°	*certainly / not stirring*
Aboute his dore syn day bigan to sprynge.°	*dawn*
"So moot I thryve,° I shall at cokkes crowe	*thrive*
Ful pryvely knokke at his wyndowe	
That stant ful lowe upon his boures wal.°	*bedroom's wall*
570 To Alison now wol I tellen al	
My love-longynge, for yet I shal nat mysse	
That at the leeste wey° I shal hire kisse;	*very least*
Som maner° confort shal I have, parfay.°	*kind of / in faith*
My mouth hath icched° al this longe day:	*itched*
575 That is a signe of kyssyng atte leeste!	
Al nyght me mette° eek I was at a feeste.°	*I dreamed / feast*
Therfore I wol goon slepe an houre or tweye	
And al the nyght thanne° wol I wake and pleye."	*then*
Whan that the firste cok° hath crowe anon,	*rooster*
580 Up rist° this joly lovere Absolon	*rose*
And hym arraieth° gay at poynt devys.[7]	*dresses*
But first he cheweth greyn° of lycorys°	*a grain / licorice*
To smellen sweete er he hadde kembd his heer.	
Under his tonge° a trewe-love[8] he beer,°	*tongue / carried*
585 For therby wende° he to ben gracious.°	*expected / attractive*
He rometh° to the carpenteres hous,	*roams*
And stille he stant° under the	*stands*
shot-wyndowe—°	*hinged window*
Unto his brist° it raughte,° it was so lowe—	*breast / reached*
And softe he knokketh with a semy soun.°	*quiet sound*
590 "What do ye, honycomb, sweete Alisoun,	
My faire bryd,° my sweete cynamone?°	*bird / cinnamon*
Awaketh, lemman myn,° and speketh to me.	*my sweetheart*
Wel litel° thynken ye upon my wo,	*very little*
That for youre love I swete° ther° I go.	*sweat / where*
595 No wonder is thogh° that I swelte° and	*is it though / swelter*
swete;	

---

[1] *They … way* For the time it takes to walk a furlong (about an eighth of a mile).

[2] *corfew tyme* Curfew, from the French for "cover your fire," announced the time when all fires had to be covered and houses were shut up for the night.

[3] *laudes* I.e., Lauds, the monastic hour of prayer that occurs very early in the morning, before dawn.

[4] *chauncel* Chancel, the area of a church or chapel near the altar.

[5] *I … Saterday* I do not know. I have not seen him work here since Saturday.

---

[6] *And … two* Abbeys usually had outlying estates, such as this one where John the carpenter is working.

[7] *at poynt devys* I.e., at point devise: perfectly.

[8] *a trewe-love* Four-leaved clover.

I moorne° as dooth° a lamb after the tete.°   *yearn | does | teat*
Ywis,° lemman,° I have swich love longynge   *indeed | sweetheart*
That lik a turtel° trewe is my moornynge.°   *turtle-dove | mourning*
I may nat ete namoore° than a mayde."   *anymore*
600   "Go fro the wyndow, Jakke fool,"° she sayde.   *Jack-fool*
"As help me God, it wol nat be 'com pa me.'°   *come kiss me*
I love another, and elles° I were to blame,   *else*
Wel bet° than thee, by Jhesu, Absolon.   *better*
Go forth thy wey, or I wol caste a ston,°   *throw a stone*
605   And lat me slepe, a twenty devel wey!"[1]
        "Allas," quod Absolon, "and weylawey,
That trewe love was evere so yvel biset!°   *ill bestowed*
Thanne kys me, syn° it may be no bet,°   *since | better*
For Jhesus love and for the love of me."
610   "Wiltow thanne go thy wey?" quod she.
        "Ye, certes, lemman," quod this Absolon.
        "Thanne make thee redy," quod she. "I come anon."
And unto Nicholas she seyde stille,°   *quietly*
"Now hust,° and thou shalt laughen al thy fille."   *shush*
615   This Absolon doun sette hym on his knees
And seyde, "I am lord at alle degrees,°   *in every way*
For after this I hope ther cometh moore.
Lemman, thy grace, and sweete bryd,° thyn oore!"°   *bird | favor*
        The wyndow she undoth° and that in haste.   *unlatched*
620   "Have do," quod she. "Com of and speed the faste,[2]
Lest that oure neighebores thee espie."°   *see you*
        This Absolon gan wype his mouth ful drie.
Dirk° was the nyght as pich° or as the cole,°   *dark | pitch | coal*
And at the wyndow out she pitte° hir hole.   *put*
625   And Absolon hym fil° no bet° ne wers,°   *fell | better | worse*
But with his mouth he kiste° hir naked ers°   *kissed | ass*
Ful savourly° er he was war° of this.   *with relish | aware*
Abak° he stirte° and thoughte it was   *backwards | jumped |*
        amys,°   *wrong*
For wel he wiste a womman hath no berd.°   *beard*
630   He felte a thyng al rough and longe yherd°   *long-haired*
And seyde, "Fy! Allas! What have I do?"°   *done*
        "Tehee!" quod she, and clapte° the wyndow to,   *slammed*
And Absolon gooth forth a sory° pas.°   *sorry | step*
        "A berd,° a berd!" quod hende Nicholas.   *beard, trick*
635   "By Goddes corpus,° this goth° faire and weel!"   *body | goes*
        This sely° Absolon herde every deel°   *foolish | part*

And on his lippe° he gan for anger byte,°   *lip | began to bite*
And to hymself he seyde, "I shall thee quyte!"°   *repay*
        Who rubbeth now, who froteth° now his lippes   *wipes*
640   With dust, with sond, with straw, with clooth, with
        chippes°   *chips (of wood)*
But Absolon, that seith ful ofte, "Allas!
My soule bitake° I unto Sathanas°   *commit | Satan*
But me were levere° than al this toun," quod he,   *rather*
"Of this despit° awroken° for to be.   *insult | avenged*
645   Allas," quod he, "Allas, I ne hadde
        ybleynt!"°   *had not restrained (myself)*
His hoote love was coold and al yqueynt.°   *quenched*
For fro that tyme that he hadde kist hir ers,
Of paramours° he sette nat a kers,[3]   *lovemaking*
For he was heeled of his maladie.
650   Ful ofte paramours he gan deffie,°   *defied*
And weepe as dooth a child that is ybete.°   *beaten*
A softe paas° he wente over the strete°   *quiet step | street*
Until° a smyth° men cleped daun°
        Gerveys,   *unto | blacksmith | master*
That in his forge smythed plough° harneys.   *plow*
655   He sharpeth shaar° and kultour° bisily.   *plowshare | plow-blade*
        This Absolon knokketh al esily°   *quietly*
And seyde, "Undo,° Gerveys, and that anon."   *open up*
        "What! Who artow?"° "I am heere Absolon."   *are you*
        "What! Absolon, for Cristes sweete tree,°   *cross*
660   Why rise ye so rathe?° Ey,° benedicitee!   *early | ah*
What eyleth° yow? Som gay gerl,° God it
        woot,°   *ails | girl | knows*
Hath broght yow thus upon the viritoot.[4]
By Seinte Note,[5] ye woot wel what I mene."
        This Absolon ne roghte nat a bene°   *did not care a bean*
665   Of al his pley. No word agayn he yaf.°   *gave*
He hadde moore tow° on his distaf[6]   *flax*
Than Gerveys knew, and seyde, "Freend so deere,°   *kind*
That hoote° kultour° in the chymenee heere,   *hot | plow-blade*
As lene° it me. I have therwith to doone,°   *lend | do*
670   And I wol brynge it thee agayn ful soone."

---

[3] *sette nat a kers* Cared nothing. (A *kers* is a watercress.)

[4] *upon the viritoot* Up and about.

[5] *Seinte Note* I.e., St. Neot, a ninth-century monk from Glastonbury who became a hermit.

[6] *distaf* I.e., distaff, a tool used in making thread to be spun into cloth.

---

[1] *a twenty devel wey* For the sake of twenty devils.

[2] *Com ... faste* "Hurry up," she said, "make haste and be quick."

Gerveys answerde, "Certes, were it gold
Or in a poke° nobles° alle untold,°   *bag / gold coins / unnumbered*
Thou sholdest have,° as I am trewe smyth.   *have (it)*
Ey, Cristes foo,° what wol ye do therwith?"   *foe*
675 "Therof," quod Absolon, "be as be may.
I shal wel telle it thee tomorwe day,"
And caughte the kultour by the colde stele.
Ful softe out at the dore he gan to stele°   *began to steal*
And wente unto the carpenteris wal.
680 He coggheth° first and knokketh therwithal   *coughs*
Upon the wyndowe right° as he dide er.   *just*
This Alison answerde, "Who is ther
That knokketh so? I warante it a theef."
"Why, nay," quod he, "God woot, my sweete leef,°   *loved one*
685 I am thyn Absolon, my deerelyng.°   *darling*
Of gold," quod he, "I have thee broght a ryng.
My mooder yaf° it me, so God me save.   *gave*
Ful fyn° it is and therto wel ygrave.°   *fine / engraved*
This wol I yeve° thee if thou me kisse."   *give*
690 This Nicholas was risen for to pisse
And thoughte he wolde amenden° al the jape: *make better*
He sholde kisse his ers er that he scape.°   *escape*
And up the wyndowe dide he hastily,
And out his ers he putteth pryvely
695 Over the buttok to the haunche bon.°   *thigh*
And therwith spak this clerk, this Absolon:
"Spek, sweete bryd,° I noot nat° where thou
    art."   *bird / do not know*
This Nicholas anon leet fle° a fart   *let fly*
As greet as it had been a thonder dent,°   *thunder-clap*
700 That with the strook he was almoost yblent.°   *blinded*
And he was redy with his iren hoot,°   *hot iron*
And Nicholas amydde the ers° he
    smoot.°   *in the middle of the ass / struck*
Of gooth° the skyn° an hande brede°
    about,   *off goes / skin / a hand-breadth*
The hoote kultour brende° so his toute,°   *burned / rear*
705 And for the smert° he wende° for to dye.°   *pain / expected / die*
As he were wood for wo, he gan to crye,
"Help, water, water, help, for Goddes herte!"
This carpenter out of his slomber sterte°   *jumped*
And herde oon crien,° "Water!" as he were wood,   *heard one cry*
710 And thoughte, "Allas, now comth Nowelis Flood!"
He sit hym up withouten wordes mo,
And with his ax he smoot the corde atwo,

And doun gooth al! He foond neither to selle,
Ne breed ne ale, til he cam to the celle[1]
715 Upon the floor, and there aswowne° he lay.   *in a faint*
Up stirte hire Alison and Nicholay,
And criden, "Out!" and "Harrow!" in the strete.
The neighebores, bothe smale and grete,°   *big*
In ronnen° for to gauren on° this man   *ran in / gape at*
720 That yet aswowne he lay, bothe pale and wan,
For with the fal° he brosten hadde° his arm.   *fall / had broken*
But stonde he moste unto his owene harm.[2]
For whan he spak, he was anon bore doun°   *shouted down*
With° hende Nicholas and Alisoun.   *by*
725 They tolden every man that he was wood.
He was agast° so of Nowelis Flood   *afraid*
Thurgh fantasie° that of his vanytee°   *fantasy / folly*
He hadde yboght° hym knedyng tubbes thre   *bought*
And hadde hem hanged in the rove° above,   *roof*
730 And that he preyde° hem for Goddes love   *asked*
To sitten in the roof par compaignye.°   *for company*
The folk gan laughen at his fantasye.
Into the roof they kiken° and they cape°   *stare / gape*
And turned al his harm unto a jape.°   *joke*
735 For what° so that this carpenter answerde,   *whatever*
It was for noght.° No man his reson° herde.   *nothing / explanation*
With othes° grete he was so sworn adoun°   *oaths / shouted down*
That he was holde° wood in al the toun,   *considered*
For every clerk° anonright heeld° with oother;   *scholar / agreed*
740 They seyde, "The man was wood, my leeve° brother."   *dear*
And every wight gan laughen of this stryf.°   *strife*
Thus swyved° was this carpenteris wyf   *made love to*
For al his kepyng° and his jalousye,   *guarding*
And Absolon hath kist hir nether° eye,   *lower*
745 And Nicholas is scalded in the towte.°   *rear*
This tale is doon, and God save al the rowte!°   *company*

HEERE ENDETH THE MILLERE HIS TALE

---

[1] *Ne ... celle* He did not find bread or ale to sell until he came to the bottom; i.e., he did not stop on his way down.

[2] *moste ... harm* This idiomatic expression has been interpreted differently. John the Carpenter must endure (or put up with, or take responsibility for) his own injury, or he must stand up for himself even though it turned out badly.

The Wife of Bath's Prologue and Tale

With the opening words of her extremely long prologue, the Wife of Bath introduces one of her central themes, the conflict between the experience of life, which for the Wife means sexual experience foremost, and "auctoritee," the written commentary of learned men on religious, moral, and philosophical issues. These men, who included both the patristic writers (such as Saints Ambrose and Jerome) and classical philosophers, have little good to say about women, whom they repeatedly depict as deceitful, quarrelsome, and lecherous. Escape from this tradition, as the Wife herself indicates in her account of the debate between the man and the lion, is not easy. Just as all paintings of lions will always be painted by men, so in classical and medieval society almost all writing, especially writing that had official authority, was done by men. The Wife herself, in one of the tale's many layers of ventriloquism, places traditional criticisms of women in the mouths of her first three husbands, whom she accuses of abusing her with these repeated insults. The criticisms can also be found in her fifth husband's book, a compilation of misogynistic texts from Jerome and others, all counseling against marriage.

The great irony is that the Wife herself is drawn from this tradition. Her character is based in part on the Old Woman in *The Romance of the Rose*, a sexually experienced cynic who teaches young people the tricks of love, and both the Wife's history and the literary shape of her prologue and tale conform to many of the traditional misogynistic stereotypes found in her husband's book. The subtle layering of the text makes its final moral elusive. Readers continue to argue whether the Wife should be taken as a moral warning against unbridled carnality or admired for her independence, courage, and vitality. The glosses in the Ellesmere manuscript tend to support the first view, but the Wife herself has some telling comments to offer on men who write glosses.

The tale that the Wife finally tells is an Arthurian romance. It follows a well-established folk-tale plot in which a knight is given a year to answer a question or die and can only get the answer from an old and ugly woman who will not give it to him unless he promises either to marry her or, as in Chaucer's version, to give her whatever she wants, which later turns out to be marriage. In several versions, including *The Tale of Florent* in John Gower's *Confessio Amantis*, the question the knight must answer is what women most desire. Chaucer modifies the familiar story in a number of ways, so that the tale contributes to the argument the Wife has been making in her prologue. The knight in the Wife's version is not innocent—he is a rapist—and he objects to the marriage not just because the woman is old and ugly, but also because she is of low birth, an objection she counters in a long disquisition on the nature of true gentility. Even the knight's final choice, which in the other versions takes the form of "foul by day and fair by night" or the reverse, is subtly altered in keeping with the Wife's interests.

Detail, opening page of the Prologue to *The Wife of Bath's Tale*, Ellesmere manuscript; see color insert for full page. (Reprinted by permission of *The Huntington Library*, San Marino, *California*. EL26C9F72r.)

THE WIFE OF BATH'S PROLOGUE

THE PROLOGUE OF THE WYVVES TALE OF BATHE

"Experience, though noon auctoritee
    Were in this world, were right ynogh to me[1]
To speke° of wo° that is in mariage.   *speak | woe*
For lordynges,° sith° I twelve yeer was of age,   *lords | since*
5 Ythonked° be God that is eterne on lyve,°   *thanked | eternally alive*
Housbondes at chirche dore° I have had fyve,°   *church door | five*
For I so ofte have ywedded° bee,°[2]   *wedded | been*
And alle were worthy men in hir° degree.   *their*
But me was toold certeyn° nat longe
    agoon° is,   *certain | not long ago*
10 That sith that Crist ne wente° nevere but onis°   *did not go | once*
To weddyng in the Cane° of Galilee,[3]   *Cana*
By the same ensample° thoughte me°   *example | it seemed to me*
That I ne sholde° wedded be but ones.°   *should not | once*
Herkne eek° which a sharpe word for the
    nones°   *listen also | for the occasion*
15 Biside° a welle Jhesus, God and man,   *beside*
Spak° in repreeve° of the Samaritan;[4]   *spoke | rebuke*
'Thou hast yhad° fyve housbondes,' quod° he,   *have had | said*
'And that man the which that hath now thee°   *who now has you*
Is noght thyn housbonde.' Thus seyde he certeyn.
20 What that he mente therby,° I kan nat
    seyn.°   *meant by this | cannot say*
But that I axe,° why that the fifthe man   *ask*
Was noon housbonde to the Samaritan?
How manye myghte she have in mariage?
Yet herde I nevere tellen° in myn age   *never heard told*
25 Upon this nombre° diffinicioun.°   *number | definition*
Men may devyne° and glosen°[5] up and doun,°   *guess | gloss | down*
But wel I woot° expres° withoute lye,°   *well I know | clearly | lie*

God bad° us forto wexe° and multiplye.[6]   *commanded | to increase*
That gentil° text kan° I understonde!   *noble | can*
30 Eek wel I woot, he seyde myn housbonde
Sholde lete fader and mooder° and take
    me.[7]   *should leave father and mother*
But of no nombre° mencioun made
    he°   *number | did he make mention*
Of bigamye° or of octogamye.°   *bigamy | marriage to eight spouses*
Why sholde men speke° of it vileynye?°   *speak | as villainy*
35 "Lo heere° the wise kyng daun° Salamon: *consider | master*
I trowe° he hadde wyves mo° than oon.°[8]   *believe | more | one*
As wolde God, it were leveful unto me[9]
To be refresshed° half so ofte° as he!   *refreshed | often*
Which yifte° of God hadde he for alle hise wyvys;°   *gift | wives*
40 No man hath swich° that in this world alyve° is.   *such | alive*
God woot,° this noble kyng, as to my
    wit,°   *knows | as far as I know*
The first nyght° had many a myrie° fit   *night | merry*
With ech° of hem,° so wel was hym° on
    lyve.   *each | them | he was so lucky*
Yblessed be God that I have wedded five![10]
45 Welcome the sixte, whanevere he shal.°   *whenever he shall arrive*
Forsothe,° I wol nat kepe me chaast in al°   *in truth | entirely chaste*
Whan myn housbonde is fro° the world ygon.°   *from | gone*
Som° Cristen° man shal wedde me
    anon,°   *some | Christian | immediately*
For thanne° th'apostle seith°[11] I am free   *then | the apostle says*

---

[1] *Experience … me* Experience, even if there were no written authority in the world, would be quite enough for me. Authority, in this sense, refers to the writings of learned men, especially the patristic writers and ancient philosophers.

[2] *For … bee* Many manuscripts have "If I so ofte myghte have ywedded be," i.e., if these multiple marriages were indeed lawful.

[3] *Cane of Galilee* See John 2.1–11.

[4] *Samaritan* See John 4.1–42.

[5] *glosen* Crucial points in the Bible, and other religious, philosophical, or legal texts were explained in glosses (comments written in the margins or between the lines).

[6] *god bad … multiplye* See Genesis 6.1.

[7] *myn housbonde … me* See Genesis 2.24.

[8] *I … oon* According to the Bible, King Solomon had seven hundred wives and three hundred concubines. See 1 Kings 11.33.

[9] *As wolde … me* If only God would permit that it should be lawful for me.

[10] *Yblessed … five* Some manuscripts contain the following six-line passage:

> "Of whiche I have pyked out the beste
> Bothe of here nether purs and of here cheste.
> Diverse scoles maken parfyt clerkes,
> And diverse practyk in many sondry werkes,
> Maken the workman parfit, sekirly;
> Of five husbandes scoleiyng am I."

John Manly and Edith Rickert suggest that these lines are "a late Chaucerian insertion," i.e., part of a late rough draft of the poem.

[11] *th'apostle seith* I.e., St. Paul. See 1 Corinthians 7.25–38.

50   To wedde, a Goddes half, where it liketh me.[1]
    He seith to be wedded is no synne:°   *sin*
    "Bet° is to be wedded than to brynne."°[2]   *better | burn*
    What rekketh me,° thogh folk seye°
        vileynye°   *what do I care | say | villainy*
    Of shrewed° Lameth[3] and of bigamye?°   *cursed | bigamy*
55   I woot wel° Abraham[4] was an hooly° man   *know well | holy*
    And Jacob eek, as ferforth as I kan,°   *as far as I know*
    And ech of hem° hadde wyves mo than two   *them*
    And many another man also.
    Whanne° saugh° ye evere in manere° age   *when | saw | any*
60   That hye° God defended° mariage   *high | forbade*
    By expres° word? I pray yow, telleth me.   *specific*
    Or where comanded he virginitee?°   *virginity*
    I woot as wel as ye,° it is no drede,[5]   *know as well as you*
    Whan th'apostel° speketh of maydenhede°   *virginity*
65   He seyde that precept° therof° hadde he
        noon.°[6]   *commandment | about | none*
    Men may conseille° a womman to been oon,°   *counsel | single*
    But conseillyng is nat comandement.
    He putte it in oure owene juggement.°   *left it to our own judgment*
    For hadde° God comanded maydenhede,   *had*
70   Thanne° hadde he dampned° weddyng with the
        dede.°   *then | condemned | in the act*
    And certein,° if ther were no seed ysowe°   *certainly | sown*
    Virginitee, wherof thanne° sholde° it growe?   *how then | should*
    Poul° ne dorste nat° comanden atte
        leeste°   *St. Paul | dared not | command at least*
    A thyng of which his maister° yaf° noon
        heeste.°   *master | gave | no command*
75   The dart[7] is set up of virginitee:

Cacche whoso may. Who renneth best, lat see![8]
  "But this word is nat taken of every
    wight,°   *does not apply to everyone*
But theras God lust gyve it of his myght.[9]
I woot wel the apostel was a mayde.°   *virgin*
80   But nathelees,° thogh° that he wroot° and
    sayde   *nevertheless | though | wrote*
He wolde° that every wight° were swich° as
    he,   *wished | person | such*
Al nys but conseil° to virginitee.   *is not but advice*
And for to been° a wyf he yaf° me leve°   *be | gave | leave*
Of indulgence,° so it is no repreve°   *by permission | reproach*
85   To wedde me if my make° dye,°   *mate | should die*
Withouten excepcioun° of bigamye.°   *objection | bigamy*
Al° were it good no womman for to touche,   *although*
He mente° as in his bed or in his couche.°   *meant | couch*
For peril is bothe fyr and tow t'assemble.[10]
90   Ye knowe what this ensample° may resemble.   *example*
This is al and som,° that virginitee   *the whole matter*
Moore profiteth than weddyng in freletee;[11]
Freletee° clepe I° but if° that he and she   *weakness | call it | unless*
Wolde lede° al hir lyf° in chastitee.   *would lead | their life*
95   "I graunte° it wel; I have noon envie,°   *grant | no envy*
Thogh maydenhede preferre bigamye.[12]
Hem liketh° to be clene,° body and
    goost.°   *they prefer | pure | spirit*
Of myn estaat° I nyl nat° make no
    boost.°   *my condition | will not | boast*
For wel ye knowe, a lord in his houshold,
100   He nath nat° every vessel al of gold.   *does not have*
Somme been of tree° and doon° hir° lord
    servyse.   *wood | do | their*
God clepeth° folk to hym in sondry wyse.°   *calls | in different ways*
And everich hath° of God a propre
    yifte°—   *everyone has | particular gift*
Som this, som that, as hym liketh shifte.°   *as he pleases to give*

---

[1] *To wedde ... me* To wed, by God's permission, wherever I wish.

[2] *Bet ... brynne* See 1 Corinthians 7.9.

[3] *Lameth* Lamech is the first to marry two wives. See Genesis 4.19.

[4] *Abraham* The patriarch Abraham, as recounted in the book of Genesis, was favored by God, yet he had more than one wife, as did his grandson Jacob.

[5] *it is no drede* Do not doubt it.

[6] *He ... noon* Paul admits that he could find no justification for his view in the Old Testament. See 1 Corinthians 7.25.

[7] *dart* A spear was sometimes given as a prize for a race in England in the Middle Ages. Many editors prefer the reading "for virginity" (found in many other manuscripts), which makes virginity the competitor rather than the prize.

[8] *Cacche ... see* Let whoever can catch it. Let us see who runs best.

[9] *But ... myght* Except where God wishes, through his might, to impose this principle (of virginity).

[10] *fyr ... t'assemble* To bring together fire and flax (flammable material of which wicks are made).

[11] *Moore ... freletee* Remaining a virgin is better than marrying through weakness.

[12] *Thogh ... bigamye* Though virginity be preferred to bigamy.

105   "Virginitee is greet perfeccioun
       And continence° eek with devocioun.°   *chastity / religious devotion*
       But Crist that of perfeccioun° is welle°   *perfection / well (source)*
       Bad° nat every wight sholde go selle   *commanded*
       Al that he hadde and gyve° it to the poore   *give*
110   And in swich wise folwe hym[1] and his foore.°   *steps*
       He spak to hem that wolde lyve parfitly.°   *wished to live perfectly*
       And, lordynges, by youre leve,° that am nat I!   *leave*
       I wol bistowe° the flour° of myn age   *will bestow / flower*
       In the actes and in fruyt° of mariage.   *fruit*
115   "Telle me also, to what conclusioun
       Were membres ymaad° of generacioun?[2]   *made*
       And for what profit° was a wight ywroght?°   *purpose / person made*
       Trusteth° right wel, they were nat maad° for
           noght.°   *believe me / not made / nothing*
       Glose whoso wole and seye bothe up and doun,[3]
120   That they were maad for purgacioun°   *releasing*
       Of uryne° and oure bothe thynges
           smale,°   *urine / our two small things (sexual organs)*
       And eek to knowe° a femele from a male,   *distinguish*
       And for noon oother cause: sey° ye no?   *say*
       The experience woot wel° it is   *experience (in general) knows well*
           noght so.
125   So that the clerkes° be nat with me wrothe,°   *theologians / angry*
       I sey yis,° that they beth maked° for
           bothe!   *say yes / are made*
       That is to seye, for office and for ese°   *pleasure*
       Of engendrure,[4] ther we nat God
           displese.°   *where we do not displease God*
       Why sholde men elles° in hir bookes sette°   *otherwise / set down*
130   That a man shal yelde to his wyf hire dette?[5]
       Now, wherwith° sholde he make his
           paiement°   *with what / payment*
       If he ne used° his sely° instrument?   *did not use / innocent*
       Thanne were they maad upon a creature

       To purge uryne° and for engendrure.°   *release urine / conception*
135   "But I seye noght° that every wight is holde°   *not / obligated*
       That hath swich harneys,° as I of tolde,   *such equipment*
       To goon° and usen hem° in engendrure.   *go / them*
       They shul° nat take of chastitee no cure.°   *shall / attention*
       Crist was a mayde° and shapen° as a man,   *virgin / formed*
140   And many a seint sith° the world bigan,   *since*
       Yet lyved they evere in parfit° chastitee.   *perfect*
       I nyl nat envye° no virginitee.   *will not envy*
       Lat hem° be breed° of pured whete°
           seed,   *let them / bread / pure wheat*
       And lat us wyves hoten° barly breed.   *be called*
145   And yet with barly breed, Mark[6] telle kan,
       Oure Lord refresshed° many a man.   *gave food to*
       In swich estaat° as God hath cleped us°   *condition / has called us*
       I wol persevere.° I nam nat precius.°   *remain / fastidious*
       In wyfhode I wol use myn instrument°   *sexual organ*
150   As frely° as my makere hath it sent.   *freely*
       If I be daungerous,° God yeve° me sorwe.   *stand-offish / give*
       Myn housbonde shal it have bothe eve and morwe
       Whan that hym list com forth and paye his dette.[7]
       An housbonde I wol have, I nyl nat lette,°   *will not stop*
155   Which shal° be bothe my dettour° and my
           thral°   *who shall / debtor / slave*
       And have his tribulacioun° withal°   *tribulation / also*
       Upon his flessh whil I am his wyf.
       I have the power durynge° al my lyf   *during*
       Upon his propre° body, and noght he.   *own*
160   Right thus the apostel[8] tolde it unto me
       And bad° oure housbondes for to love us
           weel.°   *commanded / well*
       Al this sentence me liketh every deel."[9]
           Up stirte° the Pardoner and that anon.°   *jumped / immediately*
       "Now, Dame," quod he, "by God and by Seint John,
165   Ye been° a noble prechour° in this cas!°   *are / preacher / matter*
       I was aboute to wedde a wyf, allas!

---

[1] *swich wise* Such a manner; *folwe hym* Follow him.

[2] *membres … of generacioun* Sexual organs.

[3] *Glose … doun* Let whoever wishes to do so offer an interpretation and say both up and down.

[4] *Of engendrure* Of conception. The phrase "office and ease of engendrure" means for a purpose (that is, conceiving children) and for the pleasure of procreation.

[5] *yelde … dette* Having sex. I.e., both partners owed each other a certain sexual fulfillment, lest sexual frustration drive one of them to adultery. The line is a quotation from 1 Corinthians 7.3.

[6] *And … man* The reference here is to John 6.9 and the miracle of the loaves and fishes, not to a passage in the Gospel of Mark.

[7] *Whan … dette* When he wishes to come forth and pay his debt.

[8] *the apostel* I.e., St. Paul, whose insights on marriage the Wife of Bath has been mentioning since she began to speak. In addition to the passage referred to above in note 5, Paul's other major pronouncement on marriage is in Ephesians 5.21–33.

[9] *Al … deel* All this lesson (of Scripture) pleases me, every part (of it).

What sholde I bye it on my flessh so deere?[1]
Yet hadde I levere° wedde no wyf to yeere!"°   *rather | this year*

    "Abyde,"° quod she, "my tale is nat bigonne!   *wait*

170 Nay, thou shalt drynken° of another
      tonne°   *drink | cask (of wine)*
Er that I go, shal savoure wors° than ale!   *that shall taste worse*
And whan that I have toold forth my tale
Of tribulacioun that is in mariage,
Of which I am expert in al myn age°—   *throughout my life*
175 This to seyn,° myself have been the whippe°—   *say | whip*
Than maystow chese wheither° thou wolt
      sippe°   *choose whether | will sip*
Of that tonne that I shal abroche.°   *open*
Bewar of it er thou to ny° approche,°   *too near | approach*
For I shal telle ensamples° mo° than ten.   *examples | more*
180 Whoso that wol nat bewar by othere men,[2]
By hym shul othere men corrected be.
The same wordes writeth Protholomee.°   *Ptolemy*
Rede° it in his *Almageste* and take it there!"[3]   *read*

    "Dame, I wolde praye° if youre wyl° it were,"   *ask | will*
185 Seyde this Pardoner, "as ye bigan
Telle forth youre tale. Spareth° for no man,   *spare*
And teche us yonge men of youre praktike!"°   *practice*

    "Gladly, sires,° sith it may yow like.°   *sirs | it may please you*
But yet I praye to al this compaignye,
190 If that I speke after my fantasye,°   *fancy*
As taketh it nat agrief° that° I seye,   *take it not wrong | what*
For myn entente is but for to pleye.

    "Now sire, now wol I telle forth my tale.
As evere moote° I drynken wyn or ale,   *might*
195 I shal seye sooth° of tho housbondes that I hadde,   *say the truth*
As thre of hem were goode and two were badde.
The thre men were goode and riche and olde.
Unnethe° myghte they the statut° holde   *scarcely | regulation*
In which that they were bounden° unto me.[4]   *bound*
200 Ye woot wel what I meene° of this, pardee.°   *mean | by God*
As help me God, I laughe whan I thynke

How pitously anyght° I made hem swynke!°   *at night | work*
And by my fey,° I tolde of it no stoor.°   *faith | set no store by it*
They had me yeven° hir° gold and hir
      tresoor.°   *given | their | treasure*
205 Me neded nat do lenger diligence[5]
To wynne hir love or doon hem reverence.°   *honor them*
They loved me so wel, by God above,
That I ne tolde no deyntee of hir love.[6]
A wys° womman wol sette hire evere in
      oon°   *wise | will always determine*
210 To gete hire° love theras° she hath
      noon.°   *get herself | where | has none*
But sith I hadde hem° hoolly° in myn hond,   *them | wholly*
And sith they hadde me yeven° al hir lond,°   *given | all their land*
What sholde I taken heede° hem for to plese,°   *bother | please*
But if° it were for my profit and myn ese?°   *unless | pleasure*
215 I sette hem so a werk,° by my fey,°   *to work | faith*
That many a nyght they songen° 'Weilawey!'°   *sang | alas*
The bacon was nat fet° for hem, I trowe,°   *fetched | believe*
That som° men han° in Essex at Dunmowe.[7]   *some | have*
I governed hem so wel after my lawe,
220 That ech° of hem was ful blisful° and fawe° *each | very happy | eager*
To brynge me gaye thynges° fro the fayre.°   *pretty things | fair*
They were ful glad whan I spak to hem faire,°   *nicely*
For, God it woot, I chidde hem spitously!°   *scolded them spitefully*

    "Now herkneth hou° I baar me° proprely,   *how | bore myself*
225 Ye wise wyves that kan understonde.
Thus shul ye speke and beren hem on honde.[8]
For half so boldely kan ther no man
Swere° and lye° as kan a womman.   *swear | lie*
I sey nat this by° wyves that been wyse,   *about*
230 But if° it be whan they hem
      mysavyse.°   *unless | give themselves bad advice*
A wys wyf, if that she kan hir good,°   *knows what is good for her*
Shal bere hym on hond the cow is wood[9]

---

[1] *What ... deere* Why should I pay so dearly for it with my flesh.

[2] *Whoso ... men* The one who will not be warned (by examples offered) by others.

[3] *Rede ... there* The aphorism is not found in the *Almagest*, the great astrological treatise of Claudius Ptolemy (second century CE), but in the preface to one of the translations of his work.

[4] *In ... me* I.e., the three old husbands could barely fulfill their obligation to pay the marriage debt.

[5] *Me ... diligence* I did not need to make any more effort.

[6] *ne tolde ... love* Did not put any value on their love.

[7] *The bacon ... Dunmowe* In the village of Dunmow, it was the custom to award a side of bacon to a married couple if they did not quarrel for a year.

[8] *beren hem on honde* Either to deceive them or to accuse them falsely. The Wife does both to her husbands.

[9] *A wys ... wood* A wise woman can convince her husband that a tale-telling cowbird (a kind of jackdaw) who tells him she has been unfaithful is mad and use her own maid as a witness.

And take witnesse of hir owene mayde°   *own maid*
Of hir° assent, but herkneth° how I
   sayde:°   *her / listen to / how I spoke*
235   "'Sire olde kaynard,° is this thyn array?°*fool / your way of behaving*
Why is my neighebores wyf so gay?°   *well dressed*
She is honoured over al ther she gooth.°   *wherever she goes*
I sitte at hoom. I have no thrifty clooth.°   *appropriate clothing*
What dostow° at my neighebores hous?   *are you doing*
240 Is she so fair? Artow° so amorous?   *are you*
What rowne° ye with oure mayde,° benedicite?   *whisper / maid*
Sire olde lecchour,° lat thy japes° be!   *sir old lecher / tricks*
And if I have a gossib° or a freend,°   *confidant / friend*
Withouten gilt,° thou chidest° as a feend!°   *guilt / complain / fiend*
245 If that I walke or pleye unto his hous,
Thou comest hoom as dronken as a mous[1]
And prechest° on thy bench, with yvel
   preef!°   *preach / bad luck to you*
   "'Thou seist° to me it is a greet
   meschief°   *you say / great misfortune*
To wedde a povre° womman for costage.°   *poor / expense*
250 And if she be riche and of heigh parage,°   *lineage*
Thanne seistow° it is a tormentrie°   *you say / torment*
To suffren° hire pride and hire malencolie.   *endure*
And if she be fair, thou verray knave,[2]
Thou seyst that every holour° wol hire have: *lecher*
255 She may no while in chastitee abyde°   *remain*
That is assailled upon ech a syde.°   *every side*
   Thou seyst that som folk desiren us for richesse,
Somme for oure shape, somme for oure fairnesse
And som for she kan synge and daunce
260 And som for gentillesse° and som for
   daliaunce,°   *nobility / flirtation*
Som for hir handes and hir armes smale.°   *slender*
Thus goth al to the devel,° by thy tale!   *devil*
Thou seyst men may nat kepe° a castel wal,°   *not hold / wall*
It may so longe assailled been overal!°   *everywhere*
265 "'And if that she be foul,° thou seist that she   *ugly*
Coveiteth every man that she may se.°   *see*
For as a spaynel° she wol on hym lepe,°   *spaniel / leap*
Til that she fynde som man hire to chepe.°   *to buy her*
Ne noon so grey goos gooth in the lake

270 As, seistow, wol been withoute make.[3]
And seyst it is an hard thyng for to welde,°   *control*
A thyng that no man wole his thankes helde.°   *willingly hold*
"'Thus seistow, lorel,° whan thow goost to bedde,   *fool*
And that no wys man nedeth° for to wedde,   *needs*
275 Ne° no man that entendeth unto
   hevene.°   *nor / intends to go to heaven*
With wilde thonder dynt° and firy
   levene°   *thunder claps / fiery lightening*
Moote° thy welked nekke° be
   tobroke!°   *may / withered neck / broken*
"'Thow seyst that droppyng° houses and eek smoke *dripping*
And chidyng° wyves maken men to flee   *nagging*
280 Out of hir owene houses. A, benedicitee,
What eyleth° swich an old man for to chide?   *ails*
"'Thow seyst that we wyves wol oure vices hide
Til we be fast,° and thanne we wol hem shewe.°   *secure / show*
Wel may that be a proverbe of a shrewe!°   *villain*
285 "'Thou seist that oxen, asses, hors,° and houndes,   *horses*
They been assayd° at diverse stoundes;°   *tried / different times*
Bacyns,° lavours° er that men hem bye,° *basins / bowls / buy them*
Spoones and stooles and al swich
   housbondrye,°   *household equipment*
And so been pottes,° clothes, and array.°   *pots / ornaments*
290 But folk of wyves maken noon assay°   *do not try them out*
Til they be wedded. Olde dotard° shrewe!   *foolish*
Thanne seistow we wol oure vices shewe.
   "'Thou seist also that it displeseth me
But if° that thou wolt preyse° my beautee   *unless / will praise*
295 And but° thou poure° alwey upon my face   *unless / gaze*
And clepe° me "faire dame!" in every place,   *call*
And but thou make a feeste° on thilke° day   *feast / the same*
That I was born, and make me fressh and gay,
And but thou do to my norice[4] honour
300 And to my chambrere° withinne my
   bour.°   *chambermaid / bedroom*
And to my fadres° folk° and his allyes: *father's / relatives*
Thus seistow, olde barel° ful of lyes!°   *barrel / lies*
   "'And yet of oure apprentice Janekyn,

---

[1] *dronken as a mous* It is not clear why mice are thought to be drunk, but the expression was common in medieval England.

[2] *thou verray knave* You true villain.

[3] *Ne noon ... make* Proverbial: There is no goose in the lake, no matter how grey, who does not have a mate.

[4] *norice* Nurse. Wealthy medieval people were attended to in their childhood by wet nurses, who often became, for a time, surrogate mothers.

For his crispe heer° shynynge° as gold so
　　fyn,°　　　　　　　　　　　*curly hair | shining | fine*
305　And for he squiereth° me bothe up and doun,　　*escorts*
　　Yet hastow° caught a fals suspicioun.　　*you have*
　　I wol° hym noght,° though thou were deed
　　　　tomorwe!　　　　　　　　　*want | not*
　　　　"'But tel me, why hydestow° with sorwe°　*do you hide | sorrow*
　　The keyes of my cheste° awey fro me?　　*chest (safety box)*
310　It is my good° as wel as thyn, pardee!°　　*possession | by God*
　　What, wenestow to make an ydiot of oure dame?°[1]
　　Now by that lord that called is Seint Jame,°　*Saint James*
　　Thou shalt nat bothe, thogh° thou were wood,°　*though | crazy*
　　Be maister° of my body and of my good!°　*master | possessions*
315　That oon thou shalt forgo, maugree thyne eyen!°[2]
　　What nedeth thee of me to enquere° or spyen?°　*inquire | spy*
　　I trowe thou woldest loke me in thy chiste!°[3]
　　Thou sholdest seye, "Wyf, go wher thee liste.°[4]
　　Taak youre disport!° I wol leve° no
　　　　talys.°　　　　　　　*enjoyment | believe | tales*
320　I knowe yow for a trewe wyf, Dame Alys!"
　　We love no man that taketh kepe or charge°　*takes heed or cares*
　　Wher that we goon. We wol ben at oure large.°　*free*
　　　　"'Of alle men, blessed moot° he be,　　*may*
　　The wise astrologien° Daun
　　　　Protholome°　　　*astronomer/ Master Ptolemy*
325　That seith this proverbe in his *Almageste*,
　　"Of alle men his wysdom is the hyeste°　　*highest*
　　That rekketh nevere who hath the world in honde."°[5]
　　By this proverbe thou shalt understonde:
　　Have thou ynogh, what thar thee recche or care[6]
330　How myrily° that othere folkes fare?°　*merrily | behave*
　　For certeyn, olde dotard,° by youre leve,°　*fool | leave*

Ye shul have queynte[7] right ynogh° at eve!°　*enough | at night*
He is to greet° a nygard° that wolde
　　werne°　　　　　*too great | skinflint | refuse*
A man to lighte his candle at his lanterne.
335　He shal have never the lasse° light, pardee!　　*less*
Have thou ynogh, thee thar nat pleyne thee.[8]
　　"'Thou seyst also that if we make us gay
With clothyng and with precious array,°　*expensive adornment*
That it is peril of° oure chastitee.　　*a danger to*
340　And yet with sorwe thou most° enforce
　　thee°　　　　　*must | support yourself*
And seye thise wordes in the apostles name:[9]
"In habit° maad° with chastitee and shame　*clothing | made*
Ye wommen shul apparaille yow,"° quod he　*dress yourselves*
"And noght° in tressed heer° and gay
　　perree,°　　　*not | braided hair | jewels*
345　As perles,° ne with gold ne clothes riche."　　*pearls*
After thy text° ne after thy rubriche°　*quotation | rubric*
I wol nat wirche° as muchel as a gnat!°[10]　*work*
　　"'Thou seydest this, that I was lyk° a cat.　*like*
For whoso wolde senge° a cattes skyn,　　*singe*
350　Thanne wolde the cat wel dwellen in his in.°　*lodgings*
And if the cattes skyn be slyk° and gay,　　*sleek*
She wol nat dwelle in house half a day,
But forth she wole° er any day be dawed°　*will go | dawned*
To shewe hir skyn and goon a caterwawed.[11]
355　This is to seye, if I be gay, sire shrewe,°　*sir villain*
I wol renne out my borel° for to shewe!　*cheap clothing*
　　"'Sire olde fool, what eyleth° thee to spyen?°　*ails | spy*

---

[1] *What ... dame* What, do you expect to make an idiot of our lady? I.e., the Wife herself.

[2] *That ... eyen* You must give up one of them, despite your eyes! (I.e., despite anything you can do.)

[3] *I trowe ... chiste* I believe you would lock me in your chest. Medieval merchants used large locked chests to lock up their coins and their valuables.

[4] *Thou ... liste* You should say, "Wife, go wherever you want."

[5] *That ... honde* Who does not care who possesses the world.

[6] *Have ... care* If you have enough, why do you need to bother yourself or care.

[7] *queynte* Literally meaning elegant, clever, or pleasing thing, queynte is also a medieval euphemism for the female sexual organs.

[8] *Have ... thee* If you have enough, you do not need to complain for yourself.

[9] *the apostles name* St. Paul. The following quotation is from 1 Timothy 2.9.

[10] *After thy ... gnat* I will not follow (work after) your quotation or your text in the smallest way, or, any more than a gnat would. In medieval service books and books of devotion, rubrics (whose name comes from the red ink in which they were written) were directions about how to use the texts to which they referred either in communal worship or private devotion.

[11] *caterwawed* Caterwauling, the loud noise cats make while they are mating.

Thogh thou preye Argus[1] with hise hundred eyen

To be my wardecors,° as he kan° best.   *bodyguard / knows how*

360   In feith, he shal nat kepe me but me lest!°   *unless I want to be kept*

Yet koude I make his berd,° so moot I thee![2]   *fool him*

   "'Thou seydest eek that ther been thynges thre,°   *three things*

The whiche thynges troublen° al this erthe   *trouble*

And that no wight may endure the ferthe.°   *fourth*

365   O leeve° sire shrewe! Jhesu° shorte° thy lyf!   *dear / Jesus / shorten*

Yet prechestow° and seyst an hateful wyf   *still you preach*

Yrekned is for° oon of thise

   meschances.°   *is counted as / misfortunes*

Been ther none othere resemblances

That ye may likne° youre parables to,   *liken*

370   But if a sely° wyf be oon of tho?°   *innocent / those*

   "'Thou liknest° wommenes love to helle,   *liken*

To bareyne° lond° ther° water may nat   *barren / land / where*

   dwelle.

Thou liknest it also to wilde fyr:

The moore° it brenneth,° the moore it hath

   desir°   *more / burns / desires*

375   To consumen° everythyng that brent wole be.   *consume*

Thou seyst, right as wormes° shendeth° a tree,   *grubs / harm*

Right so a wyf destroyeth hire housbond;

This knowe they that been to wyves bonde.'°   *bound*

   "Lordynges, right thus as ye have understonde

380   Baar I stifly myne olde housbondes on honde,

That thus they seyden in hir dronkenesse![3]

And al was fals, but that I took witnesse

On Janekyn and on my nece° also.   *niece*

O Lord, the pyne° I dide hem° and the wo,   *pain / to them*

385   Ful giltlees,° by Goddes sweete pyne!°   *guiltless / pain*

For as an hors I koude byte and whyne.°   *whinny*

I koude pleyne° thogh° I were in the

   gilt,°   *complain / though / guilty*

Or elles oftentyme hadde I been spilt.°   *destroyed*

Whoso comth° first to mille,° first

   grynt.°   *whoever comes / mill / grinds*

390   I pleyned first, so was oure were° ystynt.°   *war / concluded*

They were ful glad to excuse hem° blyve°   *them / quickly*

Of thyng of which they nevere agilte hir lyve.[4]

Of wenches° wolde I beren hym on honde,°   *girls / accuse him*

Whan that for syk° unnethes° myghte he

   stonde.   *sickness / scarcely*

395   "Yet tikled° it his herte,° for that° he   *tickled / heart / because*

Wende° that I hadde of hym° so greet

   chiertee.°   *thought / for him / love*

I swoor° that al my walkynge° out by

   nyghte°   *swore / walking / night*

Was for t'espye° wenches that he dighte.°   *spy / had sex with*

Under that colour° hadde I many a myrthe,°   *pretense / mirth*

400   For al swich thyng was yeven° us in oure byrthe.°   *given / birth*

Deceite, wepyng, spynnyng° God hath yeve°   *spinning / given*

To wommen kyndely° whil that they may lyve.   *naturally*

And thus of o° thyng I avaunte° me: *one / boast*

Atte° ende, I hadde the bettre° in ech

   degree°   *at the / better / instance*

405   By sleighte,° or force, or by som maner

   thyng,°   *deceit / manner of thing*

As by continueel murmure° or

   grucchyng.°   *continual murmur / complaining*

Namely° abedde° hadden they

   meschaunce;°   *especially / in bed / misfortune*

Ther wolde I chide° and do hem no plesaunce.°   *nag / pleasure*

I wolde no lenger° in the bed abyde°   *longer / remain*

410   If that I felte his arm over my syde°   *side*

Til he had maad his raunsoun° unto me.   *paid his ransom*

Thanne wolde I suffre hym do his nycetee.°   *foolishness*

And therfore every man this tale I telle:

Wynne° whoso may, for al is for to selle.°   *win / for sale*

415   With empty hand men may none° haukes° lure;   *no / hawks*

For wynnyng° wolde I al his lust endure   *profit*

And make me a feyned° appetit.   *pretended*

And yet in bacon[5] hadde I nevere delit.°   *delight*

That made me that evere I wolde hem chide,

420   For thogh the Pope hadde seten hem biside,°   *sat beside them*

I wolde nat spare hem at hir owene bord.°   *table*

For by my trouthe, I quitte hem,° word for word,   *requited them*

As° helpe me verray° God omnipotent!   *so / true*

Though I right now sholde make my testament,

425   I ne owe hem nat a word that it nys quit.°   *was not paid back*

---

1 *Argus* Hundred-eyed creature of Greek mythology hired by Hera to guard her husband Zeus's mistress Io. He was killed by Hermes.

2 *so moot I thee* I.e., indeed, or by my word.

3 *Baar … dronkenesse* I bore witness firmly to my old husbands that they said this when they were drunk.

4 *Of … lyve* Of a thing that they had never been guilty of in their lives.

5 *bacon* Old meat preserved by salting; in other words, old men.

I broghte° it so aboute, by my wit,   brought
That they moste yeve it up° as for the beste   had to give it up
Or elles hadde we nevere been in reste.°   at rest
For thogh° he looked as a wood leoun,°   although / crazy lion
430   Yet sholde he faille of his conclusion.°   intent
         "Thanne wolde I seye, 'Goodlief, taak keepe
How mekely looketh Wilkyn oure sheepe![1]
Com neer, my spouse. Lat me ba° thy cheke.   kiss
Ye sholde been al pacient and meke°   meek
435   And han° a sweete, spiced conscience,°   have / delicate conscience
Sith ye so preche° of Jobes pacience.°[2]   preach / Job's patience
Suffreth alwey,° syn ye so wel kan preche,   endure always
And but° ye do, certein we shal yow teche°   unless / teach you
That it is fair to have a wyf in pees.°   peace
440   Oon of us two moste bowen,° doutelees,°   must bow / doubtless
And sith a man is moore resonable
Than womman is, ye moste been suffrable.°   you must be patient
What eyleth yow,° to grucche° thus and
         grone?°   ails you / complain / groan
Is it for ye wolde have my queynte°
         allone?°   female sexual organs / alone
445   Wy,° taak it al! Lo, have it everydeel!°   why / every bit
Peter, I shrewe yow but ye love it weel![3]
For if I wolde selle my bele chose,[4]
I koude walke as fressh as is a rose.[5]
But I wol kepe it for youre owene tooth.°   own taste (pleasure)
450   Ye be to blame, by God, I sey yow sooth!'°   tell you the truth
         "Swiche manere wordes hadde we on honde.[6]
Now wol I speken of my fourthe housbonde.
         "My fourthe housbonde was a revelour°—   party-goer
This is to seyn, he hadde a paramour°—   lover
455   And I was yong and ful of ragerye,°   high spirits
Stibourne° and strong and joly° as a
         pye.°   stubborn / pretty / magpie

Wel koude I daunce to an harpe smale°   small harp
And synge,° ywis,° as any nyghtyngale   sing / indeed
Whan I had dronke a draughte of sweete wyn.°   wine
460   Metellius,[7] the foule cherl, the swyn,°   swine
That with a staf° birafte° his wyf hir lyf   club / stole from
For° she drank wyn, thogh I hadde been his wyf,   because
He sholde nat han daunted me fro drynke![8]
And after wyn, on Venus[9] moste I thynke.   must
465   For also siker° as cold engendreth hayl,°   as sure / causes hail
A likerous° mouth moste han° a likerous
         tayl.°   lecherous / must have / tail
In wommen vinolent is no defence.[10]
This knowen lecchours° by experience.   lechers
         "But, Lord Crist, whan that it remembreth
         me°   when I remember
470   Upon my yowthe° and on my jolitee,°   youth / gaiety
It tikleth° me aboute myn herte roote.°   tickles / heart's root
Unto this day it dooth myn herte boote°   does my heart good
That I have had my world as in my tyme.°   time
But age, allas, that al wole envenyme,°   will poison all
475   Hath me biraft° my beautee and my pith.° stolen from me / strength
Lat go! Farewel! The devel go therwith!°   with it
The flour is goon,° ther is namoore° to telle;   gone / no more
The bren° as I best kan now moste° I selle.   bran / must
But yet to be right myrie° wol I fonde.°   merry / try
480   Now wol I tellen of my fourthe housbonde.
         "I seye I hadde in herte° greet despit°   heart / great anger
That he of any oother° had delit.°   any other (woman) / delight
But he was quit,° by God and by Seint Joce![11]   punished
I made hym of the same wode° a croce.°   wood / cross
485   Nat of my body in no foul manere,°   manner
But certein I made folk swich cheere,°   hospitality
That in his owene grece° I made hym frye°   own grease / fry
For angre and for verray jalousie.°   true jealousy
By God, in erthe I was his purgatorie,°   purgatory

---

[1] *Thanne … sheepe* Then would I say, "Sweetheart, note well, how meekly Willie, our sheep (i.e., her husband) looks."

[2] *Jobes pacience* God allowed Satan to attempt to shake Job's faith through a series of terrible misfortunes. See the Biblical Book of Job.

[3] *Peter … weel* By St. Peter!, I curse you unless you love it well, i.e., do you ever love it well.

[4] *bele chose* French: beautiful thing, i.e. sexual organs.

[5] *I … rose* In other words, if I sold myself sexually, I could dress myself beautifully with the proceeds.

[6] *Swiche … honde* We were occupied by this kind of conversation.

[7] *Metellius* See *Facta et dicta memorabilia* (*Memorable Facts and Deeds*), a collection of short stories for orators, written by Valerius Maximus (1st century CE).

[8] *He … drynke* He should not have prevented me from drink.

[9] *Venus* Goddess of love.

[10] *In … defence* There is no defense in drunken women, i.e., they are defenseless.

[11] *Seint Joce* St. Judoc or St. Joyce was a seventh-century prince in Brittany who gave up his succession to the throne to become a priest. He was also famous for going on a pilgrimage to Rome.

490 For which I hope his soule be in glorie.
For God it woot,° he sat ful ofte and song°   knows it / sang
Whan that his shoo° ful bitterly hym
         wrong.°   shoe / hurt him very bitterly
Ther was no wight save God and he that wiste°   who knew
In many wise° how soore° I hym twiste.°   ways / sorely / tormented
495 He deyde° whan I cam fro°
         Jerusalem   died / came from (a pilgrimage to)
And lith ygrave° under the roode beem,[1]   lies buried
Al° is his tombe° noght so curyus°   although / tomb / elaborate
As was the sepulcre of hym Daryus,°   Darius
Which that Appeles wroghte° subtilly.°[2]   made / subtly
500 It nys° but wast to burye hym preciously.°   is not / expensively
Lat hym° fare wel! God yeve° his soule reste.   may he / give
He is now in his grave and in his cheste.°   coffin
    "Now of my fifthe housbonde wol I telle.
God lete his soule nevere come in Helle!
505 And yet was he to me the mooste shrewe.
That feele I on my ribbes° al by rewe,°   ribs / in a row
And evere shal unto myn endyng day.
But in oure bed he was ful fressh and gay.
And therwithal so wel koude he me glose,°   flatter
510 Whan that he wolde han my bele chose,
That thogh he hadde me bet° on every bon,°   beaten / bone
He koude wynne agayn my love anon.
I trowe° I loved hym best for that he   believe
Was of his love daungerous° to me.   standoffish
515 We wommen han, if that I shal nat lye,
In this matere a queynte fantasye:°   odd whim
Wayte,° what° thyng we may nat lightly   know (that) / whatever
         have,
Therafter° wol we crie al day and crave!   after it
Forbede° us thyng,° and that desiren we;   forbid / something
520 Preesse on us faste, and thanne wol we fle.°   flee
With daunger oute we al oure chaffare;[3]

Greet prees° at market maketh deere
         ware,°   crowd / expensive goods
And to greet cheepe° is holde at litel
         prys.°   too much merchandise / little price
This knoweth every womman that is wys.
525 My fifthe housbonde, God his soule blesse,
Which that I took for love and no richesse,
He somtyme° was a clerk° of Oxenford°   once / student / Oxford
And hadde left scole° and wente at hom° to
         bord°   school / home / rent a room
With my gossib,° dwellynge in oure toun.   confidant
530 God have hir soule! Hir name was Alisoun.
She knew myn herte and eek my privetee°   secrets
Bet° than oure parisshe preest, as moot I
         thee!°   better / may I thrive
To hire biwreyed° I my conseil° al.   revealed / counsel
For hadde myn housbonde pissed on a wal°   wall
535 Or doon a thyng that sholde han cost his lyf,
To hire and to another worthy wyf
And to my nece,° which that I loved weel,   niece
I wolde han toold his conseil everydeel.°   every bit
And so I dide ful often, God it woot!°   God knows it
540 That made his face ful often reed and hoot°   hot
For verray° shame, and blamed hymself, for he   true
Had toold to me so greet a pryvetee.
    "And so bifel° that ones° in a Lente[4]— it happened / once
So oftentymes I to my gossyb° wente,   confidant
545 For evere yet I loved to be gay
And for to walke in March, Averill, and May
Fro hous to hous to heere sondry talys°—   various tales
That Jankyn clerk and my gossyb Dame Alys
And I myself into the feeldes° wente.   fields
550 Myn housbonde was at Londoun al the Lente;
I hadde the bettre leyser° for to pleye   better opportunity
And for to se° and eek for to be seye°   see / seen
Of lusty folk. What wiste I wher my grace
Was shapen for to be or in what place?[5]
555 Therfore I made my visitaciouns°   visits

---

[1] *And ... beem* Her fourth husband was buried inside the local
parish church under the cross-beam of the cross near the high altar,
a place reserved for only the most influential members of a parish.

[2] *As was ... subtilly* The legendary tomb of Darius the Mede,
fashioned by the Jewish sculptor Appeles, was famous for its beauty.

[3] *With ... chaffare* Either (where we are greeted) with scorn, we
(put) out all our goods (i.e., are anxious to sell), or we (put) out all
our goods with (a show of) scorn (i.e., as if we did not care if anyone
buys them).

---

[4] *Lente* Period in the late winter and early spring when Christians
prepare for Easter by fasting and doing penance.

[5] *What wiste ... place* How could I know where or in what place
my good luck was destined to be? or possibly (to avoid the redun-
dancy) how could I know whether I was destined to have good luck,
or where?

To vigilies and to processiouns,[1]

To prechyng° eek and to thise pilgrimages,   *preaching*

To pleyes° of myracles and to mariages,   *plays*

And wered upon° my gaye scarlet gytes.°   *wore / robes*

560   Thise wormes, ne thise motthes,° ne thise mytes°   *moths / mites*

Upon my peril frete° hem never a deel,°   *eat / never a bit*

And wostow° why? For they were used weel.   *do you know*

"Now wol I tellen forth what happed me.°   *happened to me*

I seye that in the feeldes walked we

565   Til trewely we hadde swich daliance,°   *flirtation*

This clerk and I, that of my purveiance°   *foresight*

I spak to hym and seyde° hym how that he,   *said to*

If I were wydwe,° sholde wedde me.   *widowed*

For certeinly I sey for no bobance,°   *pride*

570   Yet was I nevere withouten purveiance

Of mariage n'of° othere thynges eek.   *nor of*

I holde a mouses herte° nat worth a leek   *mouse's heart*

That hath but oon hole forto sterte° to,   *escape*

And if that faille,° thanne is al ydo.°[2]   *should fail / completely done for*

575   "I bar hym on honde° he hadde enchanted me;   *accused him*

My dame° taughte me that soutiltee.°   *mother / trick*

And eek I seyde I mette° of hym al nyght: *dreamed*

He wolde han slayn° me as I lay upright,°   *killed / on my back*

And al my bed was ful of verray blood.

580   But yet I hope that he shal do me good,

For blood bitokeneth° gold, as me was taught.[3]   *signifies*

And al was fals! I dremed of it right naught.°   *not at all*

But I folwed ay° my dammes

        loore,°   *followed ever / mother's teaching*

As wel of this as othere thynges° moore.°   *matters / more*

585   "But now sire, lat me se° what I shal seyn.   *see*

Aha! By God, I have my tale ageyn!°   *again*

"Whan that my fourthe housbonde was on beere,°[4]   *bier*

I weepe algate° and made sory cheere,°   *continuously / face*

As wyves mooten,° for it is usage,°   *must / custom*

590   And with my coverchief° covered my visage.°   *kerchief / face*

But for that° I was purveyed of° a

        make,°   *because / provided with / mate*

I wepte but smal,° and that I undertake.°   *little / attest*

"To chirche° was myn housbonde born

        amorwe,°   *church / in the morning*

With neighebores that for hym maden sorwe,°   *sorrow*

595   And Jankyn oure clerk was oon of tho.°   *one of those*

As help me God, whan that I saugh° hym go   *saw*

After the beere, me thoughte he hadde a paire

Of legges and of feet so clene° and faire,°   *neat / attractive*

That al myn herte I yaf° unto his hoold.°   *gave / possession*

600   He was, I trowe,° a twenty wynter oold,   *believe*

And I was fourty, if I shal seye sooth.°   *say the truth*

And yet I hadde alwey a coltes° tooth.   *colt's*

Gat-tothed I was, and that bicam me weel;[5]

I hadde the prente° of Seint Venus seel.[6]   *print*

605   As help me God, I was a lusty oon,

And faire and riche and yong and wel bigon.°   *established*

And trewely, as myne housbondes tolde me,

I hadde the beste 'quonyam'° myghte be.   *sexual organ*

For certes, I am al venerien[7]

610   In feelynge,° and myn herte is marcien.[8]   *feeling*

Venus me yaf° my lust, my likerousnesse,°   *gave / lecherousness*

And Mars yaf me my sturdy hardynesse.°   *courage*

Myn ascendent was Taur, and Mars therinne.[9]

Allas! Allas! That evere love was synne!°   *sin*

615   I folwed° ay° myn inclinacioun°   *followed / ever / inclination*

By vertu° of my constellacioun,°   *influence / constellation*

---

[1] *To ... processiouns* To vigils and to processions. Vigils were church services held on the evening before the feast day of a saint. Ceremonial processions formed part of the service on the day itself.

[2] *I holde ... y do* The mouse who has only one hole to which it can escape appears in various proverbs as well as in the *Romance of the Rose* (line 13554), whose character La Vieille, the old woman who knows all about love, is one of the models for the Wife of Bath. Not worth a leek means worth nothing at all.

[3] *blood ... taught* Blood could serve as a token or symbol of gold, which was often described as red.

[4] *beere* Bier, i.e., in his coffin.

[5] *Gat-tothed ... weel* I was gap-toothed, and that suited me well. Women with gaps between their teeth were said to have lustful and licentious natures.

[6] *I hadde ... seel* I had the imprint of Venus's seal; in other words, Venus has given the Wife of Bath a birthmark, another supposed indication of a lascivious nature.

[7] *venerien* In astrology, one who is influenced by the planet Venus—i.e., prone to love.

[8] *marcien* In astrology, one who is influenced by the planet Mars—i.e., war-like.

[9] *Myn ... therinne* At the moment when the Wife was born the constellation of stars known as Taurus (the Bull) was coming over the horizon (ascendant) along with the planet Mars. It was believed that if a woman is born with Venus and Mars ascending together she will be unchaste.

That made me I koude noght withdrawe°   *withhold*
My chambre° of Venus from a good felawe.°   *organ / fellow*
Yet have I Martes° mark[1] upon my face—   *Mars's*
620 And also in another privee place.
For God so wys° be my savacioun,°   *wise / salvation*
I ne loved nevere° by no discrecioun   *never loved*
But evere folwed myn appetit,°   *appetite*
Al° were he short or long° or blak° or
      whit.°   *whether / tall / dark / fair*
625 I took no kepe,° so that he liked° me,   *did not care / pleased*
How poore he was ne eek of what degree.

      "What sholde I seye, but at the monthes ende,
This joly° clerk Jankyn that was so hende°   *pretty / handy*
Hath wedded me with greet solempnytee.°   *ceremony*
630 And to hym yaf° I al the lond and fee°   *gave / property*
That evere was me yeven° therbifoore.°   *given / before this*
But afterward repented me ful soore!°   *I regretted it sorely*
He nolde suffre nothyng of my list.[2]
By God, he smoot° me ones° on the lyst,°   *hit / once / ear*
635 For that° I rente° out of his book a leef,° *because / tore / page*
That of the strook° myn ere° wax° al
      deef.°   *blow / ear / grew / completely deaf*
Stibourne° I was as is a leonesse°   *stubborn / lioness*
And of my tonge° a verray°
      jangleresse.°   *tongue / true / ceaseless talker*
And walke I wolde as I had doon biforn°   *before*
640 From hous to hous, although he had it sworn.° *forbidden*
For which he often tymes wolde preche°   *preach*
And me of olde Romayn geestes[3] teche°   *teach*
How he Symplicius Gallus lefte his wyf
And hire forsook for terme° of al his lyf   *the rest*
645 Noght but for open heveded,[4] he hir say,
Lookynge out at his dore° upon a day.   *door*
      "Another Romayn tolde he me by name,
That, for° his wyf was at a someres game° *because / entertainment*
Withouten his wityng,° he forsook hire eke.   *knowledge*
650 And thanne wolde he upon his Bible seke°   *seek*

That ilke° proverbe of Ecclesiaste[5]   *same*
Where he comandeth and forbedeth faste°   *firmly*
Man shal nat suffre° his wyf go roule° aboute. *allow / wander*
Thanne wolde he seye right thus, withouten doute:
655 'Whoso that buyldeth his hous al of salwes[6]
And priketh° his blynde hors° over the
      falwes°   *spurs / blind horse / fields*
And suffreth his wyf to go seken halwes°   *shrines*
Is worthy to been° hanged on the galwes.'°[7] *be / gallows*
But al for noght! I sette noght an hawe°   *hawthorn berry*
660 Of his proverbes n'of° his olde lawe,   *nor of*
Ne I wolde nat of hym° corrected be.   *by him*
I hate hym that my vices telleth me°   *tells me about*
And so doo mo,° God woot,° of us than I.   *do more / knows*
This made hym with me wood° al outrely:°   *crazy / entirely*
665 I nolde noght° forbere° hym in no cas.°   *would not / endure / case*
      "Now wol I seye° yow° sooth,° by Seint
      Thomas,[8]   *tell / you / the truth*
Why that I rente out of his book a leef,
For which he smoot me so that I was deef.
      "He hadde a book that gladly, nyght and day,
670 For his desport° he wolde rede° alway.   *fun / read*
He cleped° it *Valerie and Theofraste*,[9]   *called*
At which book he lough° alwey ful faste.°   *laughed / very much*
And eek ther was somtyme° a clerk° at Rome,   *once / theologian*
A cardinal that highte° Seint Jerome,[10]   *was named*

---

[1] *Martes mark*   Red birthmark.

[2] *He ... list*   He would not allow anything I desired.

[3] *Romayn geestes*   Roman stories. Like the reference to Metellius above in line 460, the following are old misogynistic or anti-matrimonial stories dating back to ancient Rome.

[4] *Noght ... heveded*   Just because he saw her bare-headed.

---

[5] *That ... Ecclesiaste*   See Ecclesiasticus 25.34.

[6] *Whoso ... salwes*   Whoever builds his house of all willow branches

[7] *Whoso ... galwes*   Proverb.

[8] *Seint Thomas*   There are three possible candidates for this St. Thomas: Thomas the apostle, mentioned in the Gospels; St. Thomas Aquinas, the thirteenth-century theologian (though his second name was more often used than not); and St. Thomas Becket, whose shrine the Canterbury pilgrims are journeying to visit. Thomas the apostle was often referred to as "Thomas of India." Becket is the likely reference.

[9] *Valerie and Theofraste*   The Wife of Bath is actually referring to two separate works, often bound together into one volume in the Middle Ages—the *Dissuasio Valerii ad Rufinum* by the English scholar and courtier Walter Map (c. 1140–c. 1208) and the *Golden Book of Marriages* by Theophrastus, a supposed disciple of Aristotle. Both books were full of stories attacking women and discouraging men from marrying.

[10] *Seint Jerome*   Late fourth and early fifth centuries and was a theologian who wrote many influential works, including a translation of the Bible into Latin. *Against Jovinian*, which extolls virginity,

675 That made a book, *Agayn*° Jovinian,   *against*
In which book eek ther was Tertulan,[1]
Crisippus,[2] Trotula,[3] and Helowys[4]
That was abbesse nat fer° fro Parys,   *not far*
And eek the *Parables of Salomon*,[5]
680 Ovides° *Art*,[6] and bookes many on.°   *Ovid's | many (other) books*
And alle thise were bounden in o° volume.   *one*
And every nyght and day was his custume
Whan he hadde leyser° and vacacioun°   *leisure | opportunity*
From oother worldly occupacioun
685 To reden on this *Book of Wikked Wyves*.[7]
He knew of hem mo legendes and lyves°   *biographies*
Than been° of goode wyves in the Bible.   *there are*
For, trusteth wel, it is an inpossible°   *impossibility*
That any clerk wol speke good of wyves
690 But if° it be of hooly seintes lyves,   *unless*
Ne of noon other womman never the mo.
Who peynted the leoun,[8] tel me who?
By God, if wommen hadde writen stories
As clerkes han° withinne hire° oratories,°   *have | their | chapels*
695 They wolde han writen of men moore wikkednesse
Than al the mark of Adam° may redresse.   *male sex (i.e., men)*
The children of Mercurie and Venus[9]

Been in hir wirkyng ful contrarius.[10]
Mercurie loveth wysdam° and science,°   *wisdom | knowledge*
700 And Venus loveth ryot° and dispence.°   *parties | squandering money*
And for hire diverse disposicioun,°   *natures*
Ech falleth in otheres exaltacioun,°   *exaltation*
And thus, God woot, Mercurie is desolat
In Pisces, wher Venus is exaltat,°   *exalted*
705 And Venus falleth ther° Mercurie is reysed.   *where*
Therfore no womman of no clerk is preysed.
The clerk, whan he is oold and may noght° do   *cannot*
Of Venus werkes[11] worth his olde sho,°   *shoe*
Thanne sit he doun and writ in his dotage[12]
710 That wommen kan nat kepe hir mariage.
  "But now to purpos° why I tolde thee   *the reason*
That I was beten° for a book, pardee.°   *beaten | by God*
Upon a nyght Jankyn, that was oure sire,°   *master*
Redde on his book as he sat by the fire
715 Of Eva° first, that for hir wikkednesse   *Eve*
Was al mankynde broght to wrecchednesse,
For which Crist hymself was slayn,
That boghte° us with his herte blood agayn.   *who bought*
Lo, heere,° expres° of womman may ye fynde   *here, specifically*
720 That womman was the los° of al mankynde.   *destruction*
  "Tho° redde he me how Sampson[13] loste hise   *then | hairs*
    heres:°
Slepynge, his lemman° kitte° it with hir   *lover | cut | scissors*
    sheres,°
Thurgh° which tresoun° loste he bothe hise   *through | betrayal*
    eyen.
  "Tho redde he me, if that I shal nat lyen,°   *lie*
725 Of Hercules and of his Dianyre,[14]
That caused hym to sette hymself afyre.°   *on fire*
Nothyng° forgat he the sorwe and wo   *not at all*

is one of Chaucer's major sources for the "Wife of Bath's Prologue."

[1] *Tertulan* Early third-century theologian who wrote several treatises about the value of virginity.

[2] *Crisippus* Mentioned in Jerome's treatise, referred to in line 671, but none of his works survive.

[3] *Trotula* Female doctor who taught medicine at the University of Salerno in the eleventh century and wrote a treatise about gynecology.

[4] *Helowys* Tried to persuade her lover Abelard not to marry her, giving typical anti-matrimonial reasons. She eventually became the abbess of the Paraclete, a convent of nuns near Paris.

[5] *Parables of Solomon* Biblical Book of Proverbs.

[6] *Ovides Art* Ovid's *Art of Love* concludes with a long argument about why it is prudent to avoid love.

[7] *Book of Wikked Wyves* Title of the whole compendium volume mentioned above.

[8] *Who ... leoun* In medieval versions of the fable of Aesop, a man and a lion were having a dispute about who was the stronger. For proof, the man showed the lion a picture of a man killing a lion, and the lion then asked the man who painted the lion—implying the painting is biased. Then the lion ate the man.

[9] *The children ... Venus* I.e., scholars and lovers.

[10] *Been ... contrarius* In addition to influencing the body's humors (Cf. *General Prologue*, lines 413 ff.), the planets were thought to govern various parts of the body and various trades. Mercury was the planet of scholars and merchants, who, in their ways of doing things, are completely at odds with lovers.

[11] *Venus werkes* I.e., sex.

[12] *Thanne ... dotage* Then he sits down and writes in his old age.

[13] *Tho ... Sampson* See Judges 16.15–22.

[14] *Hercules ... Dianyre* Deianira was the wife of Hercules and inadvertently caused his death by giving him a shirt that she thought would keep him faithful. It was in fact poisoned and he had himself burned alive to escape the pain.

That Socrates hadde with hise wyves two,

How Xantippa[1] caste° pisse° upon his heed.°   *threw / urine / head*

730 This sely° man sat stille° as he were deed.°   *innocent / quietly / dead*

He wiped his heed. Namoore dorste° he seyn   *dared*

But, 'Er° that thonder stynte,° comth a reyn.°'   *before / stops / rain*

"Of Phasipha, that was the queene of Crete,

For shrewednesse° hym thoughte the tale swete.°   *nastiness / sweet*

735 Fy! Spek namoore! It is a grisly thyng,

Of hire horrible lust and hir likyng![2]

"Of Clitermystra,[3] for hire lecherye,

That falsly made hire housbonde for to dye,°   *die*

He redde it with ful good devocioun.

740 "He tolde me eek for what occasioun

Amphiorax at Thebes loste his lyf:[4]

Myn housbonde hadde a legende° of his wyf,   *story*

Eriphilem, that for an ouche° of gold   *brooch*

Hath prively° unto the Grekes told   *secretly*

745 Wher that hir housbonde hidde hym in a place,

For which he hadde at Thebes sory° grace.   *sorry*

"Of Lyvia tolde he me and of Lucye.[5]

They bothe made° hir° housbondes for to dye—   *caused / their*

That oon for love, that oother was for hate.

750 Lyvia hir housbonde upon an even° late   *evening*

Empoysoned° hath, for that she was his fo;°   *poisoned / foe*

Lucia likerous° loved hire housbonde so,   *lustfully*

---

[1] *Xantippa* I.e., Xanthippe (late fifth c. BCE) famously shrewish wife of the philosopher Socrates (469–399 BCE).

[2] *Phasipha … likyng* In Greek mythology, Queen Pasiphae of Crete had sex with a bull and gave birth to the monster Minotaur; *likyng* Desire.

[3] *Clitermystra* I.e., Clytemnestra, who with her lover Aegisthus murdered her husband Agamemnon when he returned from the Trojan war.

[4] *Amphiorax … lyf* Amphiaraus hid so he would not have to fight in war, but his hiding place was betrayed by his wife Eriphyle, and he was killed in battle.

[5] *Of … Lucye* Livia was either Augustus's wife, who poisoned several prominent Romans (including her own husband) for political gain, or Livilla, Livia's granddaughter, who poisoned her husband at the instigation of her lover Sejanus. Lucilla poisoned her husband, the Roman philosopher Lucretius (c. 99–c. 55 BCE), author of *On the Nature of Things*, with a love-potion intended to increase his desire for her.

That, for he sholde alwey upon hire thynke,

She yaf° hym swich a manere° love drynke°   *gave / type of / potion*

755 That he was deed° er it were by the morwe.°   *dead / morning*

And thus algates° housbondes han sorwe.°   *always / have sorrow*

"Thanne tolde he me how that oon Latumyus[6]

Compleyned unto his felawe° Arrius   *friend*

That in his gardyn growed swich a tree

760 On which he seyde how that hise wyves thre

Hanged hemself° for herte° despitus.°   *themselves / heart / cruel*

'O leeve° brother,' quod this Arrius,   *dear*

'Yif° me a plante° of thilke° blissed tree,   *give / seedling / that*

And in my gardyn planted it shal bee.'

765 "Of latter date of wyves hath he red,

That somme han slayn hir housbondes in hir bed

And lete hir lecchour dighte hire al the nyght,[7]

Whan that the corps lay in the floor upright,

And somme han dryve° nayles° in hir brayn[8]   *driven / nails*

770 Whil that they slepte, and thus they han hem slayn;

Somme han hem yeve poysoun in hire drynke.[9]

He spak moore harm than herte may bithynke.°   *imagine*

And therwithal° he knew of mo proverbes   *with all this*

Than in this world ther growen gras or herbes.

775 'Bet° is,' quod he, 'thyn habitacioun°   *better / dwelling place*

Be with a leoun or a foul dragoun

Than with a womman usynge° for to chyde.   *accustomed*

Bet is,' quod he, 'hye° in the roof abyde   *high*

Than with an angry wyf doun in the hous,

780 They been° so wikked and contrarious;   *are*

They haten that hir housbondes loveth ay.'[10]

He seyde, 'A womman cast° hir shame away   *throws*

Whan she cast of° hir smok.° And forthermo,   *off / undergarment*

A fair womman, but° she be chaast° also,   *unless / chaste*

785 Is lyk a gold ryng in a sowes° nose.'   *pig's*

Who wolde leeve or who wolde suppose°   *believe*

The wo that in myn herte was and pyne?°   *pain*

"And whan I saugh he wolde nevere fyne°   *finish*

To reden on this cursed book al nyght,

---

[6] *Thanne … Latumyus* The incident related below is another misogynistic story from ancient Rome, for which Chaucer's source is probably Walter Map's *Dissuasio Valerii*.

[7] *And … nyght* And let her lover have sex with her all night.

[8] *And … brayn* See Judges 4.17–22.

[9] *Somme … drynke* Some have given them poison in their drink.

[10] *They … ay* They always hate what their husbands love.

790　Al sodeynly thre leves have I plyght°　　　　　　　*plucked*
　　　Out of his book, right as he radde. And eke
　　　I with my fest° so took° hym on the cheke,　　　*fist | hit*
　　　That in oure fyr he fil° bakward adoun.　　　　　*fell*
　　　And he up stirte° as dooth a wood leoun,　　　　*jumps*
795　And with his fest he smoot me on the heed,
　　　That in° the floor I lay as I were deed.　　　　　*on*
　　　And whan he saugh how stille that I lay,
　　　He was agast° and wolde han fled his way.°　　　*afraid | away*
　　　Til atte laste out of my swogh° I breyde.°　　　　*faint | awoke*
800　'O hastow° slayn me, false theef?' I seyde.　　　　*have you*
　　　'And for my land thus hastow mordred me!
　　　Er° I be deed, yet wol I kisse thee.'　　　　　　*before*
　　　　"And neer he cam and kneled faire° adoun　　*pleasantly*
　　　And seyde, 'Deere suster° Alisoun,　　　　　　　*sister*
805　As help me God, I shal thee nevere smyte!
　　　That I have doon, it is thyself to wyte.°　　　　　*blame*
　　　Foryeve it me, and that I thee biseke!'°　　　　　*beg*
　　　And yet eftsoones° I hitte hym on the cheke　　　*once more*
　　　And seyde, 'Theef, thus muchel am I wreke.°　　　*avenged*
810　Now wol I dye. I may no lenger speke.'
　　　But atte laste, with muchel care and wo,
　　　We fille acorded° by usselven° two.　　*came to an agreement | ourselves*
　　　He yaf me al° the bridel° in myn hond　　　　*completely | bridle*
　　　To han the governance of hous and lond,
815　And of his tonge and his hond also,
　　　And made hym brenne his book anon right tho.°　　*there*
　　　And whan that I hadde geten° unto me　　　　　*gotten*
　　　By maistrie° al the soveraynetee,　　　　　　　*mastery*
　　　And that he seyde, 'Myn owene trewe wyf,
820　Do as thee lust to terme of al thy lyf:[1]
　　　Keepe thyn honour and keepe eek myn estaat.'—
　　　After that day we hadden never debaat.°　　　　*disagreement*
　　　God helpe me so, I was to hym as kynde
　　　As any wyf from Denmark unto Ynde°　　　　　*India*
825　And also trewe, and so was he to me.
　　　I prey to God that sit in magestee,
　　　So blesse his soule for his mercy deere.
　　　Now wol I seye° my tale, if ye wol heere."　　　*tell*

BIHOLDE THE WORDES BITWENE THE SOMONOUR
AND THE FRERE

　　　The Frere° lough° whan he hadde herd al this.　*friar | laughed*
830　"Now dame," quod he, "so have I joye or blis,
　　　This is a long preamble of a tale!"
　　　And whan the Somonour herde the Frere gale,°　　*speak up*
　　　"Lo," quod the Somonour, "Goddes armes two![2]
　　　A frere wol entremette hym evere mo![3]
835　Lo, goode men, a flye and eek a frere
　　　Wol falle in every dyssh and mateere![4]
　　　What spekestow° of preambulacioun?°　*what do you say | preambling*
　　　What! Amble or trotte° or pees° or go sit doun!　　*trot | pace*
　　　Thou lettest° oure disport° in this manere."　　　*spoil | fun*
840　"Ye, woltow so,° sire Somonour?" quod the
　　　Frere.　　　　　　　　　　　　　　　　　*will you say so*
　　　"Now by my feith, I shal er that I go
　　　Telle of a somonour swich a tale or two,
　　　That alle the folk shal laughen in this place!"
　　　"Now elles,° Frere, I bishrewe° thy face!"　　*otherwise | curse*
845　Quod this Somonour, "and I bishrewe me
　　　But if° I telle tales two or thre　　　　　　　　*unless*
　　　Of freres er I come to Sidyngborne![5]
　　　That I shal make thyn herte for to morne,°　　　*mourn*
　　　For wel I woot thy pacience is gon."
850　Oure Hoost cride, "Pees,° and that anon!"　　　*peace*
　　　And seyde, "Lat the womman telle hire tale.
　　　Ye fare° as folk that dronken were of ale!　　　*behave*
　　　Do, dame, telle forth youre tale, and that is best."
　　　"Alredy,° sire," quod she, "right as yow lest,°　*ready | wish*
855　If I have licence of this worthy Frere."
　　　"Yis, dame," quod he, "tel forth, and I wol heere."

HEERE ENDETH THE WYF OF BATHE HIR PROLOGE
AND BIGYNNETH HIR TALE

---

[1]　*Do ... lyf*　Do as you wish as long as you live.

[2]　*Goddes armes two*　God's two arms. This is an oath like those uniformly condemned by the Church.

[3]　*A ... mo*　A friar will always put himself in the middle of things.

[4]　*Wol ... mateere*　Will fall into every dish and matter.

[5]　*Sidyngborne*　I.e., Sittingbourne, a small town about forty miles from London on the road to Canterbury.

THE WIFE OF BATH'S TALE

In th'olde dayes of Kyng Arthour,
Of which that Britons speken greet honour,[1]
Al was this land fulfild of° fairye.[2]   *filled up with*
860 The Elf Queene with hir joly compaignye
Daunced ful ofte in many a grene mede.°   *meadow*
This was the olde opinion, as I rede°—   *read*
I speke of manye hundred yeres ago.
But now kan no man se none elves mo,°   *no more elves*
865 For now the grete charitee and prayeres
Of lymytours[3] and othere hooly° freres   *holy*
That serchen every lond and every streem,
As thikke as motes° in the sonne beem,   *dust particles*
Blessynge halles, chambres, kichenes, boures,°   *bedrooms*
870 Citees, burghes,° castels, hye toures,°   *fortified towns / towers*
Thropes,° bernes,° shipnes,°
    dayeryes°—   *villages / barns / stables / dairies*
This maketh° that ther been° no fairyes.   *causes it / are*
For theras° wont° to walken was an elf,   *where / accustomed*
Ther walketh now the lymytour° hymself   *friar*
875 In undermeles° and in morwenynges,   *early afternoons / mornings*
And seyth his matyns° and his hooly
    thynges°   *morning service / prayers*
As he gooth in his lymytacioun.°   *limited area*
Wommen may go saufly° up and doun: *safely*
In every bussh or under every tree
880 Ther is noon oother incubus[4] but he,
And he ne wol doon hem but dishonour.[5]
And so bifel° that this Kyng Arthour   *it happened*
Hadde in hous a lusty bachelor°   *young knight*
That on a day cam ridynge fro ryver,°   *from a river*
885 And happed that, allone° as he was born,   *alone*
He saugh a mayde° walkynge hym biforn,°   *maid / in front of him*
Of° which mayde anon, maugree° hir heed,°   *from / despite / will*
By verray° force birafte° hire maydenhed,   *true / stole*

For which oppressioun was swich clamour°   *outcry*
890 And swich pursute° unto the Kyng Arthour,   *appeal*
That dampned° was this knyght for to be
    deed°   *condemned / dead*
By cours of lawe, and sholde han lost his heed—
Paraventure° swich was the statut tho°—   *by chance / then*
But that the queene and othere ladyes mo
895 So longe preyden° the kyng of grace,°   *requested / mercy*
Til he his lyf hym graunted in the place
And yaf hym to the queene al at hir wille
To chese° wheither she wolde hym save or spille.°   *choose / kill*
The queene thanketh the kyng with al hir myght
900 And after this thus spak she to the knyght
Whan that she saugh hir tyme upon a day:
"Thou standest yet," quod she, "in swich array°   *condition*
That of thy lyf yet hastow° no suretee.°   *have you / certainty*
I grante thee lyf if thou kanst tellen me
905 What thyng is it that wommen moost desiren.
Bewar and keepe thy nekke boon° from iren!°   *bone / iron*
And if thou kanst nat tellen it anon,
Yet shal I yeve thee leve for to gon°   *go*
A twelf month and a day to seche° and leere°   *seek / learn*
910 An answere suffisant° in this mateere.   *sufficient*
And suretee° wol I han er that thou pace°—   *guarantee / leave*
Thy body for to yelden° in this place."   *return*
Wo° was this knyght, and sorwefully he siketh,°   *sad / sighs*
But he may nat do al as hym liketh.°   *as he wishes*
915 And at the laste he chees° hym for to wende,°   *chooses / go*
And come agayn right at the yeres° ende   *year's*
With swich answere as God wolde hym purveye,°   *provide*
And taketh his leve and wendeth forth his weye.
He seketh every hous and every place
920 Whereas° he hopeth for to fynde grace   *where*
To lerne what thyng wommen loven moost,
But he ne koude arryven in no coost°   *region*
Wheras he myghte fynde in this mateere
Two creatures accordynge° in feere.°   *agreeing / together*
925 Somme seyde wommen loven best richesse;
Somme seyde honour, somme seyde jolynesse,°   *jollity*
Somme riche array.° Somme seyden lust
    abedde°   *clothing / in bed*
And oftetyme to be wydwe° and wedde.°   *widowed / married*
Somme seyde that oure hertes been moost esed°   *refreshed*
930 Whan that we been° yflatered and yplesed.   *are*

---

[1] *Kyng Arthour … honour* Legendary British king of roughly the fifth or sixth century CE, the subject of many medieval tales and romances.

[2] *fairye* Supernatural beings known as elves or fairies.

[3] *lymytours* Friars who were licensed to preach in a limited area in a parish or county.

[4] *incubus* Devilish spirit who would appear to women in dreams and thereby impregnate them.

[5] *ne … dishonour* Will do them nothing but dishonor.

He gooth ful ny the sothe, I wol nat lye![1]
A man shal wynne us best with flaterye
And with attendance° and with bisynesse°   attention / diligence
Been we° ylymed[2] bothe moore and lesse.   we are
935   And somme seyn that we loven best
For to be free and so do right° as us lest°   just / wish
And that no man repreve us° of oure vice   complain to us
But seye that we be wise and nothyng° nyce.°   not / foolish
For trewely, ther is noon° of us alle,   none
940   If any wight° wol clawe° us on the galle,°   person / claw / a sore
That we nel kike,° for he seith us sooth.   will not kick
Assay° and he shal fynde it that so dooth.   try
For be we never so vicious° withinne,°   wicked / within
We wol been holden° wise and clene   wish to be considered
of synne.
945   And somme seyn that greet delit han we
For to been holden stable and eek secree,°   discreet
And in o° purpos stedefastly to dwelle,   one
And nat biwreye° thyng° that men us telle.   betray / something
But that tale is nat worth a rake-stele!°   handle of a rake
950   Pardee, we wommen konne nothyng hele.[3]
Witnesse on Myda.[4] Wol ye heere the tale?
Ovyde, amonges othere thynges smale,
Seyde Myda hadde under his longe heres°   hairs
Growynge upon his heed two asses eres,
955   The which vice he hydde as he best myghte
Ful subtilly° from every mannes sighte,   carefully
That save his wyf, ther wiste of it namo.°   no one else
He loved hire moost and triste° hire also.   trusted
He preyde° hire that to no creature   asked
960   She sholde tellen of his disfigure.°   disfigurement
She swoor hym nay: for al this world to wynne°   gain
She nolde° do that vileynye or synne   would not
To make hir housbonde han so foul a name.
She nolde nat telle it for hir owene shame.
965   But nathelees, hir thoughte that she dyde,°   would die
That° she so longe sholde a conseil° hyde.   if / secret

Hir thoughte it swal so soore aboute hir herte
That nedely som word hire moste asterte.[5]
And sith she dorste° telle it to no man,   dared
970   Doun to a mareys° faste by° she ran;   marsh / close by
Til she cam there hir herte was afyre.°   on fire
And as a bitore[6] bombleth° in the myre,°   calls out / mud
She leyde hir mouth unto the water doun.
"Biwreye me nat, thou water, with thy soun,"°   sound
975   Quod she. "To thee I telle it and namo:
Myn housbonde hath longe asses erys two!
Now is myn herte al hool.° Now is it oute!   whole
I myghte no lenger kepe it, out of doute."°   without doubt
Heere may ye se,° thogh we a tyme° abyde,   see / for a time
980   Yet out it moot!° We kan no conseil hyde.   must (go)
The remenant of the tale if ye wol heere,
Redeth Ovyde, and ther ye may it leere.°   learn
This knyght of which my tale is specially,
Whan that he saugh he myghte nat come therby,
985   This is to sey, what wommen love moost,
Withinne his brest ful sorweful was the goost.°   spirit
But hoom he gooth. He myghte nat sojourne.°   delay
The day was come that homward moste he tourne.
And in his wey it happed hym to ryde
990   In al this care under a forest syde
Wheras he saugh upon a daunce[7] go
Of ladyes foure and twenty and yet mo,
Toward the which daunce he drow ful yerne°   drew very eagerly
In hope that som wysdom sholde he lerne.
995   But certeinly, er he cam fully there,
Vanysshed was this daunce he nyste° where.   knew not
No creature saugh he that bar lyf,°   bore life
Save on the grene° he saugh sittynge a wyf°—   meadow / woman
A fouler° wight ther may no man devyse.°   uglier / imagine
1000   Agayn° the knyght this olde wyf gan ryse°   towards / rose up
And seyde, "Sire Knyght, heer forth ne lith° no
wey.°   lies / road
Tel me what that ye seken, by youre fey.°   faith
Paraventure it may the bettre be;

---

1 *He ... lye* He gets very near the truth, I will not lie.

2 *ylymed* Limed. Lime was used to catch birds.

3 *Pardee ... hele* By God, we women know nothing about how to keep a secret.

4 *Myda* I.e., Midas. See Ovid's *Metamorphoses*, Book 11 (although in Ovid's version it is the king's barber, not his wife, who whispers the secret).

5 *Hir thoughte ... asterte* It seemed to her that it became so sorely swollen around her heart. That by necessity some word had to burst out.

6 *bitore* I.e., bittern, a small heron.

7 *Wheras ... daunce* One way in which mortals were said to encounter elves was at night in the woods, where the elves performed a ritual dance.

	Thise olde folk kan° muchel° thyng," quod she. *know / many*
1005	"My leeve° mooder,"° quod this knyght certeyn, *dear / mother*
	"I nam but° deed but if° that I kan seyn *am as good as / unless*
	What thyng it is that wommen moost desire.
	Koude ye me wisse, I wolde wel quite youre hire."[1]
	"Plight° me thy trouthe° heere in myn hand," *pledge / word*
	quod she,
1010	"The nexte thyng that I requere° thee, *ask of*
	Thou shalt it do if it lye in thy myght,
	And I wol telle it yow° er it be nyght." *to you*
	"Have heer my trouthe," quod the knyght. "I grante."
	"Thanne," quod she, "I dar° me wel avante° *dare / boast*
1015	Thy lyf is sauf,° for I wol stonde therby. *safe*
	Upon my lyf, the queene wol seye as I.
	Lat se° which is the proudeste of hem alle *let's see*
	That wereth on a coverchief° or a calle° *kerchief / hairnet*
	That dar seye nay of that I shal thee teche.° *teach*
1020	Lat us go forth withouten lenger speche."
	Tho° rowned° she a pistel° in his ere *then / whispered / lesson*
	And bad hym to be glad and have no fere.
	Whan they be comen to the court, this knyght
	Seyde he had holde° his day as he hadde hight° *kept / promised*
1025	And redy was his answere, as he sayde.
	Full many a noble wyf and many a mayde
	And many a wydwe,° for that they been° wise, *widow / are*
	The queene hirself sittynge as justise,° *sitting as a judge*
	Assembled been° his answere for to heere, *are*
1030	And afterward this knyght was bode°
	appeere.° *commanded / to appear*
	To every wight comanded was silence
	And that the knyght sholde telle in audience° *in their hearing*
	What thyng that worldly wommen loven best.
	This knyght ne stood nat° stille as doth a
	best,° *did not stand / beast*
1035	But to his questioun anon answerde
	With manly voys,° that al the court it herde. *voice*
	"My lige° lady, generally," quod he, *liege*
	"Wommen desiren to have sovereynetee *to have sovereignty*
	As wel over hir housbond as hir love
1040	And for to been in maistrie hym above.
	This is youre mooste° desir, thogh ye me kille. *greatest*
	Dooth as yow list. I am at youre wille."
	In al the court ne was ther° wyf ne mayde *there was neither*

	Ne wydwe that contraried that he sayde,
1045	But seyden he was worthy han° his lyf. *to have*
	And with that word up stirte° the olde wyf *jumped*
	Which that the knyght saugh sittynge in the grene.
	"Mercy," quod she, "my sovereyn lady queene!
	Er that youre court departe, do me right.
1050	I taughte this answere unto the knyght,
	For which he plighte° me his trouthe° there, *promised / word*
	The firste thyng I wolde hym requere,
	He wolde it do if it lay in his myght.
	Bifore the court thanne preye° I thee, sire knyght," *ask*
1055	Quod she, "that thou me take unto thy wyf.
	For wel thou woost° that I have kept thy lyf. *know*
	If I seye fals, sey nay, upon thy fey!"° *faith*
	This knyght answerde, "Allas and weylawey!° *woe is me*
	I woot° right wel that swich° was my
	biheste.° *know / such / promise*
1060	For Goddes love, as chees° a newe requeste! *choose*
	Taak° al my good,° and lat° my body go!" *take / possessions / let*
	"Nay thanne,"° quod she, "I shrewe° us bothe two, *then / curse*
	For thogh that I be foul, oold, and poore,
	I nolde° for al the metal ne for oore° *would not / ore*
1065	That under erthe° is grave° or lith° above *earth / buried / lies*
	But if thy wyf I were and eek thy love."
	"My love!" quod he. "Nay, my dampnacioun!° *damnation*
	Allas, that any of my nacioun° *family*
	Sholde evere so foule disparaged° be!" *badly shamed*
1070	But al for noght! Th'end is this: that he
	Constreyned° was. He nedes moste hire wedde, *compelled*
	And taketh his olde wyf and gooth to bedde.
	Now wolden som men seye paraventure° *perhaps*
	That for my necligence I do no cure° *care*
1075	To tellen yow the joye and al th'array° *the arrangements*
	That at the feeste was that ilke° day *same*
	To which thyng shortly answere I shal.
	I seye ther nas° no joye ne feeste at al. *was no*
	Ther nas° but hevynesse and muche sorwe. *was nothing*
1080	For prively he wedded hire on a morwe,° *morning*
	And al day after hidde hym as an owle,
	So wo was hym, his wyf looked so foule.
	Greet was the wo the knyght hadde in his thoght
	Whan he was with his wyf abedde ybroght.[2]
1085	He walweth,° and he turneth to and fro. *writhes about*

---

[1] *Koude … hire* If you could inform me, I would pay you back well.

[2] *Whan … ybroght* It was a custom for wedding guests to escort the bride and groom to their bedroom.

His olde wyf lay smylynge° evere mo   *smiling*
And seyde, "O deere housbonde, benedicitee,°   *bless you*
Fareth° every knyght thus with his wyf as ye?   *behaves*
Is this the lawe of Kyng Arthures hous?
1090 Is every knyght of his so dangerous?°   *standoffish*
I am youre owene love and youre wyf;
I am she which that saved hath youre lyf.
And certes, yet ne dide° I yow nevere unright:°   *did not | injustice*
Why fare ye thus with me this firste nyght?
1095 Ye faren lyk a man had lost his wit.
What is my gilt?° For Goddes love, tel it,   *guilt*
And it shal been amended if I may."
"Amended!" quod this knyght. "Allas, nay! Nay!
It wol nat been amended nevere mo.°   *forever more*
1100 Thou art so loothly° and so oold° also,   *ugly | old*
And therto comen of so lough° a kynde,°   *low | lineage*
That litel wonder is thogh° I walwe° and
    wynde.°   *though | writhe | twist about*
So wolde God myn herte wolde breste!"°   *burst*
"Is this," quod she, "the cause of youre unreste?"
1105 "Ye, certeinly," quod he, "no wonder is!"
"Now sire," quod she, "I koude amende al this
If that me liste° er it were dayes thre,°   *I wished | three days*
So wel ye myghte bere yow unto me.[1]
But for° ye speken of swich gentillesse   *because*
1110 As is descended out of old richesse,
That therfor sholden ye be gentilmen,
Swich arrogance is nat worth an hen!
Looke who that is moost vertuous alway,
Pryvee and apert and moost entendeth ay
1115 To do the gentil dedes that he kan:[2]
Taak hym for the grettest gentilman.
Crist wole° we clayme° of hym oure
    gentillesse,   *desires that | claim*
Nat of oure eldres° for hire old richesse.   *ancestors*
For thogh they yeve us al hir heritage,
1120 For which we clayme to been of heigh parage,°   *lineage*
Yet may they nat biquethe° for nothyng   *bequeath*
To noon° of us hir vertuous lyvyng°   *none | living*
That made hem° gentilmen ycalled be,   *them*
And bad us folwen hem in swich degree.

1125 Wel kan the wise poete of Florence
That highte Dant° speken in this
    sentence.°   *is named Dante | matter*
Lo, in swich maner rym° is Dantes tale: *such a kind of rhyme*
'Ful selde up riseth by his branches smale
Prowesse of man.[3] For God of his goodnesse
1130 Wole° that of hym we clayme oure gentillesse.'   *wishes*
For of oure eldres may we nothyng clayme
But temporel thyng° that man may hurte and
    mayme.°   *temporal things | maim*
Eek every wight woot this as wel as I.
If gentillesse were planted natureelly°   *implanted by nature*
1135 Unto a certeyn lynage doun the lyne,°   *line (of generations)*
Pryvee nor apert thanne wolde they nevere fyne
To doon of gentillesse the faire office.[4]
They myghte do no vileynye or vice.
Taak fyr° and ber° it in the derkeste hous   *fire | carry*
1140 Bitwix this and the mount of Kaukasous°   *Caucasus*
And lat men shette the dores and go thenne:°   *go away*
Yet wole the fyr as faire lye° and brenne°   *blaze | burn*
As twenty thousand men myghte it biholde.
His° office natureel ay° wol it holde,   *its | ever*
1145 Up peril of my lyf, til that it dye.[5]
Heere may ye se wel how that genterye
Is nat annexed° to possessioun,   *linked*
Sith folk ne doon hir operacioun°   *do not behave*
Alwey as dooth the fyr, lo, in his kynde.°   *according to its nature*
1150 For God it woot, men may wel often fynde
A lordes sone do shame and vileynye,
And he that wole han° pris of° his gentrye,   *will have | esteem for*
For he was born of a gentil hous
And hadde hise eldres noble and vertuous,
1155 And nel hymselven° do no gentil dedis°   *will not himself | deeds*
Ne folwen his gentil auncestre that deed° is,   *dead*
He nys nat° gentil, be he duc° or erl,°   *is not | duke | earl*
For vileyns synful dedes make a cherl.°   *churl*
For gentillesse nys but° renomee°   *is not | renown*

---

[1] *So ... me* Provided that you might behave yourself well towards me.

[2] *Looke ... kan* Look for whoever is always most virtuous in private and in public and always strives to do the most noble deeds.

[3] *Ful ... man* The excellence of a man seldom extends to the further branches (of his family tree); i.e., the sons are seldom worthy of the father. Cf. Dante's *Convivio* 4 and *Purgatorio* 7.121.

[4] *Pryvee ... office* Then they would never stop doing the fair office of gentle deeds either in private or in public.

[5] *His ... dye* Upon my life, it will always perform its natural function (i.e., burn) until it dies.

1160 Of thyne auncestres for hire heigh bountee,° *their high goodness*
Which is a strange° thyng to thy persone. *separate*
Thy gentillesse cometh fro God allone.
Thanne comth oure verray gentillesse of grace;
It was nothyng biquethe us° with oure
place.° *bequeathed to us / social position*
1165 Thenketh how noble, as seith Valerius,
Was thilke° Tullius Hostillius,[1] *that*
That out of poverte roos° to heigh noblesse. *rose*
Reed Senek and redeth eek Boece:[2]
Ther shul ye seen expres° that no drede° is *specifically / doubt*
1170 That he is gentil that dooth gentil dedis.
And therfore, leeve housbonde, I thus conclude,
Al° were it that myne auncestres weren
rude,° *although / of low birth*
Yet may the hye° God—and so hope I— *high*
Grante me grace to lyven° vertuously. *live*
1175 Thanne am I gentil whan that I bigynne° *begin*
To lyven vertuously and weyve synne.° *avoid sin*
And theras° ye of poverte me repreeve,° *since / reproach*
The hye God on whom that we bileeve
In wilful° poverte chees° to lyve his lyf. *voluntary / chose*
1180 And certes, every man, mayden, or wyf
May understonde that Jesus Hevene kyng° *King of Heaven*
Ne wolde nat chesen° vicious lyvyng. *choose*
Glad° poverte is an honeste thyng, certeyn. *joyful*
This wole Senec and othere clerkes° seyn.° *writers / say*
1185 Whoso that halt hym payd of° his poverte, *satisfied with*
I holde° hym riche, al° hadde he nat a sherte. *consider / although*
He that coveiteth° is a povere wight, *covets*
For he wolde han that° is nat in his myght. *what*
But he that noght hath ne coveiteth have° *and does not covet*
1190 Is riche, although ye holde hym but a knave.
Verray poverte, it syngeth properly.
Juvenal[3] seith of poverte myrily,° *merrily*
'The povre man, whan he goth by the weye,° *along the road*
Bifore the theves he may synge and pleye.'
1195 Poverte is hateful good and, as I gesse,

A ful greet bryngere° out of bisynesse,° *very great bringer / busyness*
A greet amendere° eek of sapience° *improver / wisdom*
To hym that taketh it in pacience.° *patience*
Poverte is this, although it seme alenge:° *wretched*
1200 Possessioun that no wight wol chalenge.° *claim*
Poverte ful ofte, whan a man is lowe,
Maketh° his God and eek hymself to knowe. *causes*
Poverte a spectacle° is, as thynketh me, *lens*
Thurgh° which he may hise verray° freendes see. *through / true*
1205 And therfore sire, syn that I noght yow greve,° *do not grieve you*
Of my poverte namoore° ye me repreve. *no more*
Now sire, of elde° ye repreve me, *old age*
And certes, sire, thogh noon auctoritee
Were in no book, ye gentils° of honour *nobles*
1210 Seyn that men sholde an oold wight doon favour° *do honor*
And clepe° hym fader for youre gentillesse. *call*
And auctours° shal I fynden, as I gesse. *authorities*
Now ther° ye seye that I am foul and old: *where*
Than drede° you noght to been a cokewold.[4] *fear*
1215 For filthe and eelde, also moot I thee,° *might I thrive*
Been grete wardeyns upon° chastitee. *guardians of*
But nathelees, syn I knowe youre delit,° *delight*
I shal fulfille youre worldly appetit.
Chese now," quod she, "oon of thise thynges tweye:° *two*
1220 To han me foul and old til that I deye
And be to yow a trewe, humble wyf
And nevere yow displese° in al my lyf, *displease you*
Or elles° ye wol han me yong and fair *else*
And take youre aventure of the repair
1225 That shal be to youre hous bycause of me,
Or in som oother place, may wel be.[5]
Now chese yourselven wheither that yow
liketh."° *whichever pleases you*
This knyght avyseth° hym and sore siketh,° *considers / sorely sighs*
But atte laste he seyde in this manere:
1230 "My lady and my love and wyf so deere,
I put me in youre wise governance.
Cheseth youreself which may be moost plesance° *most pleasant*
And moost honour to yow and me also.
I do no fors° the wheither of the two, *I do not care*
1235 For as yow liketh, it suffiseth me."

---

1 *Valerius ... Hostillius* Tullius Hostillius started life as a peasant
and rose to become king. The story is told by the Roman writer
Valerius Maximus.

2 *Senek* I.e., Seneca, Stoic philosopher (c. 5 BCE–65 CE); *Boece*
I.e., Boethius. See his *Consolation of Philosophy*, book 3, prose 6 and
metre 3.

3 *Juvenal* Roman poet and satirist (55–127 CE).

4 *cokewold* I.e., cuckold, a man whose wife has been unfaithful to
him.

5 *And ... be* And take your chances of the visiting (i.e., by lovers)
at your house, or perhaps in some other places, in order to see me.

"Thanne have I gete° of yow maistrie,"° quod   *gotten / mastery*
   she,
"Syn I may chese and governe as me lest?"°   *as I wish*
"Ye certes, wyf," quod he, "I holde it best."
"Kys me," quod she, "we be no lenger wrothe.°   *angry*
1240 For by my trouthe,° I wol be to yow bothe.   *truth*
This is to seyn, ye, bothe° fair and good.   *indeed both*
I prey to God that I moote sterven wood°   *die crazy*
But° I to yow be also good and trewe   *unless*
As evere was wyf, syn that the world was newe.
1245 And but° I be tomorn° as fair to seene   *unless / tomorrow*
As any lady, emperice,° or queene   *empress*
That is bitwixe the est and eke the west,
Dooth° with my lyf and deth right° as yow lest.°   *do / just / wish*
Cast up the curtyn. Looke how that it is."
1250 And whan the knyght saugh verraily al this,

That she so fair was and so yong therto,
For joye he hente° hire in hise armes two.   *held*
His herte° bathed in a bath of blisse.   *heart*
A thousand tyme arewe° he gan hire kisse.   *in a row*
1255 And she obeyed hym in everythyng
That myghte doon hym plesance or likyng.°   *enjoyment*
And thus they lyve unto hir lyves ende
In parfit° joye. And Jesu Crist us sende   *perfect*
Housbondes meeke, yonge, and fressh abedde°   *in bed*
1260 And grace to t'overbyde° hem that we wedde.   *control*
And eek I pray Jhesu shorte hir lyves°   *shorten their lives*
That nat wol be governed by hir wyves.
And olde and angry nygardes° of dispence,°   *skinflints / spending*
God sende hem soone verray pestilence!

HEERE ENDETH THE WYVES TALE OF BATHE

The Merchant's Prologue and Tale

The Clerk's tale of an impossibly patient wife, Griselda, provokes the Merchant, who has been married for two months. Although he says that he will say no more about his own sorrow, his tale of January, the wealthy old knight cuckolded by his young wife and his squire, seems to represent his own disillusioning experience. The Merchant's voice is bitter and cynical, describing a world of lust and self-delusion concealing itself behind respectability.

    Like that of the Miller, *The Merchant's Tale* is a *fabliau*, and turns on the efforts of a blind man to guard his young wife and her ability to trick him into doubting his own eyes. However, it is a *fabliau* that repeatedly breaks the conventions of the genre. The business of the *fabliau* plot, centering around the lover in the pear tree, is largely confined to the last hundred lines and the bulk of the tale is given over to the discussion of marriage in theory and the description of marriage in practice. The tale makes its characters members of the knightly class, but their world is anything but chivalric. Most unattractive is January's calculation that, having spent his life in lechery, he can now save his soul and spend the rest of his days in comfort and sexual pleasure by marrying a young wife since, as he claims, a man

cannot sin with his own wife any more than he can cut himself with his own knife (line 628). This view, one that a medieval theologian would regard as utterly mistaken, is enthusiastically supported by the toadying courtier Placebo.

    The tale is set in January's castle, where Placebo triumphs over the wise Justinus, and in the enclosed garden, a symbolically charged location with ironic echoes of the garden of Paradise or the garden of love in works such as *The Romance of the Rose*. Like *The Knight's Tale*, *The Merchant's Tale* introduces a second level where the struggle of the earthly characters is echoed by the debate between the pagan gods. The debate between Pluto and Proserpina echoes the discussion of experience and authority in *The Wife of Bath's Prologue*, but the appearance of the gods in this *fabliau* world, even though they are the gods of the underworld, is disconcerting. More disconcerting still is the role of the three human lovers, especially January. His appeal to May to enter the garden, couched in language borrowed from *The Song of Songs* (l. 927–33) or his claim that he did not choose her for covetousness but for love (lines 954–56) make him a far more complex, if not necessarily sympathetic, character than the standard figure of the old cuckold in the *fabliaux*.

Opening page of *The Merchant's Tale*, Ellesmere manuscript. (Reprinted by permission of *The Huntington Library, San Marino, California*. EL26C9F72r.)

THE MERCHANT'S PROLOGUE

THE PROLOGE OF THE MARCHANTES TALE

"Wepyng° and waylyng,° care and oother
    sorwe°   *weeping / wailing / other sorrow*
I knowe ynogh° on even° and
    amorwe,"°   *enough / evening / morning*
Quod° the Marchant, "and so doon° othere
    mo°   *said / do / many others*
That wedded been.° I trowe° that it be so,   *are married / believe*
5   For wel° I woot° it fareth° so with me!   *well / know / fares*
I have a wyf,° the worste that may be,   *wife*
For thogh the feend° to hire° ycoupled°   *devil / her / married*
    were,
She wolde hym overmacche,° I dar wel swere!° *overcome / swear*
What° sholde I yow° reherce° in
    special°   *why / to you / describe / specially*
10   Hir hye° malice? She is a shrewe° at
    al.°   *her extreme / nag / completely*
Ther is a long and large difference
Bitwix Grisildis[1] grete pacience°   *great patience*
And of my wyf the passyng° crueltee.   *surpassing*
Were I unbounden,° also moot I thee,°   *released / might I thrive*
15   I wolde nevere eft° comen° in the snare *would never again / come*
We wedded men lyve in—sorwe and care.
Assaye° whoso wole,° and he shal fynde   *try / who will*
I seye sooth,° by Seint Thomas of Ynde![2]   *say truth*
As for the moore part,° I sey nat alle.°   *greater part / say not all*
20   God shilde° that it sholde so bifalle!°   *prevent / happen*
    "A,° good sire Hoost, I have ywedded bee°   *ah / been*
Thise monthes two and moore nat,° pardee,° *not more / by God*
And yet I trowe he that al his lyve°   *life*
Wyflees° hath been, though that men wolde him
    ryve°   *wifeless / stab*
25   Unto the herte,° ne koude° in no
    manere°   *heart / could not / manner*
Tellen so muchel° sorwe as I now heere°   *much / here*
Koude tellen of my wyves cursednesse!"
    "Now," quod oure Hoost, "Marchaunt, so God yow blesse,
Syn° ye so muchel knowen of that art,   *since*

30   Ful hertely° I pray yow, telle us part."   *heartily*
    "Gladly," quod he, "but of myn owene soore,
For soory herte I telle may namoore."[3]

THE MERCHANT'S TALE

HEERE BIGYNNETH THE MARCHANTES TALE

Whilom° ther was dwellynge° in
    Lumbardye°   *once / living / Lombardy*
A worthy knyght that born was of Pavye,°   *Pavia*
35   In which he lyved in greet prosperitee.
And sixty yeer a wyflees man was hee
And folwed ay° his bodily delyt°   *always followed / delight*
On wommen, theras° was his appetyt,°   *where / appetite*
As doon thise fooles that been seculeer.°   *worldly*
40   And whan that he wes passed sixty yeer,
Were it° for hoolynesse° or for
    dotage°   *whether it was / holiness / senility*
I kan nat seye, but swich a greet corage°   *desire*
Hadde this knyght to been a wedded man,
That day and nyght he dooth al that he kan
45   T'espien° where he myghte wedded be,   *to find out*
Preyinge° oure Lord to graunten° him that he *praying to / grant*
Mighte ones° knowe of thilke blisful lyf°   *once / that happy life*
That is bitwixe° an housbonde and his wyf,   *between*
And for to lyve under that hooly boond,°   *bond*
50   With which that first God man and womman bond.° *bound*
"Noon oother lyf," seyde he, "is worth a bene,°   *bean*
For wedlok is so esy° and so clene,°   *comforting / pure*
That in this world it is a Paradys."
Thus seyde this olde knyght, that was so wys.°   *wise*
55   And certeinly, as sooth° as God is kyng,   *true*
To take a wyf, it is a glorious thyng!
And namely° whan a man is oold° and
    hoor.°   *especially / old / gray*
Thanne° is a wyf the fruyt° of his
    tresor.°   *then / best part / treasure*
Thanne sholde he take a yong wyf and a feir,°   *fair*
60   On which he myghte engendren hym° an heir   *beget himself*
And lede° his lyf in joye and in solas,°   *lead / comfort*

---

[1] *Grisildis* Griselda, the subject of the previous tale by the Clerk, was a wife extolled for her patience and fidelity.

[2] *Seint Thomas of Ynde* St. Thomas of India is the Apostle Thomas of the Gospels. His legend made him the Evangelist of India.

[3] *but of … namoore* But I can tell no more of my own sorrow because of my sorrowful heart.

Whereas° thise bacheleris° synge°   *while | these young knights | sing*
   allas,
Whan that they fynden° any adversitee   *find | adversity*
In love, which nys° but childyssh vanytee.   *is nothing | foolishness*
65 And trewely,° it sit wel° to be so   *truly | is fitting*
That bacheleris have often peyne° and wo.°   *pain | woe*
On brotel ground they buylde, and brotelnesse
They fynde whan they wene sikernesse.°[1]   *expect security*
They lyve but as a bryd° or as a beest—   *bird*
70 In libertee and under noon arreest,°   *no hindrance*
Theras° a wedded man in his estaat°   *whereas | condition*
Lyveth a lyf blisful and ordinaat,°   *ordered*
Under this yok° of mariage ybounde.   *yoke*
Wel may his herte in joye and blisse habounde,°   *abound*
75 For who kan be so buxom° as a wyf?   *obedient*
Who is so trewe and eek so ententyf°   *attentive*
To kepe hym syk and hool as is his make?[2]
For wele° or wo, she wole hym nat forsake.   *wellness*
She nys nat° wery° hym to love and serve,   *is not | wearied*
80 Thogh° that he lye bedrede° til he sterve.°   *though | bedridden | die*
And yet somme clerkes° seyn it nys nat so,   *scholars*
Of whiche he, Theofraste,[3] is oon° of tho.°   *one | those*
What force° though Theofraste liste lye?°   *who cares | wants to lie*
"Ne take no wyf," quod he, "for housbondrye,°   *economy*
85 As for to spare in houshold thy dispence.°   *expenses*
A trewe servant dooth moore diligence°   *takes more care*
Thy good° to kepe° than thyn owene wyf,   *possessions | preserve*
For she wol clayme° half part al hir lyf.   *claim*
And if thou be syk,° so God me save,   *sick*
90 Thy verray freendes° or a trewe knave°   *own friends | true servant*
Wol kepe thee bet° than she that waiteth ay°   *better | ever*
After thy good° and hath doon many a day.   *possessions*
And if thou take a wyf unto thyn hoold,°   *under your protection*
Ful lightly° maystow been° a cokewold."[4]   *easily | may you be*
95 This sentence and an hundred thynges° worse   *things*
Writeth this man, ther God his bones corse!°   *curse*
But take no kepe° of al swich vanytee.   *heed*

Deffie° Theofraste and herke° me.   *defy | listen to*
   A wyf is Goddes yifte,° verraily.°   *gift | truly*
100 Alle otherere maner yiftes,° hardily,°   *kinds of gifts | certainly*
As londes,° rentes, pasture, or
   commune,°   *lands | rights to common land*
Or moebles,° alle been yiftes of Fortune   *movable property*
That passen as a shadwe° upon a wal.   *shadow*
But dredelees,° if pleynly° speke I shal,   *doubtless | plainly*
105 A wyf wol laste and in thyn hous endure°   *remain*
Wel lenger than thee list,° paraventure.°   *you wish | perhaps*
   Mariage is a ful greet° sacrement.[5]   *very great*
He which that hath no wyf, I holde hym
   shent!°   *consider him ruined*
He lyveth helplees and al desolat.
110 I speke of folk in seculer estaat.[6]
And herke° why. I sey nat° this for noght:°   *listen to | not | nothing*
That womman is for mannes helpe ywroght.°   *created*
The hye° God, whan he hadde Adam maked   *high*
And saugh hym al allone, bely-naked,°   *completely naked*
115 God of his grete goodnesse seyde than,°   *then*
"Lat us now make an helpe° unto this man   *helper*
Lyk to hymself."[7] And thanne he made him Eve.
Heere may ye se° and heerby may ye preve°   *see | prove*
That wyf is mannes helpe and his confort,
120 His Paradys terrestre° and his disport.°   *earthly | enjoyment*
So buxom° and so vertuous is she,   *obedient*
They moste nedes° lyve in unitee.   *necessarily must*
O° flessh they been, and o flessh as I gesse,   *one*
Hath but oon herte in wele° and in distresse.   *prosperity*
125 A wyf—a,° Seinte Marie, benedicite°—   *ah | bless you*
How myghte a man han° any adversitee   *have*
That hath a wyf? Certes, I can nat seye.
The blisse which that is bitwixe hem tweye,°   *them two*
Ther may no tonge° telle or herte° thynke.   *tongue | heart*
130 If he be povre,° she helpeth hym to swynke.°   *poor | work*
She kepeth his good and wasteth never a deel.°   *a bit*

---

[1] *On brotel ... sikernesse* They build on brittle (i.e., promiscuous) ground and they find brittleness when they expect security (i.e., fidelity).

[2] *Who ... make* Who is as true and attentive as his mate to take care of him when he is sick or healthy?

[3] *Theofraste* Theophrastus wrote *The Golden Book on Marriage*, a work that attacked marriage.

[4] *cokewold* Cuckold, a man whose wife has committed adultery.

---

[5] *Mariage ... sacrement* This is a quotation from Paul's Letter to the Ephesians, 5.32, "sacramentum hoc magnum est," often translated from the Latin to "This is a great mystery." By the thirteenth century marriage had come to be regarded as a sacrament by most Christian theologians.

[6] *in seculer estaat* As opposed to priests, who were forbidden to marry but, by implication, were not destroyed by celibacy.

[7] *Lat ... hymself* See Genesis 2.18.

Al that hire housbonde lust,° hire liketh
   weel;°   *desires / pleases her well*
She seith nat ones° nay whan he seith ye.   *once*
"Do this," seith he. "Al redy, sire," seith she.
135 O, blisful order of wedlok precious,
     Thou art so murye° and eek° so vertuous   *merry / also*
     And so commended and appreved° eek,   *approved*
     That every man that halt hym worth a leek[1]
     Upon his bare knees oughte al his lyf
140 Thanken his God that hym hath sent a wyf
     Or elles preye to God hym for to sende
     A wyf to laste unto his lyves ende.
     For thanne his lyf is set in sikernesse.°   *security*
     He may nat be deceyved, as I gesse,
145 So° that he werke after° his wyves reede.° *provided / follow / advice*
     Thanne may he boldely kepen up his heed,°   *head*
     They been so trewe and therwith al so wyse.
     For which, if thow wolt werken° as the wyse, *will do / wise (man)*
     Do alwey so as wommen wol thee rede.°   *advise*
150   Lo how that Jacob, as thise clerkes rede,°   *these scholars recount*
     By good conseil of his mooder° Rebekke,   *mother*
     Boond the kydes skyn° aboute his nekke,   *kid's skin*
     Thurgh which his fadres benysoun he wan.[2]
     Lo Judith, as the storie eek telle kan,
155 By wys conseil she Goddes peple kepte°   *saved*
     And slow° hym, Olofernus, whil he slepte.[3]   *killed*
     Lo Abigayl, by good conseil how she
     Saved hir housbonde Nabal whan that he
     Sholde han be slayn.[4] And looke, Ester also
160 By good conseil delyvered out of wo

The peple of God and made hym, Mardochee,°   *Mordecai*
Of Assuere° enhaunced° for to be.[5] *Ahasuerus (Xerxes) / promoted*
   Ther nys nothyng in gree superlatyf,°   *highest degree*
As seith Senek, above an humble wyf.[6]
165 Suffre thy wyves tonge, as Catoun bit:[7]
     She shal comande, and thou shalt suffren it.
     And yet she wole obeye of curteisye.
     A wyf is kepere of thyn housbondrye.°   *household*
     Wel may the sike° man biwaille° and wepe, *sick / complain*
170 Theras° ther nys no wyf the hous to kepe.   *where*
     I warne thee if wisely thou wolt wirche,°   *work*
     Love wel thy wyf, as Crist loved his Chirche.
     If thou lovest thyself, thou lovest thy wyf;
     No man hateth his flessh, but in his lyf
175 He fostreth° it.[8] And therfore bidde° I thee *nurtures / command*
     Cherisse thy wyf, or thou shalt nevere thee.°   *thrive*
     Housbonde and wyf, whatso men jape° or
       pleye,°   *whatever people say in joke / play*
     Of worldly folk holden the siker weye.°   *sure way*
     They been so knyt,° ther may noon harm
       bityde°—   *joined together / befall*
180 And namely upon the wyves syde.
     For which° this Januarie, of whom I
       tolde,°   *these reasons / told you*
     Considered hath, inwith hise dayes olde,°   *in his old age*
     The lusty° lyf, the vertuous quyete°   *vigorous / quiet*
     That is in mariage hony-sweete.°   *honey-sweet*
185 And for hise freendes on a day he sente

---

1 *halt ... leek* Holds himself worth a leek (i.e., worth anything at all).

2 *Thurgh ... wan* Through which he won his father's blessing. See Genesis 27.5–29. It also appears, along with the following examples of Judith, Esther, and Abigail, the saying misattributed to Seneca, the saying of Cato, and the passages from Paul's Letter to the Ephesians, in Albertano da Brescia's *Book of Consolation and Counsel.*

3 *Lo Judith ... slepte* The Book of Judith, in the apocryphal portion of the Bible, recounts the story of the widow Judith, who captivates Nebuchadnezzar's general Holofernes with her beauty and then, taking advantage of his drunkenness, beheads him, thus liberating the Jews of Bethulia.

4 *Lo Abigayl ... slayn* David sought vengeance upon Nabal, who had refused to help him in his time of need. Nabal's wife, Abigail, saved her husband's life by secretly meeting David and giving him provisions. See 1 Samuel 25.

5 *And looke ... be* When one of Xerxes's ministers secures a royal decree authorizing the slaughter of all the Jews, Esther, his second wife, reveals herself as a Jew and begs her husband to save her people. Xerxes overturns the decree and replaces the offending minister with Esther's own cousin and adopted father, Mordecai. See the Book of Esther.

6 *Senek* Seneca, the Stoic philosopher (c. 5 BCE–65 CE); *Ther nys ... wyf* The quotation actually comes from the *Mythologies* of Fabius Planciades Fulgentius, a late fifth-century Christian writer known for his elaborate allegorical interpretation of classical writers such as Ovid and Virgil.

7 *Suffre ... bit* Endure your wife's tongue, as Cato commanded. Cf. Cato's *Distichs* 3.23. The Roman moralist Dionysius Cato was reputed in the Middle Ages to be the author of a widely circulating collection of proverbs and wise sayings, often used for teaching Latin in schools.

8 *Love wel ... it* From Paul's Letter to the Ephesians 5.25 and 5.28–29, 33.

To tellen hem th'effect° of his entente.°   *the substance | intent*
  With face sad,° his tale he hath hem toold.   *serious*
He seyde, "Freendes, I am hoor and oold
And almoost, God woot,° on my pittes
        brynke;°   *knows | grave's brink*
190 Upon the soule somwhat moste° I thynke.   *must*
I have my body folily despended.°   *foolishly spent*
Blessed be God that it shal been amended!
For I wol be, certeyn, a wedded man—
And that anoon,° in al the haste I kan,   *at once*
195 Unto som mayde° fair and tendre of age.   *maid*
I prey° yow, shapeth° for my mariage   *ask | arrange*
Al sodeynly,° for I wol nat abyde.°   *quickly | wait*
And I wol fonde t'espien° on my syde   *attempt to find out*
To whom I may be wedded hastily.
200 But forasmuche as ye been mo° than I,   *be more*
Ye shullen° rather swich a thyng espyen   *shall*
Than I, and where me best were to
        allyen.°   *ally myself (through marriage)*
  But o thyng warne I yow, my freendes deere:
I wol noon oold wyf han in no manere.°   *no way*
205 She shal nat passe° twenty yeer, certain.   *exceed*
Oold fissh° and yong flessh wolde I have fayn.°   *fish | gladly*
Bet° is," quod he, "a pyk° than a
        pykerel,°   *better | pike | young pike*
And bet than olde boef° is the tendre veel.°   *beef | veal*
I wol° no womman thritty° yeer of age—   *want | thirty*
210 It is but benestraw and greet forage.[1]
And eek thise olde wydwes,° God it woot,   *widows*
They konne so muchel craft on Wades boot,
So muchel broken harm whan that hem lest,[2]
That with hem sholde I nevere lyve in reste,
215 For sondry scoles maken sotile clerkis.[3]
Womman of manye scoles° half a clerk° is.   *schools | scholar*
But certeynly, a yong thyng may men gye°   *guide*
Right as men may warm wex° with handes
        plye.°   *wax | manipulate*

Wherfore I sey yow pleynly° in a clause,   *plainly*
220 I wol noon oold wyf han, for this cause:
For if so were that I hadde swich myschaunce,°   *misfortune*
That I in hire ne koude han no plesaunce,°   *pleasure*
Thanne sholde I lede° my lyf in avoutrye—   *spend | adultery*
And streight unto the devel whan I dye!°   *die*
225 Ne children sholde I none upon hire geten.°   *beget*
Yet were me levere° that houndes° had me
        eten°   *I would rather | dogs | eaten*
Than that myn heritage[4] sholde falle
In straunge hand. And this I telle yow alle:
I dote nat.° I woot° the cause why   *am not senile | know*
230 Men sholde wedde. And forthermore, woot I
Ther speketh many a man of mariage
That woot namoore of it than woot my page°   *boy servant*
For whiche causes man sholde take a wyf:
Siththe° he may nat lyven° chaast his
        lyf,°   *since | live | chaste (all) his life*
235 Take hym° a wyf with greet devocioun   *let him take*
Bycause of leveful procreacioun°   *lawful procreation*
Of children to th'onour° of God above,   *the honor*
And nat oonly for paramour° or love;   *sex*
And for° they sholde leccherye° eschue   *because | lechery | avoid*
240 And yelde hir dettes whan that they ben due;[5]
Or for that ech of hem sholde helpen oother
In meschief,° as a suster° shal the brother,   *misfortune | sister*
And lyve in chastitee ful holily.°   *very devoutly*
But sires,° by youre leve,° that am nat
        I.°   *sirs | leave | I am not like that*
245 For God be thanked, I dar make avaunt:°   *boast*
I feele my lymes° stark° and suffisaunt°   *limbs | strong | capable*
To do al that a man bilongeth to.°   *is appropriate for a man*
I woot myselven best what I may do.
Though I be hoor, I fare as dooth a tree
250 That blosmeth er that fruyt° ywoxen° bee,   *fruit | ripened*
And blosmy° tree nys neither drye ne deed.   *blossom-filled*
I feele me nowhere hoor but on myn heed.
Myn herte and alle my lymes been as grene
As laurer° thurgh° the yeer is for to
        sene.°   *laurel | throughout | be seen*
255 And syn° that ye han herd al myn entente,   *since*

---

[1] *It ... forage* It is (nothing) but bean-straw and great fodder. In other words, marrying an older woman is a waste.

[2] *They konne ... lest* They have so much skill in Wade's boat (they know), so much about how to cause harm when they wish. Wade was once a famous hero, but only passing references to him survive (including one in Chaucer's *Troilus and Criseyde*, 3.164). The significance of his boat remains obscure.

[3] *For ... clerkis* For a variety of schools makes subtle scholars.

---

[4] *heritage* I.e., lands and property.

[5] *And ... due* And yield their debts when they are due. The reference here is to the marriage debt, of having sex with one's spouse. Cf. *Wife of Bath's Prologue*, line 130.

I prey yow to my wyl° ye wole assente."   *will*
　　Diverse men diversely hym tolde
Of mariage manye ensamples° olde.   *examples*
Somme blamed it. Somme preysed° it,
　　certeyn.°   *praised | certainly*
260　But atte laste, shortly for to seyn,[1]
As al day falleth altercacioun°   *disagreement*
Bitwixen freendes in disputisoun,°   *debate*
Ther fil° a stryf° bitwixe hise bretheren°
　　two,   *fell | strife | his brothers*
Of whiche that oon was cleped° Placebo;   *named*
265　Justinus[2] soothly° called was that oother.   *truly*
　　Placebo seyde, "O Januarie brother,
Ful litel nede° hadde ye, my lord so deere,   *little need*
Conseil to axe° of any that is heere,   *ask*
But that ye been so ful of sapience°   *wisdom*
270　That yow ne liketh° for youre heighe
　　prudence°   *it does not please you | wisdom*
To weyven fro° the word of Salomon.°   *depart from | Solomon*
This word seyde he unto us everychon:°   *every one*
'Wirk° alle thyng by conseil,' thus seyde he,   *work (do)*
'And thanne shaltow° nat repente° thee.'[3]   *shall you | regret*
275　But though that Salomon spak swich a word,
Myn owene deere brother and my lord,
So wysly God my soule brynge at reste,°   *bring to rest*
I holde youre owene conseil is the beste.
For brother myn, of me taak this motyf:°   *thought*
280　I have now been a court-man° al my lyf,   *courtier*
And God it woot, though I unworthy be,
I have stonden° in ful greet° degree   *stood | very high*
Abouten lordes of ful heigh estaat.
Yet hadde I nevere with noon of hem debaat;
285　I nevere hem contraried,° trewely.   *disagreed with them*
I woot wel that my lord kan moore than I.
What that° he seith I holde it ferme° and
　　stable;°   *whatever | firm | certain*
I seye the same or elles thyng semblable.°   *a similar thing*
A ful greet fool is any conseillour
290　That serveth any lord of heigh honour
That dar presume or elles thenken° it,   *think*
That his conseil sholde passe° his lordes wit.   *surpass*

Nay, lordes been no fooles, by my fay!°   *faith*
Ye han youreselven seyd heer today
295　So heigh sentence,° so holily° and weel,° *judgment | devoutly | well*
That I consente and conferme everydeel°   *every part*
Youre wordes alle and youre opinioun.
By God, ther nys no man in al this toun
Nyn Ytaille° that koude bet han sayd.   *nor in Italy*
300　Crist halt hym of this conseil ful wel apayd.[4]
And trewely, it is an heigh corage°   *act of high courage*
Of any man that stapen is in age°   *is stooped by age*
To take a yong wyf, by my fader kyn.°   *father's kin*
Youre herte hangeth on a joly pyn.°   *peg*
305　Dooth° now in the matiere right° as yow leste,° *do | just | wish*
For finally, I holde it for the beste."
　　Justinus, that ay° stille° sat and herde   *ever | quiet*
Right in this wise,° he to Placebo answerde,   *way*
"Now, brother myn, be pacient, I preye,
310　Syn ye han seyd,° and herkneth what I seye.   *have spoken*
Senek among his othere wordes wyse
Seith that a man oghte hym right wel avyse°   *be advised*
To whom he yeveth° his lond or his catel.°   *gives | possessions*
And syn I oghte avyse me right wel
315　To whom I yeve my good° awey fro me,   *possessions*
Wel muchel moore° I oghte avysed be   *all the more*
To whom I yeve my body for alwey.°   *always*
I warne yow wel, it is no childes pley
To take a wyf withouten avysement.°   *advice*
320　Men moste enquere—this is myn assent°—   *my counsel*
Wher° she be wys or sobre or dronkelewe°   *whether | drunken*
Or proud or elles ootherweys a shrewe,
A chidestere° or wastour° of thy good   *nag | waster*
Or riche or poore or elles mannyssh wood.[5]
325　Albeit so that no man fynden shal
Noon in this world that trotteth hool in al,[6]
Ne man ne beest which as men koude devyse;°   *imagine*
But nathelees, it oghte ynough suffise°   *to be enough*
With any wyf, if so were that she hadde
330　Mo° goode thewes° than hire vices badde.   *more | customs*
And al this axeth leyser° for t'enquere.   *requires time*

---

[1] *shortly ... seyn* To say it shortly (i.e., to make a long story short).

[2] *Placebo* Latin: I will please; *Justinus* Implies truth, justice.

[3] *Wirk ... thee* See Ecclesiasticus 32.24.

[4] *apayd* Christ considers himself very well paid by this counsel; i.e., it is pious.

[5] *mannysshe wood* Man-mad; i.e., either as fiercely crazy as a man or, possibly, crazy for men.

[6] *Noon ... al* There is no one in this world who trots perfectly in all respects. The metaphor is drawn from buying horses.

For God it woot, I have wept many a teere°   *tear*
Ful pryvely° syn I have had a wyf.   *privately*
Preyse° whoso wole° a wedded mannes
    lyf,   *praise / whoever wishes to*
335 Certein, I fynde in it but cost and care
And observances° of alle blisses bare.°   *duties / lacking all happiness*
And yet, God woot, my neighebores aboute,
And namely of wommen many a route,°   *crowd*
Seyn that I have the mooste stedefast wyf
340 And eek the mekeste oon° that bereth lyf.°   *meekest one / bears life*
But I woot best where wryngeth° me my sho.°   *pinches / shoe*
Ye mowe for me right as yow liketh do.[1]
Avyseth yow—ye been a man of age—
How that ye entren° into mariage,   *enter*
345 And namely with a yong wyf and a fair.
By hym that made water, erthe, and air,
The yongeste man that is in al this route
Is bisy° ynough to bryngen it aboute   *hard pressed*
To han his wyf allone,[2] trusteth me.
350 Ye shul nat plesen hire fully yeres thre°—   *for three years*
This is to seyn, to doon hire ful plesaunce.°   *do her great pleasure*
A wyf axeth° ful many an observaunce.°   *asks / attention*
I prey yow that ye be nat yvele apayd."°   *displeased*
    "Wel," quod this Januarie, "and hastow
    ysayd?°   *have you finished speaking*
355 Straw for thy Senek and for thy proverbes!
I counte nat a panyer° ful of herbes   *basket*
Of° scole termes.[3] Wyser men than thow,°   *for / you*
As thou has herd, assenteden° right now   *agree*
To my purpos. Placebo, what sey ye?"
360   "I seye it is a cursed man," quod he,
"That letteth° matrimoigne,° sikerly."°   *hinders / matrimony / surely*
And with that word they rysen sodeynly
And been assented fully° that he sholde   *completely agreed*
Be wedded whanne hym liste and where he wolde.
365   Heigh fantasye and curious bisynesse°   *elaborate concern*
Fro day to day gan in the soule impresse
Of Januarie aboute his mariage.
Many fair shape and many a fair visage°   *face*

Ther passeth thurgh his herte nyght by nyght,
370 As whoso° tooke a mirour° polisshed bryght *as if someone / mirror*
And sette it in a commune° market place,   *common*
Thanne sholde he se ful many a figure pace°   *pass*
By his mirour,° and in the same wyse°   *in his mirror / way*
Gan Januarie inwith° his thoght devyse°   *within / imagine*
375 Of maydens whiche that dwellen hym bisyde.°   *lived near him*
He wiste nat wher that he myghte abyde,°   *settle*
For if that oon have beaute in hir face,
Another stant° so in the peples grace°   *stands / favor*
For hire sadnesse° and hire benyngnytee°   *constancy / kindness*
380 That of the peple grettest voys° hath she.   *fame*
And somme were riche and hadden badde name.
But nathelees, bitwixe ernest° and game,°   *seriousness / jest*
He atte laste apoynted hym on oon°   *decided himself upon one*
And leet alle othere from his herte goon
385 And chees° hire of his owene auctoritee.°   *chose / authority*
For love is blynd° alday° and may nat see. *blind / all day (always)*
And whan that he was in his bed ybroght,
He purtreyed° in his herte and in his thoght   *imagined*
Hir fresshe beautee and hir age tendre,
390 Hir myddel smal,° hire armes longe and
    sklendre,°   *small waist / slender*
Hir wise governaunce,° hir gentillesse,°   *behavior / nobility*
Hir wommanly berynge and hire sadnesse.
And whan that he on hire was condescended,°   *decided*
Hym thoughte his choys° myghte nat ben
    amended.°   *choice / improved upon*
395 For whan that he hymself concluded hadde,°   *had decided*
Hym thoughte ech oother mannes wit° so badde, *intelligence*
That inpossible it were to repplye°   *object*
Agayn his choys. This was his fantasye.°   *delusion*
Hise freendes sente he to° at his instaunce°   *for / insistence*
400 And preyed hem° to doon hym that
    plesaunce°   *asked them / pleasure*
That hastily they wolden to hym come.
He wolde abregge° hir labour alle and
    some:°   *shorten / one and all*
Nedeth namoore for hym° to go ne ryde.°   *them / walk nor ride*
He was apoynted° ther he wolde
    abyde.°   *had decided / abide (by his decision)*
405   Placebo cam and eek hise freendes soone,
And alderfirst° he bad° hem alle a boone, *first of all / asked / favor*
That noon of hem none argumentz make
Agayn the purpos which that he hath take,
Which purpos was "plesant to God," seyde he,

---

[1] *Ye … do* You may, as far as I am concerned, do as you wish to do.

[2] *allone* I.e., to himself.

[3] *scole termes* School terms, the type of debates engaged in at the universities, and the language used in such debates.

410 And verray ground° of his prosperitee.°   *true basis | prosperity*
    He seyde ther was a mayden in the toun
    Which that of beautee hadde greet renoun;
    Al° were it so she were of smal degree,°   *although | low-born family*
    Suffiseth hym° hir yowthe and hir beautee.   *sufficed for him*
415 Which° mayde, he seyde, he wolde han to his wyf,   *this*
    To lede in ese and hoolynesse his lyf,
    And thanked God that he myghte han hire al,°   *might have her all*
    That no wight° his blisse parten° shal,   *person | share*
    And preyde hem° to laboure in this nede°   *asked them | need*
420 And shapen° that he faille nat to
         spede.°   *arrange | not fail to succeed*
    For thanne, he seyde, his spirit was at ese.°   *ease*
    "Thanne is," quod he, "nothyng may me displese,
    Save o thyng priketh° in my conscience,   *sticks*
    The which I wol reherce° in youre presence.   *relate*
425   "I have," quod he, "herd seyd ful yoore ago,°   *very long ago*
    Ther may no man han parfite blisses two.°   *two perfect happinesses*
    This is to seye, in erthe and eek in Hevene.
    For though he kepe hym from the synnes
         sevene°   *seven (deadly) sins*
    And eek from every branche of thilke tree,[1]
430 Yet is ther so parfit felicitee°   *happiness*
    And so greet ese° and lust° in mariage,   *comfort | pleasure*
    That evere I am agast° now in myn age   *afraid*
    That I shal lede now so myrie° a lyf,   *merry*
    So delicat,° withouten wo and stryf,   *delightful*
435 That I shal have myn Hevene in earthe here.
    For sith that verray Hevene is boght so deere°   *dearly*
    With tribulacioun and greet penance,
    How sholde I thane, that lyve in swich plesaunce
    As alle wedded men doon with hire wyvys,
440 Come to the blisse ther° Crist eterne° on lyve
         ys?°   *where | eternal | is alive*
    This is my drede, and ye, my bretheren tweye,
    Assoilleth° me this questioun, I preye."   *resolve*
       Justinus, which that hated his folye,°   *folly*
    Answerde anon right° in his japerye,°   *right away | mockery*
445 And for he wolde his longe tale abregge,°   *shorten*
    He wolde noon auctoritee allegge°   *quote*
    But seyde, "Sire, so ther be noon obstacle
    Oother than this, God of his hygh myracle
    And of his hygh mercy may so for yow wirche°   *work*

450 That er ye have youre right of Hooly Chirche,[2]
    Ye may repente of wedded mannes lyf
    In which ye seyn ther is no wo ne stryf.
    And elles, God forbede° but° he sente   *forbid | unless*
    A wedded man hym grace to repente
455 Wel ofte, rather° than a sengle° man.   *sooner | single*
    And therfore, sire—the beste reed° I kan°—   *advice | I know*
    Dispeire° yow noght, but have in youre
         memorie,°   *despair | keep in mind*
    Paraunter° she may be youre Purgatorie.   *perhaps*
    She may be Goddes meene° and Goddes
         whippe.°   *means | whip*
460 Thanne shal youre soule up to Hevene skippe°   *skip*
    Swifter than dooth an arwe° out of the bowe.   *arrow*
    I hope to God herafter° shul ye knowe   *after this*
    That ther nys no so greet felicitee
    In mariage ne nevere mo shal bee,
465 That yow shal lette of youre
         savacioun,°   *shall hinder your salvation*
    So that ye use, as skil° is and resoun,°   *reasonable | sensible*
    The lustes° of youre wyf attemprely°   *desires | temperately*
    And that ye plese hire° nat to° amorously   *please her | not too*
    And that ye kepe yow eek from oother synne.
470 My tale is doon, for my wit is thynne.°   *thin*
    Beth nat agast herof,° my brother deere,   *be not afraid of this*
    But lat us waden° out of this mateere!   *wade*
    The Wyf of Bathe, if ye han understonde,
    Of mariage, which ye have on honde,°   *hand*
475 Declared hath ful wel in litel space.
    Fareth now wel! God have yow in his grace!"
       And with this word this Justyn and his brother
    Han take hir leve and ech of hem of oother.
    For whan they saugh° that it moste be,   *saw*
480 They wroghten so° by sly and wys
         tretee°   *made it happen | negotiations*
    That she this mayden, which that Mayus°
         highte,°   *May | was named*
    As hastily as evere that she myghte
    Shal wedded be unto this Januarie.
    I trowe° it were to longe° yow to tarie°   *believe | too long | delay*
485 If I yow tolde of every scrit° and bond°   *contract | agreement*

---

[1] *thilke tree* The seven deadly sins were often described by preachers as the branches of a tree.

[2] *er ... Chirche* Before you receive your last rites from the Holy Church.

By which that she was feffed[1] in his lond

Or for to herknen of° hir riche array.   *hear about*

But finally ycomen is the day

That to the chirche bothe be they went°   *have they gone*

490   For to receyve the hooly sacrement.°   *holy sacrament (of marriage)*

Forth comth the preest with stole° aboute his nekke   *vestment*

And bad hire be lyk to Sarra and Rebekke[2]

In wysdom and in trouthe° of mariage   *constancy*

And seyde hir orisons° as is usage°   *prayers / customary*

495   And croucheth hem and bad God sholde hem blesse[3]

And made al siker ynogh° with hoolynesse.   *certain enough*

    Thus been they wedded with solempnitee,°   *ceremony*

And at the feeste sitteth he and she

With othere worthy folk upon the deys.°   *dais (high table)*

500   Al ful of joye and blisse is the paleys,°   *palace*

And ful of instrumentz° and of

    vitaille,°   *musical instruments / food*

The mooste deyntevous° of al Ytaille.°   *choice / Italy*

Biforn hem stooden instrumentz of swich soun°   *sound*

That Orpheus ne of Thebes Amphioun[4]

505   Ne maden° nevere swich a melodye.   *made*

At every cours° thanne cam loud mynstralcye,°   *course / music*

That nevere tromped° Joab[5] for to heere   *trumpeted*

Nor he Theodomas yet half so cleere

At Thebes whan the citee was in doute.[6]

510   Bacus[7] the wyn hem skynketh° al aboute   *pours*

And Venus[8] laugheth upon every wight°—   *person*

For Januarie was bicome hire knyght

---

[1] *feffed* Enfeoffed; i.e., she was given possession of some of his land.

[2] *Sarra and Rebekke* I.e. Sarah and Rebecca, two good wives in the Book of Genesis. The actual ceremony of marriage is performed on the church steps and is followed by a nuptial mass inside.

[3] *And croucheth … blesse* And blesses them with the sign of the cross and asked that God should bless them.

[4] *That … Amphioun* In Greek mythology, Orpheus could charm beasts, rocks, and trees and was almost able to rescue his wife Eurydice from Hades by playing his lyre. King Amphion was a famous harper who helped build Thebes by using the magical power of his harp to assemble the stones.

[5] *Joab* King David's trumpeter. See 2 Samuel 2.28.

[6] *Nor he … doute* In Greek legend, Theodomas was a Theban prophet whose pronouncements were heralded by a trumpet.

[7] *Bacus* I.e., Bacchus, Greek god of wine.

[8] *Venus* Greek goddess of love.

And wolde° bothe assayen° his corage°   *wanted / try / vigor*

In libertee and eek in mariage—

515   And with hire fyr brond° in hire hand aboute   *her fiery torch*

Daunceth biforn the bryde and al the route.°   *company*

And certeinly, I dar right wel seyn this:

Ymeneus[9] that god of weddyng is,

Saugh nevere his lyf so myrie a wedded man.

520   Hoold thou thy pees,° thou poete Marcian,[10]   *peace*

That writest us that ilke° weddyng murie°   *same / merry*

Of hire, Philologie, and hym, Mercurie

And of the songes that the Muses song![11]

To smal is bothe thy penne and eek thy tonge

525   For to discryven° of this mariage.   *describe*

Whan tendre youthe hath wedded stoupyng° age   *stooping*

Ther is swich myrthe° that it may nat be writen.   *mirth*

Assayeth it yourself. Thanne may ye witen°   *know*

If that I lye or noon° in this matiere.   *not*

530   Mayus, that sit with so benyngne° a chiere,°   *kind / face*

Hire to biholde, it semed fairye.°   *magical*

Queene Ester looked nevere with swich an eye

On Assuer, so meke° a look hath she.[12]   *meek*

I may yow nat devyse al hir beautee.

535   But thus muche of hire beautee telle I may,

That she was lyk the brighte morwe° of May,   *morning*

Fulfild of alle beautee and plesaunce.

    This Januarie is ravysshed in a traunce

At every tyme he looked on hir face.

540   But in his herte he gan hire to manace,°   *menace*

That he that nyght in armes wolde hire streyne°   *embrace*

Harder than evere Parys dide Eleyne.[13]

But nathelees, yet hadde he greet pitee

That thilke nyght offenden° hire moste he   *harm*

545   And thoughte, "Allas, o tendre creature!

Now wolde God ye myghte wel endure

Al my corage,° it is so sharpe and keene!   *sexual prowess*

---

[9] *Ymeneus* I.e., Hymen, god of marriage.

[10] *thou poete Marcian* The North African poet Martianus Capella (c. 5th century CE) wrote an allegorical account of the seven liberal arts, *The Marriage of Philology and Mercury*, i.e., the union of the science of language with eloquence, represented by the god Mercury.

[11] *Muses song* In classical mythology, the Muses were the goddesses of the arts and sciences.

[12] *Queene … she* See Esther 2.

[13] *Harder … Eleyne* Paris's seduction of Helen and their subsequent flight to Troy occasioned the Trojan war.

I am agast° ye shul it nat susteene.°   *afraid / sustain*
But God forbede that I dide al my myght!¹
550   Now wolde God that it were woxen° nyght   *turned to*
And that the nyght wolde lasten everemo!
I wolde that al this peple were ago!"°   *gone*
And finally he dooth al his labour
As he best myghte, savyng his honour,
555   To haste hem fro the mete° in subtil wyse.°   *food / subtle way*
      The tyme cam that resoun° was to ryse,   *reasonable*
And after that men daunce and drynken faste,
And spices al aboute the hous they caste.²
And ful of joye and blisse is every man—
560   Al but a squyer° highte Damyan,   *squire*
Which carf° biforn the knyght ful many a day.³   *carved*
He was so ravysshed on° his lady May,   *in love with*
That for the verray peyne° he was ny   *true pain / nearly crazy*
      wood.°
Almoost he swelte° and swowned° ther he stood,   *died / fainted*
565   So soore hath Venus hurt hym with hire brond,°   *torch*
As that she bar° it daunsynge° in hire hond,   *carried / dancing*
And to his bed he wente hym hastily.
Namoore of hym at this tyme speke I,
But there I lete hym wepe ynogh and pleyne,⁴
570   Til fresshe May wol rewen° on his peyne.   *have pity*
      O perilous fyr, that in the bedstraw⁵ bredeth,°   *breeds*
O famulier foo,° that his servyce bedeth,°   *foe / offers*
O servant traytour, false, hoomly hewe,°   *domestic color*
Lyk to the naddre° in bosom, sly, untrewe!   *snake*
575   God shilde° us alle from youre aqueyntaunce!   *shield*
O Januarie, dronken in plesance,
In mariage se how thy Damyan,
Thyn owene squier and thy born man,⁶

Entendeth for to do thee vileynye.
580   God graunte thee thyn hoomly fo° t'espye.°   *foe at home / to see*
For in this world nys° worse pestilence   *there is no*
Than hoomly foo alday in thy presence.
      Parfourned° hath the sonne° his ark diurne.⁷   *performed / sun*
No lenger may the body of hym sojurne°   *its body travel*
585   On th'orisonte° as in that latitude.   *horizon*
Night with his mantel that is derk° and rude°   *dark / rough*
Gan oversprede° the hemysperie°
      aboute,   *to spread over / hemisphere*
For which departed is this lusty route°   *energetic crowd*
Fro Januarie with thank on every syde.
590   Hoom to hir hous° lustily they ryde,   *their houses*
Whereas they doon hir thynges as hem leste,⁸
And whan they sye° hir tyme° goon to reste.   *see / their time*
Soone after that this hastif° Januarie   *impatient*
Wolde go to bedde. He wolde no lenger tarye.
595   He drynketh ypocras, clarree, and vernage⁹
Of spices hoote° t'encreessen his corage.°   *hot spices / potency*
And many a letuarie° hath he ful fyn,   *potion*
Swiche as the monk Daun Constantyn
Hath writen in his book, *De Coitu*.¹⁰
600   To eten hem alle he nas nothyng eschu,°   *by no means avoided*
And to hise privee° freendes thus seyde he,   *close*
"For Goddes love, as soone as it may be,
Lat voyden° al this hous in curteys
      wyse!"°   *empty / a courteous manner*
And they han doon right° as he wol devyse.°   *just / would have it*
605   Men drynken and the travers° drawe anon.   *curtains*
The bryde was broght abedde° as stille° as
      stoon.°   *to bed / quiet / stone*
And whan the bed was with° the preest yblessed,   *by*
Out of the chambre hath every wight hym dressed.¹¹
And Januarie hath faste° in armes take°   *firmly / taken*
610   His fresshe May, his Paradys, his make.°   *mate*

---

¹ *But … myght*   But God forbid that I should perform as powerfully as I can (i.e., because that would be too much for May).

² *And … caste*   An old marriage custom was to throw spices on the
floor during a wedding feast. This symbolized the beginning of the
marriage, because medieval floors were often bare dirt strewn with
straw and herbs. The old material would be removed before the new
was strewn about.

³ *Which … day*   One of the duties of a squire was to carve the meat
and serve his lord at dinner.

⁴ *But … pleyne*   But there I leave him weeping enough and
complaining.

⁵ *bedstraw*   Straw used for stuffing mattresses.

⁶ *Thyn … man*   Your own man, born into your service.

---

⁷ *ark diurne*   I.e., diurnal arc: the sun has set.

⁸ *Whereas … leste*   Where they go about their affairs as they wish.

⁹ *ypocras … vernage*   I.e., hypocras, clary, and vernaccia, types of
spiced wine, thought to heat the blood, i.e., increase desire.

¹⁰ *Swiche as … Coitu*   Constantine the African, who came from
Carthage and converted to Christianity, wrote a medical treatise
entitled *About Intercourse* (*De Coitu*) which, among other things,
recommends various remedies for impotence similar to those here
consumed by January.

¹¹ *Out … dressed*   Out of the room everyone has gone.

He lulleth° hire, he kisseth hire ful ofte,   *speaks softly to*
With thilke brustles° of his berd°
　　unsofte°   *those bristles / beard / rough*
Lyk to the skyn of houndfyssh° sharpe as brere.°   *dogfish / briar*
For he was shave° al newe in his manere.   *shaven*
615　He rubbeth hire aboute hir tendre face
And seyde thus: "Allas, I moot trespace°   *do wrong*
To yow, my spouse, and yow greetly offende
Er tyme come that I wil doun° descende.   *down*
But nathelees, considereth this," quod he,
620　"Ther nys no werkman what so evere he be
That may bothe werke wel and hastily.
This wol be doon at leyser,° parfitly.°   *leisure / perfectly*
It is no fors° how longe that we pleye:°   *it does not matter / play*
In trewe wedlok wedded be we tweye,
625　And blessed be the yok° that we been inne!   *yoke*
For in actes we mowe° do no synne.°   *can / sin*
A man may do no synne with his wyf
Ne hurte hymselven with his owene knyf.°   *own knife*
For we han leve to pleye us by the lawe."[1]
630　Thus laboureth he til that the day gan dawe.°   *began to dawn*
And thanne he taketh a sope in fyn clarree,[2]
And upright in his bed thanne sitteth he.
And after that he sang ful loude and cleere
And kiste his wyf and made wantowne
　　cheere.°   *behaved flirtatiously*
635　He was al coltissh,° ful of ragerye°   *like a colt / lechery*
And ful of jargon° as a flekked pye.°   *chatter / spotted magpie*
The slakke skyn aboute his nekke shaketh
Whil that he sang, so chaunteth° he and craketh.°   *sings / croaks*
But God wot° what that May thoughte in hir herte   *knows*
640　Whan she hym saugh up sittynge° in his
　　sherte,°   *sitting up / nightshirt*
In his nyght cappe, and with his nekke lene.°   *skinny*
She preyseth nat his pleyyng° worth a bene.°   *love-making / bean*
Thanne seide he thus: "My reste wol I take
Now day is come; I may no lenger wake."
645　And doun he leyde his heed and sleepe til pryme.[3]

And afterward, whan that he saugh his tyme,
Up ryseth Januarie. But fresshe May
Heeld hire chambre° unto the fourthe day,   *kept in her room*
As usage° is of wyves for the beste.   *custom*
650　For every labour somtyme moot han reste,
Or elles longe may he nat endure.
This is to seyn, no lyves creature,°   *living creature*
Be it of fyssh or bryd or beest or man.
　　Now wol I speke of woful Damyan,
655　That langwissheth° for love, as ye shul here.   *languishes*
Therfore I speke to° hym in this manere: *about*
I seye, "O sely° Damyan, allas!   *foolish*
Andswere to my demaunde,° as in this
　　cas:°   *question / situation*
How shaltow to thy lady, fresshe May,
660　Telle thy wo? She wole alwey seye nay.
Eek° if thou speke, she wol thy wo biwreye.°   *and / betray*
God be thyn helpe; I kan no bettre seye."
　　This sike° Damyan in Venus fyr°   *sick / fire*
So brenneth,° that he dyeth for desyr,   *burns*
665　For which he putte his lyf in aventure.°   *danger*
No lenger myghte he in this wise° endure,   *way*
But prively a penner° gan he borwe,[4]   *pen case*
And in a lettre wroot he al his sorwe
In manere of a compleynt or a lay[5]
670　Unto his faire, fresshe lady May.
And in a purs of sylk heng° on his sherte   *that hung*
He hath it put and leyde° it at his herte.   *laid*
　　The moone, that at noon was thilke day
That Januarie hath wedded fresshe May
675　In two of Tawr,[6] was into Cancre° glyden,°   *Cancer / glided*
So longe hath Mayus in hir chambre byden°   *stayed*
As custume is unto thise noble alle.°   *for all these nobles*
A bryde shal nat eten in the halle
Til dayes foure or thre dayes atte leeste
680　Ypassed been. Thanne lat hire go to feeste.
The fourthe day compleet, fro noon to noon,
Whan that the heighe masse was ydoon

---

[1] *For … lawe*　The law permits us to enjoy ourselves. Church law, known as canon law, governed matters of sexual morality. It actually placed many restrictions on sexual activity within marriage.

[2] *And … clarree*　And then he takes a piece of bread (soaked) in fine wine.

[3] *And … pryme*　And he put his head down and slept until prime (the first of the canonical hours, around 7 a.m.).

---

[4] *But … borwe*　But secretly he borrowed a pen case (or box with writing materials). Pen cases normally belonged to scholars or clerics. Damyan is literate but does not write very often.

[5] *compleynt … lay*　Complaints and lais were types of short poems, often expressing a lover's sorrow.

[6] *two of Tawr*　The second (degree) of Taurus (a sign of the zodiac).

In halle sit this Januarie and May,
As fressh as is the brighte someres day.
685   And so bifel how that this goode man
Remembred hym upon this Damyan
And seyde, "Seynte Marie, how may this be
That Damyan entendeth nat° to me?   *does not attend*
Is he ay syk? Or how may this bityde?"°   *happen*
690   His squieres, whiche that stooden ther bisyde,
Excused hym bycause of his siknesse,
Which letted hym° to doon his
    bisynesse.°   *prevented him | duty*
Noon oother cause myghte make hym tarye.
   "That me forthynketh,"° quod this Januarie.   *grieves*
695   "He is a gentil° squier, by my trouthe!   *noble*
If that he deyde, it were harm and routhe.°   *pity*
He is as wys, discreet, and as secree°   *private*
As any man I woot of his degree,
And therto manly and eek servysable°   *eager to serve*
700   And for to been a thrifty° man
    right able.°   *successful | very qualified*
But after mete° as soone as evere I may   *food*
I wol myself visite hym and eek May,
To doon hym al the confort that I kan."
And for that word hym blessed every
    man,°   *every man blessed him*
705   That of his bountee° and his gentillesse°   *generosity | nobility*
He wolde so conforten in siknesse
His squier, for it was a gentil dede.
"Dame," quod this Januarie, "taak good hede.°   *heed*
At afternoon ye with youre wommen alle,
710   Whan ye han been in chambre out of this halle,
That alle ye go se this Damyan.
Dooth hym disport.° He is a gentil man.   *cheer him up*
And telleth hym that I wol hym visite
Have I nothyng but° rested me a lite.   *when I have only*
715   And spede° yow faste, for I wole abyde°   *speed | wait*
Til that ye slepe faste by my syde."
And with that word he gan to hym to calle
A squier that was marchal° of his
    halle   *marshall (master of ceremonies)*
And tolde hym certeyn thynges what he wolde.°   *wanted*
720   This fresshe May hath streight hir wey
    yholde°   *immediately taken her way*
With alle hir wommen unto Damyan.
Doun by his beddes syde sit she than,
Confortynge hym as goodly as she may.

This Damyan, whan that his tyme he
    say,°   *he saw his opportunity*
725   In secree wise° his purs and eek his bille,°   *secret way | letter*
In which that he ywriten hadde his wille,°   *desire*
Hath put into hire hand withouten moore,
Save that he siketh° wonder° depe and soore,   *sighs | wondrously*
And softely to hire right thus seyde he:
730   "Mercy, and that ye nat discovere° me,   *betray*
For I am deed if that this thyng be kyd!"°   *known*
This purs hath she inwith° hir bosom hyd°   *inside | hidden*
And wente hire wey. Ye gete namoore of me.
But unto Januarie ycomen is she,
735   That on his beddes syde sit ful softe,°   *quietly*
And taketh hire and kisseth hire ful ofte,
And leyde hym° doun to slepe, and that anon.   *lay himself*
She feyned° hire as that she moste gon°   *pretended | had to go*
Theras° ye woot that every wight moot neede,   *where*
740   And whan she of this bille hath taken heede,°   *paid attention*
She rente° it al to cloutes° atte laste,°   *tore | pieces | at the last*
And in the pryvee° softely it caste.   *privy*
   Who studieth° now but faire, fresshe May?   *considers*
Adoun by olde Januarie she lay,
745   That sleepe° til that the coughe hath hym awaked.   *who sleeps*
Anon he preyde hire strepen° hire al naked: *strip*
He wolde of hire, he seyde, han som plesaunce;
He seyde hir clothes dide hym encombraunce.°   *got in his way*
And she obeyeth, be hire lief or looth.°   *whether she wished to or not*
750   But lest ye precious° folk be with me wrooth,°   *prudish | angry*
How that he wroghte,° I dar nat to yow telle,   *acted*
Or wheither that hire thoughte it Paradys or Helle.
But heere I lete hem° werken° in hir wyse   *leave them | acting*
Til evensong° rong and that they moste aryse.   *evening service*
755   Were it° by destynee or by aventure,°   *whether it were | chance*
Were it by influence° or by
    nature°   *(astrological) influence | natural cause*
Or constellacioun, that in swich estaat°   *condition*
The hevene stood that tyme fortunaat[1]
Was for to putte a bille of Venus werkes°—   *Venus's works*
760   For alle thyng hath tyme, as seyn thise clerkes°—   *scholars*
To any womman for to gete hire love,
I kan nat seye. But grete God above,
That knoweth that noon act is causelees,°   *without cause*
He deme° of al, for I wole holde my pees.   *may he judge*

---

[1] *The ... fortunaat* The heavens stood in such an arrangement that the time was fortunate, i.e., the planetary influences were favorable.

765 But sooth is this, how that this fresshe May
     Hath take° swich impressioun that day   *has taken*
     For pitee of this sike Damyan
     That from hire herte she ne dryve kan°   *cannot drive*
     The remembrance for to doon hym
          ese.°   *memory (thought) of comforting him*
770 "Certeyn," thoghte she, "whom that this thyng displese,
     I rekke noght,° for heere I hym assure   *care not*
     To love hym best of any creature,
     Though he namoore° hadde than his
          sherte."   *no more possessions*
     Lo, pitee renneth soone in gentil herte!
775   Heere may ye se how excellent franchise°   *generosity*
     In wommen is whan they hem narwe
          avyse.°   *consider things carefully*
     Som tyrant° is, as ther be many
          oon,°   *cruel woman / many a one*
     That hath an herte as hard as any stoon,
     Which wolde han lat hym storven° in the place   *die*
780 Wel° rather than han graunted hym hire
          grace,°   *much / favor*
     And hem rejoysen in hire crueel pryde[1]
     And rekke° nat to been an homycide.°   *care / murderer*
         This gentil May, fulfilled° of pitee,   *full*
     Right of hire hand a lettre made she
785 In which she graunteth hym hire verray grace.°   *true favor*
     Ther lakketh noght° oonly but day and place   *nothing*
     Wher that she myghte unto his lust
          suffise,°   *satisfy his desire*
     For it shal be right° as he wole devyse.°   *just / determine*
     And whan she saugh hir tyme,° upon a day   *opportunity*
790 To visite this Damyan gooth May,
     And sotilly° this lettre doun she threste°   *subtly / thrust*
     Under his pilwe,° rede° it if hym
          leste.°   *pillow / to read / wishes*
     She taketh hym by the hand and harde hym
          twiste°   *squeezes*
     So secrely that no wight of it wiste°   *knew*
795 And bad hym been al hool.° And forth he°
          wente   *whole / she*
     To Januarie whan that he for hym° sente.   *her*
         Up riseth Damyan the nexte morwe:
     Al passed was his siknesse and his sorwe.

     He kembeth hym.° He preyneth° hym and
          pyketh.°   *combs himself / preens / cleans*
800 He dooth al that his lady lust° and lyketh.°   *desires / likes*
     And eek to Januarie he gooth as lowe°   *meekly*
     As evere dide a dogge for the bowe.°   *bow (for hunting)*
     He is so plesant unto every man—
     For craft is al, whoso that do it kan—[2]
805 That every wight is fayn° to speke hym good,°   *glad / well of him*
     And fully in his lady grace° he stood.   *lady's favor*
     Thus lete° I Damyan aboute his nede,   *leave*
     And in my tale forth I wol procede.
         Somme clerkes° holden that felicitee   *scholars*
810 Stant° in delit, and therfore certeyn he,   *stands*
     This noble Januarie, with al his myght,
     In honeste wyse as longeth to a knyght,
     Shoope hym° to lyve ful deliciously.°   *determined / delightfully*
     His housynge,° his array as honestly°   *housing / honorably*
815 To his degree was maked as a kynges.
     Amonges othere of hise honeste thynges,
     He made a gardyn walled al with stoon.
     So fair a gardyn woot I nowher noon.[3]
     For out of doute,° I verraily suppose   *without doubt*
820 That he that wroot *The Romance of the Rose*[4]
     Ne koude of it the beautee wel devyse!
     Ne Priapus[5] ne myghte nat suffise,
     Though he be god of gardyns, for to telle
     The beautee of the gardyn and the welle°   *well*
825 That stood under a laurer° alwey grene.   *laurel tree*
     Ful ofte tyme he Pluto and his queene
     Proserpina, and al hire fairye,[6]

---

[1] *And ... pryde* And rejoice themselves in their cruel pride.

[2] *For ... kan* For cunning is all that matters, as whoever can practice it knows.

[3] *So ... noon* I do not know of so fair a garden anywhere.

[4] *The Romance of the Rose* Thirteenth-century French poem begun by Guillaume de Lorris and completed by Jean de Meun. In it is depicted the Garden of Love, where Cupid holds his court. Chaucer translated part of this very influential poem into English.

[5] *Priapus* Greek and Roman god of gardens. Priapus was also associated with male sexuality and fertility.

[6] *Pluto ... fairye* In Greek mythology, Pluto was the god of the underworld who abducted Proserpina and forcibly made her his queen. As a result, Proserpina's mother, Ceres, the goddess of the earth, caused the world to suffer perpetual winter until Pluto agreed to return her daughter. Since Proserpina had eaten some seeds from a pomegranate while in the underworld, however, she was forced to reside there for half the year. Her mother mourns when she is there,

Disporten hem and maken melodye
Aboute that welle, and daunced as men tolde.

830   This noble knyght, this Januarie the olde
Swich deyntee° hath in it to walke and pleye   *delight*
That he wol no wight suffren bere the keye°   *to have the key*
Save he hymself. For of the smale wyket
He baar alwey of silver of a clyket,[1]

835 With which whan that hym leste he it unshette.°   *unlocked*
And whan he wolde paye his wyf hir dette°   *marriage-debt*
In somer sesoun thider° wolde he go   *thither*
And May his wyf, and no wight but they two.
And thynges whiche that were nat doon abedde

840 He in the gardyn parfourned° hem and
     spedde°   *performed / succeeded*
And in this wyse many a murye° day   *merry*
Lyved this Januarie and fresshe May.
But worldly joye may nat alwey dure°   *endure*
To Januarie ne to no creature.

845   O sodeyn hape!° O thou Fortune instable,°   *chance / unstable*
Lyk to the scorpion so deceyvable°   *deceptive*
That flaterest with thyn heed° whan thou wolt
     stynge!°   *head / sting*
Thy tayl is deeth thurgh° thyn
     envenymynge.°   *through / poisoning*
O brotil° joye, o sweete venym queynte,°   *brittle / strange*

850 O monstre that so subtilly kanst peynte°   *paint*
Thy yiftes° under hewe of stidefastnesse   *gifts*
That thou deceyvest bothe moore and lesse!
Why hastow Januarie thus deceyved,
That haddest hym for thy ful° freend receyved?   *close*

855 And now thou hast biraft° hym bothe hise
     eyen,°   *taken from / eyes*
For sorwe of which desireth he to dyen.
     Allas, this noble Januarie free
Amydde his lust and his prosperitee
Is woxen° blynd, and that al sodeynly!   *grown*

860 He wepeth and he wayleth pitously
And therwithal the fyr of jalousie,
Lest that his wyf sholde falle in swich folye,°   *folly (i.e., adultery)*
So brente° his herte that he wolde fayn   *burned*
That som man bothe hym and hire had slayn.

865 For neither after his deeth nor in his lyf
Ne wolde he° that she were love° ne wyf   *he did not want / lover*
But evere lyve as wydwe° in clothes blake,   *widow*
Soul° as the turtle° that lost hath hire make.   *single / turtledove*
But atte laste, after a monthe or tweye,

870 His sorwe gan aswage, sooth to seye.
For whan he wiste° it may noon oother be,   *knew*
He paciently took his adversitee,°   *adversity (i.e., blindness)*
Save° out of doute° he may nat
     forgoon°   *except / without a doubt / stop*
That he nas jalous everemoore in oon,[2]

875 Which jalousye it was so outrageous
That neither in halle n'yn noon oother° hous   *nor in any other*
N'yn noon other place never the mo
He nolde suffre° hire for to ryde or go   *would not allow*
But if° that he had hond° on hire alway.   *unless / hand*

880 For which ful ofte wepeth fresshe May,
That loveth Damyan so benyngnely°   *kindly*
That she moot outher dyen° sodeynly   *either die*
Or elles she moot han hym as hir leste.°   *she wished*
She wayteth whan° hir herte wolde breste.   *expects that*

885   Upon that oother syde, Damyan
Bicomen is the sorwefulleste man
That evere was, for neither nyght ne day
Ne myghte he speke a word to fresshe May
As to his purpos of no swich mateere

890 But° if that Januarie moste it heere,   *except*
That hadde an hand upon hire everemo.
But nathelees by writyng to and fro
And privee signes° wiste° he what she mente,   *secret signs / knew*
And she knew eek the fyn° of his entente.   *aim*

895   O Januarie, what myghte it thee
     availle°   *what good would it do you*
Thogh thou myghtest se as fer° as shippes saille?   *far*
For as good is blynd deceyved be°   *to be deceived*
As to be deceyved whan a man may se.
     Lo Argus,[3] which that hadde an hondred eyen,

900 For al that evere he koude poure° or pryen,°   *investigate / pry*
Yet was he blent.° And God woot, so been mo   *blinded*

---

dooming the earth to winter.

[1] *For of … clyket* For he always carried the silver key to the small
wicket gate.

[2] *That … oon* Being jealous forever in one (matter).

[3] *Argus* In Greek mythology, Juno asked Argus, a shepherd with
one hundred eyes, to guard her husband's mistress, Io, to prevent
him from seeing her. Argus was killed by Mercury at Jove's request.

That wenen wisly that it be nat so.[1]
Passe over is an ese.[2] I sey namoore.

    This fresshe May that I spak of so yoore°   *long ago*
905 In warm wex° hath emprented the clyket°   *wax | key*
That Januarie bar° of the smale wyket,   *carried*
By which into his gardyn ofte he wente.
And Damyan, that knew al hire entente,
The cliket countrefeted pryvely.
910 Ther nys namoore° to saye but hastily   *is no more*
Som wonder by this clyket shal bityde,°   *happen*
Which ye shul heeren if ye wole abyde.

    O noble Ovyde, ful sooth° seystou,° God woot,   *truth | you say*
"What sleighte° is it, thogh it be long and hoot,°   *trick | hot*
915 That he nyl fynde it out in som manere?"
By Piramus and Tesbee may men leere,°   *learn*
Thogh they were kept ful longe streit
    overal,°   *long guarded most carefully*
They been accorded rownynge° thurgh a wal   *whispering*
Ther no wight koude han founde out swich a sleighte.°[3]   *trick*
920   But now to purpose. Er that dayes eighte
Were passed er the monthe of Juyl bifille,°   *July arrived*
That Januarie hath caught so greet a wille,°   *desire*
Thurgh eggyng° of his wyf, hym for to pleye   *incitement*
In his gardyn, and no wight but they tweye,
925 That in a morwe° unto this May seith he,[4]   *on one morning*
"Rys up, my wyf, my love, my lady free!
The turtle voys° is herd, my dowve sweete;   *turtledove's voice*
The wynter is goon with his reynes weete.°   *wet rains*
Com forth now with thyne eyen columbyn;°   *dove-like*
930 How fairer been thy brestes than is wyn!
The gardyn is enclosed al aboute.
Com forth, my white spouse; out of doute
Thou hast me wounded in myn herte, o wyf!
No spot of thee ne knew I° al my lyf.   *did I know*

935 Com forth, and lat us taken som disport;
I chees° thee for my wyf and my confort."   *choose*
    Swiche olde, lewed wordes used he.
On° Damyan a signe made she   *to*
That he sholde go biforn with his cliket.
940 This Damyan thanne hath opened the wyket,
And in he stirte,° and that in swich manere   *jumps*
That no wight myghte it se neither yheere,°   *see nor hear*
And stille° he sit under a bussh anon.   *quietly*
    This Januarie, as blynd as is a stoon,
945 With Mayus° in his hand and no wight mo°   *May | no one else*
Into his fresshe gardyn is ago°   *gone*
And clapte to° the wyket sodeynly.   *slammed*
    "Now wyf," quod he, "heere nys but thou and I,
That art the creature that I best love.
950 For by that Lord that sit in Hevene above,
Levere ich hadde° to dyen on a knyf   *rather I had*
Than thee offende, trewe, deere wyf!
For Goddes sake, thenk° how I thee chees,°   *think | chose*
Noght° for no coveitise,° doutelees,   *not | greed*
955 But oonly for the love I had to thee.
And though that I be oold and may nat see
Beth° to me trewe, and I shal telle yow why: *be*
Thre thynges, certes, shal ye wynne therby.
First, love of Crist, and to youreself honour,
960 And al myn heritage,° toun° and tour.°   *property | town | tower*
I yeve it yow. Maketh chartres° as yow
    leste.°   *charters (legal documents) | desire*
This shal be doon tomorwe er sonne reste,°   *before sunset*
So wisly° God my soule brynge in° blisse.   *surely | into*
I prey yow first, in covenat° ye me kisse,   *(to seal the) covenant*
965 And though that I be jalous, wyte° me noght;   *blame*
Ye been so depe enprented° in my thoght,   *deeply imprinted*
That whan I considere youre beautee
And therwithal the unlikly elde° of me,   *unsuitable old age*
I may nat, certes, though I sholde dye
970 Forbere° to been out of youre compaignye,   *bear*
For verray° love this is withouten doute.   *true*
Now kys me, wyf, and lat us rome° aboute."   *roam*
    This fresshe May, whan she thise wordes herde,
Benyngnely° to Januarie answerde,   *kindly*
975 But first and forward she bigan to wepe.
"I have," quod she, "a soule for to kepe°   *guard*
As wel as ye, and also myn honour,
And of my wyfhod thilke tendre flour°   *that tender flower*

---

[1] *And God … so* And, God knows, so are many others who believe firmly that it is not so (i.e., that they are not being deceived).

[2] *Passe … ese* To pass over something is a comfort or is the best course (i.e., what you don't know won't hurt you).

[3] *Ovyde … sleighte* The quotation is from Roman poet Ovid's *Metamorphoses*, book 4.68, in which he tells the story of the star-crossed lovers Pyramus and Thisbe. Their families forbade them to see one another, but they could whisper through a crack in the wall between their houses.

[4] *seith he* The following speech quotes from various passages from the Song of Songs in the Bible.

Which that I have assured in youre
　　hond°　　　　　　　　　　　　*given over to your control*
980 Whan that the preest to yow my body bond.°　　*bound*
Wherfore° I wole answere in this manere:　　　*therefore*
By the leve° of yow, my lord so deere,　　　　*leave*
I prey to God that nevere dawe° the day　　　*dawn*
That I ne sterve,° as foule° as womman may,　*do not die / foully*
985 If evere I do unto my kyn° that shame　　　　*my relatives*
Or elles I empeyre° so my name　　　　　　　*damage*
That I be fals. And if I do that lakke,°　　　　*offence*
Do strepe° me and put me in a sakke,°　　　　*strip / sack*
And in the nexte ryver do me drenche.°　　　　*drown*
990 I am a gentil womman and no wenche.°　*peasant girl or mistress*
Why speke ye thus? But men been evere untrewe,
And wommen have repreve° of yow ay
　　newe.°　　　　　　　　　　　*reproach / continually*
Ye han noon oother contenance,° I leeve,°　*behavior / believe*
But speke to us of untrust° and repreeve!"　　*mistrust*
995 　And with that word she saugh wher Damyan
Sat in the bussh. And coughen she bigan,
And with hir fynger signes made she
That Damyan sholde clymbe upon a tree
That charged° was with fruyt. And up he wente.　*laden*
1000 For verraily, he knew al hire entente
And every signe that she koude make,
Wel bet° than Januarie, hir owene make,°　*much better / mate*
For in a lettre she had toold hym al
Of this matere, how he werchen shal.°　*what he should do*
1005 And thus I lete hym sitte upon the pyrie°　*pear tree*
And Januarie and May romynge myrie.°　　*merrily*
　　Bright was the day and blew° the firmament.°　*blue / sky*
Phebus[1] hath of gold hise stremes° doun ysent　*beams*
To gladen every flour with his warmnesse.
1010 He was that tyme in Geminis, as I gesse,°　*guess*
But litel fro his declynacioun
Of Cancer, Jovis exaltacioun.[2]
And so bifel that brighte morwetyde°　*morning*

That in that gardyn in the ferther syde
1015 Pluto, that is kyng of Fairye,[3]
And many a lady in his compaignye,
Folwynge his wyf, the queene Proserpyne,
Ech after oother, right as a lyne,°　　　*line*
Whil that she gadered° floures in the mede.°　*gathered / meadow*
1020 In Claudyan[4] ye may the stories rede.
And in his grisly carte° he hire sette,°　*gruesome chariot / placed*
This kyng of Fairye, thanne adoun hym sette
Upon a bench of turves fressh and grene.[5]
And right anon thus seyde he to his queene:
1025 "My wyf," quod he, "ther may no wight seye nay.°　*deny*
Th'experience so preveth° every day　　　*proves*
The tresons whiche that wommen doon to man.
Ten hondred thousand tellen I kan
Notable of youre untrouthe and brotilnesse.°　*unreliability*
1030 O Salomon wys and richest of richesse,
Fulfild of sapience° and of worldly glorie,　*full of wisdom*
Ful worthy been thy wordes to memorie°　*to be remembered*
To every wight that wit and reson kan.°　*who has wit and reason*
Thus preiseth he yet the bountee° of man:　*goodness*
1035 'Amonges° a thousand men yet foond I oon,　*amongst*
But of wommen alle foond I noon.'
　　"Thus seith the kyng that knoweth youre wikkednesse.
And Jesus *filius* Syrak,[6] as I gesse,
Ne spekketh of yow but seelde° reverence.　*seldom*
1040 A wyldefyr[7] and corrupt pestilence°　*plague*
So falle upon youre bodyes yet tonyght!
Ne se ye nat° this honurable knyght,　*do you not see*
Bycause, allas, that he is blynd and old,
His owene man shal make hym cokewold?
1045 Lo, heere he sit, the lechour, in the tree!
Now wol I graunten° of my magestee　*grant*
Unto this olde, blynde, worthy knyght
That he shal have ayeyn hise eyen syght°　*eyesight*

---

[1] *Phebus* I.e., Phoebus, another name for Apollo, god of the sun in classical mythology.

[2] *He was … exaltacioun* The sun (Phoebus) is in the sign of Gemini (often represented in the Middle Ages by a couple embracing). The sun has almost entered its maximum northern declination and will reach it a few days later when it moves into the astrological sign of Cancer. Cancer is the "exaltation" of Jupiter, i.e., the astrological sign in which he was considered to be most powerful.

[3] *Pluto … Fairye* Pluto, also known as Hades, the god of the underworld in Greek mythology, is here made the king of the Celtic otherworld.

[4] *Claudyan* I.e., Roman author Claudian (c. 400 CE). His *Rape of Proserpina* recounts the story of Pluto and his queen.

[5] *Upon … grene* Medieval gardens often contained turf benches made by piling up earth and then growing grass on it.

[6] *Jesus filius Syrak* Jesus, son of Sirach (not Jesus Christ) is the author of the apocryphal or deuterocanonical Book of Ecclesiasticus.

[7] *wyldefyr* I.e., wildfire, or erysipelas, a painful skin disease.

Whan that his wyf wold doon hym vileynye.

1050 Thanne shal he knowen al hire harlotrye,

Bothe in repreve of hire and othere mo."

"Ye shal?" quod Proserpyne, "wol° ye so?   *will*

Now by my moodres sires soule[1] I swere

That I shal yeven° hire suffisant answere   *give*

1055 And alle wommen after for hir sake,

That though they be in any gilt ytake,°   *taken*

With face boold they shulle hemself excuse

And bere hem doun° that wolden hem accuse!   *bear them down*

For lakke of answere noon of hem shal dyen,°   *die*

1060 Al hadde man seyn a thyng with bothe hise eyen![2]

Yit shul° we wommen visage it hardily,°   *yet shall / outface it boldly*

And wepe and swere and chide° it subtilly,   *accuse*

So that ye men shul been as lewed° as gees.°   *ignorant / geese*

What rekketh me° of youre auctoritees?   *what do I care*

1065 I woot wel that this Jew, this Salomon,

Foond of us wommen fooles many oon.[3]

But though that he ne foond no good womman,

Yet that ther founde many another man

Wommen ful trewe, ful goode and vertuous.

1070 Witnesse on hem that dwelle in Cristes hous:[4]

With martirdom they preved° hire
        constance.°   *proved / their constancy*

The Romayn geestes° eek maken
        remembrance°   *Roman stories / also record*

Of many a verray, trewe wyf also.

But sire, ne be nat wrooth° albeit so,   *angry*

1075 Though that he seyde he foond no good womman:

I prey yow, take the sentence° of the man.   *meaning*

He mente thus: that in sovereyn bontee°   *supreme goodness*

Nis noon but God, that sit in Trinitee.

Ey,° for verray God, that nys but oon.   *ah*

1080 What make ye so muche of Salomon?

What though he made a temple, Goddes hous?

What though he were riche and glorious?

So made he eek a temple of false goddis.

How myghte he do a thyng that moore
        forbode° is?   *more forbidden*

1085 Pardee,° as faire as ye his name emplastre,[5]   *by God*

He was a lecchour and an ydolastre!°   *idolater*

And in his elde° he verray God forsook.   *old age*

And if God ne hadde, as seith the book,

Yspared hym for his fadres sake, he sholde

1090 Have lost his regne rather than he wolde.[6]

I sette right noght° of al the vileynye,   *consider nothing*

That ye of wommen write, a boterflye!°   *not a butterfly*

I am a womman. Nedes moot I° speke   *I must needs*

Or elles swelle til myn herte breke.

1095 For sithen he seyde that we been jangleresses,°   *chatterboxes*

As evere hool I moote brouke my tresses,[7]

I shal nat spare for no curteisye

To speke hym harm that wolde us vileynye!"°   *do harm to us*

"Dame," quod this Pluto, "be no lenger wrooth!

1100 I yeve° it up. But sith I swoor myn ooth,   *give*

That I wolde graunten hym his sighte ageyn,

My word shal stonde.° I warne yow certeyn   *stand*

I am a kyng. It sit me noght° to lye!"   *would not be fitting for me*

"And I," quod she, "a queene of Fairye.

1105 Hir answere shal she have, I undertake.

Lat us namoore wordes heerof make.

For sothe, I wol no lenger yow contrarie."°   *disagree with you*

Now lat us turne agayn to Januarie,

That in the gardyn with his faire May

1110 Syngeth ful murier° than the papejay,°   *much more merrily / parrot*

"Yow love I best and shal and oother noon."°   *none other*

So longe aboute the aleyes° is he goon,°   *paths / he walked*

Til he was come agayns° thilke pyrie,°   *upon / that same pear tree*

Whereas this Damyan sitteth ful myrie

1115 An heigh° among the fresshe leves grene.   *on high*

This fresshe May that is so bright and sheene°   *shining*

Gan for to syke° and seyde, "Allas my syde!°   *sigh / side*

Now sire," quod she, "for aught that may bityde,

I moste han of the peres° that I see,   *pears*

1120 Or I moot dye, so soore longeth me°   *I long*

---

[1] *moodres sires soule* Mother's father's soul. Proserpina was the daughter of Ceres, whose father Saturn was known for his wisdom but also for his destructive power.

[2] *Al ... eyen* Although a man had seen a thing with both of his eyes.

[3] *Foond ... oon* Found many a one of us women to be fools.

[4] *hem that ... hous* I.e., martyrs in Heaven.

---

[5] *emplastre* Apply a medicinal plaster over a wound, hence to plaster over or gloss over.

[6] *if God ... wolde* If God had not spared him for his father's sake, as the Bible says, he would have lost his kingdom sooner than he wished. See 1 Kings 11.12–13.

[7] *As ... tresses* As ever I enjoy my braids, i.e., as long as I am a woman.

To eten of the smale peres grene!
Help for hir love that is of Hevene queene![1]
I telle yow wel, a womman in my plit[2]
May han to fruyt° so greet an appetit   *have for fruit*
1125 That she may dyen but° she of it have!"   *unless*
    "Allas," quod he, "that I ne had° heer a
        knave°   *if only I had / servant*
That koude clymbe! Allas! Allas," quod he,
"That I am blynd!" "Ye sire, no fors,"° quod   *it does not matter*
        she.
"But wolde ye vouchesauf° for Goddes sake   *grant (or deign)*
1130 The pyrie inwith youre armes for to take[3]—
For wel I woot that ye mystruste me—
Thanne sholde I clymbe wel ynogh," quod she,
"So° I my foot myghte sette upon youre bak."   *if*
    "Certes," quod he, "theron shal be no lak,
1135 Mighte I yow helpen with myn herte blood."
He stoupeth doun, and on his bak she stood
And caughte hire° by a twiste,° and up she
        gooth—   *raised herself / branch*
Ladyes, I prey yow that ye be nat wroth:
I kan nat glose,° I am a rude° man—   *speak delicately / rough*
1140 And sodeynly anon this Damyan
Gan pullen up the smok,° and in he
        throng.°   *undergarment / thrust*
    And whan that Pluto saugh this grete wrong,
To Januarie he gaf agayn° his sighte   *gave back*
And made hym se as wel as evere he myghte.
1145 And whan that he hadde caught° his sighte agayn,   *gained*
Ne was ther nevere man of thyng so fayn,°   *eager*
But on his wyf his thoght was everemo.
Up to the tree he caste hise eyen two
And saugh that Damyan his wyf had dressed°   *treated*
1150 In swich manere it may nat been expressed
But if I wolde speke uncurteisly.
And up he yaf a roryng and a cry
As dooth the mooder whan the child shal dye.
"Out! Helpe! Allas! Harrow!"[4] he gan to crye.

1155 O stronge lady stoore,° what dostow?"°   *bold / what are you doing*
    And she answerde, "Sire, what eyleth° yow?   *ails*
Have pacience and resoun in youre mynde.
I have yow holpe on° bothe youre eyen blynde.   *helped you with*
Up° peril of my soule, I shal nat lyen:°   *on peril / lie*
1160 As me was taught,° to heele with youre
        eyen°   *was taught to me / heal your eyes*
Was nothyng bet° to make yow to see   *better*
Than strugle° with a man upon a tree.   *struggle*
God woot, I dide it in ful good entente!"
    "Strugle?" quod he. "Ye, algate in it wente![5]
1165 God yeve yow bothe on shames deth° to dyen!   *a shameful death*
He swyved thee!° I saugh it with myne eyen!   *had sex with you*
And elles be I hanged by the hals!"°   *neck*
    "Thanne is," quod she, "my medicyne fals.°   *false*
For certeinly, if that ye myghte se,
1170 Ye wolde nat seyn thise wordes unto me.
Ye han som glymsyng° and no parfit° sighte."   *glimpsing / perfect*
    "I se," quod he, "as wel as evere I myghte,
Thonked be God, with bothe myne eyen two.
And by my trouthe me thoughte he dide thee so!"
1175   "Ye maze,° maze, goode sire," quod she.   *you are dazed*
"This thank° have I, for I have maad yow see.   *this is all the thanks*
Allas," quod she, "that evere I was so kynde!"
    "Now dame," quod he, "lat al passe out of mynde.
Com doun, my lief,° and if I have myssayd,°   *dear / said wrong*
1180 God helpe me so as I am yvele apayd.°   *evilly paid back*
But by my fader soule, I wende° han seyn   *thought to*
How that this Damyan hadde by thee leyn°   *lain*
And that thy smok hadde leyn upon his brest."
    "Ye sire," quod she, "ye may wene as yow
        lest.°   *think as you wish*
1185 But, sire, as man that waketh out of his sleepe,
He may nat sodeynly wel taken keepe
Upon a thyng ne seen° it parfitly   *see*
Til that he be adawed verraily,°   *truly awakened*
Right so a man that longe hath blynd ybe°   *been*
1190 Ne may nat sodeynly so wel yse°   *see*
First whan his sighte is newe come ageyn
As he that hath a day or two yseyn.
Til that youre sighte ysatled be awhile°   *is settled for awhile*
Ther may ful many a sighte yow bigile.°   *trick*
1195 Beth war,° I prey yow for by Hevene kyng   *beware*

---

[1]   *for ... queene*   For the love of Her that is Heaven's Queen (i.e.,
the Virgin Mary).

[2]   *plit*   Plight. May obliquely refers to her pregnancy.

[3]   *The ... take*   To encircle the pear tree with your arms.

[4]   *Out! Helpe! Allas! Harrow!*   Cries to raise help when one is in
trouble.

[5]   *Ye ... wente*   Yes, it went all the way in!

Ful many a man weneth° to seen a thyng,   *thinks*
And it is al another° than it semeth.   *different*
He that mysconceyveth,° he mysdemeth."°*misperceives / misjudges*
And with that word she leepe° doun fro the tree.   *leapt*
1200   This Januarie, who is glad but he?
He kisseth hire and clippeth° hire ful ofte,   *hugs*
And on hire wombe° he stroketh hire ful softe,   *belly*

And to his palays° hoom° he hath hire
    lad.°   *palace / home / has led her*
Now goode men, I pray yow be glad;
1205 Thus endeth heere my tale of Januarie.
God blesse us and his mooder, Seinte Marie!

HEERE IS ENDED THE MARCHANTES TALE OF JANUARIE

The Franklin's Prologue and Tale

In the full *Canterbury Tales*, this tale is preceded by *The Squire's Tale*, which the Squire never manages to finish. The Franklin, a wealthy landowner with a reputation for generous hospitality, interrupts the Squire when he has reached line 672 of a tale that promises to go on for several thousand lines more, complimenting him on his eloquence (although in a rather back-handed way) and saying that he wishes his own son might learn "gentilesse" from the Squire. This prologue introduces what is clearly, for the Franklin, the main theme of his own tale. For him, the point of the tale lies in the final question: who was "most fre," that is, most liberal or magnanimous, these being qualities of a gentleman. Many readers, however, have found the behavior of all three men, the squire, the knight, and the magician, far from ideal, and that of Dorigen, who invokes at length noble women who have committed suicide rather than face dishonor and who postpones her own death indefinitely, far from heroic.

While the nature of gentilesse is the central concern of the Franklin, his tale also contributes to another major theme in *The Canterbury Tales*, the value of marriage and the nature and status of women. Earlier critics tended to see the balanced marriage of Dorigen and the knight Arveragus as the ideal resolution of a debate that pitted the Wife of Bath and her spirited defense of women's sovereignty against the views of the Merchant and the Clerk, but the resolution is not entirely assured. Dorigen's questioning of divine Providence suggests she may have had too much freedom by medieval standards' while her ultimate dependence on her husband to solve her dilemma suggests that by the end of the tale she has lost it.

The Franklin says that his tale is a Breton *lai*, a short romance of the kind told by Celtic storytellers or minstrels from Wales or Brittany. In fact, the tale comes from Boccaccio, who told it twice, once in his *Decameron* and once in the *Filocolo*. Chaucer does not always acknowledge his sources (and the modern notion of plagiarism was not part of a medieval textual culture in which works were adapted and translated freely), but in this case the misrepresentation may be significant. Casting the tale in a distant Celtic past is an important part of Chaucer's artistic strategy. Like many folktales, *The Franklin's Tale* revolves around a rash promise, in this case Dorigen's promise to sleep with the squire Aurelius if he can remove the black rocks along the coast. Arveragus decides that Dorigen must keep her promise, her truth, because it is "the highest thing that man may keep" (l. 807), and the conflict between truth and illusion is one of the tale's central concerns.

Opening page of the *Franklin's Tale*, Ellesmere manuscript. (Reprinted by permission of *The Huntington Library, San Marino, California*. EL26C9F72r.)

THE FRANKLIN'S PROLOGUE

HEERE FOLWEN THE WORDES OF THE FRANKELEYN TO THE SQUIER AND THE WORDES OF THE HOOST TO THE FRANKELEYN

"In feith, Squier, thow hast thee wel yquit°   *done well*
  And gentilly.° I preise° wel thy wit,"   *nobly | praise*
Quod° the Frankeleyn, "considerynge° thy
  yowthe.°   *said | considering | youth*
So feelyngly° thou spekest,° sire, I allowe
  the,°   *sensitively | speak | grant you*
5 As to my doom,° ther is noon° that is heere   *judgment | no one*
Of eloquence that shal be thy peere°   *be your equal*
If that thou lyve.° God yeve° thee good chaunce   *live | give*
And in vertu° sende thee continuaunce!°   *virtue | continuing*
For of thy speche I have greet deyntee.°   *delight*
10 I have a sone,° and by the Trinitee,°   *son | Trinity*
I hadde levere° than twenty pound worth lond,[1]   *rather*
Though it right now were fallen in my hond,°   *into my hand*
He were a man of swich discrecioun°   *such discretion*
As that ye been.° Fy° on possessioun,°   *are | fie | possession*
15 But if° a man be vertuous withal!°   *unless | as well*
I have my sone snybbed,° and yet shal,   *scolded*
For he to vertu listeth nat entende,[2]
But for to pleye° at dees° and to despende°   *play | dice | spend*
And lese° al° that he hath is his usage.°   *lose | all | custom*
20 And he hath levere° talken with a page   *would rather | boy servant*
Than to comune° with any gentil wight,°   *talk | noble person*
Where he myghte lerne gentillesse[3] aright."°   *properly*
  "Straw for youre gentillesse!" quod oure Hoost.
"What, Frankeleyn, pardee° sire, wel thou
  woost°   *by God | well you know*
25 That ech° of yow° moot° tellen atte
  leste°   *each | you | must | at least*
A tale or two or breken his biheste."°   *break his promise*

"That knowe I wel, sire," quod the Frankeleyn.
"I prey yow, haveth me nat in desdeyn°   *do not disdain me*
Though to this man I speke a word or two."
30   "Telle on thy tale withouten wordes
  mo."°   *without more words*
"Gladly, sire Hoost," quod he. "I wole obeye°   *obey*
Unto youre wyl.° Now herkneth° what I seye.   *will | listen to*
I wol yow nat contrarien in no wyse,[4]
As fer° as that my wittes° wol suffyse.°   *far | wits | suffice*
35 I prey to God that it may plesen yow;°   *please you*
Thanne woot° I wel that it is good ynow."°   *know | enough*

EXPLICIT[5]

THE PROLOGUE OF THE FRANKELEYNS TALE

Thise olde, gentil Britouns[6] in hir dayes°   *their days*
  Of diverse° aventures maden layes,°   *various | made songs*
Rymeyed° in hir firste° Briton tonge,°   *rhymed | original | language*
40 Whiche layes with hir° instrumentz they songe   *their*
Or elles redden hem° for hir plesaunce.   *read them*
And oon of hem° have I in
  remembraunce,°   *one of them | memory*
Which I shal seyn° with good wyl° as I kan.   *say | will*
  But sires, bycause I am a burel° man,   *uneducated*
45 At my bigynnyng first I yow biseche,
Have me excused of my rude° speche.   *rough*
I lerned nevere rethorik,° certeyn.°   *rhetoric | certainly*
Thyng that I speke,° it moot° be bare and
  pleyn.°   *what I speak | must | plain*
I sleepe nevere on the Mount of Pernaso,[7]
50 Ne lerned° Marcus Tullius Scithero.[8]   *nor did I learn*

---

[1] *twenty ... lond* Twenty pounds worth of land is that which provides an annual income of twenty pounds—a considerable sum in the late fourteenth century, equal to half a year's income for a well-off knight.

[2] *For ... entende* Because he does not want (listeth nat) to pay attention to virtue.

[3] *gentillesse* The quality that makes someone a gentleman or woman. In the Middle Ages it normally implied distinguished birth as well as refined manners and moral virtue.

[4] *I ... wyse* I will not contradict you in any way.

[5] *Explicit* Latin: here it ends.

[6] *Britouns* Bretons, who came from Brittany, the northwest corner of modern-day France. They were a Celtic people, many of whom had, almost a thousand years before Chaucer's time, fled from Britain to escape the Anglo-Saxon invaders and joined the earlier Celtic inhabitants.

[7] *Mount of Pernaso* Mount Parnassus, the home of the Muses (the goddesses of learning and the arts).

[8] *Marcus Tullius Scithero* Cicero (106–43 BCE), the famous Roman orator who wrote about rhetoric, among other subjects.

Colours[1] ne° knowe I none, withouten
    drede,°   *nor | without doubt*
But swiche° colours as growen in the mede,°   *such | meadow*
Or elles° swiche as men dye or peynte.°   *else | paint*
Colours of rethoryk been to queynte!°   *are too unusual*
55 My spirit feeleth noght° of swich
    mateere.°   *understands nothing | matter*
But if yow list,° my tale shul ye heere.°   *desire | hear*

THE FRANKLIN'S TALE

HEERE BIGYNNETH THE FRANKELEYNS TALE

In Armorik,° that called is Britayne,°   *Armorica | Brittany*
Ther was a knyght that loved and dide his
    payne°   *took pains*
To serve a lady in his beste wise,°   *manner*
60 And many a labour, many a greet emprise°   *undertaking*
He for his lady wroghte° er° she were wonne.°   *did | before | won*
For she was oon° the faireste under sonne°   *one of | sun*
And eek° therto comen of so heigh kynrede°   *also | high lineage*
That wel unnethes° dorste° this knyght for
    drede°   *scarcely | dared | fear*
65 Telle hire° his wo,° his peyne,° and his distresse. *her | woe | pain*
But atte laste, she for his worthynesse°   *worth*
And namely° for his meke obeysaunce° *especially | meek obedience*
Hath swich a pitee° caught of his penaunce°   *pity | penance*
That pryvely° she fil of his
    accord°   *secretly | fell in agreement with him*
70 To take hym for hir housbonde and hir lord—
Of swich lordshipe as men han° over hir
    wyves.°   *have | their wives*
And for to lede° the moore in blisse hir lyves,   *lead*
Of his free wyl he swoor hire° as a knyght   *swore to her*
That nevere in al his lyf he, day ne nyght,
75 Ne sholde° upon hym take no maistrie°   *he would not | control*
Agayn hir wyl° ne kithe hire° jalousie   *against her will | show her*
But hire obeye and folwe° hir wyl in al   *follow*

As any lovere to his lady shal,
Save° that the name of soveraynetee,   *except*
80 That wolde he have for shame of his
    degree.°   *lest it shame his rank*
  She thanked hym and with ful greet
    humblesse°   *great humility*
She seyde, "Sire, sith° of youre gentillesse   *since*
Ye profre° me to have so large a reyne,°   *offer | rein*
Ne wolde nevere God bitwixe us tweyne,
85 As in my gilt, were outher werre or stryf.[2]
Sire, I wol be youre humble, trewe wyf:
Have heer my trouthe° til that myn herte breste."° *pledge | burst*
Thus been° they bothe in quiete and in reste.   *are*
  For o thyng,° sires, saufly° dar I seye,   *one thing | safely*
90 That freendes everych oother° moot obeye   *each other*
If they wol longe holden compaignye.°   *remain in company*
Love wol nat been constreyned by maistrye.°   *control*
Whan maistrie comth, the god of love anon°   *immediately*
Beteth hise wynges,° and, farewel, he is gon!   *beats his wings*
95 Love is a thing—as any spirit—free.
Wommen of kynde° desiren libertee   *by nature*
And nat to been constreyned as a thral.°   *slave*
And so doon° men, if I sooth° seyen shal.   *do | truth*
Looke, who that is moost pacient° in love,   *patient*
100 He is at his avantage° al above.   *advantage*
Pacience is an heigh° vertu, certeyn,   *great*
For it venquysseth,° as thise clerkes°   *vanquishes | learned men*
    seyn,
Thynges that rigour° sholde° nevere
    atteyne.°   *harshnes | could | achieve*
For every word men may nat chide° or pleyne.°   *nag | complain*
105 Lerneth to suffre° or elles,° so moot I goon,[3]   *endure | else*
Ye shul it lerne wherso° ye wole or noon!°   *whether | not*
For in this world, certein, ther no wight° is   *person*
That he ne dooth or seith° som tyme°
    amys;   *neither does or says | sometimes*
Ire, siknesse,° or constellacioun,[4]   *sickness*

---

[1] *Colours* The colors of rhetoric were the stylistic devices and
figures of speech recommended by rhetoricians for use in effective
public speaking and writing. Despite the Franklin's protestation that
he knows no rhetoric, his tale has several ornate passages that make
heavy use of these rhetorical colors.

[2] *Ne ... stryf* May God never wish that there were (i.e., may there
never be) any quarrel or strife between us two through any fault of
mine.

[3] *So moot I gon* As I might go, an idiomatic expression meaning
roughly "By my word" or "I assure you."

[4] *constellacioun* By the influence of the stars and planets.

110 Wyn,° wo, or chaungynge° of complexioun[1]   *wine | changing*
Causeth ful ofte to doon amys or speken.°   *do or speak wrong*
On every wrong a man may nat be wreken.°   *avenged*
After the tyme moste be temperaunce[2]
To every wight that kan on governaunce.°   *knows about governing*
115 And therfore hath this wise, worthy knyght,
To lyve in ese,° suffrance hire
bihight,   *ease | promised her (his) patience*
And she to hym ful wisly gan to swere°   *swore*
That nevere sholde ther be defaute° in here.°   *fault | her*
     Heere may men seen° an humble, wys accord.   *see*
120 Thus hath she take° hir servant and hir lord—   *has she taken*
Servant in love and lord in mariage.
Thanne° was he bothe in lordshipe and servage.°   *then | service*
Servage? Nay, but in lordshipe above,
Sith he hath bothe his lady and his love—
125 His lady, certes, and his wyf also,
The which that lawe of love acordeth to.°   *agrees to*
And whan he was in this prosperitee,°   *prosperity*
Hoom° with his wyf he gooth° to his
contree,°   *home | goes | country*
Nat fer fro° Pedmark,[3] ther° his dwellyng
was,   *not far from | where*
130 Whereas° he lyveth in blisse and in solas.°   *where | comfort*
     Who koude telle, but he hadde wedded
be,°   *he who had married*
The joye, the ese,° and the prosperitee   *ease*
That is bitwixe° an housbonde and his wyf?   *between*
A yeer and moore lasted this blisful lyf,
135 Til that the knyght of which I speke of thus,
That of Kayrrud[4] was cleped° Arveragus,   *called*
Shoope hym° to goon and dwelle a yeer or
tweyne°   *prepared | two*
In Engelond, that cleped° was eek° Briteyne,   *called | also*
To seke in armes worshipe° and honour.   *knightly reputation*
140 For al his lust° he sette in swich labour—   *pleasure*
And dwelled there two yeer. The book seith thus.

---

[1] *complexioun* Temperament. Medieval medical theory maintained that what we now call "personality" was a function of the balance in the body of the four bodily fluids known as humors.

[2] *After … temperaunce* Moderation must be suited to the time or occasion.

[3] *Pedmark* Penmarch, a town in Brittany.

[4] *Kayrrud* In modern Brittany there are several towns called Kerru (from the Celtic name for red fort), but none is near Penmarch.

     Now wol I stynten° of the Arveragus,   *cease speaking*
And speken I wole of Dorigene his wyf,
That loveth hire housbonde as hire hertes lyf.
145 For his absence wepeth she and siketh,°   *sighs*
As doon° thise noble wyves whan hem
liketh.°   *do | when they like*
She moorneth, waketh, wayleth, fasteth, pleyneth![5]
Desir of his presence hire so destreyneth,°   *afflicts*
That al this wyde world she sette at noght.°   *set at nothing*
150 Hire freendes,° whiche that knewe hir hevy
thoght,°   *friends | sad thoughts*
Conforten hire in al that ever they may.
They prechen hire.° They telle hire nyght and day   *preach to her*
That causelees° she sleeth° hirself, allas!   *without cause | kills*
And every confort possible in this cas°   *case*
155 They doon to hire° with al hire bisynesse,°   *her | their efforts*
Al for to make hire leve° hire hevynesse.°   *leave | sadness*
     By proces,° as ye knowen everichoon,°   *gradually | everyone*
Men may so longe graven° in a stoon°   *engrave | stone*
Til som figure° therinne emprented° be.   *image | engraved*
160 So longe han° they conforted hire, til she   *have*
Receyved hath by hope and by resoun°   *reason*
The emprentyng° of hire consolacioun,   *imprinting*
Thurgh which hir grete sorwe gan aswage.°   *began to lessen*
She may nat alwey duren° in swich rage.°   *endure | passion*
165   And eek Arveragus in al this care
Hath sent hire lettres hoom of his welfare
And that he wol come hastily agayn,
Or elles hadde this sorwe hir herte slayn.
     Hire freendes sawe hir sorwe gan to slake°   *lessen*
170 And preyde° hire on knees, for Goddes sake   *asked*
To come and romen hire° in compaignye   *roam about*
Awey to dryve hire derke fantasye.°   *dark imaginings*
And finally she graunted that requeste,
For wel she saugh° that it was for the beste.   *saw*
175   Now stood hire castel° faste° by the see,°   *castle | close | sea*
And often with hire freendes walketh shee
Hire to disporte° upon the bank an
heigh,°   *to enjoy herself | on high*
Whereas° she many a shipe and barge seigh°   *where | sees*
Seillynge hir cours, whereas hem liste go.[6]
180 But thanne was that a parcel° of hire wo,°   *part | her woe*

---

[5] *She … pleyneth* She mourns, lies sleepless, wails, fasts, complains.

[6] *Seillynge … go* Sailing their course, where they wished to go.

For to hirself ful ofte "Allas!" seith she.

"Is ther no shipe of so manye as I se

Wol bryngen hom° my lord? Thanne were myn herte   *bring home*

Al warisshed° of hise bittre peynes smerte!"°   *cured / the hurt of its bitter pains*

185   Another tyme ther wolde she sitte and thynke

And caste hir eyen dounward fro the brynke.°   *from the brink*

But whan she saugh the grisly rokkes blake,°   *horrible black rocks*

For verray feere° so wolde hir herte quake   *true fear*

That on hire feet she myghte hire noght° sustene.°   *not / keep*

190   Thanne wolde she sitte adoun° upon the grene°   *sit down / green*

And pitously into the see° biholde°   *sea / gaze*

And seyn right thus with sorweful sikes colde,[1]

"Eterne° God, that thurgh° thy purveiaunce°   *eternal / through / foresight*

Ledest° the world by certein governaunce,   *lead*

195   In ydel,° as men seyn, ye nothyng make.   *vain*

But, Lord, thise grisly, feendly° rokkes blake   *fiendish*

That semen° rather a foul confusioun   *seem*

Of werk than any fair creacioun

Of swich a parfit,° wys° God and a stable,°   *perfect / wise / unchanging*

200   Why han ye wroght° this werk unresonable?°   *made / irrational work*

For by this werk south, north, ne° west, ne eest,   *nor*

Ther nys yfostred° man ne bryd ne beest.   *is not helped*

It dooth no good, to my wit,° but anoyeth.°   *understanding / harms*

Se ye nat, Lord, how mankynde it destroyeth?

205   An hundred thousand bodyes° of mankynde   *bodies*

Han rokkes slayn, al° be they nat in mynde,°   *although / remembered*

Which mankynde is so fair part of thy werk,

That thou it madest lyk to thyn owene merk.°   *image*

Thanne semed it ye hadde a greet chiertee°   *love*

210   Toward mankynde. But how thanne may it bee

That ye swiche meenes° make it to destroyen—   *means*

Whiche meenes do no good but evere anoyen?°   *harm*

I woot wel clerkes wol seyn as hem leste[2]

By argumentz that al is for the beste,

215   Though I kan the causes nat yknowe.

But thilke God that made wynd to blowe,

As kepe my lord! This my conclusioun.[3]

To clerkes° lete° I al this disputisoun.°   *theologians / leave / debate*

But wolde God that alle thise rokkes blake

220   Were sonken into Helle for his[4] sake!

Thise rokkes sleen° myn herte for the feere!"°   *kill / fear*

Thus wolde she seyn with many a pitous teere.°   *pitiful tear*

Hire freendes sawe that it was no disport°   *comfort*

To romen by the see, but disconfort,°   *distress*

225   And shopen° for to pleyen° somwher elles.   *arranged / play*

They leden hire by ryveres° and by welles°   *rivers / springs*

And eek in othere places delitables.°   *delightful*

They dauncen, and they pleyen at ches° and tables.°   *chess / backgammon*

So on a day, right in the morwetyde,°   *morning*

230   Unto a gardyn that was ther bisyde,°   *nearby*

In which that they hadde maad hir ordinaunce°   *their arrangements*

Of vitaille° and of oother purveiaunce,°   *food / other provisions*

They goon° and pleye hem° al the longe day.   *go / enjoy themselves*

And this was in the sixte morwe° of May—   *sixth morning*

235   Which May hadde peynted with his softe shoures°   *showers*

This gardyn ful of leves° and of floures,   *leaves*

And craft of mannes hand so curiously°   *cleverly*

Arrayed° hadde this gardyn trewely,°   *adorned / truly*

That nevere was ther gardyn of swich prys°   *value*

240   But if it were the verray Paradys.°   *Paradise itself*

The odour of floures and the fresshe sighte

Wolde han maked° any herte lighte   *have made*

That evere was born, but if to greet siknesse°   *too great sickness*

Or to greet sorwe° helde it in distresse,   *too great sorrow*

245   So ful it was of beautee with plesaunce.°   *pleasure*

At after dyner° gonne° they to daunce   *dinner / began*

And synge also—save° Dorigen allone,   *except*

Which° made alwey hir compleint °and hir moone.°   *who / lament / moan*

For she ne saugh° hym on the daunce go   *saw*

250   That was hir housbonde and hir love also.

But nathelees, she moste a tyme abyde°   *wait for a time*

---

[1]   *And … colde*   And say just like this with sorrowful, cold sighs.

[2]   *I … leste*   I know well that theologians will say as they wish.

[3]   *But … conclusioun*   (May) that same God that caused the wind to blow take care of my lord. That is my conclusion. (Dorigen closes her discussion of the theological question of God's foreknowledge with the word "conclusion," the formal term for the end of a scholastic argument.)

[4]   *his*   Refers here to her husband, Arveragus, rather than to God.

And with good hope lete hir sorwe slyde.° *go away*
  Upon this daunce, amonges othere men,
Daunced a squier biforn° Dorigen *before*
255 That fressher was and jolyer of array,° *more finely dressed*
As to° my doom,° than is the monthe of *according to | judgment*
  May.
He syngeth, daunceth passynge° any man *surpassing*
That is or was sith that the world bigan.
Therwith° he was, if men sholde hym
  discryve,° *moreover | describe*
260 Oon of the beste farynge° man onlyve°— *behaving | alive*
Yong, strong, right vertuous and riche and wys,
And wel biloved and holden° in greet prys.° *held | value*
And shortly, if the sothe° I tellen shal, *truth*
Unwityng° of this Dorigen at al *not knowing*
265 This lusty° squier, servant to Venus,[1] *vigorous*
Which that ycleped was° Aurelius, *was called*
Hadde loved hire best of any creature,
Two yeer and moore, as was his aventure.° *chance*
But nevere dorste° he tellen hire his grevaunce.° *dared | grief*
270 Withouten coppe he drank al his penaunce.[2]
He was despeyred.° Nothyng dorste he seye, *in despair*
Save in his songes somwhat wolde he wreye° *reveal*
His wo, as in a general compleynyng.° *lamenting*
He seyde he lovede and was biloved
  nothyng.° *by no means beloved*
275 Of swich matere made he manye layes,
Songes, compleintes, roundels, virelayes,[3]
How that he dorste nat° his sorwe telle *dared not*
But langwissheth° as a Furye[4] dooth° in Helle. *languishes | does*
And dye he moste, he seyde, as dide Ekko
280 For Narcisus, that dorste nat telle hir wo.[5]

In oother manere than ye heere me seye
Ne dorste he nat to hire his wo biwreye,
Save that paraventure° somtyme at daunces *perhaps*
Ther° yong folk kepen hir
  observaunces,° *where | keep their rituals*
285 It may wel be he looked on hir face
In swich a wise as man that asketh grace.° *for favor*
But nothyng wiste she of his entente.° *intent*
Nathelees, it happed er they thennes wente,[6]
Bycause that he was hire neighebour
290 And was a man of worshipe and honour
And hadde yknowen hym of tyme yore,[7]
They fille in speche,[8] and forth moore and moore
Unto° this purpos drough° Aurelius, *towards | drew*
And whan he saugh his tyme, he seyde thus:
295   "Madame," quod he, "by God that this world made,
So that° I wiste it myghte youre herte glade,° *provided | gladden*
I wolde that day that youre Arveragus
Wente over the see that I, Aurelius,
Hadde went ther. Nevere I sholde have come agayn,
300 For wel I woot, my servyce is in vayn.° *vain*
My gerdoun° is but brestyng° of myn herte. *reward | breaking*
Madame, reweth° upon my peynes
  smerte,° *have pity | sharp pains*
For with a word ye may me sleen° or save. *kill*
Heere at youre feet God wolde that I were grave!° *buried*
305 I ne have as now no leyser° moore to seye. *leisure*
Have mercy, sweete, or ye wol do me deye!"° *cause my death*
  She gan to looke upon Aurelius.
"Is this youre wyl?"° quod she. "And sey ye thus? *will*
Nevere erst,"° quod she, "ne wiste I what ye
  mente!° *before | meant*
310 But now, Aurelie, I knowe youre entente.
By thilke° God that yaf° me soule and lyf, *that same | gave*
Ne shal I nevere been untrewe wyf,
In word ne° werk,° as fer° as I have wit. *nor | deed | far*
I wol been his to whom that I am knyt.° *knit*
315 Taak this for fynal answere as of me."

---

[1] *servant to Venus* Aurelius, like Chaucer's Squire or Palamon in *The Knight's Tale*, is devoted to courtly love (Venus was the goddess of love), which was conceived of as a form of service, demanding total loyalty and subservience to one's lady.

[2] *Withouten ... penaunce* He drank his penance without a cup. The expression may suggest he suffered intensely or even eagerly (without bothering with a cup), but its exact meaning is unclear.

[3] *Songes ... virelayes* Genres of songs popular in fourteenth-century France and England.

[4] *Furye* Winged goddess.

[5] *Ekko ... wo* In Greek mythology, Narcissus looked into a well, saw his image, and fell in love with himself. Echo, who could only repeat the last words of others, loved him but died because he did

not return her love, fading away until only her voice was left. This story is told by the Roman poet Ovid (43 BCE–18 CE) in his *Metamorphoses* 3.353–407.

[6] *Nathelees ... wente* But nevertheless, it happened before they went from there.

[7] *And ... yore* And (she) had known him for a long time.

[8] *fille in speche* Fell into speech (i.e., began to talk together).

But after that in pley thus seyde she:

"Aurelie," quod she, "by heighe God above,

Yet wolde I graunte° yow to been youre love,   *grant you to be*

Syn° I yow see so pitously complayne.   *since*

320 Looke what day¹ that endelong° Britayne   *all along the edge of*

Ye remoeve° alle the rokkes, stoon by stoon,   *remove*

That they ne lette° shipe ne boot° to goon,   *hinder / boat*

I seye whan ye han maad the coost so clene°   *clear*

Of rokkes, that ther nys no stoon ysene,°   *is no stone seen*

325 Thanne wol I love yow best of any man.

Have heer my trouthe in al that evere I kan."²

   "Is ther noon oother grace° in yow?" quod he.   *no other mercy*

   "No, by that Lord," quod she, "that maked° me!   *made*

For wel I woot that it shal never bityde!°   *happen*

330 Lat swiche folies out of youre herte slyde!³

What deyntee° sholde a man han° in his lyf   *delight / have*

For to go love another mannes wyf,

That hath hir body whan so that hym
      liketh?"°   *whenever he wishes*

   Aurelius ful ofte soore siketh.°⁴   *sighs sorely*

335 Wo was Aurelie whan that he this herde,

And with a sorweful herte he thus answerde:

   "Madame," quod he, "this were an
      inpossible!°   *impossible (thing)*

Thanne moot° I dye of sodeyn° deth horrible!"   *must / sudden*

And with that word he turned hym
      anon.°   *turned away immediately*

340 Tho° coome hir° othere freendes, many
      oon,°   *then / her / a one*

And in the aleyes° romeden° up and doun,   *alleys / roamed*

And nothyng wiste of this conclusioun°   *matter*

But sodeynly bigonne° revel newe,°   *began / new revelry*

Til that the brighte sonne loste his hewe.°   *color*

345 For th'orisonte° hath reft° the sonne his
      light—   *horizon / taken from*

This is as muche to seye as it was nyght.

And hoom they goon in joye and in solas,

Save° oonly wrecche° Aurelius, allas!   *except / wretched*

He to his hous is goon with sorweful herte.

350 He seeth he may nat fro his deeth asterte.°   *escape*

Hym semed that he felte his herte colde.⁵

Up to the Hevene hise handes he gan holde,°   *raised*

And on hise knowes bare° he sette hym doun,   *bare knees*

And in his ravyng° seyde his orisoun.°   *raving / prayer*

355 For verray wo° out of his wit° he breyde.°   *true woe / mind / went*

He nyste° what he spak. But thus he seyde   *did not know*

With pitous herte. His pleynt hath he bigonne

Unto the goddes and first unto the sonne:

   He seyde, "Appollo,⁶ god and governour

360 Of every plannte, herbe, tree, and flour

That yevest° after° thy declinacioun⁷   *gives / according to*

To ech of hem his tyme and his sesoun,

As thyn herberwe⁸ chaungeth lowe or heighe,

Lord Phebus, cast thy merciable eighe°   *merciful eye*

365 On wrecche Aurelie, which am but lorn.°   *lost*

Lo, Lord, my lady hath my deeth
      ysworn°—   *sentenced me to death*

Withoute gilt° but° thy benignytee,°   *guilt / unless / kindness*

Upon my dedly° herte have som pitee.   *deathly*

For wel I woot, Lord Phebus, if yow lest,°   *wish*

370 Ye may me helpen, save° my lady, best.   *except for*

Now vouchethsauf° that I may yow devyse°   *grant / describe*

How that I may been holpen° and in what
      wyse.°   *be helped / way*

   Youre blisful suster° Lucina⁹ the sheene,°   *sister / bright*

That of the see is chief goddesse and queene—

375 Though Neptunus¹⁰ have deitee° in the see,   *divine rule*

Yet emperisse° aboven hym is she—   *empress*

Ye knowen wel, Lord, that right° as hir desir   *just*

---

¹ *Looke what day* On whatever day.

² *Have ... kan* Have here my word, as far as I am able.

³ *Lat ... slide* Let such follies slide out of your heart.

⁴ *Aurelius ... siketh* The awkward position of this line, which seems an interruption, may be an error, but it is found in many manuscripts, including both Ellesmere and Hengwrt. Three manuscripts whose readings are on the whole considered less reliable have lines 327 and 328 following after 334, which removes the problem.

⁵ *Hym ... colde* It seemed to him that he felt his heart grow cold.

⁶ *Appollo* Phoebus Apollo is the god of the sun.

⁷ *declinacioun* Angle of a planet from the celestial equator. As Walter Skeat notes in his edition, "The change of season depends on the sun's change of position (called *herbrewe* or 'harbor' in line 1035) to be high or low in the sky."

⁸ *herberwe* Harbor (i.e., position in the sky).

⁹ *Lucina* Another name for Diana, goddess of the moon. A gloss above the name Lucina provides the more familiar "Luna."

¹⁰ *Neptunus* Neptune, god of the sea.

Is to be quyked° and lightned of°   *animated / illuminated by*
   youre fir,
For which she folweth yow ful bisily,°   *eagerly*
380 Right° so the see desireth naturelly   *just*
To folwen hire as she that is goddesse,
Bothe in the see and ryveres moore° and lesse.°   *greater / lesser*
Wherfore,° Lord Phebus, this is my requeste: *therefore*
Do this miracle or do myn herte breste°—   *make burst*
385 That now next at this opposicioun,°   *opposition (of planets)*
Which in the signe shal be of the leoun,[1]
As preieth° hire so greet a flood to brynge   *ask*
That fyve fadme° at the leeste it
   oversprynge°   *five fathoms / overwhelm*
The hyeste rokke in Armorik Briteyne,°   *Armorican Brittany*
390 And lat this flood endure yeres tweyne.°   *two years*
Thanne, certes, to my lady may I seye,
'Holdeth° youre heste.° The rokkes been°   *keep / promise / are*
   aweye!'
   Lord Phebus, dooth this miracle for me!
Preye° hire she go no faster cours° than ye.   *ask / orbit*
395 I seye, preyeth youre suster that she go
No faster cours than ye thise yeres two.
Thanne shal she been evene atte fulle alway,[2]
And spryng° flood laste bothe nyght and day.   *spring*
And but she vouchesauf in swich manere
400 To graunte me my sovereyn lady deere,
Prey hire to synken° every rok adoun°   *sink / down*
Into hir owene dirke° regioun   *dark*
Under the ground, ther° Pluto dwelleth inne,[3]   *where*
Or neveremo shal I my lady wynne.
405 Thy temple in Delphos[4] wol I barefoot seke.°   *seek*
Lord Phebus, se° the teeris° on my cheke,   *see / tears*
And of my peyne have som compassioun."

---

[1] *signe … leoun* Constellation Leo (the lion), part of the zodiac. The sun's influence is strongest in this sign, which is his house or mansion. When the sun and the moon are in opposition, i.e., 180° apart, their effect on the earth is strongest and the tides highest.

[2] *evene … always* Completely even with you. Aurelius wishes the sun and moon to align in the sky for two years, thus causing abnormally high tides.

[3] *Under … inne* Pluto was the god of the underworld and husband of Persephone (Roman Proserpina), who was sometimes associated with the moon goddess, Luna.

[4] *Thy … Delphos* Apollo's oracle at the temple at Delphi provided clues from the gods to help solve difficult problems.

And with that word in swowne° he fil adoun,   *faint*
And longe tyme he lay forth in a traunce.
410 His brother, which that° knew of his penaunce,°   *who / grief*
Up caughte hym, and to bedde he hath hym
   broght°   *raised him up*
Dispeyred° in this torment and this thoght   *despairing*
Lete° I this woful creature lye.   *leave*
Chese he for me wheither he wol lyve or dye![5]
415 Arveragus, with heele° and greet honour,   *health*
As he that was of chivalrie the flour,°   *flower*
Is comen hoom and othere worthy men.
O blisful artow° now, thou Dorigen,   *are you*
That hast thy lusty° housbonde in thyne armes!   *vigorous*
420 The fresshe° knyght, the worthy man of armes,   *lively*
That loveth thee as his owene hertes lyf,
Nothyng list hym to been ymaginatyf[6]
If any wight hadde spoke whil he was oute°   *abroad*
To hire of love. He hadde of it no doute.°   *fear*
425 He noght entendeth° to no swich mateere   *pays no attention*
But daunceth, justeth,° maketh hire good cheere.   *jousts*
And thus in joye and blisse I lete hem° dwelle,   *them*
And of the sike° Aurelius I wol yow telle.   *sick*
   In langour and in torment furyus°   *extreme*
430 Two yeer and moore lay wrecche° Aurelyus   *wretched*
Er any foot° he myghte on erthe gon.°   *step / walk*
Ne confort in this tyme hadde he noon,
Save of his brother, which that was a clerk.°   *scholar*
He knew of al this wo and al this werk,°   *effort*
435 For to noon oother creature, certeyn,
Of this matere he dorste no word seyn.°   *say*
Under his brest he baar° it moore secree°   *carried / more secretly*
Than evere dide Pamphilus for Galathee.[7]
His brest was hool° withoute° for to
   sene,°   *healthy / outside / to be seen*
440 But in his herte ay° was the arwe° kene,°   *ever / arrow / sharp*
As wel ye knowe that of a sursanure[8]
In surgerye is perilous the cure,

---

[5] *Chese … dye* Let him choose, for all I care, whether he live or die.

[6] *Nothyng … ymaginatyf* He by no means wishes to be inquisitive.

[7] *Pamphilus … Galathee* Main characters in the thirteenth-century Latin romance, *Pamphilus de amore* (*Pamphilus on Love*).

[8] *sursanure* Wound healed only on outside.

But men myghte touche the arwe or come therby.[1]

His brother weepe and wayled pryvely,°   *privately*

445 Til atte laste hym fil in remembraunce°   *he remembered*

That whiles he was at Orliens° in Fraunce[2]   *Orléans*

As yonge clerkes that been lykerous°   *eager*

To reden artz° that been curious,°   *sciences / exotic*

Seken in every halke° and every herne°   *nook / corner*

450 Particuler° sciences° for to lerne,   *specialized / types of knowledge*

He hym remembred that upon a day

At Orliens in studie° a book he say°   *(a hall of) study / saw*

Of magyk natureel,[3] which his felawe°   *friend*

That was that tyme a bacheler of lawe,°   *student of law*

455 Al° were he ther to lerne another craft,°   *although / subject*

Hadde prively upon his desk ylaft,°   *left*

Which book spak° muchel° of the

operaciouns°   *spoke / much / operations*

Touchynge° the eighte and twenty mansiouns[4]   *pertaining to*

That longen° to the moone and swich folye,°   *belong / such folly*

460 As in oure dayes is nat worth a flye.°   *fly*

For Hooly Chirches feith in oure bileve

Ne suffreth noon illusioun us to greve.[5]

And whan this book was in his remembraunce,

Anon for joye his herte gan to daunce,

465 And to hymself he seyde pryvely,

"My brother shal be warisshed° hastily,   *healed*

For I am siker° that ther be sciences   *certain*

By whiche men make diverse apparences,°   *different illusions*

Swiche as thise subtile° tregetours° pleye.[6]   *clever / magicians*

470 For ofte at feestes, have I wel herd seye,°   *said*

That tregetours withinne an halle large

Have maad come in a water and a barge

And in the halle rowen up and doun.

Somtyme hath semed come a grym leoun,[7]

475 And somtyme floures sprynge° as in a mede;   *spring up*

Somtyme a vyne° and grapes white and rede,   *vine*

Somtyme a castel al of lym° and stoon,   *lime*

And whan hym lyked° voyded it°   *they wished / it disappeared*

anon.

Thus semed it to every mannes° sighte.   *man's*

480   Now thanne, conclude I thus: that if I myghte

At Orliens som oold felawe° yfynde°   *old friend / find*

That hadde this moones° mansions in mynde   *moon's*

Or oother magyk natureel above,

He sholde wel make my brother han° his love.   *have*

485 For with an apparence a clerk may make

To mannes sighte that alle the rokkes blake

Of Britaigne weren yvoyded° everichon°   *removed / every one*

And shippes by the brynke° comen and gon   *shore*

And in swich forme enduren a wowke° or two.   *week*

490 Thanne were my brother warisshed of his wo.

Thanne moste she nedes° holden hire biheste,   *necessarily*

Or elles he shal shame hire atte leeste."°   *at the least*

What sholde° I make a lenger tale of this?   *why should*

Unto his brotheres bed he comen is,

495 And swich confort he yaf hym for to gon°   *go*

To Orliens, that he up stirte° anon,   *started*

And on his wey forthward° thanne is he fare°   *forward / gone*

In hope for to been lissed° of his care.   *relieved*

Whan they were come almoost to that citee,

500 But if it were a two furlong[8] or thre,

A yong clerk romynge° by hymself they mette,   *roaming*

Which that in Latyn° thriftily° hem

grette.°   *Latin / appropriately / greeted*

And after that he seyde a wonder° thyng.   *wonderful*

"I knowe," quod he, "the cause of youre comyng."

505 And er they ferther any foote wente,

He tolde hem al that was in hire entente.°   *their intent*

This Briton clerk hym asked of° felawes,   *about*

The whiche that he had knowe in olde dawes,°   *days*

And he answerde hym that they dede were,

510 For which he weep ful ofte many a teere.

---

[1] *In … therby*   Is hard to cure in medicine, unless one can find the arrow head.

[2] *Orliens in Fraunce*   The university at Orléans, south of Paris, was famous for the study of law and had a more dubious reputation as a center for the study of magic.

[3] *magyk natureel*   Natural magic, such as that of Chaucer's Physician (see *General Prologue*, line 416), is based on a knowledge of the powers of the planets and the physical world, as opposed to black magic, which makes use of spirits or devils.

[4] *eighte … mansiouns*   The twenty-eight houses of astrology.

[5] *For … greve*   Because the faith in Holy Church (set out) in our creed does not allow any illusion to grieve us. The passage reminds us that the story ostensibly takes place in pagan times, even though the social customs are more or less those of Chaucer's day.

[6] *Swiche … pleye*   Tregetours produced special effects and illusions, often for banquets.

[7] *Sometyme … leoun*   Sometimes a fierce lion seems to come.

[8] *furlong*   Measurement equal to 220 yards.

Doun of his hors° Aurelius lighte° anon,   *horse | alighted*

And with this magicien forth is he gon

Hoom to his hous, and maden hem° wel at ese;°   *them | ease*

Hem lakked no vitaille that myghte hem plese.[1]

515   So wel arrayed hous as ther was oon

Aurelius in his lyf saugh nevere noon.[2]

    He shewed hym er he wente to sopeer°   *supper*

Forestes, parkes ful of wilde deer.

Ther saugh he hertes° with hir hornes

    hye,°   *harts (deer) | high horns*

520   The gretteste that evere were seyn with eye.

He saugh of hem an hondred slayn with houndes°   *by dogs*

And somme with arwes blede of bittre woundes.

He saugh, whan voyded° were thise wilde deer,   *gone*

Thise fauconers° upon a fair ryver,   *these falconers*

525   That with hir haukes° han the heroun slayn.   *their hawks*

    Tho saugh he knyghtes justyng° in a playn.°   *jousting | plain*

And after this he dide° hym swich plesaunce°   *gave | pleasure*

That he hym shewed his lady on a daunce,°   *at a dance*

On° which hymself he° daunced, as hym   *at | he himself*

    thoughte.°   *as it seemed to him*

530   And whan this maister° that this magyk

    wroughte°   *master (of Arts) | performed*

Saugh it was tyme, he clapte° hise handes two,   *clapped*

And, farewel, al oure revel° was ago!°   *revelry | gone*

And yet remoeved° they nevere out of the hous   *moved*

Whil they saugh al this sighte merveillous,°   *marvelous sight*

535   But in his studie theras° hise bookes be   *where*

They seten stille and no wight but they thre.°   *three*

    To hym this maister called his squier[3]

And seyde hym thus: "Is redy oure soper?°   *supper*

Almoost an houre it is, I undertake,°   *I suppose*

540   Sith I yow bad° oure soper for to make,   *commanded*

Whan that thise worthy men wenten with me

Into my studie, theras my bookes be."

    "Sire," quod this squier, "whan it liketh° yow,   *pleases*

It is al redy, though ye wol° right now."   *wish*

545   "Go we thanne soupe,"° quod he, "as for the beste.   *to eat*

This amorous folk somtyme moote han hir reste!"

    At after soper° fille° they in tretee°   *after supper | fell | negotiations*

What somme° sholde this maistres gerdoun° be   *sum | payment*

To remoeven alle the rokkes of Britayne

550   And eek from Gerounde° to the mouth of

    Sayne.°   *Gironde | Seine*

    He made it straunge° and swoor, so God   *made difficulties*

    hym save,

Lasse than a thousand pound he wolde nat have,

Ne gladly for that somme he wolde nat goon.[4]

    Aurelius with blisful herte anoon°   *immediately*

555   Answerde thus: "Fy° on a thousand pound!   *fie*

This wyde world which that men seye is round,[5]

I wolde it yeve° if I were lord of it.   *give*

This bargayn is ful dryve,° for we been knyt.°   *fully made | agreed*

Ye shal be payed trewely, by my trouthe.°   *pledge*

560   But looketh now, for no necligence° or

    slouthe°   *negligence | laziness*

Ye tarie° us heere no lenger than tomorwe."   *keep*

    "Nay," quod this clerk, "have heer my feith° to

    borwe!"°   *faith | as a pledge*

To bedde is goon Aurelius whan hym leste,°   *he wished*

And wel ny° al that nyght he hadde his reste.   *very nearly*

565   What for his labour and his hope of blisse,

His woful herte of penaunce° hadde a lisse.°   *grief | relief*

    Upon the morwe whan that it was day

To Britaigne tooke they the righte° way,   *direct*

Aurelius and this magicien bisyde,°   *as well*

570   And been descended° ther° they wolde abyde.   *are arrived | where*

And this was, as thise° bookes me remembre,°   *these | remind me*

The colde, frosty sesoun of Decembre.

    Phebus° wax° old and hewed lyk

    latoun,°   *the sun | grew | colored like brass*

That in his hoote declynacioun°   *hot declination*

575   Shoon as the burned° gold with stremes°   *polished | streams*

    brighte.

But now in Capricorn adoun he lighte,°[6]   *alights*

---

1 *Hem ... plese* They lacked no food that might please them.

2 *So ... noon* Aurelius, in his life, never saw any house so well arranged (or supplied) as the one that was there.

3 *squier* The squire is not a knight in training but a personal servant. The title nevertheless suggests that his master is a man of consequence.

4 *Ne ... goon* Nor, at that price, would he not gladly refuse the job, i.e., it was the minimum he would accept.

5 *This ... round* Contrary to popular modern belief, educated people in the Middle Ages knew the world was round.

6 *That ... lighte* The declination is the distance above or below the equator. The hot declination is the sign of Cancer, which the sun enters in June. When it was in Cancer the sun shone hot, but now in December it enters Capricorn, where it is at its lowest altitude and

Whereas° he shoon ful pale, I dar wel seyn.   *where*
The bittre frostes with the sleet and reyn°   *rain*
Destroyed hath the grene in every yerd.°   *yard*
580 Janus[1] sit by the fyr with double berd°   *beard*
And drynketh of his bugle horn° the wyn.°   *drinking horn | wine*
Biforn hym stant° brawen° of the tosked swyn,[2]   *stands | meat*
And "Nowel!"° crieth every lusty man.   *Noël*
    Aurelius in al that evere he kan
585 Dooth to his maister chiere and reverence[3]
And preyeth hym to doon his diligence°   *do his best*
To bryngen hym out of his peynes smerte,
Or with a swerd° that he wolde slitte° his herte.   *sword | pierce*
    This subtil° clerk swich routhe° had of this man   *clever | pity*
590 That nyght and day he spedde hym that he
        kan°   *tried as best he could*
To wayten° a tyme of his conclusioun.   *watch for*
This is to seye, to maken illusioun
By swich a apparence° of jogelrye°—   *an appearance | trickery*
I ne kan no termes of astrologye°—   *know no astrological jargon*
595 That she and every wight sholde wene° and seye   *think*
That of Britaigne the rokkes were aweye
Or ellis they were sonken under grounde.
So atte laste he hath his tyme yfounde°   *found*
To maken hise japes° and his
        wrecchednesse°   *tricks | wretchedness*
600 Of swich a supersticious cursednesse.
Hise tables *Tolletanes*[4] forth he brought,

Ful wel corrected, ne° ther lakked° nought,°   *nor | lacked | nothing*
Neither his collect° ne hise expans
        yeeris°   *collect (years) | expanse-years*
Ne hise rootes° ne hise othere geeris,°   *roots (dates) | equipment*
605 As been his centris° and his argumentz   *centric tables*
And hise proporcioneles convenientz°   *fitting proportionals*
For hise equacions° in everythyng.   *equations*
And by his eighte speere in his wirkyng[5]
He knew ful wel how fer Alnath[6] was shone°   *had shone*
610 Fro the heed° of thilke fixe° Aries[7] above,   *head | that fixed*
That in the ninthe speere° considered is.   *sphere*
Ful subtilly° he hadde kalkuled° al this.   *cleverly | calculated*
    Whan he hadde founde his firste
        mansioun,°   *position (of the moon)*
He knew the remenaunt° by proporcioun°   *the rest | proportion*
615 And knew the arisyng of his moone weel
And in whos face and terme[8] and everydeel°   *every part*
And knew ful weel the moones mansioun
Acordaunt to his operacioun.   *calculation*
And knew also hise othere observaunces,°   *ceremonies*
620 For swich illusiouns and swiche meschaunces°   *evil practices*
As hethen° folk useden° in thilke° dayes,   *heathen | used | those*
For which no lenger maked° he delayes,   *made*
But thurgh his magik for a wyke or tweye,
It semed that alle the rokkes were aweye.
625   Aurelius, which that yet despeired is°   *is still in despair*
Wher° he shal han his love or fare amys,°   *whether | lose out*
Awaiteth nyght and day on this myracle.
And whan he knew that ther was noon obstacle,
That voyded° were thise rokkes everychon,   *gone*
630 Doun to hise maistres feet he fil anon
And seyde, "I, woful wrecche Aurelius,
Thanke yow, lord, and lady myn Venus,

shines most faintly.

[1] *Janus* In Roman mythology, Janus is the double-faced god who represents the exit of the old year and the entrance of the new. The month of January is named after him.

[2] *tosked swyn* Boar. The roasted boar's head was a favorite meal during the twelve days of Christmas.

[3] *Dooth ... reverence* Treats the magician in a friendly and respectful manner.

[4] *tables Tolletanes* I.e., Toledan tables. astrological tables drawn up for the latitude of Toledo, Spain, in the thirteenth century by King Alfonso the Wise. The tables allow the astronomer or astrologer to predict the motions of the planets relative to the earth. Lines 1273–80 are full of the language of astrology, which Chaucer explains in his *Treatise on the Astrolabe*, the instrument used for measuring the angles of various planets. The complete calculation required adding together figures for the planet's motion during the collect years (periods of twenty to 300 years), expanse years (periods of one to twenty years), and fractions of years. Roots are quantities, such as dates or the longitude of a planet, which are used when

consulting the tables. "Centres" are probably not parts of the astrolabe but rather centric tables of plantery distances, while "arguments," are angles or arcs from which the planets' motions can be measured. Fitting proportionals are figures used when taking into account the passage of fractions of a year.

[5] *And ... wirkyng* And by the eighth sphere in his calculation. According to medieval cosmology, the universe was made up of nine concentric crystalline spheres on which the planets and stars were affixed and which moved them across the sky.

[6] *Alnath* Name of a star.

[7] *Aries* Constellation and a sign in the zodiac.

[8] *face and terme* Subdivisions of a sign of the zodiac.

That me han holpen° fro my cares° colde!"   *helped / sorrows*
And to the temple his wey forth hath he holde,°   *gone*
635 Whereas he knew he sholde his lady see.[1]
And whan he saugh his tyme, anon right hee
With dredful° herte and with ful humble
    cheere°   *fearful / manner*
Salewed° hath his sovereyn lady deere.   *greeted*
    "My righte lady," quod this woful man,
640 "Whom I moost° drede and love as I best kan   *most*
And lothest° were of al this world displese,   *most unwilling*
Nere it° that I for yow have swich disese°   *were it not / misery*
That I moste dyen heere at youre foot anon,
Noght° wolde I telle how me is
    wobigon,°   *by no means / afflicted by woe*
645 But certes, outher° moste I dye or pleyne.   *either*
Ye sle° me giltlees° for verray peyne!   *kill / guiltless*
But of my deeth, thogh that ye have no routhe,°   *pity*
Avyseth° yow er that ye breke youre trouthe.°   *consider / promise*
Repenteth yow, for thilke God above,
650 Er ye me sleen bycause that I yow love.
For, madame, wel ye woot what ye han hight°—   *promised*
Nat that I chalange° anythyng of right   *claim*
Of yow, my sovereyn lady, but youre grace°—   *favor*
But in a gardyn yond,° at swich a place,   *yonder*
655 Ye woot right wel what ye bihighten me
And in myn hand youre trouthe plighten
    ye°   *you gave your promise*
To love me best. God woot, ye seyde so,
Al° be that I unworthy am therto.   *although*
Madame, I speke it for the honor of yow
660 Moore than to save myn hertes lyf right now.
I have do° so as ye comanded me,   *done*
And if ye vouchesauf, ye may go see.
Dooth as yow list.° Have youre biheste in mynde.   *wish*
For quyk° or deed,° right there ye shal me fynde.   *living / dead*
665 In yow lith al to do me lyve or deye.[2]
But wel I woot the rokkes been aweye."
    He taketh his leve, and she astoned° stood.   *stunned*

In al hir face nas° a drope of blood.   *was not*
She wende nevere han come in swich a trappe.[3]
670 "Allas," quod she, "that evere this sholde happe!
For wende° I nevere by possibilitee°   *expected / it possible*
That swich a monstre° or merveille° myghte
    bee.   *monstrosity / marvel*
It is agayns the proces of nature!"
And hoom she goth, a sorweful creature.
675 For verray feere° unnethe° may she go.   *fear / scarcely*
She wepeth, wailleth al a day or two
And swowneth that it routhe was to see.
But why it was to no wight tolde shee,
For out of towne was goon Arveragus.
680 But to hirself she spake and seyde thus,
With face pale and with ful sorweful cheere,
In hire compleynt, as ye shal after heere:
    "Allas," quod she, "on thee, Fortune, I pleyne,
That unwar wrapped hast me in thy cheyne![4]
685 For which t'escape woot I no socour,°   *help*
Save oonly deeth or dishonour.
Oon of thise two bihoveth me° to chese.   *I am compelled*
But nathelees, yet have I levere° to lese   *rather*
My lif than of my body have a shame,
690 Or knowe myselven fals or lese my name.
And with my deth I may be quyt,° ywis.°   *freed / indeed*
Hath ther nat° many a noble wyf er this   *has not*
And many a mayde yslayn hirself, allas,
Rather than with hir body doon trespas?°   *do a wrong*
695 "Yis, certes; lo, thise stories beren witnesse:
Whan thritty tirauntz° ful of
    cursednesse°   *thirty tyrants / wickedness*
Hadde slayn Phidoun in Atthenes[5] at feste,°   *a feast*
They comanded hise doghtres for t'areste°   *to be arrested*
And bryngen hem biforn hem in despit°   *scorn*
700 Al naked to fulfille hir foul delit,
And in hir fadres blood they made hem daunce
Upon the pavement. God yeve hem
    myschaunce!°   *give them misfortune*
For which thise woful maydens ful of drede
Rather than they wolde lese hir maydenhede,°   *chastity*

---

[1] *And to ... see* In the Middle Ages lovers often used church services as an opportunity to meet. Chaucer here gives the social customs of his day a pagan coloring by having Dorigen go to the temple. Chaucer frequently alternates between the simple past (Aurelius *knew*) and present or perfect forms (Aurelius *has gone* rather than *had gone*).

[2] *In ... deye* In you lies everything to make me live or die.

[3] *She ... trappe* She never expected to come into such a trap.

[4] *That ... cheyne* That have tangled me unawares in your chain.

[5] *Whan ... Atthenes* Thirty oligarchs ruled Athens briefly in 403 BCE before being overthrown by the naval commander Thrasybulus.

705	They prively been stirt° into a welle	jumped
	And dreynte° hemselven, as the bookes telle.	drowned
	They of Mecene° leet enquere° and seke	Messene / make an inquiry
	Of Lacedomye° fifty maydens eke,	Sparta
	On whiche they wolden doon° hir lecherye.	exercise
710	But was ther noon of al that compaignye	
	That she nas slayn and with a good entente	
	Chees° rather for to dye than assente	choose
	To been oppressed° of hir maydenhede.	robbed
	Why sholde I thanne to dye been in drede?	
715	Lo eek, the tiraunt Aristoclides,	
	That loved a mayden heet° Stymphalides,[1]	named
	Whan that hir fader slayn was on a nyght,	
	Unto Dianes temple goth she right°	right away
	And hente° the ymage° in hir handes two,	grasped / statue
720	Fro which ymage wolde she nevere go.°	let go
	No wight ne myghte hir handes of it arace°	pull away
	Til she was slayn right in the selve° place.	same
	Now sith that maydens hadden swich despit	
	To been defouled with mannes° foul delit,	men's
725	Wel oghte° a wyf rather hirselven slee	ought
	Than be defouled, as it thynketh me!°	seems to me
	What shal I seyn of Hasdrubales wyf,	
	That at Cartage° birafte hirself hir lyf?[2]	Carthage
	For whan she saugh that Romayns wan° the toun,	conquered
730	She took hir children alle and skipte adoun°	jumped down
	Into the fyr and chees rather to dye	
	Than any Romayn dide° hire vileynye.	should do
	Hath nat Lucresse yslayn hirself, allas,	
	At Rome whan she oppressed was	
735	Of° Tarquyn?[3] For hire thoughte it was a shame	by
	To lyven whan she had lost hir name.°	(good) name
	The sevene° maydens of Melesie° also	seven / Miletus
	Han slayn hemself for drede and wo	

	Rather than folk of Gawle hem sholde oppresse.[4]	
740	Mo than a thousand stories, as I gesse,	
	Koude I now telle as touchynge this mateere.	
	Whan Habradate was slayn, his wyf so deere	
	Hirselven slow° and leet hir blood to glyde°	killed / flow
	In Habradates woundes depe and wyde	
745	And seyde, 'My body at the leeste way	
	Ther shal no wight defoulen, if I may.'[5]	
	"What sholde I mo ensamples heerof sayn,	
	Sith that so manye han hemselven slayn,	
	Wel rather than they wolde defouled be?	
750	I wol conclude that it is bet° for me	better
	To sleen myself than been defouled thus.	
	I wol be trewe unto Arveragus	
	Or rather sleen myself in som manere	
	As dide Demociones doghter deere,	
755	Bycause that she wolde nat defouled be.[6]	
	O Cedasus, it is ful greet pitee	
	To reden how thy doghtren deyde, allas,	
	That slowe hemself for swich manere cas![7]	
	As greet a pitee was it or wel° moore	even
760	The Theban mayden that for Nichanore	
	Hirselven slow,° right for swich manere wo.[8]	slew
	Another Theban mayden dide right so,°	the same
	For oon° of Macidonye hadde hire oppressed.	someone
	She with hire deeth hir maydenhede redressed.[9]	
765	What shal I seye of Nicerates wyf,	

---

[1] *Lo eek ... Stymphalides* Aristodides was a tyrant of Orchomenos who fell in love with a virgin called Stymphalides.

[2] *What ... lyf* Hasdrubal, king of Carthage, the North African empire that threatened Rome, committed suicide when the Romans took the city in 146 BCE, although only after his wife had rebuked him for his cowardice.

[3] *Hath ... Tarquyn* Lucretia ("Lucresse") committed suicide after being raped by Tarquinus Sextus, prince of Rome. The people then rebelled and drove the Tarquins out. The story is told by Ovid in his *Fasti* 2.685–852 and by Chaucer in his *Legend of Good Women*.

---

[4] *The sevene ... oppresse* Miletus, in Asia Minor (now Turkey) was conquered by the Galatians in 276 BCE.

[5] *Whan Habradate ... may* King Abradates of Susi was killed fighting the Egyptians, and his wife, Panthea, killed herself on his body.

[6] *As dide ... be* When she heard that her husband, the general Leosthenes, had been killed in battle, the daughter of Demotion committed suicide rather than re-marry.

[7] *O Cedasus ... cas* The daughters of Scedasus offered hospitality to two youths who then got drunk and raped them. Afterwards, the daughters stabbed each other to death; *swich manere cas* Such a situation.

[8] *The Theban ... wo* Nicanor, one of Alexander the Great's officers, fell in love with one of the captured Thebans after taking the city in 336 BCE. She killed herself rather than submit to him.

[9] *She ... redressed* She made up for (the loss of) her chastity with her death.

That for swich cas birafte hirself hir lyf?[1]
How trewe eek was to Alcebiades
His love, rather for to dyen chees
Than for to sufre° his body unburyed be.[2]   *allow*
770 Lo, which° a wyf was Alceste!" quod she.   *what*
"What seith Omer of goode Penalopee?
Al Grece knoweth of hire chastitee.[3]
Pardee, °of Lacedomya is writen thus: *by God*
That whan at Troie was slayn Protheselaus,
775 No lenger wolde she lyve after his day.[4]
The same of noble Porcia telle I may.
Withoute Brutus koude she nat lyve,
To whom she hadde al hool° hir herte yeve.[5]   *completely*
The parfit wyfhod of Arthemesie
780 Honored is thurgh al the Barbarie.[6]
O Teuta Queene, thy wyfly chastitee
To alle wyves may a mirour bee![7]
The same thyng I seye of Bilyea,
Of Rodogone and eek of Valeria."[8]

---

[1] *What ... lyf* The wife of Nicerates killed herself to escape the lust of the thirty oligarchs (the same ones that commanded Phidoun's daughters to dance before them) (*Against Jovinian* 1. 44).

[2] *How ... be* Alcibiades, the friend of Socrates, was beheaded at the command of the Spartan general Lysander. His mistress risked her life to bury him.

[3] *Lo which ... chastitee* The story of Penelope, wife of Ulysses, and how she kept her unwanted suitors at bay is told by Homer in *The Odyssey*. It was known in the Middle Ages in various translations.

[4] *Pardee ... day* Protesilaus, the husband of Lacedomia (or Laodamia) was the first of the Greeks to be killed at the siege of Troy. At her entreaty he was brought briefly back to life and when he died a second time she died with him. Ovid tells the story in *Heroides* 13.

[5] *The same ... yeve* Brutus joined the conspiracy against Julius Caesar and committed suicide when defeated by Marc Antony. Portia, Brutus's wife, committed suicide by swallowing hot coals after she learned of her husband's death.

[6] *The parfit ... Barbarie* Arthemesia built the famous mausoleum at Halicarnasus for her husband Mausolus, king of Caria, in what is now northern Greece. It was with this sepulcher that the term "mausoleum" was coined.

[7] *O Teuta ... bee* Teuta assumed the throne of Illyria, on the Dalmatian coast, on the death of her husband in 231 BCE.

[8] *The same ... Valeria* Bilyea's martyrdom consisted in enduring her husband's bad breath. When he reproached her for not having told him about it, she replied that she thought all men's breath was that foul. Rhodogune, daughter of Darius, king of Persia, killed her nurse for suggesting she remarry. The Roman Valeria also refused to

785 Thus pleyned Dorigene a day or tweye,
Purposynge° evere that she wolde deye.   *intending*
But nathelees, upon the thridde nyght
Hoom cam Arveragus, this worthy knyght,
And asked hire why that she weepe so soore.
790 And she gan wepen ever lenger the moore.
"Allas," quod she, "that evere I was born!
Thus have I seyd," quod she. "Thus have I sworn!"
And toold hym al as ye han herd bifore.
It nedeth nat reherce° it yow namoore.   *repeat*
795 This housbonde with glad chiere° in freendly wyse   *expression*
Answerde and seyde as I shal yow devyse.°   *describe*
"Is ther oght elles, Dorigen, but this?"
  "Nay, nay," quod she, "God helpe me so, as wys°   *certainly*
This is to muche, and° it were Goddes wille!"   *even if*
800   "Ye, wyf," quod he, "lat slepen that° is stille.°   *what / quiet*
It may be wel paraventure yet today.
Ye shul youre trouthe holden, by my fay!°   *faith*
For God so wisly have mercy upon me,
I hadde wel levere ystiked° for to be   *stabbed*
805 For verray° love which that I to yow have,   *true*
But if ye sholde youre trouthe kepe and save!
Trouthe is the hyeste thyng that man may kepe."
But with that word he brast° anon to wepe   *burst out*
And seyde, "I yow forbede up° peyne deeth,   *on*
810 That nevere whil° thee lasteth lyf ne breeth   *while*
To no wight telle thou of this aventure.°   *misfortune*
As I may best, I wol my wo endure.
Ne make no contenance of hevynesse°   *sadness*
That folk of yow may demen harm or gesse."[9]
815   And forth he cleped° a squier and a mayde.   *called*
"Gooth forth anon with Dorigen," he sayde,
"And bryngeth hire to swich a place anon!"
They take hir leve, and on hir wey they gon.
But they ne wiste why she thider° wente.   *there*
820 He nolde no wight tellen his entente.
  Paraventure an heepe° of yow, ywis,°   *many / indeed*
Wol holden hym a lewed° man in this,   *foolish*
That he wol putte his wyf in jupartie.°   *jeopardy*
Herkneth° the tale er ye upon hire   *listen to / cry out against her*
  crie:°

---

remarry.

[9] *That ... gesse* That people may think or guess that there is anything wrong with you.

825 She may have bettre fortune than yow semeth,° *it seems to you*
And whan that ye han herd the tale, demeth.° *judge*
   This squier which that highte Aurelius
On Dorigen that was so amorus,
Of aventure° happed hire to meete *by chance*
830 Amydde the toun, right in the quykkest° strete, *busiest*
As she was bown° to goon the wey forthright *prepared*
Toward the gardyn theras° she had hight.° *where | promised*
And he was to the gardynward also,
For wel he spyed whan she wolde go
835 Out of hir hous to any maner place.
But thus they mette, of° aventure° or grace,° *by | chance | fortune*
And he saleweth° hire with glad entente *greets*
And asked of hire whiderward° she wente. *where*
And she answerde half as she were mad,
840 "Unto the gardyn, as myn housbonde bad,° *commanded*
My trouthe for to holde, allas! Allas!"
   Aurelius gan wondren on this cas° *situation*
And in his herte hadde greet compassioun
Of hire and of hire lamentacioun
845 And of Arveragus, the worthy knyght,
That bad hire holden al that she had hight,
So looth hym was his wyf sholde breke hir trouthe.
And in his herte he caughte° of this greet routhe, *had*
Considerynge the beste on every syde,
850 That fro his lust yet were° hym levere
   abyde° *would | rather abstain*
Than doon so heigh° a cherlyssh wrecchednesse *great*
Agayns franchise° and alle gentillesse. *generosity*
For which in fewe wordes seyde he thus:
   "Madame, seyeth to youre lord Arveragus
855 That sith I se his grete gentillesse
To yow, and eek I se wel youre distresse,
That him were levere han shame—and that were° *would be | a pity*
   routhe°—
Than ye to me sholde breke thus youre trouthe,
I have wel levere evere to suffre wo
860 Than I departe° the love bitwix yow two. *separate*
I yow relesse, madame, into youre hond
Quyt every serement and every bond
That ye han maad to me as heer biforn[1]

Sith thilke tyme which that ye were born.
865 My trouthe I plighte:° I shal yow never repreve° *pledge | reproach*
Of no biheste. And heere I take my leve
As of the treweste and the beste wyf
That evere yet I knew in al my lyf.
But every wyf bewar of hire biheeste!
870 On Dorigene remembreth, atte leeste.
Thus kan a squier doon a gentil dede
As wel as kan a knyght, withouten drede."[2]
   She thonketh hym upon hir knees al bare,
And hoom unto hir housbonde is she fare° *gone*
875 And tolde hym al as ye han herd me sayd.
And be ye siker,° he was so weel apayd,° *certain | paid back*
That it were inpossible me to wryte.[3]
What° sholde I lenger of this cas endyte?° *why | relate*
   Arveragus and Dorigene his wyf
880 In sovereyn° blisse leden forth hir lyf. *highest*
Nevere eft° ne was ther angre hem bitwene. *again*
He cherisseth hire as though she were a queene,
And she was to hym trewe for everemoore.
Of thise folk ye gete of me namoore.
885   Aurelius, that his cost° hath al forlorn,° *money | lost*
Curseth the tyme that evere he was born.
"Allas," quod he, "allas that I bihighte
Of pured° gold a thousand pound of wighte° *pure | weight*
Unto this philosophre!° How shal I do? *wise man*
890 I se namoore but that I am fordo.° *ruined*
Myn heritage° moot I nedes selle *inheritance*
And been a beggere. Heere may I nat dwelle
And shamen° al my kynrede° in this place, *shame | kindred*
But° I of hym may gete bettre grace. *unless*
895 But nathelees, I wole of hym assaye
At certeyn dayes yeer by yeer to paye[4]
And thanke hym of his grete curteisye.
My trouthe wol I kepe; I wol nat lye."

---

[1] *I yow ... biforn* I release you, my lady, into your power (hand), discharged of every oath (*serement*, from Latin *sacramentum*) and pledge that you have made to me before. Aurelius is using the language of a formal legal contract.

[2] *But every ... drede* Most editors attribute lines 1541–44 to Aurelius and place the quotation marks accordingly. The lines could also be attributed to the Franklin. The medieval manuscripts leave the matter open, since they contain almost no punctuation; *drede* Doubt.

[3] *wryte* An apparent slip, since the Franklin is telling, not writing, the story.

[4] *But ... paye* But, nonetheless, I will try to get from him (an agreement) to pay back the money in fixed installments over the years.

With herte soor he gooth unto his cofre°   *money chest*
900 And broghte gold unto this philosophre,
The value of fyve hundred pound, I gesse,
And hym bisecheth of his gentillesse
To graunte hym dayes of the remenaunt°   *for the rest*
And seyde, "Maister, I dar wel make avaunt°   *boast*
905 I failled nevere of my trouthe as yit.
For sikerly,° my dette shal be quyt°   *surely / repaid*
Towardes yow, howevere that I fare
To goon a begged° in my kirtel° bare.   *begging / shirt*
But wolde ye vouchesauf upon seuretee[1]
910 Two yeer or thre for to respiten me,°   *give me respite*
Thanne were I wel, for elles° moot I selle   *otherwise*
Myn heritage. Ther is namoore to telle."
This philosophre sobrely answerde
And seyde thus whan he thise wordes herde:
915 "Have I nat holden covenant° unto thee?"   *kept (my) promise*
"Yes, certes, wel and trewely," quod he.
"Hastow nat had thy lady as thee liketh?"
"No, no!" quod he, and sorwefully he siketh.°   *sighs*
"What was the cause? Tel me, if thou kan."
920 Aurelius his tale anon bigan
And tolde hym al as ye han herd bifoore.
It nedeth nat to yow reherce it moore.
He seide, "Arveragus of gentillesse
Hadde levere dye in sorwe and in distresse
925 Than that his wyf were of hir trouthe fals."
The sorwe of Dorigen he tolde hym als,
How looth hire was to been a wikked wyf

And that she levere had lost that day hir lyf
And that hir trouthe she swoor thurgh innocence.
930 She nevere erst hadde herd speke of apparence.[2]
"That made me han of hire so greet pitee.
And right as frely as he sente hire me,
As frely sente I hire to hym ageyn!
This al and som.[3] Ther is namoore to seyn."
935 This philosophre answerde, "Leeve brother,
Everich° of yow dide° gentilly til° oother.   *each / acted / to*
Thou art a squier, and he is a knyght;
But God forbede for his blisful myght
But if° a clerk koude doon a gentil dede   *unless*
940 As wel as any of yow, it is no drede!°   *doubt*
Sire, I releese thee° thy thousand pound,   *you from*
As thou right now were cropen° out of the ground,   *had crept*
Ne nevere er now ne haddest knowen me.
For sire, I wol nat taken a peny of thee
945 For al my craft ne noght for my travaille.°   *trouble*
Thou hast ypayed wel for my vitaille;°   *food*
It is ynogh, and farewell. Have good day!"
And took his hors and forth he goth his way.
Lordynges, this questioun thanne wolde I aske now:
950 Which was the mooste fre,° as thynketh yow?   *generous*
Now teleth me er that ye ferther wende.°   *go further*
I kan° namoore. My tale is at an ende.   *know*

HEERE IS ENDED THE FRANKELYNS TALE

---

[1] *seuretee* In effect, Aurelius is here offering to mortgage his land in return for time to pay back the full thousand pounds of gold.

[2] *She … apparence* Never before had she heard (someone) speak of illusion.

[3] *This … som* This is the whole.

The Pardoner's Prologue and Tale

The Pardoner calls himself "a full vicious man," yet, paradoxically, his tale is one of the few that has a completely straightforward moral: covetousness is the root of all evil. The tale is actually a popular sermon of the kind that the Pardoner has given so often that he knows it by rote. A story of three men who go in search of death, *The Pardoner's Tale* has at its core an *exemplum*, a short and gripping story with a clear moral message. To this exemplum a preacher might add, as the Pardoner does, dramatic denunciations of the Seven Deadly Sins, supported by Biblical quotations, and calls for repentance. Medieval popular preachers were often excellent storytellers, but the level of detail in *The Pardoner's Tale* goes beyond the needs of any sermon. Like the Miller, the Pardoner is a churl, and their two tales share an interest in the concrete and seamy aspects of daily life, down to such matters as how people rented rooms or poisoned rats. Although the time period is not specified the Pardoner's story captures the brutal joys of the tavern and the grim atmosphere of England in a time of plague, with the death cart making the rounds to retrieve the bodies, as it would have done during the Black Death of 1348–49. The enigmatic old man who cannot die but knows where death is to be found further enriches the basic *exemplum*.

The Pardoner's greatest modification of a popular sermon, however, is to offer a full commentary on his own art, describing his motivation (simple covetousness) and the various tricks, including blackmail, which he uses to persuade his listeners to buy his spurious relics and pardons. By holding out false promises of salvation, the Pardoner is endangering the souls of others and his own. His character has fascinated readers, perhaps because it is so enigmatic. There has been much discussion of what drives the Pardoner to such extensive self-revelation and why, having just explained his methods to the pilgrims, he is so rash as to make a final sales pitch for his relics. In one much-discussed line in *The General Prologue*, "I trowe [I believe] he were a gelding [a castrated stallion] or a mare," the narrator indicates that he does not precisely know what to make of the Pardoner, while defining him as other than "masculine." Based on this line and other features of his depiction, some have seen the Pardoner as a tormented outsider, anxious to win group approval, others as a figure of spiritual sterility, corrupted by his own covetousness and in turn corrupting those who listen to him.

Opening page of *The Pardoner's Tale*, Ellesmere manuscript (detail). (Reprinted by permission of *The Huntington Library, San Marino, California.* EL26C9F72r.)

Opening page of *The Pardoner's Tale*, Ellesmere manuscript. (Reprinted by permission of *The Huntington Library, San Marino, California*. EL26C9F72r.)

THE INTRODUCTION TO THE PARDONER'S TALE

THE WORDES OF THE HOOST
TO THE PHISICIEN AND THE PARDONER

Oure Hoost gan to swere° as° he were
    wood.°   *began to swear | as if | crazy*
"Harrow!" quod he. "By nayles and by blood!"[1]
This was a fals° cherl° and a fals justice.°   *false | churl | judge*
As shameful deeth° as herte° may devyse°   *death | heart | imagine*
5 Come to thise° false juges° and hire
    advocatz!°   *these | judges | their lawyers*
Algate° this sely° mayde° is slayn,°
    allas!²   *but | innocent | maid | killed*
Allas, to deere° boughte she beautee!   *too dearly*
Wherfore° I seye° al day as men may see,   *therefore | say*
That yiftes° of Fortune and of nature   *gifts*
10 Been° cause of deeth to many a creature.   *are*
Of bothe yiftes that I speke of now
Men han ful ofte° moore for harm than
    prow.°   *have very often | profit*
But trewely,° myn owene maister° deere,°   *truly | master | dear*
This is a pitous° tale for to here.°   *pitiful | hear*
15 But nathelees,° passe over.° Is no
    fors.°   *nevertheless | let it pass | matter*
I pray to God so save thy gentil cors°   *noble body*
And eek thyne urynals and thy jurdones,³
Thyn ypocras° and eek thy galiones° *hypocras | galians (medicines)*
And every boyste° ful of thy letuarie.°   *box | medicine*
20 God blesse hem° and oure Lady, Seint Marie!   *them*
So moot° I theen,° thou art a propre° man   *might | thrive | fine*
And lyk° a prelat,° by Seint Ronyan!⁴ *like | prelate (high clergyman)*

Seyde I nat wel? I kan nat speke in terme,°   *in the right jargon*
But wel I woot,° thou doost myn herte to
    erme,°   *know | make my heart grieve*
25 That I almoost have caught a cardynacle.⁵
By corpus bones,° but° I have triacle⁶   *by God's bones | unless*
Or elles a draughte° of moyste° and corny°
    ale,   *drink | moist | malty (strong)*
Or but I heere anon° a myrie° tale,   *immediately | merry*
Myn herte is lost for pitee of this mayde.
30 Thou beel amy,° thou Pardoner," he sayde,   *good friend*
"Telle us som myrthe or japes° right anon."   *jokes*
  "It shal be doon!" quod he, "by Seint Ronyon!
But first," quod he, "heere at this ale-stake⁷
I wol bothe drynke and eten° of a cake."°   *eat | bread*
35 And right anon the gentils° gonne° to crye, *gentle folk | began*
"Nay, lat hym telle us of no ribaudye!°   *ribald story*
Telle us som moral thyng that we may leere°   *learn*
Som wit,° and thanne wol we gladly here."   *piece of wisdom*
  "I graunte, ywis,"° quod he. "But I moot
    thynke°   *indeed | must think*
40 Upon som honeste thyng° whil that I drynke." *respectable subject*

THE PARDONER'S PROLOGUE

HEERE FOLWETH THE PROLOGE OF THE PARDONERS TALE

Radix malorum est Cupiditas. Ad Thimotheum 6.10[8]

"Lordynges,"° quod he, "in chirches° whan I
    preche,°   *lords | churches | preach*

---

[1] *Harrow … blood Harrow* Help; *Nails and blood* By Christ's nails and by Christ's blood, i.e., alas. Medieval swearing often referred to parts of Christ's body.

[2] *Harow … alas* The tale told previously, by the Physician, involved an innocent young girl who agrees to let her father kill her in order to save her from the lewd desires of a corrupt judge.

[3] *urynals* Vessels to hold urine; *jurdones* Jars. These were both part of the equipment medieval doctors used.

[4] *Seint Ronyan* There were several medieval saints called St. Ronan—a seventh-century Scottish hermit, a Breton bishop who died in Cornwall, a Scottish bishop who helped settle a dispute about the date of Easter, and an early bishop of Caesarea, whose arm was kept as a relic at Canterbury Cathedral. Most editors state that it was the Scottish hermit to whom the Host refers here, but the last

Saint Ronan, given his association with Canterbury, seems the most likely reference, for the pilgrims are traveling to the place where his relic was kept. There may also be a pun on runnions (male sexual organs).

[5] *cardynacle* The Host means heart attack, though he blunders for the proper word, which is cardiacle.

[6] *triacle* Medicine or cordial, usually made primarily from molasses.

[7] *ale-stake* Post set up outside a house when the people who lived there had brewed up some ale and were ready to sell it to those passing by.

[8] *Radix … Cupiditas* Latin: the root of evils is cupidity. From 1 Timothy 6.10. Cupidity is often translated as avarice, or love of money, but, like the word covetousness, it can also refer to any excessive or sinful love of earthly things.

I peyne me to han° an hauteyn
    speche°   *take pains to have | dignified speech*
And rynge° it out as round° as gooth a
    belle,°   *ring | roundly | rings a bell*
For I kan° al by rote° that I telle.°   *know | by memory | say*
45 My theme[1] is alwey oon° and evere was: *always one*
Radix malorum est cupiditas.

    First I pronounce° whennes° that I come,   *say | whence*
And thanne my bulles[2] shewe I alle and some.°   *one and all*
Oure lige lordes seel° on my
    patente,°   *liege lord's (i.e., the bishop's) seal | license*
50 That shewe I first, my body to warente,°   *protect*
That no man be so boold,° ne preest ne clerk,[3]   *bold*
Me to destourbe° of Cristes hooly werk.   *disturb*
And after that thanne° telle I forth my tales.   *then*
Bulles of popes and of cardynales,°   *cardinals*
55 Of patriarkes° and bisshopes° I shewe,   *patriarchs | bishops*
And in Latyn° I speke a wordes fewe   *Latin*
To saffron with[4] my predicacioun°   *preaching*
And for to stire hem° to devocioun.   *stir them*
Thanne shewe I forth my longe cristal stones,°   *glass cases*
60 Ycrammed° ful of cloutes° and of bones.   *crammed | rags*
Relikes been they, as wenen they echoon.°   *as everyone believes*
Thanne have I in latoun° a sholder boon°   *brass | shoulder bone*
Which that was of an hooly Jewes sheepe.°   *holy Jew's sheep*
65 "Goode men," I seye, "taak of my wordes keepe.°   *heed*
If that this boon be wasshe° in any welle,   *washed*
If cow or calf or sheepe or oxe swelle°   *swell*
That any worm° hath ete° or worm
    ystonge,°   *snake | has eaten | stung*
Taak water of that welle and wassh his tonge,
And it is hool° anon. And forthermoor,   *healthy*

70 Of pokkes° and of scabbe° and every soor°   *pocks | scab | sore*
Shal every sheepe be hool that of this welle
Drynketh a draughte. Taak kepe° eek° what I
    telle!   *take heed | also*
If that the goode man that the beestes° oweth°   *beasts | owns*
Wol every wyke° er° that the cok° hym
    croweth°   *week | before | rooster | crows*
75 Fastynge° drynke of this welle a draughte,   *while fasting*
As thilke° hooly Jew oure eldres° taughte,   *that | ancestors*
Hise beestes and his stoor° shal multiplie.   *possessions*
    And sire, also it heeleth° jalousie.   *heals*
For though a man be falle° in jalous rage,   *fallen*
80 Lat maken with this water his potage,°   *stew*
And nevere shal he moore his wyf mystriste,°   *mistrust*
Though he the soothe° of hir defaute°
    wiste,°   *truth | default | knew*
Al had she taken preestes two or thre.[5]
    Heere is a miteyn° eek that ye may se.   *mitten*
85 He that his hand wol putte in this mitayn,
He shal have multipliyng of his grayn°   *grain*
Whan he hath sowen, be it whete° or otes,°   *wheat | oats*
So that he offre pens or elles grotes.[6]
    Goode men and wommen, o° thyng warne I yow: *one*
90 If any wight° be in this chirche now   *person*
That hath doon° synne° horrible, that he   *committed | sin*
Dar nat for shame of it yshryven° be,   *confessed*
Or any womman, be she yong or old,
That hath ymaked° hir housbonde cokewold,[7]   *made*
95 Swich folk shal have no power ne no grace
To offren° to my relikes in this place.   *make an offering*
And whoso fyndeth hym out° of swich
    fame,°   *is not subject to | (ill-) repute*
They wol come up and offre on° Goddes name,   *in*
And I assoille hem° by the auctoritee°   *absolve them | authority*
100 Which that by bulle ygraunted was to me.
    By this gaude° have I wonne° yeer° by yeer   *trick | gained | year*
An hundred mark sith I was pardoner.[8]

---

[1]. *theme* "Text." Medieval sermons were usually organized around a short passage from the Bible.

[2] *bulles* I.e., papal bulls (written documents which put official policy into effect). Pardoners had licenses from the Pope to raise money for charitable causes by selling indulgences (certificates that reduce the number of years the buyer must serve in Purgatory after death).

[3] *ne preest ne clerk* The term clerk can refer to students, scholars, or assistants to priests (as in *The Miller's Tale*), so neither priest nor clerk means not a member of the clergy. The parish clergy often regarded wandering preachers as interlopers.

[4] *To saffron with* To season with saffron, a very expensive yellow spice imported from the East.

[5] *Al … thre* Even if she had taken two or three priests as lovers.

[6] *So … grotes* Provided that he offers pennies or else groats (a coin worth fourpence).

[7] *cokewold* I.e., cuckold, a man whose wife has committed adultery.

[8] *An … pardoner* A hundred marks equaled over £66, making the Pardoner a wealthy man. In comparison, in 1367 Chaucer was granted an annual pension of 20 marks.

I stonde lyk a clerk° in my pulpet,   theologian
And whan the lewed peple[1] is doun yset,°   settled down
105 I preche so as ye han herd bifoore°   have heard before
And telle an hundred false japes° moore.   tricks
Thanne peyne I me° to strecche° forth the
        nekke   I take pains / stretch
And est° and west upon the peple° I bekke°   east / people / nod
As dooth a dowve° sittynge on a berne.°   sitting / barn
110 Myne handes and my tonge goon so yerne°   eagerly
That it is joye to se° my bisynesse.°   see / busyness
Of avarice and of swich cursednesse°   cursedness
Ys° al my prechyng, for to make hem free°   is / generous
To yeven hir pens°—and namely unto me.   give their pence
115 For myn entente° is nat but for to wynne°   intent / profit
And nothyng° for correccioun° of synne.   by no means / correction
I rekke° nevere whan they been beryed,°   care / buried
Though that hir soules goon a blakeberyed![2]
For certes, many a predicacioun°   sermon
120 Comth ofte tyme of yvel entencioun°—   evil intent
Som for plesance° of folk and flaterye   pleasure
To been avaunced by ypocrisye°   hypocrisy
And som for veyneglorie° and som for hate.   pride
For whan I dar noon oother weyes° debate,   in no other way
125 Thanne wol I stynge° hym[3] with my tonge
        smerte°   sting / sharp
In prechyng, so that he shal nat asterte°   escape
To been defamed falsly if that he
Hath trespased° to my bretheren or to me.   has done harm
For though I telle noght° his propre° name,   not / own
130 Men shal wel knowe that it is the same
By signes and by othere circumstances.
Thus quyte° I folk that doon us displesances.° pay back / offenses
Thus spitte I out my venym under hewe°   guise
Of hoolynesse, to semen° hooly and trewe.   seem
135   But shortly, myn entente I wol devyse:°   describe
I preche of nothyng but for coveityse.°   covetousness
Therfore my theme is yet and evere was

Radix malorum est cupiditas.

Thus kan I preche agayn° that same vice   against
140 Which that I use, and that is avarice.
But though myself be gilty in that synne,
Yet kan I maken oother folk to twynne°   turn away
From avarice and soore° to repente.   sorely
But that is nat my principal entente;°   intent
145 I preche nothyng but for coveitise.°   covetousness
Of this mateere it oghte ynogh suffise.°   should be sufficient
    Thanne telle I hem ensamples° many
        oon°   examples / many a one
Of olde stories longe tyme agoon,°   ago
For lewed peple° loven tales olde;   laypeople
150 Swiche thynges kan they wel reporte and holde.° remember
What? Trowe ye,° the whiles I may preche   do you believe
And wynne° gold and silver for I teche,°   gain / because I teach
That I wol lyve in poverte wilfully?°   willingly
Nay, nay! I thoghte it nevere, trewely.
155 For I wol preche and begge in sondry landes;° different countries
I wol nat do no labour with myne handes
Ne make baskettes and lyve therby,
Bycause I wol nat beggen ydelly.°   beg in vain
I wol noon of the apostles countrefete![4]
160 I wol have moneie,° wolle,° chese, and
        whete,°   money / wool / wheat
Al° were it yeven°of the povereste page° even if / given / poorest boy
Or of the povereste wydwe° in a village,   widow
Al sholde hir children sterve° for famyne.   die
Nay, I wol drynke licour of the vyne
165 And have a joly wenche° in every toun.   pretty girl
But herkneth,° lordynges, in conclusioun: listen
Youre likyng° is that I shal telle a tale.   pleasure
Now have I dronke a draughte of corny ale,
By God, I hope I shal yow telle a thyng
170 That shal by resoun° been at youre liking.   with reason
For though myself be a ful° vicious man,   very
A moral tale yet I yow telle kan,
Which I am wont° to preche for to wynne.   accustomed
Now hoold youre pees!° My tale I wol bigynne.   peace

---

[1] *lewed peple* Uneducated, illiterate (in the medieval sense—i.e., unable to read Latin), or simple, but it can also refer to lay people in general. It does not have the modern meaning of sexual offensiveness.

[2] *a blakeberyed* Go picking blackberries (i.e., wandering).

[3] *hym* I.e., any opponent. Pardoners were much criticized by the parish clergy and by reformers.

[4] *noon … countrefete* In the Gospels and the Book of Acts the apostles were enjoined to live in poverty so as to give surplus goods to the poor.

THE PARDONER'S TALE

HEERE BIGYNNETH THE PARDONERS TALE

175   In Flaundres° whilom° was a
    compaignye°   *Flanders | once | company*
  Of yonge folk that haunteden folye
  As riot, hasard, stywes, and tavernes,[1]
  Whereas° with harpes, lutes, and gyternes[2]   *where*
  They daunce and pleyen° at dees° bothe day and   *play | dice*
    nyght
180   And eten also and drynken over hir myght,°   *capacity*
  Thurgh which they doon the devel sacrifise° *sacrifice to the devil*
  Withinne that develes temple[3] in cursed wise°   *manner*
  By superfluytee° abhomynable.   *excess*
  Hir othes° been so grete and so dampnable°   *oaths | damnable*
185   That it is grisly° for to heere hem swere.   *horrible*
  Oure blissed° Lordes body they to-tere°—   *blessed | tear apart*
  Hem thoughte that Jewes rente hym noght ynough![4]
  And ech of hem at otheres synne° lough.°   *sin | laughed*
  And right anon thanne comen tombesteres°   *female acrobats*
190   Fetys° and smale° and yonge
    frutesteres,°   *elegant | slender | fruit-sellers*
  Syngeres with harpes, baudes,° wafereres,° *pimps | pastry-sellers*
  Whiche been° the verray devels officeres   *who are*
  To kyndle and blowe the fyr of lecherye
  That is annexed unto° glotonye.°   *allied with | gluttony*
195   The Hooly Writ° take I to my witnesse   *Bible*
  That luxurie° is in wyn° and dronkenesse.   *lust | wine*
    Lo how that dronken Looth[5] unkyndely°   *unnaturally*
  Lay by hise doghtres° two unwityngly!° *daughters | unknowingly*
  So dronke he was, he nyste° what he
    wroghte.°   *did not know | did*

200   Herodes,[6] whoso wel the stories soghte,[7]
  Whan he of wyn was replet° at his feeste,°   *most filled | feast*
  Right at his owene table he yaf° his heeste°   *gave | command*
  To sleen° the Baptist John ful giltelees.[8]   *kill*
  Senec[9] seith a good word, douteles.°   *doubtless*
205   He seith he kan no difference fynde
  Bitwix° a man that is out of his mynde   *between*
  And a man which that is dronkelewe,°   *often drunk*
  But that woodnesse,° fallen° in a
    shrewe,°   *madness | occurring | villain*
  Persevereth° lenger than dooth dronkenesse.   *lasts*
210   O glotonye, ful of cursednesse,
  O cause first of oure confusioun,
  O original of oure dampnacioun,[10]
  Til Crist hadde boght° us with his blood agayn!   *redeemed*
  Lo how deere,° shortly for to seyn,°   *expensively | say*
215   Aboght° was thilke° cursed vileynye!   *purchased | that*
  Corrupt was al this world for glotonye.
    Adam oure fader and his wyf also
  Fro° Paradys to labour and to wo°   *from | woe*
  Were dryven° for that vice, it is no drede.°   *driven | doubt*
220   For whil that Adam fasted, as I rede,°   *read*
  He was in Paradys, and whan that he
  Eet° of the fruyt deffended° on the tree,   *ate | prohibited*
  Anon he was outcast to wo and peyne.
  O glotonye, on thee wel oghte us pleyne!°   *complain*
225   O, wiste a man how manye maladyes°   *diseases*
  Folwen of excesse and of glotonyes,
  He wolde been the moore mesurable°   *temperate*
  Of his diete, sittynge at his table.
  Allas, the shorte throte,° the tendre mouth   *throat*
230   Maketh that° est and west and north and south,   *causes*
  In erthe, in eir, in water man to swynke°   *labor*
  To gete a glotoun° deyntee° mete° and
    drynke.   *glutton | delicious | meat*

---

[1] *Of yonge ... tavernes* Of young folk that gave themselves to foolish living, such as loud parties, gambling, brothels, and taverns.

[2] *gyternes* Like the harp and the lute, the medieval gittern was a plucked stringed instrument.

[3] *develes temple* I.e., a tavern.

[4] *Hem ... ynough* They thought that Jews did not tear him apart enough. The oaths figuratively tore God's body apart, according to the moralists. In the Middle Ages, Jews were usually blamed for Christ's crucifixion.

[5] *Looth* I.e., Lot. The story of how Lot, while drunk, made his daughters pregnant is recounted in Genesis 19.30–38.

[6] *Herodes* I.e., Herod, King of the Jewish people (74–3 BCE).

[7] *whoso ... soghte* As whoever consulted the stories carefully can confirm.

[8] *ful giltelees* Entirely guiltless. See Matthew 14.1–12.

[9] *Senec* I.e., Seneca, Roman playwright, orator, and philosopher (4 BCE–65 CE).

[10] *O cause ... dampnacioun* A reference to the role of gluttony in causing Adam and Eve to eat the forbidden fruit of the Tree of Knowledge in the Garden of Eden. See Genesis 2–3.

Of this matiere, O Paul,[1] wel kanstow trete:°   *can you write*
"Mete unto wombe° and wombe eek unto mete: *stomach*
235   Shal God destroyen bothe," as Paulus seith.[2]
Allas, a foul thyng is it, by my feith,
To seye this word, and fouler is the dede
Whan man so drynketh of the white and
    rede,°   *white and red wine*
That of his throte he maketh his pryvee,°   *latrine*
240   Thurgh thilke cursed superfluitee.°   *excess*
    The apostel[3] wepyng seith ful pitously,°   *pitifully*
"Ther walken manye of whiche yow toold have I.°*I have told you*
I seye it now wepyng with pitous voys:°   *pitiful voice*
Ther been° enemys of Cristes croys°   *are / cross*
245   Of whiche the ende is deeth.° Wombe is hir god."[4]   *death*
O wombe, o bely, o stynkyng cod,°   *stinking bag (stomach)*
Fulfilled of donge° and of corrupcioun,   *filled with dung*
At either ende of thee foul is the soun!°   *sound*
How greet labour and cost is thee to fynde.°   *provide for*
250   Thise cookes, how they stampe° and streyne° and
    grynde   *pound / strain*
And turnen substaunce into accident[5]
To fulfillen al thy likerous° talent!°   *lecherous / inclination*
Out of the harde bones knokke they
The mary,° for they caste° noght awey   *marrow / throw*
255   That may go thurgh the golet° softe and swoote.°   *throat / sweet*
Of spicerie° of leef and bark and roote   *spices*
Shal been his sauce ymaked,° by delit°   *made / through delight*
To make° hym yet a newer appetit.   *give*
But certes, he that haunteth° swiche delices°   *follows / delights*
260   Is deed whil that he lyveth in tho° vices.[6]   *those*
    A lecherous thyng is wyn, and dronkenesse

Is ful of stryvyng° and of wrecchednesse.   *quarreling*
O dronke man, disfigured is thy face!
Sour is thy breeth! Foul artow° to embrace!   *are you*
265   And thurgh thy dronke nose semeth the
    soun°   *the sound seems to come*
As though thou seydest ay° "Sampsoun, Sampsoun!"   *ever*
And yet, God woot,° Sampsoun drank nevere no
    wyn![7]   *God knows*
Thou fallest as it were a styked swyn.°   *stuck (i.e., speared) pig*
Thy tonge is lost and al thyn honeste cure.°   *care*
270   For dronkenesse is verray sepulture°   *tomb*
Of mannes wit and his discrecioun.
In whom that drynke hath dominacioun,
He kan no conseil° kepe, it is no drede.°   *counsel / doubt*
Now kepe yow fro the white and fro the rede
275   And namely fro the white wyn of Lepe[8]
That is to selle° in Fyssh Strete or in Chepe.[9]   *for sale*
This wyn of Spaigne° crepeth subtilly   *Spain*
In othere wynes growynge faste° by,[10]   *near*
Of which ther ryseth swich fumositee°   *such vapors*
280   That whan a man hath dronken draughtes thre°   *three*
And weneth° that he be at hoom° in Chepe,   *thinks / home*
He is in Spaigne, right at the toune of Lepe—
Nat at the Rochele ne at Burdeux toun—[11]
And thanne wol he seye, "Sampsoun, Sampsoun!"
285   But herkneth, lordes, o° word, I yow preye,   *one*
That alle the sovereyn actes, dar I seye,
Of victories in the Olde Testament
Thurgh verray° God that is omnipotent   *true*
Were doon in abstinence and in preyere.
290   Looketh the Bible, and ther ye may it leere.°   *learn*
    Looke, Attilla[12] the grete conquerour

---

[1] *Paul* I.e., St. Paul.

[2] *Shal … seith* See 1 Corinthians 6.13.

[3] *apostel* I.e., apostle, here St. Paul.

[4] *Ther walken … god* See Philippians 3.18–19.

[5] *And … accident* This distinction between the basic food and the flavors the cooks give to it draws on Aristotle's distinction between substance (essential inner reality) and its superficial qualities (accidents). This line could be read as an allusion to contemporary philosophical debates between Nominalists and Realists or to contemporary theological controversies concerning the process through which the bread and wine of the Eucharist are transformed into the body and blood of Christ.

[6] *he that … vices* Cf. 1 Timothy 5.6: "But she that lives in pleasure is dead while she lives."

[7] *And yet … wyn* As recounted in Judges 13, in which it is written that Samson's mother did not drink wine during her pregnancy.

[8] *Lepe* Town in Spain.

[9] *Fyssh … Chepe* I.e., Fish Street and Cheapside, two market districts in London.

[10] *This wyn … by* Expensive French wines, shipped through Bordeaux and La Rochelle, were often surreptitiously mixed with cheaper, but stronger, Spanish wines.

[11] *the Rochele … Burdeaux toun* I.e., La Rochelle and Bordeaux.

[12] *Attilla* I.e., Attila the Hun, a fifth-century nomadic chieftain who ravaged vast stretches of central Europe. According to medieval histories, such as those of Jordanes and Paul the Deacon, he died from drink on the night that he took a new bride.

Deyde° in his sleepe with shame and dishonour,   *died*
Bledynge° ay at his nose in dronkenesse.   *bleeding*
A capitayn° sholde lyve in sobrenesse.   *leader*
295 And over al this° avyseth yow° right wel   *above all / consider*
What was comaunded unto Lamwel.[1]
Nat Samuel[2] but Lamwel, seye I.
Redeth the Bible, and fynde it expresly°   *specifically*
Of wyn yevyng° to hem that han
    justise.°   *giving wine / have legal power*
300 Namoore of this, for it may wel suffise.
    And now I have spoken of glotonye,
Now wol I yow deffenden° hasardrye.°   *prohibit / gambling*
Hasard is verray mooder° of lesynges°   *mother / lying*
And of deceite and cursed forswerynges,°   *perjury*
305 Blasphemyng of Crist, manslaughtre, and
    wast° also   *wasteful spending*
Of catel° and of tyme. And forthermo,   *goods*
It is repreeve° and contrarie of° honour   *reproach / to*
For to ben holde° a commune hasardour.°   *be considered / gambler*
And ever the hyer° he is of estaat°   *higher / condition*
310 The moore is he holden° desolaat.°   *regarded as / vile*
If that a prynce° useth hasardrye,°   *prince / frequently gambles*
In alle governaunce and policye
He is as by commune opinioun
Yholde° the lasse° in reputacioun.   *held / less*
315 Stilboun,[3] that was a wys embassadour,
Was sent to Cornythe° in ful greet honour   *Corinth*
Fro Lacidomye° to maken hire alliaunce,   *Sparta*
And whan he cam, hym happed par chaunce[4]
That alle the gretteste that were of that lond
320 Pleyynge atte hasard he hem fond,
For which, as soone as it myghte be,
He stal hym° hoom agayn to his contree   *stole away*
And seyde, "Ther wol I nat lese° my name!   *lose*
Ne I wol nat take on me so greet defame°   *dishonor*
325 Yow for to allie° unto none hasardours.   *ally*
Sendeth otherewise° embassadours.   *other*

For by my trouthe, me were levere dye°   *rather die*
Than I yow sholde to hasardours allye.
For ye that been so glorious in honours
330 Shul nat allyen yow with hasardours,
As by my wyl,° ne as by my tretee."°   *will / treaty*
This wise philosophre thus seyde hee.
    Looke eek that to the kyng Demetrius,
The kyng of Parthes,° as the book seith° us,[5]   *Parthia / tells*
335 Sente him a paire of dees° of gold in scorn,   *dice*
For he hadde used hasard ther-biforn,°   *often gambled before this*
For which he heeld his glorie or his renoun
At no value or reputacioun.
Lordes may fynden oother maner pley°   *kinds of amusement*
340 Honeste ynough to dryve the day awey.
    Now wol I speke of othes° false and grete   *oaths*
A word or two, as olde bookes trete.
Greet sweryng° is a thyng abhominable,   *swearing*
And fals sweryng° is yet moore reprevable.°   *perjury / disgraceful*
345 The heighe God forbad sweryng at al,[6]
Witnesse on Mathew, but in special°   *specially*
Of sweryng seith the hooly Jeremye,°   *Jeremiah*
"Thou shalt seye sooth thyne othes° and nat lye   *truly your oaths*
And swere in doom° and eek in rightwisnesse."[7]   *judgment*
350 But ydel sweryng is a cursednesse.
Bihoold and se that in the firste table°   *tablet (of Moses)*
Of heighe Goddes heestes° honorable   *commandments*
Hou that the seconde heeste of hym° is this   *them*
"Take nat my name in ydel or amys."[8]
355 Lo, rather° he forbedeth swich   *earlier (in the commandments)*
    sweryng
Than homycide or any cursed thyng.
I seye that as by ordre thus it stondeth.°   *stands*

---

[1] *Lamwel* I.e., Lemuel, King of Massa, whose mother warns him not to drink wine. See Proverbs 31.4–5.

[2] *Samuel* I.e., the prophet Samuel. See 1 Samuel.

[3] *Stilboun* I.e., Chilon, an ambassador who is mentioned in John of Salisbury's *Polycraticus*, 1.5.

[4] *And … chaunce* And when he came, it happened to him by chance.

---

[5] *The kyng … us* King Demetrius of Parthia has not been securely identified, but John of Salisbury tells his story in the *Policraticus* immediately after that of Chilon.

[6] *The heighe … al* See Matthew 5.34.

[7] *Thou … rightwisnesse* See Jeremiah 4.2; *rightwisnesse* Righteousness.

[8] *Take … amys* See Deuteronomy 5.7–21. In the Middle Ages the first two commandments were normally grouped as one, making what is now considered the third commandment the second, as it is here. The tenth commandment was then broken into two to make up the difference; *amys* In vain.

This knowen that hise heestes understondeth,[1]
How that the seconde heeste° of God is
    that.   *second commandment*
360 And forther over,° I wol thee telle al plat°   *furthermore | plainly*
That vengeance shal nat parten° from his hous   *depart*
That of his othes° is to° outrageous.   *oaths | too*
"By Goddes precious herte!" and "By his nayles"°   *nails*
And "By the blood of Crist that is in Hayles,[2]
365 Sevene is my chaunce and thyn is cynk° and treye!"[3]   *five | three*
By Goddes armes, if thou falsly pleye,
This daggere shal thurghout thyn herte go!"°   *pierce*
This fruyt° cometh of the bicched bones two—[4]   *fruit*
Forsweryng,° ire,° falsnesse, homycide.   *perjury | anger*
370 Now for the love of Crist that for us dyde,
Lete° youre othes, bothe grete and smale.   *leave*
But sires, now wol I telle forth my tale.

    Thise riotours° thre of whiche I telle   *party-goers*
Longe erst er° prime° rong° of any belle   *before | early morning | rang*
375 Were set hem in a taverne to drynke.
And as they sat, they herde a belle clynke°   *ring*
Biforn° a cors° was° caried to his
    grave.   *before | corpse | that was being*
That oon of hem gan callen to his knave,°   *servant*
"Go bet,"° quod he, "and axe° redily°   *quickly | ask | eagerly*
380 What cors is this that passeth heer forby,
And looke that thou reporte his name weel."

    "Sire," quod this boy, "it nedeth never a deel.°   *it is not necessary*
It was me toold er ye cam heer two houres.[5]
He was, pardee,° an old felawe° of youres,   *by God | friend*
385 And sodeynly he was yslayn tonyght.
For dronke as he sat on his bench upright
Ther cam a privee theef° men clepeth° Deeth,   *secret thief | call*
That in this contree al the peple sleeth,
And with his spere he smoot° his herte atwo°   *cut | in two*

390 And wente his wey withouten wordes mo.
He hath a thousand slayn this pestilence.°[6]   *during this epidemic*
And maister, er ye come in his presence,
Me thynketh that it were necessarie
For to bewar of swich an adversarie.
395 Beth° redy for to meete hym everemoore.°   *be | always*
Thus taughte me my dame.° I sey namoore.".   *mother*
"By seinte Marie," seyde this taverner,°   *tavern-keeper*
"The child seith sooth, for he hath slayn this yeer
Henne° over a mile withinne a greet° village   *from here | large*
400 Bothe man and womman, child and hyne° and
    page.   *hired hand*
I trowe° his habitacioun° be there.   *believe | dwelling*
To been avysed° greet wysdom it were,   *warned*
Er° that he dide° a man a dishonour."°   *lest | cause | harm*
    "Ye, Goddes armes," quod this riotour,
405 "Is it swich peril with hym for to meete?°   *encounter*
I shal hym seke by wey° and eek by strete,°   *road | street*
I make avow° to Goddes digne° bones.   *a vow | worthy*
Herkneth, felawes, we thre been al ones.°   *are three together*
Lat ech of us holde up his hand til oother,°   *to the other*
410 And ech of us bicomen° otheres brother,   *become*
And we wol sleen this false traytour, Deeth!
He shal be slayn, which that so manye sleeth,
By Goddes dignitee er it be nyght!"
    Togidres° han thise thre hir trouthes plight°   *together | promised*
415 To lyve and dyen ech of hem for oother
As though he were his owene yborn° brother.   *born*
And up they stirte° al dronken in this rage.   *jumped*
And forth they goon towardes that village
Of which the taverner hadde spoke biforn.
420 And many a grisly° ooth thanne han they sworn,   *horrible*
And Cristes blessed body they torente.°   *tear apart (with their oaths)*
Deeth shal be deed, if that they may hym hente!°   *catch him*
    Whan they han goon[7] nat fully half a mile

---

[1] *This ... understondeth* Those who understand his commandments know this.

[2] *Hayles* I.e., Hales Abbey in Gloucestershire, a monastery that claimed to have some of Christ's blood as a relic. .

[3] *Sevene ... treye* The modern game of craps is a version of medieval hazard, in which the player rolling the dice must call out the numbers he hopes to get.

[4] *bicched bones two* Two cursed bones; i.e., the dice, which were made of bone in the Middle Ages.

[5] *It ... houres* It was told to me two hours ago, before you came here.

[6] *Ther cam ... pestilence* The reference here is doubtless to plague, the Black Death that spread from Italy across Europe, hit England in 1348, and in the space of a year killed at least a third of the population. There were further outbreaks in 1361–62, 1369, and 1375–76.

[7] *han goon* Have gone. Chaucer frequently alternates between the simple past (the rioters jumped up, the old man met with them) and the present or the perfect forms (the rioters have gone rather than had gone or went, which we would expect in modern English).

Right° as they wolde han troden over a stile,[1] *just*

425 An oold man and a povre° with hem mette.° *poor / encountered them*
This olde man ful mekely° hem grette° *meekly / greeted*
And seyde thus: "Now, lordes, God yow see!"° *watch over*
  The proudeste of thise riotours three
Answerde agayn, "What, carl,° with sory grace!° *peasant / bad luck to you*
430 Why artow al forwrapped,° save thy face? *wrapped up*
Why lyvestow° so longe in so greet age?" *live you*
  This olde man gan looke in his visage° *face*
And seyde thus: "For° I ne kan nat fynde *because*
A man, though that I walked into Ynde,° *India*
435 Neither in citee nor in no village,
That wolde chaunge his youthe for myn age.
And therfore moot I han myn age stille,
As longe tyme as it is Goddes wille.
Ne deeth, allas, ne wol nat han my lyf.
440 Thus walke I lyk a restelees° kaityf,° *restless / wretch*
And on the ground which is my moodres° gate *mother's*
I knokke with my staf° bothe erly and late *walking stick*
And seye, 'Leeve° Mooder, leet me in! *dear*
Lo how I vanysshe°—flessh and blood and skyn! *waste away*
445 Allas, whan shul my bones been at reste?
Mooder, with yow wolde I chaunge my cheste° *money box*
That in my chambre° longe tyme hath be,° *room / been*
Ye, for an heyre clowt° to wrappe me.'[2] *hair-shirt*
But yet to me she wol nat do that grace,° *favor*
450 For which ful pale and welked° is my face. *withered*
  "But sires, to° yow it is no curteisye *in*
To speken to an old man vileynye,° *insults*
But° he trespasse° in word or elles in dede. *unless / offend*
In Hooly Writ ye may yourself wel rede
455 'Agayns° an oold man hoor° upon his heed *in the presence of / gray*
Ye sholde arise.'[3] Wherfore° I yeve° yow reed:° *therefore / give / advice*
Ne dooth unto an old man noon harm now,

Namoore than that ye wolde° men did to yow[4] *desire*
In age—if that ye so longe abyde.° *live long enough*
460 And God be with yow, where° ye go° or ryde. *wherever / walk*
I moot go thider as° I have to go." *thither where*
  "Nay, olde cherl, by God thou shalt nat so!"
Seyde this oother hasardour° anon. *gambler*
"Thou partest nat° so lightly, by Seint John! *do not get away*
465 Thou spak right now of thilke traytour Deeth,
That in this contree° alle oure freendes sleeth. *country*
Have heer my trouthe:° as thou art his espye,° *on my word / spy*
Telle where he is, or thou shalt it abye,° *pay for it*
By God and by the hooly sacrement!° *holy sacrament (the Eucharist)*
470 For soothly, thou art oon of his assent° *plot*
To sleen us yonge folk, thou false theef!"
  "Now sires," quod he, "if that ye be so leef,° *desirous*
To fynde Deeth, turne up this croked wey.° *crooked way*
For in that grove I lafte hym, by my fey,° *faith*
475 Under a tree, and there he wole abyde.° *wait*
Noght for youre boost he wole him nothyng hyde.[5]
Se ye that ook?° Right there ye shal hym fynde. *oak*
God save yow that boghte agayn° mankynde[6] *redeemed*
And yow amende!"° Thus seyde this olde man. *make you better*
480 And everich° of thise riotours ran *each*
Til he cam to that tree, and ther they founde
Of floryns° fyne of gold ycoyned° rounde *florins (coins) / coined*
Wel ny° an eighte busshels, as hem thoughte.° *very nearly / it seemed to them*
No lenger thanne° after Deeth they soughte, *then*
485 But ech of hem so glad was of that sighte,
For that the floryns been so faire and brighte,
That doun° they sette hem° by this precious hoord.° *down / themselves / hoard*
The worste of hem, he spak the firste word.
  "Bretheren," quod he, "taak kepe° what I seye. *pay attention to*
490 My wit is greet, though that I bourde° and pleye. *joke*
This tresor hath Fortune unto us yeven° *given*
In myrthe and joliftee° oure lyf to lyven. *jollity*
And lightly° as it comth, so wol we spende. *easily*
Ey, Goddes precious dignitee! Who wende° *expected*

---

1 *stile* Steps to get over a wall or fence.

2 *Mooder ... me* People in the Middle Ages sometimes wore shirts made of hair, which irritated the body, expecting the pain to gain them spiritual benefit. Here the old man wishes be buried in such a shirt, exchanging it for the chest that holds his money.

3 *Agayns ... arise* See Leviticus 19.3.

4 *Namoore ... yow* Cf. the Golden Rule from Matthew 7:12: "So whatever you wish that men would do to you, do so to them."

5 *Noght ... hyde* He will not hide himself in any way because of your boasting.

6 *God ... mankynde* May God, who redeemed mankind (by sending his Son Jesus Christ to die on the Cross), save you.

495 Today that we sholde han so fair a grace?
     But myghte this gold be caried fro this place
     Hoom to myn hous, or elles unto yours—
     For wel ye woot that al this gold is oures—
     Thanne were we in heigh felicitee.°   *great happiness*
500 But trewely, by daye it may nat bee.°   *not be*
     Men wolde seyn that we were theves stronge°   *downright thieves*
     And for oure owene tresor doon us honge.°   *cause us to be hanged*
     This tresor moste ycaried be by nyghte
     As wisely and as slyly as it myghte.
505 Wherfore I rede° that cut° among us alle   *advise / lots*
     Be drawe° and lat se wher the cut wol falle,   *drawn*
     And he that hath the cut with herte blithe°   *happy*
     Shal renne to towne, and that ful swithe,°   *quickly*
     And brynge us breed and wyn ful prively.°   *secretly*
510 And two of us shul kepen subtilly°   *cleverly*
     This tresor wel. And if he wol nat tarie,°   *delay*
     Whan it is nyght we wol this tresor carie
     By oon assent° whereas us thynketh best."   *in agreement*
     That oon of hem the cut° broghte in his fest°   *lots / fist*
515 And bad hem drawe and looke where it wol falle.
     And it fil on the yongeste of hem alle,
     And forth toward the toun he wente anon.
     And also soone as that he was gon,
     That oon spak thus unto that oother:
520 "Thow knowest wel thou art my sworn brother;
     Thy profit° wol I telle thee anon.   *your advantage*
     Thou woost wel that oure felawe is agon,
     And heere is gold, and that ful greet plentee,°   *a great deal of it*
     That shal departed° been among us thre.   *divided*
525 But nathelees, if I kan shape it so,
     That it departed were among us two,
     Hadde I nat doon a freendes torn° to thee?"   *friend's turn*
        That oother answerde, "I noot hou° that   *do not know how*
        may be.
     He woot how that the gold is with us tweye.°   *two*
530 What shal we doon? What shal we to hym seye?"
        "Shal it be conseil?"° seyde the firste shrewe.°   *our plan / villain*
     "And I shal tellen in a wordes fewe
     What we shal doon and bryngen it wel aboute."
        "I graunte," quod that oother, "out of doute,°   *without doubt*
535 That by my trouthe I shal thee nat biwreye."°   *betray*
        "Now," quod the firste, "thou woost wel we be tweye,
     And two of us shul strenger be than oon.

     Looke whan that he is set, that right anoon
     Arys° as though thou woldest with hym pleye,   *arise*
540 And I shal ryve° hym thurgh the sydes tweye°   *stab / two sides*
     Whil that thou strogelest° with hym as in game,°   *struggle / jest*
     And with thy daggere, looke thou do the same.
     And thanne shal al this gold departed be,
     My deere freend, bitwixen me and thee.
545 Thanne may we bothe oure lustes° all fulfille   *pleasures*
     And pleye at dees° right at oure owene wille."   *dice*
     And thus acorded been° thise shrewes tweye   *are agreed*
     To sleen° the thridde, as ye han herd me seye.   *kill*
        This yongeste, which that wente unto the toun,
550 Ful ofte in herte he rolleth up and doun
     The beautee of thise floryns newe and brighte.
     "O Lord," quod he, "if so were that I myghte
     Have al this tresor to myself allone,
     Ther is no man that lyveth under the trone°   *throne*
555 Of God that sholde lyve so murye° as I!"   *merry*
     And atte laste the feend° oure enemy   *devil*
     Putte in his thought that he sholde poyson beye°   *buy*
     With which he myghte sleen hise felawes tweye,   *kill*
     For why the feend foond hym in swich lyvynge
560 That he hadde leve hym to sorwe brynge.[1]
     For this was outrely° his fulle entente,   *utterly*
     To sleen hem bothe and nevere to repent.
     And forth he gooth—no lenger wolde he tarie—
     Into the toun unto a pothecarie°   *apothecary*
565 And preyde hym that he hym wolde selle
     Som poysoun that he myghte hise rattes° quelle.°   *rats / kill*
     And eek ther was a polcat in his hawe,
     That, as he seyde, hise capouns hadde yslawe,[2]
     And fayn° he wolde wreke hym,° if he   *gladly / avenge himself*
        myghte
570 On vermyn that destroyed° hym by nyghte.   *harmed*
        The pothecarie answerde, "And thou shalt have
     A thyng that, also° God my soule save,   *as*
     In al this world ther is no creature
     That eten or dronken hath of this confiture°   *concoction*

---

[1] *For why ... brynge* Because the devil found him living in such a way (i.e., so sinfully) that he had permission (from God) to bring him to sorrow (i.e., damnation).

[2] *And eek ... yslawe* And also there was a polecat (a type of weasel) in his yard that, as he said, had killed his poultry.

575 Noght° but the montance° of a corn° of
          whete,   nothing | size | grain
    That he ne shal his lif anon° forlete.°   immediately | lose
    Ye, sterve° he shal, and that in lasse while°   die | less time
    Than thou wolt goon a paas° nat but a mile,   at a walking pace
    The poysoun is so strong and violent."
580   This cursed man hath in his hond yhent°   taken
    This poysoun in a box, and sith° he ran   afterwards
    Into the nexte strete° unto a man   street
    And borwed hym° large botels thre.   borrowed from him
    And in the two his poyson poured he.
585 The thridde he kepte clene for his owene drynke.
    For al the nyght he shoope° hym for to swynke° intended | labor
    In cariynge of the gold out of that place.
    And whan this riotour with sory grace°   wretched misfortune
    Hadde filled with wyn hise grete botels thre,
590 To hise felawes agayn repaireth he.
        What nedeth it to sermone° of it moore?   talk
    For right so° as they hadde cast° his deeth
          bifoore,   just as | determined
    Right so they han hym slayn, and that anon.
    And whan that this was doon, thus spak that oon:°   the first
595 "Now lat us sitte and drynke and make us merie,
    And afterward we wol his body berie."°   bury
    And with that word it happed hym par cas°   by chance
    To take the botel ther the poysoun was,
    And drank and yaf his felawe drynke also,
600 For which anon they storven° bothe two.   died
        But certes, I suppose that Avycen[1]
    Wroot° nevere in no *Canoun* ne in no fen°   wrote | chapter
    Mo wonder° signes° of
          empoisonyng°   more terrible | symptoms | poisoning
    Than hadde thise wrecches two er hir endyng.° before their death
605 Thus ended been thise homycides° two   murderers
    And eek the false empoysonere° also.   poisoner
        O cursed synne of alle cursednesse,
    O traytours° homycide, o wikkednesse,   traitorous
    O glotonye, luxurie,° and hasardrye,   lust

610 Thou blasphemour of Crist with vileynye
    And othes grete° of usage° and of pride!   great oaths | habit
    Allas, mankynde, how may it bitide°   happen
    That to thy creatour, which that the wroghte°   who made you
    And with his precious herte blood thee boghte,°   redeemed
615 Thou art so fals and so unkynde,° allas?   unnatural
        Now goode men, God foryeve yow youre trespas
    And ware° yow fro the synne of avarice!   guard
    Myn hooly pardoun may yow all warice,°   save
    So° that ye offre nobles or sterlynges[2]   provided
620 Or elles silver broches, spoones, rynges.
    Boweth youre heed under this hooly bulle.°   license
    Com up, ye wyves, offreth of youre wolle;°   wool
    Youre names I entre heer in my rolle° anon.   list
    Into the blisse of Hevene shul ye gon.
625 I yow assoille° by myn heigh power,   pardon
    As ye were born. And lo, sires, thus I preche.
    And Jesu Crist that is oure soules leche°   soul's physician
    So graunte yow his pardoun to receyve.
    For that is best; I wol yow nat deceyve.
630   "But sires, o° word forgat I in my tale.   one
    I have relikes and pardoun in my male°   pouch
    As faire as any man in Engelond,
    Whiche were me yeven° by the Popes hond.°   given | hand
    If any of yow wole of devocioun°   in devotion
635 Offren and han myn absolucioun,
    Com forth anon, and kneleth heere adoun,
    And mekely° receyveth my pardoun.   meekly
    Or elles taketh pardoun as ye wende,°   go
    Al newe and fressh at every miles ende,
640 So that ye offren alwey newe° and newe   anew
    Nobles or pens,° whiche that be goode and trewe.[3]   pence
    It is an honour to everich° that is heer   everyone
    That ye mowe° have a suffisant° pardoner   may | capable
    T'assoille yow in contree° as ye ryde   the country
645 For aventures° whiche that may bityde.°   accidents | befall
    Paraventure° ther may fallen oon or two   perhaps
    Doun of his hors and breke his nekke atwo.°   in two

---

[1] *Avycen* I.e., Avicenna or Ibn Sina (980–1037 CE), a Persian philosopher who wrote, among other things, a treatise about medicine entitled *Liber Canonis Medicinae* (*The Book of the Canon of Medicine*). The word *Canon* in the next line refers to this book. It was divided into chapters called "fens," from the Arabic word for a part of a science.

---

[2] *nobles or sterlynges* Gold and silver coins respectively.

[3] *Nobles … trewe* Forgery and also the clipping of coins (i.e., shaving off some of the silver or gold from the edges) were major concerns in Chaucer's day.

Looke which a seuretee° is it to yow alle   *guarantee*
That I am in youre felaweshipe yfalle,°   *fallen into your company*
650 That may assoille yow bothe moore and
        lasse°   *greater and lesser (of rank)*
Whan that the soule shal fro the body passe.
I rede° that oure Hoost heere shal bigynne,°   *advise / begin*
For he is moost envoluped in synne.
Com forth, sire Hoost, and offre first anon,
655 And thou shalt kisse my relikes everychon.
Ye, for a grote unbokele anon thy purs."[1]

    "Nay, nay," quod he, "thanne have I Cristes curs!°   *curse*
Lat be,"° quod he. "It shal nat be so, thee'ch!   *leave it be*
Thou woldest make me kisse thyn olde breech°   *pants*
660 And swere it were a relyk of a seint—
Though it were with thy fundement° depeint!°   *anus / stained*
But by the croys which that Seint Eleyne[2] fond,
I wolde I hadde thy coillons° in myn hond   *testicles*
Instide of relikes or of seintuarie!°   *reliquaries*
665 Lat kutte hem of!° I wol with thee hem
        carie.°   *let them be cut off / carry*

They shul be shryned° in an hogges
        toord!"°   *enshrined / hog's turd*
    This Pardoner answerde nat a word.
So wrooth° he was, no word ne wolde he seye.   *angry*
    "Now," quod oure Hoost, "I wol no lenger pleye°   *joke*
670 With thee ne with noon oother angry man!"
But right anon the worthy knyght bigan°   *began*
Whan that he saugh that al the peple lough,°   *laughed*
"Namoore of this! For it is right ynough!°   *quite enough*
Sire Pardoner, be glad and myrie of cheere.°   *merry of face*
675 And ye, sire Hoost, that been to me so deere,
I prey yow that ye kisse the Pardoner.
And Pardoner, I prey thee, drawe thee neer,
And as we diden,° lat us laughe and pleye!"   *did*
Anon they kiste and ryden forth hir weye.°   *their way*

HEERE IS ENDED THE PARDONERS TALE

---

[1] *Ye ... purs* Yes, unbuckle your purse immediately for a groat
(fourpenny coin).

[2] *Seint Eleyne* I.e., St. Helena, the mother of the fourth-century
Roman emperor Constantine. Legend had it that she went to the
Holy Land and found there the cross on which Christ was crucified.

The Prioress's Prologue and Tale

The Prioress's Tale belongs to the genre of the miracles of the Virgin, collections of stories recounting the Virgin Mary's dramatic interventions to save people who had shown her particular devotion. These melodramatic stories were enormously popular, In these miracle stories, Jews often figure as villains, and there are several in which they are depicted murdering or trying to murder a Christian child, whom the Virgin rescues or takes to Heaven. One such legend concerned the boy-saint Hugh of Lincoln. The Prioress describes his death as happening "but a little while ago" (line 686), but all Jews had been expelled from England in 1290 and Hugh was in fact killed in 1255.

Chaucer's presentation of this anti-Semitic story, a version of the so-called "blood libel," which accuses Jews of killing Christian children, has troubled modern readers, who have often debated whether Chaucer's own attitudes are to any degree distanced from those of the Prioress. The contrast between the sentimentality she is shown to display in *The General Prologue* (as a character who weeps if a man beats one of her lap dogs) and the extreme virulence of her hatred of the Jews—who are punished more savagely at the end of her tale than in other versions of the story—might suggest a narrative distancing. On the other hand, *The Prioress's Tale* was popular in the fifteenth century, and was copied separately in several manuscripts, with no reference to *The General Prologue*; the opening Hymn to the Virgin, the *Alma redemptoris*, is set above any possible parody; the Man of Law is no less hostile to Islam; and there are anti-Semitic lines in *The Parson's Tale* as well. In short, it is difficult not to think it likely that Chaucer shared substantially in the anti-Semitism that was so prevalent in fourteenth-century England.

Also of interest is the style of *The Prioress's Tale*. Written in rhyme-royal stanzas, and drawing on the language of the liturgy, it has moments of stately elegance, as the Prioress employs a high rhetorical style in formal praise of the Virgin. But it also contains lurid details of the murder and the disposal of the body in a privy which seem at odds with the Prioress's courtly manners.

The relation between the teller and the tale has attracted much critical attention. The Prioress clearly identifies with the innocent little *clergeon*, who is absolute in his devotion to the Virgin, even to the point of neglecting his education. His faith, like hers, is child-like in its innocence, or so she would have us believe. The tale can perhaps be explained as Chaucer's exploration of a particular kind of devotional story, the emotionally charged saint's life or miracle of the Virgin, which was immensely popular in his day.

Detail of the opening page of *The Prioress's Tale*, Ellesmere manuscript.
(Reprinted by permission of *The Huntington Library, San Marino, California*. EL26C9F72r.)

Opening page of *The Prioress's Tale*, Ellesmere manuscript. (Reprinted by permission of *The Huntington Library, San Marino, California*. EL26C9F72r.)

THE PRIORESS'S PROLOGUE

BIHOOLD THE MURIE WORDES OF THE HOOST TO THE SHIPMAN AND TO THE LADY PRIORESSE

"Wel seyd,° by *corpus dominus*,"[1] quod° oure
    Hoost.°   *well said / said / host*
"Now longe moote° thou saille° by the cost,°   *may / sail / coast*
Sire gentil° maister,° gentil maryneer!°   *noble / master / mariner*
God yeve° this monk a thousand last quade
    yeer!°   *give / cart-loads of bad years*
5 Aha, felawes,° beth war° of swich° a
    jape!°   *fellows / beware / such / joke*
The monk putte in the mannes hood an ape,[2]
And in his wyves° eek,° by Seint
    Austyn!°   *wife's / also / St. Augustine*
Draweth° no monkes moore unto youre
    in.°   *take / into your house*
  "But now passe over,° and lat° us seke° aboute   *on / let / seek*
10 Who shal now telle first of al° this route°   *all / company*
Another tale." And with that word he sayde
As curteisly° as it had been a mayde,°   *courteously / maid (speaking)*
"My Lady Prioresse, by youre leve,°   *leave*
So that I wiste° I sholde yow nat
    greve,°   *knew / would not distress you*
15 I wolde demen° that ye tellen sholde°   *would judge / should tell*
A tale next, if so were that ye wolde.
Now wol° ye vouchesauf,° my lady deere?"°   *will / agree / dear*
  "Gladly," quod she, and seyde° as ye shal heere.°   *said / hear*

EXPLICIT[3]

THE PROLOGUE OF THE PRIORESS'S TALE

Domine Dominus noster[4]

20 "O Lord, oure Lord, thy name how merveillous°   *marvelous*
    Is in this large world ysprad,"° quod she.   *spread about*
"For noght oonly° thy laude° precious   *not only / praise*
Parfourned° is by men of dignitee,   *proclaimed*
But by the mouth of children thy bountee°   *goodness*
25 Parfourned is, for on the brest° soukynge°   *breast / sucking*
Somtyme° shewen° they thyn heriynge.°   *sometimes / show / praise*

Wherfore° in laude, as I best kan° or may,   *therefore / know how*
Of thee and of the lylye flour°   *lily flower*
Which that° thee bar° and is a mayde°
    alway,[5]   *who / bore you / virgin*
To telle a storie I wol do my labour--
30 Nat that I may encreessen° hir honour,   *increase*
For she hirself is honour and the roote°   *root*
Of bountee, next hir sone, and soules boote.[6]

O mooder° mayde,° o mayde mooder
    free,°   *mother / maid / noble*
O bussh unbrent, brennynge in Moyses sighte,[7]
35 That ravysedest° doun° fro°   *allured, entranced / down / from*
    the Deitee,
Thurgh thyn humblesse, the goost that in th'alighte,[8]
Of whos vertu whan he thyn herte lighte[9]

---

1 *corpus dominus* Incorrect Latin: "The Lord's body"; a reference to the sacrament of the Eucharist, in which the communion bread was transubstantiated into Christ's body.

2 *The ... ape* Literally, "The monk put an ape in the man's hood." I.e., he made a fool of him (to "put an ape" was an expression meaning "to fool").

3 *Explicit* Latin: Here it ends.

---

4 *Domine Dominus noster* Latin: "O Lord, our Lord." These are the first words of Psalm 8, which the Prioress paraphrases in the first stanza of her Prologue.

5 *lylye ... alway* In medieval iconography, the Virgin Mary is presented with a lily, a symbol of her purity, by the angel Gabriel during the Annunciation of the birth of Christ.

6 *Of ... boote* Of goodness, next to her son, and the soul's help.

7 *O ... sighte* O unburned bush, burning in Moses's sight. The reference is to the encounter Moses has in Exodus 3 with God in the form of a burning bush that is unconsumed by the fire. This became a popular image for Mary, who preserved her virginity despite being a mother.

8 *Thurgh ... alighte* Through your humility, the spirit that alighted in you.

9 *Of ... lighte* Of whose power when he illumined your heart.

Conceyved° was the Fadres sapience,[1]   *conceived*
40   Helpe me to telle it in thy reverence.°   *for your honor*

Lady, thy bountee,° thy magnificence,°   *goodness | majesty*
Thy vertu,° and thy grete humylitee°   *power | great humility*
Ther may no tonge expresse in no
      science.°   *whatever its knowledge*
For somtyme,° Lady, er° men praye to thee,   *sometimes | before*
Thou goost biforn° of thy benyngnytee°   *anticipate | goodness*
45   And getest us thurgh lyght° of thy preyere°   *light | prayer*
To gyden° us unto thy Sone° so deere.   *guide | Son*

My konnyng° is so wayk,° o blisful°
      queene,   *knowledge | weak | blessed*
For to declare thy grete worthynesse,
That I ne may the weighte° nat susteene,°   *the weight | not sustain*
50   But as a child of twelf monthe oold or lesse
That kan unnethe° any word expresse,°   *can scarcely | pronounce*
Right° so fare I. And therfore I yow preye,°   *just | pray you*
Gydeth my song that I shal of yow seye."°   *tell of you*

EXPLICIT

THE PRIORESS'S TALE

HEERE BIGYNNETH THE PRIORESSES TALE

Ther was in Asye[2] in a greet cite°   *great city*
55   Amonges Cristene° folk a Jewerye°   *Christian | Jewish quarter*
Sustened° by a lord of that contree°   *sustained | country*

For foul usure° and lucre° of vileynye,[3]   *interest (rates) | profit*
Hateful to Crist and to his
      compaignye.°   *company (i.e., Christians)*
And thurgh this strete° men myghte ride or wende,°   *street | go*
60   For it was free and open at eyther ende.

A litel scole° of Cristen folk ther stood   *little school*
Doun at the ferther ende, in which ther were
Children an heepe° ycomen° of Cristen   *many children | come*
      blood,
That lerned in that scole yeer by yere
65   Swich manere doctrine° as men used there.   *such kind of teaching*
This is to seyn, to syngen° and to rede,°   *sing | read*
As smale children doon in hire childhede.°   *their childhood*

Among thise° children was a wydwes sone,°   *these | widow's son*
A litel clergeoun[4] seven yeer of age,
70   That day by day to° scole was his wone.°   *to [go to] | custom*
And eek also whereas° he saugh°
      th'ymage°   *where | saw | the image*
Of Cristes mooder, he hadde in usage,°   *he had the habit*
As hym was taught, to knele adoun and seye
His *Ave Marie*[5] as he goth by the weye.°   *goes along the road*

75   Thus hath this wydwe hir litel sone ytaught°   *taught*
Oure blisful lady, Cristes mooder deere,
To worshipe ay.° And he forgat it naught,°   *always | not*
For sely° child wol alwey soone leere.°   *innocent | learn*
But ay° whan I remembre on this mateere,   *ever*
80   Seint Nicholas[6] stant° evere in my presence,   *stands*
For he so yong to Crist dide° reverence.   *did*

[1] *Fadres sapience* Father's wisdom (i.e., Christ). Although each member of the Christian Trinity is equal, they are often associated with particular qualities. Christ, the word or logos, is associated with wisdom; the Father with power, and the Holy Spirit with love.

[2] *Ayse* Asia. In the Middle Ages, the geographical term "Asia" meant Asia Minor, which today is the country of Turkey and part of northern Greece. All Jews were expelled from England in 1290. In Chaucer's day there were some Jews living in France (from which they were expelled first in 1306 and again in 1394), some in central and eastern Europe, the Balkans and Asia Minor. There were also significant Jewish communities in Spain, Italy, North Africa, and the Middle East.

[3] *For ... vileynye* In the Middle Ages, the Church prohibited Christians from lending money at interest rates. Such commerce, increasingly necessary for the economy of the time, was engaged in by the few non-Christian peoples of Europe, especially the Jews. See the section on "Religion and Spiritual Life" elsewhere in this volume for a further discussion of this issue.

[4] *clergeoun* Term meaning pupil but also choir boy. Young boys often served in choirs in exchange for education.

[5] *Ave Marie* Latin: "Hail Mary," the words of the angel Gabriel to the Virgin at the Annunciation. His speech was set to music and frequently sung in church services in the Middle Ages.

[6] *Seint Nicholas* Fourth-century bishop of Myra in Asia Minor who became the patron saint of children. His legend maintained that as an infant he fasted on Wednesdays and Fridays by refusing his mother's breast-milk.

This litel child, his litel book lernynge,°   *learning*
As he sat in the scole at his prymer,°   *primer (school book)*
He *Alma redemptoris*[1] herde synge°   *heard being sung*
85   As children lerned hire° antiphoner.[2]   *their*
And as he dorste,° he drough hym°
    ner° and ner   *dared | drew himself | nearer*
And herkned ay° the wordes and the
    noote°   *ever listened (to) | melody*
Til he the firste vers koude° al by rote.°   *knew | by heart*

Noght wiste he° what this Latyn was to
    seye,°   *he did not know | meant*
90   For he so yong and tendre was of age.
But on a day his felawe° gan he preye°   *his friend | he began to ask*
T'expounden hym° this song in his langage,   *to explain to him*
Or telle hym why this song was in usage;
This preyde he hym to construe° and declare   *translate*
95   Ful often tyme° upon hise knowes° bare.   *very often | knees*

His felawe, which that elder was than he,
Answerde hym thus: "This song, I have herd seye,°   *heard said*
Was maked of° oure blisful lady free,°   *made for | noble*
Hir to salue° and eek hire for to preye   *honor*
100   To been° oure helpe and socour° whan we deye.°   *be | aid | die*
I kan namoore expounde in this mateere.
I lerne song; I kan° but smal° grammeere."   *know | little*

"And is this song maked° in reverence°   *made | honor*
Of Cristes mooder?" seyde this innocent.
105   "Now, certes,° I wol do my diligence°   *certainly | will work hard*
To konne° it al er Cristemasse is went,°   *learn | has passed*
Though that I for my prymer shal be shent[3]
And shal be beten° thries° in an houre.   *beaten | three times*
I wol it konne,° oure Lady for to honoure."   *will learn it*

110   His felawe taughte hym homward prively[4]
Fro day to day, til he koude it by rote.
And thanne he song° it wel and boldely   *sang*
Fro word to word, acordynge with the
    note.°   *according to the melody*
Twies° a day it passed thurgh his throte,   *twice*
115   To scoleward° and homward whan he wente;   *towards school*
On Cristes mooder set was his entente.

As I have seyd, thurghout° the Juerie   *throughout*
This litel child, as he cam to and fro,
Ful murily° wolde he synge and crie   *merrily*
120   O *Alma redemptoris* everemo.
The swetnesse his herte perced° so   *pierced*
Of Cristes mooder, that to hire° to preye   *her*
He kan nat stynte° of syngyng° by the weye.   *cannot stop | singing*

Oure firste foo,° the serpent Sathanas,°   *foe | Satan*
125   That hath in Jues herte° his waspes° nest   *Jewish hearts | wasp's*
Up swal° and seide, "O Hebrayk
    peple,° allas!   *swelled up | Hebrew people*
Is this to yow° a thyng that is honest,°   *you | respectable*
That swich a boy shal walken as hym lest°   *wishes*
In youre despit,° and synge of swich
    sentence°   *scorn of you | subject*
130   Which is agayn° oure lawes reverence?"   *against*

Fro thennes° forth the Jues han° conspired   *thence | have*
This innocent out of this world to chace.°   *chase*
An homycide° therto han they hyred   *murderer*
That in an aleye° hadde a privee° place,   *alley | secret*
135   And as the child gan forby for to pace,°   *to pass by*
This cursed Jew hym hente° and heeld hym faste   *grabbed*
And kitte° his throte and in a pit hym caste.°   *cut | threw*

I seye° that in a wardrobe° they hym threwe,   *say | latrine*
Whereas° thise Jewes purgen° hire
    entraille.°   *where | empty | bowels*
140   O cursed folk of Herodes[5] al newe,
What may youre yvel° entente° yow availle?   *evil | intent*
Mordre wol out! Certeyn, it wol nat faille,

---

[1] *Alma redemptoris* I.e., "Alma redemptoris mater" (Latin: Gracious mother of the redeemer), an antiphon used in church services in the Middle Ages during Advent.

[2] *antiphoner* Book containing the words and music of antiphons like *Alma Redemptoris*.

[3] *Though … shent* Although I shall be punished for [neglecting] my school book. Corporal punishment was the norm in medieval schools for students who were slow at learning their lessons.

[4] *His … prively* On the way home, his friend taught him privately.

[5] *O … Herodes* In Matthew 2.1–18, Herod causes all the children of the region to be murdered in his effort to kill the baby Jesus.

And namely, ther th'onour of God shal sprede.[1]
The blood out crieth° on youre cursed dede!   *cries out*

145 O martir° sowded° to virginitee,   *martyr | united*
     Now maystow° syngen, folwynge evere in
         oon°   *may you | following ever in unity*
     The white Lamb celestial,[2] quod she,[3]
     Of which the grete evaungelist Seint John
     In Pathmos wroot,[4] which seith that they that goon°   *go*
150 Biforn this Lamb and synge a song al newe
     That nevere flesshly° wommen they ne knewe.[5]   *carnally*

     This povre wydwe awaiteth° al that nyght   *waits*
     After hir litel child. But he cam noght.°   *did not come*
     For which, as soone as it was dayes lyght,
155 With face pale of drede° and bisy thoght° *for fear | hectic thoughts*
     She hath at scole and elleswhere hym soght,
     Til finally she gan so fer espie,°   *found out this much*
     That he last seyn was in the Juerie.

     With moodres pitee° in hir brest enclosed,   *mother's pity*
160 She gooth as she were half out of hir mynde
     To every place where she hath supposed
     By liklihede° hir litel child to fynde.   *it likely*
     And evere on Cristes mooder meeke and kynde
     She cride. And atte laste thus she wroghte:°   *did thus*
165 Among the cursed Jues she hym soghte.

     She frayneth,° and she preyeth pitously°   *asks | begs pitifully*
     To every Jew that dwelte in thilke place
     To telle hire if hir child wente oght forby.°   *by at all*
     They seyde nay, but Jesu of his grace

170 Yaf in hir thoght inwith a litel space,[6]
     That in that place after hir sone she cryde,
     Where he was casten in a pit bisyde.°   *nearby*

     O grete God, that parfournest° thy laude°   *proclaims | praise*
     By mouth of innocentz, lo heere° thy myght!   *behold here*
175 This gemme° of chastite, this emeraude,°   *gem | emerald*
     And eek of martirdom° the ruby bright,   *martyrdom*
     Ther° he with throte ykorven° lay
         upright,°   *where | cut | on his back*
     He *Alma redemptoris* gan to synge
     So loude that al the place gan to rynge!

180 The Cristene folk that thurgh° the strete wente   *through*
     In coomen° for to wondre upon this thyng,   *came*
     And hastily they for the provost[7] sente.
     He cam anon withouten tariyng°   *delay*
     And herieth° Crist that is of Hevene kyng   *praises*
185 And eek his mooder, honour of mankynde,
     And after that the Jewes leet he°
         bynde.°   *he commanded | to be bound*

     This child with pitous lamentacioun
     Up taken° was, syngynge his song alway,   *lifted up*
     And with honour of greet processioun
190 They carien hym unto the nexte abbay.°   *nearest monastery*
     His mooder swownynge° by his beere° lay.   *fainting | bier*
     Unnethe° myghte the peple that was theere   *scarcely*
     This newe Rachel[8] brynge fro his beere.

     With torment° and with shameful deeth°
         echon,°   *torture | death | each one*
195 This provost dooth° the Jewes for to sterve,°   *causes | die*
     That of this mordre wiste,° and that anon.°   *knew | immediately*
     He nolde° no swich cursednesse°
         observe.°   *would not | villainy | tolerate*
     Yvele° shal he have that yvele wol deserve!   *evil*

---

[1] *Mordre ... sprede* Murder will come to light. Certainly, it will not fail, and especially wherever the honor of God shall spread.

[2] *Lamb celestial* Heavenly lamb. The reference is to Revelation 14.1–5, in which Christ appears as the Lamb of God.

[3] *she* I.e., the Prioress. This line-filler reinforces momentarily the fiction that the Prioress is telling this tale on the road to Canterbury.

[4] *of which ... wroot* The writer of Revelation identifies himself as John, who was exiled for his faith on the island of Patmos off the coast of Turkey, where he had the visions that form the basis of the book of Revelation.

[5] *That ... knewe* Reference to the virginity of those who praise the Lamb.

[6] *Yaf ... space* Brought to her mind within a little while.

[7] *provost* Medieval judge who oversaw legal matters within a town.

[8] *This newe Rachel* Reference to Matthew 2.18, which quotes Jeremiah 31.15: "Rachel weeping for her children, and would not be comforted, because they are not." Rachel, according to Matthew, is a metaphor for the Jewish mothers whose children were slaughtered by Herod.

Therfore with wilde hors° he dide hem
   drawe,°   *horses | had them drawn*
200 And after that he heng° hem by° the lawe.   *hanged | according to*

Upon this beere ay lith° this innocent   *ever lies*
Biforn° the chief auter° whil the masse° laste, *before | altar | mass*
And after that the abbot with his covent°   *group of monks*
Han sped° hem for to burien° hym ful faste. *have hurried | bury*
205 And whan they hooly water on hym caste,
Yet spak° this child whan spreynd° was   *spoke | sprinkled*
   hooly water
And song° *O alma redemptoris mater.*   *sang*

This abbot, which that was an hooly man,
As monkes been° or elles oghte be,   *are*
210 This yonge child to conjure he bigan°   *began to call upon*
And seyde, "O deere child, I halse° thee   *ask*
In vertu of the Hooly Trinitee,
Tel me what is thy cause for to synge,
Sith that thy throte is kut, to my semynge."° *as it seems to me*

215 "My throte is kut unto my nekke boon,"°   *neck-bone*
Seyde this child, "and as by wey° of kynde° *way | nature*
I sholde have dyed, ye,° longe tyme agon.°   *yes | ago*
But Jesu Crist, as ye in bookes fynde,
Wil° that his glorie laste and be in mynde,° *wishes | remembered*
220 And for the worshipe of his mooder deere,
Yet may I synge *O alma* loude and cleere.

"This welle° of mercy, Cristes mooder sweete, *well (source)*
I loved alwey, as after my konnynge.° *according to my knowledge*
And whan that I my lyf sholde forlete,°   *have lost*
225 To me she cam and bad° me for to synge   *commanded*
This anthephen° verraily° in my
   deyynge,°   *antiphon | truly | dying*
As ye han herd. And whan that I hadde songe,
Me thoughte she leyde a greyn° upon my tonge.° *grain*

"Wherfore I synge, and synge I moot, certeyn,
230 In honour of that blisful mayden free,
Til fro my tonge of taken° is the greyn.   *taken off*
And afterward thus seyde she to me:

'My litel child, now wol I fecche° thee   *fetch*
Whan that the greyn is fro thy tonge ytake.° *taken*
235 Be nat agast.° I wol thee nat forsake!'"   *not afraid*

This hooly monk, this abbot, hym meene I,° *I mean him*
His tonge out caughte° and took awey the greyn, *pulled out*
And he yaf° up the goost ful softely.° *gave | very quietly*
And whan this abbot hadde this wonder seyn,° *seen*
240 Hise salte teeris° trikled doun as reyn,° *salty tears | rain*
And gruf° he fil° al plat° upon the grounde, *on his face | fell | flat*
And stille he lay as he had leyn ybounde.°   *lain bound*

The covent eek lay on the pavement,
Wepynge and heryng Cristes mooder deere.
245 And after that they ryse and forth been went° *are gone away*
And tooken awey this martir from his beere,
And in a temple of marbul stones cleere
Enclosen they his litel body sweete.
Ther he is now, God leve° us alle for to meete! *allow*

250 O yonge° Hugh of Lyncoln,[1] slayn also   *young*
With° cursed Jewes, as it is notable,°   *by | well known*
For it is but a litel while ago,
Preye eek for us, we synful folk unstable,° *unsteadfast*
That of his mercy God so merciable°   *merciful*
255 On us his grete mercy multiplie
For reverence of his mooder Marie. Amen.

HEERE IS ENDED THE PRIORESSES TALE

---

[1] *Hugh of Lyncoln* Child supposedly murdered by Jews in 1255.
He was one of the two principal saints associated with Lincoln, a
town midway up England's east coast. In 1386 Henry, Earl of Derby
(John of Gaunt's son by his first wife and the future Henry IV),
became a member of the fraternity of Lincoln Cathedral, to which
Edward III and John of Gaunt already belonged. Chaucer's wife
Philippa, who was a member of the household of John of Gaunt's
wife, Constance or Constanza of Castille, also became a member of
the fraternity at the same ceremony. Chaucer may have had a special
interest in Hugh of Lincoln because of this connection to the
Cathedral's fraternity, although he was not a member himself.

The Nun's Priest's Prologue and Tale

In the full *Canterbury Tales* this tale is preceded by *The Monk's Tale*, in which the Monk recites a long list of tragedies, which for him are simply stories of those who have fallen suddenly from great rank. This wearies the Knight, who interrupts him. When the Monk refuses to tell stories of hunting instead, the Host calls peremptorily upon the Nun's Priest. The Nun's Priest, who is not even described in the *General Prologue*, is at first almost a nonentity. By the end of his tale, however, he will have won whole-hearted admiration, at least from the rather undiscerning Host, whose response (also included here) is contained in a passage that does not appear in the Ellesmere Manuscript.

The tale offered by the Nun's Priest is a beast fable of the kind told by Aesop. It revolves around animals who are all too human in their follies, and it teaches a clear moral lesson: beware of flatterers. The Nun's Priest expands on this simple structure, beginning with a rich rhetorical evocation of the rooster Chauntecleer's crowing, which he contrasts to the austere life of the poor widow who owns him. The tale then moves into an elaborate debate on dream lore, in which the hen Pertelote speaks for the materialist for whom dreams are the result of indigestion, and Chauntecleer for those who see them as veiled prophecies. This debate alone takes up nearly half the lines in the tale. Throughout, the tale fluctuates between a world in which Chauntecleer and Pertelote are aristocratic lovers and a world in which they are just barnyard fowl. Much of the comedy lies in the elaborate rhetorical language, which is both celebrated and mocked. The Nun's Priest is clearly a master of this art, and it is typical of the tale's comic approach to the eloquence it proudly displays that he should invoke Geoffrey of Vinsauf and his basic textbook on rhetoric. This is a work that, while it is several steps up on Pertelote's only written authority, an elementary grammar drawn from the moral writings of Cato, is scarcely sophisticated. For all its comedy, the tale contains one of Chaucer's grimmest and most pointed historical references, to the rebels in 1381 who hunted down and murdered Flemish weavers.

The Nun's Priest ends by suggesting that the tale exists only for its moral, the fruit, and that we should discard the story, the chaff. All that is written, he tells us, is written for our doctrine, a line Chaucer repeats in his *Retraction*. But the Nun's Priest also tells us that his story is as true as that of Lancelot de Lake (line 445), that he speaks only in game (line 495), and that when he criticizes women his words are those of Chauntecleer (line 498). Filled with references to books and sayings, such as Chauntecleer's comment that "Mulier est hominis confusio" (Latin: Woman is man's confusion, line 397), that are misrepresented or otherwise untrustworthy, the tale does not allow such an easy distinction between literary art and moral content.

Opening page of *The Nun's Priest's Tale*, Ellesmere manuscript (detail).
(Reprinted by permission of *The Huntington Library, San Marino, California*. EL26C9F72r.)

Opening page of *The Nun's Priest's Tale*, Ellesmere manuscript. (Reprinted by permission of *The Huntington Library, San Marino, California.* EL26C9F72r.)

THE NUN'S PRIEST'S PROLOGUE

HEERE STYNTETH THE KNYGHT THE MONK OF HIS TALE[1]

THE PROLOGE OF THE NONNES PREESTES TALE

"Hoo,"° quod° the Knyght, "good sire, namoore° of
   this!   *whoa | said | no more*
That ye han seyd is right ynough, ywis,[2]
And muchel moore,° for litel
   hevynesse°   *much more | a little heaviness*
Is right ynough° to muche folk,° I gesse. *enough | many people*
5 I seye° for me it is a greet disese,°   *say | great discomfort*
Whereas° men han been in greet welthe° and
   ese,°   *where | wealth | ease*
To heeren° of hire° sodeyn fal,° allas! *hear | their | sudden fall*
And the contrarie° is joye and greet solas,° *contrary | comfort*
As whan a man hath been in povre° estaat,° *poor | condition*
10 And clymbeth° up, and wexeth° fortunate, *climbs | grows*
And there abideth° in prosperitee.   *remains*
Swich° thyng is gladsom,° as it
   thynketh° me,   *such a | pleasant | seems to*
And of swich thyng were goodly for to telle."
   "Ye,"° quod oure Hoost, "by Seint Poules belle,[3] *yes*
15 Ye seye right sooth.° This Monk, he clappeth
   lowed.°   *truth | chatters loudly*
He spak how Fortune covered with a clowde° *cloud*
I noot° nevere what, and also of a tragedie *know not*
Right now ye harde,° and, pardee,° no
   remedie°   *heard | by God | remedy*
It is for to biwaille° ne° compleyne° *bewail | nor | lament*
20 That that° is doon,° and als° it is a
   peyne,°   *which | done | also | pain*
As ye han seyd, to heere of hevynesse.° *sadness*
   "Sire Monk, namoore of this, so God yow blesse!
Youre tale anoyeth al this compaignye.
Swich talkyng is nat worth a boterflye!° *butterfly*
25 For therinne is ther no desport° ne game. *sport*

Wherfore,° sire Monk, daun° Piers by youre
   name,   *therefore | sir*
I pray yow hertely° telle us somwhat elles.°*heartily | something else*
For sikerly,° nere° clynkyng° of youre
   belles   *surely | were not | clinking*
That on youre bridel° hange on every syde, *bridle*
30 By Hevene Kyng° that° for us alle
   dyde,°   *the King of Heaven | who | died*
I sholde er° this han° fallen doun for sleepe, *before | have*
Althogh the slough° had never been so deepe. *mud*
Thanne hadde youre tale al be° toold in veyn.° *been | vain*
For certeinly, as that thise clerkes seyn,° *these scholars say*
35 Whereas° a man may have noon° audience, *where | no*
Noght helpeth it° to tellen his sentence.° *it is of no use | meaning*
And wel I woot, the substance is in me
If anythyng shal wel reported be.[4]
Sire, sey° somwhat of huntyng, I yow preye." *tell us*
40   "Nay," quod this Monk, "I have no lust° to
   pleye.°   *desire | play*
Now lat° another telle as I have toold."   *let*
   Thanne spak oure Hoost with rude speche° and
   boold°   *rough speech | bold*
And seyde unto the Nonnes Preest°
   anon,°   *Nun's Priest | immediately*
"Com neer, thou Preest. Com hyder,° thou sire John![5] *here*
45 Telle us swich thyng as may oure hertes glade.° *gladden*
Be blithe,° though thou ryde upon a jade.° *happy | bad horse*
What thogh° thyn hors be bothe foul and lene?° *though | lean*
If he wol serve thee, rekke nat a bene!° *do not care a bean*
Looke that thyn herte be murie° everemo." *merry*
50   "Yis sire," quod he, "yis, Hoost, so moot I go.° *as I may go*
But° I be myrie, ywis,° I wol be blamed." *unless | indeed*
And right anon his tale he hath attamed,° *has begun*
And thus he seyde unto us everichon,° *everyone*
This sweete preest, this goodly man, sire John.

EXPLICIT[6]

---

[1] *Heere ... Tale* Here the Knight stops the Monk from telling his
tale. The Monk's tragic tale recounted the fall of numerous people
from greatness to wretchedness and misery.

[2] *That ... ywis* What you have said is quite enough, indeed.

[3] *Seint Poules belle* I.e., the bell of St. Paul's Cathedral in London.

[4] *the substance ... be* Either I have the stuff (substance) in me (i.e.,
the power) to understand if a story is well told, or possibly, if a story
is well told, I know when I have grasped the substance of it.

[5] *thou sire John* The Host addresses the Nun's Priest with the
familiar thou, not the polite you that he uses for the Knight, the
Monk, or most of the other gentle folk.

[6] *Explicit* Latin: Here it ends.

THE NUN'S PRIEST'S TALE

HEERE BIGYNNETH THE NONNES PREESTES TALE OF THE COK AND HEN, CHAUNTECLEER AND PERTELOTE

55 A povre° wydwe° somdeel° stape° in age   *poor / widow / somewhat / advanced*
Was whilom° dwellyng° in a narwe° cottage   *once / living / small*
Biside° a grene[1] stondynge° in a dale.   *beside / standing*
This wydwe of which I telle yow my tale,
Syn° thilke° day that she was last a wyf   *since / that*
60 In pacience ladde° a ful° symple lyf,   *led / very*
For litel° was hir catel° and hir rente.°   *little / possessions / income*
By housbondrie° of swich° as God hire° sente   *frugal use / such / her*
She foond° hirself and eek° hir doghtren° two.   *provided for / also / daughters*
Thre° large sowes hadde she and namo,°   *three / no more*
65 Thre keen,° and eek a sheepe that highte°   *cows / was called*
Malle.
Ful sooty° was hir bour° and eek hir halle°   *dirty / bedroom / dining hall*
In which she eet° ful many a sklendre meel.°   *ate / meager meal*
Of poynaunt° sauce hir neded never a deel;°   *spicy / portion*
No deyntee° morsel passed thurgh hir throte.°   *dainty / throat*
70 Hir diete was accordant to hir cote.°   *in accord with her cottage*
Repleccioun° ne made hire nevere sik.°   *gluttony / sick*
Attempree° diete was al hir phisik,°   *temperate / medical remedy*
And excercise and hertes suffisaunce.°   *heart's content*
The goute lette hire nothyng for to daunce,[2]
75 N'apoplexie° shente° nat hir heed.°   *nor stroke / harmed / head*
No wyn ne drank she, neither whit ne reed.
Hir bord° was served moost with whit and blak—   *table*
Milk and broun breed, in which she foond no lak,[3]
Seynd bacoun° and somtyme an ey° or tweye.°   *smoked bacon / egg / two*

80 For she was, as it were, a maner° deye.°   *kind of / dairy farmer*
A yeerd° she hadde enclosed al aboute   *yard*
With stikkes° and a drye dych[4] withoute,   *sticks*
In which she hadde a cok° heet° Chauntecleer.[5]   *rooster / named*
In al the land of crowyng° nas° his peer.   *crowing / there was not*
85 His voys° was murier° than the murie orgon°   *voice / merrier / organ*
On messedayes that in the chirche gon.[6]
Wel sikerer° was his crowing in his logge°   *reliable / lodging*
Than is a clokke or an abbey orlogge.°   *monastery clock*
By nature he crew° ech ascencioun°   *crowed / each ascension*
Of the equynoxial[7] in thilke° toun.   *that*
90 For whan degrees fiftene weren ascended,
Thanne crew he that it myghte nat been amended.°   *could not be improved*
His coomb° was redder than the fyn° coral   *coxcomb / fine*
And batailled° as it were a castel wal.[8]   *crenellated*
His byle° was blak, and as the jeet° it shoon.°   *bill / jet (gemstone) / shone*
95 Lyk asure° were his legges and his toon,°   *azure / toes*
Hise nayles° whitter than the lylye flour,°   *nails / lily flower*
And lyk the burned° gold was his colour.   *polished*
This gentil° cok hadde in his governaunce°   *noble / control*
Sevene hennes for to doon° al his plesaunce,°   *do / pleasure*
100 Whiche were hise sustres° and his paramours°   *his sisters / lovers*
And wonder lyk° to hym as of colours,   *marvelously similar*
Of whiche the faireste hewed° on hir throte°   *colored / her throat*
Was cleped° faire damoysele° Pertelote.   *called / damsel*
Curteys° she was, discreet, and debonaire°   *courteous / gracious*
105 And compaignable,° and bar° hyrself so faire°   *friendly / behaved / well*

---

[1] *grene* I.e., green, a common area in a village used for pasturage or other agricultural pursuits that did not demand the plowing of the green into a field.

[2] *The goute … daunce* The gout (a disease affecting the feet and brought on by over-eating or drinking) by no means hindered her from dancing.

[3] *in … lak* Either defect or lack, so either: In which she found no fault, or of which she had no shortage.

[4] *drye dych* Contrasts with the moat of a castle.

[5] *Chauntecleer* From the French, "clear singer." Chauntecleer is the name of the rooster in *The Romance of Renard*, which tells the adventures of a wily fox and contains one of the best known medieval versions of the story told by the Nun's Priest.

[6] *On … gon* That go (i.e., are played—the organ, an instrument of many pipes, was spoken of as plural) in Church on feast days.

[7] *By nature … equynoxial* The sense of this passage is that Chauntecleer crows when each hourly point of the celestial equator rises past the horizon.

[8] *And … wal* The crenelation on a castle's walls is the alternation of high, squared masonry with blank spaces. This would provide cover for the archers defending the castle against the arrows of the attackers.

Syn thilke day that she was seven nyght oold,°   *nights old*
That trewely, she hath the herte in hoold°   *holds the heart*
Of Chauntecleer, loken° in every lith.°   *locked | limb*
He loved hire so, that wel was hym therwith.
110 And swich a joye was it to here hem° synge,   *them*
Whan that the brighte sonne bigan to sprynge,°   *rise*
In sweete accord,° "My Lief Is Faren in Londe."[1]   *harmony*
For thilke tyme,° as I have understonde,   *at that time*
Beestes and briddes° koude speke and synge.   *birds*
115   And so bifel° that in the dawenynge,°   *it happened | at dawn*
As Chauntecleer among hise wyves alle
Sat on his perche° that was in the halle,   *perch*
And next hym sat this faire Pertelote,
This Chauntecleer gan gronen° in his throte   *began to groan*
120 As man that in his dreem is drecched soore.°   *sorely disturbed*
And whan that Pertelote thus herde hym roore,°   *roar*
She was agast° and seyde, "O herte deere,   *afraid*
What eyleth° yow to grone in this manere?   *ails*
Ye been° a verray° slepere. Fy!° For shame!"   *are | good | fie*
125   And he answerde and seyde thus: "Madame,
I pray yow that ye take it nat agrief.°   *amiss*
By God, me thoughte I was in swich meschief°   *such trouble*
Right now, that yet myn herte is soore afright.
Now God," quod he, "my swevene recche aright,[2]
130 And kepe my body out of foul prisoun!
Me mette° how that I romed up and doun   *I dreamed*
Withinne oure yeerd, wheereas° I saugh a beest   *where*
Was lyk an hound, and wolde han maad areest°   *grabbed hold*
Upon my body and han had me deed!°   *have had me dead*
135 His colour was bitwixe yelow and reed,°   *red*
And tipped was his tayl° and bothe hise eeris°   *tail | his ears*
With blak, unlyk° the remenant of hise heeris;°   *unlike | hairs*
His snowte° smal with glowynge eyen tweye.°   *nose | two*
Yet° of his look for feere° almoost I deye.   *still | fear*
140 This caused me my gronyng, doutelees."°   *doubtless*
    "Avoy!"° quod she. "Fy on yow, herteleees!°   *shame | coward*
Allas," quod she, "for by that God above,
Now han ye lost myn herte and al my love.
I kan nat love a coward, by my faith!
145 For certes,° whatso° any womman seith,   *certain | whatever*

We alle desiren, if it myghte bee,
150 To han housbondes hardy,° wise, and free,°   *brave | generous*
And secree° and no nygard° ne no fool,   *discreet | cheapskate*
Ne hym that is agast° of every tool,°   *afraid | weapon*
Ne noon avauntour,° by that God above.   *nor any braggart*
How dorste° ye seyn, for shame, unto youre love   *dare*
That anythyng myghte make yow aferd?°   *afraid*
Have ye no mannes herte,° and han a berd?°   *man's heart | beard*
Allas, and konne ye been agast of swevenys?°   *be afraid of dreams*
155 Nothyng, God woot,° but vanitee° in swevene
      is!   *knows | foolishness*
Swevenes engendren of° replecciouns°   *are caused by | overeating*
And ofte of fume° and of complecciouns[3]   *stomach- gas*
Whan humours been° to habundant° in a
      wight.°   *are | too abundant | person*
Certes, this dreem which ye han met° tonyght   *have dreamed*
160 Cometh of greet superfluytee°   *excess*
Of youre rede colera, pardee,[4]
Which causeth folk to dreden° in hir dremes   *fear*
Of arwes° and of fyr° with rede lemes,°   *arrows | fire | red flames*
Of grete beestes that they wol hem byte,°   *will bite them*
165 Of contek° and of whelpes° grete and lyte,°   *conflict | dogs | small*
Right° as the humour of malencolie[5]   *just*
Causeth ful many a man in sleepe to crie
For feere of blake beres° or boles° blake   *black bears | bulls*
Or elles blake develes wole hem take.
170 Of othere humours koude I telle also
That werken° many a man in sleepe ful wo,°   *cause | much woe*
But I wol passe° as lightly as I kan.   *pass over*
    "Lo Catoun,[6] which that was so wys° a man,   *wise*
Seyde he nat thus: 'Ne do no fors of dremes'?[7]

---

[1] *My ... Londe* My dear one has traveled into (a foreign) land. This is the title of a popular song, one version of which, from c. 1500, has survived in a manuscript at Trinity College, Cambridge.

[2] *Now ... aright* "Now God," he said, "interpret my dream correctly."

[3] *complecciouns* I.e., complexions, or temperaments. Medieval medical theory maintained that what we now call personality was a function of the balance in the body of the four bodily fluids known as humors. If these fluids were unbalanced, disease would result.

[4] *Of ... pardee* Of your red choler, by God. Choler was one of the four bodily temperaments. It was formed by the combination of yellow bile (which was hot and dry) with blood (which was hot and moist).

[5] *malencolie* I.e., melancholy, another of the four temperaments.

[6] *Catoun* I.e., Dionysius Cato, a Roman politician who was believed in the Middle Ages to be the author of a widely-circulating collection of proverbs which was often used to teach basic Latin grammar.

[7] *Seyde ... dremes* Said he not this: "Do not pay attention to dreams"?

175 "Now sire," quod she, "whan ye flee° fro the
bemes,°   *fly down / beams*
For Goddes love, as taak som laxatyf!°   *take some laxative*
Up° peril of my soule and of my lyf,   *upon*
I conseille° yow the beste—I wol nat lye°—   *counsel / lie*
That bothe of colere° and of malencolye   *choler*
180 Ye purge yow,° and for ye shal nat
tarie,°   *yourself / so you do not delay*
Though in this toun is noon apothecarie,°   *no pharmacist*
I shal myself to herbes° techen yow,   *about herbs*
That shul been for youre heele° and for youre
prow,°   *health / profit*
And in oure yeerd° tho° herbes shal I fynde,   *yard / those*
185 The whiche han of hire propretee° by
kynde°   *their property / nature*
To purge yow bynethe and eek above.
Foryet nat this, for Goddes owene love!
Ye been ful coleryk of compleccioun.
Ware the sonne in his ascencioun
190 Ne fynde yow nat repleet of humours hoote.[1]
And if it do, I dar wel leye° a grote[2]   *bet*
That ye shul° have a fevere terciane[3]   *shall*
Or an agu° that may be youre bane.°   *ague (fever) / cause of death*
A day or two ye shul have digestyves°   *stomach medicines*
195 Of wormes, er ye take youre laxatyves[4]
Of lawriol,° centaure,° and fumetere,°   *laurel / centaury / fumaria*
Or elles of ellebor,° that groweth there;   *hellebore*
Of katapuce° or of gaitrys beryis,°   *euphorbia / rhamus berries*
Of herbe yve,° growyng in oure yeerd ther mery
is.°   *herb-ivy / where it is merry*
200 Pekke hem up right as they growe, and ete hem
yn.°   *eat them up*
Be myrie, housbonde, for youre fader kyn!°   *merry / father's kin*
Dredeth no dreem. I kan sey yow namoore."

"Madame," quod he, "*graunt mercy*[5] of youre loore!°   *advice*
But nathelees, as touchyng° daun
Catoun,°   *pertaining to / Master Cato*
205 That hath of° wysdom swich a greet renoun,°   *for / fame*
Though that he bad° no dremes for to drede,   *commanded*
By God, men may in olde bookes rede
Of many a man moore of auctorite
Than evere Caton was, so moot I thee,°   *so might I thrive*
210 That al° the revers° seyn of this sentence,   *completely / opposite*
That han wel founden° by experience   *have found out well*
That dremes been significaciouns°   *are signs*
As wel of joye as of tribulaciouns°   *troubles*
That folk enduren in this lif present.
215 Ther nedeth make of this noon argument.
The verray preeve° sheweth it in dede.   *true proof / deed*
  "Oon of the gretteste auctour[6] that men rede
Seith thus: that whilom° two felawes wente   *once*
On pilgrimage in a ful good entente,
220 And happed so° they coomen in a toun,   *it so happened*
Wheras ther was swich congregacioun°   *a gathering*
Of peple, and eek so streit of
herbergage,°   *such a shortage of lodging*
That they ne founde as muche as o° cotage   *one*
In which they bothe myghte logged bee,
225 Wherfor they mosten of necessitee
As for that nyght departen compaignye.°   *part company*
And ech of hem gooth to his hostelrye°   *lodging place*
And took his loggyng as it wolde falle.°   *would happen*
That oon of hem was logged in a stalle°   *stall*
230 Fer° in a yeerd, with oxen of the plough.   *far*
That oother man was logged wel ynough,
As was his aventure° or his fortune,   *chance*
That us governeth alle as in commune.°   *in common*
  "And so bifel that, longe er it were day,
235 This man mette in his bed, theras° he lay,   *where*
How that his felawe gan upon hym calle°   *to call*
And seyde, 'Allas, for in an oxes stalle
This nyght I shal be mordred ther I lye!
Now helpe me, deere brother, or I dye.

---

1 *Ware ... hoote* Beware that the sun when it is climbing does not find you when you are (already) full of hot humors. The movements of the planets were thought to affect a patient's balance of humors.

2 *grote* Coin equal to four pence.

3 *fevere terciane* I.e., tertian fever. Medieval people classified the types of fevers they would contract by how frequently they recurred. This one would return every third day—meaning every other day, in which the first day is counted, as is the non-fever day and the recurring-fever day. The disease is possibly malaria.

4 *laxatyves* The laxatives listed by the hen are all types of bitter herbs.

5 *graunt mercy* From the French "grand merci" or "much thanks." Chauntecleer, as an aristocrat, employs French phrases.

6 *Oon ... auctour* The Roman orator and writer (auctour) Cicero (106–43 BCE) tells the story in *On Divination*, and it is also found in the *Memorable Deeds and Sayings of Valerius Maximus* (see *The Wife of Bath's Prologue*, line 168).

240　In alle haste com to me,' he sayde.
　　This man out of his sleepe for feere abrayde,°　　　　woke up
　　But whan that he was wakened of his sleepe,
　　He turned hym° and took of it no keepe.°　　turned over / notice
　　Hym thoughte his dreem nas but a vanitee.°　　　　folly
245　Thus twies in his slepyng dremed hee,
　　And atte thridde tyme yet his felawe
　　Cam as hym thoughte and seide, 'I am now slawe.°　　slain
　　Bihoold my bloody woundes depe and wyde.
　　Arys° up erly in the morwe tyde,°　　arise / morning-time
250　And at the west gate of the toun,' quod he,
　　'A carte ful of donge° ther shaltow° se°　　dung / shall you / see
　　In which my body is hid ful prively.°　　　　secretly
　　Do thilke carte arresten boldely.[1]
　　My gold caused my mordre, sooth to sayn,'°　　　　true to say
255　And tolde hym every point how he was slayn
　　With a ful pitous face, pale of hewe.°　　　　color
　　And truste wel, his dreem he foond ful trewe.
　　For on the morwe, as soone as it was day,
　　To his felawes in° he took the way,　　　　friend's inn
260　And whan that he cam to this oxes stalle,
　　After his felawe he bigan to calle.
　　　　"The hostiler° answerde hym anon　　　　innkeeper
　　And seyde, 'Sire, youre felawe is agon.°　　　　gone
　　As soone as day he wente out of the toun.'
265　　　"This man gan fallen in suspecioun,°　　to be suspicious
　　Remembrynge on hise dremes that he mette.°　　　dreamed
　　And forth he gooth—no lenger wolde he lette°—　　delay
　　Unto the west gate of the toun and fond°　　　　found
　　A dong-carte, as it were to donge lond°　　to manure a field
270　That was arrayed in that same wise°　　　　way
　　As ye han herd the dede man devyse.°　　　　describe
　　And with an hardy herte he gan to crye,
　　'Vengeance and justice of this felonye!
　　My felawe mordred is this same nyght,
275　And in this carte heere he lith,° gapyng
　　　　upright.°　　　　lies / facing upright
　　I crye out on the ministres,'° quod he,　　　　magistrates
　　'That sholden kepe° and reulen° this citee!　　care for / rule
　　Harrow!° Allas! Heere lith my felawe slayn!'　　　help
　　What sholde I moore unto this tale sayn?
280　The peple out sterte° and caste the cart to grounde,　jumped up
　　And in the myddel of the dong they founde

The dede man that mordred was al newe.°　　　recently
　　"O blisful° God that art so just and trewe,　　　blessed
Lo how that thou biwreyest° mordre alway!　　　reveal
285　Mordre wol out.° That se we day by day.　　will be found out
　　Mordre is so wlatsom° and abhomynable°　repulsive / abominable
　　To God, that is so just and resonable,
　　That he ne wol nat suffre it heled° be,　　　　concealed
　　Though it abyde a yeer or two or thre.
290　Mordre wol out! This my conclusioun.
　　And right anon, ministres of that toun
　　Han hent° the cartere, and so soore° hym
　　　　pyned,°　　　arrested / sorely / tortured
　　And eek the hostiler so soore engyned,°　　tortured on a rack
　　That they biknewe° hire wikkednesse anon　　confessed
295　And were anhanged° by the nekke bon.°　　hanged / neck-bone
　　　　"Heere may men seen that dremes been to
　　　　drede.°　　　　are to be feared
　　And certes, in the same book I rede,
　　Right in the nexte chapitre after this—
　　I gabbe° nat, so have I joye or blis—　　　　babble
300　Two men that wolde han° passed over see°　would have / the sea
　　For certeyn cause into a fer contree,°　　distant country
　　If that the wynd° ne hadde been contrarie,　　　wind
　　That made hem in a citee for to tarie°　　　　delay
　　That stood ful myrie° upon an haven-syde.°　merrily / harbor-side
305　But on a day agayn the eventyde,°　　towards evening
　　The wynd gan chaunge and blew right as hem
　　　　leste.°　　　　they wanted
　　Jolif° and glad, they wente unto hir reste　　　jolly
　　And casten° hem ful erly for to saille.　　　　decided
　　But herkneth: to that o man fil a greet mervaille.[2]
310　That oon of hem, in slepyng as he lay,
　　Hym mette° a wonder dreem agayn the
　　　　day.°　　　dreamed / toward daybreak
　　Hym thoughte a man stood by his beddes syde
　　And hym comanded that he sholde abyde°　　　wait
　　And seyde hym thus: 'If thou tomorwe wende,°　　go
315　Thow shalt be dreynt.° My tale is at an ende.'　　drowned
　　He wook and tolde his felawe what he mette
　　And preyde hym his viage° to lette;°　　voyage / delay
　　As for that day he preyde hym to byde.°　　　wait
　　His felawe, that lay by his beddes syde,
320　Gan for to laughe, and scorned hym ful faste.°　very much

---

[1]　*Do ... boldely*　Cause that cart to be seized boldly.

[2]　*But ... mervaille*　But listen! To one man there happened a great marvel.

'No dreem,' quod he, 'may so myn herte agaste°   *frighten*
That I wol lette for to do my thynges.°   *business*
I sette nat a straw by thy dremynges!°   *dreams*
For swevenes been but vanytees° and japes.°   *nonsense / tricks*
325 Men dreme al day of owles or of apes,
And of many a maze° therwithal.°   *delusion / with it all*
Men dreme of thyng that nevere was ne shal.°   *nor shall be*
But sith I see that thou wolt heere abyde,
And thus forslewthen° wilfully thy tyde,°   *waste / time*
330 God woot, it reweth me!° And have good day!'   *I regret it*
And thus he took his leve° and wente his way.   *leave*
But er that he hadde half his cours yseyled,°   *sailed*
Noot I nat° why, ne what myschaunce° it
    eyled,   *I know not / went wrong*
But casuelly° the shippes botme° rente,°   *by chance / bottom / split*
335 And shipe and man under the water wente
In sighte of othere shippes it bisyde°   *beside it*
That with hem seyled at the same tyde.°   *tide*
And therfore, faire Pertelote, so deere,
By swiche ensamples olde yet maistow leere°   *may you learn*
340 That no man sholde been to recchelees°   *too careless*
Of dremes. For I seye thee doutelees
That many a dreem ful soore is for to drede!
    Lo in the *Lyf of Seint Kenelm*[1] I rede,
That was Kenulphus sone,° the noble kyng   *Cenwulf's son*
345 Of Mertenrike,° how Kenelm mette° a thyng   *Mercia / dreamed*
A lite er° he was mordred on a day.   *little before*
His mordre in his avysioun° he say.°   *vision / saw*
His norice° hym expowned° every deel°   *nurse / explained / part*
His swevene, and bad hym for to kepe hym
    weel°   *protect himself*
350 For traisoun.° But he nas but° sevene yeer
    oold,   *from treason / was only*
And therfore litel tale hath he toold°   *paid little attention*
Of any dreem, so hooly° is his herte.   *holy*
By God, I hadde levere than my sherte
That ye hadde rad his Legende as have I,[2]
355 Dame Pertelote! I sey yow trewely,
Macrobeus, that writ the avisioun

In Affrike of the worthy Cipioun,[3]
Affermeth° dremes and seith that they   *affirms (the validity of)*
    been
Warnynge of thynges that men after seen.°   *see afterwards*
360 And forthermoore, I pray yow, looketh wel
In the Olde Testament of Daniel,
If he heeld° dremes any vanitee.°   *considered / folly*
Reed eek of Joseph,[4] and ther shul ye see
Wher dremes be somtyme—I sey nat alle°—   *not always*
365 Warnynge of thynges that shul after falle.°   *happen*
Looke of Egipte° the kyng daun Pharao,°   *Egypt / Lord Pharoah*
His bakere and his butiller° also,   *butler*
Wher° they ne felte noon° effect in
    dremes.   *whether / did not feel any*
Whoso wol seken actes of sondry remes°   *various realms*
370 May rede of dremes many a wonder thyng.
Lo Cresus,[5] which that was of Lyde kyng,
Mette he nat° that he sat upon a tree,   *did he not dream*
Which signified he sholde anhanged° bee?   *hanged*
Lo heere Adromacha,° Ectores° wyf,   *Andromache / Hector's*
375 That day that Ector sholde lese his lyf
She dremed on the same nyght biforn
How that the lyf of Ector sholde be lorn°   *lost*
If thilke day he wente into bataille.
She warned hym, but it myghte nat availle.°   *could not help*
380 He wente for to fighte natheles,°   *nevertheless*

---

[1] *Lyf ... Kenelm*   This is a saint's life, or hagiography, of Kenelm (Cenhelm), a seven-year-old Anglo-Saxon king of Mercia who was murdered at the command of his aunt.

[2] *I hadde ... I*   I would rather that you had read this saint's life than that I had my shirt, or, as we might say, I'd give my shirt to have you read it.

---

[3] *In ... Cipioun*   The Roman writer Macrobius (c. 400 CE) wrote a commentary on the part of Cicero's *Republic* called "The Dream of Scipio." This book tells how Scipio Africanus Minor, a Roman consul, dreamed of meeting his famous ancestor, Scipio Africanus Major (so-called because he defeated Hannibal, the great general of Carthage, in North Africa) and urged him to pursue virtue for the sake of reward in a future life. Chauntecleer misinterprets his name, assuming the dream happened in Africa.

[4] *Daniel ... Joseph*   Both Daniel and Joseph were famous for their ability to interpret dreams. Daniel interpreted the dream of King Nebuchadnezzar to predict that the king would be banished for seven years (see Daniel 4). Joseph interpreted his own dream to predict that he would be lord over his brothers, interpreted the dreams of Pharaoh's butler and his baker to predict that the former would be restored to office but the latter hanged, and interpreted Pharaoh's dream to predict that Egypt would have seven years of good harvest followed by seven years of famine (see Genesis 37.5–11; 40.1–23; 41.1–32).

[5] *Cresus*   The Monk had mentioned the dream of Croesus, the fabulously rich king of Lydia who was conquered by King Cyrus of Persia, in the previous tale.

But he was slayn anon of Achilles.[1]

But thilke is al to° longe for to telle,   *too*

And eek it is ny° day. I may nat dwelle.° *near / not delay*

Shortly I seye, as for conclusioun,

385 That I shal han of this avisioun

Adversitee. And I seye forthermoor

That I ne telle of laxatyves no stoor!° *set no store in laxatives*

For they been venymes,° I woot° it weel. *venomous / know*

I hem diffye,° I love hem never a deel!° *reject them / not at all*

390 "Now lat us speke of myrthe° and

   stynte° al this.   *mirth / be silent about*

Madame Pertelote, so have I blis,°   *happiness*

Of o° thyng God hath sent me large grace,° *one / great favor*

For whan I se the beautee of youre face—

Ye been so scarlet reed° aboute youre eyen— *red*

395 It maketh al my drede for to dyen.

For also siker° as *In principio*,[2]   *as certain*

Mulier est hominis confusio.[3]

Madame, the sentence° of this Latyn is, *meaning*

'Womman is mannes joye and al his blis.'

400 For whan I feele anyght° youre softe side— *at night*

Albeit that I may nat on yow ryde,°   *ride*

For that oure perche is maad° so narwe,° allas! *made / narrow*

I am so ful of joye and of solas

That I diffye° bothe swevene and dreem!"[4] *defy*

405 And with that word he fly° doun fro the beem,° *flew / beam*

For it was day, and eek hise hennes alle,° *did also all his hens*

And with a "chuk" he gan hem for to calle,

For he hadde founde a corn lay° in the yerd. *kernel that lay*

Real° he was. He was namoore aferd,   *regal*

410 And fethered Pertelote twenty tyme

And trad as ofte er it was pryme.[5]

He looketh as it were° a grym leoun,° *as if he were / fierce lion*

And on hise toos° he rometh° up and doun. *his toes / roams*

Hym deigned nat to sette his foot to grounde.

415 He chukketh° whan he hath a corn yfounde, *clucks*

And to hym rennen thanne° hise wyves alle. *run then*

Thus roial° as a prince is in an halle   *regal*

Leve° I this Chauntecleer in his pasture, *leave*

And after wol I telle his aventure.

420 Whan that the monthe in which the world bigan,

That highte March, whan God first maked man,[6]

Was compleet, and passed were also,

Syn March bigan, thritty dayes and two,[7]

Bifel° that Chauntecleer in al his pryde, *it happened*

425 Hise sevene wyves walkynge by his syde,

Caste up hise eyen to the brighte sonne,

That in the signe of Taurus hadde yronne

Twenty degrees and oon° and somwhat *twenty-one degrees*

   moore,

And knew by kynde° and by noon oother

   loore°   *nature / teaching*

430 That it was pryme,° and crew with blisful

   stevene.°   *early morning / voice*

"The sonne," he seyde, "is clomben upon hevene

Fourty degrees and oon and moore, ywis.

Madame Pertelote, my worldes blis,

Herkneth thise blisful briddes,° how they synge, *birds*

435 And se the fresshe floures, how they sprynge.° *bloom*

Ful is myn herte of revel° and solas." *amusement*

But sodeynly hym fil° a sorweful cas,° *befell / event*

For evere the latter ende of joye is wo.

God woot that worldly joye is soone ago!° *gone*

440 And if a rethor° koude faire endite,° *rhetorician / write well*

---

[1] *Lo heere … Achilles*   The narrative of the Trojan war recounted by Dares Phrygius (one of the standard versions of the story in the Middle Ages) includes the story of the dream of Hector's wife. Homer's *Iliad*, which was not well known in western Europe at the time, does not include the episode.

[2] *In principio*   Latin: in the beginning; i.e., as certain as the Bible. These words begin both the book of Genesis and the Gospel of John.

[3] *Mulier … confusio*   Latin: woman is the confusion of man.

[4] *That … dreem*   Chauntecleer appears to distinguish between two kinds of dreams here, but it is not clear what the difference is. Medieval dream theory distinguished between prophetic dreams and those that had no special significance, but the terms swevene and dreme (and also mete) cover both.

[5] *And fethered … pryme*   He covered Pertelote with his feathers twenty times and copulated with her as often before it was the hour of prime (early morning).

[6] *That … man*   According to various medieval authorities, including Saint Basil and the English monastic writer Bede, God created the world at the spring equinox.

[7] *Was compleet … two*   The phrasing is ambiguous but the events seem to take place on May 3, when all of March and a further thirty-two days had passed. This date is in keeping with the position of the sun in the sky and the other astrological information. May 3 was considered an unlucky day and is also the day on which Palamon escapes from prison in *The Knight's Tale* (line 1462).

He in a cronycle saufly° myghte it write   *safely*

As for a sovereyn notabilitee.°   *very notable thing*

Now every wys man, lat hym herkne me.°   *listen to me*

This storie is also trewe, I undertake,°   *swear*

445   As is *The Book of Launcelot de Lake,*[1]

That wommen holde in ful greet reverence.

Now wol I come agayn to my sentence.°   *purpose*

       "A colfox° ful of sly iniquitee,°   *coal-black fox | malice*

That in the grove hadde woned° yeeres three,   *lived*

450   By heigh ymaginacioun forncast,[2]

The same nyght thurghout° the hegges°

       brast°   *through | hedge | burst*

Into the yerd ther° Chauntecleer the faire   *where*

Was wont, and eek hise wyves, to repaire,°   *retire*

And in a bed of wortes° stille° he lay   *herbs | quietly*

455   Til it was passed undren° of the day,   *dawn*

Waitynge his tyme° on Chauntecleer to falle,   *opportunity*

As gladly doon thise homycides alle°   *all these murderers*

That in await liggen° to mordre men.   *lie in wait*

O false mordrour, lurkynge in thy den!

460   O newe Scariot,° newe Genylon!°   *(Judas) Iscariot | Ganelon*

False dissymulour,° o Greek Synon,   *liar*

That broghtest Troye al outrely° to sorwe!°3   *utterly*

O Chauntecleer, acursed be that morwe

That thou into that yerd flaugh° fro the bemes!   *flew*

465   Thou were ful wel ywarned by thy dremes

That thilke day was perilous to thee,

But what that God forwoot° moot nedes

       bee,°   *foreknows | necessarily be*

After° the opinioun of certein clerkis.°   *according to | scholars*

Witnesse on hym that any parfit clerk is,[4]

470   That in scole° is greet altercacioun°   *the universities | debate*

In this mateere, and greet disputisoun,

And hath been of an hundred thousand men.[5]

But I ne kan nat bulte it to the bren[6]

As kan the hooly doctour Augustyn,°   *holy scholar Augustine*

475   Or Boece, or the Bisshope Bradwardyn—[7]

Wheither that Goddes worthy forwityng°   *foreknowledge*

Streyneth° me nedely° to doon a thyng—   *constrains | necessarily*

"Nedely" clepe° I symple necessitee—   *call*

Or elles, if free choys be graunted me

480   To do that same thyng or do it noght,

Though God forwoot it er that it was wroght,°   *done*

Or if his wityng° streyneth° never a

       deel°   *knowing | constrains | not at all*

But by necessitee condicioneel.[8]

---

4   *Witnesse ... is*   As any fully qualified scholar can testify.

5   *But what ... men*   The question of how God's foreknowledge could be reconciled with human free will was always important in medieval theology, but the debate flared up in Chaucer's day. The radical theologian John Wycliffe (d. 1394), best known for initiating the translation of the Bible into English, argued that God's omniscience gave him absolute knowledge of who would be saved or damned. This meant for Wycliffe that there was no justification for the institutions of the earthly church or for penitential practices such as confession or pilgrimage.

6   *But ... bren*   But I cannot separate (the kernels) from the bran. That is, the Nun's Priest cannot sort out the issues in the debate about God's foreknowledge.

7   *As kan ... Bradwardyn*   The great patristic writer St. Augustine (d. 430 CE), the late Roman scholar Boethius (d. 524 CE), and Thomas Bradwardine, chancellor of Oxford and very briefly Archbishop of Canterbury (who died of the Black Death in 1349), all wrote about the concept of predestination. Although stressing God's omniscience, all three were thoroughly orthodox in their insistence that humans have free will.

8   *necessitee condicioneel*   Boethius distinguishes between simple necessity and conditional necessity in his *Consolation of Philosophy* 5, prose 6, and then draws on God's status outside time to resolve the theological dilemma. To use Boethius's example, that a man must die is a matter of simple necessity. But if you know someone is walking, while he must then necessarily be walking, the necessity is only conditional; i.e., it depends on the condition of the man having decided to take a walk. From your perspective, he could have chosen not to do so. The issue here is whether God, in knowing in advance all future events and choices, necessarily removes free choice (for how can God be wrong?). The solution, proposed by Boethius, is this idea of conditional necessity: to know about an event is not

---

1   *The Book ... Lake*   This is the title of any one of a number of Arthurian romances that recount the adventures of Sir Lancelot, including his love affair with Guinevere, wife of King Arthur.

2   *By ... forncast*   Foreseen by exalted imagination. What this means is disputed. Many editors take it to refer to the mind or conception (ymaginacioun) of God, which foresees all events. Others take "ymaginacioun" as a reference, expressed in deliberately and ridiculously grandiose language, to Chauntecleer's dream, or as a reference to the plotting of the fox. In each case, the word "forncast" introduces the theme of predestination discussed in lines 467–830.

3   *O newe ... sorwe*   In the Gospel, Judas Iscariot betrayed Christ by identifying him to the Roman soldiers who came to arrest him; in *The Song of Roland*, Ganelon betrayed Roland with a plot that led to his death in the pass at Roncesvalles; and in *The Iliad*, Sinon betrayed Troy by suggesting the Greeks conceal themselves in a wooden horse to gain access to the city.

I wol nat han to do of° swich mateere.   *have to do with*

485 My tale is of a cok, as ye may heere,
That took his conseil of his wyf with sorwe
To walken in the yerd upon that morwe
That he hadde met that dreem that I of tolde.
Wommennes conseils been ful ofte colde.°   *bad*

490 Wommannes conseil broghte us first to wo
And made Adam out of Paradys to go,
Theras° he was ful myrie° and wel at ese.   *where | merry*
But for I noot° to whom it myght displese,   *since I do not know*
If I conseil of wommen wolde blame,

495 Passe over, for I seye it in my game.°   *in jest*
Rede auctours° where they trete of swich mateere,   *authors*
And what they seyn of wommen ye may heere.
Thise been the cokkes wordes and nat myne!
I kan noon harm of no womman divyne!°   *imagine*

500   Faire in the soond° to bathe hire myrily   *sand*
Lith° Pertelote, and alle hire sustres by°   *lies | nearby*
Agayn the sonne.° And Chauntecleer so free   *in the sunshine*
Soong murier° than the mermayde in the   *sang more merrily*
     see—
For Phisiologus[1] seith sikerly°   *surely*

505 How that they syngen wel and myrily—
And so bifel that as he caste his eye
Among the wortes° on a boterflye,   *herbs*
He was war° of this fox that lay ful lowe.   *aware*
Nothyng ne liste hym thanne for to crowe,[2]

510 But cride anon, "Cok! Cok!" and up he sterte
As man that was affrayed in his herte.
For natureely a beest desireth flee
Fro his contrarie° if he may it see,   *enemy*
Though he never erst hadde seyn it with his eye.

515   This Chauntecleer, whan he gan hym espye,°   *spotted him*
He wolde han fled, but that the fox anon
Seyde, "Gentil sire, allas, wher wol ye gon?

Be ye affrayed of me, that am youre freend?
Now certes, I were worse than a feend°   *fiend*

520 If I to yow wolde° harm or vileynye!   *intended*
I am nat come youre conseil for t'espye.°   *to spy on your council*
But trewely, the cause of my comynge
Was oonly for to herkne° how that ye synge.   *listen*
For trewely, ye have as myrie° a stevene°   *merry | voice*

525 As any aungel that is in Hevene.
Therwith ye han in musyk moore feelynge
Than hadde Boece[3] or any that kan synge.
My lord, youre fader, God his soule blesse,
And eek youre mooder of hire gentillesse

530 Han in myn hous ybeen to my greet ese.
And certes, sire, ful fayn° wolde I yow plese.   *very gladly*
But for men speke of syngyng, I wol yow seye—
So moote I brouke wel myne eyen tweye—[4]
Save yow,° herde I nevere man yet synge   *apart from yourself*

535 As dide youre fader in the morwenynge.
Certes, it was of herte° al that he song!   *from the heart*
And for to make his voys the moore strong,
He wolde so peyne hym° that with bothe hise eyen   *take pains*
He moste wynke°—so loude he wolde cryen—   *had to wink*

540 And stonden on his tip-toon° therwithal,°   *tip-toes | in doing so*
And strecche forth his nekke long and smal.°   *slender*
And eek he was of swich discrecioun°   *discernment*
That ther nas no man in no regioun
That hym in song or wisedom myghte passe.°   *surpass*

545 I have wel rad° in *Daun Burnel the Asse*,[5]   *read*
Among hise vers,° how that ther was a cok,   *verses*
For that° a preestes sone yaf° hym a knok   *because | gave*
Upon his leg whil he was yong and nyce,°   *silly*
He made hym for to lese his benefice.

550 But certeyn, ther nys no° comparisoun   *is no*

---

necessarily to cause it. As he says, "God sees those future events which happen of free will as present events; so that these things when considered with reference to God's sight of them do happen necessarily as a result of the condition of divine knowledge; but when considered in themselves they do not lose the absolute freedom of their nature."

[1] *Phisiologus* The supposed author of a bestiary, a book explaining the allegorical significances of various animals. According to this work, mermaids use their sweet singing to lure sailors to their deaths.

[2] *Nothyng ... crowe* He did by no means want then to crow.

[3] *Boece* Boethius not only wrote *The Consolation of Philosophy*, which Chaucer translated, but also wrote the basic university textbook on music used in the Middle Ages.

[4] *So ... tweye* So may I enjoy the use of my eyes, a common expression meaning little more than "indeed," but it is ill suited to express musical appreciation.

[5] *Daun ... Asse* Title of a twelfth-century Latin satire by Nigel Wireker about a foolish donkey, Master Brunellus, who becomes a wandering scholar. The episode described below concerns a young man who was about to be ordained and to receive a benefice. The cock, whom he had injured in his youth, took its revenge by not crowing, causing the man to oversleep and miss his opportunity for a benefice.

Bitwixe the wisedom and discrecioun
Of youre fader and of his subtiltee.°   *cleverness*
Now syngeth, sire, for Seinte Charitee!°   *Holy Charity*
Lat se, konne ye youre fader coun trefete?"°   *imitate*
555   This Chauntecleer hise wynges gan to bete°   *beat*
As man that koude his traysoun° nat espie,°   *betrayal / perceive*
So was he ravysshed with his flaterie.
Allas, ye lordes, many a fals flatour°   *false flatterer*
Is in youre courtes,° and many a losengeour°   *courts / spy*
560 That plesen yow wel moore, by my feith,
Than he that soothfastnesse° unto yow seith.   *truth*
Redeth Ecclesiaste[1] of° flaterye.   *on*
Beth war,° ye lordes, of hir trecherye!   *beware*
   This Chauntecleer stood hye upon his toos,
565 Strecchynge his nekke, and heeld his eyen cloos°   *closed*
And gan to crowe loude for the nones.°   *occasion*
And Daun Russell the fox stirte up atones°   *jumped up at once*
And by the gargat° hente° Chauntecleer   *throat / grabbed*
And on his bak toward the wode hym beer,
570 For yet° ne was ther no man that hym sewed.°   *as yet / pursued*
   O Destinee, that mayst nat been eschewed!°   *avoided*
Allas, that Chauntecleer fleigh fro the bemes!
Allas, his wyf ne roghte nat° of dremes!   *paid no attention*
And on a Friday fil al this meschaunce!
575 O Venus, that art goddesse of plesaunce,[2]
Syn that thy servant was this Chauntecleer,
And in thy servyce dide al his poweer°   *all he could*
Moore for delit than world to
     multiplye,°   *to increase the world (procreate)*
Why woldestow suffre° hym on thy day to
     dye?[3]   *would you allow*
580 O Gaufred,[4] deere maister soverayn,°   *sovereign teacher*

That whan thy worthy kyng Richard was slayn
With shot,° compleynedest° his deeth so soore,   *arrow / lamented*
Why ne hadde I now thy sentence° and thy
     loore°   *meaning / learning*
The Friday for to chide as diden ye?
585 For on a Friday soothly° slayn was he.   *truly*
Thanne wolde I shewe yow how that I koude pleyne
For Chauntecleres drede and for his peyne!
Certes swich cry ne lamentacioun
Was nevere of ladyes maad° whan Ylioun°   *made / Ilion (Troy)*
590 Was wonne,° and Pirrus° with his streite
     swerd,°   *conquered / Pyrrhus / drawn sword*
Whan he hadde hent° Kyng Priam by the berd°   *seized / beard*
And slayn hym, as seith us *Eneydos,*°   *Aeneid*
As maden alle the hennes in the clos°   *yard*
Whan they had seyn of Chauntecleer the sighte.
595 But sodeynly Dame Pertelote shrighte°   *shrieked*
Ful louder than dide Hasdrubales wyf
Whan that hir housbonde hadde lost his lyf
And that the Romayns hadde brend° Cartage.[5]   *burned*
She was so ful of torment and of rage
600 That wilfully into the fyr she sterte
And brende hirselven with a stedefast herte.
   O woful hennes, right so criden ye
As, whan that Nero[6] brende the citee
Of Rome, cryden senatours wyves,
605 For that hir housbondes losten alle hir lyves.
Withouten gilt this Nero hath hem slayn.
Now turne I wole to my tale agayn.
   This sely° wydwe and eek hir doghtres two   *innocent*
Herden thise hennes crie and maken wo,
610 And out at dores stirten they anon
And syen the fox toward the grove gon
And bar upon his bak the cok away,
And cryden, "Out! Harrow!" and "Weylaway!°   *alas*
Ha! Ha! The fox!" And after hym they ran,

---

[1] *Ecclesiaste* Ecclesiasticus 12.16 warns against deceptive enemies but does not specifically mention flattery. The reference might be a mistake for Ecclesiastes or for Proverbs, other books of the Bible that were, like Ecclesiasticus, attributed to King Solomon.

[2] *O … plesaunce* In classical mythology, Venus is the goddess of love.

[3] *Why … dye* According to medieval astrology, each of the planets had special influence on a given day of the week. Venus, who gives her name to Friday (*Veneris dies*) in Romance languages, controlled that day.

[4] *Gaufred* I.e., Geoffrey of Vinsauf, whose treatise *Poetria Nova*, a basic manual on how to write rhetorically elaborate poetry, is alluded to by Chaucer in the following lines. King Richard is Richard I, the

---

Lion-hearted, who in 1199 was wounded on a Friday while besieging a castle and later died of his wound.

[5] *Hasdrubales … Cartage* I.e., Hasdrubal (245–207 BCE), Carthaginian general, who died in battle at the Metaurus River in central Italy when he met the army of Caius Claudius Nero. Carthage was destroyed by Scipio Africanus in 146 BCE.

[6] *Nero* Nero (54–68 CE), Emperor of Rome, who had his city burned while he stood by, according to Suetonius, playing the bagpipes. In the previous tale the Monk narrates his tragedy.

615   And eek with staves° many another man;   clubs
      Ran Colle oure dogge, and Talbot and Gerland,[1]
      And Malkyn with a dystaf° in hir hand.   spinning staff
      Ran cow and calf and the verray hogges,
      So fered° for berkyng of the dogges   afraid
620   And shoutyng of the men and wommen eek.
      They ronne so hem thoughte hir herte breek;[2]
      They yolleden° as feendes° doon in Helle.   yelled / fiends
      The dokes° cryden as men wolde hem quelle,°   ducks / kill them
      The gees° for feere flowen° over the trees,   geese / flew
625   Out of the hyve° cam the swarm of bees.   hive
      So hydous° was the noyse,° a,
          benedicitee,°   hideous / noise / ah, bless us
      Certes he Jakke Straw and his meynee°   gang
      Ne made nevere shoutes half so shrille,
      Whan that they wolden any Flemyng kille,[3]
630   As thilke day was maad upon the fox.
      Of bras they broghten bemes and of box,
      Of horn, of boon, in whiche they blewe and powped,[4]
      And therwithal° they skriked° and they
          howped.°   with this / shrieked / whooped
      It semed as that Hevene sholde falle.
635   Now, goode men, I prey yow, herkneth alle.
      Lo how Fortune turneth sodeynly
      The hope and pryde of hir enemy.
      This cok that lay upon the foxes bak,
      In al his drede unto the fox he spak
640   And seyde, "Sire, if that I were as ye,
      Yet wolde I seyn, as wys° God helpe me,   wise
      'Turneth agayn, ye proude cherles° alle!   churls
      A verray pestilence upon yow falle!°   fall upon you
      Now I am come unto the wodes syde.°   border
645   Maugree youre heed,° the cok shal heere
          abyde.   despite your efforts

      I wol hym ete,° in feith, and that anon!'"   eat
          The fox answerde, "In feith, it shal be don!"
      And as he spak that word al sodeynly,
      This cok brak° from his mouth delyverly°   broke / quickly
650   And heighe upon a tree he fleigh anon.
      And whan the fox saugh that he was gon,
          "Allas!" quod he. "O Chauntecleer, allas!
      I have to yow," quod he, "ydoon trespas,°   done an insult
      In as muche as I maked yow aferd
655   Whan I yow hente° and broghte into this yerd.[5]   seized
      But sire, I dide it of no wikke° entente.   wicked
      Com doun, and I shal telle yow what I mente.
      I shal seye sooth° to yow, God help me so!"   tell the truth
          "Nay, thanne," quod he, "I shrewe° us bothe two!   curse
660   And first I shrewe myself, bothe blood and bones,
      If thou bigyle° me any ofter° than ones!°   trick / more often / once
      Thou shalt namoore thurgh thy flaterye
      Do me to synge and wynke with myn eye!
      For he that wynketh whan he sholde see
665   Al wilfully,° God lat hym nevere thee!"°   voluntarily / thrive
          "Nay," quod the fox, "but God yeve° hym
              meschaunce°   give / misfortune
      That is so undiscreet° of governaunce°   indiscreet / behavior
      That jangleth° whan he sholde holde his pees!"° chatters / peace
          Lo, swich it is for to be recchelees°   reckless
670   And necligent° and truste on flaterye!   negligent
          But ye that holden° this tale a folye°   consider / folly
      As of a fox or of a cok and hen,
      Taketh the moralite,° goode men.   moral
      For Seint Paul seith that al that writen is,
675   To oure doctrine° it is ywrite, ywis.[6]   for our teaching
      Taketh the fruyt,° and lat the chaf be
          stille.°   fruit / let the chaff alone
      Now, goode God, if that it be thy wille,

---

[1] *Colle … Talbot and Gerland* Names for dogs.

[2] *They … breek* They ran so (fast) that they thought their hearts would burst.

[3] *Certes … kille* Jack Straw was the name of one of the leaders of the Uprising of 1381; about thirty or forty Flemish merchants and weavers were murdered in London during this period of violence and rioting. This is one of the few contemporary events Chaucer mentions directly in his writings.

[4] *Of bras … powped* They brought trumpets (bemes) made of brass and boxwood and of horn and of bone, on which they blew and puffed.

---

[5] *into this yerd* This seems an obvious slip that should instead read "out of this yerd," as this line does in some manuscripts. Derek Pearsall, however, in the Variorum edition, defends "into" by suggesting that the fox is still trying to deceive Chauntecleer and so refers to the place they have come to as "this yerd" as if it were the kind of safe enclosure the rooster were used to.

[6] *For Seint … ywis* Cf. Romans 15.4. Chaucer cites the same line in his "Retraction" and it is also paraphrased at the beginning of the medieval translation and allegorical interpretation of Ovid's *Metamorphoses*, the *Ovide Moralisé*.

As seith my lord,[1] so make us alle goode men,
And brynge us to his heighe blisse. Amen!

HEERE IS ENDED THE NONNES PREESTES TALE

THE NUN'S PRIEST'S EPILOGUE[2]

680   "Sire Nonnes Preest," oure Hoost seide anoon,
      "Iblissed° be thy breche° and every
            stoon!°   *blessed / buttocks / testicles*
      This was a murie tale of Chauntecleer.
      But by my trouthe, if thou were seculer°   *a lay man*
      Thow woldest be a tredefoul[3] aright.

685   For if thou have corage° as thou hast myght,°   *spirit / power*
      The were nede° of hennes, as I
            wene,°   *you would have need of / think*
      Ya, moo° than sevene tymes seventeen!   *more*
      Se which braunes° hath this gentil° preest,   *what muscle / fine*
      So gret a nekke and swich a large breest.°   *chest*
690   He loketh as a sperhauke° with hise eyen.   *sparrowhawk*
      Him nedeth nat his colour° for to dyghen°   *complexion / dye*
      With brasile ne with greyn of Portingale.[4]
      Now sire, faire falle yow° for your tale."   *may good befall you*
      And after that he with ful murie chere
      Seide unto another as ye shuln here.

Chaucer's *Retraction*

The *Retraction* is found in all complete manuscripts of *The Canterbury Tales*, including the Ellesmere. In it Chaucer revokes most of his poems, including his early elegy *The Book of the Duchess*; his dream vision *The House of Fame*, which deals with worldly reputation; his great love poem *Troilus and Criseyde*; *The Legend of Good Women*, in which Chaucer compensates for telling the story of Criseyde's betrayal by telling of numerous good women; and those of *The Canterbury Tales* "that sownen into synne" (that tend to promote sin). Chaucer takes credit only for his translation of Boethius and for works of obvious moral or devotional content. Many critics, troubled by Chaucer's disavowal of so many of his poems as "worldly vanitees," have seen ironies in the *Retraction*. It effectively provides a list of his life's work, it does not name which of *The Canterbury Tales* it is revoking,

and it is found in manuscripts that contain all the tales, including the ones that would seem to "sownen into synne." As a confession of Chaucer's sins, however, the *Retraction* follows logically from *The Parson's Tale*, which is not a tale at all but a penitential treatise, calling for full confession and repentance. As a penitent should, Chaucer lists all his works that may be sinful, even those he cannot remember writing. The connection to *The Parson's Tale* may also explain the opening line, with its reference to those who read or hear this "lityl treatise," a description that can only rather awkwardly fit the entire *Canterbury Tales*. By this point, the tale-telling pilgrims have faded from the scene. If we accept the retraction as a sincere act of personal atonement, however, the crucial question becomes how far this act should affect our understanding of *The Canterbury Tales* as a whole.

---

[1]   *my lord* The Nun's Priest might be referring to the Archbishop of Canterbury, Christ, or, since he is attached to the nunnery at Stratford-at-Bow near London, his immediate ecclesiastical superior, the Bishop of London.

[2]   *The ... Epilogue* This epilogue is found in nine manuscripts but not in either Ellesmere or Hengwrt. It seems most likely that the epilogue is part of an earlier draft that Chaucer later abandoned, incorporating some of the lines into the Host's words to the Monk.

[3]   *tredefoul* Copulator with chickens, a rooster.

[4]   *brasile ... Portingale* Imported red dyes.

Chaucer's Retraction

Heere Taketh the Makere of this Book his Leve

Now preye° I to hem alle° that herkne° this litel tretys° or rede,° that if ther be anythyng in it that liketh hem,° that therof° they thanken oure Lord Jhesu Crist, of whom procedeth al wit and al goodnesse. And if ther be anythyng that displese hem,° I preye° hem also that they arrette° it to the defaute° of myn unkonnynge° and nat to my wyl,° that wolde° ful fayn° have seyd bettre, if I hadde had konnynge.° For oure book seith, "Al that is writen is writen for oure doctrine."[1] And that is myn entente.° Wherfore I biseke° yow mekely° for the mercy of God that ye preye for me, that Crist have mercy on me and foryeve° me my giltes,° and namely° of my translacions and enditynges° of worldly vanitees,° the whiche I revoke in my retracciouns—as is *The Book of Troilus*, *The Book* also *of Fame*, *The Book of the Five and Twenty Ladies*, *The Book of the Duchesse*, *The Book of Seint Valentynes Day of the Parlement of Briddes*,° *The Tales of Caunterbury* (thilke° that sownen into synne°), *The Book of the Leoun*,[2] and many another book (if they were in my remembrance) and many a song and many a leccherous° lay—that Crist for his grete° mercy foryeve me the synne.

But of the translacioun of Boece, *De Consolacioun*[3] and othere bookes of legendes° of seintes and omelies° and moralitee and devocioun, that thanke I oure Lord Jhesu Crist and his blisful mooder° and alle the seintes of Hevene, bisekynge hem° that they from hennes° forth unto my lyves° ende sende me grace to biwayle° my giltes and to studie° to the salvacioun of my soule and graunte me grace of verray° penitence, confessioun, and satisfaccioun to doon° in this present lyf thurgh the benigne grace of hym that is Kyng of kynges and Preest over alle preestes, that boghte° us with the precious blood of his herte,° so that I may been oon° of hem at the Day of Doome° that shulle° be saved. *Qui cum patre, etc.*[4]

Heere is Ended the Book of the Tales of Caunterbury Compiled by Geffrey Chaucer, of Whos Soule Jhesu Crist Have Mercy, Amen.

Glosses (right margin):

pray / them all / listen to / treatise/ read [it]
pleases them / for it

them / ask / ascribe / default
my ignorance / will / would / very gladly
knowledge
my intent / ask / meekly
forgive / sins
especially / writings / acts of folly

Parliament of Fowles / those
tend towards sin
lecherous
great

moral stories / homilies
mother
asking them / hence / life's / lament
take thought
true / do

redeemed / heart / one
Judgment Day / shall

---

[1] *Al … doctrine* From 2 Timothy 3.16; *doctrine* Instruction.

[2] *The … Leoun* This text, probably a translation of the *Dit de Leon* by the French court poet Guillaume de Machaut (c. 1300 –77), one of Chaucer's major early influences, does not survive.

[3] *De Consolacioun* This is *The Consolation of Philosophy*, the famous treatise of the late Roman scholar and statesman Boethius.

[4] *Qui … etc.* The full liturgical phrase is *Qui cum Patre et spiritu sancto vivit et regnat Deus per omnia secula, Amen.* Latin: Who with the Father and the Holy Spirit lives and reigns, God forever and ever, Amen.

To His Scribe Adam

Adam scriveyn,° if ever it thee bifalle   copyist
Boece or Troylus for to wryten newe,[1]
Under thy long lokkes thou most have the scalle,
But° after my makyng thow wryte more trewe;[2]   unless
5 So ofte adaye I mot° thy werk renewe,°   must / redo
It to correcte and eke° to rubbe and scrape,   also
And al is thorugh thy negligence and rape.°   haste
—1561 (WRITTEN C. 1380)

Complaint of Chaucer to His Purse[3]
A Supplication to King Henry

To yow, my purs, and to non other wight°   person
Complaine I, for ye ben my lady dere!
I am so sory, now that ye been light;°   empty
For certes, but if° ye make me hevy chere,   unless
5 Me were as lief be[4] laid upon my bier;
For which unto your mercy thus I crye,
Beth hevy ayeyn, or elles mot° I dye!   must

Now voucheth sauf° this day, or° hyt be   grant / ere
   nyght,
That I of you the blissful soun° may hear,   sound
10 Or see your colour lyk the sonne bright,
That of yelownesse had never peer.
Ye be my lyf, ye be myne hertes stere,[5]
Quene of comfort and of good companye;
Beeth hevy again, or elles mot I dye!

Ye purs, that ben to me my lyves° light   life's
And saviour, as doun in this worlde here,
Out of this towne helpe me thurgh your might,
Syn° that ye wylle nat ben my tresorere;   since
For I am shave as nye as any frere.[6]
20 But yet I pray unto youre curtesye,
Beeth hevy ayeyn, or elles mot I dye!
—1477 (WRITTEN C. 1399)

Lenvoy de Chaucer[7]

O conquerour of Brutes Albyoun,[8]
Which that by line and free eleccioun
Been[9] verray° kyng, this song to you I sende;   true
And ye, that mowen° alle our harmes amende,   may
5 Have mynde upon my supplicacioun.
—1399

from Troilus and Criseyde

Troilus's Song[10]

If no love is, O God, what feele I so?
And if love is, what thing and which is he?
If love be good, from whennes commeth my wo?
If it be wikke, a wonder thinketh me,[11]
5 Whan every torment and adversitee

---

[1] *if ever ... newe* If you ever have occasion to copy out Boethius (Chaucer's translation of Boethius's *Consolation of Philosophy*) or Troilus (Chaucer's *Troilus and Criseyde*). At the end of *Troilus* Chaucer also expresses concern about errors creeping in during the copying process, noting the "diversitee in English, and in writing of our tonge" and fearing that as a result someone may "miswrite" his book.

[2] *thou most ... trewe* May you have a scaly (or mangy) scalp if you do not follow more truly in your writing what I have made.

[3] The tradition in which this poem is written is that of courtly love; "complaints" to a lady concerning unrequited love were a staple of love poetry on French models.

[4] *Me were as lief be* I would be just as happy to be.

[5] *myne hertes stere* Rudder of my heart.

[6] *shave ... any frere* As close-cropped as any friar (i.e., with nothing left).

[7] *Lenvoy de Chaucer* The "envoy" or message at the close of a poem is addressed directly to the poem's recipient. Chaucer was requesting that the new king, Henry IV, renew the annual payments that the former monarch, Richard II, had previously authorized.

[8] *Brutes Albyoun* Geoffrey of Monmouth's claim that Britain ("Albion") had been founded by Brutus, the grandson of Aeneas, the founder of Rome, had long been accepted as true.

[9] *Which that ... Been* Who by your lineage and by choice are.

[10] *Troilus's Song* In Chaucer's long poem, Troilus composes a song on the theme of his feelings of love for Criseyde. Chaucer translated a sonnet of Petrarch's ("S'amor non è") for the purpose.

[11] *If it ... me* It if is wicked, I would be very surprised.

That cometh of him may to me savory°   *pleasant*
   thinke,°   *seem*
For ay° thurste I, the more that ich° drinke.   *always / I*

And if that at myn owene lust I breene,
From whennes cometh my wailing and my plainte?
10   If harm agree me, wherto plaine° I thenne?   *complain*
I noot, ne why unwary that I fainte.[1]
O quikke° deeth, O sweete harm so   *living*
   quainte,°   *strange*
How may of thee in me swich quantitee,[2]
But° if that I consente that it be?   *except*

15   And if that I consente, I wrongfully
Complaine; ywis,° thus possed° to and fro   *truly / tossed*
All stereless° within a boot° am I   *rudderless / boat*
Amiddde the see, bitwixen windes two,
That in contrarye stonden everemo.
20   Allas, what is this wonder maladye?
For hoot° of colde, for cold of hoot I die.   *hot*
—1483 (WRITTEN C. 1388)

---

[1] *I noot ... fainte* I do not know, any more than I know why I faint
when I am not weary.

[2] *How may ... quantitee* How can there be such a great quantity of
you in me.

Thomas Hoccleve
c. 1367? – 1426

We often know too little about the private lives of medieval authors. In Thomas Hoccleve's case, however, it seems we know too much; he is best known for the gossip his poetry seemed to spread about him. Most notoriously, a character in his *Regiment of Princes* (1410–11) says he has heard that Hoccleve was "aqueynted with Chaucer." Hoccleve certainly owes a significant literary debt to Geoffrey Chaucer, whom he eulogizes as "the firste fyndere of oure faire langage," and some of Hoccleve's work (including poetry in the website component of this anthology) even circulated as Chaucer's work. Hoccleve, however, did not see himself simply as indebted to Chaucer; his *Regiment of Princes* also laments the death of "my maister [John] Gower." Hoccleve was a contemporary of Julian of Norwich, Margery Kempe, John Lydgate, and the *Gawain* poet, though the form and content of his poetry was probably more influenced by French contemporaries such as Christine de Pizan. Hoccleve found favor in the fifteenth century: his *Regiment of Princes* appears in over forty manuscripts, a number that compares favorably with those of Chaucer's *Canterbury Tales* and Gower's *Confessio Amantis*.

Hoccleve's verse has recently begun to attract substantial attention again, and for good reason. Whether he depicts the perils of translating books or thinking heretically, offending women, or drinking excessively, Hoccleve engages with some of his day's most pressing concerns, often in a humorous and intimate—even gossipy—manner.

We know much about Hoccleve's professional life because his name appears in documents pertaining to his vocation in the Privy Seal, the writing office where he worked from 1387 until just before his death in 1426. Among other things, these documents record the payment (or delay) of his annuity, his receipt of rewards and benefices, and even authorization or reimbursement for the purchase of the tools of his trade: parchment, ink, and wax. We can only conjecture about Hoccleve's life before 1387. His name suggests that he came to London from Hockliffe, Bedfordshire. He likely progressed through all three levels of schooling available in medieval England. As a young boy in song school, he would have learned to sing the psalms and other texts for religious services. As a slightly older boy in grammar school, he would have learned Latin grammar. At the age of fourteen or fifteen, when others of his background might have gone to university, he likely began training in one of London's Inns of Chancery in order to acquire the legal knowledge and technical writing ability necessary for his vocation.

Much of Hoccleve's poetry ostensibly supplements the documents concerning his private life. In three texts, a first-person narrator named Hoccleve provides a detailed account of what purport to be the author's own life and experience. The first, commonly known as *La Male Regle* (1405–06), depicts an ill-regulated youth spent in the taverns of London and Westminster. It closes with a request for the annuity that had been due that autumn—a payment that we know was delayed. The second is

Hoccleve's longest and most popular poem, the *Regiment of Princes*, which similarly associates its narrator with the author by name and circumstance while lamenting the ill effects of poverty. The *Regiment of Princes* opens with a description of a sleepless night spent in one of the Inns of Chancery, where Privy Seal clerks lived: "Chestre Ynne, right fast by the stronde." This poem also suggests that Hoccleve was married, a claim reiterated in the third ostensibly autobiographical text, now commonly known as *The Series* (1419–21). Its account of a "wylde infirmitee" from which the narrator claims to have suffered and recovered has attracted a wide range of criticism. Some critics have tried to demonstrate its authenticity by pointing to documentary evidence for Hoccleve's activities (or lack thereof) during the period described; others have argued that it is a conventional representation of the state of sin. These three texts and the debate surrounding their relationship to Hoccleve's life have contributed a great deal to the revival of interest in his work. As his diction in the poem on the reburial of Richard II's body in Westminster (1413) suggests, Hoccleve engages with contemporary political and social discourses even—perhaps especially—when he employs first-person pronouns.

Whether we read it autobiographically or not, Hoccleve's writing was certainly influenced by his work in the Privy Seal. This work demanded fluency in Latin, French, and English; Hoccleve's English texts frequently translate from either French or Latin. Privy Seal work required that Hoccleve be conversant in legal language and immersed in political discourse; his poetry frequently employs legal and political diction. Privy Seal work demanded that he possess the technical ability to write a legible secretary script—a script that Hoccleve used in making one formulary of Privy Seal documents and three autograph verse manuscripts between 1422 and his death in 1426. (Durham, University Library, MS Cosin V.iii.9 is a copy of *The Series* dedicated to Joan Beaufort, Countess of Westmorland; San Marino, Huntington Library MSS HM 111 and 744 are collections of shorter poems.) These three verse manuscripts are significant for several reasons. First, they preserve all the poetry Hoccleve is known to have written other than the *Regiment of Princes* (surviving dedications reveal that he also made an autograph copy of that poem for John, Duke of Bedford in addition to a book of ballads for Edward, Duke of York). Several poems survive only in the two Huntington manuscripts. Second, these books reveal the varied audience Hoccleve anticipated for his poems: some are dedicated to noble men and women, others were read by Hoccleve's peers, and some may have circulated among readers of varying social levels. Finally, they provide an unparalleled insight into how one medieval author presented texts for his audience: autograph manuscripts in this period are exceptionally rare.

The texts that appear here and in the website component of the anthology have been selected because they represent a range of the verse found in the two Huntington manuscripts. Both major stanza forms that Hoccleve employ are present: the seven-line rime royal stanza (a b a b b c c) and the eight-line "monk stanza" (a b a b b c b c); the *balade* and *rondeau* form also appear. Hoccleve's linguistic play is evident throughout in two related phenomena: *paronomasia* (the pun) and *synonymia*. Puns use one word to invoke a similar-sounding one (e.g., Somer invokes the surname of Henry Somer and the name of the season). *Synonymia* uses different words to denote the same thing (e.g., "wexe and springe," which could both be glossed as "grow" in line 5 of the same poem). *Synonymia* sometimes allows for nuanced meaning; at other times, it simply allows Hoccleve to meet the demands of his decasyllabic line. Perhaps the two most challenging features of Hoccleve's poetry for new readers are his use of modern or double negatives to intensify a negative and his frequent inversion of standard English syntax. The best way to overcome these challenges is to read the sentence as a whole—aloud, if possible—before determining its meaning. Hoccleve's narrator in *The Series* insists that others should suspend their judgment of him until they have had the chance to converse with him fully. A text by Hoccleve often compels readers to judge it in the same way.

⌘ ⌘ ⌘

Ballad on the Re-Burial of King Richard II

*Ceste Balade ensuyante feust faite tost apres que les osses
du Roy Richard feurent apportez a Westmouster.*

[*The following Ballad was made shortly after the
bones of King Richard (II) were brought to Westminster (Abbey)*][1]

Whereas that this land wont° was for to be   *habitually*
Of sad° byleeve° and constant unioun,   *serious / belief*
And as that holy chirche us taghte, we
With herte buxum° lerned our lessoun,   *obedient*
5   Now han° we changid our condicioun: *have*
Allas! An heep° of us the feith   *A large number*
   werreye;°   *war against*
We waden° so deepe in presumpcioun   *wade*
That us nat deyneth° unto God obeye;   *deign (think fit)*

We rekken° nat, thogh Crystes lore deye.°   *heed / summons us*
10   The feend hath maad us dronke of the poisoun

An autograph copy of Hoccleve's Ballad on the Re-Burial of
King Richard II. (Reprinted by permission of *The Huntington
Library, San Marino, California,* MS HM 111, fol. 31v.)

Of heresie and lad° us a wrong weye   *led*
That torne° shal to our confusioun   *turn*
But if[2] that left be this abusioun.°   *corrupt practice*
And yit seur° confort haue I, thynkith me:[3]   *sure*
15   Our lige° Lord, the Kyng, is Champioun   *liege*
For holy chirche; Crystes knyght is he.

For why, o reverent goostly fadres, yee
And we your sones eek° han enchesoun°   *also / occasion*
Right greet to thanke God in Trinitee,
20   That of his grace hath sent this Regioun
So noble an heed. Looke up, thow Albioun,°   *i.e., England*

---

[1] *The following Ballad ... Abbey* This is one of nineteen Hoccleve
items included in the Huntington Library manuscript MS HM 111.
The nineteen have one thing in common: they were all initially
made to be circulated elsewhere before being compiled in MS HM
111 between 1422 and 1426. Hoccleve seems to have recognized the
need for readers to consider the context for some of these poems,
and he regularly provides detailed headings in space allocated for
them. This poem's heading indicates that it was written shortly after
the event that occasioned it: the re-burial of Richard II (1367–1400)
in Westminster Abbey following Henry V's accession to the throne
in 1413. Richard II had been deposed in 1399 and replaced on the
throne by Henry IV; he died in custody in February of 1400. The
ceremonial re-burial was likely intended both to establish publicly
Henry V's desire for reconciliation with Richard II's supporters as
well as to demonstrate clearly that the former king was indeed dead
and therefore could not provide rebels with a leader around whom
they could muster. The poem, which focuses on the figure of the
new king rather than the dead one, may have been distributed on
single parchment leaves. Such copies would have been ephemeral,
however, and the poem survives only in this manuscript. The poem's
composition took place in a period (c. 1410–15) when Hoccleve
may have held ambitions to be a kind of poet laureate promoting
Henry V's interests. Hoccleve uses the term *Balade* somewhat loosely
(cf. the following poem). This poem employs six eight-line stanzas
rhyming a b a b b c b c, superficially creating the impression that this is
a double ballad. While the poem does express a high degree of
formality by restricting its number of rhyming words to three, the fact
that it does not employ a common refrain at the end of each stanza
means that it is not a formal double ballad.

---

[2] *But if* Unless.

[3] *thynkith me* It seems to me.

God thanke and for thy cristen prince preye;
Syn he fo is to this Rebellioun,[1]
He of thy soules helthe is loke° and keye.   lock

25 What mighten folk of good byleeue° seye,   belief
If bent were our Kynges affeccioun
To the wrong part? Who sholde hem helpe
purveye?°   arrange
A Kyng set in that wrong opinioun
Mighte of our feith be the subversioun,
30 But eterne° God in persones three   eternal
Hath reyned[2] dropes of conpassioun
And sent us our good Kyng for our cheertee.°   affection

See eek° how our Kynges benignitee°   also / kindness
And louvyng herte his vertu can bywreye:°   reveal
35 Our Kyng Richard that was, yee may wel see,
Is nat fled from his remembrance aweye.
My wit souffysith° nat to peyse° and weye   suffices / measure

With what honour he° broght is to   i.e., Richard II('s body)
this toun
And with his queene[3] at Westmynstre in
th'abbeye°   the Abbey
40 Solempnely in Tombe leid adoun.°   down

Now God byseeche I, in conclusioun,
Henri the .v.°° in joie and hy   Henry the Fifth
nobleye°   nobility
Regne on us yeeres many a milion;
45 And whereas that men erren and forveye,°   go astray
Walkynge blyndly in the dirk
aleye°   passage (usually covered or bordered)
Of heresie, o Lord God, preye I thee
Enspire° hem that no lenger they   Inspire
foleie:°   behave wildly
50 To feithes path hem lede° thy pitee. Amen.   lead
—1413

The Series

*T*he *Series* is now the title commonly used to describe the compilation of texts that Hoccleve made
at some point between 1419 and 1421. He dedicated an autograph copy of it to Joan Beaufort,
Countess of Westmorland; this book survives at Durham, University Library, MS Cosin V.iii.9.

The Series is a collection of separate texts linked through a framing narrative that provides an
account of its making. It begins with the "Complaint" before it moves to a "Dialogue," where the
narrator and his friend discuss whether the first part of the text should be made public and, if so, what
else the narrator should make. The friend convinces the narrator to make up for the wrongs he has
done to women through his translation of Christine de Pizan's *Letter of Cupid* (1399) by means of
another translation: he thinks the narrator should translate the "Tale of the Emperor's Wife" from
a story collection known as the *Gesta Romanorum* (late thirteenth century). The narrator undertakes
this task and the friend returns to read it, as he had promised to do, whereupon he discovers that the
narrator has not included a moralization for the tale. The friend finds one and the narrator copies it
out in prose.

At this point, the narrator finally includes the text he claims initially to have set out to translate,
Learn to Die. He completes only one of the four projected parts, though, claiming that any more
would be beyond his capabilities. He provides in their place a brief prose version of the ninth lesson
read on All Saints' Day. He thinks to have completed the book, but the friend returns and asks him
to include one more selection for the benefit of his son, now fifteen and on his way to university. The

---

[1] *Rebellioun*   In the last year of Henry IV's reign, there were several rebellions, one involving the claim that Richard
II was living in Scotland, waiting for the signal to return to England and re-take his crown.

[2] *reyned*   Pun on reign / rain.

[3] *his queene*   Anne of Bohemia (1366–94), Richard II's first wife.

narrator demurs, saying that he does not know if he should include the requested tale, which is about a wicked woman, given the harm he has just tried to undo. The friend prevails, though, and the text gets included along with a prose moralization.

While the narrative that frames the compilation describes aspects of book production with which Hoccleve was intimately familiar, it is fictitious. Nonetheless, it is important insofar as it suggests that while these texts can be seen separately, they can also be seen as parts of the compilation—or book—that the narrator makes.

Though "Complaint" reads well on its own, reading the subsequent text may alter how we interpret "Complaint." In the "Dialogue" the narrator immediately reveals that, although he has resolved to set less store by what others say about him, he is still preoccupied by how others see him. It also becomes evident that the narrator himself is much like the man in the book he reads: other readers are invited to consider his example and amend their lives appropriately. The remainder of *The Series* provides the means to achieve this end.

---

from *The Series*[1]

"My Complaint"[2]

Aftir that hervest inned° had his   *brought in*
   sheves,°   *sheaves*
And that the broun° sesoun of Mighelmesse[3]   *brown*
Was come, and gan° the trees robbe of her leeves,   *began*
That greene had ben, and in lusty° fresshnesse,   *lively*
5   And hem into colour of yelownesse

Had died°[4] and doun thrown undir foote,   *dyed*
That chaunge sank into myn herte roote.°   *root*

For fresshly broghte it to my remembrance
That stablenesse° in this worlde is ther   *stability*
   noon:°   *none*
10   There is nothing but chaunge and variance.
How° welthy a man be or wel begoon,°   *however / surrounded*
Endure it shal not; he shal it forgoon.°   *pass away*
Deeth undir foote shal him thriste° adoun: *thrust*
That is every wightes° conclusioun,   *person's*
15   Wiche for to weyve° is in no   *waive (in a legal sense)*
   mannes might,
How° riche he be, stronge, lusty, fressh, and gay.   *However*
And in th'ende of Novembre upon a nyght,
Sighynge sore as I in my bed lay
For this and othir thoght which many a day
20   Before I took, sleep cam noon in myn ye,°   *eyes*
So vexid me the thoghtful maladie.

I sy° wel syn° I with seeknesse last   *saw / since*
Was scourgid, cloudy hath been the favour
That shoon° on me ful° bright in tymes past.   *shone / very*
25   The sonne abated° and the dirke shour°   *diminished / shower*
Hilded° doun right on me and in langour   *poured*

---

[1] *The Series* The Middle Engish text of this selection draws heavily on that prepared by J.A. Burrow for his Early English Texts Society edition (1999). All glosses, footnotes and introductory material for this and other Hoccleve selections in the anthology have been prepared by David Watt for *The Broadview Anthology of British Literature*.

[2] *My Complaint* The first part of *The Series*. Like the *Letter of Cupid*, it is a literary complaint in rime royal stanzas (a b a b b c c). As John Burrow has shown, most formal complaints in Hoccleve's formulary of Privy Seal documents consist of a complaint of an injury followed by petition for remedy addressed either to a benefactor or to someone who will act as an intercessor. The injury in this case is not that the narrator has suffered a mental illness, but that no one acknowledges his recovery. The narrator demonstrates at great length that this circumstance is injurious to him, and he becomes preoccupied by how he is seen by others. The "Complaint" closes with the narrator reading—and copying—a book in which Reason gives advice to a woeful man. By applying this advice to his own circumstances, the narrator learns to set less store by what others say about him.

[3] *Mighelmesse* Michaelmas. The Feast day of Michael the Archangel is 29 September; it is traditionally associated with the beginning of autumn and thus describes the subsequent season or term.

[4] *died* Although the primary meaning clearly refers to the changing of color, there is also a pun on the taking of life from the leaves.

Me made swymme so that my spiryt
To lyve no lust had, ne delyt.°   *delight*

The greef aboute myn herte so swal°   *swelled*
30 And bolned° evere to and to[1] so sore   *swelled*
That needes° oute I muste therwithal;°   *necessarily / with it*
I thoughte I nolde° keepe it cloos° no more   *could not / private*
Ne° lette it in me for to eelde and hore.[2]   *Nor*
And for to preeve° I cam° of a womman   *prove / came*
35 I brast° out on the morwe and thus began.   *burst*

Heere endith my Prolog, and folwith my Conpleynte.

Almighty God, as lykith his goodnesse,
Visiteth° folke al day, as men may see,   *Visits*
With los of good and bodily seeknesse,°   *sickness*
And amonge othir, he forgat nat me;
40 Witnesse upon the wylde infirmitee[3]
Whiche that I hadde as many a man wel kneew,
And which me out of myself caste and threew.

It was so knowen to the peple and kowth°   *familiar*
That conseil° was it noon, ne nat be might.   *secret*
45 How it with me stood was in every mowth,
And that ful sore my freendes affrighte.°   *frightened*
They for myn helthe pilgrimages highte
And soghte hem, some on hors and some on foote,
God yilde° it hem to gete me my boote.°   *yielded / relief*

50 But although the substance of my memorie
Wente to pleye° as for a certein space,   *play*
Yit° the lord of vertu, the kyng of glorie,   *Yet*
Of his hye° might and benigne° grace   *high / kind*
Made it for to retourne into the place
55 Whens it cam, which was at Alle Halwemesse,[4]
Was five yeer neither more ne lesse.[5]

And evere syn,° thankid be God oure lord,   *since*
Of his good reconsiliacioun,
My wit and I have been of swich° accord   *such*
60 As we were or° the alteracioun   *before*
Of it was, but by my sauvacioun°   *salvation*
That time[6] have I be sore set on fyre
And lyved in greet torment and martire.°   *suffering*

For thogh that my wit were hoom come ageyn,
65 Men wolde° it nat so undirstonde or take: *would*
With me to delen° hadde they desdeyn;   *deal*
A riotous persone I was and forsake;°   *forsaken*
Myn old frendshipe was al overshake;°   *shaken off*
No wight with me list make daliance;°   *conversation*
70 The world me made a straunge contenance,°   *countenance*

Which that myn herte sore gan to torment;
For ofte whan I in Westmynstre halle[7]
And eek° in Londoun among the   *also*
            prees° wente,   *press (i.e., crowd)*
I sy° the cheere° abaten° and   *saw / faces / lower*
            apalle°   *grow pale*
75 Of hem that weren wont° me for to calle   *accustomed*
To conpaignie: hire heed they caste awry
Whan I hem mette as° they nat me sy.°   *as if / saw*

As seid is in the psalter,° might I seye:[8]   *Book of Psalms*
They that me sy° fledden° away fro me;   *saw / fled*
80 Foryete° I was, al out of mynde aweye   *forgotten*
As he that deed° was from hertes cheertee.°   *dead / affection*
To a lost vessel likned° mighte I be,   *likened*
For many a wight° aboute me dwellynge   *person*
Herde I me blame and putte in dispreisynge.[9]

---

[1] *to and to*   More and more.

[2] *to eelde and hore*   To grow both old and gray.

[3] *the wylde infirmitee*   Some kind of sickness that the narrator has
suffered. There has been much critical discussion about the nature
of this illness, but no real consensus about it.

[4] *Alle Halwemesse*   All Saints Day (1 November).

[5] *five yeer ... ne lesse*   The precise dating suggests that this recovery
took place on 1 November 1414.

---

[6] *That time*   I.e., the past five years.

[7] *Westmynstre halle*   The great Hall in Westminster Palace; the Office
of the Privy Seal did business there and had space allocated nearby.

[8] *As seid ... might I seye*   Marginal note: "Qui videbant me foras
fugierunt a me. Oblivioni datus sum, sicut mortuus a corde. Factus
sum tanquam vas perditum; quoniam audiui vituperacionem
multorum commorancium in circuitu" (Latin: translated below as
Psalm 30.12–14).

[9] *They ... dispreisynge*   Psalm 30.12–14: "They that saw me
without fled from me. I am forgotten as one dead from the heart. I
am become as a vessel that is destroyed. For I have heard the blame
of many that dwell round about."

85 Thus spak° many oon and seide by me: *spoke*
 "Althogh from him his seeknesse savage
 Withdrawe and past as for a tyme be,
 Resorte° it wole, namly° in swich age *return / especially*
 As he is of." And thanne my visage°   *face*
90 Began to glowe for the wo and fere;°   *grief*
 Tho wordes, hem unwaar,° cam to myn ere. *unaware*

 "Whan passynge° hete is," quod they, *surpassing*
  "trustith this:
 Assaile him wole° ageyn that maladie." *will*
 And yit, pardee,° they token hem amis: *by God*
95 Noon effect at al took hir prophecie.
 Many someres been past syn remedie
 Of that. God of his grace me purveide.° *provided*
 Thankid be God it shoop° nat as they seide. *was destined*

 What falle° shal, what men so deeme° or gesse, *befall / judge*
100 To him that woot every hertes secree[1]
 Reserved is. It is a lewdenesse°   *unlearned (thing)*
 Men wyser° hem pretende than they be, *wiser*
 And no wight° knowith, be it he or she, *person*
 Whom, how, ne whanne God wole° him visyte;[2] *will*
 It happith often whan men weene° it lyte.° *expect / little*
 Sumtyme° I wende° as lyte° *At one time / expected / little*
  as any man
 For to han falle into that wyldenesse,
 But God—whan him liste—may, wole, and can
 Helthe withdrawe and sende a wight° seeknesse. *person*
110 Thogh man be wel this day, no sikirnesse° *certainty*
 To him behight° is that it shal endure; *promised*
 God hurte now can, and now hele and cure.[3]

 He suffrith° longe, but at the laste he smit.° *endures / smites*
 Whan that man is in prosperitee
115 To dreede a fal comynge it is a wit.° *wise thing*
 Whoso that takith heede ofte° may see *often*
 This worldes chaunge and mutabilitee
 In sundry wyse,° how needith nat expresse. *ways*

---

1. *To him ... secree* To God that "knoweth the secrets of the heart" (Psalms 43.22).

2. *And no wight ... him visyte* See Luke 19.44 on the time of visitation.

3. *God hurte ... hele and cure* Proverbial.

 To my mateere streight° wole I me *immediately*
  dresse.°   *address*
120 Men seide I lookid as a wylde steer° *ox*
 And so my look aboute I gan to throwe.
 Myn heed to hye° another seide I beer.° *too high / bore*
 "Ful bukkish° is his brayn, wel may I trow," *like a buck*
 Seide the thridde, "and apt is in the rowe° *row*
125 To sitte of hem that a resounless reed° *(piece of) advice*
 Can yeve:° no sadnesse° is in his heed." *give / soundness*

 Changed had I my paas,° some seide eek,° *pace / also*
 For heere and ther forth stirte I as a ro,° *roe (i.e., a deer)*
 Noon abood, noon areest, but al braynseek.[4]
130 Anothir spak, and of me seide also,
 My feet were ay° wavynge° to and fro *always / moving*
 Whan that I stonde sholde and with men talke,
 And that myn yen° soghten every halke.°[5] *eyes / corner*

 I leide an ere ay° to as I by wente *always*
135 And herde al, and thus in myn herte I caste:° *conceived*
 "Of long abydynge heere I may repente;
 Lest that of hastinesse I at the laste
 Answere amis,° best is hens hie fast,[6] *amiss*
 For if I in this prees° amis me gye° *crowd / conduct*
140 To harm wole it me torne° and to folie." *turn*

 And this I deemed° wel—and knew well eek:° *judged / also*
 Whatso that evere I sholde° answere or seye *should*
 They wolden° nat han° holde it worth a leek.[7] *would / have*
 Forwhy as[8] I had lost my tonges keye° *key*
145 Kepte I me cloos° and trussid me my weye[9] *private*

---

4. *Noon abood ... braynseek* Not resting, not stopping, but entirely brainsick.

5. *soghten every halke* This is likely an idiomatic expression meaning to look around furtively and excessively. Cf. Chaucer's *Franklin's Tale*, where a scholar is described as pursuing knowledge by reading everything: "seken in every halke and every herne."

6. *best is hens hie fast* It is best to go away quickly.

7. *leek* I.e., the vegetable, which signifies something of little value in this case.

8. *Forwhy as* Because.

9. *trussid ... weye* Took myself off along my way.

Droupynge and hevy and al wo bistad;[1]
Smal cause hadde I, me thoghte, to be glad.

My spirites laboured bisily
To peynte° contenance, cheere, and look,   *portray*
150   For that° men speke of me so wondryngly,   *because*
And for the verray shame and fere° I qwook.°   *grief / trembled*
Thogh° myn herte had be dippid in the brook   *as though*
It weet° and moist ynow was of my swoot,   *wet*
Which was now frosty cold, now fyry hoot.

155   And in my chambre at hoom whan that I was
Myself allone, I in this wyse wroghte:[2]
I streighte° unto my mirrour and my glas   *straight*
To looke how that me of my cheere° thoghte,   *expression*
If any othir were it than it oghte,
160   For fayn° wolde I, if it had nat been right,   *gladly*
Amendid it to my konnynge° and might.   *knowledge*

Many a saut° made I to this mirrour[3]   *leap, assault*
Thynkynge, "If that I looke in this maneere°   *manner*
Among folk as I now do, noon° errour   *no*
165   Of suspect look may in my face appeere.°   *appear*
This contenance, I am seur,° and this cheere   *sure*
If I foorth° use is nothyng   *from this time or place*
    repreevable°   *reprovable*
To hem that han conceites° resonable."   *thoughts*

And therwithal° I thoghte thus anoon: *subsequently*
170   "Men in hire owne cas° been blynde alday,°[4]   *case / always*
As I have herd seyn many a day agoon,
And in that same plyt° I stonde may.   *plight*
How shal I do? Which is the beste way
My troublid spirit for to brynge in reste?
175   If I wiste° how, fayn° wolde I do the beste."   *knew / gladly*

Syn° I recovered was have I ful ofte°   *Since / often*
Cause had of anger and inpacience,°   *impatience*

Where I born° have it esily and softe,°   *borne / gently*
Suffryng wrong be doon° to me and offense   *done*
180   And nat answerd ageyn° but kept silence,   *against (it)*
Lest that men of me deeme wolde° and seyn,   *would judge*
"See how this man is fallen in ageyn."

As that I ones° fro Westmynstre cam   *once*
Vexid ful grevously° with thoghtful hete,   *grievously*
185   Thus thoght I: "A greet fool I am
This pavyment adayes° thus to   *always*
    bete,°   *beat (i.e., walk upon)*
And in and out laboure faste and swete°   *sweat*
Wondrynge° and hevynesse° to   *Astonishment / sadness*
    purchace,
Syn° I stonde out of al favour and grace."   *Since*

190   And then thoghte I on that othir syde:
"If that I nat be seen among the prees°   *crowd*
Men deeme wole that I myn heed hyde[5]
And am wers° than I am, it is no lees."°   *worse / less*
O lord, so my spirit was resteless:
195   I soghte reste and I nat it fond,[6]
But ay° was trouble redy° at myn hond.   *always / ready*

I may nat lette° a man to ymagyne   *stop*
Ferre° above the moone,[7] if that him list;   *Far*
Thereby the soothe° he may nat determine,   *truth*
200   But by the preef° been thynges knowe and   *proof*
    wist.°   *known*
Many a doom° is wrappid in the mist.   *fate*
Man by his deedes and nat by his lookes
Shal knowen be, as it is write° in bookes.   *written*

By taast° of fruyt men may wel wite°   *taste*
    and knowe   *know*
205   What that it is;[8] othir preef is ther noon:
Every man woot° wel that, as that I trowe.°   *knows / trust*

---

[1]   *wo bistad* Beset by grief.

[2]   *wroghte* Literally, behaved, but *wrought* also invokes the idea of creating, shaping, or molding.

[3]   *Many a saut ... mirrour* Idiomatic: I frequently or repeatedly rushed to this mirror.

[4]   *Men in hire ... alday* Proverbial: Men always fail to see their own case clearly.

[5]   *Men deeme ... hyde* Men will judge that I hide my head.

[6]   *so my spirit ... it fond* Matthew 12.43: "And when an unclean spirit is gone out of a man, he walketh through dry places seeking rest and findeth none."

[7]   *Ferre above the moone* Proverbial: In a way that has no basis in reality.

[8]   *By taast ... it is* Matthew 7.16: "By their fruits you shall know them."

Right° so they that deemen° my wit is goon—   *Just / judge*
As yit this day ther deemeth° many oon°   *judge / a one*
I am nat wel—may as I by hem go
210 Taaste and assaye if it be so or no.[1]

Upon a look is hard men hem to grownde°   *establish*
What a man is: therby the soothe° is hid.   *truth*
Whethir his wittes seeke° been or sownde°   *sick / sound*
By contenance is it nat wist° ne kid.°   *known / made known*
215 Thogh a man harde° have ones been   *hardship*
    betid,°   *befallen*
God sheelde° it sholde on him continue   *defend*
    alway.°   *always*
By communynge° is the best assay.°   *conversation / test*

I meene to commune° of thynges mene,°   *converse / mean*
For I am but right lewde,° doutelees,   *unlearned*
220 And ignorant. My konnynge° is ful lene.   *knowledge*
Yit hoomly° resoun knew I natheles;°   *homely / nonetheless*
Nat hope I fownden be so resounlees
As men deemen°—Marie, Cryst forbeede![2]   *judge*
I can no more: preeve° may the deede![3]   *prove*

225 If a man ones° falle in dronkenesse   *once*
Shal he continue therin evere mo?°   *more*
Nay, thogh a man do in drynkynge excesse
So fer° forth that nat speke he can ne go,   *far*
And his wittes wel ny° been reft° him fro   *near / taken*
230 And biried° in the cuppe, he aftirward   *buried*
Comth to himself ageyn, elles were hard.[4]

Right° so, thogh that my wit were a plilgrym   *Just*
And wente fer° from hoom, he cam agayn.   *far*

God me voidid° of the grevous° venym   *emptied / grievous*
235 That had infectid and wyldid° my brayn.   *made wild*
See how the curteys° leche[5] soverain   *courteous / sovereign*
Unto the seeke° yeveth° medecyne   *sick / gives*
In neede and him releeveth° of his pyne.°   *relieves / pain*

Now let this passe. God woot,° many a man   *knows*
240 Seemeth° ful wys by contenance and cheere   *seems*
Which, and he taastid° were what he   *tasted, tested*
    can,°   *knows*
Men mighte likne° him to a fooles peere;[6]   *liken*
And sum man lookith in foltissh° maneere°   *foolish / manner*
As to the outward doom and jugement
245 That at the preef° discreet is and prudent.   *proof*

But algate° how so be my contenance,   *all the same*
Debat is now noon twixt° me and my wit,   *between*
Althogh that ther were a disseverance°   *separation*
As for a tyme betwixt me and it.
250 The gretter harm is myn that nevere yit
Was I wel lettrid,° prudent, and discreet;   *learned*
There nevere stood yit wys° man on my feet.   *(a) wise*

The soothe° is this: swich conceit° as I hadde   *truth / thought*
And undirstondyng—al° were it but smal—   *although*
255 Before that my wittes were unsadde°—   *unsound*
Thankid be our lord Ihesu Cryst of° al—   *for*
Swiche have I now, but blowe° is ny° overal   *blown / nearly*
The revers, wherthugh° moche° is   *through which / much*
    my mournynge,
Which causith me thus sighe in conpleynynge.

260 Syn° my good fortune hath changed hir cheere   *Since*
Hy° tyme is me to creepe into my grave.   *High*
To lyve joielees what do I heere?
I in myn herte can no gladnesse have:
I may but smal seyn, but men deeme° I rave.   *judge*
265 Syn° othir thyng than wo may I noon grype°   *Since / grip*
Unto my sepulture° am I now rype.   *sepulcher*

---

[1] *Taaste and assaye* Two puns combined with synonymia: *taaste* means taste but also sounds like *test;* assay means *test* but also sounds like *see.* Assay particularly connotes the testing of gold in a furnace to determine or produce purity. While the line initially seems to read "taste and test," it can also be read as "test and test" to emphasize the importance of testing as well as "taste and see" to emphasize the importance of the senses in this evaluative process.

[2] *Marie, Cryst forbeede!* Exclamation invoking the Blessed Virgin Mary and Christ.

[3] *deede* The term "deed" not only describes a physical act, but also a legal document.

[4] *elles were hard* Otherwise it would be harsh.

[5] *leche* God or Christ: the term leech normally refers to a physician, but here it refers to a figure who provides spiritual healing.

[6] *fooles peere* A pun on the peer (equal) and pear (a fruit proverbially associated with worthlessness because it seems good when rotten).

My wele° adieu! Farwel my good fortune! — wealth
Out of your tables me planed han yee.[1]
Syn wel ny any wight for to commune
270 With me looth is,[2] farwel prosperitee!
I am no lenger of your liveree:[3]
Yee han me put out of your retenance.° — retinue
Adieu my good aventure° and good chance! — fortune

And as swythe° aftir thus bethoghte I me: — swiftly
275 "If that I in this wyse° me despeire — way
It is purchas° of more adversitee. — purchase
What needith it[4] my feeble wit appeire° — to weaken
Syn God hath maad myn helthe hoom repeire?° — repair
Blessid be he, and what° men deeme or speke — whatsoever
280 Suffre it, thynke I, and me nat on me wreke."° — avenge

But sumdel° had I rejoisynge — somewhat
among° — at the same time
And a gladnesse also in my spiryt,
That thogh the peple took hem mis° and wrong, — amiss
Me deemynge° of my seeknesse nat — judging
qwyt,° — released
285 Yit for they conpleyned the hevy° plyt° — weighty / plight
That they had seen me in with tendreness
Of hertes cheertee,° my greef was the lesse. — affection

In hem putte I no deffaute° but oon:° — default / one
That I was hool° they nat ne deeme° kowde, — whole / judge
290 And day by day they sy° me by hem goon — saw
In hete and colde, and neither stille° or lowde° — silent / loud
Kneew they me do suspectly;[5] a dirk clowde
Hir sighte obscured withynne and withoute,
And for al that were ay° in swich a doute.° — always / doubt

295 Axid° han they ful ofte sythe° and — Asked / since
freyned° — inquired
Of my felawes° of the privee seel[6] — fellows
And preide hem to telle hem with herte
unfeyned° — undeceiving
How it stood with me, whethir evele or weel.
And they the soothe° tolde hem everydeel, — truth
300 But they heelden° hir wordes nat but lees; — held
They mighten as well have holden hir pees.° — peace

This troubly° lyf hath al to longe — troublesome
endurid;° — lasted
Nat have I wist° how in my skyn to tourne.[7] — knowledge
But now myself to myself have ensurid
305 For no swich wondrynge° aftir this to mourne — wondering
As longe as my lyf shal in me sojourne.° — reside
Of swich ymagynynge I nat ne recche:° — care
Let hem dreeme as hem list° and speke and — please
drecche.[8]

This othir day a lamentacioun[9]
310 Of a woful man in a book I sy,° — saw
To whom wordes of consolacioun
Resoun yaf,° spekynge effectuelly;° — gave / effectively
And wel esid° myn herte was therby, — eased
For whan I had a whyle in the book red° — read
315 With the speeche of Resoun was I wel fed.

The hevy man, woful and angwisshous,°[10] — full of anguish
Conpleyned in this wyse, and thus seide he:

---

[1] *Out of your ... han yee* You have planed my name off your tables. These "tables" are likely wax tablets upon which names of those in favor might have been written with a stylus; such tablets could be erased by means of planing.

[2] *Syn wel ... looth is* Since pretty much every person is reluctant to converse with me.

[3] *liveree* Livery, a distinctive badge given out to a retainer, servant, or member of a company.

[4] *needith it* Need is there for.

[5] *and neither ... suspectly* And neither silently or loudly did they know me to do anything suspicious.

[6] *my felawes ... seel* My fellows of the Privy Seal.

[7] *Nat have I ... to tourne* Proverbial: I have no idea how to live with myself.

[8] *drecche* To be troubled in sleep.

[9] *This othir day a lamentacioun* Marginal glosses in Latin throughout this section suggest that the book the narrator sees is the *Synonyma* by Isidore of Seville (c. 560–636) or an epitome (an abridged version). These glosses are almost certainly written by Hoccleve. The first one begins here: "Hic est lamentacio hominis dolentis" [Latin: Here is a lamentation of a grieving man].

[10] *The hevy man ... angwisshous* Marginal gloss: "Anima mea in angustiis est, cor meum fluctuat. Ubicunque fugero, mala mea sequntur me, sicut umbra persequitur corpus, et non possum ea fugere, etc." [Latin: My soul is in dire straits, my heart is storm-tossed. Wherever I flee, my evils follow me, just as a shadow follows a body, and I cannot escape them].

"My lyf is unto me ful encombrous,°   *burdensome*
For whidir or unto what place I flee
320 My wikkidnesses evere folwen me,
As men may see the shadwe° a body sue,°   *shadow / pursue*
And in no manere I may hem eschue.°   *shun*

"Vexacioun of spirit and torment
Lakke° I right noon: I have of hem plentee.   *Lack*
325 Wondirly° bittir is my taast and sent.°   *Wonderfully / scent*
Wo be the tyme of my nativitee;°   *birth*
Unhappy man, that evere sholde it be!
O deeth, thy strook° a salve° is of swetnesse¹   *stroke / ointment*
To hem that lyven° in swich° wrecchidnesse.   *live / such*

330 "Gretter plesance° were it me to die²   *pleasure*
By many fold° than for to lyve so.   *times*
Sorwes° so many in me multiplie   *Sorrows*
That my lyf is to me a verray fo.°   *foe*
Comforted may I nat be of my wo:
335 Of my distresse see noon ende I can;
No force³ how soone I stynte° to be a man."   *cease*

Than spak Resoun: "What meeneth°   *means*
    al this fare?°⁴   *fuss*
Thogh welthe be nat freendly to thee, yit
Out of thyn herte voide° wo and care."   *empty*
340 "By what skile,° how, and by what   *power of discrimination*
    reed° and wit,"⁵   *advice*
Seide this woful man, "mighte I doon° it?"   *do*
"Wrastle,"° quod Resoun, "ageyn°   *Wrestle / against*
    hevynesses⁶

Of the world, troubles, suffrynge, and duresses.

"Beholde how many a man suffrith disese°   *disease*
345 As greet as thow and alaway° grettere,   *in every way*
And thogh it hem pynche sharply and sese,°   *seize*
Yit paciently they it suffre and bere.°   *bear*
Thynke heeron and the lesse it shal thee dere:°   *injure*
Swich souffrance° is of mannes gilt°   *suffering / guilt*
    clensynge
350 And hem enablith to joie aylastynge.°   *everlasting*

"Wo, hevynesse, and tribulacioun⁷
Commune° arn to men alle and profitable.   *Common*
Thogh grevous° be mannes temptacioun,   *grieveth*
It sleeth° man nat to hem that been   *strikes down*
    souffrable;°   *patient*
355 And to whom Goddes strook° is acceptable   *stroke*
Purveied° joie is, for God wowndith° tho⁸   *Provided / wounds*
That he ordeyned hath to blisse° go.   *bliss (i.e., heaven)*

"Gold pourgid° is, thow seest, in the   *purged*
    fourneys°⁹   *furnace*
For the fyner° and clenner it shal be.   *more refined*
360 Of thy disese the weighte and the peys¹⁰
Bere lightly, for God to preeve° thee   *prove*
Scourgid thee hath with sharp adversitee;
Nat° grucche° and seye, 'Why   *Do not / complain*
    susteene I this?'
For if thow do, thow thee takist amis.°   *amiss*

365 "But thus thow sholdest thynken° in thyn herte   *think*
And seyn: 'To thee, lord God, I have agilt;°   *guilt*
So sore I moot° for myn offenses smerte,°   *must / suffer*

---

¹ *O deeth … swetnesse* Marginal gloss: "O mors, quam dulcis es male viventibus" [Latin: O death, how sweet you are to those whose life is bad].

² *Greeter plesance … to die* Marginal gloss: "Melius est me mori quam infeliciter vivere" [Latin: It is better for me to die than to live miserably].

³ *No force* It does not matter.

⁴ *What meeneth al this fare?* Marginal gloss: "Racio: Quare tantum frangeris in adversis? Omitte tristiciam, repelle dolorem a corde" [Latin: Reason: Why are you so broken in adversity? Abandon grief, drive sorrow from the heart].

⁵ *By what … and wit* Marginal gloss: "Homo: Qualiter? quomodo? qua racione? quo consilio, ingenio?" [Man: How? in what way? by what method? by what counsel, (or) skill?].

⁶ *Wrastle … ageyn hevynesses* Marginal gloss: "Racio: Sume luctamen contra tristicias temporales. Respice similes eventus etc." [Latin: Reason: Take up the struggles against the sorrows of the

temporal world. Consider the similar fates etc.].

⁷ *Wo, hevynesse, and tribulacioun* Marginal gloss: "Dolor et tristicia communia sunt omnibus" [Latin: Sorrow and unhappiness are common to all].

⁸ *Purveied joie … wowndith* Marginal gloss: "Hic Deus vulnerat eos quos preparat ad eternam salutem" [Latin: Here God wounds those whom he is preparing for eternal salvation].

⁹ *Gold pourgid … fourneys* Marginal gloss: "Aurum dequoquitur, purgatur in fornace, ut purius fiat" [Latin: Gold is melted, purged in the furnace, so that it may become purer].

¹⁰ *peys* Weight; specifically, the full statutory weight of a coin. This meaning is significant because the issue of under-weight currency is discussed at length in the Dialogue that follows the "Complaint" in *The Series*.

As I am worthy. O lord, I am spilt,°   *destroyed*
But thow to me thy mercy graunte wilt;
370 I am ful seur° thow maist it nat denye.   *sure*
Lord, I repente and I thee mercy crye.'"[1]

Lenger° I thoghte red° have in this book   *Longer / read*
But so it shoop° that I ne mighte naght: *was destined*
He that it oghte° ageyn it to him took,   *owned*
375 Me of his haaste unwaar.° Yit have I caght   *unaware*
Sum of the doctrine° by Resoun taght   *teaching*
To the man, as above have I said,
Whereof I holde me ful wel apaid.

For evere sythen° set have I the lesse   *since*
380 By the peples ymaginacioun,
Talkynge this and that of my seeknesse,°   *sickness*
Which cam of Goddes visitacioun.
Mighte I han be fownde in probacioun°   *testing*
Nat grucchyng,° but han take it in   *complaining*
    souffrance,°   *patience or patiently*
385 Holsum and wys had be my governance.

Farwel my sowre:° I caste it to the cok![2]   *sorrow*
With pacience I hensfoorth thynke unpyke°   *unpick*
Of swich thoghtful disese and wo the lok,°   *lock*
And lete° hem out that han me maad to syke.°   *let / sigh*
390 Heeraftir our lord God may, if him lyke,
Make al myn olde affeccioun resorte,°   *return*
And in hope of that wole° I me conforte.   *will*

Thurgh Goddes just doom° and his jugement   *judgment*
And for my beste, now I take and deeme,°   *judge*
395 Yaf° that good lord me my punysshement.   *Gave*
In welthe I took of him noon heede or yeeme°   *attention*
Him for to plese and him honure and qweeme,°   *gratify*
And he me yaf a boon° on for to gnawe,[3]   *bone*
Me to correcte, and of him to have awe.

He yaf me wit and he took it away
400 Whan that he sy° that I it mis despente,°   *saw / spent*
And yaf° ageyn whan it was to his pay.   *gave*
He grauntid me my giltes to repente
And hens forward to sette myn entente
405 Unto his deitee° to do plesance   *godliness*
And t'amende my synful governance.°   *regulation*

Laude and honour and thank unto thee be,
Lord God, that salve° art to al hevynesse: *ointment*
Thank of my welthe and myn adversitee;
410 Thank of myn elde° and of my seeknesse;°   *age / sickness*
And thank be to thyn infynyt goodnesse
For thy yiftes° and benefices alle;   *gifts*
And unto thy mercy and grace I calle.

Heere endith my Conpleynte....
—1419–21

---

1   *I thee mercy crye* I cry to you (for) mercy.

2   *I caste it to the cok* Proverbial: I throw it away.

3   *a boon on for to gnawe* Proverbial: a painful experience.

THE TRAVELS OF SIR JOHN MANDEVILLE
c. 1360

The Travels of Sir John Mandeville was among the most popular books of its time: more than 275 manuscripts survive, in 10 different languages. Despite the work's popularity and influence, however, the identity of its author remains unclear, and the veracity of the entire text has been the subject of considerable debate.

The book recounts the travels of Sir John Mandeville, whom the text identifies as an English knight from St. Albans (a town on the northern outskirts of London). Mandeville claims to have left England for a great journey in 1322, traveling first to Egypt and Palestine, and then further east to India and China. The book begins with a prologue that introduces the author and invites the reader to undertake a pilgrimage to the Holy Land; the first half of the book serves as a kind of guide for potential pilgrims on the way to Jerusalem, outlining travel routes and identifying highlights along the journey. It also contains a detailed and, for its time, fairly sympathetic description of Islamic history, customs, and beliefs.

The second half of the book contains what to us seems a fantastical account of the lands of South and East Asia—a world of hybrid creatures, half-human, half animal; cannibal nations who raise children for food; waterless seas of gravel and sand which nevertheless contain fish. Such travelogues fed the medieval hunger for information about the unknown world; Mandeville's *Travels* was in fact more widely read and accepted than what we now know is the more accurate account in Marco Polo's *Description of the World* (1298). Christopher Columbus, for example, is said to have taken a copy of Mandeville's *Travels* with him on his voyages; the popularity of Mandeville's book did not begin to wane until the later sixteenth century, when reports of the newly discovered lands to the west captured European imaginations.

Mandeville's identity went largely unexamined for 500 years. In the late nineteenth century scholars began to read the work more critically, and discovered that Mandeville's account was in fact a patchwork of allusions and borrowings from other sources. These include a pilgrimage narrative by a German Dominican monk, William of Boldensele (1336), a memoir of travels in India and China dictated by a Franciscan missionary, Orderic of Pordenone, an account of the first Crusade led by Albert of Aix in the mid-twelfth century, and the anonymous *Letter of Prester John* (c. 1165). In addition to these lengthier narratives, the work was sprinkled with excerpts gleaned from other travel books, encyclopedic works, and even from Julius Caesar's description of the Britons. Study of the surviving manuscripts also made it apparent that the original work was written in France. In light of these revelations it was widely suggested that "Sir John Mandeville" had never traveled—in fact, had never existed, except as the pen name of a resident of Liege.

In the mid-twentieth century, interest in Mandeville's *Travels* has resulted in the assertion by a number of scholars that John Mandeville, author/compiler of a work of fiction rather than a travel book, actually existed. Others have pointed out that most travelers would have embellished their adventures, and like many travelers to unknown lands (Columbus himself, for instance) the author of the *Travels* might well have seen in the East what his reading had led him to expect to see. Most modern readers accept that the matter may never be resolved with any certainty, and are content to read the *Travels* as a work of literature by an unknown author.

⌘ ⌘ ⌘

from *The Travels of Sir John Mandeville*[1]

PROLOGUE

Forasmuch as the land beyond the sea, that is to say the Holy Land, that men call the Land of Promission[2] or of Behest,[3] passing all other lands, is the most worthy land, most excellent, and lady and sovereign of all other lands, and is blessed and hallowed of the precious body and blood of our Lord Jesu Christ; in the which land it liked him to take flesh and blood of the Virgin Mary, to environ that holy land with his blessed feet; and there he would of his blessedness enumber[4] him in the said blessed and glorious Virgin Mary, and become man, and work many miracles, and preach and teach the faith and the law of Christian men unto his children; and there it liked him to suffer many reprovings and scorns for us; and he that was king of heaven, of air, of earth, of sea and of all things that be contained in them would all only be clept[5] king of that land, when he said, *Rex sum Judeorum*, that is to say, "I am King of Jews"; and that land he chose before all other lands as the best and most worthy land, and the most virtuous land of all the world: for it is the heart and the midst of all the world, witnessing the philosopher, that saith thus, *Virtus rerum in medio consistit*, that is to say, "The virtue of things is in the midst";[6] and in that land he would lead his life, and suffer passion and death of Jews, for us, to buy and to deliver us from pains of hell, and from death without end; the which was ordained for us, for the sin of our forme[7]-father Adam, and for our own sins also; for as for himself, he had no evil deserved: for he thought never evil nor did evil: and he that was king of glory and of joy, might best in that place suffer death; because he chose in that land, rather than in any other, there to suffer his passion and his death. For he that will publish anything to make it openly known, he will make it to be cried and pronounced in the middle place of a town; so that the thing that is proclaimed and pronounced may evenly stretch to all parts: right so, he that was former of all the world would suffer for us at Jerusalem, that is the midst of the world; to that end and intent, that his passion and his death, that was published there, might be known evenly to all parts of the world.

See now, how dear he bought man, that he made after his own image, and how dear he again—bought us[8] for the great love that he had to us, and we never deserved it to him. For more precious chattel[9] nor greater ransom might he put for us, than his blessed body, his precious blood, and his holy life that he thralled for us;[10] and all he offered for us that never did sin.

Ah dear God! What love had he to us his subjects, when he that never trespassed, would for trespassers suffer death! Right well ought us for to love and worship, to dread and serve such a Lord; and to worship and praise such an holy land, that brought forth such fruit, through the which every man is saved, but it be his own default. Well may that land be called delectable and

---

[1]   *The Travels ... Mandeville* The translation from the Anglo-Norman French used here is the Cotton Version. See the bibliography in the website component of this anthology for further information.

[2]   *Promission* Promise.

[3]   *Behest* Promise.

[4]   *enumber* Enshroud himself in.

[5]   *clept* Called.

[6]   Cf. Psalms 74.12: "For God is my king of old, working salvation in the midst of the earth."

[7]   *forme* Earliest in time or order.

[8]   *again—bought us* Redeemed us. Jesus's blood is supposed to seal God's second covenant with humanity, the first one being made with Abraham. Cf. Genesis 17, Luke 1.73, Romans 4.13, 15.18.

[9]   *chattel* Property, goods.

[10]   *thralled for us* Enslaved for our good.

a fructuous[1] land, that was be-bled[2] and moistened with the precious blood of our Lord Jesu Christ; the which is the same land that our Lord behight[3] us in heritage. And in that land he would die, as seised,[4] to leave it to us, his children.

Wherefore every good Christian man, that is of power, and hath whereof, should pain him with all his strength for to conquer our right heritage,[5] and chase out all the misbelieving men. For we be clept Christian men, after Christ our Father. And if we be right children of Christ, we ought for to challenge the heritage that our Father left us, and do it out of heathen men's hands. But now pride, covetise,[6] and envy have so inflamed the hearts of lords of the world that they are more busy for to dis-herit their neighbours, more than for to challenge or to conquer their right heritage before-said. And the common people, that would put their bodies and their chattels to conquer our heritage, they may not do it without the lords. For a sembly[7] of people without a chieftain, or a chief lord, is as a flock of sheep without a shepherd; the which departeth and disperpleth[8] and wit[9] never whither to go. But would God, that the temporal lords and all worldly lords were at good accord, and with the common people would take this holy voyage over the sea! Then I trow[10] well that within a little time, our right heritage before-said should be reconciled and put in the hands of the right heirs of Jesu Christ.

And forasmuch as it is long time passed that there was no general passage nor voyage over the sea, and many men desire for to hear speak of the Holy Land, and have thereof great solace and comfort, I, John Mandeville, Knight, albeit I be not worthy, that was born in England, in the town of St. Albans, and passed the sea in the year of our Lord Jesu Christ, 1322, in the day of St. Michael;[11] and hitherto been long time over the sea, and have seen and gone through many diverse lands, and many provinces and kingdoms and isles and have passed throughout Turkey, Armenia the little and the great; through Tartary, Persia, Syria, Arabia, Egypt the high and the low; through Libya, Chaldea, and a great part of Ethiopia; through Amazonia, Ind[12] the less and the more, a great part; and throughout many other Isles, that be about Ind; where dwell many diverse folk, and of diverse manners and laws, and of diverse shapes of men. Of which lands and isles I shall speak more plainly hereafter; and I shall devise you of some part of things that there be, when time shall be, after it may best come to my mind; and specially for them, that will and are in purpose for to visit the Holy City of Jerusalem and the holy places that are thereabout. And I shall tell the way that they shall hold thither. For I have often times passed and ridden that way, with good company of many lords. God be thanked!

And ye shall understand that I have[13] put this book out of Latin into French, and translated it again out of French into English, that every man of my nation may understand it. But lords and knights and other noble and worthy men that con[14] Latin but little, and have been beyond the sea, know and understand if I say truth or no, and if I err in devising, for forgetting or else, that they may redress it and amend it. For things passed out of long time from a man's mind or from his sight turn soon into forgetting, because that mind of man may not comprehend or withholden,[15] for the frailty of mankind.

---

[1] *Fructuous* Fertile.

[2] *be-bled* Bled upon.

[3] *behight* Promised.

[4] *seised* In legal possession (of it).

[5] *for to conquer our right heritage* This passage refers generally to the Crusades.

[6] *covetise* Covetousness.

[7] *sembly* I.e., assembly.

[8] *disperpleth* Scatters.

[9] *wit* Knows.

[10] *trow* Believe.

[11] *the day of St. Michael* The feast day of St. Michael the Archangel, 29 September.

[12] *Tartary* In Central Asia, anywhere from modern Armenia to Mongolia; *Persia* Modern Iran; *Chaldea* Modern Iraq; *Amazonia* Mythical land somewhere in Central Asia; *Ind* India.

[13] *I have* The English translator here inserted himself into the work's transmission. This sentence implies that one person translated the text from Latin to French and then from French to English. The French original reads at this point, "I should have written this in Latin in order to be briefer, but as I understand French better, I wrote it in French."

[14] *con* Know.

[15] *withholden* Retain.

CHAPTER 7

Of the country of Egypt; of the bird Phoenix of Arabia;
of the city of Cairo; of the cunning to know balm and
to prove it; and of the garners of Joseph

Egypt is a long country, but it is straight, that is to say narrow, for they may not enlarge it toward the desert for default of water. And the country is set along upon the river of Nile, by as much as that river may serve by floods or otherwise, that when it floweth it may spread abroad through the country; so is the country large of length. For there it raineth not but little in that country, and for that cause they have no water, but if it be of that flood of that river. And forasmuch as it raineth not in that country, but the air is alway pure and clear, therefore in that country be the good astronomers, for they find there no clouds to letten[1] them. Also the city of Cairo is right great and more huge than that of Babylon the less, and it sitteth above toward the desert of Syria, a little above the river above-said.

In Egypt there be two parts: the height, that is toward Ethiopia, and the lower, that is toward Arabia. In Egypt is the land of Rameses and the land of Goshen. Egypt is a strong country, for it hath many shrewd havens because of the great rocks that be strong and dangerous to pass by. And at Egypt, toward the east, is the Red Sea, that dureth unto the city of Coston;[2] and toward the west is the country of Libya, that is a full dry land and little of fruit, for it is overmuch plenty of heat, and that land is clept Fusthe. And toward the part meridional[3] is Ethiopia. And toward the north is the desert, that dureth unto Syria, and so is the country strong on all sides. And it is well a fifteen journeys[4] of length, and more than two so much of desert, and it is but two journeys in largeness. And between Egypt and Nubia it hath well a twelve journeys of desert. And men of Nubia be Christian, but they be black as the Moors[5] for great heat of the sun.

In Egypt there be five provinces: that one is Sahythe; that other Demeseer; another Resith, that is an isle in the Nile; another Alexandria; and another the land of Damietta. That city was wont to be right strong, but it was twice won of[6] the Christian men, and therefore after that the Saracens[7] beat down the walls; and with the walls of the tower thereof, the Saracens made another city more far from the sea, and clept it the new Damietta; so that now no man dwelleth at the rather town of Damietta. At that city of Damietta is one of the havens of Egypt; and at Alexandria is that other. That is a full strong city, but there is no water to drink but if[8] it come by conduit from Nile, that entereth into their cisterns; and whoso stopped that water from them, they might not endure there. In Egypt there be but few forcelets[9] or castles, because that the country is so strong of himself.

At the deserts of Egypt was a worthy man that was an holy hermit,[10] and there met with him a monster (that is to say, a monster is a thing deformed against kind both of man or of beast or of anything else, and that is clept a monster). And this monster that met with this holy hermit was as it had been a man, that had two horns trenchant on his forehead; and he had a body like a man unto the navel, and beneath he had the body like a goat. And the hermit asked him what he was. And the monster answered him, and said he was a deadly[11] creature, such as God had formed, and dwelt in those deserts in purchasing his sustenance, and besought the hermit that he would pray God for him, the which that came from heaven for to save all mankind, and was born of a maiden and suffered passion and death (as we well know) and by whom we live and be. And yet is the head with the two horns of that monster at Alexandria for a marvel.

In Egypt is the city of Heliopolis, that is to say, the city of the Sun. In that city there is a temple, made round after the shape of the Temple of Jerusalem. The priests of that temple have all their writings, under the

---

[1] *letten* Hinder.

[2] *city of Coston* Probably referring to Kus, a city just south of Luxor.

[3] *meridional* Of or relating to the south.

[4] *journey* Day's travel.

[5] *Moors* In Mandeville's time, natives of North Africa.

[6] *of* By.

[7] *Saracens* Medieval term used to denote Muslim Arabs.

[8] *but if* Unless.

[9] *forcelets* Small forts or castles.

[10] *an holy hermit* St. Anthony.

[11] *deadly* Mortal.

Woodcut illustrations to Chapter 7, from
Anton Sorg's second Augsburg edition (1481).

date of the fowl[1] that is clept phoenix; and there is none but one in all the world. And he cometh to burn himself upon the altar of that temple at the end of five hundred year; for so long he liveth. And at the five hundred years' end, the priests array their altar honestly,[2] and put thereupon spices and sulphur vif and other things that will burn lightly; and then the bird phoenix cometh and burneth himself to ashes. And the first day next after, men find in the ashes a worm; and the second day next after, men find a bird quick[3] and perfect; and the third day next after, he flieth his way. And so there is no more birds of that kind in all the world, but it alone, and truly that is a great miracle of God. And men may well liken that bird unto God, because that there is no God but one; and also, that our Lord arose from death to life the third day. This bird men see often-time fly in those countries; and he is not mickle[4] more than an eagle. And he hath a crest of feathers upon his head more great than the peacock hath; and his neck is yellow after colour of an oriel[5] that is a stone well shining, and his beak is coloured blue as ind;[6] and his wings be of purple colour, and his tail is barred overthwart[7] with green and yellow and red. And he is a full fair bird to look upon, against the sun, for he shineth full gloriously and nobly.

Also in Egypt be gardens that have trees and herbs, the which bear fruits seven times in the year. And in that land men find many fair emeralds and enough; and therefore they be greater cheap.[8] Also when it raineth once in the summer in the land of Egypt, then is all the country full of great mires. Also at Cairo, that I spake of before, sell men commonly both men and women of other laws[9] as we do here beasts in the market. And there is a common house in that city that is all full of small furnaces, and thither bring women of the town

their eyren[10] of hens, of geese, and or ducks for to be put into those furnaces. And they that keep that house cover them with heat of horse dung, without hen, goose or duck or any other fowl. And at the end of three weeks or of a month they come again and take their chickens and flourish them and bring them forth, so that all the country is full of them. And so men do there both winter and summer.

Also in that country and in others also, men find long apples to sell, in their season, and men clepe them apples of Paradise;[11] and they be right sweet and of good savour. And though ye cut them in never so many gobbets[12] or parts, overthwart or endlong, evermore ye shall find in the midst the figure of the Holy Cross of our Lord Jesu. But they will rot within eight days, and for that cause men may not carry of those apples to no far countries; of them men find the mountance[13] of a hundred in a basket, and they have great leaves of a foot and a half of length, and they be convenably large. And men find there also the apple tree of Adam, that have a bite at one of the sides; and there be also fig trees that bear no leaves, but figs upon the small branches; and men clepe them figs of Pharaoh.

Also beside Cairo, without that city, is the field where balm groweth;[14] and it cometh out on small trees, that be none higher than to a man's breeks' girdle,[15] and they seem as wood that is of the wild vine. And in that field be seven wells that our Lord Jesu Christ made with one of his feet, when he went to play with other children. That field is not so well closed, but that men may enter at their own list; but in that season that the balm is growing, men put thereto good keeping, that no man dare be hardy to enter.

This balm groweth in no place, but only there. And though that men bring of the plants for to plant in other countries, they grow well and fair; but they bring forth no

---

[1] *date of the fowl* I.e., the priests organize their writings by the period of the incarnation of the phoenix.

[2] *honestly* Appropriately.

[3] *quick* Alive.

[4] *mickle* Much. I.e., the bird is not much larger than an eagle.

[5] *oriel* Precious stone, unidentifiable.

[6] *ind* Indigo: a blue dye.

[7] *overthwart* Across.

[8] *greater cheap* A better bargain.

[9] *laws* I.e., religions.

---

[10] *eyren* Eggs.

[11] *long apples ... apples of Paradise* Many fruits were called apples in this period; it has been suggested that Mandeville is referring to plantains, a type of banana.

[12] *gobbets* Portions.

[13] *mountance* Amount.

[14] *field where balm groweth* Probably the garden of El-Matariyeh, near Cairo.

[15] *breeks' girdle* Breeches' belt.

fructuous thing, and the leaves of balm fall not. And men cut the branches with a sharp flintstone, or with a sharp bone, when men will go to cut them; for whoso cut them with iron, it would destroy his virtue and his nature.

And the Saracens clepe the wood *Enonch-Balse*, and the fruit, the which is as cubebs,[1] they clepe *Abebissam*, and the liquor that droppeth from the branches they clepe *Guybalse*.[2] And men make always that balm to be tilled of the Christian men, or else it would not fructify; as the Saracens say themselves, for it hath been oftentime proved. Men say also that the balm groweth in Ind the more, in that desert where Alexander spake to the trees of the sun and of the moon, but I have not seen it; for I have not been so far above upward, because that there be too many perilous passages.

And wit ye well, that a man ought to take good keep for to buy balm[3] but if he can know it right well, for he may right lightly be deceived. For men sell a gum, that men clepe turpentine, instead of balm, and they put thereto a little balm for to give good odour. And some put wax in oil[4] of the wood of the fruit of balm, and say that it is balm. And some distil cloves of gilofre[5] and of spikenard[6] of Spain and of other spices, that be well smelling; and the liquor that goeth out thereof they clepe it balm, and they think that they have balm, and they have none. For the Saracens counterfeit it by subtlety of craft for to deceive the Christian men, as I have seen full many a time; and after them the merchants and the apothecaries counterfeit it eft sones,[7] and then it is less worth, and a great deal worse.

But if it like you, I shall shew how ye shall know and prove, to the end that ye shall not be deceived. First ye shall well know that the natural balm is full clear, and of citron colour and strongly smelling; and if it be thick, or red or black, it is sophisticate, that is to say,

counterfeited and made like it for deceit. And understand, that if ye will put a little balm in the palm of your hand against the sun, if it be fine and good, ye shall not suffer your hand against the heat of the sun. Also take a little balm with the point of a knife, and touch it to the fire, and if it burn it is a good sign. After take also a drop of balm, and put it into a dish, or in a cup with milk of a goat, and if it be natural balm anon it will take and beclippe[8] the milk. Or put a drop of balm in clear water in a cup of silver or in a clear basin, stir it well with the clear water; and if the balm be fine and of his own kind, the water shall never trouble; and if the balm be sophisticate, that is to say counterfeited, the water shall become anon[9] trouble; and also if the balm be fine it shall fall to the bottom of the vessel, as though it were quicksilver,[10] for the fine balm is more heavy twice than is the balm that is sophisticate and counterfeited. Now I have spoken of balm.

And now also I shall speak of another thing that is beyond Babylon, above the flood of the Nile, toward the desert between Africa and Egypt; that is to say, of the garners[11] of Joseph, that he let make for to keep the grains for the peril of the dear[12] years. And they be made of stone, full well made of masons' craft; of the which two be marvellously great and high, and the tother be not so great. And every garner hath a gate for to enter within, a little high from the earth; for the land is wasted and fallen since the garners were made. And within they be all full of serpents. And above the garners without be many scriptures of diverse languages. And some men say that they be sepultures[13] of great lords, that were sometime, but that is not true, for all the common rumour and speech is of all the people there, both far and near, that they be the garners of Joseph; and so find they in their scriptures, and in their chronicles. On the other part, if they were sepultures, they should not be void within, they should have no

---

[1] *cubebs* Peppercorns.

[2] *Enoch-Balse ... Abebissam ... Guybalse* Unidentified.

[3] *take good keep ... balm* Be careful about buying balm.

[4] *put wax in oil ...* Mistranslation from the French original where *cire*, wax, replaced *cuire*, boil. The sentence should have read: "And some boil the oil of the wood of the fruit of the balm."

[5] *gilofre* Gillyflower.

[6] *spikenard* Aromatic substance used in the creation of expensive oils, distilled from a relative of lavender.

[7] *eftsones* Often.

[8] *beclippe* Mix with; in this case, curdle.

[9] *anon* At once (or, immediately).

[10] *quicksilver* Mercury.

[11] *garners* Granaries. See Genesis 41.49. The pyramids at Giza and in other parts of Egypt were thought to have been granaries built by Joseph.

[12] *dear* Lean (i.e., "dear years" = famine).

[13] *sepultures* Crypts.

gates for to enter within; for ye may well know, that tombs and sepultures be not made of such greatness, nor of such highness; wherefore it is not to believe, that they be tombs or sepultures.

In Egypt also there be diverse languages and diverse letters, and of other manner and condition than there be in other parts. As I shall devise you, such as they be, and the names how they clepe them, to such intent, that ye may know the difference of them and of others,—Athoimis, Bimchi, Chinok, Duram, Eni, Fin, Gomor, Heket, Janny, Karacta, Luzanin, Miche, Naryn, Oldach, Pilon, Qyn, Yron, Sichen, Thola, Urmron, Yph and Zarm, Thoit.[1]...

CHAPTER 15

Of the customs of Saracens, and of their law. And how the Soldan[2] reasoned me, author of this book; and of the beginning of Mohammet.[3]

Now, because that I have spoken of Saracens and of their country—now, if ye will know a part of their law and of their belief, I shall tell you after what their book that is clept *Alkaron*[4] telleth. And some men clepe that book *Meshaf.* And some men clepe it *Harme*, after the diverse languages of the country. The which book Mohammet took them. In the which book, among other things, is written, as I have often-time seen and read, that the good shall go to paradise, and the evil to hell; and that believe all Saracens. And if a man ask them what paradise they mean, they say, to paradise that is a place of delights where men shall find all manner of fruits in all seasons, and rivers running of milk and honey, and of wine and of sweet water; and that they shall have fair houses and noble, every man after his desert, made of precious stones and of gold and of silver; and that every man shall have four score wives all

maidens, and he shall have ado every day with them, and yet he shall find them always maidens.

Also they believe and speak gladly of the Virgin Mary and of the Incarnation. And they say that Mary was taught of the angel; and that Gabriel said to her, that she was for-chosen from the beginning of the world and that he shewed to her the Incarnation of Jesu Christ and that she conceived and bare child maiden; and that witnesseth their book.

And they say also that Jesu Christ spake as soon as he was born; and that he was an holy prophet and a true in word and deed, and meek and piteous and rightful and without any vice.

And they say also that when the angel shewed the Incarnation of Christ unto Mary, she was young and had great dread. For there was then an enchanter in the country that dealt with witchcraft, that men clept Taknia, that by his enchantments could make him in likeness of an angel, and went often-times and lay with maidens. And therefore Mary dreaded lest it had been Taknia, that came for to deceive the maidens. And therefore she conjured the angel, that he should tell her if it were he or no. And the angel answered and said that she should have no dread of him, for he was very[5] messenger of Jesu Christ. Also their book saith that when that she had childed under a palm tree she had great shame that she had a child; and she greet[6] and said that she would that she had been dead. And anon the child spake to her and comforted her, and said, "Mother, dismay thee nought, for God hath hid in thee his privities for the salvation of the world." And in other many places saith their *Alkaron* that Jesu Christ spake as soon as he was born. And that book saith also that Jesu was sent from God Almighty for to be mirror and example and token to all men.

And the *Alkaron* saith also of the day of doom[7] how God shall come to doom all manner of folk. And the good he shall draw on his side and put them into bliss, and the wicked he shall condemn to the pains of hell. And among all prophets Jesu was the most excellent and the most worthy next God, and that he made the

---

[1] *Athomis, Bimchi...Thoit*   Most manuscript copies of *Mandeville's Travels* include five alphabets: Greek, Egyptian, Hebrew, Saracen and Persian. None of these alphabets genuinely correspond to the languages they purport to represent. Here, the so-called Egyptian alphabet is corrupted past all recognition.

[2] *Soldan*   Sultan.

[3] *Mohammet*   Mohammed, revered in Islam as the final prophet of God.

[4] *Alkoran*   The Koran (al-Quran), the Holy Book of Islam.

[5] *very*   True.

[6] *greet*   Cried.

[7] *doom*   Judgment.

Woodcut illustrations to Chapter 15, from Anton Sorg's second Augsburg edition (1481).

gospels in the which is good doctrine and healthful, full of clarity and soothfastness[1] and true preaching to them that believe in God. And that he was a very prophet and more than a prophet, and lived without sin, and gave sight to the blind, and healed the lepers, and raised dead men, and styed[2] to heaven.

And when they may hold the Book of the Gospels of our Lord written, and namely *Missus est angelus Gabriel*,[3] that gospel they say, those that be lettered, oftentimes in their orisons, and they kiss it and worship it with great devotion.

They fast an whole month in the year and eat nought but by night. And they keep them from their wives all that month. But the sick men be not constrained to that fast.

Also this book speaketh of Jews and saith that they be cursed; for they would not believe that Jesu Christ was come of God. And that they lied falsely on Mary and on her son Jesu Christ, saying that they had crucified Jesu the son of Mary; for he was never crucified, as they say, but that God made him to sty up to him without death and without annoy. But he transfigured his likeness into Judas Iscariot, and him crucified the Jews, and weened[4] that it had been Jesus. But Jesus styed to heavens all quick. And therefore they say, that the Christian men err and have no good knowledge of this, and that they believe folily[5] and falsely that Jesu Christ was crucified.[6] And they say yet, that and he had been crucified, that God had done against his righteousness for to suffer Jesu Christ, that was innocent, to be put upon the cross without guilt. And in this article they say that we fail and that the great righteousness of God might not suffer so great a wrong: and in this faileth their faith. For they knowledge well, that the works of Jesu Christ be good, and his words and

his deeds and his doctrine by his gospels were true, and his miracles also true; and the blessed Virgin Mary is good, and holy maiden before and after the birth of Jesu Christ; and that all those that believe perfectly in God shall be saved. And because that they go so nigh our faith, they be lightly[7] converted to Christian law when men preach them and shew them distinctly the law of Jesu Christ, and when they tell them of the prophecies.

And also they say, that they know well by the prophecies that the law of Mahomet shall fail, as the law of the Jews did; and that the law of Christian people shall last to the day of doom. And if any man ask them what is their belief, they answer thus, and in this form: "We believe God, former of heaven and of earth, and of all other things that he made. And without him is nothing made. And we believe of the day of doom, and that every man shall have his merit, after[8] he hath deserved. And, we believe it for sooth, all that God hath said by the mouths of his prophets."

Also Mahomet commanded in his *Alkaron* that every man should have two wives, or three or four; but now they take unto nine, and of lemans[9] as many as he may sustain.[10] And if any of their wives misbear[11] them against their husband, he may cast her out of his house, and depart from her and take another; but he shall depart with her his goods.

Also, when men speak to them of the Father and of the Son and of the Holy Ghost, they say, that they be three persons, but not one God; for their *Alkaron* speaketh not of the Trinity. But they say well, that God hath speech, and else were he dumb. And God hath also a spirit they know well, for else[12] they say, he were not alive. And when men speak to them of the Incarnation, how that by the word of the angel God sent his wisdom in to earth and enumbred[13] him in the Virgin Mary, and by the word of God shall the dead be raised at the day of doom, they say, that it is sooth and that the word of

---

[1] *soothfastness* Truthfulness.

[2] *styed* Ascended, rose.

[3] *Missus est angelus Gabriel* Latin: the Angel Gabriel was sent. See Luke 1.26: "And in the sixth month the angel Gabriel was sent from God unto a city of Galilee, named Nazareth."

[4] *weened* Believed.

[5] *folily* Foolishly, madly.

[6] *Christian men err ... crucified* This is what Christians call the heresy of Docetism, the belief that Christ only appeared or seemed to be a man, rather than being both God and human at once.

---

[7] *lightly* Easily.

[8] *after* According to what.

[9] *lemans* Lovers or mistresses.

[10] *sustain* Support.

[11] *misbear* Misbehave.

[12] *else* Otherwise.

[13] *enumbred* Concealed. Cf. Luke 1035.

God hath great strength. And they say that whoso knew not the word of God he should not know God. And they say also that Jesu Christ is the word of God; and so saith their *Alkaron*, where it saith that the angel spake to Mary and said: "Mary, God shall preach thee the gospel by the word of his mouth and his name shall be clept[1] Jesu Christ."

And they say also that Abraham was friend to God, and that Moses was familiar speaker with God, and Jesu Christ was the word and the spirit of God, and that Mohammet was right messenger of God. And they say that of these four, Jesu was the most worthy and the most excellent and the most great. So that they have many good articles of our faith, albeit that they have no perfect law and faith as Christian men have; and therefore be they lightly converted, and namely those that understand the scriptures and the prophecies. For they have the gospels and the prophecies and the Bible written in their language; wherefore they ken[2] much of holy writ, but they understand it not but after the letter. And so do the Jews, for they understand not the letter ghostly,[3] but bodily; and therefore be they reproved of the wise, that ghostly understand it. And therefore saith Saint Paul: *Litera occidit; Spiritus autem vivificat.*[4] Also the Saracens say that the Jews be cursed, for they have befouled the law that God sent them by Moses; and the Christian be cursed also, as they say, for they keep not the commandments and the precepts of the gospel that Jesu Christ taught them.

And therefore I shall tell you what the Soldan told me upon a day in his chamber. He let void out[5] of his chamber all manner of men, lords and others, for he would speak with me in counsel.[6] And there he asked me how the Christian men governed them in our country. And I said him, "Right well, thanked be God!"

And he said me, "Truly nay! For ye Christian men reck right nought,[7] how untruly to serve God! Ye should give ensample[8] to the lewd[9] people for to do well, and ye give them ensample to do evil. For the commons, upon festival days, when they should go to church to serve God, then go they to taverns, and be there in gluttony all the day and all night, and eat and drink as beasts that have no reason, and wit[10] not when they have enough. And also the Christian men enforce themselves[11] in all manners that they may, for to fight and for to deceive that one that other. And therewithal[12] they be so proud that they know not how to be clothed; now long, now short, now strait, now large, now sworded, now daggered, and in all manner guises.[13] They should be simple, meek and true, and full of alms-deeds, as Jesu was, in whom they trow;[14] but they be all the contrary, and ever inclined to the evil, and to do evil. And they be so covetous, that, for a little silver, they sell their daughters, their sisters, and their own wives to put them to lechery. And one withdraweth the wife of another, and none of them holdeth faith to another; but they befoul their law that Jesu Christ betook[15] them to keep for their salvation. And thus, for their sins, have they lost all this land that we hold. For their sins, their God hath taken them into our hands, not only by strength of ourself, but for their sins. For we know well, in very sooth,[16] that when ye serve God, God will help you; and when he is with you, no man may be against you. And that know we well by our prophecies, that Christian men shall win again this land out of our hands, when they serve God more devoutly; but as long as they be of foul and of unclean living (as they be now) we have no dread of them in no kind, for their God will not help

---

[1] *clept* Called.

[2] *ken* Know.

[3] *ghostly* Spiritually.

[4] *Litera occidit … vivificat* Latin: the letter kills, but the spirit gives life. See 2 Corinthians 3.6.

[5] *let void out* Sent away.

[6] *in counsel* Privately.

[7] *reck right nought* Do not care at all.

[8] *ensample* Example.

[9] *lewd* Unlearned, common.

[10] *wit* Know.

[11] *enforce themselves* Strive.

[12] *therewithal* Moreover.

[13] *all manner guises* All kinds of ways.

[14] *trow* Believe.

[15] *betook* Gave.

[16] *sooth* Truth.

them in no wise."[1]

And then I asked him, how he knew the state of Christian men. And he answered me, that he knew all the state of all courts of Christian kings and princes and the state of the commons also by his messengers that he sent to all lands, in manner as[2] they were merchants of precious stones, of cloths of gold and of other things, for to know the manner of every country amongst Christian men. And then he let clepe in[3] all the lords that he made void first out of his chamber, and there he shewed me four that were great lords in the country, that told me of my country and of many other Christian countries, as well as they had been of the same country; and they spake French right well, and the Soldan also; whereof I had great marvel.

Alas! that it is great slander to our faith and to our law, when folk that be without law shall reprove us and undernim[4] us of our sins, and they that should be converted to Christ and to the law of Jesu by our good ensamples and by our acceptable life to God, and so converted to the law of Jesu Christ, be, through our wickedness and evil living, far from us and strangers from the holy and very belief, shall thus appeal[5] us and hold us for wicked livers and cursed. And truly they say sooth, for the Saracens be good and faithful; for they keep entirely the commandment of the holy book *Alkaron* that God sent them by his messenger Mahomet, to the which, as they say, Saint Gabriel the angel oftentime told the will of God.

And ye shall understand that Mahomet was born in Arabia, that was first a poor knave that kept camels, that went with merchants for merchandise. And so befell that he went with the merchants into Egypt; and they were then Christian in those parts. And at the deserts of Arabia, he went into a chapel where a hermit dwelt. And when he entered into the chapel that was but a little and a low thing and had but a little door and a low, then the entry began to wax[6] so great, and so large and so high, as

though it had been of a great minster[7] or the gate of a palace. And this was the first miracle, the Saracens say, that Mahomet did in his youth.

After began he for to wax wise and rich. And he was a great astronomer. And after, he was governor and prince of the land of Corodane;[8] and he governed it full wisely, in such manner that when the prince was dead, he took the lady to wife that hight Gadrige.[9] And Mahomet fell often in the great sickness that men call the falling evil;[10] wherefore the lady was full sorry that ever she took him to husband. But Mahomet made her to believe that all times when he fell so, Gabriel the angel came for to speak with him, and for the great light and brightness of the angel he might not sustain him from falling; and therefore the Saracens say that Gabriel came often to speak with him.

This Mahomet reigned in Arabia, the year of our Lord Jesu Christ 610, and was of the generation of Ishmael that was Abraham's son, that he gat upon[11] Hagar his chamberer. And therefore there be Saracens that be clept Ishmaelites; and some Hagarenes, of Hagar. And the other properly be clept Saracens, of Sarah. And some be clept Moabites and some Ammonites, for the two sons of Lot, Moab and Ammon,[12] that he begat on his daughters that were afterward great earthly princes.

And also Mahomet loved well a good hermit that dwelled in the deserts a mile from Mount Sinai, in the way that men go from Arabia toward Chaldea and toward Ind, one day's journey from the sea, where the merchants of Venice come often for merchandise. And so often went Mahomet to this hermit that all his men were wroth; for he would gladly hear this hermit preach and make his men wake all night. And therefore his men thought to put the hermit to death. And so it befell upon a night, that Mahomet was drunken of good wine,

---

[1] *wise* Way.

[2] *in manner as* Disguised as though.

[3] *let clepe in* Called back in.

[4] *undernim* Reprove.

[5] *appeal* Accuse.

[6] *wax* Grow.

[7] *minster* Large church or cathedral.

[8] *governor and prince ... Corodane* Mistranslation from the French original, "governour de la terre al prince de Corodane": governor of the land of the prince of Corodane. This land is called Khorsan in Crusade chronicles.

[9] *hight Gadrige* Was named Khadidjah.

[10] *falling evil* Possibly epilepsy.

[11] *gat upon* Fathered by.

[12] *Hagar ... Moat and Ammon* See Genesis 16 and 19.37–38.

and he fell on sleep. And his men took Mahomet's sword out of his sheath, whiles he slept, and therewith they slew this hermit, and put his sword all bloody in his sheath again. And at morrow, when he found the hermit dead, he was full sorry and wroth,[1] and would have done his men to death. But they all, with one accord, said that he himself had slain him, when he was drunken, and shewed him his sword all bloody. And he trowed that they had said sooth. And then he cursed the wine and all those that drink it. And therefore Saracens that be devout drink never no wine. But some drink it privily; for if they drunk it openly, they should be reproved. But they drink good beverage and sweet and nourishing that is made of gallamelle[2] and that is that men make sugar of, that is of right good savour, and it is good for the breast.

Also it befalleth sometimes that Christian men become Saracens, either for poverty or for simpleness,[3] or else for their own wickedness. And therefore the archflamen or the flamen,[4] as our archbishop or bishop, when he receiveth them saith thus: *La ellec olla Sila, Machomete rores Alla*; that is to say, "There is no God but one, and Mahomet his messenger."

Now I have told you a part of their law and of their customs, I shall say you of their letters that they have, with their names and the manner of their figures what they be: Almoy, Bethath, Cathi, Ephoti, Delphoi, Fothi, Garothi, Hechum, Iotty, Kaythi, Lothum, Malach, Nabaloth, Orthi, Chesiri, Zoch, Ruth, Holath, Routhi, Salathi, Thatimus, Yrthom, Azazoth, Arrocchi, Zotipyn, Ichetus. And these be the names of their a. b. c. Now shall ye know the figures.[5] … And four letters they have more than other for diversity of their language and speech, forasmuch as[6] they speak in their throats; and we in England have in our language and speech two letters more than they have in their a. b. c.; and that is þ and ȝ, which be clept thorn and yogh.

CHAPTER 20

Of the evil customs used in the isle of Lamary.[7] And how the earth and the sea be of round form and shape, by proof of the star that is clept Antarctic, that is fixed in the south

From that country[8] go men by the sea ocean, and by many divers isles and by many countries that were too long for to tell of. And a fifty-two journeys[9] from this land that I have spoken of, there is another land, that is full great, that men clepe Lamary. In that land is full great heat. And the custom there is such that men and women go all naked. And they scorn when they see any strange folk going clothed. And they say that God made Adam and Eve all naked, and that no man should shame him to shew him such as God made him, for nothing is foul that is of kindly nature.[10] And they say that they that be clothed be folk of another world, or they be folk that trow not in God. And they say that they believe in God that formed the world, and that made Adam and Eve and all other things. And they wed there no wives, for all the women there be common and they forsake[11] no man. And they say they sin if they refuse any man; and so God commanded to Adam and Eve and to all that come of him, when he said, *Crescite Et Multiplicamini Et Replete Terram*.[12] And therefore may no man in that country say, This is my wife; and no woman may say, This my husband. And when they have children, they may give them to what man they will[13] that hath companied[14] with them. And also all the land is common; for all that a man holdeth one year, another man hath it another year; and every man taketh what part that him liketh. And also all the goods of the land

---

[1] *sorry and wroth* Upset and angry.

[2] *gallamelle* Sugar cane.

[3] *simpleness* Foolishness or lack of intelligence.

[4] *flamen* Priest of any non-Christian religion.

[5] *figures* Numerals.

[6] *forasmuch as* Because.

[7] *Lamary* One of the kingdoms of the isle of Sumatra, near Aceh.

[8] *that country* The text refers to a previous chapter, on India and Southeast Asia.

[9] *journeys* Days' travel.

[10] *of kindly nature* Natural.

[11] *forsake* Reject.

[12] *Crescite et multiplicamini … terram* Latin. Cf. Genesis 9.7. "And you, be ye fruitful, and multiply; bring forth abundantly in the earth, and multiply therein."

[13] *what man they will* Whatever man they like.

[14] *companied* Had intercourse.

Woodcut illustrations to Chapter 20, from Anton Sorg's
second Augsburg edition (1481).

be common, corns[1] and all other things: for nothing there is kept in close, and nothing there is under lock, and every man there taketh what he will without any contradiction, and as rich is one man there as is another.

But in that country there is a cursed custom, for they eat more gladly man's flesh than any other flesh; and yet is that country abundant of flesh, of fish, of corns, of gold and silver, and of all other goods. Thither go merchants and bring with them children to sell to them of the country, and they buy them. And if they be fat they eat them anon. And if they be lean they feed them till they be fat, and then they eat them. And they say that it is the best flesh and the sweetest of all the world.

In that land, nor in many other beyond that, no man may see the Star Transmontane, that is clept the Star of the Sea, that is unmovable and that is toward the north, that we clepe the Lode-star.[2] But men see another star, the contrary to him, that is toward the south, that is clept Antarctic.[3] And right as the ship-men take their advice[4] here and govern them by the Lode-star, right so do ship-men beyond those parts by the star of the south, the which star appeareth not to us. And this star that is toward the north, that we clepe the Lode-star, appeareth not to them. For which cause men may well perceive, that the land and the sea be of round shape and form; for the part of the firmament sheweth in one country that sheweth not in another country. And men may well prove by experience and subtle compassment[5] of wit, that if a man found passages by ships that would go to search the world, men might go by ship all about the world and above and beneath.

The which thing I prove thus after that I have seen.[6] For I have been toward the parts of Brabant, and beholden the Astrolabe[7] that the star that is clept the

Transmontane is fifty-three degrees high;[8] and more further in Almayne and Bohemia it hath fifty-eight degrees; and more further toward the parts septentrional[9] it is sixty-two degrees of height and certain minutes; for I myself have measured it by the Astrolabe. Now shall ye know, that against the Transmontane is the t'other star that is clept Antarctic, as I have said before. And those two stars move never, and by them turneth all the firmament right as doth a wheel that turneth by his axle-tree. So that those stars bear the firmament in two equal parts, so that it hath as much above as it hath beneath. After this, I have gone toward the parts meridional, that is, toward the south, and I have found that in Libya men see first the star Antarctic. And so far I have gone more further in those countries, that I have found that star more high; so that toward the High Libya it is eighteen degrees of height and certain minutes (of the which sixty minutes make a degree). After going by sea and by land toward this country of that I have spoken, and to other isles and lands beyond that country, I have found the Star Antarctic of thirty-three degrees of height and more minutes. And if I had had company and shipping for to go more beyond, I trow well, in certain, that we should have seen all the roundness of the firmament all about. For, as I have said to you before, the half of the firmament is between those two stars, the which halvendel[10] I have seen. And of the tother halvendel I have seen, toward the north under the Transmontane, sixty-two degrees and ten minutes, and toward the part meridional I have seen under the Antarctic, thirty-three degrees and sixteen minutes. And then, the halvendel of the firmament in all holdeth not but nine score degrees. And of those nine score, I have seen sixty-two on that one part and thirty-three on that other part; that be, ninety-five degrees and nigh the halvendel of a degree. And so there ne faileth but that I have seen all the

---

[1] *corns* Grains.

[2] *Lode-star* Polaris, the North Star.

[3] *Antarctic* The star, obviously, does not exist, but acts as evidence for the assertion that the Earth is a sphere.

[4] *advice* Bearings.

[5] *compassment* Contrivance.

[6] *The which thing … seen* This (i.e., that the world is round) I prove from my own experience.

[7] *Astrolabe* Instrument used for practical astronomical purposes such as navigation.

---

[8] *degrees high* The part of the dome of the sky immediately above the observer's head is ninety degrees, descending to zero as you approach the horizon. A star like Polaris, which does not appear to move much in the night sky, can be used to determine the latitude at which a person is standing. In this passage, Brabant (the Netherlands) is at 53° North Latitude, and so on.

[9] *septentrional* Northern.

[10] *halvendel* A half part.

firmament, save four score and four degrees and the halvendel of a degree, and that is not the fourth part of the firmament; for the fourth part of the roundness of the firmament holds four score and ten degrees, so there faileth but five degrees and an half of the fourth part. And also I have seen the three parts of all the roundness of the firmament and more yet five degrees and a half. By the which I say you certainly that men may environ[1] all the earth of all the world, as well under as above, and turn again to his country, that had company and shipping and conduct. And always he should find men, lands and isles, as well as in this country. For ye wit well, that they that be toward the Antarctic, they be straight, feet against feet, of them that dwell under the Transmontane; also well as we and they that dwell under us be feet against feet. For all the parts of sea and of land have their opposites, habitable trepassable,[2] and they of this half and beyond half.

And wit well, that, after that that I may perceive and comprehend, the lands of Prester John,[3] Emperor of Ind, be under us. For in going from Scotland or from England toward Jerusalem men go upward always. For our land is in the low part of the earth toward the west, and the land of Prester John is in the low part of the earth toward the east. And they have there the day when we have the night; and also, high[4] to the contrary, they have the night when we have the day. For the earth and the sea be of round form and shape, as I have said before; and that that men go upward to one coast, men go downward to another coast.

Also ye have heard me say that Jerusalem is in the midst of the world. And that may men prove, and shew there by a spear, that is pight[5] into the earth, upon the hour of midday, when it is equinox, that sheweth no shadow on no side. And that it should be in the midst of the world, David witnesseth it in the Psalter,[6] where he saith, *Deus operatus est salutem in medio terrae*.[7] Then they that part from those parts of the west for to go toward Jerusalem, as many journeys as they go upward for to go thither, in as many journeys may they go from Jerusalem unto other confines of the superficiality of the earth beyond. And when men go beyond those journeys toward Ind and to the foreign isles, all is environing the roundness of the earth and of the sea under our countries on this half.

And therefore hath it befallen many times of one thing that I have heard counted[8] when I was young, how a worthy man departed some-time from our countries for to go search the world. And so he passed Ind and the isles beyond Ind, where be more than 5000 isles. And so long he went by sea and land, and so environed the world by many seasons, that he found an isle where he heard speak his own language, calling on oxen in the plough such words as men speak to beasts in his own country, whereof he had great marvel, for he knew not how it might be. But I say that he had gone so long by land and by sea, that he had environed all the earth; that he was come again environing, that is to say, going about, unto his own marches,[9] and if he would have passed further, till he had found his country and his own knowledge. But he turned again from thence, from whence he was come from. And so he lost much painful labour, as himself said a great while after that he was come home. For it befell after, that he went into Norway. And there tempest of the sea took him, and he arrived in an isle. And, when he was in that isle, he knew well that it was the isle where he had heard speak his own language before and the calling of oxen at the plough; and that was possible thing.

But how it seemeth to simple men unlearned, that men may not go under the earth, and also that men should fall toward the heaven from under. But that may not be, upon less than we may fall toward heaven from the earth where we be. For from what part of the earth that men dwell, either above or beneath, it seemeth always to them that dwell that they go more right than any other folk. And right as it seemeth to us that they be

---

[1] *environ* Circle around, circumnavigate.

[2] *trepassable* That may be passed through.

[3] *Prester John* Legendary priest-king from the East who headed a mighty army.

[4] *high* Exactly.

[5] *pight* Stuck.

[6] *Psalter* (Book of) Psalms.

[7] *Deus operatus ... Terrae* Latin: God has worked salvation in the midst of the earth. Cf. Psalms 73.12 (Vulgate).

[8] *counted* Told, recounted.

[9] *marches* Borders.

under us, right so it seemeth to them that we be under them. For if a man might fall from the earth unto the firmament, by greater reason the earth and the sea that be so great and so heavy should fall to the firmament; but that may not be, and therefore saith our Lord God, *Non timeas me, qui suspendi terram ex nihilo?*[1]

And albeit that it be possible thing that men may so environ all the world, natheles,[2] of a thousand persons, one might not happen to return into his country. For, for the greatness of the earth and of the sea, men may go by a thousand and a thousand other ways, that[3] no man could ready him perfectly toward the parts that he came from, but if it were by adventure and hap,[4] or by the grace of God. For the earth is full large and full great, and holds in roundness and about environ, by above and by beneath, 20,425 miles,[5] after the opinion of old wise astronomers; and their sayings I reprove nought. But after my little wit[6] it seemeth me, saving their reverence, that it is more.

And for to have better understanding I say thus. Be there[7] imagined a figure that hath a great compass. And, about the point of the great compass that is clept the centre, be made another little compass. Then after, be the great compass devised by lines in many parts, and that all the lines meet at the centre. So that in as many parts as the great compass shall be departed, in as many shall be departed the little, that is about the centre, albeit that the spaces be less. Now then, be the great compass represented for the firmament, and the little compass represented for the earth. Now then, the firmament is devised by astronomers in twelve signs, and every sign is devised in thirty degrees; that is, 360 degrees that the firmament hath above. Also, be the earth devised in as many parts as the firmament, and let every part answer to a degree of the firmament. And wit

it well that, after[8] the authors of astronomy, 700 furlongs of earth answer to a degree of the firmament, and those be eighty-seven miles and four furlongs. Now be that here multiplied by 360 sithes,[9] and then they be 31,500 miles every of eight furlongs, after miles of our country. So much hath the earth in roundness and of height environ, after mine opinion and mine understanding.

And ye shall understand that after the opinion of old wise philosophers and astronomers, our country nor Ireland nor Wales nor Scotland nor Norway nor the other isles coasting to them be not in the superficiality counted above the earth, as it sheweth by all the books of astronomy. For the superficiality of the earth is parted in seven parts for the seven planets, and those parts be clept climates. And our parts be not of the seven climates, for they be descending toward the west drawing towards the roundness of the world. And also these isles of Ind which be even against us be not reckoned in the climates. For they be against us that be in the low country. And the seven climates stretch them environing the world.

CHAPTER 29

Of the countries and isles that be beyond the land of Cathay;[10] *and of the fruits there; and of twenty-two kings enclosed within the mountains*

Now shall I say you, suingly,[11] of countries and isles that be beyond the countries that I have spoken of.

Wherefore I say you, in passing by the land of Cathay toward the high Ind and toward Bacharia,[12] men pass by a kingdom that men clepe Caldilhe,[13] that is a full fair country.

And there groweth a manner of fruit, as though it were gourds. And when they be ripe, men cut them a-two, and men find within a little beast, in flesh, in bone,

---

[1] *Non timeas me … nihilo* Latin: Do not fear me—who have suspended the earth from the void (cf. Psalms 104.5).

[2] *natheles* Nonetheless.

[3] *that* So that.

[4] *adventure and hap* Chance and fortune.

[5] *20,425 miles* In actuality, the earth is approximately 24,900 miles (40,000 km) in circumference.

[6] *after my little wit* According to my limited knowledge.

[7] *Be there* Let there be.

[8] *after* According to.

[9] *sithes* Times.

[10] *Cathay* I.e., China.

[11] *suingly* In due order.

[12] *Bacharia* Bactria, between the Hindu Kush and the Oxus.

[13] *Caldilhe* Thought to be a Tartar kingdom on the Volga.

and blood, as though it were a little lamb without wool. And men eat both the fruit and the beast. And that is a great marvel. Of that fruit I have eaten, although it were wonderful, but that I know well that God is marvellous in his works. And natheles I told them of as great a marvel to them, that is amongst us, and that was of the Bernakes.[1] For I told them that in our country were trees that bear a fruit that become birds flying, and those that fell in the water live, and they that fall on the earth die anon, and they be right good to man's meat. And hereof had they as great marvel, that some of them trowed it were an impossible thing to be.

In that country be long apples of good savour, whereof be more than an hundred in a cluster, and as many in another; and they have great long leaves and large, of two foot long[2] or more. And in that country, and in other countries thereabout, grow many trees that bear clove-gylofres and nutmegs, and great nuts of Ind, and of Canell[3] and of many other spices. And there be vines that bear so great grapes that a strong man should have enough to do for to bear one cluster with all the grapes.

In that same region be the mountains of Caspian that men clepe Uber[4] in the country. Between those mountains the Jews of ten lineages be enclosed, that men clepe Goth and Magoth,[5] and they may not go out on no side. There were enclosed twenty-two kings with their people, that dwelled between the mountains of Scythia. There King Alexander chased them between those mountains, and there he thought for to enclose them through work of his men. But when he saw that he might not do it, nor bring it to an end, he prayed to God of nature that he would perform that that he had begun. And all were it so, that he was a paynim[6] and not worthy to be heard, yet God of his grace closed the mountains together, so that they dwell there all fast

locked and enclosed with high mountains all about, save only on one side, and on that side is the sea of Caspian.[7]

Now may some men ask, since that the sea is on that one side, wherefore go they not out on the sea side, for to go where that them liketh?[8]

But to this question, I shall answer: that sea of Caspian goeth out by land under the mountains, and runneth by the desert at one side of the country, and after it stretcheth unto the ends of Persia, and although it be clept a sea, it is no sea, it toucheth to none other sea, but it is a lake, the greatest of the world; and though they would put them into that sea, they wist[9] never where that they should arrive; and also they can no language but only their own, that no man knoweth but they; and therefore may they not go out.

And also ye shall understand, that the Jews have no proper land of their own for to dwell in, in all the world, but only that land between the mountains. And yet they yield tribute for that land to the Queen of Amazonia, the which that maketh them to be kept in close full diligently, that they shall not go out on no side but by the coast of their land; for their land marcheth to[10] those mountains.

And often it hath befallen that some of the Jews have gone up the mountains and avaled[11] down to the valleys. But great number of folk may not do so, for the mountains be so high and so straight up that they must abide there, maugre[12] their might. For they may not go out, but by a little issue that was made by strength of men, and it lasteth well a four great mile.

And after is there yet a land all desert, where men may find no water, neither for digging nor for none other thing. Wherefore men may not dwell in that place, so is it full of dragons, of serpents and of other venomous beasts, that no man dare not pass, but if it be strong winter. And that strait[13] passage men clepe in that country Clyron. And that is the passage that the Queen

---

[1] *Bernakes* Bartlathes or Bernacae were mythical sea birds, supposedly related to barnacles, who began their life growing on the wool of sheep.

[2] *long* Mistranslation from the French original. The word should be "wide."

[3] *Canell* Cinnamon.

[4] *Uber* From Latin: *ubera aquilonis*, the breasts of the north wind.

[5] *Goth and Magoth* After devils Gog and Magog.

[6] *all were ... paynim* Although it was the case that he was a pagan.

[7] *Caspian* An inland sea of Central Asia.

[8] *where that them liketh* Where they please.

[9] *wist* Know.

[10] *marcheth to* Borders on.

[11] *avaled* Descended.

[12] *maugre* In spite of.

[13] *strait* Narrow.

of Amazonia maketh to be kept. And though it happen some of them by fortune to go out, they can no manner of language but Hebrew, so that they cannot speak to the people.

And yet, natheles, men say they shall go out in the time of anti-Christ, and that they shall make great slaughter of Christian men. And therefore all the Jews that dwell in all lands learn always to speak Hebrew, in hope that when the other Jews shall go out, that they may understand their speech, and to lead them into Christendom for to destroy the Christian people. For the Jews say that they know well by their prophecies that they of Caspia shall go out, and spread throughout all the world, and that the Christian men shall be under their subjection, as long as they have been in subjection of them.

And if that you will wit how that they shall find their way, after that I have heard say I shall tell you.

In the time of anti-Christ a fox shall make there his train,[1] and mine[2] an hole where King Alexander let make the gates;[3] and so long he shall mine and pierce the earth, till that he shall pass through towards that folk. And when they see the fox, they shall have great marvel of him, because that they saw never such a beast. For of all other beasts they have enclosed amongst them, save only[4] the fox. And then they shall chase him and pursue him so strait, till that he come to the same place that he came from. And then they shall dig and mine so strongly till that they find the gates that King Alexander let make of great stones, and passing huge, well cemented and made strong for the mastery. And those gates they shall break, and so go out by finding of that issue.

From that land go men toward the land of Bacharia, where be full evil folk and full cruel. In that land be trees that bear wool,[5] as though it were of sheep, whereof men make clothes and all things that may be made of wool.

In that country be many hippotaynes[6] that dwell sometime in the water and sometime on the land. And they be half man and half horse, as I have said before. And they eat men when they may take them.

And there be rivers of waters that be full bitter, three sithes[7] more than is the water of the sea.

In that country be many griffins, more plenty than in any other country. Some men say that they have the body upward as an eagle and beneath as a lion; and truly they say sooth, that they be of that shape. But one griffin hath the body more great and is more strong than eight lions, of such lions as be on this half, and more great and stronger than an hundred eagles such as we have amongst us. For one griffin there will bear, flying to his nest, a great horse, if he may find him at the point, or two oxen yoked together as they go at the plough. For he hath his talons so long and so large and great upon his feet, as though they were horns of great oxen or of bugles or of kine,[8] so that men make cups of them to drink of. And of their ribs and of the pens[9] of their wings, men make bows, full strong, to shoot with arrows and quarrels.[10]

From thence go men by many journeys through the land of Prester John, the great Emperor of Ind. And men clepe his realm the isle of Pentexoire.[11]

---

[1] *train* Burrow (?).

[2] *mine* Dig.

[3] *let make the gates* Had the gates built.

[4] *save only* Except.

[5] *trees that bear wool* Cotton trees.

[6] *hippotaynes* Hippopotami, possibly here confused with the hippocentaur.

[7] *sithes* Times.

[8] *kine* Cattle.

[9] *pens* Feathers.

[10] *quarrels* Crossbow bolts.

[11] *Pentexoire* This name has never been satisfactorily explained.

JULIAN OF NORWICH
c. 1342 – c. 1416

We know very little of Julian of Norwich, one of the great medieval English mystics. It is possible that she was trained as Benedictine nun, and some have speculated that she may have received some form of education at Carrow Priory, the school attached to the Cathedral in Norwich. Her lineage, name, and even the date of her death are unknown. Given what we do know of her, though, it seems likely that she would want her readers to focus on her meditations—her "shewings" and what they revealed about the nature of God—rather than her own life.

JULIAN OF NORWICH

Our knowledge of Julian of Norwich's life and mystical experiences is derived from the records she allowed others to keep. At the age of 30 years, on 8 May 1373, Julian of Norwich lay critically ill, her mother at her side. Her curate, called to administer the last rites, held a crucifix aloft at the foot of her bed. With her sight beginning to fail, she felt a creeping numbness spread from her toes to her waist. As her field of vision narrowed and she fixed her eyes on the crucifix near her bed, Julian reports that she suddenly saw the figure of Jesus begin to bleed from his forehead in drops that reminded her of rain falling from the eaves of a house. For several hours, while those around her presumed she was near death, Julian continued to experience what she termed a "bodely sight"—a total of sixteen visions. Soon after her recovery, Julian wrote a short narrative of her visions (the Short Text), and 20 years later, a longer and more theologically complex version (the Long Text) that incorporated the fruits of her years of intense and studied meditation on her sixteen original showings.

At some point after her miraculous recovery, Julian became an anchoress at St. Julian's church in Norwich, a bustling and thriving town in the north of England. Being an anchoress required taking a vow of seclusion, which would have meant that she lived the majority of her years in a small room within the sides of the church. This would probably have afforded her a certain autonomy; anchorites and anchoresses did not answer to any ecclesiastical authority other than the bishop. The ritual for enclosure included a Mass with prayers for the dead; as an anchoress Julian was, in effect, choosing to "die" to the world so that she could devote herself to prayer and meditation. Most anchoritic strongholds were small, perhaps no more than 12 or 15 feet square, with three windows. Through hers, Julian could view the altar and the Sacrament and hear Mass. She would have spoken to her confessor or counseled those, like Margery Kempe, who came to talk to her through this window. Another small window would have allowed access to those who saw to her physical needs, and a third, quite possibly facing the street but covered with a translucent cloth, would have allowed in light.

Although there is evidence that Julian, in her role as an anchoress, served her community for many years as a spiritual director and may have enjoyed at least a modicum of public attention, her written works did not garner much interest outside of ecclesiastical circles for over two centuries; in fact, the first time her writings are mentioned at length after her death is in the 1650s, during the Puritan Revolution. The anti-Catholic and anti-mystical temper of the political times led those who were sympathetic to her theological views to transfer their copies of her *Revelations* to several monastic houses in France, where, for all intents and purposes, her writings remained buried until the 1800s.

Early in the twentieth century the scholar Evelyn Underhill revived interest in Julian's writings, which began to be read again by lay, clerical, and academic readers. Over the last few decades, partly as the result of a growing interest in works by women, Julian's writings have become the focus of considerable critical attention. Along with her contemporaries Richard Rolle, Walter Hilton, and the anonymous author of the *Cloud of Unknowing*, Julian is now regarded as one of the great fourteenth-century English mystics.

Her writing is known for its innovative and sometimes startling theology: perhaps most strikingly, she says God is Mother as well as Father. Her meditations on her visions over the years persuaded her that God is not a vindictive God, prone to punish or rebuke, although she emphasized that she adhered to Church doctrine about sin and damnation, as about all other matters; for a woman writing in her time, it was essential to avoid the charge of heresy. Julian found herself unable to embrace the idea of eternal damnation, however, and perceived a God who saw His people through the eyes of love and through grace brought by Christ's death and resurrection. The strength of her unique vision, together with her ability to tap the deep potential for image and metaphor afforded by the Middle English of her time, make her texts a fascinating study of the intersection between affective piety and the flowering of the English language.

⌘ ⌘ ⌘

from *A Revelation of Love*[1]

CHAPTER I—A PARTICULAR OF THE CHAPTERS

The First chapter—of the number of the revelations particularly.

This is a revelation of love that Jesus Christ, our endless bliss, made in sixteen showings or revelations particular; of the which the first is of His precious crowning with thorns; and therein was contained and specified the Trinity with the incarnation and unity betwixt God and man's soul, with many fair showings of endless wisdom and teaching of love, in which all the showings that follow be grounded and joined.

The second is the discolouring of His fair face in tokening of his dear-worthy[2] passion.

The third is that our Lord God almighty, all wisdom and all love, right as verily[3] as He hath made every thing that is, also verily He doth and worketh all thing that is done.

The fourth is the scourging[4] of His tender body with plenteous shedding of His blood.

The fifth is that the fiend[5] is overcome by the precious passion of Christ.

The sixth is the worshipful thanking of our Lord God in which He rewardeth his blessed servants in heaven.

The seventh is often times feeling of wele[6] and woe—the feeling of wele is gracious touching and lightening, with true sikerness[7] of endless joy; the feeling of woe is temptation by heaviness and irkehede[8] of our fleshly living—with ghostly understanding that we are kept also sekirly[9] in love, in woe as in wele, by the goodness of God.

The eighth is the last pains of Christ and His cruel dying.

The ninth is of the liking which is in the blissful Trinity of the hard passion of Christ after his rueful dying; in which joy and liking he will that we be solaced

---

1. *A Revelation of Love*   For the present text the edition of Marion Glasscoe has been used as a copy text. Spelling and punctuation have been substantially modernized for this anthology.

2. *tokening* Signifying; *dear-worthy* Precious.

3. *right as verily* Just as truly.

4. *scourging* Whipping, beating.

5. *the fiend* Satan.

6. *wele* Well being.

7. *sikerness* Certainty.

8. *irkehede* Distastefulness.

9. *sekirly* Certainly.

and mirth with him till when we come to the fullness in[1] heaven.

The tenth is our Lord Jesus showeth in love his blissful heart even cloven in two enjoined.

The eleventh is a high ghostly showing of his dearworthy mother.

The twelfth is that our Lord is the most worthy being.

The thirteenth is that our Lord God will we[2] have great regard to all the deeds that he hath done in the great nobility of all things making, and of the excellence of man making, which is above all his works, and of the precious amends that he hath made for man's sin, turning all our blame into endless worship; where also our Lord saith: Behold and see; for by the same mighty wisdom and goodness I shall make wele all that is not wele and thou[3] shalt see it. And in this he will we keep us in the faith and truth of Holy Church, not willing to wit his privities[4] now, but as it longeth to us in this life.

The fourteenth is that our Lord is ground of our beseeching.[5] Herein were seen two fair properties: that one is rightful prayer, that other is sekir trust, which he will both be alike large; and thus our prayers liketh him and he of his goodness fullfilleth it.

The fifteenth, that we shall suddenly be taken from all our pain and from all our woe and of his goodness we shall come up above where we shall have our Lord Jesus to our mede[6] and be fulfilled of joy and bliss in Heaven.

The sixteenth is that the blissful Trinity our Maker, in Christ Jesus our Saviour, endlessly dwells in our soul, worshipfully ruling and giving all things, us mightily and wisely saving and keeping for love, and we shall not be overcome of[7] our enemy.

CHAPTER 2

The Second chapter—of the time of these revelations, and how she asked three petitions.

These revelations were showed to a simple creature that could no letter,[8] the year of our Lord 1373, the 8th day of May; which creature desired afore three gifts of God: the first was mind[9] of the passion, the second was bodily sickness in youth at thirty years of age, the third was to have of God's gift three wounds. As in the first, methought I had some feeling in the passion of Christ but yet I desired more by the grace of God. Methought I would have been that time with Mary Magdalene and with other that were Christ's lovers,[10] and therefore I desired a bodily sight wherein I might have more knowledge of the bodily pains of our Saviour, and of the compassion of Our Lady and of all his true lovers that seen that time his pains, for I would be one of them and suffer with Him.[11] Other sight nor showing of God desired I never none[12] till the soul was departed from the body. The cause of this petition was that after the showing I should have the more true mind in the passion of Christ. The second came to my mind with contrition, freely desiring that sickness so hard as to death that I might, in that sickness, undertaken all my rites[13] of Holy Church, myself wening[14] that I should die, and that all creatures might suppose the same that saw me; for I would have no manner comfort of earthly life. In this sickness I desired to have all manner pains bodily and ghostly that I should have if I should die, with all the dreads and tempests of the fiend, except the outpassing of the soul. And this I meant for I would be purged by the mercy of God and after live more to the worship of God because of that sickness; and that for the more speed in my death, for I desired to be soon with my God. These two desires of the passion and the

---

[1] *in* Of.

[2] *will we* Wishes that we.

[3] *thou* In the Middle Ages, "thou" was the term of familiar address, and "you" was the term of formal address.

[4] *wit* Know; *privities* Private secrets.

[5] *beseeching* Prayers.

[6] *mede* Reward.

[7] *of* By.

[8] *could no letter* Could not read.

[9] *mind* Remembrance, recollection.

[10] *Christ's lovers* Those who loved Christ.

[11] *one of them* See John 19.25.

[12] *desired I never none* I never desired any. Middle English often uses a double negative.

[13] *rites* The Last Rites given to the dying.

[14] *wening* Thinking.

sickness I desired with a condition, saying thus: Lord, thou woteth[1] what I would—if it be Thy will that I have it; and if it be not Thy will, good Lord, be not displeased, for I will nought but as Thou wilt. For the third, by the grace of God and teaching of Holy Church, I conceived a mighty desire to receive three wounds in my life: that is to say the wound of very[2] contrition, the wound of kind compassion and the wound of wilful longing to God. And all this last petition I asked without any condition. These two desires foresaid passed from my mind, and the third dwelled with me continually.

CHAPTER 3

Of the sickness she obtained of God by petition—Third chapter.

And when I was thirty years old and half God sent me a bodily sickness in which I lay three days and three nights; and on the fourth night I took all my rites of Holy Church and wened not to have lived till day. And after this I lay for two days and two nights. And on the third night I wened oftentimes to have passed, and so wened they that were with me. And yet, I thought great sweeme[3] to die; but for nothing that was in earth that me liked to live for, for no pain that I was afraid of, for I trusted in God of his mercy; but it was to have lived that I might have loved God better and longer time, that I might have the more knowing and loving of God in bliss of heaven. For methought all the time that I had lived here, so little and so short in reward of that endless bliss, I thought nothing. Wherefore I thought: Good Lord, may my living no longer be to Thy worship! And I understood by my reason and by my feeling of my pains that I should die. And I assented fully with all, with all the will of my heart, to be at God's will.

Thus I dured[4] till day, and by then my body was dead from the middle downwards as to my feeling.

Then was I stered[5] to be set upright, underset[6] with help, for to have more freedom of my heart to be at God's will, and thinking on God while my life would last. My curate[7] was sent for to be at my ending, and before he came I had set my eyen[8] and might not speak. He set the cross before my face and said: I have brought thee the image of thy Maker and Saviour. Look thereupon and comfort thee therewith. Methought I was well, for my eyen were set uprightward into heaven where I trusted to come by the mercy of God. But nevertheless I assented to set my eyen in the face of the crucifix if I might, and so I did, for methought I might longer endure to look even forth[9] than right up. After this my sight began to fail and it was all dark about me in the chamber as it had be night, save in the image of the cross wherein I beheld a common light, and I wist[10] not how. All that was beside the cross was ugly to me as if it had been much occupied with the fiends.

After this the other part of my body[11] began to die so far forth that scarcely I had any feeling, with shortness of wind.[12] And then I went soothly to have passed.[13] And, in this, suddenly all my pain was taken from me and I was as whole, and namely in the other part of my body, as ever I was before. I marvelled at this sudden change for methought it was a privy working of God and not of kind.[14] And yet by the feeling of this ease I trusted never the more to live; nor the feeling of this ease was no full ease to me, for methought I had lever[15] to be delivered of this world.

Then came suddenly to my mind that I should desire the second wound, of Our Lord's gracious gift, that my body might be fulfilled with mind and feeling of his blessed passion; for I would that his pains were my

---

[1] *woteth* Know.

[2] *very* True.

[3] *sweeme* Regret, grief.

[4] *dured* Endured.

[5] *stered* Moved.

[6] *underset* Supported.

[7] *curate* Priest.

[8] *set my eyen* Fixed my eyes.

[9] *even forth* Parallel to the ground.

[10] *wist* Know.

[11] *other part … body* The upper part of her body.

[12] *wind* Breath.

[13] *went … passed* Truly believed I would die.

[14] *kind* Nature.

[15] *lever* Rather.

pains with compassion, and afterward longing to God. But in this I desired never bodily sight nor showing of God, but compassion, as a kind soul might have with our Lord Jesus, that for love would become a deadly[1] man; and therefore I desired to suffer with Him. …

CHAPTER 5

How God is to us everything that is good, tenderly wrapping us; and all thing that is made, in regard to Almighty God, it is nothing; and how man hath no rest till he knoweth himself and all thing for the love of God—the Fifth chapter.

In this same time Our Lord showed to me a ghostly sight of his homely[2] loving. I saw that he is to us everything that is good and comfortable for us. He is our clothing that for love wrappeth us, halseth[3] us and all becloseth us for tender love, that he may never leave us, being to us all things that are good, as to mine understanding. Also in this he showed a little thing, the quantity of a hazelnut in the palm of my hand; and it was as round as a ball. I looked thereupon with eye of my understanding and thought: What may this be? And it was generally answered thus: It is all that is made. I marvelled how it might last, for methought it might suddenly have fallen to nought for little. And I was answered in my understanding: It lasteth and ever shall, for God loveth it; and so all things hath their being by the love of God.

In this little thing I saw three properties: the first is that God made it, the second is that God loveth it, the third, that God keepeth it. But what is to me soothly the maker, the keeper, and the lover I cannot tell; for, till I am substantially united to him, I may never have full rest nor very bliss; that is to say, that I be so fastened to him that there be right nought that is made betwixt my God and me.

It needeth us[4] to have knowing of the littleness of creatures and to nought[5] all thing that is made for to love and have God that is unmade. For this is the cause why we be not all in ease of heart and soul: for we seek here rest in these things that is so little, wherein is no rest, and know not Our God that is almighty, all wise, all good; for he is the very rest. God will be known, and Him liketh that we rest in Him; for all that is beneath Him sufficeth not us; and this is the cause why that no soul is rested till it is noughted[6] of all things that is made. When he is wilfully noughted, for love to have Him that is all, then is he able to receive ghostly rest.

Also our Lord God showed that it is full great pleasance to Him that a silly[7] soul come to Him nakedly and plainly and homely. For this is the kind[8] yearning of the soul by the touching of the Holy Ghost, as by the understanding that I have in this showing: God, of Thy goodness, give me Thyself; for Thou art enough to me and I may nothing ask that is less that may be full worship to Thee. And if I ask anything that is less, ever me wanteth, but only in Thee I have all.

And these words are full lovesome to the soul and full near touch the will of God and His goodness; for His goodness comprehendeth all his creatures and all His blessed works, and overpasseth without end, for He is the endlessness. And He hath made us only to Himself and restored us by His blessed passion and keepeth us in His blessed love. And all this is of His goodness. …

CHAPTER 7

How Our Lady, beholding the greatness of her Maker, thought herself least, and of the great drops of blood running from under the garland, and how the most joy to man is that God most high and mighty is holiest and most courteous[9]—Seventh chapter.

And to learn[10] us this, as to mine understanding, our Lord God showed Our Lady Saint Mary in the same time; that is to mean the high wisdom and truth she had

---

[1] *deadly* Mortal.

[2] *homely* Familiar.

[3] *halseth* Embraces.

[4] *It needeth us* It is necessary for us, we must.

[5] *nought* Despise.

[6] *noughted* Freed.

[7] *silly* Simple.

[8] *kind* Natural.

[9] *most courteous* The word "courtesy" had more connotations in the medieval period than it does today: it was suggestive of chivalry, goodness, moral virtue, and divine grace.

[10] *learn* Teach.

in beholding of her Maker so great, so high, so mighty and so good. This greatness and this nobility of the beholding of God fulfilled her of reverend dread, and with this she saw herself so little and so low, so simple and so poor, in reward of[1] her Lord God, that this reverend dread fulfilled her of meekness. And thus, by this ground, she was fulfilled of grace and of all manner of virtues and overpasseth all creatures.

In all the time that he showed this that I have said now in ghostly sight, I saw the bodily sight lasting of the plenteous bleeding of the head. The great drops of blood fell down from under the garland like pellets seeming as it had come out of the veins; and in the coming out it were brown red, for the blood was full thick; and in the spreading abroad it were bright red; and when it come to the brows, then it vanished; notwithstanding the bleeding continued till many things were seen and understood. The fairness and the liveliness is like nothing but the same.

The plenteousness is like to the drops of water that fall on the eaves after a great shower of rain that fall so thick that no man may number them with bodily wit. And for the roundness, it were like to the scale of herring in the spreading on the forehead.[2]

These three come to my mind in the time: pellets, for roundness, in the coming out of the blood; the scale of herring, in the spreading in the forehead, for roundness; the drops of eaves, for the plenteousness innumerable. This showing was quick and lively, and hideous and dreadful, sweet and lovely. And of all the sight it was most comfort to me that our God and Lord, that is so reverent and dreadful, is so homely and courteous. And this most fulfilled me with liking and sikerness of soul.

And to the understanding of this he showed this open example: it is the most worship that a solemn king or a great lord may do a poor servant if he will be homely with him, and namely if he shows it himself, of a full true meaning and with a glad cheer, both privately and openly. Then thinketh this poor creature thus: Ah! What might this noble lord do more worship and joy to show me, that am so simple, this marvellous homeliness? Soothly it is more joy and liking to me than he gave me great gifts and were himself strange[3] in manner. This bodily example was showed so high that man's heart might be ravished and almost forget himself for joy of this great homeliness.

Thus it fares by our Lord Jesus and by us; for soothly it is the most joy that may be, as to my sight, that He that is highest and mightiest, noblest and worthiest, is lowest and meekest, homeliest and most courteous. And truly and soothly this marvellous joy shall be shown us all when we see Him; and this will our Lord, that we believe and trust, joy and like, comfort us and solace us, as we may, with His grace and with His help, into the time that we see it verily;[4] for the most fullness of joy that we shall have, as to my sight, is the marvellous courtesy and homeliness of our Father that is our Maker, in our Lord Jesus Christ that is our brother and our Saviour. But this marvellous homeliness may no man wit in this time of life, but[5] he have it of special showing of our Lord, or of great plenty of grace inwardly given of the Holy Ghost. But faith and belief with[6] charity deserves the mede, and so it is had by grace; for in faith with hope and charity our life is grounded. The showing, made to whom that God will, plainly teaches the same, opened and declared with many privy points longing to our faith which be worshipful to known. And when the showing, which is given in a time, is passed and hid, then the faith keeps it by grace of the Holy Ghost unto our life's end. And thus by the showing it is not other than the faith, not less nor more, as it may be seen by Our Lord's meaning in the same matter by then[7] it come to the end....

CHAPTER II

The third revelation etc., how God doth all things except sin, never changing his purpose without end, for he hath made all things in fullness of goodness—Eleventh chapter.

---

[1] *in reward of* By comparison to.

[2] *in the spreading... forehead* As they spread over the forehead.

[3] *strange* Distant.

[4] *verily* Truly.

[5] *but* Unless.

[6] *with* In.

[7] *by then* By the time.

And after this I saw God in a point, that is to say, in mine understanding, by which sight I saw that He is in all things. I beheld with advisement,[1] seeing and knowing in sight with a soft dread, and thought: What is sin? for I saw truly that God doth all things be it never so little. And I saw truly that nothing is done by hap[2] nor by adventure, but all things be the foreseeing wisdom of God. If it be hap or adventure in the sight of man, our blindness and our unforesight[3] is the cause, for the things that are in the foreseeing wisdom of God been from without beginning, which rightfully and worshipfully and continually He leads to the best end as they come about, falling to us suddenly, ourselves unwitting;[4] and thus, by our blindness and our unforesight, we say these been haps and adventures; but to Our Lord God they be not so.

Wherefore me behooveth needs to grant[5] that all things that are done, are well done, for our Lord God doth all; for in this time the working of creatures was not showed, but of Our Lord God in the creature; for He is in the mid point of all things and all He doth, and I was sekir He does no sin. And here I saw soothly that sin is no deed,[6] for in all this was not sin showed. And I would no longer marvel in this, but beheld Our Lord, what He would show. And thus, as it might be for the time, the rightfulness of God's working was showed to the soul. Rightfulness has two fair properties: it is right and it is full. And so are all the works of Our Lord God; and thereto needs neither the working of mercy nor grace, for it been all rightful, wherein fails not. And in another time He showed for the beholding of sin nakedly, as I shall say, where He uses working of mercy and grace.

And this vision was showed to mine understanding, for Our Lord will have the soul turned truly into the beholding of Him, and generally of all His works; for they are full good and all His doings be easy and sweet, and to great ease[7] bringing the soul that is turned from the beholding of the blind deeming[8] of man onto the faire sweet deeming of our Lord God; for a man beholds some deeds well done and some deeds evil, but Our Lord beholds them not so; for as all that has been in kind is of God's making, so are all things that are done in property of God's doing; for it is easy to understand that the best deed is well done; and so well as the best deed is done and the highest, so well is the least deed done; and all in property and in the order that Our Lord hath it ordained to from without beginning, for there is no doer but He.

I saw full sekirly that He changes never His purpose in no manner thing, nor never shall, without end; for there was nothing unknown to Him in His rightful ordinance from without beginning, and therefore all things was set in order, or[9] anything was made, as it should stand without end; and no manner thing shall fail of that point; for He made all things in fullness of goodness; and therefore the Blessed Trinity is ever full pleased in all His works. And all this showed he full blissfully, meaning thus: See I am God. See I am in all things. See I do all things. See I left never mine hands of mine works, nor never shall, without end. See I lead all things to the end I ordained it to from without beginning by the same might, wisdom and love that I made it. How should anything be amiss? Thus mightily, wisely and lovingly was the soul examined in this vision. Than saw I soothly that me behooved needs to assent[10] with great reverence, enjoying in God. . . .

CHAPTER 27—THE THIRTEENTH REVELATION

The thirteenth revelation is that Our Lord God will that we have great regard to all His deeds that He have[11] done in the great nobleness of all of all things making and of etc., how sin is not known by the pain—Twenty-Seventh chapter.

---

[1] *beheld with advisement*   Viewed the vision contemplatively.

[2] *hap*   Chance.

[3] *unforesight*   Lack of foresight.

[4] *unwitting*   Unknowing.

[5] *wherefore me behooveth ... grant*   Thus I was compelled to admit.

[6] *no deed*   Nothing.

[7] *ease*   Rest.

[8] *deeming*   Judgment.

[9] *or*   Before.

[10] *me behooved ... assent*   I was compelled to agree.

[11] *have*   Has. Medieval verb forms have been maintained wherever the sense seems clear.

After this the Lord brought to my mind the longing that I had to Him before; and I saw that nothing letted[1] me but sin, and so I beheld generally in us all. And methought if sin had not been, we should all have been clean and like to our Lord as He made us; and thus, in my folly, before this time often I wondered why by the great foreseeing wisdom of God the beginning of sin[2] was not letted; for then, thought I, should have been well.

This stering[3] was mikel[4] to be forsaken, and nevertheless mourning and sorrow I made therefore without reason and discretion. But Jesus, that in this vision informed me of all that me needeth, answered by this word and said: Sin is behovely,[5] but all shall be well, and all shall be well, and all manner of thing shall be well. In this naked word sin our Lord brought to my mind generally all that is not good, and the shameful despite and the utter noughting[6] that He bare for us in this life, and His dying, and all His pains, and passions of all His creatures, ghostly and bodily—for we be all in part noughted,[7] and we shall be noughted following our master Jesus till we be full purged: that is to say, till we be fully purged of our deadly flesh and of all our inward affections which are not very good[8]—and the beholding of this, with all the pains that ever were or ever shall be. And with all these I understood the passion of Christ for most pain and over passing. And all this was showed in a touch and readily passed over into comfort. For our good Lord would not that the soul were afeared of this ugly sight.

But I saw not sin; for I believe it hath no manner of substance nor party of[9] being, nor it might not be known but by the pain that it is cause of; and thus pain, it is something, as to my sight,[10] for a time, for it purgeth and maketh us to know ourselves and ask

mercy; for the passion of Our Lord is comfort to us against all this, and so is His blessed will. And for the tender love that our good Lord hath to all that shall be saved He comforteth readily and sweetly, meaning thus: It is sooth that sin is cause of all this pain, but all shall be well, and all shall be well, and all manner thing shall be well.

These words were showed full tenderly, showing no manner of blame to me,[11] nor to none that shall be safe. Than were it a great unkindness to blame or wonder on God for my sin, sith[12] He blameth not me for sin.

And in these same words I saw a marvellous high privity[13] hid in God, which privity He shall openly make known to us in heaven; in which knowing we shall verily see the cause why He suffered sin to come; in which sight we shall endlessly joy in our Lord God.

CHAPTER 28

How the children of salvation shall be shaken in sorrows, but Christ enjoyeth with compassion; and a remedy against tribulation—Twenty-Eighth chapter.

Thus I saw how Christ hath compassion on us for the cause of sin. And right as I was before in the passion of Christ fulfilled with pain and compassion, so in this I was fulfilled a party with compassion of all my even[14] Christians; for that well, well beloved people that shall be saved: that is to say, God's servants, Holy Church, shall be shaken in sorrows and anguish and tribulation in this world as men shake a cloth in the wind. And as to this Our Lord answered in this manner: A great thing shall I make hereof in heaven, of endless worships and everlasting joy. Yea, so far forth I saw that Our Lord enjoyeth of the tribulations of His servants with pity and compassion; to each person that He loveth to His bliss for to bring, He leaveth upon Him something that is no lack in His sight, whereby they are lowed[15] and despised in this world, scorned, and so outcast. And this

---

[1] *letted*   Hindered.

[2] *beginning of sin*   See Romans 5.13.

[3] *stering*   Impulse.

[4] *mikel*   Much.

[5] *behovely*   Necessary. See Matthew 18.7.

[6] *noughting*   Belittling, disparagement.

[7] *noughted*   Freed.

[8] *not very good*   See Romans 6.12.

[9] *party of*   Share in.

[10] *as to my sight*   As far as I can see.

[11] *blame to me*   See John 8.10–11.

[12] *sith*   Since.

[13] *privity*   Mystery.

[14] *even*   Fellow. See I Peter 3.8.

[15] *lowed*   Humbled.

He doth for to let[1] the harm that they should take of the pomp and the vainglory of this wretched life, and make their way ready to come to heaven in His bliss without end lasting; for He saith: I shall all[2] to—break you for your vain affections and your vicious pride; and after that I shall together gather you and make you mild and meek, clean and holy, by joining to me.[3]

And then I saw that each kind compassion that man hath on[4] His even Christian with charity, it is Christ in him. That same noughting that was showed in His passion, it was showed again here in this compassion wherein were two manner of understandings in Our Lord's meaning:[5] the one was the bliss that we are bought to, wherein He wills that we enjoy. That other is for comfort in our pain; for He will that we wit[6] that it shall all be turned to worship and profit by virtue of His passion, and that we wit that we suffer not alone but with Him, and see Him our ground, and that we see His pains and His noughting pass so for all that we may suffer, that it may not be full thought. And the beholding of this will save us from grouching and despair in the feeling of our pains; and if we see soothly that our sin deserveth it, yet His love excuseth us, and of His great courtesy He does away all our blame, and He holdeth us with ruth[7] and pity, as children innocent and unlothful.[8] …

CHAPTER 50

How the chosen soul was never dead in the sight of God, and of a marvel upon the same; and three things bolded her to ask of God the understanding of it— Fiftieth chapter.

And in this deadly life mercy and forgiveness is our way and evermore leadeth us to grace.[9] And by the tempest and the sorrow that we fall in on our part, we be often dead as to man's doom in earth, but in the sight of God the soul that shall be saved was never dead nor never shall. But yet here I wondered and marvelled with all the diligence of my soul, meaning[10] thus: Good Lord, I see Thee that Thou art very truth, and I know soothly that we sin grievously all day and be much blameworthy;[11] and I may neither leave the knowing of this sooth, nor I see not the showing to us no manner of blame. How may this be? For I knew by the common teaching of Holy Church and by mine own feeling that the blame of our sin continually hangeth upon us, from the first man[12] into the time that we come up into heaven. Then was this my marvel, that I saw our Lord God showing to us no more blame than if we were as clean as and holy as angels be in heaven.[13] And atwix[14] these two contraries my reason was greatly travailed[15] by my blindness, and could have no rest for dread that His blessed presence should pass from my sight and I to be left in unknowing how He beholdeth us in our sin. For either me behooved[16] to see in God that sin were all done away, or else me behooved to see in God how He seeth it, whereby I might truly know how it longeth to me to see sin and the manner of our blame.

My longing endured, Him continually beholding, and yet I could have no patience for great awe and perplexity, thinking: If I take it thus, that we be not sinners nor not blameworthy, it seemeth as I should err and fail of knowing of this sooth. And if it be so that we be sinners and blameworthy, good Lord, how may it then be that I cannot see this soothness in Thee, which art my God, my Maker, in whom I desire to see all truths?

---

[1] *let* Prevent.

[2] *I shall all* I shall do all.

[3] *I shall together … me* See Matthew 23.37, 11.28–29, Ephesians 5.25–26.

[4] *on* For.

[5] *nothing that was … meaning* Christ's love of humanity made Him see all the pains of the Passion as nothing, and such stoicism is achieved through two means.

[6] *wit* Know.

[7] *ruth* Compassion.

[8] *unlothful* Innocent.

[9] *And in … grace* See Psalm 118.132–33.

[10] *meaning* Saying.

[11] *Good Lord … blameworthy* See Proverbs 24.16.

[12] *the first man* Adam.

[13] *I saw … heaven* See Luke 20.35–36.

[14] *atwix* Between.

[15] *travailed* Tormented.

[16] *me behooved* It was incumbent upon me.

For three points make me hardy to ask it: the first is for it[1] is so low a thing, for if it were a high I should be adread;[2] the second is that it is so common, for if it were special and privy, also I should be adread; the third is that it needeth me to wit it, as me thinketh, if I shall live here, for knowing of good and evil, whereby I may by reason and grace the more depart them asunder, and love goodness and hate evil as Holy Church teacheth.

I cried inwardly with all my might, seeking unto God for help, meaning thus: Ah! Lord Jesus, King of bliss, how shall I be eased? Who that shall teach me and tell me that[3] me needeth to wit, if I may not at this time see it in Thee?

CHAPTER 51

The answer to the doubt afore by a marvellous example of a lord and a servant; and God will abide, for it was near twenty years after ere she fully understood this example; and how it is understood that Christ sitteth on the right hand of the Father—Fifty-First chapter.

And then our courteous Lord answered in showing full mystily[4] a wonderful example of a lord that hath a servant, and gave me sight to my understanding of both; which sight was showed double in the Lord, and the sight was showed double in the servant: than one party was showed ghostly in bodily likeness, and the other party was showed more ghostly without bodily likeness.[5] For the first thus: I saw two persons in bodily likeness, that is to say, a lord and a servant; and therewith God gave me ghostly understanding. The lord sitteth solemnly in rest and in peace, the servant standeth by, before his lord reverently, ready to do his lord's will. The lord looketh upon his servant full lovely and sweetly, and meekly he sendeth him to a certain place to do his will.[6] The servant, not only he goeth, but sud-denly he starteth and runneth in great haste for love to don his lord's will. And anon he falleth in a slade[7] and taketh full great sore. And than he groaneth and moaneth and waileth and writheth, but he ne may risen[8] nor help himself by no manner way. And of all this the most mischief that I saw him in was failing of comfort; for he could not turn his face to look upon his loving lord, which was to him full near, in whom is full comfort;[9] but as a man that was feeble and unwise for the time, he intended to his feeling, and endured in woe, in which woe he suffered seven great pains. The first was the sore bruising he took in his falling, which was to him much pain. The second was the heaviness of his body. The third was feebleness following of these two. The fourth, that he was blinded in his reason and stonied[10] in his mind so far forth that almost he had forgotten his own love. The fifth was that he might not rise. The sixth was most marvellous to me, and that was that he lay alone. I looked all about and beheld, and far nor near, high nor low, I saw to him no help. The seventh was that the place which he lay on was a long, hard and grievous.

I marvelled how this servant might meekly suffer there all this woe. And I beheld with avisement to wit if I could perceive in him any default, or if the Lord should assign in him any blame, and soothly there was none seen; for only his good will and his great desire was cause of his falling; and he was as unlothful[11] and as good inwardly as when he stood afore his lord ready to do his will.

And right thus continually his loving lord full tenderly beholdeth him; and now with a double cheer:[12] one outward, full meekly and mildly with great ruth and pity, and this was of the first; another inward, more ghostly, and this was showed with a leading of my understanding into the lord, which I saw him highly enjoy, for the worshipful resting and nobleth[13] that he will and shall bring his servant to by his plenteous grace.

[1] *it* This question.
[2] *adread* Afraid.
[3] *that* That which.
[4] *mystily* Mistily, darkly.
[5] *ghostly in bodily … ghostly without bodily* This refers to the spiritual sight versus bodily sight distinction that Julian sets up in the First Revelation.
[6] *do his will* See John 17.18.
[7] *slade* Valley, dell.
[8] *ne may risen* Cannot rise.
[9] *full comfort* See 2 Corinthians 1.3.
[10] *stonied* Astonished, stunned.
[11] *unlothful* Innocent.
[12] *cheer* Countenance.
[13] *nobleth* Eminence, high standing.

And this was of that other showing. And now my understanding led again into the first, both keeping in mind.

Then saith this courteous lord in his meaning: Lo, lo, my loved servant. What harm and disease[1] he hath taken in my service for my love, yea, and for his good will! Is it not reason that I award him[2] his fright and his dread, his hurt and his maim and all his woe? And not only this, but falleth it not to me to given a gift that be better to him and more worshipful than his own whole should have been? And else methinketh I did him no grace.

And in this an inward ghostly showing of the Lord's meaning descended[3] into my soul, in which I saw that it behoveth needs to be, standing His great and His own worship, that His dear-worthy servant which he loved so much should be verily and blissfully rewarded without end above that he should have been if he had not fallen; yea, and so far forth that his falling and his woe that he hath taken thereby shall be turned into high and over-passing worship and endless bliss.

And at this point the showing of the example vanished, and our good Lord led forth mine understanding in sight and in showing of the revelation to the end. But notwithstanding all this forth-leading, the marvelling[4] of the example came never from me; for methought it was given me for an answer to my desire. And yet could I not taken therein full understanding to mine ease at that time. For in the servant that was showed for Adam, as I shall say, I saw many diverse properties that might by no manner or way be directed to single Adam.[5] And thus in that time I stood mikel in unknowing. For the full understanding of this marvellous example was not given me in that time; in which misty example three privities of the revelation be yet mikel hid, and notwithstanding this I saw and understood that every showing is full of privities. And therefore me behoveth now to tell three properties in which

I am sumdele[6] eased.

The first is the beginning of teaching that I understood therein in the same time; the second is the inward learning that I have understood therein sithen;[7] the third all the whole revelation from the beginning to the end, that is to say, of this book, which our Lord God of his goodness bringeth oftentimes freely to the sight of mine understanding. And these three are so joined, as to my understanding, that I cannot, nor may, depart them. And by these three as one I have teaching whereby I owe to believe and trust in our Lord God, that of the same goodness that he showed it, and for the same end, right so of the same goodness and for the same end he shall declare it to us when it is His will.

For twenty years after the time of the showing, save three months, I had teaching inwardly, as I shall say: It longeth to thee to taken heed to all the properties and condition that were showed in the example though thou think that they been misty and indifferent to thy sight. I assented wilfully with great desire, seeing inwardly with avisement all the points and properties that were showed in the same time, as far forth as my wit and understanding would serve; beginning mine beholding at the lord and at the servant, and the manner of sitting of the lord, and the place that he sat on, and the colour of his clothing and the manner of shape, and his cheer without, and his nobleth and his goodness within; at the manner of standing of the servant and the place where and how, at his manner of clothing, the colour and the shape, at his outward having and at his inward goodness and his unlothfulness. The lord that sat solemnly in rest and in peace, I understand that he is God. The servant that stood before the lord, I understood that it was showed for Adam, that is to say, one man was showed that time, and his falling to make that thereby understand how God beholdeth a man and his falling; for in the sight of God all man is one man and one man is all man. This man was hurt in his might and made full feeble; and he was stonied in his understanding, for he turned from the beholding of his Lord. But his will was kept whole in God's sight; for his will I saw Our Lord commend and approve, but himself was letted and blinded of the knowing of this will. And this is to him

---

[1] *disease* Distress.

[2] *award him* Remind him for.

[3] *descended* This is the only place where Julian speaks of a revelation as coming from above.

[4] *marvelling* Wonder.

[5] *to single Adam* I.e., to Adam alone.

[6] *sumdele* Somewhat.

[7] *sithen* Since.

great sorrow and grievous disease, for neither he sees clearly his loving lord, which is to him full meek and mild, nor he sees truly what himself is in the sight of his loving lord. And well I wot, when these two are wisely and truly seen, we shall getten rest and peace here in part, and the fullness of the bliss of heaven, by His plenteous grace.

And this was a beginning of teaching which I saw in the same time whereby I might come to knowing in what manner he beholdeth us in our sin. And then I saw that only pains blameth and punisheth, and our courteous Lord comforteth and sorroweth; ever He is to the soul in glad cheer, loving and longing to bring us to His bliss.

The place that our Lord sat on was simple, on the earth barren and desert, alone in wilderness. His clothing was wide and syde,[1] and full seemly as falleth to a lord; the colour of his cloth was blue as azure, most sad[2] and fair. His cheer was merciful, the colour of his face was fair brown with fulsomely[3] features; his eyes were black, most fair and seemly, showing full of lovely pity; and within him an high ward,[4] long and broad, all full of endless heavens. And the lovely looking that he looked upon his servant continually, and namely in his falling, methought it might melt our hearts for love and brest[5] them in two for joy. The fair looking showed of a seemly medlur[6] which was marvellous to beholden: that one was ruth and pity, that other was joy and bliss. The joy and bliss passeth as far ruth and pity as heaven is above earth. The pity was earthly and the bliss was heavenly.

The ruth in the pity of the Father was of the falling of Adam, which is his most loved creature. The joy and the bliss was of his dear-worthy Son, which is even[7] with the Father. The merciful beholding of his lovely cheer fulfilled all earth and descended down with Adam into hell,[8] with which continuant pity Adam was kept from endless death. And this mercy and pity dwelleth with mankind until the time we come up into heaven. But man is blinded in this life, and therefore we may not see our Father, God, as He is. And what time that He of His goodness will show Him to man, He showeth Him homely[9] as man. Notwithstanding that, I saw verily we ought to know and believe that the Father is not man. But his sitting on the earth barren and desert is this to mean: he made man's soul to be his own city and his dwelling place, which is most pleasing to him of all his works; and what time that man was fallen into sorrow and pain he was not all seemly to serven of that noble office; and therefore our kind Father would dight[10] him no other place but to sit upon the earth abiding mankind, which is meddled[11] with earth, till what time by His grace His dear-worthy Son had brought again His city into the noble fairness with His hard travail.[12]

The blueness of the clothing betokeneth his steadfastness. The brownness of his fair face with the seemly blackness of the eyen was most according to show his holy soberness. The largeness of his clothing, which were fair, flamand[13] about, betokeneth that he hath beclosed in him all heavens and all joy and bliss. And this was showed in a touch where I say mine understanding was led into the lord, in which I saw him highly enjoy for the worshipful restoring that he will and shall bring his servant to be his plenteous grace. And yet I marvelled, beholding the lord and the servant before said.

I saw the lord sit solemnly, and the servant standing reverently before his lord, in which servant is double understanding: one without, another within. Outward, he was clad simply as a labourer which were disposed to travail, and he stood full near the lord, not even for against[14] him, but in part aside, that on the left. His

---

[1] syde Ample.

[2] sad Deep or dark (blue).

[3] fulsomely Gracious.

[4] high ward Secure citadel, place of refuge. See 2 Kings 22.3, Psalm 58.17.

[5] brest Break.

[6] medlur Mixture.

[7] even Equal.

[8] into hell See Psalm 138.8–10.

[9] homely Familiarly.

[10] dight Prepare.

[11] meddled Mixed. See Genesis 2.7.

[12] travail Labor.

[13] flamand Flaming.

[14] for against In front of.

clothing was a white kirtle,[1] single, old and all defaced, dyed with sweat of his body, strait[2] fitting to him and short, as it were an handful beneath the knee, bare,[3] seeming as it should soon be worn up, ready to be ragged and rent. And in this I marvelled greatly, thinking: This is now an unseemly clothing for the servant that is so highly loved to stand afore so worshipful a lord. And inward, in him was showed a ground of love, which love he had to the lord was even like to the love that the lord had to him. The wisdom of the servant saw inwardly that there was one thing to do which should be to the worship of the lord. And the servant for love, having no reward to[4] himself nor to nothing that might fall of[5] him, hastily he started and ran at the sending of his lord to do that thing which was his will and his worship. For it seemed be his outward clothing as he had been a continuant labourer of long time. And by the inward sight that I had, both in the lord and in the servant, it seemed that he was anew, that is to say, new beginning for to travail, which servant was never sent out before.

There was a treasure in the earth[6] which the lord loved. I marvelled and thought what it might be. And I was answered in mine understanding: It is a meat[7] which is lovesome and pleasant to the lord. For I saw the lord sit as a man, and I saw neither meat nor drink wherewith to serve him; this was one marvel. Another marvel was that this solemn lord had no servant but one, and him he sent out. I beheld, thinking what manner labour it might be that the servant should do. And then I understood that he should do the greatest labour and hardest travail, that is, he should be a gardener; delving and diking,[8] swinking[9] and sweating, and turn the earth upside down, and seek the deepness, and water the plants in time. And in this he should continue his travail

and make sweet floods to run, and noble and plenteous fruits to spring, which he should bring before the lord and serve him therewith to his liking. And he should never turn again till he had dight this meat,[10] all ready as he knew that it liked the lord, and then he should take this meat with the drink, and bear it full worshipfully before the lord. And all this time the lord should sit on the same place abiding his servant whom he sent out.

And yet I marvelled from whence the servant came; for I saw in the lord that he hath within himself endless life and all manner of goodness, save that treasure that was in the earth and that was grounded in the lord in marvellous deepness of endless love—but it was not all to the worship till this servant had dight thus nobly it, and brought it before him, in himself present. And without the lord was nothing but wilderness. And I understood not all what this example meant, and therefore I marvelled whence the servant came.

In the servant is comprehended the second person in the Trinity; and in the servant is comprehended Adam, that is to say, all men. And therefore when I say the Son, it meaneth the Godhead which is even with the Father, and when I say the servant, it meaneth Christ's manhood which is rightful Adam. By the nearness of the servant is understood the Son, and by the standing on the left side is understood Adam. The lord is the Father, God. The servant is the Son, Christ Jesus. The Holy Ghost is even love which is in them both. When Adam fell, God's Son fell; for the ruthful joining which was made in heaven, God's Son might not be separated from Adam, for by Adam I understand all man. Adam fell from life to death into the slade of this wretched world and after that into hell. God's Son fell with Adam into the slade of the maiden's womb, which was the fairest daughter of Adam, and therefore to excuse Adam from blame in heaven and in earth; and mightily he fetched him out of hell.[11] By the wisdom and goodness that was in the servant is understood God's Son. By the poor clothing as a labourer standing near the left side is understood the manhood and Adam, with all the mischief[12] and feebleness that followeth; for in all this our good lord showed his own Son and Adam but one

---

[1] kirtle Tunic.

[2] strait Close.

[3] bare Threadbare.

[4] reward to Regard for.

[5] fall of Happen to.

[6] treasure in the earth See Matthew 13.44.

[7] meat Food.

[8] diking Digging ditches.

[9] swinking Toiling.

[10] dight this meat Prepared this food.

[11] he fetched ... hell Here the text alludes to the Harrowing of Hell.

[12] mischief Misfortune.

man. The virtue and the goodness that we have is of Jesus Christ, the feebleness and the blindness that we have is of Adam; which two were showed in the servant.

And thus hath our good Lord Jesus taken upon Him all our blame; and therefore our Father may, nor will, no more blame assign to us than to his own dear-worthy Son, Christ. Thus was He the servant before His coming into the earth, standing ready before the Father in purpose till what time He would send him to do that worshipful deed by which mankind was brought again into heaven; that is to say, notwithstanding that He is God, even with the Father as against[1] the Godhead, but in His foreseeing purpose that He would be man to save man in fulfilling of his Father's will, so He stood afore his Father as a servant, wilfully taking upon Him all our charge. And then He start full readily at the Father's will, and anon he fell full low in the maiden's womb, having no reward to Himself nor to His hard pains.

The white kirtle is the flesh; the singleness is that there was right naught atwix[2] the Godhood and manhood; the straitness is poverty; the eld[3] is of Adam's wearing; the defacing of sweat, of Adam's travail; the shortness showeth the servant's labour.

And thus I saw the Son standing, saying in His meaning: Lo, my dear Father, I stand before Thee in Adam's kirtle all ready to start and to run. I would be in the earth to do Thy worship when it is Thy will to send me. How long shall I desire? Full soothfastly wist the Son when it was the Father's will and how long He shall desire; that is to say, against the Godhead, for He is the wisdom of the Father. Wherefore this meaning was showed in understanding of the manhood of Christ; for all mankind that shall be saved by the sweet incarnation and blissful passion of Christ, all is the manhood of Christ; for he is the head and we be his members;[4] to which members the day and the time is unknown when every passing woe and sorrow shall have an end, and the everlasting joy and bliss shall be fulfilled; which day and time for to see all the company of heaven longeth. And all that shall be under heaven that shall come thither,

their way is by longing and desire; which desire and longing was showed in the servant standing afore the Lord, or else thus, in the Son's standing before the Father in Adam's kirtle; for the languor and desire of all mankind that shall be saved appeared in Jesus; for Jesus is all that shall be saved and all that shall be saved is Jesus; and all of the charity of God, with obedience, meekness and patience, and virtues that longen[5] to us. Also in this marvellous example I have teaching with me, as it were the beginning of an ABC, whereby I may have some understanding of our Lord's meaning; for the privities of the revelation be hid therein, notwithstanding that all the showings are full of privities.

The sitting of the Father betokeneth His Godhead, that is to say, for showing of rest and peace; for in the Godhead may be no travail. And that he showed himself as lord betokeneth to our manhood. The standing of the servant betokeneth travail; on side and on the left betokeneth that he was not all worthy to stand even right before[6] the lord. His starting was the Godhead, and the running was the manhood; for the Godhead start from the Father into the maiden's womb, falling into the taking of our kind; and in this falling he took great sore; the sore that he took was our flesh in which he had feeling of deadly pains. By that he stood dreadfully before the lord, and not even right, betokeneth that his clothing was not honest to stand in even right before the Lord; nor that might not, nor should not, be his office while he was a labourer; nor also he might not sit in rest and peace with the Lord till he had won his peace rightfully with his hard travail; and by the left side, that the Father left His own Son wilfully in the manhood to suffer all man's pains without sparing of Him. By that his kirtle was in point to be ragged and rent is understood the rods and the scourges, the thorns and the nails, the drawing and the dragging, his tender flesh rending; as I saw in some part. The flesh was rent from the head-pan,[7] falling in pieces until the time the bleeding failed; and then it began to dry again, clinging to the bone. And by the wallowing and writhing, groaning and moaning is understood that he might

---

[1] *against* Regards.

[2] *right naught atwix* Nothing at all between.

[3] *eld* Age.

[4] *we be his members* Cf. 1 Corinthians 12.12.

[5] *longen* Belong.

[6] *even right before* Directly in front of.

[7] *head-pan* Forehead.

never rise all mightily from the time that he was fallen into the maiden's womb till his body was slain and dead, he yielding the soul in the Father's hands with all mankind for whom he was sent.

And at this point He began first to show his might; for He went into hell, and when He was there He raised up the great right out of the deep deepness which rightfully was knit to Him in high heaven. The body was in the grave till Easter morrow, and from that time he lay never more. For then was rightfully ended the wallowing and the writhing, the groaning and the moaning; and our foul deadly flesh that God's Son took on him, which was Adam's old kirtle, strait, bare and short, then by Our Saviour was made fair now, white and bright and of endless cleanness, wide and syde, fairer and richer than was than the clothing which I saw on the Father; for that clothing was blue, and Christ's clothing is now of a fair, seemly medlur[1] which is so marvellous that I can it not discrien;[2] for it is all of very worships.

Now sitteth not the Lord on earth in wilderness, but He sitteth in his noblest seat which He made in heaven most to His liking. Now standeth not the Son before the Father as a servant dreadfully, unornly[3] clad, in part naked, but He standeth before the Father even right, richly clad in blissful largess, with a crown upon his head of precious riches; for it was showed that we be his crown, which crown is the Father's joy, the Son's worship, the Holy Ghost's liking, and endless marvellous bliss to all that be in heaven.

Now standeth not the Son before the Father on the left side as a labourer, but He sitteth on his Father's right hand in endless rest and peace. But it is not meant that the Son sitteth on the right hand, side by side, as one man sitteth by another in this life; for there is no such sitting, as to my sight, in the Trinity; but he sitteth on his Father's right hand, that is to say, in the highest nobleth of the Father's joys. Now is the spouse, God's Son, in peace with his loved wife, which is the fair maiden of endless joy. Now sitteth the Son, very God and man, in his city in rest and peace, which his Father

hath adyte to[4] him of his endless purpose; and the Father in the Son, and the Holy Ghost in the Father and in the Son....

Chapter 58

God was never displeased with His chosen wife; and of three properties in the Trinity; Fatherhead, Motherhead and Lordhead; and how our substance is in every person, but our sensuality is in Christ alone—Fifty-Eighth chapter.

God, the blessed Trinity which is everlasting being, right as He is endless from without beginning, right so it was in His purpose endless to make mankind; which fair kind first was dight to His own Son, the second person. And when He would, by full accord of all the Trinity, He made us all at once; and in our making He knit us and joined us to himself; by which joining we are kept as clean and as noble as we were made. By the virtue of that ilke[5] precious joining we love our Maker and liken him, praise Him and thank Him and endlessly enjoy in him. And this is the work which is wrought continually in every soul that shall be saved; which is the godly will beforesaid.

And thus in our making God almighty is our kindly Father; and God all wisdom is our kindly Mother, with the love and the goodness of the Holy Ghost; which is all one God, one Lord. And in the knitting and in the joining He is our very true spouse, and we His loved wife and His fair maiden, with which wife He is never displeased; for He saith: I love thee and thou lovest me, and our love shall never be departed on two.

I beheld the working of all the blessed Trinity, in which beholding I saw and understood these three properties: the property of the Fatherhead, the property of the Motherhead and the property of the Lordship in one God. In our Father almighty we have our keeping and our bliss as our kindly substance, which is to us by our making without beginning; and in the second person, in wit and wisdom, we have our keeping as our sensuality, our restoring and our saving; for He is our Mother, Brother and Saviour. And in our good Lord the Holy Ghost we have our rewarding and our yielding for

---

1 *medlur* Mixture.

2 *descrien* Describe.

3 *unornly* Wretchedly.

4 *adyte to* Prepared for.

5 *ilke* Same.

our living and our travail;[1] and endless overpassing all that we desire, in His marvellous courtesy, of His high plenteous grace. For all our life is in three. In the first we have our being and in the second we have our increasing and in the third we have our fulfilling. The first is kind;[2] the second is mercy; the third is grace.

For the first: I saw and understood that the high might of the Trinity is our Father, and the deep wisdom of the Trinity is our Mother, and the great love of the Trinity is our Lord; and all this have we in kind and in our substantial making. And furthermore, I saw that the second person, which is our Mother substantial, that same dear-worthy person is become our Mother sensual; for we are double of Gods making: that is to say, substantial and sensual. Our substance is the higher part, which we have in our Father, God Almighty; and the second person of the Trinity is our Mother in kind in our substantial making, in whom we are grounded and rooted, and He is our Mother in mercy in our sensuality taking. And thus our Mother is to us diverse manner working, in whom our parties are kept undeparted; for in our Mother, Christ, we profit and increase, and in mercy He reformeth us and restoreth, and, by the virtue of His passion and His death and uprising, joineth us to our substance. Thus worketh our Mother in mercy to all His children which are to Him buxom and obedient. And grace worketh with mercy, and namely in two properties as it was showed; which working longeth to the third person, the Holy Ghost. He worketh rewarding and giving; rewarding is a large giving of truth that the Lord doth to Him that hath travailed, and giving is a courtesy working which He doth freely of grace fulfil, and overpassing all that is deserved of creatures.

Thus in our Father, God Almighty, we have our being; and in our Mother of mercy we have our reforming and restoring, in whom our parties are joined and all made perfect man; and by yielding and giving in grace of the Holy Ghost we are fulfilled. And our substance is our Father, God Almighty, and our substance is our Mother, God all wisdom, and our substance is in our Lord the Holy Ghost, God all goodness; for our substance is whole in each person of the Trinity, which is one God. And our sensuality is only in the second

person, Christ Jesus, in whom is the Father and the Holy Ghost; and in Him and by Him we are mightily taken out of hell and out of the wretchedness in earth, and worshipfully brought up into heaven and blissfully joined to our substance, increased in riches and nobleth, by all the virtue of Christ and by the grace and working of the Holy Ghost....

CHAPTER 60

How we be bought again[3] and forth-spread by mercy and grace of our sweet, kind and ever loving Mother Jesus, and of the properties of Motherhead; but Jesus is our very Mother, not feeding us with milk but with Himself, opening His side unto us and challenging all our love—Sixtieth chapter.

But now behoveth to say a little more of this forth-spreading, as I understand in the meaning of our Lord, how that we be bought again by the Motherhead of mercy and grace into our kindly stead[4] where that we were made by the Motherhead of kind love; which kind love it never leaveth us.

Our kind Mother, our gracious Mother, for He would all wholly become our Mother in all things, He took the ground of His work full low and full mildly in the maiden's womb. And that He showed in the first, where He brought that meek maid before the eye of mine understanding in the simple stature as she was when she conceived; that is to say, our high God is sovereign wisdom of all, in this low place He raised him and dight him full ready in our poor flesh, himself to do the service and the office of Motherhead in all things. The Mother's service is nearest, readiest and surest, for it is most of kind.[5] This office nor might, nor could, nor never none do to the full[6] but He alone. We wit that all our Mother's bearing is us to pain and to dying; and what is that but our very Mother Jesus? He, all love, beareth us to joy and to endless living; blessed may He be! Thus He sustaineth us within himself in love, and

---

[1] *travail* Work.

[2] *kind* Nature.

[3] *bought again* Redeemed.

[4] *kindly stead* Natural place

[5] *kind* Nature.

[6] *nor might ... full* None ever might, nor could, nor did fully.

travailed into the full time that He would suffer the sharpest thorns and the grievous pains that ever were or ever shall be, and died at the last. And when He had done, and so born us to bliss, yet might not all this make a seeth[1] to His marvellous love; and that showed He in these high over passing words of love: If I might suffer more, I would suffer more. He might no more die, but He would not stint[2] of working.

Wherefore Him behooveth to feed us, for the dearworthy love of Motherhead hath made Him debtor to us. The mother may give her child suck her milk, but our precious Mother Jesus, He may feed us with himself; and doth full courteously and full tenderly with the blessed sacrament that is precious food of very life. And with all the sweet Sacraments He sustaineth us full mercifully and graciously. And so meant He in this blessed word where that He said, I it am that Holy Church preacheth thee and teacheth thee. That is to say: All the health and life of sacraments, all the virtue and grace of my word, all the goodness that is ordained in Holy Church for thee, I it am.

The mother may lay the child tenderly to her breast, but our tender Mother Jesus, He may homely lead us into His blessed breast by His sweet open side,[3] and show therein part of the Godhead and the joys of heaven, with ghostly sekirnes[4] of endless bliss; and that showed in the giving the same understanding in this sweet word where He saith: Lo how I love thee, beholding into His side, enjoying.

This fair lovely word Mother, it is so sweet and so kind of the self that it may not verily be said of none but of Him, and to her that is very Mother of Him and of all. To the property of Motherhead longeth[5] kind love, wisdom and knowing, and it is good; for though it be so that our bodily forth-bringing be but little, low and simple in regard of our ghostly forth-bringing yet it is He that doth it in the creatures by whom that it is done. The kind, loving mother that wot and knoweth the

need of her child, she keepeth it full tenderly as the kind and condition of motherhead will. And as it waxeth in age she changeth her working but not her love. And when it is waxen of more age, she suffered that it be chastised in breaking down of vices to make the child to receive virtues and graces. This working, with all that be fair and good, our Lord doth it in Him by whom it is done. Thus He is our Mother in kind by the working of grace in the lower part, for love of the higher part. And He will that we know it; for He will have all our love fastened to Him. And in this I saw that all our debt that we owe, by God's bidding, by Fatherhead and Motherhead, for God's Fatherhead and Motherhead is fulfilled in true loving of God; which blessed love Christ worketh in us. And this was showed in all, and namely in the high plenteous words where He saith: I it am that thou lovest. . . .

CHAPTER 86

The good Lord showed this book should be otherwise performed than at the first writing; and for His working [we] will thus pray, Him thanking, trusting, and in Him enjoying; and how He made this showing because He will have it known, in which knowing He will give us grace to love him; for fifteen years after it was answered that the cause of all this showing was love, which Jesus grant us. Amen—Eighty-Sixth chapter.

This book is begun by God's gift and His grace, but it is not yet performed, as to my sight. For charity pray we all to God, with God's working, thanking, trusting, enjoying; for thus will our good Lord be prayed, as by the understanding that I took in all His own meaning, and in the sweet words where He saith full merrily: I am ground of thy beseeching. For truly I saw and understood in our Lord's meaning that He showed it for He will have it known more than it is, in which knowing He will give us grace to love Him and cleave to him; for He beheld His heavenly treasure with so great love on earth that He will give us more light and solace in heavenly joy in drawing of our hearts, for sorrow and darkness which we are in.

And from that time that it was showed I desired oftentimes to wit what was our Lord's meaning. And fifteen years after and more I was answered in ghostly

---

[1]   *make a seeth*   Give satisfaction.

[2]   *stint*   Stop.

[3]   *open side*   Referring to the wound that Jesus received from a soldier's spear when he hung on the Cross. See John 19.34.

[4]   *sekirnes*   Certainly.

[5]   *longeth*   Belongeth, i.e., belongs.

understanding, saying thus: Wouldst thou wit thy Lord's meaning in this thing? Wit it well: love was His meaning. Who showed it thee? Love. What showed He thee? Love. Wherefore showed it he? For love. Hold thee therein and thou shalt wit and know more in the same; but thou shalt never know nor wit therein other thing without end.

Thus was I learned that love was our Lord's meaning. And I saw full sekirly in this and in all, that ere God made us He loved us; which love was never slaked, nor never shall. And in this love He hath done all His work; and in this love He hath made all things profitable to us; and in this love our life is everlasting. In our making we had beginning, but the love wherein He made us was in Him from without beginning; in which love we have our beginning. And all this shall be seen in God without end; which Jesus may grant us. Amen.

Thus endeth the revelation of love of the blessed Trinity showed by our Saviour Christ Jesus for our endless comfort and solace, and also to enjoy in Him in this passing journey of this life. Amen, Jesus, Amen.

I pray Almighty God that this book come not but to the hands of them that will be His faithful lovers, and to those that will submit them to the faith of Holy Church and obey the wholesome understanding and teaching of the men that be of virtuous life, sad[1] age and profound learning; for this revelation is high divinity and high wisdom, wherefore it may not dwell with him that is thrall to sin and to the devil. And beware thou take not one thing after thy affection and liking and leave another, for that is the condition of a heretic. But take everything with other and truly understand all is according to Holy Scripture and grounded in the same, and that Jesus, our very love, light and truth, shall show to all clean souls that with meekness ask perseverantly[2] this wisdom of Him. And thou, to whom this book shall come, thank highly and heartily our Saviour Christ Jesus that He made these showings and revelations for thee, and to thee, of His endless love, mercy and goodness, for thine and our safe guide and conduct to everlasting bliss; the which Jesus may grant us. Amen.

—LATE 14TH CENTURY

---

[1] *sad* Mature.

[2] *perseverantly* With perseverance.

MARGERY KEMPE

c. 1373 – 1439

Widely varying descriptions of Margery Kempe have been proposed in the past century—mystic, eccentric, feminist, lunatic, saint, fanatic, heretic, visionary—but for literary purposes, one point about her is central: hers is often considered the first extant autobiography written in English. Dictated to two different scribes, *The Book of Margery Kempe* describes the spiritual awakening and religious fervor of a medieval woman who could neither read nor write, but who had a wide and heartfelt knowledge of theology from listening to sermons and lectures. Modeling herself after various female saints (Bridget of Sweden and Katherine of Alexandria, for example), Kempe was herself on a self-described quest for sainthood; in her autobiography she describes the many obstacles that stood in her spiritual path, as well as her shrewd approaches to dealing with the impediments. Her willingness to challenge powerful men—including the Archbishop of York—and her determination to follow her calling at any cost make her story as fascinating as it is remarkable.

Margery Brunham Kempe's early life was typical of a prosperous woman of the fifteenth century. Her father was an important man in the affluent port town of Bishop's Lynn (now called King's Lynn) in Norfolk, England. John Brunham was five times mayor of the town, two times Member of Parliament, and he held various other estimable positions. At the age of 20 Margery married John Kempe, also of Bishop's Lynn; the couple had 14 children over the following 20 years. Kempe's autobiography begins with her marriage, although she mentions having committed some sin, possibly of a sexual nature, before the age of 20 and having felt deeply remorseful about it ever since; she seemed to feel that no amount of penance or atonement would redeem her. Following the difficult birth of her first child, Kempe, believing she was near death, called for a priest and attempted to confess her "crime." The priest's response was so unsympathetic and threatening that Kempe was not able to continue her confession, nor would she ever again mention her misdeed to anyone. She subsequently suffered what most modern readers would describe as a mental breakdown and experienced visions of the Devil and of Christ; she would endure many more travails before experiencing salvation.

At the age of 60, Kempe dictated an account of these travails and of the happiness she eventually found in God. Narrated in a colloquial and often non-chronological manner, her book describes her progress from a strong-willed wife who ran her own businesses to a strong-willed ascetic who renounced her family and her conjugal bed and set out on a series of pilgrimages. Kempe candidly describes the various ways in which she alienated both priests and laypeople wherever she went. Weeping and sobbing were not unusual occurrences in the medieval church, but Kempe's unrestrained crying and her obsessive discourse on religious topics annoyed many townsfolk and travelers and led some to believe that she was insane. More than once she was taken into custody as a heretic, only to use her wiles and her knowledge of Scripture to assuage (if not always win over) her accusers.

Although she had not lived with her husband for some years, when he suffered a bad accident Kempe rushed to his side and nursed him for several years until his death in 1431. While settled in

Bishop's Lynn, she claimed to have performed a miracle that prevented the town from burning down, and her claim was widely believed. The last known mention of Kempe is in the town records of 1439, so she is presumed to have died around that time. These days Kempe is often studied alongside anchoress Julian of Norwich (in fact the two had once met when Kempe went to Julian to seek spiritual guidance), who also described mystical visions in her *Revelations of Divine Love*; Kempe's autobiography, however, affords greater insights into the lives of secular women and the lay spirituality of medieval England.

⌘ ⌘ ⌘

from *The Book of Margery Kempe*[1]

THE PROEM

Here begins a short treatise, and a comforting one for sinful wretches, from which they can take great solace and comfort and understand the exalted and ineffable mercy of our sovereign Saviour Jesus Christ, whose name should be worshipped and exalted without end, who now in our time deigns to exercise His nobility and goodness upon us unworthy ones. All the works of our Savior serve as an example and instruction for us, and whatever grace He works in any creature is for our benefit, provided that a lack of charity does not hinder us.

And therefore, by leave of our merciful Lord Jesus Christ, for the exaltation of His Holy Name, Jesus, this little treatise will treat a small part of his wonderful works: how mercifully, how kindly, and how charitably He moved and stirred a sinful wretch[2] to love Him, a sinful wretch who for many years wished and intended, through the incitement of the Holy Spirit, to follow our Savior, and made great promises of fasting and many other acts of penance. And she was continually turned back from this in time of temptation, like a reed that bends with every wind and is never stable unless no wind blows, until the time when our merciful Lord Jesus Christ, taking pity and compassion on His handiwork and His creature, turned health into sickness, prosperity into adversity, honor into reproach, and love into hatred. With all these things turning upside down in this way, this creature, who for many years had gone astray and had always been unstable, was perfectly drawn and stirred to enter the way of noble righteousness, the righteous way that Christ our Savior exemplified in His own person. He trod it steadfastly and diligently prepared it.

Then this creature, whose way of life this treatise, through the mercy of Jesus, will partly show, was touched by the hand of our Lord with great bodily sickness, from which she lost her reason and her wits for a long time until our Lord restored her again by grace, as will be more clearly showed hereafter. Her worldly goods, which were plenteous and abundant at that time, shortly afterward became quite worthless and meager. Then pomp and pride were cast down and laid aside. Those who had honored her before reproached her most sharply; her kin and those who had been her friends were now her greatest enemies. Then she, considering this astonishing change, seeking help under the wings of her spiritual mother, Holy Church, went and submitted herself to her spiritual father, accusing herself of her misdeeds, and then did great bodily penance.

And in a short time our merciful Lord endowed this creature with plenteous tears of contrition, day by day, to such an extent that some men said she could weep at will, and slandered the work of God. She was so accustomed to being slandered and reproached, to being chided and rebuked by the world on account of the grace and virtue with which she was endowed through the strength of the Holy Spirit, that it was a kind of solace and comfort to her when she suffered any unhappiness for the love of God and for the grace that God worked in her. For the more slander and reproach that she suffered, the more she increased in grace and in devotion to holy meditation and deep contemplation and in the wonderful speech and conversation that our

---

[1] *The Book ... Kempe* The text has been translated from the Middle English for this anthology by Claire Waters.

[2] *a sinful wretch* Kempe refers to herself in the third person throughout her text.

Lord spoke and provided in her soul, teaching her how she would be despised for love of Him, how she should have patience, putting all her trust, all her love, and all her affection in Him alone. She knew and understood many secret and hidden things that were going to happen afterward, by inspiration of the Holy Spirit. And often, while she was engaged in such holy speech and conversation, she would weep and sob so much that many people were greatly astonished, for they little knew how much at home our Lord was in her soul. Nor could she herself ever tell the grace that she felt, it was so heavenly, so high above her reason and her bodily wits, and her body was so weak when grace was present in her that she could never express it in words as she felt it in her soul.

Then this creature was very much afraid of illusions and deceptions by her spiritual enemies. She went, at the bidding of the Holy Spirit, to many estimable learned men, both archbishops and bishops, teachers of divinity and scholars as well. She also spoke with many anchoresses[1] and showed them her way of life and the grace that the Holy Spirit, in His goodness, worked in her mind and in her soul, as well as her wits allowed her to express it. And all those to whom she showed her secrets said that she should greatly love our Lord for the grace that He showed her, and they counseled her to follow her movings and stirrings and trustingly believe they were from the Holy Spirit and not from an evil spirit.

Some of these worthy and estimable clerks accepted, on the peril of their souls and as they would answer to God for it, that this creature was inspired by the Holy Spirit, and asked her to have written and made for them a book of her experiences and her revelations. Some offered to write down her experiences with their own hands, and she would not by any means consent, for she was commanded in her soul not to write so soon. And so it was twenty years and more from the time when this creature had her first experiences and revelations before she had any of them written down. Afterward, when it pleased our Lord, He commanded and charged her that she should have her experiences and revelations and way of life written down so that His goodness might be known to all the world.

The creature had no writer who would fulfil her desire or give credence to her experiences until the time when a man living in Germany, who was an Englishman by birth and later was married in Germany and had both a wife and child there, having good knowledge of this creature and of her desire, moved, I trust, by the Holy Spirit, came to England with his wife and his belongings and lived with the aforementioned creature until he had written as much as she would tell him during the time they were together. And then he died. Then there was a priest for whom this creature had great affection, and so she conversed with him about this matter and brought him the book to read. The book was so badly written that he could do little with it, for it was neither good English nor German, and the letters were not shaped or formed as other letters are. Therefore the priest fully believed that no one would ever be able to read it, unless it were by special grace. Nevertheless, he promised her that if he could read it he would with good will copy it out and write it better.

Then there was such ill spoken of this creature and of her weeping that the priest, out of cowardice, did not dare speak with her often, and would not write as he had promised the aforementioned creature. And so he avoided and deferred the writing of this book well into the fourth year or more, despite the fact that the creature often asked him for it. At last he said to her that he could not read it, and so he would not do it. He would not, he said, put himself in danger from it. Then he advised her to go to a good man who had been well acquainted with the man who first wrote the book, on the supposition that he would be best able to read the book, for he had sometimes read letters in the other man's writing that were sent from overseas while he was in Germany. And so she went to that man, asking him to write this book down and never to let it be known as long as she lived, and granting him a large portion of goods for his labor. And this good man wrote about a page, and yet it was not much help, for he could not do much with it, the book was so badly presented and so poorly written.

Then the priest was troubled in his conscience, for he had promised her to write this book, if he could manage to read it, and had not done his part as well as he could have, and he asked this creature to get the book

---

[1] *anchoresses* Female religious ascetics who secluded themselves and devoted their lives to God.

back if she were able. Then she got the book back and brought it to the priest with a glad face, asking him to do his best, and she would pray to God for him and get him grace to read and also to write it. The priest, trusting in her prayers, began to read this book, and it was much easier, it seemed to him, than it had been before. And so he read it over in this creature's presence, every word, with her sometimes helping him when there was any difficulty.

This book is not written in order, each thing after another as it was done, but just as the material came to the creature's mind when it was being written down, for it was so long before it was written that she had forgotten the time and the order in which things happened. And therefore she had nothing written down unless she knew for certain it was really true. When the priest first began to write this book, his eyes failed him so that he could not see to form his letters, nor could he see to mend his pen. Everything else he could see well enough. He set a pair of spectacles on his nose, and then it was even worse than it had been before. He complained to the creature of his trouble. She said his enemy resented his good deed and would prevent him if he could, and she told him to do as well as God would give him grace to do, and not to stop. When he went back to his book, he could see as well, it seemed to him, as he had ever done before, by both daylight and candlelight. And for this reason, when he had written a quire,[1] he added a leaf to it, and then wrote this prologue to be clearer than the next one is, which was written before this one. *Anno domini*[2] 1436.

THE PREFACE

A short treatise of a creature living in great pomp and worldly pride, who then was drawn to our Lord by great poverty, sickness, shame, and great reproaches in many diverse countries and places, some of which tribulations will be depicted below, not in order as they happened but as the creature was able to recall them when it was written, for it was twenty years and more from the time when this creature had forsaken the world and eagerly devoted herself to our Lord before this book was writ-

ten, even though this creature was greatly advised to have her tribulations and experiences written down, and a Carmelite friar[3] offered to write them willingly, if she would agree. And she was warned in her spirit that she should not write so soon. And many years afterward she was bidden in her spirit to write. And yet then it was first written by a man who wrote neither good English nor German, so it was unreadable except by special grace, for there was so much malicious talk and slander of this creature that few people would believe her. And so at last a priest was greatly moved to write this treatise, and he could not easily read it for four whole years. And then at the request of this creature and the urging of his own conscience he tried again to read it, and it was much easier than it had been previously. And so he began to write in the year of our Lord 1436, on the day after Mary Magdalene's day,[4] according to the information of this creature.

from BOOK 1

CHAPTER 1

When this creature was twenty years old or a little more, she was married to a respected townsman and was pregnant within a short time, as nature would have it. And after she had conceived, she was afflicted with great fever until the child was born, and then, because of the labor she had in giving birth and the sickness that had gone before, she despaired of her life, believing she might not survive. And then she sent for her spiritual father, for she had something on her conscience that she had never told before that time, in all her life. For she was always prevented by her enemy, the devil, continually saying to her while she was in good health that she did not need confession but should do penance alone, by herself, and all would be forgiven, for God is merciful enough. And therefore this creature often did great penance by fasting on bread and water, and other charitable deeds with devout prayers, but she

---

[1] *quire* Four large sheets of paper folded to create eight sheets.

[2] *Anno domini* Latin: In the year of our Lord.

[3] *Carmelite friar* Monk of the religious order of Our Lady of Mount Carmel, founded in the twelfth century; Kempe refers here to Alan of Lynn.

[4] *Mary Magdalene's day* July 23rd.

would not tell it in confession. And whenever she was sick or unwell, the devil said in her mind that she would be damned, for she was not absolved of that sin. Therefore, after the child was born, she, not trusting she would live, sent for her spiritual father, as was said before, with the full intention of being absolved for her entire life, as near as she could. And when she came to the point of saying the thing that she had concealed for so long, her confessor was a little too hasty, and began sharply to rebuke her before she had said everything she meant to, and so she would say no more for anything he could do.

And then, on account of the fear she had of damnation, on the one hand, and his sharp reproofs on the other hand, this creature went out of her mind and was terribly troubled and harassed by spirits for half a year, eight weeks and some days. And in this time she saw, as it seemed to her, devils opening their mouths, all aflame with burning flames of fire as though they would swallow her in, sometimes raging at her, sometimes threatening her, sometimes pulling her and dragging her, night and day, during this time. And also the devils cried out at her with great threats and told her to forsake her Christianity, her faith, and deny her God, His mother, and all the saints in heaven, her good works and all good virtues, her father, her mother, and all her friends. And so she did. She slandered her husband, her friends and her own self; she spoke many reproving words and many harsh words; she knew no virtue or goodness; she desired all wickedness; just as the spirits tempted her to say and do, so she said and did. She would have destroyed herself many times at their instigation, and been damned with them in hell. And in demonstration of this, she bit her own hand so violently that it could be seen for the rest of her life afterward. And she tore the skin of her body above her heart with her nails pitilessly, for she had no other instrument, and she would have done worse except that she was bound and strongly restrained both day and night, so that she could not do what she wished.

And when she had been oppressed for a long time by these and many other temptations, so that no one thought she would escape or live, then at one point, as she lay alone and her keepers were away, our merciful Lord Jesus Christ, who is ever to be trusted, worshiped

be His name, never forsaking His servant in time of need, appeared to His creature, who had forsaken Him, in the likeness of the loveliest, most beauteous, most pleasing man who could ever be seen with human eye, wearing a mantle of purple silk, sitting on her bedside, looking upon her with such a blessed face that she was strengthened in all her spirits, and He said to her these words: "Daughter, why have you forsaken me, and I never forsook you?"

And at once, as He said these words, she saw truly how the air opened, as bright as any light, and He rose up into the air, not hastily or quickly, but gently and easily so that she could see Him well in the air until it closed again.

And at once the creature was confirmed in her wits and her reason as well as she had ever been before, and asked her husband, as soon as he came to her, to give her the keys of the cellar so that she could get her food and drink as she had done before. Her maids and her keepers advised him not to give her any keys, for they said she would just give away whatever goods there were, for they believed she did not know what she was saying. Nevertheless, her husband, still having tenderness and compassion for her, commanded them to give her the keys. And she ate and drank as well as her bodily strength would allow her, and recognized her friends and her household and everyone else who came to her to see how our Lord Jesus Christ had worked His grace in her, so blessed may He be who is always near in tribulation. When people think He is far from them, He is very near, by His grace. Then this creature did all the other tasks that fell to her wisely and soberly enough, but she did not truly know the ecstasy of our Lord.

CHAPTER 2

And when this creature had in this way, by grace, come to herself again, she thought she was indebted to God and that she would be His servant. Still, she would not leave the pride and pompous display that she had been accustomed to beforehand, either at her husband's or at anyone else's advice. And yet she knew full well that men said many bad things of her, for she wore ornaments of gold wire on her head and her hoods were fringed with tassels. Her cloaks were fringed as well and decorated with many colors between the fringes, so that they would be more striking to men's eyes and she herself would be more admired. And when her husband would tell her to leave her pride, she answered harshly and sharply and said that she came from such a worthy family that he could never have expected to marry her, for her father had once been mayor of the town N. and then was alderman of the noble Guild of the Trinity[1] in N., and therefore she would defend the honor of her kin whatever anyone said.

She was very envious of her neighbours if they were dressed as well as she was. All her desire was to be admired by people. She would not be warned by any chastisement nor be content with the goods God had given her, as her husband was, but always wanted more and more. And then, for pure greed and to support her pride, she began to be a brewer, and was one of the main brewers in the town of N. for three or four years until she lost a great deal of money, for she had no experience at it. For no matter how good her servants were, nor how knowledgeable about brewing, it would never ferment with them. For when the air was standing as nicely under the froth as anyone could see, suddenly the froth would fall down so that all the ale was lost, one brewing after another, so that her servants were ashamed and would not stay with her.

Then this creature thought of how God had punished her previously and she would not take the warning, and now again by the loss of her goods, and then she left it and did no more brewing. And then she asked her husband's pardon for not following his advice before, and she said that her pride and sin were the cause of all her punishment and that she would make good what she had done wrong, with good will. And yet she did not entirely leave the world, for now she thought of a new business. She had a horse-mill. She got two good horses and a man to grind people's corn and in this way she thought she would make her living. This plan did not last long, for a short while after, on the eve of Corpus Christi,[2] this marvel took place. The man was in good bodily health, and his two horses, which were

strong and healthy, had pulled well in the mill before, but now he took one of these horses and put it in the mill as he had done before, and the horse would not pull at all in the mill, for anything the man might do. The man was upset and tried with all his wits to think how he could get the horse to pull. Now he led him by the head, now he beat him, now he coaxed him, and all to no avail, for he would rather go backward than forward. Then the man set a sharp pair of spurs on his heels and rode on the horse's back to make him pull, and still it was no better. When the man saw that it was not going to work, he put the horse back in the stable and gave him food, and he ate well and heartily. And then he took the other horse and put him in the mill, and just as his companion had done, so he did, for he would not pull for anything the man might do. And then the man gave up his position and would no longer stay with the aforesaid creature.

As soon as it was reported around the town of N. that no man or beast would work for the said creature, some said she was cursed; some said God took open vengeance on her; some said one thing and some said another. And some wise men, whose minds were more grounded in a love of our Lord, said it was the divine mercy of our Lord Jesus Christ that called and cried to her from the pride and vanity of the wretched world. And then this creature, seeing all the adversity coming on every side, thought it was the scourges of our Lord that were chastising her for her sin. Then she asked God's mercy and forsook her pride, her greed, and her desire for worldly honor, and did great bodily penance, and began to enter the way of everlasting life, as will be told hereafter.

CHAPTER 3

One night, as this creature lay in bed with her husband, she heard the sound of a melody as sweet and delectable, it seemed to her, as if she had been in Paradise. And at that she jumped out of bed and said, "Alas that ever I did sin; it is full merry in heaven."

This melody was so sweet that it surpassed, beyond comparison, all the melody that could ever be heard in this world, and caused this creature, when she heard any mirth or melody after that, to experience most plenteous

---

[1] *alderman ... Guild of the Trinity* Leader of an organization dedicated to the Holy Trinity that served as a social aid group; Kempe was inducted into the Guild in the 1440s.

[2] *Corpus Christi* Feast of the Blessed Sacrament, in early summer.

and abundant tears of sincere devotion, and great sobbing and sighing after the bliss of heaven, without dreading the shame and spite of the wretched world. And after this spiritual ecstasy she always had in her mind the mirth and melody that were in heaven, so much so that she could not easily restrain herself from speaking of it. For, whenever she was in company, she would often say, "It is full merry in heaven."

And those who knew her previous behavior and now heard her speak so much of the bliss of heaven said to her, "Why do you talk in this way of the mirth that is in heaven? You do not know it, and you have not been there any more than we have," and they were angry with her because she would not hear any talk of worldly things as they did and as she had done before.

And after this time she never wished to have intercourse with her husband, for the debt of matrimony was so abominable to her that it seemed to her she would rather eat or drink slime, or the muck in the gutter, than to consent to any bodily intercourse, except out of obedience. And so she said to her husband, "I cannot deny you my body, but the love of my heart and my affection is drawn away from all earthly creatures and set only on God."

He would have his will, and she obeyed with great weeping and lamenting because she could not live chastely. And often this creature lived chastely, advised her husband to live chastely, and said that she knew well that they had often displeased God by their excessive love and the great enjoyment that they both had in sleeping together, and now it was right that they should, by the will and consent of both of them, both punish and chastise themselves deliberately by abstaining from their bodily lust. Her husband said it would be good to do so, but that he could not yet, and he would when God wished him to. And so he slept with her as he had done before, he would not restrain himself. And she continually prayed to God that she might live chastely, and three or four years later, when it pleased our Lord, her husband made a vow of chastity, as will be written hereafter by leave of Jesus.

And also, after this creature heard this heavenly melody, she did great bodily penance. She was confessed sometimes twice or three times in a day, and especially of that sin that she had so long concealed and hidden, as is written in the beginning of the book. She gave herself to great fasting and keeping vigils. She got up at two or three o'clock and went to church, and stayed there in her prayers until noontime and also all afternoon. And then she was slandered and reproached by many people because she lived so strict a life. Then she got a rough haircloth[1] from a kiln, of the kind that men use to dry malt on, and put it under her gown as craftily and secretly as she could, so that her husband would not notice it, and he did not, even though she lay by him every night in bed and wore the haircloth every day, and bore children during this time.

Then she spent three years being greatly troubled by temptations, which she bore as meekly as she could, thanking our Lord for all His gifts, and was as happy when she was reproached, scorned, or jeered at for love of our Lord, as she had been before at worldly honor— indeed, much happier. For she knew full well that she had sinned greatly against God and was worthy of more shame and sorrow than any man could do to her, and that being despised by the world was the right path to heaven, since Christ Himself chose that path. All His apostles, martyrs, confessors and virgins, and all who ever came to Heaven, passed along the path of tribulation, and she desired nothing so much as Heaven. Then she was glad in her conscience when she believed that she was entering the path that would lead her to the place that she most desired. And this creature had contrition and great remorse, with plenteous tears and many loud sobs for her sins and for her unkindness to her maker. She contemplated her unkindness since her childhood, which our Lord would many times bring to her mind. And then she, beholding her own wickedness, could only lament and weep and keep praying for mercy and forgiveness. Her weeping was so plenteous and so continual that many people thought that she could weep and stop weeping at will, and therefore many people said she was a false hypocrite and wept for show, for support and worldly good. And then a great many forsook her who had loved her before, when she was in the world, and would not acknowledge her, and she continually thanked God for everything, desiring nothing but mercy and forgiveness of sin.

---

[1] *haircloth* Coarse shirt made from animal hair and worn by penitents.

CHAPTER 4

The first two years when this creature was drawn to our Lord in this way, she had great rest in spirit with regard to temptations. She could easily endure fasting, it did not cause her suffering. She hated the joys of the world. She felt no rebellion in her flesh. She was so strong, it seemed to her, that she feared no devil in hell, for she did such great bodily penance. She thought that she loved God more than He loved her. She was struck with the deadly wound of vainglory and did not feel it, for she desired many times that the crucifix should free His hands from the Cross and embrace her as a sign of love. Our merciful Lord Jesus Christ, seeing this creature's presumption, sent her, as is written above, three years of great temptations, of which I propose to write about one of the hardest, as an example to those who come after that they should not trust in themselves or have joy in themselves as this creature had, for assuredly our spiritual enemy does not sleep, but very busily searches our characters and our dispositions, and wherever he finds us weakest, there, by our Lord's permission, he lays his snare, which no one can escape by his own power. And so he laid before this creature the snare of lechery, when she thought that all fleshly lust had been wholly quenched in her. And for a long time she was tempted with the sin of lechery, in spite of anything she could do. And yet she often went to confession, she wore the haircloth and did great bodily penance and wept many a bitter tear, and very often prayed to our Lord that he should preserve her and keep her so that she should not fall into temptation, for she thought she would rather be dead than consent to that. And all this time she had no desire to have intercourse with her husband, but found it very painful and horrible.

In the second year of her temptations it so happened that a man she loved well said to her on the eve of St. Margaret's Day, before evensong,[1] that come what may he would lie by her and have his bodily pleasure, and she would not withstand him, for if he could not have his will this time, he said, he would have it another time, she had no choice. And he did it to test what she

would do, but she thought he meant it entirely in earnest at that time, and said little in reply. So then they parted from one another and both went to hear evensong, for she attended St. Margaret's Church. This woman was so intent on the man's words that she could not hear evensong, or say her Lord's Prayer, or think any other good thought, but was more troubled than she had ever been before. The devil put it into her mind that God had forsaken her, and otherwise she would not have been so tempted. She believed the devil's persuasion and began to consent because she could not think any good thought. Therefore she believed that God had forsaken her. And when evensong was over, she went to the man and said that he should have his desire, as she thought he had wished, but he dissimulated[2] so that she did not know what he meant, and so they parted from one another for the night.

This creature was so troubled and vexed all that night that she had no idea what to do. She lay beside her husband, and having intercourse with him was so loathsome to her that she could not endure it, although it was lawful for her and at a lawful time[3] if she had wished. But she was continually thinking about the other man and about sinning with him, since he had spoken to her about it. At last she was overcome by the pressure of temptation and a lack of control, and consented in her mind, and went to the man to see if he would consent to her. And he said he would not do it for all the wealth in the world; he would rather be chopped up as small as meat for the cooking pot. She went away all ashamed and confused, seeing his stability and her own weakness. Then she thought of the grace God had given her before, how she had had two years of great rest in her soul, repentance for her sins with many bitter tears of compunction,[4] and a perfect will never to return to her sins, but to be dead rather than do so, it seemed to her. And now she saw how she had consented to do sin in her will. Then she fell half into despair. She thought she was in hell, she had such sorrow. She thought she was not worthy of any mercy because her consent was so willingly given, and not worthy to do

---

[1] *St. Margaret's Day* June 20th, feast of St. Margaret of Antioch, patron saint of pregnant women; *evensong* Vespers, or evening prayer.

[2] *dissimulated* Pretended not to understand her.

[3] *at a lawful time* I.e., not during one of the many times when sex was prohibited—feast days, etc.

[4] *compunction* Remorse.

him service because she was so false to him. Nevertheless she was absolved[1] many times and often, and did whatever penance her confessor would order her to do, and was guided by the rules of the Church. God gave this creature that grace, blessed may He be, but He did not withdraw her temptation, but instead increased it, it seemed to her. And therefore she believed He had forsaken her and dared not trust in His mercy, but was oppressed by horrible temptations of lechery and despair for almost the whole rest of the year, except that our Lord, in His mercy, as she said herself, gave her almost every day two hours of compunction for her sins, with many bitter tears. And then she was troubled by the temptation to despair, as she had been before, and was as far from feeling grace as those who never felt it at all. And that she could not bear, and therefore she continually despaired. Except when she felt grace, her troubles were so overwhelming that she could hardly manage them, but continually mourned and lamented as though God had forsaken her. …

CHAPTER II

It happened one Friday, on Midsummer Eve in very hot weather, as this creature was coming from the direction of York, carrying a bottle of beer in her hand, and her husband with a cake tucked in his coat, that he asked his wife this question: "Margery, if a man came along with a sword and was going to cut off my head unless I had natural intercourse with you as I have done before, tell me the truth of your conscience—for you say you will not lie: would you allow my head to be cut off, or would you allow me to sleep with you again as I once did?"

"Alas, sir," she said, "why do you raise this matter, we having been chaste these eight weeks?"

"Because I want to know the truth of your heart."

And then she said with great sorrow, "Truly I would rather see you be killed than that we should go back to our uncleanness."

And he said to her, "You are no good wife."

And then she asked her husband why he had not slept with her for eight weeks before, since she lay beside him every night in his bed. And he said he was so afraid when he went to touch her that he dared do no more.

"Now, good sir, amend yourself and ask God's mercy, for I told you nearly three years ago that you[2] would be killed, and here it is the third year, and still I hope I shall have my wish.[3] Good sir, I beg that you grant me what I ask, and I will pray that you may be saved through the mercy of our Lord Jesus Christ, and you will have greater reward in heaven than if you wore a hairshirt or a coat of mail. I beg you, allow me to make a vow of chastity by the hand of whatever bishop God wills."

"No," he said, "that I will not grant you, for now I can sleep with you without deadly sin, and then I could not do so."

Then she said again, "If it is the will of the Holy Spirit to fulfil what I have said, I pray God that you may consent to it; and if it is not the will of the Holy Ghost, I pray God you never consent."

Then they went on toward Bridlington in very hot weather, the aforesaid creature in a state of great sorrow and great fear for her chastity. And as they passed by a Cross, her husband sat himself down under the Cross, calling his wife to him and saying these words to her: "Margery, grant me my desire, and I shall grant you yours. My first desire is that we should continue to lie together in one bed as we have done before; the second that you shall pay my debts before you go to Jerusalem; and the third that you should eat and drink with me on a Friday as you used to do."

"Nay, sir," she said, "to break the Friday I will never grant you while I live."

"Well," he said, "then I shall sleep with you again."

She asked him to give her leave to make her prayers, and he granted it willingly. Then she kneeled down beside a Cross in the field and prayed in this manner, with a great abundance of tears: "Lord God, You know all things; You know what sorrow I have had to be chaste in my body for You these three years, and now I could have my will and I dare not for love of You. For if I were to break that custom of fasting that You commanded me to keep on Fridays, without meat or drink, I would now have my desire. But, blessed Lord, you know I will not go against Your will, and now my

---

[1] *she was absolved*   I.e., absolved of her sins through the sacrament of Confession.

[2] *you*   I.e., your sexual desire.

[3] *my wish*   To live chastely.

sorrow is great unless I find comfort in You. Now, blessed Jesus, make Your will known to me unworthy, that I may follow it and fulfil it with all my might."

And then our Lord Jesus Christ with great sweetness spoke to this creature, commanding her to go back to her husband and ask him to grant what she desired. "And he shall have what he desires. For, my most worthy daughter, this was the reason that I told you to fast, so that you should sooner obtain and get your desire, and it is granted you. I do not wish you to fast any longer, therefore I bid you in the name of Jesus, eat and drink as your husband does."

Then this creature thanked our Lord Jesus Christ for His grace and His goodness, and then rose up and went to her husband, saying to him, "Sir, if it please you, you shall grant me my desire, and you shall have your desire. Grant me that you shall not come into my bed, and I grant you to pay your debts before I go to Jerusalem. And put my body at God's disposal so that you never make any claims on me to ask me for any marriage debt after this day as long as you live, and I will eat and drink on Fridays at your bidding."

Then her husband said in reply, "May your body be as much at God's disposal as it has been at mine." This creature greatly thanked God, rejoicing that she had her desire, and asking her husband that they might say three Our Fathers in honor of the Trinity for the great grace that He had given them. And so they did, kneeling under a Cross, and then they ate and drank together in great gladness of spirit. This was on a Friday, on Midsummer Eve. Then they went on toward Bridlington and also to many other regions and spoke with God's servants, both hermits and recluses and many other lovers of our Lord, as well as many worthy clerks, doctors of divinity, and also scholars in many various places. And this creature showed to various of them her experiences and her contemplations, as she was commanded to do, to know if there were any deception in her experiences. …

CHAPTER 50

When she got to York, she went to an anchoress who had loved her well before she went to Jerusalem to find out about her spiritual progress, and also wishing, for

more spiritual conversation, to eat with the anchoress that day nothing but bread and water, for it was Our Lady's Eve.[1] And the anchoress would not receive her, for she had heard so much evil spoken of her. So she went off to other strangers and they made her very welcome for the love of our Lord.

One day, as she sat in a church in York, our Lord Jesus Christ said in her soul, "Daughter, there is much tribulation coming to you."

She was somewhat dejected and upset at that, and therefore, sitting still, she did not answer. Then our blessed Lord said again, "What, daughter, are you unwilling to suffer more tribulation for love of Me? If you do not wish to suffer any more, I will take it away from you."

And then she said in reply, "Nay, good Lord, let me be at Your will and make me mighty and strong to suffer all that You will ever wish me to suffer, and grant me meekness and patience as well."

And so, from that time forward, knowing it was our Lord's will that she suffer more tribulation, she received it willingly when our Lord wished to send it, and thanked Him greatly for it, being truly glad and merry on any day when she suffered any misfortune. And over the course of time, she was not as merry nor as glad on a day when she suffered no tribulation as on a day when she did suffer tribulation.

Then, when she was in the aforementioned Minster[2] at York, a clerk came to her, saying, "Damsel, how long will you stay here?"

"Sir," she said, "I plan to stay for the next fourteen days."

And so she did. And in that time many good men and women asked to meet her and made her warmly welcome and were very glad to hear her conversation, marvelling greatly at the fruitfulness of her speech. And she also had many enemies who slandered, scorned and despised her, of whom one, a priest, came to her while she was in the said minster and, taking her by the collar of her gown, said, "You wolf, what is this cloth that you

---

[1] *Our Lady's Eve*   The eve of the Feast of St. Mary, i.e., 1 September.

[2] *Minster*   Large church.

have on?"[1]

She stood still and would say nothing on her own behalf. Young men from the monastery who were going by said to the priest, "Sir, it is wool."

The priest was annoyed because she would not answer, and began to swear many great oaths. Then she spoke on God's behalf; she was not afraid. She said, "Sir, you should keep God's commandments and not swear so carelessly as you do."

The priest asked her who kept the commandments. She said, "Sir, those who keep them."

Then he said, "Do you keep them?"

She said in reply, "Sir, it is my will to keep them, for I am bound to do so, and so are you and every man who will be saved at last."

When he had grumbled at her for some time, he went away secretly before she was aware of it, so that she did not know what became of him.

CHAPTER 51

Another time a great clerk came to her asking how these words should be understood: "Be fruitful and multiply."[2]

She, answering, said, "Sir, these words should be understood to mean not only the bodily procreation of children, but also the attainment of virtue, which is spiritual fruit, such as by hearing the words of God, by setting a good example, by meekness and patience, charity and chastity, and other such things, for patience is worth more than miracle-working." And by the grace of God she answered that clerk in such a way that he was well pleased. And our Lord in His mercy always made some men love and support her.

And so in this city of York there was a doctor of divinity, Master John Aclom, also a canon of the Minster, Sir John Kendale, and another priest who sang by the Bishop's grace; these were her good friends among the clergy. So she remained in that city for fourteen days, as she had said before, and a little more, and on the Sundays she was absolved in the Minster

with great weeping, loud sobbing, and loud crying so that many people greatly wondered what was wrong with her. So afterward a priest came, who seemed like an honorable clerk, and said to her, "Damsel, you said when you first came here that you would stay here only fourteen days."

"Yes, sir, by your leave, I said that I would stay here fourteen days, but I did not say that I would stay here neither more nor less. But now, sir, I tell you truly that I am not going yet."

Then he set a day when he commanded her to appear before him in the chapterhouse. And she said that she would obey his order with a good will. Then she went to Master John Aclom, the aforesaid doctor, asking him to be there on her side, and so he was, and gained great favor among all of them. Another master of divinity had also promised her that he would be there with her, but he held back until he knew how things would go, whether for or against her. There were many people that day in the chapterhouse of the Minster to hear and see what would be said and done to the aforesaid creature.

When the day came, she was all ready in the Minster to answer for herself. Then her friends came to her and told her to be in good spirits. She, thanking them, said that she would. And soon a priest came very kindly and took her by the arm to help her through the crowd of people and brought her before a distinguished doctor, the one who had summoned her before to appear before him in the chapterhouse that day in York Minster. And with this doctor sat many other reverend and distinguished clerks, some of whom loved the said creature well. Then the eminent doctor said to her, "Woman, what are you doing here in this area?"

"Sir, I came on pilgrimage to make an offering here at St. William."[3]

Then he said again, "Do you have a husband?" She said, "Yes." "Do you have any letter of record?"[4]

"Sir," she said, "my husband gave me leave with his own mouth. Why do you behave like this with me more than with other pilgrims who are here, who do not have a letter any more than I have? Sir, you let them go in

---

[1] "*You wolf ... have on.*" See Matthew 7.15: "Beware of false prophets, which come to you in sheep's clothing, but inwardly they are ravening wolves."

[2] *Be fruitful and multiply.* From Genesis 1.22.

[3] *St. William* Shrine of William Fitzherbert, Archbishop of York (at the Cathedral of York).

[4] *letter of record* I.e., letter of consent to go on a pilgrimage.

peace and quiet and in rest, and I can get no rest among you. And sir, if there is any clerk among you all who can prove that I have said any word otherwise than I ought to do, I am ready to amend it with a good will. I will neither maintain error nor heresy, for it is my full will to believe as Holy Church believes and fully to please God."

Then the clerks examined her in the articles of the faith and in many other questions as they pleased, to which she answered well and truly so that they could find no excuse in her words to make trouble for her, thanks be to God.

And then the doctor who sat there as a judge ordered her to appear before the Archbishop of York and told her what day, at a town called Cawood, commanding that she be kept in prison until the day of her appearance. Then the secular people spoke for her and said that she should not go to prison, for they themselves would take responsibility for her and go to the Archbishop with her. And so the clerks said no more to her at that time, for they got up and went where they liked and let her go where she liked, praise be to Jesus. And soon afterward a clerk came to her, one of the same who had sat in judgment against her, and said, "Damsel, I beg that you not be displeased with me, though I sat with the doctor against you; he insisted so much that I did not dare do otherwise."

And she said, "Sir, I am not displeased with you for it."

Then he said, "I ask you then, pray for me."

"Sir," she said, "I will, gladly."

CHAPTER 52

There was a monk who was going to preach in York, who had heard much slander and much evil talk about the said creature. And when he was going to preach there was a great multitude of people there to hear him, and she was present with them. And so, when he was giving his sermon, he discussed many matters so openly that the people easily gathered that it was because of her, for which reason her friends who loved her well were very distressed and upset about it, and she was much happier, for she had something to test her patience and her charity, by which she hoped to please our Lord Jesus Christ. When the sermon was done, a doctor of divinity

who loved her well, along with many others, also came to her and said, "Margery, how are things with you today?"

"Sir," she said, "very well, blessed be God. I have reason to be truly merry and glad in my soul if I can suffer anything for His love, for He suffered much more for me."

Soon after there came a man who loved her well with a good will, along with his wife and others, and led her seven miles from there to the Archbishop of York, and brought her into a handsome room, and a good clerk came in, saying to the good man who had brought her there, "Sir, why have you and your wife brought this woman here? She will sneak away from you, and cause you to be disgraced."

The good man said, "I dare well say that she will remain, and be here to answer for herself with a good will."

The next day she was brought into the Archbishop's chapel, and many of the Archbishop's household came in, scorning her, calling her "Lollard"[1] and "heretic," and they swore many a horrible oath that she would be burned. And she, through the strength of Jesus, said in reply to them, "Sirs, I fear you will be burned endlessly in hell unless you improve yourselves with regard to your swearing, for you do not keep God's commandments. I would not swear as you do for all the goods of this world."

Then they went away as if they were ashamed. She then, making a silent prayer, asked grace to behave herself that day in the way that would be most pleasing to God and profit to her own soul and a good example to her fellow Christians. Our Lord, answering her, said it would be just so. At last the said Archbishop came into the chapel with his clerks, and said sharply to her, "Why do you wear white? Are you a maiden?"[2]

She, kneeling on her knees before him, said, "No, sir, I am no maiden; I am a wife."

He commanded his people to fetch a pair of shackles and said she would be shackled, for she was a false

---

[1] *Lollard* Follower of theologian John Wycliffe (1330–84), considered by some to be a heretic because of his severe criticisms of corruption in the institutional church and the failings of the clergy, as well as his views on certain church doctrines.

[2] *maiden* Virgin.

heretic. And then she said, "I am no heretic, nor shall you prove me to be one."

The Archbishop went away and let her stand there alone. Then she prayed for a long while to our Lord God Almighty to help her and support her against all her enemies, spiritual and bodily, and her flesh trembled and shuddered terribly so that she wanted to put her hands under her clothing in order that it would not be seen.

Then the Archbishop came back into the chapel with many worthy clerks, among whom was the same doctor who had examined her before and the monk who had preached against her a little while before in York. Some of the people asked whether she was a Christian woman or a Jew; some said she was a good woman and some said not. Then the Archbishop took his seat, and her clerks also, each of them according to his rank, there being many people present. And in the time while the people were gathering together and the Archbishop taking his seat, the said creature stood to the back, making her prayers with deep devotion for help and succor against her enemies, for such a long time that she melted all into tears. And at last she cried out loudly as well, so that the Archbishop and his clerks and many people were astonished at her, for they had not heard such crying out before.

When her crying had passed she came before the Archbishop and fell on her knees, the Archbishop saying rudely to her, "Why do you weep like that, woman?"

She, answering, said, "Sir, you will wish some day that you had wept as hard as I."

And shortly, after the Archbishop had put to her the articles of our faith, which God gave her grace to answer well and truly and readily without any great thought so that he could not find fault with her, then he said to the clerks, "She knows her faith well enough. What shall I do with her?"

The clerks said, "We know well that she knows the articles of the faith, but we will not allow her to remain among us, for the people have great faith in her conversation, and perhaps she might lead some of them astray."

Then the Archbishop said to her, "I hear bad reports of you; I hear tell that you are a very wicked woman."

And she said back to him, "Sir, so I hear tell that you are a wicked man. And if you are as wicked as men say, you shall never get to heaven unless you mend your ways while you are here."

Then he said very rudely, "Why, you, what do people say about me?"

She answered, "Other people, sir, can tell you well enough."

Then a great clerk with a furred hood said, "Peace! You speak of yourself and let him be."

Then the Archbishop said to her, "Lay your hand on the book here in front of me and swear that you will leave my diocese as soon as you can."

"Nay, sir," she said, "I beg you, give me leave to go back to York to take leave of my friends."

Then he gave her leave for a day or two. She thought it was too short a time, so she said again, "Sir, I cannot leave this diocese so hastily, for I must stay and speak with good men before I go, and I must, sir, by your leave, go to Bridlington and speak with my confessor, who was the confessor of the good prior who is now canonized."

Then the Archbishop said to her, "You shall swear that you will not teach or scold the people in my diocese."

"Nay, sir, I will not swear," she said, "for I shall speak of God and rebuke those who swear great oaths wherever I go, until the time that the Pope and Holy Church have ordained that no one shall be so bold as to speak of God, for God Almighty does not forbid, sir, that we shall speak of Him. And moreover the Gospel mentions that when the woman had heard our Lord preach, she came before Him with a loud voice and said, 'Blessed be the womb that bore you and the breasts that gave you suck.' Then our Lord said in reply to her, 'Truly, so are they blessed who hear the word of God and keep it.'[1] And therefore, sir, it seems to me that the Gospel gives me leave to speak of God."

"Ah, sir," said the clerks, "here we truly think that she has a devil in her, for she speaks of the Gospel."[2]

---

[1]   *Blessed be the womb ... and keep it*   From Luke 11.27–28.

[2]   *she has a devil ... Gospel*   Reading the Scriptures in English was one of the major points of debate in the Lollard conflict. The Catholic Church did not wish the Bible to be made available in the vernacular or for anyone other than the clergy to engage in Biblical interpretation. The Lollards took issue with the established Church on both counts.

At once a great clerk brought forth a book and for his part quoted St. Paul against her, that no woman should preach.[1] She, in response to this, said, "I do not preach, sir; I go into no pulpit. I use only conversation and good words, and that I will do as long as I live."

Then a doctor who had examined her previously said, "Sir, she told me the worst stories about priests that I ever heard."

The Bishop commanded her to tell that story.

"Sir, with all due respect, I spoke only of one priest by way of example, whom, as I have been told, God allowed to go astray in a wood, for the profit of his soul, until night came upon him. He, lacking in shelter, found a pleasant garden in which he rested that night, which had a lovely pear tree in the middle, all covered and adorned with flowers and blooms delightful to see, to which there came a big, rough bear, huge to behold, shaking the pear tree and knocking down the flowers. This dreadful beast greedily ate and devoured those fair flowers. And when he had eaten them, turning his tail end toward the priest, he excreted them out again from his hind parts.

"The priest, greatly disgusted at this loathsome sight, and struck with great doubt about its meaning, went on his way the next day melancholy and pensive, when it happened that it met with a handsome, aged man who looked like a palmer[2] or pilgrim, who asked the priest the cause of his melancholy. The priest, telling him what is written above, said he was struck by great fear and melancholy when he saw that loathsome beast defoul and devour such fair flowers and blooms and afterward excrete them from his backside so horribly in front of him, and that he did not understand what this could mean.

"Then the palmer, showing himself to be the messenger of God, explained it to him in this way: 'Priest, you yourself are the pear tree, partly flourishing and flowering by saying your service and administering the sacraments, though you do so undevoutly, for you pay little attention to how you say your matins[3] and your service, so long as you babble your way through it.

Then you go to your Mass without devotion, and you have little contrition for your sin. You receive there the fruit of everlasting life, the Sacrament of the altar, in a most inappropriate state of mind. Then the whole day afterward you spend your time badly, devoting yourself to buying and selling, chopping and changing, as if you were a worldly man. You sit at your ale, giving yourself over to gluttony and excess, to bodily pleasure, through lechery and uncleanness. You break God's commandments by swearing, lying, slander, and backbiting and practicing other such sins. Thus through your misconduct you, like the loathsome bear, devour and destroy the flowers and blooms of virtuous living, to your endless damnation and the detriment of many people, unless you get the grace of repentance and amendment.'"

Then the Archbishop liked the story well and commended it, saying it was a good story. And the clerk who had examined her before in the absence of the Archbishop said, "Sir, this story strikes me to the heart."

The aforesaid creature said to the clerk, "Ah, honorable sir doctor, in the place where I mostly live there is a worthy clerk, a good preacher, who boldly speaks against the misconduct of the people and will flatter no one. He says many times in the pulpit, 'If any man dislikes my preaching, let him take note, for he is guilty.' And just so, sir," she said to the clerk, "is your experience with me, God forgive you."

The clerk did not know what to say to her. Afterward the same clerk came to her and asked her forgiveness for having been so much against her. He also asked her especially to pray for him.

And then soon after the Archbishop said, "Where can I find a man who will take this woman away from me?"

At once many young men jumped up, and every one of them said, "My lord, I will go with her."

The Archbishop answered, "You are too young; I will not have you." Then a good solid man of the Archbishop's household asked his lord what he would give him if he would take her. The Archbishop offered him five shillings and the man asked for a noble.[4] The Archbishop, answering, said, "I will not spend so much on her body." "Yes, good sir," said the aforesaid creature, "our Lord shall reward you well in return." Then

---

[1] *St. Paul ... preach* See 1 Timothy 2.11–12.

[2] *palmer* Pilgrim to the Holy Land.

[3] *matins* Morning services.

[4] *noble* English gold coin worth six shillings eightpence.

the Archbishop said to the man, "See, here is five shillings, and take her quickly out of this region." She, kneeling down on her knees, asked his blessing. He, asking her to pray for him, blessed her and let her go. When she then went back to York she was welcomed by many people and worthy clerks, who rejoiced that our Lord had given her, who was unlearned, wit and wisdom to answer so many learned men without disgrace or blame, thanks be to God.

CHAPTER 53

Then the good man who was escorting her brought her out of town and then they went on to Bridlinton to her confessor, who was called Sleytham, and spoke with him and with many other good men who had entertained her previously and done much for her. Then she did not wish to stay but took her leave, to proceed on her journey. And then her confessor asked if she did not dare stay on account of the Archbishop of York, and she said, "No, indeed."

Then the good man gave her money, beseeching her to pray for him. And so she went on toward Hull. And there at one time, as they went in procession, a woman of high rank treated her with great contempt, and she said not a word. Many other people said she should be put in prison, and made great threats. And despite all their malice, a good man came and asked her to eat with him and made her very welcome. Then the malicious people who had scorned her before came to this man and told him not to be kind to her, for they believed that she was not a good woman. The next day in the morning her host led her out to the edge of town, for he did not dare entertain her any longer. And so she went to Hessle and wanted to cross the water at Humber.[1] Then she happened to find there two Dominican friars and two yeomen[2] of the Duke of Bedford. The friars told the yeomen who she was, and the yeomen arrested her as she was about to take her boat, and also arrested a man who was with her.

"For our lord the Duke of Bedford," they said, "has sent for you. And you are considered the greatest Lollard in this whole area and around London as well. And we have looked for you in many places, and we will have a hundred pounds for bringing you before our lord."

She said to them, "Sirs, I will willingly go with you where you want to take me."

Then they took her back to Hessle, and there people called her a Lollard, and women came running out of their houses with their distaffs,[3] crying out to the people, "Burn this false heretic."

And as she went on toward Beverley with the aforesaid yeomen and friars, they repeatedly met with people of that area who said, "Damsel, give up this life you are living, and go spin and card as other women do, and do not suffer so much shame and sorrow. We would not suffer so much for anything on earth."

Then she said to them, "I do not suffer as much sorrow as I wish to for our Lord's love, for I suffer only harsh words, and our merciful Lord Jesus Christ, worshipped be His name, suffered hard blows, bitter scourging, and at last shameful death for me and for all mankind, blessed may He be. And therefore what I suffer is truly nothing compared to what He suffered."

And so, as she went along with the aforesaid men, she said good things to them, until one of the Duke's men who had arrested her said, "I regret that I came upon you, for it seems to me that you say right good words."

Then she said to him, "Sir, do not regret or repent having come upon me. Do your lord's will, and I trust that all will be for the best, for I am very well pleased that you came upon me."

He said in reply, "Damsel, if ever you are a saint in heaven, pray for me."

She answered, saying to him in reply, "Sir, I hope you will be a saint yourself, and everyone that shall come to heaven."

So they went on until they came into Beverley, where the wife of one of the men who had arrested her lived. And they took her there and took her purse and her ring away from her. They prepared a pleasant room for her and a clean bed in it with the necessities, locking the door with the key and taking the key away with them. Then they took the man whom they had arrested with her, who was the Archbishop of York's man, and put him in prison. And soon after, that same day, word came that the Archbishop had come into the town

---

[1]   *Humber*   I.e., the River Humber.

[2]   *yeomen*   Attendants; men of high rank who serve a lord.

[3]   *distaffs*   Rods used for spinning wool.

where his man was in prison. The Archbishop was told of his man's imprisonment, and at once had them let him out. Then the man went angrily to the aforesaid creature, saying, "Alas that ever I knew you. I have been put in prison on your account."

She, comforting him, said, "Be meek and patient, and you will get a great reward in heaven for it."

So he went away from her. Then she stood looking out a window, saying many good words to those who wished to hear her, so that women wept hard and said with great sorrow in their hearts, "Alas, woman, why must you be burned?"

Then she asked the good woman of the house to give her something to drink, for she was ill with thirst. And the woman said her husband had taken the key away, and so she could not get to her nor give her anything to drink. And then the women got a ladder and put it up to the window and gave her a pint of wine in a pot and gave her some bread, beseeching her to put the pot and bread away secretly so that when the man of the house came he would not see it.

CHAPTER 54

The aforesaid creature, lying in her bed on the following night, heard with her bodily ears a loud voice calling, "Margery." At that voice she awoke, very frightened, and lying still in silence she made her prayers as devoutly as she could at the time. And soon our merciful Lord, who is present everywhere, comforting his unworthy servant, said to her, "Daughter, it is more pleasing to Me that you endure contempt and scorn, shame and reproof, wrongs and misfortunes than if your head were struck off three times a day, every day for seven years. And therefore, daughter, do not fear what any man may say to you; rather you have great reason to rejoice in My goodness and in the sorrows you have suffered for it, for when you come home to heaven, then every sorrow will turn to joy for you."

The next day she was brought into the chapterhouse of Beverley, and the Archbishop of York was there and many great clerks with him, priests, canons, and secular men. Then the Archbishop said to the aforesaid creature, "What, woman, have you come back? I would willingly be rid of you."

And then a priest brought her before him, and the Archbishop said, in the hearing of everyone present, "Sirs, I had this woman before me at Cawood, and there I and my clerks examined her in the faith and found no error in her. Furthermore, sirs, I have since that time spoken with good men who consider her a righteous woman and a good woman. Nevertheless, I gave one of my men five shillings to lead her out of this area to keep the people quiet. And as they were going on their journey, they were taken and arrested, my man put in prison on her account, and her gold and silver taken away from her, as well as her prayer beads and her ring, and she is brought before me again. Is there anyone here who can say anything against her?"

Then other men said, "Here is a friar who knows many things against her."

The friar came forth and said that she led everyone astray from Holy Church, and uttered many bad things about her at that time. He also said that she would have been burnt at Lynn if his order, that is, the Dominicans, had not been there. "And sir, she says that she can weep and feel contrition when she wishes."

Then the two men who had arrested her came, saying like the friar that she was Cobham's[1] daughter and was sent to carry letters around the country. And they said she had not been to Jerusalem nor in the Holy Land nor on other pilgrimages,[2] when in truth she had been. They denied all truth and insisted on what was wrong, as many others had done before. When they had said enough for a great while and a long time, they held their peace.

Then the Archbishop said to her, "Woman, what do you say to this?"

She said, "My lord, with all due respect, every word they say is a lie."

Then the Archbishop said to the friar, "Friar, these are not heretical words; they are slanderous and erroneous words."

"My lord," said the friar, "she knows her faith well enough. Nevertheless, my lord of Bedford is angry with her, and he wishes to see her."

---

[1] *Cobham* Sir John Oldcastle, Lord Cobham, one of the leaders of the Lollards in the early fifteenth century; he was executed as a heretic in 1417.

[2] *pilgrimages* Lollards did not condone pilgrimages.

"Well, friar," said the Archbishop, "then you shall take her to him."

"Nay, sir," said the friar, "it is not for a friar to lead a woman around."

"And I do not wish," said the Archbishop, "for the Duke of Bedford to be angry with me on her account."

Then the Archbishop said to his men, "Keep watch on the friar until I wish to see him again," and commanded another man to keep the aforesaid creature as well, until he wished to see her again another time at his pleasure. Then the aforesaid creature asked him by his lordship not to have her put among men, for she was a man's wife. And the Archbishop said, "No, you will not be harmed."

Then he who was entrusted with her took her by the hand and led her home to his house and asked her to sit with him at meat and drink, making her welcome. Soon afterwards many priests and other people came there to see her and speak with her, and many people felt great compassion that she was treated so badly.

Shortly afterward the Archbishop sent for her, and she came into his hall. His retinue was dining, and she was taken into his room and up to his bedside. Then she, obeying, thanked him for his gracious lordship that he had shown to her before.

"Yes, yes," said the Archbishop; "I am told worse of you than I ever was before."

She said, "My lord, if you would like to question me, I will tell the truth, and if I am found guilty, I will submit to your correction."

Then a Dominican who was a diocesan bishop[1] came forward and the Archbishop said to him, "Now, sir, say while she is present what you said to me when she was not present."

"Shall I really?" said the bishop.

"Yes," said the Archbishop.

Then the bishop said to the aforesaid creature, "Damsel, you were with Lady Westmoreland."

"When, sir?" she said.

"At Easter," said the suffragan.

She, not answering, said, "Well, sir?"

Then he said, "My lady herself was very pleased with you and liked your words, but you counselled Lady Greystoke to leave her husband, and she is a baron's wife and the daughter of Lady Westmoreland, and now you have said enough to be burnt for it." And so he spoke many harsh words in front of the Archbishop; it is not useful to repeat them.

At last she said to the Archbishop, "My lord, by your leave, I have not seen Lady Westmoreland for the past two years and more. Sir, she sent for me before I went to Jerusalem and, if you like, I will go to her again so she can attest that I never brought up any such matter."

"Nay," said those who stood about, "have her put in prison, and we will send a letter to the noble lady, and if what she says is true, let her go without any objection."[2]

And she said she was quite happy for it to be so. Then a great clerk who stood just beside the Archbishop, "Put her in prison for forty days and she will love God better all her life."

The Archbishop asked her what tale it was she had told Lady Westmoreland when she spoke with her.

She said, "I told her a good tale of a lady who was damned because she would not love her enemies and of a bailiff who was saved because he loved his enemies and forgave their trespasses against him, and yet he was considered a bad man."

The Archbishop said it was a good tale. Then his steward and many others said, crying out with a loud voice to the Archbishop, "Lord, we pray you, let her go away at this time, and if she should ever come back, we will burn her ourselves."

The Archbishop said, "I believe there was never a woman in England who was so much feared as she is and has been."

Then he said to the aforesaid creature, "I do not know what to do with you."

She said, "My lord, I pray you, let me have your letter and your seal to witness that I have defended myself against my enemies and nothing has been alleged against me, neither error nor heresy, that can be proved against me, thanked be our Lord, and have John, your man, take me back across the water."

And the Archbishop very kindly granted her all her desire, may our Lord reward him, and gave back her purse with her ring and prayer beads that the Duke of

---

[1] *diocesan bishop* Bishop suffragan: a bishop under the Archbishop's jurisdiction.

[2] *objection* I.e., resistance.

Bedford's men had taken from her before. The Archbishop was surprised that she had the means to travel around the country, and she said good men gave it to her asking her to pray for them.

Then she, kneeling down, received his blessing and took her leave in very good spirits, going out of his room. And the Archbishop's people asked her to pray for them, but the steward was angry because she laughed and was cheerful, and said to her, "Holy folk should not laugh."

She said, "Sir, I have great reason to laugh, for the more shame and contempt I suffer, the merrier I am in our Lord Jesus Christ."

Then she went down into the hall and there stood the Dominican friar who had caused her all that trouble. And so she left the town with one of the Archbishop's men, carrying the letter that the Archbishop had granted her as a witness, and the man brought her to the River Humber, and there he took his leave of her, returning to his lord and taking the letter back with him, and so she was left alone without anyone she knew. All this misfortune came to her on a Friday,[1] thanked be God of all.

CHAPTER 55

When she had crossed the River Humber she was immediately arrested as a Lollard and taken toward prison. There happened to be a person who had seen her stand before the Archbishop of York, and he obtained permission for her to go where she wished and defended her against the bailiff and vouched for her that she was no Lollard. And so she escaped in the name of Jesus. Then she met a man from London and his wife. And she went along with them until she got to Lincoln, and there she suffered much scorn and many injurious words, answering back in God's cause at once so wisely and prudently that many people marveled at her cleverness.

There were lawyers who said to her, "We have gone to school for many years, and we are still not capable of answering as you do. Where do you get such cleverness?"

And she said, "From the Holy Spirit."

Then they asked, "Do you have the Holy Spirit?"

"Yea, sirs," she said, "no one can say a good word without the gift of the Holy Spirit, for our Lord Jesus Christ said to his disciples, 'Do not worry about what you will say, for it will not be your spirit that speaks in you, but the spirit of the Holy Ghost.'"[2] And thus our Lord gave her the grace to answer them, worshiped may He be.

Another time a great lord's men came to her and swore many great oaths, saying, "We have been told that you can tell us whether we shall be saved or damned."

She said, "Yes, indeed I can, for as long as you swear such horrible oaths and knowingly break the commandment of God as you do and will not give up your sin, I dare well say you will be damned. And if you will be contrite and confess your sin, willingly do penance and give it up while you can, with no intention of returning to it, I dare well say you will be saved."

"What, can you tell us nothing else but this?"

"Sirs," she said, "this is very good, it seems to me."

And then they went away from her.

After this she went on toward home again until she got to West Lynn. Once she was there, she sent to Bishop's Lynn for her husband, for Master Robert, her confessor, and for Master Alan, a doctor of divinity, and told them in part of her difficulties. And then she told them that she could not come home to Bishop's Lynn until she had gone to the Archbishop of Canterbury to get his letter and his seal. "For when I was called before the Archbishop of York," she said, "he would not believe what I said because I did not have a letter and seal from my lord of Canterbury. And so I promised him that I would not go to Bishop's Lynn until I had my lord's letter and the seal of Canterbury."

And then she took her leave of the aforesaid clerks, asking for their blessing, and went on with her husband to London. When she got there, she was provided with her letter at once by the Archbishop of Canterbury. And so she stayed in the city of London for a long time and was made very welcome by many worthy people.

Then she went toward Ely in order to get home to Lynn, and when she was three miles from Ely a man came riding after them at great speed and arrested her husband and her as well, intending to take them to prison. He cruelly rebuked and thoroughly insulted them, saying many chiding words. And at last she asked

---

[1] *on a Friday* The day of Christ's Passion.

[2] *Do not worry ... Holy Ghost* From Matthew 10.19–20.

her husband to show him my lord of Canterbury's letter. When the man had read the letter, he spoke politely and kindly to them, saying, "Why didn't you show me your letter before?"

And so they left him and went on to Ely and from there home to Lynn, where she suffered much contempt, much reproach, many a slander, many a harsh word, and many a curse. And one time a reckless man, thinking little of his own shame, wilfully and on purpose threw a bowlful of water on her head as she came down the street. She, not at all bothered by it, said, "May God make you a good man," greatly thanking God for that, as she did for many other occasions. ...

CHAPTER 86

One time our Lord spoke to this creature when it pleased him, saying to her spiritual understanding, "Daughter, as many times as you have received the blessed Sacrament of the altar[1] with many more holy thoughts than you can speak of, just so many times will you be rewarded in heaven with new joys and new comforts. And daughter, in heaven you will know how many days you have had of devout contemplation on earth, by My gift. And though all these are gifts and graces that I have given you, still you will have the same grace and reward in heaven as if they came from your own merits, for I have given them to you freely. But I thank you earnestly, daughter, for allowing Me to work My will in you and letting Me be so familiar with you. For there is nothing that you could do on earth, daughter, that would please Me better than allowing Me to speak to you in your soul, for then you understand My will and I understand your will.

"And also, daughter, you call My mother to come into your soul and take Me in her arms and put Me to her breast and give Me suck. Also, daughter, I know your holy thoughts and the good desires you have when you receive Me[2] and the true charity that you have for Me when you receive My precious body in your soul, and also how you call Mary Magdalene into your soul to welcome Me, for daughter, I know your thoughts well enough. You think that she is worthiest in your soul,

and you have the greatest trust in her prayers next to My mother's, and well you may, daughter, for she is a very great intercessor for you with Me in the bliss of heaven. And sometimes, daughter, you find your soul so large and wide that you call all the court of heaven into your soul to welcome Me. I know well, daughter, what you say: 'Come, all twelve apostles, who were so well beloved of God on earth, and receive your Lord in my soul.'

"You also ask Katherine, Margaret, and all holy virgins to welcome Me in your soul. And then you ask My blessed mother, and Mary Magdalene, all the apostles, martyrs, and confessors,[3] Katherine, Margaret, and all holy virgins that they should adorn the chamber of your soul with many beautiful flowers and with many sweet spices so that I might rest there.

"Furthermore you imagine sometimes, daughter, that you have a cushion of gold, another of red velvet, and the third of white silk in your soul. And you imagine that My Father sits on the cushion of gold, for to Him belong power and might. And you imagine that I, the second Person,[4] your love and your joy, sit on the cushion of red velvet, for all your thoughts are for Me because I redeemed you at such cost, and you think that you can never repay Me for the love that I have shown you, even if you were slain a thousand times a day, if that were possible, for love of Me. Thus you think in your soul, daughter, that I deserve to sit on a red cushion in remembrance of the red blood that I shed for you. Moreover you imagine that the Holy Spirit sits on a white cushion, for you consider that He is full of love and purity, and therefore it becomes Him to sit on a white cushion, for He is the giver of all holy thoughts and chastity.

"And yet I know well enough, daughter, that you think you cannot worship the Father unless you worship the Son, and you cannot worship the Son unless you worship the Holy Spirit. And you also think sometimes, daughter, that the Father is all-powerful and all-knowing and all grace and goodness, and you think the same of the Son, that He is all-powerful and all-knowing and all grace and goodness. And you think that the Holy Spirit has the same properties equally with the Father

---

[1] *blessed Sacrament of the altar*   The Eucharist; Communion.

[2] *you receive Me*   In Communion.

[3] *confessors*   Those who bore witness to the faith, often referring to saints who were not martyred.

[4] *second Person*   Of the Trinity.

and the Son, proceeding from them both. Also you think that each of the three Persons in the Trinity has what the other has in His Godhead, and so you believe truly in your soul, daughter, that there are three diverse Persons and one God in substance, and that each knows what the others know, and each can do what the others can, and each wills what the others will. And daughter, this is a true faith and a right faith, and this faith you have only by My gift. And therefore, daughter, if you will consider it carefully, you have great reason to love Me well and to give Me your whole heart so that I may fully rest in it as I myself wish to, for if you allow Me, daughter, to rest in your soul on earth, believe well that you shall rest eternally with Me in heaven.

"And therefore, daughter, do not be surprised that you weep hard when you take Communion and receive My blessed body in the form of bread, for you pray to me before you receive the Sacrament, saying to me in your mind, 'As surely, Lord, as you love me, make me clean from all sin and give me grace to receive your precious body worthily, with every kind of worship and reverence.'

"And daughter, know well that I hear your prayer, for you cannot say a better word to please Me than 'as surely as I love you,' for then I fulfil my grace in you and give you many a holy thought—it is impossible to tell them all. And for the great intimacy that I show you you are all the bolder to ask Me for grace for yourself, for your husband, and for your children, and you make every Christian man and woman your child in your soul for that time, and wish to have as much grace for them as for your own children. You also ask mercy for your husband, and you think you are greatly obliged to me for having given you such a man, who would allow you to live chaste while he is still alive and in good bodily health. Truly, daughter, you think rightly, and therefore you have great cause to love me well. Daughter, if you knew how many wives there are in this world that would love Me and serve Me well and diligently, if they could be as free of their husbands as you are of yours, you would say that you were very greatly obliged to Me. And yet they are prevented from having their will and suffer great pain, and therefore they will have great reward in Heaven, for I take every good will as a deed.

"Sometimes, daughter, I cause you to feel great sorrow for your spiritual father's sins, and especially that he should have as full forgiveness of his sins as you would hope to have of yours. And sometimes when you receive the precious Sacrament, I cause you to pray for your spiritual father in this way: that as many men and women might be inspired by his preaching as you hope may be inspired by the tears of your eyes, and that My holy words might sink as deep in their hearts as you wish them to sink in your heart. And you also ask the same grace for all good men who preach My word on earth, that they might benefit all rational creatures.

"And often, on the day when you receive my precious body, you ask grace and mercy for all your friends, and for all your enemies that ever shamed you or reproached you or scorned you or mocked you for the grace that I work in you, and for all this world both young and old, with many tears of heavy weeping and sobbing. You have suffered much shame and reproach, and therefore you will have great bliss in heaven.

"Daughter, do not be ashamed to receive My grace when I will give it to you, for I will not be ashamed of you when you are received into the bliss of heaven, where for every good thought, for every good word, and for every good deed, for every day of contemplation, and for all the good desires that you have had here in this world, you will be rewarded there with Me eternally as My beloved darling, as My blessed spouse, and as My holy wife.

"And therefore fear not, daughter, though the people wonder why you weep so hard when you receive Me, for if they knew what grace I put in you at that time, they would wonder instead why your heart did not burst asunder. And so it would if I did not measure that grace myself, but you see well yourself, daughter, that when you have received Me into your soul you are in peace and at rest, and sob no longer. And the people wonder at that, but it should be no wonder to you, for you know well that I act like a husband who is going to marry a wife. Once he has married her, it seems to him that he is sure enough of her and that no man will part them asunder, for then, daughter, they can go to bed together without any shame or dread of the people and sleep in rest and peace if they wish to. And so it goes, daughter, between you and Me, for you have every week, especially on Sunday, great fear and dread in your soul about how you can be sure of My love, and how, with great reverence and holy dread, you may best receive Me for the salvation of your soul with every kind of meekness, humility, and charity, as any lady in this world is eager to receive her husband when he comes home and has been away from her a long time.

"My beloved daughter, I thank you highly for all the sick people that you have taken care of in My name, and for all the goodness and service that you have done to them in any degree, for you shall have the same reward with Me in heaven as if you had protected Me Myself when I was here on earth. Also, daughter, I think you for all the times you have bathed Me in your soul at home in your room, as if I had been present there in My humanity, for I know well, daughter, all the holy thoughts that you have shown Me in your mind. And also, daughter, I thank you for all the times you have sheltered Me and My blessed mother in your bed. For these and for all other good thoughts and good deeds that you have thought in My name and done for love of Me you shall have, with Me and with My mother, with My holy angels, with My apostles, with My martyrs, confessors, and virgins, and with all My holy saints, all manner of joy and bliss everlasting."

from BOOK TWO

…

CHAPTER 10

From London she went to Sheen[1] three days before Lammas Day[2] to get a pardon[3] through the mercy of our Lord. And when she was in the church at Sheen, she experienced great devotion and high contemplation. She had abundant tears of compunction and of compassion at the remembrance of the bitter pains and suffering that our merciful Lord Jesus Christ suffered in His blessed humanity. Those who saw her weep and heard her sob so loudly were greatly astonished and wondered what was the concern of her soul.

A young man who saw her appearance and her countenance, moved by the Holy Spirit, went to her when he was able to do so alone, with a fervent desire to understand what might be the cause of her weeping, and said to her, "Mother, if it please you, I ask that you show me the reason for your weeping, for I have not seen a person with such abundance of tears as you have, and I have, especially, never before heard anyone sob so hard as you do. And mother, though I am young, my desire is to please my Lord Jesus Christ and to follow Him as I can and may. And I intend by the grace of God to take the habit[4] of this holy religion, and therefore I beg you not to be distant with me. Show me your thoughts in a good and motherly way, as I trust in you."

She, kindly and meekly, with gladness of spirit, as it seemed right to her, commended him for his intention and told him in part that the cause of her weeping and sobbing was her great unkindness toward her Maker, by which she had many times offended His goodness, and the great disgust she felt at her sins caused her to sob and weep. Also the great and excellent charity of her Redeemer, who by virtue of suffering the Passion and shedding His precious Blood redeemed her from everlasting pain and through whom she hoped to be the inheritor of joy and bliss, moved her to sob and weep, and it was no wonder. She told him many good words of spiritual comfort, by which he was incited to great virtue, and afterward he ate and drank with her while she was there and was very glad to be in her company.

Lammas Day was the principal day of pardon,[5] and as the aforesaid creature went into the church of Sheen, she caught sight of the hermit who had led her out of Lynn when she went toward the sea with her daughter-in-law, as is written above. At once, with great joy of spirit, she presented herself to him, welcoming him with all the powers of her soul, saying to him, "Ah, Reynald, you are welcome. I trust our Lord sent you here, for now I hope that just as you led me out of Lynn, so you will bring me home again to Lynn."

The hermit had a cross face and a discouraging expression, neither wishing nor intending to bring her home to Lynn as she desired. Answering curtly, he said,

---

[1] *Sheen* Carthusian monastery founded by Henry V.

[2] *Lammas Day* Harvest festival on August 1.

[3] *pardon* Official grant by the Church for the remission of a sin after the sacrament of Penance and specified devotional duties are performed.

[4] *take the habit* Become a monk.

[5] *Lammas Day … pardon* Pardons were often associated with major feast days.

"I think you should know that your confessor has forsaken you, for you went overseas and did not tell him a word about it. You got leave to take your daughter down to the shore; you did not ask leave any further. You had no friend who knew of your plan; therefore I imagine you will find little friendship when you get back there. I pray you, get your company where you can, for I was blamed for your absence after I last escorted you; I will not do it again." She spoke to him pleasantly and asked him for the love of God not to be displeased, for those who loved her for God's sake before she went away would love her for God's sake when she came home. She offered to pay his costs along the way home. So at last he, consenting, took her back to London and then home to Lynn, to the great worship of God and the merit of both their souls. When she got home to Lynn, she submitted herself to her confessor. He spoke sharply to her, for she was under obedience to him and had taken such a journey upon herself without his knowing. Therefore he was displeased with her, but our Lord helped her so that she had as good love from him and from other friends afterward as she had before, worshipped be God. Amen.

This creature, who is spoken of above, for many years used to begin her prayers in this way. First, when she got to church, kneeling before the sacrament in worship of the blessed Trinity (Father, Son, and Holy Spirit, one God and three Persons), of the glorious Virgin, Queen of Mercy, our Lady Saint Mary, and of the twelve apostles, she said the holy hymn "*Veni creator spiritus*"[1] with all the verses belonging to it, so that God would illuminate her soul, as He did with His apostles on Pentecost Day, and endow her with the gifts of the Holy Spirit so that she might have grace to understand His will and perform it in her works, and so that she might have grace to withstand the temptations of her spiritual enemies and avoid every kind of sin and wickedness.

When she had said "*Veni creator spiritus*" with its verses, she said as follows: "I call the Holy Spirit to witness, and our Lady Saint Mary, the mother of God, all the holy court of heaven, and all my spiritual fathers here on earth, that even if it were possible for me to have all knowledge and understanding of the secrets of God by hearing them from a devil of hell, I would not do it. And as surely as I would not know, hear, see, feel, nor understand in my soul in this life more than it is God's will for me to know, may God just as surely help me in all my works, in all my thoughts, and in all my speech, eating and drinking, sleeping and waking. As surely as it is not my will nor my intention to worship any false devil as my God, nor any false faith, nor to have false belief, just so surely do I reject the devil and all his false counsel and everything that I have ever done, said, or thought on the devil's advice when I believed it to be the counsel of God and the inspiration of the Holy Spirit. If it has not been so, God, who sees into and knows the secrets of all men's hearts, have mercy on me for it and grant me in this life a well of abundantly flowing tears with which I can wash away my sins through Your mercy and goodness.

"And Lord, by Your exalted mercy, bring upon me, here on earth, all the tears that can increase my love for you and build up my merit in heaven, and help and profit the souls, lives, or deaths of my fellow Christians. Good Lord, do not spare the eyes in my head any more than You spared the Blood in Your body, which You shed abundantly for sinful mankind's soul, and grant me so much pain and sorrow in this world that I am not held back from Your bliss and the sight of Your glorious face when I pass from here.

"As for my crying, my sobbing and weeping, Lord God Almighty, as surely as You know what scorns, what shames, what contempt and blame I have had for it, as surely as it is not in my power to weep either loudly or quietly for any devotion or sweetness, but only by the gift of the Holy Spirit, just so surely, Lord, acquit me so that all this world may know and believe that it is Your work and Your gift to magnify Your name and increase other people's love for You, Jesus. And I beg You, Sovereign Lord Jesus Christ, that as many men may be inspired by my crying and my weeping as have scorned me or shall scorn me for it to the end of the world, and many more if it be Your will.

"And regarding the love of any earthly man, as surely as I would have no beloved but God to love above all things, and would love all things and all other creatures for God and in God, just so surely quench all fleshly lust

---

[1] *Veni creator spiritus* Latin: Come, Creator Spirit.

in me and in all those in whom I have beheld Your blissful body. And give us Your holy dread in our hearts for Your painful wounds. Lord, make my spiritual fathers fear You in me and love You in me, and make all the world have greater sorrow for their own sins for the sorrow that You have given me for other people's sins. Good Jesus, make my will Your will and Your will my will, so that I may have no will but Yours alone.

"Now, good Lord Jesus Christ, I ask Your mercy for all the ranks in Holy Church, for the Pope and all his cardinals, for all archbishops and bishops, and for the whole order of the priesthood, for all monks and nuns, especially those who are active in preserving and defending the faith of Holy Church. Lord, bless them of Your mercy and grant them victory over all their enemies and help them in all they do for Your worship; may God send all who are in grace at this time perseverance to the end of their lives. And make me worthy to share in their prayers, and they in mine, and each of us in others'.

"I ask Your mercy, blissful Lord, for the King of England and for all Christian kings and for all lords and ladies who are in this world. God, give them the governance by which they can most please You and be lords and ladies in heaven without end. I ask Your mercy, Lord, for the rich men of this world who have Your goods at their disposal; give them grace to spend these as it pleases You. I ask Your mercy, Lord, for Jews and Saracens,[1] and all heathen people. Good Lord, be mindful that there is many a saint in heaven who was once a heathen on earth. And as You have spread Your mercy to those on earth.[2] Lord, You say Yourself that no one shall come to You without Your help nor anyone be drawn to You without Your drawing him. And therefore, Lord, if there is any man undrawn, I pray that You draw him toward You. You have drawn me, Lord, and I never deserved to be drawn, but You have drawn me according to Your great mercy. If all this world knew all my wickedness as you do, they would marvel and wonder at the great goodness that You have shown me. I wish that all this world were worthy to thank You on my account, and as You have made unworthy creatures worthy, so make all this world worthy to thank and

praise You.

"I ask Your mercy, Lord, for all false heretics and for all misbelievers, for all false tithers,[3] thieves, adulterers, and all prostitutes, and for all who live wickedly. Lord, of Your mercy have mercy on them if it is Your will, and bring them out of their wickedness the sooner for my prayers.

"I ask Your mercy, Lord, for all those who are tempted and troubled by their spiritual enemies, and that You of Your mercy give them grace to withstand their temptations and deliver them from these when it is most pleasing to You. I ask Your mercy, Lord, for all my spiritual fathers, that You deign to spread as much grace in their souls as I would wish You to do in mine.

"I ask Your mercy, Lord, for all my children, spiritual and bodily, and for all the people in this world, and ask that You give me contrition for their sins as if they were my own sins, and forgive them as I would wish You to forgive me.

"I ask Your mercy, Lord, for all my friends and for all my enemies, especially for all who are sick, for all lepers, for all bedridden men and women, for all who are in prison, and for all creatures in the world who have spoken either good or ill of me and ever shall do to the end of the world. Have mercy on them and be as gracious to their souls as I would wish You to be to mine. And those who have said any evil of me, forgive them for it of Your divine mercy; and those who have said well, Lord, I pray You reward them, for it is through their charity and not through my merits, for even if You allowed all this world to avenge You on me and to hate me for displeasing You, You would do me no wrong.

"I ask Your mercy, Lord, for all the souls that are in the pains of purgatory awaiting Your mercy and the prayers of Holy Church[4] as surely, Lord, as they are Your own chosen souls. Be as gracious to them as I would wish You to be to me if I were in the same pain that they are in.

"Lord Jesus Christ, I thank You for all health and wealth, for all riches and all poverty, for sickness and

---

[1] *Saracens* I.e., Muslims.

[2] The manuscript seems to have some text missing at this point, leaving an incomplete idea.

[3] *tithers* Those who tithe, or donate one-tenth of their incomes to the Church.

[4] *pains of purgatory ... Holy Church* It was believed that prayer could help shorten a soul's time in purgatory.

scorns, for all the contempt and all the wrongs, and for all the various tribulations that have befallen or shall befall me as long as I live. I thank You earnestly for allowing me to suffer in this world in remission of my sins and to the increase of my merit in Heaven, as I surely have great reason to thank You.

"Hear my prayers, for even if I had as many hearts and souls enclosed in my soul as those that God without beginning knew would dwell in Heaven without end, and as there are drops of water, fresh and salt, chips of gravel, large and small stones, grasses growing in all the earth, kernels of corn, fish, birds, animals, and leaves on trees when they are most plentiful, feathers of birds or hair of animals, seed that grows into plant or weed or flower, on land or on water when they grow the most, and as many creatures as there have been on earth and ever shall be and can be by Your power, and as there are stars and angels in Your sight or other kinds of good that grow on the earth, and each were a soul as holy as our Lady Saint Mary was, who bore our Savior Jesus, and if it were possible that each could think and speak as much reverence and worship as our Lady Saint Mary ever did here in earth and now does in heaven and shall do without end, I may well think in my heart and say with my mouth at this time, to the honor of the Trinity and of all the court of Heaven and to the great shame and disgrace of Satan who fell from God's presence, and of all his wicked spirits, that all these hearts and souls could never thank God nor fully praise Him, fully bless Him nor fully worship Him, fully love Him nor fully give Him the glory, praise, and reverence that He deserves to have for the great mercy that He has shown me in earth; that I cannot and may not do.

"I ask my Lady, who alone is the Mother of God, the well of grace, the flower and fairest of all women that God ever made on earth, the worthiest in His sight, the most beloved, dear, and precious to Him, most worthy to be heard by God and the one who most truly deserved it in this life, kind Lady, meek Lady, charitable Lady, with all the reverence that is in heaven and with all Your holy saints, I ask you, Lady, to offer thanks and praise to the blissful Trinity for love of me, asking mercy and grace for me and for all my spiritual fathers and perseverance for the rest of our lives in the way of life that is most pleasing to God. I bless my God in my soul and all of you who are in heaven. Blessed may God be in you all and all of you in God.

"Blessed be You, Lord, for all the mercies that You have shown to all those in heaven and earth. And I especially bless You, Lord, for Mary Magdalene, for Mary the Egyptian, for Saint Paul, and for Saint Augustine. And as You have shown Your mercy to them, show Your mercy to me and to all who earnestly ask You for mercy. The peace and rest that You have bequeathed to Your disciples and those who love You, bequeath that same peace and rest to me on earth and in heaven without end. Be mindful, Lord, of the woman who was taken in adultery and brought before You, and as You drove away all her enemies from her and she stood alone beside You, so indeed may you drive away all my enemies from me, both bodily and spiritual, so that I may stand alone beside You and make my soul dead to all the joys of this world and alive and eager for devout contemplation in God.

"Be mindful, Lord, of Lazarus who lay dead in his grave for four days, and as I have been in that holy place where Your body was living and dead and crucified for mankind's sin and where Lazarus was raised from death to life, as surely, Lord, if any man or woman die in this hour by deadly sin, if any prayer can help them, hear my prayers for them and give them life without end. Many thanks, Lord, for all the sins You have kept me from and that I have not done, and many thanks, Lord, for all the sorrow You have given me for those I have done, for these graces and for all the other graces that are necessary to me and to all creatures on earth. And for all those who have faith and trust in my prayers, or will have faith and trust in them until the world's end, I pray You, Lord, grant them of the multitude of Your mercy such grace as they desire, spiritual or bodily, to the profit of their souls. Amen."

—1436–38

RELIGIOUS AND SPIRITUAL LIFE

CONTEXTS

Religion was so central to life in the Middle Ages that it is impossible in a section of this sort to do more than touch on a few important developments and themes.

Celtic culture forms a strong thread through the Christian culture of the early Middle Ages; several striking visual examples are included here. Among the most important developments in the transition from the Christianity of the Early to that of the High Middle Ages was a dramatic change in religious architecture; again, illustrations are provided below.

The prayers that Christians were expected to be able to recite and two excerpts from works of advice and instruction may give some sense of the reality of religious life for the laity. The Canons of the Fourth Lateran Council in 1215 were of enormous importance in regularizing Church practice throughout Western Europe; several of these are reproduced below.

Monks and friars both played vital roles in medieval Christianity generally; both are touched on here. Beginning in the eleventh century the recovery of Aristotelian and other classical texts facilitated the development of new planes of theological argument among the Scholastics; represented here is the most influential argument of the leading theologian in Britain in the Middle Ages, St. Anselm. Scholasticism of the sort practised by St. Anselm, however, existed only in pockets; much more representative of the popular cast of mind are the accounts of miracles connected to saints' lives—those associated with Thomas Becket being a leading example.

Corruption within the Church was a recurring complaint—and a recurring reality—throughout the medieval period. During the fourteenth and early fifteenth centuries it was a particularly pressing concern both for reformist clerics such as John Wycliffe and the Lollards and for lay writers such as William Langland; in both cases relevant excerpts are included below.

The regularizing of Christian practice in the later Middle Ages was accompanied by the growth of exclusionist attitudes towards those who did not follow the designated path; as several of the readings at the end of this section illustrate, attitudes towards both heretics and Jews hardened significantly.

⌘⌘⌘

Celtic Christianity

Celtic art is characterized by formal intricacy and an extraordinarily high level of decorative skill. Its most famous expressions in a Christian context are in Gospels such as the Book of Kells and the Lindisfarne Gospels, but for centuries Celtic designs also featured prominently in a variety of forms of stone and metalwork.

Decorative page from the Book of Durrow (c. 670).   Carpet page from the Lindisfarne Gospels (8th century).

First text page, Gospel of Saint Luke, from the
Lindisfarne Gospels (8th century).

St. John from The Book of Kells (9th century).

Ardagh chalice (c. 700). This extraordinarily elaborate chalice was discovered in a hoard in a ring-fort in Limerick County in Ireland.

St. John, from The Macdurnan Gospels (9th century).

Pictish memorial stone (7th century?). This stone stands at Glamis in Scotland; accompanying the "Celtic cross" are a variety of pictograms, the meaning of which is unknown.

Church and Cathedral

Greensted Church at Ongar, Essex (c. 850). Thought to be the oldest wooden church in the world, the walls of Greensted Church are formed of tree trunks split in two, erected curved-side outward.

The Norman Crypt, Canterbury Cathedral (12th c.). Round arches and heavy stone work are characteristic of Romanesque church architecture of the Norman Period.

Interior, Durham Cathedral (1093–1133). Durham is the most spare and imposing of the Norman cathedrals in England.

Roger Fenton, "Salisbury Cathedral" (1858). Salisbury Cathedral was built in the thirteenth century, with work beginning in 1220. The spire, which was completed near the end of the century, remains the tallest in England at 404 feet. Until the latter part of the nineteenth century it was one of the world's tallest structures. (From the late medieval period until the 1890s all but one of the world's tallest buildings were churches—the exception being the Pyramid of Cheops at Giza.)

Roger Fenton, *Cloisters, Westminster Abbey* (c. 1858). The cloisters date from the 13th and 14th centuries. Like Salisbury and York Minster, Westminster Abbey is built in the Gothic style, with pointed rather than rounded arches and extensive vaulting giving a stronger sense of verticality than in Romanesque architecture.

Roger Fenton, *York Minster, from the South East* (c. 1856). Built in the late thirteenth and fourteenth centuries, York Minster remains one of Britain's leading cathedrals.

Religion for All: The Apostles' Creed, the Pater Noster, and the Hail Mary

In the Middle Ages the Apostles' Creed was believed to have been jointly composed by the apostles, with each contributing one verse. Its origins are in fact unknown, though in its earliest forms the Creed almost certainly dates back to at least the fourth century. The following Latin text and English translation show the Creed divided into twelve constituent articles.

By the later medieval period all Christians were required to be able to recite the Apostles' Creed, the Pater Noster (or Lord's Prayer), and the Hail Mary in Latin rather than in the vernacular. The Pater Noster derives from two passages in the Gospels that were believed to contain Jesus's very words, Matthew 6.9–13 and Luke 11.2–4. The Pater Noster was ubiquitous throughout society, but few understood precisely what they were saying (the word "patter" derives from the sounds people made as they recited the Pater Noster quickly and without understanding); even among the clergy a working knowledge of Latin was far from universal.

The Hail Mary had come into wide use by the eleventh century, but it was not until the twelfth century that it became common for lay people to be required to be able to recite it.

The Apostle's Creed

Credo in Deum Patrem omnipotentem, Creatorem cæli et terræ.
Et in Jesum Christum, Fílium eius unicum,
    Dominum nostrum,
  qui conceptus est de Spiritu Sancto, natus ex Maria
    Virgine,
  passus sub Pontio Pilato, crucifixus, mortuus, et
    sepultus,
  descendit ad infernos, tertia die resurrexit a mortuis,
    ascendit ad cælos, sedet ad dexteram Dei Patris
    omnipotentis,
  inde venturus est iudicare vivos et mortuos.
Credo in Spiritum Sanctum,
    sanctam Ecclesiam catholicam, sanctorum
      communionem,

remissionem peccatorum,
carnis resurrectionem,
vitam æternam. Amen.

I believe in God the Father Almighty,
creator of heaven and earth,
and in Jesus Christ, His only Son, our Lord;
who was conceived by the Holy Spirit,
born of the Virgin Mary,
suffered under Pontius Pilate, was crucified, died,
and was buried.
He descended into hell; on the third day He arose
again from the dead;
He ascended into heaven and sits at the right hand
of God the Father Almighty.
From thence He shall come to judge the living and
the dead.
I believe in the Holy Spirit,
the Holy Catholic Church,
the Communion of Saints,
the forgiveness of sins,
the resurrection of the body,
and life everlasting. Amen.

The Pater Noster

Pater noster, qui es in caelis, sanctificetur nomen
tuum. Adveniat regnum tuum. Fiat voluntas tua,
sicut in caelo et in terra. Panem nostrum quotidianum
da nobis hodie, et dimitte nobis debita nostra, sicut et
nos dimittimus debitoribus nostris. Et ne nos inducas in
tentationem: sed libera nos a malo. Amen.

Our Father, who art in heaven, hallowed be Thy name.
Thy kingdom come. Thy will be done, on earth as it is
in heaven. Give us this day our daily bread. And forgive
us our trespasses, as we forgive those who trespass
against us. And lead us not into temptation, but deliver
us from evil. Amen.

[The following verse, which has never been part of the
Roman Catholic Pater Noster, began to be added by
various Protestant groups in the sixteenth century.]

For thine is the kingdom, the power and the glory, for
ever and ever. Amen.

Illuminated page, Genesis-Job volume, Lambeth Bible (c.
1150). This page illustrates the centrality of the Virgin
Mary to medieval Christianity. During the Middle Ages
the Latin words *virga* (stem) and *virgo* (virgin) were often
assumed to be related. Here the illustration shows the
stem of genealogy passing from Jesse through the Virgin
Mary to Christ, with the four prophets (lower roundels),
the four virtues of Mercy, Truth, Righteousness and Peace
(middle roundels), and Moses with representatives of the
Church Triumphant (upper roundels) looking on. In the
corners are the four apostles.

The Hail Mary

Ave Maria, gratia plena, Dominus tecum, benedicta
tu in mulieribus et benedictus fructus ventris tui.

Hail Mary, full of grace, the Lord is with thee, blessed

art thou among women and blessed is the fruit of thy womb.

[The following verse began to be added during the fifteeth and sixteenth centuries.]

Sante Maria, Mater Dei, ora pro nobis peccatoribus, nunc et in hora mortis nostrae.

Holy Mary, Mother of God, pray for us sinners now and at the hour of our death.

from Robert Manning of Brunne, *Handlyng Synne* (early 14th century)

Robert Manning (c. 1264–c. 1340) was a Gilbertine monk at an abbey near Brunne (now Bourne) in Lincolnshire. Manning's poem *Handlying Synne*, written in English but very largely a translation of a similar work in French by William of Wadding-ton, is an educational text designed to set out in everyday terms what is entailed in following the Ten Commandments, avoiding the Seven Deadly Sins, and so forth. Whereas most religious writing of the time was in Latin, Manning wrote in the vernacular for "lewd" men "that tales and rhyme will blithely hear" rather than for the educated minority who were literate in Latin. The extracts below set out specific examples of forbidden or morally question-able activities. Interestingly, miracle plays performed outside the church are included here on the list of proscribed activities—though depicting the birth and resurrection of Jesus within the church is "without danger."

… Of tournaments that are forbade
in holy church, as men do read,
of tournaments I shall prove therein,
seven points of deadly sin:
5 first is pride, as thou well know'st,
vanity, pomp, and many a boast;
of rich attire there is great flaunting,
spurring her horse with much vaunting.
Know you well this is envy
10 when one sees another do mastery,

some in words, some in deeds;
envy most of all him leads.
Ire and wrath cannot be late;
oft are tournaments made for hate.
15 If all knights loved each other well,
tournaments would never be held;
And of course they fall into slothfulness,
they love it more than God or Mass;
And truly, there can be no doubt,
20 they spend more gold thereabout—
that is, they give it all to folly—
than on any deed of mercy.
And yet be very careful lest
you forget Dame Covetousness,
25 for she shall be foolish, in all ways,
to win a horse and some harness.
And a man shall also do robbery,
or beguile his host where he shall stay.
Gluttony also is them among,
30 delicious meats do make him strong;
and gladly he drinks wine untold,
with gluttony to make him bold.
Also is there Dame Lechery;
from here comes all her mastery.
35 Many times, for women's sake,
knights these tournaments do make;
and when he goes to the tournament
she sends him some secret present,
and bids him do, if he loves her best,
40 all that he can at her behest,
for which he gets so much the worst,
that he may not sit upon his horse,
and that peradventure, in all his life,
shall he never after thrive.
45 Consider whether such tournaments
should more truly be called torments? …

It is forbidden him, in the decree,
miracle plays for to make or see,
for, miracles if thou begin,
50 it is a gathering, a site of sin.
He may in the church, through this reason,
portray the resurrection—
that is to say, how God rose,
God and man in strength and loss—

to make men hold to belief good,
that he rose with flesh and blood;
and he may play, without danger,
how God was born in the manger,
to make men to believe steadfastly
60   that he came to us through the Virgin Mary. ...

A parson is slothful in holy church
who on his sheep will not work
how they should heed his own word
and please the church and their Lord.
65   The high Shepherd shall him blame,
for how he lets them go to shame.
If he should see in anything
that they have a lack of chastising,
unless he teach them and chastise so
70   that they from henceforth better do,
for them he shall, at God's assize,
be punished before the high Justice.
Also it behooves him to pray
that God, of grace, show him the way. ...

75   Man or woman that has a child
that with bad manners grows too wild,
that will both mis-say and –do,
chastisement behooves them too;
But chastise them with all your might,
80   Otherwise you'll be in their plight.
Better were the child unborn
than lack chastising, and thus be forlorn.
Thus says the wise king Solomon
to men and women every one,
85   "If you want your children to be good,
give them the smart end of the rod;"
and teach them good manners each one;
but take care that you break no bone. ...

Everywhere I see this custom:
90   that rich men have shrews for sons—
shrews in speech and in act—
Why? They hold no one in respect.
In his youth shall he mis-say
and scorn others by the way;
95   then says the father, "This child's story
doesn't hang together—sorry!"

And if he learns guilefulness,
false words and deceitful looks,
his father shouldn't acquit him then;
100   his sly wit will be his only friend.
If he injures foes in rages,
then says his father, "He shall be courageous,
he shall be hardy, and no man dread,
he begins early to be doughty in deed."
105   But right so shall it him befall
as it did with Eli's bad sons all. ...

from William of Pagula, *Priest's Eye* (c. 1320)

William of Pagula was an English curate who wrote
a work entitled *Oculis Sacerdotis* (*Priest's Eye*)
between 1320 and 1323, intended for use as a
handbook of instruction for parish priests–many of
whom remained poorly educated. Both the full
book and excerpts taken from it circulated widely;
the following constituted a selection of twenty-one
instructions taken from the larger work and issued
independently in 1385.

1.   A parish priest should recommend as many things to
his parishioners on Sundays as seem useful to him for
their instruction, and he should repeat them often so
they will not slip from memory. First he should teach
them the formula for baptizing infants in the absence of
a priest if it becomes necessary. This is the vernacular
version: *I crysten thee in the name of the fadyr and the sone
and the holy ghost.* While saying this, sprinkle water over
the child or immerse it in water three times or at the
very least once. Anyone, whether cleric or lay person,
may baptize a child in an emergency. Even the father of
the child or its mother may do so without putting
restrictions on their conjugal relations unless there is
someone else present who knows how and wishes to do
it. And if someone must baptize a child in an emergency using the above formula, he should speak the
words distinctly and clearly only once, in no manner
repeating the words of the rite or anything like them
over the child. And if an infant baptized in this manner
recovers, it should be taken to the church, and those
who bring it should tell the priest that the child was
baptized at home so that the priest will not baptize it

again. But, excluding the immersion in water, he should perform the exorcism, the anointing, and the other customary actions that accompany baptism but were omitted. Let the priest teach his parishioners that they should baptize using only water, no other liquids. Likewise let him warn men and women who are appointed the godparents of children at baptism that, except in an emergency they should not delay having their godchildren confirmed by a bishop. They should teach them or have them be taught the Lord's Prayer and the Creed, and admonish them when they reach adulthood or are capable of learning that they should guard their chastity, love justice, and practice charity.

The baptism of children born within eight days of Easter or Pentecost should be postponed for a week if it is convenient and they may be held back without danger, and then they should be baptized.

2. He should also warn them that anyone who has children who are not confirmed should make arrangements to have them confirmed by the time they are five years old if it is possible.

3. Also he should warn them that they should never put their children in bed with them in case through negligence they should roll over and smother them, which would be reckoned a case of homicide according to canon law. Nor should they thoughtlessly bind them in swaddling clothes or leave them alone by day or by night without someone watching them because of various dangers.

4. Also the priest should teach his parishioners that a spiritual kinship is established among godparents, godchildren, and the parents of the godchildren. The same is true for sponsors at confirmation. Because of this kinship, marriage between any of these parties is prohibited. A spiritual kinship is established among ten people in baptism and the same number in confirmation.

5. He should also teach them that if a man and a woman shall have given their legitimate consent to contract a marriage by an exchange of words in the present tense, even though there has been no betrothal but only an oath, and even though, as is the custom, no carnal relations have occurred, still they have contracted a true marriage—so much so that if afterwards one of them should contract a second marriage and even have carnal relations with the new partner, they should be separated and that person should return to the first marriage. Also he should teach them that marriages should not be contracted except in the presence of a priest and legitimate witnesses. Prior to the marriage ceremony banns should be solemnly published to the people in the church on three consecutive feast days. And any cleric or priest or other person who is present at a clandestine marriage shall be suspended from his office for three years.

6. Also he should warn them that boys and girls older than seven years should not lie together in the same bed because of the danger of fornication, nor should a brother share a bed with his sister because of the danger of incest.

7. Also he should publicly announce that any member of the faithful who has reached the age of discretion [i.e, fourteen] ought to confess all his sins to his own parish priest at least once a year and he should fulfill the penance imposed on him for his vices. During Eastertide he should receive the Body of Christ unless, with the counsel of his priest, for some reason he should abstain; otherwise while he is alive he should be barred from entering a church, and when he dies he should be without Christian burial. But if anyone does not wish to confess to his parish priest for a specific and well-founded reason, he should seek and obtain permission from his own priest to confess to another suitable priest.

8. Also he should teach them that pregnant women should be confessed beforehand so that they are prepared to receive the Eucharist if life-threatening danger should arise during their delivery, since it would seem improper for the priest to stay with them [hearing confession] during the course of their labor.

9. Also he should teach his parishioners that when the Host is elevated during the consecration of the Mass, they should genuflect if they can comfortably do so,

and, adoring the Host, they should say in a low voice: "Hail salvation of the world, Word of the Father, true sacrifice, living flesh, fully God, truly man" or "Glory to you Lord who is born" or the Lord's Prayer or some other devout words. And they should also do this when they see the Body of Christ, preceded by lights and a ringing bell, carried to the sick.

10. Also he should warn his parishioners that they should faithfully pay their tithes on goods legitimately acquired. For faithfully paying tithes brings a fourfold reward: the first is an abundance of crops; the second is bodily health, according to Augustine; the third is the remission of sins; the fourth is reward in the kingdom of heaven. But those who tithe badly are punished in four ways: first because they transgress a divine commandment. Second because once they had an abundance of all things when they tithed well, but now since they tithe badly they will be forced to tithe. Third, when tithes are poorly paid, God does not ward off locusts or other harmful things, nor does he dispel plagues or bring rain, except short-lived ones. Fourth, because of a lack of tithes, men justly collect taxes and tolls from the people since what Christ does not take, taxes will. Besides, those who do not pay their tithes are cursed by God. And merchants and artisans as much as carpenters, blacksmiths, weavers, alewives and other such people, and all other hired laborers and boon laborers all ought to be admonished to pay tithes from their earnings or else reach a settlement with the rector of their church.

11. And the priest ought to announce to his people which days are feast days and which are days of fast.

12. Also he should instruct his parishioners that they should not practice the magical arts, incantations, or sorcery, since these things have no power to cure either man or beast and besides are utterly worthless and unlawful. Moreover clerics who do these things shall be degraded and lay people shall be excommunicated.

13. Also he should warn everyone not to lend money, grain, wine, oil or any other thing whatsoever by usury; namely by entering into a contract or having the intention to receive back more in repayment than he lent out.

And if a cleric shall do this he shall be suspended from office; and a lay person shall be excommunicated until he makes restitution. To be sure, usury is forbidden in both the Old and the New Testaments.

14. He should also warn his parishioners that they should not wait in order to sell their goods at a higher price, for they are obliged to repay what they have gained by this type of withholding. Likewise they should not sell their goods to travelers, pilgrims, and other wayfarers for a higher price than they charge to their neighbors or than they can receive at market.

15. Let him also warn them that if anyone shall receive land or a dwelling as a pledge for a loan of money, after deducting his expenses, he should return the pledge; and if he receives more than that, it is to be reckoned as usury.

16. Also he shall publicly announce three times yearly that all those men who wish to enjoy the privileges of the clergy shall be duly tonsured, displaying the crown of their head suitably shaved especially in the presence of their ordinaries and in churches and in congregations of the clergy.

17. Also one day during Lent he should publicly preach the Creed, that is to say, the articles of faith.

18. And he should admonish his parishioners that they should enter church humbly and devoutly and should behave reverently, peacefully, and devoutly while in it. And when they hear named the Name of Jesus they should genuflect at the very least in their hearts, or by bowing their head, or beating their breast.

19. He should admonish them that no one should cause a disturbance, or a disagreement, or hold discussions, or useless and profane conversations in a church or its graveyard; nor should they provoke disputes or fights or anything else which could interrupt the divine services or dishonor the holiness of the place. Likewise business should not be conducted in the church or its graveyard and especially not fairs or markets, nor should courts, pleas, or secular judgments be held there. And

dishonorable dances should not take place there, nor should improper songs be sung during the vigils of saints days or at other times, nor should there take place anything else by which the church or the graveyard could be dishonored.

20. Also he should instruct them that neither a husband nor a wife should make an oath swearing to practice chastity, to fast, or to go on pilgrimage (except for a vow to go to the Holy Land) without the consent of the other. For a man and a wife are to be judged as equals in this regard.

21. He should also warn his parishioners that no one should harbor or defend in his home anyone who he knows has committed a known robbery.

from The Canons of the Fourth Lateran Council (1215)

> The following selections touch on the behavior of clerics, on confession, and on regulating the display and sale of the relics of saints. The final selection, Canon 68, is an illustration of the manner in which, as the canons of the Council acted to unify and strengthen the practices of Christians, equally they strengthened Christian hostility towards non-Christians.

Canon 14. That the morals and general conduct of clerics may be better reformed, let all strive to live chastely and virtuously, particularly those in sacred orders, guarding against every vice of desire, especially that on account of which the anger of God came from heaven upon the children of unbelief so that in the sight of Almighty God they may perform their duties with a pure heart and chaste body. But lest the facility to obtain pardon be an incentive to do wrong, we decree that whoever shall be found to indulge in the vice of incontinence, shall, in proportion to the gravity of his sin, be punished in accordance with the canonical statutes, which we command to be strictly and rigorously observed, so that he whom divine fear does not restrain from evil, may at least be withheld from sin by

a temporal penalty. If therefore anyone suspended for this reason shall presume to celebrate the divine mysteries, let him not only be deprived of his ecclesiastical benefices but for this twofold offense let him be forever deposed. Prelates who dare support such in their iniquities, especially in view of money or other temporal advantages, shall be subject to a like punishment. But if those, who according to the practice of their country [i.e., the Latin East] have not renounced the conjugal bond, fall by the vice of impurity, they are to be punished more severely, since they can use matrimony lawfully.

Canon 15. All clerics shall carefully abstain from drunkenness. Wherefore, let them accommodate the wine to themselves, and themselves to the wine. Nor shall anyone be encouraged to drink, for drunkenness banishes reason and incites to lust. We decree, therefore, that that abuse be absolutely abolished by which in some localities the drinkers bind themselves in their manner to an equal portion of drink and he in their judgment is the hero of the day who outdrinks the others. Should anyone be culpable in this matter, unless he heeds the warning of the superior and makes suitable satisfaction, let him be suspended from his benefice or office.

We forbid hunting and fowling to all clerics: wherefore, let them not presume to keep dogs and birds for these purposes.

Canon 21. All the faithful of both sexes shall after they have reached the age of discretion [then accepted to be fourteen] faithfully confess all their sins at least once a year to their own [parish] priest and perform to the best of their ability the Penance imposed, receiving reverently at least at Easter the sacrament of the Eucharist, unless perchance at the advice of their own priest they may for a good reason abstain for a time from its reception; otherwise they shall be [barred from entering] the church during life and deprived of Christian burial in death. Wherefore, let this salutary decree be published frequently in the churches, that no one may find in the plea of ignorance a shadow of excuse. But if anyone for good reason should wish to confess his sins to another priest, let him first seek and obtain permission from his own priest, since otherwise the other priest cannot absolve or bind him.

Let the priest be discreet and cautious, ... carefully inquiring into the circumstances of the sinner and the sin, from the nature of which he may understand what kind of advice to give and what kind of remedy to apply, making use of different means to heal the sick one. But let him exercise the greatest precaution that he does not in any degree by word, sign, or any other manner make known the sinner, but should he need more prudent counsel, let him seek it cautiously without any mention of the person. He who dares to reveal a sin confided to him in the tribunal of penance, we decree that he be not only deposed from the priestly office but also relegated to a monastery of strict observance to do penance for the remainder of his life ...

Canon 62. From the fact that some expose for sale and exhibit promiscuously the relics of the saints, great injury is sustained by the Christian religion. That this may not occur hereafter, we ordain in the present decree that in the future old relics may not be exhibited outside of a vessel or exposed for sale. And let no one presume to venerate publicly new ones unless they have been approved by the Roman pontiff. In the future prelates shall not permit those who come to their churches [for the sake of venerating relics] to be deceived by worthless fabrications or false documents as has been done in many places for the sake of gain. We forbid also that seekers of alms, some of whom, misrepresenting themselves, preach certain abuses, be admitted, unless they exhibit genuine letters either of the Apostolic See or of the diocesan bishop, in which case they may not preach anything to the people but what is contained in those letters. We give herewith a form which the Apostolic See commonly uses in granting such letters, that the diocesan bishops may model their own upon it....

Canon 68. In some provinces a difference of dress distinguishes the Jews and Saracens from the Christians, but in others confusion has developed to such a degree that no difference is discernible. Whence it happens sometimes through error that Christians mingle with the women of Jews and Saracens, and, on the other hand, Jews and Saracens mingle with those of the Christians. Therefore, that such religious commingling

through error of this kind may not serve as a refuge for further excuse for excesses, we decree that such people of both sexes (that is, Jews and Saracens) in every Christian province and at all times be distinguished in public from other people by a difference in dress, since this was also enjoined on them by Moses. On the days of the Lamentations and on Passion Sunday they may not appear in public, because some of them, as we understand, on those days are not ashamed to show themselves more ornately attired and do not fear to amuse themselves at the expense of Christians, who in memory of the sacred passion go about attired in robes of mourning. That we most strictly forbid, lest they should presume in some measure to burst forth in contempt of the Redeemer. And, since we ought not be ashamed of him who blotted out our offenses, we command that the secular princes restrain presumptuous persons of this kind by condign punishment, lest they presume to blaspheme in some degree the one crucified for us.

Monks, Anchoresses, and Friars

from The Rule of St. Columba (6th century)

The monastic movement in Ireland in the sixth century exerted enormous influence on the spread of both Christianity and Celtic culture. Irish monks led by St. Columba (521–97) converted large areas of northern England, as well as much of Scotland, to Christianity.

Be alone in a separate place near a chief city, if thy conscience is not prepared to be in common with the crowd.

Be always naked in imitation of Christ and the Evangelists.

Whatsoever little or much thou possessest of anything, whether clothing, or food, or drink, let it be at the command of the senior and at his disposal, for it is not befitting a religious to have any distinction of property with his own free brother.

Let a fast place, with one door, enclose thee.

A few religious men to converse with thee of God and his Testament; to visit thee on days of solemnity; to strengthen thee in the Testaments of God, and the narratives of the Scriptures.

A person too who would talk with thee in idle words, or of the world; or who murmurs at what he cannot remedy or prevent, but who would distress thee more should he be a tattler between friends and foes, thou shalt not admit him to thee, but at once give him thy benediction should he deserve it.

Let thy servant be a discreet, religious, not tale-telling man, who is to attend continually on thee, with moderate labour of course, but always ready.

Yield submission to every rule that is of devotion.

A mind prepared for red martyrdom.

A mind fortified and steadfast for white martyrdom.

Forgiveness from the heart of every one.

Constant prayers for those who trouble thee.

Fervour in singing the office for the dead, as if every faithful dead was a particular friend of thine.

Hymns for souls to be sung standing.

Let thy vigils be constant from eve to eve, under the direction of another person.

Three labours in the day, viz., prayers, work, and reading.

The work to be divided into three parts, viz., thine own work, and the work of thy place, as regards its real wants; secondly, thy share of the brethen's [work]; lastly, to help the neighbours, viz. by instruction or writing, or sewing garments, or whatever labour they may be in want of, *ut Dominus ait, "Non apparebis ante Me vacuus"* [as the Lord says, "You shall not appear before me empty"].

Everything in its proper order; *Nemo enim coronabitur nisi qui legitime certaverit* [For no one is crowned except he who has striven lawfully].

Follow alms-giving before all things.

Take not of food till thou art hungry.

Sleep not till thou feelest desire.

Speak not except on business.

Every increase which comes to thee in lawful meals, or in wearing apparel, give it for pity to the brethren that want it, or to the poor in like manner.

The love of God with all thy heart and all thy strength;

The love of thy neighbour as thyself.

Abide in the Testament of God throughout all times.

Thy measure of prayer shall be until thy tears come;

Or thy measure of work of labour till thy tears come;

Or thy measure of thy work of labour, or of thy genuflexions, until thy perspiration often comes, if thy tears are not free.

from The Rule of St. Benedict (6ᵗʰ century)

By the end of the eighth century most monasteries both in Britain and on the continent were Benedictine; even many that had originally been Columban had adopted the full and precise set of rules that had been composed in the first half of the sixth century by St. Benedict.

Prologue. ... We are about to found, therefore, a school for the Lord's service; in the organization of which we trust that we shall ordain nothing severe and nothing burdensome. But even if, the demands of justice dictating it, something a little irksome shall be the result, for the purpose of amending vices or preserving charity;—thou shalt not therefore, struck by fear, flee the way of salvation, which can not be entered upon except through a narrow entrance. But as one's way of life and one's faith progresses, the heart becomes broadened, and, with the unutterable sweetness of love, the way of the mandates of the Lord is traversed. Thus, never departing from His guidance, continuing in the monastery in His teaching until death, through patience we are made partakers in Christ's passion, in order that we may merit to be companions in His kingdom.

Concerning the kinds of monks and their manner of living. It is manifest that there are four kinds of monks. The cenobites are the first kind; that is, those living in a monastery, serving under a rule or an abbot. Then the second kind is that of the anchorites; that is, the hermits—those who, not by the new fervour of a conversion but by the long probation of life in a monastery, have learned to fight against the devil, having already been taught by the solace of many. They, having been well prepared in the army of brothers for the solitary fight of the hermit, being secure now without the consolation of another, are able, God helping them, to fight with their own hand or arm against the vices of the flesh or of their thoughts.

But a third very bad kind of monks are the sarabaites, approved by no rule, experience being their teacher, as with the gold which is tried in the furnace. But, softened after the manner of lead, keeping faith with the world by their works, they are known through their tonsure to lie to God. These being shut up by twos or threes, or, indeed, alone, without a shepherd, not in the Lord's but in their own sheep-folds— their law is the satisfaction of their desires. For whatever they think good or choice, this they call holy; and what they do not wish, this they consider unlawful. But the fourth kind of monks is the kind which are called gyrovagues. During their whole life they are guests, for three or four days at a time, in the cells of the different monasteries, throughout the various provinces; always wandering and never stationary, given over to the service of their own pleasures and the joys of the palate, and in every way worse than the sarabaites. Concerning the most wretched way of living of all such monks it is better to be silent than to speak. These things therefore being omitted, let us proceed, with the aid of God, to treat of the best kind, the cenobites. ...

Concerning humility. ... The sixth grade of humility is, that a monk be contented with all lowliness or extremity, and consider himself, with regard to everything which is enjoined on him, as a poor and unworthy workman; saying to himself with the prophet: "I was reduced to nothing and was ignorant; I was made as the cattle before thee, and I am always with thee." The seventh grade of humility is, not only that he, with his tongue, pronounce himself viler and more worthless than all; but that he also believe it in the innermost workings of his heart; humbling himself and saying with the prophet, etc. ... The eighth degree of humility is that a monk do nothing except what the common rule of the monastery, or the example of his elders, urges him to do. The ninth degree of humility is that a monk restrain his tongue from speaking; and, keeping silence, do not speak until he is spoken to. The tenth grade of humility is that he be not ready, and easily inclined, to laugh. ... The eleventh grade of humility is that a monk, when he speaks, speak slowly and without laughter, humbly with gravity, using few and reasonable words; and that he be not loud of voice. ... The twelfth grade of humility is that a monk shall, not only with his heart but also with his body, always show humility to all who see him: that is, when at work, in the oratory in the monastery, in the garden, on the road, in the fields. And everywhere, sitting or walking or standing, let him always be with head inclined, his looks fixed upon the ground; remembering every hour that he is guilty of his sins. Let him think that he is already being presented before the tremendous judgment of God, saying always to himself in his heart what the publican of the gospel, fixing his eyes on the earth, said: "Lord I am not worthy, I a sinner, so much as to lift mine eyes unto Heaven."

Concerning the divine offices at night. In the winter time, that is from the Calends of November until Easter, according to what is reasonable, they must rise at the eighth hour of the night [i.e., around 2 a.m.), so that they rest a little more than half the night, and rise when they have already digested. But let the time that remains after vigils be kept for meditation by those brothers who are in any way behind hand with the psalter or lessons. From Easter, moreover, until the aforesaid Calends of November, let the hour of keeeping vigils be so arranged that, a short interval being observed in which the brethren may go out for the necessities of nature, the matins, which are always to take place with the dawning light, may straightway follow.

How many psalms are to be said at night. In the winter first of all the verse shall be said: "O God, come to my assistance; O Lord, make haste to help me." Then, secondly, there shall be said three times: "Oh Lord open my lips, and my mouth shall proclaim Thy praise." To which is to be subjoined the third psalm and the Gloria. After this the ninety-fourth psalm is to be sung antiphonally or in unison. The Ambrosian chant shall then follow: then six psalms antiphonally. These having been said, the abbot shall, with the verse mentioned, give the blessing. And all being seated upon the benches, there shall be read in turn from the Scriptures—following out the analogy— three lessons; between which also three responses shall be sung. Two responses shall be said without the *Gloria* [i.e., The doxology "Glory to the father, the Son, and the Holy Spirit, as it was in the beginning, is now, and ever shall be"]; but, after the third lesson, he who chants shall say the *Gloria.* And, when the cantor begins to say this, all shall straightway rise from their seats out of honour and reverence for the Holy Trinity. Books, moreover, of the old as well as the New Testament of Divine authority shall be read at the Vigils; but also expositions of them which have been made by the most celebrated orthodox teachers and catholic Fathers. Moreover, after these three lessons with their responses, shall follow other six psalms to be sung with the Alleluia. After this a lesson of the Apostle shall follow, to be recited by heart; and verses and the supplication of the Litany, that is the *Kyrie eleison*: and thus shall end the nocturnal vigils. …

How Divine Service shall be held through the day. As the prophet says: "Seven times in the day so I praise Thee." Which sacred number of seven will thus be fulfilled by us if, at matins, at the first, third, sixth, ninth hours [i.e., roughly 6 a.m., 9 a.m., noon, and 3 p.m.], at vesper time and at *completorium* we perform the duties of our service; for it is of these hours of the day that he said: "Seven times in the day do I praise Thee." For, concerning nocturnal vigils, the same prophet says: "At midnight I arose to confess unto thee." Therefore, at these times, let us give thanks to our Creator concerning the judgments of his righteousness; that is, at matins, etc. … and at night we will rise and confess to Him …

How the monks shall sleep. They shall sleep separately in separate beds. They shall receive positions for their beds, after the manner of their characters, according to the dispensation of their abbot. If it can be done, they shall all sleep in one place. If, however, their number do not permit it, they shall rest by tens or twenties, with elders who will concern themselves about them. A candle shall always be burning in that same cell until early in the morning. They shall sleep clothed, and girt with belts or with ropes; and they shall not have their knives at their sides while they sleep, lest perchance in a dream they should wound the sleepers. And let the monks be always on the alert; and, when the signal is given, rising without delay, let them hasten to mutually prepare themselves for the service of God—with all gravity and modesty, however. The younger brothers shall not have beds by themselves, but interspersed among those of the elder ones. And when they rise for

the service of God, they shall exhort each other mutually with moderation on account of the excuses that those who are sleepy are inclined to make. …

Concerning the amount of food. … We believe, moreover, that, for the daily refection of the sixth as well as of the ninth hour, two cooked dishes, on account of the infirmities of the different ones, are enough for all tables: so that whoever, perchance, can not eat of one may partake of the other. Therefore let two cooked dishes suffice for all the brothers: and, if it is possible to obtain apples or growing vegetables, a third may be added. One full pound of bread shall suffice for a day, whether there be one refection, or a breakfast and a supper. But if they are going to have supper, the third part of that same pound shall be reserved by the cellarer, to be given back to those who are about to sup. But if, perchance, some greater labour shall have been performed, it shall be in the will and power of the abbot, if it is expedient, to increase anything; surfeiting above all things being guarded against, so that indigestion may never seize a monk: for nothing is so contrary to every Christian as surfeiting, as our Lord says: "Take heed to yourselves, lest your hearts be overcharged with surfeiting." But to younger boys the same quantity shall not be served, but less than that to the older ones; moderation being observed in all things. But the eating of the flesh of quadrupeds shall be abstained from altogether by every one, excepting alone the weak and the sick. …

Concerning the amount of drink. Each one has his own gift from God, the one in this way, the other in that. Therefore it is with some hesitation that the amount of daily sustenance for others is fixed by us. Nevertheless, in view of the weakness of the infirm we believe that a hemina[1] of wine a day is enough for each one. Those moreover to whom God gives the ability of bearing abstinence shall know that they will have their own reward. But the prior shall judge if either the needs of the place, or labour or the heat of summer, requires more; considering in all things lest satiety or drunkenness creep in. Indeed we read that wine is not suitable for monks at all. But because, in our day, it is

[1] *hemina* About half a pint.

not possible to persuade the monks of this, let us agree at least as to the fact that we should not drink till we are sated, but sparingly. For wine can make even the wise to go astray. Where, moreover, the necessities of the place are such that the amount written above can not be found—but much less or nothing at all—those who live there shall bless God and shall not murmur. And we admonish them to this above all: that they be without murmuring. …

Concerning the daily manual labour. Idleness is the enemy of the soul. And therefore, at fixed times, the brothers ought to be occupied in manual labour; and again, at fixed times, in sacred reading. Therefore we believe that, according to this disposition, both seasons ought to be arranged; so that, from Easter until the Calends of October, going out early, from the first until the fourth hour [i.e., roughly 6–10 a.m.] they shall do what labour may be necessary. Moreover, from the fourth hour until about the sixth, they shall be free for reading. After the meal of the sixth hour, moreover, rising from table, they shall rest in their beds with all silence; or, perchance, he that wishes to read may so read to himself that he do not disturb another. And the *nona* (the second meal) shall be gone through with more moderately about the middle of the eighth hour; and again they shall work at what is to be done until Vespers. But, if the exigency or poverty of the place demands that they be occupied by themselves in picking fruits, they shall not be dismayed: for then they are truly monks if they live by the labours of their hands; as did also our fathers and the apostles. Let all things be done with moderation, however, on account of the faint-hearted. From the Calends of October, moreover, until the beginning of Lent they shall be free for reading until the second full hour. At the second hour the *tertia* (morning service) shall be held, and all shall labour at the task which is enjoined upon them until the ninth. The first signal, moreover, of the ninth hour having been given, they shall each one leave off his work; and be ready when the second signal strikes. Moreover after the refection they shall be free for their reading or for psalms. But in the days of Lent, from dawn until the third full hour, they shall be free for their readings; and, until the tenth full hour, they shall do the labour that is enjoined on them. In which days of Lent they shall all receive separate books from the library; which they shall read entirely through in order. These books are to be given out on the first day of Lent. Above all there shall certainly be appointed one or two elders, who shall go round the monastery at the hours in which the brothers are engaged in reading, and see to it that no troublesome brother chance to be found who is open to idleness and trifling, and is not intent on his reading; being not only of no use to himself, but also stirring up others.

from *The Ancrene Wisse*

> As St. Benedict expressed it, anchorites and anchoresses lived "the solitary life of the hermit." Unlike hermits of the very early days of Christianity, however, they lived in groups rather than in absolute isolation. *The Ancrene Wisse*, a set of rules for a group of English anchoresses, dates from the early thirteenth century.

[Temptations] … An anchoress thinks that she shall be most strongly tempted in the first twelve months after she shall have begun her monastic life, and in the next twelve thereafter; and when, after many years, she feels them so strong, she is greatly amazed, and is afraid lest God may have quite forgotten her, and cast her off. Nay! it is not so. In the first years, it is nothing but ball-play; but now, observe well, by a comparison, how it fares. When a man has brought a new wife home, he, with great gentleness, observes her manners. Though he sees in her some thing that he does not approve, yet he takes no notice of it, and puts on a cheerful countenance toward her, and carefully uses every means to make her love him, affectionately in her heart; and when he is well assured that her love is truly fixed upon him, he may then, with safety, openly correct her faults, which he previously bore with as if he knew them not: he becomes right stern, and assumes a severe countenance, in order still to test whether her love toward him might give way. At last when he perceives that she is completely instructed—that for nothing that he does to her does she love him less, but more and more, if possible, from day to day, then he shows her that he loves her sweetly, and does whatsoever she desires, as to one whom he loves and knows—then is all that sorrow become joy. If Jesu Christ, your Spouse, does thus to you, my dear sisters, let it not seem strange to you. For in the beginning it is only courtship, to draw you into love; but as soon as he perceives that he is on a footing of affectionate familiarity with you, he will now have less forbearance with you; but after the trial—in the end—then is the great joy....

Of sight, and of speech, and of the other senses enough was said. Now this last part, as I promised you at the commencement, is divided and separated into seven small sections.

Men esteem a thing as less dainty when they have it often, and therefore you should be, as lay brethren are, partakers of the holy communion only fifteen times a year: at midwinter [December 25]; Candlemas [February 2]; Twelfth-day [January 6]; on Sunday halfway between that and Easter, or our Lady's Day [March 25], if it is near the Sunday, because of its being a holiday; Easter Day; the third Sunday thereafter; Holy Thursday [that is, Ascension Day, forty days after Easter]; Whitsunday [that is, Pentecost, six weeks after Easter]; and Midsummer Day [June 24]; St. Mary Magdalen's Day [July 22]; the Assumption [August 15]; the Nativity [of the Virgin Mary, September 8]; St. Michael's Day [September 29]; All Saints' Day [November 1]; St. Andrew's Day [November 30]. And before all these days, see that you make a full confession and undergo discipline; but never from any man, only from yourselves. And forego your pittance for one day. And if any thing happens out of the usual order, so that you may not have received the sacrament at these set times, you may make up for it the Sunday next following, or if the other set time is near, you may wait till then.

You shall eat twice every day from Easter until the later Holyrood Day [September 14], which is in harvest, except on Fridays, and Ember Days [that is, days of fasting and prayer in each season of the year], and procession days and vigils. In those days, and in the Advent, you shall not eat any thing white, except when necessity requires it. The other half year you shall fast always, except only on Sundays.

You shall eat no flesh nor lard except in great sickness; or whosoever is infirm may eat potage without scruple; and accustom yourselves to little drink.

Nevertheless, dear sisters, your meat and your drink have seemed to me less than I would have it. Fast no day upon bread and water, unless you have permission. There are anchoresses who make their meals with their friends outside the convent. That is too much friendship, because, of all orders, this is most ungenial, and most contrary to the order of an anchoress, who is quite dead to the world. We have often heard it said that dead men speak with living men; but that they eat with living men, I have never yet found. Make no banquetings, nor encourage any strange vagabond fellows to come to the gate; though no other evil come of it but their immoderate talking, it might sometimes prevent heavenly thoughts.

It is not fit that an anchoress should be liberal with other men's alms. Would we not laugh loud to scorn a beggar who should invite men to a feast? Mary and Martha were two sisters, but their lives were different. You anchorites have taken to yourselves Mary's part, whom our Lord himself commended. "Mary hath chosen the best part. Martha, Martha," said he, "thou art much cumbered. Mary hath chosen better, and nothing shall take her part from her." Housewifery is Martha's part, and Mary's part is quietness and rest from all the world's din, that nothing may hinder her from hearing the voice of God. And observe what God saith, "that nothing shall take away this part from you." Martha has her office; let her alone, and sit with Mary stone-still at God's feet, and listen to Him alone. Martha's office is to feed and clothe poor men, as the mistress of a house. Mary ought not to intermeddle in it, and if anyone blame her, God Himself supreme defends her for it, as Holy Writ bears witness. On the other hand, an anchoress ought to take sparingly only that which is necessary for her. Whereof, then, may she make herself liberal? She must live upon alms, as frugally as ever she can, and not gather that she may give it away afterwards. She is not a housewife, but a church anchoress. If she can spare any fragments for the poor, let her send them quite privately out of her dwelling. Sin is oft concealed under the semblance of goodness. And how shall those rich anchoresses that are tillers of the ground, or have fixed rents, do their alms privately to poor neighbors? Desire not to have the reputation of bountiful anchoresses, nor, in order to give much, be too eager to possess more. Greediness is the root of bitterness: all the boughs that spring from it are bitter. To beg in order to give away is not the part of an anchoress. From the courtesy of an anchoress, and from her liberality, sin and shame have often come in the end.

Make women and children who have labored for you to eat whatever food you can spare from your own meals; but let no man eat in your presence, except he be in great need; nor invite him to drink anything. Nor do I desire that you should be told that you are courteous anchoresses. From a good friend take whatever you have need of when she offers it to you; but for no invitation take anything without need, lest you get the name of gathering anchoresses. Of a man whom you distrust, receive neither less nor more—not so much as a race of ginger. It must be great need that shall drive you to ask any thing; yet humbly show your distress to your dearest friend.

You shall not possess any beast, my dear sisters, except only a cat. An anchoress that hath cattle appears as Martha was, a better housewife than anchoress; nor can she in any wise be Mary, with peacefulness of heart. For then she must think of the cow's fodder, and of the herdsman's hire, flatter the hayward, defend herself when her cattle is shut up in the pinfold, and moreover pay the damage. Christ knows, it is an odious thing when people in the town complain of anchoresses' cattle. If, however, anyone must needs have a cow, let her take care that she neither annoy nor harm anyone, and that her own thoughts be not fixed thereon. An anchoress ought not to have anything that draws her heart outward. Carry on no business. An anchoress that is a buyer and seller sells her soul to the chapman of hell. Do not take charge of other men's property in your house, nor of their cattle, nor their clothes, neither receive under your care the church vestments, nor the chalice, unless force compel you, or great fear, for oftentimes much harm has come from such care-taking. Let no man sleep within your walls. If, however, great necessity should cause your house to be used, see that, as long as it is used, you have therein with you a woman of unspotted life day and night.

Because no man sees you, nor do you see any man, you may be well content with your clothes, be they white, be they black; only see that they be plain, and warm, and well made—skins well tawed; and have as many as you need, for bed and also for back.

Next to your flesh you shall wear no flaxen cloth, except it be of hard and coarse canvas … You shall sleep in a garment and belted. Wear no iron, nor haircloth, nor hedgehog-skins; and do not beat yourselves therewith, nor with a scourge of leather thongs, nor leaded; and do not with holly nor with briars cause yourselves to bleed without leave of your confessor; and do not, at one time, use too many flagellations. Let your shoes be thick and warm. In summer you are at liberty to go and to sit barefoot, and to wear hose without vamps, and whoever likes may sleep in them … She who wishes to be seen, it is no great wonder that she adorn herself; but, in the eyes of God, she is more lovely who is unadorned outwardly for his sake. Have neither ring, nor brooch, nor ornamented girdle, nor gloves, nor any such thing that is not proper for you to have.

I am always the more gratified, the coarser the works are that you do. Make no purses, to gain friends therewith …; but shape, and sew, and mend church vestments, and poor people's clothes. You shall give nothing away without leave from your father confessor. Assist with your own labor, as far as you are able, to clothe yourselves and your domestics, as St. Jerome teaches. Be never idle; for the fiend immediately offers his work to her who is not diligent in God's work, and he begins directly to talk to her. … An anchoress must not become a schoolmistress, nor turn her anchoress-house into a school for children. Her maiden may, however, teach any little girl concerning whom it might be doubtful whether she should learn among boys, but an anchoress ought to give her thoughts to God only.

You shall not send, nor receive, nor write letters without leave. You shall have your hair cut four times a year to unburden your head; and be bled as oft, and oftener if it is necessary; but if anyone can dispense with this, I may well suffer it. When you are bled, you ought to do nothing that may be irksome to you for three days; but talk with your maidens, and divert yourselves together with instructive tales. You may often do so when you feel dispirited, or are grieved about some worldly matter, or sick. Thus wisely take care of yourselves when you are bled, and keep yourselves in such rest that long thereafter you may labor the more vigorously in God's service, and also when you feel any sickness, for it is great folly, for the sake of one day, to lose ten or twelve. Wash yourselves wheresoever it is necessary, as often as you please.

When an anchoress does not have her food at hand, let two women be employed, one who stays always at home, another who goes out when necessary; and let her be very plain, or of sufficient age. ... Let neither of the women either carry to her mistress or bring from her any idle tales, or new tidings, nor sing to one another, nor speak any worldly speeches, nor laugh, nor play, so that any man who saw it might turn it to evil. ... No servant of an anchoress ought, properly, to ask stated wages, except food and clothing, with which, and with God's mercy, she may do well enough. ... Whoever has any hope of so high a reward will gladly serve, and easily endure all grief and all pain. With ease and abundance men do not arrive at heaven.

A Friar, preaching. Nineteenth-century copy of an illustration from British Library MS Royal XIVE (early 14th century). The friar stands barefoot, outdoors, on a portable pulpit.

Franciscan Friars

Whereas the early monastic movements embodied a Christian striving for purity and simplicity, by the twelfth century monasteries were widely regarded as sites of wealth and corruption. The friars represented in later medieval Christianity many of the same ideals that the monks professed in earlier centuries. But rather than seeking a better life by removing themselves from the world, friars aimed to travel and preach and combat heresy and heal, all the while maintaining strict vows of poverty and chastity. St. Francis (c. 1182–1226) founded the largest order of friars; excerpts from his Rule appear below.

1. In the name of the Lord, the life of the lesser brothers begins.

The rule and life of the lesser brothers is this: To observe the Holy Gospel of our Lord Jesus Christ, living in obedience without anything of our own, and in chastity. Brother Francis promises obedience and reverence to the Lord Pope Honorius and his canonically elected successors, and to the Roman Church; and the rest of the brothers are obliged to obey Francis and his successors.

2. Concerning those who wish to adopt this life.

... Let those who have promised obedience take one tunic with a hood, and let those who wish it have another without a hood. And those who must may wear shoes. All the brothers are to wear inexpensive clothing, and they can use sackcloth and other material to mend it with God's blessing.

3. Concerning the divine office and fasting; and how the brothers ought to travel through the world.

Clerics are to perform the divine office according to the rite of the Roman Church, except for the Psalter, and they can have breviaries for that purpose. Laymen are to say twenty-four "Our Fathers" at matins; five at lauds; seven each at prime, terce, sext and none; twelve at vespers; and seven at compline. They should also pray for the dead.

They should fast from the feast of all saints until Christmas. Those who voluntarily fast at Quadragessima, those forty days after Epiphany which the Lord consecrated with his own holy fasting, will themselves be blessed by the Lord; yet they are not required to do so if they do not want to. They must fast during Lent, but they are not required to do so at other times except on Fridays. In case of obvious necessity, however, they are excused from bodily fasting.

I counsel, admonish and beg my brothers that, when they travel about the world, they should not be quarrelsome, dispute with words, or criticize others, but rather should be gentle, peaceful and unassuming, courteous and humble, speaking respectfully to all as is fitting. They must not ride on horseback unless forced to so by obvious necessity or illness. Whatever house they enter, they are first to say, "Peace to this house" (Luke 10.5). According to the Holy Gospel they can eat whatever food is set before them.

4. That the brothers should not accept money.

I strictly forbid the brothers to receive money in any form either directly or through an intermediary. Nevertheless, the ministers and custodians can work through spiritual friends to care for the sick and clothe the brothers, according to place, season and climate, as necessity may seem to demand. This must be done, however, in such a way that they do not receive money.

5. On their manner of working.

Those brothers whom the Lord favors with the gift of working should do so faithfully and devotedly, so that idleness, the enemy of the soul, is excluded yet the spirit of holy prayer and devotion, which all other temporal things should serve, is not extinguished. As payment for their labor let them receive that which is necessary for themselves and their brothers, but not money. Let them receive it humbly as befits those who serve God and seek after the holiest poverty.

6. That the brothers should appropriate nothing for themselves; and on how alms should be begged; and concerning sick brothers.

The brothers should appropriate neither house, nor place, nor anything for themselves; and they should go confidently after alms, serving God in poverty and humility, as pilgrims and strangers in this world. Nor should they feel ashamed, for God made Himself poor in this world for us. This is that peak of the highest poverty which has made you, my dearest brothers, heirs and kings of the kingdom of heaven, poor in things but rich in virtues. Let this be your portion. It leads into the land of the living and, adhering totally to it, for the sake of our Lord Jesus Christ wish never to have anything else in this world, beloved brothers.

And wherever brothers meet one another, let them act like members of a common family. And let them securely make their needs known to one another, for if a mother loves and cares for her carnal son, how much more should one love and care for his spiritual son? And if one of them should become ill, let the other brothers serve him as they themselves would like to be served....

9. On preachers.

The friars must not preach in the diocese of any bishop if they have been forbidden to do so by him. And no brother should dare preach to the people unless he has been examined and approved by the minister general of his brotherhood and the office of preaching has been conceded to him. I also admonish and exhort the brothers that in their preaching their words be studied and chaste, useful and edifying to the people, telling them about vices and virtues, punishment and glory; and they ought to be brief, because the Lord kept His words brief when He was on earth.

10. On the admonition and correction of brothers.

Brothers who are ministers and servants of other brothers must visit and admonish their brothers, and they should correct them humbly and lovingly, prescribing nothing against their soul or our rule. Brothers who are subject to authority must remember that they have surrendered their own wills for the sake of God. ...

I admonish and exhort the brothers in the Lord Jesus Christ to beware of all pride, vainglory, envy, avarice, worldly care and concern, criticism and complaint. And I admonish the illiterate not to worry about studying but to realize instead that above all they should wish to have the spirit of the Lord working within them, and that they should pray to him constantly with a pure heart, be humble, be patient in persecution and infirmity, and love those who persecute, blame or accuse us. ...

11. That the brothers should not enter the convents of nuns.

I strictly order all the brothers to avoid suspicious meetings or conversations with women and to stay out of the convents of nuns except in cases where special permission has been granted by the Holy See. Nor should they be godfathers of men or women, lest it lead to scandal among or concerning the brothers.

12. Concerning those who go among the Saracens and other infidels.

Whoever should, by divine inspiration, wish to go among the Saracens and other infidels must ask permission from their provincial ministers. The ministers should grant permission only to those whom they consider qualified to be sent.

I enjoin the ministers by obedience to ask the Lord Pope for a cardinal of the Holy Roman Church to serve as governor, protector and corrector of their brotherhood so that we servants and subjects at the feet of Holy Church, firm in faith, will always observe the poverty, humility and Holy Gospel of our Lord Jesus Christ which we firmly promised.

Scholasticism

In the wake of the rediscovery of Aristotelian and other classical works of philosophy, theological discourse in the late eleventh and twelfth centuries began to become far more abstract and densely reasoned than had previously been the case; theologians were now keen to demonstrate that faith was in complete harmony with the dictates of reason. One of the most important of these university-influenced "scholastics" was St. Anselm, Archbishop of Canterbury from 1093 to 1109. Anselm's great contribution to theology was the argument that has come to be known as the "ontological proof" for the existence of God.

from St. Anselm, *Proslogion* (c. 1080)

I acknowledge, Lord, and I give thanks that you have created in me this Your image, so that I can remember You, think about You and love You. But it is so worn away by sins, so smudged over by the smoke of sins, that it cannot do what it was created to do unless You renew and reform it. I do not even try, Lord, to rise up to Your heights, because my intellect does not measure up to that task; but I do want to understand in some small measure Your truth, which my heart believes in and loves. Nor do I seek to understand so that I can believe, but rather I believe so that I can understand. For I believe this too, that "unless I believe I shall not understand."[1]

2. That God Really Exists

Therefore, Lord, You who give knowledge of the faith, give me as much knowledge as You know to be fitting for me, because you are as we believe and that which we believe. And indeed we believe You are something greater than which cannot be thought. Or is there no such kind of thing, for "the fool said in his heart, there is no God"?[2] But certainly that same fool, having heard what I just said, "something greater than which cannot be thought," understands what he heard, and what he understands is in his thought, even if he does not think it exists. For it is one thing for something to exist in a person's thought and quite another for the person to think that thing exists. For when a painter thinks ahead to what he will paint, he has that picture in his thought, but he does not yet think it exists, because he has not done it yet. Once he has painted it he has it in his thought and thinks it exists because he has done it. Thus even the fool is compelled to grant that something greater than which cannot be thought exists in thought, because he understands what he hears, and whatever is

---

[1] *unless I believe I shall not understand*   See Isaiah 7.9.

[2] *the fool said ... no God*   See Psalms 13.1, 52.1.

understood exists in thought. And certainly that greater than which cannot be understood cannot exist only in thought, for if it exists only in thought it could also be thought of as existing in reality as well, which is greater. If, therefore, that than which greater cannot be thought exists in thought alone, then that than which greater cannot be thought turns out to be that than which something greater actually can be thought, but that is obviously impossible. Therefore something than which greater cannot be thought undoubtedly exists both in thought and in reality.

3. That God Cannot Be Thought Not to Exist

In fact, it so undoubtedly exists that it cannot be thought of as not existing. For one can think there exists something that cannot be thought of as not existing, and that would be greater than something which can be thought of as not existing. For if that greater than which cannot be thought can be thought of as not existing, then that greater than which cannot be thought is not that greater than which cannot be thought, which does not make sense. Thus that than which nothing can be thought so undoubtedly exists that it cannot even be thought of as not existing.

And you, Lord God, are this being. You exist so undoubtedly, my Lord God, that you cannot even be thought of as not existing.

Truly there is a God, although the fool hath said in his heart, There is no God.

And so, Lord, do thou, who dost give understanding to faith, give me, so far as thou knowest it to be profitable, to understand that thou art as we believe; and that thou art that which we believe. And, indeed, we believe that thou art a being than which nothing greater can be conceived. Or is there no such nature, since the fool hath said in his heart, there is no God? But, at any rate, this very fool, when he hears of this being of which I speak—a being than which nothing greater can be conceived—understands what he hears, and what he understands is in his understanding; although he does not understand it to exist.

For, it is one thing for an object to be in the understanding, and another to understand that the object exists. When a painter first conceives of what he will afterwards perform, he has it in his understanding, but he does not yet understand it to be, because he has not yet performed it. But after he has made the painting, he both has it in his understanding, and he understands that it exists, because he has made it.

Hence, even the fool is convinced that something exists in the understanding, at least, than which nothing greater can be conceived. For, when he hears of this, he understands it. And whatever is understood, exists in the understanding. And assuredly that, than which nothing greater can be conceived, cannot exist in the understanding alone. For, suppose it exists in the understanding alone: then it can be conceived to exist in reality; which is greater.

Therefore, if that, than which nothing greater can be conceived, exists in the understanding alone, the very being, than which nothing greater can be conceived, is one, than which a greater can be conceived. But obviously this is impossible. Hence, there is no doubt that there exists a being, than which nothing greater can be conceived, and it exists both in the understanding and in reality. …

… For no one who understands what fire and water are can conceive fire to be water, in accordance with the nature of the facts themselves, although this is possible according to the words. So, then, no one who understands what God is can conceive that God does not exist; although he says these words in his heart, either without any, or with some foreign, signification. For, God is that than which greater cannot be conceived. And he who thoroughly understands this, assuredly understands that this being so truly exists, that not even in concept can it be non-existent. Therefore, he who understands that God so exists, cannot conceive that he does not exists. …

The Miraculous and the Strange

from *The Miracles of Thomas of Becket*

In the medieval period records of miracles associated with saints were often kept at saints' shrines. These miracles were alleged to be either a result of contact with a relic of a saint, or of the saint's direct involvement. The largest collection of such records is that associated with Thomas Becket, the Archbishop of Canterbury who was murdered (allegedly on the orders of King Henry II) in 1170.

[Miracles of 1171] Book 2, Chapter 7. Edilda, a woman from Canterbury, was left at the shrine, carried with the help of three women. It had now been about a year and half since she could stand on her foot. During that whole time she had lived as if on the brink of death, confined to bed. The disease was especially severe in her left knee, which through the contraction of the muscles prevented her from walking. Her knee reeled with pain if the woman happened to touch it even lightly with her hand. She was carried to the martyr by three women, as we said, and propped on a staff; she returned home with her pain relieved. In witness of her recovered health, before us all with her upraised fist she struck her knee a hard blow, which since the second year of her illness she could not touch because of the pain. The people saw her walking about and praising the Lord; they were filled with wonder and amazed over what had happened to her. But we refrain from discussing why she remained lame and did not regain complete health, considering it more prudent to keep totally silent about God's secret judgments than to draw rash conclusions from them.

Chapter 8. But we know that He who strengthened that woman's weak knee was capable of making her feet and soles completely firm so that she could have walked normally, just as we have no doubt that He did grant this to Wlviva, a woman from Canterbury. Satan had bound her for three years already, and she was bent over, unable to walk anywhere without a crutch. She fell down before the saint for a short prayer and, with the pain gone from her loins, she rose standing straight up without her crutch, wanting no longer to carry the thing that had once supported her. ...

Chapter 12. Robert, a blacksmith from the Isle of Thanet, also found the grace of healing, but the vision that preceded the gift of his cure is no less wonderful.

He had been blind for at least two years; the loss of his livelihood troubled him more than his lost sight. But then, after our venerable father had been called home from exile, around the time when he was called to heaven from the exile of this world [i.e., Dec. 29], this man heard this oracle in a dream: "Go, Robert, to Christ Church Canterbury; a monk will put milk in your eyes and you will recover your sight." But at first he thought he was deluded: he neither believed the promise nor obeyed the command. Yet later, when he heard that God's saint practically glittered with miracles, he recalled what he had heard and, equating this sweetest lamb's innocent blood to milk's sweetness, he began to hope for a cure. With the guidance of his wife and daughter (for we understand they accompanied him), he arrived where he had been ordered to go. After daubing his eyes with the longed-for blood of the martyr, he prostrated himself in prayer. While face-down, he felt his head racked by what seemed like a loud thunderclap and he regained his sight. Getting up, he publicly preached God's grace.

Chapter 13. But what is easier: to restore health to the body or the mind? He who restored sight to physical eyes restored sanity to the young man, Henry of Fordwich. He had been insane for some days and had accidentally wounded his friends due to his pain. With his hands bound behind him, he was dragged to the saint. He was presented to the saint even though he was struggling and shouting. He remained there insane for the whole day, but as the light of the sun waned, he started gradually to recover the light of reason. He spent the night in the church and went back home in the morning completely recovered.

Chapter 14. We received a woman from the vicinity of the same town who not only could not hear but was also troubled by an unbearable pain in the head. That universal medicine of the sick—water mixed with the blood—was poured into her stopped ears; she was also given some to drink, and then threw herself into prayer. While she prayed she suffered more bitterly than before and she thought [she heard] many twigs being snapped in pieces inside her head. She asked those standing around whether they heard the noise in her head. But while she was being racked this way, she cried out to the Lord and he heard her. For as she shouted, a great deal of matter flowed out of her ears, as if some inner abscess had ruptured. The matter was followed by blood, and the blood by the gift [of the return] of her lost hearing.

Chapter 15. Eilward, a man from Tenham, for some years had lost the pleasures of the sense of smell and could smell absolutely nothing. He entered that place where rests that good odor of the anointed one, that sweet victim, that scented tree, whose aroma the whole world now senses; but before he had reached that fragrant flower of England, there came to him the sweetest perfume filling his nostrils, and he rejoiced to recover his smell.

Chapter 16. We think that it should not be forgotten that, while many people obtained a longed-for healing, one person was denied outright. For the holy father [Becket] came to a crippled boy who had gone seeking a favor from the martyr and had fallen asleep with his head resting on top of the tomb. "Why are you lying on me?" he asked, "You certainly will not be healed. Go away. I'll do nothing for you." These words woke him up, and he told us and his mother what he had heard with great sadness of heart. Convinced by the adamancy of the [saint's] words, he had himself taken elsewhere. Still, we urged him to press on with his prayers, and he agreed; but time passed and he did not regain his health....

Book 3, Chapter 2. There was a man of the common folk, Eilward by name, in the king's town of Weston in the county of Bedford. One of his neighbors, Fulk, owed him two pennies of rent for a portion of plow-land; he had paid part but put off paying the rest until the following year with the excuse that he did not have the money. One day after the Feast of the Passion of the Blessed Martyr [Thomas] when they were both by chance going to the alehouse together (for it is the English custom to indulge in feasting and drinking on feast days, which makes them seem to be enemies and scorners of their holy days), Eilward asked for his money and Fulk swore that he did not owe him. Eilward asked him to pay half, as he was going to have some beer, and

keep the other half for himself, likewise for beer. When Fulk completely denied that he was in debt to him, the other said that he would get even with him.

After both of them got drunk at the tavern, getting up on some pretext, Eilward left before Fulk and turned aside to Fulk's cottage, tore away the bar to the door, and broke into the house, turned burglar as much through rashness as through drunkenness. Going through the house looking for what he could take, he stumbled upon a large grindstone and some gloves which country people are wont to wear on their hands to protect them from the sharp points of thorns. The poor robber stole these, both of them together scarcely worth a penny. The boys playing together in the yard of the house cried out, and running to the tavern, called out to their father to come get his property back. Striking him, Fulk wrenched the grindstone from him and, brandishing it over the robber's head, he as much broke the grindstone with Eilward's head as he smashed his head with the grindstone. Baring a sharp-pointed knife he carried, he stabbed him in the arm. Overcoming him, he bound the miserable man and led him as a thief and robber back to the house he had broken into. He summoned Fulk[1] the town beadle to find out what he should do with the prisoner. "The charge for which he has been seized," he said, "is not serious enough and insufficient. But if you make the robbery more serious by producing him loaded with other things that appear stolen, you can prosecute him to be punished for the crime." Fulk agreed and fastened around his prisoner's neck an awl, a two-edged axe, a net, and some clothes together with the grindstone and the gloves, and on the following day brought him thus before the king's officers.

Having been thus taken to Bedford, he was kept in prison there for a month. He sent for a priest, the reverend Paganus, so that, faced with the ultimate danger, he could prepare himself for death—or rather for life; and going over all the secrets of his conscience, whatever he found contrary to his salvation, he poured into the safely-sealed ears of the priest. Putting his trust in divine mercy for the deliverance of his body, he said, "Dearest sir, if I escape this moment of danger, I will go on foot to the land that the Son of God, our Lord Jesus made holy by his life on earth and death. And so I beg to have

---

[1] *Fulk* I.e., another man of the same name.

the sign of the cross branded on my right shoulder with a hot iron so that no one has the power to strip it from me even though my clothes are stripped away." The priest branded him accordingly, but also suggested that he should devoutly seek the protection of the saints, and especially of the glorious martyr St. Thomas whom the Lord magnified by such glorious signs. Moreover, he measured the length and breadth of his body with a thread with which to make a candle to be offered to the martyr for his release. He also gave him a scourge made of branches, saying, "Take these branches and five times a day before you take a little food, become your own torturer, and do not cease day and night to kneel to the martyr and call upon him except when, overcome by the annoyance of sleep, you are compelled to succumb to the weakness of human nature." Thus carefully instructing him, he left him, saying that the judges had forbidden any priest to have further access to him. However, he sent for him many times and he secretly announced himself at the window either to rouse him from negligence [in his devotions] or to further kindle his zeal. Also, Galfrid, the prior of the canons of Bedford (whose witness we have for this admirable miracle) often supplied him with needed food, visited him in prison, and—for him to have at least an hour of fresh air—took him from the jail and had him walk around under the open sky.

When four weeks had passed and the fifth begun, this poor man was led from jail and taken before the court for trial. His accuser charged him with the crime of theft; he consistently denied the charge, further objecting that he had taken none of the things hanging around his neck except for the grindstone and the gloves which he admitted taking, but only as a pledge for Fulk's debt, which had motivated the theft and the crime. The judgment was put off so he was again remanded into custody.

Brought out again in the fifth week and taken before the court, he was now charged by his accuser only with the theft of the grindstone and the gloves. For his accuser feared to undergo the trial by combat demanded by the accused, and his silence condemned all his previous charges; but—having the viscount and the judges on his side—he managed to free himself from the obligation to fight, and to arrange that the accused should be tried by the ordeal of water.

Now it was the Sabbath, and the examination was put off until the third day of the following week, he himself being kept again in prison. The cruelty of his keeper forbade him to keep vigil in the church—a right conceded by the compassion of religion to all who are to purge themselves by ordeal from criminal charge. In prison, however, he devoutly kept the watch that he was not allowed to keep in the church.

When brought out to the water [for the ordeal], he was met by the priest Paganus, mentioned earlier, who exhorted him to bear everything patiently in remission of his sins, to hold no hatred and anger in his heart, to forgive sincerely all his enemies for all they had done to him, and not to despair of God's mercy. And he replied, "May the will of God and of the martyr Thomas be done in me."

After being plunged into the water, he was found guilty. The beadle Fulk now seized him, saying, "Follow me, rascal, follow me!" "Thanks be to God," he replied, "and to the holy martyr Thomas." Dragged to the place of punishment, he was deprived of his eyes and his genitals were lopped off. As for his left eye, they at once extracted that whole; but his right eye, after being sliced and cut in pieces, was at last with difficulty gouged out. The members which they had chopped off him they hid under the sod; and—like what is read about the man who "fell in with robbers"—"after both stripping him and beating him" (as described above) "they went their way, leaving him half-dead" [Luke 10.30].

His accuser Fulk and the official of the same name (by whose suggestion and advice this man is believed to have been brought into this misery) and also two other executioners with them mutilated him. When, however, they asked pardon for the love of God and St. Thomas the martyr, he willingly forgave them, crying aloud with a wonderful faith that he would go to the martyr's memorial, blind though he was, and he would not despair of the martyr's holiness and power, knowing that it was more glorious for the martyr to restore eyes that had been taken away than to preserve them when not taken.

He was escorted only by his twelve-year-old daughter, who had also begged food for him while he was incarcerated. For all his goods were confiscated, all his friends spurned him, and there was not one of all those dear to him to console him. Such a great amount of blood gushed from his wounds that, in fear of his death, those who were present sent for a priest to whom he confessed. By degrees, however, when the flow of blood was assuaged, led by the little girl, he returned to Bedford, where he threw himself down against the wall of a house; and all that day, until evening, no man showed him kindness. But at nightfall, one Eilbrict took compassion on him, especially since the weather was inclement and he was lying there vexed by a downpour of rain. He welcomed him rejoicing into his house.

He lay there in darkness for ten days, offering prayers and vigils. But at the first watch of the tenth night, after mourning, groaning, and sighing, as he relaxed in sleep he whom he had invoked appeared to him, clothed in snow-white garments. With his pastoral staff he painted the sign of the cross on his forehead and eyeless sockets and appeared to depart in silence. Waking up and disregarding the vision, he flung himself down again and went back to sleep. A second time before dawn he, who washed his garments in the blood of the Lamb, returned dressed in white. He said to the man, "Good man, are you sleeping?" When he acknowledged that he was awake, the man in white said, "Do not sleep, do not sleep, but watch and press on with your prayers. Do not despair but put your hope in God, the Blessed Virgin Mary, and St. Thomas who comes to visit you. If, tomorrow night, you keep watch with a waxen light before the Virgin's altar in the church of the Blessed Mary close by, and devote yourself in faith to praying, and have no doubts, you shall rejoice in the restoration of your eyes." Rousing from sleep, the man silently thought about what such a vision could mean—or rather whether once the hidden meaning was uncovered, the saint's promise would be fulfilled. Mulling over such a mysterious thing, taking it as news of a good omen, the maid-servant said, "Tonight, Eilward, I dreamed that you recovered sight in both your eyes." And he said, "So it may be when it shall please God and His blessed martyr Thomas."

When it was getting on toward evening, and daylight was declining, the eyelids of his left eye started itching. In order to scratch them, he removed a wax poultice which had been applied either to draw out the purulent matter in the empty orbs, or to close the eyelids themselves. Opening his eyelids, by the marvelous power of God it appeared to him as if a bright lantern were shining on the opposite wall of the house—it was the red sunlight, since the sun was by this time verging on setting. But he, ignorant of the truth and distrusting himself about the matter, called the master of the house and pointed out to him what he thought he saw. "You are mad, Eilward, you are mad," replied his host, "Be quiet. You don't know what you are saying." "I am not the least bit mad, sir," he said, "but I do seem to see what I say with my left eye." Shaken in his mind and anxious to ascertain the truth, his host spread out his hand before his eyes and said to him, "Do you see what I'm doing?" He answered, "I think your hand is waving before my eyes, moving back and forth." Then, starting with the beginning of the first vision, he told Eilbrict step by step what he had seen and what he had been ordered and promised.

Word about this spread among the neighborhood, and this novelty of novelties attracted not a small multitude of people. The deacon Osbern, lord—or rather, minister—of the church mentioned earlier comes running. When he hears about the vision from the man, he takes him to the church, brings him before the altar of the Blessed Virgin, and instructs and strengthens his faith. Putting a light in his hand, he declares that he distinctly sees the altar cloth, then the image of the Blessed Virgin Mary, and then any other objects of smaller size.

People's amazement grows over how this man was favored with sight. Thus, when the strength of the vision in his new eyes (or rather empty sockets without pupils) proceeds to be put to the test, they detect two small pupils concealed deeply in his head, scarcely equal in size to the pupils of a small bird, which, still constantly growing, prolonged by their gradual increase in size the ineffable and incredible wonder of those beholding them.

The shouts of the people rise up to heaven; due praises are paid to God; church bells are rung; crowds flock in who were just about to go to bed, and sleepless they await the sunlight with the man restored to light.

In the morning a crowd of the whole town massed together. Closely examining him in the bright light, they noticed that one eye was parti-colored, the other quite black, though from birth both his eyes had been particolored. Now among others the priest from the church of St. John, who had heard his confession after the mutilation, ran up. Seeing this miracle of God's power he said, "Why are we waiting for papal instructions? No more delaying for me! This very moment I will begin and conduct to the end a solemn service in the name of Thomas, the glorious friend of God, indeed, the martyr beyond price. Who can hesitate to give the name martyr to one who does such mighty and such merciful deeds?" So he ran to the church, set the bells ringing, and was as good as his word.

This man, however, now no longer bereft of light but bedecked with it, as he had been dragged in disgrace through the middle of the town to be punished, so now through the self-same street, amid the praise and applause of the people, he is led back to the church of St. Paul where he also passed the eve of the Lord's Day in vigil. Departing from there he hastened on the way toward St. Thomas, the author of his healing. Wherever he passed, a great multitude of people followed him, for his fame flying along in front of him excited anyone on his way. Whatever gifts they gave him, he gave to the poor out of love for the martyr. He had completed about four miles of his journey when he started to scratch an itch on his testicle bag with his near hand, and he discovered that those members had also been restored to him, very small indeed but growing bigger, which he even did not refuse to anyone who wanted to feel them.

On his coming to London, he was received with congratulations by Hugh, Bishop of Durham, who would not let him leave him until he had sent a messenger to Bedford to make careful inquiry and had been made certain of the facts.

But even after we had received him in our house [at Canterbury], although he had been preceded by the testimony of very many witnesses, we did not feel satisfied until we heard the substance of the above-written statements confirmed by the letter and testimony of the citizens of Bedford. For they sent letters to us, the contents of which were as follows:

"The burgesses of Bedford to the convent of Canterbury and to all the faithful in Christ, greetings. Be it known to the convent of Canterbury and also to all Catholics that God has worked a wonderful and excellent miracle by the merits of the most holy martyr, Thomas. For it happened that a certain countryman of Weston by the name of Eilward was seized and taken before the viscount of Bedford and knights of the county for a theft valued at only a penny. He was publicly condemned by them and deprived of his eyes and genitals in the presence of clergy, men, and women. The chaplain of St. John of Bedford, to whom the aforesaid countryman confessed [after his mutilation] also testifies to this. And this same is testified by his host, named Eilbrict, in whose house he was afterwards received: namely that he was entirely without eyes or testicles when he was first received in his house. And afterwards, often invoking the merits of St. Thomas the martyr, by an apparition of the aforesaid martyr he was gloriously and miraculously restored to health." ...

Book 4. Chapter 45. Eilwacher of Dover was sailing to lesser Britain. A storm arose and he cast out three anchors but lost all of them through the cables breaking. However, he made it back to land after invoking the martyr. On the return of fair weather he returned with his companions to the sea to seek the anchors, for the place where he had lost them was not far from the land. For three days they searched and found nothing, so one of them said, "Let's also promise to the martyr of Canterbury a wax anchor so that he will give us back our iron ones." All agreed, and straightaway letting down into the water the instrument with which they were searching the bottom, they drew out all of the anchors. So they turned back to England and came to the martyr. They brought to him the gift they had promised. ...

Decorated box designed to hold relics of St. Thomas Becket (c. 1190). The town of Limoges, from which this box originated in the late twelfth century, became part of the territory ruled by Henry II and Eleanor of Aquitaine with their marriage in 1152. Becket is shown at the altar, being attacked from behind.

Sin, Corruption, and Indulgence

from William Langland, *Piers Plowman* (B-text, c. 1377–81)

Langland's *Piers Plowman* is one of the major English literary texts of the fourteenth century— and also one of the most important historical documents in the overlapping histories of religious and secular developments during the period. The full poem is a long and in many ways a challenging and confusing text. It is framed as a Christian allegory, with characters such as Truth and Reason pronouncing on the ills of the world, and on the way to salvation. An important thread running through the poem is the attempt of an individual soul to seek out the stages that will lead to salvation; each of the various parts of the poem is called a "passus," or "step." The poem also includes powerful elements of social satire, in which many of the ways of the fourteenth-century world are harshly criticized. Chief among these are corrupt religious practices—perhaps most notably the practice of

purchasing "indulgences" from the Church. (The principle of an indulgence was that a sacrifice of money, meant to help the Church with its financial obligations to the community, could ensure the forgiveness of the giver's sins.) Langland's text also includes wide-ranging criticisms of the greed and lack of charity that he saw as characterizing the behavior of the rich and privileged, nobles and clergy alike.

Langland did not advocate any revolutionary program to remedy society's ills and injustices; he intended to prick the consciences of the powerful to encourage them to mend their ways and carry out good works, but he did not intend to aid in any overthrow of their authority. Indeed, when it became clear that *Piers Plowman* was providing inspiration to the leaders of the uprising of 1381, Langland revised the poem in ways that made it less inflammatory.

Though Langland lived in London (he is believed to have held a modest position in the church), he eschewed the rhymed style of poetry that Chaucer and other Londoners had come to favor, preferring instead to write alliterative verse in a style reminiscent of that of Old English. (*Piers Plowman* is a key text in what scholars have come to refer to as the "alliterative revival" of the fourteenth century.) *Piers Plowman* has come down to us in many manuscripts, and exists in three versions, known as the A-, B-, and C- texts. The concise A-text and the considerably longer B-text are both more sharply critical of authority than is the C-text, which dates from after the 1381 rebellion (and in which Langland distances himself from the rebels' agenda).

Much as *Piers Plowman* is a central text of late medieval social protest, it is also a religious text and a spiritual allegory. The excerpts below give some sense both of the roots of social protest and of the degree to which what we would see as secular and religious elements are virtually inseparable in a text of this sort.

The first sixteen lines of the first Passus of the poem are provided below in the original as well as in a modernized version. As the selection from Passus 5 suggests, the poem has harsh advice for the common folk as well as for the well-to-do. But the prevailing note of criticism in the poem is of the sort seen in the excerpt below from Passus 7; these lines give some sense of the degree to which *Piers Plowman* takes in a broad sweep of the religious and social life of the fourteenth century.

from PASSUS 1

What this mountaigne bymeneth and the merke dale
And the feld ful of folk, I shal yow faire shewe.
A lovely lady of leere in lynnen yclothed
Cam doun from castel and called me faire,
5   And seide, "Sone, slepestow? Sestow this peple—

How bisie they ben aboute the maze?
The mooste partie of this peple that passeth on this erthe,
Have thei worship in this world, thei wilne no bettre;
Of oother hevene than here holde thei no tale."

10   I was afered of hire face, theigh she faire weere,
And seide, "Mercy, madame, what this to mene?"
   "The tour upon the toft," quod she, "Truthe is therinne,
And wolde that ye wroughte as his word techeth,
For he is fader of feith and formed yow alle
15   Bothe with fel and with face and yaf yow fyve wittes
For to worshipe hymn therwith while that ye ben here."

What this mountain means, and the dark dale
And the field full of folk[1] I fairly will show.
A lady, lovely of looks, in linen clothed,
Came down from a castle, and called me fairly
And said, "Son, are you sleeping? Do you see these people,
How busy they are, all thronging about?
Most of the people that pass their time on earth,

Have honor in this world, and they wish for no better
They don't care about any heaven but the one here on earth."
   I was afraid of her face, though she was fair,
And I said, "Mercy, madam, what does this mean?"
   "The tower on the hill," she said, "Truth is therein

And he would like you to do as his word teaches;
For he is Father of Faith, who formed you all
Both with flesh and with face, and gave you five senses
To worship him with, while you are here."

---

[1] *What this ... of folk*   The Prologue introduces the narrative as a dream vision, in which Piers recounts that he has seen a tower on a hilltop, and another in a valley, and a fair field full of folk between the two:
   A faire field full of folk found I there between,
   Of all manner of men, the mean and the rich ...

PASSUS 5

The king and his knights to the church went
  To hear matins of the day, and the Mass after.
Then waked I from my winking, and felt woeful
That I had not slept sounder, and so seen more.
5 But ere I had traveled a furlong, faintness so seized me
That I could not go further on foot, for lack of my
    sleep,
And I sat softly down, and said my belief,
And as I babbled on my beads,[1] they brought me asleep.
  And then saw I much more than I have already told,
10 For I saw the field full of folk that I before spoke of,
And how Reason got ready to preach to the realm,
And with a cross before the king commenced in this way
    to teach.
  He proved that these pestilences had to do purely
    with sin,
And the south-west wind on Saturday evening
15 Had plainly to do with pride, and for no point else.
Pear-trees and plum-trees were puffed to the earth
To show you people that you should do better.
Beeches and broad oaks were blown to the ground,
Their tails torn upwards, a dreadful sign
20 That at doomsday deadly sin shall be the sinners'
    undoing.
  Of this matter I may mumble at length
But I will say as I saw, God help me!
How plainly before the people Reason began to preach.
  He told Waster go work as best he could
25 And redeem himself for laziness with some sort of craft.
  And prayed that Pernele take off her costly array
And keep it in her box, in case she might need money
    later.
  Tom Stowe he taught to take two staves
And bring home Phyllis from women's punishment.
30 He warned Wat that his wife was to blame,
Saying that her hat was worth half a mark, but his hood
    cost not even a groat.
  And he bade Batt cut down a bough or even two

With which to beat Betty unless she would work.

from PASSUS 7

Truth heard what was happening, and sent word to
  Piers
To take his team and to till the earth;
And Truth provided a pardon *a poena et a culpa*[2]
For him, and for his heirs, for evermore after.
5 And told him to stay at home, and plow up his fields,
And those that helped him to plow, to plant, or to sow,
Or any other work that might help Piers–
They too were granted pardon with Piers Plowman.
  Kings and knights that keep Holy Church
10 And rightfully in realms rule over the people
Have pardon to pass through purgatory lightly,
And to join patriarchs and prophets in paradise.
Bishops are most blessed, if they be as they should, …

Merchants had many years to the good,
15 But none were pardoned a *poena et a culpa* by the pope,
For they do not always observe the holy days, as the
    Holy Church teaches, …
Under his secret seal Truth sent them a letter
Saying they should buy boldly what they liked best,
And afterwards sell again, and save their profits
20 To use in helping *maisons Dieu*,[3] and in helping folk in
    misery;
In helping to repair rotten roads, where plainly needed;
And to build up bridges that were broken down;
In helping maidens to marry, or to become nuns;
In helping poor people and prisoners find their food;
25 And helping send scholars to school, or to some other
    craft;
In helping poor religious souls, and in lowering their
    rents …

Now has the Pope power to grant the people
Remission of penance, to pass directly into Heaven:
This is our belief, as lettered men teach us:
30 … I believe loyally (the Lord forbids anything else!)

---

[1] *beads* It is the practice of Roman Catholics to say their prayers to the Virgin Mary on a set of prayer beads called a rosary. The Apostles' Creed, or the "belief," as Piers says, is one of the prayers one recites when one says his or her rosary.

[2] *a poena et a culpa* Latin: from punishment and from guilt, i.e., absolving the holder of the pardon.

[3] *maisons Dieu* French: houses of God, i.e., hospitals, houses of charity, etc.

That pardon, penance, and prayers cause people to be
   saved.
For souls that have sinned the seven deadly sins.
To trust to indulgences—truly I think
Is not so safe for the soul as it is to do well.
35   Therefore I advise all that are rich and
That trust of your treasure ...
And especially you masters, mayors, and judges,
Who are held to be wise, and have the world's wealth
Available to purchase your pardons, and the Pope's
   bulls:[1]
40 At the dreadful Doom, when the dead shall arise
And you all will come before Christ, to have it reckoned
How you have led your life, and kept His laws,
And how you behaved day by day, the doom will declare
That however many pardons ... of all the friars' orders
45 Promising two-fold indulgence—unless you have
Also good deeds to help you, I rate your patents
And pardons at one pea-pod's value!
Therefore I counsel Christians to cry to God for mercy,
And to Mary His mother to mediate for us,
50 That God grant us grace here, before that we depart,
That we may do such good works, while we are here
That after our death-day Do-well will declare
At the day of Doom that we did as he told us.

from Thomas Wimbleton, Sermon (c. 1388)

The sermon from which the following passages are
taken was preached by Thomas Wimbleton at Paul's
Cross in London; it survives in over a dozen English
(and two Latin) manuscripts.

... As I see, the first question that shall be purposed [to
a new curate or prelate] is this: how hast thou entered?
Who brought thee into this office? Truth other simony?
God or the devil? Grace or money? The flesh or the
spirit? ...
   And if we taken heed truly what abominations been
scattered in the church nowadays among priests, we

should well wit[2] that they all cometh nought into the
fold of Christ by Christ's clepynge[3] for the profit but by
other ways to get him worldly wealth; and this is cause
of many errors among the people.... When were [pride,
envy, wrath, and covetousness] so great as they are now,
and so of all other sins? ...

The second question that every curate and prelate of
holy church shall answer to is this: how hast thou ruled,
that is to say the souls of the subjects and the goods of
poor men? Give now thine account. First, how hast
thou governed God's folk that was taken thee to keep?
As a [shep]herd or as a hired man that doth all for the
love of his bodily hire? As a father [or] as a wolf that
eateth the sheep and keepeth them nought? ...

The third question that this first [curate or prelate] shall
answer to is this: how hast thou lived? What light of
holiness hast thou showed in thy living to the people?
... Reckon how thou hast lived. As a priest [or] as a lewd
man? As a man or as a beast? It is a wonder truly how
the life of priests is changed. They beith clothed as
knights; they speak as unhonestly as churls, [or] of
winning as merchants; they ride as princes; and all this
that is thus spent is of the goods of poor men and of
Christ's heritages.

Lollardy

One of the earliest movements in the direction of
the Reformation of Christianity was that of John
Wycliffe and the Lollards. Over a century before the
upheavals brought on by Martin Luther, Wycliffe
spoke out strongly against corruption and in favor of
bringing all Christians into more direct contact with
the Word of God. In Wycliffe's view the veneration
of saints and of relics, the drawing of a veil of
mystery around the Bible by refusing to authorize
translations into the vernacular, and the acceptance
of vast levels of wealth and privilege for members of
the clergy were all of a piece—and all deserved to be
brought to an end. Those who followed and

---

[1] *Pope's bulls* Declarations by the Pope; specifically in this case,
declarations providing "indulgences," granting pardon for sins in
exchange for money.

[2] *wit* Know.

[3] *clepynge* Calling, bidding.

extended Wycliffe's teachings came to be known as "Lollards"; their "heresies" were ruthlessly stamped out in the fifteenth century.

from Account of the Heresy Trial of Margery Baxter

On April 1, 1429 Johanna Clifland, wife of William Clifland, who lives in the parish of St. Mary the Less in Norwich, being cited, appeared in person before the reverend father and lord in Christ William, by the grace of God Bishop of Norwich [1426–36], holding court in his palace chapel. At the command of the bishop she placed her hand on God's Holy Gospels and swore that she would tell the truth about any and all questions asked of her that concerned matters of faith.

After swearing this oath, Johanna Clifland said that on the Friday [January 28] before the most recent feast of the Purification of the Blessed Mary, Margery Baxter, the wife of William Baxter the wright, recently living at Martham in the diocese of Norwich, was sitting and sewing near the fireplace with the witness in the witness's room. In the presence of the witness and her servants Johanna Grymell and Agnes Bethom, she told the witness and her servants that they should never swear oaths, saying in English: "Dame, beware of the bee, for every bee will sting; and therefore see that you swear neither by God nor by Our Lady nor by any other saint; and if you do the contrary the bee will sting your tongue and poison your soul."

Then the witness said Margery asked her what she did daily in church. The witness told her that as soon as she entered, after kneeling before the Cross it was her habit to say five Our Fathers in honor of the crucifix and the same number of Hail Marys in honor of Blessed Mary, the Mother of Christ. Then Margery scolded her and told the witness, "You act badly by kneeling like that and praying before images in these churches, because God has never been in such a church, and He never has gone forth from heaven nor will He ever. And He will not give or offer you any more merit for the genuflectings, and adorations, and prayers that you do in these churches than a lit candle hidden away under the cover of a baptismal font can give any light to people inside a church at nighttime." ...

Next the witness said that the aforesaid Margery told her no child or infant born of Christian parents ought to be baptized in water according to the common custom since such a child had been sufficiently baptized in its mother's womb. So the image-worshipping and idolatry these false and accursed priests do when they dip babies in fonts in churches is done solely to wrench money from people in order to maintain these priests and their concubines.

Next the witness said Margery told her there that the consent of mutual love alone between a man and a woman sufficed to make the sacrament of marriage; no other exchange of words or ceremonies in a church were necessary.

Next she said Margery told her that no faithful man or woman was obliged to fast during Lent, Ember Days, Fridays, the vigils of saints, or other days indicated by the church; and that anyone could eat meat or any other kind of food during these times and on these days; and that on fast days it was better for someone to eat scraps of meat left over from Thursday than to go to the market and run up debts buying fish ...

The witness also said Margery asked her and her servant Johanna to come secretly at night to Margery's house, and there they could hear her husband read the law of Christ to them, the law written in a book [i.e., the Bible] which her husband read to her at night; and she said her husband is an excellent teacher of Christianity.

Margery also said that she had spoken with Johanna West, a woman living near the churchyard of St. Mary-in-the-Marsh, about the law of Christ, and that Johanna is on the good road to salvation.

Furthermore, Margery said this to the witness: "Johanna, from your expression it looks like you plan to reveal what I've told you to the bishop." And the witness swore that she wished never to reveal her counsels in this regard unless Margery gave her cause to do so. Then Margery told her: "If you accuse me to the bishop, I'll do to you what I did to this Carmelite friar from Yarmouth who was the wisest friar in the land." The witness asked her what she had done to the friar. Margery answered that she had spoken with the friar, upbraiding him because he begged for his living, and telling him that it wasn't an act of charity to do good to someone or give him aid unless he himself wanted to take off his friar's habit and get behind a plow to work for a living, which would be more pleasing to God than following the way of life of some of these friars. Then the friar asked her whether she had anything else to tell him or teach him. So Margery, as the witness said, explained the Gospels to him in English. After that, the friar left Margery, so the witness said. Later this friar accused Margery of heresy. But Margery, hearing that the friar had denounced her, accused him of wanting to have sex with her, and since she would not give in to him, he accused her of heresy. Margery said this was the reason her husband wanted to kill the friar. Out of fear the friar shut up and left these parts in shame.

Margery also told the witness she had often made false confessions to the Dean of St. Mary-in-the-Fields so that he would think she led a good life. Because of this, he often gave Margery money. Then the witness asked her whether she had confessed all her sins to a priest. Margery told her she had never done harm to any priest, so she had never wanted to confess to a priest or be obedient to any priest, since a priest had no power to absolve anyone from sins; and in fact priests sinned more grievously every day than other people. Margery also said that every man and woman who shared Margery's opinion were good priests, and that the Holy Church exists only wherever all those people were who believed as she did. For that reason, Margery said she was obliged to confess only to God, not to any priest.

Next Margery told the witness that people honor the devils that fell from heaven with Lucifer who, when they fell to earth, entered into the statues standing in churches. They have dwelled in them since then and are still hiding in them, so that people who adore statues are committing idolatry.

Next the witness said Margery informed her that holy water and blessed bread were just trifles with no power, and that every church bell should be pulled down and destroyed, and that all those who set up bells in churches are excommunicated.

Margery also said that even if she were convicted of Lollardy, she shouldn't be burned because she, so the witness said, had and still has a charter of salvation in her womb.

Next Margery said she had won a judgment against the Lord Bishop of Norwich, and Henry Inglese, and the Lord Abbots associated with them.

Next the witness said she had sent Agnes Bethom, her servant, to Margery's house on the Saturday after last Ash Wednesday. Margery wasn't home but Agnes found a kitchen kettle on the fire, and boiling inside it were a piece of salt pork and oat flour—so Agnes reported to the witness.

[Margery confessed on 7 October, 1429. Her sentence included being flogged on four consecutive Sundays as she walked barefoot around her parish church.]

The Persecution of the Jews

The twelfth and thirteenth centuries were tumultuous and difficult times for Jews in Britain. Early Norman kings had encouraged the emigration of Jews from continental Europe, but in the latter part of the twelfth century attacks on Jews on the Continent by crusading Christians became common, and in Britain vicious propaganda against Jews (such as that found in Thomas of Monmouth's *Life and Miracles of St. William of Norwich*) began to be widely disseminated. Physical attacks on Jews (the most horrific of which was the massacre/mass suicide of approximately 150 Jews on 16 March, 1190, described below by Roger of Howden) became widespread in Britain in the late twelfth century. New taxes and restrictions (such as the 1194 Ordnances) began to be placed on Jews, and even more "favorable" developments (such as King John's Charter of 1201 confirming certain Jewish rights) were couched in such terms as to make clear that relations between Christians and Jews would remain entirely on an "us and them" footing. Restrictions became far more extreme with the Ordnances of Henry III, and in 1290 all Jews were expelled from the country by order of Edward I.

from Thomas of Monmouth, *The Life and Miracles of St. William of Norwich* (c. 1173)

When therefore [William] was flourishing in this blessed boyhood of his, and had attained to his eighth year [about 1140], he was entrusted to the skinners to be taught their craft. Gifted with a teachable disposition and bringing industry to bear upon it, in a short time he far surpassed lads of his own age in the craft aforesaid, and he equaled some who had been his teachers. So leaving the country, drawn by a divine urge he betook himself to the city and lodged with a very famous master of that craft, and some time passed away. He was seldom in the country, but was occupied in the city and sedulously gave himself to the practice of his craft, and thus reached his twelfth year.

Now, while he was staying in Norwich, the Jews who were settled there and required their cloaks or their robes or other garments (whether pledged to them, or their own property) to be repaired, preferred him before all other skinners. For [the Jews] esteemed him to be especially fit for their work, either because they had learnt that he was guileless and skillful, or, because attracted to him by their avarice, they thought they could bargain with him for a lower price, Or, as I rather believe, because by the ordering of divine Providence he had been predestined to martyrdom from the beginning of time, and gradually step by step was drawn on, and chosen to be made a mock of and to be put to death by the Jews, in scorn of the Lord's Passion....

For I have learnt from certain Jews, who were afterwards converted to the Christian faith, how that at that time they had planned to do this very thing with some Christian, and in order to carry out their malignant purpose, at the beginning of Lent they had made choice of the boy William, being twelve years of age and a boy of unusual innocence....

Then the boy, like an innocent lamb, was led to the slaughter. He was treated kindly by the Jews at first, and, ignorant of what was being prepared for him, he was kept till the morrow. But on the next day [Tuesday, 21 March], which in that year was the Passover for them, after the singing of the hymns appointed for the day in the synagogue, the chiefs of the Jews ... suddenly seized hold of the boy William as he was having his dinner and in no fear of any treachery, and ill-treated him in various horrible ways. For while some of them held him behind, others opened his mouth and introduced an instrument of torture which is called a teazle [a wooden gag] and, fixing it by straps through both jaws to the back of his neck, they fastened it with a knot as tightly as it could be drawn.

After that, taking a short piece of rope of about the thickness of one's little finger and tying three knots in it at certain distances marked out, they bound round that innocent head with it from the forehead to the back, forcing the middle knot into his forehead and the two others into his temples, the two ends of the rope being most tightly stretched at the back of his head and fastened in a very tight knot. The ends of the rope were then passed round his neck and carried round his throat under his chin, and there they finished off this dreadful engine of torture in a fifth knot.

But not even yet could the cruelty of the torturers be satisfied without adding even more severe pains. Having shaved his head, they stabbed it with countless thorn points, and made the blood come horribly from the wounds they made. And so cruel were they and so eager to inflict pain that it was difficult to say whether they were more cruel or more ingenious in their tortures. For their skill in torturing kept up the strength of their cruelty and ministered arms thereto.

And thus, while these enemies of the Christian name were rioting in the spirit of malignity around the boy, some of those present adjudged him to be fixed to a Cross in mockery of the Lord's Passion, as though they would say: "even as we condemned the Christ to a shameful death, so let us also condemn the Christian, so that, uniting the lord and his servant in a like punishment, we may retort upon themselves the pain of that reproach which they impute to us."

Conspiring, therefore, to accomplish the crime of this great and detestable malice, they next laid their blood-stained hands upon the innocent victim, and having lifted him from the ground and fastened him upon the Cross, they vied with one another in their efforts to make an end of him.

And we, after enquiring into the matter very diligently, did both find the house, and discovered some most certain marks in it of what had been done there....

As a proof of the truth and credibility of the matter we now adduce something which we have heard from the lips of Theobald, who was once a Jew, and afterwards a monk. He verily told us that in the ancient writings of his fathers it was written that the Jews, without the shedding of human blood, could neither obtain their freedom, nor could they ever return to their fatherland. Hence it was laid down by them in ancient times that every year they must sacrifice a Christian in some part of the world to the Most High God in scorn and contempt of Christ....

from Roger Howden, *Chronicle* (1190)

In the same month of March [1190] ... the Jews of the city of York, in number five hundred men, besides women and children, shut themselves up in the tower of York, with the consent of the sheriff, in consequence of their dread of the Christians; but when the sheriff and the constable sought to regain possession of it, the Jews refused to deliver it up. In consequence of this, the people of the said city, and the strangers who had come within the jurisdiction thereof, at the exhortation of the sheriff and the constable, with one consent made an attack upon the Jews.

After they had made assaults upon the tower day and night, the Jews offered the people a large sum of money to allow them to depart with their lives; but this the others refused to receive. Upon this, one skilled in their laws arose and said, "Men of Israel, listen to my advice. It is better that we should kill one another, than fall into the hands of the enemies of our law." Accordingly, all the Jews, both men and women, gave their assent to his advice, and each master of a family, beginning with the chief persons of his household, with a sharp knife first cut the throats of his wife and sons and daughters, and then of all his servants, and lastly his own. Some of them also threw their slain over the walls among the people; while others shut up their slain in the king's house and burned them, as well as the king's houses. Those who had slain the others were afterwards killed by the people. In the meantime, some of the Christians set fire to the Jews' houses, and plundered them; and thus all the Jews in the city of York were destroyed, and all acknowledgments of debts due to them were burnt.

from The Ordinances of the Jews (1194)

All the debts, pledges, mortgages, lands, houses, rents, and possessions of the Jews shall be registered. The Jew who shall conceal any of these shall forfeit to the King his body and the thing concealed, and likewise all his possessions and chattels, neither shall it be lawful to the Jew to recover the thing concealed.

Likewise six or seven places shall be provided in which they shall make all their contracts, and there shall be appointed two lawyers that are Christians and two lawyers that are Jews, and two legal registrars, and before them and the clerks of William of the Church of St. Mary's and William of Chimilli, shall their contracts be made.

And charters shall be made of their contracts by way of indenture. And one part of the indenture shall remain with the Jew, sealed with the seal of him, to whom the money is lent, and the other part shall remain in the common chest: wherein there shall be three locks and keys, whereof the two Christians shall keep one key, and the two Jews another, and the clerks of William of the Church of St. Mary and of William of Chimilli shall keep the third. And moreover, there shall be three seals to it, and those who keep the seals shall put the seals thereto.

Moreover the clerks of the said William and William shall keep a roll of the transcripts of all the charters, and as the charters shall be altered so let the roll be likewise. For every charter there shall be threepence paid, one moiety thereof by the Jews and the other moiety by him to whom the money is lent; whereof the two writers shall have twopence and the keeper of the roll the third.

And from henceforth no contract shall be made with, nor payment, made to, the Jews, nor any alteration made in the charters, except before the said persons or the greater part of them, if all of them cannot be present. And the aforesaid two Christians shall have one roll of the debts or receipts of the payments which from henceforth are to be made to the Jews, and the two Jews one and the keeper of the roll one.

Moreover every Jew shall swear on his Roll, that all his debts and pledges and rents, and all his goods and his possessions, he shall cause to be enrolled, and that he shall conceal nothing as is aforesaid. And if he shall know that anyone shall conceal anything he shall secretly reveal it to the justices sent to them, and that they shall detect, and shew unto them all falsifiers or forgers of the charters and clippers of money, where or when they shall know them, and likewise all false charters.

from The Charter of King John to the Jews (1201)

1. John, by the grace of God, &c. Know that we have granted to all the Jews of England and Normandy to have freely and honourably residence in our land, and to hold all that from us, which they held from King Henry, our father's grandfather, and all that now they reasonably hold in land and fees and mortgages and goods, and that they have all their liberties and customs just as they had them in the time of the aforesaid King Henry, our father's grandfather, better and more quietly and more honourably.

from The Ordinances of Henry III (1253)

The king has provided and decreed ... that no Jew dwell in England unless he do the king service, and that as soon as a Jew shall be born, whether male or female, in some way he shall serve the king. And that there be no communities of the Jews in England save in those places wherein such communities were in the time of the lord King John, the king's father. And that in their synagogues the Jews, one and all, worship in subdued tones according to their rite, so that Christians hear it not. And that all Jews answer to the rector of the parish in which they dwell for all parochial dues belonging to their houses. And that no Christian nurse hereafter suckle or nourish the male child of any Jew, and that no Christian man or woman serve any Jew or Jewess, nor eat with them, nor dwell in their house. And that no Jew or Jewess eat or buy meat in Lent. And that no Jew disparage the Christian faith, nor publicly dispute touching the same. And that no Jew have secret intercourse with any Christian woman, nor any Christian man with a Jewess. And that every Jew wear on his breast a conspicuous badge. And that no Jew enter any church or any chapel save in passing through,

nor stay therein to the dishonor of Christ. And that no Jew in any wise hinder another Jew willing to be converted to the Christian faith. And that no Jew be received in any town without the special licence of the king, save in those towns wherein Jews have been wont to dwell.

And the justices appointed to the guardianship of the Jews are commanded to cause these provisions to be carried into effect and straitly kept on pain of forfeiture

Illustration from *Flores Historianum* (14th century). Three Jews (all depicted with beards, as was customary) are attacked by a soldier.

of the goods of the Jews aforesaid. Witness the king at Westminster on the 31st day of January. By the king and council.

Edward I's Order (1290)

Edward ... to the treasurer and barons of the exchequer, greeting. Whereas formerly in our Parliament at Westminster on the quinzaine of St. Michael in the third year of our reign, to the honor of God and the profit of the people of our realm, we ordained and decreed that no Jew thenceforth should lend anything at usury to any Christian on lands, rents or other things, but that they should live by their commerce and labor; and the same Jews, afterwards maliciously deliberating among themselves, contriving a worse sort of usury which they called courtesy, have depressed our people aforesaid on all sides under color thereof, the last offense doubling the first; whereby, for

QUEM QUAERITIS
c. 970

The *Quem Quaeritis* (Latin: "Whom do you seek?") was originally a trope, or an expansive insertion into the standard text of the Mass (in this case, during Easter services). It appears to have originated in the early tenth century, taking the form of an antiphonal song, wherein two groups of the choir on opposite sides of the cathedral nave would sing in a call-and-answer form. With a few lines of rudimentary dialogue the trope dramatized the biblical account of the meeting of the three Marys and the two angels at the tomb of Christ on Easter morning described in Luke 24.1–8. In the simplest version that has come down to us (c. 950), it takes the following form:

Quem quaeritis in sepulchro, Christicolae?
Jesum Nazarenum crucifixum, o caelicolae.
Non est hic, surrexit sicut praedixerat.
Ite, nuntiate quia surrexit de sepulchro.

Whom do you seek in the sepulcher, O Christians?
Jesus of Nazareth who was crucified, O heavenly ones.
He is not here; He is risen, just as He had foretold.
Go, announce that He has risen from the sepulcher.

Although the ceremony in its most basic form bears little resemblance to a play, it quickly developed into a more overtly theatrical work. Within a few decades, a variant of the *Quem Quaeritis* with substantial "stage directions" was recorded. In the *Regularis Concordia* (c. 970), four monks act out the play, taking on the roles of the Marys and, in this case, a single angel. The altar of the cathedral is used as a set for the sepulcher, and the text includes basic costume and properties notes.

⌘ ⌘ ⌘

their crimes and to the honor of the Crucified, we have caused those Jews to go forth from our realm as traitors: we, wishing to swerve not from our former choice, but rather to follow it, do make totally null and void all manner of penalties and usuries and every sort thereof, which could be demanded by actions by reason of the Jewry from any Christians of our realm for any times whatsoever; wishing that nothing be in any wise demanded from the Christians aforesaid by reason of the debts aforesaid, save only the principal sums which they received from the Jews aforesaid; the amount of which debts we will that the Christians aforesaid verify before you by the oath of three good and lawful men by whom the truth of the matter may the better be known, and thereafter pay the same to us at terms convenient to them to be fixed by you. And therefore we command you that you cause our said grace so piously granted to be read in the aforesaid exchequer, and to be enrolled on the rolls of the same exchequer, and to be straitly kept, according to the form above noted. ...

The Quem Quaeritis[1] Ceremony

from the *Regularis Concordia* of St. Æthelwold[2]

(*When the third lesson [of the matins[3]] is recited, let four brethren[4] dress themselves. Let one, wearing an alb,[5] enter as if doing something else; and let him without being observed approach the place of the sepulcher,[6] and, holding a palm in his hand, sit there quietly. While the third responsory is being sung, let the remaining three brethren follow, all of them wearing capes and carrying thuribles[7] filled with incense. Then slowly, as if seeking something, let them move toward the place of the sepulchre. These things are to be performed in imitation of the Angel seated on the tomb, and of the women coming with spices to anoint the body of Jesus. Therefore, when the seated angel sees the three women, approaching him wandering about as if looking for something, let him begin to sing in a pleasing voice of medium pitch:*)

[ANGEL.] Whom do you seek [in the sepulcher, O followers of Christ?]

(*When he has sung this to the end, let the three respond in one voice:*)

[MARYS.] Jesus of Nazareth [who was crucified, O celestial one.]

(*He [then says] to them:*)

[ANGEL.] He is not here: He is risen, just as He foretold. Go, announce that he is risen from the dead.

(*At the word of his command, let the three turn to the Choir, and say:*)

[MARYS.] Alleluia! The Lord is risen. [Today is risen the strong lion, Christ, the Son of God.]

(*When this has been said, let the angel, again seating himself, as if recalling them, speak the antiphon.[8]*)

[ANGEL.] Come, and see the place [where the Lord was laid. Alleluia!]

(*And saying this, let him rise, and let him lift the veil and show them the place bare of the cross, except for the cloths lying there with which the cross was wrapped. Seeing this, let the women set down the thuribles they carried into the sepulcher, and let them pick up the cloth and spread it out before the clergy; and, as if making known that the Lord had risen and was not now wrapped in it, let them sing this antiphon:*)

[MARYS.] The Lord is risen from the sepulcher [Who for us hung on the cross. Alleluia!]

(*And let them place the cloth upon the altar. When the antiphon has ended, let the Prior,[9] rejoicing with them at the triumph of our King, who arose having conquered death, begin the hymn:*)

We praise you, O God.

(*When this has begun, let the bells be rung in unison.*)
—C. 970

---

[1] *Quem Quaeritis* Latin: whom do you seek?

[2] *from the ... Æthelwold* This manuscript dates from Winchester between 965 and 975 CE; it provides liturgical instructions for use in Benedictine monasteries. The *Quem Quaeritis* in this version is not a trope to be inserted into the text of the Mass but rather a ceremony to be performed at the conclusion of the service. Included in square brackets are more expansive versions of the text that are frequently found in other editions. The present text has been newly translated from the Latin text given in David Bevington, *Medieval Drama*, p. 27–28; the Latin text of the short version in the headnote on the previous page is also from Bevington, p. 26, and has been translated for this anthology.

[3] *matins* Service preceding the first Mass of the day.

[4] *brethren* Members of the religious community.

[5] *alb* Tunic of white cloth reaching to the feet.

[6] *sepulcher* A permanent or temporary structure prepared in a church for the dramatic burial of the Sacrament on Good Friday. The Holy Sepulcher refers to the cave outside Jerusalem where Christ was buried.

[7] *thuribles* Containers for incense.

---

[8] *antiphon* Verse sung before the recitation of a psalm or hymn.

[9] *Prior* Superior officer of a religious house.

THE SERVICE FOR REPRESENTING ADAM

The *Jeu d'Adam* (*Play*, or *Game of Adam*; in Latin: *Ordo Repraesentationis Ade*, or *Service for Representing Adam*) is a twelfth-century dramatic representation of the stories of the Biblical Temptation and Fall, of Cain and Abel, and of a succession of prophets who herald the coming of Christ. It is one of the oldest surviving dramas to make extensive use of the Anglo-Norman vernacular, and it marks a shift from earlier liturgical texts written and performed exclusively in Latin. Most estimates place the play's composition in the third quarter of the twelfth century, making it roughly contemporary with both the Fleury playbook (which contains ten liturgical plays that dramatize Biblical events named for the French monastery at which the plays are assumed to have been written), and other more secular Anglo-Norman dramas (such as *La Seinte Resureccion*, or *Holy Resurrection*) that were designed to be performed outside an ecclesiastical context.

The artistic flair the *Jeu d'Adam* brings to its liturgical material grows out of a larger medieval dramatic tradition. As early as the ninth century the celebration of the Mass involved elements of spectacle, with vestments, processions and responsories (chants sung during services) lending a dramatic air to liturgical proceedings. The ritual of the Mass grew in both scope and elaboration until the distinction between church service and the dramatic embellishment of liturgical subjects began to blur. The *Jeu d'Adam* is not liturgical, but it is based on the experience of the liturgy; it draws its inspiration from Biblical texts and sermons, but it was probably performed outside of churches and was independent of any particular service. The play was staged in England and France, but possibly first composed in England, where French was, after the Norman Conquest of 1066, the language of much of the ruling class and of most vernacular literary works composed in the twelfth century.

The drama might have been performed during Advent, Lent, or Christmas. The actors were likely clerics, who would have understood not just the Anglo-Norman dialogue, but also the Latin choral, costume, and stage directions. These guidelines, or *didascalia*, are quite specific, providing instructions about how the actors should modulate their voices when speaking, where they should direct their gaze, and what gestures they ought to make in order to convey the particular emotion of the scene. The *Jeu d'Adam* would probably have been staged on and around the steps of the church, with the church doors symbolizing the gates of heaven, the upper steps standing in for Paradise, and the lower steps representing worldly existence on earth. Hell would be found in the *platea*, the staging area at the bottom of the stairs, encircled by spectators. The audience would be close enough to reach out and touch the devil and his minions as they raced around in their elaborate costumes.

The author of the play is unknown, but it seems safe to assume that he was a priest or monk. The play is extant only in a relatively careless copy, MS. 927 of the Bibliothèque Municipale de Tours, which contains a miscellany of works including liturgical dramas, hymns, songs, and poems. The play ends with Nebuchadnezzer's account of his fiery vision, but the text is truncated, and its abrupt ending has led to speculation about the original conclusion of the play. Some have wondered if the final scene might explicitly link the Old and New Testaments or perhaps dramatize Christ's harrowing of Hell. Whatever finale was originally conceived, it seems likely that the last scene would typologically echo the first, since the ultimate aim of the play was clearly to encourage the audience to accept that only through Christ could they hope to redeem the consequences of both Adam's and their own sin.

⌘ ⌘ ⌘

The Service for Representing Adam[1]

[DRAMATIS PERSONAE]

Adam
Eve
Figure[2] [of God]
Devil
Responsory
Cain
Abel
Isaiah
Jew
Responsory of the King's Ministers
Nebuchadnezzar

Let Paradise be constructed in a prominently high place; let curtains and silken hangings be placed around it at such a height that those persons who will be in Paradise can be seen from the shoulders upwards; let sweet-smelling flowers and foliage be planted; within let there be various trees, and fruits hanging on them, so that the place may seem as delightful as possible. Then let our Saviour come, clothed in a dalmatic,[3] and let Adam [and Eve] be stationed before him. Let Adam be robed in a red tunic, Eve in a woman's white garment with a wimple[4] of white silk; and let them both stand before the Figure [of God]—Adam somewhat [closer with a calm expression, with Eve a little further

---

[1] *The Service for Representing Adam* Translated by David Bevington (copyright © David Bevington, 1975) from the Latin *Ordo Repraesentationis Adae*. Stage directions that appear in the original appear here in parentheses; where stage directions or other material not in the original text has been added for clarity, the added text appears in square brackets. The fifteenth-century manuscript of the play divides the text more or less as is done here, into nine-line stanzas with internal rhymes in each stanza's first four lines. (An alternative approach now widely favored by scholars is to divide the play into 13-line stanzas.)

[2] *Figure* The unusual term "Figure" for the character of God may point toward the way in which characters and events in the Hebrew Bible or Old Testament were seen, by medieval convention, as "figures" or "types" that foreshadowed characters and events in the New Testament.

[3] *dalmatic* Ecclesiastical garment with a slit on either side, and with wide sleeves, worn in the western Church by deacons and bishops on certain occasions.

[4] *wimple* Head-dress worn by women, covering the head, chin, neck, and sides of the face.

off].[5] And let this Adam be well coached when he must give answers, lest in answering he should be either too hasty or too slow. Nor him alone, but let all persons be coached thus, so that they may speak in an orderly manner and make gestures appropriate to the things of which they speak; and, in their verses, let them neither add nor subtract a syllable, but pronounce them all steadily, and speak those things that are to be spoken in their due order. Whoever will mention the name of Paradise, let him look in its direction and point it out with his hand. Then let the lesson begin:

In the beginning God created the heavens and the earth.

(*When this is finished let the choir sing:*)

RESPONSORY.   And the Lord God formed [man].[6]

(*When this is finished let the Figure [of God] say:*)

Adam! (*Who must answer:*) Sire?
FIGURE.   I have formed you
5   Of loam° of the earth.   *clay, mud*
ADAM.   I know it well.
FIGURE. I have formed you in my likeness,
[...][7]
In my image I have made you of earth.
10   You must never make war against Me.
ADAM.   I will not; but I will believe You,
I will obey my Creator.
FIGURE.   I have given you a worthy companion:
Your wife, Eve by name.
15   She is your wife and partner;
You ought to be entirely faithful to her.
Love her, and let her love you,
If you would both be mine.
Let her be subject to your commandment,
20   And both of you to My wish.
I formed her from your side;
Born of you, she is no stranger.

---

[5] *closer with ... off* The editors have slightly emended Bevington's translation in light of recent scholarship.

[6] *In the beginning ... formed [man]* See Genesis 1.1 and 2.7. This Biblical lesson (reading) and responsory (the sung response by the choir) were part of the liturgy; the play as a whole is structured around a series of such readings and responses.

[7] *[...]* Line missing from the original text.

I fashioned her from your body;
From you she issued,° not from outside.   *was born*

25   Govern her by reason.
Let no dissension come between you,
But great love and mutual obedience:
Such is the law of marriage.

[FIGURE TO EVE.]   Now I will speak to you, Eve.
30   Be heedful, do not take this lightly:
If you wish to do My will,
Cherish goodness in your heart.
Love and honor Me as your Creator,
And acknowledge Me your Lord.
35   To serve Me devote your care,
All your might and all your mind.
Love Adam, and hold him dear.
He is your husband, and you his wife.
To him be obedient at all times,
40   Do not stray from his discipline.
Serve and love him with willing spirit,
For that is the law of marriage.
If you do well as his helpmeet,°   *helpmate*
I will place you with him in glory.

45   EVE.   Sire, I will do according to Your pleasure;
I do not wish to stray from it.
I will acknowledge You as sovereign,
Him as my partner and stronger than I.
I will always be faithful to him;
50   From me he will have good counsel.
Your pleasure, Your service
I will perform, Sire, in every way.

(Then let the Figure call Adam nearer and say to him more intently:)

[FIGURE.]   Listen, Adam, and hear My judgment.
I have formed you; now I will give you this gift:
55   You may live forever, if you obey My teaching;
You may remain healthy, and not feel illness.
You will neither hunger nor thirst for need,
Feel neither heat nor cold.
You will dwell in joy, and never leave,
60   And in this pleasant state you will not taste sadness.
You will spend all your life in joy;
You will live forever, your life will not be short.
I say this to you, and wish that Eve attend;°   *listen, consider*

65   If she doesn't listen, there will be trouble.
Take dominion over all the earth,
Birds, beasts, and other riches.
Let those who envy you be held in slight regard,
For all the world will be obedient to you.
Both good and evil are in your power;
70   He who has such a choice is not bound to a stake.
Hold all in balance, weigh things equally.
Believe in my counsel, be true to Me.
Leave the evil, and hold yourself to the good;
Love your Lord, and keep with Him;
75   Do not forsake My counsel for another.
If you do this, you will be without sin.

ADAM.   Great thanks I give for Your kindness,
You who created me and give me such bounty
As to place good and evil in my power.
80   I will bestow my will in serving You.
You are my Sire, I am your handiwork;
You give me shape, I am of Your making.
My will can never be so stubborn
But that all my care will be to serve You.

(Then let the Figure point out Paradise to Adam with his hand, saying:)

85   Adam!
ADAM.   Sire?
FIGURE.   I will tell you my advice.
Do you see this garden?
ADAM.   What is it called?
90   FIGURE.   Paradise.
ADAM.   How beautiful it is!
FIGURE.   I planted it and laid it out.
He who will remain in it will be my friend.
I charge you to remain and guard it.

(Then he will send them into Paradise, saying:)

95   I set you both therein.
ADAM.   And can we stay?
FIGURE.   For your entire life, you need fear nothing here;
You can neither die nor fall sick.

(Let the choir sing.)

RESPONSORY.   And the Lord God took the man.[1]

(*Then the Figure will stretch forth his hand toward Paradise, saying:*)

100 I will tell you the nature of this garden:
You will find no lack of any delight.
There is no earthly good a creature might desire
That each cannot find to his own measure.
Here woman will receive from man no anger,
105 Nor man from woman have shame or fear.
Man is no sinner for begetting children,
Nor does woman experience pain in bearing them.
You will live forever, thus you will have a wonderful
    existence here;
Your age can never alter.
110 Death you will never fear, nor can it ever harm you.
I do not wish you to leave; here you must make your
    dwelling.

(*Let the choir sing:*)

RESPONSORY.   The Lord God said to Adam.[2]

(*Then let the Figure point out to Adam the trees of Paradise, saying:*)

Of all this fruit you may eat for your pleasure:

(*And let him show him the forbidden tree and its fruit, saying:*)

This I forbid you, do not take your enjoyment of this
    other one.
115 If you eat of it, you will experience death at once;
You will lose My love, change your fortune into bad.
ADAM. I will keep° all Your commandment.   observe
Neither I nor Eve will disobey in anything.
If for one sole fruit such an abode is lost,
120 It would be right for me to be thrown out to the wind.
If for one apple I forsake Your love,
Throughout my life, whether deliberately or foolishly,
Judge him to be a traitor

---

[1] *And ... man*   See Genesis 2.15.

[2] *The Lord ... Adam*   See. Genesis 2.16–17.

Who so perjures and betrays his Lord.

(*Then let the Figure go to the church,[3] and let Adam and Eve walk about, virtuously taking delight in Paradise. Meantime let devils run to and fro through the platea,[4] making appropriate gestures; and let them come, one after the other, close to Paradise, showing Eve the forbidden fruit, as if tempting her to eat it. Then let the devil come to Adam and say to him:*)

125 How are you doing, Adam?
ADAM.   I live in great delight.
DEVIL. Are you well?
ADAM.   I feel nothing that annoys me.
DEVIL. Things could be better.
130 ADAM.   I don't know how.
DEVIL. Would you like to know?
ADAM.   I'd like that!
DEVIL. I know how.
ADAM.   And what does that matter to me?
135 DEVIL. Why wouldn't it matter?
ADAM.   It's of no benefit to me.
DEVIL. It will benefit you.
ADAM.   I don't know when.
DEVIL. I won't hurry to tell you, then.
140 ADAM. Come on, tell me.
DEVIL.   I won't,
Until I see you weary of begging.
ADAM. I don't need to know this thing.
DEVIL. You don't deserve to be well off.
145 You have a good thing that you don't know how to
    enjoy.
ADAM. How is that?
DEVIL.   Would you like to hear?
I'll tell you confidentially.
ADAM. [I'll listen,[5]] surely.
150 DEVIL. Listen, Adam, pay attention to me.
This will be to your advantage.
ADAM.   I consent to that.
DEVIL. Will you believe me?

---

[3] *church*   I.e., God's heavenly residence, spatially represented by the church doors behind Paradise at the top of the church steps.

[4] *platea*   Open acting area at the foot of the steps, near the spectators.

[5] *I'll listen*   A few words are missing here from the text and a possible reading is supplied in brackets.

ADAM.   Yes, very well.
155 DEVIL. In everything?
ADAM.   Everything except one thing.
DEVIL. What thing?
ADAM.   I'll tell you:
I will not offend my Maker.
160 DEVIL. Do you fear Him that much?
ADAM.   Yes, indeed,
I love and fear Him.
DEVIL.   That's foolish.
What can He do to you?
165 ADAM.   Both good and evil.
DEVIL. You're starting on a very foolish business,
To fear so much that evil can come to you.
Aren't you in glory? You cannot die.
ADAM. God said to me that I shall die
170 When I transgress° His commandment.   disobey
DEVIL. What is this great transgression?
I'd like to hear this right off.
ADAM. I will tell you quite frankly.
He gave me one commandment:
175 Of all the fruits of Paradise
I may eat—so He taught me—
Except one only; that one is forbidden.
That one I will not touch with my hands.
DEVIL. Which one is that?

(*Then let Adam raise his hand and point out to him the
forbidden fruit, saying:*)

180 ADAM.   Do you see there?
That one has been forbidden to me.
DEVIL. Do you know why?
ADAM.   I? No, indeed.
DEVIL. I'll tell you the reason.
185 He doesn't care at all about the other fruit,

(*And let him point out to him the forbidden fruit with his
hand, saying to Adam:*)

Except for that one which hangs on high.
That is the fruit of knowledge:
It gives the understanding to know everything.
If you eat it, you will benefit from it.
190 ADAM. How?
DEVIL.   You'll see.

At once your eyes will be opened;
Everything to come will be revealed to you;
You will be able to do whatever you desire.
195 It will bestow many blessings upon you:
Eat it, and you'll prosper.
You'll have nothing to fear from your God;
Instead, you will be His peer in everything.
This is why He has seen fit to refuse you.
200 Will you trust me? Taste of the fruit.
ADAM. I won't do it.
DEVIL. [*Ironically.*] Well, listen to this pleasant news!
Won't you do it?
ADAM.   No.
205 DEVIL.   How stupid you are!
You will remember these words again.

(*Then let the devil withdraw; and he will go to the other
demons, and make a foray through the platea; and, after a
short delay, cheerful and rejoicing, he will return to the
tempting of Adam, and say to him:*)

Adam, how are you doing? Will you change your mind?
Are you still having foolish ideas?
I meant to tell you the other day,
210 God has made you His beneficiary,
He put you here to eat this fruit.
Have you then any other pleasures?
ADAM. Yes, I lack for nothing.
DEVIL. Don't you aspire to anything higher?
215 You can certainly consider yourself fortunate
When God has made you His gardener!
God has made you keeper of His garden;
Won't you look for other pleasures?
Did He create you solely for material appetite?
220 Didn't He wish to bestow any other honor on you?
Listen, Adam, pay attention to me:
I will counsel you in faith
How you can be without a master,
And the equal of your Creator.
225 I'll tell you the whole truth:
If you eat of the apple

(*Then he will raise his hand toward Paradise.*)

You will reign in majesty.
You can share omnipotence with God.

ADAM.   Get away from here.

230 DEVIL.   What did you say, Adam?

ADAM.   Get away from here! You are Satan.
You give evil counsel.

DEVIL.   I? How is that?

ADAM.   You would deliver me into torment,

235 Set me at odds with my Lord,
Remove me from joy, put me in sadness.
I won't trust you. Get away from here!
Don't ever be so audacious
As to come into my presence.

240 You are a traitor and without grace.

*(Then, sadly and with downcast countenance, he will
withdraw from Adam and go to the gates of hell, and hold
a conference with the other demons. Thereafter he will
make a foray among the people. Thereupon he will draw
near to Paradise, on the side where Eve is, and with a
joyful countenance, fawningly, he addresses Eve as follows:)*

DEVIL.   Eve, I have come to you.

EVE.   Tell me, Satan, why?

DEVIL.   I want to seek your profit, your honor.

EVE.   May God grant it!

245 DEVIL.   Don't be afraid.
For a long time I have known
All the secrets of Paradise.
One part of them I'll tell you.

EVE.   Begin, and I will listen.

250 DEVIL.   Will you listen to me?

EVE.   I'll do so, all right,
Nor anger you in any way.

DEVIL.   You'll keep a secret?

EVE.   Yes, by my faith.

255 DEVIL.   Will it be revealed?

EVE.   Certainly not by me.

DEVIL.   I will put me in your trust.
I wish no further assurance from you.

EVE.   You can certainly trust my word.

260 DEVIL.   You have been to a good school!—
I have seen Adam, but he is too much of a fool.

EVE.   He's a little hard.°   *obstinate*

DEVIL.   He will be soft.
He is harder than fire!

265 EVE.   He is very noble.

DEVIL.   On the contrary, he's servile.

He lacks the will to look after his best interests.
He ought to do so at least for you.
You are a delicate and tender thing,

270 And fresher than the rose;
You are whiter than crystal,
Than snow that falls on ice in the valley.
The Creator has made an ill-matched pair:
You are too tender, and he too hard.

275 But notwithstanding you are wiser;
Your mind has discovered great wisdom.
For this reason it is good to approach you.
I wish to speak with you.

EVE.   Speak truthfully, then.

280 DEVIL.   Let no one know of it.

EVE.   Who should know?

DEVIL.   Not even Adam.

EVE.   Certainly not by me.

DEVIL.   I will tell you, and you listen to me.

285 There is no one in this business but us two
And Adam over there, who doesn't hear us.

EVE.   Speak louder, he won't know anything of it.

DEVIL.   I'll acquaint you with a great plot
Laid against you in this garden.

290 The fruit God gave you
Has scarcely any goodness in it;
That one He so vehemently forbade you
Has extraordinary virtue.
In it there is the gift of life,

295 Of power and dominion,
Of knowing all things, good and evil.

EVE.   What taste does it have?

DEVIL.   Heavenly!
To your fair body, to your face

300 This fortunate event would be so well suited
That you would become mistress of the world,
Of the firmament° and of the deep,   *sky, heavens*
And know everything to come,
So that you would become the wise ruler of all things.

305 EVE.   Is the fruit of such a nature?

DEVIL.   Yes, truly.

*(Then Eve will carefully inspect the forbidden fruit, and,
after having considered it for a long while, she will say:)*

It does me good just to look at it.

DEVIL.   What will happen if you eat it?

EVE.   How should I know?

310 DEVIL.   Won't you believe me?
Take it first, and give it to Adam.
At once you will possess the crown of heaven.
You will be the equal of the Creator;
He won't be able to hide secrets from you.
315 As soon as you have eaten of the fruit,
At once your hearts will be transformed.
With God you will be, without fail,
Of equal goodness, equal might.
Taste of the fruit.
320 EVE.   I intend to.
DEVIL.   Don't trust Adam.
EVE.   I'll do it [later].
DEVIL.   When?
EVE.   … Let me [wait][1]
325 Until Adam is asleep.
DEVIL.   Eat, it, don't be doubtful!
To delay would be childish.

(*Then let the devil withdraw from Eve, and he will go to
hell. Adam will come to Eve, acting annoyed because the
devil has spoken with her, and he will say to her:*)

Tell me, wife, what was that evil Satan
Asking you about? What did he want from you?
330 EVE.   He talked to me about our advancement.
ADAM.   Don't believe the traitor! —
Yes, he is a traitor.
EVE.   I know it perfectly well.
ADAM.   How do you know?
335 EVE.   Because I have tried it out.
What's wrong with his seeing me?
[ADAM.]   He'll make you change your mind.
EVE.   No he won't, because I will believe nothing
Until I've tested him.
340 Adam.   Don't let him come near you,
For he's a fellow of very bad faith.
He wanted to betray his Sovereign
And set himself in place of Him who is highest.
I do not want a scoundrel who has done such things
345 To have access to you.

---

[1]   *[wait]*   There are some words missing here and a possible reading
is supplied in brackets.

(*Then a serpent, artfully constructed, arises alongside the
trunk of the forbidden tree. Eve will incline her ear near to
it, as if hearkening to its counsel. Hereupon Eve will accept
the apple, and offer it to Adam. But he will not accept it
yet, and Eve will say to him:*)

Eat, Adam. You don't know what it is.
Let us take this good thing that is at hand for us.
ADAM.   Is it so good?
EVE.   You will know soon,
350 But you can't know until you've tasted.
ADAM.   I'm fearful of it.
EVE.   Stop being afraid!
ADAM.   I won't do it.
EVE.   You delay out of cowardice.
355 ADAM.   I'll take it.
EVE.   Eat. Take it!
By it you will know both good and evil.
I will eat some first.
ADAM.   And I afterwards.
360 EVE.   Promise?

(*Then Eve will eat part of the apple, and say to Adam:*)

I've tasted it. My God, what flavor!
I've never savored such sweetness.
What a taste this apple has!
ADAM.   Like what?
365 EVE.   Like no mortal taste.
Now my eyes see so clearly
I am like the all-powerful God.
I know all that has been and is to come;
I am complete master of everything.
370 Eat, Adam, don't hesitate.
You will take it in a lucky hour.

(*Then Adam will take the apple from Eve's hand, saying:*)

I'll trust you in this. You are my partner.
EVE.   Eat. Don't be fearful.

(*Then let Adam eat part of the apple. When he has eaten he
will recognize his sin at once, and will bend over so that he
cannot be seen by the people. And he will strip off his festive
garments, and will put on poor clothes sewn together with*

fig leaves, and, manifesting exceedingly great sorrow he will
begin his lamentation:)

Alas, sinful wretch, what have I done?
375 Now I am dead without escape.
Without remedy I am dead,
So evil has my fortune fallen.
My fortune has changed for the worse:
Once it was auspicious, now it is harsh.
380 I have forsaken my Creator
Through the counsel of a wicked wife.
Alas, sinful one, what shall I do?
Upon my Creator how can I look?
How can I look upon my Creator
385 Whom I have forsaken through my folly?
Never have I made such a bad bargain.
Now I know what it is to sin.
O Death, why do you let me live?
Why is the world not rid of me?
390 Why do I still encumber° the world?   burden
I must experience the depths of hell.
In hell will be my dwelling,
Until the coming of one who can save me.
Thus in hell I will lead my life.
395 Whence will help come to me there?
Whence will rescue come to me there?
Who will draw me away from such sorrow?
Why did I do wrong to my Lord?
Now there is no one that should be my friend.
400 There will be no one that can avail at all.
I am lost without fail.
I have sinned so against my Lord,
I can enter no plea against Him,
For I am in the wrong, He in the right.
405 My God, what a horrible plight I'm in!
Who henceforth will remember me?
For I have sinned against the King of Glory.
Against the King of Heaven I have sinned so
That I have not the slightest claim upon Him.
410 No friend have I, or neighbor,
Who might rescue me from my accusation at last.
And whom shall I beseech to aid me,
When my own wife has betrayed me,
She whom God gave me as partner?
415 She has given me evil counsel.
Oh, Eve!

(Then he will look at Eve his wife, and say:)

Alas, foolhardy wife!
In an evil hour were you born of me!
If only that rib had been burned
420 Which has brought me to this evil pass!
If only the rib had been consumed in fire
Which has caused me such strife!
When He drew that rib from me,
Why didn't He burn it, and kill me?
425 The rib has betrayed the whole body,
Injured and maltreated it.
I don't know what to say or do.
If grace does not come to me from heaven,
I can never be rescued from pain,
430 Such is the evil that torments me.
Ah, Eve! Evil the hour—
Such terrible torment overwhelms me—
When you became my companion!
Now I am dead by your counsel.
435 By your counsel I am reduced to evil fortune,
Brought low from great height.
I will be redeemed thence by no mortal,
None save God in his majesty.
What do I say, unhappy one? Why have I named Him?
440 He help me? I have angered Him.
None will ever aid me
Except the Son who will come forth from Mary.
I don't know where to turn
Since we have not kept faith with God.
445 Then let all be as it please God:
No alternative except to die.

(Then let the choir begin:)

RESPONSORY.   While God walked [in the garden of
       Paradise[1]].

(When this has been said, the Figure will come wearing a
stole and will walk in Paradise, looking around as if
seeking to know where Adam is. But Adam and Eve will
hide in a corner of Paradise, as if knowing how wretched
they are; and the Figure will say:)

Adam, where are you?

---

1   *While God ... Paradise*   See Genesis 3.8.

(*Then both will rise, standing before the Figure, and yet not fully upright, but, through shame for their sin, somewhat bent forward and extremely sad; and let [Adam] answer:*)

ADAM.   I am here, reverend Sire.
450 I hid myself from Your wrath;
     And because I was completely naked
     I thus concealed myself here.
     FIGURE.   What have you done? How have you gone
          astray?
     Who has drawn you away from your goodness?
455 What have you done? Why are you ashamed?
     How will I settle accounts with you now?
     Until recently you had nothing
     Of which you ought to be ashamed;
     Now I see you downcast and mournful.
460 They enjoy themselves ill who live thus.
     ADAM. I am so ashamed, Sire, before You
     [...]¹
     FIGURE.   And why?
     ADAM. Such great shame entwines my body
465 That I dare not look You in the face.
     FIGURE.   Why have you transgressed My prohibition?
     Have you gained anything?
     You are My servant, and I your Lord.
     ADAM. I cannot deny it.
470 FIGURE. I created you in My own likeness;
     Why have you transgressed my commandment?
     I shaped you after My own image;
     Why have you done Me this outrage?
     You paid no attention to My prohibition;
475 Deliberately you transgressed it.
     You ate the fruit which I told you
     I had forbidden you.
     Did you think by this to be My equal?
     I didn't think you would joke this way.

(*Then Adam will stretch out his hand toward the Figure, then toward Eve, saying:*)

480 The woman you gave me,
     She first committed this trespass:
     She gave it to me, and I ate.
     Now, I see, it has turned to woe.
     I meddled rashly to eat this;

485 I have transgressed through my wife.
     FIGURE.   You trusted your wife more than me.
     You ate the fruit without my permission.
     Now I will render you the following recompense:
     The earth will be cursed
490 Where you will wish to sow your grain.
     It will fail to bear fruit,
     It is cursed beneath your hand;
     You will cultivate it in vain.
     It will deny its fruit to you;
495 It will yield you thorns and thistles.
     It will change whatever you sow;
     It will be cursed, as punishment to you.
     With grievous toil, with great exertion
     You will have to eat your bread.
500 In great torment and sweat
     You will live night and day.

(*Then the Figure will turn toward Eve, and with a threatening countenance say to her:*)

     And you, Eve, wicked woman,
     You began to make war against me:
     You held my commandments in light regard.
505 EVE. The wicked serpent deceived me.
     FIGURE. Through him did you think to become My equal?
     Have you learned how to prophesy well?
     Formerly you held sovereignty
     Over all living things;
510 How quickly you've lost that!
     Now I see you sad and dejected;
     Have you gained or lost?
     I will render you your just desert,
     I will give you this for your service:
515 Misfortune will afflict you in every way.
     In sorrow you will bring forth children,
     And in pain they will live all their lives.
     Your children will be born in sorrow,
     And will end their days in great anguish.
520 To such hardship, to such shame
     You have brought both yourself and your lineage.
     All those who will issue from you
     Will deplore your sin.

(*And Eve will answer, saying:*)

---

¹ *[...]* A space appears here in the original.

[EVE.] I have sinned, it was by my folly.
525 For one apple I will suffer great shame thus,
Because I have placed myself and my lineage in pain.
A small gain yields me a heavy toll in sorrow.
If I have sinned, it was no great marvel,
Whereas the deceiving serpent betrayed me.
530 Much he knows of evil; he certainly isn't innocent like
        a lamb.
Anyone who follows his advice is put in evil plight.
I took the apple; now I know I acted foolishly
Against Your prohibition; in that I behaved wickedly.
Evilly I tasted it; now I am hated by You.
535 For a little fruit I must lose my life.

(*Then the Figure will threaten the serpent, saying:*)

[FIGURE.] And you, serpent, be accursed!
From you I will recover my full right.
Upon your belly you shall go
All the days of your life.
540 Dust will be your daily food
In the wood, in field, on heath.
Woman will detest you;
Forever she will be an evil neighbor to you.
You will lie in wait for her heel,
545 She will pluck you by the head.
She will strike your head such a blow
That it will cause you great hardship.
She will carefully figure out
How she can be revenged on you.
550 You meddled evilly in her company;
She will bow your head.
A root will spring from her
Who will confound all your powers.

(*Then the Figure will drive them forth from Paradise,
saying:*)

Now get out of Paradise.
555 You have made an unhappy change of residence.
On earth you will have your dwelling;
You have no claim on Paradise.
You have nothing that is your due here.
Out you will go, without remedy.
560 You have nothing here to claim through judgment.
Now take some other dwelling.

Depart from bliss;
Hunger and weariness will not fail you,
Nor sorrow and pain,
565 Every day of the week.
On earth you will have an unhappy sojourn;°   *stay*
Then you will finally die;
After you have tasted death,
You will come to hell without remission.
570 Here in hell exile will afflict your bodies,
Peril daunt your souls.
Satan will have you in his power.
There is no man who could aid you:
By whom could you be rescued,
575 If I do not take pity on you?

(*Let the choir sing:*)

RESPONSORY.   In the sweat of your face.[1]

(*Meanwhile an angel will come dressed in white, bearing
a flaming sword in his hand, whom the Figure will station
at the gate of Paradise and will say to him:*)

Guard Paradise well for me
So that this outlaw may not enter there;
That he may not have the power or dominion
580 To touch the fruit of life.
With this flaming sword
Bar him the way.

(*When they are outside Paradise, as though sad and
confused they will be bowed down to the ground, bent over
to their ankles, and the Figure will point at them with his
hand, his face turned toward Paradise. And the choir will
begin.*)

RESPONSORY.   Behold, Adam is become as one [of us].[2]

(*When this is done, the Figure will return to the church.
Then Adam will have a spade and Eve a rake, and they
will begin to till the ground, and sow wheat in it. After
they have sown, they will go and sit for a while in a certain
place, as if worn out by their work, and mournfully they*)

---

[1] *In … face* See Genesis 3.18–19.

[2] *Behold … us* See Genesis 3.22.

will often look back at Paradise, beating their breasts. Meanwhile the devil will come and plant thorns and thistles in their cultivated fields, and withdraw. When Adam and Eve come to their fields and see the thorns and thistles that have sprung up, stricken with violent grief they will throw themselves down on the earth, and, remaining there, will strike their breasts and their thighs, manifesting their sorrow with their gestures. And [Adam] will begin his lamentation:)

[ADAM.]   Alas, woe is me, how evil was that hour
585   In which my sins overwhelmed me,
In which I forsook the Lord whom all adore!
Whom shall I ever implore to help me?

(Here let Adam look back at Paradise, and he will raise both his arms toward it, and, devoutly bowing his head, will say:)

O Paradise, how sweet to dwell there!
Garden of glory, what a beautiful sight you make!
590   I am thrown out for my sin, in truth;
I have lost all hope of return.
I dwelt therein, yet didn't know how to enjoy it;
I believed advice that caused me to leave it too quickly.
Now I repent; it is fitting that I am angry.
595   It is too late; my sighs avail nothing.
Where was my understanding? What became of my
        memory,
That for Satan I forsook the King of Glory?
Now I suffer for it, and have lost my self-esteem.
My sin will be written down in history.

(Then he will lift up his hand against Eve, who will have been moved away a short distance from him, and, moving his head with great indignation, will say to her:)

600   O wicked woman, full of treason,
How quickly you cast me into perdition
When you banished my understanding and reason!
Now I repent, I cannot have pardon.
Despondent Eve, how inclined you were to evil,
605   When you believed so quickly the counsel of the viper!
Through you I am dead, thus I have lost life;
Your sin will be written in the book.
Do you see the signs of terrible confusion?

The earth senses our curse:
610   We sowed corn, now thistles thrive.
[…]¹
You see the beginning of our misery;
Great is our sorrow, but greater awaits us.
We will be led to hell in heaviness;
615   No pain nor torment will be spared us.
Wretched Eve, what do you think of this?
You have won this, it has been given you for your dowry.
Nevermore can you bring man felicity,
But will be forever contrary to reason.
620   All those who will come hereafter, of our lineage,
Will feel the weight of your misdeed.
You have sinned; all those are condemned by it.
Only much later will He come by whom this will be
        changed.

(Then let Eve answer Adam:)

[EVE.]   Adam, dear lord, you have blamed me much,
625   Reviled and reproached my villainy.
If I have sinned, I suffer the weight of it.
I am guilty; I will be judged by God.
I have sinned greatly toward God and you;
My sin will long be reviled.
630   My guilt is great, my sins afflict me.
Wretched me, I have lacked all goodness!
I have no grounds whereby to defend myself against God,
That He should not find me a guilty sinner.
Pardon me, for I cannot make amends!
635   If I could, I would offer a sacrifice.
Sinner, unhappy, wretched,
For my misdeed I am overcome with shame toward God.
Take me, Death, do not permit me to live!
I am in peril, and cannot reach the shore.
640   The wicked serpent, the evil viper,
Made me eat the apple of misfortune.
I gave it to you; I thought it for the best,
And I led you into sin, for which I can't reproach you.
Why wasn't I obedient to the Creator?
645   Why, my lord, didn't I hold to your teaching?
You sinned, but I was the root of it.
For our malady, the cure is a long one.
My sin, my grave misdoing,
Our progeny will pay dearly for.

---

¹ *[…] A space appears here in the original.*

650 The fruit was sweet, the pain is hard.
It was evil to eat; ours will be the guilt.
Notwithstanding, in God is my hope.
There will be full reconciliation for this sin:
God will tend me His grace and His favor;
655 He will rescue us from hell by His might.

(*Then the devil will come, and three or four devils with him, carrying in their hands chains and iron fetters, which they will put on the necks of Adam and Eve. And certain ones will push them, others drag them to hell; still other devils will be close beside hell waiting for them as they come, and among themselves they will make a great dancing and jubilation over their damnation; and each of these other devils will point at them as they come, and will take them and put them into hell. And therein they will cause a great smoke to arise, and they will shout to one another in hell, rejoicing, and they will bang together their pots and caldrons, so that they may be heard outside. And after a short interval, the devils will issue forth, scattering across the platea; certain of them, however, will remain in hell.*

Then Cain and Abel will come. Let Cain be dressed in red garments, Abel in white, and they will cultivate ground that has been made ready.

And when he has rested from his labor for a time, let Abel speak to his brother Cain agreeably and amicably, saying to him:)

Brother Cain, we are two kinsmen
And sons of the first of men:
That was Adam, our mother was named Eve.
In serving God let us not be churlish.
660 Let us be at all times obedient to the Creator;
Let us so serve that we will win back His love,
Which our parents lost by their folly.
May there be steadfast love between us two!
So let us serve God that it will please Him always;
665 Pay Him his due, let nothing be held back.
If with willing heart we will obey Him
Our souls will have nothing to fear.
Let us pay His tithes[1] and all that is justly His due,

First-fruits, offerings, gifts, sacrifice;
670 If covetousness° impels us to hold back,   greed
We will be lost in hell, without recourse.
Between us two let there be great love;
Let there be neither envy nor dissension.
Why should there be strife between us two?
675 The entire earth has been surrendered to us.

(*Then Cain will look at his brother Abel as if mocking him, and he will say to him:*)

Dear brother Abel, you certainly know how to preach,
How to lay out and present your arguments!
If anyone paid attention to your notions,
In a few days he wouldn't have much left to give.
680 This giving of tithes has never suited me, anyway.
With your belongings you can do your good deeds,
And with mine I'll follow my own inclination.
You won't be damned by my misdeed.
Nature teaches us to love one another;
685 Between us two let's not have any dissimulation.
Whichever of us two starts an argument,
Let him pay dearly for it, for it is right that one should
     complain of this.

(*Again let Abel speak to his brother Cain, who will answer more mildly than usual; Abel will say:*)

Cain, dear brother, listen to me.
CAIN.   Gladly. Listen to what?
690 ABEL.   Something to your benefit.
CAIN.   So much the better.
ABEL.   Don't rebel against God.
Don't be proud toward Him,
I'm warning you.
695 CAIN.   That's what I want.
ABEL.   Believe my advice. Let us make offering
To the Lord God, to please Him.
If He is reconciled toward us,
Sin will not afflict us,
700 Nor sadness come upon us.
It is beneficial to secure His love.
Let us sacrifice at His altar
Such a gift as He would be pleased to look upon.
Let us pray to Him that He give us his love
705 And defend us from evil, night and day.

---

[1] *tithes* A tithe was a tenth of one's harvest or other earnings offered as a sacrifice to God.

(*Then Cain will answer as if Abel's counsel has pleased him, saying:*)

Dear brother Abel, you have said well;
You have written this sermon effectively,
And I'll heed it diligently.
Let us make offering, as is right.
710   What will you offer?
ABEL.   A lamb,
The best and fairest
That I can find in the fold.
This I'll offer, none other;
715   And I will offer him incense.
Now I've told you all my intent.
What will you offer?
CAIN.   Some of my wheat,
Such as God has given me.
720   ABEL. Your very best?
CAIN.   Certainly not.
From that I'm going to make bread for tonight.
ABEL. Such offering is not acceptable
[...]¹
725   CAIN.   That's nonsense.
ABEL. You are a rich man, and have many cattle.
CAIN. Granted.
ABEL. Why don't you count the number of head
And give a tenth of the total?
730   Thus you will make offering to God's very self,
Sacrifice to Him wholeheartedly;
That way you'll receive a fine reward.
Will you do this?
CAIN.   You're crazy.
735   [...]²
Of ten, there'll only be nine left!
This advice isn't worth an egg.
Let's make offering, each for himself
What he thinks good.
740   ABEL.   So be it.

(*Then they will go to two great stones that have been readied for the purpose. One stone will have been set at a distance from the other so that, when the Figure appears,*)

the stone of Abel will be on his right hand, the stone of Cain on his left.

Abel will offer his lamb and incense, from which smoke will arise. Cain will offer a handful of his harvest. Appearing accordingly, the Figure will bless Abel's gift but disdain that of Cain. Wherefore, after the oblation,³ Cain will make a savage face against Abel; and, when their oblations have been completed, they will go to their own places. Then Cain will come to Abel, seeking cunningly to lead him forth in order to kill him, and will say to him:)

Dear brother Abel, let us depart.
ABEL. Why?
CAIN.   To refresh our bodies
And to inspect our labor,
745   To see how the crops have grown, and whether they're
          in flower.
Then we'll go to the meadows;
We will feel refreshed afterwards.
ABEL. I'll go with you, wherever you wish.
CAIN. Come on, then; you'll do well by it.
750   ABEL. You are my elder brother;
I'll follow your wishes.
CAIN. Go ahead, I'll follow after
With unhurried steps, very leisurely.

(*Then they will both go to a place apart and, as it were, secret, where Cain, like a madman, will rush upon Abel wishing to kill him, and say to him:*)

Abel, you die.
755   ABEL.   For what?
CAIN. I will be avenged on you.
ABEL. Have I done wrong?
CAIN.   Yes, wrong enough!
You're a proven traitor.
760   ABEL. I certainly am not.
CAIN.   Do you deny it?
ABEL. I've never even thought of committing treason.
CAIN. You've done it already.
ABEL.   Me? How?
765   CAIN. You'll know soon.
ABEL.   I don't understand.
CAIN. I'll make you understand plenty soon enough.

---

¹ [...] A space appears here in the original.

² [...] A space appears here in the original.

³ *oblation* Offering or sacrifice.

ABEL.   You can't prove anything, truthfully.
CAIN.   The proof is here.
770 ABEL.   God will help me.
CAIN.   I'll kill you!
ABEL.   God will know it.

(*Then Cain will lift up a menacing right hand against him, saying:*)

Look here at this proof.
ABEL.   In God is all my trust.
775 CAIN.   He won't be of much use to you against me.
ABEL.   He could stop you, all right, if He wanted.
CAIN.   He can't save [you] from death.
ABEL.   He does with me according to His pleasure in
    everything.
CAIN.   Do you want to hear why I'm killing you?
780 ABEL.   Tell me.
CAIN.   I'll tell you:
You make yourself too much God's favorite.
Because of you He has rejected me entirely.
Because of you He refused my offering.
785 Do you think I won't pay you back for this?
I'll give you this reward for it:
You'll lie dead today on the sand.
ABEL.   If you kill me, that will be wrong.
God will avenge my death on you.
790 I haven't wronged [you], God knows it well;
I haven't slandered you to Him in anything.
On the contrary, I told you to do such deeds
That you would be deserving of His peace:
Render to Him his due,
795 Tithes, first-fruits, oblations—
Thereby you could have His love.
You didn't do this, now you're angry.
God is true; he who serves Him
Spends his time wisely, and loses nothing by it.
800 CAIN.   You've talked too much. Now you're going to die.
ABEL.   Brother, what are you saying? You led me here;
I came here trusting in you.
CAIN.   Trust won't help you.
I'm going to kill you. I defy you!
805 ABEL.   I pray God to give me mercy!

(*Then Abel will kneel to the east. And he will have a pot concealed in his garments, which Cain will strike violently,*)

as though killing Abel. Abel will lie prostrate as though dead. The choir will sing:)

RESPONSORY. Where is Abel, your brother?[1]

(*Meantime the Figure will come forth from the church to Cain, and, when the choir has finished the responsory, he will say to him [Cain] as though very angry:*)

Cain, where is your brother Abel?
Have you entered into rebellion?
You have begun to strive against Me.
810 Now show Me your brother alive.
CAIN.   How should I know, Lord, where he's gone,
Whether at home or in his fields?
Why should I find him? I am not his keeper.
FIGURE.   What have you done with him? Where have
815   you put him?
I know perfectly well, you have killed him.
His blood cries out to Me of it;
The cry has come to Me in heaven.
You have committed a grave felony;
820 You will be cursed for it all your life.
Forever you will bear a curse;
For such a misdeed, such is the reward.
Yet I desire not that any man kill you,
But that you endure your life in sorrow.
825 Whoever will kill Cain
Will pay a sevenfold penalty.
Your brother died in My faith;
Your penance will be grave.

(*Then the Figure will return to the church. The devils, coming forth, will lead Cain to hell, beating him often. They will lead Abel away more gently.*)

(*Then the prophets will be made ready, one by one, in a concealed place, as appropriate to them. Let the lesson be read in the choir:*)

You, I say, I do summon before a tribunal, O Jews.[2]

---

[1] *Where ... brother* See Genesis 4.9.

[2] *You, I say ... Jews* The opening of the pseudo-Augustinian *Sermo contra Judeos, Paganos, et Arianos*, a popular Christmas sermon that inspired the *Ordo Prophetarum* or "Procession of Prophets" in liturgical drama and supplied the structure for the concluding action in

(And let the prophets be called by name; and, when they come forward, let them proceed with dignity and announce their prophecies clearly and distinctly. Accordingly Abraham will come first, an old man with a very long beard, dressed in ample garments; and when he has sat on a bench for a little time, let him begin his prophecy in a loud voice:)

830 Your seed will possess the gates of their enemies, and in
[your] seed will all the nations [of the earth] be blessed.[1]

I am Abraham, such is my name.
Now listen to my entire message:
Let him who has good hope in God
835 Hold to his faith and his trust.
He who will have firm faith in God,
God will be with him, this I know through personal
    experience:
He tested me, I did His pleasure;
Well I accomplished His will.
840 I would have killed my own son for Him,
But by Him I was told not to.
I would have offered him for a sacrifice;
God turned me from it, in His justice.
God has promised me—and true indeed it will be—
845 Another such heir will come of my lineage
Who will conquer all His enemies;
Thus strong and mighty will He be.
He will hold their gates in His hands,
And their castles; He will be no serf.
850 Such a man will issue from my seed,
Who will commute our sentence of damnation,
And by whom the world will be ransomed.
Adam will be delivered from his pain;
The peoples of every nation
855 Will receive benison° through him.[2]   *blessing*

(When these things have been said, and after a brief interval, the devils will come and lead Abraham to hell.)

---

this play.

[1] *Your seed ... blessed* The introductory quotations (mostly, though not exclusively, from the Bible) that precede the prophets' speeches are in Latin in the original text. Missing words are supplied in brackets.

[2] *I am Abraham ... through him* For Abraham's prophecy see Genesis 12.17–18.

(Then Moses will come, bearing a rod in his right hand and the tablets in his left. When he has sat, let him say his prophecy:)

God will raise up a prophet from among your brethren;
you shall hearken to him as if to me.

That which I tell you, I saw through God:
From our own brethren, from our law
860 God will raise up a man.
He will be a prophet, and the summit of wisdom;
He will know all heaven's secrets;
You ought to believe him more than me.

(Thereupon he will be led to hell by the devil. Similarly with all the prophets [throughout the play].)

(Then Aaron will come, in bishop's apparel, bearing in his hands a rod having flowers and fruit; being seated, let him say:)

"This is the branch bearing the flower
865 Which gives the perfume of salvation.
The sweet fruit of this branch
Will expiate the sorrow of our death."[3]
This rod,[4] implanted,
Can blossom and bear fruit.
870 Such a rod will come from my lineage
Who will be Satan's nemesis,
Who, without fleshly birth,
Will bear man's nature.
This is the fruit of salvation,
875 Who will release Adam from prison.

(After him let David approach, royally accoutred and wearing a diadem, and let him say:)

Truth has sprung out of the earth, and justice has looked down from heaven. For the Lord will give goodness, and our earth will yield her fruit.

Out of the earth truth shall arise,

---

[3] *This is the branch ... our death* This quoted verse at the beginning of Aaron's speech is in Latin in the original text.

[4] *This rod* See Numbers 17.1–8 for the Biblical account of the blossoming rod.

880 And justice, from divine majesty.
God will give us goodness,
Our earth will yield her fruit;
Of her increase she will give her bread,
Which will save the sons of Eve.
885 This will be the Lord of all the earth,
This one will bring peace, end war.[1]

(*Then let Solomon come forward, with the same
adornments as those in which David advanced, except that
he should seem younger; and, being seated, let him say:*)

Being ministers of God's kingdom, you have not judged
rightly, nor kept the law of justice, nor walked according
to the will of God. [Terribly] and swiftly will He appear
890 to you, because a most severe judgment shall befall those
who rule. For to the lowly, mercy is granted.

O Jews, God gave you His law,
But you have not borne Him faith.
He made you custodians of His kingdom,
895 You were well established;
You have not judged justly,
Your verdict was against God.
You have not done His will;
Your iniquity was very great.
900 All you have done will be made manifest;
Extremely harsh vengeance will be visited
On those who were the most high:
They will take a fearful fall.
God will have pity on the lowly:
905 He will make them very happy.
This prophecy will be fulfilled
When the Son of God dies for us.
Those who are ministers of the law
Will kill Him, out of faithlessness.
910 Against all justice and reason
They will put Him on the Cross like a thief.
For this they will lose their ruling authority
That they used to have from Him, during His lifetime.
From great height they will be humbled;
915 Well may they bewail their unhappy state.
He will have pity of poor Adam,

And deliver him from sin.[2]

(*After him Balaam will come, an old man dressed in ample
garments, sitting on an ass. And he will come into the midst,
and, seated on the ass's back, will speak his prophecy:*)

A star shall rise out of Jacob, and a sceptre shall spring
up from Israel, and shall strike the chiefs of Moab, and
920 shall waste° all the children of Seth.   destroy

From Jacob a star will rise,
Red with the fire of heaven,
And a sceptre will spring up from Israel
Which will overthrow [the chiefs of] Moab
925 And will abase their pride;
For Christ will rise out of Israel,
And He will be that shining star.
All things will be illumined by Him.
His faithful ones He will safely lead,
930 His enemies He will all confound.[3]

(*Thereafter let Daniel approach, young in years, but old in
his dress. And when he has seated himself, let him speak his
prophecy, stretching out his hand toward those to whom he
speaks:*)

When the holy of holies comes, your anointing will
cease.

To you, O Jews, I deliver my sermon,
You who are excessively wicked toward God.
935 When the greatest of all the saints appears—
Of whom you will experience great misfortune—
Then your anointing will cease;
You won't be able to claim it any longer.
By this greatest of saints, I mean Christ,
940 He who wishes His people to gain eternal life through
    Him;
For them He will come to earth.
Your tribe will wage terrible war on Him,
Will subject Him to His Passion;
On this account they will lose their anointing.

---

[1] *Truth ... end war* See Psalms 85.11–12 for David's prophecy.

[2] *O Jews ... from sin* See the apocryphal Wisdom of Solomon 6.5–7.

[3] *From Jacob ... all confound* For Balaam's prophecy see Numbers 24.17.

945   Neither bishop nor king will have power;
       Thus their law will perish through their means.

(After him Habakkuk will come, an old man. And, sitting down, when he begins his prophecy, he will lift up his hands toward the church; manifesting wonder and fear, let him say:)

O Lord, I have heard your speech and was afraid; I have contemplated your works and feared greatly. Between two beasts you will become known.

950   I have heard strange tidings concerning God:
       I am most troubled in my mind about it.
       I have considered this sign so intently
       That great fear agitates my heart.
       Between two beasts He will be recognized;
955   By all the world He will be feared.
       He of whom I have such great wonder
       Will be pointed out by a star;
       Shepherds will find Him in a crib
       That will be carved out of dry stone,
960   Where beasts will eat hay.
       Then He will reveal Himself to kings;
       The star will lead the kings there;
       All three will bear offerings.[1]

(Then Jeremiah will enter, bearing a scroll in his hand; and let him say:)

Hear the Word of the Lord, all you men of Judaea, that
965   enter in at these gates to worship the Lord.

(And with his hand he will point to the doors of the church.)

Thus says the Lord of Hosts, the God of Israel: Make your ways and your doings good, and I will dwell with you in this place.

Hear the Holy Word of God,
970   All you who are of His doctrine,
       The mighty lineage of righteous Judaea,
       You who are of His household.
       By this door you will enter

---

[1]   *I have heard ... offerings*   See Habakkuk 3.2.

       To adore our Lord.
975   The Lord of Hosts summons you,
       The God of Israel, from heaven on high:
       Make good your ways,
       Let them be straight as furrows,
       And let your hearts be pure,
980   That no shame may come to you;
       Let your endeavors be good,
       Free of wickedness.
       If you do thus, God will come,
       Will dwell with you;
985   The Son of God, the glorious one,
       Will come down to earth for your sake;
       He will be among you as mortal man,
       The Lord, the cœlestial one.
       He will release Adam from prison,
990   Giving His own body as ransom.[2]

(After him Isaiah will come, bearing a book in his hand, dressed in an ample cloak. And let him speak his prophecy:)

And there shall come forth a rod out of the root of Jesse, and a flower shall rise up out of his root, and the spirit of the Lord shall rest upon it.

Now I will tell you a marvelous thing:
995   From Jesse's root will come forth
       A rod, which will bear a flower
       Worthy of great honor.
       The Holy Spirit will enclose it,
       Will rest upon this flower.[3]

(Then somebody from the synagogue will rise up, disputing with Isaiah, and will say to him:)

1000   Now answer me, Sir Isaiah:
       Is this a fable, or prophecy?
       What is this you've said?
       Did you invent it, or is it written?
       You've been sleeping, you dreamed it.
1005   Is this serious or a joke?
       ISAIAH.   This is not fable; on the contrary, it's all true.
       [JEW.]   Make us see this truth, then.

---

[2]   *Thus says ... ransom*   See Jeremiah 7.2–3.
[3]   *Now I will tell ... flower*   See Isaiah 11.1–2.

[ISAIAH.]   What I have spoken is prophecy.

[JEW.]   Written in a book?

1010 ISAIAH.   Yes, the book of life.

I did not dream it; I saw it.

[JEW.]   How?

[ISAIAH.]   By God's grace.

JEW.   You seem like an old dotard to me;

1015 Your mind is addled.

You appear to me to be senile.

You know well enough how to look in a mirror:

Now look at this hand for me, and tell

(Then he will show him his hand.)

If my heart is sick or healthy.

1020 ISAIAH.   You have the disease of wickedness,

From which you will never recover in your life.

JEW.   Am I sick, then?

ISAIAH.   Yes, of error.

JEW.   When will I get better?

1025 ISAIAH.   Never.

JEW.   Now begin your soothsaying.°   *prophesying*

ISAIAH.   What I say will not be untrue.

JEW.   Now tell your vision again,

If it was a rod, or a stick,

1030 And what will be born from its flower.

We will take you for our master,

And this generation

Will hearken to your teaching.

ISAIAH.   Then listen to this great wonder.

1035 Never has our listening heard anything so magnificent;

Never has anything so fabulous been heard

Since this world began:

Behold a virgin shall conceive in her womb and bear
a son, and His name shall be called Emmanuel.

1040 The time is near, it is not far,

It will not delay, it is at hand,

That a virgin shall conceive

And as a virgin shall bear a son.

He will have the name Emmanuel.[1]

1045 Saint Gabriel will be the messenger.

The maid will be the Virgin Mary;

Thus she will carry the fruit of life,

Jesus, our Saviour,

Who will recover Adam from his great sorrow

1050 And put him again in Paradise.

This that I speak to you, I learned from God.

And this will be fully accomplished, in truth,

And you ought to put your hope in it.

(Then Nebuchadnezzar will come, adorned like a king.)

Did we not cast three youths, bound, into the fire?

1055 RESPONSORY OF THE KING'S MINISTERS.   True, O king.

[NEBUCHADNEZZAR.]   Lo, I see four men loose, walking
in the midst of the fire, and they have no hurt, and the
form of the fourth is like the Son of God.

Hear a wondrous great miracle—

1060 No living man has heard the like—

Which I witnessed, of the three youths

Who were cast into the burning fire.

The fire was very hot and fierce,

And the flame bright and searing;

1065 The three youths rejoiced greatly

There where they were, in the burning fire.

They sang a verse so beautiful

It seemed the angels were in heaven.

When I looked there, thus I saw the fourth

1070 Who gave them very great comfort.

His face shone so resplendently

He seemed the Son of mighty God.[2]

...

—12TH CENTURY

---

[1]   *Then listen ... Emmanuel*   See Isaiah 7.14.

[2]   *Lo ... mighty God*   See Daniel 3.24–25.

The Chester Noah's Flood
c. 1422 – c. 1569

N̄oah's Flood is part of the cycle of biblical pageants from Chester, a northern English town near the Welsh border. As with other biblical plays of the period, not much is known about its author or authors. It is possible that one person wrote all of the Chester cycle; the plays demonstrate a close unity of form and style, which strongly suggests either one author or (perhaps more likely) a thorough revision of existing texts over time. Nevertheless, information about the Chester cycle is incomplete, and the cycle surely developed and changed over the one hundred and fifty years it was performed. The surviving manuscripts of the play are copies transcribed around 1600, long after it stopped being performed, and may therefore not give fully accurate information about the development of the texts.

The story of Noah, a popular subject in medieval biblical drama, encapsulates a miniature version of the broader narrative of creation, fall, and redemption. The Chester *Noah's Flood* came third in a cycle of 24 extant pageants. The cycle was performed on wagons in the city streets at Whitsun (Pentecost) in May or June, probably because the weather would then be suitable for outdoor performances. Scheduling of such performances differed from one town to another; towns such as York, for example, performed their plays eleven days later at the Feast of Corpus Christi.

Each play in the Chester cycle was assigned to a specific trade guild within the town. An existing copy of the Chester Banns, a document presumably read by a town crier to announce the impending performance, indicates that *Noah's Flood* was appropriately assigned to the "waterleaders and drawers of Dee," who drew and carried water from the river Dee, which runs through Chester. Stage directions within the text are unusually descriptive and provide useful information on how the play was staged. For example, they indicate that pictures were used to represent the animals that were brought onto the ark. As in other biblical drama of the period, minor actors wore contemporary clothing, rather than being costumed according to a conception of what people of the ancient Middle East might have worn. The actor playing God probably appeared in ecclesiastical vestments. The ark would in all probability have looked like a medieval ship.

The story of this pageant departs from the biblical narrative of Noah in several respects, perhaps most notably in the depiction of Noah's wife (who is never given a name). Here, as in many medieval versions of the story, both literary and artistic, she is shown as a strong-willed woman who resists doing her husband's bidding and is reluctant to enter the ark; her resistance contributes both to the pageant's religious lesson and to its dramatic tension.

The play's text is in a "tail-rhyme" form, an eight-line stanza with a uniform rhyming structure and pattern of stressed syllables—a form shared by all the pageants in the Chester cycle.

⌘⌘⌘

The Third Pageant of Noah's Flood [1]

CHARACTERS:

God/Deus
Noah
Noah's Wife
Sem
Cam
Jaffett
Sem's Wife
Cam's Wife
Jaffett's Wife
The Good Gossips

(*And first in some high place—or in the clouds, if it may be—God speaketh unto Noah standing without* [2] *the ark with all his family.*)

GOD. I, God, that all this world hath wrought,
　　Heaven and yearth, and all of° nought,　　　　*from*
　　I see my people in deed and thought
　　Are set foul in sinne.
5　　My goost° shall not lenge° in mone°　*spirit / linger / man*
　　That through flesh-liking [3] is my fone°　　　　*foe*
　　But till six score years be commen and gone
　　To looke if they will blynne.°[4]　　　　*cease, desist*

　　Man that I made I will distroy,
10　　Beast, worm, and fowl to fly;
　　For on yearth they do me noy,°　　　*vex, annoy*
　　The folk that are thereon.
　　It harms me so hurtefully,
　　The malice that doth now multiply,

15　　That sore it grieves me inwardly
　　That ever I made mon.°　　　　　　*man*

　　Therefore Noah, my servant free,
　　That righteous man art as I see,
　　A ship, son, thou shalt make thee
20　　Of trees dry and light.
　　Little chambers therein thou make
　　And binding sliche° also thou take;　　　*pitch*
　　Within and without thou ne slake°　*weaken, decrease effort*
　　To annoint [5] it through all thy might.

25　　Three hundred cubits [6] it shall be long
　　And fifty broad to make it strong;
　　Of height sixty. The meete° thou fong; [7]　*quantity, amount*
　　Thus measure thou it about.
　　One window work through thy wit;
30　　A cubit of length and breadth make it.
　　Upon the side a door shall shut,
　　For to come in and out.

　　Eating-places thou make also
　　Three, roofed chambers one or too,°　　　*two*
35　　For with water I think to flow
　　Mone° that I can make.　　　　　　*man*
　　Destroyed all the world shall be—
　　Save° thou, thy wife, thy sons three,　　*except*
　　And their wives also with thee—
40　　Shall fall before thy face.

NOAH. A, lord, I thank thee loud and still
　　That to me art in such will
　　And spares me and my household to spill,
　　As I now soothly° find.　　　　　　*truly*
45　　Thy bidding, lord, I shall fulfill
　　Nor never more thee grieve ne gryll,°　*irritate, offend*
　　That such grace hath sent me till
　　Amonges° all mankind.　　　　　　*amongst*

　　Have done, you men and women all.
50　　Hie° you, lest this water fall,　　*hasten, hurry*

---

[1]　*The Third Pageant of Noah's Flood* The Chester cycle of Mystery plays exists in eight whole or partial manuscript forms. For the present text, spelling and punctuation have been substantially modernized, but alterations that would affect rhythm or rhyme have (with few exceptions) been avoided. Stage directions that appear in the original appear here in parentheses. Some additional stage directions have been added for the sake of clarity; these appear in square brackets.

[2]　*without* Outside.

[3]　*flesh-liking* Attachment to the flesh, carnal sin.

[4]　*But till … they will blynne* I will give one hundred and twenty more years to see if they will turn away from sin.

[5]　*annoint* Rub with the pitch (but also punning on sense of consecration).

[6]　*cubits* Ancient form of measurement (a cubit is roughly equivalent to the length of a forearm).

[7]　*The meete thou fong* Take the measurement.

to work this ship, chamber and hall,
as God hath bidden us do.

SEM.   Father, I am already bown:°   *ready*
An axe I have, by my crown,
55   As sharp as any in all this town
For to go thereto.

CAM.   I have an hatchet wonder keen
To bite well, as may be seen;
A better ground, as I ween,°   *believe*
60   Is not in all this town.

JAFFETT.   And I can well make a pin
And with this hammer knock it in.
Go we work bowte° more din,°   *without / noise*
And I am ready bown.°   *prepared*

65   NOAH'S WIFE.   And we shall bring timber too,
For we mon° nothing else do—   *can*
Women been° weak to underfoe[1]   *are*
Any great travel.°   *travail*

SEM'S WIFE.   Here is a good hackstock;°   *chopping block*
70   On this you may hew and knock.
Shall none be idle in this flock,
Ne now may no man fable.°   *weaken*

CAM'S WIFE.   And I will go gather slytch,°   *pitch*
The ship for to clam° and pitch.°   *smear, daub / fix*
75   Anoint it must be with stitch—
Board, tree, and pin.

JAFFETT'S WIFE.   And I will gather chips° here   *woodchips*
To make a fire for you in fere,°   *together*
And for to dight° your dinner   *prepare*
80   Again° you come in.   *before*

(*Then Noah beginneth to build the ark.*)

NOAH.   Now in the name of God I begin
To make the ship that we shall° in,   *shall go*
That we may be ready for to swim
At the coming of the flood.
85   These boards I pin here together

To bear us safe from the weather,
That we may row both hither and thither
And safe be from this flood.

Of this tree will I make a mast
90   Tied with gables that will last,
With a sail-yard for each bast,[2]
And each thing in their kind.°   *place*
With topcastle[3] and bowspreete,[4]
Both cords and ropes I have all meete°   *appropriate, fitting*
95   To sail forth at the next weete°—   *rain storm*
This ship is at an ende.[5]

Wife, in this vessel we shall be kept;
My children and thou, I would ye lept.[6]

NOAH'S WIFE.   In faith, Noah, I had as leeve thou slept.[7]
100   For all thy Frenyshe fare,[8]
I will not do after thy reade.°   *command*

NOAH.   Good wife, do now as I thee bid.

NOAH'S WIFE.   By Christ, not or° I see more need,   *before*
Though thou stand all day and stare.

105   NOAH.   Lord, that women been crabbed°   *ill-tempered*
aye,°   *always*
And none are meek, I dare well say.
That is well seen by me today
In witness of you each one.
Good wife, let be all this bear°   *commotion*
110   That thou makest in this place here,
For all they weene° that thou art master—   *believe*
And so thou art, by sayncte° John.   *saint*

---

[1]   *underfoe* I.e., undertake.

[2]   *sail-yard for each bast* Spar or beam for each bast-rope.

[3]   *topcastle* Platform at the head of a ship's mast.

[4]   *bowspreete* Boom running out from the stem of a vessel to which stays are fastened.

[5]   *This ... at an ende* The ship is completed and ready.

[6]   *Wife, in this ... ye lept* Wife, we (the children, yourself, and me) will be kept in this ship; I wish you and our children would enter it.

[7]   *I had as ... slepte* I would rather you were sleeping.

[8]   *For all thy Frenyshe fare* For all your Frenchified behavior.

(*Then Noah with all his family shall make a sign as though they wrought upon the ship with diverse instruments. And after that God shall speak to Noah as followeth*:)

DEUS.[1] Noah, take thou thy meanye°   family
And in the ship hie° that ye be;   hurry
115 For none so righteous man to me
Is now on yearth living.
Of clean beasts with thee thou take
Seven and seven or° then thou slake;   before
He and she, make to make,°   mate to mate
120 Belive° in that thou bring;   quickly

Of beasts unclean two and two,
Male and female, bowt moo;[2]
Of clean fowls seven also,
The he and she together;
125 Of fowls unclean twain° and no more,   two
As I of beasts said before.
That man be saved through my lore,
Against° I send this wedder,°   Before / weather

Of meats that mon° be eaten,   may
130 Into the ship look they be getten,
For that may be no way forgotten.
And do this all bydeene°   immediately
To sustain man and beasts therein
Aye till the water cease and blynne.°   stop
135 This world is filled full of sin,
And that is now well seen.

Seven days been° yet coming;   are
You shall have space them in to bring.
After that, it is my liking
140 Mankind for to annoy.°   destroy
Forty days and forty nights
Rain shall fall for their unrights.°   misdeeds
And that° I have made through mights   that which
Now think I to destroy.

145 NOAH. Lord, at your bidding I am bain.°   ready, willing
Sithen° no other grace will gain,   since
It will I fulfill fain,°   gladly

For gracious I thee find.
One hundredth winters and twenty
150 This ship-making tarried have I,
If through ammendment thy mercy
Would fall to mankind.

Have done, ye men and women all;
Hie you lest this water fall,
155 That each beast were in stall
And into the ship brought.
Of clean beasts seven shall be,
Of unclean two; thus God bade me.
The flood is nigh, you may well see;
160 Therefore tarry you nought.

SEM. Sir, here are lions, leopards in;
Horses, mares, oxen, and swine,
Geates,° calves, sheep, and kine°   goats / cows
Here sitten thou may see.

165 CAM. Camels, asses, man may find,
Buck and doe, hart° and hind.°   male deer, stag / female deer
All beasts of all manner of kind
Here been,° as thinketh me.   are

JAFFETT. Take here cats, dogs too,
170 Otters and foxes, fullimarts° also;   polecat
Hares hopping gaily can go
Here have cole[3] for to eat.

NOAH'S WIFE. And here are bears, wolves set,
Apes, owls, maremussett,°   small monkeys
175 Weasels, squirrels, and ferret;
Here they eaten their meat.

SEM'S WIFE. Here are beasts in this house;
Here cats maken it crowse;°   lively
Here a rotten,° here a mouse   rat
180 That standen near together.

CAM'S WIFE. And here are fowls less and more—
Hernes,° cranes, and byttoer,°   herons / bitterns
Swans, peacocks—and them before
Meat for this wedder.

---

[1] *Deus* Latin: God.

[2] *bowt moo* No more.

[3] *cole* Vegetable of the cabbage family.

185 JAFFETT'S WIFE.   Here are cocks, kites,[1] crows,
    Rooks, ravens, many rows,
    Ducks, curlews, whoever knows,
    Each one in his kind.
    And here are doves, digges,° drakes,   ducks
190 Redshanks° running through lakes;   wading birds
    And each fowl that leaden[2] makes
    In this ship man may find.

    NOAH.   Wife, come in. Why stands thou there?
    Thou art ever frowarde;° that dare I swear.   difficult
195 Come, in God's name; half time it were,[3]
    For fear lest that we drown.

    NOAH'S WIFE.   Yes, sir, set up your sail
    And row forth with evil hail;[4]
    For withouten any fail
200 I will not out of this town.

    But° I have my gossips[5] everyechone,°   Unless / everyone
    One foot further I will not gone.
    They shall not drown, by sancte John,
    And° I may save their life.   If
205 They loved me full well, by Christ.
    But thou wilte let them into thy chiste,°   chest
    Elles° row forth, Noah, when thy list°   else / desire
    And get thee a new wife.

    NOAH.   Sem, son, lo thy mother is
           wraow;°   wroth, contrarious
210 By God, such another I do not know.

    SEM.   Father, I shall fetch her in, I trowe,°   trust
    Withouten any fail.
    Mother, my father after thee send
    And bids thee into yonder wend.°   turn, go
215 Look up and see the wind,
    For we been ready to sail.

    NOAH'S WIFE.   Son, go again to him and say
    I will not come therein today.

    NOAH.   Come in, wife, in twenty devils' way,
220 Or else stand there without.

    CAM.   Shall we all fetch her in?

    NOAH.   Yea, son, in Christ's blessing and mine,
    I would ye hied° you betime°   hurried / in good time
    For of this flood I stand in doubt.°   apprehension

225 THE GOOD GOSSIPS.   The flood comes fleeting in full fast,
    On every side that spredeth full far.
    For fear of drowning I am agast;
    Good gossip, let us draw near.

    And let us drink or° we depart,   ere, before
230 For oftentimes we have done so.
    For at one draught° thou drink a quart,   drink
    And so will I do or° I go.   ere

    Here is a pottell[6] full of malnesaye[7] good and strong;
    It will rejoice both heart and tongue.
235 Though Noah think us never so long,
    Yet we will drink atyte.[8]

    JAFFETT.   Mother, we pray you all together—
    For we are here, your own childer°—   children
    Come into the ship for fear of the wedder,
240 For his love that you bought.[9]

    NOAH'S WIFE.   That will I not for all your call°   outcry
    But° I have my gossips all.   unless

    SEM.   In faith, mother, yet thou shall,
    Whether thou will or not.

    [He forcibly leads her onto the boat, leaving the gossips behind.]

---

[1]   kites   Bird of prey.

[2]   leaden   Language of birds, i.e., a birdsong.

[3]   half time it were   Make it quick (in half the time).

[4]   with evil hail   With a curse on you!

[5]   gossips   In the late medieval period the noun "gossips" was used to refer to godparents, friends, or familiar acquaintances.

[6]   pottell   Measure for liquids.

[7]   malnesaye   I.e., malmsey, a sweet wine.

[8]   Though Noah … atyte   Though Noah might think we are taking ever so long, still we'll have a quick drink.

[9]   For his love … bought   For Christ's sake (anachronistically refers to the redemption of Christ's death and resurrection).

245 NOAH. Welcome, wife, into this boat.

NOAH'S WIFE. Have thou that for thy note!

[*She takes a swipe at him.*]

NOAH. Aha, marry, this is hot;
It is good for to be still.
Ah, children, me think my boat remeeves.°   *removes*
250 Our tarrying here me highly grieves.
Over the land the water spreads;
God do he as he will.

(*Then they sing, and Noah shall speak again.*)

NOAH. Ah, great God that art so good,
That workes not thy will is wood.[1]
255 Now all this world is one a flood,[2]
As I see well in sight.
This window I will shut anon,
And into my chamber I will gone
Till this water, so great one,
260 Be slaked through thy might.

(*Then shall Noah shut the window of the ark, and for a
little space within the boards he shall be silent; and afterward
opening the window and looking round about saying:*)

Lord God in majesty
That such grace hast granted me
Where all was lost, salfe° to be!   *safe, saved*
Therfore now I am boune°—   *bound*
265 My wife, my children, and my menye—
With sacrifice to honour thee
Of beasts, fowls, as thou mayest see,
And full devotion.

GOD. Noah, to me thou art full able
270 And thy sacrifice acceptable;
For I have found thee true and stable,
One thee now must I myne.°   *mention, recall*
Warry[3] yearth I will no more

For man's sins that grieves me sore;
275 For of° youth man full yore   *since*
Has been inclined to sin.

Ye shall now grow and multiply,
And yearth again to edify,
Each beast and fowl that may fly
280 Shall be feared of you.
And fish in sea, all that may fleete,°   *swim*
Shall sustain you, I thee behett;°   *command, promise*
To eat of them ye ne let°   *hesitate*
That clean been you mon know.[4]

285 Thereas° ye have eaten before   *Whereas, although*
Trees and roots since ye were bore,
Of clean beasts now, less and more,
I give you leave to eat—
Save blood and flesh both in fere°   *together*
290 Of wrauge° dead carrion that is here.   *raw*
Eat ye not of that in no manner,
For that aye° ye shall leave.   *always*

Manslaughter also aye ye shall flee,
For that is not playsante° unto me.   *pleasing*
295 They that sheden blood, he or she,
Ought-where° amongst mankind,   *Anywhere*
That blood foul shed shall be
And vengeance have, men shall see.
Therefore beware all ye,
300 You fall not into that sin.

And forward,° Noah, with thee I make   *contract*
And all thy seed for thy sake,
Of such vengeance for to slake,
For now I have my will.
305 Here I behette° thee an heeste°   *promise / promise*
That man, woman, fowl, ne beast
With water while this world shall last
I will no more spill.

My Bow between you and me
310 In the firmament[5] shall be,

---

[1] *That workes ... is wood* He who does not do your will is crazy.

[2] *one a flood* Aflood.

[3] *Warry* Lay a divine curse on.

[4] *To eat ... mon know* Do not hesitate to eat of those which you
are able to know are clean.

[5] *firmament* Arch or vault of heaven.

By very tokening that you may see[1]
That such vengeance shall cease.
The man ne woman shall never[2] more
Be wasted by water as hath before;
315   But for sin that greveth me sore,
Therefore this vengeance was.

Where clouds in the welkin° been,   sky, heaven
That ilke° bow[3] shall be seen,   same
In tokening that my wrath and teen°   annoyance
320   Shall never thus worken be.

The string is turned towards you
And towards me is bent the bow,
And such wedder shall never show;
And this behett I thee.

325   My blessing now I give thee here,
To thee, Noah, my servant dear,
For vengeance shall no more appear.
And now farewell, my darling dear.
—late 16th century

---

[1] *By very ... may see* So that you can see by a true sign.

[2] *The man ... never* Neither man nor woman shall ever.

[3] *bow* I.e., rainbow.

In Context

Biblical Source Material

Noah's Flood supplements Biblical source material, as do most other medieval plays that present Biblical stories. Below is the relevant Biblical text, in the Douay-Rheims version.

from the Douay-Rheims Bible, Genesis 6–9

CHAPTER 6

1 And after that men began to be multiplied upon the earth, and daughters were born to them,

2 The sons of God seeing the daughters of men, that they were fair, took to themselves wives of all which they chose.

3 And God said: My spirit shall not remain in man for ever, because he is flesh, and his days shall be a hundred and twenty years.

4 Now giants were upon the earth in those days. For after the sons of God went in to the daughters of men, and they brought forth children, these are the mighty men of old, men of renown.

5 And God seeing that the wickedness of men was great on the earth, and that all the thought of their heart was bent upon evil at all times,

6 It repented him that he had made man on the earth. And being touched inwardly with sorrow of heart,

7 He said: I will destroy man, whom I have created, from the face of the earth, from man even to beasts, from the creeping thing even to the fowls of the air, for it repenteth me that I have made them.

8 But Noe[1] found grace before the Lord.

9 These are the generations of Noe: Noe was a just and perfect man in his generations, he walked with God.

10 And he begot three sons, Sem, Cham, and Japheth.

11 And the earth was corrupted before God, and was filled with iniquity.

12 And when God had seen that the earth was corrupted (for all flesh had corrupted its way upon the earth,)

13 He said to Noe: The end of all flesh is come before me, the earth is filled with iniquity through them, and I will destroy them with the earth.

14 Make thee an ark of timber planks: thou shalt make little rooms in the ark, and thou shalt pitch it within and without.

15 And thus shalt thou make it: The length of the ark shall be three hundred cubits: the breadth of it fifty cubits, and the height of it thirty cubits.

16 Thou shalt make a window in the ark, and in a cubit shalt thou finish the top of it: and the door of the ark thou shalt set in the side: with lower, middle chambers, and third stories shalt thou make it.

17 Behold I will bring the waters of a great flood upon the earth, to destroy all flesh, wherein is the breath of life, under heaven. All things that are in the earth shall be consumed.

---

[1] *Noe* I.e., Noah.

18   And I will establish my covenant with thee, and thou shalt enter into the ark, thou and thy sons, and thy wife, and the wives of thy sons with thee.

19   And of every living creature of all flesh, thou shalt bring two of a sort into the ark, that they may live with thee: of the male sex, and the female.

20   Of fowls according to their kind, and of beasts in their kind, and of every thing that creepeth on the earth according to its kind; two of every sort shall go in with thee, that they may live.

21   Thou shalt take unto thee of all food that may be eaten, and thou shalt lay it up with thee: and it shall be food for thee and them.

22   And Noe did all things which God commanded him.

CHAPTER 7

1   And the Lord said to him: Go in thou and all thy house into the ark: for thee I have seen just before me in this generation.

2   Of all clean beasts take seven and seven, the male and the female.

3   But of the beasts that are unclean two and two, the male and the female. Of the fowls also of the air seven and seven, the male and the female: that seed may be saved upon the face of the whole earth.

4   For yet a while, and after seven days, I will rain upon the earth forty days and forty nights; and I will destroy every substance that I have made, from the face of the earth.

5   And Noe did all things which the Lord had commanded him.

6   And he was six hundred years old, when the waters of the flood overflowed the earth.

7   And Noe went in and his sons, his wife and the wives of his sons with him into the ark, because of the waters of the flood.

8   And of beasts clean and unclean, and of fowls, and of every thing that moveth upon the earth,

9   Two and two went in to Noe into the ark, male and female, as the Lord had commanded Noe.

10   And after the seven days were passed, the waters of the flood overflowed the earth.

11   In the six hundredth year of the life of Noe, in the second month, in the seventeenth day of the month, all the fountains of the great deep were broken up, and the flood gates of heaven were opened:

12   And the rain fell upon the earth forty days and forty nights.

13   In the selfsame day Noe, and Sem, and Cham, and Japheth his sons: his wife, and the three wives of his sons with them, went into the ark:

14   They and every beast according to its kind, and all the cattle in their kind, and every thing that moveth upon the earth according to its kind, and every fowl according to its kind, all birds, and all that fly,

15   Went in to Noe into the ark, two and two of all flesh, wherein was the breath of life.

16   And they that went in, went in male and female of all flesh, as God had commanded him: and the Lord shut him in on the outside.

17   And the flood was forty days upon the earth, and the waters increased, and lifted up the ark on high from the earth.

18   For they overflowed exceedingly: and filled all on the face of the earth: and the ark was carried upon the waters.

19   And the waters prevailed beyond measure upon the earth: and all the high mountains under the whole heaven were covered.

20   The water was fifteen cubits higher than the mountains which it covered.

21   And all flesh was destroyed that moved upon the earth, both of fowl, and of cattle, and of beasts, and of all creeping things that creep upon the earth: and all men.

22   And all things wherein there is the breath of life on the earth, died.

23   And he destroyed all the substance that was upon the earth, from man even to beast, and the creeping things and fowls of the air: and they were destroyed from the earth: and Noe only remained, and they that were with him in the ark.

24   And the waters prevailed upon the earth a hundred and fifty days.

CHAPTER 8

1   And God remembered Noe, and all the living creatures, and all the cattle which were with him in the ark, and brought a wind upon the earth, and the waters were abated.

2   The fountains also of the deep, and the flood gates of heaven were shut up, and the rain from heaven was restrained.

3   And the waters returned from off the earth going and coming: and they began to be abated after a hundred and fifty days.

4   And the ark rested in the seventh month, the seven and twentieth day of the month, upon the mountains of Armenia.

5   And the waters were going and decreasing until the tenth month: for in the tenth month, the first day of the month, the tops of the mountains appeared.

6   And after that forty days were passed, Noe, opening the window of the ark which he had made, sent forth a raven:

7   Which went forth and did not return, till the waters were dried up upon the earth.

8   He sent forth also a dove after him, to see if the waters had now ceased upon the face of the earth.

9   But she, not finding where her foot might rest, returned to him into the ark: for the waters were upon the whole earth: and he put forth his hand, and caught her, and brought her into the ark.

10   And having waited yet seven other days, he again sent forth the dove out of the ark.

11   And she came to him in the evening, carrying a bough of an olive tree, with green leaves, in her mouth. Noe therefore understood that the waters were ceased upon the earth.

12   And he stayed yet other seven days: and he sent forth the dove, which returned not any more unto him.

13   Therefore in the six hundredth and first year, the first month, the first day of the month, the waters were lessened upon the earth, and Noe opening the covering of the ark, looked, and saw that the face of the earth was dried.

14   In the second month, the seven and twentieth day of the month, the earth was dried.

15   And God spoke to Noe, saying:

16   Go out of the ark, thou and thy wife, thy sons, and the wives of thy sons with thee.

17   All living things that are with thee of all flesh, as well in fowls as in beasts, and all creeping things that creep upon the earth, bring out with thee, and go ye upon the earth: increase and multiply upon it.

18   So Noe went out, he and his sons: his wife, and the wives of his sons with him.

19   And all living things, and cattle, and creeping things that creep upon the earth, according to their kinds, went out of the ark.

20   And Noe built an altar unto the Lord: and taking of all cattle and fowls that were clean, offered holocausts upon the altar.

21   And the Lord smelled a sweet savour, and said: I will no more curse the earth for the sake of man: for the imagination and thought of man's heart are prone to evil from his youth: therefore I will no more destroy every living soul as I have done.

22   All the days of the earth, seedtime and harvest, cold and heat, summer and winter, night and day, shall not cease.

CHAPTER 9

1   And God blessed Noe and his sons. And he said to them: Increase and multiply, and fill the earth.

2   And let the fear and dread of you be upon all the beasts of the earth, and upon all the fowls of the air, and all that move upon the earth: all the fishes of the sea are delivered into your hand.

3   And every thing that moveth and liveth shall be meat for you: even as the green herbs have I delivered them all to you:

4   Saving that flesh with blood you shall not eat.

5   For I will require the blood of your lives at the hand of every beast, and at the hand of man, at the hand of every man, and of his brother, will I require the life of man.

6   Whosoever shall shed man's blood, his blood shall be shed: for man was made to the image of God.

7   But increase you and multiply, and go upon the earth, and fill it.

8   Thus also said God to Noe, and to his sons with him,

9   Behold I will establish my covenant with you, and with your seed after you:

10   And with every living soul that is with you, as well in all birds as in cattle and beasts of the earth, that are come forth out of the ark, and in all the beasts of the earth.

11   I will establish my covenant with you, and all flesh shall be no more destroyed with the waters of a flood, neither shall there be from henceforth a flood to waste the earth.

12   And God said: This is the sign of the covenant which I give between me and you, and to every living soul that is with you, for perpetual generations.

13   I will set my bow in the clouds, and it shall be the sign of a covenant between me, and between the earth.

14   And when I shall cover the sky with clouds, my bow shall appear in the clouds:

15   And I will remember my covenant with you, and with every living soul that beareth flesh: and there shall no more be waters of a flood to destroy all flesh.

16   And the bow shall be in the clouds, and I shall see it, and shall remember the everlasting covenant, that was made between God and every living soul of all flesh which is upon the earth.

17   And God said to Noe: This shall be the sign of the covenant which I have established between me and all flesh upon the earth.

18   And the sons of Noe who came out of the ark, were Sem, Cham, and Japheth: and Cham is the father of Chanaan.

19   These three are the sons of Noe: and from these was all mankind spread over the whole earth.

20   And Noe, a husbandman, began to till the ground, and planted a vineyard.

21   And drinking of the wine was made drunk, and was uncovered in his tent.

22   Which when Cham the father of Chanaan had seen, to wit, that his father's nakedness was uncovered, he told it to his two brethren without.

23   But Sem and Japheth put a cloak upon their shoulders, and going backward, covered the nakedness of their father: and their faces were turned away, and they saw not their father's nakedness.

24   And Noe awaking from the wine, when he had learned what his younger son had done to him,

25   He said: Cursed be Chanaan, a servant of servants shall he be unto his brethren.

26   And he said: Blessed be the Lord God of Sem, be Chanaan his servant.

27   May God enlarge Japheth, and may he dwell in the tents of Sem, and Chanaan be his servant.

28   And Noe lived after the flood three hundred and fifty years:

29   And all his days were in the whole nine hundred and fifty years: and he died.

THE WAKEFIELD MASTER

c. 1400 — 1450

Much is unclear about the identity of the "Wakefield Master" and about the group of plays ascribed to this individual. That group of plays is brought together in a manuscript that is believed to date from the mid-sixteenth century. Nothing is sure about its origin, but by the seventeenth century it was in the library of a well-to-do Catholic family, the Towneleys of Towneley Hall near Burnley, Lancashire, from which the Towneley manuscript (now in the Huntington Library in San Marino, CA) takes its name. The manuscript includes thirty-two short plays based largely on biblical story material.

In the manuscript the plays appear in a sequence that approximates that of the Bible, beginning with a play depicting the story of the Creation. For that reason the Towneley Plays were long assumed to represent a cycle similar to that of the York and Chester cycles, in which a sequence of pageant plays was performed once every year, with performances beginning early in the day and running until dark, and with each play mounted under the auspices of one of the trade guilds of the town. Largely because the name "Wakefield" appears on the first page of two of the plays, the assumption took root that all thirty-two plays constituted a unified group that had been performed in that town, and the Towneley plays became widely referred to as the "Wakefield Cycle." As recent scholarship has emphasized, however, the thirty-two plays form a very disparate group. The plays have a variety of sometimes incompatible staging requirements; several have been borrowed virtually intact from the York cycle of pageant plays; and several exhibit inconsistencies suggesting that they were unlikely ever to have been performed as they now appear. It is thus now thought to be entirely possible that the manuscript collection simply represents a group of plays from various sources, assembled in quasi-chronological order. Some have speculated that the collection may have been brought together in one manuscript with a view more to reading than to performance (though marks in some plays suggest a performance history, it is not clear when these were added to the manuscript). It is now regarded as highly improbable that the thirty-two were all performed together as part of a unified cycle, in Wakefield or in any other town.

Within the Towneley Plays, however, are five plays with strong points of similarity: *Noah*, the *First Shepherds' Play*, *The Second Shepherds' Play*, *Herod the Great*, and *The Buffeting of Christ*. A sixth, *The Killing of Abel*, is sometimes also linked with these five, though it is not written in the same stanzaic form as the others. The two shepherds' plays and *The Killing of Abel* (unlike other plays in the Towneley manuscript) contain textual allusions to the Wakefield area. The five maintain a strong metrical structure, presented in the manuscript in the form of nine-line stanzas, with a consistent a a a a b c c c b rhyming pattern throughout. The first four manuscript lines also contain rhyming half lines; in the light of this, recent scholarship is in agreement that an appropriate alternative to the way in which the lines are laid out in the manuscript is to read them as forming thirteen-line stanzas, rhymed a b a b a b a b c d d d c. These plays are also acknowledged to be distinguished by their lively characterization—and by the sheer skill of their composition. Since the nineteenth century they have generally been ascribed to a single author, now conventionally referred to as the "Wakefield Master." Here too, however, recent scholarship has challenged old assumptions. While the commonality of all five plays has not been questioned, we have no firm evidence as to authorship. The quotation marks placed around the name "Wakefield Master" are thus to be taken to indicate that the ascription of authorship is the product of convention rather than proven fact. All that can be said with confidence is that there seems clearly to have been a common force involved in the shaping of all five of these plays.

Whether through the medium of a single author or the shaping editorial hand of the compiler, the five plays demonstrate an extensive and sophisticated knowledge of the Bible. It is also possible that the author or editor had some knowledge of continental literature, as the structures suggest some influences from the French comic theater of the time. The plays are written in a northern dialect of Middle English.

The Second Shepherds' Play is the best known and most widely read of the English biblical pageant plays. As with all such plays, it seems to have been intended to make biblical stories interesting to a largely illiterate population. It is noteworthy, however, that the play contains a very significant amount of material that has no biblical source. The play interweaves a touching presentation of Christ's nativity (extrapolated from the biblical account) with a farcical plot involving the thief and trickster Mak. The story material that has been added has considerable entertainment value, but it also offers social commentary.

In *Herod the Great*, King Herod orders the slaughter of all male children in Bethlehem under two years of age in an attempt to kill the infant Jesus, whom he sees as a potential threat. In its dramatization of this Bible story, the play draws on several medieval literary traditions to portray Herod as an arch-villain. Taking a cue from the depiction of Herod in Matthew 2.16, medieval artists often portrayed Herod as a raving madman. (That this tradition was still familiar in Shakespeare's time is evidenced by Hamlet's advice to the players to avoid a performance that "out-Herods Herod.") The play also portrays Herod as a Muslim, another medieval literary tradition; in medieval biblical plays, Herod and his cohorts were often costumed as Saracens. For the most part, however, the play makes no distinction between first-century Palestine and fifteenth-century England. Much as in *The Second Shepherds' Play*, where characters anachronistically swear by Christ's cross and by Pontius Pilate before they know of the birth of Jesus, Herod here employs knights and receives the gift of medieval European lands.

⌘ ⌘ ⌘

The Second Shepherds' Play[1]

CHARACTERS

First Shepherd
Second Shepherd
Third Shepherd
Mak
Gill
An Angel
Mary

(*Here begins their second.*)

[1] *The Second Shepherds' Play* For the present text spelling and punctuation have been substantially modernized from the original Towneley text. The stage directions in Latin in the Towneley text are here translated into English and shown in parentheses. For clarity some other stage directions have been added; these appear in square brackets. The manuscript divides the text as is done here—into nine-line stanzas, with internal rhymes in each stanza's first four lines. (An alternative approach now widely favored by scholars is to divide the play into 13-line stanzas.)

[*A field near Bethlehem. Enter First Shepherd.*]

FIRST SHEPHERD.   Lord! what these weathers are cold!
    And I am ill-happed;°   *poorly clothed*
I am near-hand dold,° so long have I napped; *numb*
My legs they fold, my fingers are chapped;
It is not as I would, for I am all lapped° *wrapped*
5   In sorrow.
In storms and tempest,
Now in the east, now in the west,
Woe is him has never rest,
    Mid-day nor morrow.

10 But we seely husbands[2] that walk on the moor,
In faith, we are near-hands out of the door;
No wonder, as it stands, if we be poor,

[2] *seely husbands* Poor farm workers.

For the tilth of our lands lies fallow as the floor,[1]
    As ye ken.°   *know*

15 We are so hamed°   *hamstrung*
For-taxed and ramed,[2]
We're made hand-tamed
    With° these gentlery men.°   *By / gentry*

Thus they reave[3] us our rest, Our Lady them wary!°   *curse*
20 These men that are lord-fast,[4] they cause the plough tarry.
What men say is for the best, we find it contrary;
Thus are husbands° oppressed, in point to miscarry *farmers*
    In life.
Thus hold they us under,
25 Thus they bring us in blunder;°   *confusion*
It were great wonder,
    And° ever should we thrive.   *If*

For may he get a paint sleeve, or a brooch nowadays,
Woe is him that him grieve, or once again-says![5]
30 Dare no man him reprieve,° what mast'ry he   *reprove*
    makes;
And yet may no man lefe° one word that he says,   *believe*
    No letter.
He can make purveyance,[6]
With boast and bragance,
35 And all is through maintenance
    Of men that are greater.[7]

There shall come a swain,° as proud   *retainer, servant*
    as a po,°   *peacock*

He must borrow my wain,° my plough also;   *wagon*
Then I am full fain° to grant ere° he go. *delighted / before*
40 Thus live we in pain, anger, and woe,
    By night and day.
He must have if he longed,
If I should forgo it;[8]
I were better be hanged
45   Than once say him nay.

It does me good, as I walk thus by mine own,
Of this world for to talk in manner of moan.[9]
To my sheep will I stalk and hearken anon,
There abide on a balk,° or sit on a stone   *ridge*
50   Full soon.
For I trow,° pardie,[10]   *think*
True men if they be,
We get more company
    Or° it be noon.   *Before*

[*Enter Second Shepherd. He does not see the First Shepherd.*]

55 SECOND SHEPHERD. Benste[11] and Dominus! what
    may this bemean?°   *indicate*
Why fares this world thus? Oft have we not seen,
Lord, these weathers are spiteous,° and the   *nasty*
    winds full keen;
And the frost so hideous they water mine eeyen,° *eyes*
    No lie.
60 Now in dry, now in wet,
Now in snow, now in sleet,
When my shone° freeze to my feet   *shoes*
    It is not all easy.

But as far as I ken, or yet as I go,
65 We seely wed-men dre mekill woe;[12]
We have sorrow then and then, it falls° oft so. *happens*
Seely Capel, our hen, both to and fro
    She cackles;

---

[1] *the tilth ... floor* I.e., all of our land—the arable land (tilth) as much as the low-lying areas—is lying fallow; no crops are being grown there. During the fifteenth century many landowners were converting farmland to grazing land.

[2] *For-taxed and ramed* Overburdened and oppressed.

[3] *reave* Take away from.

[4] *lord-fast* Attached to lords.

[5] *For ... again-says!* For, if anyone gets a painted sleeve or a brooch (i.e., wears livery), woe to the man who gives grief to or contradicts that person! (A man in livery is a high-ranking employee of the landlord.)

[6] *purveyance* The requisition and purchase of provisions, specifically the right of the crown or of a lord to buy supplies for the household at a price set by a purveyor.

[7] *through maintenance ... greater* Through the support of those with greater power.

[8] *He must ... forgo it* If he has longed for a thing he must have it, even if I have to do without.

[9] *in manner of moan* In a complaining way.

[10] *pardie* By God (a corruption of the French "Pardieu").

[11] *Benste* Bless us (a corruption of the Latin "Benedicte"); *Dominus* Latin: Lord.

[12] *seely ... woe* We poor married men suffer a great deal.

But begins she to croak,
70   To groan or to cluck,
  Woe is him, our cock,
     For he is in the shackles.[1]

These men that are wed have not all their will;
When they are full hard stead,[2] they sigh full
    still;°   *continually*
75 God wayte° they are led full hard and full ill,   *knows*
In bower° nor in bed they say nought   *bedroom*
    theretill,°   *in reply*
     This tide.°   *time*
My part have I fun°—   *found*
  I know my lesson:
80 Woe is him that is bun°   *bound*
     For he must abide.°   *stay that way*

But now late in our lives—a marvel to me,
That I think my heart rives° such wonders to see,   *breaks*
What that destiny drives, it should so be!—
85 Some men will have two wives, and some men three,
    In store.
Some are woe° that have any;   *sad, woeful*
But so far can I,[3]
Woe is him that has many,
90   For he feels sore.

[*To the audience.*]

But young men, of wooing, for God that you bought,[4]
Be well ware of wedding, and think in your thought:
"Had I wist"° is a thing that serves of nought;   *known*
Mekill still° mourning has wedding home   *much steady*
    brought,
95   And griefs,
With many a sharp shower,°   *pang*
For thou may catch in an hour
That shall sow° thou full sour°   *grieve / bitterly*
    As long as thou liffys.°   *you live*

---

1 *Seely Capel … in shackles* The husband is in servitude to his wife, who is likened to a silly hen.

2 *full hard stead* Hard pressed, stricken by misfortune.

3 *so far can I* This much I know.

4 *you bought* Redeemed you.

100 For, as ever read I pistill, I have one to my fere[5]
As sharp as a thistle, as rough as a brier;
She is browed like a bristle, with a sour-loten°   *looking*
    cheer;
Had she once wet her whistle she could sing full clear
    Her pater-noster.[6]
105 She is as great as a whall,°   *whale*
She has a gallon of gall;
By him that died for us all,°   *i.e., Jesus*
    I would I had run to° I had lost her!   *till*

FIRST SHEPHERD. God look over the row!°   *audience*
    Full deafly ye stand.
110 SECOND SHEPHERD. Yea, the devil in thy maw, so
    tarryand!°[7]   *tarrying*
    Saw thou anywhere of Daw?
FIRST SHEPHERD. Yea, on a lea[8] land
    Heard I him blow;[9] he comes here at hand,
      Not far;
    Stand still.
SECOND SHEPHERD.   Why?
115 FIRST SHEPHERD. For he comes, hope I.
SECOND SHEPHERD. He will make° us both a lie   *tell*
    But if ° we beware.   *unless*

[*Enter Third Shepherd, a boy. He does not see the others.*]

THIRD SHEPHERD. Christ's cross me speed, and Saint
    Nicholas!
Thereof had I need, it is worse than it was.
120 Whoso could, take heed, and let the world pass:
It is ever in dread and brekill° as glass,   *brittle*
    And slithes.°   *slides away*
This world fared never so,
With marvels more and more,
125 Now in weal,° now in woe,   *well-being, prosperity*
    And all thing writhes.[10]

---

5 *as ever … fere* As surely as I read the Epistle, I have one as my companion.

6 *pater-noster* Latin: Our Father; the Lord's Prayer.

7 *maw … tarryand* Belly, for taking so long.

8 *lea* Fallow, unploughed.

9 *Heard … blow* I heard him blow (his horn).

10 *all thing writhes* Everything keeps turning.

Was never since Noah's flood such floods seen,
Winds and rains so rude, and storms so keen;
Some stammered, some stood in doubt, as I
        ween;°   *think*
130 Now God, turn all to good! I say as I mean.
            For ponder:
These floods so they drown
Both in fields and in town,
And bear all down,
135   And that is a wonder.

[*He sees the others, but at first does not recognize them.*]

We that walk in the nights, our cattle to keep,
We see sudden sights, when other men sleep.
Yet methink my heart lights—I see shrews° peep.   *villains*
Ye are two all-wights!° I will give my sheep   *monsters*
140   A turn.
But full ill have I meant;
As I walk on this bent,°   *heath*
I may lightly repent
            My toes if I spurn.[1]

145 Ah, sir, God you save, and master mine!
A drink fain would I have, and somewhat to dine.
FIRST SHEPHERD.   Christ's curse, my knave, thou art a
        lither hind![2]
SECOND SHEPHERD.   What, the boy list° rave!   *likes to*

(*To the Third Shepherd.*)

            Abide unto sine;°   *later*
        We have made it.
150 Ill thrift° on thy pate!°[3]   *luck / head*

(*To the First Shepherd.*)

Though the shrew° came late,   *rascal*
Yet is he in state
            To dine, if he had it.[4]

THIRD SHEPHERD.   Such servants as I, that sweats and
        swinks,°   *labors, toils*
155 Eats our bread full dry, and that me forthinks;[5]
We are oft wet and weary when mastermen winks,°   *sleep*
Yet comes full lately° both dinners and drinks.   *very slowly*
            But naitly°   *thoroughly*
Both our dame and our sire,
160 When we have run in the mire,°   *muck*
They can nip at our hire,[6]
            And pay us full lately.

But hear my truth, master: for the fare that ye make,
I shall do thereafter work as I take;[7]
165 I shall do a little, sir, emang ever lake;[8]
For yet lay my supper never on my stomach
        In fields.[9]
Whereto should I threap?°   *complain*
With my staff can I leap,
170 And men say "light cheap
            Litherly foryields."[10]

FIRST SHEPHERD.   Thou were an ill lad—to ride on
        wowing
With a man that had but little of spending—
SECOND SHEPHERD.   Peace, boy, I bade; no more
        jangling,°   *chattering*
175 Or I shall make thee afraid, by the heaven's king,
            With thy gauds!°   *pranks*
Where are our sheep, boy? We scorn—
THIRD SHEPHERD.   Sir, this same day at morn

---

[1] *But full ill ... spurn* The meaning here is obscure; the suggestion seems to be that a comical penance (of stubbing his toes) is to be imposed on the shepherd for having taken his fellow shepherds to be monsters.

[2] *lither hind* Wicked farm servant.

[3] *Abide ... pate* Wait a while; we have had food already—bad luck to you.

[4] *in state ... had it* Would like to eat, if he had food.

[5] *me forthinks* Upsets me.

[6] *nip at our hire* Reduce our wages.

[7] *I shall do ... take* I will only work as well as I am being paid for it.

[8] *emang ever lake* Keep playing continually.

[9] *For yet ... fields* For I have never had such a full stomach that it weighed me down in the fields.

[10] *light cheap / Litherly foryields* Proverbial: low costs yield low returns, i.e., you get what you pay for.

I left them in the corn,°   *grain*
180   When they rang Lauds;[1]

They have pasture good—they cannot go wrong.
FIRST SHEPHERD. That is right. By the rood,°   *cross*
    these nights are long!
Yet I would, ere we yode,° one gave us a song.   *went*
SECOND SHEPHERD. So I thought as I stood, to mirth
    us among.[2]
185 THIRD SHEPHERD. I grant.
FIRST SHEPHERD. Let me sing the tenory.°   *tenor*
SECOND SHEPHERD. And I the treble so high.
THIRD SHEPHERD. Then the mean° falls to me; *middle part*
    Let's see how ye chant.

(*Enter Mak, with a cloak thrown over his smock.*)

190 MAK. Now, Lord, for thy names seven, that made
    both moon and stars,
Well more than I can neven,[3] thy will, Lord, of me
    tharnys;[4]
I am all uneven,° that moves oft my harns;° *upset / brains*
Now would God I were in heaven, for there weep no
    bairns°   *children*
    So still!°   *incessantly*
195 FIRST SHEPHERD. Who is that pipes so
    poor?°   *cries so wretchedly*
MAK. Would God ye wist° how I foor!°   *knew / fared*
Lo, a man that walks on the moor,
    And has not all his will![5]

SECOND SHEPHERD. Mak, where has thou gone? Tell
    us tidings.
200 THIRD SHEPHERD. Is *he* come? Then each one take
    heed to his thing.[6]

(*Takes his cloak from him.*)

MAK. What! *Ich*[7] be a yeoman, I tell you, of the king;
The self and the some,° sent from a great lording, *same*
    Und *sich*.°   *and such*
Fie on you! Goeth hence!
205 Out of my presence!
I must have reverence.
    Why, who be *Ich*?

FIRST SHEPHERD. Why make ye it so quaint?° *affected*
    Mak, ye do wrong.
SECOND SHEPHERD. But, Mak, play ye the saint? I
    trow that ye long.[8]
210 THIRD SHEPHERD. I trow the shrew can paynt,[9] the
    devil might him hang!
MAK. I shall make complaint, and make you all to
    thwang[10]
    At a word.
And tell even how ye doth.[11]
FIRST SHEPHERD. But, Mak, is that truth?
215 Now take out that southern tooth,[12]
    And set° in a turd!   *put*

SECOND SHEPHERD. Mak, the devil in your eye! A
    stroke would I lean° you.   *give*
THIRD SHEPHERD. Mak, know ye not me? By God, I
    could teen[13] you.

[*Mak now pretends to recognize the shepherds for the first time.*]

MAK. God look you all three! Methought I had seen you.
Ye are a fair company.

---

[1] *Lauds* "Lauds" was the first hour of the Church day, and it ended with the singing of a Psalm of praise (from the Latin for praise, *laus, laudem*).

[2] *to mirth us among* To have mirth among us.

[3] *neven* Refer to, especially by name.

[4] *of me tharnys* Is unclear to me.

[5] *Lo … will* Look, I am just a man out walking, who does not know what to do; or, does not have all he wants.

[6] *Then … thing* In that case everyone should look out for his belongings.

[7] *Ich* The use of this word (together with "sich") suggests that Mak is affecting a southern English dialect.

[8] *play … long* Are you pretending to be a saint? I believe that's what you long to be.

[9] *paynt* Feign, deceive.

[10] *thwang* Be flogged.

[11] *tell … doth* I will even tell (the authorities) how you are acting.

[12] *southern tooth* Southern dialect.

[13] *teen* Vex, cause physical injury to.

220 FIRST SHEPHERD.   Can ye now mene you?[1]
SECOND SHEPHERD.   Shrew, peep!°   *look out!*
   Thus late as thou goes,
   What will men suppose?
   And thou has an ill noise
225   Of stealing of sheep.[2]

   MAK.   And I am true as steel, all men watt!°   *know*
   But a sickness I feel, that holds me full hatt°   *hot*
   My belly fares not well, it is out of estate.°   *in poor shape*
   THIRD SHEPHERD.   Seldom lies the devil dead by the
         gate.[3]
230 MAK.   Therefore
   Full sore am I and ill,
   If I stand stone still;
   I eat° not a needle   *ate*
         This month and more.

235 FIRST SHEPHERD.   How fares thy wife? By my hood,
         how fares sho?°   *she*
   MAK.   Lies weltering,° by the rood, by the fire, lo!   *sprawled*
   And a house full of brood;° she drinks well, too;   *children*
   Ill speed other good that she will do!
         But so
240 Eats as fast as she can,
   And each year that comes to man,
   She brings forth a lakan°   *baby*
         And some years two.

   But were I now more gracious, and richer by far,
245 I were° eaten out of house and of harbour;°   *would be / home*
   Yet is she a foul douce,° if ye come near.   *woman*
   There is none that trows° nor knows a worse   *believes*
         Than ken I.
   Now will ye see what I proffer?
250 To give all in my coffer
   To-morn next to offer
         Her head-mass penny.[4]

SECOND SHEPHERD.   I know so forwaked[5] is none in
         this shire:
   I would sleep if I took less to my hire.[6]
255 THIRD SHEPHERD.   I am cold and naked, and would
         have a fire.
   FIRST SHEPHERD.   I am weary, for-raked,°   *exhausted*
         and run in the mire.
         Wake thou!
   SECOND SHEPHERD.   Nay, I will lie down-by,
   For I must sleep, truly.
260 THIRD SHEPHERD.   As good a man's son was I
         As any of you.[7]

[*Lies down.*]

   But, Mak, come hither! between shall thou lie down.
   MAK.   Then might I lett you bedene of that ye would
         rowne;[8]
         No dread.
265 From my top to my toe
   Manus tuas commendo,
   Pontio Pilate![9]
         Christ's cross me speed!

(*Then he rises, while the shepherds are asleep, and says:*)

   Now were time for a man that lacks what he would,
270 To stalk privily then into a fold,°   *sheepfold*
   And nimbly to work then, and be not too bold,
   For he might aby the bargain, if it were told
         At the ending.[10]
   Now is the time to reyll°   *act quickly*
275 But he needs good counsel

---

[5] *forwaked*   Tired from lack of sleep.

[6] *I would ... to my hire*   I would take less wages if I could sleep.

[7] *As good ... any of you*   I am just as good as you are (and therefore just as deserving of a rest).

[8] *lett you ... would rowne*   Hinder your whispering round me.

[9] *Manus tuas commendo / Pontio Pilate!*   Latin: Into thy hands I commend (my spirit), Pontius Pilate! Mak misquotes Luke 23.46 ("Father, into thy hands I commend my spirit") and substitutes Pontius Pilate for God.

[10] *he might ... ending*   He (who is too bold) may pay a high price for it in the end.

---

[1] *Can ye now mene you?*   Are you now able to recognize yourself too?

[2] *And thou ... stealing of sheep*   And you have a bad reputation as a sheep stealer.

[3] *Seldom ... gate*   Proverbial: when the devil seems to lie dead, it is more likely that he is feigning.

[4] *head-mass penny*   Payment for her funeral mass.

That fain would fare well,
    And has but little spending.[1]

[*Mak casts a spell on the sleeping shepherds.*]

But about you, a circle as round as a moon!
Till I have done that I will, till that it be noon,
280 That ye lie stone-still, to° that I have done.   *till*
And I shall say there-till of good words a fayne:°   *few*
    "On height,
Over your heads my hand I lift,
Out go your eyes, fordo° your sight!"   *lose*
285 But yet I must make better shift,°   *arrangements*
    And° it be right.   *If*

[*Shepherds snore. Mak addresses the audience.*]

Lord, what they sleep hard! That may ye all hear.
Was I° never a shepherd, but now will I lere.°   *I was / learn*
If the flock be scared, yet shall I nip° near.   *come*
290 How! Draw hitherward! Now mends our cheer
    From sorrow.
A fat sheep, I dare say,
A good fleece, dare I lay.°   *wager*
Eft-whyte° when I may,   *repay*
295   But this will I borrow.

[*Carries the sheep to the door of his house.*]

How, Gill, art thou in? Get us some light.
WIFE. Who makes such din this time of the night?
I am set for to spin. I doubt that I might
Rise a penny to win; I shrew them on height!
300   So fares
A huswiff that has been
To be raced thus between![2]
Here may no note° be seen   *benefit, profit*
    For such small chares.°   *chores*

305 MAK. Good wife, open the hek!° Sees thou not   *door*
    what I bring?
WIFE. I may let thee draw the sneck.° Ah, come   *latch*
    in, my sweeting!
MAK. Yea, thou there not reck of my long standing![3]
WIFE. By the naked neck art thou like for° to   *likely*
    hang!
MAK. Do way!°   *Stop that!*
310 I am worthy my meat,
    For in a strait° can I get   *tight spot*
    More than they that swink° and sweat   *work*
        All the long day.

Thus it fell to my lot, Gill: I had such grace![4]
315 WIFE. It were a foul blot to be hanged for the case.
MAK. I have scaped, Gillot, oft as hard a glace.°   *blow*
WIFE. But so long goes the pot to the water, men says,
    At last
Comes it home broken.
320 MAK. Well know I the token,
    But let it never be spoken.
        But come and help fast.

I would he were flayn;° I list° well eat: *skinned / wish*
This twelvemonth was I not so fain of one sheep-
    meat.
325 WIFE. Come they ere he be slain, and hear the sheep
    bleat—
MAK. Then might I be ta'en: that were a cold sweat!
    Go spar°   *fasten*
The gate door.
330 WIFE.   Yes, Mak,
    For and they come at thy back—
330 MAK. Then might I buy, fro all the pack,
        The devil of the war![5]

WIFE. A good bowrde° have I spied, since thou   *trick*
    ken° none: *know*
Here shall we him hide too they be gone,
In my cradle abide. Let° me alone,   *leave*

---

1 *he needs ... spending* Someone who would like to fare better but has few resources needs to follow good advice.

2 *I am set ... between* I am all in a tizzy. I don't see how I can gain anything from this; I curse them mightily! This is how it goes for a housewife who has been interrupted like this!

3 *Yea ... standing* Yes, don't let it bother you how long I've been standing here!

4 *I had such grace* I was so blessed.

5 *Then might ... war* Then I might receive, from the pack of them, a hellishly bad experience.

335 And I shall lie beside in childbed and groan.

MAK.   Thou red°   *ready yourself*

And I shall say thou was lighted°   *delivered*

Of a knave°-child this night.   *male*

WIFE.   Now, well is me! Day bright

340   That ever I was bred!

This is a good guise and a far cast;°   *clever trick*

Yet a woman avyse° helps at the last!   *advice*

I wote never who spies; again, go thou fast![1]

MAK.   But I come ere they rise, else blows a cold blast!

345   I will go sleep.

[Mak returns to the Shepherds.]

Yet sleeps all this meneye°   *group*

And I shall go stalk privily,°   *stealthily*

As it had never been I

        That carried their sheep.

[He lies down among them. The shepherds begin to wake up.]

350 FIRST SHEPHERD.   *Resurrex a mortruis!*[2] Have hold my
        hand!

Judas carnas dominus![3] I may not well stand.

My foot sleeps, by Jesus! and I water fastand.

I thought that we laid us full near England.[4]

SECOND SHEPHERD.   Ah, yea!

355 Lord, what, I have slept well!

As fresh as an eel,

As light I me feel

        As leaf on a tree.

THIRD SHEPHERD.   Benste be herein! So me quakes,

360 My heart is out of skin; what so it makes!

Who makes all this din? So my brows blakes

———

[1] *I wote never ... fast* I don't know who may be looking; go back
(to the shepherds) again quickly!

[2] *Resurrex a mortruis* Garbled Latin: He has risen from the dead!

[3] *Judas carnas dominus* Corrupted Latin: Judas, lord of the flesh!

[4] *I water ... England* I have eaten so little that I thought we had
been lying down very close to England.

To the door will I win.[5] Hark, fellows, wake!

        We were four:

See ye anywhere of Mak now?

365 FIRST SHEPHERD.   We were up ere thou.

SECOND SHEPHERD.   Man, I give God a vow,

        That yede he nowhere.

THIRD SHEPHERD.   Methought he was lapt in a
        wolfskin.

FIRST SHEPHERD.   So are many happed now, namely,
        within.

370 THIRD SHEPHERD.   When we had long napped,
        methought with a gin°   *trap*

A fat sheep he trapped, but he made no din.

SECOND SHEPHERD.   Be still!°   *quiet*

Thy dream makes thee wood;°   *insane*

It is but phantom, by the rood.

375 FIRST SHEPHERD.   Now God turn all to good,

        If it be his will!

[They turn to wake up Mak.]

SECOND SHEPHERD.   Rise, Mak, for shame! Thou lies
        right long.

MAK.   Now Christ's holy name be us emang!°   *among*

What is this? For Saint James, I may not well go!

380 I trow I be the same. Ah, my neck has lain wrang°   *wrong*

        Enough,

Mekill thank, since yester-even.°   *yesterday evening*

Now, by Saint Stephen,

I was flayed° by a sweven°   *scared / dream*

385   My heart out of slough.°   *skin*

I thought Gill began to croak, and travail° full sad,   *labor*

Well near at the first cock,° of a young lad   *cock-crow*

For to mend our flock. Then be I never glad;

I have tow on my rok[6] more than ever I had.

390   Ah, my head!

A house full of young tharms,°   *stomachs*

The devil knock out their harns!°   *brains*

Woe is him has many bairns,

        And so little bread!

———

[5] *So my brows ... will I win* My brows furrow (out of fear at the
commotion) and I will run away.

[6] *tow on my rok* Flax on my distaff (i.e., trouble).

395 I must go home, by your leave, to Gill, as I thought.
Pray you: look up my sleeve, that I steal nought:
I am loth you to grieve, or from you take aught.
[*Exits*]
THIRD SHEPHERD.   Go forth; ill might thou cheve.°   *fare*
　　　Now would I we sought,
　　　　　This morn,
400 That we had all our store.[1]
FIRST SHEPHERD.   But I will go before.
　　Let us meet.
SECOND SHEPHERD.   　　Where?
THIRD SHEPHERD.   At the crooked thorn.

[*They leave to check on their sheep. The scene shifts to Mak's house.*]

MAK.   (*Knocking.*) Undo this door! Who is here? How
　　long shall I stand?
405 WIFE.   Who makes such a bere?° Go walk in the   *noise*
　　wanyand![2]
MAK.   Ah, Gill, what cheer? It is I, Mak, your
　　husband.
WIFE.   Then may we see here the devil in a band.°   *noose*
　　　Sir Guile!
　　Lo, he comes with a lote,°   *noise*
410 As° he were holden in° the throat.   *As if / held by*
　　I may not sit at my note°   *work*
　　　A hand-long° while.   *little*

MAK.   Will ye hear what fare she makes to get her a
　　gloze?°   *an excuse*
　　And does nought but lakys,° and claws° her   *plays / scratches*
　　toes.
415 WIFE.   Why, who wanders, who wakes, who comes,
　　who goes?
　　Who brews, who bakes? What makes me thus hose?
　　　And then
　　It is sad to behold,
　　Now in hot, now in cold—
420 Full woeful is the household
　　　That wants° a woman!   *lacks*

---

1 *Now would I ... store* Now I would (think we should) check, this
morning, that we have all our belongings.

2 *wanyand* Waning of the moon (an unlucky time).

But what end hast thou made with the herds,°   *herders*
　　Mak?
MAK.   The last word that they said when I turned my
　　back:
　　They would look that they had their sheep, all the pack.
425 I hope° they will not be well paid when they   *expect*
　　their sheep lack,
　　　Per Die!°   *By God*
　　But howso the game goes,
　　It's me they will suppose,°   *suspect*
　　And make a foul noise,
430 　　And cry out upon me.

　　But thou must do as thou hight.°   *promised*
WIFE.   　　　I accord me theretill;
　　I shall swaddle him right in my cradle.
　　If it were a greater sleight,° yet could I help till.   *trick*
　　I will lie down straight; come hap me.
MAK.   　　　I will.
435 WIFE.   Behind!
　　Come Coll and his marroo,°   *mate*
　　They will nip us full narroo.°   *pinch us hard*
MAK.   But I may cry out "Harroo!"°   *help*
　　　The sheep if they find.

440 WIFE. Hearken, aye, when they call: they will come anon.
　　Come and make ready all, and sing by thine own;
　　Sing "Lullay!" thou shall, for I must groan,
　　And cry out by the wall on Mary and John,
　　　Full sore.
445 Sing "Lullay" on fast°   *quickly*
　　When thou hears at the last;
　　And but° I play a false cast,   *unless*
　　　Trust me no more.

[*The shepherds meet in a field.*]

THIRD SHEPHERD.   Ah, Coll, good morn! Why sleeps
　　thou not?
450 FIRST SHEPHERD.   Alas, that ever was I born! We have
　　a foul blot!
　　A fat wether° have we lorn.°   *sheep / lost*
THIRD SHEPHERD.   　　Marry, Gods forbott!°   *God forbid!*
SECOND SHEPHERD.   Who should do us that scorn? That
　　were a foul spot.

FIRST SHEPHERD. Some shrew.°   *villain*
I have sought with my dogs
455 All Horbury Shrogs,[1]
And of fifteen hogs°   *young sheep*
    Found I but one ewe.

THIRD SHEPHERD. Now trow me if ye will: by Saint
    Thomas of Kent,[2]
Either Mak or Gill was at that assent!°   *was involved*
460 FIRST SHEPHERD. Peace, man, be still! I saw when he
    went.
Thou slanders him ill; thou ought to repent
    Good speed.°   *speedily*
SECOND SHEPHERD. Now as ever might I the°   *thrive*
If I should even here die,
465 I would say it were he
    That did that same deed.

THIRD SHEPHERD. Go we thither, I rede,° and   *advise*
    run on our feet;
Shall I never eat bread, the sooth till I wit.[3]
FIRST SHEPHERD. Nor drink in my head with him till
    I meet.
470 SECOND SHEPHERD. I will rest in no stead° till   *place*
    that I him greet.
    My brother,
One thing I hight:°   *promise*
Till I see him in sight
Shall I never sleep one night
475   There I do another.[4]

[*They approach Mak's house. They hear Gill groaning
and Mak singing a lullaby.*]

THIRD SHEPHERD. Will ye hear how they hack?[5] Our
    sire list croon.°   *likes to sing*
FIRST SHEPHERD. Heard I never none crack so clear
    out of tune.

---

[1] *All Horbury Shrogs* All the hedges of Horbury (a town near Wakefield).

[2] *Thomas of Kent* Thomas Becket (1118?–1170), Archbishop of Canterbury.

[3] *the sooth till I wit* Until I know the truth.

[4] *Shall I ... do another* I will never sleep in the same place two nights in succession.

[5] *hack* To break a note, i.e., sing badly.

Call on him.
SECOND SHEPHERD. Mak! undo your door soon.
MAK. Who is that spake, as it were noon,
480   On loft?°   *loudly*
Who is that, I say?
THIRD SHEPHERD. Good fellows, were it day!

[*Opening the door.*]

MAK. As far as ye may,
    Good,° speak soft,   *Good fellows*
485 Over a sick woman's head that is at malease;
I had liefer° be dead than she had any   *rather*
    disease.°   *discomfort, distress*
WIFE. Go to another stead; I may not well
    quease.°   *breathe*
Each foot that ye tread goes through my nose,
    So hee!°   *loudly*
490 FIRST SHEPHERD. Tell us, Mak, if ye may,
How fare ye, I say?
MAK. But are ye in this town today?
    Now how fare ye?

Ye have run in the mire, and are wet yit?°   *yet*
495 I shall make you a fire, if ye will sit.
A nurse would I hire—think ye on it?
Well quit is my hire—my dream, this is it!—

[*Points to the cradle.*]

    A season.[6]
I have bairns, if ye knew,
500 Well more than a few;
But we must drink as we brew,
    And that is but reason.°   *reasonable*

I would ye dined ere ye yode; methink that ye sweat.
SECOND SHEPHERD. Nay, neither mends our mood,
    drink nor meat.
505 MAK. Why, sir, ails you aught but good?[7]

---

[6] *A nurse ... season* I would like to hire a nursemaid—what do you think of the idea? I've got what was coming to me—just what I had dreamt of—another child every year.

[7] *Why, sir ... good?* Sir, does something that is not good trouble you?

THIRD SHEPHERD.   Yea, our sheep that we get
  Are stolen as they yode; our loss is great.
MAK.   Sirs, drinks!
  Had I been there,
  Some should have bought it° full sore.   *paid the price*
510 FIRST SHEPHERD. Marry, some men trows°   *believe*
      that ye *were*,
        And that us forthinks.°   *displeases us*

SECOND SHEPHERD. Mak, some men trows that it
      should be ye.
THIRD SHEPHERD. Either ye or your spouse; so say we.
MAK. Now, if ye have suspowse to° of Gill   *suspicion of*
      or of me,
515 Come and rip our house, and then may ye see
        Who had° her.   *took*
  If I any sheep got,
  Either cow or stot°—   *heifer*
  And Gill, my wife, rose not
520   Here since she laid her[1]—

  As I am both true and lele,° to God here I pray,   *loyal*
  That this be the first meal that I shall eat this day.
FIRST SHEPHERD. Mak, as I have zeal, watch out, I say;
  He learned timely to steal, that could not say nay.

[*They begin to search.*]

525 WIFE. I swelt!°   *faint*
  Out, thieves, from my wonys!°   *home*
  Ye come to rob us, for the nonce.°   *on purpose*
MAK. Hear ye not how she groans?
        Your hearts should melt.

[*They approach the cradle.*]

530 WIFE. Out, thieves, from my barn!° Nigh°   *child / approach*
      him not there!
MAK. Wist ye[2] how she had farne,° your   *labored*
      hearts would be sore.
  Ye do wrong, I you warn, that thus comes before

To a woman that has farne[3]—but I say no more!
WIFE. Ah, my middle!
535 I pray to God so mild,
  If ever I you beguiled,
  That I eat this child
        That lies in this cradle.

MAK. Peace, woman, for God's pain, and cry not so:
540 Thou spills thy brain, and makes me full woe.
SECOND SHEPHERD. I trow our sheep be slain. What
      find ye two?
THIRD SHEPHERD. All work we in vain; as well may we go.
        But hatters![4]
  I can find no flesh,
545 Hard nor nesh,°   *soft*
  Salt nor fresh,
        But° two bare platters …   *Except*

[*Nears cradle.*]

  Whik° cattle like this, tame nor wild,   *Live*
  None, as I have bliss, as loud° as he smiled.° *strongly / smelled*
550 WIFE. No, so God give me bliss, and give me joy of my
      child!
FIRST SHEPHERD. We have marked amiss; I hold us
      beguiled.
SECOND SHEPHERD. Sir, done!
  Sir, Our Lady him save!
  Is your child a knave?°   *boy*
555 MAK. Any lord might him have,
        This child, to° his son.   *as*

  When he wakens, he kipps°—what joy to see.   *grips*
THIRD SHEPHERD. In good time to his hips, and in sely![5]
  But who was his gossips,° so soon ready?   *godparents*
560 MAK. So fair fall their lips![6]
FIRST SHEPHERD. (*Aside.*)   Hark now, a lie.
MAK.   So God them thank,
  Parkin, and Gibbon Waller, I say,
  And gentle John Horne, in good fay°—   *faith*

---

1 *And Gill … laid her* And my wife Gill has not gotten up since
she lay down here.

2 *Wist ye* If you knew.

3 *Ye do wrong … has farne* I warn you, you do wrong, coming like
this before a woman who has given birth.

4 *But hatters* An exclamation, "by God's clothing."

5 *In good time … in sely* Good fortune to him, and happiness!

6 *So fair … lips* Blessings on their lips.

He made all the garray°   noise
565   With his great shank.°   legs

SECOND SHEPHERD.   Mak, friends will we be, for we
     are all one.
MAK.   [Aside.] We! Now I hold for me, for
     mends° get I none.   amends
     [To the Shepherds.] Farewell all three! [Aside again.] All
     glad were ye gone.

[They leave the house.]

THIRD SHEPHERD.   Fair words may there be, but love
     is there none
570   This year.
FIRST SHEPHERD.   Gave ye the child anything?
SECOND SHEPHERD.   I trow, not one farthing.
THIRD SHEPHERD.   Fast again will I fling—
     Abide ye me there.

[Goes back into the house.]

575   Mak, take it to no grief° if I come to thy bairn.   don't be upset
MAK.   Nay, thou does me great reprefe,° and foul   reproof
     has thou farn.°   done
THIRD SHEPHERD.   The child will it not grieve, that
     little day-star.
     Mak, with your leave, let me give your bairn
         But sixpence.
580   MAK.   Nay, do way: he sleeps.
THIRD SHEPHERD.   Methinks he peeps.
MAK.   When he wakens he weeps.
         I pray you go hence.

[First and Second Shepherds return.]

THIRD SHEPHERD.   Give me leave him to kiss, and lift
     up the clout.°   cloth

[Lifts the covering.]

585   What the devil is this? He has a long snout!
FIRST SHEPHERD.   He is marked amiss.[1] We wait ill
     about.

---

[1]   *marked amiss*   Deformed, misshapen.

SECOND SHEPHERD.   Ill-spun weft, I wis, ay comes
     foul out.[2]
         Aye, so? [Recognizes the sheep.]
     He is like to our sheep!
590   THIRD SHEPHERD.   How, Gib, may I peep?
FIRST SHEPHERD.   I trow, kind° will creep   nature
         Where it may not go.°   walk (go in a forthright way)

SECOND SHEPHERD.   This was a quaint gaud,°   cunning prank
     and a far cast°—   clever trick
     It was a high fraud!
THIRD SHEPHERD.   Yea, sirs, was't.
595   Let burn this bawd, and bind her fast. (To Gill.)
     A false skawde° hangs at the last;   scold
         So shall thou.
     Will ye see how they swaddle
     His four feet in the middle?
600   Saw I never in a cradle
         A horned lad ere now.

MAK.   Peace, bid I! What, let go your blare!
     I am he that him got, and yond woman him
     bare.°   bore him
FIRST SHEPHERD.   What devil shall ye hat° Mak?   be called
     Lo, God, Mak's heir!
605   SECOND SHEPHERD.   Let be all that. Now God give
     him care,
         I sagh.°   saw
WIFE.   A pretty child is he,
     As sits on a woman's knee;
     A dilly-down[3] par Die,
610   To gar° a man laugh.   make

THIRD SHEPHERD.   I know him by the ear-mark—that
     is a good token.
MAK.   I tell you, sirs, hark, his nose was broken.
     Afterwards, he was forspoken.°   bewitched
FIRST SHEPHERD.   This is a false work—I would fain
     be wroken:°   avenged
615   Get a weapon!
WIFE.   He was taken with° elf,   by
     I saw it myself;

---

[2]   *Ill-spun weft … foul out*   Proverbial: i.e., the deformity of the
parents comes out in the offspring.

[3]   *dilly-down*   Term of endearment.

When the clock struck twelve,
            Was he forshapen.°   deformed

620 SECOND SHEPHERD.   Ye two are well feft° same in a
            stead.°   endowed / together
     FIRST SHEPHERD.   Since they maintain their theft, let's
            do them to dead.
     MAK.   If I trespass eft,° gird° off my head!   again / cut
            With you will I be left.
     FIRST SHEPHERD.   Sirs, do my rede:°   take my advice
            For this trespass,
625 We will neither ban° nor flyte,°   curse / quarrel
     Fight nor chite,°   chide
     But have done as tight,°   quickly
            And cast him in canvas.

     [*They toss Mak up and down in a sheet, and then leave
     his house.*]

     FIRST SHEPHERD.   Lord, what! I am sore, in point for
            to brist;°   burst
630 In faith, I may no more; therefore will I rist.°   rest
     SECOND SHEPHERD.   As a sheep of seven score he
            weighed in my fist.
     For to sleep anywhere, methink that I list.
     THIRD SHEPHERD.   Now I pray you,
            Lie down on this green.
635 FIRST SHEPHERD.   On these thieves yet I mene.°   think
     THIRD SHEPHERD.   Whereto should ye tene?°   be angry
            Do as I say you.

     [*The shepherds lie down.*]
     (*An angel sings "Glory to God in the highest"; then let
     him say:*)

     ANGEL.   Rise, herdmen kind, for now is he born
            Who shall take from the fiend that which Adam had
            lorn:°   lost
640 That warlock to sheynd,° this night is he born.   destroy
     God is made your friend now at this morn.
            He behests
     At Bedlam° go see,   Bethlehem
     There lies that free°   noble one
645 In a crib full poorly,
            Betwixt two beasts.

FIRST SHEPHERD.   This was a quaint stevyn°   voice
            that ever yet I heard.
     It is a marvel to nevyn,° thus to be scared.   report
     SECOND SHEPHERD.   Of God's son of heaven, he
            spake upward.
650 All the wood on a leynn,° methought that he   lighting
            he gard°   made
            Appear.[1]
     THIRD SHEPHERD.   He spake of a bairn
            In Bedlam, I you warn.°   tell
     FIRST SHEPHERD.   That betokens yond star;
            Let us seek him there.

     SECOND SHEPHERD.   Say, what was his song? Heard ye
            not how he cracked it,
     Three breves° to a long?   short notes
     THIRD SHEPHERD.   Yea, marry, he hacked° it.   sang
     Was no crochet° wrong, nor nothing that lacked it.   note
     FIRST SHEPHERD.   For to sing us among, right as he
            knacked it,[2]
660   I can.
     SECOND SHEPHERD.   Let see how ye croon.
     Can ye bark at the moon?
     THIRD SHEPHERD.   Hold your tongues; have done!
     FIRST SHEPHERD.   Hark after, then.

665 SECOND SHEPHERD.   To Bedlam he bade that we
            should gang;°   go
     I am full fard° that we tarry too lang.°   afraid / long
     THIRD SHEPHERD.   Be merry and not sad; of mirth is
            our sang.°   song
     Everlasting glad to mede° may we fang°   reward / get
            Without noise.
670 FIRST SHEPHERD.   Hie we thither, forthy,
     If we be wet and weary,
     To that child and that lady:
            We have it not to lose.

     SECOND SHEPHERD.   We find by the prophecy—let be
            your din!—
675 Of David and Isaiah, and more than I min°—   mind
     They prophesied by clergy, that in a virgin
     Should he light° and lie, to slokyn° our sin   alight / quench

---

[1] *methought … Appear* It seemed to me that he made the whole
wood light up in a flash.

[2] *knacked it* Sang it in a lively or ornate manner.

And slake it,
Our kind from woe;
680   For Isaiah said so:
     Ecce virgo
         Concipiet[1] a child that is naked.

THIRD SHEPHERD.   Full glad may we be and
         abide° that day,   *wait for*
That Lovely One to see that all mights may.[2]
685   Lord, well were me for once and for ay,°   *always*
Might I kneel on my knee some word for to say
         To that child.
But the angel said:
In a crib was he laid,
690   He was poorly arrayed,
         Both mener° and mild.   *poor*

FIRST SHEPHERD.   Patriarchs that have been, and
         prophets beforn,°   *before now*
They desired to have seen this child that is born.
They are gone full clean;° that have they lorn.° *completely / lost*
695   We shall see him, I ween, ere it be morn,
         To° a token.   *As a*
When I see him and feel,
Then wot I full well
It is true as steel
700   That prophets have spoken:

To so poor as we are that he would appear,
First find, and declare by his messenger.
SECOND SHEPHERD.   Go we now, let us fare; the place
         is us near.
THIRD SHEPHERD.   I am ready and yare°—go we in
         fere°   *eager / together*
705   To that bright.
Lord, if thy wills be,
We are lewd,° all three;   *unlearned*
Thou grant us somekins° glee,   *some kind of*
         To comfort thy wight.°   *creature*

[*They enter the stable in Bethlehem.*]

710   FIRST SHEPHERD.   Hail, comely and clean! hail, young
         child!
Hail, Maker, as I mean, of° a maiden so mild!   *born of*
Thou has waried,° I ween, the warlock so wild,[3]   *cursed*
The false guiler° of teyn° now goes he   *deceiver / suffering*
         beguiled.
             Lo, he merries![4]
715   Lo, he laughs, my sweeting!
A well-fare meeting!
I have holden my heting°—   *kept my promise*
         Have a bob° of cherries!   *bunch*

SECOND SHEPHERD.   Hail, sovereign saviour, for thou
         has us sought!
720   Hail, freely foyde° and flower, that all thing   *noble child*
         has wrought!
Hail, full of favour, that made all of nought!
Hail! I kneel and I cower. A bird have I brought
         To my barn.
Hail, little tiny mop,°   *moppet*
725   Of our creed thou art crop!°   *harvest*
I would drink in thy cup,
         Little day-star!

THIRD SHEPHERD.   Hail, darling dear, full of godhead!
I pray thee be near, when that I have need.
730   Hail! sweet is thy cheer! My heart would bleed
To see thee sit here in so poor weed,°   *clothes*
         With no pennies.
Hail! put forth thy dall,°   *hand*
I bring thee but a ball;
735   Have and play thee withall,
         And go to the tennis.

MARY.   The Father of Heaven, God omnipotent,
That made all in seven, his son has he sent.
My name couth° he neven,° and light ere   *could / utter*
         he went.°[5]   *walked*
740   I conceived him full even, through might, as he meant;

---

[1] *Ecce virgo Concipiet* Latin: Behold, a virgin shall conceive…
(Isaiah 7.14).

[2] *That Lovely One … mights may* To see that lovely one that is able
to do all things that can be done.

[3] *the warlock so wild* I.e., the devil.

[4] *Lo, he merries!* Look, he (Christ) is merry!

[5] *and light ere he went* And he could leap before he could walk.
The allusion is to the medieval idea of the Seven Leaps of Christ,
one of which was the Incarnation: Christ was thought of as having
miraculously "leapt" down from heaven into Mary's womb.

And now he is born.
He keep you from woe!
I shall pray him so;
Tell forth as ye go,
745   And mind on° this morn.   *remember*

FIRST SHEPHERD.   Farewell, lady, so fair to behold,
With thy child on thy knee.
SECOND SHEPHERD.   But he lies full cold.
Lord, well is me! Now we go, thou behold.
THIRD SHEPHERD.   Forsooth, already it seems to be told
750   Full oft.
FIRST SHEPHERD.   What grace we have fun!°   *found*
SECOND SHEPHERD.   Come forth, now have we won.
THIRD SHEPHERD.   To sing are we bun—°   *bound*
     Let take on loft! [*They exit, singing.*]

(*Here ends the shepherds' pageant.*)
—C. 1400–1450

Opening page, *The Second Shepherds' Play*, Towneley Plays 1F.38. (Reproduced by permission of *The Huntington Library, San Marino, California*.)

IN CONTEXT

Biblical Source Material

The Second Shepherds' Play supplements Biblical source material very extensively. Here is the relevant Biblical text, in the Douay-Rheims version.

from the Douay-Rheims Bible, Luke 2.8–21

8   And there were in the same country shepherds watching, and keeping the night watches over their flock.

9   And behold an angel of the Lord stood by them, and the brightness of God shone round about them; and they feared with a great fear.

10   And the angel said to them: Fear not; for, behold, I bring you good tidings of great joy, that shall be to all the people:

11   For, this day, is born to you a Saviour, who is Christ the Lord, in the city of David.

12   And this shall be a sign unto you. You shall find the infant wrapped in swaddling clothes, and laid in a manger.

13   And suddenly there was with the angel a multitude of the heavenly army, praising God, and saying:

14   Glory to God in the highest; and on earth peace to men of good will.

15   And it came to pass, after the angels departed from them into heaven, the shepherds said one to another: Let us go over to Bethlehem, and let us see this word that is come to pass, which the Lord hath shewed to us.

16   And they came with haste; and they found Mary and Joseph, and the infant lying in the manger.

17   And seeing, they understood of the word that had been spoken to them concerning this child.

18   And all that heard, wondered; and at those things that were told them by the shepherds.

19   But Mary kept all these words, pondering them in her heart.

20   And the shepherds returned, glorifying and praising God, for all the things they had heard and seen, as it was told unto them.

21   And after eight days were accomplished, that the child should be circumcised, his name was called JESUS, which was called by the angel, before he was conceived in the womb.

Herod the Great[1]

CHARACTERS

Nuntius
Herod
1 Miles
2 Miles
3 Miles
1 Consultus
2 Consultus
1 Mulier
2 Mulier
3 Mulier

(Incipit Magnus Herodes.)[2]

[*Herod's messenger speaks directly to the audience.*]

NUNTIUS. Most mighty Mahowne° meng   *Mohammed*
    you with mirth![3]
Both of burgh° and of town, by fellys°   *city / moor, marsh*
    and by firth,°   *forest*
Both king with crown and barons of brith,°   *birth*
That radly° will rowne,° many great   *quickly / whisper*
    grith°   *protection*
5   Shall behapp.°[4]   *happen*
Take tenderly intent[5]
What sondys° are sent—   *messages*
Else harms shall ye hent,°   *receive*
    And lothes you to lap.[6]

10 Herod, the heynd° king—by grace of   *noble, gracious*
    Mahowne—
Of Jury,° surmonting° sternly with crown   *Jewry / excelling*

On life that are living in tower and in town,
Gracius° you greting, commands you be   *graciously*
    bowne°   *prepared, ready*
    At his bidding.
15 Luf him with lewté;°   *loyalty*
Drede him, that doughty!°   *virtuous, valiant*
He charges you be ready
    Lowly° at his liking.   *Humbly*

What man upon mold° menys him again[7]   *earth*
20 Tytt teyn shall be told[8]—knight, squire, or
    swain.°   *common man*
Be he never so bold, buys he that bargain
Twelve thousandfold more than I sayn,°   *say*
    May ye trast.°   *trust*
He° is worthy wonderly,[9]   *Herod*
25 Selcouthly sorry;[10]
For a boy that is borne hereby
    Stands he abast.°   *upset*

A king they him call, and that we deny.
How should it so fall,° great marvel have I.   *happen*
30 Therefore overall° shall I make a cry   *everywhere*
That ye busk° not to brail,° nor   *attempt, prepare / brawl*
    like not to lye
    This tide.°   *time*
Carpys° of no king   *Speak*
But Herod, that lording,
35 Or busk° to your building   *hurry, hasten*
    Your heads for to hide!

He is king of kings, kindly I know,
Chief lord of lordings, chief leader of law.
There watys° on his wings that bold boast   *waits*
    will blaw:°   *blow*
40 Great dukes down dingys° for his great awe[11]   *fall*
    And him lowtys.°   *revere*
Tuskane and Turky,

---

[1] *Herod the Great* For the present text spelling and punctuation have been substantially modernized from the original Towneley manuscript. Stage directions included in the original appear here in parentheses. Some additional stage directions have been added for the sake of clarity; these appear in square brackets.

[2] *Incipit Magnus Herodes* Latin: here begins Herod the Great.

[3] *meng … mirth* Make you merry!

[4] *Both of … behapp* I.e., the King's messenger is promising protection for virtually everyone.

[5] *Take … intent* Pay close attention.

[6] *And lothes … lap* And troubles will surround you.

[7] *menys him again* Complains against him.

[8] *Tytt teyn shall be told* Shall immediately be dealt out trouble.

[9] *worthy wonderly* Marvelously worthy.

[10] *Selcouthly sorry* Strangely distressed.

[11] *There watys … great awe* There wait under his protective wing those who will boldly proclaim that even great dukes bow down in awe of him.

All Inde and Italy,
Cecyll° and Surry°   *Sicily / Syria*
45   Dread him and dowtys.[1]

From Paradise to Padwa to Mount Flascon,
From Egypt to Mantua unto Kemp town,
From Sarceny to Susa to Greece it abowne,°   *above it*
Both Normondy and Norwa° lowtys°   *Norway / bow*
        to his crown.
50   His renown
Can no tongue tell,
From heaven unto hell.
Of him can none spell°   *speak, say*
        But his cousin Mahowne.

55 He is the worthiest of all barnes° that are born.   *children*
Free men are his thrall,° full teynfully torn.[2]   *servants, slaves*
Begin he to brail, many men catch scorn!
Obey must we all, or else be ye lorne°   *lost*
        At onys.°   *once*
60 Down ding of your knees,
All that him seys!°   *sees*
Displesyd he beys,
        And byrkyn° many bonys.°   *breaks / bones*

Here he commys° now, I cry, that lord I of spake!   *comes*
65 Fast afore will I hy,° radly on a rake,[3]   *hasten, hurry*
And welcome him worshipfully, laughing with lake,°   *glee*
As he is most worthy, and kneel for his sake
        So low;
Down deruly° to fall,   *promptly*
70 As rank most ryall.°   *royal*
Hail, the worthiest of all!
        To thee must I bow.

[*He kneels. King Herod enters accompanied by retainers.*]

Hail, luf lord! Lo, thy letters have I laid.
I have done I couth° do, and peace have   *could*
        I prayed—
75 Mekill° more therto openly displayed.   *Much*

But rumour is raised so, that boldly they brade°   *outburst*
        Emangys them:[4]
They carp of a king;
They cease not sich° chattering.   *such*
80 HEROD.   But I shall tame their talking,
        And let them go hang them.

Stint,° brodels,° your din°—   *Cease / wretches / noise*
        Yea, everychon!°   *everyone*
I red° that ye harkyn° to° I be gone.   *advise / listen / until*
For if I begin, I break ilka° bone   *each, every*
85 And pull fro the skin the carcass anone,°   *quickly, readily*
        Yea, Per Die!°   *by God!*
Cease all this wonder
And make us no blonder,°   *trouble, disturbance*
For I ryfe° you in sonder°   *tear, split / quickly*
90   Be ye so hardy.

Peace, both young and old, at my bidding, I red!
For I have all in wold:° in me stands life   *command, power*
        and dead.°   *death*
Who that is so bold, I brain him through the head!
Speak not or I have told what I will in this stead.
95   Ye wote° not   *know*
All that I will mefe.°   *do*
Stir not but° ye have lefe;°   *unless / permission*
For if ye do, I clefe
        You small as flesh to pot.[5]

100 My mirthes are turned to teyn,° my meekness into
        ire,°   *grief, anger / anger*
And all for one.° I weyn,° within I   *Christ / believe*
        fare° as fire!   *behave*
May I see him with eyn,° I shall give him his   *eyes*
        hire.°   *payment*
But I do as I meyn,° I were a full lewde sire   *intend*
        In wonys.°   *everywhere*
105 Had I that lad in hand,
As I am king in land
I should with this steel brand°   *sword*
        Byrkyn° all his bones.   *Break*

---

[1] *Dread him ... dowtys* Dread and fear him.

[2] *teynfully torn* Distressingly injured.

[3] *radly on a rake* Quickly on (my) way.

[4] *Emangys them* Amongst themselves.

[5] *For if ye ... to pot* For if you do, I will cleave (cut) you as small as flesh for the pot.

My name springs° far and near: the doughtiest,   *extends*
    men me call,

110 That ever ran with spear, a lord and king ryall.

What joy is me to here° a lad to seize my stall!¹   *hear of*

If I this crown may bear, that boy shall buy° for all.   *pay*
    I anger.

I wote not what devil me ails.²

115 They teyn° me so with tales   *trouble, anger*

That, by Gottys dear nails,
    I will peace no langer.³

What, devil! me think I brast° for anger and   *burst*
    for teyn.

I trow° these kings be past that here with me   *believe*
    has been.

120 They promised me full fast or now here to be seen,

For, else I should have cast an other sleght,°   *trick*
    I weyn.°   *believe*
    I tell you

A boy they said they sought,

With offering that they brought.

125 It mefys° my heart right not   *bothers, moves*
    To break his neck in two!

But be they past me by, by Mahowne in heaven,

I shall, and that in hy, set all on six and seven.⁴

Trow ye a king as I will suffer them to
    neven°   *mention, name*

130 Any to have mastery but myself full even?
    Nay, leyfe!°   *gladly*

The devil me hang and draw

If I that losell° knaw,°   *scoundrel / know, recognize*

Bot I gif him a blaw

135   That life I shall him reyfe.⁵

For perils, yit° I would wist° if they   *if / know*
    were gone.

---

¹ *to seize ... stall* To seize my throne!

² *I wote ... me ails* I know not what devil ails me.

³ *by Gotteys ... no langer* By God's dear nails (of the cross) I will no longer have peace.

⁴ *But be they ... on six and seven* But if they have passed by me, by Mohammed in heaven, I shall wreak havoc, and that in a hurry!

⁵ *The devil me hang ... shall him reyfe* The devil hang and draw me if I don't give him a blow such that I deprive him of life, if I should ever recognize that scoundrel.

And ye thereof her told, I pray you say
    anone;°   *at once, immediately*

For, and they be so bold, by God that sits in
    trone,°   *throne*

The pain cannot be told that they shall have,
    ilkon,°   *each one*

140   For ire.⁶

Such pains hard° never man tell,   *heard*

For-ugly and for-fell,°   *most bitter*

That Lucifer in hell
    Their bones shall all to-tire.

145 1 MILES.⁷ Lord, think not ill if I tell you how they
    are past;

I keep not layn, truly.⁸ Syn° they came by you last,   *Since*

Another way in hy they sought, and that full fast.

HEROD. Why, and are they past me by? We,⁹ out!
    for teyn° I brast!   *anger*
    We! Fie!

150 Fie! on the devil! Where may I bide,°   *dwell, wait*

But fight for teyn and al to-chide?°   *scold, fight furiously*

Thiefs,° I say ye should have spied   *Scoundrels*
    And told when they went by.

Ye are knights to trast! Nay, losels ye are, and thieves!

155 I wote I yield° my gast,° so sore my heart it   *give / spirit*
    grieves.

2 MILES. What need you be abast?° There are   *upset*
    no great mischiefs

For these matters to gnast.¹⁰

3 MILES. Why put ye such reprefys°   *reproofs*
    Without cause?

160 Thus should ye not thrett° us,   *threaten*

Ungainly° to bete° us,   *Impurely / beat*

Ye should not rehett° us   *rebuke, scorn*
    Without other sawes.°   *sayings*

HEROD. Fie, losels and liars, lurdans° ilkon!°   *rascals / everyone*

165 Traitors and well wars!° Knaves, but knights   *worse*
    none!

---

⁶ *For ire* Because of my anger.

⁷ *MILES* Latin: soldier.

⁸ *I keep ... truly* I will not hide it.

⁹ *We* An exclamation for attention or emphasis.

¹⁰ *There are no ... to gnast* No mischiefs have been so great as to cause you to gnash your teeth.

Had ye been worth your ears, thus had they not gone.
Get° I those land-lepers, I break ilka° bone.   *If I get / every*
   First vengeance
Shall I see on their bones.
170 If ye bide in these wonys°   *places*
I shall ding° you with stones—   *hit*
   Yea, ditizance doutance![1]

I wote not where I may sit for anger and for teyn.
We have not done all yit, if it be as I weyn.
175 Fie, devil! Now how is it? As long as I have eyn°   *eyes*
I think not for to flitt,° but king I will be seyn   *flee*
   Forever.
But stand I to quart,°   *health*
I tell you my heart:
180 I shall gar° them start,°   *make / flinch*
   Or else trust me never.

1 MILES.   Sir, they went suddenly or° any man wist,   *before*
Else had met we—yea, perdy!° and may ye trist.   *by God*
2 MILES.   So bold nor so hardy against our
   list°   *desire, inclination*
185 Was none of that company durst° met me with   *dared*
   fist,[2]
   For ferd.°   *fear*
3 MILES.   Ill durst they abide,
   But ran them to hide.
   Might I them have spied,
190   I had made them a berd.[3]

What couth° we more do to save your honour?   *could*
1 MILES.   We were ready therto, and shall be ilk hour.
HEROD.   Now, syn° it is so, ye shall have favour.   *since*
Go where ye will go, by town and by tower.
195   Goys° hence! [*The soldiers leave.*]   *Go*
I have matters to mell°   *discuss*
With my privy counsel.

[*To his attendants.*]

Clerks, ye bear the bell;[4]
   Ye must me incense.°   *enlighten*
200 One spoke in mine ear a wonderful°   *marvelous, hard to believe*
   talking,
And said a maiden should bear another to be king.
Sirs, I pray you inquire in all writing,
In Virgil, in Homer, and all other thing
   But legend.[5]
205 Sekys poece-tayllys;[6]
Lefe pistyls and grales;[7]
Mes,° matins,[8] not avails°—   *Mass / has no benefit*
   All these I defend.°   *forbid*

[*They examine various books.*]

I pray you tell, heyndly,° now what ye find.   *quickly*
210 1 CONSULTUS.[9]   Truly, sir, prophecy it is not blind.
We read thus by Isay:[10] He shall be so kinde°   *conceived*
That a madyn, sothely,° which never sinde,°   *truly / sinned*
   Shall him bear.
Virgo concipiet,
215 *Natumque pariet.*[11]
"Emanuel" is hete,°   *he is called*
   His name for to lere:°   *teach*

"God is with us," that is for to say.
2 CONSULTUS.   And other says thus, trust me ye may:
220 "Of° Bedlem° a gracious Lord   *From / Bethlehem*
   shall spray°   *spring*
That of Jury° mightius king shall be ay,   *Jewry*
   Lord mighty;
And him shall honour
Both king and emperor."[12]
225 HEROD.   Why, and should I to him cower?
   Nay, there thou lies lightly!°   *easily, readily*

---

[1] *ditizance doutance!* Without doubt!

[2] *Was none … with fist* None of that company dared meet me in a fistfight.

[3] *I had … a berd* I would have outwitted them.

[4] *ye bear the bell* You are the best.

[5] *But legend* Except scripture.

[6] *Sekys poece-tayllys* Seek tales of poetry.

[7] *Lefe pistyls and grales* Leave epistles and graduals (antiphons, hymns).

[8] *matins* Early morning prayer service.

[9] *CONSULTUS* Latin: counselor.

[10] *Isay* Isaiah (see Isaiah 7.14).

[11] *Virgo … pariet* Latin: A virgin shall conceive and bear a son.

[12] *Of Bedlem … and emperor* Cf. Micah 5.2.

Fie! the devil thee speed, and me, but I drink onys![1]
This has thou done indeed to anger me for the
    nonys.°   *occasion*
And thou, knave, thou thy mede° shall have,   *reward*
    by Cokys° dear bonus!°   *God's / bones*
230 Thou can° not half thy creed.° Out,   *know / belief*
    thiefs, fro° my wonys!°   *from / dwelling*
    Fie, knafys!°   *knaves*
Fie, dottypols,° with your books—   *fools, blockheads*
Go cast them in the brooks!
With such wiles and crooks
235   My wit away rafys.°   *strays, wanders*

Hard I never such a trant,° that a knave so sleight   *trick*
Should come like a saint and refe° me my right.   *deprive*
Nay, he shall on-slant; I shall kill him down stright.[2]
War,° I say, let me pant! Now think I to fight   *Beware*
240   For anger.
My guts will out thring°   *burst, press*
But I this lad hing.°   *hang*
Without° I have a venging,°   *Unless / vengeance*
    I may live no langer.

245 Should a carll° in a cave, but of one year age,   *peasant*
Thus make me to rafe?
  1 CONSULTUS.   Sir, peace this outrage!
Away let ye wafe° all such langage.   *put*
Your worship to safe, is he ought but a page°   *boy*
250   Of a year?[3]
We two shall him teyn°   *injure, harm*
With our wits between,°   *combined*
That, if ye do as I mean,
    He shall die on a spear.

255 2 CONSULTUS.   For dread that he reign, do as we red:
Throughout Bedlem and ilk other stead
Make knights ordain° and put unto dead   *prepare*
All knave-children of two years bred
    And within.°   *under (two years)*
260 This child may ye spill°   *slay, kill*

Thus at your own will.
HEROD.   Now thou says heretill°   *on this matter*
    A right noble gin!°   *scheme*

If I live in land good life, as I hope,
265 This dar I thee warand:° to make thee a pope.   *warrant*
O, my heart is risand° now in a glope!°   *rising / wonder, joy*
For this noble tithand° thou shall have a
    drope°   *news* / *drop*
    Of my good grace:
Marks, rents, and pounds,[4]
270 Great castles and grounds;
Through all sees° and sounds°   *kingdoms / channels*
    I give thee the chase.°   *hunting rights*

Now will I proceed and take veniance.°   *vengeance*

[*To a messenger.*]

All the flower of knighthood call to legeance,°   *allegiance*
275 Bewshere,[5] I thee bid; it may thee avance.
NUNTIUS.   Lord, I shall me speed and bring, perchaunce,
    To thy sight. (*He goes to summon the soldiers.*)
Hark, knights, I you bring
Here new tithing:
280 Unto Herod king
    Haste with all your might,

In all the haste that ye may; in armour full bright,
In your best array, look that ye be
    dight.°   *equipped, prepared*
1 MILES.   Why, should we fray?°   *attack*
285 2 MILES.   This is not all right.
3 MILES.   Sirs, withoutten delay I dread that we fight.
NUNTIUS.   I pray you,
As fast as ye may
Come to him this day.
290 1 MILES.   What, in our best array?
NUNTIUS.   Yea, sirs, I say you.

2 MILES.   Somewhat is in hand, whatever it mean.
3 MILES.   Tarry° not for to stand, there or°   *Delay / before*
    we have been.

---

1 *but I drink onys!* Unless I have a drink!

2 *he shall … down stright* He shall come to grief; I will kill him
immediately.

3 *Your worship … a year?* Saving your worship (i.e., begging your
pardon; excuse me, sir), is he not only a year-old boy?

4 *Marks … pounds* Monies.

5 *Bewshere* Beau sire (i.e., Good sir).

(*They go to Herod.*)

NUNTIUS.   King Herod all-weldand,° well be   *all-ruling*
      ye seen!
295   Your knights are comand° in armour full sheen   *coming*
      At your will.
1 MILES.   Hail, doughtiest° of all!   *strongest*
      We are comen at your call
      For to do what we shall°   *must*
300   Your lust° to fulfill.   *desire, wish*

HEROD.   Welcome, lordingys, iwis,° both great   *truly*
      and small.
      The cause now is this that I send for you all:
      A lad, a knave, born is that should be king ryall;
      But° I kill him and his, I wote I brast my gall.[1]   *Unless*
305   Therefore, sirs,
      Veniance° shall ye take   *Vengeance*
      All for that lad sake;
      And men I shall you make
            Where ye come aywhere,[2] sirs.

310   To Bedlem look ye go, and all the coste° about.   *country*
      All knave children ye slo°—and, lords, ye shall *slay*
            be stout°—   *fierce*
      Of years if they be two and within.° Of all   *under*
            that rout,°   *crowd*
      On life leave none of tho that lies in swedill-clowte,[3]
            I red° you.   *advise*
315   Spare no kin's blood,
      Let all run on flood.
      If women wax woode,°   *grow angry*
            I warn you, sirs, to speed° you.   *hurry*

      Hence, now go your way, that ye were thore.°   *there*
320   2 MILES.   I wote we make a fray; but I will go before.
      3 MILES.   A, think, sirs, I say: I mon wet like a boar.[4]
      1 MILES.   Set me before, ay good enough for a score.[5]

---

[1] *I wote … gall* I know I will burst my gall bladder (the traditional seat of bitterness).

[2] *Where ye … aywhere* Wherever you go, anywhere.

[3] *On life … swedill-clowte* Leave none of those who lie in swaddling clothes alive.

[4] *I mon … boar* I wet (my tusks, in blood) like a boar.

[5] *Set me … score* Put me in front, I'm as skillful as twenty (men).

Hail, heyndly!
      We shall for your sake
325   Make a dulfull lake.°   *painful sport*
HEROD.   Now if ye me well wrake,°   *avenge*
      Ye shall find me friendly.

[*The soldiers continue on their way.*]

2 MILES.   Go ye now till our noytt,° and   *work, profit*
      handle them well.
3 MILES.   I shall pay them on the cote,[6] begin I to
      reyll.°   *riot*

[*A woman comes toward the soldiers with her child.*]

330   1 MILES.   Hark, fellows! ye dote. Yonder comes
      unceyll.°   *misfortune*
      I hold here a grote° she likes me not well   *wager*
      By we part.[7]

[*To the woman, mockingly.*]

      Dame, think it not ill,
      Thy knave° if I kill.   *son*
335   1 MULIER.[8]   What, thief, agans° my will?   *against*
      Lord, keep him in qwarte!°   *good health*

[*The woman is held by the soldiers, but struggles.*]

1 MILES.   Abide° now, abide. No farther thou goes.   *Stop*
1 MULIER.   Peace, thief! Shall I chide and make here a
      nose?°   *noise*
1 MILES.   I shall reyfe thee[9] thy pride. Kill we these
      boyse!°   *boys*
340   1 MULIER.   Tyd may betide,[10] keep well thy nose,
      False thief! [*She hits the soldier.*]
      Have on loft on thy hode![11]
1 MILES.   What, whore, art thou woode?°   *insane*

---

[6] *I shall … the cote* I will beat them.

[7] *By we part* By the time we leave.

[8] *MULIER* Latin: woman.

[9] *reyfe thee* Take away from you.

[10] *Tyd may betide* Time brings what it will.

[11] *Have on … hode* Have a hit on your head!

[He kills the child.]

1 MULIER. Out, alas, my child's blood!
      345   Out, for represe!°   *shame*

Alas for shame and sin! Alas that I was born!
Of weeping who may blin° to see her child   *cease*
    forlorn?°   *forsaken*
My comfort and my kin, my son thus al to-torn!
Veniance for this sin I cry, both evyn° and morn!   *evening*
350 2 MILES.   Well done.

[A second woman comes toward the soldiers with her child.]

Com hedyr, thou old stry:°   *hag*
That lad of thine shall die.
2 MULIER. Mercy, lord, I cry!
    It is mine own dear son.

355 2 MILES. No mercy thou mefe.[1] It mends° thee   *profits*
    not, Mawd.
2 MULIER. Then thy scalp shall I cleave! List thou be
    clawed?[2]

[She tries to fight off the soldier.]

Lefe,° lefe, now bylefe!°   *Leave / stop*
2 MILES.   Peasse, bid I, bawd!°   *prostitute*
2 MULIER. Fie, fie, for represe! Fie, full of frawde—
360   No man!
Have at thy tabard,°   *knight's overcoat*
Harlot and holard:°   *whoremonger*
Thou shall not be sparde!
    I cry and I ban!°   *swear*

[He kills the child.]

365 Out, murder man, I say, strong traitor and thief!
Out, alas, and waloway,° my child that was me   *misery*
    lefe!°   *beloved*
My love, my blood, my play,° that never   *joy, happiness*
    did man grief!
Alas, alas this day, I would my hart should clefe° *cleave*

---

[1] *No mercy ... mefe* No mercy do you inspire.

[2] *List thou ... clawed* Does it please you to be clawed?

In sonder!°   *asunder*
370 Veniance I cry and call
On Herod and his knights all—
Veniance, Lord, upon them fall,
    And mekill° worldys° wonder!   *great / world's*

[A third woman comes toward the soldiers.]

3 MILES. This is well-wrought° gere°   *made / appearance*
    that ever may be.
375 Comes hederward° here! Ye need not to flee.   *hither*
3 MULIER. Will ye do any dere° to my child   *harm*
    and me?
3 MILES. He shall die, I thee swear. His heart blood
    shall thou see.
3 MULIER.   God forbede! *[He kills the child.]*
Thief, thou sheds my childs blood!
380 Out, I cry! I go near wood!
Alas, my heart is all on flood
    To see my child thus bleed!

By God, thou shall aby° this dede that   *pay, suffer for*
    thou has done.
3 MILES. I red° thee not, stry,° by sun   *follow / hag*
    and by moyn.°   *moon*
385 3 MULIER. Have at thee, say I! Take thee ther a
    foyn!°   *wound*

(She attacks him.)

Out on thee, I cry! Have at thy groyn°   *nose, snout*
    Anothere!
This kepe I in store.
3 MILES. Peasse now, no more!
390 3 MULIER. I cry and I rore,
    Out on thee, mans mordere!°   *murderer*

Alas, my babe, mine innocent, my fleshly
    get!° For sorrow   *offspring*
That God me dearly sent, of bales° who may me
    borrow?°   *sorrow, grief / defend*
Thy body is all to-rent! I cry, both even and morrow,
395 Veniance for thy blood thus spent: "Out," I cry, and
    "horow"![3]

---

[3] *horow!* Help (a cry of distress).

1 MILES.   Go lightly!°   *quickly*
Get out of this wonys,°   *place*
Ye trattys,° all at onys,°   *hags / once*
Or by Cokys° dear bones   *God's*
400   I make you go wightly!°   *quickly*

[*The soldiers force the women to leave.*]

They are flayd° now, I wote; they will not abide.   *frightened*
2 MILES.   Let us run foot-hot—now would I we
         hide°—   *hurry*
And tell of this lot,° how we have betide.   *fortune, occurrence*
3 MILES.   Thou can do thy note;° that have   *duty, work*
         I aspide.
405   Go forth now,
Tell thou Herod our tale.
For all our avail,
I tell you, saunce° fail,   *without*
         He will us allow.

410 1 MILES.   I am best of you all, and ever has been;
The devil have my soul but I be first seen!
It sits me to call my lord, as I wene.
2 MILES.   What needs thee to brawl? Be not so keen
         In this anger.
415 I shall say thou did best—
Save myself, as I gest.°   *thought, believed*
1 MILES.   We! that is most honest.
3 MILES.   Go, tarry no langer.

[*The soldiers go to report to Herod.*]

1 MILES.   Hail, Herod, our king! Full glad may ye be.
420 Good tithing we bring. Harkyn now to me:
We have made riding throughout Jure.°   *Jewry*
Well wit ye one thing: that murdered have we
         Many thousands.
2 MILES.   I held them full hot;°   *severely*
425 I paid them on the cote.[1]
Their dammys,° I wote,   *mothers*
         Never binds them in bands.°   *swaddling clothes*

---

[1] *I paid ... cote* I gave it to them hard.

3 MILES.   Had ye seen how I fared when I came among
         them!
There was none that I spared, but laid on and
         dang° them.   *hit, struck*
430 I am worthy of reward. Where I was among them,
I stood and I stared. No pity to hang them
         Had I.
HEROD.   Now, by mighty Mahowne,
That is good of renown,
435 If I bear this crown
         Ye shall have a lady

Ilkon° to him laid,° and wed at his will.   *Each one / presented*
1 MILES.   So have ye long said—do somwhat
         thertill!°   *for that matter*
2 MILES.   And I was never flayed, for good ne for ill.
440 3 MILES.   Ye might hold you well paid°   *satisfied, pleased*
         our lust to fulfill,
         Thus think me,
With treasure untold,
If it like that ye wold[2]
Both silver and gold
445   To give us great plenty.

HEROD.   As I am king crowned, I think it good right.
There goes none on ground that has such a wight.[3]
A hundred thousand pound is good wage for a knight;
Of pennies good and round, now may ye go light
450   With store.°   *plenty, abundance*
And ye knights of ours
Shall have castles and towers,
Both to you and to yours,
         For now and evermore.

455 1 MILES.   Was never none borne, by downs°   *hills*
         ne by dales,°   *valleys*
Nor yit us beforne, that had such avalys.°   *benefits, allowances*
2 MILES.   We have castles and corne,° much   *grain*
         gold in our malys.°   *wallets*
3 MILES.   It will never be worn,° without any   *wasted*
         tales.
         Hail, heyndly!

---

[2] *If it ... wold* If it pleases you.

[3] *wight* Soul, i.e., person; here, refers to the service the knight has given—no one on earth had such a servant.

460 Hail, lord, hail, king!
     We are forth founding.[1]
     HEROD.   Now Mahowne he you bring
         Where he is lord friendly!

[*The soldiers exit.*]

     Now in peace may I stand—I thank thee,
         Mahowne—
465 And give of my land that longs to my crown.

[*To the audience.*]

     Draw therefore nearhand,° both of burgh and   near
         of town:
     Marks, ilkon, a thousand, when I am
         bowne,°   prepared, ready
         Shall ye have.
     I shall be full fain°   happy, glad
470 To give that I sayn.
     Wait when I come again,
         And then may ye crave.°   demand it

     I set by no good, now my heart is at ease,
     That I shed so mekill blood. Peace, all my riches!
475 For to see this flood from the foot to the knees
     Mefys° nothing my mode;° I laugh that I   Moves / mood
         wheeze.
         A, Mahowne,
     So light is my soul
     That all of sugar is my gall![2]
480 I may do what I shall,
         And bear up my crown.

     I was castyn° in care, so frightly afraid!   cast, tossed
     But I there not despair, for low is he laid
     That I most dread are,° so have I him   before
         flayed.°   tortured
485 And else wonder where—and so many strayed
         In the strete—

That one should be harmeles°   unharmed
And skape away, hafles,°   helpless
Where so many childes
490   There balys° cannot bete.°   harms / mend

A hundred thousand, I watt, and forty are slain,
And four thousand. Therat me ought to be fain;
Such a murder on a flat° shall never be again.   field, meadow
Had I had but one bat° at that lurdan°   blow / rascal, wretch
495   So young,
It should have been spoken
How I had me wrokyn,°   avenged myself
Were I dead and rotten,
    With many a tongue.

500 Thus shall I teach knaves ensampyll° to take,   example
In their wits that raves, such master° to   authority
    make.°   claim
All wantones wafys!° no language ye crak!°   avoid / boast
No sufferan you savys;[3] your necks shall I shak
    In sonder!
505 No king ye on call
But on Herod the ryall,°   royal
Or else many one shall
    Upon your bodies wonder.

For if I hear it spoken when I come again,
510 Your brains bese° broken. Therefore, be ye   will be
    bain.°   ready
Nothing bese unlokyn;° it shall be so plain.   explained
Begin I to rokyn,° I think all disdain   shake, rock
    For-daunche.°   fastidious
Sirs, this is my counsel:
515 Bese not too cruel.
But adieu!—to the devil!
    I can no more Franch.° (*Exit.*)   French

(*Explicit Magnus Herodes.*)[4]
—c. 1400–1450

---

[1] *forth founding* Hurrying forth.

[2] *That all … my gall* That my anger is turned to sugar (sweetness).

[3] *All wantones … you savys* Avoid all insolence! Do not boast! No sovereign will save you.

[4] *Explicit Magnus Herodes* Latin: Here ends Herod the Great.

IN CONTEXT

Biblical Source Material

Herod the Great supplements Biblical source material, as do other mystery plays. Here is the relevant Biblical text, in the Douay-Rheims version.

from the Douay-Rheims Bible , Matthew 2

1   When Jesus therefore was born in Bethlehem of Judea, in the days of King Herod, behold, there came wise men from the east to Jerusalem.

2   Saying, Where is he that is born King of the Jews? For we have seen his star in the east, and are come to adore him.

3   And King Herod hearing this, was troubled, and all Jerusalem with him.

4   And assembling together all the chief priests and the scribes of the people, he inquired of them where Christ should be born.

5   But they said to him: In Bethlehem of Judea. For so it is written by the prophet:

6   And thou Bethlehem the land of Judea art not the least among the princes of Judea: for out of thee shall come forth the captain that shall rule my people Israel.

7   Then Herod, privately calling the wise men, learned diligently of them the time of the star which appeared to them;

8   And sending them into Bethlehem, said: Go and diligently inquire after the child, and when you have found him, bring me word again, that I also may come to adore him.

9   Who having heard the King, went their way; and behold the star which they had seen in the east, went before them, until it came and stood over where the child was.

10   And seeing the star they rejoiced with exceeding great joy.

11   And entering into the house, they found the child with Mary his mother, and falling down they adored him; and opening their treasures, they offered him gifts; gold, frankincense, and myrrh.

12   And having received an answer in sleep that they should not return to Herod, they went back another way into their country.

13   And after they were departed, behold an angel of the Lord appeared in sleep to Joseph, saying: Arise, and take the child and his mother, and fly into Egypt: and be there until I shall tell thee. For it will come to pass that Herod will seek the child to destroy him.

14   Who arose, and took the child and his mother by night, and retired into Egypt: and he was there until the death of Herod:

15   That it might be fulfilled which the Lord spoke by the prophet, saying: Out of Egypt have I called my son.

16   Then Herod perceiving that he was deluded by the wise men, was exceeding angry; and sending killed all the men children that were in Bethlehem, and in all the borders thereof, from two years old and under, according to the time which he had diligently inquired of the wise men.

17   Then was fulfilled that which was spoken by Jeremias the prophet, saying:

18   A voice in Rama was heard, lamentation and great mourning; Rachel bewailing her children, and would not be comforted, because they are not.

19   But when Herod was dead, behold an angel of the Lord appeared in sleep to Joseph in Egypt,

20   Saying: Arise, and take the child and his mother, and go into the land of Israel. For they are dead that sought the life of the child.

21   Who arose, and took the child and his mother, and came into the land of Israel.

22   But hearing that Archelaus reigned in Judea in the room of Herod his father, he was afraid to go thither: and being warned in sleep retired into the quarters of Galilee.

23   And coming he dwelt in a city called Nazareth: that it might be fulfilled which was said by prophets: That he shall be called a Nazarene.

THE YORK CRUCIFIXION

c. 1376 – 1569

The York Corpus Christi Play as we know it consists of forty-seven surviving individual plays or "pageants," including *The Crucifixion* (pageant 35), reproduced here, and *The Last Judgment* (pageant 47, included in the website component of the anthology). Together, the 47 pageants comprise a narrative concerning the Christian history of the world from the Creation to Judgment Day, with emphasis on the Passion and Resurrection of Christ. This cycle of plays was produced by the York civic government and its occupational guilds—called "crafts"—and performed annually for nearly 200 years on Corpus Christi day, a mid-summer feast with a movable date. The earliest record we have of the York play is from 1376; the last performances were in the 1560s.

A spectacular and logistically complex event, the York Corpus Christi Play as a whole required the participation of a great many of York's citizens. Each craft, or sometimes a group of crafts, was assigned a pageant for which it would be responsible every year. Individual pageants were performed on "pageant wagons," movable stages custom-built for the sponsoring craft. Each pageant played multiple times on Corpus Christi day at designated stopping places, or "stations," on a pre-determined route through the city's center, thus emphasizing the important economic, social, and religious spaces of the city. The play served both civic and religious purposes, but it was the product of the city and lay devotion, not the Church. Like *The Book of Margery Kempe* and the examples of other late medieval plays included here, the York Corpus Christi Play signifies the growing participation of lay people in devotional culture and spiritual life, and of the urban middle classes in literary culture.

What survives of the complete play is contained in one manuscript, copied some time between 1463 and 1477. This manuscript was the official "register" of the complete cycle, kept by the York civic authorities. Each guild also had a copy of its own individual pageant; all but one of these "originals" have now been lost. Since the cycle was performed annually over two centuries, the surviving register can best be seen as a kind of snapshot of the performance at a point in time. In fact, other records from the city and its crafts tell us that the play changed over time. As a living celebration, performance, and annual event, the York Corpus Christi play was subject to revision and alteration, growing and changing with the city that gave life to it.

Scholars do not know for certain who wrote the York *Crucifixion* or any of the other pageants in the cycle. Linguistic and stylistic evidence suggests that a number of the individual plays were written or at least revised by a single author. Whoever this person was, however, he did not have a hand in the entire cycle. However, there are some thematic unities, or at least continuities, in the cycle. The themes, images, and language of work, labor, manufacture, and craft culture persist throughout. Given the sponsorship of the crafts, this emphasis on work is not surprising; though the crafts or the civic government may have hired clergy or established poets to write the play, the craftsmen underwrote and authorized it.

The Pinners, who made pins, needles, and similar items, produced the *Crucifixion* play. Even though the *Crucifixion* is not about the Pinners' craft in any literal sense, the theme of work and its consequences still drives this version of the Crucifixion narrative, which draws both from Gospel accounts and from legendary and apocryphal material. The soldiers are simultaneously the Roman men who blindly obeyed orders and also late medieval workmen who seek only to get the day's work done and over with, however shoddily, regardless of its effects or consequences. Such purposeful anachronism is a technique common to late medieval art and literature, especially drama, that seeks to make Biblical narratives resonate for late medieval audiences.

Dark humor is also a common trait of medieval drama and can be found even here in this most violent of sacred episodes. Critics have debated the meaning of this cringe-inducing humor. Some have argued that it lulls audience members into unthinking identification with the soldiers until they realize their complicity in the Crucifixion, most of which occurs below a crowded audience's sight-lines until the cross is raised, making viewers belatedly aware of the target of their laughter. Others insist that the laughter heightens the violence and makes it more terrible; thus the play participates in a form of late medieval devotion known as "affective piety," whereby the audience or reader is meant to come to an understanding of God's love through deep feeling and empathy. Still others see the potential for laughter as both mocking the ignorant soldiers and also looking forward to the joy of the Resurrection; the cycle as a whole is a comedy in the classical sense, after all, ending triumphantly for Jesus and the faithful.

The York *Crucifixion* is unusual in late medieval literature, and especially drama, in its isolating the Crucifixion from other events and characters of the Passion narrative, separating it from Jesus's death on the cross and from the representation of those who mourn for him, especially from significant female figures. Contrast it, for example, with the lyric poem "Stond well, moder, under Rode."

The *Crucifixion* is written in 12-line stanzas rhyming a b a b a b a b c d c d. Only Jesus is given full stanzas; the soldiers share stanzas between them, and sometimes their dialogue stretches across stanza boundaries.

⌘ ⌘ ⌘

The York Crucifixion[1]

CHARACTERS

Soldier 1
Soldier 2
Soldier 3
Soldier 4
Jesus

(*Enter four Roman Soldiers with Jesus.*)

SOLDIER 1.   Sir knights, take heed; hither°   *come here*
in hie!°   *haste*

This deed on dergh° we may not draw.[2]   *aside*
Ye wot° yourself as well as I   *know*
How lords and leaders of our law
5 Has° given doom° that this   *Have / judgment*
     dote° shall die.   *fool*
SOLDIER 2.   Sir, all their counsel well we know.
Since we are come to Calvary[3]
Let ilk° man help now as him owe.[4]   *each*
SOLDIER 3.   We are all ready, lo,
10 That forward° to fulfill.   *contract, agreement*
SOLDIER 4.   Let° hear how we shall do,   *Let's*
And go we tite° there-til.°   *quickly / to it*

SOLDIER 1.   It may not help here for to hone°   *delay*
If we shall any worship° win.   *honor*

---

[1]   *The York Crucifixion*   Spelling and punctuation of this text have been modernized in accordance with the practices of this volume, except where that modernization would affect rhyme. Stage directions do not appear in the original text, which exists in one manuscript, the "Register" of the York Corpus Christi Play, created c. 1463–77, now a British Library manuscript. Where stage directions have been added for clarity, they are presented in rounded brackets.

[2]   *on dergh ... draw*   We may not put off.

[3]   *Calvary*   Anglicized Latin name for the place of Jesus' crucifixion. See Luke 23.33: "And when they were come to the place which is called Calvary, they crucified him there."

[4]   *him owe*   He ought to.

15 SOLDIER 2.   He must be dead needling°   *necessarily*
by none.°   *canonical hour of nones, i.e., 3 p.m.*

SOLDIER 3.   Then is good time that we begin.

SOLDIER 4.   Let ding° him down, then is he   *beat*
done.°   *finished, done for*

He shall not dere° us with his din.   *hurt*

SOLDIER 1.   He shall be set and learnèd soon,

20 With care° to him and all his kin.[1]   *sorrow*

SOLDIER 2.   The foulest death of all
Shall he die for his deeds.

SOLDIER 3.   That means cross him[2] we shall.

SOLDIER 4.   Behold, so right° he redes.°   *rightly / counsels*

25 SOLDIER 1.   Then to this work us must take heed,
So that our working be not wrong.

SOLDIER 2.   None other note° to neven°   *task / mention*
is need,°   *needed*

But let us haste him for to hang.

SOLDIER 3.   And I have gone for gear, good speed,[3]

30 Both hammers and nails large and long.

SOLDIER 4.   Then may we boldly do this deed.
Come on, let kill this traitour strong.°   *villainous*

SOLDIER 1.   Fair might ye fall in fere°   *together*
That has wrought on this wise.°[4]   *way*

35 SOLDIER 2.   Us needs not for to lere[5]
Such faitours° to chastise.   *vagrants*

SOLDIER 3.   Since ilk a thing[6] is right arrayed,°   *set in place*
The wiselier now work may we.

SOLDIER 4.   The cross on ground is goodly°   *well*
graid°   *prepared*

40 And bored even as it oweth° to be.   *ought*

SOLDIER 1.   Look that the lad on length be laid
And made° me° then   *secured / for me, i.e., at my command*
unto this tree.°   *cross*

SOLDIER 2.   For all his fare° he shall be   *actions*
flayed,°   *defeated*

That on assay° soon shall ye see.   *trial*

45 SOLDIER 3.   (*To Jesus.*) Come forth thou cursèd knave,
Thy comfort soon shall keel.°   *cool, diminish*

SOLDIER 4.   Thine hire° here shall thou   *payment, wages*
have.

SOLDIER 1.   Walk on! Now work we well.

JESUS.   Almighty God, my father free,°   *noble*

50 Let these matters be made in mind:[7]
Thou bade that I should buxom° be   *obedient*
For Adam's plight for to be pined.°   *pained, punished*
Here to dead° I oblige° me°   *death / obligate / myself*
From that sin for to save mankind,

55 And sovereignly beseech I thee[8]
That they° for° me may   *i.e., all humankind / because of*
favour find.
And from the fiend them fend,°   *defend*
So that their souls be safe
In wealth° withouten° end.   *spiritual bounty / without*

60 I keep not else to crave.[9]

SOLDIER 1.   Wey,[10] hark° sir knights, for   *listen*
Mahound's[11] blood,
Of Adam-kind is all his thought.

SOLDIER 2.   The warlow° waxes° worse   *traitor, felon / grows*
than wood,°   *insane*
This doleful° dead° ne dreadeth he not.[12]   *sorrowful / death*

65 SOLDIER 3.   Thou should have mind,° with   *remembrance*
main and mood,[13]
Of wicked works that thou hast wrought.

SOLDIER 4.   I hope° that he had been as good   *think*

---

[1] *He shall be set … his kin* He will be set straight and educated soon, with sorrow to him and all his kin (as a result).

[2] *cross him* Crucify him.

[3] *good speed* With great haste.

[4] *Fair might … on this wise* May good befall you together who have worked in this way.

[5] *Us … lere* It is not necessary for us to be taught how.

[6] *ilk a thing* Every thing.

[7] *made in mind* Considered.

[8] *And … thee* Principally I beg you.

[9] *I … crave* I desire nothing more.

[10] *Wey* Interjection for getting attention, akin to the modern "hey."

[11] *Mahound's* Mohammad (c. 570–632), prophet and founder of Islam. Medieval English texts often depict all non-Christian and non-Jewish characters as worshipping or otherwise calling on Mohammad.

[12] *ne dreadeth he not* He does not dread.

[13] *with main and mood* Fervently, with determination.

Have ceased of saws° that he up-sought.° [1]   *sayings / made up*
SOLDIER 1.   Those saws shall rue him sare [2]
70 For all his sauntering° sone.°   *babbling / sound*
SOLDIER 2.   Ill speed them [3] that° him spare   *who*
Till he to dead° be done.   *death*

SOLDIER 3.   Have done belive° boy, and make   *quickly*
thee boon,°   *ready*
And bend thy back unto this tree.

(Jesus lies down on the cross.)

75 SOLDIER 4.   Behold, himself has laid him down
In length and breadth as he should be.
SOLDIER 1.   This traitor here tainted° of treason,   *convicted*
Go fest° and fetter him then ye three;   *fasten*
And since he claimeth kingdom with crown,
80 Even as a king here hang shall he.
SOLDIER 2.   Now, certes,° I shall not fine°   *certainly / finish*
Or° his right hand be fest.°   *Ere, before / fastened*

(SOLDIER 2 stands at the right hand of the cross.)

SOLDIER 3.   The left hand then is mine—
Let see who bears him best.

(SOLDIER 3 stands at the left hand of the cross.)

85 SOLDIER 4.   His limbs° on length then shall   *i.e., legs*
I lead,
And even unto the bore° them bring.   *nail hole*

(SOLDIER 4 stands at the foot of the cross.)

SOLDIER 1.   Unto his head I shall take heed,
And with mine hand help him to hang.

[SOLDIER 1 stands at the head of the cross.]

SOLDIER 2.   Now since we four shall do this deed

90 And meddle with this unthrifty° thing,   *unprofitable*
Let no man spare for special speed [4]
Till that we have made ending.
SOLDIER 3.   This forward° may not fail;   *agreement*
Now are we right arrayed.°   *prepared*
95 SOLDIER 4.   This boy here in our bail°   *custody*
Shall bide° full bitter braid.°   *experience / blow*

SOLDIER 1.   Sir knights, say, how work we now?
SOLDIER 2.   Yis,° certes, I hope° I hold   *Indeed / think*
this hand,
And to the bore I have it brought
100 Full buxomly° withouten band.°   *obediently / rope*
SOLDIER 1.   Strike on then hard, for him thee bought. [5]
SOLDIER 2.   Yis, here is a stub° will stiffly stand,   *nail*
Through bones and sinew it shall be sought.°   *found*
This work is well, I will warrant.°   *guarantee*

(SOLDIER 2 nails Jesus's right hand.)

105 SOLDIER 1.   Say sir, how do we
thore?°   *there (i.e., at left side of cross)*
This bargain° may not blin.°   *business / cease*
SOLDIER 3.   It fails° a foot and more,   *falls short*
The sinews are so gone° in.   *shrunken*

SOLDIER 4.   I hope° that mark amiss be bored.   *think*
110 SOLDIER 2.   Than must he bide in bitter bale.°   *misery*
SOLDIER 3.   In faith, it was over-scantly°   *inadequately*
scored,°   *marked*
That makes it foully for to fail.
SOLDIER 1.   Why carp° ye so? Fast° on a cord   *talk / Fasten*
And tug him to, by top and tail. [6]

(SOLDIER 3 tugs Jesus's left hand to reach the poorly bored nail hole)

115 SOLDIER 3.   Ya, thou commands lightly° as a lord;   *easily*

---

[1] *I hope ... up-sought* I think that he would have been as good (i.e., better off) to have ceased those sayings that he made up.

[2] *shall rue him sare* He shall sorely regret.

[3] *Ill speed them* Bad luck to them.

---

[4] *Let ... speed* Let none of us refrain from all due speed.

[5] *for him thee bought* For the sake of him (i.e., Jesus) who redeemed you. Refers anachronistically to medieval Christian redemption theology, in which Jesus' death on the cross ransomed souls from eternal death.

[6] *And tug ... tail* And tug him to (the holes) from top to bottom.

Come help to haul, with ill hail.[1]

SOLDIER 1. Now certes that shall I do—
Full snelly as a snail.[2]

SOLDIER 3. And I shall tach° him to,°   *tack, nail / to (the cross)*
120 Full nemely° with a nail.   *nimbly*

(SOLDIER 3 nails Jesus's left hand to the cross.)

This work will hold, that dare I hete,°   *promise*
For now are fest fast° both his hend.°   *firmly / hands*

SOLDIER 4. Go we all four then to his feet,
So shall our space° be speedily spend.°   *time / spent*

125 SOLDIER 2. Let see what bourd° his bale might   *jest*
bete;[3]
There-to° my back now would I bend.   *To that (task)*

SOLDIER 4. Oh, this work is all unmeet!°   *unworthy*
This boring° must all be amend.   *the bore-holes*

SOLDIER 1. Ah, peace man, for Mahound,
130 Let no man wot° that   *know about*
wonder.°   *marvel (i.e., poorly bored holes)*
A rope shall rug° him down   *yank*
If° all his sinews go asunder.   *Even if*

SOLDIER 2. That cord full kindly° can I   *thoroughly*
knit,°   *tie*
The comfort of this carl° to   *churl, base fellow*
keel.°   *cool, diminish*

135 SOLDIER 1. Fest on then fast that all be fit,
It is no force how fell° he feel.   *terrible*

*(They pull down on his feet to stretch his body to fit the
incorrectly bored holes.)*

SOLDIER 2. Lug on ye both a little yet.
SOLDIER 3. I shall not cease, as I have sele.°   *bliss*
SOLDIER 4. And I shall fond° him for to hit.[4]   *test*
140 SOLDIER 2. Oh, hail!°   *heave!*

SOLDIER 4.   Ho° now, I hold it well.[5]   *Hold, stop*

SOLDIER 1. Have done, drive in that nail,
So that no fault be found.

SOLDIER 4. This working would not fail
If four bulls here were bound.

(SOLDIER 4 nails Jesus's feet to the cross.)

145 SOLDIER 1. There cords have evil° increased   *evilly*
his pains,
Or° he were till° the borings brought.   *Before / to*

SOLDIER 2. Ya, asunder are both sinews and veins
On ilk a side, so have we sought.

SOLDIER 3. Now all his gauds° nothing him gains,   *tricks*
150 His sauntering° shall with bale be bought.   *babbling*

SOLDIER 4. I will go say to our sovereigns
Of all this work how we have wrought.

SOLDIER 1. Nay sirs, another thing
Falls first to you and me—
155 They bade we should him hang
On height that men might see.

SOLDIER 2. We wot° well so° their   *know / thus, such*
words wore,°   *were*
But sir, that deed will do us dere!°   *harm*

SOLDIER 1. It may not mend° for to moot°   *help / argue*
more,
160 This harlot° must be hangèd here.   *base fellow, rogue*

SOLDIER 2. The mortise° is made   *hole (to hold base of cross)*
fit therefore.

SOLDIER 3. Fest on your fingers then, in fere.[6]

(They try unsuccessfully to lift the cross.)

SOLDIER 4. I ween° it will never come   *believe*
thore;°   *(up) there*
We four raise it not right to-year.[7]

165 SOLDIER 1. Say man, why carps° thou so?   *talk*
Thy lifting was but light.°   *little*

---

[1] *with ill hail* Bad luck to you! Interjection of displeasure and
impatience.

[2] *Full snelly as a snail* As quickly as a snail.

[3] *Let see … bete* Let's see what jest can mend his sorrow (i.e., the
soldiers treat stretching Jesus as a game to amuse him).

[4] *fond him for to hit* Test him by hitting (him).

[5] *I hold it well* I think it (i.e., the task) has been done well.

[6] *in fere* All together.

[7] *We … to-year* We four will not raise it right in a year.

SOLDIER 2. He means there must be mo°   *more (men)*
To heave him up on height.

SOLDIER 3. Now certes, I hope it shall not
          need°   *be necessary*
170   To call to us more company.
Methinks° we four should do this deed   *It seems to me*
And bear him to yon° hill[1] on high.   *yonder*

SOLDIER 1. It must be done, withouten dread.
No more, but look ye be ready,
175   And this part° shall I lift and lead.   *i.e., the head*
On length° he shall no longer lie.   *prone*
Therefore now make you boun;°   *ready*
Let bear him to yon hill.

SOLDIER 4. Then will I bear here down,°   *i.e., at the feet*
180   And tend his toes until.

SOLDIER 2. We two° shall see till   *i.e., SOLDIERS 2 and 3*
          either side,
For else this work will wry° all wrong.   *go awry*

SOLDIER 3. We are ready.

SOLDIER 4.   Good sirs, abide,°   *wait*
And let me first his feet up fang.°   *take*

185   SOLDIER 2. Why tend ye so to tales°   *talking*
          this tide?°   *time*

SOLDIER 1. Lift up!

(They try again to lift the cross.)

SOLDIER 4.   Let see!°   *Watch out!*
SOLDIER 2.   Oh, lift along.°   *lengthwise*
SOLDIER 3. From all this harm he should him° *himself*
          hide
And° he were God.   *If*
SOLDIER 4.   The devil him hang!
SOLDIER 1. For great harm have I hent°—   *received*
190   My shoulder is in-sunder.°   *asunder*
SOLDIER 2. And certes I am near shent,°   *disgraced, ruined*
So long have I borne under.[2]

SOLDIER 3. This cross and I in two must twin,°   *separate*
Else breaks my back in-sunder soon.

195   SOLDIER 4. Lay° down again and leave your *Set (the cross)*
          din,
This deed for us will never be done.

(They put the cross down.)

SOLDIER 1. Assay° sirs, let see if any gin°   *Try / device*
May help him up withouten hone,°   *hesitation*
For here should wight° men worship° win,   *strong / honor*
200   And not with gauds° all day to gone.   *nonsense*

SOLDIER 2. More wighter men than we
Full few I hope ye find.

SOLDIER 3. This bargain° will not be,   *business*
For certes me wants wind.[3]

205   SOLDIER 4. So wil° of work never we   *bewildered*
          wore.°   *were*
I hope this carl some cautels° cast.   *tricks, spells*

SOLDIER 2. My burden set me wonder sore;
Unto the hill I might not last.

SOLDIER 1. Lift up, and soon he shall be thore;°   *there*
210   Therefore fest on your fingers fast.

SOLDIER 3. Oh, lift!

(They try again to lift the cross.)

SOLDIER 1.   Wey, lo!
SOLDIER 4.   A little more.
SOLDIER 2. Hold then!
SOLDIER 1.   How now?
SOLDIER 2.   The worst is past.
SOLDIER 3. He weighs a wicked weight.

*(They reach the place where the cross will be erected on
the "hill.")*

SOLDIER 2. So may we all four say,
215   Or° he was heaved on height   *Already*
And raised in this array.°   *manner*

---

¹ *yon hill* Refers either to the pageant wagon (if the action so far
has taken place on the ground) or the opposite end of the wagon if
the nailing scene is performed on the wagon.

² *borne under* Borne under the weight of the cross.

---

³ *me wants wind* I am lacking breath; i.e., I need to catch my
breath.

SOLDIER 4.   He made us stand° as any stones,   *motionless*
So boustous° was he for to bear.   *awkward, huge*
SOLDIER 1.   Now raise him nemely° for the   *nimbly*
nones[1]

220 And set him° by this mortise here,   *i.e., Jesus on the cross*
And let him fall in all at once,
For certes that pain shall have no peer.
SOLDIER 3.   Heave up!

(*They raise the cross upright and maneuver it into the mortise.*)

SOLDIER 4.   Let down, so all his bones
Are asunder now on sides sere.[2]

(*They drop the cross into the mortise.*)

225 SOLDIER 1.   This falling was more fell°   *wicked, harmful*
Than all the harms he had.
Now may a man well tell°   *count*
The least lith° of this lad.   *limb*

SOLDIER 3.   Methinketh this cross will not
abide°   *hold steady*
230 Ne° stand still in this mortise yet.   *Nor*
SOLDIER 4.   At the first time was it made over-wide;
That makes it° wave, thou may well   *i.e., the cross*
wit.°   *perceive*
SOLDIER 1.   It shall be set° on ilk a side   *stabilized*
So that it shall no further flit.°   *move from side to side*
235 Good wedges shall we take this tide°   *time*
And fest the foot,° then is all fit.   *i.e., of the cross*
SOLDIER 2.   Here are wedges arrayed°   *laid out*
For that, both great and small.
SOLDIER 3.   Where are our hammers laid
240 That we should work withal?°   *with*

SOLDIER 4.   (*Picking up hammer.*) We have them here
even at our hand.
SOLDIER 2.   (*Picking up wedge.*) Give me this wedge, I
shall it in drive.

SOLDIER 4.   (*Picking up another wedge.*) Here is
another yet ordand.°   *ordained, prepared*
SOLDIER 3.   Do take° it me° hither   *give / to me*
belive.°   *at once*
245 SOLDIER 1.   Lay on then fast.
SOLDIER 3.   Yis, I warrant.
I thring° them same,° so mote° I thrive.   *knock / together / must*
Now will this cross full stably stand,
All° if he rave they° will not rive.°   *Even / i.e., the wedges / split*
SOLDIER 1.   (*To Jesus.*) Say sir, how likes you now,
250 This work that we have wrought?
SOLDIER 4.   (*To Jesus.*) We pray you say us how
Ye feel, or° faint ye ought.°   *before / need to*

JESUS.   (*To audience.*) All men that walk by way or street,
Take tent° ye shall no travail tine.[3]   *heed*
255 Behold mine head, mine hands, and my feet,
And fully feel now, or ye fine,°   *finish*
If any mourning may be meet,°   *matched with*
Or mischief° measured° unto mine.   *misfortune / compared*
(*He prays.*) My father, that all bales may
bete,°   *make better, put right*
260 Forgives° these men that do me pine.°   *Forgive / pain*
What they work wot they not;[4]
Therefore, my father, I crave,
Let never their sins be sought,°   *examined*
But see their souls to save.

265 SOLDIER 1.   Wey, hark, he jangles° like a jay.   *chatters*
SOLDIER 2.   Methinks he patters[5] like a pie.°   *magpie*
SOLDIER 3.   He has been doing all this day,
And made great moving° of mercy.   *prompting*
SOLDIER 4.   Is this the same that gun° us° say   *did / to us*
270 That he was God's son almighty?
SOLDIER 1.   Therefore he feels full fell° affray,°   *fierce / attack*
And deemèd° this day for to die.   *judged*

---

[1] *for the nones*   At once.

[2] *on sides sere*   Into many sections.

---

[3] *Take tent … tine*   Take heed you do not lose the work (of my suffering); i.e., do not lose the meaning and message of this.

[4] *Forgives … wot they not*   See Luke 23.34: "And Jesus said: Father, forgive them, for they know not what they do."

[5] *patters*   Chatters; but also, recites a prayer. Play on the Latin version of the Lord's Prayer, which begins "Pater noster," often used derogatively to mean mumbling prayers indistinctly.

SOLDIER 2.   Vah! qui destruis templum![1]

SOLDIER 3.   His saws were so, certain.°   *certainly*

275 SOLDIER 4.   And sirs, he said to some
            He might raise it° again.   *i.e., the temple*

SOLDIER 1.   To muster that he had no might,
            For all the cautels that he couth° cast.   *knew how to*
            All if he were in word so wight,°   *strong*
280   For° all his force now he is fest.°   *Despite / fastened, caught*
            As Pilate[2] deemed is done and dight,°   *dealt with*
            Therefore I rede° that we go rest.   *counsel, advise*

SOLDIER 2.   This race° mon° be   *action / must*
            rehearsed° right,   *reported*
            Through the world both east and west.

285 SOLDIER 3.   Ya, let him hang here still
            And make moues° on° the moon.   *grimaces / at*

SOLDIER 4.   Then may we wend° at will.   *go*

SOLDIER 1.   Nay good sirs, not so soon,

            For certes us needs another note:°   *advantage*
290   This kirtle° would I of you crave.   *tunic (i.e., Jesus's tunic)*

SOLDIER 2.   Nay, nay sir, we will look by lot°   *lottery, draw*
            Which of us four falls° it to have.   *chances*

SOLDIER 3.   I rede° we draw cut° for   *counsel / lots, straws*
            this coat.
            Lo, see how soon°—all sides to save.°   *quickly / be fair to*

295 SOLDIER 4.   The short cut shall win, that well ye wot,
            Whether it fall to knight or knave.

SOLDIER 1.   Fellows, ye thar° not flyte,°   *need / argue*
            For this mantle is mine.

SOLDIER 2.   Go we then hence tite,°   *quickly*
300   This travail° here we tine.°   *labor / lose*
            —c. 1463–77

---

[1] *Vah! qui destruis templum!* Latin: Hah! You who destroy the temple! See Mark 15.29: "And they that passed by blasphemed him, wagging their heads, and saying: Vah, thou that destroyest the temple of God, and in three days buildest it up again." See also Matthew 27.40.

[2] *Pilate* Pontius Pilate, Roman prefect (governor) of Judea (26–36? CE), before whom Jesus was brought for judgment in all four Gospel accounts and in the plays preceding this one. According to the Gospel accounts, he evaded responsibility for Jesus's final judgment, but he would have overseen executions nevertheless, and so the crucifixion is "done and dight" as "Pilate deemed."

MANKIND

*M*ankind is one of only a handful of extant "morality plays"—a form that became popular in England between 1400 and 1550, at roughly the same period as the surviving biblical pageant plays. "Morality play" is not a medieval term, but rather a term of convenience first applied to this genre in the eighteenth century. The morality play is a secular form, and unlike the cycle plays it does not tell stories from the Bible or about the lives of the saints. Most morality plays, however, have an overtly religious message and tone. Morality plays may well have developed out of the "Pater Noster" ("Our Father") prayer and its dramatic derivatives, the Pater Noster play, of which no texts have survived. These plays apparently focused on what were known as the seven cardinal virtues (prudence, justice, temperance, fortitude, faith, hope, and charity) and the seven deadly sins (pride, envy, anger, greed, gluttony, lust, and sloth), and depicted life as a *psychomachia*, or the constant struggle between good and evil within the human soul. The topic of the war between virtue and sin was also favored by popular preachers of the time, which encouraged its entrance into general public discourse. Linked to this focus on vice and virtue was an increasing interest in allegory as an artistic form, as well as a heightened attention to questions of death and the afterlife within Christian thought of the time. The morality play was one artistic result of the convergence of these interests.

Mankind can be reliably dated to the reign of Edward IV (1465–70) because of its mention of Edward and of the new coins issued in the period. The play was probably performed near Cambridge, as it alludes to villages in the area and the linguistic forms preserved in the manuscript of *Mankind* are consistent with an East Anglian dialect.

Like other morality plays, *Mankind* is an allegorical drama with a universal human character as its protagonist and with a focused moral purpose. The play's central story involves the temptation of Mankind, the play's main character, by the Vices (Mischief, along with Nought, Nowadays, and New Guise), as well as Titivillus (in Christian tradition, one of Satan's demons). These Vices are portrayed as both physically and verbally playful, in contrast to Mercy, with his more reserved behavior and ornate, Latinate language.

Mankind is distinctive among morality plays in its energetic theatricality and its clever use of language. It is unique among extant morality plays in its incorporation of a direct fundraising appeal by the players: during the play the performance is stopped until the audience is able to provide enough money to lure the devil Titivillus into appearing onstage. Formal differences in the play's stanzas distinguish between different sorts of speakers. The Vices speak in eight-line stanzas, the Virtue Mercy in four-line stanzas. When Mankind succumbs to temptation his speeches are patterned like those of the Vices; when he inclines towards virtue they are patterned like those of Mercy.

Little is known of the early performance history of morality plays such as *Mankind*; we do not know, for example, if they were frequently staged by guilds in a manner similar to that of much biblical drama of the period. In the sixteenth century we know that morality plays were sometimes performed by troupes of itinerant players. With the development in the late sixteenth century of more permanent performance spaces and of companies of players sponsored by patrons, the old form of morality play died out. Nevertheless, the form survived in its influence on later drama, most notably in the Seven Deadly Sins segment of Christopher Marlowe's *Doctor Faustus* (1588).

⌘ ⌘ ⌘

Mankind[1]

DRAMATIS PERSONAE

Mankind
Mercy
Titivillus[2]
Mischief
New-Guise
Nowadays
Nought

(*Enter Mercy.*)

MERCY. The very founder and beginner of our first creation,
Among us sinful wretches He oweth° to be magnified, *ought*
That for our disobedience He had none indignation
To send His own son to be torn and crucified.
5 Our obsequious service to Him should be applied,
Where He was Lorde of all and made all thing of nought,
For the sinful sinner to had him revived,
And, for his redemption, set His own Son at nought.

It may be said and verified: mankind was dere bought.[3]
10 By the pitious death of Jhesu he had his remedy.
He was purged of his defawte,° that wretchedly *default, sin*
had wrought,
By His glorious Passion, that blissyde° lavatory.° *blessed / purifier*
O soverence, I beseech yow° your conditions to rectify, *you*
And with humility and reverence to have a remotion
15 To this blissyde prince that our nature doth glorify,
That ye may be participable of His retribution.

I have be° the very mean° for your restitution. *been /means*
Mercy is my name, that mournith° for your offence *mourns*
Divert not yowrsilffe° in time of temptation, *yourself*
20 That ye may be acceptable to God at your going hence.
The great mercy of God, that is of most preemminence,
By meditation of Our Lady, that is ever
habundaunte° *abundant, generous*
To the sinful creature that will repent his necligence.° *negligence*
I pray God, at your most need, that mercy be your
defendawnte.° *defendant*
25 In good works I avise° yow, soverence,° to *advise / masters*
be perseveraunte° *perseverant*
To purify your sowlys,° that they be not corrupt; *souls*
For your gostly° enmy° will make his *spiritual / enemy*
avaunte,° *boast*
Your good conditions if he may interrupt.

O ye soverens that sit, and ye brothern° that *brethren, fellows*
stand right up,
30 Prick not your felicites in things transitory!
Behold not the earth, but lift your eye up!
See how the head the members daily do magnify.
Who is the head, forsoth, I shall yow certify:
I mean our Saviour, that was likynnyde° to a lamb; *likened*
35 And His saints be the members that daily He doth satisfy
With the precious rever° that runnith° from His *river / runs*
womb.

There is none such food, by water nor by londe,° *land*
So precious, so glorious, so needful to our entent;
For it hath dissolved mankind from the bitter bond
40 Of the mortal enmye,° that venomous serpent— *enemy*
From the which God preserve yow all at the Last Judgement!
For sekirly° there shall be a strait° *surely / strict, rigorous*
examination:
The corn shall be saved, the chaffe[4] shall be brente.° *burned*
I beseech yow heartily, have this in
premeditation.° *thought, meditation*

(*Enter Mischief.*)

45 MISCHIEF. I beseech yow heartily, leave your calculation!
Leave your chaffe, leave your corn, leave your
daliacion!° *idle, frivolous talk*

---

[1] *Mankind* In the present text, spelling and punctuation have been substantially modernized from the original in accordance with the practice of this anthology. Where stage directions are from the original text, they appear in parentheses. Some additional stage directions are here added for the sake of clarity; these appear in square brackets. The play survives in a single text, Folger Shakespeare Library MS Va. 354.

[2] *Titivillus* Traditionally, the name of a devil whose role was to record idle words spoken in churches and any Latin errors committed by priests, and store them in a bag for use as evidence against the speakers on Judgment Day; cf. Matthew 12.36.

[3] *dere bought* Dearly redeemed.

[4] *chaffe* Husks of corn, i.e., grain.

Your wit is little, your head is mekyll,° ye   *large*
    are full of predication.°   *preaching*
But, sir, I pray you this question to clarify:
Misse-masche, driff-draff,[1]
50   Some was corn and some was chaffe,
My dame said my name was Raffe;
On-schett° your lock and take an   *Un-shut, open*
    halpenye.°   *halfpenny*

MERCY.   Why come ye hither, brother? Ye were not desired.
MISCHIEF.   For a winter corn-thresher, sir, I have hired,
55   And ye said the corn should be saved and the chaff
    should be feryde.°   *burned*
And he provith° nay, as it schewth by this verse: *proves*
"*Corn servit bredibus, chaffe horsibus, straw firybusque.*"[2]
This is as much to say, to your lewd understanding,
As: the corn shall serve to bread at the next baking;
60   "*Chaff horsibus,*" *et reliqua,*[3]
The chaff to horse shall be good provente;°   *food*
When a man is for-colde,° the straw may   *very cold*
    be brent,
And so forth, *et cetera.*

MERCY.   Avoid, good brother! Ye ben° culpable   *are*
65   To interrupt thus my talking delectable.
MISCHIEF.   Sir, I have nother° horse nor sadle,   *neither*
Therefore I may not ride.
MERCY.   Hie° yow forth on foot, brother,   *Hurry, hasten*
    in God's name!
MISCHIEF.   I say, sir, I am come hedyr° to make   *hither*
    yow game.
70   Yet bade ye me not go out in the devil's name,
And I will abide.

MERCY.   [*Here there is a break in the manuscript; a leaf is
missing. Evidently Mischief exits during the missing section
and New-Guise, Nowadays and Nought up the banter, with
the first two exhorting Nought to dance in a more lively
fashion.*]

NEW-GUISE.   And how, minstrels, play the common
    trace!°   *dance*

---

[1] *Misse-masche, driff-draff* Sing-song nonsense.

[2] *Corn ... firybusque* Mock Latin: corn serves for bread, chaff for
horses, straw for fires.

[3] *et reliqua* Latin: and the rest.

Lay on with thy ballys° till his belly   *rod, switch for flogging*
    breste!°   *bursts*
NOUGHT.   I put case[4] I break my neck: how than?°   *then*
75   NEW-GUISE.   I give no force, by Saint Anne!
NOWADAYS.   Leppe° about lively! Thou art a   *Leap*
    wight° man.   *active, agile*
Let us be merry while we be here.
NOUGHT.   Shall I break my neck to schew° yow sport?   *provide*
NOWADAYS.   Therefore ever beware of thy report.
80   NOUGHT.   I beschrew° ye all! Here is a shrewd sort.   *curse*
Have thereat, then, with a merry cheer!

(*Here they daunce. Mercy seyth:*)

MERCY.   Do way! do way this revel, sirs, do way!
NOWADAYS.   Do way, good Adam, do way?
This is no part of thy play.
85   NOUGHT.   Yis, mary, I pray yow, for I love not this revelling.
Come forth, good fader,° I yow pray!   *father*
By a little ye may assay.
Anon,° off with your clothes, if ye will play.   *At once*
Go to! for I have had a praty° scottlinge.°   *pretty / caper*

90   MERCY.   Nay, brother, I will not dance.
NEW-GUISE.   If ye will, sir, my brother will make yow to
    prance.
NOWADAYS.   With all my heart, sir, if I may yow
    avaunce.°   *assist, help*
Ye may assay° by a little trace.   *try*
NOUGHT.   Yea, sir, will ye do well?
95   Trace not with them, by my counsel,
For I have traced somewhat too fell—
I tell you it is a narow space!

But sir, I trow, of us three I heard yow speak.
NEW-GUISE.   Christ's curse had ye therefore! for I was in
    sleep.
100 NOWADAYS.   And I had the cup in my hand, ready to
    go to mete.°   *dine, eat*
Therefore, sir, curtly great yow well.
MERCY.   Few words, few and well set!
NEW-GUISE.   Sir, it is the new guise and the new
    jett:°   *fashion, style*
Many words, and schortely° set—   *shortly, curtly*
105 This is the new guise, every dele.°   *bit, thing*

---

[4] *I put case* Assume for the sake of argument that.

MERCY.   Lady, help! How wretches delight in their
 simple ways!

NOWADAYS.   Say nought again° the new guise   *against*
 nowadays!

 Thou shall find us shrews at all assays.°   *trials*

 Beware, ye may soon like a bofett!°   *blow, strike*

110 MERCY.   He was well occupied that brought you,
 brether!°   *brother*

NOUGHT.   I harde° yow call "New-Guise, Nowadays,   *heard*
 Nought," all these three together.

 If ye say that I lie, I shall make yow to slither:°   *fall*

 Lo, take yow here a trepett!° (*Trips him.*)   *trip*

MERCY.   Say me your names. I know yow not.

115 NEW-GUISE.   New-Guise, I.

NOWADAYS.   I, Nowadays.

NOUGHT.   I, Nought.

MERCY.   By Jhesu Crist, that me dear bought,
 Ye betray many men.

120 NEW-GUISE.   Betray? Nay, nay, sir, nay, nay!

 We make them both fresh and gay.

 But of your name, sir, I yow pray,

 That we may yow ken.°   *know*

MERCY.   "Mercy" is my name by denomination.

125 I conceive ye have but a little favour in my communication.

NEW-GUISE.   Ey, ey, your body is full of English Latin!

 I am aferde° it will brest.   *afraid, scared*

 "Pravo te,"[1] quod° the bocher° onto me   *said / butcher*

 When I stale° a leg a mutton.   *stole*

130 NOWADAYS.   Ye are a strong cunning clerk;

 I pray yow heartily, worshipful clerk,

 To have this English made in Latin:

 "I have eaten a dish-full of curds,

 And I have schetun°[2] your mouth full of turds."—   *shitten*

135 Now, open your satchel with Latin words

 And say me this in clerical manner!

 Also, I have a wife—her name is Rachel—

 Betwix° her and me was a great battle,   *Between*

 And fain of yow I would here tell

140 Who was the most master.

---

¹ *Pravo te*   Latin: I curse you.

² *schetun*   To defile with excrement, to deceive.

NOUGHT.   Thy wife Rachel, I dare lay twenty lise.[3]

NOWADAYS.   Who spake° to thee, foll?° Thou art   *spoke / fool*
 not wise.

 Go and do that longith° to thine office: *belonging, fitting*
 Osculare fundamentum![4]

145 NOUGHT.   Lo, master, lo, here is a pardon belly-
 mett°—   *satisfying*

 It is granted of Pope Pocket:

 If ye will putt your nose in his wife's sokett,°   *hole, i.e., vagina*

 Ye shall have forty days of pardon.

MERCY.   This idle language ye shall repent!

150 Out of this place I would ye went.

NEW-GUISE.   Go we hence all three with one assent.

 My fadyr is irke° of our eloquence;   *irked, annoyed*

 Therefore I will no longer tarry.

 God bring you, master, and blissyd Mary,

155 To the number of the demonical friary![5]

  · · · · · ·

NOWADAYS.   Come wind, cum rain,

 Though I come never again.

 The devil put out both your eyn!°   *eyes*

 Fellows, go we hence tight.

160 NOUGHT.   Go we hence, a devil way!

 Here is the door, here is the way. (*To Mercy.*)

 Farewell, gentle Jaffrey,

 I pray God give you good night!

(*Exiant simul. Cantent.*)[6]

MERCY.   Thankyd be God we have a fayer deliverance[7]

165 Of these three onthrifty° guests!   *worthless*

 They know full little what is their ordinance.

 I preve,° by reason, they be worse than beasts: *prove*

 A best° doth after his natural institution;   *beast*

 Ye may conceive, by their disport and behaviour,

---

³ *lise*   I.e., lis. An obsolete abbreviation, li, libra for pound; i.e., the wager here is twenty pounds.

⁴ *Osculare fundamentum*   Latin: Kiss my ass!

⁵ A line is missing to complete the stanza.

⁶ *Exiant … Cantent*   Latin: Let them all go out together. Let them sing.

⁷ *a fayer deliverance*   Good riddance.

170   Their joy and delight is in derision
Of their own Christ, to His dishonour.

This condition of living, it is prejudicially—
Beware thereof! It is worse than any felony or treason.
How may it be excused before the Justice of all,
175   When for every idle word we must yield a reason?

They have great ease; therefore they will take no thought.
But how then, when the angel of heaven shall blow
        the trumpe°   trumpet
And say to the transgressors that wickedly hath wrought:
"Come forth onto your judge, and yield your account"?

180   Then shall I, Mercy, begin sore to weep.
Nother° comfort nor counsel there shall none be had,   Neither
But such as they have sown, such shall they reap.
They be wanton now, but then shall they be sad.

The good new guise nowadays I will not disallow;
185   I discommend the vicious guise. I pray have me excused,
I need not to speak of it; your reason will tell it yow.
Take that is to be taken, and leave that is to be refused.

(*Enter Mankind, carrying a spade.*)

MANKIND.   Of the earth and of the clay we have our
        propagation.
By the providence of God thus be we derivatt°—   derived
190   To whose mercy I recommend this whole congregation.
I hope, onto His bliss ye be all predestinatt!°   predestined

Every man, for his degree, I trust shall be
        participatt,°   a participant
If we will mortify our carnal condition
And our voluntary desires, that ever be
        pervercionatt°—   perverse
195   To renounce them, and yield us under God's provision.

My name is "Mankind." I have my composition
Of a body and of a soul, of condition contrary—
Betwix them tweyn° is a great division.   of the two
He that should be subject, now he hath the victory.

200   This is to me a lamentable story,
To see my flesh of my soul to have governance.

Where the good-wife is master, the goodman may be sorry.
I may both syth° and sob; this is a pituose°   sigh / piteous
        remembrance.

O thou my soul, so sotyll° in thy substance,   subtle
.   .   .   .

205   Alas, what was thy fortune and thy chance
To be associat° with my flesh, that stinking   associated
        dungehill?

Lady, help! Soverens, it doth my soul much ill
To see the flesh prosperous, and the soul trodden under foot.
I shall go to yonder man, and assay him I will.
210   I trust of gostly solace he will be my bote.°   help

(*He kneels in front of Mercy.*)

All hail, seemly father, ye be welcome to this house!
Of the very wisdom ye have participation.
My body with my soul is ever querilous;
I pray you, for Saint Charity, of your supportation!

215   I beseech yow heartily of your gostly comfort.
I am unstedfast in living; my name is "Mankind."
My gostly enmy, the devil, will have a great disport,
In sinful guiding if he may see me end.

MERCY.   Christ send you good comfort! Ye be welcome,
        my friend.
220   Stand up on your feet. I pray you, arise.
My name is "Mercy." Ye be to me full
        hende;°   courteous, gracious
To eschew vice I will yow avise.

MANKIND.   O Mercy, of all grace and virtue ye are the well!
I have heard tell, of right worshipful clerks,[1]
225   Ye be approximate to God and near of his counsel;
He hath institute you above all his works.

O, your lovely words to my soul are sweeter then honey!
MERCY.   The temptation of the flesh ye must resist
        like a man,
For there is ever a battle betwix the soul and the body:

---
[1]   *clerks* Scholars.

230   *Vita hominis est militia super terram.*[1]

Oppress your gostly enmy and be Christ's own knight!
Be never a coward again your adversary:
If ye will be crowned, ye must needs fight.
Intend well, and God will be yow adjutory.°   *helper*

235   Remember, my friend, the time of continuance:
So help me God, it is but a cherry time![2]
Spend it well. Serve God with heart's affiance.°   *trust, loyalty*
Distemper not your brain with good ale nor with wine.

"Measure is treasure"; I forbid yow not the use.
240   Measure yourself ever. Beware of excess.
The superfluous guise I will that ye refuse;
When nature is sufficed, anon that ye cease.

If a man have an horse, and keep him not too high,
He may then rule him at his own desire;
245   If he be fed over-well he will disobey
And, in happe,° cast his master in the   *perhaps*
     mire.°   *swamp, bog*

(*New-Guise, Nowadays, and Nought, who have been
listening in on the conversation, now begin to speak. They
remain hidden from Mercy and Mankind.*)

NEW-GUISE. Ye say true, sir; ye are no faitour:°   *liar, cheat*
I have fed my wife so well till she is my master!
I have a great wound on my head, lo! and thereon
     leyth° a plaster;   *lies*
250   And another there I piss my peson.°   *pease*
And my wife were your horse, she would yow all to-
     banne.°   *curse*
Ye feed your horse in measure; ye are a wise man!
I trow,° and° ye were the king's palfrey-man   *believe / if*
A good horse should be gesunne.°   *scarce*

255   MANKIND. Where speaks this fellow? Will he not come
     near?
MERCY. All too soon, my brother, I fear me, for you.
He was here right now—by him that bought me dere!—

With other of his fellows. They kan° much sorrow   *know*
They will be here right soon, if I ought depart.
260   Think on my doctrine! It shall be your defence.
Learn while I am here; set my words in heart.
Within a short space I must needs hence.[3]

NOWADAYS. (*Unseen.*) The sooner the lever, and it be
     even anon![4]
I trow your name is "Do-little," ye be so long fro° home.   *from*

265   If ye would go hence, we shall come everychon,°   *everyone*
Mo° then a good sort. Ye have leave, I dare well say;   *More*
When ye will, go forth your way.
Men have little deynte° of your play   *joy, pleasure*
Because ye make no sport.

270   NOUGHT. (*Unseen.*) Your potage° shall be for-cold, sir. *soup*
     When will ye go dine?
I have seen a man lost twenty nobles in as little time—
Yet it was not I, by Saint Quentin!
For I was never worth a potful a wortys° sithyn° *cabbage / since*
     I was born.
My name is "Nought." I love well to make merry!
275   I have be sethen° with the common tapster[5] of Bury   *before*
And played so long the fool that I am even very weary—
Yet shall I be there again to-morn.

MERCY. (*To Mankind.*) I have much care for you, my
     own friend.
Your enmys° will be here anon; they make their   *enemies*
     avaunte.
280   Think well in your heart: your name is "Mankind";
Be not unkind to God, I pray you! Be his servant.

Be steadfast in condition; see ye be not variant.
Lose not through folly that is bought so dere!
God will prove you soon; and, if that ye be constant,
285   Of his bliss perpetual ye shall be partner.

Ye may not have your intent at your first desire.
See the great patience of Job in tribulation:

---

[1] *Vita hominis … terram* Latin: The life of man on Earth is a
battle; see Job 7.1.

[2] *but a cherry time* A brief time, i.e., the duration of a cherry
harvest is brief.

[3] *needs hence* Depart.

[4] *The sooner … even anon!* The sooner the better, even if it were
right now!

[5] *tapster* Proprietor of a drinking house.

Like as the smith trieth ern in the fire,[1]
So was he tried by God's visitation.

290 He was of your nature and of your fragility.
Follow the steps of him, my own sweet son,
And say, as he said, in your trouble and adversity:
"*Dominus dedit, Dominus abstulit; sicut sibi placuit, ita
  factum est; sit nomen Domini benedictum.*"[2]

Moreover, in special I give you in charge:
295 Beware of New-Guise, Nowadays, and Nought!
Nice° in their array, in language they be large.   *Extravagant*
To pervert your conditions, all their means shall be sought.

Good son, intromitt° not yourself in their company!   *intermix*
They heard not a mass this twelmonyth,°   *twelve-month, year*
  I dare well say.
300 Give them none audience; they will tell yow many a lie.
Do truly your labour, and keep your holy day.

Beware of Titivillus—for he lesith° no way—   *loses*
That goth° invisible and will not be seen.   *goes*
He will ronde° in your ear, and cast a net before   *whisper*
  your eye.
305 He is worst of them all, God let him never then!

If ye displease God, ask mercy anon,
Else Mischief will be ready to brace yow in his bridle.
Kiss me now, my dear darling. God shield yow from
  your fon!°   *foes*
Do truly your labour, and be never idle.
310 The blessing of God be with yow and with all these
    worshipful men!   (*Exit.*)
MANKIND.   Amen, for Saint Charity, amen!

Now, blessed be Jhesu! My soul is well saciatt°   *satisfied*
With the mellifluous° doctrine of this   *sweet, honeyed*
  worshipful man.
The rebellion of my flesh, now it is
  superatt,°   *suppressed, conquered*
315 Thanking be God of the coming that I came.

Here will I sit, and tityll° in this paper   *write*
The incomparable astat° of my   *estate, nature*
  promicion.° (*Writes.*)   *promise*
(*To the audience.*) Worshipful soverence, I have written
  here
The glorious remembrance of my noble condition.

320 To have remorse and memory of myself thus written it is,
To defend me from all superstitious charms:
"*Memento, homo, quod cinis es, et in cinerem reverteris.*"[3]

(*He points to his chest.*)

Lo, I bear on my breast the badge of mine arms.

(*New-Guise comes forward.*)

NEW-GUISE.   The weather is cold. God send us good fires!
325 "*Cum sancto sanctus eris, et cum perverso perverteris.*"
"*Ecce quam bonum et quam jocundum,*" quod the devil
    to the friars,
"*Habitare fratres in unum.*"[4]

MANKIND.   I hear a fellow speak. With him I will not
  mell.°   *speak, meddle*
This earth, with my spade, I shall assay to delve.
330 To eschew idleness I do it mine own self.
I pray God send it His fusion!° (*Digs.*)   *plenty, abundance*

(*Nowadays and Nought come forward through the audience.*)

NOWADAYS.   Make room, sirs, for we have be long!
We will come give you a Cristemes song.

NOUGHT.   Now I pray all the yemandry°   *yeomanry*
    that is here
335 To sing with us, with a merry cheer!

(*He sings each line; New-Guise and Nowadays encourage the
members of the audience to sing along in response.*)

---

[1] *trieth ern in the fire*   Tries (refines, purifies) iron in the fire.

[2] *Dominus dedit … Domini benedictum* Latin: The Lord gave, and
the Lord has taken away; as it was pleasing to him, so it was done;
blessed be the name of the Lord. See Job 1.21.

[3] *Momento … reverteris* Latin: Remember man, that you are dust,
and to dust you will return; see Job 34.15.

[4] *Cum sancto … unum* Latin: With the holy you will show yourself
holy, and with the wicked you will show yourself wicked (Psalms 18.
25–26); "Behold, how good and how pleasant it is … for the
brethren to dwell together in unity" (Psalms 133.1).

It is written with a coal, it is written with a coal,

NEW-GUISE *and* NOWADAYS. It is written with a coal,
it is written with a coal,

NOUGHT. He that schitith° with his hole, he   *shits*
that schitith with his hole,

NEW-GUISE, NOWADAYS. He that schitith with his
hole, he that schitith with his hole,

340 NOUGHT. But° he wipe his arse clean, but he   *Unless*
wipe his arse clean,

NEW-GUISE, NOWADAYS. But he wipe his arse clean,
but he wipe his arse clean,

NOUGHT. On his breche° it shall be seen, on   *breeches*
his breche it shall be seen,

NEW-GUISE, NOWADAYS. On his breche it shall be seen, on
his breche it shall be seen.

(*Cantant omnes:*)[1]

Holyyke, holyke, holyke! holyke, holyke, holyke!

345 NEW-GUISE. Ey, Mankind, God speed yow with your spade!
I shall tell you of a marriage:
I would your mouth and his arse, that this made,
Were married junctly° together.   *jointly*

MANKIND. Hie you hence, fellows, with bredinge!°   *reproach*

350 Leave your derision and your japing!°   *mocking*
I must needs labour—it is my living.

NOWADAYS. What, sir? We came but late hither.
Shall all this corn grow here
That ye shall have the next year?

355 If it be so, corn had need be dear,
Else ye shall have a poor life.

NOUGHT. Alas, good fadere, this labour
fretith° you to the bone!   *frets, i.e., devours*
But, for your crop I take great mone:°   *complaint*
Ye shall never spend it alone!

360 I shall assay to get you a wife.

How many acres suppose ye here, by estimation?

NEW-GUISE. Ey, how ye turn the earth up and down!
I have be in my days in many good town,
Yet saw I never such another tilling.

365 MANKIND. Why stand ye idle? It is pity that ye were born!

NOWADAYS. We shall bargain with you, and nother
mock nor scorn:

Take a good cart in harvest, and load it with your corn,
And what shall we give you for the levinge?°   *crop*

NOUGHT. He is a good stark labourer—he would fain
do well!

370 He hath met with the good man Mercy, in a shrewd sell![2]
For all this, he may have many a hungry meal.
Yit, will ye se? He is politic:°   *prudent, careful*
Here shall be good corn—he may not miss it.
If he will have rain, he may over-piss it;[3]

375 And if he will have compost, he may over-bless it
A little with his arse, like.

MANKIND. Go and do your labour—God let you never
the!°—   *thrive, prosper*
Or with my spade I shall you ding,° by the holy   *hit, strike*
Trinity!
Have ye none other man to mock but ever me?

380 Ye would have me of your set?
Hie you forth lively, for hence I will you driffe!°   *drive*

(*He hits them with his spade.*)

NEW-GUISE. Alas, my jewels!° I shall be   *testicles*
schent[4] of my wife!

NOWADAYS. Alas, and I am like never for to thrive,
I have such a buffett!

385 MANKIND. Hence I say, New-Guise, Nowadays, and Nought!
It was said beforn,° all the means should be sought   *before*
To pervert my conditions and bring me to nought.
Hence, thieves! Ye have made many a lesinge.°   *deception, lie*

NOUGHT. Marred I was for cold, but now am I warm!

390 Ye are evill-avisyde,° sir, for ye have done harm,   *ill-advised*
By Cokkys° body sacred, I have such a pain in my arm   *God's*
I may not change a man a farthing!°   *quarter penny*

(*New-Guise, Nowadays and Nought begin to leave. Mankind
kneels down.*)

MANKIND. Now I thank God, kneeling on my knee.
Blessed be His name! He is of high degree.

---

[1] *Cantant omnes* Latin: All sing.

[2] *in a shrewd sell* At a bad time.

[3] *over-piss it* Piss over it.

[4] *schent* Free of; i.e., I shall lose my wife.

395   By the subsidy of His grace that He hath sent me,
Three of mine enmys I have put to flight. (*He holds up the
          spade.*)
Yet this instrument, soverens, is not made to defend.
David seyth, "*Nec in hasta, nec in gladio, salvat Dominus.*"[1]
NOUGHT.   (*As he is leaving.*) No, mary, I beschrew yow,
          it is *in spadibus!*[2]
400   Therefore Christ's curse come on your hedibus,°   head
To send yow less might!

(*Exiant.*)

MANKIND.   I promitt yow, these fellows will no more
          come here;
For some of them, certainly, were somewhat too near!
My fadyr Mercy avisyde me to be of a good cheer
405   And again my enmys manly for to fight.

I shall convict them, I hope, everychon.
Yet I say amiss; I do it not alone:
With the help of the grace of God, I resist my fon°   foes
And their malicious heart.
410   With my spade I will depart, my worshipful soverence,
And live ever with labour, to correct my insolence.
I shall go fett° corn for my lande. I pray yow of   fetch
          patience;
Right soon I shall revert.°   return

(*He exits. Enter Mischief.*)

MISCHIEF.   Alas, alas, that ever I was wrought!
415   Alas the will, I am worse then nought!
Sithyn I was here, by Him that me bought,
I am utterly undone.
I, Mischief, was here at the beginning of the game,
And argued with Mercy—God give him shame!
420   He hath taught Mankind, while I have be° vain,   been
To fight manly again his fon.

For with his spade, that was his weapon,
New-Guise, Nowadays, and Nought hath he all
          to-betyn°—   beaten

I have great pity to see them weeping.
425   Will ye list?° I here them cry. (*Clamant.*)[3]   listen

(*New-Guise, Nowadays, and Nought re-enter, crying.
Mischief addresses them.*)

Alas, alas, come hither! I shall be your
          borow.°   protector, guardian
Alack, alack! *Vene, vene!*[4] Come hither, with sorrow!
Peace, fair babies! Ye shall have an apple—tomorrow.
Why grete° ye so, why?   weep

430   NEW-GUISE.   Alas, master, alas, my privite!°   private parts
MISCHIEF.   A, where? Alacke, fair babe, ba° me!   kiss
Abide! Too soon I shall it see.
NOWADAYS.   Here, here, see my head, good master!
MISCHIEF.   Lady, help! Silly darling, *vene, vene!*°   come
435   I shall help thee of thy pain:
I shall smite off thy head and set it on again.
NOUGHT.   By Our Lady, sir, a fair plaster!

Will ye off with his head? It is a shrewd charm!
As for me, I have none harm—
440   I were lothe to forbear mine arm.
Ye play: *In nomine patris,*[5] chop!
NEW-GUISE.   Ye shall not chop my jewels, and I may.
NOWADAYS.   Ye, Christ's cross! Will ye smight my head away?
There, where, on and on? Out! Ye shall not assay—
445   I might well be called a fop.°   fool

MISCHIEF.   I can chop it off and make it again.
NEW-GUISE.   I had a shrewd *recumbentibus,*°   knockdown blow
          but I feel no pain.
NOWADAYS.   And my head is all save and whole again.—
Now, touching the matter of Mankind,
450   Let us have an interleccion,° sithen ye be   consultation
          come hither.
It were good to have an end.

MISCHIEF.   How, how? A minstrel! Know ye any ought?

---

[1]   *Nec in ... Dominus*   Latin: Not by the spear or sword does the
Lord save; see 1 Samuel 17.47.

[2]   *in spadibus!*   In spades!

[3]   *Clamant*   Latin: They cry.

[4]   *Vene, vene!*   Latin: Come, come!

[5]   *In nomine patris*   Latin: In the name of the Father.

NOUGHT.   I kan pipe in a Walsingham[1] whistle, I, Nought,
　　Nought.
MISCHIEF.   Blow a piece, and thou shall bring him in
　　with a flute.

(*Nought starts to play the pipe. A voice comes from offstage.*)

455　TITIVILLUS.   I come, with my legs under me!
MISCHIEF.   How, New-Guise, Nowadays, hark or I go:
　　When our heads were together, I spoke of *si dedero.*[2]
NEW-GUISE.   Ye, go thy way, we shall gather money onto—
　　Else there shall no man him see.

(*To the audience.*)

460　Now gostly° to our purpose, worshipful soverence.　　　devoutly
　　We intend to gather money, if it please your negligence,
　　For a man with a head that is of great omnipotence—
NOWADAYS.   Keep your tayll,° in goodness I pray　　　tally
　　you, good brother!
　　He is a worshipful man, sirs, saving your reverence.
465　He lovith no groats, nor pence of two-pence:
　　Give us rede reyallys,°[3] if ye will see his　　　ready royals
　　abominable presence.
NEW-GUISE.   Not so! Ye that mow° not pay the　　　may
　　ton,° pay the tother.°　　　one / other

(*They begin to take up a collection from the audience.*)

　　At the good-man of this house first we will assay.
　　God bless you, master! Ye say us ill, yet ye will not say "nay."
470　Let us go by and by, and do them pay.
　　Ye pay all alike. Well mut ye fare![4]

(*When they finish taking up the collection they return to the
stage.*)

NOUGHT.   I say, New-Guise, Nowadays, *Estis vos pecuni-
　　atus?*[5]

---

[1]　*Walsingham*   Town in Norfolk.

[2]　*si dedero*   Latin: if I give something, i.e., I expect something
(payment in return).

[3]　*He lovith … reyallys*   Groats, "pence of two pence," and "Ready
Royals" were worth 4 pence, 2 pence, and 10 shillings, respectively.

[4]　*Well mut ye fare!*   Good luck to you!

[5]　*Estis … pecuniatus?*   Latin: Are you wealthy?

　　I have cried a fayer will,[6] I beschrew your patus!°　　　heads

(*Nowadays turns to call in Titivillus.*)

NOWADAYS.   *Ita vere, magister,*[7] come forth now your
　　gatus!°　　　gate
475　He is a goodly man, sirs; make space, and beware!

(*Enter Titivillus, arrayed as a devil with a net in his hand.
He addresses the audience.*)

TITIVILLUS.   *Ego sum dominantium dominus,*[8] and my
　　name is Titivillus.
　　Ye that have good horse, to you I say "*caveatis*":[9]
　　Here is an able fellowship to trise° hem°　　　snatch / them
　　out at your gatis!°　　　gates
　　Ego probo sic:[10]

(*Loquitur ad*[11] *New-Guise.*)

480　Sir New-Guise, lend me a penny.
NEW-GUISE.   I have a great purse, sir, but I have no money:
　　By the mass, I fail two farthings of an halpeny.
　　Yet had I ten pound this night that was.

TITIVILLUS.   (*Loquitur ad Nowadays.*) What is in thy purse?
　　Thou art a stout villain.
485　NOWADAYS.   The devil have the qwitt!° I am a clean　　　reward
　　gentleman.
　　I pray God I be never worse storyde°　　　supplied, provided for
　　then I am.
　　It shall be otherwise, I hope, or this night pass.
TITIVILLUS.   (*Loquitur ad Nought.*) Hark now, I say,
　　thou hast many a penny.
NOUGHT.   *Non nobis, domine, non nobis,*[12] by Saint Deny![13]
490　The devil may dance in my purse for any penny;
　　It is as clean as a bird's arse.

---

[6]　*fayer will*   Fair while.

[7]　*Ita … magister*   Latin: Truly then, master.

[8]　*Ego sum … dominus*   Latin: I am Lord of Lords.

[9]　*caveatis*   Latin: beware.

[10]　*Ego probo sic*   Latin: I show it thus.

[11]　*loquitur ad*   Latin: He speaks to.

[12]　*Non nobis … nobis*   Latin: Not to us, O Lord, not to us; cf.
Psalms 115.1.

[13]　*Saint Deny*   Saint Denis is the patron saint of France.

TITIVILLUS.   (*To the audience*.) Now I say yet again, "*caveatis*":
Here is an able fellowship to trise hem out of your gatis!—
(*To the three rogues*.) Now I say, New-Guise, Nowadays,
    and Nought,
495 Go and search the country: anon that it be sought,
Some here, some there, what if ye may catch ought.°   *anything*

If ye fail of horse, take what ye may else.
NEW-GUISE.   Then speak to Mankind for the
    recumbentibus[1] of my jewels!
NOWADAYS.   Remember my broken head in the
    worship of the five vowels.
500 NOUGHT.   Yea, good sir, and the siatica° in my arm!   *sciatica*
TITIVILLUS.   I know full well what Mankind did to you;
Mischief hath informed me of all the matter
    thorow.°   *thoroughly*
I shall venge° your quarrel, I make God a vow.   *avenge*
Forth, and espy where ye may do harm!
505 Take William Fyde,[2] if ye will have any mo.°   *more*
I say, New-Guise, whethere art thou avisyde to go?[3]

NEW-GUISE.   First I shall begin at Master Huntington
    of Sawston.
Fro thens[4] I shall go to William Thurlay of
    Hauston,°   *Hauxton*
And so forth to Picharde of Trumpington—
510 I will keep me to these three.
NOWADAYS.   I shall go to Williham Bakere of Walton,
To Richerde Bollman of Gayton.
I shall spare Master Woode of Fullburn—
He is a "*noli me tangere*."[5]

515 NOUGHT.   I shall go to William Patrike of Massingham;
I shall spare Master Alington of Bottisham,
And Hamonde of Swoffeham,
For dread of "*in manus tuas*, qweke!"[6]

---

[1] *recumbentibus*   Heavy blow.

[2] *William Fyde*   Greg Walker notes that the names in this and the
following exchanges were most likely prominent local personalities
in the area where the play was meant to be performed.

[3] *whethere art … to go?*   Where are you thinking of going?

[4] *Fro thens*   From there.

[5] *noli me tangere*   Latin: touch me not.

[6] *in manus tuas*   Latin: into your hands (the last words spoken by
Christ on the cross); see Luke 23.46; *qweke*   Sound of a neck
breaking.

Fellows, come forth and go we hence together.
520 NEW-GUISE.   Sith we shall go, let us be well ware°   *aware*
    wither.
If we may be take, we come no more hither.
Let us con° well our neck verse, that we have   *know, learn*
    not a cheke.°   *disaster*

TITIVILLUS.   Go your way, a devil way, go your way all!
I bless you with my left hand—foul you befall!
525 Come again, I warn, as soon as I you call,
And bring your avantage° into   *advantage (i.e., spoils, booty)*
    this place.

(*Exeunt. Manet Titivillus.*[7])

To speak with Mankind I will tarry here this tide,°   *time*
And assay his good purpose for to set aside.
The good man Mercy shall no longer be his guide.
530 I shall make him to dance another trace!

Ever I go invisible—it is my jett—
And before his eye thus I will hang my net
To blench° his sight. I hope to have his   *blind*
    fote-mett!°   *take his measure*
To irk him of his labour I shall make a frame:
535 This board shall be hid under the earth
    prevely.°   *privately, secretly*

(*Titivillus hides a board beneath a thin covering of earth in
Mankind's field.*)

His spade shall enter, I hope, onredily!°   *unreadily, with difficulty*
By then he hath assayde, he shall be very angry
And lose his patience—pain of shame.
I shall menge° his corn with drawke and with durnell;[8]   *mix*
540 It shall not be like to sow nor to sell.
Yonder he commith. I pray of counsel.
He shall wene° grace were wane!°   *believe / gone*

(*Enter Mankind, carrying a heavy sack.*)

MANKIND.   Now God, of his mercy, send us of his
    sonde!°   *message*

---

[7] *Manet Titivillus*   Latin: Titivillus remains.

[8] *drawke … durnell*   Types of weeds.

I have brought seed here to sow with my land.
545   Qwhill° I over-dylve° it, here it shall stand.   *While / dig*

(*He sets the sack down, and Titivillus walks away with it
while Mankind starts to dig.*)

In nomine Patris et Filii et Spiritus Sancti,[1] now I will begin.

(*His spade strikes Titivillus' board in the earth.*)

This land is so hard it makith me unlusty° and   *tired*
      irke!°   *angry*
I shall sow my corn at venture, and let God work.

(*He turns to get his sack of grain.*)

Alas, my corn is lost! Here is a foul work!
550   I see well, by tilling little shall I win.

(*He throws down the spade.*)

Here I give up my spade, for now and forever!
To occupy my body I will not put me in dever.[2]

(*Here Titivillus goeth out with the spade.*)

I will here my evensong here, or I dissever.°   *depart*
This place I assing° as for my kirke;°   *assign / church*
555   Here, in my kerke,° I kneel on my knees.   *church*

(*Prays, using beads.*)[3]

Pater noster, qui es in caelis.[4]
TITIVILLUS.   (*Returning.*) I promise you, I have no lead
      on my heels![5]
I am here again to make this fellow irke.

---

[1]   *In nomine ... Sancti*   Latin: In the name of the Father, and the
Son, and the Holy Spirit.

[2]   *I will not ... dever*   I will not endeavor.

[3]   *beads*   Rosary beads. Each bead on the rosary represents a specific
prayer.

[4]   *Pater noster ... caelis*   Latin: Our Father who art in Heaven (the
opening of the Lord's Prayer).

[5]   *no lead on my heels*   I.e., I move quickly.

Qwhist!° Peace! I shall go to his ear and   *Quiet*
      tittle° therein.   *whisper*

(*He whispers in Mankind's ear.*)

560   A short prayer thirlith° heaven. Of thy   *pierces*
      prayer blin.°   *cease*
Thou art holier then ever was any of thy kin.
Arise and avent thee!° Nature compels.   *relieve yourself*

(*Mankind gets up.*)

MANKIND.   (*To the audience.*) I will into this yard,
      soverens, and come again soon.
For dread of the cholic, and eke° of the stone,[6]   *also*
565   I will go do that needs must be done.
My beads shall be here for whosummever° will else.   *whoever*

(*Exiat.*) (*Leaving his prayer beads.*)

TITIVILLUS.   Mankind was busy in his prayer, yet I did him
      arise;
He is conveyde°—by Christ!—from his   *removed, relieved*
      divine service.
Whithe° is he, trow ye? Iwisse,° I am wonder   *Where / Certainly*
      wise:
570   I have sent him forth to shit lesinges.°   *lies*
If ye have any silver, in happe° pure brass,   *or perhaps*
Take a little powder of Parish° and cast over his face,   *Paris*
And even in the howll-flight° let   *owl-flight, (i.e., the dark)*
      him pass.
Titivillus can learn you many praty° things!   *pretty*

575   I trow Mankind will come again soon,
Or else, I fear me, evensong will be done!
His beads shall be trisyde° aside, and that anon.   *tossed, thrown*
Ye shall a good sport, if ye will abide:
Mankind cummith° again—well fare he!   *comes*
580   I shall answer him *ad omnia quare.*[7]
There shall be set abroche° a clerical matter.   *raised*
I hope of his purpose to set him aside.

(*Re-enter Mankind.*)

---

[6]   *stone*   Kidney stone.

[7]   *ad omnia quare*   Latin: at every why (i.e., question).

MANKIND.   Evensong hath be in the saying, I trow, a fair
    while!
I am irk of it. It is too long, by one mile.
585 Do way! I will no more so oft° over the church-stile;[1]   *often*
Be as be may, I shall do another.
Of labour and prayer, I am near irk of both;
I will no more of it, though Mercy be wroth.
My head is very heavy, I tell you, forsooth.
590 I shall sleep full my belly, and he were my brother.

(*Sleeps.*)

TITIVILLUS.   (*To the audience*.) And ever ye did, for me
    keep now your silence!
Not a word, I charge you, pain of forty pens!
A praty° game shall be showed you, or ye go hence.   *crafty*
Ye may hear him snore—he is sad asleep.
595 Qwhist! Peace! The devil is dead, I shall go round in his ear.

(*He whispers in Mankind's ear.*)

Alas, Mankind, alas, Mercy stown° a mare!   *stolen*
He is run away fro his master, there wot° no man   *knows*
    where.
Moreover, he stole both a horse and a nete!°   *ox, cow*

But yet I heard say he broke his neck as he rode in France;
600 But I think he ridith on the gallows, to learn for to dance,
Because of his theft—that is his governance!
Trust no more on him: he is a married man.
Mekill° sorrow with thy spade beforn thou hast   *Much*
    wrought;
Arise and ask mercy of New-Guise, Nowadays, and Nought.
605 They can avise thee for the best. Let their good will be sought;
And thy own wife brethell,° and take thee a   *betray*
    lemman.°   *mistress*

(*To the audience.*) For-well, everychon, for I have done
    my game,
For I have brought Mankind to mischief and to shame!

(*Exit Titivillus. Mankind wakes up.*)

MANKIND.   Whope! who! Mercy hath broken his
    nekekicher,° avows,   *neck*
610 Or he hangith by the neck high up on the gallows!
Adieu, fair masters, I will hast me to the ale-house
And speak with New-Guise, Nowadays, and Nought,
And get me a lemman with a smattringe° face.   *kissable*

(*New-Guise runs in, a broken noose hanging around his neck.*)

NEW-GUISE.   (*To the audience.*) Make space, for
    Cokkys° body sacred, make space!   *God's*
615 A ha, well over-ron, Gode give him evil grace!
We were near Saint Patrick's Way, by Him that me bought;

I was twitched by the neck—the game was begun!
A grace was, the halter brast° asunder: *Ecce signum!*[2]   *burst*
The half is about my neck. We had a near run!
620 "Beware," quod the good-wife when she smote off
    her husband's head, "beware!"
Mischief is a convict, for he could° his neck-verse.   *knew*
My body gave a swing when I hinge° upon the   *hung*
    casse.°   *gallow*
Alas, he will hang such a lighly° man and a   *ready (to fight)*
    ferse°   *fierce*
For stealing of an horse—I pray God give him care!

625 Do way° this halter! What devil doth Mankind   *take off*
    here, with sorrow?
Alas, how my neck is sore, I make avowe!°   *swear*
MANKIND.   Ye be welcome, New-Guise. Sir, what cheer
    with yow?
NEW-GUISE.   Well, sir; I have no cause to mourn.
MANKIND.   What was that about your neck, so God you
    amend?[3]
630 NEW-GUISE.   In faith, Saint Audrey's holy
    bend.°   *band, necklace*
I have a little dishes,° as it please God to send,   *disease*
With a running ring-worm.

(*Enter Nowadays, carrying a number of articles belonging to
the church.*)

NOWADAYS.   Stand a-rom,° I pray thee, brother   *Stand back*
    mine!

---

[1] *church-stile* Steps over the churchyard wall, leading to the church.

[2] *Ecce signum!* Latin: Behold the proof/the sign!

[3] *so God you amend* God help you.

I have laboured all this night. When shall we go dine?

635   A church here-beside° shall pay for ale, bread,   close by
          and wine:

Lo, here is stuff will serve.

NEW-GUISE.   Now, by the holy Mary, thou art better
          marchande° then I!   merchant

(*Enter Nought.*)

NOUGHT.   Avante, knaves, let me go by!

I cannot get, and I should starve!

(*Enter Mischief, carrying fetters.*)

640   MISCHIEF.   Here cummith a man of arms! Why stand
          ye so still?

Of murder and manslaughter I have my belly-fill.

NOWADAYS.   What, Mischief, have ye been in prison? And it
          be your will,

Me semith[1] ye have scored a pair of fetters.

MISCHIEF.   I was chained by the arms—lo, I have them here.

645   The chains I brast asunder, and killed the jailer,

Yea, and his fair wife halsyde° in a corner—   embraced

A, how sweetly I kissed the sweet mouth of hers!

When I had do,° I was mine own butler: done

I brought away with me both dish and dublere.°   plate, platter

650   Here is anow for me. Be of good cheer!

(*He passes round refreshment and proposes a toast.*)

Yet well fare the new chesaunce![2]

MANKIND.   (*Kneeling.*) I ask mercy of New-Guise,
          Nowadays, and Nought.

Once with my spade I remember that I fought;

I will make you amends if I hurt you ought,

655   Or did any grievance.

NEW-GUISE.   What a devil liketh thee to be of this
          disposition?[3]

MANKIND.   I dreamt Mercy was hange°—   hanged
          this was my vision—

And that to you three I should have recourse and remotion.

Now I pray you heartily of your good will:

660   I cry you mercy of all that I did amiss.

NOWADAYS.   (*Aside.*) I say, New-Guise, Nought:
          Titivillus made all this;

As sekyr° as God is in heaven, so it is!   sure

NOUGHT.   (*To Mankind.*) Stand up on your feet! Why
          stand ye so still?

NEW-GUISE.   Master Mischief, we will you exhort

665   Mankind's name in your book for to report.

MISCHIEF.   I will not so; I will set a court.

Nowadays, make proclamation,

And do it *sub forma juris*,[4] dastarde!°   idiot

NOWADAYS.   Oy-yt, oy-yit, oyet!° All manner of   Oyez, listen
          men and common women

670   To the court of Mischief othere° come or sen!°   either / send

Mankind shall return; he is one of our men.

MISCHIEF.   Nought, come forth. Thou shall be steward.

NEW-GUISE.   Master Mischief, his side gown may be sold;

He may have a jacket thereof, and money told.

675   MANKIND.   I will do for the best, so I have no cold.

(*He takes off his gown reluctantly.*)

Hold, I pray you, and take it with yow,

And let me have it again in any wise.°   way

(*Nought scribit.*)[5]

NEW-GUISE.   I promitt yow a fresh jacket, after the new
          guise.

MANKIND.   Go and do that longith to your office,

680   And spare that ye mow!

(*New-Guise exits, taking Mankind's coat. Nought approaches
Mischief.*)

NOUGHT.   Hold, master Mischief, and read this!

MISCHIEF.   Here is (*Reads.*) "*Blottibus in blottis,
Blottorum blottibus istis.*"[6]

---

[1]   *Me semith*   It seems to me that.

[2]   *Yet well … new chesaunce!*   Good luck to the new trade!

[3]   *liketh thee … disposition*   Makes you act this way.

[4]   *sub forma juris*   Latin: in legal form.

[5]   *scribit*   Latin: writes.

[6]   *Blottibus … istis*   Nonsense Latin, implying blotted writing.

I beshrew your ears, a fair hand!
685 NOWADAYS. Yea, it is a good running fist;[1]
Such a hand may not be mist.
NOUGHT. I should have done better, had I wist.°   known
MISCHIEF. Take heed, sirs, it stoude you on hande:[2]

(*Reads.*)

"*Curia tenta generalis*,[3]
690 In a place there good ale is,
Anno regni regitalis
Edwardi nullateni,[4]
On yestern day,° in *Feverere*,° the year   yesterday / February
   passeth fully;
As Nought hath written—here is our Tully[5]—
695 *Anno regni regis nulli*."[6]
NOWADAYS. What how, New-Guise, thou makest much
   tarrying!
That jacket shall not be worth a farthing.

(*New-Guise returns through the audience, carrying
Mankind's coat, now cut smaller.*)

NEW-GUISE. (*To the audience.*) Out of my way, sirs, for
dread of fighting!
Lo, here is a feet° taill,° light to leap about!   suitable / size
700 NOUGHT. It is not schapyn° worth a morsel   shaped
   of bread!
There is too much cloth—it weighs as any lead.
I shall go and mend it, else I will lose my head.
Make space, sirs, let me go out!

(*He exits, carrying Mankind's coat.*)

MISCHIEF. Mankind, come hither—God send you the
   goute!
705 Ye shall go to all the good fellows in the country about,

---

Onto the good-wife when the good-man° is out.   husband
"I will," say ye.
MANKIND.   I will, sir.
NEW-GUISE. There arn° but six deadly sins;   are
   lechery is non,°   not one
710 As it may be verified by us brethellys° everychon.   wretches
Ye shall go rob, steal, and kill as fast as ye may gon.
"I will," say ye.
MANKIND. I will, sir.

NOWADAYS. On Sundays, on the morow early
   betime,°   in the morning
715 Ye shall with us to the ale-house early to go dine,
And forbear mass and matins, hours and prime.[7]
"I will," say ye.
MANKIND.   I will, sir.
MISCHIEF. Ye must have by your side a long *da pacem*,[8]
720 As true men ride by the way, for to onbrace° them.   cut, carve
Take their money, cut their throats! Thus
   overface° them.   overcome, overwhelm
"I will," say ye.
MANKIND. I will, sir.

(*Nought returns, carrying Mankind's coat. It has now been
cut down even further.*)

NOUGHT. Here is a jolly jacket! How say ye?
725 NEW-GUISE. It is a good jacket of fence° for a   defence
   man's body!

(*They put it on Mankind.*)

Hay, dog! hay, whoppe! whoc! Go your way lightly!
Ye are well made for to run.

(*Mercy enters from the other side.*)

MISCHIEF. Tidings, tidings! I have aspied one.
Hence with your stuff; fast we were gone!
730 I beshrew the last shall come to his home.

---

[1] *running fist* Cursive hand.

[2] *it stoude … hande* It concerns you.

[3] *Curia … generalis* Latin: The general court having been held.

[4] *Anno regni … nullateni* Latin: In the regnal year of King Edward the Nothing.

[5] *Tully* Marcus Tullius Cicero (106 BCE–43 CE), known variously as "Cicero" and as "Tully," and renowned as an orator and thinker.

[6] *Anno regni… nulli* Latin: In the regnal year of no one.

[7] *mass … prime* All terms for Christian services. Prime was the earliest of the several "hours" or short religious recitations that were supposed to be performed each day.

[8] *da pacem* Latin: peace-maker, i.e., a dagger.

(*Dicant omnes:*)[1]

ALL. Amen!

MERCY. What, how, Mankind, flee that fellowship, I
    yow pray!
MANKIND. I shall speak with thee another time—to-
    morn, or the next day.
    We shall go forth together, to keep my faders
    yer-day.°   *death anniversary*
735 A tapster, a tapster! Stow,° statt,° stow!   *come / slut*
MISCHIEF. A mischief go with! Here I have a foul fall.
    Hence, away fro me, or I shall beschitte° you all.   *shit on*
NEW-GUISE. What, how, hustler, hustler, lend us a football!
    Whoppe, whow! a-now, a-now, a-now, a-now!

(*The three exit, taking Mankind.*)

740 MERCY. My mind is dispersed,° my body   *distracted*
    trembleth as the aspen leaf!
    The tears should trickledown by my cheeks, were not your
    reverence.
    It were to me solace,[2] the cruel visitation of death!
    Without rude behaviour, I cannot express this
    inconvenience.
    Weeping, sythinge,° and sobbing were my   *sighing*
    sufficience;
745 All natural nutriment to me as caren is odibull.[3]
    My inwarde affliction yeldith° me tedious unto   *makes*
    your presence.
    I cannot bear it evenly° that Mankind is so   *calmly*
    flexible!°   *malleable*

    Man un-kind, wherever thou be! For, all this world was
    not apprehensible
    To discharge thine original offence, thraldam,°   *slavery*
    and captivity,
750 Till God's own well-beloved Son was obedient and passible.
    Every drop of his blood was shed to purge thine iniquity.
    I discommend and disallow thine often
    mutability!°   *changeability*

To every creature thou art dispectuose°   *despicable*
    and odible.°   *odious*
Why art thou so on-curtess,° so inconsiderate?   *uncourteous*
    Alas, woe is me!
755 As the fane° that turnith with the wind,   *weathervane*
    so thou art convertible.

In trust is treason; thy promise is not credible.
Thy perversiose° ingratitude I cannot rehearse!   *perverse*
To God and to all the holy court of heaven thou art
    despectible,°   *despicable*
As a noble versifier makith mention in this verse:
760 "*Lex et natura, Cristus et omnia jura*
    Damnant ingratum; lugent eum fore natum."[4]

O good Lady and Mother of Mercy, have pity and
    compassion
Of the wretchedness of Mankind, that is so wanton and
    so frail!
Let Mercy exceed Justice, dear Mother! Admit this
    supplication:
765 Equity to be leyde onparty,[5] and Mercy to prevail.

To sensual living is reproveable that is nowadays,[6]
As° by the comprehence° of this matter it   *Thus / understanding*
    may be specified.
New-Guise, Nowadays, Nought, with their
    allectuose° ways   *alluring*
They have perverted Mankind, my sweet son, I have
    well espied.

770 A, with these cursed caitiffs,° and I may,[7] he shall   *wretches*
    not long endure!
I, Mercy, his father gostly, will proceed forth and do my
    propyrté.°   *task*
Lady, help! This manner of living is a detestable pleasure.
Vanitas vanitatum,[8] all is but a vanity.

---

1 *Dicant omnes* Latin: Let all say.

2 *It were to me solace* It would be a comfort to me.

3 *to me as … odibull* Is odious as carrion to me.

4 *Lex et natura … fore natum* Latin: Law and nature, Christ and
all justice damn the ingrate, they lament that he was born.

5 *leyde onparty* Set aside.

6 *To sensual living … nowadays* What happens nowadays can be
blamed on sensual living.

7 *and I may* If I have my way.

8 *Vanitas vanitatum* Latin: Vanity of vanities.

Mercy shall never be convicte° of his oncurtes   *conquered*
condition;

775   With weeping tears, by night and by day, I will go, and
never cease.

Shall I not find him? Yes, I hope. Now God be my
protection!

(*He calls.*) My predilecte° son, where be ye?   *beloved*
Mankind, *ubi es?*[1]

(*He exits, calling "Ubi es?" Enter Mischief.*)

MISCHIEF.   My prepotent fadere, when ye sup, sup out
your mess!

Ye are all too gloried in your terms—ye make many a
less.°   *lie*

780   Will ye here? He crieth ever "Mankind, *ubi es?*"

(*Enter New-Guise. Nowadays and Nought follow a few
moments later.*)

NEW-GUISE.   Hic,[2] hic, hic, hic, hic, hic, hic, hic!

That is to say, here, here, here, ny° dead in the   *nearly*
cryke!°   *creek*

If ye will have him, go and syke,° syke, syke!   *seek*

Syke not over-long, for losing of your mind.

785   NOWADAYS.   If ye will have Mankind—how, *Domine,
Domine, Dominus!*[3]—

Ye must speak to the schrive° for a *cape corpus,*[4]   *sheriff*

Else ye must be fain to return with *non est inventus.*[5]

How say ye, sir? My bolt is schett.°   *shot*

NOUGHT.   I am doing of my nedingys;[6] beware how ye schott!

790   Fy, fy, fy! I have foul arrayed° my foot.   *foully covered*

Be wise for shooting with your takyllys,° for,   *equipment*
God wott,

My foot is foully over-schett.

MISCHIEF.   A parliament, a parliament! Come forth,
Nought, behind;

---

[1]   *ubi es?* Latin: where are you?

[2]   *Hic* Latin: Here.

[3]   *Domine, Domine, Dominus!* Latin: Lord, Lord, Our Lord.

[4]   *cape corpus* Latin: literally, take his body; an order to move him.

[5]   *non est inventus* Latin: he is not found.

[6]   *of my nedingys* Something necessary.

A counsel belive!° I am aferde° Mercy will   *quickly / afraid*
him find.

795   How say ye? And what say ye? How shall we do with
Mankind?

NEW-GUISE.   Tush, a fly's wing![7] Will ye do well?

He wenith° Mercy were hung for stealing of a mare.   *thinks*

Mischief, go say to him that Mercy sekith everywhere:

He will hang himself, I undertake, for fear.

800   MISCHIEF.   I assent thereto. It is wittily said, and well.

NOWADAYS.   Qwippe it in° thy coat; anon it   *Whip it under*
were done!

Now, Saint Gabriel's modyr° save the clothes°   *mother / shoes*
of thy schon![8]

All the books in the world, if they had be undone,

Could not a cownselde° us bett.°   *counsel / better*

(*Hic exit Mischief.*) (*He returns with Mankind, now in
despair.*)

805   MISCHIEF.   How, Mankind, come and speak with Mercy!
He is here fast by.

MANKIND.   A rope, a rope, a rope! I am not worthy.

MISCHIEF.   Anon, anon, anon! I have it here ready,
With a tree also that I have get.

(*They prepare a gallows.*)

Hold the tree, Nowadays; Nought, take heed, and be wise!

810   NEW-GUISE.   Lo, Mankind, do as I do: this is thy new guise.

Give the rope just to thy neck, this is mine avise.°   *advice*

(*New-Guise demonstrates how the noose works. Mercy enters.*)

MISCHIEF.   Help thyself, Nought! Lo, Mercy is here!

He skarith° us with a bales;° we may no longer   *scares / whip*
tarry!

(*They exit. New-Guise forgets about the noose he has been
demonstrating and begins to hang himself.*)

NEW-GUISE.   Qweke, qweke, qweke! Alas, my throat!

---

[7]   *a fly's wing* I.e., a trifling matter.

[8]   *Saint … thy schon* May the mother of Saint Gabriel save the
leather of your shoes (a proverbial expression of thanks).

I beschrew you, mary!

815   A, Mercy, Christ's coppyde° curse go with you   *abundant*
    —and Saint Davy!

Alas, my wesant!° Ye were somewhat too near.   *throat*

(*They return and rescue New-Guise.*) (*Exiant.*)
(*Mankind falls, despairing.*)

MERCY.   Arise, my precious redempt son! Ye be to me full
    dear.—

He is so timerouse,° me semith his vital   *frightened*
    sprit° doth expire.   *spirit*

MANKIND.   Alas, I have be° so bestially disposed   *been*
    I dare not appear!

820   To see your solayciose° face I am not worthy to   *comforting*
    desire.

MERCY.   Your criminose complaint[1] woundeth my
    heart as a lance!

Dispose yourself meekly to ask mercy, and I will assent.

Yield me neither gold nor treasure, but your humble
    obeisiance[2]—

The voluntary subjection of your heart—and I am content.

825   MANKIND.   What, ask mercy yet once again? Alas, it
    were° a vile petition!   *would be*

Ever to offend and ever to ask mercy, it is a
    puerility.°   *childish thing*

It is so abominable to rehearse my iterat transgression,[3]

I am not worthy to have mercy by no possibility.

MERCY.   O Mankind, my singler° solace,   *unique*
    this is a lamentable excuse!

830   The dolorous° tears of my heart, how they   *sorrowful*
    begin to a-mownt!°   *gather*

O pirssid° Jhesu, help thou this sinfull sinner   *pierced*
    to redouce!°   *be led back*

Nam haec est mutatio dexterae Excelsi: vertit impios, et
    non sunt.[4]

---

[1]   *criminose complaint*   Confession of guilt.

[2]   *obeisiance*   Obedience.

[3]   *iterat transgression*   Repeated sin.

[4]   *Nam haec … et non sunt*   Latin: For this is the change of the right
hand of the Most High; He overthrows the wicked, and they are no
more. See Psalms 77.10 and Proverbs 12.7.

Arise and ask mercy, Mankind, and be associate to me.

Thy death shall be my heaviness. Alas, tis pity it should
    be thus!

835   Thy obstinacy will exclude thee fro the glorious perpetuity.

Yet, for my love, ope° thy lips and say "*Miserere mei,*   *open*
    Deus!"[5]

MANKIND.   The egall° justice of God will   *equal*
    not permit such a sinful wretch

To be revived and restored again; it were impossible.

MERCY.   The justice of God will as I will, as himself
    doth preach:

840   *Nolo mortem peccatoris, inquit,*[6] if he will be
    reducible.°   *recoverable*

MANKIND.   Than mercy, good Mercy! What is a man
    without mercy?

Little is our part of paradise, where mercy ne were.°   *is not*

Good Mercy, excuse the inevitable objection of my
    gostly° enmy.   *spiritual*

The proverb seyth, "The truth tryeth° the self." Alas,   *tests*
    I have much care!

845   MERCY.   God will not make yow privy unto his Last
    Judgement.

Justice and equity shall be fortified,° I will not deny;   *strong*

Truth may not so cruelly proceed in his straight argument

But that Mercy shall rule the matter, without
    controversy.°   *doubt*

Arise now, and go with me in this deambulatorye.°   *cloister*

850   Incline your capacity; my doctrine is convenient.

Sin not in hope of mercy! That is a crime notary.°   *notorious*

To trust overmuch in a prince, it is not expedient.

In hope, when ye sin, ye think to have mercy: beware
    of that aventure!°   *approach*

The good Lord said to the lecherous woman of
    Chanaan°—   *Canaan*

855   The holy Gospel is the autorite,° as we read in   *authority*
    Scripture—

---

[5]   *Miserere mei, Deus!*   Latin: Have mercy on me, God!

[6]   *Nolo mortem … inquit*   Latin: I do not wish the sinner's death, he
said; cf. Ezekiel 33.1.

"Vade, et iam amplius noli peccare."[1]

Christ preserved this sinful woman taken in avowtry;° *adultery*
He said to her these words, "Go and sin no more."
So to you: "Go, and sin no more." Beware of vain
    confidence of mercy!
860 Offend not a prince on trust of his favour, as I said before.

If ye feel yourself trapped in the snare of your gostly enmy,
Ask mercy anon;° beware of the continuance!   *at once*
While a wound is fresh, it is proved curable by surgery,
That, if it proceed overlong, it is cause of great grievance.

865 MANKIND. To ask mercy and to have, this is a liberal[2]
    possession.
Shall this expeditious petition ever be allowed, as ye have
    insight?[3]
MERCY. In this present life, mercy is plenty,°   *readily available*
    till death maketh his division.
But, whan ye be go,° *usque ad minimum*   *gone*
    quadrantem[4] ye shall reckon your right.

Ask mercy, and have, while the body with the soul
    hath his annexion;°   *is united*
870 If ye tarry till your decease, ye may hap of your desire to miss.
Be repentant here! Trust not the hour of death. Think
    on this lesson:
Ecce nunc tempus acceptabile, ecce nunc dies salutis.[5]

All the virtue in the world if ye might comprehend,
Your merits were not premiabyll to° the   *deserving of*
    bliss above—
875 Not to the least joy of heaven, of your proper effort to ascend.
With mercy, ye may. I tell you no fable; Scripture doth
    prove.

MANKIND. O Mercy, my suavius° solas° and   *sweet / sole*
    singular recreatory,°   *restorer*

---

[1] *Vade ... noli peccare* Latin: Go, and sin no more.

[2] *liberal* Freely and generously given.

[3] *Shall this ... insight* So far as you can judge, will this hasty request be granted?

[4] *usque ad ... quadrantem* Latin: unto the smallest farthing.

[5] *Ecce nunc ... dies salutis* Latin: Behold, now is the accepted time, now is the day of salvation. See Corinthians 6.2.

My predelect° special! Ye are worthy to have my love. *beloved*
For, without desert and means supplicatory,
880 Ye be compacient° to my inexcusable   *compassionate*
    reprove.°   *shame*

A, it swemith° my heart to think how unwisely   *grieves*
    I have wrought!
Titivillus, that goeth invisible, hing° his net   *hung*
    before my eye,
And by his fantastical visions sediciously sought,°   *led*
To New-Guise, Nowadayis, Nowght caused me to obey.

885 MERCY. Mankind, ye were oblivious of my doctrine
    monitory:°   *warning*
I said before, Titivillus would assay yow a bronte.° *attack you*
Beware fro hensforth of his fables delusory!°   *deceitful*
The proverb seyth: *"Jacula praestita minus laedunt."*[6]

Ye have three adversaries and he is master of hem all:
890 That is to say, the Devil, the World, the Flesh and the
    Fell.°   *Skin*
The New-Guise, Nowadayis, Nowgth, the "World"
    we may hem call;
And properly Titivillus signifeth the Fiend of hell;

The Flesh—that is the unclean concupiscence of your body.
These be your three gostly enemies, in whom ye have
    put your confidence.
895 They brought you to Mischief, to conclude your
    temporal glory—
As it hath be showed before this worshipful audience.

Remember how ready I was to help you;
    fro swheche° I was not dangerous.   *from such*
Wherefore, good son, abstain fro sin evermore after this!
Ye may both save and spill your soul, that is so precious;
900 *Libere welle, libere nolle*[7] God may not deny, iwis.° *certainly*

Beware of Titivillus with his net, and of all his envious will,
Of your sinful delectation that grieveth your gostly substance.
Your body is your enmy. Let him not have his will!
Take your leave whan ye will—God send you good
    perseverance!

---

[6] *Jacula ... laedunt* Latin: Familiar darts sting less.

[7] *Libere ... nolle* Latin: Freely to will, freely not to.

MANKIND.   Sith I shall depart, bless me, fader, here then I go.
905   God send us all plenty of his great mercy!
MERCY.   *Dominus custodit te ab omni malo!* [1]
      In nomine Patris, et Filii, et Spiritus Sancti. [2] Amen.

      (*Hic exit Mankind.*)

      (*To the audience.*) Worshipful soverens, I have do my
          property:°   *done my work*
910 Mankind is delivered by my faverall
          patrocinye.°   *benevolent protection*
      God preserve him fro all wicked capitivity,
      And send him grace his sensual conditions to mortify!

Now, for His love that for us received His humanity,
      Search your conditions with due examination!
915 Think and remember the world is but a vanity,
      As it is proved daily by diverse transmutation.

Mankind is wretched, he hath sufficient
          prove;°   *sufficiently proven*
      Therefore God grant you all *per suam misericordiam* [3]
      That ye may be pley-ferys° with the angels above, *companions*
920 And have to your portion *vitam aeternam. Amen!* [4]

      (*Finis.*)
      —1465–70

---

[1] *Dominus ... malo!* Latin: The Lord shall preserve thee from all
evil. See Psalms 121.7.

[2] *In nomine ... Sancti* Latin: In the name of the Father, and the
Son, and the Holy Spirit.

[3] *per suam misericordiam* Latin: by his mercy.

[4] *vitam aeternam* Latin: eternal life.

SIR THOMAS MALORY

c. 1405– 1471

Thomas Malory's place in English literary history rests on one great work, his *Morte Darthur* (*The Death of Arthur*), the first major prose work of the English language. Malory's version is the basis for the Arthurian mythology that endures to the present day. Malory drew on various sources, both French and English, but crafted those sources to provide a full narrative of the life of Arthur and the Knights of the Round Table. Tennyson's *Idylls of the King* is perhaps the best known of the works inspired by *Morte Darthur*, but Malory's work has also strongly influenced the writings of Spenser, Milton, and Arnold, the paintings of Rossetti and Watts, and the music of Wagner.

The facts of Malory's life are few, his story a matter of conjecture and dispute, but the available information suggests that he led an extraordinary life. There were several individuals with the name Thomas Malory in the fifteenth century. The one who is most commonly, though by no means certainly, identified with the author of the *Morte Darthur* was born to John Malory and Philippa Chetwynd of Newbold Revell, Warwickshire, near the beginning of the fifteenth century. John Malory was a man of some distinction, having served as a sheriff, a Member of Parliament, and a Justice of the Peace in Warwickshire.

The records that survive, however, give John's son Thomas a rather dubious reputation. The political intrigues of the 1450s eventually led to the Wars of the Roses, the battle for the English throne that was carried on by the families of York and Lancaster, and Thomas Malory appears to have been a participant in the turmoil. Surviving records show that he was charged with significant crimes during the 1450s including extortion, theft, horse stealing, and rape. It is possible that Malory's political activities earned him some enemies who engaged in a slander campaign against him, or he may indeed have been responsible for the crimes for which he was charged. In 1451 a warrant was issued for Malory's arrest. He was imprisoned at Coleshill, Warwickshire, but escaped; in 1452 he was recaptured and put in jail in London, where he spent most of the next eight years awaiting trial.

By the mid-1450s the Wars of the Roses were in full force. Malory's loyalty seems to have wavered between the two warring houses, and his fortunes rose and fell on that basis. While in prison, Malory was pardoned by the Duke of York; the Lancastrian court, however, dismissed the pardon. When the Yorkists overthrew the Lancastrians, Malory was pardoned and released. He then fought against the Lancastrians in a number of key battles. Malory seems then to have changed sides in the dispute—in 1468 his name appeared on a list of men allied with the Lancastrians. He was arrested by the Yorkists for his support of the Lancastrians, and again imprisoned in London. During these last years of imprisonment, Malory wrote *Morte Darthur*, describing himself in the text as a "knight presoner."

Malory's primary source for the *Morte Darthur* was the French Arthurian Prose Cycle (1225–30), but he also borrowed from Geoffrey of Monmouth's *History of the Kings of Britain* (1136–39) and two anonymous English works of the later fourteenth century, the alliterative *Morte Arthure* and the stanzaic *Morte Arthur*. Some of the details of the narrative are purely Malory's own inventions, but he nevertheless takes care to ascribe each of his additions to "the Freynshe booke."

Morte Darthur is vast in its scale. Malory tells eight tales over 21 books with 507 chapters. Malory originally titled the work *The Book of King Arthur and his Noble Knights of the Round Table;* William Caxton, the printer who published the book in 1485, changed the title to *Morte Darthur.* Caxton also made a significant number of editorial changes, as was discovered in 1934, when a manuscript copy of Malory's work that was significantly at variance with Caxton's text came to light. It became clear that Caxton had brought together what had been eight separate romances into twenty-one books, making alterations so as to give the appearance of a more unified text. Caxton had also deleted the personal remarks with which Malory concluded each romance.

Within a year of the completion of *Morte Darthur*, the Lancastrians briefly returned to power, and Malory was once again released from prison. He died six months later and was buried in Greyfriars Church, in London.

⌘ ⌘ ⌘

from *Morte Darthur*

from MERLIN

So in the greatest church of London, whether it were Paul's[1] or not the French book[2] maketh no mention, all the estates[3] were long ere day[4] in the church for to pray. And when matins[5] and the first mass was done there was seen in the churchyard, against the high altar, a great stone four square,[6] like unto a marble stone, and in midst thereof was like an anvil of steel a foot on high, and therein stuck a fair sword naked[7] by the point, and letters there were written in gold about the sword that said thus: "WHOSO PULLETH OUT THIS SWORD OF THIS STONE AND ANVIL IS RIGHTWISE[8] KING BORN OF ALL ENGLAND." Then the people marvelled and told it to the Archbishop.

"I command," said the Archbishop, "that ye keep you within your church and pray unto God still; that no man touch the sword till the high mass be all done."

So when all masses were done all the lords went to behold the stone and the sword. And when they saw the scripture some essayed,[9] such as would have been king, but none might stir the sword nor move it.

"He is not here," said the Archbishop, "that shall achieve the sword, but doubt not God will make him known. But this is my counsel,"[10] said the Archbishop, "that we let purvey[11] ten knights, men of good fame,[12] and they to keep[13] this sword."

So it was ordained, and then there was made a cry[14] that every man should essay that would for to win the sword. And upon New Year's Day the barons let make a jousts and a tournament, that all knights that would joust or tourney there might play. And all this was ordained for to keep the lords together and the commons,[15] for the Archbishop trusted that God would make him known that should win the sword.

So upon New Year's Day, when the service was done, the barons rode unto the field, some to joust and some to tourney. And so it happed[16] that Sir Ector, that had great livelihood[17] about London, rode unto the jousts, and with him rode Sir Kay, his son, and young Arthur that was his nourished brother;[18] and Sir Kay was made knight at All Hallowmass[19] afore. So as they rode

---

[1] *Paul's* Church of St. Paul. This church stood on the site of the present-day St. Paul's Cathedral.

[2] *French book* Unnamed French source from which Malory supposedly takes his material, actually a group of thirteenth-century Old French texts.

[3] *estates* Clergy, nobility, and commoners.

[4] *long ere day* Long before dawn.

[5] *matins* Church service conducted at daybreak.

[6] *four square* Having four equal sides.

[7] *naked* Unsheathed.

[8] *Rightwise* Rightfully.

[9] *essayed* Tried.

[10] *counsel* Advice.

[11] *let purvey* Appoint.

[12] *fame* Reputation.

[13] *keep* Guard.

[14] *cry* Request.

[15] *commons* Commoners.

[16] *happed* Happened.

[17] *livelihood* Property from which income is derived.

[18] *nourished brother* Foster brother.

[19] *All Hallowmass* All Saint's Day, Christian holy day celebrated on 1 November.

to the jousts-ward[1] Sir Kay had lost[2] his sword, for he had left it at his father's lodging, and so he prayed[3] young Arthur for to ride for his sword.

"I will well," said Arthur, and rode fast after the sword.

And when he came home the lady and all were out to see the jousting. Then was Arthur wroth,[4] and said to himself, "I will ride to the churchyard and take the sword with me that sticketh in the stone, for my brother Sir Kay shall not be without a sword this day." So when he came to the churchyard Sir Arthur alight and tied his horse to the stile,[5] and so he went to the tent and found no knights there, for they were at the jousting. And so he handled the sword by the handles, and lightly and fiercely[6] pulled it out of the stone, and took his horse and rode his way until he came to his brother Sir Kay and delivered him the sword.

And as soon as Sir Kay saw the sword he wist[7] well it was the sword of the stone, and so he rode to his father Sir Ector and said,

"Sir, lo here is the sword of the stone, wherefore[8] I must be king of this land."

When Sir Ector beheld the sword he returned again and came to the church, and there they alight all three and went into the church, and anon[9] he made Sir Kay to swear upon a book[10] how he came to that sword.

"Sir," said Sir Kay, "by my brother Arthur, for he brought it to me."

"How got ye this sword?" said Sir Ector to Arthur.

"Sir, I will tell you. When I came home for my brother's sword I found nobody at home to deliver me his sword, and so I thought my brother Sir Kay should not be swordless, and so I came hither eagerly[11] and pulled it out of the stone without any pain."[12]

"Found ye any knights about this sword?" said Sir Ector.

"Nay," said Arthur.

"Now," said Sir Ector to Arthur, "I understand ye must be king of this land."

"Wherefore[13] I?" said Arthur, "and for what cause?"

"Sir," said Ector, "for God will have it so, for there should never man have drawn out this sword but he that shall be rightwise king of this land. Now let me see whether ye can put the sword thereas[14] it was and pull it out again."

"That is no mastery,"[15] said Arthur, and so he put it in the stone. Therewithal[16] Sir Ector essayed to pull out the sword and failed.

"Now essay," said Sir Ector unto Sir Kay. And anon he pulled at the sword with all his might, but it would not be.

"Now shall ye essay," said Sir Ector to Arthur.

"I will well," said Arthur, and pulled it out easily.

And therewithal Sir Ector kneeled down to the earth and Sir Kay.

"Alas!" said Arthur, "my own dear father and brother, why kneel ye to me?"

"Nay, nay, my lord Arthur, it is not so. I was never your father nor of your blood, but I wot[17] well ye are of an higher blood than I weened[18] ye were." And then Sir Ector told him all, how he was betaken[19] him for to nourish him and by whose commandment, and by Merlin's deliverance.[20]

Then Arthur made great dole[21] when he understood that Sir Ector was not his father.

"Sir," said Ector unto Arthur, "will ye be my good and gracious lord when ye are king?"

---

[1] *jousts-ward*   Toward the jousting-place.

[2] *lost*   Realized he had forgotten.

[3] *prayed*   Asked.

[4] *wroth*   Angry.

[5] *stile*   Turnstile entrance to the churchyard.

[6] *lightly and fiercely*   Easily and boldly.

[7] *wist*   Knew.

[8] *lo*   Behold; *wherefore*   For which reason.

[9] *anon*   Immediately.

[10] *a book*   I.e., a copy of the Bible.

[11] *hither eagerly*   Here quickly.

[12] *pain*   Difficulty.

[13] *Wherefore*   Why.

[14] *thereas*   Where.

[15] *mastery*   Action requiring great skill.

[16] *Therewithal*   That being done.

[17] *wot*   Know.

[18] *weened*   Understood, knew.

[19] *betaken*   Entrusted to.

[20] *deliverance*   Delivery.

[21] *dole*   Sorrow.

"Else were I to blame," said Arthur, "for ye are the man in the world that I am most beholding[1] to, and my good lady and mother your wife that as well as her own hath fostered me and kept. And if ever it be God's will that I be king as ye say, ye shall desire of me what I may do, and I shall not fail you. God forbid I should fail you."

"Sir," said Sir Ector, "I will ask no more of you but that ye will make my son, your foster brother Sir Kay, seneschal[2] of all your lands."

"That shall be done," said Arthur, "and more, by the faith of my body, that never man shall have that office but he while he and I live."

Therewithal they went unto the Archbishop and told him how the sword was achieved and by whom. And on Twelfth-day[3] all the barons came thither[4] and to essay to take the sword who that would essay, but there afore them all there might none take it out but Arthur. Wherefore there were many lords wroth, and said it was great shame unto them all and the realm to be over-governed with a boy of no high blood born. And so they fell out[5] at that time, that[6] it was put off till Candlemas,[7] and then all the barons should meet there again; but always the ten knights were ordained to watch the sword day and night, and so they set a pavilion over the stone and the sword, and five always watched.

So at Candlemas many more great lords came hither for to have won the sword, but there might none prevail. And right as Arthur did at Christmas he did at Candlemas, and pulled out the sword easily, whereof the barons were sore aggrieved[8] and put it off in delay till the high feast of Easter. And as Arthur sped[9] afore so did he at Easter. Yet there were some of the great lords had indignation that Arthur should be king, and put it off in a delay till the feast of Pentecost.[10] Then the Archbishop of Canterbury, by Merlin's providence,[11] let purvey then of the best knights that they might get, and such knights as Uther Pendragon[12] loved best and most trusted in his days, and such knights were put about Arthur as Sir Baudwin of Britain, Sir Kaynes, Sir Ulfius, Sir Brastias; all these with many other were always about Arthur day and night till the feast of Pentecost.

And at the feast of Pentecost all manner of men essayed to pull at the sword that would essay, but none might prevail but Arthur, and he pulled it out afore all the lords and commons that were there. Wherefore all the commons cried at once,

"We will have Arthur unto[13] our king! We will put him no more in delay, for we all see that it is God's will that he shall be our king, and who that holdeth against[14] it we will slay him!"

And therewithal they kneeled at once, both rich and poor, and cried Arthur mercy[15] because they had delayed him so long. And Arthur forgave them, and took the sword between both his hands and offered it upon the altar where the Archbishop was, and so was he made knight of the best man that was there. . . .

---

[1] *beholding* Bound in duty.

[2] *seneschal* Steward, official overseeing the administration of a king's lands and court.

[3] *Twelfth-day* Twelfth day after Christmas, or the Feast of the Epiphany, celebrating the visit of the three wise men Jesus and their recognition of his divinity.

[4] *thither* There.

[5] *fell out* Quarreled.

[6] *that* So that.

[7] *Candlemas* Holy day commemorating the purification of the Virgin Mary after the birth of Jesus and the presentation of Christ at the Temple, celebrated on 2 February.

[8] *aggrieved* Distressed.

[9] *sped* Succeeded.

[10] *Pentecost* Christian celebration commemorating the descent of the Holy Spirit on the apostles, at which time they were given the gift of tongues, which would allow them to spread Christianity to other lands. The Feast of Pentecost is celebrated on the seventh Sunday after Easter.

[11] *providence* Arrangement.

[12] *Uther Pendragon* King of Britain before the action of the story and Arthur's true father.

[13] *unto* As.

[14] *holdeth against* Holds out against his acclamation.

[15] *cried ... mercy* Begged Arthur's forgiveness.

THE DEATH OF KING ARTHUR
OR THE MOST PITEOUS TALE OF THE
MORTE ARTHUR SAUNZ GUERDON[1]

I

SLANDER AND STRIFE

In May, when every heart flourisheth and burgeoneth (for as the season is lusty[2] to behold and comfortable,[3] so man and woman rejoiceth and gladdeth[4] of summer coming with his fresh flowers, for winter with his rough winds and blasts causeth lusty[5] men and women to cower and to sit by fires), so this season it befell in the month of May a great anger and unhap that stinted[6] not till the flower of chivalry of all the world was destroyed and slain.

And all was long upon two unhappy knights[7] which were named Sir Agravain and Sir Mordred,[8] that were brethren unto Sir Gawain.[9] For this Sir Agravain and Sir Mordred had ever a privy[10] hate unto the Queen, Dame Guinevere, and to Sir Lancelot;[11] and daily and nightly they ever watched upon Sir Lancelot.

So it misfortuned Sir Gawain and all his brethren[12] were in King Arthur's chamber, and then Sir Agravain said thus openly, and not in no counsel,[13] that many knights might hear:

"I marvel that we all be not ashamed both to see and to know how Sir Lancelot lies daily and nightly by the Queen. And all we know well that it is so, and it is shamefully suffered of us all[14] that we should suffer so noble a king as King Arthur is to be shamed."

Then spoke Sir Gawain and said,

"Brother, Sir Agravain, I pray you and charge you,[15] move no such matters no more[16] afore me, for wit[17] you well, I will not be of your counsel."[18]

"So God me help," said Sir Gaheris and Sir Gareth, "we will not be known of[19] your deeds."

"Then will I!" said Sir Mordred.

"I lieve[20] you well," said Sir Gawain, "for ever unto all unhappiness, sir, you will grant.[21] And I would[22] that ye left all this and made you not so busy, for I know," said Sir Gawain, "what will fall[23] of it."

"Fall whatsoever fall may,"[24] said Sir Agravain, "I will disclose it to the king!"

"Not by my counsel," said Sir Gawain, "for, an[25] there arise war and wrake[26] betwixt Sir Lancelot and us, wit you well, brother, there will many kings and great lords hold[27] with Sir Lancelot. Also, brother Sir Agravain," said Sir Gawain, "ye must remember how oftentimes Sir Lancelot has rescued the king and the queen; and the best of us all had been full cold to the heart-root[28] had not Sir Lancelot been better than we, and that has he proved himself full oft.[29] And as for my

---

[1] *Saunz Guerdon* Old French: without reward.

[2] *lusty* Here, joyful.

[3] *comfortable* Pleasant.

[4] *gladdeth* Are glad.

[5] *lusty* Here, strong, healthy.

[6] *unhap that stinted* Misfortune that ceased.

[7] *long upon … knights* Because of two ill-fated knights.

[8] *Sir Mordred* Arthur's son from his accidental incestuous union with Morgause, his half-sister.

[9] *Sir Gawain* Arthur's nephew and one of the chief knights of the Round Table.

[10] *privy* Secret.

[11] *Dame Guinevere … Lancelot* The Queen has been in a love-affair with Lancelot, the foremost knight of Arthur's court, universally acclaimed for his prowess in battle.

[12] *brethren* Gawain's brothers are Agravain, Gaheris, Gareth and Mordred.

[13] *not … counsel* Not in private.

[14] *it … us all* It is shameful to us that we should allow.

[15] *pray … you* Beg you and order you.

[16] *move … more* Suggest no such thing any more.

[17] *wit* Know.

[18] *I … counsel* I will not go along with you.

[19] *not … of* We do not wish to be associated with your plans.

[20] *lieve* Believe.

[21] *grant* Go with, agree with.

[22] *would* Wish.

[23] *fall* Happen.

[24] *Fall … may* Whatever may happen.

[25] *an* If.

[26] *wrake* Strife.

[27] *hold* Side.

[28] *full … heart-root* Dead.

[29] *full oft* Often.

part," said Sir Gawain, "I will never be against Sir Lancelot for one day's deed, and that was when he rescued me from King Carados of the Dolorous Tower and slew him and saved my life. Also, brother Sir Agravain and Sir Mordred, in like wise[1] Sir Lancelot rescued both you and three score and two[2] from Sir Tarquin. And therefore, brother, methinks such noble deeds and kindness should be remembered."

"Do you as ye list,"[3] said Sir Agravain, "for I will lain[4] it no longer."

So with these words came in Sir Arthur.[5]

"Now, brother," said Sir Gawain, "stint[6] your strife."

"That will I not," said Sir Agravain and Sir Mordred.

"Well, will ye so?" said Sir Gawain. "Then God speed[7] you, for I will not bear of your tales, neither be of your counsel."[8]

"No more will I," said Sir Gaheris.

"Neither I," said Sir Gareth, "for I shall never say evil by that man that made me knight."

And therewithal they three departed, making great dole.[9]

"Alas!" said Sir Gawain and Sir Gareth, "now is this realm wholly destroyed and mischieved,[10] and the noble fellowship of the Round Table shall be disparbled."[11]

So they departed, and then King Arthur asked them what noise they made.[12]

"My lord," said Sir Agravain, "I shall tell you, for I may keep it no longer. Here is I and my brother Sir Mordred break[13] unto my brother Sir Gawain, Sir Gaheris and to Sir Gareth—for this is all, to make it short—how that we know all that Sir Lancelot holdeth

your queen, and hath done long, and we be your sister's sons, we may suffer it no longer. And all we wote[14] that you should be above Sir Lancelot; and ye are the king that made him knight, and therefore we will prove it that he is a traitor to your person."

"If it be so," said the king, "wit you well, he is none other. But I would be loth[15] to begin such a thing but[16] I might have proofs of it, for Sir Lancelot is an hardy[17] knight, and all you know that he is the best knight among us all, and but if he be taken with[18] the deed he will fight with him that bringeth up the noise,[19] and I know no knight that is able to match him. Therefore, an it be sooth[20] as ye say, I would that he were taken with the deed."

For, as the French book saith, the king was full loath that such a noise[21] should be upon Sir Lancelot and his queen; for the king had a deeming[22] of it, but he would not hear thereof, for Sir Lancelot had done so much for him and for the queen so many times that wit you well the king loved him passingly well.

"My lord," said Sir Agravain, "ye shall ride to-morn an-hunting, and doubt ye not, Sir Lancelot will not go with you. And so when it draweth toward night ye may send the queen word that ye will lie out all that night, and so may ye send for your cooks. And then, upon pain of death, that night we shall take[23] him with the queen, and we shall bring him unto you, quick[24] or dead."

"I will well," said the king. "Then I counsel you to take with you sure[25] fellowship."

"Sir," said Sir Agravain, "my brother Sir Mordred and I will take with us twelve knights of the Round Table."

---

[1] *like wise* Similar fashion.

[2] *three ... two* Sixty-two.

[3] *list* Please.

[4] *lain* Hide.

[5] *Sir Arthur* I.e., King Arthur.

[6] *stint* Cease.

[7] *speed* Help.

[8] *neither ... counsel* Nor will I participate in your plans.

[9] *dole* Sorrow.

[10] *mischieved* Brought to ruin.

[11] *disparbled* Dispersed.

[12] *what noise they made* What had upset them, why they were upset.

[13] *break* Make known.

[14] *wote* Know.

[15] *loth* Reluctant.

[16] *but* Unless.

[17] *hardy* Strong.

[18] *but if ... with* Unless he be caught at.

[19] *bringeth up the noise* Presents the accusation.

[20] *sooth* True.

[21] *noise* Accusation.

[22] *deeming* Suspicion.

[23] *take* Catch.

[24] *quick* Alive.

[25] *sure* Trustworthy.

"Beware," said King Arthur, "for I warn you, ye shall find him wight."[1]

"Let us deal,"[2] said Sir Agravain and Sir Mordred.

So on the morn King Arthur rode an-hunting and sent word to the queen that he would be out all the night. Then Sir Agravain and Sir Mordred got to them twelve knights and hid themselves in a chamber in the castle of Carlisle. And these were their names: Sir Colgrevance, Sir Madore de la Porte, Sir Guingalen, Sir Meliot de Logres, Sir Petipace of Winchelsea, Sir Galeron of Galway, Sir Melion de la Mountayne, Sir Ascomore, Sir Gromorsom Eriore, Sir Cursessalain, Sir Florence, and Sir Lovell. So these twelve knights were with Sir Mordred and Sir Agravain, and all they were of Scotland, other else[3] of Sir Gawain's kin, other well-willers[4] to his brother.

So when the night came Sir Lancelot told Sir Bors how he would go that night and speak with the queen.

"Sir," said Sir Bors, "ye shall not go this night by my counsel."[5]

"Why?" said Sir Lancelot.

"Sir, for I dread me ever of Sir Agravain that[6] waits upon you daily to do you shame and us all. And never gave my heart against no going that ever ye went to the queen so much as now,[7] for I mistrust that the king is out this night from the queen because peradventure[8] he has lain some watch for you and the queen. Therefore I dread me sore of some treason."

"Have you no dread," said Sir Lancelot, "for I shall go and come again and make not tarrying."[9]

"Sir," said Sir Bors, "that me repents,[10] for I dread me sore that your going this night shall wrath[11] us all."

"Fair nephew," said Sir Lancelot, "I marvel me much why you say thus, since the queen has sent for me. And wit you well, I will not be so much a coward, but she shall understand I will see her good grace."

"God speed you well," said Sir Bors, "and send you sound and safe again!"

So Sir Lancelot departed and took his sword under his arm, and so he walked in his mantle,[12] that noble knight, and put himself in great jeopardy. And so he passed on till he came to the queen's chamber, and so lightly[13] he was had into the chamber. For, as the French book says, the queen and Sir Lancelot were together, and whether they were abed other at other manner of disports me list not thereof make no mention,[14] for love at that time was not as love is nowadays.

But thus as they were together there came Sir Agravain and Sir Mordred with twelve knights with them of the Round Table, and they said with great crying and scaring voice,

"Thou traitor, Sir Lancelot, now art thou taken!" And thus they cried with a loud voice, that all the court might hear it. And these fourteen knights all were armed at all points,[15] as they should fight in a battle.

"Alas!" said Queen Guinevere, "now are we mis-chieved both!"

"Madame," said Sir Lancelot, "is there here any armour within you that might cover my body withal?[16] And if there be any, give it me and I shall soon stint their malice, by the grace of God!"

"Now, truly," said the queen, "I have none armour, neither helm, shield, sword, neither spear, wherefore I dread me sore our long love is come to a mischievous end. For I hear by their noise there be many noble knights, and well I wot they be surely armed, and against them ye may make no resistance. Wherefore ye are likely to be slain, and then I shall be brent![17] For an ye might escape them," said the queen, "I would not

---

[1] *wight* Strong and courageous.

[2] *deal* Take action.

[3] *other else* Or else.

[4] *other well-willers* Or well-wishers.

[5] *counsel* Advice.

[6] *I ... that* I fear always Sir Agravain, who.

[7] *And ... now* Never before now did my heart warn me so much against your visiting the Queen.

[8] *peradventure* Perhaps.

[9] *make not tarrying* Not delay.

[10] *me repents* Distresses me.

[11] *wrath* Bring to disaster.

[12] *mantle* Cloak.

[13] *lightly* Quickly.

[14] *disports* Amusements; *me ... mention* I do not wish to discuss.

[15] *armed ... points* Fully armed.

[16] *withal* With.

[17] *brent* Burned at the stake.

doubt but that ye would rescue me in what danger that I ever stood in."

"Alas," said Sir Lancelot, "in all my life thus was I never bestrad[1] that I should be thus shamefully slain for lack of mine armour."

But ever Sir Agravain and Sir Mordred cried,

"Traitor knight, come out of the queen's chamber! For wit thou well thou art beset[2] so that thou shalt not escape."

"Ah, Jesu mercy!" said Sir Lancelot, "this shameful cry and noise I may not suffer, for better were death at once than thus to endure this pain."

Then he took the queen in his arms and kissed her and said, "Most noblest Christian queen, I beseech ye, as you have been ever my special good lady, and I at all times your poor knight and true unto my power and as I never failed you in right nor in wrong since the first day King Arthur made me knight, that you will pray for my soul if that I be slain. For well I am assured that Sir Bors, my nephew, and all the remnant of my kin, with Sir Lavain and Sir Urry, that they will not fail you to rescue you from the fire. And therefore, mine own lady, recomfort yourself,[3] whatsoever come of me, that ye go with Sir Bors, my nephew, and Sir Urry, and they all will do you all the pleasure that they may, and you shall live like a queen upon my lands."

"Nay, Sir Lancelot, nay!" said the queen. "Wit thou well that I will not live long after thy days. But an you be slain I will take my death as meekly as ever dead martyr take his death for Jesu Christ's sake."

"Well, madame," said Sir Lancelot, "sith[4] it is so that the day is come that our love must depart, wit you well I shall sell my life as dear as I may. And a thousandfold," said Sir Lancelot, "I am more heavier[5] for ye than for myself! And now I had liefer[6] than to be lord of all Christendom that I had sure armour upon me, that men might speak of my deeds or ever I were slain."[7]

"Truly," said the queen, "an it might please God, I would that they would take me and slay me and suffer you to escape."

"That shall never be," said Sir Lancelot, "God defend me from such a shame! But, Jesu Christ, be thou my shield and mine armour!"

And therewith Sir Lancelot wrapped his mantle about his arm well and surely; and by then they had gotten a great form[8] out of the hall, and therewith they all rushed at the door.

"Now, fair lords," said Sir Lancelot, "leave[9] your noise and your rushing, and I shall set open this door, and then may ye do with me what it liketh you."[10]

"Come off, then," said they all, "and do it, for it availeth thee not to strive against us all! And therefore let us into this chamber, and we shall save thy life until thou come to King Arthur."

Then Sir Lancelot unbarred the door, and with his left hand he held it open a little, that but one man might come in at once. And so there came striding a good knight, a much[11] man and a large, and his name was called Sir Colgrevance of Gore. And he with a sword struck at Sir Lancelot mightily, and so he put aside the stroke, and gave him such a buffet[12] upon the helmet that he fell grovelling[13] dead within the chamber door.

Then Sir Lancelot with great might drew the knight within the chamber door. And then Sir Lancelot, with help of the queen and her ladies, he was lightly armed in Colgrevance[14] armour. And ever stood Sir Agravain and Sir Mordred, crying,

"Traitor knight! Come forth out of the queen's chamber!"

"Sirs, leave your noise," said Sir Lancelot, "for wit you well, Sir Agravain, ye shall not prison me this night! And therefore, an ye do by my counsel, go ye all from this chamber door and make you no such crying and

---

[1] *bestrad* Attacked.

[2] *beset* Surrounded.

[3] *recomfort yourself* Take courage.

[4] *sith* Since.

[5] *more heavier* More sorrowful.

[6] *liefer* Rather.

[7] *or ... slain* Before I was killed.

[8] *form* Bench.

[9] *leave* Cease.

[10] *what ... you* What pleases you.

[11] *much* Big.

[12] *buffet* Stroke.

[13] *grovelling* Upon his belly.

[14] *Colgrevance* I.e., Colgrevance's.

such manner of slander[1] as ye do. For I promise you by my knighthood, an ye will depart and make no more noise, I shall as to-morn appear afore you all and before the king, and then let it be seen which of you all, other else ye all,[2] that will depreve[3] me of treason. And there shall I answer you, as a knight should, that hither I came to the queen of no manner of *mal engin*,[4] and that will I prove and make it good upon you with my hands."

"Fie[5] upon thee, traitor," said Sir Agravain and Sir Mordred, "for we will have thee maugre thine head[6] and slay thee, an we list![7] For we let thee wit we have the choice of King Arthur to save thee other slay thee."

"Ah, sirs," said Sir Lancelot, "is there none other grace with you? Then keep[8] yourself!"

And then Sir Lancelot set all open the chamber door, and mightily and knightly he strode in among them. And anon at the first stroke he slew Sir Agravain, and anon after twelve of his fellows. Within a while he had laid them down cold to the earth, for there was none of the twelve knights might stand Sir Lancelot one buffet. And also he wounded Sir Mordred, and therewithal he fled with all his might. And then Sir Lancelot returned again unto the queen and said,

"Madame, now wit you well, all our true love is brought to an end, for now will King Arthur ever be my foe. And therefore, madame, an it like you[9] that I may have you with me, I shall save you from all manner adventurous[10] dangers."

"Sir, that is not best," said the queen, "meseems,[11] for now ye have done so much harm it will be best that ye hold you still[12] with this. And if ye see that as to-morn they will put me unto death then may ye rescue me as ye think best."

"I will well," said Sir Lancelot, "for have ye no doubt, while I am a man living I shall rescue you."

And then he kissed her, and either of them gave other a ring, and so the queen he left there and went until[13] his lodging.

When Sir Bors saw Sir Lancelot he was never so glad of his home-coming.

"Jesu mercy!" said Sir Lancelot, "why be ye all armed? What meaneth this?"

"Sir," said Sir Bors, "after ye were departed from us we all that been of your blood and your well-willers were so adretched[14] that some of us leapt out of our beds naked, and some in their dreams caught naked swords in their hands. And therefore," said Sir Bors, "we deemed there was some great strife on hand, and so we deemed that we were betrapped with some treason; and therefore we made us thus ready what need that ever ye were in."

"My fair nephew," said Sir Lancelot unto Sir Bors, "now shall ye wit all that this night I was more hard bestad than ever I was days of my life. And thanked be God, I am myself escaped their danger." And so he told them all how and in what manner, as ye have heard toforehand.[15] "And therefore, my fellows," said Sir Lancelot, "I pray ye all that you will be of heart good, and help me in what need that ever I stand, for now is war coming to us all."

"Sir," said Sir Bors, "all is welcome that God sendeth us, and we have taken much weal[16] with you and much worship,[17] we will take the woe[18] with you as we have taken the weal." And therefore they said, all the good knights, "Look you take no discomfort! For there is no band of knights under heaven but we shall be able to grieve[19] them as much as they may us, and therefore discomfort not yourself by no manner. And we shall gather together all that we love and that loves us, and

---

[1] *sclander* Slander.

[2] *other else ye all* Or else you all.

[3] *depreve* Accuse.

[4] *mal engin* Old French: ill intent.

[5] *Fie* Shame.

[6] *maugre … head* In spite of your head, i.e., despite all you can do.

[7] *an … list* If we wish.

[8] *keep* Defend.

[9] *an … you* If it pleases you.

[10] *adventurous* Here, accidental.

[11] *meseems* It seems to me.

[12] *hold … still* Be content.

[13] *until* Unto, i.e., to.

[14] *adretched* Troubled.

[15] *toforehand* Beforehand.

[16] *weal* Prosperity.

[17] *worship* Praise, honor.

[18] *woe* Misfortune.

[19] *grieve* Injure.

what that you will have done shall be done. And therefore let us take the woe and the joy together."

"Grantmercy,"[1] said Sir Lancelot, "of your good comfort, for in my great distress, fair nephew, ye comfort me greatly. But this, my fair nephew, I would that ye did in all haste that you may or it is far days past:[2] that ye will look in their lodging that been lodged nigh here about the king, which will hold with me and which will not. For now I would know which were my friends from my foes."

"Sir," said Sir Bors, "I shall do my pain,[3] and or it be seven of the clock I shall wit of such as ye have doubt for,[4] who that will hold with you."

Then Sir Bors called unto him Sir Lionel, Sir Ector de Maris, Sir Blamour de Ganis, Sir Bleoberis de Ganis, Sir Gahalantin, Sir Galyhodin, Sir Galihud, Sir Menaduke, Sir Villiers the Valiant, Sir Hebes le Renown, Sir Lavain, Sir Urry of Hungary, Sir Neroveous, Sir Plenorius (for these two were knights that Sir Lancelot won upon a bridge, and therefore they would never be against him), and Sir Garry le Fitz Lake, and Sir Selises of the Dolorous Tower, Sir Melias de Lisle, and Sir Bellengere le Beuse, that was Sir Alexander le Orphelin's son; because his mother was Alice la Belle Pellerine, and she was kin unto Sir Lancelot, he held with him. So came Sir Palomides and Sir Saphir, his brother; Sir Clegis, Sir Sadok, Sir Dinas and Sir Clarius of Cleremont.

So these two-and-twenty[5] knights drew them together, and by then they were armed and on horseback they promised Sir Lancelot to do what he would. Then there fell to[6] them, what of North Wales and of Cornwall, for Sir Lamorak's sake and for Sir Tristram's sake, to the number of a seven score[7] knights. Then spoke Sir Lancelot:

"Wit you well, I have been ever since I came to this court well-willed unto my lord Arthur and unto my lady Queen Guinevere unto my power.[8] And this night because my lady the queen sent for me to speak with her, I suppose it was made by[9] treason; howbeit I dare largely[10] excuse her person, notwithstanding I was there by a forecast nearhand slain but as[11] Jesu provided for me."

And then that noble knight Sir Lancelot told them how he was hard bestad in the queen's chamber, and how and in what manner he escaped from them.

"And therefore wit you well, my fair lords, I am sure there is but war unto me and to mine. And for cause I have slain this night Sir Agravain, Sir Gawain's brother, and at the least twelve of his fellows, and for this cause now am I sure of mortal war. For these knights were sent by King Arthur to betray me, and therefore the king will in this heat[12] and malice judge the queen unto brenning, and that may not I suffer that she should be brent for my sake. For an I may be heard and suffered and so taken,[13] I will fight for the queen, that she is a true lady[14] until her lord. But the king in his heat, I dread, will not take[15] me as I ought to be taken."

"My lord, Sir Lancelot," said Sir Bors, "by mine advice, ye shall take the woe with the weal, and take it in patience and thank God of it. And since it is fallen as it is, I counsel you to keep yourself, for an ye will yourself,[16] there is no fellowship of knights christened that shall do you wrong. And also I will counsel you, my lord, that my lady Queen Guinevere, an she be in any distress, insomuch as she is in pain for your sake, that ye knightly rescue her; for an you did any other wise all the world would speak you shame to the world's end. Insomuch as ye were taken with her, whether you did right other wrong, it is now your part to hold with the

---

1 *Grantmercy* Thank you.

2 *or ... past* Before too many days go by.

3 *I ... pain* I will strive to do so.

4 *ye ... for* You are uncertain of.

5 *two-and-twenty* As some editors have pointed out, this may be a scribal error; there are twenty-five knights in total.

6 *fell to* Joined with.

7 *seven score* One hundred and forty.

8 *unto ... power* As far as it was in my power.

9 *made by* Arranged by.

10 *largely* Wholly.

11 *by a forecast ... but as* By a pre-arrangement nearly slain had not.

12 *heat* Anger.

13 *so taken* Accepted (as Guinevere's protector).

14 *true lady* Faithful wife.

15 *take* Accept.

16 *an ye will yourself* I.e., as you must accept yourself ("if you will").

queen, that she be not slain and put to a mischievous death. For an she so die, the shame shall be evermore yours."

"Now Jesu defend me from shame," said Sir Lancelot, "and keep and save my lady the queen from villainy and shameful death, and that she never be destroyed in my default.[1] Wherefore, my fair lords, my kin and my friends," said Sir Lancelot, "what will ye do?"

And anon they said all with one voice, "We will do as ye will do."

"Then I put this case unto you," said Sir Lancelot, "that my lord King Arthur by evil counsel will to-morn in his heat put my lady the queen unto the fire, and there to be brent, then, I pray you, counsel me what is best for me to do." Then they said all at once with one voice,

"Sir, us thinks best that ye knightly rescue the queen. Insomuch as she shall be brent, it is for your sake; and it is to suppose, an ye might be handled,[2] ye should have the same death, other else a more shame-fuller death. And, sir, we say all that you have rescued her from her death many times for other men's quarrels; therefore us seems it is more your worship that you rescue the queen from this quarrel, insomuch that she has it for your sake."

Then Sir Lancelot stood still and said,

"My fair lords, wit you well I would be full loath that my lady the queen should die such a shameful death. But an it be so that ye will counsel me to rescue her, I must do much harm or I rescue her, and perad-venture I shall there destroy some of my best friends, and that should much repent me.[3] And peradventure there be some, an they could well bring it about or disobey my lord King Arthur, they would soon come to me, the which[4] I were loath to hurt. And if so be that I may win the queen away, where shall I keep her?"

"Sir, that shall be the least care of us all," said Sir Bors, "for how did the most noble knight Sir Tristram?[5]

By your good will, kept not he with him La Beale Isode[6] near three year in Joyous Gard,[7] the which was done by your althers advice?[8] And that same place is your own, and in like wise may ye do, an ye list, and take the queen knightly away with you, if so be that the king will judge her to be brent. And in Joyous Gard may ye keep her long enough until the heat be past of the king, and then it may fortune you to bring the queen again to the king with great worship, and peradventure you shall have then thank for your bringing home, whether other may happen to have maugre."[9]

"That is hard for to do," said Sir Lancelot, "for by Sir Tristram I may have a warning: for when by means of treatise[10] Sir Tristram brought again La Beale Isode unto King Mark from Joyous Gard, look ye now what fell on[11] the end, how shamefully that false traitor King Mark slew him as he sat harping afore his lady, La Beale Isode. With a grounden glaive[12] he thrust him in behind to the heart, which grieveth sore me," said Sir Lancelot, "to speak of his death, for all the world may not find such another knight."

"All this is truth," said Sir Bors, "but there is one thing shall courage[13] you and us all: you know well that King Arthur and King Mark were never like of condi-tions,[14] for there was never yet man that ever could prove King Arthur untrue of his promise."

But so, to make short tale, they were all conde-scended[15] that, for better other for worse, if so were that the queen were brought on that morn to the fire, shortly they all would rescue her. And so by the advice of Sir Lancelot they put them all in a bushment[16] in a wood as nigh Carlisle as they might, and there they abode[17] still to wit what the king would do.

---

1. *in my default* Because of my failure, because I am not there.

2. *handled* Captured.

3. *that ... me* I.e., I would be sorry about that.

4. *the which* Whom.

5. *how ... Tristram* What did the most noble knight Sir Tristram do?; *Tristram* Knight who fell in love with Iseut, the wife of his uncle Mark. Malory recounts this episode in *The Book of Sir Tristram de Lyones*.

6. *La Beale Isode* The Beautiful Iseut, Tristram's lover.

7. *Joyous Gard* Lancelot's castle.

8. *your ... advice* The advice of you all.

9. *whether ... maugre* Even if some may dislike it.

10. *treatise* Negotiation.

11. *fell on* Happened in.

12. *grounden glaive* Sharpened spear or lance.

13. *courage* Encourage.

14. *like of conditions* Similar in disposition, character.

15. *condescended* In agreement.

16. *bushment* Ambush.

17. *abode* Waited.

Now turn we again, that when Sir Mordred was escaped from Sir Lancelot he got his horse and mounted upon him, and came to King Arthur sore wounded and all forbled,[1] and there he told the king all how it was, and how they were all slain save himself alone.

"Ah, Jesu, mercy! How may this be?" said the king. "Took ye him in the queen's chamber?"

"Yea, so God me help," said Sir Mordred, "there we found him unarmed, and anon he slew Sir Colgrevance and armed him in his armour."

And so he told the king from the beginning to the ending.

"Jesu mercy!" said the king, "he is a marvellous knight of prowess. And alas," said the king, "me sore repenteth that ever Sir Lancelot should be against me, for now I am sure the noble fellowship of the Round Table is broken for ever, for with him will many a noble knight hold. And now it is fallen so," said the king, "that I may not with my worship but[2] my queen must suffer death," and was sore amoved.[3]

So then there was made great ordinance in this ire,[4] and the queen must needs be judged[5] to the death. And the law was such in those days that whatsoever they were, of what estate or degree, if they were found guilty of treason there should be none other remedy but death, and other the menour[6] other the taking with the deed should be causer[7] of their hasty judgement. And right so was it ordained for Queen Guinevere: because Sir Mordred was escaped sore wounded, and the death of thirteen knights of the Round Table, these proofs and experiences caused King Arthur to command the queen to the fire, and there to be brent. Then spake Sir Gawain and said,

"My lord Arthur, I would counsel you not to be over-hasty, but that ye would put it in respite,[8] this judgement of my lady the queen, for many causes. One is this, though it were so that Sir Lancelot were found in the queen's chamber, yet it might be so that he came thither for none evil. For you know, my lord," said Sir Gawain, "that my lady the queen has oftentimes been greatly beholden[9] unto Sir Lancelot, more than to any other knight; for oftentimes he hath saved her life and done battle for her when all the court refused the queen. And peradventure she sent for him for goodness and for none evil, to reward him for his good deeds that he had done to her in times past. And peradventure my lady the queen sent for him to that intent that Sir Lancelot should come privily[10] to her, weening that it had be best in eschewing[11] and dreading of slander; for oftentimes we do many things that we ween for the best be, and yet peradventure it turns to the worst. For I dare say," said Sir Gawain, "my lady, your queen, is to you both good and true. And as for Sir Lancelot, I dare say he will make it good upon any knight living that will put upon him[12] villainy or shame, and in like wise he will make good for my lady the queen."

"That I believe well," said King Arthur, "but I will not that way work with Sir Lancelot,[13] for he trusteth[14] so much upon his hands and his might[15] that he doubteth[16] no man. And therefore for my queen he shall nevermore fight, for she shall have the law. And if I may get[17] Sir Lancelot, wit you well he shall have as shameful a death."

"Jesu defend me," said Sir Gawain, "that I never see it nor know it!"

"Why say you so?" said King Arthur. "For, pardy,[18] ye have no cause to love him! For this night last past he slew your brother, Sir Agravain, a full good knight, and almost he had slain your other brother, Sir Mordred, and also there he slew thirteen noble knights. And also remember you, Sir Gawain, he slew two sons of yours, Sir Florence and Sir Lovell."

---

[1] *forbled* Covered with blood.

[2] *I may ... but* I may not keep my honor unless.

[3] *amoved* Moved to emotion.

[4] *ordinance ... ire* Preparation in this wrath.

[5] *must needs ... judged* Must be condemned.

[6] *menour* Manner, behavior.

[7] *taking ... causer* Being caught in the act is the reason for.

[8] *respite* Delay.

[9] *beholden* Obligated, in debt.

[10] *privily* Privately.

[11] *eschewing* Avoiding.

[12] *put ... him* Accuse him of.

[13] *I ... Lancelot* I will not deal in that manner with Sir Lancelot.

[14] *trusteth* Has confidence in.

[15] *might* Strength.

[16] *doubteth* Fears.

[17] *get* Capture.

[18] *pardy* By God.

"My lord," said Sir Gawain, "of all this I have a knowledge, which of their deaths sore repents me. But insomuch as I gave them warning and told my brother and my sons afore-hand what would fall on the end, and insomuch as they would not do by my counsel, I will not meddle me thereof, nor revenge me nothing of their deaths; for I told them that there was no boot to strive[1] with Sir Lancelot. Howbeit I am sorry of the death of my brother and of my two sons, but they are the causers of their own death; and oftentimes I warned my brother Sir Agravain, and I told him of the perils the which be now fallen."

Then said King Arthur unto Sir Gawain,

"Make you ready, I pray you, in your best armour, with your brethren, Sir Gaheris and Sir Gareth, to bring my queen to the fire and there to have her judgement."

"Nay, my noble king," said Sir Gawain, "that will I never do, for wit you well I will never be in that place where so noble a queen as is my lady Dame Guinevere shall take such a shameful end. For wit you well," said Sir Gawain, "my heart will not serve me for to see her die, and it shall never be said that ever I was of your counsel[2] for her death."

"Then," said the king unto Sir Gawain, "suffer your brethren Sir Gaheris and Sir Gareth to be there."

"My lord," said Sir Gawain, "wit you well they will be loath to be there present, because of many adventures that is like to fall,[3] but they are young and full unable to say you nay."

Then spake Sir Gaheris and the good knight Sir Gareth unto King Arthur,

"Sir, you may well command us to be there, but wit you well it shall be sore against our will. But an we be there by your straight commandment, ye shall plainly hold us there excused: we will be there in peaceable wise, and bear none harness[4] of war upon us."

"In the name of God," said the king, "then make you ready, for she shall have soon her judgement."

"Alas," said Sir Gawain, "that ever I should endure to see this woeful day!"

So Sir Gawain turned him and wept heartily, and so he went into his chamber. And so the queen was led forth without Carlisle, and anon she was despoiled into her smock.[5] And then her ghostly father[6] was brought to her to be shriven[7] of her misdeeds. Then was there weeping and wailing and wringing of hands of many lords and ladies; but there were but few in comparison that would bear any armour for to strength[8] the death of the queen.

Then was there one that Sir Lancelot had sent unto that place, which went to espy what time the queen should go unto her death. And anon as he saw the queen despoiled into her smock and shriven, then he gave Sir Lancelot warning anon. Then was there but spurring and plucking up[9] of horse, and right so they came unto the fire. And who that stood against them, there were they slain; there might none withstand Sir Lancelot.

So all that bore arms and withstood them, there were they slain, full many a noble knight. For there was slain Sir Belias le Orgulous, Sir Segwarides, Sir Griflet, Sir Brandiles, Sir Aglovale, Sir Tor, Sir Gauter, Sir Gillimer, Sir Reynold, three brethren, and Sir Damas, Sir Priamus, Sir Kay l'Estrange, Sir Driant, Sir Lambegus, Sir Herminde, Sir Pertolip, Sir Perimones, two brethren which were called the Green Knight and the Red Knight.

And so in this rushing and hurling,[10] as Sir Lancelot thrang[11] here and there, it misfortuned him to slay Sir Gaheris and Sir Gareth, the noble knight, for they were unarmed and unawares. As the French book saith, Sir Lancelot smote[12] Sir Gareth upon the brain-pan, where-through that[13] they were slain in the field. Howbeit in very truth Sir Lancelot saw them not. And so were they found dead among the thickest of the press.[14]

---

[1] *no boot to strive* No use in quarreling.

[2] *I ... counsel* I was in agreement with you.

[3] *adventures ... fall* Perils likely to happen.

[4] *harness* Gear.

[5] *despoiled ... smock* Stripped to her undergarment.

[6] *ghostly father* Confessor.

[7] *shriven* Confessed and given absolution.

[8] *for ... strength* To assist in.

[9] *plucking up* Spurring forward.

[10] *rushing and hurling* Pushing and dashing violently.

[11] *thrang* Thrust (his weapon) about.

[12] *smote* Struck.

[13] *brain-pan ... that* Skull by means of which.

[14] *press* Crowd.

Then Sir Lancelot, when he had thus done, and slain and put to flight all that would withstand him, then he rode straight unto Queen Guinevere and made cast a kirtle[1] and a gown upon her, and then he made her to be set behind him and prayed her to be of good cheer. Now wit you well the queen was glad that she was at that time escaped from the death, and then she thanked God and Sir Lancelot.

And so he rode his way with the queen, as the French book saith, unto Joyous Gard, and there he kept her as a noble knight should. And many great lords and many good knights were sent him, and many full noble knights drew unto him. When they heard that King Arthur and Sir Lancelot were at debate[2] many knights were glad, and many were sorry of their debate.

2

THE VENGEANCE OF SIR GAWAIN

Now turn we again unto King Arthur, that when it was told him how and in what manner the queen was taken away from the fire, and when he heard of the death of his noble knights, and in especial Sir Gaheris and Sir Gareth, then he swooned for very pure sorrow. And when he awoke of his swough, then he said,

"Alas, that ever I bore crown upon my head! For now have I lost the fairest fellowship of noble knights that ever held Christian king together. Alas, my good knights be slain and gone away from me, that now within this two days I have lost nigh forty knights, and also the noble fellowship of Sir Lancelot and his blood,[3] for now I may nevermore hold them together with my worship. Now, alas, that ever this war began!"

"Now, fair fellows," said the king, "I charge you that no man tell Sir Gawain of the death of his two brethren, for I am sure," said the king, "when he heareth tell that Sir Gareth is dead, he will go nigh out of his mind. Mercy Jesu," said the king, "why slew he Sir Gaheris and Sir Gareth? For I dare say, as for Sir Gareth, he loved Sir Lancelot of[4] all men earthly."

"That is truth," said some knights, "but they were slain in the hurling as Sir Lancelot thrang in the thickest of the press. And as they were unarmed he smote them and wist not whom that he smote, and so unhappily they were slain."

"Well," said Arthur, "the death of them will cause the greatest mortal war that ever was, for I am sure that when Sir Gawain knoweth thereof that Sir Gareth is slain, I shall never have rest[5] of him till I have destroyed Sir Lancelot's kin and himself both, other else he to destroy me. And therefore," said the king, "wit you well, my heart was never so heavy as it is now. And much more I am sorrier for my good knights' loss than for the loss of my fair queen; for queens I might have enough, but such a fellowship of good knights shall never be together in no company. And now I dare say," said King Arthur, "there was never Christian king that ever held such a fellowship together. And alas, that ever Sir Lancelot and I should be at debate! Ah, Agravain, Agravain!" said the king, "Jesu forgive it thy soul, for thine evil will that thou hadst and Sir Mordred, thy brother, unto Sir Lancelot has caused all this sorrow."

And ever among these complaints the king wept and swooned.

Then came there one to Sir Gawain and told him how the queen was led away with Sir Lancelot, and nigh a four-and-twenty knights slain.

"Ah, Jesu, save me my two brethren!" said Sir Gawain. "For full well wist I," said Sir Gawain, "that Sir Lancelot would rescue her, other else he would die in that field; and to say the truth he were not of worship but if he had rescued the queen, insomuch as she should have been brent for his sake. And as in that," said Sir Gawain, "he has done but knightly, and as I would have done myself an I had stood[6] in like case. But where are my brethren?" said Sir Gawain, "I marvel that I see not of them."

Then said that man, "Truly, Sir Gaheris and Sir Gareth be slain."

"Jesu defend!" said Sir Gawain, "For all this world I would not that they were slain, and in especial my good brother, Sir Gareth."

"Sir," said the man, "he is slain, and that is great pity."

"Who slew him?" said Sir Gawain.

[1] *kirtle* Petticoat, under-skirt.
[2] *at debate* At odds.
[3] *blood* Kin.
[4] *of* Above.
[5] *rest* Peace.
[6] *stood* Been.

"Sir Lancelot," said the man, "slew them both."

"That may I not believe," said Sir Gawain, "that ever he slew my good brother, Sir Gareth, for I dare say, my brother loved him better than me and all his brethren, and the king both. Also I dare say, an Sir Lancelot had desired my brother Sir Gareth with him, he would have been with him against the king and us all. And therefore I may never believe that Sir Lancelot slew my brethren."

"Verily,[1] sir," said the man, "it is noised that he slew him."

"Alas," said Sir Gawain, "now is my joy gone!"

And then he fell down and swooned, and long he lay there as he had been dead. And when he arose out of his swough he cried out sorrowfully, and said,

"Alas!"

And forthwith[2] he ran unto the king, crying and weeping, and said,

"Ah, mine uncle King Arthur! My good brother Sir Gareth is slain, and so is my brother Sir Gaheris, which were two noble knights."

Then the king wept and he both, and so they fell on-swooning. And when they were revived, then spake Sir Gawain and said,

"Sir, I will go and see my brother Sir Gareth."

"Sir, you may not see him," said the king, "for I caused him to be interred and Sir Gaheris both, for I well understood that you would make overmuch sorrow, and the sight of Sir Gareth should have caused your double sorrow."

"Alas, my lord," said Sir Gawain, "how slew he my brother, Sir Gareth? I pray you tell me."

"Truly," said the king, "I shall tell you as it hath been told me: Sir Lancelot slew him and Sir Gaheris both."

"Alas," said Sir Gawain, "they bore none arms against him, neither of them both."

"I wot not how it was," said the king, "but as it is said, Sir Lancelot slew them in the thick press, and knew them not. And therefore let us shape a remedy for to revenge their deaths."

"My king, my lord, and mine uncle," said Sir Gawain, "wit you well, now I shall make you a promise which I shall hold by my knighthood, that from this day forward I shall never fail[3] Sir Lancelot until that one of us have slain that other. And therefore I require you, my lord and king, dress you unto the war,[4] for wit you well, I will be revenged upon Sir Lancelot; and therefore, as ye will have my service and my love, now haste you thereto and assay[5] your friends. For I promise unto God," said Sir Gawain, "for the death of my brother, Sir Gareth, I shall seek Sir Lancelot throughout seven kings' realms, but I shall slay him, other else he shall slay me."

"Sir, you shall not need to seek him so far," said the king, "for as I hear say, Sir Lancelot will abide me and us all within the castle of Joyous Gard. And much people draweth unto him as I hear say."

"That may I right well believe," said Sir Gawain; "but, my lord," he said, "assay your friends and I will assay mine."

"It shall be done," said the king, "and as I suppose I shall be big enough to drive him out of the biggest[6] tower of his castle."

So then the king sent letters and writs throughout all England, both the length and the breadth, for to assummon all his knights. And so unto King Arthur drew many knights, dukes, and earls, that he had a great host, and when they were assembled the king informed them how Sir Lancelot had bereft him[7] his queen. Then the king and all his host made them ready to lay siege about Sir Lancelot where he lay within Joyous Gard.

And anon Sir Lancelot heard thereof and purveyed him of[8] many good knights; for with him held many knights, some for his own sake and some for the queen's sake. Thus they were on both parties well furnished and garnished[9] of all manner of things that longed unto[10] the war. But King Arthur's host was so great that Sir Lancelot's host would not abide him in the field. For he was full loath to do battle against the king; but Sir Lancelot drew him unto his strong castle with all manner of victual plenty, and as many noble men as he might

---

[1]   *Verily*   Truly.

[2]   *forthwith*   Immediately.

[3]   *fail*   Stop pursuing.

[4]   *dress … war*   Prepare for war.

[5]   *assay*   Appeal to.

[6]   *big*   Powerful; *biggest*   Strongest.

[7]   *bereft him*   Robbed him of.

[8]   *purveyed … of*   Provided himself with.

[9]   *garnished*   Provided.

[10]   *longed unto*   Were required for.

suffice[1] within the town and the castle.

Then came King Arthur with Sir Gawain with a great host and laid siege all about Joyous Gard, both the town and the castle. And there they made strong war on both parties, but in no wise Sir Lancelot would ride out, nor go out of the castle, of long time; and neither he would not suffer none of his good knights to issue out, neither of the town neither of the castle, until fifteen weeks were past.

So it fell upon a day in harvest time that Sir Lancelot looked over the walls and spake on height[2] unto King Arthur and to Sir Gawain:

"My lords both, wit you well all this is in vain that ye make at this siege, for here win ye no worship, but maugre and dishonour. For an it list me to come myself out and my very good knights, I should full soon make an end of this war."

"Come forth," said King Arthur unto Sir Lancelot, "an thou darest, and I promise thee I shall meet thee in midst of this field."

"God defend me," said Sir Lancelot, "that ever I should encounter with the most noble king that made me knight."

"Now, fie upon thy fair language!"[3] said the king, "for wit thou well and trust it, I am thy mortal foe and ever will to my death-day; for thou hast slain my good knights and full noble men of my blood, that shall I never recover again. Also thou hast lain by my queen, and holden her many winters, and sithen, like a traitor, taken her away from me by force."

"My most noble lord and king," said Sir Lancelot, "ye may say what ye will, for ye wot well with yourself I will not strive. But thereas ye say that I have slain your good knights, I wot well that I have done so, and that me sore repenteth; but I was forced to do battle with them in saving of my life, other else I must have suffered them to have slain me. And as for my lady, Queen Guinevere, except your person of your highness and my lord Sir Gawain, there is no knight under heaven that dare make it good upon me that ever I was traitor unto your person. And where it please you to say that I have holden my lady, your queen, years and winters, unto

that I shall ever make a large[4] answer, and prove it upon any knight that beareth the life, except your person and Sir Gawain, that my lady, Queen Guinevere, is as true a lady unto your person as is any lady living unto her lord, and that will I make good with my hands. Howbeit[5] it hath liked her good grace to have me in favour and cherish me more than any other knight; and unto my power again[6] I have deserved her love,[7] for oftentimes, my lord, you have consented that she should have been brent and destroyed in your heat, and then it fortuned[8] me to do battle for her; and or I departed from her adversary they confessed their untruth, and she full worshipfully excused.[9] And at such times, my lord Arthur," said Sir Lancelot, "you loved me and thanked me when I saved your queen from the fire, and then you promised me for ever to be my good lord. And now methinketh you reward me evil for my good service. And, my lord, meseemeth I had lost[10] a great part of my worship in my knighthood an I had suffered my lady, your queen, to have been brent, and insomuch as she should have been brent for my sake; for sithen I have done battles for your queen in other quarrels than in mine own quarrel, meseemeth now I had more right to do battle for her in her right quarrel. And therefore, my good and gracious lord," said Sir Lancelot, "take your queen unto your good grace, for she is both true and good."

"Fie on thee, false recreant[11] knight!" said Sir Gawain. "For I let thee wit: my lord, mine uncle King Arthur shall have his queen and thee both maugre thy visage,[12] and slay you both and save you, whether it please him."[13]

"It may well be," said Sir Lancelot, "but wit thou well, my lord Sir Gawain, an me list to come out of this

---

[1] *suffice* Provide for.

[2] *on height* Loudly.

[3] *fair language* Courteous speech.

[4] *large* Bold.

[5] *Howbeit* Nevertheless.

[6] *unto ... love* To the best of my ability in return.

[7] *I ... love* I have tried to deserve her love.

[8] *fortuned* Fell to.

[9] *worshipfully excused* Honorably acquitted.

[10] *meseemeth I had lost* It seems to me I would have lost.

[11] *recreant* Cowardly, villainous (a particularly insulting term).

[12] *maugre ... visage* In spite of your face, i.e., in spite of all that you can do.

[13] *whether ... him* Whichever might please him.

castle you should win me and the queen more harder[1] than ever you won a strong battle."

"Now, fie on thy proud words!" said Sir Gawain. "As for my lady the queen, wit thou well I will never say of her shame. But thou, false and recreant knight," said Sir Gawain, "what cause hadst thou to slay my good brother, Sir Gareth, that loved thee more than me and all my kin? And alas, thou madest him knight thine[2] own hands! Why slewest thou him that loved thee so well?"

"For to excuse me," said Sir Lancelot, "it boteneth me not,[3] but by Jesu, and by the faith that I owe unto the high Order of Knighthood, I would with as good a will have slain my nephew Sir Bors de Ganis at that time. And alas, that ever I was so unhappy," said Sir Lancelot, "that I had not seen Sir Gareth and Sir Gaheris!"

"Thou liest, recreant knight," said Sir Gawain, "thou slewest them in the despite of me![4] And therefore wit thou well, Sir Lancelot, I shall make war upon thee, and all the while that I may live be thine enemy!"

"That me repents," said Sir Lancelot, "for well I understand it boteneth me not to seek none accordment[5] while ye, Sir Gawain, are so mischievously set.[6] And if ye were not, I would not doubt to have the good grace of my lord King Arthur."

"I lieve well, false recreant knight, for thou hast many long days overlaid[7] me and us all, and destroyed many of our good knights."

"Sir, you say as it pleaseth you," said Sir Lancelot, "yet may it never be said on me[8] and openly proved that ever I by forecast of treason[9] slew no good knight as ye, my lord Sir Gawain, have done;[10] and so did I never but

in my defence, that I was driven thereto in saving of my life."

"Ah, thou false knight," said Sir Gawain, "that thou meanest by Sir Lamorak.[11] But wit thou well, I slew him!"

"Sir, you slew him not yourself," said Sir Lancelot, "for it had been overmuch for you, for he was one of the best knights christened of his age. And it was great pity of his death!"

"Well, well, Sir Lancelot," said Sir Gawain, "sithen thou enbraidest me[12] of Sir Lamorak, wit thou well, I shall never leave thee till I have thee at such avail[13] that thou shalt not escape my hands."

"I trust you well enough," said Sir Lancelot, "an ye may get me, I get but little mercy."

But the French book saith King Arthur would have taken his queen again and to have been accorded with Sir Lancelot, but Sir Gawain would not suffer him by no manner of mean.[14] And so Sir Gawain made many men to blow upon[15] Sir Lancelot, and so all at once they called him "false recreant knight." But when Sir Bors de Ganis, Sir Ector de Maris and Sir Lionel heard this outcry they called unto them Sir Palomides and Sir Lavain and Sir Urry with many more knights of their blood, and all they went unto Sir Lancelot and said thus:

"My lord, wit you well we have great scorn of the great rebukes[16] that we have heard Sir Gawain say unto you; wherefore we pray you, and charge you as you will have our service, keep us no longer within these walls, for we let you wit plainly we will ride into the field and do battle with them. For you fare as a man that were afeard, and for all your fair speech it will not avail you, for wit you well Sir Gawain will never suffer you to accord with King Arthur. And therefore fight for your life and right, an ye dare."

---

[1] *win ... harder*   Get me and the queen at a greater price.

[2] *thine*   With your.

[3] *For ... not*   It is of no use for me to offer explanations.

[4] *in ... me*   Purposefully to harm me.

[5] *accordment*   Reconciliation.

[6] *mischievously set*   Bent on destruction.

[7] *overlaid*   Overpowered.

[8] *on me*   About me.

[9] *forecast ... treason*   Premeditated betrayal.

[10] *as ... done*   In "The Tale of Sir Tristram de Lyones," Malory recounts how Gawain, Gaheris, Agravain and Mordred conspire to murder Sir Lamorak for sleeping with their mother, Morgause.

Lamorak is conventionally considered Arthur's third best knight, after Lancelot and Tristram.

[11] *that ... Lamorak*   You speak of Sir Lamorak.

[12] *sithen ... me*   Throw in my face the matter.

[13] *avail*   Disadvantage.

[14] *by ... mean*   By no means.

[15] *blow upon*   Discredit.

[16] *rebukes*   Insults.

"Alas," said Sir Lancelot, "for to ride out of this castle and to do battle I am full loath."

Then Sir Lancelot spake on height unto King Arthur and Sir Gawain:

"My lord, I require you and beseech you, sithen that I am thus required and conjured[1] to ride into the field, that neither you, my lord King Arthur, neither you, Sir Gawain, come not into the field."

"What shall we do then?" said Sir Gawain. "Is not this the king's quarrel to fight with thee? And also it is my quarrel to fight with thee because of the death of my brother, Sir Gareth."

"Then must I needs unto battle,"[2] said Sir Lancelot. "Now wit you well, my lord Arthur and Sir Gawain, ye will repent it whensomever I do battle with you."

And so then they departed either from other; and then either party made them ready on the morn for to do battle, and great purveyance[3] was made on both sides. And Sir Gawain let purvey many knights for to wait upon Sir Lancelot, for to overset him and to slay him. And on the morn at underne[4] King Arthur was ready in the field with three great hosts.

And then Sir Lancelot's fellowship came out at the three gates in full good array;[5] and Sir Lionel came in the foremost battle, and Sir Lancelot came in the middle, and Sir Bors came out at the third gate. And thus they came in order and rule as full noble knights. And ever Sir Lancelot charged[6] all his knights in any wise[7] to save King Arthur and Sir Gawain.

Then came forth Sir Gawain from the king's host and proffered to joust. And Sir Lionel was a fierce knight, and lightly he encountered with him, and there Sir Gawain smote Sir Lionel throughout the body, that he dashed to the earth like as he had been dead. And then Sir Ector de Maris and other mo bare[8] him into the castle.

And anon there began a great stour,[9] and much people were slain; and ever Sir Lancelot did what he might to save the people on King Arthur's party. For Sir Bors and Sir Palomides and Sir Saphir overthrew many knights, for they were deadly knights, and Sir Blamour de Ganis and Sir Bleoberis, with Sir Bellengere le Beuse, these six knights did much harm. And ever was King Arthur about Sir Lancelot to have slain him, and ever Sir Lancelot suffered him and would not strike again. So Sir Bors encountered with King Arthur, and Sir Bors smote him; and so he alight and drew his sword, and said to Sir Lancelot,

"Sir, shall I make an end of this war?" (For he meant to have slain him.)

"Not so hardy,"[10] said Sir Lancelot, "upon pain of thy head, that thou touch him no more! For I will never see that most noble king that made me knight neither slain nor shamed."

And therewithal Sir Lancelot alight of his horse and took up the king and horsed him again, and said thus:

"My lord the king, for God's love, stint this strife, for ye get here no worship an I would do mine utterance.[11] But always I forbear[12] you and ye nor none of yours forbeareth not me. And therefore, my lord, I pray you remember what I have done in many places, and now am I evil rewarded."

So when King Arthur was on horseback he looked on Sir Lancelot; then the tears brast out of his eyen,[13] thinking of the great courtesy that was in Sir Lancelot more than in any other man. And therewith the king rode his way, and might no longer behold him, saying to himself, "Alas, alas, that ever yet this war began!"

And then either party of the battles withdrew them to repose them, and buried the dead, and searched[14] the wounded men, and laid to their wounds soft salves;[15] and thus they endured that night till on the morn. And on the morn by underne they made them ready to do

---

1 *conjured* Begged.

2 *Then ... battle* Then it is necessary that I go into battle.

3 *purveyance* Preparation.

4 *underne* Ecclesiastical third hour of the day, i.e., early morning.

5 *array* Military precision.

6 *charged* Ordered.

7 *in ... wise* At any cost.

8 *other mo bare* Many more bore.

9 *stour* Battle.

10 *Not ... hardy* Not so fast!

11 *utterance* Utmost.

12 *forbear* Spare.

13 *brast ... eyen* Burst out of his eyes.

14 *searched* Examined.

15 *salves* Healing ointments.

battle, and then Sir Bors led the vaward.[1]

So upon the morn there came Sir Gawain, as brim[2] as any boar, with a great spear in his hand. And when Sir Bors saw him he thought to revenge his brother, Sir Lionel, of the despite Sir Gawain gave him the other day.

And so, as they that knew either other, fewtred[3] their spears, and with all their might of their horses and themselves so fiercely they met together and so felonously[4] that either bare other through, and so they fell both to the bare earth.

And then the battle joined, and there was much slaughter on both parties. Then Sir Lancelot rescued Sir Bors and sent him into the castle, but neither Sir Gawain neither Sir Bors died not of their wounds, for they were well holpen.[5]

Then Sir Lavain and Sir Urry prayed Sir Lancelot to do his pain[6] and fight as they do:

"For we see that ye forbear and spare, and that doth us much harm. And therefore we pray you spare not your enemies no more than they do you."

"Alas," said Sir Lancelot, "I have no heart to fight against my lord Arthur, for ever meseemeth I do not as me ought to do."

"My lord," said Sir Palomides, "though ye spare them never so much all this day they will never con you thank;[7] and if they may get you at avail ye are but a dead man."

So then Sir Lancelot understood that they said him truth. Then he strained himself more than he did toforehand, and because of his nephew, Sir Bors, was sore wounded he pained[8] himself the more. And so within a little while, by evensong[9] time, Sir Lancelot's party the better stood; for their horses went in blood past the fetlocks,[10] there were so many people slain.

And then for very[11] pity Sir Lancelot withheld his knights and suffered King Arthur's party to withdraw them inside. And so he withdrew his meiny[12] into the castle, and either parties buried the dead and put salve unto the wounded men. So when Sir Gawain was hurt, they on King Arthur's party were not so orgulous[13] as they were toforehand to do battle.

So of this war that was noised through all Christian realms, and so it came at the last by relation[14] unto the Pope. And then the Pope took a consideration of the great goodness of King Arthur and of the high prowess of Sir Lancelot, that was called the most noblest knight of the world. Wherefore the Pope called unto him a noble clerk that at that time was there present (the French book saith it was the Bishop of Rochester), and the Pope gave him bulls under lead,[15] and sent them unto the king, charging him upon pain of interdicting[16] of all England that he take his queen again and accord with Sir Lancelot.

So when this Bishop was come unto Carlisle he showed the king his bulls, and when the king understood them he wist not what to do: but full fain[17] he would have been accorded with Sir Lancelot, but Sir Gawain would not suffer him. But to have the queen, he thereto agreed; but in no wise he would suffer the king to accord with Sir Lancelot; but as for the queen, he consented. So the Bishop had of the king his great seal and his assurance, as he was a true and anointed king, that Sir Lancelot should go safe and come safe, and that the queen should not be said unto of[18] the king, neither of none other, for nothing done of time past. And of all these appointments[19] the Bishop brought with him sure

---

[1] *vaward* Vanguard, first troops.

[2] *brim* Fierce.

[3] *fewtred* Set firmly.

[4] *felonously* Cruelly.

[5] *holpen* Helped.

[6] *pain* Utmost.

[7] *never ... thank* No matter how much you spare them, they will never be able to thank you.

[8] *pained* Exerted.

[9] *evensong* Ecclesiastical office taking place just before dusk.

[10] *fetlocks* Tufts of hair above and behind horses' hooves.

[11] *very* True.

[12] *meiny* Retinue.

[13] *orgulous* Haughty.

[14] *relation* Report.

[15] *bulls under lead* Mandates sealed with lead.

[16] *charging ... interdicting* Ordering him upon pain of excommunication.

[17] *fain* Gladly.

[18] *said ... of* Rebuked by.

[19] *appointments* Conditions.

writing[1] to show unto Sir Lancelot.

So when the Bishop was come to Joyous Gard, there he showed Sir Lancelot how he came from the Pope with writing unto King Arthur and unto him. And there he told him the perils, if he withheld the queen from the king.

"Sir, it was never in my thought," said Sir Lancelot, "to withhold the queen from my lord Arthur, but I keep her for this cause: insomuch as she should have be[2] brent for my sake, meseemed[3] it was my part to save her life and put her from that danger till better recover[4] might come. And now I thank God," said Sir Lancelot, "that the Pope hath made her peace. For God knoweth," said Sir Lancelot, "I will be a thousandfold more gladder to bring her again than ever I was of her taking away, with this I may be sure to come safe and go safe, and that the queen shall have her liberty as she had before, and never for nothing that hath be surmised afore this time that she never from this stand in no peril. For else," said Sir Lancelot, "I dare adventure me to keep her from an harder shour[5] than ever yet I had."

"Sir, it shall not need you," said the Bishop, "to dread thus much, for wit you well, the Pope must be obeyed, and it were not the Pope's worship neither my poor honesty[6] to know you distressed neither the queen, neither in peril neither shamed."

And then he showed Sir Lancelot all his writing, both from the Pope and King Arthur.

"This is sure enough," said Sir Lancelot, "for full well I dare trust my lord's own writing and his seal, for he was never shamed of[7] his promise. Therefore," said Sir Lancelot unto the Bishop, "ye shall ride unto the king afore and recommend me unto his good grace, and let him have knowledging that this same day eight days,[8] by the grace of God, I myself shall bring the queen unto him. And then say ye to my redoubted[9] king that I will say largely for the queen;[10] that I shall none except[11] for dread neither for fear but the king himself and my lord Sir Gawain, and that is for the king's love more than for himself."[12]

So the Bishop departed and came to the king to Carlisle, and told him all how Sir Lancelot answered him; so that made the tears fall out at the king's eyen. Then Sir Lancelot purveyed him an hundred knights, and all well clothed in green velvet, and their horses trapped[13] in the same to the heels, and every knight held a branch of olive in his hand in tokening of peace. And the queen had four-and-twenty gentlewomen following her in the same wise. And Sir Lancelot had twelve coursers[14] following him, and on every courser sat a young gentleman; and all they were arrayed in white velvet with sarpes of gold about their quarters,[15] and the horse trapped in the same wise down to the heels, with many ouches iset[16] with stones and pearls in gold, to the number of a thousand. And in the same wise was the queen arrayed, and Sir Lancelot in the same, of white cloth of gold tissue.[17]

And right so as you have heard, as the French book maketh mention, he rode with the queen from Joyous Gard to Carlisle. And so Sir Lancelot rode throughout Carlisle, and so into the castle, that all men might behold them. And there was many a weeping eyen. And then Sir Lancelot himself alight and voided[18] his horse, and took adown the queen, and so led her where King Arthur was in his seat; and Sir Gawain sat afore him, and many other great lords.

So when Sir Lancelot saw the king and Sir Gawain, then he led the queen by the arm, and then he kneeled down and the queen both. Wit you well, then was there many a bold knight with King Arthur that wept as

---

1   *sure writing* Guarantees in writing.

2   *be* Been.

3   *meseemed* It seemed to me.

4   *recover* Rescue.

5   *I ... shour* I would dare risk myself to protect her by fighting a harder battle.

6   *were not ... honesty* Would not be to the Pope's honor or my humble credit.

7   *shamed of* Untrue to.

8   *same ... days* Eight days from today.

9   *redoubted* Noble.

10   *I ... queen* I will speak wholly in defense of the queen.

11   *none except* Except no one from my challenge to trial by combat.

12   *himself* I.e., Gawain.

13   *trapped* Adorned.

14   *coursers* Powerful horses.

15   *sarpes ... quarters* Chains of gold around their thighs.

16   *ouches iset* Jeweled ornaments set.

17   *gold tissue* Gauzy cloth of gold.

18   *voided* Dismounted.

tenderly as they had seen all their kin dead afore them! So the king sat still and said no word. And when Sir Lancelot saw his countenance he arose up and pulled up the queen with him, and thus he said full knightly:

"My most redoubted king, ye shall understand, by the Pope's commandment and yours, I have brought to you my lady the queen, as right requireth. And if there be any knight, of what degree that ever he be of, except your person, that will say or dare say but that she is true and clean to you, I here myself, Sir Lancelot du Lake, will make it good upon his body that she is a true lady unto you.

"But, sir, liars ye have listened,[1] and that hath caused great debate betwixt you and me. For time hath been, my lord Arthur, that ye were greatly pleased with me when I did battle for my lady, your queen; and full well you know, my most noble king, that she hath be put to great wrong or this time. And sithen it pleased you at many times that I should fight for her, therefore meseemeth, my good lord, I had more cause to rescue her from the fire when she should have been brent for my sake.

"For they that told you those tales were liars, and so it fell upon them: for by likelihood, had not the might of God been with me, I might never have endured with fourteen knights. And they were armed and afore purposed,[2] and I unarmed and not purposed;[3] for I was sent unto my lady, your queen, I wot not for what cause, but I was not so soon within the chamber door but anon Sir Agravain and Sir Mordred called me traitor and false recreant knight."

"By my faith, they called thee right!" said Sir Gawain.

"My lord, Sir Gawain," said Sir Lancelot, "in their quarrel they proved not themselves the best, neither in the right."

"Well, well, Sir Lancelot," said the king, "I have given you no cause to do to me as ye have done, for I have worshipped you and yours more than any other knights."

"My lord," said Sir Lancelot, "so ye be not displeased, ye shall understand that I and mine have done you oftentimes better service than any other knights have done, in many diverse places; and where ye have been full hard bestad diverse times, I have rescued you from many dangers; and ever unto my power I was glad to please you and my lord Sir Gawain. In jousts and in tournaments and in battles set, both on horseback and on foot, I have often rescued you, and you, my lord Sir Gawain, and many mo of your knights in many diverse places.

"For now I will make avaunt,"[4] said Sir Lancelot: "I will that ye all wit that as yet I found never no manner of knight but that I was overhard for him an I had done mine utterance, God grant mercy! Howbeit I have been matched with good knights, as Sir Tristram and Sir Lamorak, but ever I had favour unto them and a deeming what they were.[5] And I take God to record, I never was wroth nor greatly heavy with[6] no good knight an I saw him busy and about to win worship; and glad I was ever when I found a good knight that might anything[7] endure me on horseback and on foot. Howbeit Sir Carados of the Dolorous Tower was a full noble knight and a passing strong man, and that wot ye, my lord Sir Gawain; for he might well be called a noble knight when he by fine force pulled you out of your saddle and bound you overthwart[8] afore him to his saddle-bow.[9] And there, my lord Sir Gawain, I rescued you and slew him afore your sight. Also I found your brother, Sir Gaheris, and Sir Tarquin leading him abounden[10] afore him; and there also I rescued your brother and slew Sir Tarquin and delivered three score and four[11] of my lord Arthur's knights out of his prison. And now I dare say," said Sir Lancelot, "I met never with so strong a knight nor so well-fighting as was Sir Carados and Sir Tarquin, for they and I fought to the uttermost. And therefore," said Sir Lancelot unto Sir Gawain, "meseemeth ye ought of right to remember this; for, an I might have your

---

[1] *liars ... listened* You have listened to liars.

[2] *afore purposed* Had planned ahead of time.

[3] *not purposed* Unprepared.

[4] *I ... avaunt* I will make a boast..

[5] *I had ... were* I went easy on them because I suspected who they were (i.e., friends he did not want to harm).

[6] *greatly ... with* Too hard upon.

[7] *anything* At all.

[8] *overthwart* Lying across.

[9] *saddle-bow* Front part of saddle.

[10] *abounden* Bound up.

[11] *delivered ... four* Rescued sixty-four.

good will, I would trust to God for to have my lord Arthur's good grace."

"Sir, the king may do as he will," said Sir Gawain, "but wit thou well, Sir Lancelot, thou and I shall never be accorded while we live, for thou hast slain three of my brethren. And two of them thou slew traitorly and piteously,[1] for they bore none harness against thee, neither none would do."

"Sir, God would they had been armed," said Sir Lancelot, "for then had they been on life.[2] And wit ye well, Sir Gawain, as for Gareth, I loved no kinsman I had more than I loved him, and ever while I live," said Sir Lancelot, "I will bewail Sir Gareth his death, not all only for the great fear I have of you, but for many causes which causeth me to be sorrowful. One is that I made him knight; another is, I wot well he loved me above all other knights; and the third is, he was passing noble and true, courteous and gentle and well-conditioned.[3] The fourth is, I wist well, anon as I heard that Sir Gareth was dead, I knew well that I should never after have your love, my lord Sir Gawain, but everlasting war betwixt us. And also I wist well that you would cause my noble lord King Arthur forever to be my mortal foe. And as Jesu be my help, and by my knighthood, I slew never Sir Gareth neither his brother by my willing; but alas that ever they were unarmed that unhappy day!

"But this much I shall offer me to you," said Sir Lancelot, "if it may please the king's good grace and you, my lord Sir Gawain: I shall first begin at Sandwich, and there I shall go in my shirt, bare-foot; and at every ten miles' end I shall found and gar make[4] an house of religion, of what order that you will assign me, with an holy convent, to sing and read day and night in especial for Sir Gareth and Sir Gaheris. And this shall I perform from Sandwich until Carlisle; and every house shall have sufficient livelihood.[5] And this shall I perform while that I have any livelihood in Christendom, and there is none of all these religious places but they shall be performed, furnished and garnished with all things as an holy place ought to be. And this were fairer and more holier and more parfit[6] to their souls than ye, my most noble king, and you, Sir Gawain, to war upon me, for thereby shall you get none avail."[7]

Then all the knights and ladies that were there wept as they were mad, and the tears fell on King Arthur's cheeks.

"Sir Lancelot," said Sir Gawain, "I have right well heard thy language and thy great proffers. But wit thou well, let the king do as it pleaseth him, I will never forgive thee my brothers' death, and in especial the death of my brother Sir Gareth. And if mine uncle, King Arthur, will accord with thee, he shall lose my service, for wit thou well," said Sir Gawain, "thou art both false to the king and to me."

"Sir," said Sir Lancelot, "he beareth not the life that may make it good![8] An ye, Sir Gawain, will charge me with so high[9] a thing, ye must pardon me, for then needs must I answer you."

"Nay, nay," said Sir Gawain, "we are past that as at this time, and that causeth the Pope,[10] for he hath charged mine uncle the king that he shall take again his queen and to accord with thee, Sir Lancelot, as for this season, and therefore thou shalt go safe as thou came. But in this land thou shalt not abide past a fifteen-days, such summons[11] I give thee, for so the king and we were condescended and accorded ere thou came. And else," said Gawain, "wit thou well, thou should not a-comen here but if it were maugre thine head. And if it were not for the Pope's commandment," said Sir Gawain, "I should do battle with thee mine own hands, body for body, and prove it upon thee that thou hast been false unto mine uncle, King Arthur, and to me both; and that shall I prove on thy body, when thou art departed from hence, wheresomever that I find thee!"

Then Sir Lancelot sighed, and therewith the tears fell on his cheeks, and then said he thus:

"Most noblest Christian realm, whom I have loved above all other realms! And in thee I have gotten a great part of my worship, and now that I shall depart in this

---

[1] *piteously* Sadly.

[2] *on life* Alive.

[3] *well-conditioned* Of a pleasant disposition.

[4] *gar make* Order to be made.

[5] *livelihood* Endowment, possessions.

[6] *parfit* Perfect, right.

[7] *avail* Disadvantage.

[8] *he ... good* There is no one alive who can prove that.

[9] *charge ... high* Accuse me of so serious.

[10] *causeth ... Pope* Because of the Pope.

[11] *summons* Terms.

wise, truly me repents that ever I came in this realm, that I should be thus shamefully banished, undeserved and causeless. But fortune is so variant, and the wheel so mutable[1] that there is no constant abiding. And that may be proved by many chronicles, as of noble Hector of Troy[2] and Alexander,[3] the mighty conqueror, and many more other: when they were most in their royalty, they alight passing low.[4] And so fareth it by me," said Sir Lancelot, "for in this realm I had worship, and by me and mine all the whole Round Table hath been increased more in worship, by me and mine, than ever it was by any of you all.

"And therefore wit thou well, Sir Gawain, I may live upon lands as well as any knight that here is. And if ye, my most redoubted king, will come upon my lands with Sir Gawain to war upon me, I must endure you as well as I may. But as to you, Sir Gawain, if that ye come there, I pray you charge me not with treason neither felony, for an ye do, I must answer you."

"Do thou thy best," said Sir Gawain, "and therefore hie[5] thee fast that thou were gone! And wit thou well we shall soon come after, and break the strongest castle that thou hast, upon thy head!"

"It shall not need that," said Sir Lancelot, "for an I were as orgulous set[6] as ye are, wit you well I should meet you in midst of the field."

"Make thou no more language," said Sir Gawain, "but deliver the queen from thee, and pike thee lightly[7] out of this court!"

"Well," said Sir Lancelot, "an I had wist of this shortcoming,[8] I would 'a advised me[9] twice or that I had come here. For an the queen had been so dear unto me

---

[1] *fortune … mutable* Fortune so variable, and the Wheel of Fortune so changeable.

[2] *Hector of Troy* Heroic prince of Troy, killed by Achilles in Homer's *Iliad*.

[3] *Alexander* Famed conqueror (356–323 BCE) of Greece, Egypt, and Persia.

[4] *alight … low* Fell to the bottom. (Ever changeable, the Wheel of Fortune might raise up those who were low and cast down those who were at the top.)

[5] *hie* Hasten.

[6] *orgulous set* Proudly determined.

[7] *pike thee lightly* Quickly get yourself.

[8] *shortcoming* Unfortunate situation.

[9] *'a advised me* Have thought.

as ye noise her, I durst have kept her from the fellowship of the best knights under heaven."

And then Sir Lancelot said unto Queen Guinevere, in hearing of the king and them all,

"Madam, now I must depart from you and this noble fellowship for ever. And sithen it is so, I beseech you to pray for me, and I shall pray for you. And tell ye me, an if ye be hard bestead by any false tongues, but lightly, my good lady, send me word; and if any knight's hands under the heaven may deliver you by battle, I shall deliver you."

And therewithal Sir Lancelot kissed the queen, and then he said all openly,

"Now let see whatsomever he be in this place that dare say the queen is not true unto my lord Arthur, let see who will speak an he dare speak."

And therewith he brought the queen to the king, and then Sir Lancelot took his leave and departed. And there was neither king, duke, earl, baron, nor knight, lady nor gentlewoman, but all they wept as people out of mind, except Sir Gawain. And when this noble knight Sir Lancelot took his horse to ride out of Carlisle, there was sobbing and weeping for pure dole of his departing.

And so he took his way to Joyous Gard, and then ever after he called it the "Dolorous Gard." And thus departed Sir Lancelot from the court forever.

And so when he came to Joyous Gard he called his fellowship unto him and asked them what they would do. Then they answered all wholly together with one voice, they would do as he would do.

"Then, my fair fellows," said Sir Lancelot, "I must depart out of this most noble realm. And now I shall depart, it grieveth me sore, for I shall depart with no worship; for a fleamed[10] man departeth never out of a realm with no worship.[11] And that is to me great heaviness,[12] for ever I fear after my days that men shall chronicle upon me that I was fleamed out of this land. And else, my fair lords, be ye sure, an I had not dread shame, my lady Queen Guinevere and I should never have departed."

---

[10] *fleamed* Banished.

[11] *no worship* Any honor. Middle English often uses the double negative for additional emphasis.

[12] *heaviness* Sadness.

Then spake noble knights, as Sir Palomides and Sir Saphir, his brother, and Sir Bellengere le Beuse, and Sir Urry with Sir Lavain, with many other:

"Sir, an ye will so be disposed to abide in this land we will never fail you; and if ye list not abide in this land, there is none of the good knights that here be that will fail you, for many causes. One is, all we that be not of your blood shall never be welcome unto the court. And sithen it liked us to take a part with you in your distress in this realm, wit you well it shall like us as well to go in other countries with you, and there to to take such part as you do."

"My fair lords," said Sir Lancelot, "I well understand you, and as I can, I thank you. And you shall understand, such livelihood as I am born unto I shall depart with you in this manner of wise: that is for to say, I shall depart[1] all my livelihood and all my lands freely among you, and myself will have as little as any of you; for, have I sufficient that may long unto my person,[2] I will ask none other riches neither array. And I trust to God to maintain you[3] on my lands as well as ever you were maintained."

Then spake all the knights at once: "Have he shame that will leave you! For we all understand in this realm will be no quiet, but ever debate and strife now the fellowship of the Round Table is broken. For by the noble fellowship of the Round Table was King Arthur upborne, and by their noblesse[4] the king and all the realm was ever in quiet and rest. And a great part," they said all, "was because of your most noblesse, Sir Lancelot."

"Now, truly I thank you all of your good saying! Howbeit, I wot well that in me was not all the stability of this realm, but in that I might I did my dever.[5] And well I am sure I knew many rebellions in my days that by me and mine were peased;[6] and that I trow we all shall hear of in short space, and that me sore repenteth. For ever I dread me," said Sir Lancelot, "that Sir Mordred will make trouble, for he is passing envious, and applyeth him much to trouble."

And so they were accorded to depart with Sir Lancelot to his lands. And to make short this tale, they trussed, and paid[7] all that would ask them; and wholly an hundred knights departed with Sir Lancelot at once, and made their avows they would never leave him for weal ne[8] for woe.

And so they shipped at Cardiff, and sailed unto Benwick: some men call it Bayan[9] and some men call it Beaune, where the wine of Beaune is. But say the sooth, Sir Lancelot and his nephews was lord of all France and of all the lands that longed unto[10] France; he and his kindred rejoiced[11] it, all through Sir Lancelot's noble prowess.

And then he stuffed and furnished and garnished all his noble towns and castles. Then all the people of those lands came unto Sir Lancelot on foot and hands.[12] And so when he had 'stablished all those countries, he shortly called a parliament; and there he crowned Sir Lionel king of France, and Sir Bors he crowned him king of all King Claudas' lands, and Sir Ector de Maris, Sir Lancelot's younger brother, he crowned him king of Benwick and king of all Guienne, which was Sir Lancelot's own lands. And he made Sir Ector prince of them all.

And thus he departed his lands and advanced[13] all his noble knights. And first he advanced them of his blood, as Sir Blamour, he made him duke of Limousin in Guienne, and Sir Bleoberis, he made him duke of Poitiers. And Sir Gahalantin, he made him duke of Auvergne; and Sir Galyhodin, he made him duke of Saintonge; and Sir Galihud, he made him earl of Perigord; and Sir Menaduke, he made him earl of Rouergue; and Sir Villiers the Valiant, he made him earl of Bearn; and Sir Hebes le Renown, he made him earl of Comminges; and Sir Lavain, he made him earl of Armagnac; and Sir Urry, he made him earl of Astarac; and Sir Neroveous, he made him earl of Pardiac; and Sir Plenorius, he made him earl of Foix; and Sir Selises of

---

[1] *depart* Divide.

[2] *for ... person* For if I have what I need.

[3] *maintain you* Provide for you.

[4] *noblesse* Noble quality.

[5] *in ... dever* Insofar as I could, I did my duty.

[6] *peased* Reconciled.

[7] *trussed ... paid* Equipped themselves and hired.

[8] *ne* Nor.

[9] *Bayan* Bayonne.

[10] *longed unto* Belonged to.

[11] *rejoiced* Possessed.

[12] *on ... hands* Submissively.

[13] *advanced* Promoted in station.

the Dolorous Tower, he made him earl of Marsan; and Sir Melias de Lisle, he made him earl of Tursan; and Sir Bellengere le Beuse, he made him earl of the Landes; and Sir Palomides, he made him duke of Provence; and Sir Saphir, he made him duke of Languedoc. And Sir Clegis, he gave him the earldom of Agen; and Sir Sadok, he gave him the earldom of Sarlat; and Sir Dinas le Seneschal, he made him duke of Anjou; and Sir Clarrus, he made him duke of Normandy.

Thus Sir Lancelot rewarded his noble knights, and many more meseemeth it were too long to rehearse.

3

The Siege of Benwick

So leave we Sir Lancelot in his lands and his noble knights with him, and return we again unto King Arthur and unto Sir Gawain that made a great host aready to the number of three-score thousand. And all thing was made ready for shipping to pass over the sea, to war upon Sir Lancelot and upon his lands. And so they shipped at Cardiff.

And there King Arthur made Sir Mordred chief ruler of all England, and also he put the queen under his governance: because Sir Mordred was King Arthur's son, he gave him rule of his land and of his wife.

And so the king passed the sea and landed upon Sir Lancelot's lands, and there he brent and wasted, through the vengeance of Sir Gawain, all that they might over-run. So when this word was come unto Sir Lancelot, that King Arthur and Sir Gawain were landed upon his lands and made full great destruction and waste, then spake Sir Bors and said,

"My lord Sir Lancelot, it is shame that we suffer them thus to ride over our lands. For wit you well, suffer ye them as long as ye will, they will do you no favour an they may handle[1] you."

Then said Sir Lionel that was ware[2] and wise, "My lord, Sir Lancelot, I will give you this counsel: let us keep our strong-walled towns until they have hunger and cold and blow on their nails; and then let us freshly[3] set upon them and shred them down as sheep in a fold,

that ever after aliaunts[4] may take ensample[5] how they land upon our lands!"[6]

Then spoke King Bagdemagus to Sir Lancelot and said, "Sir, your courtesy will shend[7] us all, and your courtesy hath waked all this sorrow; for an they thus override our lands, they shall by process bring us all to nought while we thus in holes us hide."

Then said Sir Galihud unto Sir Lancelot, "Sir, here been knights come of king's blood that will not long droop and dare[8] within these walls. Therefore give us leave, like as we been knights, to meet them in the field, and we shall slay them and so deal with them that they shall curse the time that ever they came into this coun-try."

Then spake seven brethren of North Wales which were seven noble knights; for a man might seek seven kings' lands or he might find such seven knights. And these seven noble knights said all at once,

"Sir Lancelot, for Christ's sake, let us ride out with Sir Galihud, for we were never wont[9] to cower in castles neither in noble towns."

Then spake Sir Lancelot, that was master and governor of them all, and said, "My fair lords, wit you well I am full loath to ride out with my knights for shedding of Christian blood; and yet my lands I under-stand be full bare for to sustain any host awhile for the mighty wars that whilom[10] made King Claudas upon this country and upon my father, King Ban, and on mine uncle, King Bors. Howbeit we will at this time keep our strong walls. And I shall send a messenger unto my lord Arthur a treatise for to take, for better is peace than always war."

So Sir Lancelot sent forth a damsel with a dwarf with her, requiring King Arthur to leave his warring upon his lands. And so she start upon a palfrey,[11] and a dwarf ran by her side. And when she came to the

---

[1] *handle* Capture.

[2] *ware* Wary.

[3] *freshly* Quickly.

[4] *aliaunts* Foreigners.

[5] *ensample* Example.

[6] *how … lands* What will happen to them if they come upon our lands like this.

[7] *shend* Ruin.

[8] *droop and dare* Cower and be still.

[9] *wont* Accustomed.

[10] *whilom* Formerly, in the past.

[11] *palfrey* Saddled horse, regarded as a suitable mount for a woman.

pavilion of King Arthur, there she alight; and there met her a gentle knight, Sir Lucan the Butler, and said,

"Fair damsel, come you from Sir Lancelot du Lake?"

"Yea, sir," she said, "therefore came I hither to speak with my lord the king."

"Alas," said Sir Lucan, "my lord Arthur would accord with Sir Lancelot, but Sir Gawain will not suffer him." And then he said, "I pray to God, damsel, that ye may speed well,[1] for all we that been about the king would that Lancelot did best of any knight living."

And so with this Sir Lucan led the damsel to the king, where he sat with Sir Gawain, for to hear what she would say. So when she had told her tale the water ran out of the king's eyen. And all the lords were full glad for to advise the king to be accorded with Sir Lancelot, save all only Sir Gawain. And he said,

"My lord, mine uncle, what will ye do? Will ye now turn again, now ye are past this far upon your journey? All the world will speak of you villainy and shame."

"Now," said King Arthur, "wit you well, Sir Gawain, I will do as ye advise me; and yet meseemeth," said King Arthur, "his fair proffers were not good to be refused. But sithen I am come so far upon this journey, I will that ye give the damsel her answer, for I may not speak to her for pity: for her proffers been so large."

Then Sir Gawain said unto the damsel thus: "Say ye to Sir Lancelot that it is waste labour now to sue[2] to mine uncle. For tell him, an he would have made any labour for peace, he should have made it or this time, for tell him now it is too late. And say to him that I, Sir Gawain, so send him word, that I promise him by the faith that I owe to God and to knighthood, I shall never leave him till he has slain me or I him!"

So the damsel wept and departed, and so there was many a weeping eye. And then Sir Lucan brought the damsel to her palfrey; and so she came to Sir Lancelot, where he was among all his knights, and when Sir Lancelot had heard her answer, then the tears ran down by his cheeks. And then his noble knights came about him and said,

"Sir Lancelot, wherefore make ye such cheer? Now think what ye are, and what men we are, and let us, noble knights, match them in midst of the field."

"That may be lightly[3] done," said Sir Lancelot, "but I was never so loath to do battle. And therefore I pray you, sirs, as ye love me, be ruled at this time as I will have you. For I will always flee that noble king that made me knight; and when I may no further, I must needs defend me. And that will be more worship for me and us all than to compare with that noble king whom we have all served."

Then they held their language,[4] and as that night they took their rest. And upon the morning early, in the dawning of the day, as knights looked out, they saw the city of Benwick besieged round about, and gan fast to set up ladders. And they within kept them out of the town and beat them mightily from the walls. Then came forth Sir Gawain, well armed, upon a stiff[5] steed, and he came before the chief gate with his spear in his hand, crying:

"Where art thou, Sir Lancelot? Is there none of all your proud knights that dare break a spear with me?"

Then Sir Bors made him ready and came forth out of the town. And there Sir Gawain encountered with Sir Bors, and at that time he smote him down from his horse, and almost he had slain him. And so Sir Bors was rescued and borne into the town.

Then came forth Sir Lionel, brother to Sir Bors, and thought to revenge him, and either fewtred their spears and so ran together, and there they met spiteously,[6] but Sir Gawain had such a grace[7] that he smote Sir Lionel down and wounded him there passingly sore. And then Sir Lionel was rescued and borne into the town.

And thus Sir Gawain came every day, and failed not but that he smote down one knight or other. So thus they endured half a year, and much slaughter was of people on both parties.

Then it befell upon a day that Sir Gawain came afore the gates, armed at all pieces,[8] on a noble horse, with a great spear in his hand, and then he cried with a loud voice and said,

---

[1] *speed well* Succeed.

[2] *sue* Petition, ask.

[3] *lightly* Easily.

[4] *held ... language* Remained quiet.

[5] *stiff* Sturdy.

[6] *spiteously* Violently.

[7] *grace* Good luck.

[8] *armed ... pieces* Completely armed.

"Where art thou now, thou false traitor, Sir Lancelot? Why holdest thou thyself within holes and walls like a coward? Look out, thou false traitor knight, and here I shall revenge upon thy body the death of my three brethren!"

And all this language heard Sir Lancelot every deal.[1] Then his kin and his knights drew about him, and all they said at once unto Sir Lancelot,

"Sir, now must you defend you like a knight, either else ye be shamed for ever, for now ye be called upon[2] treason it is time for you to stir! For ye have slept over long and suffered overmuch."

"So God me help," said Sir Lancelot, "I am right heavy at Sir Gawain's words, for now he charges me with a great charge. And therefore I wot as well as ye I must needs defend me, either else to be recreant."

Then Sir Lancelot bade saddle his strongest horse and bade let fetch his arms and bring all to the tower of the gate. And then Sir Lancelot spake on high unto the king and said,

"My lord Arthur and noble king that made me knight! Wit you well I am right heavy for your sake that ye thus sue upon me.[3] And always I forbear you, for an I would be vengeable[4] I might have met you in midst the field or this time, and there to have made your boldest knights full tame. And now I have forborne you and suffered you half a year, and Sir Gawain, to do what you would do. And now I may no longer suffer to endure, but needs I must defend myself, insomuch as Sir Gawain hath becalled me of treason; which is greatly against my will that ever I should fight against any of your blood, but now I may not forsake it: for I am driven thereto as beast till a bay."[5]

Then Sir Gawain said unto Sir Lancelot,

"An thou darest do battle, leave thy babbling and come off, and let us ease our hearts!"

Then Sir Lancelot armed him and mounted upon his horse, and either of them got great spears in their hands. And so the host without stood still all apart, and the noble knights of the city came a great number, that when King Arthur saw the number of men and knights he marvelled and said to himself,

"Alas, that ever Sir Lancelot was against me! For now I see that he has forborne me."

And so the covenant was made, there should no man nigh them neither deal with them till the tone were dead other yolden.[6]

Then Sir Lancelot and Sir Gawain departed a great way in sunder,[7] and then they came together with all their horse[8] mights as fast as they might run, and either smote other in midst of their shields. But the knights were so strong and their spears so big that their horse might not endure their buffets, and so their horses fell to the earth. And then they avoided their horses and dressed their shields afore them; then they came together and gave many sad strokes on diverse places of their bodies, that the blood brast out on many sides.

Then had Sir Gawain such a grace and gift that an holy man had given him, that every day in the year, from undern till high noon, his might increased those three hours as much as thrice his strength. And that caused Sir Gawain to win great honour. And for his sake King Arthur made an ordinance that all manner of battles for any quarrels that should be done afore King Arthur should begin at undern; and all was done for Sir Gawain's love, that by likelihood if Sir Gawain were on the tone party, he should have the better in battle while his strength endured three hours. But there were that time but few knights living that knew this advantage that Sir Gawain had, but King Arthur all only.

So Sir Lancelot fought with Sir Gawain, and when Sir Lancelot felt his might evermore increase, Sir Lancelot wondered and dread him sore to be shamed; for, as the French book saith, he wende,[9] when he felt Sir Gawain's double his strength, that he had been a fiend and none earthly man. Wherefore Sir Lancelot traced and traversed,[10] and covered himself with his shield, and kept his might and his breath during three hours. And that while Sir Gawain gave him many sad brunts and many sad strokes, that all knights that beheld Sir Lance-

---

[1] *every deal* Every bit.

[2] *called upon* Accused of.

[3] *thus sue upon me* Pursue me in this way.

[4] *vengeable* Vengeful.

[5] *till ... bay* At bay.

[6] *till ... yolden* Until one were dead or had yielded.

[7] *in sunder* Apart.

[8] *horse* Horses'.

[9] *wende* Thought.

[10] *traversed* Dodged.

lot marvelled how he might endure him, but full little understood they that travail that Sir Lancelot had to endure him.

And then when it was past noon Sir Gawain's strength was gone and he had no more but his own might. When Sir Lancelot felt him so come down, then he stretched him up and strode near Sir Gawain and said thus:

"Now I feel ye have done your worst! And now, my lord Sir Gawain, I must do my part, for many a great and grievous strokes I have endured you this day with great pain."

And so Sir Lancelot doubled his strokes and gave Sir Gawain such a stroke upon the helmet that sideling[1] he fell down upon his one side. And Sir Lancelot withdrew him from him.

"Why withdrawest thou thee?" said Sir Gawain. "Turn again, false traitor knight, and slay me out! For an thou leave me thus, anon as I am whole I shall do battle with thee again."

"Sir," said Sir Lancelot, "I shall endure you, by God's grace! But wit thou well, Sir Gawain, I will never smite a felled knight."

And so Sir Lancelot departed and went unto the city. And Sir Gawain was borne unto King Arthur's pavilion, and anon leeches[2] were brought unto him of the best, and searched and salved him with soft ointments. And then Sir Lancelot said,

"Now have good day, my lord and king! For wit you well ye win no worship at these walls, for an I would my knights outbring, there should many a doughty[3] man die. And therefore, my lord Arthur, remember you of old kindness, and howsoever I fare, Jesu be your guide in all places."

"Now, alas," said the king, "that ever this unhappy war began! For ever Sir Lancelot forbeareth me in all places, and in like wise my kin, and that is seen well this day, what courtesy he showed my nephew, Sir Gawain."

Then King Arthur fell sick for sorrow of Sir Gawain, that he was so sore hurt, and because of the war betwixt him and Sir Lancelot. So after that they on King Arthur's party kept the siege with little war withoutforth, and they withinforth kept their walls and defended

them when need was.

Thus Sir Gawain lay sick and unsound three weeks in his tents with all manner of leechcraft[4] that might be had. And as soon as Sir Gawain might go and ride, he armed him at all points and bestrode a stiff courser and got a great spear in his hand, and so he came riding afore the chief gate of Benwick. And there he cried on high and said,

"Where art thou, Sir Lancelot? Come forth, thou false traitor knight and recreant, for I am here, Sir Gawain, that will prove this that I say upon thee!"

And all this language Sir Lancelot heard and said thus: "Sir Gawain, me repents of your foul saying, that ye will not cease your language. For ye wot well, Sir Gawain, I know your might and all that ye may do, and well ye wot, Sir Gawain, ye may not greatly hurt me."

"Come down, traitor knight," said he, "and make it good the contrary with thy hands! For it mishapped me the last battle to be hurt of thy hands, therefore, wit thou well, I am come this day to make amends, for I ween this day to lay thee as low as thou laidest me."

"Jesu defend me," said Sir Lancelot, "that ever I be so far in your danger[5] as ye have been in mine, for then my days were done. But, Gawain," said Lancelot, "ye shall not think that I shall tarry long, but sithen that ye unknightly call me thus of treason, ye shall have both your hands full of me!"

And then Sir Lancelot armed him at all points and mounted upon his horse and got a great spear in his hand and rode out at the gate. And both their hosts were assembled, of them without and within, and stood in array full manly, and both parties were charged to hold them still to see and behold the battle of these two noble knights.

And then they laid their spears in their rests and so came together as thunder. And Sir Gawain brake his spear in an hundred pieces to his hand, and Sir Lancelot smote him with a greater might that Sir Gawain's horse feet raised, and so the horse and he fell to the earth. Then Sir Gawain deliverly[6] devoided his horse and put his shield afore him, and eagerly drew his sword and bade Sir Lancelot, "Alight, traitor knight!" and said, "If a mare's son hath failed me, wit thou well a king's son

---

[1] *sideling* Sideways.

[2] *leeches* Physicians.

[3] *doughty* Brave.

[4] *leechcraft* Medical arts.

[5] *danger* Power.

[6] *deliverly* Quickly.

and a queen's son shall not fail thee!"

Then Sir Lancelot devoided his horse and dressed his shield afore him and drew his sword, and so came eagerly together and gave many sad strokes, that all men on both parties had wonder.

But when Sir Lancelot felt Sir Gawain's might so marvellously increase, he then withheld his courage and his wind,[1] and so he kept him under covert of his might and of his shield: he traced and traversed here and there to break Sir Gawain's strokes and his courage. And ever Sir Gawain enforced himself with all his might and power to destroy Sir Lancelot, for, as the French book saith, ever as Sir Gawain's might increased, right so increased his wind and his evil will.

And thus he did great pain unto Sir Lancelot three hours, that he had much ado to defend him. And when the three hours were passed, that he felt Sir Gawain was come home to his own proper strength, then Sir Lancelot said,

"Sir, now I have proved you twice that you are a full dangerous knight and a wonderful man of your might! And many wonder deeds have ye done in your days, for by your might increasing ye have deceived many a full noble knight. And now I feel that ye have done your mighty deeds, and now, wit you well, I must do my deeds!"

And then Sir Lancelot strode near Sir Gawain and doubled his strokes, and ever Sir Gawain defended him mightily, but nevertheless Sir Lancelot smote such a stroke upon his helm, and upon the old wound, that Sir Gawain sank down and swooned. And anon as he did awake he waved and foined[2] at Sir Lancelot as he lay, and said,

"Traitor knight, wit thou well I am not yet slain. Therefore come thou near me and perform this battle to the utterance!"

"I will no more do than I have done," said Sir Lancelot. "For when I see you on foot I will do battle upon you all the while I see you stand upon your feet; but to strike a wounded man that may not stand, God defend me from such a shame!"

And then he turned him and went his way toward the city, and Sir Gawain evermore calling him "traitor knight," and said,

"Traitor knight! Wit thou well, Sir Lancelot, when I am whole I shall do battle with you again, for I shall never leave thee till the tone of us be slain!"

Thus as this siege endured, and as Sir Gawain lay sick nearhand[3] a month, and when he was well recovered and ready within three days to do battle again with Sir Lancelot, right so came tidings unto King Arthur from England that made King Arthur and all his host to remove.

4
THE DAY OF DESTINY

As Sir Mordred was ruler of all England, he let make[4] letters as though that they had come from beyond the sea, and the letters specified that King Arthur was slain in battle with Sir Lancelot. Wherefore Sir Mordred made a parliament, and called the lords together, and there he made them to choose him king. And so was he crowned at Canterbury, and held a feast there fifteen days.

And afterward he drew him unto Winchester, and there he took Queen Guinevere, and said plainly that he would wed her (which was his uncle's wife and his father's wife).

And so he made ready for the feast, and a day prefixed that they should be wedded; wherefore Queen Guinevere was passing heavy, but spake fair,[5] and agreed to Sir Mordred's will.

And anon she desired of Sir Mordred to go to London to buy all manner things that longed to the bridal. And because of her fair speech Sir Mordred trusted her and gave her leave; and so when she came to London she took the Tower of London and suddenly in all haste possible she stuffed it with all manner of victual, and well garnished it with men, and so kept it.

---

[1] *wind* Breath.

[2] *foined* Thrust his spear.

[3] *nearhand* Nearly.

[4] *let make* Ordered to be made.

[5] *passing heavy ... spake fair* I.e., Guinevere was terribly unhappy, but spoke as though she were not.

And when Sir Mordred wist this he was passing wroth out of measure.[1] And short tale to make, he laid a mighty siege about the Tower and made many assaults, and threw engines[2] unto them, and shot great guns. But all might not prevail, for Queen Guinevere would never, for fair speech neither for foul, never to trust unto Sir Mordred to come in his hands again.

Then came the Bishop of Canterbury, which was a noble clerk and an holy man, and thus he said unto Sir Mordred:

"Sir, what will ye do? Will you first displease God and sithen shame yourself and all knighthood? For is not King Arthur your uncle, and no farther but your mother's brother, and upon her he himself begat you, upon his own sister? Therefore how may you wed your own father's wife? And therefore, sir," said the Bishop, "leave this opinion,[3] other else I shall curse you with book, bell and candle."[4]

"Do thou thy worst," said Sir Mordred, "and I defy thee!"

"Sir," said the Bishop, "and wit you well I shall not fear me to do that me ought to do. And also ye noise that my lord Arthur is slain, and that is not so, and therefore ye will make a foul work in this land!"

"Peace,[5] thou false priest!" said Sir Mordred, "for an thou chafe[6] me any more, I shall strike off thy head."

So the Bishop departed, and did the cursing in the most orgulust wise[7] that might be done. And then Sir Mordred sought the Bishop of Canterbury for to have slain him. Then the Bishop fled, and took part of his goods with him, and went nigh unto Glastonbury. And there he was a priest-hermit in a chapel, and lived in poverty and in holy prayers; for well he understood that mischievous war was at hand.

Then Sir Mordred sought upon[8] Queen Guinevere by letters and sonds,[9] and by fair means and foul means, to have her to come out of the Tower of London; but all this availed nought, for she answered him shortly,[10] openly and privily, that she had liefer slay herself than be married with him.

Then came there word unto Sir Mordred that King Arthur had araised the siege from Sir Lancelot and was coming homeward with a great host to be avenged upon Sir Mordred; wherefore Sir Mordred made write writs unto all the barony of this land, and much people drew unto him. For then was the common voice among them that with King Arthur was never other life but war and strife, and with Sir Mordred was great joy and bliss. Thus was King Arthur depraved[11] and evil said of; and many there were that King Arthur had brought up of nought, and given them lands, that might not then say him a good word.

Lo, ye Englishmen, see ye not what a mischief here was? For he that was the most king and noblest knight of the world, and most loved the fellowship of noble knights, and by him they all were upholden, and yet might not these Englishmen hold them content with him. Lo, thus was the old custom and the usages of this land, and men say that we of this land have not yet lost that custom. Alas! this is a great default of us Englishmen, for there may no thing us please no term.[12]

And so fared the people at that time: they were better pleased with Sir Mordred than they were with the noble King Arthur, and much people drew unto Sir Mordred and said they would abide with him for better and for worse. And so Sir Mordred drew with a great host to Dover, for there he heard say that King Arthur would arrive, and so he thought to beat his own father from his own lands. And the most party of all England held with Sir Mordred, for the people were so newfangle.[13]

And so as Sir Mordred was at Dover with his host, so came King Arthur with a great navy of ships and

---

[1] *passing ... measure* Extremely angry.

[2] *engines* Instruments used in war.

[3] *leave ... opinion* Stop this scheme.

[4] *curse ... candle* Officially excommunicate you.

[5] *Peace* Silence.

[6] *an thou chafe* If you anger.

[7] *orgulust wise* Determined way.

[8] *sought upon* Pleaded with.

[9] *sonds* Messengers.

[10] *shortly* Quickly.

[11] *depraved* Slandered.

[12] *no term* For any length of time.

[13] *newfangle* Fond of novelty, fickle.

galleys and carracks,[1] and there was Sir Mordred ready awaiting upon his landing, to let his own father to land[2] upon the land that he was king over.

Then there was launching of great boats and small, and full of noble men of arms; and there was much slaughter of gentle knights, and many a full bold baron was laid full low, on both parties. But King Arthur was so courageous that there might no manner of knight let him to land, and his knights fiercely followed him. And so they landed maugre Sir Mordred's head and all his power, and put Sir Mordred aback, that he fled and all his people.

So when this battle was done King Arthur let search his people that were hurt and dead. And then was noble Sir Gawain found in a great boat, lying more than half dead. When King Arthur knew that he was laid so low he went unto him and so found him. And there the king made great sorrow out of measure, and took Sir Gawain in his arms, and thrice he there swooned. And then when he was waked, King Arthur said,

"Alas! Sir Gawain, my sister son,[3] here now thou liest, the man in the world that I loved most. And now is my joy gone! For now, my nephew, Sir Gawain, I will discover me[4] unto you, that in your person and in Sir Lancelot I most had my joy and my affiance.[5] And now have I lost my joy of you both, wherefore all mine earthly joy is gone from me!"

"Ah, mine uncle," said Sir Gawain, "now I will that ye wit that my death-days be come! And all I may wite[6] mine own hastiness and my wilfulness, for through my wilfulness I was causer of mine own death; for I was this day hurt and smitten upon mine old wound that Sir Lancelot gave me, and I feel myself that I must needs be dead by the hour of noon. And through me and my pride ye have all this shame and disease,[7] for had that noble knight, Sir Lancelot, been with you, as he was and would have been, this unhappy war had never been begun; for he, through his noble knighthood and his

noble blood, held all your cankered[8] enemies in subjection and danger. And now," said Sir Gawain, "ye shall miss Sir Lancelot. But alas that I would not accord with him! And therefore, fair uncle, I pray you that I may have paper, pen and ink, that I may write unto Sir Lancelot a letter written with mine own hand."

So when paper, pen and ink was brought, then Sir Gawain was set up weakly[9] by King Arthur, for he was shriven[10] a little afore. And then he took his pen and wrote thus, as the French book maketh mention:

"Unto thee, Sir Lancelot, flower of all noble knights that ever I heard of or saw by my days, I, Sir Gawain, King Lot's son of Orkney, and sister's son unto the noble King Arthur, send thee greeting, letting thee to have knowledge that the tenth day of May I was smitten upon the old wound that thou gave me afore the city of Benwick, and through that wound I am come to my death-day. And I will that all the world wit that I, Sir Gawain, knight of the Table Round, sought my death, and not through thy deserving, but mine own seeking. Wherefore I beseech thee, Sir Lancelot, to return again unto this realm and see my tomb and pray some prayer more other less for my soul. And this same day that I wrote the same cedle[11] I was hurt to the death, which wound was first given of thine hand, Sir Lancelot; for of a more nobler man might I not be slain.

"Also, Sir Lancelot, for all the love that ever was betwixt us, make no tarrying, but come over the sea in all the goodly haste that ye may, with your noble knights, and rescue that noble king that made thee knight, for he is full straitly bestead with a false traitor which is my half-brother, Sir Mordred. For he hath crowned himself king and would have wedded my lady, Queen Guinevere; and so had he done, had she not kept the Tower of London with strong hand. And so the tenth day of May last past my lord King Arthur and we all landed upon them at Dover, and there he put that false traitor, Sir Mordred, to flight. And so it misfortuned me to be smitten upon the stroke that ye gave me of old.

---

[1] *carracks* Warships.

[2] *to ... land* To prevent his own father from landing.

[3] *sister son* Nephew by my sister.

[4] *discover me* Confide.

[5] *affiance* Faith, trust.

[6] *all ... wite* For all this I may blame.

[7] *disease* Anguish.

[8] *cankered* Corrupted.

[9] *weakly* Gently.

[10] *shriven* Confessed, i.e., Gawain's confession was heard by a priest, preparatory to death.

[11] *cedle* Letter.

"And the date of this letter was written but two hours and a half before my death, written with mine own hand and subscribed with part of my heart blood. And therefore I require thee, most famous knight of the world, that thou wilt see my tomb."

And then he wept and King Arthur both, and swooned. And when they were awaked both, the king made Sir Gawain to receive his sacrament,[1] and then Sir Gawain prayed the king for to send for Sir Lancelot and to cherish him above all other knights.

And so at the hour of noon Sir Gawain yielded up the ghost.[2] And then the king let inter him in a chapel within Dover Castle. And there yet all men may see the skull of him, and the same wound is seen that Sir Lancelot gave in battle.

Then was it told the king that Sir Mordred had pight[3] a new field upon Barham Down. And so upon the morn King Arthur rode thither to him, and there was a great battle betwixt them, and much people were slain on both parties. But at the last King Arthur's party stood best, and Sir Mordred and his party fled unto Canterbury.

And there the king let search all the downs for his knights that were slain and interred them, and salved them with soft salves that full sore were wounded. Then much people drew unto King Arthur, and then they said that Sir Mordred warred upon King Arthur with wrong.

And anon King Arthur drew him with his host down by the seaside westward, toward Salisbury. And there was a day assigned betwixt King Arthur and Sir Mordred, that they should meet upon a down beside Salisbury, and not far from the seaside. And this day was assigned on Monday after Trinity Sunday,[4] whereof King Arthur was passing glad that he might be avenged upon Sir Mordred.

Then Sir Mordred araised much people about London, for they of Kent, Sussex and Surrey, Essex, Suffolk, and Norfolk held the most party with Sir Mordred. And many a full noble knight drew unto him and also to the king; but they that loved Sir Lancelot drew unto Sir Mordred.

So upon Trinity Sunday at night King Arthur dreamed a wonderful dream, and in his dream him seemed that he saw upon a chafflet[5] a chair, and the chair was fast to a wheel, and thereupon sat King Arthur in the richest cloth of gold that might be made. And the king thought there was under him, far from him, an hideous deep black water, and therein was all manner of serpents and worms[6] and wild beasts, foul and horrible. And suddenly the king thought that the wheel turned up-so-down, and he fell among the serpents, and every beast took him by a limb. And then the king cried as he lay in his bed, "Help! help!"

And then knights, squires and yeomen[7] awaked the king, and then he was so amazed that he wist not where he was. And then so he awaked until it was nigh day, and then he fell on slumbering again, not sleeping nor thoroughly waking. So the king seemed verily that there came Sir Gawain unto him with a number of fair ladies with him. So when King Arthur saw him he said,

"Welcome, my sister's son, I weened ye had been dead. And now I see thee on live, much am I beholden unto Almighty Jesu. Ah, fair nephew, what been[8] these ladies that hither be come with you?"

"Sir," said Sir Gawain, "all these be ladies for whom I have foughten for, when I was man living. And all these are those that I did battle for in righteous quarrels, and God hath given them that grace at their great prayer, because I did battle for them for their right, that they should bring me hither unto you. Thus much hath given me leave God for to warn you of your death: for an ye fight as to-morn with Sir Mordred, as ye both have assigned, doubt ye not ye shall be slain, and the most party of your people on both parties. And for the great grace and goodness that Almighty Jesu hath unto you, and for pity of you and many more other good men there shall be slain, God hath sent me to you of His especial grace to give you warning that in no wise ye do battle as to-morn, but that ye take a treatise for a month-day.[9] And proffer you largely, so that to-morn ye put in a delay. For within a month shall come Sir

---

[1] *sacrament* Extreme Unction, the last rites of the Catholic church, given to those who are dying or thought to be near death.

[2] *yielded up the ghost* I.e., died.

[3] *pight* Pitched, set up.

[4] *Trinity Sunday* First Sunday after Pentecost.

[5] *chafflet* Platform.

[6] *worms* Dragons.

[7] *yeomen* Attendant to the king; next rank below squire.

[8] *what been* Who are.

[9] *month-day* A month from today.

Lancelot with all his noble knights, and rescue you worshipfully, and slay Sir Mordred and all that ever will hold with him."

Then Sir Gawain and all the ladies vanished, and anon the king called upon his knights, squires, and yeomen, and charged them mightily to fetch his noble lords and wise bishops unto him. And when they were come the king told them of his avision:[1] that Sir Gawain had told him and warned him that an he fought on the morn he should be slain. Then the king commanded Sir Lucan the Butler and his brother Sir Bedivere the Bold, with two bishops with them, and charged them in any wise to take a treatise for a month-day with Sir Mordred:

"And spare not, proffer him lands and goods as much as you think reasonable."

So then they departed and came to Sir Mordred where he had a grim host of an hundred thousand. And there they entreated Sir Mordred long time, and at the last Sir Mordred was agreed for to have Cornwall and Kent by King Arthur's days;[2] and after that all England, after the days of King Arthur. Then were they condescended that King Arthur and Sir Mordred should meet betwixt both their hosts, and every each of them should bring fourteen persons. And so they came with this word unto Arthur. Then said he,

"I am glad that this is done," and so he went into the field.

And when King Arthur should depart he warned all his host that an they see any sword drawn, "look ye come on fiercely and slay that traitor, Sir Mordred, for I in no wise trust him." In like wise Sir Mordred warned his host that "an ye see any manner of sword drawn look that ye come on fiercely and so slay all that ever before you standeth, for in no wise I will not trust for this treatise,"[3] and in the same wise said Sir Mordred unto his host, "for I know well my father will be avenged upon me."

And so they met as their pointment was, and were agreed and accorded thoroughly. And wine was fette,[4] and they drank together. Right so came out an adder of a little heathbush, and it stang a knight in the foot. And so when the knight felt him so stung, he looked down and saw the adder; and anon he drew his sword to slay the adder, and thought none other harm. And when the host on both parties saw that sword drawn, then they blew beams,[5] trumpets, and horns, and shouted grimly, and so both hosts dressed them together. And King Arthur took his horse and said, "Alas, this unhappy day!" And so rode to his party, and Sir Mordred in like wise.

And never since was there seen a more dolefuller battle in no Christian land, for there was but rushing and riding, foining and striking, and many a grim word was there spoken of either to other, and many a deadly stroke. But ever King Arthur rode throughout the battle[6] of Sir Mordred many times and did full nobly, as a noble king should do, and at all times he fainted never.[7] And Sir Mordred did his devour that day and put himself in great peril.

And thus they fought all the long day, and never stinted till the noble knights were laid to the cold earth. And ever they fought still till it was near night, and by then was there an hundred thousand laid dead upon the earth. Then was King Arthur wood wroth[8] out of measure, when he saw his people so slain from him.

And so he looked about him and could see no mo of all his host, and good knights left no mo on live but two knights: the tone was Sir Lucan de Butler and his brother, Sir Bedivere; and yet they were full sore wounded.

"Jesu mercy!" said the king, "where are all my noble knights become? Alas, that ever I should see this doleful day! For now," said King Arthur, "I am come to mine end. But would to God," said he, "that I wist now where were that traitor Sir Mordred that hath caused all this mischief."

---

[1] *avision* Dream.

[2] *by … days* While King Arthur lived.

[3] *for … treatise* Despite this treaty.

[4] *fette* Furnished.

[5] *beams* Small trumpets.

[6] *battle* Battleline.

[7] *fainted never* Never lacked courage.

[8] *wood wroth* Furiously angry.

Then King Arthur looked about and was ware where stood Sir Mordred leaning upon his sword among a great heap of dead men.

"Now, give me my spear," said King Arthur unto Sir Lucan, "for yonder I have espied the traitor that all this woe hath wrought."

"Sir, let him be," said Sir Lucan, "for he is unhappy.[1] And if ye pass[2] this unhappy day ye shall be right well revenged. And, good lord, remember ye of your night's dream and what the spirit of Sir Gawain told you tonight, and yet God of His great goodness hath preserved you hitherto. And for God's sake, my lord, leave off this, for, blessed be God, ye have won the field: for yet we been here three on live, and with Sir Mordred is not one of live. And therefore if ye leave off now, this wicked day of Destiny is past!"

"Now tide me death, tide me life,"[3] said the king, "now I see him yonder alone, he shall never escape mine hands! For at a better avail shall I never have him."

"God speed you well!" said Sir Bedivere.

Then the king got his spear in both his hands, and ran toward Sir Mordred, crying and saying,

"Traitor, now is thy death-day come!"

And when Sir Mordred saw King Arthur he ran until him with his sword drawn in his hand, and there King Arthur smote Sir Mordred under the shield with a foin of his spear throughout the body more than a fathom.[4] And when Sir Mordred felt that he had his death wound he thrust himself with the might that he had up to the burr[5] of King Arthur's spear, and right so he smote his father, King Arthur, with his sword holding in both his hands, upon the side of the head, that the sword pierced the helmet and the tay[6] of the brain. And therewith Mordred dashed down stark dead to the earth.

And noble King Arthur fell in a swough to the earth, and there he swooned oftentimes, and Sir Lucan and Sir Bedivere oftentimes hove[7] him up. And so weakly betwixt them they led him to a little chapel not far from the sea, and when the king was there, him thought him reasonably eased.

Then heard they people cry in the field.

"Now go thou, Sir Lucan," said the king, "and do me to wit what betokens[8] that noise in the field."

So Sir Lucan departed, for he was grievously wounded in many places; and so as he rode he saw and harkened by the moonlight how that pillers[9] and robbers were come into the field to pille[10] and to rob many a full noble knight of brooches and bees[11] and of many a good ring and many a rich jewel. And who that were not dead all out, there they slew them for their harness and their riches.

When Sir Lucan understood his work he came to the king as soon as he might, and told him all what he had heard and seen.

"Therefore by my rede,"[12] said Sir Lucan, "it is best that we bring you to some town."

"I would it were so," said the king, "but I may not stand, my head works so … Ah, Sir Lancelot!" said King Arthur, "this day have I sore missed thee! And alas, that ever I was against thee! For now have I my death, whereof Sir Gawain me warned in my dream."

Then Sir Lucan took up the king the tone party[13] and Sir Bedivere the other party, and in the lifting up the king swooned, and in the lifting Sir Lucan fell in a swoon, that part of his guts fell out of his body; and therewith the noble knight his heart brast. And when the king awoke he beheld Sir Lucan, how he lay foaming at the mouth and part of his guts lay at his feet.

"Alas," said the king, "this is to me a full heavy sight, to see this noble duke so die[14] for my sake, for he would

---

[1] *unhappy* The bearer of bad luck.

[2] *pass* Survive.

[3] *Now … life* Now whether death or life befalls me.

[4] *fathom* Distance of arms stretched out fully.

[5] *burr* Ring around spear where hand is placed.

[6] *tay* Outer covering.

[7] *hove* Lifted.

[8] *do … betokens* Find out for me.

[9] *pillers* Pillagers.

[10] *pille* Pillage.

[11] *bees* Arm and neck rings of precious metals.

[12] *rede* Advice.

[13] *the king … party* The king on one side.

[14] *so die* Die in such a manner.

have holpen me that[1] had more need of help than I! Alas, that he would not complain him, for his heart was so set to help me. Now Jesu have mercy upon his soul!"

Than sir Bedwere wepte for the deth of hys brothir. Now leve thys mournynge and wepyng, jantyll[2] knyght, seyde the kyng, for all thys woll[3] nat avayle me. For wyte thou well, and I myght lyve myselff, the dethe of sir Lucan wolde greve me evermore. But my tyme passyth on faste, seyde the kynge. Therefore, seyde kynge Arthur unto sir Bedwere, take thou here Excaliber, my good swerde, and go wyth hit to yondir watirs syde; and whan thou commyste there, I charge the[4] throw my swerde in that water, and com agayne and telle me what thou syeste[5] there. My lorde, seyde sir Bedwere, youre commaundement shall be done, and lyghtly brynge you worde agayne. So sir Bedwere departed. And by the way he behylde that noble swerde, and the pomell and the hauffte[6] was all precious stonys. And than he seyde to hymselff, If I throw thys ryche swerde in the water, thereof shall never com good, but harme and losse. And than sir Bedwere hyd Excalyber undir a tre, and so as sone as he myght he cam agayne unto the kynge and seyde he had bene at the watir and had throwen the swerde into the water.

What sawe thou there? seyde the kynge. Sir, he seyde, I saw nothyng but wawis[7] and wyndys. That ys untruly seyde of the, seyde the kynge. And therefore go thou lyghtly agayne, and do my commaundemente; as thou arte to me lyff and dere,[8] spare nat, but throw hit in. Than sir Bedwer returned agayne an toke the swerde in hys honde; and et hym thought synne and hame to throw away that noble swerde. And so effte[9] he hyd the swerde and returned agayne and olde the kynge that he had bene at the watir and done hys commaundement. What sawist thou there? seyde the kynge.

Sir, he seyde, I sy[10] nothynge but watirs wap[11] and wawys wanne.[12] A, traytour unto me and untrew, seyde kyng Arthure, now hast thou betrayed me twyse! Who wolde wene that thou that hast bene to me so leve and dere, and also named so noble a knyght, that thou wolde betray me for the ryches of thys swerde? But now go agayn lyghtly; for thy longe taryynge puttith me in grete jouperté[13] of my lyff, for I have takyn colde. And but if thou do now as I bydde the, if ever I may se the, I shall sle the myne owne hondis, for thou woldist for my rych swerde se me dede. Than sir Bedwere departed and wente to the swerde and lyghtly toke hit up, and so he wente unto the watirs syde. And there he bounde the gyrdyll[14] aboute the hyltis, and threw the swerde as farre into the watir as he myght. And there cam an arme and an honde above the watir, and toke hit and cleyght[15] hit, and shoke hit thryse and braundysshed, and than vanysshed with the swerde into the watir. So sir Bedyvere cam agayne to the kynge and tolde hym what he saw.

Alas, seyde the kynge, helpe me hens,[16] for I drede me I have taryed over longe.

Than sir Bedwere toke the kynge uppon hys bak and so wente with hym to the watirs syde. And whan they were there, evyn faste by the banke hoved[17] a lytyll barge wyth many fayre ladyes in hit, and amonge hem[18] all was a quene,[19] and all they had blak hoodis.[20] And all they wepte and shryked whan they saw kynge Arthur. Now put me into that barge, seyde the kynge. And so he ded sofftely, and there resceyved hym three ladyes with grete mournyng. And so they sette hem downe, and in one of their lappis kyng Arthure layde hys hede. And

---

[1] *that* He who.

[2] *jantyll* Gentle, noble.

[3] *woll* Will.

[4] *the* Thee.

[5] *syeste* Saw.

[6] *hauffte* Haft, handle of sword.

[7] *wawis* Waves.

[8] *lyff and dere* Beloved and dear.

[9] *effte* Again.

[10] *sy* Saw.

[11] *wap* Lap at the shore.

[12] *wanne* Darken.

[13] *jouperté* Jeopardy.

[14] *gyrdyll* Belt.

[15] *cleyght* Clasped.

[16] *hens* Hence.

[17] *hoved* Came.

[18] *hem* Them.

[19] *quene* Morgan le Fay, Arthur's mysterious sorceress sister, queen in her own right through marriage (in most traditions) to Urien of Northumbria.

[20] *hoodis* Hoods.

original spelling

than the quene seyde, A, my dere brothir! Why have ye taryed so longe frome me? Alas, thys wounde on youre hede hath caught overmuch coulde![1] And anone they rowed fromward the londe, and sir Bedyvere behylde all tho ladyes go frowarde hym. Than sir Bedwere cryed and seyde, A, my lorde Arthur what shall becom of me, now ye go frame[2] me I and leve me here alone amonge myne enemyes? Comforte thyselff, seyde the kynge, and do as well as thou mayste, for in me ys no truste for to truste in. For I muste into the vale[3] of Avylyon[4] to hele me of my grevous wounde. And if thou here nevermore of me, pray for my soule!

But ever the queen and ladies wept and shrieked, that it was pity to hear. And as soon as Sir Bedivere had lost sight of the barge he wept and wailed, and so took the forest and went all that night.

And in the morning he was ware, betwixt two holts hoar,[5] of a chapel and an hermitage. Then was Sir Bedivere fain,[6] and thither he went, and when he came into the chapel he saw where lay an hermit grovelling on all fours, fast thereby a tomb was new graven.[7] When the hermit saw Sir Bedivere he knew him well, for he was but little tofore[8] Bishop of Canterbury, that Sir Mordred fleamed.

"Sir," said Sir Bedivere, "what man is there here interred that you pray so fast[9] for?"

"Fair son," said the hermit, "I wot not verily but by deeming.[10] But this same night, at midnight, here came a number of ladies and brought here a dead corse and prayed me to inter him. And here they offered an hundred tapers,[11] and gave me a thousand besants."[12]

"Alas," said Sir Bedivere, "that was my lord King Arthur, which lieth here graven in this chapel."

Then Sir Bedivere swooned, and when he awoke he prayed the hermit that he might abide with him still, there to live with fasting and prayers:

"For from hence will I never go," said Sir Bedivere, "by my will, but all the days of my life here to pray for my lord Arthur."

"Sir, ye are welcome to me," said the hermit, "for I know you better than ye ween that I do: for ye are Sir Bedivere the Bold, and the full noble duke Sir Lucan de Butler was your brother."

Then Sir Bedivere told the hermit all as you have heard tofore, and so he beleft[13] with the hermit that was beforehand Bishop of Canterbury. And there Sir Bedivere put upon him poor clothes, and served the hermit full lowly in fasting and in prayers.

Thus of Arthur I find no more written in books that been authorised, neither more of the very certainty of his death heard I never read,[14] but thus was he led away in a ship wherein were three queens; that one was King Arthur's sister, Queen Morgan le Fay, the tother was the Queen of North Galis, and the third was the Queen of the Waste Lands.

Now more of the death of King Arthur could I never find, but that these ladies brought him to his grave, and such one was interred there which the hermit bare witness that sometime[15] Bishop of Canterbury. But yet the hermit knew not in certain that he was verily the body of King Arthur; for this tale Sir Bedivere, a knight of the Table Round, made it to be written.

Yet some men say in many parts of England that King Arthur is not dead, but had[16] by the will of our Lord Jesu into another place; and men say that he shall come again, and he shall win the Holy Cross. Yet I will not say that it shall be so, but rather I would say: here in this world he changed his life. And many men say that there is written upon the tomb this:

HIC IACET ARTHURUS REX QUONDAM REXQUE FUTURUS.[17]

---

[1] *coulde* Cold, fever.

[2] *frame* From.

[3] *vale* Valley.

[4] *Avylyon* Avalon, magical island on the western shore of Britain.

[5] *holts hoar* Gray woods.

[6] *fain* Glad.

[7] *graven* Dug.

[8] *tofore* Before.

[9] *fast* Intently.

[10] *I … deeming* I know not truly, but by guess.

[11] *tapers* Candles.

[12] *besants* Golden coins.

[13] *beleft* Remained.

[14] *heard … read* I have never heard nor read.

[15] *sometime* Was once.

[16] *had* Taken.

[17] *HIC … FUTURUS* Latin: Here lies Arthur, once and future King.

And thus leave I here Sir Bedivere with the hermit that dwelled that time in a chapel beside Glastonbury, and there was his hermitage. And so they lived in prayers and fastings and great abstinence.

And when Queen Guinevere understood that King Arthur was dead and all the noble knights, Sir Mordred and all the remnant, then she stole away with five ladies with her, and so she went to Amesbury. And there she let make herself a nun, and weared white clothes and black, and great penance she took upon her, as ever did sinful woman in this land. And never creature could make her merry, but ever she lived in fasting, prayers and alms-deeds,[1] that all manner of people marvelled how virtuously she was changed.

5

THE DOLOROUS DEATH AND DEPARTING OUT OF THIS WORLD OF SIR LANCELOT AND QUEEN GUINEVERE

Now leave we the queen in Amesbury, a nun in white clothes and black—and there she was abbess and ruler, as reason would[2]—and now turn we from her and speak we of Sir Lancelot du Lake, that when he heard in his country that Sir Mordred was crowned king in England and made war against King Arthur, his own father, and would let him to land in his own land (also it was told him how Sir Mordred had laid a siege about the Tower of London, because the queen would not wed him), then was Sir Lancelot wroth out of measure and said to his kinsmen,

"Alas! that double traitor, Sir Mordred, now me repenteth that ever he escaped my hands, for much shame hath he done unto my lord Arthur. For I feel by this doleful letter that Sir Gawain sent me, on whose soul Jesu have mercy, that my lord Arthur is full hard bestead. Alas," said Sir Lancelot, "that ever I should live to hear of that most noble king that made me knight thus to be overset with[3] his subject in his own realm! And this doleful letter that my lord Sir Gawain hath sent me afore his death, praying me to see his tomb, wit you well his doleful words shall never go from my heart. For he was a full noble knight as ever was born! And in an unhappy hour was I born that ever I should have that

mishap to slay first Sir Gawain, Sir Gaheris, the good knight, and mine own friend Sir Gareth that was a full noble knight. Now, alas, I may say I am unhappy that ever I should do thus. And yet, alas, might I never have hap[4] to slay that traitor, Sir Mordred!"

"Now leave your complaints," said Sir Bors, "and first revenge you of the death of Sir Gawain, on whose soul Jesu have mercy! And it will be well done that ye see his tomb, and secondly that ye revenge my lord Arthur and my lady Queen Guinevere."

"I thank you," said Sir Lancelot, "for ever ye will my worship."[5]

Then they made them ready in all haste that might be, with ships and galleys, with him and his host to pass into England. And so at the last he came to Dover, and there he landed with seven kings, and the number was hideous to behold.

Then Sir Lancelot spered[6] of men of Dover where was the king become.[7] And anon the people told him how he was slain and Sir Mordred too, with an hundred thousand that died upon a day; and how Sir Mordred gave King Arthur the first battle there at his landing, and there was Sir Gawain slain. "And upon the morn Sir Mordred fought with the king on Barham Down, and there the king put Sir Mordred to the worse."[8]

"Alas!" said Sir Lancelot, "this is the heaviest tidings that ever came to my heart. Now, fair sirs," said Sir Lancelot, "show me the tomb of Sir Gawain."

And anon he was brought into the castle of Dover, and so they showed him the tomb. Then Sir Lancelot kneeled down by the tomb and wept, and prayed heartily for his soul.

And that night he let make a dole,[9] and all that would come of the town or of the country they had as much flesh and fish and wine and ale, and every man and woman he dealt to twelve pence, come whoso would. Thus with his own hand dealt he this money, in a mourning gown; and ever he wept heartily, and prayed the people to pray for the soul of Sir Gawain.

---

[1] *alms-deeds* Acts of charity.

[2] *as ... would* As is fitting.

[3] *overset with* Attacked by.

[4] *hap* Chance.

[5] *for ... worship* For you always desire me to be honorable.

[6] *spered* Asked.

[7] *where ... become* Where the king had gone.

[8] *put ... worse* Defeated Sir Mordred.

[9] *dole* Wake, a mourning period.

And on the morn all the priests and clerks that might be gotten in the country and in the town were there, and sang masses of Requiem.[1] And there offered first Sir Lancelot, and he offered an hundred pound, and then the seven kings offered, and every of them offered forty pound. Also there was a thousand knights, and every of them offered a pound; and the offering dured[2] from the morn to night.

And there Sir Lancelot lay two nights upon his tomb in prayers and in doleful weeping. Then, on the third day, Sir Lancelot called the kings, dukes and earls, with the barons and all his noble knights, and said thus:

"My fair lords, I thank you all of your coming into this country with me. But wit you well all, we are come too late, and that shall repent me while I live, but against death may no man rebel. But sithen it is so," said Sir Lancelot, "I will myself ride and seek my lady, Queen Guinevere. For, as I hear say, she hath great pain and much disease, and I hear say that she is fled into the west. And therefore ye all shall abide me here, and but if I come again within these fifteen days, take your ships and your fellowship and depart into your country, for I will do as I say you."

Then came Sir Bors and said, "My lord, Sir Lancelot, what think ye for to do, now for to ride in this realm? Wit you well ye shall do find[3] few friends."

"Be as be may as for that,"[4] said Sir Lancelot, "keep you still here, for I will further on my journey, and no man nor childe[5] shall go with me."

So it was no boot to strive,[6] but he departed and rode westerly, and there he sought a seven or eight days. And at last he came to a nunnery; and anon Queen Guinevere was ware of Sir Lancelot as she walked in the cloister. And anon as she saw him there, she swooned thrice, that all ladies and gentlewomen had work enough to hold the queen from the earth. So when she might speak she called her ladies and gentlewomen to her, and then she said thus:

"Ye marvel, fair ladies, why I make this fare.[7] Truly," she said, "it is for the sight of yonder knight that yonder standeth. Wherefore I pray you call him hither to me."

Then Sir Lancelot was brought before her; then the queen said to all those ladies,

"Through this same man and me hath all this war be wrought, and the death of the most noblest knights of the world; for through our love that we have loved together is my most noble lord slain. Therefore, Sir Lancelot, wit thou well I am set in such a plight to get my soul-heal.[8] And yet I trust, through God's grace and through His Passion[9] of His wounds wide, that after my death I may have a sight of the blessed face of Christ Jesu, and on Doomsday[10] to sit on His right side; for as sinful as ever I was now are saints in heaven. And therefore, Sir Lancelot, I require thee and beseech thee heartily, for all the love that ever was betwixt us, that thou never see me no more in the visage.[11] And I command thee, on God's behalf, that thou forsake my company. And to thy kingdom look thou turn again, and keep well thy realm from war and wrack;[12] for as well as I have loved thee heretofore, mine heart will not serve now to see thee; for through thee and me is the flower of kings and knights destroyed. And therefore go thou to thy realm, and there take thee a wife, and live with her with joy and bliss. And I pray thee heartily to pray for me to the Everlasting Lord that I may amend my misliving."

"Now, my sweet madam," said Sir Lancelot, "would ye that I should turn again unto my country, and there to wed a lady? Nay, madam, wit you well that I shall never do, for I shall never be so false unto you of that I have promised. But the self[13] destiny that ye have taken you to, I will take me to, for the pleasure of Jesu, and ever for you I cast me[14] specially to pray."

"Ah, Sir Lancelot, if ye will do so and hold thy

---

[1] *masses ... Requiem* Masses for the dead.

[2] *dured* Lasted.

[3] *ye ... find* You shall find.

[4] *Be ... that* Be that as it may.

[5] *childe* Young knight or squire.

[6] *no ... strive* No use to argue.

[7] *fare* Commotion.

[8] *soul-heal* Salvation.

[9] *Passion* Christ's suffering on the cross, for which, according to Christian doctrine, humanity has been cleansed of original sin.

[10] *Doomsday* Judgment Day.

[11] *visage* Face, i.e., in person.

[12] *wrack* Ruin.

[13] *self* Same.

[14] *cast me* Resolve.

promise! But I may never believe you," said the queen, "but that ye will turn to the world again."

"Well, madam," said he, "ye say as it pleaseth you, for yet wist ye me never false of my promise. And God defend but that I should[1] forsake the world as ye have done! For in the quest of the Sankgreal[2] I had that time forsaken the vanities of the world, had not your love been. And if I had done so at that time with my heart, will and thought, I had passed[3] all the knights that ever were in the Sankgreal except Galahad, my son.[4] And therefore, lady, sithen ye have taken you to perfection, I must needs take me to perfection, of right. For I take record of God, in you I have had mine earthly joy; and if I had found you now so disposed, I had cast me to have had you into mine own realm. But sithen I find you thus disposed, I ensure[5] you faithfully, I will ever take me to penance and pray while my life lasts, if that I may find any hermit, either gray or white, that will receive me. Wherefore, madam, I pray you kiss me, and never no more."[6]

"Nay," said the queen, "that I shall never do, but abstain you from such works."[7]

And they departed; but there was never so hard an hearted man but he would have wept to see the dolour that they made, for there was lamentation as they had be stung with spears, and many times they swooned. And the ladies bare the queen to her chamber.

And Sir Lancelot awoke, and went and took his horse, and rode all that day and all night in a forest, weeping. And at last he was ware of an hermitage and a chapel stood betwixt two cliffs; and then he heard a little bell ring to mass. And thither he rode and alight, and tied his horse to the gate, and heard Mass. And he that sang Mass was the Bishop of Canterbury. Both the Bishop and Sir Bedivere knew Sir Lancelot, and they spake together after Mass. But when Sir Bedivere had told his tale all whole, Sir Lancelot's heart almost brast for sorrow, and Sir Lancelot threw his arms abroad, and said, "Alas! Who may trust this world?"

And then he kneeled down on his knee and prayed the Bishop to shrive him and assoil[8] him; and then he besought the Bishop that he might be his brother.[9] Then the Bishop said, "I will gladly," and there he put an habit[10] upon Sir Lancelot. And there he served God day and night with prayers and fastings.

Thus the great host abode at Dover. And then Sir Lionel took fifteen lords with him and rode to London to seek Sir Lancelot; and there Sir Lionel was slain and many of his lords. Then Sir Bors de Ganis made the great host for to go home again, and Sir Bors, Sir Ector de Maris, Sir Blamour, Sir Bleoberis, with mo other of Sir Lancelot's kin, took on them to ride all England overthwart and endlong[11] to seek Sir Lancelot. So Sir Bors by fortune rode so long till he came to the same chapel where Sir Lancelot was. And so Sir Bors heard a little bell knell,[12] that rang to Mass; and there he alight and heard Mass. And when Mass was done the Bishop, Sir Lancelot and Sir Bedivere came to Sir Bors, and when Sir Bors saw Sir Lancelot in that manner clothing, then he prayed the Bishop that he might be in the same suit. And so there was an habit put upon him, and there he lived in prayers and fasting.

And within half a year there was come Sir Galihud, Sir Galyhodin, Sir Blamour, Sir Bleoberis, Sir Villiars, Sir Clarrus, and Sir Gahalantin. So all these seven noble knights there abode still. And when they saw Sir Lancelot had taken him to such perfection they had no lust[13] to depart, but took such an habit as he had.

Thus they endured in great penance six year. And then Sir Lancelot took the habit of priesthood of the Bishop, and a twelve-month he sang Mass. And there was none of these other knights but they read in books and holp for to sing Mass, and rang bells, and did lowly all manner of service. And so their horses went where

---

[1] *God ... should* God forbid that I should not.

[2] *Sankgreal* Holy Grail, the chalice used by Christ at His Last Supper, the quest for which was undertaken by the Knights of the Round Table.

[3] *had passed* Would have surpassed.

[4] *Galahad, my son* Lancelot's son by Elaine, daughter of King Pelles. Galahad was generally regarded as the most perfect knight, body and soul.

[5] *ensure* Promise.

[6] *never ... more* Never again.

[7] *works* Behavior.

[8] *assoil* Absolve, forgive.

[9] *be ... brother* Become a monk.

[10] *habit* Monk's clothing.

[11] *overthwart and endlong* Across and from one end to the other.

[12] *knell* Toll.

[13] *lust* Desire.

they would, for they took no regard of no worldly riches; for when they saw Sir Lancelot endure such penance in prayers and fastings they took no force what pain they endured, for to see the noblest knight of the world take such abstinence that he waxed[1] full lean.

And thus upon a night there came a vision to Sir Lancelot and charged him, in remission of his sins, to haste him unto Amesbury: "And by then thou come there, thou shalt find Queen Guinevere dead. And therefore take thy fellows with thee, and purvey them of an horse bier,[2] and fetch thou the corse of her, and bury her by her husband, the noble King Arthur."

So this avision came to Lancelot thrice in one night. Then Sir Lancelot rose up or day and told the hermit.

"It were well done," said the hermit, "that ye made you ready and that ye disobey not the avision."

Then Sir Lancelot took his seven fellows with him, and on foot they yede[3] from Glastonbury to Amesbury, the which is little more than thirty mile, and thither they came within two days, for they were weak and feeble to go.

And when Sir Lancelot was come to Amesbury within the nunnery, Queen Guinevere died but half an hour before. And the ladies told Sir Lancelot that Queen Guinevere told them all or she passed that Sir Lancelot had been priest near a twelve-month: "and hither he cometh as fast as he may to fetch my corse, and beside my lord King Arthur he shall bury me." Wherefore the Queen said in hearing of them all, "I beseech Almighty God that I may never have power to see Sir Lancelot with my worldly eyen!"

"And thus," said all the ladies, "was ever her prayer these two days till she was dead."

Then Sir Lancelot saw her visage, but he wept not greatly, but sighed. And so he did all the observance of the service himself, both the Dirige,[4] and on the morn he sang Mass. And there was ordained[5] an horse-bier, and so with an hundred torches ever brenning about the corse of the queen and ever Sir Lancelot with his eight fellows went about the horse-bier, singing and reading

many an holy orison,[6] and frankincense[7] upon the corse incensed.[8]

Thus Sir Lancelot and his eight fellows went on foot from Amesbury unto Glastonbury; and when they were come to the chapel and the hermitage, there she had a Dirige, with great devotion. And on the morn the hermit that sometime was Bishop of Canterbury sang the Mass of Requiem with great devotion, and Sir Lancelot was the first that offered, and then all his eight fellows. And then she was wrapped in cered[9] cloth of Rennes, from the top to the toe, in thirtyfold;[10] and after she was put in a web[11] of lead, and then in a coffin of marble.

And when she was put in the earth Sir Lancelot swooned, and lay long still while the hermit came and awaked him, and said,

"Ye be to blame, for ye displease God with such manner of sorrow-making."

"Truly," said Sir Lancelot, "I trust I do not displease God, for He knoweth mine intent: for my sorrow was not, nor is not, for any rejoicing of sin, but my sorrow may never have end. For when I remember of her beauty and of her noblesse, that was both with her king and with her, so when I saw his corpse and her corpse so lie together, truly mine heart would not serve to sustain my careful[12] body. Also when I remember me how by my default, mine orgule and my pride that they were both laid full low that were peerless that ever was living of Christian people, wit you well," said Sir Lancelot, "this remembered, of their kindness and mine unkindness, sank so to mine heart that I might not sustain myself." So the French book maketh mention.

Then Sir Lancelot never after ate but little meat, nor drank, till he was dead, for then he sickened more and more and dried and dwined[13] away. For the Bishop nor none of his fellows might not make him to eat and little

---

[1] *waxed* Grew.

[2] *horse bier* Coffin carrier drawn by a horse.

[3] *yede* Went.

[4] *Dirige* Dirige, Office of the Dead in the Catholic funeral Mass.

[5] *ordained* Prepared.

[6] *orison* Prayer.

[7] *frankincense* Aromatic tree resin used for incense.

[8] *incensed* Perfumed.

[9] *cered* Waxed.

[10] *thirtyfold* Wrapped around her thirty times.

[11] *web* Sheet.

[12] *careful* Filled with care, sorrowful.

[13] *dwined* Wasted.

he drank, that he was waxen by a cubit[1] shorter than he was, that people could not know him. For evermore, day and night, he prayed, but sometime he slumbered a broken sleep. Ever he was lying grovelling[2] on the tomb of King Arthur and Queen Guinevere, and there was no comfort that the Bishop nor Sir Bors nor none of his fellows could make him, it availed not.

So within six weeks after, Sir Lancelot fell sick, and lay in his bed. And then he sent for the Bishop that there was hermit, and all his true fellows. Then Sir Lancelot said with dreary steven,[3]

"Sir Bishop, I pray you give to me all my rites that longeth to a Christian man."

"It shall not need you,"[4] said the hermit and all his fellows. "It is but heaviness of your blood. You shall be well mended by the grace of God to-morn."

"My fair lords," said Sir Lancelot, "wit you well my careful body will into the earth, I have warning more than now I will say. Therefore give me my rites."

So when he was houseled and anealed[5] and had all that a Christian man ought to have, he prayed the Bishop that his fellows might bear his body to Joyous Gard. (Some men say it was Alnwick, and some men say it was Bamborough.)

"Howbeit," said Sir Lancelot, "me repenteth sore, but I made mine avow sometime that in Joyous Gard I would be buried. And because of breaking of mine avow,[6] I pray you all, lead me thither."

Then there was weeping and wringing of hands among his fellows.

So at a season[7] of the night they all went to their beds, for they all lay in one chamber. And so after midnight, against day,[8] the Bishop that was hermit, as he lay in his bed asleep, he fell upon[9] a great laughter. And therewith all the fellowship awoke and came to the Bishop and asked him what he ailed.[10]

"Ah, Jesu mercy!" said the Bishop, "why did ye awake me? I was never in all my life so merry and so well at ease."

"Wherefore?" said Sir Bors.

"Truly," said the Bishop, "here was Sir Lancelot with me, with mo angels than ever I saw men in one day. And I saw the angels heave up Sir Lancelot unto heaven, and the gates of heaven opened against him."[11]

"It is but dretching of swevens,"[12] said Sir Bors, "for I doubt not Sir Lancelot aileth nothing but good."[13]

"It may well be," said the Bishop. "Go ye to his bed, and then shall ye prove the sooth."

So when Sir Bors and his fellows came to his bed they found him stark dead; and he lay as he had smiled, and the sweetest savour about him that ever they felt. Then was there weeping and wringing of hands, and the greatest dole they made that ever made men.

And on the morn the Bishop did his Mass of Requiem, and after the Bishop and all the nine knights put Sir Lancelot in the same horse-bier that Queen Guinevere was laid in tofore that she was buried. And so the Bishop and they all together went with the body of Sir Lancelot daily till they came to Joyous Gard; and ever they had an hundred torches brenning about him.

And so within fifteen days they came to Joyous Gard. And there they laid his corpse in the body of the choir,[14] and sang and read many psalters[15] and prayers over him and about him. And ever his visage was laid open and naked, that all folks might behold him; for such was the custom in those days that all men of worship should so lie with open visage till that they were buried.

And right thus as they were at their service, there came Sir Ector de Maris, that had seven year sought all England, Scotland, and Wales, seeking his brother, Sir Lancelot. And when Sir Ector heard such noise and light in the choir of Joyous Gard, he alight and put his horse from him and came into the choir. And there he saw

---

[1] *cubit* Unit of measurement equal to the distance between elbow and fingertips.

[2] *grovelling* Face downward.

[3] *steven* Voice.

[4] *It ... you* You do not need this.

[5] *houseled and anealed* Given communion and anointed.

[6] *And ... avow* So that I do not break my vow.

[7] *at a season* At the proper time.

[8] *against day* Just before daybreak.

[9] *fell upon* Began.

[10] *he ailed* Ailed him.

[11] *against him* At his arrival.

[12] *dretching of swevens* Torment of dreams.

[13] *aileth ... good* Feels well.

[14] *choir* Area of church where services are performed.

[15] *psalters* Psalms.

men sing and weep, and all they knew Sir Ector, but he knew not them.

Then went Sir Bors unto Sir Ector and told him how there lay his brother, Sir Lancelot, dead. And then Sir Ector threw his shield, sword and helm from him, and when he beheld Sir Lancelot's visage he fell down in a swoon. And when he waked, it were hard any tongue to tell the doleful complaints that he made for his brother.

"Ah, Lancelot!" he said, "thou were head of all Christian knights! And now I dare say," said Sir Ector, "thou Sir Lancelot, there thou liest, that thou were never matched of[1] earthly knight's hand! And thou were the courteoust knight that ever bare shield! And thou were the truest friend to thy lover that ever bestrad[2] horse, and thou were the truest lover of a sinful man[3] that ever loved woman, and thou were the kindest man that ever strake with sword. And thou were the goodliest person that ever came among press of knights, and thou was the meekest man and the gentlest that ever ate in hall among ladies, and thou were the sternest knight to thy mortal foe that ever put spear in the rest."[4]

Then there was weeping and dolour out of measure.

Thus they kept Sir Lancelot's corpse on-loft[5] fifteen days, and then they buried it with great devotion. And then at leisure they went all with the Bishop of Canterbury to his hermitage, and there they were together more than a month.

Then Sir Constantine, that was Sir Cador's son of Cornwall, was chosen king of England. And he was a full noble knight, and worshipfully he ruled this realm. And then this King Constantine sent for the Bishop of Canterbury, for he heard say where he was. And so he was restored unto his Bishopric, and left that hermitage. And Sir Bedivere was there ever still hermit to his life's end.

Then Sir Bors de Ganis, Sir Ector de Maris, Sir Gahalantine, Sir Galihud, Sir Galihodin, Sir Blamour, Sir Bleoberis, Sir Villiars le Valiant, Sir Clarrus of Clermount, all these knights drew them to their countries. Howbeit King Constantine would have had them with him, but they would not abide in this realm. And there they all lived in their countries as holy men.

And some English books make mention that they went never out of England after the death of Sir Lancelot—but that was but the favour of makers.[6] For the French book maketh mention—and is authorised—that Sir Bors, Sir Ector, Sir Blamour and Sir Bleoberis went into the Holy Land, thereas Jesu Christ was quick and dead, and anon as they had established their lands. For, the book saith, so Sir Lancelot commanded them for to do or ever he passed out of this world. And these four knights did many battles upon the miscreants, or Turks. And there they died upon a Good Friday for God's sake.

HERE IS THE END OF THE WHOLE BOOK OF KING ARTHUR AND OF HIS NOBLE KNIGHTS OF THE ROUND TABLE, THAT WHEN THEY WERE WHOLLY TOGETHER THERE WAS EVER AN HUNDRED AND FORTY. AND HERE IS THE END OF *THE DEATH OF ARTHUR*.

I PRAY YOU ALL GENTLEMEN AND GENTLEWOMEN THAT READETH THIS BOOK OF ARTHUR AND HIS KNIGHTS FROM THE BEGINNING TO THE ENDING, PRAY FOR ME WHILE I AM ON LIVE THAT GOD SEND ME GOOD DELIVERANCE. AND WHEN I AM DEAD, I PRAY YOU ALL PRAY FOR MY SOUL.

FOR THIS BOOK WAS ENDED THE NINTH YEAR OF THE REIGN OF KING EDWARD THE FOURTH, BY SIR THOMAS MALORY, KNIGHT, AS JESU HELP HIM FOR HIS GREAT MIGHT, AS HE IS THE SERVANT OF JESU BOTH DAY AND NIGHT.

—1485

---

[1] *of* By.

[2] *bestrad* Sat astride.

[3] *of ... man* Among sinful men.

[4] *rest* Area on armor for stabilizing a spear during a charge.

[5] *on-loft* On display.

[6] *favor ... makers* Fancy of the authors.

IN CONTEXT

Early Editions of *Morte Darthur*

CAXTON'S PREFACE[1]

After that I had accomplished and finished diverse histories, as well of contemplation as of other historical and worldly acts of great conquerors and princes, and also certain books of ensamples[2] and doctrine, many noble and diverse gentlemen of this realm of England came and demanded me many and oft times, wherefore that I have not do made and imprint[3] the noble history of the Saint Grail,[4] and of the most renowned Christian king—first and chief of the three best Christians—and worthy, King Arthur, which ought most to be remembered among us Englishmen to-fore all other Christian kings.

For it is notourly[5] known through the universal world, that there be nine worthies[6] and the best that ever were, that is to wit, three Paynims, three Jews, and three Christian men. As for the Paynims, they were tofore the Incarnation of Christ, which were named, the first Hector of Troy, of whom the history is comen both in ballad and in prose, the second Alexander the Great, and the third Julius Caesar, Emperor of Rome,[7] of whom the histories be well known and had. And as for the three Jews, which also were tofore the Incarnation of our Lord, of whom the first was duke Joshua which brought the children of Israel into the land of behest, the second David King of Jerusalem, and the third Judas Maccabeus,[8] of these three the Bible rehearseth all their noble histories and acts. And since the said Incarnation have been three noble Christian men, stalled[9] and admitted through the universal world into the number of the nine best and worthy. Of whom was first the noble Arthur, whose noble acts I purpose to write in this present book here following. The second was Charlemagne,[10] or Charles the Great, of whom the history is had in many places, both in French and in English. And the third and last was Godfrey of Bouillon,[11] of whose acts and life I made a book unto the excellent prince and king of noble memory, King Edward the Fourth.

---

[1] *Caxton's Preface* William Caxton (1422?–91), first printer in England; Caxton printed nearly 100 works, many of which he translated from French and Dutch. In addition to Malory's work, his most notable books include Chaucer's *Canterbury Tales* and *Troilus and Criseyde* and John Gower's *Confessio Amantis* ("*Confession of a Lover*"). The *Morte Darthur* was printed in 1485.

[2] *ensamples* Stories depicting examples of behavior that should be followed or avoided.

[3] *do … imprint* Have made and printed.

[4] *Saint Grail* Holy Grail.

[5] *notourly* Notoriously, publicly.

[6] *nine worthies* See Jean de Longuyon's *Voeux du Paon* (*Vows of the Peacock*), a fourteenth-century book that addresses the nine leaders who best embodied chivalric values. The triads represent Pagan ("Paynim") Law, Old Testament (Jewish) Law and Christian Law, respectively.

[7] *Hector of Troy* Trojan Prince famed for his battle prowess, killed by Achilles in Homer's *Iliad*; *Alexander the Great* Conqueror of Greece, Egypt and Persia (356–323 BCE); *Julius … Rome* Roman general and ruler (100–44 BCE) who was murdered by political rivals.

[8] *Joshua* Successor to Moses as Israel's leader; *land of behest* Land belonging to Israel by right of God's promise; *David … Jerusalem* Biblical figure who defeated the giant Goliath and became King of Jerusalem; *Judas Maccabeus* Jewish military leader.

[9] *stalled* Installed.

[10] *Charlemagne* Charles I (768–814), King of the Franks and Emperor of much of Western Europe. His court became the center of a renaissance of art and culture.

[11] *Godfrey of Bouillon* One of the leaders of the First Crusade (1058–1100).

The said noble gentlemen instantly[1] required me to imprint the history of the said noble king and conqueror King Arthur, and of his knights, with the history of the Saint Grail, and of the death and ending of the said Arthur; affirming that I ought rather to imprint his acts and noble feats, than of Godfrey of Bouillon, or any of the other eight, considering that he was a man born within this realm, and king and emperor of the same, and that there be in French diverse and many noble volumes of his acts, and also of his knights.

To whom I answered that diverse men hold opinion that there was no such Arthur, and that all such books as been made of him be feigned and fables, because that some chronicles make of him no mention, nor remember him nothing,[2] nor of his knights.

Whereto they answered, and one in special said, that in him that should say or think that there was never such a king called Arthur might well be aretted[3] great folly and blindness. For he said that there were many evidences of the contrary. First ye may see his sepulchre in the monastery of Glastonbury. And also in *Polychronicon*,[4] in the fifth book the sixth chapter, and in the seventh book the twenty-third chapter, where his body was buried, and after found, and translated[5] into the said monastery. Ye shall see also in the history of Bochas, in his book *De Casu Principum*,[6] part of his noble acts, and also of his fall. Also Galfridus in his British book[7] recounteth his life: and in diverse places of England many remembrances be yet of him, and shall remain perpetually, and also of his knights. First in the Abbey of Westminster, at St. Edward's shrine, remaineth the print of his seal in red wax closed in beryl,[8] in which is written, Patricius Arthurus, Britannie, Gallie, Germanie, Dacie, Imperator.[9] Item[10] in the castle of Dover ye may see Gawaine's skull, and Cradok's mantle; at Winchester the Round Table; in other places Lancelot's sword and many other things. Then all these things considered, there can no man reasonably gainsay but there was a king of this land named Arthur. For in all places, Christian and heathen, he is reputed and taken for one of the nine worthy, and the first of the three Christian men. And also, he is more spoken of beyond the sea, more books made of his noble acts, than there be in England, as well in Dutch, Italian, Spanish, and Greek, as in French. And yet of record remain in witness of him in Wales, in the town of Camelot, the great stones and the marvellous works of iron lying under the ground, and royal vaults, which diverse now living have seen. Wherefore it is a marvel why he is no more renowned in his own country, save only it accordeth to the Word of God, which saith that no man is accepted for a prophet in his own country.

---

[1] *instantly*   Pressingly.

[2] *remember ... nothing*   Record nothing of him.

[3] *aretted*   Reckoned, considered.

[4] *Polychronicon*   Long chronicle that strives to couple universal history with theology, written in Latin by Ranulf Higden (1299–1363) and translated into English by John Trevisa (in 1387), printed by Caxton in 1482.

[5] *translated*   Transferred.

[6] *Bochas*   Giovanni Boccaccio (1313–75), Italian writer, author of the *Decameron* and various other works; *De Casu Principum*   Probably *De Casibus Virorum Illustrium* (*On the Downfalls of Famous Men*), a biographical work written by Boccaccio between 1357 and 1363 that recounts the stories of great men who fell from the heights of success and happiness.

[7] *Galfridus*   Geoffrey of Monmouth (1100?–1155), early British chronicler; *British book*   Geoffrey's *Historia Regum Britanniae* (*History of the Kings of Britain*), completed c. 1138, which begins in a legendary past and continues up to Cadwallader, the last "British" king.

[8] *beryl*   Emerald.

[9] *Patricius ... Imperator*   Latin: noble Arthur, Emperor of Britain, Gaul, Germany, and Dacia.

[10] *Item*   Also.

Then all these things aforesaid alleged, I could not well deny but that there was such a noble king named Arthur, and reputed one of the nine worthy, and first and chief of the Christian men. And many noble volumes be made of him and of his noble knights in French, which I have seen and read beyond the sea, which be not had in our maternal tongue.[1] But in Welsh be many and also in French, and some in English but nowhere nigh all. Wherefore, such as have late[2] been drawn out[3] briefly into English I have after the simple conning[4] that God hath sent to me, under the favour and correction of all noble lords and gentlemen, enprised[5] to imprint a book of the noble histories of the said King Arthur, and of certain of his knights, after a copy unto me delivered, which copy Sir Thomas Malory did take out of certain books of French, and reduced[6] it into English.

And I, according to my copy, have done set it in imprint,[7] to the intent that noble men may see and learn the noble acts of chivalry, the gentle and virtuous deeds that some knights used in those days, by which they came to honour, and how they that were vicious were punished and oft put to shame and rebuke; humbly beseeching all noble lords and ladies, with all other estates of what estate or degree[8] they been of, that shall see and read in this said book and work, that they take the good and honest acts in their remembrance, and to follow the same. Wherein they shall find many joyous and pleasant histories, and noble and renowned acts of humanity, gentleness, and chivalry. For herein may be seen noble chivalry, courtesy, humanity, friendliness, hardiness, love, friendship, cowardice, murder, hate, virtue, and sin. Do after the good and leave the evil, and it shall bring you to good fame and renown.

And for to pass the time this book shall be pleasant to read in, but for to give faith and belief that all is true that is contained herein, ye be at your liberty; but all is written for our doctrine,[9] and for to beware that we fall not to vice nor sin, but to exercise and follow virtue, by which we may come and attain to good fame and renown in this life, and after this short and transitory life to come unto everlasting bliss in heaven; the which He grant us that reigneth in heaven, the blessed Trinity. Amen.

Then to proceed forth in this said book, which I direct unto all noble princes, lords and ladies, gentlemen or gentlewomen, that desire to read or hear read of the noble and joyous history of the great conqueror and excellent king, King Arthur, sometime king of this noble realm, then called Britain; I, William Caxton, simple person, present this book following, which I have enprised to imprint, and treateth of the noble acts, feats of arms of chivalry, prowess, hardiness, humanity, love, courtesy, and very gentleness, with many wonderful histories and adventures.

---

[1] *maternal tongue*   Mother tongue, i.e., English vernacular.

[2] *late*   Lately.

[3] *drawn out*   Translated.

[4] *conning*   Knowledge, understanding.

[5] *enprised*   Undertaken.

[6] *reduced*   Translated.

[7] *done ... imprint*   Caused it to be printed.

[8] *estate or degree*   Social class or position.

[9] *doctrine*   Instruction. See Romans 15.4.

Illustrating *Morte Darthur*

The first edition of Malory's work, printed by William Caxton in 1485, was not illustrated; however, in the next edition (1498), Wynkyn de Worde added a number of woodcut illustrations. Two of these are reproduced below.

Balin unsheathing Excalibur (after Arthur and various of his knights have failed to do so).

The Battle of Salisbury Plain.

Reading Poetry

WHAT IS A POEM?

Most of us know what a poem is when we see one. Still, even poets find it difficult to define a poem, or poetry. In a lecture on "The Name and Nature of Poetry" (1933), the English poet A.E. Housman stated that he could "no more define poetry than a terrier can define a rat"; however, he added, "we both recognize the object by the symptoms which it provokes in us." Housman knew he was in the presence of poetry if he experienced a shiver down the spine, or "a constriction of the throat and a precipitation of water to the eyes." Implicit in Housman's response is a recognition that we have to go beyond mere formal characteristics—stanzas, rhymes, rhythms—if we want to know what poetry is, or why it differs from prose. Poetry both represents and *creates* emotions in a highly condensed way. Therefore, any definition of the genre needs to consider, as much as possible, the impact of poetry on us as readers or listeners.

Worth consideration too is the role of the listener or reader not only as passive recipient of a poem, but also as an active participant in its performance. Poetry is among other things the locus for a communicative exchange. A section below deals with the sub-genre of performance poetry, but in a very real sense all poetry is subject to performance. Poems are to be read aloud as well as on the page, and both in sensing meaning and in expressing sound the reader plays a vital role in bringing a poem to life, no matter how long dead its author may be; as W.H. Auden wrote memorably of his fellow poet W.B. Yeats, "the words of a dead man / Are modified in the guts of the living."

For some readers, poetry is, in William Wordsworth's phrase, "the breath and finer spirit of all knowledge" ("Preface" to the *Lyrical Ballads*). They look to poetry for insights into the nature of human experience, and expect elevated thought in carefully-wrought language. In contrast, other readers distrust poetry that seems moralistic or didactic. "We hate poetry that has a palpable design upon us," wrote John Keats to his friend J.H. Reynolds; rather, poetry should be "great & unobtrusive, a thing which enters into one's soul, and does not startle it or amaze it with itself but with its subject." The American poet Archibald MacLeish took Keats's idea a step further: in his poem "Ars Poetica" he suggested that "A poem should not mean / But be." MacLeish was not suggesting that a poem should lack meaning, but rather that meaning should inhere in the poem's expressive and sensuous qualities, not in some explicit statement or versified idea.

Whatever we look for in a poem, the infinitude of forms, styles, and subjects that make up the body of literature we call "poetry" is, in the end, impossible to capture in a definition that would satisfy all readers. All we can do, perhaps, is to agree that a poem is a discourse that is characterized by a heightened attention to language, form, and rhythm, by an expressiveness that works through figurative rather than literal modes, and by a capacity to stimulate our imagination and arouse our feelings.

THE LANGUAGE OF POETRY

To speak of "the language of poetry" implies that poets make use of a vocabulary that is somehow different from the language of everyday life. In fact, all language has the capacity to be "poetic," if by poetry we understand a use of language to which some special importance is attached. The ritualistic utterances of religious ceremonies sometimes have this force; so do the skipping rhymes of children in the schoolyard. We can distinguish such uses of language from the kind of writing we find in, say, a computer user's manual: the author of the manual can describe a given function in a variety of ways, whereas the magic of the skipping rhyme can be invoked only by getting the right words in the right order. So with the poet: he or she chooses particular words in a particular order; the *way* the poet speaks is as important to our understanding as what is said. This doesn't mean that an instruction manual couldn't have poetic qualities—indeed, modern poets have created "found" poems from even less likely materials—but it does mean that in poetry there is an intimate relation amongst language, form, and meaning, and that the writer deliberately structures and manipulates language to achieve very particular ends.

THE BEST WORDS IN THE BEST ORDER

Wordsworth provides us with a useful example of the way that poetry can invest quite ordinary words with a high emotional charge:

> No motion has she now, no force,
> She neither hears nor sees;
> Rolled round in earth's diurnal course
> With rocks, and stones, and trees.

To paraphrase the content of this stanza from "A Slumber Did My Spirit Seal," "she" is dead and buried. But the language and structures used here give this prosaic idea great impact. For example, the regular iambic meter of the two last lines conveys something of the inexorable motion of the earth and of Lucy embedded in it; the monosyllabic last line is a grim reminder of her oneness with objects in nature; the repeated negatives in the first two lines drive home the irreparable destructiveness of death; the alliteration in the third and fourth lines gives a tangible suggestion of roundness, circularity, repetition in terms of the earth's shape and motion, suggesting a cycle in which death is perhaps followed by renewal. Even the unusual word "diurnal" (which would not have seemed so unusual to Wordsworth's readers) seems "right" in this context; it lends more weight to the notion of the earth's perpetual movement than its mundane synonym "daily" (which, besides, would not scan here). It is difficult to imagine a change of any kind to these lines; they exemplify another attempted definition of poetry, this time by Wordsworth's friend Samuel Taylor Coleridge: "the best words in the best order" (*Table Talk*, 1827).

POETIC DICTION AND THE ELEVATED STYLE

Wordsworth's diction in the "Lucy" poem cited above is a model of clarity; he has chosen language that, in its simplicity and bluntness, conveys the strength of the speaker's feelings far more strongly than an elaborate description of grief in more conventionally "poetic" language might have done. Wordsworth, disturbed by what he felt was a deadness and artificiality in the poetry of his day, sought to "choose incidents and situations from common life" and to describe them in "a selection of language really used by men" ("Preface" to *Lyrical Ballads*). His plan might seem an implicit reproach of the "raised" style, the elevated diction of epic poetry we associate with John Milton's *Paradise Lost*:

> Anon out of the earth a fabric huge
> Rose like an exhalation, with the sound
> Of dulcet symphonies and voices sweet,

> Built like a temple, where pilasters round
> Were set, and Doric pillars overlaid
> With golden architrave; nor did there want
> Cornice or frieze, with bossy sculptures graven;
> The roof was fretted gold.
>   (*Paradise Lost* I.710–17)

At first glance this passage, with its Latinate vocabulary and convoluted syntax, might seem guilty of inflated language and pretentiousness. However, Milton's description of the devils' palace in Hell deliberately seeks to distance us from its subject in order to emphasize the scale and sublimity of the spectacle, far removed from ordinary human experience. In other words, language and style in *Paradise Lost* are well adapted to suit a particular purpose, just as they are in "A Slumber Did My Spirit Seal," though on a wholly different scale. Wordsworth criticized the poetry of his day, not because of its elevation, but because the raised style was too often out of touch with its subject; in his view, the words did not bear any significant relation to the "truths" they were attempting to depict.

"PLAIN" LANGUAGE IN POETRY

Since Wordsworth's time, writers have been conscious of a need to narrow the apparent gap between "poetic" language and the language of everyday life. In much of the poetry of the past century, especially free verse, we can observe a growing approximation to speech—even to conversation—in the diction and rhythms of poetry. This may have something to do with the changed role of the poet, who today has discarded the mantle of teacher or prophet that was assumed by poets of earlier times, and who is ready to admit all fields of experience and endeavor as appropriate for poetry. The modern poet looks squarely at life, and can often find a provoking beauty in even the meanest of objects.

We should not assume, however, that a greater concern with the "ordinary," with simplicity, naturalness, and clarity, means a reduction in complexity or suggestiveness. A piece such as Stevie Smith's "Mother, Among the Dustbins," for all the casual and playful domesticity of some of its lines, skilfully evokes a range of emotions and sense impressions defying simple paraphrase.

IMAGERY, SYMBOLISM, AND FIGURES OF SPEECH

The language of poetry is grounded in the objects and phenomena that create sensory impressions. Sometimes the poet renders these impressions quite literally, in a series of *images* that seek to recreate a scene in the reader's mind:

> Only a man harrowing clods
> In a slow silent walk
> With an old horse that stumbles and nods
> Half asleep as they stalk.
>
> Only thin smoke without flame
> From the heaps of couch-grass;
> Yet this will go onward the same
> Though Dynasties pass.

Yonder a maid and her wight
Come whispering by:
War's annals will cloud into night
Ere their story die.

(Thomas Hardy, "In Time of 'The Breaking of Nations'")

Here, the objects of everyday life are re-created with sensory details designed to evoke in us the sensations or responses felt by the speaker viewing the scene. At the same time, the writer invests the objects with such significance that the poem's meaning extends beyond the literal to the symbolic: that is, the images come to stand for something much larger than the objects they represent. Hardy's poem moves from the presentation of stark images of rural life to a sense of their timelessness. By the last stanza we see the ploughman, the burning grass, and the maid and her companion as symbols of recurring human actions and motives that defy the struggles and conflicts of history.

IMAGISM

The juxtaposition of clear, forceful images is associated particularly with the Imagist movement that flourished at the beginning of the twentieth century. Its chief representatives (in their early work) were H.D. and Ezra Pound, who defined an image as "that which represents an intellectual and emotional complex in an instant of time." Pound's two-line poem "In a Station of the Metro" provides a good example of the Imagists' goal of representing emotions or impressions through the use of concentrated images:

The apparition of these faces in the crowd,
Petals on a wet, black bough.

As in a Japanese *haiku,* a form that strongly influenced the Imagists, the poem uses sharp, clear, concrete details to evoke both a sensory impression and the emotion or the atmosphere of the scene. Though the Imagist movement itself lasted only a short time (from about 1912 to 1917), it had a far-reaching influence on modern poets such as T. S. Eliot, and William Carlos Williams.

FIGURES OF SPEECH

Imagery often works together with figurative expression to extend and deepen the meaning or impact of a poem. "Figurative" language means language that is metaphorical, not literal or referential. Through "figures of speech" such as metaphor and simile, metonymy, synecdoche, and personification, the writer may alter the ordinary, denotative meanings of words in order to convey greater force and vividness to ideas or impressions, often by showing likenesses between unlike things.

With *simile,* the poet makes an explicit comparison between the subject (called the *tenor*) and another object or idea (known as the *vehicle*), using "as" or "like":

It is a beauteous evening, calm and free,
The holy time is quiet as a Nun
Breathless with adoration. ...

In this opening to a sonnet, Wordsworth uses a visual image of a nun in devout prayer to convey in concrete terms the less tangible idea of evening as a "holy time." The comparison also introduces an emotional dimension, conveying something of the feeling that the scene induces in the poet. The simile can thus illuminate and expand meaning in a compact way. The poet may also extend the simile to elaborate at length on any points of likeness.

In *metaphor*, the comparison between tenor and vehicle is implied: connectives such as "like" are omitted, and a kind of identity is created between the subject and the term with which it is being compared. Thus in John Donne's "The Good-Morrow," a lover asserts the endless joy that he and his beloved find in each other:

> My face in thine eye, thine in mine appears,
> And true plain hearts do in the faces rest;
> Where can we find two better hemispheres,
> Without sharp north, without declining west?

Here the lovers are transformed into "hemispheres," each of them a half of the world not subject to the usual natural phenomena of wintry cold ("sharp north") or the coming of night ("declining west"). Thus, they form a perfect world in balance, in which the normal processes of decay or decline have been arrested. Donne renders the abstract idea of a love that defies change in pictorial and physical terms, making it more real and accessible to us. The images here are all the more arresting for the degree of concentration involved; it is not merely the absence of "like" or "as" that gives the metaphor such direct power, but the fusion of distinct images and emotions into a new idea.

Personification is the figure of speech in which the writer endows abstract ideas, inanimate objects, or animals with human characteristics. In other words, it is a type of implied metaphorical comparison in which aspects of a non-human subject are compared to the feelings, appearance, or actions of a human being. In the second stanza of his ode "To Autumn," Keats personifies the concept of autumnal harvesting in the form of a woman, "sitting careless on a granary floor, / Thy hair soft-lifted by the winnowing wind." Personification may also help to create a mood, as when Thomas Gray attributes human feelings to a hooting owl in "Elegy Written in a Country Church-Yard"; using such words as "moping" and "complain," Gray invests the bird's cries with the quality of human melancholy:

> … from yonder ivy-mantled tow'r
> The moping owl does to the moon complain
> Of such, as wand'ring near her secret bow'r,
> Molest her ancient solitary reign.

In his book *Modern Painters* (1856), the English critic John Ruskin criticized such attribution of human feelings to objects in nature. Calling this device the "pathetic fallacy," he objected to what he saw as an irrational distortion of reality, producing "a falseness in all our impressions of external things." Modern criticism, with a distrust of any notions of an objective "reality," tends to use Ruskin's term as a neutral label simply to describe instances of extended personification of natural objects.

Apostrophe, which is closely related to personification, has the speaker directly addressing a non-human object or idea as if it were a sentient human listener. Blake's "The Sick Rose," Shelley's "Ode to the West Wind" and his ode "To a Sky-Lark" all employ apostrophe, personifying the object addressed. Keats's "Ode on a Grecian Urn" begins by apostrophizing the urn ("Thou still unravish'd bride of quietness"), then addresses it in a series of questions and reflections through which the speaker attempts to unravel the urn's mysteries.

Apostrophe also appeals to or addresses a person who is absent or dead. W. H. Auden's lament "In Memory of W. B. Yeats" apostrophizes both the earth in which Yeats is to be buried ("Earth, receive an honoured guest") and the dead poet himself ("Follow, poet, follow right / To the bottom of the night …"). Religious prayers offer an illustration of the usefulness of apostrophe, since they are direct appeals from an earth-bound supplicant to an invisible god. The suggestion of strong emotion associated with such appeals is a common feature of apostrophe in poetry also, especially poetry with a religious theme, like Donne's "Holy Sonnets" (e.g., "Batter My Heart, Three-Personed God").

Metonymy and *synecdoche* are two closely related figures of speech that further illustrate the power of metaphorical language to convey meaning more intensely and vividly than is possible with prosaic statement. *Metonymy* (from the Greek, meaning "change of name") involves referring to an object or concept by substituting the name of another object or concept with which it is usually associated: for example, we might speak of "the Crown" when we mean the monarch, or describe the U.S. executive branch as "the White House." When the writer uses only part of something to signify the whole, or an individual to represent a class, we have an instance of *synecdoche*. T. S. Eliot provides an example in "The Love Song of J. Alfred Prufrock" when a crab is described as "a pair of ragged claws." Similarly, synecdoche is present in Milton's contemptous term "blind mouths" to describe the "corrupted clergy" he attacks in "Lycidas."

Dylan Thomas employs both metonymy and synecdoche in his poem "The Hand That Signed the Paper":

> The hand that signed the paper felled a city;
> Five sovereign fingers taxed the breath,
> Doubled the globe of dead and halved a country;
> These five kings did a king to death.
>
> The mighty hand leads to a sloping shoulder,
> The finger joints are cramped with chalk;
> A goose's quill has put an end to murder
> That put an end to talk.
>
> The hand that signed the treaty bred a fever,
> And famine grew, and locusts came;
> Great is the hand that holds dominion over
> Man by a scribbled name.
>
> The five kings count the dead but do not soften
> The crusted wound nor stroke the brow;
> A hand rules pity as a hand rules heaven;
> Hands have no tears to flow.

The "hand" of the poem is evidently a synecdoche for a great king who enters into treaties with friends and foes to wage wars, conquer kingdoms, and extend his personal power—all at the expense of his suffering subjects. The "goose quill" of the second stanza is a metonymy, standing for the pen used to sign the treaty or the death warrant that brings the war to an end.

Thomas's poem is an excellent example of the power of figurative language, which, by its vividness and concentrated force, can add layers of meaning to a poem, make abstract ideas concrete, and intensify the poem's emotional impact.

THE POEM AS PERFORMANCE: WRITER AND PERSON

Poetry is always dramatic. Sometimes the drama is explicit, as in Robert Browning's monologues, in which we hear the voice of a participant in a dialogue; in "My Last Duchess" we are present as the Duke reflects on the portrait of his late wife for the benefit of a visitor who has come to negotiate on behalf of the woman who is to become the Duke's next wife. Or we listen with amusement and pity as the dying Bishop addresses his venal and unsympathetic sons and tries to bargain with them for a fine burial ("The Bishop Orders His Tomb at St. Praxed's"). In such poems, the notion of a speaking voice is paramount: the speaker is a personage in a play, and the poem a means of conveying plot and character.

Sometimes the drama is less apparent, and takes the form of a plea, or a compliment, or an argument addressed to a silent listener. In Donne's "The Flea" we can infer from the poem the situation that has called it forth: a lover's advances are being rejected by his beloved, and his poem is an argument intended to overcome her reluctance by means of wit and logic. We can see a similar example in Marvell's "To His Coy Mistress": here the very shape of the poem, its three-paragraph structure, corresponds to the stages of the speaker's argument as he presents an apparently irrefutable line of reasoning. Much love poetry has this kind of background as its inspiration; the yearnings or lamentations of the lover are part of an imagined scene, not merely versified reflections about an abstraction called "love."

Meditative or reflective poetry can be dramatic too. Donne's "Holy Sonnets" are pleas from a tormented soul struggling to find its god; Tennyson's "In Memoriam" follows the agonized workings of a mind tracing a path from grief and anger to acceptance and renewed hope.

We should never assume that the speaker, the "I" of the poem, is simply a voice for the writer's own views. The speaker in W. H. Auden's "To an Unknown Citizen," presenting a summary of the dead citizen's life, appears to be an official spokesperson for the society which the citizen served ("Our report on his union"; "Our researchers ..." etc.). The speaker's words are laudatory, yet we perceive immediately that Auden's own views of this society are anything but approving. The speaker seems satisfied with the highly regimented nature of his society, one in which every aspect of the individual's life is under scrutiny and subject to correction. The only things necessary to the happiness of the "Modern Man," it seems, are "A phonograph, a radio, a car, and a frigidaire." The tone here is subtly ironic, an irony created by the gap between the imagined speaker's perception and the real feelings of the writer.

PERFORMANCE POETRY

Poetry began as an oral art, passed on in the form of chants, myths, ballads, and legends recited to an audience of listeners rather than readers. Even today, the dramatic qualities of a poem may extend beyond written text. "Performance poets" combine poetry and stagecraft in presenting their work to live audiences. Dramatic uses of voice, rhythm, body movement, music, and sometimes other visual effects make the "text" of the poem multi-dimensional. For example, Edith Sitwell's poem-sequence *Façade* (1922) was originally set to music: Sitwell read from behind a screen, while a live orchestra played. This performance was designed to enhance the verbal and rhythmic qualities of her poetry:

Beneath the flat and paper sky
The sun, a demon's eye
Glowed through the air, that mask of glass;
All wand'ring sounds that pass

Seemed out of tune, as if the light
Were fiddle-strings pulled tight.
The market-square with spire and bell
Clanged out the hour in Hell.
　　(from *Façade*)

By performing their poetry, writers can also convey cultural values and traditions. The cultural aspect of performance is central to Black poetry, which originates in a highly oral tradition of folklore and storytelling. From its roots in Africa, this oral tradition has been manifested in the songs and stories of slaves, in spirituals, in the jazz rhythms of the Twenties and the Thirties and in the rebelliousness of reggae and of rap. Even when it remains "on the page," much Black poetry written in the oral tradition has a compelling rhythmic quality. The lines below from Linton Kwesi Johnson's "Mi Revalueshanary Fren," for example, blur the line between spoken poetry and song. Johnson often performs his "dub poetry" against reggae or hip-hop musical backings.

yes, people powa jus a showa evry howa
an evrybady claim dem democratic
but some a wolf an some a sheep
an dat is problematic

The chorus of Johnson's poems, with its constant repetitions, digs deeply into the roots of African song and chant. Its performance qualities become clearer when the poem is read aloud:

Husak
e ad to go
Honnicka
e ad to go
Chowcheskhu
e ad to go
Just like apartied
will av to go

To perform a poem is one way to see and hear poetry as multi-dimensional, cultural, historical, and often also political. Performance is also another way to discover how poetic "meaning" can be constructed in the dynamic relation between speaker and listener.

TONE: THE SPEAKER'S ATTITUDE

In understanding poetry, it is helpful to imagine a poem as having a "voice." The voice may be close to the poet's own, or that of an imagined character, a *persona* adopted by the poet. The tone of the voice will reveal the speaker's attitude to the subject, thus helping to shape our understanding and response. In speech we can indicate our feelings by raising or lowering our voices, and we can accompany words with physical actions. In writing, we must try to convey the tonal inflections of the speaking voice through devices of language and rhythm, through imagery and figures of speech, and through allusions and contrasts.

THE IRONIC TONE

Housman's poem "Terence, This Is Stupid Stuff" offers a useful example of ways in which manipulating tone can reinforce meaning. When Housman, presenting himself in the poem as "Terence," imagines himself to be criticized for writing gloomy poems, his response to his critics takes the form of an ironic alternative: perhaps they should stick to drinking ale:

> Oh, many a peer of England brews
> Livelier liquor than the Muse,
> And malt does more than Milton can
> To justify God's ways to man.

The tone here is one of heavy scorn. The speaker is impatient with those who refuse to look at the realities of life and death, and who prefer to take refuge in simple-minded pleasure. The ludicrous comparisons, first between the brewers who have been made peers of England and the classical Muse of poetry, then between malt and Milton, create a sense of disproportion and ironic tension; the explicit allusion to *Paradise Lost* ("To justify God's ways to man") helps to drive home the poet's bitter recognition that his auditors are part of that fallen world depicted by Milton, yet unable or unwilling to acknowledge their harsh condition. The three couplets that follow offer a series of contrasts: in each case, the first line sets up a pleasant expectation and the second dashes it with a blunt reminder of reality:

> Ale, man, ale's the stuff to drink
> For fellows whom it hurts to think:
> Look into the pewter pot
> To see the world as the world's not.
> And faith, 'tis pleasant till 'tis past:
> The mischief is that 'twill not last.

These are all jabs at the "sterling lads" who would prefer to lie in "lovely muck" and not think about the way the world is. Housman's sardonic advice is all the more pointed for its sharp and ironic tone.

POETIC FORMS

In poetry, language is intimately related to form, which is the structuring of words within identifiable patterns. In prose we speak of phrases, sentences, and paragraphs; in poetry, we identify structures by lines, stanzas, or complete forms such as the sonnet or the ode (though poetry in complete or blank verse has paragraphs of variable length, not formal stanzas: see below).

Rightly handled, the form enhances expression and meaning, just as a frame can define and enhance a painting or photograph. Unlike the photo frame, however, form in poetry is an integral part of the whole work. At one end of the scale, the term "form" may describe the *epic,* the lengthy narrative governed by such conventions as division into books, a lofty style, and the interplay between human and supernatural characters. At the other end lies the *epigram*, a witty and pointed saying whose distinguishing characteristic is its brevity, as in Alexander Pope's famous couplet,

> I am his Highness' dog at Kew;
> Pray tell me sir, whose dog are you?

Between the epic and the epigram lie many other poetic forms, such as the sonnet, the ballad, or the ode. "Form" may also describe stanzaic patterns like *couplets* and *quatrains*.

"FIXED FORM" POEMS

The best-known poetic form is probably the sonnet, the fourteen-line poem inherited from Italy (the word itself is from the Italian *sonetto*, little song or sound). Within those fourteen lines, whether the poet chooses the "Petrarchan" rhyme scheme or the "English" form (see below in the section on "Rhyme"), the challenge is to develop an idea or situation that must find its statement and its resolution within the strict confines of the sonnet frame. Typically, there is an initial idea, description, or statement of feeling, followed by a "turn" in the thought that takes the reader by surprise, or that casts the situation in an unexpected light. Thus in Sonnet 130, "My Mistress' Eyes Are Nothing Like the Sun," William Shakespeare spends the first three quatrains apparently disparaging his lover in a series of unfavorable comparisons—"If snow be white, why then her breasts are dun"—but in the closing couplet his point becomes clear:

> And yet, by heaven, I think my love as rare
> As any she belied with false compare.

In other words, the speaker's disparaging comparisons have really been parodies of sentimental clichés which falsify reality; his mistress has no need of the exaggerations or distortions of conventional love poetry.

Other foreign forms borrowed and adapted by English-language poets include the *ghazal* and the *pantoum*. The *ghazal*, strongly associated with classical Urdu literature, originated in Persia and Arabia and was brought to the Indian subcontinent in the twelfth century. It consists of a series of couplets held together by a refrain, a simple rhyme scheme (a/a, b/a, c/a, d/a…), and a common rhythm, but only loosely related in theme or subject. Some English-language practitioners of the form have captured the epigrammatic quality of the ghazal, but most do not adhere to the strict pattern of the classical form.

The *pantoum*, based on a Malaysian form, was imported into English poetry via the work of nineteenth-century French poets. Typically it presents a series of quatrains rhyming *abab*, linked by a pattern of repetition in which the second and fourth lines of a quatrain become the first and third lines of the stanza that follows. In the poem's final stanza, the pattern is reversed: the second line repeats the third line of the first stanza, and the last line repeats the poem's opening line, thus creating the effect of a loop.

Similar to the pantoum in the circularity of its structure is the *villanelle,* originally a French form, with five *tercets* and a concluding *quatrain* held together by only two rhymes (aba, aba, aba, aba, aba, abaa) and by a refrain that repeats the first line at lines 6, 12, and 18, while the third line of the first tercet reappears as lines 9, 15, and 19. With its interlocking rhymes and elaborate repetitions, the villanelle can create a variety of tonal effects, ranging from lighthearted parody to the sonorous and earnest exhortation of Dylan Thomas's "Do Not Go Gentle Into That Good Night."

STANZAIC FORMS

Recurring formal groupings of lines within a poem are usually described as "stanzas." Both the recurring and the formal aspects of stanzaic forms are important; it is a common misconception to think that any group of lines in a poem, if it is set off by line spaces, constitutes a stanza. If such a group of lines is not patterned as one of a recurring group sharing similar formal characteristics, however, then it may be more appropriate to refer to such irregular groupings in the way we do for prose—as paragraphs. A ballad is typically divided into stanzas; a prose poem or a poem written in free verse, on the other hand, will rarely be divided into stanzas.

A stanza may be identified by the number of lines and the patterns of rhyme repeated in each grouping. One of the simpler traditional forms is the *ballad stanza*, with its alternating four and three-foot lines and its *abcb* rhyme scheme. Drawing on this form's association with medieval ballads and legends, Keats produces the eerie mystery of "La Belle Dame Sans Merci":

> I saw pale kings and princes too,
> Pale warriors, death-pale were they all;
> They cried—"La Belle Dame sans Merci
> Hath thee in thrall!"

Such imitations are a form of literary allusion; Keats uses a traditional stanza form to remind us of poems like "Sir Patrick Spens" or "Barbara Allen" to dramatize the painful thralldom of love by placing it within a well-known tradition of ballad narratives with similar forms and themes.

The four-line stanza, or *quatrain*, may be used for a variety of effects: from the elegiac solemnity of Gray's "Elegy Written in a Country Churchyard" to the apparent lightness and simplicity of some of Emily Dickinson's poems. Tennyson used a rhyming quatrain to such good effect in *In Memoriam* that the form he employed (four lines of iambic tetrameter rhyming *abba*) is known as the "In Memoriam stanza."

Other commonly used forms of stanza include the *rhyming couplet, terza rima, ottava rima, rhyme royal,* and the *Spenserian stanza*. Each of these is a rhetorical unit within a longer whole, rather like a paragraph within an essay. The poet's choice among such forms is dictated, at least in part, by the effects that each may produce. Thus the *rhyming couplet* often expresses a complete statement within two lines, creating a sense of density of thought, of coherence and closure; it is particularly effective where the writer wishes to set up contrasts, or to achieve the witty compactness of epigram:

> Of all mad creatures, if the learn'd are right,
> It is the slaver kills, and not the bite.
> A fool quite angry is quite innocent:
> Alas! 'tis ten times worse when they repent.
>
> (from Pope, "Epistle to Dr. Arbuthnot")

Ottava rima, as its Italian name implies, is an eight-line stanza, with the rhyme scheme *abababcc*. Like the sonnet, it is long enough to allow the development of a single thought in some detail and complexity, with a concluding couplet that may extend the central idea or cast it in a wholly unexpected light. W.B. Yeats uses this stanza form in "Sailing to Byzantium" and "Among Schoolchildren." Though much used by Renaissance poets, it is particularly associated with George Gordon, Lord Byron's *Don Juan*, in which the poet exploits to the full its potential for devastating irony and bathos. It is long enough to allow the development of a single thought in some detail and complexity; the concluding couplet can then, sonnet-like, turn that thought upon its head, or cast it in a wholly unexpected light:

Sagest of women, even of widows, she
   Resolved that Juan should be quite a paragon,
And worthy of the noblest pedigree
   (His sire was of Castile, his dam from Aragon).
Then for accomplishments of chivalry,
   In case our lord the king should go to war again,
He learned the arts of riding, fencing, gunnery,
And how to scale a fortress—or a nunnery.

(Don Juan I.38)

FREE VERSE

Not all writers want the order and symmetry—some might say the restraints and limitations—of traditional forms, and many have turned to *free verse* as a means of liberating their thoughts and feelings. Deriving its name from the French "vers libre" made popular by the French Symbolistes at the end of the nineteenth century, free verse is characterized by irregularity of metre, line length, and rhyme. This does not mean that it is without pattern; rather, it tends to follow more closely than other forms the unforced rhythms and accents of natural speech, making calculated use of spacing, line breaks, and "cadences," the rhythmic units that govern phrasing in speech.

Free verse is not a modern invention. Milton was an early practitioner, as was Blake; however, it was the great modern writers of free verse—first Walt Whitman, then Pound, Eliot, and William Carlos Williams (interestingly, all Americans, at least originally)—who gave this form a fluidity and flexibility that could free the imagination to deal with any kind of feeling or experience. Perhaps because it depends so much more than traditional forms upon the individual intuitions of the poet, it is the form of poetic structure most commonly found today. The best practitioners recognize that free verse, like any other kind of poetry, demands clarity, precision, and a close connection between technique and meaning.

PROSE POETRY

At the furthest extreme from traditional forms lies poetry written in prose. Contradictory as this label may seem, the two have much in common. Prose has at its disposal all the figurative devices available to poetry, such as metaphor, personification, or apostrophe; it may use structuring devices such as verbal repetition or parallel syntactical structures; it can draw on the same tonal range, from pathos to irony. The difference is that prose poetry accomplishes its ends in sentences and paragraphs, rather than lines or stanzas. First given prominence by the French poet Charles Baudelaire (*Petits Poèmes en prose*, 1862), the form is much used to present fragments of heightened sensation, conveyed through vivid or impressionistic description. It draws upon such prosaic forms as journal entries, lists, even footnotes. Prose poetry should be distinguished from "poetic prose," which may be found in a variety of settings (from the King James Bible to the fiction of Jeanette Winterson); the distinction—which not all critics would accept—appears to lie in the writer's intention.

Christan Bok's *Eunoia* is an interesting example of the ways in which a writer of prose poetry may try to balance the demands of each medium. *Eunoia* is an avowedly experimental work in which each chapter is restricted to the use of a single vowel. The text is governed by a series of rules described by the author in an afterword; they include a requirement that all chapters "must allude to the art of writing. All sentences must accent internal rhyme through the use of syntactical parallelism. The text must exhaust the lexicon for each vowel, citing at least 98% of the available repertoire...." Having imposed such constraints upon the language and form of the work, Bok then sets himself the task of showing that "even under such improbable conditions of duress, language can still express an uncanny, if not sublime, thought." The result is a surrealistic narrative that blends poetic and linguistic devices to almost hypnotic effect.

THE POEM AS A MATERIAL OBJECT

Both free verse and prose poetry pay attention in different ways to the poem as a living thing on the printed page. But the way in which poetry is presented in material form is an important part of the existence of almost any form of poetry. In the six volumes of this anthology the material form of the poem is highlighted by the inclusion of a number of facsimile reproductions of poems of other eras in their earliest extant material form.

RHYTHM AND SCANSION

When we read poetry, we often become aware of a pattern of rhythm within a line or set of lines. The formal analysis of that rhythmic pattern, or "metre," is called *scansion*. The verb "to scan" may carry different meanings, depending upon the context: if the *critic* "scans" a line, he or she is attempting to determine the metrical pattern in which it is cast; if the *line* "scans," we are making the observation that the line conforms to particular metrical rules. Whatever the context, the process of scansion is based on the premise that a line of verse is built on a pattern of stresses, a recurring set of more or less regular beats established by the alternation of light and heavy accents in syllables and words. The rhythmic pattern so distinguished in a given poem is said to be the "metre" of that poem. If we find it impossible to identify any specific metrical pattern, the poem is probably an example of free verse.

QUANTITATIVE, SYLLABIC, AND ACCENTUAL-SYLLABIC VERSE

Although we owe much of our terminology for analyzing or describing poetry to the Greeks and Romans, the foundation of our metrical system is quite different from theirs. They measured a line of verse by the duration of sound ("quantity") in each syllable, and by the combination of short and long syllables. Such poetry is known as *quantitative* verse.

Unlike Greek or Latin, English is a heavily accented language. Thus poetry of the Anglo-Saxon period, such as *Beowulf*, was *accentual:* that is, the lines were based on a fixed number of accents, or stresses, regardless of the number of syllables in the line:

Oft Scyld Scefing   sceapena þreatum
    monegum maegþum   meodosetla ofteah.

Few modern poets have written in the accentual tradition. A notable exception was Gerard Manley Hopkins, who based his line on a pattern of strong stresses that he called "sprung rhythm." Hopkins experimented with rhythms and stresses that approximate the accentual quality of natural speech; the result is a line that is emphatic, abrupt, even harsh in its forcefulness:

I caught this morning morning's minion, kingdom of daylight's dauphin, dapple-dawn-drawn
    Falcon, in his riding

Of the rolling level underneath him steady air ....

(from "The Windhover")

Under the influence of French poetry, following the Norman invasion of the eleventh century, English writers were introduced to *syllabic* prosody: that is, poetry in which the number of syllables is the determining factor in the length of any line, regardless of the number of stresses or their placement. A few modern writers have successfully produced syllabic poetry.

However, the accentual patterns of English, in speech as well as in poetry, were too strongly ingrained to disappear. Instead, the native accentual practice combined with the imported syllabic conventions to produce the *accentual-syllabic* line, in which the writer works with combinations of stressed and unstressed syllables in lines of equal syllabic length. Geoffrey Chaucer was the first great writer to employ the accentual-syllabic line in English poetry:

> Ther was also a Nonne, a Prioresse,
> That of hir smiling was ful simple and coy.
> Hir gretteste ooth was but by sainté Loy,
> And she was clepéd Madame Eglantine.

(from *The Canterbury Tales*)

The fundamental pattern here is the ten-syllable line (although the convention of sounding the final "e" at the end of a line in Middle English verse sometimes produces eleven syllables). Each line contains five stressed syllables, each of which alternates with one or two unstressed syllables. This was to become the predominant metre of poetry in English until the general adoption of free verse in the twentieth century.

IDENTIFYING POETIC METER

Conventionally, meter is established by dividing a line into roughly equal parts, based on the rise and fall of the rhythmic beats. Each of these divisions, conventionally marked by a bar, is known as a "foot," and within the foot there will be a combination of stressed and unstressed syllables, indicated by the prosodic symbols / (stressed) and x (unstressed).

> I know | that I | shall meet | my fate
> Somewhere | among | the clouds | above ...

(from *Yeats*, "An Irish Airman Foresees His Death")

To describe the meter used in a poem, we must first determine what kind of foot predominates, and then count the number of feet in each line. To describe the resultant meter we use terminology borrowed from classical prosody. In identifying the meter of English verse we commonly apply the following labels:

iambic (x /): a foot with one weak stress followed by one strong stress

> ("Look home | ward, Ang | el, now, | and melt | with ruth")

trochaic (/ x): strong followed by weak

> ("Ty | ger! Ty | ger! bur | ning bright")

anapaestic (x x /): two weak stresses, followed by a strong

    ("I have passed | with a nod | of the head")

dactylic (/ x x): strong stress followed by two weak

    ("Hickory | dickory | dock")

spondaic (/ /): two strong stresses

    ("If hate | killed men,| Brother | Lawrence,
      God's blood,| would not | mine kill | you?")

We also use classical terms to describe the number of feet in a line. Thus, a line with one foot is *monometer*; with two feet, *dimeter*; three feet, *trimeter*; four feet, *tetrameter*; five feet, *pentameter*; and six feet, *hexameter*.

    Scansion of the two lines from Yeats's "Irish Airman" quoted above shows that the predominant foot is iambic (x /), that there are four feet to each line, and that the poem is therefore written in *iambic tetrameters*. The first foot of the second line, however, may be read as a trochee ("Somewhere"); the variation upon the iambic norm here is an example of *substitution*, a means whereby the writer may avoid the monotony that would result from adhering too closely to a set rhythm. We very quickly build up an expectation about the dominant meter of a poem; the poet will sometimes disturb that expectation by changing the beat, and so through substitution create a pleasurable tension in our awareness.

    The prevailing meter in English poetry is iambic, since the natural rhythm of spoken English is predominantly iambic. Nonetheless, poets may employ other rhythms where it suits their purpose. Thus W.H. Auden can create a solemn tone by the use of a trochaic meter (/ x):

    Earth, receive an honoured guest;
    William Yeats is laid to rest:
    Let the Irish vessel lie
    Emptied of its poetry.

The same meter may be much less funereal, as in Ben Jonson's song "*To Celia*":

    Come, my Celia, let us prove,
    While we may, the sports of love.
    Time will not be ours forever;
    He, at length, our good will sever.

The sense of greater pace in this last example derives in part from the more staccato phrasing, and also from the greater use of monosyllabic words. A more obviously lilting, dancing effect is obtained from anapaestic rhythm (x x /):

    I sprang to the stirrup, and Joris, and he;
    I galloped, Dirck galloped, we galloped all three.
    "Good speed!" cried the watch, as the gatebolts undrew;
    "Speed!" echoed the wall to us galloping through.
      (from *Browning*, "How They Brought the Good News from Ghent to Aix")

Coleridge wittily captured the varying effects of different meters in "Metrical Feet: Lesson for a Boy," which the poet wrote for his sons, and in which he marked the stresses himself:

> Trochee trips from long to short;
> From long to long in solemn sort
> Slow Spondee stalks; strong foot! yet ill able
> Ever to come up with Dactyl trisyllable.
> Iambics march from short to long:—
> With a leap and a bound the swift Anapaests throng....

A meter which often deals with serious themes is unrhymed iambic pentameter, also known as *blank verse*. This is the meter of Shakespeare's plays, notably his great tragedies; it is the meter, too, of Milton's *Paradise Lost*, to which it lends a desired sonority and magnificence; and of Wordsworth's "Lines Composed a Few Miles above Tintern Abbey," where the flexibility of the meter allows the writer to move by turns from description, to narration, to philosophical reflection.

RHYME, CONSONANCE, ASSONANCE, AND ALLITERATION

Perhaps the most obvious sign of poetic form is rhyme: that is, the repetition of syllables with the same or similar sounds. If the rhyme words are placed at the end of the line, they are known as *end-rhymes*. The opening stanza of Housman's "To an Athlete Dying Young" has two pairs of end-rhymes:

> The time you won your town the *race*
> We chaired you through the market-*place*;
> Man and boy stood cheering *by*,
> And home we brought you shoulder-*high*.

Words rhyming within a line are *internal rhymes*, as in the first and third lines of this stanza from Coleridge's "The Rime of the Ancient Mariner":

> The fair breeze *blew*, the white foam *flew*
> The furrow followed free;
> We were the *first* that ever *burst*
> Into that silent sea.

When, as is usually the case, the rhyme occurs in a stressed syllable, it is known as a *masculine rhyme*; if the rhyming word ends in an unstressed syllable, it is referred to as *feminine*. The difference is apparent in the opening stanzas of Alfred Tennyson's poem "The Lady of Shalott," where the first stanza establishes the basic iambic meter with strong stresses on the rhyming words:

> On either side the river *lie*
> Long fields of barley and of *rye*,
> That clothe the wold and meet the *sky*;
> And through the field the road runs *by*
> To many-towered Camelot ...

In the second stanza Tennyson changes to trochaic lines, ending in unstressed syllables and feminine rhymes:

> Willows whiten, aspens *quiver*,
> Little breezes dusk and *shiver*
> Through the wave that runs *forever*
> By the island in the *river*
> Flowing down to Camelot.

Not only does Tennyson avoid monotony here by his shift to feminine rhymes, he also darkens the mood by using words that imply a contrast with the bright warmth of day—"quiver," "dusk," "shiver"—in preparation for the introduction of the "silent isle" that embowers the Lady.

NEAR RHYMES

Most of the rhymes in "The Lady of Shalott" are exact, or "*perfect*" rhymes. However, in the second of the stanzas just quoted, it is evident that "forever" at the end of the third line is not a "perfect" rhyme; rather, it is an instance of "*near*" or "*slant*" rhyme. Such "*imperfect*" rhymes are quite deliberate; indeed, two stanzas later we find the rhyming sequence "early," "barley," "cheerly," and "clearly," followed by the rhymes "weary," "airy," and "fairy." As with the introduction of feminine rhymes, such divergences from one dominant pattern prevent monotony and avoid a too-mechanical sing-song effect.

More importantly, near-rhymes have an oddly unsettling effect, perhaps because they both raise and frustrate our expectation of a perfect rhyme. Their use certainly gives added emphasis to the words at the end of these chilling lines from Wilfred Owen's "*Strange Meeting*":

> For by my glee might many men have laughed,
> And of my weeping something had been left,
> Which must die now. I mean the truth untold,
> The pity of war, the pity war distilled.
> Now men will go content with what we spoiled,
> Or, discontent, boil bloody, and be spilled.

CONSONANCE AND ASSONANCE

In Owen's poem, the near-rhymes "laughed / left" and "spoiled / spilled" are good examples of *consonance*, which pairs words with similar consonants but different intervening vowels. Other examples from Owen's poem include "groined / groaned," "hall / Hell," "years / yours," and "mystery / mastery."

Related to consonance as a linking device is *assonance*, the echoing of similar vowel sounds in the stressed syllables of words with differing consonants (lane/hail, penitent/reticence). A device favored particularly by descriptive poets, it appears often in the work of the English Romantics, especially Shelley and Keats, and their great Victorian successor Tennyson, all of whom had a good ear for the musical quality of language. In the following passage, Tennyson makes effective use of repeated "o" and "ow" sounds to suggest the soft moaning of the wind as it spreads the seed of the lotos plant:

> The Lotos blooms below the barren peak,
> The Lotos blows by every winding creek;

All day the wind breathes low with mellower tone;
Through every hollow cave and alley lone
Round and round the spicy downs the yellow Lotos dust is blown.

(from "The Lotos-Eaters")

ALLITERATION

Alliteration connects words which have the same initial consonant. Like consonance and rhyme, alliteration adds emphasis, throwing individual words into strong relief, and lending force to rhythm. This is especially evident in the work of Gerard Manley Hopkins, where alliteration works in conjunction with the heavy stresses of *sprung rhythm*:

Brute beauty and valour and act, oh, air, pride, plume, here
Buckle! AND the fire that breaks from thee then, a billion
Times told lovelier, more dangerous, O my chevalier!

(from "The Windhover")

Like assonance, alliteration is useful in descriptive poetry, reinforcing an impression or mood through repeated sounds:

Thou on whose stream, 'mid the steep sky's commotion,
Loose clouds like Earth's decaying leaves are shed,
Shook from the tangled boughs of Heaven and Ocean ....

(from Percy Shelley, "Ode to the West Wind")

The repetition of "s" and "sh" sounds conveys the rushing sound of a wind that drives everything before it. This effect is also an example of *onomatopoeia*, a figure of speech in which the sound of the words seems to echo the sense.

RHYME AND POETIC STRUCTURE

Rhyme may play a central role in the structure of a poem. This is particularly apparent in the *sonnet* form, where the expression of the thought is heavily influenced by the poet's choice of rhyme-scheme. The "English" or "Shakespearean" sonnet has three quatrains rhyming *abab, cdcd, efef*, and concludes with a rhyming couplet, *gg*. This pattern lends itself well to the statement and restatement of an idea, as we find, for example, in Shakespeare's sonnet "That time of year thou mayst in me behold." Each of the quatrains presents an image of decline or decay—a tree in winter, the coming of night, a dying fire; the closing couplet then relates these images to the thought of an impending separation and attendant feelings of loss.

The organization of the "Italian" or "Petrarchan" sonnet, by contrast, hinges on a rhyme scheme that creates two parts, an eight-line section (the *octave*) typically rhyming *abbaabba*, and a concluding six-line section (the *sestet*) rhyming *cdecde* or some other variation. In the octave, the writer describes a thought or feeling; in the sestet, the writer may elaborate upon that thought, or may introduce a sudden "turn" or change of direction. A good example of the Italian form is Donne's "Batter My Heart, Three-Personed God."

The rhyming pattern established at the beginning of a poem is usually followed throughout; thus the opening sets up an expectation in the reader, which the poet may sometimes play on by means of an unexpected or surprising rhyme. This is especially evident in comic verse, where peculiar or unexpected rhymes can contribute a great deal to the comic effect:

> I shoot the Hippopotamus
> with bullets made of platinum,
>   Because if I use leaden ones
> his hide is sure to flatten 'em.
>   (*Hilaire Belloc,* "The Hippopotamus")

Finally, one of the most obvious yet important aspects of rhyme is its sound. It acts as a kind of musical punctuation, lending verse an added resonance and beauty. And as anyone who has ever had to learn poetry by heart will testify, the sound of rhyme is a powerful aid to memorization and recall, from helping a child to learn numbers—

> One, two,
> Buckle my shoe,
> Three, four,
> Knock at the door—

—to selling toothpaste through an advertising jingle in which the use of rhyme drives home the identity of a product:

> You'll wonder where the yellow went,
> When you brush your teeth with Pepsodent.

OTHER FORMS WITH INTERLOCKING RHYMES

Other forms besides the sonnet depend upon rhyme for their structural integrity. These include the *rondeau*, a poem of thirteen lines in three stanzas, with two half lines acting as a refrain, and having only two rhymes. The linking effect of rhyme is also essential to the three-line stanza called *terza rima*, the form chosen by Shelley for his "Ode to the West Wind," where the rhyme scheme (*aba, bcb, cdc* etc.) gives a strong sense of forward movement. But a poet need not be limited to particular forms to use interlocking rhyme schemes.

THE POET'S TASK

The poet's task, in Sir Philip Sidney's view, is to move us to virtue and well-doing by coming to us with

words set in delightful proportion, either accompanied with, or prepared for, the well-enchanting skill of music; and with a tale forsooth he cometh unto you, with a tale which holdeth children from play, and old men from the chimney corner; and pretending no more, doth intend the winning of the mind from wickedness to virtue: even as the child is often brought to take most wholesome things by hiding them in such other as have a pleasant taste.

(The Defence of Poesy, 1593)

Modern poets have been less preoccupied with the didactic or moral force of poetry, its capacity to win the mind to virtue; nonetheless, like their Renaissance counterparts, they view poetry as a means to understanding, a point of light in an otherwise dark universe. To Robert Frost, a poem "begins in delight and ends in wisdom":

It begins in delight, it inclines to the impulse, it assumes direction with the first line laid down, it runs a course of lucky events, and ends in a clarification of life—not necessarily a great clarification, such as sects and cults are founded on, but in a momentary stay against confusion.

("The Figure a Poem Makes," *Collected Poems,* 1939)

Rhyme and metre are important tools at the poet's disposal, and can be valuable aids in developing thought as well as in creating rhythmic or musical effects. However, the technical skills needed to turn a good line or create metrical complexities should not be confused with the ability to write good poetry. Sidney wryly observes in his *Defence of Poesy* that "there have been many excellent poets that never versified, and now swarm many versifiers that need never answer to the name of poets. . . . it is not rhyming and versing that maketh a poet, no more than a long gown maketh an advocate." Technical virtuosity may arouse our admiration, but something else is needed to bring that "constriction of the throat and ... precipitation of water to the eyes" that A.E. Housman speaks about. What that "something" is will always elude definition, and is perhaps best left for readers and listeners to determine for themselves through their own encounters with poetry.

Maps

COUNTIES
OF THE
BRITISH ISLES

THE BRITISH ISLES

THE LONDON AREA

EPPING FOREST

Finchley

Harrow

Twyford Abbey

London   Tower

Westminster

Chelsea

Woolwich

Greenwich

Richmond

Battersea

Deptford

Twickenham

Dartford

Kingston   Wimbledon

Sydenham

Hampton Court

Merton

LONDON

- - - - Boundary of the walled city

········· Boundary of Elizabethan London

1. Lambeth Palace
2. Westminster Bridge
3. Westminster Abbey
4. Whitehall
5. Tyburn
6. Covent Garden
7. The Temple
8. Blackfriar's Bridge
9. Swan Theatre
10. Bear Garden
11. Globe Theatre
12. London Bridge
13. St. Paul's Cathedral
14. Fortune Theatre
15. The Theatre
16. Bethlehem Hospital ("Bedlam")
17. The Tower

TOTTENHAM COURT RD.

GRAY'S INN RD.

ALDERSGATE

BISHOPSGATE

HOLBORN

OXFORD ST.

DRURY LANE

FLEET ST.

CHEAPSIDE

THAMES ST.

STRAND

Thames

HYDE PARK

PICADILLY

PALL MALL

GREEN PARK

ST. JAMES'S PK.

CHELSEA RD.

CHELSEA

Thames

Monarchs and Prime Ministers of Great Britain

MONARCHS

House of Wessex

Egbert (Ecgberht)	829–39
Æthelwulf	839–58
Æthelbald	858–60
Æthelbert	860–66
Æthelred I	866–71
Alfred the Great	871–99
Edward the Elder	899–924
Athelstan	924–40
Edmund I	940–46
Edred (Eadred)	946–55
Edwy (Eadwig)	955–59
Edgar	959–75
Edward the Martyr	975–78
Æthelred II (the Unready)	978–1016
Edmund II (Ironside)	1016

Danish Line

Canute (Cnut)	1016–35
Harold I (Harefoot)	1035–40
Hardecanute	1040–42

Wessex Line, Restored

Edward the Confessor	1042–66
Harold II	1066

Norman Line

William I (the Conqueror)	1066–87
William II (Rufus)	1087–1100
Henry I (Beauclerc)	1100–35
Stephen	1135–54

MONARCHS

PLANTAGENET, ANGEVIN LINE

Henry II	1154–89
Richard I (Coeur de Lion)	1189–99
John (Lackland)	1199–1216
Henry III	1216–72
Edward I (Longshanks)	1272–1307
Edward II	1307–27
Edward III	1327–77
Richard II	1377–99

PLANTAGENET, LANCASTRIAN LINE

Henry IV	1399–1413
Henry V	1413–22
Henry VI	1422–61

Henry VIII

PLANTAGENET, YORKIST LINE

Edward IV	1461–83
Edward V	1483
Richard III	1483–85

HOUSE OF TUDOR

Henry VII	1485–1509
Henry VIII	1509–47
Edward VI	1547–53
Mary I	1553–58
Elizabeth I	1558–1603

HOUSE OF STUART

James I	1603–25
Charles I	1625–49

Mary I

(The Commonwealth)	1649–60
Oliver Cromwell	1649–58
Richard Cromwell	1658–59

MONARCHS

HOUSE OF STUART, RESTORED

Charles II	1660–85
James II	1685–88

HOUSE OF ORANGE AND STUART

William III and Mary II	1689–94
William III	1694–1702

HOUSE OF STUART

Anne	1702–14

HOUSE OF BRUNSWICK, HANOVER LINE

George I	1714–27
George II	1727–60
George III	1760–1820

George, Prince of Wales,
Prince Regent

PRIME MINISTERS

George III

Sir Robert Walpole (Whig)	1721–42
Earl of Wilmington (Whig)	1742–43
Henry Pelham (Whig)	1743–54
Duke of Newcastle (Whig)	1754–56
Duke of Devonshire (Whig)	1756–57
Duke of Newcastle (Whig)	1757–62
Earl of Bute (Tory)	1762–63
George Grenville (Whig)	1763–65
Marquess of Rockingham (Whig)	1765–66
William Pitt the Elder (Earl of Chatham) (Whig)	1766–68
Duke of Grafton (Whig)	1768–70
Frederick North (Lord North) (Tory)	1770–82
Marquess of Rockingham (Whig)	1782
Earl of Shelburne (Whig)	1782–83
Duke of Portland	1783
William Pitt the Younger (Tory)	1783–1801
Henry Addington (Tory)	1801–04
William Pitt the Younger (Tory)	1804–06
William Wyndham Grenville (Baron Grenville) (Whig)	1806–07

MONARCHS

George, Prince of Wales, Prince Regent	1811–20
George IV	1820–30
William IV	1830–37
Victoria	1837–1901

Victoria

HOUSE OF SAXE-COBURG-GOTHA

Edward VII	1901–10

HOUSE OF WINDSOR

George V	1910–36

PRIME MINISTERS

Duke of Portland (Whig)	1807–09
Spencer Perceval (Tory)	1809–12
Earl of Liverpool (Tory)	1812–27
George Canning (Tory)	1827
Viscount Goderich (Tory)	1827–28
Duke of Wellington (Tory)	1828–30
Earl Grey (Whig)	1830–34
Viscount Melbourne (Whig)	1834
Sir Robert Peel (Tory)	1834–35
Viscount Melbourne (Whig)	1835–41
Sir Robert Peel (Tory)	1841–46
Lord John Russell (later Earl) (Liberal)	1846–52
Earl of Derby (Con.)	1852
Earl of Aberdeen (Tory)	1852–55
Viscount Palmerston (Lib.)	1855–58
Earl of Derby (Con.)	1858–59
Viscount Palmerston (Lib.)	1859–65
Earl Russell (Liberal)	1865–66
Earl of Derby (Con.)	1866–68
Benjamin Disraeli (Con.)	1868
William Gladstone (Lib.)	1868–74
Benjamin Disraeli (Con.)	1874–80
William Gladstone (Lib.)	1880–85
Marquess of Salisbury (Con.)	1885–86
William Gladstone (Lib.)	1886
Marquess of Salisbury (Con.)	1886–92
William Gladstone (Lib.)	1892–94
Earl of Rosebery (Lib.)	1894–95
Marquess of Salisbury (Con.)	1895–1902
Arthur Balfour (Con.)	1902–05
Sir Henry Campbell-Bannerman (Lib.)	1905–08
Herbert Asquith (Lib.)	1908–15
Herbert Asquith (Lib.)	1915–16

MONARCHS		PRIME MINISTERS	
		Andrew Bonar Law (Con.)	1922–23
		Stanley Baldwin (Con.)	1923–24
		James Ramsay MacDonald (Labour)	1924
		Stanley Baldwin (Con.)	1924–29
		James Ramsay MacDonald (Labour)	1929–31
		James Ramsay MacDonald (Labour)	1931–35
		Stanley Baldwin (Con.)	1935–37
Edward VIII	1936	Neville Chamberlain (Con.)	1937–40
George VI	1936–52	Winston Churchill (Con.)	1940–45
		Winston Churchill (Con.)	1945
		Clement Attlee (Labour)	1945–51
		Sir Winston Churchill (Con.)	1951–55
Elizabeth II	1952–	Sir Anthony Eden (Con.)	1955–57
		Harold Macmillan (Con.)	1957–63
		Sir Alex Douglas-Home (Con.)	1963–64
		Harold Wilson (Labour)	1964–70
		Edward Heath (Con.)	1970–74
		Harold Wilson (Labour)	1974–76
		James Callaghan (Labour)	1976–79
		Margaret Thatcher (Con.)	1979–90
		John Major (Con.)	1990–97
		Tony Blair (Labour)	1997–

Winston Churchill

GLOSSARY OF TERMS

Accent: the natural emphasis (stress) speakers place on a syllable.

Accentual Verse: poetry in which a line is measured only by the number of accents or stresses, not by the number of syllables.

Accentual-Syllabic Verse: the most common metrical system in traditional English verse, in which a line is measured by the number of syllables and by the pattern of accented (stressed) and unaccented (unstressed) syllables.

Aesthetes: members of a late nineteenth-century movement that valued "art for art's sake"—for its purely aesthetic qualities, as opposed to valuing art for the moral content it may convey, for the intellectual stimulation it may provide, or for a range of other qualities.

Alexandrine: a line of verse that is 12 syllables long. In English verse, the alexandrine is always an iambic hexameter: that is, it has six iambic feet. The most-often quoted example is the second line in a couplet from Alexander Pope's "Essay on Criticism" (1711): "A needless Alexandrine ends the song / That, like a wounded snake, drags its slow length along." See also *Spenserian stanza*.

Allegory: a narrative with both a literal meaning and secondary, often symbolic meaning or meanings. Allegory frequently employs personification to give concrete embodiment to abstract concepts or entities, such as feelings or personal qualities. It may also present one set of characters or events in the guise of another, using implied parallels for the purposes of satire or political comment, as in John Dryden's poem "Absalom and Achitophel."

Alliteration: the grouping of words with the same initial consonant (e.g., "break, blow, burn, and make me new"). The repetition of sound acts as a connector. See also *assonance* and *consonance*.

Alliterative Verse: poetry that employs alliteration of stressed syllables in each line as its chief structural principle.

Allusion: a reference, often indirect or unidentified, to a person, thing, or event. A reference in one literary work to another literary work, whether to its content or its form, also constitutes an allusion.

Ambiguity: an "opening" of language created by the writer to allow for multiple meanings or differing interpretations. In literature, ambiguity may be deliberately employed by the writer to enrich meaning; this differs from any unintentional, unwanted, ambiguity in non-literary prose.

Amphibrach: a metrical foot with three syllables, the second of which is stressed: x / x (e.g., sensation).

Analogy: a broad term that refers to our processes of noting similarities among things or events. Specific forms of analogy in poetry include *simile* and *metaphor* (see below).

Anapaest: a metrical foot containing two unstressed syllables followed by one stressed syllable: xx / (e.g., underneath, intervene).

Anglican Church / Church of England: formed after Henry VIII's break with Rome in the 1530s, the Church of England had acquired a permanently Protestant cast by the 1570s. There has remained considerable variation within the Church, however, with distinctions often drawn among High Church, Broad Church, and Latitudinarian. At one extreme High Church Anglicans (some of whom prefer to be known as "Anglo-Catholics") prefer relatively elaborate church rituals not dissimilar in form to those of the Roman Catholic Church and place considerable emphasis on church hierarchy, while in the other direction Latitudinarians prefer relatively informal religious services and tend far more towards egalitarianism.

Antistrophe: from Greek drama, the chorus's countermovement or reply to an initial movement (strophe). See *ode* below.

Apostrophe: a figure of speech (a trope; see figures of speech below) in which a writer directly addresses an object—or a dead or absent person—as if the imagined audience were actually listening.

Archetype: in literature and mythology, a recurring idea, symbol, motif, character, or place. To some scholars and psychologists, an archetype represents universal human thought-patterns or experiences.

Assonance: the repetition of identical or similar vowel sounds in stressed syllables in which the surrounding consonants are different: for example, "shame" and "fate"; "gale" and "cage"; or the long "i" sounds in "Beside the pumice isle..."

Aubade: a lyric poem that greets or laments the arrival of dawn.

Ballad: a folk song, or a poem originally recited to an audience, which tells a dramatic story based on legend or history.

Ballad Stanza: a quatrain with alternating four-stress and three-stress lines, rhyming *abcb*. A variant is "common measure," in which the alternating lines are strictly iambic, and rhyme *abab*.

Ballade: a fixed form most commonly characterized by only three rhymes, with an 8-line stanza rhyming *ababbcbc* and an envoy rhyming *bcbc*. Both Chaucer and Dante Gabriel Rossetti ("Ballad of the Dead Ladies") adopted this form.

Baroque: powerful and heavily ornamented in style. "Baroque" is a term from the history of visual art and of music that is sometimes also used to describe certain literary styles, such as that of Richard Crashaw.

Bathos: an anticlimactic effect brought about by a writer's descent from an elevated subject or tone to the ordinary or trivial.

Benedictine Rule: set of instructions for monastic communities, composed by Saint Benedict of Nursia (died c. 457).

Blank Verse: unrhymed lines written in iambic pentameter, a form introduced to English verse by Henry Howard, Earl of Surrey, in his translation of parts of Virgil's *Aeneid* in 1547.

Bombast: inappropriately inflated or grandiose language.

Broadside: individual sheet of paper printed on only one side. From the sixteenth through to the eighteenth centuries broadsides of a variety of different sorts (e.g., ballads, political tracts, short satires) were sold on the streets.

Broken Rhyme: in which a multi-syllable word is split at the end of a line and continued onto the next, to allow an end-rhyme with the split syllable.

Burlesque: satire of a particularly exaggerated sort, particularly that which ridicules its subject by emphasising its vulgar or ridiculous aspects.

Caesura: a pause or break in a line of verse occurring where a phrase, clause, or sentence ends, and indicated in scansion by the mark II. If it occurs in the middle of the line, it is known as a "medial" caesura.

Canon: in literature, those works that are commonly accepted as possessing authority or importance. In practice, "canonical" texts or authors are those that are discussed most frequently by scholars and taught most frequently in university courses.

Canto: a sub-section of a long (usually epic) poem.

Canzone: a short song or poem, with stanzas of equal length and an envoy.

Carpe Diem: Latin (from Horace) meaning "seize the day." The idea of enjoying the moment is a common one in Renaissance love poetry. See, for example, Marvell's "To His Coy Mistress."

Catalexis: the omission of unstressed syllables from a line of verse (such a line is referred to as "catalectic"). In iambic verse it is usually the first syllable of the line that is omitted; in trochaic, the last. For example, in the first stanza of Housman's "To an Athlete Dying Young" the third line is catalectic: i.e., it has dropped the first, unstressed syllable called for by the poem's iambic tetrameter form: "The time you won your town the race / We chaired you through the market-place; / Man and boy stood cheering by, / And home we brought you shoulder-high."

Catharsis: the arousal through the performance of a dramatic tragedy of "emotions of pity and fear" to a point where "purgation" or "purification" occurs and the feelings are released or transformed. The concept was developed by Aristotle in his *Poetics* from an ancient Greek medical concept, and adapted by him into an aesthetic principle.

Chiasmus: a figure of speech (a scheme) that reverses word order in successive parallel clauses. If the word order is A-B-C in the first clause, it becomes C-B-A in the second: for example, Donne's line "She is all states, and all princes, I" ("The Sun Rising") incorporates this reversal (though with an ellipsis).

Classical: originating in or relating to ancient Greek or Roman culture. As commonly conceived, *classical* implies a strong sense of formal order. The term *neoclassical* is often used with reference to literature of the Restoration and eighteenth century that was strongly influenced by ancient Greek and Roman models.

Closet Drama: a play (typically in verse) written for private performance. The term came into use in the first half of the nineteenth century.

Colored Narrative: alternative term for *free indirect discourse*.

Comedy: as a literary term, used originally to denote that class of ancient Greek drama in which the action ends happily. More broadly the term has been used to describe a wide variety of literary forms of a more or less light-hearted character.

Commedia dell'arte: largely improvised comic performances conducted by masked performers and involving considerable physical activity. The genre of *commedia dell'arte* originated in Italy in the sixteenth century; it was influential throughout Europe for more than two centuries thereafter.

Commonwealth: from the fifteenth century, a term roughly equivalent to the modern "state," but tending to emphasize the commonality of interests among all citizens. In the seventeenth century Britain was named a commonwealth under Oliver Cromwell. In the twentieth century, the term came to be applied to associations of many nations; the British Commonwealth became the successor to the British Empire.

Conceit: an unusually elaborate metaphor or simile that extends beyond its original tenor and vehicle, sometimes becoming a "master" analogy for the entire poem (see, for example, Donne's "The Flea," and Robert Frost's sonnet "She is as in a field a silken tent"). Ingenious or fanciful images and comparisons were especially popular with the metaphysical poets of the seventeenth century, giving rise to the term "metaphysical conceit."

Concrete Poetry: an experimental form, most popular during the 1950s and 60s, in which the printed type itself forms a visual image of the poem's key words or ideas. See also *pattern poetry, assonance*.

Connotation: the implied, often unspoken meaning(s) of a given word, as distinct from its denotation, or literal meaning. Connotations may have highly emotional undertones and are usually culturally specific.

Conservative Party: See *Political Parties*.

Consonance: the pairing of words with similar initial and ending consonants, but with different vowel sounds (live/love, wander/wonder). See also *alliteration*.

Convention: aesthetic approach, technique, or practice accepted as characteristic and appropriate for a particular form. It is a convention of certain sorts of plays, for example, that the characters speak in blank verse, of other sorts of plays that characters speak in rhymed couplets, and of still other sorts of dramatic performances that characters frequently break into song to express their feelings.

Couplet: a pair of rhyming lines, usually in the same meter. If they form a complete unit of thought and are grammatically complete, the lines are known as a closed couplet. See also *heroic couplet* below.

Dactyl: a metrical foot containing one strong stress followed by two weak stresses: / xx (e.g., muttering, helplessly). A minor form known as "double dactyls" makes use of this meter for humorous purposes, e.g., "Jiggery pokery" or "Higgledy Piggledy."

Denotation: See *connotation* above.

Devolution: process through which a degree of political power was transferred in the late twentieth and early twenty-first centuries from the British government to assemblies in Scotland and in Wales.

Dialogue: words spoken by characters to one another. (When a character is addressing him or her self or the audience directly, the words spoken are referred to as a *monologue*.)

Diction: word choice. Whether the diction of a literary work (or of a literary character) is colloquial, conversational, formal, or of some other type contributes significantly to the tone of the text as well as to characterization.

Didacticism: aesthetic approach emphasizing moral instruction.

Dimeter: a poetic line containing two metrical feet.

Dirge: a song or poem that mourns someone's death. See also *elegy* and *lament* below.

Disestablishmentarianism: movement opposing an official state-supported religion, in particular the Church of England in that role.

Dissonance: harsh, unmusical sounds or rhythms which poets may use deliberately to achieve certain effects.

Dramatic Irony: this form of irony occurs when the audience's reception of a speech by a character on the stage is affected by the possession by the audience of information not available to the character.

Dramatic Monologue: a lyric poem that takes the form of an utterance by a single person addressing a silent listener. The speaker may be an historical personage (as in some of Robert Browning's dramatic monologues), a figure drawn from myth or legend (as in some of Tennyson's), or an entirely imagined figure, as in Webster's "A Castaway."

Dub Poetry: a form of protest poetry originating in Jamaica, with its roots in dance rhythms, especially reggae, and often accompanied in performance by drums and music. See also *rap* and *hip-hop*.

Duple Foot: A duple foot of poetry has two syllables. The possible duple forms are iamb (in which the stress is on the second of the two syllables), trochee (in which the stress is on the first of the two syllables), spondee (in which both are stressed equally), and pyrrhic (in which both syllables are unstressed).

Eclogue: now generally used simply as an alternative name for a pastoral poem. In classical times and in the early modern period, however, an *eclogue* (or *idyll*) was a specific type of pastoral poem—a dialogue or dramatic monologue involving rustic characters. (The other main sub-genre of the pastoral was the *georgic*.)

Elegiac Stanza: a quatrain of iambic pentameters rhyming *abab*, often used in poems meditating on death or sorrow. The best-known example is Thomas Gray's "Elegy Written in a Country Churchyard."

Elegy: a poem which formally mourns the death of a particular person (e.g., Tennyson's "In Memoriam") or in which the poet meditates on other serious subjects (e.g., Gray's "Elegy"). See also *dirge*.

Elision: omitting or suppressing a letter or an unstressed syllable at the beginning or end of a word, so that a line of verse may conform to a given metrical scheme. For example, the three syllables at the beginning of Shakespeare's sonnet 129 are reduced to two by the omission of the first vowel: "Th' expense of spirit in a waste of shame." See also *syncope*.

Ellipsis: the omission of a word or words necessary for the complete grammatical construction of a sentence, but not necessary for our understanding of the sentence.

End-Rhyme: See *rhyme*.

End-stopped: a line of poetry is said to be end-stopped when the end of the line coincides with a natural pause in the syntax, such as the conclusion of a sentence; e.g., in this couplet from Pope's "Essay on Criticism," both lines are end-stopped: "A little learning is a dangerous thing; / Drink deep, or taste not the Pierian spring." Compare this with *enjambement*.

Enjambement: the "running-on" of the sense from one line of poetry to the next, with no pause created by punctuation or syntax. (The more commonly found alternative is referred to as an *end-stopped line*.)

Envoy (Envoi): a stanza or half-stanza that forms the conclusion of certain French poetic forms, such as the *sestina* or the *ballade*. It often sums up or comments upon what has gone before.

Epic: a lengthy narrative poem, often divided into books and sub-divided into cantos. It generally celebrates heroic deeds or events, and the style tends to be lofty and grand. Examples in English include Spenser's *The Faerie Queene* and Milton's *Paradise Lost*.

Epic Simile: an elaborate simile, developed at such length that the vehicle of the comparison momentarily displaces the primary subject with which it is being compared.

Epigram: a very short poem, sometimes in closed couplet form, characterized by pointed wit.

Epigraph: a quotation placed at the beginning of a discourse to indicate or foreshadow the theme.

Epiphany: a moment at which matters of significance are suddenly illuminated for a literary character (or for the reader), typically triggered by something small and seemingly of little import. The term first came into wide currency in connection with the fiction of James Joyce.

Episodic Plot: plot comprising a variety of episodes that are only loosely connected by threads of story material (as opposed to plots that present one or more continually unfolding narratives where successive episodes build one on another).

Epithalamion: a poem celebrating a wedding. The best-known example in English is probably Edmund Spenser's "Epithalamion" (1595).

Eulogy: text expressing praise, especially for a distinguished person recently deceased.

Euphemism: mode of expression through which aspects of reality considered to be vulgar, crudely physical, or unpleasant are referred to indirectly rather than named explicitly. A variety of euphemisms exist for the processes of urination and defecation; *passed away* is often used as a euphemism for *died.* (The word *euphemism* has the same root as *Euphuism* (see below), but has taken on a different meaning.)

Euphony: pleasant, musical sounds or rhythms—the opposite of dissonance.

Euphuism: In the late sixteenth century John Lyly published a prose romance, *Euphues*, which employed a style that featured long sentences filled with balanced phrases and clauses, many of them adding little to the content. This highly mannered style was popular in the court of Elizabeth I for a few years following the publication of Lyly's famous work, and the style became known as *Euphuism.*

European Union: (EU) Group of nations formed in 1993 as the successor to the European Economic Community (Common Market). Britain first applied for membership in the latter in 1961; at first its efforts to join were blocked by the French government, but in 1973 Prime Minister Edward Heath successfully negotiated Britain's entry into the group. Britain has resisted some moves towards full integration with the European community, in particular retaining its own currency when other European nations adopted the Euro on 1 January 2002.

Exchequer: In earlier eras, the central royal financial office, responsible for receiving and keeping track of crown revenues. In later eras, part of the bureaucracy equivalent to the Ministry of Finance in Canada or the Treasury in the United States (the modern post of Chancellor of the Exchequer is equivalent to the American post of Secretary of the Treasury, the Canadian post of Minister of Finance or the Australian post of Treasurer).

Exposition: the setting out of material in an ordered form, either in speech or in writing. In a play those parts of the action that do not occur on stage but are rather recounted by the characters are frequently described as being presented in exposition. Similarly, when the background narrative is filled in near the beginning of a novel, such material is often described as having been presented in exposition. Somewhat confusingly, however, the term "expository prose" is usually used with reference not to fiction but to the setting forth of arguments or descriptions in the context of essays or other works of prose non-fiction.

Eye-Rhyme: See *rhyme* below.

Feminine Ending: the ending of a line of poetry on an "extra," and, especially, on an unstressed syllable. See, for example, the first line of Keat's "Ode on a Grecian Urn": "A thing of beauty is a joy forever," a line of iambic pentameter in which the final foot is an amphibrach rather than an iamb.

Feminine Rhyme: See *rhyme* below.

Figures of Speech: deliberate, highly concentrated uses of language to achieve particular purposes or effects on an audience. There are two kinds of figures: schemes and tropes. Schemes involve changes in word-sound and word-order, such as *alliteration* and *chiasmus*. Tropes play on our understandings of words to extend, alter, or transform meaning, as in *metaphor* and *personification*.

First-Person Narrative: narrative recounted using *I* and *me*. See also *narrative perspective*.

Fixed Forms: the term applied to a number of poetic forms and stanzaic patterns, many derived from French models, such as *ballade, rondeau, sestina, triolet,* and *villanelle*. Other "fixed forms" include the *sonnet, rhyme royal, haiku,* and *ottava rima*.

Folio: largest of several sizes of book page commonly used in the first few centuries after the introduction of the printing press. A folio size results from sheets of paper of at least 14 inches by 20 inches being folded in half (a folio page size will thus be at least 7 inches by 10 inches). When the same sheet is folded twice a quarto is produced, and when it is folded 3 times an octavo.

Foot: a unit of a line of verse which contains a particular combination of stressed and unstressed syllables. Dividing a line into metrical feet (*iambs, trochees,* etc.), then counting the number of feet per line, is part of *scansion*. See also *meter*.

Franklin: in the late medieval period, a landholder of free status, but ranking below the gentry.

Free Indirect Discourse: in prose fiction, commentary in which a seemingly objective and omniscient narrative voice assumes the point of view of one or more characters. When we hear through the third person narrative voice of Jane Austen's *Pride and Prejudice*, for example, that Mr. Darcy "was the proudest, most disagreeable man in the world, and every body hoped that he would never come there again," the narrative voice has assumed the point of view of "every body" in the community; we as readers are not meant to take it that Mr. Darcy is indeed the most disagreeable man in the world. Similarly, in the following passage from the same novel, we are likely to take it to read it as being the view of the character Charlotte that marriage is "the only honourable provision for well-educated young women of small fortune," not to take it to be an objective statement of perceived truth on the part of the novel's third person narrative voice:

> [Charlotte's] reflections were in general satisfactory. Mr. Collins to be sure was neither sensible nor agreeable; his society was irksome, and his attachment to her must be imaginary. But still he would be her husband. Without thinking highly either of men or of matrimony, marriage had always been her object; it was the only honourable provision for well-educated young women of small fortune, and however uncertain of giving happiness, must be their pleasantest preservative from want.

The term free indirect discourse may also be applied to situations in which it may not be entirely clear if the thoughts expressed emanate from the character, the narrator, or some combination of the two. (In the above-quoted passage expressing Charlotte's thoughts, indeed, some might argue that the statement concerning marriage should be taken as the expression of a belief that the narrative voice shares, at least in part.)

Free Verse: poetry that does not follow any regular meter, line length, or rhyming scheme. In many respects, though, free verse follows the complex natural "rules" and rhythmic patterns (or cadences) of speech.

Gaelic: Celtic language, variants of which are spoken in Ireland and Scotland.

Genre: a particular literary form. The concept of genre may be used with different levels of generality. At the most general, poetry, drama, and prose fiction are distinguished as separate genres. At a lower level of generality various sub-genres are frequently distinguished, such as (within drama) comedy and tragedy, or, at a still lower level of generality, Elizabethan domestic tragedy, Edwardian drawing-room comedy, and so on.

Georgic: (from Virgil's *Georgics*) a poem that celebrates the natural wealth of the countryside and advises how to cultivate and live in harmony with it. Pope's *Windsor Forest* and James Thomson's *Seasons* are classed as georgics. They were often said to make up, with eclogues, the two alliterative forms of pastoral poetry.

Ghazal: derived from Persian and Indian precedents, the ghazal presents a series of thoughts in closed couplets joined by a simple rhyme-scheme: *ab bb cb eb fb*, etc.

Gothic: in architecture and the visual arts, a term used to describe styles prevalent from the twelfth to the fourteenth centuries, but in literature a term used to describe work with a sinister or grotesque tone that seeks to evoke a sense of terror on the part of the reader or audience. Gothic literature originated as a genre in the eighteenth century with works such as Horace Walpole's *The Castle of Otranto*. To some extent the notion of the medieval itself then carried with it associations of the dark and the grotesque, but from the beginning an element of intentional exaggeration (sometimes verging on self-parody) attached itself to the genre. The Gothic trend of youth culture that began in the late twentieth century is less clearly associated with the medieval, but shares with the various varieties of Gothic literature (from Walpole in the eighteenth century, to Bram Stoker in the early twentieth, to Stephen King and Anne Rice in the late twentieth) a fondness for the sensational and the grotesque, as well as a propensity to self-parody.

Guilds: non-clerical associations that arose in the late Anglo-Saxon period, devoted both to social purposes (such as the organization of feasts for the members) and to piety. In the later medieval period guilds developed strong associations with particular occupations.

Haiku: a Japanese form, using three unrhymed lines of five, seven, and five syllables. Conventionally, it uses precise, concentrated images to suggest states of feeling.

Heptameter: a line containing seven metrical feet.

Heroic Couplet: a pair of rhymed iambic pentameters, so called because the form was much used in seventeenth and eighteenth-century poems and plays on heroic subjects.

Hexameter: a line containing six metrical feet.

Home Rule: movement dedicated to making Ireland politically independent from Britain.

Horatian Ode: inspired by the work of the Roman poet Horace, an ode that is usually calm and meditative in tone, and homostrophic (i.e., having regular stanzas) in form. Keats's odes are English examples.

House of Commons: elected legislative body, in Britain currently consisting of six hundred and fifty-nine members of Parliament. See also *Parliament*.

House of Lords: the "Upper House" of the British Houses of Parliament. Since the nineteenth century the House of Lords has been far less powerful than the elected House of Commons. The House of Lords is currently made up of both hereditary peers (Lords whose title is passed on from generation to generation) and life peers. As a result of legislation enacted by the Labour government of Tony Blair, the role of hereditary peers in Parliament is being phased out.

Humors: The four humors were believed in until the sixteenth and seventeenth centuries to be elements in the makeup of all humans; a person's temperament was thought to be determined by the way in which the humors were combined. When the *choleric* humor was dominant, the person would tend towards anger; when the *sanguine* humor was dominant, towards pleasant affability; when the *phlegmatic* humor was dominant, towards a cool and calm attitude and/or a lack of feeling or enthusiasm; and when the *melancholic* humor was dominant, towards withdrawal and melancholy.

Hymn: a song whose theme is usually religious, in praise of divinity. Literary hymns may praise more secular subjects.

Hyperbole: a *figure of speech* (a trope) that deliberately exaggerates or inflates meaning to achieve particular effects, such as the irony in A.E. Housman's claim (from "Terence, this is stupid stuff") that "malt does more than Milton can / To justify God's ways to man."

Iamb: the most common metrical foot in English verse, containing one unstressed syllable followed by a stressed syllable: x / (e.g., between, achieve).

Idyll: traditionally, a short pastoral poem that idealizes country life, conveying impressions of innocence and happiness.

Image: the recreation in words of objects perceived by the senses, sometimes thought of as "pictures," although other senses besides sight are involved. Besides this literal application, the term also refers more generally to the descriptive effects of figurative language, especially in *metaphor* and *simile*.

Imagism: a poetic movement that was popular mainly in the second decade of the twentieth century. The goal of Imagist poets (such as H.D. and Ezra Pound in their early work) was to represent emotions or impressions through highly concentrated imagery.

In Memoriam Stanza: a four-line stanza in iambic tetrameter, rhyming *abba*: the type of stanza used by Tennyson in *In Memoriam*.

Incantation: a chant or recitation of words that are believed to have magical power. A poem can achieve an "incantatory" effect through a compelling rhyme scheme and other repetitive patterns.

Interlocking Rhyme: See *rhyme*.

Internal Rhyme: See *rhyme*.

Irony: a subtle form of humor in which a statement is understood to convey a quite different (and often entirely opposite) meaning. A writer achieves this by carefully making sure that the statement occurs in a context which undermines or twists the statement's "literal" meaning. *Hyperbole* and *litotes* are often used for ironic effect. *Sarcasm* is a particularly strong or crude form of irony (usually spoken), in which the meaning is conveyed largely by the tone of voice adopted; something said sarcastically is meant clearly to imply its opposite.

Labour Party: See *Political Parties*.

Lament: a poem which expresses profound regret or grief either because of a death, or because of the loss of a former, happier state.

Language Poetry: a movement that defies the usual lyric and narrative conventions of poetry, and that challenges the structures and codes of everyday language. Often seen as both politically and aesthetically subversive, its roots lie in the works of modernist writers like Ezra Pound and Gertrude Stein.

Liberal Party: See *Political Parties*.

Litotes: a *figure of speech* (a trope) in which a writer deliberately uses understatement to highlight the importance of an argument, or to convey an ironic attitude.

Liturgical Drama: drama based on and/or incorporating text from the liturgy—the text recited during religious services.

Lollard: member of the group of radical Christians that took its inspiration from the ideas of John Wyclif (c. 1330–84). The Lollards, in many ways precursors of the Protestant Reformation, advocated making the Bible available to all, and dedication to the principles of evangelical poverty in imitation of Christ.

Luddites: protestors against the mechanization of industry on the grounds that it was leading to the loss of employment and to an increase in poverty. In the years 1811 to 1816 there were several Luddite protests in which machines were destroyed.

Lyric: a poem, usually short, expressing an individual speaker's feelings or private thoughts. Originally a song performed with accompaniment on a lyre, the lyric poem is often noted for musicality of rhyme and rhythm. The lyric genre includes a variety of forms, including the *sonnet*, the *ode*, the *elegy*, the *madrigal*, the *aubade*, the *dramatic monologue*, and the *hymn*.

Madrigal: a lyric poem, usually short and focusing on pastoral or romantic themes. A madrigal is often set to music.

Masculine Ending: a metrical line ending on a stressed syllable. *Masculine Rhyme*: see *rhyme*.

Masque: an entertainment typically combining music and dance, with a limited script, extravagant costumes and sets, and often incorporating spectacular special effects. Masques, which were performed before court audiences in the early seventeenth century, often focused on royal themes and frequently drew on classical mythology.

Mass: Within Christianity, a church service that includes the sacrament of the Eucharist (Holy Communion), in which bread and wine are consumed which are believed by those of many Christian denominations to have been transubstantiated into the body and blood of Christ. Anglicans (Episcopalians) are more likely to believe the bread and wine merely symbolizes the body and blood.

Melodrama: originally a term used to describe nineteenth-century-plays featuring sensational story lines and a crude separation of characters into moral categories, with the pure and virtuous pitted against evil villains. Early melodramas employed background music throughout the action of the play as a means of heightening the emotional response of the audience. By extension, certain sorts of prose fictions or poems are often described as having melodramatic elements.

Metaphor: a *figure of speech* (in this case, a trope) in which a comparison is made or identity is asserted between two unrelated things or actions without the use of "like" or "as." The primary subject is known as the *tenor*; to illuminate its nature, the writer links it to wholly different images, ideas, or actions referred to as the *vehicle*. Unlike a *simile*, which is a direct comparison of two things, a metaphor "fuses" the separate qualities of two things, creating a new idea. For example, Shakespeare's "Let slip the dogs of war" is a metaphorical statement. The tenor, or primary subject, is "war"; the vehicle of the metaphor is the image of hunting dogs released from their leash. The line fuses the idea of war with the qualities of ravening bloodlust associated with hunting dogs.

Metaphysical Poets: a group of seventeenth-century English poets, notably Donne, Cowley, Marvell, and Herbert, who employed unusual difficult imagery and *conceits* (see above) in order to develop intellectual and religious themes. The term was first applied to these writers to mark as far-fetched their use of philosophical and scientific ideas in a poetic context.

Meter: the pattern of stresses, syllables, and pauses that constitutes the regular rhythm of a line of verse. The meter of a poem written in the English accentual-syllabic tradition is determined by identifying the stressed and unstressed syllables in a line of verse, and grouping them into recurring units known as feet. See *accent, accentual-syllabic, caesura, elision,* and *scansion*. For some of the better known meters, see *iamb, trochee, dactyl, anapaest,* and *spondee*. See also *monometer, dimeter, trimeter, tetrameter, pentameter,* and *hexameter*.

Methodist: Protestant denomination formed in the eighteenth century as part of the religious movement led by John and Charles Wesley. Originally a movement within the Church of England, Methodism entailed enthusiastic evangelism, a strong emphasis on free will, and a strict regimen of Christian living.

Metonymy: a *figure of speech* (a trope), meaning "change of name," in which a writer refers to an object or idea by substituting the name of another object or idea closely associated with it: for example, the substitution of "crown" for monarchy, "the press" for journalism, or "the pen" for writing. *Synecdoche* (see below) is a kind of metonymy.

Mock-heroic: a style applying the elevated diction and vocabulary of epic poetry to low or ridiculous subjects. An example is Alexander Pope's "The Rape of the Lock."

Monologue: words spoken by a character to him or herself or to an audience directly.

Monometer: a line containing one metrical foot.

Mood: This can describe the writer's attitude, implied or expressed, towards the subject (see *tone* below); or it may refer to the atmosphere that a writer creates in a passage of description or narration.

Motif: an idea, image, action, or plot element that recurs throughout a literary work, creating new levels of meaning and strengthening structural coherence. The term is taken from music, where it describes recurring melodies or themes. See also *theme*.

Narrative Perspective: in fiction, the point of view from which the story is narrated. A first-person narrative is recounted using *I* and *me*, whereas a third person narrative is recounted using *he, she, they*, and so on. When a narrative is written in the third person and the narrative voice evidently "knows" all that is being done and thought, the story is typically described as being recounted by an "omniscient narrator."

Neoclassical: adapted from or substantially influenced by the cultures of ancient Greece and Rome. The term *neoclassical* is often used to describe the ideals of Restoration and eighteenth-century writers and artists who looked to ancient Greek and Roman civilization for models.

Nobility: privileged class, the members of which are distinguished by the holding of titles. Dukes, Marquesses, Earls, Viscounts, and Barons (in that order of precedence) are all holders of hereditary titles—that is to say, in the British patrilineal tradition, titles passed on from generation to generation to the eldest son. The title of Baronet, also hereditary, was added to this list by James I. Holders of non-hereditary titles include Knights and Dames.

Nonconformist: general term used to describe one who does subscribe to the Church of England.

Nonsense Verse: light, humorous poetry which contradicts logic, plays with the absurd, and invents words for amusing effects. Lewis Carroll is one of the best-known practitioners of nonsense verse.

Octave: also known as "octet," the first eight lines in an Italian/Petrarchan sonnet, rhyming *abbaabba*. See also *sestet* and *sonnet*.

Octosyllabic: a line of poetry with eight syllables, as in iambic tetrameter.

Ode: originally a classical poetic form, used by the Greeks and Romans to convey serious themes. English poetry has evolved three main forms of ode: the Pindaric (imitative of the odes of the Greek poet Pindar); the Horatian (modeled on the work of the Roman writer Horace); and the irregular ode.

The Pindaric ode was an irregular stanza in English, has a tripartite structure of "strophe," "antistrophe," and "epode" (meaning turn, counterturn, and stand), modeled on the songs and movements of the Chorus in Greek drama. The Horatian ode is more personal, reflective, and literary, and employs a pattern of repeated stanzas. The irregular ode, as its name implies, avoids a recurrent stanza pattern, and is sometimes irregular in line length also (see, for example, Wordsworth's "Ode: Intimations of Immortality").

Onomatopoeia: a *figure of speech* (a scheme) in which a word "imitates" a sound, or in which the sound of a word seems to reflect its meaning.

Ottava Rima: an 8-line stanza, usually in iambic pentameter, with the rhyme scheme *ababababcc*. For an example, see Byron's *Don Juan*, or Yeats's "Sailing to Byzantium."

Oxymoron: a *figure of speech* (a trope) in which two words whose meanings seem contradictory are placed together, a paradox: for example, the phrase "darkness visible," from Milton's *Paradise Lost*.

Paean: a triumphant, celebratory song, often associated with a military victory.

Pale: in the medieval period, term for a protective zone around a fortress. As of the year 1500 three of these had been set up to guard frontiers of territory controlled by England—surrounding Calais in France, Berwick-upon-Tweed on the Scottish frontier, and Dublin in Ireland. The Dublin Pale was the largest of the three, and the term remained in use for a longer period there.

Pantoum: a poem in linked quatrains that rhyme *abab*. The second and fourth lines of one stanza are repeated as the first and third lines of the stanza that follows. In the final stanza the pattern is reversed: the second line repeats the third line of the first stanza, the fourth and final line repeats the first line of the first stanza.

Parliament: in Britain, the legislative body, comprising both the House of Commons and the House of Lords. Since the eighteenth century, the most powerful figure in the British government has been the Prime Minister rather than the monarch, the House of Commons has been the dominant body in Parliament, and members of the House of Commons have been organized in political parties. Since the mid-nineteenth century the effective executive in the British Parliamentary system has been the Cabinet, each member of which is typically in charge of a department of government. Unlike the American system, the British Parliamentary system (sometimes called the "Westminster system," after the location of the Houses of Parliament) brings together the executive and legislative functions of government, with the Prime Minister leading the government party in the House of Commons as well as directing the cabinet. By convention it is understood that the House of Lords will not contravene the wishes of the House of Commons in any fundamental way, though the "Upper House," as it is often referred to, may sometimes modify or reject legislation.

Parody: a close, usually mocking imitation of a particular literary work, or of the well-known style of a particular author, in order to expose or magnify weaknesses. Parody is a form of satire—that is, humor that may ridicule and scorn its object.

Pastiche: a discourse which borrows or imitates other writers' characters, forms, style, or ideas. Unlike a parody, a pastiche is usually intended as a compliment to the original writer.

Pastoral: in general, pertaining to country life; in prose, drama, and poetry, a stylized type of writing that idealizes the lives and innocence of country people, particularly shepherds and shepherdesses. Also see *eclogue, georgic, idyll*, above.

Pastoral Elegy: a poem in which the poet uses the pastoral style to lament the death of a friend, usually represented as a shepherd. Milton's "Lycidas" provides a good example of the form, including its use of such conventions as an invocation of the muse and a procession of mourners.

Pathetic Fallacy: a form of personification in which inanimate objects are given human emotions: for example, rain clouds "weeping." The word "fallacy" in this connection is intended to suggest the distortion of reality or the false emotion that may result from an exaggerated use of personification.

Pathos: the emotional quality of a discourse; or the ability of a discourse to appeal to our emotions. It is usually applied to the mood conveyed by images of pain, suffering, or loss that arouse feelings of pity or sorrow in the reader.

Pattern Poetry: a predecessor of modern concrete poetry, in which the shape of the poem on the page is intended to suggest or imitate an aspect of the poem's subject. George Herbert's "Easter Wings" is an example of pattern poetry.

Penny Dreadful: Victorian term for a cheap and poorly produced work of short fiction, usually of a sensational nature.

Pentameter: a line of verse containing five metrical feet.

Performance Poetry: poetry composed primarily for oral performance, often very theatrical in nature. See also *dub poetry* and *rap*.

Persona: the assumed identity or "speaking voice" that a writer projects in a discourse. The term "persona" literally means "mask." Even when a writer speaks in the first person, we should be aware that the attitudes or opinions we hear may not necessarily be those of the writer in real life.

Personification: a *figure of speech* (a trope), also known as "prosopopoeia," in which a writer refers to inanimate objects, ideas, or animals as if they were human, or creates a human figure to represent an abstract entity such as Philosophy or Peace.

Petrarchan Sonnet: the earliest form of the sonnet, also known as the Italian sonnet, with an 8-line octave and a 6-line sestet. The Petrarchan sonnet traditionally focuses on love and descriptions of physical beauty.

Phoneme: a linguistic term denoting the smallest unit of sound that it is possible to distinguish. The words *fun* and *phone* each have three phonemes, though one has three letters and one has five. (Each makes up a single syllable.)

Pindaric: See *ode*.

Plot: the organization of story materials within a literary work. The order in which story material is presented (especially causes and consequences); the inclusion of elements that allow or encourage the reader or audience to form expectations as to what is likely to happen; the decision to present some story material through exposition rather than in more extended form as part of the main action of the narrative—all these are matters of plotting.

Political Parties: The party names "Whig" and "Tory" began to be used in the late seventeenth century; before that time members of the House of Commons acted individually or through shifting and very informal factions. At first the Whigs and Tories had little formal organization either, but by the mid-eighteenth century parties had acknowledged leaders, and the leader of the party with the largest number of members in the House of Commons had begun to be recognized as the Prime Minister. The Tories evolved into the modern Conservative Party, and the Whigs into the Liberal Party. In the late nineteenth century the Labour Party was formed in an effort to provide better representation in Parliament for the working class, and since the 1920s Labour and the Conservatives have alternated as the party of government, with the Liberals reduced to third-party status. (Since 1988, when the Liberals merged with a breakaway faction from Labour known as the Social Democrats, this third party has been named the Liberal Democrats.)

Pre-Raphaelites: originally a group of Victorian artists and writers, formed in 1848. Their goal was to revive what they considered the simpler, fresher, more natural art that existed before Raphael (1483-1520). The poet Dante Gabriel Rossetti was one of the founders of the group.

Presbyterian: term applied to a group of Protestants (primarily English and Scottish) who advocated replacing the traditional hierarchical church in which bishops and archbishops governed lower level members of the clergy with a system in which all presbyters (or ministers) would be equal. The Presbyterians, originally led by John Knox, were strongly influenced by the ideas of John Calvin.

Prose Poem: a poetic discourse that uses prose formats (e.g., it may use margins and paragraphs rather than line breaks or stanzas) yet is written with the kind of attention to language, rhythm and cadence that characterizes verse.

Prosody: the study and analysis of meter, rhythm, rhyme, stanzaic pattern, and other devices of versification.

Protagonist: the central character in a literary work.

Prothalamion: a wedding song; a term coined by the poet Edmund Spenser, adapted from "epithalamion" (see above).

Public School: See *schools* below.

Pun: a play on words, in which a word with two or more distinct meanings, or two words with similar sounds, may create humorous ambiguities. Also known as *paranomasia*.

Puritan: term, originally applied only in a derogatory fashion but later widely accepted as descriptive, referring to those in England who favored religious reforms that went beyond those instituted as part of the Protestant Reformation, or, more generally, who were more forceful and uncompromising in pressing for religious purity both within the Church and in society as a whole.

Pyrrhic: a metrical foot containing two weak stresses: xx.

Quadrivium: group of four academic subjects (arithmetic, astronomy, geometry, and music) that made up part of the university coursework in the Middle Ages. There were studied after the more basic subjects of the *Trivium*.

Quantitative Meter: a metrical system used by Greek and Roman poets, in which a line of verse was measured by the "quantity," or length of sound of each syllable. A foot was measured in terms of syllables classed as long or short.

Quantity: duration of syllables in poetry. The line "There is a Garden in her face" (the first line from the poem of the same name by Thomas Campion) is characterized by the short quantities of the syllables. The last line of Thomas Hardy's "During Wind and Rain" has the same number of syllables as the line by Campion, but the quantities of the syllables are much longer—in other words, the line take much longer to say: "Down their carved names the rain drop ploughs."

Quatrain: a four-line stanza, usually rhymed.

Quintet: a five-line stanza. Sometimes given as *quintain*.

Rap: originally coined to describe informal conversation, "rap" now usually describes a style of performance poetry in which a poet will chant rhymed verse, sometimes improvised and usually with musical accompaniment that has a heavy beat.

Realism: as a literary term, the presentation through literature of material closely resembling real life. As notions both of what constitutes "real life" and of how it may be most faithfully represented in literature have varied widely, "realism" has taken a variety of meanings. The term *naturalistic* has sometimes been used a synonym for *realistic*; *naturalism* originated in the nineteenth century as a term denoting a form of realism focusing in particular on grim, unpleasant, or ugly aspects of the real.

Refrain: one or more words or lines repeated at regular points throughout a poem, often at the end of each stanza or group of stanzas. Sometimes a whole stanza may be repeated to create a refrain, like the chorus in a song.

Reggae: a style of heavily-rhythmic music from the West Indies with lyrics that are colloquial in language and often anti-establishment in content and flavor. First popularized in the 1960s and 1970s, reggae has had a lasting influence on performance poetry, rap, and dub.

Rhetoric: in classical Greece and Rome, the art of persuasion and public speaking. From the Middle Ages onwards, the study of rhetoric gave greater attention to style, particularly figures of speech. Today in poetics, the term rhetoric may encompass not only figures of speech, but also the persuasive effects of forms, sounds and word choices.

Rhyme: the repetition of identical or similar sounds, usually in pairs and generally at the ends of metrical lines.

    End-rhyme: a rhyming word or syllable at the end of a line.

    Eye Rhyme: rhyming that pairs words whose spellings are alike but whose pronunciations are different: for example, though/slough.

Feminine Rhyme: a two-syllable (also known as "double") rhyme. The first syllable is stressed and the second unstressed: for example, hasty/tasty. See also *triple rhyme* below.

Interlocking Rhyme: the repetition of rhymes from one stanza to the next, creating links that add to the poem's continuity and coherence. Examples may be found in Shelley's use of *terza rima* in "Ode to the West Wind" and in Dylan Thomas's villanelle "Do Not Go Gentle Into That Good Night."

Internal Rhyme: the placement of rhyming words within lines so that at least two words in a line rhyme with each other.

Masculine Rhyme: a correspondence of sound between the final stressed syllables at the end of two or more lines, as in grieve/leave, arr-ive/sur-vive.

Slant Rhyme: an imperfect or partial rhyme (also known as "near" or "half" rhyme) in which the final consonants of stressed syllables match but the vowel sounds do not. E.g., spoiled / spilled, taint / stint.

Triple Rhyme: a three-syllable rhyme in which the first syllable of each rhyme-word is stressed and the other two unstressed (e.g., lottery / coterie).

True Rhyme: a rhyme in which everything but the initial consonant matches perfectly in sound and spelling.

Rhyme Royal: a stanza of seven iambic pentameters, with a rhyme-scheme of *ababbcc*. This is also known as the Chaucerian stanza, as Chaucer was the first English poet to use this form. See also *septet*.

Rhythm: in speech, the arrangement of stressed and unstressed syllables creates units of sound. In song or verse, these units usually form a regular rhythmic pattern, a kind of beat, described in prosody as *meter*.

Romanticism: a major social and cultural movement, originating in Europe, that shaped much of Western artistic thought in the late eighteenth and nineteenth centuries. Opposing the ideal of controlled, rational order of the Enlightenment, Romanticism emphasizes the importance of spontaneous self-expression, emotion, and personal experience in producing art. In Romanticism, the "natural" is privileged over the conventional or the artificial.

Rondeau: a fifteen-line poem, generally octosyllabic, with only two rhymes throughout its three stanzas, and an unrhymed refrain at the end of the ninth and fifteenth lines, repeating part of the opening line.

Sarcasm: See *irony*.

Satire: literary work designed to make fun of or seriously criticize its subject. According to many literary theories of the Renaissance and neoclassical periods, the ridicule through satire of a certain sort of behavior may function for the reader or audience as a corrective of such behavior.

Scansion: the formal analysis of patterns of rhythm and rhyme in poetry. Each line of verse will have a certain number of fairly regular "beats" consisting of alternating stressed and unstressed syllables. To "scan" a poem is to count the beats in each line, to mark stressed and unstressed syllables and indicate their combination into "feet," to note pauses, and to identify rhyme schemes with letters of the alphabet.

Scheme: See *figures of speech*.

Schools: In the sixteenth and seventeenth centuries the different forms of school in England included Cathedral schools (often founded with a view to the education of members of the choir); grammar schools (often founded by towns or by guilds, and teaching a much broader curriculum than the modern sense of "grammar" might suggest, private schools, operated by private individuals out of private residences; and public schools, which (like the private schools and the grammar schools) operated independent of any church authority, but unlike the grammar schools and private schools were organized as independent charities, and often offered free education. Over the centuries certain of these public schools, while remaining not-for-profit institutions, began to accept fee-paying students and to adopt standards that made them more and more exclusive. In the eighteenth and nineteenth century attendance at such prestigious public boarding schools as Eton, Westminster, and Winchester had become almost exclusively the preserve of the upper classes; by the nineteenth century such "public" schools were the equivalent of private schools in North America. Though a few girls attended some early grammar schools, the greater part of this educational system was for boys only. Though a number of individuals of earlier periods were concerned to increase the number of private schools for girls, the movement to create a parallel girls' system of public schools and grammar schools dates from the later nineteenth century.

Septet: a stanza containing seven lines.

Serf: in the medieval period, a person of unfree status, typically engaged in working the land.

Sestet: a six-line stanza that forms the second grouping of lines in an Italian / Petrarchan sonnet, following the octave. See *sonnet* and *sestina*.

Sestina: an elaborate unrhymed poem with six 6-line stanzas and a 3-line envoy.

Shire: originally a multiple estate; since the late medieval period a larger territory forming an administrative unit—also referred to as a county.

Simile: a *figure of speech* (a trope) which makes an explicit comparison between a particular object and another object or idea that is similar in some (often unexpected) way. A simile always uses "like" or "as" to signal the connection. Compare with *metaphor* above.

Sonnet: a highly structured lyric poem, which normally has fourteen lines of iambic pentameter. We can distinguish four major variations of the sonnet.

> **Italian/Petrarchan:** named for the 14th-century Italian poet Petrarch, has an octave rhyming *abbaabba*, and a sestet rhyming *cdecde*, or *cdcdcd* (other arrangements are possible here). Usually, a turn in argument takes place between octave and sestet.

Miltonic: developed by Milton and similar to the Petrarchan in rhyme scheme, but eliminating the turn after the octave, thus giving greater unity to the poem's structure of thought.

Shakespearean: often called the English sonnet, this form has three quatrains and a couplet. The quatrains rhyme internally but do not interlock: *abab cdcd efef gg*. The turn may occur after the second quatrain, but is usually revealed in the final couplet. Shakespeare's sonnets are the best-known examples of this form.

Spenserian: after Edmund Spenser, who developed the form in his sonnet cycle *Amoretti*. This sonnet form has three quatrains linked through interlocking rhyme, and a separately rhyming couplet: *abab bcbc cdcd ee*.

Speaker: in the late medieval period, a member of the Commons in Parliament who spoke on behalf of that entire group. (The Commons first elected a Speaker in 1376.) In later eras the role of Speaker became one of chairing debates in the House of Commons and arbitrating disputes over matters of procedure.

Spenserian Stanza: a nine-line stanza, with eight iambic pentameters and a concluding alexandrine, rhyming *ababbcbcc*.

Spondee: a metrical foot containing two strong stressed syllables: // (e.g., blind mouths).

Sprung Rhythm: a modern variation of accentual verse, created by the English poet Gerard Manley Hopkins, in which rhythms are determined largely by the number of strong stresses in a line, without regard to the number of unstressed syllables. Hopkins felt that sprung rhythm more closely approximated the natural rhythms of speech than did conventional poetry.

Stanza: any lines of verse that are grouped together in a poem and separated from other similarly-structured groups by a space. In metrical poetry, stanzas share metrical and rhyming patterns; however, stanzas may also be formed on the basis of thought, as in irregular odes. Conventional stanza forms include the *tercet*, the *quatrain*, *rhyme royal*, the *Spenserian stanza*, the *ballad stanza*, and *ottava rima*.

Stream of Consciousness: narrative technique that attempts to convey in prose fiction a sense of the progression of the full range of thoughts and sensations occurring within a character's mind. Twentieth-century pioneers in the use of the stream of consciousness technique include Dorothy Richardson, Virginia Woolf, and James Joyce.

Stress: See *accent*.

Strophe: the first stanza in a Pindaric ode. This is followed by an *antistrophe* (see above), which presents the same metrical pattern and rhyme scheme, and finally by an *epode*, differing in meter from the preceding stanzas. Upon completion of this "triad," the entire sequence can recur. *Strophe* may also describe a stanza or other subdivision in other kinds of poem.

Sublime: a concept, most popular in eighteenth-century England, of the qualities of grandeur, power, and awe that may be inherent in or produced by undomesticated nature or great art. The sublime was thought of as higher and loftier than something that is merely beautiful.

Subplot: a line of story that is subordinate to the main storyline of a narrative. (Note that properly speaking a subplot is a category of story material, not of plot.)

Substitution: a deliberate change from the dominant pattern of stresses in a line of verse to create emphasis or variation. Thus the first line of Shakespeare's sonnet "'Shall I compare thee to a summer's day?' is decidedly iambic in meter (x / x / x / x / x /), whereas the second line substitutes a trochee (/ x) in the opening foot: "Thou art more lovely and more temperate."

Subtext: implied or suggested meaning of a passage of text, or of an entire work.

Syllabic Verse: poetry in which the length of a line is measured solely by the number of syllables, regardless of accents or patterns of stress.

Syllable: vocal sound or group of sounds forming a unit of speech; a syllable may be formed with a single effort of articulation. Some syllables consist of a single phoneme (e.g., the word *I*, or the first syllable in the word *u*-ni-ty) but others may be made up of several phonemes (as with one-syllable words such as *lengths*, *splurged*, and *through*). By contrast, the much shorter words *ago*, *any*, and *open* each have two syllables.

Symbol: a word, image, or idea that represents something more, or other, than for what it at first appears to stand. Like metaphor, the symbol extends meaning; but while the tenor and vehicle of metaphor are bound in a specific relationship, a symbol may have a range of connotations. For example, the image of a rose may call forth associations of love, passion, transience, fragility, youth and beauty, among others. Depending upon the context, such an image could be interpreted in a variety of ways, as in Blake's lyric, "The Sick Rose." Though this power of symbolic representation characterizes all language, poetry most particularly endows the concrete imagery evoked through language with a larger meaning. Such meaning is implied rather than explicitly stated; indeed, much of the power of symbolic language lies in the reader's ability to make meaningful sense of it.

Syncope: in poetry, the dropping of a letter or syllable from the middle of a word, as in "trav'ler." Such a contraction allows a line to stay within a metrical scheme. See also *catalexis* and *elision*.

Synecdoche: a kind of *metonymy* in which a writer substitutes the name of a part of something to signify the whole: for example, "sail" for ship or "hand" for a member of the ship's crew.

Tercet: a group, or stanza, of three lines, often linked by an interlocking rhyme scheme as in *terza rima*. See also *triplet*.

Terza Rima: an arrangement of tercets interlocked by a rhyme scheme of *aba bcb cdc ded*, etc., and ending with a couplet that rhymes with the second-last line of the final tercet (for example, *efe, ff*). See, for example, Percy Shelley's "Ode to the West Wind."

Tetrameter: a line of poetry containing four metrical feet.

Theme: the governing idea of a discourse, conveyed through the development of the subject, and through the recurrence of certain words, sounds, or metrical patterns. See also *motif*.

Third-Person Narrative: See *narrative perspective*.

Tone: the writer's attitude toward a given subject or audience, as expressed though an authorial persona or "voice." Tone can be projected through particular choices of wording, imagery, figures of speech, and rhythmic devices. Compare *mood*.

Tories: See *Political Parties*.

Tragedy: in the traditional definition originating in discussions of ancient Greek drama, a serious narrative recounting the downfall of the protagonist. More loosely, the term has been applied to a wide variety of literary forms in which the tone is predominantly a dark one and the narrative does not end happily.

Transcendentalism: a philosophical movement that influenced such Victorian writers as Thomas Carlyle and Robert Browning. Also a mode of Romantic thought, Transcendentalism places the supernatural and the natural within one great Unity and believes that each individual person embodies aspects of the divine.

Trimeter: a line of poetry containing three metrical feet.

Triolet: a French form in which the first line appears three times in a poem of only eight lines. The first line is repeated at lines 4 and 7; the second line is repeated in line 8. The triolet has only two rhymes: *abaaabab*.

Triple Foot: poetic foot of three syllables. The possible varieties of triple foot are the anapest (in which two unstressed syllables are followed by a stressed syllable), the dactyl (in which a stressed syllable is followed by two unstressed lines), and the mollossus (in which all three syllables are stressed equally). English poetry tends to use duple rhythms far more frequently than triple rhythms.

Triplet: a group of three lines with the same end-rhyme, much used by eighteenth-century poets to vary or punctuate the flow of couplets. See also *tercet*.

Trivium: group of three academic subjects (dialectic, grammar, and rhetoric) that were part of the university curriculum in the Middle Ages. Their study precedes that of the more advanced subjects of the *quadrivium*.

Trochee: a metrical foot containing one strong stress followed by one weak stress: / x (heaven, lover).

Trope: any figure of speech that plays on our understandings of words to extend, alter, or transform "literal" meaning. Common tropes include *metaphor*, *simile*, *personification*, *hyperbole*, *metonymy*, *oxymoron*, *synecdoche*, and *irony*. See also *figures of speech*, above.

Turn (Italian "volta"): the point in a *sonnet* where the mood or argument changes. The turn may occur between the octave and sestet, i.e., after the eighth line, or in the final couplet, depending on the kind of sonnet.

Unities: Many literary theorists of the late sixteenth through late eighteenth centuries held that a play should ideally be presented as representing a single place, and confining the action to a single day and a single dominant event. They disapproved of plots involving gaps or long periods of time, shifts in place, or subplots. These concepts, which came to be referred to as the unities of space, time, and action, were based on a misreading of classical authorities (principally of Aristotle).

Vers de societé: French: literally, "verse about society." The term originated with poetry written by aristocrats and upper-middle-class poets that specifically disavows the ambition of creating "high art" while treating the concerns of their own group in verse forms that demonstrate a high degree of formal control (e.g., artful rhymes, surprising turns of diction).

Vers libre (French):   See *free verse* above.

Verse: a general term for works of poetry, usually referring to poems that incorporate some kind of metrical structure. The term may also describe a line of poetry, though more frequently it is applied to a stanza.

Villanelle: a poem usually consisting of 19 lines, with five 3-line stanzas (tercets) rhyming *aba*, and a concluding quatrain rhyming *abaa*. The first and third lines of the first tercet are repeated at fixed intervals throughout the rest of the poem. See, for example, Dylan Thomas's "Do Not Go Gentle Into That Good Night."

Whigs: See *Political Parties*.

Workhouse: public institution in which the poor were provided with a minimal level of sustenance and with lodging in exchange for work performed. Early workhouses were typically administered by individual parishes. In 1834 a unified system covering all of England and Wales was put into effect.

Zeugma: a *figure of speech* (trope) in which one word links or "yokes" two others in the same sentence, often to comic or ironic effect. For example, a verb may govern two objects, as in Pope's line "Or stain her honour, or her new brocade."

Permissions Acknowledgments

Exeter Book Riddles: from THE OLD ENGLISH RIDDLES OF THE 'EXETER BOOK' edited by Craig Williamson. Copyright © 1977 by the University of North Carolina Press. Used by permission of the publisher.

Monmouth, Geoffrey. From THE HISTORY OF THE KINGS OF BRITAIN, translated and edited by Michael A. Faletra. (Broadview Press, 2008). Reproduced with permission of the translator and editor.

The Service for Representing Adam: from MEDIEVAL DRAMA, edited by David Bevington. (Boston: Houghton Mifflin Company, 1975). Reproduced with permission of the publisher.

Sir Orfeo: from THE MIDDLE ENGLISH BRETON LAYS, edited by Anne Laskaya and Eve Salisbury (Kalamazoo, MI: TEAMS, Medieval Institute Publications, 1995). Reproduced with permission of the publisher.

Gower, John. From CONFESSIO AMANTIS, edited by Russell A. Peck, with Latin translations by Andrew Galloway. (Kalamazoo, MI: TEAMS, Medieval Institute Publications, 2004). Reproduced with permission of the publisher.

Illustration Credits

Cover: Reproduced by permission of The Trinity College Library, Dublin. Page 245: Reproduced by permission of the Trustees of the National Library of Scotland. Page 364: Reproduced by permission of the British Library. Page 366: Reproduced by permission of the British Library. Page 380: Reproduced by permission of the Huntington Library. Page 398: Reproduced by permission of the Huntington Library. Page 415/16: Reproduced by permission of the Huntington Library. Page 449: Reproduced by permission of the Huntington Library. Page 462: Reproduced by permission of the Huntington Library. Page 483: Reproduced by permission of the Huntington Library. Page 502: Reproduced by permission of the Huntington Library. Page 518/19: Reproduced by permission of the Huntington Library. Page 531/32: Reproduced by permission of the Huntington Library. Page 538/39: Reproduced by permission of the Huntington Library. Page 557: Reproduced by permission of the Huntington LibraryPage 713: Reproduced by permission of the Huntington Library.

Information on all translations used is provided in footnotes at the beginning of selections. Copyright permission to reproduce material translated or edited for this anthology and material reproduced or adapted here that originally appeared in other books published by Broadview Press may be sought from Broadview.

The publisher has endeavored to contact rights holders of all copyright material and would appreciate receiving any information as to errors or omissions.

Index of First Lines

Index of Authors and Titles

Plate 1. MARTHA ALF (b. 1930; American). *Two Pears No. 3. (for Michael Blankfort).* c. 1982. Pastel pencil on paper, 12 × 18" (31 × 46 cm).
The Museum of Contemporary Art, Los Angeles, CA.

Plate 2. JEANETTE PASIN SLOAN (b. 1946; American). *Silver Bowl Still Life.* c. 1978. Acrylic and colored pencil on board, 28 1/2 × 38 1/2" (72 × 98 cm).
Security Pacific National Bank, California.

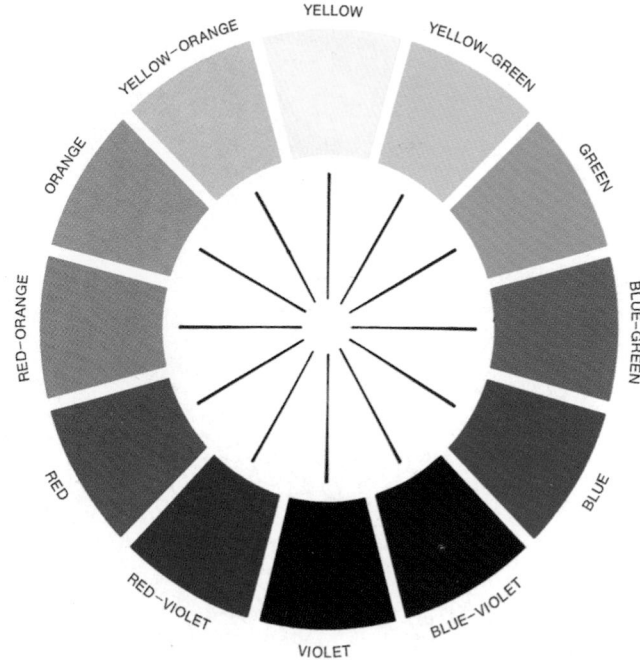

Plate 3. Color wheel with primary, secondary, and tertiary colors. The Birren Color Chart. By Alexander.

Plate 4. EDMOND-FRANÇOIS AMAN-JEAN (1860–1935; French). *Les Confidences.* c. 1898. Pastel on blue paper affixed to canvas, 4′ × 3′2″ (1.22 × .97 m).
Achenbach Foundation for Graphic Arts, Mildred Anna Williams Fund, The Fine Arts Museums of San Francisco.

Plate 5. WILLEM DE KOONING (1904–1997). *Two Women's Torsos.* c. 1952. Pastel, 18 7/8 × 24″ (48 × 61 cm).
© The Art Institute of Chicago.

Plate 7. ALANSON APPLETON (1922–1985; American). *David Roinski.* c. 1976. Pen and ink with pastel, 10 × 8 1/2″ (25 × 22 cm). Collection of Mrs. Alanson Appleton, San Mateo, California.

Plate 6. WILLIAM BERRY (b. 1933; American). *Self Portrait with Lamp.* c. 1988. Graphite and colored pencil on colored paper, 16 1/2 × 12 1/2″ (42 × 32 cm). Courtesy of the artist.

Plate 8. WAYNE THIEBAUD (b. 1920; American). *Pastel Scatter.* c. 1972. Pastel on paper, 26 × 20 1/8″ (66 × 51.1 cm). Private collection.

Plate 9. EMMI WHITEHORSE (b. 1957; Native American; Navajo). *The Conversion*. 1992. Pastel, oil, paper on canvas, 51 × 78" (129.7 × 198.3 cm).
Courtesy of LewAllen Gallery, Santa Fe, New Mexico.

Plate 10. DUANE WAKEHAM (b. 1931; American). *Russian River, Spring Afternoon*. Pastel on paper, 19 × 29" (48.3 × 73.7 cm). Collection of Lila Gold, New York City.

Sixth Edition

A Guide to Drawing

Daniel M. Mendelowitz
Late of Stanford University

Duane A. Wakeham
Professor Emeritus, College of San Mateo

David L. Faber
Wake Forest University

THOMSON

WADSWORTH

Australia • Canada • Mexico • Singapore • Spain • United Kingdom • United States

To my father, a gentle-hearted guardian of the land,
who taught me how to draw a black line across a textured
field with a plow—and in memory of my mother, a
musician of sacred song, who taught me the difference
between the solo and the accompaniment in life.

THOMSON
™
WADSWORTH

Art and Humanities Editor: John R. Swanson
Senior Development Editor: Stacey Sims
Assistant Editor: Amy McGaughey
Editorial Assistant: Rebecca Fay Green
Technology Project Manager: Melinda Newfarmer
Marketing Manager: Mark D. Orr
Advertising Project Manager: Vicky Chao
Project Manager, Editorial Production: Kathryn M. Stewart
Print Buyer: Tandra Jorgensen
Production Service: Greg Hubit Bookworks

Text Designers: Serena Manning; John Edeen
Photo Researcher: Shirley Webster
Copy Editor: Jamie Fuller
Cover Designer: Brittney Singletary
Cover Image: Leonardo da Vinci, *The Virgin and
    Child with Saint Anne and Saint John the Baptist*
    (detail), 4'-6 3/4" × 3' × 3'-3 3/4", National Gallery.
Cover Printer: Transcontinental Printing
Compositor: Thompson Type
Printer: Transcontinental Printing

Printed in Canada
1 2 3 4 5 6 7 06 05 04 03 02

Wadsworth/Thomson Learning
10 Davis Drive
Belmont, CA 94002-3098
USA

Asia
Thomson Learning
5 Shenton Way #01-01
UIC Building
Singapore 068808

Australia
Nelson Thomson Learning
102 Dodds Street
South Melbourne, Victoria 3205
Australia

Canada
Nelson Thomson Learning
1120 Birchmount Road
Toronto, Ontario M1K 5G4
Canada

Europe/Middle East/Africa
Thomson Learning
High Holborn House
50/51 Bedford Row
London WC1R 4LR
United Kingdom

Latin America
Thomson Learning
Seneca, 53
Colonia Polanco
11560 Mexico D.F.
Mexico

Spain
Paraninfo Thomson Learning
Calle/Magallanes, 25
28015 Madrid, Spain

For more information about our products,
contact us at:
Thomson Learning Academic Resource Center
1-800-423-0563
For permission to use material from this text,
contact us by:
Phone: 1-800-730-2214
Fax: 1-800-730-2215
Web: http://www.thomsonrights.com

Library of Congress Control Number 2002110045
ISBN 0-15-506210-7

Contents

103858

PART 5
SYNTHESIS IN DRAWING

Preface

In the mid-1960s the late Professor Daniel Mendelowitz of Stanford University perceived that although "drawing as it had been practiced in the past seemed about to disappear" and had "almost ceased to exist as a significant part of the curricula of art schools and of college and university art departments" during the previous two decades, "certain of the traditional disciplines were again emerging as functional and necessary elements in the training of artists." His reaction was to write *Drawing*, which combined a survey of the history of drawing, an analysis of the elements of art, and an explanation of the principal media used in drawing. In an accompanying *Study Guide*, Professor Mendelowitz presented a series of projects intended to provide a range of basic drawing experiences appropriate for either classroom or independent study. Nine years later the most important elements from the two previous volumes were combined in *A Guide to Drawing*, which in its various revisions has remained one of the most respected and widely used books in its field. Now, thirty-five years after *Drawing* was originally published, *A Guide to Drawing* appears in a newly revised sixth edition.

It should be well noted that Professor Wakeham has masterfully steered the development of the text through three revisions and at each juncture has advanced the text significantly by responding to expressed pedagogical needs and expanding the applications as necessary in the last two decades. His contributions have been timely, well orchestrated, and significant in a major way to the continued success and life of the book. As artist and teacher, Wakeham's voice speaks formidably alongside that of Daniel Mendelowitz, introducing new issues to complement the former states of the book. It has been my intent to remain faithful to both Professors Mendelowitz and Wakeham's original concept for the book: providing a comprehensive and systematic introduction to the art of drawing by focusing on the understanding of form and the mastery of traditional skills as the basis for descriptive and expressive drawing.

Because it is meant to be comprehensive, *A Guide to Drawing* includes much more material than can be covered in any one course, and it is unlikely that anyone—student or instructor—will choose to adhere strictly to the sequence as presented. Instead, all are encouraged to dip in and help themselves to that which interests them or seems appropriate to their needs.

The book, designed for use in beginning, intermediate, and advanced classes, as well as for specialized advanced courses such as life drawing, offers an introduction to the breadth and range of subjects, media, and techniques that provide a framework for developing individual ideas and approaches, with *seeing skills* and modes of *expression* as the primary artistic goals. Each topic is accompanied by a rich selection of master drawings as well as a progression of studio project assignments designed to allow beginning students, working alone or under the direction of a teacher, to master basic skills, and to encourage more advanced students to use those skills creatively and expressively. The assignments have been made as flexible as possible so that they will serve the needs of many studio situations and creative intentions.

While not intended to provide a history of drawing, as the original volume did, the inclusion of such references and the selection of drawings for the book reflect the collectively shared desires of Professors Mendelowitz, Wakeham, and myself to arouse in students both curiosity and awareness about the long tradition of drawing. Time limitations generally discourage drawing instructors from attempting to include a full survey of the history of drawing in studio curricula, and the subject generally receives only minimal attention in art history survey courses. While many metropolitan and university museums boast of large collections of drawings, very few of those works are ever on exhibit at any one time, making it difficult for even the most avid student to see and study original drawings from the past. Looking at reproductions is not the same as viewing original works of art; however, for most of us, books and catalogues are our most convenient resource for beginning to appreciate the great range and wealth of drawings that have been preserved.

Perhaps the only great drawing that remains on constant view to the public is Leonardo da Vinci's *Madonna and Child with Saint Anne* (Fig. 17-5) at the National Gallery in London, where it is housed in its own room with light and temperature carefully monitored. For that reason, it seemed an appropriate choice to illustrate the cover of this new edition. It is a remarkably large drawing for its time. The cover focuses on the figure grouping of the Holy Family with its splendid array of lines, textures, colors, and tonal vestiges describing the figurative forms in space. As I see it, in the affirming and provocatively upward-pointing hand of Saint Anne, Leonardo beckons us to engage our creative wills and acts of faith in learning how to draw—and to draw with greater skill than ever before.

This new edition includes 102 new drawings in black and white and seven new color plates. It reproduces three images in both black-and-white and as color plates to illustrate the reduction of color to black-and-white tonal contrasts. Approximately 60 percent of the 408 drawings reproduced are twentieth-century examples and so can only hint at the richness and the diversity that exists historically in the field of drawing. As in previous editions, the harvesting of new drawings and the reorganization of many works carried over from the previous edition have resulted in substantial rewriting in almost every chapter. Whenever possible, I have selected appropriate new drawings related in subject but different in technique or expression to accompany the discussion of the topic so that students begin to develop an awareness of some of the various approaches to drawing that are available to them and which have been proven by the old masters and contemporary artists as well.

Two large groups of the new drawings selected came from two major collections: The Jalane and Richard Davidson Collection of Contemporary American Realist Drawings at the Chicago Art Institute and the very well-known major collection of drawings at the National Gallery of Art in Washington, D.C. From the Davidson Collection alone twenty-two new drawings were selected spanning three decades—the oldest, a drawing by Philip Pearstein dating from 1974. What I find most attractive about the drawings in this relatively young collection is their adherence to the timeless and traditional methods of media application and technical handling, bearing significant evidence of the great number of contemporary artists involved in creating drawings using the same proven materials that have been in use for centuries.

I have also included many old-master drawings selected from much older collections such as the British, Albertina, and Ashmolean museums, the Rijksmuseum, and the Royal Collection at Windsor Castle to name a few. A formidable list of old masters' names, many familiar to previous editions of the book, although through different drawings, are Leonardo da Vinci, Albrecht Dürer, Raphael, Jacopo da Pontormo, Francesco Primaticcio, Pieter Bruegel the Elder, Jacques De Gheyn II, Peter Paul Rubens, and Gerbrandt Van Den Eeckhout. From this highly respected stable of artists, the student should be able to clearly observe the conceptual parallels as well as media associations between the old masters and contemporary artists working today.

Seeing and drawing go hand-in-hand, and the depth to which artists learn to see contributes to greater heights of interpretation and expression. For that reason, a new theme—the importance of seeing—has been introduced in this edition and now runs throughout the book. Seeing is continually discussed as a critical part of artistic activity, and the project assignments have been written and designed to remind students that the act of seeing comes before the act of drawing, whether with the *eye of the mind* or with the *physical eye*. Several new project assignments have been added to the book to develop seeing skills, and new critique questions ask students to apply those skills to their own work and their own development as artists. First-time critiques for beginning students can be intimidating experiences, but these questions clearly focus on the objectives of the assignment, and I hope they will thereby ease any apprehension or discomfort and instead instill a sense of confidence. When properly done, self-critiques can be immensely constructive, even intellectually enjoyable experiences.

The sixth edition now includes a new Chapter 18, Expressive Mixed Media, which provides twenty new illustrations to assist the student in identifying the concept of mixed media usage through drawing's long history. It calls on student experiences with various techniques and materials presented in the previous chapters and serves as a culmination of everything they have learned in the course.

Finally, the new edition now provides a glossary of approximately 250 terms, and marginal glosses appear on the pages where the terms are first introduced. These new features should make it more convenient for students to identify and reference major terms and their definitions.

It has been my intent that all the various features of the sixth edition be designed to emphasize the importance of drawing not only as an act of seeing subject matter deeply, but also as an approach to creative thinking and creativity itself.

Acknowledgments

I would like to acknowledge and thank a number of people for their steadfast assistance, which has contributed greatly to the book's final form. My thanks go out first of all to the many capable editors at Wadsworth: to John R. Swanson, Acquisitions Editor, for his initial telephone call in June of 2000 inviting and encouraging me to consider the co-authorship; to Stacey Sims, Senior Developmental Editor, who soon engaged me in the logistics of the revision process with constant encouragement, answers, and advice; to Shirley Webster, Photo Researcher and Permissions Editor, who orchestrated the granting of many permissions of spectacular new images in record time; to Preston Thomas, Associate Art Director, and his freelance staff, who designed the beautiful cover of the new edition; my hearty thanks for your important role in helping to create the first image that people will see when they approach the book; to Kathryn Stewart, Senior Production Project Manager, who masterfully oversaw the placing of illustrations with text while steering the book's new formation through its final courses; to Greg Hubit, of Bookworks and "longtime publishing pro," as he is referred to by his colleagues, thanks for the many details of the book's final format that you so capably directed and for the great arrangements of the text passages and their illustration groupings; to Jamie Fuller, Copy Editor, whose invaluable assistance helped bring this revised text, along with the newly added Chapter 18, into its final form; to Alma Bell of Thompson Type; and to Joy Westberg for her assistance with the text layout on the back cover.

My thanks also to Dr. Eric Denker, Curator of Prints and Drawings at the Corcoran Gallery of Art, and Senior Lecturer in the History of Art at the National Gallery of Art, both in Washington, D.C., for his many kindnesses in inviting me to Washington and providing a place for me to stay while I studied the collections, collected books, and harvested new images, and to Mark Pascale, Associate Curator of Prints and Drawings at the Chicago Art Institute, who directed me to the recent publication of "Contemporary American Realist Drawings" of the Jalane and Richard Davidson Collection at the Art Institute of Chicago. Thanks also to my colleagues in the Art Department at Wake Forest University: Margaret Supplee Smith, Chair; Millie Herrin, Administrative Assistant; Martine Sherrill, Visual Resources Librarian and Print Curator; Kendra Weaver, Visual Resources Technician; and Paul Marley, Instructional Technology Specialist, for their timely assistance and organizational skills.

Finally, I owe much to the former author, Professor Emeritus Duane Wakeham, of the College of San Mateo. Duane wrote me a kind letter of invitation early on in the project sharing many of the things he had learned during his years as author of three revisions. He sent me materials and expressed his availability to me at any time I might need counsel. He also expressed to me his understanding of this very private and often solitary process of revision writing, and I have appreciated the respect he has shown me as new author. His direct connection to, and long friendship with Daniel Mendelowitz, has for me, enriched the passing of this book through his very capable hands into my comparatively inexperienced hands. His openness in sharing his seasoned thoughts, feelings, and aspirations for the book helped set a contextual tone for the revision process and gave me a place to start. And on a more personal note, Duane's kind and instructive voice on the phone has always reminded me of that of my former teacher, Professor Emeritus David Driesbach of Northern Illinois University. These two artists and teachers will remain very important mentors in my life.

The success of *A Guide to Drawing* depends in large part on the illustrations. I am most grateful to the many artists, collectors, and institutions that have enthusiastically given permission to reproduce their drawings. It has been an honor to work with all of you.

DAVID L. FABER

The Nature of Drawing 1

*Drawing . . . is the necessary beginning of
everything in art, and not having it, one
has nothing.*

—Giorgio Vasari

Drawing is the progenitor of art. The fundamental theme of this text is that the unique fine art medium of drawing is inseparable from the act of seeing. In fact, the acts of seeing and drawing are so intertwined that the diminishment of one or the other disturbs the symbiotic balance between the two, lessening their expressive powers. To draw is to **visualize** a subject through reinvention, using selected graphic media that possess highly descriptive capabilities. From this exquisite act of visualization comes the formative and visually expressive result that we call a drawing—the essential by-product of seeing deeply. Hence, responding to a subject through this pleasurable process of intense scrutiny is the *genesis of drawing.*

Drawing is unique from all other visual art forms in that it is the major boulevard leading to the avenues of painting, printmaking, sculpture, mixed media, illustration, and certainly architecture. The widely varied acts of seeing and drawing are embedded within the confines of these different disciplines. Since the *act of seeing* is paramount to the *act of drawing,* the consequence of *seeing deeply* is the harvesting and attainment of detailed information, which leads to more highly descriptive and expressive states of rendering. Above all else, drawing is a visual language—an eloquently expressive as well as graphic form of visual communication. As one develops the ability to visualize, one becomes more engaged in the thorough investigation of subject matter, inviting more articulately **rendered** visual forms, whether they are "live" or "still," "improvised" or "premeditated."

We characterize the acts of drawing and drawings themselves as "intimate," "delightful," "spontaneous," "immediate," "provocative,"

drawing
A division of the fine arts in which the artist makes a descriptive graphic mark of line, tone, texture, or value, by pulling or dragging a tool across a receptive surface or background—usually a piece of fine-quality grained or toothed paper.

visualize
To enact a mental picture or image not present to the sight; in the act of drawing, to give tangible form to what is imagined.

rendered
Drawn, usually with a high degree of representation.

1

1-1. KÄTHE KOLLWITZ (1867–1945; German). *Self-Portrait with Pencil.* 1935. Charcoal on gray paper, 16 x 17″ (40.6 × 43.2 cm). National Gallery of Art, Washington, D.C. (Rosenwald Collection).

Do I let myself do this?

"spiritual," "direct," "unlabored," "weightless"—these adjectives carry special implications of the affection that many critics and connoisseurs feel for this extraordinary form of visual artistic utterance. Part of the reason for this fondness must certainly reside in the very informal and personal nature of the body of master drawings that comprise our legacy from the past. Unlike more elaborately finished works, drawings offer an intimate contact with the act of creation and thereby permit the viewer insights into the artist's personality. Like entries in a diary, drawings often present direct notation made by the artists for themselves alone, free of artificial elaboration or excess finish.

In her *self-portrait* (Fig. 1-1), Käthe Kollwitz not only represents herself at the drawing board but also allows the viewer to experience both the mental and physical process of drawing in the powerfully kinetic zigzag line that moves along the length of the arm connecting the eye, mind, and hand. The length of the piece of charcoal she grasps in her fingers is equal to the width of the bold strokes in the drawing. Perhaps nowhere has the act of drawing been more graphically illustrated.

If we compare a master painting with one of its preliminary sketches, not only do we see the different approach and manner of execution characteristic of the two processes, but we also find hints of the artist's progress in conceptualization as we begin to sense the impulses that formed the final work (Figs. 1-2, 1-3). An incomplete or fragmentary work, precisely because it does not provide a fully developed statement, may evoke a greater play of the observer's imagination than does a more finished expression. A sketchy work can be interpreted and becomes meaningful as we supply unspecified details in terms of our own individual experience. By contrast, the closure of a carefully finished, fully detailed work largely excludes such imaginative wanderings on the part of the viewer.

What Is Drawing?

In both a historical and a conceptual sense, the words *genesis* and *drawing* are very similar. In the beginning, drawing is about "first sightings"; it is the initial approach to a subject through the pathways of both the physical and inner eyes; it is the first glimpse, the unfettered and artful penetration into the understanding of form that naturally invites a response. As *drawing* begins with *seeing*, our visual history begins with drawing. The oldest human records are the vividly lifelike images of animals drawn on cave walls between 10,000 and 20,000 years ago. Prehistoric drawings predated the written word, and the emergence of civilization, as we generally think of it, is linked to the invention of writing, which originated in easily recognized object drawings known as pictographs. Drawing has been present in all cultures throughout history—sometimes in the form of **naturalistic representation,** sometimes as stylized **abstract symbols.** Drawing is a visual barometer of a culture's given modes of expression.

The word *drawing* implies making a mark by pulling or dragging a graphic tool across a receptive background or surface, usually a piece of paper. Drawing, however, goes beyond the act of simply making marks; it is making marks that communicate visual language and

1-2. *above, left:* JEAN AUGUSTA DOMINIQUE INGRES (1780–1867; French). *Study for the Portrait of Mme. d' Haussonville.* c. 1843. Graphite on white wove paper, 234 × 196 mm.
Courtesy of the Fogg Art Museum, Harvard University, Cambridge, Massachusetts. Bequest of Meta and Paul J. Sachs.

1-3. *above, right:* JEAN AUGUSTE DOMINIQUE INGRES. *La Comtessa d' Haussonville.* 1845. Oil on canvas, 57 7/8 × 36 1/4" (147 × 92.1 cm).
The Frick Collection, New York.

naturalistic representation
The depiction of subject matter in its most natural and unaltered state.

abstract symbols
Symbols that have been visually simplified or rearranged to create visual impact and enhance meaning; they are often specific to certain cultures or political eras that represent a quality or circumstance.

share pictorially by the most immediate means an artist's responses to perceptions and experiences. Additionally, thought, feeling, and judgment are essential to the process if drawing is to be more than mere representation. The simultaneous and intertwined acts of seeing and drawing, when fully operational, produce a combination of intellect, skill, instinct, and impulse that reveal the inaudible language of the artist's soul.

A quick glance through the illustrations of this book will reveal that drawing encompasses a potentially endless variety of media and techniques. While it is perhaps more common to think of drawing in terms of black marks on white paper, many drawings include color, even a full spectrum of colors. In recent years, contemporary drawing exhibitions have come to include almost any works done on paper, adhering to the concept that it is sometimes impossible to separate drawing techniques from the methodologies of painting and printmaking. There has been an expansion of the traditional drawing repertoire of materials and tools to include all types of wet media formerly relegated to watercolor or painting. Likewise, all forms of painting media are now seated onto a variety of different paper surfaces instead of the traditional cotton duck canvas, unbleached linen, and wooden panels. However, in the purest sense, the acts of drawing, painting, and printmaking are still singularly recognizable as the individually creative modes they have always been. It's just that now they are more likely than in previous periods of art history to interact with each other as a result of greater artistic experimentation and investigation with materials common to all three disciplines.

Nonetheless, categorization has become decreasingly important; the lines separating one area of creative endeavor from another have blurred, with some artists evidencing more concern about achieving a desired effect than about the process that is used. This has produced a myriad of hybrid drawings often referred to as **mixed-media** works that take the richness of drawing and combine it with the visual attributes of other materials not necessarily associated with the traditional assortment of drawing tools. In Michael Mazur's *Self-Portrait* (Fig. 1-4), the artist achieves a splendid effect by laying mixed-media drawing techniques over the tonal foundation of a previously made **monotype.** This image has evolved through a highly emotional process of realization and response, on the part of the artist, to the mixing of media. For a time during the execution of the piece, there was an ongoing process of action and response, acceptance and refusal, until the image attained its own clarity and the artist was no longer needed. By bringing together these various and seemingly incongruous elements, Mazur has produced a state of visual freshness free of mannerism and overworked convention.

Drawings are no longer limited in size, as they were for centuries, by the dimensions of sheets of handmade paper. Both professional-grade and good-quality student-grade drawing papers are now available in rolls that make possible drawings on a scale previously associated with works on canvas. A photograph of Chuck Levitan standing before his drawing *Lincoln Split* (Fig. 1-5) clearly establishes the monumental size of his images. Without such reference, it is only by reading captions and taking note of dimensions that we can begin to fathom the scale of individual works, which in a book such as this, are all reduced to images of much the same size.

mixed media
A variety of different materials used in a creative process for the purpose of heightening surface effects and increasing the visual complexity of an image.

monotype
As a unique impression, a one-time drawing with printer's inks on a flat metal plate, which is then transferred to dampened paper with the use of a press. The French artist Edgar Degas is well known for his use of the monotype medium.

1-4. MICHAEL MAZUR. *Self-Portrait.* 1986. Pastel and charcoal with smudging over monotype on gray wove paper. 841 × 762 mm (33 1/2 × 30"). The Jalane and Richard Davidson Collection; © The Art Institute of Chicago.

1-5. CHUCK LEVITAN (b. 1942; American). *Lincoln Split.* 1976. Charcoal pencil on paper, each panel 6 x 10' (1.83 × 3.05 m). Courtesy of the artist.

Types of Drawings

For an introduction to the art of drawing we should define the term *drawing* from its origins, then briefly touch upon the various types of drawings and functions they can perform. Drawing is defined most basically as the art of representing something by lines made on a surface with a pencil or pen. How simple, how fundamental, and yet how true! To expand this definition we might identify three broad categories—drawings that describe what is seen **(descriptive drawings),** that visualize what is imagined **(visualized drawings),** and that symbolize ideas and concepts **(symbolic drawings).**

To many people, drawing means recording that which is seen. This may entail a quick linear sketch or a carefully observed study, greatly

descriptive drawings
Usually highly detailed drawings whose images articulately describe what is seen.

visualized drawings
Drawings whose images represent realities of sight or cause the viewer to visualize or see what is imagined in the mind of the artist.

symbolic drawings
Drawings whose images directly symbolize ideas and concepts.

1-6. KENT BELLOWS. *Self-Portrait, Resting.*
1989. Charcoal with stumping and erasing,
and white crayon, on white wove paper.
610 × 813 mm (24 × 32″).
The Jalane and Richard Davidson Collection.
© The Art Institute of Chicago.

eye of the mind
That which perceives subjectively apart
from what the physical eye sees objectively or concretely. Often referred to as
"the eye of the soul."

abstract vision
The imagined essence of premeditated
forms arising in the mind of the artist
whose intent it is to interpret a subject
by analyzing and altering its recognizable forms and features by reassembling them into a nonrecognizable
state with little or no reference to the
original forms.

detailed and nearly photographic in its accuracy, as in Kent Bellows's
Self-Portrait, Resting (Fig. 1-6). By using charcoal with stumping, white
crayon, and erasing, the artist has ingeniously created as near a photo
state as possible combing the human figure with botanical forms.

Drawing can also visualize through representation a nonexistent
situation or an object conceived in the imagination of the artist, in the
eye of the mind. Greg Colfax, a Native American artist of the Makah
tribe of Neah Bay, Washington, works to preserve tribal traditions and
symbols, while at the same time going beyond to introduce change
through artistic invention. After completing the preliminary design for a
hand drum (Fig. 1-7), he decided to use only the portion enclosed within
the inner circle for the completed drum (Fig. 1-8). Although Colfax chose
to focus on the eagle and the human head, he incorporated curvilinear
abstract elements that represented whale, sea, and wind motifs in his
original sketch into his final evolved composition.

As Paul Klee implies in his statement, "Art does not render the visual, but art renders visual," visualization is not limited to representational images. Klee shared with his colleagues of the Blaue Reiter
movement his desire "to reveal the reality that is visible behind things."
He explained that it is art itself which makes visible, and "it is the lines
of the draftsman, which are going for a walk, that can lead to the land
of deeper insight." Drawing can also be an **abstract vision,** such as
Philip Guston's *ink drawing* (Fig. 1-9). This work gives few clues to its
figurative origins—if needed, these origins certainly do exist on a spiritual level—but with its lines and shapes offering an expressive character
of their own, the drawing seems to soar into a far more transcendent
realm than mere representational depiction may allow. Latin American

artist Rafael Soriano expands representation into the **eldritch** sphere of dreaming, imagining, and remembering with ambiguous figure and landscape references that preclude literal interpretation (Fig. 1-10). Richly rendered in conté crayon, Soriano's untitled drawing offers an evocative fusing of light and shadow, forms and space. There is a softness of quality as well as a translucency of visual presence within the drawing that does not rely upon the seemingly forceful strengths of highly representational interpretation.

The third category of drawings is based upon the use of symbols as enigmatic shorthand for nonliteral communication. Objects, ideas as concepts, and qualities can be presented as symbols that may or may not resemble the symbolized subject. The subject may, in fact, be a mere suggestion of a provocative idea, so transient in nature that only the viewer's interpretation at the moment of seeing gives the work any

eldritch
A word describing an unexpectedly rare and eerie quality or an unforgettable, otherworldly presence, usually conspicuously out of place when and wherever found.

1-10. RAFAEL SORIANO (b. 1920; Cuban). *Untitled.* 1987. Conté crayon, 30 × 40″ (76.2 × 101.6 cm). Courtesy of the artist.

meaning. The stylized representations of the various forms in both Colfax's preparatory drawing and the drum itself are derived from symbols that are part of his tribal tradition. In David Suter's drawing, work gloves and a lunch bucket, which in themselves are blue-collar symbols, assume additional significance when cleverly anthropomorphized to illustrate the effect of unemployment for a magazine article entitled "A More Severe Slump" (Fig. 1-11).

The three categories need not be treated independently. Often elements of all three may flow together as one presence in the same drawing, producing a formidable conceptual structure of representational, imaginary, and symbolic icons that collectively depict an artist's sense of heightened awareness or spiritual prowess. In each category, however, drawings can range from simplified, preliminary indications of form and ideas to complex and intricately detailed, finished drawings. The effectiveness and completeness of any drawing as visual language depend not so much on elaborate development as on the degree to which the drawing conveys the artist's intent. By the same token, a drawing is both finished and effective, and may even be considered infinitely successful, when the intent of the artist is clearly and poignantly seen and felt even through the complex layers of media that suggest a careful and laborious execution.

Expressive Drawing

All drawings as visual language are expressive to greater or lesser degrees. Through their own specified modes of communication, they all tell us something. Drawings exist because they have their beginnings in the interactive, nonverbal dialogues between artists and their subjects that give rise to the responsive and expressive evidences of artistic creation. Visual expression is not something that can ever be explicitly defined. Nor can it be predicted or fully understood through the concrete meanings of words. Artistic expression is nonetheless an ever-present force that manifests itself within the artist's heart, mind, and soul. Like

1-11. DAVID SUTER (b. 1949; American). Illustration for "A More Severe Slump," *Time* Magazine. 1980. Felt-tip pen, 10″ (25.4 cm) square. Courtesy of the artist.

dormant seeds stored in a pod that eventually germinate in the presence of fertile soil, moisture, and sunlight, artistic expression is born from seeing, which gives rise to response and ultimate visual communication.

Gertrude Stein stated quite emphatically that Pablo Picasso was born knowing everything there was to know about drawing. In contrast, art historian John Rewald described Vincent van Gogh as a person with no natural talent who became an artist through sheer determination. Whether either assessment is completely accurate or not, they both acknowledge different degrees of innate ability.

Persons of "no natural talent," but having an interest in learning to draw, plus the willingness and persistence to master some basic skills, can develop the ability to record what they see with a certain degree of accuracy. Again, learning to see, and thereby learning to see deeply, is all-important to being able to draw. It is the eye that leads the hand in the act of drawing what is seen, not the other way around. Often beginning students (along with more advanced drawing students who have never learned the proper way to let the eye lead the hand) will draw with their hands, and then judge with their eyes instead of first judging with their eyes, then drawing with their hands. Furthermore, drawing, as suggested by the examples reproduced in this book, involves more than making an accurate rendering of a subject, just as it requires more than the skillful manipulation of media and technique. Drawing is primarily about content: it presents a point of view, interpretation, and expression unique to the individual artist.

As viewers we respond to those works that not only draw us closest to the artist by allowing us to share an interest, emotion, or insight, but also allow us to project our own experiences, thoughts, and feelings. We find most appealing drawings that offer more than an ordinary depiction of a subject, drawings that reveal qualities about the artist as well as the subject. What is most fascinating about Henry Moore's drawing *Sheep in Landscape* (Fig. 1-12) is his abiding interest in the size and scale-relationships between sheep and other elements of the landscape such as trees, fence posts, even his own sculpture. He once said, "I like

1-12. HENRY MOORE (b. 1898; British). *Sheep in Landscape.* 1972. Ballpoint pen, 8 1/4 × 9 7/8″ (21 × 25.1 cm). Private collection, U.K.; The Henry Moore Foundation.

1-13. LARRY RIVERS (b. 1923; American). *Portrait of Edwin Denby.* 1953. Pencil, 16 3/8 × 19 3/4″ (41.7 × 50.2 cm). The Museum of Modern Art, New York. Given anonymously.

1-14. KÄTHE KOLLWITZ (1867–1945; German). *Woman with Dead Child.* 1903. Black chalk and charcoal heightened with white on two sheets of green paper, 390 × 480 mm (15 1/8 × 18 7/8 in.). Private collection.

the size of sheep in relation to my sculptures as part of the overall landscape. Horses or cows would be too large, but sheep seem to be just the right size to be immersed into their surroundings." In this drawing Moore uses a variety of linear techniques to describe the forms of the sheep and their grassy surroundings into a unified whole.

Less literal, though nonetheless compelling, is Larry River's *Portrait of Edwin Denby III* (Fig. 1-13), which combines vigorous drawing in graphite with a keen sense of selectivity evident in the subtractive eraser whites and the tonal smudge marks. Equally effective in conveying not only a strong but also a powerful sense of humanity is Käthe Kollwitz's *Woman with Dead Child* (Fig. 1-14). In this drawing, Kollwitz has used the elements of line, tone, texture, and value as vehicles for the expression of anguish over the mother's loss of her little child. Käthe Kollwitz devoted her life to caring for the poor and needy. As the wife of a physician, she was no stranger to human suffering and death. Much of her expressive and highly emotional graphic work was influenced by the lives of people who needed compassion.

Comparing the works of these three artists, we can see that while the choice of medium and technique contributes significantly to the effectiveness of the drawings, it is the individual sensitivity, character, and intention of the artist that give unique expressive character to each of the works. It also becomes highly evident that artists select specific media in combination with a variety of techniques for emotional reasons in order to enhance the conceptual strengths of their images.

The Role of Drawing Today

Like much else in our artistic heritage, our conceptions about the role of drawing in the arts come to us largely from the Renaissance. During the early years of that period, drawing as we now practice it became established as the foundation of training in the arts. In the traditional master-student relationship, long-term apprenticeships called for drawing from nature as well as copying studies executed by known master artists and eventually prepared students for their profession. In later centuries this system, with only slight alteration, continued as the accepted means of artistic training.

In the twentieth century this procedure was seriously challenged. The impact of abstract drawings, collages, paintings, and prints, along with other contemporary movements, tended to make the arduous discipline of earlier times seem irrelevant to the formal training of later students. Many artists and teachers believed that highly structured training inhibited the development of original and innovative forms of expression by requiring that students depend on trite and outworn formulas, rather than allowing their inner resources free play. In light of this statement, one must remember that the human creative spirit is a mysterious and powerful entity filled with inner determination. The potent will of the artist to see, respond, and act is irrepressible. When given proper encouragement and sound pedagogy, this artistic force will thrive according to the established art conventions of the day. When artistic will is left to its own devices, it will still appear in one form or another. Also, it is important to mention that throughout history, the various established traditions and standards of artistic acceptance have not always served as a true and accurate measuring stick for an individual's talent. There have always been those artists who have chosen to go against the accepted standards of their times, and in doing so, have left the art world a legacy of renowned works well respected for their unprecedented daring and ambition. Who, other than the artists of the day, are better qualified to uproot the commonplace in search of something more profound and ethereal?

For example, the early training of artists as diverse as Pablo Picasso, Henri Matisse, Paul Klee, Josef Albers, and Joseph Stella—all schooled in the conventional regimen—would seem, as evidenced by their later and more mature works, to contradict this attitude of the necessity of requiring students to follow suit with the high and lofty academic training of the Renaissance. In addition to the early academic *Standing Male Nude* by Picasso (Fig. 1-15), this book includes some

1-15. PABLO PICASSO. (1881–1973; Spanish-French). *Standing Male Nude.* 1896–1897. Charcoal and crayon on light tan paper, 18 5/8 × 12 1/2" (47.3 × 31.8 cm). Museo Picasso, Barcelona.

expressionism

The visual traits or character of a work of art that communicates emotions and feelings as opposed to only being concerned with the *objective* and *subjective* realms; the way in which a work of art was conceived and made, as occurs in an *expressionistic response* to a subject by a particular artist.

abstraction

The extraction of an essence; an analytical study of an object or the formation of an idea apart from its tangible or recognizable form, as of the characteristics of an object or idea, whereby the virtues of an insightful rearrangement of form are substituted for exact representation.

abstract expressionism

An American movement in the field of painting that began in the late nineteen-forties and emphasized a nonrepresentational style. The movement broke into two branches: *action painting* and *color field painting*.

rather surprising early drawings by Albers and Stella that are very different from the images with which they are so closely identified. However, one must understand that academic training is a fortifying element in the way an artist ultimately chooses to compose and that as stylistic changes occur throughout an artist's career, the work still reflects the essence of that training.

In a letter dated 1948, Matisse wrote:

> I am afraid the young, seeing in my work only the apparent facility and negligence in the drawing, will use this as an excuse for dispensing with certain efforts I believe necessary.

While the rigidly maintained academic procedures taught in the ateliers of past masters no longer seem appropriate, a program of introducing instruction and guidance remains vital to skillful and artistic development. The initial experiences of the beginner leave an indelible imprint upon subsequent development. Although making accurate descriptive drawings may not be the ultimate goal, learning to see size, shape, and spatial relationships, along with surface textures within a play of lights and darks, is necessary for representing any formal idea, whether it be realistic, imaginary, or symbolic. Another vital part of artistic training is the development of discipline and control so that the artist can convincingly translate what is seen onto a piece of paper, thereby establishing a basic and essential working vocabulary with which to speak a visual language effectively (Fig. 1-15). Having acquired that vocabulary, the artist is then free to choose to draw in whatever style is pleasing and seems appropriate to what is being expressed (Fig. 1-16). Picasso is reported to have commented that if he could draw as well as Raphael, as some observers suggested, he should be allowed to draw as he chose.

As artists are confronted with new technologies, they are finding that drawing is more important today than ever before as a way of seeing, understanding, and responding to forms in space. Rather than abandoning the discipline of drawing as irrelevant to contemporary art, we will choose to reinterpret the craft in terms of today's artistic standards and artists' needs, which accept an increased variety of styles and a much wider range of **expressionism** than in the past. **Abstraction** (Fig. 1-9) flourishes side by side with the most disciplined realism (Fig. 1-6) or with powerful emotion (Fig. 1-14). Our increased catholicity of taste is, to an equal extent, the result of a greater understanding of the psychology of human beings and a consequent sympathy toward a broader range of expression.

Reveling in the glorious freedoms to mix and manipulate traditional as well as experimental media in whatever manner they choose, many artists, representing all levels of artistic maturity, now feel challenged to work with media in more traditionally disciplined ways. For some who came of age during the heyday of **abstract expressionism,** using traditional, even "academic," drawing techniques in the pursuit of naturalistic and highly representational imagery, sometimes in the monumental scale characteristics of other contemporary styles, has been and remains a truly novel experience. For present-day artists who regard draftsmanship as important, however, revived interest in representational styles and figure drawing is a welcome change.

Until this century drawing was viewed as a prerequisite to painting and sculpture. It provided the initial training for young artists, who then continued to draw primarily as a preparatory step in the realization of a more major work (Figs. 1-2, 1-3). Although drawings have been collected and admired since the sixteenth century, they were thought of as studies that would ultimately inform something else, rather than as complete and independent works in themselves. During the twentieth century, and now into the beginnings of the twenty-first century, drawing has come to be accepted as the unique and major art form that it has always been, although unrecognized as such. Because of the uniqueness of drawing (and all that drawing captures), it is no surprise that drawing has continued and will continue to serve artistic pursuits as a means to an end; often that end comes when the drawing is finished and it stands fully on its own, emitting all the visual power and drama present in other works of art. Since the 1960s, there has been, within the artists' community, a reemphasis on the directness of drawing and the intimacy an artist has with drawing media. Drawing has not only regained some of the identity it seemed to have lost, but it has taken on a new and more far-reaching identity that artists around the world have benefited from. Drawing, even during its low periods, has never needed a justification for its existence, since its justification is inherent in the act of drawing itself; rather, it has always led practicing artists to an increased understanding of form as well as to the development and conceptualization of their deepest expressions. Drawing is, as mentioned early in this chapter, the progenitor of art, as well as providing a means to an end in itself. Drawing has a continuing and an essential role to play in our world. Perhaps it is truly an art of the twenty-first century.

2 Initial Experiences

[I]t is essential for both hand and eye to grasp the form, and it is only by much drawing, drawing everything, drawing unceasingly that one fine day one is very surprised to find it possible to express something in its true spirit. . . .

—Camille Pissarro

This 1883 letter of Camille Pissarro to his son Lucien expresses the basic concept of *A Guide to Drawing*. Drawing is a matter of training the eye as well as the hand—the hand responds to what the eye sees. While learning to see is a major topic of Chapter 3, the essential relationship between observation and representation—the act of faith between the eye and the hand—will be a recurring theme throughout the book.

The subject chapters that follow have been structured around a series of projects with specific instructions for novice artists. Generally speaking, the exercises increase in difficulty throughout the book, although there is no rigid adherence to this scale. You are encouraged not only to read each project carefully but also to execute all of the project assignments in order to more fully understand the concepts presented.

Making Drawings

The purpose of the assignments is not solely to make beautiful drawings or even necessarily to make successful drawings. The purpose is to learn to draw by making drawings. Michelangelo is supposed to have said that his work contained 99 percent hard work and 1 percent genius. The value of each drawing experience that is to be derived from each individual assignment can be measured only by the discipline and dedication that the student is willing to invest.

Beginners can expect to make some awful drawings. Mistakes will be frequent, but they can be corrected and changed. The realization of why a mistake is a mistake is the first significant step toward learning how to draw. Success cannot be determined on the basis of just one experience, one drawing. Anything, whether it be playing a musical instrument, meditating, or drawing, becomes easier and more effective with continued practice, and practice contributes to increased technical competence, control, and eventual mastery.

Most drawings fail not from lack of skill but from lack of planning. Many artists and students mistakenly believe that planning automatically destroys freshness and spontaneity when, in fact, the contrary is more often true. Knowing what one intends to do allows one to enter into the drawing process directly and spontaneously. The uncertainty and confusion that accompany lack of planning frequently result in overworking a drawing, since the searching process never had a legitimate directive from the beginning. In such instances, once the drawing problems have been solved, it is advantageous to redo the drawing to achieve the desired freshness. Students are urged not to discard any of their drawings, since development and improvement become self-evident when later works are compared with the earlier attempts.

With increasing development of skills and confidence, the student may wish to concentrate on one type of drawing, one medium, or one variety of subject matter. This natural tendency should be fully exploited, since creative growth and expressionistic depth are important to artistic maturity. It is also true that any serious and intensive activity eventually demands an expansion of horizons with media usage and approach. Often, the beginner finds it all too compelling to act repeatedly on minor successes and finds it difficult to forge onward into the discoveries of other strengths and capacities. The directness of interpretive exploration that successful drawing requires keeps the artist honest and the art student humble, qualities that only lead to legitimate—even profound results.

The work of most mature artists reveals periods of intensive concentration within a narrow framework of special problems alternating with periods of experimentation. It is not only wise but also essential for the beginner to travel a similar path, focusing on areas of particular interest as long as they remain challenging. However, when success comes too easily, it is imperative to move on to new explorations.

Before one is familiar with the materials and has experience in using them, any new medium, technique, or subject may seem difficult, even for the accomplished artist. Serious art students, however, soon discover that the understanding and discipline leading to acquired skills in one area are directly applicable to other areas, and although success is not always immediate or insured, each project, each new experience contributes to creative growth and establishes the basis for eventual, mature artistic expression.

Looking at Drawings

In Chapter 4, and throughout this book, learning to draw by studying the works of other artists is appropriately emphasized and encouraged. *A Guide to Drawing* is richly illustrated with master drawings, both past and present, selected to acquaint you with creative uses of media and techniques and to introduce you to different approaches to handling form, composition, and subject matter. Understanding the ways in which master artists see expands your own abilities to see deeply. There is little value in copying any of the drawings line for line in order to produce a facsimile; however, the powers of seeing developed through your study of the masters will foster a unique reinterpretation that will become evident in your own usage of line, tone, texture, and value. (The tradition of copying is discussed in Chapter 4.)

Presentation of Drawings

Drawings done as learning experiences are not necessarily intended to be exhibition pieces. There will be occasions, however, when more finished drawings will be exhibited, if only for classroom critiques, at which time it will be appropriate to consider how the work is to be presented and how best an individual drawing might be visually enhanced. Smudged, torn, wrinkled drawings pinned to a wall make much less of an impression than clean, neatly bordered, and obviously cared-for drawings. Critiques may not always require that drawings be matted, but when mats are called for, they should be clean, well cut, and as unobtrusive as possible so that the focus is on the drawings rather than what surrounds them. Naturally, white or off-white mats are recommended over colored mats, which tend to detract attention from the work of art. Mat knives or utility knives are satisfactory for cutting simple mats of four-ply thickness, whereas X-acto knives are suitable for the lighter-weight two-ply thickness. Beveled mats require a mat cutter that holds the cutting blade securely at an angle. For safety reasons, never use razor blades as they are too difficult to hold and control simultaneously. A metal straightedge or T-square offers the best cutting edge, and it helps significantly if two people work as a team, one holding the straightedge firmly down to avoid slippage, the other cutting the straight line. Always position the straightedge on the mat side of the line to be cut so that if the knife were to slip, it would cut into the center portion to be discarded rather than into the mat. Make sure that all surfaces are clean and free from any materials that might cause smudges or scuff marks.

The widths of mats can vary greatly and are often a matter of personal preference; however, the minimum width should be no less than three to four inches (7.7 to 10.2 centimeters) for the sides and top, and no less than four to five inches (10.2 to 12.8 centimeters) for the bottom (these measurements can be proportionally increased for much larger-scale drawings). The borders of your drawing will lie under the mat's overlapping perimeter with only the image exposed through the mat's opening. In determining the outer dimensions of the mat and the size of the opening to be cut, lay a clean straightedge ruler down across your drawing, allowing it to overhang each side. Determine the width of the image and add a minimum of three inches for the width of the mat on each side, or six inches plus the width of the image. This measurement represents the outer dimensions of the width measurement. Follow the same procedure of measuring for the height of the drawing, remembering to add an extra inch for the width of the bottom portion of the mat, which will give you the outer dimensions of the height measurement of your mat. After carefully measuring and cutting the mat, attach it along the top edge only to a piece of strong backing material such as acid-free foam-core board (with the identical outer dimensions), using acid-free linen tape. Lift the window mat from the backing board enough to position the drawing inside, then close the mat back down, loosely covering the edges of the drawing. Shift the drawing slightly—up, down, side to side, until it is correctly centered in relation to the window opening, securing it with a paperweight (resting on a clean paper towel on top of the drawing). Then open the mat and hinge the drawing's top edge securely to the backing surface with two or three one-inch lengths of linen tape (the taped edge will be concealed under the top width of the mat when it is fully closed).

It is always best to use acid-free board for both the mat and backing, and linen tape for the hinges, particularly for permanent matting projects. A sheet of acetate may be cut to the identical size of the outer dimensions and slipped inside the mat and over the drawing's surface to prevent rubbing when drawings are to be stored on top of one another in flat file drawers. It is also a good idea to place clean sheets of paper in between the matted drawings when they are stacked in drawers.

Students who develop the habit of doing full-sheet drawings can prepare two standard mats—one vertical, one horizontal—for classroom presentation. Diagrams of matting and information on portfolio preparations are discussed at the end of Chapter 16, Illustration.

And now you are ready to begin the adventure of learning how to draw.

Beginner's Media

Adolphe William Bouguereau made the following statement to Matisse: "[B]ut first you must learn how to hold a crayon. . . ."

There is a universal familiarity with pens and pencils the world over, and it is strangely curious to suddenly enlist these common mark-making tools into the deeply profound mystery of drawing. Yet pens and pencils, along with charcoal and brush and ink, have always been the humblest and most easily obtained drawing tools for artists throughout most of recorded art history. The timeless familiarity with these ever common, yet highly expressive indelible tools is deepened by the drawing experience. Every artist, sooner or later, comes to realize that a particular drawing tool resonates in the hand, and in combination with a chosen working surface, produces an organically expressive marriage of materials.

As one approaches drawing for the first time, it is important to concentrate on the drawing media that are least demanding. One must pay attention to the drawing tools and the variety of ways they may be held, each producing a different effect, and then draw as freely and uninhibitedly as possible, so that the transmission of impressions, ideas, and impulses will be direct and un-self-conscious. Charcoal, pencil, ballpoint pen, felt-tip pen, and brush and ink should meet initial needs and provide ample possibilities for expression. The following equipment and materials are generally standard and suffice to commence working. Other materials and tools can be added later.

> drawing board (basswood or Masonite), 20 × 26 inches
>   (51 × 76 cm)
> thumbtacks (to use with basswood board)
> masking tape (to hold sheets of paper to Masonite board)
> pad of multipurpose drawing paper, suitable for pencil, charcoal,
>   and ink, 18 × 24 inches (46 × 61 cm)
> heavy clips (to hold drawing pad to the board)
> HB, 2B, 4B, 6B, and 8B graphite drawing pencils
> large, soft pencil erasers of different kinds

stick charcoal (soft) and compressed charcoal (0 or 00)
kneaded eraser
blending chamois, shading stump (*tortillon* or *estompe*)
fixative in pressurized cans (to be used with ventilation only)
ballpoint and felt-tip pens (medium and wide point)
India ink and dilution tray for washes
medium-size pointed brush (No. 10), of the best quality you can
    afford (not an oil painting brush)
Optional:
heavy-weight paper, charcoal paper, vellum
fine sandpaper sharpening pads for graphite
assorted gray crayons/pastels (available in boxes of 12 from
    Conté, NuPastel, or Weber Costello)
6B stick graphite
graphite powder
Conté crayon

Charcoal   Charcoal, because it is easy to apply and equally easy to re-move, provides a rich and versatile medium for the beginner. Depending on the angle of the stick and the pressure exerted upon it, charcoal lines can be pale or dark, of uniform or varying widths, creating a vast and dramatic repertoire for line drawings. Line, which will be discussed often throughout this text as it pertains to different media and expres-

2-1. PABLO PICASSO (1881–1973; Spanish-French), *Still Life.* c. 1919. Charcoal on white paper, 28 × 20 3/4″ (71.2 × 52.7 cm). Private collection.

sion, is particularly important in the use of charcoal. The swelling and tapering of a charcoal line created by varying amounts of pressure is the descriptive lifeline of expression. Charcoal is an extremely responsive medium, and the effects of a live and pulsing line are easily attained. The discovery process of the descriptive qualities of line that ensue as the beginner draws is quite profound. In Pablo Picasso's *Still Life* (Fig. 2-1), we see this descriptive life in the line as it courses about the picture plane identifying the contours of each object. It is a delight to the eyes to be entertained by both the subtlety and boldness of the charcoal as if the line itself were breathing. A wide range of values from light gray to black can be produced by the application of parallel or cross-hatched lines (Figs. 2-2, 2-3) or by dragging the stick on its side, as demonstrated by Kollwitz in Figure 1-1. When grays of minimum texture are desired, tonal areas can be fused by rubbing the surface gently with the fingers, with soft paper, or with a paper stump known as a **tortillon** or **estompe.**

Project 2.1

Familiarize yourself with the nature of charcoal by drawing lines using varying amounts of pressure and changing the angle at which you hold the charcoal stick. Practice building tones with rapidly drawn clusters of diagonal parallel lines and cross-hatched lines. With the side of a piece of charcoal, lay down a smooth gradation of tone from black to very light gray. Do the same with lines fused by your fingers, reinforced by subsequent applications of charcoal and rubbing. Notice that excessive rubbing or rubbing with any slight presence of moisture on the surface can

2-2. *above, left:* JUAN GRIS (1887–1927; Spanish). *Le Moulin à Café.* 1911. Charcoal, 18 3/4 × 12 1/2". The Brooklyn Museum.

2-3. *above, right:* ROBERT HENRI (1865–1929; American). *Portrait Head of a Woman.* Crayon, 6 1/2 × 4 1/2" (16.5 × 11.4 cm). Susan and Herbert Alder Collection.

tortillon
A paper shading stump used in combination with dry media for blending tones.

estompe A paper stump used for shading or blending tones.

2-4. FREDERICK W. MACMONNIES (1863–1937; American). *Head of a Man.* 1884. Charcoal, 22 11/16 × 15 7/8" (57.8 × 40.3 cm). The Cleveland Museum of Art.

result in the loss of freshness and perhaps a marked disturbance of the tooth of the paper. In these preliminary exercises you will quickly become aware that while charcoal can be easily blended, it can be just as easily smudged, which necessitates learning how to draw without resting your hand on the paper. To steady your hand for precise details, reach across and grasp the opposite side of the board with your other hand, using that arm to support your drawing hand.

The drawings in Figures 2-1 to 2-4 are all extensions of the exercises suggested in Project 2.1. Picasso's *Still Life* (Fig. 2-1) is drawn with a line of essentially uniform width. By wiping out rather than erasing completely, he allows us to see how carefully he has considered the exact shape and placement of each form. The drawing, which at first glance seems deceptively simple, suggests that it is unimportant that a line or shape be correct as first drawn as long as you can change it. Furthermore, as the artist orchestrated the composition through these changes, the vestiges of former lines add richness and soft vulnerability to each altered form. *Le Moulin à Café* by Juan Gris (Fig. 2-2) is a line drawing very much like Picasso's, augmented by diagonally hatched shading to create a greater illusion of volume and space. The added tone creates richness and a more formidable presence of the objects drawn.

The gradations in tone in Robert Henri's *Portrait Head of a Woman* (Fig. 2-3)—a crayon drawing identical in effect to the charcoal drawing—result from variations in pressure rather than from blending. Notice how the obvious diagonal stroking of the left half of the drawing changes to a more even tone on the right side. Henri gives definition to the figure by reinforcing his broad tonal areas with a few selected, expressive lines. Figures 2-3 and 2-4 are amazingly similar drawings that differ only in execution. Whereas the Henri drawing exhibits a loose yet descriptive directness and spontaneity, *Head of a Man* by Frederick W. MacMonnies (Fig. 2-4) is a more fully rendered portrait in which the details of form are defined through tonal variations created by dragging the side of the charcoal stick across the surface of the paper. Notice how the linear accents of the clothing appear to have been made by dragging the charcoal vertically and in the direction of the fabric lines it is describing. There is some blending of tone and also subtraction of the darks to create subtle highlights by the use of an eraser; this gives the drawing a spatially dynamic force setting it apart from the Henri work. Most of the grain, or surface characteristics, evident in these drawings derives from the texture or tooth of the paper itself.

A luxurious advantage of stick charcoal is that it can be easily manipulated through both additive and subtractive methods. Large areas can be wiped away with a piece of chamois; more precise corrections can be made with a kneaded eraser that can be shaped to a rather sharp point and used to lift off an undesired mark or area of tone. Broad strokes of highlights can be created with either a plastic or rubber eraser in the opposite fashion that dark strokes are created using the side of a charcoal stick. Be aware that erasing with excessive pressure can damage the surface of some papers and make it difficult to draw back into an area without the erasure marks being visible. The eventual accumulation of charcoal dust can be removed from a chamois by snapping it against something solid or by washing it, while charcoal picked up by the eraser disappears in the process of kneading and reshaping the eraser.

A

B

C

D

2-5. Tonal study in charcoal using chamois and kneaded eraser as drawing implements.
A. Light-colored objects, middle-value background, light source from side.
B. Middle-value charcoal tone on paper; middle lights lifted with chamois.
C. Darks added to further establish forms.
D. Kneaded eraser used for highlights and lightest tones; additional darks for detailing.

The concepts of both additive and subtractive elements in the activity of drawing are extremely important to the overall degree of finish and complexity of any drawing. In addition to their usefulness for making corrections, both chamois and a variety of different erasers can serve as drawing implements to create a wide-ranging tonal study in charcoal. As demonstrated in Figure 2-5, working into a homogenous middle value tone laid down with soft stick charcoal, a chamois is used to lift out middle light tones and an eraser is used for the lightest tones. Darks are easily added with direct applications of charcoal in selected areas.

Project 2.2

Place a few simple objects of light value against a middle value background. Provide a source of light above and to one side. Using stick charcoal, cover a sheet of smooth, good-quality paper with middle value tone. To achieve a uniform tone, blend the charcoal with a tissue, cotton puff, or a foam cosmetic blender. Establish the size, shape, and position of the objects by sketching them in very lightly with charcoal. Study the composition to determine what areas to lift out with the chamois, which lights to erase, and where to add darker tones. Be alert to patterns of light and shadow on the various objects, gaining a sense of the lightest and the darkest areas. Begin to be aware of the sharp edges that separate objects as well as the soft edges where light turns to shadow. Work as directly and deliberately as

CH. 2 Initial Experiences **21**

possible and avoid overworking the paper surface in order to maintain a state of freshness. One reason for introducing this tonal approach to drawing as one of the first projects is to provide beginners with an early awareness that drawing doesn't have to begin with lines.

Compressed charcoal is charcoal ground to a powder and compressed into chalklike sticks. It is a far more saturated and potent black and offers deeper, richer darks than stick charcoal, but it is more difficult to erase, as are the gray crayons listed as optional materials.

Protecting Charcoal Drawings   Spraying finished charcoal drawings with a protective coating of fixative will prevent smudges and help hold the charcoal powders to the paper surface. "Workable" fixative allows you to spray the working paper surface at intervals while continuing to work back into the drawing after it has been fixed. To apply, position the drawing in a well-ventilated area, hold the can about nine to twelve inches from the drawn surface, and spray with a back-and-forth motion, making sure to cover the entire drawn area. In the past, if ventilation was not available, spraying the drawing outside in the open air was recommended. This, however, is not very effective in terms of evenly coating the paper and doesn't ensure that stray vapors will not be inhaled. Always use spray fixative in a ventilated area intended for that purpose, such as a spray booth. Also, the spray should never be used near an open flame.

Pencil   Pencil, or **graphite,** comes in varying degrees of hard and soft, and although not as flexible as charcoal, it is also an excellent beginning drawing medium, having the virtues of familiarity and relative cleanliness. Graphite, found in nature, is a soft, black, and lustrous material mixed with a binding material and compressed to form a wide range of light to dark effects. These light to dark effects are analogous to their manufactured hard to soft physical properties, ranging from 9H as the hardest and lightest, to 9B as the softest and darkest. The complete range of graphite grades starting with the hardest and working toward the softest is: 9H, 8H, 7H, 6H, 5H, 4H, 3H, 2H, H, F, HB, B, 2B, 3B, 4B, 5B, 6B, 7B, 8B, 9B.

We learn to handle pencils early in childhood, if not for drawing, then certainly for writing. As noted at the beginning of this chapter, there is a universal familiarity with pencils, along with several other common drawing instruments. But when a pencil graduates from its use as a primarily utilitarian tool to that of a fine art tool, it resonates differently in the hand of the artist, just as it will begin to in the hand of the beginning student. Holding a pencil in an upright position as for writing produces an essentially uniform line (Fig. 2-6) and encourages finger control most appropriate for working on small details. Although beginners generally feel most comfortable holding the pencil and other drawing tools in this conventional manner, the results are often small, cramped, and centralized images. Drawing on full sheets of paper with the intent to use the entire paper surface as the working picture plane, along with using broader movements of both the hand and arm, will result in looser, freer drawing.

Many artists let the pencil resonate by holding it under the hand (Fig. 2-7) because it permits easier variations in the thickness and darkness of the line. A slight shift in the hand position utilizes either the point or the side of the graphite to produce a line of greater interest and

graphite
A soft form of carbon found in nature and used as lead in pencils. It is manufactured in a wide range of soft to hard states and produces a lustrous, black, or gray-black mark when dragged against a receptive surface. The softer states produce darker, richer blacks than harder versions. It is also available in stick, chunk, or powdered form.

2-6. Line made by pencil held in handwriting position.

2-7. Line made by pencil held under the hand.

in turn greater potential to describe the object being drawn. The latter position encourages a freer drawing, since neither the hand nor the arm rests on the paper and more of the artist's upper body is engaged in the act of drawing. It also prevents smudging when working with softer graphite, charcoal, and other media that tend to smear easily.

2-8. VINCENT VAN GOGH (1853–1890; Dutch). *Mill on the Hill.* 1887. Pencil, 11 × 20″ (28 × 50.8 cm). Vincent van Gogh Foundation/Vincent van Gogh Museum, Amsterdam.

Project 2.3

Before starting to draw specific things, spend a little time playing with the pencil in your hand so that you begin thinking of it as a drawing tool rather than as a writing implement. Observe the quality of the line produced by the point of the pencil and by the side of the graphite as you scribble freely on your paper. Also note the difference in line quality achieved by holding the pencil in the writing position (Fig. 2-6) and by holding it between the thumb and forefinger but under your hand (Fig. 2-7).

Practice with a soft pencil, a 4B, 6B, or 8B, by drawing parallel lines in either a vertical or horizontal fashion from one edge of the paper to the other. As you draw, concentrate on changing the amount of downward pressure that you exert on the pencil, creating lines that swell and darken with more pressure and taper and lighten with lighter pressure. Fill the entire surface of the paper with these ever-changing lines. Notice how they seem to recede by dropping back into space and project forward as they weightlessly lift themselves off the page.

Project 2.4

As you have just discovered in the previous project, it is possible using a soft pencil to create a full range of light to dark tones (values) and rich, dark blacks by increasing or decreasing the pressure, as evidenced in Vincent van Gogh's *Mill on the Hill* (Fig. 2-8) and George Bellows's *Tennis at Newport* (Fig. 2-9). Fill in a series of six two-inch (five-centimeter) squares both with even tones of varying degrees of darkness and with gradations of tone, using broad strokes made with the side of the graphite rather than with the point. It is not necessary to work for a smooth blending without any visible strokes as long as you achieve the effect of a uniform tone.

Drawing with the point of the pencil, develop even gray tones of different values using closely spaced parallel and cross-hatched lines. Explore different directional strokes and patterns—regular and uniform, also random and spontaneous—to create gradations, even gray tones, and the suggestion of textural differences. You will discover that the successful laying down of tones depends upon learning to control pressure. Care must be given not to tear the paper by bearing down too heavily in the attempt to achieve stronger darks.

Five pencil drawings of the human head (Figs. 2-10 to 2-14) begin to suggest the range of visual interest that evolves from using a variety of line, tone, texture, and value, rather than relying on the uniform line weight that results from drawing as though writing. In each of the drawings, we remain conscious of the pencil as an implement that produces lines, but in each example it is the difference both in the quality of the line and the way in which the line is drawn that should be examined.

Jack Beal's *Self-Portrait* (Fig. 2-10) comes closest to the pure line drawing. The variation within individual lines that results from such factors as differing degrees of pressure, varying directions of movement, or positions of the hand in the act of drawing gives energy to the image and contributes to establishing the visual character of the artist. Looking at the deeper nature of the drawing, as a self-portrait statement, we notice that the thickening of the lines on the right side of the face and the strong, dark accent under the nose introduce a suggestion of light and shadow as a means of revealing three-dimensional form. Here, in the swelling and tapering of the line, there exudes a pulsing life that is inextricably fused with the power of varied and singularly expressive line.

To describe Paul Cézanne's small pencil drawing of Delacroix (Fig. 2-11)—done from a photograph—as "impetuous" is not to imply that the drawing is undisciplined. The foundation tone, or underdrawing, serving as enrichment and support for the superimposed bold, slashing, descriptive darks, is vitally necessary for the life and power of this small drawing. Notice how skillfully he gave form to the left cheek with a quick curve crossed by a number of equally quick diagonals. Cézanne's drawing and Alberto Giacometti's *Head* (Fig. 2-12) share much of the same sense of energy and expression that accompanies the viewer's being able to experience the physical act of manipulating the pencil. It is easy to imagine that Giacometti may have never lifted his pencil from the paper as he "scribbled" his image. The visual excitement of the drawing is indicative of the obvious presence of adrenaline

2-11. PAUL CÉZANNE (1839–1906; French). *Portrait of Delacroix.* c. 1870. Black pencil on white paper, 5 1/2 × 5 1/8" (13.9 × 13 cm). Musee Calvet, Avignon.

2-12. ALBERTO GIACOMETTI (1901–1966; Swiss-French). *Head.* 1946. Pencil, 5 7/8 × 4 1/4" (15 × 11 cm).

2-13. *above, left:* JOHN LUKE
(1906–1975; Irish). *Self Portrait.* Pencil on
white paper, 16 3/8 × 11 1/2″
(41.7 × 29 cm).
National Self Portrait Collection, Ulster
Museum (no. 2526).

2-14. *above, right:* JAMES VALERIO
(b. 1938; American). *Portrait of Tom (Study
for "Tom's Choice"),* 1991. Pencil on paper,
28 1/2 × 13″ (72.5 × 33 cm).
The Arkansas Arts Center Foundation
Collection.

at work in the artist's mind, body, and spirit. Here, the pencil resonated
in the hand of the artist quite differently than it did in either Cézanne's
or Beal's portrait.

The most restrained and traditional of the five drawings so far is
John Luke's *Self Portrait* (Fig. 2-13), in which line and tone are separate
but skillfully integrated. In contrast to the ghostlike implication of the
clothing and only slight interest in the hair, the features of the face, especially the eyes, are delineated with greater detail and with an intensi-
fication of shading done with carefully controlled diagonal hatching.
The effectiveness and expressiveness of the drawing are attributable to
Luke's use of selective emphasis and to his expert handling of the
medium.

Finally, the most involved and labored pencil drawing is James
Valerio's *Portrait of Tom* (Fig. 2-14). Here we see a full-blown repertoire
of graphite handling at its very best, and it is the most complex of the
five portrait drawings. Many of the descriptive uses of graphite and
wide-ranging qualities of line of the previous drawings exist in Valerio's
work, albeit on a highly revised level of refinement.

Project 2.5

Explore some of the approaches to developing lines, values, tones, and textures similar to those seen in Figures 2-8 to 2-14, using a soft pencil to depict subjects of
your own choice. You might find it informative to work with the same subject, or
choose a subject of your own such as a friend who agrees to pose for a portrait
drawing. To break into other subject matter with this same approach, choose something as ordinary as a paper bag and draw it in the manner of each artist. Only Figures 2-13 and 2-14 seem to have been drawn with a well-sharpened pencil, while
the heavier lines of the other three examples suggest the use of a pencil with a

blunted point or, more likely, one in which the graphite was exposed with a knife rather than by a mechanical sharpener. Whether exposed by a knife or a mechanical device, graphite can easily be sharpened to a broad chisel point or to a sharp point with fine-tooth sandpaper (sandpaper sharpening pads are available in most art supply stores).

Project 2.6

The range of graphite from hard to soft is also available in stick form in the soft "B" grades. Try several of the same drawing explorations of the previous project, but substitute a graphite stick for the pencil and see what expressionistic differences occur. This will bring back similar sensations of working with the charcoal sticks, and you will readily discover that the graphite stick can be manipulated in the exact same way as the charcoal stick. Draw by holding the soft graphite stick up on its end, using one of the four flat edges to make a wide line; then roll it slightly and draw with one of the corner points at the end of the stick to produce a narrow line. Finally, lay the stick down on its side to produce wide areas of tone of varying values by exerting different amounts of pressure. Through all of these assignment explorations, you will become aware of the vast array of mark making that can be obtained from each single tool. Artists think of this as an extended *vocabulary of marks*; and the word *vocabulary* in the context of art introduces to us the concept of *visual language*.

Ballpoint and Felt-Tip Pens   The familiar, easy-to-use ballpoint, fiber-tip, and felt-tip pens are capable of producing a variety of line widths. They therefore provide the beginner with a graceful transition from pencil and charcoal to brush and ink. Some **inks** are insoluble; others are water soluble and can be smeared with a wet thumb or a brush with water to introduce a painterly quality.

When directed to draw with any tool that is associated with writing, there is a natural inclination to first draw in outline before considering texture or tone. Feliks Topolski's pen-and-ink drawing *E. M. Forster and Benjamin Britten* (Fig. 2-15) suggests a method, easily duplicated with ballpoint pen, that avoids strict outlining.

inks
Any fluid or semifluid drawing or printing materials that may be used in conjunction with various pens, brushes, brayers, or rollers. They are available in a wide range of colors. Some are soluble in solvents such as mineral spirits and turpentine; others are soluble in water.

2-15. FELIKS TOPOLSKI (b. 1907; Polish). *E. M. Forster and Benjamin Britten.* Pen and brown ink, 9 3/4 × 7 3/4" (24.7 × 19.7 cm). Sotheby's.

2-16. PABLO PICASSO (1881–1973; Spanish-French). *L' Amour Masque.* January 5, 1954. Brush and ink, 12 1/2 × 9 3/8" (31.7 × 23.8 cm). Galerie Louise Leiris, Paris.

Project 2.7

Experiment using ballpoint and felt-tip pens of varying widths, taking full advantage of the unique linear strengths and rich textures these pens produce. The techniques suggested for pencil drawing are easily adapted to this assignment. Thumbing through the book and looking at examples of pen-and-ink drawings will suggest other drawing styles as well. Think of the inherent variety and endless possibilities of visual translation when substituting a pen for a pencil with any subject matter. There are some newly developed drawing pens of high quality available in art supply stores today that were not in use ten to fifteen years ago. Their pigments are permanent, lightfast, waterproof, and fast-drying. They will not bleed on most artists' papers and work especially well for underdrawing on surfaces that will receive watercolor washes. The pens come in black along with a variety of colors and points ranging from fine to wide.

Brush and Ink   Brush and ink demand a certain assurance of execution, since lines and shapes cannot be erased. The bold, fluid lines that result from the free play of brush and India ink give a certain authority to a drawing, and a sense of self-confidence emerges from the deliberate, successful use of the brush. The flexibility of the pointed brush allows for rich variation in lines and their multiple effects. Drawing with brush and ink is immediate and dramatic, and allows for ultimate spontaneity and highly descriptive and expressive occurrences with a wide variety of subject matter.

The choice of line contributes to the expressive character of a brush drawing. The impression of lightness and aliveness in Picasso's brush drawing (Fig. 2-16) results, in part, from the contrast between the long, flowing lines of the figure and the broad, individual strokes of the vegetation. Using an almost weightless line, and without shading, Picasso subtly introduces a sense of volume through the swelling and tapering of the contour line. Notice also the dramatic diagonals created by the contours of the figure within the composition. Our eyes can't help but dance playfully along the contours and diagonals of this light and airy composition.

Hans Hoffman's *Seated Nude* (Fig. 2-17), executed with such directness and force, initially appears to be very different from Picasso's drawing, but going beyond the immediate visual impact we become aware of strong similarities, most noticeable by comparing Picasso's winged figure of Love with the left arm of Hoffman's figure. Looking deeper, we see that the physical act of manipulating the brush to produce long continuous lines looping about and changing direction is nearly identical. Hoffman's line that begins at the elbow, sweeps over the shoulder, curves across the upper chest, and ends with a swirling line at the chin imparts a certain delicacy to an otherwise blunt, graceless, and seemingly immovable figure.

Considering the large size of Henri Matisse's *Nude with Black Fern* (Fig. 2-18), the thinnest of his lines are at least equal in thickness to the heaviest black brush strokes in the much smaller Picasso and Hoffman drawings. In fact, there is much less distinction between line and brushed shapes in the Matisse drawing: everything is primarily broad bold brush work with few subtle variations to suggest volume or light

2-17. *above, left:* HANS HOFFMAN (1880–1966; German). *Seated Nude.* c. 1935–1940. Brush and India ink on paper, 11 × 8 1/2" (28 × 21.6 cm.). Chrysler Museum.

2-18. *above, right:* HENRI MATISSE (1869–1954; French). *Nude with Black Fern.* 1948. Brush and ink. 41 1/4 × 29 1/2" (105 × 75 cm.). Musee National d'Art Moderne, Paris.

and shadow. In contrast to the fragmented, frenetic patterning of light and dark introduced by Hoffman, Matisse has deliberately layered dark against light against dark to define space.

These three drawings remain essentially two-dimensional because of the domination of pure black and white and the absence of internal modeling. Matisse, in *Nude in a Folding Chair* (Fig. 2-19), breaks away from two-dimensionality, suggesting volume by introducing modeling within the figure and thereby creating a three-dimensional illusion. Furthermore, Matisse creates space by combining broad areas of tone with linear patterns to produce a variety of different values along with interesting painterly effects. The textural patterns and more descriptive suggestions of modeling are done with a fully loaded brush. The ink flows most easily and fastest just after the brush has been newly charged with ink. There is also a subtle, but nonetheless true, element of variation that results when the brush is used with varying amounts of downward pressure. The greater the downward pressure, the wider the line as the brush even bends as it courses across the paper. The lesser the downward pressure, the thinner the resulting line will be. The absolute thinnest line is produced when the longest hairs of the brush, at its very point, delicately touch the surface.

Project 2.8

To commence drawing, dip your brush in India ink and then press it against the side of the bottle neck to remove excess ink and create a point by slightly swirling the brush hairs against the bottle as you lift it out. Begin by exploring the different kinds of lines you can make with the brush—lines similar to those illustrated, lines that change from thin to thick and back to thin by increasing and decreasing the pressure with which the brush is applied to the paper. Practice this several times, keeping your hand, wrist, and arm relaxed and take full advantage of the springing action of the brush against the paper surface. Observe the results created by gently bouncing the brush while dragging it over the paper.

Your first attempts may seem hesitant and awkward and forced. Gradually, your attempts will become more refined and descriptive in a gesture-producing way. There is much to be gained from the wet drawing media in terms of spontaneity and fluidity. As you begin to feel more comfortable with the brush, you will also begin to develop the control necessary to give meaning and expression to the subject matter of your brush drawings.

2-20. EMIL NOLDA (1867–1956; German). *Harbor.* c. 1900. Brush and ink, 323 × 465 mm.
© The Art Institute of Chicago.

Project 2.9

Make a number of drawings of the same subject or object using different kinds of lines for each drawing. Repeat individual drawings until you are satisfied that the quality of the line is effective and controlled. A good test is to ask yourself whether you would find the drawing interesting if someone else had done it. Next, do a group of drawings that will allow you to introduce solid and broken areas of tone and shape. Note the contrasting visual effects of the solid and broken shapes with the line variation in your drawings. How do they enhance and support each other visually?

Dragging a less-than-fully loaded brush lightly across a piece of drawing paper, especially one that has some texture or tooth to it, produces an irregular or broken brush stroke known as **drybrush,** which is useful in creating tonal and textural effects. In Emile Nolde's *Harbor* (Fig. 2-20), the drybrush passages begin to soften the harshness of the pure black

drybrush
The irregular or broken brush stroke effects of ink that ultimately diminish, created by dragging a less-than-fully-loaded brush lightly across a piece of drawing paper—especially one with some surface variation or high degree of tooth.

2-21. GERBRAND VAN DEN EECKHOUT (1621–1674; Dutch). *A Boy Lying Down.* Rijksmuseum, Amsterdam.

and to establish a sensation of atmosphere, space, and even reflections in this wonderful and powerful composition.

Project 2.10

To produce drybrush effects, wipe excess ink from the brush on paper toweling or a clean rag before dragging the brush lightly over the paper. Also try loading the brush with ink and drawing a vertical line through the paper. Then quickly remove excess ink from the brush and with quick horizontal strokes, drag the brush in a perpendicular direction over and through the vertical line. Notice how the semidry brush picks up and redeposits the ink from the still wet vertical line at right angles to the vertical line. Observe how the amount of ink quickly diminishes on the paper as the brush moves further away from the wet line.

The tonal effects in Figures 2-19 and 2-20 were created with full-strength black ink. Gerbrand van den Eeckhout (Fig. 2-21) has diluted his ink with water proportionally to create a wide range of light-to-dark wash values. In his drawing *A Boy Lying Down,* created exclusively by brushed applications of ink wash, we see a beautifully descriptive work of high spatial complexities and definition of form all within the human figure as it reclines before us. The variations of value within the tones are achieved by working back into the still-wet areas of the clothing particularly in the blanket draped over the left arm and in the low-cast shadow on the wall to the right of the figure. There are also areas where the wash was allowed to dry completely before later washes were added. Notice how delicately the artist has described the scarf sash around the figure's neck and the ribbing of folds in the sleeve of the right arm supporting the head. As the artist progressed with this brilliant work, there evolved a deeper and more profound expression of the fabric life and weight of the blanketed, clothed figure. This adds a high degree of definition and volume to the drawing.

Project 2.11

A simple still life of light objects placed against a middle-value background and lighted from the side, as in Project 2.2, would be an appropriate subject for the first experiments with ink wash drawings. Plan carefully as you view the lights and darks of the still life; find the positions of extreme lights and use the open white paper to represent those lightest areas of the composition. Keep the shapes and washes as simple as possible while still being descriptive yet spontaneous. Limit yourself to three to five grays plus black and white. At first, and as you are learning to control the medium, allow each wash to dry before adding the next to prevent them from bleeding into one another and negating individual values.

Summary

It is not important if the exercises done for the assignments in this chapter are not of exhibition quality. If you did more than a single drawing for each assignment, you probably began to experience, perhaps only in a limited sense, that practice contributes to the gaining of competence and control. Above all, remember that you have begun to speak a personal visual language with fine art tools. How far you take this language is up to you. But the rudiments of these techniques and the explanations of these drawing tools presented in this book will serve you well as a reference guide for your future endeavors in drawing.

Further explorations into the uses of media and technique will elaborate on these preliminary experiences. Other approaches to drawing and other techniques will be examined throughout the remaining chapters of this drawing text; Chapters 10 and 11 discuss various media and their uses.

3 Learning to See

[T]here's something that's very intense about the experience of sitting down and having to look at something in the way that you do in order to make a drawing or a painting of it.

By the time you've done that, you feel that you've really understood what you were looking at . . . and somehow it becomes a method of possessing the experience in a unique way.

—Robert Bechtle

The most fundamental discipline involved in drawing is learning to record what one sees, which contrary to popular misconceptions is not primarily a matter of manual skills. In fact, the physical requisites for drawing are minimal: average sight and average manual dexterity. The well-worn adage "seeing is believing" is well suited here since drawing is a matter of seeing and seeing deeply with both the physical eye and the "eye of the believing mind." There is a distinct difference between the physical eye and what it sees and the inner eye and what it envisions, and yet the two most often work together in a seamless symbiosis. But more important, successful drawing requires that one have the will to *extract an image* from a subject, and that this extracted image be self-sustaining, no longer needing its source. It has little or nothing to do with 20-20 vision and deft fingers, but rather, it is a process of internalizing form, then releasing that form in a new and uniquely translated tangible state—the physical state we call "a drawing."

Basically, a person who can look at an object, analyze the relationships of size, shape, value, and texture, and then create an analogous set of relationships on paper as a graphic record of those visual perceptions has made a drawing. Learning to draw necessitates learning to see in a new, more penetrating way. It is essential that we learn to see through all our senses rather than simply looking with our eyes alone. Seeing comes before speaking, and from earliest childhood our hands, our bodies, and most of all our eyes—placed in our swivel-pivoting heads—appraise objects in terms of their three-dimensional character and our relationship to them in space. This is how we recognize them and know their distinctive qualities. Consequently, rather than looking at the object and drawing only what can be seen, the beginner frequently draws according to a preconception or remembrance of the object—and often cannot see the difference between the preconceived and the actual object.

When we commence to draw, we are surprised to discover the degree to which any object, except a sphere, presents a different appearance each time we change the position of our eyes in relation to it. Since actual spatial depth is absent from the surface of the drawing paper, three-dimensional reality must be interpreted as a two-dimensional pattern. *Descriptive drawing is an illusion.* Therefore, much of learning to draw consists of discovering how things *appear* rather than how they are, and it is not until we begin to draw that most of us realize the tremendous difference between what we *know* about objects and what we *see*.

Learning to draw, then, demands a reevaluation of visual experience, a new dependence on visual cues about the appearance of objects and their relationships in space. Most of us are familiar with the art of children, which is based upon concepts of how things are—near forms are placed at the bottom of the page, and more distant objects appear higher on the page. Daniel Mendelowitz, the original author of *A Guide to Drawing,* was interested in the psychology of children's perceptions when they looked at the world around them, and as a result, had a keen appreciation for the art of children. In his very first book, *Children are Artists,* he states:

> First the child selects the objects that constitute his world (most of the drawings done by children between the ages of four and six are of human beings). Then these objects are reduced to what constitute the essential elements for the child (a human for a five-year-old is usually a head plus arms and legs). Because the child's range of experience is very limited, many objects are unfamiliar to him and therefore are incomprehensible. The child cannot portray what he cannot comprehend. Studies have shown that a five-year-old can draw a circle best if it has two eyes, a nose, and a mouth in it: the child can understand the circle head but the abstract circle meaning nothing is difficult to understand and therefore difficult to draw.

Folk artist and traditional Oriental artists often employ the same devices for representing spatial depth. Most people in Western cultures, however, readily accept two other concepts relating to forms in space: (1) one object placed in front of another partially obscures the object behind (think how you shift your head in a movie theater to prevent the relatively small head immediately in front of you from obscuring most of the giant screen); (2) objects appear to diminish in size when seen at a distance. In Jan Matulka's still life (Fig. 3-1) the effect of overlapping shapes is evident, but no significant diminishing in size occurs because the space depicted is so shallow. In contrast, the deep exterior space in Henri de Toulouse-Lautrec's *The Laundress* (Fig. 3-2) results in extreme discrepancies in size relationships judging from what the viewer knows to be the actual size of the subjects. Although the basket the woman carries is indeed large, it does not approach the size of the carriage at the left, and yet the two shapes are drawn as measurably equal in size. The head of the laundress appears to be as large as the carriage behind her on the right, and twice the size of the full figure

3-1. JAN MATULKA (1890–1972; Czech-American). *Still Life with Guitar, Pears, Wine Pitcher, and Glass.* c. 1925. Charcoal, 18 × 12″ (45.7 × 30.5 cm).
Susan and Herbert Alder Collection.

perspective drawing
The systematic method of representing and describing forms as they appear to recede in space through the use of converging lines that meet at a central vanishing point located on the horizon line. Also, the depiction of forms as they appear to the eye relative to distance or depth.

foreshortening
A term that applies to organic and anatomical forms seen in radical perspective, as in the portrayal of lines being shorter than they actually are, in order to create the illusion of correct size-and-shape relationships in space.

farther to the right. While those comparisons refer only to the relative size of shapes drawn on a flat sheet of paper, it is precisely because the artist was thinking in terms of shapes, rather than heads and carriages, that he was able to transform a two-dimensional surface into the illusion of three-dimensional space. Without careful comparison of the size relationships as observed, the beginner probably would draw the individual forms in some other scale and sacrifice the powerful illusion of deep space.

Perspective, Foreshortening

The considerable difference in size of things of the same measure in Toulouse-Lautrec's drawing and the converging of what are assumed to be the parallel curbs of the narrow street are aspects of **perspective drawing,** which relates to the changes that occur in the appearance of three-dimensional forms—specifically, geometric and architectural objects—when seen from a variety of viewpoints. Drawing in perspective can be accomplished by following a system of rules (see Chapter 9). **Foreshortening,** the term that applies to organic and anatomical forms

3-2. HENRI DE TOULOUSE-LAUTREC (1864–1901; French). *The Laundress.* 1888. Brush and black ink, with opaque white on cardboard, 30 × 24 3/4″ (76.3 × 63 cm). Cleveland Museum of Art.

seen in perspective, such as the horse in Figure 3-2, depends on the careful observation of overlapping shapes and diminishing scale rather than on a set of rules.

PROJECT 3.1

The perspective of simple rectangular forms can be introduced by making some drawings of a sheet of paper. The sheet will appear as a perfect rectangle only if held vertically at eye level or placed flat on a table and viewed directly from above. In any other position it becomes a rectangle seen in perspective and requires a non-rectangular shape.

As you draw the sheet in a number of different positions seen from varying viewpoints, do not think of it as either a sheet of paper or a rectangle. See it simply as a shape enclosed within four straight lines—lines that sometimes appear to be parallel, sometimes appear to converge. Though you know the actual shape and proportions of the rectangle, draw just what you see, even when what you know to be the narrow width of the rectangle appears to be much greater than its length. You will become aware that visual analysis of a geometric shape is unrelated to determining the exact dimensions of the object; it is a matter of establishing relative proportions. A more systematic development of perspective will be undertaken in Chapter 9.

3-3. CHARLES WHITE (b. 1918; American). *Preacher.* 1952. Ink on cardboard, 21 3/8 × 29 3/8″ (54.3 × 74.7 cm). Whitney Museum of American Art.

Charles White's *Preacher* (Fig. 3-3) demonstrates the exaggerated foreshortening that occurs when a person is viewed at close range. Giovanni Paolo Lomazzo's study in foreshortening (Fig. 3-4) poses the figure somewhat theatrically well above the eye level of the viewer, as determined by the line defining the ledge on which he stands. If the full shapes of the bottom of the feet were shown, it would also be possible to read the drawing as a man lying down, which would establish the viewer's eye level as above the figure. This points out the importance of providing all the visual clues necessary to ensure a correct reading not only of forms in space but also of our relationship to those forms. In constructing his figure, Lomazzo simplified the arms into blocks. The head, trunk, and legs suggest anatomical features superimposed over a geometric substructure—imagined if not actually drawn.

Just as the rectilinear sheet of paper assumed different shapes when seen at different angles, so do all other objects. Consider a leafy plant or a simple branch with several leaves. A tracing of a single leaf pressed flat will provide one description of the leaf, but one having little to do with its actual appearance and as it exists in space (Fig. 3-5). As similar as they may be in size and shape, no two leaves will be seen as the same shape, nor will any single leaf retain the same appearance when viewed from a different angle, as demonstrated in Project 3.1 with the sheet of paper. Drawing the complex undulations of large leaves involves a careful analysis of the twistings and turnings of foreshortened forms in multiple directions toward, to the side, and away from the viewer. The emphasis is on seeing as deeply as possible—seeing more intensely than one has ever seen before. Most drawing mistakes occur from not looking intently at the model and not seeing its well-kept visual secrets. If we draw what we think the shape should be rather than what we see, our intellects are working against our eyes and we have defeated the purpose of truly seeing. Our physical eyes tell us what we see, our intellects tell us what we think we see—and these can be at war with each other in the creative process. Experienced artists use their physical eyes to give them accurate and highly detailed information. The inner eye—the eye of the soul—then, if desired, embellishes the information given by the physical eye. This is called expression, and at this stage, has nothing to do with intellect.

PROJECT 3.2

Take a branch with three or four leaves on it—magnolia, avocado, or maple leaves are excellent. Draw the cluster of leaves from several different angles, noticing the constantly changing relationships of shape, size, and proportions. Remember that it is most important to base your drawings on visual analysis. Draw exactly what you see with the abiding sense that you are seeing accurately and deeply. As thoughts creep in of what you know about leaves and what you think they should look like, immediately disregard those wanderings and focus back on what you actually see! You will discover that you produce more accurate descriptions of the forms selected by steadfastly attending to the lines, shapes, and proportions than by thinking about drawing leaves.

CRITIQUE (Project 3.2)   Compare your drawings to the corresponding actual positions of the leaves and branch. How accurately have you portrayed the actual visible reality of the subject? Did you have difficulty focusing on what you saw instead of what your intellect told you to see? If so, try the same exercise several more times, continually changing the position of the object until the pure act of seeing becomes more natural. It is extremely important that you develop a sense of confidence in relying upon your physical eyes to give you accurate and complete information. This sense of confidence will occur and grow with practice.

3-4. GIOVANNI PAOLO LOMAZZO (1538–1600; Italian). *Foreshortened Nude Man with Arms Uplifted Looking Up.* Pen and brown ink, 7 1/2 × 4 3/4" (19 × 12 cm). Art Museum, Princeton University.

3-5. ELLSWORTH KELLY (b. 1923; American). *Five-Leaved Tropical Plant.* Pencil on paper, 18 × 24" (45.8 × 61 cm). Collection John Berggruen Gallery.

Mechanical Aids to Perception

A rectangle drawn in simple perspective without reference to anything else appears simply as a four-sided shape. Leaves drawn as a clump take on an identity, whereas one leaf drawn in isolation with an unembellished contour line might appear simply as an interesting irregular shape. In their singularity of form, neither shape provides any particular visual interest; however, it is the ability to abstract the object, be it rectangle or leaf, to a new shape and draw that *extracted shape* accurately that is the basis of representational drawing, no matter what the subject.

In the last two projects you were directed to base your drawings of the rectangles and leaves on careful visual analysis of shapes. In the critique of Project 3.2, you were asked to compare your drawings with the actual visual realities of the objects drawn. You should be interested in discovering how accurate your visual analysis and subsequent drawings are. With the leaves, deviations would be relatively unimportant. It is important, however, to adopt the attitude that "it needs to be right" in order to fully develop the discipline of seeing accurately. Once you have developed the ability to masterfully draw what you actually see, you will then be free to choose how you actually want to draw.

There are some simple methods for checking the accuracy of your previous drawings, methods that will play an increasingly significant role as you are challenged by more complex forms. Although the ultimate goal is to develop the eye, mind, and hand coordination, there are a number of simple mechanical aids that can help ascertain size and shape relationships and help determine the correct position or angle of a line. Sometimes such devices help to guide initial judgments at the start of a drawing; they also help to identify mistakes throughout the process of drawing.

The use of these aids will be discussed in relation to John Singer Sargent's *Reclining Nude Figure* (Fig. 3-6). While the foreshortened view of a reclining figure is a complex shape, the apparent clarity and simplicity of Sargent's drawing attest to his enviable visual acuity. Yet it is important for the beginner to notice that in spite of the artist's legendary drawing and painting skills, the drawing reveals faint traces of adjustments that were made in determining proportions and positions. These faint, visual vestiges of altered line and tone are referred to as **pentimento** (because the artist "repented," or changed his mind). At close examination we see that the right leg was longer, the right foot longer at the heel, the left leg shorter at the knee, the right buttock fuller, the head either wider or positioned farther to the side, the right elbow lower with a line suggesting that the arm was originally in a different position. Sargent perhaps made all those changes based solely on direct observation, or possibly he extended his arm to its full length and sighted along his stick of charcoal to determine critical vertical and horizontal alignments and to establish correct proportions. And what of the remaining faint lines that were deliberately altered? These are to be regarded as evidence of the creative process and not as mistakes. They were necessary in the ultimate establishing of correctness. Furthermore, with regard to the vulnerability of the human hand engaged in the act of drawing, this pentimento adds richness and authenticity to the finality and wholeness of the work of art. It is vitally important to understand that these vestiges, these remembrances of line, cannot be faked or con-

pentimento
From the Italian meaning "to repent," a subtle or radical revision made by an artist when he changes his mind, or *repents* during the execution of a drawing, painting, or print. The vestiges of the previous image, whether totally concealed or not, either become more apparent through the fading of the outer surface, or have remained apparent and bear evidence of the abandoned creative intent.

3-6. JOHN SINGER SARGENT (1856–1925; American). *Reclining Nude Figure.* Charcoal on paper, 24 1/2 × 19" (62.2 × 48.3 cm). Wadsworth Atheneum.

trived for the sake of adding richness to a drawing—because, for an artist or student to do so is grossly inauthentic and has nothing to do with the *birthing act* of drawing. But the "changes of mind" that the artist goes through in order to achieve "rightness" come as part of the natural struggle inherent in any genuine creative process.

Certain poses and gestures are frequently employed to identify particular activities. To mimic an artist at work, one has only to choose one eye and sight along an upright thumb extended at arm's length. In truth, this gesture depicts one of the most useful aids to perception. It is an action that even the most experienced artists employ to great advantage, especially during the preliminary stages of drawing, painting, and printmaking from life. Figures 3-7 and 3-8 illustrate how to hold a pencil to check critical vertical and horizontal alignments. Held in the same manner, it also serves as a measuring device to determine proportional relationships.

Vertical and Horizontal Alignments Leonardo da Vinci, who examined and commented on everything having to do with drawing and painting—and almost everything else as well—included the following instruction in one of his notebooks: "To draw a nude figure from nature, or anything else, hold a plumb line in your hand to enable you to judge the relative position of objects." Leonardo specified drawing from life, from an actual form existing in space. Successful figurative artists would all agree that there is no substitute for drawing from life. Looking at a drawing or at a reproduction of a drawing is not the same thing as looking at and studying the live model because the eye works in an entirely different way. When looking at a live model, the eye perceives forms as they exist in either shallow or deep space. When you look at a drawing or its reproduction, a three-dimensional form has already been flattened out into a series of marks on a two-dimensional surface.

3-7. Held in a vertical position, a pencil serves as a plumb line to determine vertical alignments.

3-8. Held as a true horizontal, a pencil helps to determine horizontal alignments.

However, because of the masterful way in which Sargent creates the illusion of three-dimensionality describing the volumetric aspects of the live figure on a two-dimensional surface, it would be easier for a beginner to make a successful copy of the Sargent drawing than to do a successful drawing of a live figure in the same pose, since the beginner does not yet know how to create illusion. Furthermore, there would be no value in introducing a photograph of a model in the same pose as the basis of discussion, because that, too, would be a flat representation, also lacking the heightened three-dimensional quality of Sargent's drawing. Making a copy from an already existing drawing or photograph is two generations removed from the live form and would not be considered an original drawing. Also, the element of struggle to find the "rightness" of the three-dimensional form would not be present—certainly not in an authentic and professional way.

Your immediate assignment is to visualize a model before you. He appears to recline on a flat surface, the upper body arched and slightly elevated on pillows, the left knee held a little higher than the right as it drops over the edge of the platform. Though all of that is observable in the model and can be made evident in the drawing, that is not what you would set out to draw. Instead, you would begin to find alignments, both vertical and horizontal, between a series of points on what just happens to be the body of a man. Although you are urged to think only of the shapes rather than of the body, the following discussion will be clearer if the parts of the body are referred to by name.

In Figure 3-7 the pencil, used as a plumb line, allows you to begin to establish vertical alignments that will determine where to begin blocking in the figure. Make sure the entire length of the figure from top to bottom falls within the length of the vertical pencil. You will immediately notice the visual elements of the figure that align themselves vertically. These vertical relationships can be thought of as the established givens with respect to the particular position of the figure. Once you've established the outer contour of the figure on your paper according to the established givens of the plumb line, place a pencil or straightedge vertically against the drawing and move it slowly from left to right across the drawing, noticing how things line up one above the other. (Check your drawing for accuracy against the plumb line of the vertical pencil held up once again over the figure and make any appropriate corrections.) Looking at both Figures 3-7 and 3-8, we can find several good examples of triangular-shaped alignments. First, the legs of the folding chair give us strong directional lines with which to align other elements of the figure. The two parallel legs that are in line with the back of the chair also run parallel to the right side of the torso. Notice the two adjacent triangles with their longest sides touching (forming the middle vertical) that together form the shoulders, chest, and stomach areas down to the point where the left buttock meets the chair seat. The center vertical line that separates the two triangles is parallel and to the left of the vertical plumb line. In Figure 3-8, the point of the left heel is in direct vertical alignment with the left hip joint and the left armpit, and also splits in half the downward contour line of the left shoulder. Notice also in Figure 3-7, the equilateral triangle formed by the left leg with its left side not only parallel but synonymous with the vertical plumb line, and the other equilateral triangle formed by the right arm with its right side parallel to the back of the chair. When no alignments exist, the plumb line and the horizontal line allow you to determine whether one form appears to the left or right, or above or below the adjacent forms.

The pencil held in true horizontal position (Fig. 3-8) makes it possible to ascertain whether that detail should be drawn above or below some other feature. Above or below refers to placing a mark higher or lower on the page. There are two implications that can be drawn from the form's position on the page—distance from the viewer and elevation. The head, drawn highest on the paper, is farthest away, but by being connected to the figure is not elevated; the figure's left knee, although drawn higher on the page than the right knee, is nearer the viewer than all of the torso and is higher in actual space than the seat of the chair. The assumed crooked right wrist with the hand hanging downward is higher than the invisible left wrist, and closer to the viewer.

In addition to checking vertical and horizontal alignments, it is also possible to get a sense of the correct angle of a line or form by judging the degree relative to vertical or horizontal, as we touched on in our analysis of the triangles in Figure 3-7. Another approach is to locate and connect the points of termination of the major diagonal lines. For example: the angle of the lower leg follows a line connecting the figure's left knee to a point at the bottom of the imaginary vertical middle line; projecting a line from the same knee upward to the established midpoint provides the relative angle for the shape that becomes the left leg.

Proportional Relationships   In spite of what we actually see, it is startling to discover how much our perception, unchecked, is influenced by what we know about an object—it is a form of built-in prejudice and it is hard to let go of the power of that influence. When we know that in physical reality one dimension is greater than another, our natural inclination is to draw it that way, being convinced that we also see it that way. Developing the habit of using the pencil as a measuring device to establish relative proportions is one of the most important aids in learning to see—thus learning to draw.

Looking again at Figures 3-7 and 3-8, you might have difficulty in determining the proportion of height to width of the overall figure or of its individual parts, or in determining the relative sizes of shapes. Holding the pencil horizontally at full arm's length and allowing the tip of the pencil optically to "touch" the outer point on the left of the figure, you can mark the overall width of the figure on the pencil by moving your thumbnail to the point corresponding to the extreme right point of the figure. Being certain to keep your thumbnail in place on the pencil, turn the pencil vertically to see how close the height is to the width. What is calculated and measured as height is an imaginary vertical line that corresponds to the distance between a horizontal line drawn at the bottom of the toes of the right foot and one touching the exact top of the head, which as you view the figure is naturally above everything else. The height is just slightly greater than the width. Remember that consistent measurements depend on holding the instrument at arm's length, since any change in distance between the pencil and the eye destroys the accuracy of the measurement. Also, closing one eye eliminates double vision. Having established the overall proportional relationship of height to width, you can begin to determine the size and placement of major subdivisions. The bottom of the buttock is just below the midpoint vertically; horizontally the halfway mark occurs exactly where the curve of the thigh ends and the hip line begins, and also at the leftmost point of the left heel. Extending the two midpoints of the vertical and horizontal measurements places the midpoint of the overall image at the inside point of the left elbow. It is very likely that without measuring, most people would believe the midpoint to be higher and to the left.

Measurements and alignments need not be pinpointed down to fractions of an inch, nor do they have to be plotted out completely and with absolute precision on your paper. Although described as mechanical aids, they need not be adhered to rigidly. Their purpose is to provide assistance and guidance in establishing the approximate correct size, proportion, and shape relationships and in determining the placement of the shapes.

PROJECT 3.3

"Drawing without drawing" is an activity that requires no actual drawing materials, just your eyes and your finger as a substitute for a pencil to check vertical and horizontal alignments and make measurements. You simply take advantage of free moments wherever you are to look at things around you. Use your finger or thumb, or combination of fingers and thumb from both hands, to determine size and shape relationships, check angles and relative positions of above and below and right and left, and visualize how you would draw them.

PROJECT 3.4

If you do not have a model available to you, or if you would rather practice first using a similar inanimate object, a straight-back wooden chair would prove appropriate. Place it in front of you in a number of different positions: facing you, turned away from you, sideways, at an angle, on its side, turned upside down, and tilted. Note how the size and shape relationships between its parts change with each new and different position. Use your pencil and thumb in the manner described to locate and align major points, to determine correct angles, and to estimate relative proportions.

When you begin to feel comfortable using the pencil as an aid in perceiving the chair, do a number of drawings of the chair in various positions, letting your pencil serve you both as measuring device and drawing instrument. Objects of even greater complexity can be depicted with amazing accuracy when the pencil is used to search out the essential visual clues. You will be pleased at how well this simple method of measurement will assist you and your eye in quickly establishing an overall structure and correct placement of forms.

Proportional Rectangles   Any single form or group of objects can be drawn in correct proportion by first drawing a rectangle that corresponds to the maximum height and width of the subject (Fig. 3-9). Lightly sketch a rectangle of that proportion on your paper and connect the four right angle corners of the rectangle with two diagonal lines. Divide the rectangle into quarters by adding a vertical and horizontal line through the point where the diagonals of the rectangle intersect. Locate the midpoint of the subject to determine what part of the subject fits into each section of the rectangle. Block in the major shapes—the main structure—before getting involved with details. If the subject is complex, individual quarters can be subdivided with diagonal or vertical and horizontal lines.

Fitting objects into proportional rectangles requires that you study each form carefully. Again the emphasis is on *seeing* intently, and drawing objects as the shapes you *see* rather than as specific, identifiable

viewfinder
A flat, rectangular, usually black cardboard sheet with a cut-away center in the shape of a square or rectangle through which one looks to frame a composition. It functions the same way as a viewfinder apparatus in a camera.

positive line, shape, form
Established line, shape, or form that serves as the subject of a drawing and carries the intended visual dominance or subject meaning of a composition—whether representational or nonrepresentational. In figure-ground relationships it is defined by its opposite negative shapes.

negative space or area(s)
In figure-ground relationships, the spaces or areas surrounding the positive shapes that may also be referred to as ground, empty space, field, or void space. The negative spaces cause the positive shapes or forms to project forward, creating a three-dimensional illusion within a composition.

things. Drawing the shapes well is evidence of seeing well and results in more accurate representation.

3-9. Use divided proportional rectangle to block in major shapes.

Defining Forms with Negative Space

A **viewfinder** created by cutting a small square or rectangle opening in a piece of lightweight cardboard or stiff paper serves as another aid to perception. It can be used to study vertical, horizontal, and proportional relationships, and if cut to the same proportions of the drawing paper, it can be used like the viewfinder of a camera to *frame* a composition. If taped to something transparent, such as Plexiglas or clear acetate on which a grid has been drawn, it can be used in a manner similar to that of a divided proportional rectangle.

Another function is illustrated in Figure 3-10, in which the viewer is held at a distance that permits the entire object (**positive shape**) to be seen through the aperture. By allowing the object to fill as much of the square as possible, it will be necessary to let the object touch the edges of the opening. The **negative space** (the shaded areas that surround the object) become defined as closed shapes between the outer edges of the aperture and the contour edges of the object. Often it is possible to draw an object more correctly by delineating the negative space rather than the object itself, since an artist generally has fewer understood concepts about the shape of the surrounding space as compared with what is known about the object.

3-10. A simple viewing square cut from black cardboard or stiff paper enables the artist to see vertical, horizontal, and proportional relationships, and permits analysis of negative space.

PROJECT 3.5

Cut a two-inch square (five-centimeter) opening in a piece of black cardboard or stiff paper of at least 8 1/2 × 11 inches to use as your frame (black because by contrast the viewed object will appear more luminous). Look through the viewer at a

3-11. EGON SCHIELE (1890–1918; Austrian). *Organic Movement of Chair and Pitcher.* Pencil and watercolor, 18 7/8 × 12 1/8" (48 × 31 cm). Albertina, Vienna.

chair placed in a number of different positions. Do a drawing of the negative spaces—which, as mentioned above, are the areas left between the edges of the open square and the contour of the chair. Then, draw as shapes the internal spaces of the chair between the rungs, legs, stretcher bars, and any other openings. Even a simple wooden chair provides an excellent exercise in drawing, since it consists of a number of parts of varied shapes. It is also something extremely familiar to us yet poses a variety of different forms: geometric but not strictly geometric, subtle but not as subtle as anatomical or organic forms. Therefore, to be able to see it and reduce it to a mere group of shapes, irrespective of what we know or think about how it should look, is a positive advancement in learning how to see and draw. For additional drawings, arrange the chair so that it is viewed from an unusual angle—tipped on its side, turned upside down, or rotated to an unfamiliar position. Manipulating its position, or for that matter the position of any object, heightens aspects of seeing by posing unconventional visual possibilities. An unconventional view of objects is well demonstrated in Austrian artist Egon Schiele's pencil and watercolor drawing *Organic Movement of Chair and Pitcher* (Fig. 3-11).

PROJECT 3.6

As a variation of the previous assignment, and to get more involved with the drawing materials and an increase in scale, use masking tape to tape an 18 × 24-inch sheet of Strathmore or Rives BFK drawing paper with a moderate amount of tooth (do not use a slick-toothed paper) onto a hard surface such as your drawing table or a portable panel of masonite. Make sure the tape runs around the entire perimeter of the sheet and is pressed down firmly. With a soft, compressed charcoal stick lying on its side, darken the entire surface area of the drawing paper right to the taped edge by rubbing the charcoal stick with considerable pressure. With a piece of chamois hide, rub the charcoal further into the surface until you've created a rich black rectangle. Select one of your previous chair studies, or select a new position with the same chair, and with a white plastic eraser begin to erase the shape of the chair in the dark field, creating a light positive image against the dark negative space. You need not worry about erasing the shape of the chair back to the original white of the paper; instead, allow some of the marks resulting from the erasing activity to remain in the drawing as tonal, even textural, elements. The chair will dramatically emerge out of the darkness as a powerful three-dimensional illusion on the paper's flat surface. This illusion is a vital visual presence.

Make several of these drawings over a period of time to improve your seeing skills to the point of producing more accurate proportions of the chair form in space.

3-12. JAKE LEE (1915–1991; Chinese-American). *Boatyard.* Brush and ink, 5 × 7″ (12.7 × 17.8 cm).
Collection Dolores Pharr Smith, Stockton, California.

CRITIQUE (Project 3.6)   The four critical visual elements at work in these drawings are (1) the breakup of the picture plane into interesting positive and negative shapes; (2) the contrast of lights and darks between positive and negative shapes; (3) the tonal richness of the erased or subtracted positive forms; and (4) the increased degree of interest, even mystery, evoked by the black negative shapes that create a push/pull effect with their positive counterparts. How effectively have you dealt with each of these elements as a means of strengthening your visual effects? Is the breakup of space interesting? Are the contrasts between the lights and darks dramatic? Is there visual richness in the erased areas? Do elements of both positive and negative shape simultaneously and or interchangeably advance and recede?

The process discussed in Project 3.6 is exemplified in Jake Lee's *Boatyard* (Fig. 3-12). Notice again the increased degree of mystery and drama evoked by the different black negative shapes, except that in this drawing several of the dark negative shapes function as both positive and negative elements. While far more complex than the chair in Figure 3-10, the drawing utilizes the same concept of defining forms by delineating the space that surrounds them. The picket fence, the foreground boat, the post and beam framework of the shed are positive shapes defined by the bold dark patterns of the surrounding negative space. The power pole, the shadow side of the boat and the shadowed areas of the shed, as well as the cast shadows on the ground, are seen as dark shapes in white negative space.

Once again we see the alternating patterns of light against dark and dark against light create an effect of three-dimensional space.

Negative space also plays a significant role in the drawings and paintings of Fairfield Porter. *Study* (Fig. 3-13) might appear at first glance to be a sheet of six separate landscape sketches in which one is uncertain whether Porter has drawn shapes or spaces. When the viewer becomes aware that the intervals between the individual parts are the window frames of a screened porch, what seemed to be negative space is transformed into positive shapes. The drawing defines both indoor and outdoor space, and a very noticeable shift in focus is necessary to move from interior to exterior. It is almost impossible to see foreground and background at the same time. Even though there is no variation in the line or any attempt to create space through the use of light and dark, once the notion of space is suggested, it cannot be ignored. If, however, you choose to overlook the clues such as the ends of the roof beams that cut notches into the tops of the upper rectangles, and think of the panels as drawings or prints hanging on a wall, everything, including the landscapes, becomes a three-dimensional illusion on a flat surface and no refocusing is required.

3-13. FAIRFIELD PORTER (1910–1975; American). *Study.* Ink on paper, 13 1/2 × 10 1/4″ (34.3 × 26 cm). Whitney Museum of American Art, New York.

Right Brain, Left Brain

Using a pencil or any other implement for measuring and as vertical and horizontal guides, using a cutout rectangle or square as a viewer and grids to clarify relationships of parts, and focusing on negative spaces to define positive shapes are valuable aids to perception because each activity isolates seeing and drawing from knowing and identifying. What is drawn becomes the result of perception (seeing intently), rather than conception (thinking intellectually). A drawing's beauty, poetry, and expressive impact collectively form the visual language that transcends the logic of human reason. When art emerges as the inaudible language of the soul, a situation of visual intrigue is captured and suspended in time. It is the extraction of an image from a subject that transcends the subject itself and creates this sought-after state of visual intrigue.

As a teacher of drawing, Betty Edwards, author of *Drawing on the Right Side of the Brain* (J. P. Tarcher, Inc., 1978), was puzzled as to why some students found it easy to draw when for others it was difficult, and why certain drawing activities produced better results than did others. The answer, she was convinced, related to different methods by which the two hemispheres of the brain process information—the left brain controlling verbal and analytical processing, the right brain controlling that which is intuitive, spatial, and relational, all that is part of visual processing, of seeing/perceiving.

In her classes, and in her book, Edwards provides drawing experiences that tap into the special functions of the right hemisphere of the brain. For some people the mental shift into what Edwards calls "right-mode" happens automatically; they are the persons who draw easily. For others, the process can be learned. The various activities that have been discussed in this chapter as aids to perception are all part of the process. They are methods that experienced artists use, part of what Edwards describes as "the magical mystery of drawing ability."

Seeing—More Than Physical Sight

From this chapter we've learned that seeing is a multifaceted activity and certainly involves more than just the penetration of an object with our physical eyes. However, the kind of seeing required of artists is not exclusive to artists alone, nor do all artists see to the depth that perhaps they should see when conceptualizing and making art. The revision author, as artist and teacher, is convinced that there are several types of seeing modes that people engage in, either naturally or otherwise. First, there are those for whom the gift of seeing is inherent in their makeup and they have exercised this ability since early childhood. Second, there are those who understand the need to see artistically and have been trained to see beyond their natural abilities. Finally, there are those people who do not have the ability or the desire to see any differently. They have trouble believing that the world around them is an environment of visual language. They see what they see and sincerely believe in the absolutes of what their physical eyes tell them—there is nothing beyond the concrete, physical object that they can prove the existence of by merely holding it in their hands. This is hollow expression.

However, life is filled with rich potential for both tangible and intangible forms of expression, and mysteriously, but not surprisingly, the arts respond to these facets of life. The artist's main expressive tools are *seeing* and *sight,* and they can be comprised of either natural or learned ability, or both. The physical eye assesses and establishes the rudiments of compositional structure, along with formal technique, which is what has been discussed in this chapter. Then, the eye of the mind (soul) intercedes, penetrates, and prevails in places uninhabitable by the physical eye alone.

Often, it is those who have not had much exposure to the arts who eventually experience an epiphany in which a sunset, the wistful fragrance of violets, a particular passage of music, or a work of art stirs and transports them to where they have never been before. To be caught up in a moment of startling awareness, even to be overtaken by an unexpected impulse to respond in some way that is completely out of character for us is a remarkable thing. When this happens to an artist, the artist's perception is established as the impervious catalyst of an ensuing creative force, unaffected by our negligence of it and immune to critical words and disbelief.

The point is that everyone is capable of being moved by something visual, whatever it may be and whatever his or her level of exposure is to the arts. The fine arts reach places in the human being where no other catalyst reaches, and often, the activity of drawing is the first, certainly the most direct, symptom of some stimulating occurrence that successfully tugs at the heartstrings of the once artless personality. When we encounter what we cannot verbally explain, we draw it—we communicate it in a way independent of words, and the artist's audience receives it in silence—after all the words have been spoken and their meanings exhausted, for words are of no use at a certain point in the process of perceiving, creating, and interpreting a work of art.

This chapter closes with a poem written by Lisel Mueller entitled "Monet Refuses the Operation." In this imagist poem, the French Impressionist Claude Monet is confronted by his eye doctor, who is convinced that Monet needs eye surgery in order to correct what the physician feels are flaws in his painting. Keep in mind that Impressionist painting, as a movement in the art world in the latter half of the nineteenth century, was bucking the established aesthetic standards of the day. The name *impressionism* itself came from a painting by Monet exhibited in 1874, catalogued as *Impression Sunrise.* According to the physician, the deviation in Monet's painting from the accepted standard of ultrarepresentational art was something Monet could not help because of the assumed eye impairment. He simply could not paint well because he could not see well, thought the well-meaning doctor. It had not occurred to the physician that Monet's creative path had led him to paint deliberately in a still unknown style that often blurred images instead of striving for intricate detail in a hyperrealist or classicist fashion. It is important to point out that Monet had also allowed his inner eye to begin to speak and play a role in the creative decision-making process of his painting, as evidenced by Monet's reply to his doctor in the poem.

This poem is fictitious; nonetheless, it makes a clear point about the difference between the domain of *physical sight* and an artist's *inner vision*—or the paradox that the physical eye and the inner eye are antithetical. The physician believed in the concrete world—the world of the absolute where only those things that could be held in the hand and proven to exist had significance, and he had never considered the possibility of anything felt or perceived through the senses other than those over which logic and reason prevailed. The act of creating is an act of faith, and faith is antithetical to logic and reason. Therefore, the intellect, by itself, would never have come to any conclusion other than one based on total absolutes.

MONET REFUSES THE OPERATION

Doctor you say there are no haloes
around the street lights of Paris
and what I see is an aberration
caused by old age, an affliction.
I tell you it has taken me all my life
to arrive at the vision of gas lamps as angels,
to soften and blur and finally banish
the edges you regret I don't see;
to learn that the line I called the horizon
does not exist and sky and water,
so long apart, are the same state of being.
It was fifty-four years before I could see
that the Rowen Cathedral is built
of parallel shafts of sunlight,
and now you want to restore
my youthful errors: fixed
notions of top and bottom,
the illusion of three-dimensional space,
wisteria separate from the bridge it covers.
What can I say to convince you that
the Houses of Parliament dissolve
night after night to become
the fluid dream of the Thames?
I will not return to a universe
of objects that don't know each other,
as if islands were the lost children
of one great continent. The world
is flux, and light becomes what it touches,
becomes water, lilies on water,
above and below water,
becomes lilac and mauve and cerulean lamps,
small fists passing sunlight
so quickly to one another
that it would take long streaming hair
inside my brush to catch it!
Our weighted shapes, these verticals;
burn to mix with air
and change our bones, skin, cloths
to gases. Doctor if only you could see
how Heaven pulls earth into its arms
and how infinitely the heart expands
to claim this world, blue vapor without end.
                                —Lisel Mueller

4 Copying, Sketching, and the Power of Influences

I have always, undoubtedly for a number of reasons, wanted to copy and taken pleasure in copying, either from originals, but above all from reproductions, every work of art that touched my feelings or stirred my enthusiasm or just interested me particularly.

—Alberto Giacometti

The Tradition of Copying

When artist Mauricio Lasansky came from Buenos Aires to New York City in 1943 on a Guggenheim Fellowship, he spent most of his time at the Museum of Modern Art looking at every print in the collection to learn about the field of printmaking. He felt the only way he could develop his technical vocabulary, as well as his insights into what the artists were thinking, feeling, and trying to express, was to look deeply at their work. There were, at that time, over 150,000 prints in the collection, and it is said that he studied every one of them.

In reading what artists say about their own work, one is struck by how much they acknowledge looking at, being influenced by, and learning from the work of other artists. Contemporary American painter Wayne Thiebaud credits most of his training to reading about artists and studying reproductions of their works in library books. He explains that art history remains a primary source for his paintings, and he acknowledges that he continues to make copies of paintings and drawings in order to learn from them.

Copying, in its various forms, is a legitimate activity, not for the purpose of imitation, but as a means of learning—learning to see, learning about styles and techniques—as well as stimulating the imagination through experiencing the expressive spirituality in the work of other artists. During the Renaissance, drawings existed primarily as preparatory studies for paintings and as patterns to be copied by apprentice artists as part of their training. It was not until the sixteenth century that drawings came to be considered works of art to be collected. At that time monarchs and wealthy families, usually of the aristocracy, began amassing impressive collections of drawings, but their collections were generally inaccessible except to those artists directly favored with their patronage. Museums and galleries as we know them did not come into existence until the early nineteenth century. Today, we are all the benefactors of this cultural facet of our society in that we do have access to the viewing of thousands of works of art, both historical

copying
The exact imitation of the drawings of the old masters strictly for the purpose of learning to see, learning technique, and learning about styles. The view is widely held that the most beneficial learning about drawing occurs from having as direct an experience of emulating the old masters as possible.

52

4-1. REMBRANDT VAN RIJN (1606–1669; Dutch). *Copy of Leonardo da Vinci's "Last Supper."* Red chalk on paper, 14 × 18 1/4" (35.6 × 46.3 cm). The Metropolitan Museum of Art, New York.

and contemporary, in public museums and commercial galleries. In addition, we have unprecedented access to art through reproductions in books, catalogs, and periodicals. There has never been more art reproduced in print than exists today, and we tend to forget how difficult it was in the past for artists to see and study masterworks with the convenience and regularity that we enjoy today.

During the seventeenth century, the only place where Rembrandt was able to see and study masterworks was in auction houses. At the age of fourteen, he was sent to Leyden University and soon afterward became a painter's apprentice. Three years later he moved to Amsterdam, where under the tutelage of Pieter Lastman he learned Italian *chiaroscuro*. He was fortunate in that Amsterdam had become the world capital for trading art and that many major Italian collections were sent there to be sold. Rembrandt went to auctions not just to look but also to buy. Kenneth Clark describes him as an "eager and extravagant" collector, explaining that "certain works of art were absolutely necessary to him. He needed to possess them not simply to enjoy them, but to learn from them." Whenever he could not afford to buy, he made sketches of pieces that interested him. Clark, in tracing Rembrandt's debt to the Italian Renaissance, notes that "all great artists have studied the work of their predecessors and borrowed from it, if they felt the need." Rembrandt, for example, knew Leonardo da Vinci's *Last Supper* from engravings and made various studies based upon that work (Fig. 4-1).

4-2. *above left:* EDGAR DEGAS
(1834–1917; French). *Sketch after Ingres's
"Bather."* 1855. Pencil on paper, 6 × 4 1/8"
(15.2 × 10.5 cm).
Bibliotheque Nationale, Paris.

4-3. *above right:* BARTOLOMMEO
PASSAROTTI (1529–1592; Italian). *Copy
after Michelangelo's "Dawn."* Brown ink
and red chalk, 17 3/8 × 11 1/2"
(44.1 × 29.2 cm).
The Nelson-Atkins Museum of Art,
Kansas City, Mo.

Nineteenth-century French artist Edgar Degas described his own art as "the result of reflection and study of the great masters." Like Rembrandt, Degas was an avid collector. His interest was focused primarily on Ingres, Delacroix, and Daumier, whom he regarded as the "three best draftsmen" of the nineteenth century. He owned 20 paintings and 90 drawings by Ingres, 13 paintings and 190 drawings by Delacroix, and 6 paintings and drawings, plus 1,800 lithographs, by Daumier. Degas made direct copies of the works he admired (Fig. 4-2) and frequently introduced ideas adopted from other artists' work into his paintings as an act of tribute.

It is important to distinguish between the benefits of copying for the sake of learning and copying in order to enhance or build upon an artist's idea through reinterpretation—as both of these activities are prevalent, meaningful, and essential in the art world. Copying for the purpose of learning the artist's technique must be done in such a way that the actual and perceived spirit of the artist is tapped into as much as is possible by the one attempting to copy. Experiences and perceptions revolving around a common subject vary greatly among artists and make it all the more challenging to attempt to copy a masterwork. Nonetheless, one must try to relive the situation as closely as possible in order to understand the original artist's creative experience both technically and conceptually. If this fails to occur, the creative experience as well as the resulting product is diminished. In essence, one steps into the artist's shoes.

Ancient and Renaissance sculpture, in the original or in plaster replicas similar to those still found in art schools, introduced the human figure to countless generations of art students and provided them with acceptable standards for "noble physiques" and "eloquent poses." Bartolommeo Passarotti's *Copy after Michelangelo's "Dawn"* (Fig. 4-3) shows particular interest in the left foot of one of the sculptured figures from the Medici tombs in the Church of San Lorenzo in Florence. Passarotti's drawing technique is patterned after that of Michelangelo (Fig. 14-5). In a similar manner, when Eugène Delacroix made studies of two pairs of legs and an arm from a painting by Rubens (Fig. 4-4), he employed a vigorous pen technique sometimes used by Rubens himself.

Looking at a drawing done from Greek sculpture, it is interesting to identify Giacometti's free-flowing, searching analysis of the exaggerated and complex movement of *The Laocoön* (Figs. 4-5, 4-6).

4-4. *top:* EUGENE DELACROIX (1798–1863; French). *Study after Rubens.* Reed pen and ink. © The Art Institute of Chicago.

4-5. *above, left:* ALBERTO GIACOMETTI (1901–1966; Swiss-French). *The Laocoön* (Vatican Museums, Rome). Ballpoint pen on paper, 8 1/4 × 11 1/2″ (20.9 × 29.2 cm). Collection Louis Clayeux, Paris.

4-6. *above, right:* AGESANDER, ATHENODORUS, AND POLYDORUS OF RHODES. *Laocoön Group.* c. 150 B.C. Marble, height 8′ (2.44 m). Vatican Museums, Rome.

Giacometti copied from everything, tracing lines with his fingers when he had no pen or pencil in hand. He explained that in the evening and during periods of waiting he would open art books at random and make copies. For him, copying was a means of clarifying his knowledge about what he was seeing, not by a slavish line-for-line duplicating of the work or the photograph, but by feeling form, rhythm, and placement with his, pen, pencil, or finger.

Rico Lebrun's *Study from Goya's Portrait of Maria Luisa* (Fig. 4-7), taken almost directly from Goya's *Portrait of Charles IV and His Family* in the Prado, and John Piper's very similar ink-wash value study of Giorgione's *Tempest* (Fig. 4-8) both offer an analysis of the use of light and dark as an important aspect of pictorial composition.

The well-worn adage "art comes from art," is certainly true and validates the power of influence that is both universally generated and felt by artists in the creative disciplines throughout history. Furthermore, whether one is an artist, art student, or audience member, the power of inspiration takes us deeply into the source of that inspiration. Therefore, copying, both as a means of learning and as an expression of admiration for another's work is common practice in all the creative arts. It is perhaps the most apparent in music, where composers throughout history have learned and been inspired by studying the works of their predecessors and contemporaries, sometimes introducing themes from works they admire into their own compositions. Performance artists often acknowledge not only their teachers but also other artists whose styles they have studied.

Most writers will admit to the necessity of learning the rules of grammar, while stressing that you learn to write by studying what others have written. A much-heralded event in the world of fiction was the 1991 publication of the sequel to *Gone with the Wind,* fifty-five years after the famed novel was published and forty-two years after the death of its author, Margaret Mitchell. When Alexandra Ripley was selected to write the long-awaited sequel, she prepared for the task by copying lengthy sections of the original novel in longhand, explaining that she did so to get a better sense of Mitchell's style than could be gained by numerous rereadings of the book, even though her intention was not to imitate the earlier writer.

The purpose of copying, as discussed in this chapter, is to provide an understanding of how someone has done something, rather than to produce a duplicate of what that person has done. However, in the case of appropriating an exact copy for purposes of artistic restatement, as a matter of ethics, the appropriating artist must acknowledge the original authorship. In other words, even the most convincing facsimile must be acknowledged as a copy because to misrepresent it as anything else is unethical and will destroy the integrity of the artist's intention and restatement.

Copying Activities   Each of the drawings illustrated in this chapter thus far represents an aspect of copying, but not one of them is an exact copy, nor are you encouraged to attempt to copy any drawing line for line. It would be appropriate and beneficial, however, to practice drawing in the manner of some of the many examples reproduced in this book, which have been selected to acquaint you with a variety of creative uses of media and techniques, and to introduce you to different approaches to handling form, composition, and subject matter. In doing

4-7. RICO LEBRUN (1900–1964; Italian-American). *Study from Goya's "Portrait of Maria Luisa."* 1958. Pen and brush, black carbon ink, and watercolor on white paper, 25 × 18 15/16" (63.6 × 48.2 cm). Worcester Art Museum.

4-8. JOHN PIPER (b. 1903; English). *Copy of Giorgione's "Tempest."* 1952. Black ink and gray wash over purple crayon on white paper, 15" (38 cm) square. The Fogg Art Museum, Harvard University, Cambridge.

so, you will begin to gain an understanding of why an artist chooses a particular medium with which to work. Every medium has its own inherent expressive qualities that the trained artist recognizes and selects specifically in order to produce a desired effect. When an artist chooses several different media to work with in the same drawing, he does so in an effort to produce a multiplicity of effects, as evident in Figures 4-7 and 4-8, where Rico Lebrun and John Piper use both wet and dry media to produce their gloriously rich compositions. Again, the emphasis is on "seeing," and naturally, copying activities require that you look closely and see deeply in order to recognize how the various drawing media blend to form their unique and even eldritch effects. This begins to touch on the subject of mixed-media drawing and how it offers up a unique set of expressive circumstances. Mixed media will be discussed in Chapter 18.

Along with this text, use other art books and museum catalogs as well to study and broaden your pictorial vocabulary of the vast history of drawing. In the process of looking, seeing, and copying, do not allow yourself to become intimidated if your drawings do not exhibit the same mastery of media and technique—it is highly unlikely that they will, at least at first. Keep in mind that what you are looking at has been generated only through years of discipline and hard work that eventually enable an artist to acquire a high degree of skill and mastery over not only the subject but the media as well.

Looking at reproductions, however, is a poor substitute for studying original works. Try to see original drawings whenever possible. If it is not convenient to copy directly from them, make a mental picture of them by studying them line for line, detail by detail, as you would if you were making a copy directly on paper.

The Tradition of Sketching

The late-nineteenth-century French painter Gustave Moreau stunned his more conservative teaching colleagues at the École des Beaux-Arts in Paris by sending his students, including Henri Matisse, into the streets to observe and sketch life around them. While it might not have been deemed an appropriate academic procedure, sketching in the streets was certainly not a new concept. Just as artists throughout history have copied, so too have they done quick drawings from life, frequently in the streets and in the marketplaces where people gather. Here they acted as visual reporters witnessing and recording everyday occurrences. The images in these marketplace drawings came directly from sketches, or from mental sketches if pencil and paper were not readily available.

An artist whose work illustrates the daily myriad of human activity in the marketplace is Pieter Brueghel the Elder. The seven compositions of his series *The Seven Virtues,* although highly abstract, portray surroundings familiar to people of his day. The pen and dark-brown ink drawing entitled *Prudentia* (Prudence) (Fig. 4-9), done in 1559, illustrates the layered density of the artist's mind. Whether the images are derived from sketchbooks or mental pictures and recollections, they find merit in the complex orchestration of Brueghel's marketplace scenes. As a visual composer, Brueghel was a progenitor of a variety of potent theatrical treatments of his main characters. In the drawing *Prudentia,* he embellishes both the common and uncommon in the context of an everyday scene depicting the chores of life: harvesting, butchering, storing, and repairing, even tending to the sick and elderly as we see in the middle right-hand side of the composition.

 Reminiscent of Pieter Brueghel the Elder is David Driesbach's engraving *The Everyday Occurrence* (Fig. 4-10), which in similar fashion exemplifies the collective array of street and marketplace activities that produce rich and varied statements of form and space within the composition. These fictitious accounts of human interaction recall motifs from much earlier periods in art history, although, metaphorically, they occur today with as much unpredictability as in the past. Driesbach chose to freeze this imaginative frame of improvised activities to reflect his own personal symbolism. In his work, the marketplace serves as the

4-9. *top:* PIETER BRUEGHEL (1525/30–1569/70; Flemish). *Prudentia (Prudence).* 1559 Pen and dark-brown ink on paper. Musees Royaux de Beaux-Arts de Belgique. Koninklijke Musea voor Schone Kunsten van Belgie, Brussels.

4-10. *above:* DAVID DRIESBACH (b. 1922; American); *The Everyday Occurrence.* 1973. Engraving on copper printed on white wove paper, 23 3/4 × 35 3/8" (60.3 × 90 cm). Collection courtesy of David Faber.

CH. 4 Copying and Sketching **59**

main stage of daily activities where everything appears to be in motion simultaneously. As in Brueghel's drawing, the characters in Driesbach's engraving seem to be engaged with, yet strangely unaware of, each other. Upon viewing it, one begins to anticipate the unexpected within the incidental, everyday occurrences of this energized and highly symbolic composition. The revision author of this book was a student of the artist, and he remembers the ease with which his professor engraved on a copper plate using a burin as if it were merely a pencil on paper. For his work *The Everyday Occurrence* there were no preliminary sketches, but only mental pictures generated from the artist's imagination. He started with the man wearing the top hat seated at the table in the lower left-hand corner—meant to be a self-portrait. Uniquely, every subsequent image in this engraving radiated outward from the self-portrait as if coming directly from Driesbach's imagination or recollection, and was sliced into the copper with all the mastery and skill of an improvisational film director working on his set.

Human activity provided the emotional force behind the drawings of crowded street scenes, and often the artist worked unobserved. For instance, the denizens of Union Square in New York City—unemployed men standing and sitting about in the street during the Depression, young working women perched on stools in drugstore soda fountains— became the unsuspecting models of Isabel Bishop. For drawings such as *Men, Union Square* (Fig. 4-11), she was forced to work rapidly before the men altered their poses.

Sketchbooks   Leonardo da Vinci suggested: "You will be glad to have by you a little book of leaves [pages] . . . and to note down notions in it with a silverpoint . . . when it is full, keep it to serve your future plans, and take another and carry on with it." Leonardo's "little book of leaves," what we refer to as a sketchbook, is one of an artist's most important tools. As Leonardo indicated, a primary purpose of the sketchbook is collecting information and recording ideas, either jotted down quickly or explored and developed more fully, depending on the occasion. A second purpose of perhaps greater importance, particularly for beginners, is that the ongoing activity of sketching helps train the eye and the hand. Degas did as Leonardo directed. Preserved in the Bibliotheque Nationale in Paris are thirty-eight of Degas's notebooks containing more than 2,000 pages of sketches, studies, and copies.

A sketchbook can be of any form—bound, spiral, a loose-leaf binder, even loose sheets carried in a folder or envelope. While some sketchbooks are manufactured with quality drawing paper that can be used with a variety of media, an adequate and inexpensive substitute is a bound or spiral notebook with blank pages, commonly available in college bookstores. The obvious advantage of a bound or spiral book is that both eliminate the problem of losing individual sheets. A disadvantage of a bound book is the inevitability of wanting to discard one or more pages and not being able to. A sketchbook, however, is not meant to be a book of finished drawings with the book itself being considered a work of art. Anyone looking through the pages of Degas's notebooks immediately perceives that he did the drawings only for himself, yet in spite of the inclusion of bad drawings, false starts, and seemingly meaningless doodles, the collection represents a remarkable record of creative activity.

4-11. ISABEL BISHOP (1902–1990; American). *Men, Union Square.* Pencil on paper, 12 1/2 × 12 3/4″ (31.8 × 32.3 cm).
Courtesy Midtown Galleries, New York.

sketch
A drawing done quickly with minimal or no elaboration but that may use scribbled lines or tones to suggest form, texture, and shadow.

Approaches to Sketching The term **sketch** generally implies a drawing done quickly with minimal or no elaboration, using scribbled lines and tones to suggest form, texture, and shadow. Sketching successfully requires that one have the ability to see quickly and clearly, to concentrate and make judgments—to glean only what is essential from a particular subject or scene.

The activity of sketching is essential for both amateur and professional artists in collecting and recording information. The regular practice of sketching contributes to continuous development, so that in time the response of the hand to the eye becomes spontaneous. Frequent sketching does for the artist what daily workouts do for the athlete—it not only keeps the artist's eye and hand in shape, but also strengthens the artist's ability to see and understand form. But sketches are of little value as reference unless the lines, shapes, and forms have meaning. George Luks, a member of the early twentieth-century "Ash Can School" who depicted the turbulence and vigor of life in New York City, achieved an amazing degree of energy in his *River Junkmen* (Fig. 4-12). In this sketch, he captures effects of light, sound, texture, movement, and space, using only soft graphite and zigzag lines seemingly drawn without taking time to think too consciously, but instead feeling the subject and space instinctively. Jim Westergard's sketch of an aerial view of the Canadian Prairie, *Trespass* (Fig. 4-13), depicts a sense of light, depth of field, atmospheric airiness, and deep pictorial space accentuated by the increasing scale change of the footprints coming toward us as if made by an outdoorsman in the snow.

Rembrandt's *Three Studies of Women, Each Holding a Child* (Fig. 4-14), sketched directly with a fast-moving pen, reveals that clarity of concept is not dependent on completeness or detail. Even without drawing full figures, the artist presents a strong sense of life and human caring. As an intended bonus, Rembrandt includes a sketch, full of character, of a bearded man in a large fur hat. The incongruity of the different subjects of the man and three women perhaps indicates that Rembrandt's attentions were divided between two concepts. Nonetheless, the pages of artists' sketchbooks are often visually interesting because of their composite nature—their multiple, singular concepts forming compositional complexities on a single page. In the mind's eye, however, one can see that the lone figure of the bearded man might work well by itself and that the drawings of the three women without the man could form an equally interesting but entirely different composition. Regardless of his intent, Rembrandt's drawings were done mostly on individual sheets that he filed according to subject for later use in his painting and prints.

Somewhat similar to Rembrandt's example of a group of separate sketches assembled on a single sheet is Picasso's *Scene de Bar* (Fig. 4-15). The various studies are related only in that, as the title indicates, they depict figures observed in a bar. Individual heads and figures are placed wherever space is available rather than to establish a composition. Although it is barely definable, in the center of the page Picasso suggests what appears to be a tangled party of inebriates struggling to hold each other upright. The figure in the lower right corner is indicated in a very simplified manner, while the woman at the left is defined with greater detail and individuality. Picasso maintained a daily routine of sketching as evidenced by the 175 sketchbooks discovered following his death in 1973. As with many of the old masters, sketching was for Picasso as important and sustaining an activity as anything else he did in life.

The Camera as a Tool   It is unfortunate that in the twentieth century the camera came to be accepted as a kind of substitute for the sketchbook. It is true that the camera is useful in gathering and recording information, which was traditionally a function of the sketchbook, but its inventors never intended the camera to replace an artist's need for the

4-14. REMBRANDT VAN RIJN (1606–1669; Dutch). *Three Studies of Women, Each Holding a Child.* Pen and brown ink, 7 3/8 × 5 7/8″ (18.7 × 14.8 cm). Pierpont Morgan Library, New York.

4-15. PABLO PICASSO (1881–1973; Spanish-French). *Scene de Bar,* page of studies. c. 1900. Conté, 5 × 8 1/8″ (12.7 × 20.6 cm). Courtesy Christie, Manson & Woods, Ltd.

4-16. JEAN FRANÇOIS MILLET
(1814–1875; French). *Morning.* Black crayon
on paper, 6 3/4 × 10" (17.1 × 25.4 cm.).
Louvre, Paris.

visceral activity of seeing, understanding, and drawing. However, the camera, albeit far advanced from its earlier days, has established itself as a ubiquitous tool in all fields of the fine arts, and in particular, photographic processes of all kinds have come to be of great assistance to visual artists in widening their scope of media involvement. The camera, as a tool, should no longer be regarded a threat to the act of drawing, for it has become an important means in the making of art, not strictly a means to an end, as traditional artists once might have feared. The camera is "art friendly" and has enabled artists to reach greater heights, especially in the areas of scale manipulation. As we forge deeper into the twenty-first century, we can expect photographic technology to afford artists even more advanced methods of manipulating imagery, but none of this takes the place of the joy, the sensation, or the power inherent in the act of drawing.

What a camera cannot do is perform a second function of much greater value to the beginning artist—that of training the eye, mind, and hand. It is precisely that training, gained through years of sketching, which permitted Jean François Millet, in his crayon sketch *Morning* (Fig.4-16), to suggest the strong, steady, yet graceful movement of the donkey with lines, some tentative and searching, some direct and assertive, some not even drawn. The effectiveness and beauty of the sketch lie in the skill and sensitivity with which he responded to the moment of vision with the appropriate choice of lines. Even though awkwardly drawn, the stride of the figures provides an interesting visual contrast to that of the animal. It seems unlikely that a drawing done from a photograph of the same grouping would have produced so satisfying an image—a testimonial to the fact that an artist needs to witness life in order to capture its essence. This is often where photographs fall short.

4-17. HENRI DE TOULOUSE-LAUTREC (1864–1901; French). *Vintages a Celeyran.* 1883. Pen and ink, 9 3/8 × 13 3/4″ (23.8 × 34.9 cm.). Musee Toulouse-Lautrec, Albi.

Toulouse-Lautrec lived at a time when cameras and photography were becoming popular and sometimes used photographs as a source for his work (Figs. 14-29, 14-30), but he also sketched obsessively. According to one writer, "He had a sketchbook everywhere he went, and his pen or pencil was always running in nervous fluid lines through it, or on any other surface that was handy. . . ."

Defining Style through Sketching   Individual artists evolve their own style or styles of sketching by sometimes using different techniques, depending on the subject being depicted and the medium used. Many artists are drawn to a particular medium that seems right or comfortable to them and through which they can display their virtuosity by working with a particular motif or subject. This marriage of individual strength and mastery of skill decidedly enhance the subject, causing it to reach newfound, even sublime, heights of translation or reinvention. The translation of an image through an artist's channels often establishes an indelible relationship between artist and subject matter, as in the case of Pablo Picasso (Fig. 2-16) or Philip Pearlstein (Fig. 5-14), where the image of the human figure becomes readily identifiable as a result of the authentic, technical handling of the figure by each artist. Style, the ever-changing and elusive gown that works of art wear, is what separates the look of one artist from that of another. In decided contrast to the quiet, gentle mood created by Millet, Toulouse-Lautrec's *Vintages a Celeyran* (Fig. 4-17) depicts energy and power with a pen line equal in strength and intensity to that of the straining animals.

Sketches are not intended to be highly detailed, finished drawings, and yet they exude a remarkable amount of information that may, at times, surpass that of a highly detailed drawing because of the infinite power of line energy, as exemplified in Toulouse-Lautrec's work (Fig. 4-17). The degree to which individual sketches are developed is determined by time limitations, the purpose for which the sketch is intended, and the amount of information needed. There is little doubt that Charles Movalli's shorthand-like landscape notation (Fig. 4-18) represents for him a more vivid visual experience than would a photograph of the scene. While Theodore Rousseau's *Forest Landscape* (Fig. 4-19) provides only a summary indication of shapes and masses, his years of accumulated experience as a landscape painter would allow him to extract the necessary information from such a simplified sketch. Rousseau's sketch, however, might well seem useless to someone such as Thomas Cole, one of America's first important landscape painters. Cole would hike into the beckoning wilderness with a sketchbook in his backpack to make highly detailed drawings, including written statements and notations, for paintings to be done in his studio during the winter months (Fig. 4-20).

4-20. THOMAS COLE (1801–1848; English-American). *Maple, Balsam Fir, Pine, Shaggy Yellow Birch, White Birch.* 1828. Pencil, 10 3/4 × 14 1/2". (27 × 37 cm.). Detroit Institute of Arts.

4-21. JOHN SLOAN (1871–1951; American). *Sketch for "McSorley's Bar."* 1912. Pencil, 6 × 6 1/2" (15.2 × 16.5 cm.). Huntington Library and Art Gallery, San Marino, California.

Remember that sketches are not meant to be finished drawings; more often they are merely notations in which an artist records a visual impression of something seen, remembered, or imagined. Often, an impulse to depict something he has seen occurs from deep within the artist. When an experienced artist receives a signal, even on impulse, it is time to act. John Sloan's *Sketch for "McSorley's Bar"* (Fig. 4-21), which was developed into one of his finest paintings, was drawn on two overlapping scraps of paper, apparently all that he could rummage together as he stood at the bar. Perhaps he had never expected to come away from the bar with a potent idea in hand, but the moment took him by surprise and culminated in the birth of a wonderful work of art.

Sketchbooks for artists are like journals for writers. They provide a continuous source of motifs and ideas for compositions as well as an entertaining record of the past. Sketchbooks provide the artist with an ever-growing repository of images, and whenever an artist has the choice of selecting an idea from a host of different possibilities, the concluding choice could be thought of as a "proven concept" that has stood the test of time against a myriad of other images.

PROJECT 4.1

Choose to follow Leonardo's guidance and carry a sketchbook with you at all times and draw in it whenever you have a few free moments, sketching anything and everything—people, animals, things around you that you'd ordinarily not think to draw. Objects that do not seem "artistic" can prove intriguing to draw. Whether it is intriguing or not, draw whatever you see before you. It will eventually become clear that every drawing you do is a learning experience regardless of subject matter.

The more you practice drawing in your sketchbook, the more visually trained your eye will become. As you confront an unpredictable variety of subjects, your eye, mind, and hand will learn to adapt to the different requirements of various subjects that present themselves to you unannounced.

CRITIQUE (Project 4.1) It may seem superfluous to critique a sketchbook, but it is important to consider how the experience of sketching frequently throughout your daily life has benefited you and increased your seeing, your sketching, and ultimately your drawing skills. Has the notion of sketching something unpredictable at a moment's notice become more natural to you? Have you found that you have captured common objects in interesting ways? Do you have a sense that even the act of sketching can endow certain subjects with renewed visual importance, even intrigue?

Line 5

Everyone knows that even a single
line may convey an emotion.

—Piet Mondrian

A line is a dot that takes a walk.

—Paul Klee

Throughout art history **line** has been the most important of all the descriptive graphic elements employed by the visual artist. Line possesses the inherent life contained within any work of art. It is the circulatory system of visual composition. Line can be used objectively to record visual observations and to describe forms in space, or subjectively to suggest, evoke, and imply an endless variety of experiences, conceptions, and intuitions. Line is the visual pathway for the eye to travel along as one looks at art, whether it is a drawing or an etching, a painting or a sculpture. There is almost nothing that cannot be symbolized or reinvented with line. The student learning to draw soon discovers what is involved in assuming control over so powerful a tool.

Line, even in its simplest form, possesses the power to suggest direction and describe contour, define and divide space, and capture motion. It is a highly descriptive force with its varied repertoire of length, width, tone, value, and texture. As soon as a line begins to change direction—to move in curved or angular fashion, to fluctuate in width, and to have rough or smooth edges—its active and descriptive powers increase many times. Every mark made on paper, whether it be a consciously determined line or just a scribble, will inevitably convey something of the maker as well as the subject to the sensitive observer. It is therefore possible for the viewer to conclude that Robert Blum's lively, energized sketch of the painter and teacher William Merritt Chase (Fig. 5-1) is as revealing of the temperament of the artist as it is expressive of the nature of the subject. We see the power of line in an entirely different way in Jasper Johns's drawing *Flag, 1955* (Fig. 5-2), where again a revelation of the temperament of the artist is evident, but in this case line is used to describe the flag in an unconventional

line
The pathway of a moving point; the trail of deposited material or a scratch resulting from dragging a drawing tool or stylus over a surface. A line is usually made visible by contrasts in value or surface.

5-1. ROBERT BLUM (1857–1903; American). *William Merritt Chase.* Pencil on buff paper, 6 3/4 × 4 1/2" (17.2 × 11.4 cm).
Collection of Paul Magriel. The Arkansas Arts Center Foundation Collection.

5-2. JASPER JOHNS (b. 1930, American). *Flag,* 1955. Graphite pencil and lighter fluid on paper, 8 7/16 × 9 7/16" (21.4 × 24 cm) sight.
© Jasper Johns/licensed by VAGA, New York, N.Y. Collection of the artist. Photo by Harry Shunk.

5-3. REMBRANDT VAN RIJN (1606–1669; Dutch). *Self-Portrait.* Red chalk, 5 1/8 × 4 3/4″ (13 × 12.1 cm). National Gallery of Art, Washington, D.C., Rosenwald Collection.

way. This is a beautiful and sensitive drawing composed entirely of line and the building up of linear density into a formidably descriptive, tonal, and textural presence. Let's look at the use of line once more in the work of Rembrandt van Rijn's *Self-Portrait* in red chalk (Fig. 5-3), where the tonal and textural qualities of line are once again uniquely descriptive. Here the capabilities of the drawing material, the temperament of the artist, and the characteristics of the subject (the artist) come together succinctly as one essential expression.

The Contour Line

Line is a convention that artists use to translate three-dimensional images into visual symbols on a flat, two-dimensional surface. As we observe forms, we do not see lines; we see edges or **contours** of forms that produce lines. As the subject moves or is moved, as the position of the artist as viewer changes in relation to the subject, other aspects of the form and new edges are revealed. Lines that delineate the edges of forms, separating each volume or area from neighboring ones, are termed **contour lines.**

To develop sensitivity and skill at **contour drawing,** the student tries to master an exact and almost unconscious correspondence between the movement of the eye as it traces the precise indentations and undulations of the edge of a form and the movement of the hand holding the drawing instrument. You will find that a pencil or pen will be more responsive and more articulate than charcoal. The development of this faculty of eye-hand coordination is invaluable in all drawing activities because it relies once again upon the penetration and accuracy of sight and seeing. The eye tells the artist what the line should reveal before it is drawn by the hand. In Henri Gaudier-Brzeska's *Standing Female from the Back* (Fig. 5-4), the contour line, at

contour
The outermost extremities or limits of a shape, whether two-dimensional or three-dimensional, as in the skin or shell of an object, form, or volume; contour may be associated with the outline of a subject and may change with different viewing positions.

contour lines
Lines that delineate the very edges of forms and separate each volume, mass, or area from its adjacent or neighboring forms.

contour drawing
Drawing that focuses on capturing in a highly descriptive way the extreme edges of a shape, form, or object, depicting it as separate from its adjacent or neighboring forms.

5-4. HENRI GAUDIER-BRZESKA
(1891–1915; French). *Standing Female
from the Back.* Pen and blue ink on paper,
14 5/8 × 10" (37.1 × 25.4 cm).
The Art Museum, Princeton University
(Acc. No. 48-137).

its most expressive, appears to follow the artist's eye as it perceives the edge of the form.

Project 5.1

Any soft graphite pencil such as 4B or 6B is best for beginning contour drawing because it produces a firm, relatively unmodulated line. Erasing is not encouraged in this assignment because the point of the assignment is not to make proportionally accurate drawings but to produce line drawings of high description. Contour drawings can be made of any object, but geometric forms are not as interesting to draw as irregular subjects such as a shoe or boot, a book bag, a baseball mitt, or your own hand or foot. Strictly symmetrical objects are not good because beginners are likely to be discouraged by the inevitable deviations from symmetry that occur.

Start drawing at some clearly defined point, attempting to work about life size. Look only at the subject, not at your drawing—this is referred to as **blind contour.** Remember that your hand must follow your eye—not the reverse. (If you position the object so that you must turn away from your paper to see it, you will be less tempted to keep glancing at your paper.) This will be difficult at first because looking at your paper will be involuntary and you must break the habit of naturally looking back and forth from subject to paper. Let your eye move slowly along the contour of the form; do not let your eye get ahead of your pencil. Both looking and drawing should be slow and deliberate; speed is not your goal. As your eye moves, follow that movement with your hand and the pencil. Imagine that the exact point of eye

blind contour

A drawing process where the eye is trained to follow the contours of what is being drawn, looking only at the subject, not at the paper. In this process, the hand moves the drawing tool in synchronization with the movements of the eye.

contact on the edge of the form is the same as the pencil point on your paper and that your hand exactly follows your eye movements. Try to respond to each indentation and bulge with an equivalent hand movement. When you come to a point where the contour being followed disappears behind another or flattens out to become part of a larger surface, stop drawing. You may, if necessary, glance back at your pencil and drawing surface to determine another starting point.

You will discover that contour drawings done with minimum reference to the paper often grow wildly out of proportion, but as mentioned earlier, this is not the primary concern; rather, contour drawing is an exercise in coordinating the eye and the hand.

Change the position of your subject and repeat the procedure. Placing objects in other than their usual position and seeing them in a different perspective forces you to look more carefully and to see the object more intimately than before.

Project 5.2

As a challenge and a valuable exercise, close your eyes and draw the object from memory by re-creating the visual and physical sensations. In your mind's eye, see the entire picture plane of the paper in front of you and note through sensation the distance between your hand and the edges of the picture plane. The process of stimulating visual recall is more important than the results. This provides the basis for drawing from memory.

Project 5.3

Do a contour drawing of a more complex form or group of objects—a bunch of bananas, celery, beets, or carrots; a basket with onions or leeks, or other vegetables or fruits of irregular shape. Because it is more important to be drawing than searching for the perfect objects, just draw whatever is readily available to you. Kitchen utensils such as an eggbeater or electric mixer are familiar, inanimate objects that make interesting drawings. Remember that very ordinary objects increase in visual interest when tipped on their sides or seen in other than their customary positions. Why have artists had a long fascination with still-life objects? Because they live with them—they are always around and artists have always had an interest in giving uncommon life to common objects through artistic reinvention.

As you look at your still-life objects, begin with the closest form or the most forward part. Try to draw all around each form or part without looking at your drawing. Draw with long, continuous lines rather than short sketchy lines; do not be concerned about making corrections. The inevitable distortions that will occur might well contribute an expressive character to your drawing. Later you may deliberately choose to select and introduce a similar kind of distortion into other drawings.

Sketchbook Activities

Practice contour drawing in your sketchbook, establishing the habit of looking at the subject rather than at your drawing. Effective drawing depends upon learning to see accurately and deeply. When you are not drawing, continue to practice looking at objects as if you were engaged in drawing them by letting your eye slowly examine every fraction of an inch of contour. Later, try drawing those objects from memory.

Contour and Line Variety

Line variation in and of itself is a powerfully expressive tool. The swelling and tapering characteristics of line command the interplay of spatial relationships as well as descriptive contours. A continuous contour line of uniform width and weight results in a persistently two-dimensional effect. By introducing variations in thickness and weight, you can make a line appear to advance and recede in space. In this sense, line controls the activation of spatial relationships as it describes form in space and establishes the illusion of three-dimensionality of form. Thick and thin lines made from a variety of different drawing materials used with varying amounts of pressure produce varying degrees of dark and light, a key factor in understanding volume. The variations that result from changing the pressure of the hand can be in response to a particular visual stimulus such as a descriptive detail, to a shift in the direction of a contour, or perhaps to an overlapping of forms. The decisions affecting the use of light and dark are artistically provoked with the intent to be visually expressive. Often the subject itself will initiate a certain artistic response; at other times the artist deliberately chooses to infuse the subject with specific, selected linear elements that transcend mere academic description. Let's look ahead for a moment at a more complex and transcendent drawing where the artist made obvious choices using line and line variation in order to enhance, even exaggerate, form. We see this in Peter Paul Rubens's wonderfully composed *Study of Cows* (Fig. 5-5), where the quality of line variation is extensive and hits on a number of different levels of tonal, textural, and even atmospheric effects. In this drawing, Rubens has carried the manifestation of expressive contour line into the interior of the volume of the cows' bodies. There is an undeniable spatial dynamism occurring from form to form within the picture plane, and the lines, like the composition itself, are deliberately strong, highly descriptive, and graceful. Look at the symphony of acutely descriptive linear work in the head, neck, and shoulder region of the largest cow. These levels of complexity will be revisited later in this chapter, but for the moment let's return to the simplicity of line as a descriptive force.

The very act of drawing, involving as it does such factors as varying directions of movements or modifications in hand position, produces thicker and thinner lines. In fact, the overall physical action of the artist's body comes into play and determines the fluidity and gracefulness of line quality. The viewer is very much aware of the physical manipulation of the pen and changing positions of the artist's hand in Philip

5-5. PETER PAUL RUBENS (1577–1640). *Study of Cows.* Pen and ink, 13 3/8 × 20 1/2″ (34 × 52.2 cm). Reproduced by the courtesy of the Trustees of the British Museum, London.

5-6. PHILIP GUSTON (1913–1980; American). *Untitled.* 1966. Ink on paper, 19 × 25″ (48.3 × 63.5 cm). Minnesota Museum of Art, Saint Paul.

Guston's untitled still-life drawing (Fig. 5-6). Aesthetically and conceptually speaking, placing the individual forms so that they just touch or nearly touch adds tension and drama to otherwise ordinary subject matter. Guston has been both selective and deliberate in the choices he made to artfully infuse a common subject with a fresh visual curiosity.

Project 5.4

To explore the use of contour line that varies in width, select a subject that has overlapping forms—a house plant with broad distinctive leaves, leaf lettuce, a bunch of beets or radishes. Alter pressure on the pencil to describe overlapping forms, darkness of shadow, movement in space, weight, and any other aspects of form that can be implied by changes in the width and darkness of line. Vary the pressure on the drawing instrument in accordance with your instinctive appreciation of the importance of each contour, rather than changing line widths in a consciously calculated manner.

Critique (Project 5.4)   Now, in the form of a self-critique, observe the results. Does the drawing seem to hold together as a unit? Are there distinct levels of space described by the darks and lights of line variation? Do some of the darker lines seem to project forward simply by virtue of their profound darkness, or do they recede? Do the lighter, more delicate lines seem to recede because of their translucency, or do they appear to be floating off the surface? It is important to notice that these situations can be different from one drawing to the next, and we may assume or perhaps have been taught that dark lines always recede and lighter lines project. But sometimes the reverse is true. Dark, heavy lines often project outward in a composition simply because of their boldness, whereas light, ethereal lines may seem to drift into the distance, falling back in space. Much of the spatial definition of a composition depends upon the position and placement of these lines within the particular picture plane of a given drawing.

Rembrandt van Rijn and Josef Albers offer two very different and expressive personal approaches to contour drawing. Rembrandt's *Saskia Sleeping* (Fig. 5-7) depicts an intimate moment of quiet observation in the life of the artist through the contours of an intrinsically expressive composition done with pen, brush, and ink. The drawing is highly descriptive and charged with emotion and feeling, and these qualities are

5-7. REMBRANDT VAN RIJN (1606–1669; Dutch). *Saskia Sleeping*. Pen, brush, and ink, 5 1/8 × 6 3/4″ (13 × 17.1 cm). The Pierpont Morgan Library, New York. I, 180.

5-8. JOSEF ALBERS (1888–1976; German-American). *Self-Portrait VI*. c. 1919. Brush and ink, 11 1/2 × 7 3/4″ (29.2 × 19.7 cm). Collection Anni Albers and the Josef Albers Foundation, Inc.

heightened by Rembrandt's efficient use of line. Every line is visually poignant and describes the forms in space in a meaningful way. We observe that, in keeping with Rembrandt's mastery over the medium, there are no extraneous lines. In Albers's *Self-Portrait VI* (Fig. 5-8), we see the efficient use of radically different lines to make a minimum number of strokes, which are highly descriptive. Here Albers selected a bold brush line—the inside and outside edges of which are distinctly different and seem almost a contradiction to the subtle perception of form evident in the drawing. Instead of drawing a contour line of the face, he has actually drawn the negative space that in turn defines the contour of the form. The few strokes of the hair drawn in a more usual manner provide a variation that serves to heighten visual description. We see from this that drawings have greater interest when lines, and the edges they define, receive different treatment.

Project 5.5

If someone you know is willing to be a model, you might feel ready to attempt a contour drawing of the human figure. Be assured that contour drawings can be made from clothed, as well as unclothed, models. If no one is available, be your own model. Sit before a mirror and draw a self-portrait. An arrangement of two mirrors will allow you to see yourself from other than a head-on frontal view. Focus your efforts on creating a sense of volume with descriptive lines that vary in width, weight, and value (the degree of light and dark that will be dealt with in the next chapter). This is an assignment not about achieving an exact likeness but about assessing form and volume in space expressively.

Critique (Project 5.5) As you study your results, do you perceive a sense of shallow and deep space in the composition? Are your limbs positioned in space in a logical way in relation to your torso? Does the drawing portray sensitivity to your likeness, albeit not an exact likeness? Finally, is your line descriptive and expressive?

Lost and Found Edges

When we view forms we do not always perceive visible edges as complete contours, depending on the light the form receives and its relationship to surrounding objects. A strong light falling on a smooth, unbroken surface; overlapping forms of the same or similar value; the turning away of a form—all can result in the disappearance of the separating contour line. The edge becomes lost only to reappear when another condition exists. Leaving out the line when it cannot actually be seen duplicates, in part, the effect that causes the line to disappear. Therefore, omitting a line in a drawing can become a highly useful tool to depict a hot spot or the unanimous convergence of several planes into one. The condition of an absent line, but an implied edge, is a powerful visual force that describes through absence the actual presence of an important contour necessary to complete the form. This begins to be evident in Rene Bouche's portrait of Frederick Kiesler (Fig. 5-9). Departing from simple outline, Bouche produces a splendid example of selected emphasis of features and details that both conveys the thoughtful attentiveness of the sitter and transforms the paper into the light, air, and space in which the form exists apart from the surface upon which it is drawn.

It is also possible to "lose a line" by stopping it short before it passes behind another form, thereby creating a sense of space between forms. Broken or discontinuous contours should not provide a problem

5-9. RENÉ ROBERT BOUCHÉ (1905–1963; Czech-American). *Frederick Kiesler.* 1954. Pencil on paper, 25 × 19″ (63.5 × 48.3 cm). The Museum of Modern Art, New York.

for the viewer because the eye of the mind is perfectly capable of completing the outline.

Project 5.6

Using lost and found edges effectively depends on training your eye to be aware of the conditions that allow a line to disappear and those that demand that a line be drawn. As you look at forms and draw them, notice when an edge seems to disappear. Begin to rely on your understanding of that form to know that the edge, although not visible, is still there. As your understanding of form strengthens, try to determine when you can appropriately leave a line out, knowing that the absence of the line has a powerful visual effect. Furthermore, as you begin to trust your sense of form, you will be less inclined to dispense with lines randomly.

The Searching Line

The approach to contour drawing that has been discussed depends first of all upon the penetrating and accurate ability to see. The artist's eye is then able to carefully delineate form as structure. In any successful work of art, an understanding of structure becomes evident through the subtle nuances of media handling, as portrayed in the pen, ink, and wash drawing by Isabel Bishop, *Waiting* (Fig. 5-10). Notice the tremendously descriptive elements of the contrasting ink lines with their corresponding wash tones. Here we see an extended and masterful visual vocabulary of mark making that purely excites the eye. The sense of weight of the child's head and shoulder resting in the mother's lap is astoundingly real and at the same time highly sensual. The line variation and repeated contours of the child's legs imply there has been recent movement—a shift in the child's position perhaps in a semi-wakeful state—which brings us to consider another technique that encourages greater freedom and spontaneity: the use of a **searching line.** The artist's deliberate use of a searching line is clearly demonstrated in Honoré Daumier's *Man on a Horse* (Fig. 5-11). It is an approach to drawing in which the hand and drawing instrument move freely and quickly across the surface of the paper, either in continuous rhythm or in a series of more broken lines, sometimes following contour, at other times drawing through, around, and across form **(cross-contour)** to find the gesture and major lines of movement of the form. In cross-contour, the contour line has graduated from a primarily external descriptive force to both external and internal graphic pathways for the eye.

Unlike contour drawing with its singularly descriptive outline, the searching line results in a multiplicity of line generally suggestive of energy and vitality. The rapid movement and frequent directional changes produce variations in pressure, line width, and degree of darkness that automatically produce accents plus a feeling of volume. The sincerity of the searching line is another uniquely expressive force. It is not to be construed as undisciplined, meaningless scribbling as the untrained eye might at first assume it to be, but rather it is a fluid, linear gesture that captures and defines form. As a technique for capturing the wholeness of form, it requires that you begin to see, feel, and draw the total experience of that form, rather than isolated details.

Project 5.7

For beginning students the searching line works best with pencil, ballpoint pen, graphite stick, Conté crayon, or chalk. Select any readily available subject. Although

searching line

An approach to drawing in which the hand and drawing instrument move freely and quickly across the paper surface either in continuous rhythms or in a series of broken lines. Sometimes they follow contour; at other times they draw through, around, even across form in order to find the gesture and major lines of movement within the form.

cross-contour

Lines that are drawn through, around, over, under, and across form to find the gesture and major lines of movement within the form.

we are all inclined to want to draw things that interest us, realize that these projects are meant as learning exercises and that the subjects need not be chosen for any particular aesthetic value. Furthermore, try to select subjects that you've never before selected or wouldn't ordinarily choose to draw.

Before you begin drawing, spend some time looking at the object you have chosen. Without stopping to focus on any one part, let your eye roam freely around, through, and over the form. Become conscious of the continual movement of your eyes, and then begin to feel, describe, and draw with just your fingertips, allowing your hand the same freedom of movement. The relaxed movement of both your eyes and hand should be much swifter than the slow, deliberate pace of your initial contour drawings.

When you actually take up the pencil, draw as Giacometti did in his *Laocoön* study (Fig. 4-5), using one continuous line without lifting your pencil from the paper. Look at the object as you draw, glancing at your paper only when necessary. The purpose in drawing without looking at your paper is to develop a direct connection between seeing and drawing, trying not to think about how to record what you see or whether you have drawn it correctly.

Repeat this assignment frequently, eventually drawing the human figure or other living forms. Remember that mirrors allow you to be your own model. Try to re-create the experience of drawing with your eyes closed, as in Project 5.2.

Project 5.8

If possible, visit a park where people are out with their dogs, or a zoo where you have visual access to a variety of living forms. Select an animal to draw both in a stationary position and in movement. Sit and observe the animal for a few moments before drawing. Begin drawing, incorporating the procedures of Project 5.7. You may be tempted to hurry the drawing, not knowing how long the animal will remain posed. Make this necessity to hurry work for you by trying to capture as much information about the form in as little time as possible. You may be amazed at the length of time the animal actually remains posed, but more important, you'll become aware of your increased ability to capture more information in less time the more you practice drawing from life.

5-10. *above, left:* ISABEL BISHOP (1902–1988). *Waiting* (1935). Ink on paper (pen, ink, and wash), 7 1/8 × 6" (18.1 × 15.2 cm). Collection of the Whitney Museum of American Art, New York.

5-11. *above, right:* HONORÉ DAUMIER (1808–1879; French). *Man on a Horse.* Pen and ink, 19 × 17" (48.2 × 43.2 cm). Vincent Van Gogh Foundation, Vincent Van Gogh Musuem, Amsterdam.

The Modeled Line

Artists frequently feel the need to reinforce pure outline or single-line contours with suggestions of modeling, since many subtleties of form cannot be revealed by the single line, even one of varying thickness. There is a natural tendency when drawing to amplify differences in line width by means of additional lines, hatchings, or other graduated tonal values to help describe the complexity of form perceived in the model.

The drawings by Edgar Degas (Fig. 5-12) and Raphael (Fig. 5-13) reveal remarkable similarity in form, concept, and compositional handling, and yet they are stylistically and expressively quite different. Both artists have augmented a degree of lost and found contour with modeling to give the figures greater plasticity. In Degas's drawing, *Three Studies of Manet,* the contour line is almost nonexistent in places while the modeling maintains a delicate boldness and strength. Through tonal and textural variations in his modeling of the figure, Degas has used line to define his subject in space, leaving the viewer with a sense of

5-12. EDGAR DEGAS (1834–1917; French). *Three Studies of Manet.* Pencil on paper.
Reunion des Musées Nationaux/Art Resource, New York.

5-13. RAPHAEL (1483–1520; Italian).
Apollo Playing a Violin, Study for "Parnassus."
Pen and ink, 10 5/8 × 7 7/8" (27 × 20 cm).
Musee des Beaux-Arts, Lille.

the importance of **analytical sight.** Likewise, in Raphael's drawing, *Apollo Playing the Violin,* we see the same precision in the modeling of the figure carried to a slightly higher degree of discipline. In both drawings, the lost and found effects result from giving some contours greater weight and definition than others, as in the more detailed handling of Manet's facial features, beard, and tie versus the more ephemeral handling of his folded hands. We see the same antithetical visual effects in Raphael's figure by simply comparing the areas of high detail with those of lesser definition.

analytical sight

Scrutiny; the impetus for drawing only what the artist actually sees; the opposite of intuitive or instinctive drawing. All works of art are to varying degrees analytical.

Project 5.9

Select a subject of some complexity, one that seems to call for more than contour or cross-contour. Employ your practiced methods of seeing the form deeply. Draw it freely in outline, allowing your hand to move easily so that the lines are not rigid. Continue to observe the form carefully as you draw, letting your line be sensitive to roundness, flatness, and meeting of surfaces. When the initial drawing is complete, shade the form near the contour with groups of light, parallel lines that curve according to the direction the form seems to take. Study the edges carefully, and modify the curvature of the shading lines in any way that seems to describe the form more fully.

Develop your facility with this method of using line by drawing many different objects. Do not attempt full modeling in light and shadow—merely add supplementary lines, tones, and textures to reinforce the contours to create a fuller sense of form than can be achieved by pure contour outline.

Critique (Project 5.9) Does your drawing show more surface life and character than your previous drawings? Are you more aware of linear, tonal, and textural variations in the way you draw? Has your mark-making vocabulary increased? Has this increase broadened your visual language skills? Are your drawings more descriptive in general?

Hatching, Cross-Hatching, and Scribbled Tones

At the beginning of this chapter, the author refers to the important role line has played throughout art history. As this chapter has progressed, we have seen the many creative possibilities of line. Artists must believe in the infinitude of expressive possibilities contained within line which keeps them searching and constantly exploring these possibilities in their search for new forms of expression.

Line has a role to play that is not limited to defining contours, as became apparent with the introduction of modeling in Figures 5-12 and 5-13. Line used as **hatching** (parallel lines), **cross-hatching** (crisscrossing patterns of parallel lines), and **scribbling** (random, multidirectional lines) builds tones and spatially defines surface texture, shape, and volume.

Philip Pearstein uses line hatching very effectively to describe form and volume in his *Male and Female Models on Iron Stool and Bench* (Fig. 5-14). There is a beautiful display of continual tonal and textural variety throughout the drawing manifested in the use of line hatching. The light and dark patterns created by different grades of graphite and varying amounts of applied pressure not only define the forms as they exist in space but also enhance the spatial relationships of the forms within the picture plane. **Contour hatching** (curved lines that follow the turning of form) allows a more descriptive modeling of cylindrical and spherical subjects. The Italian artist Domenico Beccafumi (Fig. 5-15) demonstrates the use of **cross-contour hatching** to define volume and reveal anatomical details in his *Studies of Legs and Male Nudes*. While simple hatching and cross-hatching are easy to use, meaningful and successfully creative cross-contour hatching demands careful analysis of the form followed by intellectually conceived and deliberate drawing, as in the example of Leonardo da Vinci's pen-over-chalk drawing *Outcrop of Stratified Rock* (Fig. 5-16).

John Singer Sargent's selection of graphite as the medium for his *Nude Man* (Fig. 5-17) permits him to build both the descriptive airiness and the density of varied tonal transitions more subtly than the pen-and-ink examples do. While his hatching does not appear to be particularly complex, the directional changes reveal an enviable understanding of form. In Jacques de Gheyn's pen-and-ink drawing *Woman on Her Death Bed* (Fig. 5-18), there is a convincingly effective use of scribble drawing embodied once again in varied linear, tonal, and textural manifestations. The act of scribble drawing requires one to be somewhat facile in the handling of media, for the act of scribbling must be both immediate and precise in order to successfully capture the trueness of the form. It takes much devoted practice for the beginner to be able to consistently produce beautiful and at the same time strikingly descriptive scribbles.

Project 5.10

Make an arrangement of several relatively simple objects that possess a fullness of form—two or three apples, pears, or tomatoes grouped together on a slightly ruffled tablecloth surface. Do separate drawings using hatching, cross-hatching, and scribbling to define forms and produce tonal differences. Vary both the thickness of the line and the spacing between lines to produce different tones. Experiment with a variety of drawing tools—crayon, pen and ink, as well as pencil. After having done several drawings with these media, shift to a more radically different drawing tool—a bamboo skewer or dried wooden stick dipped in ink. The scale of the forms and sizes of your drawing will in part be determined by the drawing medium selected.

---

hatching

Repeated parallel strokes with a drawing tool that produce clusters of lines creating compositional values and tonal variations usually descriptive of form or surface.

cross-hatching

A series or cluster of parallel lines, whether continuous or broken, that traverse other clusters of the same kinds of lines creating tonal and textural variations within a composition.

scribbling

Random, multidirectional lines used to build varied tones, textures, and densities and to define surface qualities, shape, and volume, or to capture gesture or movement as in a searching line.

contour hatching

Curved lines that follow the outer contours of the turning of form, allowing a more descriptive modeling of cylindrical and spherical subjects.

cross-contour hatching

Hatched lines existing on multiple planes that follow and describe the outer extremities of the three-dimensional surface undulations of a form.

5-14. *above:* PHILIP PEARLSTEIN (American born). *Male and Female Models on Iron Stool and Bench*, 1976. Graphite on ivory wove paper, 571 × 724 mm (22 1/2 × 28 1/2″).
The Jalane and Richard Davidson Collection. © The Art Institute of Chicago.

5-15. *left:* DOMENICO BECCAFUMI (1486–1551; Italian). *Studies of Legs and Male Nudes.* Pen and brown ink, 8 7/16 × 5 3/4″ (21.4 × 14.6 cm). The Art Museum, Princeton University. Elsa Durand Mower Collection.

5-16. LEONARDO DA VINCI (1452–1519; Italian). *Outcrop of Stratified Rock.* Pen over chalk, 7 1/4 × 10 9/16" (18.5 × 26.8 cm).
Royal Collection, Windsor Castle.

5-17. JOHN SINGER SARGENT (1856–1925; American). *Nude Man.* Graphite on paper, 9 7/8 × 7 3/4" (25.1 × 19.7 cm).
Wadsworth Atheneum.

Project 5.11

Line hatching can exist independently from contour drawing, as in Harold Altman's *Matriarch* (Fig. 5-19), where a rather hefty woman appears to be seated amidst a symphony of undulating forms. Choose an appropriate subject that interests you and lay out the drawing with a very light contour pencil line. Then develop the forms using hatched lines within the contour lines without actually relying on the contour. Try this again several times, each time relying less on the initial contour line. Eventu-

5-18. *above:* JACQUE DE GHEYN (1565–1629; Flemish). *Woman on Her Death Bed.* Pen and ink, 5 3/4 × 7 5/8" (14.6 × 19.4 cm). Rijksmuseum, Amsterdam.

5-19. *left:* HAROLD ALTMAN (b. 1924; American). *Matriarch.* 1961. Felt-tip pen, 16 1/2 × 20" (41.9 × 50.8 cm). Philadelphia Museum of Art.

ally you'll be able to describe a form interestingly and accurately with just the use of hatched lines. Notice how different the character of an object becomes in the drawing as the hatching describes the surface while devoid of any graphic contour presence. Remember to always use varying amounts of pressure when drawing with these tools so as to increase your range of light and dark patterns.

Critique (Project 5.11) As you observe these project drawings, make a note to yourself of how far you've come with your understanding and use of a simple line. You should begin to have a sense of the magnitude of possibilities of linear expression as evidenced in a small way by your own early explorations of line drawings set before you. Do the natures of the objects or subjects used begin to take on a visual retranslation of their forms? Are the forms themselves evident to you in a transformed way? Are there identifiable passages within the forms that have been heightened in visual importance by the varied use of descriptive line? As your range of lights and darks increases, do the spatial relationships become more pronounced? Is there a greater sense of spatial depth in your picture planes?

The Calligraphic Line

calligraphy
Beautiful writing. In western culture it is done with a pen, in Chinese and Japanese cultures with a brush.

calligraphic line
Beautiful line. In the visual arts, when writing, drawing, engraving, etching, and painting, the beauty of line becomes a major aesthetic aim.

Calligraphy is defined as "beautiful writing." When, in writing, drawing, engraving, and painting, the beauty of line becomes a major aesthetic aim, the result is a true **calligraphic line,** as seen in Figure 5-20, a collaboration of two Japanese masters—the underpainting by Sotatsu, who needed no more than two or three deft brush strokes to place a crane in flight; the calligraphy by Koetsu.

Rico Lebrun's *Seated Clown* (Fig. 5-21) and Willem de Kooning's *Woman* (Fig. 5-22) are splendid examples of the calligraphic virtuosity of Western artists. It should be noted that the de Kooning drawing, as well as Philip Guston's *Ink Drawing* (Fig. 1-9) and Frans Kline's *Untitled* (Fig. 8-8), which also are calligraphic, have their origin in abstract expressionism.

Beautiful and meaningful calligraphic line demands more than taking brush in hand to make lines of varying thickness. The beginner, without months, perhaps even years, of practice, cannot hope to do more than become aware of the factors involved. Variations of line width, which characterize a calligraphic line, are determined by the gesture with which the line is made, in combination with the amount of pressure with which the brush, by tradition held in an upright position, is applied to the drawing surface. For example, a sweeping stroke—made rapidly, commenced while the hand is in motion in the air, and finished by lifting the hand while still in motion—usually creates a tapered line that reveals both the action by which the line was drawn and the variation in pressure. In the work of an experienced draftsman, such gestures, far from being self-conscious and deliberate, result naturally from the action of drawing. It might be mentioned that calligraphers of the world value beauty of line, flourish of execution, and individuality more than legibility.

Beyond the gesture of execution, the character of a calligraphic line results from the medium used, for medium, to a degree, controls the gesture. A pointed brush with ink permits the greatest fluidity (Fig. 5-21); a flat bristle brush produces a more abrupt, slashing change from thick to thin (Fig. 5-22). Pencil, charcoal, and chalk also respond to the differing emphasis and reflect the movement of the hand in changes of width and value when these media are held under the hand, as illustrated in Figure 2-7; lines become progressively fuller and darker with increased pressure. Holding your pencil or charcoal parallel to the direction of your line will make a narrow mark; turning it at right angles to the direction of the line increases the width.

Project 5.12

As an introduction to drawing with calligraphic line, either with brush or ink, or with soft pencil, charcoal, or chalk, choose a subject that offers undulating contours—running shoes, a backpack, a cluster of large leaves, potted geraniums and other

5-20. *above, left:* UNDERPAINTING BY NONOMURA SOTATSU (1576–1643; Japanese), calligraphy by Honnami Koetsu (1558–1637; Japanese). *Poem, with Birds in Flight.* Ink on gray-blue paper, gold-flecked; 7 5/8 × 6 5/8" (19.4 × 16.8 cm). Nelson Gallery-Atkins Museum, Kansas City, Mo.

5-21. *above, right:* RICO LEBRUN (1900–1964; Italian-American). *Seated Clown.* 1941. Ink and wash, with red and black chalk; 39 × 29" (99.1 × 73.6 cm). Santa Barbara Museum of Art, California

5-22. *left:* WILLEM DE KOONING (b. 1904; Dutch-American). *Woman.* 1961. Brush and ink on paper, 23 3/4 × 18 3/4" (60.3 × 47.6 cm). Hirshhorn Museum and Sculpture Garden, Smithsonian Institution, Washington, D.C.

plants, or a few vegetables. Spend some time looking at the subject, seeing it in terms of both contour and searching line; then begin to draw freely, allowing variations in line width to grow and develop from the act of drawing. Keep your drawing sufficiently large so that your gestures can be free and unconstricted. Learn to work as quickly as you can while keeping in mind the importance of immediacy and spontaneity of mark making. Since drawings of this type should be executed quite rapidly, repeat this procedure and do several drawings in succession.

Critique (Project 5.12)   Compare the drawings to determine which have the most linear character and best express the character of the subject, the nature of the brush and ink, and the quality of immediacy in the act of drawing. As you look at the works, select several of the most visually exciting passages, and then relive the sensations of making them in your mind and spirit. Do these sensations recall any other moments in previous drawing experiences?

Experiencing Different Line Qualities

Line functions objectively to define and describe shapes, spaces, volumes, surfaces, gestures, and movements; line used subjectively focuses on the expressive and spiritual qualities of drawing.

The expressiveness of a drawing is determined not only by the choice of drawing instrument, materials, and technique, combined with skill and manipulation, but also by the artist's emotional and intellectual attitude. If line were not expressive of the individual artist, all drawings would be very much alike—and yet the drawings selected to illustrate this chapter are all very different from one another in their quality of line. They are expressive of the individual personalities of the artists whose reflected feelings and emotions, attitudes, and points of view are made tangible and manifested in the wholeness of the drawings. These drawings are so intensely reflective of their human inventors that they describe, define, and speak a visual language that may be both academic and spiritual. Artists, as cultural problem solvers, find ways of working that are challenging, satisfying, exhilarating, and "right" for their temperaments. Note, for example, the contrast between the two drawings of trees by Jacques de Gheyn and Vincent Van Gogh (Figs. 5-23, 17-15). Where de Gheyn relies on cross-contour hatching and delicacy of mark making, Van Gogh creates a rich, linear density of branches with a wide range of contrasting values highly descriptive of dormant trees in the bleak of winter. We see intrinsic merit in the characteristically unique representation of these two trees not only because they were done by accomplished artists, but because they need no justification for their existence beyond our own acceptance and appreciation of them. These different presentations offer us a glimpse into the distinct personalities of the two artists and the visual choices they made. In consideration of line, diversity is what gives artists their individual styles of expression and audiences their joy of interpretation.

Project 5.13

Using the medium of your choice, explore some of the different ways to handle line that you have observed in these illustrations. Draw in the manner of the examples rather than engaging in self-conscious copying. It does not matter what your subject is or how accurately you draw it. The most important thing is to gain a feeling for how the artist worked. The flow of adrenaline and the release of the chemical dopamine in the brain occur spontaneously during the experiencing of a pleasant and creative activity. The feelings of exhilaration and joy are a welcome accompa-

5-23. JACQUE DE GHEYN (1565–1629; Flemish). *Chestnut Tree with a Man Sitting on the Roots.* Pen and ink over black chalk, 14 1/4 × 9 3/4" (36.2 × 24.8 cm). Rijksmuseum, Amsterdam.

niment to the creative acts of drawing. Gain a sense of exhilaration through your own drawing activities, and realize that this is an essential part of creativity—part of the vehicle of personal expression, and often the catalyst that pushes works of art to greater heights of expressive power.

As you draw, you will discover that certain kinds of line movements come naturally to your hand. Be aware of that and continue experimenting. Work to develop familiarity and versatility with the various drawing media you are using. When you have also developed a familiarity with a variety of line qualities, make your own selection of subject matter that appears appropriate to each way of working, trying not to limit yourself to subjects similar to those illustrated.

Project 5.14

Acknowledging that expressiveness is to be found in choice of line as well as in subject matter, develop a series of drawings of the same subject, allowing the quality of line to convey different moods. The nature of the subject is less important than the handling of the line. As you draw, make sure to keep your focus on line and the expressiveness of the line you are presently making. Generally speaking, as you become more and more skillful and creatively assertive with your use of line, your depiction of the nature of subject matter will often become freer and possibly more natural.

Whatever subject you select, consider the placement of your drawing on the paper. Avoid letting images float in the middle of an essentially blank page by drawing large and using as much of the full sheet as possible.

Critique (Project 5.14)   As you observe the last drawings you've done for this chapter, take an overall account of your use of line. By now you should feel as though you've used line in previously unimaginable ways. You should detect within yourself a newfound excitement over the descriptive and expressive use of line, knowing that you've worked hard and that this dedication has afforded you new creative opportunities. You may only begin to see an emerging style or personal characteristic about the line you make, and this may change often as you continue to draw—after all, remember that you have just begun a venture that artists spend a lifetime investigating. If you do begin to recognize "personal line traits," this sensitivity, unique to you, may be the route through which deeper expressions will ultimately flow.

Conclusion

Whenever you commence drawing, think about the kind of line that seems equally right for the subject, for the medium, and for your own artistic temperament as you know it thus far. Gradually, you will discover that you have developed an intuitive sensitivity to line, as well as to the other art elements, and that choices need not always occur at a conscious level. The most important goal now is to work freely, instinctively, experimentally, even playfully, realizing that impulse and feeling remain the catalysts for creative activity, along with intellect and skill.

Art critic and writer Joshua C. Taylor in his essay on Robert Rauschenberg's work wrote the following: "The provocation of unsettling alertness . . . to sense, to association, to memories and the flexibility of the mind . . . renders the inert alive, and gives voice to what might otherwise remain mute."

Value 6

*If I could have had my own way
I would have confined myself
entirely to black and white.*

—Edgar Degas

In the visual arts the term **value** denotes degrees of light and dark. White under brilliant illumination is the lightest possible value, black in shadow the darkest. Between these two extremes occurs a range of intermediate grays. Pure black, white, and gray seldom occur in the natural world, for almost every surface has some local coloration, which in turn is influenced by the color of the source of illumination. Every surface, however, no matter what its color, possesses a relative degree of lightness or darkness that the artist can analyze and record as value.

While line adequately represents the contours of an object, subjects as a rule display characteristics and suggest moods that cannot be described fully by contour alone. Values clarify and enrich the space defined by simple line in five readily identifiable ways.

1. Three-dimensional form becomes apparent through the play of light and shadow, represented by shading.
2. The degree of value contrast determines the placement and relationships of form in space. Forms can be made to advance or recede through the degree of value contrast employed.
3. Value provides a fundamental element for creating pattern, for modulating and describing surface texture.
4. The pervasive mood of a drawing—dark and ominous, light and cheerful—derives from the artist's emphasis on tones at either end of the value scale. The emotional impact of a highly descriptive drawing can be delineated through value alone without the supporting influences of line.

value
Degrees of light and dark; the light and dark characteristics of color; the amount of light reflected by a particular color.

91

6-1. Value scale with nine progressions.

6-2.
RODOLFO ABULARACH (b. 1933; Guatemalan). *Circe*. 1969. Ink on paper, 23 × 29″ (58.4 × 73.6 cm). San Francisco Museum of Modern Art.

value scale
A progressive range showing the incremental and consistent steps of change between extreme light and extreme dark.

5. Value contrasts convey dramatic power. Strong contrasts of light and dark, for example, can be manipulated to create points of accent in a composition and so draw attention to areas in terms of their importance.

The Value Scale

Learning to see relationships of value is essential to producing convincing visual images. The full range of values that exist in nature cannot be duplicated, which means that an artist can only approximate the effect of natural light. A **value scale** of nine steps (Fig. 6-1) duplicates the number of value changes that most people can distinguish.

Perception of value depends upon a number of factors: (1) the actual coloration of the subject, (2) its lightness or darkness relative to its surroundings, and (3) the degree to which the subject is illuminated or in shadow. (Compare Figures 6-22, 8-15, and 18-20 with Plates 4, 9, and 19.)

Beginners often lose sight of value, seeing only color instead. Yet color has value, which must be analyzed as to its relative lightness or darkness, not only when being translated into a black and white drawing, but also for drawing in color. The apparent value of an area is relative to the area that surrounds it. The white, middle gray, and black dots superimposed on the value scale (Fig. 6-1) reveal the optical variations that occur in the apparent lightness or darkness of the same value when seen in relation to tones of greater or lesser contrast. The optical effects of contrast are powerfully descriptive tools that when used effectively are capable of extreme distortion and exaggeration.

Rodolfo Abularach's fine pen-and-ink drawing *Circe* (Fig. 6-2), with its rich range of values from the heavily cross-hatched, deep black pupil to the gleaming white, central highlight provided by the exposed paper ground, duplicates the value scale in a pictorial form. Notice how the highlight and dark of the pupil are intensified by being placed side by side and against the low dark of the iris.

The artist must learn to see value relationships, rather than be influenced by what is known to be the **local value,** which can be perceived only when seen free from the effect of light and shadow. Under illumination, local values are lightened or darkened depending upon the degree of light. In Sidney Goodman's double portrait *Ann and Andrew Dintenfass* (Fig. 6-3), the only local value that can be identified with any degree of certainty is the darkness of the young woman's hair. Notice, however, that the highlights of her hair and the lighted portion of her face are the same value, while the shadowed areas of the face and arm are nearly as dark as her hair. The local value of the young man's hair and pants might be either light or dark as influenced by intense sunlight. The novice often fails to acknowledge such effects by thinking of a white form as entirely light (although its shadowed areas appear as medium or dark values) or representing a dark surface as dark even though it is brilliantly illuminated. Only with experience do artists attain a sharply analytical sense of value as they are affected by color and lighting. (Note that having chosen white paper, Goodman used charcoal to draw everything that appears dark; on black paper he would have drawn everything that appears light with white pencil, pastel, or chalk.)

Part of an artist's basic vocabulary is the ability to utilize an extended range of value through the control of dry and wet media (Chapters 10 and 11). Another vitally important element of an artist's working knowledge is that of the receptive surfaces upon which the artist draws. Every combination of drawing tool and particular paper will produce a different effect. It is only through experimentation and experience that

6-3. SIDNEY GOODMAN (b. 1936; American). *Ann and Andrew Dintenfass.* 1971. Charcoal, 27 × 32 1/2″ (68.6 × 82.5 cm). Courtesy Terry Dintenfass Gallery, New York.

local value
The actual, known value of objects perceived only when seen free from the effects of strong light and shadow.

the artist is able to make specific choices in order to attain desired visual effects. Therefore, the artistic choices extend beyond mere selection of drawing tools.

Because of the vigorous range of lights and darks that can be created from all media, either charcoal, Conté crayon, or soft graphite stick (4B or 6B) will prove sufficient for many of the activities suggested in this section (Conté crayon and stick graphite are cleaner to work with and smudge less easily than charcoal). Assorted gray crayons would also be appropriate for many of the suggested projects, but it would be unwise to rely completely on manufactured grays instead of developing the control necessary to produce your own grays with charcoal, Conté crayon, or graphite. Charcoal, Conté crayon, and soft graphite stick all make it easier to move from contour drawing into full three-dimensional modeling of form. They also seem to encourage drawing in a larger scale than does pencil, pen and ink, or ballpoint pen, partly because the drawing process seems faster than that from the fine points of pencils or pens. However, the dimensions of Figure 6-2 suggest that the use of pen and ink is not limited to small-scale works.

For projects using charcoal, Conté, or graphite stick, you may wish to use **charcoal paper** because of its more interesting surface texture, referred to as **active tooth,** or select another drawing or printmaking paper that has a good weight and an active tooth rather than using anything too smooth. It is best to try several different papers and learn to distinguish among them according to their weight and tone (white, off-white, cream, or buff) and their amount of active tooth, whether rough or smooth.

Project 6.1

Assemble or arrange four or five objects of different colors. Study the value relationships and do a drawing of corresponding tones—a drawing that, in effect, would duplicate a black and white photograph of the objects. Limit your concern to general shapes rather than details; apply tones flatly rather than introducing gradations of value to reveal volume. (Assorted gray crayons would be perfect for this preliminary exercise in matching relative values.) Placing the forms in direct sunlight (Fig. 6-3) or introducing artificial light will alter the value relationships. (Small, high-intensity reading lamps provide strong illumination and offer adjustable positioning as well as ease in moving.) Each repositioning of the light source, each regrouping of the objects, will alter the relationships. Focusing just on the objects by squinting at them through a cardboard viewfinder will allow you to determine the tonal differences more accurately.

Form Defined by Light

Every object has a specific three-dimensional character that constitutes its **form.** The simplest forms are spheres, cylinders, cubes, cones, and pyramids; humans, animals, and botanical forms, in contrast, are forms of greater three-dimensional complexity. We are made aware of the unique aspects of each form as it is defined by **light** and **shadow,** and by changes of value. Direction of light determines what portions of a form will be lighted. Surfaces at right angles to the direction of the light source receive the most light; those areas that turn away from the light and are hidden from receiving direct rays of light fall into shadow, possibly receiving softer reflected light from neighboring objects or surfaces. Changing the position of the source of illumination can greatly

charcoal paper
Textured paper abrasive to charcoal because of its hardness of tooth. In the drawing act, it receives a deposition of black carbon charcoal particles that adhere to its relief as well as fall into its recesses; available in different weights in white, gray tones, and muted colors; also for use with chalk, Conté crayon, and pastels.

active tooth
The degree to which a paper's surface texture retains particles of dry drawing media and influences the resulting surface qualities of those media. An artist will choose a particular paper because of its active grain in order to attain the desired expressive results.

form
The positive aspect or complement of space; the visible or recognizable configuration or shape of any object existing in atmospheric space; any structural art element separate from color, line, texture, material, etc.

light
The illumination of an object; a major component of chiaroscuro helping to define forms in space within a composition; that which makes sight possible.

shadow
The state of being blocked or partially blocked from directional light or illumination; a precise area of shade cast by an object intercepting directional rays of light.

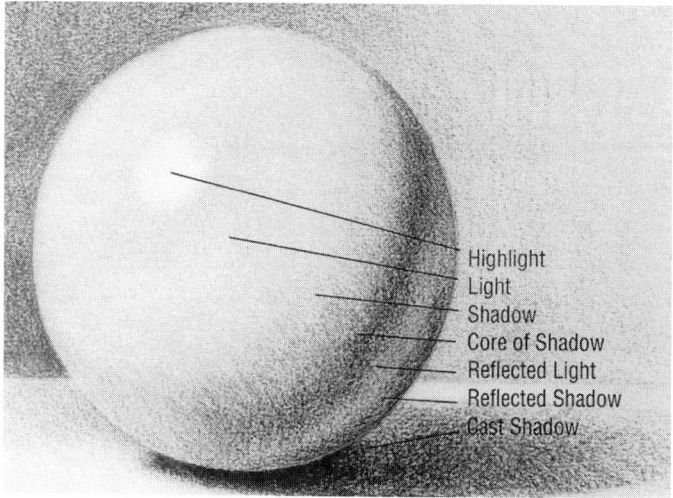

Highlight
Light
Shadow
Core of Shadow
Reflected Light
Reflected Shadow
Cast Shadow

alter the appearance of any object, the formation of cast shadows, and the degrees of illumination of reflected surfaces. Angular forms result in abrupt changes from light to dark (Fig. 6-4); spherical forms are defined as subtle gradations of tone (Fig. 6-5).

6-4. Polyhedron with value planes suggesting illumination from a single source of light.

6-5. Sphere showing the value gradations of traditional chiaroscuro.

Project 6.2

Place a white or very light-colored geometric form (a cube or other polygonal shape) on a piece of white paper or a light surface, positioned so that it receives strong light from above and to one side. (Most drawing departments in college and university art departments will have a series of geometric, three-dimensional forms made from white illustration board that are used precisely for this purpose.)

As you position the form differently, notice how its actual form is revealed by light since the angular edges dividing its planes create sharp changes of value. (If you do not have access to white geometric forms, a small cardboard carton with flaps opened at varied angles would be suitable.) Observe the object and its **cast shadow** carefully. Begin drawing by using any suitable technique to build gradations in value corresponding to the separate planes of the form. Leave the white paper for the lightest surface, defining that plane by surrounding it with continuous gray areas of tone that define adjacent planes rather than merely outlining each separate plane with a contour line (Fig. 6-4). The darkest value will be the shadow cast by the object.

Notice how the edges of each plane appear either darker or lighter, depending on the value of the adjoining planes. (The same optical illusion can be detected between the steps of the value scale.) Creating a slight exaggeration of the light and dark values where planes join results in a stronger feeling of three-dimensionality.

cast shadow
A shadow cast or thrown by an object onto an adjacent plane; one of the value gradations of traditional chiaroscuro. A cast shadow is darker than the core of the shadow.

Project 6.3

Do a series of quick studies depicting the changes that occur as the form is lighted from different angles—side, three-quarter view, front, overhead, behind, and below. Notice the shifting position of the cast shadow as the direction of light changes (see Chapter 9, Perspective).

In this and other project assignments, draw the objects as large as is practical for the medium you have chosen. Learn to use the full sheet of paper. Students have a tendency to draw too small, partly because smaller scale seems easier to master. A pencil drawing may be too large when it becomes difficult to build values of even texture; a charcoal, Conté crayon, or graphite stick drawing is too small when the stick seems clumsily oversize.

Chiaroscuro

chiaroscuro

From *chiaro* (light) and *oscuro* (dark), the continuous gradations of value, to create the illusion of three-dimensional form; systematic changes of value that produce visual states of high or low contrast in the depiction of forms as they exist in pictorial space or atmosphere.

highlights

The lightest values present on the surface of an illuminated form, occurring on very smooth or shiny surfaces; the intense spots of light that appear on the crest of the surface facing the light source.

core of shadow

The most concentrated area of dark on an illuminated sphere; one of the value gradations of traditional chiaroscuro; the core of the shadow receives no illumination.

reflected light

Light bouncing back from reflective surfaces; functions as fill-in light, making objects appear rounded by giving definition to the core of the shadow; one of the value gradations of traditional chiaroscuro.

reflected shadow

A shadow that bounces back from a nearby surface or object; one of the elements of the system of chiaroscuro. A reflected shadow is never as dark as a cast shadow.

Since the Renaissance, artists have employed **chiaroscuro,** or continuous gradations of value, to create the illusion of three-dimensional form in space or atmosphere. Chiaroscuro, which combines the Italian words *chiaro* (light) and *oscuro* (dark), involves systematic changes of value, easily identified in Figure 6-5, which shows a sphere under strong illumination. Study Figure 6-5, and notice that the elements of the system are highlight, light, shadow, core of the shadow, reflected light, reflected shadow, and cast shadow. **Highlights,** the lightest values present on the surface of an illuminated form, occur on very smooth or shiny surfaces that in turn bounce light directly off themselves since very light, shiny, ultrasmooth surfaces cannot absorb light. They are the intense spots of light that appear on the crest of the surface directly facing the light source (compare with Fig. 6-4). Light and shadow are the intermediate values between the more defined areas of highlight and the **core of shadow,** which is the most concentrated area of dark on the sphere itself. Being parallel to the source of light, the core of the shadow receives no illumination. **Reflected light**—light bounced back from nearby surfaces—functions as fill-in light, making objects appear rounded by giving definition to the core of the shadow. Reflected light is never lighter than the shadow area on the lighted portion of the form. Often there is a visibly darker portion of shadow existing on the extreme edge of an object that we refer to as **reflected shadow.** Reflected shadow defines that portion of the object farthest from the light source and is caused by the effects of the reflected, extreme darkness of the cast shadow bouncing back to the object's edge. The value of the reflected shadow lies between that of reflected light and cast shadow. Shadows thrown by objects onto adjacent planes are known as cast shadows and are always darker than the core of the shadow.

Sculptor Isamu Noguchi, possibly influenced by the years he spent as an assistant to Brancusi, presents his *Standing Nude* (Fig. 6-6) as simplified volumetric forms defined by chiaroscuro, the right buttock being almost identical to Figure 6-5.

Project 6.4

Place a white or light-colored sphere, such as a beach ball or Styrofoam ball, on a light surface. Provide strong illumination angling downward from above—a single light source plus reflected light is best, since multiple light sources create confusion. Study the form carefully before you begin to draw, observing relative values. The shadow becomes intensified as the form turns away from the light, with the core of the shadow receiving neither direct nor reflected light. No portion of the surface in the shadow is as light as the part that receives direct light. The light reflecting up into the shadowed portion of the sphere from the tabletop is lighter than the core of the shadow but darker than the lighted surface of the sphere.

Proceed with your drawing, using the method you prefer to create smooth gradations of value. If the surface of the sphere is shiny, reserve the white of the paper for the highlight. Adding a light gray background will intensify the effect of brilliant illumination.

The amount of the sphere's surface that is lighted or in shadow and the position of the cast shadow depend on the placement of the light source. If positioned directly at the side, one half of the sphere will be lighted and one half in shadow, with the core of the shadow perpendicular to

6-6. ISAMU NOGUCHI (1904–1990; American). *Standing Nude.* c. 1930. Pencil and charcoal, 19 1/4 × 12 3/8" (48.9 × 31.4 cm). Gallery of American Art, Philips Academy, Andover, Mass.

the angle of light. **Rim lighting** occurs when light from behind illuminates only the outer edge of a form, as demonstrated in Martha Alf's *Two Pears No. 3* (Pl. 1). Alf's drawing also allows us to see chiaroscuro interpreted in color.

rim lighting
Illumination of only the outer edge of an object or form by light from behind the object or form.

Project 6.5

Make a number of simplified drawings of a sphere indicating the relative amounts of light and shadow as the direction of light changes, giving emphasis to the core of the shadow. Pay attention as well to the shape and position of the cast shadow.

George Biddle's portrait of Edmund Wilson (Fig. 6-7) follows the same system used for the sphere, modeling form with broad areas of light and shadow separated by a clearly defined core of shadow. Although there are no highlights, small areas of cast shadow under the nose and chin help define the form, while the absence of dark accents at the back of the neck and ear causes the form to recede. A sense of luminosity results from the drawing's generally light tone in combination with the broad simplification of light and shadow. Biddle's handling of the shadow side of the face reveals that it is not necessary to render everything you see. Notice also how the same tonal area just to the right of the core of the

6-7. GEORGE BIDDLE (1885–1973; American). *Edmund Wilson.* 1956. Charcoal, 13 × 11 1/2″ (33 × 29.2 cm). Sotheby's.

shadow nearly reads as though there is a modeled depression in the side of the head. This is an example of how effectively an artist can create and define form with either subtle or bold value changes.

Project 6.6

Try drawing a head from life using value, rather than line, to define form. If you are self-conscious about asking a friend to pose, do a self-portrait working with a mirror. However, agreeing to exchange poses with a friend is more advantageous than a self-portrait approach at this point. Above all, do not draw from a photograph.

Position your model so that the play of light and shadow from a light source above and to the side clarifies the structure of the head. Work for solidarity of form, rather than concentrating on achieving a likeness. Do not be overly concerned with details. Just as you did in the geometric assignment (Project 6.2) to eliminate the use of a line that defines edges, remember to lay in a gray tone next to the lighted side of the face to eliminate once again the need for a contour line.

Studies for a Figure of St. Carlo Borromeo by Carlo Maratta (Fig. 6-8) illustrates how artists employ chiaroscuro to describe a complex form with broadly established areas of light, shadow, reflected light, and cast shadows. The core of the shadow functions effectively to delineate the division between light and shadow and combines with the reflected light to give sculptured fullness to the folds. Since most cloth, other than silk and satin, does not have a shiny surface, rendering of fabric rarely requires highlights.

Project 6.7

Pin a light-colored piece of fabric (a napkin or a handkerchief will do) to a wall or vertical surface. Gather and drape the fabric to create folds of some complexity. Add a strong light source to provide definition to the forms of the folds. As you draw with charcoal or graphite, pay particular attention to the way in which the core of the shadow, reflected light, and cast shadow cause the folds to stand out in bold relief. Once again, remember to delineate the edges with value changes rather than contour line.

98   PART 3   The Art Elements

6-8. CARLO MARATTA (1625–1713; Italian). *Studies for a Figure of St. Carlo Borromeo* (?). Red chalk, heightened with white, on blue-gray paper, 16 1/4 × 10 5/8" (41.3 × 26.9 cm). Kunstmuseum, Dusseldorf, Lambert Krahe Collection.

6-9. KENT BELLOWS (b. 1949; American). *Angela, Full Standing.* 1988. Pencil, 30 × 12" (76.2 × 30.4 cm). Toledo Museum of Art.

Qualities of Light

Value changes can be gradual or abrupt, depending on the character of the form and the suddenness with which it turns away from the light (Figs. 6-4, 6-5). The degree of value change, or contrast between light and shadow, also depends on the source of illumination. Brilliant light in Kent Bellows's graphite drawing *Angela, Full Standing* (Fig. 6-9) results in strong light-dark contrasts with sharply defined dark shadows (Fig. 6-3). This drawing is an excellent example of the chiaroscuro system of lights and darks defining form, and upon close examination, you can locate each element of the system: highlight, light, shadow, core of the shadow, reflected light, reflected shadow, and cast shadow. Even rim lighting occurs on the model's legs from the knees downward, where the contour edges of the legs are illuminated by reflected light bouncing off the wall from behind. Figure 6-9 illustrates the dramatic effects of the positioning of artificial light. Nine years later Bellows did another drawing in graphite pencil with touches of erasing (or subtractive drawing) of a figure showing the high contrasts of natural lighting (*Nicole, March 1997,* Fig. 6-10). Here we also see the system of chiaroscuro at work defining form in what appears to be an outdoor setting that is reminiscent of a black and white photograph taken in a garden.

A different light, one of a diffused nature in Martha Mayer Erlebacher's *Male Back* (Fig. 6-11), produces less contrast and softened cast shadows. Because of the amount of reflected light in nature, shadows cast by sunlight are generally lighter and more luminous than those created by artificial light. To maintain consistency in a drawing such as is illustrated in Figures 6-9, 6-10, and 6-11, an artist must skillfully consider the source and quality of light with regard to the desired compositional definition of form.

When we consider the abundance, intensity, and ever-changing properties of light found in nature, along with its unique effects on natural forms, we become aware of what a powerful, expressive, and necessary tool light is to the artist. Sunlight changes day to day, season by season, and continuously redefines the forms it illuminates. Artists are irretrievably attracted to the particular presentations of light in nature, never knowing entirely what they may find. Artificial light, on the other hand, is a powerfully expressive tool that gives the artist control over the amount, quality, and directional source of light to meet the desired compositional and expressive needs.

Form and Space

Space is the existing atmosphere surrounding and enveloping all form. In a compositional sense, space equals negative, form equals positive; therefore, space is generally understood as the negative aspect, or complement, of form. Space can have finite or infinite properties in the visual world as well as in the physical realm. Space is also a vehicle for illusion. Space, like form, is defined by light, which artists re-create in terms of value. Value not only defines objects, it also places and sepa-

6-10. *above:* KENT BELLOWS (b. 1949; American). *Nicole; March,* 1997. Graphite with touches of erasing on ivory wove paper, 32 1/2 × 14 1/2" (826 × 369 mm). The Jalane and Richard Davidson Collection. © The Art Institute of Chicago.

6-11. *right:* MARTHA MAYER ERLEBACHER (b. 1937; American). *Male Back.* 1980. The Arkansas Art Center Foundation Collection.

space
The negative aspect or complement of form; the atmosphere surrounding forms or objects.

6-12. RICHARD DIEBENKORN (1922–1993; American). *Seated Woman with Hat.* 1967. Pencil and ink wash, 14 × 17″ (35.6 × 43.2 cm). Courtesy of the artist.

rates forms in space. Using boldly simplified patterns of light and dark with almost no modeling of tone, Richard Diebenkorn creates both volume and space in his drawing of a woman seated in bright sunlight (Fig. 6-12). The strong light-dark contrast between the figure's right arm and her upper garment makes the arm appear to project; less contrast in value between the face and the background places the head deeper in compositional space than the arm. The brim of the sun hat exists between the arm and face, and as it shades the side of the face, this also sends it deeper into the picture plane, creating a spatial dynamic as it defines this human form.

Project 6.8

Do a drawing in which you establish spatial relationships by attending to the principle that light forms advance and dark forms recede. Arrange a group of simple, familiar objects such as cups, jars, canisters, and pots so that by their placement you are aware of space. Define space through the deliberate manipulation of value, using the lightest value for the closest object and increasingly darker values as the forms recede in space. Reserve the darkest value for the background. A strong light seen against a bold dark will appear to project more than the same light against a less contrasting value.

Use drawing media that produce wide-ranging values and do several different drawings, stopping occasionally to rearrange the objects while drawing them from different viewpoints as well. Strive for high contrasts and dynamic spatial results. The wider the value range, the greater the contrasting elements of the defined forms in space.

Critique (Project 6.8)   As you assess your drawings from Project 6.8, can you see how important value is to their compositional structure? Do they contain wide-ranging values? Are the contrasting elements visually interesting? Do the drawings have visual impact because of the way in which you used value? What do you feel are the weakest elements? How would you improve upon these drawings? Would you say these drawings look decidedly different from the drawings in previous assignments?

Sketchbook Activities

In your general approach to subject matter of all kinds, begin to see form and space as defined by light and shadow. In your sketchbook, instead of beginning a drawing with contour outlines, try to avoid any use of line and draw with masses of dark and light values whether you are drawing an object, figure, or landscape. Approach even the shadow shapes by blocking them in with areas of appropriate tonal value without depending on preliminary contour lines. If at first this seems awkward, persist and you will eventually find that you can define forms more quickly by relying on shapes of tonal value than by first establishing lines as boundaries for shapes. Even a complicated object can be reproduced with amazing accuracy when the artist concentrates on duplicating patterns of shapes and value rather than trying to draw the object itself. Learn to simplify! You do not have to define everything.

Pattern

pattern
Any compositionally repeated element or regular repetition of a design or single shape; pattern drawings in commercial art may serve as models for commercial imitation.

The term **pattern** has a number of connotations as it relates to drawing, painting, printmaking, and even sculpture. When the Diebenkorn drawing (Fig. 6-12) was described as "simplified patterns of light and dark," the term referred to all of the individual shapes, defined by changes of value, that combine to construct form and space within the composition. Perhaps a more common use of the term is as it applies to the regular repetition of a design or shape. While subtle variations in size and spacing do much to prevent the repeated shape in *Six Persimmons* (Fig. 6-13) from becoming monotonous, it is the arbitrary changes in value that Mu-Ch'i has introduced that make the piece so distinctive.

Pattern, in addition to defining form and space, can also function decoratively. Flat, unmodulated surfaces of dark and light produce pattern rather than form. We see the shape of an area and are conscious of its silhouette, but the sense of volume is minimized. Pure silhouette, whether black on white or white against black, provides the greatest possible value simplification, yet by itself is not sufficiently complex to be very entertaining. We can see how Aubrey Beardsley's elaboration of

6-13. MU-CH'I (13th century; Chinese). *Six Persimmons.* Ink on paper, 14 1/2 × 11 1/4" (36.8 × 28.6 cm). Ryoko-in, Daitokuji, Kyoto.

6-14. AUBREY BEARDSLEY (1872–1898; English). *The Peacock Skirt, from Salome.* 1894. Pen and ink, 9 1/8 × 6 5/8" (23.2 × 16.8 cm). Fogg Art Museum, Harvard University, Cambridge, Mass.

pattern in *The Peacock Skirt* (Fig. 6-14) increases the visual interest of his illustration. In the lower portion of the composition the pattern design is white against a black shape that is further silhouetted against a white background. The peacock fan and the headdress use black patterns and lines on a white ground, while other elements in the composition, such as the woman's face and the bodies of both figures, are dark outlines creating the effect of white pattern against white ground. The stippled border of the fan and the linear complexity of the man's garment and head wear further enrich the decorative scheme.

Texture

Choice of value and manner of application are important in creating the illusion of different textures and surfaces. Value permits the depiction of characteristics that cannot be described by line alone, such as the smooth sheen of heavy brown wrapping paper in Claudio Bravo's *Package* (Fig. 6-15). In fact, the powerful descriptive effects of the drawing

6-15. *above, left:* CLAUDIO BRAVO (b. 1936; Chilean). *Package.* 1969. Charcoal, pastel, and sanguine, 30 7/8 × 22 1/2" (78.4 × 57.2 cm). Baltimore Museum of Art.

6-16. *above, right:* PETER PAUL RUBENS (1557–1640; Flemish). *Lioness.* c. 1618. Black, white, and yellow chalk, 15 5/8 × 9 1/4" (39.7 × 23.5 cm). British Museum, London.

media with its subtle but poignant value changes transcend the tactile properties of mere brown wrapping paper by emulating another smoother material such as oilcloth or perhaps a rubber apron. Even gradations of tone best describe hard, smooth, polished objects, while broken patterns of light and dark are appropriate to surfaces with stronger textural characteristics, as exemplified in Peter Paul Rubens's drawing *Lioness* (Fig. 6-16), done with black, white, and yellow chalk. These two drawings are almost identical in the use of value, exhibiting strong light patterns integrated into large areas of predominantly darker values while using high contrast as a means of defining form dramatically and implying a definite light source. While the gradations of tone in the drawing by Rubens are less smooth, the major difference in effect results from the superimposed patterns of hatched lines on the animal's coat.

Project 6.9

It is possible to develop a rich variety of textures and surfaces, smooth or rough, hard or soft, by drawing on middle-value gray charcoal paper, using white chalk to build lights, even highlights, and adding dark with charcoal or Conté crayon as in Figure 6-16. Reserve the gray of the paper for all middle values; avoid mixing the chalk and charcoal to produce gray tones as this destroys the freshness of surface effects. By building the light and dark tones separately, you will make your drawing appear cleaner, crisper, and more certain.

Explore a number of different subjects that offer textural contrasts. A starched napkin, folded and pressed, provides an interesting pattern of crumpled angularity and soft flowing surfaces when pinned to a wall. A very different quality characterizes silk, satin, or taffeta, which require exaggerated highlights. The broad flat planes of a fresh new paper bag must be rendered differently from those of a used, limp sack that has been worn and crushed. Try to distinguish between a transparent object such as a glass or jar and the polished reflective surface of something metallic (Pl. 2). In doing so, you'll become aware of the vast difference in visual effects between transparent and reflective objects when at first glance you may have thought them to be very similar.

Project 6.10

Make your own gray paper by laying an even tone of charcoal over a full sheet of white paper, using either a soft charcoal or crushed compressed charcoal, which can be applied by rubbing gently with a soft cloth or chamois hide. Avoid using a paper towel that may be too stiff, as it will tend to form streaks, causing the tone to be uneven. Choose a subject in the landscape with a potentially interesting value and textural range and begin composing. Darker values are drawn in with compressed charcoal, while lighter tones and whites can be lifted out with a clean chamois and kneaded eraser. Try to work quickly and directly, not overdrawing areas that may seem fussy or problematic. Let the defining abilities of the drawing media become expressively alive without overemphasizing detail. The subject of landscape will be dealt with in depth in Chapter 13.

Critique (Projects 6.9, 6.10)   When you look at your drawing from Projects 6.9 and 6.10, is it apparent that value is the major factor in defining and creating interesting textural surfaces on a variety of different objects? How descriptive are your surfaces? Do they satisfactorily emulate the objects you've drawn? Do they emphasize or exaggerate any aspects of your chosen subjects? Is this emphasis or exaggeration visually pleasing? Does it heighten the visual statement in an interesting and provocative way? Does your handling of the medium begin to emulate surfaces other than those you've attempted to draw?

In the landscape drawing from Project 6.10, is there a visually readable space within the composition? Were you able to manipulate the media well by laying down definitive darks and also subtracting tone by erasing to create vibrant lights, even whites? Starting from the middle-value gray of the paper, do the drawings show an interesting range of added darks and lights?

Range of Values and Expressive Use of Value

Value assumes a dominant role in determining the expressive mood of a drawing and allows all aspects of the drawing to work together as a "**visual whole.**" A work that exploits full contrasts of value may convey a feeling of visual life and conceptual vigor (Fig. 6-14). However, if some aspect of composition fails in its unified attempt at visual communication, the potential sense of life and vigor may be stunted or destroyed. Furthermore, compositions in which close value relationships dominate while contrasts are minimized may create a sense of quiet, soothing restfulness or of introspection and brooding subjectivity, provided that all elements of the drawing are working together. Predominantly light compositions may carry a feeling of illumination, clarity, and perhaps a rational, optimistic outlook. On the other hand, compositions predominantly dark in value often suggest night, darkness, mystery, and even fear. Keep in mind however, that the sheer mysteries of drawings may preclude any reasonable attempt at categorizing them or their visual effects in this way. To observe a drawing in a museum or gallery exhibition, or for that matter on a wall in someone's home, is to be immersed in the mysterious circumstance of responding and interpreting according to your own level of exposure and command of a visual language. Every successful drawing is different; each has its own origin and personality. Additionally, the viewer brings another important element to the interpretation of a drawing—his or her perspective regarding mood.

visual whole
The quality of a unified compositional state brought about by the correct degrees of balance, contrast, pattern, rhythm, etc., that produce oneness.

Often the most interesting drawings reject any attempt to discover in them a specific mood or feeling, but drawings, like all works of art, are self-defining mysteries, without the need for categorization or justification. This is precisely what keeps us coming back to look at them, time and time again.

Consider how lighting is used to establish mood for films and television—popular television comedies are brightly lighted while darkness lends a heightened sense of theatricality to serious dramas. Consider also the multifaceted qualities of light and their vastly different emotive effects in black and white and in color films. Light, when used in modes of high contrast, still produces the greatest visual impact, as we saw in Figure 6-3.

High Key, Middle Key, Low Key   An artist selects and chooses from the value scale (Fig. 6-1) in much the same manner that a composer works with scales and keys to give mood and expressive character to a musical composition. For example, consider the expressive differences of minor chords as compared with major chords and how they affect you emotionally. In visual art, as in music, the terms *high key, middle key, low key,* and *full range* are used to describe the general tonality of a drawing, etching, lithograph, painting, or woodcut. They each have their intrinsic powers of provoking emotive responses and are used by artists for that purpose.

Drawings categorized as high key, middle key, and low key are those based upon a limited number of closely related values. **High key** refers to the light values—white through middle gray on the value scale, in which case the darkest value is no darker than middle gray. This is evident in *Still Life with Shadows* by William A. Berry (Fig. 6-17). The various faces of what appear to be pieces of folded cardboard, and the diffused shadows they cast as they stand upright on a box or table draped with a cloth that falls into full folds at the corners, allow Berry to translate the upper half of the value scale into a very complete drawing of lyrical beauty. This is further accomplished by building up his repertoire of middle- to light-range values with slow, deliberate, mechanical crosshatching. That something as ordinary and seemingly uninteresting as six

high key
The lightest values—white through middle gray on the value scale, in which case the darkest value is no darker than middle gray.

6-17. WILLIAM A. BERRY (b. 1933; American). *Still Life with Shadows.* 1988. Colored pencil, 30 × 40″ (76.2 × 101.6 cm). Courtesy of the artist.

6-18. WILLIAM BAILEY (b. 1930; American). *Still Life—Via dell' Oca.* 1985. Graphite on cream wove paper, 406 × 476 mm (16 × 18 1/4″).
The Jalane and Richard Davidson Collection.
© The Art Institute of Chicago.

pieces of folded cardboard could be the subject of such a poetic drawing might well surprise students who find it difficult to believe that it doesn't really matter what you draw—only how you choose to draw it. Although the drawing is done in colored pencil, Berry's primary concern is value. Here again we see that when a color work is reduced to black and white, its contrasting values, whether high-, middle-, or low-key, are the overriding factors that produce visual impact.

Another beautiful example of a high-key drawing with even less contrast and slightly more softened shadows than in Figure 6-17 is William Bailey's graphite drawing *Still Life—Via dell'Oca* (Fig. 6-18). In this subtle but powerful work we see the chiaroscuro system of defining forms in space limited to light, shadow, core of shadow, reflected shadow, and cast shadow. There are no discernible elements of highlight or reflected light. Because Bailey produced this drawing on not white but cream wove paper, he could have used white chalk or white pencil to add highlights, but chose not to.

A **middle-key** drawing such as Frank Pietek's *Abstract Configuration #2* (Fig. 6-19) includes the five values in the middle of the scale equidistant between extreme light and dark; the dark half of the scale provides the **low key** (Fig. 6-15). In practice, it is the overall tonality, rather than an exact duplicating of specific values, that determines the key of any drawing.

Project 6.11

Select a subject appropriate to a high-key (light value) rendering—for example, a still life devoid of strong darks and extensive shadow areas, perhaps one composed of basically light forms, such as eggs or lemons in a white bowl; a white paper bag resting on a well-lit draped white sheet; a sunlit landscape of ripened wheat fields or an open meadow in winter. As a greater challenge, you can transpose any subject, no matter what its actual tonality, into a high-key drawing. To do so, establish what will be the lightest and darkest values and work within that range. It will be

middle key
On a nine-step value-range scale, the five values in the middle of the scale.

low key
The darkest half of the value scale with the lightest value being no lighter than middle gray.

6-19. FRANK PIATEK (b. 1944; American). *Abstract Configuration #2*, 1987–1890. Gesso, graphite, white lead, and oil on paper, 46 × 60 1/2" (116.9 × 153.7 cm). The Arkansas Arts Center Foundation Collection.

necessary to simplify the values you see in order to compress them into the allowable number of values stages.

Determine size and shape relationships quickly, lightly, and without elaboration; block in broad value patterns as simply as possible; then study and define edges of forms, adding dark accents and highlights.

To produce a similar effect, create a drawing surface of an even tone of pale gray by rubbing a small amount of powdered graphite into the tooth of a sheet of paper (soft graphite in stick form can easily be powdered on sandpaper). Use a fairly hard graphite pencil (2H or 3H) to delineate your composition, add middle and darker values with pencil or rub in more graphite, and erase out lights. If you need darker accents, draw them with a soft pencil (4B or 6B). Selecting a very fine white paper such as Bristol board results in a pale tonality of great elegance.

Project 6.12

Select a theme that would lend itself to a predominantly dark (low-key) composition. Night subjects are, or course, ideal, but a wide variety of less obvious representational or symbolic concepts can be given a special character when presented in low key. A subject as radiant as a bouquet of summer flowers can be transformed into something ominous and mysterious through a change of value. You may wish to work on gray charcoal paper, allowing the value of the paper to determine your lightest light.

full range
A complete gradation of tones from the lightest to the darkest values.

Full Range   As the term implies, a drawing with a **full range** of values is one that uses a complete gradation of tones from white to black. Full range does not require equal distribution of all values. As in Charles Sheeler's *Interior, Bucks County Barn* (Fig. 6-20), many of the tones play only a supporting role to the feature values, black and white.

In developing any drawing, it is a valuable practice to determine the lightest light and darkest dark as a gauge from which to work. As a student, Paul Cézanne is said to have determined his values in relation to a black hat and a white handkerchief that he placed beside his models. Without establishing some reference points, it is easy to overwork an area. It is generally advisable to err on the side of lightness since it is easier to darken an area than to lighten it. Many student

6-20. CHARLES SHEELER (1883–1965; American). *Interior, Bucks County Barn.* 1932. Conté, 15 × 18 3/4″ (38.1 × 47.6 cm). Whitney Museum of American Art, New York.

drawings intended as full-range drawings lack interest because strong lights have been lost through overworking the surface while the darks have not been made rich enough. This practice of additive and subtractive drawing (both laying down tone and erasing it) allows the artist to test the tenacity of the drawing materials—to push them to their limits. In doing so, one becomes very familiar with what a particular paper can withstand.

Value Contrasts for Emphasis

Strong contrasts of light and dark, along with linear movements, create **focal points** that can direct the viewer's attention to parts of the composition according to their relative significance. Emphasis through dramatic value contrasts works equally well whether a composition is representational (Fig. 6-20) or abstract (Fig. 6-21). In Elizabeth Murray's *Untitled* work in charcoal and colored chalks on paper, we experience the quintessential drama of high contrasting values on an irregularly shaped picture plane, which adds to the overall complexity.

focal points
The elements or portions of a composition that form the main thrust or central emphasis and are visually supported or fortified by all other surrounding compositional elements.

Project 6.13

Review the various drawings you have done for the projects in this chapter. Could some forms be made to appear more solidly three-dimensional by stronger modeling in light and dark? Could objects be made to exist more convincingly in space by increasing the light-dark contrasts to make forms project, or lessening contrast to make them recede? Do the weakest drawings lack interest because everything is presented with equal emphasis? Or are the strongest drawings as strong as they could be?

It is possible, by intensifying focus on some forms or areas, to produce a greater sense of drama, visual interest, and emotive impact. Make whatever changes seem appropriate by altering value relationships through darkening and lightening. In some cases the paper surfaces may be fatigued through overworking, and you may prefer to make a new drawing of the same or similar subject. Rarely are problems solved or techniques mastered with a single drawing.

6-21. ELIZABETH MURRAY (b. 1940; American). *Untitled*, 1984. Charcoal and colored chalks on paper, 37 1/4 × 38" (94.7 × 96.6 cm). The Arkansas Arts Center Foundation Collection.

Color and Value

Although **color** can be considered a separate element, it is introduced in this chapter because it is so closely linked to value. All that has been discussed about value as black and white is applicable to drawing/painting/printmaking in color.

Almost every beginning student eventually feels limited working in black and white and longs to discover the beauty and excitement of color. To draw in black and white requires translating color into corresponding tones of gray; to draw in color demands perceiving color in terms of light and dark instead of thinking of it only in terms of **local color.** Seeing only local color, failing to notice value relationships within and between colors, is the most common error that is made in moving from black and white into color. The test of an artist's success in using color as value is revealed when a full-color drawing, painting, etching, or lithograph is photographed in black and white. The introduction of color into a drawing does not negate the fact that variations in degrees of dark and light provide one of the most effective means for giving definition to forms in space, yet many students seem reluctant to accept the concept that the success of a drawing in color depends more on correct values than on correct colors. Defining and separating forms require more than simply a color change.

Color Assembling objects for a drawing in black and white requires no particular concern or even thought about color. However, making drawings, prints, and paintings in color is another matter. Not everyone has access to a variety of objects harmonious in color, and consequently, duplicating the colors of one's assembled objects might not produce a pleasing balance of color. Artists are free, however, to alter color and create variations in hues as they choose.

color
In its purest sense, the condition produced by white light passing through a glass prism. A spectrum of color is the visual evidence of refracted or dispersed light rays of different wavelengths that stimulate the retina to see the different hues. The hue red produces the longest wavelengths; violet produces the shortest. Chromatic color is distinguished by qualities of hue: red, blue, and yellow as the primary colors; violet, green, and orange as the secondary colors.

local color
The true color or hue of a surface as seen free from the effects of light and shadow; under illumination. Local hues are lightened or darkened depending upon the degree of lightness or darkness.

Dimensions of Color   Color has three dimensions: hue, value, and intensity. **Hue** corresponds to local color. It is the quality that distinguishes one color from another—redness, blueness. The quality of color warmness pertains to the red hues and all hues related to red, and color coolness pertains to blue hues and all hues related to blue. In the context of color, **value** refers to the lightness or darkness of a color in comparison with white and black. **Intensity** describes degrees of strength and brilliance—the brightness or dullness of a color. Value and intensity can be changed, but the hue remains. Although light red might commonly be referred to as pink, it is actually a light-value red; "shocking pink" would suggest a high-intensity light red.

Hue   The basic hues—violet, blue, green, yellow, orange, and red—and their intermediate gradations are designed as primary, secondary, or tertiary colors. **Primary colors**—red, yellow, and blue—are so called because they are pure colors that cannot be obtained by mixing together any other hues. **Secondary colors**—orange, green, and purple (violet)—are derivative hues produced by mixing two primaries. **Tertiary colors** are the intermediate steps between the six basic hues. They are given hyphenated names—blue-green, yellow-orange, and red-violet. (Ordinarily the primary color is named first, followed by the secondary hue. A reversal, as in "orange-red," implies that the hue contains more orange than red.)

When arranged in a circle to form a color wheel (Pl. 3), hues opposite each other are called **complementary colors.** Yellow and violet are complementary, as are red and green, blue and orange. Complementary tertiary hues also face each other across the color wheel. The role of complementary colors will be discussed in relation to intensity.

Value   Each color has its own value; it also has its own range of values. Yellow is the lightest, violet the darkest; orange, blue, red, and green all cluster near the middle of the value scale, with orange just above the middle, blue just below, and red and green generally corresponding to middle gray. Each color can be lightened to a **tint** (high value or high key) by the addition of white, or darkened to a **shade** (low value or low key) by adding black. The value of a color will appear to change when it is placed against different backgrounds, in the same way that spots of white, gray, and black are seen to change in the value scale (Fig. 6-1). Value is always relative. It is imperative to begin to see and analyze color in terms of value, determining whether what is seen is lighter or darker than something else, not just a different hue. Many aspects of color value are evident in comparing Edmond-François Aman-Jean's richly developed pastel drawing *Les Confidences*, as reproduced both in black and white (Fig. 6-22) and color (Pl. 4).

When you work in color, degrees of value contrast are equally important in creating and describing volume and space within a composition. Greater contrast projects forms forward and tends to create dynamic spatial relationships of "push and pull" between forms; less contrast causes forms to recede and tends to flatten space. Along with spatial interplays produced by contrasting variants, there are dramatic effects and states of mood that are also influenced by the range of values employed. Aman-Jean has skillfully manipulated value both to define space and to establish mood. Although he has chosen a very limited range of values, subtle light-dark differences serve to define three-

hue
Local color; the quality that distinguishes one color from another.

value
Degrees of light and dark; the light and dark characteristics of color; the amount of light reflected by a particular color.

intensity
The degree of strength or brilliance; as related to color, the strength or saturation of a pigment; the brightness of a color.

primary colors
Red, yellow, and blue; called *primaries* because they are pure colors and cannot be obtained by mixing together any other hues.

secondary colors
Violet, orange, and green. The three colors resulting from the pairing and mixing of any two of the three primary colors: blue and red produce *violet;* red and yellow produce *orange;* yellow and blue produce *green.*

tertiary colors
The intermediate steps between the six basic hues—the three primary and three secondary colors; colors obtained by mixing two secondary colors.

complementary colors
Hues opposite one another on the color wheel; yellow and violet; red and green; blue and orange. Complementary tertiary hues also face each other across the color wheel.

tint (high key value)
Any color that has been lightened by the addition of white.

shade
A lessened degree of light caused by the blockage or partial blockage of directional light rays; as pertaining to color (low value), any color that has been darkened by the addition of black.

6-22. EDMOND-FRANÇOIS AMAN-JEAN (1860–1935; French). *Les Confidences.* c. 1898. Pastel on blue paper affixed to canvas, 48 × 38″ (1.22 × .97 m). Achenbach Foundation for Graphic Arts, the Fine Arts Museums of San Francisco.

dimensional forms and space in a more subtle way, bringing into play the power of subtlety. The separation of the seated figure's left shoulder from the foliage results from change of value as much as from color change. The highlight on her right shoulder indicates fullness of form. The ribbon of the hat and the slats of the garden bench provide the strongest light-dark accents to project that part of the bench forward, whereas darker and closer values place the back of the bench deeper in space. Value differences in the leafy background are almost imperceptible. The closeness of values and the lack of bold contrasts contribute significantly to the mood of gentle reverie.

The power of subtlety within a relatively tight range of values, aside from the light and dark accents, is also seen in Warrington Colescott's *God Destroys Bourbon Street* (Fig. 6-23). This large watercolor translated into black and white is highly definitive in its spatially descriptive powers of subtlety encased within its predominantly middle-range value scheme.

It is not necessary to be conspicuously conscious of the subtle handling of color, value, and intensity to respond to the beauty of Aman-Jean's drawing or Warrington Colescott's watercolor; but as art students, you should sharpen your awareness by studying all such drawings carefully and thoroughly.

Intensity   Looking once again at the Aman-Jean drawing, you will see that the colors in the lower half of the drawing are generally stronger and brighter than those above. The foreground colors have somewhat

6-23. WARRINGTON COLESCOTT
(b. 1921; American). *God Destroys Bourbon
Street*, 1995. Watercolor on paper,
40 1/4 × 59 3/4″ (102.3 × 151.8 cm).
The Arkansas Arts Center Foundation
Collection.

greater intensity, which combines with aspects of value to reveal space. The dominant red-orange of the seated figure's dress is obvious. It is perhaps more interesting, however, to compare the rose on the hat with the dress of the standing figure. Although they are almost identical in value, the light area of the sleeve is almost colorless in contrast to the more vibrant color of the rose. It is also important to note that the hair of the standing woman is the same hue as the dress of the seated figure—red-orange, but of a darker value and lower intensity.

The intensity of color is affected by light and by its surroundings. Color seen in strong direct light, either natural or artificial, is more brilliant and vibrant than the same color viewed in subdued light or on a gray day. The degree of believability and articulate representation in art not only derives from but is dependent upon the ability to accurately read color. Color is rarely seen in isolation but rather is influenced by neighboring colors. Colors of similar intensity placed alongside one another hold together, whereas contrast produces separation. The higher the intensity of a color, the more it appears to project; the lower the intensity, the more a color recedes.

Project 6.14

Although Willem de Kooning's *Two Women's Torsos* (Pl. 5) is a decidedly different interpretation of figures juxtaposed with each other than that of Aman-Jean's figures in the landscape (Pl. 4), careful examination of the two drawings reveals strong similarity in the way in which color has been employed. Analyze de Kooning's use of color—hue, value, and intensity. Determine the points of similarity between the two

Altering the intensity of a hue by adding white or black is, in and of itself, of limited effectiveness, since the addition of either also results in changing the value. In painting and printmaking, most pigments (whether paint or ink) are at their most intense as they come from the container. Blue and violet are the exceptions; their brilliance increases slightly by adding a small amount of white. It is possible to alter a color's intensity by adding some other color, but not without changing the hue as well.

Color Schemes

A number of **color schemes** have been formulated to provide a sense of color harmony and unity. An understanding of the three most widely recognized color schemes provides a point of departure for selecting and combining colors.

Monochromatic Color Scheme   A **monochromatic** scheme involves varied hues (colors) and varying intensities in value of a single hue. For example, a wide-ranging monochromatic color scheme can be created with any hue by adding prescribed amounts of white to form progressively lighter stages known as tints of the hue. Conversely, prescribed amounts of black can be added to the same hue, forming progressively darker stages known as shades of the same hue or color. Both black and white, not being colors, are deliberately introduced without violating the one-hue limitation, which precipitates a "pure" monochromatic situation.

Analogous Color Scheme   An **analogous** color scheme employs unlimited values and intensities of neighboring hues on the color wheel, the range not to exceed the bounds of two consecutive primary colors. Analogous character is most emphatic when a single primary hue dominates. Though more animated than the monochromatic scheme, the analogous scheme can also create a harmonious and quiet mood due to the close relationship of its component hues. Martha Alf's *Two Pears No. 3* (Pl. 1) is suggestive of analogous color.

Complementary Color Scheme   Contrasting hues are the basis of the **complementary** color scheme. The addition of other hues is permitted, as long as they do not overwhelm the requisite pair of complementaries (Pl. 4).

Two pairs of complementary colors, such as blue and orange plus red and green, comprise a **double-complementary** scheme. Willem de Kooning's *Two Women's Torsos* (Pl. 5) introduces yet a third pair, yellow and violet producing a **triple-complementary** color scheme.

A **split-complementary** scheme poses one hue against the two hues flanking its complement; an example would be yellow with red-violet and blue-violet.

According to Henri Matisse, the quality of color is determined by the quantity of color. Some color theorists who advocate a proportional use of color suggest that a balance between complementaries requires equal amounts of red and green, two times as much blue as orange, and three times as much violet as yellow. (Plate 4 comes close to meeting the red-green specifications.)

---

color schemes
Systems of color combinations that provide a sense of color harmony and unity.

monochromatic color scheme
A color scheme in which an entire composition is composed of the descriptive value ranges of a single color with its shades and tints.

analogous color scheme
A color scheme comprised of any combination of adjacent colors on the color wheel as the main color statement of a work of art.

complementary color scheme
A color scheme that poses two pairs of complementary colors, such as blue and orange plus red and green, working together in the same work of art.

double complementary color scheme
A color scheme that poses two pairs of complementary colors, such as blue and orange plus red and green, working together in the same work of art.

triple complementary color scheme
A color scheme that poses three pairs of complementary colors, such as blue and orange, red and green, and yellow and violet, all working together in the same work of art.

split complementary color scheme
A color scheme that poses one hue against the two hues flanking its complement; an example would be yellow with red-violet and blue-violet.

Project 6.15

While most artists settle for a pleasing balance of color, it is instructive to experiment with various color schemes. To experience the interaction of color, use graph paper with a quarter-inch grid and colored pencils or pastels to create images, even portraits, by filling in individual squares with a single color. Let gradations of color and tonal variations result from changing colors in adjacent squares. The completed drawing will resemble Figure 15-15. The mosaic or needlepoint effect will soften and disappear when viewed at some distance. Do a drawing, again on quarter-inch grid paper, in which the juxtaposition of the three primary colors of red, yellow, and blue creates the secondary colors orange, green, and violet.

Project 6.16

Do a drawing based on the proportional balancing of complementary colors. It is not necessary to have equal amounts of each pair of colors; you may allow one set to be dominant. Value and intensity changes will contribute to a more painterly effect, as will **broken color,** which eliminates color purity by introducing more than one color into a specific shape or object through mixing.

Complementary colors play two roles: they can either nullify or intensify each other. In theory, true complements combined in the correct proportions will produce a neutral or colorless gray. However, in practice it is difficult to find exact complementaries, and the resulting mixture usually retains traces of one of the two colors. Placed in juxtaposition, complementaries increase the apparent intensity of each other, or truly "complement" each other; the effect is called **simultaneous contrast.** A spot of low-intensity orange placed against a surrounding field of high-intensity blue will appear distinctly more intense. When orange and blue of corresponding high intensities are placed together, the colors will appear to vibrate almost to the point that the eye can barely discern a precise separation. (This fact is borne out in the color vibration paintings of the Pop and Op Art movements.)

Warm and Cool Colors   As alluded to earlier in this chapter, color temperature has psychological and spatial impact. The hues of one side of the color wheel (Pl. 3)—yellow, orange, red, and their neighboring tertiaries—are called **warm** colors; the hues on the opposite side of the wheel—green, blue, violet, and the intermediate tertiaries—are termed **cool.** Warm colors seem to project forward in space; they are considered aggressive, psychologically arousing, and stimulating. Cool colors, in contrast, tend to recede in space, seem quiet, and add a sense of restfulness to a composition. The effects of warm and cool are more evident when seen together. Temperature is relative, and any color can be made to appear either warm or cool, or both, as evidenced in the hair, shadowed face, and hat of the seated woman in Plate 4. The color of any object or surface is influenced by the temperature of the light, as are shadows. Warm light casts cool shadows; cool light casts warm shadows.

Temperature also plays an important role in color mixing. In theory, secondary colors or hues can be produced by mixing two primary colors; but in practice, special consideration must be given to the temperature of the primary colors if the resulting secondary colors are to be clean and bright. Because pure primary colors are unavailable, it is necessary to work with both warm (w) and cool (c) reds, yellows, and blues. Recommended colors for producing the purest and brightest

broken color

A color scheme where more than one color is introduced into a shape or object to produce varied painterly effects. Also, a pure color that has been altered by the invasion of another color.

simultaneous contrast

A visual effect produced when complementary colors are placed in juxtaposition, which increases the apparent intensity of both so that they truly complement each other.

warm color

A hue on one side of the color wheel—yellow, orange, red, and their neighboring tertiary colors; any color opposite the cool colors on the color wheel.

cool color

A hue on one side of the color wheel—green, blue, violet, and their intermediate tertiary colors; any color opposite the warm colors on the color wheel.

secondary colors are Alizarin Crimson (c) and French Ultramarine Blue (w) for violet, Pthalo Blue (c) and Lemon Yellow (c) for green, and Cadmium Yellow (w) and Cadmium Red (w) for orange, because each of the two primaries suggested already contains some of the other color. Other combinations will produce dull or subdued variations of the secondary colors—mixtures that might be appropriate when purity of color is not the goal.

Drawing in Color

Aman-Jean's use of color in his drawing (Pl. 4) is so fully developed that it might well rival the color usage in painting, yet it remains a drawing. Drawing is one of the purest acts of visual creativity an artist can hope to engage in. When color is introduced, the distinction between drawing and painting may be arbitrary; however, painting is a second-generation image of which the pure act of drawing is the progenitor. Color mixing is generally more related to painting than drawing, and although drawing is conceived as employing less than full modulations of color, an acute familiarity with the components of color is immeasurably useful to the artist in the act of drawing.

To explore the use of color in drawing, it will be necessary to expand your supply of materials. Today there is an unparalleled supply of colored drawing materials that provide extensive ranges of hues, values, and intensities equal to that available to painters and printmakers with their paints and inks of tremendous versatility. Colored chalks, pastels, colored pencils, colored pens, oil crayons, and colored inks—all readily available, relatively inexpensive, and easy to use—will equip the beginner for an adventure in the use of color. Although at some time you will want to experiment with a variety of media and techniques, any one of the suggested media will be sufficient for initial excursions into color. (See Chapters 10 and 11, covering drawing media.)

Adopting a technique that first came into use in Italy in the early sixteenth century, William Berry introduced a limited sense of color in *Self Portrait with a Lamp* (Pl. 6) by drawing with black and white on colored paper, adding reddish touches on the nose, cheeks, and lips. The color of the paper provides the middle value; the white and black are never blended together. Colored paper is most effective when the color and tone of the paper are incorporated into the drawing, as Berry has done. The same technique would accommodate the substitution of drawing materials of a lighter-value warm color for the white pencil, and a darker-value cool color for the graphite or black pencil.

Red chalk (red or iron oxide) is one of the oldest pigments known; the color warmth, intensity, and accessibility made it a popular medium for over four hundred years, and it remains so today. But it did not become popular as a drawing medium until the late fifteenth/early sixteenth century. Because it is partially composed of iron oxide, it produces chromatically strong marks on receptive surfaces. Used for **monochromatic** value studies, red chalk alone imparts a certain vitality to figure drawing because of its closeness in hue to the color of flesh.

Adding first black and then white to red expanded the range of color possibilities, as demonstrated in Alanson Appleton's portrait study (Pl. 7). Appleton chose to combine pen and ink with pastel in place of chalk, but the color concept remains unchanged, except for the addition of blue for the eyes. Examine this work as the pure act of drawing that

monochromatic
A word describing a hue or chromatic variation of shades and tints of the same color attained by adding black to create shades or white to create tints.

it is, and you will notice how it possesses the true life and expressive vitality of drawing at its best.

The addition of yellow ochre to red, black, and white makes possible an even fuller range of color. Drawing with these four colors of chalk or crayon on medium gray paper permits the approximation of a full spectrum of color. Ochre and red combine to make orange; ochre and black make green; seen in relation to the other colors, black and white produce bluish-gray; red and black, similarly, result in violet. None of the colors match their pure-spectrum counterparts, but seen within the context of the drawing, the effect is of a full spectrum of color. All the color mixtures will be of a low intensity, even more so if the component colors have been blended, which tends to deaden the color and also eliminates the sense of the directness of drawing. Chalk and pastel drawings have greater vibrancy and vitality when color is applied directly as areas of unmodulated color (Pl. 1) and juxtaposed strokes of pure color (Pl. 4). The separate strokes of color are mixed by the eye/mind of the viewer, not by the thumb of the artist, to create **optical color.** Lights and darks are achieved by selecting light- and dark-value chalks, rather than by adding white or black to a middle-value color.

The popularity of colored pencils as a drawing medium has increased, partly because they are cleaner and less susceptible to smudging, but perhaps more because of their versatility (Pls. 2, 6). Drawing with colored pencils is similar in a way to drawing with graphite pencils in that value and intensity are determined by pressure. Light pressure produces marks that are light in value and color that lacks brilliance; greater pressure produces darker, more intense color. Colored pencils also have a degree of transparency. Applying one color over another, on a quality drawing paper with adequate tooth, produces a third color, which is often richer and more interesting than either of the originals, since individual colors may tend to be somewhat harsh. A color can also be lightened by applying white or some other lighter color, or darkened with black or other darker colors. (An age-old question remains about the permanency of color. In spite of manufacturers' claims, art conservation laboratories caution artists that the color in pencils tends to fade because of ultraviolet rays and should be tested for permanency by controlled exposure to light.)

optical color
Color effects that are seen and read optically; the actual color the eye reads and the mind understands; tiny strokes of "pure red" in close proximity to tiny strokes of "pure blue" will be read and mixed by the eye to produce violet.

Project 6.17

Select one of the color media—pastels, colored pencils, pen and colored ink, possibly in combination with chalk—and adopt the various techniques discussed and illustrated to subjects of your own choosing. (Characteristics of individual media and suggested methods for using each are the subject of Chapters 10 and 11.) As you commence to draw, use limited color at first before launching into full color, gaining a sense of the hue, value, and intensity of each color and how it handles. Gradually increase the numbers of colors with thoughtful selection and usage, again being cognizant of qualities of value and intensity, as well as hue.

Project 6.18

Arrange a group of several objects into a still life and light them. Ignore the color that you see; draw only the values that you see and translate them into pure hues. Use yellow for the lightest areas, violet for the darkest, and middle-value hues for the intermediate areas, depending on the value of each and the value to be matched. (Hues become increasingly darker as you move in either direction on the color wheel away from yellow toward violet.) Consider color temperature in relation to both light and shadow and advancing and receding forms. Actual individual objects in the still life will be multicolored. Although the colors in the drawing will not correspond to what you see before you, the values should, and if they do, the sense of volume and space should be well defined, producing a visually convincing composition—a drawing in color.

Color, whether used literally or more expressively, can describe form and create the illusion of space, if attention is given to all three dimensions of color—hue, value, and intensity. Such concern is not limited to representational drawing, painting, or printmaking; it is a consideration for abstractionists as well.

Color carries the expressive power and vitality of light, as manifested in the value scale from intense to weak. Its ability to describe forms with provocative brilliance or somber elegance will be realized in many different venues, provided the artist uses color with thoughtful directness and assertive deliberateness. Drawing in color introduces you to the realms of painting and printmaking and expands the expressive potential of drawing to the other studio disciplines. Perhaps also, drawing in color helps students realize anew the expressive power and provocative beauty of the numerous traditional black and white compositions and the major role they play in art history.

Texture 7

In real life one did not see a high gloss on nature; it had roughness and textural variety. Constable represented these qualities. . . .

—Diana Hirsh

When we look at the world around us, we are conscious not only of form, color, space, light, dark, volume, and atmosphere, but also of tactile qualities, a sense of the feel of surfaces, of roughness and smoothness, hardness and softness—**texture.** Texture, whether actual or illusional, is a catalyst for the senses. It is, in fact, one of the things that catches our eye, that makes us notice something and causes us to reach out and touch it. Skillfully used, texture can contribute significantly to descriptive expressiveness; lacking a decisive sense of texture, a drawing tends to appear flaccid, weak, or generally uninteresting. The textural character of a drawing is determined by several factors: the particular surface portrayed, the drawing materials employed, including the tooth or slickness of the paper surface used, the method of application, and the artist's sense of invention.

texture
The surface character or the tactile qualities experienced through touch; a sense of the "feel" of surfaces, of roughness and smoothness, hardness and softness; the illusion of tactility as in the illusion of a drawn texture albeit on a smooth two-dimensional surface.

Familiar Surfaces

The convincing duplication of surface texture—the actual visible and tactile surface characteristics of an object—lends a sense of authenticity to representational drawing. In drawing we are concerned primarily with reproducing the visual aspects of texture, yet we know that our most immediate experiences with texture are tactile.

Most children, at one time or another, have reproduced the images that appear in relief on coins by placing a piece of paper over a coin and rubbing it with the flat side of a pencil lead. Robert Indiana's *The American Eat* (Fig. 7-1) was created by exactly the same method. The technique is called **frottage,** a rubbing process that takes an articulate

frottage   The technique of placing a sheet of paper over an actual, physical texture and rubbing the topside of the paper with the side of a graphite stick or Conté crayon, producing a positive impression of the relief of the physical texture. Artist Max Ernst was the first to use the technique in the production of a work of art.

119

impression from a relief texture. The beauty of Indiana's drawing lies not so much in the letters of the brass relief stencil as in the variety and richness of the undulating dark and light tones created by his hatching with Conté crayon.

Max Ernst was perhaps the first artist to use the frottage technique to create a work of art. In the charcoal drawing *La Forêt Pétrifiée* (Fig. 7-2), he superimposed rubbings made from various pieces of weathered plank. Although the natural patterns of the wood grain are perceptible, the drawing seems to be of, but not necessarily about, wood. Whatever his intention, he has produced texture that is both visual and tactile. Not only do we see texture, we also experience what it would be like to touch it, because the texture no longer seems to reside in the wood, but in the drawing. Another beautiful example of the extremely tactile quality the frottage technique can offer is Ernst's *Wheel of Light* (Fig. 7-3), done with graphite. Here we see an altogether different presentation of a delicate and more refined surface delineation. Notice the well-orchestrated linear textures that are so descriptive of the eye surface and create a powerful illusion of three-dimensionality.

The wood grain patterns in Rene Magritte's *The Thought Which Sees* (Fig. 7-4) resemble those in Figure 7-2, but beyond that, the character of the two drawings is very different. Unlike Ernst's frottage works, Magritte employs a variety of complex, obviously drawn linear patterns

7-3 MAX ERNST (1891–1976 ; German). *Wheel of Light*. 1925. Graphite frottage, 10 × 16″ (25.4 × 40.6 cm). Musée National de l'Art Moderne, Centre Georges Pompidou, Paris.

to suggest texture. The pattern chosen for the wood grain texture is appropriately the most descriptive, since it defines the only element in the drawing that is not ambiguous.

The precisely ruled vertical and horizontal ink lines of Ilya Bolotowsky's *Blue and Black Vertical* (Fig. 7-5) can be seen as texture of elegant richness, suggestive of, though not representing, sections of beautifully finished fine-grained wood. Whether or not the Bolotowsky drawing actually depicts wood, if for the moment you think of it as such, it allows a valuable comparison with Figures 7-2 and 7-4. Of the three examples, the first offers the most authentic description of wood texture because it was lifted directly from pieces of real wood, while the suggestion of texture in the other two is based on linear patterns. In each drawing the character of line conveys specific visual and tactile qualities of the texture. Thinness and regularity of ruled ink lines create the sensation of smoothness, and variations in darkness suggest the sheen of

7-4 *above, left:* RENE MAGRITTE (1898–1967; Belgian). *The Thought Which Sees.* 1965. Graphite, 15 3/4 × 11 3/4" (40 × 29.8 cm).
The Museum of Modern Art, New York.

7-5 *above, right:* ILYA BOLOTOWSKY (1907–1981; Russian-American); *Blue and Black Vertical.* 1971. Pen and ink, 30 × 22" (76.2 × 55.9 cm).
Private collection.

polished wood in the black and white reproduction of Bolotowsky's drawing, in contrast to the rough, weathered feeling of the heavy, irregular patterns of Ernst's charcoal rubbing. In spite of pattern variations, Magritte's repetitious use of short vertical lines creates a wall nearly devoid of character. However, Magritte has provided sufficient variety in the wood grain pattern to avoid monotony and also to form an interesting textural variation between the night-and-day depictions of the sky and the lapping waves of the shoreline contained within the silhouetted figures.

Project 7.1

Rubbings, as in the technique of frottage, do not produce reversed images, as in the pulling of an impression from an etching plate or woodblock, because the frottage image is created on the top side of the paper—not the underside that rests against the textured surface. We often become more conscious of the visual qualities of texture when we see them presented as a pattern of marks on a sheet of paper, isolated from the object or surface itself. This project is intended to integrate the visual with the tactile, to increase visual awareness of familiar textures through seeing them translated into images on a sheet of paper.

Use a soft pencil, graphite stick such as a 2B or 4B, or a black crayon with bond paper or any lightweight, relatively smooth drawing paper. Make rubbings comprising an area of several square inches by placing the paper over textured surfaces in your immediate area (making sure to hold the paper securely to avoid slippage). Select a variety of different textures that are from either interior or exterior surfaces, natural or manufactured, hard or soft, fine or rough. The possibilities multiply in relation to your awareness and sensitivity. As you study the samples, you will be aware that more durable materials result in stronger, even crisper-looking patterns than soft materials such as fabric, a distinction that provides you with a clue about rendering textural differences. Rubbing methodically while holding the paper steadily in place will produce an effect close to that of the actual surface. Remember to use varying amounts of pressure that will yield a range of lighter and darker patterns as you rub the surface of the paper. A freer, irregular approach will result in a more visually interesting, tonally blurred, perhaps even double texture, as in the effects of Figure 7-1.

Critique (Project 7.1) Observe your results and assess the crispness and/or softened effects that resulted from the different suggested ways of performing the frottage technique. Have you produced some successful results? Which do you find most visually interesting? Note how the harder surfaces you selected produce a more clearly defined texture than do the softer surfaces, which yield more tonal results with a somewhat obscured ghostly essence of texture.

Rendering Textures

Representational drawing demands a more three-dimensional **rendering** of different surface characteristics than does the relatively two-dimensional pattern of texture created by rubbing. The word *render* often is used as a synonym for *draw* or *represent,* but in the context of this discussion it refers to a convincing duplication—an exact re-creation, even a heightening, of the visual effects of surfaces, textures, and details. Joseph Stella's *Tree Trunk* (Fig. 7-6), in which **raking light** from the side reveals both texture and volume, presents a reality very different from the stylized linear description of a similar subject by Jacques de Gheyn in Figure 5-23.

7-6 *above, left:* JOSEPH STELLA (1877–1946; Italian-American). *Tree Trunk.* Pencil and crayon, 17 × 11 1/2″ (43.2 × 29.2 cm). New Jersey State Collection, Trenton.

7-7 *above, right:* YASUHIRO ESAKI (b. 1941; Japanese-American). *Blue Sheet No. 9.* 1979. Pencil and acrylic on paper, 28 7/8 × 21 1/2″ (73.3 × 54.6 cm). Courtesy of the artist.

rendering
A drawing displaying a high degree of detailed representation, interpretation, rendition, and other specific information about a subject; the word *render* is often used as a synonym for *draw* or *represent.*

raking light
The planned, controlled, and directed position of a lighting source that causes a "washing over" of illumination, producing a specified lighting effect usually limited to one side of an object or form.

trompe l'oeil
Rendering in its most meticulous form (from a French term meaning "deceive the eye"); usually applies to still life where the creation of poignant illusions convinces the viewer that he is looking at the actual object or objects represented.

Rendering in its most meticulous form is called **trompe l'oeil** (fool the eye). An example is Yasuhiro Esaki's *Blue Sheet No. 9* (Fig. 7-7), one of a series of full-page drawings produced over a five-year period in which the artist explored the wrinkled and folded surface of a bedsheet, transforming the soft cloth into both a topographical map and a lyrical abstraction. The textural character that Esaki achieves is very different from the sheen of smooth paper rendered by Claudio Bravo (Fig. 6-15).

Project 7.2

Enlarging the scale of a surface provides an excellent means of becoming aware of its exact character. Close examination of the texture of many familiar surfaces—a natural sponge, the skin of a cantaloupe—proves visually fascinating. Select a familiar textured surface and light it sharply from above and to one side (a raking light) to emphasize and clarify its texture. Using an HB or 2B graphite, fill a 4- by 5-inch (10- by 13-centimeter) rectangle with a pencil rendering of the surface magnified many times, using varying degrees of pressure and dark and light values to create a maximum sense of its texture. Next, using a wider variety of soft and hard graphite pencils on Bristol board, duplicate the texture as accurately as possible. Plan to spend several hours on this project, working slowly and methodically in whatever intervals your patience allows.

Project 7.3

Do a pencil rendering that contrasts the smooth polished surface of an apple with the subtle texture of the rind of an orange or lemon. Include a slice of the orange or lemon as another element in your composition. Light the forms to show chiaroscuro.

Critique [Projects 7.2 and 7.3]   These are the most involved and time-consuming drawings you've done so far from this drawing text. Assess the descriptive qualities of your drawings. Do they appear to portray texture in an enormous and significant way? Do they describe the surfaces of the objects by their textures in an articulate way? Has this exercise helped you become more aware of texture and its fascinating descriptive nature? Have you successfully employed the methods of differing amounts of pressure along with using a variety of different hard and soft graphite pencils? Does the drawing stand on its own as an interesting surface composition irrespective of what the subject was?

Textures of the Artist's Media

Different drawing media produce vastly different textural results according to how they lie on, and fuse with, the surface of paper. The way in which drawing media are applied to a surface—even by the hand of a particular artist, and the textural or "toothy" variations of paper are also important main ingredients in the creation of a drawing. For example, crayon or coarse chalk on rough paper renders greatly contrasting results to fine graphite on smooth paper, and an artist makes definitive choices as to what materials to use according to what desired effects are to be attained. The textural pattern of George Seurat's *The Artist's Mother* (Fig. 7-8) is determined solely by choice of materials. Uniformly textured paper and soft Conté crayon applied without indication of direction of stroke combine to create an impersonal surface. The drawing is more concerned with materials and technique than with a description of the subject. Nevertheless, as with all art that exhibits integrity of materials, there is an emerging character that flows from the work.

Textural quality, as determined by various combinations of media and paper, significantly influences the expressive character of a

7-8 *left:* GEORGES SEURAT (1858–1891; French). *The Artist's Mother.* Conté crayon on paper, 12 1/2 × 9 1/2" (31.7 × 24.2 cm). The Metropolitan Museum of Art, New York.

7-9 *below, left:* KÄTHE KOLLWITZ (1867–1945; German). *Self-Portrait.* 1911. Chalk, 13 3/4 × 12 1/8" (34.9 × 30.8 cm). Kupferstich Kabinett, Staatliche Kunstsammlungen, Dresden.

7-10 *below, right:* DANIEL M. MENDELOWITZ (1905–1980; American). *Portrait of Annie.* 1963. Rubbed graphite pencil and eraser, 16 × 12" (40.7 × 30.5 cm). Collection of Mrs. Daniel Mendelowitz, Stanford, California.

drawing. In both Käthe Kollwitz's *Self-Portrait* (Fig. 7-9) and Daniel Mendelowitz's *Portrait of Annie* (Fig. 7-10), there is an appropriate fusion between the choices of paper (rough, smooth), media (coarse

CH. 7   Texture   **125**

chalk, pencil), and method of application (bold, forceful; gentle, caressing) that contributes to the haunting beauty of each woman. Once the images are created, it is impossible to conceive of reversing them. Once viewed, they are impossible to forget—such is the power of art.

Project 7.4

To explore the effects produced from different combinations of media and papers it is necessary to gather papers of varying roughness, smoothness, and surface grain, referred to as "paper tooth" (see Chapter 10), as well as collect different grades of graphite pencils and sticks, charcoal, chalk, crayons, color pencils, ink, and assorted pens, brushes, and sponges. To minimize individual expense, consider sharing the cost of several sheets of large-size paper that can be halved or quartered. Experiment on both sides of the paper to extend the paper supply even further. Draw with both the sides and points of dry media; cross-hatch and stipple in both dry and wet media; combine all types of pens, sponges, brushes, and so forth. The tendency will be to overwork the drawing surfaces with so many different media at your disposal, and this can happen before you realize it. Try not to overwork the individual surfaces by working on several different drawings simultaneously and consciously refrain from using too many media on any one surface, allowing the developing images to breathe.

Project 7.5

Explore the expressive potential of texture by doing two drawings of the same subject, perhaps a still life with some textural variety, using two contrasting combinations of media and paper. Do not make meticulously detailed renderings, but devote some attention to suggesting textural differences. Try to draw with as much textural variation as possible, employing tonal ranges of lights and darks throughout.

Critique (Project 7.5)   Study your completed drawings and determine the effectiveness of each in relation to the subject. Are the drawings highly descriptive of the surface textures of the subjects drawn? Is there an expressive quality created by the textures that transcends the mere description of the subjects?

Take account of which subjects, materials, and techniques seem to be the most satisfying to use and seem to be the most successfully descriptive combinations, and repeat them with several new drawings, aiming at improvement with each new attempt.

Actual and Uniform Texture

Actual texture is texture that represents a real surface and can be experienced through the sense of touch. In the act of drawing, **simulated texture** is texture that emulates an actual surface. **Uniform texture** is the overall surface quality that results from a particular drawing medium and the relief texture or character tooth of the paper. The graphic characteristics of the drawing medium and the nature of the paper surface produce the total visual effects, and the masterful control and consistency with which an artist deliberately works produce the uniformity of effects.

Actual or uniform texture, whether deliberately drawn or determined by a particular combination of medium and paper, introduces a prevailing pattern. This pattern is often determined by the materials and is generally abstract in character rather than dictated by the nature of the subject matter. For example, an artist working in the style of photo realism with a high degree of fine detail will find a considerable diminishment in the quality of detail when coarser drawing materials and heavier-toothed papers are used to render an image in the same style. The visual effect arising purely from the nature of materials tends to em-

actual texture
A texture that is a real surface and can be experienced through the sense of touch; often used in collage or mixed-media works where the actual textured material is applied to the work of art and left unaltered by the artist—as in the art of the found object.

simulated texture
A drawn textural illusion that emulates an actual texture or surface quality and is dependent upon the degree of illusion for its various visual effects.

uniform texture
Texture or textures that appear to be very similar and together create a tight harmony or an overall consistent quality, regularity, and oneness within a composition.

7-11 THEOPHIL GROELL (b. 1932; American). *Rivers End*. 1981. Litho pencil on textured paper, 20 1/4 × 20″ (51.4 × 50.8 cm). Collection Rita Rich. Courtesy of the artist.

phasize the formal aspects of drawing, as is evident in Seurat's portrait of his mother (Fig. 7-8). Here we see that certain formidable characteristics of materials and paper surfaces produce mannered effects as uniform textures and may seem best suited for stylized modes of expression.

Theophil Groell deliberately uses uniform texture as an overall pattern of small dots by applying lithographic pencil (litho crayon) with a light touch to the rough surface of handmade papers, making no textural distinction between rocks, fallen tree trunks, and tangled thicket (Fig. 7-11). Groell has developed the technique as a visual metaphor for expressing beliefs about "the process of decay and renewal" in nature. By comparison, we see in the work of Jack Beal a similar visual situation that is highly textural in his *Study for "Wisconsin Still-Life"* (Fig. 7-12), but the objects in the still life are texturally treated as individual entities.

7-12 JACK BEAL (b. 1931; American). *Study for "Wisconsin Still Life."* 1979. Lithographic crayon on frosted Mylar, 571 × 764 mm (22 1/2 × 30 1/8").
The Jalane and Richard Davidson Collection.
© The Art Institute of Chicago.

Beal's method of drawing with lithographic crayon, as Groell did, only on frosted Mylar instead of handmade paper, exhibits greater surface description and variation.

Project 7.6

Select an appropriate subject or plan a composition permitting a range of values using one uniform texture throughout. Simplify your forms by relegating them to the same surface treatment with your selected media. Work to achieve a maximum sense of volume and space. The size of your drawing should be influenced and determined by the scale of the texture chosen. Identify the presence of actual textures that are a result of the particular medium and paper surface used.

Some suggested ways of working are (1) scribbling in curved and circular movements; (2) scribbling in angular and straight-line movements; (3) cross-hatching; (4) stippling, using dots or commalike marks; and (5) combining or modifying one or more of the above methods.

Project 7.7

Select an alternative surface to paper such as frosted Mylar, easily obtained from an art supply store in the paper section, and draw with a variety of different, but soft-grade graphite pencils. Try the same textural assignment procedures with these materials and do several drawings utilizing different subjects. By using variations in pressure you'll find that the frosted surface of the Mylar takes the soft graphite very well, resulting in rich depositions of descriptive light and dark sensual marks. You'll notice that drawing with graphite against frosted Mylar produces a different sensation than drawing with graphite on paper. This sensual difference will undoubtedly give your drawings a different look of vigor, sumptuousness, and expressionism resulting from the combination of a different mark-making tool and drawing surface.

7-13 GIORGIO MORANDI (1890–1964; Italian). *Large Still Life with Coffee Pot.* 1933. Etching on copper, 10 × 13 11/16″ (253 × 347 mm). © The Art Institute of Chicago.

Critique (Projects 7.6 and 7.7)   Examine your results from Projects 7.6 and 7.7. Identify the passages of both uniform and actual textures. Do you have an understanding of how each came to be what it is? Do you have a sense of accomplishment from your methods of using the various drawing media to create texture on the two-dimensional surface of the paper or Mylar? Would you say that the power of the illusion of texture is strong? Have you used the illusion of texture to create volumetric forms that describe the three-dimensional properties of those forms effectively? Do the works stand alone as powerful visual forces irrespective of their subjects?

Invented or Synthetic Texture

Creating uniform textures, other than those derived from the combination of materials, calls forth a sense of invention. **Invented textures** are created textures whose only source is the imagination of the artist. Giorgio Morandi's etching on copper, *Large Still Life with Coffee Pot* (Fig. 7-13), and Josef Albers's *Pine Forest in Sauerland* (Fig. 7-14) are examples of both uniform and invented texture, as is Mark Tobey's *Long Island Spring* (Fig. 7-15). Although the hatching and cross-hatching used by Morandi suggests light flickering on the surfaces of the still-life objects, it is a formal device that he employs to define shape and mass, no matter what his subject. In this case, tonal hatching is also texturally descriptive. Albers, on the other hand, seems to have chosen (invented) his linear texture deliberately to describe the appearance and feeling of a pine forest, while Mark Tobey's abstract spattering and flecking explode with the vibrancy of new growth.

invented texture
A fictional or improvised texture created to heighten the imagined and descriptive forces of the surface quality of objects or forms within a composition.

Expressive Use of Texture

To summarize, the textural character of a drawing is influenced by the nature of the surface being depicted, the choice of materials, and the manner in which they are used, plus the inventiveness of the artist. Collectively, then, expressiveness is determined by the textural character of each artist's style. Vincent van Gogh's *Tree in a Meadow* (Fig. 7-16) and Jean Dubuffet's *Garden* (Fig. 7-17), each employing essentially the same medium (although van Gogh's ink drawing was done over a charcoal sketch), have responded to somewhat similar subjects with uniquely expressive textural drawings.

7-14 *above, left:* JOSEF ALBERS
(1888–1976; German-American). *Pine Forest
in Sauerland.* c. 1918. Pen and ink on paper,
12 5/8 × 9 5/8″ (32.1 × 24.5 cm).
Collection Anni Albers and the Josef Albers
Foundation, Inc.

7-15 *above, right:* MARK TOBEY (1890–
1976; American). *Long Island Spring.* 1957.
Sumi ink, 24 × 19 1/2″ (61 × 49.5 cm).
Private collection.

7-16 *right:* VINCENT VAN GOGH
(1853–1890; Dutch-French). *Tree in a
Meadow.* Reed pen, black and brown ink
over charcoal sketch on ivory wove paper,
19 1/8 × 24 (48.6 × 61 cm).
© The Art Institute of Chicago.

The beginner frequently shows conscious preferences for one master's way of working and very often gives legitimate expression to these
preferences by following the manner of the master. As the student ma-
tures as an artist, gaining assurance and independence from admired
models, a unique and personal style of working will evolve. Later in an

artist's career a highly developed mature style becomes the abiding trademark of an artist's work, as in Henry Moore's *Women Winding Wool* (Fig. 7-18). What an absolutely beautiful use of both uniform and invented texture, executed by a well-seasoned artist in midcareer.

7-17 JEAN DUBUFFET (1901–1985; French). *Garden.* 1952. Pen and carbon ink on glazed white wove paper, 18 3/4 × 23 3/4″ (47.6 × 60.3 cm). © The Art Institute of Chicago.

Project 7.8

Study drawings with texture, not just the ones included in this chapter. From the drawings you've studied, select ways of working that achieve descriptive, vigorous, appealing textural character, and adapt the methods to objects and subjects of your own choosing; perhaps you might want to reinterpret some of your earlier drawings as a means of revisiting an idea and improving on it through reinvention. To become familiar with any one technique, it will be necessary that you do numerous drawings in the same manner. At first you will want to refer to the master drawing; then as you acquire a feeling for the technique, put aside the model and go solo with the subject, the media, and the technique. It is important to work with the same, or at least similar, materials if you wish to achieve similar effects. Van Gogh's patterns and textures, for example (Fig. 7-16), depend upon the quality of line produced by a reed pen, for which a bamboo pen offers a suitable substitute. Let it be your intention to learn to use a technique, not to make a copy. Feel the mood of the style and the manner in which it was carried out, whether slowly and methodically or rapidly and impulsively, whether with small finger strokes or with large hand movements. Allow deviations to occur. It is important to discover the most satisfying ways of developing texture with a minimum of self-consciousness so that it becomes an integral element of your compositions, contributing to expressiveness.

7-18
HENRY MOORE (1898–1986; English).
Women Winding Wool. 1949. Crayon
and watercolor, 13 1/4 × 25″. (33.7 ×
63.5 cm).
Collection of the Museum of Modern Art,
New York. Reproduced by permission of the
Henry Moore Foundation.

Orchestration

With each new chapter of study in this drawing textbook, it is the revision author's desire that you begin to attain a level of orchestrational skill over the increasingly complex project assignments. The activity of creative drawing itself is complex—it is a *highly emotional process of realization* where the artist seeks to metaphorically write the visual statements that he or she desires to speak. The repertoire of possible materials, subject matter, and technical methodology increases with each new project. It is important that you begin to gain a sense of balance and harmony between these visual elements, and that you see yourself as sitting in the director's chair calling those elements into play at the appropriate time. We will visit the subject of artist as orchestrator several times throughout this book, particularly in Chapter 18.

Composition 8

Composition . . . alters itself according to the surface to be covered. If I take a sheet of paper of given dimensions I will jot down a drawing which will have a necessary relation to its format—I would not repeat this drawing on another sheet of different dimensions.

—Henri Matisse

The success of a drawing evolves in part from the appropriate matching of medium to subject matter and from the artist's skills of visual planning and orchestration within a selected picture plane. Effective drawing, however, requires more than learning how to choose and manipulate media successfully to produce a satisfying representation of an object, for neither choice of subject nor beauty of technique is sufficient if the artist has not also been concerned with composition. At its height of *aestheticism,* the Greek civilization used the word *form* in much the same way as we use the word *composition.* They defined form as having three distinct aspects: (1) the idea or concept an artist starts with, (2) the media and technical method an artist chooses, (3) that which fuses the idea and media together as one.

In a broader sense, **composition** is the **structure** of a picture as separate from both subject and style, and is essentially an underlying matrix of abstract design. It is the selection and organization of line, shape, value, texture, pattern, and color into an aesthetically pleasing arrangement embodying such principles of design as balance, harmony, rhythm, repetition and variation, dominance and subordination, and focus. The final desired effect of composition is a sense of unity—a oneness. It has been suggested that good composition supports the image so discreetly that it is never noticed.

Principles of composition are not hard-and-fast rules, never to be broken. They should be considered guides or suggestions that have been recognized and used effectively by successful artists for centuries. The same artists felt free to interpret the principles, and you are urged to do the same, as long as the result justifies whatever you choose to do. To break rules effectively, it is first necessary to know what they are.

composition
The structure of a picture as separate from both subject and style; the essential abstract design; the selection and organization of line, shape, value, texture, pattern, and color into an aesthetically pleasing arrangement embodying such principles of design as balance, harmony, rhythm, repetition and variation, dominance and subordination, and focus.

structure
The inner core that determines, identifies, and organizes outward form; the planned or methodical network that serves as a matrix supporting and delineating the organizational elements in a work of art.

133

8-1. THEODORE GERICAULT (1791–1824; French). *Sketchbook Page, Chicago Album: Sketches for Calvary Battle; a Mounted Officer.* Pen and dark brown wash, 6 1/2 × 8 15/16" (16.5 × 22.7 cm). © The Art Institute of Chicago.

A drawing, engraving, etching, painting, or sculpture (music, or literature as well) is composed of three elements—subject matter, form or composition, and content. Each of these three elements possesses force, and collectively they generate the total impact and longevity of sustained visual language. Subject matter alone is not a sufficient condition for a work of art. The significance of any work lies in its content or meaning. The meaning given to a subject depends largely upon its characteristic form, or composition selected by the artist. Beyond having the skill to reproduce the likeness of an object and control media, the artist must know the principles of composition and be able to use the art elements expressively to ensure full meaning to every drawing.

The focus of this chapter will be on composition as the underlying matrix, or abstract structure, of drawings, painting, printmaking, and sculpture, with attention given to subject, style, and content only as they relate to pictorial design. The projects will be represented primarily as design problems that, depending on individual preference, can be approached abstractly or representationally.

Many drawings fail from lack of planning. Compositional studies made from quick "thumbnail roughs" allow you to consider different alternatives and to solve many major compositional problems in advance. In a sketchbook page of rough sketches (Fig. 8-1) for what appear to be two separate paintings, it is evident that for Theodore Gericault the distribution of light and dark is as critical to composition as the placement of forms. Boldly simplified shapes of light and dark provide an effective visualization of his dramatic talent.

Sketchbook Activities

When you visit museums, and as you look at drawings, paintings, prints, and sculpture reproduced in art books and periodicals, analyze the compositions of various works. Develop the habit of making rough thumbnail sketches of the works. Although they need be no more complete than Figure 8-1—forms reduced to bold shapes, values simplified to white, black, and middle gray—it is important that the proportions of your study match those of the original. If you are enrolled in an art history class, you have the perfect opportunity to engage in this activity. Doing such sketches will make you more aware of how the elements of composition are integrated into a finished work of art.

Selecting Format

Composition begins with the size and shape of paper, referred to as the **picture plane,** with the edges of the paper becoming the first four lines of the drawing. Composition is the arranged relationship of all lines, shapes, and elements to the four edges as well as to one another.

Students have a tendency to start drawing without regard for the size of the paper, sometimes drawing objects so large that they run off the sheet or picture plane, but more frequently drawing forms so small that wide borders of blank paper are left. It is very important to learn to use the full size of the paper. If a drawing is to be smaller than the full sheet, four lines can be drawn to define the perimeter of the picture plane and establish the format of the composition—a rectangle being the most common. When working from nature or life, you will find it helpful to use a viewfinder with a rectangular opening to select what and how much to include in the composition. Moving the viewfinder closer to your eye or holding it farther away controls how much you see. Use it exactly as you would the viewfinder of a camera to find the most interesting view of the subject and to determine whether a horizontal or vertical format is more appropriate. Two artists might well arrive at totally different compositions, both equally satisfying and strong, particularly in the presence of each other.

While photographers are limited essentially to what they see in the viewfinder, artists have the option of shifting objects around, adding or eliminating forms to achieve better balance, create stronger visual interest, and improve composition according to what it is they want to say with the picture.

Closed and Open Composition

Within the format selected, elements can be arranged into a **closed composition,** in which the forms seem well contained by the edges of the picture plane, or into an **open composition,** in which images appear unrelated to the size of the paper, creating the impression that the composition, unlimited by the outer edges, extends beyond the boundaries of the picture plane. "Open" implies something free, expansive, flowing, unrestrained, spacious, magnified, undefined; "closed" suggests images that are contained, controlled, compact, reduced, complete. (See the discussion on separation and integration in the section on value, later in this chapter.)

Balance

Among the principles of composition, balance is given first consideration. In fact, composition is defined as the balancing of the elements of design. **Balance** exists within the confines of either symmetry or asymmetry; there is no other visual situation.

picture plane
The area of a flat surface defined by its outer borders on which an artist creates an image; often the picture plane, out of necessity, becomes transparent, allowing the artist to create three-dimensional forms and objects that exist in both deep and shallow space as three-dimensional illusions.

closed composition
Compositional format in which the art elements of form and structure are visually well contained by the edges of the picture plane.

open composition
Compositional format in which the images of form and structure appear unrelated to the size of the paper, creating the impression that the composition, unlimited by the outer edges, exceeds the boundaries of the picture plane.

balance
A major underlying principle of composition that unifies all the elements of design. It can be either symmetrical or asymmetrical.

8-2. *above, left:* REMBRANDT VAN RIJN (1606–1669; Dutch). *Canal and Bridge beside a Tall Tree.* Pen and brown ink, brown wash, 5 5/8 × 9 5/8" (14.3 × 24.4 cm). Pierpont Morgan Library, New York.

8-3. *above, right:* GEORGES SEURAT (1859–1891; French). *The Lighthouse at Honfleur.* 1886. Conté crayon heightened with white gouache, 9 13/16× 12 1/8" (24.9 × 30.7 cm). The Metropolitan Museum of Art, New York (Lehman Collection)

symmetrical balance
The dividing of a composition into two equal halves with seemingly identical elements on each side of a vertical axis.

asymmetrical balance
Balance based upon a visual sense of equilibrium that can be felt more than it can be measured. There are no specific rules for asymmetrical balance except that of diversity.

Symmetrical balance calls for dividing the composition into two halves with seemingly identical elements on each side of a vertical axis. Rembrandt's *Canal and Bridge beside a Tall Tree* (Fig. 8-2) demonstrates that the two sides need not be exactly identical as long as a feeling of balanced is maintained. The freshness of the pen line and the degree of variation between the two halves of the drawing prevent the composition from seeming stiff and static, which can be an effect of symmetrical balance. Symmetry, while it may lend an aura of dignity and formality to a composition, may lack a sense of mystery or provocative visual tension.

Most artists, agreeing that diversity offers greater interest than sameness, prefer **asymmetrical balance.** There are no precise rules for asymmetrical balance; it is based upon a visual sense of equilibrium that can be felt more than it can be measured. It can be likened to a teeter-totter. For children of the same size the board is placed with one half on each side (symmetrical), whereas with a small child and a larger person it becomes necessary to shift the position of the board to provide more weight for the smaller of the two (asymmetrical). In Seurat's *The Lighthouse at Honfleur* (Fig. 8-3) the fulcrum shifts to a point near the right edge of the sail as it intersects the horizon. The lighthouse with its accent of pure white, the flanking buildings, and the four figures, plus the light area in the lower right corner, all combine to offset the weight of the simplified dark mass at the left. Curiously, what remains if you crop everything at the left is an almost perfect symmetrical balance within the composition, very similar to the Rembrandt example.

Asymmetrical balance offers the artist greater compositional freedom. The composing process itself is one of organic origins surrounding an idea and naturally not predisposed to symmetry either concretely or abstractly. For most artists—Seurat being an exception—asymmetry is more flexible, more dynamic, and more exploratory. It allows the introduction of greater movement, greater action, and greater possibilities for resolution of a working composition.

Directional Lines

Line fulfills a number of compositional functions: It defines shapes; divides space; sets up movement, rhythm, and pattern; provides structure, and is one of the definitive elements of textural description.

Learning to control the placement of each line, and the patterns created by combinations of line, provides a means of adding expression to a composition.

While any composition incorporates various linear elements, a dominant mood can be established by placing the emphasis on **directional lines.** Long, relatively unbroken, horizontal lines are calm and restful, suggestive of peace, tranquility, infinity, and serenity, while vertical lines convey a feeling of dignity, stateliness, stability, and strength. Combining vertical and horizontal elements produces a solid, confident, and orderly sense of structure similar to architectural construction. Diagonal lines are dynamic, suggestive of action, and highly complementary to both horizontal and vertical lines. Broken patterns of diagonals can result in confusion and disorder; opposing diagonals create conflict and strife. Diagonal compositions are generally more forceful and disturbing than those based on a vertical and horizontal organization. While the apparent inertness of Wayne Thiebaud's scattered pastel sticks (Pl. 8) seems to belie such description, the composition offers strong hints of the characteristics mentioned, particularly when the calming empty horizontal bands at the top and bottom are cropped. However, because of the presence of the upper and lower areas of compositional rest, the forms appear spontaneously contained as well as unified within the picture plane.

Curved lines are associated with grace, elegance, and gently flowing movement, while more complicated patterns of curves with frequent reversals produce greater animation, even agitation (Fig. 8-1). By combining arcs and diagonal lines, Charles Sheeler's drawing *Yachts* (Fig. 8-4) and Cy Twombly's oil on canvas *Untitled* (Fig. 8-5) create strongly contrasting moods, the first gentle and relaxing as if one were being consoled by a playful breeze, the second expressing turbulence and a sense of heaviness characteristic of diagonal lines, which often radiate a downward thrust.

Directional lines, or directional compositional thrusts, can be introduced without actually being drawn, as evidenced in the invisible

directional lines
Compositional linear treatment that establishes a particular or dominant mood or emotion from its linear emphasis through a variety of different line treatments yielding a visual sense of compositional weight and balance. The linear treatments may flow in the same direction or in opposite directions, each conveying different feelings.

8-4. CHARLES SHEELER (1883–1965; American). *Yachts*. 1924. Lithograph, 8 1/4 × 9 3/4" (21 × 25 cm).
National Museum of American Art, Smithsonian Institution, Washington, D.C.

8-5. CY TWOMBLY (b. 1929; American). *Untitled.* 1972. Oil on canvas. 4' 9 3/8" × 6' 4" (1.47 × 1.95 m). Collection Nicola Roscio, Rome. Courtesy of the artist.

8-6. HENRI MATISSE (1869–1954; French). *The Plumed Hat.* 1919. Pencil on paper, 29 7/8 × 14 3/8" (75.9 × 36.5 cm). Detroit Institute of Arts.

shape
The flat, two-dimensional aspects of form as opposed to three-dimensional volume; when a three-dimensional form is reduced to a silhouette, the viewer is conscious only of its shape.

though unmistakable verticality of Matisse's *The Plumed Hat* (Fig. 8-6). Although softened by the rich pattern of loops and gracefully undulating curves, it is the figure's almost rigidly upright pose that evokes such playful and sensual effects of directional lines.

Shapes

Shape refers to the flat, two-dimensional aspects of form as opposed to volume. Donald Sultan's drawing *Three Lemons and an Egg* (Fig. 8-7) illustrates beautifully that when a three-dimensional form is reduced to silhouette, we become conscious only of its shape. Silhouetted shape

8-7. DONALD SULTAN (b. 1951; American). *Three Lemons and an Egg.* 1986. Ink and pencil on paper, 15 × 16″ (38.1 × 40.6 cm). The Arkansas Arts Center Foundation Collection: The Stephens Inc. City Trust.

can therefore be a powerful illusion for three-dimensionality. Shapes can be defined by contour line and by changes of value, texture, and color, alone or in combination.

Project 8.1

One shape drawn on a piece of paper immediately sets up a relationship between it and the paper. Select a single shape, either a geometric shape such as a circle or triangle or the simplified silhouette of a familiar object like a cup or pitcher. In a series of thumbnail studies explore the relationship between the shape and the surrounding space as you move that shape by drawing it in different positions within the areas of the small picture planes. Enlarge and reduce the size of the shape by letting the shape dominate the space; then let the space dominate the shape. Create visual situations of both pleasing balance and disturbing tension. Introducing a second shape will introduce a new set of relationships that must be balanced. Each shape that is added sets up other conditions requiring adjustments to previous solutions—decisions about placement, keeping forms separate, letting them touch, maintaining equilibrium, or allowing one shape to dominate and overlap another. Figure 5-6 presents another variation of this project.

Critique (Project 8.1)   Have you created some interesting relationships between your shapes and the surrounding space within the picture plane? Are there some studies in which the configurations of the remaining space are more interesting than the shape itself? How would you define the effects of balance in your resulting thumbnail drawings? How would you define the effects of **visual tension** in the same drawings?

A shape cannot exist alone in a drawing; it can be seen only in relation to adjacent shapes and the space that surrounds it. Composition, therefore, involves positive shapes defined by negative space, and negative shapes defined by the spaces that positive shapes occupy (see Chapter 3). It is as necessary to compose negative space as it is to be concerned with positive shapes; in fact, there is an undeniable synergy between the two in any strong composition.

visual tension
A visual situation within a composition where the elements of shape, pattern, balance, harmony, and contrast all interact to produce interesting imbalances or cacophonies; some of the elements may be more pronounced than others, which creates a higher level of compositional interest.

8-8. FRANZ KLINE (1910–1962; American). *Untitled.* 1960. Ink on paper, 8 1/2 × 10 1/2" (21.6 × 26.7 cm). Whitney Museum of Art, New York.

The interlocking of positive and negative is perhaps the most apparent when represented in the extremes of black and white (Fig. 8-8). Franz Kline's intention was "to create definite positive shapes with the whites as well as with black." It is surprising, considering the force of his gesture and the scale of his brush strokes, to realize that his drawing is only slightly larger than the page size of this book.

Project 8.2

With a series of sketches, or studies, not larger than 4 × 6, or 5 × 5 inches, explore positive shapes and negative space. Using an X-acto knife, begin by cutting five shapes inward from the edges of the rectangle or square picture plane. The shapes may be large or small and of any type—amorphous or geometric—although similar shapes result in a more unified design. Using charcoal or soft graphite stick, shade either the remaining shape or the cut-away segments to emphasize positive and negative by contrasting light and dark. Experiment with symmetrical and asymmetrical balance by doing several small studies of each; then do several utilizing *dominance* and *subordination*. Try leaving one, two, or even three edges of several small picture planes unbroken to create different visual tensions.

Rotate your drawings to view them from another angle to alter the compositional impact. Artists frequently look at their works in progress upside down, or view them in reverse in a mirror to determine compositional weaknesses, particularly regarding aspects of balance, compositional weight, and lateral and longitudinal tensions.

Critique (Project 8.2)   As you look at your small positive-negative studies, it should be readily evident whether or not you achieved interesting relationships of equality and balance, dominance or subordination, even tension and calm within your compositions. Which drawings are of greatest intrigue to you as positive-negative studies: the symmetrical or asymmetrical drawings?

Do you have a deeper understanding of the aspects of composition after having performed these thumbnail exercises? Can you see how these fundamental compositional theories can be applied to nearly every work of art that has ever been created?

Visit an art museum or gallery exhibition and scrutinize the compositions of the works you see before you. Try to apply every fundamental exercise that you performed as a study to the works of art you see in the professional setting.

repetition
The unifying visual sense of regularity in the appearance of similar elements—lines, shapes, patterns, textures, colors, values, and movements within a composition.

unity
That ephemeral quality suggesting compositional "wholeness"; the quality of harmony, balance, and cogency of the art elements within a composition.

Repetition-Pattern

The **repetition** of similar visual elements—lines, shapes, patterns, textures, and movements—contributes to a sense of **unity.** The purposeful repetition of a shape or other visual element to create or suggest an overall harmonious design is **pattern.**

Pattern need not be limited to either regularly or identically repeated design. The crows on the seventeenth-century Japanese screen (Fig. 8-9) create the impression of a strongly decorative pattern, yet very few of the shapes have been repeated in identical fashion, and the groupings are highly irregular. The birds, which in reproduction appear as silhouettes, are seen in bold value contrast to the gold-leafed background.

Variation-Contrast

To prevent the repetition of any element from becoming either too obvious or too monotonous, variety can be introduced to provide **contrast.** Looking at a work of Karen Kunc, *Tumbleweed* (Fig. 8-10), we see a delightful repetition of circular and amorphous shapes, almost all boasting some uniquely tonal and textural embellishments.

Unified compositions are not built on sameness. There can and must be **variety;** yet with each element introduced, with each principle considered, the determining factor is always balance. Observe again the drawing *Tumbleweed.* Notice how Kunc uses an ever-changing value range of textural lights and darks to emphasize important visual details such as the abstract tumbleweed branch. She pulls every drawn mark as an orchestrated element into a unified whole in support of the tumbleweed form as it courses through the midsection in a powerful downward arch as if trellised by the strong dark vertical pole.

That which applies to two-dimensional design applies equally to compositions built around recognizable subject matter rendered three-dimensionally. Students too frequently think of design as existing apart from representational drawing, when in fact the two are inseparable, as

8-9. ANONYMOUS (early seventeenth century; Japanese). *The Hundred Black Crows,* one of a pair of six folded screens. Gold leaf and black ink with lacquer on paper, height 5′ 1 3/4″ (1.57 m). Seattle Art Museum.

pattern
Any compositionally repeated element or regular repetition of a design or single shape; pattern drawings in commercial art may serve as models for commercial imitation.

contrast
The visual effect of a striking difference between art elements creating a condition of compositional intrigue; opposites or complementary art elements that through their visual forces *set each other off* or draw attention and focus to each other or to particular areas within a design.

variety
A generic or specific condition of established diversity; descriptive term used to identify any number of conditional states of ranging multiplicities in a work of art; the antithesis of what is obvious or monotonous.

8-10. KAREN KUNC (b. 1952; American). *Tumbleweed.* 1997. Graphite on frosted mylar, 36 × 18″ (91.5 × 45.7 cm). Wake Forest University Art Department Collection, Winston-Salem, North Carolina.

evidenced by the work of Sidney Goodman in his charcoal drawing *Model on a Draped Table* (Fig. 8-11). This drawing is laden with powerfully contrasting elements of lights and darks, positive shapes and negative spaces laced together with the vestiges of partially drawn, once acknowledged form. There is a tremendous sense of push-pull to the composition with its spatial dynamic and strangely compelling visual tensions of shape variation and contrast. This is an undeniably powerful embodiment of asymmetrical design, representation, readable content, visual poetry, and mystery at its best.

Dominance-Subordination

In successful composition certain visual elements assume more importance than others. As a center of interest, such elements become dominant; all other parts are subordinated to them, as in Figure 8-10. Although the artist wants the viewer to be conscious of everything in the drawing and to look at every detail, attention ultimately focuses on a dominant element. However, when the dominant element becomes so strong that it overwhelms everything else, it then throws the composition out of balance. In symmetrical composition the center of interest will be placed in the middle of the composition. Generally, the **focus** of interest will not be centered in asymmetrical composition.

Movement

A picture with only one center of interest not only bores the viewer but also shows the artist's lack of compositional understanding of what it takes to invigorate the eye of the audience. Like a dramatist, novelist, or composer, an artist introduces secondary focal points—subplots, as it were—leading the eye of the viewer from one to another, eventually directing attention back to the dominant focal point. The artist determines the sequence in which the eye moves from one area to the next, ultimately focusing on the center of interest. Often during the execution of a work of art, the artist begins to discover the pathway that the eye takes, regardless of what he may have intended, and builds on the strengths of how his eye is directing him. He or she may not be consciously aware of this at the time it is occurring. Frequently, it is only after a work is finished that full realization of the degrees of compositional success become apparent. Elements of movement within a composition are powerfully engaging, and once an artist fully learns to trust his eye, he is ready to meet the demands of the composing visual elements. He learns where the eye will confidently lead and responds trustingly.

In Edward Hopper's *Study for "Evening Wind"* (Fig. 8-12), the viewer's gaze seems to focus first on the white rectangle of the open window, as does that of the woman in the drawing. But the viewer's attention does not remain fixed there. That space is essentially empty and devoid of any real visual interest. Instead, it is the woman, particularly

8-11. SIDNEY GOODMAN (b. 1936; American). *Model on a Draped Table.* 1977–1978 Charcoal. 29 × 41″. (73.6 × 104.2 cm).
Photo courtesy of Terry Dintenfass, Inc., New York.

focus
The prime center of visual importance within a composition to which all other visual elements yield; it holds the viewer's attention because of its attractive and dominant influence on its surroundings.

8-12. EDWARD HOPPER (1882–1967; American). *Study for "Evening Wind."* 1921 Conté and charcoal on paper, 10 × 13 7/8" (25.4 × 35.7 cm). Whitney Museum of American Art, New York.

her head, nearly centered on the page, that is the focal point. The contour of her head silhouetted against the curtain is the most sharply delineated detail in the drawing. The curtains billowing into the room and the circling back of the bed covers direct attention to the figure. A seemingly incidental detail—the dimly suggested pitcher and washbasin at the left—contributes to compositional balance and functions as a secondary focal point pulling the viewer back into the room.

Just as the flow of traffic can be programmed, so, too, the way the eye of the viewer moves through a composition can be controlled by a skillful artist who follows the dictates of his own eye when drawing. When looking at art, our eye tends to move rapidly between large shapes, moving more slowly through small, complicated passages as it pauses to examine details. What appears as casual disarray in Richard Diebenkorn's *Still Life/Cigarette Butts* (Fig. 8-13) is actually a very thoughtful traffic flow pattern in disguise created from the highly credible clues his own eye gave him during the execution of the drawing. As we further examine this creation in pencil and ink, we can recognize both the power of subtlety and the intrigue of complexity contained within the compositional elements that cause the eye to playfully course over the tremendously varied surface of the drawing.

Project 8.3

Determine the compositional details in the drawing that set up eye movement. When you focus on the center of the picture plane, the eye tends to travel in a counter-clockwise direction, taking in the expressive variations of media handling so skillfully performed by the artist. Notice that the most dramatic compositional elements are the two sheets of white drawing paper lying next to each other. They define the visual impact of the tonal range by providing the extreme whites of the drawing in contrast to the darks that comprise most of the remaining surface area.

It would be instructive to do a diagram of the composition. Begin by drawing a pair of lines corresponding to the left and bottom edges of the white shape (sheet of drawing paper) centered at the right, continuing both lines across the full width and height of the drawing. Repeat with the bottom and right edges of the white shape at top center. (Notice how we previously identified the white shapes as the representative sheets of white paper that they are. However, we now refer to them as shapes, thereby neutralizing their significance as representative objects so that

8-13. RICHARD DIEBENKORN (b. 1922–1993; American). *Still Life/Cigarette Butts.* 1967. Pencil and ink, 14 × 17" (35.6 × 43.2 cm). Courtesy of the artist. National Gallery of Art, Washington, D.C.

we can separate the literal object from its visual function in the work of art. As you finish drawing the lines corresponding to the two sheets of paper, indicate all elements that fall into alignment with those four major compositional lines by drawing them in contour fashion. Then add the important diagonals, curves, and circles. Notice how masterfully Diebenkorn has integrated all aspects of composition thus far discussed in this chapter into this one drawing.

From this kind of analytical study, it becomes apparent that there is need for a governing matrix or superstructure within composition, as Diebenkorn so well exemplifies.

Project 8.4

Using simple soft graphite pencil or charcoal, break up the space of a picture plane by dividing a rectangle of any size (from 4 to 6 inches to a full sheet of paper) into shapes that are interesting both individually and in relation one to another. The shapes should be varied in size and outline and at the same time provide elemental areas of both simplicity and complexity. The design can be derived from straight lines, curved lines, irregular and/or free-formed shapes, or a combination of forms. Remember that similar shapes create unity, but variety contributes to pictorial interest.

Next, introduce white and black, plus an intermediate value, to establish centers of interest. Simplify shapes or engage in additional breaking up of space as you develop a flow of movement through the composition. Allow directional lines, linear patterns, and the repetition of shapes, spaces, intervals, and values to set up pathways of eye movement. Try several of these and incorporate as many principles of design as possible into your compositions.

Critique (Project 8.4)   As you observe your designs, describe the directional movement of your eyes. Then, consider the following concepts: Is there a focal point? If so, where is it? Where does your eye tend to focus first? What design details cause your eye to move away from the focal point? What design details cause your eye to keep moving from point to point? What part does the element of value contrast play in the direction of eye movement?

8-14.
MARK TOBEY (1890–1976; American).
Mountains. 1952. Crayon on paper
mounted on cardboard, 37 3/8 × 47"
(95 × 119.5 cm).
Private Collection.

rhythm
The visual manifestation and flow of
repetition, variation, patterning, harmony
of form, and movement within a composition; a flowing and regular recurrence
of the art elements within the compositional structure of a work of art.

Rhythm

Repetition, variation, and movement combine to create **rhythm** in both musical and pictorial composition. The word *rhythm* automatically seems to evoke an image of consecutively flowing lines, as evident in Mark Tobey's crayon drawing (Fig. 8-14), yet it is not limited to curvilin-ear forms. Undulating patterns of both straight and curved lines with at-tention to the repetition of groupings and intervals of similar forms as well as direction of lines also establish compositional rhythm. All the vi-sual attributes of a well-composed drawing, etching, painting, or sculp-ture play into varying manifestations of visual rhythm. In the mixed-media work by Navajo artist Emmi Whitehorse entitled *The Con-version* (Fig. 8-15 and Pl. 9), we see a definite matrix of underlying com-positional structure utilizing all the aforementioned attributes of rhythm; the artist has fused drawing and painting media so well that we are al-most unaware of the incidental intricacies of the different media. They flow and blend, and they are welded together into an undeniable or-ganic unity. It is a large work, measuring 51 × 78 inches, and there is much to visually analyze in order to determine its compositional merits and strengths. The subtle use of contrasting values, amorphous and geo-metric shapes, irregular patterns, and multilayered compositional forms that exist between deep and shallow space keeps the eye moving. The viewer pauses only momentarily to focus on the intriguing strangeness of a particular form before moving on to the next one.

Project 8.5

Develop a composition with a rhythmic pattern created by only vertical, horizontal, and diagonal lines. Let each straight line intersect two borders of the paper or rectangle with no change in direction (keep them straight) within any single line. Establish rhythm through changes in spacing and density of lines. Concentrate on creating an interesting composition with balance and centers of interest, employing what you have learned to date about media variation and line. Try to avoid repetitious pattern, yet at the same time establish an interesting structural pattern that will serve as the compositional skeleton or superstructure.

Project 8.6

Follow the same instructions for the last assignment, substituting curved lines. Reverse curves or S-curves can be used, as they easily establish a pattern of curving lines, and when you enhance them with line variation, you can create a spatially dynamic illusion on the two-dimensional surface of the paper.

Critique (Projects 8.5, 8.6)   Do your drawings exhibit an immediate and interesting breaking up of the picture plane? Are the individual shapes curious or even mysterious? Is there a center point of focus? Are there several centers of focus? How would you assess the balance within each composition? Do the patterns seem to flow, allowing the eye to move with ease and delight around the picture plane? In your later drawings employing curved lines, does the pictorial space become more alive? Can you readily distinguish between what appears to be shallow and deep space?

Depth

In both two-dimensional design and three-dimensional representation, overlapping forms suggest spatial depth, as in Edgar Degas's *Six Friends* (Fig. 8-16). We automatically see the figures as being one in front of another in space. The effect is heightened when overlapped shapes also diminish in scale. When two similar shapes are represented in different scale, we are inclined to see the larger form as being closer. That interpretation comes from our actual experience of seeing how similar forms of the same size become different in size according to their distance from us when we view them. Illusionist art plays on the reality of actual experience and allows the artist to create dynamic spatial relationships between forms and the viewer on a two-dimensional surface. We never view as flat a room we are sitting in or the space around us as we walk through a park or meadow. We are continually experiencing the motion of our three-dimensional bodies within three-dimensional space, and we navigate by judging the size and scale of objects according to the distance between the objects and ourselves. Thus, our experiences in day-to-day seeing and moving in space provide us with the instincts of being able to create those three-dimensional illusions on a two-dimensional surface.

Project 8.7

Select several interestingly shaped objects, including a teapot or some similar form that has both positive and negative elements inherent in its design. Line them up on a table without grouping them into a composition. Study each form and see it as a flat shape. It will be helpful to do a simple contour drawing of each object.

Create a composition representing the objects as two-dimensional shapes, overlapping the forms to suggest spatial depth. Explore different ways of overlapping the shapes so that partially revealed forms are interesting as shapes apart from the objects they depict. Organize the objects to provide visual interest to the surrounding space. Develop the drawing further by creating flat areas of light, dark, and intermediate values, using contrast as a means of providing focus. Overlapping shapes of the same value will result in new shapes, which may enhance the

8-15. EMMI WHITEHORSE (b. 1957; Native American: Navajo). *The Conversion.* 1992. Pastel, oil, paper on canvas, 51 × 78″ (129.6 × 198.2 cm). Courtesy of LewAllen Gallery, Santa Fe, New Mexico. Photography by Dan Morse.

composition overall. As long as the original shapes of the forms and the new shapes created by the overlapping of forms can be understood and do not interfere with spatial relationships, they need not be separated. Remember that a balance of simplicity and complexity contributes to an interesting composition.

Value

Value, as we learned in Chapter 6, is an essential element in pictorial composition. It functions to define and separate forms in space, establish balance, provide movement, maintain spatial unity, and introduce expressiveness. A common failure in many pictures by inexperienced artists is a lack of purpose in their tonal structure. An artist who understands how to control value, rather than being bound to a literal copying of what is seen, can rearrange, reverse, or intensify patterns of light and dark to strengthen a composition and create a new visual statement, whether working from life or from imagination.

Distribution of Value   The impact of a work of art is based to a large degree on the distribution of light and dark. Strong patterns of dark against light and light against dark (Fig. 8-16) create a much different effect than light and dark used with middle-value grays (Fig. 8-15). Even against middle values the impression of white and black depends upon whether they are separated, appear side by side, or are surrounded one by the other.

Project 8.8

Arrange three simple shapes (squares) in a rectangle so that one shape is completely surrounded by two shapes that appear to float in front of the background.

This will appear as three squares of different sizes—the smaller squares inside the largest and all inside the rectangle. A good example of this is Josef Albers's *Homage to a Square* series (Fig. 8-18), where the center of focus is the smallest square contained inside all other larger squares. Using compressed charcoal or assorted gray crayons, fill in each separate area with a different value—white, light gray, dark gray, and black. Repeat the exercise four times, using each of the values as the background and altering the values of the other shapes. Observe the changes in visual impact.

Project 8.9

Compose a second, more elaborate composition using either abstract or representational shapes. Plan a major center of interest and two minor ones. Develop the composition in different values using the previous assignment as reference. Areas of greater contrast create focal points and spatial separation; subtle value changes provide transition and subordination.

Critique (Projects 8.8 and 8.9) Identify the center points of focus in all the drawings you've made and consider the degree of eye movement that occurs in each drawing. Do the drawings with multiple focus points of interest create more or less eye movement? How do you feel about your ability to create more or less eye movement in an image? How does eye movement enhance your image? How does it strengthen a visual statement?

Defining Space with Value Forms are made to advance and recede through degrees of value contrast. Against a dark background, light shapes advance to the degree of their brilliance; against a white background, light tones are held closer to the background while dark shapes are projected forward as in the value scale (Fig. 6-1) and David Faber's monotype entitled *Aberdeen Headlands* (Fig. 8-19). (A monotype is a drawing done with printer's ink on a blank plate and then transferred to paper with the use of an etching press.) (Monotype will be discussed further in Chapter 11.) In this work we see a defined spatial separation

8-16. EDGAR DEGAS (1834–1917; French). *Six Friends*. c. 1885. Pastel and black chalk, 45 1/2 × 28" (115.6 × 71.1 cm).
Rhode Island School of Design, Providence (Museum Appropriation).

8-17. IRWIN TEPPER (b. 1947; American). *Third Cup of Coffee*. 1983. Charcoal on paper, 39 7/8 × 40 7/8" (111.1 × 130.8 cm).
The Arkansas Arts Center Foundation Collection, 1984.

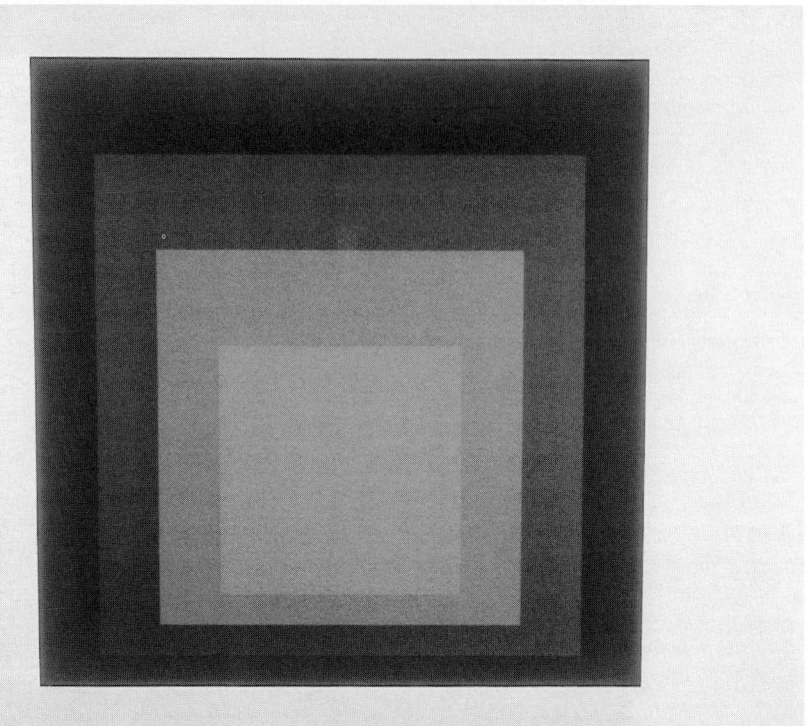

8-18. *above:* JOSEF ALBERS (1888–1976; German-American). *Homage to a Square* c. 1955. Four-color silkscreen, ed. 8/100. Reynolds House Museum of American Art, Winston-Salem, North Carolina.

8-19. *right:* DAVID FABER (b. 1950; American). *Aberdeen Headlands.* 1988. Monotype with etching and litho inks on gray wove paper, 39 3/4 × 26 7/8" (101.1 × 68.3 cm). Collection of the artist.

8-20. JOSEPH RAFFAEL (b. 1933; American). *Hyacinth*. 1975. Ink and ink wash, 22 1/2 × 30″ (57.2 × 76.2 cm). Courtesy of Nancy Hoffman Gallery.

between the black center rectangle and the lighter, ethereal outer portion of the composition. This separation phenomenon causes the dark rectangle to hover in an advanced position in front of the lighter outer background. In the reverse situation a lighter center will advance against and in front of a dark background. The stronger the contrast, the more a form advances. When contrast is lessened, forms appear to recede. These are powerful visual tools that artists use to endow their compositions with both subtle and bold spatial dynamics.

Separation and Integration   In opposite fashion to Faber's dark-against-light monotype, Joseph Raffael solves the problem of defining and separating light shapes against other light shapes by creating dark halos where the flower petals overlap in his drawing *Hyacinth* (Fig. 8-20). Shapes separated in this manner may take on a strongly decorative character, yet notice the way the petals stand out in relief. Charles Sheeler employed a similar technique in Figure 8-4, as did Richard Ziemann in his graphite drawing *Behind the Garden* (Fig. 8-21).

Project 8.10

Using such objects as teakettles, cups, jars, and other familiar objects, develop a composition in which shapes of similar value are made to stand out in bold relief one from another through the method of separation described above. The method is spatially most effective when it combines both sharp and softened edges.

Closed form, in which a value is confined within the contour or silhouette of an object, stresses separation. **Open form,** in which a value blends into a similar surrounding area without any obvious separation, allows the integration of various elements as well as producing a feeling of aliveness. When the same or similar values are placed side by side, edges begin to disappear and forms begin to merge. Such transitions serve to introduce movement by permitting the eye to flow from one area to another.

closed form
The area of a composition where a color, value, tone, or texture is confined within the contour or silhouette of an object or shape and thereby stresses visual separation from its surrounding elements.

open form   A form whose value or values blend into the similar surrounding areas of the composition without noticeable or obvious separations; also, a form that allows the integration of various compositional elements, producing a feeling of movement and vitality.

The same value came be made to function as both foreground and background without any loss of spatial depth, as seen in Elmer Bischoff's *Girl Looking in a Mirror* (Fig. 8-22). The figure and its reflection are joined together where the reflected foot becomes one with the upper leg of the figure, allowing the eye to move from the foreground into the space of the mirror. Bischoff has used value contrast to separate the figure from the background in some areas; in other areas closely related values allow the figure to merge into the background. The eye is invited to move freely into and out of the picture space. Notice that volume is suggested through relatively flat areas of tone without extensive modeling.

Project 8.11

In a series of charcoal or wash studies, explore the use of limited value to establish the effect of movement both into and out of space. Reserve white and black values for accents. Use broad, simplified shapes to describe the subject and its surrounding areas. Use contrast to separate forms and focus attention, letting closely related values provide transition. It is important to let light and dark flow from one area to another in order to provide movement and to prevent individual shapes from becoming too isolated. Avoid equal emphasis on light and dark; balance does not depend upon an even distribution of values. In each study, let one value predominate. You will discover that a limited number of values, well handled, can convey the impression of many tones.

Expressive Use of Value The choice of value scale determines the expressive tone of each drawing. Although it is difficult to exactly categorize emotional responses to works of art, generally, light pictures suggest vitality or exuberance, while dark pictures can evoke a sense of heaviness, or perhaps gloom and even despair. In drawings, prints, and paintings, the exaggerated use of chiaroscuro (discussed in Chapter 6) contributes to a heightened sense of theatricality.

Point of View

Even after careful consideration and application of the principles of composition, a drawing might well seem dull and uninteresting simply because the subject has been presented from a very ordinary point of view.

Artists, not just students, frequently let themselves become trapped into relying upon a single point of view, either out of habit or because of a deeply set mannerism often referred to as an "artist's rut." Other factors that play into artistic monotony are the restrictions imposed because of studio space or the environment in which an artist must work. In drawing classes, instructors often confront space limitations when arranging setups, which must be visible to everyone in the room. Because it is rarely possible to provide a rich variety of viewpoints, students must take the initiative to find interesting positions from which to draw. They should not, however, select one drawing bench or easel and remain there for the entire semester, so that every still life or figure tends to be viewed from exactly the same eye level and distance away.

Compositions need not and should not be monotonous if the point of view is varied. Develop the habit of making quick thumbnail sketches to examine possibilities for expanding your compositional vocabulary. Add variety, drama, and interest by shifting to high or low eye levels; even an eccentric viewpoint can be well orchestrated and produce fresh new results from the most common of subjects. Try to see beyond a mere academic approach to subject matter by allowing your sense of instinct and impulse to clue you into different approaches, to different points of view.

A composition can be enhanced either by cropping or by opening up and adding more space than actually exists. When the will arises, let radical alterations happen and begin to direct your sense of compositional instinct by looking for only the unconventional approach or viewpoint. Everything must be planned by the artist's skills and working knowledge, whether the creation results in a deliberate and academically true representation or an altogether unconventional reassembling of the subject into a nonrepresentational or abstract composition. Therefore, be certain that if cropping is used as a technique, it is intentional and not the result of poor planning. Thumbnail sketches allow you to consider different alternatives, as in Figure 8-1.

8-23. GINO SEVERINI (1883–1966; Italian). *Self-Portrait in Straw Hat.* 1912. Charcoal, 21 1/2 × 21 5/8" (54.6 × 54.9 cm). © The Art Institute of Chicago.

Multiple Points of View Representational drawing traditionally assumes a consistent point of view—each object drawn from the same eye level, each object occupying its own space—yet no single fixed viewpoint exists for either the artist or viewer. Our visual perceptions of three-dimensional form and space depend upon continuous eye movement. Interestingly, to experience a drawing, the eyes of the viewer must shift from one area to another in exactly the same manner that the eyes of the artist move around objects to draw them.

Acknowledging this aspect of seeing has resulted in a freer approach to drawing, which introduces movement through the use of multiple points of view. Paul Cézanne, recognizing that no object could be fully explained when drawing from one viewpoint, chose to look at individual objects from different vantage points. By combining the various views into a composite image, he strengthened the sense of volume and structure.

Unlike Cézanne, the cubists used multiple viewpoints to shatter the solidity of three-dimensional form. Objects were broken into fragments, which were reassembled in such a manner as to tell the viewer more about the original object than could be visible from a single point of view, as in Gino Severini's *Self-Portrait in Straw Hat* (Fig. 8-23).

Project 8.12

A cubist approach involves juxtaposing segments of three or more separate views—top, front and/or back, and side—into a composite drawing, creating the impression of movement around the object in space. On separate sheets of clear acetate, using a black design marker (made for use in impervious surfaces), draw at least four different views of the same object, keeping all the drawings in the same scale. Place the drawings one over the other. By shifting them slightly, incorporate the most interesting sections into a single drawing that reveals the character of the object as fully as possible and suggests movement around it. There will be many interesting and vastly different possibilities of depicting the object when using this method. Do not attempt to maintain a literal representation with a recognizable contour. Begin to respond more to the total visual effects of the overlying sheets of acetate, allowing those image variations to be your creative guide. Allow for distortion that will require the viewer to reassemble the fragments of information. Use shading and variations in heavy pressure and release of pressure to emphasize important contours and to suggest volume and space. Integrate the form into a complete composition, allowing the appropriate lines to run to the edge and off the sheet of paper. Remember that the first and most important lines of a picture plane are its borders. The initial planning of the composition can be done on acetate or tracing paper. Select a good-quality drawing paper and do a finished drawing in a medium of your own choosing.

Critique (Project 8.12)   Consider your drawing a finished statement, and one that is perhaps the most complex of any drawing you have done to date. Is there a sense of life and vitality in the representation of your subject? To what do you attribute this vitality? Did you feel reluctant to depart from the representational elements into the abstract realm of image rearrangement and restatement? Are you intrigued by the ultimate recognition of what the object has become through an entirely unique approach? Do you sense that the resultant composition is the object itself? Are you able to glean a great deal of visual information about the object or subject matter from the drawing? Do you have the sense that you are looking at your drawing from many different viewpoints simultaneously?

Does the composition hold together as a unit? Do you have a sense that this drawing exists on its own visual merits regardless of its derivation? Would you consider the drawing a visual generation once removed from the subject matter? Was there a decisive moment when you knew that the drawing was flying on its own compositional strengths? At what point did you stop drawing, and when did you realize that the drawing didn't need you any longer? Was this the mark of its being finished? How well do you feel your choice of media fits the statement?

How do you feel about this drawing, knowing that it is your creation? How would you feel about it if someone else had done it?

Summary

The principles of composition outlined in this chapter apply to other creative disciplines as well. Artists who make images can be thought of as "visual poets" and poets can be thought of as "literal imagists." Both are composers. Musicians and lyricists are both composers and poets, evoking images with sounds, rhythms, and cadences that call up memories and transmit emotions. In the arts, the common threads that weave the different disciplines together are as visually tangible and spiritually provocative as they are literally contextual. Each artist in his or her own discipline strives for unity, harmony, and oneness between concept and material. One of these most important common threads is that of composition, which all artists use.

9 Perspective

To create depth on a flat surface is to create an illusion. Much of the success of illusionistic art depends upon the successful use of perspective.

—Duane Wakeham

linear perspective
A scientific method of determining the correct placement of forms in space and the degree to which such forms appear to diminish in size at a given distance.

Linear perspective is a scientific method of determining the correct placement, scale, and spatial relationships of forms in space and the degree to which such forms appear to diminish in size at a given distance. Early in the fifteenth century young Italian Renaissance artists, who were seeking a logical means of creating unified, measurable space, formulated the system of perspective based on a set of visual principles. Filippo Brunelleschi's interest in perspective stemmed from direct observation and analysis of visual phenomena. His original experiment involved painting a building on a small panel into which he drilled a peephole at a point corresponding to the eye level of the artist. Rather than looking directly at the painting, people viewed its reflection in a mirror by peering through the peephole from the back of the panel. By confining the image to what could be seen with one eye through the small hole, Brunelleschi restricted vision to precisely the fixed point of view upon which linear perspective is predicated.

With the invention of the camera, photographs duplicating views previously depicted by artists (Figs. 9-1, 9-2) verified the system devised by the Florentines—the lens of a camera being a single eye in a fixed position. In both Giovanni Battista Piranesi's eighteenth-century etching *Interior of St. Paul Outside the Walls, Rome* and a photograph of the same structure, the converging horizontal lines and regular diminution of equally spaced elements create the illusion of vast, deep interior space on a flat, two-dimensional surface. (Many aspects of perspective, as they will be discussed in this chapter, can be seen in Figures 9-1 and 9-2.)

9-1. *above:* GIOVANNI BATTISTA PIRANESI (1720–1778; Italian). *Interior of St.Paul Outside the Walls, Rome.* c. 1749. Etching, 16 × 23 3/4" (40.6 × 60.3 cm). Reprinted from *Views of Rome Then and Now* by Herschel Levit.
Published by Dover Publications, Inc., 1976

9-2. *left:* Interior of St. Paul Outside the Walls, Rome. Photograph.

9-3. ADOLPH MENZEL (1815–1905; German). *Interior of the Rolling Mill at Konigshutte.* Pencil, 8 3/4 × 12" (22.3 × 30.4 cm). Berlin, Staatliche Museen, Nationalgalerie, Sammlung der Handzeichnungen (271).

empirical perspective
Perspective, that, unlike **linear perspective,** relies upon direct observation rather than a set of rules.

Empirical perspective, unlike linear perspective, relies upon direct observation rather than on a set of rules. An artist with a well-trained eye for seeing shape, size, and scale relationships, who can determine angles by sighting against verticals and horizontals, can create convincing and relatively accurate perspective without having to engage in the mechanical construction of space on a large drawing board using T-squares, triangles, and thumbtack vanishing points. Adolph Menzel displays this ability to accurately sight visual relationships in his drawing of an iron-rolling mill (Fig. 9-3).

Fixed Viewpoint and Cone or Vision

fixed point of view
A mandatory rule for linear perspective; an established, unchanging position from which an object or scene is viewed that enables the rules of linear perspective to be enacted.

The rules of linear perspective are dependent upon a single **fixed point of view,** when in fact we almost never view anything under that condition. At the location depicted in Dominique Papety's *Via Gregoriana* (Fig. 9-4) for example, it is possible to look into the two converging streets from the same spot, but only by moving your head. Even when we hold our heads in a fixed position, our eyes are almost constantly in motion. Perspective drawing, in theory, demands that you not shift the position of your head or the direction of your gaze.

cone of vision
The shape of containment of all that can be seen from one stationary position without moving the eyes.

All that can be seen without moving your eyes is contained within a **cone of vision.** The limits of your cone of vision—between 60 and 80 degrees—are easily determined by extending your arms and inscribing within a vertical circle all that can be seen clearly as you look directly forward. Only a small portion of the immediate foreground falls within your lines of sight in contrast to the expansive distant view.

picture plane
The area of a flat surface defined by its outer borders on which an artist creates an image; often the picture plane, out of necessity, becomes transparent, allowing the artist to create three-dimensional forms and objects that exist in both deep and shallow space as three-dimensional illusions.

Picture Plane

The **picture plane** is an imaginary vertical line that slices through the cone of vision. If you placed a sheet of glass before you with the intention of drawing just what you see through the glass, the glass would represent the picture plane. Substitute a sheet of drawing paper for the glass, and the paper becomes the picture plane. How much is seen through the glass and represented on the paper picture plane depends on how close you stand to the picture plane.

9-4. DOMINIQUE PAPETY (1815–1849; French). *Via Gregoriana.* c. 1838. Graphite pencil with blue ink wash, on gray paper, 13 × 17 3/4". (33 × 45.1 cm). Musée Fabre, Montpellier.

9-5. LORRAINE SHEMESH (b. 1949; American). *Paint Box.* c. 1983. Graphite on paper, 22 1/4 × 30 1/8" (56.5 × 76.5 cm). Glenn C. Janss Collection. Courtesy of the Allan Stone Gallery.

The closer an object is to the picture plane, the larger it will be projected. Lorraine Shemesh creates an almost overwhelming sense of immediacy as well as monumentality by placing the front edge of the paint box right at the line of the picture plane (Fig. 9-5).

Horizontal Line, Ground Plane

The **horizon line** indicates where sky and earth would appear to meet if the ground were perfectly flat and nothing blocked the view. It also corresponds to the eye level of the viewer. In perspective drawing, as the viewer is elevated higher above ground level, the horizon line rises on the picture plane to reveal more of the ground (Fig. 9-6); the closer to the ground level, the lower the horizon line (Fig. 9-4). It is the artist who determines eye level; the viewer has no choice but to accept it. No matter how you look at David Macauley's pen-and-ink drawing of the Gothic cathedral under construction (Fig. 9-6), whether holding it above your head or at waist level, you cannot change the point of view he has

horizon line
A line that corresponds to the eye level of the viewer in linear perspective; the line where sky and earth appear to meet (provided the earth is perfectly flat and nothing blocks the view). The vanishing point (VP), central vanishing point (CVP), and the furthest end point of the center line of vision are all located on this line.

9-6. DAVID MACAULAY (20th century; English-American). *Constructing a Gothic Cathedral.* Pen and ink. From *Cathedral* by David Macaulay. Copyright 1973 by David Macaulay.
Reproduced by permission of Houghton Mifflin Company.

ground plane
A flat horizontal plane on which the viewer stands that extends to the horizon. In drawings of interior spaces it is referred to as the floor plane.

floor plane
Same as ground plane albeit for interior spaces.

table plane
Same as ground plane or floor plane, a term used to denote the flat plane of a drawing table surface when drawing objects on a table.

central line of vision
An imaginary line centered in the cone of vision, extending from the eye and meeting the horizon line at a right angle.

center of vision
Same as the **central vanishing point;** the point of intersection of the central line of vision and the horizon line.

central vanishing point
The point of intersection of the line of vision on the horizon line; same as the point of the **center of vision.**

selected. The placement of the horizon line determines the angles from which all objects are viewed, and its location must be established even when it does not appear on the picture plane.

The **ground plane** is a flat horizontal plane that extends to the horizon. It is also called the **floor plane** in drawings of interior spaces and the **table plane** when drawing objects on a table. Only when drawn at eye level will the back edge of a floor plane or table plane coincide with the horizon line.

Line of Vision, Central Vanishing Point

The **central line of vision,** centered in the cone of vision, is an imaginary line from the eye to the horizon line. Anything, such as the edge of a table, a line between floorboards, or a curb line, that lies exactly in the line of vision will appear as a vertical line. Extended, it will meet the horizon line at a right angle. The point of intersection, the **center of vision,** or **central vanishing point** (CVP), lies directly opposite the viewer.

One-Point Perspective

Parallel lines by definition always remain equidistant, yet in our common visual experience they appear to converge as they recede. The basis of one-point perspective is that all lines parallel to our line of vision, whether to the side, above, or below, will appear to meet at the CVP, as in Robert Bechtle's charcoal drawing (Fig. 9-7). One-point perspective seems most effective when the central vanishing point is placed near the center of the horizon line. In one-point perspective, lines parallel to the picture plane are drawn parallel to the horizon line. When three-dimensional forms are set at some distance from the viewer, there is no problem with our visual perceptions of them, but a natural, visual distortion occurs when the forms are at close range.

Establishing a Grid   A series of "seeing" exercises, starting with direct observation of forms in space, then moving to some basic drawings with horizon lines and vanishing points (VPs), will demonstrate a system of determining the position and scale of objects in space. *Understanding how to draw just one square in perspective is really all that is necessary to create complex perspective studies.*

Project 9.1

An 8-inch (20 centimeter) square of heavy paper or cardboard appears perfectly square only when you look at it directly from above or held vertically in front of your eyes with the horizon line in the exact center of the square. From all other points of view it is a square in perspective. Held horizontally at arm's length, which forms a line that is square to your body, it will appear as a single line at eye level but will change as you move it above or below eye level. Move it from side to side, viewing it without turning your head. Make similar observations with the card held vertically and parallel to your line of vision. Although the shape enclosed by its four edges changes with each different position, if you hold it horizontally while maintaining it at arm's length, the dimensions of the front and back edges will remain constant while the length of the sides will change. They will become longer as the square is raised and lowered from eye level (the horizon line) and when it is moved out to the left or right sides (away from the CVP).

9-7. ROBERT BECHTLE (b. 1932: American). *Parking Garage with Imapla.* Charcoal, 9 1/2 × 14″ (24.1 × 35.6 cm). Courtesy of the Gallery Paule Anglim.

Project 9.2

While sitting down, study the square lying on a table surface in front of you placed at arm's length, square to and centered on your line of vision. Hold your pencil also at arm's length to determine the measurable vertical distance between the front and back edges (depth of the square) as compared with the width of the front edge. Calculate the angle at which the sides converge by checking them against the vertical of your pencil held at arm's length. Since the back edge of the square is farther away from you, it is shorter than the front edge. The difference in these lengths divided by two will equal the distance the back edge comes inward from each side of the front edge of the square.

Using graphite, draw the shape empirically as observed through sight and pencil calculations; then, using ballpoint pen, T-square, and triangle, overdraw it on the graphite drawing according to your mechanical measurements to see how accurately your eye recorded the square. The depth measurement is critical; be as accurate as possible. Center the square near the bottom of a full sheet of newsprint, letting the front edge be approximately 3 inches (8 centimeters) in length. The result will be a **foreshortened square**—or a square seen in perspective. Locate the CVP by extending the side edges until they meet. Draw the horizon line through that point. Visual believability and visual accuracy can be two distinctly different things to the beginner. However, the more you practice seeing and drawing objects in perspective, the more accurate your eye will become. Using a T-square and triangle to check the accuracy of your empirical drawing and making adjustments or corrections when necessary will give a good indication of how your sights skills are improving.

Project 9.3

Moving the cardboard square one full width to either side places it in a new perspective. The overall shape changes as the back edge shifts in relation to the front edge and the side edges both angle somewhat in the same direction. Each additional move will continue to alter the shape enclosed by the lines representing the four edges.

On the basis of the one square drawn empirically, it is possible, using linear perspective, to develop an elaborate drawing in one-point perspective without having to move, study, or draw the cardboard square. All necessary measurements have already been established; no further decisions need be made.

Project 9.4

Extend the lines of the front and back edges of the original square horizontally across the page. Mark off equal widths of the front edge of the original square along the bottom line, connecting each mark to the CVP to create a full row of squares. Although the shapes are different, each represents a foreshortened square in perspective. Notice that the units of measurement representing the back edges of the squares are also equal.

Project 9.5

To continue adding rows of squares is relatively simple, but first draw a 2-inch (5-centimeter) grid on the 8-inch cardboard square (creating four 2-inch squares per side) and add a diagonal line connecting two opposite corners. If you have measured accurately, the diagonal line will intersect the opposite corners of each of four squares. Place the square back on your table and return to your drawing.

Starting from the lower outside corner of one of the end squares, draw a diagonal through the square and extend it to cut across all of the converging lines.

foreshortened square

A square seen in perspective while lying flat on the ground plane whose parallel sides converge into the central vanishing point on the horizon line.

Add a horizontal at each point of intersection to create a grid as many units deep as it is wide. The width of all the squares has already been established, and since the diagonals of equal squares are equal, the diagonal establishes the depth for each additional row (Fig. 9-8).

Repeating the procedure using one of the squares in the back row allows you to continue extending the grid toward the horizon line. The grid can be expanded to either side by extending all horizontal lines across the width of the picture plane and repeating the horizontal measurement of any line laterally.

Project 9.5 demonstrates that *once the depth of the first unit has been determined, the depth of all other units of equal size is automatically established.* No additional decisions are necessary; therefore, it is imperative that the first unit be measured and drawn as accurately as possible. When creating perspective from imagination, it is necessary to have a keen sense of how much depth would be seen at the eye level selected.

Project 9.6

To construct a matching vertical grid, add exact vertical lines where each horizontal intersects one of the outer receding ground lines. Transfer the unit of measurement from one horizontal line to its adjoining vertical; complete the vertical grid by connecting each mark to the CVP (Fig. 9-9).

Equal units of measurement on adjoining horizontal and vertical lines that are parallel to the picture plane remain constant. Equal units diminish only on lines that recede from the picture plane. Such observations will aid you in seeing and understanding foreshortened forms as you draw from life and will allow you to draw convincingly from imagination.

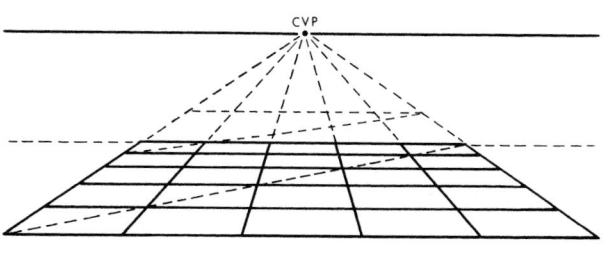

9-8. Use of diagonal to establish horizontal grid in one-point perspective.

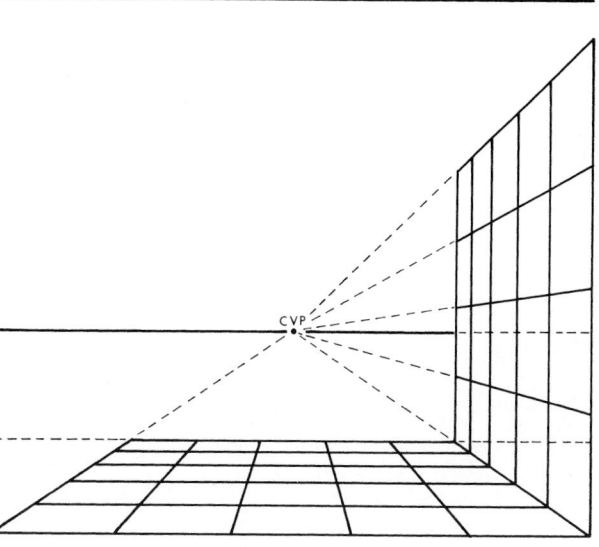

9-9. Constructing vertical grid in one-point perspective.

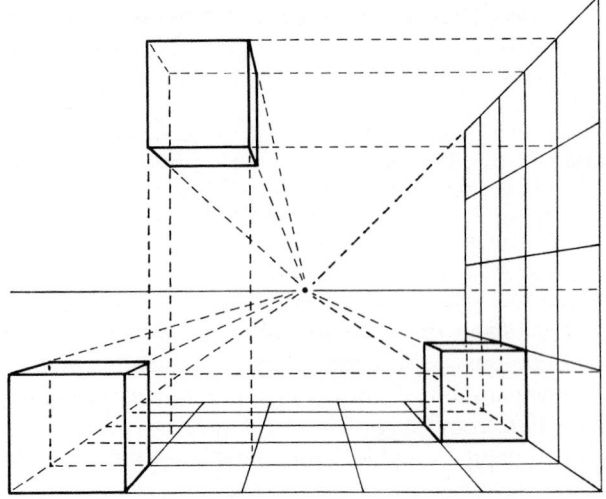

Horizontal grids can be raised or lowered to any level; vertical grids can be swung to the left or right. As the horizontal plane approaches eye level (the horizon line), you will see less space between the lines defining the front and back edges of each row until it reaches exact eye level and becomes a single line identical with the horizon. The same changes occur as the vertical plane swings toward the CVP, where it eventually becomes identical with the vertical central line of vision.

Project 9.7

Diagonals of the squares of a grid are parallel lines and, as such, appear to converge at common points—on the horizon for those of the horizontal plane, on a vertical line drawn through the CVP for those of the vertical plane. Draw one or two diagonals in each direction on both grids to verify this. (The horizontal diagonals will become the basis for two-point perspective; the diagonals of the vertical grid will become the means for determining the perspective of inclined planes.)

Almost everything else included in this chapter will be but a variation on what you have already done.

Project 9.8

Three-dimensional solids, such as cubes and blocks, are merely a series of contiguous vertical and horizontal planes. To create a cube, add vertical lines from each corner of a square on the horizontal grid. Carry a line across from the vertical grid to establish the height for one corner, and complete the cube with the help of the CVP (Fig. 9-10).

Project 9.9

You now have the information necessary to create a one-point perspective "fantasy image" constructed out of solid square blocks and units composed of multiples of blocks. Spread the blocks across the width of the page, push them deep into space, stack them, and let some of them float above the ground plane, as in Figure 9-10. You might prefer to do these drawings on tracing paper in order to preserve the grids so that you may reuse them for future drawings. If so, lay the sheets of tracing paper over the grid drawings and proceed. Include only the horizon lines with each drawing, not all of the grid lines. Simple shading of the cubes will increase the sense of solidity and volume. (Later you will be able to add cast shadows; see p. 174.)

Establishing Scale; Using Diagonals to Establish Depth   Scale is established by assigning a specific dimension to the length of one side of one square. The dimension may be changed for different drawings done from the same grids as long as the scale remains constant within any single drawing.

The illusion of depth is particularly noticeable when objects of the same size recede into space at regular intervals, such as the columns in Figures 9-1 and 9-2. Using the grids developed in the preceding projects, it would be possible to contrast a facsimile of the church interior. Linear perspective also provides alternatives for determining size and distance that are not dependent upon a complete grid system.

A relatively simple method employing the use of diagonal lines might well be the manner in which Jacopo Bellini determined the spacing of the figures in *Funeral Procession of the Virgin* (Fig. 9-11). The system is based on the principle that diagonals cross at the exact center of a plane; lines drawn through the center point divide the plane into equal halves, as demonstrated in Figure 9-12.

Project 9.10

Draw a set of converging lines more or less corresponding to the heads and feet of the figures in Figure 9-11. Add vertical lines to represent the first two figures in the procession. Forgetting for a minute about people, notice that the verticals and converging horizontals create a plane seen in perspective. Locate the center of that plane by connecting the four corners with diagonals. A line from that center point to the VP will establish the midpoint of any additional verticals. A diagonal line from the top of the first vertical through the midpoint of the second to the base line establishes the position for a third vertical spaced at the same interval (Fig. 9-12).

The use of diagonals allows for the repetition of any regularly spaced elements—vertical or horizontal. Notice, however, that the spacing of figures in Bellini's *Procession* (Fig. 9-11) is not mechanically repetitious; the distance between the last two figures in the first group is almost double that between the other figures, which adds a note of visual interest to the composition.

Calculating Scale and Distance   *An object or form whose size can be comprehended establishes the scale for everything else in a perspective drawing.* It is possible, for example, judging by the height of an average human figure, to state with some accuracy that the city wall in Bellini's drawing (Fig. 9-11) is just over 30 feet in height (9 meters) and lies

9-11. JACOPO BELLINI (c. 1400–1471; Italian). *Funeral Procession of the Virgin.* Pen and brown ink over black chalk underdrawing on tan paper, 3 3/4 or 8 1/8 × 11 7/8" (9.5 or 20.6 × 30.2 cm).
The Fogg Art Museum, Harvard University, Cambridge, Massachusetts.

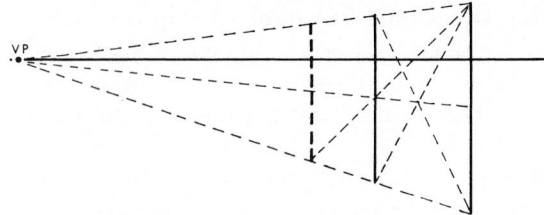

9-12. Use of diagonals to determine spacing of repeated intervals.

approximately 120 feet (37 meters) from the viewer, and that the procession passes between 15 and 20 feet (5–6 meters) to the right. These dimensions can be calculated by placing a figure against the wall seen between the two figures at the far right. The height of such a figure has already been established; since all the figures in the drawing are viewed at eye level, his eyes would fall on the horizon line, his feet at the base of the wall. Repeating the height of the figure (probably less than 6 feet [1.8 meters]) vertically gives us the height of the wall; marking off the same unit of measurement on a horizontal line projected from his feet to a point immediately below the CVP (just outside the left edge of the drawing) provides the other dimension.

The logical systems of perspective are an extremely valuable and creative tool, as is evident in this chapter. Once the systems are established, an artist can compose spatially by defining forms as true and accurate in relationship to their surroundings. Like attempting to solve a puzzle with a few preliminary but significant clues, the visual mystery of defining subject matter in space by applying the principles of perspective becomes clearly evident and irrefutable at the drawing board. One portion of visual definition generates the definition of successive forms. For example, it was possible, without a grid, to add a distant figure of equal size to the Bellini drawing because scale, ground plane, and eye level were already established. When all three conditions are known, a figure can be placed at any spot within perspective space with the assurance that the size of the figure will be correct at the distance selected.

Two-Point Perspective

Learning to draw cubes in perspective provides the raw material for constructing almost any form, since very few objects exist that cannot be enclosed within a square or rectangular container. Blocks or cubes placed square to the picture plane (one side parallel to the picture plane) are drawn in **one-point perspective;** blocks set at an angle necessitate the introduction of **two-point perspective.** Nineteenth-century American painter Thomas Eakins, a dedicated practitioner of linear perspective, uses both one-point and two-point perspective in his study for *Chess Players* (Fig. 9-13). The drawing also illustrates how simple blocks below began to be transformed into detailed specific forms above.

Project 9.11

The characteristics of two-point perspective can be studied empirically by placing a cube or square box just close enough to you that you can reach out and move it easily. A clear plastic cube, such as those used for displaying photos, would be particularly effective.

Begin with the cube directly in front of you, square to your line of vision. Observe the changes that occur as you slowly rotate the cube clockwise. The front, ver-

one-point perspective
A visual condition where all lines parallel to our central line of vision, whether to the side, above, or below, appear to meet at the central vanishing point (CVP).

two-point perspective
The system of drawing objects not set square to the picture plane but set at an angle; it requires the use of both left and right vanishing points (LVP and RVP).

9-13. THOMAS EAKINS (1844–1916; American). *Perspective Drawing for Chess Players.* c. 1876. Pencil and ink on cardboard, 24 × 19″ (61 × 48.3 cm). The Metropolitan Museum of Art, New York.

tical surface becomes the left side as the right side appears as the front; the configuration of the top begins to change, and the bottom edges are seen as diagonal lines. As the rotation continues and you see less of the left side and more of the right, the measurable height dimension of the left corner begins to diminish, and that of the right outer corner increases. The less you see of a side, the greater will be the angle between the base of that side and the horizontal of a pencil held at arm's length. When the cube reaches a 45-degree angle, you see equal amounts of both side planes receding at the same angle, the front and back corners in exact vertical alignment. Until that moment, the back corner was to the left of the front corner; rotated beyond 45 degrees, it will move to the right. Depending on the size of the cube, you might be able to detect the convergence of the sets of parallel lines delineating the separate planes.

Drawing a cube in two-point perspective requires two VPs. For a cube sitting at a 45-degree angle, both VPs will be equidistant from a CVP. At any other angle, the less you see of a side, the closer its VP will be to the CVP; the more you see of a side, the farther away will be its VP.

Project 9.12

Draw a series of cubes rotated to different angles seen above, at, and below eye level in relation to one horizon line. You might want to compare your drawing with the plastic cube. When one cube is positioned at random angles to the others, it must have its own set of VPs.

Do a second drawing of a number of cubes spread across the width of the paper, with each constructed in relation to just one set of VPs placed near the outer ends of the horizon line. A single set of VPs automatically positions the cubes square to one another.

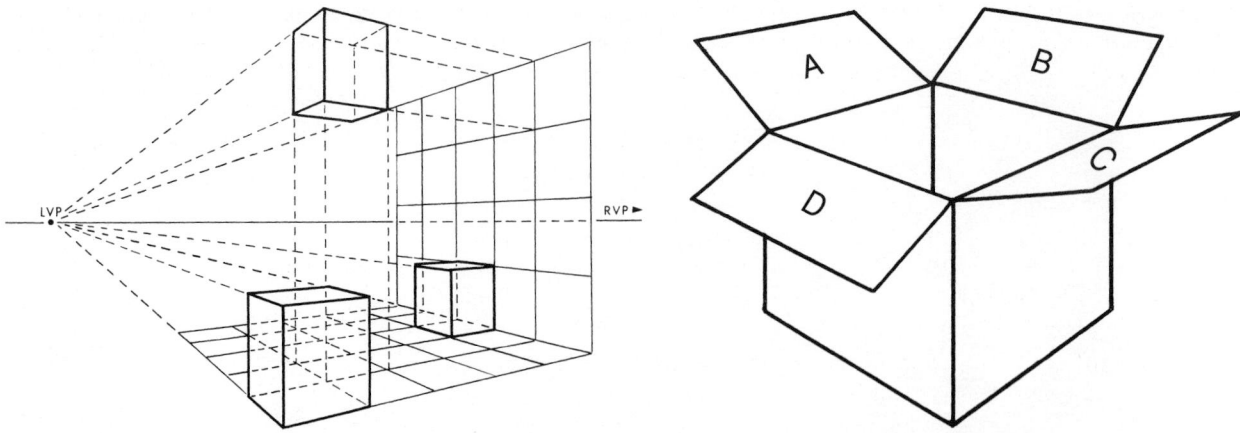

9-14. *above, left:* Figure 9-10 seen in two-point perspective.

9-15. *above, right:* Drawing inclined planes: box with flaps.

inclined planes
Planes not parallel to the ground or floor planes whose vanishing points exist on vertical lines that pass through the corresponding vanishing point on the horizon line.

ascending planes
Planes not parallel to the ground or floor planes whose vanishing points appear above the horizon line.

descending planes
Planes not parallel to the ground or floor planes whose vanishing points fall below the horizon line.

Project 9-13

Either on tracing paper or as a new drawing, select one cube positioned below eye level and extend it in both directions, using the system of parallel lines from Project 9.10 to determine the depth of each additional cube. Extending the top or bottom edges of all the cubes in the two rows to the VPs will produce a horizontal grid drawn in two-point perspective. Vertical grids can be constructed exactly as in Project 9.5. Figure 9-14 rotates Figure 9-10 into two-point perspective.

Inclined Planes   Look at Figure 9-15. The flaps of the box represent **inclined planes**—planes not parallel to the ground plane.

Project 9.14

Make a tracing of Figure 9-15. Use a straightedge to locate the VPs for all planes of the box, including the flaps. Draw the horizon line through the VPs of the sides. Notice that because they are parallel to the ground plane, the long edges of the flaps vanish at those points on the horizon line, while the short sides of the flaps converge at different VPs above or below the horizon line.

VPs on the horizon line relate only to lines and planes parallel to the ground plane. Here we see how the flaps, being inclined planes, are not parallel to the floor or to the ground plane. They have VPs on vertical lines that pass through the corresponding VP on the horizontal line. VPs for **ascending planes** appear above the horizon; those for **descending planes** fall below the horizon. (Review Project 9.6.) Ascending planes angle upward away from the viewer, as in flaps A and B; descending planes angle downward from the viewer, as in flap C. Flap D might appear as a descending plane because it falls below the rim of the box, but extending its short sides reveals that they converge upward. Viewed from the opposite side of the box while being closer to the inside long edge, flap D would be seen as a descending plane.

Uphill and Downhill Streets   Inclined planes are to be found with surprising frequency in landscapes and cityscapes. Pitched roofs, for example, are inclined planes, as are uphill and downhill streets and roads.

You may experience total confusion the first time you are confronted with the challenge of representing an uphill or downhill street lined with buildings. Until you have attempted to draw such a scene, it is very probable that you have never really looked at buildings on a hill in terms of perspective. The scene becomes easier to draw when you remember that in spite of the inclined street plane, houses are built with level floors and vertical corners. All horizontal elements, such as the flat roof of the house in the left foreground of Wayne Thiebaud's *Ripley*

Ridge (Fig. 9-16), are drawn to VPs on the horizon line, always at eye level of the observer, whereas lines of inclined planes— sidewalks, curbs, and objects parallel to the street, such as automobiles—will converge at VPs either above (looking uphill) or below (looking downhill) the true horizon line. Thiebaud has placed the VP so far above the horizon that the street appears to be nearly vertical, which is precisely the impression many first-time visitors have of San Francisco's hills. Rarely can an uphill or downhill street be drawn as one continuous inclined plane since the roadbed levels out at street crossings, as it does in the immediate foreground of Figure 9-16, where the surface of the intersection must be drawn to true horizon.

A puzzling phenomenon occurs when you do a drawing looking downhill. The imaginary horizon line is below the VP of the converging lines of the street curbs, but the angle of ascent is less than for lines representing a level plane; thus VPs of downhill street lines appear below the true horizon line. In fact, only in a drawing of the underside of a descending plane, viewed from below, would the edges converge downward.

Three-Point Perspective

Blocks or cubes placed square to the picture plane are drawn in one-point perspective, or one vanishing point, as in Figure 9-10. Blocks or cubes set at an angle necessitate the introduction of two-point perspective utilizing two vanishing points, as illustrated in Figure 9-14; and finally, **three-point perspective** requires three vanishing points in order to accommodate forms both distant and near that are positioned at different angles to one another in space.

In perspective, vertical lines remain vertical as long as the head is held level while viewing. The corners of a rectangular object placed above or below eye level continue to appear vertical if the object is viewed from sufficient distance (Fig 13-24). When the same object is viewed from such close range that you must tip your head to look up or down at it, the corners appear to converge at a VP above or below. Looking up or down, by itself, does not create three-point perspective unless the object, as in Charles Scheeler's *Delmonico Building* (Fig. 9-17), is also placed at an angle. In this age of skyscrapers, when we have frequent opportunities to view great heights from both above and below, three-point perspective has become a familiar visual experience for most people—whether they realize it or not. Figure 16-17 provides an exaggerated bird's-eye view of three-point perspective.

Project 9.15

In Figure 9-14 one cube floats above eye level. Imagine all three hovering above your head at different angles and draw them in three-point perspective. You will need a third VP for the vertical corners of the cubes. If you locate it above the left front corner of the floating cube in Figure 9-14, that corner and the hidden back corner of the lower cube in front will be drawn as vertical lines—or, as the figure illustrates, it is the same vertical line. In three-point perspective, all other corners will converge to the VP above.

First, try drawing the cubes as you think they might appear. Do a second drawing using the grid system to establish location and size. Be aware that in three-point perspective equal units of measure diminish as they move in the direction of all three VPs. Turn your finished drawing upside down to view cubes floating below eye level.

9-16. WAYNE THIEBAUD (b. 1920; American). *Ripley Ridge.* c. 1976. Pencil on paper, 22 × 15″ (55.9 × 38.1 cm). Collection Robert A. Rowan, Pasadena, California. Courtesy of the artist. © Wayne Thiebaud/licensed by VAGA, New York, N.Y.

three-point perspective
A system for drawing three-dimensional objects in space on a two-dimensional plane that requires three vanishing points: both the left and right vanishing points of two-point perspective where lines recede on the horizon, and a third vertical vanishing point where lines parallel and vertical to the ground appear to converge.

9-17. CHARLES SHEELER (1883–1965; American). *Delmonico Building.* c. 1927. Lithograph, 9 3/4 × 6 3/4" (24.8 × 17.2 cm). Library of Congress, Washington D.C.

Critique (Project 9.15) How well are you able to envision the aspects of one-, two-, and three-point perspectives in your drawings? Has the study of perspective thus far helped you in your understanding of the relationships of forms in nature, in the landscape, in the cityscape? Has perspective helped you better understand space? How accurately do you measure when drawing with a straightedge? How accurately are you able to draw forms in their correct proportions and spatial relationships to one another? Has this chapter deepened your understanding of the importance of seeing?

Circles in Perspective

A look at the rims and bases of bowls, cups, and other circular objects in the drawings of most students, and even those of some advanced artists, indicates that the perspective of a circle is little understood. The three most frequent errors are re-created in Figure 9-18: (1) outer edges drawn as points, (2) front and back edges flattened, (3) upper circle drawn too full as compared with lower circle.

A circle seen in perspective assumes the shape of an ellipse (compare examples 1 and 2 in Figure 9-18 with the circles in the floor pattern of Figure 9-2). The exact shape of an ellipse can best be visualized as a circle inscribed within a square projected into perspective—or a foreshortened square.

Project 9.16

Figure 9-19 provides the necessary clues for drawing an ellipse. In the foreshortened square provided, draw diagonals to locate the centered lines accurately. The correct positioning of the points where the circle crosses the diagonals can be deter-

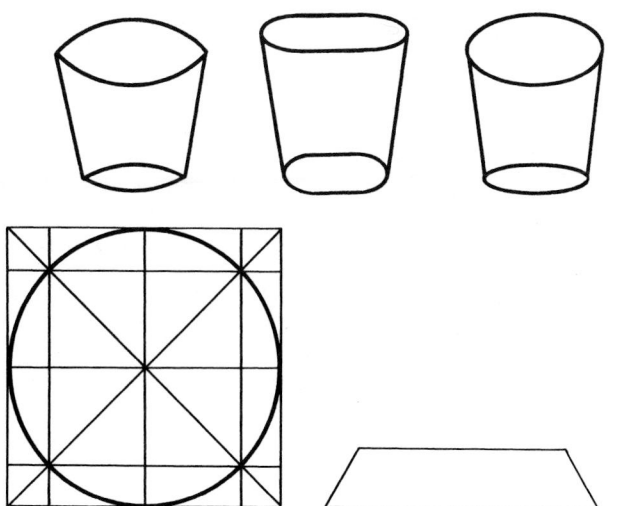

9-18. Drinking glasses with circular edges drawn in faulty perspective.

9-19. Diagram: determining circle drawn in perspective.

mined by transferring the measurements from the bottom edge of the diagram to the front edge of the square and drawing lines to the CVP. Draw the circle/ellipse so that it touches each of the eight reference points. Make certain that it is a continuous and consistently curved line with no points and no straight passages.

The center point of a circle, inscribed within a square drawn in perspective, is not equidistant between the front and back edges. The widest dimension of the ellipse, however, is tangent to the side edge of the square at points equidistant between the front and back edges, making the front half of the circle—if drawn correctly—measurably larger and fuller than the back portion.

Ellipses in Varying Perspective The third common error—mismatched ellipses—creates an effect of a shifting point of view (Fig. 9-18). The fullness or openness of an ellipse is determined by eye level (Fig. 9-20). Viewing the rim of a drinking glass in a sequence of positions from well below eye level to high above will allow you to duplicate the diagram three-dimensionally. Hold a transparent drinking glass vertically in your hand in front of your face so that the top is a perfect horizon line at eye level. Keep your eyes focused on the top plane of the glass and raise the glass slowly and vertically, letting your eyes follow upward while viewing the top plane of the glass begin to form an acute ellipse. As you raise the glass higher, the ellipse opens up more and more. Then, lower the glass and watch the ellipse close down back to the horizontal plane of the top of the glass. Continue lowering the glass and observe again how the top opens up into an ellipse. By turning the glass sideways so that the top of the glass forms a vertical plane, move it from left to right and observe the same progression of the formation of the ellipse as though it were a circle standing vertically or a disk rotated on a vertical axis.

Drawing Circular Objects Cups, plates, bowls, glasses, bottles, teakettles, coffee pots, pans, flowerpots, baskets, lamp shades, records, computer disks, wheels—the list of circular objects in our immediate environment available for drawing is not easily limited. When drawing a circular object from life, the correct degree of openness for an ellipse can be determined by using your drawing tool as a measuring device (discussed in Chapter 3) to calculate the proportional relationship of the vertical measurement between the front and back midpoints of the ellipse as compared with its maximum width.

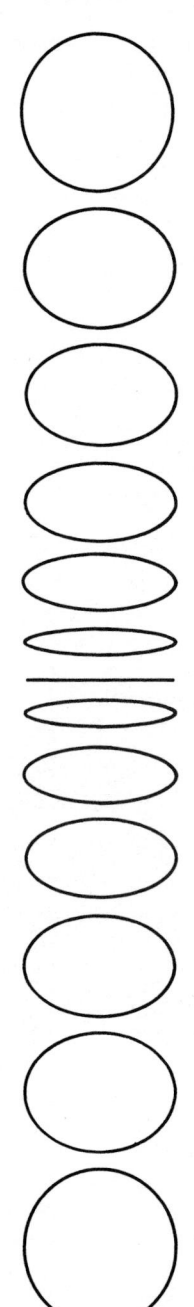

9-20. Ellipses drawn in varying perspectives.

Project 9.17

To draw two circles of the same size in perspective, one above the other, and ensure that they are correctly foreshortened, first draw a cube in one-point perspective. Add circles to the top and bottom planes using diagonals and center lines as in Figure 9.19.

Connect the two circles with vertical lines at the outer edge to create a cylinder. The verticals should join the lower ellipse just behind its widest point to create the fullest effect of roundness. The width of the cylinder, as drawn, will be greater than the dimension of the center line of the circle, but less than the full width of the front plane of the cube because of the large corner segments that are cut away.

Project 9.18

Do a tracing that includes the complete upper ellipse, the two connecting verticals, and only the front portion of the lower ellipse. The cylinder will appear more three-dimensional. Notice that the curve of the bottom rim is fuller than the curve of the upper rim. When students cannot see the full ellipse, they have a tendency to draw the bottom curve flatter than it should be.

Do a series of tracings in which you treat the cylinder first as hollow, then solid, and with various vertical sections cut out. Remove a full quarter of the cylinder, various quarters, one diagonal half. For each separate image, trace only those portions of the upper and lower ellipses that would be visible, adding necessary verticals and connecting lines.

Project 9.19

Turning the paper sideways transforms the drawing into a cylinder resting on its side at eye level. Practice drawing vertical ellipses and cylinders resting on their sides, seen from both above and below. Using the one-point and two-point grids from earlier projects and the diagram from Figure 9-19 will allow you to place cylindrical forms both parallel to the picture plane and at angles.

Few circular objects we see and draw are plain cylinders. In profile the sides curve, bulge, or flare, sometimes all in the same object, so that circles of various diameters are involved. To draw such objects correctly, you must center all the ellipses one above the other.

Project 9.20

Small plastic glasses with tapered sides are perfect for studying forms with ellipses of different sizes. Observe how the space between the upper and lower ellipses changes when a glass is viewed from the same eye level, but at different distances. As you pull the glass toward you, the ellipses get fuller and closer together until they overlap. Draw the glass as it appears at various distances and when held at different levels. In each drawing the upper and lower ellipses must be centered on each other. Remember to calculate proportional relationships, not only of the separate ellipses, but also of the overall dimensions of the glass.

While the tapered forms that you have drawn could also represent flowerpots, the reason for using the plastic glass is that the transparency of the glass allows the lower ellipse to be seen. Although glass or flowerpots best serve their function when maintained in an upright position, they become interesting and challenging drawing problems when resting on their sides.

Project 9.21

Study a plastic glass or flowerpot tipped on its side. In profile, neither the top nor the bottom is vertical, nor is an imaginary center line connecting top and bottom horizontal. Be aware, however, that both the top and bottom are at right angles to a center line. Slowly rotate the object. The ellipses open as you look more directly into the container and become narrower as it approaches profile position. Make freehand drawings of the object in several positions.

Ellipses in an Architectural Setting   Arches, circular windows, the capitals and bases of columns, domes, and towers—all involve the perspective of circles and partially circular forms. These curvilinear elements usually appear in conjunction with rectangular forms, and if the two are not handled consistently, the drawing will be weakened. It is frequently helpful to use divided squares as a basis for constructing elliptical forms (Fig. 9-19).

Two mid-eighteenth-century architectural fantasies, both of which project a series of arched forms into planes at various eye levels, provide an interesting comparison. Piranesi's *Monumental Staircase Leading to a Vaulted Hall* (Fig. 9-21) is an imaginative freehand study, admirable for its directness and its vigorous, expressive drawing rather than for accuracy, since neither the architectural forms nor the spatial relationships can withstand careful analysis in search of formal accuracy.

Equally imaginative is Giuseppe Galli Bibiena's architectural perspective design for the theater (design for painted stage scenery) with its tiers of arcades and endless corridors (Fig. 9-22). Meticulously constructed in two-point perspective, the design combines a beckoning and brilliant use of scale with the repetition of architectural elements to create a feeling of spaciousness that cannot be contained within the frame. With the view of the inner courtyard seen through the arch at the left comes the realization

9-21. *above, left:* GIOVANNI BATTISTA PIRANESI (1720–1778; Italian). *Staircase Leading to a Vaulted Hall.* c. 1755. Pen and brown ink over red chalk with brown wash, 15 × 10 1/2″ (38.1 × 26.7 cm). British Museum, London.

9-22. *above, right:* GUISEPPE GALLI BIBIENA (1696–1757; Italian). Architectural perspective design for the theater. From *Architectural and Perspective Design* (Vienna, 1740). Republished by Dover Publications, Inc., 1964.

that the columns partially visible at the top of the drawing are but the bottom half of another story towering above. Except for the staggering amount of intricate architectural detail, careful analysis of the perspective—basically two sets of parallel planes set at right angles—reveals that the drawing is merely an elaboration of the assignments in this chapter.

Shadows

Both Piranesi and Bibiena recognized the importance of using light and shadow artistically in establishing volume and creating drama in their perspective fantasies. It appears that Piranesi introduced his shadows somewhat arbitrarily, no doubt for the sake of compositional effects, while Bibiena calculated his as methodically as he graphically constructed the architecture. Whether or not to adhere to the accuracy of mechanical means, is, of course, the artist's decision. It is important, however, to note that an artist must have a full working knowledge of perspective in order to use it more freely and to his advantage regarding compositional elements of exaggeration and distortion.

All objects in direct light (regardless of the direction of the light source) cast shadows that can be determined by perspective. Three factors govern the drawing of shadows.

1. The **source of light** may be either natural or artificial. Natural light produces parallel rays; artificial light creates radiating rays. It is true that light radiates from the sun, but from a distance of about 92 million miles away, the rays are virtually parallel when they reach the earth.
2. The **direction of light** determines the direction in which shadows fall. When the source of light is to one side, shadows are cast to the opposite side. In a standing position, with the light at your back, shadows are darkest at your feet and begin to lighten slightly as they fall away from you frontally. When you look into the light, shadows are cast behind you and fall away from your back.
3. The **angle of light** determines the length of shadows. A high-positioned source of light creates short shadows; a low-positioned light produces long shadows.

Drawing Designs in Perspective

Complex patterns and designs whether actual or imaginative—geometric paving tiles, the patterns of Oriental rugs, curvilinear designs, lettering, and even fluid text—can be drawn into one- or two-point perspective on horizontal, vertical, or inclined planes, or even on a curved surface, by squaring off the design and transferring it to a grid, properly scaled and drawn in correct perspective. The smaller the scale of the grid, the easier it is to transfer complicated designs.

Seeing and Using Perspective

Perspective need not be restrictive. Used imaginatively, it offers an artist great freedom, serving as a valuable aid to creative interpretation, playful distortion, and visually penetrating expression. As with any academic stricture of any technique in the arts, to learn it well better prepares the artist to expressionistically alter its manifestation in pursuit of the sought-

---

source of light
Light that may be either natural or artificial. Natural light produces parallel rays; artificial light creates radiating rays. It is true that light radiates from the sun, but from a distance of 93 million miles, the rays are virtually parallel when they reach the earth.

direction of light
The position of light that determines the direction in which shadows fall. When the source of light is to one side, shadows are cast to the opposite side. With the light at your back, shadows fall away from you. When you look into the light, shadows of objects before you are cast toward you.

angle of light The proximity, position, and direction of a light source in relation to an object that determines the length of shadows. A highly positioned source of light creates short shadows; a low light position produces long shadows.

9-23. RACKSTRAW DOWNES (b. 1939; English-American). *The IRT Elevated Station at Broadway and 125th St.* c. 1982. Graphite on paper, 19 × 35" (48.3 × 89 cm). Collection of Glenn C. Janss. Courtesy of Hirshl & Adler Modern.

after effects. Freshness and spontaneity of expression, whether premeditated or impulsively executed, is an artist's springboard to visual impact.

We can identify elements of one-, two-, and three-point perspective in Rackstraw Downes's graphite drawing *The IRT Elevated Station at Broadway and 125th St.* (Fig. 9-23). A panoramic view of upper Manhattan sweeps from left to right in an arc so broad that it reveals the curvature of the earth and seems to include a broader view than would fall within the usual cone of vision. It is the subtle shift and tilt of perspective that causes us to notice the interpretive expression of Downes. We pause at this—we even marvel at how it entertains, provokes, and pleases our sense of sight. Downes's provocative approach to the picture plane is even more emphasized in Figures 13-18 and 13-19, where the panoramic view is hyperextended even beyond that of Figure 9-23.

Continuous practice in perspective drawing sensitizes the eye, so you will readily perceive errors. By studying the diagrams and doing projects, you are better able to see forms as they exist in space and can avoid the errors most commonly made. You will be able to see when objects do not appear to rest on the same ground plane and when they are drawn incorrectly out of scale.

Sketchbook Activities

In your sketchbook do perspective drawings from observation and from theory, and do drawings of forms both simple and complex. A partially open door, a jumbled array of drawing benches and easels in an art classroom, the confusion of plates and cups and textbooks on a table in the cafeteria all offer opportunities to consider size, shape, and space relationships. Draw objects from memory or imagination. Construct large general forms first; then modify them creatively by using value and texture as expressionistic forces. Remember that most objects can be placed in boxes, which can be visually transformed by cutting away a portion of the box. Incorporate every opportunity to instill good composition practices in your drawings.

With much looking and much drawing, your uncertainties will become less frequent, your drawings more accurate.

10 Dry Media

*I recall how I loved the material itself, how
the colors and crayons were especially
alluring, beautiful and alive.*

—Vassily Kandinsky

newsprint
An inexpensive paper made of wood
pulp used by art students for all types
of practice drawing and expedient
classroom studies such as gesture, contour, blind contour, etc. It has a smooth
surface, yellows badly due to its acid
content, and is most appropriately used
with soft graphite pencil, charcoal,
Conté crayon, and chalk.

charcoal paper
Textured paper abrasive to charcoal
because of its hardness of tooth. In the
drawing act, it receives a deposition of
black carbon charcoal particles that adhere to its relief as well as fall into its
recesses; available in different weights
in white, gray tones, and muted colors;
also for use with chalk, Conté crayon,
and pastels.

tooth
The abrasive texture of paper that makes
drawing with dry media possible by enabling graphite, charcoal, chalk, crayon,
or pastel to adhere when dragged
across the surface, leaving rich deposits
of drawn marks.

soft sketching papers
Papers manufactured with a smooth
tooth for use with soft graphite pencils,
ballpoint and felt-tip pens, and colored
crayon.

As a prelude to this chapter on dry media, as well as to the remaining
chapters of this text, a discussion regarding artistic sensitivity to the different drawing materials and papers most commonly used by professional artists is in order. A feeling for media, an intuitive awareness of
their intrinsic beauty and expressive potential, and a delight in manipulating them are part of the creative sphere of most artists. For the novice,
it is essential to discover the medium best suited for one's temperament
and talents; exploration is the first step toward discovery. Since pleasure
in the craft is an important component of the artistic temperament, the
joyful savoring of the particular qualities inherent in each material and
each surface contributes to the total effect.

There are many different artistic personalities. Artists who enjoy
working patiently and methodically naturally gravitate to those media
that demand precise control, disciplined manual dexterity, and careful
manipulation of difficult and demanding tools. At the other extreme are
the artists who cannot put down ideas with sufficient speed; they can
formulate and express an idea in a brief burst of creative energy. To facilitate this rush of enthusiasm, the ideal medium is one that demands
neither great precision nor extensive preparation, one that encourages
rapid visualization and realization, one that can be worked and modified easily without seeming to imply a lack of technical skill. Between
the two extremes lie a host of talents, temperaments, and artistic wills—
all of which can be accommodated by the wide range of available
media. In fact, any attempt to define or limit the use of a medium to

176

one type of temperament suggests a categorizing inherently false to the need for experimentation and self-discovery.

Chapter 2 introduced the media most commonly employed by beginning drawing students. Chapters 10 and 11 will explore a fuller range of drawing materials, some more sophisticated and requiring greater skill than others. While the accompanying projects have been designed to encourage students to experiment with a wide range of materials, esoteric methods and recipes have been purposefully avoided. Unduly detailed directives about the use of media, tools, and materials have also been avoided since step-by-step instructions frequently encourage self-conscious and mechanical procedures that interfere with direct and vigorous natural expression. In general, after accepting certain fundamental and very general procedures, artists work out their own methods. Students are urged to play freely with media before embarking upon their use, for only by a free and inventive manipulation of materials, whether wet or dry, on a variety of different receptive surfaces, do artists discover and develop their personal preferences and characteristic methods of working.

It is suggested that you first read through the chapters on media and then select those media and exercises that sound interesting. When you fix upon a medium or technique that proves uniquely satisfying, it is wise to explore it rather fully before moving to another. Single cursory encounters with a wide variety of materials and methods can result in confusion, while the creation of works that satisfy the artist remains the greatest encouragement and stimulus toward further development.

Papers

Before exploring the categories of dry and wet media, a brief survey of standard drawing papers will afford the student a basic reference. **Newsprint,** manufactured from wood pulp, is the cheapest paper; it has a smooth surface, yellows badly because of its acid content, and is appropriate only for quick sketching in pencil, charcoal, Conté crayon, and chalk. **Charcoal paper** has considerably more **tooth** (degree of roughness created by an embossed texture imprinted in combination with fine sand) and is available in white, gray tones, and muted colors for use with charcoal, chalk, Conté crayon, and pastels. **Soft sketching papers** are manufactured for use with soft pencils, ballpoint and felt-tip pens, and colored crayons. **Handmade Oriental papers** (mistakenly referred to as rice paper), are the traditional surfaces for Oriental brush-and-ink drawings, and provide a soft, very absorbent ground. **Bond papers,** familiar as stationery and typing or computer paper, are smooth, relatively hard-surfaced, lightweight papers appropriate for use with pencil or pen and ink; they are available by pad or in bulk in various sizes. The serious artist, however, will avoid using bond papers; since they have a rather uninteresting surface, they are limited in their expressive capabilities and considered inferior to the more professional rag papers. **Bristol board,** a very fine, hard-surfaced paper, is manufactured in two finishes: **Kid finish,** by virtue of its very slight tooth, facilitates fine pencil work and rubbed pen-and-graphite combinations; **smooth (plate) finish** encourages elegant studies in pen and ink or very hard pencil. It is available in different weights. **Illustration board** is manufactured by mounting papers of different surfaces onto a cardboard backing for stability. While relatively expensive, illustration board tends to justify its price in

handmade Oriental papers
Papers that are made by manually pulling a flat screen or sieve up through a water vat containing finely shredded mulberry fibers. The fibers come to rest in a flat, consistent sheet on the screen, which allows the water to drain through. The fibers are extracted from the inner, white bark layer of the mulberry tree.

bond paper
Familiar as stationery and computer paper, a lightweight, relatively smooth paper with a hard surface and tight grain appropriate for use with graphite or colored pencils, ballpoint pen, or pen and ink. It is available in pads or in bulk in various sizes.

Bristol board
A very fine, hard-surfaced paper, manufactured in two finishes: *kid finish,* by virtue of its very slight tooth, facilitates fine graphite pencil work of medium hardness and rubbed pen and graphite combinations; *smooth (plate) finish,* a very finely toothed paper, encourages elegant studies in pen and ink or very hard graphite pencil and is available in different weights.

kid finish paper
Bristol board paper with a slightly toothed surface; it facilitates fine graphite pencil work and rubbed pen-and-graphite combinations.

smooth (plate) finish
Bristol board paper with an extremely fine tooth that encourages elegant and detailed studies in pen and ink or very hard graphite pencil, and is available in different weights.

illustration board
A medium made by mounting different papers of relatively fine quality onto cardboard backing; available in three standard surface finishes: *rough,* which has the most active tooth; *cold press,* a versatile, medium-toothed surface; and *hot press,* the smoothest and least absorbent surface that is excellent for very refined, controlled techniques. It is expensive but highly durable and resists wrinkling when wet.

watercolor paper

As the name indicates, paper used primarily for watercolor or wash techniques. It is an acid-free, cotton-fiber paper available in a variety of different weights and degrees of sizing with an active grain or tooth that comes in three standard finishes: *rough,* a surface produced in the highest-quality papers not by mechanical graining but as the result of the hand-manufacturing process and best adapted to splashy, spontaneous techniques; *cold press,* a moderately textured matte surface paper; and *hot press,* the smoothest and least absorbent surface, excellent for very refined, controlled techniques. The different finishes come with varying capabilities of absorption and wet strengths, according to the weight and degree of sizing.

rough tooth

A characteristic of heavily toothed papers with a readily visible and pronounced surface texture as in charcoal or some watercolor papers.

cold press

Paper with a moderately textured, matte surface, softer and toothier than "hot press" paper.

hot press

One of the three standard grades of illustration board and watercolor paper characterized as having a hard surface that has been ironed and press-cured with heat and weight and possesses the smoothest and least absorbent surface; excellent for very refined, controlled techniques.

its durability and resistance to buckling when wet. **Watercolor papers,** as the name indicates, are used primarily for ink wash and watercolor drawings and paintings. The heavier the weight of the paper, the more expensive it will be. However, heavier weights are more absorbent and less likely to wrinkle or buckle when wet. There are three standard finishes for watercolor paper and illustration board. **Rough tooth,** a surface characteristic of the highest-quality papers endemic to the hand-manufacturing process, is best adapted to the spontaneous and expressionistic techniques attained by all types of wet media. **Cold press** is moderately textured matte surface. **Hot press,** the smoothest and least absorbent surface, is excellent for very refined, controlled techniques.

Papers made of 100 percent cotton rag are the most permanent and the most expensive and should be used whenever serious drawing is to be undertaken. Avoid using inferior papers. They will not yield the degree of expression and surface qualities that most artists are after, nor will they withstand the rigors of media exploitation and experimentation as well as paper of higher quality. The cost of supplies is an understandable concern for beginning students, particularly when they are asked to explore a variety of drawing materials; however, there are some good-quality student-grade papers available that afford the student the experience of working on high-percentage rag papers at a lower cost. It is important when learning technique and exploring different drawing media that the student have the best possible results from the tools at hand. The resulting difference in surface quality between the cheaper wood pulp papers and rag papers is immediately apparent; therefore, students are not encouraged to spend time attempting to develop their skills with inferior materials. As one's drawing abilities improve, works intended to be finished drawings should be done only on pure cotton rag papers.

Drawing Media

The dry media—vine and compressed charcoals, chalks, pastels, Conté crayon, wax crayon, grease crayon, color pencils, graphite, and silverpoint—are materials that leave granular deposits when they are drawn across a receptive surface.

Charcoal

The Nature of Charcoal Charcoal, probably the oldest drawing medium, is a crumbly, versatile material that readily leaves a mark when rubbed against any but a very smooth, nontoothed surface. With it, tentative lines can be put down to establish positions of form and subsequently erased or permanently drawn over. The same piece of charcoal can generate subtle, sensitive, and dramatic line drawings, or, turned on its side, it can produce broad tonal areas and even dark, intense masses, as in Käthe Kollwitz's drawing (Fig. 1-1). Charcoal is equally suited to sketches and rapidly executed compositional plans or to fully developed, large-scale drawings as value studies (Figs. 10-1, 3-1). The nature of charcoal is such that it can be easily smeared by careless movements of the hand or arm across the drawing surface, which, to the artist, is a disadvantage. However, this smearing ability can serve the artist advantageously as well. Because the material is not deeply imbedded or fused into the ground surface, its propensity to smear can be utilized to create full-scale ranges of tone. In Willem de Kooning's charcoal drawing *Two Women* (Fig. 10-2), it is evident that the artist used smears of tone to en-

10-1. JOSEPH STELLA (1877–1946; Italian-American). *Miners.* Charcoal, 15 × 19 5/8" (38.1 × 49.8 cm). Yale University Art Gallery, New Haven, Conn.

10-2. WILLEM DE KOONING (1904–1997; Dutch-American). *Two Women.* c. 1952. Charcoal, 22 1/2 × 28 1/2" (572 × 724 mm). National Gallery of Art, Washington, D.C.

hance the forms and movements of the two figures. Note how tonal areas of smearing tend to soften the forms, and coupled with the darkest lines add richness to the overall spatial effects of the drawing. To minimize the occurrence of unwanted smears, however, it is recommended that a workable spray fixative (use only in a well-ventilated area) be used at intervals during the execution of a charcoal drawing to help seal the carbon particles to the paper surface; but keep in mind that spraying alone does not eliminate the occurrence of smearing. One must also take precautions against anything rubbing across the drawing surface—a good practice regardless of the drawing medium.

In a passage from James Watrous's book *The Craft of Old Master Drawings,* he states:

During the seventeenth and eighteenth centuries charcoal was extensively used, although it was not necessarily preferred by many of the artists. However, as the use of natural chalks declined, and in the nineteenth century was ultimately abandoned, it became the principal medium for figure studies. And in the academies, it was the traditional tool for life drawing exercises, a preference which is still common today.

The methods of preparing charcoal were quite simple and had few variations over the several centuries during which artists produced their own drawing sticks. Although vine charcoal was used in the nineteenth and twentieth centuries, the manuals of the preceding centuries suggested that woods were the common source. The favorite wood was willow (or sallow, a species of willow), but linden, plum, "dogge-woode," and spindle wood were also recommended. The charcoal was made by carbonizing the wood in heated chambers from which air was excluded in order that the sticks would not burn and be reduced to ashes. Cennino described how the artist formed bundles of willow wood slips by binding them with iron or copper wire, placed them in a casserole, the cover of which was luted with clay to make it airtight. The vessel was put into a baker's oven or under the hot ashes of a fire and left overnight to produce carbonization. Borghini, at the end of the sixteenth century, paraphrased these directions of Cennino but added a third method which made use of linden wood placed in an iron box whose cover and lock had to be luted before the baking took place. And Volpato, in the late seventeenth century, suggested the use of an iron tube, into which plum or willow sticks were placed, the ends of the tube being carefully covered with ashes to exclude the air.

During these early centuries there was no simple method by which artists could control precisely the softness or hardness of their charcoal sticks as is done in the manufacturing processes of today. But Cennino and Volpato were aware that the longer one left the wood slips within their airless chambers in the hot oven or under the ashes, the softer the charcoal became.

Types of Charcoal Today, in a similar fashion, **stick charcoal** is made by heating or firing sticks of wood about 1/4 inch (.6 centimeter) in diameter in kilns until the organic materials have burned away through high-heat evaporation, leaving only dry carbon behind. The finest quality, known as **vine charcoal,** comes in varying diameters and is made in very thin sticks or rods of an even, soft texture. Much of the willow wood used for this fine-quality vine charcoal is grown and harvested from the wetlands of southeastern England. Manufacturers classify charcoal in four degrees of hardness: (4B) very soft, (3B) soft, (2B) medium, and (HB) hard. **Compressed charcoal** is different from stick or vine in that it results from pulverizing the charcoal to powder, then mixing it with varying amounts of binder and compressing it into chalklike round or 4-sided sticks about 3/8 inch in diameter. Compressed charcoal is also graded according to hardness, ranging from 00, the softest and blackest, through 0 to 5, which contains the most binder and is consequently the palest and hardest. In general, because compressed char-

stick charcoal
Charcoal made by heating sticks of wood about one-quarter inch in diameter in kilns until the organic materials have evaporated and only the dry carbon remains. The finest quality of the stick form is called **vine charcoal.**

vine charcoal
The highest quality of stick charcoal. Named for plant vines from which it is made and extracted through heating.

compressed charcoal
A substance made by grinding charcoal into powder and compressing it with a binding material into chalklike sticks that are then labeled according to hardness ranging from 00, the softest and blackest, through 5, the hardest and palest.

coal is less easily erased, it is not well suited to beginners' needs. It is most effective for quick, dramatic sketches, or for large-scale drawings when rich darks are desired. **Powdered charcoal** is simply pulverized charcoal left in a "powder state" which produces deep, rich blacks by rubbing it into the paper surface.

Charcoal pencils, made by compressing charcoal into thin rods and sheathing them in paper or wood, offer cleanliness but lack the versatility and flexibility of stick charcoal because only the point can be used effectively. (The same criticism applies to using metal holders with stick charcoal.) Charcoal pencils are graded: 6B (extra soft), 4B (soft), 2B (medium), and HB (hard). White charcoal pencils are also available.

Charcoal Techniques   There are four common methods of working with stick or compressed charcoal. The direct spontaneous attack, using both the point and side of the charcoal stick, offers maximum flexibility of stroke and tone without the time-consuming fussiness of more labored or refined modes (Fig. 1-1). An alternative process, involving a disciplined and relatively "pure" application of charcoal, is to build value relationships through systematically hatched and cross-hatched lines drawn with a pointed stick of charcoal (Fig. 10-1), or using line hatching as a shading technique (Fig. 3-1). A third manner of applying charcoal is the standard academic technique of the nineteenth century, which produces graduated tones through repeated application of charcoal rubbed into paper with dry fingers or a tortillon (shading stump). Craig Marshall Smith's imaginative *Chimerical Friend* (Fig. 10-3) combines aspects of the academic method of building and controlling tone with a fourth method of working with charcoal (introduced in Chapter 2) that relies heavily on wiping and erasing. In addition to rubbing, Smith uses a chamois to wipe away unsatisfactory charcoal lines and tones and an eraser to eliminate small areas of tone, sharpen edges, pick out small light accents, and clean up smudges. We see the same combined methods of charcoal handling techniques and their effects used by Chuck Levitan in Figure 1-5.

Jim Cogswell's *Face and Hands #2* (Fig. 10-4) appears to have been drawn in the same manner. However, his gray tones were produced by applying turpentine (or an odorless solvent) with a cotton rag, and in the process, dissolving what was the initial drawing done in compressed charcoal. This technique produces a "wash look" similar to that of wet media ink or watercolor washes used in conjunction with dry media. Because only limited erasing is possible after the solvent evaporates, Cogswell uses gesso (a white gypsum ground used to size canvas in painting) to reestablish whites—most evident along the left side of the head. He arrives at his final image by working back and forth, in a mixed-media fashion with black, gray, and white in a painterly way.

Rich and varied effects are possible by spraying, wiping, and brushing charcoal—and all other dry media—with turpentine or odorless mineral spirits, or water. These techniques will be dealt with in greater depth in Chapter 18, Mixed-Media Expression.

Charcoal can be applied to many different kinds of drawing and printmaking papers—Arches, Bristol, Fabriano, Rives, Somerset, Stonehenge, Strathmore, Twinrocker, and Zerkall are the major professional paper brand names and companies. (These may be purchased at artist supply stores, although you may not find as extended a variety as if you order by catalog.) Newsprint suffices for quick sketches and

powdered charcoal
Charcoal in a powdered state that produces intense blacks and is used in combination with a chamois to produce rubbed areas of rich darks.

charcoal pencils
Thin rods of compressed charcoal encased in paper or wooden sheaths that offer cleanliness but lack the flexibility of stick charcoal because only the point can be used. Charcoal pencils come in different grades: 6B (extra soft), 4B (soft), 2B (medium), and HB (hard). (White charcoal pencils are also available.)

10-3. *above, left:* CRAIG MARSHALL SMITH (b. 1947; American). *Chimerical Friend.* c. 1988. Charcoal, 40 × 30″ (101.7 × 76.2 cm).
Courtesy of the artist.

10-4. *above, right:* JIM COGSWELL (b. 1949; American). *Face and Hands #2.* c. 1989. Charcoal and gesso, 30 × 22″ (76.2 × 55.9 cm).
Courtesy the artist. Collection of Michael Spivak, Houston, Texas.

studies that do not demand erasing or the careful buildup of smooth tones, mixed media, or permanence. Coarse drawing papers also provide acceptable grounds for quick sketches with all types of charcoal. The texture of paper—its coarseness or smoothness—is referred to as grain or tooth and is the main consideration when choosing an appropriate paper. The textures or grains of the coarser papers are visible to varying degrees with dry drawing materials, particularly graphite sticks, chalks, and charcoals when used on either their sides or their blunt points. Figure 10-5 shows a microphotographic enlargement of a detail of *Study for a Portrait of Diego Martelli* by Edgar Degas. These charcoal strokes made from the end of a charcoal stick illustrate the manner in which weightless carbon particles fall into the pits or depressions of the grain or tooth of paper. Little holds them there until they are sealed with a workable spray fixative, shellac, or varnish recommended for drawings on paper.

Regular charcoal paper, a tenacious surface allowing repeated erasures and rubbing without losing its grain, is best for sustained studies. In Picasso's *Two Fashionable Women* (Fig. 10-6) we see a high-quality drawing paper surface that obviously held up well while worked in both additive and subtractive methods; the artist used charcoal with extensive pressure to achieve the rich darks and subtracted tone with an eraser to achieve the lightest whites. This drawing is a testament to Picasso's virtuoso sense of composition and power of line done at the young age of nineteen.

Compressed charcoal can be used effectively on relatively smooth bond or printmaking papers with slightly more grain. Heavier-weight hot-press papers, charcoal, printmaking papers such as Murillo, and Bristol boards are recommended when working with solvents. Most charcoal papers are manufactured in the standard 18-by-24-inch (46-by-

10-5. Microphotographic enlargement of a detail of *Study for a Portrait of Diego Martelli* by Degas. Charcoal strokes illustrating the manner in which the weightless carbon particles tend to fall in the pits of the grain of paper (from James Watrous's *The Craft of Old-Master Drawings*).
The Fogg Museum, Harvard University, Cambridge, Mass.

61-centimeter) size. Other suitable drawing papers are available in larger sheets or by the roll, which accommodates the needs of contemporary artists such as Chuck Levitan (Fig. 1-5), who works in charcoal on a more monumental scale.

Project 10.1

Select a subject that encompasses a wide range of value relationships—a complex still life, a self-portrait, or an abstraction of a winter landscape on an overcast day. Before embarking on a high finished drawing, establish a preliminary visualization of the linear and tonal patterns as thumbnail sketches on a piece of newsprint (Fig. 8-1), using the side of a short piece of charcoal to lay in the darks. Having determined the value pattern, develop a large-scale, full-value-range, finished drawing on charcoal paper. While it is possible to combine techniques, take care to achieve a consistency of handling throughout the drawing. Endeavor not to overwork any area—keep it freshly executed.

Chalk The word **chalk** covers a variety of drawing materials ranging in texture from coarse to fine, from hard to soft and crumbly, and from dry to greasy, shaped into rounded or square sticks. It is impossible to

chalk

The term *chalk* covers a wide variety of materials ranging in texture from coarse to fine, from hard to soft and crumbly, and from dry to greasy, shaped into rounded or square sticks. It was originally obtained from natural colored earths that were cut or sawed into sticks. Fabricated chalk is made with prepared pastes of water-soluble binding media mixed with dry pigments and sometimes with additional substances such as inert clays, then rolled, pressed into sticks, and dried.

10-6. PABLO PICASSO (1881–1973; Spanish-French). *Two Fashionable Women,* c. 1900 or 1901. Charcoal, 16 1/4 × 9 5/8″ (413 × 244 mm). National Gallery of Art, Washington, D.C.

establish the point at which chalk becomes crayon or pastel, and the dividing line between chalk and compressed charcoal is equally tenuous.

This is due to the many ambiguities handed down from historical literature as to the descriptions of chalks, pastels, and crayons. To a great extent, this ambiguity still exists simply because artists do not know or have never been taught the basic categories of these materials: where they come from (whether in natural or manufactured state), how they are presently manufactured, and what their ingredients are that make them distinctively different as drawing tools.

Natural chalks (black, red, and white) were harvested and made from colored earths containing minerals. The natural earth substances of black and red chalk were not pure minerals, but amorphous compositions that contained a natural binder—clay. The pigmentation of these earths had to possess enough density and saturation to produce the strong effects sought by artists. The deposits of natural red and black chalks were distributed over different parts of Europe; however, these lodes have been mined out and become extinct, along with any present knowledge as to the whereabouts of these mines. They simply no longer exist as direct sources of these natural, amorphous pigments. However, in the United States, in peninsular Michigan near Negaunee, there are deposits of red chalk referred to as "red ochre variety of hematite" that possess the correct natural blending of substances (iron oxide and clay) to render it an excellent drawing chalk.

Today, fabricated chalks or pastels are made by mixing dry pigments and pastes together with binding media and allowing them to dry. One major and notable difference between fabricated color sticks and natural chalks is that since most available dry pigments are used in the preparation of these fabricated chalks, the range of available colors is much greater than that of the natural chalks.

Chalk affords the artist a technical versatility similar to that of charcoal. Like compressed charcoal, chalk is somewhat difficult to erase, but it offers ample compensation with the potential for richer, darker lines and solid masses. The numerous and satisfying visual possibilities are evident in the open, energetic swirls of Lovis Corinth's black chalk drawing *Mrs. Hedwig Berend, 1923* (Fig. 10-7), where the subject looks directly at the viewer, showing a tinge of self-consciousness as though she is aware she is being sketched. Other examples are seen in Picasso's mixed-media self-portrait, using black chalk with watercolor (Fig. 10-8), and in the carefully finished drawing of Annibale Carracci's *Portrait of Mascheroni, the Lute Player* in red chalk highlighted with white chalk (Fig. 10-9). The chalk medium's chief advantage is color, permitting enriched hue and tonal and compositional relationships.

Project 10.2

Using black and white or dark-colored and light-colored chalks on a middle-value paper facilitates both rapid visualization of tonal relationships and finished drawings of great beauty (Fig. 10-9). Select a subject that will allow a full range of values—a piece of drapery or a rumpled paper bag would be appropriate, or if you want to tackle something more ambitious, a well-lighted nude, costumed model, or a head

10-7. *above, left:* LOVIS CORINTH (1858–1925; German). *Mrs. Hedwig Berend.* c. 1923. Black chalk, 12 7/16 × 10" (316 × 254 mm).
National Gallery of Art, Washington, D.C.

10-8. *above, right:* PABLO PICASSO (1881–1973; Spanish-French). *Self-Portrait.* c. 1901/1902. Black chalk with watercolor, 12 × 9 3/8" (304 × 238 mm).
National Gallery of Art, Washington, D.C.

10-9.
ANNIBALE CARRACCI (1560–1609; Italian). *Portrait of Mascheroni, the Lute Player.* Red chalk highlighted in white chalk, 16 1/8 × 11 1/8″ (40.9 × 28.2 cm). Albertina, Vienna.

pastels

Pure powdered pigments mixed with just enough clay, gum, or resin to bind them into stick form; except for differing amounts of wax and grease, they are similar to crayons and especially to chalks in composition. Pastels come in soft, hard, and oil versions in a wide range of colors. Pastel drawings tend to be fragile and require care in storing as their surfaces are easily abraded. Spray fixative may help preserve the surface but may also dull the color with too much use.

soft pastels

Pastels made from dry pigments mixed with an aqueous binder and compressed into cylindrical form. They are soft and crumbly and nonadhesive, requiring use on a paper of decided tooth.

hard pastels

Pastels made from dry pigments mixed with a higher proportion of aqueous binder than in soft pastels, which makes them harder with a firmer texture. They are compressed into square sticks; their flat side planes afford rapid coverage of broad areas; the sharp corners make them effective for detailing and accenting. They can be sharpened with a razor blade and are also manufactured in pencil form.

oil pastels

Drawing media that are similar to hard pastels except that oil has been added to the binder, creating a semihard state that adheres more readily to paper. Because oil pastels are not easily smudged, they work well for outdoor sketching. They are not easily erased.

analogous color scheme

A color scheme comprised of any combination of adjacent colors on the color wheel as the main color statement.

and face of an elderly person. Place your subject against a middle-value background and draw on toned paper of a comparable value. Letting the paper provide the transitional middle-tones, as demonstrated in Plate 4, rather than mixing light and dark to create intermediate tones, will result in a fresh, spatially alive drawing instead of a muddied dead flatness.

Pastels **Pastels** are high-quality chalks of fine, even texture, available in a wide range of hues of graduated value and intensity (color saturation). **Soft pastels** consist of dry pigment mixed with an aqueous gum or binder, usually compressed into cylindrical form. Soft and crumbly, this type of pastel is nonadhesive and thus requires paper of decided tooth. **Hard pastels,** which contain more binder than soft pastels, are compressed into square sticks with a firm texture. The flat side planes provide rapid coverage of broad areas, and the sharp corners make them effective for detailing and accenting. They can be sharpened with a razor blade. Pastels are also manufactured in pencil form. Oil added to the binder allows semi-hard **oil pastels** to adhere more readily to paper. Because oil pastels are not as easily smudged, they work well for outdoor sketching. Both semi-hard and hard pastels are difficult to erase, so it is wise to make a small preliminary color sketch before commencing on a large-scale composition. This can be done more quickly with colored pencils of hues and values similar to those of the pastels.

Pastels, with more than five hundred distinct colors and values available, permit the artist to revel in the directness of drawing while immersed in a total color involvement. The greatest richness of color results from the direct application of analogous or complementary colors side by side or with cross-hatching (Pl. 1), letting the color mix optically. Excessive blending of colors through rubbing and overapplication produces lifeless color and uninteresting surfaces. The generally recommended procedure is to lay in middle and dark values first, then work toward light, saving details and accents for last. In this way, the artist controls the process of building up value ranges and color, form, and space simultaneously. Artist Duane Wakeham, former coauthor of this text, is an accomplished pastel artist. In his composition *Russian River, Spring Afternoon* (Pl. 10), we see a vibrantly orchestrated value scale, which defines light and dark passages of a well-mastered spatial dynamism in the landscape. We cannot help but look at the spatial infinity beyond the intersecting horizon lines of the two mountain ranges in the distance, while being equally soothed by the gentle roll of the hills before us as we bring our eyes back to the immediate foreground—a dichotomous and pleasurable feast for the eyes. Notice the presence of both analogous and complementary colors in Wakeham's work.

"Fixing" pastels with spray fixative provides some protection, but at the cost of surface freshness. Without it, colors stay brighter, but pastel drawings smudge easily and color (pigment) falls off. To store pastel drawings, place a slip-sheet of **glassine,** a frictionless and translucent barrier sheet, over the drawing and secure a sheet of newsprint as a cover sheet over the glassine with masking tape. This will prevent the drawing from shifting and thereby rubbing against another surface, causing the pastel particles to disengage from the grain of the paper.

Any of the exercises in the sections on chalk and Conté crayon afford practice in the use of pastel.

Conté Crayon   Conté crayon is a semi-hard chalk of fine texture containing sufficient oily material in the binder to adhere readily and more or less permanently to smooth paper. Conté crayons, 1/4 inch (.6 centimeter) square, and 3 inches (8 centimeters) in length, come in three degrees of hardness—No. 1 (HB, hard), No. 2 (B, medium), No. 3 (2B, soft)—in white, black, brown, and **sanguine** (Venetian red), which is the most popular color. (Lithographic crayons are similar to Conté crayons, albeit far waxier and greasier.) In *Girl Seated* (Fig. 10-10), Maurice Sterne has made advantageous use of the square format of the crayon, using both the thickness and the flat side to create broad strokes of graduated tone, while making sharp accents with its corners. On textured paper, Conté crayon produces the interesting granular effect seen in Seurat's study of his mother (Fig. 7-8). Conté, which is also available in pencil form, erases with difficulty and consequently best serves the needs of the sure and experienced draftsman.

Project 10.3

Break a stick of Conté crayon into two or three pieces. Work on an 18 × 24-inch newsprint pad and do a series of rapid, full sheet drawings of any subject that appeals to you—posed figures, animals, trees, plant forms, a casual grouping of fruit or vegetables. Work for a broad representation of essential forms and movements. When you view your subject through half-closed eyes, details fall away and you see basic forms as simplified patterns of light and dark. Use the side of the crayon to block in the shadow shapes; then add linear accents with the sharp corners of the crayon. Practice drawing contours and accents with the corner held flat to the paper rather than raised. Experiment with shifting from the corner to the flat edge of the crayon within a single stroke, both for interesting line quality and to describe the contours of three-dimensional forms.

glassine
An ultra-thin, frictionless, and translucent paperlike material used to "slip sheet" in between stacked works of art on paper—drawings, prints, or watercolors—protecting them from smears or surface abrasions.

Conté crayon
A semi-hard chalk of fine texture containing sufficient oily material in the binder to adhere readily and more or less permanently to smooth paper. It comes in sizes of ¼ inch (.6 centimeter) square and 3 inches (8 centimeters) long, in three degrees of hardness— No. 1 (hard), No. 2 (medium), and No. 3 (soft)—and in four colors—white, black, brown, and sanguine (Venetian red), which is the most popular.

sanguine
Natural red chalk ranging from the color of blood to a brownish-red used for drawing and first discovered prior to the fifteenth century in European mine deposits; its first documented usage came in the late fifteenth century around the time of Leonardo da Vinci and other Renaissance artists; its usage spread shortly thereafter to other countries.

10-10. MAURICE STERNE (1878–1957; Latvian-American). *Girl Seated.* c. 1912. Conté crayon and graphite pencil, 17 × 12″ (43.2 × 30.5 cm). Susan and Herbert Adler Collection.

The fine texture of Conté crayon lends itself to the creation of carefully finished drawings of high refinement and with a full range of value, as evidenced in Charles Sheeler's *Feline Felicity* (Fig. 10-11). Conté crayon is greasy enough that it does not rub off easily, yet its softness allows smooth, homogenous gradations of dark to light.

Project 10.4

Choose a subject for a highly finished drawing in Conté crayon; plan your composition from a series of rough layouts on newsprint. When you arrive at a composition you are satisfied with, select a smooth, firm paper. Lay in your initial lines lightly, and then develop the drawing to full value. You may wish to strengthen drawings done in brown or red Conté with black accents and white highlights. Push this drawing to a greater degree of finish than perhaps you have ever done before. Concentrate on the freshness of the look of the medium as it joins with the paper surface. Avoid overworking the surface.

Critique (Project 10.4)   Have you arrived at a state of finish that surpasses your previous drawings? If not, how can you achieve this? Assess your composition, remembering what you learned from Chapter 8. Is the composition a striking one? If not, how might you improve it? Assess the value ranges in relation to the textural and tonal ranges. Are they visually interesting? If not, how might you rework or

10-11. CHARLES SHEELER (1883–1965; American). *Feline Felicity.* c. 1934. Conté crayon on white paper, 21 3/4 × 17 7/8" (55.7 × 45.4 cm). The Fogg Art Museum, Harvard University, Cambridge, Massachusetts.

recompose these ranges more interestingly in the next drawing you do? Would you say your drawing is expressive? What does it say?

How would you feel about the drawing if someone else had done it?

Wax Crayons   Inexpensive, brightly colored **wax crayons** manufactured for children are familiar to everyone. The waxy substance adheres firmly to most paper surfaces—there are no powdery fugitive particles to worry about—and so presents a relatively clean medium to handle. Some artists find wax crayons appropriate only for sketching and preliminary color planning; others produce handsome finished drawings. It is the artist who decides which particular medium or tool can best express what he or she wants to say. You may have already experienced a sense of resonation when you hold a particular drawing tool in your hand. The tool says something to you—it transmits an impulse to strive for that unusual mark which may be unfamiliar to you.

Lithographic crayons (because of their grease content and variable grades from very soft to hard) when applied to heavyweight papers with considerable tooth or grain yield vigorous, clearly defined textures and richness of values, as seen in the works of Eduardo Iglesias and Jack Beal (Figs. 10-12, 7-12). The disadvantages of crayons are that they do not erase or allow lines to be blurred easily as with charcoal or pastel. However, on firm, smooth paper (less tooth), it is possible to retrieve light areas and even highlights by scratching or scraping with an X-acto knife or razor blade. This must be done carefully and gradually so as not to cause visible damage in the form of a blemish to the surface of the drawing.

Graphite Pencils   The graphite pencil, in its manufactured form, has been an important and versatile drawing medium since the end of the eighteenth century. Graphite, although discovered much earlier in its natural form, did not come into common use until the mid-seventeenth

wax crayons
Inexpensive and brightly colored crayons made from dry pigments and waxy binders that adhere firmly to most paper surfaces, making them a relatively clean medium to handle.

lithographic crayons
Greasy crayons in both pencil and stick form that produce rich blacks and are made from carbon black, animal fat, wax, and soap. They come in a variety of hard and soft grades ranging from No. 00 (softest) through 5 (hardest). The softest crayons contain the most grease, making them adhere well to most paper surfaces.

10-12. EDUARDO IGLESIAS (b. 1940; Brazilian). *Florista*. Lithographic crayon and black pencil on cream paper. 12 1/2 × 8 1/2″ (31.8 × 21.6 cm). Courtesy of the artist.

century, and up until the invention of cartridge pens, it was the most commonly used implement for drawing and sketching both inside and outside the studio. According to James Watrous, the "lode" that provided all of Europe with its finest quality graphite was discovered around 1560 at Burrrowdale, Cumberland, England. For nearly three centuries it remained the most sought after and highly prized European deposit—jealously guarded at the source, and also by severe export restrictions.

Webster's dictionary defines graphite as "a soft, black, lustrous form of carbon found in nature and used as lead in pencils." The term *lead,* however, is misused, as it is a carryover term from the early days of lead-alloy metal point drawings. When the graphite pencil succeeded the lead-alloy metal point, the term *lead pencil* continued to be used. James Watrous writes:

> Although the basic mixtures of graphite pencil manufacture were established in the late eighteenth and early nineteenth centuries by Conté, Brookman, and Hardmuth, materials in addition to graphite and clay were sometimes introduced to vary the type of product. These included antimony, spermaceti and other waxes, shellac, rosin, gums, and at times, undoubtedly to produce a greater blackness, lampblack.

The word **pencil** in general refers to a variety of mark-making substances formed into long, slender rods that have been sheathed in wood, or in the case of lithographic pencils, paper. Along with the most popu-

pencil
A wooden or paper cylindrical tool encasing a graphite, charcoal, crayon, or colored pigment rod of a wide variety of hard and soft grades; the most important and versatile drawing instrument since the end of the eighteenth century and the most commonly used drawing implement until the invention of the cartridge pen.

lar graphite pencil, we have an astonishing variety of other types—carbon charcoal, Conté, lithographic, and grease—and a wide range of colors, both soluble and insoluble, each offering a particular quality that renders it valuable in the attainment of certain effects. Specifically, the common graphite pencil is composed of a crystalline form of carbon having a greasy texture. Graphite pencils are manufactured in as many as twenty degrees of hardness—9B, the softest, possesses the highest graphite content; 9H, the hardest, contains the greatest proportion of clay. The range of graphite from hardest to softest is: 9H, 8H, 7H, 6H, 5H, 4H, 3H, 2H, H, F, HB, B, 2B, 3B, 4B, 5B, 6B, 7B, 8B, 9B (also mentioned in Chapter 2, Beginner's Media). The so-called carpenter's pencil, with its wide (3/16 inch, or .5 centimeter), flat, soft graphite that must be sharpened with a razor blade or knife, is useful for laying in broad areas of tone, while the corner allows fine line work. It is also possible to buy drawing leads, for lack of a better term, to be inserted into metal holders, eliminating the need for sharpeners, knives, or razor blades as they can be sharpened on a draftsman's sandpaper pad.

Soft Graphite Pencil Soft pencils (9B to 2B) are particularly well suited for contour drawings or other primarily linear notations. Soft graphite lends itself beautifully to line variations by responding to the artist's handling variations of applied pressure and release of pressure when drawing, producing a line that rhythmically swells and tapers. Soft graphite also lends itself to informally applied parallel hatchings and loosely executed cross-hatching, as seen in Claes Oldenburg's *Colossal Fagend in Park Setting* (Fig. 10-13), where the artist used soft graphite with

10-13. CLAES OLDENBURG (b. 1929; American). *Colossal Fagend in Park Setting.* c. 1967. Graphite and water color, 30 × 22 1/8″ (762 × 562 mm). National Gallery of Art, Washington, D.C.

10-14. JOSEPH PICCILLO (b. 1941; American). *Horse Study.* c. 1979. Graphite with erasing on ivory wove paper, 30 × 40″ (762 × 1,016 mm).
The Jalane and Richard Davidson Collection.
© The Art Institute of Chicago.

watercolor. Notice the variety in Oldenburg's vocabulary of line: Its thickness, density, value, and energetic character all contribute to the finished impact of the drawing. In stark contrast to Oldenburg, Joseph Piccillo's graphite drawing *Horse Study* (Fig. 10-14) shows the artist's masterful ability to use graphite and eraser in an almost photo-realistic way by creating a sumptuous dark background that projects the horse forward as a decidedly three-dimensional form in motion. Piccillo's technique involves laying down graphite tone, then erasing light passages to intricately describe not only the volumetric aspects of the horse, but also the folds of the skin and flexing of muscle as the horse runs. As one studies this work, the rich density and beauty of soft graphite are easily recognized and accounted for.

Working with soft pencils, it is possible to produce elegant tones using various techniques: direct application, smudging (stumping) with a paper stomp or rag, dissolving graphite into a wash with solvent, or brushing water over a drawing surface done with water-soluble pencils.

Project 10.5

Make a drawing of tonal and linear marks on good-quality, smooth paper, producing a full range of values with soft pencils, either by using the same pencil and changing pressure, or by selecting different grades of graphite for different strokes and changing pressure when necessary. The softer grades (9B is softer than 2B) provide richer darks but are not well suited for fine details as they lose their points too quickly. Less-soft grades are better for linear detail but require more pressure to build up dark tones, sometimes resulting in a shiny, mottled surface marked with indentations from repeated strokes and excessive pressure.

Project 10.6

Select a pencil or pencils with the degree of softness most pleasing to you and make some drawings of any subject you choose. Frequently, whatever just happens to be in your field of vision has a fresh appeal and visual interest because it has not been carefully selected and arranged. A pair of hiking boots or running shoes, a friend sprawled in a chair, or a shirt and jeans tossed on a bed or carelessly draped over the back of a chair provide apt, ready-made subjects for this kind of drawing.

Try to focus on what you've learned thus far about concepts of variation and compositional interest and let your drawings be free and gestural. Define shapes by tonal changes without relying on outlines. Block in forms and shapes lightly so that the lines will disappear as you introduce stronger, darker patterns of strokes and values. Provide several dark accents, but only enough to begin to give definition to the objects, and only after general value relationships have been established. Experiment with different methods of producing tones and linear passages.

Project 10.7

Create patterns of directional strokes to indicate the shifting angles of planes and tonal variations of a group of paper bags, a broad-leafed plant, or other interesting objects. Define forms by changes in the direction and value of the pencil strokes, rather than with outlines.

Critique (Projects 10.5, 10.6, 10.7)   Have you accomplished an extremely full range of values by manipulating the graphite well? Are the marks and tones interesting visually? Do they possess visual life? Were you able to transfer that vital and extreme range of values to the subject matter? How well have you defined shapes without relying on line? Has this helped you begin to see shapes and the visual power of shapes more than seeing mere outlines? How well were you able to define different angles and shifting planes with strokes?

How would you improve upon these drawings?

Hard Graphite Pencil: The Modeled Line   The clean-cut, silvery tone of hard graphite pencil (2H to 9H) can yield effects of great elegance, either used as pure line or augmented with light shading to convey a fuller sense of form than can be suggested by outline alone. The delicacy and sensitivity with which forms can be modeled and details rendered are nowhere more evident than in the figure studies, portraits, and architectural renderings of Jean Auguste Dominique Ingres, the acknowledged master of pencil drawing (Fig. 10-15).

Rendering, as a drawing technique, demands the most precise depiction of form, texture, and value in its quest for verisimilitude. Hard pencil is well adapted to that purpose. Bill Richards, described as a "meticulous realist," uses a full range of hard pencils, from 2H to 9H, in his rendering *Blinn Valley* (Fig. 10-16).

Project 10.8

The darkest dark of a hard pencil is considerably lighter than the richest darks of the softer B grades. The delicately interlocked petals of a single rose provide a perfect subject for this medium, as do intricate glass objects or other multifaceted forms. Life drawings, portraits, costumed figures—in fact, almost any subjects—are appropriate, provided the artist concentrates on outline reinforcement with only a suggestion of modeling. Since a degree of pressure is necessary when using hard graphite pencil, a firm, not too thin paper such as kid-finish Bristol board is recommended to avoid an excessively engraved paper surface. (Take some time to find the right combination of graphite grade with the right paper.) Drawings in hard pencil are best if kept small; if they are too large, the pale lines and tones lack visual presence and do not carry well as a visual statement.

Colored Pencils   Contemporary artists in both fine and commercial art, architects, engineers, and medical illustrators have used colored pencils for a long time alone and in combination with other media, for works ranging from sketches to highly detailed renderings. Color has proven to have its advantages for the commercial designer in that color-coding can be utilized to illustrate common and different parts. Think about maps and how color is used to locate different elevations and geographical terrains.

To the fine-art artist, colored pencils, which respond in a manner similar to that of graphite pencil, provide a plethora of color usage. A uniform method of loose cross-hatching is used to define shapes and values, and to create optical color in Jennifer Bartlett's colored pencil drawing *In the Garden #122* (Pl. 11). Bob Ziering employs a more studied and tighter hatching, "layering" one color over another to produce blurred color that instills the effect of rapid movement (Pl. 12). The secondary colors—green, violet, and orange—emerge from the layering of the three primary colors—yellow, blue, and red.

The overwhelming illusion of patterned fabric, molded plastic forms, and mirror-like metallic surfaces in Jeanette Pasin Sloan's acrylic and colored pencil on board drawing *Silver Bowl Still Life* (Pl. 2) is created, in part, by the artist's use of colored pencils to give increased definition to the acrylic washes. Pencil lends itself to a precise delineation of contour and to the skillfully controlled rendering that differentiates between the subtlety of the reflections in the plastic surfaces and the crisp clarity of the reflections in the silver bowl.

Drawing Method for Colored Pencils   Paper texture, pencil pressure, and even shape of the point of the pencil influence the quality and intensity of the color granules deposited on and into the surface material. Colored pencils seem to work most effectively on medium-grained paper, but it is always best to experiment with any new paper before initiating a full drawing. Applied with light pressure, color touches only the raised portions of the paper's texture, resulting in a granular, light tone because the open, white, depressed portions of the paper texture still show through the color. Applied with greater pressure, the color begins to fill in the hollows, eliminating the white of the paper and producing a more continuous, solid, darker, and richer tone. A sharp point contributes to stronger color because it gets into the depressions, whereas a blunt point glides across the paper's surface.

Bartlett's open cross-hatching (Pl. 11) demonstrates a linear approach to creating strong color and varied tonal hues—the effects being lyrical and seemingly weightless. Using a fine point, and by varying the directions of the strokes with greater density so there is little or no space between the lines, produces linear textures of more intense color. Medium pressure with frequent directional changes in stroking gives the greatest uniformity of tone.

As you look at the Bartlett drawing, notice the presence of all the primary and secondary colors harmoniously working together. Observe also the occurrence of a **triple complementary color scheme** similar to that of Willem de Kooning's *Two Women's Torsos* (Pl. 5), where all three pairs of complementary colors—blue and orange, red and green, and yellow and violet—occur in the same composition. To further heighten the effects of light and shadow, and in turn strengthen the spatial dynamic within the picture plane, Bartlett has created *shades* of several colors by fluidly superimposing black pencil lines over selected color lines.

The semitransparency of colored pencils permits colors to be changed by deliberately applying one color over another. A color used alone has a degree of rawness; combining colors by layering produces richer, more luminous colors. The maximum darkness of an individual colored pencil is that of the colored shaft material itself. If a darker-value pencil is not available, a color may be deepened by lightly applying a layer of black over the previous color. Using any other dark-value color will change the color as well as the value. Layering with white or some other light-value color both lightens the value and brightens the intensity of a color without sacrificing solid tone. The intensity of a color can be diminished by either layering with neutral gray or using the complement of the color.

triple complementary color scheme
A color scheme found within a single composition where three pairs of complementary colors work together contributing to the visual statement in a pronounced and harmonious way.

Project 10.9

Experiment with building tones and changing colors, values, and intensities. Begin by making several squares of the same color such as yellow. Then alter all the squares but one by layering with different colors. Because yellow is a light-value color to begin with, changes in value and intensity will readily occur.

burnishing
The excessive layering of various drawing media under pressure resulting in **wax bloom,** which can be corrected πor lifted by pressing a kneaded eraser against the burnished surface, eliminating the polished appearance.

fixative spray (workable)
A type of fine, granular mist that dries quickly, forming a semiprotective, porous coating, and *fixes* or *holds* the fine particles of graphite, charcoal, chalk, and pastel in place yet allow the surface to be reworked.

wax bloom
An undesired foggy quality on a drawing's surface created by the repeated layering of colored pencils under pressure, which usually can be eliminated by rubbing the surface of the drawing lightly with a soft cloth; it is usually preventable by a light application of spray fixative.

The surface quality of a drawing changes with increased layering of color. The most noticeable change occurs when white or other light colors are applied to a darker color using heavy pressure. The result is a smooth, polished surface; the technique is called **burnishing.** (Burnished areas can be lifted and lightened by pressing a kneaded eraser against the surface.) If the surface becomes too slick, making it difficult to add more color, apply a light spray of **fixative spray** (workable)—the fixative will dry, forming minute granules of texture on the surface and allowing further application of colored pencil.

Repeated layering of color under heavy pressure can produce a foggy quality called **wax bloom,** which usually can be eliminated by rubbing the surface of the drawing lightly with a soft cotton cloth or chamois. Provided it does not alter the color, a light application of spray fixative can be used to prevent bloom also.

Some colored pencils are water-soluble and can be used to create effects similar to watercolor. Almost all colored pencils are soluble in turpentine, and although the result is not as fluid in appearance as that of water-soluble pigments, turpentine as a solvent has the advantage of drying almost immediately.

Project 10.10

Practice various drawing techniques, ranging from loose sketches to carefully finished drawings. Explore the possibilities of the medium in a series of small studies before undertaking a large-scale composition. Practice following the methodical approach of lightly laying in the shapes of your chosen composition with a light-value colored pencil such as a flesh or light-yellow hue instead of graphite. (Note that if you begin laying in contours with graphite and then apply colored pencil over the graphite contours, the graphite will tend to smear or drag under the strokes of colored pencil and be difficult or impossible to remove.)

Critique (Project 10.10) Assess your colored-pencil drawings in terms of their compositional soundness coupled with the added degree of interest created by color ranges of value and intensity. Also, assess the surface condition of your drawings. Often beginners end up with overworked areas that are either burnished or wax-bloomed beyond hope of correcting.

Do the surfaces appear technically well handled, fresh, and alive, or are there areas that seemed to get away from you through too much stroking and too much color material being pushed around on the surface? How would you assess your drawings in terms of color statements? Has color helped in describing form, or has it detracted from the form? Is there an obvious necessity for the color you chose, or does it appear to be mere decoration? Is the color range of values a broad and exciting range, or too mute?

Graphite in Stick, Powdered, and Oversized Pencil Form Graphite is available in other than the familiar and conventional-sized pencil form. Stick graphite, available in grades of softness from B to 6B, lends itself to drawing in an open, sketchy manner on a large scale in a similar way to Conté crayon, square chalks, and even charcoal (although the softest

10-17. MAURICIO LASANSKY (b. 1914; Argentine). *The Nazi Drawings #11.* c. 1961–1966. Graphite pencil, water-soluble red earth wash, and turpentine wash, 74 × 45″ (188.1 × 114.4 cm). The University of Iowa Museum of Art. (On long-term loan to The Cedar Rapids Art Museum, Cedar Rapids, Iowa)

stick graphite is much harder than the hardest charcoal). Look again at the beautifully poetic, bold, and varied hatched strokes of graphite in Oldenburg's drawing (Fig. 10-13). Here we see graphite functioning as the main character—so tonally descriptive, so direct, so luscious, and so responsive to the sensitivities of pressure and paper surface that we almost assume it to be a more extravagant material—yet it is the common, plentiful, and inexpensive material we have used since childhood.

Regarding Mauricio Lasansky's famed series *The Nazi Drawings* (Fig. 10-17, Pl. 13), the artist stated the following:

> I tried to keep not only the vision of the Nazi Drawings simple and direct, but also the materials I used in making them. I wanted the drawings to be done with a tool used by everyone everywhere— from the cradle to the grave—meaning the graphite pencil. I felt if I could use a tool like that, this would keep me away from the temptations that would arise from the virtuosity that a more sophisticated medium would demand.

One cannot overlook the expressive power of Lasansky's *Nazi Drawings* done with water-soluble red earth powder, graphite, and turpentine wash—materials so humble yet with such a riveting impact. Upon seeing the drawings, one finds it hard to look away; and yet looking away, one cannot help but see them again in the mind's eye. In large part, their richness is attributed to what happens when graphite meets a dissolving agent—such as an organic or hydrocarbon solvent like turpentine.

10-18. DANIEL MENDELOWITZ (1905–1980; American). *Wild Radish.* c. 1965. Hard graphite pencil and rubbed graphite, 15 1/2 × 21 1/2″ (39.4 × 54.5 cm). Collection Mrs. Daniel Mendelowitz, Stanford, California.

Technically, when soft graphite is used on paper that has been soaked or sprayed with turpentine, the solvent momentarily dissolves the graphite, causing the graphite stick to glide across the paper with liquid ease, leaving a heavy, rich, black, linear deposit in its wake. The turpentine dries very quickly, and the rich black line is permanently absorbed into the paper rather than merely residing on the surface. (This will be explained further in Chapter 11 on Wet Media as a wash technique.)

Graphite in either stick or pencil form, of any hardness or softness, can be powdered on sandpaper and applied to paper with a finger, soft cloth, or chamois to provide a smoothly textured tone that contrasts effectively with sharply drawn lines, a combination particularly descriptive and elegant in the modeling of life forms—such as the human figure or animals. When the need for a larger quantity exists, finely ground, powdered graphite, prepared for drawing, can be purchased from art supply stores or graphic supply distributors in 6-ounce jars or larger containers.

Also available in yet other forms are large-diameter (5.6 mm) graphite shafts called "woodless pencils" (graphite shafts coated with a thin plastic skin) along with "graphite chunks" in 8-ounce pieces. (Mechanical holders designed to hold larger-diameter graphite shafts are available from the same supply source and prevent breakage.)

For many years artists have purchased graphite powder packaged in squeeze tubes (used for lubrication) from hardware stores. Harder than stick graphite, it produces a pale, even, silvery tone of great beauty when rubbed onto a kid-finish Bristol board with a soft cloth or chamois. Daniel Mendelowitz, the original author of this book, used this silvery graphite powder to develop such a toned background in his *Wild Radish* (Fig. 10-18). He drew the images of foliage using medium-hard and hard graphite pencil lines with white highlights recovered through erasure. The technique is well suited to drawings meant to convey a sense of elegance and delicacy evident in Mendelowitz's work.

Project 10.11

Leafy plants (Fig. 10-18), portraits (Fig. 7-10), glass or metallic objects with reflective surfaces (Fig. 12-6), or an abstraction of organic forms will prove workable for this assignment.

Rub powdered graphite into kid-finish Bristol board until you have a smooth tone of light gray. Begin drawing with light pencil lines using a hard grade of graphite; add darker shading with softer graphite and erase out whites. A firm eraser cut to a fine, sharp edge (with a razor blade) allows you to lift out narrow white lines and small, precise areas of light. Plan and work carefully since all marks, whether penciled darks or erased lights, show on the gray background. Working with an extra piece of paper under your hand will prevent smudging. Use workable fixative only after all erasures are completed.

Silverpoint As has already been pointed out in this chapter, lead-alloy metal points preceded graphite pencils as drawing implements. They were, in fact, used for that purpose in ancient Rome. Over the centuries silver has seemed to provide the most satisfactory metal point, its lovely gray tone oxidizing to a gray-brown hue with the passing of time. A stout, silver wire (available at jewelry and craft supply stores) not more than 1 inch (2.5 centimeters) long, and made pointed by rubbing on sandpaper, provides a fully adequate tool for **silverpoint.** For ease of handling, the wire can be inserted into a drafting-pencil holder, a mechanical pencil, or a wooden stylus. Mount all four edges of a two-ply sheet of Bristol board on a drawing board with masking tape and coat the paper with at least four thin applications of gesso, thinned to the consistency of cream. When a smooth opaque surface has accumulated and the gesso has been burnished with a soft cotton cloth, the ground is ready for silverpoint.

Silverpoint yields a thin line of even width, like that of a hard pencil. Lines executed in silverpoint will not blur; hence, gradations of value must be achieved through systematic diagonal shading, clusters of lines, or cross-hatchings, evident in Alphonse Legros's *Head of a Man* (Fig. 10-19). Since silverpoint does not erase, students are advised to do a preliminary study in hard graphite pencil, perhaps 4H. Silverpoint is most rewarding to individuals who enjoy methodical procedures and painstaking workmanship to produce drawings of exquisite finish. Although students are encouraged to work relatively small while they are developing a familiarity with the medium, silverpoint drawings need not always be limited in scale, as evidenced by Howard Hack's *Silverpoint #97, Lily #6* (Fig. 10-20), which measures 30 by 40 inches (76 by 101 centimeters). Rather than duplicate the natural light-and-dark relationship between blossoms and leaves, Hack focuses on the complexity of the combined forms seen almost as a reverse silhouette against the soft, gray-toned background.

Project 10.12

Prepare a piece of Bristol board with four coats of gesso applied thinly to avoid brush strokes. Let each coat dry thoroughly between applications. Brush alternate layers in opposite directions with a good-quality brush and a "feather-touch" handling (light pressure). Select relatively simple forms for your first attempt. Avoid subjects that call for rich, dark tones. One or two yellow apples, lemons, or pears, or an egg placed on a saucer or in a small bowl would be fine. For greater interest, consider cutting a wedge or two out of a piece of fruit—drawing an apple doesn't require that it be left whole. A partially peeled lemon or orange with the strip of peel

silverpoint
A methodical drawing procedure where a thin rod of silver (about the size of a graphite shaft) is inserted into a mechanical pencil and used to draw on an elaborately prepared gesso surface. The silver metal point, which may be sharpened on sandpaper, yields a thin line of even width with a lovely gray color oxidizing to a grayish-brown with the passing of time. A highly recommended pencil-style mechanical holder is the Faber-Castell E-Motion Mechanical Pencil.

10-19. ALPHONSE LEGROS (1837–1911; French). *Head of a Man.* Silverpoint on white ground.
The Metropolitan Museum of Art, New York.

10-20. HOWARD HACK (b. 1932; American). *Silverpoint #97, Lily #6.* c. 1980. Silverpoint, 30 × 40″ (76.2 × 101.7 cm). Courtesy of the artist.

still attached offers interesting possibilities. Do not neglect the cast shadows of any object. Have patience; be willing to build your forms and values slowly.

Critique (Project 10.12) How well did you prepare the board with gesso coatings? Were there visible brush strokes either before or after you began silverpoint drawing? If so, next time you may want to use some extra-fine sandpaper with light pressure on the gesso ground before drawing.

How descriptive is your drawing? Have you utilized what you've learned about light and shadow to define forms in space? How would you assess your line quality? Does it appear deliberate or overrehearsed, free or tentative? Were you able to manipulate the silverpoint enough to create subtle variations in line character?

How does the composition work? How would you feel about the drawing if someone else had done it?

Wet Media 11

*A truly sensitive artist does not find the
same image in two different media,
because they strike him differently.*

—Odilon Redon

Any fluid preparation an artist chooses to use could conceivably be termed a "wet" medium. For instance, artists sometimes draw in brush and oil paint or in printer's ink. Our primary interest, however, will be liquid **drawing inks**—full strength or diluted for **wash** techniques.

Inks, applied with pen or brush, were used for writing and drawing in Egypt, China, and elsewhere long before the beginning of the Christian era. Although inks can take paste or solid form, the most distinguishing quality of ink is fluidity. Inks are identified by their purpose (relief, intaglio, lithographic, calligraphic, writing, and drawing); by special qualities (indelible, soluble, transparent, opaque); by color; and also according to place of origin (India, China, even specific cities like Frankfurt or Chicago). While most writing inks tend to be too thin and pale for other than sketching purposes, the deep, velvety black of India ink has long been prized as an artistic medium. Inks can be diluted to provide a tonal range in a drawing and can simulate watercolor effects. Because of the liquidity of ink, drawn marks extended into brush strokes, fluid linear qualities produced by a variety of pen nibs, or even spatter techniques all add to the mark-making vocabulary of drawing as a fine art form.

Pen and Ink

For its elegance and clarity, the medium of pen and ink is unexcelled. It is a linear medium that demands precise and subtle control and does not indulge mistakes (Fig. 11-1). Michelangelo is reported to have acknowledged that it was a greater art to draw masterfully with the pen than with the chisel. Although the beginning student will probably have

drawing inks
Saturated liquid pigments possessing great fluidity that may be used full strength with various types of pen nibs (points) for linear effects, or diluted with water to varying degrees of transparency, producing washes applied by brush to enhance pen-and-ink drawings. Among the most popular are India ink, China ink, sumi ink (all black), and various other quality colored inks such as Walnut, Koh-I-Noor, and Windsor-Newton brands.

wash
Ink diluted with varying amounts of water or solvent that produces a broad range of transparent or semi-transparent tonal effects when brushed against a receptive surface, usually an absorbent paper.

11-1. GERALD P. HODGE (b. 1920; American). *The External Anatomy of the Eye.* c. 1980. Pen and ink, 8 1/2 × 11" (21.6 × 27.9 cm). Courtesy of Gerald P. Hodge, University of Michigan.

11-2. Pen nibs and the lines they produce (top to bottom); turkey quill; reed pen; bamboo pen; two drawing pens with metal points; two lettering pens, with flat and round metal nibs; "crow quill" pen; Rapidograph pen; nylon-tip pen; felt-tip marker and pen; ballpoint pen.

to tolerate initially clumsy results before achieving expertise, ink is a medium that allows the development of distinctly personal styles (Figs. 2-15, 4-14, 5-15, 5-16, 7-14, 7-16, 11-3, 11-10, 11-11, 17-15, 17-16). (An added benefit is that ink, once dry, does not smear or smudge in a sketchbook as do pencil and other dry media.)

Pen Types   The requirements of a pen are that it be pointed and also have a tubular body to hold the ink that will flow from its hollow reservoir through the point to the paper (Fig. 11-2). To a much greater extent than with any other media, the choice of **pen nib** (specialized split pen point) determines the style of drawing.

Quill and reed pens have been in use for both drawing and writing since ancient times. **Quill pens,** cut from the heavy pinion feathers (the largest feathers with the thickest shafts near the leading edges of the wings are preferred) of large birds (goose, swan, crow) and shaped to a sharp or angular, coarse or fine point, respond readily to variations in touch and pressure to produce a responsive, smooth, and flexible line. Today, traditionally trained calligraphers are more inclined than artists to make and use quill pens.

Reed pens are hewn from tubular reeds or the hollow wooden stems of certain shrubs and cut to suit the user's taste. (Japanese and bamboo reeds are the most common and make good pens.) In general, reed pens are stiff; their nibs, or points, are thick and fibrous. The lack of supple responsiveness results in a bold, generally wide line. Because the reed pen does not glide easily across the paper surface, it contributes to a deliberate or even awkward strength of handling that tends to challenge the artist and thus inhibit overfacility and technical display. Interestingly, it seems to have been the favored drawing tool of Vincent van Gogh (Figs. 11-3, 7-16, 13-23, 17-16). In comparison, one notices a slight similarity of surface stroking character between his drawings and paintings.

Contemporary artists who value similarly strong, brittle qualities of line draw with **bamboo pens,** a specific type of reed pen imported from the Orient (Fig. 11-4). Bamboo pens can be greatly varied in diameter— some even thick and "stalky," which contributes to the strong character and organic quality of line. Reed and bamboo pen nibs wear out quickly but can be resharpened fairly easily.

The **metal pen** point first appeared at the end of the eighteenth century. Used on very smooth, partially absorbent paper, the steel pen can be more completely controlled than either of its precursors as the vehicle for sharp detailed observation, as demonstrated by Gerald P. Hodge's *The External Anatomy of the Eye* (Fig. 11-1). Nibs of varying sharpness, pointedness, and angularity permit almost any desired effect to suit the artist's purpose. Every artist has a particular preference for specifically designed nibs according to his or her own mode of operation, etc.

The multiplicity of steel pens available for drawing demands much experimentation and exploration. For general sketching purposes, many artists prefer a penholder and interchangeable nibs. **Lettering pen** points come with round, straight, or angular nibs raging in width from 1/10 millimeter to more than 1/4 inch (.6 centimeter). The straight-nibbed lettering pen yields a line that in its stiff regularity recalls the reed pen. Wide lettering pens allow the rapid filling in of large areas. **Fountain pens** are generally more convenient for sketchbook drawing—once filled, they eliminate frequent recourse to a bottle of ink (always a risk when being transported as unwanted drips on the artwork may occur). Two general fountain-pen types are specifically manufactured for sketching and drawing: **quill-style pens,** which dispense India ink for a sustained period of time without clogging or dripping, and **stylus-type pens,** generally termed **Rapidograph pens,** with a central cylindrical point that enables the artist to move the pen in all directions

pen nib
The point of a pen whether *quill, reed, bamboo,* or *steel,* which comes in a variety of different types and sizes and is used with fluid drawing ink; the nib itself acts as the ink reservoir and controls the flow and dispersing of the ink on paper; the style and width of the nib determine line quality.

quill pens Pens cut from the heavy pinion feathers of geese, swans, or wild turkeys, hardened by tempering with wet, heated sand, and shaped to a sharp or angular, coarse or fine point. They respond readily to variations of touch or pressure, producing a responsive, smooth, and flexible line. Today traditionally trained calligraphers are more inclined than artists to make and use quill pens.

reed pens

Pens hewn from tubular reeds or the hollow wooden stems of certain shrubs and cut with various points to suit the user's taste. In general, reed pens are stiff; their nibs, or points, are thick and fibrous. The lack of supple responsiveness results in a bold line.

bamboo pen

A type of *hollow* reed pen imported from the Orient.

metal pen

A pen that first appeared at the end of the eighteenth century; when used on very smooth, partially absorbent paper, the steel pen can be more completely controlled than its predecessors (quill, reed, bamboo pens) as the vehicle for sharp, detailed observation.

lettering pens

As the name implies, pens used for lettering; they are available with round, straight, or angular nibs ranging in width from 1/10 millimeter to more than ¼ inch (.6 centimeter). Straight-nibbed lettering pens yield a line that in its stiff angularity recalls the line made by a reed pen. Wide lettering pens allow the rapid filling in of large areas.

fountain pens

Pens that are generally more convenient for sketchbook drawing—once filled, they eliminate frequent recourse to the bottle of ink (always a risk as dripping may occur when the pen is transported). The two types of fountain pens manufactured for drawing are the *quill-style* pen and *stylus-type* pen, generally termed *Rapidograph*.

quill-style pen

One of several types of fountain pens. See **fountain pens.**

stylus-type pen

A type of fountain pen. See **Rapidograph pens.**

without varying the line width. The latter must be held perpendicular to the drawing surface for the ink to flow evenly. Thorough cleaning of pens—their nibs and reservoirs—after usage greatly prolongs their effective life. Rapidograph pens, in particular, should be flushed out frequently in accordance with the manufacturer's instructions to prevent irreparable clogging of their delicate internal mechanisms. (It is also wise to use manufacturer-specified ink.)

For sketching purposes, nylon, felt-tip, ballpoint, and marking pens offer convenient substitutes for traditional pen and ink. Some dispense black, indelible ink very similar to India ink; some use water-soluble ink. Some have replaceable ink cartridges; others are to be thrown away when the ink supply is exhausted. Although they lack the flexibility of a metal pen, their bold, simple lines have a special character (Figs. 1-12, 11-2). Illustrators producing artwork for reproduction rely upon them heavily, but uncertainty as to the performance of their inks after prolonged exposure to strong light limits their use for fine art.

Simple Line Drawings   Pure, direct, and abbreviated, a black ink line drawn with an open pen on a white paper creates with incisive brilliance and energy a kind of shorthand impression of reality by recording only what the artist considers absolutely essential, eliminating all distracting details. *Femme à la Blouse Russe* (Fig. 11-5) demonstrates what Matisse acknowledged as a seeming liberty of line, contour, and volume that "does not depend on the exact copying of natural forms, nor on the patient assembling of exact details." The virtuosity evident in Matisse's line drawings resulted from making one drawing after another in rapid succession until he was satisfied that he had achieved maximum simplicity, fluidity, and freshness.

Picasso approached pen and ink, as he did with all other media, with authority. *El Tio Pepe Don Jose* (Fig. 11-6) reveals a direct, bold, and brilliant use of the conventional flexible pen. The variations in the thickness of line are doubly descriptive—first, in revealing the physical mass of the circus clown; second, in describing the process of drawing by documenting the pressure with which each stroke was made.

Today artists have more varieties of paper to choose from than ever before; in selecting the right one, they may consider size, weight, tone, color, degree of grain/tooth, naturally deckled edges, whether or not it contains sizing (a binding starch), and so forth. Selecting paper is a matter of personal choice. Smooth paper is generally recommended, since metal pen points tend to pick up the raised paper fibers of heavier-grained papers. Bond paper is satisfactory for preliminary studies; for finished pen-and-ink drawings, smooth-finished Bristol board provides a brilliant white, takes ink well, and permits pen lines of fine quality. You are encouraged to try a heavy-grained paper to experience a different line quality and surface absorbency of ink. Fluid ink lines drawn on unsized or unstarched papers will tend to bleed slightly, creating a velvety line quality, whereas those drawn on sized papers will tend to remain crisper and more true to the way they were drawn. In an untitled drawing done as a student, Andy Warhol (Fig. 11-7) created a slightly blurred, irregular transfer image by blotting freshly inked lines with a second sheet of paper. It was a technique he relied on during his years as an illustrator.

Ink drawing offers little opportunity for revision, other than in quick sketching, making it necessary to consider each line/mark before touching pen to paper. Take care not to overload the pen with ink; wipe the point against the side of the bottle before starting to draw, or the pen may deposit a large drop of ink when it first touches the paper. Should you have such an accident when drawing on good-quality Bristol or illustration board, allow the ink to dry, gently scrape away the excess ink with a razor blade, and then remove any remaining vestiges with an ink eraser. If you attempt to draw over the scraped portion, the ink may bleed even more drastically into the disturbed surface. Except for drawings intended for reproduction, resist any temptation to block out mistakes or smudges with white paint, as the paint will always be far more obvious than the mistake or the correction made by scraping.

Project 11.1

Explore variations of line using simple pen-and-ink techniques in a series of line drawings—line for line's sake. With a small sheet of Bristol board (9 × 12″), begin at the top edge of the sheet, making lines that traverse the entire width of the surface. As you move the pen, practice changing hand positions and angles as you draw. Use rapid and slow movements and differing amounts of pressure, being sensitive to the changes in line character as you go. Fill the entire picture plane with lines of all kinds.

Set up a simple still life of organic forms. Vegetables, fruits, leaves, or even flowers make logical subjects, since deviations in contours from those of the actual model are insignificant (Fig. 5-6). Portraits and figure studies present greater difficulties for the same reason but may compensate with increased interest. You will find it valuable to follow Matisse's lead and make a number of drawings of the same subject, one after another.

11-5. *above, left:* HENRI MATISSE (1869–1954; French). *Femme à la Blouse Russe.* c. 1936. Ink, 15 1/8 × 11 1/8″ (38.4 × 28.3 cm).

11-6. *above, right:* PABLO PICASSO (1881–1973; Spanish-French). *El Tio Pepe Don Jose.* c. 1905. Black ink on cream paper, 10 × 8″ (25.4 × 20.3 cm). Collection Lee A. Ault, New York.

Rapidograph pens

Types of fountain pens that hold a supply of ink and have a central cylindrical point enabling the artist to move the pen in all directions without varying the line width; must be held perpendicular to the drawing surface for the ink to flow evenly.

11-7. ANDY WARHOL (1928–1987; American). *Untitled.* c. 1948–1949. Pen and ink on paper, 29 1/16 × 23 1/16″ (73.8 × 58.6 cm). The Carnegie Museum of Art, Pittsburgh, Pa.

11-8. CANALETTO (1697–1768; Italian). *Veduta Ideata: A Fountain on the Shrine of a Lagoon.* Pencil, pen and ink, black pencil, pen, and brown ink; 7 1/2 × 10 3/4″ (19.1 × 27.3 cm). Royal Library, Windsor Castle, England.

engraving A form of intaglio print-making where line or stipple textures are cut into the surface of a copper plate, or other suitable surface, with a tool called a burin. The burin's lozenge point cuts and removes the surface material, leaving a relatively smooth V-gouge or depressed groove in its wake. Printer's ink is forced into the grooves. The effect is a crisp line quality similar to that of certain pen-and-ink drawings.

Value, Texture, Pattern Because pen and ink is essentially a linear medium, dark values must be built up line by line or dot by dot. Two standard methods for building pen-and-ink values are hatching, the system of parallel lines seen in Canaletto's *Veduta Ideal* (Fig. 11-8), and cross-hatching, the crisscrossed patterns of parallel lines of Jacques Villon's engraving *Jeune Fille* (Fig. 11-9). At first glance, there is a similarity between the lines of an **engraving** and a pen-and-ink drawing; however, to the trained eye the two are quite different in line quality. There is a richness of surface in the engraving that differs extensively from that of an ink drawing: In an ink drawing, the line of absorbed ink is flat, or planographic, with the paper surface, whereas on the engraving surface the lines of ink are actual berms or ridges of ink raised in relief on the paper surface.

Both hatching and cross-hatching can be executed with painstaking, evenly spaced lines or with bold patterns of lines that move in many directions (Fig. 11-10), sometimes as cross-contours (Fig. 11-11), or by scribbling (Fig. 4-5).

Initial attempts at pen-and-ink cross-hatching inevitably seem stilted, but in time, each artist develops a personal style. The beginner need not be unduly concerned with blotches and mistakes; fluent, consistent, unmarred pen-and-ink lines come only with much practice and experience.

11-12. PAUL KLEE (1879–1940; Swiss-German). *A Garden for Orpheus.* c. 1926. Pen and ink, 15 1/2 × 12 1/2" (39.4 × 31.8 cm).
Paul Klee-Stiftung, Kunstmuseum, Bern.

It is important to have a fine-quality, smooth paper for cross-hatching (lest the surface tear from repeated applications of the pen, or become blurred). Cross-hatching actually appears crisper and cleaner when one set of directional lines is allowed to dry before the next set is applied. To reiterate, it is important to work on good-quality paper to be able to experience the best possible results and not waste time and energy with a material whose visual and expressive offerings are limited.

Project 11.2

Practice cross-hatching until you gain some measure of control; then select a few simple objects and proceed to model them in dark and light. Do one drawing in the manner of Figure 11-11. In a second drawing, let the forms suggest the directional pattern for your lines (Fig. 11-10; Pl. 7).

At the beginning, draw brightly illuminated, simple forms with clearly defined areas of shading and minimum surface texture. When you are ready to attempt a more complex study, you might find it profitable to translate some of your pencil drawings from earlier project assignments into pen and ink, having already established a familiarity with those subjects.

Pen and ink is well suited to drawings in which clearly defined patterns are desired for their descriptive, expressive, and decorative values. Van Gogh made extensive use of pattern—both descriptive and decorative—to impart vitality to his drawings (Figs. 7-16, 11-3, 17-15, 17-16). Paul Klee has fancifully embroidered a system of essentially straight lines into an entertaining complexity of pattern and texture (Fig. 11-12).

Project 11.3

Approach this assignment as if you were doodling with pen and ink. Using lines of all types and directions—straight, curved, meandering—begin to invent patterns, letting them evolve, perhaps into an imaginary landscape.

In *The Survivor* by George Grosz (Fig. 11-13), a rich array of textural patterns has been employed both to characterize form and surfaces and for expressive effects. The patterns reveal many different uses of the pen (as you practiced in Project 11.1), while some textures appear to result from pressing fabrics or other materials dampened with ink against paper, a form of "wet frottage."

Project 11.4

Develop a pen-and-ink drawing in which you introduce textural patterns for descriptive or expressive purposes. Textures can be suggested rather than meticulously rendered. While some hatching and cross-hatching is inevitable, incorporate a variety of linear patterns. Rocks, brambles, weeds, weathered wood, a derelict truck in a field offer interesting surfaces and textures (Figs. 7-16, 7-17). Introduce a range of values in addition to textural variations.

Take note of the fact that the more inventive you become with line, the more visual life your drawings will have, and the greater the possibilities of arriving at a higher plane of creative and descriptive visual power and expression. This is when an artist's particular style may first begin to emerge.

Project 11.5

While we tend to think of ink drawings as rich black lines against a white background, try drawing with black and white ink on a medium gray or middle-value paper.

11-13. GEORGE GROSZ (1893–1959; German-American). *The Survivor.* c. 1936. Pen and India ink, 19 × 24 3/4″ (48.3 × 62.8 cm). © The Art Institute of Chicago.

11-14. BRYONY CARFRAE (20th century; British). *Stone Crab.* c. 1977. Pen and ink, life-size; 2 × 3 3/4″ (5.1 × 9.5 cm). Courtesy of the artist.

In highly detailed ink drawings, especially in scientific illustrations such as Bryony Carfrae's *Stone Crab* (Fig. 11-14), **stippling** (patterns of dots) serves to describe the very smooth gradations of value that define form, texture, or color modulation. Even the sharpest photograph would not reveal the details of form, texture, and surface patterns with the clarity of this drawing, for in a photograph reflected lights and shadows would be intrusive. Stippling takes time and patience; the pattern of dots should be random, inventive, varied, but never careless. It is the size of the pen, not the pressure, that determines the size of the dots; it is the density of the dots that produces darker tones. Rapidograph pens are ideal for stippling, but any pen can be used as long as the dots are kept uniform.

stippling

The building up of surface and tonal descriptions through the concentrated use of tiny dots; the dots when closer together produce darker passages; further apart, lighter tones.

Project 11.6

In an earlier assignment you were asked to make a pencil rendering of a familiar surface, duplicating the texture as accurately as possible according to its exact character (Project 7.2). Do a similar rendering of a familiar object, emphasizing and clarifying its character using pen and ink stippling to delineate a textured surface or object in as disciplined a manner as possible. A detailed preliminary pencil study will prove useful.

Once you've gained confidence, begin drawing directly with pen and ink, remembering to be inventive with line, line hatching, and stippling to create passages of varying values that become more and more visually descriptive.

Pen, Brush, and Ink

Pen and ink, amplified by brush, provides an obvious transition from pure pen-and-ink to brush-and-ink drawing. The surrealistic superimposing of images in Pavel Tchelitchew's *The Blue Clown* (Fig. 11-15)—possibly the elaboration of a doodle—demonstrates how a pen allows linear detailing, while a brush facilitates lines of greater width than can be obtained with pen nib, as well as extended areas of dark. Attempting to fill in large areas with a pen produces a scruffy and uneven surface, not to mention the uninteresting look of an overly deliberate surface.

Project 11.7

Depict a subject with bold contrasts of dark and light—perhaps a self-portrait illuminated by strong light from one side—combining pen outlines and brushed ink masses to create transitional values and textures.

Brush and Ink

The narrowness of line produced by pen and ink gives it its crisp bite and energy and at the same time limits its degree of flexibility and painterliness. When artists wish to expand the scope of mark making beyond line, they pick up a brush (Fig. 11-16).

All kinds of brushes can be used with ink. Each brush imparts its particular character to a drawing—a stiff bristle oil-painting brush produces brusque, angular lines, often with heavy dry-brushed edges (Fig. 11-17); the long, very pointed Japanese brush is more responsive to pressures of the hand and so creates lines of unusually varied widths (Fig. 11-18); a red sable brush, while not as flexible as a Japanese brush, can be used in somewhat the same manner. Frequent and thorough rinsing of brushes, as well as careful storage (especially important so that brush fibers maintain their proper shape) ensures continued quality and

11-15. PAVEL TCHELITCHEW (1898–1957; Russian-American). *Study for "The Blue Clown."* c. 1929. Pen and brush and ink, 16 × 10 1/2" (40.6 × 26.7 cm). The Museum of Modern Art, New York.

11-16. JOSEF ALBERS (1888–1976; German-American). *Two Owls.* c. 1917. Brush and ink, 19 7/8 × 28 1/2" (50.5 × 72.4 cm). Collection Anni Albers and the Josef Albers Foundation, Inc.

11-17. EMIL NOLDE (1867–1956; German). *Landscape with Windmill*. Brush and black printer's ink on tan paper, 17 1/2 × 23 1/4" (44.5 × 59.1 cm). Private collection.

11-18. SESSON (1504–1589?; Japanese). *Grapes and Bamboo*. Ink on paper, 12 1/2 × 17 1/2" (31.7 × 44.5 cm). Collection Kurt Gitter, New Orleans.

dependability of the materials. Manufacturers have produced a brush designed like a fountain pen with an ink cartridge and cap that facilitates impromptu sketching and drawing with brush and ink without having to carry a bottle of ink. It offers much of the flexibility of the Japanese brush.

Different types of papers' textures, weights, whether sized or unsized, also have much to do with the quality of line in brush-and-ink drawing (see pp. 177–178). Soft, absorbent papers (unsized), like handmade Japanese papers such as Mulberry, soak up ink the moment the brush strokes touch them and so create lines that vary considerably in width and the character of the edge (Figs. 11-16, 11-17). Hard-surfaced papers (sized), on the other hand, absorb a minimum of ink from the brush, and this contributes to continuity of line and clean-cut edges (Figs. 1-9, 8-8). A dry-brush effect inevitably occurs when a very rough, textured paper is used as the brush skims the uppermost relief surface of the textured paper; conversely, it is almost impossible to achieve an interesting dry-brush quality on a very smooth paper.

Other media—gouache, printer's inks, watercolor, tempera, acrylics, and oils—are appropriate for brush drawings. Many experienced printmakers and painters prefer to draw with tools and materials they use for printmaking and painting to facilitate developing drawings into monotypes, prints, and paintings on paper. In such cases, the activity of drawing is extended and becomes naturally embodied within other creative realms, dictated by the use of other tools and materials.

Project 11.8

Explore the use of brush and ink using whatever brushes you may have available. Larger (2-inch) household paintbrushes as well as smaller 1-inch acrylic brushes down to the smallest watercolor and oil paint brushes should be used.

India ink is excellent to start with. First, experiment with small pieces of a variety of different papers of differing textures, taking note of how each receives the ink along with the type of line and stroke qualities they offer. On a larger sheet size, practice with altering amounts of downward pressure as you draw with brush and ink, keeping your arm, wrist, and hand loose and held above the paper while moving freely about the surface. Concentrate on making a variety of different marks.

Oriental Calligraphy   Among the most sophisticated and beautiful brush-and-ink drawings are those of the Oriental masters (Figs. 5-20, 6-13, 11-18, 11-19, 14-28). There has always been a particularly close relationship between the arts of writing and drawing in China and Japan, since the techniques involved in manipulating the brush are the same, and in both, the ornamental character of the line produced by skillful brush handling, known as **calligraphy,** has been highly prized. Long

calligraphy
Beautiful writing. In western culture it is done with a pen, in Chinese and Japanese cultures with a brush.

11-19. CHU TA (1626–1705; Chinese). *Bird, from an Album of Flowers, Birds, Insects, and Fish.* Brush and ink on paper, 10 1/16 × 9 1/16″ (25.5 × 23 cm).
Courtesy of the Smithsonian Institution, Freer Gallery of Art, Washington, D.C.

years of copying the works of acknowledged masters and mastering an exact vocabulary of strokes constituted an arduous apprenticeship for the Oriental artist. In the drawings of such masters as Japanese artist Sesson (Fig. 11-18) and Chinese artist Chu Ta (Fig. 11-19), one is aware of pure virtuosity of technique and decorative charm.

Oriental-brush master artists employ **sumi**, a stick of carbon ink that is ground and mixed with water on a shallow stone or ceramic block. This procedure permits great control over the density of tones. The brush itself is held in a vertical position above a flat ground, neither hand nor wrist being allowed to touch the paper or table support. By raising and lowering the hand and loading the brush with ink in different ways— using the side of the brush or the tip alone, or combining heavy black ink in the tip with very thin, watery ink in the body of the brush—the artist can regulate an extensive repertoire of strokes. Since the traditional Japanese paper and silk fabrics are very absorbent, lines cannot be altered or deleted, and a skilled craftsman never repeats a line.

11-20. *above, left:* GIOVANNI BATTISTA TIEPOLO (1696–1779; Italian). *The Rest on the Flight into Egypt.* Pen and brown wash (bistre), 16 7/8 × 11 3/8". (42.8 × 28.9 cm). The Fogg Art Museum, Harvard University, Cambridge, Mass.

11-21. *above, right:* GIOVANNI DOMENICO TIEPOLO (1727–1804; Italian). *Abraham Visited by the Angels.* Sepia, wash drawing, 15 3/4 × 11" (40 × 28 cm). The Metropolitan Museum of Art, New York.

sumi

A stick of solid carbon ink that is ground and mixed with water on a shallow stone with a water well. This procedure permits great control over the density of tones.

Project 11.9

A Japanese brush, watercolor paper, or Mulberry paper, water-soluble India ink, and a saucer and water will allow you to explore the technique. For an initial experience, study Figure 11-18 to gain a sense of the hand and brush movements and the changes in pressure required for each stroke. Practice one stroke at a time rather than attempting to copy the entire drawing.

Remember the techniques used in Project 11.8. Try to employ them here as skillfully as you can and also in a more expressive manner.

11-22. Demonstration of simple wash technique described in Project 11.10. Drawings by Duane Wakeham.

Critique (Projects 11.8, 11.9) Simply assess your line and stroke qualities. Are strokes clean and unrehearsed-looking? Is there freedom of expression with your brushed marks? Are you able to note the differences in tonal variations between different strokes, and are those variations expressive? Are they descriptive of form? How do they exist in space?

Wash Drawing

wash drawing
A drawing created exclusively by the use of ink washes of differing concentrations and dilutions applied to the paper surface with brushes.

A **wash drawing** offers an instructive transition between drawing and painting, and, in fact, often serves as a preliminary value study for a monotype or painting. Unlike brush-and-ink drawing, which depends for its effectiveness on more or less solid black contrasting with white, in wash drawing the medium is freely diluted with water to produce a wide range of grays. Both the brush and the diluted medium are extremely flexible vehicles that encourage an unusually fluid play of lines, values, and textures (Figs. 11-20 through 11-22).

Two undisputed masters of wash drawing were the eighteenth-century Venetian father-and-son duo Giovanni Battista Tiepolo and Giovanni Domenico Tiepolo. The father's dexterous handling of pale translucent washes, light-value pen lines, dark accents of brushed ink, and large areas of untouched white paper in *Rest on the Flight into Egypt* (Fig. 11-20) produces an image of amazing radiance. As we examine his son's more fully developed tonal study *Abraham Visited by the Angels* (Fig. 11-21), less is left to our imaginations. Domenico's greater use of middle and middle-light values and his focusing of light and dark on the figure of Abraham introduces an element of drama in contrast to the lyrical mood created by the pervasive light in his father's drawing. Hence, the father's work appears more open and artfully mysterious with its absence of overly defined forms, the son's more illustrative in its assertion of the absolutism of defined forms.

Wash commonly refers to ink or watercolor that has been thinned with water to various value gradations. It can also encompass **gouache** (opaque watercolor), tempera, acrylics, oil paints, and printer's inks thinned with turpentine, although these later media tend to be less fine-grained than ink or watercolor. Whatever the pigment or color, it is the principle of dilution that characterizes wash drawing.

The equipment needed for wash drawing is modest: brush, ink, black watercolor or tempera, and heavier absorbent paper. Because good-quality watercolor paper and illustration board will not wrinkle or buckle when wet, it is an excellent ground for wash drawings. Illustration board can be thumbtacked to your drawing board surface; watercolor paper is best mounted. To mount or stretch watercolor paper, wet it thoroughly on both sides with water in a spray bottle; then lay it on the drawing board for about five minutes or until the water has been absorbed, smooth it out slightly, and fasten the edges with paper tape (not masking tape). Allow the paper to dry, shrink, and stretch to a perfectly flat state. (If the paper is still buckled once dry, repeat the procedure of wetting and taping until a perfect flat sheet is achieved.)

You will need a quantity of clean water and absorbent rags. A natural sponge will prove helpful for wetting the paper or for soaking up areas of wash that appear too saturated. A white saucer, plate, watercolor palette, or glass slab can serve as a container/surface on which to mix your pigments.

Flat Washes   While the medium encourages free, spontaneous handling, a rather more cautious and systematic procedure demonstrated in

gouache
From the French word "wash," opaque watercolors used in painting whose pigments contain a *gum binder* and filler of *opaque white* such as clay that give a chalky appearance to the surface of the painting.

Figure 11-22 and described in Project 11.10 is recommended for those with no experience in wash or watercolor drawing.

Project 11.10

For your first wash drawing, select a subject with clearly defined planes of light and dark. If you have any sketches or drawings of buildings, they would be appropriate, as would the by-now-familiar cardboard boxes and paper bags. Keep to a modest size, no larger than 9 by 12 inches. Make a preliminary outline drawing. Plan the distribution of values, leaving pure white paper for the lightest areas. Place a couple of teaspoons of water in your saucer or palette and add enough ink to make a light gray. Load your brush with this light gray wash tone and spread it over all the paper (right to the taped edges) except those areas that are to be left white. Be patient and allow the first wash to dry thoroughly before applying a second wash to the areas that are intended to be the next darkest value. Laying one wash over a partially dry surface inevitably results in an ugly or uncontrolled mottled effect. To achieve deeper tones and darker values much more quickly, add more pigment to your wash.

Modulated Areas: Wash and Other Media   Wash is particularly suitable for producing free, fluid effects, and also produces a semitransparent ground that is receptive to yet other drawing media. Wash tones can be applied directly to paper without preliminary drawing or can be combined with graphite or colored pencil, pen and ink, charcoal, or chalk. When wash is augmented by other media, it is up to the artist to decide whether the wash precedes or follows the pencil, pen, or charcoal lines and to determine the amount and strength of linear support.

In Francesco Primaticcio's *Hercules and Omphale* (Fig. 11-23), the artist uses a relatively subtle yet rich value range that reveals a dramatic definition of volume and space through the combined use of pen and ink and **bistre** wash (a transparent brown pigment made by boiling soot). Käthe Kollwitz employs an even greater range of values with her brush-and-ink washes in *Mother and Child by Lamplight at the Table* (Fig. 11-24). She relies almost completely on a painterly wash technique to create extremes of light and dark that depict the effects of lamplight, introducing pen line only to detail the forms and features of the two heads and the chair's structure. (Compare Figure 11-24 with Figure 2-21, taking note of how the artist of the latter drawing built up its rich and varied value range almost exclusively with brush and ink wash.)

Project 11.11

To develop a painterly approach to wash drawing, mix a puddle of middle-value gray ink wash in your palette. Proceed to paint, adding water to the middle-value gray when you want lighter tones and concentrated pigment to yield darker tones. Do not strive for flat washes or smoothly toned effects, as this is antithetical to the wash process. Permit your brush strokes and the gradations of value to show (Figs. 2-21, 11-20 through 11-24). Work into the washes only while they are still fresh. While an area is still wet, it is possible to recover lights by squeezing or pressing all the water from a rinsed brush with your fingers or a rag and lifting out the desired light with the brush. Once the washes have begun to dry, allow them to become completely dry before introducing additional washes. For clearly defined edges, apply the wash to a dry surface; for softened contours, wet the paper with clear water before applying the wash.

After experimenting freely with this technique, select a subject that lends itself to a more fluid handling of form. Choosing a subject already drawn from an earlier project not only allows you to work with familiar forms but also offers you the opportunity to see clearly the differences that occur in treating the same subject in dissimilar media.

bistre

A transparent brown pigment used to produce wash tones in pen and ink drawings obtained by boiling soot.

11-23. *above:* FRANCESCO PRIMATICCIO (1504–1570; Italian). *Hercules and Omphale.* Pen and ink, with bistre wash, 11 1/2 × 17 7/8″ (29.2 × 45.4 cm). Albertina Museum, Vienna.

11-24. *left:* KÄTHE KOLLWITZ (1867–1945; German). *Mother and Child by Lamplight at the Table* (self-portrait with son, Hans?). c. 1894. Pen and ink with brush and wash, 8 × 10 5/8″ (20.3 × 27 cm). Courtesy Deutsche Fototek Dresden.

Project 11.12

An interesting variation of traditional wash drawing is to draw with ink or concentrated pigment (oil paint, printer's inks) on wet paper. Wet another piece of paper with clear water. Because the paper surface is wet, there will be some resistance between the oil paints and printer's inks and the water, leading to some interesting reticulation textures between these antithetical elements. The unpredictable runs, spottings, and granular deposits create evolving textures and lines quite unlike the limpid fluidity of typical wash drawings.

Another variation is to draw with pen and ink on dry paper, and then, while the lines are still wet, to touch them with a water-filled brush. This will allow for an

monotype

As a unique impression, a one-time drawing with printer's inks on a flat metal plate, which is then transferred to dampened paper with the use of a press. The French artist Edgar Degas is well known for his use of the monotype medium.

printer's ink

A heavy-bodied, oil-based, saturated ink made of carbon blacks or color pigment powders mixed with plate oil (derived from linseed oil). Printer's inks can be diluted with solvents so that they will flow from a brush to produce the painterly effects of monotype or ink wash.

subtractive method

In the dark-field manner, the gradual removal of the dark drawing materials from within a black field creating shapes, forms, tones, or textures of lighter values by allowing light to enter into the composition; the building of light-value visual forms from within an initial dark field.

dark field manner

A technique in which the artist prepares a dark field on a picture plane and proceeds to remove the darks, allowing light to enter the field. This creates a composition of lighter passages that describe forms or objects existing within the dark pictorial space. It is the opposite of **light field manner.**

additive method

The drawing activity of beginning with a white or blank surface and building up positive marks as lines, tones, textures, values; working from light to dark by the progressive addition of tonal marks.

light field manner

A technique in which the artist begins with a light surface and progressively builds up an image by adding darker forms or shapes comprised of line, tone, texture, and value. Opposite of **dark field manner.**

irregularly interesting swelling of the line and yet offer some control of the direction and the extent to which the ink spreads. Experimentation with this procedure will provide a method by which the character of lines can be altered in future ink drawings.

Project 11.13

Colored wash reinforced by colored inks, pencils, chalks, and the other tinted media offers an excellent vehicle by which students can make the transition to painting or printmaking. Do a number of drawings with colored media calling forth various wash and line techniques. Limit the selection to two colors for your initial experience—sepia brown as a warm color, French ultramarine blue as a cool color. Applying a wash of one color over the other or allowing the colors to blend will create a range of colors. Colored inks are brilliant and seem to retain their brightness even when they are mixed; however, to maintain the purity of the color in each bottle, avoid dipping an ink-filled brush from one bottle into another (it is advisable to use a separate brush for each color, then rinse and dry the brushes with a rag when necessary).

Drawing and Monotype

Monotype is a "hybrid medium" that combines the elements of drawing, printmaking, and painting into one immediate act. Because of its dependence upon the drawn, graphic, and painterly activities, it is a medium that artists from all disciplines use in producing works of great virtuosity that, in the end, possess a uniquely identifiable immediacy and directness.

Further defined, **monotype** is a drawing made with thinned **printer's ink** on a blank surface, such as a Plexiglas or metal plate or a heavy sheet of acetate. In the **subtractive method,** or **"dark field manner,"** the artist uses small inking rollers (called brayers), brushes, rags, or tarlatans (starched cheesecloths) to cover the entire surface of the plate with ink. Wooden dowel rods (used as drawing sticks), Q-tips, cotton balls, rags, brushes, fingertips, and solvents—anything that will remove the ink and create the desired compositional effects—may be utilized to create a design in the ink film. Then the image is transferred to dampened, heavy rag paper with the use of an etching press.

Another approach to monotype, referred to as the **additive method,** or **"light field manner,"** is to create the design by adding ink directly to a blank plate with brushes or rags, then building up and supplementing the image with full ranges of tones and textures by continually adding ink. The image is then transferred to dampened paper with a press, as with the subtractive method.

Because the flat surface is either metal, Plexiglas, or acetate (all nonabsorbent materials), the inks can be as easily removed as they were laid down. In fact, dramatic highlights are quickly obtained by wiping the ink away, partially or entirely, creating tonal areas of lighter values or extreme whites.

Well-known Washington, D.C., artist Jack Boul applied the dark field manner in his monotype *Cow in a Barn* (Fig. 11-25), a tonally rich drawing executed in highly descriptive films of thinned printer's inks. Notice how amazingly luminous the very lightest films of ink are on the cow's body—and the highlights of the rear udder and right hipbone so sensitively orchestrated through the subtle manipulation of tone. Artist Nancy Hersch Ingram, once a student of Jack Boul's, employed the additive method to produce *Cow Skull #1* (Fig. 11-26), a monotype of rich and delicate proportions. Notice the reticulated textures and the grain of the ink washes coupled with the deep rich black of saturated ink in Ingram's drawing. Boul's and Ingram's choices of both the subtractive and additive methods (the dark and light field manners) yield wonderfully sensitive interpretations—a strong testament to these artists' abilities to

11-27. EDGAR DEGAS (1834–1917; French). *La Toilette (Le Bain), The Bath.* Monotype in black ink on heavy white laid paper in the dark field manner. 12 3/8 × 11" (31.2 × 27.7 cm). © The Art Institute of Chicago, The Clarence Buckingham Collection.

see deeply, then translate what they see into these tonally varied and exquisitely expressive drawings.

Edgar Degas, a master at the technique of monotype, employed extreme darks and lights to emphasize his figurative composition in *La Toilette (Le Bain)* (Fig. 11-27). In this intimate scene the French master's use of extended tonal ranges—from the intense blacks of the interior's receding spaces to the projecting white linear highlights of the woman's hair—poses a formidable yet delicate definition of the human form in space. As she rises from her bath, the viewer gleans a powerful sense of this *ethereal* presence mysteriously infused within the atmospherically thin, vulnerable films of ink.

These stellar works by Boul, Ingram, and Degas, created by skilled and potent acts of drawing, are so indicative of artistic sensitivity to the ephemeral plasticity of the less-than-paper-thin films of ink. The hypersensitive penetrations into both the *dark and light field manners,* resulting in this mastery of interpretation of subject, bears evidence to these artists' skills as draftsmen and visual poets. Their fluidly drawn marks are palpable to the point that one can almost identify the tools used in making the different strokes and descriptive textures of these willfully poetic impressions (Figs. 11-25 through 11-27 and 17-8).

Still Life 12

*Common objects become strangely
uncommon when removed from their
context and ordinary ways of being seen.*

—Wayne Thiebaud

A certain artist in ancient Greece prided himself on the ability to paint
fruits so convincingly that birds would peck at them. With comparable
enthusiasm, artists of fifteenth-century Flanders reveled in the skill with
which they could depict glass, ceramics, fabrics, wood, and fruits.
Throughout the Renaissance and Baroque periods artists repeatedly
drew upon still-life materials to create an atmosphere of everyday reality in their works. The emergence of a bourgeois society in the seventeenth century, with its glorification of middle-class values, made the
portrayal of material wealth a major thematic concern. In Flanders, artists
depicted tables laden with fruit, vegetables, fish, poultry, and meat in
what to our more health-conscious age seems a gluttonous display. The
Dutch masters of the period added flowers to their repertoire, painting
prodigious arrangements complete with sparkling drops of dew and insects. Early nineteenth-century American still-life painters patterned their
works after Dutch precedents; late-nineteenth-century American ***trompe
l' oeil*** artists William Harnett and John Peto originated a brilliant style of
still-life painting employing very shallow space, clearly defined cast
shadows, and a meticulous rendering of surface textures.

    An interesting development of the second half of the twentieth cen-
tury is the realistic representation of still-life subjects in enormously oversized close-up views, such as Mary Ann Currier's *Turnips* (Fig. 12-1). The
concept derives in part from Georgia O'Keeffe, who in the 1920s—possibly influenced by close-up photography—began to produce drawings
and paintings of greatly enlarged images of flowers, bleached animal
skulls, and shells (Fig. 12-2). Additionally, the contemporary large-scale
close-up was spawned by the Pop Art movement, which owed much of
its genesis to the omnipresent American billboard.

trompe l'oeil
Rendering in its most meticulous form
(from a French term meaning "deceive
the eye"); usually applies to still life
where the creation of poignant illusions
convinces the viewer that he is looking
at the actual object or objects
represented.

12-1. MARY ANN CURRIER (b. 1927; American). *Turnips.* 1985. Oil pastel on museum board, 39 × 56 1/4″ (99.1 × 142.9 cm).
Courtesy of the artist.

12-2. GEORGIA O'KEEFE (1887–1986; American). *Shell.* c. 1925. Charcoal, 19 × 25″ (48.3 × 63.5 cm).
National Gallery of Art, Washington, D.C.

Advantages of Still Life

Still-life drawing presents a number of advantages, which have determined the preponderance of still-life subjects suggested in the preceding projects. Working alone in a quiet studio, the artist is free from many of the problems that accompany portraiture, life drawing, and landscape drawing. There is no need to schedule sittings with models or portrait subjects. The artist can ignore the caprices of weather and work uninhibited by wind, rain, changes in light, and all the other unpredictable elements that go with working out of doors. And the studio and equipment demands for the still life are minimal; any quiet room with good light, whether natural or artificial, will serve.

For the novice, still life has yet another advantage. The subject, as the name clearly indicates, does not move. Thus, the beginning student has ample time to observe, absorb, and learn to portray the tremendous variety of surface qualities that characterize all objects. Once again, the all-important activity of learning to see deeply, and to develop the skills involved in depicting the appearances of what is seen, is of paramount importance to the challenging and successful portrayal of the visually potent and highly detailed curiosities of still-life objects. The rendering of form, light and shadow, texture, color, and such subtle phenomena as luster and transparency can all be attempted at an unhurried pace. Problems of perspective and foreshortening, both elementary and complex, will arise, and these problems can be worked on at the student's leisure. If the arrangement is placed where it need not be moved for some time, and if the subject is not susceptible to withering or decay (an old boot, for instance, in contrast to fruit or flowers), the student can experiment in as many media as desired over a longer period of time, perhaps allowing artistic growth and development to be evident in works done from the same still life.

Finally, still life involves little expense. Every home is filled with potential still-life subjects. You need only glance at the illustrations in this section to see that anything from old clothing to edibles, from tableware to cooking utensils, even sections of rooms and furniture, can serve as subject matter for the artist with imaginative vision and a sense of composition, as in Catherine Murphy's *Still Life with Pillows and Sunlight* (Fig. 12-3). It is the sympathetic observation of familiar objects, accompanied by the capacity to project these observations into arresting and revealing works of art, that characterizes the true still-life artist.

Jane Lund's drawing entitled *Still Life* (Fig. 12-4) portrays an elegant display of interestingly different household items of hard and soft, smooth and textured, inanimate and perishable. It is an astonishingly accomplished work done in graphite, with stumping (blending) and erasing, on ivory wove paper. (The word *wove* refers to the woven fabric used as the sieve or screen, which is stretched flat inside a rectilinear

12-3. CATHERINE MURPHY (b. 1946; American). *Still Life with Pillows and Sunlight.* 1976. Pencil, 8 5/8 × 12 1/2" (21.9 × 31.7 cm). Courtesy Lennon, Weinberg, Inc., New York. Private collection.

12-4. JANE LUND (b. 1939; American). *Still Life.* 1980–1981. Graphite with stumping and erasing on ivory wove paper, 13 × 16 1/2″ (330 × 419 mm). The Jalane and Richard Davidson Collection. © The Art Institute of Chicago.

frame (as a pane of glass exists inside a window frame). The wet paper fibers settle on the screen as the water drains through it, leaving a flat, wet sheet of paper pulp on top. When the wet sheet dries, it carries the imprint of the woven pattern of the fabric sieve as its own surface texture or tooth. (Wove paper has the finest and most consistent surface, devoid of any lines or thinner textural patterns that may have resulted from the type of screen used.)

The trained artist's eye finds interesting compositions almost everywhere, as is suggested by the Wayne Thiebaud quote at the beginning of this chapter. It is the still-life artist's role in society to endow the common with uncommon interest—to pull something out of context and give it significance. This is what draws an audience, and this is what holds audience attention. Therefore, an interesting composition need not be complicated or even "artistically arranged"; often interesting compositions are found in the simplest of casual arrangements that happen from life and not from anything contrived. Learn to recognize that almost every object or group of objects can be interpreted in an interesting way through an artist's eyes.

Project 12.1

Select a few ordinary, nonperishable household items. Once the objects have been arranged, if that is necessary, it is essential to place the lighting from above and slightly to one side. Daylight has no particular advantage over artificial light, as long as the artificial light is brilliant. Often, high-intensity reading lamps work well because of their flexible design. Once the set is established, concentrate on form and texture, light and shadow, and employ as many of the drawing skills as have been discussed thus far, using different drawings of the same still life to perform the different techniques.

Critique (Project 12.1) Observe the results of Project 12.1 and assess the degree of visual interest that comes from each individual object, as well as from the entire composition. Is there a sense of uncommon importance given to the common objects? Has the context of the subject(s) changed in the drawing from the real-life arrangement? Have you employed your imaginative forces; and is there strong evidence of your skills of reinterpretation?

Still-life Forms and Value Studies

Much early training in nineteenth-century academics of art in Europe and America was devoted to techniques of rendering forms through traditional chiaroscuro. Still-life compositions provided ideal subjects for the study of value gradations and the elements of chiaroscuro—highlights, light, shadow, core of the shadow, and reflected light (see the section on chiaroscuro in Chapter 6). Smooth white plaster casts used as still-life objects allowed for easy observance and analysis of chiaroscuro and all its effects. Martha Alf's *Still Life #6* (Fig. 12-5) is in that tradition, but beyond technique her drawing is distinguished by a deceivingly simple elegance that results from concern for the "visual organization" of shapes and spaces. Note that the subtle shadows cast onto the backdrop appear almost landscape in quality.

Catherine Murphy (Fig. 12-3), Jane Lund (Fig. 12-4), and Akira Arita (Fig. 12-6) display similar virtuosity of technique and vision. All reveal form solely by value change with dramatic value contrasts in some areas to define forms in space. Arita has chosen brilliant back lighting to silhouette simple cylindrical shapes that have been given specific definition by the way the light picks out the rims of the open cans and by the handles. The drawing is admirable for Arita's skill in rendering the smooth, hard, reflective surfaces of the paint cans and the juxtaposition of the radiating shadows and reflections on the tabletop. Equally enviable is his sense of composition—the grouping of the cans, the repetition of the ellipses, and the variations of the upright handles.

Project 12.2

Compose a still-life arrangement containing rather simple forms, closely related in value and preferably light so that the use of chiaroscuro will not be complicated by differences in color or extreme value differences. Lemons, yellow apples, or white onions, for example, would be well suited for this project rather than items of darker colors. Illuminate the objects with a strong light from above and to one side. Place a simple background, neutral in value such as light gray, close enough behind the grouping so that the shadows cast by the objects fall on the background, while the background surface reflects light into the shadowed portions of the objects. Develop the drawing with one of the dry media. Sketch the objects in light outline to establish size and shape relationships; then proceed to model the forms in dark and light.

Study the shapes of the cast shadows carefully and render them as thoughtfully as you do the actual objects, paying particular notice to their degree of darkness as compared with the darkest shadow on the objects themselves. To the mature artist, all aspects of the visual experience are significant; the shadows cast by objects provide interesting elements of pattern equal in importance to the objects. If these delicacies of cast shadow are overlooked, the composition suffers greatly in terms of visual dynamic and power of subtlety.

Critique (Project 12.2) The main question to ask in the aftermath of this assignment is, How modeled and volumetric are the forms? Any slight underemphasis in the play of lights and darks dramatically decreases the solidity of form and readability of the objects as they exist in space. Consider these questions: Are the forms technically well drawn? Are they believable as they exist in relation to each other and in space? Are the light source and its directional flow well evident? Have you used as extensive a range from light to dark as possible without overdramatizing the drawing?

Schematic Form

One of the basic problems in drawing is learning to create a convincing sense of solid, three-dimensional form, particularly when a solid object is translated into a series of lines, shapes, and shadings on a flat, two-dimensional sheet of paper. It is not uncommon for initial drawing assignments to be based upon simplified forms that require learning how to perceive size, shape, and space relationships by using the measuring techniques described in Chapter 3, as well as learning how to use chiaroscuro. Mastering such simple geometric shapes virtually assures equal success with even the most complex subjects, provided the same basic approach is followed—looking, measuring, duplicating shapes rather than drawing objects. Learning to see complex shapes schematically—reducing objects to their nearest geometric equivalents—is one of the most successful methods of understanding and representing three-dimensional form. When drawing overlapping objects, it is essential that you understand and depict the amount of space that each requires. It is not uncommon for beginners to do drawings of a group of objects that viewed from above would reveal some forms occupying the same space. One senses immediately that each paint can in Figure 12-6 exists in its own space.

Project 12.3

Notice in Figure 12-6 and in Plates 1 and 2 how conscious we are of the basic structure of all the objects depicted. Set up a still life containing objects with clearly structured forms, but not necessarily only those objects that are simple geometric shapes—in fact, there should be some slight deviation from pure geometric form. Your assignment is to reveal the structural relationships of objects by simplifying them into basic geometric shapes or interrelated combinations of shapes, and to intensify the sense of volume with bold chiaroscuro. For instance, a pear can be reduced to a sphere and a cylindrical cone. Now use the power of chiaroscuro to intensify the presence of sphere and cylindrical cone.

In this assignment, to be able to see the geometric forms contained within each object is the first step of seeing; the second step is to be capable of reducing the objects through the process of seeing and drawing. Again, remember to focus on the geometric shapes contained within the forms.

Critique (Project 12.3) You should notice that the objects in your drawings reflect an emphasis on geometric form—perhaps even exaggerated geometric form. In fact, the objects may seem to have been constructed from parts highly descriptive of their nearest geometric equivalents. Have you drawn them that way? Or are you still too focused on the common shape of the object and unable to reduce the object to a geometric shape? This takes practice; if you haven't fully succeeded, try again. It may require that you divorce your thought processes from anything having to do with the context of the shapes of familiar objects, and in doing so, allow yourself to see geometric shape beyond the shape and meaning of the original form.

Composition and Treatment

The selection of subject matter is a problem for many beginning students, who are reluctant to relinquish the concept that what they draw must be "artistic." It can truly be said that subject matter is unimportant. It is the way in which an artist approaches any given subject matter that brings artistic life or death to the subject. Throughout the history of art, significant subjects have been rendered meaningless, while seemingly meaningless subjects have been elevated to great artistic significance. While expression remains a critical determinant of significance, subject matter achieves coherence and interest through the artist's sense of composition, intent, or viewpoint, and the chosen method of treatment, which is enhanced by the artist's unique skills of portrayal.

The most popular main characters of still life—fruits and vegetables, pots, plates, bowls, flowers, tablecloths, and so on—all relatively unimportant subjects, might seem trite, but still-life artists, past and present, have transformed them into drawings of fresh and original effect. After all, this is the point of artistic challenge—to elevate the common into new and provocative heights. Although Piet Mondrian is most familiar as a nonrepresentational geometric abstractionist, recent growing attention has been focused on his drawings and paintings of single flowers. The flower head of *Chrysanthemum* (Fig. 12-7) is drawn in the analytical manner of realism approaching that of a medical or scientific illustration: the shapes of a few leaves are accurately described, but without elaboration, while others are merely suggested by a scribbled line that seems to disintegrate as it approaches the bottom of the sheet.

12-7. PIET MONDRIAN (1872–1944; Dutch). *Chrysanthemum.* 1906. Charcoal, 14 1/4 × 9 5/8" (36.2 × 24.4 cm). The Museum of Modern Art, New York.

Mondrian was obviously being selective while fully aware of the points of articulate elaboration he chose through the use of chiaroscuro. First of all, he introduced enough background tone to spotlight the blossom and to make it project off the page, creating the illusion of a three-dimensional sphere on the flat surface. Then he used the light and dark of chiaroscuro to delineate the intricacies of each convoluted petal. Each of these effects is visually palpable. It is interesting to see this early work as part of the lineage that led to what Mondrian did later in his career. He, like nearly every old master, had a profound understanding of form.

Project 12.4

Do a close-up drawing of a single flower. Choose one at first that is not too complex. Define each petal, using light and dark chiaroscuro techniques to describe the three-dimensionality of the blossom. Thumbnail roughs will assist you in developing an interesting composition.

Let's look at an artist who vitalizes objects with imagination and heightened embellishment. In James Valero's *Still Life with Flowers and Mirror* (Fig. 12-8) we see the use of multiple blossoms displayed with various inanimate objects against a background of floral patterned fabric. Notice the positioning of the mirror to include a reflected image of one of the blossoms, and the placement of the comb in relation to the mirror. The darkest blacks are those of the mirror frame and comb that together define an extended range of lights and darks throughout the composition. Notice also the elegant and plush textures of the fabric as it cascades from the top of the picture plane to the bottom. A triangular portion of the cloth reveals the reverse side of the fabric texture as quite mute compared with the top side. These are things that are infinitely familiar to us, and yet we've never really witnessed their delicate sub-

12-8. JAMES VALERO (b. 1938 ; American). *Still Life with Flowers and Mirror.* 1983. Graphite with touches of stumping and erasing on ivory wove paper, 29 1/2 × 41 1/2" (749 × 1,054 mm). The Jalane and Richard Davidson Collection. © The Art Institute of Chicago.

12-9. JIM BUTLER (b. 1945; American). *Still Life with Glass and Clay.* Lithograph. 1995. 24 × 34" (61 × 86.4 cm). Collection of the artist.

tleties as poignantly as we do in Valero's work because of the artistic decisions that he made.

Another artist whose work lives in the transcendent and sublime nature of the object and its surroundings is Jim Butler. His **lithograph** entitled *Still Life with Glass and Clay* (Fig. 12-9) gives us a sense of standing before a shrine in reverance of not only the objects on the table but also Butler's arrangement of them. In *Burnished Sky/River Mist* (Pl. 14) the buildings, silos, and groves of trees positioned in the landscape are draped with texture and washed with light and shadow. Valero's and Butler's works have similarities, to be sure, but each is visually provocative in its own recondite way and each is orchestrated to be the deliberate visual language of the artist acting on his passions.

A study of the works of Giorgio Morandi reveals the harmony and sensitivity with which he was able to rearrange the same objects over

lithograph

A print made from a drawing done with greasy lithographic crayons greasy inks on Bavarian limestone.

12-10. TONY HEPBURN (b. 1942; English-American). *Workbench*. 1986. Charcoal on paper, 60 × 84″ (152.4 × 213.4 cm). The Stephens Inc. City Trust Grant, 1986. The Arkansas Arts Center Foundation Collection.

and over again (Fig. 7-13). The viewer soon develops a familiarity with Morandi's bottles, pitchers, tin boxes, and canisters, which appear so deceptively unarranged each time they are regrouped. The simplification of shapes and the integrity with which they are rendered lend a monumental dignity to very ordinary objects in a texturally different way than they do to the objects of Valero and Butler, yet each artist skillfully and poignantly elevates the common object to ephemeral heights, allowing us to see it differently, magically.

Project 12.5

Arrange several objects in close proximity so that they take on a group identity without losing their sense of individuality. Use a range of graphite pencils and employ varying amounts of pressure to emphasize dark and light passages. Utilize uniform texture as you draw, and subordinate surface details and patterns to concentrate on volume and space. Regroup the same objects into yet another configuration and make a second drawing. Do additional drawings with different media and techniques using Conté crayon, pen and ink, and ballpoint or felt-tip pen. Explore the use of closely related values—high-key and low-key—to create contrasting moods, as discussed in Chapter 6.

Bowls, cups, pitchers, and bottles are frequent victims of cliché, but need not be. There is also a host of other tools and implements as familiar still-life objects from our everyday routines that artists use to carry fresh and unprecedented messages to the viewer, as we see in Tony Hepburn's *Workbench* (Fig. 12-10). Here we see an orchestrated gathering of tools as objects portrayed as if each were defined by means of a two-dimensional floor plan rendered in charcoal on paper with all the richness of visual poetry produced by the deliberate and playful vestiges of the drawing process. These objects are used in an extraordinarily unannounced way—a way that we wouldn't expect.

Project 12.6

Do a number of thumbnail compositional sketches in which you see how many different ways you can group three to five familiar objects. Pay particular attention to the space intervals between forms if they are separated, and to the overlapping and degree of touching if they are clustered. Do not limit yourself to the same vantage point. Select the most interesting compositions and develop them more fully, using a variety of media and techniques. By now you have developed a sufficient repertoire of drawing techniques so that you can range beyond straightforward descriptive drawing. Begin to let the vestiges or remembrances of earlier laid marks continue to exist on the drawing surface.

Critique (Project 12.6)   As you look at the drawings, do you see a uniform handling of the different objects, shapes, and compositional segments throughout the drawing? Does the composition overall exhibit cogency? Are you struck by the unconventional portrayal of the familiar objects? Has the drawing caused the individual objects to lose their conventional identities? Is there indeed something transcendent about the objects drawn? Has the drawing taken on an organic force? Would you consider it opposite of anything cliché?

A pair of scissors, a knife, a spoon, and a fork—common utensils, ordinary in design, of no particular artistic qualities, and without any real significance—provide the subject matter for a wash drawing by Richard Diebenkorn (Fig. 12-11). Though the objects are seemingly casual in arrangement, careful analysis reveals the skill with which Diebenkorn has produced a sense of drama through the precise positioning of each of the four forms.

Like Diebenkorn, Frantisek Lesak is "interested in observing an isolated object and its relationship to other objects." In a drawing of almost undecipherable complexity (Fig. 12-12), spoons, forks, plates, cups, bottles, and bottle openers, numerous beyond counting, are defined in the most precise perspective. Lesak explains the drawing as an accumulation of many separate studies of the same objects shifted to many different locations on the table.

12-11. RICHARD DIEBENKORN (1922–1993; American). *Untitled.* Ink wash, 9 1/2 × 12" (24.1 × 30.5 cm). Collection of Theophilus Brown.

12-12. FRANTISEK LESAK (b. 1943 ; Czech). *Untitled.* 1974. Pencil on paper, 4′ 9″ × 5′ 8 1/2″ (1.45 × 1.74 m). Stedelijk Museum, Amsterdam.

Project 12.8

Choose a few kitchen utensils or household tools. Do one drawing of the most interesting grouping of the objects selected, with major emphasis on positive shapes and negative spaces. Make a second drawing of multiple images of the objects seen in perspective, as in Figure 12-12. Let the placement be random in order to avoid the suggestion of patterned design by rotating the sheet of drawing paper every fifteen minutes or so as you draw. As you rotate the paper, pay as little attention as possible to the previously drawn marks—responding as though you were drawing on a fresh, clean sheet of paper each time you rotate the image.

Transparency and Reflective Surfaces

Attention to the surface qualities of objects—rough or smooth textures, shininess, transparency—remains one of the prime concerns of many still-life artists. Glassware arranged on and reflected in sheets of plate glass in *Three Restaurant Glasses* fascinates Janet Fish as a subject for both drawings and paintings (Fig. 12-13). The images are depicted and executed with exaggerated patterns and drawn in pastel with a crisp clarity. The artist deliberately complicated her task by working with objects filled with water to distort the shapes of forms that stand behind.

Distortion and cropping transform strict representation into near abstraction in David Kessler's virtuoso rendering of the reflections seen in the highly polished surface of a new car (Fig. 12-14). A more gentle handling of reflective surfaces is evident in Walter Murch's *Study for the Birthday* (Fig. 12-15). There is a quiet, provocative appeal through the use of diffused light, softened shadows, controlled light and dark accents, and broad areas of generalized texture produced by the interaction of wet and dry elements on the surface that heightens the effect of this mixed-media drawing.

Project 12.9

Eggplants, bell peppers, apples, and other smooth-surfaced vegetables or fruits, if polished and brightly lighted, can provide subject matter for studying reflection and highlights on shiny surfaces of different value. An eggplant is a rather simple shape; peppers can be far more complex.

Shine, transparency, and translucence are perhaps the most subtle and intriguing of all surface qualities. Although glass and metal objects are generally thought to be difficult to draw, careful analysis of shapes, patterns, and values, divorced from any concept of what they are supposed to represent, is the key to rendering such effects (Pl. 2). You are rendering the actual reflective visual situation you are looking at and not making a picture of the utilitarian context of the item.

Concentrate your first efforts on a single relatively simple object—one spoon, a stainless steel or copper bowl, or a tin can, for example—and then proceed to more complicated subjects. Glass objects that are both reflective and transparent present one problem; highly polished metallic objects, such as a toaster, that reflect whatever is nearby (even the artist), offer a greater challenge. Analyze the quality of the surface and the nature of the reflections to determine the most effective combination of media and technique. Think of the areas of reflection as compositions in themselves and focus on drawing those compositions without regard for the entire

12-13. *above:* JANET FISH (b. 1938; American). *Three Restaurant Glasses.* 1974. Pastel, 30 1/4 × 16" (76.8 × 40.6 cm). Minnesota Museum of Art, Saint Paul. © Janet Fish/licensed by VAGA, New York, N.Y.

12-14. *left:* DAVID KESSLER (b. 1950; American). *Cadillac #2 Reflection Off Cadillac Fin.* 1975. Colored pencil, 36 3/4 × 24 3/4" (93.4 × 62.8 cm). Minnesota Museum of Art, Saint Paul.

12-15. WALTER MURCH (1907–1967; Canadian). *Study for the Birthday.* 1963. Crayon, pencil, and wash on paper, 23 × 17 1/2" (58.4 × 44.5 cm). Whitney Museum of American Art, New York.

immediate object. Drawing the proportioned areas of the reflective surfaces correctly within the object begins to define the shape of the object almost by default. Try making several drawings with graphite on a relatively durable, smooth-toothed paper. As the reflective surface descriptions begin to take form, use an eraser in the highlight areas to enhance the reflective brightness of the surface. Often through the course of working a drawing, stray smudges may develop over the surface. Using an eraser to eliminate unwanted smears in the intended lighter areas is especially helpful. This is referred to as both additive and subtractive drawing, where the media are added to the surface, then removed for special effect.

Critique (Project 12.9) Assess the reflective nature of the drawings you've made. Are they relatively accurate according to the model? Are the overall shapes of the forms recognizable as the objects that they are? Or does the abstract nature of the reflections and distortions overpower the object? In your estimation, what are the most interesting qualities in the drawings? Is there a transcendent quality to the life of the objects in the drawings? Do the drawings possess force and visual impact? How would you feel about these drawings if someone else had done them?

Expanded Subject Matter

While our conception of appropriate subject matter for still-life drawing is apt to be limited to small objects commonly found around the house, it can logically be extended to include large pieces of furniture and rooms and other inanimate or "still" things. Catherine Murphy's *Stairs* (Fig. 12-16) and Susan Kraut's *Untitled (Studio)* (Fig. 12-17) both have as a primary concern the depiction of interior spaces with a deeply set window on the farthest wall that opens into a still deeper outdoor space. Everything rendered in these two compositions is "still" and rather realistically described according to its own surface texture and its ability to reflect light. Jacques Villon departed from the initial "real" image to create his richly textured, semi-abstract *Interior* in pen and ink, a drawing that is elegant, fresh, and light in mood (Fig. 12-18). Executed in open cross-hatching, the volumes and forms play against one another with a beautiful and luminous now-I-can-identify-it-now-I-can't ambiguity. This is a brilliant example of radical subject transformation brought about by media handling with a free yet masterful technique.

Project 12.10

Rooms that have been "accessorized" for magazine photographs are very different from the rooms we occupy daily. Without changing the position of anything in your room, study areas through a viewfinder and select a few interesting compositions. Sketch and or draw them in the medium of your choice. Look at Edouard Vuillard's *Interior of the Artist's Studio* (Fig. 17-7). As you draw, use all the facets of media variation in order to heighten visual effects and artistic expression.

Other frequently overlooked interior sources include closets, utility rooms, garages, basements, workshops, greenhouses, and deserted drawing studios with easels and drawing horses in disarray before plaster casts and still-life setups. Try to find these places and select them to draw as they are; something is lost when you contrive a certain look to a "lived in" or "worked in" space.

Critique (Project 12.10)   The main feature to assess in your drawings is how the media usage and the surface concerns you've created have transformed the "still space" into a statement that stands on its own. What essential visual differences are there between your drawings and the actual spaces you've drawn? Did you perhaps find it irresistible to embellish a particular aspect of the interior through a total transformation or exaggeration of the textural surface? How well have you defined the existing actual textures within the space? How well have you defined the existing space? How well have you defined deep space? Is space something that you find to be a beckoning visual element awaiting your methods of alteration or distortion in order to enhance a particular statement you are trying to make?

Landscape 13

Once Leonardo established that the structure of landscape was interesting, other artists too were fascinated by the subject, and landscape drawing was thereafter done for its own sake.

—Winslow Ames

When one surveys the drawing and painting of the Orient, western Europe, and America one realizes that landscape provides a major stimulus for artistic expression. Its potentialities are infinite; variations of weather, seasonal changes, the thrilling expanse of great stretches of distance and space, the beauty and fascinating complexity of patterns and textures revealed in close-up details—all contribute to the diversity that inspires and evokes artistic response the world over.

Carol Graham's pencil drawing *Garden, Ballywater* (Fig. 13-1), a study in light, texture, and stillness, reveals an intense love of nature and its moods, as well as the "sensation" of overgrown grasses and twisted trees. Tangled yet graceful patterns of tree trunks and branches contrast with the geometric backdrop of the house. Graham intensifies the pure white of the paper by the addition of a full range of pencil tones and textures to produce a brilliant raking light that defines volumes and textures and the positions of natural forms in space. The beautiful and eldritch play of light and shadow on the compositional rhythms of the trees and grasses provides a sense of atmosphere and aliveness that conceals a slow and meticulous rendering technique.

Karl Schrag's ink drawing *Tall Grasses* (Fig. 13-2) is altogether different in feeling as well as technique. Patterns of thick and thin ink lines partially describe the plant forms in space and partially symbolize the textures of nature in the landscape.

Needs of the Landscapist

It is important for the landscape artist to be as comfortable as possible, for drawing *en plein air* (out of doors) can involve many discomforts.

13-1. *above:* CAROL GRAHAM (b. 1951; Irish). *Garden, Ballywater.* 1982. Pencil on white paper, 11 × 12 1/2″ (28 × 31.8 cm.).
Collection of Arts Council of Northern Ireland, Ulster Museum, Belfast. Courtesy of the artist.

13-2. *right:* KARL SCHRAG (b. 1912; German-American). *Tall Grasses.* c. 1970. Ink on paper, 11 1/2 × 15 1/2″ (29.2 × 39.4 cm.).
Minnesota Museum of Art, St. Paul.

Heat, cold, glare, wind, precipitation, human and animal intruders, insects, and changing lights and shadows are only a few of the problems. The famed nineteenth-century portrait painter John Singer Sargent, who painted landscapes as a welcome change from the demands of his portrait commissions, was able to hire a servant to accompany him and carry a great umbrella, a solid stool and easel, and other pieces of equipment that enabled him to work in comfort.

Few of us today can afford such luxury, so we have to care for our own needs. Dark glasses, gray rather than colored, will help cut the glare of bright sunlight on white paper. Some artists are perfectly comfortable seated on the ground holding drawing boards on their laps. For others, a firm stool and lightweight easel are important. A small toolbox provides a convenient carryall for pencils, charcoal, blending stumps, erasers, a small sketch pad, and other miscellaneous items particular to the individual artist's needs. A portable lightweight drawing board is essential for other than working in a sketchbook.

The most logical media for the landscapist are those which permit one to work rapidly and easily to produce drawings that can be transported back to the studio without smearing or other damage that may occur out of doors. Pencils, various pens and brushes equipped with their own ink supply, and oil pastels allow the beginner to draw out of doors with a minimum of difficulty. It may be advisable to have a plastic bag that can be used to cover the drawings when transporting them back to the protection of an indoor studio.

Landscape Imagery

While we tend to associate the term *landscape* with a panoramic view, artists often choose to focus upon a single facet of the landscape, both as an approach to understanding landscape texture and composition as a whole and as a rich source of particularly expressive forms.

Cesare da Sesto's handsome study of a tree (Fig. 13-3) reveals sensitivity to detail, but while the drawing is most certainly accurate, it is not a slavish copy of nature. The artist has sought instead to define the tree's essence by focusing a selective eye on the characterizing joints, bumps, and movements of branches, and shadow accents. Except that Graham (Fig. 13-1) defines her forms with greater particularity and strangeness of light, it is possible to visualize Cesare's tree in the garden at Ballywater.

Mid-nineteenth-century American landscape painters working in the Hudson River School tradition were expected to be able to draw trees so that both their species and individuality were identifiable. Charles H. Moore's *Pine Tree* (Fig. 13-4) more than satisfies the requirements. It is a large (slightly larger than a standard sheet of drawing paper) rendering of meticulous detail and superb draftsmanship, providing greater clarity than one would expect from a photograph. Nothing has been suggested, nothing has been generalized; media have been totally subordinated to the image. Few artists possess the patience and stamina necessary to undertake such a rendering; however, to hyperextend the realism of nature is one of the most challenging and rewarding approaches for many artists.

Trees can be identified by their shape (silhouette) and by their foliage. Landscape drawing calls for an awareness of the characterizing features of both. In Moore's *Pine Tree* we see first the silhouette, then

13-3. *above, left:* CESARE DA SESTO (1477–1523; Italian). *Study of a Tree.* Pen and ink over black chalk on blue paper, 15 1/2 × 10 3/8″ (39.4 × 26.3 cm.). Royal Library, Windsor Castle, England.

13-4. *above, right:* CHARLES HERBERT MOORE (1840–1930; American). *Pine Tree.* Pencil with pen and black ink, 24 7/8 × 19 3/4″ (63.2 × 50.2 cm.). Art Museum, Princeton University, N.J.

13-5. *right:* PIET MONDRIAN (1872–1944; Dutch). *Trees by the River Gein.* c. 1907. Charcoal on canvas, 18 7/8 × 24 1/2″ (48 × 62.2 cm). © The Art Institute of Chicago.

the foliage patterns. In *Trees by the River Gein* (Fig. 13-5), Mondrian presents only a simplified silhouette, but he has broken and softened the edges and provided enough variations of tone so that it does not appear to be a two-dimensional cutout. Describing a painting by Leonardo da Vinci, Kenneth Clark wrote, "[T]he black trees silhouetted against the gray evening sky are one of those effects which first, in our childhood,

13-6. LI K'AN (1245–1320; Chinese). *Ink Bamboo*, detail. 1308. Hand scroll, ink on paper; entire work 1' 2 5/8" × 7' 8 5/8" (.38 × 2.38 m.). Nelson Gallery-Atkins Museum, Kansas City, Missouri.

made us feel the poetry and, as it were, the closeness of nature." Mondrian's drawing evokes similar feelings.

Nature was one of the major themes of Chinese poetry and painting, landscape having first appeared as a major subject in painting in China. The calligraphic kinship of writing and painting has already been noted. Chinese and Japanese artists, in fact, can be said to "write" their paintings. A feeling of poetry is present in a section of a hand scroll by the fourteenth-century Chinese artist Li K'an, who shows a deft, masterful handling of the conventionalized Oriental vocabulary of brush-and-ink strokes to describe the appearance and nature of bamboo (Fig. 13-6). The subtle gradations of value, which prevent the leaves from appearing flat and decorative, achieve a gentle effect of atmospheric space.

How an artist perceives and treats individual elements of the landscape obviously has much to do with the overall sense of a landscape drawing. Richard Wilson's *Study of Foliage* (Fig. 13-7) pays close attention to the characterizing edges of individual leaves, which are made to stand out in relief by combining linear detail and accents with a suggestion of texture within the tonal areas. Much of the beauty of the drawing derives from the gentle mood Wilson created, which contrasts with the greater drama of the equally beautiful Mendelowitz drawing *Wild Radish* (Fig. 10-18). Although the two drawings differ in both technique and effect, it is interesting to note how similar they are.

Project 13.1

Select a close-up detail from the landscape around you—a cluster of rocks, a section of foliage, the complex branching patterns that become visible when you look up into a tree from below or into the interior of a bush, or the structure of a patch of wild weeds. Decide which media and techniques would permit the most effective and sympathetic interpretation of the subject. Concentrate on the most characterizing attributes of your subject and attempt to convey its uniqueness. Do several drawings; they will take time, so remember to equip yourself with everything you'll need

13-7. RICHARD WILSON (1713–1782; English). *Study of Foliage.* Black chalk heightened with white, 11 3/8 × 17 1/8" (28.9 × 43.5 cm.). National Gallery of Scotland, Edinburgh.

for an extended drawing session. After you've done several drawings, try changing media and do several more drawings.

Critique (Project 13.1) Examine your collection of drawings and determine whether the media were right for the subject. Have you infused your drawings with a certain amount of descriptive detail? Did the experience of outdoor drawing seem somewhat natural and even comfortable to you, or were there unavoidable distractions? Did the experience of drawing in a specific place inspire you to want to return to the same location? If so, this is an indication that upon seeing and examining your subjects closely, you found a plethora of drawing material from nature in a particular spot of interest. The more we study nature, the more we see.

Texture and Pattern

The textures of landscape and the patterns they compose in conjunction with the play of light have fascinated artists for centuries. As explained in Chapter 6, the overall textural interest of a drawing derives from both the depiction of actual surface qualities in the subject and the medium employed—that is, the medium's own texture and the way in which it is applied. While not precisely rendered, Asher B. Durand's *Sketch from Nature* (Fig. 13-8) is a rather detailed depiction of the texture of bark while excluding other descriptive forces contained in the immediate vicinity of the tree. In contrast, the total effect of texture in a drawing as seemingly detailed as Camille Corot's *Forest of Compiègne* (Fig. 13-9) is based on impression and suggestion. It is constructed with masses of hatching and cross-hatching in combination with quick, short, gesture marks and strokes of varying tonal range that give definition and character to the foliage. Treated as light patterns, the lacy foliage stands out in relief against the rich dense darkness of the trees beyond.

Winslow Homer's *Study for "Waverly Oaks"* (Fig. 13-10) introduces a reverse order of dark against light to define the foliage masses by attending to the animated broken patterns of sky seen through the tree. The drawing is done in graphite pencil and white gouache on

13-8. *above, left:* ASHER B. DURAND (1796–1886; American). *Sketch from Nature.* n.d. Pencil on gray paper, 14 × 11" (35.5 × 28 cm.). The Metropolitan Museum of Art, New York.

13-9. *above, right:* JEAN BAPTISITE CAMILLE COROT (1796–1875; French). *The Forest of Compiègne, with Seated Woman.* c. 1840. Crayon and pen on white paper, 15 5/8 × 10 1/2" (39.7 × 26.7 cm.). Musée Beaux-Arts, Lille.

13-10. *left:* WINSLOW HOMER (1836–1910; American). *Study for "Waverly Oaks."* 1875–1878. Pencil, white gouache on brown paper, 5 7/8 × 8 1/8" (15 × 20.7 cm.). Cooper-Hewitt Museum, the Smithsonian Institution's National Museum of Design, New York.

brown paper. The subtle variations in linear detailing and tonal enhancement with both graphite and gouache combine to create a sense of volume and space that counteracts the silhouette effect, and of course the use of the tree form's increased scale to compositionally divide the picture plane negates any possibility of the tree's assuming a silhouette shape.

13-11. *above, left:* JOHN LOFTUS (b. 1921; American). *Dark Landscape #1.* Charcoal, 25 × 19″ (63.5 × 48.3 cm.). Philadelphia Museum of Art.

13-12. *above, right:* JEAN FRANÇOIS MILLET (1814–1875; French). *The Curtain of Trees.* Black crayon, 7 1/4 × 11 1/8″ (18.4 × 28.3 cm.). Louvre, Paris.

Except for some slight tonal variations within the main dark masses, most evident at the bottom right of the drawing, John Loftus has relied almost completely on silhouette in creating his powerful and evocative *Dark Landscape* (Fig. 13-11). He has used compressed charcoal to cover nearly half the full sheet with a dense velvety black. Running across the top and middle of the page is an irregular, organic pattern of white shapes broken by boldly drawn angular lines that gives definition to the trees, separating the viewer from the open space beyond. The scale of the trunk and branch pattern, plus the indication of treetops along the upper edge of the drawing, gives evidence that the thicket of trees is at some distance removed from the spot where the viewer stands in what can be imagined as an open but dark field. As the artist "feels the sense of place," he transmits the passionate and emotive qualities that are so wonderfully apparent in this stellar work. Loftus beautifully demonstrates the degree of simplification that is possible without loss of information. It should be further noted that, although not precisely defined, as in an academic sense, the configuration of the branches reveals keen observation of the characteristic branching patterns, and this alone is adequate to portray the artist's visceral response to the place.

Millet's *The Curtain of Trees* (Fig. 13-12) bears a certain similarity to the previous drawing. In both examples, foreground and background are separated by a row or cluster of trees, and in both there is a feeling of fading evening light. However, Millet's trees offer no real barrier, and his light is gentle and poetic. He has suggested texture and pattern with amazing economy, and every line is necessarily and actively engaged in expression. His broad, broken horizontal strokes describe rough, barren fields lying fallow until the next season, thin verticals echo the tall slender trunks of poplars, and lines deviating from the vertical describe the vulnerable laciness of branches.

13-13. RICHARD ZIEMANN (b. 1932; American). *Back Field III*. Brush and black ink over graphite on white wove paper, 27 × 38 1/2″ (686 × 078 mm.). The Jalane and Richard Davidson Collection. © The Art Institute of Chicago.

In Richard Ziemann's drawing *Back Field III* (Fig. 13-13), done with brush and black ink over graphite, we see the tonally descriptive placement of a deeper dimension of trees that seem to exist far behind the spatially intermediate row of leafless trees that take our full attention. Ziemann has used brush and ink very effectively to bring the live but dormant branches of the middle-range trees into articulate focus, establishing them clearly in front of the deepest row of trees, while simultaneously, the same articulated trees separate the foreground from the deeper tonal space where the farthest trees exist in the picture plane.

Project 13.2

Texture and pattern in landscape drawing, as evidenced in the foregoing illustrations, can be, and should be, as rich as the textures of landscape itself, depending upon the temperament of the artist, the media chosen, and the effect desired. As an ongoing assignment, explore the complete range of media and techniques, alone and in combination, to realize the fullest degree of expressive possibilities in the depiction of landscape. The task might well take a lifetime, as evidenced by the lifelong pursuits of landscape artists. The purpose of this is to go beyond mere representation, beyond manipulation, trickery, and technical dexterity, to ultimately draw with expression and feeling—to create an image that stands on its own expressive merits as something mysteriously extracted from the landscape.

Spatial Relationships in Nature

The conventional linear perspective devices of converging lines, diminishing scale, and overlapping forms are often sufficient to create the illusion of space in landscape drawing. Artists who wish to display a greater degree of spatial complexity in their landscape drawings, original prints, and paintings introduce **aerial,** or **atmospheric perspective** to reinforce the illusion of depth initially mapped out by linear perspective. Atmospheric perspective is based on two observations: (1) contrasts of value diminish as objects recede into the distance, with lights becoming less light, darks less dark, until all value contrasts merge into a uniform, medium-light tone; (2) color contrasts also diminish and gradually assume the bluish color of the air (more of a concern for the painter or

aerial perspective
A drawing technique that reinforces the illusion of depth (initially mapped out by the rules of linear perspective) where contrasts of color and value diminish as objects recede into the distance, with lights becoming less light, darks less dark, until all contrasts merge into one uniform, medium-light tone.

atmospheric perspective
A drawing technique pertaining to landscape where the attributes of linear perspective are viewed through special atmospheric effects created by the artist in order to display a greater degree of spatial complexity uniquely altering the vision of perspective by reinforcing the illusion of depth.

printmaker). If J. Francis Murphy's *Untitled Drawing* (Fig. 13-14) were presented as pure line drawing, the illusion of space would be a factor of linear perspective. The addition of tonal gradations—lights to dark, then back to light—suggests not only light and shadow but also atmospheric space—hence, the operative of atmospheric perspective is in play.

John Singer Sargent's *View of Ponte Vecchio, Florence* (Fig. 13-15) moves from the deep, rich, shadowed foreground to a fully lighted middle distance to a broken pattern of halftones beyond. It seems likely that Sargent developed the dark tones first in order to determine how to fully develop the intermediate values, preserving the pure light tone of the paper for the sunlit buildings beyond the bridge. The full and convincing illusion of light and space results from the skillful combining of aerial and linear perspective. We see the same phenomenon occurring in the more modern work of Sidney Goodman in his blended charcoal drawing *East River Drive* (Fig. 13-16). This is another excellent example of both linear and aerial perspective at work as the tonal gradations

13-14. J. FRANCIS MURPHY (1853–1921; American). *Untitled Drawing*. Date unknown. Pencil, 5 3/4 × 8 1/4″ (14.6 × 21 cm.). Private collection.

13-15. JOHN SINGER SARGENT (1856–1925; American). *View of the Ponte Vecchio, Florence*. 1870–1872. Pencil on cream wove paper, 3 3/4 × 5 3/4″ (9.5 × 14.6 cm.). Corcoran Gallery, Corcoran Museum of Art, Washington, D.C.

13-16. SIDNEY GOODMAN (b. 1936; American). *East River Drive,* 1976. Charcoal with smudging and erasing on ivory wove paper, 29 1/2 × 41 1/2" (74.9 × 105.4 mm.).
The Jalane and Richard Davidson Collection.
© The Art Institute of Chicago.

13-17. JOSEPH STELLA (1887–1945; American). *Bridge.* c. 1908. Charcoal on laid paper, 14 9/16 × 23 1/2" (37 × 59.7 cm.).
Carnegie Museum of Art.

move from light to dark and back to light again, all encased in the defining structure of linear perspective as the trees and buildings shrink in size and recede into the distance.

In Joseph Stella's *Bridge* (Fig. 13-17), drawn in Pittsburgh early in the century, simplified silhouettes of structures seem to dissolve into fog and smoke. Nothing is delineated with the clarity seen in Sargent's Florentine view. Stella used an eraser to recover the white of the snow-covered foreground, but his strongest light and dark remain separated by transitional gray tones of poetic atmosphere. Even within the density of atmosphere, Stella produced a powerful spatial relationship between structures in this evocative transformation of the industrial city.

The diminishing of values that creates the effect of aerial perspective is not dependent solely upon the graduated tones that can be achieved with graphite or charcoal. Canaletto's *Veduta Ideata* (Fig. 11-8) demonstrates the use of **optical grays** that result from varying pressure and spacing of ink lines. The atmospheric effects of bleakness, stillness,

optical grays
The actual gray values that the eye sees resulting directly from a variety of drawing techniques, usually involving dry media that can be blended for heightened atmospheric effects.

13-18. *top:* RACKSTRAW DOWNES (b. 1939; English). *The Searsport Docks,* 1979. Graphite with touches of smudging and erasing on ivory wove paper, 12 × 40 1/2" (305 × 1,028 mm). The Jalane and Richard Davidson Collection. © The Art Institute of Chicago.

13-19. RACKSTRAW DOWNES (b. 1939; English). *The East River with Gracie Mansion and the Triborough Bridge.* Graphite with smudging and erasing on gray wove paper, 13 3/8 × 49 7/8" (340 × 1,266 mm). The Jalane and Richard Davidson Collection. © The Art Institute of Chicago.

and isolation are the emotively powerful attributes of Rackstraw Downes's *The Searsport Docks* (Fig. 13-18), where the ivory wove paper serves as sky, sea, and land separated only by an almost nonexistent horizon line; nonetheless, the horizon line is strongly implied in the extreme panoramic format of the landscape composition.

We see the same effects of linear and atmospheric perspective in another work by Downes, *The East River with Gracie Mansion and the Triborough Bridge* (Fig. 13-19) as an eminently tangible visual portrayal of foreground, middle ground, and deep space defined once again by the descriptive properties of linear and aerial or atmospheric perspective. There is striking clarity in these two drawings, each atmospheric in its own way. Notice the distortion of the implied, arched horizon lines giving the viewer a greater sense of seeing from a distance while the artist simultaneously renders a high degree of detail and articulation as if the viewer were actually closer to the subjects, particularly in Figure 13-18.

Project 13.3

Select a landscape scene encompassing numerous levels of distance, and do a drawing in which you attempt to delineate clearly a sense of deep space. Remember that the boldest darks and the whitest highlights occur in the foreground. As you look at your landscape, see how as the scene moves into the distance, the light and dark contrasts merge into neutral gray tones. For the sake of creating a greater sense of drama in your drawing, keep in mind that there is still a slight, but ever-present, subtle value range within the distant space you are defining. To overlook this facet of deep space description is to somewhat deaden the spatial poignancy and mystery of the composition.

Next, try a brush-and-ink technique using full-strength blacks contrasting with white paper in the immediate foreground. Dry media such as charcoal, chalk, or crayon, and the wet medium of pen and ink work equally well to create bold textures in the foreground to contrast with paler textures in the distance.

Critique (Project 13.3) Compare your drawings with the actual landscapes you selected. Is there a convincing sense of extracted space in your drawn descriptions of those landscapes? Is the visual impact of the spatial dynamic you created greater or lesser than the actual sense of space you "feel" as you are standing while looking at the landscape? What media seemed to serve you most effectively? What visual attributes did each different medium contribute to the overall effects of your drawings? Can your drawings stand alone as successful visual extractions of the landscape? If so, what do you attribute this to? If not, what changes might you bring into effect to improve the drawings?

When first beginning to draw landscapes, artists often overlook the importance of cloud configurations in determining the overall character of the scene. Clouds, like land, trees, and buildings, are also subject to the laws of linear and aerial perspective; the size and distance between forms diminish as the clouds recede, as does the contrast between light and dark. Clouds are visually elusive and can be difficult to describe in the context of a landscape. Skies, however, because of clouds, are very easy to draw attention to, and one must remember not to overdraw cloud formations.

Project 13.4

Do a series of skies with different cloud types—cumulus, cirrus, stratus, and so on. (You may need to look up the different images of various cloud formations in order to recognize them as such.) Rub charcoal or powdered graphite into your paper to produce a graduated gray ground, darker at the top of the page, lighter as you near the intended horizon. Wipe out cloud patterns with a chamois or eraser. You will soon discover that the difference between clear sky and clouds is often ethereal, and you may not always fully realize whether you are drawing clouds, sky, or some of both. This searching activity in the drawing process will tend to give character and animation not only to your depictions of clouds but also to the drawing surface. Consider also that clouds tend to appear more rounded overhead, becoming progressively flatter and more horizontal as they near the horizon.

Try another set of drawings where you purposefully give more attention to sky and cloud features than to the landscape elements. Try using an extremely low-positioned horizontal line on the page, devoting at least 80 percent of the picture plane to sky area. Again, this is not to overdraw the clouds but to focus more deeply on their subtleties and the way they are constructed. This will deepen your understanding of the immeasurable spatial factors that play into the use of sky elements when drawing landscapes.

Critique (Project 13.4) Have you described space effectively in your cloud drawings? Do the clouds intended to be overhead appear closer (as if they were the foreground of the sky) than the clouds intended to diminish gradually as they get closer to the horizon line?

How effectively did you use the media? Did you find the processes of addition (initially laying down the grays) and subtraction (performed with the eraser) to be a satisfying way to create?

Cityscape

Whereas nineteenth-century artists often chose to represent the picturesque charm of old or foreign cities, such as in Sargent's *View of the Ponte Vecchio, Florence* (Fig. 13-15), twentieth-century American artists sought to depict and give dignity to the raw, intense vigor of the modern industrial city. The city itself, with its bridges, buildings, rooftops, fire escapes, streetlights, fire hydrants, underpasses, and outdoor advertising, becomes the subject, instead of just providing a background for human activity (Figs. 9-16, 9-17, 13-22).

The repetition of strong vertical shapes in contrast to the firm horizontal line across the foreground in Edward Hopper's *Study for Manhattan Bridge Loop* (Fig. 13-20) gives solidity to both subject and composition. The position in space and the volume of the buildings are emphasized through the broad simplification of linear perspective and light and shadow, respectively. Hopper partially relieved the severity of the geometry and perhaps mundane quality of the scene by giving prominence to the curvilinear design of the street lamp in the foreground and by utilizing the positive-negative aspects of the lamp, bridge structure, and broken roofline as they are silhouetted against the clear, strong light of the sky. There is some ambiguity, however, in each extreme side of the composition. Were these elements deliberately left only partially observed and drawn by the artist, or was his intent to carry the eye away from the less important focus of the lamp in the foreground while establishing the bridge structure and corner building solidly in the middle ground?

Robert Cottingham explains that he "got turned on to art" at the age of twelve when he saw a painting of an urban scene by Edward Hopper (Fig. 13-20) at the Whitney Museum. Cottingham's *Ideal Cleaners* (Fig. 13-21) reveals his fascination with what he describes as "that magic combination of neon, chrome, brick, and glass" of outdoor signs. A photo-realist, Cottingham uses his camera as a sketchbook to provide the slides from which he works. Before making a painting, he makes a preliminary drawing to establish a value scale.

Yvonne Jacquette, in her charcoal drawing *Park Row Aerial—Black and White* (Fig. 13-22), has adopted an idiosyncratic bird's-eye view of inner-city landscapes at night in which the forms of buildings are defined by patterns of lighted windows and life is depicted by the headlighted vehicles moving antlike through an intricate web of parallel and intersecting beams of lights.

13-20. EDWARD HOPPER (1882–1967; American). *Study for Manhattan Bridge Loop,* detail. Lithographic crayon on paper, entire work 8 5/8 × 11 1/8″ (21.9 × 28.3 cm). Addison Gallery of American Art, Philips Academy, Andover, Mass.

13-21. ROBERT COTTINGHAM (b. 1935; American). *Ideal Cleaners.* 1979. Pencil on vellum, 15 1/2″ (39.4 cm) square. Courtesy of the artist.

Project 13.5

While you may not have a metropolitan view outside your window, do not neglect the urban setting in your search for subject matter. In older communities that have not been completely transformed by urban renewal, commercial buildings, particularly those facing away from the street, often provide considerable visual interest for artists. Rooftops and window designs of older apartment buildings are always interesting, as are the peculiarly structured buildings in industrial areas. Notice the pattern of light and shadow as the sunlight washes across the facade of a building. Often the sheer drama of light and shadow as it streams between buildings in early morning or near sunset provides a powerful source of artistic material. These types of subjects are not necessarily picture-postcard material. On the other hand, as artists search for these inner-city peculiarities and visually reinvent them, audiences become more appreciative of moments of light and shadow, even in the most unlikely places.

Draw from the most interesting sights you find with the intent to give importance to the visual effect of a place, rather than visual effect to the importance of a place. Try this first with any dry media, establishing a wide and interesting range of lights to darks. Don't hesitate, if you feel the impulse, to exaggerate the play of lights and darks and use this as a major compositional and structural device. The point is to see acutely the details in the ranges of value changes and shifts of light on surfaces that are ubiquitous to city life in an effort to draw out the beauty from within, just as any landscape artist would do with the countryside.

Seascape

Throughout time, water and the ocean have fascinated human beings and challenged the expressive powers of artists. The "sense of place" that we discussed earlier in this chapter is often what draws individuals to a particular spot along a shoreline. Part of the attraction lies in the

13-22. YVONNE JACQUETTE (b. 1934; American). *Park Row Aerial—Black and White*. Compressed and vine charcoal, 55 × 42" (139.8 × 106.8 cm). Collection of Mr. And Mrs. Harry W. Anderson, Atherton, California. Stanford University Museum of Art.

complexities of water: Its transparency and reflections, its unceasing movement, its color and moods, the turbulent excitement of its surface in storms, and its capacity to yield patterns of calm repose or unsettling tension have proved to be endlessly intriguing to all kinds of people. Artists are certainly not immune to this kind of spiritual attraction. In fact, it is the very thing that deepens an artist's desire to give visual tangibility to those visceral feelings. It is interesting to note how closely Van Gogh's bold reed-pen patterning (Fig. 13-23) parallels that in Vija Celmins's photo-realist study of waves (Fig. 13-24), and yet they are so different in size and scale, and media expression. Both works observe the gradual diminishment or lightening of tonal values as the space recedes.

Abstraction

The landscape serves as a basic artistic resource even for those artists whose concerns lie in abstracting relationships of form and space. We have discussed how linear and aerial perspective can provide the means for representing space in a somewhat orderly fashion. Michael Mazur, however, prefers to abstract landscapes by treating them as "ambiguous

13-23. VINCENT VAN GOGH
(1853–1890; Dutch-French). *Boats of Saintes-Maries.* 1888. Reed pen and ink, 9 1/2 ×
12 5/8″ (24.1 × 32.1 cm).
Justin K. Thannhauser Collection, Solomon R.
Guggenheim Museum, New York.

13-24. VIJA CELMINS (b. 1939; Latvian-
American). *Untitled (Big Sea #1).* 1969.
Graphite on paper, 34 3/8 × 45 1/2″
(87.3 × 115.6 cm).
Chermayeff and Geismar Inc. New York.

spatial illusions." The pastel drawing *Yard, November III* (Pl. 15), one of Mazur's many drawings and paintings of the view from his studio, reveals his preference for color rather than pattern and texture. Much of the spatial ambiguity results from the placement of color. In the immediate foreground an unbroken element—a corner post of the porch—extends from the top to the bottom of the drawing. Its color is violet; the adjacent color on the left is yellow. By choosing intense violet and very dull yellow, Mazur has reversed basic color theory of yellow as the most advancing color and violet as the most recessive. Another spatially puzzling element is that the strongest dark—the tree trunk at the right—appears in the middle of an area of color that is softened as though viewed through screens.

Let's look at another Mazur drawing, a black and white work in charcoal with smudging and erasing entitled *Landscape—Ossabow* (Fig. 13-25). This work is not nearly as ambiguous as the pastel in terms of its readability and descriptive qualities. Yet in a sense it is very

abstract. Mazur's devotion to the technical manipulation of his media
has given us an interesting depiction of plant life as if seen through a
thick glass. The ambiguity rests with portions of the image going in and
out of focus, although we are assured of their positions in space within
the picture plane. These are both masterful works—works that teach as
well as stimulate our sensations.

Philip Pearlstein's *Ridged Rock* (Fig. 13-26) demonstrates that the
term *abstraction* does not in itself preclude representational drawing.
As he does with the human figure (Figs. 5-14, 14-14), Pearlstein transforms a strongly literal study (here of rock formations) into an abstract
composition by cropping the subject to eliminate necessary clues that
would allow the viewer to relate the shapes to a specific location. Probably everyone has experienced the inability to recognize a very familiar
object as seen out of context and without certain critical details that
would permit immediate identification. This is a testament to the visual
power of analytical abstraction, where we see form only, not meaning,
association, or context.

13-26. PHILIP PEARLSTEIN (b. 1924; American). *Ridged Rock*. 1956. Ink wash on paper, 18 3/4 × 24 3/4" (47.6 × 62.9 cm).
Courtesy of the artist.

Project 13.6

Abstraction involves analysis, alteration, simplification, and reorganization, all without losing the essence of the subject. Do some drawings that evoke a feeling of growth in nature without relying upon naturalistic or obviously symbolic representation of landscape elements. Study the structure of bare trees or look up into a tree from below and make a series of drawings suggested by the branching patterns, attending to the negative spaces as well as the branches. Develop drawings that are rich in line, pattern, texture, and value without concern for specific details. Think of this series also as the development of more sophisticated visual attributes that evoke a spiritual sense of dynamic space, of atmosphere and atmospheric layering, of a sense of "place." Use whatever media and techniques seem expressionistically appropriate and right for the subject.

Critique (Project 13.6)   These are appropriately more abstract questions than in earlier critiques. Try to follow suit with the development of your thought processes just as you are developing technical procedures for abstracting images.

What kinds of essences do these drawings emit? Are there signs, indications of what these images were construed from? What degree of abstraction would you say works best for these images as convincing drawing compositions? Is there a strong sense of connection between the image and its source? Do you feel that there needs to be some visible connection or not? Is there a sense of emotion transmitted from these visual statements? Is there a sense of meaning or association that helps define a new context for these images? And finally, the familiar question: How would you feel about these drawings if someone else had done them?

14 Figure Drawing

The nude figure does not simply represent the body, but relates it, by analogy, to all structures that have become part of our imaginative experience.

—Kenneth Clark

scale

A proportional system of measurement set in accordance with an established standard; on a one-inch standard, an object whose height is one inch that is drawn in one-fourth scale will be drawn one-fourth the size of its original stature, or one-fourth inch in height.

spatial

Existing in space; surrounding objects and defining their proximal relationships to one another.

anatomical drawings

Drawings that portray and make explicit the human anatomy, illustrating the interrelationships of skin, muscle, bone, and joint structures, all with proportional correctness to the human body.

The human figure was depicted in prehistoric cave art as a crudely simplified symbol compared with the extraordinary realistic images of bison, cattle, horses, and deer. We see this early form of human stick figure animation in the hunt scene (Fig. 14-1), where slightly greater detail, sense of three-dimensionality, and more correct proportion, particularly about the head and horns, is given to the body of the bull. As early civilizations evolved, the human figure came to be represented according to stylized conventions dictated by concepts of life and spirituality. Figures in Egyptian art, based on conceptual images rather than on direct observation, combined profile and frontal views into the same image (Fig. 14-2); differences in **scale** designated degree of importance rather than **spatial** relationships. Later, Greek and Roman artists developed remarkable skill in depicting the complex form of the human body, mastering the proportional relationships of its parts and the principles of foreshortening (Fig. 14-3). With the emergence of Christian art in the fourth century, and for almost a thousand years thereafter, **anatomical drawings** of the human figure were replaced by more symbolic, even stylized forms stressing the spiritual rather than the physical qualities of its visual presence. By the beginning of the fifteenth century, the human figure reappeared to become the dominant theme in Renaissance art and established a tradition that continues to absorb experienced and inexperienced artists.

Anatomical Drawings

In the years of the European Renaissance with its heightened focus on the visual, the need to understand natural phenomena and their

14-1. *above, left:* Facsimile of neolithic rock painting: A fight, apparently for possession of a bull. Khargur Table, Libyan Desert. Frobenius-Institut, Frankfurt am Main.

14-2. *above, right:* Duck hunting and fishing scene, detail of wall painting from tomb of Nakht, Sheikh abu el Qurna. c. 1425. Copy in tempera.
The Metropolitan Museum of Art, New York.

14-3. *left:* Karneia painter. *Detail of red-figure lerater.* Ceglie del Campo, c. 410 B.C. Terra Cotta.
Museo Nazionale, Toronto.

14-4. *above:* Attributed to Raphael (RAFFAELLO SANGIO, 1483–1520; Italian). *The Virgin Supported by the Holy Women,* anatomical study for the Borghese Entombment. c. 1500–1507. Pen and brown ink over black chalk, 17 7/8 × 12″ (45.4 × 30.5 cm). British Museum, London.

14-5. *right:* MICHELANGELO (1475–1564; Italian). *Figure Study.* Pen and ink. Louvre, Paris.

interrelationships led to the inevitable merging of artistic and scientific inquiry—the catalyst for the development of linear perspective (Chapter 9) and the study of human anatomy. Not satisfied with mastering outward appearance, artists developed a curiosity about the underlying structure of the body and by the late fifteenth century were engaging in the clandestine dissection of cadavers. Raphael's rather scrutinizing study is evidenced in a preliminary sketch entitled *The Virgin Supported by the Holy Women* (Fig. 14-4).

Only meticulous study of anatomy with the resultant understanding of the forms of muscles, bones, and tendons, as they interlock and combine below the surface to create projections and hollows could have made possible the superhuman figures with which Michelangelo populated his world (Fig. 14-5). These powerfully muscled bodies—with their small heads, hands, and feet, and their great torsos, thighs, and arms— are convincing because they are based on a profound, studied knowledge of bone and muscle structure. The musculature clearly articulated in these drawings is less evident when one looks at a living nude figure. Nonetheless, the grandeur of Michelangelo's figures was such that they established a stylistic ideal that was perpetuated throughout the Baroque period and into modern times.

With their new understanding of the human body, Renaissance artists moved from direct observation to creating ideal figures by establishing

14-6. LEONARDO DA VINCI (1452–1519; Italian). *Vitruvian Man*, the study of human proportions.
Venice, Gallerie dell' Accademia.
ARS, New York.

a system of proportions as the ancient Greeks had done. Leonardo da Vinci's drawing relating the male body to the perfect geometric forms of the square and circle is the best known example of this systematic approach to human proportions (Fig. 14-6). C. Bruce Morser has transformed Leonardo's study into an exceptional medical illustration (Fig. 14-7) that includes bone and muscle structure as well as diagrammatic illustrations of the movements of the body parts.

Project 14.1

Studying and drawing the nude figure permits one a clearer understanding of proportion and construction. Have a model take a standing pose, feet slightly apart, one arm hanging at the side and the other hand on the hip. While away from drawing class assignments, or if no model is available, use a full-length mirror in which you can see your reflection from head to feet. (Renaissance artists depended upon their students and apprentices as models; hence the preponderance of male nudes in the art of that period.)

Measure the distance from the chin to the crown of the head (use the system of optical measuring described in Chapter 3); calculate the number of "head heights" composing the total height of the figure. Use that same unit of measurement to determine the placement of nipples, naval, groin, knees, ankles, elbows, and so on. Draw in charcoal or soft graphite to facilitate erasures and changes.

Critique (Project 14.1)   Is there a natural sense of proportion to your first figure drawings? Having a good amount of experience with the dry media thus far, are you now better able to use the charcoal or graphite descriptively, through additions and subtractions (erasures)?

The papers of sculptor Adolf Alexander Weinman indicate that two times a week for two years he drew from skeletons and cadavers in a class in anatomy for artists at Columbia University's College of Physicians and Surgeons. Anatomical study from one of Weinman's sketchbooks (Fig. 14-8) shows the muscles of the left arm viewed from the back (left) and from the front (right). Once an integral part of life-drawing classes, the study of anatomy is only occasionally incorporated into today's curriculum, sometimes as a series of anatomy plates to be executed. Some instructors, however, continue to lecture on the subject, drawing diagrams on the chalkboard and pointing out on obliging models the relationship between tense, bulging muscles and the bony protrusions of the body (shoulders, elbows, ribs, knees, ankles, and so forth), helping students analyze what they see. An awareness of the body's basic construction is of obvious assistance in drawing the human form, since inner structure influences outward appearance. It is the intention of this chapter that you become highly aware of the beauty of the live human form so that you can apply what you've learned about the natural movements of the body to other life forms as well. As a supplement to this chapter, you will find value in looking at one of the standard artists' anatomy books while drawing from a live model (Peck, Stephen Rogers, *Atlas of Human Anatomy for the Artist*, New York: Oxford University Press, 1951; Brown, Clint and Cheryl McLean, *Drawing from Life*, Fort Worth: Harcourt Brace Jovanovich, 1992).

14-7. *page 260:* C. BRUCE MORSER (b. 1954; American). Copyright 1987 by Bruce Morser.

14-8. *above:* ADOLPH ALEXANDER WEINMAN (1870–1952; American). *Anatomical study*, (sketchbook page). Ink on lined paper, 4 × 14 3/4″ (10.2 × 37.5 cm). Adolph Alexander Weinman Papers, Archives of American Art, Smithsonian Institution.

Project 14.2

Almost every art department can provide a skeleton, or a plastic replica of one, for study purposes. Although such skeletons are generally seen hanging from a stand in a decidedly lifeless manner, it is possible to move the limbs into positions approximating those of a living figure. Study the skeleton to become familiar with the underlying structures of the body. As you look at the different positions assumed by the skeleton, replicate those same positions with your own body to feel the sense of musculature and the various tensions placed on the limbs and joints to gain an intuitive sense of movement, flexibility, and gravitational weight of your own body. This exercise greatly aids the development of one's artistic instinct and helps provide a working understanding of the human body.

Having just mimicked the movements and different positions of the skeleton, continue to consider your own inherent skeletal structure with regard to twisting, turning, stretching, bending, and the general ease and grace with which you move. Sense the way each shoulder can be moved independently; feel the rotation of your upper arm in the shoulder socket as you extend your arm over your head. Notice the simple change that occurs by turning your hand front to back as your arm hangs at your side. Extend your arm, palm up, and then as you reverse the position of your hand, palm down, notice how the two bones of the lower arm respond.

Project 14.3

Do a drawing using dry media, again preferably charcoal or soft graphite, of the skeleton in a more interesting and challenging pose. Place the skeleton in a seated position on a wooden ladder-back chair with one leg crossed over the other and one arm raised and resting on the top corner of the chair's back. Position the head in a slightly turned pose in either direction. You may have to use white string to temporarily tie the limbs in these positions and to stabilize the seated skeleton on the chair's seat against any sudden gravitational shifts with the arms or legs, etc. Select an interesting viewing position, not too far away, and study what you see before you. Take your time and draw everything, including the chair supporting the skeleton. Describe the forms as they exist in space and in relationship to each other. Draw the entire forms of chair and skeleton as if the skeleton were transparent; if your vantage point is from the back side of the chair, draw the entire forms of skeleton and chair as if the chair were transparent, allowing full visual description of each.

Later, it will be useful and further challenging to superimpose over your original a drawing, perhaps in colored pencil or red Conté crayon, of a nude model seated in the same position as the skeleton on the same chair. Using a colored medium for the seated live nude will help avoid linear confusion by distinguishing what you are presently drawing from what you've already drawn. You should notice your drawing becoming dimensionally alive, spatially active, and powerfully illusionistic. Practice this procedure several times, changing the positions of chair and skeleton. As you continue working in this way over a period of time, your understanding of different forms and their interrelationships will deepen significantly.

Life Drawing—The Nude Model

life drawing

The act of drawing from live models in order to record the movement, gesture, and essential physical capabilities of the human body as an aesthetically pleasing art form. Also, drawing from life in order to gain a mechanical as well as visual understanding of live forms and how they exist and move in space.

Drawing from a live model—**life drawing**—serves as the principal discipline whereby students acquire knowledge of and sensitivity to the intricacies of the human form. The vitality that results in drawing from a live model cannot be duplicated when drawing from plastic models, plaster casts, or photographs.

In most life-drawing sessions, quick poses held for one to five minutes provide the student with a warming-up period and a chance to relax in the studio arena. Quick poses are generally more animated than longer poses. Note the stellar capturing of movement and exuberant expression of the human figure in Jacopo da Pontormo's gesture drawing *Dancing Figure* done in red chalk (Fig. 14-9). No matter how brief the pose, it is valuable to devote the first seconds or minute to looking at and projecting oneself into the pose before beginning to draw. Quick gesture sketches, using charcoal or soft stick graphite, are beneficial and best executed on an 18 × 24-inch newsprint pad allowing for larger drawings and greater utilization of the picture plane. Since gesture drawings are done rapidly, the pages can be easily flipped for frequent starts on fresh pages. In a soft graphite gesture drawing far more complex than Pontormo's single dancing figure, Susan Rothenberg has utilized the gesture line to build density into her untitled figurative composition (Fig. 14-10). Note the extended vocabulary of line variation and how descriptive of movement and rhythm the linear elements become throughout the composition..

The figure studies in Figure 14-11—drawn by Käthe Kollwitz, probably when she was a student—are typical of twenty- or thirty-minute poses, which usually follow the *warm-up gesture* and *quick drawing* periods and permit more fully developed drawing with some modeling of forms in dark and light masses in addition to some indication of anatomical details. Except for one pose, Kollwitz has avoided outlining the figure. Instead, she has introduced background tones to establish contours, in some areas allowing the outer contour to disappear by merging shadows on the figure with the background as tones of the same value. While the diagonal marks slashed across the sheet suggest some dissatisfaction with the drawings, we can learn much by studying her use of lights and darks to define volumes and their placements in space. It is also interesting to notice her sense of proportional logic along with her understanding of the underlying structures of the different figures in their respective positions. Notice in particular the standing figure's left leg—the knee in a locked position—defined by dark accents at the hip and the knee.

Jacopo da Pontormo's *Study for the Pieta* (Fig. 14-12) suggests the kind of drawings a skillful student could accomplish in thirty minutes. Pontormo assertively develops a chalk drawing of three human forms with line variations and blending of tones to delineate musculature, bone, and flexibility of joint movements, all poignantly described and deriving expressive life from the dry medium.

After the longer sketching period, the model generally assumes one pose for the remainder of the session. It is a good idea to take breaks at timed intervals for the benefit of both model and student when drawing from an extended pose. Repeating the same pose at successive class meetings allows the student to complete a more fully developed drawing over a longer period of time.

Whereas college and university art departments and art schools provide regularly scheduled life-drawing classes as part of the curriculum, students working independently often have only limited access to models. The cost of employing a professional model is generally

14-9. *above, left:* JACOPO DA PONTORMO (1494–1556/7; Italian). *Dancing Figure.* Red chalk. The Metropolitan Museum of Art; Gift of Cornelius Vanderbilt, 1880.

14-10. *above, right:* SUSAN ROTHENBERG (b. 1945; American). *Untitled.* 1987. Graphite on paper, 22 3/8 × 31" (57 × 78.8 cm). Collection of Charles Lund.

14-11. KÄTHE KOLLWITZ (1867–1945; German). *Four Female Nude Studies.* 1888–1889. Charcoal (55.4 × 42.2 cm). Cologne District Savings Bank, Käthe Kollwitz Collection.

14-12. JACOPO DA PONTORMO (1494–1556; Italian). *Studies for the Pieta.* Chalk, 7 × 9 3/8″ (17.8 × 23.8 cm). Museum Boymans-van Beuningen, Rotterdam.

prohibitive for most art students. Even professional artists who enjoy and find value in weekly life-drawing sessions join together to share the expense of engaging models. Some adult education programs provide figure-drawing classes that attract both beginners and professional artists; local art associations sometimes organize life-drawing sessions for their members. The models' fees are generally divided among the participants so that the cost to each person is minimal. While individuals have little control over the model and length of pose, a variety of poses and lengths of time should be incorporated to facilitate the needs of everyone.

From Renaissance times to the present, artists have taken pleasure in enacting the beautiful drawings of the human figure, sometimes as studies for projected paintings, prints, or sculptures, but just as frequently for their own sense of satisfaction. The figurative tradition multifariously continues in drawings ranging from the lyric classicism of Paul Cadmus (Fig. 14-13) to the articulate realism of Philip Pearlstein (Fig.14-14) and on to the metaphorical and melodramatic images of Alfred Leslie (Fig. 14-15).

14-13. *above, left:* PAUL CADMUS (1904–1999; American). *Male Nude NM 50.* Crayon, 24 × 18 1/8". (61 × 46 cm). Private collection.
Courtesy of Midtown Payson Galleries, New York.

14-14. *above, right:* PHILIP PEARLSTEIN (b. 1924; American). *Nude Sitting on a Chair.* Brush and brown wash on white wove paper, 22 3/8 × 30 1/4" (568 × 769 mm).
The Jalane and Richard Davidson Collection.
© The Art Institute of Chicago.

Project 14.4

The novice in life drawing derives the greatest benefit from working no more than half an hour on a single pose. Approach a thirty-minute drawing in exactly the same manner as the quick gesture—the five-, ten-, and fifteen-minute poses— using the preliminary contour lines to indicate the essential shape of the full figure. Then, as in Project 14.5, begin to establish general size-and-shape relationships of all the individual parts by laying in tone, using the measuring devices described in Chapter 3. Be alert to the formation of the negative spaces as they define the positive shapes.

Beginning students have a natural tendency to start by drawing the head, then slowly working their way down the figure, often running out of paper before they reach the feet. Learn to utilize the full sheet of paper for the full figure by studying the

14-15. *above, left:* ALFRED LESLIE (b. 1927; American) *Santa Barbara.* c. 1977. Graphite with smudging and erasing on white wove paper. 40 × 30″ (1,016 × 762 mm). The Jalane and Richard Davidson Collection. © The Art Institute of Chicago.

14-16. *above, right:* GIOVANNI BATTISTA TIEPOLO (1696–1770; Italian). *Nude Back.* Chalk on tinted blue paper, 13 9/16 × 11″ (34.4 × 28 cm). Staatsgalerie, Stuttgart.

model and then visualizing the entire figure on the page before you start drawing. Start with a lightly drawn sketch to determine the overall height and width of the figure, and then begin to break up the space, locating the shoulders, hips, knees, and so on. Remember to check the width of each form in relation to its length. Sometimes, even when the length is correct, an arm or leg will appear too long or too short because it has been drawn too thin or too wide. As before, incorporate broadly simplified patterns of light and dark to provide a sufficient indication of volume.

Project 14.5

As you become more skilled, you will benefit by increasing the time spent on individual drawings of the figure. Begin to broaden your use of dry media. For more fully developed studies from longer poses, use a harder graphite stick or black Conté crayon as these will not smear as easily, they permit reworking, and they can be used successfully in conjunction with each other. (To incorporate a simple color, try red and black Conté crayon with hard graphite on the same drawing.)

You will want to work on good quality charcoal paper, heavy drawing vellum, or Bristol board (something with enough tooth or grain to take the particles of the dry media successfully (Fig. 10-5). Have your model assume a comfortable, seated pose, since you might well spend a total of three or four hours developing a finished drawing. Illuminate your subject with a strong light to reveal the anatomical forms. A muscled back, properly lighted, offers an interesting play of convexities and concavities (Fig. 14-16). Study the model carefully and build a sense of form through the use of chiaroscuro. Use empty areas on your paper to make separate studies of difficult forms, as suggested in Figures 14-4, 14-11, 14-12).

Hands and Feet—Foreshortening   The Austrian artist Herbert Boeckl is quoted as instructing his life drawing students, "Draw the feet—draw the hands—the rest is easy." Feet and hands, perhaps the most complex and problematic parts of the body, rarely receive sufficient attention in most student drawings. Because they are more complex body forms, they are more difficult to draw, and students often avoid them by allowing them to disappear off the edge of paper. In a simplified sense, a leg or an arm is a similar, jointed, flexible form, only much larger than a finger or toe. An instructional sheet of drawings of feet by Agostino Carracci (Fig. 14-17) and a study of hands, wrists, and forearm foreshortening by Leonardo da Vinci (Fig. 14-18) reveal a concern with mastering the complexities of form present in the extremities, recognizing that the hands in particular (Michelangelo and Leonardo) fulfill a significant expressive function. No matter how well the head and torso are drawn, poorly drawn hands and feet substantially diminish the effectiveness of the figure. (The accumulation of details seen in Figures 14-17 and 14-18—in particular, the Carracci feet drawn over an earlier study of an *Annunciation*—suggests that during earlier periods, when all paper was handmade, it was not only scarce, but a precious commodity.)

Project 14.6

Select a dry medium and do extended studies of hands, feet, and heads of differing sizes, filling several entire sheets of paper. The foreshortening of hands and feet presents a major challenge (keep in mind, as has been mentioned often throughout this text, that seeing intently and accurately is imperative to understanding form in order to draw it well). If no model is available, use yourself. Figure 14-19 appears to be a drawing of Degas's own leg and foot. Remember that your task will be simplified if you concentrate on drawing size-and-shape relationships, rather than thinking about drawing hands and feet. Do several drawings until you see improvement and have gained confidence in this important area of drawing.

14-17. *above, left:* AGOSTINO CARRACCI (1557–1602; Italian). *Feet, over an earlier sketch for an Annunciation.* c. 1595. Pen and brown ink, 10 1/4 × 6 3/8″ (26 × 16 cm). Royal Library, Windsor Castle, England.

14-18. *above, right:* LEONARDO DA VINCI (1452–1519; Italian). *Study of Arms and Hands,* based on Verrocchio's *Lady with a Bunch of Flowers.* c. 1475. Royal Library, Windsor Castle, England.

One of the most challenging aspects of life drawing is that almost any view of the figure involves some degree of foreshortening—and indeed, the most interestingly descriptive drawings possess well-rendered views of foreshortened body parts (Figs. 3-3, 3-4, 3-6, 5-13, 5-14, 14-19, 14-20, 14-32, 17-24). An understanding of the figure based on a simple frontal standing pose is not sufficient to allow you to handle a more complex— and more visually interesting—pose. Initially it will be difficult to draw a figure seen at an unusual angle; but it will be easier if you concentrate on drawing *shapes* rather than *body parts,* and also if you use alignments and other visual aids to clarify what you see. If you were looking at the model for Ludovico Gimignani's *Hercules* (Fig. 14-20) rather than his drawing, you might not be aware that the figure's right shoulder appears at nearly the same level as his mouth, the top of the right hand is one head length below the chin, the extended lower left arm is a full arm's width lower than its counterpart, the thickness of the body at the waist is equal to the length of the head, the right knee appears higher in space than the bottom of the left buttock, and the left knee and right heel are centered under the chin. Such observations—similar to those made for Figure 3-6—are made as you study the model either before you commence drawing or when you pause to check alignments and proportions as you draw. Although the body parts were named for this analysis, you are urged to think only of shapes as you draw.

Project 14.7

To do a drawing that involves maximum foreshortening, pose the model in a reclining position so that you see the body from head to toe or vice versa. Allow the model to lie in a relaxed pose, perhaps with one arm extended above the head. For a more

14-20. LUDOVICO GIMIGNANI (1643–1697; Italian). *Study for the Figure of Hercules.* Red chalk, heightened with white. Rome, Gabinetto Nazionale delle Stampe.

visually interesting composition, view the figure from a slight angle. Focus again on drawing size-and-shape relationships as you *see* them, not as you *think* them to be.

Project 14.8

Degas recommended platforms of various heights so that by switching positions, the artist could view the model from above or below. Sitting on the floor below a model standing on a desk or solid table, or vice versa (you standing on the table looking down at the model standing on the floor), will provide you with an exaggerated foreshortening of the figure.

Do several studies from these various positions until you have a greater understanding of the foreshortened positions of the human figure's parts and their correct size-and-shape relationships.

Critique (Projects 14.7, 14.8)   The most important thing to assess in your foreshortening drawings is whether you've attained a convincing image of the figure read as a foreshortened image. In Project 14.6 you were instructed to pay attention to the size-and-shape relationships of the figure as you saw them, not as you know them to be. Were you able to set aside preconceptions of the human figure well enough to draw a convincingly foreshortened form? Did you find several good compositional views of the figure as you repositioned yourself or the figure between drawings? Does the foreshortened element in your drawing lend itself to a more dramatic reading of compositional space? Do you detect any exaggeration or distortion of the foreshortened forms? Finally, are your drawings expressive? Do they display skilled media handling along with sound compositional elements that you've learned in previous projects?

14-21. RAPHAEL (1483–1520 ; Italian). *Preliminary Study for "The Disputa."* Pen and ink, 11 × 16 3/8″ (28 × 41.5 cm). Stadelsches Kunstinstitut, Frankfurt am Main.

Figure Groupings   Students may become skilled at depicting single figures but remain unable to compose a successful group of related figures collectively, largely because the problem is rarely addressed and the actual opportunity to do so never exists. Economic limitations restrict most life-drawing classes to a single model; only occasionally do two models pose together. One must realize, however, that large-scale paintings from history, often done with a cast too numerous to count, were composed from individual figure studies, combined with imagination, visual memory, and accumulated knowledge and experience (Figs. 4-1, 9-11, 14-21).

Project 14.9

The problem of integrating three or more figures into a single composition will be somewhat simplified if you work with two models, since certain spatial relationships can be directly observed. If only one model is available, consider carefully the placement and scale of each figure. Since figures must not appear to occupy the same floor space and also must appear to be drawn from a consistent point of view, an understanding of perspective will prove useful (Fig. 9-11). Without changing your position, relocate the model in space to conform to the composition; chalk marks on the floor will assist you in this. Include reclining, semireclining, standing, and foreshortened figures by positioning them in a variety of the necessary poses displaying foreshortened figural forms. Work on good-quality paper and in charcoal or graphite stick so that confusing overlaps can be erased or reworked suitably. It is possible to construct a multifigure composition from an accumulation of individual figure studies done at different times, as with the old masters, but unless all were drawn from the same eye level, an inconsistency in point of view will probably occur.

Gesture Drawing

Life drawings can appear lifeless and without vitality if the figure is treated only as an academic accumulation of parts and details rather than as a complete form having within it an essential line of movement called **gesture.** Having touched upon it previously in this chapter, let's explore the concept of gesture more thoroughly.

First of all, movement or gesture is not limited to "motion" in the sense of physical action. It is also the inherently intrinsic grace of movement of the human figure—and the provocation of the artist's sensibilities embodied in graphic form that stirs us deeply in response to the live, expressive human body. Raphael (Fig. 14-21), for example, has drawn the figure in multiple standing poses, yet not one shows the figure standing rigidly at attention. Each pose has a unique sense of movement, a gesture that characterizes the attitude of the figure. Looking at any figure, we tend to perceive the essential gesture before we become aware of anything else. In fact, the eye, more often than not, makes a rapid sweeping movement that corresponds to that gesture since we are naturally inclined to look at the whole before we proceed to examine the parts.

In **gesture drawing** the hand and the medium follow the same sweeping movements of the eye in setting down the gesture that sums up the pose or action. It might be accomplished with just a single line; sometimes the "searching line" discussed in Chapter 5 is more appropriate. Peter Paul Rubens's pen and brown ink with ink wash (Fig. 14-22)

gesture
The essential line or depicted state of movement of a live form.

gesture drawing
A drawing done for the sole purpose of studying gesture whose objective is to capture the essential, descriptive movements of live forms in space, whether human or animal.

14-22. PETER PAUL RUBENS (1577–1640; Flemish). *Studies for "The Presentation in the Temple."* Brown ink and wash, 8 3/8 × 5 1/2" (21.4 × 14 cm). The Metropolitan Museum of Art, New York.

14-23. *above, left:* GIOVANNI BATTISTA PIRANESI (1720–1778; Italian). *Figure.* Black pencil and sanguine, 8 1/2 × 8 1/4" (21.6 × 20.9 cm). Louvre, Paris.

14-24. *above, right:* FRANCESCO FONTEBASSO (1709–1768/69; Italian). *Male Nude Standing and Gesturing and a Second Reclining.* Pen, dark brown ink, brown and gray wash over black chalk; 15 × 10 1/2" (38 × 26 cm). Art Museum, Princeton University.

combines the two approaches—one continuous brush stroke summarizes gesture and movement, not only of the models, but also of the hand and eye of the artist, while the searching pen line begins to give definition to the figures. What splendid visual poetry there is in these master works of figure drawing.

Quick thirty-second to one-minute poses allow for little more than a line or two to establish the gesture. Using the flat side of a piece of charcoal or crayon or a fully loaded brush allows mass to be suggested at the same time. Structure, contour, and detail follow after, depending on the length of the pose. Figures 14-22 through 14-24 are identical in concept, differing only in degree of definition and refinement. Francesco Fontebasso's greater attention to chiaroscuro produces a fuller sense of volume (Fig. 14-24). To see the gesture of the pose, one need only look at the core of the shadow as it moves from the back of the head to the left shoulder, then sweeps down the back, pausing slightly to describe the buttock before continuing down to the right ankle.

As we see in these masterful illustrations (exemplified by Leonardo da Vinci on the cover of this book and in Figure 17-5), the ability to capture gesture is what makes a drawing live.

Project 14.10

With your 18 × 12-inch newsprint pad and a stick of compressed charcoal, make several gesture sketches of the nude model. Gesture drawings resemble scribbled drawings that assume a descriptive form usually depicted in motion such as twisting, stretching, or bending. A gesture drawing should be done as quickly as possible from the entire visual impression the artist takes from the model. If the drawing becomes labored or too calculated, the gesture impression is lost. Think of the model as a hollow vessel inside of which a fast-moving marble is bouncing continually off the sides of the outer skin from head to toe. Then think of the pathway of the marble as a continuous line made with your charcoal in response to the form of the figure posed before you.

For beginners at gesture drawing, the tendency will be to draw with too much focus on the outline of the figure and not the interior mass, which ultimately describes the volume, movements, and positions of the gesturing figure. If your drawings look too much like outlined figures, stop drawing and concentrate on the fast-moving marble bouncing inside the imagined shell (skin) of the hollow figure. The marble moves every possible way—laterally, longitudinally, through deep and shallow space, from extreme top to absolute bottom. Imagine the marble moving inside your own body. Then try drawing again; draw quickly—each gesture should take no longer than twenty to thirty seconds before the model assumes a new pose that describes motion.

Expect your gesture drawings to exhibit a highly energized and varied line, and be highly descriptive of the motion while revealing a powerful essence of the figure's different positions.

Project 14.11

After doing several quick warm-up gesture drawings on newsprint, draw a nude model in five-minute, ten-minute, and fifteen-minute poses. Use a more substantial paper this time with a short stick of compressed charcoal or soft graphite stick— 1 inch or 1 1/2inches in length (2.4 to 3 centimeters). Keep the flat side of the dry medium against the paper and build broad areas of dark rapidly with a back-and-forth motion. You might well begin your drawings as a slightly expanded version of the simplified skeletal drawings in Project 14.2. Establish the essential lines of movement—the gesture—followed by an indication of volume and size-and-shape relationships. As you become more confident, pay greater attention to patterns of light and dark. Leave the contour line until last and draw it in only as time allows.

Avoid the temptation to plunge into drawing without taking time to look at the figure and glean its essence. Your drawing activity will be better served if you would spend the first half of each pose studying the model—drawing with your eyes—before setting charcoal or graphite to paper.

Critique (Projects 14.10, 14.11) Do your gesture drawings come alive in describing the positions and movements of the human figure? Have they improved in their lifelike and descriptive qualities with the added experience of continually doing them?

How lifelike and descriptive are your five-, ten-, and fifteen-minute posed drawings? Do the tonal ranges and light and dark patterns you've established provide adequate definition of the human forms in space?

What might you improve about each of the above?

For longer poses and more detailed drawings, it is particularly advantageous to lay in a light gesture drawing first to provide an inner line of movement for the figure, as well as locating it on the paper. Without that initial indication of gesture, size, and position, it is all too easy to get caught up in drawing the figure piece by piece, losing in the process the rhythm, movement, and unity of the pose and the symbiotic, proportional relationships of the different parts of the body.

The Figure in Action

Depicting the figure in action successfully depends upon the ability to isolate and represent the essential underlying gesture of that action (Fig. 14-25). Life drawing presupposes a model's holding a pose without moving, if only for a short time, even when the pose is meant to convey an action or motion. No matter how skilled the model, the mere act of assuming a pose transforms animation and movement into a frozen and static form. It is in short one-minute (or less) poses that the model can most successfully convey the impression of movement, which means that quick sketches have a significance beyond that of warming-up exercises.

14-25. *above, left:* JACOPO DA PONTORMO (1494–1556; Italian). *Three Walking Men, Study for the "Story of Joseph" Series.* Red chalk, 16 1/8 × 10 5/8" (41 × 27 cm). Musée des Beaux Arts, Lille.

14-26. *above, right:* GUERCINO (1591–1666; Italian). *Mars and Cupid.* c. 1645. Pen and brown ink on paper, 10 × 7 1/8" (25.4 × 18.1 cm). Allen Memorial Art Museum, Oberlin College, Ohio.

Many artists, skillful in depicting posed figures, cannot communicate a visually convincing sense of movement. One solution is to practice gesture drawing at every opportunity, always searching for the essential line or lines of movement that characterize a pose or action. Draw live figures in action as often as possible, projecting yourself into the action, re-creating as much as possible the physical sensation of performing the action (refer back to Project 14.10). Perhaps most important is honing one's perception of the way the structure of the body influences visible form. The slightest movement affects the whole figure; the slightest gesture results from a muscular response; the slightest change in position can alter the vitality of the image.

Observing master drawings may suggest how to approach the problems involved in representing figures in action. The figure of Mars that emerges out of the almost frenzied searching line of Giovanne Guercino's pen-and-brown ink drawing (Fig. 14-26) conveys the impression of sequential movement that is the basis of film animation.

Sweeping, curving lines implying both motion and transparent draperies carry the eye in an unbroken flow of visual movement from the dancer's ankles to her upraised arms in Matisse's fine drawing *Le Guignon* (Fig. 14-27). In delightful contrast to the smooth graceful arc of Matisse's dancer, Hokusia's *Mad Poet* leaps about with wild, carefree abandon (Fig. 14-28), his head, arms, and legs projecting at unexpected angles from a complex swirl of drapery and cascading pages of poems. It should be noted, however, that in spite of the poet's expansive gesticulations, the parts of the body have been thoughtfully positioned to ensure the effect of equilibrium.

It is interesting to compare Toulouse-Lautrec's poster image Jane Avril (Fig. 14-29) with the photograph of the famed Parisian entertainer herself

(Fig. 14-30). The photograph is obviously posed, since late-nineteenth-century cameras were not sufficiently sophisticated to capture a figure in motion. The poster reveals Toulouse-Lautrec's amazing ability to animate the figure through exaggeration of gestures and shapes, most evident in his drawing of the legs and feet, creating an image far more convincing than the photograph. The sense of equilibrium conveyed is similar to that of Hokusai's *Mad Poet*. This sense of the greater presence of life in a drawing than in a photograph is particularly evident in the field of **medical illustration** (Chapter 16), where it is important to portray more than a single, outer layer of vision. A drawing has a special ability to enhance a physician's understanding of three-dimensional forms within the human body.

Project 14.12

Draw figures engaged in relatively simple, repetitive motions—walking, running, or bending—beginning with quick gestural sketches to establish the lines of action. Next, attempt drawing a series of successive movements as overlapping images to suggest flowing, progressive movement. When you feel ready, undertake more dynamic movements. While dancers and athletes seem to be obvious subjects, their movements are generally much too rapid for a beginning artist. "Freeze framing" a videotaped sports event will allow you to study, perceive, identify with, and draw a sequence of movements. Avoid the temptation to spend too much time on individual images. As soon as you have indicated the essential gesture, advance the tape to reveal the figure/figures in the next slightly different pose (Fig. 14-25). Notice how Guercino (Fig. 14-26) employs directional line patterns to suggest roundness and describe weight and mass as well as movement.

14-27. *above, left:* HENRI MATISSE (1869–1954; French). *Illustrations for Mallarmé's "Le Guignon."* c. 1930–1931. Graphite pencil, 13 × 10 1/8" (33 × 26 cm). Baltimore Museum of Art (Cone Collection).

14-28. *above, right:* HOKUSAI (1760–1849; Japanese). *Mad Poet,* detail from a page of drawings. Ink on paper, entire page 15 5/8 × 10 3/8" (39.7 × 26.8 cm). Bristish Museum, London.

medical illustration

A type of illustrational drawing that offers visual clarity to medical conditions or anatomical circumstances, whether normal or abnormal, beyond that of a photograph since drawings have the capability to contain far more information than a camera is able to capture in an instant.

14-29. *above, left:* HENRI DE TOULOUSE-LAUTREC (1864–1901; French). *Jane Avril, Jardin de Paris.* 1893. Lithograph, 4' 2 3/4″ × 3' 5/8″ (1.3 × 0.94 m). Musée Toulouse-Lautrec, Albi.

14-30. *above, right:* Jane Avril, c. 1892. Photograph. Reprinted from *Lautrec by Lautrec,* by Huisman and M. G. Dortu. Published by Edita, S. A. Lausanne.

Critique (Project 14.12) Do your drawings evoke a sense of logical movement relative to the descriptive elements of your figure drawings? Do your drawings express a figural sense of having evolved from a previous state of movement through their present state and onward toward a future state of slightly altered movements? How might you improve upon them? Have the chosen media amplified the visual effects or detracted from them? How might you improve upon this aspect?

Drawing the Clothed Figure

Mastery in drawing the clothed figure equals the depiction of the nude form in importance but is often neglected in the training of beginning artists. The clothed figure represents a double challenge for the artist: drawing the body and the drapery. Solid background in anatomy and figure drawing gave a particular authenticity to Renaissance artists' treatment of costumed figures (Figs. 11-23, 14-22). We see another beautiful treatment of draped fabrics in the two clothed figures in Raphael's Renaissance masterpiece *Figures of the Greek Philosophers Plato and Aristotle* (Fig. 14-31). We have seen Raphael's skeletal study for his *Virgin Supported by the Holy Women* (Fig. 14-4); similar nude studies for paintings of the Madonna by Raphael also exist.

Skeletal and muscular details strongly influence the way clothing drapes on the body. Folds and creases are determined by the structure of the body, and it is important that they be accurately observed and rendered if the body inside is to be believable. While clothing can conceal as well as reveal, it is the later effect that is important. Still-life studies of cloth of various weights and textures draped over protrusions or layered by

14-31. RAPHAEL (1483-1520; Italian). *Figures of the Greek Philosophers Plato and Aristotle.* The School of Athens, painted in 1510–1512, in the Stanza della Segnatura in the Vatican.
Art Resource, New York.

falling into complex, natural folds, so often part of the basic drawing curriculum, provide valuable and necessary background for drawing the clothed figure, but as Robert Henri cautioned his students, "Without knowledge and sense of the body, wrinkles and folds remain wrinkles and folds."

Theophilus Brown's succinct graphite drawing *Seated Man* (Fig. 14-32) conveys a remarkable sense of physical presence—each fold and crease of the clothes lends emphasis to the weight and structure of the body underneath. The full weight of the figure settles solidly into the chair, the feet merely resting on the floor. Every logical and weighted fold of the clothing is familiar to us, as we have assumed the same seated position while having worn the same clothing.

Toulouse-Lautrec (Fig. 14-33), through the stance of his figure—the feet widely and firmly placed—allows no doubt that the weight of the man is on his feet. Whereas Brown delineated the patterns of folds with a certain precision, Toulouse-Lautrec offers only a few hints, a few directional, gestural lines describing the enveloping of the standing figure—coattail swung backward, flaring directionally off the contour of the right buttock while the trouser fabric projects forward, concealing but defining the volume of the hand in the pocket. By attending to the silhouette and selecting only a few details, he gives character to both the man and his well-worn suit. The heavy confluence of contour lines providing the sharp dark accent at the outer edge and bottom of the belly reveals more about the man's body than any other part of the drawing. Eliminating or changing those contours would considerably alter the character of the body. Significant also are the positions of the feet with toes pointing outward as if to express an air of security along with a sense of contented approval over something he sees—hence, the portrayal of the figure's *psychological state.*

14-32. *above, left:* THEOPHILUS BROWN (b. 1919; American). *Seated Man.* Graphite pencil. 14 1/2 × 11 1/2" (36.8 × 29.2 cm).
Courtesy of the artist.

14-33. *above, right:* HENRI DE TOULOUSE-LAUTREC (1864–1901; French). *Portrait of a Man.* 1899. Crayon, 19 1/4 × 11 3/4" (49 × 30 cm).
Louvre, Paris.

visual

That which is seen or takes form in the "seeing" process; also, one of the two extreme poles of artistic personality (the other being **haptic**) where visual people concern themselves primarily with the visible environment instead of their feelings, emotions, or bodily sensations.

Project 14.13

Practice drawing the clothed figure as often as you can, both inside and outside the studio. Make it a practice to take sketchbook and pencils along wherever you go and anticipate the act of drawing in unlikely places, as discussed in Chapter 4. Include the clothed figure as part of your ongoing drawing regimen. Since you are so constantly in the presence of other people, the possibilities are limitless—on campus, in the cafeteria, library, and classrooms, at shopping centers and outdoor cafes, at sporting events, even in church, wherever people congregate. Be continuously aware of the body inside the clothes and concentrate on revealing the physical, even psychological stance or gesture of the figures. (To study a variety of visual relationships between fabric texture, weight, and body mass, refer to figures 3-2, 3-3, 4-11, 8-6, 14-32, 14-33, 15-17, 15-21, 15-22, 15-23, 16-9, 16-10, 17-1, 17-5, 17-10, 17-13, 18-3, and 18-15.) In longer studies, learn to simplify the clothing, emphasizing lines, folds, and details that most poignantly define the body form. Refer again to the aforementioned list of figure examples and determine which of them use clothing in a simplified but highly descriptive way.

Temperament and the Human Figure

Viktor Lowenfeld, one of the most systematic students of the development of pictorial expression, perceived that various types of personalities react to visual experiences in different ways. He theorized that there are two main types of expression representing two extreme poles of artistic personality: the **visual** and the **haptic.** Visual people concern themselves primarily with the visible environment; their eyes constitute their primary instrument for perception, and they react as spectators to experience. Haptic, or nonvisual, people, on the other hand, relate their expression to their own bodily sensations and the subjective experiences in which they become emotionally involved; they depend more on touch, bodily feelings, muscular sensations, and emphatic responses to verbal descriptions or dramatic presentations.

The suggested projects in this chapter encourage both visual and haptic approaches to the figure. Some assignments stress concern with the visual appearance of form; others urge students to project themselves into the pose of the model; many combine the two forms of expression into a more encompassing visual statement.

Synesthesia

The provocative nature of various stimuli and our resulting sensations give rise to the need to visually express our responses as a work of art. More specifically, when an artist receives an impression through one of the senses—seeing, hearing, smelling, tasting, or feeling— and then channels the impression through the outlet of another sense, the artist has practiced **synesthesia.**

Webster defines synesthesia as "a sensation felt in one part of the body when another part is stimulated; a process in which one type of stimulus produces a secondary, subjective sensation, as when a color evokes a specific smell." The provocative response of a stimulus by one of the five senses triggering a response from another one of the senses was a practice used by the artists of Dada and the Abstract Impressionism movements. In fact, it occurred in the caves of the prehistoric artist, when after witnessing a herd of bison or elk, he painted the scene as the news of the day, for his fellow huntsmen, as the visual language that predated the written word.

Synesthesia is haptic in nature. Almost no one is completely haptic or visual in orientation. But one or the other, or a combination of both, is necessary to the creation of a profound, sensual, and mysterious work of art.

More than ever before, contemporary artists are exploring their experiences through senses and sources other than their eyes. Rico Lebrun's anguished image *Running Woman with Child* (Fig. 14-34) forcefully re-creates the physical "truth" of the bodily sensation of running, which we, having seen this image, feel in our own beings as a synesthetic response. The rhythmic movement of Irmagean's *Emerging* (Fig. 14-35) conveys a strong haptic response to dancing figures while the handling of the voluminous drapery suggests an equally strong visual response. Forms that at one moment seem to define individual dancers suddenly disappear into broad sweeping strokes of charcoal that duplicate the actual movements of dancers' arms and bodies in time and space.

Imagination and the Figure

In our discussion, we have emphasized seeing deeply as a fundamental factor in learning to draw and have taken an essentially representational approach to figure drawing. Once you develop your perceptive abilities and gain technical proficiency with media and techniques, you are free to begin interpreting what you see that transcends the truth of the actual visual subject. While subject matter, choice of media, and technique all contribute to the effectiveness of a drawing, it is the imaginative and

haptic

A word describing one of two extreme poles of artistic personality (the other being **visual**). Haptic, or nonvisual, people relate all forms of their expression to their feelings, bodily sensations, and subjective experiences in which they become emotionally involved.

synesthesia

In art, a subjective sensation that occurs when one type of stimulus or response to a subject evokes another reaction or secondary response. In psychological terms, a specific color, for example, may evoke a specific smell, or a specific smell may arouse a particular memory.

14-34. RICO LEBRUN (1900–1964; Italian-American). *Running Woman with Child.* Ink on gray paper, 18 3/4 × 25 3/8″ (47.6 × 64.5 cm). Sheldon Memorial Art Gallery, University of Nebraska, Lincoln.

14-35.

IRMAGEAN (b. 1947; American). *Emerging.* c. 1980. Charcoal on paper, 24 1/2 × 42 1/8″ (62.2 × 107.1 cm). Courtesy of the artist.

expressive qualities that the artist most enjoys and to which the viewer most responds.

It is easy to settle into certain pleasing habits of drawing and neglect other avenues for perceiving and recording the rich and complex form, the human figure. The use of distortion and abstraction, for example, lends zest and variety to modern interpretations of the figure (Pl. 5, Figs. 8-23, 10-2, 14-35, 15-15). To the degree that one remains receptive to a wide variety of stimuli, and learns to respond unreservedly, a rich and diverse imagination develops.

Project 14.14

Distortion, fragmentation and discoloration, ambiguity, analytical rearrangement, shifting points of view, juxtaposition of multiple images, stylization, and flat patterning are all means of approaching the abstraction of any subject. De Kooning sometimes used the process of shuffling drawings on sheets of tracing paper placed one over the other to create new images. Working with some of the drawings done for other projects in this chapter, experiment with abstracting the human figure while exploring a variety of media and techniques.

You might begin by selecting several of your previous drawings that resemble each other, considering their likenesses and differences, then combining them into a new working drawing, not giving too much attention to any one particular drawing—let them all play a role in the new visual arrangement. Then select several images that are very different and allow their unique visual forces to join together into a new composition. Again, do not overemphasize any one drawing; treat them as equally as possible, giving importance to the individual attributes that each drawing brings to the composite image.

Critique (Project 14.14) Consider the provocative aspects of your new drawings. Do they speak independently of their origins yet indicate a genetic connection to their sources? How have the individual visual statements of the former drawings changed after having been assimilated into the new compositions? How would you assess the visual impact of your abstracted works? Is the content of greater emotional or spiritual impact? Do the images prompt and lead the imaginations of the viewer? How would you assess the presence of visual and haptic expression?

Finally, how have your compositional skills grown throughout the study of this book? Do you feel well equipped to handle the complexities of richer compositions and deeper associations of meaning and content? As genuine visual language, do your images speak clearly and convey meaning or sensation? What do they say? Are you overtaken by the impulse to create successive images that hint at further meanings?

15 The Portrait

Do portraits of people in familiar and typical attitudes; above all, give to their faces the same choice of expression given to the body.

—Edgar Degas

portraiture
The art of portrayal; any of many wide-ranging approaches to the art of preserving a physical likeness whether truthful, idealized, psychological, or intended as caricature.

The face has long been an object of scrutiny for artists, because through its myriad expressions pass all the fleeting thoughts, emotions, and vicissitudes of human experience. From earliest times the making of portraits has been a means whereby human beings have tried to achieve some degree of immortality. Until the invention of the camera in the early nineteenth century, **portraiture,** whether sculpted, painted, engraved, or drawn, was the only way that physical likenesses could be preserved.

The illustrations in this chapter and elsewhere in the book reveal the tremendous variety of approach to portraiture by individual artists from different historical periods. Some portraits strive for exact replication of every bump and hollow in the face (Fig. 15-1, 15-2); others go even further by describing individual hairs of the eyebrows as well as pores of the skin on the face with hyperrealistic detail (Fig. 2-14). In still others, there is a revealing selectivity (Figs. 15-3, 2-10, 2-11). Stylization sometimes becomes caricature, at other times idealization, and more often than not sidesteps the importance of seeing and recording accurately. It is a matter of dispute whether the portrait involves psychological perceptions made and incorporated in the work by the artist or whether the telling irregularities constituting the "psychological" element—particularly those that convey tension, strain, and lack of inner quietude—are "read into" the drawing by the viewer. Because of the inordinate complexity and expressive potential of the subject matter, no field of drawing is more demanding, and perhaps rewarding, than the portrait.

The impersonal, idealized portrait in which distinctive aspects of appearance are sacrificed to a bland, generalized version of the sitter has long been the accepted standard for "official" portraiture. Con-

15-2. *below:* PAULA MODERSON-BECKER (1876–1907; German). *Portrait of a Peasant Woman.* c. 1900. Charcoal on buff wove paper, 17 1/8 × 25 1/2" (43.5 × 64.8 cm).
© The Art Institute of Chicago.

versely, too great a likeness can be as much at fault as too little, depending on what the expressive overtones are intended to be. Nearly all respected portrait artists, at some point in their careers, have had to

15-3. *above, left:* GIOVANNI BATTISTA TIEPOLO (1696–1779; Italian). *Study after Vittoria's "Bust of Giulio Contarini."* Weimar, Schlossmuseum.

15-4. *above, right:* HOWARD WARSHAW (1920–1977; American). *Skull.* 1964. Silverpoint on paper, 12 × 8 7/8″ (30.5 × 22.5 cm). Mark Ferrer, Executor, Estate of Howard Warshaw.

structure
The inner core that determines, identifies, and organizes outward form; the planned or methodical network that serves as a matrix supporting and delineating the organizational elements in a work of art.

superstructure
The usually unseen inner armature or skeletal network that directly supports and defines the shapes and outer forms of a subject or form; for example, the skeleton is the superstructure for the internal organs, muscles, and skin of the human body.

wrestle with issues of aesthetic virtue versus commercial appeal, and more often than not, they've had to operate within the constraints of a commission. The drawings reproduced here, however, have been chosen for their aesthetic and expressive interest rather than their commercial acceptability. Each work by a great portrait artist manifests a characteristic emphasis, a personal touch that constitutes the artist's genius and distinguishes such work from the thousands of adequate but merely routine likenesses that predominate in conventional portraiture.

Form and Proportion

A problem beginning students experience in drawing the head is conveying a convincing sense of **structure.** Too frequently, even though accurately positioned, the features viewed frontally appear to float on the surface of the paper rather than existing as part of a three-dimensional **form.** An awareness of the skull's structure and the acknowledgment of it as the underlying form, or **superstructure,** of the external features is essential to drawing the head effectively, as evidenced by a comparison of Tiepolo's *Giulio Contarini* (Fig. 15-3) with Warshaw's **silverpoint** on paper, *Skull* (Fig. 15-4).

Despite the fact that we are constantly observing faces as we move about and meet people, and given the vast amount of time we spend looking into each other's faces, most of us have surprisingly little knowledge of the general proportions and relationships between parts of the face. Perhaps because we attend to the individuality of each person, which is the basis of portraiture, we fail to be alert to the general system of proportions that determines the placement of features. Familiarity with some of the general rules of proportion enables us to avoid the mistakes most commonly seen in unskilled drawings of the head.

Alanson Appleton's classically rendered portrait of David Roinski (Pl. 7), combines a masterful knowledge of proportions and underlying anatomical structure with thoughtful observation to create a sense of solidity and individuality. Careful analysis reveals how closely the drawing adheres to the system of proportions presented in Figure 15-5 while at the same time concentrating on the uniqueness of the individual. John Singer Sargent's elegant profile portrait of Mme. Pierre Gautreau (Fig. 15-6), although based on observation rather than on rules of proportion, closely matches Figure 15-5 and the measurements listed in Project 15.2.

The Frontal View

Project 15.1

Study the general proportions diagrammed in Figure 15-5 and compare them with your own reflected image in a mirror. Then use a pencil for a measuring device (as explained in Chapter 3) and study the following eight points of facial proportions as they apply to your own face. We gain much vital understanding from the associations of these proportional rules through the study and sensations of our own bodies as three-dimensional forms.

1. Hold a pencil in front of your nose to create a vertical center line. The eyebrows, eyes, base of the nose, and mouth can be seen as horizontal lines perpendicular to it. When you incline your head to the left or right, your features remain at right angles to the center line. As you tip your head forward or backward, the feature lines are seen as downward or upward curves corresponding to the curvature of the skull.
2. Accurate proportion of the head width to height is a critical factor in portrait drawing if the features are to assume their correct relationships.
3. The line of the eyes lies about halfway between the top of the skull and the base of the chin. It might appear to be lower depending on the fullness of your hairstyle. With infants the eyebrows mark the halfway point, with the eye line dropping approximately one quarter into the lower half (Fig. 15-7).
4. The distance between the hairline and the chin is divided roughly into thirds by the eyebrows and the base of the nose. The lower section may be slightly greater.
5. The center line of the lips, like a flattened letter M, falls approximately one-third of the way between the nose and chin—sometimes more than a third, but always less than half.

15-5. *above, left:* ALANSON APPLETON (1922–1985; American). *General Proportions of the Head; Frontal and Profile.* Pen and ink, 8 1/2 × 11" (21.6 × 28 cm). Permission of Mrs. Alanson Appleton, San Mateo, California.

15-6. *above, right:* JOHN SINGER SARGENT (1856–1925; American). *Mme. Pierre Gautreau.* c. 1883. Pencil, 12 5/8 × 8 1/4" (32.1 × 21 cm). The Metropolitan Museum of Art, New York.

form
The positive aspect or complement of space; the visible or recognizable configuration or shape of any object existing in atmospheric space; any structural art element separate from color, line, texture, material, etc. See **space.**

silverpoint A methodical drawing procedure where a thin rod of silver (about the size of a graphite shaft) is inserted into a mechanical pencil and used to draw on an elaborately prepared gesso surface. The silver metal point, which may be sharpened on sandpaper, yields a thin line of even width with a lovely gray color oxidizing to a grayish-brown with the passing of time. A highly recommended pencil-style mechanical holder is the Faber-Castell E-Motion Mechanical Pencil.

15-7. PAUL CÉZANNE (1839–1906; French). *Portrait of His Son,* detail from sheet with *Self-Portrait.* Pencil on white paper, entire page 4 7/8 × 8 1/2″ (12.4 × 21.6 cm). © The Chicago Art Institute.

6. The tops of the ears align with the eyebrows; the bottoms of the ears fall just below the bottom of the nose.
7. The distance from the side of the head to the outer corner of the eye, the width of the eye, and the space between the eyes are all nearly equal measurements.
8. The width of the nostrils corresponds to the distance between the eyes.

The Profile View

Project 15.2

It is possible to study your profile by using two mirrors. While the frontal view of the head resembles an upright egg, in profile it appears as a tilted egg. Again, it is important to increase your knowledge through the study of and familiarity with your own facial features. Your most convenient model is yourself.

1. A common error in drawing the head in profile is placing the eye too close to the forehead plane and the nose.
2. The ear is located in the back half of the head. The distance from the outer corner of the eye to the back edge of the ear is about equal to one-half the height of the head.
3. The measurement from the ear hole to the tip of the nose and the distance from the chin to the eyebrows are equal. (In the frontal view the distance between the ear holes is equal to the measurement from the chin to the eyebrows.)
4. The earlobe indicates the position of the jawbone.

Project 15.3

Observe heads wherever you are. Notice how consistently the placement of the features adheres to the general proportions as seen in Figure 15-5 and as listed. The greatest deviation will occur in the width of heads.

Project 15.4

A plaster head—a standard fixture in most art departments—provides an excellent means for studying general proportions of the head and relationships between its parts. A plaster cast has the virtue of remaining motionless, thus permitting leisurely and accurate observation. It can be repositioned easily so that it can be viewed from above and below eye level, as well as in frontal, profile, and three-quarter views. While most portraits are drawn at eye level, there may be occasions to represent the head viewed from above or below, or to draw the head tilted up or down (Fig. 15-8), in which case the features must follow the curvature of the front of the skull.

Use your pencil or stick of charcoal for comparative measuring and to establish the correct alignment of features.

Project 15.5

Three-dimensional form becomes most apparent through the use of light and shadow. In a line drawing it is possible to impart a degree of three-dimensionality through overlapping shapes and lines and to introduce light and shadow by gradations in the thickness of lines. When the study of form is intended, adequate directional light is essential.

Working from a plaster head or your own reflected image, lighted from above and to one side, do two drawings—one in line and tone, the other fully modeled in light and dark tonal areas, using line only to clarify those areas where tone is insufficient. As you begin the first drawing, as you look, see deeply, compose, and draw, strive for the development of solid, three-dimensional, descriptive form. Emphasize bone structure, cheekbones, depressions of the eye sockets, the turn of the forehead from frontal plane to side plane, bony protuberances in the nose, and so forth. Concentrate on revealing the form rather than creating a likeness. Make sure that the front surfaces of the eyes appear to sit within the socket and not on the same plane as the forehead or cheekbones.

For the second drawing, done primarily in tone, begin by sculpting the basic form with patterns of light and dark before turning your attention to defining and detailing the features (Fig. 15-9). Drawing the head is very similar to modeling it out of clay. First you create the general form by establishing the mass and volume, then you move to the details. Establishing the mass and volume correctly makes the subsequent establishing of the general proportions and detail refinements much easier. Charcoal, white chalk, graphite stick with erasing, or any combination of light and dark colors, on a middle-value paper works well for portrait studies, as evidenced in David Hardy's elegantly understated drawing (Fig. 15-10).

15-8. *above, left:* GIOVANNI BATTISTA TIEPOLO (1696–1779; Italian). *Head of a Young Man.* Red chalk over traces of black chalk heightened with white chalk on blue paper, 8 3/4 × 6″ (22.2 × 15.3 cm). Cleveland Museum of Art.

15-9. *above, right:* JEAN FRANÇOIS MILLET (1814–1875; French). *Man's Head in Three-Quarter View to the Left.* Black crayon, 6 1/4 × 4 5/8″ (16 × 12 cm). Louvre, Paris.

The Features

Once correct relationships of form and features are firmly settled in the beginning artist's perception, and there emerges a sense of skillful interplay between artist, media, and subject, the symbiotic activity of drawing can fully begin. Depending completely on your sight skills and your newfound sense of proportion, achieving a likeness derives from the accurate analysis of a set of individual features to be superimposed over the preliminary plan. Seeing is paramount to successful results, and the most common errors result from failure to look at the shape of each feature, drawing instead what one thinks to be the shape of that feature, and not what is actually seen. The novice, for example, has a tendency to represent the eye as an almond shape with the upper and lower lids as matching curves meeting at symmetrically equal points at each end. Careful observation of the eye reveals that it is more irregular in shape—the high point of the curve of the upper lid occurs closer to the nose; the low point of the lower lid is nearer to the outer corner of the eye. At the inner corner the lids come together to form the tear duct; at the outer corner the upper lid overlaps the lower lid. Eyelids also have thickness, though the assumption might be they are paper-thin. The iris of the eye appears to rest on the lower lid, while the upper portion is partially hidden by the upper lid. In profile view, the eye appears as the letter V with slightly curved lines lying on its side; the upper lid projects beyond the lower lid, overlapping it with its outer corner; the inner corner of the upper lid also lies forward of the outer corner of the lower lid (Fig. 15-5).

Lips also present a problem for beginners, who are inclined to outline them, when the only actual line is between the lips. What we think of as the upper and lower lip lines are really changes in coloration, texture, and directional planes. Notice in Figure 15-11 that the bottom of the lower lip is defined only by the shadow centered beneath it. Moving toward the corners of the mouth, the lips tend to flatten, almost to disappear, except for the tonal difference.

Project 15.6

You must understand a form before you can draw it. Study your own features carefully at close range (a handheld mirror is recommended). You are urged not to work from photographs for this assignment, since the flattened image does not adequately

15-11. RAPHAEL SOYER (1899–1987; American). *Self-Portrait with the Artist's Father.* Pencil, 9 3/4 × 12 1/8″ (25 × 31 cm). Sotheby's.

convey the three-dimensional form. Practice by drawing separately your eyes, nose, lips, and ears, in frontal, profile, and three-quarter views. You will probably discover that your eyes are not identical in size and shape and that your mouth is not the same on both sides (Fig. 15-11). Making additional studies by drawing the individual features of other persons will increase your awareness of differences that exist, pointing to the absolute necessity of drawing exactly what you see.

Remember that the head and face with its features are antithetical to anything flat. Try to avoid any semblance of flatness. Do not just outline shapes. A single light source above and to the side will reveal the strongest sense of three-dimensional form.

Project 15.7

Drawing someone with a distinctly unusual face is a good exercise in developing sensitivity to the peculiarities of likeness. When confronted with this challenge, even certain proportional rules may not be adequate. The unusual in nature often has no precedent; therefore, stress all departures from regularity, differences between eye shapes, and the length and structure of the nose, mouth, lips, and chin. Notice wrinkles, muscularity or flabbiness of flesh, heaviness of eyebrows and lashes, and quality of hair and the direction of its growth. Although it may not please your model, you are encouraged to be as accurately analytical as possible in depicting truth. The compromising of any distinct irregularity only produces an inaccurate and flaccid likeness.

The Self-Portrait

The **self-portrait** may serve either as an opportunity for serious exploration or merely as a chance to work one's technical prowess on an obliging model. A glance at the following group of drawings will suggest that self-portraits can span a considerable range of disparate styles and approaches. For the beginning student, the self-portrait offers decided advantages. First, the sitter is always available and easily manipulated. Second, there is no need to worry about offending the sitter's "self-image," and no need to apologize for any unflattering drawing.

Raphael Soyer's drawing (Fig. 15-11) reveals a most subtle study of himself accompanied by his father. The self-portrait's thoughtful

self-portrait
An artist's portrayal of himself or herself using artistic expression to underscore temperaments or emotions related to his or her unique individual traits. The self-portrait has two functions: it allows the artist to use a cheap and available model, and it serves as a means of self-immortalization—often in an idealized way.

expression, the slight irregularity of eye shape and size, the sensitive mouth and furrowed brow all bespeak the introspective artist. Soyer displays skillful use of selectivity as he emphasizes some features more than others. In contrast, most beginners feel obliged to delineate every detail with equal clarity, not realizing that the overpronouncement of one visual aspect can imply powerful yet subtle nuances of expression. The prominence given to his eyes and the intensity of their gaze seem to underscore the essential linkage of drawing to seeing. In spite of the almost elusive nature of the modeling, except around the eyes, the head is strongly structured. The divisions of the head and the placement of the features correspond almost exactly to the general proportions diagrammed in Figure 15-5. The head of Soyer's father mimics that of the artist in structure but is less well defined in form and may well have been done from memory. The application of middle grays produced by the hatched lines positions his father behind and deeper in space, perhaps implying his father's continuing presence with him after his passing.

In his self-portrait *Myself Paranoiac* (Figure 15-12), it is evident that John Wilde's penetrating observation of himself has led to a heightened state of visual poetry with a host of nuances perhaps only partially understood. Art historian Gerald Nordland wrote of Wilde: "His watchword is *discipline*, which is observed in the careful rendering of the most telling angle and incident in realizing his frolicsome, sympathetic, and sometimes profound subject matter." Wilde's work has been further characterized as having a kinship with the Surrealists, the artists of the Italian Renaissance, and fifteenth-century Flemish masters.

15-12. JOHN WILDE (B. 1919 ; American). *Myself Paranoiac.* c. 1944. Pencil on wove paper, 16 1/4 × 12 1/2″ (41.3 × 31.8 cm). The Arkansas Art Center Foundation Collection.

In a comparison of portraits by artists John Wilde and Jonathan Thomas (Figs. 15-12, 15-13), we see two highly contemplative poses, one head centered, the other done in the upper half of the picture plane in such a way that the remaining pictorial space is completely activated by the implied presence of the figure's torso. Each artist has been selective in his composing, giving us the necessary visual information and stripping away any extraneous elements. In Wilde's *Myself Paranoiac* (Fig. 15-12) we see a sensually charged depiction of a man's face where the handling of pencil on paper is not only texturally and tonally alive but also highly descriptive. In Thomas's etching *Bed Head* (Fig. 15-13), drawn on a copper plate with etching needle, the long arms, hanging like pendulums, suggest a heavy mood, while the facial features reinforce a feeling of momentary uncertainty—even surprise. The vertical position of the figure implies that she has just risen from sleep but is not yet not fully awake, and there is a sense of unexpected confrontation.

15-13. JONATHAN THOMAS (b. 1973; American). *Bed Head*. c. 2001. Etching on copper printed on German Hahnemulhe paper. 17 3/4 × 11 7/8″ (45.2 × 30.2 cm).
Courtesy of the artist.

Project 15.8

Learning to draw heads and portraits is one thing—endowing them with unique expression is quite another. Take full advantage of your availability as a model and do several portraits in which, by relentlessly concentrating on the forms you see before you, you strive for a drawing that is not merely a portrait likeness but an expressive interpretation of yourself. Käthe Kollwitz left a lifelong record of herself in self-portraits (Figs. 1-1, 7-9). To achieve expression will require drawing your own face frequently, using various media, techniques, lighting effects, and unconventional poses. Two mirrors will allow you to draw the more interesting but difficult three-quarter view without the awkward "eyes to the side" look. Proceed from structure to features, then to expression. For your drawing to achieve a state of mystery, which usually happens more unconsciously than consciously, observe the expression—not just facial expression, but the *expressive whole* of the drawing. Everything plays a role in the total effects of the drawings.

Critique (Project 15.8) What would you describe as the most powerful visual elements of your drawings? How would you characterize their effects? What single-word adjectives would you use as synonyms for each drawing? If you have a friend or classmate who is working on the same project exercises, exchange drawings so that the two of you can write a critical analysis or review of each other's work. Discuss media handling—citing specific techniques used—effects of lighting, and positioning of the subject, and finally, describe the resulting visual impact of the drawings. Be honest and candid, knowing that criticism is not to be either doled out or received in a personal way.

The Objective Approach

Since "pure" objectivity exists only as a theoretical state of mind, in terms of artistic endeavor an objective approach involves depicting exactly that which is observed, free from distortion and interpretation. Josef Albers offers a straightforward depiction of a man, unidentified but with a strong sense of individuality (Fig. 15-14). Albers has used a line that matches in firmness and clarity the chiseled profile of his model. The essentially planar treatment of the hair contributes to a sculptured effect, while the lighter values lend softness to the beard.

William Michael Harnett's charcoal drawing *Portrait of a Young Girl* (Fig. 15-1) exemplifies the best qualities of nineteenth-century academic tradition—solidly realized form and modeling of exceptional delicacy. The nuances of texture have been rendered with amazing fidelity,

15-14. *above, left:* JOSEF ALBERS (1888–1976; German-American). *Man in Profile.* c. 1914. Pencil, 14 3/8 × 10″ (36.5 × 25.4 cm).
Collection of Anni Albers and the Josef Albers Foundation, Inc.

15-15. *above, right:* CHUCK CLOSE (b. 1940; American). *Self-Portrait/Conté Crayon.* 1979. Conté crayon on paper, 29 1/2 × 22″ (75 × 56 cm). Private Collection.
Courtesy of the Pace Gallery.

the softness of skin, hair, and wool shawl contrasting with the sharply defined profile and the accented clarity of the eye. Without deviating from his intended objectivity, Harnett has created an image of haunting intensity that is somewhat similar to the drawings of John Wilde and Jonathan Thomas in Figures 15-12 and 15-13, although it is a profile view in a more tonally developed picture plane.

We often equate pure objectivity with photographic likeness, and indeed the meticulous realism of Wilde, Thomas, and Harnett bears strong similarities to a photograph. Chuck Close's *Self-Portrait* (Fig. 15-15) can appropriately be termed a photographic likeness since it is a transcription of a photograph. Working with two grids—one superimposed over a photograph he selected to reproduce, the other an enlarged grid on a sheet of drawing paper—Close methodically analyzes and summarizes the tonal value of each square of the photograph, then duplicates it with a scribbled or hatched line tone. He has created several similar grid portraits with dots the size of the end of a round pastel crayon. The resulting images bear strong resemblance to the device used by television stations to blur and disguise the identity of individuals who wish to remain anonymous. This methodical, scrutinizing approach is called *modular analysis*.

Project 15.9

For an exercise in objective portraiture, you might find the weathered face of an older model more interesting to draw than the smooth features of a young person. Find a black and white photograph or photo magazine portrait illustration of an interesting head and face. With an acetate page the same size as the selected image, draw a one-half-inch grid with a design marker (one that will dry immediately and not bead up on the acetate surface) over the entire acetate page. Superimpose this grid over the photographic image that has been attached to a large white or off-white sheet of good drawing paper or illustration board. With the image centered on the large page, draw two flanking outlines of the same dimensions as the image—one to its left, one to its right. Then with very hard graphite pencil (4H or 6H), very lightly draw the identical grid in each flanking outline. Once this has been accomplished, you may want to spray the light grids with fixative in a well-ventilated area (even though the graphite is of a hard nature, there may still be slight smearing over the long period of time it will take to complete this drawing).

Have at your disposal a complete set of graphite pencils ranging from 9H (hard) to 9B (soft) and begin drawing the value study. If you are right-handed, do the value study to the left of the image; left-handed, to the right of the image. Observe each single module one at a time, very closely avoiding visual interference from the neighboring modules. Determine the average value of the module and evenly shade in the corresponding module on the value study side. As the value drawing progresses, step back periodically to witness the formation of the image—the farther back you stand, the clearer the image forms itself. Use workable fixative periodically to avoid smearing.

Begin the rendering upon completion of the value study by studying each single modular again, one at a time, and render in as highly a descriptive way as you are able. Think of each module as a composition unto itself while divorcing all thoughts of the surrounding modules. Again, use workable fixative periodically to avoid smearing.

This assignment with its analytical approach to any subject will prove to be highly efficacious. In fact, you may be pleasantly surprised at how well you've seen your subject, and how articulately you've depicted what you saw.

Critique (Project 15.9)   Carefully pin your drawing to the wall in a studio or large room and stand back a good distance from it (at least twenty feet). Compare the two flanking drawings with your selected image in the center, and then compare them with each other. If your drawing technique exemplifies lively variations with interesting textural and tonal finesse, along with wide-ranging descriptive values of extreme lights and darks, the two drawings will each bear a much stronger illusion of three-dimensionality than the selected image.

If you feel your drawings are a bit anemic, needing more life and power, determine the areas of visual weakness and rework the necessary portions, staying within the working method of a single module at a time.

The Idealized Portrait

Idealization in portraiture can take many forms but, in general, it means a restructuring of features to conform to a concept of perfection and a minimizing of all irregularities.

The major challenge of drawing an **idealized portrait** is to achieve a resemblance that satisfies the sitter as a "likeness" and at the same time irons out the less-than-ideal aspects of the face. Ingres had this amazing capacity, as evidenced in his portrait of Doctor Robin (Fig. 10-15); it creates the illusion of an objective likeness, exact and precise, yet careful examination reveals clear idealization—perfect symmetry of features, smooth sculptured form, and flawless skin.

Although David Hockney's *Celia in a Black Dress with White Flowers* (Fig. 15-16) seems to emphasize the positive-negative aspects of the richly varied interlocking shapes of the flowers and dress, attention ultimately centers on the delicately drawn head with its blending of likeness and idealization.

The British Museum's *Portrait of Andrea Quaratesi* (Fig. 15-17) is one of the few portraits believed to have been drawn by Michelangelo.

idealized portrait
A portrait that achieves a satisfactory resemblance to the sitter while simultaneously eliminating the physical imperfections of the face.

It seems probable that the image reflects both the unblemished beauty of youth and Michelangelo's tendency toward idealization.

Project 15.10

Draw an idealized portrait, of either yourself or a sympathetic friend (Figs. 15-16, 15-17). Determine how best to flatter your model without loss of likeness. Anyone harboring a desire to be a professional portrait artist would be well advised to focus particular attention on this project. Combine your newfound skills of objective sight from Project 15.9 with your notions of idealization. Be sure to use a flexible and easily erasable medium such as soft graphite, charcoal, or chalk (do not use crayon in any form). None of the idealized portraits discussed are large drawings, and because each includes the body, the heads are relatively small. Should you also want to include the figure, it is suggested that you first practice drawing just the head, making it large enough so that the features are not small and cramped.

The three idealized portraits discussed have been enriched by including specific details of clothing—plus architectural forms as in the Ingres drawing—and the suggestion of an interior space, with a still life, in the Hockney drawing. Be alert to opportunities to include such elements, not only for additional visual and compositional interest, but also as a means of revealing character.

The Psychological Portrait

Some drawings seem to mostly record externals (Fig. 10-10), while others create the illusion of penetrating the surface to reveal inner as-

psychological portrait
Beyond the revealing likeness, the portrayal of a person's inner personality or temperament made visually tangible through the artistic treatment of the facial features, tilt of head, relaxed quality, or stiffness of shoulders, neck, and head.

pects of personality—tensions, withdrawn self-sufficiency, or warmth and sociability. Many of the portraits already seen have included visual clues that explore character as well as appearance. The variety with which artists are able to reveal personality traits, their own and others', is one of the most fascinating aspects of portraiture.

Walter Sickert portrayed the famous English caricaturist Max Beerbohm as a warm, sympathetic observer of life (Fig. 15-18). The raised eyebrows, heavy-lidded eyes, and slightly open mouth all seem to describe an inner life as much as they do external appearances. The raised hand adds an accent as though Beerbohm needed a gesture to give full meaning to his words.

The very turbulence of the crayon scribbles with which Oscar Kokoschka has drawn his *Portrait of Olda* (Fig. 15-19) creates a disturbing mood or at least one of quandary, which is intensified by the abstracted look in the eyes, the crooked mouth, and the thoughtful pose. The rather unusual combination of free execution, suggesting the artist's spontaneous approach to the act of drawing, and the sense of the subject as a tense, withdrawn personality seem paradoxical. The sensitivity of Kokoschka's perception is evidenced in his selective delineation of features, the hair and collar being drawn more emphatically than the subject's eyes. Olda's introspective nature, in contrast to Sir Max Beerbohm's outward focus, is immediately apprehended.

Alice Neal draws with power and subtlety. In her portrait of Adrienne Rich (Fig. 15-20), the bright, alert eyes and the controlled smile

15-18. *above, left:* WALTER SICKERT (1860–1942; English). *Sir Max Beerbohm.* Pencil on cream paper. Sotheby's.

15-19. *above, right:* OSCAR KOKOSCHKA (1886–1980; Austrian). *Portrait of Olda.* 1938. Blue crayon, 17 1/4 × 13 7/8" (43.8 × 35.3 cm). Allen Memorial Art Museum, Oberlin College, Ohio. ARS, New York.

provide a clue to the tenor of the subject's thoughts. The entire pose, reinforced by the loose, easy drawing suggests a relaxed bemusement. In contrast, Mark Adams's *Margery* (Fig. 15-21) conveys a mood of melancholy quietude.

Project 15.11

Figures 15-20 and 15-21 are similar in subject, but the character and mood of the drawings are very different and can be credited only in part to the individuality of the subjects. To a much greater extent, the difference derives from the ability of each artist to recognize the most natural pose and revealing expression and to select media and technique suited to both subject and mood. Study the three drawings, noting the total appropriateness of media and treatment and the inevitable expressiveness of each subject.

As you gain confidence in your ability to render a likeness objectively, begin to introduce a note of subjectivity, allowing your drawings to reflect more than the external characteristics of your subject. Try to find the means to respond to the personality of your model in ways that are visually expressive.

Critique (Project 15.11)   What personality traits or human characteristics are expressed in your drawings? What contributions do the media and your technical handling of the media make to the overall visual statement? Are there instances where the drawings appear to be less expressive than the actual subject? Or are there drawings that seem to exaggerate the actual expressive nature of the person you are drawing? Have lights and darks offered definitive modes of expression? Does texture or spontaneity play an expressive role in the visual language of your drawings? Have you created any paradoxical situations, as in Figure 15-19?

Often the personality of an individual is revealed as much through body language—posture and gestures—as through facial characteristics. One knows in looking at Catherine Murphy's drawing *Harry Roseman Working on Hoboken and Manhattan* (Fig. 15-22) that the model builder possesses the patience to sit for endless hours engaged in the most detailed work. Interestingly, Murphy's drawing technique demonstrates the same kind of dedication and patience.

Theophilus Brown apparently found greater visual interest in the pose of fellow artist Mark Adams drawing the figure (Fig. 15-23) than in the very ordinary seated pose of the model alone (Fig. 15-21). With little more than a simple, direct contour drawing of the figure in silhouette, Brown provides an immediate, recognizable, full-length portrait of Mark Adams standing at his easel in a pose of unaffected naturalness and ease, but also one of total concentration on the act of drawing. The drawing communicates a strong sense of individuality even to those who do not know Adams. Notice how the head of Adams in Brown's drawing is so similar to the aforementioned "tilted egg-shape" that characterizes a head in profile in Josef Albers's *Man in Profile* (Fig. 15-14).

A drawing that appears to be the culmination of many of the portrait topics discussed in this chapter is Leonardo da Vinci's pen and brown ink drawing *Five Grotesque Heads* (Fig.15-24), certainly a psychological depiction in portraiture. The impact of the expressionistic aura of the five heads and faces is so well established here that we find it difficult to look away—as when we were children and were taught about the impropriety of staring. Leonardo gives us ample opportunity to stare with abandon. We have the frontal view, the three-quarter view, and the profile, as well as the tilted upward and slightly downward poses—a brilliant composition of well-rendered forms whose faces exude a myriad of emotion. Each

15-20. *above, left:* ALICE NEEL (1900–1984; American). *Adrienne Rich.* 1973. Ink heightened with Chinese white, 30 × 22″ (76.2 × 55.9 cm). Courtesy of Robert Miller Gallery, New York.

15-21. *above, right:* MARK ADAMS (b. 1925; American). *Margery.* 1980. Pencil, 24 × 19″ (61 × 48.3 cm). Courtesy of the artist.

15-22. CATHERINE MURPHY (b. 1946; American). *Harry Roseman Working on Hoboken and Manhattan.* 1978. Pencil, 13 3/4 × 11" (35 × 28 cm). Courtesy of Lennon, Weinberg, Inc., New York.

15-23. THEOPHILUS BROWN (b. 1919; American). *Mark Adams Drawing.* 1985. Pencil, 11 1/2 × 14 1/2" (29.2 × 36.8 cm). Courtesy of the artist.

respective torso is compositionally well established in space—a personal touch and attribute from a true master of visual composing. Note how line variation, the buildup of tonal and textural areas, and the placement of each form in space work together in a poignantly descriptive way.

Caricature

Webster's dictionary defines **caricature** as "a picture in which certain features or mannerisms are exaggerated for satirical effect." While in many kinds of portraiture the minor eccentricities and idiosyncratic details of feature and expression are either minimized or completely eliminated (as in the idealized portrait), such elements provide the very essence of caricature. Caricature demands a special talent for selecting, sharpening, and unveiling the most convincing details of feature, head shape, posture, and particularly facial expression. Many portrait artists cannot caricature while many caricaturists cannot do a "straight" portrait.

Like all satire, caricature can be humorous and kindly, mordant and biting, or almost ribald in the gusto with which it depicts its subject. Visual recognition remains the essential ingredient for successful caricature, and for that reason most caricaturists focus their attention on well-known personalities, particularly politicians, who are often almost savagely caricatured in the printed news media.

The particular genius of the caricaturist has rarely received more brilliant expression than in the drawings of David Levine (Fig. 15-25). Less than a month after the 1980 presidential election, Levine's interpretation of the victorious Ronald Reagan preparing to assume the presidency beamed from the cover of a national periodical. The eyes, cheeks, and expansive crooked smile could be recognized immediately, yet there was something unfamiliar about the image. Levine, obviously responding to the repeated jokes about the true color of Reagan's hair, has depicted him white-haired and wrinkled, seated before a theatrical

15-24. *above, left:* LEONARDO DA VINCI (1452–1519; Italian). *Five Grotesque Heads.* Pen and brown ink, 10 1/4 × 8 1/2" (26 × 21.6 cm). The Royal Library, Windsor Castle, England.

15-25. *above, right:* DAVID LEVINE (b. 1926; American). *Ronald Reagan.* 1980. Reprinted with permission from *The New York Review of Books.*

caricature
An exaggerated portrayal of the characteristic features or mannerisms usually of a well-known personage, intended for satirical effect.

mirror, an ample assortment of makeup containers before him. Symbolic of Reagan's years as an actor, the delicacy with which the lipstick is held perhaps suggests the deftness with which the makeup is to be applied. Levine's use of cross-hatching to emphasize features and create volume and three-dimensionality has been widely imitated.

Entertainers have always provided a special attraction for artists and public alike. Toulouse-Lautrec's drawings, lithographs, and paintings immortalized the colorful and eccentric Parisian music hall performers who were his friends (Fig. 14-29). "For Heaven's sake, don't make me so atrociously ugly," pleaded the horrified cabaret singer Yvette Guilbert when she first saw Toulouse-Lautrec's sketch for her show poster (Fig. 15-29). Later, when critics praised his interpretation and she realized the value of the poster to her continued success and popularity, her wounded vanity was considerably healed. The sketch reveals the artist's fascination with Yvette's ugly grace as he captures every nuance of feature and gesture. One cannot but take delight in the contrast between her almost clown-like makeup and the affected elegance of her pose.

Project 15.12

If you have never attempted a caricature, do so now. Regular features allow less potential for exaggeration than do strongly distinctive or irregular features. Distortion or exaggeration of one's particular physical characteristics or flaws often serves as the basis for caricature and certainly makes the subject easily recognizable.

Do several caricatures with a desired medium of your own choosing. Strive to re-create a fugitive yet recognizable image within the actual visual context of the person.

Illustration 16

Illustration is as old as civilization itself, writing having originated in easily recognized object drawings known as pictographs.

Perhaps the most encompassing definition that can be given for **illustration** is "interpretive visual language." If we accept that definitive meaning, then, any drawing, etching, lithograph, woodcut, painting, photograph, or sculpture that communicates descriptive information, ideas, or feelings could be labeled illustration. Art that emphasizes storytelling is often described—and sometimes dismissed—as being "illustrative." In essence, however, any picture, whether fine art or illustration, awakens something deep inside us and therefore has expressive merit.

Illustration Versus Fine Art

A distinction between illustration and fine art developed early in this century out of the clash between the traditional literalism of illustration and the modern art movement. The art of illustration has developed more or less independently from fine art for nearly a century. The difference between the two fields was perhaps the greatest during the late 1940s and 1950s, which were dominated by nonrepresentational art—the height of **abstract expressionism** and the advent of action painting. Today there are more influential movements afloat in the art world domain than ever before, and without a doubt, illustration reflects a full range of contemporary art styles at the same time that fine art evidences a renewed interest in the figurative and representational.

The apparent blending of the fine and illustrational arts seemed also to have started in the sixties, when leading pop artists began to introduce elements of illustration into their drawings, paintings, and prints,

illustration
Usually a highly detailed image that communicates a message, offers visual description, or portrays an episode (as in a story) through visual means.

abstract expressionism
An American movement in the field of painting that began in the late forties and emphasized a nonrepresentational style. The movement broke into two branches: *action painting* and *color field painting*.

301

16-1. VAN HOWELL (b. 1948; American). *Rothko.* 1980–1982. Pen and ink, 9 3/4 × 7 1/2" (25 × 19 cm.)
Courtesy of the artist.

MARK ROTHKO   VAN HOWELL

and major corporations began to use works by prominent contemporary artists in their advertising. Van Howell has cleverly blended the two—fine art and illustration—by allowing the head and hand of artist Mark Rothko to emerge from the familiar meditative and hovering rectangles typical of Rothko's work (Fig. 16-1).

Many drawings done as illustrations fit easily into the category of fine art and are exhibited and collected as such. Why, then, the notion that illustration and fine art must be viewed as separate, and not necessarily equal, art forms? Many major artists have worked as illustrators. Edouard Manet, a pivotal figure in the history of modern art who demanded for artists the freedom to work in the style of their own choosing, did illustrations for a French translation of Edgar Allen Poe's "The Raven"; Eugène Delacriox produced a series of lithographs to illustrate Goethe's *Faust* (Fig. 16-2). Among Toulouse-Lautrec's best-known works are the cabaret and music hall posters he designed. More than a century later, Jane Avril (Fig. 14-29), Yvette Guilbert (Fig. 15-26), and other such colorful, often eccentric entertainers continue to draw capacity audiences—not to the theaters, but to auction houses whenever original impressions of his posters come up for sale, and to museum bookstores, where sales of reproductions of the posters flourish.

16-2. EUGÈNE DELACROIX (1798–1863; French). *Mephistopheles Flying,* illustration for Goethe's *Faust.* 1828. Lithograph, 10 3/4 × 9" (27.3 × 22.8 cm.). The Metropolitan Museum of Art, New York.

A technical distinction between "illustration" and "fine art" is that the former is created expressly for the purpose of commercial reproduction. Being concerned primarily with reproduction, illustrators often select media and techniques according to how inexpensively they will reproduce, rather than from any consideration of permanence. The circumstances under which commercial works are created also contribute to the notion of poetic and spiritual separation. While the fine artist works independently and from other driving motivations, choosing when, what, and how to draw, generally without having to please anyone else, the commercial illustrator works under the guidance of an art director and must be concerned about how the work will reproduce expediently. All of this creative activity must be funneled into the confines of a time limit and deadline shadowed by the responsibility of having to please the client. Beyond that, the illustrator must create an image that will be satisfying and understood by the greatest number of viewers. "You've got to please both the art editor and the public," lamented the legendary Norman Rockwell. "This makes it tough on the illustrator as compared with the fine artist, who can paint any object any way he happens to interpret it." (It seems appropriate to point out, however, that until late in the nineteenth century, most artists could be considered commercial artists in that they worked by commission and were responsible for satisfying their patrons.)

One additional significant difference is that most illustrations are represented with text in some form, whether it be an article, story, or advertising copy. Although illustrations can be appreciated for imagery and technique, they cannot always stand alone when viewed out of context. Fine art, in contrast, while it might refer to something outside itself, is meant to be complete in itself. Furthermore, with fine art there are heightened, mysterious elements that make us want to return to the art museums for repeated looks and visual experiences. Granted, powerful advertisement images exist—but, unlike the works in permanent museum collections, they have yet to stand the test of time.

Clearly, however, artistic prowess holds an equal footing in both arenas. Generally speaking, the best illustrators were successful fine artists first; the weakest fine artists were never good illustrators—an interesting convoluted relationship, one as mysterious as the two definitions themselves.

Types of Illustration

The purpose of this chapter is to provide an introduction to illustration, the area of commercial art most closely related to fine art. A survey of different types of illustration, including a brief discussion of the purpose and requirements of each, will reveal that *A Guide to Drawing* offers a basic prerequisite course for illustrators as well as for fine artists. The illustrations reproduced are but a sampling of the remarkable range of drawings done in this diverse field. No attempt has been made to select only recent examples; like fine art, what is fashionable changes from year to year. For an expanded look at the richness and variety of contemporary illustration, you will want to linger over the illustration yearbooks that are published annually and skim through all the current magazines in the school library each month to keep yourself informed about what is happening in the field.

Commercial illustration in its various forms now appears to be divided between drawing and painting on the one hand and photography and computer/digital imaging on the other, with an apparent increase in the use of drawing—the medium that has always been most closely related to the act of seeing with the human eye and creating with the hand. There are four major categories of illustration—editorial, advertising, medical, and scientific—making its own demands on the artist. While versatility is an asset, most professional illustrators select an area of specialization.

Editorial Illustration Editorial illustrations accompany stories and articles in books, magazines, and newspapers. Although guided by an art director, the illustrator must have an awareness of the content and structure of each story, article, and story line of each to ensure that the choice of imagery, style, and technique is compatible with the text and grasps the essential meaning of the piece. In this case, the story precedes the image.

Book Illustration Nineteenth-century novels were almost always illustrated; today adult books rarely are. Illustrations are confined mostly to book jackets, special limited editions designed for book collectors, and what might be considered "children's books for adults," such as those created by Edward Gorey (Fig. 16-3) and David Macaulay (Fig. 9-6).

16-3. EDWARD GOREY (20th century; American). *"The summer she was eleven, Drusilla went abroad with her parents."* Illustration for *The Remembered Visit* (Simon and Schuster, 1965).

16-4. BARRON STOREY (20th century; American). *Captain Ahab.* Illustration for *The Great White Whale.* (Reader's Digest Association, Inc.). 1978.

Book jackets, originally called "dust jackets," were intended simply to protect the covers of books. Today they are designed to attract the attention of buyers and promote sales. Some covers use only type;

others add illustration, combining the talents of graphic designers and illustrators to suggest the essence of the book through visual means effectively, truthfully, and with immediate impact.

Contemporary book illustrations often depict character and establish mood rather than portray specific episodes from the narrative. One of Barron Storey's illustrations for *The Great White Whale* (Fig. 16-4) provocatively captures the mood of the book, suggesting the insane obsession of Captain Ahab, who stands defiantly erect against the battering forces of the sea, his ivory leg planted firmly on deck. Storey's handling of pen-and-ink cross-hatching remains very much in the tradition of nineteenth-century illustrations reproduced by the **wood-engraving** medium.

Artist Barry Moser, renowned illustrator for *An Illustrated Folio Edition of the King James Bible,* published by Pennyroyal Caxton Press in 1999, has revived wood engraving as his present-day expressive and illustrational technique (Fig. 16-5) in *Behold The Man* from the Gospel of John, 19:2. Many contemporary illustrators use this age-old technique because black and white line drawings are highly descriptive and are the easiest and most economical to reproduce. Note how Moser uses

wood engraving The technique of engraving done as a relief process on end-grain blocks of various hard woods such as maple, pear, or apple; the engraved lines are cut with a burin, receive no ink, and subsequently print as the white of the paper or negative spaces. The uncut, relief or raised surface of the woodblock receives the ink and transmits the positive image to paper when the engraving is printed.

16-5. BARRY MOSER (b. 193?; English). *Behold the Man.* Wood engraving. From the illustrated folio edition of the King James Bible. Published 1999 by Pennyroyal Caxton Press. Courtesy of the artist.

16-6. MAURICE SENDAK (b. 1928; American). Illustration for "The Three Feathers" from *The Juniper Tree and Other Tales from Grimm,* translated by Lore Segal and Randall Jarrell.

the white of the paper as enhancement to illustrate the glistening of the blood dripping down the chest of Christ in Figure 16-5.

Illustration originates with and must be true to the words of the author. Good illustration should amplify the text but should not depend upon a literal caption to explain its meaning. The interdependence of text and image would seem to require that good illustrators also be good readers.

Children's Books   Children's books, by tradition, are richly illustrated. In fact, much of the success of a children's book depends upon the contribution of the illustrator, since a child's imagination is activated through the combination of verbal and visual imagery. Text and illustrations go hand in hand; effective illustrations both follow and advance the story.

A survey of children's book illustrations reveals great diversity of styles. Literalness in representation assures visual identification, but this can be accomplished without sacrificing imagination and invention. While children's literature frequently incorporates fantasy and make-believe, skillful illustrators are able to treat the commonplace with whimsy, vividness, and excitement (Fig. 16-6).

Children are an appreciative but critical audience who expect drawings to be faithful to the text. While free to select style, the illustrator is not free to reinterpret even the most elemental detail of the text, as anyone who has ever attempted to satisfy a child's questioning can attest.

Anyone interested in illustrating children's books should become familiar with both what has been done and what is being done. Collected works of many of the best-known nineteenth- and early-twentieth-century illustrators of children's books are available in paperback editions. The illustrations of Maurice Sendak (Fig. 16-6) have been the subject of a major study; they were also the focus of a New York auction in 1987.

Magazine and Newspaper Illustration   While certain book illustrators like Edward Gorey (Fig. 16-3), Barry Moser (Fig. 16-5), and Maurice Sendak (Fig. 16-6), develop a personal style that remains relatively constant from book to book, illustrators of stories and articles for magazines and newspapers are expected to be able to change style virtually from one assignment to the next. Change is inherent in all aspects of contemporary life, particularly in the field of mass communication, in which capturing the largest percentage of public attention is, of necessity, the prime consideration.

The illustrator or photographer is often called on to provide a single major illustration to attract the attention of the reader and establish the character of a story or article in an effective and substantially truthful manner. Such images may tend to be symbolic, with their meanings immediately perceived when seen in relation to the titles of the articles. Because magazines and newspapers focus upon topics of current interest, there is the additional demand of meeting deadlines.

The range of articles printed in popular periodicals requires illustrators capable of working with a variety of subjects and also versatile in employing different media and their respective techniques without allowing technique to become more important than content. Doug Griswold's illustration of the earth seen as a skull (Fig. 16-7) suggests the boldness that is required for drawings to be reproduced on the newsprint used for daily newspapers.

Spot Drawings   Spot drawings attract the attention of readers and provide visual interest for articles and stories that do not feature a major illustration. They are often related to the subject in a general way rather than being specific, as for example, David Suter's drawing of a lunch pail and work gloves for an article about unemployment (Fig. 1-11).

Spot drawings are often used as "fillers"—that is, simply to fill unused space as well as to introduce visual interest to a page. Since the need for fillers cannot be anticipated, they usually are unrelated to the surrounding text and merely exist as a charming or whimsical bonus of no intended importance.

Sports Illustration   The ability to depict movement, excitement, and atmosphere is essential to successful sports illustration, which tends to be a highly specialized field. The sports illustrator must understand sports and be able to represent the human figure convincingly in action. Although the camera is able to freeze the image of figures in motion, photographs often fail to convey the quality of movement and excitement associated with sports precisely because the action has been frozen. In most instances, top sports illustrators are better able than photographers to suggest the feeling of energy and movement that fans associate with sports whether seen live or viewed on television. While sports illustrators frequently use photographs for reference, they have the skill to inject a sense of aliveness, vitality, and extraordinary physical accomplishments through clarification, simplification, and exaggeration. Witness the palpable energy, rhythmic motion, and extreme sense of movement, along with acceleration and speed, in Jason Howard's woodcut depiction of a bicycle race (Fig. 16-8). The image, with its left-to-right, white, slashed markings made by the quickly executed, lateral cutting of the wood depicting the streaming hair of the athletes, is so powerful that one can almost feel the parting winds as the bicyclers pass by. Similarly, Bob Ziering's colored pencil drawing of runners (Pl. 12) combines fragments of multiple images and dissolving contours to suggest rapid, rhythmic movement with the stronger delineation of selected features to reveal both the concentration and physical effort involved in competitive racing. The drawing's captivating sense of movement, heightened by subtle gradations of color that define both the figures and the currents of air that surround them, far surpasses the static expression of a photograph. Aspiring sports illustrators should avail themselves of as much life drawing as possible, with particular emphasis upon quick sketching and gesture drawing.

Editorial Cartoons and Caricature   There is a long and continuing tradition of political **cartoons** and caricatures as illustrations in popular periodicals. These brilliant, biting looks at the antics of national and world leaders have won Pulitzer prizes for some of their creators.

cartoon
A newspaper or magazine drawing or illustration that caricatures or symbolizes a person, event, or situation of popular interest, such as a politician or political party, usually in a humorous or satirical way.

CH. 16   Illustration   **309**

16-8. JASON HOWARD (b. 1972; American). *The Bicycle Race.* Woodcut on pine printed on white wove paper, 12 3/4 × 19 3/8″ (32.4 × 49.2 cm). Collection of David Faber.
Courtesy of the artist.

The impact of editorial cartoons generally results from the successful combination of visual image and caption, sometimes supplemented with dialogue. Political cartoonists depend almost entirely on broadly exaggerated caricature. Since their topics must be as current as yesterday's news, editorial cartoonists work under extreme pressure deadlines.

Feeding the public's insatiable appetite for information about the famous remains a primary function of popular periodicals. In addition to the ever-present photographs of such personalities, some magazines and newspapers continue the tradition of using caricatures of familiar politicians (Fig. 15-25), literary figures, and entertainers.

Advertising Illustration   A second area of commercial illustration embraces everything done for advertising purposes. Fashion, product, and travel illustrations all rely upon visual flattery to arouse customer interest. Advertising illustrations generally are integrated into a layout that includes headings, copy, and the client's name. Unless the illustrator is also responsible for the layout, it is necessary to learn to work within a prescribed format to create a visually stimulating ad.

Fashion Illustration   Fashion drawing falls into two categories: **reporting** and **advertising drawings.** Fashion reporting treats fashion as news. It is directed toward revealing new trends in fashion in drawings that convey the general characteristics of forthcoming styles rather than depicting specific garments in detail. Advertising drawings are designed to sell merchandise, and though often highly stylized, they are rendered with considerable concern for accurate detail (Fig. 16-9).

Because the style of representing fashion changes as rapidly as fashion itself, illustrators must be versatile, flexible, and imaginative. Not only must they be up to date, but they must also be able to anticipate and initiate change. Strictly literal representation, no matter how well drawn, lacks buyer appeal. In addition to his extraordinary renderings of garments, the drawings of George Stavrinos are distinguished by his ability to invent visually exciting settings for his models (Fig. 16-9). Ranaldi's drawing with its emphasis on sculptured planes of light and dark (Fig. 16-10) bears certain similarities to Figures 1-16, 8-4, 8-23, and 10-10.

reporting drawings
Drawings that make visually tangible an event or occurrence by communicating what happened. In fashion design, reporting drawings treat fashion as news.

advertising drawings
Drawings done by commercial illustrators and designed to promote and sell merchandise; though often highly stylized, they are rendered with considerable concern for detail.

16-9. GEORGE STAVRINOS.
Courtesy of Linda Stavrinos.

In the fashion field, competition between artists and photographers is keen. Artists have greater freedoms to change scale, exaggerate style, dramatize contrasts, and contextualize fashion. They also embellish, simplify, add, subtract, or eliminate according to the dictates of the industry. A skilled artist, working from any model, can totally transform the character of the figure at will.

The training for a fashion artist should include drawing from both nude and clothed models. There should be a keen understanding of anatomy as a precedent to knowing how the body works in motion, and understanding how the figure is constructed will permit effective visual distortion. Figures in fashion illustrations, while rarely realistic, must appear to have an underlying sense of structure, proportion, and balance. Pose, gesture, and movement, while exaggerated, must be convincing and plausible in order for the public to identify with the model—as if he or she were wearing the garment being modeled. Both structure and pose determine how a garment drapes, as do the weight and character of the fabric (Figs. 16-9, 16-10). A garment must appear to fit; it must follow the contours of the body and appear to move with the body. Although still-life studies of pieces of draped cloth perhaps seem uninspiring, fabric is the stuff that fashions are made of, and the human body the armature for the fashioned garment.

The ability to suggest and render different materials and textures in a variety of media and techniques is a basic requirement for fashion artists. Fashion illustrators generally specialize in drawing women, men,

16-10. RANALDI. Advertisement for Caumont from *Gentlemen's Quarterly*. 1985.

or children; only rarely do drawings of one include either of the other two. The category of fashion accessories provides an additional area of specialization in fashion illustration. Hats, bags, shoes, scarves, belts, and jewelry are, in effect, the province of the fashion still-life artist, who is expected to make such objects stylish and appealing without obvious falsification. This specialty requires an artist skilled at depicting detail and rendering textures and materials with a sense of flair.

Perhaps more than in any other field, one learns about fashion illustration by studying fashion drawings, fashion magazines, and window displays of fashionable stores. It is valuable to accumulate a file of outstanding fashion drawings that employ interesting and varied media techniques, as well as photographs of figures for reference.

Product Illustration   The area known as "product illustration" includes almost anything that can be manufactured and offered to the customer. The illustrator is expected to depict commonplace objects with style to make them attractive or alluring to the public. While the objects cannot be falsified (truth in advertising), they can be idealized and dramatized. An unusual perspective can be introduced to intensify the form, while bold modeling in light and dark, the contrasting of descriptive patterns, and the dramatic rendering of surface and textures complete the effect.

Standard still-life experiences provide the basis of learning a variety of techniques useful for many product illustrations.

While in the most literal sense product illustration would seem restricted to depicting objects, illustrations created for catalog covers, CD and DVD albums, and to advertise movies, television programs, and other entertainment events are product- or episode-related. Kam Mak cleverly adapted images from ancient Egyptian wall paintings (Fig. 14-2) into a catalog cover for a purveyor of contemporary travel clothing (Fig. 16-11). Rich low-keyed color and an equally rich rhythmic pattern of shapes combine to produce a visual counterpart to the sounds of the Mississippi Delta Blues Festival (Pl. 16). According to illustrator Gary Kelley, "Some of my all-time favorite music has come from the Mississippi Delta, so this was a very personal expression for me. It's an extra treat when sound and image can connect for me like it does here."

16-11. KAM MAK. Catalog cover for Banana Republic Travel Clothing. Courtesy of the artist.

16-12. ANGELO K. BILDER (1898–1998; Greek-American). *A Cargo of Milk.* c. 1941. Graphite on cream wove paper, 20 × 16″ (50.8 × 40.6 cm). Courtesy of Dorothea Bilder.

Angelo K. Bilder, an accomplished Chicago illustrator who immigrated to the United States in 1913 and worked in all media, recalls the ships and shipping yards of his youth in the graphite illustration *A Cargo of Milk* (Fig. 16-12). His skillful use of the medium and his compositional acumen, coupled with his ability to see forms in space while invoking meaning and association, give this drawing an air of intrinsic beauty and expressive value that distinguishes it from most illustrational art. To use these drawings as preliminary studies for fully developed color advertisements sets them apart in yet another way. The inherent elements of symbolic meaning and human association the artist struck early on in the drawings transcend the mere commercial reasons for their existence.

Travel Illustration   The extensive advertising program of the travel industry requires illustrations ranging from elaborate full-color paintings to spot drawings. Styles and techniques are as varied as the services provided; subject matter embraces figure, landscape, and architecture. Albert Lorenz relies upon extreme exaggeration of three-point perspective (discussed in Chapter 9) to lift his viewers high above midtown Manhattan and then focuses their attention on his client's hotel by darkening the buildings that surround it (Fig. 16-13).

16-13. ALBERT LORNEZ (20th century; American). *Grand Bay Hotel, New York City.* 1990. Pen and ink with watercolor, 20 × 22" RYP.
Robinson, Yesawich & Pepperdine, Inc., Orlando, Florida.

Medical Illustration   Medical illustration is "the graphic representation of any medical subject made for the purpose of communicating medical knowledge." Medical illustrators need to have scientific background as well as extensive art training. Since absolute accuracy is imperative, even critical, the artist must possess highly trained powers of observation and meticulous draftsmanship (Fig. 11-1). The artist is called upon to do what a camera cannot do—clarify and simplify, select what is essential, eliminate the unnecessary to communicate effectively and completely.

Illustrations for articles published in medical journals are prepared in collaboration with surgeons, often from sketches made on location in the operating room as the surgeon describes to the illustrator what is to be revealed. The artist must have both the knowledge and imagination to visualize what is desired and to find the most effective means to communicate that information. The surgeon, as imagist, must also be able to describe accurately the extreme details of three-dimensional forms in relation to each other as they are revealed during surgical procedures. Judy Morley worked with graphite dust on Mylar to achieve the subtle chiaroscuro of the exposed eyeball and the sheen of metal surgical tools (Fig. 16-14). A number of major university medical schools offer specialized training in medical illustration, which includes learning to work

16-14. JUDY MORLEY (20th century; American). *Orbitotomy.* Graphite dust on Mylar.
Courtesy of the artist.

with surgeons in the operating room. Admission requirements include completion of a premed program. Interested art students can prepare by taking classes in life drawing, anatomy, still life, perspective, design, composition, rendering, watercolor, airbrush, and mixed media.

Scientific Illustration   Each of the scientific disciplines has its unique needs for illustrative materials. The qualities required for all scientific drawings are accuracy, clarity, and neatness (Figs. 11-1, 11-14, 16-14). Details of form and surface characteristics must be carefully observed and meticulously rendered. Forms must be lighted evenly without obscuring shadows. Stippling, because of its propensity for articulation of detail, is the most common method used for hyperrealistically descriptive shading (Fig. 11-14).

Art Directors

Illustrators need to be familiar with the traditional areas of subject matter and the art elements; they must use media and technique imaginatively and expressively (Figs. 16-1 through 16-14). It is also necessary to know about different methods of visual reproduction in order to best prepare drawings or paintings suitably for the reproductive process to be used.

Without a firmly established reputation, an illustrator cannot expect to be granted complete independence in making creative decisions. It is the art director who has the major responsibility for determining what an illustration will be and how it will be used. For this reason it is important that art students, especially those who might want to become illustrators, learn to follow assignments, accept criticism and suggestions made by instructors (acting as art directors), be willing to make suggested changes, and complete projects on time. Since most illustrators are required to submit preliminary portfolios of sketches for approval, students are urged to adopt the habit of making rough working drawings before starting out to do the finished presentation piece. By doing several sketches, the illustrator can cull ideas of lesser impact early in the creative process and identify the strongest compositional possibilities.

Research Resources

Professional illustrators often are called upon to provide drawings for subjects that lie beyond their own personal experience. They must learn to use reference materials to search for information that will provide authenticity to their work. It is of incalculable value to know how to use the resources of libraries. Particularly useful to illustrators are picture collections maintained by major libraries. Several indexes also assist in locating published illustrations (drawings, paintings, photographs, prints) on specific subjects. *Illustration Index* (Volume 8) compiled by Marsha C. Appel (Scarecrow Press, 1998) has a cultural and historical orientation. It is of particular value because it indexes eight periodicals likely to be available in most libraries—*American Heritage, Ebony, Holiday, National Geographic, National Wildlife, Natural History, Smithsonian,* and *Sports Illustrated.*

Preparing a Portfolio

If you seek employment as an illustrator, it is essential to prepare and maintain a portfolio with examples of your best and perhaps latest work to show agencies, art directors, and potential clients. Never include any drawing with which you are not totally satisfied; it is better to include a few drawings of high quality than many of poorer quality. Be extremely selective. Play an objective role by putting aside any sentimental attachments you have to particular drawings, and include only your very best. It is also important that you keep your portfolio up to date. It is naturally unwise to show the same drawings if you make return visits to the same people.

Your portfolio should demonstrate both variety and consistency. Select pieces using different media and techniques, but be certain that your own sense of style is evident throughout. If you know what types of accounts an agency or art director handles, you can select pieces that most closely meet those needs.

Include any examples of your work that have been reproduced. If your illustrations have never been reproduced, it is possible and beneficial to have some pieces commercially photographed with prints made at a slightly reduced size from the original drawings. A sample of a preliminary rough with the corresponding finished drawing provides an indication of your ability to follow through.

Concentrate upon making the best possible presentation. All drawings should be clean and well matted. Use mats of uniform outer dimensions with window openings appropriate to the individual size of each drawing; smaller drawings can be grouped attractively in a single mat. Attach the drawings, with acid-free linen tape, to an acid-free backing board that is the same size as the outer dimensions of the mat and has been hinged to the mat along one side only with acid-free linen tape. Covering each drawing with a cut-to-size sheet of acetate is less troublesome than placing protective tissue paper over the entire mat.

Put as much thought and effort into preparing your portfolio as you did into doing the drawings. While it is the art that counts, art directors are influenced by the quality and degree of imagination evident in your presentation. Remember that art directors, as your potential

top

window to be cut out

bottom

straight edge–
cut along window side
A. Cutting mat board.

mat–
face down   tape

top of mat   tape   backing
B. Hinging the mat.

additional
tape

fold
C. Hinging the mat.

bottom of
mat   top of mat

drawing   hinged at top only
D. Hinging drawing at the top.

employers, have little patience with any hint of sloppiness or careless-ness regarding the way you treat and display your work.

Figure 16-15 exemplifies the professional formation and method of assembling the backing board and window mat for a work of art on paper. Acid-free materials are easily obtained and are considered the only professional way to display your work in today's marketplace. A general rule of thumb to abide by is that anything that comes into con-tact with the work of art over a long period of time should be acid-free (a neutral pH of 7.0) in order to prolong the life of the paper.

Expressive Drawing 17

If the subjects I have wanted to express have suggested different ways of expression, I have never hesitated to adopt them. . . .

—Pablo Picasso

The arts are the harbors for creative mystery and the vehicles for human expression. Just as composers are able to transform the sounds they hear around them into symphonies and other musical forms, so, too, do visual artists use the experience of *seeing* to create visually tangible impressions of the world through line, tone, and texture. Frequent mention has been made throughout the preceding chapters of the expressive qualities of drawing in the context of specific topics—the elements of art, media, and subject matter. The selection of the drawings reproduced, in fact, was prompted as much by degree of expressiveness as by topic considerations and approach to subject matter. Drawings, like prints, paintings, and sculptures, never fit into a single context, and although some drawings fit neatly into specific academic slots, their individual expressive natures reach far beyond those common attributes that may bind them together. Most of the drawings in this book could have been reassigned with equal effect to other chapters, and almost all could be included in this chapter, titled "Expressive Drawing."

Except for purely technical drawings, in which all suggestion of individual style is deliberately avoided, a degree of expressiveness remains evident even in what is intended as a completely objective drawing—admittedly more so in some than others. What distinguishes one drawing from another is the uniqueness of each artist's use of different media. Another factor that identifies certain drawings as more profound than others is the degree to which viewers respond beyond mere recognition. This in turn relates to the degree to which the artist goes beyond simple description of form and subject to reveal an attitude or emotion, not only about the subject but also about the experience of seeing and

319

the process of manipulating media. The old adage "The heart has reasons it knows not of" applies to audience response in all the arts, for it is the arts, after all, that provide a means by which we identify and experience mystery.

Some suggest that there is a distinction between representational and expressive drawings; others, while agreeing that all representational drawings are not expressive and that all expressive drawing need not be representational, can see no reason to separate the two. Drawings can be, and frequently are, both.

Empathy

The legendary early-twentieth-century American painter-teacher Robert Henri pointed out to his students that "artists have been looking at Rembrandt's drawings for three hundred years," and in spite of all the "remarkable drawings" done since then, we are not yet done looking at them. Henri's suggestion that "the beauty of Rembrandt's lines, . . . rests in the fact that you do not realize them as lines, but are only conscious of what they state of the living person," is beautifully demonstrated in *Two Women Teaching a Child to Walk* (Fig. 17-1). The drawing reveals Rembrandt's sensitivity to human gesture and the extraordinary economy with which he reveals subtle and tender emotions. Every line is *expressive* as well as *descriptive*—no line is extraneous. This is what is meant by "Rembrandt's extraordinary economy of line."

Rembrandt, a dedicated observer of humanity, rarely depicted anything that could not be found within a few hundred feet of his doorstep, but within that microcosm existed a whole spectrum of human drama that he recorded with a sensitivity, honesty, and integrity that transcend time and place. Rembrandt drew, etched, and painted out of **empathy,** which is characterized as the capacity to identify with the subject, to conceive and share feelings and experiences, and to project this sympathetic attitude through the work of art. Rembrandt had the ability to fuse emotion with art to the point that his art became emotion itself.

Empathetic drawing extends beyond the response to subject, whether people, places, events or experiences; it also embraces the

empathy
The state of identifying with someone through the projection of oneself into that person in order to gain a better understanding of that person's character; a reaching out usually through an emotional channel that is perpetuated by tenderness and deep feelings of sympathy or compassion.

empathetic drawing
A drawing that bears evidence of the sympathy for, and understanding of, one person by another through visual portrayal.

17-1. REMBRANDT VAN RIJN (1606–1669; Dutch). *Two Women Teaching a Child to Walk.* c. 1640. Red chalk, 4 × 5″ (10.2 × 12.7 cm). British Museum, London.

17-2. DAVID FINN (b. 1952; American). *Child Drawing a Chalk Line on the Ground.* c. 1988?. Ink wash on white wove paper, 22 1/2 × 30″ (57.2 × 76.3 cm). Collection of David Faber. Courtesy of the artist.

artist's response to the media selected and to the very emotional act of drawing. It is impossible for someone knowledgeable about art not to respond to the unlabored quality of Rembrandt's line, and to delight in the process of drawing, as did the artist himself.

David Finn's drawing of a little child drawing a chalk line on the ground (Fig. 17-2) infuses the media of **ink wash** and charcoal on a large, white paper surface, evoking the artist's empathetic response to a child's playful yet determined activity. The drawing portrays a child transforming his space into an atmosphere that has a special meaning for him beyond anything the adult world could comprehend. Indeed, it may capture a moment in the life of the child within the artist himself. Note the singularly expressive and translucent quality of the ink wash medium Finn selected to depict his sensitive interpretation of the weight-less bodies of the little children. As with Rembrandt's line, Finn's work exhibits a mastery over ink wash—an economical use of material sending forth every possible nuance and force of expression.

It was pointed out in Chapter 12 that students frequently struggle needlessly with the belief that what they draw must be "artistic," which is indicative of a misunderstanding of the word *artistic.* They confront a corresponding dilemma with the concept of "expressive," often confusing it with "emotional." No subject is ever artistic until the artist infuses it with the necessary ingredients of selection, perception, response, subject reinterpretation, skillful media handling, and expression.

The images of Käthe Kollwitz mirror the sorrow of her life and times with such intensity that one is easily tempted to say categorically: "Käthe Kollwitz *is* expressive drawing." *The Homeless* (Fig. 17-3) reveals her deep compassion for people who suffer, while the impenetrable black symbolizes a despair known to all homeless people. As an image it is universal and timeless—one, that upon seeing it, is hard to put aside. Kollwitz was also capable of sharing moments of great tenderness, such as in *Peter Reading in Bed* (Fig. 17-4), in which the features and tones are drawn with a pencil that seems barely to have touched the paper.

Leonardo da Vinci can be credited with introducing delicacy of tone and subtle chiaroscuro as expressive elements. Until he realized and demonstrated the potential of light and shadow in establishing an

ink wash

A dilution of ink in water or solvent, applied by brush, most often used with pen-and-ink drawings to enhance the composition by creating varying degrees of semitransparent tonal ranges.

17-3. KÄTHE KOLLWITZ (1867–1945; German). *The Homeless*. c. 1909. Charcoal and wash, 13 3/4 × 12 1/2" (35 × 32 cm). National Gallery of Art, Washington, D.C.

17-4. KÄTHE KOLLWITZ (1867–1945; German). *Peter Reading in Bed*. c. 1908. Graphite pencil, 10 1/2 × 14 1/2" (26.5 × 36.8 cm). Cologne District Savings Bank, Käthe Kollwitz Collection.

cartoon

A newspaper or magazine drawing or illustration that caricatures or symbolizes a person, event, or situation of popular interest, such as a politician or political party, usually in a humorous or satirical way. Also, a large drawing created to establish life-size scale for frescoes. Artists later used the technique to transfer large-scale images for paintings, tapestries, stained glass, and other large works (a cartoon was indispensable in the process of making stained glass).

sfumato

An Italian word meaning "smoked." The gradual, almost imperceptible blending of tones from light to dark in paintings or drawings; a technique used by Renaissance artists in combination with chiaroscuro for the visual enhancement of the overall tones within a composition.

emotional tone in such a magnificent drawing as the **cartoon** for *Madonna and Child with St. Anne* (Fig. 17-5), chiaroscuro had functioned solely to describe form and volume. Leonardo transformed chiaroscuro further by softening all hard edges so that light seemed to flow from one form to another, producing the effect of atmosphere and movement in space. As used by Leonardo, it is called **sfumato**—Italian for "smoked."

Drawings can be expressive, not solely because they are highly charged emotional statements, but also because they communicate an individual point of view and purpose. In Jim Westergard's "oil drawing" on paper titled *Insomnia* (Pl. 17), the artist visually narrates his feelings of vulnerability, loneliness, and the yearning for sleep on a seemingly endless international night flight, where finding it impossible to sleep, he roams the aircraft cabin and amuses himself by looking out at the

17-5. LEONARDO DA VINCI (1452–1519; Italian). *Cartoon for Virgin and Child with St. Anne and the Infant St. John.* c. 1497–1499. Charcoal and white chalk on paper, 4′ 6 3/4″ × 3′ 3 3/4″ (1.39 × 1.01 m). National Gallery, London.

etching

The action of a corrosive material, such as an acid, incising a design into metal, as in *copper plate etching.* One of the techniques of *fine art printmaking* that falls into the category of *intaglio,* where lines and textures are incised into and below the original surface of metal plates forming grooves and rough textures that will hold ink that can then be transferred to dampened paper with the use of an etching press.

lithograph

A type of print created by one of the four major divisions of *fine art printmaking* involving a *direct drawing process* on Bavarian limestone (calcium carbonate) or aluminum plates. The process, in its entirety, engages the *antithesis of grease and water* where images are drawn with greasy crayons on the stone or metal plate, then etched with acid, effecting a process of chemical stabilization whereby the image remains grease-loving or oleophilic, and the nonimage becomes water-loving or hydrophilic repelling grease. Through a rhythmic process between *printer* and *sponger,* the litho surface is kept wet by sponging with water, then inked with printer's inks alternately, and finally printed on paper with a litho press. *Lithograph* is from a Greek term meaning "stone writing."

airliner's wing. Upon looking at the drawing, one experiences the tremendous sense of foreshortening, yet simultaneously the incomprehensible length of the plane's wing that symbolizes Westergard's sense of being held captive inside the plane over a long period of time.

Lacking as it may any visible sense of drama or emotion, Giorgio Morandi's *Still Life* (Fig. 17-6) might not readily be accepted as "expressive." It is, in fact, difficult to convince beginning students that an expressive drawing, **etching, lithograph,** painting, or sculpture can be made from so little, from objects of such apparent insignificance—yet Morandi, with his unique and quiet talent, has done just that. Drawing out of deep respect for and attachment to the humble objects with which he shared his creative life, Morandi created expressive images as free of pretension and ostentation as he was himself.

What one feels about a subject need not be emotional. It might be interest in the space that a subject occupies or a response to line, movement, volume, or patterns of light and dark—whatever offers the greatest visual interest, with individual artists reacting differently to the same subject. Edouard Vuillard, for example, saw his studio—described as "a jumble of furniture, household objects, half-finished works and other Paraphernalia" that included a full-size cast of the Venus de Milo—with an empathy that no other person could have because it was his own (Fig. 17-7). The open, meandering soft-graphite pencil lines, drawn "with a hand that is as sure as it is light," according to one critic of the period, reveal much about the artist and his feelings. The French author

17-6. GIORGIO MORANDI (1890–1964; Italian). *Still Life.* c. 1954. Graphite pencil, 9 × 12″ (23 × 31 cm). Private collection.

17-7. EDOUARD VUILLARD (1868–1940; French). *Interior of the Artist's Studio.* c. 1897. Graphite pencil, 4 1/2 × 7″ (11.5 × 17.8 cm). Courtesy of Richard L. Feigen & Co., Inc., New York.

Andre Gide said, "I know few works where one is brought more directly into communication with the artist," and went on to describe Vuillard's style as "caressingly tender, I might even say timid."

Jack Boul's monotype *Venetian Light* (Fig. 17-8) reflects Vuillard's sentiments about the importance of interior space, in this case demonstrating the effects of light. In the "dark field manner," Boul removes black ink until his soft, swelling light folds in through the Venetian windows, causing the objects within to melt in a composition of reflective brilliance as they are washed in light.

Representation and Abstraction

Some artists, teachers, and critics believe strongly that visual reality is irrelevant, concentrating instead on abstract concepts of form and color—an argument that does not hold true and invites disagreement. Specifically, if they mean it is a matter of representation *or* abstraction, there is equally strong disagreement. If, however, what they intend is that in representational drawing the exact appearance of the subject is less important than the abstract principles of composition, there should be no disagreement. The former author, this revision author, and many others prefer not to view drawing as either representation *or* abstrac-

17-8. JACK BOUL (b. 1927; American). *Venetian Light.* c. 1996. Monotype, 8 × 11″. Gift of the Friends of the Corcoran Gallery of Art. Courtesy of the artist.

tion, seeing it instead as a combination of representation *and* abstraction unified as a visual statement. Paul Klee said, "Art does not reproduce the visual; rather, it makes visible." This statement seems to put to rest any taking of sides in the matter and upholds the fact that artists do not choose representation or abstraction—artists simply choose to create. Even though all of the drawings discussed thus far in this chapter can be described as representational, is it not possible—even imperative—for us as artists and students to look beyond subject matter, realizing that no matter what the subject—representational, abstract, or nonobjective—each line, shape, value, texture, and color are part of the underlying abstraction that *is* the composition of each drawing? And is it not possible, for example, to find and appreciate a similar creative impulse in the handling of the rhythmic, gestural, linear patterns by Käthe Kollwitz (Fig. 17-4) and Cy Twombly (Fig. 8-5), even though one offers representation and the other abstraction?

The selected media that artists choose to work with produce the visual symptoms of that wonderful, yet fully unrealized variety, and everything visual artists do is an abstraction from the actual object, subject, or mere concept. The artist has the ability to identify any subject as worthy and then to extract the essential elements needed for a particular expression.

Many artists and artist/teachers, although not all, believe that until you learn to draw and depict things as they are (representation), until you have a strong grounding in composition (abstraction), and until you

17-9. SUSAN ROTHENBERG (b. 1945; American). *Untitled.* c. 1984. Charcoal, 47 1/2 × 31" (120.6 × 78.7 cm). Private collection.
Courtesy of Sperone Westwater, New York.

intuitive drawing
Drawing activity controlled by instinct, feelings, emotions, bodily sensations, and visceral responses, as in the case of a haptic person; a drawing based on an intuitive response to a subject.

understand and master, to some degree, media and technique, as beginning artists you do not have the means or the freedom to explore your own creativity and expression successfully.

Susan Rothenberg describes her drawing *Untitled* (Fig. 17-9) as one made "with not much thought in mind other than it would be a figure partially dissolved by light." She further explains that the process was **intuitive drawing,** that the image emerged as she moved her hand over the paper, laying down bold strokes of charcoal, building rich dark shapes, smudging and erasing the lines and tones with her hand. The direct and uninhibited creative activity that can produce a drawing of such power and visual excitement becomes possible only after the artist has absorbed the fundamentals of drawing and knows about media and techniques—all of which can be taught. From that knowledge and experience comes the freedom to respond intuitively and explore, interpret, and express oneself in unique, individual ways. While an instructor can encourage such activity by equipping students with the tools, methods, and techniques with which to act, personal expression cannot be taught. Artists and students who think too much about what they are doing often find their work lacking vitality and excitement.

Theophilus Brown tells that when he was living and painting in New York in the early 1950s, Willem de Kooning visited his studio and after looking at some of his paintings suggested that Brown was "pushing style too hard." Picking up a pencil and a piece of paper from a table, de Kooning went to the window and began to make a drawing of a tree in the park across the street. "It's very simple. Draw what you see in front of you. Don't bother about style. Just observe what you are drawing very carefully. That's the way to work." De Kooning (Pl. 5, Figs. 5-22, 10-2, 17-14) was not advocating that the purpose of drawing was to imitate, but rather that you must understand what you see before you and be able to depict it accurately before you are free to interpret it.

Similarly, responding to the surprise of a young visitor at seeing a series of traditional still-life drawings pinned up around his studio, Georges Braque, who with Picasso is credited with inventing **cubism,** explained, "I have always found it necessary in all periods of my life to go back to fact so that invention does not become stale."

Of Degas it has been said, "To put it simply, he drew so well," whereas, of a successful young artist of the 1980s a national art critic commented, "He never learned to draw, and probably never will." He went on to explain that the artist traced projected images. The criticism was not that slides were used to project images, but that the quality of the line was without interest since the act of drawing became so mechanical—nothing more than a means to an end. In the beginning, and as you are learning your own way of image investigation, whether you choose representation or abstraction, choose to draw well.

Artist or Dilettante?

Learning to draw requires a host of accomplishments: learning to see intently, learning to perceive size, shape, and space relationships, learning to manipulate and control media and technique, and finally, mastering the basic skills of drawing as a graphically visual means to achieving expression.

Once these requirements have been met, drawing successfully involves dedication and hard work while developing an attitude of professionalism—first as a student and then as a practicing artist. The professional artist holds firm to the convictions that every experience related to drawing is a valuable pursuit, and the attitude that respects both the tools and the process of drawing is paramount to the final expression. It is important, even if you are a beginning student, to decide whether you are willing to make a commitment to becoming an artist or whether you are content to be a dilettante—one who dabbles in art. As with every profession, there can be fine lines of distinction between the truly committed and the dabbler, and yet there is an easily discernible difference between a professional artist and one who only plays the role of a professional artist.

The collection of drawings in this book represents the product of intense involvement by artists whose mastery over the means of drawing allows them freedom of expression in responding to all that they experience visually, physically, emotionally, and imaginatively—both inside and outside their studios. These artists have learned that life itself provides the linear, tonal, and textural ingredients of visual expression—and that they are the trained, sensitive receptors to life's clues, the visual technicians who perform the surgical fusions of meaning and association with media. In this sense, the artist is the visual initiator of his own responses, the shepherd of the creative processes, and progenitor of all

cubism
A style of painting originated by Picasso and Braque between 1907 and 1914 that uses multiple views of an object to emphasize its three-dimensionality yet acknowledges the two-dimensional surface of the picture plane.

17-10. EDGAR DEGAS (1834–1917; French). *Two Studies of Mary Cassatt or Ellen Andree in the Louvre.* c. 1879. Charcoal and pastel on gray paper, 18 3/4 × 24 3/4″ (48 × 63 cm). Private collection.

that we see hanging in museums, galleries, artists' studios, and homes of private collectors.

A critic commented that Degas seemed "continually uncertain about proportions" when he drew the human figure. The artist agreed that the criticism described exactly what he experienced as he drew. Although recognized as one of the supreme figure artists of his age, Degas knew no easy formulas for drawing the figure. Each drawing demanded total concentration on the tilt of the head, the lift of the shoulder, the manner in which the book is held, the way in which only a portion of a figure's weight is supported by an umbrella, the silhouette of a coat (Fig. 17-10). Perception? Most certainly, and also empathy, but an empathy that was rarely tendered toward the subject in a personal sense, as in the work of Kollwitz, but tendered only to the human figure as a form to be drawn. Degas explained, "There is love, and there is work, and we have but a single heart." His life was dedicated primarily to his art. (That his art was untouched by the depth of emotion that shaped the art of Käthe Kollwitz is evident in comparing Figures 17-3 and 17-10.)

What impresses us is the number of drawings that serious artists do, many of which no one but the artist ever sees. The Bibliothèque Nationale in Paris houses, in addition to his 38 notebooks, more than 500 individual sheets of drawings by Degas. Cézanne left over 1,200 drawings; Rembrandt, 1,500. It is said that Modigliani did as many as 150 drawings in a day. Giacometti, we are told, drew constantly—drawing was a way of life for him.

When Jennifer Bartlett rented a "memorably hideous" villa in the south of France during what proved an unpleasantly cold, wet winter, it was the inner need to be creatively involved rather than external inspiration that prompted a remarkable series of drawings. After rejecting the idea of attempting to paint under such conditions, Bartlett purchased a stock of paper (each sheet approximately 20 by 26 inches, or 51 by 66 centimeters), plus a full array of wet and dry drawing media. One day she picked up a pencil and, having nothing particular to draw, made a drawing of the villa's dilapidated garden, which she could see from a full-length window in the dining room. It was to be the first of almost two hundred drawings of the garden that she did during the next fifteen months. Plate 11 is #122 from that series.

Responding Subjectively

The subjective depths of Mauricio Lasansky's *The Nazi Drawings* carry this identifiable element of human vulnerability even deeper as the artist indicates strong empathy with his subjects, capturing their character. Lasansky's aim was to portray the horror of the Nazis' treatment of prisoners in its concentration camps insofar as he, the artist, could respond to that horror and reinterpret it (Fig. 10-17, Pl. 13).

Just as some people learn to play musical instruments with technical facility, but without feeling or warmth, so, too, do some artists develop the necessary proficiency to draw well, but their drawings lack personal expression and interpretation. Once perceptive abilities have been developed and the required technical proficiency gained, one is free to begin drawing subjectively rather than objectively, although this isn't as easy as simply switching conceptual gears from the purely academic to the sublime. It takes practice to be able to recognize the shift. In fact, in the case of highly gifted drawing students, often the establishment of skillful interpretation, media handling and technical prowess leads naturally, perhaps even involuntarily, to more subjective interpretations of subject matter—sometimes even before the student becomes aware of it. When this occurs, it is important that the student not be too overtaken by the powers of subjectivity alone lest other elements of the drawing act begin to suffer. Subjective expression must be combined with sound drawing skills, developed through persistence and dedication. The ultimate expressive goal for the artist is to respond naturally and intuitively, without consciously having to decide how to respond.

Making Choices

Whistler decried "the purposeless copying" of every detail; Matisse cautioned, "What does not add to a drawing detracts from it." Selection and discrimination are an important part of expressive drawing; every line, shape, form, tone, texture, value, and color requires judgment and thought *before* the pencil is put to paper as well as throughout the process of drawing and after the work is finished.

Any creative act depends upon the making of choices. The intent of *A Guide to Drawing* is to introduce the student to a broad range of options and provide an awareness of how to exercise those options (these last two chapters deal most specifically with the artist's expansion of awareness.) Deciding what choices to make is up to the artist alone and cannot be taught. Too frequently, students plunge into drawing without taking time to question themselves about the best viewpoint, the most appropriate media and technique, or how they feel about the subject emotionally and what they want the drawing to convey. A few minutes of thought and observation before actually beginning to make marks on the paper will greatly influence the end product, but not dictate it. It is possible to begin drawing with a fully formed concept, only to discover other ideas emerging along with the images on paper. This is a natural part of the creative process, and mature artists remain ever alert and receptive to such impulses that call intuition and imagination into play.

17-11. *above, left:* WAYNE THIEBAUD (b. 1920; American). *Standing Figure.* c. 1964. Graphite pencil.
Courtesy of Allan Stone Gallery, New York.
© Wayne Thiebaud/licensed by VAGA, New York, N.Y.

17-12. *above, right:* MANUEL NERI (b. 1930 ; American). *Mary Julia.* c. 1973–1975. Dry pigments, water, charcoal, and Conté pencil on paper, 41 3/4 × 30 1/4″ (106 × 77 cm). Private collection. Courtesy of the artist.

Looking at how three contemporary American artists—Wayne Thiebaud, Manuel Neri, and Willem de Kooning—depict a centrally placed female figure in a standing frontal position allows us to see how different individual responses can be to the same subject, pose, and composition. Thiebaud's *Standing Figure* (Fig. 17-11) appears, at first glance, to be a straightforward objective drawing. Thiebaud acknowledges an "academic" approach to figure drawing—his skillful use of traditional chiaroscuro creates three-dimensional solidity; the cast shadow anchors the figure firmly to the ground plane even though the space itself remains unidentified, while strong dark accents isolate the figure from an almost pure white background. The drawing, however, is not "purely objective." He has made certain choices that make the drawing uniquely expressive. Perhaps the most interesting is the distance at which he has positioned the woman behind the picture plane. Whether a deliberate or intuitive choice, it sets up a spatial condition—a psychological distance that involves the viewer in a very different way than does Manuel Neri's drawing *Mary Julia* (Fig. 17-12). Neri's faceless woman, thrust against the picture plane, creates an almost overwhelming sense of physical and psychological proximity, the impact made all the more emphatic by the dramatic black background creating deep space behind the figure. Neri explains that he draws, "to put down ideas for sculpture—gestures, positions, proportions." It is difficult to determine whether the arms of his figure are placed behind her back, or whether, like a piece of ancient Greek sculpture, she is armless. Neri's expressionistic style permits such **ambiguity,** whereas Thiebaud's figure would appear incomplete without arms.

The physical presence of a model is so strongly felt in both drawings that the viewer can easily identify the combined activity of looking and drawing. The figure in Willem de Kooning's *Woman* (Fig. 5-22) serves only as a point of departure for his powerful, gestural calligraphy. Paul Cummings of the Whitney Museum of American Art points out that de Kooning "does not produce presentation drawings, that is, refined, complete pages made for their own sake. Most of his drawings occur in the process of evolving a vocabulary of images and strokes to be used in his paintings." Cummings added that de Kooning's "mastery of media allows him to concentrate on the act of drawing."

By constantly making drawings, artists gain an understanding and control of their means that allow complete freedom and certainty in their response to visual stimuli. While some people learn to draw with less effort than others, very few artists can claim to have been born knowing everything about art, as Gertrude Stein suggested of Picasso (which is easily refuted by looking at the various stages of Picasso's work to see the development of his compositional techniques). Even those who think they were born with unprecedented abilities and insights must learn to focus and discipline their natural talents. For others it requires a more conscious and systematic dedication to mastering basic skills that provide the means for expression. Matisse commented that he always wanted his work "to have the lightness and joyousness of a springtime which never lets anyone know the labors it has cost." The facility to draw seemingly without effort is, in effect, the reward for those labors.

More Than Technique

Mastery of different media and techniques only begins to facilitate expressive drawing. Drawing is dependent on more than flashy, accomplished technique and compositional cleverness. The artist must fuse intelligence, emotional response, instinct, and impulse with compositional skill and technical facility over time to produce a personal style, one that will continue to evolve. Choosing to adopt the style of someone else only results in self-conscious and mannered drawing that is a falsehood; attempting to be "artistic" often results in an equally self-conscious and contrived drawing.

It is particularly important, however, for students to be continually receptive to new ways of seeing and new ways of drawing in order to avoid repetition in their own work. Studying the methods of others and working as they do in pursuit of one's own eventual style, as has been suggested before, is a valid learning experience that introduces new ways of seeing, perceiving, and thinking. Young artists are cautioned that while style and technique can be imitated quite easily, imagination, intuition, emotions, attitudes, and accumulated knowledge and experience cannot, and it is precisely from those intangible and elusive elements that individual style and expression are born. Style is more than talent, skill, and sleight of hand; it evolves from an individual's own being. Style is not dependent on complete originality, but upon total individuality, manifested in a unique image that reveals a subject as it is perceived by one artist alone. As Picasso explained, he either chose or invented a style appropriate to what he wanted to express. The diversity

ambiguity
A state of visual uncertainty created by intentionally ignoring or distorting accepted compositional methods; the unconventional visual effects that result from the apparently purposeful attempt to create a sense of imbalance.

17-13. *above, left:* EUGÈNE DELACROIX (1798–1863; French). *Arab Dancer.* c. 1832. Pen and ink, 7 1/2 × 6" (19 × 15 cm). Museum Boymans-van Beuningen, Rotterdam.

17-14. *above, right:* WILLEM DE KOONING (1904–1997; Dutch-American). *Man.* c. 1974. Charcoal and traces of oil paint on paper mounted on canvas, 4' 3 3/4" × 3' 5 1/2" (1.31 × 1.05 m).

metaphor
In a work of art, a concept, symbol, or motif that carries an implied comparison or is used in place of some other idea in order to draw heightened attention to the visual statement for the purpose of enhancing its meaning.

of his styles is suggested, at least in part, by the variety of his drawings selected for this edition of *A Guide To Drawing.*

A comparison of Eugène Delacriox's *Arab Dancer* (Fig. 17-13) and Willem de Kooning's *Man* (Fig. 17-14) reveals an almost identical handling of line—Delacroix's dancer an image of lightness, fluidity, and grace; de Kooning's man clumsy, his movements uncontrolled. Philip Guston's *Ink Drawing* (Fig. 1-9) shares the same character of line without any apparent reference to recognizable subject matter.

Although Van Gogh's letters to his brother Theo document the struggle he endured in learning to draw, his early pieces have an intensity of expression in spite of, or perhaps because of, their seeming awkwardness and lack of facility. Yet, because of their unprecedented and strangely unique expressive nature, they have lasted as milestones of an evolving personal style.

Van Gogh approached all subjects—landscapes, still lifes, figures—with equal fervor, and with a sense of total identification. In a drawing dating from his early dark Dutch period, Van Gogh describes the stark and barren *Winter Garden at Neunen* (Fig. 17-15) in an essentially literal way, in sharp visual contrast to the frenzied convolutions of *Grove of Cypresses* (Fig. 17-16). The unique and articulate characteristics present in these two drawings are pure invention—the expression of his loneliness and personal torment.

Visual Metaphor

A powerfully expressive device employed by artists in all disciplines is the use of **metaphor,** which is an implied comparison of one subject with another. As applied to the visual realm, an artist may depict a particular subject that substitutes for, or symbolizes, another subject. For example, in 1504 Leonardo da Vinci received a commission to paint a large mural in the council chamber of the Palazza della Signoria. He chose the famous Florentine Battle of Anghiari as his subject, for which he produced a series of preliminary drawings. In one of the drawings from that series, a highly expressive work in red chalk entitled *A Rearing Horse* (Fig. 17-17), Leonardo's ability to use metaphorical meanings that launch out in many directions is clearly evident. Leonardo chose to use the powerful gesture of the horse tossing its head as a metaphor for the spirit of battle. Notice how the physical characteristics of the drawing change from the highly descriptive musculature of the horse's hindquarters to the eventual animation and writhing gestures of the tossing head. Leonardo exhibits his stellar mastery over live anatomical forms so beautifully that one can almost hear the sounds of the battlefield.

In Greg Murr's graphite and pastel drawing entitled *Predicament* (Fig. 17-18), the artist has skillfully chosen dry media with expressive powers of both subtlety and density, high contrast, and three-dimensionality. The dogs appear to be suspended from their vertical leashes in midair like puppets controlled by a puppeteer who places them on an accompanying receptive stage or surface—in this case, that of white wove paper. From the drawing's poignancy and the visual elements of density, contrast, and weight, we glean the profound impact of Murr's subjective handling of the four dogs in a public park, unfamiliar to each other, suddenly meeting their fellow canines for the first time—being unexpectedly thrust together as their owners casually traverse each other's routine walk paths. It is without warning that the dogs find themselves suddenly in each other's territory, both invading and invaded—hence, the title.

17-15. *above, left:* VINCENT VAN GOGH (1853–1890; Dutch-French). *Winter Garden at Neunen.* Pen and brown ink with white heightening, 20 1/4 × 15″ (51.5 × 38.1 cm).
Museum of Fine Arts, Budapest.

17-16. *above, right:* VINCENT VAN GOGH (1853–1890; Dutch-French). *Grove of Cypresses.* c. 1889. Reed pen and ink over graphite pencil, 24 5/8 × 18 1/4″ (62.6 × 46.4 cm).
© The Art Institute of Chicago.

17-17. *above, left:* LEONARDO DA VINCI (1452–1519; Italian). *A Rearing Horse, Study for "The Battle of Anghiari."* c. 1504. Red chalk, 6 × 5 9/16″ (15.3 ″ 14.2 cm). Royal Library, Windsor Castle, London.

17-18. *above, right:* GREG MURR (b. 1971; American). *Predicament.* c. 1999. Graphite and pastel on paper, 22 × 23 7/8″ (55.9 × 60.8 cm). Wake Forest University Permanent Collection. Courtesy of the artist.

cacophony
A sudden, unexpected, often disharmonious visual aspect of a composition that arouses the viewer's immediate attention; an obvious and interestingly noticeable visual disharmony used in a positive way to strengthen or enhance a visual statement.

imagination
In art, the act or ability to envision fictitious, mental images that are present in the mind's eye but not in actual life; also, the artistic power to create images of a fanciful nature as metaphors for unrealized experiences that may, however, have meaning and association in real or actual life.

What a powerful human metaphor is expressed here in the feelings of surprise, uncertainty, curiosity, fear, shyness, and the territorial need for establishing instant domination. As we decipher the artist's composition, the individual position and distinctive body language of each dog conveys a uniquely different personality associated with a different set of visual sensations that respond to each other in completely different ways. In Murr's own affirmation of the metaphor, he states, "[T]here is an awkward beauty in our condition, a precariousness about the way we negotiate our environment and the means by which we interact with each other." Murr's drawing is an expressive work, a powerful comparison and exchange of meaning and association, a metaphor for the initial awkward **cacophony** of the unexpected—yet forced—interaction.

Imagination and Expression

Van Gogh stated that he never drew *from* **imagination,** but he always drew *with* imagination. Just as the external world provided the basis for Van Gogh's imaginative interpretations through his own experience and emotional responses, so, too, can the art elements—line, tone, texture, pattern—stimulate imaginative activity. Invention, improvisation, and imagination assume a greater role in Joan Miró's *Self-Portrait* (Fig. 17-19) than does observation. Although depicting himself with serious demeanor, Miró engages in imaginative play as a legitimate artistic expression. Any familiar shape or object can provide the subject for visual improvisation in the same way that a simple melodic theme can initiate elaborate musical invention.

Imagination and expression are manifested not only in *how* and *what* one draws, but also in *what* one draws. Artists have been encouraged to explore new uses and combinations of materials by the great expansion of media resulting from modern technological developments. Everything challenges artists' inventive powers if they allow technology to play a role in their creative undertakings. However, the abundance of new materials and the inventive attitude of techniques so characteristic

17-19. JOAN MIRÓ (1893–1986; Spanish). *Self-Portrait.* c. 1938. Graphite pencil on canvas, 4′ 9 1/2″ × 3′ 2 1/4″ (1.46 × .97 m).
The Museum of Modern Art, New York.

of today is not an unmixed blessing. An undue concern with invention, with new materials and techniques, can distract one from more profound visual statements. Often when a technological process displaces the physical act of creation, it leaves a sterile, expressively cold, or even expressionless result in its wake. It is easy to become enamored of superficial surface qualities of slickness without giving thought to deeper levels of interpretation and meaning that constitute the major significance of works of art. It is also possible to flit from one fascinating material to the next without ever fully exploring the potential of any one. A period of exploration and experimentation is necessary, however, for every artist, because only by such a process does one find the materials best suited to one's individuality and temperament.

In Derek Besant's relief-intaglio print *All Around Us Birds Had Fallen Silent* (Fig. 17-20), a metaphor for a storm, we see a computer-generated image born of technology as Besant utilized the cutting precision of a laser surgical arm (the same computerized laser apparatus used in eye surgery) to cut the photo-image into the mipolan (linoleum) surface. Besant, a Canadian artist, wanted to combine technology with

17-20. DEREK BESANT (b. 1950; Canadian). *All Around Us Birds Had Fallen Silent.* c. 1997. Relief-intaglio print, 14 7/8 × 29 1/4″ (37.8 × 74.3 cm). Wake Forest University Permanent Collection. Courtesy of the artist.

traditional tools to both draw and incise the image onto the linoleum plate. In the print we see the elements of artistic imagination, invention, mode of expression, and metaphorical references to the effects of the storm: young woman fearfully clutching the blanket as she crouches beside the bed; a stricken bird, its wing flapping against the window in an effort to find shelter—all of which form a complete visual statement in Besant's original print.

Mastery of Craft

Imagination and invention are of little value to artists if they have not mastered their craft sufficiently to provide visual realization for their concepts. If Picasso was not born knowing how to draw, he acquired the requisite technical skills early in life that allowed him to give form to all the inventions of his fertile imagination.

Chapters 17 and 18 reiterate, as was stated in Chapter 1, that expressive drawing requires more than an accurate rendering of form and skillful manipulation of media and technique. There are, unfortunately, no foolproof formulas or successful mechanical approaches to drawing with expression, nor are there predetermined standards by which to judge when a drawing is finished other than to consider it complete when it conveys exactly what was intended and when it can no longer be developed for the better. Hans Hoffman, one of the abstract expressionist painters, offered this metaphor that references the "act of parenting" when he said, "I know a work is finished when it doesn't need me anymore."

In the creative act, the artist must enact the beginning of the process and call a halt when the appropriate clues reveal it is completed. This is a huge responsibility. You must also decide what media and methods work best for you, and what approach is the most expressive according to what you want to convey.

The degree of detachment necessary in determining whether a drawing is successful is difficult to maintain while engaged in the process of drawing. It calls for the artist, in effect, to become another person in order to judge whether what was intended has actually been accomplished, and to decide whether technique and composition fully support and communicate the idea. The most difficult but most important question to ask is the by-now-familiar, "Would the drawing be interesting if it had been done by someone else?" Failing an honest positive answer, the artist should be willing to redo the drawing. Complacency contributes very little to expressive drawing—in fact, it defeats it. Starting a drawing over can produce new interests along the way, creating the potential for the outcome to be better, richer, and even more expressive than the first attempt.

Self-portraits offer endless possibilities for exploring various avenues leading to expressive drawing. Lacking the availability of other subject matter, one has only to look into a mirror. Fantin-Latour found in himself "a model who was always ready, offering all the advantages; he comes on time, he does what you tell him, and you already know him before you start to draw him." As a student, after he returned from copying at the Louvre, Fantin would sit before a mirror and draw self-portraits from five until eight in the evening. Figure 17-21 provides an example of that concentrated activity. Fantin favored black chalk or charcoal for building the dense rich black tones that contribute significantly to the dramatic and expressive impact of his studies. He experimented with the placement of the source of light for heightened theatricality. Positioned directly overhead, the lamp creates deep pools of blackness from which his eyes burn with hypnotic intensity.

William Beckman's *Self-Portrait* (Fig. 17-22), drawn under a less harsh overhead light and with softer modeling, appears to project from the picture plane like a piece of low relief sculpture. The head and bust seem firm, yet not fully three-dimensional because of the flattening effect of the emphatic dark outline. The strict frontality and calculated symmetry of the pose are broken only by the irregular shape of the hair and points of the shirt collar. The overall effect is both compelling and disquieting.

17-21. *above, left:* HENRI FANTIN-LATOUR (1836–1904; French). *Self-Portrait.* c. 1854–1856. Black chalk and stumping, 11 3/4 × 9 1/2" (30 × 24 cm). Detroit Institute of Arts.

17-22. *above, right:* WILLIAM BECKMAN (b. 1942; American). *Self-Portrait.* c. 1983. Charcoal on paper, 29 1/8 × 24 3/4" (74 × 62 cm). Courtesy Frumkin/Adams Gallery, New York.

17-23. M. C. ESCHER (1898–1972; Dutch). *Self-Portrait in Shaving Mirror.* c. 1943. "Scratch" drawing, brown lithographic crayon, 9 3/4 × 10 1/16" (24.9 × 25.6 cm).
Haags Gemeentemuseum, the Hague.

While artists rarely acknowledge the mirror in their self-portraits, viewers become conscious of the presence of an unseen mirror in William A. Berry's *Self-Portrait With Lamp* (Pl. 6), for example, because he has depicted the act of looking as part of the process of drawing. In contrast, M. C. Escher (Fig. 17-23) and Sigmund Abeles (Fig. 17-24) each chose to include the mirror itself in the drawing. The circular shape of Escher's shaving mirror and highlights on its frame are repeated not only in the irises of his eyes, but also in the eyelids and thin folds between the eyelids and eyebrows. Escher has successfully created the illusion, purely through inventive drawing, that his nose is pressed against the mirror surface. While artists often have built their compositions around models positioned in front of mirrors (Figs.1-2, 1-3, 8-22). Abeles depicts himself standing on a seemingly endless mirror. The drawing offers a curious juxtaposition between what is above the mirror (below in the drawing) and what is below or reflected (above in the drawing). The foreshortening is wonderfully strange and ambiguous—the head appears to grow out of his waist and he seems to be wearing his shoes upside down. We see no arms, which adds to the ambiguity of the foreshortening. The artist appears to be extremely tall, with his arms blocked from view by his decidedly wider hips, which are closer to the viewer than the shoulders.

While most people by nature are inclined to repeat what they can do successfully, a willingness to experiment leads to development of a stronger style and artistic growth in general. That does not mean that every drawing must be different; it merely suggests that you should avoid prolonged repetition of only those things that you are comfortable doing. In your quest for creative growth, remember that neither imagination nor style demands complete originality. When pursued for its own sake, originality, as we have seen, need be nothing more than your own unique interpretation and expression of seeing, perceiving, and feeling.

In Jim Dine's *Nine Self-Portraits with a Very Long Beard* (Fig. 17-25),

the artist invites us to view his tremendous facility for creating variations

17-24. SIGMUND ABELES (b. 1934; American). *Self-Portrait on Mirror.* c. 1970. Charcoal, 28 1/2 × 22 1/2" (72.4 × 57.2 cm). Collection of Dr. and Mrs. Joseph B. Barron.
Courtesy of the artist.

in the handling of a single drawing medium, graphite, with the accompaniment of an eraser to produce elaborately undulating tonal expressions from portrait to portrait. Notice the repetition, yet the differing positions on the paper of each head as a separate visual adventure. (We can well imagine how monotonous the series of drawings would be were each head in exactly the same position on each sheet of paper.) Notice how much variety there is in the nine beautiful reinterpretations of the artist's face and beard. The nine individual personalities conveyed seem estranged from one another, and yet there is no doubt that they are all the same face.

Expanding Expressive Awareness

It is not uncommon to hear students say, "All I want to do is draw" (or etch or paint or sculpt or throw pots). If one chooses to be an artist, commitment is important, even imperative, and commitment is reflected in the eagerness, willingness, and persistence to do more than just settle for the easiest and most obvious solution to a project.

At the same time, however, art students are responsible for far more than just mastering the craft of drawing (or etching, painting, and so on). They must be willing to expand their awareness of other areas

17-25. JIM DINE (b. 1935; American). *Nine Self-Portraits with a Very Long Beard.* c. 1977. Graphite and erasers on paper, each of nine sheets 30 × 22" (762 × 559 mm). Promised gift of the artist to the National Gallery of Art, Washington, D.C.

of learning and experiences beyond the studio environment in order to stimulate creative growth in their choice of and approach to different subject matter. Artists from all walks of life and different periods in history, as evidenced by this text on drawing, are some of the greatest "problem solvers" in the world. The process of making art has taken them on an expressive journey of discovering, investigating, finding solutions, solving visual dilemmas, and speaking a visual language that is cogent, succinct, descriptive, meaningful, and profoundly expressive of the human heart and mind.

The noted science fiction writer/author Ray Bradbury, when asked, said that he had never experienced "writer's block," because he had spent his life "feeding the muse." Looking, seeing, reading, and being aware of and sensitive to life are essential to all creative people; they are as necessary to an artist as learning to draw.

In the next and final chapter of this book, we will look even more closely at possibilities of expressive drawing by considering the complexities of joining together different drawing media.

Expressive Mixed Media 18

*Exploration in breadth combined with
concentration in depth requires the
particular discipline which characterizes the
artist: an inner discipline in which deep
satisfactions and dynamic dissatisfactions
alternate to stimulate continual growth.
Through such a discipline the art student
discovers and reveals himself and thereby
establishes the basis for becoming an artist.*

—Daniel Mendelowitz

At the beginning of every semester, the author of this revised text asks his students these questions: "Are your experiences silent? Do your lives have texture? Does your expression have form?"

There is a density and an inevitable multiplicity in life. In fact, in the broadest sense, our environments are laden with mixed media and myriad influences that teach and form us from childhood. There are multiple reasons for asking these questions. In answering them students learn to think more deeply about their creative potential and to recognize the importance of all our senses and their responses to stimuli in our daily lives. The sights, sounds, smells, tastes, and textures, along with all the other forms of expression in our environments that provoke our emotional responses, are the seeds of new expression awaiting the fertile soils of the student/artist's will to create. Wayne Thiebaud has said, "For the past 45 years I have been teaching drawing and painting and introducing students to the deep pleasure of learning how to draw."

This chapter on mixed media is an appropriate way to end this text, and it is only fitting that as students read it, they reflect on and review the drawings illustrated in the former chapters, as many of them are the results of more than just a single search in a single medium. Most, in fact, are mixed-media works done on a variety of different surfaces at a variety of different times in art history, and the one thing they have in common is the expression of the human heart. The artists who created these many wonderful drawings listened to their experiences, they felt deeply the textures of their lives, and they recognized the forms of their own expression.

341

Landscape of Mixed Media

When we consider the visual arena of the natural world, we readily see the effects of multiple complexities. As the artist sees, perceives, and extracts the essences of that world, he or she translates those complexities into visual expression by a variety of creative means. Often the complexity of subject engenders complexity of creative means.

The phrase *mixed media* implies far more than just the coming together of two or more materials on a multivaried surface. It also suggests the use of varied methods to create a rich and complex drawing that cannot be produced from a single medium on a common surface. Since the beginning of time artists have identified certain media as having the capabilities to produce certain desired effects. From the most primitive tools to the most complex, artists have specified the materials and techniques that will best fulfill their artistic goals.

Applying Sight Skills   The underlying theme of this text is learning how to see more intently and describe through reinvention as the eyes direct the hand. Drawing is about extracting the visual vocabulary found in the simplest objects as well as in the most complex life forms. We can enhance this vocabulary through the use of mixed media.

For the most part, seeing has been addressed in terms of scrutinizing the subjects we are drawing. Now it's time to apply the same degree of passionate scrutiny to the surfaces upon which we draw. Applying our sight skills to our drawings is the follow-up exercise and has already been put into practice through the added feature of the critiques at the end of the appropriate project assignments in this revised edition. When our sight skills approach the level of our technical facility with drawing media, our images carry more expression.

Combining Materials   The intrigue of mixed media begins with the blending of materials and technical methods of all kinds as inspiring processes in themselves. The studio, whether indoors or outdoors, is the artists' proving ground for converting their unrealized yearnings into tangible expression. Often the artist is inspired by the environment itself, or the environment may evoke a particular response not directly related to the environment but to another thought or feeling. Critic Joshua C. Taylor eloquently describes artistic inspiration in writing about layered complexities in the work of Robert Rauschenberg: "The provocation of unsettling alertness . . . to sense, to association, to memories and the flexibility of the mind . . . , renders the inert alive, and gives voice to what might otherwise stay mute."

Along with the technical explanations and projects in this chapter that will engage the student with a mixed media focus, it is also the intent to provide technical and conceptual unity to concepts discussed in previous chapters so that the student can approach mixed media both analytically and critically and learn the skills of visually deciphering his or her own avenues of creative expression in a more than fundamental way. Seeing and responding, orchestrating and refining, are an artist's most provocative activities, and will be the prescribed activities as well for studio classroom assignments in mixed media expression.

Expressionism and Media Considerations

As has been discussed through this text, drawing is about selecting the right tool and bringing it together with the right subject, then reinventing that subject onto a specifically chosen surface. Artists have discovered that there can be a powerfully expressive connection between the choice of material and the choice of subject; the choice of material can be critical to the success of an idea. Often, the desire to create a specific thing leads us to select a material or medium that seems best suited to the statement we desire to make. The attributes of line, tone, texture, color, shape, and the activation of the elements in space are the fundamental tools with which any artist attempts to give form to his inspiration. Drawing, being the most direct of all visual art disciplines, is often where we start.

The Specificity of Materials   The longing to make a graphic mark by dragging a tool across a receptive surface has been with us since the beginning of time. When we expand that effort by adding other materials, we put into play more elements of potential expression. In the hands of a master artist, any tool in combination with a viable surface can become powerfully expressive. Even humble materials can produce an emotionally charged drawing, as evidenced in the work of Mauricio Lasansky (Figs. 18-1, 10-17, Pl. 13), leading us to the conclusion that our expression itself is an irrepressible force. In these mixed media works, Lasansky chose graphite pencils, red earth pigments, and turpentine washes for his repertoire. In his own words, "I tried to keep not only the vision of The Nazi Drawings simple and direct but also the materials I used in making them. I wanted them to be done with a tool used by everyone everywhere. From the cradle to the grave, meaning the pencil. I felt if I could use a tool like that, this would keep me away from the temptations that would arise from the virtuosity that a more sophisticated medium would demand."

The Nazi Drawings delve deeply into the human consciousness exposing the guilt of the religious community in the aftermath of the Nazis' slaughter. Lasansky says of drawing 23 (Fig. 18-1),

> And so in the twenty-third drawing they reappear: the bishop with the horror slowly disappearing from his face and giving way to a guilt-evaporating incredulity, and the infant corpse held shield-like against his chest. The dead infant with a skull-helmet covering its features has clearly become identical with the Christ figure it had been merging with in the previous drawing. The falcons have returned to perch symmetrically, unmenacingly, at four corners on the two crossbars. The bishop's cope is a collage made of pages out of Exodus, the same pages that line his mitre.

Artist as Orchestrator   When a single medium is not enough to provide the variety of expression the artist seeks, he or she chooses additional tools that will create the intended effect. As an orchestrator, the artist strives for a harmonious balance among all the media applied to the surface, the ultimate challenge being to keep everything in play while being aware that changing any element, even in a minor way, will alter the total effects in either a positive or negative way.

In Robert Stackhouse's *Inside a Passage Structure* (Fig. 18-2, Pl. 18), we see a careful blending of wet and dry media on an expansive surface

18-1. *above, left:* MAURICIO LASANSKY (b. 1914; Argentinian). *Nazi Drawing #23.* Graphite pencil, red earth pigments, and turpentine wash with collage. 67 × 46". The University of Iowa Museum of Art. (On long-term loan to the Cedar Rapids Art Museum, Cedar Rapids, Iowa.)

18-2. *above, right:* ROBERT STACKHOUSE (b. 1942; American). *Inside a Passage Structure.* c. 1986. Watercolor, charcoal, and graphite on paper. 89 1/2 × 120". The Arkansas Arts Center Foundation Collection.

of nearly symmetrically descriptive forms that take us not only into the deep space, but into the internal spaces of the drawing as we find our eyes wandering among the vertical beams to the left and right of the central passageway. This is an extremely powerful illusion of three-dimensionality on a large two-dimensional surface. Stackhouse has done this so convincingly that we feel as though we could simply walk into the space, perhaps even get lost in its depths.

Media of Previous Centuries

By comparison with the wide variety of artist supplies available today, the tools and materials available to the Renaissance artist were very limited. Between the fourteenth and sixteenth centuries, the Renaissance masters produced highly expressive works by ingeniously exploiting the few tools they had to reach immeasurable heights of creativity. We see this in Raphael's beautifully depicted red chalk drawing *Two Riders* (Fig. 18-3), in which the artist uses a single medium so skillfully that nothing is visually lacking. Albrecht Dürer's *An Oriental Ruler on a Throne* (Fig. 18-4), done in pen and ink, displays every kind of linear hatching, cross-hatching, and cross-contour hatching described in this book. The media are simple, and yet the drawing lacks nothing. One could easily assess that from Durer's pen flowed the inks of an unprecedented creative mystery.

Probably the first *dry* mixed-media drawing was one in which the artist used white chalk over charcoal to create the illusion of highlights. An example of this is Peter Paul Rubens's *Study for the Figure of Christ on the Cross* (Fig. 18-5). Notice the skilled attention paid to anatomy and the adroit placement of the figure within the picture plane.

Economy of Mark   What we have been discussing in the works of these three artists is an "efficiency of means"— an economy of mark making so descriptive and expressive that few if any works since have surpassed their visual impact. When this efficiency is transferred to more complex compositional structures, the expressive potential magnifies.

Often artists who attempt to magnify expression simply by using multiple materials fail because they lack the well-orchestrated harmony that must necessarily exist between the parts of the whole. Thus we can see that the effectiveness of a mixed-media work is directly proportional to the harmony of its visual elements. Look again at Raphael, Dürer, and Rubens. These works have continued to hold our attention for several centuries because of their inherent beauty and association to the lives and times of the artists who created them. They also inspire us to further exploration of the multimedia possibilities at our disposal.

Preliminary Mark as Gesture   Another example of the use of dry mixed media is Raphael's *Combat of Nude Men* (Fig. 18-6), where we see an image done in red chalk over preliminary stylus work. Note the attention given to the anatomical structure of the human body and the gestural movements of the figures involved in battle. There was a significant moment when Raphael decided to enhance the preliminary stylus work with red chalk—a creative decision that has stood the test of time.

The preliminary marks that an artist lays down are often the determinants of the direction a work will take. Therefore, it is vitally important that initial drawing on a surface to which other materials will later be added be made with a distinct sense of purpose and sureness.

Experimentation

Choosing the right materials and combinations of materials is based largely on artists' existing knowledge about the characteristics of different media. However, in incorporating these multiple elements into a

18-3. *above, left:* RAPHAEL (1483–1520; Italian). *Two Riders.* Red chalk. 11 1/4 × 8″ (28.6 × 20.3 cm). Albertina Museum, Vienna.

18-4. *above, right:* ALBRECHT DÜRER (1471–1528; German). *An Oriental Ruler on a Throne.* Pen and black ink. 11 7/8 × 7 5/8″ (30.2 × 19.3 cm). National Gallery of Art, Washington D.C.

18-5. *above, left:* PETER PAUL RUBENS (1577–1640; Flemish). *Study for the Figure of Christ on the Cross.* Charcoal heightened by white. 20 1/4 × 15 1/2″ (51.4 × 39.4 cm).
The British Museum, London.

18-6. *above, right:* RAPHAEL (1483–1520; Italian). *Combat of Nude Men.* Red chalk over preliminary stylus work. 14 7/8 × 11 1/8″ (37.7 × 28.3 cm).
Ashmolean Museum, Oxford.

drawing there is always a danger of overdoing—a costly error that sends many potentially successful works of art to the incinerator. To avoid this outcome, it is useful to experiment—to see what visual effects may occur when certain elements are brought together on the working surface without previous knowledge of what the results will be—and then to direct those elements into a well-composed drawing.

The Working Process   It is easy to ebb and flow with the working processes, particularly when multiple elements are interacting in such an interesting way, not noticing whether the work itself is straying away from technical virtuosity, resulting in nothing more than an experimental exercise that failed. On the other hand, there is always something to be learned from a failure—this is indeed part of the process of learning. One must be thoughtfully selective in the choice of tools and envision how they will respond to each other. Then proceed with the process of investigating and experimenting to see how they react with each other and what kinds of visual effects are derived from the marriage of materials you've selected.

Material's Relationship to Material   The artist using multiple elements on the same surface must continually consider whether the addition of a single mark, area of tone or texture, or even an entire surface change enhances the whole expression or detracts from it. The variety of media and the wide-ranging expression of linear, tonal, textural, and spatial circumstances beckon the artistic mind into action, but it is important to maintain an objective view about what is taking place on the working surface. The artistic act is one of deep exploration, and what the artist is after is that unfettered, **recondite** state of poignant expression that upon seeing it for the first time, startles even the artist himself.

But it is easy for artists to get lost in the process of creating and lose sight of what they are after. They often ask one another the question, Do you get what you want, or do you want what you get? For artists to achieve precisely what they are after requires striking a balance between yielding to the demands of particular media and remaining true to their objectives.

Project 18.1

Let's begin with something that is relatively simple, yet different from all previous projects in this book. Select a strong white paper of moderate tooth and of medium size. Using red and black Conté crayon, draw a still life, using black to establish the contours of the objects within the composition. Remember to incorporate as much expression as possible in the form of line variation by using varying amounts of pressure, creating a line that swells and tapers. Then use the red Conté crayon to further define the objects by drawing cross-contour lines describing the "turn of surface" of the individual forms in the still life. Also in red, develop the drawing still further by drawing hatched and cross-hatched lines where appropriate to further define the individual forms.

Take a blending stump and blend the red with the black Conté crayon. This mixing of the red and black particles will occur for the most part near the contour edges of the forms.

Critique (Project 18.1) The most important thing to assess is the distinctive roles that the red and black Conté crayons play in the drawing. They are individual media but of the same material, and they speak visually with different expressive voices in the composition. Previous projects have also involved the use of different media, but perhaps this is the first time you've considered the distinct differences of expression between two different-looking materials because of the red and black— even though they are the same material and respond in very much the same way.

Do the effects of the different crayons support each other in the drawing? Is the dominant role of one material apparent? Do you have a sense that the two need each other in the drawing? What if the red and black were reversed? How would this change the look of the individual objects as well as the entire composition?

In the final analysis, did you achieve what you wanted in the drawing?

Strengths of Single Tools

There are not only multitudes of tools available to artists, but also multiple variations of each tool. The twenty different grades of graphite alone as delineated in Chapter 10, Dry Media, give the artist greater expressive potential with a single medium than ever before. Kent Bellows and John Wickenberg exemplify this "purist" involvement in their drawings *Portrait of Rachel* (Fig. 18-7), and *MIA (Dead Bird)* (Fig. 18-8). Drawing exclusively in graphite, these two artists show us how one can achieve great expressive heights with a simple, inexpensive, and commonly used tool. Graphite as a single medium remains one of the most popularly used tools in drawing, and one is amazed at how different graphite drawings can look because of the wide range of draftsmanship skill of the different artists represented in this book (Figs. 5-14, 6-10, 10-14, 10-18, 12-4, 12-8, 13-18, 13-19, 18-7, 18-8, 18-9, 18-16). However, graphite is also applicable as a mixed-media component with both wet and dry drawing materials, and one often finds it in combination with a host of other mark-making tools. Richard Ziemann's use of brush and black ink

recondite
A term describing the quality of being indescribably strange and curious without means of explanation or evidence of reason. As applied to art, it describes a profound visual situation the comprehension of which is beyond the grasp of the ordinary mind.

18-7. *above, left:* KENT BELLOWS (b. 1949; American). *Portrait of Rachel.* c. 1985. Graphite with smudging and touches of erasing on ivory wove paper. 19 × 17″ (483 × 432 mm).
The Jalane and Richard Davidson Collection.
© The Art Institute of Chicago.

18-8. *above, right:* JOHN WICKENBERG (b. 1944; American). *MIA (Dead Bird).* c. 1985. Graphite on cream wove paper, 16 1/2 × 26″ (419 × 660 mm).
The Jalane and Richard Davidson Collection.
© The Art Institute of Chicago.

18-9. *right:* GREGORY PAQUETTE (b. 1947; American). *Rabbits (Flayed).* c.1982. Graphite and charcoal with smudging and erasing on ivory wove paper. 36 1/2 × 35 1/4″ (927 × 895 mm).
The Jalane and Richard Davidson Collection.
© The Art Institute of Chicago.

over graphite (Fig. 13-13) shows us an example of using graphite with a wet medium; in Gregory Paquette's *Rabbits (Flayed)* (Fig. 18-9) it is used with another dry medium, charcoal.

Surface

Drawing tools are not the only consideration in mixed media—the variety of different receptive surfaces for the media is important as well. Artists today have the luxury of not only an extensive array of drawing media but also a wide variety of surfaces. The ways in which particular surfaces absorbed drawing media have concerned artists for centuries. We may speculate that even the prehistoric artist instinctively chose the most desired portion of a rock wall's surface for the necessary picture plane that was to eventually become a completely developed composition (Fig. 18-10).

Project 18.2

Combine graphite line with pen and black ink line in the same drawing of a still life. Begin with graphite and draw until you have a sense of wanting to change media. Then switch to the pen and black ink and continue drawing. Complete the contour portions of the drawing with a relatively high level of finish, including a generous amount of descriptive line hatching, again using the medium you feel directed to use—either graphite or pen and black ink. It is important that you begin to develop an instinct about what is appropriate to use for different aspects of a drawing. It is also important to be as experimental as possible with media so as to develop a sense of their interacting capabilities and resulting visual effects. Allow the ink to completely dry and go back into the drawing with a variety of sepia (brown) wash tones and brush, covering over with wash the areas of darker passages as described by the line hatching. Allow the lighter washes to overlap the hatching lines onto the surfaces of some of the still-life objects. Try to develop a painterly sense of the wet media applications, allowing the brush strokes to leave their expressive marks.

When the drawing is dry, assess the lighter areas in particular—the lightest wash areas and the open paper surface. (There should still be portions of the white paper showing in the composition.) Using white Conté crayon or white chalk, emphasize certain linear aspects of the still life, allowing the composition to become more abstracted as you draw in white. Notice how even through applications of graphite, pen and ink, and ink wash, the tooth of the paper still takes on the white Conté crayon or chalk extremely well. Ink on paper, when dry, does not resist further applications of either wet or dry drawing materials.

Repeat this exercise several more times drawing other forms—the figure, the landscape, even a self-portrait using a mirror. The more familiarity you have with different media, the more trustworthy your instincts will become.

Critique (Project 18.2) How do the different media act together to form the wholeness of expression? How would the drawing change if any single medium were removed? Are you able to ascertain the proportional effects of each medium? Do they seem well proportioned? Would you increase or decrease the use of any of the media? What might happen if you reversed the order of application in the next drawings? Is there a logistical reason for the order of application? How might the expressionism change by altering the application process in any way?

18-11. *above, left:* HENRY MOORE (1898–1986; English). *Four Grey Sleepers.* c. 1941. Pencil, white wax crayon, watercolor wash, crayon, pen and black ink. 16 5/8 × 19 3/4″ (42.5 × 50.2 cm). City Art Gallery, Wakefield. Photo courtesy of the Henry Moore Foundation.

18-12. *above, right:* HENRY MOORE (1898–1986; English). *Pink and Green Sleepers.* Pencil, white wax crayon, watercolor wash, crayon, pen and black ink. 15 × 22″ (38.1 × 55.9 cm). The Tate Gallery, London. Photo courtesy of the Henry Moore Foundation.

mixed-media drawing
A drawing created by the interaction of a few or many different drawing materials that come to rest on a surface or on multiple variations of a surface. The artist selects different materials in order to enhance a visual statement and create visually interesting surface effects that cannot be produced by a single medium.

Invention of Surface As one plans to begin a **mixed-media drawing** of some complexity, such as Henry Moore's *Four Grey Sleepers* (Fig. 18-11) (created with graphite pencil, white wax crayon, watercolor wash, colored crayon, and pen and black ink), what approach should be taken? How do you determine where to start? How do you achieve the greatest degree of expression from the media you select? A look at another of Henry Moore's works (Fig. 18-12) affirms that the artist simply moves upon instinct with deliberate clarity and skill of media usage so that the visual statement is never weakened or jeopardized. In Moore's *Pink and Green Sleepers,* we see clearly the efficiency of drawing that allows every medium to be expressive. Be aware that there is a distinct difference between "surface richness" and "surface buildup"; the latter usually results when too much material is worked on the surface and the artist is out of control with the media. In Figures 18-11 and 18-12, notice the unique tactile surface qualities of each of the figurative forms existing in space, and how identifiably different they are from the immediate forms surrounding them. This is a truly brilliant work—a mixed-media masterpiece—a testament to what happens when a master artist speaks his language with multiple materials.

Project 18.3

Select a sheet of fairly heavy, absorbent drawing paper approximately 9 by 12 inches. Lay out your media: grease crayons (#1 litho crayons will do nicely), colored wax crayons (including white), graphite pencil, colored pencils, charcoal, pen and black ink, and sepia ink wash. Both the grease and wax crayons will repel the water-soluble inks, and if the crayons are applied to the paper first, the later applications of ink washes will not be absorbed in those areas.

Begin a drawing from a subject of your choice by laying out the forms in graphite. (The graphite can be thought of as a method of laying down preliminary lines; however, think of it as an integral part of this drawing.) Then follow the graphite with charcoal, emphasizing important contour lines by making them darker. Apply hatched lines inside several selected forms with the white wax crayon, knowing that these lines will remain white (having sealed the paper with the wax content of the crayon). You might decide to use the white crayon in the portions of the drawing you intend to remain the lightest. In a painterly and descriptive way, apply several different sepia wash tones to the drawing in the areas intended for tone, allowing the brush strokes to be expressive and indicative of the wet media process. Notice how the wash tones pull away from the wax crayon lines. Notice also that in areas where the crayon seems porous by not completely covering the paper, the wash tones penetrate the openings in the crayon line, forming speckled effects of tone on the paper surface.

When the wash tones are dry, work back into the drawing, emphasizing form and the structural elements of the composition with pen and black ink and black grease or litho crayon to achieve a wide variety of linear blacks. Finish by adding conservative touches of color with the colored crayons or colored pencils.

Take your time and do several of these drawings in order to get acquainted with the media interactions and the evolving surface effects.

Critique (Project 18.3)   What assessment can you make of the overall effects of the mixed media? Does the drawing seem cogent? Do the proportions of the different media seem to blend well, or are there certain aspects of one or two media that overpower the drawing? How did you feel about the execution of the work—the way one medium went down in relationship to another? How might you alter the order of applications in the next drawing?

What is the strongest aspect of the drawing? What is the weakest? What will you do differently next time using the same combination of media? How would you feel about this drawing if someone else had done it?

Evolving Surface   It is a delightful experience to look at the surface of a highly involved mixed-media work, whose totality of techniques and interplay of materials cannot be easily deciphered, even by the trained eye. For some drawings a few different media can appear as many on the surface; conversely, other drawings can appear less involved when in actuality they have many materials and techniques in play. The point of any mixed-media involvement should be to strive for an economy of means regardless of how many tools and materials are used. There should be a cleanness and a clarity with regard to the use of any media as opposed to an overworked, fatigued surface that appears too heavily laden with material, causing one to wonder how many mistakes were covered over with further media applications.

Efficiency of Surface   An example of one of the most well-orchestrated and efficient surfaces is Jasper John's *0 through 9, 1961* (Pl. 19), where the artist combines the two simple dry media of charcoal and pastel to build up a surface of spatial power and richness that conceptually identifies it as the synthesis of several centuries of art history. An earlier drawing of the artist's number series *0 through 9, 1960* (Fig. 18-13), a charcoal work on cream paper, refers us to a much earlier stage in the development of number series, indicating a state before the pastel was applied and before any blending or erasing techniques occurred. The drawing of the image in Plate 19 began in much the same way as Figure 18-13, with a few preliminary dry marks that developed into the complex weave of illusional textures that we see in one of the artist's largest drawings, in fact, the largest drawing he had executed at that time. As viewers, our perceptions of this intriguing drawing are that the size of *numbers* we are accustomed to is usually smaller than in this unusually large depiction. This powerful reinvention of numerals transparently placed in deep space, enabling us to see the number forms through one another on a two-dimensional surface, fuses the elements of fifteenth-century **grisaille** with the analytical cubism of Picasso and Braque from the early twentieth century. We are struck by the richness of surface attained in part by the (frottage) rubbing of a charcoal-laden rag over the paper surface while the drawing was hanging on a roughly textured wall of Johns's studio. In addition to the black and tonal gray ranges, there

grisaille
A monochrome drawing and painting technique using grays or grayish colors that was popular in the Renaissance as a way of emulating sculpture. The effects are sometimes heightened with gold.

are eraser marks that produce modeling of forms, along with touches of color: yellow, red, and blue lines in the upper right and lower left with the lower right bearing an area of lavender pastel blended with charcoal.

Expressive Surface   Nan Rosenthal and Ruth Fine say of Jasper Johns's drawings, "Jasper Johns' virtuosity as a draftsman may be known to the public through his prints, but the scale, impressiveness, intellectual challenge, and beauty of his drawings, and their centrality to his work, may come as a revelation." Figure 18-14, a mixed-media work in watercolor, charcoal, and crayon on two sheets of joined paper, informs us of the even deeper limits of his prowess as a draftsman.

In Isabel Bishop's *Two Girls* (Fig. 18-15), listed by the artist as simply a mixed-media work, we are intrigued by what she used and are forced to rely on our knowledge of materials and the clues that their effects offer us in order to arrive at some determination of how the artist achieved the effects created. Regardless of what materials were used, the results derive from the total effects of the surface.

Specially Prepared Surfaces   This physiology of materials has long intrigued artists and has been the source of many stellar works of art relating to the interactive relationships of both conventional and unconventional tools and materials. In Jim Butler's drawings on gesso-coated wooden panels (Fig. 18-16, Pl. 14), the artist prepares wooden panels by applying between twenty and thirty coats of **gesso,** sanding the surface between coatings of gesso in preparation to receive the graphite. Butler uses a variety of tools to apply the powdered graphite and employs intermittent scraping with razor blades and sandings with fine sandpaper as a subtractive method until he begins to establish the desired forms. He then develops the tonal ranges of lights and darks that

gesso
A material used, generally in several thin layers, to prime wood panel or canvas surfaces in preparation for painting. It is made from plaster (dehydrated calcium sulphate prepared by firing gypsum or alabaster) mixed with sizing material.

allow a visual *pushing* and *pulling* of the various compositional forms as he adjusts them in space.

Project 18.4

On four 9-by-12-inch sheets of Arches cover paper, either white or buff, make some drawings on a prepared surface by first stapling the papers to a heavy-duty drawing board. Place the staples 2 inches apart and at least 1/2 inch in from the edge CH. 18   Expressive Mixed Media   **353**

18-16. JIM BUTLER (b. 1945; American).
Sugar Cane. c. 1996–1998. Graphite on
wooden panel, left panel: 14 × 18″;
right panel: 14 × 23″.
Collection of the artist; courtesy of the artist.

of the paper sheets. Apply several thin coats of gesso to the entire surfaces of the
four sheets. (The papers may buckle slightly as they absorb the moisture of the gesso
wash, but will flatten again as they dry.) When they are completely dry, sand them
lightly with fine sandpaper and a sanding block to ensure evenness. Apply several
more thin coats of gesso and repeat the sanding procedure—gently.

With both graphite pencils and powdered graphite begin drawing, using the
pencils first to become familiar with the effects of graphite on the gesso surface. Experiment with different grades of graphite pencil and different amounts of pressure,
drawing on the tactile surface until you feel somewhat confident with pencil. Then
apply powdered graphite with a fingertip to the surface by rubbing it on and blending it into the gesso coat. It may help to cover your fingertip with a piece of chamois
hide to act as a barrier between the graphite and your finger, particularly if your fingertips tend to be moist. Rub with varying amounts of pressure and with varying
amounts of graphite powder.

Try erasing with a white plastic eraser. You should get some immediately interesting results by erasing, depending on how smoothly you sanded the surface before applying the graphite. Try also scraping with a razor blade or an X-acto knife
to create lighter passages on the graphite surface.

Make drawings on all the gesso-coated sheets, continually experimenting
with different variations of graphite application. Later, try stretching several larger
sheets of Arches and make some additive and subtractive drawings in graphite of
subjects of your choice. In the beginning it may be advisable to select a drawing
from a previous assignment and translate it into a graphite drawing on the gesso
surface.

Critique (Project 18.4) How adaptable were you to something approached
in a completely different way? Do you enjoy the indirect process of step-by-step
methods, and of having to first prepare a surface at relatively great lengths even before you can begin to draw? Are you a meticulous person, one who requires a certain standard of professionalism when preparing to do something? Do you enjoy
labored processes that require much time and steady devotion? Did your gesso surface work well? Was it receptive to the graphite and did you find it to be a consistently smooth surface to work on? Were there any uneven areas on the surface?

How descriptive of form are your drawings? Have you utilized the process
to its fullest at this point? Were there inhibiting factors that interfered with your
desired methods of graphite application? How would you approach this differently the next time you work in this manner? Do you have the sense of wanting to
greatly expand the size of your picture planes? Are you encouraged by the aspect
of being able to continue the drawings by simply adding and subtracting more
graphite as you continually refine the elements of your compositions? Do you have
the urge to try colored pencils, charcoal, even watercolor and ink washes on the
gesso surface?

18-17. HENRY MOORE (1898–1986; English). *Forest Elephants.* c. 1977. Charcoal and black chalk. 12 × 15 1/4" (30.7 × 38.6 cm). The Henry Moore Foundation.

Often, what ends up being a mixed-media work is not planned as such from the outset. There are many mixed-media works of art whose beginnings were relatively simple. That is, they began with a single medium, and only later, through the play-by-play decision-making process of the artist, became more and more media involved. An artist begins working and responds throughout the entire process to what is happening on the surface. In response to the preliminary marks he makes, the artist instinctively reaches for other tools or materials with which to amplify those initial strokes on the fledgling surface. For instance, what made Henry Moore choose two nearly similar media—black chalk and charcoal—in his drawing *Forest Elephants* (Fig. 18-17)? Can you detect any distinction between the media as you study the illustration? The softer charcoal is blacker than the black chalk—the chalk also appears to be slightly warmer and lighter, perhaps even grayish in tone in comparison with the cold rich blackness of the charcoal in the drawing. As Raphael decided to enhance his preliminary stylus work with red chalk (Fig. 18-6), so, too, Henry Moore made the decision to use charcoal and black chalk together purely for the linear and textural effects they gave him

Directness and Indirectness   In the work of David Faber there is yet another rather extravagant method of surface preparation upon which the artist then draws. In his prints taken from etched and engraved copper and zinc **intaglio** plates, Faber often elects to use alternative materials to receive the printed images. One of these materials is plaster or gypsum, which is alkaline in nature and highly receptive to oily printer's inks.

   In Faber's *Red Holstein Factor* (Fig. 18-18), he inked an etching plate with a variety of differently colored printer's inks that were mixed with varying amounts of reducing oils. After drawing some marks on the plate's surface, he poured wet plaster onto the plate, which was positioned inside a framework, forming the plaster into a tablet about 3/4-inch thick. During the chemically induced heating stage caused by hydration, the plaster hardens and the oils in the printer's inks act as a releasing agent, allowing the plate to break free from the plaster tablet.

intaglio
One of the major media divisions of fine art printmaking where the lines, tones, and textures of a design have been cut, scratched, or incised into a metal plate, either by hand or with acid. The linear grooves and textural depressions on the metal surface hold printer's ink, which when passed through an etching press transfers the design to paper. Intaglio is an umbrella term that includes engraving, drypoint, etching, mezzotint, aquatint, etc.

In this rather immediate process the alkaline gypsum and the oily inks fuse, causing the articulate transfer of the inked intaglio image on the plate to the plaster slab. After the plaster cures and is completely dry, Faber works back into the surface of the plaster with drawing tools, both adding and subtracting marks and enhancing the printed image in a unique way.

Variations of working back into prints utilizing drawing methods are prevalent among printmakers who are not always content to leave the printed image as the sole process. To have an intimate encounter with the printed surface by means of drawing seems the true finalizing act, and one that also affords great uniqueness and eldritch surface qualities impossible to attain from the printed image alone.

Visual Order

In Guillaume Apollinaire's *Aesthetic Meditations,* he states,

> Without poets, without artists, humanity would soon weary of nature's monotony. The sublime idea men have of the universe would collapse with dizzying speed. The order which we find in nature, and which is only an effect of art, would at once vanish. Everything would break up in chaos. There would be no seasons, no civilization, no thought, no humanity; even life would give way, and the impotent void would reign everywhere.
>
> Poets and artists plot the characteristics of their epoch, and the future docilely falls in with their desires.

18-19. GREG MURR (b. 1973; American). *Thirteen Ribbons.* c. 1999. Graphite and pastel on paper. 68 × 111″. Collection of the artist; courtesy of the artist.

The pursuit of order is and has always been one of the most important, if not the foremost, objective in the artist's longing for creative resolution— the works of art being the symptomatic side effects of that longing. And like the surfer who awaits the next wave, anticipating the exhilaration of the next ride . . . hoping it will be different from all other rides, the artist poises himself in the studio amidst an array of media, anticipating the next wave, and an unknown ride into waters yet uncharted.

When an artist feels a creative force, he must rely on a plan, a scheme, a sense of order with which to explore new terrain. In Greg Murr's work *Thirteen Ribbons* (Fig. 18-19), he found himself confronted with a large span of paper surface that required him to respond. He chose the dry media of pastel and graphite with blending and erasing techniques to massage the tooth of the paper, leaving it permanently changed as a record of his aesthetic visitation upon the surface.

When artist Nancy Ingram launched her materials investigation that led to the large-scale mixed-media drawing entitled *Veneration of the Oracle: The Triumph of Iago* (Fig. 18-20), she responded to the suggestion of doing a type of mixed-media work she had never done before. In creating a statement about domination and subordination, she established a clear irony in the highly symbolic work, regarding herself as ruler over the array of recalcitrant materials that she carefully and determinedly called into play. In taking this unfamiliar approach to making an image, she metaphorically established herself as victor over an unknown force driven by the known universal laws of expansion and contraction, which inevitably worked against her at times during much of the execution of the large and ambitious work. In the end, as we observe Ingram's sense of visual order, we can see that she remained the victor.

Sketchbook Activities

Sketch subjects you wish to apply to the more complex projects of this chapter on mixed media. What kinds of subject choices are needed and have the most mixed-media potential?

As you continue to sketch, you'll notice improvements in the way you see, the way you understand form, and the way you depict forms with greater descriptive

18-20. NANCY INGRAM (b. 1930; American). *Veneration of the Oracle: The Triumph of Iago.* c. 1998. Mixed media: Chine collé of drypoint print from plexiglass matrix, litho crayon, collage of paper cutouts, acrylic paint, acrylic polymer medium, Arches cover white and buff papers, Japanese **mulberry** paper on stretched raw linen, 46 1/2 × 107 1/8″ (118.2 × 272.5 cm). Collection of the artist; courtesy of the artist.

mulberry
The type of tree from which are extracted the white fibers of the inner bark that when steam-cooked and shredded become the main fiber ingredient of many handmade Oriental papers used in calligraphy and for drawing, painting, and printmaking.

life. It would also be a good time to look back over the pages of your sketchbook to note the evolutionary changes in the way you draw at present as compared with several months ago. You'll no doubt notice areas of improvement along with those that still need work. Do not allow yourself to become discouraged—keep sketching and drawing and remember that no one ever reaches the point of having learned everything there is to know about seeing and drawing. There are always deeper levels of insight and skills to acquire. Drawing is a lifelong pursuit.

Summary

Essentially, every surface an artist works on is reinvented from its former state. From the prehistoric cave painter's rock canvas to Nancy Ingram's portable stage, artists have discovered, developed, and selected the media of their choice for thousands of years. The many images in this text have exposed you to a plethora of different approaches, choices of material, visual effects, and styles with which to proceed, as Wayne Thiebaud so well stated, "in the deep pleasures of drawing."

Return to this book often for guidance and review of the methods and procedures outlined. Continue to use your sketchbooks as a diary into which you enter sketches as notes from the array of visual stimuli that you will continue to encounter during your daily routines. And remember, it is important to set aside a time to draw. Continue to be disciplined in this.

Glossary

abstract expressionism An American movement in the field of painting that began in the late forties and emphasized a nonrepresentational style. The movement broke into two branches: *action painting* and *color field painting.*

abstract symbols Symbols that have been visually simplified or rearranged to create visual impact and enhance meaning; they are often specific to certain cultures or political eras that represent a quality or circumstance.

abstract vision The imagined essence of premeditated forms arising in the mind of the artist whose intent it is to interpret a subject by analyzing and altering its recognizable forms and features by reassembling them into a nonrecognizable state with little or no reference to the original forms.

abstraction The extraction of an essence; an analytical study of an object or the formation of an idea apart from its tangible or recognizable form, as of the characteristics of an object or idea, whereby the virtues of an insightful rearrangement of form are substituted for exact representation.

active tooth The degree to which a paper's surface texture retains particles of dry drawing media and influences the resulting surface qualities of those media. An artist will choose a particular paper because of its active grain in or-der to attain the desired expressive results. See also **paper grain** and **tooth.**

actual texture A texture that is a real surface and can be experienced through the sense of touch; often used in collage or mixed-media works where the actual textured material is applied to the work of art and left unaltered by the artist—as in the art of the found object.

additive method The drawing activity of beginning with a white or blank surface and building up positive marks as lines, tones, textures, values; working from light to dark by the progressive addition of tonal marks.

advertising drawings Drawings done by commercial illustrators and designed to promote and sell merchandise; though often highly stylized, they are rendered with considerable concern for detail.

aerial perspective A drawing technique that reinforces the illusion of depth (initially mapped out by the rules of linear perspective) where contrasts of color and value di-minish as objects recede into the distance, with lights becoming less light, darks less dark, until all contrasts merge into one uniform, medium-light tone. See **atmospheric perspective.**

ambiguity A state of visual uncertainty created by intentionally ignoring or distorting accepted compositional methods; the unconventional visual effects that result from the apparently purposeful attempt to create a sense of imbalance.

analogous colors Those colors adjacent to each other on the color wheel; any colors existing side by side on the color wheel.

analogous color scheme A color scheme comprised of any combination of adjacent colors on the color wheel as the main color statement of a work of art.

analytical sight Scrutiny; the impetus for drawing only what the artist actually sees; the opposite of intuitive or instinctive drawing. All works of art are to varying degrees analytical.

anatomical drawings Drawings that portray and make explicit the human anatomy, illustrating the interrelationships of skin, muscle, bone, and joint structures, all with proportional correctness to the human body.

angle of light The proximity, position, and direction of a light source in relation to an object that determines the length of shadows. A highly positioned source of light creates short shadows; a low light position produces long shadows.

ascending planes Planes not parallel to the ground or floor planes whose vanishing points appear above the horizon line.

asymmetrical balance Balance based upon a visual sense of equilibrium that can be felt more than it can be measured. There are no specific rules for asymmetrical balance except that of diversity.

atmospheric perspective A drawing technique pertaining to landscape where the attributes of linear perspective are viewed through special atmospheric effects created by the artist in order to display a greater degree of spatial complexity uniquely altering the vision of perspective by reinforcing the illusion of depth. See **aerial perspective.**

balance A major underlying principle of composition that unifies all the elements of design. It can be either symmetrical or asymmetrical.

bamboo pen A type of *hollow* reed pen imported from the Orient.

bistre A transparent brown pigment used to produce wash tones in pen and ink drawings obtained by boiling soot. See **wash** and **wash drawing.**

blind contour A drawing process where the eye is trained to follow the contours of what is being drawn, looking only at the subject, not at the paper. In this process, the hand moves the drawing tool in synchronization with the movements of the eye.

bond paper Familiar as stationery and computer paper, a lightweight, relatively smooth paper with a hard surface and tight grain appropriate for use with graphite or colored pencils, ballpoint pen, or pen and ink. It is available in pads or in bulk in various sizes.

Bristol board A very fine, hard-surfaced paper, manufactured in two finishes: *kid finish,* by virtue of its very slight tooth, facilitates fine graphite pencil work of medium hardness and rubbed pen and graphite combinations; *smooth (plate) finish,* a very finely toothed paper, encourages elegant studies in pen and ink or very hard graphite pencil and is available in different weights.

broken color A color scheme where more than one color is introduced into a shape or object to produce varied painterly effects. Also, a pure color that has been altered by the invasion of another color.

burnishing The excessive layering of various drawing media under pressure resulting in **wax bloom,** which can be corrected or lifted by pressing a kneaded eraser against the burnished surface, eliminating the polished appearance.

cacophony A sudden, unexpected, often disharmonious visual aspect of a composition that arouses the viewer's immediate attention; an obvious and interestingly noticeable visual disharmony used in a positive way to strengthen or enhance a visual statement.

calligraphic line Beautiful line. In the visual arts, when writing, drawing, engraving, etching, and painting, the beauty of line becomes a major aesthetic aim.

calligraphy Beautiful writing. In western culture it is done with a pen, in Chinese and Japanese cultures with a brush. See **calligraphic line.**

caricature   An exaggerated portrayal of the characteristic features or mannerisms usually of a well-known personage, intended for satirical effect.

cartoon   A newspaper or magazine drawing or illustration that caricatures or symbolizes a person, event, or situation of popular interest, such as a politician or political party, usually in a humorous or satirical way. Also, a large drawing created to establish life-size scale for frescoes. Artists later used the technique to transfer large-scale images for paintings, tapestries, stained glass, and other large works (a cartoon was indispensable in the process of making stained glass).

cast shadow   A shadow cast or thrown by an object onto an adjacent plane; one of the value gradations of traditional chiaroscuro. A cast shadow is darker than the core of the shadow.

center of vision   Same as the **central vanishing point;** the point of intersection of the central line of vision and the horizon line.

central line of vision   An imaginary line centered in the cone of vision, extending from the eye and meeting the horizon line at a right angle.

central vanishing point   The point of intersection of the line of vision on the horizon line; same as the point of the **center of vision.**

chalk   The term *chalk* covers a wide variety of materials ranging in texture from coarse to fine, from hard to soft and crumbly, and from dry to greasy, shaped into rounded or square sticks. It was originally obtained from natural colored earths that were cut or sawed into sticks. Fabricated chalk is made with prepared pastes of water-soluble binding media mixed with dry pigments and sometimes with additional substances such as inert clays, then rolled, pressed into sticks, and dried.

charcoal paper   Textured paper abrasive to charcoal because of its hardness of tooth. In the drawing act, it receives a deposition of black carbon charcoal particles that adhere to its relief as well as fall into its recesses; available in different weights in white, gray tones, and muted colors; also for use with chalk, Conté crayon, and pastels.

charcoal pencils   Thin rods of compressed charcoal encased in paper or wooden sheaths that offer cleanliness but lack the flexibility of stick charcoal because only the point can be used. Charcoal pencils come in different grades: 6B (extra soft), 4B (soft), 2B (medium), and HB (hard). (White charcoal pencils are also available.)

chiaroscuro   From *chiaro* (light) and *oscuro* (dark), the continuous gradations of value, to create the illusion of three-dimen-

sional form; systematic changes of value that produce visual states of high or low contrast in the depiction of forms as they exist in pictorial space or atmosphere.

closed composition   Compositional format in which the art elements of form and structure are visually well contained by the edges of the picture plane.

closed form   The area of a composition where a color, value, tone, or texture is confined within the contour or silhouette of an object or shape and thereby stresses visual separation from its surrounding elements.

cold press   Paper with a moderately textured, matte surface, softer and toothier than "hot press" paper.

color   In its purest sense, the condition produced by white light passing through a glass prism. A spectrum of color is the visual evidence of refracted or dispersed light rays of different wavelengths that stimulate the retina to see the different hues. The hue red produces the longest wavelengths; violet produces the shortest. Chromatic color is distinguished by qualities of hue: red, blue, and yellow as the primary colors; violet, green, and orange as the secondary colors.

color schemes   Systems of color combinations that provide a sense of color harmony and unity. (See **analogous, complementary, double complementary, triple complementary, monochromatic,** and **split complementary** schemes.)

complementary colors   Hues opposite one another on the color wheel; yellow and violet; red and green; blue and orange. Complementary tertiary hues also face each other across the color wheel.

composition   The structure of a picture as separate from both subject and style; the essential abstract design; the selection and organization of line, shape, value, texture, pattern, and color into an aesthetically pleasing arrangement embodying such principles of design as balance, harmony, rhythm, repetition and variation, dominance and subordination, and focus.

compressed charcoal   A substance made by grinding charcoal into powder and compressing it with a binding material into chalklike sticks that are then labeled according to hardness ranging from 00, the softest and blackest, through 5, the hardest and palest.

cone of vision   The shape of containment of all that can be seen from one stationary position without moving the eyes.

Conté crayon   A semi-hard chalk of fine texture containing sufficient oily material in the binder to adhere readily and more or less permanently to smooth paper. It comes in sizes of ¼ inch (.6 centimeter) square and 3 inches (8 centimeters) long, in three degrees of hardness—No. 1 (hard), No. 2 (medium), and No. 3 (soft)—and in four colors—white, black, brown, and sanguine (Venetian red), which is the most popular.

contour   The outermost extremities or limits of a shape, whether two-dimensional or three-dimensional, as in the skin or shell of an object, form, or volume; contour may be associated with the outline of a subject and may change with different viewing positions.

contour drawing   Drawing that focuses on capturing in a highly descriptive way the extreme edges of a shape, form, or object, depicting it as separate from its adjacent or neighboring forms.

contour hatching   Curved lines that follow the outer contours of the turning of form, allowing a more descriptive modeling of cylindrical and spherical subjects.

contour lines   Lines that delineate the very edges of forms and separate each volume, mass, or area from its adjacent or neighboring forms.

contrast   The visual effect of a striking difference between art elements creating a condition of compositional intrigue; opposites or complementary art elements that through their visual forces *set each other off* or draw attention and focus to each other or to particular areas within a design.

cool color   A hue on one side of the color wheel—green, blue, violet, and their intermediate tertiary colors; any color opposite the warm colors on the color wheel.

copying   The exact imitation of the drawings of the old masters strictly for the purpose of learning to see, learning technique, and learning about styles. The view is widely held that the most beneficial learning about drawing occurs from having as direct an experience of emulating the old masters as possible.

core of shadow   The most concentrated area of dark on an illuminated sphere; one of the value gradations of traditional chiaroscuro; the core of the shadow receives no illumination.

cross-contour   Lines that are drawn through, around, over, under, and across form to find the gesture and major lines of movement within the form.

cross-contour hatching   Hatched lines existing on multiple planes that follow and describe the outer extremities of the three-dimensional surface undulations of a form.

cross-hatching   A series or cluster of parallel lines, whether continuous or broken, that traverse other clusters of the same kinds of lines creating tonal and textural variations within a composition.

Cubism   A style of painting originated by Picasso and Braque between 1907 and 1914 that uses multiple views of an object to emphasize its three-dimensionality yet acknowledges the two-dimensional surface of the picture plane.

dark field manner   A technique in which the artist prepares a dark field on a picture plane and proceeds to remove the darks, allowing light to enter the field. This creates a composition of lighter passages that describe forms or objects existing within the dark pictorial space. It is the opposite of **light field manner.**

descending planes Planes not parallel to the ground or floor planes whose vanishing points fall below the horizon line.

descriptive drawings Usually highly detailed drawings whose images articulately describe what is seen.

directional lines Compositional linear treatment that establishes a particular or dominant mood or emotion from its linear emphasis through a variety of different line treatments yielding a visual sense of compositional weight and balance. The linear treatments may flow in the same direction or in opposite directions, each conveying different feelings.

direction of light The position of light that determines the direction in which shadows fall. When the source of light is to one side, shadows are cast to the opposite side. With the light at your back, shadows fall away from you. When you look into the light, shadows of objects before you are cast toward you.

double complementary color scheme A color scheme that poses two pairs of complementary colors, such as blue and orange plus red and green, working together in the same work of art.

drawing A division of the fine arts in which the artist makes a descriptive graphic mark of line, tone, texture, or value, by pulling or dragging a tool across a receptive surface or background—usually a piece of fine-quality grained or toothed paper.

drawing inks Saturated liquid pigments possessing great fluidity that may be used full strength with various types of pen nibs (points) for linear effects, or diluted with water to varying degrees of transparency, producing washes applied by brush to enhance pen-and-ink drawings. Among the most popular are India ink, China ink, sumi ink (all black), and various other quality colored inks such as Walnut, Koh-I-Noor, and Windsor-Newton brands.

drybrush The irregular or broken brush stroke effects of ink that ultimately diminish, created by dragging a less-than-fully-loaded brush lightly across a piece of drawing paper—especially one with some surface variation or high degree of tooth.

drypoint Intaglio printmaking technique where a metal plate is drawn on with a steel point that produces a *scratch* or *ditch* with a continuous or broken line of upraised metal *burrs*. When the line is inked, the burrs hold a slight residue of ink around them that produces a velvety line quality when printed.

eldritch A word describing an unexpectedly rare and eerie quality or an unforgettable, otherworldly presence, usually

conspicuously out of place when and wherever found.

empathetic drawing A drawing that bears evidence of the sympathy for, and understanding of, one person by another through visual portrayal.

empathy The state of identifying with someone through the projection of oneself into that person in order to gain a better understanding of that person's character; a reaching out usually through an emotional channel that is perpetuated by tenderness and deep feelings of sympathy or compassion.

empirical perspective Perspective, that, unlike **linear perspective,** relies upon direct observation rather than a set of rules.

engraving A form of intaglio printmaking where line or stipple textures are cut into the surface of a copper plate, or other suitable surface, with a tool called a burin. The burin's lozenge point cuts and removes the surface material, leaving a relatively smooth V-gouge or depressed groove in its wake. Printer's ink is forced into the grooves. The effect is a crisp line quality similar to that of certain pen-and-ink drawings.

estompe A paper stump used for shading or blending tones. See **tortillon.**

etching The action of a corrosive material, such as an acid, incising a design into metal, as in *copper plate etching.* One of the techniques of *fine art printmaking* that falls into the category of *intaglio,* where lines and textures are incised into and below the original surface of metal plates forming grooves and rough textures that will hold ink that can then be transferred to dampened paper with the use of an etching press.

expressionism The visual traits or character of a work of art that communicates emotions and feelings as opposed to only being concerned with the *objective* and *subjective* realms; the way in which a work of art was conceived and made, as occurs in an *expressionistic response* to a subject by a particular artist.

eye of the mind That which perceives subjectively apart from what the physical eye sees objectively or concretely. Often referred to as "the eye of the soul."

figure-ground Within a picture plane, a compositional circumstance where the figurative elements read as the *positive shapes* and project forward from the background, which is read as the *negative space.*

fixative spray (workable) A type of fine, granular mist that dries quickly, forming a semiprotective, porous coating, and *fixes* or *holds* the fine particles of graphite, charcoal, chalk, and pastel in place yet allow the surface to be reworked.

fixed point of view A mandatory rule for linear perspective; an established, unchanging position from which an object or scene

is viewed that enables the rules of linear perspective to be enacted.

floor plane Same as ground plane albeit for interior spaces. See **ground plane.**

focal points The elements or portions of a composition that form the main thrust or central emphasis and are visually supported or fortified by all other surrounding compositional elements.

focus The prime center of visual importance within a composition to which all other visual elements yield; it holds the viewer's attention because of its attractive and dominant influence on its surroundings.

foreshortened square A square seen in perspective while lying flat on the ground plane whose parallel sides converge into the central vanishing point on the horizon line.

foreshortening A term that applies to organic and anatomical forms seen in radical perspective, as in the portrayal of lines being shorter than they actually are, in order to create the illusion of correct size-and-shape relationships in space.

form The positive aspect or complement of space; the visible or recognizable configuration or shape of any object existing in atmospheric space; any structural art element separate from color, line, texture, material, etc. See **space.**

fountain pens Pens that are generally more convenient for sketchbook drawing—once filled, they eliminate frequent recourse to the bottle of ink (always a risk as dripping may occur when the pen is transported). The two types of fountain pens manufactured for drawing are the *quill-style* pen and *stylus-type* pen, generally termed *Rapidograph.*

frottage The technique of placing a sheet of paper over an actual, physical texture and rubbing the topside of the paper with the side of a graphite stick or Conté crayon, producing a positive impression of the relief of the physical texture. Artist Max Ernst was the first to use the technique in the production of a work of art.

full range A complete gradation of tones from the lightest to the darkest values.

gesso A material used, generally in several thin layers, to prime wood panel or canvas surfaces in preparation for painting. It is made from plaster (dehydrated calcium sulphate prepared by firing gypsum or alabaster) mixed with sizing material.

gesture The essential line or depicted state of movement of a live form.

gesture drawing A drawing done for the sole purpose of studying gesture whose objective is to capture the essential, descriptive movements of live forms in space, whether human or animal.

glassine An ultra-thin, frictionless, and translucent paperlike material used to "slip sheet" in between stacked works of art on paper—drawings, prints, or watercolors—protecting them from smears or surface abrasions.

gouache   From the French word "wash," opaque watercolors used in painting whose pigments contain a *gum binder* and filler of *opaque white* such as clay that give a chalky appearance to the surface of the painting.

graphite   A soft form of carbon found in nature and used as lead in pencils. It is manufactured in a wide range of soft to hard states and produces a lustrous, black, or gray-black mark when dragged against a receptive surface. The softer states produce darker, richer blacks than harder versions. It is also available in stick, chunk, or powdered form.

grisaille   A monochrome drawing and painting technique using grays or grayish colors that was popular in the Renaissance as a way of emulating sculpture. The effects are sometimes heightened with gold.

ground plane   A flat horizontal plane on which the viewer stands that extends to the horizon. In drawings of interior spaces it is referred to as the floor plane. See **floor plane.**

handmade Oriental papers   Papers that are made by manually pulling a flat screen or sieve up through a water vat containing finely shredded mulberry fibers. The fibers come to rest in a flat, consistent sheet on the screen, which allows the water to drain through. The fibers are extracted from the inner, white bark layer of the mulberry tree.

haptic   A word describing one of two extreme poles of artistic personality (the other being **visual**). Haptic, or nonvisual, people relate all forms of their expression to their feelings, bodily sensations, and subjective experiences in which they become emotionally involved.

hard pastels   Pastels made from dry pigments mixed with a higher proportion of aqueous binder than in soft pastels, which makes them harder with a firmer texture. They are compressed into square sticks; their flat side planes afford rapid coverage of broad areas; the sharp corners make them effective for detailing and accenting. They can be sharpened with a razor blade and are also manufactured in pencil form.

hatching   Repeated parallel strokes with a drawing tool that produce clusters of lines creating compositional values and tonal variations usually descriptive of form or surface.

high key   The lightest values—white through middle gray on the value scale, in which case the darkest value is no darker than middle gray.

highlights   The lightest values present on the surface of an illuminated form, occurring on very smooth or shiny surfaces; the intense spots of light that appear on the crest of the surface facing the light source.

horizon line   A line that corresponds to the eye level of the viewer in linear perspective; the line where sky and earth appear to meet (provided the earth is perfectly flat and nothing blocks the view). The vanishing point (VP), central vanishing point (CVP), and the furthest end point of the center line of vision are all located on this line.

hot press   One of the three standard grades of illustration board and watercolor paper characterized as having a hard surface that has been ironed and press-cured with heat and weight and possesses the smoothest and least absorbent surface; excellent for very refined, controlled techniques.

hue   Local color; the quality that distinguishes one color from another.

idealized portrait   A portrait that achieves a satisfactory resemblance to the sitter while simultaneously eliminating the physical imperfections of the face.

illustration   Usually a highly detailed image that communicates a message, offers visual description, or portrays an episode (as in a story) through visual means.

illustration board   A medium made by mounting different papers of relatively fine quality onto cardboard backing; available in three standard surface finishes: *rough,* which has the most active tooth; *cold press,* a versatile, medium-toothed surface; and *hot press,* the smoothest and least absorbent surface that is excellent for very refined, controlled techniques. It is expensive but highly durable and resists wrinkling when wet.

imagination   In art, the act or ability to envision fictitious, mental images that are present in the mind's eye but not in actual life; also, the artistic power to create images of a fanciful nature as metaphors for unrealized experiences that may, however, have meaning and association in real or actual life.

inclined planes   Planes not parallel to the ground or floor plane whose vanishing points exist on vertical lines that pass through the corresponding vanishing point on the horizon line.

inks   Any fluid or semifluid drawing or printing materials that may be used in conjunction with various pens, brushes, brayers, or rollers. They are available in a wide range of colors. Some are soluble in solvents such as mineral spirits and turpentine; others are soluble in water.

ink wash   A dilution of ink in water or solvent, applied by brush, most often used with pen-and-ink drawings to enhance by creating varying degrees of semitransparent tones.

intaglio   One of the major media divisions of fine art printmaking where the lines, tones, and textures of a design have been cut, scratched, or incised into a metal plate, either by hand or with acid. The linear grooves and textural depressions on the metal surface hold printer's ink, which when passed through an etching press transfers the design to paper. Intaglio is an umbrella term that includes engraving, drypoint, etching, mezzotint, aquatint, etc.

intensity   The degree of strength or brilliance; as related to color, the strength or saturation of a pigment; the brightness of a color.

intuitive drawing   Drawing activity controlled by instinct, feelings, emotions, bodily sensations, and visceral responses, as in the case of a haptic person; a drawing based on an intuitive response to a subject.

invented texture   A fictional or improvised texture created to heighten the imagined and descriptive forces of the surface quality of objects or forms within a composition.

kid finish paper   Bristol board paper with a slightly toothed surface; it facilitates fine graphite pencil work and rubbed pen-and-graphite combinations.

laid finish paper   Subtle paper texture characterized by faint lines visible when the paper is held up to strong light and caused by the structural elements, or the sieve, of the paper-making screen. Unlike the screen of wove paper, the laid screen is intricately hand sewn into the mold frame. See **wove finish paper.**

lettering pens   As the name implies, pens used for lettering; they are available with round, straight, or angular nibs ranging in width from 1/10 millimeter to more than ¼ inch (.6 centimeter). Straight-nibbed lettering pens yield a line that in its stiff angularity recalls the line made by a reed pen. Wide lettering pens allow the rapid filling in of large areas.

life drawing   The act of drawing from live models in order to record the movement, gesture, and essential physical capabilities of the human body as an aesthetically pleasing art form. Also, drawing from life in order to gain a mechanical as well as visual understanding of live forms and how they exist and move in space.

light   The illumination of an object; a major component of chiaroscuro helping to define forms in space within a composition; that which makes sight possible.

light field manner   A technique in which the artist begins with a light surface and progressively builds up an image by adding darker forms or shapes comprised of line, tone, texture, and value. Opposite of **dark field manner.** See **additive drawing.**

line   The pathway of a moving point; the trail of deposited material or a scratch resulting from dragging a drawing tool or stylus over a surface. A line is usually made visible by contrasts in value or surface.

linear perspective A scientific method of determining the correct placement of forms in space and the degree to which such forms appear to diminish in size at a given distance.

lithograph A type of print created by one of the four major divisions of *fine art printmaking* involving a *direct drawing process* on Bavarian limestone (calcium carbonate) or aluminum plates. The process, in its entirety, engages the *antithesis of grease and water* where images are drawn with greasy crayons on the stone or metal plate, then etched with acid, effecting a process of chemical stabilization whereby the image remains grease-loving or oleophilic, and the nonimage becomes water-loving or hydrophilic repelling grease. Through a rhythmic process between *printer* and *sponger,* the litho surface is kept wet by sponging with water, then inked with printer's inks alternately, and finally printed on paper with a litho press. *Lithograph* is from a Greek term meaning "stone writing."

lithographic crayons Greasy crayons in both pencil and stick form that produce rich blacks and are made from carbon black, animal fat, wax, and soap. They come in a variety of hard and soft grades ranging from No. 00 (softest) through 5 (hardest). The softest crayons contain the most grease, making them adhere well to most paper surfaces.

local color The true color or hue of a surface as seen free from the effects of light and shadow; under illumination, local hues are lightened or darkened depending upon the degree of lightness or darkness of the source of illumination.

local value The actual, known value of objects perceived only when seen free from the effects of strong light and shadow.

low key The darkest half of the value scale with the lightest value being no lighter than middle gray.

manière noire French for "in the dark manner." See **dark field manner.**

medical illustration A type of illustrational drawing that offers visual clarity to medical conditions or anatomical circumstances, whether normal or abnormal, beyond that of a photograph since drawings have the capability to contain far more information than a camera is able to capture in an instant.

metal pen A pen that first appeared at the end of the eighteenth century; when used on very smooth, partially absorbent paper, the steel pen can be more completely controlled than its predecessors (quill, reed, bamboo pens) as the vehicle for sharp, detailed observation.

metaphor In a work of art, a concept, symbol, or motif that carries an implied comparison or is used in place of some other idea in order to draw heightened attention to the visual statement for the purpose of enhancing its meaning.

middle key On a nine-step value-range scale, the five values in the middle of the scale.

mixed media A variety of different materials used in a creative process for the purpose of heightening surface effects and increasing the visual complexity of an image.

mixed-media drawing A drawing created by the interaction of a few or many different drawing materials that come to rest on a surface or on multiple variations of a surface. The artist selects different materials in order to enhance a visual statement and create visually interesting surface effects that cannot be produced by a single medium.

mold-made paper High-quality paper possessing characteristic beauty and elegance, usually with a natural deckled edge, whose sheet size, texture, and weight are characterized by the uniqueness of a particular molded framework with a mesh of finely woven cloth or wire.

monochromatic A word describing a hue or chromatic variation of shades and tints of the same color attained by adding black to create shades or white to create tints.

monochromatic color scheme A color scheme in which an entire composition is composed of the descriptive value ranges of a single color with its shades and tints. See **shade** and **tint.**

monotype As a unique impression, a one-time drawing with printer's inks on a flat metal plate, which is then transferred to dampened paper with the use of a press. The French artist Edgar Degas is well known for his use of the monotype medium.

mulberry The type of tree from which are extracted the white fibers of the inner bark that when steam-cooked and shredded become the main fiber ingredient of many handmade Oriental papers used in calligraphy and for drawing, painting, and printmaking. See **handmade Oriental papers.**

multiple The term applied to the regular appearance of shapes or forms in a pattern. Also refers to fine art processes where it is possible to produce a series of consecutive images. In printmaking, for example, an edition is a series of "multiple originals."

naturalistic representation The depiction of subject matter in its most natural and unaltered state.

negative shape(s) In two-dimensional figure-ground relationships, the remaining or unoccupied shapes within a composition

surrounding or aside from the positive shapes that maintain a visual importance equal to that of the positive shapes.

negative space or area(s) In figure-ground relationships, the spaces or areas surrounding the positive shapes that may also be referred to as ground, empty space, field, or void space. The negative spaces cause the positive shapes or forms to project forward, creating a three-dimensional illusion within a composition.

newsprint An inexpensive paper made of wood pulp used by art students for all types of practice drawing and expedient classroom studies such as gesture, contour, blind contour, etc. It has a smooth surface, yellows badly due to its acid content, and is most appropriately used with soft graphite pencil, charcoal, Conté crayon, and chalk.

oil pastels Drawing media that are similar to hard pastels except that oil has been added to the binder, creating a semihard state that adheres more readily to paper. Because oil pastels are not easily smudged, they work well for outdoor sketching. They are not easily erased.

one-point perspective A visual condition where all lines parallel to our central line of vision, whether to the side, above, or below, appear to meet at the central vanishing point (CVP).

opaque watercolor Gouache; water color pigments containing a gum binder and or filler of clay that when painted, create a chalky, opaque effect.

open composition Compositional format in which the images of form and structure appear unrelated to the size of the paper, creating the impression that the composition, unlimited by the outer edges, exceeds the boundaries of the picture plane.

open form A form whose value or values blend into the similar surrounding areas of the composition without noticeable or obvious separations; also, a form that allows the integration of various compositional elements, producing a feeling of movement and vitality.

optical color Color effects that are seen and read optically; the actual color the eye reads and the mind understands; tiny strokes of "pure red" in close proximity to tiny strokes of "pure blue" will be read and mixed by the eye to produce violet.

optical grays The actual gray values that the eye sees resulting directly from a variety of drawing techniques, usually involving dry media that can be blended for heightened atmospheric effects.

paper grain Same as paper tooth; the surface texture of a paper; the degree of roughness or smoothness of a paper. See **tooth.**

pastels   Pure powdered pigments mixed with just enough clay, gum, or resin to bind them into stick form; except for differing amounts of wax and grease, they are similar to crayons and especially to chalks in composition. Pastels come in soft, hard, and oil versions in a wide range of colors. Pastel drawings tend to be fragile and require care in storing as their surfaces are easily abraded. Spray fixative may help preserve the surface but may also dull the color with too much use. See **soft, hard,** and **oil pastels.**

pattern   Any compositionally repeated element or regular repetition of a design or single shape; pattern drawings in commercial art may serve as models for commercial imitation.

pen nib   The point of a pen whether *quill, reed, bamboo,* or *steel,* which comes in a variety of different types and sizes and is used with fluid drawing ink; the nib itself acts as the ink reservoir and controls the flow and dispersing of the ink on paper; the style and width of the nib determine line quality.

pencil   A wooden or paper cylindrical tool encasing a graphite, charcoal, crayon, or colored pigment rod of a wide variety of hard and soft grades; the most important and versatile drawing instrument since the end of the eighteenth century and the most commonly used drawing implement until the invention of the cartridge pen.

pentimento   From the Italian meaning "to repent," a subtle or radical revision made by an artist when he changes his mind, or *repents* during the execution of a drawing, painting, or print. The vestiges of the previous image, whether totally concealed or not, either become more apparent through the fading of the outer surface, or have remained apparent and bear evidence of the abandoned creative intent.

perspective drawing   The systematic method of representing and describing forms as they appear to recede in space through the use of converging lines that meet at a central vanishing point located on the horizon line. Also, the depiction of forms as they appear to the eye relative to distance or depth.

picture plane   The area of a flat surface defined by its outer borders on which an artist creates an image; often the picture plane, out of necessity, becomes transparent, allowing the artist to create three-dimensional forms and objects that exist in both deep and shallow space as three-dimensional illusions.

plasticity   The physical body characteristics of a material or substance, whether liquid or solid, that determines its use as an art material; also the characteristics of form, concept, and compositional handling of subject matter. For example, a subject may be drawn in such a way as to increase its mass or volume and thereby increase its plasticity.

portraiture   The art of portrayal; any of many wide-ranging approaches to the art of preserving a physical likeness whether truthful, idealized, psychological, or intended as caricature.

positive line, shape, form   Established line, shape, or form that serves as the subject of a drawing and carries the intended visual dominance or subject meaning of a composition—whether representational or nonrepresentational. In figure-ground relationships it is defined by its opposite negative shapes. See **negative shape** and **negative space or area.**

powdered charcoal   Charcoal in a powdered state that produces intense blacks and is used in combination with a chamois to produce rubbed areas of rich darks.

primary colors   Red, yellow, and blue; called *primaries* because they are pure colors and cannot be obtained by mixing together any other hues.

printer's ink   A heavy-bodied, oil-based, saturated ink made of carbon blacks or color pigment powders mixed with plate oil (derived from linseed oil). Printer's inks can be diluted with solvents so that they will flow from a brush to produce the painterly effects of monotype or ink wash.

psychological portrait   Beyond the revealing likeness, the portrayal of a person's inner personality or temperament made visually tangible through the artistic treatment of the facial features, tilt of head, relaxed quality, or stiffness of shoulders, neck, and head.

quill pens   Pens cut from the heavy pinion feathers of geese, swans, or wild turkeys, hardened by tempering with wet, heated sand, and shaped to a sharp or angular, coarse or fine point. They respond readily to variations of touch or pressure, producing a responsive, smooth, and flexible line. Today traditionally trained calligraphers are more inclined than artists to make and use quill pens.

quill-style pen   One of several types of fountain pens. See **fountain pens.**

raison d' être   French for "reason to be." In the art context the term is used when referring to the purpose of a work of art as a necessary means of communicating *language* as visual statement.

raking light   The planned, controlled, and directed position of a lighting source that causes a "washing over" of illumination, producing a specified lighting effect usually limited to one side of an object or form.

Rapidograph pens   Types of fountain pens that hold a supply of ink and have a central cylindrical point enabling the artist to move the pen in all directions without varying the line width; must be held perpendicular to the drawing surface for the ink to flow evenly.

recondite   A term describing the quality of being indescribably strange and curious without means of explanation or evidence of reason. As applied to art, it describes a profound visual situation the comprehension of which is beyond the grasp of the ordinary mind.

reed pens   Pens hewn from tubular reeds or the hollow wooden stems of certain shrubs and cut with various points to suit the user's taste. In general, reed pens are stiff; their nibs, or points, are thick and fibrous. The lack of supple responsiveness results in a bold line.

reflected light   Light bouncing back from reflective surfaces; functions as fill-in light, making objects appear rounded by giving definition to the core of the shadow; one of the value gradations of traditional chiaroscuro. See **core of shadow.**

reflected shadow   A shadow that bounces back from a nearby surface or object; one of the elements of the system of chiaroscuro. A reflected shadow is never as dark as a cast shadow. See **cast shadow.**

relief   The raised surface in the printmaking medium of woodcuts where the negative shapes are cut away leaving the raised or uncut surface of the wood in relief; the relief surface catches the ink from a brayer and prints as the positive image when transferred to paper.

rendered   Drawn, usually with a high degree of representation.

rendering   A drawing displaying a high degree of detailed representation, interpretation, rendition, and other specific information about a subject; the word *render* is often used as a synonym for *draw* or *represent.*

repetition   The unifying visual sense of regularity in the appearance of similar elements—lines, shapes, patterns, textures, colors, values, and movements within a composition.

reporting drawings   Drawings that make visually tangible an event or occurrence by communicating what happened. In fashion design, reporting drawings treat fashion as news.

rhythm   The visual manifestation and flow of repetition, variation, patterning, harmony of form, and movement within a composition; a flowing and regular recurrence of the art elements within the compositional structure of a work of art.

rice paper   A misnomer for Oriental papers made by hand predominantly from the inner fibers of the mulberry and other plants and having no relation to rice. It is a flexible writing and drawing paper used in China primarily for sumi painting.

rim lighting   Illumination of only the outer edge of an object or form by light from behind the object or form.

rough tooth A characteristic of heavily toothed papers with a readily visible and pronounced surface texture as in charcoal or some watercolor papers.

sanguine Natural red chalk ranging from the color of blood to a brownish-red used for drawing and first discovered prior to the fifteenth century in European mine deposits; its first documented usage came in the late fifteenth century around the time of Leonardo da Vinci and other Renaissance artists; its usage spread shortly thereafter to other countries.

scale A proportional system of measurement set in accordance with an established standard; on a one-inch standard, an object whose height is one inch that is drawn in one-fourth scale will be drawn one-fourth the size of its original stature, or one-fourth inch in height.

scribbling Random, multidirectional lines used to build varied tones, textures, and densities and to define surface qualities, shape, and volume, or to capture gesture or movement as in a searching line. See **searching line.**

searching line An approach to drawing in which the hand and drawing instrument move freely and quickly across the paper surface either in continuous rhythms or in a series of broken lines. Sometimes they follow contour; at other times they draw through, around, even across form in order to find the gesture and major lines of movement within the form.

secondary colors *Violet, orange, and green.* The three colors resulting from the pairing and mixing of any two of the three primary colors: blue and red produce *violet*; red and yellow produce *orange*; yellow and blue produce *green*.

self-portrait An artist's portrayal of himself or herself using artistic expression to underscore temperaments or emotions related to his or her unique individual traits. The self-portrait has two functions: it allows the artist to use a cheap and available model, and it serves as a means of self-immortalization—often in an idealized way.

sfumato An Italian word meaning "smoked." The gradual, almost imperceptible blending of tones from light to dark in paintings or drawings; a technique used by Renaissance artists in combination with chiaroscuro for the visual enhancement of the overall tones within a composition.

shade A lessened degree of light caused by the blockage or partial blockage of directional light rays; as pertaining to color (low value), any color that has been darkened by the addition of black.

shade lines Contour lines of the shapes of shadows; lines that separate the areas of light and shade on an object, in a still life, or in the landscape.

shadow The state of being blocked or partially blocked from directional light or illumination; a precise area of shade cast by an object intercepting directional rays of light.

shape The flat, two-dimensional aspects of form as opposed to three-dimensional volume; when a three-dimensional form is reduced to a silhouette, the viewer is conscious only of its shape.

silverpoint A methodical drawing procedure where a thin rod of silver (about the size of a graphite shaft) is inserted into a mechanical pencil and used to draw on an elaborately prepared gesso surface. The silver metal point, which may be sharpened on sandpaper, yields a thin line of even width with a lovely gray color oxidizing to a grayish-brown with the passing of time. A highly recommended pencil-style mechanical holder is the Faber-Castell E-Motion Mechanical Pencil.

simulated texture A drawn textural illusion that emulates an actual texture or surface quality and is dependent upon the degree of illusion for its various visual effects.

simultaneous contrast A visual effect produced when complementary colors are placed in juxtaposition, which increases the apparent intensity of both so that they truly complement each other.

sketch A drawing done quickly with minimal or no elaboration but that may use scribbled lines or tones to suggest form, texture, and shadow.

smooth (plate) finish Bristol board paper with an extremely fine tooth that encourages elegant and detailed studies in pen and ink or very hard graphite pencil, and is available in different weights.

soft pastels Pastels made from dry pigments mixed with an aqueous binder and compressed into cylindrical form. They are soft and crumbly and nonadhesive, requiring use on a paper of decided tooth.

soft sketching papers Papers manufactured with a smooth tooth for use with soft graphite pencils, ballpoint and felt-tip pens, and colored crayon.

source of light Light that may be either natural or artificial. Natural light produces parallel rays; artificial light creates radiating rays. It is true that light radiates from the sun, but from a distance of 93 million miles, the rays are virtually parallel when they reach the earth.

space The negative aspect or complement of form; the atmosphere surrounding forms or objects. See **form.**

spatial Existing in space; surrounding objects and defining their proximal relationships to one another.

split complementary color scheme A color scheme that poses one hue against the two hues flanking its complement; an

example would be yellow with red-violet and blue-violet.

spontaneous drawing Drawing activity performed as an instantaneous response to a subject or stimulus, as with gesture drawing intended to capture the essential movement or to depict an artist's immediate and unique mode of expression.

stick charcoal Charcoal made by heating sticks of wood about one-quarter inch in diameter in kilns until the organic materials have evaporated and only the dry carbon remains. The finest quality of the stick form is called **vine charcoal.**

stippling The building up of surface and tonal descriptions through the concentrated use of tiny dots; the dots when closer together produce darker passages; further apart, lighter tones.

structure The inner core that determines, identifies, and organizes outward form; the planned or methodical network that serves as a matrix supporting and delineating the organizational elements in a work of art.

stylus-type pen A type of fountain pen. See **Rapidograph pens.**

subtractive method In the dark-field manner, the gradual removal of the dark drawing materials from within a black field creating shapes, forms, tones, or textures of lighter values by allowing light to enter into the composition; the building of light-value visual forms from within an initial dark field. See **dark-field manner.**

sumi ink A stick of solid carbon ink that is ground and mixed with water on a shallow stone with a water well. This procedure permits great control over the density of tones.

superstructure The usually unseen inner armature or skeletal network that directly supports and defines the shapes and outer forms of a subject or form; for example, the skeleton is the superstructure for the internal organs, muscles, and skin of the human body.

symbolic drawings Drawings whose images directly symbolize ideas and concepts.

symmetrical balance The dividing of a composition into two equal halves with seemingly identical elements on each side of a vertical axis.

synesthesia In art, a subjective sensation that occurs when one type of stimulus or response to a subject evokes another reaction or secondary response. In psychological terms, a specific color, for example, may evoke a specific smell, or a specific smell may arouse a particular memory.

table plane Same as ground plane or floor plane, a term used to denote the flat plane of a drawing table surface when drawing objects on a table. See **ground plane** and **floor plane.**

tertiary colors The intermediate steps between the six basic hues—the three primary and three secondary colors; colors obtained by mixing two secondary colors.

texture The surface character or the tactile qualities experienced through touch; a sense of the "feel" of surfaces, of roughness and smoothness, hardness and softness; the illusion of tactility as in the illusion of a drawn texture albeit on a smooth two-dimensional surface.

three-point perspective A system for drawing three-dimensional objects in space on a two-dimensional plane that requires three vanishing points: both the left and right vanishing points of two-point perspective where lines recede on the horizon, and a third vertical vanishing point where lines parallel and vertical to the ground appear to converge.

tint (high key value) Any color that has been lightened by the addition of white.

tooth The abrasive texture of paper that makes drawing with dry media possible by enabling graphite, charcoal, chalk, crayon, or pastel to adhere when dragged across the surface, leaving rich deposits of drawn marks. See **paper grain.**

tortillon A paper shading stump used in combination with dry media for blending tones.

triple complementary color scheme A color scheme found within a single composition where three pairs of complementary colors work together contributing to the visual statement in a pronounced and harmonious way.

trompe l'oeil Rendering in its most meticulous form (from a French term meaning "deceive the eye"); usually applies to still life where the creation of poignant illusions convinces the viewer that he is looking at the actual object or objects represented.

two-point perspective The system of drawing objects not set square to the picture plane but set at an angle; it requires the use of both left and right vanishing points (LVP and RVP).

uniform texture Texture or textures that appear to be very similar and together create a tight harmony or an overall consistent quality, regularity, and oneness within a composition.

unity That ephemeral quality suggesting compositional "wholeness"; the quality of harmony, balance, and cogency of the art elements within a composition.

value Degrees of light and dark; the light and dark characteristics of color; the amount of light reflected by a particular color.

value scale A progressive range showing the incremental and consistent steps of change between extreme light and extreme dark.

variety A generic or specific condition of established diversity; descriptive term used to identify any number of conditional states of ranging multiplicities in a work of art; the antithesis of what is obvious or monotonous.

viewfinder A flat, rectangular, usually black cardboard sheet with a cut-away center in the shape of a square or rectangle through which one looks to frame a composition. It functions the same way as a viewfinder apparatus in a camera.

vine charcoal The highest quality of stick charcoal. Named for plant vines from which it is made and extracted through heating. See **stick charcoal.**

vision That which the artist sees with either the physical eye or the **eye of the mind,** as in conceptualizing an idea, feeling, emotion, or premonition before or during the act of drawing.

visual That which is seen or takes form in the "seeing" process; also, one of the two extreme poles of artistic personality (the other being **haptic**) where visual people concern themselves primarily with the visible environment instead of their feelings, emotions, or bodily sensations.

visualize To enact a mental picture or image not present to the sight; in the act of drawing, to give tangible form to what is imagined.

visual tangibility The proven aspect of visual reality; the ability to see an idea that has taken visual form.

visual tension A visual situation within a composition where the elements of shape, pattern, balance, harmony, and contrast all interact to produce interesting imbalances or cacophonies; some of the elements may be more pronounced than others, which creates a higher level of compositional interest.

visual whole The quality of a unified compositional state brought about by the correct degrees of balance, contrast, pattern, rhythm, etc. that produce oneness.

visualized drawings Drawings whose images represent realities of sight or cause the viewer to visualize or see what is imagined in the mind of the artist.

warm color A hue on one side of the color wheel—yellow, orange, red, and their

neighboring tertiary colors; any color opposite the cool colors on the color wheel.

wash Ink diluted with varying amounts of water or solvent that produces a broad range of transparent or semi-transparent tonal effects when brushed against a receptive surface, usually an absorbent paper.

wash drawing A drawing created exclusively by the use of ink washes of differing concentrations and dilutions applied to the paper surface with brushes.

watercolor paper As the name indicates, paper used primarily for watercolor or wash techniques. It is an acid-free, cotton-fiber paper available in a variety of different weights and degrees of sizing with an active grain or tooth that comes in three standard finishes: *rough,* a surface produced in the highest-quality papers not by mechanical graining but as the result of the hand-manufacturing process and best adapted to splashy, spontaneous techniques; *cold press,* a moderately textured matte surface paper; and *hot press,* the smoothest and least absorbent surface, excellent for very refined, controlled techniques. The different finishes come with varying capabilities of absorption and wet strengths, according to the weight and degree of sizing.

wax bloom An undesired foggy quality on a drawing's surface created by the repeated layering of colored pencils under pressure, which usually can be eliminated by rubbing the surface of the drawing lightly with a soft cloth; it is usually preventable by a light application of spray fixative.

wax crayons Inexpensive and brightly colored crayons made from dry pigments and waxy binders that adhere firmly to most paper surfaces, making them a relatively clean medium to handle.

wood engraving The technique of engraving done as a relief process on end-grain blocks of various hard woods such as maple, pear, or apple; the engraved lines are cut with a burin, receive no ink, and subsequently print as the white of the paper or negative spaces. The uncut, relief or raised surface of the woodblock receives the ink and transmits the positive image to paper when the engraving is printed.

wove finish paper Paper whose surface texture appears woven and is produced by the mesh of the mold, which is made of finely woven cloth or wire and evinces no lines or other embossed marks that are characteristic of the mold structure.

Index

Illustration Credits

Figure 1-1 National Galllery of Art,Washington, D.C. (Rosenwald Collection); 1-2 Fogg Art Museum, Harvard University, Cambridge, MA (bequest of Meta and Paul J. Sachs); 1-3 Frick Collection, New York; 1-4 Art Institute of Chicago, all rights reserved; 1-5 Courtesy of the artist; 1-6 Pierpont Morgan Library, New York; 1-7 Courtesy of the artist; 1-8 Courtesy of the artist; 1-9 Whitney Museum of Art, New York; 1-10 Courtesy of the artist; 1-11 Courtesy of the artist; 1-12 Henry Moore Foundation (private collection, U.K.); 1-13 Museum of Modern Art, New York (given anonymously); 1-14 Bristish Museum, London (photo Art Resource); 1-15 Museo Picasso, Barcelona; 1-16 Metropolitan Museum of Art (Alfred Steiglitz Collection).

Figure 2-1 Private collection; 2-2 Brooklyn Museum (purchased with funds provided by Henry and Cheryl Welt); 2-3 Susan and Herbert Adler Collection; 2-4 Cleveland Museum of Art (gift of Mrs. Henry White Cannon); 2-8 Vincent van Gogh Foundation, Vincent van Gogh Museum, Amsterdam; 2-9 Arkansas Art Center Foundation Collection (anonymous loan , 1980); 2-10 Art Institute of Chicago, all rights reserved. (gift of Mr. and Mrs. Douglas Kenyon); 2-11 Musée Calvet, Avignon; 2-13 National Self Portratit Collection, Ulster Museum (no. 2526); 2-14 Arkansas Art Center Foundation Collection; 2-15 Sotheby's; 2-16 Courtesy of Galerie Louise Leiris, Paris; 2-17 Chrysler Museum; 2-18 Musée National d'Art Moderne, Paris; 2-19 Art Institute of Chicago, all rights reserved (gift of Potter Palmer, 1944); 2-20 Art Institute of Chicago, all rights reserved; 2-21 Ricjksmseum, Amsterdam.

Figure 3-1 Susan and Herbert Adler Collection; 3-2 Cleveland Museum of Art (gift of Hanna Fund); 3-3 Whitney Museum of American Art, New York (purchase); 3-4 Art Museum, Princeton University (gift of Frank Jewitt Mather, Jr.); 3-5 Collection of John Bergruen Gallery; 3-6 Wadsworth Atheneum (gift of Miss Emily Sargent and Mrs. Francis Ormond 1930.314); 3-11 Albertina, Vienna; 3-12 Collection of Dolores Pharr Smith, Stockton, CA; 3-13 Whitney Museum of American Art. New York (gift of Alex Katz).

Figure 4-1 Metropolitan Museum of Art (Robert Lehman Collection); 4-2 Bibliothèque Nationale, Paris; 4-3 Nelson-Atkins Museum of Art, Kansas City MO (Nelson Fund 39-37); 4-4 Art Institute of Chicago, all rights reserved (Charles and Mary F. S. Worcester Collection); 4-5 Collection of Louis Clayeus, Paris; 4-6 Vatican Museum; 4-7 Worcester Art Museum; 4-8 Fogg Art Museum, Harvard University, Cambridge (bequest of Meta and Paul J. Sachs; 4-9 Musées Royaux des Beaux-Arts de Belgique Koninklijke Musea voor Schone Kunsten van Belgie, Brussels; 4-10 Coutesy of the artist; 4-11 Courtesy of Midtown Galleries, New York; 4-12 University of Michigan Art Museum; 4-13 Courtesy of the artist; 4-14 Pierpont Morgan Library, New York; 4-15

Courtesy of Christie, Manson & Woods, Ltd.; 4-16 Louvre, Paris; 4-17 Musée Toulouse-Lautrec, Albi; 4-18 Collection of Dolores Pharr Smith, Stockton, CA; 4-19 Museum of Fine Arts, Budapest: Majovsky Collection; 4-20 Detroit Institute of Arts; 4-21 Huntington Library Art Gallery, San Marino, CA (gift of Virginia Steele Scott Collection).

Figure 5-1 Arkansas Arts Center Foundation Collection (collection of Paul Magriel); 5-2 Licensed by VAGA, New York, N.Y. Collection of the artist; 5-3 National Galllery of Art Washington, D.C. (Rosenwald Collection); 5-4 Art Museum, Princeton University (acc. no. 48-137); 5-5 Bristish Museum, London; 5-6 Minnesota Museum of Art, (given in memory of Warrren Towel Mosman, 68.20.11); 5-7 Pierpont Morgan Library, New York; 5-8 Collection Anni Albers and the Josef Albers Foundation, Inc; 5-9 Museum of Modern Art, New York (gift of the artist); 5-10 Whitney Museum of American Art, New York, (purchase); 5-11 Vincent van Gogh Foundation, Vincent van Gogh Museum, Amsterdam; 5-12 ARS; 5-13 Musée des Beaux-Arts, Lille; 5-14 Art Institute of Chicago, all rights reserved; 5-15 Art Museum, Princeton University (gift of Mrs. Margaret Mower for the Elsa Durand Mower Collection); 5-16 Royal Collection, Windsor Castle; 5-17 Wadsworth Atheneum (bequest of George A. Gay); 5-18 Rijksmuseum, Amsterdam; 5-19 Philadelphia Museum of Art (gift of Dr. and Mrs William Wolgin); 5-20 Nelson Gallery-Atkins Museum, Kansas City, MO (gift of Mrs. George H. Bunting, Jr.); 5-21 Santa Barbara Museum of Art (gift of Mr. and Mrs. Arthur B. Sachs); 5-22 Hirshhorn Museum and Sculpture Garden, Smithsonian Institution, Washington, D.C.; 5-23 Rijksmuseum, Amsterdam.

Figure 6-2 San Francisco Museum of Modern Art (gift of the San Francisco Women Artists); 6-3 Courtesy of Terry Dintenfass Gallery, New York; 6-6 Addison Gallery of American Art, Phillips Academy, Andover, MA (gift of Winslow Ames); 6-7 Sotheby's; 6-8 Kunstmuseum, Düsseldorf (Lambert Krahe Collection); 6-9 Toledo Museum of Art; 6-10 Art Institute of Chicago, all rights reserved; 6-11 Arkansas Art Center Foundation Collection; 6-12 Courtesy of the artist; 6-13 Ryoko-in, Daitokujo, Kyoto; 6-14 Fogg Art Museum, Harvard University, Cambridge, MA (Greenville L. Winthrop Bequest); 6-15 Baltimore Museum of Art (Thomas E. Benesch Memorial Collection); 6-16 British Museum, London; 6-17 Courtesy of the artist; 6-18 Art Institute of Chicago, all rights reserved; 6-19 Arkansas Art Center Foundation Collection; 6-20 Whitney Museum of American Art, New York, (purchase); 6-21 Arkansas Art Center Foundation Collection; 6-22 Achenbach Foundation for Graphic Arts, Mildred Anna Williams Fund, Fine Arts Museum of San Francisco; 6-23 Arkansas Art Center Foundation Collection.

Figure 7-1 Yale University Art Gallery, New Haven, CT (lent by Richard Brown Baker); 7-2 Musée National d'Art Moderne, Centre Georges Pompidou, Paris; 7-3 Musée National d'Art Moderne, Centre Georges Pompidou, Paris; 7-4 Museum of Modern Art, New York (gift of Mr. and Mrs. Charles B. Benenson); 7-5 Private collection; 7-6 New Jersey State Museum, Trenton, NJ; 7-7 Courtesy of the artist; 7-8 Metropolitan Museum of Art, New York (purchase of Joseph Pulitzer Bequest); 7-9 Kupferstich Kabinett, Staatliche Kunstsammlungen, Dresden; 7-10 Collection of Mrs. Daniel Mendelowitz, Stanford, CA; 7-11 Courtesy of the artist (collection of Rita Rich); 7-12 Art Institute of Chicago, all rights reserved; 7-13 Private collection, Milan; 7-14 Collection of Anni Albers and Josef Albers Foundation, Inc; 7-15 Private collection; 7-16 Art Institute of Chicago, all rights reserved; 7-17 Art Institute of Chicago, all rights reserved; 7-18 Museum of Modern Art, New York (gift of Mr. and Mrs. John Pope in honor of Paul J. Sachs). Photo Henry Moore Foundation.

Figure 8-1 Art Institute of Chicago, all rights reserved (gift of Tiffany and Margaret Blake, 1947.35). 8-2 Pierpont Morgan Library, New York; 8-3 Metropolitan Museum of Art. New York (Lehman Collection); 8-4 National Museum of American Art, Smithsonian Institution, Washington, D.C.; 8-5 Courtesy of the artist; 8-6 Detroit Institute of Arts (bequest of John S. Newberry); 8-7 Arkansas Art Center Foundation Collecton; 8-8 Whitney Museum of American Art, New York (gift of Mr. and Mrs. Benjamin Weiss); 8-9 Seattle Art Museum (Eugene Fuller Memorial Collection); 8-10 Courtesy of the artist; 8-11 Photo courtesy of Terry Dintenfass Inc. New York; 8-12 Whitney Museum of American Art. New York; 8-13 National Gallery of Art, Washington, D.C. Courtesy of the artist; 8-14 Private collection; 8-15 Courtesy of Lew Allen Gallery, Santa Fe, NM. Photography by Dan Morse; 8-16 Rhode School of Design, Providence, RI; 8-17 Arkansas Art Center Foundation Collection; 8-19 Coutesy of the artist; 8-20 Courtesy of the Nancy Hoffman Gallery; 8-21 Art Institute of Chicago, all rights reserved; 8-22 San Francisco Museum of Modern Art; 8-23 Art Institute of Chicago, all rights reserved.

Figure 9-3 Berlin, Staatliche Museen, Nationalgalerie, Sammlung der Handzeichnungen; 9-4 Musée Fabre, Montpellier; 9-5 Courtesy of the Allan Stone Gallery (Glenn C. Janss Collection); 9-6 Reproduced by permission of Houghton Mifflin Co; 9-7 Courtesy of the Gallery Paule Anglim; 9-11 Fogg Art Museum, Harvard University, Cambridge, MA (bequest of Charles A. Loeser); 9-13 Metropolitan Museum Art, New York (Fletcher Fund, 1942); 9-16 Courtesy of the artist; 9-17 Library of Congress, Washington, D.C.; 9-21 British Museum, London;

9-23 Courtesy of Hirschl & Adler Modern (collection of Glenn C. Janss).

Figure 10-1 Yale University Art Gallery, New Haven, CT (John Heinz III Fund); 10-2 National Gallery Art, Washington, D.C. (promised gift of Robert and Jane Meyerhoff); 10-3 Courtesy of the artist; 10-4 Courtesy of the artist (Collection of Michael Spivak, Houston, TX); 10-5 Fogg Art Museum, Harvard University, Cambridge, MA; 10-6 National Gallery of Art, Washington, D.C. (intended gift of the Woodner Collections); 10-7 National Gallery of Art, Washington, D.C. (Ailsa Mellon Bruce Fund, 1974); 10-8 National Gallery of Art, Washington, D.C. ; 10-9 Albertina, Vienna; 10-11 Fogg Art Museum, Harvard University, Cambridge, MA (purchase, Louise E. Betterns Fund); 10-12 Courtesy of the artist; 10-13 National Gallery of Art, Washington, D.C. (gift of Robert and Jane Meyerhoff); 10-14 Art Institute of Chicago, all rights reserved; 10-15 Art Institute of Chicago, alll rights reserved (gift of Emily Crane Chadbourne, 1953); 10-16 Courtesy of Nancy Hoffman Gallery, New York; 10-17 Courtesy of the artist; 10-18 Collection of Mrs. Daniel Mendelowitz, Stanford, CA; 10-19 Metropolitan Museum of Art, New York; 10-20 Courtesy of the artist.

Figure 11-1 Courtesy of the artist; 11-3 Vincent van Gogh Foundation, Vincent van Gogh Museum, Amsterdam; 11-4 Courtesy of the artist; 11-7 Carnigie Museum of Art, Pittsburgh (gift of Russel G. Twiggs, 6825.1); 11-8 Royal Library, Windsor Castle; 11-9 Courtesy of the Boston Public Library, Print Dept; 11-10 Courtesy Galerie St. Etienne, New York; 11-11 Museum of Fine Arts, Budapest; 11-12 Paul Klee-Stifung, Kunstmsuem, Bern; 11-13 The Art Institute of Chicago, all rights reserved (gift of the Print and Drawing Club); 11-14 Courtesy of the artist; 11-15 Museum of Modern Art, New York (Mrs. Simon Guggenheim Fund); 11-16 Collectionof Annie Albers and the Josef Ablers Foundation, Inc; 11-17 Private collection; 11-18 Collection Kurt Gitter, New Orleans; 11-19 Courtesy of the Smithsonian Institution, Freer Gallery of Art, Washington, D.C.; 11-20 Fogg Art Museum, Harvard University, Cambridge, MA (Meta and Paul J. Sachs Collection); 11-21 Metropolitan Museum of Art, New York (Rogers Fund); 11-23 Albertina, Vienna; 11-24 Courtesy of Deutsch Fototek, Dresden; 11-25 Courtesy of the artist; 11-26 Courtesy of the artist; 11-27 Chicago Art Institute of Art, all rights reserved.

Figure 12-1 Courtesy of the artitst; 12-2 National Gallery of Art, Washington, D.C. (anonymous gift); 12-3 Courtesy Lennon Weinberg, Inc., New York (private collection); 12-4 Art Institute of Chicago, all rights reserved; 12-5 Courtesy of the artist; 12-6 Museum of Modern Art, New York (gift of Abby AldrichRockefeller); 12-7 Museum of Modern Art, New York (gift of Mr. and Mrs. Armand P. Bartos); 12-8 Art Institute of Chicago, all rights reserved; 12-9 Courtesy of the artist; 12-10 Arkansas Art Center Foundation Collection; 12-11 Collection of Theophilus Brown; 12-12 Stedlijk Museum, Amsterdam; 12-13 Minnesota Museum of Art, Saint Paul (Action Fund Purchase 75.43.08). Licensed by VAGA, New York; 12-14 Minnesota Museum of Art, St. Paul (gift in memory of Ruth F. Lien Miller 74.45.13); 12-15 Whitney Museum of American Art, New York (Neysa McMean Purchase Award); 12-16 Chicago Art Institute of Art, all rights reserved; 12-17 Chicago Art Institute of Art, all rights reserved;

12-18 Modern Art Museum, New York (gift of John S. Newberry Collection).

Figure 13-1 Collection Arts Council of North Ireland, Ulster Museum. Courtesy of the artist; 13-2 Minnesota Museum of Art, St. Paul, MN (acquisition Fund Purchase (71.05.39); 13-3 Royal Library, Windsor Castle; 13-4 Art Museum, Princeton Universtiy (gift of Elizabeth Huntington Moore); 13-5 Art Institute of Chicago, all rights reserved; 13-6 Nelson Gallery-Atkins Museum, Kansas, MO; 13-7 National Gallery of Scotland, Edinburgh; 13-8 Metropolitam Museum of Art, New York (gift of Mrs. John D. Sylvester, 1936); 13-9 Musée des Beaux-Arts, Lille; 13-10 Cooper-Hewitt Museum, the Smithsonian Institution's National Museum of Design, New York; 13-11 Philadelphia Museum of Art; 13-12 Louvre, Paris; 13-13 Art Institute of Chicago, all rights reserved; 13-14 Private collection; 13-15 Corcoran Gallery, Washington, D.C. (gift of Miss Emily Sargend and and Mrs. Violet Sargemd Ormond); 13-16 Art Institute of Chicago, all rights reserved; 13-17 Carnigie Museum of Art (Howard N. Eavenson Memorial Fund, 58.62); 13-18 Art Intsitute of Chicago, all rights reserved; 13-19 Art Institute of Chicago, all rights reserved; 13-20 Addison Gallery of American Art, Phillips Academy, Andover, MA (anonymous gift); 13-21 Courtesy of the artist; 13-22 Stanford Museum of Art; 13-23 Solomon R. Guggenheim Museum, New York (Justin K. Thannhauser Collection); 13-24 Chermayeff and Geismar, Inc., New York; 13-25 Art Institute of Chicago, all rights reserved; 13-26 Courtesy of the artist.

Figure 14-1 Frankfort am Main; 14-2 Metroprolitan Museum of Art, New York; 14-3 Museo Nazionale, Toronto; 14-4 British Museum, London; 14-5 Louvre, Paris; 14-6 Gallerie del'Academia, Venice; 14-7 Copyright 1987 Bruce Moser; 14-8 Adolph Alexander Weinman papers, Archives of American Art, Smithsonian Institution, Washington, D.C.; 14-9 Metropolitan Museum of Art, New York; 14-11 Cologne District Savings Bank, Käthe Kollwitz Collection; 14-12 Museum Boymans-van Beuningen, Rotterdam; 14-13 Courtesy of Midtown Payson Galleries, New York; 14-14 Art Institute of Chicago, all rights reserved; 14-15 Art Institute of Chicago, all rights reserved; 14-16 Staatgalerie, Stuttgart; 14-17 Royal Library, Windsor Castle; 14-18 Royal Library, Windsor Castle; 14-19 Bibliotheque Nationale, Paris; 14-20 Gabinetto Nazionale delle Stampe, Rome; 14-21 Stadelsches Kunstinstitute, Frankfurm-am-Main; 14-22 Metropolitan Museum of Art, New York; 14-23 Louvre, Paris; 14-24 Art Museum, Princeton University; 14-25 Musée des Beaux, Arts, Lille; 14-26 Allen Memorial Art Museum, Oberlin College, OH; 14-27 Baltimore Museum of Art (Cone Collection); 14-28 British Museum, London; 14-29 Musée Toulouse-Lautrec, Albi; 14-31 Art Resource, New York; 14-32 Courtesy of the artist; 14-33 Louvre, Paris; 14-34 Sheldon Memorial Art Gallery, University of Nebraska; 14-35 Courtesy of the artist.

Figure 15-1 Fogg Art Museum, Harvard University, Cambridge, MA (bequest of Meta and Paul J. Sachs); 15-2 Art Institute of Chicago, all rights reserved (gift of the Donnelley Family, 1978.26); 15-3 Schlossmuseum,Weimar; 15-4 Mark Ferrer, Executor, Estate of Howard Warshaw; 15-5 Permission of Mrs. Alanson Appleton, San Mateo,CA; 15-6 Metropolitan Museum of Art, New York; 15-7 Art Institute of Chicago, all righs reserved; 15-8 Cleveland Museum of Art; 15-9 Louvre, Paris; 15-10

Courtesy of the artist; 15-11 Sotheby's; 15-12 Arkansas Art Center Foundation Collection. ; 15-13 Courtesy of the artist; 15-14 Collection of Anni Albers and Josef Albers Foundation, Inc; 15-15 Private Collection. Photograph courtesy of the Pace Gallery. 15-16 © David Hockney, 1972; 15-17 Bristish Museum, London; 15-18 Sotheby's; 15-19 Allen Memorial Art Museum, Oberlin College, Ohio (R. T. Miller, Jr., Fund); 15-20 Courtesy of Robert Miller Gallery, New York; 15-21 Courtesy of the artist; 15-22 Courtesy of Lennon,Weinberg, Inc., New York; 15-23 Courtesy of the artist; 15-24 Royal Library, Windsor Castle; 15-25 New York Review of Books. Copyright © 1980 Nyrev, Inc; 15-26 Musée Toulouse-Lautrec, Albi.

Figure 16-1 Courtesy of the artist; 16-2 Metropolitan Museum of Art, New York (Rogers Fund, 1917); 16-3 Copyright © 1965 by Edward Gorey; 16-4 Reader's Digest Association, Inc. (copyright 1978 and 1981 Barron Storey); 16-5 Courtesy of the artist; 16-6 Reprinted by permission of Farrar, Straus & Giroux, Inc.; 16-7 Courtesy of the artist; 16-8 Courtesy of the artist; 16-9 Courtesy of Lydia Stavrinos; 16-10 Grinta International Corp., Copyright Ranaldi 1985. Illustration Ralph Steadman; 16-11 Courtesy of the artist; 16-12 Courtesy of Dorothea Bilder; 16-13 Robinson, Yesawich & Pepperdine, Inc. Orlando, FL; 16-14 Courtesy of the artist.

Figure 17-1 British Museum, London; 17-2 Courtesy of the artist; 17-3 National Gallery of Art, Washington, D.C.; 17-4 Cologne District Savings Bank, Käthe Kollwitz Collection; 17-5 National Gallery, London; 17-6 Private collection; 17-7 Courtesy of Richard L. Feigen & Co., Inc. New York; 17-8 Corcoran Gallery of Art, Washington, D.C. Courtesy of the artist; 17-9 Courtesy of Sperone Westwater, New York; 17-10 Private collection; 17-11 Courtesy of Allan Stone Gallery, New York. Licensed by VAGA, New York; 17-12 Courtesy of the artist; 17-13 Museum Boymans-van Beuningen, Rotterdam; 17-15 Museum of Fine Art, Budapest; 17-16 Art Institute of Chicago, all rights reserved. ; 17-17 Royal Library, Windsor Castle; 17-18 Collection of the artist; 17-19 Museum of Modern Art, New York; 17-20 Courtesy of the artist; 17-21 Detroit Institute of Arts; 17-22 Courtesy Frumkin-Adams Gallery, New York; 17-23 Haags Gemeentemuseum, The Hague; 17-24 Courtesy of the artist; 17-25 National Gallery of Art, Washington, D.C. (promised gift of the artist).

Figure 18-1 Courtesy of the artist; 18-2 Arkansas Art Center Foundation Collection; 18-3 Albertina, Vienna; 18-4 National Gallery of Washington, D.C.; 18-5 Bristish Museum, London; 18-6 Ashmolean Museum, Oxford; 18-7 Art Institute of Chicago, all rights reserved; 18-8 Art Institute of Chicago, all rights reserved; 18-9 Art Institute of Chicago, all rights reserved; 18-10 Private collection; 18-11 Henry Moore Foundation; 18-12 Tate Gallery, London; 18-13 Licensed by VAGA, New York; 18-15 Butler Institute of American Art, Youngstown, OH; 18-16 Courtesy of the artist; 18-17 Henry Moore Foundation; 18-18 Corcoran Gallery of Art, Washington, D.C.; 18-19 Courtesy of the artist.

Color Plates

Plate 1 Museum of Contemporary Art, Los Angeles, CA; **2** Security Pacific National Bank, CA; **4** Achenbach Foundation fo Graphic Arts, Fine Arts Museum of San Francisco, CA (Mildred

Plate 11. JENNIFER BARTLETT (b. 1941; American). *In the Garden # 122*. c. 1980. Colored pencil on paper, 26 × 19 3/4" (66 × 50 cm).
Collection of Chase Manhattan Bank. Courtesy of Paula Cooper, Inc.

Plate 12. BOB ZIERING (20th century; American). Courtesy of the artist. First part of a triptych.

Plate 13. MAURICIO LASANSKY (b. 1914; Argentinian). *The Nazi Drawings # 19.* c. 1961–1966. Graphite pencil, red earth pigments, and turpentine wash on paper, 76 × 45" (193.2 × 114.4 cm).
The University of Iowa Museum of Art. (On long-term loan to the Cedar Rapids Art Museum, Cedar Rapids, Iowa.)

Plate 14. JIM BUTLER (b. 1945; American). *Burnished Sky/River Mist.* c. 1993. Graphite on panel, 40 × 82" (101.7 × 208.5 cm). Collection of the artist.

Plate 15. MICHAEL MAZUR (b. 1935; American). *Yard, November III.* c. 1984. Pastel, 29 1/2 × 29 1/2" (75.2 × 75.2 cm). Rita Rich Collection. Courtesy of Barbara Krakow Gallery.

Plate 16. GARY KELLEY (20th century; American). Promotion for the Mississippi Delta Blues Festival. c. 1989. Pastel, 24 × 14". Courtesy of the artist.

Plate 17. JIM WESTERGARD (1939; American-Canadian). *Insomnia.* c. 1990. Oil paint drawing on white wove paper, 23 1/16 × 32 3/16" (58.7 × 81.8 cm). Courtesy of the artist. Collection of David L. Faber.